HANDBOOK
OF
SOCIAL
AND
CULTURAL
ANTHROPOLOGY

Contributors

Alexander Alland, Jr., *Columbia University*
James N. Anderson, *University of California, Berkeley*
Mary B. Black, *Royal Ontario Museum*
Erika Bourguignon, *Ohio State University*
Robert L. Carneiro, *American Museum of Natural History*
Ronald Cohen, *Northwestern University*
Benjamin Colby, *University of California, Irvine*
Scott Cook, *University of Connecticut*
Harold E. Driver, *Indiana University*
Marshall Durbin, *Washington University*
Frederick O. Gearing, *State University of New York, Buffalo*
John Gulick, *University of North Carolina, Chapel Hill*
Robert A. Hackenberg, *University of Colorado*
Charles Hudson, *University of Georgia*
John G. Kennedy, *University of California, Los Angeles*
Richard W. Lieban, *University of Hawaii*
Bonnie McCay, *Columbia University*
Nancy D. Munn, *University of Massachusetts, Amherst*
Laura Nader, *University of California, Berkeley*
Keith F. Otterbein, *State University of New York, Buffalo*
James L. Peacock, *University of North Carolina, Chapel Hill*
Gretel H. Pelto, *University of Connecticut*
Pertti J. Pelto, *University of Connecticut*
Richard H. Robbins, *State University of New York, Plattsburgh*
Joan Rubin, *Tulane University*
Harold W. Scheffler, *Yale University*
Bob Scholte, *New School for Social Research*
Pierre L. van den Berghe, *University of Washington*
Fred W. Voget, *Southern Illinois University*
Douglas R. White, *University of Pittsburgh*
Norman E. Whitten, *University of Illinois, Urbana*
Alvin W. Wolfe, *University of Wisconsin, Milwaukee*
Barbara Yngvesson, *Hampshire College*

HANDBOOK OF SOCIAL AND CULTURAL ANTHROPOLOGY

Edited by

John J. Honigmann
University of North Carolina,
Chapel Hill

RAND McNALLY COLLEGE PUBLISHING COMPANY • CHICAGO

RAND McNALLY ANTHROPOLOGY SERIES
Edgar F. Borgatta, Advisory Editor

Human Evolution: An Introduction to the New Physical Anthropology
   J. B. Birdsell

Make Men of Them: Introductory Readings for Cultural Anthropology
   Charles C. Hughes, ed.

Handbook of Social and Cultural Anthropology
   John J. Honigmann, ed.

Current printing   (last digit)
15   14   13   12   11   10   9   8   7   6   5   4   3   2

Preface

It looks as if the period that began about 1951 will be known for its preoccupation with surveying and synthesizing anthropological concepts and knowledge. In that year planning began for an international symposium organized by the Wenner-Gren Foundation for Anthropological Research, with the aim of assessing the accomplishments of anthropology. The assessment appeared in an "encyclopedic inventory" called *Anthropology Today,* edited by A. L. Kroeber and published in 1953. Since then other editors have pulled together ideas and discoveries in all or some of the four major subfields of anthropology, and an imposing handbook concerned exclusively with method has recently been published. One reason for so much effort at intellectual integration is the explosion of anthropological knowledge following World War II, making it more difficult than it used to be for professional people and graduate students to know what others who specialize in new lines of research are up to. Although such specialization may not be closely related to one's own interests, it yet forms part of the discipline with which anthropologists identify themselves. When Edgar Borgatta

asked me, on behalf of Rand McNally and Company, whether I would undertake to assemble a comprehensive handbook of cultural and social anthropology, my first thought was how useful such a book would be in bringing together up-to-date work in the field, the way the Wenner-Gren Foundation did in the early fifties.

Upon accepting the assignment, I wrote to about twenty friends in the profession in the United States and Canada, soliciting suggestions for topics that ought to be represented in the handbook as well as authors suitable to write on those topics. Acting on their suggestions and my own ideas, I prepared a tentative list of chapters and prospective authors, to whom I then sent invitations to contribute to the project. My letter said that the book would assess the current status of social and cultural anthropology. Each chapter should be objective and comprehensive, though the authors need not forget their own standards and personal preferences while giving other significant points of view a fair hearing. Early views on a topic should be dealt with to the extent that they still serve a purpose in graduate education or make subsequent developments more comprehensible than they otherwise would be. Handbooks, I pointed out, are most useful when subjects are treated from wide perspectives; that is, when they include reviews of relevant literature broad enough so that a graduate student or professional unfamiliar with a subject can become acquainted with it through his own efforts. I suggested a few ground rules. Each chapter should constitute a comprehensive review of a topic, including where relevant a history of what has been accomplished, major subdivisions or lines of work, unresolved issues, and future prospects. Articles should be substantive rather than programmatic. References should furnish a reliable guide to the topic.

Most of the persons whom I invited to contribute are represented in this volume. There would have been six more had not various vicissitudes prevented them from carrying out their plans. In relation to the roles of the contributors, my own role has been a modest one, comparable to that of the waiter who merely offers the delectable dishes created and prepared by skilled chefs. Unlike most waiters, however, I have tasted the dishes, and the experience convinces me that they are good.

Despite the broad range of topics treated in the book, readers will doubtless discover omissions. I regret that I could not induce someone to cover certain subjects suggested by my informal panel of advisers. There is no chapter that goes into current knowledge about the biological determinants of social behavior. I had also hoped for a chapter that would review what primate studies have contributed to our knowledge of the foundations of behavior. Perhaps it is still too early to expect substantive reviews, as distinguished from programmatic essays, on those topics.

Once again I thank the contributors for joining Rand McNally and me in this venture and for cooperating graciously in meeting deadlines and patiently enduring my queries and reminders of due dates. The vast job of writing letters, following up on manuscripts, and keeping track of permissions was carried out by Irma Honigmann, whose assistance was simply indispensable.

JOHN J. HONIGMANN
University of North Carolina
Chapel Hill, N.C.

Contents

CHAPTER 1 The History of Cultural Anthropology

FRED W. VOGET

Anthropology may be separated into two major divisions, physical and cultural. The relations of these two segments converge at certain points, but the focus on the human constitution and on culture respectively has frequently provided a basis for contradictory and conflicting interpretations of human behavior, and has made for restricted intellectual and methodological exchange. Starting from concern with the biological basis of human behavior, interpretation may be extended to include race as the variable upon which ethnic and national character and cultural achievements rest. In contrast, cultural anthropologists, who begin with socially learned behavior, have been inclined to take the biological as a constant that must assume a specific quality as culture varies. In this contrast nature traditionally has been opposed to nurture. The anthropological intent is not to polarize, however, but to examine the interrelations of generic variables and their specific factors, which converge to energize and regularize human activity in a biological, social, cul-

tural, and ecological context. The viewing of human behavior in a total context has been a constant commitment of anthropologists, frequently expressed as the "holistic approach."

FIELDS OF CULTURAL ANTHROPOLOGY

Specialization has resulted in the differentiation of a number of subfields or specializations within cultural anthropology. Specialization is largely a matter of problem definition, to which a "subject matter" and methodological techniques logically may be attached. Within cultural anthropology specialization has been carried to the point where it embraces the total range of any culture, cross-comparisons of cultures, and the study of culture processes. Below is one way in which the specializations of cultural anthropology may be outlined (see Marshall 1967; Hoebel 1966):

1. Prehistory or archaeology (descriptive and comparative)
2. Ethnology (descriptive and comparative)

1

a. Ethnography (description and analysis of specific cultures)
b. Ethnohistory (ethnic history, mixture, migration, conquest, etc.)
c. Ethnolinguistics (anthropological linguistics)
d. Ethnopsychology (psychological anthropology)
e. Ethnoeconomics (economic anthropology, technics and ethnoecology)
f. Ethnosociology (social anthropology)
g. Ethnojurisprudence (ethnography of law)
h. Ethnopolitics (political anthropology)
i. Ethnoesthetics (anthropology of art, ethnomusicology)
j. Ethnophilosophy (morals, religion, metaphysics, epistemology)
3. Social and cultural systematics (configurational and functional integration of cultures and societies)
4. Culture change
   a. Culture history
   b. Cultural evolution
   c. Acculturation
5. Applied anthropology

CULTURE: A CENTRAL CONCEPT

The concept of culture has always been central to the distinction between anthropology and other disciplines, notably sociology. It was also used at the beginning of anthropological studies in the eighteenth century to denote a state of refinement and polish equated with civilization. E. B. Tylor (1874, 1:1) was the first to assign the task of studying "culture or civilization" unequivocally to "ethnography." His definition of culture or civilization as that "complex whole which includes knowledge, belief, art, morals, law, custom, and any other capabilities and habits acquired by man as a member of society" (1874, 1:1) has received wide currency (see Stocking 1963). But it was American culture historians following Franz Boas, notably Lowie, who refined the concept for scientific purposes.

The adjectival use of the word "culture" in such terms as "culture traits" and "culture complexes" by museum ethnologists in both the United States and Germany contributed to its popularization and to its scientific use in defining artifacts, customs, beliefs, ceremonies, and the wide range of distinguishably human social features without regard to value judgments. Such definition is essential to any scientific usage. Culture may be used in both generic and specific ways. Broadly speaking, culture may refer to any product of the social life of man, either in the past or in the present. Again, any group that has maintained historic continuity can be said to possess a culture. Linton (1945:32) offered the following definition of a specific culture: "A culture is the configuration of learned behavior and results of behavior whose component elements are shared and transmitted by the members of a particular society." Culture generally has been considered the unique possession of man, although recent studies of non-human primates have challenged this view, pointing to their very rudimentary use of tools and social communication that may involve imitative learning.

The culture concept has continued to guide the theoretical orientation of American and German ethnologists. British and French social anthropologists have inclined to distinguish the social and cultural and to confine the latter, after Radcliffe-Brown (1965a:5), to the "learnt ways of thinking, feeling, and acting" that form a part of the "social process." The important dimension for social anthropologists turns on social structure, conceived to be the orderly arrangement of persons in the society according to their status rights and obligations. American ethnologists during the thirties also were moved to make a clear distinction between the social and cultural; but, unlike the social anthropologists, they assumed that social organization existed by virtue of definitions that utilized historic-cultural principles of classification—age and sex, occupation, prestige ranking, interest groups (Linton 1945). While American anthropologists viewed the social order through the integrative values and purposes implicit in or explicitly voiced in the culture patterns, British and French social anthropologists searched the social order for the principles of organization implicit or explicit in the social system, and by virtue of which individuals were assigned roles that symbolized a concord with principles. American culturalists thus came to view a culture as a value-oriented design for living, and the social structure as a reflection of the orderly arrangement of people pointed to realization of this design. British social anthropologists, on the other hand, reasoned that men and women are organized in societies according to special principles that allow them to continue their existence in an orderly fashion through a specialized cooperation of parts in the service of the whole. In some ways American culturalists betray a romantic idealism traceable to nineteenth-century German sources, while the British social anthropologists seem to draw upon the sober strength of English jurisprudence.

Despite the difference, British social anthropologists and American ethnologists at times have found themselves making distinctions more semantic than real. When, for example, Radcliffe-Brown (1965a:10-11) defines "institutions" as the "established norms of conduct" or "rules" that specify and guide proper behavior for a type or class of social relationships and interactions (e.g., husband and wife, king and subject), he obviously is talking about the "ideal patterns" of Linton (1936: 102-103). Reciprocities rooted in rights and duties define any social system, but

these reciprocals of behavior are guided by "ideal patterns . . . carried in the minds of individuals . . . [defining] what the behavior between individuals or classes of individuals should be." While the social and cultural can be distinguished usefully for an analytic purpose, at this point in time it is clear that understanding their interrelations in the complex human environment is more to the point than attempting to derive one from the other.

ANTECEDENTS TO ANTHROPOLOGY

Anthropology is a product of scientific developments that took place in the Western world. In the vital continuity of its tradition, Western civilization owes much to the scientific, political, moral, religious, philosophic, and aesthetic formulations of the Greek and Roman civilizations, and to the revival of interest in them during the Renaissance. The Greeks and Romans may be said to have laid the foundations for anthropology as they did for ethics, aesthetics, metaphysics, logic, history, and other intellectual pursuits.

THE ANCIENT WORLD

If a case for the beginnings of anthropology among the ancients is to be made, it must rest on their humanistic orientation, their interest in history, and their curiosity about natural science. In the fifth century B.C. Herodotus, a political exile from Halicarnassus in Ionia, set out to describe the war between Persia and Greece in order to get at its causes and to record its never-to-be-forgotten deeds of heroism. He did much more than that, however; he described the customs of the Persians and nearby peoples, including dress, armaments, boats, food taboos, and religious ceremonials. Herodotus (1942:105, 106) must be credited with being a shrewd observer and a narrator sensitive to dramatic contrast of custom, as the following passages reveal:

Concerning Egypt ... there is no country that possesses so many wonders, nor that has such a number of works which defy description. Not only is the climate different from that of the rest of the world, and the rivers unlike any other rivers, but the people also, in most of their manners and customs exactly reverse the common practice of mankind. The women attend the markets and trade, while the men sit at home at the looms; and here, while the rest of the world works the woof up the warp, the Egyptians work it down; the women likewise carry burdens upon their shoulders, while the men carry them upon their heads. They eat their food out of doors in the streets, but retire for private purposes to their houses, giving as a reason that what is unseemly, but necessary, ought to be done in secret, but what has nothing unseemly about it, should be done openly. A woman cannot serve the priestly office, either for god or goddess, but men are priests to both; sons need not support their parents unless they choose; but daughters must, whether they choose or not.

In other countries the priests have long hair, in Egypt their heads are shaven; elsewhere it is customary, in mourning, for near relations to cut their hair close; the Egyptians, who wear no hair at any other time, when they lose a relative, let their beards and the hair on their heads grow long. All other men pass their lives separate from animals, the Egyptians have animals always living with them; others make barley and wheat their food; it is a disgrace to do so in Egypt, where the grain they live on is spelt, which some call *zea*. Dough they knead with their feet; but they mix mud, and even take up dirt, with their hands. They are the only people in the world — they at least, and such as have learnt the practice from them — who use circumcision. Their men wear two garments apiece, their women but one. They put on the rings and fasten the ropes to sails inside; others put them outside. When they write or calculate, instead of going, like the Greeks, from left to right, they move their hand from right to left; and they insist, notwithstanding, that it is they who go to the right, and the Greeks who go to the left. They have two quite different kinds of writing, one of which is called sacred, the other common.

Herodotus wrote history spiced with the appeal of strange customs and foreign lands, and it is unfortunate that later Greek scholars turned to a narrower history of war and politics. The only other full-length description of the customs of a people came from the pen of the Roman Tacitus, writing on Germany and its tribes. Tacitus (1942) credited the Germans with excellent customs supporting the family and morality and noted their government by a warrior nobility, but he found them lacking in moderation and thus fated to be "overcome by their own vices as easily as by the arms of an enemy."

The moral drawn from the principle of moderation was long entrenched in Greco-Roman thought by the time Tacitus (*ca.* A.D. 98) composed his essay on the untutored Germans to the north for the edification of the Romans of his day. Hippocrates, writing from a physician's point of view, formulated what probably were rather current thoughts in his time. No doctor, he observed, should go into an area without taking note of climate, seasonal changes, sources of water, and the mode of life of the people; for these will affect constitution and leave people open to particular diseases. Uniformities in climate and in land surface produce a similar unity in physical type, and people so molded by a uniform climate and land will be found inferior to those living where sharp environmental contrasts are found, as in Europe. Contrast brings diversity in "physique, in character, and in constitution" (Hippocrates 1962:135). But contrast is one thing, extremes of climate are another. Climate and terrain that are hot and uniform induce a "tameness" of mind, while "frequent shocks to the mind impart wildness, destroying tameness and gentleness. For this reason, I think, Europeans are also more courageous than Asiatics [peoples of Asia Minor]. For uniformity engenders slackness, while variation fosters endurance in both body and soul; rest and slackness are food for cowardice, endurance and exertion for bravery" (p. 133).

The kinds of customs and institutions peoples have can also be traced to the climate and land, which shape their characters and physiques. Wherever climate is moderate, there one finds the best of peoples and customs; people exhibit courage, are more inclined to respond to the rule of reason, and often need less government and are less willing to accept an absolute ruler. Concern with war and politics made Greeks and Romans interested in the ways in which custom is related to national grandeur or decay. The Greek hostage Polybius (1889), embarking on an integrated history of the Mediterranean area — the whole world of his day — believed that harmony and balance so characterized Roman institutions and government that here must lie their success in ruling others. He noted, too, how custom was supported by divine sanctions, and how the youth were inspired to cultivate courage and strength and to follow the noble example of illustrious patriots.

The commitments of the Greeks and Romans to lands and peoples, political histories, natural science, and philosophy militated against their focusing directly on custom. Custom thus became more of an afterthought or by-product of a major interest, and the "science of custom" had to wait upon an awakening at a later day. Greco-Roman contributions tend to be generalized, as in the humanistic orientation, or theoretically specific, as in the alleged relationship between climate, land, national character, and institutions, especially the political institution. The Greco-Roman equation frequently derives the institution from a national character, which in turn must be traced to geographic conditions. Had the equation been reversed, deriving national character from traditional institutions, the basis for a science of culture would have existed, and the Greeks and Romans would have to be considered founders of a true science of man, culture, and society. Nonetheless, they formulated a rich philosophic and scientific tradition, to which the following propositions were fundamental:

1. Everything has a form that determines its purpose.
2. All things are in a state of flux, cycling between integration and disintegration.
3. Every form is a structure whose parts are of different orders of importance; i.e., there is a natural hierarchy in the arrangement of parts.
4. The design of each part is to contribute to the proper functioning of the total system through actualization of its own potential.
5. The general strain in every system is toward a balanced harmony wherein each part fulfills its potential activity according to its purposive form.
6. Any change in the ranking of parts in the system will disrupt the flow of proper action and result in disharmony and end in decay.
7. Change is largely a result of internal modifications as one part expands at the expense of other parts, inducing disequilibrium, which is then countered by strong exertions to reestablish the harmonious state.

The above propositions enunciate the fundamentals of a structural-functional mode, one usually derived from a humanistic or organic analogy, and one that would find recurrent utility in both utopian and scientific theories of society (see, for example, Plato's *Republic* [1888], Montesquieu's *The Spirit of the Laws* [1949], Adam Smith's *An*

Inquiry into the Nature and Causes of the Wealth of Nations [1937], and Spencer's *Principles of Sociology* [1900]). Of equal importance were theories regarding climate, physique, and character, which could readily be adapted to mechanistic interpretation. Finally there was the intellectual confrontation with the problem of how to accumulate knowledge – the importance of factual observation, classification, and careful control over analysis (induction and deduction) in the assignment of causes. Here Aristotle left his mark in defining cause as an actualization (entelechy) based on material (material cause), on something affecting this material (efficient cause), on the form taken in movement (formal cause), and on the end or purpose of the activity (final cause).

THE RENAISSANCE

The Greco-Roman intellectual and scientific heritage of Western civilization was largely muted under Christianity; but through the stimulus of Arabic contacts and the revival of trade, Greek humanism began to arouse fresh and sympathetic interest in man and his works, eventuating in the creative and innovative stimulus of the Renaissance. The later Renaissance also witnessed new advances in the natural sciences, especially with regard to astronomy and biology, which gradually freed scientific thought from limitations imposed by theology and Aristotelian science. Voyages of discovery and conquest brought knowledge of unrecorded peoples to challenge the traditional interpretation of "divine history." Accounts of these new lands and peoples became popular knowledge through the narratives of explorers, conquistadors, voyagers, administrators, travelers, and missionaries (see, for example, Díaz del Castillo's chronicles of 1562 [1908], Acosta's account of 1590 [1963], Oviedo's "natural history" of 1535 [1885], Landa's narrative of 1565 [1941], Dobrizhoffer's account of 1774 [1822], and the *Jesuit Relations* of 1610-1791 [Thwaites, ed., 1959]).

For exploitation of natural and human resources, practical descriptions of a population, settlements, roads, armaments, subsistence, trade, craft, religious and political leadership, and special customs are essential, whether for government, missionary, fur trader, or settler. But aside from practical advantages, personal interest in a good yarn and curiosity about the exotic also stimulated interest in descriptions of the peoples of the New World, the first area to be explored, conquered, and permanently settled in the wake of discovery since the days of the Phoenicians. Some interest in other peoples and their customs may have been generated among the Spaniards by such Italian scholars as Ciriaco de Pizzicolli and Flavio Biondo, who brought the Roman background of Italy into focus for their contemporaries (Rowe 1965; cf. Hodgen 1964).

There were other reasons for an interest in exotic peoples. In their untutored state they mirrored the golden age to which classical writers were wont to refer. Their relative simplicity and directness underscored the artificialities and sophistries of civilized life, especially those perpetrated in the name of religion, as Montaigne (1946) emphasized in 1580. With the rise of political controversy over the divine right of kings and the matter of natural rights, limited knowledge of the "savages" of the New World led to hypotheses about the natural state of man (see Hobbes 1958, Locke 1947). The important thrust of scholarly interest, however, was contributed by churchmen, eager to bring into the context of Christian history peoples to whom no reference could be found in the Bible. José de Acosta (1963), writing in 1588 and 1589, considered the inhabitants of the New World to have migrated from the Old, and enumerated various customs that linked them to the Jews. The Jesuit priest Joseph Lafitau (1774), who spent the years 1712-1717 with the Iroquois mission of Caughnawaga near Montreal, also sought to discover how the indigenous Americans were related to the ancient world and the Jews. He hoped to uncover customs of the New World inhabitants which pointed directly to ancient times and offered hints as to ways in which God had revealed himself to the ancients. In the process, as Fenton (1969) has pointed out, he described much of Iroquois life in perceptive detail and must be credited with uncovering the "classificatory" qualities of Iroquois kinship. In his vision of a "science of custom," dedicated to unraveling the relations of mankind according to Scripture, Lafitau defined more clearly than others what amounted to a "Christian ethnohistory." Similarities could always be traced back to the ancient Holy Land and the dispersions associated with the flood and Moses. Moving out from that center, migrants penetrated the vastness of the New World, carrying some ancient features unchanged while modifying others according to environment and losing some in transit across varying environmental zones. Diversity in custom thus was attributed to modification of an archetype, a process usually designated as degeneration or a falling away.

It would appear that Renaissance historians stood at the threshold of anthropology but were barred from passing the barrier to science by their concern for universal Christian history. To this end they brought a new, if not sympathetic, interest in the customs of exotic peoples. In assembling material for their comparisons in order to show relationships between the apostate savages and their ancient holy state, they began to collect facts drawn largely from the ancient world and the savage societies. To draw out similarities they compared forms—musical instruments, dress, custom, and ceremony. Christian ethnohistorians joined Acosta in deciding that the American Indians had migrated to the New World, but their reasons for this conclusion were widely different from those set forth by archaeologists and physical anthropologists of a later day, who based their conclusions on research on fossil forms, types, and hunting sites attributable to early man.

FOUNDATIONS OF SOCIAL SCIENCE AND ANTHROPOLOGY: PROGRESS AND EVOLUTION

The beginning of social science, the generalized base on which both anthropology and sociology would be erected, seems best located in the eighteenth century. Here for the first time one finds a strong desire to discriminate a natural history of the species from traditional history. One discerns a special theoretical orientation in the idea of progress, the accumulation of new facts stressing group rather than individual action and achievement, and a distinctive methodology later referred to as the "comparative method." From its beginnings early in the century, about 1725, this stage in anthropological development can be divided into two phases, the first ending about 1840 and the second around 1890. The first phase is dominated by the humanistic ideal of man's progressive advancement through reason; but after 1840, as biological evidence mounted to produce the idea of species variability and directional change through natural selection, the human sociocultural process came to be viewed as an extension of the biological process. After 1840 controversy over the biological basis for personal and group achievement also accelerated, ultimately implicating sociocultural explanation in a Lamarckian psychobiological inheritance, viewed in the fearsome context of the survival of the fittest. The rise of nationalism also strengthened the hands of those who saw civilization as the mark of biological superiority. Comte's *Positive Philosophy* (1893), the first volume of which appeared in 1830, marks the end of the intellectual stimulus of the idea of progress, while the writings of Herbert Spencer describe the high tide of a biopsychological interpretation of social and cultural phenomena.

PHASE I:
GENERAL SOCIAL SCIENCE
(*ca.* 1725-1840)

The idea of progress, with its vision of man realizing the full potential of his human nature as he creates civilized society, represented a flowering of a combined humanistic and scientific impulse that began during the Renaissance. During the eighteenth century there was a widespread conviction that reason, the human faculty, was the key to human nature, and that man stood at the threshold of a new millennium. He was on the eve of a new realization of self, to be perfected through new social arrangements. The basic thrust of the idea of a progressive advancement in human knowledge was carried by the French, receiving its early formulation at the hands of Fontenelle in 1688 (Bury 1920). The scientific and technological revolutions of the eighteenth century, and the social and political revolutions that accompanied other widespread changes accumulating beneath the surface of society, aided in the popular diffusion of the idea. The upgrading of man and reason resulted in a highly critical review of religion and in the growth of secularism. But though religion might be attacked for its sophistries and the chain of superstition by which it bound the mind of man, advocates of bald materialism were not very common except in France, where the struggle against *l'infâme,* as Voltaire called the ecclesiastical polity of the *ancien régime*, was felt more intensely than in England or in Germany (Holbach 1853, Condorcet 1955). But even in France it was not unusual to concede that religion was essential to human nature and development. Through logic, the human mind would create a natural religion that would grasp the true meaning of divinity and supplant the artificial and gross superstition of organized priestly religions. The scientific orientation of the Age of Reason promoted a view of the universe wherein "natural law" prevailed, and where man was just as subject to these laws as all other things in the universe, inorganic and organic. Behind the ordered universe run by natural law was Deity, the supreme mechanic.

Natural Law

Natural law is a necessary corollary for the inevitable advancement and perfectability of mankind. The processes of the human mind likewise must be subject to natural law. If man is to use his mind as the prime instrument for his advancement, then it follows that humans everywhere have the same potential, even though they may differ in their ideological achievements. In short, human nature everywhere must be the same. It is capable of discriminating perceptions and ordering them by logic, and mankind possesses the impulse to improve, to share a life rooted in moral sentiments, to respond to exemplary behavior, and to seek refinements in aesthetic and intellectual experience. All mankind shares social tendencies and is sensitive to the rewards conveyed through social life regulated by law, competition, and individualized freedom of property and of choice (so long as freedom is without detriment to others and to society as a whole). Such were the important basic assumptions about the nature of the world and of man that regulated the thoughts of those who were studying the development of the human mind. The significance of these assumptions and the supportive role of science can be grasped from the impassioned plea of Condorcet in 1795 (1955:193):

If man can, with almost complete assurance, predict phenomena when he knows their laws, and if, even when he does not, he can still, with great expectation of success, forecast the future on the basis of his experience of the past, why, then, should it be regarded as a fantastic undertaking to sketch, with some pretence to truth, the future destiny of man on the basis of his history? The sole foundation for belief in the natural sciences is this idea, that the general laws directing the phenomena of the universe, known or unknown, are necessary and constant. Why should this principle be any less true for the development of the intellectual and moral faculties of man than for the other operations of nature?

The Idea of Progress

A focus on ideas directed more attention to group achievements than to the doings of individual kings, heroes, and scheming blackguards of traditional history. Now there was a call to write a "people's history," as it were, depending not on the distorted accounts of historians, but on nature's scripture. Voltaire (1926), in *The Age of Louis XIV,* which appeared in 1752, intended to present neither a biography of the king nor the annals of his reign, but a "history of the human mind," in which

developments in the arts and sciences held an important status along with political history. In France, though Rousseau (1962) questioned the correlation between civilization and progress in 1755, belief in progress as realized in a civilized state prevailed. In 1750 Turgot produced *Two Discourses on Universal History* (Teggart 1960), in which he held forth on the benefits of Christianity and the progress of the human mind. The jurist Goguet (1775) pursued his interest *On the Origin of Laws, Arts, and Sciences, and Their Progress Among the Most Ancient Nations* (Phoenicia, Egypt, Rome, Greece, etc.), and determined that mankind had been launched on its metallurgical career by agriculturists working with the softer and more malleable ores of silver, gold, and copper. Before using metals, mankind used stones for tools. In 1784 the German cleric Herder (1952) described man in a natural and cosmic context and traced man's course to civilization to an inbuilt creative force designed to fulfill the divine plan. A professor of philosophy at Göttingen, Christoph Meiners, in 1785 published his *Foundations for the History of Mankind,* outlining the materials that should be assembled for a study of *Völkerkunde* (literally, "people's study" or ethnology).

In Scotland a number of philosophically and legally trained moralists also sought to define a "natural science of mankind" within the framework of progress (David Hume, Adam Ferguson, Adam Smith, William Robertson, James Millar, Henry Home or Lord Kames, and James Burnett or Lord Monboddo). Ferguson (1789), Robertson (1822), Millar (1806), Lord Kames (1761, 1779), and Lord Monboddo (1779-1799) dedicated themselves more than Hume or Smith to demonstrating the advance to civilization. Nonetheless, Hume (1854) did publish an essay " . . . of the Rise and Progress of the Arts and Sciences" in 1742 and a book on the *Natural History of Religion* in 1757. In his economic theory Adam Smith (1937), according to Dugald Stewart (1858:37), attempted

to illustrate the provisions made by nature in the principles of the human mind, and in the circumstances of man's external situation, for a gradual and progressive augmentation in the means of national wealth; and to demonstrate that the most effectual plan for advancing a people to greatness, is to maintain that order of things which nature has pointed out; by allowing every man, as long as he observes the rules of justice, to pursue his own interests in his own way, and to bring both his industry and his capital into the freest competition with those of his fellow-citizens.

The Comparative Method

The nature of human progress developed by the Scottish natural historians found them in essential agreement with their continental colleagues. They pictured the savage as a representative of an early stage in the history of mankind and succeeded in formulating a methodological statement of what later would be termed the comparative method. With regard to his continuity of human development, Ferguson (1789:13-14) noted how

the latest efforts of human invention are but a continuation of certain devices which were practiced in the ancient ages of the world, and in the rudest stage of mankind. What the savage projects, or observes, in the forest, are the steps which led nations, more advanced, from the architecture of the cottage to that of the palace, and conducted the human mind from the perceptions of sense to the general conclusions of science ... to a progress in which the savage, as well as the philosopher, is engaged; in which they have made different advances, but in which their ends are the same.

Savages in their rudimentary hunting state were everywhere the same in mode of life and in character. Looking backward, according to Ferguson (1789:6-7),

the Romans might have found an image of their own ancestors in the representations they have given of ours. . . . It is in their present [savage] condition, that we are to behold, as in a mirror, the features of our own progenitors; and from thence we are to draw our conclusions with respect to the influence of the situation. What should distinguish a German or a Briton, in the habits of his mind or his body, in his manners or apprehensions, from an American [Indian], who, like him, with his bow and his dart, is left to traverse the forest; and in a like severe or variable climate is obliged to subsist by the chace [*sic*]?

If contemporary people, according to their respective states of development, could serve as stand-ins for the past of more advanced historic peoples, the task was clear. One had to assemble factual data that would give testimony to this advancement, drawing upon the vast storehouse of mankind. This would mean, as Lord Kames (1761:22-23) pointed out, that, as in the instance of

tracing the [natural] history of criminal law, we must not hope that all its steps and changes can be drawn from the archives of any one nation. In fact many steps were taken, and many changes made, before archives were kept, and even before writing was a common art. We must be satisfied with collecting the facts and circumstances as they may be gathered from the laws of different countries; and if these put together make a regular system of causes and effects, we may rationally conclude that the progress has been the same among all nations, in the capital circumstances at least; for accidents, or the singular nature of a people, or of a government, will always produce some peculiarities.

In this statement Kames outlines the essence of what later nineteenth-century developmentalists would call the comparative method. Such a procedure was possible if mankind were assumed to be psychologically everywhere alike and of equal potential. What created differences between savages, barbarians, and the polished nations were the circumstances of life; hence the crucial significance of society in providing the proper stimulus for human advancement. Society makes the man, and for those who believed in progress by reason, education held an important place in the transformation of man.

As the century drew to a close, the foundations for researching the development of man in his social setting, ideas, and customs or institutions had been laid. The "natural science of the species," to use Kames's phrase, had been discriminated from traditional history with its sordid accounts of greed, rivalry, brutality, and chicanery. In its place would be substituted the clear and triumphant march of human reason and morality. Facts would be drawn from custom, legal practices, principles of government. For the vagaries of individual action would be substituted the regularities of a human nature shared by all mankind. Natural law governed mankind, but this did not mean that men and animals were subject to the same laws. On the contrary, man was supra-organic and the proud possessor of that unparalleled human faculty. Thanks to the uniform processes of the human mind, which moved from concrete representations to the abstract, it would be possible to construct the chain of logic directing human advancement from a rude and simple beginning to a complex and refined state. Here the method outlined by Kames, the comparative method of a later day, would serve admirably.

The Science of Man

When all these developments are added together, it is evident that progressivists in the eighteenth century fulfilled basic requirements for the presence of a new discipline: (1) special-problem subject matter, (2) theory (assumptions relating to progress and natural law), (3) special kinds of facts (customs, ideas, principles), and (4) unique method (comparative method). The whole would produce new kinds of knowledge, generalizations concerning the origins and development of institutions—technology, family, law, morality, political organization, religion, and the fine arts—rather than a history of nations and "great men." The new knowledge would be scientific, since it was rooted not in the accidents of history but in the regularities that defined man's irreversible course from savagery to barbarism and then to civilization.

Such was the vision of a science of man that inspired humanists and evolutionists alike for upward of 175 years, from about 1725 to 1890. Neither savage nor barbarian would hold a central place in this study. To that estate belonged civilization, the harbinger of man's future. Nonetheless, this generalized social science created a basis for including savage and barbarian contributions in the development of mankind, a purpose for researching their modes of life to determine origins, rather than seeing them as degenerate descendants of the sons of Noah. While the savage and his life could never be preferred, he could be seen more clearly than before for what he was and had been in the life of mankind. Though running a laggard's race, and childlike in his mental abilities and control of feelings, the contemporary savage, with the tutelage of the educated, could become a mature, civilized man. After Darwin, the biologically informed evolutionists would no longer grant this capability to the savage; for, being less evolved, he would be poorly formed for civilization and incapable of meeting its challenges.

Related Findings

The years between general acceptance of the new science of mankind in the last quarter of the eighteenth century and the termination of this preliminary thrust about 1840 were filled with momentous social and political events, and findings in related fields that bore directly on the development of a science dedicated to the study of primitive man and his works.

Systematic Classification. In biology and zoology, a basis for showing structural relationships had been achieved through systematic classification under the leadership of Swedish-born Karl Linnaeus. Hewing strictly to taxonomic principles, Linnaeus incorporated man among the primates. By the last quarter of the eighteenth century Johann Blumenbach (1865) had classified man into five types, using crania collected from distant regions as well as paintings of human types. However, he separated man from his primate relatives.

Geological Stratification. In geology William Smith (1815), writing in 1794, and later Georges Cuvier and Alexandre de Brongniart (1811) worked out the principles of stratification with the aid of fossil molluscs. In his travels through Siberia in the seventies, Peter Simon Pallas stirred the scientific imagination with his account of extinct elephantine forms; and Cuvier, working with the bones of fossil amphibians and mammals, succeeded in developing basic principles for restoring the skeletons of these long-gone life forms.

Extinction and Succession of Life Forms. By 1833 Sir Charles Lyell (1830-1832) had published the first charting of geological epochs and life eras from the Cenozoic, a task that would be completed in 1874. The possibility that extinct forms of man might have lived in Europe in association with extinct mammoths and rhinoceroses and cave bears appealed to the imaginative minds of a postal clerk, J. Boucher de Perthes (1864), the priest J. MacEnery (1859), and the surgeon P. C. Schmerling (1833-1834), who searched caves and gravel pits for the common association of tools and the remains of extinct humans and animals. That man, like earth, may have altered through uniform processes connecting one stage with the next also excited the minds of some zoologists, especially Lamarck, who proposed change through environmental modification of inheritance (acquired characteristics). Cuvier, however, accepting a lead from Charles Bonnet, stoutly countered transmutation with catastrophism. Species were ever fixed through preformation, and extinction of forms was due to great regional or widespread cataclysms. The destruction of life, however, was not complete, and forms surviving in secluded areas would enter the devastated areas, initiating new sequences with their different shapes. Apparent discontinuities in the succession of life forms provided the rationale for catastrophism.

Evolution. In England, however, Sir Charles Lyell had demonstrated through his percentages that there was a relative continuity of life forms during the Cenozoic, and it was there that consensual interest eventuated in the proof for evolution at the hands of Darwin (1936), whose *Origin of Species* appeared in 1859. The establishment of a technological sequence, beginning with stone and followed by bronze and then iron, provided a parallel to biological evolution (Thomsen 1848, Nilsson 1868; cf. Lubbock 1865).

Discovery of Early Tools. The new-won principles of classification, the principle of geological stratification, acceptance of the extinction and succession of life forms, and the emergent theory of evolution all conspired to alter perspective on the world and its life, including man. Added to this were the rude tools belonging to a very remote period to which John Frere (Heizer 1962) had called attention in 1797, the significance of which would not be realized until 1859 (Lyell 1863), when British geologists concurred that roughhewn hand axes had been found in association with the bones of extinct mammals.

Philology and Folklore. Developments in philology and in folklore also contributed to the broadening of the disciplinary bases converging on the study of man. The Danish and German philologists Rasmus Rask (1818), Franz Bopp (1816), and Jakob Grimm (1837) assembled proofs for the historical connection of Sanskrit, Greek, Latin, Celtic, Germanic, and Gothic, confirming the earlier statement of Sir William Jones (1969), who declared in 1786 that these languages were interrelated. Philology introduced a new tool for showing historical relations, and through the study of language, as Wilhelm von Humboldt pointed out, one could observe the processes of human thought. Etymological analysis of mythologic forms also led to the unmasking of the great nature gods of storm, sun, earth, wind, and water, and to the demonstration, as the Grimm brothers (Grimm 1837) thought at the time, that German divinities were Greek and Roman nature gods in linguistic disguise.

PHASE 2: EVOLUTIONISM
(*ca.* 1840-1890)

It was the differentiation of fields like geology, paleontology, philology, folklore, archaeology, and physical anthropology that was largely responsible for drawing together those who had a more general interest in the variety of mankind and acceptance of a common human destiny (Tax 1955). This can be seen partially in the founding of ethnological societies, first in Paris (1839), then in London (1841) and New York (1842). The ethnological science, as it was now conceived, would trace historic relations by comparison of human physiques, languages, and customs while testing for similarities and differences of intellectual and moral character. This was a time when racial differences were brought to the forefront of controversy by the issue of slavery and when a burgeoning nationalism fed upon ethnic origins and the heroic legends of folk literature. It was the perfect time for *The Ring of the Niebelungen,* which Wagner re-created in musical drama.

The strength of the current ran heavily to the study of man as a physical-psychological being, and this biological emphasis tended to draw those members of the ethnological societies experienced in medicine and anatomy. Hence the formation of "anthropological" societies (Paris, 1859; London, 1863), and the call for a new science of man, an anthropological science that would probe deeply into his past. Paul Broca, anatomist and physical anthropologist, speaking to the Anthropological Society of Paris in 1862, declared:

To describe and classify the actual races, point out their analogies and differences, to study their aptitudes and manners, to determine their filiation by blood and language, is no doubt to run over much ground in the field of anthropology; but there remain higher and more general questions. All the human races, in spite of their diversity, form a great whole, a great harmonic group, and it is important to examine the group in its *ensemble*, to determine its position in the series of beings, its relations with other groups of nature, its common character, whether in the anatomical and physiological, or in the intellectual order. It is not less necessary to study the laws which preside in maintaining or changing these characters. . . . . Finally, in a more elevated sphere, and without venturing to attain the regions which conceal the problem of origin (a fascinating and, perhaps, insoluble problem), our science eagerly searches for the first traces of man's appearance on earth, it studies the most ancient remains of his industry, and gradually descending from incalculably remote epochs towards the historical period, it follows humanity in its slow evolution, in the successive stages of its progress, in its inventions, in its struggles with the organic world, and its conquests over nature. . . . [Cited in Tax 1955:318; cf. Waitz 1863, Huxley 1896.]

Early Anthropological Societies

About the time that Darwinian evolutionary theory burst upon the world, there was a growing feeling that zoology, anatomy, physiology, philology, paleontology, archaeology, and geology were now well enough advanced to support a general science of man. The strain toward unity consolidated physical anthropology and prehistory at an international congress held in Switzerland in 1866. In England the ethnological society and the anthropological society joined hands in 1871 to form the Royal Anthropological Institute of Great Britain and Ireland, following by two years the founding in Berlin of a Society for Anthropology, Ethnology, and Prehistory through the cooperation of Adolf Bastian, ethnologist, and Rudolf Virchow, pathologist and anthropometrist. The Anthropological Society of Washington, established in 1879, laid broad claims to the human domain, but it was not until 1902 that the American Anthropological Society, a national organization, was founded. In the meantime, the American Society for the Advancement of Science accorded anthropology a place in Section H in 1882.

"Dynamic" Sociology

Other striking efforts to delineate a comprehensive study of man departed from concepts of the social and cultural. Both Comte (1893), whose six-volume *Course of Positive Philosophy* appeared in France from 1830 to 1842, and Spencer (1857, 1862, 1900) developed systematic treatises in which three orders of reality were discriminated, the "inorganic," "organic," and "super-organic," and related the science of society, or sociology, to the latter. Both again divided their sociologies into "static" and "dynamic" varieties. The former studied the structural relations of society, while the latter viewed society in change. Curiously, both decided that dynamic sociology was to be preferred, for in Spencer's words (1874:iv), "The thing it really concerns us to know is, the natural history of society." To accomplish this purpose would require knowledge of special social facts—institutions, conduct of daily life, technical, educational, and aesthetic accomplishments, morality, laws, habits, and customs regulating relations between classes. Sociology, then, was raised on facts different from history, and in final analysis they were the intrinsic facts of merit. In Spencer's view (1874:iv), "the highest office which the historian can discharge is that of so narrating the lives of nations as to furnish materials for a Comparative Sociology, and for the subsequent determination of the ultimate laws to which social phenomena conform." For this social development or evolution that Comte and Spencer hoped to chart, ideas would supply the cutting edge of change.

The Science of Culture

Taking his cue from Gustav Klemm's (1843-1851) continued used of the German word *Kultur,* Tylor (1874,1:1) determined that what in 1881 he called anthropology (1937) should be a "science of culture":

Culture or Civilization, taken in its wide ethnographic sense, is that complex whole which includes knowledge, belief, art, morals, law, custom, and any other capabilities and habits acquired by man as a member of society. The condition of culture among the various societies of mankind, insofar as it is capable of being investigated on general principles, is a subject apt for the study of laws of human thought and action. On the one hand, the uniformity which so largely pervades civilization may be ascribed, in great measure, to the uniform action of uniform causes; while on the other hand its various grades may be regarded as stages of development or evolution, each the outcome of previous history, and about to do its proper part in shaping the history of the future. To the investigation of these two great principles in several departments of ethnography, with special consideration of the civilization of the lower tribes as related to the civilization of the higher nations, the present volumes are dedicated.

Tylor would construct the history of mankind according to the logic of the human mind. Owing to the uniformity of mental processes throughout the human family, one would be able to trace a rather uniform course from savagery to barbarism to civilization. The science of culture would not be history in the usual sense, for Tylor intended to write "not [the history] of tribes or nations, but of the condition of knowledge, religion, art, custom, and the like among them" (1874,1:5). Much of his source material could not be found in historic documents, but must be drawn from narratives produced by missionaries, explorers, travelers, traders and others who had lived among the "rude peoples."

Similarities of Progressivists and Evolutionists

Like Comte and Spencer, Tylor shared with eighteenth-century natural historians a desire to assemble materials for interpretation without himself being inclined to proceed into the field. The aim was synthesis, not collection. And there are other similarities linking eighteenth-century progressivists with the self-styled sociologists and cultural ethnographers or anthropologists of the later nineteenth century:

Progress. There was the urgent need to develop a discipline that would chart man's progress as a rational and moral being.

Natural Law. There was common insistence that the universe was governed by natural laws, and that man was not excluded from the operations of these laws, thereby assuring uniformities in development.

Reason. There was the consensus that man's supreme faculty, reason, distinguished him from the rest of nature and removed him from the brutish processes to which animals were subject. Darwinian evolution, it is true, exerted an intellectual influence that viewed man both in body and in mind as related to the higher apes and primates. Indeed, Huxley (1896) went to some pains in 1863 to disprove alleged structural differences between the human brain and that of primates, supporting Darwin's contention that man shared certain instincts, emotional responses, and intellectual reasoning processes with animals, differing only in point of degree. Though at the "very summit of the organic scale," Darwin (1936:920) reminds us, "man still bears in his bodily frame the indelible stamp of his lowly origin." In placing man among the primates, Linnaeus had been equally explicit about his conviction that there was little separating "the most foolish ape . . . from the wisest man" (cited in 1785 by Blumenbach [1865:163-64]. Lord Monboddo (Lovejoy 1933:289), back in the eighteenth century, also had denied any differences other than those of degree between man and other animals. "There is no *natural* difference between our minds and theirs and the superiority we have over them is adventitious. ..." But up to the time of Darwin, Blumenbach's assignment of man to a distinct *bimanous order* had prevailed, supporting with physical structure the contention that a human faculty separated man from animals. Man, Blumenbach had declared, was a more generalized creature, ill equipped to answer to the instincts commanding animal behavior. Now, after Darwin, distinction of the social and cultural as products of the human mind again would hold a barrier between man and animals. One could ascribe a social instinct to animals and insects, but what happens to degrees of similarity if, as Spencer (1900) argued in 1876, man's sociality advanced to new heights through incorporating the effects of social experience into human inheritance? Intellectual and moral capacities would increase likewise through phyletic inheritance. In the course of evolution the mind, both as organ and as process, advanced to new levels of complexity through differentiation of functions.

Spencer's mechanisms were Lamarckian, in as much as the newly won complexity was acquired as a result of activity and then became a base for new improvements by being incorporated into inheritance. His position drew substance from Ernst Heinrich Haeckel's recapitulation theory. Darwin himself could be quoted in support of the process of change through acquired modifications. Only as the theory of acquired characteristics lost ground through the genetic researches of August Weismann, Gregor Mendel, and Thomas Hunt Morgan would this theory relating body and mind to social

processes be dropped for more certain channels of investigation. If man's accelerated pace had drawn him ahead of his animal relations, it made little difference whether one admitted or denied his clear structural connection to animals, or whether one admitted to transmutation of the species or held that man from the start was qualitatively different from animals. The effect was the same. There came a point where the continuity in degree seemed to crash a real barrier of difference. The gap between animal and man at the intellectual and moral level was so vast, Huxley admitted (1896:152, 155-56), that

whether *from* them or not, he [man] is assuredly not *of* them. . . . Our reverence for the nobility of manhood will not be lessened by the knowledge that Man is, in substance and in structure, one with the brutes; for, he alone possesses the marvellous endowment of intelligible and rational speech, whereby, in the secular period of his existence, he has slowly accumulated and organised the experience which is almost wholly lost with the cessation of every individual life in other animals; so that, now, he stands raised upon it as on a mountain top far above the level of his humble fellows, and transfigured from his grosser nature by reflecting, here and there, a ray from the infinite source of truth.

If anyone succeeded in anchoring psychological and social processes to biological processes, the credit must go to Spencer. Social evolution advanced through the hard winnowing of natural selection. Only the fittest survived in consequence of their superiority in body, mind, and the organization of society, and Spencer expected the less evolved savages to perish at every confrontation with civilization. They just were not equipped bodily and psychologically to cope with a civilized mode of life; only evolution would bring this about (Spencer 1897:258; cf. Bagehot 1875). Spencer's influence pervaded both the continent and the New World, stimulating Lippert (1931) in 1886, Letourneau (1881), and Ward (1883). However, as the humanistic progressivists of the eighteenth century, along with Comte (1893) and Bastian (see Lowie 1937:35-36), had demonstrated, belief in the fixity of the human species did not contradict a developmental process in human intellectual, moral, social, and cultural status. The cumulation of culture following the uniform processes of the mind could serve the advancement of mankind just as readily as any process of biological inheritance, once the status *Homo sapiens* had been attained.

Sociology vs. Traditional History. Both eighteenth-century progressivists and nineteenth-century evolutionists felt the need to discriminate their natural history, sociology, or science of culture from traditional history.

Sociology as an Aid to Man. Under the inspiration of advancement according to natural law, progressivists and evolutionists shared the idea that the new science could and should be applied in the interests of mankind. In sociology, as in the science of culture (Tylor 1874,1:159), ". . . we are to study savages and old nations to learn the laws that under new circumstances are working for good or ill in our own development." There was this difference in theory, if not in practice, between humanistic progressivists and the biologically oriented evolutionists: human advancement under biological evolution was not inevitable. The key to measurement was natural law. Whatever was natural was right and correct; whatever violated this naturalness was deemed artificial. If Spencer thundered at legislation that violated natural selection by extending protective welfare, so Adam Smith challenged the artificial restraints of trade that held captive the creativity engendered by free competition. Thus Smith wrote in 1776 (1937:508):

The natural effort of every individual to better his own condition when suffered to exert itself with freedom and security, is so powerful a principle, that it is alone, and without any assistance, not only capable of carrying on the society to wealth and prosperity, but of surmounting a hundred impertinent obstructions with which the folly of human laws too often incumbers its operations; though the effect of these obstructions is always more or less either to encroach upon its freedom, or to diminish its security.

At every turn the natural would prevail, as it must, if it be law.

The Perfectability of Man. By and large, progressivists and evolutionists agreed that man's existence was a purposive realization of self. The common vision was a perfected humanity dwelling in regulated and law-abiding societies, where individuals were relatively free to pursue their own ends. Beyond the oppressive military society that continuously threatened to hurl man back into barbarism, Spencer discerned the industrial type of society where voluntary cooperation prevailed in the interests of all, including the relations of nations. But for Spencer, the supreme architect of social evolution, the course of development was "not linear but divergent and re-divergent" (1900, 3:331). Moreover, the model of natural selection made it apparent that not all divergent variations were adaptively functional. Rare were the occasions when "a new combination of factors produced . . . a step in social evolution"; but when a new social type did appear, it possessed a drive to expand, and in extending itself the "less-evolved societies" would be forced into "unfavourable habitats . . . [with resultant] decrease of size, or decay of structure, or both" (1900,1:96-97).

Spencer's conception of structure as an energy system straining between integration and dissolution also influenced his charge that the evolutionary process was not inevitably purposeful and unilinear. When he gave examples, however, it was evident that his exceptions were species or varieties—empires or societies that had declined. But when addressing himself to mankind as a genus, he could trace the ideological steps in good unilinear fashion. Religion must begin with ghost theory and move on to clearer and progressive conceptions of spiritual beings "until in developed mythologies, they are specifically, and even individually, distinguished by attributes precisely stated" (Spencer 1900,1:434). The evolutionary mode also moved from the simple to the complex, from the generalized to the individuated, and when it came to the logic of ideas, Spencer was as much inclined as others to describe a direct chain of logical advancement.

The Comparative Method. Developmentalists in both the eighteenth and nineteenth centuries, whether progressivists or evolutionists, applied the comparative method in order to chart the general logic by which human institutions had taken their origin and growth from savagery to civilization.

Differences Between Progressivists and Evolutionists

There were, however, some rather striking differences and points of emphasis between the progressivist and evolutionist orientations:

Historical vs. Prehistorical Orientations. Definitions of anthropology after mid-century concentrated the discipline's role in the early history of mankind. Peoples outside the pale of civilization came to focus anthropological interest.

Discoveries of fossil men (Neanderthal in 1856, Cro-Magnon in 1868) and the opening of the vast perspective of the Paleolithic tool development during the Pleistocene (Lyell 1863, Breuil 1912, Lubbock 1865, Mortillet 1872) aided in concentrating attention on primitive man.

Race and Culture. The influence of biological evolution led to the merging of race and culture, with emphasis on differences in the capacities of races. Primitive man was cast as less evolved, as the alleged lesser size of his brain case demonstrated. Whereas progressivists of the eighteenth century had used the term "childlike" as a simile when referring to the rudimentary culture, intellectual capabilities, and character of savages, evolutionists were inclined to turn the simile into biological reality. The savage was a child-man as it were, and he would never surrender this quality except through the process of natural selection. Savages thus were lost to the mainstream of biological and cultural development. They were like living fossils, and if there were any hope in raising them from their immediate condition, it would lie in race mixture. In 1853 Gobineau (1915; see also Galton 1962, Nott and Gliddon 1857, Chamberlain 1912) argued, however, that mixture diluted the bloodline of the superior, and turned them into a decline. Quatrefages (1879), on the other hand, pointed out that all the great civilizations were products of racially mixed peoples. At any rate, education could not be trusted to improve the lot of the savage, because, as Spencer (1897; see also Letourneau 1881, Réclus 1891, Hartland 1909) and others argued, his mental capacities seemed to be fixed at puberty, which was not the case among the advanced races. The notion that primitive man was childlike in his mental and emotional capacities made its impression on psychiatry in Freud's *Totem and Taboo* (1918), where one also finds acceptance of phyletic inheritance (see also Jung 1916). Evolutionism thus introduced a less optimistic note for the improvement of uncivilized peoples, for their inferiorities could be eradicated only through alteration in their biology, tempered, like steel, through natural selection. In this view of race and culture, the "white man's burden" held real significance. The civilized, in their natural superiority, must serve as custodians not only of civilization, but of the uncivilized.

Documentation and Data. Evolutionists held clear advantages in the documentation of knowledge that accompanied the specialized differentiation of scientific fields. This is what permitted the assembly of partial disciplines, as it were, to form anthropology, drawing enthusiasts together at professional meetings and furnishing through publication a means for exchanging ideas and putting new data on record. The progress of anthropology can be recognized in the appointment of E. B. Tylor in 1884 as reader in anthropology at Oxford, hailing the dawn of a new professional, the anthropologist.

The fresh image of anthropology as a science dealing with primitive culture undoubtedly aided in projecting a scientific personality for the discipline. Demonstrating that anthropology also could extend mathematical controls to its data, Tylor (1889) applied statistical probability association to residence and avoidance practices and other features. There also was the task of collection of primary data. Lewis H. Morgan, who knew the Iroquois with some intimacy, was alerted to the fact that the mode of life of these contemporary ancestors had all but passed into history. The urgency of rescuing the primitive substance before it dissolved under the hard blows of civilization was a point stressed by Morgan (1877), and one that would be repeated by every generation of anthropologists. This would call for fieldwork. But Morgan's *League of the Iroquois* (1954), first published in 1851 and the first ethnography to appear, was not the result of any inspiration to engage in the scientific task of collecting data at firsthand. Morgan was led to his Iroquois researches because of a youthful romantic interest in these Indians who were his neighbors in central New York, and because he wished to sustain their cause against a land company that was seeking to dispossess them. In the Cambridge Expedition to the Torres Straits (1898), headed by A. C. Haddon, zoologist turned anthropologist, the natural science ideal of field collection did hold an important place. Yet field investigation was hardly the leitmotiv of evolutionary ethnology, even though in archaeology and in human paleontology, as in physical anthropology, the source for data could be found nowhere but in the field. The image of the anthropologist as fieldworker belonged to the next stage in development.

Distinctive Contributions of Developmentalists

To progressivists belongs the credit for sketching the basis for a general social science that later evolutionists would formulate as a science of man, rooted essentially in physical anthropology, ethnology, and prehistory, with linkages to philology and folklore. It is in the second phase that the core vocabulary of anthropometry, human paleontology, prehistory, and ethnology was formulated. For the latter subfield McLennan (1865) coined the terms "exogamy" and "endogamy," and Morgan (1871) detailed "descriptive" and "classificatory" systems of consanguinity. Drawing upon Greek and Latin social and legal usage, the "gens" as a group of "agnates" was distinguished from a female descent group, the "clan"–distinctions that no longer hold. Other terms that came into frequent usage were patrilineal, matrilineal, patriarchy, matriarchy, stem family, marriage class, patrilocal, matrilocal, phratry, animism, totemism, and survival, among others. To these developmentalists also belong the first efforts to conceptualize the social or cultural as a distinct level of reality, a conceptualization that would provide the substance for a science of society or culture. There was, however, no clear distinction of the social vis-à-vis the cultural, and both sociologists and culturalists devoted themselves to the same problem: uncovering the psychological origins of ideas by which mankind organized the natural and social world of experience.

When they turned to the problem of the origin and development of human institutions, later developmentalists presented a more differentiated and controversial set of theories than are to be found among the eighteenth-century progressivists. A shared psychological materialism linked the two centuries, and both emphasized summative principles (for example, logical progress of the human mind); but there are alternative principles for interpretation. Bachofen (1861), for example, delineated an opposition between male and female principles, associating each with a distinct mode of life, social organization, and philosophy, and offered evidence from the classic civilizations that a matriarchal society had preceded the patriarchal one so well known through the Romans. The drama of human cultural development thus was marked by conflict between light and darkness, between thought and feeling, and between sky and earth, epitomized by the male and female principles. But before either of these organized states, mankind had lived in a state of promiscuity.

Marriage and the Family. Ten years after publication of Bachofen's *Das Mutterrecht*, Morgan (1871) published a landmark study of kinship entitled *Systems of Consanguinity and Affinity of the Human Family.* Arguing from the classificatory terms of relationship gathered among 139 tribes throughout the world, Morgan inferred a direct connection between relationship terms and social organization, notably type of family and marriage rules. However, it was marriage that shaped the family, which then determined the terms of relationship, and not vice versa. Morgan found that he could organize his sets of terms in a series that moved from terms that included whole categories of kin to a terminological system with narrow and specific definitions. Thus he distinguished three major kinship systems, beginning with the most general, the Malayan, Turanian/Ganowanian, and Aryan. The Malayan must be the earliest, he concluded, since ego called all his cousins brothers or sisters. These cousins obviously must be the children of the paternal generation, all of whom were called father or mother. Now this paternal generation must be composed of marriage partners who were real and classificatory brothers and sisters; hence his conclusion that the first family arrangement, the consanguine family, must have been based on a modified promiscuity, uniting a set of brothers to a set of sisters as communal spouses. Before the consanguine arrangement, outright promiscuity prevailed. The system of marriage classes among the Australians (e.g., Kamilaroi) was a suggestive if not duplicate witness to this system of communal marriage and terminology. Subsequent marriage systems arose as mankind moved toward the "monogamian" family, with its descriptive Aryan terminological system. With the emergence of the clan in the upper status of savagery and its role in regulating marriage, the range of membership in the consanguine family was further restricted. Considerations of property had greatly aided the rise of the monogamian family, for descriptive terms aided in denoting heritors, and wealth used in the acquisition of brides carried a contractual agreement of chastity. With the amassing of wealth in the later period of barbarism came the transition from female to male descent as agnates collected to inherit their shares.

Primitive Promiscuity. In supporting primitive promiscuity in the wake of Bachofen, Morgan had resuscitated an old classical theory, but for different reasons and with fresh and challenging evidence. Eighteenth-century progressivists had rejected promiscuity as an original family state, pointing to a natural tendency toward pairing, reinforced by difficulties in supporting more than a simple family with the rudimentary techniques of those times (Robertson 1822, Ferguson 1789, Herder 1952, Goguet 1775). The description of the role of property in agnation and in promoting chastity through bride purchase had been sketched by Millar (1806) and Maine (1861).

The Patriarchal Family. In *Ancient Law,* representing legal researches inspired by a stay in India, Maine offered the thesis, contradictory to Bachofen's, that a patriarchal type of family had been the cell with which Aryan and Semitic social history had begun. Maine argued that male dominance would lead to a patriarchal arrangement, with women being excluded from property and descent rights.

The Matriarchal Family. Maine was contradicted by another lawyer, John F. McLennan (1865), who argued that under a condition of primitive promiscuity, the mother alone would be visibly attached to her children, and hence the concept of ancestress and the principle of descent would inhere in her. From this relation of mother to child would arise a concept of descent through the female bloodline, or matrilineal descent. McLennan visualized the earliest social unit as a local horde (stock) united by a common concern for food, protection, and sexual interests. At the time there was no idea of relationship, and promiscuity reigned until the idea of maternal descent was achieved.

Exogamy and Endogamy. Out of this ambiguous and communal stock came some rather signal developments. Living in a state of constant raid and counterraid, the group was held together by a concern for mutual safety and food; for pervasive hostility was so great that food sufficient to the group members' needs could not be gained. Hence they practiced female infanticide, and then found themselves forced to capture brides from another group. In time this practice became a rule, exogamy, to be applied first to the female and later to the male bloodlines. Endogamy, marriage within the group, was a practice of proud warrior castes, but as their supply of nonrelated spouses came to be exhausted, they too were forced into the exogamous practice by way of bride capture (McLennan, 1865).

Property and the Family. Theories about the origin and development of the family illustrate the limited possibilities of explanation. One could begin, as eighteenth-century progressivists preferred, with a biological unit, and see it as gradually enlarging by retaining the children, usually males and their spouses, by virtue of economic interest. Or, as in the instance of Morgan and McLennan, one could begin not with individual units (biological families), but with a community, and trace the gradual differentiation of the family from this generalized base. Both processes, additive and differentiative, could operate at different times, as Spencer (1862) seemed to recognize (but without modifying his definition of evolutionary development: from an unorganized homogeneity to a differentiated and organized heterogeneity). As far as the stimulus for change in family organization was concerned, agreement was general that wealth promoted a patrilineal organization with associated bride contract and the rise of a new sexual morality requiring chastity. Wealth through inheritance and private ownership was also the catalyst for individualization, giving rise to the monogamous family by cracking the ancient jurisdiction of kin. Unlike Rousseau, developmentalists were inclined to see private property not as a crime against humanity, but as the prime instrument in freeing the individual from communal and patriarchal family bounds and guaranteeing personal rights and liberties. At the end of *Ancient Society* (1877) Morgan cautioned that man could not realize himself through property alone, and looked for a restoration of liberties associated with the ancient gens organization. In 1884, drawing upon Morgan, Marx and Engels (Engels 1942) inserted primitive communism into their theory of economic determinism to show how control over the means of production had been unnaturally distorted by capitalistic enterprise.

The Individual and the Group. The problem of the relationship of the individual to his fellows in society and to the regulations imposed through custom, law, religious sanctions, and state organization was ever prominent in the developmentalists' speculations about human advancement. Early society came to be defined by evolutionists as a communal community in which individual freedom was severely restricted by custom and obligations to kin. Indeed, "consanguinity or kinship," as Maine (1875:64-65) pointed out, had determined citizenship in these early societies. "The most profound difference between modern and ancient organization," observed Vinogradoff (1920, 1: 299), a student of ancient legal systems, "consists in the fact that modern society starts from individuals and adjusts itself primarily to the claims of the individual, whereas ancient society starts from groups and subordinates individual interests to the claims of these groups."

Religion and Citizenship. That religion may have served as the primary symbol for ancient rights of citizenship, thereby aiding in defining and reinforcing consanguinity, was the thesis of Fustel de Coulanges's *The Ancient City* (1956), which appeared in 1864. Greek and Roman history, in Fustel's view, had been marked by social and political struggles to attain the right to participate in the religious community, since civil rights followed religious rights. Once the plebs had attained their sacred-civil rights, government inclined to the secular, and practical politics took precedence over religious considerations. The trend to modernity was thus marked by the decline of the sacred community and the rise of the secular, individualized community.

In two articles published in 1869 and 1870, McLennan (1896) hypothesized that his ambiguous "stocks" required a religious bond to hold the group in unity. He therefore proposed that, in speculating about their relationship, members would agree that they had come from some ancestor, and, following their primitive psychology of association, would fix upon some totem plant or animal. When maternal descent was conceived, animal worship became associated with the bloodline and gave added sanction to exogamy when that rule was invoked.

In 1885 and 1889, W. Robertson Smith (1903, 1957), friend of McLennan and a professor of Arabic, extended McLennan's formula to the ancient Semites. There, in sacrifice of the kin animal (totem) and the communion meal, Smith located the important symbolism and sentiment of the Semitic community, and of primitive societies generally. By eating flesh together, the kin worshipers would "cement and seal their mystic unity with one another and their god" (W. R. Smith 1957: 313). The ancient community was a totemic clan grounded in the ritual of sacrifice and communion. In the ancient world of Greece and Rome, religion and society retained that integral relation (1957:256):

Civil and religious morality have one and the same measure, and the conduct which suffices to secure the esteem of men suffices also to make a man perfectly easy as to his standing with the gods. . . . All antique morality is an affair of social custom and customary law, and . . . in the more primitive forms of ancient life the force of custom is so strong that there is hardly any middle course between living well up to the standard of social duty which it prescribes, and falling altogether outside the pale of the civil and religious community.

The political evolutionist Bagehot (1875) popularized the primitive "cake of custom" and the conservative quality of savage life with full support from anthropologists of the day (Lubbock 1870, Tylor 1874, Waitz 1863, Spencer 1900).

Religion as a Universal Idea. It is evident that developmentalists were aware of the interrelations of institutions and sought to show how law, morality, religion, and the state shaped the nature of society through their interconnections. Their essays in this regard were limited, however, and their efforts were directed more strongly toward describing the origins of institutions in the mental states of savages and tracing the development of those ideas until they were brought to fruition in civilization. Bastian (1860, 1895) postulated certain universal ("elemental") ideas shared by all mankind, out of which had grown corresponding universal institutions, though varying in form according to local environmental adaptations. Religion held first place because primitive man's initial philosophy and the nature of early society were based on supernatural premises. Primitive man could be conceived as reacting to the impressive forces in nature. He anthropomorphized these forces into nature deities. The mythologies produced ample evidence of the impact of nature on man's perceptual apparatus. On the other hand, as Tylor (1874) and Spencer (1900) argued, man's psychic experience in the presence of death and dreams produced a notion of duality in his own person, and he then projected this duality on nature in spiritual beings. The source of religion thus lay in animism (Tylor) or ghost theory (Spencer). From a generalized spiritism one could trace the differentiation of polytheistic deities, and see a strain toward monotheism. Frazer (1900) thought that he could detect in magic a more primitive philosophy, one in which man sought to manipulate an impersonal power to fill his own needs. Only later, through perception of the indeterminism of his actions, did he realize that he must petition a transcendent spirit. Marett (1909) resuscitated the anthropomorphic argument, which the theory of animism had superseded, and coined the term "pre-animistic religion." What prompted the challenge to animism was the concept of mana, recently propagated by the missionary Codrington (1891) in an account of peoples of Melanesia. In a survey of Australian materials, the classicist Andrew Lang (1898) pointed to ethically involved deities, who were in the nature of great men who had been magnified to the proportions of gods.

Religion and Ethics. Tylor and Spencer and later Frazer, who set the tone for the study of primitive religion, were not inclined to see any connection between ethics and religion in the thought of the "lower races." Even after morality and religion were joined, as Hobhouse (1925) observed in 1904, morality was so tied to ritual and the glorification of god that it did not find its way into human relations, where it was needed.

Religion and Secular Developments. It was through the emergence of science and a secular idealism that man would advance in the future. Religion, like the communal life, had served man well in these early days, but both must now be given up. The charge against religion, in Frazer's (1913) judgment, echoed the charge of the eighteenth-century exponents of a religion of reason ("natural religion"): orthodox religion was riddled with superstition and therefore restricted man's intellectual development. Like Marx, Frazer concluded that religion was something of a palliative for the masses. Like Comte, who also traced a development in knowledge from rank spiritism (fetichism) to theological and then to scientific (positi-

vistic) stages, the evolutionists saw a trend toward science and secularism.

What held for knowledge also held for other institutions. Law in former times had been infused with religious belief and practice and inspired with divine sanction as a gift of divinity (Maine 1861). So with the domestication of animals, according to Hahn (1896): The waxing and waning of the moon was conceived by early men to be associated with a cycle of growth. When it was noted that the female menstrual cycle coincided with the moon's phases, the idea of fertility came to be associated with the moon as well as with woman, and the moon emerged as a fertility goddess with horns. The association with cattle was unmistakable. At this point men concluded that cattle belonged to the goddess, who desired men to make sacrifices to her. If they did not do so, the goddess would punish them. So to avoid the risk of having to displease her during lean years, a small herd was corralled; and thus confined, wild cattle entered into servitude to man. As they reproduced and white cows appeared, their color reminiscent of the silvery moon, they were singled out as most holy. Attention now was drawn to milk, which at first was a holy product used in ceremonies in honor of the moon goddess. The domesticated ox, the wheel, and the plow all derived from a religious context, and were united into a complex associated with a fertility goddess (cf. Wundt 1928, Bachofen 1861).

Art also was brought under the purview of religion (Stolpe 1927, Haddon 1895, Steinen 1894, Balfour 1893). Besides developing a trend from the sacred to the profane, artistic design revealed how primitive man had followed his uncultivated sensory perception, producing a realistic representation that only later assumed a conventionalized and abstract mode.

Even the biological antitheses of maleness and femaleness and of youth and age, to which Schurtz (1902; cf. Webster 1932) pointed in his account of age classes, were anciently given social importance through religious ritual. Like Bachofen (1861), Schurtz (1902:39) considered "that the whole history of culture is to burst the narrow and clumsy natural associations [built upon the female principle] in order to construct a freer, progressive and better adapted group."

STRUCTURALISM AND THE RISE OF SOCIAL AND CULTURAL DETERMINISM (*ca.* 1890-1940)

In founding a science dedicated to the early history of mankind and distinguished by the comparative method, progressivists and evolutionists also assembled a corpus of factual materials, problems, and theories that future anthropologists could challenge and upon which they could build. Spencer's *Principles of Sociology* (1900), Frazer's *Golden Bough* (1900), Wundt's *Völker-Psychologie* (1928), Tylor's *Primitive Culture* (1874), and Westermarck's *History of Human Marriage* (1922) illustrate the massive and impressive collection of data for the developmental discourse. In opting for a dynamic anthropology, these men neglected structural-functional problems, and their evolutionary orientation prejudiced them in their use of historic materials, including data on the geographic distribution of culture elements. Devoted to synthesis, they had no serious commitment to collection of data in the field. Tentative efforts in this direction came later, and did not take hold until the natural science image had been written into the anthropological definition (Haddon 1901-1935, Spencer and Gillen 1899). Ethnographic description was often the artifact of a curious and humanistically

rooted person drawn from, or more usually assigned to, a primitive location. The United States, engaged in making arrangements for Indian nations displaced by the thrust of frontier settlement, proved to be exceptional in stimulating ethnographic research and gathering data on population, location, economy, leadership, and special customs useful in dealing with the Indians. The burden of gathering such materials was initially carried by government explorers like Lewis and Clark and USGS parties. With the end of the frontier near at hand, the U.S. government established a Bureau of American Ethnology under supervision of Major John Wesley Powell. Powell and his associates succeeded in producing a linguistic map of North American Indians north of Mexico in 1891, and in their accounts of Omaha sociology, Tusayan katchinas, technology, architecture, mythology, sign language, mortuary customs, pottery, textiles, and the like, assembled a rich storehouse of ethnographic Americana.

As the nineteenth century drew to a close, a critical reaction appeared as geographers like Friedrich Ratzel (1896-1898) began to call attention to cultural similarities throughout the areas on the Pacific rim. Increasing dissatisfaction was also voiced over the speculative quality of developmentalist interpretations, especially with regard to the primary sources for primal ideas that allegedly served to organize human institutions. Psychological explanations of elementary ideas not only varied from one author to another, but were virtually impossible to test. The assumption that the human mind accounted for uniformities in near and distant societies also seemed very doubtful when cast in the framework of historic contacts. More and more it appeared essential, if adequate controls were to be achieved, to look to the social and cultural for explanations of social and cultural phenomena, rather than to a generalized human psychology. Tracing social and cultural products to a racial psychology was equally suspect.

The moment had come to raise the social and the cultural to a distinct level of causal reality. This task primarily occupied sociologists and cultural anthropologists during approximately the next fifty years, from about 1890 to 1940. During this time strenuous efforts were directed to understanding the nature of the social and the cultural, and pointing out ways by which society and culture molded human behavior through conventionalization (patterning). The driving forces behind recognition of the social and cultural as independent domains were Émile Durkheim (1926, 1938) and Franz Boas (1940a, 1940c, 1940f, 1940g). Each attracted a coterie of devoted students and succesfully established publication channels for disseminating their views. Those associated with Durkheim included Henri Hubert, Henri Beuchat, and especially Marcel Mauss, his nephew. Boas hand-picked a number of outstanding scholars in the persons of Alfred Kroeber, Alexander Goldenweiser, Robert Lowie, Edward Sapir, Leslie Spier, and Melville Herskovits, all of whom made special contributions to the concept of culture or to the historical analysis of cultural elements. While neither Clark Wissler nor Roland Dixon was a student of Boas, both came to be associated with the American Museum of Natural History while Boas was curator of ethnology there, and devoted themselves to formulating cultural-historical constructions based on geographic distributions.

It is curious that the major thrust in exploring the social took a theoretical orientation stressing structure and function, while exploration of the cultural focused on the intercultural transmis-

sion of elements. This was true not only in the United States but on the continent, where German ethnologists and the *Kulturkreislehre* concentrated their attention on culture traits and complexes. There was, however, another approach to the elucidation of culture, one that sought to see it as connected directly to human needs, both biological and psychological. This was the tack taken by Bronislaw Malinowski, who drew much of his theoretical inspiration from Edward Westermarck. Malinowski styled himself a functionalist, and unlike A. R. Radcliffe-Brown, who drew upon the sociological image cast by Durkheim, he conceived a theory of culture rather than a theory of society.

The lead in fieldwork was taken early by Boas, who had been trained as a natural scientist. Through the zoologist Haddon and the psychologist W. R. R. Rivers, whom Haddon recruited, British anthropology also made advances in fieldwork. It was carried forward by Radcliffe-Brown and Malinowski, especially the latter. German ethnology transmuted into the *Kulturkreis* theory did not inspire a special emphasis on field investigation, and the same can be said for French sociology, at least until the late 1920s.

SOCIAL ANTHROPOLOGY AND SOCIAL STRUCTURALISM

Durkheim made a most determined effort in 1895 to establish the social fact as an independent causal domain. The unique characteristic of a social fact is its derivation. It cannot be conjured up by any individual; it can be originated only by a number of individuals in social interaction that generates a common or social feeling. This is the primal social fact, a sociopsychological state from which arise symbolic actions and emblems that renew the strength of social sentiment in social ceremony. The purpose toward which any social fact is pointed constitutes its function, and here the importance of the fact can be read. The ultimate function of social facts is to reinforce social solidarity.

Durkheim sought to prove the validity of this thesis in an analysis of the elementary religious and social forms of the Australian aborigines (1926). Here he attempts to show that only social facts can explain social facts. To grasp the meaning of the social as cause, the individual must be eliminated from analysis. The hallmarks of society are collective representations (ideas) and collective symbols. Anyone giving psychological causes to social phenomena is in gross error.

Social Structuralism: The French View

Under French tutelage, social anthropology, as it was later popularized by the British, assumed a structural posture. Every social arrangement took on the nature of a system, straining toward a state of integrative equilibrium, with social solidarity the functional purpose of all system operations. Through their special publication, *L'Année sociologique,* Durkheim and his associates set forth descriptive analyses that controverted psychological or economic or geographic causes by tracing cause to the type of social structure. For example, Mauss and Beuchat (1906), in considering seasonal variation as it affects Eskimo society, conclude that the alternation of summer and winter activities produce entirely different social arrangements, with concomitant variations in economy, legal norms, and religious ceremonial. Mauss and Hubert (1899), in their study of magic, set out to prove that magic in both ideology and practice is a social rather than personal psychological phenomenon.

Social Integration and Institutions. The French sociologists looked forward to uncovering types of social structures that could be arranged in developmental series, revealing correlations with other features, such as law and morality, ideology and political organization. While inclined to stress system and to relate phenomena in the context of integrative total social facts (Lévi-Strauss 1945), they made no attempt to achieve a detailed analysis of the social system of any single group. Their social morphology was directed more toward institutions like magic, religion, gift exchange, and the division of labor. With regard to exchange, Mauss (1954, Durkheim and Mauss 1963) points out how, in the simpler societies, exchange of goods and services links families, clans, phratries, and tribes; and he suggests that the sense of obligation attached to these exchanges might be rooted in a social sentiment or in the sacred. These are not utilitarian exchanges, but seem to be carried out for their own sake. Back of the social type, then, one can locate a social sentiment and an associated idea (collective representation) whose organizational presence can be detected in any reciprocity. In the final analysis, the exchange of the goods is nothing more than the outward manifestation of the inner reality, the social sentiment.

Psychological Theory. Contemporary theorists like Lucien Lévy-Bruhl and Arnold Van Gennep, who explained the mental operations of primitive peoples (Lévy-Bruhl 1910) and initiation rites (Van Gennep 1960) in psychological or biopsychic terms, were not acceptable to Durkheim and his followers, even though they might have arrived at similar conclusions about primitive society. Like the developmentalists, these theorists agreed that primitive society was heavily communalized and regulated by custom pervaded by religious mysticism. Mankind shared similar psychic processes that produced uniformities in response, and the trend in time demonstrated the rise of the secular over the sacred. Moreover, they were in agreement that human behavior was rooted in sentiment, but believed that the sentiments binding people and organizing activities in primitive societies were decidedly different from those by which complex societies in the Western world were organized.

Social Structuralism: The British View

British social anthropology developed under the intellectual aegis of A. R. Radcliffe-Brown, who rewrote his original field description of *The Andaman Islanders* (1922) under the acknowledged inspiration of French sociological theory as early as 1914. He summarized his scientific credo as follows (1922:233-34):

(1) A society depends for its existence on the presence in the minds of its members of a certain system of sentiments by which the conduct of the individual is regulated in conformity with the needs of the society. (2) Every feature of the social system itself and every event or object that in any way affects the well-being or the cohesion of the society becomes an object of this system of sentiments. (3) In human society the sentiments in question are not innate but are developed in the individual by the action of the society upon him. (4) The ceremonial customs of a society are a means by which the sentiments in question are given collective expression on appropriate occasions. (5) The ceremonial (i.e., collective) expression of any sentiment serves both to maintain it at the requisite degree of intensity in the mind of the individual and to transmit it from one generation to another. Without such expression the sentiments involved could not exist.

Using the term "social function" to denote the effects of an institution (custom or belief)

insofar as they concern the society and its solidarity or cohesion, the hypothesis of this chapter may be more briefly resumed in the statement that the social function of the ceremonial customs of the Andaman Islanders is to maintain and to transmit from one generation to another the emotional dispositions on which the society (as it is constituted) depends for its existence.

In short, the basic social feelings of the individual are imparted through a process of conditioning. The individual as part of a larger order occupies a special status with defined rights and obligations strengthened by legal, religious, and moral sanctions. Society is considered analogous to an organism, and social processes are compared to physiological processes that fulfill conditions or needs essential to system maintenance.

Radcliffe-Brown addressed himself to the basic problem of formal structure much as cultural anthropologists in the United States described ideal patterns as typical for behavior generally. He had little interest in variation or change, though he did see certain avoidance practices as smothering conflict through ritualized reciprocity (Radcliffe-Brown 1965*d*).

Comparative Sociology. Radcliffe-Brown was devoted to the image of a scientific comparative sociology, and he made constant reference to uncovering the social laws by which various social structures are organized and function. He located a number of social kinship types, noting how certain structural principles (e.g., unity of the sibling group, generation, sex, and lineage) lead people to arrive at particular terminological distinctions and marriage practices, such as the levirate and sororate (Radcliffe-Brown and Forde, eds., 1962). It is the lineage principle that separates tribal societies into descent groups, whose corporate nature is extended through joint ownership of lands and ceremonial rites.

Value Sentiment and Reciprocal Obligations. Radcliffe-Brown was peripatetic, sojourning in South Africa, Australia, and the United States as well as in England, where he seeded the minds of a number of followers with his social structural approach. On his return to England in 1937, reputation well established, he succeeded in influencing many students trained by Malinowski (e.g., Raymond Firth, Audrey Richards, Monica Hunter Wilson, E.E. Evans-Pritchard, Isaac Schapera, Meyer Fortes, Lucy Mair, Hilda Kuper, and Siegfried F. Nadel). In the United States Radcliffe-Brown trained and influenced Fred Eggan, Sol Tax, John Provinse and Kalervo Oberg. Through their own field experiences, various of these British and American social anthropologists came to doubt the biocultural orientation of Malinowski, especially in regard to social units larger than the family. They found Radcliffe-Brown's insistence on a value sentiment as the anchor for social structure most congenial for understanding African political systems. The ritualization of the value sentiment furnished the "ideological superstructure of political organization" (Fortes and Evans-Pritchard, eds., 1940:17). The presence of this value sentiment was but dimly apprehended by the members of a social system, but myth, dogma, ritual, and legal and moral norms brought it into the open and translated it into an intellectual language that could be comprehended. Unconscious and conscious processes thus were joined.

Like the culture constructs of Boas, Radcliffe-Brown's theoretical orientation and his suggestive definitions of problems permeated the fieldwork of those who studied under him. They concentrated on formal structure, with a view to showing how the system constitutes a dynamic equilibrium through the reciprocal obligations discharged by the several social segments in the functional operations of the whole, and how ritualization of reciprocities is used to control and accommodate conflicting interests within the group in the interests of social stability (see, for example, Fortes 1949, Gluckman 1955, Evans-Pritchard 1940). Since their efforts were directed to extracting the meaning of relations linking statuses within a social structure, they were more inclined to analyze legal and moral norms and reciprocities than custom. Hence the concept of culture plays a secondary role in their work, and the details of ceremony and custom are incidental to their other descriptions (see Murdock 1951 for a critical review and Firth 1951 for a reply). Like American culture theorists, however, they felt that implicit value assumptions serve as the unconscious integrates of human behavior, guaranteeing continuity to structure. With the concentration on value sentiments and the conscious conceptualization of value in myth and ritual, British social anthropologists have been inclined to avoid interpretations that stress economic or geographic differences. Use of the comparative method extolled by Radcliffe-Brown has not been pressed systematically on a cross-societal basis (see, for example, Fortes and Evans-Pritchard, eds., 1940; Radcliffe-Brown and Forde, eds., 1962), and statistical manipulation of data has likewise not been cultivated. Though sensitive to changes overtaking African societies, social structuralists until the postwar period were inclined to concentrate on a timeless analysis of the social system. Field research devoted largely to description of kinship, law, descent groups, marriage, and economic and political organization constitutes a major contribution of British social anthropologists.

BIOCULTURAL FUNCTIONALISM

Bronislaw Malinowski, who moved from Poland to England in 1910, was inspired to become an anthropologist by reading Frazer's *Golden Bough*. Influenced by Westermarck and Seligman, Malinowski used his field experience among the Trobriand Islanders to expound a biopsychic theory of culture that he called "functionalism" (see Firth, ed., 1957). Malinowski's reputation as a theorist and expert field researcher was built upon studies designed to contradict then current theories regarding primitive economics (1961*a*), marriage and the family (1929), law (1926), and magic and religion (1935, 1948*a*).

Biology and Cultural Instrumentalities

Malinowski (1944) developed his theory of culture around institutions connected to biological and psychological imperatives. Seven basic needs are distinguished: metabolism, reproduction, bodily comforts, safety, movement, growth, and health. Each is linked to an institution: maintenance of body metabolism to food-getting activities, survival and safety to defensive practices, including war, and the like. Malinowski notes some essential conditions without which no society can survive (cf. Radcliffe-Brown 1965*a*), notably economic organization, conventionalization of behavior by adoption of norms, formal transmission of knowledge and skills through education, and an executive or political organization. Malinowski's basic needs and principles of integration, which give special distinction to tribal institutions in accordance with their local emphasis, are not always clearly distinguished. For example, reproduction, a basic need, also operates as a principle in institutions like the family, courtship organization, and matrilineal or patrilineal clan organization. Other basic integrational principles he calls the territorial, physiological, voluntary associational, occupational and professional, rank and status, and comprehensive. The territorial principle relates to localized groups, including villages, neighborhoods, and districts, while the comprehensive principle refers to integration at the level of region and nation.

The biology of man provides the need base for behavior, directing activity instrumentally in pursuit of fulfillment. Cultural instrumentalities become invested with pleasure or pain associated with the physiological experience accompanying their instrumental success or failure. Such primary reinforcement of the cultural response through physiology moves the response into a central position for human motivation, so that in many instances cultural instrumentalities exert greater influence than physiological drives.

Institutions

Malinowski considers every institution must have a charter by which the personnel are organized according to conventionalized rules (or norms). The personnel make use of material apparatus to carry out activities having a function (1944:52-53). Function, to all intents and purposes, is the equivalent of need.

Malinowski insists that the institution is the concrete isolate for research, and his books are based upon descriptive analyses of institutions. Where cultural change is concerned, he underscores the point that all sociologically relevant impact and interaction are organized; that is, they occur between institutions (1961*b*). It was this institutional focus that guided his students in their initial African and Polynesian researches (see Richards 1932, Mair 1965, Hogbin 1934, Firth 1929).

Primitive Exchange and Religious Motivations

While Malinowski is inclined to universalize the basic structure of human nature as well as the institutions to which it gives rise, he draws a distinction between the motivations of men in primitive and civilized societies. At all times his Trobriand experience is in the foreground of interpretation. In describing the *kula*, Malinowski (1961*a*) concludes that utilitarian motives do not regulate primitive exchange. This means, in his view, that the construct of economic man utilized by economic theorists will not hold. In accenting noneconomic values and reciprocities he agrees with the position of Radcliffe-Brown.

Like Radcliffe-Brown and others before him, Malinowski (1948*b*) regards primitive society as a highly sacralized order in which "religion needs the community as a whole so that its members may worship in common its sacred things and its divinities, and society needs religion for the maintenance of moral law and order." Religion is founded on the instinct of self-preservation, which man shares with animals, and which is evoked by threats to his person, especially when faced with death. Through ritualization of death men lay to rest the anxieties generated by threats to their persons and to the community. Religious ceremony stimulates social unity and maintains it.

Anxiety and Ritual. In their respective theories of anxiety and its relation to ritual, one can grasp the distinct approaches of Malinowski and Radcliffe-Brown, as Homans (1941) has pointed out. For Malinowski, anxiety is a common human response in the face of danger; magic and religion are cultural instrumentalities that relieve anxiety. Radcliffe-Brown, on the other hand, sees anxiety as a social derivative—individuals are inculcated with anxiety when the social needs of the group require it. The view of culture as an instrument developed by man in his own service leads Malinowski to insist that he is not a structuralist. However, he seems to accept the determinism of custom and insists that native peoples are unaware of the causes of their actions. At the same time he insists that personal variation, as instanced in breaches of legal norms, are ever present in savage society.

Psychoanalytic vs. Biocultural Interpretations

The biopsychic foundation of cultural institutions found by Malinowski probably contributed to his interest in psychoanalytic interpretations of culture. In *Sex and Repression in Savage Society* (1927), however, he challenged the universality of the Freudian Oedipus complex by pointing out that among the Trobrianders, it is not the father that is pitted against the son in authoritarian competition, but maternal uncle and nephew. The hostilities and anxieties bred of the Freudian reactive syndromes offer poor support for social norms, which in Malinowski's judgment must be strengthened through some positive human impulse. The Freudian view of culture and the individual sees the latter straining against the former, whereas Malinowski describes culture as the instrument that aids and abets man in moments of trial. The cumulative effect of Malinowski's orientation is to relate the individual-as-human-being to culture, and in directing our attention to the ways by which private disposition comes under the influence of custom he contributed to the rise of culture and personality studies among American ethnologists.

The transfer of Malinowski's theoretical influence to the New World was paralleled by its decline among his former students as they centered their interest in social structure under the guidance of Radcliffe-Brown. Yet certain of his students, notably Nadel (1951, 1952), attempted to accommodate the linguistic and psychological leads of Malinowski's functionalism to social anthropology. Of his students, M. F. Ashley-Montagu (1950) alone attempted to extend the biocultural synthesis outlined by Malinowski.

CULTURE HISTORIANS: AMERICAN, BRITISH, GERMAN

Culture serves as the central concept for those who direct their energies to tracing the migration of peoples and the diffusion and exchange of inventions and ideas through contact. Interest in the problem of culture diffusion arose almost simultaneously in the United States, England, and Germany, and each produced its own solutions to the historic problem. Culture historians generally were more aggressively opposed to the developmentalists' psychocultural evolutionism than were social structuralists. While, in theory, social or cultural evolution was admitted as a possibility, the historians claimed that attention must first be directed to historical problems. The *a priori* unilinear development of culture constructed by evolutionists should be winnowed through the sieve of accumulated facts. In short, anthropologists should permit generalizations to grow inductively out of facts rather than selectively organizing facts to fit deductive propositions. The schools of culture historians may be designated as American culture historicism, German-Austrian *Kulturkreis* theory, and British migrationism.

Paralleling the social structuralists,

the culture historians insist that only cultural facts can explain cultural facts. They cannot accept psychological causes or any other noncultural basis for culture—the stimulus of geographic environment, for example. Adoption of the historical method was advocated by each school, but the British migrationists were less inclined than the American and German culture historians to see man subject to laws comparable to those uncovered by natural scientists. British migrationists held to their own deterministic notion of "individual human beings exercising their wills to change the direction of human thought and action, or . . . natural catastrophes forcing men of insight to embark on new enterprises" (G. Elliot Smith 1930:60).

Though concentrating on unique events, culture historians ultimately arrived at a deterministic position with regard to culture. This theoretical posture was defined most clearly by the Americans as they came to see culture anchored in unconscious patterning (see Boas, ed., 1911; Kroeber 1944, 1952*a*; Kroeber and Kluckhohn 1963; Benedict 1934; Sapir 1958*a*; Herskovits 1948; Linton 1945; Lowie 1924; White 1949). Owing to Boas' interest in the ideological basis of linguistic categories, and to influences stemming apparently from Bastian's concept of elementary ideas, psychological interpretation was always closely joined to the cultural. However, Boas never admitted a psychological origin for custom or social tradition. He asserted that "the psychological problem is contained in the results of the historical inquiry" (1940*c*). Yet comparative linguistics afforded a rare opportunity to penetrate the psychological laws governing the growth of human culture, in as much as the forms of thought uncovered through investigating the language categories of primitive peoples had "grown up entirely outside the conditions which govern our thoughts" (Boas 1940d). The strength of the linguistic model for understanding culture processes was equally stressed by Sapir (1958a) and Whorf (1956). The omnipresent concern for psychological processes, which are at best only dimly apprehended by the individuals concerned, prepared American culture theorists to accept Freudian explanations of the unconscious and to focus on the relation of personality and culture.

For the British migrationists, notably Elliot Smith and W. J. Perry, man was launched toward civilization and held on course by his search for the elixirs of life, which would enable him to overcome death. "The never-ending pursuit of this elusive aim was responsible for the creation of civilization, with most of its arts and crafts, its essential customs and beliefs" (G. E. Smith 1930:24).

American Culture Historians

The most exacting theoretical statement and exploration of the concept of culture belongs to American culture historians. Beginning with problems in the diffusion of culture elements, they advanced to investigate the integrative qualities of cultures and the impact of culture on the patterning of personality.

Franz Boas (for special critiques on his life and work see Kroeber et al. 1943, Goldschmidt 1959, Herskovits 1953, Rohner 1966, White 1963) gave immediate direction to American culture historicism. He was trained in natural science and fulfilled a boyhood enthusiasm for exotic lands and peoples by spending a year (1883-1884) in exploratory mapping of Baffin Island. Here he came to know the Eskimo. Later he dedicated himself to the Indians of the northwest coast, notably the Kwakiutl. Beginning in 1896 Boas attacked the comparative method and called for ethnologists to abandon that most speculative procedure for the more controlled historical method. He proposed to dedicate the "science of anthropology . . . [to] the history of human society" (1938:3) which he conceived as having developed largely through culture contact. His immediate research, like that of his first students, was directed to gathering field data that would refute evolutionary hypotheses, especially with regard to mythology (1916), art (1927), and primitive thought (1938). He worked constantly to dispel what he considered to be popular fallacies supported by scientific error, such as the implied connection between race, psychology, and culture.

Cultural Diffusion and Psychic Processes. From his orientation toward historic variation and from analysis of mythic elements in their geographic distributions, Boas became convinced that the historic process involved the diffusion of single traits rather than integrated complexes. Any particular people, according to the structure of their culture, are inclined to take up cultural features and to rework them according to taste and requirements of compatibility. Boas' demands for controlled analyses were so rigorous that he limited himself to no more than suggestions regarding the probable source of culture traits among culturally similar tribes in contiguous areas. Only occasionally did he indulge in a statement of relative age of features.

Evolutionary fallacies resting on psychological laws defined many of Boas' problems; hence much of his research had to center in primitive thought. Art was held to develop from concrete representation to the abstract. In his work on the designs of Alaskan needle cases (1940e), Boas offered a refutation and a warning that "a considerable number of . . . psychic processes must be taken into consideration if we desire to obtain a clear insight into the history of art." A fearsome antagonist of established theory, he avoided substituting his own, and thus presented his students with a challenge to be overcome rather than with a theoretical system to be imitated. More than theory, what he apparently wished to convey to his students and to anthropology was a deep respect for methodological rigor, and in this he was successful.

The Influence of Boas' Cultural Dynamics. Boas apparently had a design for anthropology. "When I thought that these *historical* methods [acculturation and dissemination] were firmly established," he wrote (1940*h*), "I began to stress, about 1910, the problems of cultural dynamics, of integration of culture and of the interaction between individual and society." The broad outlines of the development he describes can be followed in the problem definitions of his early students. Kroeber (1901, 1907) undertook a dissertation relating to art and symbolism, and consistently maintained interest in cultural dynamics as well as in theory and method (see, e.g., Kroeber 1939, 1952*b*; Kroeber and Richardson 1940). When Goldenweiser (1933) analyzed totemism, he concluded that the elements of which it was constituted varied regionally and that it was not possible to define any universal or archetypal totemistic complex, as many had assumed on the basis of Australian materials. The best one could say was that as a process "totemism is the specific socialization of emotional values" that had been generally "realized in the course of the association of man with nature" (Goldenweiser 1933). Sapir, whose major contributions lay in linguistics (1955) and in stimulating a concern for

culture and personality (1958*a*), addressed himself early to the role that linguistics might play in historic reconstruction (1958*a*). Leslie Spier (1921) analyzed the sun dance of the Plains Indians while Ruth Benedict (1923) attempted to show that the guardian-spirit complex varied regionally in North America and that there was no organic connection linking any of the several traits. Entering the Boasian mainstream at an intermediate point, Melville J. Herskovits (1928, 1942; Herskovits and Herskovits 1934) set out to unravel the physical and cultural processes of African-American contact, and was the first American ethnologist to carry out fieldwork in Africa (1938*a*). Robert Lowie analyzed the test theme in North American mythology, and in *Primitive Society* (1920) and *Primitive Religion* (1924) used the historical method to excise the cancer of scientific orthodoxy.

Both Clark Wissler (1914, 1922, 1923) and Roland Dixon (1928), though not so directly influenced by Boas as these others, also made special contributions to cultural-historical analysis. Wissler was the architect of the age-area hypothesis and of the conceptualization of culture forms as traits, complexes, areas, centers, and types. The work of John Swanton (1942, 1946) in the Southeast and of Frank Speck (1935) in the Northeast illustrates how the ethnography of heavily acculturated areas can be salvaged through historic records used in combination with fieldwork.

Cultural Description. Controlled analysis modeled on inductive science possesses the virtue of arriving at an objective appraisal, but to Paul Radin (1933), American culture historians with their historical method simply manipulated traits and complexes, disregarding the individuals who used them.

Moreover, he considered that the proper use of the historical method was "to describe a specific culture . . . without any reference to what has preceded or what is to follow" (1933:32). In short, what Radin pointed to is a description of a culture as it is lived. Hence he introduced autobiographical materials to illustrate and bring meaning to the cultural events he was able to witness (1920, 1923). This timeless method drew Radin into line with the views of social anthropologists and biocultural functionalists. His humanistic orientation also led him (1927) to defend the philosophic speculations of primitive man and to ground his theory of culture on personality types (the thinker and the practical types). At the same time he traced an evolutionary course for religion that correlated its organizational complexity with economic conditions. The aristocratic and priestly elite, made possible by economic advances, emerged as wealthy literati who concentrated on intellectual creativity. The correlation of leisure and creativity based on economic conditions was an ancient thesis; what Radin added was a dash of economic determinism and exploitation.

German-Austrian *Kulturkreis* Theory

German-Austrian culture-historical theory, like the approach of American historicists, derived from the work of geographers, notably Friedrich Ratzel. The stimulus of geographic descriptions of the distribution of inventions, domesticated animals, house types, and social and political organizations, aroused the anticipation that these features could be traced to a few regional sources, and that a relative chronology could be established. If a relatively uniform rate of diffusion is assumed, the wider the distribution of a trait, the greater the age. Where similar traits occur at distant points, with sporadic distribution among intervening ethnic enclaves, one again might assume the trait to be old. And what if no enclaves between the two occurrences harbor the feature? Again, with proper application of criteria of form, quantity, and complexity (quality), the conclusion might be drawn that a continuous distribution had existed much earlier, but had been broken by more recent migrants bearing a different culture.

As in the United States, German-Austrian culture historians worked with museum collections. The *Kulturkreislehre* never developed any impulse for fieldwork and consequently never explored the wide range of cultural problems that engaged the Americans. Leo Frobenius, a student of Ratzel's, first coined the term *Kulturkreis* to define the spread of a culture tradition, as instanced by the Malayo-Nigritian, by which he accounted for similarities between Indonesia and the African continent. Frobenius, however, did not pursue historical studies in this vein, but turned to problems of culture morphology, much as social structuralists addressed themselves to social morphology (cf. Jensen 1963). Richard Thurnwald converged theoretically on both cultural-historical relations and functional interrelations when dealing with types of economic and social systems and processes of change (Thurnwald 1932, 1935, 1937).

The major thrust of German ethnology was carried by culture historians who picked up Frobenius' lead and sought to formulate a rigorous methodology. The initial statement was made by Fritz Graebner in 1911 *(Methode der Ethnologie)* after he had published an article detailing the culture traditions and culture strata of Oceania (1905; cf. Ankermann 1905). Taken up by Wilhelm Schmidt, *Kulturkreis* studies shifted their center to Vienna.

Many of the principles of interpretation and of criteria to determine historic relations developed by the *Kulturkreislehre* paralleled those of American culture historians, like Wissler. For example, they assumed that diffusion proceeded from a center and moved outward to areas where the old traits remained in the possession of marginal peoples (age-area principle). Again, they assumed that they could detect the centers of diffusion because there they would find a more complex manifestation of traits than existed among the marginal peoples. Unlike the Americans, however, they addressed themselves to world history, and attempted to describe a succession of culture traditions on a grand scale. Thus, according to Schmidt (1935), the primitive hunting cultures of North and South America (residual examples: Fuegians, Algonkins) were united in a gigantic *Kulturkreis* that extended across Arctic Asia, including the Samoyeds, Koryaks, Ainu, and the palaeo-Eskimo.

As the guiding genius of *Kulturkreis* dogma, Schmidt was able to inspire a number of followers to research his favorite theories—that the pygmies represented the earliest culture, and that the conception of a high god was present among the pygmies and the primitive hunting cultures. Thus both Wilhelm Koppers (1924) and Martin Gusinde (1931-1939) were sent off to the tip of South America to uncover traces of the primitive culture tradition among the Yaghan, Ona, and Alacaluf. Paul Schebesta (1929,1936,1938-1950) followed the tropical spoor of the pygmies in Malaysia and the African Congo, where he too uncovered a moral high god and otherwise substantiated Schmidt's thesis that these people were possessors of a distinct variant of primitive culture and not users of a hodgepodge of features derived from their cultivating neighbors, as scholars believed.

Schmidt remained at home, synthesizing data regarding primitive cultures and high gods in twelve volumes (1912-1955).

Their knowledge of European history, sometimes corroborated in the field, as in Melanesia, led the *Kulturkreislehre* to associate culture traditions with ethnic and racial migrants. The diffusion of culture followed lines of migration and was transmitted *en bloc,* as it were, from one continent to another, making due allowance for modifications forced by environmental adaptation. This position conflicted with that of Boas, who insisted that culture traits had diffused independently from one people to another without migration. By the time of Schmidt's death in 1954, it was evident that *Kulturkreis* theory had entered a decline (Heine-Geldern 1964) and that, if we may judge by the speculative nature of their conclusions, much of their energy had been wasted.

British Migrationists

British migrationists G. Elliot Smith and W. J. Perry traced the organization of human energy, as expressed in the interests of culture and civilization, to an unconscious impulse to unlock the secret of never ending life. The stage for the new turn in British ethnology had been set by the conversion of the eminent W. H. R. Rivers to the view that historic contact was the fundamental cause of culture growth (see Rivers 1914, 1926).

G. E. Smith, an eminent zoologist and craniologist, was led to develop his theory of civilization when writing a history of mummification in Egypt (1915). Extending his observations on mummification practices, Smith came to the conclusion that Egypt, in possessing cultivation, technical arts, the calendar, and mummification, must be the hearth of civilization. Mummification encapsulated a philosophy of life as well as integrating a host of crafts, including bricklaying, stonemasonry, metalwork, carpentry, embalming, and priestcraft, to assure that the pharaoh, the god-king, would live. About mummification, then, there gathered a complex of belief, practice, and organization. "It is no exaggeration to claim," wrote Smith (1933:216), "that the arts and crafts, the social and political organization and the innermost beliefs and the symbolism of the whole world were largely shaped by the practice of embalming." Once this complex had formed in Egypt, it was conveyed through trade and colonization to adjacent lands, where some features were lost or modified. But the essentials or the core structure, as it were, remained intact, to be conveyed from one outpost to another as trading colonies were established in the never ending quest for precious stones and metals that symbolized the life-giving elixir. Pushing eastward through India to Cambodia, on to Polynesia, and finally to the New World, these trading colonies aroused the uncivilized to civilize themselves after the Egyptian original, once or thrice removed. Invention was the seed for change in that it stimulated new needs and the compounding of inventions. Thus, once irrigation had been invented, skill in measurement followed naturally.

Like the German culture historians, the British migrationists believed that change came about as migrants carried their modes of life to other regions. Unlike the Germans, however, the British not only traced the origins of civilization back to a single center, Egypt, but also concluded that the primitive groups surrounding these ancient secondary centers of civilization had degenerated as the centers were rent by internal conflict and declined. Yet the primitive groups preserved traces of the passage of the civilizers. In the instance of the totemic clan system, for example, the three main elements (grouping of clans for representation in council, perpetual reincarnation of members through initiation ceremonies, and association of each clan with some animal, plant, or material) were to be found as integral elements of the pharaoh's coronation ritual. Actual distribution of these several features showed that they varied independently, and that only in Egypt were they firmly bound in a unified complex.

The [totemic clan] system, therefore, has been brought into existence through the amalgamation of at least three distinct cultural elements, none of which have any real interrelationship, and all of which can exist in complete independence of the others; and it is only in the archaic civilization that these cultural elements appear to be in their proper setting [Perry 1927].

With this statement Perry seemed to be in essential agreement with Boas' contention that culture elements were independently diffused, and that only through acceptance into a local culture did the traits become interrelated with other features. Any complex of traits thus was a finite cultural-historical product.

In positing a single center for the origin of civilization, the British migrationists found themselves with an archetype from which all historic variants must be degenerations. This was the same model followed by Christian ethnohistorians when dealing with the dispersion of mankind from the Holy Land. Their historicism thus not only contravened evolutionary theories regarding the role of primitive culture as ancestral to civilization favored in the eighteenth and nineteenth centuries, but also resuscitated the long-dead model of the archetype used by zoologists and comparative anatomists (Blumenbach, for example) to explain subspecies differences.

It is a curious and interesting fact that with the passing of each of the prime generators of the culture-historical method in the United States, Germany and Austria, and England, the impulse for such studies dwindled. By 1930 the study of culture history through geographic distributions and culture strata had virtually ended.

SPECIALIZATIONS AND CONVERGENCES (*ca.* 1940 TO PRESENT)

The period from 1940 to the present has been characterized by a general reassessment of anthropological purposes in the light of anthropological history and accomplishments. This has produced three important intellectual thrusts. (1) Social and cultural determinism was brought under scrutiny in company with increased concern for explaining variation and the relation of variation to structure. (2) Strong efforts were made to redesign anthropology, with some advocating a position that may be characterized as historical idealism, while others called for anthropology to follow the behaviorist sciences. The former position derived its impulse from history and linguistics, while the latter was inspired by a mathematical-statistical formulation. (3) Specialization proliferated, producing independent concentrations in acculturation, applied anthropology, social and cultural integration, ethnohistory, ethnoeconomics, juridical and political anthropology, and ethnosociology.

All these developments were interrelated and supported a broadened intellectual floor. Fresh relations with sister disciplines followed, including the introduction of new techniques: formal analysis according to the canons of logic; mathematicized formulations of symbolic logic, probability statistics,

use of models for heuristic purposes, psychological tests, scalograming, and the like. The product showed much sophisticated concern for methodological rigor and for the basic assumptions upon which procedures and classifications rested. In short, anthropologists became more "theoretical," filling a void in their field which had been the target of criticism by more sophisticated students like Kluckhohn as well as by sociologists.

The new interest in anthropological possibilities led to a review of the anthropological past, revaluation of old problem areas formerly left fallow, and new perspectives applied to cultural evolution, history and anthropology and culture and ecology. In this process, inevitably, ambiguous and contradictory theories proliferated and lines of cleavage in theoretical posture became sharper; e.g., in the conflict of economic materialism and the idealist posture that had been traditional. During this period of transition the image of anthropology as a unified science also came under review (see, for example, Gillin 1954, Thompson 1961 and 1967, Hultkrantz 1968, Marshall 1967), and the role of anthropology in rapidly changing world affairs was debated in the light of scientific objectivity and neutrality (see, for example, Barnett 1956, Bunzel and Parsons 1964, Diamond 1964, O. Stewart 1964, Macquet 1964, Mair 1969, Berreman 1968, Gjessing 1968, Gough 1968).

REAPPRAISING DETERMINISM AND CAUSALITY

The challenge to social and cultural determinism ran counter to the twin assumptions that the tendency in social and cultural systems was toward integration and that individuals in their motivations had been molded to conform to society and culture. Lurking in the background were philosophic problems of free will and questions of the relation of variation to structure and of history to evolution. Unconscious and conscious processes also were involved, for structural determinists commonly assumed a social and cultural press of unconscious conditioning. Malinowski's biocultural functionalism and psychoanalytic theory had provided a basis for considering individual variation within the context of structure. Both in theory and in their accounts of culture history, Boas and Lowie denied the overpowering rule of custom in primitive society by citing individual variants—but they were variations on a central theme, as in the instance of variation in mythologic narratives. In a more formal analysis, Linton (1936, 1945; cf. Kluckhohn 1941) pointed out alternatives in culture patterns, while Kluckhohn described compulsory, preferred, typical, and sexually or socially restricted types of patterns. Opler (1945; cf. Kaplan 1954) attacked Benedict's thesis of a logically consistent integration by noting that cultures may express contradictory themes about the world, human nature, and social roles. If cultures could not be considered wholly consistent integrations, the same must be said for personality. "Personality is not always 'a whole'; that is, it is seldom perfectly integrated (completely unified)" (Kluckhohn, Murray, and Schneider, eds., 1953:31).

Application of the linguistic model to explain culture soon disclosed that the linguist did not predict as much as describe the rules by which acceptable sounds and constructions were made. Hence the ethnographer would not set out to predict behavior, but would endeavor to "state the rules of culturally appropriate behavior" according to situation (Frake 1964a:133; cf. Burling 1969, Hammer 1966, Wallace

1965). The equation of need and function in structural-functional analyses presented a problem in causality in that cause tended to dissolve into the purpose of an activity. The laws extracted from organized and reciprocal relations must not be expected to conform to necessity. The best to be achieved, according to Nadel (1951:287), would be a definition

in terms of a reciprocal interdependence between modes of action or events co-varying simultaneously. Thus we can do little with the concepts of antecedent and consequent. Their relevance does not disappear altogether; we still think of the ends as causing the means. But this relation can no longer be translated into a concrete time sequence, nor into an unequivocal nexus between determinants and things determined. Modern anthropologists are well aware of this ambiguity and, like the physicists, and partly for the same reason, tend to abandon the old irreversible nexus of cause-and-effect for the reversible and reciprocal relation of mere "functional" interdependence. . . .

Reviewing the so-called laws derived by social anthropologists, Evans-Pritchard (1964:152; see also 1949) counseled a different course:

The thesis I have put before you, that social anthropology is a kind of historiography and therefore ultimately of philosophy or art, implies that it studies societies as moral systems and not as natural systems, that it is interested in design rather than in process, and that it therefore seeks patterns and not scientific laws, and interprets rather than explains. . . .

The position assumed by Evans-Pritchard recalls that of Kroeber (1935, 1944), who pointed to anthropological concern for pattern as analogous to the historian's goal of descriptive integration. In effect, Evans-Pritchard, like Kroeber and Kluckhohn (1963), advocated a search for underlying meaning in value commitments; that is, in the formal normative structure. "This basic structure, and with it the significant functions, are much more nearly given by the so-called ideal culture than by the actual one." The structural anthropology that Lévi-Strauss (1963) anchored in the linguistic model illuminated the unconscious patterning in social organization, myth, and ritual by focusing on the use of permutating contrasts. Indeed, when it came to distinguishing history and anthropology, according to Lévi-Strauss (1963), "History organizes its data in relation to conscious expressions of social life, while anthropology proceeds by examining its unconscious foundations." The search for an unconscious configuration simply reaffirmed the traditional anthropological view, despite its statement in a new key; and Lévi-Strauss pointed back to Boas as the first to draw out the meaning of unconscious process for cultural phenomena. Like Boas, but unlike his French sociological antecedents, Durkheim and Mauss, Lévi-Strauss sought the bases of cultural phenomena in the organizational properties of the human mind.

REDESIGNING ANTHROPOLOGY: CULTURE AS COMMUNICATION

The steady influence of linguistic theory can be read in views of culture as a system of communication (Hall 1961). Edward Sapir and his student Benjamin Whorf reaffirmed the importance of language categories and modes of thought as providing the link between custom and the psychological foundations of behavior (see Whorf 1956; Hoijer, ed., 1954). Whorf pointed out two clear implications following from the relation of language to logic: first the arrangement of meaning in grammar very likely would be replicated in the arrangement of meaning in art and other symbolic forms; and second, this pattern could be reduced to

mathematical logic (Whorf 1952; cf. Greenberg 1954, Lenneberg 1953). Lévi-Strauss (1963; cf. Aberle 1957) contrasted the loose methodology of cultural anthropologists with the hope inspired by the rigorous controls achieved by linguists:

For centuries the humanities and the social sciences have resigned themselves to contemplating the world of the natural and exact sciences as a kind of paradise which they will never enter. And all of a sudden there is a small door which is being opened between the two fields, and it is linguistics which has done it.

The method that Lévi-Strauss extolled was nothing less than formal logic, by which elements are graded according to specific attributes that either allow them to be included in a category or exclude them from it. Once a common set is reduced from the multiplex variety, the basic principles ordering their relations by similarity and difference can be stated.

Ethnolinguistics and Structural Models

The productive efforts of linguistically based ethnologists found their primary substance in "folk taxonomies." That is, they sought to uncover the principles by which things were classified: concepts of diseases, plants, animals, colors, myth, religion (see, e.g., Conklin 1955; Frake 1961; Gumperz and Hymes, eds., 1964; Romney and D'Andrade 1964; Hammel, ed., 1965; A. G. Smith, ed., 1966; and Tyler, ed., 1969). Kinship terminology provided substance for a proliferation of "componential analyses" pioneered by Goodenough (1951, 1956) and Lounsbury (1956).

Those who followed the linguistic path of structural analysis viewed their efforts as reorienting ethnographic purpose and spoke to the "new ethnography" and to "ethnoscience" (Goodenough 1957, Sturtevant 1964, Frake 1964*a*). They rejected the methods of behavioral psychology for understanding culture and questioned the use of quantification and social-structural analyses for grasping the psychological reality of cultural meanings. They strained toward what Pike (1966*b*) had discriminated as the "emic approach": "Emic descriptions provide an internal view, with criteria chosen from within the system. They represent to us the view of one familiar with the system and who knows how to function within it himself." An "etic" approach remained foreign to any local system because a researcher's intention to make cross-cultural comparisons led him to construct his categories. The view from within enunciated by Pike in effect accented a structural-functional orientation and contrasted inner meaning and basic reality (emics) with manifest expression (etics). In their definition of a "semantic domain" emicists laid out a natural context for analysis, analogous to Malinowski's conception of the "institution," as the proper unit for research. The closest correspondence with any of Malinowski's institutions, however, is the domain of kinship; and here the concern is narrowed, as Goodenough (1956:195) puts it, to "What do I have to know about A and B in order to say that A is B's cousin? "

As a methodological procedure, componential analysis proves more suggestive than precise in its results, despite the elegant, parsimonious, and productive (i.e., generating anticipated effects) quality of the analysis (Burling 1964*a*, with comments by Hymes and Frake, and 1964*b*; Hammer 1966; Wallace and Atkins 1969). It is apparent that formal analysis of kinship terminology can produce several models, each of which is predictive of terminological usage. However, the question remains

as to which holds psychological saliency for the native informants (Wallace 1965:235).

Though logical analysis does not succeed in solving the complex human-culture equation, there have been a number of important side effects. For one thing, the patterning of human behavior is no longer viewed as anchored in unconscious processes, and a greater range of activity is admitted to the conscious domain. New linkages have been forged with semiotics and epistemology and with mathematics through the medium of symbolic logic. The view of language and culture as a communications system lends itself to the use of message models and cybernetics (Wiener 1948, 1950).

Mechanical and Statistical Models. Discrimination of mechanical and statistical models by Lévi-Strauss (1953; see Nutini 1965) contrasts tightly integrated and coherent systems with pluralistic ones. In the former there is a close correspondence between stated premises and behavior, while in the latter more alternatives and contradictions are present. Some systems, of course, mix the two. Implicitly the mechanical and statistical models pose the question of the relation of normative and behavioral patterns, the ideal and the real, and draw attention to the fact that some areas of activity are organized to produce specific results with little tolerance for variation. This relationship is illustrated in the distinction of prescriptive and preferential marriage and their respective connection to mechanical and statistical models (Lévi-Strauss 1969:xxxv):

Fundamentally, the sole difference between prescriptive marriage and preferential marriage is at the level of the model. It corresponds to the difference which I have since proposed between what I call a "mechanical model" and a "statistical model"; i.e., in one case, a model the elements of which are on the same scale as the things whose relationships it defines: classes, lineages, degrees; while in the other case, the model must be abstracted from significant factors underlying distributions which are apparently regulated in terms of probabilities.

Mechanical prescriptive systems tend to replicate themselves in a kind of segmentary process of fission, and hence are ill suited to historical and evolutionary analysis. In short, from the standpoint of structure they tend to be static. The relatively open statistical systems are more subject to variation, and hence are better models for the study of change processes. The goal of ethnography and social anthropology must be the construction of "mechanical models, while history (together with its so called 'auxiliary' disciplines) and sociology end ultimately in statistical models" (Lévi-Strauss 1963). *The Elementary Structures of Kinship* (Lévi-Strauss 1969) was designed to clarify the distinction between mechanical and statistical social types, and to show that the basic organization of society, simple and complex, centers in reciprocal alliances for the exchange of women. The prescriptive designation of matrilateral or patrilateral cross-cousin marriage casts societies into different cycles of exchange and of social integration:

A human group need only proclaim the law of marriage with the mother's brother's daughter for a vast cycle of reciprocity between all generations and lineages to be organized, as harmonious and ineluctable as any physical or biological law, whereas marriage with the father's sister's daughter forces the interruption and reversal of collaborations from generation to generation and from lineage to lineage.

The bilateral, matrilateral, and patrilateral types comprise the three elemen-

tary structures of exchange upon which primitive societies have developed their distinctive forms. Yet as constructs they have been "always present to the human mind, at least in an unconscious form," and it was not possible for the human mind to recall one without discriminating the others in opposition (Lévi-Strauss 1969).

Universal Ideas. In addressing himself in a philosophic mode to anthropological research, Lévi-Strauss anticipated the recovery of unconscious apprehensions of ideas universal to mankind. His goal recalls the accent on elementary ideas formulated by Bastian, and explains why Lévi-Strauss (1963) cites Boas as the first to have clarified the unconscious nature of cultural phenomena and to have grasped the nature of structural problems despite his stress on historic variation. However, Lévi-Strauss, viewing these elementary universal ideas in the dynamics of history, translates their interplay into the Marxian dialectic, seeking "to reintegrate the anthropological knowledge acquired during the last fifty years into the Marxian tradition." Thus the culture of any society discloses various orders unified by an underlying value meaning, but usually masked by the formal oppositions by which they are consciously organized. Conscious models or norms are poor fellows to follow, since they are more apt to be rationalizations of the system they are designed to perpetuate. Viewed in a historic-geographic perspective, adjacent societies can be found sharing cultural features that turn out to be permutative inversions of central ideas or value meanings (Lévi-Strauss 1963, chaps. 11 and 13). Human culture history thus is a musical score in syncopated rhythm, whose basic meaning, if it can be captured in the term "progress," implies a deepening self-awareness for individual and group.

ACCULTURATION

The appearance of "A Memorandum for the Study of Acculturation," drawn up by Robert Redfield, Ralph Linton, and Melville Herskovits (1936), coincided with the appearance of works concentrating on the contacts of peoples under colonial rule (e.g., Schapera, ed., 1934; Thurnwald 1935; M. Hunter 1936; Elkin 1937; Linton, ed., 1940) and signaled a new interest in cultural modification as a live process.

Guided by the culture concept, American ethnologists endeavored to view change in the context of form and meaning, to which Linton (1936) added use and function. Following Linton, Barnett (1940, 1942, 1953) found that innovations, especially inventions, sometimes used new principles to attain established purposes, or that a traditional principle might be used to renovate a new form. Barnett (1940:31, 47) stressed the "stability and the determinative nature of form" in the acceptance, rejection, or reinterpretation of novel traits, and noted that form and meaning were joined as a unit (complex) that satisfied "the social, biological, or psychic requirements of a specific occasion." The effort to uncover the sociopsychological basis for acceptance or rejection soon turned to unconscious processes to explain the retention of culture pattern or structure (e.g., Kluckhohn 1943, Herskovits 1948; cf. Kroeber 1944). The emergent focus on the value integration of culture and its relation to personality, both topics resting in theory on the dynamics of unconscious processes, found a ready application in acculturative studies (see, e.g., Mead 1932; Thompson and Joseph 1944; Thompson 1950; Leighton and Kluckhohn 1947; Beaglehole and Beaglehole 1946; Ford 1941; Hallowell 1955*b*; Macgregor 1946; F. Kluckhohn and Strodtbeck, eds., 1961).

Nativistic Movements

Acculturation studies have correlated cultural disorganization with personality conflicts and with retention of traditional value commitments and cultural goals that no longer can be realized. In nativistic movements, as Linton (1943) observed, one can detect rational efforts to revive or perpetuate selected aspects of culture (see Lesser 1933, La Barre 1938, P. Nash 1955; cf. Slotkin 1952 and 1956, Aberle 1966, Lommel 1953, Voget 1956, Worsley 1968, Wallace 1956). From a general theory of deprivation, first clearly formulated by P. Nash (1955), subsequent research focused on primary deprivations, threats to economic security, loss of ethnocultural identity, and loss of autonomy. As Aberle (1966) observed, deprivation experienced relative to a level of expectations may underpin a social movement; but whether people set forth to renovate society or themselves is largely a matter of social context. "It would seem that transformative movements [changing society] are likely when groups are being forced out of the socioeconomic or ecological niches they occupy into more marginal niches; whereas redemptive movements [changing the individual] are likely to appeal when groups are forced into new niches in a larger social framework" (Aberle 1966). Increasingly, by virtue of comparative surveys and classification, nativistic movements were seen as purposeful efforts directed toward socioeconomic and political ends. They might, as in the instance of the Paliau movement (Mead 1961, Schwartz 1962), involve magico-religious phases; but the "essential rationality of Melanesian thought and action," commented Worsley

(1968; cf. Balandier 1965*a*) after surveying cargo cults in the area, "is shown on a larger scale by the directional tendency of the movements, the transition from magical to political action."

Urbanization

In Africa the use of migrant labor on farms and in cities, urbanization of Africans, participation of Africans in labor unions, and government labor policies under colonial rule early focused attention on white-black relations; but it was not until the imminent release of Africans from European control that research on processes of urbanization gathered strength. Malinowski (1961*b*) provided the initial theoretical framework by pointing to the institutionalized contacts between the European and African societies. Every cultural institution, he said, is organized by a statement of goals and procedures (charter), norms regulating personnel using a material apparatus in organized activities for fulfillment of a function (need). The meeting of European and African institutionalized groups produced, in Malinowski's judgment, an accommodative field of interrelations, a third institutionalized pattern linking the European and indigenous institutions. Stimulated by Malinowski, the Wilsons (1945) developed a theory of institutional linkage that integrated economic, social, and political change into the structured field of interactions. Like Steward (1951), the Wilsons concluded that as one moves up through the integrative levels, autonomy in action diminishes.

Biculturalism

Gluckman (1965*a*), rather than seeing Africans developing tribal accommodations in the urban environment which formed the basis of a third culture order, stresses their biculturalism. When on the reserve they live out the pattern of life there, but in the city they follow specifications for urban living (see Epstein 1958). Gluckman's situational orientation can be translated readily into reference-group theory (see Merton 1957), which has also been applied to American Indian acculturation (e.g., French 1961, Dozier 1961). It also parallels Fortes' (1949) demonstration of the ways in which the general principles structuring Ashanti society—seniority, paternity, matrilineal descent, jural authority, and social affiliation—are accommodated to a varying social context. That Malinowski's theory of an intermediate accommodative culture might not be wholly wrong has been revealed by the emergence of a "recognized body of urban 'customary' law in terms of which urban African litigants present their claims" (Epstein 1958:221). To cope with the ethnocultural heterogeneity of their African litigants, magistrates need to be guided by the common core of understandings regulating social relationships, the primary focus of tribal law and custom. The extension, with functional modifications, of traditional types of family and mutual aid associations into the urban environment also indicates that African urban culture is not a mirror image of that of the industrialized West (see, e.g., Balandier 1962; Little 1957; van den Berghe, ed., 1965). The fact that Xhosa townsmen in East London, Republic of South Africa, distribute themselves in exclusive groups that either live as real townsmen, maintain their tribal traditions despite the urban environment, or follow the image instilled through their mission education, suggests that something more complicated than a simple biculturalism is involved, and that the cultural force of the rural reserve continues to exert a considerable effect on urban migrants (Mayer 1961; cf. Little 1951, Spindler 1955, Hurt 1961-1962).

In a dynamically changing Africa, the viability of traditional institutions in meeting the strenuous challenges of rapid modernization could be an important datum. Apter (1961) viewed the disintegration of colonialism as a rich opportunity for African institutions to renew their own sociopolitical development, interrupted by the period of European control. The ritualization of value in Ghana had so structured their institutional arrangements that, under the guidance of Nkrumah, they were forced to renovate their system from top to bottom. In the instance of Buganda, however, their approach to institutions had been instrumental. Apter (1961:475-76) described their state as a "tiny figure of continuity and tradition" in the midst of the "turmoil and distress of a mighty continent in motion..." (cf. Gutkind 1963, Mead 1961).

As events have proved in Africa, India, and Indonesia, instant adaptation to the pressing functional demands of modernization has been exceedingly difficult for traditional political systems variously eroded as a result of colonial modifications and the spread of European ideologies through education and Christianity. At the same time, political renovations modeled on Western lines have proved ineffective in rapidly modifying the face of village tradition and custom.

Following up his general treatment of the transformation of the folk society in the process of urbanization, Redfield (1941, 1950, 1953) revisited Chan Kom in Yucatan to see how successful the people there had been at modernizing themselves through harmonizing tradition with modernity. Their progress in facing into the future, he concluded, was a partial success in that they had brought their "traditional moral conceptions and the traditional scheme of society" to bear on the "new economic and political opportunities" available to them (Redfield 1950:167; cf. Goldkind 1965). Like Apter, Redfield (cf. Mead 1961, Erasmus 1961) is inclined to stress the conscious application of traditional moral and social "capital" to the solution of economic and political problems.

The Culture of Poverty

Foster (1965; cf. Wolf 1955), on the other hand, views peasant conditions as being founded on anxious competition with others for the limited scarcities that sustain life. Living according to the principle of limited good, peasants are not positively conditioned to be cooperative or friendly or trusting. On the contrary, they tend to be envious, suspicious, and individualistic. As Wolf (1955) points out in a typological survey of Latin American peasantry, communities in their present form are the historic-cultural product of the Spanish conquest, and their backwardness is in large part a product of their institutionalized poverty. In his researches in Mexico, Lewis (1961, 1969) has detailed through family life histories how urban life is lived under the culture of poverty, using the term to call attention to the fact that people in poverty seem to share uniformities in their mode of life. Viewed in the context of change, peasants and their urban counterparts of the ghetto are seen as undernourished and deprived substrata of a larger system. The structural-functional view of those living in a culture of poverty (see Valentine 1968 and commentaries in *Current Anthropology* 10 [1969]:181-201) echoes an earlier theoretical statement by Adam Smith, as interpreted by Dugald Stewart (1858: liv):

Every system of policy which endeavours, either by extraordinary encouragements to draw towards a particular species of industry a greater share of the capital of the society than what would naturally go to it, or, by extraordinary restraints, to force from a particular species of industry some share of the capital which would otherwise be employed in it, is, in reality, subversive of the great purpose which it means to promote.

Social Interaction

Stress on group relations as essential to understanding structure is a prime criterion for a meaningful typology of peasant societies (Wolf 1955, 1957). A change in situation is followed by an altered social interaction. In a historic-cultural description of Yaqui acculturation, Spicer (1961) has determined a succession of interactional communities. Intensive acculturation experienced under the Jesuit missionaries early in the seventeenth century produced a culture heavily loaded with Spanish organizational features and forms heavily suffused with Yaqui meanings. Cultural fusion went forward during a long period of discontinuous contact with the Spanish and later Mexican administrations, when the Yaquis were able to act with a high degree of autonomy (*ca.* 1740-1887). The result was, in the words of Spicer (1961:88; cf. Redfield 1941), a "new folk culture" that proved to be a "tightly organized system of cultural behavior . . . extremely resistant to further fundamental change," even when the Yaquis were dispersed under Mexican policy. As resettlement brought some Yaquis back to their Sonoran homeland, they found themselves in the presence of Mexicans, and a "dual society and culture developed in the reestablished communities." However, the "general tendency . . . was toward an increasing rigidity of the revived folk culture" (Spicer 1961:88).

APPLIED ANTHROPOLOGY

From its start in the eighteenth century, anthropology was conceived as an aid to the improvement of society and the quality of human life. The specific application of anthropology to social problems, however, remained a matter for individual concern or for private organizations (see McNickle 1961-1962) until the thirties, when governments intensified their invitations for anthropological participation in colonial programs of change and administration. Then anthropologists faced up to the task of applying their knowledge to directed change among subject peoples (see, e.g., Brown and Hutt 1935; Malinowski 1961b; Keesing 1945; Mekeel 1944; Kennard and Macgregor 1953; Forde 1953; Metraux 1953; Thompson 1951; Mead, ed., 1955). With the formation of the Society for Applied Anthropology (1941), an agency was established which could cooperate, through consultation and research, with governmental agencies. World War II drew anthropologists into direct cooperation with government as they provided ethnological data on peoples in the Pacific and guides to understanding the cultural psychology of the enemy. Termination of the war brought continued participation of anthropologists in the trust territories and in government programs such as Point 4, designed to improve the economic base of the developing nations.

Anthropology Applied to Governmental Programs

Participation in programs designed to implement government policy raised serious moral issues and also called into question the anthropological purpose as science (see Barnett 1956; Mair 1969). The moral and scientific issues became even more sharply divisive as tension in the cold war heightened with the rise of popular social movements in Asia and Latin America.

The practical lessons based on research which anthropologists drew to the attention of administrators were not always congenial to the politics of administration. Also, administrators found much of the content of anthropological research only distantly relevant to their urgent requirements. The failure of programs could be traced to insensitivity to the customs, organizational procedures, and covert commitments in which people's life styles were anchored. A corollary of this was the governmental purpose of organizing the goals and procedures for people undergoing change without providing for their participation, assuring their cooperation, or allowing them to design their own destiny and grow in self-realization (see, e.g., Spicer, ed., 1961; Gearing, Netting, and Peattie, eds., 1960; Foster 1962; Brokensha and Hodge 1969; Erasmus 1961; Arensberg and Niehoff 1964; Miniclier 1964; Schaedel 1964; Boggs 1964; M. Nash 1958). At Vicos in the Andes, Holmberg and his associates (Holmberg 1955, 1958; Holmberg and Dobyns 1962) succeeded over a span of ten years in renovating the community with agricultural innovations, a broadened educational base, and a local leadership that eventuated in an autonomous community; but it is evident that without the benign cooperation of government, the effort to draw the *vicosinos* into a broader network of relations in a self-reliant and independent manner would have been frustrated, owing to the nature of the socioeconomic structure.

Anthropology Applied to Industry

The application of anthropology to industry and other institutions (e.g.,

hospitals) grew up in association with structural-functional theory under Malinowski and Radcliffe-Brown. The Australian psychiatrist Elton Mayo, sensitized to the anthropological approach, conducted studies on fatigue that pointed to the immense significance of human relations for aspiration and for the slowing of productivity because of fatigue (Mayo 1933; also Roethlisberger and Dickson 1939). Subsequent stress on industrial organization as a system of interactions and communication moderated by a human factor opened new understandings about productivity, poor workmanship, absenteeism, and innovations in production (Richardson 1961, Savage 1964, Chapple and Arensberg 1940, Chapple 1953).

SOCIAL AND CULTURAL INTEGRATION, ACCULTURATION, AND PERSONALITY

The reality problem for culture, as for most phenomena, is presented in the form of a generalized structure and variations with regard to this structure. When Wissler (1923) described the universal culture pattern (cf. Murdock 1945) as including family, religion, economics, war, and the like, he outlined the generic structure of any culture, simple or complex. Malinowski (1944), with his biological and functional imperatives, had attacked the same problem as Radcliffe-Brown (1965a), who noted the functional prerequisites for maintaining any society (cf. Aberle et al. 1950). The aims of social structuralists were directed to elucidating those fundamental social operations, and to explaining social morphology. Hence Radcliffe-Brown's oft-repeated injunction that social anthropology must employ the comparative method (but not as employed by developmentalists) and his call for a general theory of society. With regard to social integration, Radcliffe-Brown was perceptive enough to distinguish two types: functional consistency and logical consistency. Functional consistency applies to basic conditions affecting the existence of any society; it is here that one must search for sociological laws, just as Malinowski searched for his laws in the generic biological and psychological needs of man, which he regarded as functional prerequisites for culture.

Malinowski's and Radcliffe-Brown's primary concern with generic requirements and general theory did not deal with the problems of variation, whereas the concern for unique events, prompted by Boas' stress on tracing the ways in which culture elements are reshaped in passing from one culture to the next, focused on the diversity of cultures and their uniqueness resulting from historic contacts.

Personality and Cultural Variation

Following an early lead of Boas, Benedict (1934, 1946) showed how, in a well-integrated culture, the most ill-assorted acts become characteristic of its peculiar goals, often by the most unlikely metamorphoses. Sapir (1958b) opened up broad philosophical issues when discussing genuine and spurious types of cultures, and suggested that a realistic typology of culture would be psychological in character. His influence on Benedict, according to Mead (1959), was considerable, and added support for her definition of Apollonian and Dionysian styles of life. In *Patterns of Culture* (Benedict 1934) an integrated culture became the product of a historical selection of a temperamental type (cf. Mead 1950 and Mead, ed., 1937).

The appeal to temperament to explain the integration of cultures never attracted wide support among anthropologists. Nonetheless, the attack on

cultural integration prompted Linton (1936) to discuss the institutionalized orientations of cultures, and Herskovits (1948) to define the focus of a culture as an area of primary interest, activity, and elaboration. Rather common agreement that covert value sentiments focused human activity prompted a continuing search for unconscious value commitments in the structural backgrounds of cultures (Bateson 1965, Opler 1945, Redfield 1941 and 1953, Kluckhohn 1949, Honigmann 1949; cf. Collier 1947, M. Wilson 1963, Vogt 1951, Smith and Roberts 1954, Albert 1956, F. Kluckhohn and Strodtbeck 1961).

Turning their attention to the situation of American Indians concentrated on reservations, researchers endeavored to discover the relation between values, cultural integration, and personality integration. They concluded that the disintegration of culture, through the shedding of values underpinning important institutionalized patterns, contributed conflict and disorientation to personality (Macgregor 1946, Thompson 1951, Kluckhohn and Leighton 1962, Hallowell 1951, 1955c).

The Psychoanalytic Approach

Stress on the unconscious patterning of behavior to which American students of culture were committed led easily to Freudian interpretation of personality in relation to culture. Here the psychoanalyst Abram Kardiner, together with Ralph Linton, Clyde Kluckhohn, and Cora Du Bois, took the initiative (Kardiner 1939, 1945; Linton 1945; Du Bois 1944). The Freudian conception of the unconscious was rooted in the repression of deep-seated reactions to frustration, whereas the anthropological approach had anchored unconscious motivation to positive conditioning based on a stimulus-response model. While both were joined in the culture-and-personality emphasis that emerged, the weight of interpretation favored the Freudian view of unconscious processes deriving from frustrative experiences rooted in biopsychic processes, notably feeding, toilet training, and sex (e.g., Whiting and Child 1962). Translated into a theory of culture, the psychodynamics of personality and culture develop a basic personality structure organized by feeling states derived from primary institutions. These primary institutions include "family organization, in-group formation, basic disciplines, feeding, weaning, institutionalized care or neglect of children, anal training, and sexual taboos including aim, object, or both, subsistence techniques..." (Kardiner 1939:471). Secondary institutions are found in taboo systems, religion, rituals, folk tales, and techniques of thinking. In Kardiner's view, the primary institutions provide the basis for deep-rooted anxiety and aggressive motivations, which are relieved through the secondary institutions. In other words, religion and mythology can be expected to house and release inner tensions arising from deprivation, providing fulfillment that has had to be forgone because of the reality situation. Religion and mythology are prime illustrations of unconscious projective systems.

There are various ways, including lengthy psychoanalysis, to get at the unconscious basis for shared behavior, but the use of free association techniques in the form of projective tests seemed to offer the fieldworker effective controls and a way of substantiating immediate observation. Hence the use of Rorschach and Thematic Apperception Tests, despite doubts concerning their validity for cross-cultural comparisons (Hallowell 1945, W. E. Henry 1947, J. Henry and Spiro 1953, Kaplan

1954, Du Bois 1944; see also Honigmann 1954; Hsu, ed., 1961; Barnouw 1963).

Sex Roles. The intellectual career of Margaret Mead discloses the timely trend to the psychoanalysis of culture. On investigating the process of growing up in Samoa (1928) and Manus (1930), Mead (1950) attempted to show that temperamental differences commonly assumed to be distinctive of the sexes were not of signal importance in determining the status personalities fixated by cultural definition. By cultural definition men could act just as maternally as women were thought naturally to be, and women could be just as aggressive as the masculine stereotype of Western civilization. By 1945 Mead had reviewed her field data dealing with seven societies in the South Seas and translated the whole into psychoanalytic terms. Yet, like Benedict, Mead continued to hold the view that human nature was exceedingly malleable and that the vast majority of individuals were shaped in the cultural mold. Again following Benedict, she used temperament to appeal for a relaxing of cultural intolerance for biologically engendered differences and standards that placed persons of certain temperamental types in positions of intolerable conflict, thereby damaging their personalities and restricting creativity.

Unconscious Processes. Freudian-based conceptions of personality processes expanded the anthropological conception of unconscious processes and of their origins. It pointed to early childhood as the timely moment when emotional commitments were laid down and pointed out that the link between culture and personality might rest on a rather ambiguous and contradictory base. "The transmission of culture ... must be thought of as part of a very complicated and symbolically mediated learning process in which mechanisms like conflict and repression play their role in the total integrative structure that we call the human personality" (Hallowell 1955c). Hence the profound stimulus to review the balance between cultural demands and compensatory satisfactions for the growing child, on the one hand, and the expression of modalities in national character in art, literature, religion, and mythology on the other. (For a considered bibliography, see Honigmann 1967; see also Mead and Metraux 1953).

Strengths and Weaknesses of Psychoanalytic Theory. Applied to acculturation, psychoanalytic theory, in conjunction with the projective techniques, seemed to provide confirmation of the anthropological view that the covert commitments supporting culture patterns are long enduring (Kluckhohn 1943, Hallowell 1955a). At the same time, it drew attention to the signal importance of interpersonal relations in tripping responses filled with anxiety, aggression, and fantasy which cannot alter so long as interpersonal relations remain the same (Caudill 1949, Barnouw 1950, Spindler 1955, Wallace 1952, Friedl 1956). However, in the search for the integrates of cultures, the psychoanalytic approach proved restrictive in that a typology must be anchored to oral, anal, and genital fixations. The individual is forever pitted against culture norms that frustrate. In their explanations psychoanalytically oriented anthropologists found themselves restricted to a part, not the whole, of culture and society. They were more at home in religion, mythology, and art, fields that could provide suggestive answers for bizarre customs.

Also, analysis of functional correlates corresponding to a human biopsychic structure necessarily omitted any reference to historic processes.

However, psychoanalytic theory did provide a basis for an evolutionary view of man's emergence as a self-conscious, socialized being. Freud had grounded psychoanalysis in biopsychic processes, the most important of which had become internalized through a kind of phylogenetic inheritance. This emphasis was dropped by neo-Freudians like Kardiner. Nonetheless, there remained the challenging problem of man's evolution and the transition from an animal to a human base, not only with regard to constitution, but with regard to awareness of self and the relation of self to others. The human milieu, according to Hallowell (1955c; cf. Spiro 1954, La Barre 1954, J. Henry 1959), is unique in that man, through his capacity to symbolize, to judge himself as self, and to experience unconsciously the irrepressible twinges of guilt and anxiety, is able to respond to socialization and become a social person. It was not hand, foot, cortical additions to the brain, or even the presence of tool-using that forecast man, but rather the human personality and the social milieu through which it developed.

ETHNOHISTORY

Use of documentary materials to describe selected aspects of ancient life is a practice of long standing among historians. Spanish documents had served to interpret the Aztec and Inca cultures, and the *Jesuit Relations* and allied documents (Thwaites, ed., 1959) had provided a rich background for the history of the Northeast. For ethnologists geared to the collection of ethnographic materials in the field, historic materials were limited to a secondary role. Only as historic documents presented themselves as primary evidence did they gain an advantage over data collected in the field. Fenton (1951: 296) observes how field and library are joined in the study of cultures, and how, in the instance of Iroquois studies, the trend has been to the library. "Perhaps," he adds, "this trend from field to library reflects the direction in which American studies are moving as they mature from a century of collecting and field reporting to a new era of maturer synthesis." Fenton (1940) broke new ground by uniting ethnological and historical data to expose cultural-geographical differentiations among the Iroquois. When assembling ethnographic descriptions of the Caddo Indians and the tribes of the Southeast, Swanton (1942, 1946) was forced to rely on historical documents for his primary sources. Cultural-historical interest, ethnographic description, and reconstruction of the aboriginal culture also promoted the use of documentary sources, as in the instance of Spier's (1935) effort to find the source for the Ghost Dance that swept through the Plains tribes in 1890, taking to new extremes an aboriginal prophet tradition among the interior plateau tribes of the Northwest. Demands for documentary evidence substantiating tribal locations and land use in Indian land claims cases drew ethnologists into ethnohistoric research, much as archaeologists were led to the use of historic materials when tying their sequences to protohistoric and historic periods (e.g., Newell and Krieger 1949, Wedel 1959). Starting from an ethnological base of inference, Eggan (1937; cf. Spoehr 1941, Hickerson 1956 and 1967) searched historic documents for evidence revealing the presence of a Crow type of kinship system among various Muskogean-speaking peoples of the Southeast. Ethnohistoric problems thus served to draw prehistorians, eth-

nologists, and historians into a common enterprise.

ETHNOECONOMICS

Malinowski's (1922) description of the *kula* ring of the Southern Massim and Mauss's (1961a) analysis of the meaning of gift exchange marked the beginning of a fresh consideration of economic organization and process in primitive societies. Reciprocities intermingled with kinship and ritual obligations seemed to remove the exchange arrangements of primitive societies from the model of market exchange characteristic of industrialization. Like Malinowski and Mauss, Firth (1929), Thurnwald (1932), and Herskovits (1940; cf. 1952) distinguished the non-market economies of primitive peoples from the market economy of the West, and held that primitive economic behavior was so embedded in a matrix of social and religious institutionalizations that nothing like the "economic man" of classic economic theory would apply.

Support for the distinction of primitive or archaic economies from the industrial exchange system was contributed by Karl Polanyi (1947, 1957), an economic historian. The significance of Polanyi's work lies in the fact that it has alerted anthropologists to the importance of primitive and archaic economies for general theory. Like Radcliffe-Brown and Malinowski, he stresses beginning empirically with the kinds of relations or transactions that appropriately can be ascribed to economics. In this perspective he distinguishes three "main patterns . . . reciprocity, redistribution, and exchange" (1968: 149). Each of these transactive modes can be found in primitive, archaic, and industrialized socioeconomic systems. The primitive societies, however, are more often integrated by reciprocity;

the archaic, such as the Dahomey (Polanyi and Rotstein 1966), by redistribution; and heavily industrialized societies by market exchange. Thus Polanyi challenges the universalizing of the classic conception of economic behavior as the allocation of scarce means to alternative ends in a rational-pragmatic fashion. On the contrary, he casts economic behavior in primitive and archaic societies against a broader context of social and moral meanings. In so doing he conforms to the anthropological intent of seeking the range of economic types and economic behavior and of deriving principles of organization, process, and meaning by induction. Part of this operation, as Firth (1939) and Herskovits (1952) indicate, consists in measuring the application of generic economic theory against the facts of primitive economies to see to what extent they apply.

Much of the theoretical debate that followed Polanyi's statement and the statements of Dalton (1960, 1961, 1963, 1965a, 1965b)—Burling (1962), Cook (1969), Le Clair (1962), and Harris (1959)—centered on the pseudo-problem of contrasting the archetypes of primitive and industrial economic man. In the judgment of the ethnographer Pospisil (1963; see Tax 1953, Belshaw 1955 and 1965), some primitive societies, such as the Papuan Kapauku, must be classed with Western capitalism; others, like the Trobriand Islanders, must be distinguished from both primitive and industrial systems.

The differences confronted by economic anthropologists recall the difficulties faced by taxonomists of fossil man: viewed in the narrow taxonomy of form and the relations of parts, *Homo habilis* might very well be viewed anatomically as belonging to the genus *Australopithecus;* but viewed in the perspective of an evolutionary potential, *H. habilis* justifiably might be classified under the genus *Homo* (Reed 1967). The fact that exchange transactions are to be found in all societies—although in lesser degree in the primitive and archaic archetypes, according to Polanyi and Dalton—establishes a base for comparing these systems with the industrial and supports Herskovits' (1952) judgment that the "distinctions to be drawn between literate and nonliterate economies are . . . those of degree rather than of kind."

JURIDICAL AND POLITICAL ANTHROPOLOGY

The differentiation of juridical anthropology owes much of its impulse to the appearance of Malinowski's *Crime and Custom in Savage Society* in 1926. Here he presents law in primitive society as a social process by which individuals are bound together in traditional obligations resting on the principle of reciprocity. Malinowski's intent is to show that primitive peoples are not slaves to custom, and to dispel the view that the sanctions for primitive behavior rest on fear and especially on supernaturalized taboos. For Malinowski, social behavior rests on a more secure foundation, and he discovered this social base in reciprocity.

Radcliffe-Brown's attempt to determine the functional prerequisites for societies led him to study law, religion, and morality as three ways of controlling human conduct in the interests of social solidarity and continuity (Radcliffe-Brown 1965e). His treatment of patrilineal and matrilineal succession (1965c) stressed the corporate nature of the descent group in the exercise of legal rights and duties over persons and things and their transfer through marriage and succession. Any individual was a legal person, in effect, holding a "status . . . defined as the totality of all his rights and duties as recognized in the social usages (laws and customs) of the society to which he belongs." Law and custom, like status, morality, religion, and property, were interrelated and collected the power of authorities in political organization. Here, according to Radcliffe-Brown (1940:xiv), "we have to deal with the maintenance or establishment of social order, within a territorial framework, by the organized exercise of coercive authority through the use, or the possibility of use of physical force."

The interrelations of law, property, and politics had long been recognized, and many students of politics, as Nader (1965:10) observed, "assumed . . . judicial behavior . . . [to be] a part of political behavior." The relation of law and political organization was described for the Comanche by Hoebel (1940), for the Nupe by Nadel (1942), for the Yap by Schneider (1957), for the Barotse by Gluckman (1965b), and for the Tiv by Bohannan (1957). An important consideration turned on the relation between law and custom. Malinowski (1926) defined law as any normative behavior requiring reciprocity; but this is such a general statement that the substance of law and of legal process can hardly be recognized. While custom as law involves normative statements, law itself, according to Bohannan (1965:34-36), gathers together a body of custom and institutionalizes it for the express purpose of settling "disputes . . . and counteract[ing] any gross and flagrant abuse of rules" in the several institutionalized activities. That is, "A social norm is legal if its neglect . . . is regularly met, in threat or fact, by the application of physical force by an individual or group possessing the socially recognized privilege of so acting" (Hoebel 1954:28). Whether the conceptual apparatus of Western jurisprudence can be used serviceably in categorizing and analyzing folk law raises a long-standing issue in anthropology

(e.g., Gluckman 1962b; cf. Ayoub 1961)—one echoed in the classic distinction of economic man and the etic and emic distinction reemphasized by Pike (1966b).

The extent to which law may reflect a basic value commitment sets the stage for Hoebel's *The Law of Primitive Man: A Study in Comparative Legal Dynamics* (1954; see also 1965; cf. W. Smith and Roberts 1954). Here Hoebel attempts to state the basic postulates underlying the legal ways of the Eskimo, Ifugao, Trobriand, Ashanti, Comanche, Kiowa, and Cheyenne peoples. In evolutionary perspective, Hoebel describes a trend from status to contract very much like that of Maine (1861; cf. Barton 1919), while stressing the submergence of legal process in the organized judicial processes of the state.

Descriptions of the interrelations of legal and political institutions as instruments for social control neatly fit with structural-functional emphases on order as symbolizing social solidarity (see, e.g., Fortes and Evans-Pritchard, eds., 1940; Gluckman 1955; Gulliver 1963). Like American culture theorists, British social anthropologists viewed the integration of the social system as a function of a value sentiment. More than other aspects of the social structure, the political order seizes the mystical symbols by which people unconciously experience their affiliation; hence the dominance of the political over other aspects of the social order (Fortes and Evans-Pritchard, eds., 1940:23). Social, economic, judicial, religious, and political symbols cluster around African kingship, drawn into focus by the rituals of accession and public welfare. The strain toward the ritualization of value, which Radcliffe-Brown made the keystone of his theory of social integration, might be productive of certain conflicts in group interests, and these conflicts, he suggests, might then themselves be ritualized (as in joking relationships) in the interest of unity. It is the latter structural theme that Gluckman (1955; cf. Bohannan 1958) explores in ceremonial role inversions and in licensed behavior expressing hatred and covetousness toward established authority. Again, a delicate integration can be reached through a balance of segmentary oppositions, as described for the Nuer by Evans-Pritchard (1940). The alternation of fission and fusion characteristic of Nuer segmentary organization, however, is translated into secession and conquest among the more populous Bantu of South Africa (cf. Schapera 1967).

From the evidence of East African societies distinguished by minimal or a diffuse popular authority (Mair 1962; cf. Cohen and Middleton, eds., 1967), it becomes clear that the larger unities of lineages, territorial groups, and tribes are controlled by ritualists or prophets, who, like the "man of cattle" among the Nuer, hold the traditional right to organize the initiation of young men into age grades (cf. Huntingford 1953 for the Nandi). Command over the most fundamental symbols uniting groups without a state organization thus seems to gravitate into the hands of religious specialists. In the rise of kingly states the principle of territoriality operates to divert the activities of lineage members into territorial forms of organization, with consequent restrictions on judicial and political functions attached to descent groups (Mair 1962). However, this historic cultural change must have engendered strain and conflict between the patterned interactions and the ideological framework on which they rested, much like the strain confronting the African chief subjected to the rationalization of government under colonial administration (Fallers 1956, Busia 1951).

Because of a bias for integrative processes in stuctural-functional analysis, processes of change tended to be overlooked in the interests of equilibrium strains and the ritualizing of conflict in the interests of group solidarity. The handling of contemporary economic, social, and political transformations witnessed in the developing nations, often fraught with conflict and confrontation, seemed to require a more dynamic model of societies in transition. Omitted from the usual structural-functional analysis, as Geertz (1957:52-53) pointed out, was a concern for the historic-cultural context, for appreciation of real differences in the relation between the existing "cultural framework of meaning and the [emergent] patterning of social interaction." In the instance of Modjokuto, situated in central Java, for example, modernization brought an increase in secularization that challenged the villager's mode of life, so filled with religious ceremony and obligation. Again the network of relationships restricted to a section of the village was challenged in the town by alignments of class, occupation, and political affiliation. In the town the villager's traditional values and associations encountered sharp discontinuities.

Thus, in addition to creating cultural ambiguity, the attempt to bring a religious pattern from a relatively less differentiated rural background into an urban context also gives rise to social conflict simply because the kind of social integration demonstrated by the pattern is not congruent with the major patterns of integration in the society generally [Geertz 1951:52; but cf. Bruner 1961, Ames 1963].

What Geertz pointed to was a cultural lag between the mystical values of the traditional system and the relatively pragmatic and politically organized activities accompanying the emergence of Indonesia as a nation. It was not the structural-functional method that needed to be faulted when applied to problems of change, however, but the investigators who restricted themselves to special theoretical issues.

ETHNOSOCIOLOGY

The differentiation of ethnosociology or social anthropology had been initiated by Durkheim and carried forward by Radcliffe-Brown in Britain. It was not until the thirties, however, that Radcliffe-Brown's message of a structural-functional social anthropology began to gain wide acceptance. The 1940s were a time of consolidation for Radcliffe-Brown and for those under his influence, a time for researching and applying his functional theory of social integration, beginning with Evans-Pritchard's (1940, 1951) research on the Nuer and culminating in Fortes' (1945, 1949) studies of kinship among the Tallensi (see also Fortes and Evans-Pritchard, eds., 1940, and Radcliffe-Brown and Forde, eds., 1962). Except for Nadel (1951), who undertook the task of developing a synthetic statement of the aims and methods of social anthropology, social structuralists were inclined to clue their hypotheses and functional-causal explanations to monographs and special articles. Much of the novelty of their analyses came in the inversion of the psychological-sociological relation in explanation. For example, when taking up the problem of incest, Evans-Pritchard (1951:91) noted:

Nuer say that marriage to persons standing in certain relationships is forbidden because it would be . . . incestuous. Speaking sociologically, I think we may reverse this statement and say that sexual relations with persons standing in these relationships are considered incestuous because it would be a breach of the marriage prohibitions to marry them. . . .

British social anthropologists became so wedded to the concept of social equilibrium and the structuring of society by principles of organization that even contrastive variations (e.g., a high rate of divorce) were held to be witnesses for the tensile strength of the organizing principles (e.g., Gluckman 1962a).

The distinction of the social and the cultural which Radcliffe-Brown enunciated when calling for a comparative sociology was followed by a similar trend in the United States, led by Ralph Linton (1936). Linton, however, considered the social system a part of the total culture, while Radcliffe-Brown saw culture as a derivative of the social structure. Yet both the American culturalists and the British social anthropologists converged on value principles as the source of the distinctive attributes of various social and cultural systems and as essential to organized social living (see, e.g., Kroeber and Kluckhohn 1963, Radcliffe-Brown 1965f). There was a sharp difference, however. Whereas British social anthropologists viewed social structure in terms of certain functional needs, American ethnologists under Linton were inclined to approach social structure from the standpoint of the individuals operating within it. Nonetheless, neither Radcliffe-Brown nor Linton could avoid a common discourse on status and role, rights and obligations, reciprocities, and legal and social sanctions.

Social Classification

Differentiation within anthropology turned investigators aside from the problem of a generic theory of society or of culture, which first concerned Radcliffe-Brown, Malinowski, and : Linton, and pointed research to social classification. The refinement of taxonomy with regard to social groups and their underlying principles of organization originally stressed unilineal and bilineal descent arrangements, owing to the rich supply of materials offered by the African researches of British social anthropologists. These processes of fission and accretion have been described as producing a hierarchic arrangement of segmentary units (see Fortes 1953; Radcliffe-Brown and Forde, eds., 1962). However, research in Southeast Asia and Oceania have focused attention on determination of membership in groups by other factors: economic and prestige (see, e.g., Firth 1929, 1957; Goodenough 1955; Freeman 1958; Davenport 1959). In short, membership is not so much a matter of ascription as of filiation (Fortes 1959).

Filiation defines the bilateral "relationship created by the fact of being the legitimate child of one's parents" (Fortes 1959:206), and properly must be considered universal to all social organization at the domestic level. Locality and relations to land, as Firth (ed., 1957) observed, presents the context in which we must understand the descent and kinship relations of the Maori, among whom choice is as much involved as assignment. Pointing out that "at least a third of the societies of the world are not unilineal, in the sense that they do not employ either patrilineal or matrilineal descent as a major organizing principle in the grouping of kinsmen," Murdock (ed., 1960:2) proposed the term "cognatic" to cover societies of this order. Some affiliations apparently were ego-centered and ramified bilaterally to include a variable and diffuse set of consanguineal and affinal relations, and this arrangement focused attention on the kindred (Freeman 1961; Goodenough 1955; Murdock, ed., 1960:10-12) as distinct from the ramage (Firth 1957, Davenport 1963), which involves relationship to an ancestor. Any descent group, unilineal or cognatic, exists by virtue of functions discharged in the interests of its members. Some are united by virtue of shar-

ing a material estate, privileged distinctions, or other incorporeal properties (Murdock, ed., 1960:4-5; cf. Leach 1961b), while others never operate as units but nonetheless serve to define the boundaries of individual obligations and reciprocities. The former can be distinguished as corporate groups, the latter as noncorporate or, in Murdock's phrase, "circumscriptive kin groups."

Following the lead of Radcliffe-Brown, Africanists of British social anthropological persuasion have accented the way the jural definition of relations supports the kinship system and produces segmentary or lineage groups that maintain their continuity through time. In *African Systems of Kinship and Marriage* (Radcliffe-Brown and Forde, eds., 1962), Radcliffe-Brown summarizes the essence of his findings on social organization, distinguishing four ideal types: father right, mother right, purely cognatic systems, and double lineage systems. He observes that cognatic systems are rare because they do not permit an easy functional definition of a corporate group that can maintain continuity. In a broad comparative work, *Social Structure*, Murdock (1949) attempts to establish a number of social types based on kinship, descent, residence, and other attributes. He then traces to changes in residence those modifications "in economy, technology, property, government, or religion [that] first alter the structural relationships of related individuals to one another, giving an impetus to subsequent modifications in forms of the family, in consanguineal and compromise kin groups, and in kinship terminology" (p. 202). Murdock's work is unique in that he states a general postulate and derives from it theorems that then are tested through statistical correlation. In a work edited by Schneider and Gough (1961) the nature of matrilineal systems is subjected to descriptive analysis in terms of hypotheses stressing the nature of tensions generated (Schneider) and level of productivity (Gough), while Aberle attempts cross-cultural correlations with regard to marriage, stratification, political organization, subsistence, and other factors coded in Murdock's "World Ethnographic Atlas" (1962).

Marriage as Reciprocity:
Mechanical and Statistical Models

Beginning with the assumption that rules are essential to the organization of society for survival, Lévi-Strauss (1969) viewed the incest rule as a collective intervention that forces groups to surrender their women in reciprocal exchanges. Through this elemental exchange, as in the instance of the Nambikwara, "a continuous transition exists from war to exchange, and from exchange to intermarriage, and the exchange of brides is merely the conclusion to an uninterrupted process of reciprocal gifts, which effects the transition from hostility to alliance, from anxiety to confidence, and from fear to friendship" (Lévi-Strauss 1969:67-68). Beyond this, he finds that the prescription of marriage with cross-cousins is the perfect model for an exchange that maintains an equivalent access to spouses. And in the cycling of reciprocities, marriage to the mother's brother's daughter promotes a more continuous and wide-ranging circle of exchange than marriage with the patrilateral cross-cousin. Exchange systems are of two orders, restricted and generalized. In the former, exchange relations are in pairs or in multiples of two, while generalized exchange is variable. A restricted exchange system is more formally structured by rules designed to produce an anticipated effect, and hence it presents an analogue to a mechanical model, whereas the generalized exchange is the analogue to a statistical model. The mechanical model describes a more static process in which alterations are little more than arithmetical increases expressing a constant structural arrangement, while the statistical model can accommodate historic variation and change in structure (cf. closed and open societies). In a broad effort to cast analysis within a context of total social facts (i.e., a primary integrate), Lévi-Strauss describes the apparent correlation of a number of social features, including the incest-exogamic rule, dual organization, unilineal descent, terminological distinctions of lineal and collateral relations, and distinction of parallel and cross-cousins. He points out (1969:98) that in the presence of an exogamic dual system, cross-cousins "are the first collaterals with whom marriage is possible."

Marriage Patterns:
A Psychological Interpretation

The structural mathematical analysis based on jural reciprocity formulated by Lévi-Strauss has drawn a counterthrust from Homans and Schneider (1955). Their psychological thesis is derived from Radcliffe-Brown (1956b), who argued that the focus of power in the hands of either the matrikin or patrikin led to formalized relations with those wielding power and to a countercurrent of friendly and protective sentiments directed to the opposite kin. Hence the male mother image associated with the mother's brother occurred in a patrilineal society in conjunction with the image of the female father associated with the father's sister. Lévi-Strauss' position regarding matrilateral or patrilateral cross-cousin prescriptions in no way depends upon type of unilineal descent. Indeed, the prevalence of matrilateral cross-cousin prescription, considering the numerical preponderance of patrilineal societies, seemed to deny any relationship with descent. On the other hand, Homans and Schneider hold that the generation of sympathetic sentiments in a matrilineal society directs individual marital choice to the patrilateral cross-cousin, while in a patrilineal society the sentiment of choice runs to the mother's brother's daughter. The greater frequency of patrilineal societies explains the prevalence of matrilateral cross-cousin preferential marriage.

Alternative Approaches

These contradictory theories, as Lounsbury (1962) perceptively observes in reviewing R. Needham's (1962) vigorous effort to refute Homans and Schneider, pose an old issue: "sociological *vs.* psychological explanation." He adds one other critical note—that the exercise of a right might be more crucial in marital arrangements than obligation, and that people might maneuver economic and political advantage when contracting marriages (cf. Leach 1960). Should that be the case, the quantification of cases to prove the validity of the jural prescriptive model might miss the point, for in the exercise of jural rights, as among the Toba Batak (Bruner 1959), not every lineage marriage must be contracted with a matrilateral cross-cousin to maintain the right in force. Mechanical models, as Lévi-Strauss has pointed out, are not subject to statistical validation and do not require it; hence the turn "to structural linguistics, logic, and mathematics, rather than to techniques for quantification and the use of statistics ... for new analytic and comparative models" that would elicit the structure and modal operations of social units (Davenport 1963:218).

QUANTIFICATION AND THE WORLD ETHNOGRAPHIC SAMPLE

The development of quantitative methods in ethnology came slowly, despite the early attempt of Tylor (1889) and the frequency percentages utilized by Hobhouse, Wheeler, and Ginsberg (1965) to document the growth in complexity of institutions with a concomitant increase in ethical judgment. In 1911 Czekanowski applied statistical correlation to the alleged historical associations of *Kulturkreis* theorists. In California, Kroeber sparked an attempt to see whether correlation coefficients of cultural traits would reveal ethnic clusterings and also assist in reconstructing the history of ethnic units (see the Culture Element Distribution Series of the University of California). Beginning with a collection of data on over 250 tribal societies (Human Relations Area Files, Yale University), G. P. Murdock (1962) gradually assembled coded materials on over 1,100 societies. Aside from bias in classification, differences in definitions, and uneven data, the construction of a random sample presented serious difficulties owing to the danger that historic contact had led to similarities not only between neighboring tribes, but throughout regions (see Naroll 1961, 1964, 1965; Naroll and D'Andrade 1963; Driver and Massey 1957; Driver 1970; Köbben 1967). Abandoning the strategy of a random sample, Murdock and White (1969) attempted to isolate as sampling provinces those societies whose geographic contiguity and cultural similarities suggested historic contact (cf. Greenbaum 1970).

Statistical correlation rests on the assumption of a functional-causal relation and therefore is not oriented toward historic-causal relations. Nonetheless, armed with a hypothesis that calls for a graduated integration of features through time, it is possible to use statistical correlations as checks on the hypothesized evolutionary developments. Thus Driver and Massey (1957), using data from 280 Indian tribes of North America, were able to offer partial confirmation of the general hypothesis that division of labor (e.g., association of cultivation with women) led to fixation of a corresponding form of nuptial residence (e.g., matrilocal or patrilocal). Once entrenched, a preferred residence pattern was followed by a type of descent congruent with the division of labor and residence, and finally came development of kinship terminology consistent with all three factors (Murdock 1949). However, as Driver (1966, Driver and Massey 1957) noted in an attempt to determine the relevance of psychofunctional and geographical-historical factors for affinal avoidances (mother-in-law-son-in-law, etc.), "significant correlations . . . with culture areas, language families, and kinship terminology" mean that historical factors are probably more responsible for the distribution of avoidances than other factors.

It became readily apparent that statistical correlations are no better than the logic of the hypothesis that a researcher brings to his study. Without selecting relevant factors according to the logic of the anticipated results, a researcher stands in danger of proving a correlation between specific avoidances and bows and arrows. The strenuous effort of Whiting and Child (1962) to link psychoanalytic and stimulus-response theory in cross-cultural correlations of hypotheses drawn from psychoanalysis also ran into an obstacle fundamental to all correlations. The "correlational method used in cross-cultural research," Whiting admits (1964:524; cf. Boas 1940a), "cannot . . . show the direction of causation." The same problem dogs the graduated

scalograms that Carneiro (1962, 1968) has drawn to describe evolutionary development from the simple to the complex.

If items are brought together in broad categories for correlation, the probability of association can usually be increased, but this does not guarantee that the result has a strengthened validity (see Murdock 1949; Driver 1966, 1970). One must be careful, too, that the mathematical manipulations do not mask relations that the simpler mathematics of frequency distribution might reveal.

Despite problems of control and of causal determination, during this time of specialization and convergence it is apparent that the application of quantitative methods can be useful in checking hypotheses, generating new hypotheses, and establishing typologies. Thus, in archaeology, Deetz (1965), through computerized control of typological change in pottery, has been able to relate these changes to turns in the historical situation of the Arikara and to suggest that the growing variability in shape and in design is correlated with the disintegration of the matrilocal extended family (cf. Binford 1962, 1963; Robinson 1951; also Clarke 1968). The use of the computer appears essential for disclosing the permutative combinations of forms to which Lévi-Strauss (1969; cf. Hymes, ed., 1965) addresses himself in the study of kinship and myth, and in which he considers laws might be unveiled (1963: 228).

RETURN TO EVOLUTIONARY AND
ECOCULTURAL PROBLEMS

In the study of culture history, archaeology has always held an advantage in uniting historic and evolutionary processes. In 1936 the English prehistorian V. Gordon Childe (1951a) described the grand subsistence and technological revolutions that advanced man's capacity to survive, thereby accelerating population growth, leading to stratified societies, and ushering in the accumulation of inventions and knowledge that would find their way into the mainstream of human advancement. Assembling evidence to show that the rise of civilization in Mesopotamia, Egypt, China, Mesoamerica, and Peru followed a similar course, Steward (1949) describes how societies became integrated through religious patterns but lost strength as militaristic expansion and secularization altered the functional requirements of the state. While the relation of militarism to population pressures and to state-directed expansion of irrigation is not clear, the final step in the rise of civilization, the "era of conquest," brought important social, technical, and religious changes. The towns became cities, a true military class appeared in the social hierarchy, and warrior-priests came to rule. At the same time war gods became prominent in the pantheon. Distinctions between classes were sharpened and strong differentiation appeared in occupational groups. Codification of laws, systematization of learning, standardization of art, and mass production of goods also indicate increasing regimentation of culture (Steward, 1949:22).

Steward's final stage describes a dynamic structural-functional-interactional model in which a number of factors (ecology, technology, social organization, military technology, administration, population growth and density) contribute to the enlargement of the interactional field (empire) to a point of maximum growth and equilibrium, whereupon disjunction among the factors provoke increasing disequilibrium and conflict (cf. Braidwood and Willey, eds., 1962; Adams 1966; Wittfogel 1957).

For Leslie White, ethnologist, the proper study of mankind must center not in temporal, spatial, or formal processes, but in the "temporal-formal . . . evolutionary, or developmental process" (1949:11). Like Comte and Spencer, White opted for a dynamic rather than a static study of process and clued his cultural evolution to the "amount of energy harnessed and put to work per capita per year" (1949:381). As energy per capita increased, it precipitated an increase in "technological and social differentiation and specialization [with] . . . evolution and progress [the] result" (1959:157). Following the biological and thermodynamic analogues drawn by their mentor, Sahlins and Service (Sahlins 1958, Service 1962, Sahlins and Service 1960) were encouraged to trace the differentiation of social and political organization as a concomitant of technological differentiation. In *Social Stratification in Polynesia* (1958; cf. Goldman 1955), Sahlins followed the thesis that the degree of stratification and restricted control of economic resources was a function of productivity. Ecologic relations on the islands also influenced the type of social organization, in as much as "ramage systems were associated with scattered distribution of rich resource zones, a tendency toward familial specialization of production, and, usually, scattered settlement; descent-line systems were associated with clustered exploitation zones, familial self-sufficiency, and village settlement" (Sahlins 1958:252). In charting the rise of social and political complexity in Polynesia and Africa, from band to tribe and chiefdom, Service (1962; cf. Fried 1967) found the model of redistributive economic integration formulated by Polanyi (1957) to be especially useful in describing the role of chiefs in stratified societies.

The "generic" evolution of culture

formulated by White on the model of earlier developmentalists was based on a comparison of classes of data (e.g., ideas or institutions), and stood in contrast with the parallel evolutionary sequences defined by Steward (1955). Steward clued his cultural evolution to the stimulus value of ecological conditions, viewing parallels in cultures and in sequences as due to similarities in relation to environmental resources or to the ethnoecology of the region. This approach he dubbed "multilineal evolution," and he saw it as more empirical then the self-generating evolution described by White and his associates; but Steward did not deny the signal importance of technology for social differentiation and increasing organizational complexity. In his statistical survey of kinship systems and related social forms, Murdock (1949) took a critical position with regard to the generic evolution of culture and society, while stating the focal importance of residence rules in filtering forces stimulating modifications in social organization. Yet parallels in the independent origins of specific types of social organization are possible (Murdock 1949:200):

The evidence from our 250 societies supports the contention of the American historical anthropologists, against the evolutionists, that there is no inevitable sequence of social forms nor any necessary association between particular rules of residence or descent or particular types of kin groups or kinship terms and levels of culture, types of economy, or forms of government or class structure. On the other hand, it supports the evolutionists, against the several schools of historical anthropology, in the conclusion that parallelism or independent invention is relatively easy and common in the field of social organization, and that any structural form can be developed anywhere if conditions are propitious.

To avoid the pitfall of unilineal evolution, White, Sahlins, and Service underscore Spencer's statement that the evolutionary process is divergent. However, this statement ignores the fact that generic evolution must be carried by a straightforward progression and that the branches, as in the analogy of a tree, draw their strength from the stage of development attained by the trunk at the time of differentiation.

Cautious in their approach to cultural evolution, archaeologists nonetheless found themselves assembling their components, sites, phases, and traditions in temporal sequences that called for the merging of local and regional manifestations into a generic type of development. Surveying the American continents, Willey and Phillips (Phillips and Willey 1953, Willey and Phillips 1955 and 1965; cf. Beardsley et al. 1956) described five sequential stages of culture growth: lithic, archaic, formative, classic, and postclassic. Their sequence described an increasing complexity, from simple hunting and gathering encampments through village farming communities to stratified urban centers, the latter being confined to nuclear America. Sensitive to technico-ecological relations, prehistorians have moved toward an explanation that stresses the stimulus value of relations among peoples who, though living close to each other, nonetheless dwell in different habitats (Willey 1962; Sanders 1962; Braidwood and Willey, eds., 1962; Clark 1952). Natural and cultural diversification are interpreted as essential to building a network of exchange that includes products, techniques, and ideas that in time produce a common tradition uniting various regions and providing a common stimulus platform for further development and unification through conquest (see, e.g., Braidwood and Willey, eds., 1962; Willey 1961; Bennett 1948).

In stressing the concomitance of natural and cultural variations and the transformation of variation into a higher order of integration through a network of interactional relations, archaeologists do not always distinguish clearly the precedence of cultural or ecological factors, though they recognize that growth in the technological base (e.g., cultivation and craft production) lessened the impact of environment on human response. The problem can be translated readily into an old issue, however: the extent to which technico-ecological factors limit cultural potential or release growth, and the extent to which historic-cultural factors are instrumental in stimulating development beyond ecological limitations (see, e.g., Caldwell 1958; Meggers, 1954, 1960; E. Leacock, ed., 1963; cf. Opler 1964, Piggott 1960).

Drawing upon a bio-ecological model, Laura Thompson (1949, 1961) describes a generalized cultural evolution in which local cultures move purposefully through a series of expanding interactional universes until a mature ecocultural supersystem is reached. The cultural succession, straining toward a homeostatic community, is very much the analogue to a biotic succession. Like Malinowski, Thompson turns to the biopsychic base for an understanding of the organization and change of cultures (1961:171-72):

Every distinctive culture system is created or re-created, maintained, transformed, and transmitted by a group of human organisms who are ultimately biologically oriented [and who] tend naturally, although not always successfully, to use their built-in culture-creating and culture-maintaining propensities to move actively in the direction of goals of maintenance, reproduction, and self-actualization of the group, as part of a total communal event. The biological goals are keyed to the long-range aims of completing the life cycle of individual components, generation after generation, and thus actualizing and perpetuating the life of the community.

These concerns for evolutionary developments and ecological relations form part of a growing consensus in which prehistorians and ethnologists have erected a theory anchored in a combined synchronic-diachronic-structural-interactional orientation. In 1948 Walter Taylor had already pointed to a new structural-functional interpretation in archaeology that in the 1960s eventuated in a systems approach (Binford 1962, Clarke 1968; cf. Rappaport 1968). In ethnology Walter Goldschmidt (1959, 1966) reiterated the same combination of temporal and structural-functional processes as part of the trend toward a social-interactional-field analysis (see, e.g., Lesser 1961; Leeds 1961; Spoehr 1960; Vayda, Leeds, and Smith 1961; Spicer, ed., 1961; Gulliver 1960; Hickerson 1962; Richardson 1961).

BASIC ISSUES IN THE DEVELOPMENT OF ANTHROPOLOGY

The history of any discipline discloses a trend toward an expanding comprehension of the organization and regularities of what is to be explained—that is, the reality problem for the discipline. At its inception the discipline must be distinguished from other fields according to (a) problem definition and subject matter, (b) conceptual inventory and methodology, (c) accumulation of special and distinctive factual data for analysis, and (d) a body of theoretical propositions that explain the orderly relations of facts. At any one point in time theory will include not only what is accepted as clearly validated, but a number of unstated assumptions governing interpretation which are outside the bounds of immediate experimental control. Such is the speculative side of theory, the meta-theory, which frequently produces an imaginative grand design and intuitions of a lesser order that stimulate new problem definitions and advancement, often by provoking counterproposals (see Bidney 1967, Harris 1968, Lowie 1937, Penniman 1965).

Understanding the nature of the thing to be explained (reality problem) centers in determining the parts that structure the reality and the kinds of relations that bind the parts into systems of reciprocities. Reality parts usually can be divided into generic and specific variables or factors. In singling out the "science of culture or civilization" for themselves, early anthropologists selected one of the generic variables now recognized as a part of the human reality. Sociologists elected another generic variable, the social, and psychologists reserved the psychological. Each discipline has been exercising its ingenuity to uncover the nature and explanatory range of the cultural, social, and pyschological; in consequence, their interests in the mutual relations of these variables have proved secondary. Yet at any one time, these and other generic variables (notably the ecological) and their factors are operative in the human situation. For anthropology this has meant a most complex confrontation, for it has involved the search for a way to disengage the social from the cultural in a way that would be analytically useful.

The relation of the social and the cultural to human nature, both in its psychological and in its "instinctual" organization, has evoked anxious concern that the social and the cultural should not be dissolved in the common human motivations and needs of the individual. If it turned out that the social and cultural were nothing more than extensions of individual psychological processes, their autonomy as independent causal variables would be lost, and anthropology and sociology could conceivably become branches of psychology. Preoccupation with reduc-

tionism grew out of a conceptualization of a stratified reality, stretching from the inorganic to the organic, then to the psychological, social, and cultural. The problem can be practically resolved by concentrating on the interrelations and mutual influences of the psychological, social, cultural, and ecological, leaving to particular circumstances questions of the weight that any variable will carry. Human nature turns up again in the contrast between conscious and unconscious motivation and the importance each may hold for social action.

The relationship between individual and group, which the contrast of psychology and culture poses, finds an echo in the opposition between historic interpretation and social or cultural interpretation. The historian's concern for an explanation, traceable to individual actions in accordance with situational circumstances, is not congenial to an interpretation that locates "cause" in a group action or in the demands of a culture pattern operating through a psychological process of conditioning. The same problem appears in the polarization of history and evolution, or traditional history and culture history. Behind these issues lies the fundamental relation between *variation* and *structure*.

The interpretation of cause represents another enduring issue, and in the instance of anthropology, as for related disciplines, the interpretation of causality has responded to developments in the natural sciences, notably physics and mathematics, and in philosophy. Causality engages the problems of determinism, probability, and accident insofar as invariance, a high degree of constancy, or inconstancy may be characteristic of relations between events. Determinism again relates to the problem of variability, and becomes vital when one considers the extent to which individuals are able to act with some independence of their social and cultural milieu.

Free will is as vitally implicated in sociocultural determinism as in a theology of predestination. Again, the problem of choice and sociocultural determinism connects logically with the controversy over absolute and relative values and value judgments. To trace the source of personal and group action to sociocultural determinants in place of psychological motivations drawn from human nature may be a matter of methodological relativism, but it is also deeply involved in the problem of personal and group responsibility. Where traditional sociocultural values of great contrast are held, judgment of the rightness or wrongness of accepting them as legitimate alternatives can be translated quickly into an absolutist-relativist argument. It is interesting to note that Benedict (1934) stressed the "unconscious canons of choice" by which culture governed individual relativity in pleading the case of those personalities whose temperament (a biological determinant) overrode the commands of cultural conformity. The contrast of ideal patterns and preferred or typical alternatives (Kluckhohn 1941) with behavioral patterns also addressed the relativist-absolutist issue, and so does the question of the extent to which the determinism of the sociocultural system is mitigated by alternatives (see also Barnett 1956; Bidney 1967; Herskovits 1948, 1958; Ginsberg 1953b; Opler 1964; Redfield 1953).

The relationship between observable form and intrinsic meaning, a problem more or less relevant to the cause of patterned behavior, has also proved an enduring hurdle for defining method and for admitting evidence to the bar of interpretation. Anthropologists generally have held the view that the culture reality was structured by an inner core of meaning, and that it was this cultur-

al genotype, as it were, that brought regularities to the "cultural phenotypic" behavior witnessed in individuals. This, of course, raises the issue of behavioral empiricism versus empirical idealism—the use of regularities in external form versus an inferred structure. A similar issue had been drawn in psychology by Watson when he initiated behaviorism in reaction to the mentalism of introspective psychology. The problem of the validity of data in exposing the "real" has surfaced in anthropology in a number of distinctions: ideal versus behavioral patterns, covert versus overt culture, and emic versus etic linguistic description. It is the argument of the behaviorist that he is working with objective data and that his inductions directly reflect the nature of what can be observed and recorded. The idealist, on the other hand, must deal with an abstraction—a value motivation, for example—which he imputes to the individual in order to explain his behavior. In short, the idealist, in the behavioral view, is at best an empiricist once removed.

SUMMARY

The emergence of anthropology as a humanistic discipline and as a science has been an exercise in growth of understanding with regard to human reality. The process of growth has involved anthropologists in a set of recurring problems, variously stated as the relation of structure and variation, of evolution and history, of history and science, of descriptive integration and process, of particular and whole, of description and causal explanation, of mechanical and statistical models, of levels of causal reality and configurated reality, of social-cultural determinism and individual variation, of social-cultural and psychological explanations, of ideal and real (or behavioral), of formal and informal structuring, of etics and emics, of overt and covert culture, of form and meaning, of unconscious and conscious motivation, and the like.

The humanistic-descriptive and scientific-processual strains in anthropology have resulted in a schizoid personality of sorts, but the major thrust has been toward the humanistic end of the spectrum. The model of linguistics, with its emphasis on conceptual categories and cognitive processes, has been a constant and persuasive influence in maintaining an emphasis on pattern, or mode of life. At the same time, anthropological comprehension has expanded with each new turn in theoretical focus and problem interest, aided by the accompanying differentiations in specialization which brought new information and stimulated fresh relations with established disciplines. Throughout its career, anthropology, by virtue of its synthetic focus, has not been a generator of methodological techniques; rather, its strength has lain in generating problems. Present trends accept a view of the human reality that stresses a configurated interrelation of elements that combine to produce an event, and which, through relations with other configurated units, bring contextual events into an organized process to maintain continuity and induce change. In this view, individuals in any social and cultural system are seen as actors in an interactional field responding to personal and social interests and norms, accommodating their own interests to the limitations of the situation, and seeking to manipulate resources to maximize their purposes.

REFERENCES

Aberle, David F.
1957 The Influence of Linguistics on Early Culture and Personality Theory. In *Essays in the Science of Culture,* ed. G. Dole and R. Carneiro, pp. 1-29. New York: Crowell.
1966 *The Peyote Religion Among the Navaho.* Chicago: Aldine.
Aberle, D. F., A. K. Cohen, A. K. Davis, M. J. Levy, Jr., and F. X. Sutton
1950 The Functional Prerequisites of a Society. *Ethics* 60:100-11.
Acosta, José de
1963 *The Natural and Moral History of the Indians,* ed. Clements Markham. New York: B. Franklin. Originally published 1590; reprinted from the English translation of Edward Grimston, 1604.
Adams, Robert M.
1966 *The Evolution of Urban Society.* Chicago: Aldine.
Albert, Ethel
1956 The Classification of Values: A Method and Illustration. *American Anthropologist* 58:221-48.
Ames, Michael
1963 Ideological and Social Change in Ceylon. *Human Organization* 22:45-53.
Ankermann, Bernard
1905 Kulturkreise und Kulturschichten in Afrika. *Zeitschrift für Ethnologie* 37: 54-91.
Apter, David E.
1961 *The Political Kingdom in Uganda.* Princeton: Princeton University Press.
Arber, Edward
1885 *The First Three English Books on America.* Birmingham: Turnbull & Spears.
Arensberg, Conrad M., and Arthur H. Niehoff
1964 *Introducing Social Change: A Manual for Americans Overseas.* Chicago: Aldine.
Ashley-Montagu, M. F.
1950 *On Being Human.* New York: H. Schuman.
Ayoub, V.
1961 Review: The Judicial Process in Two African Tribes. In *Community Political Systems,* ed. Morris Janowitz. New York: Free Press of Glencoe, Macmillan.
Bachofen, J.
1861 *Das Mutterrecht: Eine Untersuchung über die Gynaikokratie der alten Welt nach ihrer religiosen und rechtlichen Natur.* Stuttgart: Krais & Hoffmann.

Bagehot, W.
1875 *Physics and Politics; or Thoughts on the Application of the Principle of "Natural Selection" and "Inheritance" to Political Society.* New York: Appleton.

Balandier, Georges
1962 *Sociologie actuelle de l'Afrique noire.* Bibliothèque de Sociologie Contemporaine. Paris: Presses Universitaires de France. Originally published 1955.
1965a Messianism and Nationalism in Black Africa, trans. Pierre van den Berghe. In *Africa: Social Problems of Change and Conflict,* ed. P. van den Berghe, pp. 443-60. San Francisco: Chandler. Originally published 1953.
1965b Traditional Social Structures and Economic Changes, trans. Pierre van den Berghe. In *Africa: Social Problems of Change and Conflict,* ed. P. van den Berghe, pp. 383-95. San Francisco: Chandler. Originally published 1960.

Balfour, H.
1893 *The Evolution of Decorative Art.* London: Percival.

Barnett, Homer G.
1940 Culture Processes. *American Anthropologist* 42:21-48.
1942 Invention and Cultural Change. *American Anthropologist* 44:14-30.
1953 *Innovation: The Basis of Cultural Change.* New York: McGraw-Hill.
1956 *Anthropology in Administration.* Evanston, Ill.: Row, Peterson.

Barnouw, Victor
1950 *Acculturation and Personality Among the Wisconsin Chippewa.* Memoir no. 72, American Anthropological Association. Washington, D.C.
1963 *Culture and Personality.* Homewood, Ill.: Dorsey Press.

Barton, R. F.
1919 Ifugao Law. *University of California Publications in American Archaeology and Ethnology* 15:1-186.

Bastian, Adolf
1860 *Der Mensch in der Geschichte: Zur Begründung einer psychologischen Weltanschauung,* 3 vols. Leipzig.
1881 *Der Völkergedanke im Aufbau einer Wissenschaft von Menschen.*

1895 *Ethnische Elementargedanken in der Lehre von Menschen.* Berlin: Weidmannsche Buchhandlung.

Bateson, Gregory
1965 *Naven: A Survey of the Problems Suggested by a Composite Picture of the Culture of a New Guinea Tribe Drawn from Three Points of View.* Stanford: Stanford University Press. Originally published 1936.

Beaglehole, E., and P. Beaglehole
1946 *Some Modern Maoris.* Wellington: New Zealand Council for Educational Research.

Beals, Ralph L.
1964 The Uses of Anthropology in Overseas Programs: Introduction. *Human Organization* 23:185-86.

Beardsley, Richard K., et al.
1956 Functional and Evolutionary Implications of Community Patterning. In *Seminars in Archaeology,* pp. 131-57. Menasha, Wis.: Society for American Archaeology.

Belshaw, Cyril S.
1955 *In Search of Wealth.* Memoir no. 80, American Anthropological Association, Washington, D.C.
1964 *Under the Ivi Tree.* Berkeley: University of California Press.
1965 *Traditional Exchange and Modern Markets.* Englewood Cliffs, N.J.: Prentice-Hall.

Benedict, Ruth
1923 *The Concept of the Guardian Spirit in North America.* Memoir no. 29, American Anthropological Association. Washington, D.C.
1934 *Patterns of Culture.* Boston: Houghton Mifflin.
1946 *The Chrysanthemum and the Sword: Patterns of Japanese Culture.* Boston: Houghton Mifflin.

Bennett, Wendell C.
1948 The Peruvian Co-tradition. In *A Reappraisal of Peruvian Archaeology,* ed. Wendell C. Bennett, pp. 1-7. Memoir no. 4, Society for American Archaeology. Menasha, Wis.

Berreman, Gerald D.
1966 Anemic and Emetic Analyses in Social Anthropology. *American Anthropologist* 68:346-54.
1968 Is Anthropology Alive? : Social Re-

sponsibility in Social Anthropology. *Current Anthropology* 9:391-96.

Bidney, David
1967 *Theoretical Anthropology,* 2nd ed. New York: Schocken Books. Originally published 1953.

Binford, Lewis R.
1962 Archeology as Anthropology. *American Antiquity* 28:217-25.
1963 A Proposed Attribute List for the Description and Classification of Projectile Points. In *Anthropological Papers of the American Museum of Anthropology,* no. 19, pp. 193-221. Ann Arbor: University of Michigan.

Blumenbach, Johann
1865 De generis humani veritate nativa. In *The Anthropological Treatises of Blumenbach and Hunter,* trans. T. Bendyshe, pp. 145-46. London: Anthropological Society of London. Originally published 1785.

Boas, Franz
1916 Tsimshian Mythology. In *Thirty-first Annual Report, 1909-1910, Bureau of American Ethnology.* Washington, D.C.: Smithsonian Institution.
1927 *Primitive Art.* Cambridge: Harvard University Press.
1938 *The Mind of Primitive Man.* New York: Macmillan. Originally published 1911.
1940a *Race, Language, and Culture.* New York: Macmillan.
1940b The Aims of Ethnology. In ibid., pp. 628-38. Originally published 1888.
1940c The Limitations of the Comparative Method of Anthropology. In ibid., pp. 270-80. Originally published 1896.
1940d Advances in Methods of Teaching. In ibid., pp. 621-25. Originally published 1899.
1940e Decorative Designs of Alaskan Needlecases: A Study in the History of Conventional Designs, Based on Materials in the U.S. National Museum. In ibid., pp. 564-92. Originally published 1908.
1940f The Methods of Ethnology. In ibid., pp. 281-89. Originally published 1920.
1940g The Aims of Anthropological Research. In ibid., pp. 243-59. Original-

ly published 1932.
1940h History and Science in Anthropology: A Reply. In ibid., pp. 305-11. Originally published 1936.

Boas, Franz, ed.
1911 *Handbook of American Indian Languages,* pt. 1, Introduction, pp. 1-83. Bulletin no. 40, Bureau of American Ethnology. Washington, D.C.: Smithsonian Institution.
1938 *General Anthropology.* Introduction, pp. 1-6. Boston & New York: Heath.

Boggs, Stephen
1964 The Organization of Anthropology in Action. *Human Organization* 23: 193-95.

Bohannan, Paul
1957 *Justice and Judgment Among the Tiv.* London: Oxford University Press.
1958 Extra-Processual Events in Tiv Political Institutions. *American Anthropologist* 60:1-12.
1965 The Differing Realms of Law. In *The Ethnography of Law,* ed. Laura Nader. *American Anthropologist* 67: 33-42 (special publication).

Bopp, Franz
1816 *Über das conjugations System der Sanskrit Sprache in Vergleichung mit Jenem der griechischen, lateinischen, persischen, und germanischen Sprache.* Frankfurt.

Boucher de Perthes, J.
1864 *Antiquités celtiques et diluviennes,* 3 vols. Paris: Treuttel & Wurtz. Originally published 1847.

Braidwood, Robert J., and Gordon R. Willey, eds.
1962 *Courses Toward Urban Life: Archeological Considerations of Some Cultural Alternates.* Viking Fund Publications in Anthropology, no. 32. New York: Wenner-Gren Foundation for Anthropological Research.

Breuil, Henri
1912 Les subdivisions du paléolithique supérieur et leur signification. In *Congrès international d'anthropologie et d'archéologie préhistoriques* (14th session), pp. 165-238. Geneva.

Brokensha, David, and Peter Hodge
1969 *Community Development: An Interpretation.* San Francisco: Chandler.

Brown, G. G., and A. Hutt
1935 *Anthropology in Action.* London: Oxford University Press.

Bruner, Edward M.
1959 Kinship Organization Among the Urban Batak of Sumatra. In *Transactions of the New York Academy of Sciences,* series 2, vol. 22, no. 2, pp. 118-25.
1961 Urbanization and Ethnic Identity in North Sumatra. *American Anthropologist,* 63:508-21.

Bunzel, Ruth L., and Anne Parsons, with comment by Margaret Mead and Rhoda Metraux.
1964 Report on Regional Conferences. *Current Anthropology* 5:430, 437-42.

Burling, Robbins
1962 Maximization Theories and the Study of Economic Anthropology. *American Anthropologist* 64:802-21.
1964a Cognition and Componential Analysis: God's Truth or Hocus-Pocus. *American Anthropologist* 66:20-28.
1964b Burling's Rejoinder. *American Anthropologist* 66:120-22.
1969 Linguistics and Ethnographic Description. *American Anthropologist* 71:817-27.

Bury, J. B.
1920 *The Idea of Progress.* London: Macmillan.

Busia, K. A.
1951 *The Position of the Chief in the Modern Political System of the Ashanti.* London: Oxford University Press.

Caldwell, Joseph R.
1958 *Trend and Tradition in the Prehistory of the Eastern United States,* Memoir no. 88, American Anthropological Association. Washington, D.C.

Carneiro, Robert L.
1962 Scale Analysis as an Instrument for the Study of Cultural Evolution. *Southwestern Journal of Anthropology* 18:149-69.
1968 Ascertaining, Testing, and Interpreting Sequences of Cultural Development. *Southwestern Journal of Anthropology* 24:354-74.

Caudill, William
1949 Psychological Characteristics of Acculturated Wisconsin Ojibwa Children. *American Anthropologist* 51:409-27.
1953 Applied Anthropology in Medicine. In *Anthropology Today,* ed. A. L. Kroeber, pp. 771-806. Chicago: University of Chicago Press.

Chamberlain, Houston S.
1912 *Grundlagen des neunzehnten Jahrhundert,* 2 vols., trans. John Lees. London: John Lamp. Originally published 1899.

Chapple, Eliot D.
1953 Applied Anthropology in Industry. In *Anthropology Today,* ed. A. L. Kroeber, pp. 819-31. Chicago: University of Chicago Press.

Chapple, Eliot D., and Conrad M. Arensberg
1940 Measuring Human Relations: An Introduction to the Study of the Interaction of Individuals. *Genetic Psychology Monographs,* no. 22, pp. 3-147.

Childe, V. Gordon
1951a *Man Makes Himself.* New York: New American Library. Originally published 1936.
1951b *Social Evolution.* New York: Schuman.

Clark, J. G. D.
1952 *Prehistoric Europe: The Economic Basis.* London: Methuen.

Clarke, David L.
1968 *Analytical Archaeology.* London: Methuen.

Codrington, R. H.
1891 *The Melanesians: Studies in Their Anthropology and Folklore.* Oxford: Clarendon Press.

Cohen, Ronald, and John Middleton, eds.
1967 *Comparative Political Systems: Studies in the Politics of Pre-Industrial Societies.* American Museum Sourcebooks in Anthropology. Garden City, N.Y.: Natural History Press.

Collier, John
1947 *The Indians of the Americas.* New York: Norton.

Comte, Auguste
1893 *The Positive Philosophy of Auguste Comte,* 2 vols., trans. Harriet Martineau, 3rd ed. London: Kegan Paul,

Trench, Trubner. Condensed from 6 vols. Originally published 1830-1842.

Condorcet, M.
1955 *Sketch for a Historical Picture of the Progress of the Human Mind*, trans. J. Barraclough. London: Weidenfeld & Nicholson. Originally published 1795.

Conklin, Harold C.
1955 Hanunóo Color Categories. *Southwestern Journal of Anthropology* 11: 339-44.

Cook, Scott
1969 The "Anti-Market" Mentality Reexamined: A Further Critique of the Substantive Approach to Economic Anthropology. *Southwestern Journal of Anthropology* 25:378-406.

Cuvier, Georges, and Alexandre de Brongniart
1811 *Essai sur la géographie minéralogique des environs de Paris, avec une carte géognostique, et des coupes de terrain*. Paris: Baudouin. Originally published 1808.

Dalton, George
1960 A Note of Clarification on Economic Surplus. *American Anthropologist* 62:483-90.
1961 Economic Theory and Primitive Society. *American Anthropologist* 63: 1-25.
1963 Economic Surplus, Once Again. *American Anthropologist* 65:389-94.
1965a Primitive Money. *American Anthropologist* 67:44-65.
1965b Primitive, Archaic, and Modern Economies: Karl Polanyi's Contribution to Economic Anthropology and Comparative Economy. In *Essays in Economic Anthropology: Proceedings of the 1965 Annual Spring Meeting of the American Ethnological Society*, ed. June Helm, pp. 1-24. Seattle: University of Washington Press.

Dalton, George, ed.
1968 *Primitive, Archaic, and Modern Economies: Essays of Karl Polanyi*. Garden City, N.Y.: Anchor Books, Doubleday.

Darwin, Charles
1936 *The Origin of Species by Means of Natural Selection, or the Preservation of Favored Races in the Struggle for Life; and The Descent of Man and Selection in Relation to Sex*. New York: Modern Library. Originally published 1859 and 1871, respectively.

Davenport, William
1959 Nonunilinear Descent and Descent Groups. *American Anthropologist* 61:557-72.
1963 Social Organization. In *Biennial Review of Anthropology*, ed. B. J. Siegel, pp. 178-227. Stanford: Stanford University Press.

Deetz, James F.
1965 *The Dynamics of Stylistic Change in Arikara Ceramics*. Urbana: University of Illinois Press.

Diamond, Stanley
1964 Anthropology and World Affairs as Seen by U.S.A. Associates: A Revolutionary Discipline. *Current Anthropology* 5:432-41.

Díaz del Castillo, Bernal
1908 *The True History of the Conquest of New Spain*, 5 vols., trans. A. P. Maudslay. London: Hakluyt Society. Originally published 1562.

Dixon, Roland B.
1928 *The Building of Cultures*. New York: Scribner.

Dobrizhoffer, Martin
1822 *An Account of the Abipones, an Equestrian People of Paraguay*, 3 vols. London: J. Murray. Originally published in Latin, 1774.

Dole, Gertrude, and Robert Carneiro
1960 *Essays in the Science of Culture in Honor of Leslie A. White*. New York: Crowell.

Dozier, Edward P.
1961 The Rio Grande Pueblos. In *Perspectives in American Indian Culture Change*, ed. Edward Spicer, pp. 94-186. Chicago: University of Chicago Press.

Driver, H. E.
1966 Geographical versus Psycho-Functional Explanations of Kin Avoidances. *Current Anthropology* 7:132-82.
1970 Statistical Refutation of Comparative Functional-Causal Models. *South-*

western Journal of Anthropology 26: 25-31.

Driver, H. E., and William C. Massey
1957 Comparative Studies of North American Indians. *Transactions of the American Philosophical Society* 47, pt. 2. Philadelphia.

Du Bois, Cora
1944 *The People of Alor.* Minneapolis: University of Minnesota Press.

Durkheim, Émile
1926 *Elementary Forms of the Religious Life,* trans. J. W. Swain. New York: Macmillan. Originally published 1915.
1938 *The Rules of Sociological Method,* ed. George E. G. Catlin. Chicago: University of Chicago Press. Originally published 1895.

Durkheim, E., and M. Mauss
1963 *Primitive Classification,* trans. Rodney Needham. Chicago: University of Chicago Press. Originally published 1903.

Eggan, Fred
1937 Historical Changes in the Choctaw Kinship System. *American Anthropologist* 39:34-52.

Eggan, Fred, ed.
1955 *Social Anthropology of North American Tribes,* rev. ed. Chicago: University of Chicago Press. Originally published 1937.

Elkin, A. P.
1937 The Reaction of Primitive Races to the White Man's Culture. *Hibbert Journal* 35:537-45.

Engels, Friedrich
1942 The Origin of the Family, Private Property, and the State in the Light of the Researches of Lewis H. Morgan. In *Works of Marxism-Leninism,* vol. 22. New York: International Publishers.

Epstein, Arnold Leonard
1958 *Politics in an Urban African Community.* Manchester: Manchester University Press.

Erasmus, Charles
1961 *Man Takes Control: Cultural Development and American Aid.* Minneapolis: University of Minnesota Press.

Evans-Pritchard, E. E.
1940 *The Nuer.* Oxford: Clarendon Press.

1949 *The Sanusi of Cyrenaica.* Oxford: Clarendon Press.
1951 *Kinship and Marriage Among the Nuer.* Oxford and New York: Clarendon Press.
1964 *Social Anthropology and Other Essays.* New York: Free Press, Macmillan.

Fallers, Lloyd A.
1956 *Bantu Bureaucracy: A Study of Integration and Conflict of the Political Institutions of an East African People.* Cambridge: Heffer.

Fenton, William N.
1940 Problems Arising from the Historic Northeastern Position of the Iroquois. In *Essays in Historical Anthropology of North America,* ed. J. H. Steward, pp. 159-252. Smithsonian Miscellaneous Collections, vol. 100. Washington, D.C.: Smithsonian Institution.
1951 Iroquois Studies at the Mid-Century. *Proceedings of the American Philosophical Society* 95:296-310.
1969 J. F. Lafitau (1681-1746), Precursor of Scientific Anthropology. *Southwestern Journal of Anthropology* 25: 173-87.

Ferguson, A.
1789 *An Essay on the History of Civil Society.* Basel: J. J. Tourneisen. Originally published 1769.

Firth, Raymond
1929 *Primitive Economics of the New Zealand Maori.* London: Routledge.
1939 *Primitive Polynesian Economy.* London: Routledge.
1951 Contemporary British Social Anthropology. *American Anthropologist* 53:474-89.
1957 *We, the Tikopia: A Sociological Study of Kinship in Primitive Polynesia.* London: Allen & Unwin. Originally published 1936.

Firth, Raymond, ed.
1957 *Man and Culture: An Evaluation of the Work of Bronislaw Malinowski.* London: Routledge & Kegan Paul.

Ford, Clellan S.
1941 *Smoke from Their Fires: The Life of a Kwakiutl Chief.* New Haven: Yale University Press.

Forde, Daryll

1953 Applied Anthropology in Government: British Africa. In *Anthropology Today*, ed. A. L. Kroeber, pp. 841-65. Chicago: University of Chicago Press.

Fortes, Meyer
1945 *The Dynamics of Clanship Among the Tallensi, Being the First Part of an Analysis of the Social Structure of a Trans-Volta Tribe.* London: Oxford University Press.
1949 *The Web of Kinship Among the Tallensi: The Second Part of an Analysis of the Social Structure of a Trans-Volta Tribe.* London: Oxford University Press.
1953 The Structure of Unilineal Descent Groups. *American Anthropologist* 55:17-41.
1959 Descent, Filiation, and Affinity. *Man* 59:193-97, 206-12.

Fortes, Meyer, and E. E. Evans-Pritchard, eds.
1940 *African Political Systems.* London: Oxford University Press.

Foster, George M.
1962 *Traditional Cultures and the Impact of Technological Change.* New York: Harper & Row.
1965 Peasant Society and the Image of Limited Good. *American Anthropologist* 67:293-315.

Frake, Charles O.
1961 The Diagnosis of Disease Among the Subanum of Mindanao. *American Anthropologist* 63:113-32.
1964a Notes on Queries in Ethnography. In *Transcultural Studies in Cognition*, ed. A. K. Romney and R. G. D'Andrade. *American Anthropologist* 66, no. 3, pt. 2:132-45 (special publication).
1964b Further Discussion of Burling. *American Anthropologist* 66:119.

Frazer, Sir James G.
1900 *The Golden Bough*, 3 vols. London: Macmillan. Originally published 1890.
1913 *Psyche's Task: A Discourse Concerning the Influence of Superstition on the Growth of Institutions.* London: Macmillan.

Freeman, J. D.
1958 The Family System of the Iban of Borneo. *Cambridge Papers in Social Anthropology* 1:15-52.
1961 On the Concept of the Kindred. *Journal of the Royal Anthropological Institute* 91, pt. 2.

French, David
1961 Wasco-Wishram. In *Perspectives in American Indian Culture Change*, ed. Edward Spicer, pp. 337-430. Chicago: University of Chicago Press.

Freud, Sigmund
1918 *Totem and Taboo: Resemblances Between the Psychic Lives of Savages and Neurotics*, trans. A. Brill. New York: Moffat, Yard. Originally published 1913.

Fried, Morton H.
1967 *The Evolution of Political Society: An Essay in Political Anthropology.* New York: Random House.

Friedl, Ernestine
1956 Persistence in Chippewa Culture and Personality. *American Anthropologist* 58:814-25.

Fustel de Coulanges, Numa Denis
1956 *The Ancient City: A Study on the Religion, Laws, and Institutions of Greece and Rome.* Garden City, N.Y.: Anchor Books, Doubleday. Originally published 1864.

Galton, Sir Francis
1962 *Hereditary Genius: An Inquiry into Its Laws and Consequences.* Cleveland & New York: Meridian Books. Originally published 1869.

Gearing, Fred, Robert McC. Netting, and Lisa R. Peattie, eds.
1960 *Documentary History of the Fox Project, 1948-1959: A Program in Action Anthropology*, dir. Sol Tax. Chicago: University of Chicago Press.

Geertz, Clifford
1957 Ritual and Social Change: A Javanese Example. *American Anthropologist* 59:22-54.

Gillin, John
1954 *For a Science of Social Man: Convergences in Anthropology, Psychology, and Sociology.* New York: Macmillan.

Ginsberg, Morris
1953a *The Idea of Progress: A Revaluation.* Boston: Beacon Press.
1953b On the Diversity of Morals. *Journal of the Royal Anthropological Insti-*

tute 83:117-35.

Gjessing, Gutorm
1968   The Social Responsibility of the So-
       cial Scientist. *Current Anthropology*
       9:397-402.

Gluckman, Max
1955   *Custom and Conflict in Africa.* Ox-
       ford: Blackwell.
1962*a* Kinship and Marriage Among the
       Lozi of Northern Rhodesia and the
       Zulu of Natal. In *African Systems of
       Kinship and Marriage,* ed. A. R. Rad-
       cliffe-Brown and Daryll Forde, pp.
       166-206. London: Oxford University
       Press.
1962*b* African Jurisprudence. *Advancement
       of Science* 75:439-54.
1965*a* Tribalism in Modern Central Africa.
       In *Africa: Social Problems of Change
       and Conflict,* ed. P. van den Berghe,
       pp. 346-60. San Francisco: Chandler.
       Originally published 1960.
1965*b* *Politics, Law, and Ritual in Tribal
       Society.* Chicago: Aldine.

Gobineau, Joseph Arthur Comte de
1915   *The Inequality of Human Races,*
       trans. Adrian Collins. New York:
       Putnam. Vol. 1 only of original 4
       vols., first published 1853-1855.

Goguet, Antoine Yves, and A.C. Fugère
1775   *On the Origin of Laws, Arts, and
       Sciences, and Their Progress Among
       the Most Ancient Nations,* 3 vols.,
       trans. Robert Henry, D. Dunn, and
       Alexander Spearman. Edinburgh: G.
       Robinson. Originally published 1758.

Goldenweiser, A. A.
1933   Totemism: An Analytical Study. In
       History, Psychology, and Culture,
       pp. 213-332. New York: Knopf.
       Originally published 1910.

Goldkind, Victor
1965   Social Stratification in the Peasant
       Community: Redfield's Chan Kom
       Reinterpreted. *American Anthropol-
       ogist* 67: 863-84.

Goldman, Irving
1955   Status Rivalry and Cultural Evolu-
       tion in Polynesia. *American Anthro-
       pologist* 57:680-97.

Goldschmidt, Walter
1959   *Man's Way: A Preface to the Under-
       standing of Human Society.* New
       York: Holt.

1966   *Comparative Functionalism.* Berke-
       ley: University of California Press.

Goodenough, Ward H.
1951   *Property, Kin, and Community on
       Truk.* Yale University Publications in
       Anthropology, no. 46. New Haven:
       Yale University Press.
1955   *A Problem in Malayo-Polynesian So-
       cial Organization. American Anthro-
       pologist* 57:71-83.
1956   Componential   Analysis   and   the
       Study of Meaning. *Language* 32:
       195-216.
1957   Cultural Anthropology and Linguis-
       tics. In *Report of the Seventh An-
       nual Round Table Meeting on Lin-
       guistics and Language Study,* ed. Paul
       L. Garvin, pp. 167-73. Washington:
       Georgetown University Press.

Goodenough, Ward H., ed.
1964   *Explorations in Cultural Anthropolo-
       gy: Essays in Honor of George Peter
       Murdock.* New York: McGraw-Hill.

Gough, Kathleen
1968   New Proposals for Anthropologists.
       Current Anthropology 9:403-407.

Graebner, Fritz
1905   Kulturkreise und Kulturschichten in
       Ozeanien. *Zeitschrift für Ethnologie*
       37:28-53.
1911   *Methode der Ethnologie.* Heidelberg:
       C. Winter.

Greenbaum, Lenora
1970   Evaluation of a Stratified Versus an
       Unstratified Universe of Cultures in
       Comparative Research. With com-
       mentaries by R. Naroll and H. Driver.
       Behavioral Science Notes 5:251-81.

Greenberg, Joseph
1954   Concerning Inferences from Linguis-
       tic to Nonlinguistic Data. In *Lan-
       guage in Culture,* ed. Harry Hoijer,
       pp. 3-19. Memoir no. 79, American
       Anthropological Association. Wash-
       ington, D.C.

Grimm, Jakob
1837   *Deutsche   Grammatik.*   Göttingen:
       Dietrichsche Buchhandlung. Origi-
       nally published 1819.
1844   *Deutsche Mythologie,* 2 vols. Göt-
       tingen: Dietrichsche Buchhandlung.
       Originally published 1835.

Gulliver, Philip H.
1960   Incentives in Labor Migration. *Hu-*

man Organization 19:159-63.

1963 Social Control in an African Society: A Study of the Arusha, Agricultural Masai of Northern Tanganyika. London: Routledge & Kegan Paul.

Gumperz, John J., and Dell Hymes, eds.
1964 *The Ethnography of Communication. American Anthropologist* 66, no. 6, pt. 2 (special publication).

Gurvitch, G., and W. I. Moore, eds.
1945 *Twentieth-Century Sociology.* New York: Philosophical Library.

Gusinde, Martin
1931- *Die Feuerland-Indianer,* 3 vols. Möd-
1939 ling, Austria: Anthropos Institut.

Gutkind, Peter C.
1963 *The African Administration of the Kibuga of Buganda.* The Hague: Mouton.

Haddon, Alfred C.
1895 *Evolution in Art: As Illustrated by the Life Histories of Designs.* London: Walter Scott.

1901- *Reports of the Cambridge Anthropo-*
1935 *logical Expedition to Torres Straits,* 6 vols. Cambridge: At the University Press.

Hahn, Eduard
1896 *Die Haustiere und ihre Beziehungen zur Wirtschaft des Menschen: Eine geographische Studie.* Leipzig: Duncker & Humboldt.

Hall, Edward
1961 *The Silent Language.* New York: Fawcett Publications. Originally published 1959.

Hallowell, A. Irving
1945 The Rorschach Technique in the Study of Personality and Culture. *American Anthropologist* 47:195-210.

1951 The Use of Projective Techniques in the Study of the Sociopsychological Aspects of Acculturation. *Journal of Projective Techniques* 15:27-44.

1955a Some Psychological Characteristics of the Northeastern Indians. In *Man in Northeastern North America,* ed. Frederick Johnson. Papers of the R. S. Peabody Foundation for Archeology 3:195-225. Originally published 1946.

1955b *Culture and Experience.* Philadelphia: University of Pennsylvania Press.

1955c Personality Structure and the Evolution of Man. In ibid. Originally published 1950.

Hammel, E., ed.
1965 *Formal Semantic Analysis. American Anthropologist* 67, no. 5, pt. 2 (special publication).

Hammer, Muriel
1966 Some Comments on Formal Analysis of Grammatical and Semantic Systems. *American Anthropologist* 68:362-73.

Harris, Marvin
1959 The Economy Has No Surplus? *American Anthropologist* 61:185-200.

1968 *The Rise of Anthropological Theory: A History of Theories of Culture.* New York: Crowell.

Hartland, E. Sidney
1909- *Primitive Paternity: The Myth of Su-*
1910 *pernatural Birth in Relation to the History of the Family,* 2 vols. Publications of the Folk-Lore Society, vols. 65 and 67. London: David Nett.

Heine-Geldern, Robert
1964 One Hundred Years of Ethnological Theory in the German-Speaking Countries: Some Milestones. *Current Anthropology* 5:407-18.

Heizer, R. F., ed.
1962 *Man's Discovery of His Past: Literary Landmarks in Archaeology.* Englewood Cliffs, N.J.: Prentice-Hall.

Helm, June, ed.
1965 *Essays in Economic Anthropology: Proceedings of the 1965 Annual Meeting of the American Ethnological Society.* Seattle: University of Washington Press.

1966 *Pioneers of American Anthropology: The Uses of Biography.* Monograph no. 43, American Ethnological Society. Seattle: University of Washington Press.

Henry, Jules
1959 Culture, Personality, and Evolution. *American Anthropologist* 61:221-26.

Henry, Jules, and Melford E. Spiro
1953 Psychological Techniques: Projective Tests in Fieldwork. In *Anthropology Today,* ed. A.L. Kroeber, pp. 417-29. Chicago: University of Chicago Press.

Henry, William E.
1947 *The Thematic Apperception Technique in the Study of Culture-Personality Relations.* Genetic Psychology Monographs, no. 35.

Herder, Johann Gottfried
1952 *Zur Philosophie der Geschichte,* 2 vols. Berlin: Aufbau-Verlag. Originally published 1784-1791.

Herodotus
1942 *The Persian Wars,* trans. George Rawlinson. Vol. 1 of *The Greek Historians,* ed. Francis R. B. Godolphin. New York: Random House.

Herskovits, Melville J.
1928 *The American Negro: A Study in Racial Crossing.* New York: Knopf.
1930 *The Anthropometry of the American Negro.* Vol. 11 of *Columbia University Contributions to Anthropology.* New York: Columbia University Press.
1938a *Dahomey: An Ancient West African Kingdom,* 2 vols. New York: Augustin.
1938b *Acculturation: The Study of Culture Contact.* New York: Augustin.
1940 *The Economic Life of Primitive Peoples.* New York: Knopf.
1942 *The Myth of the Negro Past.* New York: Harper.
1948 *Man and His Works.* New York: Knopf.
1952 *Economic Anthropology.* New York: Knopf.
1953 *Franz Boas: The Science of Man in the Making.* New York: Scribner.
1958 Some Further Comments on Cultural Relativism. *American Anthropologist* 60:266-73.

Herskovits, Melville J., and Frances S. Herskovits
1934 *Rebel Destiny: Among the Bush Negroes of Dutch Guiana.* New York: Whittlesey House.

Hickerson, Harold
1956 The Genesis of a Trading Post Band: The Pembina Chippewa. *Ethnohistory* 5:289-345.
1962 *The Southwestern Chippewa: An Ethnohistorical Study.* Memoir no. 92, American Anthropological Association. Washington, D.C.
1967 Some Implications of the Theory of the Particularity, or "Atomism" of Northern Algonkians. *Current Anthropology* 8:313-28; Commentary and Reply, 328-43.

Hippocrates
1962 *Airs, Water, Places,* trans. W. H. S. Jones. Cambridge: Harvard University Press.

Hobbes, Thomas
1958 *Leviathan.* New York: Liberal Arts Press. Originally published 1651.

Hobhouse, Leonard T.
1925 *Morals in Evolution,* 5th ed. London: Chapman & Hall. Originally published 1906.

Hobhouse, Leonard T., G. D. Wheeler, and M. Ginsberg
1965 *The Material Culture and Social Institutions of the Simpler Peoples: An Essay in Correlation.* New York: Humanities Press. Originally published 1915.

Hodgen, M.
1964 *Early Anthropology in the Sixteenth and Seventeenth Centuries.* Chicago: University of Chicago Press.

Hoebel, E. A.
1940 *The Political Organization and Lawways of the Comanche Indians.* Memoir no. 54, American Anthropological Association. Washington, D.C.
1954 *The Law of Primitive Man: A Study in Comparative Legal Dynamics.* Cambridge: Harvard University Press.
1965 Fundamental Cultural Postulates and Judicial Lawmaking in Pakistan. In *The Ethnography of Law,* ed. Laura Nader. *American Anthropologist* 67, no. 6, pt. 2:43-56, (special publication).
1966 *Anthropology: The Study of Man.* New York: McGraw-Hill.

Hogbin, H. I.
1934 *Law and Order in Polynesia: A Study of Primitive Legal Institutions.* London: Christophers.

Hoijer, Harry, ed.
1954 *Language in Culture: Proceedings of a Conference on the Interrelations of Language and Other Aspects of Culture.* Memoir no. 79, American Anthropological Association. Washington, D.C.

Holbach, Baron de

1853 *The System of Nature,* trans. H. Robinson. Boston: Mendum. Originally published 1770.

Holmberg, Allan R.
1955 Participant Intervention in the Field. *Human Organization* 14:23-26.
1958 The Research and Development Approach to the Study of Change. Values in Action: A Symposium. *Human Organization* 17:12-16.

Holmberg, Allan R., and Henry F. Dobyns
1962 The Process of Accelerating Community Change. Community and Regional Development: The Joint Cornell-Peru Experiment. *Human Organization* 21:107-109.

Homans, George C.
1941 Anxiety and Ritual: The Theories of Malinowski and Radcliffe-Brown. *American Anthropologist* 43:164-72.

Homans, George C., and D. M. Schneider
1955 *Marriage, Authority, and Final Causes: A Study of Unilateral Cross-Cousin Marriage.* Glencoe, Ill.: Free Press.

Honigmann, John J.
1949 *Culture and Ethos of Kaska Society.* Yale University Publications in Anthropology, no. 40. New Haven: Yale University Press.
1954 *Culture and Personality.* New York: Harper.
1967 *Personality in Culture.* New York: Harper & Row.

Hsu, Francis L. K., ed.
1961 *Psychological Anthropology: Approaches to Culture and Personality.* Homewood, Ill.: Dorsey Press.

Hultkrantz, A. K.
1968 The Aims of Anthropology: A Scandinavian Point of View. *Current Anthropology* 9:289-96, 306-308.

Hume, David
1854 *The Philosophical Works of David Hume,* 4 vols. Boston: Little, Brown.

Hunter, Joannes
1865 Disputatio inauguralis: Quaedam de hominum varietatibus, et harum causis exponens. In *The Anthropological Treatises of Blumenbach and Hunter,* trans. T. Bendyshe, pp. 359-94. London: Anthropological Society of London. Originally published 1785.

Hunter, Monica (see also Wilson, Monica)
1936 *Reaction to Conquest: Effects of Contact with Europeans on the Pondo of South Africa.* London: Oxford University Press.

Huntingford, G. W. B.
1953 *The Nandi of Kenya: Tribal Control in a Pastoral Society.* London: Routledge & Kegan Paul.

Hurt, Wesley R., Jr.
1961- The Urbanization of the Yankton
1962 Indians. In *American Indians and Their Economic Development,* ed. Fred Voget. *Human Organization* 20:226-31 (special issue).

Hymes, Dell, ed.
1965 *The Use of Computers in Anthropology.* The Hague: Mouton.

Huxley, Thomas H.
1896 *Man's Place in Nature and Other Anthropological Essays.* New York: Appleton.

Janowitz, Morris, ed.
1961 *Community Political Systems.* New York: Free Press, Macmillan.

Jensen, A. E.
1963 *Myth and Cult Among Primitive Peoples,* trans. Marianna Tax Cholden and Wolfgang Weissleder. Chicago: University of Chicago Press. Originally published 1951.

Jespersen, Otto
1923 *Language: Its Nature, Development, and Origin.* New York: Holt.

Jones, Sir William
1969 Third Anniversary Discourse of the President of the Royal Asiatick Society ("On the Hindus"). In *On Language: Plato to von Humboldt,* ed. Peter H. Salus, pp. 167-72. New York: Holt, Rinehart & Winston.

Jung, Carl G.
1916 *The Psychology of the Unconscious,* trans. Beatrice M. Hinkle. New York: Moffat, Yard.

Kames, Lord (Henry Home)
1761 *Historical Law Tracts.* Edinburgh: Kincaid & Bell. Originally published 1757.
1779 *Sketches of the History of Man,* 2 vols. Dublin: J. Williams. Originally published 1774.

Kaplan, Bert
1954 A Study of Rorschach Responses in Four Cultures. *Papers of the Peabody Museum of Anthropology, Archaeol-*

ogy, and Ethnology 42, no. 2. Cambridge: Harvard University Printing Office.

Kardiner, Abram

1939 *The Individual and His Society.* New York: Columbia University Press.

1945 *The Psychological Frontiers of Society.* New York: Columbia University Press.

Keesing, Felix M.

1945 *The South Seas in the Modern World.* New York: John Day. Originally published 1941.

Kennard, Edward A., and Gordon Macgregor

1953 Applied Anthropology in Government: United States. In *Anthropology Today,* ed. A. L. Kroeber, pp. 832-40. Chicago: University of Chicago Press.

Klemm, Gustav F.

1843-   *Allgemeine   Kulturgeschichte   der*
1851   *Menschheit,* 10 vols. Leipzig: Teubner.

Kluckhohn, Clyde

1941 Patterning as Exemplified in Navaho Culture. In *Language, Culture, and Personality,* ed. Leslie Spier. Menasha, Wis.: Sapir Memorial Publication Fund.

1943 Covert Culture and Administrative Problems. *American Anthropologist* 45:213-27.

1949 The Philosophy of the Navaho Indians. In *Ideological Differences and World Order,* ed. F. S. C. Northrop. New Haven: Yale University Press.

Kluckhohn, Clyde, and Dorothea Leighton

1962 *The Navaho.* Garden City, N.Y.: Doubleday. Originally published 1946.

Kluckhohn, Clyde, H. A. Murray, and D. Schneider, eds.

1953 *Personality in Nature, Society, and Culture.* New York: Knopf.

Kluckhohn, Florence R., and Fred Strodtbeck, eds.

1961 *Variations in Value Orientations.* Evanston, Ill.: Row, Peterson.

Köbben, A. J. F.

1967 Why Exceptions? : The Logic of Cross-Cultural Analysis. *Current Anthropology* 8:3-34.

Koppers, Wilhelm

1924 *Unter Feuerland-Indianern.* Stuttgart: Strecker & Schröder.

Kroeber, A. L.

1901 Decorative Symbolism of the Arapaho. *American Anthropologist* 3:308-36.

1907 The Arapaho. *Bulletin of the American Museum of Natural History* 18, pt. 1:1-150. Originally published 1902.

1935 History and Science in Anthropology. *American Anthropologist* 37:539-69.

1939 Cultural and Natural Areas of Native North America. *University of California Publications in American Archaeology and Ethnology* 38. Berkeley: University of California Press.

1944 *Configurations of Culture Growth.* Berkeley: University of California Press.

1952 *The Nature of Culture.* Chicago: University of Chicago Press.

1953 The Superorganic. In *Anthropology Today,* ed. A. L. Kroeber. Chicago: University of Chicago Press. Originally published 1917.

Kroeber, A. L., ed.

1953 *Anthropology Today.* Chicago: University of Chicago Press.

Kroeber, A. L., et al.

1943 *Franz Boas, 1858-1942.* Memoir no. 61, American Anthropological Association. Washington, D.C.

Kroeber, A. L., and Clyde Kluckhohn

1963 *Culture: A Critical Review of Concepts and Definitions.* New York: Vintage Books. Originally published 1952.

Kroeber, A. L., and Jane Richardson

1940 Three Centuries of Women's Dress Fashions: A Quantitative Analysis. *Anthropological Records* 5, no. 2, pp. i-iv, 111-53. Berkeley: University of California Press.

Lafitau, J.

1774 *Moeurs des sauvages amériquains comparées aux moeurs des premiers temps,* 4 vols. Paris: Saugrain l'Aine. Originally published 1724.

La Barre, W.

1938 *The Peyote Cult.* Yale University Publications in Anthropology, no 19.

New Haven: Yale University Press.
1954 *The Human Animal.* Chicago: University of Chicago Press.
Lamarck, J.
1801 *Système des animaux sans vertèbres.* Paris.
Landa, Diego de
1941 *Landa's Relación de las cosas de Yucatán,* ed. A. M. Tozzer. Peabody Museum Publications 18. Cambridge: Harvard University Press.
Lang, Andrew
1898 *The Making of Religion.* London: Longmans, Green.
Leach, E. R.
1960 The Sinhalese of the Dry Zone of Northern Ceylon. In *Social Structure in Southeast Asia,* ed. G. P. Murdock, pp. 116-26. Viking Fund Publications in Anthropology, no. 29. New York: Wenner-Gren Foundation for Anthropological Research.
1961a *Rethinking Anthropology.* London School of Economics Monographs on Social Anthropology, no. 22. London: Athlone Press.
1961b *Pul Eliya, A Village in Ceylon: A Study of Land Tenure and Kinship.* Cambridge: At the University Press.
Leacock, Eleanor, ed.
1963 Introduction. In Lewis Henry Morgan, *Ancient Society.* New York: Meridian Books.
Leacock, Seth
1954 The Ethnological Theory of Marcel Mauss. *American Anthropologist* 56: 58-73.
Le Clair, Edward E., Jr.
1962 Economic Theory and Economic Anthropology. *American Anthropologist* 64:1179-1203.
Leeds, Anthony
1961 The Port-of-Trade in Pre-European India as an Ecological and Evolutionary Type. In *Symposium: Patterns of Land Utilization and Other Papers,* ed. Viola E. Garfield. American Ethnological Society. Seattle: University of Washington Press.
Leighton, Dorothea, and Clyde Kluckhohn
1947 *Children of the People.* Cambridge: Harvard University Press.
Lenneberg, Erich

1953 Cognition in Ethnolinguistics. *Language* 29:463-71.
Lesser, Alexander
1933 The Pawnee Ghost Dance Hand Game. *Columbia University Contributions to Anthropology* 16:1-137. New York: Columbia University Press.
1961 Social Fields and the Evolution of Society. *Southwestern Journal of Anthropology* 17:40-48.
Letourneau, Charles-Jean-Marie
1881 *Sociology Based upon Ethnography,* trans. H. M. Trollope. London: Chapman & Hall. Originally published 1800.
Lévi-Strauss, Claude
1945 French Sociology. In *Twentieth Century Sociology,* ed. G. Gurvitch and W. E. Moore, pp. 503-37. New York: Philosophical Library.
1953 Social Structure. In *Anthropology Today,* ed. A. L. Kroeber, pp. 524-53. Chicago: University of Chicago Press.
1963 *Structural Anthropology,* trans. Claire Jacobson and Brooke Schoepf. New York: Basic Books. Originally published 1958.
1964 *Mythologiques: Le cru et le cuit.* Paris: Plon.
1969 *The Elementary Structures of Kinship,* ed. Rodney Needham. London: Eyre & Spottiswoode. Originally published 1949.
Lévy-Bruhl, Lucien
1910 *Les fonctions mentales dans les sociétés inférieures.* Paris: F. Alcan.
Lewis, Oscar
1961 *The Children of Sánchez.* New York: Random House.
1969 *A Death in the Sánchez Family.* New York: Random House.
Linton, Ralph
1936 *The Study of Man: An Introduction.* New York: Appleton-Century.
1943 Nativistic Movements. *American Anthropologist* 45:230-40.
1945 *The Cultural Background of Personality.* New York: Appleton.
Linton, Ralph, ed.
1940 *Acculturation in Seven American Indian Tribes.* New York: Appleton-Century.

1945 *The Science of Man in the World Crisis.* New York: Columbia University Press.

Lippert, Julius
1931 *The Evolution of Culture,* trans. G. P. Murdock. New York: Macmillan. Originally published 1886-1887.

Little, Kenneth
1951 *The Mende of Sierra Leone.* London: Kegan Paul.
1957 The Role of Voluntary Associations in West African Urbanization. *American Anthropologist* 59:579-96.

Locke, John
1947 *Two Treatises of Government.* New York: Hafner. Originally published 1690.

Lommel, Andreas
1953 Der Cargo-Kult in Melanesien: Ein Beitrag zum Problem der Europaisierung der Primitiven. *Sonderdruck: Zeitschrift für Ethnologie,* supplement 78, 1:2-63.

Lounsbury, Floyd
1956 A Semantic Analysis of the Pawnee Kinship Usage. *Language* 32:158-94.
1962 Review of Structure and Sentiment: A Test Case in Social Anthropology by Rodney Needham. *American Anthropologist* 64:1302-10.

Lovejoy, A.
1923 The Supposed Primitivism of Rousseau's Discourse on Inequality. *Modern Philology* 21:165-86.
1933 Monboddo and Rousseau. *Modern Philology* 30:275-96.

Lowie, Robert H.
1920 *Primitive Society.* New York: Boni & Liveright.
1924 *Primitive Religion.* New York: Boni & Liveright.
1929 *Culture and Ethnology.* New York: Peter Smith. Originally published 1917.
1937 *The History of Ethnological Theory.* New York: Farrar & Rinehart.

Lubbock, Sir John
1865 *Pre-Historic Times, as Illustrated by Ancient Remains and the Manners and Customs of Modern Savages.* London: Williams & Norgate.
1870 *The Origin of Civilization and the Primitive Condition of Man: Mental and Social Condition of Savages.* London: Longmans, Green.

Lyell, Sir Charles
1830- *The Principles of Geology: An Attempt to Explain the Former Changes of the Earth's Surface by Reference to Causes Now in Operation,* 2 vols. London: J. Murray.
1832
1863 *The Geological Evidences of the Antiquity of Man With Remarks on the Origin of Species by Variation.* London: J. Murray.

MacEnery, J.
1859 *Cavern Researches: Discoveries of Organic Remains and of British and Roman Reliques in the Caves of Kent's Hole, Anstis Cave, Chudleigh, and Berry Head,* ed. from MS. notes by E. Vivian. London: Simkin, Marshall.

Macgregor, Gordon
1946 *Warriors Without Weapons: A Study of the Society and Personality of the Pine Ridge Sioux.* Chicago: University of Chicago Press.

McLennan, John F.
1865 *Primitive Marriage: An Inquiry into the Origin of the Form of Capture in Marriage Ceremonies.* Edinburgh: Adam & Charles Black.
1896 *Studies in Ancient History: Comprising an Inquiry into the Origin of Exogamy.* London: Macmillan.

McNickle, D'Arcy
1961- Private Intervention. In *American Indians and Their Economic Development,* ed. Fred Voget. *Human Organization* 20:208-15 (special issue).
1962

Macquet, Jacques J.
1964 Review of *Objectivity in Anthropology: Papers in Honor of Melville Herskovits. Current Anthropology* 5:47-55.

Maine, Sir Henry S.
1861 *Ancient Law: Its Connection with the Early History of Society and Its Relation to Modern Ideas.* London: J. Murray.
1875 *Lectures on the Early History of Institutions.* New York: Holt.

Mair, Lucy
1962 *The Nyasaland Election of 1961.* London: Athlone Press.

1965 *An African People in the Twentieth Century.* London: Routledge & Kegan Paul. Originally published 1934.
1969 *Anthropology and Social Change.* London: Athlone Press.

Malinowski, Bronislaw
1926 *Crime and Custom in Savage Society.* London: Kegan Paul, Trench, Trubner.
1927 *Sex and Repression in Savage Society.* New York: Humanities Press.
1929 *The Sexual Life of Savages in North-Western Melanesia: An Ethnographic Account of Courtship, Marriage and Family Life Among the Natives of the Trobriand Islands, British New Guinea.* New York: Harcourt, Brace.
1935 *Coral Gardens and Their Magic: A Study of the Methods of Tilling the Soil and of Agricultural Rites in the Trobriand Islands,* 2 vols. London: George Allen & Unwin.
1944 *A Scientific Theory of Culture and Other Essays.* Chapel Hill: University of North Carolina Press.
1948a Baloma: Spirits of the Dead in the Trobriand Islands. *Journal of the Royal Anthropological Institute* 46: 353-430. Originally published 1916.
1948b *Magic, Science, and Religion.* Boston: Beacon Press.
1961a *Argonauts of the Western Pacific.* New York: Dutton. Originally published 1922.
1961b *The Dynamics of Culture Change: An Inquiry into Race Relations in Africa.* New Haven: Yale University Press. Originally published 1945.

Mandelbaum, David C., ed.
1958 *Selected Writings of Edward Sapir in Language, Culture, and Personality.* Berkeley: University of California Press.

Marett, R. R.
1909 *The Threshold of Religion.* London: Methuen.

Marshall, Donald Stanley
1967 General Anthropology: Strategy for a Human Science. *Current Anthropology* 8:61-66.

Mauss, Marcel
1954 *The Gift: Forms and Functions of Exchange in Archaic Society,* trans.

Ian Cunnison. London: Cohen & West. Originally published 1925.

Mauss, Marcel, and Henri Beuchat
1906 Essai sur les variations saisonnières des sociétés eskimos. *L'année sociologique* 9:39-132.

Mauss, Marcel, and Henri Hubert
1899 Essai sur la nature et la fonction du sacrifice. *L'année sociologique, deuxième année (1897-1898),* pp. 22-138. Paris.

Mayer, Philip
1961 *Townsmen or Tribesmen: Conservatism and the Process of Urbanization in a South African City.* Cape Town: Oxford University Press.

Mayo, Elton
1933 *The Human Problems of an Industrial Civilization.* New York: Macmillan.

Mead, Margaret
1928 *Coming of Age in Samoa.* New York: Morrow.
1930 *Growing Up in New Guinea.* New York: Morrow.
1932 The Changing Culture of an Indian Tribe. *Columbia University Contributions in Anthropology* 15:1-313. New York: Columbia University Press.
1950 *Sex and Temperament in Three Primitive Societies.* New York: Mentor Books, New American Library. Originally published 1935.
1961 *New Lives For Old: Cultural Transformation—Manus, 1928-1953.* New York: Mentor Books, New American Library. Originally published 1956.

Mead, Margaret, ed.
1937 *Cooperation and Competition Among Primitive Peoples.* New York: McGraw-Hill.
1955 *Cultural Patterns and Technical Change.* New York: Mentor Books, New American Library.
1959 *An Anthropologist at Work: Writings of Ruth Benedict.* Boston: Houghton Mifflin.

Mead, Margaret, and Rhoda Metraux
1953 *The Study of Culture at a Distance.* Chicago: University of Chicago Press.

Meggers, Betty J.
1954 Environmental Limitation on the De-

velopment of Culture. *American Anthropologist* 56:801-24.

1960 *The Law of Cultural Evolution as a Practical Research Tool.* In *Essays in the Science of Culture in Honor of Leslie A. White,* ed. Gertrude Dole and Robert Carneiro, pp. 302-16. New York: Crowell.

Meiners, C.

1785 *Grundriss der Geschichte der Menschheit.* Lemgo: Meyerschen Buchhandlung.

Mekeel, Scudder

1944 An Appraisal of the Indian Reorganization Act. *American Anthropologist* 46:209-17.

Merton, Robert

1957 *Social Theory and Social Structure.* Glencoe, Ill.: Free Press.

Metraux, Alfred

1953 Applied Anthropology in Government: United Nations. In *Anthropology Today,* ed. A. L. Kroeber, pp. 880-94. Chicago: University of Chicago Press.

Millar, J.

1806 *The Origin of the Distinction of Ranks: or, an Inquiry into the Circumstances Which Give Rise to Influence and Authority in the Different Members of Society.* Edinburgh: W. Blackwood. Originally published 1771.

Miniclier, Louis

1964 The Use of Anthropologists in the Foreign Aid Program. *Human Organization* 23:187-89.

Monboddo, Lord (J. Burnett)

1779- *Ancient Metaphysics: or, The Science*
1799 *of Universals,* 6 vols. Vols. 4 and 5, *The History of Man.* Edinburgh: J. Balfour.

Montaigne, Michel de

1946 *The Essays of Montaigne,* trans. E. J. Trechmann. New York: Modern Library, Random House. Originally published 1580.

Montesquieu, Baron de

1949 *The Spirit of the Laws,* trans. Thomas Nugent. New York: Hafner. Originally published 1749.

Morgan, Lewis H.

1871 *Systems of Consanguinity and Affinity of the Human Family.* In Smithsonian Contributions to Knowledge, vol. 17. Washington, D.C.: Smithsonian Institution.

1877 *Ancient Society, or Researches in the Lines of Progress from Savagery Through Barbarism to Civilization.* New York: Holt.

1954 *League of the Ho-De-No-Sau-Nee or Iroquois,* 2 vols. New Haven: HRAF Press. Originally published 1851.

Mortillet, Gabriel de

1872 Classification des diverses périodes de l'age de la pierre. *Revue d'anthropologie* 1:432-42.

Murdock, George P.

1945 The Common Denominator of Cultures. In *The Science of Man in the World Crisis,* ed. Ralph Linton, pp. 123-42. New York: Columbia University Press.

1949 *Social Structure.* New York: Macmillan.

1951 British Social Anthropology. *American Anthropologist* 53:465-73.

1962 World Ethnographic Atlas. *Ethnology* 1:113-34.

Murdock, George P., ed.

1960 *Social Structure in Southeast Asia.* Viking Fund Publications in Anthropology, no. 29. New York: Wenner-Gren Foundation for Anthropological Research.

Murdock, George P., and Douglas R. White

1969 Standard Cross-Cultural Sample. *Ethnology* 8:329-69.

Nadel, Siegfried F.

1942 *A Black Byzantium: The Kingdom of Nupe in Nigeria.* London: Oxford University Press.

1951 *The Foundations of Social Anthropology.* London: Cohen & West.

1952 Witchcraft in Four African Societies: An Essay in Comparison. *American Anthropologist* 54:18-29.

Nader, Laura, ed.

1965 *The Ethnography of Law. American Anthropologist* 67, no. 6, pt. 2 (special publication).

Naroll, Raoul

1961 Two Solutions to Galton's Problem. *Philosophy of Science* 28:15-39.

1964 A Fifth Solution to Galton's Problem. *American Anthropologist* 66:863-67.

1965 Galton's Problem: The Logic of Cross-Cultural Analysis. *Social Research* 32:428-51.

1970 What Have We Learned from Cross-Cultural Surveys? *American Anthropologist* 72:1227-88.

Naroll, Raoul, and Roy G. D'Andrade
1963 Two Further Solutions to Galton's Problem. *American Anthropologist* 65:1053-67.

Nash, Manning
1958 *Machine Age Maya.* Memoir no. 87, American Anthropological Association. Glencoe, Ill.: Free Press.

Nash, Philleo
1955 The Place of Religious Revivalism in the Formation of the Intercultural Community on Klamath Reservation. In *Social Anthropology of North American Tribes,* ed. Fred Eggan, pp. 377-444. Chicago: University of Chicago Press. Originally published 1937.

Needham, Joseph, ed.
1928 *Science, Religion, and Reality.* New York: Macmillan. Originally published 1925.

Needham, Rodney
1962 *Structure and Sentiment: A Test Case in Social Anthropology.* Chicago: University of Chicago Press.

Newell, H. Perry, and Alex D. Krieger
1949 *The George C. Davis Site, Cherokee County, Texas.* Memoir no. 5, Society for American Archaeology. Menasha, Wis.

Nilsson, Sven
1868 *The Primitive Inhabitants of Scandinavia: An Essay on Comparative Ethnography, and a Contribution to the History of the Development of Mankind; Containing a Description of the Implements, Dwellings, Tombs, and Mode of Living of the Savages in the North of Europe During the Stone Age,* ed. Sir John Lubbock. London: Longmans, Green. Originally published 1838.

Nott, J. C., and G. R. Gliddon
1857 *The Indigenous Races of the Earth.* Philadelphia: Lippincott.

Nutini, Hugo G.
1965 Some Considerations on the Nature of Social Structure and Model Building: A Critique of Claude Lévi-Strauss and Edmund Leach. *American Anthropologist* 67:707-31.

Opler, Morris E.
1945 Themes as Dynamic Force in Culture. *American Journal of Sociology* 5:198-206.

1964 Morgan and Materialism: A Reply to Thomas G. Harding and Eleanor Leacock. *Current Anthropology* 5:110-14.

Oviedo y Valdés, Gonzalo Fernández de
1885 The Natural History of the West Indies. In *The First Three English Books on America,* ed. Edward Arber, pp. 205-42. Birmingham: Turnbull & Spears. Originally published 1535.

Penniman, Thomas K.
1965 *A Hundred Years of Anthropology.* London: Duckworth. Originally published 1935.

Perry, W. J.
1927 *The Children of the Sun: A Study in the Early History of Civilization.* London: Methuen. Originally published 1913.

Phillips, Philip, and Gordon Willey
1953 Method and Theory in American Archaeology: An Operational Basis for Culture-Historical Integration. *American Anthropologist* 55:615-33.

Piggott, Stuart
1960 Prehistory and Evolutionary Theory. In *The Evolution of Man: Man, Culture, and Society,* ed. Sol Tax, pp. 85-98. Chicago: University of Chicago Press.

Pike, Kenneth
1966a *Language in Relation to a Unified Theory of the Structure of Human Behavior.* The Hague: Mouton.

1966b Etic and Emic Standpoints for the Description of Behavior. In *Communication and Culture,* ed. Alfred Smith, pp. 152-63. New York: Holt, Rinehart & Winston.

Plato
1888 *The Republic,* trans. Benjamin Jowett. Oxford: Clarendon Press.

Polanyi, Karl
1947 Our Obsolete Market Mentality. *Commentary* 13:109-17.

1957 *The Great Transformation.* Boston:

Beacon Press. Originally published 1944.

1968   *Primitive, Archaic, and Modern Economies: Essays of Karl Polanyi,* ed. George Dalton. Garden City, N.Y.: Anchor Books, Doubleday.

Polanyi, Karl, and A. Rotstein
1966   *Dahomey and the Slave Trade: An Analysis of an Archaic Economy.* Monograph no. 42, American Ethnological Society. Seattle: University of Washington Press.

Polybius
1889   *The Histories of Polybius,* 2 vols., trans. Evelyn S. Shuckburgh. New York: Macmillan.

Pospisil, Leopold
1963   *Kapauku Papuan Economy.* Publications in Anthropology, no. 67. New Haven: Yale University Press.

Quatrefages de Breau, Armand de
1879   *The Human Species.* International Scientific Series, vol. 27. New York: Appleton-Century.

Radcliffe-Brown, A. R.
1922   *The Andaman Islanders.* Cambridge: At the University Press.

1940   Preface. In *African Political Systems,* ed. M. Fortes and E. E. Evans-Pritchard. London: Oxford University Press.

1950   Introduction. In *African Systems of Kinship and Marriage,* ed. A. R. Radcliffe-Brown and Daryll Forde, pp. 269-70. London: Oxford University Press.

1965a   *Structure and Function in Primitive Society.* New York: Free Press, Macmillan. Originally published 1952.

1965b   The Mother's Brother in South Africa. In ibid., pp. 15-31. Originally published 1924.

1965c   Patrilineal and Matrilineal Succession. In ibid., pp. 32-48. Originally published 1935.

1965d   On Joking Relationships. In ibid., pp. 90-104. Originally published 1940.

1965e   Religion and Society. In ibid., pp. 153-77. Originally published 1945.

1965f   On Social Structure. In ibid., pp. 188-204.

Radcliffe-Brown, A. R., and Daryll Forde, eds.
1962   *African Systems of Kinship and Marriage.* London: Oxford University Press. Originally published 1950.

Radin, Paul
1920   The Autobiography of a Winnebago Indian. In *University of California Publications in American Archaeology and Ethnology,* no. 16, pp. 381-473.

1923   The Winnebago Tribe. In *Thirty-seventh Annual Report of the United States Bureau of American Ethnology,* pp. 35-550. Washington, D.C.: Smithsonian Institution.

1927   *Primitive Man as a Philosopher.* New York: Appleton.

1933   *The Method and Theory of Ethnology: An Essay in Criticism.* New York: McGraw-Hill.

Rappaport, Roy A.
1968   *Pigs for the Ancestors: Ritual in the Ecology of a New Guinea People.* New Haven: Yale University Press.

Rask, Rasmus
1818   *Undersögelse om det gamle Nordiske eller Islandske sprogs oprindelse.* Copenhagen: Gyldendal.

Ratzel, Friedrich
1896-   *The History of Mankind,* 3 vols.,
1898   trans. A. J. Butler. New York: Macmillan.

Réclus, Elie
1891   *Primitive Folk: Studies in Comparative Ethnology.* London: Walter Scott.

Redfield, Robert
1941   *The Folk Culture of Yucatan.* Chicago: University of Chicago Press.

1950   *A Village That Chose Progress: Chan Kom Revisited.* Chicago: University of Chicago Press.

1953   *The Primitive World and Its Transformation.* Ithaca: Cornell University Press.

Redfield, Robert, Ralph Linton, and Melville J. Herskovits
1936   Memorandum for the Study of Acculturation. *American Anthropologist* 38:149-52.

Reed, Charles A.
1967   The Generic Allocation of the Hominid Species Habilis as a Problem in Systematics. *South African Journal of Science* 63:3-5.

Richards, Audrey I.
1932 *Hunger and Work in a Savage Tribe: A Functional Study of Nutrition Among the Southern Bantu.* London: Routledge.

Richardson, F. L. W.
1961 *Talk, Work, and Action.* Monograph no. 3, Society for Applied Anthropology. Ithaca: Cornell University Press.

Rink Heinrich J.
1875 *Tales and Traditions of the Eskimo, with a Sketch of Their Habits, Religion, Language, and Other Peculiarities.* Edinburgh & London: Blackwood. Originally published 1866.

Rivers, W. H. R.
1914 *The History of Melanesian Society,* 2 vols. Cambridge: At the University Press.
1926 *Psychology and Ethnology.* London: Kegan Paul, Trench, Trubner.

Robertson, W.
1822 *The History of America,* 2 vols. Philadelphia: Robert & Thomas Desilver. Originally published 1777.

Robinson, W. S.
1951 A Method for Chronologically Ordering Archaeological Deposits. *American Antiquity* 16:293-301.

Roethlisberger, F. J., and W. J. Dickson
1939 *Management and the Worker: An Account of a Research Program Conducted by the Western Electric Company, Hawthorne Works, Chicago.* Cambridge: Harvard University Press.

Rohner, Ronald
1966 Franz Boas: Ethnographer on the Northwest Coast. In *Pioneers of American Anthropology,* ed. June Helm, pp. 149-222. Monograph no. 43, American Ethnological Society. Seattle: University of Washington Press.

Romney, K., and R. G. D'Andrade, eds.
1964 *Transcultural Studies in Cognition. American Anthropologist* 66, no. 3, pt. 2 (special publication).

Rousseau, Jean Jacques
1962 *The Political Writings of Jean Jacques Rousseau,* 2 vols., ed. C. Vaughan. New York: Wiley. Originally published 1755.

Rowe, John
1965 The Renaissance Foundations of Anthropology. *American Anthropologist* 67:1-20.

Sahlins, Marshall D.
1958 *Social Stratification in Polynesia.* American Ethnological Society. Seattle: University of Washington Press.

Sahlins, Marshall D., and Elman R. Service, eds.
1960 *Evolution and Culture.* Ann Arbor: University of Michigan Press.

Salus, Peter H., ed.
1969 *On Language: Plato to von Humboldt.* New York: Holt, Rinehart & Winston.

Sanders, William T.
1962 Cultural Ecology of Nuclear Mesoamerica. *American Anthropologist* 64:34-43.

Sapir, Edward
1917 Do We Need a "Superorganic"? *American Anthropologist* 19:441-47.
1955 *Language: An Introduction to the Study of Speech.* New York: Harcourt, Brace & World. Originally published 1921.
1958a Time Perspective in Aboriginal American Culture: A Study in Method. In *Selected Writings of Edward Sapir in Language, Culture, and Personality,* ed. David C. Mandelbaum, pp. 389-462. Berkeley: University of California Press. Originally published 1916.
1958b Culture, Genuine and Spurious. In ibid., pp. 308-31. Originally published 1924.

Savage, Charles H., Jr.
1964 *Social Reorganization in a Factory in the Andes.* Monograph no. 7, Society for Applied Anthropology.

Schaedel, Richard
1964 Anthropology in AID Overseas Missions. *Human Organization* 23:190-92.

Schapera, Isaac
1967 *Government and Politics in Tribal Societies.* New York: Schocken Books. Originally published 1956.

Schapera, Isaac, ed.
1934 *Western Civilization and the Natives of South Africa: Studies in Culture Contact.* London: Routledge.

Schebesta, Paul
  1929   *Among the Forest Dwarfs of Malaya,*
          trans. A. Chambers. London: Hutch-
          inson.
  1936   *My Pygmy and Negro Hosts.* Lon-
          don: Hutchinson.
  1938- *Die Bambuti-Pygmäen vom Ituri,*
  1950   vols. 1, 2, 4. Brussels: Institut Royal
          Colonial Belge, Classe de Sciences
          Morales et Politiques, Mémoires.
Schmerling, P. C.
  1833- *Recherches sur les ossements fossiles*
  1834   *découverts dans les cavernes de la*
          province de Liège, 2 vols. Liège: Col-
          lardin.
Schmidt, Wilhelm
  1912- *Der Ursprung der Gottesidee: Eine*
  1955   *Historisch-Kritische und Positive Stu-*
          die, 12 vols. Münster: Aschendorff.
  1935   *The Origin and Growth of Reli-*
          gion: Facts and Theories, trans. H. J.
          Rose. London: Methuen. Originally
          published 1931.
Schneider, David M.
  1957   Political Organization, Supernatural
          Sanctions, and the Punishment for
          Incest on Yap. *American Anthropol-*
          ogist 59:791-800.
Schneider, David M., and Kathleen Gough,
  eds.
  1961   *Matrilineal Kinship.* Berkeley: Uni-
          versity of California Press.
Schurtz, Heinrich
  1902   *Alterklassen und Männerbunde: Eine*
          Darstellung der Grundformen der Ge-
          sellschaft. Berlin: G. Reimer.
Schwartz, Theodore
  1962   The Paliau Movement in the Admiral-
          ty Islands, 1946-1954. In *Anthropo-*
          logical Papers 39, no. 2. New York:
          American Museum of Natural His-
          tory.
Service, Elman R.
  1962   *Primitive Social Organization: An*
          Evolutionary Perspective. New York:
          Random House.
Siegel, Bernard J., ed.
  1963   *Biennial Review of Anthropology.*
          Stanford: Stanford University Press.
Slotkin, J. S.
  1952   Menomini Peyotism: A Study of In-
          dividual Variation in a Primary
          Group with Homogeneous Culture.

          Transactions of the American Phil-
          osophical Society, vol. 42, pt. 4.
          Philadelphia.
  1956   *The Peyote Religion: A Study in In-*
          dian-White Relations. Glencoe, Ill.:
          Free Press.
Smith, Adam
  1937   *An Inquiry into the Nature and Caus-*
          es of the Wealth of Nations, ed. E.
          Cannan. New York: Modern Library.
          Originally published 1776.
Smith, Alfred G., ed.
  1966   *Communication and Culture: Read-*
          ings in the Codes of Human Inter-
          action. New York: Holt, Rinehart &
          Winston.
Smith, Grafton Elliot
  1915   *The Migrations of Early Cultures: A*
          Study of the Significance of the Geo-
          graphical Distribution of the Practise
          of Mummification as Evidence of the
          Migrations of Peoples and the Spread
          of Certain Customs and Beliefs. New
          York: Longmans, Green.
  1930   *Human History.* London: Jonathan
          Cape.
  1933   *The Diffusion of Culture.* London:
          Watts.
Smith, W. Robertson
  1903   *Kinship and Marriage in Early Ara-*
          bia, ed. Stanley A. Cook. London: A.
          & C. Black. Originally published
          1885.
  1957   *The Religion of the Semites: The*
          Fundamental   Institutions.   New
          York: Meridian Books. Originally
          published 1889.
Smith, Watson, and J. M. Roberts
  1954   *Zuñi Law: A Field of Values.* Pea-
          body Museum Papers, vol. 43. Cam-
          bridge: Harvard University Press.
Smith, William
  1815   *Stratigraphical System of Organized*
          Fossils, with Reference to the Speci-
          mens of the Original Geological Col-
          lection in the British Museum . . . A
          Memoir to the Map and Delineation
          of the Strata of England and Wales,
          with Part of Scotland. London:
          J. Carey. Originally published 1794.
Speck, Frank Gouldsmith
  1935   *Naskapi: The Savage Hunters of the*
          Labrador Peninsula. Norman: Univer-

sity of Oklahoma Press.

Spencer, Baldwin, and P. J. Gillen
1899 *The Native Tribes of Central Austra-lia*. London: Macmillan.

Spencer, Herbert
1857 Progress: Its Laws and Causes. *Westminster Review* 67:445-85.
1862 *First Principles*. London: Williams & Norgate.
1874 *The Study of Sociology*. New York: Appleton.
1897 *Social Statics*, abr. and rev. New York: Appleton. Originally published 1850.
1900 *Principles of Sociology*, 5 vols. New York: Appleton. Originally published 1876.

Spicer, Edward, ed.
1961 *Perspectives in American Indian Culture Change*. Chicago: University of Chicago Press.

Spier, Leslie
1921 The Sun Dance of the Plains Indians: Its Development and Diffusion. *American Museum of Natural History Anthropological Papers* 16: 451-527.
1935 *The Prophet Dance of the Northwest and Its Derivatives: The Source of the Ghost Dance*. General Series in Anthropology, no. 1. Menasha, Wis.: George Banta Publishing Co.

Spier, Leslie, ed.
1941 *Language, Culture, and Personality*. Menasha, Wis.: Sapir Memorial Fund.

Spindler, George D.
1955 *Sociocultural and Psychological Processes in Menomini Acculturation*. Publications in Culture and Society, vol. 5. Berkeley: University of California Press.

Spiro, Melford
1954 Human Nature in Its Psychological Dimensions. *American Anthropologist* 56:19-30.

Spoehr, Alexander
1941 Camp, Clan, and Kin Among the Cow Creek Seminole. *Field Museum of Natural History Anthropological Series* 33:1-27.
1960 Port Town and Hinterland in the Pacific Islands. *American Anthropologist* 62:586-92.

Steinen, Karl von den

1894 *Unter den Naturvölkern Zentral-Brasiliens: Reiseschilderung und Ergebnisse der Zweiten Schingu-expedition, 1887-1888*. Berlin: D. Reimer.

Steward, Julian H.
1949 Cultural Causality and Law: A Trial Formulation of the Development of Early Civilization. *American Anthropologist* 51:1-27.
1951 Levels of Sociocultural Integration: An Operational Concept. *Southwestern Journal of Anthropology* 7: 374-90.
1955 *Theory of Culture Change: The Methodology of Multilinear Evolution*. Urbana: University of Illinois Press. Originally published 1951.

Steward, Julian H., ed.
1940 *Essays in Historical Anthropology of North America*. Smithsonian Miscellaneous Collections, vol. 100. Washington, D.C.: Smithsonian Institution.

Stewart, Dugald
1858 Account of the Life and Writings of Adam Smith. In *The Collected Works of Dugald Stewart*, ed. Sir William Hamilton, vol. 10. Edinburgh: T. Constable.

Stewart, Omer
1964 Anthropology and World Affairs as Seen by U.S.A. Associates: The Need to Popularize Basic Concepts. *Current Anthropology* 5:431-32.

Stocking, George W., Jr.
1963 Matthew Arnold, E. B. Tylor, and the Uses of Invention. *American Anthropologist* 65:783-99.

Stolpe, Hjalmar
1927 *Collected Essays in Ornamental Art*. Stockholm: Aftonbladets Tryckeri. Originally published 1890.

Sturtevant, William C.
1964 Studies in Ethnoscience. In *Transcultural Studies in Cognition*, ed. A. Kimball Romney and Roy G. D'Andrade, pp. 99-131. *American Anthropologist* 66, no. 3, pt. 2 (special publication).

Swanton, John R.
1942 *Source Material on the History and Ethnology of the Caddo Indians*. Bulletin no. 132, Bureau of American

Ethnology. Washington, D.C.: Smithsonian Institution.

1946 *The Indians of the Southeastern United States.* Bulletin no. 137, Bureau of American Ethnology. Washington D.C.: Smithsonian Institution.

Tacitus
1942 *The Complete Works of Tacitus,* ed. A. T. Church and W. J. Brodribb. New York: Modern Library, Random House.

Tax, Sol
1953 *Penny Capitalism: A Guatemalan Indian Economy.* Institute of Social Anthropology, pub. no. 16. Washington, D.C.: Smithsonian Institution.

1955 The Integration of Anthropology. In *Yearbook of Anthropology, 1955,* ed. W. L. Thomas, Jr., pp. 313-28. New York: Wenner-Gren Foundation for Anthropological Research.

Tax, Sol, ed.
1960 *Evolution After Darwin,* vol. 2. of *The Evolution of Man: Man, Culture, and Society.* Chicago: University of Chicago Press.

Taylor, Walter
1948 *A Study of Archeology.* Memoir no. 69, American Anthropological Association. Washington, D.C.

Teggart, Frederick J.
1960 *Theory and Processes of History.* Berkeley: University of California Press.

Thomas, W. L., Jr., ed.
1955 *Yearbook of Anthropology, 1955.* New York: Wenner-Gren Foundation for Anthropological Research.

Thomsen, Christian
1848 *Ledetraad til Nordisk Oldkyndighed.* Royal Danish National Museum guidebook, trans. Lord Ellesmere under title *A Guide to Northern Antiquities.*

Thompson, Laura
1949 Relations of Men, Animals, and Plants in an Island Community (Fiji). *American Anthropologist* 51:253-67.

1950 *Culture in Crisis: A Study of the Hopi Indians.* New York: Harper.

1951 *Personality and Government: Findings and Recommendations of the Indian Administration Research.* Mexico City: Instituto Indigenista Interamericano.

1961 *Toward a Science of Mankind.* New York: McGraw-Hill.

1967 Steps Toward a Unified Anthropology. *Current Anthropology* 8:67-91.

Thompson, Laura, and Alice Joseph
1944 *The Hopi Way.* Chicago: University of Chicago Press.

Thurnwald, Richard C.
1932 *Economics in Primitive Communities.* London: Oxford University Press.

1935 *Black and White in East Africa.* London: Routledge.

1937 Cultural Rotation, Its Propulsion and Rhythm: A Contribution Towards an Analysis of the Mechanism of Cultures. *American Sociological Review* 2:26-42.

Thwaites, R. G., ed.
1959 *The Jesuit Relations and Allied Documents: The American West,* 73 vols. in 36. Chicago: Loyola University Press. Originally published 1896-1901.

Tyler, Stephen A., ed.
1969 *Cognitive Anthropology.* New York: Holt, Rinehart & Winston.

Tylor, E. B.
1874 *Primitive Culture: Researches into the Development of Mythology, Religion, Language, Art, and Custom,* 2 vols. Boston: Estes & Lauriat. Originally published 1871.

1889 On a Method of Investigating the Development of Institutions; Applied to Laws of Marriage and Descent. *Journal of the Royal Anthropological Institute of Great Britain and Ireland* 18:245-69.

1937 *Anthropology,* 2 vols. London: Watts. Originally published 1881.

Valentine, Charles A.
1968 *Culture and Poverty: Critique and Counter-Proposals.* Chicago: University of Chicago Press.

Van den Berghe, Pierre L., ed.
1965 *Africa: Social Problems of Change and Conflict.* San Francisco: Chandler.

Van Gennep, Arnold
1960 *The Rites of Passage,* trans. Monika

B. Vizedom and Gabrielle L. Caffee. London: Routledge & Kegan Paul. Originally published 1908.

Vayda, A. P., A. Leeds, and D. B. Smith
1961 The Place of Pigs in Melanesian Subsistence. In *Symposium: Patterns of Land Utilization and Other Papers,* ed. Viola E. Garfield. Seattle: University of Washington Press.

Vinogradoff, Sir Paul
1920 *Outlines of Historical Jurisprudence,* 2 vols. London: Oxford University Press.

Voget, Fred W.
1956 The American Indian in Transition: Reformation and Accommodation. *American Anthropologist* 58:249-63.

Voget, Fred W., ed.
1961- *American Indians and Their Econom-*
1962 *ic Development. Human Organization* 20, no. 4 (special issue).

Vogt, Evon
1951 Navaho Veterans: A Study of Changing Values. *Papers of the Peabody Museum of American Archaeology and Ethnology* 41, no. 1. Cambridge: Harvard University Press.

Voltaire, François M. Arouet de
1926 *The Age of Louis XIV,* trans. Martyn Pollack. New York: Dutton. Originally published 1752.

Waitz, Theodor
1863 *Introduction to Anthropology,* trans. of vol. 1 of *Anthropologie der Naturvölker,* with additions by J. Collingwood. London: Longman, Green, Longman. Originally published 1859.

Wallace, Anthony F. C.
1952 *The Modal Personality Structure of the Tuscarora Indians, as Revealed by the Rorschach Test.* Bulletin no. 150, Bureau of American Ethnology. Washington, D.C.: Smithsonian Institution.
1956 Revitalization Movements. *American Anthropologist* 58:264-81.
1965 The Problem of the Psychological Validity of Componential Analyses. In *Formal Semantic Analysis,* ed. E. Hammel. *American Anthropologist* 67:229-48 (special publication).

Wallace, Anthony F. C., and John Atkins
1969 The Meaning of Kinship Terms. In

Cognitive Anthropology, ed. Stephen A. Tyler, pp. 345-69. Originally published 1960.

Ward, Lester
1883 *Dynamic Sociology; or Applied Social Science as Based upon Statical Sociology and the Less Complex Sciences.* New York: Appleton.

Webster, Hutton
1932 *Primitive Secret Societies: A Study in Early Politics and Religion.* New York: Macmillan. Originally published 1908.

Wedel, Waldo R.
1959 *An Introduction to Kansas Archeaology.* (With Description of the Skeletal Remains from Doniphan and Scott Counties, Kansas, by T. D. Stewart.) Bulletin no. 174, Bureau of American Ethnology. Washington, D.C.: Smithsonian Institution.

Westermarck, Edward A.
1922 *The History of Human Marriage,* 5th ed. 3 vols. New York: Allerton. Originally published 1889.

White, Leslie
1938 Science Is Sciencing. *Philosophy of Science* 5:369-89.
1949 *The Science of Culture.* New York: Grove Press.
1959 *The Evolution of Culture.* New York: McGraw-Hill.
1963 *The Ethnography and Ethnology of Franz Boas.* Texas Memorial Museum Bulletin no. 6. Austin: University of Texas.

Whiting, John W.
1964 Effects of Climate on Certain Cultural Practices. In *Explorations in Cultural Anthropology,* ed. W. Goodenough, pp. 511-44. New York: McGraw-Hill.

Whiting, John W., and Irvin L. Child
1962 *Child Training and Personality: A Cross-Cultural Study.* New Haven: Yale University Press. Originally published 1953.

Whorf, B.
1952 *Collected Papers on Metalinguistics.* U.S. Department of State, Foreign Service Institute. Washington, D.C.: U.S. Government Printing Office.
1956 *Language, Thought, and Reality: Se-*

lected Writings of Benjamin Lee Whorf, ed. John B. Carroll. New York: Wiley.

Wiener, Norbert
1948 *Cybernetics; or, Control and Communication in the Animal and the Machine.* New York: Wiley.
1950 *The Human Use of Human Beings: Cybernetics and Society.* Boston: Houghton Mifflin.

Willey, Gordon
1961 Developments in the Archaeology of Nuclear America, 1953-1960. *American Antiquity* 27:46-55.
1962 The Early Great Styles and the Rise of the Pre-Columbian Civilization. *American Anthropologist* 64:1-14.

Willey, Gordon, and Philip Phillips
1955 Method and Theory in American Archaeology. II: Historical Developmental Interpretation. *American Anthropologist* 57:723-819.
1965 *Method and Theory in American Archaeology.* Chicago: University of Chicago Press. Originally published 1958.

Wilson, Godfrey, and Monica Wilson
1945 *The Analysis of Social Change, Based on Observations in Central America.* Cambridge: At the University Press.

Wilson, Monica (see also Hunter, Monica)
1963 *Good Company: A Study of Nyakyusa Age-Villages.* Boston: Beacon Press. Originally published 1951.

Wissler, Clark
1914 The Material Culture of North American Indians. *American Anthropologist* 16:447-505.
1922 *The American Indian.* New York and London: Oxford University Press. Originally published 1917.
1923 *Man and Culture.* New York: Crowell.

Wittfogel, Karl A.
1957 *Oriental Despotism.* New Haven: Yale University Press.

Wolf, Eric
1955 Types of Latin American Peasantry: A Preliminary Discussion. *American Anthropologist* 57:452-71.
1957 Closed Corporate Peasant Communities in Mesoamerica and Central Java. *Southwestern Journal of Anthropology* 13:1-14.

Worsley, Peter
1968 *The Trumpet Shall Sound: A Study of "Cargo" Cults in Melanesia.* New York: Schocken Books. Originally published 1957.

Wundt, Wilhelm
1928 *Elements of Folk Psychology: Outlines of a Psychological History of the Development of Mankind,* trans. Edward Leroy Schaub. New York: Macmillan. Originally published 1912.

CHAPTER 2 The Four Faces of Evolution

ROBERT L. CARNEIRO

It has taken a hundred years, but cultural evolutionism has finally come full circle. The guiding principle of anthropology when it emerged as a science in the 1860s, evolutionism began to decline around 1900 and went into an eclipse that lasted nearly half a century. Around the mid-1940s, however, evolutionism began to reassert itself,[1] and today it has once more assumed its rightful place among the valid and fruitful approaches to the study of culture.

Nonetheless, many aspects of evolutionism remain unclear. Current discussions of unilinear, universal, and multilinear evolution, for example, often fail to differentiate these modes precisely. It is my aim here to distinguish the major types of evolution from one another, and to clarify their interrelationships. Before discussing the different forms of evolution, however, I would like to make clear my notion of evolution as a general process.

Without going into the many concepts of evolution that have been offered, I shall simply state that the one I have found most useful is the one first proposed. This was the formulation of the concept made by Herbert Spencer in *First Principles* in 1862.[2] Spencer defined evolution as "a change from an indefinite, incoherent homogeneity to a definite, coherent heterogeneity; through continuous differentiations and integrations" (1862:216). He later modified this definition by changing it to read "relatively indefinite" and "relatively definite" in order to make it clear that evolution need not begin with absolute homogeneity nor

---

[1] I would date the resurgence of cultural evolutionism from 1943, the year in which Leslie A. White's "Energy and the Evolution of Culture" appeared in the *American Anthropologist*.

---

[2] Contrary to popular belief, it was not Charles Darwin who introduced, or even popularized, the term "evolution." The word, in fact, does not even appear in the first five editions of *The Origin of Species*. It was not until the last edition of the book in 1872, long after Spencer's discussion of evolution in *First Principles* had given the term wide currency, that Darwin saw fit to work "evolution" into his text. Even then, he used it no more than half a dozen times, and made no attempt to define it (Darwin 1872:201, 202, 424; Peckham 1959:264, 265, 751).

end in absolute heterogeneity (Spencer 1898:353).[3]

In addition to this modification, made by Spencer himself, I would suggest another: the substitution of "successive" for "continuous" in describing differentiations and integrations. The effect of this alteration is to recognize changes that have given rise to differentiations and integrations as evolutionary, even if these changes have not been continuous and uninterrupted.

Our modified Spencerian definition of evolution now reads:

Evolution is a change from a relatively indefinite, incoherent homogeneity to a relatively definite, coherent heterogeneity, through successive differentiations and integrations.

Before proceeding further let us note what, according to this view, evolution is *not*. First of all, it is not simply change, although many biologists, and even anthropologists, consider change of any kind to be evolutionary. Likewise, it is not merely adaptive change. To be sure, most evolutionary change (as here defined) *is* adaptive; that is to say, it enhances a society's adjustment to the conditions of existence and thus increases its chances of survival. But adaptive change is not always, or necessarily, evolutionary in

our sense of the term. Indeed, it can be just the opposite. Since this point is seldom made in discussions of evolution, let me attempt to explain it with a concrete example.

During the nineteenth century the Amahuaca Indians of the Peruvian *Montaña* were subject to raids by stronger tribes like the Conibo and Piro, and to exploitation of their territory by rubber gatherers. In defending themselves against these incursions, the Amahuaca appear to have split their settlements into smaller ones and to have moved them more often than before. That is to say, they attempted to cope with attack by means of dispersion and evasion rather than by concentration. In making this adjustment, their social, political, and ceremonial organization appears to have undergone simplification, so that today they lack even headmen and shamans, and engage in ceremonialism only occasionally.

But while reduced in numbers and simplified in social life, the Amahuaca have survived. Had they attempted to remain in larger and more permanent settlements and to stand and fight, they might well have been exterminated. Thus the change undergone by the Amahuaca was clearly adaptive. However, it was also a change in the direction of simplification and dispersion, rather than toward increased complexity and integration. Accordingly, while the change was adaptive, it was not (in our terms) evolutionary.[4] In-

---

[3] Actually, Spencer had previously modified his formula of evolution in another important respect. In the second and later editions of *First Principles* (1880:407) the definition was changed to read: "Evolution is an integration of matter and concomitant dissipation of motion; during which the matter passes from an indefinite, incoherent homogeneity to a definite, coherent heterogeneity; and during which the retained motion undergoes a parallel transformation." The "integration of matter and concomitant dissipation of motion" was introduced in order to increase the applicability of the definition to evolution in the inorganic realm, where changes in the distribution of matter and motion were especially evident. My own feeling, however, is that for cultural evolution at least, and probably for all of evolution, Spencer's original formulation is superior to his revision.

[4] Of course, most adaptive changes ocurring in societies also tend to make them more complex. And similarly, few changes in the direction of increased complexity are not also adaptive. So that, by and large, increases in adaptation and in complexity go hand in hand in the course of evolution. The clearest recognition of this interrelationship that I have seen is by Thomas Munro in his *Evolution in the Arts* (1963). Munro distinguishes two major concepts of evolution, one emphasizing increasing complexity, the other emphasizing adaptive modification. The former he traces to Herbert Spencer and the latter to

deed, it might well be termed *devolutionary.*

As used here, then, evolution specifies a direction in which change must proceed if it is to qualify as evolutionary. This direction is toward increased definiteness, heterogeneity, and integration; in a word, toward increased complexity.[5]

With a working definition of evolution in hand, we may now turn to an examination of various manifestations of evolution in culture.

UNILINEAR EVOLUTION

A reasoned and sympathetic treatment of unilinear evolution is made difficult by the exaggerated and distorted picture we have of it from the hands of its critics. Unilinear evolution is usually said by such critics to be that line of cultural development which *all* societies have followed in every particular throughout their history.[6]

If unilinear evolution must mean this, and nothing less, then admittedly

---

Charles Darwin. He sees no necessary opposition between them: "The two ideas are not inconsistent, and can be regarded as indicating complementary aspects of the same process. One way to combine them would be to say that evolution *in the full sense* has *both* characteristics, while a process having only one is only partly evolutionary" (1963:219; emphasis Munro's). Cultural evolutionism in its totality Munro would characterize as "*the belief that present cultural forms have come into existence through a long process of descent with gradual, adaptive modification, the origination of new types of form, and a tendency to increasing complexity*" (1963:220; emphasis Munro's).

[5] Julian Steward (1953:314), however, maintains that "complexity as such is not distinctive of the evolutionary concept. ..."

[6] Thus Julian Steward (1953:324) asserted that "the historical reconstructions of the nineteenth-century unilinear evolutionists are distinctive for the assumption that *all* cultures pass through parallel and genetically unrelated sequences" (emphasis Steward's). (See also Gillin 1948:600; Linton 1936:314).

---

no such evolution has taken place, and anyone who argues that it has is lost. But are we really obliged to conceive of it in its full strictness? Can we not think of unilinear evolution as that line of development which a *preponderant number* of societies have followed *most* of the time? It seems to me that we can do so without straining the essential meaning of the term. Certainly the classical evolutionists, with whom unilinear evolution is most commonly associated, were content with sequences supported by a substantial majority of cases, and did not demand absolute unanimity (see, e.g., Morgan 1909:9; Frazer 1905:151).

With unilinear evolution thus defined, the shoe is now on the other foot. No longer can opponents of evolutionism reject a sequence simply because they have found an exception to it. It is now a matter of *preponderances,* and to determine these one has to examine a large number of cases. To the question "Is there an evolutionary sequence through which a substantial majority of human societies have passed?" the only answer can be "Let us look closely at the record and see."

During most of the twentieth century this question was not asked, and therefore never answered. Anti-evolutionism was firmly in the saddle and was not easily to be unhorsed. But as Leslie A. White (1960:vii) observed, "the concept of evolution ... proved itself to be too fundamental and fruitful to be ignored indefinitely by anything calling itself a science." Thus it was that around the mid-1940s a resurgence of evolutionism began to occur in American ethnology, with White himself playing the major role.

But there was another, less well-known side to this resurgence, and it occurred in the field of archaeology. Since it ultimately came to have a special bearing on the question of unilinear evolution, let us consider it in some detail.

By the mid-1940s archaeologists working in Peru and Mesoamerica were becoming increasingly impressed by the enormous degree of cultural development that had occurred in the two regions. At the bottom of their sequences they found simple villages, and at the top, complex civilizations. If these sequences revealed anything at all, they revealed evolution. And if archaeologists were to make sense of these sequences in terms of process and causation, they would have to do so by means of an evolutionary framework.

The issue between the old and the new archaeological perspectives was first joined in the matter of terminology. What terms were to be used in designating archaeological periods? The traditional and purely historical method was to name periods after pottery styles. These styles were good time markers, but did not necessarily reflect anything about the general level of culture of the periods they defined. The time had come, some archaeologists felt, to supplant, or at least supplement, period names such as "White-on-Red," "Interlocking," and "Proto-Nazca"—terms that failed to suggest evolutionary stages—with terms that did.

The pioneer in this endeavor was the Peruvian archaeologist Rafael Larco Hoyle. By 1946 Larco had drawn up a synoptic chart in which the cultural development of the Chicama Valley of northern Peru was divided into the following stages: (1) Preceramic, (2) Early Ceramic, (3) Formative (*Evolutiva*), (4) Florescent (*Auge*), (5) Fusion, and (6) Imperial (Larco Hoyle 1948:10; 1966:11). This evolutionary framework was designed "as a substitute for and an improvement on the use of an ever-increasing and overlapping list of pottery type and cultural horizon designations" (Bird 1964:ix-x). It was Larco's

feeling that the subdivision of Peruvian culture history "cannot be merely a subdivision in time, but must, at each stage, reflect the state of development of the different cultures" (1966:12).

Larco's new classification was presented at the Chiclín Conference held in Trujillo, Peru, in August 1946. The time was ripe for it. Most of the archaeologists assembled for the conference were then working in the neighboring Virú Valley on a program of survey and excavation designed to reveal the broadest aspects of cultural development in northern Peru (Willey 1953:xvii-xix). Thus they were quick to recognize the need for such a terminology[7] and to support and even copy Larco's efforts toward this end (Willey 1946:133-34; Bird 1964:x; Larco Hoyle 1948:7 and 1966:11).

The next important step along these lines was the Viking Fund conference on Peruvian archaeology held in New York the following year. At this meeting, several so-called functional-developmental terminologies were proposed, especially by Wendell C. Bennett[8] and William Duncan Strong[9] for Peru, and

---

[7] A decade later, in commenting on the long delay in the introduction of this type of archaeological terminology, Willey and Phillips (1958:64) wrote: "Possibly because of the strong reaction in this country against what is disdainfully referred to as 'nineteenth-century evolutionism,' overt developmental classifications are comparatively new in American archaeology."

[8] Bennett (1948:6) proposed the following sequence of stages for Peru: (1) Cultists, (2) Experimenters, (3) Master Craftsmen, (4) Expansionists, (5) City Builders, and (6) Imperialists. This sequence was later included in *Andean Culture History* with two additional stages, Hunters and Early Farmers, preceding Cultists (Bennett and Bird 1949:112). (Note how the criteria for labeling the various stages shift from subsistence to religion to technology to militarism to architecture and back to militarism.)

[9] Strong's (1948:98) stages for Peru—(1) Pre-Agricultural, (2) Developmental, (3) Formative, (4)

Pedro Armillas for Mesoamerica.[10] It is worth noting, in passing, that these "functional-developmental" terminologies were nothing less than *evolutionary* terminologies. But the taboo against using the word "evolution" was still so strong that a clumsy euphemism was adopted in its stead.[11]

Although not an archaeologist himself, Julian H. Steward was known for his interest in American culture history, and was invited to the conference and asked to present a synthesis of the major ideas proposed there.[12] In doing so, Steward went beyond the evolutionary formulations suggested for Peru and Mesoamerica separately, and proposed a single sequence of developmental stages that applied to both of them at

once (Steward 1948:104). His functional-developmental classification was as follows:

1. Pre-agricultural
2. Basic agricultural beginnings
3. Regional developmental or formative
4. Regional florescent
5. Empire and conquest

The characteristics of each stage were specified in terms of subsistence, settlement patterns, population density, technology, craft specialization, social stratification, political organization, religious institutions, and the like. This scheme generalized into a single sequence the course of development that had occurred in those areas of aboriginal America where civilization had been attained.

Having taken this significant step, Steward saw the possibility of taking an even greater one. This he did two years later (1949), in his memorable article "Cultural Causality and Law: A Trial Formulation of the Development of Early Civilizations." In this essay Steward showed that the six areas of the world where civilization had arisen independently—Mesopotamia, Egypt, India, China, Peru, and Mesoamerica—had passed through the same series of stages. These stages, slightly modified and elaborated over those he had proposed for native America, were:

1. Hunting and gathering
2. Incipient agriculture
3. Formative
4. Regional florescence
5. Initial conquests
6. Dark ages
7. Cyclical conquests[13]

Florescent, (5) Fusion, and (6) Imperial—were almost identical with Larco's. (See Larco Hoyle 1948: 7.)

[10] For Mesoamerica, Armillas' (1948:105-108) stages were (1) Basic, (2) Formative, (3) Florescent, and (4) Militaristic.

[11] This taboo is evidently still with us. Thus, for example, Willey and Phillips, referring to their series of stages—(1) Lithic, (2) Archaic, (3) Formative, (4) Classic, and (5) Post-Classic—designed to portray cultural development in aboriginal America, suddenly startle us by saying: " . . . ours is not an evolutionary scheme" (1958:70). It is, they tell us, a "historical-developmental sequence" (1958:64). When Rouse proposed the chronological classification of Paleo-Indian, Meso-Indian, and Neo-Indian for the Caribbean area, he noted that his periods corresponded to Willey and Phillips' Early Lithic, Archaic, and Formative, but added that, "unlike the latter, they refer to time rather than to degree of cultural evolution" (Rouse 1964:392). Thus Rouse correctly grasps the evolutionary nature of Willey and Phillips' sequence, but at the same time is careful to dissociate himself from it.

[12] Steward already had considerable experience in organizing a large mass of data along evolutionary lines. In editing the *Handbook of South American Indians* he had arranged the native cultures of that continent into four categories—Marginal, Tropical Forest, Circum-Caribbean, and Andean—which, besides designating different culture types, also represented successive levels of development.

[13] There are certain inconsistencies in the two charts in "Cultural Causality and Law" in which Steward presents his sequence. On Chart I (1949:8), Peru and Mesoamerica are shown to have passed through an "Initial Conquest" stage, but not through a "Dark Ages" or a "Cyclical Conquests" stage. On

Now this "trial formulation" was essentially an exercise in *unilinear* evolution. Steward, however, was not really aware of it. In fact, he stated that "the formulation here offered excludes all areas except the arid and semi-arid centers of ancient civilizations" (1949:17). In other words, he made no claim that his sequence applied to civilizations that had arisen in other types of environment. Thus, if anything, Steward felt he was doing *multilinear* evolution, even though he did not use the term. As we shall see in a moment, however, Steward's formulation was of more general application than he was ready to assert.

First, though, let us see why Steward restricted his formulation to arid and semi-arid regions. The reason was simple enough: he believed that such areas required irrigation to support intensive agriculture, and in irrigation, he thought, lay the causal mechanism that accounted for the rise of the state and civilization. While Steward never made it completely explicit, he was operating with Karl Wittfogel's "hydraulic hypothesis" in mind. According to this theory, the political machinery of the state came into being when "a number of farmers eager to conquer [agriculturally] arid lowlands and plains [were] forced to invoke the organizational devices which . . . offer[ed] the one chance to success; they . . . work[ed] in cooperation with their fellows and subordinate[d] themselves to a directing authority" (Wittfogel 1957:18).

Thus, according to Wittfogel, the requirements of irrigation did more than simply increase the power of the state; they actually brought the state into being. It is clear that Steward accepted this tenet of Wittfogel's hypothesis. If he did so only by implication in 1949, he was quite explicit in 1955 when he wrote: "state authority *originated* with hydraulic control . . ." (Steward 1955a: 66; emphasis mine).

The hydraulic theory was the only theory of state formation that Steward openly subscribed to in "Cultural Causality and Law." By means of it he felt he could explain the rise of civilization. Without it, he apparently thought he could not.

However, something unanticipated occurred. Despite Steward's demurral, his sequence of stages seemed to fit the development of civilization in areas where irrigation was not practiced, as well as those in which it was. Steward had never actually said that civilization in humid areas had not gone through the same stages as those he had proposed for arid areas. Now he found that Yucatan, a region of tropical rain forest, "appears to fit the formulation made for the more arid areas to the extent that its sequences were very similar to those of Mesoamerica generally" (1949:17). Already, then, there was an indication that Steward's stages might apply beyond the limits he had originally set for them.

The publication of "Cultural Causality and Law" was a landmark in the history of evolutionism. The paper aroused great interest and provoked intense debate. As a result of all the attention it received, a symposium was held at the annual meetings of the American Anthropological Association in 1953, at which specialists on Peru, Mesoamerica, Mesopotamia, and China gathered to discuss the applicability of Steward's formulation to their respective areas.

During the course of this symposium a number of discrepancies between Steward's interpretations and the archaeo-

Chart II (1949:9), however, no "Initial Conquest" stage is shown for the two areas, but a "Cyclical Conquests" stage is shown for both. These inconsistencies were not resolved when the article was revised and reprinted as a separate chapter in Steward's *Theory of Culture Change* (1955b: 189-90).

logical record were brought to light. The one that seemed most serious to him was the apparent lack of irrigation in the semi-arid valleys of Mesoamerica during Formative and even Florescent times (Steward 1955a:61). Here, then, was a second instance of state origins without a hydraulic impetus. Moreover, it now began to appear that northern China was not semi-arid after all, but had a climate that had permitted rain-fall agriculture (Steward 1955a:59; see also Gernet 1968:47, 74). Exceptions to the hydraulic hypothesis were thus beginning to mount. The notion that the organizational requirements of irrigation lay at the root of the state was becoming more difficult to sustain.[14]

But whatever the causal factors underlying Steward's sequence of stages might be, the symposium brought forth no substantial evidence that the sequence itself was not still of general applicability. Steward, however, failed to distinguish clearly between his theory and his sequence. He reacted as if the weakening of the former cast serious doubt on the validity of the latter.

Some members of the symposium, noting that except for the apparent absence of irrigation in its earlier stages, Mesoamerican civilization still seemed to adhere to Steward's trial formulation, asked him, "Why throw out the baby with the irrigation water?" (Steward 1955a:63). But Steward was more concerned with the failure of his theory than with the success of his stages. In fact, he was quite ready to sacrifice the

universality of his sequence to a new theory of state formation, which he now proposed for Mesoamerica.

Believing that there had been an "absence of either military or strictly secular political authority" in Mesoamerica prior to the late Militaristic period, Steward suggested that "religious leaders perhaps assumed power over the distribution of goods" (1955a:62). Such theocratic control over trade, he thought, might have "cause[d] these centers to develop and become cohesive in the absence of irrigation" (1955a: 63). The political unit that emerged from this process Steward called the "Ceremonial Trade State."

As Steward himself admitted, this *ad hoc* developmental scheme was highly speculative. Indeed, he felt it to be "so provisional that it will be as readily withdrawn as it is offered if further research invalidates it" (1955a:63). The significant thing, though, was not that Steward was so ready to withdraw it, but that he had been so ready to propose it. But by now proliferation of special explanations to account for individual discrepancies took precedence in Steward's mind over the attempt to discover and elaborate a single theory that might account for all cases.

This change in attitude on Steward's part is striking and worth emphasizing. In 1949 he had written that "to stress the complexity or multiplicity of the antecedents or functional correlates of any institution makes it impossible to isolate the true causes of the institution . . ." (1949:5). He therefore opposed the use of "convergent [multilinear?] evolution rather than parallel [unilinear?] evolution," feeling that recourse to the former might be "another means of denying the possibility of isolating cultural regularities . . ." (1949: 5). By 1953, however, Steward was more inclined to accept diversities at face value, and less inclined to try to

---

[14] I do not mean to imply that the construction and maintenance of a large irrigation system did not significantly increase the power of the state. This aspect of Wittfogel's hypothesis, as far as I know, stands unchallenged. The issue here, though, is whether irrigation is a *prerequisite* of state formation, and on this point I think the hydraulic hypothesis cannot be upheld (see Adams 1960:281; Gernet 1968:92; Carneiro 1970b:733, 738).

ferret out the regularity that might underlie them. Thus from an implicit unilinearity Steward had moved to an explicit multilinearity.

Had Steward not become so predisposed to take a multilinear view, he
might have set irrigation aside and
looked elsewhere for some other single
cause for the developmental regularity
he had found. He might, for example, have looked to warfare under
conditions of population pressure as
such a cause (see, e.g., Carneiro 1970*b*).
But Steward was not very much impressed with the overriding political effects of war. Thus, while he noted that
Robert Rands's study of Classic Maya art
had revealed, contrary to the prevailing
notion, that warfare was common
among the ancient Maya, he failed to
make the most of this fact. Commenting on it, he noted only that Maya
warfare "must have had a functional
difference than that of the Andes"
(1955*a*:68). So while he recognized
that warfare had contributed to state
formation in the Andes, he was not
prepared to do so for the Maya.

Steward's growing preoccupation
with plurality and diversity appeared
again and again. When comparing warfare among the Circum-Caribbean chiefdoms and the Inca empire, for example,
he noted that while the Caribbean peoples were content to take prisoners of
war, the Inca also incorporated conquered territory within their empire. But
instead of seeing this as a difference in
evolutionary stages, as he should have,
he saw it only as a difference in *societal
types* (Steward 1955*a*:68-69).

Thus confronted by discrepancies
that could have been accommodated
into his system of stages with relatively
minor patching and mending, Steward
nevertheless chose to retreat from the
scheme he had so boldly and brilliantly
proposed only four years before. So it
was that without ever realizing he had

practiced it, Steward turned his back
on unilinear evolution and cast his lot
with that mode of evolution he came to
call multilinear.

Now let us go back and pick up the
thread of our earlier discussion. The
great advance of functional-developmental terminologies such as Steward's
was in taking particular archaeological
periods and converting them into general
evolutionary stages. By this act a historical chronology, devoid of dynamic
significance, was transformed into
a developmental sequence indicating
both determinism and direction. Moreover, the stages of this sequence were
so conceived and expressed that they
might be represented anywhere in the
world that civilization had evolved.
With this step, archaeology made a major advance beyond the particularizing
approach of history, toward the generalizing approach of science.

For all their advantages over previous
archaeological nomenclatures, however,
functional-developmental terminologies
were not without their defects and limitations. For one thing, the labels applied to stages—Formative, Florescent,
Experimenter, Classic, etc.—often
lacked objectivity and precision. What
does "Formative" really mean when, in
an evolving society, new traits and complexes are being formed all the time?
Or again, what is meant by "Florescent" when a developing culture may
"flower" over and over? [15]

---

[15] The vagueness and ambiguity of these terms has
in fact led to disagreement, confusion, and qualification among archaeologists. See, for example,
Wauchope (1964:335), Ford (1966:782), Bird
(1964:x-xii), and Lanning (1967:23). However,
when Lanning goes so far as to state that "the
principal difficulty with developmental stages as an
organizing principle is their assumption that similar
events happened at about the same time and in the
same sequence all over ancient Peru," it is time to
object. No such "assumption" is implicit in the con-

Still another criticism may be raised. It is true that by employing six or seven stages instead of the traditional three of Savagery, Barbarism, and Civilization, functional-developmental terminologies have improved our ability to distinguish significant levels of cultural advance. Nonetheless, a sequence of only six or seven stages can reveal nothing more than the gross anatomy of the evolutionary process. Stages limited to this small number are simply too few and too broad to reveal the fine grain of cultural development.[16]

Yet it is precisely this fine grain that we need in order to fill in the evolutionary picture. Broad contrastive stages highlight the major phases of evolution, and by so doing perform a useful function. But they also tend to obscure the actual step-by-step mechanics of the process. By and large, evolution occurs, not by saltation, but by cumulation. Small steps follow one another in close succession until a qualitatively new level is attained and one type of sociocultural system is transformed into another.

It is the successive development of cumulating traits that I have focused on in attempting to work out evolutionary sequences. The results obtained in this study so far show what I would not hesitate to call unilinear regularities (see Carneiro and Tobias 1963; Carneiro 1968, 1970a). However, in a paper devoted to a discussion of the general aspects of evolution rather than to specific evolutionary sequences, I

can do no more than merely allude to their existence.

UNIVERSAL EVOLUTION

The term "universal evolution" was coined by Julian Steward to label the evolutionism of Leslie A. White and V. Gordon Childe. Aware that nineteenth-century unilinear schemes of development were untenable, Steward says, White and Childe tried to keep the concept of evolutionary stages alive by having it apply not to particular societies, but to culture as a whole (Steward 1953:316).

Now what does it mean to say that a certain sequence of development applies to "culture as a whole"? Does it mean that such a sequence is somehow unrelated to the culture history of particular societies? How are evolutionary sequences applying to "culture as a whole" formulated in the first place? Very little discussion of these questions has appeared in print, and even Steward himself does not make it perfectly clear what he means by the "universal evolution" he has christened.

There are, it seems to me, two possible meanings to the notion of an evolutionary sequence that applies to "culture as a whole." One of them I will call the initial-appearance meaning, and the other the predominance-of-cases meaning.

THE INITIAL-APPEARANCE VIEW

The initial-appearance view may be expressed as follows: When it is said of two traits, A and B, that in the evolution of culture as a whole A evolved before B, what is meant is that the *first appearance* of A, wherever it occurred, preceded the first appearance of B. What the relative order of appearance of these two traits may have been in other societies at some later date is

---

cept of evolutionary stages. If a particular archaeologist has made this assumption for Peru, we invite Lanning to identify him so that we may all join in criticizing and correcting him. In the meantime, let the record show that no responsible contemporary evolutionist would assume this.

[16] For a discussion of this objection as it applies to a sequence of stages proposed for Mesoamerica, see Bernal (1964:561).

irrelevant. All that matters is that the first development of *A* preceded the first development of *B*.

The initial-appearance interpretation has an obvious weakness. Suppose, for example, that after *A* and *B* appear in a society for the first time, they are both reinvented independently in a number of other societies. And suppose further that in about half of these societies, *B* precedes *A* instead of following it. Now if the weight of examples shows that *B* is just as likely to precede *A* as to follow it, then the fact that *A* preceded *B* the very first time they developed turns out to have little intrinsic significance. This order might just as easily have been the reverse. Thus the first instance of their joint appearance affords no real clue as to whether *A* or *B* can be expected to arise first as these traits develop anew in other societies. Indeed, where such developmental irregularity exists, we can scarcely speak of a definite evolutionary sequence at all.

There is one circumstance, though, in which the initial-appearance view of the evolution of culture as a whole is appropriate and defensible. This is when there is a relationship of *functional prerequisiteness* between the two traits involved—that is, when the existence of one of the traits can be shown to be a necessary precondition for the development of the other.[17] If such a relationship holds between traits *A* and

B, then the fact that *A* preceded *B* the first time they appeared *would* be significant. Their order of appearance in this instance would not be a matter of chance, then, but of evolutionary determinism.[18] And the sequence *A→B* would thus be expected to recur in any society where indigenous evolution gave rise to both *A* and *B*.

Diffusion, of course, might make it possible for some societies to adopt *B* without ever having developed *A*. Yet this fact would in no way invalidate the argument that in the evolution of culture as a whole *A* preceded *B*. Let us attempt to make this point clearer by considering an actual example.

It seems reasonably certain that wherever iron metallurgy first arose, it was preceded by the working of bronze. The reason for this supposition is that a mastery of the problems involved in bronzemaking was apparently necessary for the solution of the more difficult problems faced in smelting and working iron.[19] Thus we can say that in the evolution of culture as a whole a bronze stage preceded an iron stage because of functional necessity. The fact that, once invented, ironworking could and did diffuse to peoples who had never worked bronze does not alter the matter. In fact, the evolutionary sequence bronze→iron holds even if those societies that learned ironworking through diffusion without ever having worked bronze themselves far outnumbered the societies that worked bronze before developing iron. Indeed, it would hold even if those societies that

---

[17] The first formal discussion of this concept in anthropology that I know of was by Edward Sapir. Sapir called it the principle of necessary presupposition, and wrote (1916:15): "The first principle of chronologic reconstruction to observe is that elements which are presupposed by other elements or complexes are necessarily earlier in age than the latter." In his pioneer article "Evolution in Social Anthropology" (1952), Alexander Lesser made extensive and impressive use of the principle of functional prerequisiteness in arguing for the existence of a regular sequence of development among many pairs of traits (pp. 142-44).

[18] Or at least of *semi*-determinism, in the sense that, while *B* must be *preceded by A*, it does not have to *follow A*. (For a further discussion of this point see Carneiro 1962:160-61; 1968:368n.)

[19] Even if it were not strictly true in this case—and Kroeber (1948:727) has expressed a certain skepticism—the fact remains that there are many pairs of traits between each of which a relationship of functional prerequisiteness does hold.

learned ironworking by diffusion were to borrow bronzeworking at a later date, thus reversing the general sequence.

It is theoretically possible, then, as a result of diffusion, that a stage that at least one society had to go through might be skipped by all other societies. The skipping of stages, such as the bypassing of a Bronze Age by most of Negro Africa in going from a Stone Age to an Iron Age, does not therefore invalidate the general sequence Stone Age→Bronze Age→Iron Age in the development of culture as a whole. In the Near East, where iron metallurgy began, bronze preceded iron out of functional necessity. But wherever iron metallurgy was then carried, there was no necessity for all of the antecedent steps to have been taken. [20]

While the skipping of stages by individual societies does not nullify the validity of the concept of stages in general, it does make it necessary to distinguish between two distinct types of evolutionary sequences. Curiously enough, these two types of sequence have not hitherto been explicitly recognized or named.

If two or more societies have gone through every stage of a given sequence of development, we can say that their evolution has been *isosequential.* If, however, the societies have not passed through all the same stages, but if those stages through which they have passed were passed in the same order, then their evolution can be said to be *isodirectional.* [21] Thus, with regard to

technology, the evolution of Negro Africa and of the Near East was not isosequential, but it was isodirectional. The two areas did not go through all the same stages, Africa south of the Sahara having skipped a Bronze Age, but they did evolve in the same direction, since in both areas an Iron Age followed a Stone Age. [22]

THE PREDOMINANCE-OF-CASES VIEW

According to the predominance-of-cases view, in deciding on what constitutes an evolutionary sequence the important consideration is not the relative order of development of traits A and B the first time they appeared, but rather the *proportion of cases* in which A preceded B (or B preceded A) among all societies in which the two traits developed. Clearly this interpretation is especially well suited to instances in which neither A nor B is a functional prerequisite of the other.

Let us illustrate this interpretation. Take, for example, the two traits "taxation" and "markets," neither of which is, in any clear and direct way, a necessary precondition for the other. Concerning these two traits we ask: In the evolution of culture as a whole, which came first? Suppose we have historical evidence that in the first society ever to develop both traits, markets arose before taxation, but that in the next ten societies to develop them, taxation arose before markets. Which are we then to consider the "true" sequence in the evolution of culture as a whole: markets→taxation or taxation → markets?

---

[20] For an incisive discussion of this whole question showing how Boasian critics were too easily led astray by a simplistic notion of evolution, see White (1945:343-45).

[21] Strictly speaking, all sequences which are isosequential are also isodirectional. But I am restricting the latter term here to sequences in which the societies involved did not all go through each of the same stages.

---

[22] There is another distinction to be made between types of evolutionary sequences. Thus we can say that some sequences are *cumulative,* while others are *supplantive.* A cumulative sequence would be $A→A+B→A+B+C$. A supplantive sequence would be $A→B→C$. In the former, stages are *aggregated;* in the latter, they are *transcended.*

It seems to me that a numerical-preponderance view is better suited to instances of this type than an initial-appearance view. After all, if each of our eleven cases of the development of taxation and markets is independent, as we have stipulated, why should the appearance of markets before taxation in one society carry more weight than the reverse order in the other ten societies, just because the one case happened to be the very first instance of the development of both traits? Being independent, the cases should be coequal, and the order of development occurring in ten societies should outweigh the order occurring in only one. Consequently, the sequence taxation→markets should have a much stronger claim to being considered the "normal" sequence of development than the opposite one.[23]

In summary, the evolution of culture as a whole can have two quite different meanings. Each is to be preferred over the other under certain circumstances. Where a relationship of functional prerequisiteness exists between two traits, the initial-appearance view seems generally preferable. But where neither trait is a necessary precondition for the other, then in any attempt to determine the proper evolutionary sequence for them the predominance-of-cases view seems more applicable.

Perhaps it might be well to add, and even to emphasize, that both of these

interpretations of evolutionary sequences are based solidly on historical, archaeological, and ethnological facts. Evolutionary sequences, even those meant to apply to culture as a whole, are not somehow totally distinct from the culture history of particular peoples. They are generalizations based on a study of individual histories. Evolutionary sequences may not apply to each particular culture—in fact, they may not apply to any one particular culture[24] —but they are nonetheless distillations from the collected culture histories of individual societies. Indeed, evolutionary sequences can have no other source than this and still remain within the realm of scientific constructs.[25]

---

[24] To see how the evolutionary sequence 1→2→ 3→4 could occur without being exemplified by any one society, examine the following diagram:

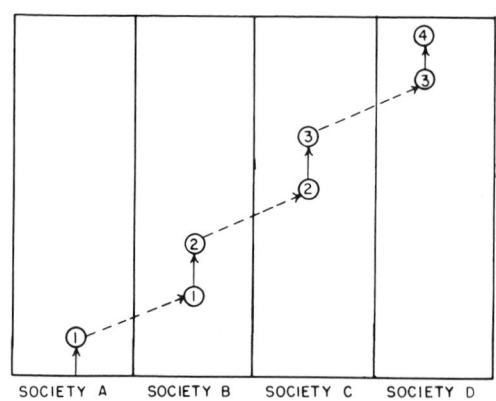

Society A invents trait 1, which diffuses to society B, which then invents trait 2, which diffuses to society C, which then invents trait 3, and so on.

---

[23] Naturally, if the relative order of appearance of traits A and B is about evenly divided in all known cases, then, as I indicated earlier, we cannot assert that either normally precedes the other. The only thing we can say then is that in the evolution of culture as a whole, B is about as likely to develop before A as A is to develop before B. Nor is this a damaging admission for the evolutionist to make. After all, who ever argued that cultural evolution had to be completely regular in all its manifestations?

[25] I stress this point because White's statement (1945:343) that "the cultural formulas [of the evolutionists] have nothing to do with [particular] peoples" has sometimes been interpreted—I would say misinterpreted—as indicating a mystical or metaphysical view of the evolution of culture (cf. Bidney 1953:170-72). In the article containing this passage White deals entirely with sequences manifesting functional prerequisiteness, in which, therefore, the logical necessity of the sequences is obvious and compelling.

MULTILINEAR EVOLUTION

Although the term "multilinear evolution" was not coined by Julian Steward,[26] the concept is most closely associated with his name. Accordingly, let us begin our discussion of it by noting what Steward has had to say about it.

For Steward, "multilinear evolution is essentially a *methodology* based on the *assumption* that significant regularities in cultural change occur . . ." (1953:318; emphasis mine). Now this is a remarkable statement. It is remarkable, first, because it views multilinear evolution as a "methodology," and second, because it states that multilinear evolution "assumes" the existence of significant regularities.

I would be inclined to consider this mode of expression an isolated slip of the pen on Steward's part were it not for the fact that he repeats this view elsewhere in the same article, referring again to multilinear evolution as a "methodology," and saying that it "postulates" parallel developments among historically unrelated cultures (1953:315). Moreover, two years later (1955b:14, 18), in revising this article for inclusion in a volume of his selected essays, Steward chose to retain this phrasing intact. Thus we must regard these expressions as Steward's considered opinion.

As an evolutionist, I find these asser-

tions unacceptable. In the first place, to say that multilinear evolution is a "methodology" is to confound the *object* of study with the *method* of study. As one critic, Thomas Munro (1963: 168n.), has observed, "It is . . . confusing to call 'evolution' a method or methodology, and to say that it 'deals with' sequences or 'searches for parallels.' Evolution itself, unilinear or multilinear, *is a process or supposed process in the historical phenomena themselves*" (emphasis mine).[27]

Even less acceptable is Steward's statement that multilinear evolution "assumes" or "postulates" developmental regularities. How could this be? Such regularities cannot be postulated, they must be *demonstrated*. If multilinear evolution can be said to be a methodology at all, surely one of its cardinal principles must be that the existence of evolutionary sequences is to be discovered empirically, not posited logically.

Turning to Steward's characterization of multilinear evolution, again I find myself unable to agree. According to Steward, multilinear evolution differs from unilinear evolution in "searching for parallels of limited occurrence instead of universals" (1953: 315). Elsewhere in the same article (p. 318) Steward reiterates that multilinear evolution "deals only with . . . limited parallels of form, function, and sequence . . ."

But why should the evolutionist so restrict himself? Is this not like tying one hand behind one's back at the outset? Should not our aim as scientists always be to formulate propositions about culture having the widest possible generality? And if this is true, why should we begin by stating flatly that we are going to ignore the search for

---

Thus it is not surprising that he should choose to emphasize the abstract nature of evolutionary sequences rather than their concrete realization in actual societies. But I do not see that in stressing the former, White denies the latter. I would not expect him to object to the assertion that an evolutionary sequence must be exemplified by at least one society or a combination of societies somewhere in the world before it can be said to exist at all.

[26] I do not know who originated the expression "multilinear evolution," but it was used at least as early as 1905 by the sociologist Edward A. Ross (1905:62).

[27] Others have also balked at this notion. See, for example, Marvin Harris (1968:656).

such broad generalizations, and confine ourselves to regularities of only limited occurrence? [28]

Moreover, how do we *know* that a generalization is of only limited occurrence unless we have examined enough cases to be sure it is not universal or nearly so? And suppose that during this examination we find that it *is* in fact a universal regularity. What is the multilinear evolutionist to do then— turn his back on it? [29]

Only after searching for the broadest regularities and failing to find them can we then talk about limited regularities. Thus the actual "methodology" of multilinear evolution, if there be such a thing, requires us to start by examining a wide spectrum of comparative data and to extract from it all the regularity we can. Multilinear evolution, then, is the *residue* left after we have attempted to find unilinear evolution and discovered exceptions. To put the matter even more metaphorically, limited sequences are the "heavy fraction" left in the "fractionating column" of evolution after the lighter unilinear "fractions" have come to the surface and been drawn off.

MULTILINEAR EVOLUTION IN RELATION TO UNILINEAR EVOLUTION

Let us look more closely at the relationship between multilinear and unilinear evolution. The two forms of evolution are by no means antithetical or opposed. Indeed, they may occur closely intertwined in the same historic sequence. At certain stages in their development, cultures may evolve similarly, while at other stages they may diverge and follow separate paths. An alternation between divergence away from a main stem and convergence back to it may even be a normal pattern of historical development.

In Figure 1 I have tried to show the relationship between these two phases

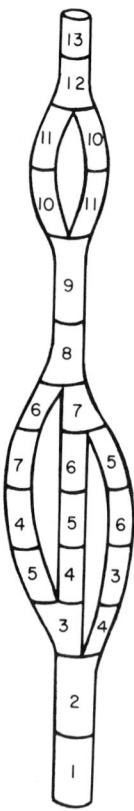

Figure 1. Evolutionary tree showing schematically the relationship between unilinear and multilinear evolution by means of branchings out from and back to the main stem. The numbers in the sections represent successively developed traits.

[28] In calling Steward to task for this, William C. Smith (1961:50) wrote: "Surely, generalizations (or 'parallels') pertaining to all societies are as valuable as those pertaining only to some societies; and the range of generalizations we seek from a given body of data should be regarded as a matter to be decided by empirical inquiry—not as an *a priori* limitation upon inquiry."

[29] Pointing to Steward's excessive wariness in this regard, Leslie A. White (1957:541) commented: "Steward resembles one who discovers that this river and that flow down hill but is unwilling to go so far as to assert that 'rivers flow down hill.' "

of evolution in a simple and schematic way. The numbers on the "evolutionary trunk" represent successively developed culture traits, while the trunk and its branchings represent groups of societies developing through time. If we consider all 13 traits, then for the societies represented in the figure evolution cannot be said to have been unilinear. However, if we consider only traits 1, 2, 8, 9, 12, and 13, then we *can* say that as far as these traits are concerned, evolution *has* been unilinear. This is so because all the societies in question have adopted these six traits in the same order. Thus the lesson of this diagram should be clear: We must not be stopped short when we encounter multilinearity; we must be ready to look for the less obvious unilinearity that may be concealed within it.

An actual instance of this blending of unilinear and multilinear evolution has recently come to light. It is the sequence of development of basic color terms discovered by Brent Berlin and Paul Kay (1969) among a considerable sample of human societies. This sequence of stages, which was arrived at by means of Guttman scale analysis was found to hold with remarkable regularity. The sequence is shown in Figure 2.

It is not possible to say whether a term for white or a term for black arose first, since every society studied by Berlin and Kay had both. But a term for red was the next one to be developed by all societies. Multilinearity comes into the picture with the following two stages, III and IV. Some societies de-

veloped a term for green first, and then a term for yellow. The remaining societies reversed the sequence, developing a term for yellow first and then one for green. After that the sequence proceeds unilinearly again, with blue the next term to arise, followed by brown. The sequence becomes multilinear once more at Stage VII, with societies developing terms for purple, pink, orange, and gray in no single order (Berlin and Kay 1969:4).

Now let us look next at Figure 3, which depicts more fully multilinear development. From a common stem representing a total of eighteen societies,

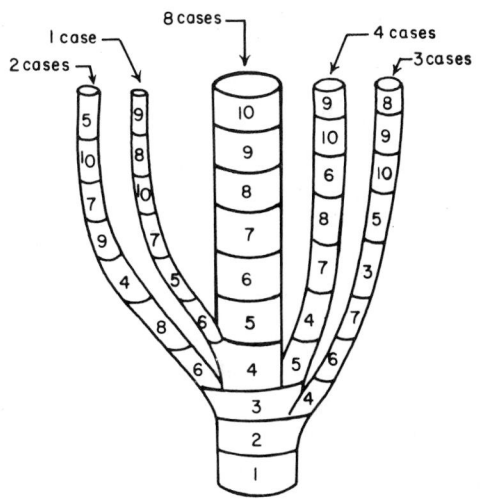

Figure 3. Evolutionary tree showing multilinear evolution as a divergence of branches away from a central stem. The thickness of the stem and of the branches is proportional to the number of societies contained in each. The numbers in the sections represent successively developed traits.

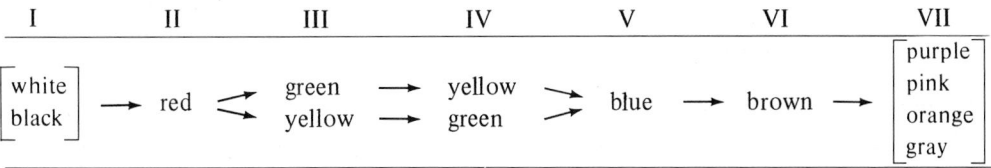

I	II	III	IV	V	VI	VII
white black	→ red	green → yellow →	yellow green	blue	→ brown →	purple pink orange gray

Figure 2. Sequence of development of basic color terms (after Berlin and Kay 1969).

multiple branchings occur after trait 2 is developed, and thereafter the various societies develop the remaining eight traits (numbers 3 through 10) in five different sequences.

In summary, then, it seems to me that the more carefully the comparative history of societies is studied, the more multilinear *and* unilinear sequences are likely to be discovered.

DIFFERENTIAL EVOLUTION

Two distinct manifestations of evolution can be labeled differential evolution. Let us look at each of them.

Differential evolution, in one sense, is the tendency of societies to evolve the various aspects of their culture—economic, social, political, legal, etc.—at various rates and to different degrees. In introducing the term with this meaning some years ago (Carneiro and Tobias 1963:204n.) I was following a similar usage by Earnest A. Hooton some forty years earlier. Noting that during hominid evolution not all parts of the human body had evolved to the same degree, Hooton (1925:126, 127) called this phenomenon "asymmetrical evolution." When I first began to consider the analogous disparity in cultural development, I was reminded of Hooton's discussion. However, the term "asymmetrical" seemed ill suited to describe the difference in the evolution of the various spheres of culture; it sounded too strictly morphological. In casting about for a better term, the word "differential" readily came to mind.

While the term "differential evolution" may be recent, the concept is not. As early as 1871 E. B. Tylor observed that "even granting that intellectual, moral, and political life may, on a broad view, be seen to progress together, it is obvious that they are far from advancing with equal steps"

(1871,1:25).[30] And fifty years later Robert H. Lowie (1927:3) wrote that "it is a commonplace of ethnology that people may advance very unevenly in different phases of civilization."

The expression "differential evolution" may be applied to another aspect of cultural development: the difference in degree to which *entire societies* have evolved. In this sense also, differential evolution was recognized early in the history of anthropology. Sir Henry Maine, for example, noted that "societies do not advance concurrently, but at different rates of progress..." (1871:116).[31]

It is the occurrence of differential evolution in this second sense that has produced the enormous differences in culture level that we observe in existing societies. As John F. McLennan (1896: 9) expressed it, " ... the variety of forms of life—of domestic and civil institution[s]—is ascribable mainly to the unequal development of the different sections of mankind." Indeed, the very basis for applying the comparative method to the making of evolutionary reconstructions was the coexistence of cultures at many different levels of development, each of which could be taken as representing a stage in a general evolutionary process.

We see, then, that there was early and ample recognition of differential evolution, whether of the several

---

[30] Another early evolutionist, Herbert Spencer, noted the same phenomenon. In his *Principles of Sociology* (1878:640), Spencer wrote: " The evidence, then, does not allow us to infer . . . that advance in the forms of the sexual relations [forms of the family, etc.] and advance in [other aspects of] social evolution, are constantly and uniformly connected."

[31] Somewhat later, James G. Frazer (1913:169) wrote that "mankind . . . advances in *échelons;* that is, the columns march not abreast of each other but in a straggling line, all lagging in various degrees behind the leader."

aspects of a culture or of entire cultures. What was lacking, though, was an objective specification of the extent to which differential evolution (in either sense) had occurred in human societies. The reason for this lack is not hard to find. Before we can measure differences in evolution within a culture or between cultures, we must have some objective yardstick for measuring culture level generally. However, the ascendancy of cultural relativism in anthropology during the first half of this century discouraged any attempt to develop such a yardstick. It was not, in fact, until very recently that one was finally constructed. I refer to the formulation by Raoul Naroll (1956) of his Index of Social Development.[32] This index was the first objective, quantitative, precise, and practical means of assessing and expressing cultural complexity.

Naroll's pioneer effort opened the door, and others have followed after him. My own work in cultural evolution led me to propose a measure of development that I call the Index of Cultural Accumulation.[33] This index permits the rating of individual societies, and thus enables one to compare societies with one another objectively and numerically.

Now if entire societies can be compared in this way, there is no reason why their separate parts cannot be compared also. If we can gauge how far society X as a whole has evolved, we can also gauge how far its economic organization, its legal system, or its architecture has evolved. By the same token, we can compare the development of society X in any one of these fields with the development of society Y or Z in the same field.

In making such comparisons, though, not all traits will serve. To measure differential evolution reliably we need to use traits that show cumulation. A cumulating trait is one that, once adopted by a society, tends to be retained indefinitely while other traits are being developed.[34] For years anthropologists have asserted that "culture is cumulative." In attempting to rate cultures objectively I have merely seized upon this fact and put it to work.

Let me interject at this point that cumulation is not all there is to evolution. Evolution is not only *cumulative,* but also *supplantive.* Along with the retention of some traits, there is occasional replacement of others. And if this replacement of one trait by another makes a society more complex— as it often does—then we must regard change of this type as evolutionary also.

My own work in cultural evolution has dealt largely with cumulating traits, and it is these that I have used in assessing cultural development. Guttman scale analysis has made it possible to show that certain traits manifest considerable evolutionary regularity. They arise in most societies at about the same general level of development, and once in existence tend to be preserved indefinitely. With such a body of traits we can construct a scale that permits us to rank societies objectively and quantitatively: the more of these cumulating traits a society has, the more evolved it is. Elsewhere I have presented a scale in

---

[32] Leslie White had suggested as early as 1943 the use of energy harnessed per capita per year as an index of culture level (1943:355). However, the difficulty of specifying the magnitude of energy expenditure for various societies has so far impeded the application of this index.

[33] This index was first used in Carneiro and Tobias (1963:201), but was not formally named at that time.

[34] Strictly speaking, individual traits show *retentiveness*; it is only groups of traits developed successively, and each retained once developed, that show *cumulation.*

which 100 societies representing a worldwide sample are ranked in this manner (Carneiro 1968:facing p. 354).

If such a scale can rank societies as wholes, then, as I have said before, selected traits from this scale representing, say, economics or law or architecture should enable us to gauge the relative degrees of complexity or evolution of individual societies in these and other sectors of culture. If a society has evolved further in economics than in law, then this fact should be reflected in the society's having substantially more cumulating economic traits than legal ones.

The simplest way to illustrate this is by means of a bar graph in which the height of each bar is proportional to the number of traits in the category it represents. When applied to several aspects of culture together, a bar graph provides us with a "cultural profile" of a society. Such a profile not only gives us a means of comparing one aspect of a society's development with another, but also permits us to compare that society's development, category by category, with that of some other society.

In Figure 4 we see the cultural profile of two societies, the Kayan of Borneo and Acoma Pueblo. These societies have nearly the same total number of traits for the seven categories of traits represented on the bar graph, and thus can be considered to be at approximately the same general level of culture. There is, however, a rather marked difference between them in the way in which traits are distributed among the seven categories. The Kayan and Acoma appear to have evolved differen-

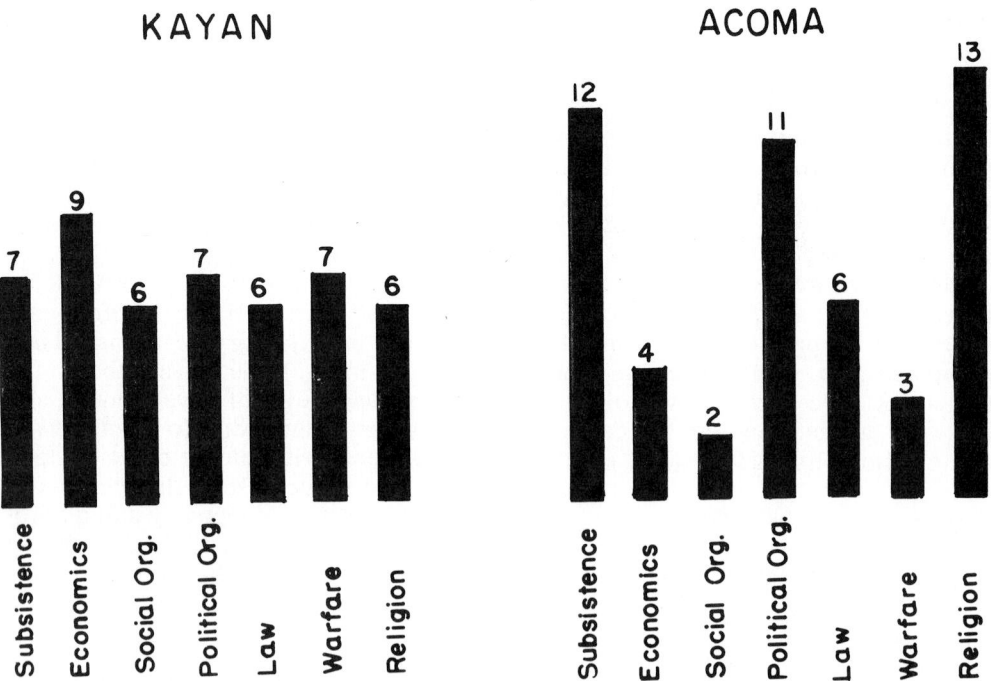

Figure 4. Bar graph showing the cultural profiles of two societies based on the number of traits they possess in each of seven selected categories of culture.

tially with regard to several aspects of their culture. For example, Acoma is more evolved than the Kayan in the field of religion, while the Kayan are more evolved than Acoma in economics.

Diagrams such as Figure 4, while useful in their own way, nevertheless present only a static picture of differential evolution. Let us see if we can depict the

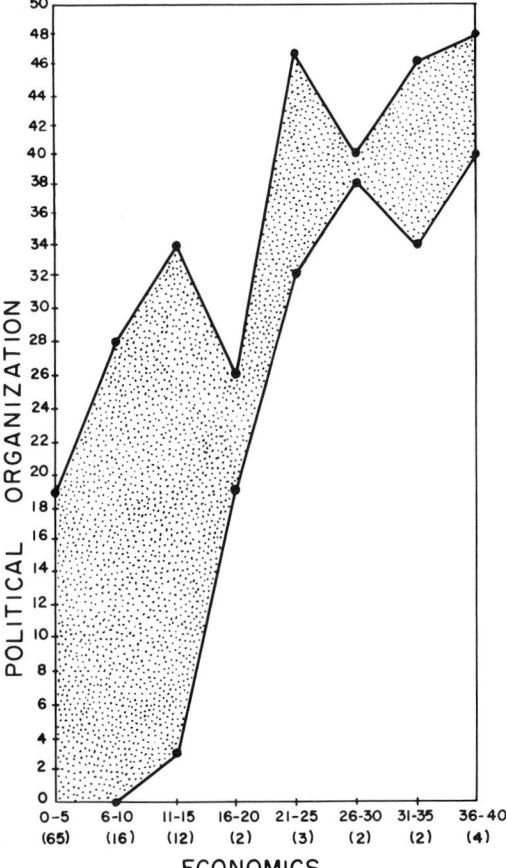

Figure 5. Graph showing the largest (upper line) and smallest (lower line) number of political organization traits present among 106 societies grouped by class intervals of 5 according to number of economics traits possessed. The figure shown in parentheses beneath each class interval indicates the number of societies having the number of economics traits included within that class interval.

process more dynamically. Figure 5 attempts to do this by relating the number of cumulating traits that societies have in economics to the number they have in political organization.

The horizontal axis of this graph shows the economic traits possessed by the 106 societies used in this study. On this scale, the societies are grouped by class intervals of 5 traits, according to how many economic traits they have— 0-5, 6-10, 11-15, and so on. The vertical axis of the graph shows the number of traits the same societies have in the field of political organization, but here the number of traits is given in exact figures rather than by class intervals.

The graph thus shows the largest and the smallest number of political traits present among societies in the various class intervals of economic traits. For example, the 16 societies that have between 6 and 10 economic traits ranged between 0 and 28 in their number of political traits. To take another example, the 2 societies falling into the class interval of 16-20 economic traits ranged between 19 and 26 in political traits.

If societies with 0-5 economic traits had 0-5 political traits, and if those with 6-10 economic traits had 6-10 political traits, and so on, then we could say that economic evolution and political evolution had proceeded in close articulation. No really significant differential evolution between these two sectors of culture would then be apparent. What the graph actually shows, though, is a considerable amount of play between developments in the economic and political spheres. Up to a point, economic organization appears able to evolve without carrying political organization along with it, and vice versa.

What is true of these two categories is true of others as well. However, the degree of fit between various sectors of culture may vary. Political organization and law, for example, may be expected to evolve in closer conjunction than, say, architecture and warfare.

But while it is important to recognize that differential evolution exists, it is also important to note that it has its limits. Completely free play between the various segments of culture does not occur. The number of cumulating traits a society has in economics *does* set limits to the number of traits it can have in political organization. Thus if we look again at Figure 5 we shall see, for example, that of societies having between 21 and 25 economic traits, none had fewer than 32 nor more than 47 political traits. This, I would say, is a significant degree of constraint.

A sociocultural system may be likened to a train of gears in which each gear represents a different sphere of culture. In the operation of this system the gears are generally in mesh. The gears differ, however. Some are larger than others, some have finer teeth, some turn faster, etc. Moreover, some are drive gears and engender motion in others, while other gears are passive and do not impart motion of their own, but merely transmit the motion they receive.

The gears also vary in the closeness with which they engage one another. If the mesh between any two were perfect and continuous, then the movement of one would automatically produce a corresponding and equivalent movement in the other. But in sociocultural systems the gears never engage perfectly *or* continuously. Now and then a gear slips out of mesh and may move forward half a turn without causing perceptible motion in the others.

Yet, by and large, the train of gears moves together. A certain position of one gear is not compatible with just any position of some other gear. Thus, leaving our metaphor aside and looking at sociocultural systems directly, we cannot imagine, for example, divine kingship fitting with cave dwellings, trial by jury with percussion flaking, parliamentary procedure with human sacrifice, or cross-cousin marriage with nuclear reactors. When culture advances significantly in one sphere, other spheres do not long remain unaffected. They tend to advance with it; not always immediately or at the same rate, to be sure, but basically together, as a single coordinated system.

It is this movement of societies, projected over long intervals of time, that constitutes evolution. When one examines it closely, as we have tried to do here, evolution does not appear simple and unitary. Rather, it manifests itself in a variety of modes. And if we are to understand the evolutionary process in its entirety, we must discriminate its various components, submit each to careful scrutiny, and assess their respective contributions to the process as a whole.

REFERENCES

Adams, Robert M.
   1960 Early Civilizations, Subsistence, and Environment. In *City Invincible,* ed. Carl H. Kraeling and Robert M. Adams, pp. 269-95. Chicago: University of Chicago Press.
Armillas, Pedro
   1948 A Sequence of Cultural Development in Meso-America. In *A Reappraisal of Peruvian Archaeology,* assembled by Wendell C. Bennett, pp. 105-11. Memoir no. 4, Society for American Archaeology.
Bennett, Wendell C.
   1948 The Peruvian Co-Tradition. In *A Reappraisal of Peruvian Archaeology,* assembled by Wendell C. Bennett, pp. 1-7. Memoir no. 4, Society for American Archaeology.
Bennett, Wendell C., and Junius B. Bird
   1949 *Andean Culture History.* Handbook

Series no. 15. New York: American Museum of Natural History.

Berlin, Brent, and Paul Kay
1969 *Basic Color Terms, Their Universality and Evolution.* Berkeley and Los Angeles: University of California Press.

Bernal, Ignacio
1964 Concluding Remarks. In *Prehistoric Man in the New World,* ed. Jesse D. Jennings and Edward Norbeck, pp. 559-66. Chicago: University of Chicago Press.

Bidney, David
1953 *Theoretical Anthropology.* New York: Columbia University Press.

Bird, Junius B.
1964 Preface to Second Edition. In Wendell C. Bennett and Junius B. Bird, *Andean Culture History*, pp. vii-xii. Garden City, N.Y.: American Museum Science Books, Natural History Press.

Carneiro, Robert L.
1962 Scale Analysis as an Instrument for the Study of Cultural Evolution. *Southwestern Journal of Anthropology* 18:149-69.
1968 Ascertaining, Testing, and Interpreting Sequences of Cultural Development. *Southwestern Journal of Anthropology* 24:354-74.
1970a Scale Analysis, Evolutionary Sequences, and the Rating of Cultures. In *Handbook of Method in Cultural Anthropology,* ed. Raoul Naroll and Ronald Cohen, pp. 834-71. Garden City, N.Y.: Natural History Press.
1970b A Theory of the Origin of the State. *Science* 169:733-38.

Carneiro, Robert L., and Stephen F. Tobias
1963 The Application of Scale Analysis to the Study of Cultural Evolution. *Transactions of the New York Academy of Sciences,* ser. 2, vol. 26, pp. 196-207.

Darwin, Charles
1872 *The Origin of Species,* 6th ed. London: John Murray.

Ford, James A.
1966 Early Formative Cultures in Georgia and Florida. *American Antiquity* 31: 781-99.

Frazer, James G.

1905 *Lectures on the Early History of Kingship.* London: Macmillan.
1913 *Psyche's Task,* 2nd ed. London: Macmillan.

Gernet, Jacques
1968 *Ancient China from the Beginnings to the Empire,* trans. R. Rudorff. London: Faber & Faber.

Gillin, John
1948 *The Ways of Men.* New York: Appleton-Century-Crofts.

Harris, Marvin
1968 *The Rise of Anthropological Theory.* New York: Crowell.

Hooton, Earnest A.
1925 The Asymmetrical Character of Human Evolution. *American Journal of Physical Anthropology* 8:125-41.

Lanning, Edward P.
1967 *Peru Before the Incas.* Englewood Cliffs, N. J.: Prentice-Hall.

Larco Hoyle, Rafael
1948 Cronología Arqueológica del Norte del Perú. Buenos Aires: Sociedad Geográfica Americana.
1966 *Peru,* trans. James Hogarth. Cleveland & New York: World Publishing Co.

Lesser, Alexander
1952 Evolution in Social Anthropology. *Southwestern Journal of Anthropology* 8:134-46.

Linton, Ralph
1936 Error in Anthropology. In *The Story of Human Error,* ed. Joseph Jastrow, pp. 292-321. New York: Appleton-Century.

Lowie, Robert H.
1927 *The Origin of the State.* New York: Harcourt, Brace.

McLennan, John F.
1896 *Studies in Ancient History,* 2nd series. London: Macmillan.

Maine, Henry Sumner
1871 *Ancient Law.* New York: Scribner.

Morgan, Lewis H.
1909 *Ancient Society.* Chicago: Charles H. Kerr.

Munro, Thomas
1963 *Evolution in the Arts and Other Theories of Culture History.* Cleveland: Cleveland Museum of Art.

Naroll, Raoul

1956 A Preliminary Index of Social Development. *American Anthropologist* 58:687-715.

Peckham, Morse
1959 *The Origin of Species by Charles Darwin: A Variorum Text.* Philadelphia: University of Pennsylvania Press.

Ross, Edward A.
1905 *Foundations of Sociology.* New York: Macmillan.

Rouse, Irving
1964 The Caribbean Area. In *Prehistoric Man in the New World,* ed. Jesse D. Jennings and Edward Norbeck, pp. 389-417. Chicago: University of Chicago Press.

Sapir, Edward
1916 *Time Perspective in Aboriginal American Culture: A Study in Method.* Canada Department of Mines, Geological Survey, Memoir no. 90, Anthropological Series no. 13.

Smith, William C.
1961 Some Misconceptions of Multilinear Evolution. *Kroeber Anthropological Society Papers,* no. 24, pp. 49-54.

Spencer, Herbert
1862 *First Principles.* London: Williams & Norgate.
1878 *The Principles of Sociology,* vol. 1. New York: Appleton.
1880 *First Principles,* 4th ed. New York: Appleton.
1898 What Is Social Evolution? *Nineteenth Century* 44:348-58.

Steward, Julian H.
1948 A Functional-Developmental Classification of American High Cultures. In *A Reappraisal of Peruvian Archaeology,* assembled by Wendell C. Bennett, pp. 103-104. Memoir no. 4, Society for American Archaeology.
1949 Cultural Causality and Law: A Trial Formulation of the Development of Early Civilizations. *American Anthropologist* 51:1-27.
1953 Evolution and Process. In *Anthropology Today,* ed. A. L. Kroeber, pp. 313-26. Chicago: University of Chicago Press.

1955a Some Implications of the Symposium. In *Irrigation Civilizations: A Comparative Study.* Social Science Monographs, no. 1, pp. 58-78. Washington, D.C.: Pan American Union.
1955b *Theory of Culture Change.* Urbana: University of Illinois Press.

Strong, William Duncan
1948 Cultural Epochs and Refuse Stratigraphy in Peruvian Archaeology. In *A Reappraisal of Peruvian Archaeology,* assembled by Wendell C. Bennett, pp. 93-102. Memoir no. 4, Society for American Archaeology.

Tylor, Edward B.
1871 *Primitive Culture,* 2 vols. London: John Murray.

Wauchope, Robert
1964 Southern Mesoamerica. In *Prehistoric Man in the New World,* ed. Jesse D. Jennings and Edward Norbeck, pp. 331-86. Chicago: University of Chicago Press.

White, Leslie A.
1943 Energy and the Evolution of Culture. *American Anthropologist* 45:335-56.
1945 "Diffusion vs. Evolution": An Anti-Evolutionist Fallacy. *American Anthropologist* 47:339-56.
1957 Review of Julian H. Steward's *Theory of Culture Change: The Methodology of Multilinear Evolution. American Anthropologist* 59:540-42.
1960 Foreword. In *Evolution and Culture,* ed. Marshall D. Sahlins and Elman R. Service, pp. v-xii. Ann Arbor: University of Michigan Press.

Willey, Gordon R.
1946 The Chiclín Conference for Peruvian Archaeology, 1946. *American Antiquity* 12:132-34.
1953 *Prehistoric Settlement Patterns in the Virú Valley, Peru.* Bureau of American Ethnology Bulletin no. 155.

Willey, Gordon R., and Philip Phillips
1958 *Method and Theory in American Archaeology.* Chicago: University of Chicago Press.

Wittfogel, Karl
1957 *Oriental Despotism.* New Haven: Yale University Press.

CHAPTER 3 The Historical Approach in Anthropology

CHARLES HUDSON

A survey of the role of historical research in anthropology must address itself to two seemingly contradictory problems.[1] In addition to examining the kinds of empirical research anthropologists have done in the past and continue to do in the present, such a survey must also examine the various attitudes anthropologists have had toward the relevance of historical research to anthropology. This latter aspect is essentially the issue of whether anthropology is itself a kind of history or, on the contrary, a kind of science. Although this problem of the historical or scientific status of anthropology has been discussed and argued at great and

often tedious length, the issue is perhaps more alive and important today than in the past. Whether one regards anthropology as a kind of science or as a kind of history is not simply a matter of terminology; it is a choice involving a fundamental difference in point of view, and as such it has important implications for the kinds of research anthropologists undertake, the manner in which they conduct their research, the results that may be expected, and the relationships between anthropology and other fields of knowledge.

To someone who is not an anthropologist it must seem peculiar that even when we include anthropologists whose research is historical by almost any definition, only a small number of anthropologists themselves feel that anthropology is a kind of history and therefore belongs alongside such fields as philosophy, literature, art, and of course history itself. Most anthropologists feel that anthropology belongs with the social sciences and that its methodology should be positivistic. Some anthropologists who have taken this position

[1] A survey of a field of research of this magnitude must inevitably contain biases. Perhaps these biases will at least be more understandable when I explain that I am a social anthropologist trained in America but sympathetic to British and French social anthropology, and that for some years I have been engaged in historical ethnographic studies on the Indians of the southeastern United States.

I am grateful to David Hally, Michael Olien, and Joyce Rockwood Hudson, my wife, for reading and criticizing this paper.

have insisted that it is nonsense to say that anthropology is a kind of history because primitive people have no history (Lowie 1917, Radcliffe-Brown 1965). Others, taking a less extreme position, recognize the fact that preliterate people possess oral traditions and that the pasts of many of them were documented in greater or lesser degree by European explorers, missionaries, and colonial administrators, but they take the view that these traditions and documents provide the anthropologist with materials not for a history, but for an "ethnohistory," thus plucking preliterate people from the province of history.[2] The reason for this neologism seems to be that to a positivist the writing of history is all right as an amusement, but it is not worth the labor of a lifetime. By consigning preliterate peoples to "ethnohistory," however, we remove them from the class of humanity to which we ourselves belong. The positivists have been placed in an increasingly uncomfortable position as intellectuals in the Third World have become increasingly critical of Western scholarship. They argue, quite expectably, that if Western scholars write histories of China, Korea, India, and Iran, why not of the rest of the non-Western world?

Granting for the moment the legitimacy of historical research in anthropology, how are we to define history? It turns out that historians themselves have rather different views on the nature of history and on the way it should be defined. The scientific historians define history as a chronicle of events, and see the task of the historian

as merely to describe events in the past, in the words of Leopold von Ranke, "as they really were." In this view the historian-observer approaches his materials of study with complete objectivity and reconstructs the past from the facts alone. This scientific view has often been held by historians who lived in periods of social stability, as, for example, the naively optimistic historians of Victorian England (Carr 1964).

In contrast we find the idealist view of history, represented in the works of Wilhelm Dilthey, Benedetto Croce, and R. G. Collingwood; Collingwood in particular argued that the past can be understood only when the historian can reenact it in his own mind. Here, obviously, the historian does not stand apart from his object of study, but tries to participate in it imaginatively. In this view, the historian sees the past through the concerns of the present, and he plays a frankly creative role in the writing of history. In its most extreme form, the historical idealist claims that all history is the history of thought, and history becomes what the historian makes of it.

The fault of the scientific view of history is that it sometimes produces a mere scissors-and-paste chronicle, while the fault of the idealist view of history is that it sometimes degenerates into mere propaganda for one point of view or another. Many historians prefer a position between these two extremes. E. H. Carr (1964:30), for example, defines history as "a continuous process of interaction between the historian and his facts, an unending dialogue between the present and the past." Marc Bloch held a similar view of history. According to Bloch, the historian respects facts, submitting them to critical scrutiny, while frankly recognizing that he himself has a point of view, and that it is through his point of view that facts about the past take on meaning. Bloch

---

[2] We shall presently see that this terminological schizophrenia also shows up when an account of the life of a preliterate person is called a life history instead of a biography. Using this curiously inverted terminology, one writes a history of a preliterate individual but an ethnohistory of a preliterate society.

(1964:43-47) insists that the present and the past interact: the past enables the historian to explain contemporary social facts, while contemporary society provides the historian with the "vibrance of human life," enabling him to breathe life into old texts.

Bloch's view of history is as appropriate for anthropologists as it is for historians. Indeed, it is remarkably close to the kind of science of man for which E. E. Evans-Pritchard (1962a, 1962b) has called—one combining synchronic and diachronic points of view. In Bloch's words (1964:47): "There is, then, just one science of men in time. It requires us to join the study of the dead and of the living."

THE RELEVANCE OF HISTORY

The attitudes anthropologists have held toward history and historical research have been extraordinarily complex. To begin at the beginning, the evolutionists were assured that anthropology was a science, but that the aim of anthropology was to reconstruct the "prehistory" of man by the use of theories and methods that were later shown to be erroneous. Next came the diffusionists, who took the contrary view that anthropology was a kind of history, but the theories and methods they used were scarcely more sound than those of the evolutionists. Then the American empiricists came along, arguing that anthropology was either a kind of history or partly history and partly science, but with few exceptions they did little bona fide historical research except in a highly inferential way. And more recently all of these theoretical orientations have been more or less displaced by positivistic psychological and sociological theories that assume that anthropology is a science and hence not concerned with the reconstruction of history.

It is important to realize that regardless of these theoretical changes, some anthropologists occupied themselves with historical research from the very outset and still do. It is only in recent years, however, that anthropologists have worked out an adequate intellectual charter to legitimize historical research and at the same time have begun to develop the historical skills necessary to bring research to an acceptable standard.

THE EVOLUTIONISTS

While a concept of "savage" society existed quite early in Europe, the concept of prehistory as we know it was developed by anthropologists in the middle of the nineteenth century, and it rapidly came into usage among educated people (Daniel 1964, Hodgen 1964). This dramatic innovation in European historical thinking made a profound impression on both scholars and laymen. John Lubbock's *Prehistoric Times,* first published in 1856, quickly became a best seller and subsequently went through seven editions. Prior to this, Europeans conceived of a span of human history divided into ancient, medieval, and modern periods, and these were preceded by natural history or biblical times, or both, depending upon one's religious convictions. Now the concept of prehistory enabled people to conceive of a new period of historical time. However, this new field of study came into its own before there was much direct archaeological evidence from which to infer this particular kind of knowledge. But the demand to know the past was great, and the nineteenth-century evolutionists stepped in to satisfy it with an evolutionary theoretical skeleton that they attempted to flesh out with inferential evidence.

Taking their departure from the Darwinism of the time, nineteenth-century evolutionists such as Edward Tylor, Lewis Henry Morgan, and James Frazer thought of anthropology as a kind of scientific history. More precisely, it was a kind of "nonarchaeological prehistory" in which man was believed to have progressed from savage to civilized, from infancy to manhood, through a fixed series of discrete stages (Daniel 1964:65). These stages of cultural and social progress could also be used to classify living preliterate peoples, and the cultures of these people in turn yielded further information about the nature of the stages themselves. Whatever the differences among them, all the evolutionists conceived of human societies as isolated natural systems, and the aim of anthropology was to establish laws about these systems (Evans-Pritchard 1962a). Godfrey Lienhardt (1966:7) has suggested that this Victorian obsession with stages was an ideological reflex of the social system in which these scholars lived. That is, they lived in a society divided into clearly demarcated strata: the lower, middle, and upper classes. Moreover, one may make the observation that another conceptual obsession of the Victorians, their version of the idea of progress, was perhaps a reflex of social mobility, another social phenomenon of the Victorian period, a time when many self-made men rose from poverty to wealth.

The historical reconstructions of the Victorian evolutionists suffered not only from the imposition of ethnocentric social categories upon the data, but also from a faulty use of comparative method. Although the evolutionists believed that their task was to write a history of man, they intended to accomplish this by means of a strictly scientific methodology. The final product was to be a kind of taxonomy, encompassing all culture traits arranged in evolutionary order and in geographi-

cal perspective (Tylor 1958:8). Their interest in comparative method seems to have been conditioned by the success of the method as it was used by the historical linguists, who earlier in the nineteenth century had startled the intellectual world by reconstructing languages that had existed only in the remote past and which had never been written down. But in the hands of the evolutionists, the comparative method was actually a kind of illustrative method. First they arrived at a thesis by deduction, usually taking a social institution from their own society as the highest form and imagining an inversion of it as the lowest form (e.g., monogamy/promiscuity). Then they filled in the gap between with a series of stages, using ethnographic facts from various parts of the world as illustrations (Evans-Pritchard 1965:13). When exceptions turned up, they explained them away as oddities, evolutionary tricks.

Although the evolutionists often claimed to be interested in explaining cultural variation on a worldwide basis, it now seems clear that they were more interested in reconstructing their own prehistory. They thought they were doing scientific history, but their methods were almost unimaginably bad. They had a poorly developed critical apparatus for judging the accuracy or veracity of ethnographic facts; they drew their evidence out of context from all parts of the world; and they classed all primitive people together, assuming that when you've seen one savage, you've seen them all. As time went on, the anthropology practiced by the evolutionists split into two parts. Prehistory increasingly became the province of archaeologists, who gradually developed a refined methodology for reconstructing the past, while living primitive people became the subject matter of social anthropologists.

DIFFUSIONISTS AND CULTURE HISTORIANS

The evolutionists, with their optimistic view of man and their belief in progress, explained cultural similarities in distant parts of the world as having been produced by the similar workings of men's minds. Man is basically inventive, and men in different societies kept coming up with similar inventions. In opposition to this point of view, the diffusionists took the position that man is basically uninventive, so that similar cultural traits in different parts of the world were almost always to be explained as having been invented by one culture and then borrowed by others. Like the evolutionists, the diffusionists were basically historical in outlook.

The English Diffusionists

In England diffusionism was vigorously set forth by Elliot Smith and W. J. Perry (Daniel 1964:91), who argued that all of the inventions that underlie civilized life originated in Egypt, and were diffused from there to every civilized part of the world. Like the evolutionists, the diffusionists wrote a kind of nonarchaeological prehistory. At some point Smith and Perry became "hyperdiffusionists," losing all semblance of scientific or historical method, so that all contrary cases were swept aside and ignored. After Smith and Perry lost their following, both diffusionistic theory and historical anthropology declined in England and virtually died out. Like the evolutionists, the diffusionists were replaced by archaeologists and social anthropologists.

The German *Kulturkreiselehre* and Culture Historians

Diffusionism enjoyed a longer career in Germany. The first clear exposition of diffusionism in Germany was in Friedrich Ratzel's *Völkerkunde,* published in 1885-1888. In the hands of the Germans, the concept of diffusion stimulated research on particular culture complexes by men like Heinrich Schurtz, Leo Frobenius, and Eduard Hahn.

In 1904 German diffusionism assumed a more specific form when Fritz Graebner and Bernard Ankermann formally defined and used the concepts of *Kulturkreise*[3] (culture circles) and *Kulturschichten* (culture strata), attempting to devise a methodology that could be used to reconstruct the history of preliterate people (Kluckhohn 1936, Heine-Geldern 1964:412). Examining ethnographic data from all over the world, they attempted to discern culture complexes that were presumed to have originated in one place and later diffused to other places, forming a culture circle. For example, one culture circle was thought to consist of the plow, the wheel, domesticated animals, and certain other traits. When these culture circles were put in chronological order, one after the other, they became "culture strata." Like the Victorian evolutionists before them, these *Kulturkreislehre* thought of anthropology as a kind of history, and they also tried to use rigorous methodology to produce yet another kind of nonarchaeological prehistory. And like the evolutionists and the hyperdiffusionists, Graebner became increasingly dogmatic about his theory, ignoring data that disconfirmed his ideas.

The *Kulturkreis* theory was next taken up by an Austrian, Father Wilhelm Schmidt, a Catholic priest of the Society of the Divine Word. From

---

[3] The world *Kulturkreis* was first used in a technical sense by Leo Frobenius, but he subsequently abandoned it, arguing that research should be done on smaller, more manageable cultural units.

about 1911 until his death Schmidt defended the *Kulturkreis* theory; he stuck by it even when direct archaeological evidence obviously disproved it. Like many before him, Schmidt became increasingly dogmatic, and eventually he lost all caution and his anthropology degenerated to a kind of medieval scholasticism. In time he began to lose favor among his Austrian and German contemporaries, until even his own student Wilhelm Koppers renounced *Kulturkreis* theory. Aside from the youthful Clyde Kluckhohn (1936), all of the prominent American anthropologists of the time, including Franz Boas, Roland B. Dixon, A. L. Kroeber, and R. L. Lowie, were highly critical of Schmidt's theory. On the other side of the Atlantic, British opinion was shaped by A. R. Radcliffe-Brown, who rejected all "conjectural history," with Bronislaw Malinowski more or less agreeing with him.

The German anthropologists who rejected the *Kulturkreis* theory have nevertheless continued to do research in the culture historical tradition. The *Kulturmorphologie* of A. E. Jensen (1963), for example, is basically historical and diffusionist in outlook. Jensen has been concerned with forms of religious belief and expression among primitive people, arguing that there are a discrete number of basic religious forms that can be recovered and reconstructed by analyzing myths. While some European anthropologists regard Jensen's work as an original synthesis, others have pointed out various technical faults. Like others before him, he is still trying to explain the present in terms of a past that is presumed to have existed. Others say that Jensen's theory is too speculative, too intuitively worked out. Even though they might criticize Jensen and the other historical theorists, however, European anthropologists, particularly in Scandinavia and

the other Germanic-speaking countries, have continued in the tradition of historical scholarship.

In contrast, the Americans, the French, and the British, under the influence of Freud and Durkheim, have taken a completely different tack, so that today there is very little interchange between the two scholarly traditions. For example, French, British, and American anthropologists usually try to explain religious behavior as a function of something else, such as a psychological variable, or as a reflection of social structure, while the German and Scandinavian anthropologists are much more inclined to explain religious behavior in terms of the beliefs that lie behind it. In Germany and Scandinavia anthropology is firmly placed among the humanities and has become increasingly historical since the close of the nineteenth century. Both the highly specialized regional European ethnology and the more generalized *Völkerkunde* have a basically historical character (Hultkranz 1967a:38-39).

The American Empiricists

The attitudes of American anthropologists toward historical research have been particularly complex. Virtually all of the early ethnographic work by American anthropologists focused upon the American Indian and was done from a common-sense historical point of view. That is, they assumed that the historical approach is as appropriate for Indians as for any other human beings. This approach can be traced all the way back to Thomas Jefferson, who did research on the Indians of Virginia and encouraged Lewis and Clark and others to do similar research elsewhere. He even prepared a questionnaire for them to use for this purpose, and thus set a precedent for later government sponsorship of anthropological research on Indians (Hallowell 1960).

The American empirical tradition begins with Henry R. Schoolcraft, who collected large amounts of linguistic and ethnographic information and published it in several volumes. Schoolcraft was more a literary man than a historian, and he edited Indian myths rather freely to make them conform to prevailing canons of literary taste. After Schoolcraft broached the subject, the real beginning of ethnological research came in 1879 with the formation of the Bureau of American Ethnology. Under the directorship of John Wesley Powell several distinguished publication series were initiated, and most of the monographs and reports published in them were basically historical in point of view. For example, Frank Hamilton Cushing lived with the Zuñis for five years, acquiring a superb knowledge of their language and culture. Unlike many American anthropologists who came later, Cushing treated Zuñi oral traditions seriously, as historical documents. James Mooney combined historical research on documentary sources with firsthand ethnographic information, producing classic works on the Ghost Dance and on the culture of the Cherokee Indians. Two of the most prolific contributors to the BAE publications were themselves Indians: J. N. B. Hewitt, a Tuscarora, and Francis La Flesche, an Omaha. Both left enormously detailed studies of Indian cultures. The most prolific of all the early BAE workers was John R. Swanton, who worked mainly among the Indians of the southeastern United States, writing five long essays for the BAE annual reports and fifteen bulletins. Like Mooney, Swanton combined documentary information with information he collected in the field (Judd 1967).

As I have said, this early empirical research by these American anthropologists was largely guided by a common-sense historical point of view. Although John Wesley Powell occasionally wrote abstract essays on various topics, his colleagues generally ignored them; consequently, no theory grew out of this empirical research. The earliest theoretical focus in America developed not in the Bureau of American Ethnology, but in the work of Franz Boas, who established anthropology as an academic subject in America. The problem in any discussion of Boas is that it is extremely difficult to say just what his theoretical position was. Although he sometimes claimed that anthropology was basically historical in character, he in fact discouraged his students from attempting to reconstruct culture history and, apparently contradicting himself, insisted that anthropology had the eventual goal of discovering laws of "cultural process" (Hultkranz 1967b:98-99).

Actually, neither Boas nor his students did much historical research in the sense that the BAE staff did; in most of their work they adopted a later phase of the diffusionist point of view, and their history was largely inferential. Boas himself ventured into historical research only to disprove various evolutionary and hyperdiffusionist schemes, and some have pointed out that the historical work he carried out possesses a one-dimensional quality. His students Clark Wissler, Robert Lowie, Leslie Spier, and A. L. Kroeber carried this kind of research much further, attempting to produce syntheses of culture history. But Boas criticized them all, without exeption, for reaching their conclusions too soon.

At one point A. L. Kroeber (1935: 544) bravely attempted to clarify Boas' theory, saying that his training in physics made his approach basically "scientific" and "only rarely and hesitantly historical." He said that although Boas used historical methods, examining cultures in great detail, keeping as much context as possible, he did not actually write histories. Kroeber also made the point that Boas tried to use scientific method on materials that had previously been studied only historically. Characteristically, Boas (1936) quickly denied most of what Kroeber said, slapping the hand of his student, saying that the only kind of work Kroeber would identify as history was the "flight of unbridled imagination."

Thus the entire first generation of academic American anthropologists was rather schizophrenic with respect to historical research. Most of the early empirical research was done by fundamentally historical BAE workers who seldom felt a need to go beyond common sense. Theory, on the other hand, grew up around Boas, who shared the historian's assumptions but did not write histories; who said that the aim of anthropology was to formulate generalizations about "process," but discouraged any of his students who were rash enough to venture any generalizations. The reason for this apparent confusion seems to have been that although Boas and his students had their closest intellectual affinities with the German culture historians, American social science in the early decades of this century was already hostile to the historical approach. Above all else, in America one had to be scientific; savages, as objects, were to be explained. Mere historical research was not regarded as a significant intellectual achievement (Hultkranz 1967b). It is certainly striking that those who came after this first generation of American anthropologists, who were at least ambivalent about historical research, generally adhered to some kind of theory, usually psychological and more rarely sociological.

PSYCHOLOGICAL AND SOCIOLOGICAL THEORIES

After the nonarchaeological prehistory of the evolutionists and the diffusionists was discredited, anthropologists in France, England, and the United States turned away from historical research and the historical point of view. This abandonment of history occurred in France in the opening decades of this century with Durkheim's sociological theory, and with some modifications Durkheim subsequently influenced the work of A. R. Radcliffe-Brown and Bronislaw Malinowski in England. In America the change came somewhat later, beginning in the 1930s, and the interest was more in psychological than in sociological theory.

Although Durkheim is often regarded as the apotheosis of nonhistorical structural functionalism, he in fact advocated that sociologists and social anthropologists do historical research. Even in his earliest writings under the influence of his teacher, the great historian Fustel de Coulanges, Durkheim emphasized the mutual relevance of history and sociology (Bellah 1959). He insisted that history and sociology were two points of view rather than two separate disciplines, history being concerned with the particulars and sociology with types and laws. Although Durkheim was most concerned with explaining social facts in terms of synchronic variables, he made the point that these can often be understood only through a knowledge of their history. Indeed, he argued that it is through the study of the history of a society that one comes to perceive structural features that may be relatively invisible in the present. He even argued that comparative studies would profit from having a time dimension. Thus Durkheim argued that there is only one truly adequate means of social explanation, and it is at once sociological and historical. As we have already seen, this point of view has more recently been advanced by both Marc Bloch and E. E. Evans-Pritchard.

Although Durkheim did not conceive of sociology or social anthropology apart from history, he himself did no significant historical research (Evans-Pritchard 1962*b*). This is perhaps the reason that many of those who were inspired by Durkheim's thought did not share his attitude toward history. More than anyone else, A. R. Radcliffe-Brown established social anthropology as a "nomothetic" field of study whose aim is to establish acceptable generalizations. Like Durkheim, Radcliffe-Brown (1965) argued that both historical and theoretical explanations were valid. But for some reason he argued that anthropologists cannot do historical research because primitive people lack writing. This of course is nonsense, if only for the fact that all societies have some form of oral tradition. In the very beginning of historical scholarship, Herodotus used both documentary information and oral traditions in his historical research (Rawlinson 1859:29-56). Moreover, even in Radcliffe-Brown's day anthropologists had begun to study societies on which considerable historical documentation was available (M. G. Smith 1962:73).

Actually, in his concept of "function" Radcliffe-Brown was probably influenced more by Herbert Spencer than by Durkheim. Armed with functionalism, he rejected the "conjectural history" of earlier anthropologists, ruling out history as a proper object of study for anthropologists. M. G. Smith (1962:77) attributes to Radcliffe-Brown "the fallacy of the ethnographic present"; that is, by initially excluding change, whether in the past or in the present, he misleads himself into believing that change does not occur. Like the evolutionists, Radcliffe-Brown was strongly committed to the concept of society as a natural system. When Radcliffe-Brown and Malinowski did study the traditional notions of history in a primitive society, they regarded them as ideological by-products of the society, a reflex of social structure—that is, as myths or charters (I. M. Lewis, ed., 1968:xi).

Many anthropologists in the United States turned to various psychological theories, in part as a result of Boas' interest in "process," which he seems to have thought of as a psychological phenomenon. Increasingly in the 1930s American anthropologists such as Edward Sapir, Margaret Mead, and Ruth Benedict used psychological concepts descriptively (Kroeber 1935:555-56). They attempted to describe cultures as wholes, and they did so by speaking of them as individuals writ large, so that the characters of cultures could be indicated by the use of concepts from personality psychology.[4] As time went on, the psychological anthropologists became more and more psychological, and the most important research done by Americans in the 1940s and 1950s were studies of culture and personality and of "acculturation," or combinations of both. Acculturation studies were fundamentally historical in character, with most of the information on any particular "acculturation sequence" coming from documentary and archival sources. But the word "history" was carefully avoided.

In retrospect it would seem that the interest of the French, British, and American anthropologists in sociolog-

---

[4] Interestingly, in Kroeber's opinion this use of psychological concepts still qualified as historical research because it was a way of achieving "descriptive integration," and this in Kroeber's opinion was the essential ingredient of history.

ical and psychological theory was partly a function of an attempt to establish an identity for social anthropology apart from history. It should be remembered, however, that throughout this period of theoretical hostility toward history, some empirical historical research continued to be done both in the United States and in England. In America the diffusionist school never quite died out, and Harold Driver (1969) in particular continued to do distributional studies of culture traits, inferring history from them. Melville Herskovits (1941) also did significant historical research. Some museum studies of material culture continued to be done, and the Bureau of American Ethnology continued to publish historical studies by John R. Swanton, Frank G. Speck, John C. Ewers, and others (Hultkranz 1967*b*:115). Something of the same thing occurred in England, where some of the social anthropologists did historical research in spite of what their mentors said (Schapera 1962).

THE RETURN TO HISTORY

Historical research in anthropology never really ceased; it simply became increasingly separated from theory. The turning point in this separation of theory and research came in the 1950s, when prominent anthropologists in the United States, France, and England advocated a stronger role for historical research and attempted to give anthropology a stronger historical identity.

The Historical Approach in America: Fred Eggan

In the United States a medium for historical studies came with the founding of the journal *Ethnohistory* in 1953, but the theoretical charter came in Fred Eggan's presidential address to the American Anthropological Association in the same year. Eggan was influenced by Radcliffe-Brown, who taught at the University of Chicago for a brief period in the early 1930s, but his first fieldwork was done among the Mississippi Choctaws (Eggan 1966: 15-44), and we recall that through the efforts of John R. Swanton historical studies were unusually strong in the southeast. Both of these influences show up in Eggan's address (1954:745), particularly when he states that we need to "adopt the structural-functional approach of British social anthropology and integrate it with our traditional American interest in cultural process and history." Repeating almost exactly what Durkheim had said earlier, Eggan (1954:747) argues that culture patterns can most clearly be seen when they are traced through time, and that comparative method should consist of a detailed comparison of small numbers of cases drawn from a restricted area. It must be said, however, that Eggan's advocacy of a combination of the historical approach with the theory of social structure went largely unheeded among his American colleagues.

The Historical Approach in France: Claude Lévi-Strauss

In France a plea for a closer rapprochement between history and anthropology came from Claude Lévi-Strauss (1963) in his introduction to *Structural Anthropology*, the French edition of which appeared in 1958. He differs from Eggan in his assessment of the achievements of the structural-functionalists, saying that they failed because the generalizations at which they arrived always turn out to be truisms; their value, in fact, declines with their generality. Rather, Lévi-Strauss says, we should realize that history and ethnography are really quite similar; both, for example, are concerned with societies other than the one in which the researcher lives,[5] and their goals are quite similar.

All that the historian or ethnographer can do, and all that we can expect of either of them, is to enlarge a specific experience to the dimension of a more general one, which thereby becomes accessible *as experience* to men of another country or epoch. And in order to succeed, both historian and ethnographer must have the same qualities: skill, precision, a sympathetic approach, and objectivity [1963:17].

Nor is there a great deal of difference in method, though ethnographers collect more information by observation than historians do. The basic difference between history and anthropology, he argues, is that history concentrates on the conscious expression of social life while anthropologists examine the "unconscious foundations" (1963:18). But one could point out that even this is probably a consequence of the kinds of societies studied by historians and anthropologists. Historians have traditionally studied societies culturally similar to our own, with whom we share many unconscious assumptions, while anthropologists have traditionally studied exotic societies whose basic assumptions are quite different from ours.

Although Lévi-Strauss, like Durkheim before him, argues for a closer rapprochement between history and anthropology, he is also like Durkheim in not undertaking any significant historical research himself. Indeed, he seems to be saying that the distinctive task of anthropology is to discern the unconscious activity of the mind, and that this can more easily be discerned through the use of historical data,

which permit the researcher to perceive the underlying structural features that remain constant while actual cultural manifestations change. The goal of the anthropologist is to penetrate

beyond the conscious and always shifting images which men hold, the complete range of unconscious possibilities. These are not unlimited, and the relationships of compatibility and incompatibility which each maintains with all the others provide a logical framework for historical developments, which while perhaps unpredictable, are never arbitrary [1963:23].

In this view, history and anthropology are inseparable.

The Historical Approach in England: E. E. Evans-Pritchard

The most forceful argument for a historical point of view in social anthropology has come not from the United States or France, but from E. E. Evans-Pritchard in England. The first statement of his position came in his Marett lecture of 1950, in which he argued that conceiving of societies as natural systems and of social anthropology as a science has undesirable theoretical implications. Instead, social anthropologists should model themselves after the historians, and they should consider anthropology to be one of the humanities—a kind of philosophy or art. According to Evans-Pritchard (1962a:22), social anthropology is a kind of historiography, in which research occurs in three phases. In the first phase the anthropologist goes to live in an exotic society, mastering the language and observing daily life for some months and years, taking copious notes and making other records of his observations. In the next phase he returns home and rethinks his experience in terms of *our* concepts and values—he "translates" from one culture to

---

[5] Kroeber indepently advocated a rather similar point of view (1963).

another. In carrying out this translation, he will inevitably abstract a structural pattern out of what he has observed. In the third phase he makes comparisons between the society he has studied and societies studied by other anthropologists. According to Evans-Pritchard, only in the first phase is the social anthropologist's research of a different sort than a historian's; that is, he observes people at firsthand, creating a "document" in the process. Thus Evans-Pritchard says that social anthropology and history differ not in methods or aims, but only in technique. In opposition to positivistic anthropologists, he argues (1962a:28) that there is

an older tradition than that of the Enlightenment with a different approach to the study of human societies, in which they are seen as systems only because social life must have a pattern of some kind, inasmuch as man, being a reasonable creature, has to live in a world in which his relations with those around him are ordered and intelligible.

Some ten years later Evans-Pritchard (1962b) elaborated on this argument, listing some of the unfortunate consequences of a breach between social anthropology and history. He maintains, for example, that in the course of their education few social anthropologists acquire the critical skills necessary to exploit documentary sources effectively, and in many parts of the world today this is the only way one can study indigenous social institutions. Another consequence is that a failure to treat preliterate societies historically gives the impression that they are static and unchanging, and this is false. Furthermore, the breach between history and social anthropology has meant that anthropologists have generally failed to examine an interesting series of problems having to do with "incapsulated history" or folk history: the factors that govern a society's choice of the events that are to be committed to tradition. There has been a similar failure to examine a series of interesting problems having to do with the distinction between "history, myth, legend, anecdote, and folklore" (1962b:51-53).

For reasons that are not entirely clear, the critical reaction to Evans-Pritchard's statements about history has been more heated than the reaction to Eggan or Lévi-Strauss.[6] For example, M. G. Smith (1962:80) is critical of Evans-Pritchard's contention that social anthropology is a kind of art or philosophy, fearing that anthropology will degenerate into a mere literary game and that anthropologists will be sidetracked from their true purpose, the search for social regularities. To counter Evans-Pritchard, Smith (1962:82) attempts to develop a diachronic methodology that retains the notion of society as a system, though in a more open sense, allowing for social conflict. Additional critical remarks have come from Ian Schapera (1962), who denies Evans-Pritchard's assertion that Radcliffe-Brown and Malinowski were hostile toward history, pointing out that some of their students used historical information in their research.[7] His sharpest disagreement with Evans-Pritchard is his insistence that a society can be understood apart from its history, and that Evans-Pritchard has himself produced studies that show that this is so. What Schapera and some of the other critics seem to be missing is the

---

[6] The intellectual controversy between Lévi-Strauss and Sartre was about more abstract issues, such as the meaning of historical action in the Third World (Abel 1966). It has thus far had little effect on empirical research in social anthropology.

[7] I. M. Lewis (1968:xiv) has more recently made the same point, with the difference that he points out that the historical research done by these anthropologists was neither very extensive nor very deep.

fact that Evans-Pritchard is talking about a point of view—a view that sees preliterate people as having a history in much the same sense that we do, and not as a special class of humanity. Evans-Pritchard does not deny the possibility of synchronic studies by anthropologists or anyone else; indeed, he even points out that historians have done such studies, citing Jacob Burckhardt's *Civilization of the Renaissance in Italy* in the nineteenth century. Some of the British anthropologists have refused to take sides with this positivist-humanist controversy, enunciated by Radcliffe-Brown on the one hand and Evans-Pritchard on the other. I. M. Lewis, for example (1968:xiii-xiv), has chosen to steer a middle course very much like E. H. Carr's middle-ground notion of history.

The Historical Approach in Anthropological Journals

These theoretical charters for historical research by anthropologists have fortunately been accompanied by the founding of several journals in the past two decades. In addition to *Ethnohistory,* mentioned earlier, historical studies by anthropologists regularly appear in *Comparative Studies in History and Society, History and Theory,* and the *Journal of Social History.* In addition, many journals concerned with specific culture areas have been founded, such as the *Journal of African History, African Historical Studies, The Indian Historian,* and *Ethnologia Europaea,* to name just a few.

VARIETIES OF HISTORICAL RESEARCH IN ANTHROPOLOGY

The decline of historical research in anthropology has ended, partly because of the theoretical contributions of Fred Eggan, Claude Lévi-Strauss, E. E. Evans-Pritchard, and others, and partly because of social and political factors in the modern world that are now in progress and hence imperfectly understood. The volume of historical research that has found its way into print since the late 1950s is now so great that no one person can be familiar with all of it. It is possible, however, to classify this research into four main areas: (1) studies of inferential history and material culture; (2) historical research by archaeologists; (3) various forms of historical research by social anthropologists; and (4) research on folk history, the beliefs about history held by people in exotic cultures. Some of this research is a continuation of older lines of anthropological thought and some of it has been stimulated by recent thinking. Because the volume of research in some of these areas is great, it will be possible to cite only a few representative samples of each of them.

INFERENTIAL HISTORY AND STUDIES OF MATERIAL CULTURE

Inferential history is based on the analysis of information not associated with absolute or relative dates. That is, it is derived from data or phenomena that do not yield up their historical content directly; their significance must be extracted from them by making one or more inferences. This area of research has its roots in the work of the European diffusionists and was carried on by the first generation of American anthropologists, including Clark Wissler, R. B. Dixon, and A. L. Kroeber. The basic methodological principles of inferential history were set out in great detail by Edward Sapir (1951) in "Time Perspective in Aboriginal American Culture: A Study in Method," a paper that in many respects is as useful today as it was when it was first published in 1916.

Inferences about history can be made from three kinds of data: biological data on man and the plants and animals he uses, linguistic data, and cultural data. In general, inferences based on biological and linguistic data can be made with more confidence than those based on cultural data (Sturtevant 1966:35). Because of the specialized nature of modern physical anthropology and linguistics, however, only one or two examples of each will be mentioned here, while inferences from cultural data will be discussed more fully.

Inferences from Biological and Linguistic Data

Inferences drawn from biological data can have striking impact, as William Pollitzer (1970) has made clear with his genetic research on various racial and ethnic groups in the southeastern United States and its implications for social and cultural isolation. Linguistic data are useful in making inferences about cultural relations because people who share the same language generally (but not always) share the same culture. Language is more compact and self-contained than other parts of culture, and it changes slowly and with great regularity. Sapir shows in intricate detail the kinds of inferences that can be made both from the cultural associations and geographical distribution of single linguistic elements and from the geographical distribution of whole languages and language groups. Because languages change and diversify through time, they can be classified into linguistic stocks and arranged in treelike taxonomies and one can make the inference that the greater the diversity within a linguistic stock, the greater the time elapsed. In another kind of reconstruction, it is sometimes possible to infer an earlier homeland of a linguistic stock by analyzing the

meanings of words, particularly archaic forms. For example, linguists who have reconstructed plant and animal names in Proto-Indo-European have advanced some much disputed hypotheses about the location of the original Proto-Indo-European speakers in the late Neolithic era (Lehmann 1962:207-209), and Sapir (1936) found linguistic evidence that the Navajos once lived in an area far to the north of their present location.

Inferences from Cultural Data

Inferences from cultural data must be made with great care, but they are of more value than has often been assumed. Typically, but not necessarily, these studies concentrate on material culture and are therefore often called "museum studies." One of the simplest kinds of inference from cultural data is what Sapir (1951:400f) calls "cultural seriation." It rests upon the assumption that culture traits develop from the simple to the complex, and simpler cultural forms are therefore presumed to be older than complex cultural forms. Another way to use cultural data is to plot the geographical distribution of a trait and make inferences from this. Since the diffusion of a trait takes time, one infers that the larger the area in which a trait is found, the older the trait must be. For example, the virtually worldwide distribution of swaddling and the use of cradle boards must mean that it is an extremely old cultural complex (Hudson and Phillips 1968:14-16). (It should, of course, be obvious that this sort of assumption cannot be made in the case of such recent phenomena as Coca-Cola bottles.) There are several persistent problems in this kind of inferential history. For one thing, the criteria for proving that two traits are genetically related are often subjective or inconclusive. Also, if two traits do seem similar, one must prove that they are not products of convergent development. And mere typological similarities, whether in kinship or language structure, must be discounted (Trigger 1968:33).

Although this form of research was once popular in the United States, little has been done with it in the recent past. A notable exception is the work of Harold Driver (1969), who has done extensive distributional studies on the Indians of North America, exploring paths first charted by A. L. Kroeber. Some very good work continues to be done in Europe. Geza de Rohan-Csermak's *Sturgeon Hooks of Eurasia* (1963) is a fine example. The sturgeon, a fish of truly enormous size and one whose flesh is considered a great delicacy, has been caught by a variety of specialized techniques in Europe and Asia since the Mesolithic era. Rohan-Csermak documents this technology from the Iron Age to the present, concluding that it probably originated in northern Europe or Eurasia.

What many anthropologists do not realize is that not all studies of material culture need be done for the sole purpose of inferring chronology, and that it is possible to use both inferential and direct evidence in the same piece of research. Material culture contains great amounts of congealed information that can be exploited in a variety of ways. Rohan-Csermak (1963), for example, goes far beyond an examination of the morphology of sturgeon hooks and their occurrence in space and time. He remarks, for example, on the extreme stability through time of one particular hook, the Samolov hook, and suggests that its functional isolation from hooks of other types explains its stability. In addition, he documents in some detail the diffusion of the Samolov hook along the lower and middle Danube River and the diffusion of sturgeon

fishing from the central Eurasian river systems to the Black Sea and the Caspian Sea.

As another example of the kind of research that can be done on material culture, one can cite Peter J. Ucko's (1970) richly detailed study of penis sheaths, in which he shows that the morphology and distribution of the penis sheath is only a part of the significance of this interesting artifact and culture complex. In the course of his investigation he not only presents the standard distribution maps and makes inferences about diffusion and independent invention, but also explores techniques of manufacture, autochthonous explanations, values associated with nakedness and nudity, and the social contexts in which penis sheaths are important. Moreover, Ucko (1970:60-61) treats his research as a case study, showing how an investigation of material culture leads to many spheres of anthropological interest and pointing out that it is therefore unfortunate that anthropologists have allowed studies of material culture to languish.

Museum research on material culture can be a stimulus to further documentary research, as Rohan-Csermak and Ucko demonstrate, and also to further field research. For example, photographs of museum specimens can be carried to the field for the purpose of eliciting new information. William Fenton (1966) has discussed several instances in which he has done this successfully. He tells, for example, of writing a paper on Iroquois masks based on various private and museum collections. He then went into the field with photographs of these masks, gathering from the Iroquois additional information on various carving styles, the artists who carved the masks, and their role in ritual. Fenton was also able to observe modern carvers at work and the use of the masks in rituals. He then wrote up this new information, and when the Iroquois read a draft of the article they gave him even more information.

HISTORY AND ARCHAEOLOGY

Although not all archaeologists concur, archaeology can be defined as a set of methods whose purpose is to recover, analyze, and document the material remains of man's past (Daniel 1964:13). Closely associated with these methods, but distinct from them, are a series of inferential methods by means of which history is extracted from the material remains recovered by archaeologists. The advantages of these inferential methods over the ones discussed above are that they permit the archaeologist to arrange his material remains in stratified series, to know the cultural context in which they were found, and to establish exact dates and acquire other kinds of information by a variety of physical means at his disposal. Thus conceived, archaeology is a set of techniques that can be used in a variety of cultural contexts ranging from the fully prehistoric to the fully historic. When the context is prehistoric, the only avenue to human meaning and significance is through inferential methods, and the product is prehistoric archaeology or prehistory proper (Trigger 1968). Protohistoric archaeology, on the other hand, is the archaeology of sites for which we have some historical documentation, but for which most of the evidence is archaeological. And finally, archaeology can be used on sites for which there is full historic documentation; here archaeology adds details to an already full historic record. It will be obvious to archaeologists that the definitions of protohistoric and historic archaeology used here differ somewhat from their own.

Prehistoric Archaeology

Of all these varieties of archaeology, prehistoric archaeology or prehistory is the variety that is most distinct from history. However, prehistoric archaeologists do utilize historical information when they familiarize themselves with cultures and societies existing in historic times for the purpose of making inferences. That is, in order to interpret the material remains of a particular prehistoric society, the prehistorian implicitly or explicitly searches the ethnographic record for a society of similar social complexity.[8] The methodological problem that sets prehistory apart from history is the problem of the degree to which material culture reflects other parts of culture, such as beliefs and values. To what degree does an archaeological phase correspond to a real social or cultural group? The fact is that archaeologists know of many historically documented cases in which considerable variation in material culture exists within a single society or culture. Because of this difficulty, Bruce Trigger (1968) has argued that the basic unit of analysis in prehistoric archaeology should be the "component"—a particular set of culture traits at a particular site. Here one presumably deals with the culture of a particular community of people.

Prehistorians are at their best when reconstructing economic systems; when the economic system is known, one can often make limited inferences about other parts of culture (Gabel 1967). Food sources can be determined in a variety of ways. Archaeologists recover desiccated plant remains and carbonized seeds, pollen, and human feces,

---

[8] More recently, prehistoric archaeologists have been trying to develop models of primitive society, composed variously of the organic analogy and computer and communication system analogies (Trigger 1968: 5, Hole and Heizer 1969:353f).

all of which yield information about the plants that were important in the economy. Animal bones likewise yield up their information. Putting all the data together, the prehistorian can often reconstruct a picture of the food resources, the seasonal cycle, the methods of storing and preserving food, and the ways in which various kinds of food were prepared. In some cases patterns of land use can be reconstructed.

Protohistoric Archaeology

In protohistoric archaeology, history is usually the handmaiden of archaeology.[9] The first and probably the most dramatic instance of protohistoric archaeology was Heinrich Schliemann's discovery and excavation of Troy in 1871—a striking demonstration that the unrecorded past is not lost forever. Less spectacularly but with more sophisticated methods, George F. Will and H. J. Spinden (1906) did protohistoric archaeological studies of the Mandan Indians. They first acquainted themselves with the historical documentation of the Mandans and with museum collections of Mandan artifacts. Then they excavated a known historic Mandan site. Surprisingly, in America little else was done with this approach until the late 1930s, when some of the methodological details of the direct historical approach were spelled out by William Duncan Strong (1936, 1940), Julian Steward (1942), and Robert Heizer (1941).

The advantage to the archaeologist of information from documentary sources is that it throws historical light on the prehistoric past, enabling him to proceed from that which is better

known to that which is less well known (Steward 1942:337). A good example of protohistoric archaeology is Robert S. Neitzel's (1965) work on the Fatherland Site, the main village of the Natchez Indians of the lower Mississippi River. Neitzel used historical sources to locate and prove that a site on the Fatherland Plantation near Natchez, Mississippi, was the site of the Grand Village of the Natchez Indians from 1682 to 1729, when the French established a settlement there. Fortunately, the Natchez had been relatively well documented by the French, and Neitzel used this documentation to identify their temple, the chief's house, the probable burial site of the Great Sun, the principal chief of the Natchez, and the probable burial sites of those who had been sacrificed at his funeral in 1725. One noteworthy feature of Neitzel's report is that it reveals some rather startling discrepancies between what his reading of history had led him to expect and what he actually found. For example, the site itself turned out to be a village with mounds fronting on a plaza, as expected, but the site contains three mounds and not two, as reported by French observers (Neitzel 1965:62). Thus the relationship between history and protohistoric archaeology is not completely one-sided: archaeology can occasionally correct and amplify the historic record.

Documentary and archaeological information can be combined in various proportions. For example, Frederica de Laguna (1960) has given us a study of a Tlingit community, using some data from archaeology but more from historical documents and from Tlingit oral traditions. One outstanding feature of this study is its detailed analysis of Tlingit folk history, which reveals that for the Tlingit, history and geography are closely connected, and both of them are connected with Tlingit kin-

---

[9] According to William Fenton (1966:71), ethnohistory had its origin when the skills and interests of the historical ethnologist were united with those of the protohistoric archaeologist.

ship organization. Laguna (1960:205) found evidence that at least some Tlingit oral traditions contain fairly accurate accounts of events that occurred a century and a half or more in the past.

Historical Archaeology

In protohistoric archaeology, history serves archaeology, but in historical archaeology the relationship is reversed. Here the archaeologist works in a fully historical context, to which archaeology adds a further dimension. The period covered by historical archaeology varies from one country to another. In the United States it begins with earliest colonization and runs through the nineteenth century. In Great Britain, on the other hand, the Society for Post-Medieval Archaeology takes as its province history occurring after 1485, the year that marks the end of the period studied by the Society for Medieval Archaeology, and ending with the Industrial Revolution in the eighteenth century (Hume 1969:6).

Historical archaeology has developed rather slowly in the United States, primarily because the impulse behind American archaeology has grown out of the Indian cultures that we first destroyed and then looked back on with puzzlement, nostalgia, and at long last shame. In addition, we have all been inclined to assume that anything one needs to know about the historic past can be learned from documents. But as Neitzel's Natchez research has shown us, the material remains of human experience sometimes contain information that contradicts the documents, and historical archaeologists increasingly encounter instances in which the material remains survive while the documents perish.

The archaeologist working on a protohistoric site can usually get by with-out much training as a historian, but this is not the case with historical archaeologists, who must be as adept at library research as at archaeological fieldwork (see Nicholson 1955). Moreover, they must have a reasonably good knowledge of the period and society with which they are working. A historical archaeologist can sometimes take a piece of pottery the size of one's fingernail and determine the date of its manufacture, the factory where it was made, the way it was shipped, the amount of money it was worth, and sometimes even the name of the person who owned it. This kind of expertise allows for very fine differentiations among strata, and it is obviously a far different thing than the typological classification of pottery by prehistoric archaeologists (Noël-Hume 1969:13). As examples of historical archaeology one can cite John L. Cotter's (1958) work at Jamestown, Bernard L. Fontana's (1962) excavation of a late nineteenth-century homesite in the West, J. C. Harrington's (1962) excavations at Fort Raleigh, North Carolina, Ivor Noël-Hume's (1963) work in Virginia, and Hale Smith's (1965) excavations at Santa Rosa Island near Pensacola. Because of their detailed knowledge of material culture, historical archaeologists often serve as consultants in the re-creation of historic sites (Deetz 1969).

Industrial Archaeology. The most recent form of historic archaeology is industrial archaeology, founded in the early 1950s in England, where the Industrial Revolution began. The aim of industrial archaeology is to document the eighteenth-century and early nineteenth-century factories and other sites before they are all torn down (K. Hudson 1964, 1967). Industrial archaeologists do little excavating; rather they make drawings, photographs, and maps of buildings, canals, bridges, aqueducts, machines, and other facilities still standing. They also collect oral history from people who worked in now defunct industries. The industrial archaeologists are even interested in the environmental blight produced during the Industrial Revolution. The slag heaps in Cornwall and Lancashire are now being eradicated by a newer form of "progress," though the British industrial archaeologists are trying to document them and to preserve some of them intact (K. Hudson 1964:66-67).

HISTORICAL RESEARCH IN
SOCIAL ANTHROPOLOGY

Although modern social anthropologists came round to historical research unevenly and slowly, in the past decade they have made up for their earlier neglect by producing so much work it is impossible to survey it comprehensively in the space available here.

Research Methods

The methods used by social anthropologists in working with oral and written materials are basically the same as those used by historians, but with some differences. We do not yet have a comprehensive manual of historical methods for social anthropologists. The most useful works so far are Harold Hickerson's *The Chippewa and Their Neighbors* (1970) and Daniel McCall's *Africa in Time-Perspective* (1964). Although both contain much of general import, Hickerson's book is a case study of historical research and McCall's is specifically meant to aid historical research on African cultures. Hickerson's book has the virtue of discussing historical reconstruction by means of both unwritten and written sources, while McCall's book is limited to the use of unwritten sources.

Oral Traditions. Some unwritten sources of history—those used in inferential history and archaeology—have already been discussed. But for the social anthropologist a far more important source is the oral tradition, and we are fortunate in having Jan Vansina's (1965) detailed examination of methods for working with oral traditions. For people in preliterate societies and for illiterate people in literate societies, oral traditions are the only avenues to the past. Vansina examines the way in which oral traditions are transmitted from one generation to another, some of the ways in which error and deliberate falsification are introduced into them, and finally the means by which historical information can be extracted from them. Before Vansina's book, much of our thinking about oral traditions came from folklorists, classicists, historians, and others; Vansina's important innovation has been to collect materials at firsthand from peoples who still have socially meaningful oral traditions, thus avoiding many of the errors of earlier scholars, who dealt mainly with oral traditions that had been committed to writing somewhere along the line. Vansina makes it plain that effective research on the oral traditions of a society requires the same mastery of that society's culture and language as is required by historians who work with written sources of literate societies.

With the exception of those connected with the Oral History Office at Columbia University, historians began to work with oral sources only relatively recently, in part because scholars are partial to the written word. In 1967, however, a number of historians, archivists, and others organized the Oral History Association, which now gives leadership to a rapidly growing field of research. The association publishes a newsletter and the proceedings of its annual colloquia, both of which contain much that is directly relevant to social anthropology. Since the founding of the association, the growth of research in oral history by historians has been astonishing, and the interest in this work by scholars and the general public has been equally impressive (Shumway 1971). T. Harry Williams (1969), for example, has won a Pulitzer Prize and a National Book Award for his biography of Huey Long, and Studs Terkel (1967, 1970) has authored two best sellers from oral sources. Moreover, historians are doing research on topics that could just as well be covered by social anthropologists, as William Lynwood Montell's (1970) recent study of an unusual enclave of racially mixed people in Kentucky amply illustrates.

Written Documents. For methods appropriate to the interpretation of written documents, the social anthropologist can refer to standard works on historical method. The English edition of Langlois and Seignobos (1898), long a standard book in many history departments, is still useful, and the work of one of their intellectual descendants, Marc Bloch (1964), can also be read with profit. Bloch is particularly relevant to anthropology, perhaps because of his research on feudal society, since the feudal period of European history is almost as alien to us as many of the exotic cultures studied by contemporary anthropologists. Bloch's study of the material remains of feudal society, particularly the field systems, would do justice to an archaeologist. Reminiscent of the social anthropologist's insistence on field experience, Bloch emphasizes that the historian's direct human experience with his fellow man is an important source of historical understanding and criticism. Bloch also insists, arguing with great ingenuity, that much of a firsthand observer's information is as

indirect as that of a historian working with documents; that is, much of what a fieldworker "sees" comes to him through the eyes of others. Many other useful works on historical method are available (e.g., Barzun and Graff 1962, Gottschalk 1950, Gustavson 1955). One particularly valuable book is Philip C. Brooks' *Research in Archives* (1969); in little more than a hundred pages he makes available knowledge that used to come only after years of experience in archival research.

Like the anthropologist working with oral traditions, the anthropologist working with written documents should master the language and customs of the society whose history he is reconstructing. Unfortunately, in the case of poorly documented preliterate societies, such as many of the extinct Indian cultures of the southeastern United States, it is not possible to do this. But here as elsewhere a general knowledge of social anthropology can be an aid in historical interpretation, particularly in sensitizing one against ethnocentrism and cultural bias (Sturtevant 1966:12-13). Probably the ideal research is documentary research done by an anthropologist on the earlier history of a people he has previously studied at firsthand. William Sturtevant, for example (1966:14), tells about a historian's disbelief concerning the Seminole leader Coacoochee's use of medicinal roots to reduce his weight so he could escape through a small window of his cell in the fort at St. Augustine. In light of his firsthand knowledge of Seminole medicinal practices, however, Sturtevant was able to conclude that the report was probably reliable, at least as far as the use of the roots was concerned. Of course, the efficacy of the roots in doing what they were supposed to do is another matter.

Although one can draw a methodological distinction between research based on oral traditions and on written sources, in practice both kinds of evidence are frequently used in the same piece of research. Indeed, in historical research one is usually willing to use *any* source of information on the past.

Types of Research

Contemporary social anthropologists are doing a variety of types of historical research, some similar to the kinds of research that historians do and others dictated by the traditional interests of social anthropology. In reviewing research in this area, one can separate the work of social anthropologists from that of historians and scholars in other fields only in the most arbitrary fashion, and rather than do this it has seemed wiser to include some work by nonanthropologists.

Life Histories. Biographies of individuals in exotic societies probably constitute the most concrete and obvious kind of historical research in social anthropology. There were, of course, many examples of this kind of biography before anthropology existed in a formal sense. Many biographies of American Indians were written in the nineteenth century, most of them coming out at about the same time that the last remaining American Indians lost their autonomy (Langness 1965: 5-7). Most of these biographies have been ignored by anthropologists, quite unjustly, on the grounds that they are too literary.

The writing of biographies enjoyed a brief period of popularity among American anthropologists, though they called them "life histories." This interest was aroused in 1926 with the publication of Paul Radin's *Crashing Thunder*. Research on life histories did not become popular, however, until the 1930s and 1940s, through the influence of Edward Sapir and Clyde Kluckhohn; and perhaps as a result of their influence life histories were distinctly psychological in point of view. In recent years, however, a number of excellent biographies of people in other cultures have been published which are not at all historical. One need only mention Oscar Lewis' *The Children of Sánchez* (1961) and *Pedro Martínez* (1964) and Theodora Kroeber's incomparable *Ishi* (1961). In addition to being a legitimate and useful means of documenting life in other cultures from an individual perspective, the biographical form is an effective means of communicating to the layman what anthropology has to teach.

Biographies and Time Depth. Collecting biographies can also be used as a research technique in anthropological fieldwork (Langness 1965:20-46), and is particularly useful in fieldwork that attempts to add time depth to a synchronic study. There are two principal ways of doing this: the extended case method and the developmental cycle method (Olien 1967). In the extended case method, the fieldworker follows a single set of persons through time, using the incidents in which they become involved as a means of clarifying the relationships among them. The fieldworker observes the behavior of the group of persons over an extended period of time, collects their oral accounts of events in the past, and consults any written records that may be available (Mitchell 1956, Gluckman 1961). In the developmental cycle method, the interest is in the statistical properties of groups that have a life cycle, a regular course of development (Fortes 1949, Goody 1958). When the developmental cycle method is used, it often turns out that seemingly different types of domestic groups are simply different stages of a single structure that changes through time. In both of these methods biographical information is quite useful. The two methods can be combined in the same piece of research, as was done by John Middleton in his *Lugbara Religion* (1960).

Fieldwork and 'Documentary Data. These firsthand field studies that incorporate time depth shade imperceptibly into studies that combine field data with documentary data. The use of documentary records has been particularly useful in working out complicated variables governing succession to office in tribal societies (I. M. Lewis, ed., 1968:xvi-xvii). In tribal politics and in many other areas of social life it is becoming apparent that a flat, synchronic analysis misses much. For example, in the light of a purely synchronic study a social institution might appear to be defunct, only to appear later in changed social conditions as a fully viable social form. An example of just this kind of thing has been found by E. R. Cregeen (1968) in his historical study of Scottish clanship. In light of this, we see that Durkheim's realization of the value of historical research in sociological studies was especially prophetic.

Ethnohistory. Ethnohistory, or historical ethnology, bases its research primarily on the study of documentary information. There are as many varieties of historical ethnology as there are kinds of history. Following the precedent of historians, social anthropologists produce critical editions of primary historical documents, which, thus edited, become accessible to the general reader and more useful to the scholar. Examples are John C. Ewers' edition (1967) of George Catlin's *O-kee-pa*, a Mandan religious ceremony Catlin witnessed in 1832, and his edition of Jean Louis Berlandier's (1969) description of Indians in Texas in 1830. Along this same line are critical editions of documents by literate members of exotic cultures, such as León-Portilla's (1962) version of the Aztec account of the conquest of Mexico and James Mooney and Frans Olbrechts' (1932) version of the Swimmer manuscript, a notebook written by a Cherokee medicine man in the Sequoyah syllabary.

The kinds of research done by historical ethnologists is similar to anthropologists' analyses of their field data on particular social institutions or aspects of culture. Any selection from the works in this category is bound to be arbitrary. One can mention Lancaster's (1958) study of the bilateral kinship system of the Anglo-Saxons and Maurice Freedman's (1958) study of lineage organization in China. Nor is kinship the only subject of interest to historical ethnologists. There have been historical studies of political organization (Evans-Pritchard 1949, M. G. Smith 1960), economics (Obeysekere 1967), and belief systems (León-Portilla 1963).

As historical equivalents of traditional, holistic ethnographies, many fine historical ethnographies of societies in most of the major areas of the world have been produced by anthropologists in recent years. Selecting a few arbitrarily, for Africa we have Argyle's (1966) work on the Fon of Dahomey and Alagoa's (1964) history of the Nembe people of the Niger Delta. For North America we have Hickerson's (1962, 1970) work on the Chippewa, Tooker's (1964) ethnography of the early seventeenth-century Huron Indians, and Weltfish's (1965) reconstruction of a year in the life of the Pawnee Indians. For Latin America we have Ronald Spores' book on the Mixtec of northwestern Oaxaca in Mexico, derived from archaeological, ethnographic, and historical sources.

One further topic on which historical ethnologists have done research is the relationship between European colonial powers and preliterate people. In some instances the interest is in episodes in this history, as in James Mooney's (1896) classic study of the Ghost Dance and a more recent study of the same phenomenon in a different setting by Henry Dobyns and Robert Euler (1967). Much of the great quantity of research done by anthropologists on acculturation and culture change would fall in this category. A particularly ambitious work is Edward Spicer's (1962) study of the relationships between Spain, Mexico, the United States, and the Indians of the southwestern United States. One should also mention the much neglected collection of papers on Puerto Rico edited by Julian Steward (1956). Historians have been as active in this field as anthropologists have, and much of their work is relevant to anthropology; two fine examples are William Hagan's (1966) study of government-sponsored Indian police and judges on reservations in the nineteenth century and Charles Gibson's (1964) comprehensive study of Spanish rule over the Aztecs.

One further genre of historical ethnology is the history of the small community in preindustrial and industrial societies. This grows directly out of the American preoccupation with community studies, pioneered by Robert Redfield and others. One example of this kind of research is Clifford Geertz's (1965) social history of a town in Indonesia from the middle of the nineteenth century until the middle of the twentieth. A further example, less exotic than Geertz's town, is Wissous, a village near Paris studied by Robert and Barbara Anderson (1965). This kind of research is similar to what the historians call "local history," a genre that is frequently (but not invariably) under-

taken by amateurs (Parker 1944). The fact is, however, that local histories often become valuable historical documents in future generations. William Bradford's *History of Plymouth Plantation* is far more important today than many of the more ambitious books written in the same period (Parker 1944:ix). In the hands of a good historian, local history can assume stature and significance far beyond its scope, as for example Sumner Chilton Powell's *Puritan Village* (1965).

Folk History

One further form of historical research in anthropology has been termed "folk history," the study of the historical notions of people in exotic societies (C. Hudson 1966). Since the main concern here is with beliefs about history and with their relationship with other beliefs, this kind of research is more akin to the sociology of knowledge than it is to orthodox historical scholarship. Here the task is not to produce a history according to our historiographic canons of validity and credibility, but to grasp in their own terms the view of history held by people in an exotic society. This kind of research is comparable to the research a Western scholar might do on the philosophy of history of other literate societies, or on the philosophy of history of remote periods of European history (see Hall, ed., 1961).

Although the difference between the philosophy of history of other literate societies and the philosophy of history of preliterate societies is one of degree, a difference nevertheless exists. The crux of the difference is that preliterate people carry all they know, their entire world view, in their heads along with their remembered history. For this reason their categories of historical understanding are strongly colored by other

beliefs and categories and are continually adjusted with respect to them. Thus
in a society with strong lineage organization, the remembered history is laid
out along genealogical lines and it is
adjusted with respect to the social relations obtaining among kinship groups
in the present (Bohannan 1952). In
societies in which travel is important,
particularly among seafarers, the
remembered history is commonly associated with various locations and
places (Laguna 1960). In plural societies, the various sociocultural segments
commonly have rather different versions of the "same" history, and the
differences among them are socially
significant (C. Hudson 1970:105-27,
Barnes 1951).

Students of folk history should not
lose sight of the fact that traditional
histories do contain information about
the past that meets our critical standards, and the degree and manner in
which this operates is of some importance. Thus in studying folk history it
is worthwhile to reconstruct the past
from information from independent
sources if possible, because stories that
appear to have a mythological cast may
nevertheless contain historical truths,
while "facts" that seem clearly historical may refer to events that never happened (I. M. Lewis, ed., 1968:xvii).
And the historical value of a body of traditional knowledge may vary from one
part to another. Both Cunnison (1951)
and Bohannan (1952) have shown how
genealogies are telescoped and manipulated to keep them in tune with existing social conditions, but this should
not obscure the fact that other parts of
these genealogies do actually represent
historical facts.

Thus the oral traditions of other cultures may be seen in the light of two
philosophies of history—our own and
theirs. The most important problems in
this area of research are whether there

are significant similarities among the
philosophies of history of preliterate
peoples and whether there are significant differences between their philosophies of history and ours. According to
Jack Goody and Ian Watt (1962), this
indeed seems to be the case. That is, it
is only in literate cultures, where written records can be compared with each
other, that historical criticism in the
sense in which we know it can exist.

PROBLEMS AND PROSPECTS

The greatest problem faced by an
anthropologist doing historical research
is that of acquiring competence in both
fields of study. The problem is as great
for the archaeologist as it is for the
social anthropologist. Even the most
methodologically expert prehistoric
archaeologist is not competent to ex-
cavate an eighteenth-century site unless
he knows a fair amount of the history
of the period and place in question
(Noël-Hume 1969:12-15). It is difficult
to train a person in both fields, partly
because the structure of our universities
puts barriers in the way of interdisciplinary studies and partly because of
the mutual distrust between archaeologists and historians. The historian
thinks of the archaeologist as a dreary
collector of old objects, while the archaeologist thinks of the historian as a
woolly-minded humanist interested in
small facts about the past. The unfortunate consequence is that historical
ethnography is all too often written
either by a historian who has a nineteenth-century concept of "primitive
man" or by a social anthropologist
whose competence at historical research fails to meet minimal standards
set by historians (Fenton 1966:72-73,
Berkhofer 1971).

Another problem is that the social
anthropologist who undertakes extensive historical research, like the over-

zealous fieldworker, sometimes runs the risk of losing his identity as an anthropologist (Fenton 1966:76). There is no doubt that as anthropologists do more and more historical research this problem will increase. One solution, of course, is to reexamine and redefine the ideals to which social anthropologists should conform. That is, perhaps the time has come for social anthropologists to stop feeling guilty because they cannot duplicate Malinowski's fieldwork.

In another vein, one might argue that this individual loss of identity is simply a part of a larger process—that anthropology is merely a phase in Western intellectual history, an epiphenomenon of colonialism. And because social anthropology was ideologically connected with colonialism, whether supporting it or covertly opposed to it, the demise of colonialism left it in an awkward position (Hooker 1963). Thus the argument is that anthropologists will eventually be absorbed into two fields: some will turn to the study of developing and newly emerging nations and be absorbed into sociology and political science, while others will study dead or dying preliterate societies and become historians.

Whether social anthropology disappears entirely at some time in the future is an open question, though some anthropologists have seriously argued that it will (Goody 1966, Worsley 1966).[10] It does seem that if anthropologists want to continue working with exotic cultural materials, it is almost inevitable that they will increasingly do historical research. Indeed, we have seen indications that there may even be a resurgence of museum studies. Along with increased historical research, closer identification with historians may very well cause anthropologists to be less enamored of abstract theorizing and more tolerant of explanation at the common-sense level (I. M. Lewis, ed. 1968:x). As used here, "common sense" does not mean a return to ethnocentrism, but simply a frank recognition that our primary means to understanding another culture is through the stock of categories, beliefs, and values we acquire as members of our own culture.[11] This is what Evans-Pritchard means by "translation." In these terms, anthropological expertise is not a matter of learning a great body of technical concepts and theories, but rather a heightened ability to set unfamiliar beliefs and customs into understandable terms. And in these terms, anthropology, like history, would be measured against literary standards. Some of the implications of this common-sense point of view have already been worked out by Robin Horton (1968).

Conceiving of anthropology as a kind of history is an alternative to positivism; it is a wholly different point of view, requiring the anthropologist to rethink some of his basic assumptions. For example, along with the historian he must be prepared to admit frankly that he is not immune to socially conditioned ideological points of view, and that these views have their effects on his work (Washburn 1971). In fact, this possibility has recently been considered by Eric Wolf (1969) in a paper on changes in theory in American anthropology in the past hundred years.

Many feel that Western civilization—certainly the United States—is nearing a

---

[10] The future of archaeology is more secure. If the destruction of archaeological sites continues at the rate with which it is proceeding today, however, archaeologists have cause for alarm—unless, of course, they begin digging last Saturday's garbage heaps. Some archaeological purists feel that this is precisely what the historical and industrial archaeologists are already doing.

[11] Most historians adhere to common-sense theory, but for an exception see Berkhofer (1969).

turning point in its history, and that anthropology along with everything else
will be transformed. Perhaps anthropologists would do well to pay attention to some of the younger historians
who are calling for a reexamination of
our history (Bernstein 1968). It could
be that the most important contribution that anthropology can make at this
point is of a historical nature: the anthropological point of view could be of
great service in the reexamination of
the way the modern world as a whole
got to be the way it is today.[12]

REFERENCES

Abel, Lionel
　1966　Sartre vs. Lévi-Strauss. *Commonweal*
　　　　84:364-68.
Alagoa, Eblegberi Joe
　1964　*The Small Brave City-State: A His-
　　　　tory of Nembe-Brass in the Niger
　　　　Delta.* Madison: University of Wis-
　　　　consin Press.
Anderson, Robert T., and Barbara Gallatin
　　　　Anderson
　1965　*Bus Stop for Paris: The Transfor-
　　　　mation of a French Village.* New
　　　　York: Doubleday.
Argyle, W. J.
　1966　*The Fon of Dahomey: A History and
　　　　Ethnography of the Old Kingdom.*
　　　　Oxford: Clarendon Press.
Bandelier, Adolph F.
　1966　*The Southwestern Journals of
　　　　Adolph F. Bandelier,* ed. Charles H.
　　　　Lange and Carroll L. Riley. Albuquer-
　　　　que: University of New Mexico Press.
Barnes, J. A.
　1951　The Perception of History in a Plural
　　　　Society: A Study of an Ngoni Group
　　　　in Northern Rhodesia. *Human Rela-
　　　　tions* 4:295-303.
Barzun, Jacques, and Henry F, Graff

　1962　*The Modern Researcher.* New York:
　　　　Harcourt, Brace & World.
Bellah, Robert N.
　1959　Durkheim and History. *American
　　　　Sociological Review* 24:447-61.
Berkhofer, Robert F.
　1969　*A Behavioral Approach to Historical
　　　　Analysis.* New York: Free Press,
　　　　Macmillan.
　1971　The Political Context of a New In-
　　　　dian History. *Pacific Historical Re-
　　　　view* 40:357-82.
Berlandier, Jean Louis
　1969　*The Indians of Texas in 1830,* ed.
　　　　John C. Ewers. Washington, D.C.:
　　　　Smithsonian Institution Press.
Bernstein, Barton J., ed.
　1968　*Towards a New Past: Dissenting Es-
　　　　says in American History.* New York:
　　　　Pantheon Books.
Bloch, Marc
　1964　*The Historian's Craft,* trans. Peter
　　　　Putnam. New York: Vintage Books.
　　　　Originally published 1953.
Boas, Franz
　1936　History and Science in Anthropolo-
　　　　gy: A Reply. *American Anthropolo-
　　　　gist* 38:137-41.
Bohannan, Laura
　1952　A Genealogical Charter. *Africa* 22:
　　　　301-15.
Brooks, Philip
　1969　*Research in Archives: The Use of Un-
　　　　published Primary Sources.* Chicago:
　　　　University of Chicago Press.
Carr, E. H.
　1964　*What is History?* Harmondsworth:
　　　　Penguin Books.
Catlin, George
　1967　*O-kee-pa: A Religious Ceremony and
　　　　Other Customs of the Mandans,* ed.
　　　　John C. Ewers. New Haven: Yale
　　　　University Press.
Cotter, John L.
　1958　*Archaeological Excavations at James-
　　　　town, Virginia.* U.S. National Park
　　　　Service Archaeological Research
　　　　Series no. 4. Washington, D.C.: U.S.
　　　　Government Printing Office.
Cregeen, E. R.
　1968　The Changing Role of the House of
　　　　Argyll in the Scottish Highlands. In
　　　　History and Social Anthropology, ed.
　　　　I. M. Lewis. A.S.A. Monograph no. 7.

---

[12] As this was going to press, an unusually good
guide to historical research for social anthropologists
came to hand: David C. Pitt's *Using Historical
Sources in Anthropology and Sociology* (1972).

London: Tavistock Publications.

Cunnison, Ian
1951 *History on the Luapula: An Essay on the Historical Notions of a Central African Tribe.* Rhodes-Livingston Papers, 21.

Daniel, Glyn
1964 *The Idea of Prehistory.* Baltimore: Penguin Books.

Deetz, James
1969 The Reality of the Pilgrim Fathers. *Natural History* 78, no. 9:32-45.

Dobyns, Henry F., and Robert C. Euler
1967 *The Ghost Dance of 1889 Among the Pai Indians of Northwestern Arizona.* Prescott, Ariz.: Prescott College Press.

Driver, Harold E.
1969 *Indians of North America,* 2nd ed., rev. Chicago: University of Chicago Press.

Eggan, Fred
1954 Social Anthropology and the Method of Controlled Comparison. *American Anthropologist* 56:743-63.
1966 *The American Indian: Perspectives for the Study of Social Change.* Chicago: Aldine.

Evans-Pritchard, E. E.
1949 *The Sanusi of Cyrenaica.* Oxford: Clarendon Press.
1962a Social Anthropology: Past and Present. In *Essays in Social Anthropology.* London: Faber & Faber.
1962b Anthropology and History. In ibid.
1965 The Comparative Method in Social Anthropology. In *The Position of Women in Primitive Societies and Other Essays in Social Anthropology.* New York: Free Press, Macmillan.

Fenton, William N.
1966 Field Work, Museum Studies, and Ethnohistorical Research. *Ethnohistory* 13:71-85.

Fontana, Bernard L.
1962 Johnny Ward's Ranch. *Kiva* 28, nos. 1-2.

Fortes, Meyer
1949 Time and Social Structure: An A-shanti Case Study. In *Social Structure: Studies Presented to A. R. Radcliffe-Brown,* ed. Meyer Fortes. Oxford: Clarendon Press.

Freedman, Maurice
1958 *Lineage Organization in Southeastern China.* London School of Economics Monographs on Social Anthropology, no. 18. London: Athlone Press.

Gabel, Creighton
1967 *Analysis of Prehistoric Economic Patterns.* New York: Holt, Rinehart & Winston.

Geertz, Clifford
1965 *The Social History of an Indonesian Town.* Cambridge: M.I.T. Press.

Gibson, Charles
1964 *The Aztecs Under Spanish Rule: A History of the Indians of the Valley of Mexico, 1519-1810.* Stanford: Stanford University Press.

Gluckman, Max
1961 Ethnographic Data in British Social Anthropology. *Sociological Review* 9:5-17.

Goody, Jack, ed.
1958 *The Developmental Cycle in Domestic Groups.* Cambridge Papers in Social Anthropology, no. 1. Cambridge: At the University Press.
1966 The Prospects for Social Anthropology. *New Society* 13:574-76.

Goody, Jack, and Ian Watt
1962 The Consequences of Literacy. *Comparative Studies in Society and History* 5:304-45.

Gottschalk, Louis
1950 *Understanding History.* New York: Knopf.

Gustavson, Carl
1955 *A Preface to History.* New York: McGraw-Hill.

Hagan, William T.
1966 *Indian Police and Judges: Experiments in Acculturation and Control.* New Haven: Yale University Press.

Hall, D. G. E., ed.
1961 *Historians of Southeast Asia.* London: Oxford University Press.

Hallowell, A. Irving
1960 The Beginnings of Anthropology in America. In *Selected Papers from the American Anthropologist, 1888-1920,* ed. Frederica de Laguna. Evanston, Ill.: Row, Peterson.

Harrington, J. C.
1962 *Search for the Citie of Ralegh, North Carolina.* U.S. National Park Service

Archaeological Research Series, no.
6. Washington, D.C.: U.S. Government Printing Office.

Heine-Geldern, Robert
1964 One Hundred Years of Ethnological Theory in the German-Speaking Countries: Some Milestones. *Current Anthropology* 5:407-16.

Heizer, Robert F.
1941 The Direct Historical Approach in California Archaeology. *American Antiquity* 7:98-122.

Herskovits, Melville J.
1941 *The Myth of the Negro Past.* New York: Harper.

Hickerson, Harold
1962 *The Southwestern Chippewa: An Ethnohistorical Study.* American Anthrological Association Memoir no. 92, vol. 64, no. 3, pt. 2.
1970 *The Chippewa and Their Neighbors: A Study in Ethnohistory.* New York: Holt, Rinehart & Winston.

Hodgen, Margaret T.
1964 *Early Anthropology in the Sixteenth and Seventeenth Centuries.* Philadelphia: University of Pennsylvania Press.

Hole, Frank, and Robert F. Heizer
1969 *An Introduction to Prehistoric Archaeology.* New York: Holt, Rinehart & Winston.

Hooker, James R.
1963 The Anthropologists' Frontier: The Last Phase of African Expansion. *Journal of Modern African Studies* 1:455-59.

Horton, Robin
1968 Neo-Tylorianism: Sound Sense or Sinister Prejudice? *Man* 3:625-34.

Hudson, Charles
1966 Folk History and Ethnohistory. *Ethnohistory* 13:52-70.
1970 *The Catawba Nation.* University of Georgia Monograph no. 18. Athens: University of Georgia Press.

Hudson, Charles, and Helen Phillips
1968 Rousseau and the Disappearance of Swaddling Among Western Europeans. In *Essays on Medical Anthropology*, ed. Thomas Weaver. Southern Anthropological Society Proceedings, 1:13-22. Athens: University of Georgia Press.

Hudson, Kenneth
1964 *Industrial Archaeology: An Introduction.* Philadelphia: Dufour Editions.
1967 *A Handbook for Industrial Archaeologists.* London: John Baker.

Hultkranz, Ake
1967a Some Remarks on Contemporary European Ethnological Thought. *Ethnologia Europaea* 1:38-44.
1967b Historical Approaches in American Ethnology: A Research Survey. *Ethnologia Europaea* 1:96-116.

Jensen, Adolf E.
1963 *Myth and Cult Among Primitive Peoples,* trans. Marianna Tax Choldin and Wolfgang Weissleder. Chicago: University of Chicago Press.

Judd, Neil M.
1967 *The Bureau of American Ethnology: A Partial History.* Norman: University of Oklahoma Press.

Kluckhohn, Clyde
1936 Some Reflections on the Method and Theory of the Kulturkreislehre. *American Anthropologist* 38:157-96.

Kroeber, A. L.
1935 History and Science in Anthropology. *American Anthropologist* 37:539-69.
1963 *An Anthropologist Looks at History.* Berkeley: University of California Press.

Kroeber, Theodora
1961 *Ishi in Two Worlds: A Biography of the Last Wild Indian in North America.* Berkeley: University of California Press.

Laguna, Frederica de
1960 *The Story of a Tlingit Community.* Bureau of American Ethnology Bulletin no. 172. Washington, D.C.: Smithsonian Institution.

Lancaster, Lorraine
1958 Kinship in Anglo-Saxon Society. *British Journal of Sociology* 9:230-50, 359-77.

Langlois, Charles V., and Charles Seignobos
1898 *Introduction to the Study of History.* New York: Henry Holt.

Langness, L. L.
1965 *The Life History in Anthropological Science.* New York: Holt, Rinehart & Winston.

Lehmann, Winfred P.

1962 *Historical Linguistics: An Introduction.* New York: Holt, Rinehart & Winston.

León-Portilla, Miguel
1963 *Aztec Thought and Culture: A Study of the Ancient Nahuatl Mind.* Norman: University of Oklahoma Press.

León-Portilla, Miguel, ed.
1962 *The Broken Spears: The Aztec Account of the Conquest of Mexico.* Boston: Beacon Press.

Lévi-Strauss, Claude
1963 Introduction: History and Anthropology. In *Structural Anthropology,* trans. Claire Jacobson and Brooke Grundfest Schoepf, pp. 1-27. New York: Basic Books.

Lewis, I. M., ed.
1968 *History and Social Anthropology.* A.S.A. Monograph no. 7. London: Tavistock Publications.

Lewis, Oscar
1961 *The Children of Sánchez.* New York: Random House.
1964 *Pedro Martínez.* New York: Random House.

Lienhardt, Godfrey
1966 *Social Anthropology,* 2nd ed. London: Oxford University Press.

Lowie, Robert
1917 Oral Tradition and History. *Journal of American Folklore* 30:161-67.

McCall, Daniel
1964 *Africa in Time-Perspective.* Boston: Boston University Press.

Middleton, John
1960 *Lugbara Religion: Ritual and Authority Among an East African People.* London: Oxford University Press.

Mitchell, James Clyde
1956 *The Yao Village: A Study in the Social Structure of a Nyasaland Tribe.* Manchester: Manchester University Press.

Montell, William Lynwood
1970 *The Saga of Coe Ridge: A Study in Oral History.* Knoxville: University of Tennessee Press.

Mooney, James
1896 *The Ghost-Dance Religion and the Sioux Outbreak of 1890.* 14th annual report of the Bureau of American Ethnology. Washington, D.C.: Smithsonian Institution.

Mooney, James, and Frans M. Olbrechts
1932 *The Swimmer Manuscript: Cherokee Sacred Formulas and Medicinal Prescriptions.* Bureau of American Ethnology Bulletin no. 99. Washington, D.C.: Smithsonian Institution.

Neitzel, Robert S.
1965 *Archaeology of the Fatherland Site: The Grand Village of the Natchez.* Anthropological Papers of the American Museum of Natural History, vol. 51, pt. 1. New York: American Museum of Natural History.

Nicholson, H. B.
1955 Native Historical Traditions of Nuclear America and the Problem of Their Archaeological Correlation. *American Anthropologist* 57:594-613.

Noël-Hume, Ivor
1963 *Here Lies Virginia.* New York: Knopf.
1969 *Historical Archaeology.* New York: Knopf.

Obeyesekere, Gananath
1967 *Land Tenure in Village Ceylon: A Sociological and Historical Study.* Cambridge: At the University Press.

Olien, Michael D.
1967 Diachronic Analysis in Current British Social Anthropology. *Working Papers in Sociology and Anthropology* 1, no. 2:58-68. Athens: University of Georgia.

Parker, Donald Dean
1944 *Local History: How to Gather It, Write It, and Publish It,* rev. and ed. Bertha E. Josephson. New York: Social Science Research Council.

Pitt, David C.
1972 *Using Historical Sources in Anthropology and Sociology.* New York: Holt, Rinehart & Winston.

Pollitzer, William S.
1970 Some Interactions of Culture and Genetics. In *Current Directions in Anthropology.* Bulletins of the American Anthropological Association, vol. 3, no. 3, pt. 2:69-86.

Powell, Sumner Chilton
1965 *Puritan Village: The Formation of a New England Town.* New York: Anchor Books.

Radcliffe-Brown, A. R.

1965 *Structure and Function in Primitive Society.* New York: Free Press, Macmillan. Originally published 1952.

Radin, Paul
1926 *Crashing Thunder: The Autobiography of an American Indian.* New York: Appleton.

Rawlinson, George
1859 *The History of Herodotus,* vol. I. New York: Appleton.

Rohan-Csermak, Geza de
1963 *Sturgeon Hooks of Eurasia.* Viking Fund Publications in Anthropology, no. 35. New York: Wenner-Gren Foundation.

Sapir, Edward
1936 Internal Linguistic Evidence Suggestive of the Northern Origin of the Navaho. *American Anthropologist* 38:224-35.
1951 Time Perspective in Aboriginal American Culture: A Study in Method. In *Selected Writings of Edward Sapir,* ed. David G. Mandelbaum. Berkeley: University of California Press. Originally published 1916.

Schapera, Ian
1962 Should Anthropologists Be Historians? *Journal of the Royal Anthropological Institute* 92:143-56.

Shumway, Gary L.
1971 *Oral History in the United States: A Directory.* New York: Oral History Association.

Smith, Hale G.
1965 *Archaeological Excavations at Santa Rosa Pensacola. Notes in Anthropology,* vol. 10. Tallahassee: Florida State University.

Smith, M. G.
1960 *Government in Zazzau, 1800-1950.* London: Oxford University Press.
1962 History and Social Anthropology. *Journal of the Royal Anthropological Institute* 92:72-85.

Spicer, Edward H.
1962 *Cycles of Conquest: The Impact of Spain, Mexico, and the United States on the Indians of the Southwest, 1533-1960.* Tucson: University of Arizona Press.

Spores, Ronald
1967 *The Mixtec Kings and Their People.*

Norman: University of Oklahoma Press.

Steward, Julian
1942 The Direct Historical Approach in Archaeology. *American Antiquity* 7:337-43.

Steward, Julian, ed.
1956 *The People of Puerto Rico.* Urbana: University of Illinois Press.

Strong, William D.
1936 Anthropological Theory and Archaeological Fact. In *Essays in Anthropology in Honor of A. L. Kroeber,* ed. Robert H. Lowie, pp. 359-70. Berkeley: University of California Press.
1940 From History to Prehistory in the Northern Great Plains. In *Essays in Historical Anthropology,* pp. 353-94. Smithsonian Miscellaneous Collections, vol. 100.

Sturtevant, William C.
1966 Anthropology, History, and Ethnohistory. *Ethnohistory* 13:1-51.

Terkel, Studs
1967 *Division Street: America.* New York: Pantheon Books.
1970 *Hard Times.* New York: Pantheon Books.

Tooker, Elizabeth
1964 *An Ethnography of the Huron Indians, 1615-1649.* Bureau of American Ethnology Bulletin no. 190. Washington, D.C.: Smithsonian Institution.

Trigger, Bruce
1968 *Beyond History: The Methods of Prehistory.* New York: Holt, Rinehart & Winston.

Tylor, Edward Burnett
1958 *Primitive Culture,* 2nd ed. New York: Harper Torchbook. Originally published 1873.

Ucko, Peter J.
1970 Penis Sheaths: A Comparative Study. Curl Prize Lecture, 1969. *Proceedings of the Royal Anthropological Institute for 1969,* pp. 27-67.

Vansina, Jan
1965 *Oral Tradition: A Study in Historical Methodology.* Chicago: Aldine. Originally published 1961.

Washburn, Wilcomb
1971 The Writing of American Indian His-

tory: A Status Report. *Pacific Historical Review* 40:261-81.

Weltfish, Gene
   1965   *The Lost Universe.* New York: Basic Books.

Will, George F., and H. J. Spinden
   1906   The Mandans: A Study of Their Culture, Archaeology, and Language. *Peabody Museum of American Archaeology and Ethnology Papers,* vol. 3, no. 4. Cambridge: Harvard University Press.

Williams, T. Harry

   1969   *Huey Long.* New York: Knopf.

Wolf, Eric R.
   1969   American Anthropologists and American Society. In *Concepts and Assumptions in Contemporary Anthropology,* ed. Stephen A. Tyler. Southern Anthropological Society Proceedings no. 3. Athens: University of Georgia Press.

Worsley, P.
   1966   The End of Anthropology. *Proceedings, Sixth World Conference of Sociology.*

CHAPTER 4

The Concept of Adaptation in Biological and Cultural Evolution

ALEXANDER ALLAND, JR.
BONNIE McCAY

A discussion of adaptation must be set in the context of evolutionary theory. In anthropology such theory has developed somewhat independently of Darwinian biology, although of course it has been influenced by it. White (1959) has stated that theories of social evolution owe more to Spencer than to Darwin. While this may be the case historically, it is our opinion that a fruitful review of the concept of adaptation must begin with the place of this term in biology before any attempt is made to demonstrate the value of the concept for cultural anthropology.

As evolutionists and behavioral scientists we are concerned with (*a*) those processes and mechanisms that act to maintain systems in balance with their environment and (*b*) those processes and mechanisms that act to produce change in systems. We are dismayed

that most anthropological literature dealing with culture change and acculturation generally ignores evolutionary theory in both biology and anthropology (there are notable exceptions, which will be discussed later). Such indifference to a vast body of literature apparently derives from the historical orientation of many anthropologists interested in change. Some of these anthropologists are largely concerned with so-called nonrecurring events, which make up the data of ethnohistory as they conceive it. An evolutionist views the dichotomy between ethnohistory and behavioral science as unnecessary. In his view those mechanisms that maintain stability and those that operate in changing systems function only in the context of specific environments and depend, at least in part, on random events. These two factors account for historical differences. The study of evolution is most emphatically *not* the study of history writ large, but rather the search for those underlying factors that drive systems of human behavior.

This paper could not have been written without the inspiration of Paul Collins and the incessant conversations and debates among students and colleagues at Columbia University.

Bonnie McCay is the author of the greater part of the section on biological adaptation.

The major problems involved in making the concept of adaptation useful consist of (*a*) arriving at a definition of adaptation conjunctive with the theory of evolution apart from the tautology that what is there is adaptive, that what is adaptive is there, and (*b*) finding an empirical measure of adaptation which fits that definition and opens the way for comparisons between organic and cultural processes.

THE CONCEPT OF ADAPTATION IN BIOLOGY

The concept of adaptation has been used at least since the early seventeenth century to refer to the state of being fit, apt, or suitable to some condition, and since the end of the eighteenth century to refer to the process of modifying something so as to fit new conditions. Charles Darwin (1859) appeared to have the seventeenth-century view in mind when he wrote: "In the water-beetle, the structure of its legs, so well adapted for diving, allows it to compete with other aquatic insects, to hunt for its own prey, and to escape serving as prey to other animals." But Darwin's major contribution to biology was his specification of the causes of the second dictionary meaning of "adaptation": the process of modification to suit new conditions. Those causes are variability and natural selection.

When adaptation is taken to mean homeostatic response to short-term variations in the environment (such as adaptations to temperature change), the definition is appropriate within the discipline of physiology. Such response capabilities, however, evolve — that is, change transgenerationally in the direction of better environmental fit — and also change "to meet new conditions." It is therefore useful to distinguish between adaptation as the physiological response of organisms and transgenera-tional adaptation as an outcome of the evolutionary process.

In anthropology, the concept of adaptation has been invoked to describe the fitness of customs and societies to their settings, as implied in the phrase "cultural ecological adaptations" (Steward 1958). However, although some lip service has been given to Darwinian evolutionary theory, few anthropologists have tried to understand the *process* of adaptation in terms of Darwin's postulates of variation and natural selection. An early exception is the neglected work of Keller (1915); more recently Harris (1960), Collins (1969), Campbell (1965), and Alland (1970) have considered the problems and implications of using Darwinian selection theory in studying processes of human sociocultural adaptation and evolution.

THE MEANING OF THEORETICAL NOTIONS

The semantics of theoretical concepts is rather rigidly determined by the logical structure of basic theoretical postulates, which may or may not have been explicitly formulated in any given case. Philosophers of science have carefully examined the logical structure of Newtonian mechanics, for instance, but the structure of Darwinian selection theory remains at present less well understood. Some beginnings have been attempted by Sommerhoff (1950), Williams (1966), Levins (1968), and others, but the task. is by no means simple, nor have biologists been in universal agreement. Let it suffice here to state the conditions for establishing the meaning of theoretical terms.

First, theories contain "primitive" terms, such as the Newtonian "mass," "length," and "time," which are only implicitly defined by their relations to each other (Nagel 1961:90f). Perhaps the analogous primitive terms in selection theory are "variation" and "differential reproduction" (Collins 1969). Next there are terms that receive meaning from derivation from primitive terms and their relations; "velocity" is, for example, a theoretical term derived from the primitive terms of Newtonian theory, and "adaptation" may be similarly derived from the primitive terms of selection theory: a variation that is differentially reproduced is adaptive (Collins 1969).

Theoretical concepts have structural but not substantive meaning (Nagel 1961:93), and thus they must be linked with the world of observable phenomena. To say that an observed biological or cultural trait is adaptive requires a leap from the semantics of observation, experience, and ordinary language to that of theory.[1] The leap is made possible in science by rules of interpretation or correspondence between theoretical and experimental concepts (Nagel 1961:93), which may not be explicitly formulated but which nonetheless are implicit in all scientific inquiry. Such rules are flexible, and may be revised or discarded with changes in experimental instrumentation or extension of areas of inquiry. As we shall see, such as yet imprecise rules in biology allow for a great variety of operational definitions of adaptation, but do not define the theoretical concept itself.

One reason for our concern with the philosophy of scientific theory is that the concept of adaptation has often been referred to as a tautology (Waddington 1960; Burnett and Eisner 1964; Harris 1960). Burnett and Eisner refer to the supposedly "self-evident" characteristic of biological adaptation: "organisms are surviving because they are adapted, and they are adapted because they are surviving." The tautology is implied in Simpson's argument (1953:166-67) that all structures probably have "adaptive value," which, although not immediately demonstrable, must be considered so in principle because they exist. The logical consequence is that in order to prove that a way of life or morphological feature or gene is adaptive one need only show that it exists and is relatively durable, "thereby obviating any need to look for evidence beyond the mere existence of the trait itself, in order to confirm the prediction of the theory of natural selection" (Harris 1960). If, however, a distinction is maintained between an operational definition of adaptation, such as population survival, and the theoretical meaning of the concept, then no such tautology exists, and proof of adaptation will require further evidence and subsumption under laws derived from the postulates of selection theory. The danger of vacuity and tautology arises not only from the lack of distinction between theoretical and operational or experimental concepts, but—more commonly in anthropology—from inattention to the distinction between common usage and theoretical meanings. As a result, Cancian, for one (1968:34-35), advises throwing the concept of adaptation out of anthropology because of its vagueness and the tautologies behind its use. We believe, however, that it would be more useful to explore the assumptions behind the use of adaptation in selection theory, understand the restrictions and implications of its use, and from those logical implications derive testable hypotheses by which anthropologists can decide whether or not the Darwinian

---

[1] Objectivity, and the consequent ability to test and evaluate theories continually, is maintained by the distinction in semantic domains; without such distinction, the argument can be made that a scientist's theory completely controls his observations and that his findings are subjective. See Scheffler (1967) for the objectivity-subjectivity debate.

concept of adaptation should be jetti-soned.

USES OF THE CONCEPT OF ADAPTATION IN BIOLOGY

Adaptation has been variously re-ferred to as the key concept, the cen-tral problem, and the principal explana-tory concept in evolutionary biology. Biological adaptation has been referred to metaphorically as "design and pur-pose" (Simpson, Pittendrigh, and Tif-fany 1957:34), and as "the appearance of design" (Waddington 1960:386). The connotation of design and purpose derives most clearly from the usage of adaptation as "some feature of the or-ganism which serves a proximate end that the observer believes he can discern fully . . ." (Pittendrigh 1958:392). Thus the water beetle was observed by Dar-win to have legs structured for the pur-pose of diving (Darwin 1859). Goal-directed traits are, by definition, orga-nized or nonrandom traits, and thus the loose Darwinian sense of adaptation as suitability or effectiveness (Nicholson 1960) may be amended to the more specific meaning of "nonaccidental ap-propriateness" (Sommerhoff 1950:51).

Nonaccidental organization "is an improbable state in a contingent . . . universe; and as such it can not be merely accepted, it must be explained" (Pittendrigh 1958:395). Some biolo-gists, however, offer no more explana-tion for the improbability of an orga-nized state than its survival: "organisms are surviving because they are adapted, and they are adapted because they are surviving" (Burnett and Eisner 1964). Others refer to the vernacular sense of "fitness"–that is, general well-being–and loosely state that adaptation is "any aspect of the organism that pro-motes its welfare, or the welfare of the species to which it belongs, in the en-vironment it usually inhabits" (Simp-son, Pittendrigh, and Tiffany 1957: 434). These statements leave unan-swered the pertinent questions of (a) the goal of a particular organization and (b) the origin of the information that underlies and causes the organi-zation[2] (Pittendrigh 1958:396).

The emphasis on reproductive suc-cess as an index to or synonym for adaptation frees the study of adapta-tion from the clichés of survival and struggle, and approaches explanation: "Organisms are said to be adapted to their environment, because they are built and act in ways which enable them to survive and to propagate their kind in the environment in which they normally occur" (Dobzhansky 1942: 391). And "Adaptations are those as-pects of the living thing . . . that serve the end of efficient reproduction" (Simpson, Pittendrigh, and Tiffany 1957:35). Elsewhere Simpson (1953) explores the possibility of replacing the notion of adaptation with that of reproductive success.[3]

It is only since the advent of popu-lation genetics in the 1930s that *differ-ential* reproductive success is clearly seen as the process of adaptation. Fitness is defined in accordance with the con-tribution made to the genes of the succeeding generation, and selection produces differential fitness by operat-

---

[2] Or, as Pittendrigh says (1958:397), "How has the information content of the genotype accumulat-ed in face of the universal tendency to maximize entropy?"

[3] Although he is reluctant to do so because "most of the characteristics generally considered to be adaptive seem to be so in the old Darwinian sense of promoting survival of the individual and seem to have little or nothing to do with population repro-duction *per se*" (Simpson 1953:20). His reluctance is probably justified, although for the very different reasons of (1) maintaining the distinction between the theoretical meaning of adaptation and its opera-tional definition, and (2) the open question as to whether the individual or the population is the unit of adaptation.

ing either on factors that determine whether the organism survives to the time of reproduction or on the factors that determine efficiency of reproduction (McKusick 1964:117). Differential reproduction results in "a change, within a population, of the proportions of individuals exhibiting some advantageous trait under a given environment" (Wallace and Srb 1964). Adaptation is thus a consequence of *"heritable variation in different directions . . . followed by differential survival and multiplication of the variants"* (Muller 1949). Focus on differential reproductive success is important in introducing the notion of the relativity of reproductive success, usually relative to other traits or individuals within a population, ideally a Mendelian population.

Selection is thus the complement of fitness, and is essential in the study of adaptation. As Fisher (1954) points out, the selectionist need not demonstrate that all characters are adaptive. In rejecting alternative theories like Lamarckism or special creation, however, he must be prepared to claim that all genuinely adaptive characters are acquired through selection. Thus the only general answer to the questions about the goals and origins of adaptation is "natural selection." Fisher states that selection is a device for generating a high degree of improbability, through differential reproductive success (cited in Pittendrigh 1958:397).

Natural selection is, of course, a result of the setting of populations that increase according to Malthusian principles in environments that are limited by nature: not all organisms can succeed, given limited resources. Most authors have made it clear that adaptation must always be understood in relation to the environment. To Dobzhansky (1962: 16), adaptation is "the harmony between the organism and its environments." Earlier (1942:395) he wrote, "The general

fitness of a genotype, its adaptive value, is evidently a function of its response in different environments." To Prosser (1960:577), adaptation is "the unique fitness of a species to its environment"; to Dansereau (1957:204), "the response of various forms of life to the *stimuli* and *compulsions* of the environment." But a statement about the relation between an organism and its environment may be misleading. All these statements tend to obscure the "fundamental asymmetry of the relationship, the fact that the essential nonrandomness of adaptation is due entirely to the organism's (not the environment's) capacity to accumulate and retain information both phylogenetically and ontogenetically" (Pittendrigh 1958:391). And Nicholson (1960:510-11) argues that adaptation is not some kind of balance between organisms and their environments, or a phenotypic optimum. "The adaptation of an organism as a whole should rather be regarded as an obligatory compromise resulting from the various selection pressures to which it is subject and from varying degrees of resistance to adaptation in different directions." The picture is not simple, and Levins (1968) points out that adaptations do not always relate to *particular* environments, but in many instances to the *pattern* of the environment. But all Darwinian biologists agree that the environment is a major variable, perhaps *the* major variable:

If Darwin's natural selection is more than the tautology — "What survives, survives" — it is an emphasis on environment as the major variable; organisms are passively chosen or rejected by it—like souls on a Calvinistic judgment day. Lamarck emphasized the organism as the major variable; organisms actively achieve their adaptations—as salvation is won by good deeds. Both factors, of course, operate . . . [Gerard 1960:256]

The "Roman Catholic" view of adaptation—that organisms win their salvation by good deeds—may be justified when biologists use the concept of adaptation as system-specific adjustment. To Wallace and Srb (1964) adaptation is "an individual affair, as the clever physiological or morphological alteration made under environmental stress." For Dansereau (1957:204) it is "achieved through an adjustment of [the] requirements and tolerances [of the organism] to the elements of the habitat(s)." Ashby (1960:58) says, "A form of behaviour is adaptive if it maintains the essential variables . . . within physiological limits." And Sommerhoff (1950:195) states: "The value of a biological variable is "adapted" to the value of another variable if both variables are directively correlated and an antecedent value of the latter variable figures as a coenetic variable in this correlation."

The ability or capacity to adjust within a system may be adaptive in the selectionist ("Calvinist") sense, and in fact often is, for the ability to do so may be heritable and thus subject to natural selection; and directively correlated adjustments are generally adaptive because "in being made they increase the chances that the individual will survive in his new surroundings" (Wallace and Srb 1964). However, it is important to understand this system-specific concept of adaptation as belonging to general systems theory rather than to selection theory. Adaptation or adjustment within systems belongs properly to formal functional analysis, which may tell us *how* something works, but not *why*. A full explanation requires deduction from theoretical postulates and laws, which in evolutionary biology are supplied by the Darwinian theory of natural selection.

Adaptation is properly a technical term in selection theory, although many of the statements we have quoted are models or metaphors. Muller (1949) makes clear the technical meaning of the concept: "*heritable* variation in *different* directions . . . followed by *differential* survival and *multiplication* of the variants." Williams (1966) also provides a technical definition of adaptation, as the consequence of differential selection among alternative alleles or individuals in a Mendelian population. Pittendrigh (1958:397) also makes clear the role of the postulates of variation and differential reproduction:

As novelty is thrust into the inherited message by mutation and recombination, there is a slow net gain by the population gene pool of information with respect to reproductive efficiency. Alternative versions of the inherited message make larger or smaller contributions to the ancestry of future generations in proportion to their effect on the efficiency of the genotype to perpetuate itself by reproduction.

Thus, to quote Samuel Butler, "a hen is only an egg's way of making another egg" (cited in Pittendrigh 1958:398). We might here add that neither selection theory nor Samuel Butler says anything about the hen's role in perpetuating a population or species. Her egg-laying success will contribute information to the gene pool relative to that contributed by other hens, but her theoretically important role, and that of the rooster that fertilized her egg, is simply to see that the egg from which she herself was hatched results in another egg. If the traits she possesses result, over several generations, in increased progeny relative to those of other hens in the population, then they may be adaptive.

OPERATIONAL DEFINITIONS AND MEASUREMENT OF ADAPTATION

The theoretical notion of adaptation is defined by its derivation from the abstract postulates of selection theory:

an adaptive trait is one that reproduces itself. As we have already seen, theoretical notions are empty of substance. If theoretical notions are to be useful in explaining anything, they must somehow relate to the real world, to phenomena we try to understand and about which we try to make true statements. The scientist must use operational definitions in order to measure empirical things.

The basic problem in this area for evolutionary biologists appears to be that the easily measured variables are not always the theoretically important ones (Williams 1966:106). If the theoretical meaning of adaptation is differential reproduction of variations, then the logical way to measure it would be to count the second- or third-generation descendants of an organism with a supposedly adaptive trait and compare this count with the mean of its contemporaries' descendants. Even this technique does not give a true measure of adaptation, for it depends on correlation with the factor of reproductive success, which may be affected by chance elements such as natural disasters and, in small populations, genetic drift. But "more often than not, a highly successful organism would have been of above average fitness" (Williams 1966:103).

Measurements of comparative population success are more common than measurements of individual adaptation, and more difficult to achieve. It takes more time and more energy to measure the reproductive success of most populations over several generations than to note the current apparent success of a population. A common measure of current success is the numbers of individuals, adjusted by comparisons of ecologically equivalent types, equal areas, similar stages in the life cycle, and so on. But there are real problems connected with this technique, problems of which anthropologists should be aware,

since they often advocate it (e.g., Harris 1960). For instance, if the diatom populations of the North Atlantic are larger and denser than those of Lake Geneva, are they better adapted? Where do we stop in bringing in correction factors (Williams 1966:103)?

One alternative is to measure the current rate of change in the size of a population, with the assumption that a better adapted population will increase more rapidly than another population (Odum and Allee 1956). Others, however, particularly the proponents of group selection, argue that a reduction in number, population regulation, or numerical stability might be a better measure of adaptation (e.g. Wynne-Edwards 1962, Dunbar 1960). On the other hand, Brown (1958) believes that wide fluctuations in number rather than population stability should be the measure of adaptation.

Lewontin (1958) suggests that the fitness of populations be measured by the degree of ecological versatility, the number of environments in which a population can survive. But this would depend as much "on the classification of habitats as on the properties of populations" (Williams 1966:106), and the populations of some amphibious animals would have to be considered better adapted than the great majority of birds and mammals.

The degree of assurance of long-term population survival has been offered as a measure of population fitness (Thoday, cited in Williams 1966:106), but no objective measurement has been offered beyond the measurement of current population success by demographic variables and the imperfect correlation of the results with long-term survival and extinction. Large and increasing populations may very well have greater chances of surviving over time than small and decreasing ones, but the predictions are extremely unreliable

(Williams 1966:106). Furthermore, it may not be correct to assume that natural selection always promotes the long-term survival of populations, for in cases of increasing ecological specialization, adaptation might be concomitant with increasing vulnerability to extinction. Williams cites an example of decrease in numbers brought about by the evolution of the slave-making instinct in certain groups of ants (Emerson 1960).

In discussing organisms, Stern (1970:44) defines adaptation as "any transmissible characteristic of an organism that by its presence permits an interaction with the environment that causes its possessors to produce, on the average, more offspring than would be produced in its absence." He goes on to caution against using the concept of survival in determining the fitness of organisms, and would remove it altogether from the definition of adaptation. He defines the adaptation of a *population* (1970:56) as any characteristic of that population which causes, on the average, a higher rate of increase in size than would occur in its absence. Williams maintains that such characteristics are to be distinguished from those of the individuals within the population. In fact, the members of a group comprise the characteristics of that group.

Other problems emerge when population survival is used as a criterion of adaptation (for proponents of this criterion, see Burnett and Eisner 1964, Dobzhansky 1942:391, Wallace and Srb 1964, Huxley 1954:3). The development of an adaptation is no evidence that it was necessary to the survival of a population or species (Williams 1966:28). Thus, although the white coat of the polar bear may be advantageous in its snowy environment, it may not be necessary to the survival of the species. If a hypothetical mutation should result in the birth of some polar bears with pink coats, they might not survive *as well* as those with white coats, but if a few pink polar bears stayed alive and reproduced themselves, albeit poorly, there are no grounds for precluding further adaptations, such as hunting for longer periods of time or at night, and a declining population may in fact eventually increase in numbers. There *are* "necessary" adaptations, such as the polar bear's lungs, but the argument remains that the mere presence of an adaptation does not signal its necessity, either for the individual or for the population. "It is evidence only that during the evolutionary development of the adaptation the genes that augmented its development survived *at a greater rate* than those that did not" (Williams 1966:29).

The presence of an adaptive trait does often cause the species or population to be more numerous and widespread than it would be without it. Nicholson (1956, 1960), however, believes that improved adaptation may have only a slight effect on numbers, because even slight increases in population may greatly intensify the negative-density factors that normally check population growth. Thus a population that survived in certain numbers might eventually be replaced by a population with an advantageous trait, but there is no reason to assume that the latter population would survive in greater numbers.

One common method of determining the adaptiveness of traits, rather than of population per se, is to show parallel variation in space or time for several species, assuming constant environment, and to relate traits to features of the environment, such as size to temperature, color to substrate, or hunting behavior to type of prey (Levins 1968:10). A good example of this technique in anthropology is the study of fur trappers and rubber tappers (Murphy and Steward 1956). However, many characteristics of organisms and populations are not explicable as adaptations to particular environments—degree of homeostasis, amount of polymorphism, extent of spatial differentiation, sensitivity to natural selection, and so on. Levins (1968:11) suggests that these and other traits may be regarded as "adaptations to the *pattern* of the environment in space and time, to temporal variability, to environmental uncertainty. . . . Levins' approach is to develop theoretical models of adaptive strategies for a variety of environmental patterns. If such models proved to be successful, their predictions might be matched against observed strategies, and the degree of adaptation might be seen as the degree of fit to the optimal adaptive strategy generated by the model. For example, anthropologists might use the model of hunting behavior suggested by the work of MacArthur and Pianka (1966) to measure the adaptiveness of human hunting behaviors. For hunters who must chase their game but need not search for it, it is advantageous to specialize in the choice of food. For those who must search for their game, advantage lies in pursuing any capturable prey that can be caught quickly; "But if pursuit is long compared to search, the energy invested in pursuit might be better invested in searching for the preferred items" (Levins 1968:30). The use of models of adaptive strategy to measure adaptation awaits empirical testing and subsequent refinement of the models. However, this approach may avoid the problems inherent in trying to measure population adaptations by comparing populations with each other; instead, a population's adaptive strategy may be compared with a model derived from some of the theoretical notions of selection theory.

The measurements of adaptation outlined here, regarded in a sense as operational definitions of a theoretical concept, are varied and at times contradictory. Their variety should not worry us, for it is common in all domains of science for the connections between theoretical concepts and experimental notions to be many and flexible, reflecting the differing experimental techniques and instruments of the observers and the ranges of their subject matter. The contradictions, however—such as that between measuring rate of change of size versus measuring the degree of population stability—do reflect differing understandings of the theoretical meaning of adaptation. By exploring one major difference in interpretation—or degree of strictness in the use of the theoretical postulates of selection theory—within biology, we hope to provide some help to anthropologists in their study of cultural adaptation and evolution.

Units, Levels, and Goals of Adaptation

. . . Adaptation is a special and onerous concept that should be used only where it is really necessary. When it must be recognized, it should be attributed to no higher a level of organization than is demanded by the evidence. In explaining adaptation, one should assume the adequacy of the simplest form of natural selection, that of alternative alleles in Mendelian populations, unless the evidence clearly shows that this theory does not suffice [Williams 1966:4-5].

A source of conceptual confusion in biology, perpetuated in anthropology, is the failure to define properly the units, levels, and goals of adaptation within the framework of selection theory, and to restrict the use of that concept appropriately. A focus of the confusion has been the argument over group versus individual selection and adaptation. Two central questions (Williams 1966) are: (1) Are individual mechanisms designed to promote their own reproductive success or that of a larger group, such as a population or species? (2) Do populations or species have adaptive mechanisms of their own, or is such apparent organization merely a statistical result of individual adaptations? In other words, is there a conceptual difference between a population of adapted bumblebees and an adapted population of bumblebees?

Williams (1966) has provided a substantial argument against group selection, showing that, given the postulates of selection theory—variation and differential reproduction within a population—there is no need to look beyond the level of individual reproductive units for explanations of adaptation, and hence individual organisms, not populations or species, are the units of adaptation. Those who argue for populations or species or even local groups of unrelated individuals as the units of adaptation forget that the contribution of population genetics to the study of evolution and adaptation has been its concern with variation, selection, and adaptation *within* populations, not *between* populations (Lewontin 1958).

In biological selection theory the primary unit is the gene rather than the genotype or phenotype. It is the gene that is potentially immortal, whereas genotypes and phenotypes disappear with the death of the individual organism. Selection, of course, acts on phenotypes only. *Gene* may be defined as "that which segregates and recombines with appreciable frequency" (Williams 1966:23-24). Genes are quite stable: although they may have a mutation rate of 10^{-4} to 10^{-10} per generation, there is evidence for selection coefficients in nature that exceed mutation rates by 1 to many multiples of 10, and thus the selective accumulation of genes in nature provides a good deal of stability. "In evolutionary theory, a

gene could be defined as any hereditary information for which there is a favorable or unfavorable selection bias equal to several or many times its rate of endogenous change" (Williams 1966:25). Genes have a phenotypic effect on fitness in that if individuals bearing gene A replace themselves by reproduction to a greater extent than those with gene A', and if the population is so large that we can rule out chance as the explanation, the individuals with A would be, as a group, more fit than those with A' (Williams 1966:25). The mean effect on individual fitness of A would be favorable and of A' unfavorable. Thus mean individual fitness is maximized, although in some cases a gene might be favorably selected not because "its phenotypic expression favors an individual's reproduction, but because it favors the reproduction of close relatives of that individual" (Williams 1966:26). (We shall have occasion to discuss this complication of selection later.)

According to this theory, an adaptation is a mechanism "designed to promote the success of an individual organism, as measured by the extent to which it contributes genes to later generations of the population of which it is a member" (Williams 1966:97). (Hamilton [1964] has termed this measurement "inclusive fitness.") The unit of adaptation is thus the individual organism and its offspring, or, strictly, the genes carried by them.

Group selection (Wynne-Edwards 1962) concerns alternative groups or populations made up of individuals that need not be closely related. Group selection results in what Williams calls "biotic adaptation," and what we shall refer to as group adaptation; that is, a mechanism designed to promote the success of a biota, either a community, a taxonomic group, or, most often, a single population. As a corollary the natural selection of individuals might be opposed to or compromise the development of group-related adaptations. Examples of group-adaptive mechanisms are frequently population-limiting devices, purportedly designed to keep the population size below the carrying capacity of the environment, or "social adaptations" such as "altruistic" behavior, supposedly designed not to perpetuate the reproduction of one's own young but to aid other, unrelated individuals.

It is important to distinguish between the goals of an adaptation and any incidental effects it might have on the population or species or individual. An example of misattributed adaptation may be seen in the hypothetical case of a fox on its way to the henhouse for the first time after a heavy snowfall. It makes a path through the snow with its feet, and on subsequent occasions uses that path to get back to the henhouse, saving a lot of time and energy, and thus perhaps ensuring its survival through the period of its reproduction and care for its young. The fox's feet are adaptive for running and walking, but there are no grounds for assuming that they are adaptive for efficient trail-blazing. The fact that they do actually blaze a trail very efficiently is an accident as far as the fox's feet are concerned; but the sensory mechanisms by which the fox perceives the most familiar and least obstructed routes and its motivation to follow the path of least effort might indeed be adaptive mechanisms (Williams 1966:12-13). Likewise, and more central to our argument, the interactions between a parent and its offspring may be adaptive mechanisms "directly concerned with reproductive survival of the parent and the somatic survival (for later reproduction) of the young [but] there is no need to postulate an additional function of survival of the species" (Wil-

liams 1966:161). The survival of the species may be an incidental effect of the adaptation, but it should in no sense be seen as its goal, any more than the goal of Newton's famous apple was to make a contribution to his theory of physics.

But what about the so-called social adaptations, or cooperative and altruistic behavior among unrelated individuals? Is it not necessary to invoke some higher level of adaptive organization than the reproductive unit? One frequently cited example of social adaptation is the self-sacrifice of sterile workers in a bee colony. Williams points out, however, that social insects typically live in colonies consisting of one or both parents, or sisters, together with numerous offspring of various ages, in effect a very extended family. The workers may be sterile, but those they help are their siblings, who carry the same genes. The permanent sterility of a large proportion of individuals may be explained by selection for a gene that augments "altruistic" care of younger offspring by older siblings; this behavior might be favorably selected for in certain conditions because the aid provided would go to other individuals with the same genes (see Williams 1966: 197-98).

Thus the altruistic behavior of worker bees is adaptive in the theoretical sense, for it facilitates the reproduction of the information it expresses. But how about behavior that is directed toward clearly unrelated individuals? One example of this is the "helper" phenomenon among certain California woodpeckers. Helpers are unmated birds who assist breeding pairs, apparently unrelated to them, in nest construction and other chores. Is this helper trait a mechanism for the reproduction of the population rather than of the individual with the trait? Williams points out that the behavior exhibited includes only those traits or elements that form part of the normal reproductive behavior of the species. It may be interpreted as misplaced parental care, one example of "irrelevant" reproductive behavior found widely in nature (others include homosexuality and prepubertal mating). "The helper phenomenon can be attributed to selection pressures for the maintenance of a certain pattern of parental behavior, with a less-than-perfect system of timing mechanisms for regulating this behavior" (Williams 1966:208). It may be a consequence of a certain economy in the information load of the organism: it is more efficient in some cases to have available a variety of stimuli, relatively unspecific as to timing. The general behavior *is* adaptive when the individual reproduces itself and cares for its own, but it is *not* an adaptive mechanism for the goal of the survival of the population or species.

Similarly, the warning signals of deer and rabbits in flight have been regarded as social adaptations designed for the reproductive success of the population. Do they not serve to warn other individuals in the area of possible danger and thus reduce the pressures of predation? It is possible to see those raised tails of the deer as mechanisms designed to warn dependent young and to divert the attention of a possible predator; it may be only an incidental effect of living in close proximity to other members of the species that such behavior results in reduced rates of predation on populations, some members of which may be "accidentally" alerted by the raised tails of deer protecting their young. That the consequences of helpful behavior may in fact contribute to the survival of the population does not ensure the continuance of the genes of those helpful individuals, and thus cannot, given the meaning of adaptation in selection theory, be considered adap-

tive for the end of population fitness.

Williams suggests, however, that cooperative and altruistic behavior among human beings and perhaps other mammals such as some primates and porpoises may be due to the evolution of systems of personal friendships and animosities that transcend the limits of family relationship. Certainly in primitive societies reproductive success depends on stable interactions of personalities, facilitating food and mate exchange. Altruistic behavior is not completely self-sacrificing or unrelated to survival and reproductive success, for although a man is not necessarily consciously motivated to help unrelated others in hopes of future payment, such behavior may be selected for if his help is occasionally reciprocated by others. A person who maximizes his friendships and minimizes his antagonisms will have an evolutionary advantage, selection favoring those characters that promote the capacity to optimize personal interrelationships. The behavior is indeed group-related, and its immediate goal is the well-being of some other individual, often genetically unrelated. But ultimately it should not be seen as an adaptation for group benefit, but rather an adaptation developed by the differential survival of individuals, designed for the perpetuation of the genes of the individual providing the benefit to another, working through the probability of later repayment (Williams 1966:93-96).

The concept of organization is no less troublesome in animal biology than it is in anthropology. Central to proponents of group selection is the notion that some groups are more adaptively organized than others, or simply that groups or populations have adaptive organization. However, statistical organization, as evidenced by the maintenance of population parameters such as mean size, weight, age distribution, and so on, does not necessarily imply functional or adaptive organization, and many supposed group adaptations may be seen as the statistical summation of individual adaptations. For example, the gregariousness of wolf packs is not a feature of adaptive organization, facilitating the reproductive success of the pack, but rather a consequence of the necessary conditions for the fulfillment of individual wolf food preferences (Williams 1966:218): it takes more than one wolf to bring down an elk.

Dominance-subordinance hierarchies may also be viewed as statistical consequences of "a compromise made by each individual in its competition for food, mates, and other resources. Each compromise is adaptive, but not the statistical summation" (Williams 1966: 218). And what appears to be a functional division of labor in large herds of mammals, such as musk ox and caribou herds, in which adult males appear to sort themselves in order to protect others in the group, may be interpreted rather as statistical sorting of thresholds to various internal and environmental stimuli (Williams 1966:218): older males may be more likely to stand their ground or behave in some other "defensive" manner than younger animals and females. Adaptive divisions of labor do exist within families and colonies of social insects, and in certain human organizations, but it remains to be demonstrated that group selection results in populations adapted because of division of labor.

Another supposedly adaptive feature of populations is their ability to limit their size by periodic reproductive failure: organisms are infertile or produce abnormal offspring with little chance of survival, mothers neglect their young, lemmings run into the sea. Is reproduction, then, adjusted through some adaptive mechanism to the needs of the population? Is high fecundity a response to

high mortality rates and low fecundity to low mortality rates, thus maintaining population stability? This assumption, which is related to the notions of group selection, has been criticized by Lack (1954), who, in analyzing clutch sizes among birds, showed rather that mortality is dependent upon fecundity. High fecundity in a limited environment is checked by carrying capacity or some other factor, and thus high fecundity beyond or approaching a certain point simply increases the number of individuals that must die without issue, given limited environmental and parental resources. Lack's work shows that decreased resources per zygote results in increased mortality rates in birds and in mammals, among which both death rates and litter sizes increase.

That population size may be checked by density-dependent factors (Nicholson 1960) does not in any way prove that populations are adapted. That something is beneficial to a population does not mean that it is the purpose of an adaptation. Here we take issue with Stott's (1962) conclusion that such factors as reproductive failure following stress during pregnancy among human populations are "mechanisms which have been evolved to obviate" the calamities of overpopulation. We agree that changes in fertility due to stress or other density-dependent factors may occur in human populations, but we disagree with Stott's conclusion that this has been selected for. How could it be, when selection for something—the adaptive process—requires its maximization of mean reproductive success relative to other alternatives within the population? And here we have a case of minimization of mean reproductive success: those people adversely affected by density-induced stress reproduce themselves less than other people do, and thus their genes diminish in relation to those of the total population. His argument might be saved by empirical demonstration that a decrease in the number of viable babies produced by an individual better ensured the survival of those offspring, through an ultimately beneficial change in the ratio of people to resources, but it is theoretically wrong to say that decreased fecundity is a mechanism evolved to obviate the calamities of overpopulation for the population as a whole.

Adaptations can be simply and elegantly explained by reference to the postulates of selection theory: "Natural selection arises from a reproductive competition among the individuals, and ultimately among the genes, in a Mendelian population. A gene is selected on one basis only, its average effectiveness in producing individuals able to maximize the gene's representation in future generations" (Williams 1966:251). If these kinds of adaptations can be used to explain group and population survival, as an incidental and statistical result of individual adaptations, then there is no need to refer to group selection and adaptation. Furthermore, an advantage of looking to selection within populations, rather than among populations, is that the Mendelian population can itself be seen as a major part of the environment, providing for each individual some resources, competition for other resources, a social structure favoring the possession of specific social adaptations, and other aspects of the demographic environment (such as age-related probability distributions of death, of sex ratios among social contacts, and so on). And finally, speciation may be important taxonomically and in considerations of evolutionary change through the development of barriers to genetic recombination, but it has no special significance for the study of adaptation. A species is not an adapted unit any more than a population

tion is—probably less so—and there are no mechanisms that function for the survival of the species. "The only adaptations that clearly exist express themselves in genetically defined individuals and have only one ultimate goal, the maximal perpetuation of the genes responsible for the visible adaptive mechanisms" (Williams 1966:252).

Units and levels of adaptive organization are especially problematic in anthropology. In many instances it is quite difficult to adhere to Williams' model of variation and differential reproduction as applied to the parent-offspring unit of adaptation, and to argue against the existence of human altruistic behavior—whether shamanistic or medical healing or chiefly distribution of food during periods of scarcity—which is designed to benefit much larger groups of people than one's own relations. We shall discuss this problem in more detail shortly.

GENERAL AND SPECIFIC ADAPTATION

Anthropological evolutionary theory has generally been limited to the progressive course of evolution. White, however (1949, 1959), has made a distinction between general and specific evolution. The same distinction has been made in biology. General adaptation commonly refers to an improvement in the effectiveness of adaptation of species in general over time (Brown 1958; Waddington 1961; Huxley 1954). The anthropologist Leslie White (1949) measures such improvement in terms of increased efficiency in energy utilization, as do Yehudi Cohen (1968), and Marvin Harris (1971), and Sahlins and Service (1960). According to Thoday (1953, 1958), such general adaptation serves in the long run to make populations less susceptible to extinction. Other long-term trends in general adaptation include specialization, adaptive radiation, and, according to Huxley (1954), in most cases restriction and stabilization.

The features of general adaptation are invoked as evolutionary theories, but in most cases the stories they tell are just that: narratives that, eliminating exceptions and environmental variables, tell how, by and large, things go. This kind of narrative is not a theory, for it has no logical structure from which observed events may be deduced. The features of general adaptation might be useful indices of the theoretical notion of adaptation if they were empirically demonstrated—which Williams (1966) says is not the case in biology, and which has not been convincingly done in anthropology. To refer to a feature of the course of biological or cultural evolution as adaptation really begs the question, ignores the postulates of selection theory, and tells us nothing about why particular adaptations have evolved and persisted. This last question is the one to ask if we are to have recourse to the explanatory power of Darwinian selection theory, and are to test that theory in order to justify its further use.

THE CONCEPT OF ADAPTATION IN ANTHROPOLOGY
EVOLUTIONISTS

Shortly after the publication of *The Origin of Species* in 1859 many of Darwin's contemporaries noted that the idea of evolution had been in the air for some time. And so it had. Darwin's grandfather Erasmus and the poet Goethe both published theories of evolution, and surely no student can forget Lamarck, whose error (the inheritance of acquired characteristics) is used as a negative example when Darwinian theory is discussed. But Lamarck himself was an evolutionist.

It is well known among sociologists that Herbert Spencer was the author of the phrase "survival of the fittest."

Darwin, Spencer, and A. R. Wallace, who independently discovered the principle of natural selection, were the three great evolutionists of the nineteenth century.

Darwin and Wallace found the mechanisms in nature responsible for speciation and thus elevated evolutionism from philosophical speculation to a powerful explanatory theory. Briefly, they noted that organisms produce more offspring than can survive in a given environment and that such offspring display inherent variation that is likely to be differentially advantageous in a specific environmental context. They saw variation arising in organisms, and selection as an environmental process operating on this variation.

Spencer's phrase "survival of the fittest" would appear to meet these criteria of natural selection, for it suggests struggle, but Spencer was a universalist who saw evolution as an inevitable process. All matter shall proceed in time from the simple to the complex, from the unordered to the highly ordered. Such a process is of necessity independent of environmental variation. It should be noted, however, that Spencer, impressed with Darwin's theory, modified his own position on evolution after the publication of *The Origin of Species* and *The Descent of Man.* Much of Spencer's writing on social evolution bears witness to this influence.

Spencer, along with Durkheim, is responsible for the concept of the superorganic in sociology and anthropology. The concept is useful when it is limited to an examination of social networks and behavioral systems as systems (culture and society tend to follow certain internal rules), but it has proved dangerous and limited when it is misapplied, as it has been (particularly by White in the United States and the structural-functionalists in England). White in particular sees culture as an emergent form that is *sui generis* and subject only to its own rules. Thus he would have anthropologists follow the golden rule of Durkheim: social facts can be derived only from social facts; or, in American terms, culture can be explained only by culture. Such a view has until recently inhibited a true ecological approach to human behavior, although for many years White, joined only by Childe in England, kept the idea of evolution alive in anthropology.

A model of progressive evolution was applied to anthropological phenomena by L. H. Morgan (1877). Although Harris (1968) and other authors have attempted to show that Morgan was not a unilineal evolutionist, his scheme was similar to Spencer's in its failure to provide mechanisms for change and its general neglect of natural selection. Social development proceeds in a relatively set track. The driving force in Morgan's evolution is some kind of metaphysical entity, although from time to time he demonstrated an awareness that the environment plays a role in selection. He noted, for example, differences in cultural development in the Old and New Worlds, and recognized the role of diffusion in the distribution of similar traits in different geographical areas.

Tylor (1871) too was an evolutionist. At times he adhered rather strictly to the model of Spencer, Darwin, and Morgan, but his interest in material culture and diffusion drew his attention more strongly to the influence of various societies on the general development of behavioral systems. For all early evolutionists, however, natural selection in the context of a specific ecological niche was, at the very least, secondary to the overall process of evolution, which proceeds independently of outside forces. For these scholars adaptation was an axiom of the system

rather than the outcome of some interactive process between organisms or populations and their environments.

V. Gordon Childe (1936, 1951) stands out among those anthropologists who have been labeled unilineal evolutionists. Although he was a Marxist, his view of the evolutionary process was quite close to the Darwinian model. Childe recognized evolution as a process in which the carrying capacity of an environmental niche was raised through technological innovation so that it could support an increased number of people. He labeled these changes "technological revolutions." Thus, like the Darwinians, Childe saw evolutionary outcomes in demographic terms. He also suggested that significant evolutionary developments that were to have wide-ranging consequences for the species as a whole were likely to occur only under certain environmental conditions. Childe's theory accounts for the difference between sites of origin of particular social forms and their later appearance elsewhere. Thus while his focus was unilineal (he was interested in sequences of increasing complexity), his theory suggests that the process of cultural adaptation is the result of natural selection. There is much to criticize in Childe's specific schemes, but in general his theoretical contribution to evolutionary theory within the framework of anthropology remains outstanding.

Leslie White (1949, 1959, and many other publications) has steadfastly adhered to the evolutionary model of Spencer, Tylor, and Morgan. White has been concerned with progressive unilineal evolution measured by the amount of surplus energy produced by a society. His orientation is primarily technological rather than environmental. White has also concerned himself with correlations among technological growth, population increase, and internally adaptive social forms. He has been followed in this by Service (1962) and Dole (1960). The cumulative aspect of evolution has been investigated by Robert Carneiro (1962, 1963, 1966, 1967), who in several papers has attempted to construct scales that demonstrate the order of priority among technological and social forms. The evolution of political organization has been investigated by Service (1962) and Fried (1960, 1968). Fried has been particularly concerned with political evolution and has drawn a distinction between pristine and secondary states, more or less following Childe's concept of the site of origin and diffusion. In a series of papers Marshall Sahlins (1957, 1958) has investigated relationships between economic organization and social structure, particularly family structure. He has also suggested (1961) that the segmentary lineage, a structural form limited to a few African societies (Sahlins restricts the term to the Nuer and Tiv), is an adaptive device for what he refers to as predatory expansion.

Karl A. Wittfogel (1957) has argued that a form of autocratic society (oriental despotism) develops in irrigation societies in which large-scale waterworks operate to distribute water over the cropping area. Such waterworks, he claims, require precision and control over both manpower and resources, leading to the formation of bureaucracies that come increasingly under the control of an autocratic central power. This theory, which has been widely supported as well as attacked, is Marxist in the sense that social and political organization is seen as the outcome of the productive process and the control of scarce resources. The scheme, however, allows for multilineal evolution, for oriental despotism is seen as only one of several possible adaptations to

certain ecological conditions, one specific possible outcome of the evolutionary process.

Julian Steward is unique among anthropologists in the forties and fifties in his advocacy of multilineal evolution based on what he calls cultural ecology (see Steward 1937, 1958). He has concerned himself with the development of levels of sociocultural integration in the context of similar (not identical) environments. He attempts to pick out specific features of the ecological setting which interact with the social system to produce types of exploitive organization (see in particular Murphy and Steward 1956). His major focus is on social organization associated with environmental exploitation and its relation to what he calls the cultural core. The cultural core, a flexible concept, concerns those aspects of culture and social organization that are tied more or less directly to technology.

Steward sees levels of sociocultural organization as persistent forms. Many levels may occur together in technologically complex societies. His method of analysis is in many ways close to that of Marx, although Marx emphasized a unilineal scheme, primarily because of his major interest, the development of European society. Steward's multilinearity places him nearer to Darwin than the other social evolutionists discussed so far (with the exception of Childe), but his reliance on the superorganic and his extreme selectiveness in choice of ecological variables removes him from the camp of those ecologists who adhere closely to the Darwinian framework.

Among archaeologists B. J. Meggers has been the strongest advocate of White's view of evolution and adaptation. This is clear both in her 1960 article "The Law of Cultural Evolution as a Practical Research Tool" and in the earlier (1954) "Environmental Limitations on the Development of Culture." Meggers attempts to show that increases in energy output produce an alteration in the general cultural product, and that a decline in such resources results in a decline in cultural complexity. Finally she introduces data on the Basin Plateau tribes to show that cultures with limited food resources remain primitive. Since evolution involves increased efficiency in environmental exploitation, Meggers' analysis is by no means without merit, but it fails to provide any information on the processes that are involved in what she would call progression, regression, or stability.

Meggers' approach to the environment is typical of what we have already noted among most anthropologists who place themselves within the evolutionary school. Calling forth the still puzzling case of the growth and decline of the Mayan civilization, Meggers (1954: 815) suggests that it can be explained by her law of environmental limitation on culture: "the level to which a culture can develop is dependent upon the agricultural potentiality of the environment it occupies." She goes on to note that in areas in which the discovery or invention of new techniques does not occur, and when such cultures are far from centers of diffusion, a culture may stabilize at a level lower than that set by environmental limitations. The Maya are seen as a group that developed a complex civilization under one set of environmental conditions and then migrated to an area that could not support the attained cultural level. Thus the Maya represent a case of cultural regression.

While Meggers' analysis of the rise and fall of Mayan civilization has been criticized, we think successfully, from many standpoints, her theoretical position deserves discussion. Such a position rests on the notion of carrying capacity, the demographic level attainable by a population under specific environmental and technological conditions. Meggers' emphasis on the limiting effect of the environment on the population, however, blinds her to the active role played by environmental factors in natural selection.

With the exception of Steward, the anthropologists discussed so far have emphasized general (that is, unilineal) evolution, although most are aware that local adaptations to environment are part of the evolutionary process. They are concerned with general historical development of the human species and abstract those technological trends that in White's terms allow for greater energy production. Such emphasis on the cumulative aspect of evolution places them in a position analogous to that of paleontologists, who attempt to derive evolutionary sequences from fossil material. Their tendency to ignore specific trends in relation to ecological conditions, however, removes them from the kind of reconstruction that paleontologists would ideally like to make: the reconstruction of temporal sequences of emergent forms *in relation to environmental selection*. The unilineal approach forces one to factor out environmental influences.

It must be admitted that such an approach has some merit in the investigation of human social development. Human beings belong to a single species, come more and more to occupy a single niche, are capable of changing cultural behavior through diffusion, and to some extent are masters over their own development. On the other hand, the discovery of those mechanisms that underlie change requires careful attention to rather specific evolutionary episodes. The grand overview commits the sin of omission and risks superficiality.

Sahlins and Service (1960) have distinguished between what they call general and specific evolution, and Sahlins at least (1957, 1958, 1964) has offered several interesting analyses of social organization under varying ecological conditions. In their 1960 work they attempt to identify certain principles that act as mechanisms of change and retardation in cultural development. The most interesting of these are the "law of cultural dominance" (high comparative efficiency leads to greater all-round adaptability) and the "law of evolutionary potential" (less specialized cultures have a greater potential for change than those that are highly specialized). These laws are analogous to laws in evolutionary biology and are clearly inspired by them, but the book in general is not intended as an analogy to Darwinian theory. White's rather than Darwin's measure of adaptation is employed.

As we pointed out earlier, the great question in evolution concerns the second dictionary meaning of the word, the process of modification to fit new conditions, and those mechanisms that cause such modification. The cultural paleontological approach is capable only of showing that the process has occurred, but even the laws of cultural dominance and evolutionary potential tell us little of the dynamics of the process. The progressive evolutionary approach, which stresses universal or unilineal evolution, tells us nothing about sources of variation. The rejection of natural selection which accompanies most versions of unilineal evolution, with no substitute mechanism for the maintenance or rejection of traits, reduces such theories to mere catalogues of significant parts of the developmental process. The failure to use comparative population as an index of adaptation (a method not without difficulty) takes these cultural-evolutionary models just

that much further from the Darwinian model.

NONEVOLUTIONARY ANTHROPOLOGISTS

Kroeber (1939) was one of the first anthropologists to examine the relationship between environment and culture. The main objective of his work is the analysis of historical relationships among cultures, but Kroeber lists environmental relationships as one major line of inquiry. His bias is clear when he suggests that the concept of a culture area is a means to the end of understanding the historic events of a specific culture. Nonetheless, Kroeber admits that every society is conditioned by its subsistence base. Environment is seen as a stabilizer of culture. It holds it fast in the sense that certain aspects of culture must be adapted to the environment. The environment tends to inhibit new variation because once an adaptation has occurred it becomes difficult to change. In addition, adaptation to a specific environment will make it difficult for a culture to enter another environment. If for some reason a social group does enter a new territory, it is then subject to change.

Kroeber's study compares culture areas modified from the original scheme published by Wissler in 1917. His natural areas are based upon vegetation zones, which reflect climate and soil, support local fauna, and are strictly empirical.

The work is particularly interesting for its attempt to review demographic data in relation to natural areas and subsistence. Kroeber notes, for example, that coastal residence in most cases is related to increased density, while agriculture alone does not increase density. Density is also correlated with regions of culture climax.

Kroeber then goes on to discuss the possible effects of specific environmental factors upon culture. A decisive and variegated local landscape is corre-lated with diversification of related cul-tural groups. Natural vegetation appears to be much more closely related to culture areas in the West than in the East. Climate limits the development of culture. Available water exerts a strong limiting effect on population growth. Adequate water provides a good sub-sistence opportunity, which in turn may be linked to population increase.

The book concludes with a dis-cussion of the concept of culture cli-max. Each culture area can be viewed not only in relation to its environment, but in relation to its intensity or level of development in comparison with other cultures. An intensive culture is one that contains not only more mate-rials than others (is richer), but also more materials that are peculiar to it. These materials are also interrelated to a great-er extent than those of less integrated cultures. The main thrust of the conclu-sion is that the historical aspect of the climax should be studied; ecological aspects are given little attention.

Kroeber, as well as many other an-thropologists, described the environ-ment as a limiting rather than selecting agency. Boas took a similar view of environment-culture relations. The ear-ly anthropologists' united front was a necessary defense against biological and environmental determinism. Cultural studies left no doubt that neither racial nor environmental factors could be shown to be the direct *cause* of a partic-ular behavioral system or cultural trait. On the other hand, we know today that arguments that lump evolutionists within the camp of environmental determinists fall wide of the mark. For most cultural evolutionists, change orig-inates on the level of the culture itself (the superorganic), and is selected by the culture in a process of functional accommodation within the system. For the biologically oriented ecologist-

evolutionist, change originates on the level of the individual, is restricted by the behavioral system *qua* system, and is selected by the environment.

Clyde Kluckhohn apparently had little to say about adaptation, yet he employed the term "cultural evolu-tion" to indicate some sort of vague process analogous to biological evolu-tion. He says (1959:53): "Of the causes of culture growth and decay little more can be said at present than that they are complicated." And (p. 52): "The course of cultural evolution both re-sembles and differs from that of biologi-cal evolution. In culture change there are sudden spurts reminiscent of those abrupt alterations in hereditary ma-terials that biologists call mutation." And (p. 54): "Cultural development re-sembles organic evolution . . . in its un-even character and in following certain directional trends."

Although unassociated with any evo-lutionary school, Margaret Mead (1964) has published a long work that is con-cerned with change rather than "prog-ress," and thus is more Darwinian than the works of many other social evolu-tionists. Mead's view is particularly idiosyncratic in its focus on communi-cation theory in the context of social networks. She accepts macro-evolution as a process, but chooses to examine micro-evolution at the level of the indi-vidual or small group. On this level "the properties of individuals which are of potential evolutionary significance may then be defined as those properties which are most peculiar to a member of those groups which possess the greatest leverage either for the perpetuation of the status quo or for innovation in a specified social unit of any size" (p. 181).

The structure and ideology of these groups may have a profound effect upon the success or failure of the ge-nius or geniuses within it. Thus the family's beliefs about the genius of its most gifted members can create an atmosphere of acceptance or rejection. If there is only one outstanding member of a group, the absence of any others with whom he or she might communicate may inhibit innovation or its acceptance.

Murdock's *Social Organization* (1949) is not ostensibly about evolution, but his analysis of the relationships among sets of social variables adds up to a kind of cyclical model in which the direction of change in particular cases can be predicted from shifts in key aspects of social structure. Eggan's (1954, 1966) method of controlled comparisons follows a similar model, reflecting a happy blend of social anthropology with ethnohistory. Both Eggan and Murdock are concerned with adaptation—or better, perhaps, accommodation—within a functional system. They are therefore relatively unconcerned with the effects of the natural environment on the direction of change.

In a paper entitled "How Culture Changes" (1960), however, Murdock comes very close to the Darwinian model. First of all he states:

From the point of view of cultural change . . . actual or observable behavior is of primary importance. Whenever social behavior persistently deviates from established cultural habits in any direction, it results in modification first in social expectation, and then in customs, beliefs, and rules. Gradually in this way, collective habits are altered and the culture comes to accord better with the new norms of actual behavior.

Murdock no doubt was influenced by the work of his predecessors at Yale (see Sumner and Keller 1927). These authors, in turn influenced by the work of Spencer, developed a model of evolution based in part upon the selective retention of adaptive culture traits.

This idea has been picked up most recently by Campbell (1965).

Murdock has always stressed the nonrepetitive aspect of specific change and no doubt sees himself primarily as an ethnohistorian. Nonetheless he admits that similar events occurring in different places and at different times can produce parallel effects, and he admits that both the historical (particularistic) and scientific (generalizing) approaches to culture change are valid. His model of change recognizes the stimulating effect environmental change may have on culture, but he does not emphasize its selective effect on change, which results in the sorting out of specific traits within the system. In this sense he is true to his major interest, the internal dynamics of culture. His rather strict adherence to Hullian rather than Skinnerian learning psychology tends to obscure (as we shall see later) the relationships between the process of organic evolution and learning. Murdock's (1960:255) major deviation from modern Darwinian evolution comes with his introduction of the concept of "selective elimination": "Every innovation . . . enters . . . into a competition for survival. The process superficially resembles that of natural selection in organic evolution." The focus on elimination rather than retention reflects Hullian psychology, and denies us the chance to see how close the model can come to the biological process of adaptation.

THE ECOLOGICAL APPROACH TO THE ANALYSIS OF CULTURE

Recently several anthropologists, particularly in the United States, have turned to careful analyses of relations between the environmental setting of a particular population and its behavioral system (see Vayda and Leeds 1965, Vayda 1969, Sahlins 1964). Vayda in particular has noted that certain aspects of the environment may enter into an adaptive system, operating as part of a negative feedback system in which component variables can be extracted from both behavior and setting. The approach is natural historical in scope, for it tends to concentrate on individual adaptations limited to particular situations. Such studies prepare the way for future syntheses out of which the mechanisms of cultural evolution will emerge. They have already corrected our view of the development of technologically advanced civilization and provided a model for a nontautological analysis of functional systems in which the concept of negative feedback plays an important role.

One of the key papers in the ecological approach is "Ecological Relationships of Ethnic Groups in Swat, North Pakistan," by Frederick Barth (1956). Noting that "the importance of ecologic factors for the form and distribution of cultures has usually been analyzed by means of a culture area concept," Barth (1956:1079) attempts "a more specific ecological approach to a case study of distribution by utilizing some of the concepts of animal ecology, particularly the concept of a *niche*—the place of a group in the total environment, its relations to resources and competitors."

Barth goes on to demonstrate how, within a single broad geographical area, three different ethnic groups have come to occupy special segments (niches) of the environment—those to which they have adapted in their cultural behavior.

Six years earlier Barth (1950:338) had noted the utility of the ecological niche:

. . . In archeology one has a continuous record of cultural change. By regarding this change as a process of adaptation to a specific ecologic niche, the patterns of change should

make as much sense to the archeologist as do structural changes to the paleontologist. . . . Thus cultural change may be described in terms of the ecologic adaptation towards which it is moving since this is a major controlling factor of the change.

Note here that Barth, in contrast to cultural evolutionists, sees the environment as the controlling (rather than limiting) factor in change. Adaptation is the result of a dialectic between the culture (producing variation) and the environment (which selects from this variation).

Coe and Flannery (1966) employ the micro-environmental approach suggested by Barth, and as archaeologists attempt to answer specific processual questions about the development of sedentary village life as a step toward civilization. Three questions are asked (p. 348):

1. What factors favored the early development of food production in Mesoamerica as compared with other regions of the hemisphere?
2. What was the mode of life of the earlier hunting and collecting peoples in Mesoamerica and in exactly what ways was it changed by the addition of cultivated plants?
3. When, where, and how did food production make it possible for the first truly sedentary villages to be established in Mesoamerica?

While Barth concentrates on three niches exploited by three separate ethnic groups, Coe and Flannery concentrate on the multiple exploitation of a range of niches by two single homogeneous populations, not ethnically identical to each other but very closely related, which inhabited areas with widely differing available natural resources: the people of the Tehuacán valley in Mexico and those of coastal Guatemala. Parallel adaptive movements from micro-environment to micro-environment were noted until the development of irrigation in the Tehuacán valley allowed for the beginning of full-time agriculture and permanent settlement.

A similar analysis for Mesopotamia is offered by Flannery. But in this case, in addition to noting geographical zones of exploitation, Flannery (1969:303-304) shows how different ethnic groups settled in different niches all contributed to a *single* food-producing revolution.

The food-producing revolution in Southwestern Asia is here viewed not as the brilliant invention of one group or the product of a single environmental zone, but as the result of a long process of changing ecological relationships between groups of men (living at varying altitudes and in different environmental settings) and the locally available plants and animals which they had been exploiting on a shifting, seasonal basis. In the course of making available to all groups the natural resources of every environmental zone, man had to remove from their natural contexts a number of hard-grained grasses and several species of ungulates. These species, as well as obsidian and native copper, were transported far from the biotopes or "niches" in which they had been at home. Shielded from natural selection by man, these small breeding populations underwent genetic change in the environment to which they had been transplanted . . . .

The three articles discussed so far show three variations on the same theme. Barth stresses ethnic differentiation in relation to specific niches. Coe and Flannery emphasize multiniche exploitation by single ethnic groups, and finally Flannery attempts to show how different groups exploiting different niches through time make a combined contribution to the development of a more complex and highly evolved system of exploitation.

The dialectic does not end here, however. In a recent book that attempts to find parallels between the evolution of civilization in Mesoamerica and in Mesopotamia, Adams (1969) employs the multiniche, multigroup model but attempts as well to indicate how certain features of social structure developing in the context of ecological adjustment contributed the major share to the process of change. For Adams (1969:2) "the independent emergence of stratified politically organized societies based upon a new and more complex division of labor is clearly one of those great transformations which have punctuated the human career rarely, at long intervals." Adams finds the preconditions for stratification in early Mesopotamia and Mesoamerica in the existence of conical clans (unilineal kin groups in which certain members considered closer to the central line because of primogeniture have greater status and/or greater access to common property than others). Such groups serve differentially and contribute to the development of a fully stratified society in the context of increasing technological complexity and political control. While the two areas are distinct in many respects, the evolutionary thrust of both contributed to a similar processual core.

Adams is highly critical of Wittfogel's irrigation theory as well as of hypotheses that relate social change to population pressure. He is Stewardian in the sense that his main focus is on social institutions as they relate to the process of production, but he is interested in the process of transformation rather than the development of levels of sociocultural integration. His awareness of the role of multiple ecological zones in the slow development of stratified society keeps him within the camp of those evolutionists who view the environment as active in selection, but like so many other anthropologists, he is led to minimize the overall interaction process between culture and the environment by his desire to focus on function and change within the behavioral system itself.

Sanders and Price (1968:9) take an opposing view. They believe that urban civilization is based on demographic factors. "Technological change as the basic causal factor is, we feel, significant only where such change results in a substantial increase in the numbers and densities of human beings, or in the markedly increased efficiency of the individual human producer."

Sanders and Price see a definite relation between increased population and increased political complexity. The factors that limit density are, however, first and foremost ecological. Much of the variation among agricultural populations in South America, for example, is due to protein availability.

The second factor they relate to political evolution is competition between families and communities (1968:95):

One factor that promotes competition is the ratio between man-hours of work and crop production. In this critical ratio swidden agriculture is actually more productive than most labor intensive systems of agriculture. . . . Only extreme population pressure . . . will force farmers to shift from swidden to more intensive patterns of land use.

Population pressure produces a series of positive responses. These include (1) changes in technology related to productivity per unit of land or increases in the percentage of land cultivated; (2) changes in social and economic structure which contribute to increased economic efficiency; (3) development of specialization by both individuals and communities for the production of specific goods; (4) political control of surplus food by central authority rather than local producing groups; (5) local migrations and segmentations of communities; (6) warfare, which acts to re-

duce or stabilize population; and (7) the development of other checks on population.

Other authors have emphasized the role of population pressure in the process of adaptation, employing it as the mechanism that drives the evolutionary process forward. Carneiro (1967:239) has long emphasized the relationship between complexity and population density:

The thesis advanced here is not that societies become more complex only by growing larger, or that as they grow larger they invariably become more complex. Rather the contention is that if a society does increase significantly in size, and if at the same time it remains unified and integrated, it must elaborate its organization.

For Carneiro the elaboration of social structure is a systemic response to stress generated by the multiplication of units.

Boserup (1965) attacks the whole foundation of Malthusian theory. Her suggestion, simply put, is that agricultural techniques respond adaptively to population pressure. Increases in population are met more or less automatically by shifts toward increasingly labor-intensive forms of production. The driving force behind cultural evolution therefore is population pressure.

The same approach has been taken recently by Harner (1970:67):

Growth of population pressure is postulated to be a major determinant of human social evolution through the mechanism of competition for increasingly scarce subsistence resources. In terms of a model for societies practicing agriculture, inter- and intra-group competition for such natural resources is seen as leading to the evolution of more competitively successful cooperative units in descent (in classless societies) and in political structure, and the evolution of class stratification.

Harner has constructed a scale for the measurement of population pressure based on an inverse relation between the degree of dependence on hunting and gathering and the degree of population pressure. Fishing dependence is also predicted to show a positive correlation with an increase in the scarcity of land resources. When the scale is tested in relation to political complexity and social differentiation, very high correlations are found between the index of population growth and social evolution.

Alland (1970) has related adaptation to population increase. He notes that adaptation in the sense of system stability means an accommodation between a system of economic exploitation and the carrying capacity of the environment. As long as the technological system remains stable, population increase is acceptable only so long as it does not degrade the environment; when it exceeds this limit, the social system eventually regresses. Adaptation is the outcome of technological change that increases the carrying capacity of the environment and is measured by population increase. Carrying capacity is related to both agricultural potential in the context of a particular technological system and to such population-reducing factors as disease and nutritional limitations.

Dumond (1961, 1965) has examined the relationship between civilization and demographic density on the one hand and population growth on the other. In the earlier paper, dealing specifically with Meggers' hypothesis relating Maya decline to swidden agriculture, Dumond suggests that centralization may predate intensive agriculture, and that heavy population growth stimulates expansion of subsistence activity and a tightening of social organization. He notes, however, that when expansion of subsistence activity is impossible or difficult and when the welfare of the population is threatened, a population has two choices open to it: (1) population control and (2) a decreased standard of living with increased threat of famine. Thus, according to Dumond, population growth appears favorable to, but is not a sufficient cause of, social centralization and the improvement of subsistence and commerce. Both may in fact encourage the growth of population. Population growth (a natural outcome of human fertility) stimulates a set of responses that produce an adaptation to increased numbers, but this adaptation is often capable of supporting a much expanded population, and so the increase may accelerate under changed technical and social conditions.

Other authors, particularly Harris (in a personal communication), appear to favor the idea that technological change precedes population increase, which is then followed by changes in social structure in the direction of increasingly complex political organization, the formation of centralized authority, and eventually the state. Harris has noted in an unpublished paper that the number of man-hours put into subsistence activities is about the same in hunting and gathering societies and in various types of agricultural systems. Technological innovation leads to an increase in per-capita output, particularly with the advent of industrialization. An interesting point made earlier by Sahlins (1968) is that, economically speaking, hunters and gatherers are not really marginal, locked in a daily struggle for food. Lee (1966) has demonstrated quantitatively that !Kung Bushmen have ample time for leisure, and that the population-limiting factor in their environment is water rather than food. Harris notes that large increases in man-hour input come only with the rise of the state, and are highest in technologically advanced Western societies. Surplus output is then exploited by those segments of the population in control of the politicotechnological system. Harris comes down very strongly against the point made by Boserup (1965) that natural increase of population in so-called backward areas may stimulate what might be termed healthy technological change. We find Harris' criticism of Boserup well taken, for she apparently ignores the role of centralized authority in production and the distribution of goods, as well as the stimulation of input without benefit to the producers themselves. Far from adapting to increased numbers, such a population may become, in Geertz's (1963) term, involuted; that is, directed into a kind of productive system dependent upon increased labor, with little technological change. This, according to Geertz, is the case in Java, where the peasants have been consistently exploited by either the colonial system or the urban centers. Labor intensification occurred not as an adaptation to local demographic and ecological conditions, but under the forced stimulation of an elite.

Population growth was also stimulated during the Industrial Revolution in England as well as other parts of Europe to meet an increasing demand for workers. It is interesting to note that it is only with the advent of automation that national planners have begun to talk about population control.

Anthropologists' rather extensive discussion of the role of population in adaptation is related to the interesting question of the forces that drive the evolutionary machine. A group of anthropologists, particularly from Columbia University and the University of Michigan, have concerned themselves with stable ecological systems and the role of behavioral variables in maintaining a balance between population and the natural environment. Vayda (1970) and Rappaport (1968) have also examined the effect of disruption on these systems. Vayda and Collins (1969) have come to be associated with neofunctionalism, which applies functional analysis to the operation of self-regulating systems in which variations in environmental parameters are offset by predictable changes in behavior. A case for this kind of system has been made by Piddock (1965) for the potlatch system of the American northwest coast, following an idea first presented by Suttles (1960) and Vayda (1961). The most comprehensive ecological study employing the notion of stable systems is Rappaport's (1968) *Pigs for the Ancestors.* In this detailed ethnographic monograph Rappaport attempts to demonstrate how the ritual cycle of pig slaughter can be coupled to demographic changes in both the human and pig populations. Rappaport suggests that an element of culture that some might assume to be removed from a direct role in ecological adjustment is central to the maintenance of the system. Such a system is seen, therefore, as an adaptation equivalent to homeostatic adjustment, and is analogous to adaptation in the physiological sense.

In a more recent set of as yet unpublished papers Rappaport has extended his examination of ritual and the concept of sanctity as they operate as communication systems within and among populations. Such a notion is exciting for three reasons: (1) it suggests how ritual performances may operate to spread ecologically adaptive information from group to group within an interacting set of populations; (2) it offers an explanation for the truth value of sacred rituals—that is, the truth of secular information transmitted on ritual occasions is validated by the participants' acceptance of the sacredness (and hence the truth) of the ritual ceremonies; and (3) it provides a link between ecological studies and the work of structural anthropologists and others concerned with myth and ceremony, such as Claude Lévi-Strauss, Edmond Leach, and Victor Turner.

The ecological school has raised the question of non-Malthusian population controls. Rappaport himself has drawn analogies between ritual and epidictic displays in birds and other infrahuman animals. Stott (1962) was among the first to suggest that the adaptation of populations to a limited environment may include biological and cultural mechanisms that bring populations into equilibrium before the intervention of disease or famine, and within the limitations of a particular carrying capacity. It seems to us that such conclusions are highly suspect. As we noted earlier, such mechanisms generally call into play the dubious concept of group selection.

According to more recent information on the Maring area (the set of populations that include the Tsembaga, studied by Rappaport), population is checked well below carrying capacity (Georgeda Buchbinder; personal communication). This discovery raises the immediate question of how such a hypothetical adaptation could arise through natural selection. Population stability in this case and many others might be due rather to the scarcity of a single natural resource, which by itself sets limits on the population. Carneiro has already suggested that protein availability is responsible for low population densities in lowland South America, and Lee has pointed out that it is limitations of water resources rather than food that keep the !Kung Bushman population at its present level. If this is the case, we can say that those populations that operate below carrying capacity (as an estimate of total potential productivity of the environment within the context of a particular technology) will survive at a predictable demographic level, but that such survival in relation to environmental resources is merely an artifact of a limiting factor that in fact is Malthusian. To say that such population stability is an "adaptation" to the environment is to beg the question and fall victim to the classical evolutionary tautology.[4]

It should be clear that the assumption of a negative feedback system when a population exists well below carrying capacity is open to criticism. This is not to say that functional systems do not exist. If the model of adaptation we are about to present is to work at all, accommodations to the environment will occur, and many will

---

[4] A factor producing a Malthusian check can operate in a system to limit population, but it *may or may not itself* be affected by population shifts. Take water as an example: Increased population might produce pollution, which at a certain level will prove toxic. If this is the case, reduction in population and/or changes in use patterns will produce an adaptive response and the resource will return to its nonpolluted state. On the other hand, water can act as a check on population growth merely by means of its total availability. It may do this directly or indirectly by affecting the amount of available game or vegetation. Population increase will not degrade the water supply, but the supply will limit population growth. Stable population brought about in this way is not the same as a specific systematic adjustment that operates below carrying capacity to maintain a stable environment. In the former case we can say that the adjustment is passive and in the latter case that it is active. An active adjustment should be hypothesized only after a careful investigation shows that no passive adjustment is occurring. It is the passive adjustment that might make a population look as if it were adjusting to a more complex set of variables. In this sense the complex adjustment is an artifact. No non-Malthusian checks should be hypothesized until all possible Malthusian checks have been investigated.

It should also be noted that carrying capacity is not an easy concept to apply. Its measurement is complicated and involves many variables, including local conditions of soil and climate, natural vegetation, technological level, and trade with other communities (see Street 1969).

be homeostatic in nature. But it must be remembered that purely Malthusian mechanisms can produce demographic stability across generations. Demographic loss at times of stress may act to bring populations once again into balance with their environment.

SOME TENTATIVE NOTIONS ABOUT ADAPTATION AND CULTURAL EVOLUTION

Simpson (1961) suggested some years ago that culture was man's species-specific means of adaptation to the environment. While such a generalization fails to provide clues to the specific mechanisms involved, it does have the virtue of setting anthropology on the Darwinian path. That is, if culture is seen (1) as the outcome of natural selection and (2) as the behavioral means by which human populations accommodate to the environment, then the equation cultural variation plus selection (in the context of a specific natural environment) equals evolution brings the study of cultural evolution within the biological context. Anthropology may then come to owe more to Darwin than to Spencer! Before this hope can materialize, however, other criteria must be met.

First of all, we must recognize that the source of variation is organismic rather than superorganic. Selection is a complex process that is ultimately determined by the environment, but heuristically, at least, one can speak of internal and external selection (see Goodman 1963, Radcliffe-Brown 1952). Internal selection is the process whereby internally consistent homeostatic systems evolve. The generation of a system *qua* system demands that the units be functionally compatible. Lack of such compatibility will lead to reduced efficiency in external selection, which is in effect the interaction of the system with the environment. Thus some theoretically efficient mechanisms might in fact have low survival value in systems with which they were not compatible. This explains why so many culture-change schemes fail in practice when they are applied indiscriminately in a variety of environmental and cultural settings. A division of the selective process into internal and external selection has the philosophical gain of eliminating the need for free will with the assertion that variation occurs on the level of the individual. What is *selected* is constrained by the existing system *and* the pressure of the environment on the evolving behavioral system. Indeed, variation itself is constrained by the behavioral and ecological setting at any particular point in time.

Second, we must assume, as do modern geneticists, that evolution as a process takes place on the level of the population, for this aggregate of organisms interacts as a unit with the environment. At the same time we must not assume that the population is some metaphysical entity. The formulae of population genetics deal with potential average outcomes of genes. One predicts what chance such-and-such an individual with a specific genetic constitution has of producing a certain number of offspring in relation to individuals with other genetic constitutions in the same population.

Third, we must not fall victim to analogies that falsely equate such phenomena as mutation with innovation, diffusion with gene flow, and differences in culture with differences in species. While the process of evolution is biological in nature (all organisms face the problem of survival), culture provides man with special mechanisms through which adaptation takes place. Innovation is perhaps partially dependent upon chance, but man also thinks, and he can think about change. The ability to construct theories and test them can speed up the process of adaptation, which in lower animals is dependent on chance factors alone. The term "culture" should be restricted to traditional behavior. Human social groups should be seen always as populations of the same species. Competition, when it occurs, is intraspecific.

Fourth, Darwinian measures should be applied to the Darwinian process. Energy output (transformation is a better term) is meaningless as far as evolution is concerned unless it is translated into the number of organisms that can be supported by the environment. In the case of man, this number will always be related to a particular level of technology, including both productivity and disease control, for these are opposite sides of the same demographic problem. Stern (1970) has suggested that adaptation is a single-generation phenomenon; that is, selective coefficients apply synchronically. One should not worry about what will happen to a certain phenotype some generations hence. This is true for genetic studies, but from the viewpoint of the evolutionary process we must ask what a species—particularly the human species—is doing to its environment. Overexploitation of the niche can lead only to eventual destruction and population reduction. For cultural evolutionary studies, therefore, it is necessary to consider the relation between particular behavioral strategies, the maintenance of the environment, and the maximal population level supportable in the total technoenvironmental setting. Nicholson (1956) has cautioned against using increased population as a criterion of adaptation, because one species can be replaced by another without a total gain in numbers. The use of numbers in biology is generally restricted to coefficients that

reflect relative intrapopulational fertility. During the process of species replacement, however, the dominant species comes to outnumber the less well-adapted species until it replaces it in the niche. When a new species occupies a niche, interspecific comparative data no longer exist. The same stricture should apply to human populations in competition, or to the replacement of culture traits within a population. But in transgenerational terms it does in fact make sense to speak of conditions for population growth and to view these as adaptations by which population comes to exploit the environment more and more efficiently. Diachronically evolutionary adaptation is the process whereby environmental energy is converted into organisms with increased efficiency.

In biological evolution, variation on the level of the organism (occurring as the result of chemical change in gene structure or some form of chromosomal recombination) is selected out by the environment. Better endowed organisms produce a greater number of viable offspring than less well-endowed organisms. The process is similar to a game in which a population is one player and the environment the other. The organisms produce variation and the natural environment selects (favors) certain moves over others. The process can also be profitably cast in terms of learning theory, particularly the operant conditioning theory of B. F. Skinner. In operant conditioning a naive animal to be trained in a specific task is allowed to make random moves. When by chance the organism moves in the direction of the desired response, it is immediately rewarded. After a time the behavior takes on a pattern that is shaped to the goals of the experimenter. Random moves are extinguished and responses become highly ordered. In evolution the environment plays the role of the experimenter shaping the responses of the organism (the moves are random mutations). This analogy not only is useful in explaining adaptation, but allows us to see the connection between genetic and cultural evolution. For behavior (either genetically influenced or learned) is shaped by the environment in the same way as a somatic trait. The learned adaptive responses of man can be transmitted culturally. The adaptive gain of a single individual can be transmitted to others independently of genes.

Random behaviors are bound to occur in the cultural stream. Some of these may have reward value (i.e., they are adaptive). Seen in this light, cultural adaptation need not be a conscious process. Shaping (natural selection) can occur without subjective awareness. This does not mean, however, that all depends upon random behavior. Humans, because they think, may be stimulated to think about environmental problems.

While much of cultural evolution might be the outcome of random behavior fixed through environmental rewards, we do not mean to suggest that this is the only way humans can adapt to the environment. Theory construction may increase the speed of adaptation. The discovery of penicillin was accidental, but observations and theory based on this discovery rapidly led to the development of many other antibiotics. Theories can, however, retard adaptation as well. Poor theories may produce blocks to the solution of very simple problems. In such cases parts of the behavioral stream that are not tied to some specific theory may adapt more rapidly than those that are. Alland (1970) has suggested that primitive medicine provides a case in which bad theory may retard the development of useful therapeutic devices. He has also suggested that preventive medical practices may occur outside the medical system in disparate areas of behavior, and be selected out from among random responses. In the case of disease prevention, the rewards would often be rapid and direct. Preventive medicine (in the Western sense) in primitive societies is frequently underdeveloped as a systematic part of culture, but measures that work medically nevertheless exist.

It might be noted in passing that one of the biological bases of adaptation in which the environment is constantly tested may lie in exploratory behavior, which is common and widespread among mammalian species. Such behavior is not instinctual, at least not in man, but the capacity for such behavior appears to be part of the human biological heritage. Active exploration is one way in which variation and testing are maximized and left open for the intervention of natural selection.

Assuming that the model presented so far works, let us now examine various possibilities that can occur as a population interacts with its environment (including other populations).

When a population is stabilized in a niche with a level of energy of extraction below that of carrying capacity, it can continue to persist at that level. Such stability may be due to a single limiting factor in the environment, such as water or some essential nutrient. Stabilization in this case is an artifact of natural limitation and not an adaptation in the dynamic sense of the term.

It is also possible that population size can be fixed below carrying capacity through the adaptive process. When environmental variation is relatively severe in relation to the existing technological system, population stability below carrying capacity can provide a buffer against bad years. This type of adaptation will be difficult to demonstrate empirically, however.

When a population exists at an extraction level equal or close to carrying capacity, one can look for a negative feedback system that acts to maintain a balance between demographic factors and natural conditions. It is also possible, however, that such a population is in a state of growth, and after a number of generations will surpass the carrying capacity and degrade the environment. Such stress on the environment and/or the population (increased disease frequency, lowered nutritional standards) may stimulate individuals within the population to seek new modes of environmental accommodation. Under all conditions environmental stress will eventually lead to a demographic crisis, which in turn should stimulate a phase of innovation (indigenous or borrowed). Often as not contemporary "primitive" populations will already be familiar with subsistence techniques capable of producing higher caloric output than their own.

When it is not possible to alter carrying capacity, a population may decline to a level below its previous one, making do in what has become a marginal environment. If space is available, a population might migrate to a new area of virgin land and continue its subsistence mode unchanged. It is also possible that only a segment of a population will migrate to new territory (a common occurrence in parts of Africa).

Adaptations that increase carrying capacity indirectly are also possible. A population might develop new methods of warfare and social organization that would allow it to expand and hence to extend its territory, either incorporating or destroying those populations lying in the path of conquest.

When it is impossible to raise carrying capacity either directly or through territorial expansion, forms of population control may evolve to produce a stable system—infanticide, birth control, and gerontocide, as well as social practices that indirectly affect fertility levels.

It should be clear that we ourselves are committed to the proposition that increased population is one of the major mechanisms involved in evolutionary change. Thus we go part-way with Boserup, Harner, Carneiro, and others who see a rather strict correlation between size of population, stress on the environment, and culture change. It should be noted, however, that we consider Boserup's solution to contemporary problems rather naive. The direct relationship between population growth and *adaptive* change should occur only so long as the distribution of both caloric and noncaloric goods (produced with surplus calories) is relatively equal. That is to say, the kind of adaptive mechanism we have been talking about works in egalitarian societies. Once distribution comes under the control of elites, particularly with the development of the state, other factors intervene to produce culture change.

Harris has some interesting if tentative data that shed light on this particular point. He notes that the amount of man-hours going into subsistence production does not go up significantly no matter what type of economic (agricultural) system is employed. He suggests that there is no basis for Boserup's assumption that labor intensification occurs with changes in technology. Harris says rather that input remains at relatively the same level, but that output is increased. Thus he notes that labor intensification (in terms of man-hours expended per year) increases significantly only in advanced industrial societies or their colonial satellites. Thus it is modern Americans who work hard, not primitive men. Unfortunately Harris refers to those technological advances that increase surpluses as "labor-saving devices." The choice of terms would not be worth quibbling about except that it obscures the fact that the man-hour input remains stable. In other words, though people may be producing more without working more, still they are working no less than before. This is a key to the process, for it begs the question: Why produce more with the same work rather than reduce input? The most sensible answer is that people are stimulated to produce more when there are more mouths to feed. Thus Harris' data, if correct, supports the contention that population growth is a stimulus to change.

We cannot say that growth is both the cause and the measure of adaptation without some explanation. Actually the process is rather simple. Population stress increases the chance that behavioral variation will be rewarded— the reward being increased carrying capacity, which can itself be expressed in terms of potential population. Diachronically this potential can be measured, as ideally it should be, in terms of actual population increase. Energy production is not acceptable as a measure of adaptation because it tells us nothing about its consumption or the effect of extraction on the environment. In addition, such a measure would remove cultural evolution from the Darwinian realm.

Improvements in the "quality of life," so popular as a measure of progress in the West, fail as indices of adaption, since they involve value judgments inadmissible in science.

REFERENCES

Adams, R. M.
1969 *The Rise of Urban Society.* Chicago: Aldine.
Alland, A., Jr.
1970 *Adaptation in Cultural Evolution:*
An Approach to Medical Anthropology. New York: Columbia University Press.
Ashby, W. R.
1960 *Design for a Brain,* 2nd ed. New York: Wiley.
Barth, F.
1950 Ecologic Adaptation and Cultural Change in Archeology. *American Antiquity* 15:338-39.
1956 Ecologic Relationships of Ethnic Groups in Swat, North Pakistan. *American Anthropologist* 58:1079-89.
Boserup, E.
1965 *The Conditions of Agricultural Growth.* Chicago: Aldine.
Brown, W. L., Jr.
1958 General Adaptation and Evolution. *Systematic Zoology* 7:157-68.
Burnett, A. L., and T. Eisner
1964 *Animal Adaptation.* New York: Holt, Rinehart & Winston.
Campbell, D. T.
1965 Variation and Selective Retention in Socio-Cultural Evolution. In *Social Change in Developing Areas,* ed. H. Barringer, pp. 19-49. Cambridge, Mass.: Schenkman.
Cancian, F. M.
1968 Functional Analysis: Varieties of Functional Analysis. *International Encyclopedia of the Social Sciences* 6:29-43.
Carneiro, R.
1962 Scale Analysis as an Instrument for the Study of Cultural Evolution. *Southwestern Journal of Anthropology* 18:149-69.
1963 The Application of Scale Analysis to the Study of Cultural Evolution. *Transactions of the New York Academy of Science.* Series 21, 26: 196-207.
1966 On Determining the Probable Rate of Population Growth During the Neolithic. *American Anthropologist* 68:177-81.
1967 On the Relationship Between Size of Population and Complexity of Social Organization. *Southwestern Journal of Anthropology* 23:234-43.
Childe, V. G.

1936 *Man Makes Himself.* London: Watts.
1951 *Social Evolution.* New York: Schuman.
Coe, M., and K. V. Flannery
1966 Micro Environments and Mesoamerican Prehistory. In *New Roads to Yesterday,* ed. J. Caldwell, pp. 348-57. New York: Basic Books.
Cohen, Y. A.
1968 Culture as Adaptation. In *Man in Adaptation: The Cultural Present,* ed. Y. A. Cohen, pp. 40-60. Chicago: Aldine.
Collins, P. W.
1964 The Logic of Functional Analysis in Anthropology. Unpublished Ph. D. dissertation, Columbia University.
1965 Functional Analyses in the Symposium Man, Culture and Animals. In *Man, Culture, and Animals: The Role of Animals in Human Ecological Adjustments,* ed. A. Leeds and A. P. Vayda, pp. 271-282. Washington, D.C.: American Association for the Advancement of Science.
1969 Talk on adaptation given to the University Seminar on Ecological Systems and Cultural Evolution, Columbia University, November 10, 1969.
Collins, P. W., and A. P. Vayda
1969 Functional Analysis and Its Aims. *Australian and New Zealand Journal of Sociology* 5:153-56.
Dansereau, P.
1957 *Biogeography: An Ecological Perspective.* New York: Ronald Press.
Darwin, C.
1859 *The Origin of Species by Means of Natural Selection, or the Preservation of Favored Races in the Struggle for Life.* London: J. Murray.
Dobzhansky, T.
1942 Biological Adaptation. *Scientific Monthly* 55:391-402.
1962 *Mankind Evolving.* New Haven: Yale University Press.
Dole, G. E.
1960 The Classification of Yankee Nomenclature in the Light of Evolution in Kinship. In *Essays in the Science of Culture in Honor of Leslie White,* ed. G. E. Dole and R. Carneiro, pp.

162-78. New York: Crowell.
Dumond, D. E.
1961 Swidden Agriculture and the Rise of Maya Civilization. *Southwestern Journal of Anthropology* 17:301-16.
1965 Population Growth and Culture Change. *Southwestern Journal of Anthropology* 21:304-24.
Dunbar, M. J.
1960 The Evolution of Stability in Marine Environments: Natural Selection at the Level of the Ecosystem. *American Naturalist* 94:129-36.
Eggan, F.
1954 Social Anthropology and the Method of Controlled Comparisons. *American Anthropologist* 56:743-63.
1966 *The American Indian.* Chicago: Aldine.
Emerson, A. E.
1960 The Evolution of Adaptation in Population Systems. In *Evolution After Darwin,* ed. S. Tax, vol. 1, pp. 307-48. Chicago.: University of Chicago Press.
Fisher, R. A.
1954 Retrospect of Criticisms of the Theory of Natural Selection. In *Evolution as a Process,* ed. J. Huxley. London: Allen & Unwin.
Flannery, K. V.
1969 The Ecology of Early Food Production in Mesopotamia. In *Environment and Cultural Behavior,* ed. A. P. Vayda, pp. 283-307. New York: Natural History Press.
Fried, M.
1960 On the Evolution of Social Stratification and the State. In *Culture in History,* ed. S. Diamond. New York: Columbia University Press.
1968 *The Evolution of Political Society.* New York: Random House.
Geertz, C.
1963 *Agricultural Involution.* Berkeley: University of California Press.
Gerard, R. W.
1960 Becoming: The Residue of Change. In *Evolution After Darwin,* ed. S. Tax, vol. 2. Chicago: University of Chicago Press.
Goodman, M.
1963 Man's Place in the Phyllogeny of the

Primates as Reflected in Serum Proteins. In *Classification and Human Evolution,* ed. S. Washburn, pp. 204-34. Chicago: Aldine.

Hallowell, A. I.
1960 Self, Society, and Culture in Phylogenetic Perspective. In *Evolution After Darwin,* ed. S. Tax, vol. 2, pp. 309-71. Chicago: University of Chicago Press.

Hamilton, W. D.
1964 The Genetical Evolution of Social Behavior. *Journal of Theoretical Biology* 7:1-52.

Harner, M. J.
1970 Population Pressure and the Social Evolution of Agriculturists. *Southwestern Journal of Anthropology* 26:67-86.

Harris, M.
1960 Adaptation, Function, Selection in Cultural and Biological Evolution. Paper read before the New York Academy of Sciences, Division of Anthropology, October 24, 1960.
1968 *The Rise of Anthropological Theory.* New York: Crowell.
1971 *Culture, Man, and Nature.* New York: Crowell.

Hempel, C. G.
1965 *Aspects of Scientific Explanation, and Other Essays in the Philosophy of Science.* New York: Free Press, Macmillan.

Huxley, J.
1954 The Evolutionary Process. In *Evolution as a Process,* ed. J. Huxley. London: Allen & Unwin.

Keller, A. G.
1915 *Societal Evolution.* New York: Macmillan.

Kluckhohn, C.
1959 *Mirror for Man.* New York: Fawcett World Library.

Kroeber, A. L.
1939 *Cultural and Natural Areas of Native North America.* Berkeley: University of California Press.

Lack, D.
1954 The Evolution of Reproductive Rates. In *Evolution as a Process,* ed. J. Huxley. London: Allen & Unwin.

Lee, R. B.
1966 !Kung Bushman Subsistence: An Input-Output Analysis. In *Ecological Essays: Proceedings of the Conference on Cultural Ecology.* Ottawa: National Museum of Canada.

Levins, R.
1968 *Evolution in Changing Environments: Some Theoretical Explorations.* Princeton: Princeton University Press.

Lewontin, R. C.
1958 The Adaptations of Populations to Varying Environments. *Cold Spring Harbor Symposia on Quantitative Biology* 22:395-408.

MacArthur, R., and E. Pianka
1966 On the Optimal Use of a Patchy Environment. *American Naturalist* 100:603-19.

McKusick, V. A.
1964 *Human Genetics.* Englewood Cliffs, N. J.: Prentice-Hall.

Mead, M.
1964 *Continuities in Cultural Evolution.* New Haven: Yale University Press.

Meggers, B. J.
1954 Environmental Limitation on the Development of Culture. *American Anthropologist* 56:801-24.
1960 The Law of Cultural Evolution as a Practical Research Tool. In *Essays in the Science of Culture,* ed. G. Dole and R. Carneiro, pp. 302-16. New York: Crowell.

Morgan, L. H.
1877 *Ancient Society.* London: Macmillan.

Muller, J.
1949 The Darwinian and Modern Conceptions of Natural Selection. *Proceedings of the American Philosophical Society* 93, no. 6:459-70.

Murdock, G. P.
1949 *Social Structure.* New York: Macmillan.
1960 How Culture Changes. In *Man, Culture, and Society,* ed. H. Shapiro, pp. 247-60. New York: Galaxy Books.

Murphy, R. F., and J. H. Steward
1956 Tappers and Trappers: Parallel Process in Acculturation. *Economic Development and Cultural Change* 4:335-53.

Nagel, E.
1961 *The Structure of Science.* New York:

Harcourt, Brace & World.

Nicholson, A. J.
1956 Density-Governed Reaction, the Counterpart of Selection in Evolution. *Cold Spring Harbor Symposia on Quantitative Biology* 20:288-93.
1960 The Role of Population Dynamics in Natural Selection. In *Evolution After Darwin*, ed. S. Tax, vol. 1. Chicago: University of Chicago Press.

Odum, H. T., and W. C. Allee
1956 A Note on the Stable Point of Populations Showing Both Interspecific Cooperation and Disoperation. *Ecology* 35:95-97.

Piddocke, S.
1965 The Potlatch System of the Southern Kwakiutl: A New Perspective. *Southwestern Journal of Anthropology* 21: 244-64.

Pittendrigh, C. S.
1958 Adaptation, Natural Selection, and Behavior. *Behavior and Evolution*, ed. A. Roe and G. G. Simpson. New Haven: Yale University Press.

Prosser, C. L.
1960 Comparative Physiology in Relation to Evolutionary Theory. In *Evolution After Darwin*, ed. S. Tax, vol. 1, pp. 569-94. Chicago: University of Chicago Press.

Radcliffe-Brown, A. R. N.
1952 *Structure and Function in Primitive Society*. Glencoe, Ill.: Free Press.

Rappaport, R. A.
1968 *Pigs for the Ancestors*. New Haven: Yale University Press.

Sahlins, M. D.
1957 Land Use and the Extended Family in Moala, Fiji. *American Anthropologist* 59:449-62.
1958 *Social Stratification in Polynesia*. American Ethnological Society. Seattle: University of Washington Press.
1961 The Segmentary Lineage: An Organization of Predatory Expansion. *American Anthropologist* 63:322-45.
1964 Culture and Environment: The Study of Cultural Ecology. In *Horizons in Anthropology*, ed. S. Tax, pp. 132-47. Chicago: Aldine.
1968 Notes on the Original Affluent Society. In *Man the Hunter*, ed. R. Lee

and I. De Vore. Chicago: Aldine.

Sahlins, M. D., and E. R. Service
1960 *Evolution and Culture*. Ann Arbor: University of Michigan Press.

Sanders, W. T., and B. Price
1968 *Mesoamerica: The Evolution of a Civilization*. New York: Random House.

Scheffler, I.
1967 *Science and Subjectivity*. Indianapolis: Bobbs-Merrill.

Service, E. R.
1962 *Primitive Social Organization: An Evolutionary Perspective*. New York: Random House.

Simpson, G. G.
1949 *The Meaning of Evolution*. New Haven: Yale University Press.
1953 *The Major Features of Evolution*. New York: Columbia University Press.
1961 Comments on Cultural Evolution. *Daedalus* 90:514-18.

Simpson, G. G., C. S. Pittendrigh, and L. H. Tiffany
1957 *Life: An Introduction to Biology*. New York: Harcourt, Brace.

Sommerhoff, G.
1950 *Analytical Biology*. London: Oxford University Press.

Stern, J. J.
1970 The Meaning of "Adaptation" and Its Relation to the Phenomenon of Natural Selection. In *Evolutionary Biology*, ed. T.H. Dobzhansky, vol. 4, pp. 39-66. New York: Appleton-Century-Crofts.

Steward, J.
1937 Ecological Aspects of Southwestern Society. *Anthropos* 32:87-104.
1949 Cultural Causality and Law: A Trial Formulation of the Development of Early Civilizations. *American Anthropologist* 51:1-27.
1958 *Theory of Culture Change*. Urbana: University of Illinois Press.

Stott, D. H.
1962 Cultural and Natural Checks on Population Growth. In *Culture and the Evolution of Man*, ed. M. F. Ashley-Montagu. New York: Columbia University Press.

Street, J.
1969 An Evaluation of the Concept of Car-

rying Capacity. *Professional Geographer* 21:104-107.

Sumner, W. G., and A. G. Keller
1927 *The Science of Society*. New Haven: Yale University Press.

Suttles, W.
1960 Affinal Ties, Subsistence, and Prestige Among the Coast Salish. *American Anthropologist* 62:296-305.

Thoday, J. M.
1953 Components of Fitness. *Symposium of the Society for Experimental Biology* 1:96-113.
1958 Natural Selection and Biological Progress. *A Century of Darwin,* ed. S. A. Barnett, pp. 313-33. London: Heinemann.

Tylor, E. B.
1871 *Primitive Culture*. London: J. Murray.

Vayda, A. P.
1961 A Re-examination of Northwest Coast Economic Systems. *Transactions of the New York Academy of Sciences,* series 2, vol. 23:618-24.
1969 *Environment and Cultural Behavior*. New York: Natural History Press.
1970 Maoris and Muskets in New Zealand: Disruption of a War System. *Political Science Quarterly* 85:560-84.

Vayda, A. P., and A. Leeds
1965 *Man, Culture, and Animals*. Publication no. 78. Washington,

D.C.: American Association for the Advancement of Science.

Waddington, C. H.
1960 Evolutionary Adaptation. In *Evolution After Darwin,* ed. S. Tax, vol. 1, pp. 381-402. Chicago: University of Chicago Press.
1961 *The Nature of Life*. London: Allen & Unwin.

Wallace, B., and A. M. Srb
1964 *Adaptation,* 2nd ed. Englewood Cliffs, N. J.: Prentice-Hall.

White, L.
1949 *The Science of Culture. New York:* Farrar, Straus & Cudahy.
1959 *The Evolution of Culture.* New York: McGraw-Hill.

Williams, G. C.
1966 *Adaptation and Natural Selection: A Critique of Some Current Evolutionary Thought.* Princeton: Princeton University Press.

Wittfogel, K. A.
1957 *Oriental Despotism.* New Haven: Yale University Press.

Wright, S.
1968 *Evolution and the Genetics of Populations,* vol. 1: *Genetic and Biometric Foundations.* Chicago: University of Chicago Press.

Wynne-Edwards, V. C.
1962 *Animal Dispersion in Relation to Social Behavior.* Edinburgh: Oliver & Boyd.

CHAPTER 5

Ecological Anthropology and Anthropological Ecology

JAMES N. ANDERSON

INTRODUCTION

In his introduction to *Anthropology Today*, the first great inventory of the study of man, A L. Kroeber (1953:xiv) portrayed anthropology as an integrating discipline *par excellence.*

It is evident that anthropology—however specific it may often be in dealing with data—aims at being ultimately a co-ordinating science. . . . It tries to understand in some measure how Chinese civilization and economies and human heredity, and some dozens of other highly developed special bodies of knowledge, do indeed interrelate in being all parts of "man"–flowing out of man, centered in him, products of him. . . .

Since Kroeber wrote these words, anthropology has greatly prospered. It has expanded exponentially the number of

I wish to acknowledge the valuable efforts of Leonard Charles, Ruth-Inge Heinze, and David Tyler, each of whom provided bibliographical assistance, helpful criticism, and fruitful ideas during the preparation of this chapter. Anne Brower provided much appreciated editorial assistance. Of course, I bear sole responsibility for the views expressed.

its practitioners, its literature, and its intellectual influence. Inevitably such burgeoning growth encouraged tendencies toward diversification, fragmentation, and specialization within the discipline. These trends are characteristic of the development of all sciences; specialization particularly is a concomitant of scientific refinement. Is it nostalgia for a more humanistic period of anthropology, then, that is responsible for the perpetuation of the ideal of a holistic anthropology by many anthropologists, especially those in the United States? I think there are many indications not only that a holistic anthropology is possible, but also that it is a matter of practical and theoretical priority that anthropologists seek to integrate knowledge of the interrelated systems that bear on man and to develop the strategy of synthesis.

Kroeber (1953:xiv) concluded his statement of the ultimate goal of anthropology on a prophetic note: " . . . the principle of culture already gives anthropology a viewpoint of enormous range, a center for co-ordination of most phenomena that relate to man. And we anthropologists feel that this is only a beginning." Yet, despite its range and its integrative powers, the concept of culture is nonetheless too narrow to serve as the central coordinating concept for the sciences that bear on man.

THE SYSTEMS APPROACH

Beginning in biology and spreading rapidly to other fields, a new synthetic view encompassing life and its consequences provides a concept of greater coordinating value than the concept of culture. This "organismic revolution" saw its modern development in the work of Ludwig von Bertalanffy (1952, 1962). In his words (1962:177-78):

We now believe that the solution to this antithesis in biology is to be sought in an *organismic* or *system theory* of the organism which, on the one hand, in opposition to machine theory sees the essence of the organism in the harmony and co-ordination of the processes among one another, but on the other hand, does not interpret this co-ordination as Vitalism does, by means of a mystical' entelechy, but through the forces immanent in the living system itself. [Italics in original.]

This view, now generally known as the "systems approach," provides a holistic view of nature, a recognition of reciprocal relations among the various systems of an organism and of interactions among organisms.

Research on the acknowledged themes of anthropology—man's biobehavioral evolution and the elaboration and diversification of human culture—requires, as Kroeber noted, that knowledge and principals be drawn from other life sciences and social sciences. To date, however, despite their avowed concern for the integration of knowledge, anthropologists have taken little more than superficial account of the systems mode of thought. I am convinced that the study of many anthropological problems can profit from this emerging unitary conception of the world, but whether anthropologists will adopt the concept systematically remains to be seen. Will new attempts at integration dominate the interests of anthropologists in the coming decade, or will they narrow their focus by increased specialization? My own view is that integration must be a central goal of anthropology; and if in fact some anthropologists devote themselves to the integration of human knowledge as a major task, systems thinking will undoubtedly become their primary synthetic tool.

An Ecology of Man

My aim here is to consider only one area—albeit a central and broadly encompassing one—in which a systems framework can be applied toward a fuller understanding of man. Specifically, I shall consider principal aspects of the study of man from the perspective of an ecology of man.

Ecology is the study of living systems as integrated complexes. Ecological studies of numerous animal species suggest the necessity of studying the interrelations of morphology, physiology, and behavior in any given ecological adaptation against a broad background of contingent environmental relationships. Such a strategy is nowhere more applicable than in the study of man. Man's basic biocultural adaptations emerged in reciprocal relationships with technology and social organization. The manifold biocultural adaptations of human populations today continue to interrelate complexly with characteristics of the gene pool, population numbers and structure, energy transactions, tools, behavioral strategies, institutional orders, and ideological commitments—to list only a few components of human ecosystems. The character of ecological research is thus so synthetic and complex that, if we defined "ecology" broadly, it could be stretched to include the whole range of anthropological studies.

The task of reviewing the scope, accomplishments, lines of thought, and unresolved issues in the ecological work of anthropologists is therefore enormous. Moreover, even an extensive review would exclude relevant studies in related fields that bear directly or indirectly upon anthropological problems.

TOWARD AN EVALUATION OF WORK
ON THE ECOLOGY OF MAN:
LIMITS AND FOCUSES

As I see it, it is possible to review and evaluate studies of man's ecological relations only by limiting and focusing one's attention in four ways. First, I do not attempt here to provide an inventory of all work by anthropologists on the ecology of man. Second, I define the field of research and teaching of man's ecological relations both more narrowly and more broadly than is generally done. Third, I treat only briefly those specific components of human ecological studies that fall clearly into categories discussed elsewhere in this volume. Finally, my understanding of ecology persuades me that there is a more immediate need to be served here than the provision of a standard review of what remains to date a "nonfield." A crisis of monumental proportions is taking shape, the consequence of unparalleled rates of demographic, technological, economic, organizational, ideological, and ecological change. Anthropology is one of the many disciplines that can contribute to possible solutions of the crisis in which nothing less than man's survival is at stake. Since each of

the four limitations I have applied to my task critically affects my treatment of the subject, I shall elaborate on each of them briefly.

Inventories

I feel free to reject a standard survey-inventory-prospectus treatment because a number of highly perceptive reviews of the literature are readily available. These reviews were written from a number of perspectives, and together they constitute an adequate inventory of most of the work accomplished to date in the broad area of man-environmental studies. They are required reading for anyone interested in the ecological relationships of man. Several excellent surveys are directed specifically to social and cultural anthropologists. These include articles or chapters in books by Marston Bates (1953), Clifford Geertz (1963), Marvin Harris (1968), June Helm (1962), Marshall Sahlins (1964), Julian Steward (1955, 1968), and Andrew Vayda and Roy Rappaport (1968). Some sociologists whose thinking has moved beyond the analogic "human ecology" of earlier days have contributed valuable reviews, in particular Otis Duncan (1959, 1964), Otis Duncan and Leo Schnore (1959), Amos Hawley (1944, 1968), and John Kunkel (1967). Medical anthropologists and human biologists have also surveyed major problems and reviewed work on human biocultural adaptations; for example, Alexander Alland (1970), Paul T. Baker (1962), P. Baker and J. S. Weiner (1967), Stephen Polgar (1962), and J. S. Weiner (1964). Finally, Marvin Mikesell (1967) has provided a cultural geographer's appraisal of "cultural ecology" and Åke Hultkrantz (1968) has reviewed the ecological perspective in the study of religion. Several recent essays, collections of articles, and reports on symposia also provide access and some guidance to literature on the ecology of man (Bresler, ed., 1966, 1968; Buckley 1968; Damas 1969; Hazen, ed., 1964; Vayda, ed., 1969; Watson and Watson 1969).

Definition

The second limitation of this presentation, the definition of the review area, is required by the inclusiveness of the subject matter of man's ecological relationships. Ecology is by no means an anthropological subdiscipline, nor is it now a standardized approach in anthropology. For most anthropologists it is scarcely even the "pervasive point of view" that Bates (1953) suggested might constitute its most useful function. In common usage, studies that deal in any way with man-environmental relations are labeled "ecological." Since much of the research of anthropologists concerns the relations of the groups they study with some aspect of the environment, ecological anthropology becomes by this logic the most comprehensive of subdisciplines. Such research ranges from natural-history descriptions to systematic attempts to explain social phenomena by reference to natural events. A range so broad is quite ineffective in guiding inquiry.

A succinct definition of ecology is difficult, the more so when it includes man, and the problem was exacerbated in 1971, the third year of general enthusiasm for "ecology." Recent public concern about environmental degradation has given rise to distorted usages that tend, by treating culture and environment as independent of each other, to lead away from an ecological perspective. First steps toward a workable definition must therefore begin with what ecology is not. It is not equivalent to environment, although it is frequently used in this sense by some an-

thropologists and a large part of the lay public. It does not, in any strict sense, refer to the unforeseen consequences of many of man's activities, as in the phrase "ecological disaster"; neither is it synonymous with conservation, narrowly construed. In fact, the standard dictionary definition of ecology—"the study of relations between organisms and their environment"—is itself misleading if it is not understood as requiring a holistic, reciprocal mode of thought. When ecology had as its subject matter the study of botanical relationships, a focus upon individual organisms and their environment sufficed; but when ecology extends its concern to more complex sets of reciprocal interdependencies, the dualism of this definition can perpetuate a limited view that can have unfortunate consequences for research. One hundred years of development (regrettably all too discrete), first in plant ecology, then in animal ecology, in the study of biotic communities, and finally in human ecology, have led to a conception of ecology less as a subject matter than as a point of view.

Accordingly, we can define ecology as the study of entire assemblages of living organisms and their physical milieus, which together constitute integrated systems. This definition has the advantage of providing a framework that includes the study of all species. Moreover, environment in this view is seen not as external, but as an integral component of the total system—the "givens" of the system. The definition thus avoids the unfortunate dualism of thought—man versus environment—that has encouraged man's often despoiling intrusions into the world's ecosystems and which has hindered adequate conceptualization of ecological problems.

"Ecology" and "Economy." The holistic emphasis in this definition is in keeping with the meaning of the Greek

root of the world "ecology." *Oîkos* (house) connoted the web of social interdependency that existed among members of the household. According to their common Greek root, economics (discourse on the household) and ecology (management of the household) should be very similar sciences (Bates 1961), and in fact since its first use the term "ecology" has been interchanged with that for the older study, "economy." Haeckel (1870) described ecology as "the body of knowledge concerning the economy of nature." Elton (1927) defined ecology as "scientific natural history," dealing with the "sociology and economics" of animals. Bates (1960*a*) subtitled one of his books *A Look at the Economy of Nature and the Ecology of Man*. Nonetheless, in modern usage economics and ecology are usually thought to have little in common. The dualism that separates the study of the "natural environment" from the study of "human environment" has effectively isolated the two sciences. Recent discussions (Boulding 1966, Hardin 1970) and reports concerning disastrous unforeseen ecological consequences of human actions (e.g., Carson 1962, Commoner 1966) suggest not only that the two *eco* studies have much to learn from each other, but also that narrow economic analysis will eventually be subordinated to ecology. Man's survival seems dependent upon an adequate cost accounting and evaluation of his transactions in the ecosphere, undertaken prior to action rather than in postmortem critiques. The essence of ecology, then, is the study of the complex whole of reticulate interactions taking place within the living system under consideration. For E. P. Odum (1963) the study of these interactions reveals the structure and function of nature in that system. Systems may vary in scale and complexity, but on whatever scale, the system is maintained by the mutually dependent interactions of its multiple components—organic, inorganic, and sociocultural.[1]

The Ecosystem Concept

The holistic concept of "ecosystem" has gained wide acceptance as a key tool for the study of ecology. As a type of general system, it is capable of including the activities of man within its purview. The ecosystem framework suggests a synthetic focus upon an organized unit in which transactions of production, distribution, consumption, and material recycling are structured and function. Thus the ecosystem conceptually unites the biology, behavior, organization, and functioning of man, other animals, plants, and inorganic components within a single framework in which the interaction of the components may be studied. Utilization of the concept of ecosystem shifts emphasis from specific, one-to-one relationships (the focus of earlier "cultural ecological" studies) to the nature and functioning of the holistic system. The structure and functional interrelations of an ecosystem emerge from the study of circular exchanges between living and nonliving components (i.e., biogeochemical cycles) and include noncircular energy and information transactions (E. P. Odum 1971, Duncan 1964). The study of ecosystems that include man seeks to understand the structure and functioning of this systemic whole composed of linked subsystems. Human ecosystemic studies thus are the meeting ground for all the disciplines concerned with man. Anthropology,

---

[1] The arrogant ideas concerning the relative independence of sociocultural subsystems, best developed in the technologically "highly advanced" nations, are severely challenged by the economics of the causes and consequences of ecosystem degradation.

the most holistic science and, according to many, the "coordinating science," should benefit greatly from the application of the ecosystem concept. With its aid, the ambitious goal of anthropology may be more closely approached. The ecosystem's dual roots, firmly established in the natural and the social sciences, now may be utilized as a single nutrient source.

The Compass of an Ecology of Man

My conception of ecology comprises all aspects of man as a biocultural animal as they are subsumed within the structure and functioning of ecosystems, including human morphology, reproduction, population genetics, stress physiology, nutritional requirements, the ecology of health and disease, and human adaptability. It also encompasses human population ecology—that is, population processes: fertility, mortality, migration and population structure—the feedback between biological and cultural factors (technological, economic, organizational) in populations, spatial and economic distribution, and ecological consequences of population trends. Individual biological and population processes are interrelated with ecological perceptions, environmental cognition, language as cultural codification, ideology, creative thinking, planning, and decision-making. Finally, this holistic conception of ecology includes the adaptiveness *and* nonadaptiveness of human behavior and institutions viewed in their widest context. It poses the questions of the degree to which technological, economic, social, political, ritual, aesthetic, and ideological organizations are adaptive and maladaptive; whether the feedback of human behavior and institutions on the earth's ecosystems is positive or negative, and to what degree; and whether ethics, purposive policy, and planning

are ecologically beneficial or detrimental. It is concerned with problems of urban-industrial ecosystems, environmental aesthetics, design and planning, government-citizen interactions, and environmental law and policy-making. So defined, the study of human ecosystems touches on many of the chapters of this handbook and is capable of integrating them within a single framework.

Recognition of Crisis

I am well aware that my decision to advocate an interdisciplinary role for anthropology in working to solve the ecological crises brought about by accelerated demographic, technological, economic, ideological, and ecological changes may place me on controversial ground. But as Zelinsky (1970:500) has written in an important recent piece, "Given the choice between grappling with small immediacies . . . or with larger forces and questions (and some profoundly interesting technical questions) that cannot be evaded more than a few years longer, the decision for audacity was not difficult to make."

ACHIEVEMENTS: TOWARD A SYSTEMIC INTERACTIONALISM

Anthropologists, never conservative in the range of factors they have included in descriptions, analyses, interpretations, and explanations, frequently refer to the environmental relations of the people they study. One of anthropology's principal contributions to knowledge is its record of holistic descriptions of human diversity and similarity. Anthropology's emphasis upon both the physical and the cultural sides of man, upon intensive studies of small localized populations, upon the broad context of human life, upon the functionally interrelated aspects of culture, upon humanism, together with the emphasis of its two early attempts at synthesis, "evolution" and "history," should have made anthropology among the most ecologically oriented of the social sciences.

These promises and these pretensions to the status of coordinator among the sciences of man have so far failed to materialize. Despite the appearance of the word "ecology" in the title or in the text of a burgeoning literature by anthropologists, most of it is not ecological; it fails to meet the minimum definition of the study of holistic functional transactions in man-occupied ecosystems. It is proper to ask, therefore: Given the dominant concerns of anthropology and given too the obvious and fundamental importance of man-environmental transactions in the understanding of any people, why is it that until very recently anthropologists have given so little systematic consideration to the ecology of man? We can best answer this question first by reviewing briefly the major formulations of man-environmental relations and the major problems that anthropologists have posed in their research, and then by analyzing the recurrent limiting perspectives that have hindered more productive conceptions of the ecological relationships of man.

LIMITED PERSPECTIVES: ENVIRONMENTALISM AND POSSIBILISM

The necessity to view man within the framework of his habitat tended toward the adoption of two fruitless positions that long dominated the thought of anthropologists. With some simplification these positions can be seen as extremes on a continuum, one pole being environmental determinism and the other cultural determinism. Their less extreme versions are known by the terms "environmentalism" and "possibilism."[2]

These views tend to separate man and his culture from his environment (and behavior from biology); in fact, they tend to treat them as opposing entities. At one extreme of the continuum culture is viewed as passive and the environment as an active force molding culture to its pattern. At the other extreme, culture is viewed as the active force reshaping the passive environment.[3] A relatively clear division thus developed between those who viewed environment as dominant in the relationship and those who viewed culture as dominant. These views, environmentalism and possibilism, although much diluted, still have their adherents.

INTERACTIONAL VIEWS

Contrasting with both these views and standing intermediate between them is a reciprocal or interactional phrasing of man-environmental relations. It assumes that neither man nor environment is necessarily dominant. Reciprocation is assumed to exist not between abstract culture and environment, but between men living and behaving in local populations and the organic and inorganic components with which they interact. In this holistic view, man (including his biology and his cultural behavior) and his specific environment are mutually dynamic; they constitute an organized system including other populations and inorganic components. Such an ecological perspective, a holistic interactionalism, has only recently begun to gain supporters in the social sciences. Dominated in their teaching and research by the con-

---

[2] See Sprout and Sprout 1965 for a recent summary treatment of these contrastive positions of man's relationship with nature.

[3] See also Geertz 1963, Sahlins 1964, Vayda and Rappaport 1968.

cepts of culture and society, and having helped crush simplistic environmental determinism and Spencerian evolutionism, cultural and social anthropologists embraced almost to a man the plausible, if uninformative, possibilist position. Combined with new interests in American anthropology then emerging, the adoption of this position had the effect of discouraging detailed consideration of the evidently noncausal factors of the environment. In Kroeber's (1939:3) words,

... most attention came to be paid, accordingly, to those parts of culture which readily show self-sufficient forms: ceremonial, social organization, art, mythology; somewhat less to technology and material culture; still less to economics and politics, and the problem of subsistence. Much of the anthropology practiced in this country in the present century has been virtually a sociology of native American culture; strictly historic or geographic interests have receded into the background, except where archaeological preoccupations kept them alive.[4]

Indeed, except in the work of archaeologists and a few ethnologists and social anthropologists (such as Birket-Smith 1929, Evans-Pritchard 1940, Forde 1934, Gayton 1946, Kroeber 1939), genuine concern for establishing regular relationships between specific aspects of cultures and their environments did not reemerge until Steward revitalized thinking concerning ecological relations of human populations (Steward 1933, 1936, 1937, 1938, 1955; Steward, ed., 1946-1950; Steward et al. 1956). Steward's basic notion of "adaptive interaction" (1955:82), which is the basis for his cultural ecology, remains a legacy that informs the dominant stream of interactional-analytical thinking regarding the relationships of culture and environment.[5]

With the renewed interest in describing and seeking understanding of interactions among a local population, its culture, and its environment, three broad subclasses of interactional or ecological thought are perceptible. I shall label these "cultural ecology," "ethnoecology," and "quasi-population" or "systemic ecology."

The three main lines of interactional thought are not inclusive and certainly are not water-tight categories. They serve roughly to segregate the major theoretical and methodological interests of anthropologists in ecology. I should mention two other categories that qualify as quasi-ecological, although I shall not deal with them in detail. The first can be called "incidental ecology"—that is, the occasional or partial use of ecological concepts by scholars who are aware of ecology and who utilize it in a particular article or as part of an argument, because ecological relations cannot be dismissed in their research or because they illuminate an interesting point. Certain ethnoecological studies might be included in the category of incidental ecology insofar as their concern for ecological relations is the epiphenomenon of the development of a rigorous ethnographic method. The second category of studies utilizes an "ecological point of view," varying from a fine to a coarse focus in recognizing ecological principles and methods and in employing degrees of artistry, sensitivity, holism, and forcefulness. This designation is by no means a deprecatory one; some of the most

---

[4] For Kroeber's own view of culture-environmental relations, see Kroeber 1939:205.

[5] M. Harris (1968:654-87) provides a perceptive review of the sociology of cultural ecological knowledge. Vayda and Rappaport (1968:483-99) have also provided a critique of Steward's approach (see also Geertz 1963, Helm 1962, Freilich 1963, Mikesell 1967, and Netting 1968).

impressive ecological studies in anthropological literature are of this sort (e.g., Geertz 1963, Oliver 1962, and Thompson 1949). However, neither incidental ecology nor the ecological point of view is theoretically oriented. Both are essentially depictive; neither makes any attempt to develop ecology as a rigorous approach or as a set of general principles.[6]

Cultural Ecology

"Cultural ecology" is used here to denote the interactional analysis of environmental-cultural relationships, an essentially deterministic position that has developed under the leadership of Julian Steward (1955). The original statement of his concept and method was developed in connection with the theory of multilinear evolution, and although cultural ecology now enjoys a separate status somewhat apart from that theory, many of its assumptions and implications remain. The definitive characteristics of the cultural ecological approach are these:

1. "Adaptation" is the major process of cultural change.

2. The analysis of sociocultural-environmental adaptations serves to uncover variables that explain the origin of particular cultural features or structures in similar environmental conditions.

3. The degree and kind of functional interdependence among the parts of culture are not equal; "core" features, those closely interrelated with subsistence activities and economic arrangements, have causal priority over "secondary" features. Thus similar subsistence problems (relevant environmental and technoeconomic relationships) "may require social adaptations which have far-reaching consequences" (Steward 1955:38).[7] Both culture and environment are divided into relevant and essentially irrelevant parts.

4. The functional relationship of relevant environmental factors causes certain organizational relationships, which in turn give rise to other relevant aspects of the culture; that is, causation is simple, linear, and one-to-one. Analysis is confined to the investigation of the environment and subsistence concerns; that is, to the "relevant" or "effective" environment of the culture core.

5. The creative cultural core-environmental nexus is usually conceived as intracultural and is little affected by historical factors and intersocietal relationships (although see Steward et al. 1956).

6. The foci of study are the equilibrium plateaus of sociocultural-environmental systems. Even in diachronic analysis stable adaptations are assumed to exist; the environment is seen for the most part as stable and the result of adaptation is a stable culture core.

In its latest version (Steward 1968; see also Netting 1965) the language of cultural ecology is modern, the scope of the factors considered has grown,

---

[6] A good example of the difficulty of classifying ecological concerns is provided by Marvin Harris. As an ecological position Harris' cultural-materialist position (1968) appears to have one foot in cultural ecology and the other in quasi-systemic ecology (1966). In fact, however, his single minded concern for material causation, utilizing the "principle of techno-environmental and techno-economic determinism," and his abhorrence of any hint of particularism weaken his frequently insightful intuitive ecological grasp. Ecology, in Harris' hands, actually is subordinated to the dogma of cultural materialism.

[7] A serious problem in making this approach operative is the identification of the special environmental and core cultural features. Steward's technique is intuitive; it follows from a consideration of productive relations (1955:40-42). No objective basis is provided. Steward's *a priori* assumption regarding the priority of economic factors in change is unjustified (see Geertz 1963:11, Freilich 1963).

and intersocietal relations are also considered. But the basic scheme is unchanged, and cultural ecology remains essentially a generalizing endeavor, an attempt to explain contingent structural and processual regularities in space or time.

Ethnoecology

Ethnoecology, by contrast, is an ethnographic endeavor. It has its roots in efforts to develop rigorous methods that will upgrade the quality of cultural description. Deriving inspiration from concepts of structural linguistics, it emphasizes the analysis of verbal behavior and assumes that "culture consists of an inventory of precepts and concepts—of ideational forms—and a set of principles ordering them" (Goodenough 1969:330). Variously called ethnoscience, ethnographic semantics, or cognitive ethnography, it focuses on the task of adequately describing some domain of the culture bearers' tacit theory of the world. Before describing this development further, I would like to cast the question of ecological perceptions in its proper perspective.

Bates (1960a:140), in a compelling description of the difficulty of studying mosquito behavior, makes an important and now widely accepted point. It may be referred to as the organism-oriented view:[8] "To gain any understanding of behavior, we have to know something about the stimuli, which leads up again directly to the problem of environment and to the ways in which parts of the environment are perceived." (1960a: 141). Bates goes on to define the

"environment" in three ways: first, as the elements perceived by the organism; second, as elements, perceived or not, that affect the organism; and third, as all elements, influential or not, that are detectable or inferrable. The first may be called the "perceptual environment" of the organism, the second the "effective environment," and the third the "total reality." The ecologist emphasizes the effective environments of the organism, population, or ecosystem under study. The behavioralist emphasizes the perceptual environment of the organism. "These two kinds of environment are probably similar for most animals: they need to be if the animal is to get along in the world." The differences between the two for populations of men may be considerable, however. Thus, on the one hand, *both* the perceptual and the effective environments of any human group are relevant to the understanding of its behavior and ecology. On the other hand, the degree of fit between perceptual and effective environments is for every human group an empirical question.

Ethnoecologists have emphasized the description of the perceptual or "cognitized" (Rappaport 1963) environments of specific cultures as a primary research strategy. Their goal is first to describe what people know about nature and second to describe how people use this knowledge to get along in the world. In fact, the second goal has rarely been attained. Ethnoecologists rely principally upon verbal eliciting techniques to tap classifications of the structure of specific analytically discrete cognitive domains. The research perspective is normative and narrowly analytical. A people's linguistic classification of its environment is an important datum of research that seeks to reveal ecological processes in man-occupied ecosystems. It is an essential initial step in such research. This is something less

---

[8] Further discussion of the implications of the organism-oriented view of the environment is reserved for a later section of this chapter. In philosophy it finds perceptive expression in John Dewey (1938: 25-36).

than the implication sometimes left that the folk classification of the perceptual environment indeed provides a description of the human population's effective environment (Frake 1962).[9]

The importance of the perceptual environment of a people is well established in anthropology and geography. In the form of the idea of *genres de vie* it is traceable to Ratzel and Vidal de la Blanche (Sorre 1962). The perceptual environment has been of special interest to scholars favoring culture-dominant, possibilist views.[10] This orientation and the dominant theoretical concern in anthropology with the understanding of the nature and functioning of culture and society lead away from the examination of effective environment and of objective behavior relations (M. Harris 1964, 1968) and from explicit recognition of the dynamic influence of human populations in altering their objective environments. It is to the credit of some who favor this perspective that they have sought a complementary view of the relationship of perceptual and effective environments (see Conklin 1954*a*, 1954*b*, 1955, 1957, 1959, 1960, 1961, 1967; Berlin, Breedlove, and Raven 1966, 1968; Blaut 1959; Brookfield 1969; Evans-Pritchard 1940; Forde 1934, 1956; Fox 1952; Glacken 1956, 1967; Griaule and Dieterlen 1954; Hallowell 1951; Lowenthal 1961; Lowenthal, ed., 1967; Redfield 1952; Sapir 1912; Spoehr 1956). However, the general focus of ethnoecological studies (and of

many cultural ecological studies as well) is similar to that of the *genre de vie* concept; these studies do not attempt to account for the complex interactional nature of ecological relationships. The consequences for other aspects of an ecosystem of cognitive and behavioral regularities are not considered. Analysis implicitly or explicitly utilizes and is restricted to narrow conceptions of "niche" and "adaptation." Niche in this sense, as an organism's or (by extension) a culture's immediate "occupation," leaves aside its functional interrelationships in a wider system. The focus on adaptation, too, emphasizes only one aspect, the benefits to the organism or culture; it fails to examine the consequences of the adaptation for other parts of the system.

We can summarize the characteristics of ethnoecology as follows:

1. Its emphasis upon perceptual environment and its general lack of serious consideration of interactions between cognitive domains or with the effective environment result in the narrowest and least interactional of modern approaches. (Harold Conklin's research is an exception in this respect. See also Vayda and Rappaport 1968:491 and M. Harris 1968:602-603.)

2. It aims at adequate emic description of cultural domains, including the perceptual environment, principally by means of formal semantic analysis.

3. Its analysis is restricted to intracultural ecological relationships.

4. Insofar as it deals with the effective environment it seeks to evaluate and predict the effects of various behavioral possibilities on the participants' microenvironment, that environment frequently being restricted to other people (see also Sprout and Sprout 1965:118-20).

5. It makes assumptions of a high degree of homogeneity and stability in cultural categorization.

---

[9] See Vayda and Rappaport (1968:479-83) and Sprout and Sprout (1956, 1965:83-141) on this point.

[10] Thus concern with the perceptual environment is closely linked with philosophical idealism as well as with pragmatism (see Hofstadter 1955:32, 123-25), cultural relativism, and a folk-teleology approach.

Quasi-Population and Systems Ecology

The choice of the term "quasi-population and systems ecology" for the third category of interactionalist research is not meant to demean the impressive research accomplished to date in implementing a population or systems ecology that includes man. The label seems justified on the grounds of the small volume of work and the caution with which it has proceeded. As late as 1968 Vayda and Rappaport advanced the notion of "the possibility and desirability of a single science of ecology with laws and principles that apply to man as they do to other species" (1968:492). This idea is promoted in this chapter. But simplistic mechanical transferral of concepts and principles will not do. Concepts from general ecology require modification and refinement when applied explicitly to human populations and systems. Nonetheless, I believe that before the decade is out, varieties of systems ecology will have synthesized all the various adjectival ecologies in the social sciences.

The movement from autonomous ecologies (social, cultural, human, etc.) toward systems ecology[11] may be viewed as a development from analogical toward homological thinking. The intellectual roots of a systemic ecology are diverse and complex. It is the indirect feedback of multiplex lines rather than any assignable direct line that provides the grounds for an ecological synthesis now emerging. Therefore, I shall not attempt to assess the relative importance or temporal priority of the various lines of thought. As an indication of the diverse lines that ought to be considered in a sociology of ecological knowledge in anthropology, I offer

the following admittedly incomplete list. It is apparent that developments external to anthropology generally occurred prior to those within the subdisciplines, and I shall start with these.[12]

1. Some ecologists[13] have been interested in including man in ecological studies. They recognize that the simplifying assumption that "natural" systems can be isolated for study is untenable.

2. Important and sophisticated developments occurred in the human ecologies of geography[14] and sociology.[15] Ecology today occupies a central place in both of these disciplines, although their approaches are quite different (compare, for example, Stoddart 1966 and Duncan 1964). Interesting developments have also occurred in psychology (Barker 1960; Barker, ed., 1963) and history (Malin 1950).

3. An indirect and highly diffuse impact on ecology has come from developments in general systems theory and information theory.[16] Buckley (1967,

---

[11] Schultz (1967) has proposed the term "ecosystemology" for this field. He advocates development of qualitative as well as quantitative systems approaches.

[12] Citations for each of these lines represent my impression of some of the high points in the literature of each.

[13] E.g., E. Adams 1935; Bates 1953, 1960a, 1960b, 1961, 1962; Bews 1935; Charter 1962; Cole 1964, 1966; Commoner 1966; Dansereau 1964, 1966; Darling 1951, 1955-1956; Darling and Milton, eds., 1966; Dice 1955; Dubos 1964, 1967; Elton 1927; Hutchinson 1948; Kendeigh 1965; Klopfer 1962; E. Odum 1969; H. Odum 1962; Schultz 1967; Sears 1954, 1955, 1956, 1957, 1966; Watt 1968; Winterbottom 1945; Wynne-Edwards 1962.

[14] E.g., Ackerman 1963; Brookfield 1964; Carter 1950; Clarkson 1970; English 1968; Eyre and Jones 1966; Glacken 1956, 1967; Morgan and Moss 1965; Sauer 1952, 1956, 1967; Sorre 1943; Stewart 1954, 1956; Stoddart 1965, 1966; Thornthwaite 1940.

[15] E.g., Duncan 1959, 1961, 1964; Duncan and Schnore 1959; Gibbs and Martin 1959; Hawley 1950; Kunkel 1967; Schnore 1957-1958; Theodorson 1961.

[16] E.g., Ackoff 1960; Ashby 1958a, 1958b; Attneave 1967; Bertalanffy 1968; Boulding 1956;

1968) has argued articulately the value of modern systems theory for sociology (see also Berrien 1968).

4. Rapid developments have been made toward an integration of social science.[17]

5. Although environment was never completely neglected by archaeologists, the postwar period saw a revitalization of emphasis upon contextualization and upon cultural reconstructions informed by knowledge of ecological relationships.[18] Close communication between archaeologists and ethnographers has, if anything, increased (e.g., Chang 1967, Gjessing 1963), and has recently proved of great value in a review and reorientation of studies of hunting and collecting populations (Lee and De Vore 1968).

6. Studies concerned with environmental degradation and with aesthetic degradation[19] have argued for the necessity of seeking a balance between technology, human population, and environment. Research in environmental planning has also witnessed rapid growth.[20]

7. Rapidly expanding knowledge of human adaptability, nutrition, epidemiology, and health has demonstrated the necessity of considering broad interrelationships of man, culture, and environment.[21]

8. A resurgence of interest in problems of origins in sociocultural evolution, and especially in the concept of sociocultural adaptations, brought ecological questions to the fore again.[22]

9. Development and implementation of the method of controlled comparison (Eggan 1950, 1954) provided a near experimental framework for microanalysis of ecological, historical, and functional relationships.[23] These

---

Buchler and Nutini 1969; Churchman 1968; Foote and Greer-Wooten 1968; Hall and Fagen 1944; Hempel 1951; McClelland 1962; Margalef 1957; Marney and Smith 1964; Rapoport 1956, 1968; Van Dyne 1969.

[17] E.g., Bennett 1954; Bennett and Wolff 1955; Berelson and Steiner 1964; Boulding 1953, 1968; Dogan and Rokkan, eds., 1969; Forde 1959; Kuhn 1963; Lewin 1951; Sherif and Sherif 1969.

[18] E.g., Ascher 1959; Butzer 1964; J. D. Clark 1952, 1960, 1963, 1965; J. G. D. Clark 1945, 1952, 1953, 1967; J. G. D. Clark et al. 1954; M. D. Coe and Flannery 1967; Coles 1963; Cowgill and Hutchinson 1963; Cressman 1960; Cushing and Wright 1967; Flannery 1965; Fowler and Parmalee 1959; Heizer 1955, 1960; Hiernaux 1963; Howell and Bourlière, eds., 1963; Iversen 1941, 1949, 1960; Lanning 1965, 1967; McCarthy 1963; MacNeish 1964; MacNeish et al. 1968; Meighan 1959; Meighan et al. 1958; Sanders 1962, 1965; Sanders and Price 1968; Sears 1953; Steward 1937; Taylor 1948; Troels-Smith 1960a, 1960b; Wedel 1941, 1953, 1957; West 1965.

[19] E.g., Borgstrom 1965, 1969; Brown 1954; Burton 1968; Carson 1962; Ehrlich and Ehrlich 1970; Gutkind 1953; Hardin 1968; Leopold 1949; Mumford 1961; Nicholson 1959; Osborn 1948; Platt 1969; Rasmussen 1967; Rostlund 1954-1955, 1961;

Shepard and McKinley 1969; Simmons 1966; Sternberg 1964, 1968; W. L. Thomas, ed., 1956.

[20] E.g., Caldwell 1963; Firey 1945, 1946, 1960; Hubbert 1964; Huxley 1963; Jouvenel 1957; MacKaye 1940; Meier 1956; Simmons 1966.

[21] E.g., P. T. Baker 1962, 1969; P. T. Baker and Weiner, eds., 1966; Banks 1950; Banks and Hislop 1956; Bates 1956, 1959; Burnet 1962; Cameron 1958; Castro 1952; Cockburn 1963, 1971; Corwin, eds., 1949; Dubos 1959, 1967; Fiennes 1964; Gordon 1952; Honigmann 1962; Hudson 1965; Hunter 1967; Livingstone 1958; May 1959, 1961, 1965; Newman 1962; Otten 1967; Polgar 1962, 1964; Prothero 1964, 1965; Richards 1939; Rogers 1960, 1962; Sorre 1962; Stamp 1964.

[22] E.g., R. Adams 1966; Alland 1967; Barth 1950, 1964, 1968; Dole and Carneiro, eds., 1960; Fried 1952; Goldschmidt, ed., 1965; Greenberg 1959; Hallowell 1959; Hockett and Ascher 1964; Kroeber 1960; Lenneberg 1960; Lesser 1952; Mead 1964; Meggers 1954; Nicholaisen et al. 1964; Sahlins 1957, 1958, 1961, 1964; Sahlins and Service 1960; Service 1962; Steward 1955, 1960; Steward and Shimkin 1961; Tax, ed., 1960; L. A. White 1960; Wolf 1964; Yengoyan 1966.

[23] E.g., Eggan 1966; Goldman 1955; Gulliver 1955; Hackenberg 1962; Levy 1961; Nadel 1952;

closely controlled comparative studies have yielded some of the most provocative and soundly based statements of ecological relationships.

10. Concern within social and cultural anthropology for processes of sociocultural change or with the transactional aspect of social interaction[24] and recent developments in economic anthropology have refocused interest on social and material transactions.[25]

11. Results in new findings and redirection of interest in human biobehavioral evolution, including especially new knowledge of primate social behavior, have stimulated interaction between physical and social-cultural anthropology. Ecology has been a bridge in such interaction.[26]

Characteristics of Studies of Human Population and Systems Ecology. The major assumptions or characteristics of studies of human population ecology or

---

Nicholas 1963; Oliver 1962; Sahlins 1958, 1961; Secoy 1953; Steward et al. 1956.

[24] E.g., J. N. Anderson 1970; Barth 1963, 1966, 1967; Blau 1964; Boissevain 1968; Burling 1962; Cancian 1966; Colson 1962; Firth 1964b; Homans 1961; Leach 1954, 1961; Oliver 1965; Salisbury 1962; Scudder 1962; Thompson 1961.

[25] E.g., Barth 1963, 1967; Belshaw 1965; Cook 1966; Dalton 1967, 1969; Firth 1964a; Firth, ed., 1967; Forde 1956; Geertz 1963, 1964; M. Harris 1959; Herskovits 1952; Le Clair and Schneider 1968; Nash 1966; Orans 1966; Pearson 1957; Sahlins 1965; Vayda 1967; Wolf 1966.

[26] E.g., Brace 1962; Brues 1959; Campbell 1966; J. D. Clark 1960; J. D. Clark and Howell 1966; Count 1958; De Vore 1965; Dobzhansky 1962, 1963; Evernden and Curtis 1965; Garn 1965; Hallowell 1961; Hockett and Ascher 1964; Howell and Bourlière, eds., 1963; Jay, ed., 1968; Lasker 1969; Lee and De Vore 1968; Livingstone 1958, 1969; Medawar 1960; Roe and Simpson, eds., 1958; Simpson 1962; Tax, ed., 1960; Washburn 1953; Washburn, ed., 1961, 1963; Washburn and Howell 1960; Washburn, Jay, and Lancaster 1965.

of holistic studies of ecosystems that include human populations are these:

1. Human populations are an integral part of most, if not all, present ecosystems. Ecosystems are as they are at present because of man, his numbers, his varying behavior, and his use of energy.

2. The nature and structure of local ecosystems is everywhere relatively recent. Although most biota predate man's entry into specific ecosystems, some biota are more recent than human invaders of various niches of the ecosystem. For instance, man himself provides new niches for parasites and microorganisms; his behavior diverts energy flows and creates artifacts (Audy 1965, 1971), thus providing other potential new niches.

3. Men, as individuals and in populations, are involved in profound reticulate transactions with physical elements of their environment as well as with biotic ones. This is readily detectable in soil and watershed characteristics.

4. Man's transactional relations with an ecosystem can be treated from analytical and synthetic standpoints, just like those of other major components of its biota. The difference between man and other living things is relative. Human populations are more dynamic, more manipulative, and more dominant than other species in ecosystems. Man's complex sociocultural behavior enables him to collapse the time span required for biological adaptations, and has permitted an unparalleled explosive adaptive radiation into virtually all the earth's biomes.

5. Human populations and their complex sociocultural behaviors are in constant flux. It is unnecessary to determine *if* a specific population and its behavior are changing, but only to determine the rate or nature of change. The rate of change is relative. Thus an explicit assumption of equilibrium may

be permissible for populations of Pleistocene hunters, in order to simplify the demographic model, but such an assumption becomes increasingly tenuous in the construction of models of human populations following plant and animal domestication and subsequent forms of agricultural intensification.

6. The dynamic transactions of human populations in ecosystems reverberate essentially through the entire ecosystem, affecting the structure of energy flow and the functioning of natural control (feedback) systems. Causation is not simple or linear; it is complex and, to select a more heuristic metaphor, is circular or spiraling.

7. Of critical importance in the study of ecosystems that include human populations is the study of man's role in energy flow. Man drastically alters energy flow, simplifying ecosystems for his own use. Man's faculty as highly efficient capturer, converter, utilizer, and especially transporter of energy is closely interrelated with his symbolic behavior or tool-manufacturing ability, and is as uniquely human a property.[27]

8. Finally, although this should scarcely come as news to any anthropologist, we must never lose sight of the fact that an observer's presence *always* has an effect upon the objects of his observations within an ecosystem.

ANTHROPOLOGICAL PROBLEMS INVOLVING ECOLOGY

It is possible to outline major works in the literature and learn much about the status of ecology in anthropology by focusing on the specific kinds of ecological problems with which anthropologists have dealt. Therefore I shall

---

[27] I owe the notion of the uniqueness of energy transport from one part of an ecosystem to another part, or from one ecosystem to another, to David Tyler.

list below what I perceive to be the major problems and the major works representing them. But first I must refer to two aspects of problems in research. The first is succinctly put by Kaplan (1964:381-82): "Values enter into science . . . as a basis for the selection of problems, the order in which they are dealt with, and the resources expended on their solution. . . . Values make for bias, not when they dictate problems, but when they prejudge solutions." The second is just as aptly put by Merton (1959:ix): " . . . the experience of scientists is summed up in the adage that it is often more difficult to find and to formulate a problem than to solve it."

Both of these aspects of problems are illustrated in the research on ecology by anthropologists. We shall encounter the former reflected in recurrent modes of thought resting often on unexamined values that in turn affect the selection and priority of problems; we shall even encounter biases. We see the latter aspect—the difficulty in identifying problems—in the fact that many so-called problems are little more than questions of descriptive fact or of correlations between descriptive facts. Anthropological problems, then, are frequently the important but initial steps in the intensification and statement of a scientific problem. Topics of interest often stem from philosophical perspectives and general theoretical viewpoints at this early stage of inquiry. Not infrequently the initiating question is not even explicitly framed. All this reflects the low level of development of problem-forming, not to speak of problem-solving, with respect to the man-environmental relationships that constitute ecology.

For our purposes here, I define ecological questions or problems as those that include interactional consideration of external contingent factors of the topic under study as relevant variables in the explanation of sociocultural or biological phenomena. These relevant factors may be other people–demographic, interpersonal, and intergroup transactions–or may be nonhuman characteristics of the population's environment: biotic, edaphic, and climatic factors, for instance (Wallace, ed., 1969). In fact, these characteristics of the environment are not easily separated. Both human and nonhuman factors are involved in complementary transactions with the population under study and its behavioral artifacts (technology, social organization, and ideology, not to mention its collective biology).

Two more preliminaries: First, I hope that in the following outline of questions or problems I have adequately perceived and depicted the issues that are reflected in the research. Classification is always arbitrary to some degree. The classifier only hopes that his categories make some sense of events. When the events are ideas, perhaps the difficulties are greater than usual, especially at the general level at which this outline is pitched.[28] Second, I urge the reader to ask himself these questions: Why are these problems pursued? How are they phrased? Why these specific questions and phrasings, and not others? What do we need to know to answer these questions? How do we collect the information needed? How do we go about answering the question or explaining the matter at issue?

Finally, I hope the outline of major problems will enable the reader to assess the kind of ecological knowledge that anthropologists have contributed. Most of these problems are included in the central practical concerns of anthropology, those of describing, analyzing, and explaining similarities and differences among ethnic groups.

POPULATION AND DEMOGRAPHIC FACTORS

Although this fundamental dimension of ecological studies remains an area seriously neglected by anthropologists, concern for demography and for broader population studies has entered the work of some anthropologists either explicitly or implicitly. Development of this area holds promise for significant advances for an ecology that includes man. The general question is how sociocultural (including technological) and other ecological factors relate to the distribution and numbers of human populations.[29] There are several subproblems within studies of human population ecology. The relationship between population density or population size and sociocultural development has long attracted attention.[30] By contrast, little attention has been paid to the relationships between specific demographic trends (fertility, mortality, and migration) or population structure and aspects of social structure or behavior. Exceptions are studies examining the sizes and demographic rates of prehistoric and protohistoric popula-

---

[28] The classification that follows reflects my judgment of the ways in which the specific studies cited contribute to ecology. Since many studies do not make their ecological contributions explicit, a systematic author-oriented depiction is not possible. Besides, most citations could easily fall into more than one category. I have categorized each work on the basis of the principal question addressed. A few studies representing outstanding examples are cited in more than one category.

[29] E.g., Barth 1956, 1959; Baumhoff 1963; Binford 1968; Birdsell 1953, 1958; Carneiro 1956, 1961; Halbwachs 1960; Hallowell 1949; Keyfitz 1966a; Livingstone 1958, 1962; Steward 1936, 1955; Weisenfeld 1967.

[30] E.g., Boserup 1965; Braidwood and Reed 1957; Carneiro 1967, 1970; Childe 1951; Deevey 1960a, Dumond 1965; Luten 1969; Mead and Granger 1965; Meggers 1954; Ooi 1958; Sanders and Price 1968; Service 1962.

tions,[31] postcontact changes in social organization connected with drastically increased mortality,[32] migration, and distribution,[33] and the effect of social organization (and disorganization) on population trends, or of population trends on social organization.[34] Interest in the question of the role of environmental factors in structuring populations has also lagged.[35] Studies of the ecological concomitants, including population, of disease and nutrition constitute a major exception.[36] The general topic of ethnodemography[37] deserves a great deal more attention by anthropologists in the future. New studies should routinely examine the demographic status of the population studied (McArthur 1970). Much can also be done by utilizing techniques of ethno-history and formal demography to reconstruct population trends and structure for populations otherwise well known in the ethnographic literature.

At present, anthropological literature lacks adequate ecological and demographic contextualization. Most populations studied by anthropologists were at the time of investigation undergoing severe though frequently unreported ecological, demographic, and (we must assume) sociocultural dislocations as a result of the colonial and modernizing experience. Not a few "sociocultural adaptations," generally viewed as pristine, may be related to such dislocations (e.g., Wolf 1957) or to effects of temporary reduction in human numbers and in the intensity of human use on a local ecosystem.

HUMAN BIOBEHAVIORAL EVOLUTION

Studies of human biobehavioral evolution have employed varying degrees of ecological thinking. Some ecological rules have been applied to morphological adaptations.[38] Extrapolation from principles of mammalian ecology to protohominid ecology proved useful in the reconstruction of protohominid evolution.[39] Ecological concepts such as ecological barriers, limiting factors, territoriality, food web, biomass, and carrying capacity, as well as sophisticated ecological reasoning, have been applied to the population ecology of hunters and collectors.[40] Studies of the social behavior and of the ecology of

[31] E.g., Birdsell 1958, Borah and Cook 1963, Carneiro and Hilse 1966, Deevey 1960a, Laughlin 1968, McArthur 1970, Neel 1970.

[32] E.g., J. R. Baker 1928, Birdsell 1970, Blasingham 1956, Hogbin 1930, Lantis 1957, Lessa 1955, Lipschutz 1966, Service 1962, Smith 1970, Wagley 1940.

[33] E.g., Bohannan 1954; Colson 1960; Geisler 1967; Lowenthal and Comitas 1962; L. Mason 1950, 1957; Pelzer 1940.

[34] E.g., Benedict 1970; Birdsell 1971; Cook 1946, 1947; Davis 1951; Davis and Blake 1956; Douglas 1966; Hackenberg 1966; Hitchcock 1967; Hulse 1961; Keyfitz 1966b; Kunstadter et al. 1963; Lantis 1953, n.d.; Lorimer et al. 1954; Reed 1955; Roberts 1957; Schneider 1955; Slater 1959; Stevenson 1968; Stott 1962; United Nations 1953; Wertheim 1959; Yengoyan 1968.

[35] E.g., Aschmann 1959; Birdsell 1953, 1958; Cole 1957; Eichenwald and Fry 1969; Spuhler 1959; Whiting 1964.

[36] E.g., Gerlach 1965; Gladson, ed., 1960; Gordon 1952; May 1959, 1961, 1963, 1965, 1966, 1967; Newman 1962, 1964; Richards 1932, 1939.

[37] E.g., P. Brown and Winefield 1965, Dorjahn 1958, C. S. Ford 1964, Hainline 1965, Krzywicki 1934, McArthur 1967, Nag 1962.

[38] E.g., Coon 1950, 1954, 1959; Coon, Garn, and Birdsell 1950; Newman 1953; Schreider 1963, 1964.

[39] E.g., Bartholomew and Birdsell 1953, Hockett and Ascher 1964.

[40] E.g., Birdsell 1953, 1958, 1968; Knight 1965; Lee 1963, 1965, 1969; Lee and De Vore 1968; Lyman and Scott 1967.

free-ranging subhuman primate populations are contributing importantly to the reconstruction of hominid biobehavioral evolution.[41] The recognition and study of the selective effects of sociocultural behavior upon the evolution of man's biology (Hallowell 1956; Washburn 1950, 1960), together with an understanding of the importance of biological factors in the origin of cultural behavior,[42] have done much to develop knowledge of human evolution. Fundamental to these studies is the assumption that the underlying behavior of the entire primate order rests upon homologous evolutionary mechanisms. The concept of adaptation to changing environmental conditions provides a basic link between ecological and evolutionary studies.

SYNTHESIS OF CULTURAL EVOLUTION, ARCHAEOLOGY, AND ECOLOGY

The old question of the reconstruction of the development of specific cultures and general culture has brought forth attempts to synthesize concepts of cultural evolution, archaeology, and ecology (e.g., Butzer 1964, D. Harris 1969). Concepts such as levels of sociocultural integration and developmental sequences[43] have been combined with concepts that translate cultural artifacts into indices of social systems (population size and density, degree of stratification, etc.) and with ecological concepts such as symbiosis, demographic dynamics, type of agricultural system, and so on.

---

[41] E.g., De Vore 1965; Howell and Bourlière, eds., 1963; Jay 1965; Jay, ed.. 1968; Washburn, ed., 1961; Washburn, Jay, and Lancaster 1965.

[42] E.g., Hallowell 1960, Lesser 1961, Steward 1960.

[43] E.g., Byers, ed., 1967; Sanders and Price 1968; Service 1962; Steward 1955; Willey and Phillips 1958.

A persistent general problem concerns the nature and functioning of various types of broad sociocultural adaptations or strategies. The study of those adaptations that are most obviously dominated by environmental factors have tended to yield the most explicit ecological analysis. Ecological studies of hunters and gatherers,[44] swidden cultivators,[45] and pastoralists[46] are better developed than those of peasants[47] or postpeasants and farmers (Bennett 1969).

ECOLOGICAL RELATIONS OF SOCIAL ORGANIZATION

Another very general concern of ecological studies is the question of ecological relationships of forms of social organization. One specific question concerns the effect of features of the habitat, through the medium of productive organization, upon the organization of groups, stratification, leadership, and other social institutions.[48] The question has been refined by the employment of the ecological concept of niche.[49] Structural regularities in

---

[44] E.g., Tindale 1959; Tobias 1964; Watanabe 1964, 1966; for bibliography see Lee and De Vore 1968.

[45] E.g., Barrau 1958, Brookfield and Brown 1963, Conklin 1961, Gourou 1956, Harding 1967, J. E. Spencer 1966.

[46] E.g., Barth 1960, 1968; Johnson 1969; Krader 1955, 1957; Marx 1967; Nicholaisen 1963; Paine 1958, 1964; Stenning 1957; Wilbert, ed., 1961.

[47] E.g., Beardsley 1964, Blaut 1959, Clarkson 1968, Evans 1956, Mencher 1966, Nicholas 1963, Parrack 1969, Shimkin 1964, Steward et al. 1956, Wolf 1966.

[48] E.g., Bennett 1944, Iijima 1964, Sahlins 1958, Service 1962, R. Spencer 1959, Steward 1955, Steward et al. 1956.

[49] E.g., Barth 1956, 1959, 1968; Geertz 1963.

socioeconomic adaptations have been suggested for populations profoundly affected by acculturation situations.[50] The limiting effect of environmental conditions upon settlement pattern has been frequently studied.[51] Some studies have related the relative inflexibility of constraints of the habitat to the tightness of rules of the social order.[52] More generally, the hypothesis of the adaptation of human populations to specific environmental conditions by means of sociocultural institutions or behavior has been widely employed and has produced interesting interpretations.[53] Disagreement exists, however, about the degree to which sociocultural features can or should be regarded as adaptations (e.g., Bennett 1967; Collins 1965; M. Harris 1960, 1966; Millon 1962).

Studies focusing upon the ways in which particular sociocultural features or complexes originate or function (mainly the latter) in ecosystems have demonstrated how fruitful the assumption of adaptation can be.[54] Several of the most sophisticated and thoroughgoing studies utilize concepts from animal ecology and attempt to show how sociocultural features (such as rituals) serve as homeostatic mechanisms maintaining a wider system. Many of these studies adopt an intuitive ecological point of view, sometimes brilliantly. They are perceptive, but are usually insufficiently holistic, and permit alternative functional interpretations. Thus they are subject to refutation by further study (as, for example, Drucker and Heizer's [1967] refutation of Piddocke [1965]).

LATENT FUNCTIONS AND DYSFUNCTIONS

Ecological hypotheses are also proposed regarding the functions served by animals in human populations (Leeds and Vayda, eds., 1965), and regarding the functions or causes of conflict, raiding, and warfare.[55] Studies of dysfunctions of sociocultural features and of positive feedback are fewer in number than those of functional and equilibrium mechanisms. The search for dysfunctions should be prosecuted with equal vigor. Moreover, in light of recent worldwide ecological degradation, there is greater need for knowledge of deviation-suppressing processes than deviation-amplifying processes (though see Maruyama 1963:164). The entire range of consequences of social institutions and behavior is also badly in need of study, especially when serious ecosystem dysfunctions may ensue, in an ecologically informed judgment. For instance, the prime role of the family in much of man's biobehavioral evolution—reproduction—may be judged more dysfunctional than functional in a world threatened by a population avalanche. Or consider the dysfunctions of the state in today's world.

FOLK CONCEPTIONS AND DECISION-MAKING

The general problem of folk conceptions of environmental or ecosystem relations and the impact of these con-

---

[50] E.g., Fried 1952, Hoffman 1964, Murphy and Steward 1956, Wolf 1957.

[51] E.g., Carneiro 1956, Frake 1962.

[52] E.g., Berthoud 1967, Burns 1961.

[53] E.g., Cohen, ed., 1968; Fortier 1957; Frake 1956; Gerlich 1965; Goldschmidt, ed., 1965; M. Harris and Morreu 1966; R. Harris 1962; Howard 1966; Sahlins 1962, 1964; Steward 1955; Strehlow 1965; Tindale 1959.

[54] E.g., Bohannan 1954; Moore 1957; Piddocke 1965; Sahlins 1961; Suttles 1960a, 1960b; Vayda 1961b, 1969; Vayda, Leeds, and Smith 1961; Vayda and Rappaport 1963.

[55] E.g., Ekvall 1961, Hickerson 1965, Sweet 1965, Vayda 1961a.

ceptions on behavior have been mentioned. It is of increasing interest in this connection to discover the rules of decision-making toward achievement of behavioral goals. Changes in knowledge, in technology, and in the organization of rules have been found to be frequently related to alternative sociocultural behavior and to changes in ecosystem relations.[56] Some excellent progress has been made on the problem of describing folk biosystematics.[57]

BEHAVIORAL AND BIOLOGICAL LIMITATIONS

Still other studies have begun to investigate the cultural definitions of interpersonal and intergroup spacing and their ecological implications.[58] Studies relating to environment, conceptions of spacing, high density conditions, social tension, and physiological stress in laboratory animals suggest possible application in the study of human populations.[59] Further, it has been demonstrated that settlement morphology and forms of social organization are often implicitly linked to ecological factors;[60] the interesting possible correspondence of cultural frontiers with ecological boundaries has also been raised.[61]

The related question of environmental limitation of sociocultural devel-

opment has elicited a very large literature, and the thesis of Meggers (1954, 1957) has stimulated a fruitful series of refutations and rebuttals.[62]

CONTROLLED COMPARISONS

Comparison has always been a basic tool of anthropology. The method of controlled comparison (Eggan 1954) has stimulated some of the best studies in the ecological literature.[63] Since controls are exercised over significant ecological, historical, and organizational variables, the likelihood of isolating critical relationships and underlying processes is heightened.

RECENT POPULATION AND SYSTEMS ECOLOGY STUDIES

A few intensive descriptive and analytical studies of specific human populations and their environments as systems have been attempted by anthropologists.[64] The best of these have been longitudinal in nature, have collected quantitative data and utilized them to investigate aspects of biosocial process, and have involved interdisciplinary team research to some degree. These studies have focused to date on maintenance processes of the particular subsistence system that keep crucial variables within an adaptive range. The level of description and of methodological sophistication achieved in these works is exceptional. All assume functionally integrated systems in long-term equilib-

---

[56] E.g., Brookfield 1968, Davenport 1960, Gould 1963, Hoffman 1969.

[57] E.g., E. N. Anderson 1967; Bailey 1968; Berlin et al. 1966, 1968; Bulmer 1967; Conklin 1954*a*, 1955; Frake 1962; Wyman and Bailey 1965.

[58] E.g., Deevey 1960*b*, E. Hall 1966, Wagley 1951.

[59] E.g., Calhoun 1962; Christian 1950, 1963; Christian and Davis 1964.

[60] E.g., R. Adams 1965, Chang 1958.

[61] E.g., Lattimore 1951, 1962; Wolf 1962.

[62] E.g., Carneiro 1961; W. Clark 1966; Coe 1957; Dumond 1961, 1965; Ferdon 1959; Meggers 1957; Porter 1965. See also Mikesell's (1967) review of the literature on this question.

[63] E.g., Oliver 1962, and Sahlins 1958.

[64] E.g., Carneiro 1956; Conklin 1957, 1961, 1967; Lee 1965, 1969; Nelson 1969; Netting 1968; Rappaport 1967*b*; Scudder 1962.

rium. Specific findings resulting from meticulous application of systematic methods have raised fundamental questions that have challenged heretofore established dogmas about types of hunters and collectors and swidden or terrace cultivators. Studies of such subsistence economies have been revitalized, if not revolutionized; they have greatly stimulated further research. Generally, these accomplishments were achieved by sound anthropological fieldworkers who used principles and methods of population or systems ecology for the study of human groups.

Conklin (1954a, 1954b, 1967) carefully applies ecological principles in his goal of describing and analyzing broad types of subsistence agriculture: swidden and irrigation. This goal and his primary concern for the perceptual environment help explain his lack of interest in explicit consideration of theoretical questions in ecological research. Conklin's treatment of features of the natural environment in ecological terms is comprehensive and skillful, but his strict separation of environmental features from cultural (technological, social, ethnoecological) and contingent demographic features detracts from a fully systemic approach. Conklin produces detailed and highly perceptive scientific and folk analyses of specific ecological arrangements of the subsistence system. But his useful data on food webs, energetics, demography, succession, labor efficiency, and temporal relationships generally are dealt with apart from and external to cultural features (such as aspects of social grouping). Linkages between ecosystem and sociocultural subsystem are incomplete, and the uniqueness of the sociocultural system requires separate methods of analysis, although Conklin produces a sound general depiction of the costs and benefits of the subsistence types.

Lee (1965, 1969) and Rappaport (1967a, 1967b) have contributed perhaps the most rigorous studies of the ecology of human populations yet attempted. These studies, like those of Carneiro, Conklin, Scudder, and Netting, are more descriptive than theoretical, as one must expect at this state of knowledge. These are admirable studies worthy of emulation by other investigators. Especially significant are the attempts by Lee and Rappaport to measure caloric and protein intake, energy inputs and outputs, to estimate productivity and carrying capacity and the effects of animal populations on ecosystems, and to describe the numbers and kinds of floral and faunal species. Lee's broad ethnographic research also deals specifically with limiting factors, organizational flexibility, and energetics. Rappaport's specific concerns are with marriage and other exchanges, and intergroup conflict and land tenure in relation to stress physiology and territoriality. In brief, Rappaport's thesis suggests that the ritual slaughter of pigs serves as a negative feedback control upon the sociocultural-ecological system.

Despite their high level of accomplishment, these studies exhibit several weaknesses that can be avoided in subsequent studies. Subtle problems are raised by Rappaport's use of "ecosystem," his nutritional physiology, his mathematical treatment, and his treatment of energetics:

First, although the application of the ecosystem concept is most appropriate to these studies, and although Rappaport demonstrates its value and contributes to operationalizing the concept, he seems to have applied synecological concepts with an autecological approach, thus reducing the power of the ecosystem concept. Rappaport defines the ecosystem exclusively by trophic relationships, and since boundaries of ecosystems are always somewhat arbitrary, he selects a small local unit convenient for quantitative and other analysis. However, trophic exchanges represent only one type of relationship existing in an ecosystem (physical cycles and other biologic parameters are also influential and usually limiting). Insistence that an ecosystem must be nearly a closed system is unwarranted. The larger local system within which land is redistributed (probably more satisfactorily "the ecosystem" in an order of ecosystems) is, as Rappaport notes, a hierarchical extension of the relatively arbitrary subsystem under analysis. Rappaport appears at best to be applying the concept of community rather than that of ecosystem.

Second, Rappaport's treatment of the complex problems of nutritive needs has been challenged by nutritionists and physiologists, leaving the thesis open to the charge of overinterpretation.

Third, mathematical and cybernetic analyses are useful tools in ecology. Rappaport's quantitative data and mathematical calculations and estimates are descriptive. They are interesting and useful for comparison, but they lack a link with theory and cannot be used to study or simulate human processes with available models. Moreover, his discussion could be clarified and supplemented by use of a flow chart— to some a prerequisite for a serious systems study. Rappaport's qualitative analysis of the cybernetic aspects of ritual for certain components of the ecosystem studies is impressive, but it reflects a still incomplete application of qualitative systems concepts.

Fourth, this work might have been more successful were it not for another weakness. Rappaport does not fully depict the role of energy flow in an ecosystem. Energy is basic to all biological transactions. Moreover, one of man's unique properties in his technological and organizational capacity for exploiting, transforming, and transporting external energy sources. It is this property that gives man such awesome ecological impact, and it cannot be neglected in ecological research. Energy flow is channeled by food webs and by energy transport and exchange (Lee 1969:48). Energy flow for man is significantly intraspecific as well as interspecific. The intraspecific aspects of energy flow are not adequately accounted for in Rappaport's analysis.

Only the initial results of Lee's studies have appeared to date. (This is true also of Rappaport's, Conklin's, and Netting's studies.) Lee's research on the !Kung Bushman subsistence deals with such problems as the origin and development of human energy relations and the measurement and evaluation of the precariousness or the security of the hunter-collector strategy. Lee's works represent a high level of achievement in providing rich data on a broad range of demographic and nutritional factors and functional interrelationships. One hopes that subsequent research will permit calculation of age-specific fertility and mortality and rates of growth, and consideration of protein nutrition and vitamin and mineral needs and intakes similar to that provided for caloric intake and expenditure. Application of concepts of productivity, predation, and energy flow to an ecosystemic treatment of the Dobe !Kung would also prove interesting. Questions that have not yet been considered concern the factors that regulate population growth (since Lee has shown that food is not limiting); the effects that displacement of adjacent Bushman groups have had on succession; the impact of such nonindigenous variables as Bantu cattle-keeping on flora, water resources, and contingent factors; and the impact of trade on the ecosystem under study. As yet Lee has applied no synecological thinking in his Kalahari studies.

The excellent ecological descriptions of Scudder (1962) and Netting (1968) are less quantitative than Lee's. Scudder's work is especially thorough, an outstanding qualitative treatment of ecological relationships. All these studies are autecological in approach, although they range widely to investigate significant contingent factors of the local subsistence systems studied. In general, the problem of how to deal with relevant factors of wider systems that impinge upon the local ecosystem has not been solved. The study of energy flow and ecological transactions is confined to those within the system of the small local population studied.

Such questions as I have raised about these excellent studies are possible only because of the strides that these scholars have made.

CONCEPTUAL OBSTACLES TO AN ECOLOGICAL APPROACH

We begin with a paradox: as ideas sow a harvest of knowledge, they also reap its limitations; that is, the heuristic success of philosophical perspectives, theoretical viewpoints, methodological strategies, and research techniques are inevitably accompanied by counterproductive consequences. I think it useful to review here certain perspectives, viewpoints, strategies, and techniques that are quite general in Western thought—in the social sciences and anthropology in particular—and which, while contributing to knowledge, have also discouraged development of a systematic ecology including man.

Basic philosophical perspectives of any people—their world view—inevitably affect folk theories. Such perspectives invade even the systematic theories of science. Pelto (1970:118) has noted that a metatheory of anthropology can be abstracted from the work of American anthropologists. Its assump-

tions generally go unconsidered and are only rarely challenged in print (Batalla 1966, Hickerson 1967). One of the responsibilities of the anthropologist, as scientist, is to make explicit and to examine his underlying perspectives and metatheories. It is important that he go beyond the examination of personal assumptions, which is conventional in the methodological literature, to specify the seldom considered though highly influential collective assumptions concerning human nature and values that underlie his experience.

MAN AGAINST NATURE

I know of no more pertinent example of the powerful and far-reaching influence of an idea than the Western conception of "man against nature." Since Glacken (1967, 1970) and L. White, Jr. (1962, 1967), hace recently traced the roots, the development, and the general consequences of this dichotomy. I shall confine my discussion here to its direct and indirect impact on ecology. Although the notion of man against nature is not monolithic in Western thought, so far it has nonetheless effectively withstood the periodic challenges of intellectual countercurrents. Glacken (1970) attributes the lasting strength of this "outmoded idea" to its adoption in modern times as the basis for a secular philosophy of history that views cultural evolution as a process of reversing the early dominance of nature over man by man's "conquest" over nature. In this view the progressive improvement of the human condition and the eventual humanization of the earth rests in the development of the arts and sciences. Thus man is placed above and separate from the realm of nature. Nature is placed at the disposal of man, not to be preserved, but to be used as man's rationality and purposes dictate. Man's manipulation of nature, it follows, inevitably gives rise to unlimited progress. Despite the Darwinian counterrevolution, the separation of man and nature, if somewhat compromised, remains with us. In the words of L. White, Jr. (1967:1206), "Despite Darwin, we are *not*, in our hearts, part of the natural process."

The world view of man separate from and in conflict with nature encouraged the separation of the humanities from the sciences, epitomized in the idea of the "two cultures" (Snow 1959), and encouraged the fusion of science and technology, a combination that has carried forward the "conquest" of nature so efficiently and so often mindlessly that the functioning of the entire encosphere is drastically threatened.

In anthropology the man-nature dichotomy is mirrored in the divisions made between human biology and human behavior, between scientist and humanist, between theory and application (Thompson 1967:68). Recognition that this dichotomy exists helps us comprehend the folly of a would-be value-neutral study of man that confines itself to means and excludes all consideration of ends. A detached laissez-faire scientism becomes the justification for the evasion of social responsibility (Leach 1968). Even more subtly this dichotomy encourages anthropologists to confine their study of man's behavior to his functioning within the framework of human institutions, or to explicate behavior only in terms of social phenomena. Although on one level the unity of mankind and the notion of cultural relativism are anthropological dogmas, at another level "progress" is assumed to imply the existence of a gap between "primitive" peoples and modern peoples, and is explained as a result of modern peoples' superior rational command over nature. The vast majority of modern men, even

the most radical, do not question that growth and "development" are normal processes, destined eventually to "improve" the condition of all mankind. (For a minority opinion, see Illich 1969.)

But these considerations could take us far afield. The man-against-nature perspective is only one of a complex of ideas that variously intrude into scientific thought. I can touch here on only a few of the ways in which some of the implications of these ideas have led anthropologists away from the ecological legacy of Darwin—the concept of the unity and harmony of all of nature, including man.

THE NATURE-NURTURE CONTROVERSY

There is the question of the locus of the determinants of human behavior. Though all would readily agree that behavior is a complex biosocial phenomenon, most scholars would also insist that the study of behavior requires us to make some simplifying assumptions. A major simplifying assumption finds its origin in the nature-nurture question, which also is deeply rooted in Western thought. The analysis of behavior is thus allocated to different specialists, those who study its physiological base and those who study its cultural manifestations. Unfortunately, the division leaves us largely ignorant of a crucial middle ground. The controversy as it is phrased in biology is not dead; environmentalists argue that external factors determine biological trends, whereas hereditarians argue that factors internal to the organism are the sole determinants of biological traits.

Although it is widely recognized that the dichotomous phrasing of the issue—environment versus genetics—is simplistic and seriously limits inquiry, the viewpoint nonetheless has its impact on scientific theory.[65] In this century more attention and more spectacular success have attended molecular biology (the study of the physiochemical basis of life) and genetics (the study of inheritance) than classical biology (the study of complex living systems in their environmental contexts). In Commoner's words (1966:45), "The dominance of the molecular approach in biological research fosters increasing inattention to the natural complexity of biological systems." Furthermore, studies of complex living systems at the population or community levels are, as might be expected, the least developed, even within classical biology. And even those studies that focus on ecosystems rarely include man, their focus being upon "natural" wholes (e.g., Allee et al. 1949, Shelford 1963). Similarly, students of human behavior also phrase the problem in terms of nature versus nurture. Physical and social-cultural anthropologists have generally tended to maintain the pretense that each deals with a discrete part of man. Since man's biology is *almost* exclusively physical and man's behavior is *almost* exclusively learned, the division of labor appears efficient and supposedly leaves little out of consideration. Consequently, for much of this century, the fact that morphology and behavior are outcomes of the continuous interaction of biology and culture was neglected (see criticism by P. T. Baker 1962, Count 1958, Laughlin 1962, Vayda and Rappaport 1968, Washburn 1950, Washburn and Avis 1958). Only recently, some anthropologists (those

just mentioned, among others) have reframed the question in a form allowing research to focus on the whole biocultural nexus, so basic in the evolution of man.

On another level, the nature-nurture conception enters into the phrasing of problems by students of human biology and of human culture, the former adopting approaches similar to those of other biologists and the latter tending to consider that behavior may be determined by either culture or environment. In this latter view, culture is the superorganic extension of man's evolved nature and also part of his nurture, and environment is the nurturing constraints of nature. Since no anthropologist is a thoroughgoing environmental determinist and most have eschewed psychological reductionism, culture or society has been explicable only in terms of itself. Physical environment, as we saw earlier, when it was considered at all, was treated as an external limiting factor, not as a part of the culture or the society. At best, it is generally viewed as slowly changing, little influenced by man and having little influence on him; it has played a small role in anthropological explanation (e.g., Hsu 1963:147-49).

CONCEPTIONS OF STABILITY AND CHANGE

Technology and Progress

Technology, an outcome of social behavior, in contrast to environment, is treated as the chief cause of sociocultural change and as a key factor in man's ascendancy over nature. Although the thought is seldom explicitly stated by anthropologists in deterministic terms, technology—the corollary of man-against-nature, the handmaiden of progress, the dynamo of civilization—is for many a basic factor in social

---

[65] Pastore (1949) suggests further that the positions of a sample of scholars with respect to nature and nurture were highly correlated with their sociopolitical views; environmentalists were liberals or radicals and hereditarians were conservatives.

and cultural explanations.[66] A related notion is seen in what has been referred to as the "technological fix" (A. Weinberg 1966); this is the assumption that the solution to *all* problems—environmental, scientific, and social—lies in technological developments. This Western folk view regarding the fundamental causal and "progressive" role of technology has now been projected across the entire globe.

"Development," with its attendant process "growth," is today the goal of all nations. Growth and development are accepted as normal, even inevitable processes, although they may frequently be locally and temporarily retarded. However, although development is considered the normal condition of modernizing industrializing states, at the same time, by a dichotomization so familiar in the West, it is considered abnormal for the so-called folk societies (Redfield 1952). Societies of this type—highly self-sufficient, small in scale, relatively isolated, technologically simple, preliterate, essentially undifferentiated, and reputedly typically nondynamic—have constituted the principal object of anthropological study and a dominant model of nonindustrial societies for more than one century. Whether validly or not, folk societies have generally been viewed as relatively stable—that is, well adjusted to external conditions or essentially in states of equilibrium. Various concepts and procedures used in the conduct of research, however militate against verification of the equilibrium hypothesis in most societies studied. Culture was viewed as relatively homogeneous and highly stable, "norms being highly prescriptive in a wide range of activities—i.e., few alternative courses of action are available to members of the system" (Sjoberg

---

[66] Cottrell 1955, Ogburn 1933, Ribiero 1969, White 1959.

1960:9). Changes were usually seen as unusual events, ordinarily the results of the diffusion of technological traits or, more rarely, of technological or organizational innovations.

The Organismic Model

The "organism analogy" is an important source of the assumption of sociocultural equilibrium and of a return to a balanced state following change. Since the time of Herbert Spencer, the organism has been a dominant model, for the most part an implicit one, in the thinking of social scientists. Society or culture, treated in analogy with an organism, is assumed to have an internal integrity and a life of its own. The organismic analogy is deeply imbedded in superorganic, culturalogical, structural-functionalist, cultural-psychological, and cultural-ecological theories.[67]

My concern is with the ways in which views of the environment are influenced by the organismic model. Because culture was assumed to be in equilibrium, environment too was assumed to be constant, in perfect equilibrium. Dynamic change was a property of modern societies; primitive man's role as an ecological agent was ignored (Heizer 1955). Environment was a limiting and generally nondynamic factor. In some studies—especially of hunters, swidden cultivators, and pastoralists—the impact of seasonal changes, the severity of environmental conditions, crucial relationships between features of the environment and social behavior were too evident to be treated casually, and in such studies the close dependency of the human population

---

[67] It is interesting to note that early in this century influential ecologists, in discussing the characteristics of plant succession and the nature of the biotic community, also found a model for both in the individual organism and the organism's life cycle (see Clements 1916).

on the land and on the seasons was stressed. Thus, for instance, Evans-Pritchard (1940) described the "ecological time" of the Nuer and the basic relations of man, animals, and space. In many ethnographic descriptions and comparative studies there remained, usually implicit, the notion that the level of cultural development was basically a function of the degree of dependence on or mastery over the environment. When anthropologists studied cultures that were technologically more advanced, environmental factors, less immediate and more complex, faded from consideration as variables facilitating understanding of social behavior. F. Thomas (1925:311) clearly expresses this view:

However men [scholars] differ regarding the importance of geographical factors in social causation, they seem to agree that their operation is most effective on primitive peoples, and that advancing civilization is characterized by a diminishing importance of physical influences and an increasing importance of psychological and cultural factors.

The same notion was emphasized by Robert Redfield late in his career. Redfield (1960:29-31) went on to suggest why the ecosystem approach was inadequate for the study of man in complex societies:

The ecological system of the naturalist is a system of organisms in a natural environment, not a mental environment. . . . Human mental life has a structure of its own. It is difficult to describe it in terms of its connections with the land and the rain and the trees. The things that men think and feel are only partly connected with adaptation for survival.

Thus, for the study of complex societies, which in his view are essentially environmentally autonomous, Redfield recommends the analogic human ecology—the spatial sociology—of Robert Park (1936) and his colleagues.

THE ETHNOGRAPHIC PRESENT

Another convention of ethnographic description that has unfortunate consequences for the development of systemic ecological studies is the use of the concept of the "ethnographic present." The convention was partly rooted in the early interest of philosophers of the Enlightenment in recording the natural state of man and his stages of development. In part too it represented a convenient simplifying concept, employed first by explorers and then by anthropologists whose goals were the depiction of the "natural" precontact customs of exotic peoples. Two unwarranted assumptions were involved. On the one hand, it was assumed that the remembered, precontact culture was a "genuine" culture—a stable, coherent way of life unpolluted by alien influence; this assumption tended to justify and to encourage the use of accounts of informants in reconstructing culture as against the anthropologist's observations of overt behavior. On the other hand, it was assumed that the stable sociocultural system exists in harmony with a stable environment. When studies of European intrusions upon indigenous populations, of rapidly changing cultures, and of microdynamics became respectable, they became part of separate subdisciplines. "Acculturation" and "culture change" thus are separate subjects of study, as if change were an abnormal state and stability normal. As man was considered apart from nature, statics became divorced from dynamics.

The unvalidated hypotheses underlying the ethnographic present could remain unchallenged only so long as anthropologists disregarded available micro- and macrohistorical sources and ecological relationships. Convenient simplifying assumptions of earlier periods die slowly. The complex of ideas constituting the ethnographic present seems to be in part responsible for a long-standing devaluation of studies of peoples undergoing drastic change. (Emphasis upon small, relatively isolated communities also is a major contributing factor.) At any rate, a preference for isolated, alien, "primitive" subjects and an antipathy for the rapidly changing plural segments of complex modern societies remain dominant attitudes.

ANALYSIS VS. SYNTHESIS

Yet another hindrance to development of studies of human ecosystems is the dominant strategy of analysis favored by social and cultural anthropologists. The few brilliant departures from the analytical strategy are considered as works of art that captured the integrative spirit of culture rather than works of science (Redfield 1953:734). We have noted that biosocial reality has been segmented in order to be understood. This is only one of a series of analytical operations that characterize current anthropological inquiry. Consequently, in the best "cultural ecological" studies the environment is generally separated out as a discrete component to be further analyzed and eventually related to other discrete cultural components—economy, religion, social structure, and the like. This highly productive "scientific" strategy of analysis assumes that the best or only way to understand a complex whole is to take it apart, investigate the parts, and then reassemble them. To date, attempts by anthropologists to utilize the strategy of synthesis to understand an integral biocultural reality are rare, but the breadth and depth of human understanding appear likely to be increased by a shift to such a strategy.

As Dubos (1968:27) has noted, since the seventeenth century the dominant strategy in the pursuit of knowledge by scientific methods has been the separation of phenomena into their ultimate discrete components. The success of atomistic science has witnessed the neglect of integrated science.

The most pressing problems of humanity, however, involve relationships, communications, changes of trends—in other words, situations in which systems must be studied as a whole in all the complexity of their interactions. This is particularly true of human life. When life is considered only in its specialized functions, the outcome is a world emptied of meaning. To be fully relevant to life, science must deal with the responses of the total organism to the total environment.

The survival of mankind may depend upon development of a new scientific humanism (see also Commoner 1966, Ehrlich and Ehrlich 1970).

Structural Functionalism

Some readers may respond that although modern social anthropology has indeed relied exclusively upon analysis, it has nonetheless performed its analysis within a systemic framework. They will point to the dominance of structural-functionalist thought. While structural functionalism employs the concept of system, albeit in the limited sense of social system and subsystem, it emphasizes a static structural relationship of the parts. Fraser Darling (1951:245) cogently expresses the point of difference:

I was once asked by a social anthropologist what human ecology was that social anthropology was not. This was a very right and proper question, to which the reply should be that there is no difference. But I ventured to say that human ecology deals essentially with *process*. The value of the ecologist in society will be his power and accuracy in elucidating causes and forecasting consequences.

The understanding of process has never been a concern of structural functionalism, and therefore it comes as no surprise that it is incapable of dealing with anything but maintenance processes such as socialization (Firth 1964*b*). Its goal is to discover universal (or contingent) laws of structural relations. The results are modest, generally involving the clarification of sociocultural phenomena by showing their culturally specific interrelationships with other sociocultural phenomena. In almost all social science research, this focus on the study of reality as discrete parts (structural components) connected by interrelations or dependent functions (usually unitary) essentially excludes the possibility of the perspective necessary to a view of the constant interaction of the components in complex human systems.

The dominance of the analytical strategy, together with assumptions of equilibrium (including ecological equilibrium), the "ethnographic present," the "order" or "consensus" perspective, the neglect of available history, the "explanation" of society by social functions of structural parts, and the relative lack of interest in change, all militate against any adequate coming to grips with process. The most exemplary works concerned with process deal with homeostatic equilibrium—as dynamic oscillations in structure in highland Burma, for instance (Leach 1954). Unfortunately, concerns and concepts that contribute to heuristic views of process, especially the long-standing ideas of Raymond Firth, were coolly and unenthusiastically received until very recently.

The structural-functionalist approach and its dominant strategy of analysis encourage the treatment of ecology (generally meaning "environment") as a discrete component among other institutional components. Thus most ethnographies or problem-oriented studies begin with a chapter on the physical environment—the gross natural setting of the sociocultural investigation. Since the contents of the chapter are seldom referred to subsequently, we infer that such information is viewed as a backdrop, discretely separated from the primary components of the study. Nash (1967:249) speaks for a large group of anthropologists when he says, "But ecology is just that: a setting, a framework, a ground for the weaving of a figure determined by other than ecological factors. In my view, ecology is a sub-social, or exogenous factor in relation to the social system."

LINEAR CAUSATION AND REDUCTIONIST ANATHEMA

Efforts to trace functional interrelationships or to infer causal relations between environmental and sociocultural phenomena are usually conducted on a one-to-one basis. For example, aspects of environments are related in a simple causal chain to aspects of economic production, which are in turn related to group organization or authority (Sahlins 1958, Steward 1955, Wittfogel 1957). Causation is treated almost exclusively as simple and linear (see, for example, Whiting 1964). In fact, if an aspect of environment enters as an explanatory factor at all, it is treated, as we have seen, as an external factor or a background factor influencing the system under study—the social or cultural system—but not as part of it. That is to say, most studies confine their explanatory factors to those that exist on the same emergent level as the phenomenon to be explained, thus avoiding the bogey of reductionism. But to avoid reductionism it is not necessary to consider factors only on the emergent level upon which one is focusing. To paraphrase Feibleman's (1954: 59-66) "laws" of integrative levels, it is impossible to reduce a higher level (e.g., a population) to a lower one (e.g., an organism), since each level organizes the level below it plus one emergent property; in any organization the higher level (the population) depends on the lower one (organisms) for its continuance, but the lower is directed by the higher; thus for any organization its "mechanism" lies at the level below and its "purpose" at the level above. In other words, a sociocultural phenomenon is understood only by examining its level (e.g., population), the level below (organism), and the level above (ecosystem). Therefore, for instance, the fears implied in Redfield's position (1960), noted previously, that to grant intrusion of the physical environment upon man's "mental environment" is to reduce culture to biology and man to a mere animal are unwarranted. A systems approach permits the integration within a single framework of interrelated phenomena across levels as well as within a level.

FIELDWORK PROCEDURES

Certain standard procedures of anthropological fieldwork have had a mixed effect on the treatment of ecological relations. The normal tendency of investigators to work alone rather than in teams excludes virtually any possibility of a truly holistic consideration of the lifeways of a population. With respect to the unit of study, the usual tendency is to focus research upon a single small local community. Although this universe occasionally constitutes a somewhat natural unit, some arbitrary decisions must usually be made about boundaries. Ideally, the community offers the possibility of including the study of environmental relations within and without the bounded unit of study. For reasons already mentioned, even local environmental relations seldom receive intensive consideration. The recording of the range of relevant

spatial relations within the community frequently is lax. Furthermore, though Steward (1950), among others, long ago attacked the practice, the community is normally treated as if it were a narrow self-contained structural and functional whole, to be understood in terms of itself.

Participant observation in the research community, and especially research in the same community over several years, has sometimes stimulated the fieldworker to notice ecological and sociocultural dynamics. But the other standard technique of data collection—interviewing key informants—although a potentially useful instrument for exploring a people's subjective perceptions of dynamics, is usually employed to reconstruct moribund ways of life and to elicit the ideal culture of the present. Definitions of "cultural" and "social" behavior have generally emphasized subjective (covert, dispositional) behavior relations over objective (overt, motor) behavior relations. This emphasis is in agreement with the emphasis upon qualitative rather than quantitative statements in ethnographic descriptions.

Bennett and Thaiss (1968:273) have rightly noted the benefits of the "holistic depiction"—Kroeber's "descriptive integration" (1952:4-7)—which is more closely linked with qualitative than with quantitative concerns. This "holism," however, is usually restricted to man's cultural environment, and further, although holism has been reflected in attempts to depict the functional interrelationships of the parts of the assumed sociocultural whole, other commitments have tended to narrow the achievement of this ideal. Both the personal interests of the investigator and the cultural concerns of the people studied are unquestioned justifications for narrowing the scope of inquiry. Of course, the goals of the research—

descriptive or generalizing—also enter importantly into its conduct. The so-called emic-etic controversy, which has deep philosophical roots (Chomsky 1966), thus also expresses its influence.

THE UNITY OF CULTURE AND ENVIRONMENT

The image of environment as an external, discrete, and essentially static entity, to be subdued by culture in the course of human progress, has had disastrous practical and theoretical consequences, as noted earlier. I therefore consider it essential to suggest an alternative view, one that helps overcome some conceptual obstacles to an adequate view of nature, including man. In this view, the culture and the environment of a particular population are seen as constituting a functionally inseparable unity that may be analyzed but cannot be divided. The environment is not *for* the population (or ecosystem), but in a real sense it is *of* the population (or ecosystem). In this view of population and environment as a single system, if either component could be separated, the other could not exist in its present form. The population and environment not only are mutually interdependent, but form a subsystem within a larger system of contingent populations-environments, all of which are in constant flux, however imperceptible. Variables of the system are linked in continuous, dynamic feedback (Buckley 1967:78-80), so that any specific variable may be viewed as causal only at a precise instant. Ultimately all interdependent variables in the system are causally significant. This conceptualization of the role played by variables in systems is at the core of the ecosystem concept. Ecosystem constructs envision the interaction of *all* interdependent variables. All are important, but, as any sufferer from hay fever will affirm, not all are of equal magnitude, nor do all operate maximally during any selected time span. Analysis of such systems does not require us to treat all interdependent variables equally. It does require us to seek out the parameters of the "effective environment" as a practical delimitation of the environment (Bates 1960a: 141).

So much for the outline of the alternative ecosystems view. Now to the argument that underlies it:

In ecology, studies have been differentiated by the level of organization emphasized. Thus autecology focuses upon the study of an organism and its interrelationships with its environment; population ecology focuses upon the more abstract relationships between a population and its environment; synecology focuses upon a biocenosis (community) or an ecosystem and regards the organic and inorganic components as a functional whole or an ecosystemic unit.

HABITAT, NICHE, AND ENVIRONMENT

Reflecting the prominence of autecological studies, three concepts have tended to become standard usages among ecologists to designate the external relationships of individual organisms. From general to specific, these are "habitat," "niche," and "environment." "Habitat" is defined as the place where the organism of the species lives—its "address." "Niche" refers to the role that the organism plays in a wider network of mutual dependencies, thus implying interrelationships in a community or ecosystem. Niche is equivalent to Darwin's "place of an animal in the economy of nature," and has been translated by Elton as its "occupation." Since niche emphasizes the functional role of the organism, the general role of the population (the state-space [Hutch-

inson 1957]) of the species in a wider
system is implied. "Environment,"
for the nonecologist the most general
term for external contingent factors, is
for many ecologists today the most specific of the three concepts (although I
do not wish to imply that agreement is
general on this point). In this usage
each organism has a unique environment. This microenvironment is assumed to change constantly whether the
organism is mobile or at rest; only the
rate of change varies. Including both
temporal and spatial dimensions, the
"environment" becomes those external
contingent factors of the organism at
any point in time.

Environment and the Organism

The organism and its environment are
intimately interrelated. As the individual organism changes in age, in morphology, in physiology, in experience,
and so on, its environmental factors
also change. And as the organism's environmental factors change diurnally,
seasonally, climatically, biotically, and
geologically, the organism must accommodate to the changes. The organism
and the environment are "in a constant
state of flux on account of changes in
the various ecological factors concerned" (Dowdeswell 1961:16).

A review of usage of the concept of
environment by Mason and Langenheim (1957:332) reflects this idea of
interaction. By their definition,

the environment of an organism is the logical
class composed of the sum of those phenomena that enter a *reaction system* of the organism or otherwise directly impinge upon it to
affect its mode of life at any time throughout
its life cycle *as ordered by the demands* of the
ontogeny of the organism or as ordered by
another condition of the organism that alters
its environmental demands. [Emphasis added.]

Similarly, in Bertalanffy's (1952:

184) "systemic" definition, environment

denotes the total system of influences acting upon the organism, a system that depends
on the specific organization of the organism,
and at the same time makes possible its maintenance. Therefore, *Umwelt* [environment] includes not only the things that can act as
stimuli, but also the whole complex of conditions necessary to the maintenance of the
organism.

Earl Count (1960:581-82) takes up
the same point:

. . . an organism is no *tabula rasa* where an
environment writes as it pleases. It is the peculiar constitution of the organism itself that
converts energies into *"stimuli."* There is
nothing intrinsic about a lightwave that makes
of it the source of visual experience; it does
not compel eyes into existence; the intrinsi-
cality of vision resides in the organism. Organisms . . . can *elect* to *ignore* or *give attention*
to certain energies and phenomena which they
are quite capable of perceiving. . . . Thus out
of the natural surroundings, an animal organizes a world within which it acts.

Thus an individual organism in a very
real sense *defines* its environment. This
is certainly true of man, who possesses
the most complex perceptual views of
the world. Man's world view, the definition of those features of environment
that are of significance to the group,
also depends upon his technological, social, organizational, and ideological relations. But we have a problem here.

Since "environment" is oriented to
the individual, the conception "environment of a population" apparently
becomes so abstract and complex a notion as to be unusable. However, this
concept of environment is capable of
transfer from the organism level of
system to the population level of system,
or to even higher levels. Schwerdtfeger
(1963:24, 438-40; 1968) has employed
the term *Mitwelt*, "a characteristic of
the collective organisms," for this usage.

THE ECOLOGY OF HUMAN POPULATIONS

The ecology of social and cultural anthropologists, as I have noted, has been almost exclusively autecological to date. Increasing interest is now directed toward the study of the ecology of human populations. The goal of this chapter is to elicit greater interest on the part of anthropologists in synecology. At each level (organism, population, ecosystem), adequate concepts of man's environment, niche, and habitat are important. At each of these levels man and environment can be viewed as a subsystem. Thus the organization of a population, like the organization of the individual, selects those external factors that are of significance to it, as expressed in statistical behavior. With respect to this "effective environment" of a human population, its numbers, density, structure, distribution, technology, social organization, perceptual ideology, and interactions with other human populations (Barth 1956, Helm 1962, Sahlins 1964) specify its relevant external contingencies. This idea has practical as well as methodological importance. Methodologically, we can find in it part of the answer to the question: How does an ecologist establish workable boundaries around the complexity that he studies, short of the entire ecosphere? The answer is that the study of the adaptations that maintain the place of a population in a system need not involve the interactions of *every* part in the system, but only those of certain relevant parts and in certain relevant ways. In other words, the study of the environment of a population is a limited empirical inquiry expressed in the study of energy relations and significant interactions. Each human group's own definition of its environment is obviously of very great importance in any study of the ecology of human populations. If there is a direct or indirect relationship between the organization of techniques for production, social relations, perceptions, and values, on the one hand, and the relevant physical and cultural environment, on the other, then a change in that organization or in that environment requires a reaction in the other. The two conceptually separable spheres are inextricably bound up in a single system. Furthermore, any such system is in flux as behavior and traditions change, thus altering the environment and requiring a readaptation of parts of the sociocultural sybsystem to the new environment.

When we turn a practical eye to the situation, we must recognize that man's complex symbolic processes exhibit both adaptive and maladaptive aspects. There is always a difference between the *actual* environment of a specific human population and that population's *perceptions* of significant environmental features. It is precisely this gap between the cognitized environment of the populations of the United States and their actual objective environment that is at the root of what is called the ecological crisis.

TOWARD AN ANTHROPOLOGICAL ECOLOGY

The present is thus a most appropriate time for us to review the past and to look toward the future of ecological perspectives. Actually, although some excellent initial work exists and new directions are visible, little has been resolved and much of importance has not even been considered. In 1953 Bates saw a preoccupation with facts and a wariness of speculation as characteristics of the biological and social sciences. He viewed these as handicaps and called for "a certain amount of bold speculation" aimed at relating contemporary man and his environment. Bates (1953:711) went on to assess the status of knowledge of man's ecological relations: "Our information about man's relations with his environment seems, at every point, to be meager indeed; but it also seems to be scattered and unrelated. Perhaps more than new information, we need a consolidation and relation of these facts that have been so diversely garnered. . . ."

Despite some enlightened speculations and some additional fact-collecting, Bates's assessment of status of ecological anthropology remains substantially correct, A period of building has commenced, even stirrings of a possible movement beyond an ecological anthropology toward an anthropological ecology (or "ecosystematology" [Schultz 1967]) are perceptible. A few anthropologists have envisioned the possible contributions of such an anthropological ecology. What directions lie ahead? What are the urgent problems of anthropological ecology? What assets can anthropologists provide toward such a multidisciplinary development?

Wolf (1964:94) has said that the goal of anthropology is "the creation of an image of man that will be adequate to the experience of our time." Such an image of man today must take cognizance of the experience of man within the context of the whole biosphere. Men, like all life forms, are part of an extremely complex network of interrelationships. They will survive only so long as the network is respected and an adequate balance among system components is maintained. In modern societies, with the decline of reliance on God, man's ultimate imperative changes from individual salvation to the collective survival of mankind. Survival is the key concern in the experience of our times. What contribution has an anthropological ecology to make to a rele-

vant image of man and to a more adequate science of man?

Today we hear a great deal about "relevant" science, "urgent" anthropology and ecology. Areas of modern science are indicted for producing technological applications that contribute little to human welfare or even threaten it. Such recent "science" is defended by the claims that only nonnormative science is truly scientific and that the use of information generated by scientists lies outside the realm of science. Despite these assertions, science is never value-neutral; values have always been a part of science (Kaplan 1964:370f). Indeed, today it is more critical than ever to recognize explicitly the values that actually operate in various scientific disciplines. Scientists must seek to keep bias from entering into their solutions of their problems, but they also must become aware of the values expressed in problem selection and of the misuses to which research may be put. The various sciences are subcultures; as such they affect and are affected by other subcultures in society. The problems valued in the social sciences are particularly closely linked to changing conceptions of social relevance in other sectors of society. A science of man especially must seek to integrate a concern for human ends with the scientific mode of thought, which owes its success to its emphasis upon means. It ought to deal with scientific problems that are related to real human needs.

The calls heard for greater concern with crucial social and biological issues are certainly justified. In developing a new scientific humanism, the anthropologist should fuse the scientist's commitment to truth and the humanist's commitment to human welfare. In an adequate scientific humanism the scientifically relevant and the humanly relevant should coincide. But the criteria that the anthropologist uses to judge relevance must also be sufficiently broad. Judgments based on parochialism of any stripe cannot adequately direct the focus of social inquiry, nor can they suggest the proper application of knowledge to alleviate human problems. Ultimately only the broadest perspective toward man, one that will specify an adequately inclusive frame of inquiry and will specify the range of likely consequences of alternative actions, will suffice. An ecological perspective, including an adequate ecological ethic, may provide the soundest basis for judging social relevance and for defining the frame of scientific inquiry. This is perhaps the strongest argument for adopting a thoroughgoing "ecological point of view" or an ecosystemic approach for a humanistic science of man.

In the light of a comprehensive understanding of survival, which necessarily involves the survival of whole ecosystems (Lack 1965, Odum 1969), it may be possible to evaluate effectively the costs and benefits of specific actions and plans. An anthropological ecology could help provide a more objective basis for restating and judging moral questions as well as material ones. Such an approach could become a touchstone of relevance.

Although free of ideological bias, an anthropological ecology would nonetheless be a radical development. The collective welfare and ultimately the survival of mankind with any reasonable quality of life will demand a drastic reordering of every modern socioeconomic system. The more modern and growth-oriented the society, the more fundamental the reordering will be. It is for this reason that ecology has been called the "subversive science." A humanistic ecology would subvert the present orders of both capitalism and socialism. It is the revolution of revo-lutions—it would humanize aspects of the science-technology approach that presently are geared almost exclusively to expansion; it would focus greatest attention upon the most challenging technological, sociological, and psychological problems of the present, which are basically ecological (population control, food, environmental deterioration, health and well-being, and so on); it would substitute a world view of gradually evolving, well-articulated systems for the fragmented physical science-technological view that prevails today over most of the globe. Moreover, humanistic ecology is a revolution that is certain to come, whether it arrives as a result of gradual planning and reordering of economic and social systems and ecosystems to increase diversity and complementarity, or is forced by major disasters that must attend continuing growth trends.

Despite these implications, I do not suggest that ecology is the only relevant focus of anthropological study, although I believe that ecological awareness can throw light on many problems and can help us avoid many methodological pitfalls. Neither do I advocate only a synthetic strategy for the study of man. All inquiry is subject to what Kaplan (1964:30) has called "existential dilemmas," which pull in opposite directions: theory or observation, general laws or individual cases, synthesis or analysis. All inquiry, of course, requires both theory and data, general laws and individual cases, synthesis and analysis, and we might add ends and means. As Gjessing (1968:401) put it, ". . . the alteration between synthesis and analysis, between wholes and parts [is a] mode of thought absolutely necessary to any holistic approach, since the basic postulate of holism is that the whole is more than the sum of the parts."

If anthropology—which long has claimed to be a study that encompasses man the animal, man the member of society, and man the culture-bearing human being—adopted an adequate conception of ecology, it *could* play an enormous role in the humanistic science of man to come; at least in providing an ecological consciousness, at best much more. Indeed, anything less than such a holistic scope probably dooms the vision of anthropology as the coordinating science. Not even an integrated social science will permit scholars to anticipate the ecologically relevant consequences of social behavior and social institutions. Yet it is absolutely necessary that we seek optimum knowledge of probable consequences if plans for the survival of man are to be made. Both ecology and anthropology today require increased attention to the strategy of synthesis, but they also require a continuing strategy of analysis. Scholars may emphasize either, according to the problems on which they focus and the state of knowledge attained with respect to them. Whichever they emphasize at any point, researchers must be more explicitly guided by a fuller consideration of the ends of inquiry and the wider contextualization of research than they have been heretofore (see Commoner 1966, Dubos 1968, Gjessing 1968:401-402). I agree heartily with Gjessing's conclusion: "The social responsibility of science is not to our own or to any other particular social class, or to the nation, but rather to mankind as a whole."

His compromise of this position one paragraph later, while supportable in the term he uses, is, I believe, unnecessary. In a world full of intergroup conflict, Gjessing seemingly finds it impossible to serve the interests of all simultaneously, and therefore sees his foremost responsibility as the interests of the oppressed. Our instinct serves us well. It is proper for an anthropologist to help those peoples he has learned to know in the solution of their problems by any means he can. Yet we need not "choose between the immediate *interests* of the oppressed and the oppressor" (emphasis added). An ecosystemic approach puts the disparity of interests among international social strata in proper perspective. Moreover, immediate interests are a poor guide for understanding the needs of a specific population or of mankind as a whole. Ultimately the anthropologist serves the oppressed best by helping them to understand the real alternatives open to them over the long term and to anticipate as best they can the fullest consequences of the actions they may take before they take them. A conflict model of society is useful in arriving at an understanding of dynamics in society, past and present, but it is madness to adopt it today as a program for the solution of the world's problems. Without any question, if it becomes more widely embraced, it will be the final solution. As Berreman (1964:11) has put it so perceptively, "A society organized on complementary behavior alone cannot long survive; certainly a world community so based cannot. . . . Fundamental common values must be the ultimate goal if the frontiers of fear and the dangers they hold are to recede."

There is an immediately related point here. Whatever a humanized ecology might become—perhaps even a touchstone for relevance—in the political realities of today it is variously viewed as a panacea, a cop-out, or a passing fad. Ecology is not a panacea, although it seems from present perspective to provide a ray of hope; it is dangerous to oversell today's ecology—and tomorrow's ecology is barely visible. Ecologists have little more than sensed the challenge. Embraced as something that will not require any reshaping of the socioeconomic system, a spurious "ecology" (narrowly construed environmental pollution) is for many either a cop-out or a passing fad. It is unquestionably a cop-out for certain interests in government and in politics, a means of diverting attention from war, inequality, urban crisis, and general social tension. As such, it is properly resented by those who suffer further as attention is thus shifted away from their immediate problems. Inevitably, ecology is also a passing fad from which some opportunists may gain quick benefits.

Fortunately, as cop-out and fad, spurious ecology will not last long. What will remain? A humanistic ecology is the latest in a series of attempts to understand broad interrelationships, attempts that date back to antiquity.[68] The number of its adherents is relatively small, but it is growing rapidly. Moreover, they are strongly committed to this valid perspective for the study of interrelationships. It is to be hoped that those who suffer from the cop-out and those left disappointed by the fad will come to see that their problems are not separate from a genuine ecology, but rather are part of a wider network of ecological relations (see, e.g., Illich 1969). Social causes are also ecological causes, except in the narrowness of our thinking. Only in the narrow sociology and economics of the midcentury are the full social and ecological consequences and costs of war, racism, urban sprawl, social disorganization, and alienation not counted; in the world of reality they take their full toll.

Mankind is in trouble. Anthropology can lend its strength toward the solution of some aspects of that trouble; it can at the same time fulfill one of its aspirations. But as I noted earlier, a systemic anthropological ecology is

problematic. The problem is whether some anthropologists in close communication with colleagues in related fields will contribute significantly to the generation of a humanistic ecology. If they do not, ecological anthropology is likely to remain an occasional, mainly intuitive point of view for subtle interpretations of aspects of sociocultural systems. With those colleagues who opt for an interdisciplinary humanistic ecology, I am enrolling in Kenneth Boulding's (1964:193) "invisible college."

Like any other commitment, joining the invisible college of the transition implies a change from the unexamined life to the examined life. What the results of this examination will be, however, and even what constitutes a good grade, is hard to predict for any particular person. What is certain is that we shall see and do even old things in a new light and in a more examined manner.

By enrolling we do not surrender our birthright; we only share it.

REFERENCES

Ackerman, E. A.
1963 Where Is a Research Frontier? *Annals of the American Association of Geographers* 53:429-40.
Ackoff, R. L.
1960 Systems, Organizations, and Interdisciplinary Research. *General Systems* 5:1-8.
Adams, E.
1935 The Relation of General Ecology to Human Ecology. *Ecology* 16:316-35.
Adams, R. M.
1965 *Land Behind Baghdad*. Chicago: University of Chicago Press.
1966 *The Evolution of Urban Society: Early Mesopotamia and Pre-Hispanic Mexico*. Chicago: Aldine.
Alland, A., Jr.
1967 *Evolution and Human Behavior*. Garden City, N.Y.: Natural History Press.

---

[68] I am grateful to Clarence Glacken for helping to sharpen this and other ideas presented in this essay.

1970 *Adaptation in Cultural Evolution: An Approach to Medical Anthropology.* New York: Columbia University Press.

Allee, W. C., A. E. Emerson, et al.
1949 *Principles of Animal Ecology.* Philadelphia: W. B. Saunders.

Anderson, E. N.
1967 The Ethnoichthyology of the Hong Kong Boat People. Unpublished Ph.D. dissertation, Department of Anthropology, University of California at Berkeley.

Anderson, J. N.
1970 Interpersonal Bridges Across Social Chasms: Personal Intermediation in the Philippines. Unpublished manuscript.

Ascher, R.
1959 A Prehistoric Population Estimate Using Midden Analysis and Two Population Models. *Southwestern Journal of Anthropology* 15:168-78.

Aschmann, H.
1959 The Central Desert of Baja California: Demography and Ecology. *Ibero-Americana* 42.

Ashby, W. R.
1958a General Systems Theory as a New Discipline. *General Systems Yearbook* 3:1-6.
1958b *An Introduction to Cybernetics,* 3rd ed. New York: Wiley.

Attneave, F.
1967 *Applications of Information Theory to Psychology: A Summary of Basic Concepts, Methods, and Results.* New York: Holt, Rinehart & Winston.

Audy, J. R.
1965 The Environment in Human Ecology: Artifacts—the Significance of Modified Environment. In *Environmental Determinants of Community Well-Being.* Scientific Publication no. 123. Washington, D.C.: Pan American Health Organization.
1971 The Ipsefact: In Ecology, Ethology, Parasitology, Sociology, and Anthropology. In *Behavior and Environment,* ed. A. H. Esser. New York: Plenum Press.

Bailey, K. D.
1968 Human Ecology: A General Systems Approach. Unpublished Ph.D. dissertation, University of Texas.

Baker, J. R.
1928 Depopulation in Espiritu Santo, New Hebrides. *Journal of the Royal Anthropological Institute* 58:279-303.

Baker, P. T.
1962 The Application of Ecological Theory to Anthropology. *American Anthropologist* 64:15-22.
1969 Human Adaptation to High Altitude. *Science* 163:1149-56.

Baker, P. T., and J. S. Weiner, eds.
1966 *The Biology of Human Adaptability.* London: Oxford University Press.

Banks, A. L.
1950 *Man and His Environment.* Cambridge: At the University Press.

Banks, A. L., and J. A. Hislop
1956 Sanitation Practices and Disease Control in Extending and Improving Areas for Human Habitation. In *Man's Role in Changing the Face of the Earth,* ed. W. L. Thomas, pp. 817-30. Chicago: University of Chicago Press.

Barker, R. G.
1960 Ecology and Motivation. In *Nebraska Symposium on Motivation,* ed. M. R. Jones, pp. 1-49. Lincoln: University of Nebraska Press.

Barker, R. G., ed.
1963 *The Stream of Behavior: Explorations of Its Structure and Content.* New York: Appleton-Century-Crofts.

Barrau, J.
1958 Subsistence Agriculture in Melanesia. Bernice P. Bishop Museum Bulletin no. 219. Honolulu: Bishop Museum.

Barth, F.
1950 Ecological Adaptation and Cultural Change in Archaeology. *American Antiquity* 15:338-39.
1952 The Southern Mongoloid Migration. *Man* 22, no. 2:5-8.
1956 Ecologic Relationships of Ethnic Groups in Swat, North Pakistan. *American Anthropologist* 58:1079-89.
1959 The Land Use Pattern of Migratory Tribes of South Persia. *Norsk Geografisk Tidsskrift* 17:1-11.
1960 Nomadism in the Mountain and Plateau Areas of South West Asia. In

Problems of the Arid Zone: Proceedings, pp. 341-55. Paris: UNESCO.

1963 *The Role of the Entrepreneur in Social Change in Northern Norway.* Bergen and Oslo: Norwegian Universities Press.

1964 Competition and Symbiosis in North East Baluchistan. *Folk* 6:15-22. Copenhagen: Danish Ethnographical Association.

1966 *Models of Social Organization.* Royal Anthropological Institute Occasional Paper no. 23.

1967 On the Study of Social Change. *American Anthropologist* 69:661-69.

1968 *Nomads of South Persia.* Boston: Little, Brown.

Barth, F., ed.
1969 *Ethnic Groups and Boundaries.* Boston: Little, Brown.

Bartholomew, G. A., Jr., and J. B. Birdsell
1953 Ecology and the Proto-Hominids. *American Anthropologist* 55:481-98.

Batalla, G. B.
1966 Conservative Thought in Applied Anthropology: A Critique. *Human Organization* 25, no. 2:89-92.

Bates, M.
1953 Human Ecology. In *Anthropology Today,* ed. A. L. Kroeber, pp. 700-13. Chicago: University of Chicago Press.

1956 Man as an Agent in the Spread of Organisms. In *Man's Role in Changing the Face of the Earth,* ed. W. L. Thomas, pp. 788-806. Chicago: University of Chicago Press.

1959 The Ecology of Health. In *Medicine and Anthropology,* ed. I. Galdston. New York: International Universities Press.

1960a *The Forest and the Sea: A Look at the Economy of Nature and the Ecology of Man.* New York: Random House.

1960b Ecology and Evolution. In *Evolution After Darwin,* ed. S. Tax, vol. 1, pp. 547-68. Chicago: University of Chicago Press.

1961 *Man in Nature.* Englewood Cliffs, N.J.: Prentice-Hall.

1962 The Human Environment. Berkeley: Horace M. Albright Conservation Lectureship, University of California.

Baumhoff, M.
1963 *Ecological Determinants of Aboriginal California Populations.* Berkeley: University of California Press.

Beardsley, R. K.
1964 Ecological and Social Parallels Between Rice-Growing Communities in Japan and Spain. In *Proceedings of the 1963 Annual Spring Meeting of the American Ethnological Society,* ed. V. E. Garfield, pp. 51-63. Seattle: University of Washington Press.

Belshaw, C. S.
1965 *Traditional Exchange and Modern Markets.* Englewood Cliffs, N.J.: Prentice-Hall.

Benedict, B.
1970 A Review of Social Regulation of Fertility. In *Demography and the Biological and Social Structure of Human Populations.* Burg Wartenstein Symposium no. 50, pp. 22-30.

Bennett, J. W.
1944 The Interaction and Environment in the Smaller Societies. *American Anthropologist* 46:461-78.

1954 Interdisciplinary Research and the Concept of Culture. *American Anthropologist* 56:169-79.

1967 On the Cultural Ecology of Indian Cattle (and reply by M. Harris). *Current Anthropology* 8:251-53.

1969 *Northern Plainsmen: Adaptive Strategy and Agrarian Life.* Chicago: Aldine.

Bennett, J. W., and G. Thaiss
1968 Sociological Anthropology and Survey Research. In *Survey Research in the Social Sciences,* ed. C. Glock. New York: Russell Sage Foundation.

Bennett, J. W., and K. W. Wolff
1955 Toward Communication Between Sociology and Anthropology. In *Current Anthropology,* ed. W. L. Thomas, pp. 329-54. Chicago: University of Chicago Press.

Berelson, B., and G. A. Steiner
1964 *Human Behavior: An Inventory of Scientific Findings.* New York: Harcourt, Brace & World.

Berlin, B., D. E. Breedlove, and P. H. Raven
1966 Folk Taxonomies and Biological Classification. *Science* 154:273-75.

1968 Covert Categories and Folk Taxonomies. *American Anthropologist* 70: 290-99.

Berreman, G. D.
1964 Fear Itself: An Anthropologist's View. *Bulletin of the Atomic Scientist* 20, no. 9:8-11.

Berrien, F. K.
1968 *General and Social Systems.* New Brunswick: Rutgers University Press.

Bertalanffy, L. von
1952 *Problems of Life.* New York: Harper.
1962 *Modern Theories of Development.* New York: Harper. Originally published 1933.
1968 *General Systems Theory: Foundations, Development, Applications.* New York: Braziller.

Berthoud, G.
1967 *Changement économique et social de la montagne: Vernamiège en valais.* Berne: A. Francke.

Bews, J. W.
1935 *Human Ecology.* London: Oxford University Press.

Binford, L. R.
1968 Post-Pleistocene Adaptations. In *New Perspectives in Archaeology,* ed. Binford and Binford. Chicago: Aldine.

Birdsell, J. B.
1953 Some Environmental and Cultural Factors Influencing the Structuring of Australian Aboriginal Populations. *American Naturalist* 87:171-207.
1958 Some Population Problems Involving Pleistocene Man. In *Population Studies: Animal Ecology and Demography. Cold Spring Harbor Symposia on Quantitative Biology* 22:47-69.
1959 On Population Structure in Generalized Hunting and Collecting Populations. *Evolution* 12:189-205.
1968 Some Predictions for the Pleistocene Based on Equilibrium Systems Among Recent Hunter-Gatherers. In *Man the Hunter,* ed. R. B. Lee and I. De Vore. Chicago: Aldine.
1970 Local Group Composition Among the Australian Aborigines: A Critique of the Evidence from Fieldwork Conducted Since 1930. *Current Anthropology* 11:115-42.
1971 Ecology, Spacing Mechanisms, and Adaptive Behavior Among Australian Aborigines. In *Land Tenure in the*

South Pacific, ed. R. C. Crocombe. New York: Oxford University Press.

Birket-Smith, K.
1929 The Caribou Eskimos: Material and Social Life and Their Cultural Position. *Report of the 5th Thule Expedition, 1921-23,* vol. 5. Copenhagen.

Blasingham, E. J.
1956 The Depopulation of the Illinois Indian. *Ethnohistory* 3:193-224.

Blau, P.
1964 *Exchange and Power in Social Life.* New York: Wiley.

Blaut, J. M.
1959 The Ecology of Tropical Farming Systems. In *Plantation Systems of the New World.* Social Science Monograph no. 7, pp. 83-97. Washington, D.C.: Pan American Union.

Bohannan, P.
1954 The Migration and Expansion of the Tiv. *Africa* 24:2-16.

Boissevain, J.
1968 The Place of Non-Groups in the Social Sciences. *Man* 3:542-46.

Borah, W., and S. F. Cook
1963 The Aboriginal Population of Central Mexico on the Eve of the Spanish Conquest. *Ibero-Americana* 45.

Borgstrom, G.
1965 *The Hungry Planet.* New York: Macmillan.
1969 *Too Many.* New York: Macmillan.

Boserup, E.
1965 *The Condition of Agricultural Growth.* Chicago: Aldine.

Boulding, K. E.
1953 *The Organizational Revolution.* New York: Harper.
1956 *The Image.* Ann Arbor: University of Michigan Press.
1964 *The Meaning of the Twentieth Century.* New York: Harper & Row.
1966 Economics and Ecology. In *Future Environments of North America,* ed. F. F. Darling and J. P. Milton, pp. 225-34. New York: Natural History Press.
1968 *Beyond Economics: Essays on Society, Religion, and Ethics.* Ann Arbor: University of Michigan Press.

Brace, C. L.
1962 Cultural Factors in the Evolution of

Human Dentition. In *Culture and the Evolution of Man,* ed. A. Montagu, pp. 343-54. New York: Galaxy Books, Oxford University Press.

Braidwood, R. J., and C. A. Reed
1957 The Achievement and Early Consequences of Food-Production: A Consideration of Archaeological and Natural-Historical Evidence. In *Population Studies: Animal Ecology and Demography. Cold Spring Harbor Symposia on Quantitative Biology* 22:19-31.

Bresler, J. B., ed.
1966 *Human Ecology: Collected Readings.* Reading, Mass.: Addison-Wesley.
1968 *Environments of Man.* Reading, Mass.: Addison-Wesley.

Brookfield, H. C.
1964 Questions on the Human Frontier of Geography. *Economic Geography* 40:283-303.
1968 The Money That Grows on Trees: The Consequences of an Innovation Within a Man-Environment System. *Australian Geographical Studies* 6:97-119.
1969 On the Environment as Perceived. *Progress in Geography* 1:53-80.

Brookfield, H. C., and P. Brown
1963 *Struggle for Land: Agriculture and Group Territories Among the Chimbu of the New Guinea Highlands.* Melbourne: Oxford University Press.

Brown, H.
1954 *The Challenge of Man's Future.* New York: Viking Press.

Brown, P., and G. Winefield
1965 Some Demographic Measures Applied to Chimbu Census and Field Data. *Oceania* 35:175-90.

Brues, A.
1959 The Spearman and the Archer: An Essay on Selection in Body Build. *American Anthropologist* 61:457-69.

Buchler, I. R., and H. Nutini, eds.
1969 *Game Theory in the Behavioral Sciences.* Pittsburgh: University of Pittsburgh Press.

Buckley, W.
1967 *Sociology and Modern Systems Theory.* Englewood Cliffs, N.J.: Prentice-Hall.
1968 *Modern Systems Research for the Behavioral Scientist.* Chicago: Aldine.

Bulmer, R.
1967 Why Is the Cassowary Not a Bird? A Problem of Zoological Taxonomy Among the Karam of the New Guinea Highlands. *Man* 2, no. 1:5-25.

Burling, R.
1962 Maximization Theories and the Study of Economic Anthropology. *American Anthropologist* 64:802-21.

Burnet, Sir F. M.
1962 *Natural History of Infectious Disease.* Cambridge: At the University Press.

Burns, R. K.
1961 The Ecological Basis of French Alpine Peasant Communities in the Dauphin. *Anthropological Quarterly* 34:19-34.

Burton, I.
1968 The Quality of the Environment: A Review. *Geographical Review* 58:472-81.

Butzer, K. W.
1964 *Environment and Archaeology: An Introduction to Pleistocene Geography.* Chicago: Aldine.

Byers, D., ed.
1967 *The Prehistory of the Tehuacán Valley,* vol. 1: *Environment and Subsistence.* Austin: University of Texas Press.

Caldwell, L. W.
1963 Environment: A New Focus for Public Policy? *Public Administration Review* 23:132-39.

Calhoun, J. B.
1962 A Behavioral Sink. In *Roots of Behavior,* ed. E. L. Bliss, chap. 22. New York: Harper & Row.

Cameron, T. W. M.
1958 Parasites of Animals and Human Disease. *Annals of the New York Academy of Science* 70:564-73.

Campbell, B.
1966 *Human Evolution.* Chicago: Aldine.

Cancian, F.
1966 Maximization as Norm, Strategy, and Theory: A Comment on Programmatic Statements in Economic Anthropology. *American Anthropologist* 68:465-69.

Carneiro, R. L.

1956 Slash-and-Burn Agriculture: A Closer Look at Its Implications for Settlement Patterns. In *Men and Cultures,* ed. A. F. C. Wallace, pp. 229-34. Philadelphia: University of Pennsylvania Press.

1961 Slash-and-Burn Cultivation Among the Kuikuru and Its Implications for Cultural Development in the Amazon Basin. In *The Evolution of Horticultural Systems in Native South America: Causes and Consequences,* ed. J. Wilbert, pp. 47-68. Caracas: Sociedad de Ciencias Naturales La Salle.

1967 On the Relationship Between Size of Population and Complexity of Social Organization. *Southwestern Journal of Anthropology* 23:234-43.

1970 A Theory of the Origin of the State. *Science* 169:733-38.

Carneiro, R. L., and D. F. Hilse
1966 On Determining the Probable Rate of Population Growth During the Neolithic. *American Anthropologist* 68: 177-80.

Carson, R.
1962 *Silent Spring.* Boston: Houghton Mifflin.

Carter, G.
1950 Ecology, Geography, Ethnobotany. *Scientific Monthly* 70:73-80.

Castro, J. de
1952 *The Geography of Hunger.* Boston: Little, Brown.

Chang, K. C.
1958 Study of the Neolithic Social Grouping: Examples from the New World. *American Anthropologist* 60:298-334.

1967 Major Aspects of the Interrelationship of Archaelogy and Ethnology. *Current Anthropology* 8:227-43.

Charter, S. P. R.
1962 *Man on Earth: A Preliminary Evaluation of the Ecology of Man.* Sausalito, Calif.: Contact Editions.

Childe, V. G.
1951 *Man Makes Himself.* New York: Mentor Books, New American Library.

Chomsky, N.
1966 *Cartesian Linguistics: A Chapter in the History of Rationalist Thought.* New York: Harper & Row.

Christian, J. J.

1950 The Adreno-Pituitary System and Population Cycles in Mammals. *Journal of Mammalology* 31:247-59.

1963 The Pathology of Overpopulation. *Military Medicine* 128, no. 7:571-603.

Christian, J. J., and D. E. Davis
1964 Endocrines, Behavior, and Population. *Science* 146:1550-60.

Churchman, C. W.
1968 *The Systems Approach.* New York: Dell.

Clark, J. D.
1952 Environment and Culture-Contact in Prehistoric Africa South of the Sahara. In *Proceedings of the Second Pan-African Congress on Prehistory,* sec. 3. Algiers.

1960 Human Ecology During Pleistocene and Later Times in Africa South of the Sahara. *Current Anthropology* 1:307-24.

1963 Ecology and Culture in the African Pleistocene. *South African Journal of Science* 59:353-66.

1965 Culture and Ecology in Prehistoric Africa. In *Ecology and Economic Development in Tropical Africa,* ed. D. Brokensha, pp. 13-28. Berkeley: Institute of International Studies, University of California.

Clark, J. D., and F. C. Howell, eds.
1966 Recent Studies in Paleo-Anthropology. *American Anthropologist* 68, no. 2, pt. 2.

Clark, J. G. D.
1945 Farmers and Forests in Neolithic Europe. *Antiquity* 19:57-71.

1952 *Prehistoric Europe: The Economic Basis.* London: Methuen.

1953 The Economic Approach to Prehistory. *Proceedings of the British Academy* 34:215-38.

1967 *The Stone Age Hunters.* New York: McGraw-Hill.

Clark, J. G. D., et al.
1954 *Excavations at Star Carr.* Cambridge: At the University Press.

Clark, W. C.
1966 From Extensive to Intensive Shifting Cultivation: A Succession from New Guinea. *Ethnology* 5:347-59.

Clarkson, J. D.
1968 The Cultural Ecology of a Chinese

Village: Cameron Highlands, Malaysia. University of Chicago Department of Geography research paper no. 114.

1970   Ecology and Spatial Analysis. *Annals of the Association of American Geographers* 60:700-716.

Clements,
1916   *Plant Succession: An Analysis of the Development of Vegetation.* Washington, D.C.: Carnegie Institution.

Cockburn, T. A.
1963   *The Evolution and Eradication of Infectious Disease.* Baltimore: Johns Hopkins University Press.
1971   Infectious Diseases in Ancient Populations. *Current Anthropology* 12:45-62.

Coe, M. D., and K. V. Flannery
1967   *Early Cultures and Human Ecology in South Coast Guatemala.* Smithsonian Contributions to Anthropology, no. 3. Washington, D.C.: Smithsonian Institution Press.

Coe, W. R.
1957   Environmental Limitation on Maya Culture: A Re-examination. *American Anthropologist* 59:328-35.

Cohen, Y. A., ed.
1968   *Man in Adaptation: The Biosocial Background.* Chicago: Aldine.

Cole, L. C.
1957   Sketches of General and Comparative Demography. In *Cold Spring Harbor Symposia on Quantitative Biology* 22:1-15.
1964   The Impending Emergence of Ecological Thought. *Bioscience* 14:30-32.
1966   Man's Ecosystems. *Bioscience* 16:243-48.

Coles, J. M.
1963   Environmental Studies and Archaeology. In *Science and Archaeology*, ed. D. Brothwell and E. Higgs, pp. 93-98. London: Thames & Hudson.

Collins, P. W.
1965   Functional Analyses in the Symposium on Man, Culture, and Animals. In *Man, Culture, and Animals: The Role of Animals in Human Ecological Adjustments*, ed. A. Leeds and A. F. Vayda, pp. 271-82. Washington, D.C.: American Association for the Advancement of Science.

Colson, E.
1960   Migration in Africa: Trends and Possibilities. In *Population in Africa*, ed. F. Lorimer and M. Karp, pp. 60-87. Boston: Boston University Press.
1962   *The Social Organization of the Gwembe Tonga: Kariba Studies.* Manchester: Manchester University Press.

Commoner, B.
1966   *Science and Survival.* New York: Viking Press.

Conklin, H. C.
1954a   The Relation of the Hanunoo Culture to the Plant World. Unpublished Ph.D. dissertation, Department of Anthropology, Yale University.
1954b   An Ethnoecological Approach to Shifting Agriculture. *Transactions of the New York Academy of Sciences*, ser. 2, 17:133-42.
1955   Hanunoo Color Categories. *Southwestern Journal of Anthropology* 11:339-44.
1957   *Hanunoo Agriculture in the Philippines.* Forestry Development paper no. 12. Rome: Food and Agricultural Organization of the United Nations.
1961   The Study of Shifting Cultivation. *Current Anthropology* 2:27-61.
1967   Some Aspects of Ethnographic Research in Ifugao. *Transactions of the New York Academy of Sciences*, ser. 2, 30:99-121.

Cook, S.
1946   Human Sacrifice and Warfare as Factors in the Demography of Pre-Colonial Mexico. *Human Biology* 18:81-100.
1947   The Interrelation of Population, Food Supply, and Building in Pre-Conquest Central Mexico. *American Antiquity* 13:45-52.
1966   The Obsolete "Anti-Market" Mentality: A Critique of the Substantive Approach to Economic Anthropology. *American Anthropologist* 68:323-45.

Coon, C. S.
1950   Human Races in Relation to Environment and Culture with Special Reference to the Influence of Culture upon Genetic Changes in the Human Population. In *Origin and Evolution*

of Man. Cold Spring Harbor Symposia on Quantitative Biology 15: 247-58.

1954 *Climate and Race.* Smithsonian Report for 1953, pp. 277-98.

1959 Race and Ecology in Man. In *Cold Spring Harbor Symposia on Quantitative Biology* 24:153-59.

Coon, C. S., S. M. Garn, and J. B. Birdsell

1950 *Races: A Study of the Problems of Race Formation in Man.* Springfield, Ill.: Charles C. Thomas.

Corwin, E. H. L., ed.

1949 *The Ecology of Health.* New York: Commonwealth Fund.

Cottrell, F.

1955 *Energy and Society.* New York: McGraw-Hill.

Count, E. W.

1958 The Biological Basis of Human Sociality. *American Anthropologist* 60: 1049-85.

1960 Myth as World View. In *Culture in History,* ed. S. Diamond, pp. 580-630. New York: Columbia University Press.

Cowgill, U. M., and G. E. Hutchinson

1963 Ecological and Geochemical Archaeology in the Southern Maya Lowlands. *Southwestern Journal of Anthropology* 19:267-86.

Cressman, L. S.

1960 The Dalles. *American Philosophical Society Transactions* 50, pt. 10. Philadelphia.

Cushing, E. J., and H. E. Wright, Jr.

1967 *Quarternary Paleoecology.* New Haven: Yale University Press.

Dalton, G.

1967 *Tribal and Peasant Economies: Readings in Economic Anthropology.* Garden City, N.Y.: Natural History Press.

1969 Theoretical Issues in Economic Anthropology. *Current Anthropology* 10:63-102.

Damas, D., ed.

1969 Contributions to Anthropology: Ecological Essays. National Museums of Canada Bulletin no. 230, Anthropological Series no. 86. Ottawa: Queen's Printer for Canada. Reviewed in *American Anthropologist* 72:1471-74.

Dansereau, P.

1964 The Future of Ecology. *Bioscience* 14, no. 7:20-23.

1966 Ecological Impact and Human Ecology. In *The Future Environments of North America,* ed. F. F. Darling and J. P. Milton, pp. 425-62. Garden City, N.Y.: Natural History Press.

Darling, F. F.

1951 The Ecological Approach to the Social Sciences. *American Scientist* 39: 244-54.

1955- The Ecology of Man. *American*
1956 *Scholar* 25:38-46.

Darling, F. F., and J. P. Milton, eds.

1966 *Future Environments of North America: Transformation of a Continent.* Garden City, N.Y.: Natural History Press.

Davenport, W.

1960 *Jamaican Fishing: A Game Theory Analysis.* Yale University Publications in Anthropology no. 59.

Davis, K.

1951 *The Population of India and Pakistan.* Princeton: Princeton University Press.

Davis, K., and J. Blake

1956 Social Structure and Fertility: An Analytic Framework. *Economic Development and Cultural Change* 4:211-35.

Deevey, E. S., Jr.

1960a The Human Population. *Scientific American* 203:144-205.

1960b The Hare and the Haruspex. A Cautionary Tale. *American Scientist* 48: 415-30.

De Vore, I.

1965 *Primate Behavior.* New York: Holt, Rinehart & Winston.

Dewey, J.

1938 *Logic: The Theory of Inquiry.* New York: Holt.

Dice, L. P.

1955 *Man's Nature and Nature's Man: The Ecology of Human Communities.* Ann Arbor: University of Michigan Press.

Dobzhansky, T.

1962 *Mankind Evolving.* New Haven: Yale University Press.

1963 Anthropology and the Natural Sciences: The Problem of Human Evolution. *Current Anthropology* 4:146-48.

Dogan, M., and S. Rokkan, eds.
1969 *Quantitative Ecological Analysis in the Social Sciences.* Cambridge: M.I.T. Press.

Dole, G. E., and R. L. Carneiro, eds.
1960 *Essays in the Science of Culture in Honor of Leslie White.* New York: Crowell.

Dorjahn, V. R.
1958 Fertility, Polygyny, and Their Interrelations in Temne Society. *American Anthropologist* 60:838-60.

Douglas, M.
1966 Population Control in Primitive Groups. *British Journal of Sociology* 17:263-73.

Dowdeswell, W. H.
1961 *Animal Ecology,* 2nd ed. New York: Harper & Row.

Drucker, P., and R. F. Heizer
1967 *To Make My Name Big: A Re-examination of the Southern Kwakiutl Potlatch.* Berkeley: University of California Press.

Dubos, R.
1959 *Mirage of Health.* New York: Anchor Books, Doubleday.
1964 Environmental Biology. *Bioscience* 14:11-14.
1967 *Man Adapting.* New Haven: Yale University Press.
1968 *So Human an Animal.* New York: Scribner.

Dumond, D. E.
1961 Swidden Agriculture and the Rise of Maya Civilization. *Southwestern Journal of Anthropology* 17:301-16.
1965 Population Growth and Cultural Change. *Southwestern Journal of Anthropology* 21:302-24.

Duncan, O. D.
1959 Human Ecology and Population Studies. In *The Study of Populations,* ed. P. Hauser and O. D. Duncan, pp. 678-715. Chicago: University of Chicago Press.
1961 From Social System to Ecosystem. *Sociological Inquiry* 31:140-49.
1964 Social Organization and the Ecosystem. In *Handbook of Modern Sociology,* ed. R. E. Faris, pp. 36-82. Chicago: Rand McNally.

Duncan, O. D., and L. F. Schnore
1959 Cultural, Behavioral, and Ecological Perspectives in the Study of Social Organization. *American Journal of Sociology* 65:132-50.

Eggan, F.
1950 *The Social Organization of the Western Pueblos.* Chicago: University of Chicago Press.
1954 Social Anthropology and the Method of Controlled Comparison. *American Anthropologist* 56:743-63.
1966 The Cheyenne and Arapaho in the Perspective of the Plains: Ecology and Society. In *The American Indian: Perspectives for the Study of Social Change,* ed. F. Eggan. Chicago: University of Chicago Press.

Ehrlich, P. R., and A. H. Ehrlich
1970 *Population, Resources, Environment: Issues in Human Ecology.* San Francisco: W. H. Freeman.

Eichenwald, H. F., and P. C. Fry
1969 Nutrition and Learning. *Science* 163:644-48.

Ekvall, R. B.
1961 The Nomadic Pattern of Living Among the Tibetans as Preparation for War. *American Anthropologist* 63:1250-63.

Elton, C.
1927 *Animal Ecology.* New York: Macmillan.

English, P.
1968 Landscape, Ecosystem, and Environmental Perceptions: Concepts in Cultural Geography. *Journal of Geography* 67:198-205.

Evans, E. E.
1956 The Ecology of Peasant Life in Western Europe. In *Man's Role in Changing the Face of the Earth,* ed. W. L. Thomas, pp. 217-39. Chicago: University of Chicago Press.

Evans-Pritchard, E. D.
1940 *The Nuer.* Oxford: Clarendon Press.

Evernden, J. F., and G. H. Curtis
1965 Potassium-Argon Dating of Late Cenozoic Rocks in East Africa and Italy. *Current Anthropology* 6:342-431.

Eyre, S. R., and G. R. Jones
1966 *Geography as Human Ecology.* New York: St. Martin's Press.

Feibleman, J. K.
1954 Theory of Integrative Levels. *British*

Journal of the Philosophy of Science 5:59-66.

Ferdon, E. N., Jr.
1959   Agricultural Potential and the Development of Cultures. *Southwestern Journal of Anthropology* 15:1-19.

Fiennes, R.
1964   *Man, Nature, and Disease.* New York: New American Library.

Firey, W.
1945   Sentiment and Symbolism as Ecological Variables. *American Sociological Review* 10:140-48.
1946   Ecological Considerations in Planning Urban Fringes. *American Sociological Review* 11:411-23.
1960   *Man, Mind, and Land: A Theory of Resource Use.* New York: Free Press of Glencoe, Macmillan.

Firth, R.
1964a Capital, Saving, and Credit in Peasant Societies: A Viewpoint from Economic Anthropology. In *Capital, Saving, and Credit in Peasant Societies,* ed. R. Firth and B. Yamey, pp. 15-34. Chicago: Aldine.
1964b *Essays on Social Organization and Values.* London: Athlone Press.

Firth, R., ed.
1967   *Themes in Economic Anthropology.* A.S.A. monograph no. 6. London: Tavistock.

Flannery, K. V.
1965   The Ecology of Food Production in Mesopotamia. *Science* 147:1247-56.

Foote, D. C., and B. Greer-Wooten
1968   An Approach to Systems Analysis in Cultural Geography. *Professional Geography* 20:86-91.

Ford, C. S.
1964   *A Comparative Study of Human Population.* New Haven: HRAF Press.

Forde, C. D.
1925   Values in Human Geography. *Geography* 13:216-21.
1934   *Habitat, Economy, and Society: A Geographical Introduction to Ethnology.* New York: Dutton.
1956   Primitive Economics. In *Man, Culture, and Society,* ed. H. L. Shapiro, pp. 330-44. New York: Oxford University Press.
1959   The Anthropological Approach in Social Science. In *Readings in Anthropology,* ed. M. Fried, vol. 2, pp. 59-78. New York: Crowell.

Fortier, D. H.
1957   The Chinese in British North Borneo: Ecological Factors in Culture Change. *Transactions of the New York Academy of Science,* ser. 2, 19:571-80.

Fosberg, F. R., ed.
1963   *Man's Place in the Island Ecosystem: A Symposium.* Tenth Pacific Science Congress, Honolulu, Hawaii, 1961. Honolulu: Bishop Museum Press.

Fowler, M. L., and P. W. Parmalee
1959   Ecological Interpretation of Data on Archaeological Sites: The Modoc Rock Shelter. *Transactions of the Illinois State Academy of Science* 53, nos. 3 and 4:109-19.

Fox, R. B.
1952   The Pintubo Negritos: Their Useful Plants and Material Culture. *Philippine Journal of Science* 81:173-414.

Frake, C. O.
1956   Malayo-Polynesian Land Tenure. *American Anthropologist* 58:170-78.
1962   Cultural Ecology and Ethnography. *American Anthropologist* 64:53-60.

Freilich, M.
1963   The Natural Experiment, Ecology and Culture. *Southwestern Journal of Anthropology* 19:21-39.

Fried, M. H.
1952   Land Tenure, Geography, and Ecology in the Contact of Cultures. *American Journal of Economics and Sociology* 11:391-417.

Galdston, I., ed.
1960   Human Nutrition: Historic and Scientific. New York Academy of Medicine monograph no. 3. New York: International Universities Press.

Garn, S.
1965   *Human Races,* 2nd ed. Springfield, Ill.: Charles C. Thomas.

Gayton, A. H.
1946   Culture-Environment Integration: External References in Yokuts Life. *Southwestern Journal of Anthropology* 2:252-68.

Geertz, C.
1963   *Agricultural Involution: The Processes of Ecological Change in Indonesia.* Berkeley: University of Califor-

nia Press.
1964 *Peddlers and Princes.* Chicago: University of Chicago Press.

Geisler, P.
1967 Some Different Factors Affecting Population Movement: The Nubian Case. *Human Organization* 26, no. 3:164-77.

Gerlach, L. P.
1965 Nutrition in Its Sociocultural Matrix. In *Ecology and Economic Development in Tropical Africa.,* ed. D. Brokensha, pp. 245-68. Berkeley: Institute of International Studies, University of California.

Gibbs, J. P., and W. T. Martin
1959 Toward a Theoretical System of Human Ecology. *Pacific Sociological Review* 2:29-36.

Gjessing, G.
1963 Socio-archaeology. *Folk* 5:103-12.
1968 The Social Responsibility of the Social Scientist. *Current Anthropology* 9, no. 5:397-402.

Glacken, C.
1956 Changing Ideas of the Habitable World. In *Man's Role in Changing the Face of the Earth,* ed. W. L. Thomas, pp. 70-92. Chicago: University of Chicago Press.
1967 *Traces on the Thodian Shore: Nature and Culture in Western Thought from Ancient Times to the End of the Eighteenth Century.* Berkeley: University of California Press.
1970 Man Against Nature: An Outmoded Concept. In *The Environmental Crisis,* ed. H. W. Halfrich, Jr., pp. 127-42. New Haven: Yale University Press.

Goldman, I.
1955 Status, Rivalry, and Cultural Evolution in Polynesia. *American Anthropologist* 57:680-97.

Goldschmidt, W., ed.
1965 Variation and Adaptability of Culture: A Symposium. *American Anthropologist* 67, no. 2:400-47.

Goodenough, W. H.
1969 Frontiers of Cultural Anthropology: Social Organization. *Proceedings of the American Philosophical Society* 1113:329-35

Gordon, J. E.

1952 *Ecologic Investigation of Disease.* New York: Milbank Memorial Fund.

Gould, P. R.
1963 Man Against His Environment: A Game Theoretic Framework. *Annals of the Association of American Geographers* 53:290-97.

Gourou, P.
1956 The Quality of Land Use of Tropical Cultivators. In *Man's Role in Changing the Face of the Earth,* ed. W. L. Thomas, pp. 336-49. Chicago: University of Chicago Press.

Greenberg, J. H.
1959 Language Evolution. In *Evolution and Anthropology,* ed. B. Meggers, pp. 61-75. Washington, D.C.: Anthropological Society of Washington.

Griaule, M., and G. Dieterlen
1954 The Dogon. In *African Worlds: Studies in the Cosmological Ideas and Social Values of African Peoples,* ed. C. D. Forde, pp. 83-110. London: Oxford University Press.

Gulliver, P. H.
1955 *The Family Herds: A Study of Two Pastoral Tribes in East Africa, the Jie and Turkana.* London: Routledge & Kegan Paul.

Gutkind, E. A.
1953 *Community and Environment: A Discourse on Social Ecology.* Bungay, Suffolk: Philosophical Library, Richard Clay.

Hackenberg, R. A.
1962 Economic Alternatives in Arid Lands: A Case Study of the Pima and Papago Indians. *Ethnology* 1:186-96.
1966 An Anthropological Study of Demographic Transition: The Papago Information System. *Milbank Memorial Fund Quarterly* 44:470-94.

Haeckel, E.
1870 Über Entwicklungsgang und Aufgabe der Zoologie. *Jenaische Zeitschrift für Medizin und Naturwissenschaft* 5:353-70.

Hainline, J. L.
1965 Culture and Biological Adaptation. *American Anthropologist* 67:1174-97.

Halbwachs, M.
1960 *Population and Society: Introduction to Social Morphology,* trans.

C. D. Duncan and R. W. Pfautz. New York: Free Press of Glencoe.

Hall, A. D., and R. E. Fagen
1944 Definition of Systems. *Social Forces* 22:399-404.

Hall, E. T.
1966 *The Hidden Dimension.* Garden City, N.Y.: Doubleday.

Hallowell, A. I.
1949 The Size of Algonkian Hunting Territories: A Function of Ecological Adjustment. *American Anthropologist* 51:35-45.
1951 Cultural Factors in the Structurization of Perception. In *Social Psychology at the Crossroads,* ed. J. S. Rohrer and M. Sherif. New York: Harper.
1956 The Structural and Functional Dimensions of a Human Experience. *Quarterly Review of Biology* 31:88-101.
1959 Behavioral Evolution and the Emergence of the Self. In *Evolution and Anthropology: A Centennial Appraisal,* pp. 36-60. Washington, D.C.: Anthropological Society of Washington.
1960 Self, Society, and Culture in Phylogenetic Perspective. In *Evolution After Darwin,* ed. S. Tax, vol. 2, pp. 309-71. Chicago: University of Chicago Press.
1961 The Protocultural Foundations of Human Adaptation. In *Social Life of Early Man,* ed. S. L. Washburn, pp. 235-55. Chicago: Aldine.

Hardin, G.
1968 The Tragedy of the Commons. *Science* 162:1243-48.
1970 To Trouble a Star: The Cost of Intervention in Nature. *Bulletin of the Atomic Scientists,* 26, no. 1:17-20.

Harding, T. G.
1967 Ecological and Technical Factors in a Melanesian Gardening Cycle. *Mankind* 6:403-408.

Harris, D.
1969 Agricultural Systems, Ecosystems and the Origins of Agriculture. In *The Domestication and Exploitation of Plants and Animals,* ed. P. J. Ucka and G. W. Dimbleby, pp. 3-15. London: Duckworth.

Harris, M.
1959 The Economy Has No Surplus? *American Anthropologist* 61:185-99.
1960 Adaptation in Biological and Cultural Science. *Transactions of the New York Academy of Sciences,* ser. 2, 23:59-65.
1964 *The Nature of Cultural Things.* New York: Random House.
1966 The Cultural Ecology of India's Sacred Cattle. *Current Anthropology* 7:51-66.
1968 *The Rise of Anthropological Theory.* New York: Crowell.

Harris, M., and G. Morreu
1966 The Limitations of the Principle of Limited Possibilities. *American Anthropologist* 68:122-27.

Harris, R.
1962 The Influence of Ecological Factors and External Relations on the Mbembe Tribes of Southeast Nigeria. *Africa* 32:38-52.

Hawley, A.
1944 Ecology and Human Ecology. *Social Forces* 22:398-405.
1950 *Human Ecology: A Theory of Community Structure.* New York: Ronald Press.
1968 Human Ecology. In *International Encyclopedia of the Social Sciences* 4: 328-37.

Hazen, W. E., ed.
1964 *Readings in Population and Community Ecology.* Philadelphia: Saunders.

Heizer, R. F.
1955 Primitive Man as an Ecological Factor. *Kroeber Anthropological Society Papers* 13:1-31.
1960 Physical Analysis of Habitation Residues. In *The Application of Quantitative Methods in Archaeology,* ed. R. F. Heizer and S. F. Cook, pp. 93-124. Chicago: Quadrangle Books.

Helm, J.
1962 The Ecological Approach in Anthropology. *American Journal of Sociology* 17:630-39.

Hempel, C. G.
1951 General Systems Theory and the Unity of Science. *Human Biology* 23: 313-22.

Herskovits, M. J.
1952 *Economic Anthropology: A Study of Comparative Economics.* New York:

Knopf.

Hickerson, H.
1965 The Virginia Deer and Inter-Tribal Buffer Zones in the Upper Mississippi Valley. In *Man, Culture, and Animals: The Role of Animals in Human Ecological Adjustments*, ed. A. Leeds and A. P. Vayda, pp. 43-66. Washington, D.C.: American Association for the Advancement of Science.
1967 Some Implications of the Theory of the Particularity or "Atomism" of Northern Algonkians. *Current Anthropology* 8:313-43.

Hiernaux, J.
1963 Some Ecological Factors Affecting Human Populations of Sub-Saharan Africa. In *African Ecology and Human Evolution*, ed. F. C. Howell and F. Bourlière, pp. 534-46. Viking Fund Publications in Anthropology no. 36.

Hitchcock, J. T.
1967 Fatalistic Suicide Resulting from Adaptation to Asymmetrical Sex Role. *Eastern Anthropologist* 20: 133-42.

Hockett, C. P., and R. Ascher
1964 The Human Revolution. *Current Anthropology* 5:135-68.

Hoffman, H.
1964 Money, Ecology, and Acculturation Among the Shipibo of Peru. In *Explorations in Cultural Anthropology*, ed. W. H. Goodenough, pp. 259-76. New York: McGraw-Hill.
1969 A Linear Programming Approach to Cultural Intensity. In *Game Theory in the Behavioral Sciences*, ed. I. R. Buchler and H. Nutini. Pittsburgh: University of Pittsburgh Press.

Hofstadter, R.
1955 *Social Darwinism in American Thought*. New York: Braziller.

Hogbin, E. I.
1930 The Problems of Depopulation in Melanesia Applied to Ontong Java. *Journal of the Polynesian Society* 39:43-66.

Homans, G. C.
1961 *Social Behavior*. New York: Harcourt, Brace & World.

Honigmann, J. J.
1962 *Foodways in a Muskeg Community:* *An Anthropological Report on the Attawapiskat Indians*. Ottawa: Northern Co-ordination and Research Center, Department of Northern Affairs and National Resources.

Howard, J. H.
1966 *The Dakota or Sioux Indians: A Study in Human Ecology*. South Dakota Museum Anthropological Papers no. 2. Vermillion: University of South Dakota.

Howell, F. C., and F. Bourlière, eds.
1963 *African Ecology and Human Evolution*. Chicago: University of Chicago Press.

Hsu, F.
1963 *Clan, Caste, and Club*. Princeton, N.J.: Van Nostrand.

Hubbert, M. K.
1964 Earth Scientists Look at Environmental Limits of Human Ecology. *National Research Council News Report* 14:58-60.

Hudson, E. H.
1965 Treponematosis and Man's Social Evolution. *American Anthropologist* 67:885-901.

Hulse, F. S.
1961 Warfare, Demography, and Genetics. *Eugenics Quarterly* 8:185-97.

Hultkrantz, A.
1966 An Ecological Approach to Religion. *Ethnos* 31:131-50.
1968 The Aims of Anthropology: A Scandinavian Point of View. *Current Anthropology* 9:289-310.

Hunter, J. M.
1967 The Social Roots of Dispersed Settlement in Northern Ghana. *Annals of the Association of American Geographers* 57:339-49.

Hutchinson, G. E.
1948 Teleological Mechanisms: Circular Causal Systems in Ecology. *Annals of the New York Academy of Science* 50:221-46.
1957 Concluding Remarks. In *Cold Spring Harbor Symposia on Quantitative Biology* 22:415-27.

Huxley, A.
1963 The Politics of Ecology: The Question of Survival. Occasional paper on the free society. Chicago: Center for the Study of Democratic Institu-

tions.

Iijima, S.
1964 Ecology, Economy, and Social System in the Nepal Himalayas. *Developing Economies* 2:91-105.

Illich, I.
1969 Outwitting the Developed Countries. *New York Review of Books* 12, no. 8:20-24.

Iversen, J.
1941 Land Occupation in Denmark's Stone Age. *Geological Survey of Denmark*, ser. 21, vol. 2, no. 66.
1949 The Influence of Prehistoric Man on Vegetation. *Danmarks Geologiske Undersogelse* 3:5-25.
1960 Problems of the Early Post-Glacial Forest Development in Denmark. *Geological Survey of Denmark*, ser. 4, vol. 4, no. 4.

Jay, P. C.
1965 Field Studies of Monkeys and Apes. In *Behavior of Nonhuman Primates,* ed. A. M. Schrier and H. F. Harlow. New York: Academic Press.

Jay, P. C., ed.
1968 *Primates: Studies in Adaptation and Variability.* New York: Holt, Rinehart & Winston.

Johnson, D.
1969 The Nature of Nomadism. Department of Geography Research Paper no. 18, University of Chicago.

Jouvenel, Bertrand de
1957 From Political Economy to Political Ecology. *Bulletin of the Atomic Scientists* 13:287-91.

Kaplan, A.
1964 *The Conduct of Inquiry.* San Francisco: Chandler.

Kendeigh, S. C.
1965 The Ecology of Man, the Animal. *Bioscience* 15:521-23.

Keyfitz, N.
1966a The Impact of Technological Change on Demographic Patterns. In *Industrialization and Society,* ed. B. F. Hoselitz and W. E. Moore, pp. 218-36. Mouton: UNESCO.
1966b Population Density and the Style of Social Life. *Bioscience* 16:868-73.

Klopfer, P. H.
1962 *Behavioral Aspects of Ecology.* Englewood Cliffs, N.J.: Prentice-Hall.

Knight, R.
1965 A Re-examination of Hunting, Trapping, and Territoriality Among the Algonkin Indians. In *Man, Culture, and Animals: The Role of Animals in Human Ecological Adjustments,* ed. A. Leeds and A. P. Vayda, pp. 27-42. Washington, D.C: American Association for the Advancement of Science.

Krader, L.
1955 Ecology of Central Asian Pastoralism. *Southwestern Journal of Anthropology* 2:301-26.
1957 Culture and Environment in Interior Asia. In *Studies in Human Ecology,* ed. A. Palmer et al., pp. 115-38. Washington, D.C.: Pan American Union.

Kroeber, A. L.
1939 *Cultural and Natural Areas of Native North America.* Berkeley: University of California Press.
1952 *The Nature of Culture.* Chicago: University of Chicago Press.
1953 Introduction. In *Anthropology Today,* ed. A. L. Kroeber, pp. xiii-xv. Chicago: University of Chicago Press.
1960 Evolution, History, and Culture. In *Evolution After Darwin,* ed. S. Tax, vol. 2, pp. 1-16. Chicago: University of Chicago Press.

Krzywicki, L.
1934 *Primitive Society and Its Vital Statistics.* London: Macmillan.

Kuhn, A.
1963 *The Study of Society: A Unified Approach.* Homewood, Ill.: Dorsey Press.

Kunkel, J.
1967 Some Behavioral Aspects of the Ecological Approach to Social Organization. *American Journal of Sociology* 73:12-29.

Kunstadter, P., R. Buhler, F. F. Stephan, and C. Westoff
1963 Demographic Variability and Preferential Marriage Patterns. *American Journal of Physical Anthropology,* n.s. 21:511-20.

Lack, D.
1965 Evolutionary Ecology. *Journal of Ecology* 53:237-345.

Lanning, E. P.
1965 Early Man in Peru. *Scientific Ameri-*

can 213, no. 4:68-76.

1967 *Peru Before the Incas.* Englewood Cliffs, N.J.: Spectrum Books, Prentice-Hall.

Lantis, M.
1953 *Research on Human Ecology of the American Arctic.* Washington, D.C.: Arctic Institute.

1955 Problems of Human Ecology in the North American Arctic. *Arctic* 7: 307-20.

1957 American Arctic Populations: Their Survival Problems. In *Arctic Biology,* ed. Henry P. Hansen. Corvallis: Oregon State University Press.

Lasker, G. W.
1969 Human Biological Adaptability. *Science* 166:1480-86.

Laslett, P.
1965 The History of Population and Social Structure. *International Social Sciences Journal* 27:582-93.

Lattimore, O.
1951 The Steppes of Mongolia and the Characteristics of Steppe Nomadism. In *Inner Asian Frontiers of China.* American Geographical Society Research Series, no. 21.

1962 *Studies in Frontier History: Collected Papers, 1928-1958.* London: Oxford University Press.

Laughlin, W. S.
1962 Correspondences in Human Biology and Culture. *Centennial Review* 6: 98-119.

1968 Guide to Human Population Studies. *Arctic Anthropology* 5, no. 1:32-47.

Leach, E. R.
1954 *Political Systems of Highland Burma.* Cambridge: Harvard University Press.

1961 *Pul Eliya: A Village in Ceylon.* Cambridge: At the University Press.

1968 *A Runaway World?* New York: Oxford University Press.

Le Clair, E. E., Jr., and H. K. Schneider
1968 *Economic Anthropology: Readings in Theory and Analysis.* New York: Holt, Rinehart & Winston.

Lee, R. B.
1963 The Population Ecology of Man in the Early Upper Pleistocene of Southern Africa. *Proceedings of the Prehistoric Society,* n.s. 29:235-57.

1965 Subsistence Ecology of !Kung Bush-

men. Unpublished Ph. D. dissertation, Department of Anthropology, University of California, Berkeley.

1969 !Kung Bushman Subsistence: An Input-Output Analysis. In *Environment and Cultural Behavior,* ed. A. Vayda. Garden City N.Y.: Natural History Press.

Lee R. B., and I. De Vore.
1968 *Man the Hunter.* Chicago: Aldine.

Leeds, A., and A. Vayda, eds.
1965 *Man, Culture, and Animals: The Role of Animals in Human Ecological Adjustments.* Washington, D.C.: American Association for the Advancement of Science.

Lenneberg, E.
1960 Language, Evolution, and Purposive Behavior. In *Culture in History,* ed. S. Diamond, pp. 869-93. New York: Columbia University Press.

Leopold, A.
1949 *A Sand County Almanac.* New York: Oxford University Press.

Lessa, W. A.
1955 Depopulation on Ulithi. *Human Biology* 27:151-83.

Lesser, A.
1952 Evolution and Social Anthropology. *Southwestern Journal of Sociology* 8:134-46.

1961 Social Fields and the Evolution of Society. *Southwestern Journal of Anthropology* 17:40-48.

Levy, J. E.
1961 Ecology of the South Plains: The Ecohistory of the Kiowa, Comanche, Cheyenne, and Arapaho, 1830-1870. In *Symposium on Patterns of Land Utilization and Other Papers,* ed. V. E. Garfield, pp. 18-25. *Proceedings of the 1961 Annual Spring Meeting of the American Ethnological Society.* Seattle: University of Washington Press.

Lewin, K.
1951 *Field Theory in Social Science.* New York: Harper.

Lipschutz, A.
1966 La depoblación de las Indias después de la conquista. *América Indígena* 26:229-47.

Livingstone, F. B.
1958 Anthropological Implications of

Sickle-Cell Gene Distribution in West Africa. *American Anthropologist* 60:533-62.

1962 Population Genetics and Population Ecology. *American Anthropologist* 64:44-53.

1969 Genetics, Ecology, and the Origins of Incest and Exogamy. *Current Anthropology* 10:45-62.

Lorimer, F., et al.
1954 *Culture and Human Fertility*. UNESCO Population and Culture Series. Paris: UNESCO.

Lowenthal, D.
1961 Geography, Experience, and Imagination: Towards a Geographical Epistemology. *Annals of the Association of American Geographers* 51:241.

Lowenthal, D., ed.
1967 Environmental Perception and Behavior. Geography Research Paper no. 109. Chicago: University of Chicago, Department of Geography.

Lowenthal, D., and L. Comitas
1962 Emigration and Depopulation: Some Neglected Aspects of Population Geography. *Population Review* 6:83-94.

Luten, D. B.
1969 Empty Land, Full Land, Poor Folk, Rich Folk. *Yearbook of the Association of Pacific Coast Geographers* 31:133-38.

Lyman, S. M., and M. B. Scott
1967 Territoriality: A Neglected Sociological Dimension. *Social Problems* 15:236-49.

McArthur, N.
1967 *Island Populations of the Pacific*. Canberra: Australian National University Press.

1970 The Demography of Primitive Populations. *Science* 167:1097-1101.

McCarthy, F. D.
1963 Ecology, Equipment, Economy, and Trade. In *Australian Aboriginal Studies: A Symposium of Papers Presented at the 1961 Research Conference, Australian Institute of Aboriginal Studies*. Canberra: Oxford University Press.

McClelland, C. A.
1962 General Systems and the Social Sciences. *Etc.: A Review of General Semantics* 18:449-68.

MacKaye, B.
1940 Regional Planning and Ecology. *Ecological Monthly* 10:349-53.

MacNeish, R. S.
1964 Ancient Mesoamerican Civilization. *Science* 143, no. 3606.

MacNeish, R. S., et al.
1968 *Reports of the Tehuacán Archaeological-Botanical Project*, 6 vols. Austin: University of Texas Press.

Malin, J. C.
1950 Ecology and History. *Scientific Monthly* 70:296.

Margalef, R.
1957 Information Theory in Ecology. *General Systems Yearbook* 3:36-71.

Marney, M. C., and N. M. Smith
1964 The Domain of Adaptive Systems: A Rudimentary Taxonomy. *General Systems Yearbook* 9:107-33.

Maruyama, M.
1963 The Second Cybernetics: Deviation Amplifying Mutual Causal Processes. *American Scientist* 51:164-79.

Marx, E.
1967 *Bedouin of the Negev*. Manchester: Manchester University Press.

Mason, H. L., and J. H. Langenheim
1957 Language Analysis and the Concept Environment. *Ecology* 38:325-40.

Mason, L.
1950 The Bikinians: A Transplanted Population. *Human Organization* 9:5-15.

1957 Ecologic Change and Culture Pattern in the Resettlement of Bikini Marshallese. In *Cultural Stability and Cultural Change*, ed. V. F. Ray, pp. 1-6. New York: American Ethnological Society.

May, J. M.
1959 *The Ecology of Human Disease*. New York: MD Publications.

1961 *The Ecology of Malnutrition in the Far and Near East*. New York: Hafner.

1963 *The Ecology of Malnutrition in Five Countries of Eastern and Central Europe*. New York: Hafner.

1965 *The Ecology of Malnutrition in Middle Africa: Ghana, Nigeria, Republic of the Congo, Rwanda, Burundi, and the Former French Equatorial Africa*. New York: Hafner.

1966 *The Ecology of Malnutrition in Central and Southeastern Europe.* New York: Hafner.
1967 *The Ecology of Malnutrition in Northern Africa.* New York: Hafner.
Mead, M.
1964 *Continuities in Cultural Evolution:* New Haven: Yale University Press.
Mead, M., and E. B. Granger
1965 Social Aspects of Density. *Ekistics* 28:214-15.
Medawar, P. N.
1960 *The Future of Man.* New York: Mentor Books.
Meggers, B.
1954 Environmental Limitations on the Development of Culture. *American Anthropologist* 56:301-24.
1957 Environment and Culture in the Amazon Basin: An Appraisal of the Theory of Environmental Determinism. In *Studies in Human Ecology,* pp. 71-90. Social Science Monographs no. 3. Washington, D.C.: Pan American Union.
Meier, R. L.
1956 *Science and Economic Development: New Patterns of Living.* Cambridge: M.I.T. Press.
Meighan, C.
1959 The Little Harbor Site, Catalina Island: An Example of Ecological Interpretation in Archaeology. *American Antiquity* 34:383-405.
Meighan, C., et al.
1958 Ecological Interpretation in Archaeology. Part 1: *American Antiquity* 34: 1-23. Part 2: *American Antiquity* 34: 131-50.
Mencher, J. P.
1966 Kerala and Madras: A Comparative Study of Ecology and Social Structure. *Ethnology* 5, no. 2:135-71.
Merton, R. K.
1959 Notes on Problem-Finding in Sociology. In *Sociology Today,* ed. R. K. Merton, L. Broom, and L. S. Cottrell, vol. 1, pp. ix-xxxiv. New York: Basic Books.
Mikesell, M.
1967 Geographical Perspectives in Anthropology. *Annals of the Association of American Geographers* 57:617-34.
Millon, R.

1962 Variations in Social Responses to the Practice of Irrigation Agriculture. In *Civilization in Desert Lands,* ed. R. B. Woodbury, pp. 56-88. Salt Lake City: University of Utah Press.
Moore, O. K.
1957 Divination: A New Perspective. *American Anthropologist* 59:69-74.
Morgan, W. B., and R. P. Moss
1965 The Concept of the Community and Its Relationship to Environment. *Annals of the Association of American Geographers* 55:339-50.
Mumford, L.
1961 *The City in History.* New York: Harcourt, Brace & World.
Murphy, R. F., and J. H. Steward
1956 Tappers and Trappers: Parallel Process in Acculturation. *Economic Development and Cultural Change* 4: 335-55.
Nadel, S. F.
1952 Witchcraft in Four African Societies: An Essay in Comparison. *American Anthropologist* 54:18-29.
Nag, M.
1962 *Factors Affecting Human Fertility in Nonindustrial Societies: A Cross-Cultural Study.* Yale University Publications in Anthropology no. 96. New Haven: Yale University Press.
Nash, M.
1966 *Primitive and Peasant Economic Systems.* San Francisco: Chandler.
1967 Reply to reviews of *Primitive and Peasant Economic Systems. Current Anthropology* 8, no. 3:246, 249.
Neel, J. V.
1970 Lessons from a "Primitive" People. *Science* 170:815-21.
Nelson, R. K.
1969 *Hunters of the Northern Ice.* Chicago: University of Chicago Press.
Netting, R. McC.
1965 A Trial Model of Cultural Ecology. *Anthropological Quarterly* 38:81-96.
1968 *Hill Farmers of Nigeria: Cultural Ecology of the Kofyar of the Jos Plateau.* Seattle: University of Washington Press.
Newman, M. T.
1953 The Application of Ecological Rules to the Racial Anthropology of the Aboriginal New World. *American*

Anthropologist 55:311-27.

1962 Ecology and Nutritional Stress in Man. *American Anthropologist* 64: 22-34.

1964 Ecology and Medical Anthropology. *Anthropos* 22:351-54.

Nicholaisen, J.

1963 *Ecology and Culture of the Pastoral Tuareg: With Particular Reference to the Tuareg of Ahaggar and Ayr.* Leiden: E. J. Brill.

Nicholaisen, J., et al.

1964 Ecological and Historical Factors. *Folk* 6, no. 1:75-82. Copenhagen: Danish Ethnographical Association.

Nicholas, R. W.

1963 Ecology and Village Structure in Deltaic West Bengal. *Economic Weekly* 15:1185-96.

Nicholson, M. H.

1959 *Mountain Gloom and Mountain Glory: The Development of Aesthetics of the Infinite.* Ithaca: Cornell University Press.

Odum, E. P.

1963 *Ecology.* New York: Holt, Rinehart & Winston.

1969 The Strategy of Ecosystem Development. *Science* 164:262-70.

1971 *Fundamentals of Ecology,* 3rd ed. Philadelphia: Saunders.

Odum, H. T.

1962 *Man and the Ecosystem: Proceedings of the Lockwood Conference on Suburban Forestry and Ecology.* New Haven Agricultural Experiment Station Bulletin no. 652:57-75.

1971 *Environment, Power, and Society.* New York: Wiley.

Ogburn, W. F.

1933 *Social Change.* New York: Viking Press.

Oliver, S. C.

1962 *Ecology and Cultural Continuity as Contributing Factors in the Social Organization of the Plains Indians.* Berkeley: University of California Press.

1965 Individuality, Freedom of Choice, and Cultural Flexibility of the Kamba. *American Anthropologist* 67: 421-28.

Ooi, J.

1958 The Distribution of Present-Day Man in the Tropics: Historical and Ecological Perspective. In *Proceedings of the Ninth Pacific Congress* (Bangkok), no. 20.

Orans, M.

1966 Surplus. *Human Organization* 25:24-32.

Osborn, F.

1948 *Our Plundered Planet.* Boston: Little, Brown.

Otten, C. M.

1967 On Pestilence, Diet, Natural Selection, and the Distribution of Microbial and Human Blood Group Antigens and Antibodies. *Current Anthropology* 8:209-26.

Paine, R.

1958 Change in the Ecological and Economic Bases in a Coast Lappish Environment. *Southwestern Journal of Anthropology* 14:168-88.

1964 Herding and Husbandry: Two Basic Distinctions in the Analysis of Reindeer Management. *Folk* 6, no. 1:83-88. Copenhagen: Danish Ethnographical Association.

Park, R. E.

1936 Human Ecology. *American Journal of Sociology* 42:1-15.

Parrack, D. W.

1969 An Approach to the Bioenergetics of Rural West Bengal. In *Environment and Cultural Behavior,* ed. A. Vayda. Garden City; N.Y.: Natural History Press.

Pastore, N.

1949 *The Nature-Nurture Controversy.* New York: King's Crown.

Pearson, H.

1957 The Economy Has No Surplus. In *Trade and Market in the Early Empires,* ed. K. Polanyi, C. Arensburg, and H. Pearson, pp. 320-41. Glencoe, Ill.: Free Press.

Pelto, P. J.

1970 *Anthropological Research: The Structure of Inquiry.* New York: Harper & Row.

Pelzer, K.

1940 *Pioneer Settlement in the Asiatic Tropics.* American Geographical Society Publication no. 29.

Piddocke, S.

1965 The Potlatch System of the Southern

Kwakiutl: A New Perspective. *Southwestern Journal of Anthropology* 21: 244-64.

Platt, J.
1969 What We Must Do. *Science* 166: 1115-21.

Polgar, S.
1962 Health and Human Behavior. *Current Anthropology* 3:159-205.
1964 Evolution and the Ills of Mankind. In *Horizons of Anthropology*, ed. S. Tax, pp. 200-211. Chicago: Aldine.

Porter, P. W.
1965 Environmental Potentials and Economic Opportunities: A Background for Cultural Adaptation. *American Anthropologist* 67:409-20.

Prothero, R. M.
1964 Geographical Factors and Malaria Eradication: The Case of Morocco. *Pacific Viewpoint* 5:183-204.
1965 *Migrants and Malaria in Africa.* London: Longmans.

Rapoport, A.
1956 The Promise and Pitfalls of Information Theory. *Behavioral Science* 1: 303-15.
1968 General Systems Theory. In *International Encyclopedia of the Social Sciences* 15:452-58.

Rappaport, R. A.
1963 Aspects of Man's Influence upon the Island Ecosystem: Alteration and Control. In *Man's Place in the Island Ecosystem*, ed. F. R. Fosberg, pp. 155-74. Honolulu: Bishop Museum Press.
1967a Ritual Regulation of Environmental Relations Among a New Guinea People. *Ethnology* 6:17-30.
1967b *Pigs for the Ancestors.* New Haven: Yale University Press.

Redfield, R.
1952 *The Primitive World and Its Transformation.* Ithaca: Cornell University Press.
1953 Relations of Anthropology to the Social Sciences and to the Humanities. In *Anthropology Today*, ed. A. L. Kroeber et al., pp. 729-38. Chicago: University of Chicago Press.
1960 *The Little Community.* Chicago: University of Chicago Press.

Reed, S. W.

1955 Culture Dynamics and Demographic Change in Preliterate Societies. In *Proceedings of World Population Conference, 1954,* 6:187-97. New York: United Nations.

Ribiero, D.
1969 *The Civilizational Process.* Washington, D.C.: Smithsonian Institution Press.

Richards, A. I.
1932 *Hunger and Work in a Savage Tribe: A Functional Study of Nutrition Among the Southern Bantu.* London: Routledge.
1939 *Land and Labor and Diet in Northern Rhodesia.* London: Oxford University Press.

Roberts, G. W.
1957 *The Population of Jamaica.* Cambridge: At the University Press.

Roe, A., and G. G. Simpson, eds.
1958 *Behavior and Evolution.* New Haven: Yale University Press.

Rogers, E. S.
1960 *Human Ecology and Health: An Introduction for Administrators.* New York: Macmillan.
1962 Man, Ecology, and the Control of Disease. *Public Health Reports* 77: 755-62.

Rostlund, E.
1954- The Changing Forest Landscape.
1955 *Landscape* 4:30-35.
1961 Training Trees. *Bulletin of the Atomic Scientists* 17:326-33.

Sahlins, M. D.
1957 Differentiation by Adaptation in Polynesian Societies. *Journal of the Polynesian Society* 66:291-300.
1958 *Social Stratification in Polynesia.* Seattle: University of Washington Press.
1961 The Segmentary Lineage: An Organization of Predatory Expansion. *American Anthropologist* 63:322-45.
1962 *Moala: Culture and Nature on a Fijian Island.* Ann Arbor: University of Michigan Press.
1964 Culture and Environment: The Study of Cultural Ecology. In *Horizons of Anthropology*, ed. S. Tax, pp. 132-47. Chicago: Aldine.
1965 On the Sociology of Primitive Exchange. In *The Relevance of*

Models for Social Anthropology, ed. M. Banton, pp. 139-236. A.S.A. Monograph no. 1. London: Tavistock.

Sahlins, M., and E. R. Service
1960 *Evolution and Culture.* Ann Arbor: University of Michigan Press.

Salisbury, R. F.
1962 *From Stone and Steel.* Melbourne: Melbourne University Press.

Sanders, W. T.
1962 Cultural Ecology of Nuclear Meso-America. *American Anthropologist* 64:34-44.
1965 *The Cultural Ecology of the Teotihuacán Valley.* University Park: Pennsylvania State University Press.

Sanders, W. T., and B. J. Price
1968 *Mesoamerica: The Evolution of a Civilization.* Part 1: Civilization as an Ecological System, pp. 37-100. New York: Random House.

Sapir, E.
1912 Language and Environment. *American Anthropologist* 14:226-42.

Sauer, C.
1952 *Agricultural Origins and Dispersals.* New York: American Geographical Society.
1956 The Agency of Man on Earth. In *Man's Role in Changing the Face of the Earth,* ed. W. L. Thomas, Jr., pp. 49-68. Chicago: University of Chicago Press.
1967 *Land and Life: A Selection from the Writings of Carl O. Sauer,* ed. John Leighly. Berkeley: University of California Press.

Schneider, D.
1955 Abortion and Depopulation on a Pacific Island. In *Health, Culture, and Community,* ed. B. D. Paul, pp. 211-35. New York: Russell Sage Foundation.

Schnore, L. F.
1957- *Social Morphology and Human Ecol-*
1958 *ogy. American Journal of Sociology* 63:620-34.

Schneider, E.
1963 Physiological Anthropology and Climatic Variations. In *Environmental Physiology and Psychology in Arid Conditions: Proceedings of the Lucknow Symposium, 1962.* Paris: UNESCO.

1964 Ecological Rules, Body-Heat Regulation, and Human Evolution. *Evolution* 18:1-9.

Schultz, A. M.
1967 The Ecosystem as a Conceptual Tool in the Management of Natural Resources. In *Natural Resources: Quality and Quantity,* ed. S. V. Ciriacy-Wantrup and J. J. Parsons, pp. 139. 61. Berkeley: University of California Press.

Schwerdtfeger, F.
1963 *Autökologie.* Hamburg and Berlin: Verlag Paul Parey.
1968 *Demökologie.* Hamburg and Berlin: Verlag Paul Parey.

Scudder, T.
1962 *Kariba Studies,* vol. 2: *The Ecology of the Gwembe Tonga.* Manchester: Manchester University Press.

Sears, P. B.
1953 The Interdependence of Archaeology and Ecology, with Examples from Middle America. *Transactions of the New York Academy of Science,* ser. 2, 15:113-17.
1954 Human Ecology: A Problem in Synthesis. *Science* 120: 959-63.
1955 Changing Man's Habitat: Physical and Biological Phenomena. In *Current Anthropology,* ed. W. L. Thomas, Jr. Chicago: University of Chicago Press.
1956 The Processes of Environmental Change. In *International Symposium on Man's Role in Changing the Face of the Earth,* pp. 471-84. Chicago: University of Chicago Press.
1957 *The Ecology of Man.* Eugene: University of Oregon Press.
1966 *The Biology of the Living Landscape.* New York: Basic Books.

Secoy, F. R.
1953 *Changing Military Patterns of the Great Plains.* American Ethnological Society Monograph no. 21. Locust Valley, N.Y.: J. J. Augustin.

Service, E. R.
1962 *Primitive Social Organization.* New York: Random House.

Shelford, V. W.
1963 *The Ecology of North America.* Urbana: University of Illinois Press.

Shepard, P., and D. McKinley

1969 *The Subversive Science: Essays Toward an Ecology of Man.* Boston: Houghton Mifflin.

Sherif, M., and C. W. Sherif
1969 *Interdisciplinary Relationships in the Social Sciences.* Chicago: Aldine.

Shimkin, D. B.
1964 National Forces and Ecological Adaptation in the Development of Russian Peasant Societies. In *Process and Pattern in Culture,* ed. R. A. Manners, pp. 237-47. Chicago: Aldine.

Simmons, I. G.
1966 Ecology and Land Use. *Transactions of the Institute of British Geographers* 38:59-72.

Simpson, G. G.
1962 Comments on Cultural Evolution. In *Evolution and Man's Progress,* ed. U. Hoagland and R. W. Burhoe, pp. 104-108. New York: Columbia University Press.

Sjoberg, G.
1960 *The Pre-industrial City: Past and Present.* New York: Free Press, Macmillan.

Slater, M. K.
1959 Ecological Factors in the Origin of Incest. *American Anthropologist* 61:1042-59.

Smith, C. T.
1970 Depopulation of the Central Andes in the Sixteenth Century. *Current Anthropology* 11:453-64.

Snow, C. P.
1959 *The Two Cultures and the Scientific Revolution.* Cambridge: At the University Press.

Sorre, M.
1943 *Les fondements de la géographie humaine,* vol. 1: *Les fondements biologiques: Essai d'une écologie de l'homme.* Paris: Colin.
1962 The Concept of *Genre de Vie.* In *Readings in Cultural Geography,* ed. Wagner and Mikesell, pp. 399-415. Chicago: University of Chicago Press.

Spencer, H.
1925 *The Principles of Sociology.* New York: Appleton. Originally published 1876.

Spencer, J. E.
1966 *Shifting Cultivation.* Berkeley: University of California Press.

Spencer, R.
1959 *The North Alaskan Eskimo: A Study in Ecology and Society.* Bureau of American Ethnology Bulletin no. 171. Washington, D.C.: Smithsonian Institution.

Spoehr, A.
1956 Cultural Differences in the Interpretation of Natural Resources. In *Man's Role in Changing the Face of the Earth,* ed. W. L. Thomas, Jr., pp. 93-102. Chicago: University of Chicago Press.

Sprout, H., and M. Sprout
1956 *Man-Milieu Relationship Hypothesis in the Context of International Politics.* Princeton: Center for International Studies.
1965 *The Ecological Perspective on Human Affairs.* Princeton: Princeton University Press.

Spuhler, J. N.
1959 Physical Anthropology and Demography. In *The Study of Population,* ed. Philip Hauser and Otis Duncan. Chicago: University of Chicago Press.

Stamp, L. D.
1964 *The Geography of Life and Death.* London: Collins.

Stenning, D. J.
1957 Transhumance, Migratory Drift, Migration: Patterns of Pastoral Fulani Nomadism. *Journal of the Royal Anthropological Institute* 87:57-75.

Sternberg, H. O'R.
1964 Land and Man in the Tropics. *Latin American Trends* 27:11-21.
1968 Man and Environmental Change in South America. In *Biogeography and Ecology of South America,* ed. W. Junk, pp. 413-45. The Hague: Junk.

Stevenson, R. F.
1968 *Population and Political Systems in Tropical Africa.* New York: Columbia University Press.

Steward, J. H.
1933 *Ethnography of the Owens Valley Paiute.* University of California Publications in American Archaeology and Ethnology. Berkeley: University of California Press.
1936 The Economic and Social Basis of Primitive Bands. In *Essays in Honor*

of A. L. Kroeber, ed. Robert H. Lowie, pp. 331-50. Berkeley: University of California Press.

1937 Ecological Aspects of Southwestern Society. *American Anthropologist* 39:87-104.

1938 *Basin-Plateau Aboriginal Sociopolitical Groups.* Bureau of American Ethnology Bulletin no. 137. Washington, D.C.: Smithsonian Institution.

1950 *Area Research: Theory and Practice.* Social Science Research Council Bulletin no. 63.

1955 *Theory of Culture Change.* Urbana: University of Illinois Press.

1960 Evolutionary Principles and Social Types. In *Evolution After Darwin,* ed. S. Tax, vol. 2. Chicago: University of Chicago Press.

1968 Cultural Ecology. In *International Encyclopedia of the Social Sciences* 4:337-44.

Steward, J. H., ed.

1946- *Handbook of the South American In-*
1950 *dians,* 6 vols. Bureau of American Ethnology Bulletin no. 143. Washington, D.C.: Smithsonian Institution.

Steward, J. H., et al.

1956 *The People of Puerto Rico.* Urbana: University of Illinois Press.

Steward, J. H., and D. Shimkin

1961 Some Mechanisms of Socio-Cultural Evolution. *Daedalus,* September.

Stewart, O. C.

1954 The Forgotten Side of Ethnogeography. In *Method and Perspective in Anthropology,* ed. R. F. Spencer, pp. 221-48. Minneapolis: University of Minnesota Press.

1956 Fire as the First Great Force Employed by Man. In *Man's Role in Changing the Face of the Earth,* ed. W. L. Thomas, Jr., pp. 115-33. Chicago: University of Chicago Press.

Stoddart, D. R.

1965 Geography and the Ecological Approach: The Ecosystem as a Geographic Principle and Method. *Geography* 50:242-51.

1966 Organism and Ecosystem as Geographical Models. In *Models in Geography,* ed. Chorley and Haggett. London: Methuen.

Stott, D. H.

1962 Cultural and Natural Checks on Population Growth. In *Culture and the Evolution of Man,* ed. M. F. Ashley-Montagu. New York: Oxford University Press.

Strehlow, T. G. H.

1965 Culture, Social Structure, and Environment in Aboriginal Central Australia. In *Aboriginal Man in Australia: Essays in Honor of Emeritus Professor A. P. Elkin,* ed. R. M. and C. H. Berndt, pp. 121-45. Sydney: Angus & Robertson.

Suttles, W.

1960*a* Variation in Habitat and Culture on the Northwest Coast. *International Congress of Americanists* 34:522-37.

1960*b* Affinal Ties, Subsistence, and Prestige Among the Coastal Salish. *American Anthropologist* 62:296-305.

Sweet, L. E.

1965 Camel Raiding of North Arabian Bedouin: A Mechanism of Ecological Adaptation. *American Anthropologist* 67:1132-50.

Tax, S., ed.

1960 *Evolution After Darwin.* Chicago: University of Chicago Press.

Taylor, W. W.

1948 *A Study of Archaeology.* Memoir no. 69, American Anthropological Association.

Theodorson, G. A., ed.

1961 *Studies in Human Ecology.* Evanston, Ill.: Row, Peterson.

Thomas, F.

1925 *The Environmental Basis of Society: A Study of the History of Sociological Theory.* Century Social Science Series. New York: Johnson Reprint Corp.

Thomas, W. L., Jr., ed.

1956 *Man's Role in Changing the Face of the Earth.* Chicago: University of Chicago Press.

Thompson, L.

1949 Relations of Men, Animals, and Plants in an Island Community. *American Anthropologist* 51:544-56.

1961 *Toward a Science of Mankind.* New York: McGraw-Hill.

1967 Steps Toward a Unified Anthropology. *Current Anthropology* 8:67-77.

Thornthwaite, C. W.

1940 *The Relation of Geography to Human Ecology.* Ecological Monographs 10:343-48.

Tindale, N. B.
1959 Ecology of Primitive Aboriginal Man in Australia. In *Biography and Ecology in Australia,* ed. W. Junk, pp. 36-51. The Hague: W. Junk.

Tobias, P. V.
1964 Bushman Hunter-Gatherers: A Study in Human Ecology. In *Ecological Studies in Southern Africa,* ed. D. H. S. Davis, pp. 67-86. The Hague: W. Junk.

Troels-Smith, J.
1960a The Muldbjerg Dwelling Place: An Early Neolithic Archaeological Site in the Aamosen Bog, West-Zealand, Denmark. In *Smithsonian Report for 1959,* pp. 577-601. Washington, D.C.: Smithsonian Institution.
1960b *Ivy, Mistletoe, and Elm: Climate Indicators—Fodder Plants.* Geological Survey of Denmark, ser. 4, vol. 4, no. 4.

United Nations
1953 Determinants and Consequences of Population Trends. Population Studies no. 17. U.N. Department of Social Affairs, Population Division. New York: United Nations.

Van Dyne, George M., ed.
1969 *The Ecosystem Concept in Natural Resource Management.* New York: Academic Press.

Vayda, A. P.
1961a Expansion and Warfare Among Swidden Agriculturalists. *American Anthropologist* 63:346-58.
1961b A Re-examination of Northwest Coast Economic Systems. *Transactions of the New York Academy of Science,* 2nd ser., 23:618-24.
1967 On the Anthropological Study of Economics. *Journal of Economic Issues* 1:86-90.
1969 An Ecological Approach in Cultural Anthropology. *Bucknell Review* 17:112-19.

Vayda, A. P., ed.
1969 *Environment and Cultural Behavior: Ecological Studies in Cultural Anthropology.* Garden City, N.Y.: Natural History Press.

Vayda, A. P., A. Leeds, and D. B. Smith
1961 The Place of Pigs in Melanesian Subsistence. In *Proceedings of the 1961 Annual A.E.S. Meetings,* ed. V. E. Garfield, pp. 69-77. Seattle: University of Washington Press.

Vayda, A. P., and R. A. Rappaport
1963 Island Cultures. In *Man's Place in the Island Ecosystem,* ed. F. R. Fosberg, pp. 133-44. Honolulu: Bishop Museum Press.
1968 Ecology: Cultural and Non-Cultural. In *Introduction to Cultural Anthropology,* ed. J. A. Clifton, pp. 476-98. Boston: Houghton Mifflin.

Wagley, C.
1940 The Effects of Depopulation upon Social Organization as Illustrated by the Tapirape Indians. *Transactions of the New York Academy of Sciences,* ser. 2, vol. 3:12-16.
1951 Cultural Influences on Population: A Comparison of Two Tupi Tribes. *Revista do Museu Paulista* 5:95-104.

Wallace, W. A., ed.
1969 *Sociological Theory: An Introduction.* Chicago Aldine.

Washburn, S. L.
1950 The Analysis of Primate Evolution with Particular Reference to the Origin of Man. In *The Origin and Evolution of Man. Cold Spring Harbor Symposia on Quantitative Biology* 15:67-68.
1953 The Strategy of Physical Anthropology. In *Anthropology Today,* ed. A. L. Kroeber, pp. 714-27. Chicago: University of Chicago Press.
1960 Tools and Human Evolution. *Scientific American* 203:63-75.

Washburn, S. L., ed.
1961 *Social Life of Early Man.* Viking Fund Publications in Anthropology no. 31. New York: Wenner-Gren Foundation.
1963 *Classification and Human Evolution.* Chicago: Aldine.

Washburn, S. L., and V. Avis
1958 Evolution of Human Behavior. In *Behavior and Evolution,* ed. Roe and Simpson, pp. 421-36. New Haven: Yale University Press.

Washburn, S. L., and F. C. Howell
1960 Human Evolution and Culture. In

Evolution After Darwin, ed. S. Tax, vol. 2, pp. 35-56. Chicago: University of Chicago Press.

Washburn, S. L., P. C. Jay, and J. Lancaster
1965   Field Studies of Old World Monkeys and Apes. *Science* 150:1541-47.

Watanabe, H.
1964   The Ainu: A Study of Ecology and the System of Social Solidarity Between Man and Nature in Relation to Group Structure. *Journal of the Faculty of Science,* sec. 5, "Anthropology." Tokyo: University of Tokyo.
1966   Die sozialen Funktionen des Bärenfestes der Ainu und die ökologischen Faktoren in seiner Entwicklung. *Anthropos* 61:708-26.

Watson, R. A., and P. J. Watson
1969   Man and Nature: An Anthropological Essay. In Richard A. Watson and Patty Jo Watson, *Human Ecology.* New York: Harcourt, Brace & World.

Watt, K.
1968   *Ecology and Natural Resource Management.* New York: McGraw-Hill.

Wedel, W. R.
1941   *Environment and Native Subsistence Economics in the Central Great Plains.* Washington, D.C.: Smithsonian Institution.
1953   Some Aspects of Human Ecology in the Central Plains. *American Anthropologist* 55:499-514.
1957   The Central North American Grassland: Man-Made or Natural? In *Studies in Human Ecology,* ed. Palerm et al., pp. 39-70. Social Science Monographs. Washington, D.C.: Pan American Union.

Weinberg, A.
1966   Can Technology Replace Social Engineering? *Bulletin of the Atomic Scientists* 22:6-10.

Weinberg, D.
1965   Models of Southern Kwakiutl Social Organization: General Systems. *Yearbook of the Society for General Systems Research* 10:169-81.

Weiner, J. S.
1964   Human Ecology. In *Human Biology: An Introduction to Human Evolution, Variation, and Growth,* ed. G. A. Harrison et al. New York: Oxford University Press.

Weisenfeld, S. L.
1967   Sickle-Cell Trait in Human Biological and Cultural Evolution. *Science* 157: 1134-40.

Wertheim, W. F.
1959   Sociological Aspects of Inter-Island Migration in Indonesia. *Population Studies* 12:184-201.

West, R. D., ed.
1965   *Natural Environment and Early Cultures:* vol. 1, *Handbook of Middle American Indians.* Austin: University of Texas Press.

White, L. A.
1959   *The Evolution of Culture.* New York: McGraw-Hill.
1960   Four Stages in the Evolution of Minding. In *Evolution After Darwin,* ed. S. Tax, vol. 2, pp. 239-53. Chicago: University of Chicago Press.

White, L. A., Jr.
1962   *Medieval Technology and Social Change.* Oxford: Oxford University Press.
1967   The Historical Roots of Our Ecological Crisis. *Science* 155:1203-1207.

Whiting, J. W. M.
1964   Effects of Climate on Certain Cultural Practices. In *Explorations in Cultural Anthropology,* ed. W. H. Goodenough, pp. 511-44. New York: McGraw-Hill.

Wilbert, J., ed.
1961   *The Evolution of Horticultural Systems in Native South America: Causes and Consequences: A Symposium.* Caracas: Sociedad de Ciencias Naturales La Salle.

Willey, G. R., and P. Phillips
1958   *Method and Theory in American Archaeology.* Chicago: University of Chicago Press.

Winterbottom, J. M.
1945   Ecology of Man and Plants in Northern Rhodesia. *Rhodes-Livingstone Institute Journal* 3:33-44.

Wittfogel, K.
1957   *Oriental Despotism.* New Haven: Yale University Press.

Wolf, E. R.
1957   Closed Corporate Peasant Communities in Mesoamerica and Central Java. *Southwestern Journal of Anthropology* 13:1-18.

1962 Cultural Dissonance in the Italian Alps. *Comparative Studies in Sociology and History* 5:1-14.

1964 *Anthropology.* Englewood Cliffs, N.J.: Prentice-Hall.

1966 *Peasants.* Englewood Cliffs, N.J.: Prentice-Hall.

Wrigley, E. A.
1969 *Population and History.* New York: McGraw-Hill.

Wyman, L. C., and F. Bailey
1965 *Navaho Indian Ethnoentogeology.* University of New Mexico Publications in Anthropology no. 12.

Wynne-Edwards, V. C.
1962 *Animal Dispersion in Relation to Social Behavior.* Edinburgh: Oliver & Boyd.

Yengoyan, A. A.
1966 Ecological Analysis and Agriculture. *Comparative Studies in Society and History* 9:105-17.

1968 Demographic and Ecological Influences on Aboriginal Australian Marriage Sections. In *Man the Hunter,* ed. R. Lee and I. De Vore, pp. 185-99. Chicago: Aldine.

Zelinsky, W.
1970 Beyond the Exponentials: The Role of Geography in the Great Transition. *Economic Geography* 46: 498-535.

CHAPTER **6** Ethnography:
The Fieldwork Enterprise

PERTTI J. PELTO
GRETEL H. PELTO

INTRODUCTION

In 1800 a young French philosopher, Citizen Joseph-Marie Degérando, wrote what was probably the first field guide for ethnographers. His *Considerations on the Various Methods to Follow in the Observation of Savage Peoples* was intended as a guide for members of the Société des Observateurs de l'Homme as they embarked on expeditions to Africa and Australia. Degérando (1969: 70) discussed the principal weaknesses in the ethnographic observations of earlier explorers, and argued that "the first means to the proper knowledge of the Savages, is to become after a fashion like one of them; and it is by learning their language that we shall become their fellow citizens."

Degérando was especially clear about the importance of studying primitive peoples within the context of their social systems. The following are among the topics that he listed for the study of social organization (Degérando 1969:88-89, 91):

Does the father have any authority? On what

principle does it appear to the based? . . . What respect have young people for the old? . . . What is the force and character of the bond between brothers? Is there any precedence of age among them? To what point do the relations of kinship extend and keep any influence? In what way are they observed? Do the members of a single family unite for work, for hunting, for food? Then what law and order is observed among them? . . . What are the internal bonds of society, and the foundations on which rests the unity of its members?

In addition to giving detailed suggestions concerning ethnographic observations, Degérando (1969:101) notes:

We are aware that the totality of problems here posed . . . calls for a huge amount of work. . . . We are aware that this work is surrounded by all kinds of difficulties, and that one must expect to meet great obstacles in the first relations that one wishes to establish with the Savages.

Degérando's excellent fieldwork instructions had little effect on the French explorers he intended to influence, and his *Considerations* was totally unknown to the ethnographers of the nineteenth century. The fieldwork profession that grew into a major enterprise toward the end of the last century nonetheless made use of some methodological principles similar to those he laid down, although it can be argued that the kind of fieldwork he envisioned did not become a significant reality until well into the twentieth century.

We do not intend to review the history of ethnographic fieldwork, but the long-forgotten suggestions of Degérando, along with some comments about earlier decades of ethnographic work, provide us with a perspective from which to view contemporary ethnographic activities. It is especially important to note that Degérando's guidelines to fieldwork called for observations of ongoing sociocultural behavior. It is also significant that his methodology assumed rather little in the way of *a priori* theoretical prejudices concerning "native" peoples, and based itself mainly on an inductive, empirical approach to non-Western cultures.

NINETEENTH-CENTURY TECHNIQUES: HISTORICAL RECONSTRUCTION

The methods and techniques of many nineteenth-century ethnographers suffered from the pervasive, taken-for-granted presence of an evolutionist theory that favored the collection of only certain types of data, and predisposed anthropologists to look for broad "stages" of past culture history, rather than to concentrate on the systematic characteristics of the life and thought of the people they encountered during their fieldwork. Even those fieldworkers who were relatively unconcerned with general cultural evolution had historical interests that blunted their observations of the here-and-now among the peoples they studied. For example, the work of many European ethnographers was directed toward recon-struction of the past histories of Indo-European, Finno-Ugric, and other proto-groups from combined evidence of their linguistic characteristics and the lists of traits found in their customs and folklore.

The reconstruction of history as a major goal of field ethnography endured into the early decades of the twentieth century. Evolutionist theories of Morgan, Tylor, Lubbock, and others had given way to the culture historicalism of Boas and his students and of the *Kulturkreis* school in Vienna, but diachronic studies that sought "origins" and "periods" remained a major focus of attention affecting the methods and techniques of the profession.

Informant-Oriented Studies

In North America most ethnographers who went out to study "primitive peoples" found themselves confronted with Indian peoples whose cultural behavior had been drastically altered by the rapid incursions of the white man's way of life. Fieldworkers usually defined their task as that of recording for posterity the details of an "aboriginal" culture and social system that had already largely disappeared by the time the anthropologist arrived on the scene. Of necessity the ethnographic method in this situation consisted mainly of lengthy interview sessions with a few key informants—older members of the population who remembered in rich (and sometimes romanticized) detail the ways of life they had enjoyed in earlier decades. Exaggerated characterizations of this research method sometimes place the fieldworker in a hotel bar with his informants, who recall their glorious past for the ethnographer and afterward use their hourly pay to dissolve in alcohol the memories of defeats, exploitation, and the white man's greed. The great importance of individual key informants in this type of research is epitomized in a fieldwork description by Cornelius Osgood (1940), who logged some five hundred hours of interviewing with one well-informed Ingalik Indian.

Strictly historical anthropology, when it is concerned with a people's cultural past, does not necessitate very much living among, or identifying with, the "natives." In considering the past history of the ethnographic work it is interesting to note instances in which the fieldworker's daily tasks were actually hindered by the "cultural present" of the research population. Franz Boas, for example, while working in the field among the Kwakiutl in 1886, wrote in a letter dated October 12-13:

I had a miserable day today. The natives held a big potlatch again. I was unable to get hold of anyone and had to snatch at whatever I could get. Late at night I did get something [a tale] for which I had been searching—"The Birth of the Raven." ... The big potlatches were continued today, but people found time to tell me stories ... [Rohner, ed., 1969:38].

It is apparent from this comment by one of the father figures of American anthropology that there can be a great difference between informant-oriented and observation-oriented fieldwork styles. Most anthropologists today would be overjoyed at the prospect of observing a full-blown potlatch and would assume that crucially important social structural and cultural data could be extracted from details of the ceremony.

TWENTIETH-CENTURY TECHNIQUES: PARTICIPANT OBSERVATION

Fieldwork that involves living in close contact with a research population in order to observe their daily routines, ritual and social acts, economic activities, and other aspects of cultural behavior assumed methodological prominence with the rise of interest in an ahistorical, "structural-functionalist" study of human social systems. This sharp reorientation of ethnographic interests began in the decade of 1915-1925, particularly following the appearance in 1922 of major theoretical works by A. R. Radcliffe-Brown and Bronislaw Malinowski.

Malinowski is often credited with being the originator, or at least the major developer, of the style of fieldwork that involves intensive and long-term immersion in the daily lives of native peoples. Even though the recent publication of his private diary (Malinowski 1967) casts some new light on his attitudes and interactions with the Trobrianders, it cannot be doubted that he observed their daily rounds and activities over a long period of time, and from this experience he developed a program and rationale for "functionalist" fieldwork that has had a powerful influence on ethnographic work both in Europe and in North America. Gluckman (1967:xii) has noted that Malinowski's field methodology of extensive immersion in the daily lives of native communities produces a new level of information, much more elaborated and complex than had been typical of earlier ethnographic work:

A new technique of observation may virtually create a new discipline, as Leeuwenhoek's improvements of the microscope, and later creation of radio-telescopes did. I consider that Malinowski's field researches had this effect on anthropology, partly because of his long residence in the Trobriand Islands, partly because he worked through the Trobriand language, and partly because his temperament led him to a deep involvement with the people he was studying.

Some anthropologists before Malinowski worked in the native language and also became deeply involved emotionally with the people they studied. The ethnographer Frank Cushing lived for five years (1880-1885) at Zuñi pueblo, participating fully in Zuñi daily life. He was initiated into one of the secret religious fraternities, and later into the War Chief Society (Mead and Bunzel 1960: 204-205). Nonetheless, modern fieldwork, with its strong emphasis on participant observation, owes much to the Malinowskian example.

Community Studies

If ethnographic methodology after Malinowski became more and more oriented to what can be called "community study," there is at least one other important source of this direction in fieldwork. At about the same time that Malinowski was developing his functionalist ideas, sociologists in Chicago, notably Robert Park, were embarking on a paradigm of sociological research which had important interrelationships with anthropological work. Maurice Stein (1960:15) has noted that the Chicago sociologists,

like the large majority of the population of the time, had spent their early years in small towns. This was the form of community living with which they were most familiar and it provided a frame of reference within which the highly dissimilar features of Chicago social life were perceived and evaluated.

Their research tended toward holistic, qualitative descriptions of life in face-to-face communities.

Among the persons influenced by the Chicago sociologists was Robert Redfield, who married Robert Park's daughter. During the middle 1920s he embarked on a holistic study the Mexican village of Tepoztlán, near Cuernavaca (see Redfield 1930). Redfield's fieldwork is one of the earliest community studies by anthropologists, and probably was influenced more by the Chicago

sociologists than by the methodological and theoretical writings of Malinowski.

The community study, whether sociological or anthropological, is in part a natural development from the idea of intensive, long-term fieldwork. The fieldworker who takes up residence within a research population finds himself becoming a member of a particular community (town, village, band, or other local social unit). He develops close friendships and working ties with its members. Often he is assigned ties of fictive kinship within the social network and is expected to show local loyalties vis-à-vis "foreigners" from other such communities.

The often difficult tasks of personal maintenance—preparing food; keeping washed, groomed, and laundered; getting firewood, fuels, and other supplies; and the far more difficult chores of keeping order within one's system of social relations—all exert such influences on the ethnographer that he can hardly help becoming a specialist in the life and times of "his" community. In an earlier period, when ethnographers were more interested in bygone culture history, all this special knowledge about a community seemed to serve no useful anthropological purpose. But as theoretical interests turned increasingly toward analysis of society and culture as an integrated, living system, the community of research became the basic unit of study. The importance of the community as research unit was further emphasized as more ethnographers in the post-World War II era began increasingly to study peasant peoples—populations too large to pretend that one could adequately describe the "whole culture." Acknowledging the great variations to be found among regions and communities of peasants, fieldworkers converted the fact of living in a particular community from a necessity to a methodological virtue and produced holistic community studies.

Not all ethnographic studies are community studies, of course. One notices, though, that in many studies that at first seem to deal generally with a "whole culture," much of the descriptive material actually comes from a particular community or small region—the locale of the anthropologist's fieldwork. In addition to most studies of peasants, whether in Europe, Latin America, India, or elsewhere, many recent studies of Indian and Eskimo groups in North America are explicitly focused on communities.

Most recently, a number of ethnographic works concerning segments of urban populations have begun to appear: Liebow's *Tally's Corner* (1968), Keiser's *The Vice Lords* (1969), Peattie's *The View from the Barrio* (1968), and Nash's *A Community in Limbo* (1970), among others. It is probably fair to say that the community-as-research-unit mode of ethnographic investigation is especially prevalent among American researchers, although it is by no means unknown among ethnographers in other parts of the world.

Although our review of contemporary ethnographic activities will make community-oriented studies a central aspect of modern fieldwork, there is a growing interest in studies that seek to escape the limitations of single-community data organization. Sampling in a research region, comparisons among a carefully selected series of communities, and various kinds of specialized study involving other types of research units are becoming increasingly important in ethnographic investigation. Among these the specialized research that is characteristic of the so-called New Ethnography represents a return to intensive interviewing of a few key informants. In these studies, using techniques of "componential analysis" or

other specialized "emic" analysis of taxonomic categories, the unit of research is usually the "culture" as expressed in a particular language.

The Humanistic-Scientific Dilemma

The fieldwork method that was adumbrated in Citizen Đegérando's farsighted *Considerations* and then rediscovered by Malinowski in his long stay among the Trobriand Islanders contains an inherent dilemma that is a source of unending debate for anthropologists and their critics. The dynamic conflict involves the seeming contradictions between the necessity for humanistic, empathic "understanding" of the way of life of a people, which is generated in part through the fieldwork process itself, and the equally important matter of developing scientifically objective, verifiable modes of observation. Some anthropologists have resolved this dilemma by pronouncing the entire enterprise to be a humanistic *verstehen* discipline. Others feel that the humanistic, impressionistic side of ethnographic work must be eliminated; that all field data must be operationalized and quantified. The more usual attitude in recent anthropological writing seeks an amalgam, a judicious mixture of the two aspects of the research enterprise. Gerald Berreman (1968:368) has expressed this view effectively:

The question I see is not whether to be scientific or humanistic, but how to be both. That is, the ethnographer must strive to make his observations and analyses more rigorous than those of a casual observer and he must do so without losing the fundamental insights that are obtained by perceptive non-scientists (for instance, novelists). The humanistic view tends to overlook the advantages of rigor—especially of verifiability of findings; the scientistic view tends to overlook the advantages of insight. The humanist ignores the fact that findings are only as good as the theories and methods by which they are derived and are only convincing if they can be verified; the scientist ignores the fact that studying human social events is in itself a social event. . . .

The solution to the problem of achieving an effective balance between the scientific and humanistic sides of fieldwork may be sought, Berreman feels, "through making explicit and public the procedures by which research is accomplished and derived. This requires . . . a description of exactly how ethnography is done, how insights are derived, how judgments about data are made" (Berreman 1968:368-69). In the following materials we shall treat both aspects of the fieldwork enterprise, in order to examine the ways in which contemporary ethnographers seek to resolve the humanistic-scientific dilemma by means of an eclectic, qualitative-quantitative mix of fieldwork methods.

New Fieldwork Literature

Fortunately, much new material has been published recently concerning ethnographers' field experiences and methods. A collection of papers edited by Epstein (1967) is primarily concerned with an assessment of some main research tools employed by social anthropologists. Jongmans and Gutkind (1967) have edited a collection of methodological papers under the title *Anthropologists in the Field;* the Holt, Rinehart and Winston methodological series now includes personalized descriptions of ethnographic experiences by Beattie (1965), Middleton (1970), and Williams (1967). In the same series, *Stress and Response in Field Work,* edited by Henry and Saberwal (1969), contains interesting analyses of psychological and social aspects of the ethnographer's experience; and a recent addition to this series is a collection of fieldwork narratives by thirteen au-

thors, entitled *Being an Anthropologist* (Spindler, ed., 1970).

The special role conflicts, problems, and advantages experienced by female fieldworkers have been examined in detail in *Woman in the Field* (Golde, ed., 1970). Hortense Powdermaker's excellent *Stranger and Friend* (1966) provides an extended autobiography of some three decades of fieldwork and illustrates how the ethnographic enterprise has changed during this period. Elenore Bowen's *Return to Laughter* (1964; first published in 1954) gives a quasi-fictitious view of a West African research experience, emphasizing the complex interactions between the fieldworker and the people studied. Other descriptions of the research experiences of female ethnographers are included in the several collections of fieldwork narratives that have recently appeared.

Gerald Berreman's (1962, 1968) theoretical discussions about methods and techniques of fieldwork have been illustrated by a vivid description of his own research in a north Indian village, in which he portrays the ethnographer and villagers in dramaturgical terms as "both performers and audience to each other." Each side seeks to present a certain image of self, but the audience (especially the ethnographer) "will attempt to glimpse the back region [of the theatrical scene] in order to gain new insights into the nature of the performance and the performers" (Berreman 1968:362).

A number of other autobiographical narratives appeared during the 1960s, of which the book-length accounts by Lévi-Strauss (1965) and Maybury-Lewis (1965) are noteworthy. *Marginal Natives: Anthropologists at Work*, edited by Morris Freilich (1970), contains descriptions of fieldwork by ten anthropologists, each of whom compares the methods, problems, and results of two research trips. Freilich himself has added an interesting analysis of the fieldwork process, as well as a practical training guide for graduate students. Several of the papers in Freilich's volume give special emphasis to the scientific side of fieldwork, although they do not neglect humanistic aspects. There are many other recent works that treat one or another aspect of fieldwork, so that we can no longer complain, as we did a few years ago, of the paucity of information about the ethnographic enterprise.

Besides making use of the available published materials, we shall draw to a limited extent on our own fieldwork experiences, on those of our working colleagues, and on responses to a questionnaire that we sent to a random sample of anthropologists listed in the 1969 *Guide to Graduate Departments of Anthropology* published by the American Anthropological Association. The responses to our questionnaire provide an interesting statistical supplement to published accounts of ethnographic work. It might be argued that people who publish autobiographical accounts of their own fieldwork are

somehow different from the average ethnographer. Of course, the fifty-one questionnaire respondents cannot be taken as fully representative of the profession (unknown biases are introduced by the fact that only 45 percent of the original sample returned the questionnaire). Nevertheless, these data are probably somewhat more representative of the profession as a whole than are the published personal accounts. The information about these respondents contained in Tables 1, 2, and 3 demonstrates the range of variation in our sample.

TABLE 1
Culture Area of Most Recent Fieldwork

Area	Number
U.S. and Canada (including Indian groups and urban studies)	7
Europe and Mediterranean	6
Caribbean	2
Mesoamerica	7
South America	3
West Africa	7
East and South Africa	5
Middle East	1
South and Southeast Asia	5
East Asia	5
Oceania	3

TABLE 2
Institution From Which Highest Degree Received

Institution	Number
University of Arizona	1
University of California:	
Berkeley	4
Los Angeles	4
Catholic University of America	2
University of Chicago	5
Columbia University	3
Cornell University	3
Florida State University	1
University of Georgia	1
University of Illinois	1
Indiana University	1
University of London	2
London School of Economics	1
University of Michigan	3
Michigan State University	1
Northwestern University	4
Ohio State University	1
University of Oregon	2
Oxford University	2
University of Pennsylvania	1
Stanford University	2
University of Washington	1
University of Wisconsin	2
Yale University	1
No response	2

TABLE 3
Year of Most Recent Degree

Year	Number	Year	Number
1938	2	1961	2
1939	1	1962	3
1946	1	1963	2
1950	1	1965	6
1951	2	1966	2
1953	1	1967	5
1954	1	1968	4
1955	3	1969	4
1958	1	1970	5
1959	1	1971	2
1960	1	NR	1

THE ETHNOGRAPHER AS MARGINAL NATIVE

Although Degérando urged that ethnographers live like the people they seek to study, we should understand clearly at the outset that the fieldworker does not assume a role that is fully "native" in all respects. Nor do the "natives" come to think of the anthropologist as a completely assimilated member of the local social order. The fieldworker is always a marginal person, an outsider who, if he is successful, is permitted relatively free access to the backstage area of the local social scene. This is true even though the anthropologist is often "adopted" into the society he is studying and is assigned social roles that seem appropriate within the framework of the host culture.

Morris Freilich has suggested that the fieldworker moves back and forth between "going native" and reasserting his role as ethnographer. "As the anthropologist slips out of the role of fieldworker and into one of several roles available to him (friend, neighbor, blood brother, or whatever), a closeness develops with some natives which cannot be achieved while in the role of fieldworker" (Freilich, ed., 1970:533). He argues that such moments of tempo-

rary identification with the local people are essential to effective fieldwork.

An interesting glimpse of the dual role of the fieldworker is captured in Hortense Powdermaker's (1966:115) account of research in Lesu: "Although I enjoyed those brief moments of feeling at one with the woman dancers at the initiation rites and although I was fairly involved in this Stone-Age society, I never fooled myself that I had 'gone-native.' I participated rather freely, but remained an anthropologist."

A striking instance of role conflict occurred when Powdermaker's best friend lay seriously ill after her baby was stillborn. "I sat around the bed with the women, went back to my house, wrote up everything, wandered back to Pulong's bed again. The fact that I was getting good data did not take away my restlessness. I felt all wrong during this crisis: outside it, though emotionally involved" (1966:116).

Maintenance of the ambiguous "marginal native" role permits the ethnographer to move relatively freely in different sectors of the social system. His position is not fixed immutably in any particular ascribed cluster of obligations and expectations. On the other hand, in all fieldwork the anthropologist develops certain main channels of social relations; he usually makes a few enemies, wittingly and unwittingly; some parts of the society remain virtually closed to him; and all of these social facts influence the patterning of the information he is able to collect. Berreman (1962, 1968a) has given a compelling description of the way in which social contacts with high-caste families (because of the social origins of his interpreter-assistant) colored his perceptions of the entire community. When illness forced his Brahmin assistant to leave the community, Berreman acquired a Muslim (low-status) research associate. This change in social identification of the fieldwork team opened up many new avenues of information-gathering, particularly among the lower caste members of the village. "Not long after Mohammed's arrival villagers found that he indulged in both [meat and liquor] and that I could be induced to do so. Thereafter we became aware of frequent meat and liquor parties, often of an intercaste nature. . . . Rapport increased notably" (Berreman 1968:360).

INTRODUCTION TO THE COMMUNITY

Hans Buechler (1969:19), in looking back over his role as ethnographer in a Bolivian community, noted that his information-gathering was much influenced by the particular pathways and contacts he chose early in his fieldwork:

Had I introduced myself into the community through the teachers, I would probably not have gotten very far, since most of them are strangers with few ties with community members. Had I employed Pedro instead of Paz as an interpreter, my insight into sectional divisions might have been reduced but I might have attained deeper understanding of the life of migrants. . . .

Whatever role negotiations follow later, the very first step in fieldwork is the introduction of oneself and one's research intentions to the people. Usually the anthropologist has had prior contact with the research area, perhaps through government officials whose permission he has obtained to make a study. Naturally it is highly desirable that all available information be studied concerning the proposed research site, so that the fieldworker has some general knowledge about the size and composition of the local population, the state of communications and transportation systems, and (most important) some idea of "who runs the place"; that is, who are the constituted *local* authorities whose permission (or at least indifference) one must secure if a full-scale research project is to be carried out.

William Schwab (1970:83) had the approval of higher governmental authorities for his study of the Yoruba town of Oshogbo; nonetheless, he recalls:

I did not begin investigations in the town proper until I had the consent of the ruling hierarchy. The approval of the chiefs and other literate and influential members of the community did not ensure the approval and cooperation of the people, but it was a necessary pre-requisite to gaining the confidence of the community at large.

In some cases the ethnographer nears the field situation on a bus, train, car, ship, or other conveyance that is carrying some members of the local population home from travels in the wider world. These returning travelers can be the anthropologist's initial contacts in the community. Nelson Graburn (1969:1-2) gives an example of such a situation in describing his arrival at Sugluk, in the central Canadian arctic:

The ship carried a number of Eskimos from the tuberculosis sanatoria "down south" back to their scattered settlements. . . . Day by day I met a few more—those who were younger and came on deck more often. . . . A few spoke a little English and the older children were the least shy. . . . Luckily I met one or two residents of Sugluk on the ship who were later able to introduce me to their families when we arrived there. People from other settlements chatted about places I was to visit only years later. None of them ever forgot our short conversations, though, and those, too, were good introductions in later years.

Fieldwork in relatively complex sub-communities within our own society often is not officially cleared through constituted authorities, although such officials usually should be notified of research activities. As a general rule, the fieldworker should make clear to *some* legitimate authorities (the police, local school authorities, or the Chamber of Commerce, for example) that research activities are being undertaken. However, contact with such authorities often is relatively remote from the realities of the day-to-day scene. Elliot Liebow (1968:240-41) has described some of the processes by which his research among black street-corner men in Washington, D.C., was "legitimated" where it counted most:

Back on the street, I ended up in the Downtown Café, this time by way of the morning's now very drunk owner of the puppy, who was standing in the entrance. The puppy was our bond and we talked about him with enthusiasm. ... Then, still drinking beer at the bar stool, I met two other men in quick succession. ... The other was a surly man in his middle thirties who initiated contact by taking the stool next to me and asking what kind of work I did. ... I told him briefly what my job was. "Well, if you hang around here you'll see it all. Anything can happen and it does happen here. It can get rough and you can get your head knocked in. You'll be okay though, if you know one or two of the right people."
"That's good to know," I told him, guessing (and hoping) that he was one of the "right people." He left me with the impression that he was being friendly and, in a left-handed sort of way, was offering me his protection.

In Liebow's case the mutual interest in and activity with a newly acquired puppy (the fieldworker paid for the milk to feed it) provided part of the rationale for initial contacts with the men around "Tally's Corner."

Approach to "Deprived" Groups

In the contemporary world, the conflicts produced by racial, ethnic, and other social differentiations are of great importance and complexity. Ethnographers often study groups that are defined as socially (and economically) marginal or "deprived" in relation to national social systems. Entry into their communities is often made difficult by the established relationships between the racial or ethnic community and persons of the (supposedly) dominant social category, of which the anthropologist is usually a member. In some instances it may be that *any* style of initial interaction between the would-be fieldworker and the intended research community is "wrong," and will create problems. That is, formal behavior and language, especially when acted out through the official (superordinate-subordinate) channels, may be regarded as necessary by both officialdom and "the people," yet they stamp the fieldworker as associated with the superordinate social system. Bypassing the usual, "legitimate" channels of entry into communities, on the other hand, can lead to suspicions among the local populace, even though the fieldworker feels he has thereby avoided the negative image caused by direct association with the local authorities or government officials.

Norman Whitten (1970:370-71) has described the problems of getting started in fieldwork in a Negro community in Nova Scotia. Although he describes this set of events as a series of "mistakes," it is probable that at the point of entry into the community anything he did would have been interpreted somewhat negatively:

Within the first week of research we had blundered in such a manner as to alienate the person with whom we presumably had to make friends if we were to work in the area of our choice. We later found that we had made two basic errors. First, when Nova Scotians tell one to first call the official responsible for a community, they are paying due respect to the official, but they do not expect the investigator to take this advice. They expect that the investigator will establish an enduring contact with someone who can introduce him to the official. Crucial to this procedure is that the investigator is first known to the person who will make the introduction, for the middleman may be held responsible for the investigator's mistakes.... Second, it is not expected that one will use the term *Negro* in referring to Nova Scotians ethnically identified as colored. The use of ethnic terminology (including the term *colored*) is reserved for those who are already part of the system.... The most effective way to approach an official, we found, is to recognize no ethnic distinctions whatsoever, thereby forcing the official to make the preliminary distiction (e.g., between colored community and white community).

THE ETHNOGRAPHER AT WORK

In discussions about the beginnings of fieldwork we sometimes have a tendency to list a series of moves and countermoves, as if fieldwork can be described and proscribed like a game of chess. Probably nothing could be further from the facts. It is more likely that the successful fieldworker will make all kinds of mistakes; he will offend members of the local community and will experience all kinds of emotional setbacks during fieldwork; yet he emerges from the experience with full notebooks and with tales of great rapport and undying friendship with many of his best (and worst) informants. What happened in the meantime?

The answers are complex, yet some points stand out. To achieve Degérando's directive of "living like the people" (whether "savage" or "civilized"), the most successful fieldworkers have had a personal flexibility, humility, and sensitivity that we sincerely believe are universally recognized, regardless of custom or occasion. Some courage enters into the picture, too. But in the most general terms (we submit this for general discussion and debate in our profession), successful fieldworkers have been those who were able to meet the research community on the basis of face-to-face, human universals—although these are hard to define.

Acceptance of Local Food and Drink

It seems to us that choices of food and drink are among the most sensitive indicators of differential status, ethnicity, and economic position. Over and over again fieldworkers have reported that their willingness to accept local food and drink was a first step to fieldwork rapport. In a great many instances the anthropologist immediately establishes himself as a different kind of person from government officials, wealthy traders, or other outsiders simply by eating or drinking with the local people. Middleton (1970:20-21) describes the effects of his first dinner invitation among the Lugbara:

... I had shown that unlike other Europeans in their experience I was willing to eat with them.... Secondly, I had shown that I trusted my hosts not to poison me.... To share food is the epitome of kinship and to eat of a man's salt shows that one accepts the relationship of kinship that cannot later be denied.... As with food, my willingness and indeed my love of drinking beer (which I admit was a simulated affection) was taken as a sign that I was willing to accept my neighbors as equals....

In many instances the fieldworker must overcome some squeamishness with regard to both flavor and sanitation when he accepts food and drink in the field. Middleton's (1970:21) observations on beer-drinking appear to be in accord with the experiences of a great many ethnographers in Africa:

At first I admit that I found it difficult to drink the beer in any quantity due to its strong smell and the amount of dirt and foreign matter in it; also I found it difficult to drink from a calabash that had just been cleaned by the woman who was offering it to me having licked the rim before filling it. But I soon realized that to refuse beer would be both an absurdity and an insult, and as far as I know I never came to any harm from doing so.

In Mexico fieldworkers have encountered the same sort of situation with regard to *pulque* (fermented from the sap of the maguey plant), sometimes with consequences not quite so benign as those reported by Middleton. Decisions about when and where to accept food and drink are not simple in the field—but more about this later. At any rate, the sharing of food and drink has symbolic significance that goes beyond conventional standards of politeness, so that in *any* field situation the ethnographer can assume that identification with the local population will involve some common meals and/or drinking.

We do not intend to make a psychoanalytic point concerning the pan-human symbolism of oral sharing, but it is interesting to note that several other oral acts have social and emotional significance in many parts of the world. Some fieldworkers have found it useful to take up smoking because of the symbolic value of tobacco sharing. In the South American highlands, chewing coca can have some of the same importance in establishing and maintaining social contact.

Use of the Local Language

When Degérando suggested that fieldwork among "savages" necessitates learning their language, he was probably concerned mainly with the practical problems of communication, as well as with the fact that the structure and content of languages constitute an important body of information about the stuff of cultural behavior. Modern anthropologists, too, appear to emphasize the directly instrumental side of language use, although most fieldworkers are well aware of the symbolic, social-solidarity aspects of language use.

We feel that the attribution of positive social value to (hence putative solidarity with) persons who "talk like us" is universal in human cultures. For the fieldworker this usually means in practice that his first groping attempts to learn the local vernacular are important steps toward the building of rapport.

In places where the people speak a language that not only is unwritten but also is foreign to the officials who govern them and the entrepreneurs who trade with them, the fieldworker can in a few days establish a positive image of himself as different from "those others" by making obvious attempts to acquire the local idiom. Frequently the attitude of the local people is expressed as "Who would bother to learn our unimportant tongue?" Of course they don't in the least regard it as unimportant, and the rare stranger who makes the effort to learn it must obviously be a pretty good guy.

Powdermaker (1966:66) observed reactions of this sort among the people of Lesu: "Although my competence in the language increased, I never became expert in it. But my friends were so pleased at my trying to learn their language that they exaggerated my ability to use it."

Occasionally we hear accounts of people who appear to be ambivalent about the use of their language by outsiders, but we are convinced that a sincere interest in learning the local idiom can be an excellent rapport-builder in practically all human groups. Research on these matters is woefully inadequate at this time, but it seems to us that the use of language as a symbol of social closeness also involves the selection of intonations and general dialectic style. Thus the fieldworker whose research involves some nonacademic segment of his own culture will consciously or unconsciously modify his speech style as he becomes more closely identified with the particular subcultural group he is studying. Simply as a matter of communicational effectiveness he drops more and more of his college-bred vocabulary as he takes on some of the speech patterns and "ungrammatical" usages of the local community. It is important, however, that such linguistic identification with a local community not be rushed. If the fieldworker too quickly begins to imitate local inflection and grammatical forms, his presentation of self may be taken as presumptuous or patronizing. This same point sometimes applies to clothing style as well.

Participation in the Local Social Scene

Fieldwork descriptions nowadays are full of references to ethnographers' participation in the daily activities of their research communities, and most fieldworkers since Malinowski's time have emphasized the great importance of participant observation as a vital fieldwork technique. Malinowski (1961: 21-22) said:

... It is good for the Ethnographer sometimes to put aside camera, note book and pencil, and to join in himself in what is going on. He can take part in the native games, he can follow them on their visits and walks, sit down and listen and share in their conversations. ... Out of such plunges into the life of the natives—and I made them frequently not only for study's sake but because everyone needs human company—I have carried away a distinct feeling that their behavior, their manner of being, in all sorts of tribal transactions, became more transparent and easily understandable than it had been before.

While most discussions of this aspect of fieldwork emphasize the practical, observational advantages, immersion in the activities of the local people is also essential for achieving a satisfactory role as marginal native. Through participation in activities the ethnographer signals the fact that he *wants* to be identified as an insider. (Through nonparticipation, other types of visitors to the local scene—officials, teachers, merchants, etc.—signal their intention to remain apart from social interactions.)

The people of the community have an important part in this role-shaping, of course. If they permit the newcomer to take part, they thereby signify their willingness to consider him (tentatively) a candidate for local membership. Naturally this negotiating of an insider role is closely tied to the matters of language use and food-and-drink behavior mentioned earlier.

It should be noted that some aspects of behavior are relatively harmless—even outsiders can join in—while other action scenes imply greater penetration toward social acceptance. The ethnographer begins his role negotiations by participating in the marginal, nonthreatening scenes, and tries to move from this behavioral periphery toward participation in activities that symbolize increased integration with the group. Often, however, such participation requires learning certain skills, such as dancing, singing, playing ball, herding animals, or other complex motor behaviors. If the fieldworker happens to be adept at this sort of thing before his arrival in the field, he may be able to speed the process of social acceptance. Morris Freilich (1970:214) provides us with a good example:

My rapport-getting was much facilitated by my ability to play an adequate game of cricket. The British had introduced cricket to Trinidad, and the sport was popular with young and old. My knowledge of the game soon brought me into contact with Mr. Ed ...

[whose] house was a hang-out for many of the Creole peasants. . . . After cricket practice we would all stop at Ed's house. . . .

In a similar vein, Buechler (1969:17) found his panpipe-playing ability very important in establishing an insider role in an Aymará community. At one point he had suffered a serious setback in rapport, but "things began to improve when I was asked to dance in the annual folklore festival in Compi. I declined the invitation since I was not able to attend the practice sessions, but I did play the panpipes with a dance group after the main presentation."

Often the fieldworker can communicate his interest in being considered an insider by participating in activities that entail danger, arduous travel, sleepless nights, or other inconveniences. Also, carrying on visible productive work, such as a bit of gardening or working with the herdsmen, conveys a message that is translated into positive rapport. Melvin Perlman (1970:306) writes: "Like my neighbors [in Uganda] I worked in my garden, and many people appreciated that and 'thanked me for working' . . ."

Many of the societies studied by anthropologists identify themselves with one of the major religious faiths, and usually the fieldworker is not an active adherent of the religious faith professed by the people in his research community. One of the first major role problems for many fieldworkers comes when they must decide whether to participate actively in the local religious services, and whether to lie about their own religious backgrounds. Peggy Golde (1970:72) reported very favorable results from her early participation in religious ritual in a Mexican village:

My first public act was to present two very expensive, highly decorated candles to the larger-than-life-sized figure of the Virgin, the village "patron saint.". . . The day I left the village the women reassured themselves and me that I would someday return because I had given candles to the Virgin.

Probably many anthropologists who are asked their religious affiliation try to convey an impression that their religious background is basically similar to that of the local people. Some anthropologists, on the other hand, have found that admission of a religious affiliation different from that of the local people is not necessarily destructive of rapport. Laura Nader (1970:109) describes the following experience during fieldwork in Lebanon:

I was at first asked by the family with whom I stayed about my religion; when I said I was a Christian, they advised me to say that I was Moslem if asked by the other villagers. I answered simply that I was not in the habit of lying. When that story circulated about the village, I was treated with an openness and respect that I had not expected.

Fieldworkers sometimes find themselves in positions in which effective in-group membership even for the marginal native implies some acceptance of the reality and efficacy of witchcraft, sorcery, and shamanistic healing. George and Louise Spindler (1970:279) have described an instance in which they gained rapport with a Menominee medicine man and his people by asking for magical protection from sorcery. They note that an ethical question is involved in this action, and their resolution of this problem involves an interesting expression of cultural relativism:

Our explanation, to him and to others, was that we were not sure that the shooting by the medicine bag had made George ill, and that we did not know whether anything Shumaysen fixed up could protect one from harm. But apparently they believed that it worked. We were on their land, in their community, and while there would try to do things their way, so we would need to learn what those ways were. Further, we found it possible, as we became more and more deeply involved with the native-oriented group and their thinking, to accept what they did and believe on their terms without worrying about whether it was "true" or not. We came to regard their culture as a complex metaphor that was neither true nor false, just as we have come to regard our own. We think that some such position is essential in direct and prolonged participant observation.

The majority of fieldworkers follow Malinowski's advice and participate actively in the daily rounds of work, ritual, and recreation of the people they study. This often necessitates temporary suspensions of systematic observations and note-taking, but these losses are offset by the fact that through active participation in events the fieldworker negotiates his way into a role that permits at least a partial entry into the backstage scenes and facts of community life. At the same time, the participation frequently contributes a great deal to his understanding of "how it all fits together" in the sociocultural system.

Avoidance of Authoritarian and Judgmental Behavior

It is extremely difficult to document or even to describe some of the subtle proxemic behavior that the successful ethnographer employs in conveying an essentially egalitarian impression to the people he studies. Of course, it involves the matters of eating, drinking, language use, and other social participation already outlined, but there are many other elements that are essential to successful presentation of a nonauthoritarian, nonharmful image. The fieldworker often indicates behaviorally that he is not afraid of dirt, that he is willing to sit, squat, lie down, or stand in the same kinds of places and positions as local people. He shakes hands with farmers, workers, or artisans whose hands are dirty; he does not recoil from physical contact with persons whom he suspects might be carrying contagions or at least discomfort-producing fleas or lice. This all sounds a bit patronizing and artificial—and it is a very inadequate account of extremely subtle aspects of behavior—but it is certainly true that the proxemic and paralinguistic behavior of excellent fieldworkers *looks different* from that of other nonnatives. In some cases (we wish someone would do research on this) we suspect that the fieldworker in conversation or other interaction allows his body rhythms to harmonize or interrelate with the movements of the local people in a manner that is avoided by those outsiders who keep their social distance. Of course, there certainly are fieldworkers whose performances with regard to nonauthoritarian behavior are rather poor; and there are many nonethnographic persons whose proxemic and paralinguistic presentation of self would outshine that of most fieldworkers.

Closely related to the matter of nonauthoritarian presentation of self is the ethnographer's ideology of cultural relativity, in accordance with which he generally eschews negative value judgments concerning the morality, goodness, or aesthetic worth of behavior encountered in the research community. The ideology of cultural relativity (however difficult to realize in many situations) has generally meant in practice that the fieldworker accepts as culturally defensible some types of behavior that his own Judeo-Christian background would condemn as "lazy," "sexually promiscuous," "drunken," and "improvident." John Honigmann's (1970:22) recollections from fieldwork among the Kaska are a good example of the fieldworker's attitudes toward certain types of behavior:

To some extent I shared their positive attitudes toward drinking and regarded as recreational some of its accompanying behaviors. I also accepted permissively the Kaska's sexual behavior, viewing it as indicative of a non-puritan society which, from the wide arc of human possibilities, had chosen a considerable measure of premarital sexual freedom.

Usually the fieldworker does not maintain an attitude of absolute neutrality toward certain behaviors that are considered delinquent in our own culture. Rather, he regards the behavior as appropriate, or even laudatory, *if the local cultural norms are positive toward the behavior.* Sometimes the ethnographer's cultural relativity may be tinged with a need to revolt against his own cultural background. In considering his attitudes toward the behavior of the Kaska, Honigmann (1970:49) noted:

Perhaps the field trip allowed me, at the age of thirty, to work off unresolved elements of revolt against the conventions of my own culture, or to release other expressive components of my personality. Undoubtedly my attitudes toward sex, drinking, and similar aspects of Kaska life also sprang from the spirit of cultural relativity I had cultivated since first encountering it in 1940.

There is another aspect of cultural relativism that is not usually recognized in anthropologists' abstract writing about this concept. In negotiating the fieldworker's role as marginal native, the local people come to regard the cultural behavior of the anthropologist as a "complex metaphor" that is "neither true nor false," to use the Spindlers' apt expression. The medicine man and his people do not really believe that the anthropologist has literally internalized their beliefs in sorcery, but his metaphorical enactment of this cultural belief is treated as a socially valuable sig-

nal of his identification with the local community.

The Spindlers, it seems to us, appear to have some misgivings about the culturally relativistic behavior and attitudes that came so naturally during the fieldwork enterprise. And their post-hoc explanation reflects the ambiguities of the fieldworker's role. Perhaps even the ethnographer often fails to realize the full import of the bargain he has struck with the people he studies. The local people (medicine man included) often *force* the ethnographer to affirm beliefs or engage in practices that they *know* he does not fully believe in. (In modern times the fieldworker more and more frequently encounters individuals within cultural groups who privately deny the validity of the practices they publicly support.)

All of these things are understandable when we realize that both sides in the role negotiations regard the ethnographer's performance as a complex metaphor. The attitudes on the "native" side to this ambiguous bargain are perhaps more apparent in those cases in which the metaphor takes the form of a kinship role assigned to the fieldworker. An example from John Middleton's (1970:18) work among the Lugbara makes clear that the local people, too, see the fieldwork bargain in complex terms:

I was expected to behave to other people as if I were a member of that lineage by the giving of proper gifts and so on, and I did my best to carry out my expected role. . . . I noticed that on many occasions when observing a death dance, or sitting in a beer house, or attending a sacrifice, that if I did not stand near the people of Nyio sooner or later someone would gently remind me that that was where I should be. . . . Of course my position had the disadvantage that other people were perhaps not so willing as they might have been to regale me with their pieces of scandalous and confidential information about the people of Nyio. Yet in fact they would usually do so since *in that situation they realized that I was not a "true" member of Nyio.* I also found out very soon that it was necessary sometimes to stand well outside the situation. [Emphasis added.]

The ethnographer's cultural relativism takes the form of a positive attitude toward the behavior he encounters in the research community because he perforce becomes partly identified with those behavioral patterns. Part of the "contract" of the marginal native is that he accepts as reasonable and moral the activities of the people in the community he has joined.

Flexibility

In reviewing all these points and sifting through examples of "successful" fieldwork behavior, we realized that they might be interpreted as a list of do's and don'ts of proper fieldwork style. The essential point is that no such list of do's and don'ts is possible, except as a general schema around which the fieldworker builds up his social relationships. The successful fieldworker, we believe, does not seek to apply particular rules of procedure, but rather trains himself to be a sensitive receiver of social feedback (both negative and positive), by means of which he constantly adjusts his behavior to suit the styles and modes of conduct of the local community. This means that the fieldworker is in part being "trained" by the people with whom he works. In some exceptional situations the ethnographer secures a very able and sensitive local assistant who takes an active part in shaping the fieldwork strategy. Steve Schensul reports (in a personal communication) that when he embarked on fieldwork in Uganda, he was fortunate to find an assistant who had had experience with previous anthropologists, and so had acquired a

good deal of lore about proper ways to go about the business of ethnography.

Friendship as a Strategy of Fieldwork

We believe, then, that the essence of successful ethnography is a form of behavior that makes the fieldworker a "friend" of the community he studies, and a special friend of a number of persons within it. Further, we suggest that the behavior involved in successful fieldwork presents a model for a pan-humanly applicable style of friendship. This style of friendship (involving relationships with individuals and also with the community as a whole) is not necessarily congruent with definitions of friendship within local communities. Quite the contrary. Often the friendship offered by the fieldworker is successful precisely because it is *different* from the expected patterns of affiliation current in the research community. Ethnographers have reported on many societies in which close friends are not expected to really trust one another, and where no local models exist for the modes of interaction that the fieldworker adopts.

It is important to note that the friendship offered by the fieldworker is inevitably different, because he is not competing for the scarce resources within the local scene. He is not seeking to gain land or other capital resources; he is not (except in rare instances) going to compete for desirable local mates; above all, he will after a time leave the community and scene of competition. And he is different too from most other outsiders, because he is neither exercising governmental authority over the local people, seeking material gains through commercial transactions, teaching them something that other outsiders have unilaterally decided they ought to know, or trying to save their souls.

Altruism. One aspect of the ethnographer's "friend" role that is perhaps least understood is that from the point of view of the local populace, his behavior has the appearance of legitimate altruism. We needn't delve into the philosophical complexities of altruism, but it is useful to mention two important and frequently expressed points that pose a seeming contradiction: *(a)* the fieldworker is not competing for the *locally* defined scarce resources, yet *(b)* field research transactions can be seen as processes of exchange.

Usually the ethnographer's key informants are fully aware of an exchange relationship in which the value they deliver to the fieldworker takes the form of information (including the time it takes to give the information). The values that the fieldworker gives in return are quite varied. Sometimes it is money. Often he gives other useful goods as "gifts." His local friends and informants often translate his friendship and companionship into prestige in the community. Other "trade goods," to name only a few main types, include medical care, transportation, various communication services (especially writing letters and contacting governmental officials), and in recent times the free-handed distribution of photographs. So far, so good. The transaction is an exchange of values, hence there is nothing particularly altruistic involved.

In spite of the fact that his social interactions involve exchanges of recognized values, the ethnographer-as-friend appears to be altruistic from the point of view of the research community for one very simple reason: the "value" he seeks from his informants is for *practical purposes* a free good. The information—the cultural data—that he systematically elicits does not cost the informant anything exept time. (Information as an economic good has the unusual characteristic that "giving" quanti-

ties of it to certain individuals does not diminish the giver's available supply.) We must hasten to add that from the anthropologist's point of view there is nothing altruistic in the transaction: the information he receives is directly translatable into economic, professional, and social advantage—*when he gets home.* But that's the point—the fieldworker usually exchanges some sort of socially valuable goods or actions in return for information that costs the local people practically nothing and does not adversely affect the community's structure of scarce resources. On the contrary: in almost all instances of fieldwork the presence of the ethnographer enlarges the total economic resources of the community in some ways. His Jeep or Land Rover (which often becomes the village bus), his medical supplies, his money for paid informants, and his imported equipment—these and other items raise the total "gross national product" of the local populace. Often the fieldworker brings very useful new information about the outside world, and ethnographers usually are not loath to advise local people on possibilities of economic and social gain. Many fieldworkers have gone far beyond this brief list of local socioeconomic inputs.

This explanation is not offered as an apology to the critics of the ethnographic enterprise, but rather as the beginnings of explanation for the fact that ethnographers have "invaded" countless local communities during the past decades and have emerged with unbelievably extensive data—all this with an amazingly low rejection rate. Some anthropologists have had to leave their research communities because of local opposition, but the percentage of such rejections is very small. Until recent times, when international policies and tensions have greatly complicated the picture, most anthropologists have in most instances been welcomed, feted, loved, and remembered. This is a fact to be reckoned with, considering the equally important fact that anthropologists are in no wise more altruistic or noble than other people. Their seeming altruism is a *structural* characteristic that deserves our careful attention.

Observer Effects. As already noted, the role of the anthropologist as friend is closely related to the fact that the fieldworker participates actively in the social events of the community he studies. From time to time social scientists and others have criticized this characteristic, suggesting that the community is "not the same" because of "investigator effects." However, the patterns of behavior in all communities are constantly changing, and since there are many other outsiders besides the anthropologist (administrators, vendors, and so on) who interfere in the affairs of local communities, the fieldworker is usually not greatly concerned about the fact that his presence has some effects on the community. He should, of course, make careful note of the situations in which his presence appears to influence patterns and outcomes of events.

John Bennett's (1967b:vii) description of research among the Hutterian Brethren illustrates the type of situation in which the anthropologist intentionally introduces changes in the community, even though his main purpose is *not* "applied anthropology":

My resident study was participative, insofar as I engaged in the normal activities connected with farm and construction labor, shared the Brethren's regular meals, attended their church services, sat in on their policy discussions, and on one memorable occasion acted as a boss of the women's house-painting crew.... I became an informal agricultural extention advisor to one colony and helped to design an agricultural regime more suited to their specialized resources. I made many close

friends among the Brethren in the colony where I resided....

The Myth of Total Acceptance. Ethnographers are sensitive people, and we often read in the prefaces of monographs that the fieldworker is indebted to everyone in the community he studied, and he considers them all to be his friends. For the beginning fieldworker, it may be something of a disappointment, then, to discover that in reality not everyone really likes the ethnographer, and that he does not really like all of them. In fact, he may have some enemies. Aram Yengoyan (1970: 436) has written in realistic terms about the matter:

My initial desire to be accepted by the Mandaya evaporated soon after the debacle with the females and the Muslim proselytizer. It was at this point that I realized that the ideal of being completely accepted by a particular group is a romantic myth. In most cases one ends up with a handful of warm friends with whom communication is easy. Like most populations, the Mandaya had a segment of people who did not like me and who made no attempt to hide their contempt....

The ethnographer who feels he is a special personality who must be accepted and "liked" by all the members of the group he is working with is fairly naive. No one is liked and accepted by everyone, even in his own culture, so there is no reason why he should be completely accepted in an alien society.

Probably a great many first-time ethnographers would have avoided some feelings of guilt and depression if they had started into the field with the attitudes Yengoyan suggests, rather than with the romantic notion that all the "natives" are going to accept them as good friends and associates.

The Success of Friendship. In summary, we suggest that the marginal native role of the ethnographer is successful because fieldworkers have adopted patterns of behavior that amount to an apparently panhumanly successful friendship role. Anthropologists have carried out fieldwork successfully in a very wide variety of human communities (and in a few nonhuman groups as well), and this fact requires some explanation. The pattern of friendship that ethnographers have so often enacted is not necessarily preordained to invariant success in all future situations; but at the moment we are concerned with the way it has worked until now. Also, this pattern of behavior never ensures that everyone in the research community will be the ethnographer's friend—that probably never happens. Nonetheless, fieldworkers still go out every year and come back with amazing amounts of detailed data, gathered from people who in general appear to have feelings of enduring friendship toward the stranger who came into their midst and pried into their lives.

SELF-MAINTENANCE IN FIELDWORK: FOOD AND HEALTH

There are many aspects of fieldwork that should be discussed in detail in any thorough summary of the ethnographic enterprise. Problems of clothing, food, drink, shelter, relief from psychological tensions, vacations from fieldwork, storage and maintenance of equipment and data, and scheduling of work form only a partial list of important topics. Instead of trying to treat all of these, we shall concentrate on two closely related aspects of self-maintenance: food and health. Among the complexities of fieldwork management the problems of adequate food and health perhaps involve the most complicated adaptations. A romanticized myth has the fieldworker totally indifferent to the germ theory of disease, and the mystique of fieldwork usually has the anthropologist eating with the "natives,"

becoming completely accustomed not only to their food, but to the amount they eat, the way they eat, and the times at which they eat. Any teenaged exchange student knows better.

FOOD

While many fieldworkers do arrange to take their meals with local families, most ethnographers set up their own households and prepare their own meals. Usually the ethnographer doesn't have to bring large supplies of food with him to the field. There are stores, markets, or trading posts in many fieldwork locations, and researchers can often buy food from the local people—especially meat, eggs, and fresh produce. Napoleon Chagnon's (1968: 6-7) description of food arrangements during his research among the Yanomamö constitutes one of the more striking exceptions to general ethnographic practice, for he not only brought most of his food supplies with him, but also steadfastly refused to participate in local food-sharing patterns:

Meals were a problem in another way. Food sharing is important to the Yanomamö in the context of displaying friendship. "I am hungry" is almost a form of greeting with them. I could not possibly have brought enough food with me to feed the entire village, yet they seemed not to understand this. All they could see was that I did not share my food with them at each and every meal. Nor could I enter into their system of reciprocities with respect to food. . . .

Chagnon found that food preparation was a very time-consuming process:

It is appalling how complicated it can be to make oatmeal in the jungle. First, I had to make two trips to the river to haul water. Next, I had to prime my kerosene stove with alcohol and get it burning, a tricky procedure when you are trying to mix powdered milk and fill a coffee pot at the same time. . . .

Eating three meals a day was out of the question. I solved the problem by eating a single meal that could be prepared in a single container. . . . Frequently, my single meal was no more complicated than a can of sardines and a package of crackers. But at least two or three times a week I would do something sophisticated, like make oatmeal or boil rice and add a can of tuna fish or tomato paste to it. . . .

Nelson Graburn (1969:4-5) brought supplies of food with him to the Eskimo community of Sugluk, but these were soon exhausted because he had to share them with the local inhabitants:

I learned that the community had been short of many vital foods. Within the first week at least 120 Eskimos came to visit and to share my food. . . . Very soon my supply of foods ran low and the tables were turned . . . I found that just as I had not excluded them, so they never excluded me from such sharing at any time of day or night.

Food and Morale

The kinds of foods we eat and our success in maintaining a personally satisfying food regimen appear to have powerful effects on our psychological well-being. Numbers of ethnographers have reported that they found eating (especially special foods from home) to be very important in relieving the tensions and anxieties of fieldwork. (It is interesting that peanut butter is often mentioned as a particularly satisfying treat.)

Jean Briggs's (1970:23) description of tense relationships with her adopted Eskimo family includes the comment that "the evening was a time for recuperation—a time to read Jane Austen, to indulge in secret feasts of half-frozen dates and chocolate. . . . Books, food, and thoughts all provided a much needed link with the world I had left behind."

Those fieldworkers who, like Chagnon, suffered through long periods in which the daily diet consisted mainly of oatmeal, canned sardines, biscuits, or other psychologically unrewarding camp rations can be rightfully envious when reading about research cuisines like those of Norma Diamond (1970: 121) in a Taiwanese village:

. . . village meals were sparse and dull except at festivals. . . . Luck intervened again, this time in the form of a woman [cook] who had worked for me for a time in Tainan. . . . Overnight, our diet improved, as we explored the delights of Szechuanese, Shanghai, and Peking specialties, and our morale increased as mealtimes became times for recreation. . . .

The following items from a variety of field situations give something of the flavor of fieldworkers' food quests:

Melanesia:

Sinbanimous was just right as a cook. He did not aspire to doing fancy dishes, but he knew the basic facts about cooking and he baked an excellent loaf of bread. When we occasionally had eggs, he made a delicious creme caramel [Powdermaker 1966:70].

Australia:

The settlement was established in 1961 . . . [the] settlement store sells basic staples to the locals and fresh beef is sold three times a week. . . . We bought most of our canned food from the local store; fresh vegetables and fruits were flown in on the Saturday mail plane from Alice Springs [Yengoyan 1970:425].

East Africa:

. . . I interviewed several men, some with excellent references, before engaging Yositasi (Eustace); and it is worth recording that ability as a cook was only one—perhaps not the most important of the qualities I was looking for. I knew that I and the man I took on would be living in quite close companionship in the bush for long periods, and that at least in the early stages of my work I would be dependent on him for much more than just food; for helping me in my initial contacts with the local people, for example, and for advice on matters of etiquette.... Yositasi certainly had these qualities.... He was also a brilliant raconteur and mimic. . . [Beattie 1965:12].

South America:

I spent the whole morning trying to persuade a woman to sell me a chicken.... Finally I persuaded her to let me have it for five shillings and my only spare shirt on condition that she gave me an egg as well. I took the fowl back to Suzaure's household and told them that I wanted it cooked for supper, when they were all welcome to share it with us. I also stipulated that I wanted a lot of the gravy to make a chicken broth for my wife [who was ill with a high fever]. That was the best that I could do in the way of a Christmas dinner for her [Maybury-Lewis 1965:128].

Types and Sources of Food

These quotations illustrate, among other things, the fact that ethnographers usually arrange for their own food preparation. There appear to be several reasons for this practice. Fieldworkers often establish their own cooking facilities in order to protect their physical health. It is still the exceptional research community in which the local populace maintains standards of sanitation and nutritional balance adequate for a health-conscious ethnographer. To ensure that water is boiled before use, that meat and other foods are stored and cooked under sanitary conditions, and to keep use of seasoning and other additives within his range of tolerance, the ethnographer usually finds it advisable to take on the often complex problems of managing his own kitchen and commissary establishment.

In many societies food reciprocities are essential for maintaining good social relationships, and the ethnographer needs to have his own facilities for the preparation of special meals. As already mentioned, the matter of keeping up fieldwork morale through psychologically satisfying foods is also significant. Wintrob (1969) has recently commented on the patterning of psychological stresses in fieldwork and notes the role of food in relieving tensions.

As we mentioned earlier, we received data from fifty-one fieldworkers who replied to a questionnaire we sent to a random sample of anthropologists. Their replies to questions on food habits in the field are shown in Tables 4 and 5.

It is a bit surprising to find that nearly half of the fieldworkers (twenty-four) did not report that they had been fed by local hosts. At first glance this would appear to run counter to our earlier suggestions concerning the importance of eating and drinking with the local people in order to establish rapport. We see, however, that the majority of these ethnographers were eating local food. By far the largest part of these fieldworkers' food was purchased in local stores and markets. Thus, although they ate the same food as the local people, they frequently cooked it themselves. This is related to the fact that thirty-two of the fifty-one respondents were accompanied by their wives or husbands.

More light is thrown on the eating and living styles of fieldworkers if we

TABLE 4
Type of Food Eaten by Ethnographer

Same as local people (except occasional treats)	33
Same as upper class (except occasional treats)	6
Brought own "city food"	4
Other	4
No response	4
Total	51

TABLE 5
Sources of Food During Fieldwork

	None	1-15%	16-30%	>30%	Mentioned but % Not Specified
Brought or shipped from home	35*	6	5	3	0
Purchased in local stores, markets	9	4	5	24	4
Purchased from local people	34	6	4	7	0
Gifts from local people	37	14	0	0	0
Own crops and animals	50	1	0	0	0
Own hunting, gathering, fishing	49	2	0	0	0
Local hosts	24	8	3	8	4
Local restaurants	28	11	2	2	2
Restaurants outside local area	36	5	0	0	0
Other (ate at university guesthouse)	0	0	0	1	0

*Number of ethnographers mentioning this category.

examine the kinds of living quarters they establish in the field. Table 6 shows these data for our sample.

TABLE 6
Habitation During Fieldwork*

Rented house or apartment in local community	29
Lived with local family	16
Commuted from nearby town or city	11
Lived in tent, trailer, or other makeshift dwelling	1
Natives built me a house	7
Lived in school or other special building	3
Lived in outbuilding of local family (barn, storeroom, boat, etc.)	3

*Total is more than 51 because some fieldworkers reported more than one type of living quarters during field stay.

The typical fieldworker, then, is accompanied by his or her spouse (but usually no children), and rents a house or apartment in the local community. His food usually consists of meals prepared from products purchased locally in stores and markets or from neighbors. In short, the ethnographer sets up a separate household and thereby becomes a member of the local community. Nonetheless, about a third of these anthropologists (sixteen) did live at least part of the time with local families. Naturally these were among the fieldworkers whose food supplies consisted to a large extent of meals served by their hosts.

Of the eleven fieldworkers who reported commuting from a nearby town or city, only four maintained the pattern throughout the fieldwork period. The other seven had some kind of residence in the fieldwork community during part of their research.

HEALTH

Most fieldworkers carry with them a very considerable supply of medicines. Even though a period of from ten to fifteen months sounds like ample time in which to accomplish an extensive study, the fieldworker finds that time is precious at every stage of his work, and illness can seriously damage one's chances of getting enough data for a meaningful study. Many ethnographers have had their fieldwork so marred by illness that they have been unable to publish significant portions of their data because of gaps in information. Others have been able to complete their data-gathering only by making extreme efforts while suffering from debilitating illnesses. The late Allan Holmberg's (1969) account of serious illness during fieldwork among the Siriono provides a striking example of the problems that can beset fieldworkers in tropical and subtropical areas, especially in locations far from population centers.

Norman Whitten (1970:396) reports that during fieldwork in Ecuador he became extremely ill for a time and suffered considerable weakness from dysentery and fever. Robert Maxwell (1970:474-75) experienced serious illness during his fieldwork in Samoa:

Another reason I didn't get more done was that I was sick during much of this period. I had already gone through the usual problems of pinworms, fungus, and digestive disorders. But a few months after the testing began I contracted a relatively severe virus infection that stayed with me for more than a month. I had hardly recovered from it when I found my ear was infected as a complication of the virus. Not long after that cleared up I caught some sort of skin disease that involved both my neck and my ears. It smelled bad and looked worse, and I was too embarrassed to work in public.

Robert Pehrson's promising anthropological career was cut short at the age of twenty-nine by his death from illness during fieldwork in Pakistan. Many other fieldworkers have suffered serious long-term debilities brought about by illnesses contracted in the field. These casualties are not surprising when one realizes that ethnographic fieldwork often entails relatively long periods in areas where modern medical services are not available.

The Fieldworker as Medical Aide

The typical modern ethnographer, especially when working in areas far removed from doctors and hospitals, generally takes along a fairly elaborate array of antibiotics, salves, bandages, and other medical supplies. These supplies are, of course, primarily intended for the maintenance of the ethnographer's own health, but medical supplies and services are also dispensed to the local people as the need arises. Sometimes medical care is one of the major services the anthropologist gives to the people. John Middleton's (1970:22-23) example is instructive:

Lugbara were always sick, with malaria, dysentery, sores, yaws, wounds of many kinds, and the more serious illnesses such as leprosy, meningitis, and sleeping sickness. . . . The local government doctor . . . supplied me with a few simple drugs. . . . Every day people would come to me to ask for medicine. All I could do was give aspirin and to dress the more dreadful-looking sores and cuts brought to me. I soon realized that the flood of patients was unending, so I set aside an hour each morning to give what help I could. This meant that from seven until eight each day I would help, as best I could, several dozen people. The favorite medicines were iodine and acroflavin, a yellow liquid intended primarily for dressing burns. . . .

Modern antibiotics, especially the sulfa drugs and penicillin, have recently done much to help fieldworkers maintain their health. Even in areas where some expert medical services are available, ethnographers usually maintain small kits of medicines for intestinal disorders, symptom-relieving drugs for viral infections, and ample supplies of aspirin for headaches, hangovers, and other minor aches and pains. Tranquilizers and other psychiatric drugs are less usual in the fieldworker's medical kit, but can be useful in maintaining states of mind that promote effective work.

Psychological Disturbances

In addition to physical illness, psychological stress can also take its toll in reducing the fieldworker's effectiveness. Sometimes there is an initial culture shock during the first days of fieldwork. Loneliness, inability to communicate effectively with the local people, difficulties in finding housing and arranging other practical concerns, plus the confusion of figuring out where to start all contribute psychological hazards in the beginning phase of research. Even after the ethnographer has been at work for some months, the complexities of the marginal native role, unexpected difficulties in getting data from key informants, and a variety of other common problems of fieldwork can bring about periods of depression, discouragement, and general anxiety.

Among the ethnographers responding to our survey, eight of the fifty-one mentioned *serious* psychic distress in connection with their most recent fieldwork. Some of their comments illustrate the fact that the sources of psychological stress in fieldwork are varied:

" . . . periodic and temporary depression . . . considered it normal for the fieldwork situation [Melanesia] where it was impossible to 'get away' physically except for a two-week holiday once in fifteen months . . . no local nonnatives or outsiders resident in area. . . ."

" . . . vomiting in local market at animal sacrifice . . . constant hassle with local government . . . and language problems. . . ."

"[Culture shock] complicated by lack of oxygen at [high altitude] . . . ."

" . . . drunk several weeks in a row . . . not working for three of four days at a time, just reading novels . . . anxiety over feelings of bewilderment and incompetence. . . ."

" . . . the last two months of fieldwork . . . mental fatigue. . . ."

In addition to the eight fieldworkers reporting serious stress, nineteen others reported "some psychological tensions." Thus about half of our sample

TABLE 7
Ethnographers' Psychological and
Physical Experiences

Culture shock	8
Some psychological tension	19
General excitement, relaxation, enjoyment	30
Much physical illness	1
Some illness	27
No illness	10
Frequent tiredness	1

TABLE 8
Psychological Tensions in Fieldwork in Relation to Therapy, Training,
Presence of Spouse, and Field Experience

	Psychological Tensions Reported	No Psychological Tensions Reported
Therapy received prior to fieldwork	4	3
No prior therapy	23	21
Field techniques/methodology training prior to fieldwork	11	16
No prior research training	16	8
Spouse in field	16	14
No spouse in field	11	10
First field trip	4	2
Not first field trip	22	23

TABLE 9
Field Training in Relation to Degree of Quantification

Research Orientation	Had Training in Techniques and Methods Prior to Fieldwork		Total
	Yes	No	
Quantifiers	12	7	19
Intermediates	6	13	19
Nonquantifiers	9	4	13

of ethnographers reported at least moderate psychological problems in fieldwork. Physical illnesses were reported by most of our respondents; only ten of the fifty-one reported "no illness."

Some of the apparent correlates of reported psychological tensions are quite interesting. Tables 7 to 12 give the results of testing a number of hypotheses. The presence of one's spouse in the field site does not appear to account for differences between the stress group and the no-stress group. Also, the fact that the fieldworker has been on several previous field expeditions does not appear to be related to psychological stresses and anxieties.

Several anthropologists have suggested that some form of psychotherapy might be helpful in preparing a person to adjust to the fieldwork situation, but, as Table 8 indicates, those few persons (seven) in our sample who had had therapy previous to fieldwork were just as likely as the others to report culture shock and other stresses.

Effect of Research Training. Another frequently mentioned aid to mental health in fieldwork is that of adequate training in research and techniques. It is curious that previous field *experience* does not predict freedom from psychic stresses, but previous research *training* does. In Table 8 we note that the people who reported no significant fieldwork tensions tended to be those who had had some sort of coursework or other training in field methods.

Research Orientations. But there is another element in the pattern. We asked the sample of ethnographers to report on the data-collection methods used in their most recent research and the amount of time devoted to each method. We then grouped the respondents into three categories on the basis of their data-collection reports:

1. Quantifiers. Report large investment of fieldwork time in collection of census materials, formal interviews, questionnaires, tests.
2. Intermediates. Report some collection of quantified data, but not a major time investment in comparison to time devoted to more qualitative techniques.
3. Nonquantifiers. Report no data-gathering techniques involving quantification.

Table 9 indicates the relationship of these three groups to training in field methods and techniques prior to actual work in the field. And as we can see in Table 10, previous research training

TABLE 10
Psychological Tensions in
Relation to Research Orientation

Research Orientation	Psychological Tensions Reported	
	Yes	No
Quantifiers	13	6
Intermediates	10	9
Nonquantifiers	4	9

seems to be quite strongly related to an absence of significant stresses among the nonquantified anthropologists. On the other hand, as Table 11 indicates, the intermediates and quantifiers do not appear to gain much tension reduction from courses in techniques and methodology.

TABLE 11
Psychological Tensions in Relation
to Research Training and
Research Orientation

	Research Training	
	Yes	No
Psychological tensions		
Quantifiers	7	6
Intermediates	3	7
Nonquantifiers	1	3
Total	11	16
No psychological tensions		
Quantifiers	5	1
Intermediates	3	6
Nonquantifiers	8	1
Total	16	8

It is also important to note that the quantifiers more frequently report psychological tensions than do the nonquantifiers (see Table 10). From our own fieldwork experiences, plus informal conversations with other ethnographers, we feel that these data reflect an important element in fieldwork. It is our impression that fieldworkers who put heavy emphasis on quantified data very often have a clearly stated research plan that specifies types of survey data, questionnaires, and other materials necessary for testing particular hypotheses. Such quantified fieldwork is generally carried out *in addition to* more informal modes of data collection. Thus the quantifier has extra pressures; he often experiences anxiety concerning the numbers of interviews he has yet to carry out. Also, the administering of structured interviews—especially to a random sample of persons or households—frequently arouses suspicion and hostility among the local people. The nonquantifier, on the other hand, generally does not conduct long and tension-producing interviews with people he does not know very well. He can more easily adjust his interviewing and other data-collection techniques to avoid interpersonal antagonism.

Courses in fieldwork techniques and methodology apparently do not remove these sources of tension for the quantified fieldworker. They may even increase his anxieties by raising his standards concerning "hard data." Ethnographic fieldwork is apparently becoming more and more quantified and "operationalized" in orientation, as we shall see shortly; hence we might expect psychological tensions to be increasing among fieldworkers, if our argument here is sound.

Culture Shock. The type of data-gath-

TABLE 12
Fieldwork Location in Relation to Psychological Tensions

Location	Psychological Tensions Reported	No Psychological Tensions Reported
North America (including Caribbean)	0	9
Latin America	6	4
Africa	8	4
Asia	6	4
Europe and Middle East	5	2

ering orientation is not the only contributor to fieldwork tensions, of course. We might easily surmise that culture shock and other stresses are most likely to occur in cultural contexts that are very different from our own. Table 12 demonstrates strikingly that this is so. In our sample, all nine of the persons whose fieldwork took place in North America (including the Caribbean area) report no significant psychological tensions. Even ethnographers working with Indian groups (some of whom have developed notable hostilities toward anthropologists) indicated no tensions or anxieties. Given the vast increase in transportation facilities, we may suggest that any fieldworker in North America (except in the high arctic) is close enough to home base and in contact with major segments of familiar cultural patterns that he need not experience serious psychological tensions. It is also important to note that fieldwork in North America is almost always carried out at least partly in English nowadays.

Dennison Nash (1963, 1970) has suggested that a major factor in the psychological experiences of fieldworkers is the initial anomie as one confronts a cultural scene much different from anything one is accustomed to. Thus the ethnographer experiences the shock of suddenly finding himself a stranger in a strange land. Our data lend strong support to Nash's hypothesis.

From our survey of ethnographers' statements about psychological tensions, we may suggest that the strains and anxieties of later phases of fieldwork are of a different order from the initial shock of anomie. There may be continuing loneliness, difficulties with local politics, increasing demands of one kind or another from the local people, and anxieties over work still to be done. Very often the researcher sees the end of his fieldwork time (and

money) approaching at a point where it seems as if his understanding of the local community is still in chaos and his data are still full of awful gaps. Some fieldworkers report that the final weeks of research are the most trying ones, even though problems of communication, self-maintenance, and social relationships may be nicely under control.

The Return of the Marginal Native. The return from fieldwork is often cause for another culture shock. Many anthropologists have commented on their feelings of anomie—the sense of being strangers—in returning home from the field. Allan Beals (1970:55), recalling his return from India, has written:

Where in Gopalpur there was a feeling of stability, timelessness, and adaptation to nature, even the houses and buildings in the United States seemed to express instability, sterility, and a kind of opposition to nature. Everyone seemed to be rushing toward the mystical doom of atomic destruction, all the while pretending that nothing was the matter. We had returned to civilization. We were suffering from culture shock. In time we would get used to it. We would never forget that once we lived in a world that had not yet gone mad.

Often the shock of reentry to one's home culture is sharpened by any illness and distress suffered in the field. Helen Codere (1970:163) said of her return from fieldwork in Africa, "The year in Rwanda was a hard one physically and emotionally, and I was sick for over a month when I got home: physical fatigue, virus pneumonia, and mental fatigue. It all took some mending and time."

THE SCIENCE OF FIELDWORK

We have dealt at considerable length with the essentially personalized, highly variable matter of the way in which the ethnographer goes about becoming a marginal native. Much of the essence of our profession is based on the assumption that we must enter into close social interaction with the people in our research communities if we are to succeed in gathering significant information on their culture and social organization. This is the humanistic side of fieldwork. At this point some critics would claim that the personalized, emotionally involved fieldwork situation automatically prevents any possibility of objective, scientific method.

We feel, however, that the matter of establishing a role in the field situation can be conceptually separated from the complex problems of making objective observations on life styles and behavior patterns. Everything we have discussed in the previous section can be considered a brief essay on "how to put oneself in a position to get useful data"; the problem yet to be discussed is how to collect the data, assuming one is successful in establishing satisfactory relationships with the local populace.

The recent literature on fieldwork clearly indicates a growing tendency toward quantified, "operationalized" observations. In the volume *Marginal Natives: Anthropologists at Work* (Freilich, ed.,1970), for example, almost all of the twenty fieldwork accounts (two per author) involve some use of surveys, questionnaires, psychological tests, or other quantified data-collection methods.

John Honigmann (1970:51) administered Rorschach inkblot tests to twenty-eight adults and children among the Kaska Indians, and in the research among Eskimos in Frobisher Bay the Honigmanns embarked on an extensive series of interviews for census purposes. William Schwab (1970:78) reported that fieldwork in a complex urban African setting necessitated the use of some "sociological" methods: "Question-

naires, field guides, random sampling, and other sociological devices had to be employed." Robert Maxwell (1970: 473) kept a wall chart of his progress in the administration of questionnaires, motor tests, psychological tests, and other methods of collecting quantifiable data. "As the week passed I gleefully watched the X's [completed responses] march across the chart."

COMBINING OF RESEARCH STYLES

Extensive collection of quantified data does not signify the abandonment of qualitative data-gathering methods among a new generation of ethnographers. Many fieldworkers employ an eclectic mixture of research styles in order to maximize the advantages of hard and soft data gathering.

As Table 9 has shown, nineteen of our sample of fifty-one ethnographers, or about 37 percent, reported extensive use of quantified research methods; the same number devoted approximately as much time to qualitative research as to the collection of quantified data. Only thirteen, or about 25 percent, could be described as nonquantifiers.

Nonquantified data-gathering techniques are thus still very important, and most of the fifty-one fieldworkers reported considerable reliance on participant observation, casual interviewing, and key-informant interviewing. Table 13 shows the relative degree of utilization of these techniques as reported by our sample of ethnographers.

We feel that these data are in accord with our general impressions of the state of ethnographic methodology at the present time. There has been so much criticism of impressionistic, nonquantifiable field methods that many anthropologists are making a considerable effort to produce more "credible" ethnographic reports. It would appear

TABLE 13
Use of Nonquantified Techniques of Data-Gathering

Time Spent on Each Activity	Participant Observation	Casual Interviewing	Key-Informant Interviewing
Little or none	11	3	8
Moderate amount	21	24	22
Extensive amount	19	24	21

that the majority of contemporary ethnographers employ a research strategy that involves a quantitative-qualitative mix of data-gathering techniques. They seek to obtain replicable, representative information that is backed up by and interpreted in accordance with a great variety of nonquantified materials. As William Schwab (1970:79-80) puts it:

Our emphasis on quantifying devices was not an attempt to reduce social relations to mere statistics, but rather a recognition of the fact that statistics and other quantifying mechanisms when used properly can be excellent research tools. Statistical data . . . can add the substantive flesh to the theoretical skeleton. . . . I hoped that by combining survey and statistical methods with traditional anthropological field techniques we would be able to collect data representative of the entire community and at the same time be able to provide cultural insights, details, and nuances.

SCIENTIFIC OBSERVATIONS IN FIELDWORK

In common-sense terms, the major scientific task of the ethnographer is to translate the stuff of people's daily lives—their things, activities, and interactions—into a coherent, organized set of descriptive statements. To be scientifically useful, the systematic observations and inferential steps in this work must be reliable and valid—that is, they must be credible. A variety of techniques are employed by ethnographers in their efforts to achieve this goal. We must warn the reader, however, that we can offer only a partial and general summary of these techniques here; for further details he must go to texts on methodology.

Mapping, Inventories, and Census

Mapping. Most ethnographers begin fieldwork with some kind of mapping operation in order to locate major features of the physical and social landscape. Although some anthropological theorists have tended to lay such heavy emphasis on cognitive, psychological, and ideal-cultural constructs that the physical world is scarcely present in their conceptual models, the description of village streets and paths, locations of fields, forests, and sources of water, and inventories of the material things in the research setting are generally essential preliminaries to all other aspects of field study. The mapping of residence patterns usually leads the ethnographer into aspects of kin relations, and therefore often to the collection of genealogical data.

Williams (1967:17) has suggested that the first weeks of field research should

involve a plan of work which will allow you to be seen as regularly and widely as possible, and which will provide details of the physical and social arrangements in the village. These aims can be met in mapping the community, making a household census, cataloging food and technology, and collecting genealogies.

John Middleton's (1970:8) first days of research among the Lugbara were aimed at getting a mental image of the local landscape:

I started this merely by walking, some ten miles or so each day, with a companion, so as to see the kind of life that went on in the homesteads and fields that I could see from my ridge. Each day I would set out in a different direction, and this served the purpose of introducing me to large numbers of people. . . .

For the anthropologist, mapping involves both the notation of physical and topographical features and the recording of information about the people who occupy the physical spaces. Middleton (1970:32-33) writes:

I therefore decided that I had to begin by mapping the layout of the compounds over a reasonably small area and then to put down the genealogies of all the people who lived in them. I chose two areas, one on either side of where I lived, mapped them. . . . The mapping was extremely rough and resulted merely in two sketch maps with approximate distances between compounds and the main topographical features that seemed to have ecological and social significance for my informants. . . .

Very often the "mapping" of socially relevant groups and relationships is best carried out by means of the standard genealogical method that was first set forth in detail by W. H. R. Rivers (1910). More recently Barnes (1967) has discussed the uses of genealogical techniques of inquiry.

In some situations genealogical data may prove to be the key to understanding the whole social system. C. W. M. Hart (1970:160) noted that he was gaining very little understanding of the Australian Tiwi social system until he began to collect extensive genealogical data:

. . . My own judgment is that the genealogical method was not just useful but absolutely essential for the anthropologist . . . which makes one wonder why it is not used more often. The interminable disputes about the Murngin, for instance, might be readily settled

if Warner had only given us some complete and detailed genealogies.

While some fieldworkers have suggested that the genealogical method of inquiry is important in practically any type of society, it is probable that many fieldworkers do not rely very much on genealogical data, particularly in complex societies where kinship is not a chief element in the structuring of day-to-day social interaction. In urban studies involving thousands of people, any genealogical inquiry would necessarily be very imcomplete and fragmentary, possibly concentrated on certain important families such as the "royal line," a small coterie of notables, or a group of leading merchants.

Aerial photographs are nowadays available for many areas of the world. Archaeologists have frequently used them for mapping purposes, but it appears that the use of aerial photographs in ethnographic work has been slow to develop. Young and Bury (1966) have described ways in which very important information can be gained from the bird's-eye view of one's research area.

The importance of mapping in ethnographic work has come more sharply into focus with the growth of interest in studies of territoriality and territorial behavior. Recent debates about the territorial behavior of hunting and gathering peoples have highlighted the fact that much earlier ethnographic work has been deficient in this respect, and urban studies such as *The Vice Lords* (Keiser 1969) and *The Social Order of the Slum* (Suttles 1968) illustrate territorial behavior in slum areas and thus the importance of social-physical mapping in modern urban settings. In both cases the behavior in question is that of teenage street gangs, whose concepts of territory or "turf" suggest that ethnographic studies of peoples in settings of high population density should include careful attention to the relationship between the utilization of physical space and social processes. Edward T. Hall's discussion of spatial behavior in *The Hidden Dimension* (1966) suggests that the micromapping of behavioral settings can contribute new insights on cultural behavior.

The relationship between physical space and social interaction is probably always reflected in individuals' personal cognitive maps of behavioral settings. Gulick (1963) asked his Lebanese informants to draw maps of the city of Tripoli; the maps they produced revealed significant variations in social features and aspects of spatial conceptualization.

Inventories of Material Goods. Although the study of material culture and technology has been seriously neglected by anthropologists during the past twenty to thirty years, it appears that the growth of a general ecological perspective has encouraged a return to careful ethnographic observations of physical things. Detailed study of the characteristics of boats, vehicles, tools, equipment, buildings, utensils, and other items is usually necessary if man-environment transactions are to be systematically explored. Often ethnographers have found that they can accomplish quite a lot in early phases of fieldwork through inventorying and describing material culture, even though their language skills are not yet developed to a point where complicated interviewing is possible.

In addition to simple lists and descriptions of material goods, most field studies include information about differential ownership. Some people of the community have radios, cars, and bicycles, while others do not. Some households have a nearly complete supply of equipment and furnishings, while other families have practically nothing. Paul

Kay (1964) found in Tahiti that durable consumer goods (bicycles, radios, kerosene or gas stoves, automobiles) were differentially distributed in the local population in such a way that a Guttman scalogram of ownership could be constructed. Such a scalogram, or other index of material-goods ownership, can be quite useful in revealing patterns of socioeconomic differentiation.

Schensul (1969) used this technique for establishing the range of variation in material styles of life in villages in northern Minnesota and Uganda. In both cases he found that differences in material life styles were significantly related to variations in cognitive orientations and other individual characteristics. G. Pelto (1970) used a similar material life style index in a study of northern Minnesota communities and found that this indicator of socioeconomic status was effective in predicting psychological difficulties, especially tendencies to depression.

Robbins and Kilbride (1972) have recently studied the effects of "microtechnological" items (flashlights, radios, wristwatches, bicycles, lanterns, cameras) on the behavior of Baganda peasant farmers. They found that some of these items facilitated an expansion of people's social networks by providing longer hours of light (facilitating social gatherings), greater contact with information about the outside world, and greater possibilities for traveling.

The Census and Numerical Data. As we noted earlier, most anthropologists nowadays make use of techniques of data collection that produce quantifiable materials. Usually this takes the form of a "census"—a structured interview administered to each household, with questions about family composition; age, education, marital status, and other data about family members; occupations and sources of income; landholdings and other economic assets; and other basic social information. Sometimes the fieldworker includes a few questions about opinions or attitudes along with the basic demographic and social items. Beattie (1965) and Colson (1967) have described field census operations in detail. Mitchell's (1967) review of quantified techniques in social anthropology and a summary of survey techniques by Bennett and Thaiss (1967) provide useful discussions of the place of quantified data in ethnographic fieldwork.

Bennett and Thaiss note some problems that have arisen in ethnographic comparisons because of lack of numerical data. They cite as an example Gallaher's (1961) restudy of "Plainville, U.S.A.," fifteen years after James West's (1945) research in that community. In the earlier study, a fairly clear system of social classes was described; Gallaher denied that such a pattern of stratification existed at the time of the later study. The differences between the two studies would represent a very important demonstration of social change if we could be sure that they did not simply reflect differences in theoretical orientations. Bennett and Thaiss (1967:283) feel that the two ethnographic studies

suggest a criticism of field methods in which a needed survey-type discipline is lacking. The ambiguity in the differences between the two approaches to stratification and status is due in part to the fact that structured instruments apparently were not used in either study, alone or in combination with the observational field methods. . . . The case illustrates the potential usefulness of a combination of the extensive survey approach with intensive field investigation.

Since more and more studies now include numerical data, future ethnographic restudies may provide more credible demonstrations of cultural and social change.

There are two chief purposes for numerical data in ethnographic work. As Clyde Mitchell (1967:43) notes:

The various demographic measures such as birth rates, death rates, replacement rates, divorce frequencies, age distributions, tables of the frequencies of kinship categories found in villages, ownership of cattle, and income distribution, are [descriptive data about village or regional composition]. These the anthropologist uses as he thinks necessary to supplement his verbal descriptions. Quantitative data may also be used, however, to express the underlying relationship between phenomena either by assessing them against some theoretical model developed on the basis of probability theory or by computing one of the various measures of correlation or association.

Mitchell's own work with the Yao provides some illustrations of the use of statistical analysis to examine the patterning of social characteristics. He found through numerical analysis that "the size of the village and the headman's kinship with the chief are the main factors that influence the possession of marks of prestige" (Mitchell 1967:45).

Frank Cancian's (1965:115-17) analysis of the *cargo* system in Zinacantan (Mexico) is an example of the examination of numerical data in relation to a postulated theoretical model. The *cargos* (religious offices) were ranked by Cancian according to their presumed prestige (estimated from the costs and relative authority incurred by those who held them). By gathering information about the *cargo* careers of a sample of individual Zinacantecans and analyzing it statistically, Cancian was able to show that there is a coherent system of stratification among the Zinacantecans: sons tend to follow the lead of their fathers in achievement of *cargos,* and marriages are likely to be contracted between families of similar *cargo* ranking.

Meggitt's (1962) study of the Walbiri tribe of central Australia is another good example of the use of extensive statistical analysis to support generalizations about social patterns. His statistical tables include data on remarriage of Walbiri widows, selection of midwives, observance of patrimoiety ceremonial divisions, adherence to marriage rules, and many other social patterns. All of these tables examine reported social behavior of individuals in relation to the ideal cultural norms of the Walbiri people. This kind of numerical examination of the relationships of real to ideal behavior is unfortunately still rare in anthropological studies.

In some instances, detailed counting of behavioral items has led to important revisions in our ethnographic knowledge. Richard Lee (1968:37). made painstaking counts of time expenditures and food yields among the !Kung Bushmen. These data produced the striking information that

in all, the adults of Dobe camp worked about two and a half days a week. Since the average working day was about six hours long, the fact emerges that !Kung Bushmen of Dobe, despite their harsh environment, devote from twelve to nineteen hours a week to getting food. Even the hardest working individual in the camp, a man named ≠oma who went out hunting on sixteen of the twenty-eight days, spent a maximum of thirty-two hours a week in the food quest.

Furthermore, Lee was able to demonstrate quantitatively that this group of Bushmen are able to maintain a quite satisfactory level of nutrition, since they attain an intake of an estimated 2,140 calories per day, with approximately 93 grams of proteins per adult.

Other recent studies of a similar nature give added support to the radical new view that hunting and gathering

provide a much more leisurely and secure life than had been believed on the basis of earlier, more impressionistic descriptions (see Sahlins 1968:85-89). In general, ethnographic studies have been seriously lacking in data on time expenditures and comparative productivity. Very few studies of peasants, for example, give any data about work schedules, hours of effort per week, or productivity per unit of crop yield.

The quantitative extreme in the continuum of ethnographic styles is represented by studies that consist mainly of statistical testing of theoretical constructs. Some anthropologists, we suppose, would not consider these works to be "ethnographic" in any sense. However, these studies are often focused on particular communities; they include nonquantified descriptive data as general background; and they thus present a highly refined and specialized portion of cultural data that can be regarded as a legitimate segment of the ethnographic range of variation. The monograph entitled *Society, Personality, and Deviant Behavior* by Jessor, Graves, et al. (1968) is a recent example of this highly specialized end of the field research continuum. (Of the authors, only Graves is an anthropologist, but many of the fieldworkers in their large-scale project were anthropologists).

The hallmark of this kind of study is that the researchers' attention is focused on testing a theoretical system rather than on describing a particular community. Nonetheless, the data were collected in a single community, in this case a tri-ethnic community that included Spanish-American, Anglo-American, and Indian subpopulations. In a methodological discussion on "minimizing inferential ambiguity" the authors made clear that they intended to maintain careful, objective control over the processes of observation and to provide clear, replicable guides to the processes of inference from data. Control of observations and inferences was maintained through *(a)* careful *selection* of observational units (cases), *(b)* *standardization* of observations (interview schedules, etc.), *(c)* use of *theory* as the explicit frame of reference for data-gathering, *(d)* "*construct validation*" of results, and *(e)* use of "*multiple converging studies*" (Jessor, Graves, et al. 1968:140-49).

The tri-ethnic project illustrates a type of study that may be of growing importance in anthropology. The work of Rodgers and his associates in the Bahamas (see Rodgers and Long 1968) fits this category. Also, Robbins and his associates appear to be concerned mainly with quantifiable observations in their work in Uganda (see Robbins et al. 1969, Robbins and Kilbride 1972).

THE CASE-STUDY METHOD AND SITUATIONAL ANALYSIS

One of the significant trends in recent ethnographic work is the increased attention to case study as a research method (see Van Velsen 1967; Epstein, ed., 1967; Turner 1967; and a number of other recent discussions). As Van Velsen points out, earlier social anthropological fieldwork often focused on a few key informants and their accounts of the abstract "rules" or "patterns" of social relationships. Such fieldwork was usually predicated on assumptions about the homogeneity and equilibrium of the social systems studied. The case-study method focuses instead on "actors" and their patterns of decision-making in a variety of significant social situations. Probably the most conspicuous use of the case method occurs in studies of legal systems. In this domain the patterned behavior to be studied often consists of repeatable rules and canons of jurisprudence in a series of

legal situations. Actually, law cases generally provide two kinds of patterned cultural behavior: statements of rules to be applied in particular kinds of cases and tabulations of particular types of legal outcomes in relation to other social data.

Leopold Pospisil's study of the *Kapauku Papuans and Their Law* (1964) is based on a corpus of 176 cases in a New Guinea tribe. Analysis of these cases permitted Pospisil to set forth the main rules that the Kapauku apply in settlement of disputes. The following example illustrates his method (Pospisil 1964:244-45):

Rule 117 (Paniai region): An ungenerous wealthy man should be executed, preferably by his son, brother, or paternal parallel cousin.

Case 170.
  Place: Madi, Paniai region
  Date: August 3rd, 1955
  Parties:
    (a) *Defendant:* Mo Juw of Madi, Paniai region, a wealthy man and village headman
    (b) *Killers:* Mo Jow of Madi, the defendant's eldest son; two FaBroSons of the defendant and two unrelated men

Facts:
  Juw was a very wealthy man but he failed to lend out his property in proportion to his fortune. People of his village, dissatisfied with the state of affairs, spoke to the paternal parallel cousins of the man and persuaded them to kill the culprit. They, in turn, talked to the man's eldest son who agreed to join them in the execution of his own father. He was promised a pig and 20 Km for his participation.

Outcome:
  When the rich man was working in his garden, five men approached him and started to discharge their bamboo-tipped arrows into his body. His son was the first who shot him. . . . The killers divided the dead man's property among themselves.

The case-study method is particularly suited to the study of social behavior associated with classes of events that recur frequently enough to provide a substantial sample: ceremonial enactments, curing practices, marriage settlements, commercial transactions, hunting expeditions (e.g., division of game), and many other behavioral domains. (It is quite important for the fieldworker to specify which cases he himself observed and which were related to him by informants.) As Van Velsen (1967: 147) has pointed out, in extended case-method and situational analysis

one seeks interconnected cases within a small area involving a limited number of *dramatis personae*. Such cases should later be presented in the analysis in their social context as part of a social process and not [simply] as isolated instances illustrating, more or less aptly, a particular generalization.

Collecting a series of cases permits the fieldworker to employ numerical analysis to support his generalizations. Thus the case method in fieldwork has the dual advantage of permitting extended analysis of social processes (actual ongoing behavior in social situations) *and* statistical manipulation of the data. In her analysis of Zapotec law cases, Laura Nader (1964) makes extensive use of situational and social structural analysis of individual cases, but the body of court cases also permits numerical observations such as the following (pp. 412-13):

...We learn, for example, that men and women use the courts to an approximately equal degree. In 22 of our cases the plaintiff is a female, and in 17 a male. The men, however, seek judicial remedies mainly in conflicts with nonkin. Of 17 cases initiated by men, 15 were with nonkin and two with affinal kin. On the other hand, of the 22 cases initiated by women, 14 were with kin and only eight with nonkin. From a cross-cultural view the number of women who contest cases in the court is extraordinarily high. Upon investigation of these 22 female plaintiffs it was found that more than two-thirds lacked a male relative (father, father-in-law, husband) who might have defended them.

The collection of cases and the attendant situational analysis clearly require great effort and endurance on the part of the fieldworker. Often he must shift his attention rapidly from one actor to another in a complex, multiperson social event. He needs to transcribe verbal performances in detail (sometimes use of a tape recorder ensures recall of most of the spoken action), but he must also remember to record details of physical setting, movements of persons, and other factors affecting the interactions. In studying complex social events, therefore, it is a great advantage for a number of field researchers to work together, so they can compare their observations after the event has ended. Epstein (1967:223) has described his solution to the problem:

The procedure I have myself adopted has been to train an assistant to record the case in the vernacular as it proceeded or, where this was not possible, to prepare a text on it as soon as possible thereafter. At the same time I myself took notes of the hearing, recording passages or phrases verbatim in the vernacular. The two records were then checked against each other, discussed and clarified, and combined into a final typed record of the case.... The record served as a springboard to further inquiry....

THE FIELDWORK TEAM: SPOUSES, COLLEAGUES, ASSISTANTS

Every field of scientific investigation has experienced a remarkable growth in the complexity of its technology and observational techniques during recent decades. Our brief and incomplete review of research techniques should make clear that ethnographic work is no exception to this generalization. The result is that properly executed fieldwork is an exhausting and time-demanding activity, although most researchers still report that the experience is pleasurable. The image of the lone fieldworker strolling about the village, casually interviewing informants and watching their daily activities, has come less and less to resemble the realities of the fieldwork enterprise. The average fieldworker is constantly harassed by the realization that there are not enough hours in the day to finish the task he has assigned himself, not enough hours in the night to get all the field notes typed up, and worse still, not enough time even to take in all the goings-on about him. Too many things are happening at the same time. At any point in the day there may be three or four or more important events taking place—and all the time there is the realization that the dull routine of structured interviewing must go on if one's sample is to be adequate.

At the very least one needs to have some assistants in the field. Most fieldworkers (thirty-two of the fifty-one in our sample) have their wives or husbands with them in the field, but often the wife, even when she is herself a professional, finds herself spending an unconscionable amount of time coping with the complexities of maintaining a household in an unfamiliar setting. There appears to be an increase in the number of research expeditions involving fieldwork teams—often with interdisciplinary participation, although about half of the reported projects involved only one fieldworker plus an assistant or two.

The data in Tables 14-17 indicate the use of assistants and colleagues in the field by our fifty-one respondents.

Tables 16 and 17 show the interesting fact that those fieldworkers who are quantitatively oriented require more field assistance than nonquantifiers.

Of those anthropologists who had assistants in the field with them, only

TABLE 14
Use of Assistants and Colleagues in Fieldwork

Composition of Fieldwork Unit	Number
Lone fieldworker	6
Fieldworker and nonprofessional spouse	9
Fieldworker and assistants	10
Fieldworker, nonprofessional spouse, and assistants	8
Husband-wife professional team	7
Team of professional social scientists other than husband and wife	11

TABLE 15
Types of Assistants in Field Teams

Source of Assistants	Number
Home university	9
Other U.S. institutions	14
Local university	11
Local community:	
educated	12
uneducated	7

TABLE 16
Use of Field Assistants in Relation to Research Orientation

Research Orientation of Fieldworker	Assistants Employed	
	Yes	No
Nonquantifiers	5	8
Intermediates	8	10
Quantifiers	17	2
Total	30	20

TABLE 17
Use of Collaborators or Assistants (Exclusive of Spouse) in Relation to Research Orientation

Research Orientation of Fieldworker	Collaborators or Assistants Employed	
	Yes	No
Nonquantifiers	6	7
Intermediates	11	6
Quantifiers	17	2

nine reported bringing assistants from their home universities. Four others reported obtaining assistants from other universities or institutions in the United States. The more typical field assistant is an educated native of the local research area (twelve cases). Nearly as frequently (eleven cases in this sample) the fieldworker hires an assistant from a college or university in the nation where he carries out his fieldwork. Only seven anthropologists in our sample reported that they hired local uneducated assistants. It is interesting that six of these seven are quantitative ethnographers. It appears that the gathering of census materials or other quantified data can be routinized to such an extent that intelligent but uneducated local persons may be trained to carry out the tasks.

In most parts of the world there are few or no anthropology students in the local universities who could serve as assistants; but there are growing numbers of sociologists and other types of social scientists in most parts of Africa, Latin America, and throughout much of the Far East. Thus, it is becoming more and more feasible to hire assistants who have some background and interests in social research.

Sometimes the very best assistants are relatively untrained and uneducated persons who have unusual perceptions and knowledge about their own local cultural and social systems. These local field assistants may be important as much for their special social ties as for their research abilities. During fieldwork in Nepal, John Hitchcock (1970: 172-73) hired a young man, Hem, who was the son of an important headman. "The day after our arrival in Banyan Hill, Hem's father had sent messengers to all quarters of the multivillage community where Banyan Hill was located, and on the following day a large gathering had appeared and listened while

Hem and I explained why we were there." In the collection of villagers' estimates of harvest yields, Hem's social position was of great significance: "People knew that Hem would know—and if not Hem, his father—when estimates were very far off. It was the same with debts, usually a most difficult item. Here we were assured of accuracy because Hem's father was the principal money lender."

Many ethnographers would point out that the presence of more than three or four people in the research group presents large problems of rapport maintenance (too many outsiders in the village), and requires complex organization of supplies and work schedules. Training field assistants and supervising their work can be a very time-consuming and emotionally arduous task. Anthropologists are often loath to invest valuable time in training and maintaining a field crew at the expense of time spent in direct, personalized contact with informants.

But there are a number of trends in modern fieldwork that create pressures toward expanding the fieldwork crew. Besides the general tendency toward increased quantification in field operations, there is the important fact that ethnographers today very frequently study peasant societies or even urban communities instead of simpler (or at least smaller) villages and bands of tribal, nonliterate peoples. It comes as no surprise, then, to find that of our fifty-one respondents, fifteen of them had field teams of five or more persons, and six of these field expeditions involved teams of *more than ten members.*

The field team with five or more members obviously has more eyes and ears than the traditional lone fieldworker. A large and complex scene such as a village festival, a county fair, or some sort of public ceremonial can be much more fully and effectively covered by a team of fieldworkers, each of whom observes only a few aspects of the event, than by one person who tries to be everywhere and see everything at once.

When several persons are in the same fieldwork scene, it is usually good practice for them to become individually involved in different subgroups, or different "ecological niches" within the local social system. One fieldworker might develop special ties with the poorest segment of the community, while another cultivates relationships with the local elite, and so on. If the community is sharply divided along religious, ethnic, or racial lines, the fieldworkers should, if possible, divide their zones of concentration accordingly. In this way the multiperson team may be able to portray neutrality in the field situation, even though each individual researcher becomes personally involved with particular segments of the divided society.

Multiperson field teams appear to enhance their effectiveness if they hold frequent field "seminars" in which they compare notes, resolve differences in interpretations of events, and allocate observational assignments. Frequent discussion of theoretical and methodological problems helps to keep members of the team in contact with the scientific objectives of the research and also helps to reduce some of the psychological tensions of fieldwork. The fieldworker who encounters various difficulties in rapport maintenance and data organization is usually a bit relieved when he finds that most of the rest of the crew is experiencing the same kinds of problems. On the other hand, the presence of other professional fieldworkers can sometimes prove too effective as an escape mechanism, allowing an individual to avoid intensive personal relationships with the local people.

TRENDS IN CONTEMPORARY ETHNOGRAPHIC WORK

As we review all these data and observations on recent ethnographic work, certain trends become apparent. We offer the following generalizations tentatively, keeping in mind that more descriptions and studies of ethnographic procedures are needed before a full picture of our professions can be developed. Most of these recent changes in fieldwork objectives, techniques, and styles are evident in the many autobiographical accounts of ethnographers that have recently appeared.

1. Quantification of field observations and increasingly sophisticated "operationalizing" of field data have become more usual in ethnographic investigations than they were earlier.

2. Much ethnographic research is now focused on urban social systems, complex segments of peasant societies, and other types of "nonprimitive" literate populations.

3. The study of social change, modernization, and social processes looms large in contemporary research, partly overshadowing earlier concerns with static, "equilibrated" social and cultural systems.

4. The tendency of ethnographers to identify with "their people" and to find positive values in their cultural practices has continued, but more and more anthropologists now go beyond this passive partisanship, seeking to foster social changes that would improve the socioeconomic situations of their research communities. This trend is related to a series of ethical questions with which we shall deal in the concluding section of this chapter.

5. In connection with the tendency to press for social action, some contemporary ethnographers are begin-

ning to see themselves as carrying out research *for* the local communities themselves, rather than simply for their academic peers and perhaps for governmental agencies. Thus some anthropologists have assumed the responsibility of making their research results relevant for and available to the people whose ways of life they have studied. This tendency is evident, for example, in the Cree project carried out by Norman Chance (1969).

6. Although there continues to be a large number of general, descriptive ethnographic studies, many fieldworkers focus their data-gathering on one specialized aspect of the sociocultural system, or on some one theoretical problem. Cancian's (1965) study of the Zinacantan system of religious *cargos* is a good example of a specialized topical orientation. The tri-ethnic project of Jessor, Graves, et al. (1968) exemplifies a research effort focused on a particular theoretical question.

7. A general ecological orientation is becoming more common in ethnographic work, bringing with it a much-needed re-emphasis on physical and biological environment; it also promotes the possibilities for theoretical interrelating of the biological (including genetic) with the sociocultural aspects of local populations. Defining local research units as populations rather than as "cultures" is one important indicator of this trend.

8. The focusing of research on culture change, modernization, social processes, and individual decision-making, together with the trends toward quantification of data, has diminished the importance of key informants as main sources of data. Structured interviews with samples of respondents, observation of significant behavioral settings, and collection of "cases" (court cases, divinations, divorces, marriage settlements, land conflicts, and so on) have become increasingly important as field techniques.

9. Although the study of local subgroups (clans, lineages, voluntary associations, and the like) and their interrelationships is still very important in ethnographic research, the focus on ecological adaptations, social processes, decision-making, and individual differences has led to increased concern with individuals and their social networks.

10. Those same trends also have led anthropologists to give increased weight to intracommunity or intracultural differences. The ethnographer's research targets are more heterogeneous now than they were two or three decades ago, but the research techniques now being employed provide him with effective tools for dealing with these heterogeneous and complex research areas.

11. The psychological and pragmatic attractions of the community study, as well as the continuing strong theoretical interests of anthropologists in the community as a sociocultural system, are reflected in the prominence of this type of study in contemporary research efforts. At the same time, a growing number of researchers are engaged in regional or intercommunity studies, frequently stating as rationales for such studies the methodological and theoretical advantages to be gained in a multicommunity research design (see Tables 18 and 19).

12. There appear to be increasing numbers of multiperson, interdisciplinary research projects. These team

TABLE 18
Organization of Fieldwork
and Conceptualization of
Materials in Relation to Research Unit*

Research Unit	Number
Single community (village, band, town, etc.)	17
2, 3, or more communities (comparative studies)	16
Region	13
Culture (Navajo, Yoruba, etc.)	8
Neighborhood or other segment of larger community	5
Series of households	2
Other	5

*Some respondents checked more than one category.

projects seem to reflect a convergence of several factors: it is increasingly common for economists, sociologists, psychologists, and other social scientists to be interested in field research as a mode of investigation; the skills and research capabilities required in full-scale ecological studies demand team research; and increased sensitivity to problems of quantification and sampling, along with the trend toward multicommunity research designs, adds many hours of work to the anthropologist's task. These and other factors encourage the development of a team approach to ethnographic research.

13. Self-conscious concern and writing about the techniques of field research must also be considered a significant characteristic of the contemporary ethnographic scene. As we mentioned earlier, autobiographical accounts of field experiences are mainly a phenomenon of the last ten years, and the three most comprehensive collections of essays about fieldwork appeared in 1970.

POSTLOGUE

THE FUTURE OF ETHNOGRAPHIC WORK: PROBLEMS OF ETHICS AND RELEVANCE

Into each life, it is said, some rain must fall. Some people have bad horoscopes, others take tips on the stock market. McNamara created the TFX and the Edsel. Churches possess the real world. But Indians have been cursed above all other people in history. Indians have anthropologists.

* * *

The implications of the anthropologist, if not for all America, should be clear for the Indian. Compilation of useless knowledge "for knowledge's sake" should be utterly rejected by the Indian people. We should not be objects of observation for those who do nothing to help us. During the crucial days of 1954, when the Senate was pushing for termination of all Indian rights, not one single scholar, anthropologist, sociologist, historian, or economist came forward to support the tribes against the detrimental policy.[1]

---

[1](From *Custer Died for Your Sins: An Indian Manifesto* by Vine Deloria, Jr. [1969: 78, 94]. The author is from the Standing Rock Sioux Reservation.)

TABLE 19
Type of Society Studied by Ethnographers

Type of Society	Number	Type of Society	Number
Peasant	20	Urban	4
Tribe	15	Factory workers	1
Hunting-gathering	2	National	1
"Pueblo"	1	Folk	1
Postpeasant	1	Postindustrial (U.S.)	1
Urban-peasant	3	Reservation	1

During the past few years anthropologists have come under attack from several quarters, as both the ethics and the relevance of fieldwork have been sharply questioned. Deloria's statement is a sample of the growing body of opinion that challenges the *relevance* (to social problems and to the communities studied) of ethnographic research. Other writers have denounced ethnographic activities on other grounds, particularly when field activities have appeared to be related in some way to U.S. foreign policy matters.

During the middle 1960s the involvement of some American anthropologists in the ill-starred Project Camelot in Chile brought the matter of "imperialism" and professional ethics into sharp focus. Project Camelot was funded by the Department of Defense and was widely regarded, by Latin Americans and others, as a thinly disguised espionage venture. More recently similar questions have arisen in connection with government-sponsored ethnographic activities in Southeast Asia, where anthropologists have been accused of participating, in effect, in U.S. counterinsurgency programs.

Complex ethical and practical questions are posed by anthropologists' involvements in research related to American foreign policy:

1. Are such research activities actually or potentially detrimental to the local populations involved?

2. Is it likely that other populations will act to prevent ethnographers from entering their communities for fieldwork purposes?

3. If social research is to be relevant, who is to judge what is relevant, and to whom is it to be relevant?

4. If relevance frequently involves political and ideological partisanship, what kind of balance can be struck between relevance and scientific neutrality?

While many anthropologists have been as sharply critical and as deeply concerned about these issues as our "outside" critics, they have also, understandably, felt strong emotional reactions of anger, hurt, and perplexity at increasingly hostile attitudes toward anthropology. In numerous ways anthropologists have tried to be helpful to the people they study. In addition to setting up informal medical clinics, writing innumerable letters to Congressmen, the Bureau of Indian Affairs, and other authorities, and providing information and encouragement in various local projects, ethnographers have testified before congressional committees and pleaded on behalf of Indian communities and other groups in many contexts. But the ethnographer is usually as powerless as the people themselves in the face of the massive impersonality of government bureaucracy and commercial and industrial enterprises; he is as poorly equipped, financially and otherwise, as any other individual without political power.

Many fieldworkers have suggested that "in the long run" they can have the most impact by "telling the truth" (as they see it) in books and articles about the people they study. In writing of tribes, peasant villages, or hunting and gathering bands, they serve most effectively, they suggest, by educating people to an appreciation of ways of life different from their own. Over and over again anthropologists have defined the prime goals of their teaching in these ways, and most members of the profession would argue that anthropological teaching and writing have had an enormous effect on European and North American attitudes during the past fifty years.

It would appear that the "contract" between the fieldworker and his research community has frequently been appreciated by the people themselves, for in many instances they have been proud to display, and even quote from, the monographs about their communities, and have sometimes found these anthropological works of practical use—for example, in putting together the details of a half-forgotten ritual they seek to revive. Most people are proud to see themselves in print, especially if the description is, on the whole, a favorable interpretation of their lives. People in host communities have often said, "It will be good for our grandchildren to read about the way we used to live." This part of the bargain may be of less relevance now, when ethnographers no longer deal with the halcyon days before the white man took over.

Looking back, the anthropologist may feel that he has not betrayed the friendships he formed in the course of fieldwork. Very possibly the task of general data-gathering was justified by its contributions to the general body of social science knowledge. Times change, however, and it may be that the old justifications are no longer adequate in many cases.

Frequently the people who demand "relevance" and practical benefits from social research in their communities are the new leaders and activists who have newly acquired political and social power. Unlike the people studied in earlier years, they can indeed make use of social data for practical ends. The political and social power inherent in local action movements is now richly evident—to national leaders as well as to the people themselves. The effectiveness of such movements, according to our time-honored social theory, can be increased if the people involved in them have adequate information—data and ideas about the social system they seek to manipulate. (One of the most tragic moments in the history of twentieth-century social movements occurred

when the two charismatic leaders of the Mexican Revolution, Pancho Villa and Emiliano Zapata, met in Mexico City and found they had neither the social information nor an ideological program with which to translate their military alliance into effective political power (see Wolf 1969:37).

Because of many pressures both within and outside the profession, fieldworkers will have to devise new kinds of "contracts" with their research communities. And that will often require new kinds of research, as well as some changes in our role relationships in field situations. Of course, there is room for much debate and disagreement on the matter, but there is some evidence that the most relevant and useful field research would often consist of a fairly prosaic, methodologically sound description of the social and cultural facts in a particular community or region. Effective political or social action often depends on knowledge that is essentially the same as the basic survey data from which the best monographs are built—income and occupation data, inventories of material possessions and facilities, behavior of people in regard to "social articulation to the wider society," and so on. In fact, some demands made to ethnographers by local leaders have been for just this sort of aid. They need those statistical descriptive data in order to shape the requests, demands, or charges they propose to present to the agencies in Washington!

Urban court cases involving slum housing conditions, sanitation problems, and other forms of bureaucratic neglect also require well-organized, methodologically sophisticated numerical data, backed up by some effective contextualization and explicit illustrative cases, explored in depth. Action projects in the community or on the reservation require a variety of types of descriptive data—the very sort of data that social scientists, including anthropologists, are accustomed to gathering and organizing.

While doing research in a Mexican district in Chicago, Schensul (1970) and his associates found that the local community action organization was quite interested in data on the ethnic composition of the neighborhood; the extent of knowledge among the people about social agencies and recent local issues; and a tabulation of social characteristics of persons who took active part in a rezoning protest. All of these data were available from a household survey that was conducted in the neighborhood immediately after the rezoning protest took place.

Relevance in fieldwork is often not so much a matter of the type of study, but the form in which the data are made available. Frequently the most serious charge leveled against ethnographers is that the field data are published only in anthropological journals (relatively inaccessible to the research subjects), and are not available until two or three years after the research is completed. Moreover, the language and style in which the data are presented make their use most difficult for non-anthropologists.

Ethnographers who seek to make their research relevant to local action groups and individuals will need to develop forms of communication that are much more rapid and informal than our customary modes of transmission. Schensul (1970) and his associates have printed leaflets, prepared posters, and presented informal talks to interested community groups in the course of their Chicago research. Norman Chance (1969) and his associates from McGill have transmitted research results to Cree communities through meetings with local Indian leaders, as well as through reports translated into written Cree.

The transmission of useful information to people who want it is often best accomplished through a fairly long-term dialogue between the researcher and his audience, during which the forms of information transmission and the interpretations of the data are negotiated. This negotiation will involve much trial and error. In the period immediately after World War II a number of anthropologists learned about the difficulties of negotiating information exchange between researchers and government officials (Barnett 1956). With local community leaders and groups as their clients, fieldworkers have a chance to try again the difficult job of transforming social data into forms that are understandable and useful to nonacademicians.

Relevant research involves several levels of abstraction and many levels of utility. Fieldworkers who communicate their results to local "clients" will also transmit their data in a more formal form to professional colleagues and other readers. We have also to face the difficult problem of making ethnographic data more relevant and useful to colleagues in other disciplines. All of these brief comments concentrate on our relationships to the primary research communities and their spokesmen because of the simple fact that our work becomes ethically and practically impossible if we cannot do right by those people whose friendship makes our fieldwork possible.

There are certain kinds of research topics that are likely to become increasingly frequent as a result of the push for relevance. For example, ethnographers have often virtually ignored the political and economic relationships that subordinate local communities to the more powerful and dominant sectors of their social systems. The structuring of "microcosm-macrocosm relationships," as John Bennett (1967a) has described them, is often of great importance for local programs of social action, and fieldworkers will need to develop their conceptual and methodological apparatus to a degreee of sophistication adequate for dealing with this aspect of power alignments and patterns.

The closely related problems of ethics and relevance came sharply into focus during the 1960s. In the decade of the 1970s ethnographers will have to find solutions for these problems in order to continue to do research in other people's communities. It is in the nature of modern social problems that no single, clear solution to these questions will be found. The forms that ethnographic fieldwork takes, and their relationships to current social problems, will be varied. In some areas ethnographers will be able to carry out fieldwork pretty much as it was practiced in the past. And the local people will for the most part enjoy and approve the activities.

In other cases, though, fieldworkers will be acceptable to the local populace only if there is direct return of useful information *and* the assurance that the fieldworker is not an agent of some segment of "the establishment" whose concerns may run counter to their own perceived interests. Probably many ethnographic activities will continue to be seen as ethically justified by the researchers involved but denounced as unethical and immoral by persons with other ideological views.

REFERENCES

American Anthropological Association
1969 *Guide to Graduate Departments of Anthropology.* Washington, D.C.
Barnes, J. A.
1967 Genealogies. In *The Craft of Social Anthropology,* ed. A. L. Epstein. London: Tavistock.
Barnett, Homer G.
1956 *Anthropology in Administration.* Evanston, Ill.: Row, Peterson.
1970 Palauan Journal. In *Being an Anthropologist,* ed. G. Spindler. New York: Holt, Rinehart & Winston.
Beals, Alan R.
1970 Gopalpur, 1958-1960. In *Being an Anthropologist,* ed. G. Spindler. New York: Holt, Rinehart & Winston.
Beattie, John
1965 *Understanding an African Kingdom: Bunyoro.* New York: Holt, Rinehart & Winston.
Bennett, John W.
1967a Microcosm-Macrocosm Relationships in North American Agrarian Society. *American Anthropologist* 69:441-54.
1967b *Hutterian Brethren.* Stanford: Stanford University Press.
Bennett, John W., and Gustav Thaiss
1967 Sociocultural Anthropology and Survey Research. In *Survey Research in the Social Sciences,* ed. Charles Y. Glock. New York: Russell Sage Foundation.
Berreman, Gerald
1962 *Behind Many Masks: Ethnography and Impression Management in a Himalayan Village.* Society for Applied Anthropology Monograph no. 4. Ithaca, N.Y.
1968 Ethnography: Method and Product. In *Introduction to Cultural Anthropology,* ed. James Clifton. Boston: Houghton Mifflin.
Boissevain, Jeremy
1970 Fieldwork in Malta. In *Being an Anthropologist,* ed. G. Spindler. New York: Holt, Rinehart & Winston.
Bowen, Elenore S.
1964 *Return to Laughter.* Garden City, N.Y.: Doubleday. Originally published 1954.
Briggs, Jean
1970 Kapluna's Daughter. In *Women in the Field,* ed. P. Golde. Chicago: Aldine.
Buechler, Hans
1969 The Social Position of an Ethnographer in the Field. In *Stress and Response in Field Work,* ed. F. Henry and S. Saberwal. New York: Holt, Rinehart & Winston.
Cancian, Frank
1965 *Economics and Prestige in a Maya*

Community. Stanford: Stanford University Press.

Chagnon, Napoleon
1968 *Yanomamö: The Fierce People.* New York: Holt, Rinehart & Winston.

Chance, Norman A.
1969 The Anthropologist as Informant: Problems of Feedback in Anthropological Research. Paper presented at the annual meeting of the American Anthropological Association, New Orleans.

Codere, Helen
1970 Field Work in Rwanda, 1959-60. In *Women in the Field,* ed. P. Golde. Chicago: Aldine.

Colson, Elizabeth
1967 The Intensive Study of Small Sample Communities. In *The Craft of Social Anthropology,* ed. A. L. Epstein. London: Tavistock. Originally published 1954.

Degérando, Joseph-Marie
1969 *The Observation of Savage Peoples,* trans. and ed. F. C. T. Moore. Berkeley: University of California Press. Originally published 1800.

Deloria, Vine, Jr.
1969 *Custer Died for Your Sins.* Toronto: Collier-Macmillan.

Diamond, Norma
1970 Fieldwork in a Complex Society: Taiwan. In *Being an Anthropologist,* ed. G. Spindler. New York: Holt, Rinehart & Winston.

Epstein, A. L., ed.
1967 *The Craft of Social Anthropology.* London: Tavistock.

Freilich, Morris
1970 Mohawk Heroes and Trinidadian Peasants. In *Marginal Natives,* ed. M. Freilich. New York: Harper & Row.

Freilich, Morris, ed.
1970 *Marginal Natives: Anthropologists at Work.* New York: Harper & Row.

Gallaher, Art, Jr.
1961 *Plainville Fifteen Years Later.* New York: Columbia University Press.

Gjessing, Gutorm
1968 The Social Responsibility of the Social Scientist. *Current Anthropology* 9:397-402.

Gluckman, Max
1967 Introduction. In *The Craft of Social*

Anthropology, ed. A. L. Epstein. London: Tavistock.

Golde, Peggy
1970 Odyssey of Encounter. In *Women in the Field,* ed. P. Golde. Chicago: Aldine.

Golde, Peggy, ed.
1970 *Women in the Field.* Chicago: Aldine.

Graburn, Nelson
1969 *Eskimos Without Igloos.* Boston: Little, Brown.

Gulick, John
1963 Images of an Arab City. *Journal of American Institute of Planners* 29:179-98.
1970 Village and City Field Work in Lebanon. In *Marginal Natives,* ed. M. Freilich. New York: Harper & Row.

Hall, Edward T.
1966 *The Hidden Dimension.* Garden City, N.Y.: Doubleday.

Hart, C. W. M.
1970 Fieldwork Among the Tiwi, 1928-1929. In *Being an Anthropologist,* ed. G. Spindler. New York: Holt, Rinehart & Winston.

Henry, Frances, and Satish Saberwal, eds.
1969 *Stress and Response in Field Work.* New York: Holt, Rinehart & Winston.

Hitchcock, John T.
1970 Fieldwork in Ghurka Country. In *Being an Anthropologist,* ed. G. Spindler. New York: Holt, Rinehart & Winston.

Holmberg, Allan
1969 *Nomads of the Long Bow: The Siriono of Eastern Bolivia.* Garden City, N.Y.: Natural History Press. Originally published 1950.

Honigmann, John J.
1970 Field Work in Two Northern Canadian Communities. In *Marginal Natives,* ed. M. Freilich. New York: Harper & Row.

Jessor, Richard, Theodore D. Graves, et al.
1968 *Society, Personality, and Deviant Behavior.* New York: Holt, Rinehart & Winston.

Jongmans, D. C., and P. C. W. Gutkind, eds.
1967 *Anthropologists in the Field.* New York: Humanities Press.

Kay, Paul

1964 A Guttman Scale Model of Tahitian Consumer Behavior. *Southwestern Journal of Anthropology* 20:160-67.

Keiser, Lincoln
1969 *The Vice Lords: Warriors of the Streets.* New York: Holt, Rinehart & Winston.
1970 Fieldwork Among the Vice Lords of Chicago. In *Being an Anthropologist,* ed. G. Spindler. New York: Holt, Rinehart & Winston.

Lee, Richard B.
1968 What Hunters Do for a Living, or, How to Make Out on Scarce Resources. In *Man the Hunter,* ed. R. B. Lee and I. De Vore. Chicago: Aldine.

Lévi-Strauss, Claude
1965 *Tristes Tropiques.* New York: Atheneum.

Liebow, Elliot
1968 *Tally's Corner.* Boston: Little, Brown.

Malinowski, Bronislaw
1961 *Argonauts of the Western Pacific.* New York: Dutton. Originally published 1922.
1967 *A Diary in the Strict Sense of the Term.* New York: Harcourt, Brace & World.

Maxwell, Robert J.
1970 A Comparison of Field Research in Canada and Polynesia. In *Marginal Natives,* ed. M. Freilich. New York: Harper & Row.

Maybury-Lewis, David
1965 *The Savage and the Innocent.* New York: World.

Mead, Margaret, and Ruth Bunzel
1960 *The Golden Age of American Anthropology.* New York: Braziller.

Meggitt, M. J.
1962 *Desert People.* Chicago: University of Chicago Press.

Middleton, John
1970 *The Study of the Lugbara: Expectation and Paradox in Anthropological Research.* New York: Holt, Rinehart & Winston.

Mitchell, J. Clyde
1967 On Quantification in Social Anthropology. In *The Craft of Social Anthropology,* ed. A. L. Epstein. London: Tavistock.

Nader, Laura

1964 An Analysis of Zapotec Law Cases. *Ethnology* 3:404-19.
1970 From Anguish to Exaltation. In *Women in the Field,* ed. P. Golde. Chicago: Aldine.

Nash, Dennison
1963 The Ethnologist as Stranger: An Essay in the Sociology of Knowledge. *Southwestern Journal of Anthropology* 19:149-67.
1970 *A Community in Limbo.* Bloomington: Indiana University Press.

Norbeck, Edward
1970 Changing Japan: Field Research. In *Being an Anthropologist,* ed. G. Spindler. New York: Holt, Rinehart & Winston.

Osgood, Cornelius
1940 *Ingalik Material Culture.* London: Oxford University Press.

Peattie, Lisa
1968 *The View from the Barrio.* Ann Arbor: University of Michigan Press.

Pelto, Gretel
1970 Life on the Upper Mississippi: Psychological and Social Adaptations in a Marginal Rural Region. Unpublished Ph. D. dissertation, University of Minnesota.

Perlman, Melvin
1970 Intensive Field Work and Scope Sampling: Methods for Studying the Same Problem at Different Levels. In *Marginal Natives,* ed. M. Freilich. New York: Harper & Row.

Pospisil, Leopold
1964 *Kapauku Papuans and Their Law.* New Haven: HRAF Press.

Powdermaker, Hortense
1966 *Stranger and Friend.* New York: Norton.

Redfield, Robert
1930 *Tepoztlán: A Mexican Village.* Chicago: University of Chicago Press.

Rivers, W. H. R.
1910 The Genealogical Method of Anthropological Inquiry. *Sociological Review* 3:1-12.

Robbins, Michael C., et al.
1969 Factor Analysis and Case Selection in Complex Societies. *Human Organization* 28:227-34.

Robbins, Michael C., and Philip L. Kilbride
1972 Microtechnology in Rural Baganda.

In *Technology and Social Change,* ed. H. R. Bernard and P. J. Pelto. New York: Macmillan.

Rodgers, William B., and John M. Long
1968 Male Models and Sexual Identification: A Case from the Out Island Bahamas. *Human Organization* 27: 326-31.

Rohner, Ronald, ed.
1969 *The Ethnography of Franz Boas.* Chicago: University of Chicago Press.

Sahlins, Marshall
1968 Notes on the Original Affluent Society. In *Man the Hunter,* ed. R. B. Lee and I. De Vore. Chicago: Aldine.

Schensul, Stephen L.
1969 Marginal Rural Peoples: Behavior and Cognitive Models Among Northern Minnesotans and Western Ugandans. Unpublished Ph.D. dissertation, University of Minnesota.
1970 Action Anthropology: Aspects of Applied Research in a Mexican Community in Chicago. Paper presented at the meeting of the Society for Applied Anthropology, Boulder, Col.

Schwab, William B.
1970 Comparative Field Techniques in Urban Research in Africa. In *Marginal Natives,* ed. M. Freilich. New York: Harper & Row.

Spindler, George, ed.
1970 *Being an Anthropologist.* New York: Holt, Rinehart & Winston

Spindler, George, and Louise Spindler
1970 Fieldwork Among the Menomini. In *Being an Anthropologist,* ed. G. Spindler. New York: Holt, Rinehart & Winston.

Stein, Maurice R.
1960 *The Eclipse of Community.* New York: Harper Torchbooks.

Stocking, George W.
1968 *Race, Culture, and Evolution.* New York: Free Press, Macmillan.

Suttles, Gerald D.
1968 *The Social Order of the Slum.* Chicago: Chicago University Press.

Turner, Victor
1967 Aspects of Saora Ritual and Shamanism: An Approach to the Data of Ritual. In *The Craft of Social Anthropology,* ed. A. L. Epstein. London: Tavistock.

Van Velsen, J.
1967 The Extended-Case Method and Situational Analysis. In *The Craft of Social Anthropology,* ed. A. L. Epstein. London: Tavistock.

West, James
1945 *Plainville, U.S.A.* New York: Columbia University Press.

Whitten, Norman
1970 Network Analysis and Processes of Adaptation Among Ecuadorian and Nova Scotian Negroes. In *Marginal Natives,* ed. M. Freilich. New York: Harper & Row.

Williams, Thomas R.
1967 *Field Methods in the Study of Culture.* New York: Holt, Rinehart & Winston.

Wintrob, Ronald M.
1969 An Inward Focus: A Consideration of Psychological Stress in Field Work. In *Stress and Response in Field Work,* ed. F. Henry and S. Saberwal. New York: Holt, Rinehart & Winston.

Wolf, Eric
1969 *Peasant Wars of the Twentieth Century.* New York: Harper & Row.

Yengoyan, Aram
1970 Open Networks and Native Formalism: The Mandaya and Pitjandjara Cases. In *Marginal Natives,* ed. M. Freilich. New York: Harper & Row.

Young, Frank, and Ernest Bury
1966 Farm Structure and Field Operations: An Aerial Photographic Study. *Rural Sociology* 31:320-32.

Genealogical Method in Social Anthropology: The Foundations of Structural Demography

ROBERT A. HACKENBERG

> ... There is a limited number of common
> human problems for which all peoples at all
> times must find some solution ... All variants
> of all solutions are in varying degrees present
> in all societies at all times [Kluckhohn
> 1963:221].

THE GALILEIAN PROBLEM IN SOCIAL ANTHROPOLOGY

Political Systems of Highland Burma (Leach 1954) ended an era in the theory and method of social anthropology. It is no longer possible to accept Pareto's assumption (Henderson 1936) that communities or societies are systems of institutions seeking stable equilibrium (Henry 1955, Easton 1956, Cadwallader 1959, Gouldner 1959) in an unchanging environment. Normative functionalism, which provided the rationalization for stability, is likewise being discarded (Merton 1957, Dahrendorf 1958, Hempel 1959, Moore 1960, Nagel 1961, Deutsch 1963, Firth 1964), and along with it presumptions of interdependence and integration, which comprise the intellectual heritage of Benedict, Kroeber, and Linton, as well as of Malinowski and Radcliffe-Brown.

Evolution is beginning to replace involution as the central process in anthropological theory once more, but fortunately it bears none of the polemical attributes by which in was characterized in the nineteenth century. Evolution today refers to the partially integrated and continuously changing configurations of interacting social, psychological, physiological, and environmental variables that join with cultural elements to form the "open system" of the modern community (Cassel, Patrick, and Jenkins 1960; Vogt 1960).

Gouldner (1959) has convinced us that a community consisting of institutions that are totally interdependent is totally vulnerable. The community's capacity to adapt responsively to environmental change and external threat resides in the partial autonomy of its parts—that is, groups. If old values are only partially maintained and old groupings only partially interconnected, the community's capacity to transform itself adaptively is not impaired. The community's evolutionary potential resides in its *variability*, then, and not in its *conformity*.

Instead of assuming that a community represents a self-maintaining set of interconnected components, anthropologists now see *maintenance* and *connectedness* as central problems for investigation. As Lewin (1936) observed about psychology, Leach has shifted anthropology from a timeless Aristotelian world, in which our concern was with classes of events (cultures), to a confrontation with a restless Galileian world, whose primary feature is change and in which our concern must be with variables and relationships.

The community today presents to us a "society of trends" (Meadows 1957) undergoing alteration at unequal rates. The methodological implication is clear: our research must be diachronic instead of synchronic, though we admit that cross-sectional studies were adequate for the Paretian models featuring restorative equilibrium, as Leach (1954:4-10) affirms. But methods focused upon variation require data collected on something other than the nominal scale of observation, which reports presence or absence of behavior only (Coombs 1953:473-74). To record variation, either at one point or through time, the ordinal and interval scales of observation must be utilized (Coombs 1953:474-83). And to inquire into the ways in which the community maintains, connects, and transforms itself, time-series observations appear to be obligatory.

The years since publication of *Political Systems* have not stimulated a new era of anthropological research based on the alternative assumptions about the social order which are now generally accepted. Measurement procedures, previously thought to be nonessential, have been slow to develop. Models to incorporate the measures, once collected, have been even less prodigal. While Leach (1961a) has pointed the way by writing, in *Pul Eliya*, a monograph in the probabilistic mode, it has fallen short of the goals specified in his programmatic statements (Leach 1961b).

The confrontation with change presents the research anthropologist with a host of problems. Some, such as the representativeness of the unit measured, the size of the unit to be observed, and attrition in the unit of study through time, have been treated elsewhere (Goldfarb 1960; Duncan, Cuzzort, and Duncan 1961; Hackenberg 1967; Colson 1967). Others are more properly artifacts of the situation within which the anthropologist conducts his research than issues of general methodology.

COLLECTION OF TIME-SERIES DATA

Time-series data may be collected in one of three ways: (1) *prospectively,* by initiating a baseline or benchmark study, and then keeping the unit of study under continuous surveillance for a suitable interval; (2) *retrospectively,* by reconstructing past events in sufficient depth and individual detail to gain temporal perspective on the present; (3) *cross-sectionally,* by various techniques (such as cohort analysis) for converting older and younger members of a population, described at one point in time, into a sequence of classes.[1]

[1] The conceptual distinction between the second and third procedures is not complete. Treating age-

From the standpoint of reliability and validity, these procedures are given in descending order, from the most to the least desirable.

Extracting processual insights from cross-sectional data is a perilous procedure, and serious constraints restrict the applicability of the alternatives. Prospective data must be compiled for a period of years, and items pertaining to individuals in the study population must be linked across the entire interval—at least a generation for most types of inquiry. The cost, logistics, and continuity of administration of such an effort, combined with problems of data linkage and processing, present formidable obstacles to individual investigators, although institutional research of this sort has been initiated (Hackenberg 1970).

Efforts at retrospectively based studies of change have most frequently employed historical documents to recapture the past (Smelser 1959, Glass and Eversley 1965, Anderson 1971). When information on individuals over time or quantitative data are sought, the retrospective inquiry has usually

been confined to census books, church records, vital statistics, and government reports. This observation is tinged with irony for most anthropologists, since gathering suitable information "in a non-western setting almost seems to require the institutional structure associated with the elimination of the subject to be studied" (Hackenberg 1966:471-72). If these historical record systems were adequate and accurate, the group they described would already have completed its modernization experience, and its usefulness for understanding the most critical features of recent evolution would be lost.

The dimensions of the methodological problem confronting us, after the abandonment of stable equilibrium models, now stand in sharper outline, and perhaps the uncertainty and self-examination so characteristic of recent anthropological discussion can be better appreciated. But there are solutions at hand—and uniquely anthropological ones, at that. Neglected elements of the genealogical method, as first described by Rivers (1900, 1906, 1910) and recently revised by others (Romney n.d., Conklin 1964, Barnes 1967, Hackenberg 1967), offer one promising solution. Curiously, Rivers anticipated three-quarters of a century ago the methodological dilemma we have just begun to experience today: *the need to establish intracultural and intercultural variation along dimensions common to all persons at all points in time which are independent of the beliefs of the participants.*

But it was Leach, after placing us in this dilemma, who advised that "rethinking" was the proper way out of it. We shall follow his advice and devote the remainder of this essay to rethinking one aspect of Rivers' genealogical procedure: its potential for constructing a description that incorporates retrospective enumeration and establishes

---

specific events within the same population as though they had time-series implications is a retrospective method of sorts, because events occurring to older members of the population are retrieved from memory. This procedure is biased by survivorship, since the information from various cohorts is usually obtained by cross-sectional census interview at one point in time. Also, the span of time bracketed for analysis is limited to decades intervening between the youngest adults participating in a critical experience (such as marriage) and the oldest adults who are not significantly depleted by death. In practice, this may mean comparison across no more than twenty years (the group aged twenty to twenty-four with the group aged forty to forty-four, for example) in a premodern population. The argument to be presented here is that the enumerative genealogical method, which is purely retrospective and not restricted to census counts, can compensate for survivorship and introduce much greater time depth into the analysis. The cohort method (Ryder 1965*a*) can be utilized *either* prospectively, retrospectively, or cross-sectionally with good results.

the baseline for prospective quantitative studies. Its utility for research will be illustrated from various studies of recent writers.

FUNDAMENTALS OF GENEALOGICAL METHOD

INTRODUCING STRUCTURAL DEMOGRAPHY

Variation in the social behavior of a human population is manifested quantitatively in proportions, rates, and trends. These may be subjected to measurement through two quite different techniques: *net change* and *turnover* studies (Goldfarb 1960). The study of net change may be exemplified by intercensal comparison (or by the comparison of any two cross-sectional measurements of characteristics in the same community at two points in time). By superimposing the proportions of those employed, of those married, of the educated, of the young and old at T_2 on those of T_1, we may infer trends. But the characteristics are those of the community, and not of the individuals it contains. There is no basis for presuming that the bearers of attributes described at T_2 are either the same as or the descendants of the bearers of attributes at T_1.

Turnover studies, on the other hand, follow the fates of specific individuals over time, recording their entry into and exit from the community as well as changes in the status of those who remain. In addition to collecting data on emigration and immigration, turnover studies report alterations in family size, marital status, household composition, employment and income, property ownership, and group membership. They yield records of the demographic and social mobility of identified individuals.

As Bogue (1952) points out, a number of questions pertaining to social

dynamics can be answered only by turnover research: (1) Which persons *initiate* change? (2) Which persons *participate* in change? (3) What is the rate of change at its greatest intensity, and when and where is this peak attained? (4) Is a change achieved by a single type of behavior or by a great variety of alterations that contribute to a net result?

These considerations suggest an obvious but not a trivial conclusion: frequency distributions that link individuals, attributes, and events are the essential data for the description and analysis of social variation, and therefore of all models based on assumptions other than those of stable equilibria. Construction of such distributions requires the investigator to compile and analyze information obtained from *each member* of the community or society—whichever has been established as the unit to which conclusions will be generalized.

Formulations from these data, according to Lévi-Strauss (1963:292-93, 295), may be used to create a kind of *structural demography*—a model constructed from elements of social continuity and discontinuity which, when placed in a temporal configuration, define evolution:[2]

---

[2] The vexed question of mechanical versus statistical models, which relates to the ideal versus actual behavior controversy, does not need to intrude into Lévi-Strauss's formulation of evolutionary analysis. Cultural norms and ideals—especially those pertaining to marriage, descent, inheritance, and property rights—are instruments utilized by each member of the group, who deals with them manipulatively to further his individual goals, which may or may not be those of the culture. A mechanical model of norms and ideals could be constructed, and if it were it would define a mythical St. Francis of Assisi or the George Washington of our childhood "history" books. Once we realize that *normative statements can be used to validate either the observance of a rule or the violation of it* (as in claiming that a murder was actually self-defense, or that a theft was really collection of a debt), the issue is clarified. The

Another approach which may lead more directly to a mathematical expression of social phenomena starts with the numerical properties of human groups. . . . It is only recently that a few scholars . . . have begun to elaborate a kind of qualitative demography, that is, dealing . . . with significant discontinuities evidenced in the behavior of groups considered as wholes and chosen on the basis of these discontinuities. This "sociodemography" . . . is "on a level" with social anthropology, and it is not difficult to foresee that in the very near future it will be called upon to provide firm grounds for any kind of anthropological research. . . . There is an obvious relation between the functioning and even the durability of the social structure and the actual size of the population. . . . These should be the first to be assessed and taken into account in an interpretation of other properties.

Next come numerical properties expressing, not the group size taken globally, but the size and interaction of subsets of the group which can be defined by significant discontinuities. . . .

It seems that both the reality and the autonomy of the concept of culture could better be validated if culture were treated, from an operational point of view, in the same way as the geneticist and demographer treat the closely allied concept of "isolate." What is called a "culture" is a fragment of humanity which, from the point of view of the research at hand . . . presents significant discontinuities in relation to the rest of humanity. . . . Accordingly, the same set of individuals may be considered to be parts of many different cultural contexts: universal, continental, national, regional, local, etc., as well as familial, occupational, religious, political, etc. This is true as a limit; however, anthropologists usually reserve the term "culture" to designate a

_____

role of mechanical models is to *legitimize,* and appear to make *socially relevant,* behavior performed for *personal goals.* Consequently, statistical models alone can describe behavior. This argument has been extended and clarified by two little-known works on social motivation (Gerth and Mills 1953:112-25; Devereaux 1961:227-42), and paves the way for consideration of sociopsychological models of evolutionary dynamics such as Wallace (1970) has introduced through his concept of equivalence structures.

group of discontinuities which is significant on several of these levels at the same time. That it can never be valid for all levels does not prevent the concept of "culture" from being as fundamental for the anthropologist as that of "isolate" for the demographer.

Discovery procedures for delimiting a unit of culture "from an operational point of view," according to Lévi-Strauss (1963:296) include the location of boundaries to the circulation and exchange of (1) marriage partners, (2) goods and services, and (3) messages. While the thresholds at which "the rates and forms of communication, without waning altogether, reach a much lower level" may not be congruent for each of these three, the *degree* of congruence is an indicator of the nature of maintenance and connectedness within the unit under study.

INTRODUCING GENEALOGICAL METHOD

W. H. R. Rivers (1900, 1906, 1910) is entitled to recognition as anthropology's first structural demographer. As a member of the Cambridge Torres Straits Expedition, and later among the Toda, Rivers (1906) confronted the problems of describing composition and variation, conformity and deviance, persistence and change in an undefined social unit. He solved these problems this way:

1. The unit of relevance to social analysis of the Toda was defined as the universe within which all marriages contracted by members of the tribe took place (p. 508).

2. Dimensions of composition and variation were measured in terms of marriage choices, clan membership, age, sex, fertility, divorce, residence, property ownership, and ceremonial participation (pp. 504-509).

3. Dimensions of conformity and deviance were measured by describing kin terms, behavioral expectations among

relatives, and preferential and proscribed marriages. The frequency with which preferred marriages took place was then measured, together with the occurrence of forbidden intraclan, outgroup, and incestuous marriages (p. 512).

4. Dimensions of persistence and change were measured by contrasting customs of ancestors with those of descendants in regard to polyandry, infanticide, and ceremonial practices. Ancestral data were obtained in connection with genealogical inquiry, and completed through four ascending generations among the Toda (pp. 461-62).

Rivers was aware that fieldwork presented a problem of conceptual translation. His interest was in issues that could not be expressed in direct interrogation (1910:9):

The genealogical method makes it possible to investigate abstract problems on a purely concrete basis. It is even possible by its means to formulate laws regulating the lives of people which they have probably never formulated themselves. . . . Endless misunderstandings are avoided . . . which have their source in differences of outlook and in the lack of appreciation on one side or the other of the niceties of the language, whether European or native, which is serving as the means of communication.

Those who have not employed the method as Rivers intended may have a distorted view of its operational content. For example, a recent text (Bock 1969:323) advises, "Extensive genealogies are collected from several reliable informants, and supplemented by interviews with others." On the contrary, Rivers' procedure consists of the exhaustive recording of the pedigrees of all adult members of the community or tribe, together with their remote ancestors, descendants, affines, and collaterals, to the limit of the memory of

each. By interrogation of the individual members of each relationship set, overlapping networks of carefully identified individuals are constructed throughout the tribe or community. When redundancy is removed, the composition of all these networks equals the total population, including both living and recent dead, immigrants and emigrants. While much of the information contributed by each informant duplicates that secured from others, an essential methodological purpose is served by repetition: it builds reliability into the procedure. Since there is usually no external criterion for evaluating genealogical networks, redundancy is essential.

The genealogical interviews, conducted initially for the purpose of identifying and locating all members of the population within a common network of relationships, were expanded to include other material (Rivers 1910:2-3):

A most important feature of the method is to record as far as possible the social condition of each person recorded in the pedigrees. The locality to which each person belongs should be obtained. . . . If the people have a totemic organization the names of the totem or totems of each person should be recorded, or if there are non-totemic clans or other social divisions, these should be taken in the same way. . . . Especial care should be taken to record the localities of those who have married into the community from other tribes and places. If adoption exists . . . both real and adoptive parents should be recorded.

Among the Toda, Rivers (1906) also obtained years of birth and death and records of property ownership.

From the genealogies, Rivers (1910: 8) extracted quantitative descriptions concerning

the proportions of the sexes, the size of the family, the sex of the first-born child, the proportion of children who grow up and marry to the total number born, and other similar subjects which can be studied statistically by the genealogical method. We have in the pedigrees a large mass of data of the utmost value for the exact study of various demographic problems. . . .

One of the demographic problems that was of interest to Rivers, and which is critically important to the study of community microevolution, is migration (Rivers 1910:7):

Another line of application which is occasionally of great value is in the study of migrations. Thus in many parts of Melanesia there has taken place during the last fifty years a change from life in the bush to life on the sea-coast, and the information given by the localities of successive generations may throw much light on the nature of such migration.

Moving from biosocial to cultural issues, Rivers saw his procedure as an inductive device for constructing generalizations concerning systems of relationship independent of the beliefs of the participants. So he inquired further into kinship terminology (1910:3-4):

My procedure is to ask my informant the terms which he would apply to the different members of his pedigree, and reciprocally the terms which they would apply to him. . . . It is . . . only exceptionally that a complete set of terms of relationship can be obtained from a single pedigree, and even if this were possible it is not advisable to do so, for there is always the chance of some double relationship . . . which may mislead, and I am never wholly content with a kinship system unless each of the relationships has been obtained from three separate pedigrees.

His next interest was in the regulation of marriage, for which the kinship data were combined with that identifying marriage partners (1910:6):

If the pedigrees of the whole of the population have been collected as I have been able to do in several cases, we have in them a register of the marriages which have taken place in the community, reaching back perhaps for 150 years. . . . We can see not only what marriages have been allowed or enjoined and what marriages have been prohibited, but we can express statistically the frequency of different kinds. . . . Furthermore, the method enables us to determine how far the marriage regulations of a people are being actually followed in practise, and a study of the marriages in successive generations may reveal a progressive change in the strictness with which any given regulation has been observed.

Furthermore, descent and inheritance could be investigated with the same data base (Rivers 1910:7):

. . . In the sample pedigree . . . each person belongs to the clan of his mother . . . illustrating the matrilineal descent of this part of the Solomon Islands. The mode of succession of chiefs can be exactly studied in the same manner, while the method is especially important in studying the inheritance of property. Thus it is possible to take a given piece of land and inquire into its history . . . from the time it was first cultivated.

One other point on which Rivers was quite specific was the incorporation of time perspective into genealogical inquiry (1910:11). He considered its importance to be "sufficient to make its use essential even if there were no others."

It is almost impossible at the present time to find a people whose culture, beliefs and practises are not suffering from the effects of European influence . . . which has been especially active during the last fifty years. To my mind the greatest merit of the genealogical method is that it often takes us back to a time before this influence had reached the people. It may give us records of marriage and descent and other features of social organization 150 years ago, while events a century old may be obtained in abundance in all the communities with whom I have myself worked. . . . Further, the course of the pedigrees is itself sometimes sufficient to demonstrate the gradual effect of the new influences which have affected the people.

While the time depth for which he claims reliability of recall is no doubt excessive, his emphasis on the utility of genealogical inquiry as a tool for retrospective study is not.

Rivers was clearly aware that there are both qualitative and quantitative aspects of genealogical reporting. The qualitative element is *semantic:* the meanings of kin terms and behaviors appropriate among relatives (as in ceremonial and ritual exchanges, of which he gives several examples). The quantitative element is in part *demographic,* in the broad sense in which Lévi-Strauss (and French sociologists such as Mauss and Halbwachs) employs the term: with reference to the biosocial events of birth, death, residence, and migration, and also to the proportions of occupants of various status positions and their combinations into groupings of greater or lesser exclusiveness, which are sociocultural elements.[3]

In Rivers' usage, as well as in his presentation, the semantic and demographic aspects of genealogical method are seen to be inseparable, even though the procedure used for inquiry into terminology is much less comprehensive than that used to delimit the population and compile individualized attributes. While systems of kin terms could be established by interrogating three reliable informants on the proper definition of each term, other matters required interrogation of all members of the population. In the next several decades, the interdependence of the semantic and demographic parts of the

method was destroyed, and this fact may explain the light regard in which the method is held by many social anthropologists today. This issue will be given greater consideration in the following section.

RECENT ISSUES IN GENEALOGICAL METHOD

While the recent elaboration of methodology for elicitation and semantic classification of kin terms greatly exceeds the development of the demographic component, the latter has not been neglected. The research worker interested in using genealogical procedures will find guidance in several sources. After a concise description of genealogical recording techniques, *Notes and Queries* (Committee of the Royal Anthropological Institute 1960: 79-88) follows with "the application of the genealogical method to the study of kinship systems," emphasizing the behavior appropriate to each set of reciprocal terms. It advises particular attention to joking relationships, avoidance, respect relationships, and patterns of duty and privilege. A parallel statement on recording techniques has been published by Barnes (1967).

Technical Aids in Genealogy Construction

A genealogy, unlike a survey, is a *contextual document.* Since each person it contains, even a stillborn child, is embedded in a kinship matrix, the information obtained on the individual is the product of *coordinated multiple reports* (Rivers 1910:3):

---

[3] This is reminiscent of the discussion by Wilson and Wilson (1949) concerning the quantitative aspects of *social categories* (occupants of statuses or bearers of specific skills or attributes) as opposed to quantitative aspects of *social groups*; e.g., tailors are a social category, but the International Ladies Garment Workers Union is a social group. This distinction is also similar to that made by Levy (1952) between analytical and concrete social units.

In collecting the pedigrees of a whole community there will be much overlapping; people who belong to the paternal stock of one informant will come in the maternal stock of another, and in the wife's ancestry of a third, and there will thus be ample opportunity of testing the agreement of the accounts of different informants.

Since references to kinship networks are employed as an orientation and identification device by non-Western peoples everywhere, and since the procedure requires nothing more than recognition of the biological facts of birth and death and the social facts of paternity and maternity, "one really can collect a genealogy from any people . . . and expand that genealogy as far as the informant's memory will carry him" (Schneider 1968:13-14). Hence the universality of kin-based networks as a context for individual identification and placement may be assumed. Claims made for the versatility of the method are premised on this assumption.

Because of the presence of coordinated multiple reports, one of the most forbidding problems confronting the investigator has been the processing of the accumulated mass of materials. A system of algebraic notation for consolidating data has been developed by Romney (n.d.), and a more recent unpublished method has been devised by Collier (n.d.). Another computer program for linking genealogically connected members of populations of up to six hundred persons was also developed by Coult and Randolph (1965). Hackenberg's (1967) numerical indexing system provides another approach to establishing a computerized data bank for statistical analysis of genealogically ordered data. It is now employed for storage, access, and retrieval of individualized data on the Papago tribe, currently including more than 24,000 persons.

A number of computerized edit procedures are customarily employed to improve the quality of the contents of large population data banks. These may utilize comparison of different reports on the same person, retrieving all disagreements for field verification or logic testing. They may also utilize logic checks that identify two types of errors: (1) attributes that fall outside predetermined parameters (births prior to a base year; ages greater than 100; incomes higher than maximum reportable; grain yields beneath subsistence level, etc.) and (2) attributes apparently contradictory to others reported for the same person (births to women below fifteen or above forty-five years of age, male "housewives" or females in "male" occupations, professionals lacking educational qualifications, etc.).

To some extent, then, genealogical demographic inquiry is self-correcting and relatively culture-free. Its accuracy may be improved upon, however, when information obtained during the course of genealogical construction may be measured against a population-wide and external criterion that does not depend solely upon the memory of any informant. In the Papago study, for example, all houses either occupied or abandoned, located within territory historically utilized by ancestors of the Papago tribe, were identified through a presurvey. Through preliminary interrogation, the builder of each house was identified and his name entered on a founder's list. Each founder served as a reference point for genealogical construction (Hackenberg 1961:16-18; 1967:490n), and the entire population, operationally defined, consisted of the universe of descendants of these founders, regardless of present residence.

The importance of external reference points as controls in genealogical fieldwork cannot be overestimated. Parallel use of lists of landownership (in Chiapas) and terrace construction (in Ifugao) has been reported by Vogt (1969) and Conklin (1967). In all three cases—Papago, Mayan, and Ifugao—cultural features that could be linked with individuals (houses, fields, terraces) were described with the assistance of aerial photography. (The use of aerial photography as an ethnographic technique is more fully described in a forthcoming volume [Vogt, in press]). Since knowledge of the local terrain is significant information possessed by hunters, gardeners, and agricultural peasants alike, it represents a vast unexploited resource for genealogical inquiry.

Demographic Dimensions of Genealogical Method

Minimally, both anthropologist and demographer are involved in the precise description of age, sex, birth, death, and migration. Where the demographer has relied upon the household census and registration of vital statistics to provide insights, the anthropologist has coordinated three procedures. These are exemplified in Firth's original investigation of Tikopia, which attempted a "superimposition of the genealogical record of the community upon a residential plan of it" (1957:56) together with a household census (the "alimentary approach") of the total population (1957:107-108). On the issue of the household census, the interests of the genealogical anthropologist and the demographer converge.

Since it is a prominent aspect of the unique identification of the individual and the demographic description of the community, the problem of age determination in field studies deserves special consideration. The reckoning of age in years presumes calendrical knowledge and arithmetic skills beyond those possessed by most of the non-Western world. Christian missionary emphasis upon baptism and marriage tends to reinforce consciousness of these events, and also initiates record-keeping among client populations, which may include death registers as well. But even where such records are present, immigration and emigration detract from their completeness, and many artifacts of record-keeping detract from their accuracy.[4]

Age determination in non-Western parts of the world is largely a matter of estimation. F. G. Rose (1960, 1968) developed procedures that incorporated a self-correcting mechanism for his work among the Australian aborigines of Groote Eylandt. Roberts (1956) used dentition to estimate Dinka ages. This method is described with references in Weiner and Lourie (1969:17-23). Powdermaker (1931) defined generation intervals for age placement within lineages. Fortes (1954:271-73) was one of many investigators to employ an event calendar (reproduced as Appendix B, pp. 338-39, of his report). Fortes also devised a maturation scale for dating the births of children of less than one year, a technique that might merit more general use.[5]

Event calendars for determining relative ages may be based upon historical-political events (terms of office of local politicians can be even more useful than wars, revolts, and other more dramatic occurrences), but natural phenomena are often more useful among preliterates: earthquakes, volcanic eruptions, floods, typhoons, tidal waves, eclipses, meteoric showers. An arrangement of these phenomena in a dated sequence provides a frame of reference for locating individual births and deaths. Birth order and birth interval

---

[4] June Helm's (1968:216-17) discovery of a century of mission records (1860-1956) for the Hare Indians of western Canada, a population of approximately three hundred, suggests that more data of an acceptable degree of precision may exist than is usually admitted. Since these data have been analyzed only for consanguineal marriages, however, their utility for age determination is unproven.

[5] Firth (1957) utilized a crude classificatory scheme based on historical events to estimate Tikopian ages during his 1929 field trip. For the potentials and limitations of this procedure when the data are analyzed by a professional demographer, see Borrie, Firth, and Spillius (1957).

are valuable tools for interpolating dates of vital events falling between the years defined by the event calendar. Further assistance is provided by the United Nations' (1967) manual of estimating techniques.

In some respects, the collection of genealogies could be improved through the use of pregnancy rosters (Bogue and Bogue 1970), which must also cope with problems of age determination and the reporting of infant deaths. These instruments for obtaining reproductive histories employ interview formats that best protect against omissions and falsifications by the informant, and it would be wise to consult them in preparing for all genealogical inquiries intended for use in reporting population statistics. A typical pregnancy roster, now widely adapted for local use, is that of the International Union for the Scientific Study of Population (IUSSP), which appears in the family planning survey manual of the Population Council (1970).

Further technical assistance from demographers is available in the form of the "Brass technique"—a device for verifying the results of fertility data obtained by survey methods, pregnancy rosters, or genealogical construction. In a population of determined age, the procedure requires only two information items: number of children (living and dead) ever born to each woman, and all children born to each woman during the previous year. The rationale has been concisely stated by Brass and Coale (1968:90):

The two types of measure can be used to detect and allow for errors in the data because of the logical relationship between them. As a cohort of women moves through life the mean number of children ever born at each exact age equals the cumulative total of age-specific fertility rates to that age, if it can be assumed that the women dying have the same fertility as those surviving. If the fertility of the population is constant, the age-specific rates of each cohort will be the same as the "current" ones and the relationship will hold for all ages of women. These theoretical results will apply approximately to the actual population if fertility rates have not been subject to a marked trend. The mean number of children ever born per woman at each age calculated from the current data can be compared with the corresponding retrospective data. If the two sets of indices agree at every age the evidence for accuracy is strong.

Brass has developed mathematical correctives to compensate for two types of error appearing in both genealogies and fertility surveys: (1) in reporting births during the previous year, errors usually involve the duration of the reference period; (2) in reporting children ever born, errors usually involve omission of births by older women.

Death reporting is more often neglected by anthropologists than fertility data. Where vital registration has been long established, as in Guatemala, mortality data may be analyzed (Early 1970a, 1970b) and relationships between mortality and fertility established (Hinshaw, Pyeatt, and Habicht 1972; Barnett, Jackson, and Cann 1971). While mortality reports and causes of death (especially infant mortality) are very significant social indicators (Hauser 1959, Stockwell 1960), the field studies conducted by anthropologists seldom last long enough to provide a meaningful series of observations on a prospective basis. Retrospective death reporting through genealogical inquiry needs further testing in the field.

There is a parallel Brass technique for estimating mortality among children and infants (Brass and Coale 1968). It is based upon comparison between current mortality (deaths taking place during the year preceding the survey) and cumulative mortality (all deaths occurring among children ever born). The assumption is that age-specific current mortality should sum to a figure approximately equal to the cumulative rate. However, because of the under-reporting of deaths of infants and young children, substantial mathematical correction is required.

Brass and Coale (1968) also briefly discuss the use of regional life tables and stable population models developed earlier by Coale and Demeny (1966) to improve estimates of births and deaths based on incomplete data. The discussion is somewhat technical, however, and there is disagreement among anthropologists concerning applicability (Early 1970a:176-77). For additional discussion of the Brass technique, see Brass (1953, 1954, 1960) and Brass and Coale (1968). Use of life tables is also described in the United Nations' Manual 4 (1967).

Migration is the neglected variable in both demographic and anthropological research. Population studies frequently assume that a community may be considered "closed" (characterized by neither emigration nor immigration). But anthropologists who make this assumption bias their research by neglecting one of the most sensitive indices of adaptation. The movement of peoples characterizes urbanization, assimilation, territorial expansion, environmental deterioration, colonization, and many other vital evolutionary processes.

Studies of migration by anthropologists have not been numerous (Lowenthal and Comitas 1962, Khuri 1967, Kunstadter 1970, Hackenberg and Wilson 1972), nor have conceptual developments been very abundant (E. S. Lee 1966, Hackenberg 1971). Since gross trends in population redistribution are readily abstracted from intergenerational data on residence contained in genealogies, this method is well suited for the study of migration.

Many of the issues in the preceding pages have already been confronted in a series of studies completed under the most adverse conditions by the geneticist James V. Neel and his associates among the Xavante and Yanomamö tribes of the Brazilian Mato Grosso. The Yanomamö ethnography recently published by Chagnon (1968), based on genealogical inquiry, was one component of the research program. The impressiveness of the results derive both from the extreme primitiveness of the human subjects and from the internal consistency of the multidimensional data accumulated (sociological, physiological, genetic, and demographic). Among the corpus of publications, several papers contain demographic materials (Neel, Salzano, et al. 1964; Salzano, Neel, and Maybury-Lewis 1967; Neel and Chagnon 1968). Interpretations of the program and a bibliography of earlier work are contained in Neel and Salzano (1967).

Quality of Genealogical Data

Recent efforts by demographers to acquire fertility and mortality data by retrospective inquiry through survey methods have shed some doubt on the utility of genealogical inquiry for this purpose. Mauldin (1966:652) concludes a recent review with the ominous judgment: "Single retrospective surveys cannot be depended upon to provide valid or reliable estimates of births and deaths." There is growing reluctance to accept the results of survey inquiry if the data cannot be validated by an external criterion.

The genealogical researcher must admit that his technique is subject to certain biases, most of which were known to Rivers (1906:468-70):

Of course in so large a mass of material there are mistakes. . . . A man would often know all about the members of a given family in the past, but, living perhaps at some distance from the family in question, he was often hazy as to the exact number and names of the children recently born, and it is the record of children under five years of age which I know to be deficient. . . .

Like all people at a low stage of culture, the Todas are very uncertain about their ages. . . . Every Toda knows, however, whether he is older or younger than another, this fact determining the names and salutations which they give each other. . . . With a knowledge of the relative ages of different members of the community, it became possible to arrive at estimates which probably do not deviate very widely from the correct ages. . . .

A specific reference to the problem identified by Mauldin appears in Rivers (1900:76):

There would be occasional discrepancies in such details as the exact order of birth of several children, the omission of a child who died young, and rarely the omission of a childless marriage, but on the whole the agreement between different accounts was extraordinarily close.

In Rivers' defense, his own comment should be reported (1906:468):

There is . . . a deficiency entirely due to my own carelessness. . . . In my absorption in the records of the past, I have often neglected the present and have omitted to ascertain carefully the children of families at present in process of growth. . . . I had one excuse for this in . . . that I had to obtain my information about a given family from people of some other family.

Unlike more recent ethnographers who have employed the genealogical method, such as Firth (1957) and Goodenough (1951), Rivers was limited to field trips of very short duration, and his genealogies were frequently constructed at a distance from the community in which the subjects resided.

Genealogical records for demograph-ic uses may suffer from three problems, quite familiar to those acquainted with vital registration or with population registers (Wolfenden 1954: 60-67): overenumeration, underenumeration, and false enumeration. Underenumeration, the problem with which Rivers was concerned, results from insufficient attention to recent births, to persons absent from the community, to infant deaths, and to children of divorced spouses. Because of high mortality during the first year of life, infant deaths present a particularly difficult problem in maintaining the accuracy of a genealogical record.

Overenumeration results from failure to remove decedents from the record. Accurate death reporting is probably inversely proportional to the distance between the informant and the persons described. False enumeration is the result of the "alias problem," which was reported first from the Torres Straits (Rivers 1900:77), and by every subsequent investigator. Name changing and the use of nicknames, together with frequent alternate names, are prevalent throughout the world (Collier and Bricker 1970). One may advocate coordination of multiple reports as a field technique that ensures reliability, but if the same individuals are constantly being reported under various names by different informants, the technique may ensure chaos instead.

These observations lead to a conclusion that might seem trivial without them. The unique identification of each member of the population is a basic problem of the genealogical demographer. It can be solved only by the description of each individual through a set of invariant attributes other than name: "The lifetime fixity of kinship position, place of origin, sex, year of birth and birth order . . . tends to overcome overenumeration and false enumeration . . . through misidentification based upon names" (Hackenberg 1964a:6). When subsequent information sources are to be used to update the genealogical record, it has been demonstrated by Newcombe (Newcombe et al. 1959, Newcombe and Rhynas 1962) that computer matching on the basis of attributes is a more efficient linkage procedure than reliance upon names (Hackenberg 1966:480-83).

One final caution may be distilled from the cumulative experience of a number of fieldworkers: only the foolhardy would consider that different cultural interpretations of kinship would produce identical genealogical capabilities. Just as some individuals possess more genealogical information than others, some cultures permit and stimulate greater depth and precision in the recall of kinsmen than others.

Evans-Pritchard (1940:199) found that Nuer clans claim knowledge of ten to twelve generations, but recall of actual ancestral names is uncertain for more than five or six. Fortune (1932: 30-31) asserted that Dobuans were unable to reproduce more than several generations with accuracy. Firth (1957) reported genealogical plates from Tikopia with twelve or more generations of named lineage members, however. Bohannan (1952) has reported falsification of genealogies among the Tiv for the purpose of legitimizing recent political alliances by a semblance of linkage with the past. While this practice is not infrequently reported, it is usually confined to the mythological level, at a point in time too remote for reference to actual ancestors (Fortes 1953:27, 31).

These accounts confirm that the genealogical capability of any particular people must be treated as a variable. To account for the variance, Salisbury (1956) compared two New Guinea highland groups and concluded that genealogical depth was a function of ter-

ritorial stability. Among the Siane, with very short genealogies (three ascending generations), there is permanent residence and congruity between descent and residence groups. Among the Mbowomb, on the other hand, there are genealogies eight or nine generations in depth; this tribe is mobile and characterized by increasing population. Salisbury concludes that Siane territorial divisions, to which descent groups attach themselves, provide a geographical image of social organization, making precise genealogical reckoning superfluous. But since the Mbowomb have no land-based stability, they maintain instead a genealogical image of social organization identifying subdivisions with genealogical segments. This interpretation, of course, suggests the kinship-versus-territory distinction advanced by Maine a century ago in *Village Communities of East and West.*

In addition to recent genealogical technique, the anthropologist wishing to qualify as a structural demographer should avail himself of all the demographic lore that he can master to improve the quality of his information. As a genealogist, however, he has additional control over the field situation. Demographic survey procedures never use the overlap among kin groups as a verification technique. Other things being equal, then, the genealogical method that incorporates demographic survey instruments should be superior to the use of those instruments alone.

One can only suggest that the coordinated mapping, census interview, and genealogical techniques of the social anthropologist might compensate for the lack of the bureaucratic social structures upon which academic demography appears to depend. If the suggestion proves unwarranted, much of the world may remain *terra incognita* until it has been transformed from tropical rain forest to asphalt jungle.

HISTORICAL DEVELOPMENT OF THE GENEALOGICAL METHOD

In Rivers' thinking, the semantic and demographic components of genealogical procedure were inseparable: the former provided the definition of significant units of organization and the latter gave their proportionate distribution. A contemporary example of their complementarity is Goodenough's (1956) investigation of Trukese residence rules, which would have been impossible without both classes of data. Since the separation of the two components is unquestionable, and no explanation appears in the literature, an examination of the fate of genealogical method in the decades since Rivers' publications may be illuminating.

MALINOWSKI AND RADCLIFFE-BROWN

The bifurcation was initiated in the early part of the century by Malinowski and Radcliffe-Brown. The semantic emphasis was seized by Radcliffe-Brown, while Malinowski concerned himself with quantification. The methodological discontinuity appears in their basic volumes of ethnography on the Andaman Islanders and the people of the Trobriands. Radcliffe-Brown (1922:72) admits that "inexperience in the use of the genealogical method . . . made this branch of my investigation a failure," while Malinowski (1922: 14-15) observed:

... The genealogical census of every community, studied . . . in detail, extensive maps, plans and diagrams, illustrating ownership in garden land, hunting and fishing privileges, etc., serve as the more fundamental documents of ethnographic research.

A genealogy is nothing else but a synoptic chart of a number of connected relations of kinship. . . . As a document its value consists in that it gives a number of authenticated data, presented in their natural grouping. . . . This method could be called *the method of statistical documentation by concrete evidence.*

Examples of this ambitious field program may be seen in the work of Malinowski's students Firth (1957) and Powdermaker (1933), if not in his own.

The methodological distinction was captured in a statement of Kaberry's (1957:75):

... The difference in approach is nowhere more evident than in their ethnographic monographs. If, in Malinowski's, the people are always with us (and, some would say, too much with us), in Radcliffe-Brown's they are conspicuous by their absence; they are the invisible facts. One explanation lies not so much in Radcliffe-Brown's preoccupation with structure, but rather in the nature of the "effects" which he thought most significant. They are . . . the more remote effects upon the social cohesion and continuity. . . . Malinowski in his Trobriand monographs concentrated on the more immediate effects, the analysis of institutional interdependencies.

Radcliffe-Brown's later use of the semantic component of genealogical inquiry as a separate tool for research reflects his theoretical commitment to Durkheimian assumptions (Lowie 1937:221-29). Principal among these was the concept of society as a moral order worked out in behavioristic form (Leach 1961a:296-97). In fact, the cohesion of the society ("solidarity" in Radcliffe-Brown's terms) and its continuity depend on this (Radcliffe-Brown 1922:401):

For a culture to exist at all, and to continue to exist, it must conform to certain conditions. It must provide a mode of subsistence adequate to the environment and the existing density of population; it must provide for the continuance of the society by the proper care of children; it must provide means for maintaining the cohesion of the society. All these things involve the regulation of conduct in certain definite ways; they involve, that is, a certain system of moral customs.

This statement, from the conclusion of *The Andaman Islanders,* was illustrated by the ceremonials, myths, and legends that embodied the moral code of the Andamanese. Later, through the semantic genealogical method, Radcliffe-Brown located the essential constraints within the kinship system of the Kariera and its reciprocal sets of rights and duties in which each person was embedded at birth. Both examples point to Radcliffe-Brown's belief in a societal control mechanism represented by a set of logically integrated and consistent principals that both provided the norms and explained them.[6]

Radcliffe-Brown visited the Kariera of western Australia in 1910. While he inferred cross-cousin marriage in this tribe from genealogical evidence (Radcliffe-Brown 1913:156), he did not compile quantitative marriage preferences like Rivers (1906:504-509), asserting instead that "in nearly every case where such a marriage was possible it had taken place." We are left to wonder about the cases where such a marriage was *not* possible, since among the Toda (Rivers 1906:512), who also preferred cross-cousin marriage, only 11.8 percent of the marriages were "correct."[7]

The inference of principles of social organization from kin terms was initiated by Radcliffe-Brown (1913:157) in three assertions from the Kariera genealogies:

1. The relationship system of the Kariera tribe is not only a system of names or terms of address, but is pre-eminently a system of reciprocal rights and duties.
2. It is based on actual relations of consanguinity and affinity that can be traced by means of the genealogical knowledge preserved by the old men and women.
3. The recognition of relationships is so extended that everyone with whom an individual comes in contact in the ordinary course of social life is his relative.

The limiting case to which these principles might be applied would be a society in which *all* the essential rights and duties are implied by its kinship terminology.[8]

---

[6] Radcliffe-Brown is actually postulating a cultural level of ideational or symbolic behavior which is superimposed upon the institutions of society and gives meaning to them. Since the ideational propositions that control behavior also explain the relationship between the society and its environment, the argument is quite compelling. If only it did not require a Ptolemaic social universe, it would be convincing as well.

[7] Our curiosity about possible variation in Australian marriage choices is intensified by other statements in this account. While close conformity between norm and practice is asserted for the Kariera, they were apparently exceptional in this respect: "In many Australian tribes ... irregular marriages are ... permitted. ... I have obtained good evidence, by means of genealogies, that in a number of tribes of Western Australia, such irregular marriages took

place before the country was occupied by white men. In the Kariera tribe ... there is not a single instance of such a marriage taking place before 1860." Recent studies by Yengoyan (1968*a*, 1968*b*, 1970) establish the minimum population within which an Australian section system could operate effectively by providing appropriate mates for eligible males. His genealogical data show that, while the Pitjandjara today have over 80 percent conforming marriages (Yengoyan 1970:88-89), this high level of normative observance is made possible by recent population growth and infant mortality reduction. He concludes, "The working of any socio-ceremonial rules ... is a function of a viable population size as indicated by the Pitjandjara and Walbiri."

[8] In a later Australian publication, Radcliffe-Brown (1930:123) claimed that "the terminology of kinship has a real and very close correlation with the social organization. Secondly ... throughout Australia it is the actual genealogical individual relationships resulting from the family that are the significant thing and form the basis of the whole social structure." Again, in 1924, Radcliffe-Brown (1952:29) asserted that "the characteristic of most of those societies that we call primitive is that the conduct of individuals to one another is very largely regulated on the basis of kinship, this being brought about by the formation of fixed patterns of behavior for each recognized kind of kinship relation." In later papers he made it clear, however, that Australian society

Thus, to Radcliffe-Brown and his disciples (particularly Fortes and Evans-Pritchard), the kinship system became a model for the organization of the society (Leach 1961b:103-104). The genealogical method, as a semantic instrument to define kin terminologies and to elicit the behavioral norms appropriate to each pair of terms, gained popularity. Since this short form of inquiry obviated the need for enumerative induction, demographic uses of the genealogical method were quite rare during the 1920s and 1930s.

After periods of service in South Africa and Australia, Radcliffe-Brown arrived at the University of Chicago in 1931. Acceptance of his views by his students is signified in the memorial volume prepared for him upon his departure for Oxford in 1937 (Eggan 1954): American researchers studying the Indian tribes of the Plains and Southwest were dealing with "badly deteriorated societies," much altered by the impact of acculturation. By learning to employ informants' recitals of terminology, and through these to arrive at systematic statements of the associated behavior patterns, they mastered the art of ethnographic salvage. Since they were usually dealing with aged informants, it would have served no purpose to enumerate marriage choices, clan strengths, demographic composition, and land transactions. Tax, almost alone, directed his inquiries at communities that were going concerns and not "memory cultures."[9]

But the semantic aspect of the genealogical method did not eclipse the demographic component completely. Malinowski also had students, and they heeded his advice to utilize the "method of statistical documentation by concrete evidence." As we would suspect, data derived from different procedures provided different inferences. Enumerative methods that permitted behavioral variability to intrude on the abstract symmetry and logical coherence of the kinship system disclosed conflicts, oppositions, and a precarious equilibrium maintained by a balance of conflicting interests. Where the semantic view of society presented an appearance of unshakable consistency and stability, the demographic view presents the image of an uneasy reconciliation of forces about to come unstuck.

THE SECOND GENERATION: FIRTH AND WARNER

These distinctions between the two masters were amplified in the works of their students, two of whom performed studies in the western Pacific in the same year, 1929. Warner (1937) extended the earlier inquiry of his professor, Radcliffe-Brown (1913), with new research on the Murngin of northern Australia. Firth (1957) intended to clarify the observations of his professor,

---

was an extreme example of the total exemplification of the social structure by the kinship system and its extensions.

[9] Even though it did not use enumerative methods, one genealogical study of kinship terms, which treated Indian communities as functioning units rather than as survivals, produced exemplary results. This was the work performed by Spoehr (1941, 1942, 1944, 1947) on the Seminole, Creek, Cherokee, and Choctaw. Two groups of Seminole (a traditional camp in Florida and a progressive group in Oklahoma) were compared to discern effects of acculturation, and three adjacent groups in Oklahoma were arranged along an implicit acculturation continuum from conservative to modern (Creek, Cherokee, and Choctaw) for the same purpose. In both cases, family type was shown to have changed from consanguineal to conjugal, while terminology changed from Crow type to generational. Spoehr's (1947: 216-30) interpretation of these changes, in which economic factors are seen as independent variables, is in the Malinowskian mode. Summaries of Spoehr's work appear in Eggan (1966:41-44) and Murdock (1949:199-200).

Malinowski, on the Trobriands by a new investigation of Tikopia. Warner's methodological emphasis was on the formal (semantic-terminological) aspects of social structure, into which he made genealogical inquiry. Firth made intensive use of the demographic genealogical techniques: mapping, overlapping genealogical inquiry, and the household census survey.

Firth's description of the Tikopia is lodged in a matrix of "real time" associations. In addition to historical notes, there is a vivid description of the acculturation status of the island and the extent of missionary activity, together with recent population trends, as of 1929. Real time is complemented by real space: village maps, household diagrams, garden plots and their complexities of tenure, residential distribution of members of particular kin groups— all these and more are included. Lodged among these space-time coordinates are real people: named members of actual households whose behavior, emotions, decisions, and problems are so vividly presented that one may empathize with them.

Beneath the "slice of life" realism of his narrative, there is a rigorous method that requires (1957:57) "the superimposition of the genealogical record upon a residential plan of it." Firth's statements are supported throughout with "statistical documentation": the membership of an entire village is analyzed (1957:55-64); variations in household composition are provided (1957:108-14); distribution of clan members is traced throughout every village (1957:67), and clan strengths are reported (1957:321); distribution of land among individuals is described (1957:342-46); and much more.

From all this emerges the essential premise concerning Tikopian society: it is characterized by the functional integration of cross-cutting membership groups divided by claims of locality, affinity, descent, and rank (Firth 1957: 64, 88-89, 313-16). But it is an equilibrium tending toward instability, and it must be constantly restored. Frictions and conflicts are continuously generated in daily interaction, but are resolved by joint membership of the disputants in cooperative activities at another level.

The operation of the social system is continuously threatened by disequilibrium between the population and its limited resource base (Firth 1957:367-76). Firth provides one of the few ethnographic accounts concerning processes through which population stability is maintained, and frequently observes that there is a relationship between high population density and the organization of the entire system (Firth 1957:57, 486-87).

The substance of Tikopian life is represented as individual interaction, mediated through group membership, but certainly not restrained by it (Firth 1957:116): "Where the act of an individual diverges from the structural norm it may be regarded with approval, it may be ignored or it may be counteracted by a mechanism serving the express function of handling such breach of continuity."

The essence of Firth's presentation is *variation within sets of limits*, both *structural* and *environmental*. Through his adherence to enumerative genealogical procedures, he is able to show both the individual and group contexts of Tikopian life, and the centrifugal and centripetal interplay among them, from which an uneasy stability emerges.

Real time has no place among the Murngin; Warner describes neither historical nor acculturational contact. The time described is the ethnographic present, and the only chronological sequences are cyclical (generational and maturational). Real space is lacking also. Schematic diagrams replace maps, and in place of real people, the social group or the impersonal occupant of a social status is ever present.[10]

In place of enumerative methods that lead to recognition of variation, friction, and groups in opposition, Warner (1937:47-48) uses the genealogical method for specification of terms and related "sociological" components:

The whole kinship system of the Murngin people is made up of fundamental kinship reciprocals, such as brother and sister, father and son, maternal uncle and sister's son. Every ... term represents a complex nexus of social behavior which creates a well defined social personality.

And later (1937:94) Warner asserts that "Ego ... is an extremely complex social personality. We must remember that he is a member of a tribe, a clan, and moiety; of a totemic system, of an economic group; of a system of mythology, ceremony and belief; and of many other mechanisms." To these, age grade and subsection might be added.

It is the major premise of Warner's presentation that these multiple memberships are mutually reinforcing and contribute to overall group solidarity. Each element of the social personality is consistent with all other elements, and the entire system is rationalized by the ideological institutions, which include mythology, magic, and totemic ritual and belief.

Warner clearly intends us to understand that the Murngin system mani-

fests *cultural* integration. The elements of the kin, clan, moiety, and subsection conform to the logic of classes and relations, but the ideological elements are grouped separately in a section entitled "absolute logics," which "integrate the group and relate each of the separate parts of the society and of nature into a larger and general unity" (1937:11). The obvious parallels with the final chapters of *The Andaman Islanders* need not be stressed.[11]

When the Murngin are seen in this way, locked into a complex framework of logically consistent categories, all deviations from which are condemned by mythology and punished by lethal forms of black magic, the absence of variation in their behavior is readily explained by the ethnographer. However, Warner's methods did not permit variability to enter into his formulations.

SEMANTIC OR DEMOGRAPHIC GENEALOGICAL METHOD?

The Murngin and Tikopia studies suggest that the semantic and demographic genealogical methods provide

---

[10] Instead of individuals, Warner deals in "social personalities," a concept later incorporated by Radcliffe-Brown (1952) into his essay on social structure. The social personality refers to the behavior of an individual as the occupant of a status. "As a male social personality, a man is part of the totem, and in all his social relations with the male part of his group he is identified with the totem. This is true for all other individuals in his adult age grade, so that the totality of the males' individual relations forms the whole of totemic behavior" (Warner 1937:380-81).

[11] The common heritage of Warner and Radcliffe-Brown derives from Durkheim. Each of the three following paragraphs is a paraphrase of major premises taken from *Rules of Sociological Method, Elementary Forms of Religious Life,* and *Division of Labor,* respectively. They are quoted from Warner (1937:220, 381, 385):

"A prerequisite of social conditioning is a normal organism, normal not only in biological fact but in the values of the group. The normal human being ... is the 'well' person."

"It is the sacred tradition of the clan groups, as held in the minds of the individuals of the adult male age grade ... which forms the totemic configuration. The group in this sense does unconsciously worship itself."

"The totemic system provides, first, a final set of absolute sanctions for the society which places a pressure on all the members to perform the acts dictated by the rules of the social organization; and, second, a set of concepts organized into a unified system which provides a mechanism for group integration."

different points of view toward society. The first relates social groupings to ideological components and leads to the rationalizing of behavior. It recalls Sorokin's logicomeaningful integration, which, because it is symbolic in substance, is properly restricted to the cultural level of analysis. The second relates social groupings to their temporal and spatial correlates, emphasizing their interactive and processual aspects. It corresponds to Sorokin's causal-functional model of interdependence, which has the unique property of uniting social phenomena with biological and environmental organization (Sorokin 1957:1-13).

There is a misleading tendency to strike postures in the recent literature indicating intransigent adherence to *either* semantic *or* demographic procedures. The source of this tendency rests largely in efforts to score points by the two leading members of the Cambridge anthropology department's intramural debate team. Fortes (1969) seems to pledge irrevocable commitment to categorical models based on social norms, while Leach (1960, 1961*a*) with surpassing fierceness advocates distributional models based on choice.

Only the uninitiated will be surprised to learn that Leach's *Political Systems* (1954) is an essay in social categories (*gumsa* and *gumlao*) and their normative implications, while (perversely) it is Fortes (1954) who performed demographic surveys among the Ashanti. In actuality, the work of Leach (1961*a*) and Fortes (1949), like that of Firth (1957), Goodenough (1951, 1956), and Rivers (1906) himself, rests upon *both* elements of the genealogical method, viewed as complementary discovery procedures.

An inquiry into the kinship terminology of a community elicits patterns that are *perceived* by the participants themselves. These verbalized patterns,

embodying the conventional wisdom of the community, Lévi-Strauss (1963: 281-82, 312-13) designates as "homemade models" or "lived-in orders." Concepts derived from these perceptions provide the *counting units* into which later enumerative observations will be sorted. Unless he pays strict attention to ethnic classification in the establishment of the concepts employed in social measurement, the anthropologist engages in the quantification of essentially biological events: births, deaths, and terrestrial movement. In other words, *he becomes a demographer, but not a structural demographer.*

Conversely, inquiring only into ethnic classification by semantic-categorical procedures, without confronting the issues of situational variability, will produce an ethnography of culture patterns, of norms and rules for deciding what is *appropriate* (Frake 1964:133). This ideational configuration of ground rules, devoid of the "strategy rules" (Buchler and Selby 1968:311-17) through which each person manipulates the culture patterns for his own ends, tells us very little about social behavior. It is the difference between a treatise on the rules of baseball and a descriptive analysis of the seventh game of the World Series.[12] A person who engages in compiling "vocabularies of different kinds of forms and a syntax or set of rules for their composition into . . . sequences of social events" (Goodenough 1965:1) *becomes a structuralist* (Lane

----

[12] Defenders of the presentation of ethnography as culturally appropriate behavior sometimes observe that it provides the outsider with the information necessary to behave in a fashion which will gain him acceptance as a member of the culture. This argument merits Moerman's (1968:22) rejoinder that such information "can hardly be expected to interest anyone except those who may be dropped among them by black parachute in the dead of night."

1970:11-39), *but certainly not a structural demographer.*[13]

It is through the quantitative treatment of natively perceived patterns, as Leach (1961*a*) demonstrated in *Pul Eliya,* that covert patterns emerge—patterns of which the participants themselves are unaware. Only enumerative inquiry discloses organizational components of community life that either (1) fall beyond the perceptions of the participants or (2) appear to conflict with them.[14] Clearly, anthropological method must provide for the articulation of both perceptions and practices in the description of social organization.

Utilization of the comprehensive genealogical method, including both semantic and demographic components, is methodologically neutral. Fortes (1949), in a classic exposition of the essentials of structural demography, compared Ashanti norms concerning household formation and found that a conflict existed between the injunctions that a man should (1) establish an independent neolocal household for his wife and children and (2) support the attempt of his mother, as female lineage head, to establish her own household by living with her. By matching genealogical and quantitative residential and demographic data, he discovered that both sets of norms were observed alternatively: nuclear households with male heads were formed during the childbearing years; subsequently the household dissolved and both partners returned to reside with their lineage mates.

This probabilistic model demonstrates normative observance of patterns of which the participants are unaware. By the same method, Leach (1960) demonstrates the opposite. In tracing patterns of inheritance and marriage over a half century, he discovered in Pul Eliya that the strategy of marriage choice frustrated the cultural norm favoring bilateral descent. Here the probabilistic model disclosed violations of normative observances of which the participants were unaware. Commitment to investigate variability does not *entail* the discovery of instability, disorganization, or change, but it admits the *possibility.* And this is the critical difference between the Tikopia and Murngin examples.

---

[13] The points rather superficially skimmed in this paragraph have been richly described and knowledgeably interpreted by Van Velsen (1967) in his discussion of *situational analysis,* which he presents as an alternative to structural analysis. Since it is a qualitative procedure for gaining information on strategy rules and variation in the observance of cultural norms, it falls outside the scope of this paper. However, the notion of gaining insights into the workings of a society by examining situations in which norm conflicts are resolved (Van Velsen 1964) appears to warrant the designation "post-structuralist" given to it by its author.

[14] Firth (1964:47-48) provides an example of covert patterning in Tikopian interclan marriage choices, which follow no conscious preference, and have proved to be stable over three decades. Freeman's (1958) study of residential preference among the *bilek* (longhouse) groups of the Iban disclosed statistical patterning explicable in terms of anticipated inheritances, again in the absence of residence rules. Necessity for both semantic and demographic inquiry is confirmed by interpretations of recent New Guinea data (Sahlins 1965) which hold that descent-group membership (a semantic category) postulates nothing about residence-group membership (a demographic category). Langness (1964) asserts that, for tribes such as the Bena Bena, residence determines kinship rather than the reverse! Meggitt (1965) asserts an inverse relationship between amount of garden land available and degree of conformity between descent group and residence group. Schapera's (1950) treatment of Tswana marriages discloses covert patterns that conflict with verbal norms.

STRUCTURAL DEMOGRAPHY: MODELS FOR INQUIRY

When social theories based on equilibrium assumptions are abandoned, the maintenance of social units and the connectedness of their components become critical research problems. The capacity of communities to survive and to evolve is inherent in these attributes. Since biophysical elements and other social units making up the environment are implicated in these problems, an open systems approach is required. Relationships among components at different levels may be measured and cross-tabulated (Bogue 1959) with conventional indices (migration rates, crop yields, net population changes, nutritional densities) if appropriate individualized data have been collected.

If we are to avoid the criticism of presenting ground rules without strategy rules, however, we must be more specific in relating these theoretical considerations to the operations of the genealogical method. For this purpose we shall present specific variables and relationships through which the problems of maintenance and connectedness may be explored.

Let us focus attention upon natural social settings, such as the community (Arensberg 1961), which harbor evolutionary potential. To initiate discussion we must make certain assumptions. It must be possible to isolate the community from its societal context through the definition of its membership. The community's identity is based on the temporal continuity of this membership, rather than on its spatial separation from surrounding communities, for it is a social rather than a geographical entity.

While the rationale for the community's existence lies in its provision of certain necessities to its membership (including, perhaps, mates, goods and services, and information) through its subsidiary groups, their *continuing* participation rests upon their expectation that these necessities will be forthcoming from the community in the future as well as in the present. Temporal continuity defines the community from the viewpoints of both the observer and the observed.

We are accustomed to think of the functional interdependence of community activities from a cross-sectional or instantaneous point of view, and to infer from their relationship the conclusion that the social unit is integrated, and therefore viable. But our definition of community requires us to think about functional interdependence from a *longitudinal* rather than a cross-sectional viewpoint. For every real community, like every real society, "is a process in time" (Leach 1954:5).

Of what must temporal integration consist? For its maintenance and connectedness—that is, its viability—most certainly depend on this notion of integrity. The key concept is that of *replacement*. Replacement subsumes three types of requirements, each of which must be replenished at a rate at least equal to consumption and removal, or resignation from the community: (1) environmental materials, (2) population, and (3) status occupants in specific proportions.

The mechanisms or constraints of the environment, surrounding social units, or the community itself must facilitate replacement within critical limits if the community is to maintain itself. Deficits in replacement will force the community below the limit beneath which it cannot survive without radical adjustments such as "dedifferentiation" (Gouldner 1959:262-63). But excessive replacement may lead to penetration of an upper limit above which the community cannot operate in its preexistent form.

The clearest example of this situation is overpopulation, but Moore (1960) also calls attention to changes in patterns of scarcity and status recruitment as change initiators. Excessive replacement may lead to systemic breakdown or to "shifts in levels of integration" of the sort tending to increase density, complexity, energy consumption, and heterogeneity (Steward 1956). In either case, the adequacy of replacement can be assured only through time-series observations.

Much has been written at an abstract level about controls and feedback mechanisms that counteract these tendencies (Ashby 1956, 1960), and a recent paper has attempted to identify them at the village level in a rapidly developing rural area (Hackenberg 1971). Temporal processes generating variation beyond the limits of the community to sustain were recognized as schismogenesis (Bateson 1958) and deviation amplification (Maruyama 1963).

Functional mechanisms that stabilize population processes, soil fertility, incentive systems, distribution processes, and social mobility must be treated as temporal variables (Deutsch 1963:48):

In biology, every qualitative statement about the function of this or that structure or process implies from the outset also a quantitative statement. To say that, in an organism, structure "x" fulfills the function "y" is to raise three obvious quantitative questions. *How much* does this structure ... have to contribute of what kind of output in order to perform what kind of function at the minimum level required for the continuation of the organism? Second, how much does it in fact contribute? And third, precisely what happens when the kind of its contribution remains the same but the quantity is varied to just what extent?

It is now quite clear that belief in social norms and sanctions as community regulators is utopian (Dahrendorf 1958). The study of temporal integration—that is, of the limits of tolerable variation and the mechanisms of self-regulation (Nadel 1953) tending to constrain behavior within them—may now begin.[15]

With this additional clarification, the dependence of structural demography upon time series observations of the relations between communities and their environments may be appreciated. As an instrument for initiating these observations we advocate the comprehensive genealogical method, containing inductive procedures for (1) delimiting the unit of study, (2) identifying elements of social structure and property, and (3) following rates and trends in participation through time by turnover analysis.

While genealogical methods may document the human use of the earth and human occupation of it, they are inadequate by themselves for evaluating resource replacement. In the realm of biosocial variables, however, they afford quantified observations concerning population replacement and status recruitment. To understand the specific observations needed, let us examine a biosocial model of these variables accessible with genealogical tools.

SAMSARA: AN INTERGENERATIONAL MODEL

The Samsara model is derived from earlier work by sociologists and demographers which attempts to identify vari-

[15] My indebtedness to S. F. Nadel for many of the ideas in this section will be apparent. It was he who advanced the propositions that causal analysis requires the observation of change in social systems (1951:101-104); that open systems inquiries need the incorporation of variables from different levels (1951:209-19); that implicit probability assumptions underlie all anthropological assertions concerning structure (1951:246-55; 1957:138-39); that there are quantitative dimensions to all social institutions (1951:111-17, 128, 187); that temporal observations play an important role in functional analysis (1957:125-52); and much more. The interwoven theoretical fabric to which Nadel, Firth, Leach, and Fortes are all contributors provides, in a more general sense, the framework for the entire discussion. Despite this, Nadel never made a quantitative study to my knowledge, and never used the genealogical method. His contributions have been largely logical rather than methodological.

ables and infer relationships responsible for premodern patterns of population growth and composition. In part, these relationships are suggested by the theory of demographic transition (Ryder 1957, Stolnitz 1964, Freedman 1965), by hypotheses connecting specific sociocultural variables and fertility (Davis and Blake 1956; Freedman 1961; Davis 1962, 1963, 1967), and by papers in demographic method (Coale 1957, Hauser 1962, Ryder 1965*b*).

Samsara is the concept of an infinite series of births and deaths, introduced into northern India through the Upanishads in the ninth century B.C. The Samsara model seeks to identify community institutions that determine reproduction. Since population changes are the products of temporal trends, Samsara should comprehend intergenerational fertility patterns.

A preliminary grasp of how Samsara operates may be gleaned from following a hypothetical cohort through a sequence of stages:

1. If we begin with a generation (G_1) of young adults who are potential parents, we may observe that the community interposes constraints that produce an asymmetrical pattern of marriages.

2. Within the marriages completed, opportunities for procreation may be unevenly apportioned, yielding a sharply skewed distribution of numbers of children born to married couples.

3. Among children born, survivorship and emigration may introduce further differential attrition.

4. As the remaining children approach maturity, they will be selectively recruited into adult statuses and become a generation (G_2) of potential parents, thus completing the cycle.

However, because of the assumptions concerning differentiation and selection that are built into the model, the distribution of G_2 personnel occupying adult statuses, and their numerical

strength within them, may differ significantly from that of the G_1 generation. This, in turn, will alter the reproductive performance of the G_2 generation.

If fertility differentials, or net reproductive increases, extend over several generations, the community may be forced to alter its system of constraints or its pattern of environmental adaptation. Perhaps it is not too much to hope that a small number of ethnographers may collect data sufficient for a G_1 and G_2 comparison of the type illustrated in Figure 1.

Figure 1 exemplifies the opportunities for positive or negative feedback between fertility differentials and the total context of the community (represented by status organization and marriage regulation). Computer simulation may be employed to develop implications of cross-sectional data over time, and to supplement incompletely quantified observations (Kunstadter et al. 1963, Coale 1965).

Figure 1 provides the frame of reference within which an ethnographic approach to demographic analysis can be fitted. An expanded version of Samsara

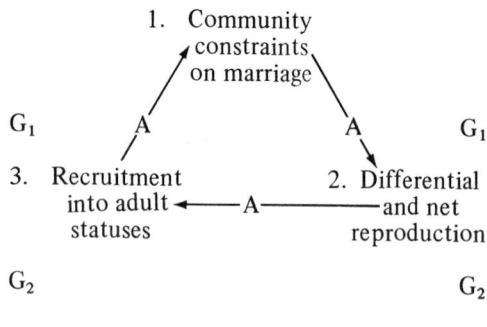

A = continuous mediation of differential mortality, emigration, and immigration

Figure 1. Samsara model for comparison of intergenerational reproductive patterns.

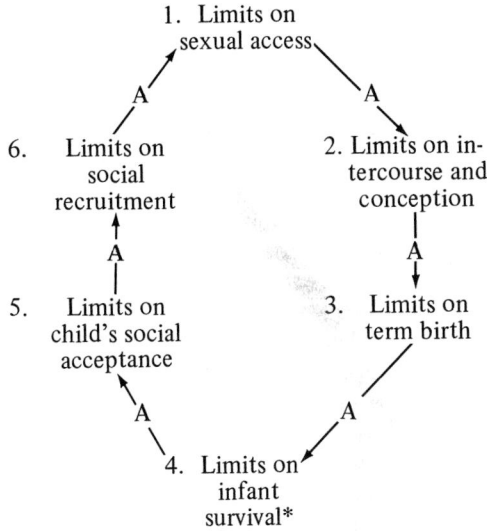

1. Limits on sexual access

A

A

6. Limits on social recruitment

2. Limits on intercourse and conception

A

A

5. Limits on child's social acceptance

3. Limits on term birth

A

A

4. Limits on infant survival*

* All forms of infant death, but especially infanticide

A = continuous mediation of differential mortality, emigration, and immigration

Figure 2. Expanded Samsara model of intergenerational reproductive patterns as sequential set of limits.

is outlined in Figure 2 as a sequential *set of limits,* each of which tends to reduce both the size of a birth cohort and the proportion of its members reaching adult procreative status.

Samsara: The Determinants

Each set of limits may be imposed with differential intensity by a particular society, and through either simple or elaborate social machinery. Each term of the model can be varied separately, yet if its value is changed, it will implicate all the others. It remains to give an "ethnographic definition" to each set of limits.

1. *Limits on sexual access.* This refers specifically to limits on access to partners for heterosexual relations. It points to the possible existence of restraints on premarital sex behavior, definitions of incest and kin-based marriage regulations, physical availability of suitable partners, presence of property ownership or bride-price requirements, prevalence of divorce and other factors relating to duration of marital unions, possibilities for extramarital relations and plural marriage, and so on.

2. *Limits on intercourse and conception.* This refers to limits on pregnancy within sexual unions permitted by the society. It points to possible periodic absence of one partner, or periodic abstinence required for ritual or hygienic reasons, the presence of contraceptive practices and frequency of sterility, and so on.

3. *Limits on term birth.* This refers to limits on the normal fetal span of development to live birth. It points to frequency of miscarriage, abortion, and stillbirth—in other words, all causes of fetal mortality, both natural and induced. Children escaping these limits will be considered live births and should be counted to determine fertility levels.

4. *Limits on infant survival.* This refers to all forms of infant mortality, but particularly to infanticide. It points to the possible sex differential leading to disposal of female children, beliefs about twins, albinos, birth defects, children born during eclipses or at other inauspicious times of the year, and various social practices that tend to limit infant survival.

5. *Limits on social acceptance of children.* This refers to the desire for children in particular societies and the reasons for desiring or not desiring them, and especially to their "cost-benefit" status. Where children are desired and possess sufficient marginal utility, they may be adopted from other communities or social strata. Where children are considered liabilities, they

may be sold, abandoned, given away, or hired out for labor or prostitution.

6. *Limits on social recruitment.* This refers to the ascriptive-achievement aspect of the child's transition from adolescence to adulthood, and the relative advantages or disadvantages of his prospects. Where inheritances, property settlements, or instruction in skills are ascriptively distributed among children, stratification will be created. Competition in achievement-oriented communities may reach an analogous outcome by a different route. Population excesses must exert different kinds of pressures on systems in which status is ascribed than on systems in which it is achieved, however.

As in Figure 1, the cycle of components included in Figure 2 possesses positive or negative feedback potential. If sufficient data are available or can be simulated, it should be possible to demonstrate that both the population and the organization of the community must change through time, and in directions that can be predicted.

A model of a temporal event sequence, forming a feedback loop with regulatory or transformational properties and incorporating biosocial and environmental properties at the community level has not yet been grounded in ethnographic observations. Laughlin (1968*a*) presents a conceptual scheme that includes many of the determinants of Samsara, is linked with the circumstances of hunting and gathering cultures, and possesses regulatory properties. However, until such a model is reproduced empirically, with actual variables measured intergenerationally, our insights must remain hypothetical.

A comment of Lévi-Strauss (1963: 286-87) may help to place the models of structural demography in a unique perspective:

Anthropology uses a mechanical time, re-

versible and non-cumulative. . . . On the contrary, historical time is statistical; it always appears as an oriented and non-reversible process. . . . The elements to be organized into an evolutionary process cannot be borrowed from the level of cultural typology which consists of mechanical models. They should be sought at a sufficiently deep level to insure that these elements will remain unaffected by different cultural contexts . . . and can accordingly permit the drawing of long statistical runs. . . . The evolutionists would find it easier to regain their position if they consented to substitute statistical for mechanical models, that is, models whose elements are independent of their combinations and which remain identical through a sufficiently long period of time.

The elements of genealogical method, combined into variables through models such as Samsara, will yield this sort of outcome.

Research on the scale projected may appear impractical for the present. Our conventional "one man, one village, one year" field trips do not normally yield such a rich harvest of facts. Yet those who skeptically veto these proposals need to be reminded of one man (Firth), one village (Tikopia), and one year (1929). For the future, there are monitoring systems, record-linkage programs, and computerized data banks, and these technical aids to longitudinal studies will arrive considerably in advance of "1984" (Hackenberg 1970). But unless we reorient some of our recent efforts, technical capability may develop much more rapidly than our capacity to design significant research.

FOUNDATIONS OF STRUCTURAL DEMOGRAPHY: RECENT RESEARCH RESULTS

Structural demography incorporates inductive discovery procedures, based on accumulation of individualized demographic and social data through time, for the purpose of charting stability and change in institutions and communities at various levels of social structure. It may be used with equal effectiveness to investigate the family, the community, or the region. Only the scale of observation needs to be changed. It relies upon the genealogical method, including the charting of pedigrees, the mapping of residences, and the completion of household census surveys. With the exception of technical aids that have come into existence since his death, it is substantially the method of W. H. R. Rivers.

The tools of structural demography are discovery procedures. Let new observations, then, permit new questions to be raised. They will not be slow in coming, and some are already taking shape. Two examples of retrospective and prospective inquiry are Hackenberg's (1961) Papago Indian research of the past decade, which provides illustrations of the results of retrospective method, and Firth's (1957, 1959) observations of Tikopian behavior—spanning three decades—which illustrate the value of prospective studies. Both exemplify the possibilities inherent in temporal observation of a defined population.

The population of Papago Indians, long residents of southern Arizona and northern Mexico, was defined by retrospective genealogical methods (Hackenberg 1961, 1967) as of 1960. In the environmental-ecological domain, historical demography has located the origin villages of the present-day Papago, and differentiated them by size and subsistence pattern (Mark 1960, Hackenberg 1964b, Jones 1969). These studies have helped to document the interplay between environmental change and technological intervention (Hackenberg 1962, Padfield and van Willigen 1969), and rapid redeployment of population subsequent to each ecological adjustment.

Biomedical and demographic research has provided insights into changes in health status related to modernization (Tyroler 1965) and in frequency and causes of death (Tyroler and Patrick 1972). Impact of culture change upon breeding isolates has been investigated by genetic methods (Niswander et al. 1970, Lamb 1969, Workman and Niswander 1970) and by quantifying mate selection (Zimmerly 1968). Culture change relationships with migration have been measured (Hackenberg and Wilson 1972), and an initial study of fertility has been completed (Uhlmann 1972).

Sociocultural change studies have developed indices of modernization (Patrick and Tyroler 1972), community and tribal microevolution (Hackenberg 1965, 1968), and have conceptualized and quantified a folk-urban continuum model for the assessment of cross-sectional variation within the total population (Hackenberg 1963). The existence of the genealogically defined population base has motivated a wide range of cross-disciplinary inquiries, which now provide the opportunity for a summary treatment of the modernization process from the triangular perspective of environmental, genetic-demographic, and social organization transformations.

For centuries the Papago have resided in an ethnic corridor, in frequent contact with representatives of other non-Western cultures: Pima, Seri, Sobaipuri, Apache, and Mohave. Their relationships with these groups have ranged from intermarriage and employment as farm workers through trade to continuous warfare and slave-taking. Interaction has been further complicated since the seventeenth century by the intrusion of Europeans, who have made administrative, economic, military, and genetic contributions of their own. Viewed from the three perspectives recurrent throughout this discussion—

environmental, demographic, and socio-cultural—the Papago tribe has maintained itself under "open system" conditions, in free exchange of resources, population, and culture content with its surroundings. Since each Papago community has alternately incorporated and been incorporated into elements of adjacent territory and society, the maintenance of specific social units and the connectedness of their components have not been critical to the survival of the membership. Yet through three centuries, according to ethnohistoric and genealogical evidence, they have maintained a separate identity.[16]

The research program initiated by Firth on his visit to Tikopia in 1929 and extended on his return in 1952 (Firth 1957, 1959) provided the opportunity for a range of time-series analyses. The analysis of social change included quantitative assessment of population growth and marriage choice, lineage membership and differential replacement, property owned and exchanged, densities and pressures on arable land, and shifts in patterns of subsistence.

Spillius (1957), who participated in the restudy, made a special assessment of the response of the Tikopian community to a disastrous drought and hurricane. Technical assistance in the evaluation of demographic data was ob-

[16] The lack of congruence between the boundaries within which Papago mate-selection, economic, and residential institutions were located lends support to Owen's (1965) interpretation of the interdependence of tribal groups at the level of the patrilineal band. While politically it would be necessary to locate the Papago somewhere between a band and a tribe, their organization tended to oscillate between these organizational levels (Hackenberg 1962). It is quite possible that, as they approached higher levels of organization, the degree of congruence between behavioral subsystems increased, as Owen predicts. This would have been complemented by reduced dependence upon surrounding tribes for mates, subsistence, and allies in warfare.

tained (Borrie, Firth, and Spillius 1957). Migration and recent culture change on Tikopia has been described through a third census-based inquiry in 1965 (Larson 1966). This latter project, concentrating on the "colonization" phase of Tikopian population growth and expansion, includes the expatriate community of Nukufero, whose social organization is compared with that of the parent island. Larson also investigated the quality of the environment by soil testing.

The wealth of data, judicious comparisons, and abundant insights derived from Firth's work underline the immense value of quantified time-series data from an island ecosystem considered as a natural isolate. The theoretical significance of the natural isolate for genetic research (Lasker 1956, Shapiro 1957, Sutter and Tran-Ngoc-Toan 1957), for ecological inquiry (Odum 1969), and for social and cultural studies (Redfield 1947) is widely recognized.

The Tikopia represent a population in which the boundaries of culture patterns, group membership, trade, language, and genetic exchange are all *coterminous.* Redfield (1947) spoke of the folk society as a hypothetical limiting case, or "zero point," from which deviations from autonomy, homogeneity, and traditionalism could be measured; Tikopia approximates such a limit in actuality.

The insights into stresses and constraints operating within such a closed system whose environmental relationships are sharply circumscribed represent a position almost diametrically opposed to that of the Papago Indians mentioned earlier. Tikopia embodies a situation in which the alternative to maintenance is extinction, and connectedness must be at its maximum.

Comparative significance of the Tikopian case can be enhanced by reference to other studies of semi-isolated island communities in recent years utilizing comparable methods (Goodenough 1951; Lessa 1955, 1964, 1966; Danielsson 1956; Lessa and Meyers 1962; Sahlins 1962).

In concluding a review of social anthropology's oldest method, it is perhaps unjust to leave the impression that its systematic use is just beginning. Yet the apparent bias must remain, if for no other reason than that all of the excellent work published since Rivers' time cannot be included in a paper of this length. Some significant African studies in the tradition of Fortes' Ashanti research have been unreasonably neglected, particularly the research on village stability among the Tonga (Colson 1962) and the Ndembu (Turner 1957).

In the western Pacific, insufficient mention has been made of Scheffler's (1965) genealogically based inquiry into the way descent groups "really work" among the Choiseulese; his account gives substance to the concept of strategy rules in social organization. In the same region, Meggitt's (1965) account of the Mae-Enga lineage system approximates an open system analysis involving surrounding peoples and ecological considerations. Rappaport's (1967) Maring project, while more ecological than genealogical, evaluates demographic stresses and environmental responses in a quantified model with cybernetic implications. His viewpoint is clearly akin to that identified here as structural demography.

Obviously, genealogical methods for the study of social processes have been utilized asymmetrically. The uneven geographical distribution is apparent. Southeast Asia, sub-Saharan Africa, and the western Pacific, including Australia, are best represented. North and South America and eastern and southern Asia have been much less favored, though the Mexican inquiry by Nutini (1968) and a Caribbean study by M. G. Smith (1962) deserve mention.

Asymmetry is also present in the types of societies that have been investigated by genealogical procedures. Gardening and farming peoples are strongly represented, while societies higher or lower in the scale of complexity are poorly described. However, studies of hunting and gathering tribes of Australia (Rose 1960, Yengoyan 1970), the Amazon region (Chagnon 1968), and the Kalahari Desert (R. B. Lee 1966) have been published. It would be difficult to find three urban areas about which the same could be said!

In urban investigations, however, it is evident that "social network" studies are gaining in popularity as a methodological device (Mitchell 1969). The many analogies between constructing a network and building a genealogy are recognized by some of the users of the former concept. Since urban residence is synonymous with the demise of kin-based associations, an analogous device, such as the network, may be the appropriate substitute.

Asymmetric selection of subject matter also occurs in this inventory. Preference has been given to genealogical studies that view community members from a demographic-ecological perspective. Genealogical inquiry is not so tightly circumscribed. Cognitive aspects of group formation and variability in perceptions of membership have recently been investigated from a genealogical point of view by Sankoff (1970a, 1970b), using New Guinea data.

Structural demography is concerned with comparative research, which imposes a logical constraint on study design. Data must be compiled from different groups but the same dimensions must be employed, and degrees of variation must be recorded with precision through observations that may be replicated. Unoriginal as these stipulations may be, few studies that purport to employ comparison adhere to them. By observing them, we may eventually escape from the admonition of Adams (1960:47): "To assume that a form, because it is a variant, is abnormal is to evade the task before us. The first job of science is, after all, to study what *is*, not what *might*, or *could*, or *should* be." The development of structural demography, through the use of the genealogical method, is one path toward that objective.

REFERENCES

Adams, Richard N.
1960 An Inquiry into the Nature of the Family. In *Essays in the Science of Culture,* ed. Gertrude E. Dole and Robert L. Carneiro, pp. 30-49. New York: Crowell.

Anderson, Robert T.
1971 *Traditional Europe: A Study in Anthropology and History.* Belmont, Calif.: Wadsworth.

Arensberg, Conrad
1961 The Community as Object and as Sample. *American Anthropologist* 63:241-64.

Ashby, W. Ross
1956 *Introduction to Cybernetics.* London: Chapman & Hall.
1960 *Design for a Brain,* 2nd ed. New York: Wiley.

Barnes, J. A.
1967 Genealogies. In *The Craft of Social Anthropology,* ed. A. L. Epstein, pp. 101-28. London: Tavistock.

Barnett, Clifford R., Jean Jackson, and Howard M. Cann
1971 Childspacing in a Highland Guatemala Community. In *Culture and Population: A Collection of Current Studies,* ed. Steven Polgar, pp. 139-50. Chapel Hill, N.C.: Carolina Population Center.

Bateson, Gregory
1958 *Naven,* 2nd ed. Stanford: Stanford University Press.

Bock, Philip K.
1969 *Modern Cultural Anthropology.* New York: Knopf.

Bogue, Donald
1952 The Quantitative Study of Social Dynamics and Social Change. *American Journal of Sociology* 57:565-68.
1959 Population Distribution. In *The Study of Population,* ed. Philip Hauser and O. D. Duncan, pp. 383-99. Chicago: University of Chicago Press.

Bogue, Donald, and Elizabeth J. Bogue
1970 *Techniques of Pregnancy History Analysis.* Family Planning Research and Evaluation Manual no. 4. Chicago: Community and Family Study Center, University of Chicago.

Bohannan, Laura
1952 A Genealogical Charter. *Africa* 22:301-15.

Borrie, W., Raymond Firth, and James Spillius
1957 The Population of Tikopia, 1929 and 1952. *Population Studies* 10:229-52.

Brass, William
1953 The Derivation of Fertility and Reproduction Rates from Restricted Data on Reproductive Histories. *Population Studies* 7:137-66.
1954 The Estimation of Fertility Rates from the Ratios of Total to First Births. *Population Studies* 8:74-87.
1960 The Graduation of Fertility Distributions by Polynomial Functions. *Population Studies* 14:148-62.

Brass, William, and Ansley Coale
1968 Methods of Analysis and Estimation. In *The Demography of Tropical Africa,* ed. William Brass et al., pp. 88-139. Princeton: Princeton University Press.

Buchler, Ira, and Henry Selby
1968 *Kinship and Social Organization.* New York: Macmillan.

Cadwallader, Mervyn
1959 The Cybernetic Analysis of Change in Complex Social Organizations. *American Journal of Sociology* 65:154-57.

Cassel, John, Ralph Patrick, and David Jenkins
1960 Epidemiological Analysis of the Health Implications of Culture Change: A Conceptual Model. *Annals of the New York Academy of Science* 84:938-49.

Chagnon, Napoleon

1968 *Yanomamö: The Fierce People.* New York: Holt, Rinehart & Winston.

Coale, Ansley
1957 How the Age Distribution of a Human Population Is Determined. *Cold Spring Harbor Symposia on Quantitative Biology* 22:83-89.
1965 Birth Rates, Death Rates, and Rates of Growth in Human Populations. In *Public Health and Population Change,* ed. Mindel Sheps and Jean Ridley, pp. 221-41. Pittsburgh: University of Pittsburgh Press.

Coale, Ansley, and Paul Demeny
1966 *Regional Life Tables and Stable Population Models.* Princeton: Princeton University Press.

Collier, George
n.d.   KINPROGRAM. Stanford: Department of Anthropology, Stanford University.

Collier, George, and Victoria R. Bricker
1970 Nicknames and Social Structure in Zinacantan. *American Anthropologist* 72:289-302.

Colson, Elizabeth
1962 Residence and Village Stability Among the Plateau Tonga. In *The Plateau Tonga of Northern Rhodesia,* pp. 102-21. Manchester: University of Manchester Press.
1967 The Intensive Study of Small Sample Communities. In *The Craft of Social Anthropology,* ed. A. L. Epstein, pp. 3-16. London: Tavistock.

Committee of the Royal Anthropological Institute
1960 *Notes and Queries in Anthropology,* 6th ed. London: Routledge & Kegan Paul.

Conklin, Harold
1964 Ethnogenealogical Method. In *Explorations in Cultural Anthropology,* ed. W. H. Goodenough, pp. 25-56. New York: McGraw-Hill.
1967 Some Aspects of Ethnographic Research in Ifugao. *Transactions of the New York Academy of Science* 2, no. 30:99-121.

Coombs, Clyde H.
1953 Theory and Methods of Social Measurement. In *Research Methods in the Behavioral Sciences,* ed. Leon Festinger and David Katz, pp. 471-535. New York: Dryden Press.

Coult, Allan, and Richard Randolph
1965 Computer Methods for Analyzing Genealogical Space. *American Anthropologist* 67:21-29.

Dahrendorf, Ralf
1958 Out of Utopia: Toward a Reorientation of Sociological Analysis. *American Journal of Sociology* 64:115-27.

Danielsson, Bengt
1956 *Work and Life on Raroia.* London: Allen & Unwin.

Davis, Kingsley
1962 The Role of Class Mobility in Economic Development. *Population Review* 6:67-75.
1963 Theory of Change and Response in Modern Demographic History. *Population Index* 29:345-66.
1967 Population Policy: Will Current Programs Succeed? *Science* 158:730-39.

Davis, Kingsley, and Judith Blake
1956 Social Structure and Fertility: An Analytic Framework. *Economic Development and Cultural Change* 4: 221-35.

Deutsch, Karl
1963 *The Nerves of Government.* New York: Free Press, Macmillan.

Devereaux, George
1961 Two Types of Modal Personality Models. In *Studying Personality Cross-Culturally,* ed. Bert Kaplan, pp. 227-41. Evanston, Ill.: Row, Peterson.

Duncan, Otis D., Ray Cuzzort, and Beverly Duncan
1961 *Statistical Geography.* New York: Free Press, Macmillan.

Early, John D.
1970a Demographic Profile of a Maya Community: The Atitecos of Santiago Atitlán. *Milbank Memorial Fund Quarterly* 58:167-78.
1970b The Structure and Change of Mortality in a Maya Community. *Milbank Memorial Fund Quarterly* 58:179-201.

Easton, David
1956 The Limit of the Equilibrium Model in Social Research. *Behavioral Science* 1:96-105.

Eggan, Fred
1954 *Social Anthropology of North Amer-*

ican Tribes, 2nd ed. Chicago: University of Chicago Press.

1966   *The American Indian.* Chicago: Aldine.

Evans-Pritchard, E. E.
1940   *The Nuer.* London: Oxford University Press.

Firth, Raymond
1957   *We, the Tikopia,* 2nd ed. Boston: Beacon Press.

1959   *Social Change in Tikopia.* London: Allen & Unwin.

1964   *Essays in Social Organization and Values.* Monographs on Social Anthropology no. 28. London: London School of Economics.

Fortes, Meyer
1949   Time and Social Structure. In *Social Structure: Studies Presented to A. R. Radcliffe-Brown,* ed. Meyer Fortes, pp. 54-84. New York: Russell & Russell.

1953   The Structure of Unilineal Descent Groups. *American Anthropologist* 55:17-41.

1954   A Demographic Field Study in Ashanti. In *Culture and Human Fertility,* ed. Frank Notestein, pp. 253-319. Paris: UNESCO.

1969   *Kinship and the Social Order.* Chicago: Aldine.

Fortune, Reo
1932   *Sorcerers of Dobu.* New York: Dutton.

Frake, Charles
1964   Notes on Queries in Ethnography. *American Anthropologist* 66, no. 4, pt. 2:132-45.

Freedman, Ronald
1961   The Sociology of Human Fertility: A Trend Report and Bibliography. *Current Sociology* 10-11, no. 2.

1965   The Transition from High to Low Fertility: Challenge to Demographers. *Population Index* 31:417-35.

Freeman, J. D.
1958   The Family System of the Iban of Borneo. In *The Developmental Cycle in Domestic Groups,* ed. Jack Goody, pp. 15-52. Cambridge Papers in Social Anthropology no. 1. Cambridge: At the University Press.

Gerth, Hands, and C. Wright Mills
1953   *Character and Social Structure.* New York: Harcourt, Brace.

Glass, D. V., and D. E. C. Eversley
1965   *Population in History.* Chicago: Aldine.

Goldfarb, Nathan
1960   *Longitudinal Statistical Analysis.* New York: Free Press, Macmillan.

Goodenough, Ward
1951   *Property, Kin, and Community on Truk.* Yale University Publications in Anthropology no. 46. New Haven: Yale University Press.

1956   Residence Rules. *Southwestern Journal of Anthropology* 12:22-37.

1965   Rethinking Status and Role: Toward a General Model of the Cultural Organization of Status Relationships. In *The Relevance of Models for Social Anthropology,* ed. Michael Banton, pp. 1-22. New York: Praeger.

Gouldner, Alvin
1959   Reciprocity and Autonomy in Functional Theory. In *Symposium on Sociological Theory,* ed. L. Gross, pp. 241-70. Evanston, Ill.: Row, Peterson.

Hackenberg, Robert A.
1961   *Papago Population Study.* Tucson: Bureau of Ethnic Research, University of Arizona.

1962   Economic Alternatives in Native Lands: A Case Study of the Pima and Papago Indians. *Ethnology* 1:186-96.

1963   Demographic Measurement of Sociocultural Change: The Papago Folk-Urban Continuum. Paper read at 61st annual meeting, American Anthropological Association, San Francisco.

1964a *A Navajo Population Register.* Tucson: Bureau of Ethnic Research, University of Arizona.

1964b Papago Indian Aboriginal Land Use and Occupancy. Tucson: Bureau of Ethnic Research, University of Arizona.

1965   Community Organization and Population Structure. Paper read at annual meeting, Society for Applied Anthropology, Lexington.

1966   An Anthropological Study of Demographic Transition: The Papago Information System. *Milbank Memorial Fund Quarterly* 44:470-94.

1967   Parameters of an Ethnic Group: A Method for Studying the Total Tribe. *American Anthropologist* 69:478-92.

1968 Cultural Microevolution in a South-western Indian Reservation Community. Paper read at 66th annual meeting, American Anthropological Association, Seattle.

1970 The Social Observatory: Time Series Data for Health and Behavioral Research. *Social Science and Medicine* 4:343-57.

1971 The Cybernetic Village. *Southeast Asian Journal of Sociology* 4:5-25.

Hackenberg, Robert A., and C. Roderick Wilson
1972 Reluctant Emigrants: The Role of Migration in Papago Indian Adaptation. *Human Organization* 31:171-86.

Hauser, Philip
1959 Demographic Indicators of Economic Development. *Economic Development and Cultural Change* 7:98-116.

1962 On Design for Experiment and Research in Fertility Control. In *Research in Family Planning,* ed. Clyde Kiser, pp. 463-74. Princeton: Princeton University Press.

Helm, June
1968 Statistics of Kin Marriage: A Non-Australian Example. In *Man the Hunter,* ed. Richard Lee and Irven De Vore, pp. 216-17. Chicago: Aldine.

Hempel, Carl G.
1959 The Logic of Functional Analysis. In *Symposium on Sociological Theory,* ed. L. Gross, pp. 271-310. Evanston, Ill.: Row, Peterson.

Henderson, Lawrence J.
1936 *Pareto's General Sociology.* Cambridge: Harvard University Press.

Henry, Jules
1955 Homeostasis, Society, and Evolution: A Critique. *Scientific Monthly* 81: 300-309.

Hinshaw, Robert, Patrick Pyeatt, and Jean Pierre Habicht
1972 Environmental Effects on Child-Spacing and Population Increase in Highland Guatemala. *Current Anthropology* 13:100-114.

Jones, Richard D.
1969 An Analysis of Papago Communities, 1900-1920. Ph.D. dissertation, Department of Anthropology, University of Arizona.

Kaberry, Phyllis
1957 Malinowski's Contribution to Field Work Methods and the Writing of Ethnography. In *Man and Culture: An Evaluation of the Work of Malinowski,* ed. Raymond Firth, pp. 71-92. London: Routledge & Kegan Paul.

Khuri, Fuad I.
1967 A Comparative Study of Migration Patterns in Two Lebanese Villages. *Human Organization* 26:206-13.

Kluckhohn, Florence R.
1963 Some Reflections on the Nature of Cultural Integration and Change. In *Sociological Theory, Values, and Sociocultural Change,* ed. E. A. Tiryakian, pp. 217-48. New York: Free Press, Macmillan.

Kunstadter, Peter
1970 Natality, Mortality, and Migration in Upland and Lowland Populations in Northwestern Thailand. In *Culture and Population: A Collection of Current Studies,* ed. Steven Polgar, pp. 46-60. Carolina Population Center Monograph no. 9. Chapel Hill, N.C.

Kunstadter, Peter, et al.
1963 Demographic Variability and Preferential Marriage Patterns. *American Journal of Physical Anthropology* 21:511-19.

Lamb, N. P.
1969 Papago Population Biology: A Study of Microevolution. Ph.D. dissertation, Department of Anthropology, University of Arizona.

Lane, Michael
1970 *Introduction to Structuralism.* New York: Basic Books.

Langness, L. L.
1964 Some Problems in the Conceptualization of Highlands Social Structures. *American Anthropologist* 66, no. 4, pt. 2:162-82.

Larson, Eric H.
1966 Nukufero: A Tikopian Colony in the Russell Islands. Eugene: Department of Anthropology, University of Oregon.

Lasker, Gabriel
1956 Small Isolated Human Breeding Populations and Their Significance for the Process of Racial Differentiation. In *Men and Cultures,* ed. A. F. C. Wallace, pp. 684-91. Philadelphia: University of Pennsylvania Press.

Laughlin, William
1968a Hunting: An Integrating Bio-Behavior System and Its Evolutionary Importance. In *Man the Hunter,* ed. Richard Lee and Irven De Vore, pp. 304-20. Chicago: Aldine.
1968b Guide to Human Population Studies. *Arctic Anthropology* 5:32-47.
Leach, Edmund R.
1954 *Political Systems of Highland Burma.* Cambridge: At the University Press.
1960 The Sinhalese of the Dry Zone of Northern Ceylon. In *Social Structure in Southeast Asia,* ed. G. P. Murdock, pp. 116-26. Viking Fund Publications in Anthropology no. 29. Chicago: Quadrangle Books.
1961a *Pul Eliya: A Village in Ceylon.* Cambridge: At the University Press.
1961b *Rethinking Anthropology.* Monographs on Social Anthropology, no. 22. London: London School of Economics.
Lee, Everett S.
1966 A Theory of Migration. *Demography* 3:47-57.
Lee, Richard B.
1966 !Kung Bushman Subsistence: An Input-Output Analysis. In *Conference on Cultural Ecology,* ed. D. Damas. National Museum of Canada Bulletin no. 230, Ottawa.
Lessa, William
1955 Depopulation of Ulithi. *Human Biology* 27:161-83.
1964 The Social Effects of Typhoon Ophelia (1960) on Ulithi. *Micronesia* 1:1-47.
1966 *Ulithi: A Micronesian Design for Living.* New York: Holt, Rinehart, & Winston.
Lessa, William, and George C. Myers
1962 Population Dynamics of an Atoll Community. *Population Studies* 15:244-57.
Lévi-Strauss, Claude
1963 *Structural Anthropology.* New York: Basic Books.
Levy, Larion J.
1952 *Structure of Society.* Princeton: Princeton University Press.
Lewin, Kurt
1936 The Conflict Between Aristotelian and Galileian Modes of Thought in Contemporary Psychology. In *A Dynamic Theory of Personality,* ed. Kurt Lewin, pp. 1-42. New York: McGraw-Hill.
Lowenthal, David, and Lambros Comitas
1962 Emigration and Depopulation: Some Neglected Aspects of Population Geography. *Population Review* 6:83-94.
Lowie, Robert H.
1937 *History of Ethnological Theory.* New York: Rinehart.
Malinowski, Bronislaw
1922 *Argonauts of the Western Pacific.* London: Routledge.
Mark, Albyn K.
1960 Description of and Variables Relating to Ecological Change in the History of the Papago Indian Population. M.A. thesis, Department of Anthropology, University of Arizona.
Maruyama, Magoroh
1963 The Second Cybernetics: Deviation-Amplifying Mutual Causal Processes. *American Scientist* 51:164-79.
Mauldin, W. Parker
1966 Estimating Rates of Population Growth. In *Family Planning and Population Programs,* ed. Bernard Berelson et al., pp. 635-53. Chicago: University of Chicago Press.
Meadows, Paul
1957 Models, Systems, and Science. *American Sociological Review* 22:3-9.
Meggitt, M. J.
1965 *The Lineage System of the Mae Enga of New Guinea.* New York: Barnes & Noble.
Merton, Robert K.
1957 *Social Theory and Social Structure.* Glencoe, Ill.: Free Press.
Mitchell, J. Clyde
1969 *Social Networks in Urban Situations.* Manchester: Manchester University Press.
Moerman, Michael
1968 *Agricultural Change and Peasant Choice in a Thai Village.* Berkeley: University of California Press.
Moore, Wilbert E.
1960 A Reconsideration of Theories of Social Change. *American Sociological Review* 25:810-18.
Murdock, George P.

1949   *Social Structure.* New York: Macmillan.

Nadel, S. F.
1951   *Foundations of Social Anthropology.* Glencoe, Ill.: Free Press.
1953   Social Control and Self-Regulation. *Social Forces* 31:265-73.
1957   *Theory of Social Structure.* Glencoe, Ill.: Free Press.

Nagel, Ernest
1961   *Structure of Science.* New York: Harcourt, Brace.

Neel, J. V., and Napoleon Chagnon
1968   The Demography of Two Tribes of Primitive Relatively Unacculturated American Indians. *Proceedings of the National Academy of Sciences* 59:68-689.

Neel, J. V., and F. M. Salzano
1967   Further Studies on the Xavante Indians: Some Hypotheses-Generalizations Resulting from These Studies. *American Journal of Human Genetics* 19:554-74.

Neel, J. V., F. M. Salzano, et al.
1964   Studies on the Xavante Indians of the Brazilian Mato Grosso. *American Journal of Human Genetics* 16:52-140.

Newcombe, H. B., et al.
1959   Automatic Linkage of Vital Records. *Science* 130:954-59.

Newcombe, H. B., and P. O. W. Rhynas
1962   Family Linkage of Population Records. In *The Use of Vital and Health Statistics for Genetic and Radiation Studies,* pp. 135-53. United Nations Publication no. 61. New York: United Nations.

Niswander, J. D., et al.
1970   Population Studies on Southwestern Indian Tribes: 1. History, Culture, and Genetics of the Papago. *American Journal of Human Genetics* 22:7-23.

Nutini, Hugo
1968   *San Bernardino Contla: Marriage and Family Structure in a Tlaxcalan Municipio.* Pittsburgh: University of Pittsburgh Press.

Odum, Eugene P.
1969   The Strategy of Ecosystem Development. *Science* 164:262-70.

Owen, Roger

1965   The Patrilocal Band: A Linguistically and Culturally Hybrid Social Unit. *American Anthropologist* 67:675-90.

Padfield, Harland, and John van Willigen
1969   Work and Income Patterns in a Transitional Population: The Papago of Arizona. *Human Organization* 28:208-16.

Patrick, Ralph, and H. A. Tyroler
1972   Papago Indian Modernization: A Community Scale for Health Research. *Human Organization* 31:127-36.

Population Council
1970   *A Manual for Surveys of Fertility and Family Planning.* New York.

Powdermaker, Hortense
1931   Vital Statistics of New Ireland as Revealed in Genealogies. *Human Biology* 3:351-75.
1933   *Life in Lesu.* London: Williams & Northgate.

Radcliffe-Brown, A. R.
1913   Three Tribes of Western Australia. *Journal of the Royal Anthropological Institute* 43:143-94.
1922   *The Andaman Islanders.* Glencoe, Ill.: Free Press.
1930   *The Social Organization of Australian Tribes.* Oceania Monographs no. 1. Melbourne.
1952   *Structure and Function in Primitive Society.* Glencoe, Ill.: Free Press.

Rappaport, Roy A.
1967   *Pigs for the Ancestors.* New Haven: Yale University Press.

Redfield, Robert
1947   The Folk Society. *American Journal of Sociology* 52:293-308.

Rivers, W. H. R.
1900   A Genealogical Method of Collecting Social and Vital Statistics. *Journal of the Royal Anthropological Institute* 30:74-82.
1906   *The Todas.* New York: Macmillan.
1910   The Genealogical Method of Anthropological Inquiry. *Sociological Review* 3:1-12. Reissued as Bobbs-Merrill Reprint Series in the Social Sciences no. A-190.

Roberts, D. F.
1956   A Demographic Study of a Dinka Village. *Human Biology* 28:323-49.

Romney, A. Kimball

n.d. The Processing of Genealogical Data. Stanford: Department of Anthropology, Stanford University.

Rose, F. G.
1960 *Classification of Kin, Age Structure, and Marriage Amongst the Groote Eylandt Aborigines.* Berlin: Akademie Verlag.
1968 Australian Marriage, Land-Owning Groups, and Initiations. In *Man the Hunter,* ed. Richard Lee and Irven De Vore, pp. 200-208. Chicago: Aldine.

Ryder, Norman B.
1957 The Conceptualization of the Transition in Fertility. *Cold Spring Harbor Symposia on Quantitative Biology* 22:91-96.
1959 Fertility. In *The Study of Population,* ed. Philip Hauser and O. D. Duncan, pp. 400-36. Chicago: University of Chicago Press.
1965a The Cohort in the Study of Social Change. *American Sociological Review* 30:843-61.
1965b The Measurement of Fertility Patterns. In *Public Health and Population Change,* ed. Mindel Sheps and Jean Ridley, pp. 287-305. Pittsburgh: University of Pittsburgh Press.

Sahlins, Marshall
1962 *Moala.* Ann Arbor: University of Michigan Press.
1965 On the Ideology and Composition of Descent Groups. *Man,* no. 97.

Salisbury, Richard
1956 Unilineal Descent Groups in the New Guinea Highlands. *Man,* no. 2.

Salzano, Francisco M., J. V. Neel, and D. Maybury-Lewis
1967 Further Studies on the Xavante Indians: Demographic Data on Two Additional Villages: Genetic Structure of the Tribe. *American Journal of Human Genetics* 19:463-89.

Sankoff, Gillian
1970a Surface and Underlying Levels in Cognitive Models: Buang Social Organization. Paper read at 69th annual meeting, American Anthropological Association, San Diego.
1970b Cognitive Variability and New Guinea Social Organization: The Buang Dgwa. Unpublished MS.

Schapera, I.
1950 Kinship and Marriage Among the Tswana. In *African Systems of Kinship and Marriage,* ed. A. R. Radcliffe-Brown and Daryll Forde, pp. 140-65. London: Oxford University Press.

Scheffler, Harold W.
1965 *Choiseul Island Social Structure.* Berkeley: University of California Press.

Schneider, David
1968 Rivers and Kroeber in the Study of Kinship. In W. H. R. Rivers, *Kinship and Social Organization,* pp. 7-16. Monographs on Social Anthropology, no. 34. London: London School of Economics.

Shapiro, Harry L.
1957 The Population Unit and Culture. *Cold Spring Harbor Symposia on Quantitative Biology* 22:409-14.

Smelser, Neil
1959 *Social Change in the Industrial Revolution.* Chicago: University of Chicago Press.

Smith, Michael G.
1962 *Kinship and Community in Carriacou.* New Haven: Yale University Press.

Sorokin, Pitirim
1957 *Social and Cultural Dynamics.* Boston: Porter Sargent.

Spillius, James
1957 Natural Disaster and Political Crisis in a Polynesian Society. *Human Relations* 10:3-28, 113-25.

Spoehr, Alexander
1941 Camp, Clan, and Kin Among the Cow Creek Seminole of Florida. *Field Museum of Natural History Anthropological Series,* vol. 33, no. 1:1-27. Chicago: University of Chicago Press.
1942 Kinship System of the Seminole. *Field Museum of Natural History Anthropological Series,* vol. 33, no. 2: 29-113. Chicago: University of Chicago Press.
1944 The Florida Seminole Camp. *Field Museum of Natural History Anthropological Series,* vol. 33, no. 3:115-50. Chicago: University of Chicago Press.

1947 Changing Kinship Systems. *Field Museum of Natural History Anthropological Series,* vol. 33, no. 4:151-235. Chicago: University of Chicago Press.

Steward, Julian
1956 *Theory of Culture Change.* Urbana: University of Illinois Press.

Stockwell, Edward G.
1960 The Measurement of Economic Development. *Economic Development and Cultural Change* 8:419-32.

Stolnitz, George
1964 The Demographic Transition: From High to Low Birth Rates and Death Rates. In *The Vital Revolution,* ed. Ronald Freedman, pp. 30-46. Garden City, N.Y.: Doubleday.

Sutter, Jean, and Tran-Ngoc-Toan
1957 The Problem of the Structure of Isolates and of Their Evolution Among Human Populations. *Cold Spring Harbor Symposia on Quantitative Biology* 22:379-83.

Turner, Victor
1957 *Schism and Continuity in an African Society.* Manchester: Manchester University Press.

Tyroler, H. A.
1965 Blood Pressure Studies of the Papago Indian. Paper read at American Heart Association Conference on Epidemiology of Cardiovascular Diseases, Chicago.

Tyroler, H. A., and Ralph Patrick
1972 Epidemiologic Studies of Papago Indian Mortality. *Human Organization* 31:163-70.

Uhlmann, Julie M.
1972 The Impact of Modernization upon Papago Indian Fertility. *Human Organization.* 31:149-62.

United Nations
1967 *Methods of Estimating Demographic Measures from Incomplete Data.* Manual 4. ST/soa/series A 42.

Van Velsen, J.
1964 *The Politics of Kinship.* Manchester: Manchester University Press.
1967 The Extended Case Method and Situational Analysis. In *The Craft of Social Anthropology,* ed. A. L. Epstein, pp. 129-52. London: Tavistock.

Vogt, Evon Z.

1960 On the Concepts of Structure and Process in Cultural Anthropology. *American Anthropologist* 62:18-33.
1969 Some Unexpected Uses of Aerial Photography for Ethnographic Research in the Highlands of Chiapas. Paper read at 69th annual meeting, American Anthropological Association, New Orleans.

Wallace, Anthony F. C.
1970 *Culture and Personality,* 2nd ed. New York: Random House.

Warner, William L.
1937 *A Black Civilization.* New York: Harper.

Weiner, J., and J. Lourie
1969 *Human Biology.* International Biological Programme, Handbook no. 9. Philadelphia: F. A. Davis.

Wilson G., and M. Wilson
1949 *Analysis of Social Change.* Cambridge: At the University Press.

Wolfenden, Hugh H.
1954 *Population Statistics and Their Compilation.* Chicago: University of Chicago Press.

Workman, P. L., and J. D. Niswander
1970 Population Studies on Southwestern Indian Tribes: II. Local Genetic Differentiation in the Papago. *American Journal of Human Genetics* 22:24-49.

Yengoyan, Aram
1968a Demographic and Ecological Influences on Aboriginal Australian Marriage Sections. In *Man the Hunter,* ed. Richard Lee and Irven De Vore, pp. 185-99. Chicago: Aldine.
1968b Demography, Social Structure, and Ritual in Central Australia. Paper read at 67th annual meeting, American Anthropological Association, Seattle.
1970 Demographic Factors in Pitjandjara Social Organization. In *Australian Aboriginal Anthropology,* ed. R. M. Berndt, pp. 70-91. Perth: University of Western Australia Press.

Zimmerly, David
1968 Changing Patterns of Mate Selection Among the Papago Indians. Paper read at 67th annual meeting, American Anthropological Association, Seattle.

CHAPTER 8   Cross-Cultural Studies

HAROLD E. DRIVER

Any study that compares the cultures of two or more societies may be said to be a cross-cultural study. The largest number of societies compared so far is about a thousand, but most researchers are content with a smaller sample. Such a sample may deal with a few adjacent peoples, or with a larger number in a culture area, a continent, a hemisphere, or the entire world. The cultural content to be compared may vary from a single detail, such as avoidance between a man and his mother-in-law, to a wide variety covering many aspects of culture, such as those listed by Murdock (1967).

Naroll (1968:236-39) has divided all cross-cultural studies into two kinds: idiographic and nomothetic. Idiographic studies concentrate on particularistic details localized in time and space, while nomothetic studies attempt to make lawlike generalizations about all human societies in all times and places. I prefer to regard the two as conceptually opposite poles of a continuum. A field report on a single society is rarely completely idiographic, as Lévi-Strauss and some of the British structural-functional school have made clear in their formulation of universal laws of human behavior from data on a single society. Furthermore, comparative studies of small numbers of societies may also interpret data in accordance with lawlike principles. My recent review (Driver 1970d) of statistical studies of continuous geographical distributions reveals interpretations based on lawlike concepts as well as particular details on the particular societies involved. When the regional study covers a large continent, some of the generalizations arrived at may match those derived from a world sample and thus be nomothetic. This was true of most of my generalizations about North American Indian kinship and social organization (Driver 1956; Driver and Massey 1957:421-39). The postulated multiple independent origins of all of the variables in this study can be explained only by nomothetic principles of an ecological, social, and causal-evolutionary kind. In this case I had Lowie's (1920) and Murdock's (1949) work to fall back on and found few reasons to differ with them on the main issues of interpretation.

Naroll (1968:240-42) calls a comparative study in a small region a concomitant variation study. The methods employed in such studies are close to what Eggan (1954) has called the method of controlled comparison. Here the researcher knows almost all of the culture inventory and the ecological and archaeological bases shared by all the peoples in the study; he has only to explain the relatively few differences. In such a study the investigator has less chance to distinguish an idiographic relationship from a nomothetic one than does the researcher covering a continent. My emphasis here will be on worldwide cross-cultural studies.

McEwen (1963) classifies studies in social anthropology into three principal categories: (1) illustrative, where only one or a few positive instances are cited to support a preconceived or ex post facto hypothesis; (2) typological, where a number of societies classified into types are compared, often in the form of a cross-classification table, but without any definition of universe sampled, sampling method, or use of statistics; (3) statistical, where the universe and sampling method are specified and statistical tests are run to measure strength of relationship and its significance. My main concern here is with the third group.

The arrangement of data for cross-cultural comparisons takes the form of a cross-classification table with the societies (ethnic units) listed on one axis and the culture traits or behaviors on the other. Table 1 gives a small portion of the data in Murdock's *Ethnographic Atlas* (1967:64). Column 1 gives the area code of each society, with A signifying Africa. Column 3 gives an arbitrary code number (assigned in order of inclusion in the atlas) and the name of the society. Columns 42 to 62 give the dominant sexual division of labor for as many kinds of economic and technological activity: 42, metalworking; 44, weaving; 46, leather working; 48, pottery making; 50, boat building; 52, house construction; 54, gathering food, principally wild plants; 56, hunting; 58, fishing; 60, animal husbandry; 62, agriculture. The capital letters in the body of the table have the following definitions: D, differentiation of specific tasks by sex but approximately equal participation by both sexes in the total activity; E, equal participation by both

TABLE 1
Cross-Classification Table of Data

Societies (Ethnic Units)		Sets of Culture Traits or Behaviors										
1	*3*	*42*	*44*	*46*	*48*	*50*	*52*	*54*	*56*	*58*	*60*	*62*
Aa1	1: Kung	O	O	M	O	O	F	G	M	O	O	O
Aa2	101: Dorobo	O	O	F	O	O	F	G	M	O	O	O
Aa3	102: Nama	M	O	G	F	O	D	F	M	M	D	O
Aa5	202: Mbuti	O	O	O	O	O	G	G	N	E	O	O
Aa6	301: Sandawe	.	.	.	.	.	.	F	M	F	M	G
Aa7	636: Naron	O	O	M	O	O	F	F	M	O	O	O
Aa9	726: Hatsa	O	O	.	.	O	.	F	M	O	O	O
Ab1	2: Herero	Mc	O	M	.	O	.	F	M	O	E	O
Ab2	3: Swazi	Mc	O	M	.	.	E	F	M	O	M	G

Source: George P. Murdock, *Ethnographic Atlas*, p. 64. (Pittsburgh: University of Pittsburgh Press.)

sexes without marked or reported differentiation in specific tasks; F, females alone perform the activity, male participation being negligible; G, both sexes participate, but females appreciably more than males; I, sex participation irrelevant, especially where production is industrialized; M, males alone perform the activity, female participation being negligible; Mc, craft specialization by males, with no female participation; N, both sexes participate, but males do appreciably more than females; O, the activity is absent or unimportant in the particular society; P, the activity is present, but sex participation is unspecified in the sources consulted. A dot indicates no data of any kind in the sources consulted.

HISTORY OF
CROSS-CULTURAL STUDIES

NINETEENTH-CENTURY COMPARISONS
OF TRENDS IN CULTURAL EVOLUTION

Cross-cultural comparisons were well launched by the second half of the nineteenth century. The greatest figures of this period wrote books that attempted to sum up the major worldwide trends in cultural evolution, which was often regarded as unilinear. The general method of this period was to conjure up generalizations in some intuitive manner and then cite as many positive instances as the author could find to bolster the preconceived theory or hypothesis. Ethnic units and subject units generally were not well defined, nor was there mention of the total universe being described or any explicit method of drawing a sample.

The one exception was Tylor (1889), who assembled detailed data on social organization for some 350 ethnic units. His simple statistics distinguished between obtained and expected frequencies for a part of his data, but he never

assembled his material in one or more cross-classification tables or computed the probability of the differences arising by an accident of sampling. This came a decade later when Karl Pearson discovered chi square and the formula for its sampling distribution. But most of Tylor's correlations have since been confirmed with more accurate data and better samples. His assumption of unilinear evolution, from matrilineal to patrilineal to bilateral descent, is generally considered unproven today. Tylor's paper will be discussed in more detail in a later section, "The Galton Problem."

EARLY TWENTIETH-CENTURY STUDIES:
CULTURAL EVOLUTION VS. DIFFUSION

The next important study was that of Hobhouse, Wheeler, and Ginsberg (1930). They classified some six hundred societies around the world according to method of obtaining food, and arranged them in the following sequence: lower hunters, higher hunters, agriculture I, pastoral I, agriculture II, pastoral II, agriculture III. The evolutionary scale was given on the horizontal axis, and the percentage of ethnic units in each class possessing each social institution being studied was plotted on the vertical axis. This study stopped at the descriptive level; it included no tests for significant differences between or among the proportions. Most of the cultural variables (institutions) showed an upward trend on the evolutionary scale, but a few revealed a downward trend or leveled off. Some of the variables that showed what we could call today a positive correlation with the subsistence scale were tribal government, a regular system of public justice, bride purchase, polygamy, and social stratification. Although the sample has been criticized on the grounds that almost all the lower hunters are located in Australia and the higher hunters in North America, most of its generalizations about evolutionary trends are accepted today and have been confirmed by later research.

The extreme diffusionists of the *Kulturkreis* school never employed statistics to support their assertions, but two such regional tests were made by Czekanowski (1911) and Kroeber and Holt (1920). The former supported the diffusion theory but the latter refuted it. These studies too are discussed in greater detail in the later section called "The Galton Problem."

Between 1926 and 1941 a number of statistical regional studies, aimed principally at establishing areal classifications and postdicting historical relationships, were done under Kroeber at the University of California at Berkeley. These have largely been ignored by the worldwide nomothetic school, but will be shown below to have relevance to lawseeking studies. I have recently reviewed these and other statistical studies of continuous geographical distributions (Driver 1970*d*).

CURRENT COMPARATIVE STUDIES

The dominant group of worldwide cross-cultural studies today began with G. P. Murdock at Yale. His doctoral thesis was a translation from German to English of Julius Lippert's *Evolution of Culture* (1931) and was done under the direction of A. G. Keller in the sociology department at Yale. Murdock received a joint appointment in anthropology at Yale when that department was founded in 1931. By 1937 Murdock had made a printed announcement of his new cross-cultural files and edited a volume of essays in honor of Keller (Murdock, ed., 1937). This volume included two correlation studies, one by Murdock (1937) and the other by Simmons (1937). Each of these was based

on purposive or judgmental samples of fewer than a hundred societies, and was concerned with social organization.

Murdock's *Social Structure,* based on 250 societies, appeared in 1949. It was criticized severely by reviewers in anthropology, whose orientation was largely antievolutionary and antistatistical, but it was hailed as a major advance by other behavioral scientists and later took its place as a milestone of progress within anthropology. This was followed soon by Whiting and Child's (1953) *Child Training and Personality,* which launched a long series of comparative studies in this field.

The Yale Cross-Cultural Files were converted into the multi-university Human Relations Area Files (HRAF) in 1949, and since that time this organization has been the rallying point for cross-cultural research. Some idea of the great number of such studies since this date can be gathered from the bibliographies in Marsh (1967) and O'Leary (1969). Other review articles comparable to this one are Cohen (1968), Naroll (1968, 1970*a*), and Whiting (1968). Marsh (1967) reviews at book length comparative studies in sociology and political science as well as in anthropology and gives 1,146 titles in his bibliography. Two readers published by the HRAF Press, edited by Moore (1961) and Ford (1967), give examples of article-length cross-cultural studies.

THE ETHNIC UNIT

The most common technique of analysis of cross-cultural data is the correlation of pairs of culture traits or behaviors. The ethnic units (societies) are the cases counted. The classic objection to this method is that one is counting a mixed assemblage of cherries, olives, apples, oranges, grapefruits, watermelons, papayas, and pumpkins. A common answer to this criticism is that all the things counted are plant foods and comparable enough on this general level. This cavalier attitude toward ethnic units does not satisfy those social scientists whose position is somewhere between the poles of extreme historical particularism and extreme scientific abstraction.

Recent discussions of the ethnic unit problem by Naroll (1964b, 1970b), Helm (1968), and Cohen (1969) are informative but have failed to establish a uniform set of ethnic units generally accepted by cross-cultural researchers. When it is remembered that the human populations in ethnic unit vary from a couple of dozen persons in the smallest "primitive" groups to the 700 million in China, and from the simplest levels of subsistence exclusively on wild plants and animals to the wide choice of nationally marketed foods in the United States, it is easy to see why anthropologists and other social scientists are not very happy with the great variety of ethnic units used so far in statistical studies.

Where language units have been used largely as ethnic units, as for North American Indians, the skin of each ethnic unit is easy to determine. Where two or more languages meet, persons almost always speak one or the other, not a mixture of two or more. Not so with culture, which tends to blend under similar circumstances. The reason so-called tribal maps are about 90 percent language maps is because it is impossible or next to impossible to determine where one culture-bearing unit stops and another begins on the basis of culture alone. The skin of a culture is extremely difficult to find. Where there are sharp differences in physical type, as between Pygmies and larger blacks in Africa, these are often used to distinguish ethnic units, and become meaningful if correlations between

physical type and culture are run. It is true that language families or phyla are rarely coterminous with culture areas or racial types, but at the lowest level in the classification, the group that communicates internally with a single language and within which most marriages are endogamous is most often the culture-bearing group described by the ethnographer.

Anthropologists have always maintained a natural science attitude toward the size of human populations. No biological taxonomist would ever weight his various species according to their numbers at any given time. Thus the Australian duck-billed platypus, with only a handful of individuals left today, is included as a distinct animal in every taxonomy, and is accorded no less space on the list than man, who numbers over three billion. Similarly, no anthropologist so far has weighted his societies according to size of population in any comparative study.

The analogy between biological species and ethnic units should not be pushed too far because, once biological forms are far enough apart to be classed in separate genera, they can no longer cross-breed. Not so for societies. Contact between the most advanced modern nation and an isolated ethnic unit in the middle of New Guinea always involves some cultural exchange and, if the contact lasts a long time, a drastic transformation of the tribal society is the rule. Because every society in the world, except the Polar Eskimo for a few centuries, has had contact with neighbors, all cultures are hybrids rather than pure types. In addition to descent from common ancestors, every culture is highly cross-bred by acculturation, diffusion, and other kinds of outside contact.

Within each society there are always individual differences in behavior, and these multiply enormously as societies increase their population sizes and their levels of cultural complexity. A single society may even be regarded as a stratum in a stratified sample, and a group of societies as an assemblage of strata, each one of which should be randomly sampled from within. This, of course, cannot be done from a structural-functional kind of field report that treats the society as a whole. Detailed data on a representative sample of individuals within each society are required and can be achieved in the future in studies of ongoing "peasant" societies.

Murdock, Whiting, Naroll, and others have urged that comparativists choose a single community rather than a larger tribe or nation when data are available on the community. This often works well where the family or kinship unit tends to be self-sufficient economically or to control the major norms of behavior toward other communities, such as a rule of exogamy. But if one wishes to study political organization of a large African tribe, or international relations of a group of such large tribes or kingdoms, he must go beyond the data on any single community. Therefore, in a system with a hierarchy of such units, there is no single size of ethnic unit that is best for all purposes. Furthermore, although comparative data should also be pinpointed in time, there is also no single time period that is ideal for all purposes; but because most data apply to the last hundred years, this is the most fruitful time period. For causal inferences a minimum of two time periods is required, and more are still better.

A practical solution to the ethnic unit problem, which no cross-cultural researcher has used so far, is to accept the wide range of variation that everyone knows exists in ethnic units and add variables describing the most obvious kinds of variation to every cross-cultural study. This I have already suggested (Driver et al. 1966:158). Even though such a list might come to 100 attributes grouped into 15 or 20 sets or variables, a matrix reduction technique, such as factor analysis, would probably reduce such variables to four or five factors, which could then be treated as factor variables and included in every cross-cultural study. Every new variable would thereby be placed in a meaningful ethnic unit context. This would rule out bivariate comparisons in favor of multivariate analyses and raise standards of cross-cultural research enormously.

Naroll's (1964b, 1970b) typology of cult units (Hopi, Flathead, Aztec, and Aymará) is better than no division at all, but seems to me to be less adequate than my proposal above. A more lengthy discussion of ethnic units is not very rewarding because the cross-cultural researcher is forced to use the units that hundreds of fieldworkers have chosen for him in advance. He can only modify these a little and must learn to live and work with them.

SAMPLING ETHNIC UNITS

How do we choose a sample of ethnic units from the thousands on which desired information may be available? If the data chosen for study are restricted to a single region, the question of the extent to which a sample is representative of all human societies in all parts of the world and over all periods of time does not exist. Thus one may make a comparative study of the Sun Dance of the Plains Indians and include every tribe that is known to have presented this ceremony up to the terminal time of the study (Spier 1921, Clements 1931, Driver and Kroeber 1932, Driver 1939). Regional studies of wider topical coverage sometimes create a problem as to where to delimit the region, but as long as the area is continuous, the limits set have not tended to draw much flak from critics. Worldwide samples are another matter, however, and there has been much argument about them over the years.

It is impossible to draw a simple random sample from a roster of all human societies because no such list exists. If the standard is lowered to a universe of all societies adequately described, a closer approach to an operational parameter is achieved, but the unevenness of such descriptions still makes it impossible to draw a simple random sample and obtain the desired information on every society drawn. If a researcher finds the information he is seeking on half the societies he chooses, he is doing well. When the data sought are especially rare, some researchers have made universal generalizations about human behavior from fewer than fifty societies around the world (see Textor 1967, where the number of cases are given for all relationships in eight pounds of computer printout). A description of some of the worldwide samples of the last twenty-five years will bring out the issues involved.

Murdock (1949) used a sample of 250 societies from all major areas of the world in his *Social Structure*. Most of them were the so-called tribal societies studied by anthropologists, but some were communities in modern nations in Europe and America. In spite of overemphasis on North American Indians and to a lesser extent on Africans, and repeated criticism of the sample at later dates by Murdock himself, practically all of the statistical generalizations made in 1949 have withstood the criticism of the years. This was definitely a purposive or judgmental sample; the researcher chose the societies to give as even a representation as possible to all the varieties of social structure known to him at the time.

Whiting and Child (1953) initially chose a world sample of seventy-five societies, but field reporting was so uneven that their statistics were based on a range of from twenty to forty societies. Cross-cultural data on child training and personality were so scarce at that time that they used whatever was available, and managed to include at least a few cases from every major area of the world. In spite of this severe sampling limitation, many of their statistical generalizations have been confirmed by later research.

Murdock (1957) published a world ethnographic sample of 565 ethnic units and 210 culture traits grouped into 30 sets or variables. This was about six times the size of his 1949 sample because it contained about twice as many ethnic units and three times as many culture categories. Time periods, however, are more mixed: e.g., the Aryans of 800 B.C. are included. He and others considered this sample of ethnic units more representative of all the known human societies than the one of 1949, but it was still based on his judgment rather than on an explicit sampling technique. Swanson (1960) was the first to use a stratified random sample, and it was drawn from this one.

Marsh (1967:329-74) combined 467 societies from Murdock's 1957 sample and 114 contemporary national societies not included by Murdock. He scaled all of these societies according to their amount of "differentiation," based on degree of political integration and degree of social stratification for the part derived from Murdock, and on the percentage of males engaged in nonagricultural pursuits and gross energy consumption in megawatt hours per capita per year for the nations added. All of the ethnic units chosen from Murdock (1957) were regarded as less differentiated than any of the modern nations, and ranged from 1 to 7 on the scale. The modern nations ranged from 8.6 (Portuguese Guinea) to 109.4 (U.S.A.). Marsh apparently added all the modern nations on which he could get enough information to scale, but the judgmental character of the majority chosen by Murdock tends to place the entire sample in this general category. To the best of my knowledge, Marsh's sample has not yet been used by any cross-cultural researcher.

Murdock began publishing additional data coded on a still larger number of ethnic units in *Ethnology* in 1962, and in 1967 assembled them in a book entitled *Ethnographic Atlas*. The total number of societies was 863, but some of these were so close to others in geographical, linguistic, or cultural · space that they were combined into 412 "clusters," some with multiple members and others with only a single member. This was done to eliminate some of the resemblances due to common cultural heritage or diffusion. Where membership was multiple, a single society was chosen to represent the group, resulting in another judgmental sample of 412 units.

Murdock (1968) combined the 412 clusters of this study into 200 "provinces" and suggested that the first ethnic unit listed under each province be chosen to represent the type in a new "standard" world sample.

Murdock and White (1969) drew a sample of 186 societies that closely resembled the 200 provinces of Murdock's 1968 sample. In this study Murdock completely abandoned the hope of eliminating all historical influence by choosing ethnic units some distance apart in geography, culture, and language. He joined White in the application of a partly new "Galton problem" (see below) technique to measure the amount of influence of common history on a given correlation coefficient.

Their conclusion was that if the effects of historical influence were totally eliminated from the correlations computed, there would be only twenty provinces left from which to choose a sample of historically independent societies, a smaller number than any cross-cultural researcher would care to work with.

Naroll (1968:254-58) mentioned the Northwestern University Permanent Ethnographic Probability Sample. He first constructed a universe of well-described societies in which each ethnographer spent at least a year in the field, made some claim to knowing the native language, and published a chapter or article on each of ten two-digit categories in the *Outline of Cultural Materials* (Murdock et al. 1961). From this universe he originally drew a simple random sample.

Naroll (1967) and Anonymous (1967) produced another probability sample. The point of departure was a universe of 206 societies "stratified" (grouped) into 60 macroclusters by Murdock (1957, 1967). The number of societies in each macrocluster varied from none to eight, and these were rated A or B quality according to quality control criteria devised largely by Naroll. When the number of societies in group A was only one, that society was chosen; when the number was more than one, one was selected from a table of random numbers. If there were no A quality societies and more than one of B quality, one of the B group was chosen from a table of random numbers. Although such a sample is a probability sample as defined by Kish (1965:20, 75-106), it differs in two important respects from most of the social survey samples Kish discusses: (1) it has sixty strata, instead of the three to ten that Kish (1965:102) says are desirable; (2) each stratum is not weighted in proportion to the number of societies within it, whereas most of Kish's (1965:75-106) sociological strata are weighted according to the number of families or individuals within each. When sixty strata are determined judgmentally, judgment looms larger than it does when only three to ten strata are involved. Regardless of Kish's classification of all stratified samples as probability samples, Naroll's probability sample is a mixture of judgments and probabilities and not completely unbiased. A more objective way to determine groups of societies for stratified sampling will be discussed shortly.

Chaney and Ruiz Revilla (1969) computed the same correlations from seven world samples containing 48, 60, 112, 400, 412, 565, and 863 societies respectively. Their most general conclusion was that the three smaller samples gave more significant differences with each other and with the larger four than did the larger four among themselves. In short, small samples are more volatile than large samples—a conclusion known a century ago, but important today also.

Many significant differences between small samples and large samples are shown in a paper by Tatje, Textor, and Naroll (1970), summarized below in the section on "Reliability and Quality Control."

Greenbaum (1970) compared correlation results from a simple random sample drawn from Murdock's 1967 sample of 863 societies with a "stratified" sample of 412 societies drawn randomly from those clusters that had two or more member societies. But because 217 of the clusters contained only one member, the random selection applied to fewer than half. The general conclusion was that there was little or no significant difference in correlations computed from the two samples.

A discussion of sampling at the Second HRAF Cross-Cultural Research Conference in November 1969 (Anonymous 1970) will reflect some of the issues currently being discussed. Frank Moore mentioned that when the HRAF probability sample of sixty societies was drawn in 1967, files on all but seventeen societies had already been compiled. Since 1967, twelve new files have been added and five remain to be done. Then Naroll criticized Murdock's clusters and provinces as being too subjective. Murdock countered with the criticism that one pair of societies in the HRAF probability sample, chosen largely by Naroll, were so close together geographically that they shared too much common history. Moore replied that the societies in this pair had been put in two separate clusters by Murdock, and for this reason both were eligible for the probability sample and happened to be drawn by an "accident" of sampling. Roberts then made the point that a single sample cannot determine the effectiveness of a sampling design because a very large number of specifically different samples may be drawn with a single design. Ember, who has chosen small random samples from Murdock's large samples on several occasions, recommended that two such random samples be chosen for the same study and the same statistics run on each. If the two samples agree, this gives the researcher more assurance than he can get from a single sample. Murdock next criticized the HRAF probability sample of sixty societies for not giving any representation at all to forty-six (25 percent) of his sampling provinces. A number of persons at this conference agreed that no one sample is the answer to every researcher's prayer. To this I heartily subscribe.

Turning to the field of glottochronology and substituting linguistic distance or proximity for cultural distance or proximity, as Whiting and Ayres (1968) have done, is better than making no attempt at all to gauge cultural distance or proximity, but it is hardly the perfect solution because it rests on the assumption that there is a perfect correlation between language and culture. Although Jorgensen (1969) found a relatively high correlation between linguistic and cultural proximity within the Salish language family, such a relationship among multiple language families would be lower and the prediction of cultural proximity from linguistic proximity quite low. To note a single example of lack of relationship between linguistic and cultural proximity, consider the Yurok, K'arok, and Hupa, neighbors in California, whose cultures are extremely close (Driver and Schuessler 1957), but whose languages are not only in separate families, but also in separate phyla.

Although Murdock's division of the world into major areas, provinces, clusters, and societies has given great impetus to cross-cultural research, the ad hoc nature of these units becomes clear when they are examined critically. For the major areas, North and South America are sufficiently distinct geographically and culturally to satisfy everyone, and Insular Pacific is also quite distinct from other Old World areas. But the division of the mainland Old World into Africa south of the Sahara, Circum-Mediterranean, and East Eurasia is more arbitrary and subjective. When it is noted that each of these six areas was further subdivided into ten provinces, it is obvious that such uniformity in numbers would not happen if an explicit technique of numerical classification had been employed. Therefore no high order of objectivity can be claimed for the determination of the "strata," and any probability sample drawn from such strata is far from ideal. Furthermore, Murdock's design, beginning with the largest areal units, then splitting these into ten

subdivisions, and finally dividing these into smaller clusters, reflects the fundamentally subjective nature of the operation. Biological science begins with the smallest units and progressively combines these into larger taxa (Sokal and Sneath 1963).

Areal classification of human societies is best done with a Q-type analysis that expresses the relationship between pairs of societies in terms of the proportion of common cultural inventory shared. The lexicostatistics used in glottochronology is a Q-type analysis applied to lists of words. Boas (1894) was the first anthropologist to make such a comparison (for folklore), and many other examples from the California school of comparative ethnology were published between 1926 and 1941 (Driver 1970d). The two largest and most informative examples of areal classification from California are those of Klimek (1935) and Driver (1941), although the latter is based on a single topic rather than a broad spectrum of culture inventory. A more recent regional study that groups both languages and cultures into taxa with the Q-type technique is that of Jorgensen (1969). In none of these empirical demonstrations is the number of societies at a lower level uniform with respect to the next higher level, as are Murdock's ten macroclusters in each of his six major areas.

Although all of the interrelationships among a thousand or more societies cannot be grouped in a single computer run, the techniques given by Sokal and Sneath (1963), Driver (1965), and Jorgensen (1969) could be adapted to Murdock's largest sample (1967). However, Murdock's subject content was chosen primarily to determine functional-causal-evolutionary intertrait relationships and is not ideal for an areal taxonomy, in which historical relationships are normally sought; a Q-type analysis applied to his data would yield a more accurate and meaningful taxonomy of societies than his ad hoc intuitive schemes. Naroll's introduction of a little randomization at the lowest level does not make his probability stratified sample a completely satisfactory random sample, but, like many other samples, it is good enough to use until further refinements in sampling are achieved.

Historical relationships are best postdicted from a sample of more specific trait categories than those of Murdock (1967), and the sample should ideally include a larger proportion of nonfunctional relationships (see below). The addition of sections on technology would add to the historicity of such a sample because this subject contains many alternative and arbitrary ways of manufacture and use of material objects. Naroll (1970d) suggests that this type of analysis should control for functional "contamination," just as the Galton problem techniques control for historical "contamination."

In light of Greenbaum's (1970) and Chaney and Ruiz Revilla's (1969) work, the pragmatic thing to do at present is to use any large sample or a simple random sample from it. The notion that small samples are better than large samples, now being circulated by some of the younger men, reflects ignorance of the advisability of using measures of strength of relationship (e.g., phi or gamma) in addition to measures of significance (e.g., chi square). I am skeptical of results from any worldwide sample of fewer than one hundred cases, unless it is randomly chosen from one of Murdock's large samples.

To the best of my knowledge, all anthropologists who have done cross-cultural research have used statistical formulas designed for simple random samples drawn from infinite universes of cases. When a simple random sample is chosen from a finite sample of four hundred or fewer, it would be a little more accurate to use finite sample formulae. For a discussion of other sampling designs at a not too difficult level, see Naroll (1970c) and Lazerwitz (1968).

When correlations are high they can tolerate a large amount of error and will show up as significant in almost any sample; the error present is likely to affect only their magnitudes, not their signs. When correlations are low, they may not pass a significance test when the same amount of error is present. Sampling becomes critical for lower correlations, increasingly so as smaller samples are used.

As Naroll (1970c) points out, the sampling error formulas built into practically all statistics measure only random error arising from accidents of sampling. For a discussion of systematic errors, see the section on "Reliability and Quality Control" below. Should significance tests designed for simple random samples be used for nonrandom judgmental samples? The answer is yes. They give the minimum amount of error: that arising from random sampling. If no test of significance is made, a few cases are as good as a thousand, which everyone knows is nonsense. If a relationship passes a significance test, one can still worry about the nonrandomness of the sample or the systematic errors; but if it fails to pass a significance test it may be dismissed as unproven until retested with a "better" or larger sample.

It is apparent that cross-cultural researchers are still largely dependent on purposive or judgmental samples, and that Naroll's introduction of randomization within strata makes them more impartial, but does not eliminate the judgments used in choosing the large number of strata. However, the drawing of judgmental samples or "strata" has been greatly improved by the bibliographic work of Murdock (1960), the world roster of societies by Murdock (1963), by other bibliographies published by the HRAF, and by Naroll's Permanent Ethnographic Probability Sample, done at Northwestern University. For more detail on the last, see the section on "Reliability and Quality Control."

The most novel sampling idea of recent years is the grid method of McNett and Kirk (1968). A grid of squares the size of five degrees of longitude along the equator is superimposed on an equal-area projection map of the world. Then each intersection of the coordinate lines is numbered by its coordinates. A random sample of these points is next chosen from a table of random numbers and the culture closest to each point is chosen, providing it is sufficiently well described. So far this system has not been used. Although it introduces some randomness into the sampling procedure, the choice of each society also depends on the fullness and accuracy of its data, and that is always a matter of judgment even with quality control criteria. McNett and Kirk (1968) cite an earlier grid sample chosen by Naroll (1961b) but not published.

THE GALTON PROBLEM

The now famous paper by Tylor (1889) was aimed at establishing causal-evolutionary sequences from worldwide data on 350 ethnic units. His interculture-trait comparisons of presence-absence dichotomies fell short of twentieth-century methods, but he was the first to apply probability theory to this kind of data by computing expected frequencies for some of the cells of the cross-classification tables and comparing them with the observed frequencies.

Of more importance than Tylor's paper are the questions raised about it by Sir Francis Galton. Galton asked about the comparability of the ethnic units and their historical independence, and suggested that the mapping of the data would aid interpretation. Tylor gave unsatisfactory answers or none at all to these questions and never even listed the ethnic units, much less the entire geographical distributions of the various culture elements of the study, in the published version; nor did he even give a bibliography of sources used.

Galton's question about the historical independence of the ethnic units introduced confusion that still persists in cross-cultural research. It is generally believed that statistical treatment is invalid unless the historical independence of the ethnic units can be established. This is nonsense. The independence of cases in statistics refers only to the drawing of the sample. A simple random sample is one in which each case in the total parameter has an equal chance of being drawn and the selection of each case is independent of every other case. Sample drawing has nothing to do with the historical independence of ethnic units in cross-cultural research. Historical independence is necessary only if the researcher is trying to establish a causal-evolutionary sequence. This is exactly what Tylor was trying to do and is the main goal of cross-cultural research today, but it is not the only one.

It is necessary to distinguish three types of interculture-trait relationships: functional, dysfunctional, and nonfunctional. The relation between patrilocal residence and patrilineal descent is functional because the two concepts align members of a society in a parallel fashion. The relation between patrilocal residence and matrilineal descent is dysfunctional because the two groupings align members in opposing ways. The relation between patrilocal residence and coiled basketry is nonfunctional because neither trait reinforces or opposes the other. Cross-cultural studies done in the United States have been almost wholly concerned with functional and dysfunctional relationships and the arrangement of the former into causal-evolutionary sequences. But the German *Kulturkreis* school looked for nonfunctional relationships to establish diffusion or migration. The form criterion of this school demanded that the culture variables (originally material objects) have resemblances in form not caused by the materials from which they were made or the uses to which they were put. The greater the quantity of such resemblances among a number of societies, the greater the probability of diffusion or migration. For instance, Czekanowski (1911) computed Q coefficients between seventeen traits of material culture among forty-seven African ethnic units from data compiled by B. Ankerman. When clustered, these coefficients fell into two distinct clusters, which were interpreted as historical as well as geographical units. Kroeber and Holt (1920), finding a zero correlation between masks and moieties in native North America, concluded that there was no historical relationship between the two traits of this nonfunctional pair. These studies measured historical dependence in this way: the higher the correlation, the greater the probability that the relationship was determined by some historical process. However, this interpretation applies only to relationships conceded to be nonfunctional.

Nonfunctional relationships have been recognized recently by Naroll (1965, 1968), who notes the association in aboriginal California of patrilinear totemic clans with flageolets, carrying frames of sticks and cords, oval plate pottery, a particular kind of fish scoop, a squared muller, and a high regard for twins. I (Driver et al. 1966: 157) mentioned the nonfunctional correlations between a man's avoidance of his mother-in-law and three other items: dog eating, hafted mauls used to grind food, and both hard- and soft-soled moccasins in native North America. Such relationships are probably more numerous than functional and dysfunctional relationships among the culture inventories available now, but they have largely been ignored by most cross-culture researchers, who have been trying until very recently (Murdock and White 1969) to sweep the dirt of diffusion under the rug. Murdock's (1959) *Africa: Its Peoples and Their Culture History* is full of diffusion and migration, but it is not a quantitative cross-cultural study that intercorrelates cultural variables. For a review of diffusion theory and methods for establishing it, see Driver (1973). While nonfunctional correlations are perhaps more numerous in limited regions, many also may be found for the world, as I have suggested. I (Driver 1967) have postulated, but not actually computed, positive correlations for the world among the true arch, the wheel, the plow, the seven-day week, the milking of domesticated animals, ordeals as part of legal procedure (Roberts 1965), and the alphabet. These seem to be nonfunctionally related.

Statistical techniques aimed at measuring the Galton effect, or the influence of historical factors on correlations, have been applied or discussed by Naroll (1961a, 1964a, 1965, 1968), Naroll and D'Andrade (1963), Driver et al. (1966), Jorgensen (1966), Murdock and White (1969), Driver and Chaney (1970), and Chaney et al. (n.d.). All of these techniques demonstrate that all cultural variables so far tested, taken singly or in pairs, are not randomly distributed over the face of the earth, but tend to form nonrandom geographical clusters. Naroll (1961a) demonstrated this for Murdock's 1957 sample, in which the societies had been deliberately separated in geographical, cultural, and linguistic space to minimize such clustering. All of these authors have assumed that the nonrandom clustering was due to diffusion or some other historical process. Naroll (1961a) distinguished between hyperdiffusional, semidiffusional, and undiffusional relationships. His hyperdiffusional correlation corresponds to my nonfunctional category; his semidiffusional category refers to a functional correlation for which both of a pair of traits are found in the same geographical clusters; and his undiffusional relationship refers to a correlation in which the positive instances are randomly distributed with no tendency toward areal clustering. Nearly all relationships so far tested by cross-cultural researchers are semidiffusional.

Driver and Chaney (1970) were the first to divide pairs of societies into adjacent and distant pairs for the matched-pair technique originally introduced by D'Andrade (Naroll and D'Andrade 1963). We found that areal clustering (diffusion) was significantly more frequent among adjacent pairs, and that functional relationship was significantly more frequent among distant pairs. Our other major conclusion was that semidiffusional relationships were far more frequent among adjacent pairs than the hyper- or undiffusional, and accounted for more than half of the total variance. Chaney et al. (n.d.) divided pairs of societies into four groups according to geographical distance. They found that the effect of diffusion diminished with distance and that of function increased in proportion to diffusion, thus confirming and refining the main conclusion of Driver and Chaney (1970).

Although cultural variables may differ enormously in the number and density of their geographical clusterings, taken singly or in combinations of two or more, it now seems established that none are likely to be randomly distributed; they are partly determined by ecological and historical factors.

Goodenough (Anonymous 1970: 181) suggested at the Second HRAF Cross-Cultural Research Conference that the dichotomy between common ancestry and diffusion was false: language, religious cults, metallurgical traditions, ceramic traditions—each has its own historical pedigree and could be grouped in its own genetically related family, and a number of such families may cross-cut one another without sharing any or much common history. Within the best researched language family, Indo-European, the distinction between genetically inherited material and diffused (loaned) items is quite sharp and the dichotomy very real. In language families with no documentary depth, such as those of American Indians, this distinction is more difficult to make, but it has nevertheless been done for the best researched of them. Culture on the whole is so much less structured than language that it is much more difficult to assign cultural similarities to genetic heritage or to more recent diffusion. I agree that each cultural domain may have a history partly or totally independent of that of another domain. The problem is how to determine indirectly whether this is so in any particular case from largely synchronic data. The only reason for trying to correlate cultural data with language families or human biological types is that the data exist with which to do it. Where cultural domains do not match linguistic or biological classes, one must make a detailed regional study or a series of such studies, as I have done for girls' puberty rites (Driver

1941). In this study I distinguished between diffusion, migration, convergence, and other historical and evolutionary processes. It thus seems clear that worldwide cross-cultural studies cannot stand on their own feet, but need the support of regional studies of various sorts, including those aimed at postdicting history as well as evolution.

SUBJECT UNITS: CODING AND SCALING

The enormous variation in terminology in ethnographies around the world, even in English, makes it impossible to compare hundreds of societies by quoting exact words from each field report. The comparativist must code all the data in order to get it organized into categories that have universal or near universal application to the primary data. Codes range all the way from the most direct kinds of concepts, such as those of population statistics, to concepts for which no direct evidence is ever given, such as castration anxiety. The information on kinship and social structure coded by Murdock lies somewhere between the extreme poles of most direct and most indirect.

Marsh (1967:271-72) distinguishes between formal and functional equivalence. For instance, if two societies on the northwest coast of North America use strings of dentalium shell beads as the material most frequently exchanged for a bride, this would be formal equivalence; but if an African society's bride price consists principally of cattle, cattle in Africa are the functional but not formal equivalent of dentalium shells on the northwest coast.

A recent development in the United States called the new ethnography, ethnoscience, or ethnosemantics, but better labeled ethnoepistemology, asserts that a componential analysis of a semantic domain in a native language produces a cognitive map of the way everyone in the society thinks about a subject (Sturtevant 1964, Colby 1966, Wallace 1965). It is claimed that such semantic information obtained from one informant can be replicated practically 100 percent from any other informant. So far the ethnoepistemologists have not been able to agree even on the components of English kinship terminology, and recent research suggests enormous individual differences in the United States in this domain alone (Sanday 1968). No one has yet shown a way to take a number of componential analyses of the same domain in as many languages and code the material in a way that makes comparison possible. So far ethnoepistemology has been a retreat into a cave of particulars, but it has succeeded in warning the cross-cultural researcher about the enormous variation in concepts he faces in his worldwide comparisons.

Naroll (1968:268) mentions the wide range of concepts subsumed under cannibalism. Human flesh may be sold in the marketplace, eaten only for magical purposes to obtain the desirable personal qualities of a slain man, eaten primarily to humiliate a slain enemy, eaten in small quantities only by a mourner at a funeral. Therefore, to code cannibalism merely as present or absent is a nearly meaningless oversimplification.

In the realm of social structure Murdock's (1949) work has led the field. He chose variables for their relevance to the relation of the semantics of kinship terminology to social structure. His variables were the major forms of marriage, residence, descent, and kinship terminology coded as present or absent. About 180 correlations with tests of significance were computed from the distributions of the frequencies of pairs of variables in the 2 x 2 table. Since that time there has been a general tendency to split the subject units in this domain into finer and finer units. On the whole, more detailed subject units produce lower correlations than broader categories, as I have shown. However, such detailed subject units may always be combined in various ways, and experience shows that such combinations tend to raise correlations (Coult and Habenstein 1965, Driver 1970*a*).

Coding always involves scaling, although the so-called nominal scale may not be a true scale but an arbitrary arrangement of categories that must only be mutually exclusive and account for all of the cases. Presence and absence are the most commonly used nominal categories, and when each of two variables is split near the median so that about 50 percent of the cases are present and the other 50 percent absent, the resulting 2 x 2 table is almost as meaningful as an ordinal or interval scale of more steps. When the dichotomy is highly asymmetrical, however, it distorts all statistical measures applied to it. For instance, if the asymmetry is 95:5 in one variable and 5:95 in the other, the maximum value that phi can attain is 0.05. Naroll (1970*e*) shows that such asymmetry in opposite directions alters the sampling distribution of chi square, so that fewer than 5 percent of the samples will reach a 5 percent or lower significance level. In correlating language family membership with culture area membership for 260 ethnic units in native North America, I (Driver et al. 1966:172-73) actually found a comparison where phi maximum was 0.05. Under ideal conditions where the marginal totals are identical (in direction as well as in amount of asymmetry), phi maximum is ± 1.00. The ratio of both dichotomies does not have to be 50:50 to achieve unity, as Textor (1967:16) claims. The number of different coefficients for the 2 x 2 table totals about thirty; the most fashionable one at this time is the gamma of Goodman and Kruskal (1954), which may also be used for cross-classification tables with any number of rows and columns. For a short discussion of the Q coefficient, see Driver (1961).

A common kind of ordinal scale used in cross-cultural comparisons is the Guttman scale. This is a cumulative scale that arranges the culture traits in order of frequency among the societies, and at the same time arranges the societies in the order of frequency of the total number of culture traits possessed by each. The perfect form of this scale appears as a sort of right triangle, a figure with two straight sides and a curved "hypotenuse," with all the symbols for presence appearing solidly within every cell of the triangle and those for absence filling the space in the complementary triangle. An example of such a scale applied to cross-cultural data is the evolutionary scale of Carneiro (1968). He finds that the documented first appearance of many of his traits in England matches the order of their postdicted appearance on his scale from evidence of synchronic distribution alone. However, he had to select both his culture traits and his societies to get his scale; neither is a random sample of any larger corpus of material, and either may be estimated to include only about 10 percent of comparable traits and societies available in field reports and about 1 percent (0.10 times 0.10) of the total number of bits of data available. Other examples of Guttman scales may be found in Freeman and Winch (1957), Schwartz and Miller (1964), and Young and Young (1962).

A point emanating from Guttman scale applications to evolutionary postdictions is that when only two variables are correlated, the direction of causation is strengthened when the cause is more widespread (more frequent) than the result. I (Driver 1970c) made this point in a criticism of Judith K. Brown's (1963) assertion from a test of significance alone that matrilocal residence caused girls' puberty rites. From Brown's data the cause, matrilocal residence, was present in only nineteen societies, while the result, girls' puberty rites, occurred in forty-two societies. Brown must postulate the earlier presence and subsequent loss of matrilocal residence in twenty-three instances if her hypothesis is to be maintained.

Other studies have operated on the assumption that a single scale of evolutionary development is an oversimplification and that multiple uncorrelated scales are to be anticipated. One of these is that by Gouldner and Peterson (1962), who used a small corpus of 109 culture traits in 71 societies compiled by Simmons (1945). They computed a principal axes factor analysis with varimax rotation and found two orthogonal factors, hence two dimensions of evolutionary growth. Bowden (1969), using the same data, applied Thurstone's latent-distance model, described in Torgerson (1958), and came up with three dimensions of evolution. The ten factors found by Sawyer and Levine (1966) and the twelve factors isolated by Driver and Schuessler (1967), both from Murdock's 1957 sample, suggest as many independent lines of cultural evolution, or no evolution for some of the factors. These techniques have yet to be applied to the larger body of data in Murdock (1967). Presumably such techniques would yield still more dimensions of evolution. Recent computer programs for multiple scalogram analysis have refined methods for determining how many independent scalograms can be derived from a corpus of data.

A number of cross-cultural researchers have assumed that ordinal scales were interval scales and applied parametric measures to such data. The best known example of this technique is Whiting and Child (1953), who used a t test to determine significant differences between ordinal scales. Those differences significant at the 0.01 level or lower would surely have remained significant had an ordinal test for differences been used, but some of the higher probabilities might have failed to pass an ordinal significance test.

For Murdock's 1957 world sample, the scales of up to four steps of Sawyer and Levine (1966) gave higher correlations, on the average, than the modal dichotomies of Driver and Schuessler (1967) (see also Driver 1970a). When factor analysis was done, the total amount of variance extracted by the first ten factors was 0.74 for Sawyer and Levine and 0.64 for Driver and Schuessler. This suggests that scales of three and four steps are more efficient or more powerful statistically than dichotomies, as would be anticipated on theoretical grounds. Textor (1967: 20-25) reduced every variable to a dichotomy, but in a variety of ways, such as contrasting the two ends in a trichotomy and dropping out the middle, or lumping two ordinal categories at one end of the scale and opposing them to the remainder. He did not consistently oppose the modal category to the others, as Schuessler and I did.

At the Second HRAF Cross-Cultural Research Conference (Anonymous 1970:162) Roberts brought up the problem of curvilinear relationships, which may be lost if linear measures are the only ones used. I mentioned a recent computer program for making bivariate scatter diagrams that reveal curvilinear relationships intuitively to the educated eye, and also suggested some curvilinear measures to employ, such as Karl Pearson's eta.

Other techniques of scaling are given

in Whiting (1968:710-20) and in Torgerson (1958). See Marsh (1967:261-86) for a critical review of coding and scaling.

RELIABILITY AND QUALITY CONTROL

Reliability refers to the amount of agreement between two coders, ethnographers, or informants working independently and is usually measured by correlating the responses of pairs of such persons. If agreement is perfect, the reliability coefficient is 1.00; if it is less than perfect, the result may be any value down to 0.00. The first statistical study of reliability is the one I published in 1938, which compared multiple informant responses to interview schedules or multiple ethnographers' field reports on a few ethnic units in California. I made a Q type of comparison with the tetrachoric r coefficient and found a range of from 0.87 to 0.97, but discounted the highest value as likely to have been biased. Nevertheless, the reliability of the California culture element survey was proven to be quite satisfactory. I also mentioned that a satisfactory level of reliability required the intrasocietal coefficients to be higher than the intersocietal ones.

Whiting and Child (1953) used three coders for much of their work and tended to accept agreement of two out of three as sufficient, although resolution of particular differences was also achieved by rereading the same sources. Since that time most studies by Whiting and his followers have measured coding reliability in some manner. Swanson (1960:222-26) used two students to code part of his data and tested the reliability of the results. His reliability coefficients ranged from 1.00 to -0.15, but 72 percent passed a significance test.

The best recent study of reliability is that of Rohner and Katz (1970). They assembled ratings by two coders on six variables in a single matrix, which showed the intervariable coefficients of each of two raters in separate sections as well as the intravariable coefficients between the two raters in another section. Their conclusion was that unless the intravariable correlations are significantly higher than the intervariable ones, the distinctness of the variables is unproven and those that do not pass this test should be dropped from the study.

Spearman (1907) assumed that most errors in the psychological testing of that time were random. He demonstrated that random errors in any corpus of data tend to lower all correlations. This he called attenuation, and he devised a formula for correcting obtained intervariable correlation coefficients upward to their true values on the basis of the intravariable reliability coefficients. I cited his study (Driver 1938) and have since said that cross-cultural comparisons based on field reports written by a hundred or more fieldworkers were likely to contain more random errors than systematic or biased errors.

Validity refers to the amount of agreement between obtained results and some more direct representation of the true results. The latter is rarely known and must be estimated from reliability or some other indirect means. Roberts and Sutton-Smith (1962) found that cross-cultural correlations based on about fifty societies from every major world area were supported by correlations of similar variables based on 1,900 schoolchildren in the United States. In short, an intercultural relationship matched an intracultural relationship: differences in child training of boys and girls around the world tended to match those within the United States and accounted, at least in part, for the different games played by the two sexes.

Minturn and Lambert (1965) found that factors obtained from a six-culture correlational analysis of mother roles were supported by intracultural analyses of a similar type. However, Przeworski and Teune (1970) gave many examples of the lack of agreement between intersocietal and intrasocietal relationships among political behaviors in Europe (see the section below on "Causality, Evolutionary, and Historical Postdictions"). Although cross-cultural correlations may sometimes throw light on relationships among personalities within a single society, as Whiting, Child, and their followers have often asserted, one cannot be sure that this will hold in every case, and testing within single societies is called for.

Naroll (1960, 1962, 1968, 1970e) has introduced the concept of data quality control, and has made the point that this technique searches for systematic errors that are not random, not measured by conventional significance tests, and not affected by sample size. Another point of difference is that systematic errors may raise as well as lower correlations.

Naroll's principal hypotheses tested in the 1962 book were: (1) field reports that give actual individual cases are better than those that give only generalizations about the whole society; (2) reports giving direct observations or participant observations are better than those that rely exclusively on informants' verbal responses; (3) reports based on research done during a stay of more than one year in the field are better than those based on shorter stays; (4) reports that make use of the native language, or make reasonable claims of doing so, are better than those that do not; (5) reports by professionally trained ethnographers or native authorities on their own cultures are better than those written by amateurs, such as missionaries or colonial administrators or natives who have not specialized in their own traditions; (6) reports that are very explicit and detailed are better than ones that are not.

Naroll (1962) found no significant relation between drunken brawling and any of the six criteria of quality listed above. The same was true of defiant homicide; and protest suicide showed only one significant relationship with criterion 6, although a few others were borderline cases. Witchcraft attribution, however, showed a significant positive relation with criterion 3, length of stay, and a nearly significant positive relation to 4, use of native language. Naroll (1968:267) added the following criteria for future testing: (7) the longer the report, the better; (8) publication date might be significant—e.g., for the reporting on sex in the nineteenth versus the twentieth century; (9) number of native helpers used by fieldworkers.

Naroll (1970e) lists a total of twenty-five factors that he investigated for quality control in his study of war, stress, and culture. About the same number, but arranged differently, were listed earlier by Koh (1966).

Tatje, Textor, and Naroll (1970) have made a quality control study from Textor's (1967) A Cross-Cultural Summary. Textor's huge eight-pound computer printout is based on a Murdock judgmental sample of 400 societies, plus smaller samples from 36 additional cross-cultural studies. It gives correlations that pass a significance test among 480 dichotomized substantive variables plus 56 methodological variables. A total of 113,443 correlations is presented among the substantive variables; and for each set of raw frequencies in each 2 x 2 table, a phi, chi square, the probability derived from it, or Fisher's exact probability is given.

The methodological variables include the nine nationalities of the leading ethnographers, ten randomly chosen nonsense variables, thirty-six variables to match the thirty-six cross-cultural studies used, and one variable for date of publication (before or after 1930). When the ten random nonsense variables were intercorrelated with some of the substantive variables, the number expected to fall at the 0.01 level or lower was twenty-five, but the actual number that fell in this "rejection" tail of the probability curve was only seven. Two reasons for this were given: (1) When the total number of cases (N) in the 2 x 2 table is very small (seven in the example given), a perfect correlation gives a Fisher's exact probability of 0.025; lower values cannot occur in such small samples. (2) When N is small, sometimes all the cases fall on one side of the dichotomy of the random variable, making it impossible to compute a correlation at all. These two factors therefore reduce the number of correlations that pass a conventional significance test to well below the number expected when larger samples are used. Those that do pass the test are more significant than the test indicates.

Nationality of the ethnographer showed no significant error bias, nor did date of publication (before or after 1930), but the selection of the thirty-six samples showed many strong biases. In addition, the thirty-six samples fell into several schools of cross-cultural research, the most dominant of which was that of Whiting and Child. Many of their students and followers used the data precoded by previous investigators in the group and added one or two newly coded variables. The result was a considerable number of biased samples of fewer than a hundred societies not chosen randomly or even judgmentally for representativeness around the world, but simply because of the availability of precoded data on a related topic. The percentage of false relationships asserted in these studies is probably higher than in those made from Murdock's large samples, but they still may be correct in a substantial majority of correlations, at least in the sign of the relationship if not in its magnitude.

Quality control studies so far have revealed few systematic errors except when small availability samples have been used. Naroll's educated guess is that the total amount of such error is under 5 percent. If this is true, random error surely looms larger, but because random error lowers correlations, it errs on the conservative side. Therefore, we may rest assured that correlations that pass a significance test in world samples of four hundred or more are likely to be correct and confirmed by future research.

There was considerable discussion at the Second HRAF Cross-Cultural Research Conference (Anonymous 1970: 142-64) on professional versus naive coders. Whiting repeated his rule of many years that it is best to employ naive coders who do not know enough about theories and hypotheses to anticipate relations between variables and slant their codings in those directions. This method requires very explicit coding instructions by the researcher. When the data coded are of such narrow range that only a few variables are coded at one time, such a method is feasible. On the other hand, when hundreds of categories grouped into about fifty variables are coded at the same time, as in Murdock's 1967 sample, only an expert can do it at all. Coding instructions explicit enough for a naive person to replicate Murdock's codings would fill volumes and would be the equivalent of his lifetime experience at this task. My experience has been that the coding of difficult and poorly reported subjects, such as postnuptial residence, requires the coder to read many sections in field reports and fit the pieces together in a meaningful way. A naive person cannot do this.

At the above-mentioned conference Goodenough stressed the necessity for the fieldworker to begin with emic concepts and later convert them to etic codes for comparison. Rohner countered with the view that observations of manifest behavior can be rated directly on etic codes without going through the emic stage, and Naroll and Carneiro concurred. Carneiro cited the proportion of waking hours spent in subsistence activity, which no nonliterate society ever keeps track of, as an example of an etic variable without emic basis. Goodenough admitted that one might observe this even though it was not a part of native culture. Most participants in the conference seemed ready to use etic concepts whether or not they existed anywhere in the emics of individual societies. It seems quite obvious to me that the entire history of science shows a regular and progressive substitution of etic concepts for culture-bound and language-bound emic ones.

At the same conference Murdock reported that a recent attempt to resolve all the differences among multiple coders in a pilot sample by rereading the sources and redefining categories and variables was 100 percent successful; all differences were resolved. These coding refinements were then ready to be applied to the entire sample. Davenport and Casagrande challenged this resolution technique on the grounds that it might introduce bias in the coding, but Naroll and Whiting approved of the technique. Ember argued that replication of an entire study with a second sample (presumably both samples being chosen randomly from one of Murdock's large samples) was cheaper and better than ironing out differences among coders for a single sample.

At the same conference Naroll (Anonymous 1970:162-64) emphasized the need to use ordinal measures of strength of relationship for ordinal scales and mentioned Goodman and Kruskal's gamma, M. G. Kendall's tau, and Robert H. Somers' Dxy. He showed that one may obtain a high level of significance from a cross-classification table of more than two rows and columns using chi square, when there is no linear or curvilinear relationship between the variables. For instance, if the greatest differences between obtained and expected frequencies fall in the four corner cells of a 4 x 4 table, this fact can be highly significant yet indicate no correlation whatsoever between the variables.

I (Driver 1970b:60), in a review of "Folk Song Style and Culture" by Alan Lomax (1968), found seven examples where the order of the steps in one ordinal scale was altered to make the gamma larger and a closer match to a high level of significance obtained from chi square. I criticized this as a violation of the assumptions of the gamma coefficient and suggested that Harald Cramèr's V^2 would have been a preferable measure of strength of relationship, because it is not limited to linear or slightly curvilinear relationship, as gamma is. Like chi square, however, it measures the proportion of difference (squared) between the obtained and expected values regardless of the cells in which they occur. Cramèr's V^2 was used by Driver and Schuessler (1967:334-35), who found that only 8 percent of the relationships among Murdock's thirty variables (1957 sample) were significant at the 5 percent level or lower. Because 5 of the 8 percent might occur by chance, only 3 percent of the relationships are certain to have passed this significance test.

In conclusion, it is worth repeating

that small world samples of fewer than a hundred cases not chosen randomly from a judgmental sample of four hundred or more are likely to contain considerable sampling error.

PRECODED VS. NEWLY CODED DATA

At the Second HRAF Cross-Cultural Research Conference in November 1969 (Anonymous 1970:164-77), Roberts led off the discussion with the comment that if a researcher uses data previously coded by another comparativist for one variable and then correlates it with a second variable newly coded by himself or his assistants, the relationship is likely to be less biased than if one person did all the coding; or at least it would reflect two different biases of two researchers rather than a single bias of one. He mentioned making dozens of unpublished experiments with precoded data and small numbers of cases as a preliminary to more careful and costly research. He further commented that cross-cultural study is one of the few fields of cultural anthropology where there is a definite progressive accumulation of knowledge.

Robert O. Lagacé described a field trip aimed at checking data on a single society previously coded for comparative purposes. His list of errors uncovered included the following: (1) incorrect ratings; (2) faulty spacial or temporal localization of data; (3) ignoring of differences between subgroups in the society, such as differences between social strata and religious groups; (4) the selecting of the second most frequent alternative as the type instead of the first, when multiple alternatives occurred; (5) failure of the data to fit the trait definition of the code; (6) general poor quality of a field report, with frequent contradictions and ambiguities. Goodenough mentioned that the

time period coded is important for many societies in which differences over time are known. He also thought the lumping together of uncles and aunts and other kin categories in Murdock's *Ethnographic Atlas* (1967) was too rough, and that the treating of linguistically related but nevertheless distinct kin terms as equivalents was not always acceptable. He raised the question "Coded for what?," implying that different theories and hypotheses require different coding.

Murdock agreed that his 1967 coding was not careful enough about time period and mentioned that the October 1969 issue of *Ethnology* contained finer time distinctions. He asked everyone who found errors to send them in to *Ethnology,* which would print the corrections. He emphasized how important this was to nonanthropological behavioral scientists, who must rely wholly on what anthropologists print.

Ember expressed the optimistic opinion that some amount of error was inevitable and that if most of it is random a valid correlation can be obtained in spite of it. I might repeat here that if a correlation is very high, the obtained value can tolerate a large amount of error; but if it is low, the same amount of error would reduce it to a value so low that it would not pass a significance test.

Naroll next emphasized the need for more careful documentation of coded data with page references for every entry, more attention to time period, and more use of data quality control to uncover systematic errors. Textor followed with a plea for more quality control.

William Davenport made the point that some of the generalizations about single societies in field reports are contradicted by other data on other pages of the same report, and that the coder should read the entire work before final-izing his coding. Whiting supported Davenport and said that the genealogical data collected by Evans-Pritchard on the Nuer do not support his generalization that residence is patrilocal.

Rohner summed up his views on some sources of error in cross-cultural studies: (1) mistakes in the ethnographic collecting that end up in the written report; (2) the weakness of sampling procedure when the entire parameter cannot be specified; (3) coder bias resulting from a status difference among coders working together, such as professor and student; when a difference occurs, the student tends to defer to the professor.

Naroll made an educated guess that no more than 5 percent of the conclusions of all cross-cultural research are biased by the circumstances he outlined, as I noted earlier, but that this should be reduced to one-tenth of 1 percent. I am less optimistic and believe that if it could be kept within 5 percent we could still live with it.

Murdock expressed confidence in the progress made in cross-cultural methodology and said that, in spite of the "terrible" sample used in his *Social Structure* (1949), few of his conclusions based on correlations have been overthrown by subsequent research.

Carneiro made a plea for more explicit descriptions of coding procedures with more careful documentation of each entry. Murdock followed with the pragmatic view that many of the societies used in cross-cultural comparisons are no longer functioning and cannot be further investigated in the field; that one must learn to live with these far from ideal data and code them the best one can. Goodenough countered with the opinion that better fieldwork in the future would shed light on the limitations of much of the field data today.

Naroll asked if the HRAF organization was ready to prepare a more de-

tailed field manual than the *Outline of Cultural Materials* (Murdock et al. 1961), which would encourage fieldworkers to get data with a higher comparability for the cross-cultural investigator. Whiting concluded the discussion with the parallel point that cross-cultural research should feed back into fieldwork and improve it in the future.

It is worth repeating that much of the precoded data used by Whiting, Child, and their followers contain sizable amounts of sampling error because the samples are chosen on the basis of availability of the precoded data rather than randomly from a larger judgmental sample of four hundred or more societies (Tatje, Textor, and Naroll 1970).

CAUSALITY, EVOLUTIONARY, AND HISTORICAL POSTDICTIONS

Because most of the cross-cultural data used by anthropologists have been collected in the last century, they are deficient in time depth, and causal-evolutionary sequences must be postdicted from largely synchronic data. An exception is the use of documents by Carneiro (1968), who found a close agreement between the postdicted sequence of Carneiro and Tobias (1963) and the documented sequence in England in the last thousand years. Histories of science and technology alone contain a vast amount of documentation that, when added to the more recently and accurately dated archaeological sequences, is capable of lending a great deal of support to the evolutionary and historical orientations in cultural anthropology. These documents are largely unused at the present time by cultural anthropologists, who prefer to follow the romantic tradition of fieldwork in faraway places with strange-sounding names rather than library work among the archives.

Most cross-cultural studies to date have computed only bivariate correlations to test hypotheses involving causality. If the correlation is zero, no causal relationship can be claimed and the case is closed. If the correlation is significant on the positive side, and the hypothesis asserts that one variable tends to cause the other, most authors interpret this as support of the hypothesis. From the correlation coefficient alone it is impossible to determine causality, much less its direction, as I mentioned earlier in connection with Judith K. Brown's assertion that matrilocal residence caused girls' puberty rites. However, when one variable is extracultural, such as limited moisture in the Southwest, the investigator is safe in assuming that this scarcity of water caused the Indians to plant their hills of corn far apart. If Indians in the tropical lowlands of Middle or South America planted their corn in hills far apart, no reader of this article would claim that such behavior would cause the precipitation to diminish to the water level of the Southwest.

In other instances, when archaeological evidence or historical documentation has shown that one variable appeared earlier than another, we may reasonably hypothesize that the earlier variable may have played some causal role in the appearance of the later one.

Thus the domestication of animals and plants was at least a partial cause of increased settlement size and all the other ramifications of culture that led to the development of what we call civilization.

In still other instances, when a first variable is more widespread and frequent than a second, the case for the causal role of the first vis-à-vis the second is strengthened, as was mentioned earlier under "Subject Units: Coding and Scaling." Exceptions to this rule come about when a trait is lost or re-

placed by another. Thus bronze was at one time dominant in tools and weapons and a determiner of success in technology and war. It was later replaced by iron, which spread much farther than bronze had done and replaced bronze entirely (at least for certain purposes) in many localities. Thus the most widespread trait at a particular time is not always the older.

The best evidence for diffusion, derived from documents, recent dating methods of archaeology, and laboratory analyses of physical, chemical, and biological materials, clearly shows that the building blocks that formed the progressive steps up the evolutionary stairway were almost invariably invented once or a few times and spread by diffusion to the vast majority of societies possessing them at a given time. Thus corn was first domesticated in Middle America and was relayed or carried by migrating men to the St. Lawrence River on the north and to latitude $-43°$ on Chiloe Island on the south before A.D. 1492; after that time it was taken by man to the Old World. In the Old World, wheat was first domesticated in the fertile crescent of the Middle East and later spread to the Atlantic on the west, the Pacific on the east, and, after A.D. 1492, to the New World. The important metals have similar histories, as do writing systems (a single origin for the alphabet) and a hundred other things.

For nonmaterial variables describing human behavior, which leave no physical evidence for the archaeologist to unearth and the modern scientific laboratory to test, little is known about their evolution, history, or causal relationships. I (Driver 1956; Driver and Massey 1957:421-39; Ford, ed., 1967: 259-90) employed a series of correlation matrices to test against North American Indian data a general causal chain model of social organization postulated by Murdock (1949). Murdock's hypothesis asserted this causal chain: dominant sexual division of labor in subsistence activities $\longrightarrow$ postnuptial residence $\longrightarrow$ descent $\longrightarrow$ semantics of kinship terminology. The three alternative chains were: (1) matridominant food production $\longrightarrow$ matrilocal residence $\longrightarrow$ matrilineal descent $\longrightarrow$ bifurcate merging uncle and aunt terms $\longrightarrow$ Crow cousin terms; (2) patridominant food production $\longrightarrow$ patrilocal residence $\longrightarrow$ patrilineal descent $\longrightarrow$ bifurcate merging uncle and aunt terms $\longrightarrow$ Omaha cousin terms; (3) balanced food production $\longrightarrow$ bilocal or neolocal residence $\longrightarrow$ bilateral descent $\longrightarrow$ lineal or generation uncle and aunt terms $\longrightarrow$ Hawaiian or Eskimo cousin terms.

Although my correlations were in the middle and lower range, they tended on the whole to support Murdock's causal chain. This was not the customary cumulative scale of evolution, because any society at any time could change the sexual divison of labor for its extraction or production of food by migrating to a new environment or by accepting a new domesticated plant or animal in the old environment. The same society could conceivably be bicentered at one period in its history or evolution, patricentered at another, and matricentered at still another time. This was a theory of cycles of change rather than evolution.

Blalock (1960), at the suggestion of David Aberle, applied a causal analysis to four of the six variables in my matricentered group: (1) matridominant division of labor; (2) matrilocal residence; (3) matricentered land tenure; (4) matrilineal descent. (The sixth variable, not listed in the paragraph above, was land tenure. I added this to Murdock's original five.) Blalock found that, in addition to the causal chain direction of influence, there was some direct in-

fluence from 1 to 3 and 4, and some direct influence from 2 to 4. This produced a square model, which was a better fit than my linear model. Some of this effect may have been caused by feedback from the later members of the chain to earlier members, as I had suggested in my original article (Driver 1956).

I later found that when land tenure was left out and kinship terminology added to conform to Murdock's original sequence, the fit to the causal chain model was much improved. This was true for all three sex-centered variables, matricentered, patricentered, and bicentered, with the fit closest for the last. Averages of the corresponding coefficients in the three matrices are given in Table 2, together with the actual and expected values according to Blalock's method. The fit is unbelievably close. Therefore the causal chain model is a good one for Murdock's original sequence. Such a model, however, cannot give the direction of change. This must be inferred from other evidence. Such a model does not give the actual sequence that a particular society experienced; it can only postulate it.

Blalock (1964) developed his causal models further and in a later theoretical

TABLE 2
Average Phi Coefficients
for Matricentered, Patricentered, and
Bicentered Variables

	Division of Labor	Residence	Descent	Kin Terms
Division of labor	—	0.24	0.11*	0.00†
Residence		—	0.36	0.13‡
Descent			—	0.43
Kin terms				—

*Expected value, 0.09 = (0.24) (0.36)
†Expected value, 0.04 = (0.24) (0.36) (0.43)
‡Expected value, 0.15 = (0.36) (0.43)

article (1968) summarized his views to that date. In the same volume in which the latter article appeared, Boudon (1968) adds still other statistical ramifications involved in causal models. The principal limitation of such models is that their number increases at a geometric ratio as the number of variables is increased. Few actual applications have dealt with more than five variables. Furthermore, all such causal models assume that the system is closed, that no other variables have any influence (correlation) on the variables isolated for study. Although the employment of such techniques is a great advance over dealing with only two variables at a time, causal determination is still a very debatable issue. Causality is never certain from synchronic data, and postdictions about it do not tell us how close the actual diachronic sequence was to the inferred one.

I believe that in the present stage of cross-cultural research in anthropology, descriptive studies that package a large number of variables in the same matrix are the most instructive. Rivalry between psychological and sociological hypotheses about causes of a given phenomenon can be resolved by exhibiting all the variables in the same matrix, which often will show that both kinds of causes are at work and are correlated with each other. With recent refinements in matrix reduction techniques, hundred variables are not too many one to analyze in one operation.

Aberle (1961) listed the following variables that tend to discourage matrilineal descent and encourage bilateral or patrilineal descent: increased importance of male labor; increased importance of male-owned property, such as domesticated animals; increased male control of tools of production, such as the plow and the potter's wheel; nonkinship control of political organization; large political units; segmentary

descent groups; and advanced technology and high level of productivity. Matrilineal systems, in contrast, seem to have arisen in tropical or subtropical areas where the wild plant foods gathered by women were more abundant than game that could be readily caught by men, or, at a later date, from hand farming and ownership of farm plots by women in the same environments. Later, as the increased population brought about by this early stage of farming exhausted the game and further reduced the importance of hunting, men turned to farming and craftwork and gradually invented techniques of production superior to those formerly used by women. This was not because male hormones automatically produced superior mentality in males, but because childbearing, child care, and the multitude of household tasks performed by women made it impossible for them to be the full-time specialists who became the innovators. If this reconstruction is correct, the nineteenth-century evolutionists were right about the main trend of the sequence, but nowhere near all peoples of the world were ever matrilineal because ecological factors in the higher latitudes were never right for such a system. Such an evolution was neither universal nor inevitable, as many nineteenth-century writers thought, nor was the initial matrilineal stage brought about by promiscuity and a universal failure to recognize paternity.

In a provocative paper called "Why Exceptions? The Logic of Cross-Cultural Analysis," Köbben (1967) lists a number of sources of exceptions to generalizations to which the majority of instances conform: mistakes in field reporting; mistakes in coding by the comparativist; multicausality; parallel causality; unawareness of functional equivalence; intervening variables; diffusion; cultural lag; personality; and disturbing coincidences. This bare list does not do justice to Köbben's thoughtful contribution. However, it should be pointed out that all but the first two factors are heuristic ones and are not logically independent of one another. A single correlation may include exceptions that are a combination of all of these, as Jorgensen has pointed out (in a personal communication).

In the six-culture study of Minturn and Lambert (1965) the roles of mothers were first defined by a factor analysis that yielded ten factors or roles; then these roles were correlated with residence patterns, household size and structure, extended kin groups, and patterning of sex roles. A general finding was that intracultural and cross-cultural results supported each other, but that intracultural variations appeared to be more important than cross-cultural variations in accounting for the totality of differences among the 133 mothers interviewed in the six cultures.

A recent book by Przeworski and Teune (1970) presents some new statistical techniques, not yet used by any anthropologist, which show relations of variables within single societies and among groups of societies. Their method requires census-type data, in which the individual is the unit of observation in all the societies. Their principal conclusion is that relationships within societies may not hold across societies. They deal with European nations, which they call "systems" throughout the book. These authors offer the following six types of relationship, with actual examples for each: (1) all within-system regressions have the same slope, which is also the same for the regression of the means among systems and the total covariance; (2) within-system regressions are the same for all systems and are approximately equal to zero, but the slope of the regression of system means among systems is different from zero; (3) the among-system regres-sion (of means) equals zero but the within-system regressions are different from zero; (4) the among-system regression has a different sign (direction of slope) than the within-system regressions; (5) the among-system regression is curvilinear because the within-system regressions that determine parts of the curve are positive, zero, and negative; (6) the among-system regression is curvilinear but the within-system regressions are linear and share the same sign but differ in magnitude of slope.

AREAL DIFFERENCES

The problem created by areal differences was mentioned by Murdock more than thirty years ago (1940:369):

A valid cross-cultural hypothesis should hold true in any area. If, however, some areas are discovered to yield negative coefficients, it must be concluded that the apparent statistical confirmation of the hypothesis is fictitious and accidental, and the hypothesis must either be rejected entirely or modified and tested again.

This principle must be modified to be of any use, because only a perfect correlation could pass the test if small areas were considered. Areas to be tested for such differences should be fairly large, should be continuous, and should conform to natural geographical divisions or the major cultural groups in a Q type of numerical classification made from long lists of cultural inventory.

Whiting and Child (1953) and Landauer and Whiting (1964) divided the world into a few major regions (the six of Murdock's in the 1964 study) and ran the same correlations for each region separately. They found that the magnitude of the correlations was "substantially the same" in each of the areas. This finding supports their nomothetic functional-causal interpretation and rules out a nonfunctional historical association. This method requires a fairly large sample in order to have enough cases in each area to pass a significance test.

One of Kimball Romney's students tested Murdock's 1949 correlations by continental areas and found that, while all held for some of the areas, none held for all of the areas.

Sawyer and Levine (1966:719-27) and Driver and Schuessler (1967:336-47) found many significant differences among the six major regions of Murdock's 1957 sample. These were explained as due to different ecological and historical circumstances in the various areas. Diffusion within each of the areas was assumed but not measured, but diffusion between or across the most similar areas, which were in the tropics, was denied as a dominant explanation by Driver and Schuessler, especially diffusion across the Pacific Ocean. The greater similarity of South America than North America to the Pacific islands, East Asia, and Africa south of the Sahara was explained in terms of parallel and independent ecological and social adaptation to generically similar tropical or subtropical environments; in other words, parallel or convergent cultural evolution.

Textor (1967) correlated everything in his samples of up to four hundred societies not only with the same six areas, but also with latitude, language families, and natural environment. He found some significant correlations with each of the categories within these variables, but he gave no explanations of them.

When a more empirically determined set of world culture areas, ranging from areas of continental size down to the smallest clusters, has been achieved, all interculture-trait correlations could be tested for areal differences and, when possible, new variables substituted for the proper names of the areas. One of the goals of cross-cultural method is the substitution of variables for proper nouns referring to places or time periods. It seems likely that in the future most correlations will exhibit significant areal differences, in magnitude if not in sign.

Worldwide researchers who ignore areal differences are treating human societies as if they were inorganic particles racing around in a cyclotron or inorganic objects of other kinds that do not interact with each other. Just as human individuals interact with others with whom they come in contact, so societies interact via their individual members with other societies with which they have contact. It is impossible to rule out external influences where human social groups are concerned, as numerical areal classifications and "Galton problem" studies have shown. Galton suggested in 1888 (Tylor 1889) that cross-cultural data be mapped. Maps can reveal intuitively a host of nonrandom areal clusterings that are so obvious that precise measurement is scarcely called for Driver and Massey 1957). Richard Chaney (personal communication) has recently written a computer program to map any and all of the data in Murdock's 1967 sample. He finds that all data mapped so far tend to group in nonrandom areal clusters.

SOME RESULTS

So far this review has been concerned principally with methodology. It is time now to attempt to summarize the major results achieved by cross-cultural studies. There are two sources that summarize a wider range of results than the others: Marsh (1967) and Naroll (1970a). Because most of Marsh's findings are included in Naroll's paper, I shall rely more heavily on the latter.

KINSHIP AND SOCIAL ORGANIZATION

What Naroll (1970*a*) calls "main sequence" kinship theory is the cycling from dominant division of labor in subsistence to residence to descent to kinship terminology, described earlier in the section on "Causality, Evolutionary, and Historical Postdictions." Murdock's 1949 view has been modified by Tatje (n.d.), who found with a Galton problem test that about half of the variance in Murdock's correlations was due to diffusion, rather than all of it to functional factors operating in historically isolated societies. Tatje (n.d.), Aberle (1961), and Driver (1956) all show that the relation of food extraction and production to the other variables holds strongly for North America; but Tatje and Aberle find that it does not hold for Africa, where other variables seem to override the ecological ones. Nevertheless, the relations between residence, descent, and kinship terminology apparently hold for all major areas.

A distinctive feature of Murdock's 1949 work is that it tests a whole network of interrelated hypotheses. Such a research design is much stronger than one centered around a single hypothesis, and the total results are much more convincing. Although some of Murdock's individual correlations failed to pass a conventional significance test, collectively the fact that all but a couple were positive lends overwhelming support to the entire network of hypotheses.

In the Americas, unilineal and exogamous descent systems seem to have flourished at an intermediate level of cultural evolution. Lowie, Murdock, I, and others agree that the first Indian immigrants to the New World probably used a bilateral descent system, and that there were multiple historically independent developments of both patrilineal and matrilineal systems. In Middle America (except among the Mayas) and in the central Andes, unilineal descent had largely disappeared by the time of the Spanish conquest, suggesting that the centralized governments of the nations in these areas had taken over most of the functions of former clans and sibs. But this generalization fails to hold for other areas of the world. The Australians at a late Paleolithic level of subsistence and technology had one of the most strongly developed unilineal and double descent systems in the world; at the other end of the scale, civilized peoples such as the Arabs, Hindus, Chinese, and Japanese have retained patrilineal clans or sibs down to the twentieth century. In Europe, however, most of them were phased out as much as two thousand years ago. No society as civilized as the four above has a matrilineal descent system. See my reference to Aberle (1961) in the section on "Causality, Evolutionary, and Historical Postdictions" for probable reasons for this.

KIN AVOIDANCES

The combined work of Tylor (1889), Stephens and D'Andrade (1962), Sweetser (1966), Driver et al. (1966), and Jorgensen (1966) on kin avoidances is not very conclusive because Tylor never even listed his ethnic units, Stephens and D'Andrade and Sweetser used small samples that were probably biased, I limited my work to North America, and Jorgensen's correlations were rarely significant. However, such avoidances are probably related to incest taboos, and to unilineal and exogamous descent systems that sharply differentiate the members of each of such groups from the others. The highest correlation I found for avoidance was with bifurcation in kinship terminology, but the correlation with culture areas was still higher, suggesting that diffusion explained more of the variance than did any structural-functional variable.

CULTURAL EVOLUTION IN GENERAL

The strongest evidence for cultural evolution in the past two million years comes from archaeology, with documentary history adding precision in the past five thousand years. A few evolutionary scales postdicted from the largely synchronic data of ethnography have been mentioned earlier under "Causality, Evolutionary, and Historical Postdictions." The most common way to construct a short evolutionary scale is to follow the plan of Hobhouse, Wheeler, and Ginsberg (1930), who classified the peoples of the world according to the way they obtained their food, with hunters and gatherers at the early and low end of the scale, and plow farmers with both plants and animals domesticated at the later and higher end. Marsh (1967) used social stratification and political complexity for most of the societies in Murdock's 1957 sample and then extended the scale further by adding 114 modern nations on the later and higher end. More recent evolutionary scales, relying heavily on Murdock's large samples, are better based than the earlier ones.

It should be remembered, however, that if enough evolutionary detail were known about each of a thousand societies, we would have a hard time indeed finding two of them that evolved through exactly the same sequence for a thousand or so items of culture. None of the cultures of the hunters and gatherers have remained changeless over the last ten thousand years or so. All

that evolutionary postdictions from synchronic nonmaterial culture can show is the very broad general trend of societies as a whole. A recent study of twentieth-century cultural evolution in Mexico (Graves et al. 1969) showed that rank-order correlations between two postdicted evolutionary sequences derived from Guttman scales and the actual documented sequences varied from 1.00 to −0.63 among forty Mexican towns. The average was about 0.40 for one scale and 0.60 for the other, which reveals a very modest amount of conformity to the postdicted scales. I doubt if any other set of evolutionary postdictions for as many localities would average much better, although Carneiro's (1968) study shows a higher relationship in England. The other interesting feature of the Graves study is that none of the innovations discussed originated in any of the Mexican towns; all were introduced from the outside—originally even from outside Mexico.

POPULATION DENSITY AND SIZE OF LARGEST SETTLEMENT

The most common estimate of total world human population at the end of the Paleolithic is 10 million, with all societies subsisting on wild animals and wild plants; in A.D. 1492 the total is estimated at 350 million, with hunting and gathering societies constituting 1 percent; at present the total is between three and four billion, with hunters and gatherers representing only .001 percent (Lee and De Vore, eds., 1968: frontispiece). From these figures and a mountain of other evidence, it is obvious that the large increase in population in the past ten thousand years has been due partly to domestication of plants and animals. The size of any society's largest settlement has also increased along with density of population.

GROSS NATIONAL PRODUCT AND SPECIALIZATION OF LABOR

The per capita gross national (or tribal) product has increased in parallel fashion, and so have the specialization of labor needed to produce it, the organization of work (Textor 1967:FC 115-24, Naroll 1956, Freeman and Winch 1957, Udy 1959), and, along with these, the total amount of knowledge possessed by the society. The number of distinct statuses and roles in a given society has shown an equally spectacular upward trend, as has the number of team organizations in single societies and general societal complexity (Textor 1967:FC 84-101, Naroll 1956, Carneiro 1967).

WRITING

The dissemination of knowledge increased with the advent of writing, especially after the alphabet was achieved and widely diffused to most of the world's societies. Word inventory has shown an enormous increase since the alphabet began to document it, and today many modern languages have more loan words than genetically derived words (Swadesh 1971). Printing, first developed in China and later diffused to Europe, greatly facilitated the spread of knowledge and increase in word inventory.

ART

Fischer (1961) found a strong positive correlation between level of social stratification and four major characteristics of art style. Artists of highly stratified societies produced more complex designs, crowded more material into a given space, produced less sym-metrical figures, and more often enclosed their works within borders than artists of societies in which there was less social stratification. Wolfe (1969) found a positive correlation between degree of development of graphic and plastic arts in Africa and a number of other variables reflecting position on an evolutionary scale. The principal other variables were degree of sodality elaboration, degree to which community sovereignty overrides kinship authority, and degree of social stratification.

MUSIC

Lomax (1968) constructed two subsistence scales on the order of the one done by Hobhouse, Wheeler, and Ginsberg (1930), but based on Murdock's better samples, and found positive correlations between these scales and wordiness of song texts, precision of articulation of words in song texts, frequency of solo singing, narrowness of melodic intervals, absence of repetition, complexity of rhythms, presence of heterophony and counterpoint, and degree of embellishment. In addition he classified the world's song styles into areal types and explained many of the similarities in terms of diffusion, migration, military and religious conquest, and other historical processes.

GAMES

Roberts, Arth, and Bush (1959) found that games of strategy are correlated with social classes and high political integration; that games of chance more often occur in societies that are high in benevolence and low in aggression, and which also believe in their ability to coerce spiritual beings; and that numbers of games of physical skill are negatively correlated with numbers of games of chance. Games of physical skill are also more frequent in latitudes more than 20 degrees from the equator, suggesting that climate or diet may be involved. In this and other cross-cultural studies Roberts admits that diffusion may influence correlations, and he makes no claim that his cases are historically independent.

CONSENSUAL VS. AUTHORITATIVE LEADERSHIP

Consensual leadership is found in so-called acephalous societies, in which authority is minimal and is vested in kinship groups or simply in public opinion. Authoritative leadership is far from minimal and is vested in officers who can force compliance by means of fines, corporal punishment, or death. The main evolutionary trend has been from consensual to authoritative leadership (Textor 1967:FC 138-40; Hobhouse, Wheeler, and Ginsberg 1930; Barry, Child, and Bacon 1959; Schwartz and Miller 1964; Naroll 1970a).

THE ROLE OF THE ELITE

Any large society must have an elite group to lead it and manage its affairs. This is true of both the most capitalistic and most communistic of modern nations. Small societies can get along without an elite or without any social stratification at all. Therefore the principal evolutionary trend has been toward increasing power and authority in the hands of the elite (Textor 1967:FC 110; Russett et al. 1964:237-47; Naroll 1970a).

WEALTH SHARING AND WEALTH HOARDING

Polanyi (1962) asserts that "primitive" societies tend to have reciprocal exchange systems, so-called ceremonial exchanges of gifts and brides, which tend to distribute wealth evenly throughout a society; higher civilizations, in contrast, tend to have market or redistributive (taxation, socialism) exchange systems, which concentrate wealth in the hands of a few. Both capitalism and socialism fall within the latter system. In spite of much criticism of Polanyi's view, largely by citations of individual exceptions, Textor (1967:FC 132) supports him.

WAR

There has been a general evolutionary trend from small-scale fighting, revolving around defense of the most economically productive parts of the landscape, revenge for former losses in fights, and the raising of prestige, toward large-scale warfare aimed at conquering territory, gaining control of the conquered people, and either exploiting them or acculturating them to the way of life of the conquerors (Otterbein 1968a, 1968b; Naroll 1970a; Textor 1967:FC 416-22). There has probably been no correlation between the size of the military operation and the mortality and suffering per capita per annum (Driver 1969:328). Every civilized society has been extremely warlike at some time in its history. A large amount of internal feuding is associated with societies made up of patrilocal residence groups, which constitute the rival factions, while those with matrilocal residence are more likely to fight with a different linguistic or political group (Ember n.d.).

RELIGION

Some of the principal conclusions from Swanson (1960) are: (1) monotheism is positively related to the presence of a hierarchy of three or more sovereign (decision-making) groups in a society; (2) polytheism (belief in multiple superior gods) is correlated with social classes; (3) belief in active ancestral spirits is correlated with importance of kinship groups; (4) belief in reincarnation is correlated with small and nomadic settlement patterns (in spite of its high frequency in India, a highly evolved group of societies with many large settlements); (5) belief in witchcraft is most common in societies with few or no other kinds of social controls; (6) supernatural sanctions for interpersonal relations are most frequent in societies with interpersonal differences in wealth.

CHILD TRAINING AND ADULT CULTURE

The scarcity of data on this subject in most field reports has resulted in small and biased samples (see "Reliability and Quality Control," above), and indirect coding is common (see "Subject Units: Coding and Scaling," above). Nevertheless, some of the relationships discovered are so strong that many scholars accept them, and the sign of the correlation is probably correct in a majority of such studies, even though its magnitude may be significantly off and the causal explanations open to challenge. All other studies made from small nonrandom samples are subject to the same criticism. Whiting (1968) lists in his bibliography more cross-cultural studies in this field done by psychologists than by anthropologists.

Whiting and Child (1953) divided severity of socialization into the following five aspects, each of which was rated separately: anal, oral, sexual, dependence, aggression. The ratings on these five aspects were intercorrelated and the highest positive correlation turned out to be that between the oral and dependent aspects. The amount of oral socialization anxiety showed a high positive degree of relationship to presence of oral explanations of illness. On the other hand, they found no relation between anal socialization anxiety and anal explanations of illness.

The general thesis of Whiting, Child, and their followers is that the varying forms of child training have their origins in the varying forms of cultural maintenance systems. These maintenance systems lead to particular kinds of child-training practices, and the latter lead to particular kinds of adult personality and ideological projective systems.

A basic report on the relation of cultural maintenance systems and child-training practices is that of Barry, Child, and Bacon (1959), who found that societies with large accumulations of subsistence resources (farmers) tend also to place emphasis on obedience training and responsibility in children, while societies with little or no food surplus (hunters and gatherers) emphasize individual initiative, self-reliance, and independence of action in children.

Yehudi Cohen (1961) reported that early food indulgence of children is correlated with generous food-sharing practices of adults. Others have suggested that both of these variables are more characteristic of hunting and gathering societies, where food supply is less regular than among farmers.

Apple (1956) found that grandparents who are kind and indulgent to children are more frequent in societies where the grandparents have little or no authority over the parents.

Barry, Bacon, and Child (1957) found that the training of girls emphasized nurturance, obedience, and responsibility, while that of boys placed more stress on achievement and self-reliance.

Landauer and Whiting (1964) reported a correlation between amount of infantile stimulation and adult stature, and cited a rat experiment with parallel results. I am skeptical of the causal relationship they postulate, and the wide variety of practices coded as infantile stimulation can hardly be considered to be functional equivalents.

Whiting, Kluckhohn, and Anthony (1958) found a positive correlation between male initiation ceremonies at puberty and patrilocal residence, exclusive mother-infant sleeping arrangements, a long postpartum sex taboo, and a long lactation period. Their explanation was that the resulting strong attachment to the mother had to be broken by an initiation rite that separated the boy from his mother entirely and prepared him for an adult masculine role.

Young (1965:41) says:

The dramatization of sex role—initiation rites—is functionally necessary for maintaining the solidarity of the men. Such ritualization calls attention to the boy's change in status and gives him access to the intimate communication of the group. In this new sector, the boy quickly consolidates his role and the stability of the community's age-sex status classification is preserved.

This sociogenic explanation does not contradict the psychogenic interpretation of Whiting et al.; it complements it.

Cohen (1964:549-50) interprets ·initiation rites as

one of the ways—and the lesser in importance—by which the society manipulates the child in relation to the boundaries of his nuclear family and kin group in order to implant a social-emotional identity and values consonant with the culture's articulating principles. More importantly than by initiation ceremonies, the society carries these out at a point of greater psychological vulnerability through the practice of extrusion and/or brother-sister avoidance.

Thus Cohen uses both a sociogenic and a psychogenic interpretation.

ALCOHOLISM

High insobriety ratings were more frequent among societies with hunting and gathering economies, small and temporary settlements, weak political organization, little or no social stratification, bilateral descent, neolocal residence, nuclear family households, absence of male initiations ór sodalities, and indulgence of infants and children (Horton 1943, Field 1962, Naroll 1970a). Child, Bacon, and Barry (1965) found that nineteen variables on alcoholism grouped into four factors that accounted for 80 percent of the total variance. These factors, in order of the amount of variance for which each accounts, are (1) integrated drinking in religion and ceremony, (2) degree of inebriety, (3) degree of hostility, and (4) frequency and quantity of drinking. Their general conclusion is that high levels of the use of alcohol are in part motivated by a need to relieve frustrated or conflicted dependency needs.

CRIME

Bacon, Child, and Barry (1963) found that both theft and personal assaults were more frequent in societies where there was little or no opportunity for a boy to identify with his father. Theft alone was associated with a high degree of socialization anxiety in childhood and a high degree of status differentiation in adulthood. Personal assault more than theft tended to go with a general attitude of suspicion and distrust.

SUICIDE

Naroll (1963, 1969) found that thwarting disorientation patterns were correlated with reported numbers of suicides and the amount of attention the ethnographer gives to suicide. The seven facets of thwarting disorientation tested were defiant homicide, witchcraft attribution, drunken brawling, frequent warfare, wife beating, divorce freedom, and interference by relatives with choice of spouse. These seven traits, with a few exceptions, were unrelated to each other, suggesting that a multiple correlation of the seven to suicide would produce a much higher relationship, and still higher if each of the seven correlations were weighted in consonance with its magnitude.

RIVAL EXPLANATIONS

Naroll (1970a) gives many examples of situations that are explained psychogenically by some investigators and sociogenically by others; he suggests that both explanations are probably correct, and adds biogenic and culturogenic explanations as additional major factors. If all the variables involved in all the explanations were intercorrelated and first displayed in a single matrix, the stage would be set for a multivariate analysis that could raise such controversies above the polemic level where most of them remain at present. Some of the statistical techniques mentioned earlier under "Causality, Evolutionary, and Historical Postdictions" could help solve this problem.

SOME CONCLUSIONS

Cross-cultural studies so far have done much better at listing the difficulties and controversial issues than at solving them in a manner agreeable to all researchers involved. There is at present a healthy amount of difference of opinion, which is a necessary prerequisite to a more objective solution of the problems. I see no quick solution of the ethnic unit sampling problem. On the other hand, I anticipate a better taxonomy of the world's societies, more

attention to the inferential historical influences called the Galton problem, better measurement of reliability and control of quality of data, more recognition of areal differences and the substitution of new variables for area names, and a more sophisticated attitude toward causality.

Although most cross-cultural anthropologists have much to learn from the other behavioral scientists about statistics and experimental and mathematical models, they have an obligation at the same time to help free these people from their more Western-culture-bound view of the human species. If the factor analysts have isolated eighty independent dimensions of human behavior (Guilford 1968) and anticipate forty more among English-speaking subjects in the United States, how many dimensions can we anticipate from the speakers of several thousand languages with as many cultures in other parts of the world? It is surely an astronomical number. In our cross-cultural search for generalizations that apply to all human beings in all times and places, we must not ignore the enormous range of differences among the societies we compare and among the individuals within each society. A complete science of man includes all levels of abstraction, from individuals in a single society to all known societies around the world in the past as well as the present.

REFERENCES

Aberle, David F.
    1961   Matrilineal Descent in Cross-Cultural Perspective. In *Matrilineal Kinship*, ed. David M. Schneider and Kathleen Gough, pp. 655-727. Berkeley and Los Angeles: University of California Press.
Anonymous
    1967   The HRAF Quality Control Universe. *Behavior Science Notes* 2:81-88.

1970 Transcription of Discussion at Second HRAF Cross-Cultural Research Conference. *Behavior Science Notes* 5:141-93.

Apple, Dorrian
1956 The Social Structure of Grandparenthood. *American Anthropologist* 58:656-63.

Bacon, Margaret K., I. L. Child, and H. Barry III
1963 A Cross-Cultural Study of Correlates of Crime. *Journal of Abnormal and Social Psychology* 66:241-300.

Barry, Herbert, III, M. K. Bacon, and I. L. Child
1957 A Cross-Cultural Survey of Some Sex Differences in Socialization. *Journal of Abnormal and Social Psychology* 55:327-32.

Barry, Herbert, III, I. L. Child, and M. K. Bacon
1959 Relation of Child Training to Subsistence Economy. *American Anthropologist* 61:51-53.

Blalock, Hubert, M., Jr.
1960 Correlational Analysis and Causal Inferences. *American Anthropologist* 62:624-32.
1964 *Causal Inferences in Non-experimental Research*. Chapel Hill: University of North Carolina Press.
1968 Theory Building and Causal Inferences. In *Methodology in Social Research*, ed. Hubert M. Blalock and Ann B. Blalock, pp. 155-98. New York: McGraw-Hill.

Boas, Franz
1894 *Indianische Sagen von der Nord-Pacifischen Küste Amerikas.* Berlin: Asher.

Boudon, Raymond
1968 A New Look at Correlation Analysis. In *Methodology in Social Research,* ed. Hubert M. Blalock and Ann B. Blalock, pp. 199-235. New York: McGraw-Hill.

Bowden, Edgar
1969 An Index of Sociocultural Development Applicable to Precivilized Societies. *American Anthropologist* 71:454-61.

Brown, Judith K.
1963 A Cross-Cultural Study of Female Initiation Rites. *American Anthropologist* 65:837-53.

Carneiro, Robert L.
1967 On the Relationship Between Size of Population and Complexity of Social Organization. *Southwestern Journal of Anthropology* 23:234-43.
1968 Ascertaining, Testing, and Interpreting Sequences of Cultural Development. *Southwestern Journal of Anthropology* 24:354-74.

Carneiro, Robert L., and Stephen F. Tobias
1963 The Application of Scale Analysis to the Study of Cultural Evolution. *Transactions of the New York Academy of Sciences*, ser. 2, vol. 26, no. 2:196-207.

Chaney, Richard P., K. Morton, and T. Moore
n.d. The Tylor-Galton Problem: A Reply to Naroll.

Chaney, Richard, and Rogelio Ruiz Revilla
1969 Sampling Methods and Interpretation of Correlations: A Comparative Analysis of Seven Cross-Cultural Samples. *American Anthropologist* 71:597-633.

Child, Irvin, M. K. Bacon, and H. Barry III
1965 A Cross-Cultural Study of Drinking. *Quarterly Journal of Studies on Alcohol,* Supplement no. 3.

Clements, Forrest E.
1931 Plains Indian Tribal Correlations with Sun Dance Data. *American Anthropologist* 33:216-27.

Cohen, Yehudi A.
1961 Food and Its Vicissitudes: A Cross-Cultural Study of Sharing and Nonsharing. In *Social Structure and Personality: A Casebook*, ed. Yehudi Cohen, pp. 312-50. New York: Holt, Rinehart & Winston.
1964 The Establishment of Identity as a Social Nexus: The Special Case of Initiation Ceremonies and Their Relation to Value and Legal Systems. *American Anthropologist* 66:529-52.
1968 Macroethnology: Large-Scale Comparative Studies. In *Introduction to Cultural Anthropology: Essays in the Scope and Methods of the Science of Man*, ed. James A. Clifton, pp. 402-48. Boston: Houghton Mifflin.
1969 Social Boundary Systems. *Current Anthropology* 10:103-26.

Colby, B. N.

1966 Ethnographic Semantics: A Preliminary Survey. *Current Anthropology* 7:3-32.

Coult, Allan D., and Robert W. Habenstein
1965 *Cross Tabulations of Murdock's World Ethnographic Sample.* Columbia: University of Missouri Press.

Czekanowski, Jan
1911 Objective Kriterien in der Ethnologie. *Korrespondenzblatt der Deutschen Gesellschafft für Anthropologie, Ethnologie und Urgeschichte* 42:1-5.

Driver, Harold E.
1938 The Reliability of Culture Element Data. *University of California Anthropological Records* 1:205-19.
1939 The Measurement of Geographical Distribution Form. *American Anthropologist* 41:583-88.
1941 Girls' Puberty Rites in Western North America. *University of California Anthropological Records* 6:21-90.
1956 An Integration of Functional, Evolutionary, and Historical Theory by Means of Correlations. *Indiana University Publications in Anthropology and Linguistics,* Memoir no. 12:1-35.
1961 Introduction to Statistics for Comparative Research. In *Readings in Cross-Cultural Methodology,* ed. Frank W. Moore, pp. 303-31. New Haven: HRAF Press.
1965 Survey of Numerical Classification in Anthropology. In *The Use of Computers in Anthropology,* ed. Dell Hymes, pp. 301-44. The Hague: Mouton.
1967 Comment on "Why Exceptions? The Logic of Cross-Cultural Analysis," by A. J. F. Köbben. *Current Anthropology* 8:21.
1969 *Indians of North America,* 2nd ed., rev. Chicago: University of Chicago Press.
1970a Statistical Refutation of Comparative Functional-Causal Models. *Southwestern Journal of Anthropology* 26:25-31.
1970b Review of "Folk Song Style and Culture," by Alan Lomax. *Ethnomusicology* 14:57-62.
1970c Girls' Puberty Rites and Matrilocal Residence. *American Anthropologist* 71:905-908.
1970d Statistical Studies of Continuous Geographical Distributions. In *A Handbook of Method in Cultural Anthropology,* ed. Raoul Naroll and Ronald Cohen, pp. 620-40. Garden City, N.Y.: Natural History Press.
1973 Cultural Diffusion. In *Main Currents in Ethnological Theory,* ed. Raoul Naroll. New York: Appleton-Century-Crofts.

Driver, Harold E., et al.
1966 Geographical-Historical versus Psycho-Functional Explanations of Kin Avoidances. *Current Anthropology* 7:131-82.

Driver, Harold E., and Richard P. Chaney
1970 Cross-Cultural Sampling and the Galton Problem. In *A Handbook of Method in Cultural Anthropology,* ed. Raoul Naroll and Ronald Cohen, pp. 990-1003. Garden City, N.Y.: Natural History Press.

Driver, Harold E., and A. L. Kroeber
1932 Quantitative Expression of Cultural Relationships. *University of California Publications in American Archaeology and Ethnology* 31:211-56.

Driver, Harold E., and William C. Massey
1957 Comparative Studies of North American Indians. *Transactions of the American Philosophical Society* 47:165-456.

Driver, Harold E., and Karl F. Schuessler
1957 Factor Analysis of Ethnographic Data. *American Anthropologist* 59:655-63.
1967 Correlational Analysis of Murdock's 1957 Ethnographic Sample. *American Anthropologist* 69:332-52.

Eggan, Fred
1954 Social Anthropology and the Method of Controlled Comparison. *American Anthropologist* 56:743-63.

Ember, Melvin
n.d. The Conditions Favoring Matrilocal versus Patrilocal Residence.

Field, Peter B.
1962 A New Cross-Cultural Study of Drunkenness. In *Society, Culture, and Drinking Patterns,* ed. D. J. Pittman and C. R. Snyder, pp. 48-74. New York: Wiley.

Fischer, John L.
1961 Art Styles as Cultural Cognitive

Maps. *American Anthropologist* 63: 79-93.

Ford, Clellan S., ed.
1967 *Cross-Cultural Approaches.* New Haven: HRAF Press.

Freeman, L. C., and R. F. Winch
1957 Societal Complexity: An Empirical Test of a Typology of Societies. *American Journal of Sociology* 62: 461-66.

Goodman, Leo A., and William H. Kruskal
1954 Measures of Association for Cross Classifications. *Journal of the American Statistical Association* 49:732-64.

Gouldner, Alvin W., and Richard A. Peterson
1962 *Technology and the Moral Order.* Indianapolis: Bobbs-Merrill.

Graves, Theodore D., N. B. Graves, and M. J. Kobrin
1969 Historical Inferences from Guttman Scales: The Return of Age-Area Magic. *Current Anthropology* 10:317-38.

Greenbaum, Lenora
1970 Evaluation of a Stratified versus an Unstratified Universe of Cultures in Comparative Research. *Behavior Science Notes* 5:251-81.

Guilford, Joy Paul
1968 Intelligence Has Three Facets. *Science* 160:615-20.

Helm, June, ed.
1968 Essays on the Problem of Tribe. *Proceedings of the 1967 Annual Spring Meeting of the American Ethnological Society.* Seattle: University of Washington Press.

Hobhouse, Leonard T., G. C. Wheeler, and M. Ginsberg
1930 *The Material Culture and Social Institutions of the Simpler Peoples.* London: Routledge & Kegan Paul. First part originally published separately in 1915.

Horton, Donald
1943 The Functions of Alcohol in Primitive Societies: A Cross-Cultural Study. *Quarterly Journal of Studies on Alcohol* 4:199-320.

Jorgensen, Joseph
1966 Geographical Clusterings and Functional Explanations of In-Law Avoidances: An Analysis of Comparative

Method. *Current Anthropology* 7: 161-69.
1969 *Salish Language and Culture.* Indiana University Language Science Monographs no. 3.

Kish, Leslie
1965 *Survey Sampling.* New York: Wiley.

Klimek, Stanislaw
1935 The Structure of California Indian Culture. *University of California Publications in American Archaeology and Ethnology* 37:1-70.

Köbben, A. J. F.
1967 Why Exceptions? The Logic of Cross-Cultural Analysis. *Current Anthropology* 8:3-34.

Koh, Hesung Chun
1966 A Social Science Bibliographic System: Orientation and Framework. *Behavioral Science Notes* 1:145-63.

Kroeber, A. L., and Katharine Holt
1920 Masks and Moieties as a Culture Complex. *Journal of the Royal Anthropological Institute of Great Britain and Ireland* 50:452-60.

Landauer, Thomas K., and John W. M. Whiting
1964 Infantile Stimulation and Adult Stature of Human Males. *American Anthropologist* 66:1007-1028.

Lazerwitz, Bernard
1968 Sampling Theory and Proceedings. In *Methodology in Social Research,* ed. M. Blalock and Ann B. Blalock, pp. 278-328. New York: McGraw-Hill.

Lee, Richard B., and Irven De Vore, eds.
1968 *Man the Hunter.* Chicago: Aldine.

Lippert, Julius
1931 *The Evolution of Culture,* trans. G. P. Murdock. New York: Macmillan. Originally published 1886-1887.

Lomax, Alan
1968 *Folk Song Style and Culture.* Washington, D.C.: American Association for the Advancement of Science.

Lowie, Robert H.
1920 *Primitive Society.* New York: Liveright.

McEwen, William J., et al.
1963 Forms and Problems of Validation in Social Anthropology. *Current Anthropology* 4:155-83.

McNett, Charles W., Jr., and Roger E. Kirk

1968 Drawing Random Samples in Cross-Cultural Studies. *American Anthropologist* 70:50-55.

Marsh, Robert M.
1967 *Comparative Sociology*. New York: Harcourt, Brace & World.

Minturn, Leigh, and W. W. Lambert
1965 *Mothers of Six Cultures*. New York: Wiley.

Moore, Frank W., ed.
1961 *Readings in Cross-Cultural Methodology*. New Haven: HRAF Press.

Murdock, George P.
1937 Correlations of Matrilineal and Patrilineal Institutions. In *Studies in the Science of Society*, ed. G. P. Murdock, pp. 445-70. New Haven: Yale University Press.
1940 The Cross-Cultural Survey. *American Sociological Review* 5:361-70.
1949 *Social Structure*. New York: Macmillan.
1957 World Ethnographic Sample. *American Anthropologist* 59:664-87.
1959 *Africa: Its Peoples and Their Culture History*. New York: McGraw-Hill.
1960 *Ethnographic Bibliography of North America*. New Haven: HRAF Press.
1963 *Outline of World Cultures*. New Haven: HRAF Press.
1967 *Ethnographic Atlas*. Pittsburgh: University of Pittsburgh Press.
1968 World Sampling Provinces. *Ethnology* 7:305-26.

Murdock, George P., ed.
1937 *Studies in the Science of Society*. New Haven: Yale University Press.

Murdock, George P., et al.
1961 *Outline of Cultural Materials*, 4th rev. ed. New Haven: HRAF Press.

Murdock, George P., and Douglas R. White
1969 Standard Cross-Cultural Sample. *Ethnology* 8:329-69.

Naroll, Raoul
1956 A Preliminary Index of Social Development. *American Anthropologist* 58:687-715.
1960 *Controlling Data Quality*. Series Research in Social Psychology, Symposia Studies Series, vol. 4. National Institute of Social and Behavioral Sciences.
1961a Two Solutions to Galton's Problem. *Philosophy of Science* 28:15-39.
1961b Two Stratified Random Samples for a Cross-Cultural Survey. Mimeographed.
1962 *Data Quality Control*. New York: Free Press, Macmillan.
1963 Thwarting Disorientation and Suicide: A Cross-Cultural Survey. Northwestern University, Anthropology Department. Mimeographed.
1964a A Fifth Solution to Galton's Problem. *American Anthropologist* 66:863-67.
1964b On Ethnic Unit Classification. *Current Anthropology* 5:283-312.
1965 Galton's Problem: The Logic of Cross-Cultural Research. *Social Research* 32:428-51.
1967 The Proposed HRAF Probability Sample. *Behavior Science Notes* 2:70-80.
1968 Some Thoughts on Comparative Method in Cultural Anthropology. In *Methodology in Social Research*, ed. Hubert M. Blalock and Ann B. Blalock, pp. 236-77. New York: McGraw-Hill.
1969 Cultural Determinants and the Concept of the Sick Society. In *Changing Perspectives in Mental Illness,* ed. Robert B. Edgerton and Stanley C. Plog. New York: Holt, Rinehart & Winston.
1970a What Have We Learned from Cross-Cultural Surveys? *American Anthropologist* 72:1227-88.
1970b The Culture-Bearing Unit in Cross-Cultural Surveys. In *A Handbook of Method in Cultural Anthropology*, ed. Raoul Naroll and Ronald Cohen, pp. 721-66. Garden City, N.Y.: Natural History Press.
1970c Cross-Cultural Sampling. In *A Handbook of Method in Cultural Anthropology*, ed. Raoul Naroll and Ronald Cohen, pp. 889-927. Garden City, N.Y.: Natural History Press.
1970d Galton's Problem. In *A Handbook of Method in Cultural Anthropology*, ed. Raoul Naroll and Ronald Cohen, pp. 974-90. Garden City, N.Y.: Natural History Press.
1970e Data Quality Control in Cross-Cultur-

al Surveys. In *A Handbook of Method in Cultural Anthropology*, ed. Raoul Naroll and Ronald Cohen, pp. 927-46. Garden City, N.Y.: Natural History Press.

Naroll, Raoul, and Roy G. D'Andrade
1963   Two Further Solutions to Galton's Problem. *American Anthropologist* 65:1053-67.

O'Leary, Timothy J.
1969   A Preliminary Bibliography of Cross-Cultural Studies. *Behavior Science Notes* 4:95-115.

Otterbein, Keith F.
1968*a* A Cross-Cultural Study of Internal War. *American Anthropologist* 70: 277-89.
1968*b* A Cross-Cultural Study of Armed Combat. Research Monograph no. 1. *Buffalo Studies in International Conflict,* ed. Glen H. Snyder, vol. 4:91-112.

Polanyi, Karl
1962   *The Great Transformation.* New York: Rinehart.

Przeworski, Adam, and Henry Teune
1970   *The Logic of Comparative Social Inquiry.* New York: Wiley.

Roberts, John M.
1965   Oaths, Autonomic Ordeals, and Power. *American Anthropologist* 67, no. 6, pt. 2:186-212.

Roberts, John M., Malcolm J. Arth, and Robert R. Bush
1959   Games in Culture. *American Anthropologist* 61:597-605.

Roberts, John M., and Brian Sutton-Smith
1962   Child Training and Game Involvement. *Ethnology* 1:166-85.

Rohner, Ronald P., and Leonard Katz
1970   Testing for Validity and Reliability in Cross-Cultural Research. *American Anthropologist* 72:1068-73.

Russett, Bruce M., et al.
1964   *World Handbook of Political and Social Indicators.* New Haven: Yale University Press.

Sanday, Peggy R.
1968   The "Psychological Reality" of American-English Kinship Terms: An Information-Processing Approach. *American Anthropologist* 70:508-23.

Sawyer, Jack, and Robert A. Levine
1966   Cultural Dimensions: A Factor Analysis of the World Ethnographic Sample. *American Anthropologist* 68: 708-31.

Schwartz, Richard D., and James C. Miller
1964   Legal Evolution and Societal Complexity. *American Journal of Sociology* 70:159-69.

Simmons, Leo W.
1937   Statistical Correlations in the Science of Society. In *Studies in the Science of Society*, ed. G. P. Murdock, pp. 495-571. New Haven: Yale University Press.
1945   *The Role of the Aged in Primitive Society.* New Haven: Yale University Press.

Sokal, Robert R. and Peter H. A. Sneath
1963   *Principles of Numerical Taxonomy.* San Francisco: W. H. Freeman.

Spearman, Charles
1907   Demonstration of Formulae for True Measure of Correlation. *American Journal of Psychology* 18:161-69.

Spier, Leslie
1921   The Sun Dance of the Plains Indians. *American Museum of Natural History Anthropological Papers* 16:451-527.

Stephens, William N., and Roy G. D'Andrade
1962   Kin-Avoidance. In *The Oedipus Complex,* ed. William N. Stephens, pp. 124-50, 213-26. New York: Free Press, Macmillan.

Sturtevant, William C.
1964   Studies in Ethnoscience. *American Anthropologist* 66, pt. 2:99-131.

Swadesh, Morris
1971   *The Origin and Diversification of Language*, ed. Joel Sherzer. Chicago: Aldine-Atherton.

Swanson, Guy E.
1960   *The Birth of the Gods: the Origin of Primitive Beliefs.* Ann Arbor: University of Michigan Press.

Sweetser, Dorrian Apple
1966   Avoidance, Social Affiliation, and the Incest Taboo. *Ethnology* 5: 304-16.

Tatje, Terrence A.
n.d.   On Main Sequence Kinship Theory.

Tatje, Terrence A., R. B. Textor, and R. Naroll
1970   The Methodological Findings of the Cross-Cultural Summary. In *A Handbook of Method in Cultural Anthro-*

pology, ed. Raoul Naroll and Ronald Cohen, pp. 649-76. Garden City, N.Y.: Natural History Press.

Textor, Robert B.
1967 *A Cross-Cultural Summary.* New Haven: HRAF Press.

Torgerson, Warren S.
1958 *Theory and Methods of Scaling.* New York: Wiley.

Tylor, Edward B.
1889 On a Method of Investigating the Development of Institutions, Applied to Laws of Marriage and Descent. *Journal of the Royal Anthropological Institute of Great Britain and Ireland* 18:245-72.

Udy, Stanley H., Jr.
1959 *Organization of Work: A Comparative Analysis of Production Among Nonindustrial Peoples.* New Haven: HRAF Press.

Wallace, Anthony F. C.
1965 The Problem of the Psychological Validity of Componential Analysis. *American Anthropologist* 67, pt. 2: 229-48.

Whiting, John W. M.
1964 The Effects of Climate on Certain Cultural Practices. In *Explorations in Cultural Anthropology: Essays in Honor of George Peter Murdock,* ed. Ward H. Goodenough, pp. 175-95. New York: McGraw-Hill.

1968 Methods and Problems in Cross-Cultural Research. In *Handbook of Social Psychology,* 2nd ed., ed. Gardner Lindzey and Elliot Aronson, vol. 2, pp. 693-728. Reading, Mass.: Addison-Wesley.

Whiting, John W. M., and Barbara Ayres
1968 Inferences from the Shape of Dwellings. In *Settlement Archaeology,* ed. K. C. Chang, pp. 117-33. Palo Alto: National Press Books.

Whiting, John W. M., and Irvin L. Child
1953 *Child Training and Personality.* New Haven: Yale University Press.

Whiting, John W. M., Richard Kluckhohn, and Albert Anthony
1958 The Function of Male Initiation Ceremonies at Puberty. In *Readings in Social Psychology,* ed. E. E. Maccoby, T. M. Newcomb, and E. L. Hartley, pp. 359-70. New York: Holt, Rinehart & Winston.

Wolfe, Alvin W., et al.
1969 Social Structural Bases of Art. *Current Anthropology* 10:3-44.

Young, Frank W.
1965 *Initiation Ceremonies: A Cross-Cultural Study of Status Dramatization.* Indianapolis: Bobbs-Merrill.

Young, Frank W., and R. C. Young
1962 The Sequence and Direction of Community Growth. *Rural Sociology* 27:374-86.

CHAPTER 9   Mathematical Anthropology

DOUGLAS R. WHITE

INTRODUCTION

This review will introduce the general reader in anthropology to some of the uses of mathematics in the analysis of ethnographic data in order to intensify the conceptual and explanatory power of anthropological theory. Many of the problems currently modeled by mathematics are of such general relevance to anthropological theory that it is doubtful that they should be confined under the title of mathematical anthropology. What unites them under this rubric is not quantification, which covers a fraction of mathematics, but rather the common logical substructure that mathematics shares with science in the use of axiomatic reasoning.[1] The major thrust of modern mathematical thought has been to refine the logical underpinnings of mathematical systems of analysis.

Early drafts of various sections of this paper were reviewed and criticized by others, and I have tried to incorporate their criticisms and to interpret the extensive work that has been done in mathematical anthropology in light of various suggestions. I gratefully acknowledge the assistance and encouragement of William Geoghegan, Paul Kay, Robert Randall, François Lorrain, Michael Agar, Robert Kozelka, Thomas Fararo, Ira Buchler, and Michael Burton, and the critical and editorial suggestions of G. P. Murdock and Lilyan Brudner. I am also grateful to A. Kimball Romney, Roy G. D'Andrade, George Collier, Kenneth Morgan, and Bob Scholte for suggestions, contributions, and references, and to members of the Summer Seminar in Quantitative Anthropology for discussions that stimulated my thinking on the general subject.

G. P. Murdock was particularly helpful in providing information on the Natchez case, Ira Buchler provided the stimulus for the Kapauku analysis, William Geoghegan provided the solution to the Purum case and generously went over his field material on the Samal address system, and Robert Randall graciously allowed me to use the American kin-terms example from his unpublished work on kinship algebra. My professors at the University of Minnesota, E. Adamson Hoebel, Pertti J. Pelto, and Eldin Johnson, contributed encouragement to the exploration of mathematical anthropology; professors in mathematical psychology at the University of Michigan, including Clyde Coombs, Frank Harary, Louis Guttman, James Lingoes, and Robert Hefner, provided an important part of my training.

[1] In the twentieth century, modern mathematicians have shown that all mathematics is based upon axiomatic reasoning in which four basic concepts are involved: (1) a specification of primitive notions; (2) a presentation of relevant definitions built up from

Axiomatic reasoning is central not only to mathematics, but also to the growth and development of modern sciences. It provides a logical skeleton upon which systems of explanation and verification are constructed. A model derived from an axiomatic theory contains a logical structure of equivalence between the set of axioms and the set of consequences derived from the axioms. An interpretation of such a model with respect to a body of data allows logical explanation, such that if an axiom set is true, a consequence set derived from it must also be true (i.e., logical extension from known facts), and also allows indirect falsification, such that if the consequence set contains a false statement, the axiom set cannot be true (i.e., indirect invalidation of first premises). Axiomatic models differ from the conventional and looser use of the term "model" in social science research. The latter usage provides no formal system of explanation and falsification, since here the term "model" refers simply to an analogous relationship between one phenomenon and another.

In this review we shall be concerned with models in the narrower sense—models derived from mathematized axiomatic theory. Rather than attempt to trace the developments that encouraged the use of mathematical reasoning in anthropology, the present frame of reference is designed to allow the resultant accomplishments to represent themselves and be judged largely on their own merits. The frame of reference is organized in terms of several important types of general anthropological problems that are modeled.

This review examines theoretical contributions of mathematical anthropology in (1) processual analysis, (2) optimization analysis, (3) structural analysis (graph theory), and (4) ethnographic decomposition. Other areas of mathematization in anthropology, such as data reduction through matrix and statistical analysis, and inferential generalization through statistical analysis and inference, will not be discussed here. These omissions are due partly to limitations of space and partly to the fact that these areas are highly developed and their anthropological applications are therefore better known than the various topics I shall be discussing (but see Burton 1970 and Romney, Shepard, and Nerlove 1972 on new developments in scaling theory).[2]

The four types of mathematical modeling that will be discussed, viewed in conjunction, provide a framework for explanatory theories of behavior in relation to anthropological data. Processual analysis and optimization analysis focus on the development of theories and models of social process. The processual models (section 1) deal with

---

the primitives; (3) a statement of axioms containing only primitives and auxiliary definitions; and (4) logical derivation of theorems from the preceding elements, such that if the axioms are true, the theorems necessarily follow (for a rigorous anthropological example, see Geoghegan 1971; for an earlier use of the logicodeductive or postulational method, see Murdock 1949).

[2] Previous reviews and readings on mathematical anthropology can roughly be divided into six categories, with selected references, as follows:

1-2. Processual and optimization analysis (Buchler and Selby 1968a, Buchler and Nutini 1969, Buchler and Kozelka n.d.).
3. Structural analysis (graph theory) (Barnes 1969, Flament 1963).
4. Algebraic or ethnographic decomposition (White 1963; Hoffmann 1970 [general review article]; Kay, ed., 1971 [also includes items under 5 and 6]).
5. Quantification, statistics, probability (Mitchell 1963, 1967; Hammel and Freedman n.d.; Driver 1953, 1961, 1965; D'Andrade 1959).
6. Data reduction via matrix analysis and computer analysis (Burton 1970; Romney, Shepard, and Nerlove 1972; Hymes, ed., 1965).

Only items 1 through 4 are included in the present review.

the limits and contingencies of social systems, providing a quantitative and somewhat mechanistic model of a behavioral system. The optimization models (section 2) add the element of goal-directed behavior, broadening processual analysis to include choice and learning behavior. Structural analysis and ethnographic decomposition begin with theories of modeling data by axiomatic methods. They search for pattern, structure, and regularity in ethnographic data, translating insight about structural properties of anthropological data into formal axiomatic structures. Structural analysis through graph theory (section 3) is useful in developing models of structural properties, and in examining the fit between these theoretical principles and complex bodies of data about empirical structures. Ethnographic decomposition (section 4) applies primarily to the qualitative and symbolic areas of rule systems in culture, including rules of appropriateness, ordering rules, decision rules, transformation rules, and the like. Structural analysis and ethnographic decomposition, as part of an integrated approach to data analysis, provide a basis on which theoretical statements about human behavior can be constructed, secure in both empirical adequacy and a self-consistent logical structure. Processual and optimization analysis provide a more general and theoretical account of sociocultural and behavioral systems.

1. PROCESSUAL ANALYSIS

Social anthropology is concerned with explaining similarity and diversity of forms of social life. The focus on explanation in anthropology, which builds upon and supersedes description and classification, represents a shift from the study of forms of social life to the investigation of the generative relationship between social processes and social forms. The need for a generative approach to social organization and structure was suggested by Murdock (1955) and others, and articulated in greater detail by Barth (1966:2):[3]

Patterns are generated through processes of interaction and in their form reflect the constraints and incentives under which people act. I hold that this transformation from constraints and incentives to frequentative patterns of behavior in a population is complex but has a structure of its own, and that by an understanding of it we shall be able to explain numerous features of social form. Indeed . . . the processes which effect that transformation are our main field of study as social anthropologists.

In this section we shall examine the uses of mathematical models in the investigation of social processes, focusing chiefly on the problems of relating the principles of social behavior at the individual level (residence, marriage alignment, recruitment to social groups, acceptance of innovation, etc.) to social forms and frequencies of behavior at the group level. The social processes are mediated by a large number of contingencies. Numbers of people in the sys-

---

[3] Murdock (1955:361), for example, stated: "However useful, and indeed indispensable, is this task of classification, it is by no means the ultimate goal of science. Any typological system is, by its very nature, static in character. It takes on full meaning only when scientists are able to demonstrate the dynamic processes which give rise to the phenomena thus classified. The Linnaean system, for example, came alive only after Darwin had discerned the processes of variation and natural selection, and especially after the geneticists had laid bare the dynamic mechanisms of heredity."

Similarly, Barth (1966:2) stated: "Explanation [of social forms] is not achieved by a description of patterns of regularity, no matter how meticulous and adequate, nor by replacing this description by other abstractions congruent with it, but by exhibiting what *makes* the pattern, i.e., certain processes. To study social forms, it is certainly necessary but hardly sufficient to be able to describe them. To give an explanation of social forms, it is sufficient to describe the processes that generate the form."

tem (i.e., demographic factors), distribution of resources (e.g., ecological and economic factors), and other contingencies mitigate the effect of cultural rules or individual motives and strategies. They constitute the framework or ground rules within which a social system operates (Buchler and Selby 1968*a*). The study of social process can be viewed from the perspective of statistical factors in demography, resource distribution, situations, etc., or from the perspective of the interaction between statistical factors and cultural or jural rules.

Until recently there was no foundation in anthropology for a systematic investigation of various types of social process. Earlier processual accounts— for example, of marriage systems—"had few theoretically determined base lines from which to draw conclusions regarding the differential effect of ecological, demographic, and cultural variations on social organization" (Gilbert and Hammel 1966:72). Recently, mathematical models, including computer simulation, have provided the needed framework for the analysis of interactions between complex sets of variables. These models have been applied to problems such as residential patterns, marriage choice, recruitment patterns, and diffusion of information as well as material artefacts. Formal theories pertinent to these phenomena allow models to be derived which can be compared with actual ethnographic data. The criterion of a well-formed theory in such cases is the extent to which a logical structure of explanation of the process is provided, and how well the model of the theory can match actual data.

Mathematical models that may be utilized in processual analysis include the probabilistic (e.g., stochastic or time-dependent statistical processes) and the deterministic (e.g., linear or difference equations). Computer simulations provide a mathematical model through numerical computation when a general mathematical solution to a problem is not already worked out. Simulations may be either probabilistic or deterministic. A decision tree may also be used as a processual model if a population (defined in terms of variable situations of individuals within it) is "mapped" by the tree into a set of outcomes. This model may again be either deterministic or probabilistic, depending on whether the outcomes are certain or probable.

In comparison to a body of ethnographic data, axiomatic mathematical theories and derived models provide a much greater number of theoretical possibilities than are contained in a finite body of data. The data used to test various models may be statistical distributions or observations over time. The models may be tested at those points where data are available, but they may also help clarify other areas of the theoretical problem for future research. They may serve as a guide to the collection of new data needed to test and refine the theory or model. This provides the research with a paradigmatic quality (Kuhn 1962), in that past, present, and future data can be related to a formal model or theory, and findings can feed back to modify the general theoretical framework.

In the choice of a model for a theory, the distinction between probabilistic and deterministic models is important and should be understood. Deterministic systems, exemplified by Newton's laws, assume that the entire future of the system can be predicted given sufficient information about the past. Probabilistic systems, such as statistical mechanics, can predict only the probabilities of certain future occurrences (Kemeny and Snell 1962:5), usually becoming less accurate as the time span lengthens. Probabilistic models are suited to a host of contingency factors that play important parts in social processes. Deterministic models come into play either as approximations of the probability model (e.g., exact calculation of the most likely or expected outcome) or else as an approximate representation of a set of cultural rules. It is highly unlikely that the social sciences will ever approach deterministic laws in the Newtonian sense of strict prediction. As we shall see, deterministic models that do take social contingencies into account and may predict behavior very accurately at a given point in time have been developed; these models will not, however, explain change in the system—that is, they do not predict well over time. The closer we come to an exact model of the structure of social behavior, the less we are able to account for change, and the more we are able to deal with change (e.g., through probabilities), the less exact our knowledge of the structure. There is thus no possibility (or humanistic "danger") of reducing human behavior to a set of mathematical predictions, although mathematics may help to make both process and structure understandable as aspects of human behavior. A review of anthropological uses of processual mathematical models may show the potential complementarity of probabilistic and deterministic models.

A. PROBABILISTIC MODELS

Stochastic or probabilistic approximation models represent one of the modern developments in statistics, in the statistical modeling of empirical phenomena. In a processual model, or stochastic process, a phenomenon is represented as a set of states that are maintained over time or altered in accordance with a set of transition prob-

abilities. Finite state probability models have only recently begun to be used in anthropology, but they have proved useful in relation to questions of change and stability, and in the analysis of unintended consequences of social processes.

Buchler and Selby (1968a:58-68) have suggested that studies of developmental cycles and change in residential patterns can benefit from stochastic modeling. Residential patterns were one of the first ethnographic phenomena to be modeled processually (see Fortes 1945, 1949). Fortes' work stimulated others (e.g., Mitchell 1956, Smith 1956) to study residential patterns developmentally in terms of household composition. The emphasis on process also led to new conceptual interests in decision processes underlying residential choice (Goodenough 1956b).

A major problem in the developmental studies of residence and of household affiliation and composition (e.g., Goody, ed., 1958, Hammel 1961, Fortes 1962, and Miller 1964 for the former; Fischer 1958, Barnes 1960, and Romney n.d. for the latter) was in gauging the effects of vital rates, reproductive ages, segmentation processes, and so forth on household composition. A stochastic model can, in effect, handle all of these factors simultaneously by setting appropriate transition probabilities for household composition types over time. Buchler and Selby (1968a:63-66) show how such a model could be constructed using the example of Freeman's (1958) data on the Iban *bilek* family system. If the various demographic factors are relatively constant over time, it is possible to assume that the transition probabilities representing the normal frequencies of maintenance and change in household types are also constant. A stochastic process with stable transition probabilities, called a Markov process, has an important mathematical property: it can be proved that the expected frequencies in successive states of the system, as computed by the transition probabilities, approach a limiting set of values or an equilibrium vector. Regardless of the initial set of frequencies of the system, the same limiting vector will be reached for a given matrix of transition probabilities. I shall attempt to illustrate a mathematical model of such a system using Otterbein's (1970) data on residence changes on Andros Island.

Otterbein (1970:1414) has classified Andros Island households into nine types. These have been relabeled in Figure 1 to show basic family types and their composition in terms of principal adult members. The arrows on the diagram indicate the traditional developmental cycle from a married couple (Z_2) to a nuclear family (X_2) to an extended family (Y_2), followed by a decline of the family; typically the grandfather dies first (leaving type Y_1), and finally the children and grandchildren move away, leaving the grandmother alone (Z_1). Migration from the island, however, has been increasing,

and has disrupted this cycle: young men and women move off the island for wage labor, and often send their children back to be cared for by grandparents. In comparing two successive censuses (1961 and 1968), Otterbein found that the actual patterns of maintenance or change in household composition differed considerably from the normative developmental cycle in the past. The types and numbers of changes can be indicated in a finite-state diagram (Figure 2). The numbers to the right of the diagram indicate formation of new families and dissolution of old families (new/old).

In spite of the small numbers in this sample, the frequencies of stability and change give a fairly accurate indication of the relative frequency or probability of the transition processes during the seven-year period. The transition probability matrix can be computed for these data to show transitions for the three types of families (nuclear, extended, adult) as well as for the category D, which stands for the demographic processes of formation of new households from the demographic pool of unmarried adults, etc. (Df), and dissolution of households through death or

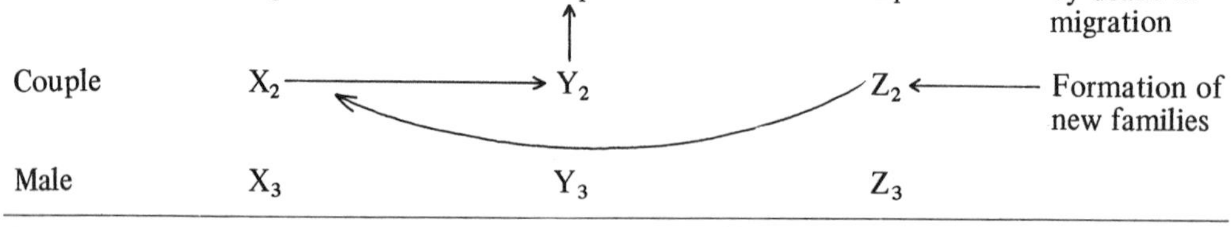

Basic Family Types				
Principal Adult Members	Nuclear (with Children)	Extended (with Grandchildren)	Adults Only	Demographic Factors
Female	X_1	$Y_1 \longrightarrow$	$Z_1 \longrightarrow$	Dissolution by death or migration
Couple	$X_2 \longrightarrow$	Y_2	$Z_2 \longleftarrow$	Formation of new families
Male	X_3	Y_3	Z_3	

Figure 1. Normal developmental cycle among household types in traditional Andros society.

Frequency data: Numbers of households of each type.

	X_1	X_2	X_3	Y_1	Y_2	Y_3	Z_1	Z_2	Z_3
1961	4	25	1	9	15	2	11	8	10
1968	4	17	0	11	20	1	7	5	8

Diagram: Transitions for the nine household types, including demographic factors of formation and dissolution of households.

	X	Y	Z	Df/Dd (formation/dissolution)		
	$1\left(X_1 \xrightarrow{-2} \overset{3}{\underset{?}{}} Y_1 \xleftarrow{-2} \overset{2}{\underset{?}{}} Z_1\right)2$			3/1	4/3	1/7
	$14\left(X_2 \xrightarrow{-6} \overset{1}{\underset{11}{}} Y_2 \xleftarrow{-1} \overset{1}{\underset{2}{}} Z_2\right)4$			3/4	1/1	0/1
	$X_3 \quad {}_1\!\left(Y_3 \xrightarrow{-1} Z_3\right)4$			0/1	0/0	0/6

Reduced state diagram:

$$15\left(X \xrightarrow[16]{-8} Y \xleftarrow[12]{-6} Z\right) \qquad 6/6 \qquad 5/4 \qquad 1/14$$

Reduced state matrix (corresponding to reduced state diagram:

	X	Y	Z	Dd
X	15	8	1	6
Y	0	16	6	4
Z	0	3	12	14
Df	6	5	1	0

Figure 2. Construction of transition matrix from Andros household censuses for 1961 and 1968.

migration (Dd). The approximate transition probabilities, computed from the reduced state matrix in Figure 2, are as follows:

		X	Y	Z	Dd

To: later time period

		X	Y	Z	Dd
From: earlier time period	X	0.5	0.3	0.0	0.2
	Y	0.0	0.6	0.2	0.2
	Z	0.0	0.1	0.4	0.5
	Df	0.5	0.5	0.0	0.0

We see from the matrix, for example, that there is an 0.5 probability that a type X household in 1961 will remain so in 1968, an 0.3 probability that it will change to type Y, 0.0 to type Z, and 0.2 that it will disappear. If these transition probabilities are stable, the same will be true for any seven-year period in the future.

Given the matrix, the operation of the stochastic (Markov) process on a population for successive time intervals can be illustrated. We will start with a hypothetical population of eighty households in 1961, plus a pool of potential householders (category D, which also in this hypothetical case represents the number of out-migrants), distributed to correspond to the census data figures for 1961 for the household types X, Y, and Z. We shall assume that the numbers for the various types of families in 1961 are $X = 28$, $Y = 25$, $Z = 27$, and that in category D there are 20 potential households. The expected values for household distributions for 1968 can then be computed, for example:

$$X(1968) = 0.5X(1961) + 0.0Y(1961)$$
$$+ 0.0Z(1961) + 0.5D(1961)$$
$$= 0.5 \times 28 \qquad + 0.5 \times 20$$
$$= 14 + 10 = 24$$

The equilibrium vector can be computed by solving a set of linear equations where X, Y, Z, and D have the same value before and after transitional probabilities are computed. The values at successive time intervals can then be compared with the final equilibrium values:

	1961	1968	1975	1982	... Equilibrium
X	28	24	24	22	20
Y	25	36	42	44	45
Z	27	16	14	14	15
D	20	24	20	20	20

The equilibrium point (20, 45, 15, 20) will be the same regardless of the initial frequencies. In this case, the initial frequencies, after two intervals, lead to expected values that approach within 4 percent of the equilibrium vector, and are in three intervals within 2 percent of equilibrium values. Thus, whereas the past domestic cycle on Andros Island may have involved a low percentage of extended families (e.g., about 20 percent), the new conditions would stabilize within fifteen years, when the frequency of extended families approaches 45 percent. By the use of the stochastic model, then, aspects of processes of stability and change can be evaluated more precisely. As Buchler and Selby (1968a:67) state:

This perspective opens up a variety of approaches and poses a series of questions relevant to process and change. Consider one example: residence rules. We may say that a given society is "matrilocal," typologize residential processes (Fischer 1958), or consider the decision processes underlying residential choice (Goodenough 1956b). But ... it is of considerable importance to construct and examine a transition matrix in order to determine the stability of the . . . tendency, to compute a limiting vector that may well indicate a drift. . . . Here, then, is a new way of coming at the problem of process.

Equilibrium conditions in a Markov process model have also been used to analyze age-grade systems of the type in which sons must go through the same cycle or set of grades as their fathers (Hoffmann 1965, 1971). In the Shoa Galla system, for example, in which the age-grade cycle is forty years long (five grades at eight-year intervals), stability would represent a problem if the age span between father and son were much less or much greater than forty years.[4] Hoffmann's (1971) assumption that a Markov process model is applicable to this case is questionable, because the transition probabilities cannot be assumed to approximate stability. On the contrary, the likelihood of a son's entering his father's grade at the same age as his father did obviously depends on the age of the father when the son was born.

Unless the conditions for the use of stochastic or Markov models are fulfilled (i.e., satisfaction of the assumptions of the axioms of the model and nonarbitrary determination of transition probabilities), the use of these models simply replicates initial faulty assumptions without providing better understanding of the mechanisms involved. The decision to use a stochastic or Markov process model should be based upon the plausibility of assumptions that can be made about the phenomenon being modeled, and, as far as its predictive adequacy is concerned, on the extent to which (1) the actual

_____

[4] This is an example of the more widespread *Gada,* or cycling, system in North Africa (Murdock 1959:326). Entrance into the system is crucial for adult status, so stability of the system is a real question.

Hoffmann (1965, 1971) shows that stability of the system can be expressed in an equation, where D_n is defined as the difference in age at entry of a descendant, "n" generations hence, the length of the cycle is denoted by "k" (in this case, forty years), and the average reproductive age by "P." Then $D_n = n \cdot k - \sum_i^n P_i$. If P is greater than 40, D_n is negative; if P is less than 40, D_n is positive. The system will be stable only when $D_n = 0$, which occurs when P is equal to 40.

transition probabilities can be logically derived or estimated from known data and (2) the model can be tested against time-sequence data for goodness of fit.

Marriage choice is another area of traditional anthropological interest that has only recently been studied processually. Models of marriage choice phenomena within cultural, social, and demographic constraints are so complex as to require mathematical treatment. This represents the first major area in anthropology in which computer simulation has been used (Kunstadter et al. 1963; Coult and Hammel 1963; Randolph and Coult 1968; Gilbert and Hammel 1965, 1966), although later refinements have made use of stochastic processes as well (Morgan 1969, 1970). In general, the operation and consequences of a cultural rule or marriage preference is studied by constructing a model of a population of a given size, with specified vital rates and probabilities of choice within a range of social categories.

For example, in exploring Ayoub's (1959) view that patrilateral parallel cousin marriage was an "epiphenomenon of a general tendency toward kin-group endogamy," Gilbert and Hammel (1966:72) took advantage of the experimental potential of the computer by simulating a territorially subdivided population with specific marriage rules (e.g., incest prohibition, territorial preference for mates), residence rules (patri-virilocal), and demographic factors (average reproductive age, age matching in marriage, etc.). They hypothesized that the resultant pattern of patrilateral parallel cousin marriage could be accounted for "as an epiphenomenon of territorial endogamy alone, without necessarily specifying kinship-phrased preference."

After logical clarification of the kinship preference problem was obtained through simulation, Gilbert and Hammel developed a formal mathematical model of the probability of cousin marriages as a function of the probability of endogamous marriage, and they were able to compare the results of the two models.[5] The close fit between the formal mathematical model and the computer simulation tended to confirm the conceptual validity of each.

Models of the type used by Gilbert and Hammel can be adapted to similar studies in other societies. Variables such as territorial marriage preferences, residence rules, and demographic factors can be changed without affecting the basic structure of the problem, so that their effects upon expected marriage frequencies may be observed. Through the use of experimental models (probabilistic equations and simulations) it is possible to examine relationships between variables, and to evaluate the kinds of empirical data that would be needed to test or falsify the hypotheses involved.

Computer simulation was used by Kunstadter et al. (1963) for analysis of the effect of demographic constraints on an ideal pattern of marriage: preferential matrilateral cross-cousin marriage. In construction of the demographic model, the factors allowed to vary were population size and marriage probability by age (which in turn affected average age at marriage and at

---

[5] The mathematical equation for the probability that Ego will marry FBD is: $Pr(FBD) = (Pr(ENDOG) \times Pr(FBD|ENDOG)) + (Pr(EXOG) \times Pr(FBD|EXOG))$. In ordinary language, the probability that a man will marry his father's brother's daughter is equal to the sum of the probability of his choosing her from among the marriageable girls within the village (the probability of endogamy times the probability of his marrying his father's brother's daughter if he marries within the village) plus the probability of his choosing her from among the marriageable girls outside the village (the probability of exogamy times the probability of his marrying his father's brother's daughter if he marries outside the village) (Gilbert and Hammel 1966:80).

childbirth, average number of children, and the growth and size of the population). The results showed the impossibility of prescriptive marriage of this type in relatively small populations. The maximum frequency of the marriage type in populations of about a hundred persons is generally between 15 and 24 percent for the simulation model, and generally between 31 and 45 percent for initial populations of two to three hundred which are expanding. The authors note that in societies with larger populations and with a matrilateral cross-cousin marriage preference, it is often a problem to explain why the actual frequency of this marriage type is lower than might be expected from their model.

Baseline models and overlay models are effectively utilized to study interacting effects in complex systems (Coleman 1964:519-22). The two examples of simulation of marriage choice illustrate a means by which complex phenomena can be broken down into simpler subsystems by the use of baseline (i.e., given demographic conditions) and overlay (i.e., marriage preference) models. More sophisticated baseline models can be constructed in which variance in the baseline model is simulated to help understand the effect upon the overlay phenomenon (e.g., marriage rules).

Morgan (1969) uses a model of demographic constraints, including different marriage rules (Morgan 1970), to study the survival possibilities of small, closed populations. He uses a demographic baseline model where the vital rules (e.g., birth, death) are set by a stochastic process. A computer simulation utilizes the stochastic process in such a way that the population undergoes successive demographic transitions governed by random fluctuation in the vital rates as determined by the transition probabilities. The use of a random generating process is known as Monte Carlo simulation. In simulating small populations, this process introduces a realistic fluctuation in population size over time, and successive runs of the program can be used to establish general trends as well as the probabilities of a society's being reduced to extinction. By the use of this baseline model, overlay modifications in terms of different marriage rules can be introduced into the program to determine their effect upon population growth or decline. By this method, Morgan (1970) found that for a model where population tends to slight natural increase without specified marriage rules (random mating), the introduction of incest prohibitions (without consideration of deleterious inbreeding effects) tended slightly to augment population growth, while the effects of clan endogamy tended to lead to dying out of a population in about four hundred years, because of restrictions in the availability of mates.[6]

The use of a stochastic process in Monte Carlo simulation to estimate the chances that a society (or household type or age grade) will die out under certain conditions is one of the important contributions of stochastic models (Coleman 1964:527-28). Gilbert and Hammel (1966:87), in their model, noted that Monte Carlo simulation "allows one to speak of the dispersion of the results." The suitability of stochastic models for analysis of "survival chances" of the components of social

---

[6] The conditions for the baseline population model were found to be stable in the earlier simulations (Morgan 1969), and correspond to low-fertility, low-mortality demographic rates. Thus the results of this simulation are not necessarily generalizable to other conditions. High-fertility, high-mortality rates in small populations were found to exhibit such a degree of random fluctuation that they tended to become extinct in the absence of any marriage rules after an average span of about four hundred years.

systems was not considered by Buchler and Selby (1968*a*) or Hoffmann (1971) in their models of the changing composition of households or age grades, but certainly would be relevant to the problems of estimating the stability of a given sociodemographic system.

Transmission of cultural information can also be studied probabilistically, and constitutes a focus of Hägerstrand's (1967) studies of migration, diffusion, and spatial distributions. Since his work is not widely known, it should be brought to anthropologists' attention. The acceptance of an innovation and the decision to move or to marry are subject to the limits of information available to the individual decision-maker. Information is transmitted through an individual's social network (Pred 1967:300). Hägerstrand has developed a representation of an information network in which probabilities of interpersonal contact are represented spatially in a "private information field." Within a given area, the private information fields of various individuals can be averaged to give a "mean information field." A mean information field can serve as a model to predict a variety of phenomena: rates of migration, of marriage, of innovation or diffusion, etc. Where mean information fields are fairly regular (i.e., not spatially contorted), precise mathematical equations can be derived which estimate rates of transmission within the field.[7] If the mean information field of an area or of neighboring areas is highly irregular (spatially contorted), however, computer simulation using Monte Carlo

methods may give better prediction of a distributional phenomenon.

Hägerstrand's own work on information transmission as it affects socioeconomic factors is meticulously based upon decades of empirical research using data on agricultural parishes in Sweden. The usefulness of his mathematical models of information fields for prediction of marriage and migration rates can be seen in Morrill and Pitts's (1967) studies of a network of Japanese villages. The anthropological value of this type of processual model, which is useful in examining theories of the spread and movement of people and artefacts, is enhanced by the fact that it is explicitly modeled upon social interaction networks, and anthropological field data may be the basis for constructing such models.

B. DETERMINISTIC MODELS

Deterministic equations may serve as approximate models of social phenomena but will never predict social behavior in the sense of behavioral determinism. A deterministic model may be useful as a formalization of an idealized system, or may be useful in the initial formulation of a model where the variables are presumed to be correlated as approximate mathematical functions of one another. While deterministic models are useful at a conceptual stage of investigation, the equations that result from deterministic models may be interpreted as mean tendencies, indicating that a more precise formulation of the problem is required. The final formulation may require a probabilistic

---

[7] One of the best examples of such an equation from Hägerstrand's work is his formula expressing the frequency of migration between two points, O and R: $M_{O-r} = k \cdot Vr \cdot Ir/Pr$. K stands for a constant, Vr for the number of vacancies in R, Ir for the number of contacts of potential migrants in O with R, and Pr for the population of R. Thus, the number of migrations from O to R in a given time period is a

function of drawing power (vacancies) and density of informational contacts (Ir/Pr). The equation, according to Pred (1967:301), "did account for, or 'overlap' with, 96.2% of the actual destinations from a single parish over a five-year period," in comparison to an 84 percent prediction of an alternate model using the same data.

model. One example of the conceptual use of hypothetical systems of variables is George Homans' (1950, 1961) model of "elementary social behavior." Simon (1954:408-11) provided a mathematization of the verbal model using one linear equation, held to express the relationships among group interaction, friendliness, and group activity, and two differential equations that state the conditions under which friendliness and group activity will increase or decrease. Gullahorn and Gullahorn (1963) studied the same problem using computer simulation. Chapple (1970, 1971) also attempted to use deterministic equations to describe social interaction.

Deterministic equations rarely provide precise models of social behavior. They can provide a set of statements of theoretical relationships in the form of equations that help to determine what variables are required to develop an adequate model of the actual empirical phenomenon. As Kay (1971:1) points out, "mathematics is the language par excellence in which it is difficult to say something that you do not intend . . . the entire level of precision is many removes from anything that can be achieved in a natural language." Deterministic equations have a useful function in anthropology, for they may be used to trace out the consequences and logical relationships that are implicit in a verbal model. They may be valuable in verifying or checking the outcomes that would be generated from a verbal statement of a cultural rule system.

The Natchez paradox provides one of the more fascinating examples of the use of deterministic equations in modeling a complex problem. Mathematical models played an instrumental role in the formulation of the "paradox" and the history of attempted solutions.

The statements of French contemporaries of the Natchez in the period 1700-1731 were reviewed and collated by Swanton (1911:100-108) in his reconstruction of the Natchez social classes, including rules of marriage and hereditary class membership. In his interpretation, there were three ranks or classes of nobility, the Suns, the Nobles, and the Honored People, and a fourth class of commoners, referred to as the Stinkards. The nobility had obligatory class exogamy; that is, they were obliged to marry Stinkards, although the numerically preponderant Stinkards presumably also married among themselves. Swanton stated that the rule of descent was matrilineal, except that the children of Sun fathers were Noble and the children of Noble fathers were Honored.

Hart (1943:375-76) noted that under Swanton's reconstruction of the Natchez system, the Stinkard population would rapidly dwindle. Swanton's model of the marriage and descent system "cannot but result in a situation wherein a large number of female Stinkards are debarred from bearing Stinkard children by reason of the fact that these women must marry aristocratic husbands and hence . . . are required to produce aristocratic children." This outcome of the set of rules for the Natchez social classes has been known as the Natchez paradox because Swanton's rules allow the proliferation of the Noble and especially the Honored segments at the expense of the Stinkards. Hart noted that in all other known cases of segmented social systems, demographic symmetry is built into the rules of marriage and descent.

Hart's analysis of the paradox has been formalized by Goldberg (1958:238-41) in a textbook on difference equations, using reasonable simplifications of the reproductive process and Swanton's rules as axioms in the model. Goldberg shows by formal proof from the axioms that the system was demographically unstable; that is, Noble and

Honored classes would grow out of proportion until the rules became unworkable.

Hart (1943:382) attempted the first solution of the Natchez paradox "in the same trial and error spirit as one approaches an incorrect algebraic equation." He suggested that if Swanton's exceptions to matrilineal descent applied only to males, but descent for females was consistently matrilineal, the paradox would disappear. Asymmetric descent for male and female children of Sun and Noble fathers would thus provide a solution to the paradox with least modification of Swanton's original formulation of the descent rule. He found some support in the French sources for asymmetric descent of children of Noble fathers, but his hypothesis was contradicted by the sources in regard to the children of Sun fathers; the early authorities seemed to agree that both sons and daughters of a Sun male were Nobles.

Fischer (1964:54) gave an apt description of the problem that had been raised by Hart: "In the event that a mathematical model derived from an ethnographic description proves self-contradictory or contradicts other ethnographic data, there are two major possibilities: either the model is inadequate, or the ethnographic reports are mistaken." Hart had suggested that Swanton's ethnographic interpretation was mistaken. Quimby (1946) had accepted Hart's analysis of the paradox, but suggested that the class system in its present form had not been long in existence and that the problems of imbalance raised by the model were ameliorated by the assimilation of lesser tribes into the class of Stinkards. Brain (1971) essentially repeated this argument. Fischer (1964) suggested an ameliorative solution that would retain Swanton's model by postulating that the reproductive rates for Noble and

Honored women were lower than the rate for Sun women, and that the Stinkard women had the highest reproductive rate. Fischer's modified mathematical model described the reproductive system by four equations with five unknown variables. Solving these equations for equilibrium conditions among social segments yielded an infinite number of solutions, but all are constrained by the inequalities in reproductive rates expressed above.

The problem with the ameliorative solutions to the Natchez paradox (Quimby, Fischer, Brain) is that they are all based upon inferences that cannot readily be substantiated. None is based upon firm evidence. The inferences of the mathematical models are equally strong, since they identify the rule of descent for the lesser nobility, for which Swanton's formulation was only hypothetical, as the source of demographic imbalance. Hart's hypothesis, however, also suffers from his failure to try to reconcile it with the statements of the French authorities.

Murdock (1950, chap. 12:11-12), in an unpublished paper, uncovered distributional evidence supporting, at least in part, Hart's hypothesis of asymmetric descent. He noted Swanton's (1931: 204-206; 1946:655) ethnographic report of asymmetric descent among the neighboring Caddo, with whom the Natchez had close prehistoric connections:

The possibility of different rules of descent for the two sexes, advanced as an hypothesis by Hart, is converted into a strong probability by the existence of precisely such a differentiated rule among the neighboring Caddo. In this tribe . . . the children of a union between parents of different status groups were affiliated with the mother's group unless that of the father was of higher rank, in which case daughters followed their mothers but sons were classed with their fathers.

When Murdock brought this distributional evidence to my attention, it became apparent that the source of inconsistency identified by the mathematical models of Hart, Goldberg, and Fischer might be rectified by a rule of asymmetric descent for lesser nobility and that the original French sources were in need of restudy. The results are reported by White, Murdock, and Scaglion (1971).

Reanalysis showed that in contrast to all other categories in the descent system, there was no mention whatever of Honored women in the French sources, either as translated by Swanton (1911) or in the original. Analysis also showed consistent sexual asymmetry in the French sources in reference to the children of Noble males. Swanton, it was found, had simply inferred the existence of Honored women, as well as the rule that the daughters of Noble males were Honored, and the rule that the children of Honored women were Honored. On the basis of our analysis of the internal evidence of the French authorities and the distributional evidence from the Caddo, we concluded that (1) Honored status by birth was exclusively for males, (2) there were no Honored women other than the wives of Honored men (a rank that was open by achievement to Stinkard men as well as ascribed to sons of Noble men), and (3) descent for children of Noble males was asymmetric, the sons being Honored and the daughters being Stinkards. In addition, we found abundant evidence to support a hypothesis by MacLeod (1924) that (4) the Suns were not a class but a royal family, collateral lines of which were demoted to the Noble class after three generations. By extension, (5) Noble matrilines also degenerated after three generations to commoner status (Stinkard status for women, Honored rank for men).

It is not necessary here to demonstrate that these rules for the Natchez

class and descent system constitute an equilibrium solution to the Natchez paradox. White, Murdock, and Scaglion (1971) show that even with different rates of reproduction for the various marriage types, with achievement of Honored rank by Stinkard men and of Noble rank by men of Honored birth, and with polygyny of the Sun and Noble men, assuming constant rates, a stable ratio among social segments will be reached under these rules.

In the Natchez case, deterministic models pointed to inconsistencies in the classic and widely accepted ethnographic description of the class system, and led to the reevaluation of the evidence. Our reformulation of the evidence for a two-class system of nobility and commoners, with a special rank for the royal family (Sun rank) and with recognition of distinction achieved by commoners by raising them to Honored rank, is consistent with the principles of stratification in other societies with a class of nobility.

Mathematical models of the reproductive implications of rules of marriage and descent can also help to show the greater vulnerability of smaller social segments, such as the Sun family among the Natchez, to biological extinction. This is a frequent concern of royalties and is for the Natchez Sun family, which maintained a delicate balance of power. The Natchez case also raises the question of why demographic symmetry of the rules of marriage and descent should be so nearly universal in segmentary social systems (Hart 1943). The answer lies in the conditions by which agreement on common cultural rules is hammered out in the conflict of interest between potentially conflicting social segments.

For the problem of conflict of interest as well as the question of whether individual behavior can be accurately portrayed as following normative cultural rules, the use of simple processual models is not adequate. The types of rules we have discussed for the Natchez are idealized or normative; we do not know to what extent they were honored in the breach. If we recognize that rule-breaking occurs but assume that it is essentially a random phenomenon, then probabilistic processual models could take into account random deviation from the norm, and deterministic models would serve as useful approximations to the central tendencies of the more precise probabilistic models. But nonrandom or strategic rule-breaking, like conflict of interest, cannot be modeled as an essentially mechanical process ·of the sort we have discussed: we must introduce the elements of choice and decision-making. Leach (1962a:133) states the need for choice-making models categorically: "In all viable systems there must be an area where the individual is free to make choices so as to manipulate the system to his own advantage."

There are two approaches to the study of choice-making. One is the study of choice as a process of optimization, assuming that the social actor attempts to maximize according to his values or preferences. Another is to recognize that when ethnographers speak of "cultural rules," they generally refer only to the gross level of cognitive recognition of patterned alternatives by social actors, and that the actual cognitive rules utilized in decision-making are more complex, specifying contingencies, subrules, and rules for breaking rules. At the level of more detailed cognitive models of cultural rules, mathematical models may again be formulated which have a deterministic structure, if only in the cognitive sense of indicating expected or appropriate behavior.

Geoghegan (1969a) and Fjellman (1969) have developed methods for analyzing residence patterns as the outcomes of decision rules that take situational contingencies into account. Rather than being models of normative rules, these models indicate residential modes as outcomes that are regarded as expected or appropriate by social actors under the possible varieties of circumstances, no matter how infrequent the outcomes. The deterministic model is that of the decision tree, which Geoghegan has used to analyze residential choice among the Tagtabon Samal and which Fjellman has utilized for the Kangundo Akamba. Each ethnographer elicited from informants the ways in which they assessed information in predicting the residential choices of others and in making residential choices themselves. The form of a typical decision tree is given in Figure 3, simplified from Geoghegan (1969a). A more formal basis for the ethnographic construction of decision trees is given in the fourth part of this paper. What is important for the present discussion is that since the various assessments in this decision tree represent statuses or resources of social actors, knowledge of the frequency and distribution of these attributes in the population will serve to predict the distribution of residential modes in the population. Thus the model indicates not only the most likely choice of an appropriate residential mode for an individual actor, but the most likely societal residence distribution as well. On this basis, Geoghegan and Fjellman found their predictions of residential patterns to be 95-98 percent accurate. A decision tree used to predict societal distributions becomes a processual model when changes in the independent variables or assessments predict changes in the dependent variables or outcomes.

Processual models based on indigenous decision rules or assessment rules will generally give more accurate and

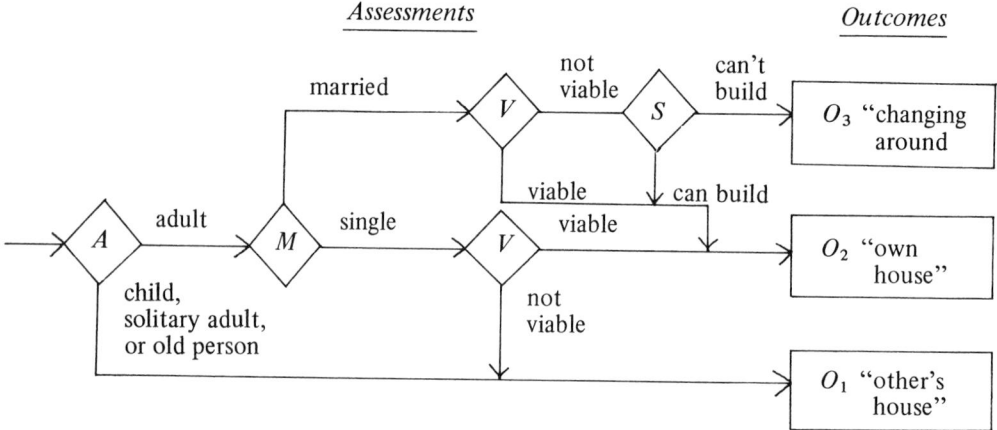

Figure 3. Typical decision tree: a simplification of Geoghegan's "Decision-Making and Residence on Tagtabon Island."

theoretically satisfying accounts of social behavior than statistical analysis of variables that are defined without reference to the particular cultural system. Goodenough (1956b) illustrated this principle in his comparison of his and Fischer's (1958) classification of Trukese residence patterns from census records and auxiliary cultural data. For the Tagtabon Samal, Geoghegan (1969a:3) reports that "considering the census data alone, a matrilineal principle or bias appears to dominate the selection of residence locations. . . . This would certainly seem to go against the strict bilaterality observed in other domains of social organization." The decision rule analysis shows that "this apparent matrilineal tendency is an artefact of the rule which Tagtabon Samal use in making decisions about residence—a rule, moreover, which makes no reference to any matrilineal principle and is quite consistent with their professed bilateral ideology." Thus processual models of cultural rules in the form of cognitive information processing and decision-making rules have considerable power in the analysis of the ways in which social forms are generated and may lead to new theoreti-

cal insights into the structure of social phenomena. To summarize, mathematical systems, even of the simplest variety, are built up from axioms and derived theorems in order to provide a logical structure from which models or interpretations can be derived for the analysis of empirical cases. The usefulness of these systems relates to the general elucidation of problems which is provided by mathematical reasoning. The cases presented here have shown that selection of axioms is of greatest importance in applying mathematical rigor to ethnographic problems. Selection must be made from a wide perspective on the field of inquiry as well as by the strict criterion of consistency with such facts as can be definitively established.

Most importantly, mathematization of a problem demands well-defined concepts, as well as analogs of the concepts in empirical situations and measures, so that a problem can be analyzed empirically. These factors are in short supply in the initial phases of formal theoretical development within any discipline. Because of its single-minded logic and literalness, mathematical formulation may provide theoretical breakthroughs that are both concrete and general. For the same reasons, mathematization used improperly may have a pernicious influence, for it can hide as well as expose weaknesses in our use of various theories and models. Stochastic processes, for example, may only replicate our ignorance of a process without increasing our understanding of the phenomenon modeled. Attempts to define a system by linear equations may show the impossibility of finding mathematically well-defined functions for the phenomenon modeled. Mathematization may show the gaps in our knowledge of a particular system, as in the Natchez case, where, fortunately, these gaps could then be filled in by a reexamination of evidence.

Nonetheless, mathematical formulations quite frequently have the advantage of demonstrating their own lacunae, and those in the assumptions of the investigator, so that a problem can be reevaluated either on its own terms or comparatively. Imprecise and non-mathematical formulations cannot be properly evaluated for their very lack of explicitness. The explication and test of a limited problem in a formally logical manner may contribute more to a general solution to a set of problems (as in the Gilbert and Hammel case) than a set of quasi-theoretical statements that lack formal logical precision and relation to operational definitions. As we shall see, carefully constructed and tested mathematical models can also be linked together by virtue of their explicit attention to different aspects of larger theoretical problems.

2. OPTIMIZATION ANALYSIS

A general processual account can model only the gross regularities in sociocultural processes. Within a population there is variation with respect to learning, strategy, and choice. Individual variability is conditioned by cultural rules, individual or situational constraints, contingencies, and other external factors. Optimization analysis can be viewed as a more precise focus within processual analysis upon the social actor, his conscious goals or plans, and his conscious or unconscious values as they enter into the actual contexts of choice.

Optimization encompasses many alternative criteria of value and goals and has become one of the widely accepted explanatory concepts in the social sciences. It incorporates a host of related behavioral and cognitive concepts: economizing, decision-making, adaptation, competition, and the like. Models of optimization processes are constructed to test and refine through comparative analysis the various theories hosted by the concept of optimization.

Optimization problems were first approached mathematically by the use of classical mathematics in the form of deterministic equations (the calculus of continuously measurable, functionally related phenomena). These approaches were not immediately or directly useful to the analysis of anthropological data. Human behavior is not necessarily representable as continuously measurable or deterministic phenomena. It was not until the development of qualitative or finite mathematics in the past two decades (game theory, graph theory, linear programming, flows in networks, etc.) and until anthropology prepared the groundwork within its own domains that optimization analysis of anthropological data could be approached through mathematization.

An adaptive and dynamic perspective in such fields as social structure (see Murdock 1955), and subsequently in economic anthropology, political anthropology, legal anthropology, psychological anthropology, and other fields, was parallel to the perspective that led to developments in the mathematization of "social economy" by von Neumann and Morgenstern (1947:41):

Let the physical basis of a social economy be given—or, to take a broader view of the matter, of a society. According to all tradition and experience human beings have a characteristic way of adjusting themselves to such a background. This consists not of setting up one rigid system of apportionment ... but rather a variety of alternatives, which will probably express some general principles but nevertheless differ among themselves in many particular respects. This system ... describes the "established order of society."

Game theory was suggested as an indispensable tool to anthropology as early as 1953 by Lévi-Strauss, who also suggested a number of situations in which it is particularly applicable. O. K. Moore responded to the potential of the "natural laboratory" of ethnography for exploring von Neumann and Morgenstern's theory of competitive strategies. Moore's background and experimental work on human problem-solving had led him (1957:73) to consider those situations in which a "randomizing strategy" is an efficacious means of problem-solving, for it may allow actors "to avoid unwitting regularities in their behavior which can be utilized by adversaries."

Moore focused on the divinatory scapulimancy practices of the Montagnais-Naskapi, a tribe that relied on deer as a stable food source. Using the ethnographic data of Speck (1935), Moore (1957:74) determined that the practice of divination was used during periods of food shortage when in fact an adaptive randomizing strategy would be important in avoiding regularities of behavior that might jeopardize the success of the hunt. Divination served much as might a "table of random numbers" in

determining the direction the hunters might take. Other techniques of magic and divination, Moore suggested, might be considered in this light as possible efficacious problem-solving devices using a chance mechanism.

Roberts, Arth, and Bush (1959) were heavily influenced by the conceptual content of the theory of games as a framework for studying the cultural system in relation to the "expressive" components of actual games, as well as the practical value of games as training or learning devices for culturally appropriate types of skills and strategies. They introduce into anthropology von Neumann and Morgenstern's distinction between games of physical skill, games of chance, and games of strategy. As expressive models, they suggest, types of games should be related to variables that "figure in expressive or projective mechanisms" (Roberts et al. 1959: 399):

... Games of strategy which are models of social interaction should be related to the complexity of the social system; games of chance which are models of interaction with the supernatural should be linked with the supernatural; and ... games of physical skill may be related to aspects of the natural environment.

Barth's (1959) article on segmentary opposition was important in placing optimization analysis centrally within the study of social organization, although he did not lean heavily on mathematization. Davenport's (1960) excellent but provocative article on Jamaican fishing strategies, which he characterized as a zero-sum game, was also an important early contribution. In an article written in 1962 Fortes also advocated the use of game theory. Barth's (1966) article on models of social organization introduced processual and optimization concepts further into the mainstream of anthropological discourse, altough his discussion was largely programmatic and suggestive. In 1966 an anthropological conference was held on the subject, the results of which were published in a 1969 volume (Buchler and Nutini, eds., 1969). Subsequently, Buchler and various colleagues have made extensive use of game theory and related techniques (Buchler and Selby 1968a, Buchler and Kozelka n.d.), focusing on the mathematization of anthropological theory and drawing upon the theory of games as an important stimulus for the new phase of conceptualization in anthropology. As von Neumann and Morgenstern (1964:7) state:

The great progress in every science came when, in the study of problems which were modest as compared with ultimate aims, methods were developed which could be extended further and further. . . . The sound procedure is to obtain first utmost precision and mastery in a limited field, and to proceed to another, somewhat wider one, and so on.

Buchler and Selby (1968a:311) conclude their review of the new approaches to social organization with the remark:

It would be . . . misleading to assert that modern anthropology has achieved utmost precision and mastery in even the most limited fields; but aspects of the . . . study of kinship and social organization appear to be on the threshold of the development of a theory based on the interpretation of "ethnological facts." This stage will ultimately be marked by the transition from unmathematical plausibility considerations to the formal procedures of mathematics, and "the theory finally obtained must be mathematically rigorous and conceptually general."

In exploring the mathematical models of optimization, let us begin by considering how the axioms of the classical models of rational or "economic man" have been gradually relaxed in the new

mathematics until they are now applicable to anthropological data. Optimization models are tested and the theories refined by examining the empirical adequacy of consequence sets or derived theorems, whose adequacy is traced back so that the adequacy of the axioms may be inferred. Thus optimization models are necessarily accompanied by experimental work in matching mathematical models against a variety of "realistic" situations. Anthropology to date has contributed only in a limited degree to the empirical refining of the theories of optimization, even though anthropological fieldwork provides the best of possible natural laboratories for such work. This lack of feedback and an incomplete grasp of the analytical orientation in testing logico-deductive theory are blocks to theoretical development within anthropology as well as to dialogue with related disciplines working along parallel lines.

The unwillingness of anthropologists to utilize classical optimization models of economics, however, is completely justified when we consider that these models require axioms that afford the decision-maker (1) perfect knowledge of the existing situation so that he can predict exact outcomes for each of his possible actions, (2) complete sensitivity to information in the form of linear functions for strategic commodities (e.g., exact knowledge of the current shape of supply and demand curves), (3) ability to rank-order outcomes in terms of some criterion as to maximization or optimization of his goal (i.e., a rank-ordering of the utilities of outcomes), and (4) knowledge that whatever his choice, it will not affect the operation of the system (i.e., there will be no feedback between actors or between an actor and the system). This is a model for decision-making under certainty (d.m.u.c.) of outcomes, and for anthropological purposes all but axiom 3 are patently absurd. Axiom 3 assumes that actors know their preferences and act to optimize goals, but does not specify what is maximized. Axiom 3 is a subject for anthropological investigation.

In an article on the strategies and canons for constructing mathematical models in social science, Herbert Simon (1954:388-415) suggests that the concept of rationality can be retained while the rigid assumptions of classical economic man are thrown out by relaxing each of the three objectionable axioms in the theory of optimization so that they may apply to more realistic situations. Even in the classic model, he points out, change in rational behavior is studied as a function of existing conditions and the decision-maker's knowledge of the consequences of his options under these conditions. Also, what is rational to one actor may be nonrational to another. These "bounds" of rationality are specified in part by the decider's definition of his goals or his criterion for selecting an outcome, and by his information about existing conditions and about functions that predict outcomes. "Improvement in the model of rational behavior will come primarily through careful attention to the boundaries of the area of rationality" (p. 394).

The newer models of optimization are generated by relaxing the classical axioms of rationality. The first axiom of perfect knowledge of outcomes can be relaxed by having outcomes contingent upon risk. It would then read that the decider must know in advance the probabilities of different outcomes for each of his possible actions (decision-making under risk, d.m.u.r.). Whereas classical economic man was required only to rank-order his preferences among outcomes (an ordinal measure of utilities), the "risky choice" involves rank-ordering probability combinations of outcomes (Edwards 1967: 28-29). Von Neumann and Morgenstern (1947) show a formal proof that the ordering of such probability combinations can be used to construct a cardinal measure (interval scale) of utility. Multiplying this measure by the probability of each outcome and summing the results for all the outcomes under each possible choice of action produce a measure of expected utility for each choice. Thus maximization of expected utility is possible for d.m.u.r. or "risky" choices. Once this simple mathematical model has been developed, maximization hypotheses can be given much broader empirical testing.

In the case where the outcomes, in a model of choice, are not only risky but uncertain—i.e., even the likelihood of different outcomes cannot be estimated in advance—the first axiom in optimization theory is relaxed further. It is modified so that the decider knows the set of possible outcomes, but does not know their relative probabilities. This is decision-making under uncertainty (d.m.u.u.), and presents a problem in that expected utilities cannot be computed without knowing exact probabilities of risk. One possibility for maximization under these circumstances is that in the absence of information, minimum regret of loss or the difference between the best and worst outcomes is the criterion for choice (Savage 1951). Another possibility is that over successive trials, the decision-maker will attempt to maximize on the use of information gained in each trial about the possibilities of different outcomes. Bayesian statistics (see Wald 1950, Chernoff and Moses 1959) is essentially the study of the optimum use of information on successive trials to estimate expected gain. In the d.m.u.u. (Bayesian) model, utility or expected gain is again the maximization criterion.

We have now seen that by relaxation of the first axiom covering d.m.u.c. situations to those covering d.m.u.r. and d.m.u.u. (Bayesian) situations, it is possible to derive comparable models of the maximization of utility. Thus the first axiom may be modified to fit any of the possible levels of knowledge which an actor may have of the consequences of his actions. It is also possible to maximize other criteria besides utility, as in the case of d.m.u.u. (regret).

The second classical axiom falls away simply in shifting from continuous to finite mathematics (see Edwards 1967: 14). The troublesome remaining axiom is the fourth: no anthropologist (or economist, for that matter) would unconditionally agree that individuals do not affect one another's behavior (via knowledge or prediction of one another's choices) or the social systems of which they are part. It is on this point—interaction between the players in a system—that von Neumann and Morgenstern (1947) erected the mathematical theory of games. Dropping this fourth axiom altogether, they allow for strategic competition, in which each player may try to outguess his opponent or opponents. In a zero-sum game, where one player's gain is another's loss, choice of a strategy that contains a maximal payoff, or any kind of decision function to compute maximal expected payoffs, may be detected by the other player and used to one's disadvantage. Rather than maximize utility, then, players who assume their opponent to be capable of "second guessing" may turn to the strategy that maximizes security: assuming that the worst can happen, the player chooses that course of action which is the "best" among the worst outcomes. If both players use the minimax loss strategy, there are two possible outcomes: their choices may coincide (in which

case a saddle point or stable solution exists) or they may make different choices (an unstable solution). In the unstable case, game theory states that there will be a stable equilibrium solution to the game consisting of one or more best "mixed" strategies (all of equal and optimal value) for each player. This equilibrium solution is precisely the kind of "statistical" or randomizing strategy that O. K. Moore (1957) discussed in connection with those cultural situations in which a chance mechanism such as divination is employed in choice-making.

A general conceptual and mathematical solution was thus introduced by von Neumann and Morgenstern in their *Theory of Games and Economic Behavior*, defining at least one type of plausible optimization for situations of pure competition. Now, by different combinations of the strict or relaxed axioms (removing axiom 2 altogether), we may attempt to account "realistically" for the different types of decision situations. Mathematical models for each of the types of situations may be tested empirically for their adequacy: classical for d.m.u.c. situations; expected utility for d.m.u.r.; minimal loss for d.m.u.u. (regret); expected gain for d.m.u.u. (Bayesian); and minimax loss for d.m.u.u. with opponents (game theory).

The predictions of each of these types of mathematical models may be examined for their goodness of fit with one of the best described applications of decision theory in anthropology, Davenport's (1960) description of Jamaican fishing strategies. Fishing close to shore (inside) can be done with less expensive boats than deep-water fishing requires, but yields fish that are worth less on the market than fish caught beyond the shallows (outside). Classical analysis (d.m.u.c.) is ruled out in this situation because of the uncertainty of the current, which runs about 25 percent of the time by informants' estimates and may result in the loss of fishing pots in the outside banks. The other models, involving risk or uncertainty, may apply to the situation, but there is no *a priori* reason to select one of the axiom sets above the other. Each model makes different assumptions about what is maximized. Read and Read (1970:351-54) criticize Davenport for not examining the model of maximization of expected value (d.m.u.r.) and for simply assuming that game theory applies because it predicts the frequencies of different fishing strategies. One may criticize Read and Read on their own grounds, in that maximization of expected values is not the only alternative model. Kozelka (1969) has shown how the problem may be approached through Bayesian statistical analysis, assuming that the fishermen try to utilize information each day to predict whether the current will flow, and that they choose their fishing location accordingly. Thus there are two models that assume maximization of expected value or expected gain, but which differ in the use of information: (1) the Bayesian model makes the greatest use of information on a day-to-day basis to predict whether or not the current will flow; (2) the expected utility (d.m.u.r.) or "risk" model uses the information on the statistical average of nature's behavior. The two other models make successively even less use of available information, but also begin to maximize on security factors in the face of uncertainty: (3) in the uncertainty-with-opponent or game theory model, the "security level" or minimax value is sought, assuming that nature is doing its best to make life difficult for the fishermen (which is, in a sense, a "predictive" assumption); (4) in the uncertainty-without-opponent model, which

assumes that nature is unpredictable, the best that can be achieved is the minimization of "regret" or of the difference between the best and the worst outcome under each strategy.

The differences in predictions of these four models, as computed from Davenport's data, are shown in Table 1. The four strategies are ranked in order of their assumptions about the use of information. The optimum strategies for allocation of fishing pots, the expected or minimax values for these strategies, and the expected actual payoffs, given the frequency of the current, are shown in the columns of the table. The first or Bayesian strategy has been computed on the assumption that the fishermen are able to predict successfully when the current runs two-thirds of the time, and to predict two-thirds of the time as well when it does not run. (The computations here can be derived by reversing the calculations of Kozelka [1969], who assumed that the fishermen could predict the current only one-third of the time.) The expected gain of the Bayesian strategy is £15.70.[8]* The second or expected utility strategy (d.m.u.r.) has been calculated by Read and Read (1970), and the expected value is £14.35. The third or game theory strategy is calculated by Davenport (1960), and has an expected minimax security level of £13.30, but owing to the fact that the current flows somewhat less than this model predicts, the average payoff would be £13.60. The fourth or regret criterion leads to a guaranteed minimal payoff of at least £11.50, but averaged over time the actual payoff would be £12.95.

If the solutions in Table 1 are ranked according to risk rather than information (2,1,3,4), it is apparent that the risky outside strategies have the highest payoffs, and the conservative inside strategies have lower payoffs. But a fishing captain who followed the risky

*Footnote 8 may be found on p. 417.

TABLE 1
Four Optimization Models, Showing Their Predictions
for Jamaican Fishing Strategies

	%Allocations of Fishing Pots, by Boat			Value of Strategy	Value Corrected for Actual Current
	Inside*	In-Out†	Outside		
1. D.m.u.u. with "prediction": Bayesian expected gain (Kozelka 1969)	25%		75%	£15.70	£15.70
2. D.m.u.r.: expected utility (Read and Read 1970)			100	14.35	14.35
3. D.m.u.u. with "opponent": game theory (Davenport 1960)	67	33		13.30	13.60
4. D.m.u.u., "no information": regret (Savage 1951)	100			at least 11.50	12.95

*Actual % boats used inside, 69%; pots placed inside, 79%.
†Actual % boats used in-out, 31%; pots placed outside, 21%.

strategy could be ruined by a bad month. In the choice of maximization criteria, then, we must distinguish the use of information from the attitude toward risk. The fact that the fishermen avoid the high-risk strategies may mean that they actually view nature as an opponent, or act as if this were true, or else it may simply mean that they place more emphasis on security factors than on expected payoffs over time per se. It is impossible to decide between these two alternative interpretations of "rational" behavior without further information on the way the fishermen actually utilize information, and their actual attitude toward risk.

This analysis points up that Davenport's use of game theory leads to indeterminate results without more field data: the fit between the predictions of his data and a game theory model may or may not be coincidental, but of the four models examined, only the mini-max criterion provides accurate predictions of the outcomes. However, all four of these models assume that the payoffs of each strategy are invariant with respect to the frequencies of captains who choose each strategy. They assume that the fishermen compete against nature, both as individuals and as a group, in an effort to derive maximal value from fishing production. However, in another sense they also compete with one another. They sell their fish on the market, and an overall reduction in the price of fish will result if the market is glutted with "outside" or "inside" fish exclusively. In addition, the canoes enter into market considerations, since the used canoes from outside fishing are put to use in inside fishing, and a shift to predominant outside fishing will affect this balance of price and use as well (Read and Read 1970). Thus the overall distribution of strategies affects the payoffs of particular strategies as well as the joint income of the fishermen. Read and Read (1970) suggest a more complex mathematical model for calculating expected utilities, taking market factors (prices, costs, wages, life cycle of canoes, etc.) into account.

In entering the problem of individual versus joint or group optimum values and strategies, however, the situation may arise where optimal strategies at these two levels conflict. In the Jamaican case, this could occur when the best individual strategy is high-risk but the best group strategy is conservative. The problem then becomes one of how the fishermen decide whether or not to cooperate, and what sanctions will be taken against those that do not cooperate. Non-zero-sum games can be a starting point for the analysis of this type of situation. For example, an analogous conflict between individual optimization and joint optimization exists in the classic problem of the non-zero-sum game "The Prisoner's Dilemma" (Rap-

oport and Channah 1965). The situation can be stated in a verbal payoff matrix, Figure 4, representing two prisoners accused of a crime who are being interrogated by the police. Given this payoff matrix, A will prefer to confess if he uses a minimax loss criterion, since at worst he will go to prison for one year or so, which is better than the ten-year sentence he might get if he does not confess. The situation is the same for B. In each case, the decision to confess depends on the inability to predict with certainty that the other prisoner (the accomplice) will not break down and confess. However, if the two criminals have a high mutual trust and an agreement beforehand not to confess, they may both get off free. The minimax solution is yes/yes to confess, but the optimal joint strategy is no/no, or "honor among thieves."

Non-zero-sum game situations allow for the study of cooperative and noncooperative strategies, individual versus group levels of rationality, and the de-

Prisoner A, interrogated separately

Prisoner B, interrogated separately, same question	Will you confess to the crime? If you turn state's evidence on your partner, you will be acquitted and given a reward. If you don't confess, but your partner does, you will receive a severe sentence.	
	Confess	*Not confess*
Confess	Both given light sentence, conviction by confession.	A given severe sentence, B an acquittal and reward.
Not confess	B given severe sentence, A an acquittal and reward.	Both acquitted, lack of evidence.

Figure 4. "The Prisoner's Dilemma."

velopment of formal notions of trust and justice (Braithwaite 1955, Nash 1950). Game theorists (Rapoport, ed., 1960; Bartos n.d.) have attempted to develop further mathematical models for bargaining and negotiation among players who are allowed to make verbal contracts and develop relations of trust.

The theory of coalitions, or zero-sum *N*-person majority games, was introduced into anthropology by Fredrik Barth (1959) in his analysis of Yusufzai Pathan political organization. The game theory model provides an explanation of certain aspects of the political system, since the features of competition within the game model define "the necessary and sufficient conditions for the emergence of a two-bloc system" (Barth 1959:15). The competitive features of the model involve control of land and resources, persisting opposition of interests over joint estates between collaterals in the agnatic descent system, and the existence of "unrestricted freedom for the units of the system to form coalitions on the basis of strategic choices." The majority coalition principle, derived from game theory (von Neumann and Morgenstern 1947:332), predicts that a minimal winning coalition will be to the advantage of the dominant coalition, since it can then extract values from a maximal number of players in the minority coalition. The dominant coalition will also discourage shifting of sides, according to the model. By the simple nature of opposition and shifting alliances, the model predicts the formation of a two-party system, although there may be many more than two players. Thus the first part of Barth's explanation is provided by game theory. "The system of two blocs does not depend on a recognition of the nature or function of duality, but emerges through the separate self-interested decisions of the persons in the system" (p. 16). The second part

of his explanation demonstrates why it is to the advantage of a dominant bloc leader to define strategic restraints on the exploitation of a minority bloc leader (p. 18):

If he extracts too much from his weaker rival, one of his own lieutenants, who by virtue of his private following holds the balance of power, will be [enticed by the willingness of the minority bloc leader to abdicate] to become the leader of the other faction. That faction thus becomes the stronger bloc, and the leader of the formerly stronger bloc will suffer a loss.

Thus optimization analysis can prove exceedingly useful in providing an explanatory framework for viewing the interrelation of interest groups in a society, jural rules and economic factors, and the system of social segments and political affiliations. Southwold (1969) demonstrates a similar utility of the theory of coalitions in zero-sum *N*-person games as applied to African politics, especially problems of succession and secession. These studies, backed by the work of Riker (1962), Schelling (1960), and other political scientists who have used game theory to study conflicts and coalitions, have begun to reorient basic anthropological perspectives on the structure of sociopolitical systems.

Striking instances of two-party political coalitions can be treated within a game theory framework. Murdock (1956), for example, showed a parallel between democratic two-party systems and local and political moieties. Haas (1940) and Spoehr (1941) discovered that shifting alliances between Creek towns of the Red and White political moieties were regulated by means of a formal gaming situation (Murdock 1956:140):

Any town which lost four successive lacrosse matches to a particular opponent was compelled to shift its political moiety affiliation. . . . It had no choice, for it was deserted by all its former friends, who now regarded it as an "enemy," and would have been completely isolated if it had not accepted its old enemies as its new friends. One can scarcely conceive of a device more admirably suited to preserving the unity of the entire body politic by preventing intertown rivalries from degenerating into permanent feuds.

This and many other instances in the ethnographic literature can be placed within the larger theoretical framework of von Neumann and Morgenstern (1947:31-45), which is essentially a general theory of social organization. The essence of this theory is that it shows choice and variation within a population, yet provides models that are of great interest for comparative statements about behavior of actors in terms of cognition, cultural information, cooperation and competition, cultural values, and culture change.

Peter Gould (1965), for example, has analyzed the introduction of wheat after World War II into the Moshi and Arusha areas around Mount Kilimanjaro, Tanganyika. Like Davenport, he uses game theory to model a "game against Nature," but resolves the problem of the applicability of this model in a different way. Gould (1965:159) constructs a larger framework in which adaptive strategies are viewed as learned behavior over time:

There is the implication that the farmers regard the environment as a vindictive, minimizing player. There is the objection that such a view is unrealistically severe, but when men have to make decisions under conditions of great uncertainty, they may very well choose extremely conservative strategies or, in game theory terms, strategies according to the minimax criteria, to maximize their security level, particularly in the initial phases.

Gould couples the more conservative predictions of game theory with those of learning theory, and shows evidence

that the early years after the introduction of wheat were marked by conservative locational strategies, followed by gradual adoption of high-payoff high-risk locations. The farmers learned and utilized information about probabilities of rainfall in various locations. Given this new information, a d.m.u.r. (expected utility) model for decisions could be gradually substituted for a d.m.u.u. model (game theory) for a growing segment of the population. The farmers were also faced with a problem of severe wheat rusts, and Gould shows that the adoption of rust-resistant varieties of wheat over a twenty-year period follows the learning curve that has been developed from laboratory experiments as well as successfully applied in models of innovation and diffusion (Hägerstrand 1967).

The relationship of psychological variation within a population to the general framework of "multiple interests" in social economics (von Neumann and Morgenstern 1947:43) is also shown in Gould's study (1965:164):

One could also speculate about the psychological attitudes of the farmers, and the shapes of the utility functions associated with the attitudes. Those farmers who planted high on the mountain during the initial years might be characterized as having a "cautious attitude" with a convex utility curve which gradually straightens to the linear function of the "fair attitude" player over the years; while the initial plungers on the lower slopes may have the upward, concave utility function of the player with a "gambler's attitude."

Sutton-Smith and Roberts (1964) have done more than speculate on the relation of psychological characteristics in the population and social behavior within the framework of game theory. They found that the cross-cultural work on the correlation of games as expressive models of fortunism (games of chance), potency (games of physical skill), and strategy (games of strategy), with dimensions of supernatural, natural, and social relations, could be extended intraculturally into the area of personality differences. Children can categorize one another into types corresponding to the fortunist, the potent, the strategist, and combinations thereof, and these categorizations have some predictive relationships to success or failure in various tasks. Thus competitive styles as well as games and "rules of the game" in the larger sense of the cultural system "reflect cognitive attitudes that emerge in developmental sequence in association with specific child-training techniques" (Sutton-Smith and Roberts 1964:36).

Formulation of problems in terms of optimization theories, where appropriate, may lead to a much greater ethnological contribution to scientific theory of behavior than has been the case wherever parochial or descriptive goals have dominated anthropological thinking. Dalton's (1969) parochial assumption that optimization does not occur in societies with predominantly reciprocal or redistributive transactional modes has been attacked on logical grounds by formalists, but the detailed explanation of his point of view has rarely been examined on empirical grounds.[9]* Dalton (1969:67-68) states:

In subsistence (non-market) economies, the question of choice among real alternatives does not arise in such explicit fashion. A Trobriand Islander learns and follows the rules of economy in his society almost like an American learns and follows the rules of language in his. . . . He does not "choose" to plant yams rather than broccoli. The question does not arise in this form, but rather in the form of how much of each of very few conventional crops to plant or how to apportion a given work day to several tasks. . . .

Because a Tikopian chooses to fish today rather than to tend his garden does not mean that the economics of Tikopian fishing or gardening is usefully described by linear programming . . . [or economic optimization theory].

We shall examine this question of whether economic optimization analysis can be usefully applied to non-market societies in some detail by examining Buchler and Kozelka's (n.d.) empirical test and critique of Dalton's hypothesis, using the case of Kapauku agriculture. Although Buchler and Kozelka deal only with the sweet potato crop, our analysis of the Kapauku case will be extended to the problem of whether the ethnographic facts fit an optimization model for the major crop complexes, including taro and sugar cane as well as sweet potatoes. The problem is of interest because it exemplifies quite clearly the relevance of some of the decision models we have discussed, and also allows us to examine the technique of linear programming (which Dalton says does not apply here). Linear programming constitutes a general solution method for any of the decision problems formulated in this section. Aspects of the Kapauku problem are identical to those in economics, although the method of linear programming used here has a much wider relevance, contrary to Dalton's assertion, than simply to substantive economic problems.

The Kapauku face a strategic choice of focusing cultivation in the fertile valley lands, where yields are greater but there is risk of destruction of the sweet potato crop under heavy rains, or employing extensive slash-and-burn techniques in the mountain fields, where yields are less but heavy rains do not damage the crop. There are about four times more mountain land in the Kamu area suitable for sweet potato cultivation (more than 156 *pekas*) than valley land (35 *pekas*) (Pospisil 1963). Since the Kapauku cannot afford to fall below the subsistence requirements, the conservative minimax strategy is the only choice that will guarantee continued support of the population even in years of heavy rain. The Kapauku accordingly utilize all of the available mountain land (156 *pekas*) for sweet potato production. (Several years of dry weather induced members of one village, Botukebo, to use the more speculative high-risk high-gain strategy of planting most of their crops in the valley lands in 1959. The year proved to be a wet one, their crops were destroyed, and starvation was barely averted through exchange with neighboring villages that had planted prudently and acquired a surplus [Pospisil 1963:86]. Obviously, the minimax strategy can be learned by trial and error as well as by "second guessing.")

The guaranteed subsistence base that is taken care of by the mountain lands does not utilize the total labor supply. In addition to 29,200 man-hours spent in the mountain fields, Pospisil (1963: 423) estimates that 11,680 man-hours were spent in the valley lands. Of these hours, 90 percent (10,556 man-hours) were spent in the three major types of crop complexes: (1) intensive shifting cultivation of root crops (sweet potato, taro); (2) intensive shifting cultivation of sugar cane; and (3) intensive complex cultivation of the sweet potato. The second and crucial part of our analysis focuses on these production choices in the valley lands, where the crops vary in terms of labor input and agricultural techniques, and in yields. The problem—to us and to the Kapauku—is to find the balance of land and labor which optimizes productive effort.

Optimization of productive effort in the valley lands is a complex problem, since the high-yield crops (sugar cane and intensive complex cultivation of the sweet potato) are also more labor-

intensive than the low-yield extensively cultivated root crops. The information that is needed to assess the optimization of productive effort includes the constraints of land and labor, and, for each of the crop types, the yields (in weight) per *peka* of land, the nutritional value (in calories) per unit weight, and the hours of labor required per *peka*. The measure of caloric value of foods is used in this problem since their value cannot be measured directly in kilograms (unequal nutritional value per unit weight), and there is no way of determining the market value of the crops, since these subsistence crops are not exchanged or marketed. Indeed, one of the conditions for testing Dalton's hypothesis, that food production in societies based on reciprocity and redistribution is regulated by "custom" rather than optimization, should be the absence of a market for these goods.

With the information required for optimization analysis provided by Pospisil (1963), we can proceed to state the problem as a linear programming problem. The total land (out of the 35 *pekas* available in the valley) for the three types of crop complexes occupied 30 *pekas:* this is the land constraint. If X, Y, and Z represent the amounts of land corresponding to types 1, 2, and 3 of food production, this constraint can be written: $X + Y + Z \leq 30$ (*pekas*). The total labor has been given as 10,556 man-hours spent on the three crops. This is the labor constraint. The other information is taken from Pospisil's tables on yields, nutrition, and labor inputs, and is summarized in Table 2.

The equation for caloric food production is a function of the number of *pekas* cultivated within each of the categories X, Y, and Z, and the equation can now be written as: CP (caloric production) $= 1,200X + 1,560Y + 1,520Z$. The constraints of labor for

TABLE 2
Raw Data on Yields of the Three Major Types of
Agricultural Land Use in the Kamu Valley

	Kilogram Yields per Peka		Caloric Value per Kilogram		1,000-Calorie Yields per Peka	Hours of Labor Required per Peka
Type 1 (X): intensive, shifting cultivation of root crops*	1,200	x	1,000	=	1,200(000)	210
Type 2 (Y): intensive, shifting cultivation of sugar cane	5,200	x	300[†]	=	1,560(000)	401
Type 3 (Z): intensive, complex cultivation of sweet potatoes	1,520	x	1,000	=	1,520(000)	376

*Closely similar figures for caloric value of taro and sweet potatoes have been averaged.
[†]Estimate (see Pospisil 1963:195).

any given allocation of land can be written: $210X + 401Y + 376Z \leq 10,556$. In each of the three equations, of course, the variables X, Y, and Z are the *pekas* of land devoted to intensive shifting cultivation of root crops (X), intensive shifting cultivation of sugar cane (Y), and intensive complex cultivation of sweet potatoes (Z).

The linear optimization of the equation for *CP*, under the constraints of land and labor, can be visualized as one of the options that can be combined along three dimensions, corresponding to axes X, Y, and Z in Figure 5. Production may be increased along any of these axes, corresponding to the modes of production, or along several axes simultaneously. The limitations of land form one planar surface in Figure 5 which restricts land allocations. Limitations of labor form a second planar surface imposing a second restriction on land, even though in some cases the required land is not available. The feasible points for an optimization solution are contained in the first of the two planes encountered moving away from the

origin $(0, 0, 0)$. Calculations of the *CP* values for feasible points, as shown in Figure 5, range from 36,000 $(30, 0, 0)$ to 44,160 $(4.5, 0, 25.5)$. The latter point, a mixture of X (type 1) and Z (type 3), is the optimum use of land and labor for food production, as measured in caloric value.

How well does this compare with the actual allocation of land use in the Kamu Valley? The actual figures for Kapauku allocations (Pospisil 1963: 423) correspond to the point $(5.8, 9.6, 14.6)$: 5.8 *pekas* of type 1 (X) production, 9.6 *pekas* of type 2 (Y) production, and 14.6 *pekas* of type 3 (Z) production. The caloric production value for this allocation is 44,127 — within a hundred points of the optimum. It is also along the line of intersection between the two planes where land and labor limitations intersect. This line contains the best or optimal allocations for mixed solutions of all three types of crops. Thus if a balance of different crops is sought by the Kapauku, such that the juice or pulp of sugar cane is included in their diet,

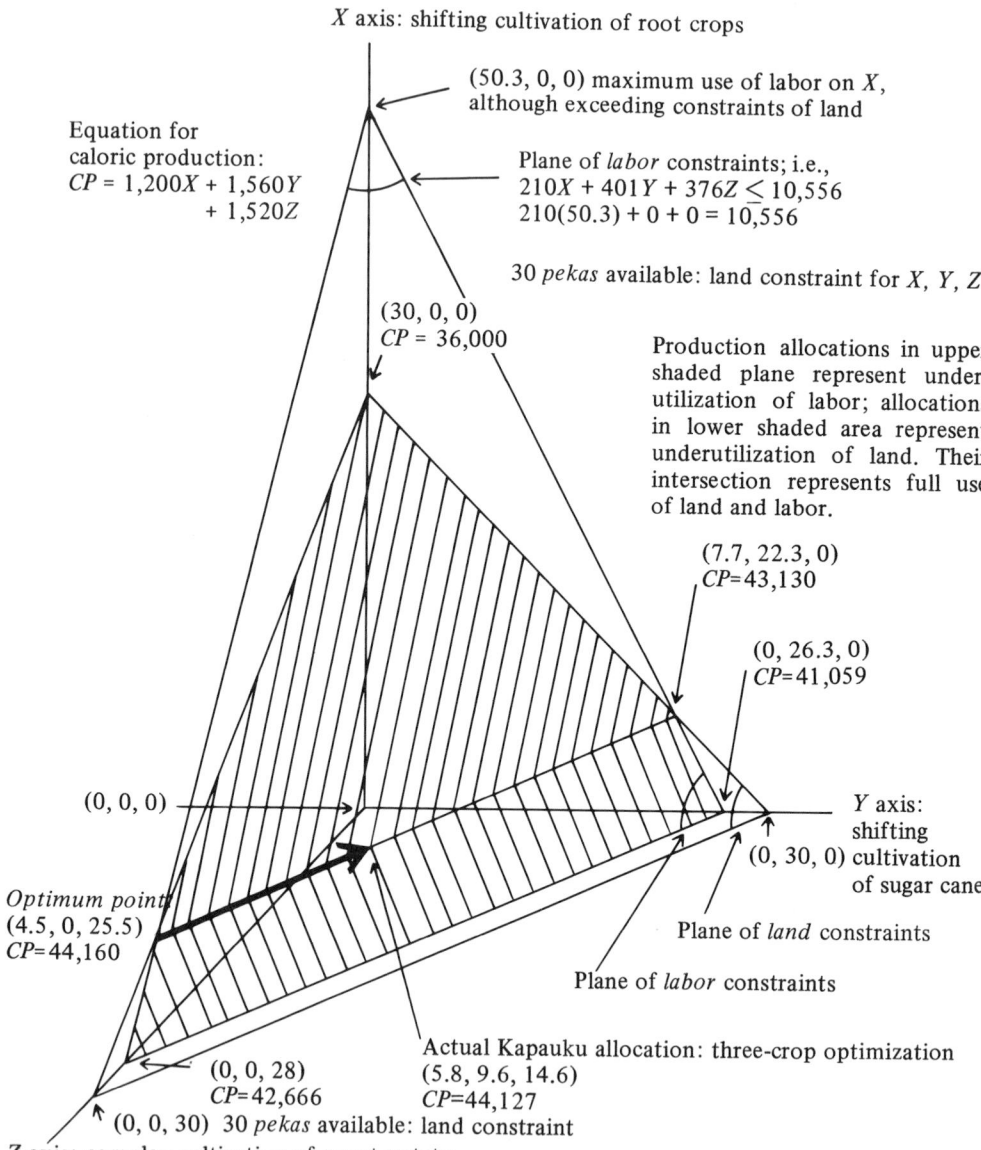

X axis: shifting cultivation of root crops

(50.3, 0, 0) maximum use of labor on *X*, although exceeding constraints of land

Equation for caloric production:
CP = 1,200*X* + 1,560*Y*
              + 1,520*Z*

Plane of *labor* constraints; i.e.,
210*X* + 401*Y* + 376*Z* ≤ 10,556
210(50.3) + 0 + 0 = 10,556

30 *pekas* available: land constraint for *X, Y, Z*

(30, 0, 0)
CP = 36,000

Production allocations in upper shaded plane represent under-utilization of labor; allocations in lower shaded area represent underutilization of land. Their intersection represents full use of land and labor.

(7.7, 22.3, 0)
CP=43,130

(0, 26.3, 0)
CP=41,059

(0, 0, 0)

Y axis: shifting cultivation of sugar cane
(0, 30, 0)

Optimum point
(4.5, 0, 25.5)
CP=44,160

Plane of *land* constraints

Plane of *labor* constraints

Actual Kapauku allocation: three-crop optimization
(5.8, 9.6, 14.6)
CP=44,127

(0, 0, 28)
CP=42,666

(0, 0, 30) 30 *pekas* available: land constraint

Z axis: complex cultivation of sweet potato

Figure 5. Kapauku optimization, showing Kamu Valley land-use problem involving shifting cultivation of root crops (*X*) and sugar cane (*Y*) and intensive complex cultivation of sweet potato (*Z*).

their optimal production strategy lies along this line, moving away from the absolute optimum in the direction shown by the heavy arrow in Figure 5. By this criterion, the Kapauku have reached an optimum production strategy.

The Kapauku agricultural problem illustrates the complex predictions that can be made by optimization analysis outside the context of a market economy. Without mathematical analysis it is not immediately apparent that Kapauku agriculture should be broken down into separable but related decision problems: one a game against nature with a minimax solution, the other a classical (d.m.u.c.) problem of the alternative use of land and labor. Determination of the optimum feasible point in the land/labor allocation in valley cultivation as a mixed weighting of the production strategies is also not apparent without mathematical analysis. Our case of the utility of linear programming, contrary to Dalton, has been established.

Optimization analysis can provide an explanatory framework for behavior in allocation problems, utilizing the concept of maximization. But it is not restricted only to those cases in which it can be shown that an optimum has been reached. It may be equally useful in examining those cases in which optimization has not been reached. A measure of how close an observed allocation comes to an optimal point can be derived by a distance function, such as the length of the heavy arrow in Figure 5. (Common approaches to linear programming, simplex methods, and distance functions are given in Dantzig 1951 and Gale 1960.) Hoffmann's (1969) article, "A Linear Programming Approach to Cultural Intensity," is essentially concerned with the possibility of measuring observed distances from theoretical optima in optimization prob-

lems. He feels that this might allow for a precise definition of the degree of adaptation a system has attained, and that concepts such as "cultural intensity" or "climax" may be measurable in terms of degree of optimization. These are speculative pronouncements. What is needed at this stage in empirical research is a more intensive analysis of cases, as data become available, to explore the behavioral implications of optimization analysis.

From a strictly mathematical point of view, linear programming has the advantage of being a fully generalizable solution technique for the variety of decision models outlined in this section, as well as others that are more complex. Programming problems can be broken down as shown in Figure 6.

Buchler and various colleagues (Buchler and Selby 1968a, Buchler and McKinlay 1969, Buchler and Kozelka n.d.) have suggestively demonstrated how optimization analysis may be applied in seemingly qualitative problems in ethnology, such as problems of social structure. From Buchler's Mexican ethnographic material, for example, he found that the way a man decides to seek or be sought as a mate is related to choices of virilocal or uxorilocal residence. There is a tradeoff of loss of status in the choice of uxorilocal residence against gain in resources by marrying into a wealthy family. In the overall optimization decision, it might be possible to say at what point a man's resources are low enough and a girl's high enough so that the low-status option becomes favorable. If this optimization problem could be solved in general terms, residential choices might then be predicted for the entire village (see Buchler and Selby 1968a:51).

Another example derives from the observation that among the Tiwi and several other Australian groups, "it is perfectly clear that men attempt to

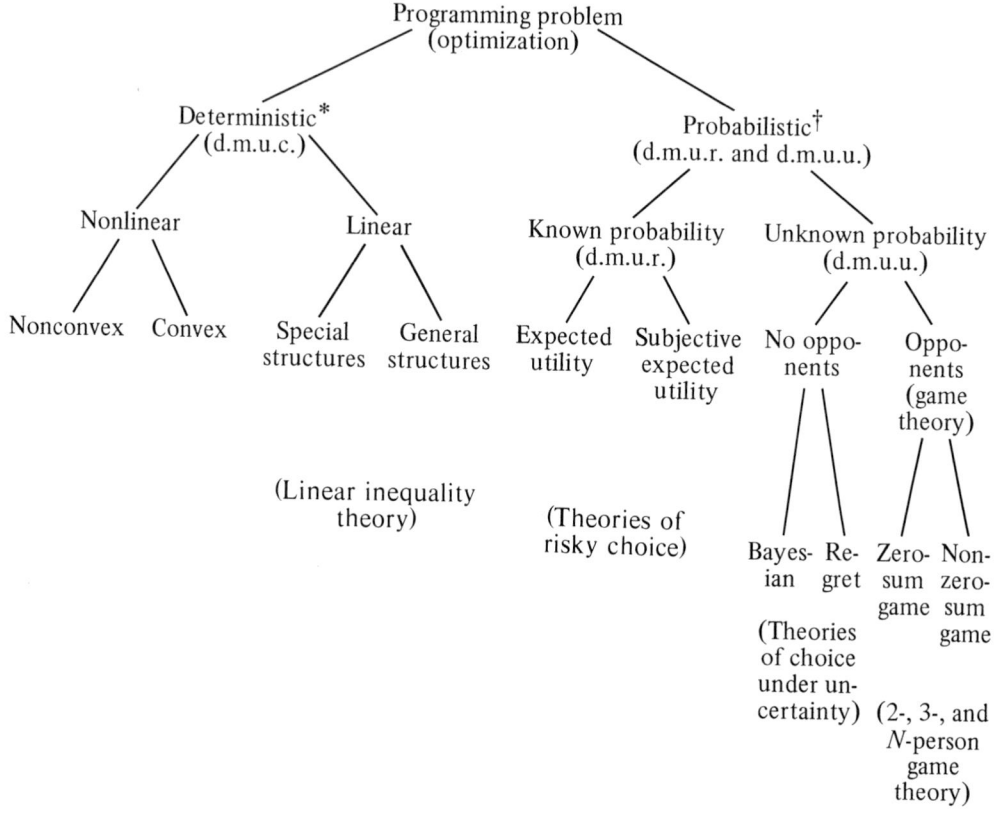

*As in the land/labor optimization of the Kapauku example, using linear inequality theory.

†As in the Jamaican example, showing alternative solutions under the assumptions of various models under the subheadings.

Figure 6. The varieties of optimization models subsumed under the general technique of programming problems. (After Dantzig 1951, Buchler and Kozelka n.d.)

maximize the objective function 'number of wives,' and at the same time, attempt to minimize a cost function involved in the acquisition of wives. . . . The decision processes underlying the maximization of this function is a linear programming problem" (Buchler and Selby 1968a:313-14). There is a much more complex (although again programmatic) statement in Buchler and McKinlay (1969:191-212) about the possibility of analyzing the Mesoamerican *cargo* system of religious posts in terms of decisions of the elders about "who shall and who shall not advance to positions of high prestige and moral rank." In this case the optimization analysis involves the most complex of the programming approaches, nonlinear equations (see Figure 6). In the particular case of the Atempan *cargo* system, the goal is to derive the weighting of the various factors that go into a decision, so that the decision rule matches the ethnographic facts. As we shall see in section 4, there may exist less difficult solutions for some problems of this sort, though these solutions are none the less mathematical in nature.

A final example of optimization analysis in the anthropological literature focuses not upon decisions and strategies and their optimal employment, but upon the rule systems that define culturally and strategically circumscribed behavior. Atkins and Curtis (1969:xii) note a difference in the conceptual interests of anthropologists and those of game theorists:

Game theory deals both with game rules per se and with rules for playing games intelligently. It has been rules of the latter sort, of course, which have claimed by far the larger share of the game theorist's attention—and quite properly so, given the motivations that guide most game-theoretic studies.

By contrast, the historically dominant and still flourishing concern of the cultural anthropologist has been with the analogues, in culture at large, of game rules in the first or narrower sense—that is, with what might be referred to as "ground rules" that have more to do with structuring the basic cultural framework within which decision-making occurs than with guiding choices among the options that this framework may allow. Indeed, one major source of difficulty in finding immediate anthropological applications for game theory lies precisely in this difference of emphasis.

For the study of game rules in culture, Atkins and Curtis show the usefulness of constructing a model that defines positions in the game, and permissible sequences, as well as the rules that define the turns of each player. They link the use of game theory to another mathematical theory, the theory of graphs, to show how the two methods of analysis can be combined to provide a broader explanatory and analytic framework. The use of graph theory will be examined in the following section.

It is not necessary to look for "dramatic" cases in which one mathematical model or another seems to apply. The raw materials for the analysis of optimization, according to the values and goals that are inherently variable in human beings, are everywhere. The impressive results of optimization analysis in anthropology have come by the use of the axiomatic method for the construction of formal models of optimization within the constraints of a particular system. The intensive study of an ethnographic case (or intensive comparative analysis of a problem) must be encompassed within the larger concerns for the explanation of human behavior. It is not the analogic use of mathematical models that helps to solve these problems, but the clarification of the logic of a problem by the construction and examination of axiomatic models. Alternative models and theories are explored until an adequate theoretical beginning is achieved—after which it may be improved upon, tested, or replaced.

Optimization analysis, including decision theory, game theory, linear programming, various types of learning theory, and the like, provide one of the bases for an integrated approach to anthropological theory. They do not, however, "solve" a problem in any final sense, nor do they suggest that a given behavior is rational or irrational. The predictions of game and decision theory in the experimental or ethnographic settings will always be controverted and then modified to account for the variability of human goal-directed behavior. What is interesting is that these models provide a test of fit between various models of highly standardized optimization criteria, such as can be expressed along a utility scale, or of fit between the stated or implied goals of actors and the outcomes of actual behavior. They do provide a means of examining the predictions of different axiomatic models of optimizing behavior, in comparison with behavioral outcomes or statistical distributions of behavior within a population. The assumptions that these models utilize in their predictions can also be matched against the various types of characteristics of actors: differences in types of optimization criteria; differences in the ways information is processed or utilized; in subjective perception (optimism/pessimism in subjective probabilities); in levels of rationality (cooperative/noncooperative); and different procedures of establishing trust, bargaining, or distributive justice.

In a sense, anthropological fieldwork provides an extension into the "natural laboratory" of the more culturally limited experimental work on human choice behavior. Ours, however, is the task of relating individual choice and variability in such a way as to show the general principles that operate in society in the interplay of multiple interests. As we shall see in the discussion that follows, the study and understanding of choice behavior must also be cognizant of cultural constraints, and may depend upon breaking the indigenous cultural code, or the systematic representation of the general principles of an indigenous cultural system as it is organized from within.

3. STRUCTURAL ANALYSIS: GRAPH THEORY

Graph theory and matrix analysis are two types of mathematical analysis that are used for anthropological data reduction. Data reduction is a process that attempts to identify the nature of ordering relations or structural properties in a body of data, and to reduce a complex body of raw data into a finished model that displays these structural properties to a maximal degree. In anthropological matrix analysis raw data are arranged into rows and columns

that are suitable for mathematical analysis. For example, reported characteristics of individuals may be arranged in such a way that individuals are listed by rows and the various characteristics are listed by columns: a particular cell in the matrix is then a datum pertaining to a specific individual.

A matrix can be represented on a graph only in the specific case where both the rows and the columns represent the same elements, and the cells contain information on the relationship between pairs of elements. For example, both the rows and the columns of a matrix may correspond to the same set of individuals or social personae, and the cells might contain information on relationships between them. In this case, the individuals could be represented by points on a graph, and the relations between them could be represented by lines, perhaps with an additional symbol used to indicate the type of relationship. Matrix analysis and graph theory are interdependent, with matrix analysis being the more general of the two types of analysis.

For the sake of simplicity in presentation of data-reduction methods, this section deals only with graph theory, and only with a small part of the broader methodologies of data reduction which are of central importance to the development of anthropological theory.

The development of axiomatic systems regarding structural properties of graphs has been one of the most significant recent innovations in mathematics. The utility of graph theory as a mode of data reduction derives partly from this attempt to provide a formal theory of structural properties of relational systems, quite apart from any specific empirical phenomenon (see Berge 1962; Harary, Norman, and Cartwright 1965; Busaker and Saaty 1965). If empirical data are fitted to the format of graph theory, however, the formal body of theorems in graph theory provide derivations for certain structural properties that may prove to be useful models of the empirical phenomenon. The interpretation that is given to these formal properties will vary, depending on the phenomenon that is modeled.

Graph theory models have an explicational use, with the goal of rendering the meanings of basic structural concepts more precisely than is otherwise possible. Berger, Cohen, Snell, and Zelditch (1962) distinguish explicational models from theoretical construct models, such as the processual or optimization models we have examined already. In these previous uses of axiomatic theory, theoretical constructs were translated into operational measures, so that a model of the theory could be interpreted with specific reference to a body of data. In graph theory, formal structural properties are derived from the internally consistent set of axioms for the types of structures that can be represented on a graph.

Anthropological matrices for data on relationships between members of a set of elements may be put into correspondence with different types of graphs. The type of graph that is appropriate depends upon the type of relational data that is contained in the matrix. If the content of the cells in the matrix represents the presence or absence of the relationship, the cells in the matrix may be coded as a binary 1 or 0 distinction, while in the corresponding graph a line between two points indicates presence, and no line between two points indicates absence of the relationship. When the matrix is symmetric—that is, when all specified relationships (x, y) are symmetric in their reciprocal form (y, x)—e.g., x is related to y implies that y is related to x—the matrix can be represented as a *simple graph*. In a nonsymmetric matrix, a relationship (x, y) may be directional rather than reciprocal: x gives to y does not imply that y gives to x. In a nonsymmetric matrix, entries of 1 or 0, for presence or absence of the relationship, may be represented by directional arrows on a "directed graph" or *digraph.*

When the relations between a pair of elements in a matrix are either positive or negative or absent $(+ 1, - 1, 0)$, this can be represented on a *signed graph,* where connecting lines between points, if any, have either positive or negative values or signs. Another possibility is the *signed digraph*, which corresponds to a nonsymmetric matrix with relations that are positive, negative, or absent $(+ 1, - 1, 0)$. Lack of symmetry in relationships on the signed digraph is again represented by directional arrows. These four types of graphs do not exhaust the possibilities for types of graphs, since obviously the type of data that may be encoded for a relational network can be too complex to be represented by signs $(+1, -1, 0)$ or by a simple binary code $(1, 0)$. In the *network graph,* for example, magnitudes are assigned to various relations between points or elements (see Harary, Norman, and Cartwright 1965, chap. 14, on networks).

Various types of measurement may be defined on a graph, although we will not dwell on the subject here. By defining lines between points we have already implicitly defined a measure of whether or not two points are adjacent. The minimal number of steps between any two points may be derived by counting successive links required to reach one point from another. Various measures may be expressed by reachability matrices, distance matrices, and measures of connectedness of the graph. Digraphs may be analyzed for hierarchical tendencies, for loops, for "sinks" that may be reached by directional paths but may not be escaped, and for many other formally defined properties. Sociometric choices may be analyzed on a matrix or graph for cliques and other patterns of group structure (e.g., Festinger, Schachter, and Back 1964:258-69). In the following examples, I shall attempt to show how the concepts and measures of graph theory can be used for various problems in modeling ethnographic data.

The Purum case is one of the most overanalyzed in anthropology (Livingstone 1969:239). Needham (1958, 1960, 1962) believed that the Purum constituted an empirical case of the ideal type of "prescriptive" marriage system (see Buchler and Selby 1968a: 125-45 on "The Positivistic Error"). Ackerman (1964, 1965) received nearly as much criticism as Needham for his use of distorted statistical procedures to show that the Purum marriage system was not what Needham said it was (see Müller 1964, 1966; Geoghegan and Kay 1964; Cowgill 1964; Wilder 1964; Needham 1964, 1966). Yet a succinct and agreed-upon analysis of the Purum marriage system has not been reached.

The lack of a satisfactory resolution for the Purum marriage system may have been due to the aura of debate, but certainly much of the remaining confusion stems from incomplete formalization of the analysis. Much of the needed conceptual clarification in distinguishing cultural rules from behavioral choices has been attained: "alliance theorists have brought culture and social structure into an ordered relationship which even Needham's gross manipulations of the Purum data cannot obscure" (Schneider 1965:79). While true at the conceptual level, it is still an open question whether this ordered relationship can be clarified in the analysis of the Purum ethnographic data on marriage choices.

Various questions in the Purum case remain obscure. If these can be clarified by graph theory and matrix analysis, as methods of data reduction, it may be of help in other and future analyses of marriage networks. How do the various normative or preferential rules of Purum marriage relate to one another? How well do actual marriage patterns fit these norms? What are the units involved in exchange, and what is the structure of their relationship? What is the effect of some units' having many women to dispose of in a system of marriages or exchange of women, and others' having few? What happens within these units by way of fission or fusion or segmentation over time?

The analysis begins where the other analyses have begun, with the data on sib and lineage intermarriages (the lineages will here be referred to as subsibs, since they are actually nonlocalized). The analysis presented here derives from the formal data-reduction techniques advanced by White (1963:130-45) and subsequently used by Geoghegan (personal communication) to reach a more complete solution to the problems posed above.

The five Purum sibs indicated in Figure 7 are Thao, Parpa, Makan, Marrim, and Kheyang (T, P, Mk, M, and K in subsequent discussion). Each sib is made up of one or more subsibs. The actual marriages recorded by Das (1945:133-38) from census and genealogical materials (four villages) are recorded in the matrix of Figure 7, indicating numbers of marriages between men of one subsib (rows) and women of another (columns). The data shown are from Ackerman's (1964) compilation of Das's materials. To simplify analysis, the sibs in Figure 7 have been arranged in order of increasing size. It can be seen from the matrix that each of the subsibs is exogamous, as are the sibs with the exception of three marriages within the Kheyang sib. Each

Wife-Givers (♀)

Wife-Takers (♂)		Thao*			Parpa	Makan		Marrim				Kheyang		
		T_1	T_2	T_4	P	Mk_1	Mk_2	M_1	M_2	M_3	M_4	K_1	K_2	
Thao-Kung	T_1				6	2								8
Thao-Run	T_2				4	10	2							16
Rangshai	T_4				2							1		3
Parpa	P							4	4		10	3	3	24
Kankung	Mk_1				2				5			18	3	28
Makan-Te	Mk_2											2		2
Rimphunchong	M_1					4						3	1	8
Rimkung	M_2	2	4											6
Rin-Ke-Lek	M_3	4												4
Pilling	M_4					1						2	1	4
Julhung	K_1	3	1	4	10		1		2		2		3	26
Aihung	K_2	4		1	1	2	2		2					12
Totals		13	5	5	23	21	5	4	13	0	12	29	11	141

* The five major divisions are sibs, the twelve minor divisions (T_1, T_2, etc.) subsibs.
Explanation: Cells indicate number of marriages between men of the subsibs on the left (rows) and women of the subsibs on the top (columns). Numbers on the right and bottom indicate total men or women married for each subsib. The total sample consists of 141 marriages or 282 individuals. Double lines indicate the divisions into sibs.

Figure 7. Raw data matrix for Purum intermarriages.

subsib and sib has a different alliance pattern.

Analysis of the relationships between sibs can be simplified by summarizing the matrix at the sib level. Figure 8 shows the simplified matrix in which the raw data have been aggregated by sib (Matrix A). Matrix A is then reduced to a directed graph (Digraph A), in which arrows show the direction of wife-giving relationships. "$M \longrightarrow P$," for example, indicates that sib M gives wives to sib P. Various operations can be seen in terms of the graph. The graph is complete, since all pairs of points are connected. Note that some points, such as K, have more arrows coming and going than other points. In fact, this measure for the total number of connections for each sib is proportional to the size of the sib. The ratio of arrows coming and going, or of wife-giving and wife-taking, is approximately the same, however, for all sibs, regardless of size.

Matrix A: Raw Frequencies

Digraph A: All Paths of Wife-Giving Relations Between Sibs

Wife-Givers (♀)

	T	P	Mk	M	K	Totals
T	0	10	16	0	1	27
P	0	0	0	18	6	24
Mk	0	2	0	5	23	30
M	10	0	5	0	7	22
K	13	11	5	6	3	38
	23	23	26	29	40	141

Wife-Takers (♂)

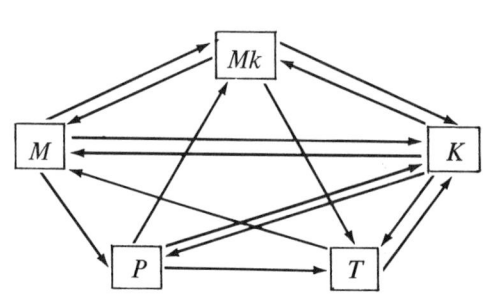

Matrix B: Livingstone's Idealization of Predominant Wife-Giving Relations (Asymmetric Paths)

Digraph B: Idealized Asymmetric Tournament

Wife-Givers (♀)

	T	P	Mk	M	K	Totals
T	0	1	1	0	0	2
P	0	0	0	1	0	1
Mk	0	1	0	1	1	3
M	1	0	0	0	0	1
K	1	1	0	1	0	3
	2	3	1	3	1	10

Wife-Takers (♂)

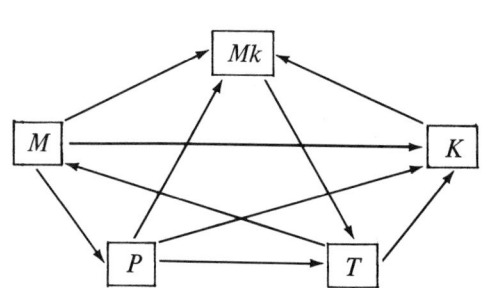

Figure 8. Matrices and graphs for Purum data, aggregated at the level of sibs. (Adapted from Ackerman 1964, Livingstone 1969.)

Livingstone (1969) classified the relationship between sibs that are predominantly either wife-giving or wife-taking on the basis of which of the two reciprocal cells has the greater frequency. His results are shown in Matrix B, an asymmetric matrix, and the corresponding graph, Digraph B. His simplification "accounts for" 88 percent of the marriages, in the sense that 114 marriages out of 141 are contained in the cells that Livingstone has marked with a "1" for predominant asymmetric rela-

tions between sibs. However, it distorts the system in giving the impression that the M and P sibs, for example, are the biggest wife-givers, each having three wife-giving relationships. Livingstone notes that the sequence of wife-giving scores for the Purum is 1, 1, 2, 3, 3. This may be compared with the score sequence for wife-giving relations among five Kachin lineages, which Livingstone states is 2, 2, 2, 2, 2. The Purum seem to have a more unbalanced or hierarchical structure of wife-giving relations than do the Kachin on the basis of this comparison. This is the type of measurement on a graph which may be defined formally. An index of hierarchy for score sequences has been devised by Landau (1951), for example. Livingstone also suggests, in addition to the hierarchy index, that the number of cyclic triples, or directional cycles composed of three arrows on the asymmetric digraph, is a useful measure of integration or connectedness. The notion of "marriage circles" that is implicit in this formal measure of integration corresponds to Lévi-Strauss' (1949) system of generalized exchange. Thus formal measures on a graph provide an explication and basis for comparison of conceptual aspects of marriage systems.

The usefulness of Livingstone's comparative analysis depends upon how accurately these models do, in fact, represent the data. In the reduction of the raw data to the graph, 88 percent of the marriages conformed to the model; 12 percent did not. In addition, cells with only two marriages ($P \longrightarrow Mk$) were weighted equally with cells containing twenty-three marriages ($K \longrightarrow Mk$). This is not a close enough fit to the Purum data to say that Livingstone's graph represents the definitive structure of marriage relationships among Purum sibs.

White (1963:130-45) provided an alternate solution for the structural reduction of the Purum marriage system, one that was ignored in the Ackerman-Needham and subsequent debates. He analyzed both the cultural and the statistical data pertaining to marriages and found a consistent pattern between the two systems: (*a*) the kinship terminology and the idealized marriage rules specified seven definitive marriage relationships between the five sibs, and (*b*) the types of marriage with the greatest frequency and consistency in the

recorded statistics on intermarriages matched the seven idealized relationships. These seven marriage relations between sibs (White 1963:139) are shown in Figure 9, Digraph C. Arrows indicate the structurally correct or ideal marriages for each of the five sibs. This pattern is consistent with an asymmetric alliance system with three consistent cycles of "marriage in a circle," *T/M/Mk*, *T/K/P*, and *T/M/P*. The graph shows that the pairs (*M*, *K* and *P*, *Mk*) are in structurally equivalent positions. *M* and *K* are positionally equivalent to *T* and *P*; *P* and *Mk* are positionally equivalent to *T* and *M*. Moreover, in the system of kinship terminology, White shows that the men in pairs *M*, *K* and *P*, *Mk* are also in a consistent position as "classificatory brothers." Thus, by separate criteria of structural equivalence and terminological equivalence, the pairs *M*, *K* and *P*, *Mk* form two classificatory descent lines, and can be folded together on the graph. Digraph D shows the reduced system with structurally equivalent sibs folded into three classificatory descent lines.

Only 72 percent of the Purum marriages conform to the seven basic marriage relations shown in Digraph C and described by White (1963:139-40). This is considerably less than the percentage of marriages that fit Livingstone's (1969) model. Matrix C shows the actual data for intermarriage between the reduced classificatory descent lines in White's model. The marriages shown in brackets are consistent with his model; the rest (forty marriages, or 28 percent) are not. White left his analysis at this point, indicating pessimistically that the "ideal" system and the actual marriages simply did not match with a high degree of consistency. Ackerman (1965:89) uses this conclusion of White's in support of his argument against Needham.

Given inequalities in the size of sibs,

Matrix C: Intermarriage Between
Reduced Classificatory Descent Lines
(Brackets indicate preferential
marriage categories)

Digraph C: Reduced Graph of
Seven Basic Marriage Relations
(White 1963:139)

	Wife-Givers			
	T	*P, Mk*	*M, K*	*Totals*
T	0	[26]	1	27
P, Mk	0	2	[52]	54
M, K	[23]	21	16	60
Totals	23	49	69	141

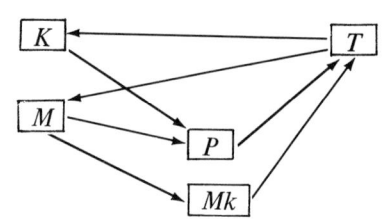

Percentage of preferential marriages = 72%

Matrix D: Optimization of Marriages
Under Preference Ordering and
Demographic Constraints

Digraph D: Reduced System
from Digraphs A and C

	Wife-Givers		
	T	*P, Mk*	*M, K*
T	0	27 (*a*)	0
P, Mk	0	0	54 (*a*)
M, K	23 (*a*)	22 (*b*)	15 (*c*)

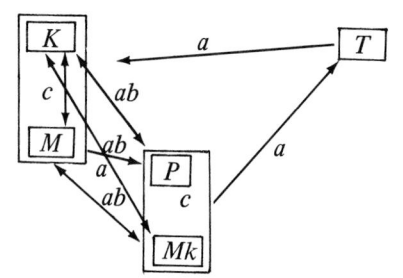

(*a*) Men marry into wife-givers
(*b*) Men marry into wife-takers
(*c*) Men marry into own classificatory
descent line

Percentage of marriages accounted for compared to actual frequencies as listed in Matrix C:
98%

Digraph E: Segmentation of Sibs
(based on data in matrix in Figure 7)

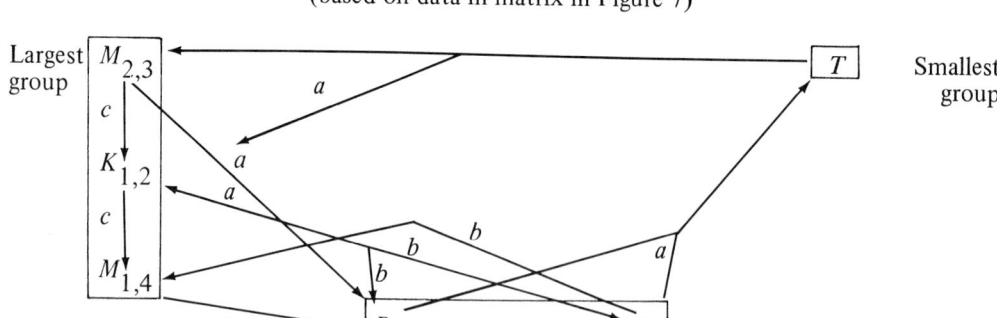

Figure 9. Reduced matrices and graphs for Purum marriage system. (Adapted from White 1963;
Geoghegan, personal communication.)

it would be impossible for the Purum to meet the specifications of their "ideal" model, as described by White, even if everyone tried to follow the rules. Geoghegan notes (in a personal communication) that the rules of marriage may include preferences as to what men from any sib should do when there are not enough women of the ideal wife-giving lineage to match the prospective husbands. Geoghegan suggests that the rules under such circumstances might also be clearly ranked in a preference ordering: (1) try to marry a woman from the wife-giving lineage; (2) if a wife is not available there, try to marry a woman from the wife-taking lineage; (3) if neither is available, marry a woman from a classificatory brother's lineage. Given the demographic imbalance, on the order of 50 adults in T, 103 in P and Mk, and 129 in M and K (282 adults, 141 marriages), it is a natural result that contingency rules 2 and 3 will be applied by the members of the larger sibs. If these rules were followed—i.e., if optimal choices were made given the demographic imbalance—the result would be as shown in Matrix D. A comparison of Matrix D with the actual data in Matrix C will show that only 3 out of the total of 141 marriages were inconsistent with the preference orderings as stated by Geoghegan. This is less than 3 percent deviation from the idealized marriage rules. Three other marriages were inconsistent with the rule of sib exogamy (within sib K). Thus reduction to the basic structural relations between Purum sibs and treatment of the problem as one of optimizing marriages ("flow" in a network) under a preference ordering and under demographic constraints show a 95 percent fit between the data and the model. The advantage of this model over Livingstone's lies not only in its higher degree of predictiveness; the fundamental

structural properties of the Purum marriage system have also been shown.

The Purum marriage patterns coincide with ideal norms once these norms are expressed as a preference ordering with dominant and contingency rules. The analysis confirms that the units of the alliance system are indeed the sibs and subsibs, and by implication that the units of alliance systems need not be localized. Boundaries of larger and smaller units in the exchange system can also be identified, as in the identification of the classificatory descent lines by their structural equivalence on the graph. It remains to show, by reference to the original data on subsibs in Figure 7, how the structure of Purum marriage relates to the process of segmentation or fission of descent groups. Digraph E in Figure 9 shows how the largest classificatory descent line (M, K) can be further broken down on the basis of evidence in Figure 7. Sib M appears to be splitting, with M_2, M_3 and M_1, M_4 showing separate alliance patterns. If we were to go into finer detail, the divergent patterns of alliance in K_1 and K_2 may indicate that they are in the process of splitting also. This is reinforced by the fact that one man of K_1 broke the rule of sib exogamy by marrying a woman of K_2, and two other exceptions to the rule resulted when their two sons married classificatory matrilateral cross-cousins. These interpretations would be consistent with a process whereby the larger sibs or subsibs segments and the smaller ones are maintained or die out or are absorbed into others. Graph theory may be useful in showing the structural cleavages by which fission occurs.

I have hoped to show in this extended example how formal and relatively exact data reduction may be attained by graph theory, matrix analysis, and optimization analysis used in combination. The Purum case is illustrative of many problems and arguments in ethnographic description and ethnological theory when premature conclusions are reached from incompletely formalized analysis. Analysis through graph theory and related methods need not stop with a superficial model of a system. Various models should be tried and tested. Livingstone's statistical reduction to an "ideal" Purum system as a complete asymmetric digraph was useful for comparative purposes, but not for an internal structural model. White's structural reduction showed the operation of a system of rules, but still appeared to be only roughly approximated in actual behavior. Geoghegan's analysis of the graph as a network with an imbalanced "flow" of marriages caused by demographic inequalities provided a final solution that was consistent with ethnographic facts, allowing small deviations from the rules.

The solution to the Purum analysis is identical in its general character to the firsthand descriptions of asymmetric alliance systems that have been offered by Leach (1962b, 1963) and Löffler (1964). They note that asymmetric alliance depends upon marriage relationships between social categories in the descent system, not upon marriage with a specific relative, such as the matrilateral cross-cousin. Prescriptive cross-cousin marriage does not exist in ethnographic fact, although a social category that is prescribed by an asymmetric marriage rule may contain the cross-cousin as one of its members.

In providing an explication model of the relations and rules of a social system, graph theory may also be a useful adjunct to the kind of optimization problem that can be represented as a game. One problem in the conventional treatment of two-person games is that the utilities of outcomes for the players are in a rectangular matrix, where outcomes are determined by the choices of the two players. Most real situations that can be represented as games—and indeed most games (e.g., tic-tac-toe, chess, checkers)—involve a number of moves and rules for defining the turns of each player. Berge (1962:52-64) has shown how the moves and turns in a game can be represented as a graph. Atkins and Curtis (1969:214) use Berge's definitions to develop a general approach to the study of rule systems, in which positions, moves, turns, preferences, strategies, and orderings or paths of permissible moves can apply in the formal solution of an ethnographic problem. In their example of Tenejapa *ladino* weddings, they show an ordered structure of "path rules" which reduces the eleven possible named events in the wedding to a simple graph of five partitions and their possible connections or "permissible paths" (Atkins and Curtis 1969:225):

These serve to differentiate the eight combinations of elements . . . that seemingly are allowed from 2,040 combinations which appear to be disallowed. These unit rules were shown also to be interrelated in such a way as to form a set of equivalence rules (reflected in the partition . . .) and a set of ordering rules (depicted in [the graph]).

Buchler and McKinlay (1969:196-97) also show how option on problems of the Atempan religious *cargo* can be represented on a "game tree" or graph. The combination of the tools of game theory with graph theory appear to be a fruitful one for anthropology. Probably Atkins and Curtis' (1969:213-20) analysis is the best general discussion of this point, although it is to date tentative.

Signed graphs have been one of the important explicational devices used in formulating theory about social structures. Balance theory was originally formulated by F. Heider (1946) to describe stability and forces acting toward stability in an individual's cognitive field (see Berger et al. 1962:135-36 and Harary, Norman, and Cartwright 1965, chap. 13). The notion of balance defined by Heider applied to a person (*P*), another person (*O*), and some third entity (*X*). If *P* has an evaluation of *O*, and *O* an evaluation of *X*, the triad *P-O-X* is balanced only if *P* has a consistent evaluation of *X*. Thus "*P* likes *O, P* dislikes *X*, and *O* dislikes *X*" is balanced (+, −, −), but "*P* likes *O, P* dislikes *X*, and *O* likes *X*" is unbalanced (+, −, +). In general, if all three relations are positive, or if two are negative and one positive, the *P-O-X* triad is balanced. Cartwright and Harary (1956) generalize the notion of cognitive balance to an arbitrary number of elements and to signed digraphs in addition to ordinary signed graphs. Festinger (1957) extended cognitive balance theory into a general theory of cognitive dissonance which could be tested experimentally. It has also been used to provide a structural model of balance in status systems and to explicate static and dynamic properties of social organization (see various articles in Berger at al. 1966, for example).

In anthropology, Lévi-Strauss (1945, 1963) used an intuitive notion of balance to characterize attitude structures in the elementary kinship unit. A formal and more parsimonious explication of this balance theory model was provided by Flamant (1963:124) in a book on applications of graph theory in social science. I shall give a more general derivation of the problem here. Briefly, the problem is to find those attitudinal structures that are balanced in the system of six dyadic relations between father (*F*), mother (*M*), son (*S*), and maternal uncle (*U*). Four nodes on the graph define six relations: husband/wife (*F/M*), father/son (*F/S*), mother/son (*M/S*), wife's brother/sister's husband (*F/U*), sister/brother (*M/U*), and

sister's son/mother's brother (*S/U*). The six relations may be shown in a simple unsigned graph:

If dyads are characterized as positive (+) for free and familiar relations, and negative (−) for hostile, antagonistic, or reserved relations (Lévi-Strauss 1963:44), then there are sixty-four possible signed graphs of attitude distributions on the same simple graph. Of these sixty-four graphs, only eight are fully balanced, while forty-eight are semibalanced and eight totally unbalanced. Balance in these graphs is measured by the extent to which each component triangle (out of four) contains signs whose product is positive (i.e., +++ and −−+ are positive; and −−− and −++ are negative products). Lévi-Strauss seems to introduce the implicit assumption that the relation between *F/U* (brothers-in-law) is universally negative, thus ruling out half of the graphs as not permissible, and reducing the number of balanced graphs to four, shown below. Positive relations are indicated by solid lines, negative by dotted lines.

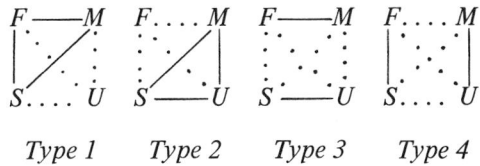

Type 1   *Type 2*   *Type 3*   *Type 4*

As for actual cases, Lévi-Strauss (1963:73) states that it is common to find arrangements of types 1 and 2, less common to find arrangements of types 3 and 4 (frequent but "often poorly developed"), and "rare, or perhaps impossible" to find arrangements of the unbalanced type, "because they would lead to the breakdown of the group. . . ." He cites examples and associated rules of descent such as Trobriand (type 1, matrilineal), Cherkess (type 2, patrilineal), Tonga (type 3, patrilineal), Siuai (type 4, matrilineal), and Lake Kutubu (type 4, patrilineal). Although he makes no point of it, by an extension of his balance theory balanced graphs for nuclear family relations can also be derived for each of his four types. In these graphs, D is introduced, for daughter, the sign of S/D being equivalent to that of M/U in the previous four graphs. Fully balanced graphs can then be derived:

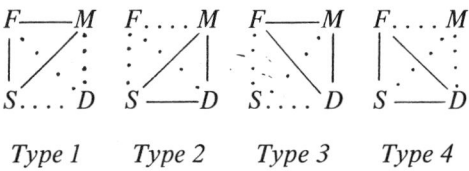

Type 1   Type 2   Type 3   Type 4

By further extension of balance theory, balanced configurations of attitudes can also be derived for the controversial cross-cousins (Homans and Schneider 1955, Needham 1962). The balance theory models of Lévi-Strauss and Homans and Schneider have never been evaluated in this manner. The analysis presented here may exemplify some of the power of abstract mathematical reasoning. Lévi-Strauss (1949) had argued that the type of unilateral cross-cousin marriage (patrilateral or matrilateral) was independent of the type of descent. Homans and Schneider argued that the likelihood of unilateral cross-cousin marriage was dependent upon a positive attitude toward either the father or the maternal uncle, and by extension to the corresponding paternal or maternal cousin. They argued that this positive attitude or sentiment would be inversely related to the line of authority, which is generally through the father in patrilineal societies, and through the

mother's brother in matrilineal societies. Thus, in their model, patrilateral cross-cousin marriage would be related to matrilineality, and matrilateral cross-cousin marriage to patrilineality. Logical flaws in their argument have been pointed out by Berting and Philipsen (1960), Needham (1962), Coult (1962), and others. Leach (1962b, 1963) states that rules of differential cross-cousin marriage do not generally require that a man marry his true cross-cousin, but that such rules may indicate a preference or prescription for marriage within a social category (e.g., Kachin, Nam) which also contains a particular cross-cousin. In developing a graph theoretical model here, we shall take Leach's point of view into account in the sense that the particular personae of cross-cousin marriage and the attitudes that pertain to them are representative of a more general set of attitudes and jural relations among members of different lineages. The "cross-cousins" in these graphs should be seen as representing the social category that contains the cross-cousin via classificatory kinship links. Given these representative personae of classificatory cross-cousin marriage, Figure 10 shows the unique balanced graphs that can be derived for the relations between these classificatory kin types, for each of the four types of balanced graph of "elementary" kinship relations. These are ideal types, and it is not expected that ethnographic reality will fall so easily into this fourfold classification of attitude configurations. In fact, K. Heider (n.d.) has shown where some of Lévi-Strauss' interpretations are faulty for the societies exemplifying the four types. This discussion is intended to be explicational and suggestive rather than ethnographically precise, since relevant data on attitude configurations have not been assembled for a comparative sample of societies.

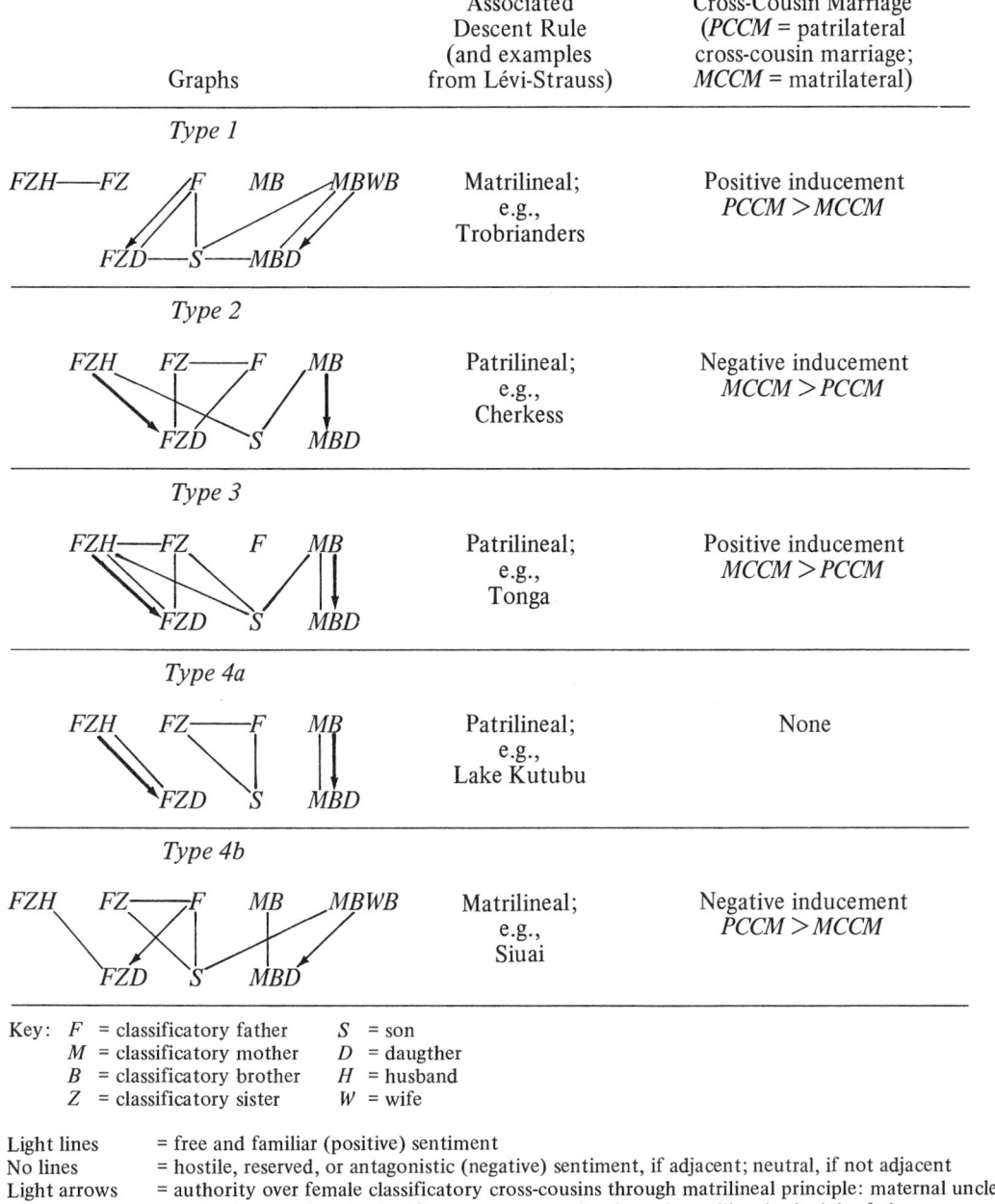

Graphs	Associated Descent Rule (and examples from Lévi-Strauss)	Conditions Favoring Cross-Cousin Marriage (*PCCM* = patrilateral cross-cousin marriage; *MCCM* = matrilateral)
Type 1	Matrilineal; e.g., Trobrianders	Positive inducement *PCCM* > *MCCM*
Type 2	Patrilineal; e.g., Cherkess	Negative inducement *MCCM* > *PCCM*
Type 3	Patrilineal; e.g., Tonga	Positive inducement *MCCM* > *PCCM*
Type 4a	Patrilineal; e.g., Lake Kutubu	None
Type 4b	Matrilineal; e.g., Siuai	Negative inducement *PCCM* > *MCCM*

Key: F = classificatory father   S = son
      M = classificatory mother   D = daugther
      B = classificatory brother   H = husband
      Z = classificatory sister   W = wife

Light lines   = free and familiar (positive) sentiment
No lines   = hostile, reserved, or antagonistic (negative) sentiment, if adjacent; neutral, if not adjacent
Light arrows   = authority over female classificatory cross-cousins through matrilineal principle: maternal uncle
Heavy arrows   = authority over female classificatory cross-cousins through patrilineal principle: father

Figure 10. Balanced graphs for classificatory cross-cousin relations.

The four ideal types of balanced graphs presented in Figure 10 illustrate the clusters of positive affect among selected relatives for each of the four elementary kinship types. Associated descent and jural authority over the two cross-cousins in relation to Ego (*S* in the diagram) has also been indicated. Since type 4 is associated with either type of descent (according to Lévi-Strauss), it has been separated into 4*a* and 4*b* to show the differences. The likelihood of Ego's marrying a classificatory cross-cousin is positively reinforced if he has positive affect with the cross-cousin as well as with the senior male who has jural authority over her. This situation, called positive inducement, exists for type 1 (matrilineal) and type 3 (patrilineal). In types 2 and 4*b*, Ego has a relation of positive affect toward the senior male who has jural authority over the cross-cousin, but neither he nor the senior male has a relation of positive affect with the cross-cousin. Ego may presume upon the authority of the senior male in order to marry a cross-cousin, but the situation is one of negative inducement as far as the affective relations with the cousin herself are concerned. In all these cases, the conditions for inducement of cross-cousin marriage on the patrilineal and matrilateral sides are symmetrical: if positive inducement exists for *PCCM*, it will exist for *MCCM*, and vice versa; the same is true for negative inducement. However, in terms of the closeness of the linking male relatives, we note that in the matrilineal cases it is the father, on the *PCCM* side, who is genealogically closer than the *MBWB* on the *MCCM* side. In view of these structural distinctions, the likelihood of *PCCM* is greater in the matrilineal cases (*PCCM* > *MCCM*), while the likelihood of *MCCM* is greater in the patrilineal cases (*MCCM* > *PCCM*). The conditions that favor cross-cousin marriage may thus be summarized from Figure 10 as follows:

Descent	*Type*	*Positive*	*Negative*
Matrilineal	1	*PCCM>MCCM*	...
	4*b*	...	*PCCM>MCCM*
Patrilineal	3	*MCCM>PCCM*	...
	2	...	*MCCM>PCCM*
	4*a*	...	...

Because of the symmetricality of conditions favoring positive or negative inducements to cross-cousin marriage, one would predict on the basis of the balance theory model that bilateral cross-cousin marriage would be more frequent than either *PCCM* or *MCCM* for all types of unilineal societies. The actual figures (from Murdock 1957: 687) are (*a*) matrilineal: *BCCM* 30 percent, *PCCM* 11 percent, *MCCM* 10 percent; (*b*) patrilineal: *BCCM* 21 percent, *MCCM* 16 percent, *PCCM* 1 percent. The model also predicts greater frequency of *PCCM* than *MCCM* for matrilineal societies, and greater frequency of *MCCM* than *PCCM* for patrilineal societies. This prediction is made on the basis of the structural relations of the affective and jural inducements— that is, on the basis of which of the cross-cousins is linked through inducements that are genealogically closer and more accessible to Ego. Thus the general empirical predictions of the balance theory model are borne out, although the specific details remain to be filled in and tested empirically.

It should be repeated that balance theory does not require that these four completely balanced types of kinship-attitudes graphs are the only types that occur empirically. They are ideal types, expressing the possible tendencies toward balanced configurations of attitudes. The theory is explicational, in that it shows how the ideal types of balanced configurations can be formally derived. Semi- or unbalanced configurations may occur empirically, and other factors may affect the stability of the system. Additional theorems or constraints would have to be added to the system of explication in this case. The power of graph theory for the analysis of this problem is that it permits formulation of an extension of Lévi-Strauss' theory of elementary kinship structures so that it is directly comparable to Homans and Schneider's model of sentiment and authority relations. From this analysis, the two seem more compatible than might otherwise be supposed.

In summary, we have seen how ethnographic data—in the Purum case—can be simplified or reduced to fit various assumptions of structural models (graph theoretic), and how the axiomatic theory of this new branch of mathematics may be used in examining derived properties that may be tested against the empirical system. With more precise and accurate techniques of data reduction (e.g., the White-Geoghegan reduction to classificatory descent lines), more of the exact properties of the system are replicated. In the final model of the Purum system, using actual marriage statistics, we were able to show that optimization of marriage selection (represented by flows or connections on the graph) could be seen to derive from three decision rules that are completely consistent with the ethnographic facts, and that the fit between the optimization model and the data was nearly 96 percent accurate. Thus we have seen how data reduction via graph theory and matrices is used in ethnographic analysis, particularly in connection with optimization models from the previous section.

Second, we have seen how games—also part of optimization analysis—may be represented on graphs, and how this analysis may correspond to the goals of ethnographic discription of cultural rule systems where alternative paths and moves are available to the social actors (Atkins and Curtis 1969).

Third, we have seen how data reduction through graph theory can abstract basic structural properties of systems, and provide structural measures of these systems which have conceptual value in the construction of ethnographic theory. There is a large literature on such applications, of which Barnes's (1969) article on the uses of graph theory in the study of connectedness in social networks is an excellent example.

Finally, we discussed the use of graph theory in the formalization of ethnographic theory. Since measurement and conceptualization of some structural aspects of systems can be formally defined by graphical representation, it is possible to formalize such theories as structural balance. Balance theory allows a high degree of empirical explication, but is lacking in formal explanation of the exact social and cognitive processes that are involved in the stability or instability of actual behavior systems. The combination of structural models with optimization theories is one of the significant frontiers of behavioral research in the social sciences.

4. ETHNOGRAPHIC DECOMPOSITION

The class of problems that fall under the heading of decomposition in anthropology involve mathematical modeling at the foundations of ethnographic theory. Decomposition problems are concerned with the analysis of qualitative ethnographic data presented in the form of statements of cultural rule systems. Ethnographic decomposition relates to the identification of the grammatical rules, ordering rules, decision rules, and transformational rules in a cultural system.

Effective decomposition has been

one of the major goals of ethnography as well as one of the central theoretical problems in other areas of scientific investigation. Decomposition is the process of reducing a complex system to a set of constituents (elements) and a set of analytical rules (operations) which specify allowable combinations of elements. Decomposition attempts to show the structural or ordering properties inherent in a complex system, and in this respect it is similar to general procedures in data reduction. It differs from data reduction in placing explicit attention on identifying the minimal set of elements that constitute the larger system, as well as in focusing on the exact principles by which elements are combined and ordered to make up the system.

One of the major shifts in modern mathematics has been toward the development of abstract and nonquantitative systems in which the power of mathematical logic (axiomatic method) reaches its fullest theoretical form. Finite mathematics (e.g., Kemeny, Snell, and Thompson 1966) and abstract algebra (e.g., Dinkines 1964) have provided the tools for a fully generalizable study of symbolic or abstract rule systems. Axiomatic systems of composition and decomposition are central to these areas of mathematics. The use of modern mathematics in the development of ethnographic theory provides a means by which many traditional concerns in ethnography can be knit together in a rigorous and explicit manner.

A classic example of decomposition in anthropology is Kroeber's 1909 article on the component attributes of kinship distinctions. Kroeber showed that the terms in any given system of kinship terminology can be decomposed by identifying the various combinations of features or attributes that distinguish the kin types to which each

kin term applies. By the use of Kroeber's notion of kinship features in a formal description it is possible to show that the range of a given kin term can be defined by those referential kin types that possess a given combination or intersection of features. A feature that is a member of a contrast set or component can be symbolized; e.g., a for age, b for lineality, c for sex. Thus the features senior, collateral, and male could be represented by the symbols a_1, b_2, c_1. The features correspond to the elements in formal decomposition. The intersection of features (as in set theory: e.g., $a_1 \cap b_2 \cap c_1$) corresponds to the operator in formal decomposition.

Componential analysis (e.g., Goodenough 1956a) represents a further step in ordering the relationships within a single semantic domain between distinctive features that define the range of terms. Like Kroeber's analysis, componential analysis of kinship terminology focuses on referential definitions of the range of terms, and uses the intersection of attributes as the basis for defining kin type and kin term classes. A system defined by intersecting components (sets of contrasting features) can be written as a Cartesian product (class product, cross product). For example, in a hypothetical system having component sets $G = \{g_1, g_2\}$ for generation and $S = \{s_1, s_2\}$ for sex of the referent, the cross product $G \times S$ is written $G \times S = \{(g_1, s_1), (g_1, s_2), (g_2, s_1), (g_2, s_2)\}$. The four ordered pairs define all possible kin types formed by the combination of features in the two components. These kin types may be mapped onto individual kin terms by an assignment, T, of one term to each kin type (e.g., as in $T = \{t_1, t_2, t_3, t_4\}$), although several kin types may be merged into one kin term (e.g., as in $T = \{t_1, t_2, t_3\}$). The assignment T, where $G \times S => T$, is an operator that maps an ordered set of n

elements (kin type n-tuples) into members in the set of kin terms.

Transformational analysis (e.g., Lounsbury 1956) represents an additional step in ordering the internal relationships of kinship terminological systems, using relative products. An example of a relative product in kinship terminology is $P'\ B = U$, "parent's brother equals uncle," the operator $'$ being the relative product operator. Sequences of permissible relative products can be written in the form of a decision tree. Cognitively relative products used in transformational analysis may correspond more closely to the verbal definitions of terms than do the referential definitions (e.g., see Burling 1970) used in componential analysis. Some of the implications of the uses of various types of rules and operators in the analysis of cultural or semantic systems will be examined later in this section.

Intersection, relative products, the assignment of class product n-tuples to new elements, and other mathematical operators, including the familiar $+$, $-$, $\times$, and $\div$ of arithmetic, are instances of composition operators. In modern algebra, the abstract notion of a composition of two elements to form a third is represented by the operator $\circ$. For example, two elements, A and B, can be composed to define a new element, $A \circ B = C$. The decomposition of C could be written $C = A \circ B$.[10*] If one starts with a set of elements and operators and attempts to develop or discover decomposition properties, however, there would seem to be a problem of an indefinite number of ways to decompose a given element C within a system. A simple arithmetic example may illustrate that this is not necessarily the case, once elements and operators have been specified. Let the operator $\circ$ stand for multiplication. The product C will be formed from any composition (multiplication) of two elements; e.g., $A \circ B = C$. Let A and B vary as positive integers greater than 1, and let C define the set of composite numbers. Numbers that are neither 1 nor composite are prime numbers. Now, a fundamental theorem of arithmetic (derived from Euclid's *Elements* and proven by Gauss in 1801) is that every composite number can be expressed as a product of prime numbers, and the set of primes into which the composite number can be decomposed is unique (e.g., $20 => 2° 2° 5$; $24 => 2° 2° 2° 3$, etc.). This example illustrates the use of formal theorems to demonstrate the structure of a mathematical system, in this case the set of integers, which can be divided into prime and composite numbers under multiplication. It also shows an instance in which *unique* decomposition theorems can be specified for a set of elements and an operator.

Modern algebra is concerned with the study of the abstract structure of mathematical systems that are constructed from elements and operators. Decomposition is central not only to modern algebra but to modern logic as well. Propositional logic concerns the analysis of compound statements (logical compositions), which can also be

---

[8] The assumption that utility can be measured in dollars has often been made, as one of convenience, in economics. But in studies of decision-making, it has recurrently been shown that people's preferences do not indicate a strict one-to-one linear relationship between currency value and utility. Friedman and Savage (1952) proposed that most persons' utility for money can be shown as a graph that is convex at the lower end, linear in the middle range, and concave at the upper end. Markovitz (1952) proposed a modification that makes the utility curve for money

relative to one's customary wealth or financial status. Altough Davenport did not investigate the preferences and utilities of his fishermen for various types of fishing hauls, it is generally true that within a limited range, most people's utility for money is approximately linear. It is on this assumption that we continue the analysis of this case.

*Footnote 10 may be found on p. 420.

represented as a decision tree. Such statements may contain a great deal of redundancy, and one of the problems of decomposition in this case is to find the most efficient or parsimonious expression of the logical statement. Again, through the use of theorems, one may wish to specify the unique set of most efficient solutions to the problem of logical decomposition. A similar problem occurs in systems design, when a number of machines or operations are to be linked into complex chains and the designer wishes to find the most efficient set of connections. The solution to these problems is identical to those that are encountered in the study of decision-making rules under natural conditions, and also resembles problems of decomposition of natural language systems into equivalence classes and transformational generative rules (see Chomsky 1963, Arbib 1968). These topics are far-reaching and entirely beyond the scope of the present paper, but they do indicate the breadth and the relevance of the type of approach under consideration.

The most systematic advances that have been made to date in ethnographic decomposition have led to innovations in the use of discrete information theory (related to propositional logic), and in the use of abstract algebra, in each case to adapt the tools of mathematics to the specific requirements of empirical research in anthropology. The major advances that will be discussed in this section are (1) Geoghegan's axiomatic theory for the analysis of discrete information processing systems in culture, (2) Boyd's and Randall's axiomatic and algebraic approaches to kinship systems and componential analysis solutions, and (3) Harrison White and François Lorrain's axiomatic and algebraic theory for the reduction of role systems and group marriage systems, including a formal algebraic and graph-

theoretical approach to social networks. Although these advances will be discussed under separate headings, important links and similarities between them will be noted.

A. NATURAL INFORMATION PROCESSING SYSTEMS

The clear separation of culture as a symbolic system from behavior as a biosocial/physical system has greatly spurred the development of anthropological theory and methodology. Within the past decade the theory of ethnography and the statement of the components of the ethnographic task have become more clearly defined. There is a growing insistence that ordering principles in ethnographic description be determined empirically from the study of indigenous expressions and behavior (Goodenough 1957). It is more widely recognized that behavior and messages are variable within a constrained diversity, and that their internal structure can be studied as "manifestations of a finite shared code, the code being a set of rules for the socially appropriate construction of messages" (Frake 1964:132). The notion of appropriateness is one of the links between behavior and cognition which allows the diversity of human behavioral expression to be formulated in terms of a cultural grammar. It is also recognized that the rules of appropriateness are not so much a solid body of custom as a set of expectations, predictions, and contingencies that are learned and which apply differentially to different members of the social group.

Sanday (1966, 1968) noted that the cognitive information processing systems of American speakers of English, in simple tasks such as listing terms for kinsmen, can be classified into two, if not more, distinct types. Wallace (1961:31-41) had also suggested that the cognitive structures of individuals within a society may be multiplex and yet intermesh in terms of expectations and predictions in a common "equivalence structure." From these and similar studies, it is clear that our description of cultural rules must be considerably more detailed than simply a description of customary behavior or the customary and shared meaning and·use of message forms.

Geoghegan's (1970, 1971) theory of natural or cultural information processing (IP) systems begins with the implications of studying "variable messages as manifestations of a finite shared code" (Frake 1964:133). Frake noted that code rules must deal with appropriate responses governed by situations, but he himself did not provide a means of identifying situational units or mechanisms by which code rules relate encoding and decoding of messages with situational contexts. How are rules of appropriate behavior generated for a situation, how are situations delimited and identified, and how is this information used by the actor? As Geoghegan (1971:5) has said:

If all we desire is to account for the relationship between situations and performances as we define and conceptualize them, then there are any number of adequate theories (and models for these theories) which could be used to accomplish the task ... If, on the other hand, the adequacy of ethnographic description is to turn on whether or not it accounts for not only what a native actor does under certain circumstances, but also how he decides what to do, then we have to know what information he is operating on and how it is being processed.

The problem of situational constraints requires that as ethnographers, "We must get inside our subjects' heads" (Frake 1964:133). This task has been one of the concerns of the new ethnography. Methods such as compo-

nential analysis, however, are only partially adequate. As Geoghegan points out (1970:11-13), componential analysis may at best provide an idealized version of a statement of competence respecting shared notions of appropriateness. Statements of the performance of a social actor, which are at present quite rare in ethnography as well as in linguistics (from whence the competence/ performance distinction arises), have certain advantages. A performance model "is capable of accounting for competence, since it can be used to generate one or more adequate competence statements" (Geoghegan 1970:12). It deals also with the problem of variability among social actors, and allows the identification of divergence from generally shared competence rules (which may be related to learning and the acquisition of competence in the life cycle, to social position, or other factors). A performance model must deal with description of the information-processing rule or system that the social actor would employ in generating the appropriate mapping from situations into culturally appropriate outputs.

In developing a theory of natural IP systems, Geoghegan has linked ethnographic description more closely to the study of human cognition, and wedded his approach to the developments in cognitive psychology, which has similar theoretical concerns with information processing (e.g., Miller et al. 1960, Hunt 1962). His focus, however, is not upon overt behavior in a decision-making model, but rather with one of the sets of ways in which information is obtained for making decisions.[11*] He is

---

[9] I appreciate the scholarly contributions of Dalton's and Polanyi's work, especially in the construction of an analytic framework and conceptual vocabulary that includes the analysis of redistribution and reciprocity as transactional modes. However, to state that this vocabulary for socioeconomic organizations cannot exist with formal analysis is

*Footnote 11 may be found on p. 421.

concerned with culturally patterned IP routines used in selecting an appropriate outcome relevant to specific sociocultural situations. In this his concerns are identical with the type of ethnographic concerns shown by Goodenough (1956*b*), for example, in his discussion of residential choice on Truk. Geoghegan has added greater focus on individual performance models through IP analysis, and the development of an axiomatic theory of the internal structure of IP routines for naturally recurrent decision-making situations.[12]* The theory has important consequences for the construction of ethnographic theory, as we shall see.

The early version of Geoghegan's axiomatic theory, written in 1965 but not published till 1971, has been replaced by a more refined treatment (Geoghegan 1970). In the later statement of the theory, assessments of a situation are defined in terms of culturally salient attributes that generate information about the appropriate alternative out of a set of possible outcomes. The culturally salient attributes are called assessment sets, each having a number of states. Ordered combinations of states (state sequences) must define outputs unambiguously in a many-to-one mapping that can be represented as a decision tree. A code

rule is constituted by the decision tree if each assessment used in the tree makes a difference in the final outcome (i.e., there is no redundant or unnecessary use of assessments). There may be equivalent code rules, each utilizing the same set of assessments and producing the same outputs but ordering the assessments differently. If a set of individuals utilizes equivalent code rules—that is, different decision trees that nonetheless lead to the same outcomes for the situations covered by the rules—this set of code rules can be subsumed under a single set of competence statements.

The question of information-processing performance asks which of the possible set of code rules for a given set of competence statements is actually used by an informant to reach statements of appropriateness. Further specification of alternative but equivalent code rules is required in the formal theory. Geoghegan defines an efficient code rule as one that utilizes the most parsimonious ordering of assessments to reach out-

---

another matter. Dalton's watershed theory, that one set of tools (substantive) is the only appropriate one for preindustrial societies, and another (formal) restricted to industrial societies, amounts to applying intellectual straitjackets to two related approaches. Only an idealization of preindustrial society can justify this watershed on *a priori* grounds. In this respect, I agree with Cook (1966) that Dalton has romanticized "primitive society" and exalted custom, failing to see the social dynamics of choice-making in the technologically least sophisticated society.

[10] Decomposition may also be defined on a graph or matrix as the partitioning of sets of elements that are not connected. A related problem,

when a graph or matrix is fully connected, is how to make the minimum number of deletions of connections between elements to decompose the structure into separate parts. This may be called the problem of minimal decomposition. It is useful in the analysis of flow in networks, or in finding the disjunctures or bottlenecks in a system.

Decomposition theorems are used in game theory as well (von Neumann and Morgenstern 1947, chap. 9). We have already seen an example in the analysis of Kapauku agriculture, where the problem of growing in mountain versus valley land was shown to be separable from the problem of which crops to grow in the valley land. A game or optimization problem, C, such as Kapauku agriculture, may be decomposed into subgames or subproblems A and B, if and only if A and B can be separated as aspects of the larger game which are independent of each other. For example, the decision of how much effort to allocate to mountain lands was made independently of the specific figures for payoffs in the valley land. Thus we can write $A^\circ B \Rightarrow C$ as a composition of subgames into the larger game, and $C \Rightarrow A^\circ B$ as a decomposition of the larger game into the smaller games.

*Footnote 12 may be found on p. 421.

comes.[13]* By definition, an efficient code rule must not be dominated by any other code rule. Dominance is defined by a formal criterion of shorter lengths of paths when the paths of two code rules are ranked by the lengths of their paths and put into one-to-one correspondence. Efficient code rules require fewer assessments on the average to reach the same outputs as equivalent but nonefficient code rules. The subset of efficient code rules within the larger set of equivalent code rules will be finite and denumerable, and denumeration can be achieved by the use of a formal algorithm derived from propositional logic. The existence of a set of efficient code rules for this type of IP system can be stated so as to constitute a uniqueness theory for solutions to this type of decomposition problem. It is an empirical question, however, as to whether actual IP routines as used in natural decision-making settings are efficiently ordered. The evidence from cognitive psychology as well as ethnography strongly suggests that one of the fundamental characteristics of natural IP systems is efficient ordering

(Geoghegan 1970:174): "If a cognitively localized IP routine can be represented accurately by a code rule, then this code rule is very likely to be efficiently ordered." What is the implication of efficient ordering of IP routines, if these results hold true? Essentially it means that the range of performance models is limited in its empirical distribution to a unique and specifiable subset out of the total range of possible code rules (decision trees) for a given set of assessments and appropriate outcomes. Individuals may share a set of competence statements about appropriate behavior, and differ in information-processing performance in a delimited number of ways. This makes the study of performance, as one of the goals of the new ethnography, more systematic and more feasible than previously supposed. This is significant in that ethnographic semantics has assumed the importance of cognitive mediation of patterned social behavior; the study of performance also brings the study of encoding and decoding of messages and behavior down to a finer level of detail and precision.

An example of a cultural IP system, simplified but not substantially altered from Geoghegan's (1970) study of Tagtabon Samal address terms, may serve to clarify the formal definitions and

---

[11] The use of an information processing routine by a social actor does not necessarily have immediate observable consequences in behavior. As the previous quote by Geoghegan illustrates, decision rules cannot always be inferred simply from behavioral observation, but require interviewing and further analysis of surface manifestations of cognitive information processing. In other words, we need to get inside our subjects' heads.

Not all types of decisions use culturally patterned information processing routines of the sort discussed by Geoghegan. A decision is a consciously selected choice between a set of contrastive alternatives. There are a number of ways of obtaining information relevant to a decision, of which a culturally patterned assessment or I.P. routine is one. Appropriateness is not always a decision-making criterion. The classical models discussed in section 2 deal with theories about maximization in decision-making, which might apply when the decision is made on the basis of graded preferences between outcomes, rather than appropriateness.

[12] For example, Geoghegan's focus on "natural" information-processing routines follows the work done in cognitive psychology (e.g., Miller, Galanter, and Pribram 1960; Hunt 1962; Hunt, Martin, and Stone 1966) in recognizing that natural problem-solving is a discrete cognitive process. By contrast, classical models of decision-making involve quantitative information processing: utility functions, probabilities, and multiplication of utility by probability, supposedly in the informant's head, to obtain expected utilities. The classical models can be reinterpreted within a "natural" information processing framework if we assume that cognitive information is generally recoded or "quantized" into discrete bundles in decision-making.

*Footnote 13 may be found on p. 422.

methods involved in an IP analysis. It will also introduce the marking rule and the recoding operator, which are factors of fundamental importance in the study of cultural systems, not taken into account by competence models (Geoghegan 1970:14). The marking rule, as opposed to a code rule, applies to the assessment situation in which there is one predominant expected outcome in spite of other possible but infrequent contingencies that would make other outcomes appropriate (see Geoghegan 1969b). The infrequent contingencies may also be special cues that assume a linguistically or behaviorally "marked" status as opposed to the more normal "unmarked" output (see Greenberg 1966 on this usage and for a general theory of marked/unmarked categories in linguistics). Thus the marking rule applies to the situation in which typically few assessments need

be made and a minimum of information need be processed to reach an appropriate outcome, unless marked cues or infrequent contingencies intervene. By contrast, the code rule habitually involves multiple assessments, since there is a variety of situationally dependent outcomes. For some areas of social choice and information processing, such as residential decisions, the code rule may be a sufficient ethnographic statement. For other areas, such as situational behavior, in a more narrow sense, as in the case of address terminology, marking rules may outnumber the code rules in the complex set of assessments in an IP system.

The Samal address system can be outlined in abbreviated form (Geoghegan 1970, personal communication):

1. There are four lexical classes of address elements:
   A: Address terms (including kinship terms)
   T: Honorifics (*tuan* for male, *dayang* for female)

---

[13] Definitions of assessment sets, states, state sequences, and mappings can perhaps best be illustrated by showing how they relate to the decision tree, in which each node represents an assessment leading to an outcome.

A. Assessments sets: A, B (represented as diamond-shaped nodes in the decision tree).

B. States: a_1, a_2 and b_1, b_2, b_3 are the states that make up the assessment sets of A and B, respectively. They are represented as the alternative paths at each node in the decision tree.

C. State sequences: $a_1 b_1$, $a_1 b_2$, $a_1 b_3$, $a_2 b_1$, $a_1 b_2$, $a_2 b_3$, all the permutations of states from A and B ordered such that the element from A always precedes that from B. Not all of the state sequences are shown on the decision tree.

D. Mappings: in the tree shown below, $a_1 b_1$, $a_1 b_2$, $a_1 b_3$, and $a_2 b_3$ go to output O_1, $a_2 b_2$ goes to O_2, and $a_2 b_2$ goes to O_3. These indicate the mappings of possible state sequences into outcomes. The first decision tree below is an efficient representation of these mappings, the second an inefficient representation.

E. Code rule: a_1 and $a_2 b_3 \rightarrow O_1$, $a_2 b_2 \rightarrow O_2$, and $a_2 b_1 \rightarrow O_3$. This is one of several possible ways of representing the mapping without redundancy. Here is another: b_3 and $b_2 a_1$ and $b_1 a_1 \rightarrow O_1$, b_2, $a_2 \rightarrow O_2$, and b_1, $a_2 \rightarrow O_3$. Note that the first is an efficient code rule.

F. Decision tree:
   The first represents the efficient code rule.

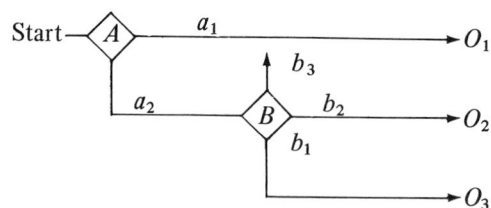

The second, leading to the same outcomes, is inefficient.

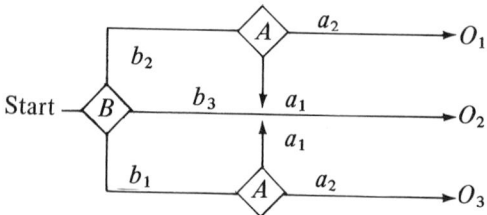

G: *Gallal* or positional terms (civil and religious titles)

N: Names and pronames

2. These combine into ten adress form types (AFTs), with linguistic glosses that can be diagrammed as cumulative additions of elements (+A, +T, +G) onto the basic element /N/, for name, or deletion (φ) of the name from the formal set of address titles. Figure 11 shows the permissible sets of transformations by which the ten AFTs are generated.

3. Specific lexical renderings for these ten AFTs are capable of generating over two hundred address forms (AFs), as well as thousands of personal name and address form combinations.

Geoghegan's description of the Samal address system is primarily concerned with the way names are gener-

ated within the specific type AFT /N/. This corresponds with the simplest class (i) in Figure 11. Working intensively with six informants, he was able to derive each of their assessments involved in the final lexical rendering of an address form (AF) within the class AFT /N/. The rules for reaching these assessment outputs take into account prior knowledge about the other person, including the habitual term that has been applied to him (none if a stranger), and the possible choices to express marked meanings of added or diminished respect in the selection of an AFT or a lexical rendering.

The seven name types in the Samal address system are (1) *TN,* a person's true name; (2) *TN',* a pronoun corresponding to *TN;* (3) *NN,* his nickname; (4) *NN',* a pronoun corresponding to *NN;* (5) *PN,* his pet name; (6) *PN',* a

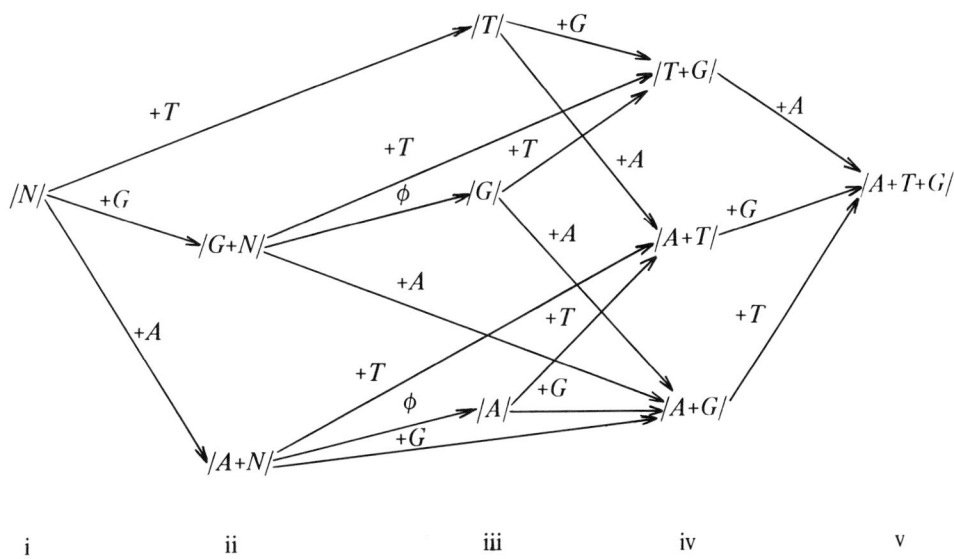

Figure 11. Directed graph of permissible sets of transformations that generate the ten address form types (AFTs) of the Samal address system. Arrows indicate the four operators (+A, +T, +G, φ) whereby AFTs are generated. Classes i-v express increasing degrees of respect, but within classes the terms differ by the type of respect.

pronoun corresponding to *PN;* and (7) *T '*, a special proname type derived from the Samal honorific.

The general IP routine for address form selection can be indicated by the operation "Select AF" (level 1). This is a complex operation that consists of two major parts (level 2): (1) "Select AFT" and (2) "Select lexical realization for AFT." Since there is an appropriate AFT for every social context, given the past interaction between the actors, the choice of an AFT may be unmarked in terms of respect, or it may be marked by disrespect or augmented respect. The choice of specific lexical realizations within the AFT may also be marked or unmarked. Operations at this level (level 2) are further broken down into several specific operations (level 3). A major operation at this level is the selection of the lexical realization of AFT /N/, which is indicated by the designation "Select N." This operation involves three major suboperations: (1) "Select unmarked name type," (2) "Apply marking rule," and (3) "Select lexical realization of N." These three suboperations (level 4) may be further broken down into more specific operations (level 5), including the input and assessment of the habitual name, which determines the unmarked type for the name, the encoding of marking cues (if any) that will alter the realization of the name type if they are present, and the selection of inputs for name types *PN*, *NN*, and *TN* and code rules for name types *T'*, *PN'*, and *TN'*.

In constructing a decision model of IP rules, the following symbols are used:

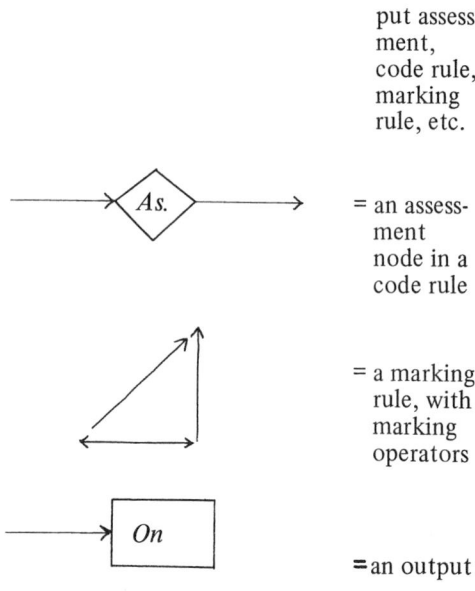

= an information-processing operation; e.g., an output assessment, code rule, marking rule, etc.

= an assessment node in a code rule

= a marking rule, with marking operators

= an output

Figure 12 shows the structure of the Samal address system, with each level (1-5) broken down into more specific operations until the actual marking rules and code rules are reached (level 5) for the name-selection operations. The relationship between these levels corresponds to the process whereby more specific assessments at a lower level are recoded as outputs, and this recoded or compacted information enters into an assessment at the next higher level.

What is the form of ethnographic statements that an IP analysis of this type allows? It provides for statements about the linkage between cognitive and situational factors. It provides for analysis of variable messages by one speaker in a single model. It provides a model for comparing the content of variable messages encoded by various speakers so that factors such as age differences, status differences, and the like can be identified vis-à-vis particular speakers. It provides a system of operations for indicating the interrelationships that link different domains in a behavioral system. It does not beg the

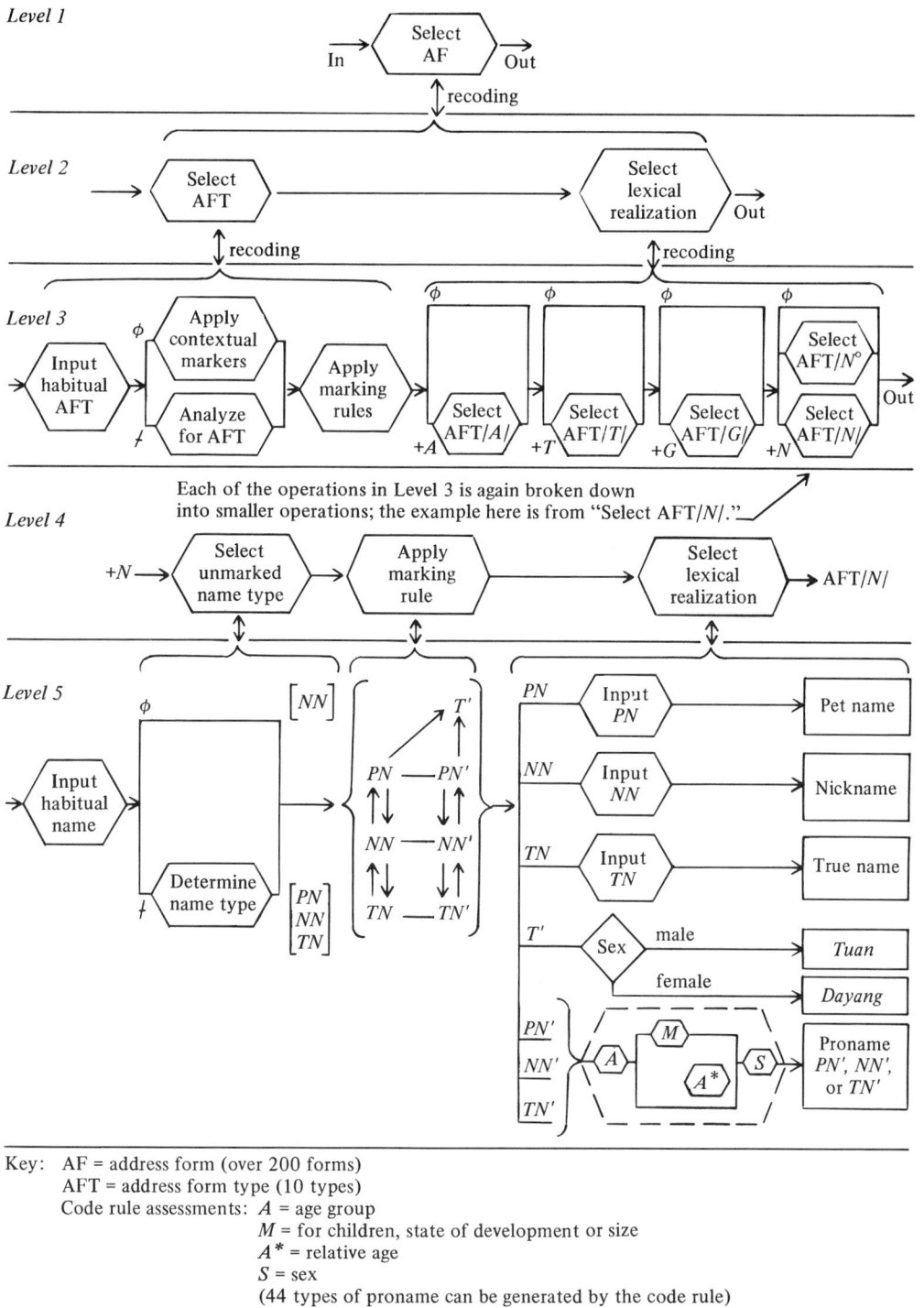

Figure 12. Samal address terms (after Geoghegan 1970).

question of logical starting points within an indigenous cognitive system and it thus provides a useful solution to an ethnographic problem mentioned by Goodenough (1951:11-12): "Characteristics by which one element of Trukese culture had to be defined were frequently other elements in the culture, which in turn required definition. . . . This experience led the writer to conclude that the empirical determination of logical starting points is a requisite for rigorous ethnographic description."

The Samal address IP routines have not yet been tested formally, as has Geoghegan's (1969a) model of Samal residential choices. The 99 percent predictive accuracy of the latter model indicates the power of the IP approach. Another IP approach has been used by Fjellman (1969) with notable success. Models of this type may provide us with very useful information on the cultural regulation of behavior in various social settings, and provide further information on the theories that view social morphology as the outcome of individual choices operating under cultural constraint (Murdock 1960:9; Leach 1960:124; Barth 1966).

There is one fundamental aspect of Geoghegan's description of IP systems that ties together the use of the newer transformational analysis of kinship (Lounsbury 1964a, 1964b) and language (Chomsky 1965), as well as the algebraic approaches to ethnographic decomposition that will be discussed next. This is the question of the limits upon human information-processing capacity. Miller (1956) has shown that the complexity of a cognitive or IP system is not limited per se, but there are limits to the amount of information and the number of units of information individuals can handle simultaneously. Thus the complexity of a cognitive system must be obtained through the phasing of operations and the recoding of information into larger chunks so that the number of units of information handled at any one time are within the span of information-processing ability (Miller 1956, Geoghegan 1971). Miller (1956:95) says that "the kind of linguistic recoding that people do seems to me to be the very lifeblood of the thought process." Any formal system of ethnographic analysis that attempts to deal with "cognitively real" operations by which cultural rules are brought into effect must deal with the problem of recoding.

Lounsbury's (1964a) "rewrite rules" or transformational operators for the analysis of systems of kinship terminology are in effect a recoding operation. The reduction equation "parent's child → sibling" (the half-sibling rule), for example, is a recoding of an ordered pair into a new single element. A person may generate in memory a long chain of kinship links, yet by applying "rewrite rules" for kinship terms at each point in the chain, he keeps a manageable number of items of information from being exceeded in memory at any time.

B. ABSTRACT ALGEBRAIC DECOMPOSITION

A recoding rule is the equivalent of the concept of an operator in modern abstract algebra. An operator maps N ordered elements into a new element. Unary, binary, or in general N-ary operators differ in the number of elements in the ordered set. For example, a unary operator maps each element in a set into new elements in another set. The mapping of an ordered pair of elements (a, b) into a new element (c) by a binary operator is the simplest form of recoding; informational complexity varies between the initial set of ordered elements and the mapping into single elements. There are two important classes of binary operators: (1) the conjunctive and disjunctive operators of set theory (corresponding to "and," "or"), such as the class intersection used in componential analysis; and (2) the relational operators (corresponding to the prepositions "of," "to," "from," etc.), such as are used in transformational analysis. Bruner (1956) has shown that these two types of binary operators correspond to two of the fundamental processes human beings use in learning, problem-solving, and cognition in general.

The rewrite rules of Lounsbury's (1964a) kinship analysis are relational operators. They may be derived from this concept in abstract algebra via transformational linguistics. A distinctive aspect of the relational operator, in constrast to conjunctive or disjunctive operators, is that it may be capable of generating infinite recursive strings from a finite number of elements. For example, starting with the primary kin types, F, M, B, Z, D, S, H, W, and the operator of linking kin types into more remote kin types, the number of relational strings defining kin types is infinite (e.g., F, FF, FFF, $FFFF$ . . . *ad infinitum*). Thus, at least for some purposes, a semantic algebra consisting of elements and relational operators may be useful in modeling cognitive and cultural domains.

Wallace (1970) has indicated how the American kinship system can be analyzed into constituent relational operators, which correspond to the way in which kinship is actually reckoned. There is a formal similarity between his relational operators, rewrite rules, and certain of the recoding operations in an information-processing framework. Where such recoding operations are cognitively valid, a relational analysis such as Wallace's (1970) analysis of American kinship may be greatly superior to the class-product approach of componential analysis. One advantage is stated by Wallace (1970:845): "It appears that in contrast to the non-uniqueness of componential solutions in general, the relational solution here proposed is unique: in its essentials it is the only relational solution for the usage of adult English-speaking Americans." Wallace suggests that relational analysis may be a useful adjunct to the current methods of kinship terminology analysis.

Burling (1964) criticized componential analysis for failing to produce criteria for selection of one solution from the many logical possibilities of representing elements as the Cartesian products of sets. His recent analysis of American kin terms (Burling 1970), like Wallace's, drops all of the notational complexities of componential analysis in favor of an eminently simple means of representing the verbal definitions of kin terms offered by informants as relative products (e.g., an uncle is "brother of a parent" or "aunt's husband"), and other operators (e.g., step-, grand-, etc.). He explains (1970: 20):

I believe that the relative product definition reflects the manner in which terms are explained to children and the manner in which terms are learned, and I would even imagine that anyone who felt concerned to produce a "cognitively real" analysis would be far happier with a version that uses colloquial words than one that uses esoteric terms and symbols.

Close examination of Burling's analysis will show that it is identical to that of Wallace (1970). As for the markedly different results of some of the componential solutions of American kinship (e.g., Wallace and Atkins 1960, Romney and D'Andrade 1964, Goodenough 1965), there is some evidence to suggest that some of the differences are due to cognitive, dialect, or ethnic differences in the American population

(Geoghegan 1963*a*, 1963*b*; Sanday 1968; Randall n.d.). If this is so, we must ask whether this affects the uniqueness properties of a relative product solution of the decomposition problem, and whether a relative product solution can be used to model intrapopulation differences. Randall (n.d.) has developed a relational system identical to that of Wallace (1970) for core terms in American kinship, but also capable of showing dialect variants in semantics for alternative types of American kinship terminology. When Americans reckon the genealogical distance of remote cousins (as in second cousin, first cousin once removed, etc.), Randall shows that there are at least three semantic variants, each using many of the same terms but with different ranges and meanings. The variants are based upon different methods of reckoning distance, measured in "steps": (1) in one variant, distance is counted upward, and FaFaBrSo, for example, is second cousin once removed; (2) in another variant, genealogical distance is counted both upward and downward, and FaFaBrSo is first cousin once removed; (3) in the common simplified American version, distance is counted downward. In the latter variant, kin terms are not generally used for remote relatives, and the speaker does not have a special term, for example, for Fa-FaBrSo, other than "cousin" or "parent's cousin."

In the relational analyses of American kinship by Randall, Wallace, and Burling, there are four primary relationships of parent, sibling, child, and affine or spouse (*P, S, C, A*)—or eight if sex is taken into account—which are concatenated to form all the derivative kin types. Wallace (1970) and Burling (1970) show how various classes of these compositions form the ranges of American kin terms. Randall's model extends this analysis by showing how attributes are compounded for the remote kin types by rules of composition of the attributes of the basic terms (*P, S, C, A*, or the eight basic terms denoting sex). The three variants in his model differ in the "generational distance" attribute, but agree in attributes of "relationship," "branch," and "generation."[14] The attributes of the basic relations *P, S, C, A*) are shown in Table 3. *P, S,* and *C*, for example, are "blood" relatives; *A* (spouse) is an "affine." *P, C,* and *A* are "lineals" ; *S* (sibling) is a "collateral."

The rules for the composition of these basic relations can be written sep-

---

[14] The "branch" attribute corresponds to the more usual attribute of "lineality" in kinship literature, but Randall has tried to retain the native glosses for each attribute.

TABLE 3
Randall's Relational Operators for American Kinship, Showing
Shared and Distinctive Attribute Systems for Three Variants

Basic Relation	Shared Attributes			Distinctive Attribute: Genealogical Distance		
	Relationship*	Branch†	Generation	Variant 1	Variant 2	Variant 3
P = parent	D	L	+1	1	1	0
S = sibling	D	K	0	0	0	0
C = child	D	L	−1	0	1	1
A = spouse	A	L	0	0	0	0

*D = descent; A = affinity.
†L = lineal; K = collateral.

arately for each attribute in the form of a composition diagram, as in Figure 13. Such a figure simply reads, as for example under relationship, $D°D = D$, or the blood relative of a blood relative is a blood relative, $D°A = A$, or the spouse of a blood relative is an affine, and so forth.

Relationship and branch form a closed set under composition; generation and degree are potentially unbounded or infinite, corresponding to the set of integers under the operation of addition.[15]

Given any composition of the basic relations (P, S, C, A) in Table 3, for example $P°P°S$, the attributes of the composite relation can be composed by following the rules of the composition tables. Thus, for variants 1 and 2, $P°P°S = (D°D°D) (L°L°K) (+1°+1°0) (1°1°0) = (D) (K) (+2) (2) = D, K, +2,$

2. But for variant 3, $P°P°S = D, K, 2, 0.$

The variants agree that parent's parent's sibling $(P°P°S)$ is a blood relation, collateral, and two generations senior to Ego, but they differ in the distance feature. In the assignment of terms to remote cousins, differences in the mode of reckoning degree manifest themselves overtly in the range of the various cousin terms (e.g., first and second cousins, once removed, twice removed, etc.). In order to show this patterned variation, the compositions for various kin types in a consanguineal genealogy (composed of relations $P, S,$ and C) have been written out in Figure 14.

The feature systems for assigning terms to cousins is shown in Table 4.

Comparison of the terms for specific kin types, in each of the three variants, is shown in Table 5. It can easily be seen that the terms "first cousin," "second cousin," and the designations "once removed," "twice removed," etc., have different ranges in the three variants. This is directly ascertainable from interviews with American English speakers, and has been, of course, frequently mentioned in the literature on American kinship. Randall's analytic

---

[15] While generation and distance are potentially unbounded, the operations actually performed by American English speakers are more limited, giving these tables an upper or outer bound. These algebraic composition tables for all four attributes, although they are bounded, do not conform to the strict algebraic definition of a monoid or semigroup, which would require that all elements in the composition table be defined.

*Relationship** *

	D	A
D	D	A
A	A	-

Branch†

	L	K
L	L	K
K	K	-

Generation

	0	+1	-1	
0	0	+1	-1	...
+1	+1	+2	0	...
-1	-1	0	-2	...

. . . .

Distance

	0	1	
0	0	1	...
1	1	2	...
2	2	3	...

. . . .

* D = descent; A = affinity.
+ L = lineal; K = collateral.

Note: Some $A°A$ and $C°C$ are undefined and ungrammatical in English.

Figure 13. Diagram of composition of basic kin relations for attributes of relationship, lineality, generation, and distance.

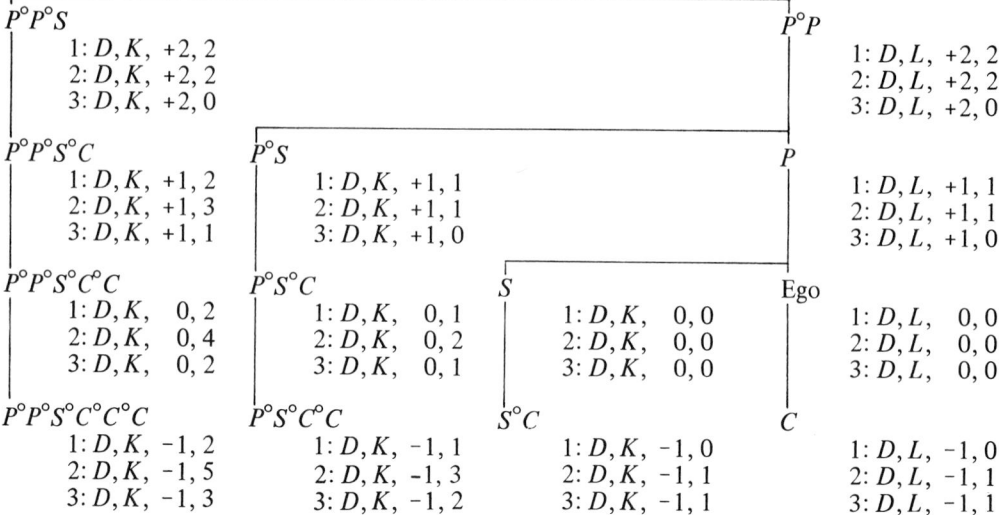

Key: See Table 3. P, S, and C are relational operators for parent, sibling, and child. When concatenated, e.g., $P^\circ P$, this simply indicates "parent's parent." D stands for blood or consanguineal relatives. K and L stand for collateral and lineal features. The pair of digits indicates the differences in composing the degree features for the three systems. Variants 1, 2, and 3 are the semantic dialect variants.

Figure 14. Randall's variants of American English kin term features (for male consanguineals).

TABLE 4
Feature Systems for Cousins in Semantic Variants

	Semantic Variant 1			Semantic Variant 2			Semantic Variant 3
	Cousin	Cousin once removed	Cousin twice removed	Cousin	Cousin once removed	Cousin twice removed	Cousin*
First cousin	0, 1	−1, 1	−2, 1	0, 2	−1, 3 +1, 3	−2, 4 +2, 4	0, 1
Second cousin	0, 2	−1, 2 +1, 2	−2, 2 +2, 2	0, 4	−1, 5 +1, 5	−2, 6 +2, 6	(−1, 2)†
Third cousin	0, 3	−1, 3 +1, 3	−2, 3 +2, 3	0, 6	−1, 7 +1, 7	−2, 8 +2, 8	(−2, 3)†

*Degree of removal is not used.
†A decriptive term such as "cousin's child" may be used, or simply "cousin."

TABLE 5
Cousin Terminology in the Three American English Variants

Kin Type	Semantic Variant 1	Semantic Variant 2	Semantic Variant 3
P°S°C	first cousin (0, 1)	first cousin (0, 2)	first cousin (0, 1)
P°S°C°C	first cousin once removed (-1, 1)	first cousin once removed (-1, 3)	second cousin (0, 2)
P°S°C°C°C	first cousin twice removed (-2, 1)	first cousin twice removed (-2, 4)	
P°P°S°C	second cousin once removed (+1, 2)	first cousin once removed (+1, 3)	
P°P°S°C°C	second cousin (0, 2)	second cousin (0, 4)	
P°P°S°C°C°C	second cousin once removed (-1, 2)	second cousin once removed (-1, 5)	
P°P°P°S°C	third cousin twice removed (+2, 3)	first cousin twice removed (+2, 4)	
P°P°P°S°C°C	third cousin once removed (+1, 3)	second cousin once removed (+1, 5)	
P°P°P°S°C°C°C	third cousin (0, 3)	third cousin (0, 6)	

model has the advantage not only of systematically accounting for these differences in usage, but also of accounting for differences that have been noted in psychological tests of association between pairs of relatives (in the triads test), and of accounting for differences between the Romney and D'Andrade (1964) and the Wallace and Atkins (1960) componential analyses of American kinship terms. Variant 2 in Randall's model is the equivalent of the Romney-D'Andrade analysis, whereas variants 1 and 3 are closer to the Wallace-Atkins analysis. The correlation between usage in cousin terminology and in psychological tests of judged similarities between kin types can be confirmed by simple experiment. Persons who use the cousin terminology of variant 2, and presumably utilize the de-

gree feature of variant 2, would be more likely to view uncle and nephew as the closest pair out of the triad uncle, nephew, grandfather. In variant 2, uncle and nephew differ only in one feature, generation. Grandfather, on the other hand, differs in branch, generation, and genealogical distance from the other two. Persons who use the cousin terminology of variant 1, however, would be more likely to judge uncle and grandfather as the closest pair in the triad, since they are closer in degree and generation, whereas both differ considerably in degree and generation from nephew. If this correlation holds, it is an indication of the "psychological reality" of the composition features of Randall's system. Results from Geoghegan (1963a, 1963b), Randall (n.d.), Romney and D'Andrade (1964), and

Wexler and Romney (n.d.) tend to confirm this model. Geoghegan (1963*a*, 1963*b*) showed a similar set of predictions for tests of judged similarities between GrFa, Br, So, and GrSo, which distinguished groups according to the Wallace-Atkins or the Romney-D'Andrade model. Wexler and Romney (n.d.) have done further research on distinguishing segments of the population according to these differences.

Randall's model does not conflict with Wallace's (1970) statement that a relational analysis will yield a unique solution to the decomposition problem for American kinship terminology and presumably others as well. His variants simply show that a more detailed investigation may identify different usages and different cognitive organization for segments of a population, but constrained by core features that are shared by all. This is consistent in a general sense with Wallace's (1961:31-41) discussion of "equivalence structures," or cognitive nonsharing, in different segments or different institutional settings within a population.

Boyd's (1968) analysis of kinship terminology presents a more abstract version of a kinship algebra of the same general type as used by Randall in the preceding example. Boyd has also found it necessary to define the basic operations in semantic domains such as kinship in terms of relational operators or recoding rules. He shows that it is possible to define the componential analysis of a relational algebra in terms of greater and lesser efficiency, in a manner somewhat analogous to Geoghegan's use of the notion of efficiency in studying IP systems. He shows that unique efficient solutions exist for problems of decomposition of a relational algebra. The formal criterion that Boyd suggests for an efficient componential solution (Boyd 1968, 1971) is the substitution property, which has roots both in descriptive linguistics and abstract algebra (Boyd 1969:57):

Two distinct objects are by definition never completely intersubstitutable. However, it is sometimes very useful to form classes that are mutually substitutable with respect to some limited criteria. For example, a syntactic word class is a class such that whenever one substitutes words from this class in a sentence, one always gets the same response to the question, "Was that sentence grammatical?" The situation is somewhat more complicated when one deals with objects such as kinship terms, that are at the same time names of relations between those same objects. In this case, one has to deal with a whole collection of classes at once; that is, with partitions. Here the partition itself determines the criteria of substitutability. That is, two elements from a block of a partition are intersubstitutable if no relation sends them into different blocks of the partition.

Boyd finds that the componential analysis of Romney and D'Andrade (1964) lacks the substitution property, while that of Wallace and Atkins (1960) passes this criterion of an efficient decomposition. Thus the formal criterion of an efficient decomposition, in the case of American kinship terms, converges with psychological criteria, linguistic criteria, and learning or language-acquisition criteria.

The finite mathematical modeling of American kinship in terms of a simple system of relational operators has broader implications for kinship and formal ethnographic analysis. Abstract algebraic decomposition, in its simplest form, may provide solutions to the problem of formal decomposition that are simultaneously (1) unique and determined by formal criteria, (2) parsimonious, readily understood and communicated, (3) linguistically valid, (4) ontogenetically valid in terms of language acquisition and learning, (5) cognitively or psychologically valid, and (6) capable of dealing with variants within the population.[16] As if these were not enough, Randall has also shown how algebraic models can be used comparatively, with appropriate modifications of the operators, when applied to the other major types of kinship systems (e.g., Hawaiian, Iroquois, Crow, Omaha, and descriptive), as defined by Murdock (1949). Since this material is currently unpublished, no further examples will be given.

Unique decomposition hypotheses and theorems in formal ethnosemantic analysis raise the possibility of new and powerful sets of tools for the analysis of culture. The development of such formal decomposition models for ethnographic description and for the foundations of ethnological theory depends upon links with linguistics and cognitive psychology that will require further investigation, as for example the question of the conditions under which efficient cognitive organization of cultural domains is achieved. It may be that the empirical occurrence of cognitive efficiency, such as might be expected from the processes by which cognitive systems evolve and adapt, provides the basis for unique and parsimonious formal decomposition of cultural systems, as well as the existence, per se, of the high degree of cultural sharing found in most societies.

Studies of rule systems using abstract

algebra have also been carried out at a much more abstract level, somewhat removed from the direct problems of cognition and ethnographic description. One of the goals of these studies has been to provide a model of the permutations of cultural rules—for example, group marriage rules—into systems or types that can serve as aids to the understanding and classification of ethnographic facts. The algebraic analysis of group marriage rules, for example, derives from André Weil's (1949) account of an Australian section system using abstract algebra. Weil's use of the theory of groups of permutations was intended "to facilitate study and classification." An extension of his analysis by Robert Bush (reprinted along with Weil's article in White 1963) showed the use of permutation matrices for the analysis of a wider range of Australian section systems. Bush suggested a means of computing the number of logical permutations of various marriage rule systems. Because of the large number of permutations and types of empirical cases, he suggested that formal mathematical analysis as a means of classification of these systems on logical grounds constituted a distinct advantage over the more usual typological approach to kinship systems.

At the outset, algebraic models seemed to be applicable to group marriage systems, or "elementary" kinship systems in Lévi-Strauss' terms, only because marriages were nonprobabilistic and the rules seemed to have definite prescriptive implications for the relationships in a closed system of groups. In this respect, these early models suffer from the same deficiencies as processual models, which assume that cultural rules "prescribe" behavior. The studies, of course, were qualified as only ideal models of marriage systems.

In tracing the development of these algebraic models, it will be noted that

---

[16] Burling (1970:15) has stated, in reference to the overformalization of componential analysis: "The other theme found in much of the work on American kinship has been a search for some sort of psychological reality, or an attempt to decide which among various formal analyses is closest to the way in which Americans actually conceive of their terms ... The possibility that these two goals might be in conflict (as would be the case if the psychologically real solution turned out not to be the most formal or abstract) does not seem to have caused concern." This difference between the most formal and abstract analysis, which may be inordinately complicated, and the simplest or most efficient analysis, may be stated mathematically as well as verbally.

the mathematical axioms and definitions are successively relaxed from an algebra that fits only closed groups and deterministic rules to a more adaptive algebra that fits open groups and actual structures with holes and inconsistencies such as are familiar in social systems.

Kemeny, Snell, and Thompson (1966:424-33) continued the development of the algebraic approach to kinship with some significant refinements in the axiomatic structure used in the Bush and Weil models. They show that from axioms that specify very basic kinship connections in a closed type of section system, a powerful theorem about the mathematical structure of these systems can be derived, to the effect that they can be represented algebraically as regular permutation groups (roughly speaking, permitting complete permutation chains in which all of the marriage classes are reachable through lineal descent links [Kemeny, Snell, and Thompson 1966:431-32]). The possibilities for combinations of marriage rules under these axioms are severely limited by this theorem. The varieties of four-section systems, for example, can be defined merely by six regular permutation groups.

Harrison White devoted fuller attention to the ideal types that are generated by a simplified algebraic system, using the equivalent of the Kemeny, Snell, and Thompson axioms. Algebraic formulation of matrilateral, patrilateral, and bilateral cross-cousin marriage and second-cousin paired-clan marriage allowed White (1963:81-82) to explore the type and number of systems allowable for different numbers of sections or clans. Some interesting sidelights emerge from the enumeration of logical possibilities, such as why second-cousin marriage (wife is *MMBDD* or *FMBSD*) with paired clans should be so unlikely theoretically yet empirically so common (see Elkin 1938:61). The theoretical aim of White's algebraic work, like that of Weil, Bush, and Kemeny et al., is concerned with problems of classification, but this goal is seen as a preliminary to further types of mathematical analysis of rule systems (White 1963: 28, 148-49):

A weakness of anthropologists' analyses of data on existing tribes may be that they try to force the data into one of the very few systems of which they are aware.

* * *

I have succeeded only in deriving the ideal types. Chance mechanisms probably must be included in a more general framework: to provide a basis for measuring mixtures of ideal systems; to allow for individual deviations from any of the recognized norms ... and to provide a basis for assessing the demographic stability of a given ideal system or mixture of systems. Once such a framework is developed one can hope to test meaningful theories, presumably of a stochastic nature, of the evolution of classificatory systems.

Connections between the two parts of White's algebraic kinship analysis have been provided by Boyd (1968, 1969, 1971). Chapter 1 of White's (1963) work dealt with kinship roles and role trees, or algebraic compositions of kinship relations. Chapters 2 and 3 of his book dealt with marriage class rules. Boyd's "group partition theorem" (1969:145-47) shows, by the method of formal proof, that the combination of permutation rules for marriage classes plus homogeneous and close-knit role systems necessarily result in consistency among the multiple role sets (e.g., social obligations, attitudes, etiquette, etc.) that make up the diffuse set of ties in the kinship system. The proof is of broad significance, since it provides a generalization of structural balance theory, discussed in section 3, to diffuse but homogeneous role systems.

Boyd (1971) has also shown that the

"substitution property" of components in decomposition of kin terminology also applies to the relational operators that define marriage class systems. The substitution property as well as the group partition theorem essentially depend upon a consistent and efficient partitioning of a domain defined by relational operators. The theorems are similar, overall, to Geoghegan's analysis of efficient code rules. In fact, the problem of efficient ordering has the same mathematical form for language systems, information processing, role systems, componential analysis problems, and other areas as well (e.g., automata theory or systems design). Boyd's major contribution is to have pointed up these convergences in a number of important areas of investigation in anthropology (1969:140):

Perhaps the strongest criticism of transformational grammars, componential analyses, and marriage class analyses] is that they are viewed as distinct. If this criticism is valid, it is partly due to a lack of rigor in their formulations. The value of the abstract mathematical approach to problems is that it can transform superficially different problems into special cases of a general theory.

Boyd also ties his work in kinship algebra back into the major currents of ethnological interest in marriage class systems, in the evolution and regional variation of these systems. By careful development of mathematical models of kinship role and marriage class systems, matching these against the ethnographic facts, he attempts to show how these systems are related diachronically, and how neighboring systems differ by transformations in this process of development. He develops an algebraic notion of "covers" (Boyd 1969:152-56) which is suitable to the task of transformational analysis in this developmental sense. A "covering" is defined as the closest asymmetric relationship between two structures: the set *abcd*, for example, "covers" *abc*, but not *ab*; nor does *abc* cover *abcd*. The formal definition of covering relationships allows an ordering of the sequences of structural similarities between different marriage class systems. If each of the structural models in this ordering is based upon an empirical case in the region, and if all cases in the region are accounted for by one of the models, then this constitutes a plausible evolutionary or transformational sequence. The logic involved in this type of mathematical modeling is similar to that used by Lévi-Strauss (1949, 1963, 1969) in his regional and transformational studies of kinship and mythological structures.

Another major synthesis of disparate areas of concern in anthropology and a major breakthrough in mathematical decomposition analysis have been developed by François Lorrain and Harrison White (1971). They have developed an algebraic approach to social networks. It stems from the first chapter of White's (1963) book, and from the stimulus of Boyd's work, and is most fully developed in its anthropological implications in various papers by Lorrain (1968, 1969a, 1969b, 1970, 1971). In these papers Lorrain provides an extension to the theoretical integration that Boyd achieved for componential analysis, group marriage systems, and generative grammar. Lorrain's work encompasses these plus many of Lévi-Strauss' ideas regarding binary opposition, hierarchies, and balance theory within a general theoretical framework.

The abstract formalization of Lorrain and White's approach to networks is already familiar from our preceding discussions. It is a relational algebra whose elements are roles (e.g., father, friend, boss) and whose composition operator allows these roles to be compounded in successive chains linked by the possessive "of": father of friend, son of brother of father (or father's brother's son), boss of boss, etc. The cultural institutionalization of role compositions is shallow in some areas and deep in others. The number of "friend of" links that can be concatenated in our own culture, for example, is limited, but father of father of father . . . and boss of boss of boss . . . are expressions that recognize institutionalized roles. Some expressions such as "boss's father" may not be institutionalized, while others such as "father's boss" are culturally recognized. Culturally recognized role compositions can be written on a composition table. Since these may have reference to specific individuals and relationships in a finite population, the composition table of roles for a given and bounded social group may be considered along with a graph of the actual primary relationships between individuals in terms of a defined set of primary roles.

By studying a role composition table (culturally defined) as well as an actual network graph of social relations (defined by social persons), Lorrain and White (1971) are able to identify systemic effects of total social networks:

In order to do justice at least in part to the bewildering complexity of social structure, it is important to take into account the possible very long and devious chain of effects propagating within concrete social systems through links of various kinds. It is partly owing to these indirect effects, together with the largely extrinsic driving force of membership renewal, that social structures and processes can so vastly transcend the consciousness of actors and investigators.

In order to achieve a formal procedure of analysis, Lorrain and White are required to loosen some of the axioms of mathematical systems that have been used to study algebraic groups and categories (systems of composition having such properties as closure, associative composition, identity, and inverse elements; consult any textbook on abstract algebra). The table of role compositions, for example, has undefined "holes" where the composition of two roles is culturally unrecognized, so that the axiom that a composition table must be everywhere defined has to be loosened to define an appropriate mathematical system for this type of analysis. On this basis, Lorrain and White proceed to define an appropriate notion of an algebraic "category," for network analysis, which consists of concrete nodes on the graph (objects, persons) plus the set of all relations in the composition table (called "morphisms"). It is also assumed that a cultural morphism (institutionalized role relationship) will not exist without at least one corresponding relationship of this type on the graph. The associative property of relations—i.e., $(RS)T = R(ST)$ for all R, S, T that can be so composed in the composition table—is also assumed to hold.

When the structure of the algebraic "category," as defined above in terms of network analysis, is analyzed, the undefined compositions in the network acquire a new significance. They may define points of cleavage, disjunction, or decoupling in the social structure. Algebraic and graph-theoretic analysis of the properties of the system can be utilized to analyze the structure of the system (for examples see section 3 on the Purum, where reduction on a graph is discussed, and the discussion of Harrison White's analysis of marriage rules). In addition, formal algebraic theorems derived from the theory of groups and categories can be utilized to derive certain structural properties of networks. This type of analysis represents an important advance over graph theory, which had been able to focus only upon sets of nodes or cycles within a graph, and to develop only a limited set of measures of the interlocking of relationships and the overall structure of a graph.

Given the definition of an algebraic category as defined in terms of a specific social network, the major task of analysis in Lorrain and White's (1971) approach is to determine how the total set of relational types in a network can be "reduced" by formal principles of structural equivalence. A reduction must satisfy the "structure-preserving" requirement of mapping a category (objects and morphisms) *onto* a new category; that is, preserving the partitions in the old category between elements in the set. The reduction applies to objects and morphisms at one and the same time, and reduction applies only if there is structural equivalence among a set of persons (objects) as well as the corresponding set of relationships (morphisms) that define their positions in the network. A number of reductions may be possible (Lorrain and White 1971):

A wider notion of *homothety* is involved here, that is, a notion of similarity of position of individuals in a social network, this similarity being relative to particular abstract "points of view" (reductions) taken on the structure. For example, homothety could correspond to clustering of individuals into disjunct interest groups, common interest being defined by similarity of position relative to some abstract, analytic perspective on the structure. . . . But, of course, in general, structural equivalence does not imply actual or conscious solidarity.

What are the uses of network reductions? The first is in identifying equivalence in networks. The distinction here is between being in the same position in the social structure (local homogeneity) as distinct from an isomorphic position, as, for example, groups in a simple exchange cycle (global homogeneity). A common but not obvious characteristic of groups and social structure is that in the global structure of a network, the extremes often become equivalent in the sense of homothetic structural relations. Second, the existence of identity morphisms of various types (e.g., the ego of kinship trees) enables consideration of a structure from the viewpoint of generic egos. Third, two special strategies are suggested (Lorrain and White 1971) for reductions that are of particular interest to anthropology. One is a cultural reduction that deals with equivalence of morphisms (roles) solely on the basis of their cultural content (e.g., the saying "A friend of yours is a friend of mine"), but enabling reduction of the network graph by such rules. The other is sociometric analysis, which utilizes the actual properties of the relationships on the network graph. This method identifies those morphisms that have common ordered pairs and those that have self-loops and symmetric ties, such that "in the reduction the nodes linked by these morphisms will become structurally equivalent and hence will be identified." Further sociometric reduction may utilize a "majority rule" (Lorrain and White 1971):

Two morphisms whose graphs have a majority of ordered pairs in common are in similar positions with the composition operation and it is reasonable to identify them in a reduction—the more so as we have already argued that two types of relation with the same graph should be considered a single type.

Other procedures of homothetic reduction are discussed by Lorrain and White for simple finite systems, and have been extended to complex cases in a paper by Heil (1970) for use with computer algorithms.

Work on network reduction is in a germinal stage, which accounts for the lack of anthropological examples in this discussion. Some of the tasks that remain to be done on network reduction methods include (1) development of unique decomposition theorems, if possible; (2) delimitation of the total range of meaningful reduction strategies relative to their uses; (3) demonstration of the mapping of important aspects of social structure by these reductions; (4) resolution of the problem of distances between nodes in a network; (5) dealing with the intensity of flows in the network; (6) dealing with diachronic problems of allocating individuals to roles and roles to individuals; (7) dealing with attributes of individuals, rather than just roles; and (8) formalization of efficient reduction criteria, e.g., "of the idea of the 'simplest' reduction within a certain structural 'distance' of an initial category" (Lorrain and White 1971).

The problems that are dealt with by Lorrain and White's categorical network theory include the reduction of formal decomposition analysis of hierarchical tree structures or role trees (as in White's 1963 analysis of kinship role trees), classificatory systems, including "classificatory kinship nomenclatures, elementary kinship structures, systems of binary oppositions, componential analysis, hierarchies with levels, and balance theory" (Lorrain and White 1971:39-40), of networks of diffusion, innovation, gossip, etc., which involve relational links, and of specific social networks with complex and interlocking systems of roles among actors. If these approaches to the mathematical decomposition of social network and cultural systems of rules and classifications, along parallel lines, can succeed in any of the ways outlined by Lorrain and White, the results will be of fundamental significance to the theory of ethnographic description, and to the development of ethnological theory.

Development not only of new mathematical applications in anthropol-ogy, but of new mathematics, should be seen in the larger context of the relationship between mathematics and fields of scientific inquiry. The work of John Boyd and Lorrain and White, like the development of the theory of games by Von Neumann and Morgenstern, represents genuine innovation in the field of mathematics as well as social science. Where the existing axiomatic systems in mathematics are not adequate for the analysis of a given problem, new mathematical systems may have to be constructed which are more appropriate to the goals of the specific scientific research task.

There will always be problems in anthropology which will appear to lie beyond the power and applicability of current mathematization. As in other scientific disciplines, when these areas are theoretically rich and empirically well described, they are an index of the sources of future growth of theoretical formalization of the field. One such area in anthropology, for example, is in the analysis of myth and oral literature; the work of Lévi-Strauss (1969), Maranda and Maranda (1971), Buchler and Selby (1968a), and others has indicated that these symbolic domains are almost within reach of mathematical formalization, awaiting the assembly of the appropriate mathematical tools. These areas may be rich sources of both anthropological theory and mathematical innovation. While most of science proceeds outside of mathematization, axiomatic reasoning and mathematical formulation are the connectives of modern science, and the feedback between anthroplogical science and mathematics is of crucial importance in the coming of age of anthropology.

The problems of ethnographic decomposition are essential to the rethinking of the elements of ethnography, and it is from these elements and the structures in which they are embedded that new ethnological theory will be constructed.

REFERENCES

Ackerman, C.
1964 Structure and Statistics: The Purum Case. *American Anthropologist* 66: 53-66.
1965 Structure and Process: The Purum Case. *American Anthropologist* 67: 83-91.

Arbib, Michael A., ed.
1968 *Algebraic Theory of Machines, Languages, and Semigroups.* New York: Academic Press.

Atkins, J. R., and L. Curtis
1969 Game Rules and Rules of Culture. In *Game Theory in the Behavioral Sciences*, ed. I. R. Buchler and H. G. Nutini. Pittsburgh: University of Pittsburgh Press.

Ayoub, M. R.
1959 Parallel Cousin Marriage and Endogamy: A Study in Sociometry. *Southwestern Journal of Anthropology* 15:266-75.

Barnes, J. A.
1960 Marriage and Residential Continuity. *American Anthropologist* 62:850-66.
1969 Graph Theory and Social Networks: A Comment on Connectedness and Connectivity. *Sociology* 3:215-32.

Barth, F.
1959 Segmentary Opposition and the Theory of Games: A Study of Pathan Organization. *Journal of the Royal Anthropological Institute* 89:5-21.
1966 *Models of Social Organization.* Occasional Papers of the Royal Anthropological Institute of Great Britain and Ireland, no. 23.

Bartos, O. J.
n.d. Negotiation Under Experimental Conditions. Forthcoming.

Berge, C.
1962 *The Theory of Graphs.* New York: Wiley.

Berger, J., B. P. Cohen, J. L. Snell, and M. Zelditch, Jr.
1962 *Types of Formalization.* Stanford: Stanford University Press.

Berger, Joseph, et al.
1966 *Sociological Theories in Progress*, vol. 1. Boston: Houghton Mifflin.

Berting, J., and H. Philipsen
1960 Solidarity, Stratification, and Sentiments: The Unilateral Cross-Cousin Marriage According to the Theories of Lévi-Strauss, Leach, and Homans and Schneider. *Bijdragen tot de Taal-, Land- en Volkenkunde* 116:55-80.

Boyd, John Paul
1968 Algebra and Consanguineal Kinship. In *Calcul et formalisation dans les sciences de l'homme.* Paris: Editions du Centre de la Recherche Scientifique.
1969 The Algebra of Group Kinship. *Journal of Mathematical Psychology* 6:139-67.
1971 Componential Analysis and the Substitution Property. In *Explorations in Mathematical Anthropology*, ed. Paul Kay. Cambridge: M.I.T. Press.

Brain, Jeffrey P.
1971 The Natchez "Paradox." *Ethnology* 10, no. 2.

Braithwaite, R. B.
1955 *The Theory of Games as a Tool for the Moral Philosopher.* Cambridge: At the University Press.

Bruner, J. S., J. J. Goodnow, and G. A. Austin
1956 *A Study of Thinking.* New York: Wiley.

Buchler, I. R., and R. Kozelka
n.d. Mathematical Thinking in Cultural Anthropology. Unpublished MS.

Buchler, I. R., and R. McKinlay
1969 Decision Processes in Culture: A Linear Programming Analysis. In *Game Theory in the Behavioral Sciences*, ed. I. Buchler and H. Nutini. Pittsburgh: University of Pittsburgh Press.

Buchler, I. R., and H. G. Nutini, eds.
1969 *Game Theory in the Behavioral Sciences.* Pittsburgh: University of Pittsburgh Press.

Buchler, I. R., and H. A. Selby
1968a *Kinship and Social Organization.* New York: Macmillan.
1968b *A Formal Study of Myth.* Monograph series no. 1, Center for Intercultural Studies in Folklore and Oral

History. Austin: University of Texas.

Burling, Robbins
1964 Cognition and Componential Analysis: God's Truth or Hocus-Pocus? *American Anthropologist* 66:20-28.
1970 American Kinship Terms Once More. *Southwestern Journal of Anthropology* 26:15-24.

Burton, Michael
1970 Computer Applications in Cultural Anthropology. *Computers and the Humanities* 5:37-46.

Busaker, R. G., and T. L. Saaty
1965 *Finite Graphs and Networks.* New York: McGraw-Hill.

Bush, R. R.
1963 An Algebraic Treatment of Rules of Marriage and Descent. Appendix 2 in H. C. White, *An Anatomy of Kinship: Mathematical Models for Structures of Accumulated Roles.* Englewood Cliffs, N.J.: Prentice-Hall.

Cartwright, D., and F. Harary
1956 Structural Balance: A Generalization of Heider's Theory. *Psychological Review* 63:277-93.

Chapple, Eliot D.
1970 *Culture and Biological Man.* New York: Holt, Rinehart & Winston.
1971 Toward a Mathematical Model of Interaction: Some Preliminary Considerations. In *Explorations in Mathematical Anthropology,* ed. Paul Kay. Cambridge: M.I.T. Press.

Chernoff, H., and L. E. Moses
1959 *Elementary Decision Theory.* New York: Wiley.

Chomsky, Noam
1963 Introduction to the Formal Analysis of Natural Languages. In *Handbook of Mathematical Psychology*, ed. R. D. Luce et al., vol. 2. New York: Wiley.
1963 *Syntactic Structures.* The Hague: Mouton.

Coleman, J. S.
1964 *Introduction to Mathematical Sociology.* New York: Free Press of Glencoe, Macmillan.

Cook, S. C.
1966 The Obsolete "Anti-Market" Mentality: A Critique of the Substantive Approach to Economic Anthropology. *American Anthropologist* 68:323-45.

Coult, Allan D.
1962 The Determinants of Cross-Cousin Marriage. *Man* 62, no. 47.

Coult, Allan D., and E. A. Hammel
1963 A Corrected Model for Patrilateral Cross-Cousin Marriage. *Southwestern Journal of Anthropology* 19:287-96.

Cowgill, G. L.
1964 Statistics and Sense: More on the Purum Case. *American Anthropologist* 66:1358-65.

Dalton, G.
1969 Theoretical Issues in Economic Anthropology. *Current Anthropology* 10:63-101.

D'Andrade, R. G.
1959 Memorandum on Statistics in Social Anthropology. Laboratory of Social Relations: Unpublished MS.

Dantzig, G. B.
1951 Maximization of a Linear Function of Variables Subject to Linear Inequalities. In *Activity Analysis of Production and Allocation*, ed. T. C. Koopmans. Cowles Commission Monograph no. 13. New York: Wiley.

Das, T. C.
1945 *The Purums: An Old Kuki Tribe of Manipur.* Calcutta: University of Calcutta.

Davenport, William
1960 Jamaican Fishing: A Game Theory Analysis. *Yale University Publications in Anthropology* 59:3-11.

Dinkines, F.
1964 *Elementary Concepts of Modern Mathematics.* New York: Appleton-Century-Crofts.

Driver, H. E.
1953 Statistics in Anthropology. *American Anthropologist* 55:42-59.
1961 Introduction to Statistics for Comparative Research. In *Readings in Cross-Cultural Methodology*, ed. F. Moore. New Haven: HRAF Press.
1965 Survey of Numerical Classification in Anthropology. In *The Use of Computers in Anthropology*, ed. Dell Hymes. The Hague: Mouton.
1971 Statistical Studies of Continuous Geographic Distributions. In *A Handbook of Method in Cultural Anthropology*, ed. R. Naroll and R. Cohen.

Garden City, N.Y.: Natural History Press.

Edwards, W.
1967 The Theory of Decision Making. In *Decision Making*, ed. W. Edwards and A. Tversky. Baltimore: Penguin Books. Originally published 1954.

Elkin, A. P.
1938 *The Australian Aborigines.* London: Angus & Robertson.

Festinger, L.
1957 *A Theory of Cognitive Dissonance.* Stanford: Stanford University Press.

Festinger, L., S. Schachter, and K. Back
1964 Patterns of Group Structure. In *Mathematics and Psychology*, ed. G. A. Miller. New York: Wiley.

Fischer, J. L.
1958 The Classification of Residence in Censuses. *American Anthropologist* 60:508-17.
1964 Solutions for the Natchez Paradox. *Ethnology* 3:53-65.

Fjellman, Stephen M.
1969 Talking About Talking About Residence: An Akamba Case. Unpublished MS.

Flament, Claude
1963 *Applications of Graph Theory to Group Structure.* Englewood Cliffs, N.J.: Prentice-Hall.

Fortes, M.
1945 *The Dynamics of Clanship Among the Tallensi.* London: Oxford University Press.
1949 Time and Social Structure: An Ashanti Case Study. In *Social Structure*, ed. M. Fortes. London: Oxford University Press.
1962 *Marriage in Tribal Societies.* Cambridge Papers in Social Anthropology, no. 3, Introduction. Cambridge: At the University Press.

Frake, Charles O.
1964 Notes on Queries in Ethnography. In *Transcultural Studies in Cognition,* ed. A. K. Romney and R. G. D'Andrade. *American Anthropologist* 66, no. 3, pt. 2:132-45 (special issue).

Freeman, J. D.
1958 The Family System of the Iban of Borneo. In *The Developmental Cycle in Domestic Groups*, ed. J. Goody.

Cambridge Papers in Social Anthropology, no. 1. Cambridge: At the University Press.

Friedman, M., and L. J. Savage
1952 The Utility Analysis of Choices Involving Risk. In *Readings in Price Theory,* ed. G. J. Stigler and K. E. Boulding. Homewood, Ill.: Richard D. Irwin.

Gale, D.
1960 *The Theory of Linear Economic Models.* New York: McGraw-Hill.

Geoghegan, W. H.
1963a A Distance Model for the American-English Kinship System. Unpublished MS.
1963b Alternative Models for the English-American Kinship System: Classification of Response Data as to Model Types. Unpublished MS.
1969a Decision-Making and Residence on Tagtabon Island. Working Paper no. 17, Language Behavior Research Laboratory. Berkeley: University of California.
1969b The Use of Marking Rules in Semantic Systems. Working Paper no. 26, Language Behavior Research Laboratory. Berkeley: University of California.
1970 Natural Information Processing Rules: Formal Theory and Application to Ethnography. Ph. D. dissertation, Stanford University. To be published by Stanford University Press.
1971 Information Processing Systems in Culture. In *Explorations in Mathematical Anthropology,* ed. P. Kay. Cambridge: M.I.T. Press.

Geoghegan, W. H., and P. Kay
1964 More on Structure and Statistics: A Critique of C. Ackerman's Analysis of the Purum. *American Anthropologist* 66:1351-58.

Gilbert, J. P., and E. A. Hammel
1965 Computer Simulation of Problems of Kinship and Social Structure. In *The Use of Computers in Anthropology,* ed. D. H. Hymes. The Hague: Mouton.
1966 Computer Simulation and Analysis of Problems in Kinship and Social Structure. *American Anthropologist* 68:71-93.

Goldberg, S.
1958 *Introduction to Difference Equations.* New York: Wiley.
Goodenough, W. H.
1951 *Property, Kin, and Community on Truk.* Yale University Publications in Anthropology, no. 46. New Haven: Yale University Press.
1956a Componential Analysis and the Study of Meaning. *Language* 32:195-216.
1956b Residence Rules. *Southwestern Journal of Anthropology* 12:22-37.
1957 Cultural Anthropology and Linguistics. In *Report of the Seventh Annual Roundtable on Linguistics and Language Study*, ed. Paul L. Garvin, pp. 167-73. Georgetown University Monograph Series no. 9.
1965 Yankee Kinship Terminology: A Problem in Componential Analysis. *American Anthropologist* 67, no. 5, pt. 2:259-87.
Goody, J., ed.
1958 *The Developmental Cycle in Domestic Groups.* Cambridge Papers in Social Anthropology, no. 1. Cambridge: At the University Press.
Gould, P.
1965 Wheat on Kilimanjaro: The Perception of Choice Within Game and Learning Model Frameworks. *General Systems* 10:157-66. Yearbook for the Society for General Systems Research.
Greenberg, J. H.
1966 Language Universals, with Special Reference to Feature Hierarchies. The Hague: Mouton.
Gullahorn, John T., and Jeanne E. Gullahorn
1963 A Computer Model of Elementary Social Behavior. In *Computers and Thought*, ed. E.A. Feigenbaum and J. Feldman, pp. 375-86. New York: McGraw-Hill.
Haas, M. R.
1940 Creek Inter-Town Relations. *American Anthropologist* 42:479-89.
Hägerstrand, Torsten
1967 *Innovation, Diffusion, and Social Process.* Chicago: University of Chicago Press.
Hammel, E. A.

1961 The Family Cycle in a Coastal Peruvian Slum and Village. *American Anthropologist* 63:989-1005.
Hammel, E. A., and M. Freedman
n.d. Review of Mathematical Anthropology. Forthcoming, UNESCO.
Harary, F., R. Z. Norman, and D. Cartwright
1965 *Structural Models: An Introduction to the Theory of Directed Graphs.* New York: Wiley.
Hart, C. W.
1943 A Reconsideration of Natchez Social Structure. *American Anthropologist* 45:374-86.
Heider, F.
1946 Attitudes and Cognitive Organization. *Journal of Psychology* 21:107-12.
Heider, K.
n.d. Notes on Lévi-Strauss's Balance Theory. Unpublished MS.
Heil, G. H.
1970 Computer-Aided Study of the Algebraic Structure of Sociograms. Unpublished honors thesis, Harvard College.
Hoffmann, H.
1965 Formal vs. Informal Estimates of Cultural Stability. *American Anthropologist* 67:110-15.
1969 A Linear Programming Approach to Cultural Intensity. In *Game Theory in the Behavioral Sciences*, ed. I. Buchler and H. Nutini. Pittsburgh: University of Pittsburgh Press.
1970 Mathematical Anthropology. In *Biennial Review of Anthropology*, ed. B. J. Siegal, pp. 41-79. Stanford: Stanford University Press.
1971 Markov Chains in Ethiopia. In *Explorations in Mathematical Anthropology*, ed. Paul Kay. Cambridge: M.I.T. Press.
Homans, George C.
1950 *The Human Group.* New York: Harcourt, Brace.
1961 *Elementary Social Behavior.* New York: Harcourt, Brace & World.
Homans, G. C., and H. Schneider
1955 *Marriage, Authority, and Final Causes.* Glencoe, Ill.: Free Press.
Hunt, Earl B.
1962 *Concept Learning.* New York: Wiley.

Hunt, E. B., J. Martin, and P. J. Stone
1966 *Experiments in Induction.* New York: Academic Press.

Hymes, Dell, ed.
1965 *The Use of Computers in Anthropology.* The Hague: Mouton.

Kay, Paul, ed.
1971 *Explorations in Mathematical Anthropology.* Cambridge: M.I.T. Press.

Kemeny, J. G., and J. L. Snell
1962 *Mathematical Models in the Social Sciences.* Boston: Ginn.

Kemeny, J. G., J. L. Snell, and G. L. Thompson
1966 *Introduction to Finite Mathematics,* 2nd ed. Englewood Cliffs, N.J.: Prentice-Hall.

Kozelka, R. M.
1969 A Bayesian Approach to Jamaican Fishing. In *Game Theory in the Behavioral Sciences,* ed. I.Buchler and H. Nutini. Pittsburgh: University of Pittsburgh Press.

Kroeber, A. L.
1909 Classificatory Systems of Relationship. *Journal of the Royal Anthropological Institute* 39:77-84.

Kuhn, T.
1962 *The Structure of Scientific Revolutions.* Chicago: University of Chicago Press.

Kundstadter, Peter, R. Buchler, R. Stephan, and C. Westoff
1963 Demographic Variability and Preferential Marriage Patterns. *American Journal of Physical Anthropology* 22:511-19.

Landau, H. G.
1951 On Dominance Relations and the Structure of Animal Society. *Bulletin of Mathematical Biophysics* 13:1-19, 245-62.

Leach, E. R.
1960 The Sinhalese of the Dry Zone of Northern Ceylon. In *Social Structure in Southeast Asia,* ed. G. P. Murdock, pp. 116-26. London: Tavistock.
1962a Notes on Some Unconsidered Aspects of Double Descent Systems. *Man* 62, no. 214.
1962b The Determinants of Differential Cross-Cousin Marriage. *Man* 62, no. 238:153.

1963 The Determinants of Differential Cross-Cousin Marriage. *Man* 63, no. 87:76-77.

Lévi-Strauss, Claude
1945 L'Analyse structurale en linguistique et en anthropologie. *Word* 1:1-21.
1949 Les structures élémentaires de la parenté. Paris: Presses Universitaires de France.
1953 Social Structure. In *Anthropology Today,* ed. A. L. Kroeber. Chicago: University of Chicago Press.
1963 Structural Analysis in Linguistics and Anthropology. Chap. 2 of *Structural Anthropology.* New York: Basic Books.
1969 *The Raw and the Cooked.* New York: Harper & Row.

Livingstone, F. B.
1969 The Applicability of Structural Models to Marriage Systems in Anthropology. In *Game Theory in the Behavioral Sciences,* ed. I. Buchler and H. Nutini, pp. 235-52. Pittsburgh: University of Pittsburgh Press.

Löffler, L. G.
1964 Prescriptive Matrilateral Cross-Cousin Marriage in Asymmetric Alliance Systems: A Fallacy. *Southwestern Journal of Anthropology* 20:218-27.

Lorrain, François
1968 Tools for the Formal Study of Networks, I. Unpublished MS. Harvard University.
1969a Tools for the Formal Study of Networks, II. Unpublished MS, Harvard University.
1969b Quelques aspects de l'interdépendance entre l'organisation réticulaire interne des systèmes sociaux et des modes culturels de classification. Ph.D. dissertation, Harvard University.
1970 Locality, Globality, and Abstractness in Social Networks. Unpublished MS.
1971 Organisation réticulaire des systèmes sociaux et modes culturels de classification. Paris (in press).

Lorrain, F., and H. White
1971 Structural Equivalence of Individuals in Social Networks. *Journal of Mathematical Sociology* 1:49-80.

Lounsbury, F. G.

1956   A Semantic Analysis of Pawnee Kinship Usage. *Language* 32: 158-94.
1964a A formal Account of the Crow- and Omaha-Type Kinship Terminologies. In *Explorations in Cultural Anthropology*, ed. W. H. Goodenough. New York: McGraw-Hill.
1964b The Structural Analysis of Kinship Semantics. In *Proceedings of the Ninth International Congress of Linguists*, ed. H. G. Lunt, pp. 1073-93. The Hague: Mouton.

MacLeod, W. C.
1924   Natchez Political Evolution. *American Anthropologist* 26: 201-29.

Maranda, Elli K., and Pierre Maranda
1971   *Structural Models in Folklore and Transformational Essays*. The Hague: Mouton.

Markowitz, H.
1952. The Utility of Wealth. *Journal of Political Ecology* 60: 151-58.

Miller, F.
1964   Tzotzil Domestic Groups. *Journal of the Royal Anthropological Institute* 94: 172-82.

Miller, G. A.
1956   The Magical Number Seven, Plus or Minus Two: Some Limits on Our Capacity for Processing Information. *Psychological Review* 63:81-97.

Miller, G. A., E. Galanter, and K. H. Pribram
1960   *Plans and the Structure of Behavior*. New York: Holt, Rinehart & Winston.

Mitchell, J. C.
1956   *The Yao Village: A Study in the Social Structure of a Nyasaland Tribe*. Manchester: University of Manchester Press.
1963   Quantitative Methods and Statistical Reasoning in Social Anthropology. *Sudan Society* 2:1-23.
1967   On Quantification in Social Anthropology. In *The Craft of Social Anthropology*, ed. A. L. Epstein, pp. 17-46. London: Tavistock.

Moore, O. K.
1957   Divination: A New Perspective. *American Anthropologist* 59:69-74.

Morgan, Kenneth
1969   Monte Carlo Simulation of Artificial Populations: The Survival of Small, Closed Populations. Unpublished MS.
1970   Monte Carlo Simulation of Artificial Populations: The Effects of Incest Prohibitions and Clan Proscriptions on the Survival and Growth of Small, Closed Populations. Unpublished MS.

Morrill, R. L., and Forrest R. Pitts
1967   Marriage, Migration, and the Mean Information Field: A Study in Uniqueness and Generality. *Annals of the Association of American Geographers* 57(2):401-22.

Müller, E. W.
1964   Structure and Statistics: Some Remarks on the Purum Case. *American Anthropologist* 66:1371-77.
1966   Critique of Ackerman. *American Anthropologist* 68:524-25.

Murdock, G. P.
1949   *Social Structure*. New York: Macmillan.
1950   American Indian Society, chap. 12. Unpublished MS.
1955   Changing Emphases in Social Structure. *Southwestern Journal of Anthropology* 11: 361-70.
1956   Political Moieties. In *The State of the Social Sciences*, ed. L. D. White, pp. 133-47. Chicago: University of Chicago Press.
1957   World Ethnographic Sample. *American Anthropologist* 59:664-87.
1959   *Africa: Its Peoples and Their Culture History*. New York: McGraw-Hill.
1960   Social Structure in Southeast Asia. *Viking Fund Publications in Anthropology* 29:1-182.
1965   *Culture and Society*. Pittsburgh: University of Pittsburgh Press.

Nash, J. F.
1950   The Bargaining Problem. *Econometrica* 18:155-62.

Needham, R.
1958   A Structural Analysis of Purum Society. *American Anthropologist* 60: 75-101.
1960   Structure and Change in a Symmetric Alliance: Comments on Livingstone's Further Analysis of Purum Society. *American Anthropologist* 62:499-503.
1962   *Structure and Sentiment*. Chicago: University of Chicago Press.

1964 Explanatory Notes on Prescriptive Alliance and the Purum. *American Anthropologist* 66:1377-86.

1966 Comments on the Analysis of Purum Society. *American Anthropologist* 68:171-77.

Otterbein, K. F.
1970 The Developmental Cycle of the Andros Household: A Diachronic Analysis. *American Anthropologist* 72:1412-19.

Pospisil, L.
1963 *Kapauka Papuan Economy.* Yale University Publications in Anthropology. New Haven: Yale University Press.

Pred, Allan
1967 Postscript. In T. Hägerstrand, *Innovation, Diffusion, and Social Process.* Chicago: University of Chicago Press.

Quimby, G. I.
1946 Natchez Social Structure as an Instrument of Assimilation. *American Anthropologist* 48:134-37.

Randall, R.
n.d. An Algebraic Approach to Systems of Kinship Terminology. Unpublished MS.

Randolph, Richard R., and A. D. Coult
1968 A Computer Analysis of Bedouin Marriages. *Southwestern Journal of Anthropology* 24:83-99.

Rapoport, A., ed.
1960 *Games, Fights, and Debates.* Ann Arbor: University of Michigan Press.

Rapoport, A., and A. M. Channah
1965 *Prisoner's Dilemma: A Study in Conflict and Cooperation.* Ann Arbor: University of Michigan Press.

Read, D. W., and C. E. Read
1970 Critique of Davenport's Game Theory Analysis. *American Anthropologist* 72:351-55.

Riker, W. H.
1962 *The Theory of Political Coalitions.* New Haven: Yale University Press.

Roberts, J. M., M. J. Arth, and R. R. Bush
1959 Games in Culture. *American Anthropologist* 61:597-605.

Romney, A. K.
n.d. *Social Structure: The Collection and Interpretation of Data.* New York: Holt, Rinehart & Winston (in press).

Romney, A. K., and R. G. D'Andrade
1964 Cognitive Aspects of English Kin Terms. In *Transcultural Studies in Cognition,* ed. A. K. Romney and R. G. D'Andrade. *American Anthropologist* 66, no. 3, pt. 2:230-42 (special issue).

Romney, A. K., R. Shepard, and S. Nerlove, eds.
1972 *Multidimensional Scaling in the Behavioral Sciences.* New York: Academic Press.

Sanday, Peggy R.
1966 The Problem of Kinship Terms and Psychological Reality: An Information Processing Approach. Ph. D. dissertation, University of Pittsburgh.

1968 The Psychological Reality of American-English Kinship Terms: An Information Processing Approach. *American Anthropologist* 70:508-23.

Savage, L. J.
1951 The Theory of Statistical Decision. *Journal of the American Statistical Association* 46:55-67.

Schelling, T.
1960 *The Strategy of Conflict.* Cambridge: Harvard University Press.

Schneider, D. M.
1965 Some Muddles in the Models, or How the System Really Works. In *The Relevance of Models in Social Anthropology,* ed. M. Banton. A.S.A. Monographs, no. 1. London: Tavistock.

Simon, Herbert A.
1954 Some Strategic Considerations in the Construction of Social Science Models. In *Mathematical Thinking in the Social Sciences,* ed. P. F. Lazarsfeld, pp. 338-415. Glencoe, Ill.: Free Press.

Smith, R. T.
1956 *The Negro Family in British Guiana: Family Structure and Social Status in the Villages.* Cambridge: At the University Press.

Southwold, M.
1969 A Games Model of African Tribal Politics. In *Game Theory in the Behavioral Sciences,* ed. I. Buchler and H. Nutini. Pittsburgh: University of Pittsburgh Press.

Speck, F. G.
1935 *Naskapi.* Norman: University of Oklahoma Press.

Spoehr, A.
1941 Creek Inter-Town Relations. *American Anthropologist* 43:132-33.

Sutton-Smith, B., and J. M. Roberts
1964 Rubrics of Competitive Behavior. *Journal of Genetic Psychology* 105: 13-37.

Swanton, J. R.
1911 *Indian Tribes of the Lower Mississippi Valley and Adjacent Coast of the Gulf of Mexico.* Bureau of American Ethnology bulletin no. 43. Washington, D.C.: Smithsonian Institution.
1931 The Caddo Social Organization and Its Possible Historical Significance. *Journal of the Washington Academy of Sciences* 21:203-206.
1946 *The Indians of the Southeastern United States.* Bureau of American Ethnology bulletin no. 137. Washington, D.C.: Smithsonian Institution.

Von Neumann, J., and O. Morgenstern
1947 *Theory of Games and Economic Behavior,* 2nd. ed. Princeton: Princeton University Press.
1964 Ibid., 3rd ed. New York: Wiley.

Wald, A.
1950 *Statistical Decision Functions.* New York: Wiley.

Wallace, A. F. C.
1961 *Culture and Personality.* New York: Random House.
1970 A Relational Analysis of American Kinship Terminology. *American Anthropologist* 72:841-45.

Wallace, A. F. C., and J. Atkins
1960 The Meaning of Kinship Terms. *American Anthropologist* 62:58-80.

Weil, André
1949 Sur l'étude algébrique de certain types de lois de mariage (système Mirngin). In Claude Lévi-Strauss, *Les structures élémentaires de la parenté,* pp. 278-85. Paris: Presses Universitaires de France. Also translated by C. White as Appendix I in H. C. White, *An Anatomy of Kinship.* Englewood Cliffs, N.J.: Prentice-Hall, 1963.

Wexler, Kenneth, and A. Kimball Romney
n.d. Individual Variations on Cognitive Structures. Paper presented at the Mathematical Social Science Board Advanced Research Seminar on Scaling and Measurement, Irvine, Calif.

White, D. R., G. P. Murdock, and R. Scaglion
1971 Natchez Class and Rank Reconsidered. *Ethnology* 10:369-88.

White, H. C.
1963 *An Anatomy of Kinship: Mathematical Models for Structures of Accumulated Roles.* Englewood Cliffs, N.J.: Prentice-Hall.

Wilder, W.
1964 Confusion vs. Classification in the Study of Purum Society. *American Anthropologist* 66:1365-71.

CHAPTER 10 Cognitive Anthropology

MARSHALL DURBIN

INTRODUCTION

The number of stimuli and their combinations in any given environment is infinite at any given time. The responses of an object (organic or inorganic) to these stimuli are likewise infinite, though they fall within a pattern of constraints.[1] These stimuli operate in conjunction with the properties of the object to produce the patterned constraints of responses. Thus a stone

falling off a cliff shatters in certain patterns and not others, depending on the height of the cliff, the amount of energy that precipitated the fall, and the direction and force of the prevailing wind current during the fall, among a host of other stimuli. It is worth noting that (1) the patterns themselves represent an infinite set of responses, and (2) they are established by the form, weight, and composition of the stone in concert with the stimuli; e.g., conditions that would cause some stones to shatter would leave other stones intact, though there undoubtedly would be responses such as heating, cooling, and so on.

All living organisms react to the stimuli in their environments in a manner similar to the one described above. All life forms process stimuli from their environments and produce observable responses by means of their biological mechanisms. The same stimuli receive different processing arrangements in different life forms as determined by the nature of the processing mechanisms. Thus stimuli are received differ-

I wish to thank Professor Dell Hymes for the many substantive comments and suggestions he made on this work. I have not incorporated all of them here. Naturally, I take full responsibility for the material and ideas presented in this chapter.

[1] The implications of this statement are that though stimuli and responses have an infinite potential, not all possible ones or possible combinations occur. The reason for this is that a stimulus does not occur singly but arrives in a bundle with others. This bundling of stimuli puts patterns or constraints on the responses. This does not preclude the patterns of responses from being infinite, just as the set of odd numbers is an infinite subset within the infinite set of real numbers. See Chomsky (1965b) for a further explication of this process as regards natural languages.

entially and processed differentially: plants produce chlorophyll, slime molds aggregate and migrate, female turkeys attempt to lure predators away from their nests, human beings discuss their kin relations, and bees engage in communal activities to produce honey. Chapple (1970:255-56) says:

Studies of animals (and humans) have demonstrated that each species seems to have particular predilections for particular perceptual configurations or stimulus complexes. Presumably this is a case of the evolutionary history of the species; in any case, there is a filtering (using the zoologist's terms) which highlights some properties of the external environment and minimizes others. . . . How specific the stimulus has to be depends on the number of factors, but seems to be a consequence of the impact of natural selection over the history of the species. Once the species begins to choose particular stimulus-complex properties, natural selection then continues the process by refining the characteristics for the species which emphasize that particular trend towards filtering. These fall within the great class of recognition symbols (or signs)— the plumage of the male grouse or the variegated color (and shape) patterns of tropical fish.

Although insects and some birds require precise synchronization of their calls, individual recognition among birds and the primates is also clearly dependent on visual cues. Among primates, the ways in which eyes, brows, mouth, ears, body, limbs, and tail (and movements thereof) combine enable their cohorts to recognize who is coming into interactional distance. But in addition, there are preferences for colors, shapes, and forms. Yellow, orange, and red colors are highly conspicuous to man and many other vertebrates, and commonly selected as distinguished signs. In addition, certain kinds of spatial patterns, particularly broken and concentric designs, are intriguing to human babies and, inexplicably, to bees.

This type of interaction between the living organism and the stimuli of the surrounding environment which produce responses is usually termed a *communication system*. This term, however, turns out to be infelicitous, since it can be applied to any response, as in the case of the falling stone mentioned earlier. The inability to formulate a definition of communication in ordinary language is well exemplified in the following definitions and comments (from Newman 1966:59-60; Weaver 1966: 15):[2]

1. Communication is a philosophical principle, undeniable because it itself is involved in the very denial.
2. Communication cannot be broadly defined without losing itself in generalities; nevertheless, let us venture to say that communication is the discriminatory response an organism makes to a stimulus. If the stimulus is ignored, there has been no communication.
3. Communication is not a response but the relationship between the transmission of a stimulus and the evocation of a response.
4. Communication is not only verbal, intentional, and explicit; it includes all the processes by which people influence one another. All actions have communicative aspects once they are perceived by human beings.
5. Communication may occur in face-to-face interaction; through reading; in man-machine relationships (e.g., reading a microscope or radar); person-to-person interaction mediated through machines, and machine-machine relationships (as in automation).
6. Communication includes verbal as well as nonverbal messages, the latter communicated paralinguistically and via kinesics. The very context of a message involves communication.

---

[2] This article originally appeared in 1960 in *Journal of Communication* 10:115-24, where references to the authors cited by Newman may be found.

7. Communication involves messages directed to a specific target person as well as undirected messages (e.g., transmitted via a public-address or broadcasting system); messages of primary content as well as messages of secondary content (consisting of the reflexive awareness of who knows what); consummatory messages, like the expression of emotion that requires no feedback, as well as instrumental messages that require feedback about the effect of the message on the recipient; phatic communication, in which the primary message is attenuated, as well as dense information, such as is conveyed in the tower talk during airport observations.
8. Communication includes all the procedures by which one mind can affect another, including music, pictures, and other methods of conveying information.

The problems and failures to define communication in ordinary language successfully are obvious. Nevertheless, the discipline of anthropology has since its inception considered the communication (in a broad sense of the word) of human beings as its rightful domain. This domain, in fact, encompasses the total range of human behavior, or what anthropologists term "culture." A broad sense of *communication* equated with the concept of *culture* is readily seen in the following passages cited by Kroeber and Kluckhohn (1963):[3]

Culture embraces all the manifestations of social habits of a community, the *reactions* of the individual as *affected* by the habits of the group in which he lives, the *products* of human activity as determined by these habits [p. 82; from Boas].

* * *

. . . the sum total of ideas, *conditio*~~nal~~ tional *responses,* and patterns of hab~~it~~ havior which the members of that society have acquired through *instruction* or *imitation* and which they share to a greater or less degree [p. 82; from Linton].

* * *

. . . and cultures are, in the last analysis, nothing more than the *organized* repetitive *responses* of a society's members [p. 119; from Linton].

* * *

A culture is the configuration of learned behavior and *results* of behavior whose component elements are shared and transmitted by the members of a particular society [p. 119; from Linton].

* * *

A culture is any given people's *way of life,* as distinct from the *life-ways* of other peoples [p. 97; from Kluckhohn and Leighton].

* * *

There are certain recurrent and inevitable human *problems,* and the ways in which man can *meet* them are limited by his biological equipment and by *certain facts of the external world.* But to most problems there are a variety of possible *solutions.* Any culture consists of the set of habitual and traditional ways of thinking, feeling, and reacting that are characteristic of the ways a particular society *meets* its *problems* at a particular point in time [p. 107; from Kluckhohn and Leighton].

* * *

Culture is those habits which humans possess because they have been *learned* (not necessarily without modification) from *other humans* [p. 113; from Hockett].

* * *

Culture is generally understood to mean learned models of behavior which are socially *transmitted* from one generation to another within particular societies and which may be *diffused* from one society to another [p. 113; from Steward].

* * *

Culture is socially *transmitted* behavior conceived as an abstraction from concrete social groups [p. 113; from Aberle].

* * *

The *interaction* of *learning* and society thus *produces* in every human group a body of socially *transmitted* adaptive behavior which *appears* super-individual because it is *shared* and because it is *perpetuated* beyond the individual life span, and because its quantity and quality so vastly exceed the capacity of any single person to achieve by his own unaided effort. The term "culture" is applied to such systems of *acquired* and *transmitted* behavior [p. 128; from Murdock].

There is little doubt that it has been as tortuous, difficult, and impossible to define "culture" as it has been to define its near synonym "communication." Still, both terms are meaningful for the anthropologist because an explicit contrastive knowledge of other animal behavior underlies his observations and analyses of human culture; that is, anthropologists have traditionally been interested in the ways in which human beings differ from other animals, particularly hominids, in processing stimuli from their environments. The assumption of anthropologists that man processes information from the surrounding environment differently from other animals represents the core of the discipline. There has been a spectacular lack of success, however, in isolating these differences or their locus. Nevertheless, anthropologists have steadfastly held to this assumption—unlike sociologists, psychologists, and other social scientists. The failure to extract meaningful differences in this area is chiefly due to the fact that all domains of human behavior (social structure, language, exchange, values, toolmaking, and even religion[4]) reflect some parallels in the

behavior of other animals. Generally, anthropologists gloss over these parallels by stating that the sum total of the domains of human behavior is not found in any other animal. This, of course, brings us back to the starting point, forcing us to ask again, "How does *Homo sapiens* process the environment differently from other animals? "

The present essay is devoted to reviewing the anthropological investigations of this problem from the standpoint of one domain—human language—during the twentieth century. This field is presently called "cognitive anthropology" (Tyler 1969a), though many other terms have also been used.

One encounters a number of pitfalls in dealing with human language as the sole representative of human behavior. A large number of communication systems (kinesics, paralanguage, music, etc.) also convey information, for example, and such systems may carry information that is unexpressed by human language. Many social anthropologists feel that a great deal of information is carried by social structures and religion which is not carried by human language. But, all in all, human language can reflect most of the cognitive categories found in other social behavior. Anthropologists recognize this either tacitly or explicitly when they insist upon using the language of the group they are studying, although it is the group's behavior rather than its language that is their concern.

If we view language as an expressive system reflecting categories of social behavior, we may define it as a mnemonic device that maps the totality of human experience by subcategorization processes. This definition is in accord with the "stimuli plus organism equals response" process mentioned above. Thus, while one can outline the shortcomings of language studies alone, lan-

---

[4] One can include religion as a parallel activity if one recalls the behavior of Gua, the Kelloggs' chimpanzee (Kellogg and Kellogg 1933), when she was frightened, or the stone that she insisted on carrying with her. I think it also appropriate here to mention the similarities of the behavior of bower birds (Marshall 1954) to human religious activities. If one defines religion as an attempt to explain the unknown, then there are a great number of animals that participate in this activity from time to time, as we can see in the behavior of house pets.

guage still represents the most encompassing aspect of human behavior.

RELATIONS TO OTHER DISCIPLINES

These endeavors in the field of American anthropology have touched upon a number of other fields: philosophy and logic, psychology, sociology, and literary criticism. Fields such as political science, economics, history, and language teaching (as distinct from linguistics) have been little concerned with this area.

PHILOSOPHY AND LOGIC

From their beginnings philosophy and logic have manifested deep concern with the ways in which *Homo sapiens* processes his environment, as is evident in Plato's dialogues, especially *Cratylus* (Hamilton and Cairns 1961:421-74). More recently, however, two dominant schools of the philosophy of language have exhibited interest in these matters (Fodor and Katz 1964:1-19; Katz 1966). The *logical positivists* approach language through a series of logical connectives. Logic used in this sense replaces what linguists generally call syntax. It accompanies a "deeply ingrained view that a language functions primarily in the statement of truths . . . a theory of sentences and sentence structures" (Fodor and Katz 1964:2-3). Carnap (1956:246-47) best exemplifies the logical positivists' attempt to arrive at all those cognitive processing systems peculiar to *Homo sapiens* when he says:

I have tried to show in this paper that in a pragmatical investigation of natural language there is not only, as generally agreed, an empirical method for ascertaining which objects are denoted by a given predicate and thus for determining the extension of the predicate, but also a method for testing a hypothesis concerning its intension (designative meaning). The intension of a predicate for a speaker x is, roughly speaking, the general condition which an object must fulfill for x to be willing to apply the predicate to it. For the determination of intension, not only actually given cases must be taken into consideration, but also possible cases, i.e., kinds of objects which can be described without self-contradiction, irrespective of the question whether there are any objects of the kinds described. The intension of a predicate can be determined for a robot just as well as for a human speaker, and even more complete if the internal structure of the robot is sufficiently known to predict how it will function under various conditions. On the basis of the concept of intension, other pragmatical concepts with respect to natural languages can be defined, synonymy, analyticity, and the like. The existence of scientifically sound pragmatical concepts of this kind provides a practical motivation and justification for the introduction of corresponding concepts in pure semantics with respect to constructed language systems.

In a footnote Carnap (1956:246) defends the lack of psychologistic connotations in his approach, and aligns himself with Bar-Hillel (1954:230-37) by defending the "concept of meaning against those contemporary linguists who wish to ban it from linguistics. . . ." Both Carnap and Bar-Hillel, as representatives of the school of logical positivism, appeal to linguists, psychologists, and analytic philosophers to construct a semantic theory based on formal logic which is free from the psychologistic character of the traditional concepts of meaning.

The *ordinary-language* analysts deny that a logistic system can capture the richness and complexity of a natural language (Fodor and Katz 1964:1). They contend that language is an extremely complicated form of social behavior and should be studied through the detailed analyses of individual words and expressions. The result is that the ordinary-language analysts work almost exclusively with words and their usage. The ordinary-language analyst and the lexicographer have much in common, as can be seen in the following passage from Quine (1960:1), though it should be noted that Quine is not properly in the realm of ordinary-language analysis, but rather bridges the two views of language:

This familiar desk manifests its presence by resisting my pressures and by deflecting light to my eyes. Physical things generally, however remote, become known to us only through the effects which they help to induce at our sensory surfaces. Yet our common-sense talk of physical things goes forward without benefit of explanations in more intimate sensory terms. Entification begins at arm's length; the points of condensation in the primordial conceptual scheme are things glimpsed, not glimpses. In this, there is little cause for wonder. Each of us learns his language from other people, through the observable mouthing of words under conspicuously intersubjective circumstances. Linguistically, and hence conceptually, the things in sharpest focus are the things that are public enough to be talked of publicly, common and conspicuous enough to be talked of often, and near enough to sense to be quickly identified and learned by name; it is to these that words apply first and foremost.

While logical positivists never concern themselves with words, there is a fringe of ordinary-language analysts that deals with both sentences and words in varying degrees, such as Quine (1960) and Wittgenstein (1953). There are, however, radical ordinary-language analysts such as Ryle (1953) who claim "that sentences are not part of language but only of speech" (Fodor and Katz 1964:11). A joining of these two opposing viewpoints has never been seriously entertained by the community of philosophers at large.

PSYCHOLOGY

The entire field of psychology might be viewed as a quest for the cognitive processes of man. However, in regard to the material presented here, there are three scholars in twentieth-century America whose works illustrate a principal concern with language as an instrument reflecting human perception patterns: R. Brown, E. Lenneberg, and G. Miller. These men's work is such that though they are properly social psychologists, they can be equally considered linguists, psycholinguists, or sociolinguists.

The idea that an undefined portion of natural language (and hence of social behavior) may reside in the human brain shows up early in the work of Miller (1951). His experiments in the mid-fifties (Miller and Selfridge 1961, Miller 1961) involved work with syntactic arrangements in the areas of verbal recall, memory, and learning. The resultant conclusions claim that context as well as meaning per se facilitates learning, and that redundancy increases the length of the string being learned but not the efficiency of information learned. By the late fifties he had begun to explore the formal properties of grammar (Chomsky and Miller 1965). Miller (1956) openly suggests a search for the processing device of man when he maintains that the human brain can hold in abeyance in the memory no more than 7 ± 2 units. More recently Miller's work has involved experimentation that seeks to validate grammatical categories posited by linguists (Miller and McKean 1964).

Roger Brown's work involves a heavy experimental approach and fewer formal analyses (Brown 1958). But underlying all his experimental work in language acquisition and phonetic symbolism there is the strong belief that learning a language is more than a rehearsal of particular sentences.

This belief is most forcefully brought out in his latest studies on the "tip of the tongue" phenomenon (TOT) (Brown and McNeill 1966). Here he investigates phonological and semantic properties utilized when an individual is attempting to recall a word that is on the "tip of the tongue." This work is an extension of his previous studies on sound symbolism (Brown 1958:110-54).

Eric Lenneberg implicitly postulates a biological matrix for the development of speech and language. He states (1964:603) that such a matrix "is tantamount to an assumption that the general morphology characteristic of the order *primates* and/or universal physiological processes such as *respiration* and *motor-coordination* have undergone specialized adaptations, making the exercise of this behavior possible." In a later work (1967) he explores more fully the biological basis of language, mainly through observations on enanocephalic dwarfs, aphasics, and brain-damaged patients.

SOCIOLOGY

In the twentieth century the field of sociology has generally been recalcitrant in examining language in relation to its field data (Micklin and Durbin 1969), in spite of early contrary pronouncements by G. H. Mead (1934) and Mills (1939). This recalcitrance may in part be due to sociologists' doubts about the lack of a formalized methodology in the fields of anthropology and linguistics. More recently the ethnomethodologists (Garfinkel 1964) have become interested in language as an instrument of representation for the social system. The new field of sociolinguistics is largely dominated by linguistics in America, as we shall see in more detail later.

LITERARY CRITICISM

The field of literary criticism has offered two critics who have continually worked on the problem under survey here. Empson (1967) attempts to examine ambiguity, emotions, and feelings, and has proposed five ways in which a work can carry a doctrine. On "feeling" in words, he says (p. 1):

Emotions, as is well known, are frequently expressed by language; this does not seem one of the ultimate mysteries; but it is extremely hard to get a consistent and usable theory about their mode of action. What an emotive use of language may be, where it crops up, and whether it should be praised there, is not so much one question as a protean confusion, harmful in a variety of fields and particularly rampant in literary criticism. It is not hard to see why there is a puzzle here. Much of thinking has to be done in a summary practical way, trusting to a general sense of the whole situation in the background; we get a feeling that the rest of the situation is within call, so that we can concentrate our attention on one aspect of it, and this feeling is often trustworthy. But we also know that our judgment is often misled by our emotions, and there seems to be nothing in the feeling itself, at any rate before we give it attention (perhaps at the expense of something else which also needs attention) to show whether it is emotive or cognitive, whether we have adequate reasons for it in the background or not. This is the basis in experience of the question, and it is then developed into philosophical or psychological issues about what an adequate reason would be, or about what an emotion is.

Empson's early *Seven Types of Ambiguity* (1930) provides a classic reference to the various functions of human language. Kenneth Burke's work (1967) follows along the same lines, though the most interesting aspect of his study is the sound-sense nexus and its implications.

I have gone on at some length regarding the relation of other disciplines to anthropology's central focus, though in reality I have only scratched the surface. In doing so I have been forced to ignore a great deal of pertinent work in other fields and have listed only certain central figures whose work is germane to the cognitive bases of social behavior and whose work is in direct accord with the material that follows.

ORIGINS OF ANTHROPOLOGICAL LINGUISTIC COGNITIVE STUDIES IN THE UNITED STATES

During the first half of the twentieth century, unlike today, the fields of anthropology and linguistics were closely allied in this country. While departments of linguistics existed apart from anthropology, most of the linguistics faculty could claim to be anthropologists as well, since most of them had been trained under Franz Boas, Edward Sapir, or their students. Thus most theoretical issues were common knowledge to the group at large. During this period there were three individuals who laid the theoretical groundwork for what was to happen from 1955 on.

The following discussion is in no way meant to slight Franz Boas' contributions to the general perspective that later developed; his "psychological approach" probably lies at the heart of this perspective. But it was Edward Sapir, Benjamin Lee Whorf, and Zellig Harris that became methodologically precise and innovative in this perspective.

EDWARD SAPIR

Sapir, mentor to Harris and Whorf, was early concerned with cognitive problems such as the psychological validity or reality of the phoneme. Writing in 1933, Sapir (1949b:46) observed, "To the naive [untrained native] speaker, and hearer, sounds (i.e., phonemes) do not differ as five-inch or six-inch entities differ, but as clubs and poles differ." This concept so permeated the field at the time that most linguists working with native speakers maintained that the data would speak for itself: a phonemic analysis would result automati-

cally from the data if the analyst were careful in gathering it and paid enough heed to his informant's intuition.

Problems were arising at both a theoretical and a practical level, however, as can be seen in Chao (1958) and Twadell (1958). The latter especially was grappling with the problem of whether the phoneme was a mental or physiological reality or a fiction. This particular problem eventually gave rise to the field of psycholinguistics (see Osgood and Sebeok 1965; Saporta, ed., 1961), with an intermediate stage called psycho-acoustics.

Sapir's faith in a psychological reality of linguistic phenomena had been manifested much earlier, as shown in the following statement (1949a:90, 101-102):

It is the vocabulary of a language that most clearly reflects the physical and social environment of its speakers. The complete vocabulary of a language may indeed be looked upon as a complex inventory of all the ideas, interests and occupations that take up the attention of the community, and were such a complete thesaurus of the language of a given tribe at our disposal, we might to a large extent infer the character of the physical environment and the characteristics of the culture of the people making use of it. It is not difficult to find examples of languages whose vocabulary thus bears the stamp of the physical environment in which the speakers are placed. This is particularly true of the language of primitive peoples, for among these culture has not attained such a degree of complexity as to imply practically universal interests.

* * *

In other words, not only will the words themselves of a language serve as symbols of detached cultural elements, as is true of languages at all periods of development, but we may suppose the grammatical categories and processes themselves to symbolize corresponding types of thought and activity of cultural significance. To some extent culture and language may then be conceived of as in a constant state of interaction and definite association for a considerable lapse of time. This state of correlation, however, can not continue indefinitely. . . . A grammatical system as such tends to persist indefinitely. In other words, the conservative tendency makes itself felt more profoundly in the formal groundwork of language than in that of culture. One necessary consequence of this is that the forms of language will in course of time cease to symbolize those of culture and this is our main thesis. Another consequence is that the forms of language may be thought to more accurately reflect those of a remotely past stage of culture than the present ones of culture itself. It is not claimed that a stage is ever reached at which language and culture stand in no sort of relation to each other, but simply that the relative rates of change of the two differ so materially as to make it practically impossible to detect the relationship. . . .

Though the forms of language may not change as rapidly as those of culture, it is doubtless true that an unusual rate of cultural change is accompanied by a corresponding accelerated rate of change in language. If this point of view be pushed to its legitimate conclusion, we must be led to believe that rapidly increasing complexity of culture necessitates correspondingly, though not equally rapid, changes in linguistic form and content. This view is the direct opposite of the one generally held with respect to the greater conservatism of language in civilized communities than among primitive peoples. . . . I am not inclined to consider it an accident that the rapid development of culture in western Europe during the last 2000 years has been synchronous with what seems to be unusually rapid changes in language. Though it is impossible to prove the matter definitely, I am inclined to doubt whether many languages of primitive peoples have undergone so rapid modification in a corresponding period of time as has the English language.

This was written in 1912. Carroll (1956:134) quotes Sapir as saying also:

Human beings do not live in the objective world alone, nor alone in the world of social activity as ordinarily understood, but are very much at the mercy of the particular language which has become the medium of expression for their society. It is quite an illusion to imagine that one adjusts to reality without the use of

language and that language is merely an incidental means of solving specific problems of communication or reflection. The fact of the matter is that the "real world" is to a large extent unconsciously built up on the language habits of the group. . . . We see and hear and otherwise experience very largely as we do because the language habits of our community predispose certain choices of interpretation.

And Lounsbury (1969:9) quotes him as saying that "the tyrannical hold that linguistic form has upon our orientation in the world . . . not only refers to experience largely acquired without its help but actually defines experience for us . . . because of our unconscious projection of its implicit expectations into the field of experience." For Lounsbury (1969:10), this "represents something of a turning point in Sapir's outlook, or else it is a crystallization of a point of view which had only gradually been taking shape." I would suspect the latter conjecture is more valid (contrary to Lounsbury's intimation), since Sapir always gave a special place to the individual in relation to his language. Sapir early formulated the influences of environment on language *(langue)* and the influence of language on the individual's speech *(parole)*, which I take to be a progressive ordering or a crystallization of a point of view rather than a turning point or revolution.

BENJAMIN LEE WHORF

During the late twenties and early thirties Sapir came in contact with Benjamin Lee Whorf (Carroll, ed., 1956). Whorf had started out with an interest in language at the level of the word or the stem. In particular, he was interested in investigating the properties of oligosynthetic languages, which he defined as follows (in Carroll 1956:12-13):

Oligosynthesis is a name for that type of language structure in which all or nearly all of the vocabulary may be reduced to a very small number of roots or significant elements, irrespective of whether these roots or elements are to be regarded as original, standing anterior to the language as we know it, or as never having had independent existence, theirs being an implicit existence as parts in words that were always undissociated wholes.... Obviously we have here a structure, a point-to-point correspondence between the path of ideation and the succession of lip, tongue, and glottal activities (i.e., consonants and vowels) that may be of great linguistic, glottogonic, and psychological significance.

Whorf's interest in the psychological attributes of words, stems, phonemes, and articulatory features, however, was soon put aside after he came into Sapir's sphere.[5] His interest in the cognitive undercurrents of language was switched to morphology and syntax (Whorf 1956c:240-41):

...segmentation of nature is an aspect of grammar.... We cut up and organize the spread and flow of events as we do, largely because, through our mother tongue, we are

parties to an agreement to do so, not because nature itself is segmented in exactly that way for all to see. Languages differ not only in how they build their sentences but also in how they break down nature to secure the elements to put in those sentences. This breakdown gives units of the lexicon.... By these more or less distinct terms we ascribe a semifictitious isolation to parts of experience.... Indeed this is the implicit picture of classical physics and astronomy—that the universe is essentially a collection of detached objects of different sizes.... The real question is: What do different languages do, not with those artificially isolated objects but with the flowing face of nature in its motion, color, and changing form; with clouds, beaches, and yonder flight of birds? For, as goes our segmentation of the face of nature, so goes our physics of the Cosmos.

Here we find differences in segmentation and selection of basic terms.

Whorf's formulations developed under Sapir's tutelage and influence are generally known as the Sapir-Whorf hypothesis. The stringent Sapir-Whorf hypothesis implies that the grammatical and semantic structure of one's native

---

[5] Whorf had started his interest in the cognitive aspects of language by studying what would now be called phonetic symbolism in roots or stems of language. He was led to this interest by Fabre d'Olivet (1921), a nineteenth-century French dramatist and mystic who died with the reputation of being a fool or a visionary (Carroll, ed., 1956). Fabre d'Olivet had executed a study of the stems of the Hebrew language in an attempt to reconstruct the original words of Moses. Whorf was intrigued by Olivet's techniques. According to Carroll (1956:16), Whorf had abandoned his ideas concerning binary grouping and oligosynthesis by 1931 under the influence of Sapir. This seems unlikely, however, in light of the facts that (1) among the papers left at his death was a brief outline of a textbook for college students dedicated to the memory of Edward Sapir and Antoine Fabre d'Olivet; (2) his "Gestalt Technique of Stem Composition in Shawnee" (1956b), first published in 1940, is very close to the idea of phonetic symbolism as Whorf viewed it, though he is quite careful not to invoke the concept of Olivet's work here; (3) it is highly doubtful that Whorf would have been able to present his attempted deciphering of the linguistic portion of the Maya hieroglyphs (1956e) without an overt heavy reliance on his knowledge that Maya was an oligosynthetic language; and (4) late in 1936 (Carroll, ed., 1956:74-

75), Whorf said of Fabre d'Olivet: "Even the greatest European grammarians of the nineteenth century did not go much beyond formal and overt structures except for riding the classical grammatical and philosophical concepts to the limits of travel in the language they studied. To this statement there is one grand exception—one of those amazing geniuses who baffle their contemporaries and leave no successors. The real originator of such ideas as rapport-systems, covert classes, cryptotypes, psycholinguistic patterning, and language as part and parcel of a culture was, so far as I can learn, a French grammarian of the early nineteenth century, Antoine Fabre d'Olivet (1768-1825).... Unfortunately for its comprehension either then or now, its author was a mystical and religious metaphysician who mingled this side of his nature with the workings of one of the most powerful linguistic intellects of any age.... His Hebrew stands on its own feet as completely as does Boas's Chinook. He reorganized the treatment of verb conjugations on a psycholinguistic basis, considered individual prefixes and suffixes from the standpoint of their meaning and function, went into the semantics of vowel patterns and the semantic coloring of vowels, and showed how many Hebrew stems can be resolved into meaningful fractions...."

language confines one to certain patterns of thinking. This further implies that translation from one language to another is nearly impossible, especially if the languages are unrelated, and sets up a very narrowly conceived type of linguistic relativism (see Lounsbury 1969). In Whorf's words (1961:465):

This fact is very significant for modern science, for it means that no individual is free to describe nature with absolute impartiality but is constrained to certain modes of interpretation even while he thinks himself free. The person most nearly free in such respects would be a linguist familiar with very many widely different linguistic systems. As yet no linguist is in any such position. We are thus introduced to a new principle of relativity, which holds that all observers are not led to the same picture of the universe, unless their linguistic backgrounds are similar, or can in some way be calibrated.

Lounsbury (1969:6) has pointed out that the Whorf hypothesis appealed to a large number of people in a wide variety of disciplines. But he states that a fair number of linguists at the present time hold that the linguistic relativity that Whorf proposed is untenable, probably because linguists tend to view the main issues of the hypothesis from vantage points that differ from those implied by Sapir and Whorf. Interestingly, Lounsbury also notes that not a few linguists would hold that Sapir and Whorf may not have believed everything they said.

Apart from linguists, there were objections from persons in other disciplines (see Lenneberg 1953). As Lounsbury points out (1969:10), not all cultural anthropologists were willing to subordinate the psychic unity of mankind to superstructures of social, cultural, and linguistic systems. Out of this attempt to subordinate all behavior to cultural and linguistic systems, there grew what Lounsbury has termed the "limited relativist" position. The limited relativist position recognizes no universal higher-order concepts and views all human behavior as a potentially infinite set of variations that are completely relative to each other.

It is probably quite true that Sapir and Whorf may not have really believed everything they seemed to be saying, nor would they believe everything that other people impute to their hypothesis. For one thing, Whorf apparently never totally abandoned his interest in the cognitive aspects of phonology (see footnote 6), and late in his writing we find statements along the following lines (Whorf 1956d:268):

My own studies suggest, to me, that language, for all its kingly role, is in some sense a superficial embroider upon deeper processes of consciousness, which are necessary before any communication, signaling, or symbolism whatsoever can occur, and which also can, at a pinch, effect communication (although not true AGREEMENT without language's and without symbolism's aid. . . . The statement that "thinking is a matter of LANGUAGE" is an incorrect generalization of the more nearly correct idea that "thinking is a matter of different tongues." The different tongues are the real phenomena and may generalize down not to any such universal as "Language," but to something better—called "sublinguistic" or "superlinguistic"—and NOT ALTOGETHER unlike, even if much unlike, what we now call "mental." This generalization would not diminish, but would rather increase, the importance of intertongue study for investigation of this realm of truth.

These statements, first published in 1941, shortly before Whorf's death, hardly imply a strict relativistic viewpoint or tyranny of words over one's total behavior. But a climate prevailed among anthropologists, linguists, and laymen alike which caused a strict relativist interpretation of what both Sapir and Whorf had posited. Linguistics was in the heydey of its descriptivism vs. prescriptivism period, and the practitioners of anthropology were firmly maintaining that all cultures are equally complex and equally "satisfactory" for the environment to which they have adapted.

By 1956 the understanding of this topic had reached the point where most persons were ready to ask along with Greenberg (1961): (1) What is the nature of the linguistic evidence (e.g., phonemes, allophones, morphemes, and so on)? (2) With what other behavioral data are the linguistic data being connected (e.g., social structure, perception, group maintenance, and the like)? And (3) what theories and methodologies of general science are being invoked to join the two types of data (causality, correlation, predictability, probability, etc.)? [6]

ZELLIG HARRIS

During the same period there existed several linguists who tended to stay out of the admiration and discussion sur-

---

[6] Another factor conditioning the two phenomena can be clearly seen in the work of Mathiot (1968:2):

"The hypothesis underlying the present approach is that the theme structure of the language is related to the theme structure of the culture. The degree to which the two structures are related constitutes the degree of integratedness of the language into the total culture. Such a hypothesis, therefore, allows for varying degrees of integratedness of a language into a culture, as may become apparent both in the synchronic comparison of different language-and-culture situational contexts and in the diachronic comparison of the same language-and-culture situational context.

"The assumption implicit in the usual interpretation of the Sapir-Whorf hypothesis is that the cognitive domain of language is directly related to culture, thus influencing cultural behavior. In the present approach, this assumption is replaced by the postulation of two separate theme structures related to each other in varying degrees. Thus, instead of direct correlations, an intermediate level is proposed. This means that language and culture relations are expected to emerge on a higher level of abstraction. This also means that no necessary determinism is postulated in the relation of language and culture."

rounding the Sapir-Whorf hypothesis. Their interests lay mainly in the structure of language. Foremost among the group is Zellig Harris, whose linguistic inquiries over the past quarter of a century have directly given rise to the present trend in anthropological linguistics, ethnolinguistics, or language and culture studies, as well as in the field of linguistics itself.

In 1945 Zellig S. Harris rephonemicized Hoijer's (1945) Navaho data. In order to illustrate the problem fully, Hoijer's version of the phonemes of Navaho are given below:

b		m	m'	s	z		dz	ts	ts'	a a·	a^n $a^{l \cdot n}$
d t	t'	n	n'	š	ž		dž	tš	tš'	e e·	e^n $e^{\cdot n}$
		ł	l				dl	tł	tł'	i i·	i^n $i^{\cdot n}$
				y	y'					o o·	o^n $o^{\cdot n}$
g k k'				x	γ						
g k k^w				x^w	γ^w						
				h					´ ` ∨ ∧ tones		
				h^w							

Harris (1945) reanalyzed the data by:
1. Establishing the nine affricates as stops by considering allophonic patterning.
2. Using syllable and stem final junctures as phonological units.
3. Considering the nasalization of vowels as an allophone of /m/.
4. Considering the length of vowels as a case of two identical vowels, /VV/.
5. Considering ∧ and ∨ as combinations of ´ + ` and ` + ´ respectively.
6. Considering a stop-making component to be present in /m, n, z, l, g, y, d/, while a devoicing, a glottalizing, and a palatalizing component are

present in /h/, /'/, and /ˇ/ respectively.

The overall effect is to rearrange the phonemes in such a way that the resulting "components cannot very well be represented in chart form, since the relations among them are distributed and complicated and cannot be fairly indicated by geometric properties of the chart" (Z. S. Harris 1945:245). A side effect is the drastic reduction of the number of phonological units that characterize Navaho, so that $z = z$, $d + z = dz$, $h + z = s$, $h + z +$ ˇ $= š$. Apparently Harris had no other interest in the matter other than structural manipulation, since he says (1945:240-41):

It is interesting to see how the stock of phonemes and their interrelations (as indicated by a chart) can be differently stated on the basis of detailed allophonic information, and the distributional information which Hoijer gives. . . . In considering here the reduction of the phonemic stock, the purpose is not to have fewer phonemes, come what may, but rather to have a simpler statement of the phonetic facts about the language. Reducing the number of phonemes, or the complexity of allophonic variation within each phoneme, often aids in this direction. Eliminating the limitations of distribution upon each phoneme is yet a greater aid. Often, these three objectives clash with one another. However, when we use the limitations of distribution of phonemes as a basis for reducing their number, we serve two purposes simultaneously.

A prelude to Harris' reorganization of the Navaho data can be seen in his 1942 analysis of morpheme alternants (1958a) and in his 1944 analysis of simultaneous components in phonology (1958b). Indeed, this methodology had a long history (Hockett 1947:258n) among members of the Prague school, particularly Jakobson (Jakobson, Fant, and Halle 1951).[7]

_____
[7] The effects of Jakobson's work and the Prague school as regards the distinctive feature (or componentializing) approach to phonology can be seen in

By 1951 Harris' technique of componentializing simultaneous features had been heavily incorporated in his book *Methods in Structural Linguistics*. The reaction to this method is fairly well summed up by Joos (1958:138):

I remember being asked more than once what Harris meant to accomplish by using components to remove limitation on the occurrence of phonemes: Why is it so important to him to remove limitations? How is description improved if it is done by introducing a complication? The answer seems to be that a worse complication is thereby removed. . . . The completed analysis yields a *phonological model* for that language. This model is purely phonological: it has nothing to do with meaning, hence nothing to do with the identities of its own. . . . Having established a phonological model for a language, one henceforth treats it as autonomous: no further regard for phonetics or for meaning is permissible while one examines the functioning of the phonological model. This allows (and forces) the examination to be abstract. The elements of the phonological model are treated as counters—as marks on paper, for instance. What can be the functioning of counters like that?

Zellig S. Harris' book (1951) was reviewed by two persons from opposite ends of the anthropological perspective: Margaret Mead and Fred W. Householder. Both show keen aware-

_____
present-day transformational phonological analyses (Chomsky and Halle 1968). It is interesting to note that Householder (1965) levels pretty much the same kind of arguments against transformational phonology that he leveled against Harris. For a reply to those arguments, see Chomsky and Halle (1965). Jakobson's work in the distinctive-feature approach to phonology has also had its effect abroad, where Claude Lévi-Strauss (1967) picked it up and gives it constant praise. I believe that at the time Lévi-Strauss first presented these analyses (1944-1957) they were quite remarkable and were considerably in advance of what was going on in America at the time. In line with the work that is being carried on now, the methodology of Lévi-Strauss could be considered very naive, though his ideas concerning universals are quite refreshing.

ness of the problem presented by Harris' analysis. Mead says (1952:258):

This particular aspect of the method—that structure must be discriminated rigorously, but that different series of discriminations may be used—raises a fundamental problem in cultural analysis, where it has been found repeatedly that the same cultural materials can be analyzed with different sets of categories, and that the essentials are: accurate recording of a contextual body of data sufficiently extensive to permit its analysis in other ways; accurate specification of the units of observations; and a type of recording that provides analysts using different categories with a set of common referents (a recorded verbatim unrearranged body [of] autobiographical materials, a sequence of photographs, the whole kinship terminology collected in some way that transcends the particular type of analysis to be used, e.g., which includes recorded terms of address and of reference used within everyday life as well as terms given in response to a genealogical chart).

Householder (1952:260-61) brings out the crux of the issue (an issue that is still with us) in the following statement:

The book (and its title) raise an interesting metaphysical question. On the metaphysics of linguistics there are two extreme positions, which may be termed (and have been) the "God's truth" position and the "hocus-pocus" position. The theory of the "God's truth" linguists (and I regret to say I am one) is that a language *has* a structure, and the job of the linguist is (a) to find out what that structure is, and (b) to describe it as clearly, economically, and elegantly as he can, without at any point obscuring the God's truth structure of the language. The hocus-pocus linguist believes (or professes to believe—words and behavior are not always in harmony) that a language (better, a corpus since we describe only the corpus we know) is a mass of incoherent, formless data, and the job of the linguist is somehow to arrange and organize this mass, imposing on it some sort of structure (which must not, of course, be in any striking or obvious conflict with anything in

the data). Now it may be that these two metaphysical viewpoints are in some sense equivalent, but I suspect that there is at least a psychological effect of the metaphysics on the linguist (and above all, on the student of linguistics). If you look upon a language as a sort of elaborate building which you must map and plan as accurately as possible, so that later visitors may rapidly find their way about it with the aid of your plan, your whole attitude will have about it a respect for the facts, a humility, a patience, a desire for perfection, which is not as likely to be there if you think of a language as a certain select portion of a large pile of shapeless rocks which you may play with and rearrange to suit your fancy (provided you don't break too many of the rocks).

Now I conceive that the term "structural" implies a God's truth metaphysics, and Harris here and there pays his respects to this point of view, but I must also assert that many, many parts of the book seem to me pure hocus-pocus. Now a certain amount of hocus-pocus is fine; hocus-pocus is, so to speak, the pure mathematics for which the God's truth linguist (like a physicist) may at some time or other find a use. I think all linguists indulge in it frequently, for fun; and it is the greatest fun of linguistics.

It is remarkable that the same questions are still being raised today, as we shall see in the next section. Householder's statement set the stage for what was to become the center of many debates and polemics in cognitive studies.

It is important to keep in mind the following points concerning this period of time before we turn to the next epoch: (1) anthropologists and linguists were keenly aware of the implications of Harris' method as well as the problem that is encountered in the Sapir-Whorf hypothesis, though the two areas had not yet reached a nexus; (2) Harris continued applying his methodology to all aspects of language, including discourse structure and the interrelation of sentences (Z. S. Harris 1964*a*,

1964*b*);[8] and (3) though Whorf had started with an interest at the level of the word, cognitive studies in anthropology at this period focused on the psychological attributes of phonological (phonemic), morphological, and syntactic processes. The *word* was to have its day much later.

DEVELOPMENTS SINCE 1955

In retrospect, we can see that around 1955 there was a turning point in the attempts of anthropology and linguistics to understand and consequently to investigate the cognitive processes of man.

By 1955 the Sapir-Whorf hypothesis, as it had previously existed, had been laid to rest. Researchers had nearly abandoned the hope of demonstrating the influence of linguistic structures on the behavior of speakers. A conference had been held in Chicago in 1953 (Hoijer 1954) principally to discuss Whorf's ideas. Most of the participants generally agreed with Greenberg's proposals (given above) incorporated in the lead article in the published version of the conference (Greenberg 1961).[9] For the most part the debate and discussions on the topic subsided shortly after 1955, though positions of extreme relativism have continued up to the present time (Lounsbury 1969).

Z. S. Harris' previous researches had stimulated work in two directions, which until recently were conceived as two opposing approaches to cognitive analysis. After Householder's (1952) review of Harris' book (1951), many people must have come to the conclu-

---

[8] These works, introduced in 1952 and 1954, were still being revised in the middle and late fifties.

[9] It is worthy of note that only one book has appeared since that time which contains just the words *language* and *culture* in its title.

sion that they were in the "God's truth" camp, and consequently stopped reading Harris' works. On this Chomsky (1957:231) says:

It is interesting that since the "God's truth"-"hocus-pocus" distinction was suggested, every linguist who has committed himself has been on the side of God's truth. One suspects that terms like "game-playing" and "hocus-pocus" are nothing more than a most unfortunate and misleading way to damn opposing views without the annoying necessity for giving reasons. ⟵

In 1952 Harris extended his methods of componential analysis to discourse structure. His interest stemmed from two problems (Z. S. Harris 1964*a*:356-57): extending structural linguistics beyond the domain of the sentence into discourse analysis and correlating nonlinguistic and linguistic behavior (i.e., language and culture). While discourse analysis as such had been thought to be in the domain of linguistics prior to this time, descriptive linguistics had never felt that language and culture studies were within their domain, and in fact had no tools for taking the social situation into account.

One can readily see that componential analysis, which had been previously applied to phonology and morphology, was extended to discourse structure in Harris' (1964*a*:355-56) statement of his method. Whereas in phonology, Harris had attempted to extend the domain of phonemes, he now began to observe the privilege of occurrence of lexical items and syntactic structures in wider domains. This will inevitably lead any analyst to question how the same meaning gets manifested in different situations, how sentences are related, and how the native speaker intuits a relationship between these sentences. This type of analysis also points out differences of structure between different persons in different styles and subject matters.

By 1954 Harris (1964*b*) had a somewhat better grasp of discourse structure and had begun to examine distributional structure in natural languages. The distributional structures that Harris proposed are roughly equivalent to *syntax*, which linguists and logical positivists attempt to study. They were direct products of discourse analysis studies. The essence of Harris' *discourse analysis* was the examination of the relationship of sentences; e.g., how do we formally account for the relationship between the two sentences "John hit Jack" and "Jack was hit by John"?

By 1957 the outcome of these investigations was transformational grammar (Z. S. Harris 1964*c*), with sole emphasis on the syntactic processes of natural languages and total neglect of semantic structures.

However, what started out as a straightforward extension of the descriptive linguistic method dedicated to an attempt to further language and culture studies came to be opposed by many linguists, anthropologists, and anthropological linguists, since it was viewed by the critics in terms of God's truth vs. hocus-pocus. Much of the subsequent work by anthropological linguists continued without the new insights provided by Harris' discourse analysis and transformational grammar.

The practitioners of descriptive linguistics during the forties and fifties had concerned themselves very little with studies of larger scope than those dealing with sentences and language as a manifestation of human behavior.[10] Consequently, the years 1955-1957 were crucial, because the descriptive linguistics of the 1940s and 1950s was

being cast aside by a small group of linguists. The first general dissatisfaction with descriptive linguistics is seen in Chomsky's review (1957) of Hockett's *A Manual of Phonology* (1955), a whole compartment in the ballast of descriptive linguistics. The flavor of transformational grammar and its new goals can be caught in the criticism he offers:

1. A machine that would produce human language cannot be built on the basis of a vast amount of statistical information (which Hockett proposed) or on the basis of the relational frequency of occurrence of morpheme sequences. Something else is needed, since native speakers constantly produce *novel sentences* that they have never heard others use.
2. A statistical base fails to account for the *relationship between sentences* which a native speaker intuits.
3. The book lacks a careful and precise definition of the theoretical concepts of linguistics.
4. Objective criteria for the *validation and justification of grammars* is needed if linguistics is to be a serious science.
5. Grammatical research must be characterized as the attempt to reconstruct precisely and explicitly the *linguistic intuition* of the native speaker.

Chomsky's chief contribution during this period was to orient the new transformational grammar developed by Harris as well as linguistics in general toward a wider and deeper base in the social sciences. He accomplished this by bringing linguistics to bear directly on matters of philosophy, logic, mathematics, and psychology. An example of this wider focus can be seen in his review of B. F. Skinner's *Verbal Behavior* (1957), representing the bulwark of S-R psychology (Chomsky 1964). In

---

[10] This occurred during the postwar heydey of language teaching institutes that served as technical schools to universities and foreign area programs. Descriptive linguists were employed in these institutes, though there was little relation between their training and the languages they taught.

this review he utilizes the concepts developed in transformational grammar up to this point to attack the mechanisms postulated by the S-R psychologists for language behavior. In particular, he points out that while reinforcement, casual observation, natural inquisitiveness, and imitation are important factors in language acquisition, the concept of inborn structure, maturation, and learning are much more important. He argues that *Homo sapiens* has an innate capacity to handle information in certain specific ways—that experience is not the prime factor in the processing of information. This innate capacity would be of overwhelming importance in language acquisition. In summary, he states that while there are known neural structures that could handle innate knowledge, there is nothing known about language acquisition at the present time that would support the S-R hypothesis that a newborn child's mind is a *tabula rasa* upon which information is etched by the environment.

Some of the results of this expansion of linguistics into other fields has already been mentioned (Miller and McKean 1964, Brown and McNeill 1966, Lenneberg 1967). By 1965 the field of linguistics dominated by transformational grammar had the following goals well in view:

1. Since a native speaker constantly produces new utterances he has not heard before, a grammar must account for the infinite set of sentences that characterize a language (its "creative aspect") by a finite set of rules.
2. A grammar must account for the relationship of sentences that is intuitively felt by a native speaker, and linguistics must determine what types of models would lead to a grammar of this nature (Chomsky 1965*b*).
3. A theory of linguistics must account for the yet unexplained process of language acquisition in children.
4. A theory of linguistics must take into consideration universal grammar, a subject almost totally ignored since the time of Humboldt (Chomsky 1966).
5. A theory of linguistics (in conjunction with psychology) must investigate the biological bases of the universal grammar which is innate (Lenneberg 1967).

Componential analysis also had a significant impact on ethnography. During the crucial two years from 1955 to 1957, ethnographers were making great strides in applying componential analysis to lexical sets. Within this period three publications paved the way for an approach to the study of meaning through the componential analysis of lexical sets, kinship sets, and color categories (Conklin 1955, Goodenough 1956, and Lounsbury 1956). The strong influence of componential analysis can, of course, be seen earlier, in Goodenough (1951) and Conklin (1954). These earlier analyses were important because they explicitly focused the goals of anthropology on man's cognitive processing mechanisms. Goodenough (1956:195) says:

What do I have to know about A and B in order to say that A is B's cousin? Clearly, people have certain criteria in mind by which they make the judgment that A is or is not B's cousin. What the expression *his cousin* signifies is the particular set of criteria by which this judgment is made.

Further, Conklin (1955:343) states:

In short, we have seen that the apparent complexity of the Hanunóo color system can be reduced at the most generalized level to four basic terms which are associated with lightness, darkness, wetness, and dryness. This intracultural analysis demonstrates that what appears to be color "confusion" at first may result from an inadequate knowledge of the internal structure of a color system and from a failure to distinguish sharply between sensory reception on the one hand and perceptual categorization on the other.

In these works and others that followed (Frake 1961, Berlin and Romney 1964, Werner 1966, Metzger and Williams 1963, Tyler 1965, Black 1963, Buchler and Selby 1968a) we can see the beginning of what was to become a different focus in anthropology (Tyler 1969b:3), which

focuses on *discovering* how different peoples organize and use their cultures. This is not so much a search for some generalized unit of behavioral analysis as it is an attempt to understand the *organizing principles underlying behavior.* It is assumed that each people has a unique system for perceiving and organizing material phenomena—things, events, behavior, and emotions. . . . The object of study is not these material phenomena themselves, but the way they are organized in the minds of men. Cultures then are not material phenomena; they are cognitive organizations of material phenomena. Consequently, cultures are neither described by mere arbitrary lists of anatomical traits and institutions such as house type, family type, kinship type, economic type, and personality type, nor are they necessarily equated with some over-all integrative pattern of these phenomena. Such descriptions may tell us something about the way an anthropologist thinks about a culture, but there is little, if any, reason to believe that they tell us anything of how the people of some culture think about their culture.

In essence, cognitive anthropology seeks to answer two questions: What material phenomena are significant for the people of some culture; and, how do they organize these phenomena. Not only do cultures differ among one another in their organization of material phenomena, they differ as well in the kinds of material phenomena they organize. The people of different cultures may not recognize the same kinds of material phenomena as relevant, even though from an outsider's point of view the same material phenomena may be present in every case.

This focus was new in contrast to the foci of the present and immediate past, but in fact was a renewal of an interest present around the end of the nineteenth century.

Up until approximately 1959, componential analyses in the field of ethnography had been carried on along the lines used by Harris (1945). The methodology was simple and straightforward. In 1956, Lounsbury (1964) began to expand the method, just as Harris had expanded it to syntax a few years earlier (1964a). Whereas Harris had gone from phonology to discourse analysis, Lounsbury (1964:1088) extended the method from single denotata to multiple denotata within a field of meaning.

Componential analyses up to this time had dealt with single denotata, whereas linguistic analysis had mainly dealt with multiple denotata and consequently had been involved in the analysis of "allo-units." There are, in essence, two ways of handling allo-units: (1) by *total* and *class definitions,* and (2) by *basic member definitions* and *supplementary rules of extensions.* Again, the former had been in the domain of general linguistics in America for some time, while the latter was well known only in Europe, for the most part in the Prague school of linguistics. This latter analysis involves setting up a few members of a class as basic, or "primitives." These extensions are derived by either expansion or reduction rules; in some senses, the idea of a metaphor is invoked. Here are some examples of Lounsbury's (1964:1089) rules:

1. Skewing Rule: *Let any woman's brother, as linking relative, be regarded as equivalent to that woman's son, as linking relative.*

$$ ♀ \text{ B} \ldots \longrightarrow ♀ \text{ s} \ldots $$

From this follows a corollary stating the consequent relationship of the reciprocals: *Any male linking relative's sister will then be equivalent to that male linking relative's mother.*

$$\ldots \, \delta \, S \longrightarrow \ldots \, \delta \, M$$

2. Merging Rule: *Let any person's sibling of same sex as linking relative be equivalent to that person himself directly linked.*

$$\delta \, B \ldots \rightarrow \delta \ldots; \, ♀ \, S \ldots \rightarrow ♀ \ldots$$

From this follows the corollary pertaining to the reciprocals: *Any linking relative's sibling of same sex as himself (or herself) will then be equivalent to that relative himself (or herself) as an object of reference.*

$$\ldots \, \delta \, B \rightarrow \ldots \, \delta; \ldots \, ♀ \, S \rightarrow \ldots \, ♀$$

3. Half-sibling Rule: *Let any child of one of one's parents be regarded as one's sibling.*

$$Fs \longrightarrow B; Fd \longrightarrow S; Ms \longrightarrow B; Md \longrightarrow S$$

This rule contains its own reciprocal corollary. Of these three, the third one is—so far as I know—universal in kinship systems; the second is widespread ... but is by no means universal; while the first of these is the one of most restricted occurrence, being peculiar to this particular subvariety of so-called "Crow" systems, but being found in quite a number of unrelated systems in many parts of the world nonetheless.

The rules constitute an unordered set. When we scan the rules for applicability in reducing a kin-type, if any is applicable, there is never more than one that is applicable at any particular step in the reduction. And if we write them as expansion rules rather than as reduction (which can be done by merely reversing the arrows), all possible orders of application of the rules must be exploited in generating a system. Since the rules cannot come into conflict, there is no basis for ordering.

Even then, Lounsbury's methodology was not particularly foreign in linguistics, since Halle had set up the same system for phonology (principally morphophonemics) as early as 1959. The similarity between the two methods can be seen by comparing Lounsbury's rules with the phonological rules found in Halle (1959). These rules, originally called morpheme structure rules and later called readjustment and phonological rules (Chomsky and Halle 1968), utilized the fewest phonological features to explain the occurrence of phonological segments in the structure of morphemes. The novelty of Lounsbury's approach was the application of this methodology (not adapted necessarily from Halle) to semantic fields, which brought certain techniques out of "pure" linguistics into general anthropological review.

It is striking to note the similarity of Harris' early transformational grammar to Lounsbury's approach. Both analysts were attempting to handle metaphor; Harris was attempting to handle the problem of the relationship between sentences in syntax and Lounsbury was grappling with the problem at the level of semantics in the relationship of kin terms. Both were attempting to handle the relationship between morphemes within a limited field. But there were differences as well as similarities: Lounsbury was positing a solution for simultaneous events of human behavior (so-called semantic features) while Harris offered an explanation of sequential events of human behavior (so-called grammatical categories). From the facts that simultaneous events turn up not only in phonology but in semantics as well, and that simultaneous phonological events fall into sequential patterns (morphemes), we begin to get our first inklings of the principles of human cognitive organization. That is, the processes involved in the organization of grammar are pretty nearly the same as the processes involved in the organization of semantics (so-called "culture"), and are interdependent.

By 1964, when a conference was

held on componential analysis, there was some confusion as to the validity of such analyses for anthropology. In addition, it was difficult to define Lounsbury's new extensions (now called "formal semantic analyses"). It was mainly methodology that defined these approaches, a methodology that was rigorous and insisted on internal form and recognition of higher determinants of the domains being analyzed. These features are not surprising if we remember that the analyses developed within the field of linguistics (Hammel 1965:v). When we begin to apply the criteria of contrast, complementary distribution, and pattern congruity to any set of behavioral data, much less to semantics, we will encounter a methodology that is rigorous and internally consistent and which recognizes a series of structured higher determinants (witness the hierarchical structure found in the concepts of the morphophoneme, allomorphophone, morphophone, morpheme, allomorph, morph, phoneme, allophone, and phone).

Though the line between the two types of analysis is still difficult to determine, the main difference lies in the formalism involved in the "formal semantic analyses." As regards their importance for anthropology, they provided anthropologists with a method by which to return to a search for universals. Lounsbury's own analyses led him (1969:26-27) to take genealogical criteria in kinship analyses as essential for primary as well as nonmetaphoric expanded senses, rather than the nongenealogical criteria as the essential attributes of the meanings of kinship terms, as most anthropologists prefer. Whereas most anthropologists regard genealogical criteria as accidental attributes of some of the referents of kinship terms, Lounsbury regards the nongenealogical attributes of kinship terms as accidental. For further work carried

on in the universality of basic kin types, see Buchler and Selby (1968b) and Durbin and Saltarelli (1967).

During the same time period in which lexicon was beginning to offer insights to anthropologists, it was causing trouble for transformational grammar (Katz and Fodor 1964, Katz and Postal 1964). As early as 1963, Katz and Fodor's work indicated that transformational grammar, with its insistence on the centrality of syntax, was beginning to flounder, though up to this point very little attention had been given to semantics or to the lexicon of a language in general. Syntax was felt to be the central domain of language, while phonology and semantics were regarded as interpretive systems.

In 1965 Chomsky outlined the necessity of utilizing semantic features (though still as an interpretive component of syntax) in a grammar. The semantics he proposed, however, was not powerful enough to account for the subcategorical processes of natural languages. This gave rise to the "neo-semanticists" within the field of transformational grammar (see McCawley 1968). The problems of a semantic (rather than a syntactic) focus of a grammar are barely realized (see the transformational papers in Darden, Bailey, and Davison 1968; Binnick et al. 1969; Bach and Harms 1968). The problem of writing a grammar that begins with a semantic approach had already been outlined by Lamb (1965), but the difficulty basically lies in a lack of understanding as to what constitutes the universal set of semantic features that will be employed in such a grammar. Are there thousands of semantic features common to all cultures or only a couple of dozen, to which each individual culture adds perhaps five hundred more semantic features that are uniquely its own, utilized by no other culture? The general feeling among both anthropological and linguistic analysts is that if inroads could be made into the semantic systems underlying natural languages, then semantics would generate universal syntax. Universal syntax, in turn, would generate the surface structure of the phonology of a given language. This type of analysis for the new cognitive anthropologist would be equivalent to a description of culture, because he feels very strongly, as Tyler (1969b:2-3, 6) points out, that all earlier anthropological studies (typologies, definitions, diffusion, change and development, static descriptions), are

an index to another feature characteristic of this period in anthropology. Anthropologists were really much more concerned with discovering what anthropology was than, for example, what an Eskimo was. In a sense anthropologists were studying only one small culture—the culture of anthropology.

* * *

Many anthropologists have expressed an interest in how the natives see their world. Yet, there is a difference in focus between the old and the new. Where earlier anthropologists sought categories of description in their native language, cognitive anthropologists seek categories of description in the language of their natives. Ultimately, this is the old problem of what do we describe and how do we describe it. Obviously, we are interested in the mental codes of other peoples, but how do we infer those mental processes? Thus far, it has been assumed that the easiest entry to such processes is through language, and most of the recent studies have sought to discover codes that are mapped in language. Nearly all of this work has been concerned with how other peoples "name" the things in their environment and how these names are organized into larger groupings. These names are thus both an index to what is significant in the environment of some other people, and a means of discovering how these people organize their perceptions of the environment. Naming is seen as one of the chief methods for imposing order on perception.

In a very real sense, the anthropologist's problem is to discover how other people create order out of what appears to him to be utter chaos.

The spectre of God's truth and hocus-pocus has unfortunately been revived (Burling 1964, 1969) during the last few years, though we may hope that Hymes (1969) and Frake (1969) have laid it to rest again forever. Wallace (1965:231) points out that *the problem is really the psychological reality of the analyses of the cognitive anthropologists.* "One or many, their psychological validity—in distinction to their sociological, mineralogical, biological or whatever objective validities may be relevant—must be established by means independent of the mechanics internal to componential analysis itself."

The failure to establish such a system by such means, of course, is also related to the failure to establish a set of universal semantic features. But it appears that the time is not yet ripe for such an independent system, in spite of Wallace's plea for anthropologists to carry on experimental programs that would test the psychological validity of their analyses. There still remains a great amount of work to be done in the areas of lexicon and grammar; there still remains the task of reexamination of a great many myths in anthropology which have not yet been touched; and there remains the cleaning out of old myths that have only recently been attacked.

SUMMARY

In America during the past fifty years we have seen interests in language and culture studies gyrate from the word (Sapir 1949a) to phonology (Sapir 1949b) back to the word (Whorf 1956b), to morphology and syntax (the Sapir-Whorf hypothesis), and most recently again to the word. Componential analysis has been utilized as the principal technique for many of the domains of language and culture studies. One of its extensions, transformational grammar, was intended primarily for syntax, but can and has been utilized also for lexicon in relation to language and culture studies (M. A. Durbin 1970) The other extension of componential analysis, formal semantic analysis, has been utilized principally for lexicon studies. However, we see its parallel has been used in phonology (Halle 1959), resulting in what might be labeled "formal phonological analysis," though it is usually called "transformational phonology" (Postal 1968).

These two new developments out of componential analysis—transformational grammar and formal semantic analysis—are so intertwined in their methodologies that it is impossible for any serious researcher in the field to ignore one or the other. Both have arrived at the point where the lexicon of a language or culture—its *words,* its *lexemes*—is the central focus. These methodologies have led researchers in both anthropology and linguistics to focus not only on the same data—lexicon—but also on the same goals. They have led us to question our myths concerning the relativity of culture and languages (Lounsbury 1969 and references therein; Tyler 1969*b*), ethnocentrism (Lounsbury 1969), and the nongenealogical bases of kinship systems (Lounsbury 1969, Tyler 1969*b*, Conklin 1969). More than ever before both fields have turned toward a search for universals. Many of the universals posited in one field of endeavor have relevance for the other (Fillmore 1968:24). The overall goal of both fields at the present time is to understand the way in which man processes information from his surrounding environment (Bolinger 1965). The proposed method in cognitive anthropology is through

the mnemonic device—human language. Tyler's (1969*b*) warning that the object we study is also the instrument of our studies must always be kept in mind. All the same, as Tyler (1969*b*:77) points out, this should not deter us or discourage us from these studies, since the "metalanguage" myths we are using at the present time are "more complete and consistent than previous myths."

The cognitive anthropological approach differs radically from prior approaches to language and culture, even though one may desire to compare it to emics and etics, ethnosemantics (M. Harris 1968:568-604), the Sapir=Whorf hypothesis, ethnolinguistics, or ethnoscience. In the first place, cognitive anthropologists simply do not care about the "psychological validity" problem because they do not believe it is knowable (Tyler 1969*b*:77). To dwell endlessly on psychological validity and God's truth versus hocus-pocus only distracts one from the goal of establishing a system that explains (not necessarily replicates) human behavior. Early transformational grammarians encountered the same problem. Descriptive linguists consistently wanted to believe "real structures" existed in the minds of speakers in the forms of transformational rules. One only has to read Z. S. Harris' (1945) reanalysis of Hoijer's (1945) Navaho to discern that psychological validity does not fall within the domain of his motivations.

Second, the search for the universals of human behavior does not imply endless lists from assorted (or all) cultures and languages in the world. Anthropologists generally are so oriented toward "lists" in their methodological and theoretical endeavors that they encounter great difficulties in understanding universals from the cognitive point of view. A universal is not an empirical fact, nor is it something as undefinable as the institution of marriage (which falls in the category of what A. L. Kroeber called a fake universal [Geertz 1970:53]). Rather, marriage is an abstract formal system that would explain the mating of couples as well as a host of other "cultural" phenomena. Furthermore, one can reveal this universal on the basis of one culture or language without necessary recourse to other systems, mainly on the grounds that the analyst himself operates within the confines and constraints of a similar system that is derived from the same underlying universals. Further, it is useless to peel off layer after layer of man in our search for universals, nor can universals be established by a consensus of all mankind (Geertz 1970). Though he starts from an entirely different approach to human behavior, Geertz (1970:56) ends up nevertheless with nearly the same concept of universals as that expressed by transformational grammarians and cognitive anthropologists:

The notion that unless a cultural phenomenon is empirically universal it cannot reflect anything about the nature of man is about as logical as the notion that because sickle-cell anemia is, fortunately, not universal it cannot tell us anything about human genetic processes. It is not whether phenomena are empirically common that is critical in science—else why should Becquerel have been so interested in peculiar behavior in uranium? —but whether they can be made to reveal the enduring natural processes that underlie them. Seeing heaven in a grain of sand is not a trick only poets can accomplish.

In short, we need to look for systematic relationships among diverse phenomena, not for substantive identities among similar ones. And to do that with any effectiveness, we need to replace the "stratigraphic" conception of the relations between the various aspects of human existence with a synthetic one; that is, one in which biological, psychological, sociological and cultural factors can be treated as variables within unitary systems of analysis.

An excellent example of the quest for universals along these lines can be seen in the universality of color categories (Berlin and Kay 1969).

The third major difference between cognitive anthropology and prior approaches lies in its methodology. Cognitive anthropology insists that mindless fact-gathering and data-collecting as ends unto themselves are useless. If new data are to be collected, then they should be collected only to satisfy the demands of the theory. Field methods proper do not lie within the domain of cognitive anthropology. Once the data have been collected, they are usually subjected to two or three levels of analysis in regard to higher-order abstractions before they are properly considered as raw data for the cognitive anthropologist. For example, the data that Lounsbury used in his studies were already at least two levels of abstraction removed from the field situation.

It is now necessary to ask whether these gyrations of the past fifty years, and particularly the past fifteen, represent a recursive feeding upon old ideas, allowing new approaches no opportunity to emerge. This would be true if (1) each new phase had been an eclectic rehashing of prior approaches, (2) the goals of the field had remained the same, and (3) no new insights had been offered by the so-called cyclic changes to the new theory. None of these are true. There has been no eclecticism. In both linguistics and anthropology there has been an outright casting aside of earlier methods and goals. We can see this first in Z. S. Harris (1964a), who cast aside the goals of linguistics but kept its methodology, while Chomsky, building on Harris' work, cast aside both the methods and the goals. The same has been true in formal semantic analysis. The goals of neither linguists nor cognitive anthropologists have remained the same during this period. It is true that we have returned to the goals of Boas, but with much sharper methods. The insights that have been offered during this period have stemmed from a growing awareness that "culture" is best seen as a set of control mechanisms—plans, recipes, rules, instructions—which are the principal bases for the specificity of behavior and an essential condition for governing it (Geertz 1970:57). The key term here is *rules*. We have become aware that rules governing behavior are of several types. Briefly, they can be reduced (though there is a continuum, no doubt) to *simultaneous* rule behavior (for a detailed explication of the formulation of simultaneous rule behavior, see Buchler and Selby 1968b:191-217) and *sequential* rule behavior. Buchler and Selby (1968b:191) point out that simultaneous rule behavior is utilized in that domain of human behavior "whose significance cannot be inferred from a knowledge of anything else in language, specifically from its grammatical structure"—i.e., the *word* or the *lexeme*. It must be remembered that in 1965 transformational grammar ran into difficulties precisely on the grounds of the lexical item whose meaning could not be milked from syntactic structures despite all of Chomsky's attempts. Simultaneous rule behavior involves a clustering of distinctive features (as seen in earlier componential analysis) which are unordered but exist in particular relations to each other (Lounsbury 1964). Neither the nature of the extent of the simultaneous features nor the logical relations between them are yet well understood.

Sequential rule behavior is better understood as exemplified by long years of work in syntax and logic. Here we have a rigidly ordered concatenation of units. Concatenation, a cover word for several types of logical relations, has been utilized in tagmemics, immediate constituent analysis, Chinese boxes, parsing, and most recently by transformational grammar, which imposed a set of formal operations (transformations) upon the concatenations. But the point previously missed in anthropology and linguistics was that human behavior is neither a bundle of simultaneous features nor a sequence of units, but a complex (not necessarily linear) interaction of units (composed of features) in a linear or time sequence. One without the other becomes a vacuous concept. Knowledge of the semantics of a kinship term outside the daily flow of life (its usage) (Tyler 1969b) or a grammar composed of syntax without the knowledge of the meanings of its words does not provide a very useful explanation of human behavior. One cannot justifiably criticize researchers in these areas for complete concentration on one area or the other, since it is exactly these in-depth independent foci that brought us the realization that the two phenomena (simultaneous rules and sequential rules) are completely interdependent. As it turns out also, the same logical relations that weld features into a unit also bind units together in a sequence; i.e., the same cement is used for syntax as for semantics. This was first brought to the attention of cognitive anthropology by Hymes (1964) in his plea for an "ethnography of communication" (sometimes called sociolinguistics, though the former term is more apt, since its special focus is the functions of language in a speech community). It is in the *functions* of language that we see most clearly the complete nexus of a total interdependence of simultaneous rules and sequential rules, though they are readily observable elsewhere. When we reduce the functions of a language to a bare minimum we simultaneously reduce its lexical items (simultaneous rule manifestation) and its syntax (sequential rule manifestation), as seen in pidgin languages. When we crank up the functions of a pidgin language, however, the complexity of its lexical items as well as of its syntax are increased, as observed in Creole languages. Hymes (1964) has stated what has been said throughout this paper, that culture and communication are the same. Hymes (1964:11) maintains that a focus on *function* must involve changes in the orientation of linguists which include emphases on the structure of speech, rather than the structure of language; function as a source of structure, rather than function as a derivative; function as a reality in ethnography, rather than postulated or ascribed; the nonarbitrariness of structures and messages in language, rather than their arbitrariness, which is now stressed; and function as a source of differential structural perspectives and organizations, among other shifts in emphasis.

Some works that typify what Hymes proposed have been recently presented: Fischer (1964), Gumperz (1964), and Bernstein (1964).

It is obvious, as Hymes notes (1964:3), that a study of this sort is tantamount to a new field that would give linguistics a much wider base than it enjoys even now. To see the field in such a wide view allows for a general science of signs, signals, symbols, codes, and communication within which all animal (including human) behavior can be viewed (Sebeok 1962; Sebeok et al., eds., 1964).[11]

For all these reasons I can say with confidence that cognitive anthropology, far from traveling in circles, has made long strides forward during the past fifty years.

In the search for universals of human behavior, one area that strongly merits the attention of anthropologists is for the most part ignored: *sound* or *pho-*

netic symbolism. In his investigations of lexicostatistics, Morris Swadesh (1964a, 1971; see also Gudschinsky 1956, Hymes 1960a) became aware of the fact that many phonologically similar consonant-vowel-consonant (-vowel) sequences were also semantically similar. These sequences occurred in various unrelated languages throughout the world. His investigations (1964b:542) led him to conclusions such as the following:

Besides indicating near and far, in space and time, apparently vowel change once represented physical form, as follows: the vowel sound *i,* more or less as in *stick,* expressed what was thin or pointed; the vowel *u,* as in *Lulu,* expressed cylindrical or round shape; vowel *a,* pronounced not as in *flat* but as in *father,* expressed what was flat or extended. One can give some examples of such words in English, but the old use must have applied to all words, so that for instance **piki* was a *pointed bone* or a *feather,* *puku a *cylindrical* or *round bone,* *paka a *flat bone.* However, there was no strong division between the names of things and actions, so that *piki might also refer to thrusting with a point, *puku with a round thing, *paka with the flat. It is possible that this system does not exist anywhere today in the form in which we have reconstructed it, but ample evidence of its existence in the past has been found, for example, in Altaic, of Asia, and Wakashan, of North America.

In some languages there has been a change of function, as in Huave, where a front vowel represents a small thing or a brief action, and a back vowel, a large thing or abundant action. In some Altaic languages the difference between *i* and *a* marks a difference of sex, except that different languages of the group show opposite sex interpretations—for example, some think of the man as broad-shouldered and the woman as slender, others of the woman as broad in the hip and the man as thin. . . . In efforts to compare widely different languages in the past, one of the great obstacles was the difficulty of getting the phonemes to match according to strict equation in the way that the comparative linguist requires in order to prove relationships. The

---

[11] The broadening of the field can be seen by the appearance of the journal *Semiotics.*

clue to the problem is now before us. It is due to the old phoneme alternation, liquidated in different fashions in different regions in the process of stretching out the root inventory of the old-type languages. Having this key in our hands, we know that we may expect to find different old variants for the same or similar meanings, like English *stick*, Nutka *tlaga-pt* tree, and Mayan *te'* tree, all based on the old archiform **teke* but with three different variants: the English on **t'ek'o* with an old *s* demonstrative as prefix, the Nutka on **taqa*, the Mayan on **taq'i*. The recognition of old alternations does not eliminate the possibility of finding exact variants but only warns us that they may show changed meanings. To give but one example, Nutka *tlaqa-pt* tree compares with Nahua *tlaka-tl* man, so called evidently because of his erect stance.

Most workers in the field (Bolinger 1950, Brown 1958, Hymes 1960*b*, and Jakobson 1960, 1965 are exceptions) feel that the matter should be dismissed immediately because of the general dictum that the relationship between sound and sense is arbitrary. But the implications of the observations made by Swadesh are too serious to be lightly dismissed. First, the phenomenon found in purely oligosynthetic languages (such as Hebrew, Arabic, Maya, Nahuatl) must be explained. Second, all languages are oligosynthetic in varying degrees (witness the stride-straddle-saddle-spraddle-spray . . . complex in English, which Bolinger [1950] calls a word-cancer). Third, how can we explain the fact that if a basic stem (non-inflectional) begins with a stop, the probability is much higher than expected that it will end with a non-plosive and vice versa in many languages of the world (particularly the purely oligosynthetic languages)? Why are there permissible sound occurrences that do not occur? Why are there non-permissible occurrences of sound and why do they differ from language to language? All these questions, I believe, are related to modes of human

perception that intimately link sound and sense. The following phonological similarities within *each* language corresponding to a general semantic field illustrate some of the potentialities of this area of research. These kinds of data are usually cast aside as "curious linguistic accidents." They are too numerous in the languages of the world to be accidents.

English:	sa*n*d	
	sa*l*t	
Spanish:	ha*r*ina	(flour)
	a*r*ena	(sand)
Gujarati:	re*ṇ*a	(sand, pollen)
	lu*ṇ*	(salt)
	lo*ṭ*	(flour)
Yucatec:	ta'ab	(salt)
Maya:	sa'am	(sand)
	ta'am	(ground limestone used for whitewash)

As Swadesh pointed out, examples of this type will not satisfy the comparative method, but the results of investigations in this area may help provide universals theory with a small working set of semantic features that would also aid in understanding individual languages as well. In the above examples,

$$\begin{bmatrix} + \text{ alveolarity} \\ - \text{ nasality} \end{bmatrix} + \begin{bmatrix} + \text{ alveolarity} \\ + \text{ nasality} \end{bmatrix}$$

generally characterize fine, grainy, powdery objects. Further, in Gujarati and Yucatecan Maya we see (in the same position) the corresponding non-nasal homorganic stop (lo*ṭ* and ta'a*b*, respectively) distinguish one item from the other two, while the mode of articulation, *l* versus *r* in Gujarati and *t* versus *s* in Yucatecan Maya, distinguishes still another category.

Observations of this nature based upon phonology will undoubtedly lead us to a better understanding of the universal perceptual categories of human beings in general as well as a better understanding of the semantics of individual languages, a goal that is much desired and in line with a search for the ways in which *Homo sapiens* processes stimuli from his surrounding environment.

REFERENCES

Bach, Emmon, and Robert T. Harms, eds.
1968 *Universals in Linguistic Theory.* New York: Holt, Rinehart & Winston.
Bar-Hillel, Yehoshua
1954 Logical Syntax and Semantics. *Language* 30:230-37.
Berlin, Brent, and Paul Kay
1969 *Basic Color Terms: Their Universality and Evolution.* Berkeley: University of California Press.
Berlin, Brent, and A. Kimball Romney
1964 The Descriptive Semantics of Tzeltal Numeral Classifiers. In *Transcultural Studies in Cognition,* ed. A. K. Romney and R. G. D'Andrade. *American Anthropologist* 66, no. 3, pt. 2:79-98 (special issue).
Bernstein, Basil
1964 Elaborated and Restricted Codes: Their Social Origins and Some Consequences. In *The Ethnography of Communication,* ed. J. Gumperz and D. Hymes. *American Anthropologist* 66, no. 6, pt. 2 (special issue).
Binnick, Robert I., A. Davison, G. M. Green, and J. L. Morgan
1969 Papers presented at the fifth regional meeting of the Chicago Linguistic Society. Department of Linguistics, University of Chicago.
Black, Mary
1963 On Formal Ethnographic Procedures. *American Anthropologist* 65:1347-51.
Bloomfield, Leonard
1933 *Language.* New York: Holt, Rinehart & Winston.
Bolinger, Dwight L.
1950 Rime, Assonance, and Morpheme Analysis. *Word* 6:117-36.

1965 The Atomization of Meaning. *Language* 41:553-73.
Brown, R. W.
1958 *Words and Things.* Glencoe, Ill: Free Press.
Brown, Roger, and David McNeill
1966 The "Tip of the Tongue" Phenomenon. *Journal of Verbal Learning and Verbal Behavior* 5:325-37.
Buchler, Ira R., and Henry A. Selby
1968a *A Formal Study of Myth.* Monograph Series no. 1, Center for Intercultural Studies in Folklore and Oral History. Austin: University of Texas.
1968b *Kinship and Social Organization: An Introduction to Theory and Method.* New York: Macmillan.
Burke, Kenneth
1967 *The Philosophy of Literary Form,* 2nd ed. Baton Rouge: Louisiana State University Press.
Burling, Robbins
1964 Rejoinder (to Hymes and Frake). *American Anthropologist* 66:120-22.
1969 Cognition and Componential Analysis: God's Truth or Hocus-Pocus? In *Cognitive Anthropology,* ed. Stephen A. Tyler, pp. 419-28. New York: Holt, Rinehart & Winston. Originally published 1964.
Carnap, Rudolph
1956 *Meaning and Necessity.* Chicago: University of Chicago Press.
Carroll, John B., ed.
1956 *Language, Thought, and Reality: Selected Writings of Benjamin Lee Whorf.* Cambridge: M.I.T. Press.
Chao, Yuen-ren
1958 The Non-Uniqueness of Phonemic Solutions of Phonetic Systems. In *Readings in Linguistics,* ed. Martin Joos, pp. 38-54. New York: American Council of Learned Societies. Originally published 1934.
Chapple, Eliot D.
1970 *Culture and Biological Man: Explorations in Behavioral Anthropology.* New York: Holt, Rinehart & Winston.
Chomsky, Noam
1957 Review of C. F. Hockett, *A Manual of Phonology.* International Journal of American Linguistics 23:223-34.
1964 Review of B. F. Skinner, *Verbal Be-*

havior. In *The Structure of Language: Readings in the Philosophy of Language,* ed. Jerry A. Fodor and Jerrold J. Katz, pp. 547-78. Englewood Cliffs, N.J.: Prentice-Hall. Originally published 1959.

1965a *Aspects of the Theory of Syntax.* Cambridge: M.I.T. Press.

1965b Three Models for the Description of Language. In *Readings in Mathematical Psychology,* ed. R. Duncan Luce, Robert R. Bush, and Eugene Galanter, vol. 2, pp. 105-24. New York: Wiley. Originally published 1956.

1966 *Cartesian Linguistics.* New York: Harper & Row.

Chomsky, N., and M. Halle
1965 Some Controversial Questions in Phonological Theory. *Journal of Linguistics* 1:97-138.

1968 *The Sound Pattern of English.* New York: Harper & Row.

Chomsky, N., and George A. Miller
1965 Finite State Languages. In *Readings in Mathematical Psychology,* ed. R. Duncan Luce, Robert R. Bush, and Eugene Galanter, vol. 2, pp. 156-71. New York: Wiley. Originally published 1958.

Conklin, Harold C.
1954 An Ethnoecological Approach to Shifting Agriculture. *Transactions of the New York Academy of Sciences,* Series 2, vol. 17:133-42.

1955 Hanunóo Color Categories. *Southwestern Journal of Anthropology* 11:339-44.

1969 Ethnogenealogical Method. In *Cognitive Anthropology,* ed. Stephen A. Tyler, pp. 93-122. New York: Holt, Rinehart & Winston. Originally published 1964.

Darden, Bill J., Charles-James N. Bailey, and Alice Davison
1968 Papers presented at the fourth regional meeting of the Chicago Linguistic Society. Department of Linguistics, University of Chicago.

Durbin, Marshall, and Mario Saltarelli
1967 Patterns in Kinship. *Anthropological Linguistics* 9:6-14.

Durbin, Mridula A.
1970 The Transformational Model of Linguistics and Its Implications for an

Ethnology of Religion: A Case Study of Jainism. *American Anthropologist* 72:334-42.

Empson, William
1930 *Seven Types of Ambiguity.* New York: New Directions.

1967 *The Structure of Complex Words.* Ann Arbor: University of Michigan Press.

Fabre d'Olivet, Antoine
1921 *The Hebraic Tongue Restored,* trans. Louise Nayan Redfield. New York: Putnam. Originally published 1815-1816.

Fillmore, Charles J.
1968 The Case for Case. In *Universals in Linguistic Theory,* ed. Emmon Bach and Robert T. Harms, pp. 1-88. New York: Holt, Rinehart & Winston.

Fischer, J. L.
1964 Some Japanese Families. In *The Ethnography of Communication,* ed. J. Gumperz and D. Hymes. *American Anthropologist* 66, no. 6, pt. 2 (special issue).

Fodor, Jerry A., and Jerrold J. Katz, eds.
1964 *The Structure of Language: Readings in the Philosophy of Language.* Englewood Cliffs, N.J.: Prentice-Hall.

Frake, Charles O.
1961 The Diagnosis of Disease Among the Subanun of Mindanao. *American Anthropologist* 63:113-32.

1969 Further Discussion on Burling. In *Cognitive Anthropology,* ed. Stephen A. Tyler, p. 432. New York: Holt, Rinehart & Winston. Originally published 1964.

Garfinkel, Harold
1964 Studies of the Routine Grounds of Everyday Activities. *Social Problems* 11:225-50.

Geertz, Clifford
1970 The Impact of the Concept of Culture on the Concept of Man. In *Man Makes Sense,* ed. E. A. Hammel and William S. Simmons, pp. 47-65. Boston: Little, Brown. Originally published 1965.

Goodenough, Ward H.
1951 *Property, Kin, and Community on Truk.* Yale University Publications in Anthropology no. 46.

1956 Componental Analysis and the

Study of Meaning. *Language* 32:195-216.

Greenberg, Joseph H.
1961 Concerning Inferences from Linguistic to Nonlinguistic Data. In *Psycho-Linguistics: A Book of Readings,* ed. Sol Saporta, pp. 468-80. New York: Holt, Rinehart & Winston. Originally published 1954.

Gudschinsky, Sarah C.
1964 The ABC's of Lexicostatistics (Glottochronology). In *Language in Culture and Society,* ed. Dell Hymes, pp. 612-22. New York: Harper & Row. Originally published 1956.

Gumperz, John J.
1964 Linguist and Social Interaction in Two Communities. In *The Ethnography of Communication,* ed. J. Gumperz and D. Hymes. *American Anthropologist* 66, no. 6, pt. 2 (special issue).

Halle, Morris
1959 *The Sound Pattern of Russian.* The Hague: Mouton.

Hamilton, Edith, and Huntington Cairns
1961 *The Collected Dialogues of Plato, Including the Letters.* New York: Bollingen Foundation.

Hammel, E. A., ed.
1965 *Formal Semantic Analysis. American Anthropologist* 67, no. 5, pt. 2 (special issue).

Harris, Marvin
1968 *The Rise of Anthropological Theory.* New York: Crowell.

Harris, Zellig S.
1945 Navaho Phonology and Hoijer's Analysis. *International Journal of American Linguistics* 11:239-46.
1951 *Methods in Structural Linguistics.* Chicago: University of Chicago Press.
1958a Morpheme Alternants in Linguistic Analysis. In *Readings in Linguistics,* ed. Martin Joos, pp. 109-15. New York: American Council of Learned Societies. Originally published 1942.
1958b Simultaneous Components in Phonology. In *Readings in Linguistics,* ed. Martin Joos, pp. 124-37. New York: American Council of Learned Societies. Originally published 1944.
1962 *String Analysis of Sentence Structure.* The Hague: Mouton.
1964a Discourse Analysis. In *The Structure of Language,* ed. Jerry A. Fodor and Jerrold J. Katz, pp. 355-83. Englewood Cliffs, N.J.: Prentice-Hall. Originally published 1952.
1964b Distributional Structure. In *The Structure of Language,* ed. Jerry A. Fodor and Jerrold J. Katz, pp. 33-49. Englewood Cliffs, N. J.: Prentice-Hall. Originally published 1954.
1964c Co-occurrence and Transformation in Linguistic Structure. In *The Structure of Language,* ed. Jerry A. Fodor and Jerrold J. Katz, pp. 155-210. Englewood Cliffs, N. J.: Prentice-Hall. Originally published 1957.

Hockett, Charles F.
1947 Componential Analysis of Sierra Popoluca. *International Journal of American Linguistics* 13:258-67.
1955 *A Manual of Phonology.* Indiana University Publications in Anthropology and Linguistics, Memoir no. 11.

Hoijer, Harry
1945 *Navaho Phonology.* University of New Mexico Publications in Anthropology no. 1. Albuquerque: University of New Mexico Press.

Hoijer, Harry, ed.
1954 *Language in Culture.* Comparative Studies of Cultures and Civilizations no. 3; Memoirs of the American Anthropological Association no. 79. Chicago: University of Chicago Press.

Hook, Sidney, ed.
1969 *Language and Philosophy.* New York: New York University Press.

Householder, Fred W., Jr.
1952 Review of Zellig S. Harris' *Methods in Structural Linguistics. International Journal of American Linguistics* 18:260-68. Bobbs-Merrill Language Reprint Series no. 51.
1965 On Some Recent Claims in Phonological Theory. *Journal of Linguistics* 1:13-34.

Hymes, Dell
1960a Lexicostatistics So Far. *Current Anthropology* 1:3-44.
1960b Phonological Aspects of Style: Some English Sonnets. In *Style in Language,* ed. T. A. Sebeok, pp. 107-31. Cambridge: M.I.T. Press.
1964 Introduction: Toward Ethnographies of Communication. In *The Ethnography of Communication,* ed. John J.

Gumperz and Dell Hymes. *American Anthropologist* 66, no. 6, pt. 2:1-34 (special issue).

1969 Discussion of Burling's Paper. In *Cognitive Anthropology*, ed. Stephen A. Tyler, pp. 428-31. New York: Holt, Rinehart & Winston. Originally published 1964.

Hymes, Dell, ed.
1964 *Language in Culture and Society.* New York: Harper & Row.

Jakobson, Roman
1960 Closing Statement, Linguistics and Poetics. In *Style in Language*, ed. T. A. Sebeok, pp. 350-77. Cambridge: M.I.T. Press.
1965 Quest for the Essence of Language. In *Problems of Language. Diogenes* 51:21-37.

Jakobson, Roman, C. Fant, and M. Halle
1951 *Preliminaries to Speech Analysis: The Distinctive Features and Their Correlates.* Cambridge: M.I.T. Press.

Joos, Martin, ed.
1958 *Readings in Linguistics: The Development of Descriptive Linguistics in America Since 1925.* New York: American Council of Learned Societies.

Katz, Jerrold J.
1966 *The Philosophy of Language.* New York: Harper & Row.

Katz, Jerrold J., and Jerry A. Fodor
1964 The Structure of a Semantic Theory. In *The Structure of Language*, ed. Jerry A. Fodor and Jerrold J. Katz, pp. 479-518. Englewood Cliffs, N.J.: Prentice-Hall. Originally published 1963.

Katz, Jerrold J., and Paul M. Postal
1964 *An Integrated Theory of Linguistic Descriptions.* Cambridge: M.I.T. Press.

Kellogg, W. N., and L. I. Kellogg
1933 *The Ape and the Child: A Study of Environmental Influence upon Early Behavior.* New York: McGraw-Hill.

Kroeber, A. L., and C. Kluckhohn
1963 *Culture: A Critical Review of Concepts and Definitions.* New York: Random House.

Lamb, Sydney M.
1965 Kinship Terminology and Linguistic Structure. In *Formal Semantic Analysis,* ed. E. A. Hammel. *American Anthropologist* 67, no. 5, pt. 2:37-64 (special issue).

Lenneberg, Eric H.
1953 Cognition in Ethnolinguistics. *Language* 29:463-71.
1964 The Capacity for Language Acquisition. In *The Structure of Language,* ed. Jerry A. Fodor and Jerrold J. Katz, pp. 579-603. Englewood Cliffs, N.J.: Prentice-Hall.
1967 *Biological Foundations of Language.* New York: Wiley.

Lévi-Strauss, Claude
1967 *Structural Anthropology,* trans. Claire Jacobson and Brooke Grundfest Schoepf. Garden City, N.Y.: Doubleday Anchor Books. Originally published 1958.

Lounsbury, Floyd G.
1956 A Semantic Analysis of the Pawnee Kinship Usage. *Language* 32:158-94.
1964 The Structural Analysis of Kinship Semantics. In *Proceedings of the Ninth International Congress of Linguists, Cambridge, Mass., 1962,* ed. Horace G. Lunt, pp. 1073-90. The Hague: Mouton.
1969 Language and Culture. In *Language and Philosophy,* ed. Sidney Hook, pp. 3-29. New York: New York University Press.

McCawley, James D.
1968 The Role of Semantics in a Grammar. In *Universals in Linguistic Theory,* ed. Emmon Bach and Robert T. Harms, pp. 124-69. New York: Holt, Rinehart & Winston.

Mandelbaum, David G., ed.
1949 *Selected Writings of Edward Sapir.* Berkeley: University of California Press.

Marshall, Alexander Jones
1954 *Bower-Birds: Their Displays and Breeding Cycles.* Oxford: Clarendon Press.

Mathiot, Madeleine
1968 *An Approach to the Cognitive Study of Language. International Journal of American Linguistics* 34, no. 1, publication 45. Bloomington: Indiana University Research Center in Anthropology, Folklore, and Linguistics.

Mead, George Herbert

1934 *Mind, Self, and Society.* Chicago: University of Chicago Press.

Mead, Margaret
1952 Review of Zellig S. Harris' *Methods in Structural Linguistics. International Journal of American Linguistics* 18:257-60.

Metzger, Duane, and G. E. Williams
1963 A Formal Ethnographic Study of Tenejapa Ladino Weddings. *American Anthropologist* 65:1076-1101.

Micklin, Michael, and Marshall Durbin
1969 Syntactic Dimensions of Attitude Scaling Techniques: Sources of Variation and Bias. *Sociometry* 32:194-206.

Miller, George A.
1951 *Language and Communication.* New York: McGraw-Hill.
1956 The Magical Number Seven, Plus or Minus Two: Some Limits on Our Capacity for Processing Information. *Psychological Review* 63:81-97.
1961 Free Recall of Redundant Strings of Letters. In *Psycholinguistics: A Book of Readings,* ed. Sol Saporta, pp. 207-13. New York: Holt, Rinehart & Winston. Originally published 1958.

Miller, George A., and K. O. McKean
1964 A Chronometric Study of Some Relations Between Sentences. *Quarterly Journal of Experimental Psychology* 16:297-308.

Miller, George A., and Jennifer A. Selfridge
1961 Verbal Context and the Recall of Meaningful Material. In *Psycholinguistics: A Book of Readings,* ed. Sol Saporta, pp. 198-206. New York: Holt, Rinehart & Winston. Originally published 1953.

Mills, C. Wright
1939 Language, Logic, and Culture. *American Sociological Review* 4:670-80.

Newman, John B.
1966 A Rationale for a Definition of Communication. In *Communication and Culture,* ed. Alfred G. Smith, pp. 55-63. New York: Holt, Rinehart & Winston. Originally published 1960.

Osgood, C. E., and T. A. Sebeok
1965 *Psycholinguistics: A Survey of Theory and Research Problems with a Survey of Psycholinguistic Research, 1954-1964, by A. Richard Diebold and the Psycholinguists by G. A. Miller.* Bloomington: Indiana University Press.

Postal, Paul
1968 *Aspects of Phonological Theory.* New York: Harper & Row.

Quine, Willard van Orman
1960 *Word and Object.* Cambridge: M.I.T. Press.

Romney, A. Kimball, and Roy G. D'Andrade, eds.
1964 *Transcultural Studies in Cognition. American Anthropologist* 66, no. 3, pt. 2 (special issue).

Ryle, G.
1953 Ordinary Language. *Philosophical Review,* 62, no. 2.

Sapir, Edward
1949a Language and Environment. In *Selected Writings of Edward Sapir,* ed. David G. Mandelbaum, pp. 89-103. Berkeley: University of California Press. Originally published 1912.
1949b The Psychological Reality of Phonemes. In *Selected Writings of Edward Sapir,* ed. David G. Mandelbaum, pp. 46-60. Berkeley: University of California Press. Originally published 1933.

Saporta, Sol, ed.
1961 *Psycholinguistics: A Book of Readings.* New York: Holt, Rinehart & Winston.

Sebeok, Thomas A., ed.
1960 *Style in Language.* Cambridge: M.I.T. Press.
1962 Coding in the Evolution of Signaling Behavior. *Behavioral Science* 7:430-42.

Sebeok, T. A., A. S. Hayes, and Mary C. Bateson, eds.
1964 *Approaches to Semiotics.* The Hague: Mouton.

Skinner, B. F.
1957 *Verbal Behavior.* New York: Appleton-Century-Crofts.

Smith, Alfred G., ed.
1966 *Communication and Culture.* New York: Holt, Rinehart & Winston.

Swadesh, Morris
1964a Linguistics as an Instrument of Prehistory. In *Language in Culture and Society,* ed. Dell Hymes, pp. 575-83. New York: Harper & Row. Originally

published 1959.

1964b Linguistic Overview. In *Prehistoric Man in the New World*, ed. Jesse D. Jennings and Edward Norbeck, pp. 527-56. Chicago: University of Chicago Press.

1971 *The Origin and Diversification of Language*, ed. Joel Sherzer. Chicago: Aldine-Atherton.

Twadell, W. Freeman

1958 On Defining the Phoneme. In *Readings in Linguistics*, ed. Martin Joos, pp. 55-79. New York: American Council of Learned Societies. Originally published 1935.

Tyler, Stephen A.

1965 Koya Language Morphology and Patterns of Kinship Behavior. *American Anthropologist* 67:1428-40.

1969a *Cognitive Anthropology*. New York: Holt, Rinehart & Winston.

1969b The Myth of P: Epistemology and Formal Analysis. *American Anthropologist* 71:71-79.

Wallace, Anthony F. C.

1965 The Problem of the Psychological Validity of Componential Analysis. In Formal Semantic Analysis, ed. E. A. Hammel, *American Anthropologist* 67, no. 5, pt. 2:229-48 (special issue).

Weaver, Warren

1966 The Mathematics of Communication. In *Communication and Culture*, ed. Alfred G. Smith, pp. 15-24. New York: Holt, Rinehart & Winston. Originally published 1949.

Werner, Oswald, ed.

1966 Studies in Ethnoscience. *Anthropological Linguistics* 8.

Whorf, B. L.

1956a A Linguistic Consideration of Thinking in Primitive Communities. In *Language, Thought, and Reality: Selected Writings of Bejamin Lee Whorf*, ed. John B. Carroll, pp. 65-86. Cambridge: M.I.T. Press. Written *ca.* 1936.

1956b Gestalt Technique of Stem Composition in Shawnee. In *Language, Thought, and Reality: Selected Writings of Benjamin Lee Whorf*, ed. John B. Carroll, pp. 160-72. Cambridge: M.I.T. Press. Originally published 1940.

1956c Languages and Logic. In *Languages, Thought, and Reality: Selected Writings of Benjamin Lee Whorf*, ed. John B. Carroll, pp. 233-45. Cambridge: M.I.T. Press. Originally published 1941.

1956d Decipherment of the Linguistic Portion of the Maya Hieroglyphs. In *Language, Thought, and Reality: Selected Writings of Benjamin Lee Whorf*, ed. John B. Carroll, pp. 173-98. Cambridge: M.I.T. Press. Originally published 1942.

1961 Science and Linguistics. In *Psycholinguistics: A Book of Readings*, ed. Sol Saporta, pp. 460-68. New York: Holt, Rinehart & Winston. Originally published 1940.

Wittgenstein, L.

1953 *Philosophical Investigations*. New York: Macmillan.

CHAPTER 11 Sociolinguistics

JOAN RUBIN

INTRODUCTION

The study of sociolinguistics offers a significant departure from the current major concerns of both linguistic and cultural anthropological theory. Traditional linguistic theory has focused upon units that were assumed to be uniform, homogeneous, or monolithic (Hymes 1962; Bright, ed., 1966; De Camp 1970). It was assumed that one could describe the speech of a region, or at least of a speech community—or at worst of a single individual—in a uniform way. Although variation was known to occur in the speech of each of these, it was considered of no importance in establishing the linguistic system. In fieldwork, one took care to find an informant who was a legitimate representative of this assumed homogeneous unit and whose speech did not have much variation. At the analytical

stage, variation within the language or dialect or idiolect was dealt with by explaining it away (as not being part of the system). Variation in an idiolect was attributed to the fact that the individual was bidialectal or that he made a mistake, or it was classified as "free" or random variation (which means that no linguistic [or other] explanation was to be found). Variation in a dialect area meant that the dialect had begun to break up into two dialects. No attempt has been made by linguistic theorists to explain how or why such variation coexists in the same area or person. Indeed, such variation could not be adequately explained or its function understood by use of a theory that insists on homogeneity. Additionally, the fact that such variation is the norm rather than the exception did not trouble analysts of "monolithic linguistics."[1] How-

I wish to thank Robert Cooper, John Macnamara, Björn Jernudd, and Munro Edmonson for their editorial comments. As always, I learned a great deal from these colleagues; however, responsibility for any errors in this paper remains mine alone.

[1] Similar assumptions are to be found in cultural theory. It is regularly assumed that there is some unit in which the cultural system is to be found—a culture area, a culture, a subculture, or the ideal informant (Back 1960). Barth (1969:9) further points out that such units are considered to have

479

ever, the explanation of just such linguistic variation or diversity is one of the major concerns of sociolinguistics. It is clear that such variation is not entirely "free," but is related to systematic sociocultural differences. In trying to understand the characteristic variation in code and speech, sociolinguistics looks to the characteristics of a culture, of a society, and of individuals as the culture-bearers acquire, use, maintain, and change their code and speech. Sociolinguists are also concerned with the influence of one speech variety on another.

Although this whole chapter will largely be an illustration of these last sentences, we can perhaps quicken our understanding by first looking at two recent sociolinguistic books. The first, Burling's *Man's Many Voices* (1970), is concerned with those variables that affect or constrain language use and change. Burling indicates that the three most important are referential meaning, social organization, and individual vari-

ability among speakers. In the three variables that Burling isolates we can see a concern with variation in code and speech as this relates to culture, society, and the individual. A second book, the new introductory volume by Fishman (1970), illustrates further dimensions of sociolinguistic concern. He isolates six goals of the field (p. 3). It seeks to:

1. Describe the linguistic and functional characteristics of language varieties.
2. Determine how much of the entire speech community's verbal repertoire is available to various smaller interaction networks within that community.
3. Trace the linguistic influences of varieties on each other.
4. Determine how changes in the fortunes and interactions of networks of speakers alter the ranges of their verbal repertoires.
5. Discover societal rules or norms that explain and constrain language behavior and the behavior toward language in speech communities.
6. Determine the symbolic value of language varieties for its speakers.

While the emphasis of Fishman's writings is more often on the sociological aspects, other writers who are more linguistically oriented tend to place greater emphasis on the value of sociolinguistic variation in changing the focus of linguistic theory (Hymes 1967; Weinreich, Labov, and Herzog 1968; Labov 1970; De Camp 1970; Bailey 1969-1970).

The literature contains several other designations that, to my mind, cover approximately the same area of interest—ethnography of communication (Gumperz and Hymes, eds., 1964), the sociology of language (Fishman, ed., 1968), and ethnolinguistics (Olmstead 1950; for an extensive bibliography see Goodell 1964; for a defense of the term

---

discrete boundaries: "Practically all anthropological reasoning rests ȯn the premise that cultural variation is discontinuous; that there are aggregates of people who essentially share a common culture, and interconnected differences that distinguish each such discrete culture from all others." Although anthropology has recognized variation (through such terms as ideal versus real, prescribed versus preferred, mechanical versus statistical), it is commonplace for the analysis of the system to ignore variation. "Note, however, that when an anthropologist describes the characteristics of a given culture, he does not mean to suggest that every person in the group behaves in the ways described. Instead, an anthropological portrayal of a culture, technically referred to as an ethnography, is a 'profile' of the behavior that is most characteristic of the members of the group" (Cohen 1968:8). The analysis of ethnoscience has come under some criticism because it assumes a single unitary structure defined by a set of organizing principles (Tyler 1969:487-88). While the interrelation between variation and system has concerned some cultural anthropologists (Geertz 1957, Wallace 1961, Goodenough 1963, Tyler 1969, and others), a productive and significant resolution is not yet in sight.

see Hymes 1965).[2] Three other designations include many of the same concerns as sociolinguistics: language and culture, anthropological linguistics, and linguistic anthropology. The first of these was more frequently used in the forties and fifties, when there was greater concern with the ways in which language allegedly influenced or determined culture (for a bibliography on the Whorfian hypothesis, the position that language constrains world view, see Miller 1968). Interest in the Whorfian hypothesis largely subsided in the 1960's, after research efforts to demonstrate the stronger version of the hypothesis proved largely futile. The Whorfian thesis assumed, along with traditional linguistics, the homogeneity of linguistic and cultural units.[3] With the greater emphasis on the importance and omnipresence of variation, concern with the problem of the linguistic determination of culture has now largely been replaced by concern with the ways in which cultural, social, and individual variation place constraints on or covary with linguistic variation. Another language and culture focus is that of zoosemiotics (Sebeok 1968; Sebeok and Ramsey, eds., 1970), or the relation of animal communication to human communication. Although of considerable interest to anthropologists, this area is not usually the concern of sociolinguistics.

THE FIELD AND ITS MAJOR FOCI

In concentrating on the nature and function of sociocultural and linguistic variation, sociolinguistics has emphasized two concepts. The first of these is a redefinition of the term "speech community" or "linguistic community," which Gumperz (1962:31) gives a conjoint focus: "a social group which may be either monolingual or multilingual, held together by the frequency of social interaction patterns and set off from surrounding areas by weaknesses in the lines of communication." An earlier definition of this term (Bloomfield 1933) emphasized the common linguistic structure and the mutual intelligibility of all the varieties for the members of the community. In looking at communication networks and their frequency, Gumperz focuses on the need to isolate types of verbal repertoires (whether similar linguistically or not)[4] and the patterns of social interaction that together form some sort of unit because of this frequency and because of the functions of the networks.

A second important concept is that of the verbal repertoire, which again Gumperz (1964:137) has defined as "the totality of linguistic forms regularly employed in the course of socially significant interaction." Each repertoire consists of varieties or variants from which the speakers select in accordance with the rules of linguistic etiquette. Such varieties may be sharply distin-

---

[2] The terms include both the description of the rules of speaking or communicative competence and the description of behaviors toward language—language maintenance and language shift, language attitudes, language values, language as social variable, and the like. While some distinction may exist between the ethnography of communication, which refers at times to the rules of speaking, and the sociology of language, which refers to behaviors toward language, the distinction does not seem to be clearly maintained.

[3] For a discussion of some of the difficulties this assumption presents, see Brown, 1958; Miller, 1968; Percival, 1966.

[4] Gumperz (1968:385) used the term "linguistic range" to distinguish "internal language distance between constituent varieties, that is, the total amount of purely linguistic differentiation that exists in a community, thus distinguishing among multilingual, multidialectal, and homogeneous communities."

guished or not—the term "compart-mentalization" is used to refer to the degree of separation. No distinctive term exists to separate the verbal repertoire of a speech community from that of a member of the community, although clearly in studying a speech community it is necessary to isolate the speech varieties and to identify those who use them, the situations and ways in which they use them, and the meanings they attach to them (Fishman 1965). It is also possible to speak of an individual or a type of individual as having a particular linguistic range (see footnote 4 for a definition of this term).

In order to understand some of the major concerns and results of sociolinguistics, it is useful to consider first the types of linguistic variation and then to focus on the social, cultural, and individual concomitants of these variations. I shall take this approach here because unfortunately many of the studies tend to focus on one set of phenomena at a time. Actually this approach is not recommended, and the best studies continuously look at both phenomena at the same time. Although for exposition purposes we shall look at one at a time, the reader should keep in mind the danger of losing sight of the important interaction between the phenomena which may be lost by this approach. In addition, I want to state clearly that this review does not pretend to cover all of the rather extensive sociolinguistic literature, but rather tries to illustrate the variables isolated in each section. Omission does not constitute a judgment of the value of a study.

We shall first focus on *what* varies linguistically: phonological, lexical, and syntactic variation and code-switching. We shall see how this linguistic variation reflects, is constrained by, or is changed by individual, social, or cultural determinants. This focus has in-cluded areas such as ethnoscience, dialectology, language change, and more recently rules of speaking.

Second, we shall focus on social, cultural, and individual determinants and concomitants of linguistic variation within a speech community. Included here are such areas as linguistic socialization, ethnography of communication (speaking), language maintenance and shift, language planning, linguistic virtuosity (Burling 1970), and language attitudes. Our focus will include *(a)* determinants or concomitants of use, *(b)* stability, maintenance, and change of language repertoires, and *(c)* acquisition of linguistic varieties. We shall be considering use, stability, and acquisition separately. Although in fact these three processes are in constant interplay, most of the literature does not consider the nature of this interaction.

Other approaches to sociolinguistic studies can be found in the several excellent collections of readings now available: Bright, ed., 1966; Burling 1970; Capell 1966; Fishman 1970; Fishman, ed., 1968; Gumperz and Hymes, eds., 1964 and 1970; Hymes, ed., 1964; Lieberson, ed., 1966; and Pride and Holmes, eds., n.d.

LINGUISTIC VARIATION

The literature over the past decade has indicated that linguistic devices of all kinds (phonological, grammatical, semantic) as well as whole languages reflect social, cultural, and individual preferences. Speech communities vary widely in the devices they use to do this. In addition, groups of linguistic devices may be combined to reflect social and cultural categorization.

Phonological Variation

An examination of the phonological variation found in a speech community indicates that variation in one feature may reflect a whole host of phenomena. Such variation may not be constrained by location (as considered in dialectology) or by some absolute characteristic of the speaker, such as class or social group (as the concept of idiolect seems to imply).

Fischer (1958:51), in a study of two different pronunciations of the suffix -ing—/in/ and /iŋ/—revealed the complex significance of the variation between them. He found that such variation was related to "sex, class, and personality (aggressive/cooperative), and mood (tense/relaxed) of the speaker, to the formality of the conversation and to the specific verb spoken." Such variation, then, reflects social constraints (sex, class, formality), individual constraints (personality, mood), and perhaps cultural constraints (verb—which reflects topic or some larger domain).

Labov (1970) distinguished two kinds of sociolinguistic variables: *indicators* and *markers*. Indicators are those linguistic features that show regular distribution over socioeconomic, ethnic, and age groups. Markers are those variables that show not only social distribution, but also stylistic differentiation.

In a brilliant study of phonological variation in New York City, Labov (1966c) demonstrated the fallacy of assuming that speakers of a particular region or dialect have a phonological system of discrete entities that can be described apart from sociocultural variables. He established that there is a consistent relationship between individual variation in several phonological features and the contextual styles in which they are used. Labov used five contexts based on different elicitation procedures—casual speech, careful speech, reading style, word lists, and minimal pairs. Moreover, Labov showed that linguistic differences between social classes are not necessarily reflected by a categorical presence or absence of given phonetic features, but rather are expressed by the frequency of occurrence of these features. An example of the type of pronunciation variation Labov found is that for orthographic *r* in final and preconsonantal position. He observed that in casual speech only the highest ranking status group showed a significant amount of *r* pronunciation. In more formal contexts, however, the *r* indexes for other groups rose sharply. In fact, one of his groups, the lower middle class, showed a marked increase. "Whereas this group is essentially *r*-less in everyday speech, it shows an average *(r)* index for the two most formal styles which is considerably greater than that of the upper middle class . . ." (Labov 1964b:172). Labov demonstrated similar quantitative relationships between social classes and contexts for other phonological variants.

Other scholars who have studied the complex relationship between phonological and sociocultural variants include Ferguson and Gumperz, eds., 1960; Levine and Crockett 1966; Ma and Herasimchuk 1968; Fishman and Herasimchuk 1968; Labov et al. 1968; Wolfram 1969; and Edwards 1970.

Although it has repeatedly been suggested that phonological variation of suprasegmental features or paralinguistic features—whining, shouting, whispering, elongation of vowels—regularly conveys social information, the systematic study of such variation in any one society has been relatively limited.[5] A list of those variables can be found in Trager (1964). They have been shown to relate to the speaker's attitude (anger, hurt, remorse) and intent (scholarly, vindictive, and the like). Labov (1966c) noted that vari-

---

[5] One extensive attempt to do so can be found in Pittenger, Hockett, and Danehy (1960).

ables such as speed of utterance and amount and kind of laughter (his so-called "channel cues" for informal casual speech) relate to the function of a conversation.

For a long time linguists have contended that phonological change could not be observed while in process. A study by Labov (1963) on Martha's Vineyard, however, did just that. Labov studied the varied pronunciations of the first elements of /ai/ and /au/ in words such as "right" and "house" and found that such variation was indicative not only of differences between social groups but also of linguistic change. He showed that those persons who strongly identified themselves with the special island tradition tended to use a more centralized position for the vowels than did the less traditional speakers. The former included people who lived in the rural areas or were dependent on fishing, those who resented or feared encroachment by the outside summer people, those people who most stubbornly defended their own way of life and fought to maintain their own identity in the face of threats from the outside. Labov also demonstrated the historical dimension reflected by the variability. In older forms, the first element of /ai/ was more centralized, but not that of /au/. In more recent times, as increasing pressures from the outside were felt, the first element of /au/ was pulled to that of /ai/. This change is said to be indicative of a desire to signal separateness from mainlanders.

A study by Bright (1960) also considers a sociological explanation for phonological change. Bright questions whether phonological change among some Kannada speakers in India is due to emulation of Brahmins by non-Brahmins or vice versa. On the whole, he concludes that it is the Brahmins that introduce new sounds from English or Sanskrit, as a result of their greater literacy. On the other hand, the non-Brahmin dialect shows more sound change within native vocabulary; this, Bright suggested, is due to the inaccurate imitation of Brahmin speech by non-Brahmins. The conservatism of Brahmins in their native vocabulary is attributed to their greater literacy.

Semantic Variation

In considering the semantic constraints on language, Burling (1970) discusses two kinds: those that relate linguistic forms directly to referential meaning and those that additionally relate them to specific sociocultural situations. The former, which Burling calls "rules of reference," are concerned with the way a language organizes reality and gives labels to this organization. Rules of reference are studied in order "to produce a formal statement that will account for or *predict* the terms that can be appropriately used in various nonlinguistically-defined circumstances" (p. 42). This area of semantics, which usually is called ethnoscience or componential analysis (and sometimes transformational analysis), is covered by other chapters of this book (Durbin 1973) and others (e.g., Tyler, ed., 1969), so we shall go on to consider the second kind of rules, those relating meaning to social context. These rules cover synonyms or near synonyms and the social constraints on their use.

The relation between lexical choice and its social significance has been discussed by several writers. Studies by Brown and Gilman (1960) and Brown and Ford (1961) on the use of pronouns and terms of address have stimulated a consideration of linguistic forms of respect (often called honorifics) around the world (Slobin 1963, Howell 1965, Friedrich 1966, Neustupný 1968a, Ervin-Tripp 1968, Das 1968, and Jain 1969, to mention only a few).

Brown and Gilman (1960) point out that where there are at least two variant forms of the second person pronoun (such as *tu* and *vous* in French), their use is related to two social dimensions: status and solidarity. They show that the form that is used depends in large part on the degree of solidarity and the status relationship that exists between the speaker and the addressee. Status, however, must be defined within a particular cultural context. In some societies, age may take preference over other status variables, such as occupation, whereas in other societies the reverse may be true. Brown and Ford (1961) point out that address forms are also related to these two dimensions. They point out that Americans will use titles plus last names with people of higher status or of great social distance, while they will use first names with individuals of lower status or of great solidarity. Further, they found that choice of address terms rests with the person of greater status. These two very provocative papers not only look at the ways in which linguistic variation reflects social categories, but also consider how such choice may change through time and how individual preferences are reflected through choice. (For a discussion of this problem see the section on "Determinants, Concomitants, and Functions of Linguistic Variation" below.)

Just as we have seen that phonological choice may reveal at one and the same time sociocultural and individual preferences, so too with lexical choice. A study by Geertz (1960) of Javanese linguistic etiquette points to complex and highly significant patterns of linguistic variation. In Javanese, Geertz points out, there are three basic levels of speech distinguished by a large number of contrasting items of vocabulary. Indeed, Geertz feels it is impossible for a Javanese to speak without selecting from among the levels, which range from plain (low) speech to very elegant (high) speech. Differences among the levels are largely marked by the choice among linked sets of lexical items. He also notes that the number of levels available to a given speaker is determined by group membership. Differences among items or levels reflect a number of things (Geertz 1960:257-58):

They include not only qualitative characteristics of the speakers—age, sex, kinship relation, occupation, wealth, education, religious commitment, family background—but also more general factors: for instance, the social setting (one would be likely to use a higher level at a wedding than in the street); the content of the conversation (in general, one uses lower levels when speaking of commercial matters, higher ones if speaking of religious or aesthetic matters); the history of social interaction between the speakers (one will tend to speak rather high, if one speaks at all, with someone with whom one has quarreled); the presence of a third person (one tends to speak higher to the same individual if others are listening).

The important point to note is the way lexical variation reflects social (age, sex, kinship, and the like), cultural (perhaps content of the conversation), and individual (history of social interaction) determinants. A natural and necessary continuation of Geertz' analysis would be some indication of the weight each of these variables should be assigned so as to allow a more formal specification of the rules of speaking.

There are a number of other papers (Kantrowitz 1967 and items mentioned in Hertzler 1965, chap. 14) which point to special vocabularies or argots used by special groups within a community. Many of these seem to fall short of the mark because they fail to specify the circumstances under which members of a group will use these terms, the frequency with which these terms are used, and the social intent with which they are used (although some indicate that command of terminology is required to underline one's right to membership in the group, other intent is rarely identified).

Although we shall not discuss the enormous literature on referential meaning, which in large part assumes homogeneity of reference, it is worth noting that some scholars of cognitive anthropology have recognized that even in referential meaning there can be variation that may be related to the sociocultural context. Tyler (1969, 500-501) has noted that the distinction between reference and situation cannot be clearly maintained:

. . . the appropriate use of Koya kin terms cannot be predicted solely on the basis of formal analysis predicated on the assumption of genealogical reckoning. There are many contextual factors to be taken into consideration. Among these are: social setting, audience composition, sex and age of speaker/hearer, linguistic repertoires of speaker/hearer, and—most difficult of all—something that might be called the speaker's intention.

Among other studies that recognize the need to consider such variation even while describing rules of reference are Swartz (1960), Foster (1964), and Schneider (1968).

Though lexical stability and change have been the sources of a great many studies, sociological explanations of differential change have thus far taken little note of the complexity of the reasons for change. In general, such studies have tended to list borrowed items and to suggest ad hoc reasons for their acceptance into a language.

Many studies of vocabulary change have used the term "interference." Inherent in the use of this term is an assumption of monolithic linguistic systems that are clearly separable (identifiable), and an assumption that it is possible and useful to indicate the influence of one system on another. The problem of identifying points of interference is in and of itself difficult. There is the question of which linguistic criteria to use. (Weinreich 1953 and Haugen 1953 and 1956 suggest several types of interference phenomena.) Then there is the question of whether it is appropriate to say that because an item clearly looks like or sounds like an item in another language, interference has indeed occurred. From a historical point of view, this is not as simple as it seems, especially today, when there are many words used by the scientific community whose real origin cannot be ascertained. Then there is the more interesting social problem that what is interference to the linguist may not be interference for the native speaker. Linguists may identify the origin of a term as foreign although the speakers themselves do not consider it foreign at all. Have we understood the communication process when we identify these items? It is well known that large parts of the English vocabulary are of French origin, but this does not make the United States and France one speech community. What we need to know is whether the members of a speech community recognize the "foreignness" of an item and whether this recognition affects the communication process. In contact situations, it would be of interest to ask such questions as: Are old terms retained in order to identify a community as unique? Are new terms adopted to help communication with another group?

The literature contains some interesting suggestions concerning processes. In a study of language change among two American Indian groups, Dozier (1956) points to the different degrees to which Spanish is accepted in the Yaqui and Tewa languages. According to Dozier, the Yaqui language and culture have indicated a general willingness to accept and incorporate the Spanish language and culture. Indeed, all aspects of the Yaqui language—lexicon, morphology, and syntax—show Spanish influence. On the other hand, the Tewa have apparently resisted Spanish influence on their language and culture. To Dozier, the fact that there are only a few Spanish loan words in Tewa indicates that Tewa resistance to Spanish pressures has been conscious. Rather than borrow Spanish words, the Tewa have coined new words and extended old meanings to cover new cultural acquisitions. The differential approach to Spanish contact which Dozier describes is intriguing; it would have been helpful if there were some indication of current reactions by both these groups to the lexical items in question.

Perhaps the most extensive study of language change in a cultural context has been achieved by Einar Haugen, who has studied the Norwegian language in Norway and in the United States over many years. His two-volume work (1953) describes the influence of living in America on the linguistic habits of Norwegian immigrants. A more recent work (1966a) is a study of the conscious changes made in the several standard varieties of the Norwegian language since independence was gained in the early nineteenth century. Haugen indicates among other things how changes in vocabulary are related to the more aristocratic or folk tendencies of the Norwegian legislators.

Grammatical Variation

Grammatical variation has also been shown to reflect sociocultural choice. An outstanding example is Martin's (1964) study of Japanese speech levels, which describes the grammatical gymnastics necessitated by the requirement that the speaker of Japanese indicate relative (speaker-addressee) age, position, sex, and group by the verb and verbal suffix chosen. In addition, Martin indicates that work by the National Language Research Institute in Japan isolated other linguistic features that reflect politeness; for example, negatives are more polite, Chinese loan words are less polite, longer utterances are more polite, and use of many dialect words is less polite.

Complex Linguistic Variation

Just as there is considerable evidence that sociocultural and individual choice are reflected in phonological, lexical, and grammatical variation, there is also ample indication that this same sort of choice may be reflected between languages. My studies of bilingualism in Paraguay (Rubin 1962, 1968b) indicate that choice of the use of Guaraní or Spanish is influenced by the location and seriousness of the discourse, the degree of formality, and the degree of intimacy. Choice of language reflects individual preferences as well—the first language learned by the speaker, the predicted linguistic ability of the addressee, and the linguistic preference of the speaker.

Scholars have increasingly given attention to the range of linguistic variation (which encompasses phonological, lexical, and grammatical variants) found in creole-speaking[6] areas, where

---

[6] A clear definition of a creole is hard to come by. Usually a pidgin language is defined as one used by speakers of a language when speaking to those who don't know the language. In this type of encounter, the pidgin is said to become a simplified version of the language. If the pidgin becomes the first language of some, then it may be called a creole. As a creole it often undergoes relexification in the process. Often the standard language from which the creole is said to have derived its grammatical struc-

changes made in linguistic forms are found to be rich indicators of a multitude of sociocultural meanings (De Camp 1961; Stewart 1963; Edwards 1970; Reisman 1970; and Hymes, ed., 1971, among others). Because of the complex relation between this variation and its social significance, the study of creoles will be an area of considerable theoretical significance in the future.

Ferguson (1959a) contributed to this whole area of the use of two or more varieties within a speech community by describing a type of speech community in which two varieties receive differential social evaluation. He notes that the one he calls the "high" variety is reserved for formal public functions, and the "low" variety is used for all other functions. Ferguson suggests that there are also characteristic linguistic differences between the two varieties: the grammatical structure of any given L variety is simpler than that of its corresponding H, and there are different vocabulary items in H and L for the same reference. Such a speech situation, to which he gives the term "diglossia," is characterized by relative stability, the two varieties sometimes being maintained by the speech communities for hundreds of years. Householder (1963), Moulton (1963), and Stewart (1963) examined *katherevusa* and *dhimotiki* Greek, standard and Swiss German, and Haitian French and Creole for some of the characteristics that Ferguson ascribed to diglossic situations.

In more recent years, Fishman (1966, 1967) has extended the meaning of the term diglossia to include not only those societies that utilize vernacular and classical varieties of the same language, but also "societies

which employ separate dialects, registers, or functionally differentiated language varieties of whatever kind," (Fishman 1970:74).[7] Fishman (1966) suggests that such a phenomenon is becoming more frequent as a consequence of modernization and growing social complexity.

Although, as we have seen, social categorization may be reflected through phonological, lexical, grammatical, or whole language differences, it is important to keep in mind Gumperz' (1970:7) statement:

Although members of all societies categorize each other through speech, groups differ in the linguistic means by which such organization is accomplished. What some groups accomplish by alternating between familiar and respectful personal pronouns, such as "tu" and "vous," others achieve by shifting between Mr. Smith and John. Still others may achieve similar ends by simply switching from a local dialect to a standard language.

It is equally true, as Gumperz (1970) points out, that in addition to the above-mentioned linguistic devices, "similar information can be conveyed through style shifting, intonation, special in-group vocabulary, topic selection, and like devices."

In the last five or six years, a number of scholars have tried to make more precise the kinds of rules that pervade conversation, narrative, and other types of communication, and to specify the sociocultural information they convey (Garfinkel 1967, Labov and Watelsky 1967, Ervin-Tripp 1968, Schegloff 1968, and Moerman 1969). Among the kinds of rules that Ervin-Tripp isolated

---

ture coexists in the same speech community as the creole, and the rules of usage as well as the linguistic relations have been shown to be very complex.

[7] While I agree wholeheartedly with Fishman that it is important to consider the coexistence of the several functionally differentiated language varieties, their concomitant values and attitudes, and their maintenance in a society, I would prefer a term that avoided the particular high/low or superimposed connotations of Ferguson's original conception.

are alternation rules, sequencing rules, and co-occurrence rules. This is an area that is receiving considerable attention and represents the combining of sociocultural and linguistic interests in a very original and creative way. Labov (1970) suggests that the isolation of these linguistic structures could not be achieved without reference to social dimensions.

Although language boundaries have often been isolated by linguists on structural criteria or criteria of mutual intelligibility, such boundaries have recently been demonstrated to be inadequate as an explanation of the changes in types of communication networks. While languages may be identified as linguistically close to each other, there may be reasons why the two social groups involved may wish to emphasize the differences between them. One of the groups might establish a set of differences in a conscious, consistent manner. This sort of activity, in which the speakers consciously set out to distinguish two linguistic varieties, has been called *Ausbau* by Kloss (1952, 1967). Stewart (1968) points out that desire for autonomy—that is, a belief in the uniqueness and independence of the linguistic system—may be sufficient to block communication between social groups.[8] Such blockage of communication is often connected with a desire to avoid political subservience; it is a resistance against the claim that if two groups speak the "same" language, one ought to incorporate the other. Other writers (Neustupný 1970, Hymes 1970, Haugen 1970) have pointed out the need to consider the contribution of language users in determining *which* linguistic differences matter *how much*. People are beginning to consider the important contribution of individual

users in determining the linguistic system.

Gumperz (1969) has shown that the boundary process between separation and identification is not simple. Where the colloquial dialects of two Indian languages—Marathi and Kannada—come into direct contact, the mutual influence has taken a very complex form. Gumperz observed that while the separation between these languages has been maintained on the lexical level, at the same time the village dialects have undergone such profound mutual grammatical influence as almost to obscure the boundaries between the two languages. Gumperz suggests that in our pursuit of the social significance of language behavior, "we go beyond popular language and simple language usage statistics" and reconsider the view that multilingualism is indicative of deep social cleavages. In the case he presents, Gumperz points to the need to explain both the retention of lexical differences and the lessening of differences on the grammatical level.

DETERMINANTS, CONCOMITANTS, AND FUNCTIONS OF LINGUISTIC VARIATION

Our discussion in this section will be divided in two ways. First of all, we shall consider (*a*) the determinants or concomitants of the use of language within speech communities, (*b*) the stability, maintenance, and change of the linguistic components within speech communities, and (*c*) the acquisition of linguistic varieties and rules of usage. Second, we shall see how each of these variables is constrained by cultural, social, and individual pressures.

I use the term "cultural" here to refer to what Goodenough (1963) calls the ideational order, particularly to those values, attitudes, and beliefs about both the society and the language which affect rules of usage and expectations

---

[8] Lunt (1959) provides such an example for Macedonia.

about social interaction. My use of the term "social" is similar to Geertz' (1957); it refers to social structure, status and role relationships, and social institutions.

The past ten years have seen a great deal of interest in isolating the many factors that operate to control rules of speaking. Although no systematic approach has been developed within which to fit these many factors, at least a great many have been isolated and applied (Mackey 1962; Ervin-Tripp 1964, 1968; Labov 1964). Hymes (1967) uses the term "communicative competence" (in contrast to the well-known term "linguistic competence") to refer to the individual's ability to know when to speak and when to remain silent, which code to use when, where, and to whom, etc. This competence must be acquired within a sociocultural setting. The task is to define the nature of this competence and the way it is acquired.

Social Determinants and Concomitants. One of the sets of constraints on linguistic usage within a speech community is the role relationship between the speaker and addressee, or social identity (Goodenough 1965). Social identities may be characterized by the dimensions of status and solidarity, isolated by Brown and Gilman (1960) and reflected in the use of the second person pronoun. Although these dimensions have been found to be significant in many cultures in constraining usage, each must be defined according to the culture itself. Thus status may be defined by relative sex, relative caste or class, relative professional ranking, and relative age. Solidarity may be defined

not only in linguistic behavior but also in nonverbal ways. Brown and Gilman have pointed out that in the United States, the degree of solidarity among women may be indicated by willingness to lend a comb or lipstick.

Higher status may be reflected not only within one language but also between languages within a single speech community. Wolff (1959) found that nonreciprocal bilingualism between two groups in Nigeria reflected the political dominance of the coastal peoples in the symbiotic relationship between coast and hinterland.

Role relationships that constrain linguistic usage may also be characterized by dimensions other than those of status and solidarity. Gumperz (1964) has suggested that there are two kinds of social interaction that are paralleled by types of social discourse. In the first type, called "transactional," the speakers enact a specific socially defined task; their speech is constrained by that task and may take on the aspects of a formula. In the second, called "personal," the speakers are free to express themselves as individuals rather than as participants in a specified socially defined task. Here the speech may be freer and open to greater manipulation. This distinction incorporates two other contrasts, formal/informal and public/private, isolated by Stewart (1962). I found in bilingual Paraguay (Rubin 1968*a*) that Spanish rather than Guaraní is used in more "formal" (transactional) sorts of relationships: lawyer to client, doctor to patient, teacher to student, mayor to constituent, and the like. The less formal relationships, however, are defined by a number of variables, among them the type of personal relationship.

Another type of role relationship may obtain between members of different ethnic or national groups. Tanner (1967), has shown the functional specialization of codes among bilinguals in Indonesia. Whereas the lower classes speak only their local ethnic language, the middle and upper classes also speak Indonesian, and the elites can speak English and Dutch as well. Tanner indicates that for those who speak more than one language, use is related to successively larger groups. Thus, Dutch is used for intraclique communication, the ethnic language is used intra-ethnically, Indonesian interethnically, and English and Dutch internationally.

Language usage has also been found to be a concomitant of the absolute social status of the speaker. Ross (1956) found a consistent difference between all upper-class British speakers and all others; he called this difference U and non-U speech. Among the Koasati, all men have variations in their speech which clearly distinguish it from that of women (Haas 1944). Religious differences may also be marked in speech. Blanc (1964) has described a dialect split among Jews, Christians, and Muslims within the city of Baghdad in their speaking of Arabic.

The relationship between absolute status and type of communication is not a simple one. While one of the styles of a speaker may be heavily marked for a status type, the speaker may also use another style that is not so clearly marked. In an intensive study of the village of Khalapur, India, Gumperz (1958) shows how differences in the village variety of Hindi are indicative of several social groupings. Variations in the village variety reflect not only caste differences, but also the village's territorial divisions. This variety is, however, not the only one known by some of the inhabitants; some can also speak the regional and standard variety of Hindi as well, and use of one of these varieties would mask such caste or territorial identification.

Several writers have indicated that persons present in the audience may influence the variety of speech used. Geertz (1960) mentions audience as one of the variables affecting the level of speech used, but he does not indicate just what the effect of audience presence is on linguistic variation. Others have pointed out that conversations that occur in public situations where the audience is not known and where one is required to represent oneself in an official or semiofficial way may affect linguistic behavior. The weight of this factor in affecting speech variation in any one social setting has not yet been well delimited.

It has long been recognized that the topic under discussion may be a determinant of linguistic behavior. Ervin-Tripp (1964) has indicated how broadly the concept "topic" may be construed: it may include not only categories such as subject matter (economics, household affairs, gossip) but also the propositional content of utterances. While Ervin-Tripp (1964) offers evidence that topic may indeed be a basic variable, Fishman (1970) questions whether topic can really be separated from situation or domain.

Another social factor that constrains linguistic usage is setting, which includes both the time and the place of interaction. In a study of an American Indian wake, Bock (1964) isolated several culturally important times: gathering time, prayer time, singing time, intermission, and mealtime, which are reflected in the speech variation of the participants. Any definition of setting must be made culturally specific. A distinction such as "rural-urban" is useless unless the cues for recognizing when a setting is considered urban by the participants themselves are made clear.

It has been suggested that some of these factors may be combined at a higher level of social abstraction. Bock

(1964) speaks about a dimension, "situation," which combines three other variables: time, space, and roles. For example, one type of cultural situation might be a class, which usually takes place during *class time* in a *school* with the roles of *teacher and pupil*. Fishman (1970) calls our attention to the fact that in situations where all three of these variables come together in a regular way, they may be reflected in certain language usage norms. He points out that there may be times when the three are not congruent yet the resulting nonverbal behavior and consequent linguistic behavior are not random or chaotic. One of the parties to the encounter may reinterpret the situation so that the congruence among the three variables is increased. When sufficient congruence has been attained, a new definition of the situation in which the interlocutors find themselves can be achieved.

At a still higher level of social abstraction, Fishman (1965) has isolated the social construct of domain, which he says results from the large-scale aggregative regularities that obtain between varieties and societally recognized functions. In general, Fishman indicates, domains show a marked paralleling with major social institutions such as government, school, home or family, and church. He sees domains as "clusters of social situations which are typically constrained by a common set of behavioral rules" and which may in any speech community be associated with a particular speech variety. In particular, Fishman singles out the diglossic situation, in which both speech varieties are also associated with a set of values and attitudes and a regular set of social functions (see Barker 1947, Fishman et al. 1968 and Labov 1968 for examples of the functioning of domains).

Cultural Determinants and Concomitants. Another set of factors that both constrain and accompany linguistic variation within a speech community is cultural. Most of the work thus far has focused on the attitudes and values that constrain both the social behavior and the linguistic variety. Hymes (1961) and Haugen (1962) have demonstrated the importance of a speech community's evaluation of a particular linguistic variety in understanding the social mobility process.[9] Labov (1966b) provides a further evaluation example demonstrating the relation between pronunciation hypercorrection and expressed desire for social mobility.

There is a growing interest in what has been called subjective reaction tests, in which speakers are asked to evaluate the social characteristics of speakers with differing speech varieties. An early but inconclusive study was that by Putnam and O'Hearne (1955). More recently, Lambert and his associates (Lambert et al. 1960, Ainsfield and Lambert 1964) have devised a technique called the matched guise, in which the attitudes toward a particular social group are assessed through an evaluation of the speech variety considered representative of that group. Respondents hear passages recorded in two varieties and are asked to rate the speakers in each of several dimensions: intelligence, sense of humor, and the like. Unknown to the respondent, the passages are recorded by the same (bilingual) speaker. As Agheyisi and Fish-

[9] This contrasts with the earlier descriptive emphasis of linguistics, which indicated that all languages were equal despite social belief to the contrary. Hymes (1961) and Haugen (1962) pointed out that one cannot throw away such evaluation if one wants to understand fully the process of communication and social interaction. Recognition of such different evaluation is also critical in establishing educational policy.

SOCIOLINGUISTICS

493

man (1970) rightly point out, the test assumes a direct correlation between the values associated with the group and the linguistic variety; other dimensions might well be interfering with the evaluation of the language variety, such as the degree of congruence between the topic and the particular linguistic variety. Any study of such attitudes must be careful to assure that other social variables are not intervening.

Labov et al. (1968) have developed an elaborate series of subjective reaction tests for the speech varieties of standard English and Negro non-standard English. Such tests include judgment of the speaker's occupation, geographic background, education, ability in fighting, desirability as a friend, amount of self-knowledge, and the like. The complex relations between other values and the results of these tests are discussed in great depth, and validated by statistical findings.

Attitudes toward one's own and other groups may encourage the expression of unity and distinctness through language. In particular, Garvin (1959) showed that a standard language may serve to unite several dialect areas into a single standard language community while at the same time allowing this community to set itself off from its neighbors. The case of the Swiss German standard, which serves both to unite all of the dialect communities and at the same time to separate the German-speaking Swiss from other German-speaking communities, is a good example. Further, although no spoken standard language may exist, a community may use a standard script to express its unification, as in the case of Chinese (De Francis 1950).

Heretofore, such evaluations and attitudes have been considered quaint by most linguists. They are coming to be recognized as significant, however, be-

cause they may well reflect trends in social mobility or other social change, or indicate trends in linguistic change. The newly evolving discipline of subjective dialectology (Grootaers 1959 and Japanese scholars at the National Language Research Institute in Japan have been working on this problem) recognizes the importance of language attitudes and subjective reactions in establishing speech communities. A major difference between the work of the earlier dialectologists and that of the subjective dialectologists is that the former used their own reactions and attitudes to establish boundaries and isoglosses while the latter place as much importance on those of the speech community.[10] Jernudd (1968b) discusses two approaches to dialectology which distinguish variety differences based on "objective" linguistic differences and variety differences based on the speaker's reaction. Neustupný (1965, 1970) adds a third approach based on verbalizations about linguistic differences, both factual statements about language and attitudes, and beliefs attached to these facts. These studies suggest a need to consider the interrelationships among all three approaches in defining boundaries. In an early study, Grootaers (1959) asked the inhabitants of a number of Japanese villages if the language differed from that of neighboring villages, and if so to what extent. Although Grootaers was disappointed in his results because they did not correspond to the linguist's absolute statement of dialect differences, the patterns that did emerge, based on folk beliefs, may in fact be more impor-

[10] I owe most of the insights stated here to a lecture given by Björn Jernudd during his visit to Djakarta in May 1970. Any errors of interpretation remain mine alone.

tant in identifying communication network patterns.

Another set of values that have been isolated are those about a language or linguistic variety per se. Such values may be expressed as feelings either about the value of a particular variety or about when it is to be used and in what way. Several writers have pointed to the symbolic value of a language for its users. In a discussion of Arabic, Ferguson (1959*b*) pointed to a common set of beliefs about the standard variety: it is held to be superior because it is beautiful, because it has grammatical symmetry, because it has a "logical" structure, because it has a vast and rich lexicon, and because it is sacred. Such evaluation affects feelings about the most appropriate times for the language to be used; those in the community who command this standard variety are held in higher esteem than those who do not.

Garvin (1959) found another value regularly associated with the standard language: awareness of norm. Speakers look to one linguistic variety as the yardstick for correctness. "Individual speakers and groups of speakers are then judged by their fellows in terms of their observance of this yardstick."

The importance of the values given to the use of the proper variety in the proper setting have not been given extensive attention. In Paraguay I found that the use of Guaraní in the classroom was laughed at because of the attitude that it didn't belong there; on the other hand, city folk who used Spanish rather than Guaraní in the countryside were considered to be putting on airs (Rubin 1968*b*). Gumperz (1966) found that in Hemnes, Norway, speakers became embarrassed when they realized they were code-switching instead of using the dialect solely. However, the evidence thus far is still only of an anecdotal kind.

Societies have been shown to hold values and beliefs regarding speaking (or not), and such values may be related to major social institutions and other cultural values. There may be rules on when to speak and when not to speak, or certain parts of speech may be considered taboo at particular times with particular persons. Perhaps the most brilliant paper thus far on values attached to speech habits is that by Albert (1964:35), which indicates that among the Burundi of Central Africa "speech is explicitly recognized as an important instrument of social life; eloquence is one of the central values of the cultural world view; and the way of life affords frequent opportunity for its exercise." Further, she indicates that there is a "constant flow of speech about speech." Linguistic skill is built into the organization of this society "as a means of gaining one's ends, as social status symbols, and as skills enjoyable in themselves." Finally, Albert indicates that indeed in this society beauty in speech usage overrides all other values, such as moral or logical principles.

Individual Determinants and Concomitants. A third set of variables that constrain usage within a speech community relates to individual preferences and skills. In his new book Burling (1970) describes a phenomenon that, although common, was previously unlabeled: "linguistic virtuosity." In all societies, members with superior linguistic skills are admired. The individual who displays these skills is considered gifted. Among the skills that have been recognized in various cultures, Burling mentions glossolalia ("speaking in tongues"), Walbiri upside-down talk (a type of secret language used by men at the time of certain rituals), street talk (found among urban black children and having a variety of expressive forms, such as rapping, shucking, running it down, signifying), oratory, and poetry. Burling also recognizes another interesting form of linguistic virtuosity: multilingualism in parts of New Guinea. Richard Salisbury (1962) notes that translation occurs far more often than practical understanding and communication needs would suggest, and that even when the audience is monolingual, a speech may be translated in order to demonstrate linguistic skills.

It is also possible to sort out differences in linguistic behavior that reflect the attitudes of individuals. Some suggestions exist in the extant literature. Brown and Gilman (1960) found that differences in pronoun usage reflect in part the democratic orientation of a particular speaker—those who have such an orientation more frequently use the pronoun of solidarity than those who are not so inclined. Friedrich's study (1966) of Russian pronoun usage in the nineteenth century clearly demonstrates that usage changed with differences in speaker attitude.

Stability, Maintenance, and Change of Linguistic Components Within Speech Communities

Social Determinants and Concomitants. Although some considerable progress has been made in the last ten years in considering the relationship among speech communities, linguistic usage, and social factors, the relationship between linguistic usage and social change is only beginning to be explored. Fishman (1966) says that linguistic maintenance and change need to be related to the more general social change theory. Gumperz (1966:27) indicates that we "still lack a theory of language and society which would explain how specific factors in the social system may lead to linguistic changes, and how linguistic structures are affected by these factors."

In order to understand the effect of social variables on constraint of lin-

guistic change and the ways in which such an effect is reflected in linguistic variation, we must try to ascertain who is more likely to change his linguistic behavior and the sorts of circumstances under which he may be expected to do so.

Some suggestions already exist in the literature. Diebold (1962) isolated social variables relating to the acquisition of Spanish in Tehuantepec, Mexico. He noted that Indian adult males whose occupations brought them into frequent contact with Spanish speakers were more frequently bilingual than others. Jernudd (1968a) demonstrated that the acquisition of Arabic among the For of the Sudan was directly related to age (young people know more Arabic than old people), sex (women do not know Arabic), residence (less Arabic is known in the mountain areas than in the foothills), and education (schools are major sources of Arabic acquisition). Fischer (1958:52) indicated that a linguistic standard is often set by the elite, and that they then tend to change the standard when the masses try to imitate it. This process he called "the protracted pursuit of an elite by an envious mass, and the consequent 'flight' of the elite." Spicer (1962, adapted from Herzog 1941), concerned with the differential effect of contact on the same group, showed that the type of vocabulary incorporated into several Indian languages in the Southwest and the changing functions of these contact languages have depended in large part on the type of contact these Indians have had with the Spanish and English speakers. He examined the differences to be found in the period of Spanish colonization and missionizing, the period of U.S. frontier expansion, and finally the reservation period, and found differences not only in the type of vocabulary but also in the process of acceptance. Weinreich (1957:212) found in India "that the incidence of bilingualism is (very roughly) inversely proportional to the relative size of the MT (mother tongue) group." He noted, however, that factors other than size—the status of a social group is one—are clearly involved in the rate of bilingualism.

Little study has been made of changes in the setting (time and place), although there exists the very general theory that changes in the degree of urbanization may affect linguistic usage.

Fishman (1966, n.d.) isolated language maintenance and change as an area of study and directed a survey of this process within several ethnic groups in the United States. The study examines the domains in which the ethnic language is still being used, considers the influence of these domains on the maintenance of ethnic languages, and suggests ways of encouraging language maintenance.

Changes in usage are clearly related to domain. Fishman (1970) suggests that some domains are more maintenance-prone than others. Since decisions about national language usage usually relate to the domains of government, school, and public administration, these domains are most susceptible to change. Studies of such decisions certainly yield information about the various patterns of domain resistance to change.

Conscious and rationalized attempts to change both the linguistic code and speech patterns of a speech community as large as a nation have been called "language planning." Language planning is deliberate change; that is "changes in the systems of language code or speaking or both that are planned by organizations that are established for such purposes or given a mandate to fulfill such purposes" (Rubin and Jernudd 1971). This sort of change is the concern largely of the new nations that have had to establish one language for use in administration, communication, and education.

In addition, they have attempted to elaborate and codify the variety selected. Policy decisions and their implementation in planning are always made and carried out within a number of speech communities, and in the process of planning, values, attitudes, and beliefs about the native language and also about the official one come to the fore. Language planning then is part and parcel of social change. As more work is done in this area,[11] the many variables that are brought to the fore in planning efforts and which constrain and affect language change will become clearer. To date, most studies of language planning have focused on the product but not on the process of change. Two recent volumes do isolate some of the sociocultural-economic-educational problems that arise in language planning and indicate the promising rewards from future work (Fishman, Ferguson, and Das Gupta, eds., 1968; Rubin and Jernudd 1971).

Cultural Determinants and Concomitants. Cultural attitudes and values are necessarily important in affecting linguistic usage within a speech community. Language attitudes may reflect attitudes and values toward social groups but they may also serve as tools for effecting change. The variety of attitudes relating social groups to speech communication in a changing situation has only begun to be isolated.

Das Gupta (1970), in analyzing the complex Indian linguistic situation, has shown how the leaders of religious

---

[11] The Language Planning Processes Project was directed and coordinated by J. Das Gupta, C. A. Ferguson, J. A. Fishman, B. Jernudd, and J. Rubin. The project studied language planning in four countries—Indonesia, India, Israel, and Sweden—from 1969 to 1972.

groups have deliberately exaggerated the differences between Hindi and Urdu to mobilize their followers and to gain cohesion among them. The linguistic differences between the two languages have been shown to be rather narrow. Wolff (1967) indicates that the awareness of ethnic identity among a group of hinterland Nigerian peoples has had linguistic repercussions: the languages learned have changed, child-naming practices have changed so that most families now give their children names drawn from the linguistic vernacular, and there is a marked increase in the use of the vernacular in church services, elementary education, and public meetings. Brown and Gilman (1960:264) suggest that the relationship between status and solidarity has changed with changes in political philosophies. "A historical study of the pronouns of address reveals a set of semantic and social psychological correspondences. The nonreciprocal power semantic is associated with a relatively static society in which power is distributed by birthright and not subject to much redistributing." They found that, after the French Revolution, when a more democratic philosophy prevailed in France, a conflict between status and solidarity arose, and the dimension of solidarity prevailed. Under extreme democratizing influences the status dimension may for a while be neutralized, and all members of a society may be considered equal. This equality is reflected in pronoun usage, as Brown and Gilman have shown.

The politics of language planning are complex indeed and reflect both intra- and intergroup values as well as patterns of power and prestige. When new nations are established, there is often a desire to establish one common language; however, the choice often reveals intergroup conflicts and differing philosophies.

In an extensive study of Norwegian language planning, Haugen (1966*b*) suggests that the creation of two national standards was motivated not only by patriotism but also by different class values. One of the varieties of standard Norwegian reflects the speech of the "official elite," who have city values; a second variety of standard Norwegian reflects the speech of the "folk elite," who embrace the values of folk life. A third linguistic model is arising with industrialization and with the introduction of many foreign words. The ideological battle between the democratic and the elitist values continues to be fought on linguistic grounds. The third variety interposes still another value often found among language planners, that of consideration of more international values.

Rubin and Wahjono (n.d.) found that conflicting values are often reflected in what might be considered minor linguistic changes. A study of the recent Indonesian attempt to equate its spelling with that of Malaysia indicated that the complicated response to a spelling change was a reflection both of the changing political situation and of the pendulum-like political relations of the two countries. The vehemence of the attack on the suggested new spelling was perhaps more closely related to the new era of democracy that arose with Suharto and to opportunities for expression than a rejection of the spelling reform per se. Nonetheless, the criticisms reflected some of the political positions of various vested interests quite well and brought to light social alliances hitherto not clearly defined.

Among other attitudes associated with linguistic varieties is that of language loyalty, which Weinreich (1953:99) defined as "the name given to the desire of a speech community to retain its language and, if necessary, to defend it against foreign encroachment." Feelings of language loyalty are aroused when there is some sort of attack on the mother tongue. Another attitude, the converse, is language antipathy, which may be found when usage of a particular language may be on the decline.

Willingness to effect changes in language may also reflect positive attitudes toward change and modernization in general. A study in progress directed and coordinated by Ferguson, Fishman, Das Gupta, Jernudd, and Rubin includes consideration of the relationship between the two (see footnote 11).

Neustupný (1968a) points out that there is a range of the means for effecting language change which may reflect a number of values. The four he mentions relate language treatment (which may not be as organized as language planning) to the degree of systematicity, theoretical elaborateness, depth, and rationality.[12] Thus, while the treatment of language problems may motivate a more formalized controlled attempt by a language planning agency, it is also common for some of the members of a society to effect change in a less systematic and rationalized fashion. The study of the values involved in solving language problems may be important in indicating direction and possibilities for change. It re-

---

[12] Neustupný defines these terms as follows: (1) systematicity refers to the way in which problems are exposed and solved—either in an ad hoc way or as an ordered system of items; (2) theoretical elaborateness refers to the meaningful basis of the treatment patterns, whether on sociological or linguistic models or both; (3) depth of treatment refers to the consideration that is taken of problems as they are reflected in folk taxonomies and native attitudes toward language or of the linguistic situation responsible for these taxonomies and attitudes; (4) rationality refers to treatments that are characterized by affective neutrality, specificity of goals and solutions, universalism, emphasis on effectiveness, and long-term objectives.

mains, however, largely unstudied as a process.

Acquisition of Speech Varieties

Although children's language acquisition has long been a field of great interest (Leopold 1952, Ervin-Tripp 1966, Slobin 1968), more recently interest has been growing in isolating universal language acquisition features (Slobin, 1968). Students of psycholinguistics have been concerned with the stages of acquisition of a particular homogeneous language. However, information on differential patterns of speech acquisition within a speech community, and the ways in which this differential acquisition pattern might reflect social, cultural, and individual constraints, has been very limited indeed.

Accompanying this interest in the universal features of language acquisition is a more recent one in linguistic socialization—an interest in considering the social and cultural concomitants of speech acquisition. A result of this growing interest is Slobin's (1967) field manual for the cross-cultural study of the acquisition of communicative competence and several doctoral dissertations (Stross 1969, Kernan 1969, Mitchell-Kernan 1969, Blount 1969). Some of the important questions raised in these dissertations are: (1) How do social settings alter the linguistic performance of children? (2) To what extent can aspects of the natural and social environment facilitate or inhibit the rate and degree of language development? (3) What beliefs and practices have a direct or indirect bearing on language acquisition? (4) How do children learn the various linguistic styles they need? Following the manual, these studies explore a number of topics: baby talk, parental correction of the child's speech, speech play and verbal games, conceptions of child development (and linguistic development), speech defects, verbal sanctions for bad behavior, linguistic taboos, and child participation in adult speech events. While the evidence indicates the importance of social setting for speech acquisition and production, the complexities involved in investigating this topic suggest that much more work will be needed.

Blount (1969:43) gives some indication of the difficulties of acquiring a full picture of the acquisition process. He recognizes that any description of competence must "follow an account of the major rules governing children's speech," and specifies that the rules for the community he studied are: (1) children do not interact with strangers, (2) children interact only ritually with visitors, (3) children interact formally with adults in the presence of other adults according to a prescribed manner, and (4) children interact "freely" (with minimum constraint) with peers." He also recognizes that he could not manipulate data collecting so as to acquire samples of speech under condition 4, which offers the best indication of acquired competency. Similar difficulties are recognized in others of these studies.

Social Determinants and Concomitants. There is a growing body of literature on the relevance of social contexts in determining the types of rules of speaking learned and the emphasis given to them in different groups. Hymes (1968) points out that cultures vary in the amount of speaking permitted to children—some insist that they speak while others insist that they be silent. This has been further elaborated by Blount (1969), who shows that the amount of speaking permitted to children is related to the social group in which the child finds himself—with his peers he is permitted free interaction, but with others rules of speech are tightly constrained. In contrast to this pattern, Labov (1969:72) notes that among the black populations he studied, a speech style not only is acquired from peers, but also achieves a dominance in use and is extended to many areas of social interaction:

But we may note that somewhere between the time that children first learn to talk and puberty, their language is restructured to fit the rules used by their peer group. From a linguistic point of view, the peer group is certainly a more powerful influence than the family. Less directly, the pressures of a peer group activity are also felt within the school.

Labov et al. (1968) indicated some of the differences between the kinds of speech learned from peer groups (story telling, word games, verbal dueling) and the kinds of speech learned at home or in school.

Philips (1970) found that among Warm Springs Indians, rules of speaking in public are constrained not by the age of the participants, but rather by an individual's assessment of his own communicative competence in a particular encounter. Use of this set of rules by Indian children in schools have led white teachers to remark that the children are too silent.

Observation of speech acquisition must be sure to take account of the rules for speaking in various contexts. If it does not, conclusions about the verbal capacity of children may be inconclusive. One of the studies that has been widely cited and emulated in the United States is that of the British scholar Basil Bernstein, who has studied the speech of various groups in England over a number of years. In his early work, Bernstein (1962, 1964, 1966) distinguished two linguistic codes—a "restricted" code by which language is used largely in formulaic and relatively predictable ways, and an "elaborated" code that emphasizes the speaker's ability to use speech creatively and permits more sublety and precision. Bernstein studied the speech of two social groups, which he called middle and lower class, and indicated that the lower class usually used only the "restricted" code while the middle class used both. He claimed that the two modes arise because the two social strata place different emphases on language potential, and that once this emphasis is placed, the resulting modes of speech progressively orient speakers toward different types of relationships to objects and persons. As Cazden (1966) has pointed out, speech is seen as both cause and effect. Bernstein seems to postulate a direct relationship between the socialization practices of the two groups and the individual's ability to express explicit relationships through speech.

More recent work carried out elsewhere has raised doubts about the validity of Bernstein's findings for other areas of the world. The work of Labov (1969) and Mitchell-Kernan (1969), among others, which used techniques to establish a less formal research situation, found that the same children who speak only in short and highly formulaic utterances (which would be characterized as "restricted" speech) in formal interviews, in school, or with strangers show themselves to be highly creative and effective communicators when they are interviewed in a setting that they perceive as culturally realistic, or when their natural interaction with peers is recorded. Thus, under the right conditions, lower-class American children have been shown to use a more elaborated code. There is little justification at this point, then, to associate absolute differences in verbal speaking with class or ethnic background. Furthermore, there is little reason to assume that differences in socialization processes are the only determinants of the language codes that children acquire.

Cultural Determinants and Concomitants. Among the cultural constraints that may affect linguistic acquisition are attitudes toward language learning and teaching. Ferguson (1964) points out that many cultures have baby talk (i.e., speech used by adults when addressing infants); others have added that this feature is presumably based on the feeling that adult speech is too difficult for young children. In contrast, Ervin-Tripp and Miller (1968:85) point out that the Hidatsa claim to use no baby talk at all because "We don't like baby talk . . . When they talk, we want them to talk just like us, right from the start." Cultures vary in the amount of verbal stimulation given to children, and it is still not clear how this affects their way of speaking. Some, Hymes (1968) points out, emphasize good speaking (the Ngoni, for example), and this presumably creates a different range of varieties. Attitudes toward the different sexes may also affect the speech acquisition process; Hymes (1968) says that the Tlingit believed that the talk of women was a source of conflict among men, and therefore an amulet was placed in a baby girl's mouth to make her taciturn. The ways in which acquisition of speech varieties and rules of speaking are related to social and cultural factors constitute a whole new area that will require a great deal more study.

SOCIOLINGUISTICS THUS FAR

The shift from a major concern with the ways in which language determines culture to examination of the ways in which language varieties reflect, are constrained by, and are changed by social, cultural, and individual determinants has proven very productive, and should profoundly affect both linguistic and sociocultural theory in the future. Labov (1964a, 1970) has argued that sociolinguistic research could be used to solve important theoretical problems within the disciplines of linguistics and sociology. For linguistics, Labov isolated important issues such as the nature of linguistic structure and of linguistic change. Neustupný (1968a) points out that the linguist's concern with language problems is only one type of treatment of language; many other kinds of treatment that are critical in affecting linguistic behavior and its significance exist in any speech community and deserve attention.

A central problem in sociolinguistics is the concern with understanding the kinds of speech communities; the types of varieties in a community and the distribution of varieties within this community; the functional allocation among the components of these varieties; the values, attitudes, beliefs, and behaviors associated with the varieties (and their components) within a speech repertoire; and the ways in which these varieties within a repertoire are patterned and changed by sociocultural and individual determinants.

It is clear that a speech community may be any of several types of populations—it may be a ward or *barrio* or group of any size (localized or not) whose members share similar communication networks. Thus ethnic groups, social classes or castes, nations and states all fall within the purview of sociolinguistics. Fishman and others (Fishman 1965, 1970; Haugen 1966a; Kloss 1967) have emphasized the need to coordinate microsociolinguistics, which Fishman (1970) calls the specification and utilization of speech acts and events, with macrosociolinguistics, which I understand to mean both the specification of higher level compo-

nents that influence speech acts and events and the community-wide functional description of varieties. By this distinction, it seems to me, Fishman is trying to find a link between social and cultural determinants that influence speech events and the larger community; that is, macrosociolinguistics includes microsociolinguistics.

The study of variation within a speech community leads to the conclusion that the study of linguistic structures apart from the social context is artifical and not very helpful to the student of social behavior or social communication. Historical relations cannot be studied or understood by concentrating on an idealized monolithic speech variety. A vocabulary list does not indicate very much unless you know who uses it with whom, with what meaning, how often, and with what intent. Although linguists may isolate structural similarities, the significance of these similarities for social processes is not at all clear-cut. The social variables of self-identity and the nature and frequency of contact have been found to affect not only intelligibility but also the definition of the language boundaries themselves. Although linguistic differences may be marked, intelligibility may be great—indeed, the members of a community may overcome the differences by adjusting their own speech variety or by learning that of another group. Creoles provide a unique form of linguistic structure that is both continuous and discontinuous at the same time. Of interest to anthropologists is the nature and meaning of the communication as speakers vary their linguistic structures at all levels.

Labov's work has shown conclusively that linguistic variables are precise indicators of socioeconomic status. His emphasis on quantitative analysis within a speech community has related linguistic variation and social indicators. His New York study (1966c) has demonstrated how variation can be regularly correlated with stylistic changes as well as with long-term changes. Labov has noted, however, that the rate of change between social values and linguistic change is not identical; in Martha's Vineyard (1963), he found that social structures and values change at a more rapid rate than relations between elements in a linguistic system.[13]

In addition to the important emphasis on the significance of quantitative analysis of variation, qualitative analysis has isolated some of the values, attitudes, and beliefs toward language and its usage which members of a speech community may share. It is clear that similar social functions can be served by different linguistic means; moreover, the same linguistic devices may serve different social functions within different speech communities. Further research is needed on the role of variables in constraining speech usage and expectations.

Thus far, sociolinguistics does not have any coherent theory. Some (Labov 1964a) argue against the establishment of sociolinguistics as a separate discipline apart from linguistics or sociology. Others (Fishman 1968) argue that there is a need for sociolinguistics as a separate field because its concerns have been neglected by both sociologists and linguists. Whether a coherent theory will result remains to be seen.

---

[13] In recent work, Labov (1970; Labov et al. 1968) has indicated that there are many *variant* relations to be found in linguistic structures. He considers (1970:78) that "a very great number of linguistic rules are not variable in the least: they are categorical rules which, given the proper input, always apply." He further indicates (1970:79) that his variable rules "depend upon, and interlock with, a number of invariant rules of grammar derived from studies of language quite apart from any social context."

One of the most important issues brought to light by the development of sociolinguistics is the need to break down the artificial units created by linguists—dialect, language, and idiolect. In their places have been substituted functional units such as speech communities, social networks, speech repertoires and varieties. Now one can begin to build a theory that includes behavioral variation and higher level units including both synchronic and diachronic interaction. The problem seems similar to the need to integrate behavioral variation, society, and culture as one system. Sociolinguistics may shed some light on similar problems in sociocultural theory.

REFERENCES

Agheyisi, Rebecca, and Joshua A. Fishman
1970 Language Attitude Studies: A Brief Survey of Methodological Approaches. *Anthropological Linguistics* 12, no. 5:137-57.
Ainsfield, E., and W. E. Lambert
1964 Evaluational Reactions of Bilingual and Monolingual Children to Spoken Language. *Journal of Abnormal and Social Psychology* 69:89-97.
Albert, Ethel
1964 "Rhetoric," "Logic," and "Poetics" in Burundi: Culture Patterning of Speech Behavior. In *The Ethnography of Communication,* ed. J. Gumperz and D. Hymes, pp. 35-54. *American Anthropologist* 66, no. 6, pt. 2 (special issue).
Back, K.
1960 The Well-Informed Informant. In *Human Organization Research,* ed. R. Adams and J. J. Priss, pp. 179-88. Homewood, Ill.: Dorsey Press.
Bailey, Charles-James
1969- Studies in Three-Dimensional Lin-
1970 guistic Theory. Working Papers in Linguistics, Department of Linguistics, University of Hawaii.
Barker, George C.
1947 Social Functions of Language in a

Mexican-American Community. *Acta Americana* 5:185-202.

Barth, Fredrik
1969 *Ethnic Groups and Boundaries.* Boston: Little, Brown.

Bernstein, Basil
1962 Social Class, Linguistic Codes, and Grammatical Elements. *Language and Speech* 5:221-40.
1964 Elaborated and Restricted Codes: Their Social Origins and Some Consequences. In *The Ethnography of Communication,* ed. J. Gumperz and D. Hymes, pp. 55-69. *American Anthropologist* 66, no. 6, pt. 2 (special issue).
1966 Elaborated and Restricted Codes: An Outline. *Sociological Inquiry* 36: 254-61.

Blanc, Haim
1964 *Communal Dialects in Baghdad.* Cambridge: Harvard University Press.

Bloomfield, Leonard
1933 *Language.* New York: Holt, Rinehart & Winston.

Blount, Benny G.
1969 Acquisition of Language by Luo Children. Unpublished Ph.D. dissertation, University of California, Berkeley.

Bock, Philip K.
1964 Social Structure and Language Structure. *Southwestern Journal of Anthropology* 20:393-403.

Bright, William
1960 Social Dialect and Language History. *Current Anthropology* 1:424-25.

Bright, William, ed.
1966 *Sociolinguistics: Proceedings of the UCLA Sociolinguistics Conference.* The Hague: Mouton.

Brown, Roger W.
1958 *Words and Things,* pp. 229-63. Glencoe, Ill.: Free Press.

Brown, Roger W., and Marguerite Ford
1961 Address in American English. *Journal of Abnormal and Social Psychology* 62:375-85.

Brown, Roger W., and Albert Gilman
1960 The Pronouns of Power and Solidarity. In *Style in Language,* ed. *Thomas A. Sebeok.* New York: Wiley.

Burling, Robbins

1970 *Man's Many Voices.* New York: Holt, Rinehart & Winston.

Cazden, Courtney
1966 Subcultural Differences in Child Language: An Inter-Disciplinary Review. *Merrill-Palmer Quarterly.*

Cohen, Yehudi
1968 *Man in Adaptation: The Cultural Present.* Chicago: Aldine.

Das, Sisir K.
1968 Forms of Address and Terms of Reference in Bengali. *Anthropological Linguistics* 10, no. 5:19-31.

Das Gupta, Jyotirindra
1970 *Language Conflict and National Development.* Berkeley and Los Angeles: University of California Press.

De Camp, David
1961 Social and Geographical Factors in Jamaican Dialects. In *Creole Language Studies,* ed. Robert Le Page, vol. 2. New York: St. Martin's Press.
1970 Is a Sociolinguistic Theory Possible? *Georgetown University Monograph Series on Languages and Linguistics* 22:157-73.

De Francis, John
1950 *Nationalism and Language Reform in China.* Princeton: Princeton University Press.

Diebold, Richard
1962 Mexican and Guatemalan Bilingualism. In *Study of the Role of Second Languages in Asia, Africa, and Latin America,* ed. Frank Rice, pp. 26-33. Washington, D.C.: Center for Applied Linguistics.

Dozier, Edward P.
1956 Two Examples of Linguistic Acculturation: The Yaqui of Sonora and Arizona and the Tewa of New Mexico. *Language* 32:146-57.

Durbin, Marshall
1973 Cognitive Anthropology. In *Handbook of Social and Cultural Anthropology,* ed. J. Honigmann. Chicago: Rand McNally.

Edwards, Jay D.
1970 Social Linguistics on San Andrés and Providencia Islands, Colombia. Unpublished Ph.D. dissertation, Tulane University.

Ervin-Tripp, Susan M.
1964 An Analysis of the Interaction Be-

tween Language, Topic, and Speaker. *American Anthropologist* 66, no. 2:86-102.

1966 Language Development. In *Review of Child Development Research*, ed. M. Hoffman and L. Hoffman, vol. 2, pp. 55-105. Ann Arbor: University of Michigan Press.

1968 Sociolinguistics. In *Advances in Experimental Social Psychology,* ed. L. Berkowitz, vol. 4. New York: Academic Press.

Ervin-Tripp, Susan M., and Wick R. Miller
1968 Language Development. In *Readings in the Sociology of Language*, ed. J. Fishman. The Hague: Mouton.

Ferguson, Charles A.
1959*a* Diglossia. *Word* 15:325-40.
1959*b* Myths about Arabic. *Georgetown University Monograph Series on Languages and Linguistics* 12:75-82.
1964 Baby Talk in Six Languages. *American Anthropologist* 66, no. 2:86-102.

Ferguson, Charles A., and John J. Gumperz, eds.
1960 Linguistic Diversity in South Asia: Studies in Regional, Social, and Functional Variation. *International Journal of American Linguistics* 26, pt. 2:3; publication no. 13, Indiana University Research Center in Anthropology, Folklore, and Linguistics.

Fischer, John L.
1958 Social Influence in the Choice of a Linguistic Variant. *Word* 14:47-56.

Fishman, Joshua A.
1964 Language Maintenance and Language Shift as Fields of Inquiry. *Linguistics* 9:32-70.
1965 Who Speaks What Language to Whom and When. *Linguistique* 2:67-88.
1967 Bilingualism with and Without Diglossia: Diglossia with and Without Bilingualism. *Journal of Social Issues* 23, no. 2:29-38.
1970 *Sociolinguistics.* Rowley, Mass.: Newbury House.
n.d. Language Maintenance and Language Shift as a Field of Inquiry (Revisited). Unpublished MS.

Fishman, Joshua A., ed.
1966 *Language Loyalty in the United*

States. The Hague: Mouton.
1968 *Readings in the Sociology of Language.* The Hague: Mouton.

Fishman, Joshua A., and Eleanor Herasimchuk
1968 The Multiple Prediction of Phonological Variables in a Bilingual Speech Community. In *Bilingualism in the Barrio,* ed. J. Fishman et al., pp. 836-58. New York: Yeshiva University Press.

Fishman, Joshua A., et al.
1968 *Bilingualism in the Barrio.* New York: Yeshiva University Press.

Fishman, Joshua A., C. A. Ferguson, and J. Das Gupta, eds.
1968 *Language Problems of Developing Nations.* New York: Wiley.

Foster, George M.
1964 Speech Forms and Perception of Social Distance in a Spanish-Speaking Mexican Village. *Southwestern Journal of Anthropology* 20:107-22.

Friedrich, Paul
1966 Structural Implications of Russian Pronominal Usage. *In Sociolinguistics,* ed. William Bright, pp. 214-59. The Hague: Mouton.

Garfinkel, Harold
1967 *Studies in Ethnomethodology.* Englewood Cliffs, N.J.: Prentice-Hall.

Garvin, Paul L.
1959 The Standard Language Problem. *Anthropological Linguistics* 1, no. 3:28-31.

Geertz, Clifford
1957 Ritual and Social Change: A Javanese Example. *American Anthropologist* 59:32-53.
1960 Linguistic Etiquette. In *Religion of Java.* New York: Free Press, Macmillan.

Goodell, R. J.
1964 An Ethnolinguistic Bibliography with Supporting Material in Linguistics and Anthropology. *Anthropological Linguistics* 6, no. 2:10-32.

Goodenough, Ward H.
1963 *Cooperation in Change.* New York: Russell Sage Foundation.
1965 Rethinking "Status" and "Role": Toward a General Model of the Cultural Organization of Social Relationships. In *The Relevance of Models*

for Social Anthropology, ed. M. Banton, pp. 1-24. New York: Praeger.

Grootaers, Willem A.
1959 Origin and Nature of the Subjective Boundaries of Dialects. *Orbis* 8:355-89.

Gumperz, John J.
1958 Dialect Difference and Social Stratification in a North Indian Village. *American Anthropologist* 60:668-82.
1962 Types of Linguistic Communities. *Anthropological Linguistics* 4, no. 1:28-40.
1964 Linguistic and Social Interaction in Two Communities. *American Anthropologist* 56, no. 2:137-53.
1966 On the Ethnology of Linguistic Change. In *Sociolinguistics,* ed. William Bright, pp. 27-38. The Hague: Mouton.
1968 The Speech Community. In *International Encyclopedia of the Social Sciences,* ed. David L. Sills. New York: Free Press, Macmillan.
1969 Communication in Multilingual Societies. In *Cognitive Anthropology,* ed. Stephen Tyler, pp. 435-49. New York: Holt, Rinehart & Winston.
1970 Sociolinguistics and Communication in Small Groups. Working Paper no. 33, Language-Behavior Research Laboratory.

Gumperz, John J., and Dell Hymes, eds.
1964 *The Ethnography of Communication. American Anthropologist* 66, no. 2, pt. 2 (special issue).
1970 *Directions in Sociolinguistics.* New York: Holt, Rinehart & Winston.

Haas, Mary
1944 Men's and Women's Speech in Koasati. *Language* 20:142-49.

Haugen, Einar
1953 *The Norwegian Language in America: A Study in Bilingual Behavior,* 2 vols. Philadelphia: University of Pennsylvania Press.
1956 *Bilingualism in the Americas: A Bibliography and Research Guide.* University, Ala: American Dialect Society.
1962 Schizoglossia and the Linguistic Norm. *Georgetown University Monograph Series on Languages and Linguistics* 15:63-69.

1966a Dialect, Language, Nation. *American Anthropologist* 68:922-35.
1966b *Language Conflict and Language Planning: The Case of Modern Norwegian.* Cambridge: Harvard University Press.
1970 Linguistics and Dialinguistics. In *Bilingualism and Language Contact: Anthropological, Linguistic, Psychological, and Sociological Aspects,* ed. James E. Alatis, pp. 1-12. Georgetown University 21st Annual Round Table. Washington, D.C.: Georgetown University Press.

Hertzler, Joyce O.
1965 *A Sociology of Language.* New York: Random House.

Herzog, George
1941 Culture Change and Language: Shifts in the Pima Vocabulary. In *Language and Personality,* ed. L. Spier, A. I. Hallowell, and S. S. Newman, pp. 66-74. Menasha, Wis.: Banta.

Householder, Fred W., Jr.
1963 Greek Diglossia. *Georgetown University Monograph Series on Languages and Linguistics* 15:109-29.

Hymes, Dell
1961 Functions of Speech: An Evolutionary Approach. In *Anthropology and Education,* ed. Fred Gruber. Philadelphia: University of Pennsylvania Press.
1962 The Ethnography of Speaking. In *Anthropology and Human Behavior,* ed. T. Gladwin and W. C. Sturtevant, pp. 13-53. Washington, D.C.: Anthropological Society of Washington.
1965 Corrigenda and Addenda to R. J. Goodell: An Ethnolinguistic Bibliography with Supporting Material in Linguistics and Anthropology. *Anthropological Linguistics* 7, no. 3: 84-87.
1967 Models of the Interaction of Language and Social Setting. *Journal of Social Issues* 23, no. 2:8-28.
1968 The Ethnography of Speaking. In *Readings in the Sociology of Language,* ed. J. A. Fishman. The Hague: Mouton.
1970 Bilingual Education: Linguistic vs. Sociolinguistic Bases. In *Bilingualism and Language Contact: Anthropolog-*

ical, Linguistic, Psychological, and Sociological Aspects, ed. James E. Alatis, pp. 69-76. Georgetown University 21st Annual Round Table. Washington, D.C.: Georgetown University Press.

1971 *Pidginization and Creolization of Languages.* Cambridge: At the University Press.

Hymes, Dell, ed.
1964 *Language in Culture and Society: A Reader in Linguistics and Anthropology.* New York: Harper & Row.

Jain, Dhanesh K.
1969 Verbalization of Respect in Hindi. *Anthropological Linguistics* 11, no. 3:79-97.

Jernudd, Björn
1968a Linguistic Integration and National Development: A Case Study of the Jebel Marra Area, Sudan. In *Language Problems of Developing Nations,* ed. J. Fishman, C. A. Ferguson, and J. Das Gupta, pp. 167-82. New York: Wiley.
1968b There Are No Subjective Dialects. *Kivung* 1, no. 1:38-42.

Kantrowitz, Nathan
1967 The Vocabulary of Race Relations in a Prison. Paper presented at meeting of American Dialect Society, Chicago.

Kernan, Keith
1969 The Acquisition of Language by Samoan Children. Unpublished Ph.D. dissertation, University of California, Berkeley.

Kloss, Heinz
1952 *Die Entwicklung neuer germanischer Kultursprachen.* Munich: Pohl.
1967 "Abstand Languages" and "Ausbau Languages." *Anthropological Linguistics* 9, no. 7:29-41.

Labov, William
1963 The Social Motivation of a Sound Change. *Word* 19:273-309.
1964a The Aims of Sociolinguistics Research. Unpublished working paper, Sociolinguistics Seminar, Indiana University.
1964b Phonological Correlates of Social Stratification. In *The Ethnography of Communication,* ed. J. Gumperz and D. Hymes, pp. 164-76. *American Anthropologist* 66, no. 6, pt. 2 (special issue).
1966a The Effect of Social Mobility on Linguistic Behavior. *Sociological Inquiry* 36:186-203.
1966b Hypercorrection by the Lower Middle Class as a Factor in Linguistic Change. In *Sociolinguistics,* ed. William Bright, pp. 84-101. The Hague: Mouton.
1966c *The Social Stratification of English in New York City.* Washington, D.C.: Center for Applied Linguistics.
1968 The Reflection of Social Processes in Linguistic Structures. In *Readings in the Sociology of Language,* ed. J. Fishman, pp. 240-51. The Hague: Mouton.
1969 The Logic of Non-standard English. In *Linguistic-Cultural Differences and American Education,* pp. 60-74. *Florida FL Reporter* 7, no. 1 (special issue).
1970 The Study of Language in Its Social Context. *Studium Generale* 23:30-87.

Labov, William, and Joshua Watelsky
1967 Narrative Analyses: Oral Versions of Personal Experience. In *Essays on the Verbal and Visual Arts: Proceedings of 1966 Annual Spring Meeting of the American Ethnological Society,* ed. June Helm, pp. 12-44. Seattle: American Ethnological Society.

Labov, William, et al.
1968 *A Study of the Non-standard English of Negro and Puerto Rican Speakers in New York City,* 2 vols. Final report, Cooperative Research Project, Office of Education, U.S. Department of Health, Education, and Welfare. Washington, D.C.: U.S. Government Printing Office.

Lambert, Wallace E., et al.
1960 Evaluational Reactions to Spoken Languages. *Journal of Abnormal and Social Psychology* 66, no. 1:44-51.

Leopold, W. F.
1952 *Bibliography of Child Language.* Evanston, Ill.: Northwestern University Press.

Levine, William L., and H. J. Crockett
1966 Speech Variation in a Piedmont

Community: Postvocalic R. *Socio-logical Inquiry* 36:204-26.

Lieberson, Stanley, ed.
1966 *Explorations in Sociolinguistics.* Bloomington: Indiana University Research Center in Anthropology, Folklore, and Linguistics.

Lunt, Horace G.
1959 The Creation of Standard Macedonian: Some Facts and Attitudes. *Anthropological Linguistics* 1, no. 5:19-26.

Ma, Roxana, and Eleanor Herasimchuk
1968 The Linguistic Dimensions of a Bilingual Neighborhood. In *Bilingualism in the Barrio,* ed. J. Fishman et al., vol. 2, pp. 638-835.

Mackey, William F.
1962 The Description of Bilingualism. *Canadian Journal of Bilingualism* 7, no. 2.

Martin, Samuel
1964 Speech Levels in Japan and Korea. In *Language in Culture and Society,* ed. Dell Hymes. New York: Harper & Row.

Miller, Robert L.
1968 *The Linguistic Relativity Principle and Humboldtian Ethnolinguistics.* The Hague: Mouton.

Mitchell-Kernan, Claudia
1969 Language Behavior in a Black Urban Community. Unpublished Ph.D. dissertation, University of California, Berkeley.

Moerman, Michael
1969 A Little Knowledge. In *Cognitive Anthropology,* ed. Stephen Tyler. New York: Holt, Rinehart & Winston.

Moulton, William G.
1963 What Standard for Diglossia? The Case of German Switzerland. *Georgetown University Monograph Series on Languages and Linguistics* 15: 133-44.

Neustupný, Jiří V.
1965 First Steps Towards the Conception of "Oriental Languages": A Contribution to the Sociology of Language. *Archiv Orientalni* 33:83-92.

1968a Basic Types of Treatment of Language Problems. Paper read at the Eighth International Congress of Anthropological and Ethnological Sci-ences, Tokyo and Kyoto.

1968b Politeness Patterns in the System of Communication. Paper read at the Eighth International Congress of Anthropological and Ethnological Sciences, Tokyo and Kyoto.

1970 Basic Types of Treatment of Language Problems. *Linguistic Communications* 1:77-98.

Olmstead, D. L.
1950 Ethnolinguistics So Far. *Summer Institute of Linguistics Occasional Papers* 2:1-16.

Percival, Keith
1966 A Reconsideration of Whorf's Hypothesis. *Anthropological Linguistics* 8, no. 8:1-12.

Philips, Susan U.
1970 Acquisition of Rules for Appropriate Speech Usage. *Georgetown University Monograph Series on Languages and Linguistics* 23:77-101.

Pittenger, Robert, Charles F. Hockett, and J. S. Danehy
1960 The First Five Minutes. Ithaca, N.Y.: Paul Martineau.

Pride, J. B., and Janet Holmes, eds.
1972 *Readings in Sociolinguistics.* Penguin Books.

Putnam, George N., and Edna M. O'Hern
1955 The Status Significance of an Isolated Urban Dialect. *Language* 31, no. 4, pt. 2.

Reisman, Karl
1970 Cultural and Linguistic Ambiguity in a West Indian Village. In *Afro-American Anthropology,* ed. N. Whitten and J. F. Szwed, pp. 120-44. New York: Free Press, Macmillan.

Ross, Allan S. C.
1956 U and Non-U: An Essay in Sociological Linguistics. In *Noblesse Oblige,* ed. N. Mitford, pp. 11-38. London: Hamish Hamilton.

Rubin, Joan
1962 Bilingualism in Paraguay. *Anthropological Linguistics* 4, no. 1:52-58.

1968a Language and Education in Paraguay. In *Language Problems of Developing Nations,* ed. J. A. Fishman et al. New York: Wiley.

1968b National Bilingualism in Paraguay. The Hague: Mouton.

Rubin, Joan, and Björn Jernudd

1971   Language Planning as an Element in Modernization. In *Can Language Be Planned: Sociolinguistic Theory and Practice for Developing Nations,* ed. Joan Rubin and Björn Jernudd. Honolulu: East-West Center Press.

Rubin, Joan, and Wahjono
n.d.   Perubahan Edjaan Bahasa, Unpublished MS.

Salisbury, Richard
1962   Notes on Bilingualism and Linguistic Change in New Guinea. *Anthropological Linguistics* 4, no. 7:1-13.

Schegloff, Emanuel A.
1968   Sequencing in Conversational Openings. *American Anthropologist* 70, no. 6:1075-95.

Schneider, David
1968   *American Kinship: A Cultural Account.* Englewood Cliffs, N.J.: Prentice-Hall.

Sebeok, Thomas, A.
1968   Zoosemiotics: A Guide to Its Literature. *Language Sciences,* no. 3:7-14.

Sebeok, Thomas A., and Alexandra Ramsey, eds.
1970   *Approaches to Animal Communication.* New York: Humanities Press.

Slobin, Dan
1963   Some Aspects of the Use of Pronouns of Address in Yiddish. *Word* 19:193-202.
1967   *Field Manual for the Cross-Cultural Study of the Acquisition of Communicative Competence.* Berkeley: University of California Press.
1968   Early Grammatical Development in Several Languages, with Special Attention to Soviet Research. Working paper no. 11, Language-Behavior Research Laboratory.

Spicer, Edward H.
1962   *Cycles of Conquest.* Tucson: University of Arizona Press.

Stewart, William A.
1962   Creole Languages in the Caribbean. In *Study of the Role of Second Languages in Asia, Africa, and Latin America,* ed. Frank Rice, pp. 34-53. Washington, D.C.: Center for Applied Linguistics.
1963   The Functional Distribution of Creole and French in Haiti. *Georgetown University Monograph Series on Language and Linguistics* 15:149-59.

1968   A Sociolinguistic Typology for Describing National Multilingualism. In *Readings in the Sociology of Language,* ed. J. A. Fishman, pp. 531-45. The Hague: Mouton.

Stross, Brian
1969   Language Acquisition by Tenejapa Tjeltal Children. Unpublished Ph.D. dissertation, University of California, Berkeley.

Swartz, Marc
1960   Situational Determinants of Kinship Terminology. *Southwestern Journal of Anthropology* 17:205-18.

Tanner, Nancy
1967   Speech and Society Among the Indonesian Elite: A Case Study of a Multilingual Community. *Anthropological Linguistics* 9, no. 3:15-39.

Trager, George L.
1964   Paralanguage: A First Approximation. *Studies in Linguistics* 13:1-12.

Tyler, Stephen A., ed.
1969   *Cognitive Anthropology,* New York: Holt, Rinehart & Winston.

Wallace, Anthony
1961   *Culture and Personality.* New York: Random House.

Weinreich, Uriel
1953   *Languages in Contact.* New York: Linguistic Circle of New York.
1957   Functional Aspects of Indian Bilingualism. *Word* 13:203-33.

Weinreich, Uriel, William Labov, and Marvin Herzog
1968   Empirical Foundations for a Theory of Language Change. In *Directions for Historical Linguistics,* ed. W. P. Lehmann and Y. Malkiel. Austin: University of Texas Press.

Wolff, Hans
1959   Intelligibility and Inter-Ethnic Attitudes. *Anthropological Linguistics* 1, no. 3:34-41.
1967   Language, Ethnic Identity, and Social Change in Southern Nigeria. *Anthropological Linguistics* 9, no. 1:18-25.

Wolfram, W. A.
1969   *A Sociolinguistic Description of Detroit Negro Speech.* Washington, D.C.: Center for Applied Linguistics.

CHAPTER 12 Belief Systems

MARY B. BLACK

INTRODUCTION

Taking "belief systems" as ideology, either we can say that they constitute all of culture (if culture is defined as knowledge of the things believed to exist in the world, their properties, and sets of rules about their ordering and manipulation) *or* we can posit an ideological level of culture complementary to a phenomenal, on-the-ground level. Either way, a problem presents itself: how to limit such a subject in undertaking a survey of this subfield of anthropology?

The subfield has variously viewed cultures as mental phenomena (Boas), codifications of reality (Bateson, Lee), underlying values and orientations that provide a more or less shared "definition of the situation" (Kluckhohn), means for cognitive orientation to the world outside the self (Hallowell), the competence of native knowers to generate acceptable performances, reactions, and judgments (Goodenough, Chomsky), and communicational systems (McQuown, White). A number of other terms have been applied over the years to models for this avenue to the study of culture: configurations, themes, genius, postulates, world view, ethos-eidos, jural rules, decision models, emic classifications, folk taxonomies, semantic structures, actor-oriented or inside-view ethnography. Please note that these are thrown together for the sake of their area of similarity, not to belabor their differences.

I propose to trace briefly the history of some of these approaches, to divide them roughly on the basis of their holism (macrosystems) or their particularism (microsystems), and to survey recent and current work, particularly of the macro kind. For it appears that those interested in studying systems of knowledge and belief have interpreted their task at varying scales of magnitude. "Belief system" connotes to some a major unifying philosophical structuring—indeed, it is sometimes identified with "religion" and/or epistemology, a society's "system of explanation" of the universe, particularly of the unknown and the unpredictable. At the other end, the term has been applied to conceptual structuring of the most minute and "trivial" domains of cultural knowledge. These latter have frequently been isolated and treated independently of their cultural contexts, in ethnoscience descriptions (or ethnosemantics, or descriptive semantics, or any of a number of other synonyms).

The present discussion will attempt to find a middle ground between these extremes, and will center on belief systems within their total culture context. It will include, among other approaches, the contemporary work of cognitive anthropologists (ethnoscience-trained) toward description of large-scale belief systems and toward interlinking of knowledge domains within a particular cultural system, and analysis of productive semantic features and relations (those that can function recurringly in many sectors of the culture). Thus, of the several responses to the charge of triviality originally directed at early ethnoscience work, this survey will document some extensions of ethnoscience ethnography to nontrivial descriptions of single cultures and their prospective significance for advancing our knowledge of culture in general. Others have already shown how ethnoscientific work has led to the discovery of universals of semantic structuring and insights to possible evolutionary development (Berlin and Kay 1969; Berlin 1969, 1970, 1971). The fact that ethnosemantic research, beginning with a deliberate concentration on rigorous emic descriptions of internal structure, has turned now to these more general considerations only after a serious and respectable compilation of descriptive data about particular systems has been clearly put forth in recent papers of Berlin (1970) and Kay (1970), as well as in their substantive work. It remains here, then, to stress

that this new generalizing does not mean the cessation of work on improving particular descriptions or of compilation of additional data. There is a need to point out some steps toward total-culture cognitive ethnographies and comparative holistic models, which have also been undergoing development as outgrowths of the ethnoscientific movement of the past two decades. This work is still incipient and is proceeding along several independent lines, some of which may not yet have come to my attention. The attempt to introduce scientific rigor to the unitary characterization of a culture has a long history and perhaps a longer future. It may indeed be ultimately impossible, in either a practical or a theoretical sense; yet the idea seems to persist among some anthropologists of each succeeding generation that it is a worthy and important task, uniquely challenging our discipline as such. And the old question of whether the *Gestalt* is not something different from the separate analyses of its parts may be an important one for belief system studies in the coming period.

The belief system goal is being approached from other starting points as well. These will be covered to the extent that they are anthropological in the larger sense, but I shall confine my comments mainly to theoretical and substantive results, omitting certain methodological issues and metaphysical conundrums inherent in the rather presumptuous goal of trying to understand other men's systems of reaction and thought. Questions of how one "gets inside" an alien belief system (or whether one ever does, or should expect to) are relevant in some contexts, and have been argued fairly extensively elsewhere, both within and without the halls of ethnoscience (see Burling 1969a; Hahn, in press). Philosophically oriented anthropologists and linguistically or anthropologically oriented philosophers have concerned themselves with the validity and status of such descriptions; they deal too in comparative epistemologies and logics and cultural philosophies. Schools of phenomenology, ethnomethodology, and work of sociologists relating to action-knowledge systems observable in our own society are also relevant. Finally, the contributions of linguists, communication scientists, and psychologists to the study of human systems of belief and cognition are not to be overlooked. It can be seen that a number of disciplines concern themselves with the subject of beliefs, and it will be necessary to keep in mind that it is *as parts of cultural systems* that belief systems will be treated.

DEFINITIONS AND HISTORICAL OVERVIEW

DEFINITIONS

"Belief" and "belief system" are terms used both popularly and technically, loosely and tightly, but generally they refer to some unseen intellectual/emotional activity of human beings. Before I outline one or two technical definitions upon which anthropological work is based, it might be useful to state that as these words are to be used here, there is no practical difference between "belief" and "knowledge." It is the "knowledge system" of an exotic people that the anthropologist describes as "beliefs." (He relegates all knowledge to the realm of belief, in order to entertain the idea of knowledge that contradicts his own.) That "belief" refers to a commitment to facts or ideas without adequate evidence (on faith, as it were) cannot be applied cross-culturally without confusion, for the idea of adequate evidence varies as well. That it implies a

greater emotional commitment (to "believe in") can be questioned too; when the chips are down, we are probably committed most deeply to those things we believe we know. The last statement may be held to demonstrate that the two words are not synonymous, one signifying a "state of mind . . . a conviction of truth," and the other an "acquaintance with fact," as Webster says. It should be noted, however, that their use will then carry a further underlying message about the speaker (or writer) and his convictions—his state of mind, if you will, about his own and others' acquaintance with fact. This is blatant in the following contrastive use: "They believe that the earth is round; (but) we know that it is flat"; but it is implied in any use that recognizes the dictionary definition. Since it is the exotic people's state of mind about their own acquaintance with fact that the belief system anthropologist seeks to describe, he may sometimes use "belief," sometimes "knowledge." If he subscribes to the dictionary distinction, however, he can hardly avoid inserting himself into his description in a confusing manner; some have solved this problem by consistently using either one word or the other, with reference both to exotic systems and to their own. Calling this chapter "belief systems" is a case in point; however, since many of those whom I would term belief system anthropologists have chosen to employ the term "knowledge system" instead, the dictionary distinction appears less than useful and will therefore be ignored. Where "belief (system)" or "believer" occurs in this paper, "knowledge (system)" or "knower" can be substituted freely. Furthermore, references to a culture-bearer's knowledge (or belief) will denote all that he "knows" of his culture's meaning structures—his "competence," in Chomsky's terms (1965:4), to use these structures for communicating with his fellows. They will not refer merely to those facts or theories about which he is able or likely to make statements, to an ethnographer or to anyone else. Belief propositions must be statable in language, but are not necessarily ever stated or even held consciously in mind. Some knowledge structures are built into the habit systems of their users. These are equally a part of cultural knowledge.

Goodenough's "Belief System"

On the premise that men need a cognitive organization of their experience, with limits on dissonance, contradiction, and chaos, Goodenough (1963, chap. 7) presents a model of beliefs which plugs them into percepts of the physical world at one end and into cultural explanations of the universe at the other. Our intake of experience starts getting organized at the level of sensory perception of the physical world; perceptual categories (shape, sound, taste, color) and their perceived arrangements vary according to cultural learning.[1] We then group and arrange our percepts to form concepts, with the aid of a coding system (e.g., language), so that many instances of recurring arrangements of percept categories may be reacted to similarly (e.g., robin, ghost); and additionally we can manipulate concepts themselves to form further concepts (e.g., bird, supernatural—including novel arrangements never actually perceived, such as unicorn and thunderbird). *Percepts* are thus defined as "the decision as to what is there" in sensory experience, and *concepts* as inferences from perceptions manipulated by a *coding system* (not perceived in direct

experience but conceived by analogy or symbolically created new arrangements of percepts). The code not only allows us to make classes and new arrangements, but is a vehicle for making statements about percepts and concept classes. This is where beliefs enter in. Even in order to classify (which is what we were doing from the beginning), we need to formulate propositions about properties and groupings. *Propositions* are statements capable of being true or false. And *beliefs* are "propositions held to be true."

Goodenough's belief system, then, consists of percepts, concepts, a code or language for manipulating them, and those propositions about the percepts and concepts that are held to be true by the believer. The *belief system* further has the properties of a system; that is, it is defined as a set of noncontradictory beliefs pertaining to the same domain (Goodenough 1963). The reduction of chaos which began with systematic perceptual distortions of physical "reality" is ultimately accomplished by explanations of the universe which are logically consistent, once assigned to appropriate domains. (Thus a behavior believed appropriate in one domain may be rejected as evil in another, without felt contradiction: an act or word may carry one message in a particular context and an altogether different message within another.) Goodenough further delineates *levels* of truths or beliefs that form a logical hierarchy: first those that are *self-evident* because rooted in everyday experience (e.g., the sun rises over the lake each day); then beliefs that can be *inferred* from the everyday ones as logically consistent (e.g., the sun arrives cooled by the water, heats up during the day to make things grow for humans, cools off again overnight); and finally there are *unifying beliefs*. These are more general postulates or axioms

---

[1] Though to what extent is being questioned by recent cross-cultural work on named color categories (Berlin and Kay 1969).

from which the self-evident and inferred truths follow (e.g., elements such as sun, moon, wind are supernatural persons who can move, have intentions, and affect human life willfully). These unifying beliefs appear to be true because they can explain so many diverse other things. They are likely to recur in a number of domains. (The properties of supernatural persons may be perceived at work in a host of everyday contexts.) We are most reluctant to question the truth of these last beliefs, because of the chaos or vacuum in which disbelief would leave us, for a change in one such belief could have the effect of destroying nearly the whole system.[2]

In turn, then, sense experience is adduced as evidence of the truth or falseness of inferred and unifying beliefs. In this model, the various levels of beliefs are seen as justifying each other, logically and in practice, *in both directions.* Conceptual and unifying beliefs are postulated to resolve contradictions or explain nonfitting experience, and in turn such beliefs have an effect on "the decision as to what is there" in further experience. Goodenough (1963:55) stresses the importance of the perceptual base, for example in accounting for differences in beliefs and belief systems of the peoples of the world:

The truth [of our beliefs], we aver, is ascertained by our senses. The entities we perceive are what we perceive them to be, and those propositions about their mutual arrangements and transformations that we are able to verify by direct observation are true. Other propositions that follow logically from these are presumably also true. . . . With such a measure, what is true and what is false is a function of our percepts, the categories in terms of which we habitually perceive things; and these, we have observed, are themselves ab-

stractions from experience and, as such, selective and arbitrary.

As an illustration, Goodenough refers to differing perceptions of the same stream of sound: "An Englishman and an Italian listening to French for the first time do not hear the same sounds." Lounsbury (1963:565-69), writing for psychologists about phonological analysis, termed it "stimulus equivalence" when a speaker fails to perceive the difference between two objectively different sound stimuli; he added it is a "learned nonperception," or "conditioned indifference," based on language structure at the sound-coding level. The speaker's language does not utilize this sound difference for distinguishing meanings, and he has learned to ignore it. Lounsbury adduced several cases of evidence from reactions of a Cayuga speaker, for whom "the rules [of the phonological system] are built into his habits already." This same type of evidence and argument was given by Sapir in his famous paper "The Psychological Reality of the Phoneme" (1949c).[3]

Goodenough points to cases in which people "see" different sensory features of the same events met in everyday experience, and thus use experience dif-

---

[2] Wallace (1961, chap. 4) discusses the effects of the loss of cognitive coherence, or disorganization of the system.

[3] The phoneme, a concept in a particular language system, represents a class of physical sound types which function equivalently in the language structure when produced as percept stimuli. At the lexical level, ease of distinguishing colors has been shown to be related to the way the color spectrum is divided by particular language and cultural organization (Brown and Lenneberg 1961), and it may be that the particular features attended to or ignored when other terminologies are used (e.g., kin terms) influence or reflect nonlinguistic cultural structure (Lounsbury 1963). Studies of these kinds have sometimes been directed toward testing the Whorf hypothesis, which maintained that language forms condition our percepts and concepts to such an extent that our thought and world view are molded and limited by the language we speak (Whorf 1956; and see Hoijer, ed., 1954).

ferently for verifying the truth of their inferred beliefs: "Differences in percept categories . . . mean that almost any event is capable of verifying different, inconsistent and even downright contradictory propositions." (He seems here to be asserting that all differences in beliefs stem from differences in perceiving; it might be argued that "the decision as to what is there" can also stem from conceptual interpretations of the *same* percept categories.[4]) Whether or not all belief differences have their roots in percept differences, the importance he places on logical and empirical *reduction* of conceptual and belief phenomena to *their cue value in the world of sense experience* is significant. This becomes more clear in his presentations of descriptive semantics, where the physically perceivable base of cultural knowledge systems has important implications for ethnographic methodology and analysis.

------

[4] It seems to me that "the decision as to what is there" can refer simply to differing concepts. Alec Everwind and I both saw the lightning hit the lake, and the shimmering movement afterward. He called it a thunderbird sending his light down for food, and lifting the wiggling fish. He knows because he saw it himself. I called it elements behaving in some nonpurposive way according to natural laws. We decided differently about "what was there," but for this our sensory perception of the physical event need not have differed, only our conceptual classification of it and attendant beliefs about class properties. Note also that Nida (1964, chap. 5) has found that taxonomies differ more across cultures at the higher levels (more general, conceptually based classes) than at the specific level (closer to that of perceptually distinguishable phenomena). It would seem that a variety of different unifying beliefs could equally "explain" certain identical sensory experiences. It is true that we may perceive the same object differently because of our learned conceptual categories, but also we may perceive similarly, yet bring different beliefs to bear in our interpretations of the event. "The decision as to what is there" is perhaps a rather ambiguous way to characterize sensory perceptions. Once named or otherwise decided about, the perceived item becomes a manifestation of a concept.

Certain other ways of defining belief system will be considered later, but the division between macro- and microsystems can best be introduced by way of Goodenough's phrasing, which also points up the significance of *context* for the investigation of cultural belief structures.

MACRO- AND MICROSYSTEMS OF BELIEF

Within ideological culture, systems relate to separate domains, according to Goodenough. That is, the rules of a system are valid and useful only within recognizably distinct contexts. It is part of our cultural knowledge to assess correctly the boundaries within which allowable or meaningful substitutions may occur or choices be made. Linguists would say that for information to be conveyed, we must be aware of the environment within which items contrast. As Frake has noted (1969a), "The three categories 'hamburger,' 'hot dog,' and 'rainbow' are mutually exclusive in membership. But in writing rules for classifying hamburgers I must say something about hot dogs, whereas I can ignore rainbows" (assuming that no unlikely lunch counter decides to offer a concoction on a split roll and call it a "rainbow"). It is only beliefs that contradict each other within the same domain that are disturbing, and then a unifying explanation or a subrule may be postulated or brought to bear to resolve the contradiction. (You can't say that a rainbow is not a sandwich and at the same time that it is a sandwich without postulating something like the unlikely lunch counter.)

Thus separate domains and unifying postulates allow resolution of contradictory beliefs, reduction of cognitive dissonance, and maintenance of tolerable degrees of coherence. In addition, beliefs at the higher unifying levels, constant through many domains, allow economy in the individual's cognitive operation. As Goodenough points out, beliefs provide the basis for the strategies by which we act, and the wider the range of situations in which the same strategy is applicable, the simpler life becomes. It is at this level, where beliefs function in larger cultural contexts than single domains (or in single largish domains encompassing embedded subdomains), that *macro belief system* may be distinguished from micro, for the purpose of this discussion. The line is not strictly drawn; it is in fact always relative. And the ultimate context yielding a total belief system ethnography may always remain merely hypothetically possible.

Macrosystem studies, then, will refer to explicit attempts to relate or synthesize the belief structures of several domains of the same culture, as well as to other approaches, past and present, for presenting "whole cultures" in terms of their cognitive[5] or conceptual organization. An overview of such approaches in the anthropological past will be given next, followed by recent and current work, most of which falls within the realm of what has been termed "the new ethnography." It is hoped that the historical sketch will serve to dissuade any reader who still takes this appellation literally. Ethnographic semantics is not a revolutionary change of direction or command, nor are the "new ethnographers" engaged in overthrowing past modes of inquiry. They are rather attempting explicit formulation and formalization, carrying on a line of earlier work that had viewed culture as the rules rather than the product and had examined methods and assumptions necessary for presenting a people's culture in terms of its own internal organization.

BRIEF HISTORY OF BELIEF SYSTEM FORMULATIONS IN ANTHROPOLOGY

Some of the anthropological studies in the current century prior to the late 1950s might be considered forerunners to one aspect or another of the belief system formulation just outlined, especially those emphasizing macrosystems ("holists" or "contextualists"),[6] or an "emic" point of view (culture as shared codification of experience seen from the culture-bearers' view).

Franz Boas

In 1911 Boas (1966) defined ethnology as "the science dealing with the mental phenomena of the peoples of the world," and placed linguistics within its field of study, language being "one of the most important manifestations of mental life." He noted the unconscious nature of speakers' use of the laws of language, and found that ethnological phenomena also showed unaware groupings or classifications of sense impressions and of concepts. This early statement about percept-concept categories and their relation to language

---

[5] This article attemps to avoid the argument, implied by use of the word "cognitive," that the rules presented by the ethnographer are or are not exactly those carried about in the heads or habit systems of the culture-bearers. "Beliefs" necessarily depend on the point of view of the believers. The God's-truth assumption that there is system in the tendency of human beings to infer propositions and hold them to be true or false is axiomatic to the studies considered.

[6] Wallace (1970) surveyed holistic analytic models, including those of psychological patterning (national character, model personality), which are omitted here. Spindler (1963: 543-44) described the contextualist anthropologist, in comparison with the psychologist: "Psychologists seem to work on isolable and limited variables and their interrelationships. But for the anthropologist, variables make sense only when seen in their natural context. . . . A real anthropologist, it might be said, never trusts a correlation or a statistically significant difference without intimate acquaintance with its ancestors, parents, marrying and nonmarrying cousins, and descendants, *in situ.*"

coding included the notion of the necessity of classification, that the infinite variability in actual experience must be grouped into discrete units: "Many different individual experiences appear to us as representative of the same category of thought . . . a trait of human thought and speech." His Introduction to the *Handbook of American Indian Languages* ends with this statement: "No attempt has been made to compare the forms of the Indian grammars with the grammar of English, Latin or even among themselves; but in each case the psychological groupings which are given depend entirely upon the inner form of each language."

Edward Sapir

Sapir (1949*b*), student of Boas and probably the most outstanding linguist-ethnologist in the United States during the 1920s, noted "unconscious patterning of behavior," both verbal and nonverbal, and gave linguistics a basic start toward structural analysis of those unconscious groupings of sounds by which all language-users convey meaning to one another, phonemes (1949*a*). Both Boas and Sapir were perhaps more concerned with micro belief system material than total-culture characterization, insisting that inferences and generalizations not be based on insufficient or nonexistent data. On the other hand, their characterization of language structure as "psychological" placed it within the habit systems of individual speakers, but they were not consistent on the question of whether these habits mold the individual's cognitive outlook and thus macro cultural themes, as Whorf later claimed.

Paul Radin

Radin (1957), another early Boas student, made another kind of attack on armchair theories about primitive mentality when he demonstrated that there are macro thinkers in every society. His interest in cultural philosophies and philosophers was by its nature macro, and he provided intensive field data on the Winnebago and related tribes (1923, 1949). His publication of raw texts and informants' verbatim reports separately from his own interpretive notes was his way of "letting the Indian speak for himself," and also reveals his concern with the role of the native language in the codification of its speakers' reality. Kluckhohn (1964) wrote, "The publication of Paul Radin's *Primitive Man as Philosopher* did much toward destroying the myth that a cognitive orientation toward experience was a peculiarity of literate societies."

Ruth Benedict

Benedict (1928, 1960) was perhaps the most extreme of the contextualists. Her configurational anthropology, taking off from *Gestalt* psychology, argued for viewing all traits (and domains) in the context of the whole configuration (individual or cultural). While applying concepts from Nietzsche to characterize the "ethos" of certain cultures (Apollonian, Dionysian), she cautioned that these were not to be used for classifying cultures, but were empirical generalizations, and she warned against the danger of starting fieldwork with any such type-models of cultural integration. As for cultures described as lacking integration, possibly the "description itself is disoriented rather than the culture . . . or the nature of the integration may be outside our experience and difficult to perceive." Benedict was opposed to "topical studies" of particular institutions (marriage, initiation, religion), "as if each is a special area of behavior which has generated its own motivations." Rather, "these are occasions that each society seizes upon to express its characteristic purposes." "The significant sociological unit . . . is not the institution but the cultural configuration." There was criticism of her oversimplified holistic characterizations and her lack of sampling, and controversy over the ethnocentrism of the Western concept labels she applied (see Honigmann 1961). However, both Kluckhohn and Bateson lent support. Kluckhohn (1960) pointed out that "configuration" was at a different level of abstraction from "pattern" and that Benedict had not made explicit that she was talking about *ideal* rather than *behavioral* patterns; only behavioral patterns require statistical norms.

Gregory Bateson

Bateson (1936) conceded that such concepts as configuration and *Zeitgeist* are difficult to define "without invoking mysticism," but pointed out that Benedict had not defined them, only illustrated them. These concepts are based on "holistic rather than crudely analytic study of the culture. . . . The thesis is that when a culture is considered as a whole certain emphases emerge." He agreed with Benedict that a culture "standardizes the psychology of the individuals," and his own characterization of the Iatmul holistic culture included the ethos, defined as "a culturally standardized system of organization of the instincts and emotions of individuals," and the eidos, "a standardization of the cognitive aspects of the personality of individuals." He used "cultural structure" as a "collective term for the coherent 'logical' system which may be constructed by the scientist fitting together the various premises of the culture." He added a note: "This exposition of eidos and the definition of social structure

are, I think, clumsy, but a more exact formulation of the matter is impossible until an adequate enquiry has been conducted into the eidoses and ethoses of various cultures," thus making it clear that he considered more emic descriptions necessary before generalizations could be fruitful.

Bateson's description of the eidos of Iatmul culture was an early attempt to tie the cultural whole in cognitive terms. While "cultural structure" was defined as constructed by the scientist, he placed the cognition within Iatmul heads (1936:219): ". . . any pervasive characteristic of the cultural structure can be referred to peculiarities of the Iatmul mind . . . we are here dealing with the cultural expression of cognitive or intellectual aspects of Iatmul personality." He discussed cultural standardization of eidos in terms of types of thought and cognitive systems that "pervade every aspect of the culture and give support to every cultural activity." In all, Bateson looked at Iatmul from several points of view, one of them "eidological," and stated that an explanation from this point of view would be in "structural terms." The other possible terms were "ethnological, economic, sociological, and developmental," and since each of these sorts of relevance is present in all behavior, a holistic picture from each point of view is possible. It was only a step from there to identifying these points of view as analytic constructs rather than divisions of culture.

Bateson added an epilogue to this work for its 1958 edition, which will be discussed in a later section along with his other more recent applications of communications theory and metacontext analysis. In 1951, however, he was already incorporating information theory, and writing of *value system* on the same level as *codification system* (Reusch and Bateson 1951, chap. 7):

"each is a system ramifying through the total world of the individual." Through their locus in the individual, such systems are thus seen in *Gestalten* terms, or we might say in terms of macrosystems. Bateson's use of "figure" and "ground" to show *contrast* as a basis for conveying information (whether such contrast is stated or implied) ties the *Gestalten* view of the importance of the whole to the (micro)analysis of meaning and definition as carried out by ethnosemanticists. In the 1950s information theory and communications notions, as well as those of structural linguistics, were commingling in the intellectual stream of the anthropologists for whom "culture" could be approached as a complex system of codes. Bateson showed also the relation of *value* to *perception,* especially as perception is influenced by value, and to *belief* in that we not only see the external world in accordance with what we wish to see, but having "seen," we must wish our information to be "true." Every man "must act in terms of what he knows . . . and when he acts he will meet with frustration and pain if things are not as he 'knows' them to be. Therefore, he must, in a sense, wish them to be as he 'knows' they are."

Clyde Kluckhohn, Ethel Albert

Kluckhohn (1952) offered a systematization of ideology in terms of values and value systems. He did not place values explicitly as code-level phenomena, but wrote of types of patterning. Values, as "conceptions of the desirable," fell under *ideal patterns,* as opposed to *behavioral patterns,* or generalizations of statistically observable events. *Configuration* represented a further level of abstraction, a unifying statement "from the point of view of the observer." However, "implicit values" (values of which the actor is not consciously aware) are also inferential constructs of the investigator, although the value is "imputed to the actor," who generally becomes aware of the rule only when it is transgressed.

Albert's (1956) model for classifying values, using Kluckhohn's definitions, showed a hierarchy of logical dependence from most concrete values to most general, somewhat analogous to Goodenough's levels of beliefs. However, it appeared that the more general the value statement, the more likely that it was inferred by the investigator, up to a level of "value orientations" that Kluckhohn had appended as a necessary foundation of the system and a bridge to basic postulates or axioms. These last are more like beliefs, as they include existential ideas about the nature of the world, underlying the "values" proper. Although the areas of "unaware structure" have a different locus from Goodenough's model (at the general rather than concrete end), it can be seen that when Kluckhohn and Albert derived ideal patterns from behavioral events, they too rooted the ideology description in sensory or observable material. It proved somewhat difficult in practice, however, to fit real data into the explicit-implicit, overt-covert dimensional classification units of Kluckhohn (Black 1960).

A major six-year values research project of Harvard University's Laboratory of Social Relations, "Comparative Study of Values in Five Cultures," was originated by Kluckhohn in 1949 in conjunction with John Roberts of Cornell, Evon Vogt, and others. Kluckhohn's early and constant interest in defining culture can be seen in his publications with Kelly in 1945 and with Kroeber in 1952, as well as in his 1941 paper (reprinted in 1960) already referred to in connection with Benedict. In 1949 he also wrote about "The Philosophy of the Navaho Indians"

(1968). He was clearly concerned with macrosystems of ideology, and faced the dilemma of trying to present the culture-participants' view at a level of integration not offered explicitly by native informants.

Lee, Whorf, Du Bois, Opler

Dorothy Lee, in writings of the 1940s and 1950s (collected in 1959), saw culture as a "codification of reality" and described cultures as different codifications of the same·reality. She used linguistic evidence in somewhat the manner of Benjamin Whorf (1956; see also Hoijer 1954), who also contributed to the ethnography of conceptual systems through investigation of linguistic structure. While Whorf's ideas of linguistic relativity and the thesis that language structure directly influences men's "thought world" came out of his association with Sapir and Boas, his writings brought forth a certain amount of criticism, and controversy still surrounds the Whorfian hypothesis and methods for testing it.

Cora Du Bois (1955), in writing of American values, laid special emphasis on the coherence of the system: no value system can encompass genuine contraries, and value changes result from the strain to remove them. Her "oppositional propositions" are similar to Goodenough's contradictory beliefs. Morris Opler (1946) developed a concept of "themes" as underlying forces affecting cultural phenomena, on a diffuse macro level.

Robert Redfield

Redfield (1952, 1953) stressed the concept of "world view," a term that has come into common usage to denote a person's or a culture's peculiar view of the world. Redfield's definition includes cultural sharing ("that outlook

upon the universe that is characteristic of a people") while at the same time locating it in the self and underlining its systematic nature:

"World view" . . . is the picture the members of a society have of the properties and characters upon their stage of action. While "national character" refers to the way these people look to the outsider looking in on them, "world view" refers to the way the world looks to that people looking out. Of all that is connoted by "culture," "world view" attends especially to the way a man, in a particular society, sees himself in relation to all else. It is the properties of existence as distinguished from and related to the self. It is, in short, a man's idea of the universe. It is that organization of ideas which answers to a man the questions: Where am I? Among what do I move? What are my relations to these things?

Rather than offering models for analyzing or describing world views, Redfield and his students generalized the concept toward *types* of world view (Redfield 1952, Wax and Wax 1962). The concept was therefore "emic," but with some outside-view comparative types emerging.

A. I. Hallowell

Hallowell cited Redfield's world view concept in his later presentations of Ojibwa ideology and taxonomy (1958), but much earlier (1942, 1955) he had argued the case for belief systems and the need to consult the knowledge of natives in order to describe cultures. In 1942 he wrote:

Human beings live in a meaningful universe, not a world of bare physical objects and events. These meanings . . . are derived from the amazingly variable belief systems of mankind. . . . [The] native belief system . . . defines the . . . environment in which they live, and no purely objective account . . . would be sufficient to account for their behavior in relation to this physical environment.

The physical environment, in fact, must be supplemented:

Thunderbirds and monster snakes ... are important items in the behavioral environment of these Indians. Since from our point of view thunder is part of their physical environment and monster snakes are not, we might be inclined to make a distinction between them. But if we do this we are making *our* categories a point of departure.

Hallowell's papers collected in 1955 contained several analyses of Ojibwa cognitive domains; contextualization came through his extensive and intensive concentration on a single culture, which no doubt led to his later presentation of large-scale Ojibwa world view categories, which we shall discuss shortly.

Linguists

Linguists McQuown (1954, 1956, 1957), Hockett (1948, 1954), and Pike (1954), among others, found close connections between linguistic and cultural structures, and defined the latter as code-level communicational systems. By 1954 Pike had worked out a unified theory for expanding the rationale and procedures of structural linguistics to include other cultural codes. As we shall see, the development of ethnographic semantics had linguistics and linguists as its acknowledged models and allies.

European and British Influences

Important influences also came from Europe and Britain, in particular those of Bronislaw Malinowski and Claude Lévi-Strauss. Malinowski was surely the great contextualist, pointing out with regard to language (1923, 1965) as well as other cultural items that meaning resides in use, and that as the context is changed (at any level), the meaning

likewise changes (that is, the results of the analysis), while enlargement or extension of context provides an analysis that is more complete for the purpose of operating appropriately in the culture. (For a review of Malinowski's work, see R. Firth 1961; for his mutual influence with linguist J. R. Firth regarding "context of situation," see Langendoen 1968.) The British social anthropologists Radcliffe-Brown (1951), Evans-Pritchard (1956), and Nadel (1951, 1957) were also influential in structural and functionalist analysis of cultures. In France, Lévi-Strauss is the outstanding figure, writing in 1945 of the parallels of "Structural Analysis in Linguistics and Anthropology" (1967*b*) and evolving a "structural anthropology" (1967*a*) applicable to any aspect of culture but applied most extensively to social structure and the symbolic codes of art and myth. Lévi-Strauss' structuralism does not take quite the inductive emic path of most of the cognitive anthropologists considered here, and his holism is directed more at the whole of man's experience than at the whole of particular cultures, but his structural work cannot be overlooked in any outline of the development of belief system analysis.

RECENT APPROACHES

As the 1950s progressed and merged into the 1960s, the same scholars entered postwar intellectual streams. Hallowell (1958, 1963, 1964) argued for descriptions of men's "cognitive orientation toward the world outside the self" and presented Ojibwa world view in essentially ethnoscientific terms (see also Black 1967), although without reference to other such work or to the more formal methods being applied to descriptions of native conceptual classifications through analysis of lexical structure. His contextualization was accomplished through his extensive knowledge of the culture and the large domain he chose to display, combined with his format of taxonomic classes with their defining attributes.

Kluckhohn (1964) found "Navaho categories" and native language referential systems a productive way to present the values and thought system of the Navaho. This paper might usefully be compared with his 1945 paper "Philosophy of the Navaho Indians" (1968), which was configurational (in his sense of the point of view of the investigator). He had also added to his values model a classification by a series of "binary oppositions": autonomy-dependence, individual-group, etc., as well as explicit-implicit, with cross-cultural comparison in mind (1956a). F. Kluckhohn (1958; F. Kluckhohn and Strodtbeck, eds., 1961) boldly systematized value orientations as an etic grid, with categories strictly configurational (orientation toward time, toward action, toward nature, and so on), rather than attempting to approach such orientations inductively as unifying propositions from the believers' point of view. C. Kluckhohn, however, followed more closely the work of the linguistic anthropologists (and anthropological linguists), and in his review (1956b) of the work emanating from the conference on the Whorfian hypothesis regarding the relations between language and culture (Hoijer 1954) he strongly approved resolving his implicit/explicit dilemma as a parallel to code/message, *langue/parole,* context/content. The progress toward formal pattern analysis of cultural materials, which was resulting at least partly from renewed cross-fertilization with linguistic work as well as from advances in communications and information theory, was given full recognition by Kluckhohn, and in fact was no doubt influenced by his own voicing of the values

dilemma over many thoughtful years.

During this same period Bateson added his 1958 epilogue to *Naven,* where he outlined the communications breakthrough of World War II, in which he had participated, and its relation to his ethnographic problems of description-explanation of the 1930s. His work with schizophrenics and emphasis on context learning at a metalevel to the learning of explicit cultural rules (1960) contributed also to the new look at ethnographic theory and practice.

Those anthropologists concerned more strictly with formal analysis of ethnographic materials, especially kinship data (Lounsbury, Goodenough, Romney, Burling), were striding ahead in the fifties and early sixties on the basis of rigor introduced into kinship studies some years ago by anthropologist-linguists Boas, Kroeber, and Sapir—a rigor underlying the new ethnography very basically and historically, for the latter grew from an extension of kinship semantics to the more general descriptive (or ethnographic) semantics, both paralleling structural linguistics. Lounsbury (1956) and Goodenough (1951, 1956) were largely responsible for the renewed application of structural principles to the semantic analysis of kin term reference systems, and began referring to this work as "componential analysis" and uncovering its implications for the study of meaning in general.

"NEW ETHNOGRAPHY"

Descriptive Semantics: Goodenough and Others

Concurrently during this period, younger anthropologists were beginning to formulate and articulate what has sometimes been dubbed "the new ethnography." Goodenough's explication of what he termed "descriptive semantics" has been perhaps the most cited, especially as to his operational definition of culture and the relation of ethnography to descriptive linguistics. Some of these ideas were presented in his Truk monograph (1951), explicitly set forth later in his "Cultural Anthropology and Linguistics" (1964b):

The proper definition of culture must ultimately derive from the operations by which we describe particular cultures. . . . A society's culture consists of whatever it is one has to know or believe in order to operate in a manner acceptable to its members. . . . [It is] the end product of learning . . . not things, people, behavior or emotions, but the organization of these things . . . that people have in their minds, their models for perceiving, relating and otherwise interpreting them.

Thus, however much this was or was not "new," the definition of culture within the new ethnography insisted (in Tyler's summary, 1969a:3) that "cultures then are not material phenomena; they are cognitive organization of material phenomena. . . . The object of study is not these material phenomena themselves, but the way they are organized in the minds of men."

Goodenough (1964b) expressed the relation of ethnography to descriptive linguistics in terms especially of the reduction to sensory cues and its implications for descriptive methodology: "Ethnographic description . . . requires methods of processing observed phenomena such that we can inductively construct a theory of how our informants have organized the same phenomena. . . . Thus viewed, it seems to me that the methodological problem of ethnography is identical with that of descriptive linguistics."

Those first citing Goodenough, and themselves providing early programmatic and substantive statements of

this point ot view, included Conklin (1964, 1969a), Lounsbury (1956), Frake (1962, 1964a, 1969b), and Metzger and Williams (1963a, 1963b). Surveys and critiques were subsequently published by Hymes (1964b:94-102), Sturtevant (1964), and Colby (1966a), with a recent summary by Tyler (1969a). These surveys should be consulted for fuller bibliographic information and background on descriptive semantics prior to 1964. Colby's paper, with its accompanying critical comment and rebuttal, is especially useful for references to European scholars. These writings show, for one thing, how more or less synonymous labels for the new ethnography had proliferated: descriptive semantics, ethnographic semantics, ethnosemantics, ethnoscience, belief and knowledge systems, structural ethnography, cognitive anthropology, linguistic anthropology. (The first five are, in fact, used as synonyms here; the others are employed with somewhat larger or different ranges of reference.)

Goodenough's definition of culture grew out of procedures employed to observe and describe cultural structure, paralleling those of the structural linguist.[7] As the linguist can work with occurring observable samples or specimens of language in use (in sign theory the concept of "iconic signs" would apply; for the linguist, these are speech utterances), so can the ethnographer

---

[7] Goodenough referred initially (1964b) to the problem that in nonlinguistic culture (including most speech acts, it might be pointed out) we have identifiable icons, but lack the equivalent of a phonetic notation. This means there are observable stimuli with which to work, such as phones for the linguist, but in many cases there is no etic inventory such as phone types. This problem has been dealt with in papers by Gardin (1965) and Pospisil (1965a, 1965b), and by the use of automatic classification computer programs (e.g., Stefflre et al. 1971), by the eliciting techniques of Metzger and Williams, and in the work of Pike (1954).

discover cultural structure through samples of behavior of informants or native actors (rather than through informants' explanations; see next paragraph). Goodenough identified iconic signs as the occurring physical stimuli observable in the scene, to which culturally structured behavior is a response. As descriptive linguistics is a "science of iconic signs," so can ethnography be. By "performing operations on icons," ethnographers can describe any cultural knowledge system (Goodenough 1964b): "any material object, event, or act to which people respond is necessarily an icon signifying a conceptual form of some kind." The ethnographer can perceive the same physical objects or events that his informants do, and can learn from their performance what features are significant in their system (see Frake 1969c, Black and Metzger 1969).

In the phrasing of Pike (1954), who had also worked out a unified theory and analytic method for extending emic distributional analysis from phonology to other cultural codes (and who derived the words "emic" and "etic" from "phonemic" and "phonetic"), one can say the ethnographer notes the various physical stimuli to which system users react as similar, and the points where they make the emic break of judging (or reacting to) two icons as significantly different when one is substituted for the other in the same environment. In Pike's formulation, verbal and nonverbal units may be analyzed within the same domain, being substitutable for each other in some communicational contexts.

Goodenough at first dealt chiefly with lexical meaning systems, but also indicated that the descriptive semantic approach can extend to other systems of cultural communication. For example (1969:311), "the cultural content of social relationships" can be seen as containing 'vocabularies' of different kinds of forms and a 'syntax' or set of rules for their combination." Thus structural analysis of nonlanguage forms can also constitute descriptions of cultural knowledge systems, within the descriptive semantic approach. These will be treated below, as nonverbal structures. The lexical meaning systems (native language terminologies) that have been most widely investigated by anthropologists are those of kinship terms, the particular nature of which allows a "componential analysis" of the semantic distinctive features employing an etic notation of kin types of universal application; this parallels most closely the technique of linguistic analysis (Lounsbury 1956). Analysis of kinship systems as such is the most sophisticated branch of descriptive semantics today. However, since most kinship studies limit themselves to descriptions of micro belief systems (kinship domain in isolation from cultural context), these are not surveyed here. Those works that relate the domain of kinship to other systems of the culture will be treated in a later section (an early example: Romney and Epling 1958).

Goodenough has now summarized and restated his contribution and position regarding cultural description in Part 4 of his recently published *Description and Comparison in Cultural Anthropology* (1970:98-119). This is certainly recommended to those who wish to acquaint themselves with his work in this area, in preference to second- or thirdhand critiques and criticisms, including this one.

Ethnography and Native Language

The above discussion relates ethnography to *linguistics*, showing parallels with linguistic analysis. The relation of *language* to descriptive semantics ought also to be clarified, with special reference to the native language of the subject culture. Goodenough pointed out that cultural behavior consists of people reacting to icons as stimuli. One kind of reaction to stimuli is *naming behavior*. It turns out that language not only represents a symbolic system that in some respects is a microcosm of culture itself, but presents lexical sets that are amenable to the distributional type of analysis regarding their semantic references (denotata) and their signification (necessary defining features). Lexical labels generally refer to cultural concepts, and the structure of their usage in contrastive situations reveals a good deal of the cultural equipment of the native knower. (This applies, of course, to sociolinguistic variation in lexical usage, as well as to the reference system; see Hymes 1964*b*:97-102). Much of the work in descriptive semantics that is best known as such has dealt with analyses of terminological systems in the native language. (But see below, "Nonverbal Codes and 'Vocabularies.'") This may account for some of the apparent misunderstanding regarding the scope and procedures of this kind of ethnography.

A major critic of the "new ethnography" has been Harris (1968, chap. 20), and his specific points have brought response and clarification, for example by Burling (1969*b*, n. 3) and most recently by Berlin (1970), Goodenough (1970:112-13), Hymes (1970: 301-304), and Kay (1970). A summary of the differences, in terms of Harris' dichotomy of "eticists" and "emicists," is to be found in a recent work by Pelto (1970, chap. 4). Pelto, however, makes basic assertions that do not seem to accord with the intent or method of ethnographic semantics as I have experienced it. As indicated above, the locus of this ethnographic approach is in *structural meaning*—as carried by

contrastive use of behavioral units, whether verbal or nonverbal—and in this sense some anthropologists can reasonably view it as synonymous with culture (i.e., code for communication; see especially Kay 1966 and Hall 1959), or at least as the major element of human communicative systems with which a cultural anthropologist is in the business of dealing. Colby (1966*a*:17) defines "ethnographic semantics" as the "semantic description of the communicative codes of a particular speech community"; thus Pelto's statement (1970:82) that "the semantics of cultures" refers to "primitive thought patterns as expressed in language" must have derived from some source other than those cited here. As used here, "semantics" is equivalent to "structural meanings." Such meanings are expressed in all behavior patterns that result from cultural learning, and are thus conveyed through other code media as well as language. These can be (and have been) described and analyzed within the realm of the new ethnography (see below). But I would say that even lexical analysis yields knowledge systems, not "thought patterns."

Another point of confusion regarding ethnographic semantics has to do with the supposed "opposition" between emic and etic units and procedures. The relation between these, as I understand it, is something different from "opposite." Ethnographic semantics makes use of a standard etic notation or grid whenever that is possible, just as the linguist does. Even when it is not possible, it is strange to hear that the type of ethnographer termed by some as "emicist" goes about collecting "verbal statements *about* human action" while an eticist is out there observing human action firsthand (Pelto 1970:83). The data of ethnosemantics consist of records of direct observations of human actions, verbal and/or nonverbal. It might be better to say "reactions," for the ethnographer is interested in formally identifying the stimulus of each observed action, in order to decipher the cultural code or knowledge system of the native actors. He is not asking the actors what their rules are. Perhaps his difference from the eticist is that he begins with etics when he can, but does not stop there. Hockett's paper "Scheduling" (1964) states this rather clearly.

Burling also, in an otherwise clear paper outlining and demonstrating some parallels of linguistic and cultural descriptions (1969b:825), states that linguists and anthropologists "typically use their informants in rather different ways," anthropologists obtaining "statements that describe behavior" while linguists "elicit examples of behavior," and he speaks as if the anthropologists' informants are giving "explicit instruction" in the learning of their culture's rules.[8] Although Burling goes on to point out that the anthropologist gets both types of data, and in the end uses both equally as material

---

[8] Burling further speaks of informants' giving the "explicit rules" formulated by natives (1969b:826). This sounds as though he refers to what have been termed "ethnomodels" by Conklin (1969b), who acknowledges, along with all practitioners of ethnosemantics, that these may have heuristic value but are not likely to coincide with the rules as analyzed by the ethnographer (the point made by Burling as well). To document the position further, Goodenough (1951:10) also stated, regarding the formulation of emic (culture-specific) definitions: "We have sought to so define the Trukese lineage that everything to which the Trukese react as such is accounted for by our definition while everything else is excluded. As products of analysis, our definitions frequently fail to coincide with those given by informants, which were usually in the nature of rules of thumb. . . . [The writer] does not intend to present it (Trukese culture) as the Trukese see it but as his analysis reveals it." Burling (1969b: 826) further seems to identify ethnomodels with the "psychological reality" question (see Burling 1969a), while at the same time presenting this as a feature that differentiates linguistic and cultural description. This is a bit confusing.

for his own analysis of rules, his remarks could be misunderstood (as they perhaps were by Pelto), and would seem to distort ethnosemantic work as I have known it, which is precisely work with "examples of behavior."

As for beliefs and their systematic arrangement, it is my experience that beliefs too are revealed in and analyzed from behavior examples. True, they are also *capable of* being expressed as propositions, although some of them probably never are, spontaneously, by native knowers. One can reason propositionally (inferentially) without making verbal statements, although the ability to do so may have to be more or less present. In actual ethnographic practice verbal and nonverbal actions in combination probably comprise the belief system data, and while some of these may be statements about behavior, they are, again, not taken at face value for their content, but rather as behavior responses to be analyzed. *Systematic* statements about behavior can represent an interesting set of behavioral data. This can be illustrated by a portion of an Ojibwa belief system of a relatively macro dimension that I elicited on a verbal level, but with valuable nonverbal contributions (Black 1967). I did not learn, for example, that it is believed dangerous to talk about the weather (in certain contexts) by being told so by informants, but rather by listening to other statements (responses) *and* observing their fear. That their belief system includes a concept that connects thunder with an avian form was not elicited as a language-expressed proposition (in fact, they denied it), but rather was revealed when they referred to a painting of a magical-looking eagle-type bird on my wall as *pinesi* (the Ojibwa word said to "mean 'thunder'"). Language has many and intricate relations to beliefs and their arrangements, and it may be employed as an entrée and a labeler as well as a vehicle for stating propositions. Getting people to name and classify the things in their world is one way to start learning some of their beliefs. And they need not *state* the semantic features to which they are attending as stimuli; they *reveal* them in their sortings. In short, the idea that ethnoscience is interested in language and linguistics for the purpose of having informants *make statements about their patterns of behavior* is rather simplistic and can be held only by those who have not done ethnosemantic work.[9] In fact, when informants do make such statements, these are treated as behavioral data, sometimes termed "ethnomodels," not as system-descriptive data (see footnote 8). This is true even in the rather radical use of purely verbal data by the formalized eliciting procedures of Metzger and Williams, to be described below.

This clarification of the relation of language to ethnosemantic description is necessary because in this article I approach belief systems through the theoretical orientation and procedures of ethnographic semantics, and furthermore I define "beliefs" in terms of language-expressible propositions, forced onto the verbal level from wherever they may reside in the native knower-actor.

BELIEF SYSTEMS WITHIN ETHNOGRAPHIC SEMANTICS

Summary of Goodenough's Contribution

For the study of macro belief systems, the triple impact of Goodenough's contribution during the 1950s consist-

[9] Bohannan (1956) defended his use of native terms not as a "linguistic approach" but as an obvious means of getting at people's conceptual categories, which is "the anthropologist's first task." He cited Malinowski as an influence.

ed in his combining the following three aspects:

1. The old concern with describing *cultural systems as ideology* (see now Goodenough 1964a:11-12 regarding ideational versus phenomenal order, as well as 1964b). In his terms, this amounts to *knowledge* of the rules (or codes) that give organization and allow communication within a particular cultural system and thus constitutes a description or theory of the way a particular system is organized internally.

2. Reduction of the structural units of belief and code to their cue value in terms of *sensory experience of the physical world;* thus, percept system (1963), iconic signs (1964b). This is seen as paralleling the phonetic grounding of structural linguistics, providing a manipulable base of physically observable stimuli which is as accessible to the ethnographer as to the informant or native actor.

3. Retention of *total-culture context,* at least in principle: first, through an explicitly meshed account of several facets of a single culture (1951, especially p. 11), and later in his repeated requirement that the test of adequacy of the ethnographic account—as well as its mode of correction and refinement—is its success in allowing one to operate appropriately in the alien culture (1951:10; 1964b; 1967:1203). The latter implies knowledge of cultural rules operative through many semantic domains and code levels, for in each ongoing scene numerous codes are simultaneously in use. When joining the action, one would soon find out the inadequacy of a structural description limited to the rules of a single domain, or to the "referential" level of coding.

Toward Belief System Ethnographies

It might seem that Goodenough as well as most others has paid only lip service to the third point, which indeed is most important for the macro belief systems we wish to consider. Through most of the 1960s descriptive semantics generated some theoretical insights of perhaps great importance, a good deal of methodological refinement and programmatic presentation, and also substantial amounts of application to actual data collecting and processing. But in few of these, particularly the last, was there more than a nod toward that complex structure of codings that a single whole culture "must be." (Exceptions, of varying degrees and kinds, will be noted later.) Indeed, the enormity—and sometimes the impossibility—of the task of producing a total-culture belief system ethnography was mentioned in the literature. Sturtevant (1964:123) concluded his survey of "Studies in Ethnoscience" with an assessment of some steps toward interrelating different domains of a culture, and decided that by the nature of ethnoscientific standards for reliability, validity, and exhaustiveness "the ideal goal of a complete ethnography is farther removed from practical attainment. The full ethnoscientific description of a single culture would require many thousands of pages published after many years of intensive field work based on ethnographic methods more complete and more advanced than are now available." Williams (1966:19) went further, having himself engaged in multilevel semantic eliciting and analysis and having taken a look at intracultural synthesis possibilities and the great complexity of even segments of a "cultural grammar": "This complexity has consequences other than making for difficulty in diagrammatic display. It makes clear, for example, that the notion of 'whole culture' descriptions is at best a useful fiction." The complexity referred to is that of culture itself. Sturtevant and Williams retain

the "ideal" of a total ethnography, but do not anticipate its realization. The middle ground that I have proposed to examine in recent and current macro belief system efforts falls somewhere between this fictional ideal and the rejection of analysis of belief system syntheses.

Thus ethnosemantic studies of native classifications and knowledge systems proceeded by analysis of domains, or segments of cultural systems. They took up the challenge of a more rigorous and more indigenously valid ethnography, demonstrating the power of a systematic search for native organization of percepts and concepts regarding the things and events believed to exist or occur in the world and their properties and ordering. Systems were discovered, ethnographically, which would have remained obscured by other descriptive models that predetermined the categories and features to be attended to or the domains to be isolated. The classic example was Conklin's (1964) finding that the Hananóo do not communicate verbally about a domain of "color" such as this English word signifies, but encode other features into their statements about the visual appearance of an object. Hue is one dimension of meaning in this coding, but so are matters of desiccation versus succulence and of fadedness versus indelibility. The premature locating of domain boundaries and characteristics remained one of the most recalcitrant problems in the study of belief systems.

Most workers applied themselves to solving that problem and others inherent in the analysis of the internal ordering of culture segments or subsystems. A variety of diverse domains were and still are being investigated by the developing formalizations: illness beliefs, medicine, curers; ethnobotany, zoology, icthyology; color, kin, weddings; persons, personality traits, sexual distance; property, lawyers, crimes; firewood, drinking, "living things"; and concepts and behaviors defining pollution and taboo, status and role, residence and home—to name just a few. Some of these show the relation of their domain to other things in the culture, others do not. On the whole, the complexity revealed in cultural segments was convincing evidence that if one wished to describe conceptual systems respectably, the notion of an integrated ethnography was a long way off, or even out of sight. Interesting things about culture could be learned by collecting and analyzing data on micro belief systems.

On the other hand, there was also the claim that the very formalization that has demonstrated that alien systems of knowledge and belief are now amenable to this type of rigorous description also promises means for the potential descriptive integration of the various systems in daily use by members of one society. This was a part of the goal all along, for some; Goodenough's 1951 monograph not only showed how formal analysis could decode small miscellaneous segments of cultural knowledge, but also showed a concern with the form of his large-scale ethnography and the ways in which the subsystems relate to each other—that is, the internal ordering of the macrostructure.

Data for Belief System Propositions: Metzger and Williams

One particular formulation for the study of belief systems within the descriptive semantic framework was developed in the early 1960s and has been cited as potentially productive of domain synthesis or macro-oriented ethnography (Frake 1969c, Keesing 1971). This was the work of Metzger, an ethnographer, and Williams, a linguist, who together formalized the collection of native-language assertions along with the native-language questions to which they were responses. The procedure makes deliberate use of language coding, not only by means of its lexical inventory and its semantic arrangements, but also by retaining the "proposition" context. It contains the statements that establish lexically labeled concepts, for one thing, and also includes the query sentences that stimulate such propositions as responses.

Colby (1966a:11,17) refers to their work as "programmed specification" and considers it important in providing a form of validation as well as an eliciting procedure. It specifies by use of substitution frames in the form of questions, with distributional properties of responses chartable against variation in terms (slot fillers). Nida (1961, 1964) also outlined use of substitution frames in eliciting semantic data, and the work of Stefflre (1963) on distributional analysis and substitution frames was of great value and is currently being applied to computational programming (Stefflre et al. 1971).

A series of substantive papers produced jointly by Metzger and Williams (1963a, 1963b, 1966, 1967) yielded systematic beliefs regarding a number of areas of cultural knowledge of the population of a Mayan village in Chiapas, Mexico. Theoretical and methodological formulations of this language-based approach were included in Black and Metzger (1969), Williams (1966), Frake (1969c), Black (1967, 1969a), and some unpublished work of Metzger (1963, 1964, 1966). In the last, Metzger first posits "assertion" as a synonym for "proposition" (true proposition), then defines belief system as "an inventory of all possible (true) answers to all possible questions that can be asked." In thus dealing only with "truth-testable statements," Metzger penetrates immediately to the level of belief, and explicitly insists that "the smallest meaningful unit in a belief system is one which can be judged by an informant as true or false."

With respect to this ethnography of systematic questions and answers, it is interesting to note the writings of philosopher R. G. Collingwood (1939, chap. 5), in which he pointed out that the basic unit of thought is not simply the proposition, but the proposition along with the question it was intended to answer (see Black 1963, Black and Metzger 1969). Collingwood added that no two propositions can contradict each other unless they are intended as answers to the same question. This clearly refers to the semanticist's *context,* or *domain,* and we see Goodenough's "belief system" consisting of "noncontradictory propositions pertaining to the same domain." The point is that we don't know much about a culture until we know what question is being answered; an act is not meaningful until one knows the context or stimulus. If all objects and behaviors observed by a field ethnographer are responses to some stimuli or answers to some unstated questions, it follows that his business is to discover the stimuli or questions to which the actions are responses. Actions may be verbal or nonverbal, but in the context of a belief system they are statable (along with their stimuli) in verbal form, and in the Metzger-Williams procedure the ethnographer forces his learning of informants' distinctions onto the verbal level. They may later be tested and validated in other than verbal contexts, of course. Belief system data have been obtained by this and related methods in the works cited above, and also by Frake (1964a), Mathiot (1964), Berlin, Breedlove, and Raven (1968), Bright and Bright (1969), Fowler and Leland (1967), Chiapas Drinking Project (n.d.),

and others. Most of these works do not attempt to report or relate more than a single ethnographic domain, but as we shall see later, the eliciting format itself provides a means for linkage of domains.

Nonverbal Codes and Vocabularies

Cultural meaning structures encoded in nonverbal forms have been observed and described by what I define here as semantic analysis. These might be divided between, first, the "language" of gestures and facial expression, body motions and placings, proximity/distance rules and other use of space, olfactory messages, and other such code media that can substitute for or supplement language in human communication; and second, acts and events, social relations, roles, etc., whose rules of distribution and decision (also a part of cultural knowledge) are derived from their contrastive or alternative use in conveying information. The inclusion of these as belief system components may be questioned, especially the first, for communication by means of these systems may be for most people, most of the time, out of their conscious awareness. Native statements of the belief-knowledge propositions underlying these communications would be furthest from realization, although behavioral responses would confirm the "cultural knowledge."[10] Since we are not differentiating belief from knowledge, I think it is appropriate to understand from Goodenough's model that

---

[10] The state of awareness (regarding the rules of meaning structures) of individual system users varies and alters, and depends partly on their past experience, especially of contrasts. It can hardly be used as a criterion for excluding some kinds of "rules," especially in view of behavioral reaction and acquired awareness when the rule is violated—i.e., when a contrast occurs—for it has been shown that awareness of a given rule can be unstable across individuals and over time.

some beliefs are unstated propositions, for at least some of the users of the system. (That is, both "knowledge" and "belief" can be placed within quotation marks—or other notation to indicate special use—to indicate the learned patterns or structures upon which the "knower" acts but does not reflect. Boas' "unconscious psychological groupings," Whorf's "background phenomena," Bateson's "metapattern" contextual learning, and Kluckhohn's "implicit values" are variations of this concept. Note now that Goodenough's belief system model begins with percept categories or habits that may be largely unconscious. When *concepts* are inferred from groupings of stimuli that the actor may not detect that he has grouped, or does not overtly label, these would be the basis for beliefs at an unaware level, since propositions can be made about any concept. Most beliefs of this type would be accepted by knower-believers once they were brought to their attention, and they are recognized by knowers especially when they are violated. See "Sociological Approaches" below.)

Our first type of nonverbal code includes such things as the study of kinesics as carried out for some years by Birdwhistell (1952, 1970). Kinesics is an analysis of body motion defined by Birdwhistell (1970:3) as "multilevel approach (physical, physiological, psychological and cultural) to the study of body motion as related to the nonverbal aspects of interpersonal communication." It includes also a special domain of "posture" analyzed by Hewes (1966), *paralanguage* or the communicational phenomena accompanying the use of language (Trager 1958, 1961), and the study of *proxemics* by Hall. Proxemics refers to the manner in which man structures space, especially interpersonal distance, or "the study of man's use of space as a

specialized elaboration of culture" (Hall 1966:1). Hall, like most of the above authors, explicitly defines culture as communication, and culture is the referent of his title *The Silent Language* (1959), while *The Hidden Dimension* (1966) refers to proxemics as a mostly unaware cultural code. (See also Hall 1963, 1968.) Meanings are systematically conveyed by these nonverbal coding systems, but the structures are considered to be transmitted "informally" and rarely brought to the conscious attention of the actor. Again, it is when the rules are violated that we take note of our own system, having otherwise encountered no contrastive situation by which to conceive of rules. Hall (1966:2) points out Whorf's reflections on the obligatory—and thus unconscious—categories of grammar, which in turn go back to Boas, and states that "the principles laid down by Whorf and his fellow linguists in relation to language apply to the rest of human behavior as well—in fact to all culture." If the unaware status of these codings makes us hesitate to view them as beliefs proper, their pervasiveness throughout many cultural domains renders them decidedly "macro." Their combination with other knowledge systems operating together in cultural scenes points up their importance to the consideration of beliefs in cultural context.

The second type of nonverbal forms or units subjected to semantic analysis consists of meaningful acts and events found to occur in contrastive distribution within relevant contexts, the selection among available alternatives representing a culturally understood message or unit of information. Rules for appropriate and meaningful selection constitute the "beliefs" that in this case, though acted out nonverbally, can often be stated in propositional form, and may be so given to the ethnographer. This framework for cultural description, sometimes called a "decision model" or "grammatical rules" framework, may be centered on fairly isolable domains of knowledge; for example, Frake's religious behavior (1969b), Metzger and Williams' weddings (1963a), Burling's rules of household composition (1969b), and Keesing's marriage contributions (1967), to name only a few of the domains to which structural emic description has been applied. In most of these cases, if not all, the delineation of "rules" governing acts and decisions cannot be accomplished without resort to cultural knowledge of other interrelated domains. Keesing makes this explicit in the last-named study, showing how in each case the principles underlying decisions about appropriate marriage contributions depend upon prior knowledge of systems of economics, age categories, kinship, prestige, etc. This demonstration of a macro quality inherent in those ethnographies that take the form of laying out the cultural rules resulting in the observed product (which most ethnographies always have done, though not so formally or explicitly; see Burling 1969b) may be one of the more important and promising signs pointing toward formalization of ethnographies of macro belief systems.

It should perhaps be added here that many studies of "single domains" of verbal behavior, even of linguistic structure, also call upon "outside" ethnographic information for their resolution; note especially Berlin's "Categories of Eating in Tzeltal and Navaho" (1967), Mathiot's comparison of linguistic and semantic classes in Papago (1964) and mine in Ojibwa (Black 1969b), and Haugen's "The Semantics of Icelandic Orientation" (1969). Frake's "How to Ask for a Drink in Subanun" (1964b) is just one example of the abundantly studied systems of verbal actions determined by social context. These sociolinguistic studies are by definition studies of cultural contextualization and synthesis.

OTHER APPROACHES

It is difficult to draw the line between approaches to belief and knowledge systems that are part of descriptive semantics (or so similar as to be identified as such for convenience) and those that have a different starting point but produce parallel results. The previous section on nonverbal codings may be an ambiguous type, and some of the following also. This problem is not surprising, and is in a sense artificial, for the mutual influence and interaction of social scientists concerned with these matters (including linguists, mathematicians, computer specialists, and communications scientists, as well as anthropologists, psychologists, sociologists, and philosophers) have been increasing dramatically since World War II and have been of considerable importance to the development of each. Current work, especially with regard to the synthesizing of macrosystems, is being carried out by interdisciplinary teams, and since present students are being trained by participation in such research and often in classrooms and departments that do not segregate one social science from another, it appears that future work will be carried out by individuals with interdisciplinary training. (This is of course already so in numerous cases.)

Communications Approaches

Early connections of communications theory with culture were made by Bateson (1958, 1966), as we have seen. Bateson brought clarity to the broad conceptual applications; the specific mathematical formulae are also being applied. For the delineation of beliefs in cultural context, a middle ground is again relevant. A volume of "readings in the codes of human interaction" titled *Communication and Culture* (Smith, ed., 1966) contains writings from a variety of social science disciplines, organized along the intersections of three types of investigation—mathematics, social psychology, and linguistic anthropology—and three divisions or levels of communication: syntactics, semantics, and pragmatics. The readings cover a diversified range of approaches to cultural knowledge which show the impact of the mathematical theory of communication of Shannon and Weaver, and Weiner's "cybernetics" or feedback concept. Several of the nonverbal codings cited above are present: Birdwhistell's kinesics, Hall on nonverbal unconscious codes in intercultural communication, Pike's "emic and etic standpoints for the description of behavior." Smith's introductory statement defines culture as a code for communication, the notion that has brought together these previously diverse fields. All are concerned with meaning and messages, in different ways. As for culture, Smith (1966:6-7) states:

> Meaning is a product of coding, and coding is a form of behavior that is learned and shared by the members of a communicating group. ... Any behavior that is learned and shared is cultural. ... To look at the world around us is a form of behavior. Each of us learns to look at it in the way that other members of our communicating group have learned to look at it. ... We look at it now through learned concepts, categories, and labels: animal, vegetable, and mineral; eatable, drinkable, and desirable; good, bad, and indifferent. Our perception is behavior that is learned and shared, and it is mediated by symbols. Culture is a code we learn and share, and learning and sharing require communication. And communication requires coding and symbols, which must be learned and shared.

Communication and culture are inseparable.

Although many of the selections are applicable, two in particular deserve attention: Colby's (1966b) "Behavioral Redundancy" and Bateson's (1966) "Information, Codification, and Communication." Colby holds that cultures have areas of both low redundancy, where choices require conscious consideration, and high redundancy, where common assumptions and understandings are taken for granted and choice is nearly automatic and often implicit. Cultures may be characterized by their areas of high and low redundancy, and Colby's dichotomy between structural redundancy and process redundancy provides a model for some comparisons on a macro basis. Bateson does somewhat the same thing when he proposes a division between two types of decision or selection which he terms selective integration and progressional integration, the first accomplished through categorization of the alternatives, the second influenced more by ongoing contextual or total-pattern-of-the-moment characteristics. He compares Balinese and Occidental cultures on the basis of the predominance of one or the other mode of decision-making in different realms or levels of activity. These types of cultural analysis can be seen to represent a synthesizing or holistic approach.

Bateson (1966:425) then speaks of propositions: "Man lives by those propositions whose validity is a function of his belief in them." Some propositions, he points out, are *about* codification; e.g., the statement "The word 'cat' stands for a certain small mammal." Such propositions are not true or false in the same sense as substantive statements (e.g., "Cats are dirty"), for they depend on an agreement between speakers that they be true. This is so of all statements about the conventions of codification, verbal or nonverbal—some of which, as we have seen, are conventions agreed upon and carried out in a mostly unaware fashion. They can nevertheless be considered belief or knowledge propositions, but on a meta-level of coding where the code rules themselves are the referent of the knowing. Bateson (1960) has pointed out that while traditionally science has proceeded by abstracting out one level or another for analysis, ignoring for the moment the effect of context, he had been doing the reverse and focusing his attention on the relationships and influences between levels. His studies of metacommunication and the learning of metapatterns (the patterns within which substantive learning takes place) are of great value to the view of culture as shared conventions of coding, especially with respect to those background patterns within which we "unknowingly" operate. The sound systems of language, percept systems in general, and a large proportion of the nonverbal codes discussed earlier contain propositions that are essential to "know" if one is to operate successfully in a cultural group, yet which are not to be obtained through explicit statements by informants (or by adults, from the point of view of the child of the culture). We learn the context pattern implicitly while learning the content explicitly.

Included in metacommunicative propositions are those about ongoing interpersonal relationships among the interacting persons, again propositions "whose truth or stability depend upon implicit or explicit agreement between the persons that the relationship is as indicated." These rules encode cues about status and role, and also cues as to the classification of the ongoing situation or action—whether it is in fun or sarcasm, a question, request, or command. For example, some conversations carry the sole message "We are in

communication," and the content could nearly as well be nonsense syllables. It is probably a graver error, indicating lack of cultural knowledge, to make a mistake on this metalevel, where classifying of the situation takes place, than to make substantive errors in content.

Further relevant coordinations of communications theory with anthropological study of beliefs are found in a collection of papers regarding epistemology in anthropology (Northrop and Livingston, eds., 1964) which will be discussed under "Philosophical Approaches."

Sociological Approaches

Some sociologists have forced the metapatterns of our own culture into awareness by a deliberate miscommunication about classification of situation. (Indeed, one need not go to professional sociologists: the old television show "Candid Camera" was based on similar grounds.) Garfinkel (1967:76) writes of our "common sense knowledge of social structures," which is an earmark of "any-bona-fide-member-of-the-society." We assume that others of our group will use the same "socially sanctioned grounds of inference and action" that we do—it is a measure of our mutual "competence," lack of which is immediately detected when the rules are violated (but presence of which is generally taken for granted and passes without notice). Garfinkel documents his thesis with certain experiments that switch the background patterns on unsuspecting subjects, who are then predictably amazed or outraged in response. ("Candid Camera" showed only those victims who were persuaded to find the situation amusing, in the end, and gave permission for telecasting.) This is similar to what Bateson (1960) and others have called a "double bind," a situation in which a person receives two contradictory messages simultaneously, so that any response he may make is bound to be "wrong." Psychiatrists are well acquainted with the double bind and the schizophrenic disturbances it can produce. Nothing is more dismaying and disorienting than to find oneself out of contact on the metalevel—literally a person without a culture. Wallace's (1970:199-206) analysis of situations of "cultural loss" is pertinent here.

Garfinkel and Sacks (1967), in noting the context determinants of meaning, and especially the metaclassifying that goes on during the course of a conversation (to use Bateson's terms, not theirs), take a look at the "machinery" used by the conversationalists in actually "doing" this metawork. They claim that it is of special interest that such work is not only done but recognized by the participants as a constituent part of the conversation being so characterized. It looks as though the probable infinite regression of contexts suggested by Bateson then poses a problem regarding the ultimate analysis of conversations (or other ongoing activities). It also looks as though whenever social scientists try looking at "everyday activities," "common talk," "real events," "dynamic interactions" (for the last two see Sarles 1966), "life *in vivo*," "situated . . . natural social life" (Moerman 1969)—in other words, when they attempt to observe whole ongoing cultural scenes—they find themselves confronting the complexities of total systems: macro in the most intricate and subtle sense. It is for this reason that studies that take metacontextual determinants into account will be treated separately, save for this work by sociologists and Bateson's cross-disciplinary researches.

Garfinkel uses also a "trouble case" entrée to some of the structures we all "know" but do not know of, by finding individuals who have had to learn "technically" what most of us have learned "informally," as Hall (1959, chap. 4) has put it. For example, Garfinkel (1967, chap. 5) gives the case of a person who had to learn how to behave as ("pass as") a girl after having been brought up as a boy, for she had been physiologically bisexual or "intersexed."

Goffman, too, has used special-case examples to lay bare our background expectations and our dependence on them; for example, the "stigmatized" person—one who possesses an attribute that is unanticipated in the category of persons to which he is for some occasion or purpose assigned (Goffman 1963:2):

Society establishes the means of categorizing persons and the complement of attributes felt to be ordinary and natural for members of each of these categories. Social settings establish the categories of persons likely to be encountered there. The routines of social intercourse in established settings allow us to deal with anticipated others without special attention or thought. When a stranger comes into our presence, then, first appearances are likely to enable us to anticipate his category and attributes, his "social identity." . . . We lean on these anticipations that we have, transforming them into normative expectations, into righteously presented demands. Typically, we do not become aware that we have made these demands or aware of what they are until an active question arises as to whether or not they will be fulfilled. It is then that we are likely to realize that all along we had been making certain assumptions as to what the individual before us ought to be.

One example: we do not generally realize that normally, in most settings, we expect our companions to be able to see. When in the company of a blind person, we are forced to revise some of our offhand, automatic behaviors that heretofore had not represented to our minds a choice among alternative behaviors. Awkwardness is one of the manifestations of the resentment that results, as Davis (1961:123) has pointed out. Whether we mention the handicap openly or try to avoid any allusion to it, our interaction with the blind person is almost wholly colored by our consciousness that he is literally in the dark, that his world is alien to us. We feel uncomfortable, and in our discomfort we speak awkwardly, stop in mid-sentence as we hear ourselves using everyday expressions that suddenly seem tactless if not taboo, rush on in compulsive bursts of words and forced laughter, and stare resolutely at everything except the blind person (as though he could know if we stared at him). And Gowman (1957) has written:

For some, there may be a hesitancy about touching or steering the blind, while for others, the perceived failure to see may be generalized into a gestalt of disability, so that the individual shouts at the blind as if they were deaf or attempts to lift them as if they were crippled.

Goffman (1961:ix-x) admits he is doing a kind of ethnography when he investigates the belief systems of special groups in our society—for example, inmates of "total institutions." He did fieldwork

to try to learn about the social world of the hospital inmate, as this world is subjectively experienced by him. . . . The world view of a group functions to sustain its members and expectedly provides them with a self-justifying definition of their own situation and a prejudiced view of nonmembers. . . . To describe the patient's situation faithfully is necessarily to present a partisan view.

To describe the patient's situation also involved, for Goffman, presenting the complementary rules of interaction and belief attending other institutional roles as well, and then seeing how these rules extend to more general social institutions within which all members of a society are unwittingly held and molded in the course of their "moral careers."

It is probably (and by definition) more difficult to detect unaware structuring in one's own cultural system than in an alien one. The work of these sociologists is by that token alone impressive. Another feature of note in their approach is the concentration on the terrible temporal "ongoingness" of actual behavior "choices" in actual scenes, where what occurs *now* is contingent not only upon the historical and the immediately preceding past, but also upon the outcome, so that judgment or classification (especially metaclassification) can in fact be deferred by participants to some future moment. Or, even more subtly, the metaclassification affects the outcome, since it is itself a part of the unfinished scene. Sensitive ethnographers surely have been aware of this nonlinear temporal aspect, but to my knowledge haven't yet the means to incorporate it into their formal descriptions.[11] Attempts to do so are on the ascendance, especially in some extensions of the "ethnography of speaking" of Hymes (1962) and in analysis of situational determinants, process rules, and scenes. Garfinkel's "common sense knowledge of social structures" is a part of belief ideology, as presented here; his gap between common-sense knowledge and scientific knowledge will, we hope, be reduced if means for deciphering this

---

[11] Perhaps this is impossible, with current means. I have seen the principle (of withholding classification until some outcome is known) as an important element in Ojibwa interaction and in their definitional (taxonomic) structure, yet could insert the information only as a footnote explaining anomolies in the taxonomy, *and* as a rule of the belief system (Black 1967).

ongoing aspect of ideology can be attained.[12]

Philosophical Approaches

In his Introduction to the volume *Cross-Cultural Understanding: Epistemology in Anthropology* (Northrop and Livingston, eds., 1964), Northrop enunciates the view that philosophy is a universal category of culture, and that "any other factor, be it universal or provincial, of a particular culture is misunderstood unless it is interpreted in terms of that particular people's specific philosophy." He was citing Kluckhohn's 1949 view as put forth in his "Philosophy of the Navaho Indians" (1968); and Kluckhohn, in turn, was supporting Radin, as we have seen. The papers of Northrop's volume are intended to bring the implications of Kluckhohn's words up to date and place them in more modern context, by showing the interdependence of science and philosophy. Part of the modern context is the contact of cultural anthropology with the sciences of communication and of neurophysiology under the pervasive influence of the cybernetics developments of modern physics. In addition, Einstein's proposal that epistemology, the science of *knowing,* must be applied to the sciences of

___

[12] I do not feel that analyses of "static" semantic structures and analysis of the other structures of ongoing interactional scenes are to be seen as antithetical. Rather, they are two parts of the descriptive process and of the knowledge systems of the users. The reference system must generally be assumed as common knowledge of participants before interaction can take place and its additional structuring can be meaningful or effective. While some proponents of the "dynamic" tend to dismiss or overlook the reference system knowledge, more and more studies are deliberately taking both into account (Basso, n.d.; Bellman 1971; Werner 1966). With regard to criticism of the narrowness of early ethnoscience endeavors, Werner replies that they could be more aptly criticized for trying to cover too much than for leaving something out.

knowing something is the key factor brought to bear on the central question of how we can know that we are knowing something about someone else's knowing.

This symposium on "the determination of the philosophy of a culture" takes a philosophical look at the culture of anthropologists and other social scientists, and at their increase in epistemological sophistication regarding their mode of knowing. Northrop suggests that Radin and Kluckhohn, while trying not to falsify the natural history data of other cultural philosophies by imposing concepts and assumptions from their own, did not have the tools with which to succeed, especially since the major portion of many primitive philosophies is not expressed but rather is covert, or implicit, having to be inferred by the investigator. Philosopher-anthropologist Maquet (1964) proposes that such inferences are constructs of the scientist, not part of the cultures described. He thus rejects on empirical grounds the proposition that cultural philosophies are universal. On the other hand, we may deductively assume that any society, if it is to survive, must have a system of explanation. If this system must be expressed in the language and concepts of the observer, he has at this point entered the deductive stage of anthropology, where the kind of *a priori* categories of description that are used depend upon the question the investigator is asking. Northrop endorses the change to deductively formulated theory and suggests that cultures be classified on the grounds of their epistemologies, as radical empiricists, naive realists, or logical realists; Maquet notes other schemes that have been proposed: Benedict's Dionysian/Apollonian, Sorokin's sensate/idealistic/ideational—the type of large *a priori* category sets that cover all the possible philosophical positions concerning the nature of reality (an etic grid, actually). Such broad classificatory categories, Maquet thinks, are not well suited to investigations of anthropological problems. If anthropologists wish to present whole-culture images such as world view or philosophy, this may be useful; their categories, however, will be closer to the data of observed societies, built up gradually from the gathering of empirical facts in a number of cultures. Hoebel's (1964:286) paper endorses "a natural growth through painstaking development of meticulously tested middle-level generalizations," and proceeds to provide some that pertain to legal spheres. Maquet (1964:25) concludes, however, that because the "facts" of anthropology, particularly in the sphere of world views, cannot be treated mathematically or statistically, and are not replicable by independent investigations, anthropology "belongs epistemologically to the sphere of the humanistic disciplines rather than to the sphere of the physico-mathematical sciences." This conclusion appears to ignore material presented in some of the other papers.

Other contributors (from a deliberately wide range of disciplines and cultural backgrounds) either (1) provide whole-culture substantive descriptions in terms of philosophies (or world view, values, national character, belief—the terms are used mostly interchangeably) (e.g., León-Portilla, Jahn, Klausner, Yamamoto); (2) suggest some theoretical constructs useful for answering particular questions of investigators (Hoebel, Sambursky, Smith); or (3) take the bent toward a hard science of cultural phenomena by applying the physico-mathematical theories of communication and information processing to culturally learned behavior (in individuals and social groups) or to the physiology of the brain or central nervous system (Braitenberg, MacKay, McCulloch,

Campbell, Hockett). Little communication among these groups is evidenced; those offering substantive descriptions proclaim their material to be satisfactorily holistic, showing the overall or central unity of the culture from which behavior and other cultural categories derive, but their validity-replicability-methodological status is largely pre-Radin and -Kluckhohn. At the other end, those dealing with the newer tools are largely programmatic and abstract, and although some of them attend to cross-cultural comparison, in all cases but one they do not try to extend their interesting models of human functioning to anything near a "whole culture" dimension.

The exception is a contribution by linguist-anthropologist Hockett (1964), whose "Scheduling" has implications for structural and quantifiable treatment of cultural data that *would* allow replication. In addition, he carries his information theory/linguistic format for calculating indeterminacy (and thus predictability) in various structured choice situations (i.e., cultural situations) to its ultimate use for a holistically oriented description (1964:141) such as "the simpler, broader and deeper characterizations (which some anthropologists make) of themes of a culture, or of its values, or of national character, model personality, or philosophy." These also "find their place within the scheduling framework." This is accomplished through extending his notation for individual states of predictability, freedom of choice, urgency, and anxiety to states of cultural systems or subsystems, so that, for example, degree of ritualization in one context is represented by a particular pattern, while the anxiety pattern predominates in another. The concept of metapattern learning, as analyzed also by Bateson, appears in Hockett's generalization to multiperson units. A culture participant learns a background pattern of states to be expected—for example, a pattern of low freedom of choice combined with high anxiety—upon repeated exposures to these states, and comes to interpret all sorts of states as though they involved little freedom and much anxiety. This pattern has an effect on social structure through its effect on personality (Hockett 1964:142): "In due time the whole community may be marked by fatalism and anxiety. Alternatively, such a combination as fatalism and anxiety might become widespread for certain cultural systems [subsystems?] only, other systems having different properties." Thus a culture might be characterized by its areas of distinctive patterns of degree of predictability, the latter being measurable mathematically. Hockett's paper is entirely programmatic, and while his parallel of ethnography with the "inside-view-outside view" of linguistic description (relations of etics and emics) has been applied substantively in descriptive semantics, I do not know of any application of his synthesizing scheme toward the analysis of an actual macro belief system.

While none of the papers in the volume refers to beliefs as such, the volume as a whole pertains to cultural knowledge and knowing; and, as Northrop (1964:202) points out, "the word 'philosophy' is but the name for the elemental concepts and assumptions in terms of which any subject matter is thought of, described, and understood." Goodenough's "belief system," at its unifying level, is then philosophy. And if concepts and assumptions have connection with percepts, as Goodenough avers, the inclusion of psychologists' studies in the Northrop volume is sensible; for example, Campbell's (1964) on "differences in perception as distinguished

from failures of communication." (This should be included in a section on "psychological approaches," but it is clear by now that a focus on belief systems leads to work by interdisciplinary teams and cross-discipline workers.) Campbell (1964:330) emphasizes again the observer's virtual inability to transcend his own emics, and concludes that Hockett's statement of the ideal of striving for an inside view shows at the same time the impossibility of doing more than approximating it, and that this is the particular bind of those who work in the field of anthropology, "where human minds provide the major instrument both for observation and for confronting theory and data." On the other hand (1964:326), complete solipsism is as inappropriate for the problem of knowing another culture as for that of knowing a second language, for while "a brain which has mapped a certain environment becomes a biased machine for mapping another environment," and an adult conditioned to the culture of one society (or to the rules of one language) has the disadvantage of having to learn to disregard well-learned discriminations while attending to the subleties of the other, it is a fact that adults have been able to learn novel languages. "The physical discriminanda available to the children of any society are also available to the anthropologist." Campbell also stresses and demonstrates the importance of a *context of similarity* before two items can be seen to contrast as different, and that such controls could be made more explicit in anthropologists' studies. The unchanging background is often unnoticed and unnoted or left implicit (by culture participant and anthropologist), but its existence is what makes it possible to compare two items, or successive states of a single item. Campbell discovers this principle in the laboratory conditions of a perception experiment, and suggests that confirmation of scientific knowledge may require very special settings, and that it is the possibility of providing such conditions in the study of the philosophies of cultures that is under scrutiny. He is not particularly optimistic about the matter.

It would seem that this is in essence the same principle recognized by linguists in their contrastive analysis of language structure, by some ethnographic theorists with regard to cultural meaning structure generally, and by Lévi-Strauss (1963) in his final analysis of totemism. Lévi-Strauss, as philosopher, finds in all the anthropological fuss over totemism the single but vital and worthy discovery (already told us by Rousseau, he states, in 1754) that the source of man's first logical operations, and thus the birth of culture, was in his apprehension of the classificatory principles of the plant and animal world, upon which he based his own subsequent social differentiation, "which could be lived out only if it were conceptualized" (1963:99). *The logic of distinctions and oppositions,* or contrasts of diversity within a unifying context, Lévi-Strauss believes began when man first apprehended himself along with other animals as sentient beings, then distinguished human from nonhuman within this field, then acquired "the capacity to distinguish himself as he distinguished them, i.e. to use the diversity of species as conceptual support for social differentiation" (1963:101). Whether or not this is the way it happened, Lévi-Strauss has identified (with Rousseau, Bergson, and also Radcliffe-Brown before him, as he points out) "a certain mode of human thought" that appears universal. "Radcliffe-Brown, though abstaining from metaphysical considerations which were foreign to his temperament, followed the same route, when he reduced

totemism to a particular form of a universal tendency, in order to reconcile *opposition* and *integration*" (1963:99). Radcliffe-Brown had found that the totems for the dual divisions in Australia were chosen as pairs of opposites, and that this comparison can be made only when the species chosen have in common at least one characteristic that permits them to be compared. Lévi-Strauss (1963:90) concludes that the structural principle, consisting of "the union of opposites," is an "elementary logic, which is like the least common denominator of all thought . . . a direct expression of the structure of the mind." He also recognizes this as the basis of language and of structural linguistics: "The ideas of opposition and correlation, and that of pair of opposites, have a long history; but it is structural linguistics and subsequently structural anthropology which rehabilitated them in the vocabulary of the humane sciences."

Lévi-Strauss' "oppositions" always take binary form. One wonders if sometimes the dual division should not refer simply to the manner of analysis (or of thought), in which contrast is known by successive pairings of the members of a contrast set. In this case they are not necessarily "opposite"—as black/white or good/bad—but simply "different" from each other, within the frame of similarity. And the set can consist of more than two (indeed, totem groupings often do, in societies other than the Australian). This does not nullify the method of contrasting pairs, but it allows the possibility of structures in the world which may be best shown as other than dual in form or membership, or with other than two-valued dimensions or differentiation.

In considering the learning of native contrast sets for belief system ethnography, Metzger (1966, n.d.) has employed some concepts from the philosophers of language and symbolic logic (Carnap, Quine, Reichenbach) to make the point that the ethnographer will replicate the native's knowledge of cultural structure only by acquiring as much information about the unstated boundaries of complete contrast sets as is represented in the competence of the native knower. Having defined belief system as an inventory of all the possible assertions (true propositions) in someone's language, Metzger uses the concept of analytic truth, or *analytic sentence,* to show that a person's belief system must include knowledge of the possible alternatives to that which has been stated or acted, since this is prerequisite to the understanding of factual propositions.[13] He states that ethnography consists of converting factual assertions to analytic assertions, the latter being those that are "true in all imaginable states of the world"—in other words, making them specify the contexts to which they apply. Quine (1960:66) suggests that "analytic sentences are those we are prepared to affirm come what may," and he adds that we must then circumscribe the "what may." The truth value, then, of analytic sentences is, in a sense, context-free. Metzger's ethnography is now redefined as "the set of all analytic assertions in some person's language."

Now, this is not the type of assertion people normally go around making to each other. It contains the elements that hearers "know" already and staters do not bother to state. It contains the things the ethnographer has got to learn. The process of converting factual assertions to analytic assertions consists, for one thing, of learning the con-

trasts of all concepts included in the statement. The native hearer has a knowledge of what specifically *is not being referred to,* what is being *specifically excluded,* when someone says, for example, "*Xs* are blue." This can be rewritten "*Xs* are blue and they are not red and they are not orange and they are not . . ." When the rewriting is complete it covers the universe of the speaker-hearers' "known or imagined 'colors' " and becomes a partially analytic sentence. (The next rewriting would be "*X* and not *Y* and not *Z* and not . . . are blue and not red . . ." etc.) This filling in of contrasts simply shows that we define things by what they are not (Kelly 1955) and within a known frame of similarity; that is, situations in which items substitute (Frake 1969a). We also define them by what they include in their reference (extensional definition), so that a comprehensive list of items that could be called *X* would also be in the ideal knower's repertoire, along with knowledge of differentiating and defining features at each level (intensional definition). Statements specifying this structural knowledge are presented here as a kind of belief; they also are data from which to analyze the system. The ethnographer "elicits a corpus of assertions that *permits the composition* of analytic sentences of the belief system" (Metzger 1966; italics mine).

This part of Metzger's argument, then, specifies the prerequisite analytic belief propositions that underlie the competence of native knowers to make correct sense of factual propositions and to utter them. It appears to be a formalized execution of the proposition structure outlined by Goodenough, for even the elementary levels of his belief system model (concepts, etc.) can be manifested in propositional form. This might be made clearer by initially separating levels: beliefs are factual propositions held to be true,

---

[13] This is somewhat similar to the question-and-answer logic of Collingwood (1939), in which a statement is not meaningful until the unstated question it answers is known, and the statement is misunderstood if the question is incorrectly inferred. "Question" refers to knowledge of context, and so does this interpretation of analyticity, as I see it.

plus propositions about the analytic substructure implied by each and "known" by native communicators; these last are true by mutual agreement.[14] Then, when all factual propositions have been converted to their full analytic statement (which now extends to knowledge of features of intensional definition, and also structured knowledge of contexts-in-which-true, omitted from most factual propositions), one can say that a belief system is "the set of all analytic assertions in some person's language." It may be objected that this is strangely like an ethnography of tautologies, for the propositions in this form are all "true by definition," as it were. This is partly so. The tautologies of the exotic culture have to be learned by the ethnographer. Until he knows them, he will "understand" native belief propositions incorrectly or incompletely. Much of the work of ethnosemantics has focused on kinds of formalization for making explicit and replicable this basic step in any attempt to observe and describe another's world of belief and knowledge.

Formalization need not extend to a specification of field procedures, but in these papers Metzger theorizes also regarding the relation of the end product of his ethnography to the ways in which the ethnographer can systematically elicit from informants the necessary assertions about concepts and their relations. He points to the simple conversion of assertions to questions, and vice versa, and to the universal property of natural languages that they can interrogate by use of a relatively limited set of question types, each specifying a particular aspect of the factual belief proposition to be analytically explored—e.g., the ranges of *where, when, who, what*, etc. of the various elements in the proposition. Analysis of questions as semantic operators is quite relevant to this type of belief system ethnography. (Note Collingwood 1939; Belnap 1963; Harrah 1960, 1961; Weinreich 1963:120-22; and Cherry 1960 for theoretical issues. Black 1967 and 1971 give an analysis of Ojibwa question constructions, worked out while doing belief system native-language eliciting.) Since the question approach leads to one means for synthesizing macro belief systems, its further review will be deferred.

Developments in symbolic logic and other language-related and mathematical philosophical inquiries have significantly affected the type of social science work under consideration here, as they have many other fields. This effect is too close to be treated separately; the same is true of "linguistic" and "psychological" approaches. Some philosophical approaches by anthropologists, which relate such things as myth to belief, will be included immediately below.

---

[14] Quine's (1961:23) second type of analyticity, which depends on extralogical synonymy, may relate to this, if extralogical can mean depending on factors outside the language rules—in his case a convention among users that two terms will be used with reference to the same object (bachelor = unmarried man). In Metzger's application to ethnographic learning, it might be considered a type of analyticity when some belief is "true in all imaginable states of the world" because, for the native user, there has been no experience of contrast. "Imaginable" here refers to the informant-believer, and must boil down to all he has imagined up to the moment of providing data. See note 10.

Approaches Through Myth and Folk Narrative

Myths and other folk narratives have been variously defined and related to belief, according to Bidney's critique (1953, chap. 10). In this brief survey I shall not try to distinguish myth from folktale. In either case, the "meaning" is symbolically portrayed, as in other forms of expressive art, and the question arises as to how analyses of these symbols by outsiders can contribute toward a knowledge of the belief systems of particular cultures.

Bidney's (1953:294, 297) own analysis of myth places it as a special kind of belief, "namely an incredible belief, or the idea of a credible impossibility. . . . Myth . . . is value-charged and implies a negative evaluation of the truth of a given belief." This statement refers to popular usage, and the "outside view" of what believers would not themselves regard as myth. Boas had characterized myths as stories that represent serious quests for an understanding and explanation of life and nature. These two views might be reconciled by regarding myths as revealing the things that people have found it useful or necessary to believe, in spite of finding them impossible to validate empirically. This conceptualization has a certain accordance with two recent usages worth mentioning: King's in "Myth, Basic Values, Ethos, and Style in Culture" (1960) and Tyler's "The Myth of P: Epistemology and Formal Analysis" (1969b).

King does not deal with any actual mythology, but rather with clarification of the concept. He locates myth in that area of life where "man postulates a reality beyond that which he can empirically control or predict." Since man is capable of transcending what is learned, he is continually apprehending and experiencing some things that are at the same time unknown, unpredictable, and therefore not amenable to manipulation or objectively verifiable explanation. This "unpredictable experience" must, however, be accommodated to the known and explained cultural world, and this is the function of myth. It is thus the locus of creativity and innovation.

The "apprehended unknown," then,

cannot by definition be *analyzed,* and King's second related point is that it therefore is learned and used as a *Gestalt,* a "global definition of man and the universe" which is "phatically and symbolically learned," and the attempt to communicate it, "because of lack of empirical [analytical?] modes of expression, must be gestalt in nature." The meaning of myths, we therefore deduce, is symbolic and hidden in the sense that it is not explicitly formulated, yet is of greatest importance to man's inherent needs. It is indeed both useful and necessary for men to "believe" their myths.

Tyler deals with a very specific mythological content. "P" is a symbol in formal analysis representing his reduction of kin term etic notation to one "primitive relation" (P stands for Parent, but as an analytic relation rather than as a kin term). Thus P, in the reference language of the analyst, is a term used to talk about the kinship terms that occur in the target language. It has only a metastatus of reality and its cognitive saliency to speakers of the target language cannot be known, or rather is irrelevant. Tyler refers to these terms of the metalanguage as "our language of mythic explanation,"—useful, but not provably real in the world outside the analyst's imposed model. As for the goal of understanding native cognition (e.g., "psychological reality" of formal analytic results), it too may never be demonstrably knowable, but may remain only mythical—a useful myth, however, in the current state of anthropological theory. Now this is an interesting use of "myth," especially in relation to Bidney's and King's definitions. Tyler's myth refers to symbolic representation of a reality apprehended but not empirically known, and also to a utility directed toward creative advances.

The symbolic content of myth, then,

may reveal what things a particular people have found it useful and necessary to believe—the new and "unexplainable" things they have creatively worked into the coherence of their already existing belief systems. The problem then arises of the valid interpretation of the symbols of a people who are alien or exotic to the culture of the interpreter, and of the level at which to relate myth manifestations to culture: surface, hidden, or whatever. A second problem in relating mythology to culture (*a* mythology to *a* culture?) is the decision about the boundaries of the culture (area) to be considered. And a third problem may arise, if one concentrates upon the ethnographic present: that of the contemporary status of "belief" in this handed-down tradition.

An approach that obviates all three questions is that which rests its case on a universal symbolism. Jung's "archetypes of the collective unconscious" are principles and forms common to all human psyches. According to Jung (1959: xvii), these archetypes have been elevated to the roles of dieties and heroes in the myths of all people, and distinctive mythologies "reflect the inner distinctive life of the psyche of any given culture." However, "tribal lore and myth" have given archetypes a specific cultural stamp—they have been modified and brought to consciousness, and this "conscious elaboration" renders them no longer true archetypes, which are unconscious and universal. Mythologists, according to Jung (1959:289), "have absolutely refused to see until now . . . the fact that myths are first and foremost psychic phenomena that reveal the nature of the soul," for they have paid attention to the material content only.

Primitive man is not much interested in objective explanations of the obvious, but he has an imperative need . . . to assimilate all outer sense experiences to inner, psychic events. It is not enough . . . to see the sun rise and set; this external observation must at the same time be a psychic happening: the sun in its course must represent the fate of a god or hero who, in the last analysis, dwells nowhere except in the soul of man. . . . The mythologized processes of nature . . . are in no sense allegories of objective experiences.

Rather they are projections from the psyche, made accessible to men's consciousness by the symbolic expression.

Lévi-Strauss (1967c) objected to Jung's "misconception" that "a given mythological pattern—the so-called archetype—possesses a certain meaning." Myth is a language, according to Lévi-Strauss, on a higher level than either *langue* or *parole,* though partaking of both, and "if there is a meaning to be found in mythology, it cannot reside in the isolated elements which enter into the composition of a myth, but only in the way those elements are combined." In the cultural interpretation of myth symbolism, then, there is a subquestion of whether to attend to content or to structure. Analysis of structure came late to the study of folklore, according to Dundes (1965); while other disciplines were taking up the "structural or pattern approach" in the twenties and thirties, there was practically no interest among folklorists "in a holistic synchronic approach," but rather an atomistic interest in lexicon and motif inventories. The great exception was Propp's *Morphology of the Folktale* (1968), which, however, was not accessible to Western scholars until thirty years after it first appeared in 1928. Thus Lévi-Strauss' 1955 emphasis on *relations* as units of meaning in myths—which he conceded to have come from the work of structural linguistics—was early among structural model approaches in this field. However, although his analyses are applied to particular bodies of folklore, there is little indication of how he came upon the particular dimensions of meaning that he uses—uses, indeed, as if they were the only ones possible in the material but without supporting evidence. His concern with holism, again, takes into account cultural context, but it emerges as culture per se, not particular cultures. His goal (1967c:220) is "to perceive some basic logical processes which are at the root of mythical thought," and he concludes that "the purpose of myth is to provide a logical model capable of overcoming a contradiction," which refers to his universal logic of oppositions mentioned earlier. Colby (1966c:1) notes that "Lévi-Strauss . . . views myths as vehicles for the expression of opposing dualities and their mediating elements (as in the opposition between sky and earth, with mist as the mediator)," and he elsewhere (1970) dismisses myth analyses of Lévi-Strauss and of Leach (1967) as intuitive and unvalidated. Dundes (1968:xiii) remarks that while most structural analyses of myths have had a lack of concern with cultural context, "Lévi-Strauss has bravely attempted to relate the paradigm(s) he 'finds' in myth to the world at large, that is, to other aspects of culture such as cosmology and world view." This approach "helped lead to the new notion of myth (and other forms of folklore) as *models*" (rather than as *charters*, as Malinowski would have it). But the "emphasis on context is rather one of application of the results of structural analysis than one inherent in the approach."[15] It is clear that some American formalists are not exactly comfort-

able with the type of formalism applied to myth texts on the other side of the Atlantic. Propp's model is more to their liking.

Keeping our focus on folk narrative as related to macro belief systems of particular cultures, we shall see that recent applications both of Lévi-Strauss and of Propp are turning their attention in this direction. Some of these, indeed, appear to be bridging the gap between the two styles of structural analysis. In 1968 Dundes outlined some possible avenues of culture application, but placed their execution largely in the future, as did Colby in 1970, noting the paucity of substantive studies. "Structural analysis is not an end in itself! " writes Dundes (1968:xiii). "The form [of the folkloristic text] must ultimately be related to the culture or cultures in which it is found." He goes on to point out that Lévi-Strauss' paradigmatic analyses tend to be speculative

---

[15] Lévi-Strauss' *The Savage Mind* (1966) gives further exposition of his work with myths. Here he characterizes myth as a system of abstract relations, which starts from structure and constructs the already conceived whole from available concrete materials (events and objects). Mythical units are halfway between percepts and concepts, tied to the concrete but, like signs, having the power of reference. Myth and science (1966: 15) are "not different stages in the development of the human mind, but rather two strategic levels at which nature is accessible to scientific inquiry," one level more tied to sensible perception than the other. In this first chapter, he places art, games, and rites along with myth in the framework of "the science of the concrete." In Chapter 5 of the same work, Lévi-Strauss concludes that the reason myths focus on natural species (a question asked by Boas) is that the notion of species, as used in myths, is not just a relation between man and the natural world, but a perceivable manifestation of the ultimate discontinuity of nature. "It is the sensible expression of an objective coding." It might be said that Chapter 5 of *The Savage Mind* begins with Lévi-Strauss' position with regard to cultural holism: all levels of classification within a particular society, he says, are equally parts of the whole, and whichever is put first must have recourse to the others, for all are formally analogous and differ from one another "only in their relative position within the whole system of reference." He then makes his special point that all systems— "whole," macro, and micro—operate "by means of a pair of contrasts: between general and particular on the one hand, and nature and culture on the other." Thus with one characteristic leap Lévi-Strauss leaves the realm of *a* culture to enter that of *all* culture.

and deductive, in contrast to the syntagmatic model of Propp, which has led to empirical and inductive application. Propp's analysis of the formal organization of a text is linear, following the chronological ordering of the sequence of action elements that he called "functions" and which he found to be limited in number and constant in sequence in the Russian fairy tales he analyzed. There is no reason, Dundes argues, that this type of structural analysis "cannot be meaningfully related to other aspects of a culture," but Propp himself did not do this, though his contribution of a structural inductive model was a necessary first step. For by providing a means for independently examining the structure of this genre in the expressive area of a culture, his model makes it possible to find similarities to or differences from the structures of other genres and other areas of the same culture. There have been preliminary studies applying similar structural models to a variety of folklore genres; for example, Köngäs and Maranda (1962). Colby (1970:189) suggests that future work may answer such questions as "Do the same expansion rules apply to a variety of genres in the same culture?" when considering studies of narrative production dynamics.

Colby (1970, n.d.) has proposed a "grammar of narrative culture" that builds on Propp's basic units and adds considerably more structural components and levels. His "dramatic component," or "highlighting structure," contains the devices for creating emphasis, underlining or framing values, behavioral modes, beliefs, and so on. Here the narrative's function as a "cultural production" and model for transmission might be found to have regularities of patterning. Other such cultural productions could be compared—for example, games, which have been studied

as culture models by Roberts (1959; Roberts and Sutton-Smith 1962; Roberts, Sutton-Smith, and Kendall 1963). However, Colby (1970:191) considers that methods are not yet available to study narrative as a culture vehicle, as this would require an experimental anthropology:

As vehicles, myths and other folk narratives present a world view, convey values and motivations, codify institutional organizations and practices, and illustrate typical strategies and other behavior (among other things). At the same time, we know that folk narratives do not mirror social life to any large extent. The relationships are indeed complex.[16]

Colby (1971) is also using mathematical and computerized methods for analyzing content and emphasis in folktales, following upon his previous work in developing a theory of "cultural templates" or cognitive patterns (1966c, 1966d). Most recently he has produced a partial narrative grammar (n.d.) based on a corpus of Alaskan Eskimo texts collected by Spencer (1959). This work is a substantive realization of his proposed narrative grammar, presented as a "theory of Eskimo folktales" which "claims some replicability and predictive power." His results yield elements and rules at several levels, which he predicts will describe the syntax of other Eskimo folktales but will distinguish them from those of neighboring peoples. A comparison

---

[16] Of course, many culture descriptions have used myth and other narrative material as evidence for their conclusions (e.g., Hallowell 1964; Radin 1923, 1949; Lessa 1966; Wax 1962; Wax and Wax 1962); most of these have used these materials as anecdotal illustrations, to support holistically oriented cultural characterizations, and generally on the side of myth content rather than structure. Note that the Waxes applied myth evidence to a culture *type* (magical world view), presumably using myths taken from cultures having the described type of belief system. Lessa looks for ways in which mythology may be a reflection of culture, and finds no clear relation.

with Propp's Russian fairy tale analysis shows them distinct at the base sequence level to which Propp limited his description. Colby has not attempted to relate the results to other aspects of Alaskan Eskimo culture, and "separating the universal from the particular (i.e., culture-specific) will have to await the study of additional narrative cultures."

The question of the particular culture or the culture area to which a body of narrative material can be meaningfully related for macro belief system study might be considered at this point. Narratives frequently occur over wide areas encompassing several cultures. Colby (n.d.) notes that the assumption of a homogeneous speech community is risky here, and that he chose Eskimo folktales because the available data came from a relatively homogeneous group. He adds, "As one deals with stories originating from users of a much more 'pluralistic' culture than that of the Eskimos . . . it is better to restrict oneself to individual storytellers with large repertoires or to very circumscribed geographical areas in order to discover regularities." When there have been enough grammars produced to make comparison possible, the narrative regularities may in return (1970: 190)

sharpen our notion of culture and culture boundaries. Patterns found in the folktale repertoire of a single person can be indicative of that person alone, of some subculture he uses, or of a culture; then more widely of a culture area and beyond. Different types of elements within a particular narrative culture may have different distributional characteristics.

We might note further that many narratives and narrative cycles are found distributed over language barriers as well. The North American "trickster

cycle" is a case in point. Radin (1956) limited himself to certain tribes in his presentation of North American trickster texts—Siouan speaking, Algonkian speaking, and several of the Northwest Coast (Tsimshian, Tlingit, Haida). Are these all to be included in one "narrative culture"? And what of the trickster tales in the rest of North America? Structural analyses would provide the answer, presumably; they also might provide significant evidence of differences in the ways in which various cultural groups have handled the "same" narratives, and thus give independent data regarding macro aspects of cultural belief systems.

Dundes (1965: 212), in fact, suggests this with regard to diffusion through acculturation (European $\rightarrow$ American Indian), but he focuses on predicting the new form of the incoming tale, and treats all of North American narrative culture as though it were a single unit with a single structure. His own *Morphology of North American Indian Folktales* (1964) may have persuaded him that this is so; in this work he applied Propp's morphological framework combined with a Pikean distributional terminology of "motifemes," "motifs," and "allomotifs," the last of which are substitutable motifs in a motifeme slot, a tale then being a sequence of motifemes (see Dundes 1962). He claims to have found structural regularities in this largely dispersed sample of cultures. Colby (1970:191) sees this selection from widely differing cultures as resulting in a loss of control, and therefore considers that Dundes' 1964 study has failed to provide a useful distributional analysis. The limited and general schemes (structural types of motifeme sequences) reported by Dundes, he says, simply describe properties of all folk narratives. It seems that this might be the natural result when one focuses on this large an area or level of cultural similarity. Training the analysis on single cultural traditions within North America, as Radin chose to do, should bring out the more complex and specific schemes distinctive of each. Radin drew it finer than that when he showed variations *within the Winnebago group,* distributed by faction (traditional versus Peyote people), in the function that a single narrative event can represent.

Radin's (1956:168-69) remarks about the overall "meaning" (or most generally accepted characteristics) of the trickster figure, and the variations and reformulations given the cycle over both space and time, are additionally suggestive:

Since this cycle has been revised, reorganized and reinterpreted for an untold period of time and since innumerable exploits have the same import as those just mentioned, many may have been attributed to Trickster that did not originally have any connection with him.... The symbol which Trickster embodies is not a static one. It contains within itself the promise of differentiation.... Every generation occupies itself with interpreting Trickster anew. No generation understands him fully but no generation can do without him.... He represents not only the undifferentiated and distant past, but likewise the undifferentiated present within every individual.... What happens to him happens to us.

This seems a rather strangely Jungian and Lévi-Straussian interpretation of myth meaning, coming on the heels of so much careful Boasian data. Trickster does lend himself to this combination; he surely could be seen as an archetype; in fact, Jung (1956:20) says so. Trickster is also productive of a great deal of textual data. On the side of Lévi-Strauss, the notion that this unclassifiable creature represents the dawn or the origin of man's logical differentiat-

ing capacities is of some interest. Some of the tales make this explicit. Savard (1970) summarizes the case of Trickster's giving the large flying creatures different names and characteristics, and in a personal communication tells of a story in which various trees have a similar differentiating history. (See also Savard 1971.)

In this connection, we might introduce now a possible mediating view between the opposing structural analysts on each side of the Atlantic. There are a number of French-Canadian structuralists at the Laboratoire d'Anthropologie Amérindienne in Montreal, headed by Rémi Savard, who have been engaged since 1967 in the collection and analysis of Algonkian myths from the Indians of northern Quebec and Labrador, with essentially a Lévi-Straussian approach. However, they have acquainted themselves closely with American "cognitive anthropology" as well, and claim to be incorporating a semantic description of the storytellers' cultural world (belief system) to support their choices of dimensions of analysis ("*axes sémantiques,*" from Greimas 1966). Savard's recent work (1969, 1970; Savard and Lachapelle 1970) attests to this, although in the first—his analysis of one version of a trickster tale—the native taxonomy is not given, and only portions of Black's (1967) Ojibwa taxonomy of the relevant domain are included where useful. More important, perhaps, he shows a connection between the syntagmatic chain and the paradigm of interimage relationships, as he describes it, and suggests that these "grammatical elements" will prove not to be isolated to the single myth but will appear in others of the same cultural group, and even in other manifestations of the same culture. The grammar, when known more completely, may in fact upset our carving of cultural boundaries. Savard finds that myths have a special place among cultural communications, using language but constituting a language as well, a metacode that talks about symbols, as it were. Myths use many codes at once, of which language is but one (although the structural principles at the base of language may be universal in human functioning). Another code is the indigenous natural science; but as with the language, so with the folk taxonomy: knowledge of them is not sufficient to enable one to understand the message of the myth. On the other hand, while mythology is not a faithful reflection of indigenous natural science, it cannot be understood without a knowledge of that science. Myth, however, has other ends of its own.[17]

In "Structures sémantiques et mythologie" (1970) Savard asks: (1) What exactly is the relation between the myths and the semantic structures of a given group? (2) Since knowledge of the indigenous natural science classifications is of value to the myth analyst, couldn't myth analysts furnish the results of their investigations to ethnosemanticists to aid them in *their* work? His hypothesis is that the trickster subcategory of myth sends back a concretized metalinguistic reflection of the semantic classifications in which the world is formed for the members of the culture of the narrator. Demonstration of this, and determination of the taxonomic placing of terms used in the myths, will await a semantic analysis of

the narrator's terminology. These questions are not yet answerable in full, he implies, but are worth beginning to explore.[18]

Mathiot's (1972) method for structural analysis of myths may also represent a mediating position, and be of particular interest for belief system study. (See Mathiot 1968 for theoretical orientation.) This method takes account of several types of structural relations and units, and of two levels, *story* and *message,* one overt, the other hidden and symbolic. The work is termed "cognitive analysis of a myth," and is intended to uncover the cognitive significance of the myth-telling; that is, what it reveals regarding "the conception of reality held by the people to whom it belongs." Structuralist method is employed, chiefly for the analysis of the story, which then leads to a revelation of the message through story units termed "key statements" —those narrative elements that convey emphasis. (This seems similar to Colby's "highlighting structure.") A sample myth is analyzed, in a very systematic manner. The culminating message could be read as a belief proposition: "With the help of magic, an undesirable state of affairs can be remedied by the same means which has brought it about in the first place." How is one to know if these

---

[17] I hope M. Savard will not object to this loose rendition of his French and summary of his statements; any misreadings are my error. I was helped by the translation of an earlier version by Dr. Charlotte Kursh.

[18] The relations between the word labels of semantic reference structures in everyday use and those same words as they occur in the telling and retelling of myths must be extremely complex, es-

pecially in view of the traveling of myths in both space and time. My Ojibwa material includes both taxonomies and myths from the same Indian community (Black 1970a, 1970b). It contains evidence that the relations of myth words to the reference content of beliefs can be such that hearing of myths is actually confusing to the believers. I have begun to document this case (Black 1972), and I hope also to consider Savard's other point regarding the uses ethnosemanticists might find in the product of myth analysis. Savard's emphasis here is on semantic features and dimensions (or "articulations" and "axes," as he terms them), and how myth material can aid in the discovery of features that have ethnographic validity. He has a notion that one function of myth may be to solve problems of feature ambiguities, and thus of communication.

beliefs can be ascribed to the story-teller's culture? Mathiot seeks corrobo-ration of the myth message in indepen-dent ethnographic information about the culture in question. The ethno-graphic data are in the form of *beliefs* reported by the ethnographer on the basis of certain observed behaviors, all of which he interpreted as directed toward restoring a desirable condition by working hard at the very things that had caused the imbalance. The steps by which he arrived at this interpretation are not made explicit, however. In light of Mathiot's interest in formally con-necting folk narratives to the culture of the storyteller and his audience, her further work on referential meaning and the cognitive analysis of language is relevant; for example, she provides a needed distinction between cognitive and semantic (1970), and some opera-tional criteria for approaching induc-tively the cognitive analysis of folk nar-ratives (n.d.), always taking into ac-count the cultural setting.

In contrast to the formalized types of narrative analysis being developed by these investigators, it may turn out to be equally important that some ethnog-raphers are utilizing a largely intuitive interpretation of narratives as an ave-nue to the description of particular cul-tural belief systems. Preston (1971*a*, 1971*b*) reveals Cree belief ideology through what he claims are Cree-like interpretations of the messages of stories, centering on their distinctive usage of metaphor "as a technical vo-cabulary for the expression of non-ordinary experience." While the met-aphors are specifically analyzed as if from the Cree point of view, the "Cree understanding" of the events in the nar-ratives (their translation by the listener into unstated primary images) is ap-parently understood by Preston through his own prior knowledge of the ideology, gained through "a carefully acquired 'feel' for the culture." He has learned to replicate the Cree's "particu-lar way of understanding events" and thus can apply a kind of *Verstehen*. I have a notion that a careful account of the operations of a good intuitive eth-nographer might very well turn up some interesting avenues of access to belief systems, and furthermore, if Pres-ton's understanding of the myth mes-sage can be shown to match that of native listeners, his report constitutes a kind of validity testing of his belief description regardless of his manner of learning it.

For another focus on metaphor, a recent book titled *Lore: An Introduc-tion to the Science of Folklore and Literature* (Edmonson 1971) surveys a wide swath of worldwide literary tradi-tions—primitive, folk, and sophisti-cated—with an emphasis on the need for systematic study of metaphor. Ed-monson opposes "the metaphoric side of culture" to the logical or denotative (metaphor being connotative and ana-logical, and definitive of what he terms "lore"). To be perpetuated, metaphor depends on specific cultural context in both space and time, and is communi-cated or diffused beyond that context with difficulty, unless "retold logi-cally," as Edmonson states Lévi-Strauss has done with his South American myth analyses, for example. These anal-yses, though, tell us more about the nature of human communication (of culture, that is) than about South America, according to Edmonson. Yet structure of metaphor is stable only *in context*, and *temporarily* (Edmonson 1971:25). This book is surely an in-triguing and stimulating impetus to-ward attempts to analyze "how meta-phors are created and transmitted" as a wedge to understanding the workings of the less tractable side of cultural knowledge systems. Its contribution toward understanding or validly describing particular systems is not too clear, but, in view of Edmonson's (1970:49-50) belief that we create metaphor out of an excess of redundancy ("we have developed as a species more communicative potential than we 'need' for environmental purposes and hence we transmit in culture an overload of highly consequential but entirely metaphorical structure"), the contribution may rest on its possible corroborating function, providing metaphorical restatement of beliefs.

This review of the field of folk narrative is by no means comprehensive, yet one can see here a valuable yet difficult and somewhat elusive approach to the study of cultural belief systems. Especially there is reason to look forward to the future development of current trends toward relating a people's narrative tradition to other genres and structures of their culture.

CURRENT FOCI ON MACROSYSTEMS OF BELIEF AND KNOWLEDGE

There are at least three vantage points from which the integration of systems can be viewed. The different levels and domains of codings can be considered as operating in and comprising *a single cultural system,* as necessary for participation in or interpretation of *a single ongoing scene of action,* or as known and used by *a single individual.* This could alternatively be stated as three ways in which to enlarge the context of a set of micro data: (*a*) by additional domains or segments of the same culture, (*b*) by additional codes and code levels operating concurrently, and (*c*) by the additional repertoire or mazeway content of the actor involved. While these are not mutually exclusive in practice (or in the work of most anthropologists), it will be useful to consider that in *a* emphasis is on the more static relationships be-

tween domains, in *b* on the dynamic relations between ongoing levels, and in *c* on the individual's sampling of both.

CULTURE FOCUS: DOMAIN LINKAGE

Theoretically, culture has been defined as a complex of symbolic codes, or as a set of interrelated propositions; for example, by Kay (1966). This view of culture would allow us to see a culture, for the moment, as a single macro belief system. Kay (1966:110-11) says, "If culture is . . . a complex, probably multi-level, symbolic code, the first thing we need is a large number of descriptive studies of as many levels and aspects of as many different cultural codes as possible." Kay is calling for the inductive analysis of many microsystems but not for their inductive cultural synthesis, and thus is not confronting the macro complexity of a single culture as such in this first step toward his stated task of discovering formal features that are common to all cultures. There may be a sense, however, in which the macro complexity is prior—if it is found, for example, that the most elegant analyses of single domains result in formal features that are culturally unlikely in terms of the elegance of the whole for users of the particular culture. (See Keesing 1971: "The briefest whole is not necessarily the sum of the briefest parts. . . . Economy is a long-run matter.") Numerous studies of micro belief systems have since been produced, as called for by Kay, and have yielded some universals of content and of process. Perhaps what is needed now is a large number of substantive studies of partial integration of subsystems within single cultures from which to derive integrative principles known to operate in these larger cultural contexts. In 1966 Stefflre outlined the problems of constructing what he termed a "behavioral dictionary" (descriptions of things, beliefs about things, behavior toward things)[19] and proposed that the real problems, not yet close to being solved, concerned the organization of the whole, its combinatorial rules and types of structures: "how to strike a belief system so it breaks up a certain way" and shows its elements and lines of formation and cleavage, "uncorrelating things that were correlated in the old world" so as to learn the principles that are productive in predicting the fate of new input.

The work of Keesing supports this position and contributes substantively. In "Formalization and the Construction of Ethnographies" (1971) he directly attacks the problem of progressing toward macro belief system descriptions. He notes that Goodenough in 1951 not only showed how we could break small segments of a cultural code, but dealt also with the empirical problems involved in the rigorous description of the macrostructure, especially the nonarbitrary ordering of subsystems. For Goodenough, certain elements in Trukese culture were found to depend for their definition upon other as yet undefined elements. He called for "a method for isolating empirically what elements are functionally linked to a given set of initial definitions to form what may be called a structural system within the larger culture." (See Goodenough 1951:11-12 for his discussion of the problem, and the entire monograph for his solution of that date.)

Keesing states that this problem of

internal ordering of macroscale descriptions has been largely delayed in favor of the analysis of segments. He examines the macro problem in some detail, with a view to possible solutions through current work in mathematical anthropology and with illustrations from Kwaio data. His inventory of some of the specific types of interdependence that will enter into a macro belief system ethnography includes (1) conceptual distinctions and dimensions of contrast that recur in several domains; (2) rules in one system that must be defined in terms of other domains (e.g., sexual distance rules use the dimension of sexuality, which in turn is defined by maturation and age categories); (3) nonarbitrary ordering of subsystems on the basis of these priorities which is not simply linear but will require complex cross-referencing back and forth in the parts of the ethnography; (4) construction of "models or paradigms that specify the outcome of many different situations or sequences," and also the sequences or strings that recur and their types of distribution; (5) relationships between conceptual categories and behavioral principles, which are not direct or derivable; (6) very general principles for behavior, which can override other more specific principles, producing a hierarchical ordering of principles in terms of levels of contrast; and (7) the fact that the maximally economical macroethnography is not necessarily a summation of maximally economical domain analyses, for the latter could employ dimensions found nowhere else in the ethnography. He notes (1971: 43):

As in a grammar, economy [in an ethnography] is a long-run matter. Our search must be for analytical breakthroughs that generalize and link domains together efficiently. Our preoccupation with little chunks of data in

---

[19] Stefflre et al. (1971) pursue some of the more modest and preliminary goals of the behavioral dictionary, characterized as "a description of the structure of meaning, belief, and normatively associated behavior of a speech community" (Kay 1971:79), with computerized methods for elicitation and distributional analysis of lexical elements or word classes.

isolation has hampered advances here, and has led us to emphasize discovery procedures at the expense of the creativity, insight, and experimentation required to construct larger-scale ethnographies.

Keesing's idea of domains is not limited to terminological systems, but includes social structural events and role relationships. He does note, however, the specific problems of relations between different terminological domains within a culture, and then also the relation of these lexical systems to the social code rules for language usage, which call for decision models of some kind. For display of these and other interlinkings, Keesing makes use of some flow diagrams such as had been worked out by Geoghegan (whose own use of them in work relevant here will be described below).

In addition to this overview of the problem of macroethnography, Keesing has produced a number of substantive studies of partial integration of Kwaio subsystems (e.g., 1967, 1968, 1969, 1970a). Each of these describes and demonstrates one or another of the types of linkage noted above, and each makes an explicit case for macro complexity. In the first of these papers, for example, after showing how the principles underlying decisions about appropriate marriage contributions depend upon prior knowledge of systems of economics, age categories, kinship, and prestige concepts, he summarizes (1967:14):

Our sketch of this decision model of Kwaio marriage contribution illustrates an interesting point about productive ethnography. An ethnographic description of a culture ramifies in a less trivial sense than that implied by Malinowski and the early functionalists. A great many principles impinge on or help to define appropriate behavior in a specific context. Thus one of the crucial factors in a particular situation might be membership in some kin group. Somewhere in the ethnography the rules that govern membership in these groups must be specified, and this in turn may require description of other cultural principles. In a full description of Kwaio culture, for example, ancestral spirits, property rights, and a number of other phenomena must be analyzed before descent-group membership can be defined. . . . An ethnography, then, becomes a complicated arrangement of interrelated statements. . . . The self-contained and exhaustive analysis of nontrivial segments or domains of a culture is difficult, if not impossible, owing to this pervasive spread and interconnection of cultural principles.

Keesing's work on integrating belief systems of kinship, social structure, and roles (1969, 1970b, n.d.), as well as Goodenough's work on social relationships (1969) and Howard's on decision-making and interpersonal relations (1963, 1964), has affinities with Metzger and Williams' "weddings" (1963a) and Frake's "religious behavior" (1969b); all these studies employ the principle of cultural knowledge in the form of distributions and definitions of acts and events. These descriptions represent partial integrations involving multiple micro belief systems, in that the cultural knowledge required for encoding and decoding the information conveyed by these selections must be drawn from many diverse subsystems of knowledge occurring on the same and different levels in the total cultural system. (This type of study can also be seen to represent systems in the total mazeway of individuals or interlinked by their concurrent use in "scenes," depending on which of the foci is chosen.)

All of Frake's work stresses the importance of cultural context, and while separate systems are described, the results are always tentative pending further knowledge of the culture in question. In other words, the ethnographic statement is always improvable by enlarging its cultural context and the amount and kinds of data for which it accounts. As Frake says (1969*d*), "The best statement is the one which most adequately accounts for the widest range of behavior." Frake is always concerned with specific linkages, even while considering large patterns, and in "Cultural Ecology and Ethnography" (1962) he shows that Subanun settlement-pattern rules link sociological and ecological belief systems in specifiable ways.

In "Notes on Queries in Ethnography" (1969*c*) Frake presents a model of interlinkage of verbally elicitable systems of cultural knowledge in the form of queries and responses. These link "categories of things in a culture" (i.e., concepts) by the various kinds of relations that may be revealed by using native-language question frames ("kind of," "part of," "ingredient of," "source of," "use of," etc.). Additionally, pairs of relations are linked through items that function as the response to one query and the topic of the next. Each concept thus becomes linked in a variety of ways with other concepts, and they are not thereby separated into domains in the overall conceptual system. The approach shows, rather, how each concept participates in a number of domains. These relational queries represent a model of empirically established indigenous semantic relationships as a synthesizing framework for macro belief system descriptions. Another road to such a model has been presented by Casagrande and Hale (1967), who analyzed a large sample of informants' native-language "folk definitions" in accordance with the types of semantic relationships they displayed—attribution, comparison, class inclusion, synonymy, and so on. This type of model has been further examined as a possible source of a set of universal semantic or

logical relationships common to all cultures, by Metzger (1967), Werner (1969*b*), and others, as well as by Casagrande and Hale themselves.

Thus it can be seen that domain linkage within a culture sometimes takes place through common logical properties or recurrent semantic features, and that models and substantive descriptions can be based upon such pervasive cultural manifestations and overall economy. For additional work along this line see D'Andrade (1970; "broad models versus narrow models" of kinship), Vogt (1965; "replication" in Zinacantan culture), Keesing (1970*a*; "cultural principles of high generality"), Black (1967; "productive semantic features" in Ojibwa belief systems), Hymes (1961; "cognitive styles"), Cohen (1969; "conceptual styles"), Glenn (1970; "cognitive-cultural styles"), Conklin (1964; "ethnomodels" of cultural explanation), and Bright and Bright (1969; resistance to strict taxonomizing).

Belief systems as learned from strictly verbal behavior are dealt with by Werner (1969*a*), Hahn (in press), and Williams (1966). Werner contrasts "whole culture" complexity as described by traditional ethnographers with that described by ethnoscience ethnographers. The macrosystem achievements of the latter "are at present much more pedestrian." Eventually, Werner believes his integrating principles will come from the tested models of universal application, which so far have established only the principles of taxonomic systems, although present work shows "that other general principles of integration of lexical domains are called for." Werner chooses to limit his overview of ethnoscience to "culture through language," although he states it need not be so limited. He is therefore dealing with "linguistic ethnoscience" only: "that part of cultural knowledge which is accessible through the language of informants." This, he thinks, allows him to put aside that oldest and horniest of the issues that have beset us, "the implicit parts of a culture," though he considers these "neither unimportant nor unnecessary; they are simply outside of the self-imposed limitations" (1969a:330).

A very recent theoretical essay by Hahn (in press), entitled "Understanding Beliefs: An Essay on the Methodology of the Statement and Analysis of Belief Systems," also sidesteps this issue by defining beliefs as "general propositions about the world (consciously) held to be true." The concept of unconsciously held beliefs, he says, "has never been adequately explicated." This seems to be the basis of his differentiation between what he calls "beliefs" and a series of other concepts he cites, including "knowledge," "ethnoscience," and "culture." His paper is so hypothetical that having *first* required, "as a vital concomitant of the study of beliefs," that the anthropologist know everything in the alien believers' world (he does not say how, except by doing a "general ethnography"),[20] Hahn then goes on to explain that alien beliefs are unknowable, owing to the metaphysics of translation, so that the best the anthropologist can achieve is an inextricable two-way overlay of natives' and observer's beliefs. (The reader then must know everything in the ethnographer's world, in order to translate

the ethnography . . . and so on.) I see little utility here for the working anthropologist. No new problems or techniques are introduced. As for intracultural synthesizing, Hahn simply names a few alternative ways to display beliefs as a system. One way, called a "net," looks interesting, as it would presumably link some domains through beliefs that reappear in different parts of the system, but no examples of such beliefs are given, nor is the question of subsystem boundaries explored. It is hard to envision this "methodology" being used to obtain or interpret real data, and it is also hard to take this author seriously when he states that he is not being solipsistic.

Williams (1966) also anticipates no total cultural ethnographies, which he labels a "useful fiction." His work underlines the *useful,* however. His effort is spent showing the ways in which careful microsystem descriptions can more closely approximate objectivity and be "indefinitely expandable" within the given cultural grammar. He discusses the rationale and procedures of his work with Metzger (Metzger and Williams 1963a, 1966, 1967). All these studies were carried out as descriptions of different segments of the same culture, but their cultural linkages are not revealed. Rather, the method is shown to lead to potential integration (as also noted by Sturtevant 1964, Colby 1966a, Frake 1964a, Keesing 1971, and others). Williams (1966:18-20) points

---

[20] A number of code levels of cultural knowledge are indicated in Hahn's necessary concomitant for studying beliefs: "In order to understand a people's symbolism, one must understand the environment of acts and artefacts with which the symbolism deals. One must also understand a people's acts and the motivations for them, in order to distinguish sincere from insincere behavior, and to distinguish . . . referential from non-referential use of language." These are to be gained by the adjunct "general ethnography" as well as the "ethnography of sincerity" and the "ethnography of symbol use," none of

which are explicated in the essay. (It might be that the macrosystem synthesis to be found in this scheme lies in the way these three ethnographies mesh with the "ethnography of beliefs"–to the extent that any of them are realizable.) Hahn leans heavily on Quine, whom it might be simpler to read directly. This paper is to be given CA* treatment (*Current Anthropology's* terminology for papers it publishes together with solicited critical comment by specialists in the field who have been provided with preprints, and the author's rebuttal); perhaps others will point out its more useful aspects.

out that "cultural grammars" will be "of an order of complexity far beyond that of the grammars of language." He diagrams a sample "query-response network" for interrelating lexical classes, which, though it goes a certain distance toward "the sort of structured interconnectedness that has generally been attributed to culture by anthropologists," is not adequate for the "quantities of structural information" that a cultural grammar would have to handle. Williams makes it clear that while he is stressing the complexities of cultural knowledge systems, "the developments discussed here are in the process of providing us access to these complexities as well as a perspective which inspires humility." A development that he proposes as possibly better able to handle the job is Lamb's (1964, 1965) stratificational view of linguistic phenomena, especially his *sememic stratum,* which Williams suggests is to be compared profitably with Goodenough's (1964a) *ideational order of culture.* Williams' rejection of the "total culture" ideal, then, provides in fact some concrete steps toward attaining limited valid syntheses.

In another forward-looking programmatic paper, Durbin (1966) outlines the full range of "partial," "entire," and pancultural descriptive goals toward which ethnoscience looks. He places the culture-synthesis step, from partial (microsystem) to entire (total-culture) descriptions, prior to that of finding universals (which does not entirely accord with the work of some ethnoscientists toward deriving universal principles of semantic structuring from examination of microsystem descriptions; see especially Berlin 1969 and 1970, Berlin and Kay 1969, Werner 1969b, and my remarks at the beginning of this section). Durbin also is one of those who invoke Chomsky's (1965) linguistic goals,[21] which he says pro-

vide a means for mapping one structure onto another in a given culture.

SCENE FOCUS: DYNAMICS

Attention has been directed lately toward situations or scenes for a more culturally valid analysis of knowledge systems in action. As far as codes are concerned, scenes are pretty complicated. An infinite regression of contexts and metacontexts is conceivable (Bateson 1960 and the earlier sections of this paper on communications approaches and sociological approaches). More modestly, partial integration of concurrently used knowledge systems is displayed, for example, by any speech usage (sociolinguistic) code, since its rules involve some element(s) of a situation plus some units of a referential, syntactic, morphemic, or phonological code. But this is only the beginning of the many-layered meaning systems controlled by the native actors of an ongoing event. To describe the totality of what is going on in any given scene seems well-nigh impossible. Yet the feeling persists that the "real" culture has not been approached until the interaction of one set of rules with another has been "situated" at some moment of time in which there is ongoing interaction of members. Such integration involves a look at concurrent codes and their dynamic relations. The complexities are immense, but they are being confronted in several ways.

Earlier Goodenough's triple impact

---

[21] Chomsky first presented his "goals of linguistic theory" in 1957, in the publication of work in which he states he had been engaged since 1951 (Chomsky 1962). These dates interestingly coincide with Goodenough's publications of 1951 and 1957 (Goodenough 1951, 1964b), which are frequently cited as introducing the goals of the "new ethnography" or descriptive semantics. The two were independent parallel developments, according to Hymes (1964a).

on the study of macro belief systems was outlined, and the third point, his test of ethnographic adequacy, was cited as indicating a macro or intraculture-synthesizing intent. The ethnographer validates his analysis by applying its rules successfully in further interactions with native knowers—that is, by operating appropriately in the subject culture. This certainly means *in the scenes of the culture,* in the final analysis, and shows Goodenough's ethnography to include the dynamic dimension. However, the learning of alien belief systems—not to mention the rules for their concurrent use—must logically and empirically begin with knowledge of the referential meaning systems they employ, and this is where descriptive semantics concentrated most of its initial attention. Denotative structures have a certain priority in the understanding of propositions or scenes. (This is not to deny that reference meanings are initially learned by encountering them in use in scenes, whether concocted or spontaneous, but neither should the basic nature of denotative knowledge be overlooked, as it sometimes is by proponents of "real situation" analysis, probably because such knowledge is taken for granted, especially when working with one's own language and culture.)

The test of a formal description has been construed less holistically than to demand successful performance in whole scenes; for example, it has been restricted to success in judging the appropriateness or "grammaticality" of a particular household's composition (Burling 1969*b*). Burling's test is simply that the analysis "work." Here he seems to be referring to a scene between the analyst and his data. To counter this it has been argued that the ethnographer is presumably dealing with situations of a real culture in which rules have developed from the

need to make certain useful distinctions. The analysis, to be ethnographically valid, must work in interaction with members of the culture in question. This may turn out to be the only way to succeed in translating what first appears to the ethnographer as chaos into the unambiguous communication it usually is for the natives (Frake 1964*a*, Conklin 1964, Burling 1969*a* with comment by Frake and Hymes). The nonethnographic kind of test that Burling safely invokes may account for some of the shallow views of ethnoscience ethnography (for example, Videbeck and Pia 1966). This is not to say that microanalyses are not valid for certain purposes, but the question arises as to what happens to the results when the cultural context is enlarged. We have seen that enlarging the context horizontally (adding or expanding domains) may affect the results of a microanalysis. If context is enlarged vertically, to include social and other determinants *that operated in the data-collection scene,* the results may again be altered, presumably increasing the overall action validity if not the elegance of the microdescription.

One wonders how often ethnographers, in some controlled way, do make the proposed adequacy test and record their progress toward appropriate participation. Goodenough (1951: 9) describes anecdotally how the ethnographer is constantly testing and correcting by participation and by instructive goofs:

Our attempts at participation also revealed unsuspected aspects of the internal organization of the extended family. Rules of conduct which informants had given frequently turned out to be inaccurate generalizations or approximate rules of thumb when the responses which the writer's behavior evoked proved quite different from those he had been told it would evoke. While in this way the writer unquestionably made a fool of himself in native eyes on more than one occasion, his faux pas provided a basis for straightening out many misconceptions which no amount of straight interviewing would have clarified. They revealed that many of his questions of informants had been beside the point, had failed to allow for necessary distinctions, or had left a confused impression as to what he was driving at.

The validity even of micro belief systems ultimately rests upon the rules' "working" in actual whole cultural context rather than in contexts that have been abstracted out by the analyst. For macrosystems, the "long-run economy" sought by Keesing may reveal itself also through the careful study of the vertical meshing of knowledge systems that takes place in any ongoing cultural scene. The following illustrations start with the most partial of vertical integration models and proceed toward those that attempt a more comprehensive display of the combinatorial rules controlled by native knowers.

To begin with the most obvious and now fairly well-studied type of vertical integration rules, we may examine the contribution of sociolinguistic studies. As we saw at the start of this discussion of the scene focus, speech usage codes link systematically some elements of a social situation with some units of language codes. At this basic level, we include both as "cultural knowledge." Any simultaneous usage of two or more knowledge systems in an interconnected manner is accomplished by a set of rules that comprise yet another knowledge system. Sociolinguistic studies state the rules that link linguistic and referential codes to their cultural situations. They may in one sense be seen as distributional analyses, showing systematic variation by social context of a set of items that have been classed as free variants in the rules of other code levels. An early example by Fischer (1964) shows that in the speech

usage of a sample of English-speaking informants, the occurrence of the "free variant" endings "-in" and "-ing" was governed by factors of sex, social class, personality type, and topic. Thus any two code levels can be interlinked when a class of "free variants" in one code becomes the focus of contrasting distribution in the next.[22] Another example is a group of referential synonyms that are in free variation with regard to their denotata (e.g., father, dad, pop, daddy, papa, pa) but which become coded as contrasting messages with regard to usage contexts. Since nothing occurs (meaningfully) without a specified or implied context, this kind of intercontext linkage probably occurs throughout the culture and could in principle be a macro integration model of wide coverage. (See Geoghegan 1971 for mathematical formulation of this type of linkage.)

Before such intercontext linkage can be seen, different code levels must be analyzed separately. It is therefore not fair—indeed, it is a mixing of levels—to criticize a microanalysis of a referential code for not taking situational conditioning into account. Furthermore, here it can be seen that referential meaning is in some sense prior or prerequisite to situational meaning; it is necessary for participants first to know the semantic reference before usage ploys or settings will carry their mes-

22 It seems not quite correct to call this "complementary distribution by social context" as Keesing has done (1968), for when the focus is on the social context code it becomes contrastive distribution. The problem here seems to lie in the place of "complementary distribution" in phonological analysis, where such a "conditioned variation" is sometimes necessary in order to demonstrate *lack of contrast*. At code levels where lack of contrast can be shown by elements outside of language (e.g., overlap of referents in the world), the complementary distribution analysis is not necessary. Referential synonyms might as well be in "free variation" *for the purposes of the semantic analysis.*

sage. The order of priority applies to analysts' operations as well. D'Andrade (1970:131) has recently covered this point with regard to kinship terms, distinguishing "semantic rules for deciding which things will get which labels" from "usage rules for deciding how one will use such labels in speech. The basic argument . . . appears to be that . . . one must first understand the genealogically based semantic rules for kin term labelling before one can understand the way in which these labels are used in speech." He refers to Hymes's "Ethnography of Speaking" (1962), which together with Gumperz and Hymes's *Ethnography of Communication* (1964) helped to bring the sociolinguistic study of dynamic usage rules into conjunction with formal semantic analysis. This may be considered a major contribution toward approaching the macro dimension of cultural belief and knowledge systems, as defined here.

Moving now toward more total descriptions of real situations, we find problems of process being confronted. (As I previously suggested, some proponents of purely situational analysis appear rather shortsighted with regard to the other codes embedded in their scenes. Their substantive studies reveal, however, that the reference code is used *as a resource* by the actors, along with linguistic codes; this fact is not always mentioned.[23]) These studies

claim to face squarely the dynamic complexities of cultural context. Sarles (1966) and Moerman (1969) have contributed two papers of note and value.

Sarles's "Dynamic Study of Interaction as Ethnoscientific Strategy" (1966:66) takes account of the static belief system codes prerequisite to the interaction, stating, "Not only must each interactant possess knowledge of a large number of domain attributes concerning more stable things, but he must have the ability to implement this in a rapidly moving situational context"; Sarles's proposed "processual model" is designed to introduce "procedural rules . . . which presumably order ongoing behavior." While he concedes that the usual definitions of ethnoscience include process rules, he asserts that present working notions (e.g., substitution frames and informant elicitation)[24] preclude this processual level

---

knowledge that referential codes are necessary and prior, when professing their own interest in usage rules (1966:71): "The question of interest is *how the knowledge is put to use*" (italics mine). Other workers, themselves doing reference-code analysis, have deplored the "serious limitations" of their own studies for not including usage-level codings. I do not think this attitude is warranted. Had they mixed code levels, their work would have been totally useless, which is likely to happen when one tries to do everything at once. Tyler's (1969c) socioanalysis of variability in kin term usage and reference is a nice example of how complex the situation can be, and would have told little if code levels had not been carefully isolated, including an initial analysis of the reference system. Sankoff's recent work (1971, 1972) measuring variability in reference codings among members of a single speech community is another such case, as is Black's (1970a) charting of possible sociodeterminants of certain referential-class alternatives as used by a small Ojibwa population. As for reports of single denotational systems, most have claimed no more than the very first step toward that ultimate goal of an ethnography that provides all the rules for appropriate participation in the (alien) culture's scenes. They should be applauded rather than criticized for patiently doing as respectable a job as possible on that first step—which was, after all, rather exciting in itself.

---

[23] Roy Turner, in a personal communication, has used this phrase to describe an ongoing situational communication setting, and included semantic classes as an integral part of his reported data, yet at the same time he dismissed "taxonomic" studies as static and failing in their goal of describing the communicational properties of speech occasions, ethnoscience having closed the door to the fulfilling of Goodenough's test of adequacy. Also, Videbeck and Pia (1966), after deploring the limitations of ethnoscience (because it analyzes one code level at a time and fails "to take into account the inherent complexity of its subject"), then turn around and ac-

and cannot lead to complex rules regarding "dynamic events." Anthropologists not merely must show classifications of "stable sets of things," but also must connect them in a way that resembles real behavior in everyday life. In dynamic events many things are happening at once and multiple contexts determine meanings and actions. Thus the movement of an actual scene requires of participants a "dynamic cognitive map," and the investigator must expand his model to account for this. Sarles gives a clear programmatic presentation of the combinatorial problem, and it will be interesting to see substantive work based upon his model.

Moerman (1969) documents his sensitive observations about adequate ethnography with a fairly detailed analysis of some levels of cultural knowledge operating in an event that took place in a Thai-Lue village. He requires records of "life *in vivo*" in order to satisfy Goodenough's test of ethnographic adequacy, and seems to consider it desirable to dispense with "fieldnotes which consist of dubiously situated answers to questions which no native ever asks another" (thus dispensing, it would appear, with all the information that members take for granted as part of each other's cultural equipment when they are interacting, but which ethnographers must learn). Moerman nicely notes that "the ethnographer's task is to freeze for analysis the bubble of situated action" which occurs in "motile and ephemeral situations" and from which it derives its native significance. In this scheme, the informants' function is to aid in rendering coherent the ethnographer's observation of "natural social life" by verifying or disqualifying the latter's rules. As a working scheme for field ethnography that focuses on scenes—and particularly with the *Gestalt* view in mind—this contribution presents a notable beginning. Moerman's use of informants resembles some of the field operations that Metzger, Kay, Berlin, Nash, et al. worked out in 1964 during the Chiapas Drinking Project (n.d.) fieldwork for interlocking informant-eliciting with ethnographer-observation techniques (see also Nash 1969).

Basso (n.d.) also presents a study showing the relation of ethnoscientific belief system knowledge to situational factors. He claims to be extending the sociolinguistic type of usage rules to nonlinguistic behavior as he examines Slave Indian decisions about traversing various kinds of ice in their subarctic environment. He says (in a personal communication) that "belief systems must be articulated with situations in order to come up with truly productive rules for action," but his work specifically shows how knowledge of "ice taxonomy" is necessary before the rules that specify the contextual restrictions of settings and timings may be appropriately applied. His study provides, first, the manner in which the Slave classify ice, and then the other decision-making criteria that affect their behavior toward ice, including categories of travel and of conveyance, of seasonal periods and weather conditions, and of degrees of danger. He also goes into the vertical intersections of these categorizations as they occur in ongoing situations. The temporally occurring combinations of several concep-

---

[24] That present eliciting methods block ethnoscience workers from confronting dynamic interlevel codes is questionable, in my view. The methods as I have used them include devices for tapping native knowers' rules about ongoing priorities, when they are aware of them, and for causing the informant to reveal the rules that operate for him at an unaware level. I would never suggest, however, that data sources should exclude the observation of other ongoing scenes than those of the informant-ethnographer interactions.

tual category systems are what Basso refers to as "situations," and it is these that determine behavior choices at a given time.

A development that may represent one kind of approach to the final step of total-scenes analysis is one that has been taking place in a deliberately interdisciplinary framework. This approach takes specific and equal account of several embedded and concurrent microcodes and involves the combined work of such specialists as phoneticians, linguists, paralinguists, nonverbal code specialists, communications scientists, psychologists, psychiatrists, and social anthropologists, each analyzing a separate code level of the same ongoing scene. The interconnections and temporal correlations between code levels constitute the contribution to macrosystem research. As indicated earlier, Bateson had been examining the relations between context levels for some time, and his work was important in laying groundwork for these studies of vertical macro belief systems. He also is a member of one group conducting the type of multilevel analysis of a single scene described above. Others in the group include Birdwhistell (kinesic code), McQuown (phonological), Hockett (linguistic), and Brosin (behavioral). When published, their work will have the title "The Natural History of an Interview" (Bateson et al., n.d.). Pittenger et al. (1960) did somewhat similar multilevel analysis of small segments of scenes in *The First Five Minutes;* and Sarles (1966:70) reports working with a group at the Western Psychiatric Institute and Clinic microanalyzing films of interactional situations. These microanalyses, however, cut their material rather fine to be directly applicable to the systems of propositions we have labeled beliefs. Their results contribute to the *percept* level of largely automatic cultural responses, which, accord-

ing to Goodenough's outline, *underlie* belief systems. They are also aimed chiefly toward psychological research, although the interdisciplinary team as such is notable, as this type of cooperation is taking place increasingly among social scientists today.

INDIVIDUAL FOCUS:
COGNITIVE MAPS AND MAZEWAYS

Another view of multiple subsystems of cultural knowledge as they work together focuses on the cognitive operations of the individual and of the "whole" as he perceives and experiences it. The concepts "cognitive map" (Tolman 1948) and "mazeway" (Wallace 1970) refer to the individual's personal organization of cultural rules. Although the locus of culture is nowhere if not in the heads, the acts, and the productions of individuals, many anthropologists prefer to avoid the claim that their analysis of rules has any necessary correspondence to the actual cognition processes of the people involved. Others have utilized this cognitive approach, in varying ways, as a basis for macro belief system models and hypotheses.

In one such application, controlled tests of cognitive task performance are given to samples of individuals to determine the "psychological reality" of the models resulting from single-domain formal analyses; e.g., kin terms in the work of Romney and D'Andrade (1969), following on Wallace and Atkins' (1969) contribution toward determining ethnographic or contextual fit of formal solutions. (See also Wallace 1965.) D'Andrade later wrote (1970) that the behavioral tests he and Romney had administered to kin term users were not so much psychological as cultural, "tests of the applicability of various content models of kinship across varieties of data." His "broad model" approach to formal kinship analyses takes cultural context into account, and settles on the solution that has proved most satisfactory in treating other data involving kin terms. These investigators are approaching macroculture and overall economy through behavioral reactions of individual culture users rather than through the comparison of results from analyses of several domains of one cultural system.

Geoghegan (1969) explicitly aims at formalizing the individual's use of cultural codes, and has devised a mathematical decision-making model that yields criteria for selection of postmarital residence. The model is expected to generate the structure of residence types through rules governing the processing of information by individuals. It requires semantic distinctions from several subsystems of cultural knowledge (some of which operate "in a large number of other domains throughout a person's life"), and uses flow diagrams expressing the outcomes of rule application. Additionally, the model provides a precise manner of considering social and cultural change quantitatively, specifying when a change has taken place in the ideational order as well as in terms of on-the-ground frequency. All decision models, of course, refer to the individual actors, and Geoghegan's is similar in many respects to those of Keesing and others. The latter, however, put more emphasis on the particular domains of the culture that become linked by their mutual contribution toward a given decision. It is also similar to such "situational" approaches as Basso's, in that both consider the users' knowledge of categories and semantic distinctions underlying their action choices. Basso, however, chooses to emphasize *the integration of systems that pertain to the same domain across different situations,* while Geoghegan emphasizes *the inte-gration of systems through the individual's store of knowledge and his economizing across domains.* These differences reflect the different ways in which anthropologists are thinking about the same problems and the same phenomena of cultural synthesis.

Studies that use the notion of "plans" also locate system meshing in the individual. Werner (1966) calls upon the work of psychologists Barker and Wright (1951) and of Miller et al. (1960) for his treatment of the individual's usage of cultural knowledge. He is here systematically extending "ethnoscience proper" to include what he calls pragmatics (know-how, or the rules for using what one knows). He thus includes among "the competences which underlie human behavior" *both* "knowledge of the universe" *and* pragmatics. The latter involves the concept of *plans* (e.g., recipes or instructions) and their storage and retrieval. Werner's data collection employs a technique whereby individual informants report activities encountered in the course of several days or projected for some hypothetical typical day. Since each individual member of a community possesses a somewhat different set of cultural competences, Werner (1966:64, 1969a:332-33) posits the "ideal native speaker-hearer" (or actor), who would incorporate the total knowledge of the culture, which no actual member has. To Werner (1969a:332) a total-culture ethnography is also an ideal: "Exhaustiveness of description is a principle which, in practice, may be only approximated to some degree." His own descriptive plan is quite comprehensive, however. It shows, among other things, how the pragmatic interpretation or decoding of members' plans includes much information assumed to be mutually known and thus not explicitly encoded; a nice example is given of a narrative in English whose "translation into, say, Bushman would require the filling in of considerable pragmatic detail"—that normally supplied by the cultural knowledge of the reader or hearer (1966:63-64). These filled-in "plans that every reader knows" consist of items of background structure of which the native actor is not consciously aware and of unstated contrasts or inclusions, showing Werner's "ethnographic dictionary" to include, at least ideally, the full range of belief system knowledge as defined here.

Hypotheses regarding the overall economy and coherence of cultural systems often spring from a consideration of the individual culture bearer. For one thing, his cognitive apparatus is generally assumed to require some economizing among the possible rules of the cultural coding systems he uses. A rule that works in many situations is likely to be kept readily accessible, to be chosen often, and to become well worn and familiar. The ethnographer, too, when he has described two or more domains or coding levels of a culture, has gained experience to allow a start at similar economizing, and this would presumably be incorporated into his further learning about the culture if he is working toward Goodenough's test of adequacy. The limitations on the human capacity for processing information have been calculated mathematically by Wallace (1961) and Miller (1956). If the individual needs economy, he also needs coherence. Goodenough's (1963) belief levels—self-evident, specific, and unifying—are presented from the point of view of the individual believers and their need for a "cognitive organization of experience." While these assumptions may be carried too far—and people's "plans" may turn out in actual fact to be less elegant than the blueprints anthropologists have drawn for them—it could perhaps safely be proposed that the dynamic source of

belief system is in the individual's need for coherence and that the *macrosystem* stems from the individual's articulation of microsystems. Nevertheless, the individual is always acting in a cultural and social situation, so that locating economy and coherence in the social situation or in the culture whole may merely represent a shift of focus.

CONTINUING PROBLEMS AND FUTURE PROSPECTS

The promise of formalized semantic ethnography, which treats culture as knowledge of code rules for human interaction, has been steadily growing and already affords a certain degree of access to the organization of the exotic worlds of others which constitute the "variable belief systems of mankind" (Hallowell 1942). Malinowski's "context of situation" must be included in any attempt to grasp the *in situ* dynamic meaning of given acts or words or combinations, and to understand the message conveyed by intracultural variability in usage. The distribution of situations within the larger context cannot then remain unattended. However, inasmuch as description of any one microsystem is immensely complex, steps toward the ethnography of total-culture belief systems have been understandably tentative. Partial macro segments or cross-sections have been examined as units and their internal ordering displayed, and an overall economy from the point of view of the individual, the interaction scene, or the culture as a whole has been deduced, but major barriers to the empirical construction of larger scale ethnographies of cultural knowledge systems remain.

A primary obstacle is the complexity of culture itself. Another is that as observers we cannot avoid using our own culture toward the understanding of another—or conversely, that our subjects are themselves observers. Yet another is that some part of everyone's observations are below the level of awareness, yet clearly direct behavior in systematic ways. There is also the matter of isolating the sets of items of a culture which cluster systematically. Then there is the matter of culture sharing: To what degree do members operate with the "same" set of rules? How safely can one generalize from the performances of the informants or subjects observed? Measures and controls of various kinds have been applied to these problems (including the decision to ignore them for the time being), but they continue to be posed. A final problem is the question of whether the analysis of segments (microsystems) hastens or blocks progress toward an eventual analysis of the whole. Support has arisen for both sides of this issue, but the question remains open and largely unexamined. Since it is an issue that determines major logistic decision with regard to future work, it might be worthwhile to try to state it more precisely, while examining current models and tools and the possibilities emerging from the intercourse of anthropology with related disciplines.

Analysis of segments has led to some elegant models that are apparently applicable to any culture and productive of the discovery of universals (e.g., taxonomic relations, kinship paradigms). If we are thus led to the nature of culture in general, do we also arrive at a general formula for fitting together the segments of particular cultures? This may be so, to the extent that macro segments have the same structural and dynamic properties as micro segments. Both linguistic and mathematical tools have shown that domains can be linked by the same type of relations as hold within a domain (e.g., Williams 1966, Geoghegan 1971). On the other hand, enlarging the particular culture context can change the results of analysis, just as the native actor's cognitive map is constantly revised as he experiences more contexts, probably in the direction of economizing his rules across the board. As the ethnographer, too, knows more of a particular culture, he can reject descriptive solutions that "work" but do not fit. It might be argued that the analysis of segments can be productive of an integrated belief system description if results are in fact kept open to revision as the new elements of cultural context are added. Few published works have been thus revised, however. I have personally had the experience (no doubt not unique) of revising previously "finished" analyses as added concepts and domains come under scrutiny. A report now in preparation will attempt to trace exactly the alterations that were necessary in the analysis of a macrodomain (Black 1967) when further formal investigation of related concepts had been carried out.[25] Of-

---

[25] I experimented in eliciting a macro-size taxonomic domain as a unit (Ojibwa *bema.diziwa.d,* "living things"), and I hope this work may provide some empirical evidence toward the question of *Gestalt* versus separate analysis of parts—that is, whether the linking of separate microsystems within this domain would have produced the same results (Black 1967: 208). These results were then considered together with a later study conducted with the same informants on a related and partially embedded domain (*maškiki,* generally glossed as "medicine"). Preliminary analysis demonstrates an alteration of results, with each study throwing new light upon the other. Other evidence will be sought to learn what happens as the context is enlarged or altered, including expansion to other code levels (e.g., situational). Additionally, the two studies encompass a content area of Ojibwa culture which includes everything that has to do with "illness" but is not confined to it; the results appear to throw doubt on the utility and universality of "medicine as an ethnographic category," as proposed and defined by Glick (1967), for from the Ojibwa results one cannot abstract "a subsystem of ideas and practices having to do with illness and with nothing else." (The argument is *not* based upon the English gloss for the *maškiki* domain). There may be relevance here for ethnoscientific and comparative studies of "disease beliefs"

ten, however, freezing of results of single-domain analyses takes place (except when other investigators present competing and differing results, notably in kinship studies). Especially when single-domain data are treated with sophisticated analytic tools, and/or compared across cultures, their original ethnographic validity (or stage of tentativeness) may not come into question. The question of the ethnographic validity of cross-cultural data will not be discussed here, but a look at some current application of mathematical tools to belief system data and to the continuing problems of macro belief system analysis seems in order.

Application of mathematics to anthropological problems connected with the study of belief systems is accelerating. Componential analysis has for some time applied an algebraic method; now so do Geoghegan's and Keesing's models for relating cultural domains and levels, which appear in the collection of studies edited by Kay (1971) entitled *Explorations in Mathematical Anthropology*. This book includes also computer methods, classical methods, and probabilistic methods, and Kay's introduction predicts that the areas of mathematics that are most likely to interest anthropologists will be abstract algebra, computer technology, probability theory, and statistics, in that order—a change in emphasis from the day when statistical tests of significance constituted the anthropologist's formal training in this field. He claims that a school of mathematical anthropology is *not* developing, but rather that a wider variety of mathematical techniques is being applied to a diversity of anthropological problems, in line with a "nascent trend to introduce greater

precision into all anthropological discourse."

The Kay volume contains several studies addressed to problems mentioned above. With regard to programs for discovering internal ordering or clustering, Stefflre et al. (1971) give a type of clumping analysis by computer for matrices of lexemes and frame contexts, one of which is termed a "belief matrix." With this computational procedure it is possible to get sets of grammatical, semantic, and "truth" word classes that show similar distributional properties according to the frames used. Roberts et al. (1971) employ quantitative measures for examining empirically the old concept of "systemic culture pattern" (a complex of culture items that persists as a system), applying it to ideological material. Their measurement of the contrastive patterning of preferences has been successfully applied to preferential family size and composition and to patterns of clothing preferences. (It is not stated whether the authors believe that macro patterning could be similarly treated; e.g., combinations of domains). Preferential pattern analysis is seen as potentially applicable to culture change, especially in the determination of high and low contrast values for particular combinations. Change would occur in low contrast areas—i.e., where there is more overlap of choices between the items of two sets and selection by association does not appear firmly fixed. (Could one not also speak, though, of revolutionary change in previously highly contrastive sets—for example, the virtual elimination today of sex contrast in style of dress and appearance by an influential segment of the younger members of our society? Contrast has changed rapidly from distinctions between the sexes to distinctions between the hip and the square, or whatever the rapidly changing termi-

---

or of "ethnomedical domains," of which there have been quite a few (Rubel 1960; Frake 1964a; Metzger and Williams 1963b; Werner 1965; Epling and Whitley 1970; D'Andrade et al., n.d.).

nology now endorses.) The dynamics of changing belief systems presently is receiving the attention of a number of workers whose future findings may be expected to enlarge our understanding in this area (Basso, n.d.; Black 1970*a*; Geoghegan 1969: Roberts et al. 1971).

Kozelka and Roberts (1971) present a mathematical measure of culture sharing. The tendency of subjects from one culture to agree among themselves on certain tasks is measured and compared across cultures, and essentially the relative degree of integration is derived. Roberts has done work on culture sharing (see Roberts et al. 1971: 223) and suggests lines of inquiry yet to be undertaken. D'Andrade also, in an unpublished report, measured intracultural agreement and disagreement regarding ideological material. One wonders if sharing at higher (more general) levels of cultural systems could be ascertained as opposed to more specific (micro) levels of the same culture—in other words, would macrosystems or microsystems tend to be more shared? Nida (1964) has reported that taxonomic organization of concepts differs more between cultures at the more general level.

Geoghegan's work has contributed mathematical formulations relevant to each of the integrative foci discussed in the section on macrosystems. His individual decision-making model has already been discussed. A second model (1970), for mapping the precise nature of relations between simultaneously used code levels, considers both referential (denotative) and usage levels, as with sociolinguistic studies. (It is discussed in detail in Chapter 9 of this volume.) The "marking rules" employed by the model contrast message forms that convey supplementary attitudinal information (such as nicknames) with those that convey no such additional information (such as the name by which an individual is generally known). This contrast is treated as a particular type of "natural information processing routine" that lends itself to mathematical formulation and allows some preliminary suggestions concerning the formal properties of marking rules in general (and thus the nature of belief system rules in general). If a formulation of this type can be developed to handle the more complex regression of contexts that is present in any ongoing scene, it could represent an extremely valuable contribution to macrosystem analysis.

Geoghegan's interest in "information processing systems in culture" is further exemplified by his paper of that title (1971), which deals with domain linkage. Kay (1971:3) describes it as an "original synthesis of the most recent results in ethnography and cognitive psychology" regarding theory of coding behavior. Using a formal device from the latter discipline (Miller 1956, Miller et al. 1960) and flow diagrams, as well as algebraic methods, Geoghegan's work is "an advance over existing methods for representing cognitive/semantic domains . . . in that it presents a natural and explicit mechanism for expressing the relations among different domains." It allows the "total formal structure of one domain to serve as an item in the structure of another domain . . . and goes a long way toward solving the ethnographic problem of interrelation of semantic domains." This application of mathematical models to cognitive as well as cultural phenomena (cognitive in the sense of information the actor is actually processing) does not sidestep the psychological reality issue and combines our domain-linkage focus with that of the individual's experience in meshing cultural knowledge systems.

Further mathematical applications are found in a current use of scaling techniques for analyzing belief systems by D'Andrade et al. (1972). The belief system material used encompasses a single domain—illness—and the several mathematical analyses are applied for the purpose of relating individual cognitive' processes to the results of a formal analysis of the rules of knowledge systems. The investigators construct a model of the cognitive and semantic structure of an illness belief system in terms of the *salient features* of a set of illness terms as reacted to by a sample of users, rather than in terms of the *defining properties* of the named types of disease. Defining properties lacked salience in this particular domain for these subjects, according to the findings of D'Andrade and his colleagues. The authors do not generalize to other domains, but state, on the basis of results obtained from studies in two cultures (and two languages), that "the defining properties of a set of terms are not always the properties which determine how people categorize or react to those terms. Thus, the categories discovered by the analysis of how disease terms distribute across beliefs do not seem to be related to the features which define those disease terms. . . ."

This study by D'Andrade et al. is of interest here for several reasons. *First,* it makes use of modern analytic tools of a kind on the ascendance in anthropological work. *Second,* it treats a single belief domain whose boundary is apparently assumed to be universal (see note 25); it does not claim ethnographic coverage even of this domain, but derives some principles of potential applicability to the study of cultural belief systems in general. *Third,* some of the principles have to do with processes of human cognition, traditionally of interest to psychologists, and thus the study represents a synthesis of some of the disciplines that have examined various aspects of the patterning

displayed by human life—a definite earmark of current and future work in the social-behavioral-biological sciences. With regard to the tools, they seem potentially powerful; yet the possibility that they might result in the freezing of ethnographic results at stages as yet unvalidated by culture context is somewhat alarming. With regard to general principles derived from subjects' reactions to a symbolic domain of disease terms, the findings regarding salient versus defining features as they relate to beliefs about disease is of interest and could be further tested. (My findings in a study of native classification by salient features of a set of Ojibwa terms for "living things" [Black 1967] were similar; however, the domain was of macro dimension and the features were seen as productive in a large-scale belief system integrating a number of microsystems, including illness. Taxonomic generic reactions were also elicitable, of course, and these were considered "beliefs" as well. There was thus a *defining properties belief system* and a salient features belief system, and their relations were explored.) Further general implications by D'Andrade et al. concern "the relationship between cognitive operations and belief systems," which presents a modern form of a continuing problem that has long troubled anthropologists. This study is an example of the kinds of analysis that can be brought to bear on quantities of systematic belief system data by a combined interest in cognitive psychology, mathematical techniques, and cultural systems of belief and knowledge. It also indicates the still tentative and preliminary stage of the scientific study of beliefs. The authors state:

It seems unlikely that people have stored in their memories huge matrices of the sort presented in miniature in this paper. . . . Nor is it apparent that people have an internal representation like the spatial plot produced by multidimensional scaling procedures. . . . Perhaps a belief system may be represented as a set of propositions, capable of generating such data matrices. At present we have little empirical evidence about the form of such propositions; our initial inclination is to use the symbolic apparatus of logic, especially first-order predicate logic, which remains relatively close to a natural language format. In any case, whatever form these propositions eventually take, the problem will be to develop decision procedures which can economically generate assessments of "truth" and "likelihood" which are the same as those made by informants.

Finally, with regard to the third point, it seems clear from many of the foregoing endeavors that increased intercourse between anthropology and other disciplines is bearing fruit for students of belief systems. In the interest of macro belief systems, a researcher seeking synthesis of a culture through individuals finds impetus, for example, from cognitive psychology and communications science; seeking synthesis through domain linkage, he may find partners in the fields of mathematics, linguistics. and philosophy; and when seeking synthesis through ongoing scenes and situations, he may team with sociologists and social psychologists. It appears likely, however, that for all time to come we alone shall have to reckon with the monster that we spawned while the bundling board still separated the sciences: that intuitively real, elusively abstract, and distressingly complex "culture whole."

REFERENCES

Albert, Ethel
1956 The Classification of Values: A Method and Illustration. *American Anthropologist* 58:221-48.
Barker, Roger G., and H. F. Wright
1951 The Psychological Habitat of Raymond Birch. In *Social Psychology at the Crossroads,* ed. J. H. Rohrer and M. Sherif. New York: Harper.
Basso, Keith H.
n.d. Ice and Travel Among the Fort Norman Slave. Scheduled for inclusion in first issue of *Language in Society.*
Bateson, Gregory
1936 *Naven.* Cambridge: Harvard University Press.
1958 Epilogue. In *Naven,* 2nd ed. Stanford: Stanford University Press.
1960 Minimal Requirements for a Theory of Schizophrenia. *AMA Archives of General Psychiatry* 2:477-91.
1966 Information, Codification, and Communication. In *Communication and Culture,* ed. A. G. Smith. New York: Holt, Rinehart & Winston. Originally published 1951.
Bateson, G., et al.
n.d. The Natural History of an Interview. Unpublished MS.
Bellman, Beryl L.
1971 Village of Curers and Assassins: On the Production of Fala Kpelle Cosmological Categories. Ph. D. dissertation, University of California, Irvine.
Belnap, Nuel D., Jr.
1963 An Analysis of Questions: Preliminary Report. Santa Monica: System Development Corporation.
Benedict, Ruth
1928 Psychological Types in the Cultures of the South-west. *Proceedings of the 23rd International Congress of Americanists,* pp. 572-81.
1960 *Patterns of Culture.* New York: Mentor Books. Originally published 1934.
Berlin, Brent
1967 Categories of Eating in Tzeltal and Navaho. *International Journal of American Linguistics* 33:1.
1969 Universal Nomenclature Principles in Folk Science. Paper presented at 67th annual meeting, American Anthropological Association, New Orleans.
1970 A Universalist-Evolutionary Approach to Ethnographic Semantics. In *Current Directions in Anthropology,* ed. Ann Fischer, pp.

3-18. *Bulletin of American Anthropological Association* 3, no. 3, pt. 2 (special issue).

1971   Speculations on the Growth of Ethnobotanical Nomenclature. Working paper no. 39. Berkeley: Language-Behavior Research Laboratory.

Berlin, Brent, Dennis E. Breedlove, and Peter H. Raven

1968   Covert Categories and Folk Taxonomies. *American Anthropologist* 70: 290-99.

Berlin, Brent, and Paul Kay

1969   *Basic Color Terms: Their Universality and Evolution.* Berkeley: University of California Press.

Bidney, David

1953   *Theoretical Anthropology.* New York: Columbia University Press.

Birdwhistell, R. L.

1952   *Introduction to Kinesics: An Annotation System for Analysis of Body Motion and Gesture.* Washington, D.C.: U.S. State Department Foreign Service Institute.

1970   *Kinesics and Context.* Philadelphia: University of Pennsylvania Press.

Black, Mary B.

1960   An Application of Albert's Scheme for Classifying Values. Paper presented at 58th annual meeting, American Anthropological Association, Minneapolis.

1963   On Formal Ethnographic Procedures. *American Anthropologist* 65:1347-51.

1967   An Ethnoscience Investigation of Ojibwa Ontology and World View. Ph. D. dissertation, Stanford University.

1969a   Eliciting Folk Taxonomy in Ojibwa. In *Cognitive Anthropology,* ed. Stephen A. Tyler. New York: Holt, Rinehart & Winston.

1969b   A Note on Gender in Eliciting Ojibwa Semantic Structures. *Anthropological Linguistics* 11:177-86.

1970a   An Ethnoscience Report on a Multicode Community. Paper presented at annual meeting of Canadian Sociological and Anthropological Association, Winnipeg.

1970b   Legends and Accounts of Weagamow Lake. *Rotunda* 3, no. 3:4-13. Toronto: Royal Ontario Museum.

1971   On Ojibwa Question Constructions. *International Journal of American Linguistics* 37:146-51.

1972   Mythes et structures sémantiques: Ambiguités referentielles au Lac Weagamow, Ontario. *Recherches Amérindiennes au Québec* 2:20-28.

Black, Mary B., and Duane Metzger

1969   Ethnographic Description and the Study of Law. In *Cognitive Anthropology,* ed. S. Tyler. New York: Holt, Rinehart & Winston. Originally published 1965.

Boas, Franz

1966   Introduction. *Handbook of American Indian Languages.* Lincoln: University of Nebraska Press. Originally published 1911.

Bohannan, Paul

1956   On the Use of Native Language Categories in Ethnology. *American Anthropologist* 58:557.

Bright, Jane O., and William Bright

1969   Semantic Structures in Northwestern California and the Sapir-Whorf Hypothesis. In *Cognitive Anthropology,* ed. S. Tyler. New York: Holt, Rinehart & Winston. Originally published 1965.

Brown, Roger, and E. Lenneberg

1961   A Study in Language and Cognition. In *Psycholinguistics,* ed. S. Saporta. New York: Holt, Rinehart & Winston. Originally published 1954.

Burling, Robbins

1969a   Cognition and Componential Analysis: God's Truth or Hocus-Pocus? In *Cognitive Anthropology,* ed. S. Tyler. New York: Holt, Rinehart & Winston. Originally published 1964.

1969b   Linguistics and Ethnographic Description. *American Anthropologist* 71:817-27.

Campbell, Donald

1964   Differences in Perception as Distinguished from Failures of Communication. In *Cross-Cultural Understanding,* ed. F. S. C. Northrop and H. H. Livingston. New York: Harper & Row.

Casagrande, Joseph, and Kenneth Hale

1967   Semantic Relationships in Papago

Folk-Definitions. In *Studies in Southwestern Ethnolinguistics,* ed. Dell Hymes and W. Bittle. The Hague: Mouton.

Cherry, Colin
1960 The Informational Analysis of Questions and Commands. In *Fourth London Symposium on Information Theory,* ed. C. Cherry. London: Butterworth.

Chiapas Drinking Project
n.d. P. Kay, D. Metzger, B. Berlin, G. E. Williams, J. Nash, C. Wilson. Unpublished report.

Chomsky, Noam
1962 *Syntactic Structures.* The Hague: Mouton. Originally published 1957.
1965 *Aspects of the Theory of Syntax.* Cambridge: M.I.T. Press.

Cohen, Rosalie A.
1969 Conceptual Styles, Culture Conflict, and Nonverbal Tests of Intelligence. *American Anthropologist* 71:828-56.

Colby, B. N.
1966a Ethnographic Semantics: A Preliminary Survey. *Current Anthropology* 7:3-32.
1966b Behavioral Redundancy. In *Communication and Culture,* ed. A. G. Smith. New York: Holt, Rinehart & Winston.
1966c Cultural Patterns in Narrative. *Science* 151:793-98.
1966d The Analysis of Culture Content and the Patterning of Narrative Concern in Texts. *American Anthropologist* 68:374-88.
1970 The Description of Narrative Structures. In *Cognition: A Multiple View,* ed. P. Garvin. New York: Spartan Books.
1971 The Shape of Narrative Concern in Japanese Folktales. In *Explorations in Mathematical Anthropology,* ed. P. Kay. Cambridge: M.I.T. Press.
n.d. A Partial Grammar of Eskimo Folktales. Unpublished MS.

Collingwood, R. G.
1939 *An Autobiography.* London: Oxford University Press.

Conklin, Harold
1964 Hananóo Color Categories. In *Language in Culture and Society,* ed. Dell Hymes. New York: Harper & Row. Originally published 1955.
1969a Lexicographical Treatment of Folk Taxonomies. In *Cognitive Anthropology,* ed. S. Tyler. New York: Holt, Rinehart & Winston. Originally published 1962.
1969b Ethnogenealogical Method. In *Cognitive Anthropology,* ed. S. Tyler. New York: Holt, Rinehart & Winston. Originally published 1964.

D'Andrade, R. G.
1970 Structure and Syntax in the Semantic Analysis of Kinship Terminologies. In *Cognition: A Multiple View,* ed. P. Garvin, pp. 87-143. New York: Spartan Books.

D'Andrade, R. G., N. R. Quinn, S. B. Nerlove, and A. K. Romney
1972 Categories of Disease in American-English and Mexican-Spanish. *Multidimensional Scaling,* vol. 2: *Applications,* ed. A. K. Romney and S. B. Nerlove. New York: Seminar Press.

Davis, F.
1961 Deviance Disavowal: The Management of Strained Interaction by the Visibly Handicapped. *Social Problems* 9:120-32.

Du Bois, Cora
1955 The Dominant Value Profile of American Culture. *American Anthropologist* 57:1232-39.

Dundes, Alan
1962 From Etic to Emic Units in the Structural Study of Folktales. *Journal of American Folklore* 75:95-105.
1964 *Morphology of North American Indian Folktales.* Helsinki: Helsinglin/ Lubekirjapainooy.
1968 Introduction to V. Propp, *Morphology of the Folktale,* 2nd ed. Austin: University of Texas Press.

Dundes, Alan, ed.
1965 *The Study of Folklore.* Englewood Cliffs, N.J.: Prentice-Hall.

Durbin, Marshall
1966 The Goals of Ethnoscience. In *Ethnoscience,* ed. O. Werner, pp. 22-41. *Anthropological Linguistics* 8 (special issue).

Edmonson, Munro
1971 *Lore: An Introduction to the Science of Folklore and Literature.* New York: Holt, Rinehart & Winston.

Epling, P. J., and Virginia Whitley
1970 Cognitive and Semantic Models of Samoan Disease Beliefs. Research fellowship grant, National Institute of Mental Health.

Evans-Pritchard, E. E.
1956 *Nuer Religion.* London: Oxford University Press.

Firth, Raymond, ed.
1961 *Man and Culture: An Evaluation of the Work of Bronislaw Malinowski.* London: Routledge & Kegan Paul. Originally published 1957.

Fischer, John
1964 Social Influence in the Choice of a Linguistic Variant. In *Language in Culture and Society,* ed. D. Hymes. New York: Harper & Row. Originally published 1958.

Fowler, C. S., and J. Leland
1967 Some Northern Paiute Native Categories. *Ethnology* 6:381-404.

Frake, Charles O.
1962 Cultural Ecology and Ethnography. *American Anthropologist* 64:53-59.
1964a The Diagnosis of Disease Among the Subanun of Mindanao. In *Language in Culture and Society,* ed. D. Hymes. New York: Harper & Row. Originally published 1961. (Also Bobbs-Merrill Reprint A-72.)
1964b How to Ask for a Drink in Subanun. In *The Ethnography of Communication,* ed. J. Gumperz and D. Hymes, pp. 127-32. *American Anthropologist* 66, no. 6, pt. 2 (special issue).
1969a The Ethnographic Study of Cognitive Systems. In *Cognitive Anthropology,* ed. S. Tyler. New York: Holt, Rinehart & Winston. Originally published 1962.
1969b A Structural Description of Subanun "Religious Behavior." In *Cognitive Anthropology,* ed. S. Tyler. New York: Holt, Rinehart & Winston. Originally published 1964.
1969c Notes on Queries in Ethnography. In *Cognitive Anthropology,* ed. S. Tyler. New York: Holt, Rinehart & Winston. Originally published 1964.
1969d Further Discussion of Burling. In *Cognitive Anthropology,* ed. S. Tyler. New York: Holt, Rinehart & Winston. Originally published 1964.

Gardin, J.-C.
1965 On a Possible Interpretation of Componential Analysis in Archeology. In *Formal Semantic Analysis,* ed. E. Hammel, pp. 9-22. *American Anthropologist* 67, no. 5, pt. 2 (special issue).

Garfinkel, H.
1967 *Studies in Ethnomethodology.* Englewood Cliffs, N.J.: Prentice-Hall.

Garfinkel, H., and H. Sacks
1967 On "Setting" in Conversation. Paper presented to American Sociological Association.

Geoghegan, William
1969 Decision-Making and Residence on Tagtabon Island. Working paper no. 17. Berkeley: Language-Behavior Research Laboratory.
1970 A Theory of Marking Rules. Working paper no. 37. Berkeley: Language-Behavior Research Laboratory.
1971 Information Processing Systems in Culture. In *Explorations in Mathematical Anthropology,* ed. P. Kay. Cambridge: M.I.T. Press.

Glenn, E. S.
1970 Cohen's "Conceptual Styles": A Comment. *American Anthropologist* 72:1448-50.

Glick, L. B.
1967 Medicine as an Ethnographic Category: The Gimi of the New Guinea Highlands. *Ethnology* 6:31-56.

Goffman, Erving
1961 *Asylums: Essays on the Social Situation of Mental Patients and Other Inmates.* New York: Doubleday Anchor Books.
1963 *Stigma: Notes on the Management of Spoiled Identity.* Englewood Cliffs, N.J.: Prentice-Hall.

Goodenough, Ward
1951 *Property, Kin, and Community on Truk.* Yale University Publications in Anthropology no. 46.
1956 Componential Analysis and the Study of Meaning. *Language* 32:195-216. (Also Bobbs-Merrill Reprint A-91.)
1963 *Cooperation in Change.* New York: Russell Sage Foundation.
1964a Introduction. In *Explorations in Cultural Anthropology,* ed. W. Good-

enough. New York: McGraw-Hill Book Company.

1964*b* Cultural Anthropology and Linguistics. In *Language in Culture and Society*, ed. D. Hymes. New York: Harper & Row. (Also Bobbs-Merrill Reprint L-29.) Originally published 1957.

1967 Componential Analysis. *Science* 156: 1203-1209.

1969 Rethinking "Status" and "Role": Toward a general Model of the Cultural Organization of Social Relationships. In *Cognitive Anthropology*, ed. S. Tyler. New York: Holt, Rinehart & Winston. Originally published 1965.

1970 *Description and Comparison in Cultural Anthropology*. Chicago: Aldine.

Gowman, A. G.
1957 *The War Blind in American Social Structure*. New York: American Foundation for the Blind.

Greimas, A. J.
1966 *Sémantique structurale*. Paris: Larousse.

Gumperz, J., and D. Hymes, eds.
1964 *The Ethnography of Communication. American Anthropologist* 66, no. 6, pt. 2 (special issue).

Hahn, Robert A.
in press   Understanding Beliefs: An Essay on the Methodology of the Statement and Analysis of Belief Systems. *Current Anthropology.*

Hall, Edward T.
1959 *The Silent Language*. Garden City, N.Y.: Doubleday.

1963 A System for the Notation of Proxemic Behavior. *American Anthropologist* 65:1003-1026.

1966 *The Hidden Dimension*. Garden City, N.Y.: Doubleday.

1968 Proxemics. *Current Anthropology* 9:83-95, 105-108.

Hallowell, A. I.
1942 *The Role of Conjuring in Saulteaux, Society*. Philadelphia: University of Pennsylvania Press.

1955 *Culture and Experience*. Philadelphia: University of Pennsylvania Press.

1958 Ojibwa Metaphysics of Being and the Perception of Persons. In *Person Perception and Interpersonal Be-*

havior, ed. R. Taguiri and L. Petrullo. Stanford: Stanford University Press.

1963 Ojibwa World View and Disease. In *Man's Image in Medicine and Anthropology*, ed. I. Galdston. New York: International Universities Press.

1964 Ojibwa Ontology, Behavior, and World View. In *Primitive Views of the World*, ed. S. Diamond. New York: Columbia University Press. (Also Bobbs-Merrill Reprint A-101.) Originally published 1960.

Harrah, David H.
1960 The Adequacy of Language. *Inquiry* 3:73-88.

1961 A Logic of Questions and Answers. *Philosophy of Science* 28:40-46.

Harris, M.
1968 *The Rise of Anthropological Theory*. New York: Crowell.

Haugen, Einar
1969 The Semantics of Icelandic Orientation. In *Cognitive Anthropology*, ed. S. Tyler. New York: Holt, Rinehart & Winston. Originally published 1957.

Hewes, Gordon W.
1966 The Domain Posture. In *Ethnoscience*, ed. O. Werner, pp. 106-12. *Anthropological Linguistics* 8 (special issue).

Hockett, Charles
1948 A Note on Structure. *International Journal of American Linguistics* 14: 269-71.

1954 Discussion. In *Language in Culture*, ed. H. Hoijer. Chicago: University of Chicago Press.

1964 Scheduling. In *Cross-Cultural Understanding*, ed. F. S. C. Northrop and H. H. Livingston. New York: Harper & Row.

Hoebel, E. A.
1964 Status and Contract in Primitive Law. In *Cross-Cultural Understanding*, ed. F. S. C. Northrop and H. H. Livingston. New York: Harper & Row.

Hoijer, H., ed.
1954 *Language in Culture: Conference on the Interrelations of Language and the Other Aspects of Culture*. Chicago: University of Chicago Press.

Honigmann, J.
1961 North America. In *Psychological An-thropology*, ed. F. Hsu. Homewood, Ill.: Dorsey Press.
Howard, Alan
1963 Land, Activity Systems, and Deci-sion-Making Models in Rotuma. *Eth-nology* 2:407-40.
1964 On the Structural Analysis of Inter-personal Relations. *Southwestern Journal of Anthropology* 20:261-77.
Hymes, Dell
1961 On Typology of Cognitive Styles in Language. *Anthropological Linguis-tics* 3:22-54.
1962 The Ethnography of Speaking. In *Anthropology and Human Behavior*, ed. T. Gladwin and W. C. Sturtevant. Washington, D.C.: Anthropological Society of Washington.
1964a Directions in Ethno-Linguistic The-ory. In *Transcultural Studies of Cog-nition*, ed. A. K. Romney and R. G. D'Andrade. *American Anthropol-ogist* 66, no. 3, pt. 2:6-56 (special issue).
1964b A Perspective for Linguistic Anthro-pology. In *Horizons of Anthropol-ogy*, ed. Sol Tax. Chicago: Aldine.
1970 Linguistic Method in Ethnography: Its Development in the United States. In *Method and Theory in Lin-guistics*, ed. P. Garvin. The Hague: Mouton.
Jung, C. G.
1956 Commentary. In P. Radin, *The Trick-ster: A Study in American Indian Mythology*. New York: Philosophical Library.
1959 Archetypes of the Collective Uncon-scious. In *Basic Writings of C. G. Jung*, ed. V. S. de Laszlo. New York: Random House.
Kay, Paul
1966 Ethnography and Theory of Culture. *Bucknell Review*, May, pp. 106-13.
1970 Some Theoretical Implications of Ethnographic Semantics. In *Current Directions in Anthropology*, ed. Ann Fischer, pp. 19-31. *Bulletin of Amer-ican Anthropological Association* 3, pt. 2 (special issue).
1971 Introduction. In *Explorations in Mathematical Anthropology*, ed. P. Kay. Cambridge: M.I.T. Press.

Keesing, Roger M.
1967 Statistical Models and Decision Mod-els of Social Structure: A Kwaio Case. *Ethnology* 6:1-16.
1968 Step-kin, In-laws, and Ethnoscience. *Ethnology* 7:59-70.
1969 On Quibblings over Squabblings of Siblings: New Perspectives on Kin Terms and Role Behavior. *South-western Journal of Anthropology* 25: 207-27.
1970a Kwaio Fosterage. *American Anthro-pologist* 72:991-1019.
1970b Toward a Model of Role Analysis. In *A Handbook of Method in Cultural Anthropology*, ed. R. Naroll and R. Cohen. Garden City, N.Y.: Natural History Press.
1971 Formalization and the Construction of Ethnographies. In *Explorations in Mathematical Anthropology*, ed. P. Kay. Cambridge: M.I.T. Press.
n.d. Descent, Residence, and Cultural Codes. In *Collected Essays in Oce-anic Anthropology*, ed. L. Hiatt and C. Jayarwardena. In preparation.
Kelly, G.
1955 *The Psychology of Personal Con-structs*. New York: Norton.
King, Arden
1960 Myth, Basic Values, Ethos, and Style in Culture. Paper presented at 59th annual meeting, American Anthro-pological Association, Minneapolis.
Kluckhohn, Clyde
1952 Values and Value-Orientations in the Theory of Action. In *Toward a Gen-eral Theory of Action*, ed. T. Parsons and E. A. Shils. Cambridge: Harvard University Press.
1956a Toward a Comparison of Value-Emphases in Different Cultures. In *The State of the Social Sciences*, ed. L. D. White. Chicago: University of Chicago Press.
1956b Review of *Language in Culture*, ed. H. Hoijer. *American Anthropologist* 58:569-74.
1960 Patterning as Exemplified in Navaho Culture. In *Language, Culture, and Personality*, ed. L. Spier, A. I. Hallo-well, and S. Newman. Salt Lake City: University of Utah Press. Originally published 1941.
1964 Navaho Categories. In *Primitive*

Views of the World, ed. S. Diamond. New York: Columbia University Press. Originally published 1960.

1968 The Philosophy of the Navaho Indians. In *Readings in Anthropology,* ed. Morton Fried, 2nd ed. New York: Crowell. Originally published 1949.

Kluckhohn, Clyde, and W. H. Kelly
1945 The Concept of Culture. In *The Science of Man in the World Crisis,* ed. R. Linton. New York: Columbia University Press.

Kluckhohn, F.
1958 Variations in the Basic Values of Family Systems. *Social Case Work* 39:63-72.

Kluckhohn, F., and Fred Strodtbeck, eds.
1961 *Variations in Value Orientations.* Evanston, Ill.: Row, Peterson.

Köngäs, Elli-Kaija, and Pierre Maranda
1962 Structural Models in Folklore. *Midwest Folklore* 12:133-92.

Kozelka, Robert M., and John Roberts
1971 A New Approach to Nonzero Concordance. In *Explorations in Mathematical Anthropology,* ed. P. Kay. Cambridge: M.I.T. Press.

Kroeber, A., and C. Kluckhohn
1952 Culture: A Critical Review of Concepts and Definitions. *Papers of the Peabody Museum of Archeology and Ethnology* 47, no. 1.

Lamb, Sydney M.
1964 Sememic Approach to Structural Semantics. In *Transcultural Studies in Cognition,* ed. A. K. Romney and R. G. D'Andrade, pp. 57-78. *American Anthropologist* 66, no. 3, pt. 2 (special issue).

1965 Kinship Terminology and Linguistic Structure. In *Formal Semantic Analysis,* ed. E. Hammel, pp. 37-64. *American Anthropologist* 67, no. 5, pt. 2 (special issue).

Langendoen, D. T.
1968 *The London School of Linguistics: A Study of the Linguistic Theories of B. Malinowski and J. R. Firth.* Cambridge: M.I.T. Press.

Leach, Edmund
1967 *The Structural Study of Myth and Totemism.* Monograph no. 5. London and New York: Association of Social Anthropologists.

Lee, Dorothy

1959 *Freedom and Culture.* Englewood Cliffs, N.J.: Prentice-Hall.

Lessa, William A.
1966 "Discoverer-of-the-Sun": Mythology as a Reflection of Culture. In *The Anthropologist Looks at Myth,* ed. M. Jacobs, pp. 3-51. *Journal of American Folklore* 79, no. 311 (special issue).

Lévi-Strauss, Claude
1963 *Totemism.* Boston: Beacon Press. Originally published 1962.

1966 *The Savage Mind.* Chicago: University of Chicago Press. Originally published 1962.

1967a *Structural Anthropology.* Garden City, N.Y.: Doubleday Anchor Books. Originally published 1958.

1967b Structural Analysis in Linguistics and Anthropology. In C. Lévi-Strauss, *Structural Anthropology.* Garden City, N.Y.: Doubleday Anchor Books. Originally published 1945.

1967c The Structural Study of Myth. In C. Lévi-Strauss, *Structural Anthropology.* Garden City, N.Y.: Doubleday Anchor Books. Originally published 1955.

Lounsbury, F.
1956 A Semantic Analysis of the Pawnee Kinship Usage. *Language* 32:158-94.

1963 Linguistics and Psychology. In *Psychology: A Study of a Science,* ed. S. Koch, vol. 6. New York: McGraw-Hill. (Also Bobbs-Merrill reprint A-322.)

McQuown, N.
1954 Analysis of the Cultural Content of Language Materials. In *Language in Culture,* ed. H. Hoijer. Chicago: University of Chicago Press.

1956 A Linguistics Laboratory Serves Cultural Anthropology. *American Anthropologist* 58:536-39.

1957 Review of K. Pike, *Language in Relation to a Unified Theory of the Structure of Human Behavior. American Anthropologist* 59:189-92.

Malinowski, B.
1923 The Problem of Meaning in Primitive Languages. Appendix to C. K. Ogden and I. A. Richards, *The Meaning of Meaning.* London: Kegan Paul.

1965 *The Language of Magic and Gardening.* Bloomington: Indiana University

Press. Originally published 1935.

Maquet, Jacques
1964 Some Epistemological Remarks on the Cultural Philosophies and Their Comparison. In *Cross-Cultural Understanding,* ed. F. S. C. Northrop and H. H. Livingston. New York: Harper & Row.

Mathiot, Madeleine
1964 Noun Classes and Folk Taxonomy in Papago. In *Language in Culture and Society,* ed. D. Hymes. New York: Harper & Row. Originally published 1962.
1968 *An Approach to the Cognitive Study of Language. International Journal of American Linguistics* 34, no. 1, pub. no. 45. Bloomington: Indiana Research Center in Anthropology, Folklore, and Linguistics, Indiana University.
1970 The Semantic and Cognitive Domains of Language. In *Cognition: A Multiple View,* ed. P. L. Garvin. New York: Spartan Books.
1972 Cognitive Analysis of a Myth: An Exercise in Method. *Semiotica* 4.
n.d. Informational Structure Versus Syntactic Structure: Segmentation Criteria. Scheduled for inclusion in *Proceedings of the Symposium on Structures and Genres of Ethnic Literature* (Palermo, April 1970).

Metzger, Duane
1963 Asking Questions and Questioning Answers in Ethnography. Paper presented at spring meetings, Southwestern Anthropological Association, Riverside, Calif.
1964 Current Trends in Ethnography. Paper presented at 62nd annual meeting, American Anthropological Association, Detroit.
1966 The Ethnography of Absolute Truth. Paper presented at spring meetings, Southwestern Anthropological Association, Davis, Calif.
1967 Folk Structures and Ethnographic Dictionaries. Paper presented at spring meetings, Southwestern Anthropological Association, San Francisco.
n.d. Semantic Procedures for the Analysis of Belief Systems. Unpublished MS.

Metzger, Duane, and G. E. Williams
1963a A Formal Ethnographic Analysis of Tenejapa Ladino Weddings. *American Anthropologist* 65:1076-1101.
1963b Tenejapa Medicine I: The Curer. *Southwestern Journal of Anthropology* 19:216-34.
1966 Procedures and Results in the Study of Native Categories: Tzeltal Firewood. *American Anthropologist* 68: 389-407.
1967 Patterns of Primary Personal Reference in a Tzeltal Community. *Estudios de cultura maya* 6.

Miller, George A.
1956 The Magical Number Seven, Plus or Minus Two: Some Limits on Our Capacity for Processing Information. *Psychological Review* 63:81-97.

Miller, George A., E. Galanter, and K. H. Pribram
1960 *Plans and the Structure of Behavior.* New York: Holt.

Moerman, Michael
1969 A Little Knowledge. In *Cognitive Anthropology,* ed. S. Tyler. New York: Holt, Rinehart & Winston.

Nadel, S. F.
1951 *The Foundations of Social Anthropology.* London: Cohen & West.
1957 *The Theory of Social Structure.* New York: Free Press, Macmillan.

Nash, June
1969 The Individual Looks at His Culture. Paper presented at 67th annual meeting, American Anthropological Association, New Orleans.

Nida, Eugene
1961 Some Problems of Semantic Structure and Translation Equivalence. In *A William Cameron Townsend en el vigésimoquinto aniversario del Instituto Lingüístico de Verano.* Cuernavaca: Typográfica Indígena.
1964 *Toward a Science of Translating.* Leiden: Brill.

Northrop, F. S. C., and H. H. Livingston, eds.
1964 *Cross-Cultural Understanding: Epistemology in Anthropology.* New York: Harper & Row.

Opler, Morris
1946 Themes as Dynamic Forces in Culture. *American Journal of Sociology* 51:196-206.

Pelto, Pertti
1970 *Anthropological Research: The Structure of Inquiry.* New York: Harper & Row.

Pike, Kenneth
1967 *Language in Relation to a Unified Theory of the Structure of Human Behavior,* 2nd revised ed., The Hague: Mouton.

Pittinger, R. E., C. Hockett, and J. J. Danehy
1960 *The First Five Minutes.* Ithaca: Martineau.

Pospisil, L.
1965a A Formal Analysis of Substantive Law: Kapauku Papuan Laws of Land Tenure. In *Formal Semantic Analysis,* ed. E. Hammel, pp. 186-214. *American Anthropologist* 67, no. 5, pt. 2 (special issue).
1965b A Formal Analysis of Substantive Law: Kapauku Papuan Laws of Inheritance. In *The Ethnography of Law,* ed. L. Nader, pp. 166-85. *American Anthropologist* 67, no. 6, pt. 2 (special issue).

Preston, Richard
1971a Cree Narration: An Expression of the Personal Meanings of Events. Ph. D. dissertation, University of North Carolina.
1971b Eastern Cree Symbolism: The Use of Metaphor in the Expression of Beliefs. Paper presented at meetings of Northeastern Anthropological Association, Albany.

Propp, V.
1968 *Morphology of the Folktale,* 2nd ed. Austin: University of Texas Press. Originally published 1928.

Quine, W. Van Orman
1960 *Word and Object.* Cambridge: M.I.T. Press.
1961 *From a Logical Point of View.* Cambridge: Harvard University Press.

Radcliffe-Brown, A. R.
1951 The Comparative Method in Social Anthropology. *Journal of the Royal Anthropological Institute* 81:15-22.

Radin, Paul
1923 *The Winnebago Tribe: 37th Annual Report, 1915-16.* Washington, D.C.: Bureau of American Ethnology.
1949 *The Culture of the Winnebago as Described by Themselves.* Memoir no.

2, *International Journal of American Linguistics* 15, no. 1 (supplement).
1956 *The Trickster: A Study in American Indian Mythology.* New York: Philosophical Library.
1957 *Primitive Man as Philosopher.* New York: Dover Publications. Originally published 1927.

Redfield, Robert
1952 The Primitive World View. *Proceedings of the American Philosophical Society* 96:30-36.
1953 *The Primitive World and Its Transformations.* Ithaca: Cornell University Press.

Reusch, J., and G. Bateson
1951 *Communication: The Social Matrix of Psychiatry.* New York: Norton.

Roberts, John M.
1959 Games in Culture. *American Anthropologist* 61: 597-605.

Roberts, John M., and Brian Sutton-Smith
1962 Child Training and Game Involvement. *Ethnology* 1:166-85.

Roberts, John M., B. Sutton-Smith, and A. Kendon
1963 Strategy in Games and Folk Tales. *Journal of Social Psychology* 61:185-99.

Roberts, John M., R. F. Strand, and E. Burmeister
1971 Preferential Pattern Analysis. In *Explorations in Mathematical Anthropology,* ed. P. Kay. Cambridge: M.I.T. Press.

Romney, A. K., and R. G. D'Andrade
1969 Cognitive Aspects of English Kin Terms. In *Cognitive Anthropology,* ed. S. Tyler. New York: Holt, Rinehart & Winston. Originally published 1964.

Romney, A. K., and P. J. Epling
1958 A Simplified Model of Kariera Kinship. *American Anthropologist* 60: 57-74.

Rubel, Arthur
1960 Concepts of Disease in Mexican-American Culture. *American Anthropologist* 62:795-814.

Sankoff, Gillian
1971 Quantitative Analysis of Sharing and Variability in a Cognitive Model. *Ethnology* 10:389-408.
1972 Cognitive Variability and New Guin-

ea Social Organization: The Buang Dgwa. *American Anthropologist* 74.

Sapir, Edward
1949a Sound Patterns in Language. In *Selected Writings of Edward Sapir,* ed. D. Mandelbaum. Berkeley: University of California Press. Originally published 1925.
1949b The Unconscious Patterning of Behavior in Society. In *Selected Writings of Edward Sapir,* ed. D. Mandelbaum. Berkeley: University of California Press. Originally published 1927.
1949c The Psychological Reality of the Phoneme. In *Selected Writings of Edward Sapir,* ed. D. Mandelbaum. Berkeley: University of California Press. Originally published 1933.

Sarles, Harvey B.
1966 The Dynamic Study of Interaction as Ethnoscientific Strategy. In *Ethnoscience,* ed. O. Werner, pp. 66-71. *Anthropological Linguistics* 8 (special issue).

Savard, Rémi
1969 L'hôte maladroit: Essai d'analyse d'un conte montagnais. *Interprétation* 3:5-52.
1970 Structures sémantiques et mythologie: Le personnage du décepteur dans la littérature orale amérindienne. Paper presented at symposium on structures and genres of ethnic literature, Palermo.
1971 *Carcajou et le sens du monde.* Série Cultures Amérindiennes, Civilization du Québec. Quebec: Ministère des Affaires Culturelles.

Savard, Rémi, and Claude Lachapelle
1970 L'Analyse des mythes et les ordinateurs. Paper presented at annual meetings of Canadian Sociological and Anthropological Association, Winnipeg.

Smith, Alfred G., ed.
1966 *Communication and Culture: Readings in the Codes of Human Interaction.* New York: Holt, Rinehart & Winston.

Spencer, Robert
1959 *The North Alaskan Eskimo.* Washington, D.C.: Smithsonian Institution Press.

Spindler, George D.
1963 Psychology and Anthropology: Culture Change. In *Psychology: A Study of a Science,* ed. S. Koch, vol. 6. New York: McGraw-Hill.

Stefflre, Volney
1963 An Outline for Study of Some Relations Between Language and Non-linguistic Behavior. Paper presented at Social Science Research Council Conference on Transcultural Studies of Cognitive Processes, Mérida.
1966 Problems of Descriptive Semantics. Paper presented at meetings of Southwestern Anthropological Association, Davis, Calif.

Stefflre, Volney, P. Reich, and M. McClaran-Stefflre
1971 Some Eliciting and Computational Procedures for Descriptive Semantics. In *Explorations in Mathematical Anthropology,* ed. P. Kay. Cambridge: M.I.T. Press.

Sturtevant, William C.
1964 Studies in Ethnoscience. In *Transcultural Studies in Cognition,* ed. A. K. Romney and R. G. D'Andrade, pp. 99-131. *American Anthropologist* 66, no. 3, pt. 2 (special issue).

Tolman, E. D.
1948 Cognitive Maps in Rats and Men. *Psychological Review* 55:189-208.

Trager, George
1958 Paralanguage: A First Approximation. *Studies in Linguistics* 13:1-12.
1961 The Typology of Paralanguage. *Anthropological Linguistics* 3:17-21.

Tyler, Stephen A.
1969a Introduction. In *Cognitive Anthropology,* ed. S. Tyler. New York: Holt, Rinehart & Winston.
1969b The Myth of P: Epistemology and Formal Analysis. *American Anthropologist* 71:71-79.
1969c Context and Variation in Koya Kinship Terminology. In *Cognitive Anthropology,* ed. S. Tyler. New York: Holt, Rinehart & Winston.

Videbeck, R., and J. Pia
1966 Plans for Coping: An Approach to Ethnoscience. In *Ethnoscience,* ed. O. Werner, pp. 71-78. *Anthropological Linguistics* 8 (special issue).

Vogt, Evon Z.

1965 Structural and Conceptual Replication in Zinacantan Culture. *American Anthropologist* 67:342-54.

Wallace, A. F. C.
1961 On Being Just Complicated Enough. *Proceedings of National Academy of Science* 47:458-64.
1965 The Problem of the Psychological Validity of Componential Analysis. In *Formal Semantic Analysis,* ed. E. Hammel, pp. 229-48. *American Anthropologist* 67, no. 5, pt. 2 (special issue).
1970 *Culture and Personality,* 2nd ed. New York: Random House. Originally published 1961.

Wallace, A. F. C., and John Atkins
1969 The Meaning of Kinship Terms. In *Cognitive Anthropology,* ed. S. Tyler. New York: Holt, Rinehart & Winston. (Also Bobbs-Merrill Reprint A-231.) Originally published 1960.

Wax, Murray
1962 The Notions of Nature, Man, and Time of a Hunting People. *Southern Folklore Quarterly* 25:175-186.

Wax, Rosalie, and Murray Wax
1962 The Magical World View. *Journal for the Scientific Study of Religion* 1:179-88.

Weinreich, Uriel
1963 On the Semantic Structure of Language. In *Universals of Language,* ed. J. Greenberg. Cambridge: M.I.T. Press.

Werner, Oswald
1965 Semantics of Navaho Medical Terms. *International Journal of American Linguistics* 31:1-17.
1966 Pragmatics and Ethnoscience. In *Ethnoscience,* ed. O. Werner, pp. 42-65. *Anthropological Linguistics* 8 (special issue).
1969a The Basic Assumptions of Ethnoscience. *Semiotica* 1:329-38.
1969b On the Universality of Some Lexical/Semantic Relations. Paper presented at 67th annual meeting, American Anthropological Association, New Orleans.

Whorf, Benjamin L.
1956 *Language, Thought, and Reality.* Cambridge: M.I.T. Press.

Williams, G.E.
1966 Linguistic Reflections of Cultural Systems. In *Ethnoscience,* ed. O. Werner, pp. 13-21. *Anthropological Linguistics* 8 (special issue).

CHAPTER **13** Symbolism in a Ritual Context:
Aspects of Symbolic Action

NANCY D. MUNN

The growing interest in symbolism in the last decade has fanned back to life an old anthropological flame: the study of ritual. In one sense, of course, this flame has never gone out: as Cohen (1969:216f) has recently stressed, ritual is one of the major institutional fields continuously accounted for by monographs in social anthropology.[1]

What distinguishes the new "acolytes" is the concern with the internal structures and meanings of symbolic processes. Ritual is being examined with fresh enthusiasm as more than a "statement" or "document" of social organization (Peacock 1968:245), or an expression of nonrational imperatives in human action. Looked at from the symbolic "inside out" (rather than the functionalist "outside in"), ritual can be seen as a symbolic intercom between the level of cultural thought and complex cultural meanings, on the one hand, and that of social action and immediate event, on the other. It is from this perspective that I propose to examine it here.

INTRODUCTION

In this paper I utilize a model for ritual action based on the view that

---

[1] A continuous if "submerged" line of interest in ritual process was also, of course, evident in other fields of anthropology as well: for example, Bateson and Mead (1942) and Belo (1949) examined it from the perspective of personality and culture studies in their well-known research in Bali. The current revival of interest, however, emerges from a confluence of various elements in the Durkheimian tradition that intersect in the problem of symbolism; it is this tradition, therefore, that forms the subject of the present account. It should be noted that although the present swing of attention toward the symbolic aspect of ritual is largely a phenomenon of the 1960s, it began to gather momentum in British an-

thropology in the latter part of the previous decade. Three major publications of this period that concentrated on ritual symbolism are Evans-Pritchard's *Nuer Religion* (1956), which includes a special chapter devoted to symbolism; Audrey Richards' *Chisungu* (1956), an account of a Bemba girl's initiation; and Monica Wilson's two-volume study of Nyakyusa ritual (1957, 1959) with its extensive data on native exegesis of symbols, as well as detailed accounts of ritual processes. These accounts are extensions of the tradition for ritual studies earlier established by Radcliffe-Brown (1964), Malinowski (1935), Firth (1940), and others discussed in this chapter.

ritual belongs to the broad category of social mechanisms that Talcott Parsons has called "generalized symbolic media of social interaction" (T. Turner 1968; Parsons 1963a, 1963b, 1964). This notion was developed by Parsons to refer to a symbolic control system in which, as in language, the media manipulated by the actors are communication vehicles that themselves have no intrinsic utility but "signify commodities that do" (Parsons 1963a:39). Parsons' paradigmatic example of generalized media is money, but he also discusses influence, power, and (in the personality system) pleasure (Parsons 1964:116) as exemplars. Recently T. Turner (1968) has suggested further modifications of the notion that make it more amenable to use in anthropology, and has extended it to include such widespread cultural phenomena as gift exchange.

An essential characteristic of a generalized symbolic medium is that it commands a battery of intrinsic values or "real utilities" matrixed in diffuse social contexts, which it symbolically manipulates in transactions freed from the spatiotemporal determinants of these contexts. The medium is thus generalized in its capacity to convert any utility within a relevant domain or category of value into a currency that circulates between actors at a new symbolic level of social interaction.

I define ritual as a generalized medium of social interaction in which the vehicles for constructing messages are iconic symbols (acts, words, or things) that convert the load of significance or complex sociocultural meanings embedded in and generated by the ongoing processes of social existence into a communication currency. In other words, shared sociocultural meanings constitute the utilities that are symbolically transacted through the medium of ritual action. The generalization of

ritual symbolism derives from its capacity to synthesize and circulate meanings from many domains and specific situational contexts through the agency of a comparatively limited number of tokens or vehicles, sometimes very simple in form, that have assumed varying degrees of semantic "multivocality" (V. Turner 1961, 1962, 1969a). By this means a complex world view or aspects of it can, in effect, be circulated within the interplay of the immediate relationships and processes of symbolic (ritual) action.

I have said that the symbol vehicles of ritual action are iconic: i.e., there is a component of likeness or perceptual continuity patterning the relationship between the vehicle's form and its meanings. In this respect, the form of the vehicle is intrinsic to the message carried, and certain qualities of the referents are put into social circulation as part of this form. Thus the symbol vehicles of ritual do carry intrinsic value at the same time that they function as generalized media of social interaction; ritual action can provide structures for expressing or "modeling" the qualities of life situations while at the same time converting them into the level of symbolic objectification.

CULTURAL CODE AND RITUAL MESSAGE SYSTEM

I distinguish in this account between the lexicon of sociocultural concepts or categories and the message system of ritual action. The ritual message system consists of all the forms and rules governing these forms that pertain to the ritual process as a mode of expressive communication (e.g., the symbols, the action sequences, and the rules governing these; the categories of participants and their modes of participation, etc.).

Ritual manipulates a lexicon of sociocultural concepts or categories that refer to the various domains of experience within a particular society and condense the meanings of these domains; for instance, categories of flora and fauna; categories of persons; body parts and fluids; color and perceptual properties like heat and cold, etc. These categories, organized through the operation of principles such as those of binary opposition and associative clustering, I shall call the cultural code.

Any given category itself constitutes an abstraction or synthesis of meanings derived from the experiential world. For instance, in a particular culture, "blood" may condense such experiences as the flowing of blood from wounds in warfare and blood flow at menstruation; it may also be associated with various qualities such as heat and anger, and convey abstract social meanings such as "blood brotherhood." Each category may also be flooded with attitudes and feelings, and often with sociomoral values.

Different ritual messages can be created through various reformulations or coinages of the same code elements, as for instance in the case of different rituals that draw on the same or similar selections of the cultural lexicon. Moreover, ritual forms may variously render the structural oppositions and relationships of the code categories, as will become clear later. In the same way, a narrative myth—which constitutes another type of message system for communicating cultural meanings[2]—may draw on the same (or similar) cultural lexicon as a particular ritual, each organizing the code elements and their relationships in its own terms.

THE SOCIAL CO-IMPLICATES OF RITUAL SYMBOLS

In his discussion of Parsons' notion of generalized media, Terence Turner (1968:122) suggests that the domain of value controlled by a particular medium itself "represents a mode of relationship between social actors." For example, the value domain relevant to money is "economic utility"; but economic utility presupposes the sort of social relationship in which actors "assume the role of buyers and sellers towards each other." Thus in any given monetary transaction this social relationship is in effect transacted as part of the "message" condensed within the symbols.

We might say that this social message is co-implied by the symbol vehicles, since in any particular instance the relevant relationship is demonstrated by the transaction itself.[3] Thus the symbol co-implies the social relationship represented by the domain of utility it commands, and manifested in any particular transaction between actors referable to that domain.

This Durkheimian-styled thesis can be adapted to a theory of ritual action. I have suggested that the value domain controlled by ritual symbols is that of shared sociocultural meanings. This do-

---

[2] For present purposes, I define myth as actions and events located in a world culturally defined as "real," but permanently distal from the living actors in time and sometimes in space. Mythic action, being only indirectly "known," must always be symbolically mediated to the living actors, for example, by verbal narration or dramatic enactment.

[3] My use of the notion of "co-implication" derives most immediately from Urban's (1951:668f) notion of the "co-implicates of experience." In his account, notions like the "self" or "other" are the necessary presuppositions of experience and communication. In any given instance, they are not the objects of experience (or the referents of the communication), but are implicitly given within it (1951:669): "These co-implicates are made known or shown forth in the very processes of communication or discourse itself."

main presupposes a relationship between actors in their roles as persons sharing *common social objectifications* that make life experience *subjectively* plausible. Ritual symbols are testaments to the joining of individuals in objective social relationships that have personal, subjective relevance and internalized normative value. Rituals "fail" when they no longer co-imply this sort of relationship; i.e., when they no longer serve the participants as a means of transacting their relationships in social terms that contain "intimations" of personal identity.

It is apparent that any particular ritual action will activate only a selection of the cultural code of meanings. The portion activated is conditioned by the particular set of specific social roles actualized in that ritual (for example, the roles of neighbor, kinsman, lineage member, etc.). In the ancestral sacrifices of a lineage, for instance, the symbols co-imply the joining of *lineage* members in subjectively meaningful social forms. The shared cultural meanings here involved presuppose a relationship between actors in their roles as lineage members sharing common objectifications of subjective significance.

THE RITUAL MODEL DEVELOPED BY
FUSTEL DE COULANGES, DURKHEIM,
AND RADCLIFFE-BROWN[4]

Fustel de Coulanges

The basis for a social theory of symbolic action was laid by N. D. Fustel de Coulanges (1956) in his remarkable study *La cité antique,* which first appeared

in 1864. For Fustel de Coulanges, certain rituals of ancient Greece and Rome functioned as what we would now call "boundary maintaining mechanisms": they expressed and sustained the corporate identity of social groups.

Implicit in Fustel's approach is the recognition, basic to any social theory of symbolism, that certain material forms and modes of organizing physical space carry messages relating to the organization of social space; regulation of behavior in the concrete sphere of social (ritual) action can express and regulate relationships in the sphere of social structure (Fustel de Coulanges 1956: 25):

In the house of every Greek and Roman was an altar; on this altar there had always to be ... a few lighted coals. It was a sacred obligation for the master of every house to keep the fire up night and day. Woe to the house where it was extinguished. ... An extinguished hearth, an extinguished family, were synonymous expressions among the ancients.

The equation of hearth and family rested on the fact that the continuity of the fire represented the continuity of the ancestors, and therefore of the social relationships constituted in the family. In Fustel's theory (1956:42), rules of behavior involving ancestral symbols form the intersection of the social and religious systems: religion "did not create the family" but "it gave it its rules."

Indeed, since social groups are constituted, in his view, by conformity to cultural rules embodied in symbolic action rather than by natural associa-

---

[4] My discussion reviews briefly some of the points made by these writers which are integral to the study of ritual from the perspective of symbol theory. Two other well-known writers who made major contributions to this ritual model, Robertson Smith (1956) and Marcel Mauss (1954), are not discussed here. Robertson Smith's influential notion

of sacrifice as a communion meal demonstrating the social bonds of the worshipers with their god and Mauss's concept of the "gift" as an assertion of the obligatory relationship binding the parties to the exchange are also excellent examples of the insights afforded by the concern of early theorists with the social co-implicates of ritual symbols.

tion or natural affection, the grounds of social order must be continuously re-created through common ritual activities. The implication of his theory is that social bonds and the structure of social units have to be perpetually reinstated in individual experience within a social process that symbolizes these bonds. Speaking of the communal repasts of the Roman senate, Fustel states (1956:158), "These old customs give us an idea of the close tie which united the members of a city. Human association was a religion; its symbol was a meal. . . . Neither interest, nor agreement, nor habit creates the social bond; it is this holy communion. . . ." This ritual maintenance of social bonds requires a particular mode of individual orientation toward society, one where the individual conscience is, in effect, lodged within external social forms that govern it, compelling it from without, almost like a "material bond" (1956: 167, 352).[5] Only when these bonds are loosened is the individual conscience detached from ritual forms. In his view, these traditional human societies developed a mode of social control involving the projection of the individual conscience into external symbolic forms that in turn functioned to express sociopolitical relationships.

Durkheim

The basic paradigm used by Durkheim to develop his theory of ritual symbolism was already available in inchoate form in the work of Fustel de Coulanges and Robertson Smith. On the one hand, this model conveyed a picture of social groups defined through concrete ritual acts regulating their internal solidarity and their external identity vis-à-vis other parallel groups; on the other hand, it depicted ritual as societal action through which the individual directly engaged in behavior expressive of social relationships entailed in group organization; and in Fustel, as we have just seen, we find the implication that the individual conscience was externalized in these ritual acts or rules.

Durkheim's signal importance for the history of ritual symbol theory is not due to the truncated functional notions often promulgated in his name—that ritual reinforces social solidarity, or that religious beliefs are symbols of social groups—but rather to his development of a theoretical model that envisages social (ritual) symbolism as the switch point between the external moral constraints and groupings of the sociopolitical order and the internal feelings and imaginative concepts of the individual actor.

In *Les formes élémentaires de la vie religieuse,* Durkheim used the notion of totemism in central Australia to work out the basic terms of this model. Thus the "totemic emblem" is viewed as the "outward and visible form" (1954:206) of the moral authority of the community;[6] through it the latter takes on concrete form in the imagination, and so enters directly into individual experience.

Since the totemic representations have their locus in the collectivity, they are external to the individual; but, as Durkheim stresses, collective representations must be continually manifested in the individual imagination so as to

---

[5] This viewpoint is a reflection of Fustel's preoccupation with the evolution of consciousness and the emergence of individual freedom, a preoccupation that is, of course, characteristic of the period. In this respect, he conceived of ritual symbolism as a kind of enslavement, since it encased individual definitions of morality in socially established, external rules of behavior.

---

[6] As Nisbet (1966:83) points out, Durkheim's concept of "society" refers essentially to *communitas* rather than *societas.*

assure their societal continuity (1954: 209, 221, passim). Ritual action functions to maintain this dialectical relationship between the individual mind and the communal order via the mediation of collective representations.

A major implication of Durkheim's thesis is that collective representations (such as the totemic emblems, or the notion of a god) automatically infuse the individual with attitudes and feelings that reflect their source in society, irrespective of what the individual himself may say about the matter; through such symbolisms the individual internalizes the imperatives of his community, while at the same time, by coming to experience these imperatives as part of himself (from within, as it were, rather than from without), he is also able to achieve a transcendence of individual identity. It is this combined experience of individual transcendence and societal imperative entering into consciousness in the form of collective representations (and so condensed within them) that constitutes, from a Durkheimian perspective, the essence of the religious experience.

Thus what Durkheim was attempting to do for the sociology of symbol theory was parallel to what Freud was attempting at about the same time for its psychology.[7] For Durkheim, society is, as it were, "primary process" and the "omnipotent background to conscious and overt mental life and behavior" (MacIntyre 1958:31; MacIntyre is referring to Freud's notion of the unconscious). Collective representations are the conceptual "shapes" taken by social relationships and imperatives in the consciousness of members of a collectivity.

Durkheim's notion of collective representations corresponds broadly to what I have called the cultural code and the symbols of the ritual message system. His fundamental concern is with demonstrating the *a priori* social conditions of individual experience, and thus the implicit entailment of societal relationships and their imperatives in collective symbols. Consequently his approach short-circuits the problem of cultural meanings, tending to reduce them to the social co-implicates of the symbols (see also Stanner 1967:235f).

Radcliffe-Brown

It is precisely the problem of specific cultural meanings that Radcliffe-Brown (1964) attempts to tackle in *The Andaman Islanders* (originally published in 1922), but from which he is diverted by the social and sociopsychological emphasis of the Durkheimian approach. I reserve discussion of Radcliffe-Brown's semantic analysis for the following section; here I wish to take up some aspects of his general ritual symbol theory.[8]

Radcliffe-Brown's basic proposal concerning the relation between ritual symbols and social relations hinges on his concept of "social value" and its subjective counterpart, "social sentiments." The latter are "emotional tendencies" (feelings of affection and attachment to others) that come to be focused in those objects of social activity affecting social well-being or forming the nexus of intensive social interaction (1964:234). Such objects then become vehicles of "social value," in that they reflect coordinated social activity or bonds of social relation. Ritual symbolism "fixes" this social value by creating a language-like form that celebrates it.

---

[7] Nisbet (1966:82f) compares Durkheim and Freud in general terms, but not specifically with reference to their symbol theories.

[8] My discussion refers to the theory as set out in *The Andaman Islanders*. Although in later studies, Radcliffe-Brown (1952a, 1957) developed his concepts of social and ritual value more explicitly, the fundamental ideas are laid down in this early work.

This point may be illustrated by Radcliffe-Brown's interpretation of special precautions taken by the Andamanese in connection with eating. He stresses that these precautions (for example, painting the body with clay designs before or after eating) must be explained in terms of the overall social contexts in which food acquisition plays a part. Because food acquisition for the Andaman Islander is a day-to-day activity (1964:270), "we may say that it is particularly in connection with food that he is made to feel that he is a member of the community, sharing with others their joys and sorrows, taking part in a common activity, often dependent upon others for the satisfaction of his hunger. . . ."

As a result, feelings of "moral obligation" and of social euphoria (food plenty) and disphoria (lack of food) come to cohere in the food objects themselves, and these experiences are synthesized and projected in the ritual form of specific precautions surrounding food consumption (1964:272): "The sense of the social value of food reveals itself as a belief that food may be a source of danger unless it is approached with circumspection, and this belief, translated into action, gives rise to the rite of painting the body after eating." "Painting the body after eating" is seen as, in effect, a translation of the diffuse social experiences generated in daily food acquisition into a coherent act that fixes in consciousness the social value of food. Ritual is envisaged as a meta-social form, a kind of projective system capable of converting social sentiments and values into communications that can "circulate" them in social action outside the specific contexts within which they are generated.[9] In this respect, we may say (utilizing the terms of the present model) that in Radcliffe-Brown's approach ritual is viewed as a generalized medium of interaction in which the utilities controlled and symbolically circulated are social values and sentiments.

Because of his interest in the daily social contexts of behavior and the social values accruing to cultural objects, Radcliffe-Brown's study draws attention to the situational contexts where the meanings of cultural elements and activities are built up, and to the related matter of the social sources of certain ritual symbols:[10] for example, some of the Andaman symbol vehicles, like fire and the hibiscus bush, are objects of prominent use in the nonritual contexts of daily life, a feature reflecting the more general fact that the symbol vehicles of ritual consist of heterogeneous cultural elements. Ritual, like myth, is a form of *bricolage,* its materials being "the remains and debris of events" (Lévi-Strauss 1966:22).

In line with Radcliffe-Brown's approach, a number of commentaries in the anthropological literature refer to continuities between ritual vehicles and nonritual media (for example, Chapple and Coon 1942:532f; Evans-Pritchard 1940:89; Firth 1967:213f; Gluckman 1965:47; Goody 1962:39f; Rosaldo 1968:526). In some instances, a symbol "language" may draw important vehicles from technology. As Evans-Pritchard (1940:89), referring to the important ritual functions of Nuer spears, remarks, objects of material culture

---

[9] Radcliffe-Brown sometimes equivocates on the relation between ritual and social value, writing as if the rites "create" the social value (e.g., 1952a:148).

This is not, however, the main thrust of the argument.

[10] Leach (1968:522) states that Radcliffe-Brown is indebted to Jane Harrison for the view that ritual objects derive their importance from secular contexts. However, an earlier precedent for conceiving of the social grounds or sources of ritual elements is to be found in Robertson Smith's view of sacrifice as a meal. He suggests that the meal is an appropriate ritual symbol of social bonds because in daily life "the very act of eating and drinking with a man was a symbol and confirmation of fellowship and mutual social obligations" (1956:269).

"are chains along which social relationships run, and the more simple is a material culture, the more numerous are the relationships expressed through it." As the "nodal points"[11] of multiple social contexts, such objects can become, as it were, detached from the diffuse flows of daily social activity and enter into the society's generalized symbolic media of social interaction. As symbols, the meanings they carry relate to the situational contexts from which they are drawn.

A well-known phenomenon is the case where the material vehicles of ritual are special forms of the same class of objects as those operative in the technology: for example, the formally elaborate, technologically useless ritual axes known from some parts of the Pacific. On the other hand, the presence of a special class of objects culturally defined as part of the ritual system, as for example the Tikopian *tapu* axes discussed by Firth (1967), does not necessarily mean that such objects are not to be used outside of ritual contexts. Firth (1967:222) points out that for some categories of *tapu* ax, the "ritual qualities . . . could be turned on and off, as it were, according to need." This was the case with a particular type of steel ax: one of its symbolic uses was (metaphorically) to cut down a thief, but it could also be used for ordinary work.

Still another sort of continuity can be exemplified from the central Australian Walbiri, where, according to my own data, certain secret oval boards

exclusive to male cult are commonly identified with the traditional wooden containers for food, water, and babies. The secret boards have special Walbiri names and are usually decorated with totemic designs, but their oval shapes are similar to those of the ordinary containers and men sometimes refer to them directly by the terms for these utilitarian objects. It is as if the ceremonial objects substitute for the containers in the domain of symbolic action, providing them with representative forms on this plane.

The relationship between the forms of particular ritual acts and daily social behavior may also be considered. For instance, Rosaldo (1968:526) points to much of the behavior of the Zinacantan *cargo* ritual for the Christ of Esquipulas as being a "condensed elaborate version of daily social intercourse . . . in particular of the various ways in which individuals signal their recognition of difference in age. In drinking, the eldest male is served first, then the next oldest, and so on; in cargo ritual it is the highest ranking official who drinks first."

We may isolate various forms of continuity (and discontinuity) between symbolic vehicles and their social sources, but the general problem is the manner in which objects or acts utilized on one plane or level of action are "translated" into the plane of symbolic functioning, whether this translation is direct or involves displacement, or whether the vehicles are specialized to the symbolic plane.

In sum, the Durkheimian tradition led to the establishment of a framework for the study of ritual symbolism as a special form of social action. The issues raised include, on the one hand, the relationship between ritual and other forms of social activity, and on the other, the messages about social relationships among ritual participants

---

[11] Freud (1938:323). Freud's discussion of the "dream-work" provides a parallel at the level of the personality system. See his discussion of the dream of the botanical monograph (1938:323): "the elements 'botanical' and 'monograph' were taken up into the dream-content because they were able to offer the most numerous points of contact with the greatest number of dream-thoughts, and thus represented *nodal points* at which a great number of the dream-thoughts met together. . . ."

carried by the symbols; i.e., what I have called the social co-implicates of the symbols. The Durkheimian tradition defines the sociopsychological functions of ritual as the mediation of normative social relationships to the individual, but the model it develops does not adequately handle the complex sociocultural meanings that are condensed and circulated in the symbols. Nevertheless, the problem of these meanings is inherent in the framework for dealing with rite as symbolic expression referable to the ongoing social order, a feature illustrated by Radcliffe-Brown's attempts to cope with it, and by his interest in the social contexts where meanings are built up in experience.[12]

MEANING AND THE CULTURAL CODE

It was the linguist Saussure (1966:17) who suggested that rites should be studied as part of "a science of semiology," and his views may well have influenced Radcliffe-Brown. Radcliffe-Brown (1964:viii) conceived of ritual as a system of "expressive signs," and suggested an analogy between morphemes and the units of ritual.

In his early Andaman study, Radcliffe-Brown (1952a:146) proposed his well-known method for semantic analysis, one that he himself never consistently applied. It consists, in essence, of tracing the symbols of a rite through different contexts of use, on the assumption that "when, in a single society, the same symbol is used in different contexts or on different kinds of occasions there is some common element of meaning, and . . . by comparing together the various uses we may

be able to discover what the common element is. . . ."

It is significant that Radcliffe-Brown's linguistic analogues for rite are confined to the morphological rather than the grammatical aspects of language (see Radcliffe-Brown 1964:ix; 1952a:146). On the one hand, the examination of ritual semantics in Radcliffe-Brown's social anthropology involved a study of the minimal (morpheme-like) units of rite involving objects such as food or fire or acts such as embracing or washing; on the other hand, it stressed a single, broad meaning common to all the usages of each symbolic unit, rather than chains of associations or complex multiple meanings that can be built into a symbol.[13] In this respect, this approach contrasts with the current emphasis of Victor Turner (1969a) on the "multivocal" meanings of ritual symbols, but both approaches are focused in "vocabulary" and merely stress different aspects of symbol semantics.

In his Introduction to Srinivas' (1952) study of the Coorgs of southern India, Radcliffe-Brown (1952b:vi) wrote: "In any system of ritual each ritual action has its meaning, and the totality of such meanings constitutes the idiom of that system." Such an approach lends itself to descriptions of lists of symbols, a feature illustrated by Srinivas' (1952:70-123) discussion of the Coorg "ritual idiom," in which the various contextual frames of Coorg ritual symbols (e.g., the bath, the white robe, the sprinkling of rice, etc.) are carefully set out, but the interrelationships of these elements as components of a cultural code with its own internal "logic" remain unanalyzed. Despite its limita-

---

12 The Durkheimian tradition is, of course, multiplex, and I have dealt here with only one part of it. Later I discuss another framework for ritual theory which emerged from a second strand of thought in this tradition.

13 Radcliffe-Brown did, however, recognize the importance of "associations," but in his general statement of method he is concerned with the establishment of a common strand of meaning in different contexts.

tions, Radcliffe-Brown's theory constituted the first recognition that the ritual system of a given society makes use of a limited number of symbolic vehicles (acts and objects) that may be ramified through a range of specific ceremonial contexts and variously assembled in a number of rituals. As Srinivas (1952:70) states: "Certain ritual acts forming part of the body of ritual repeat themselves constantly." (See also M. Wilson 1957:5.)

In addition, Radcliffe-Brown drew attention to the importance of the contextual method in ritual analysis. An important implication of this method is that while informants' explanations of meanings are critical parts of the anthropological data, the analyst's semantic determinations are to be based not simply on these statements, but on an examination of the sociocultural matrices in which different symbolic elements appear; that is to say, on an examination of cultural usage and not alone on informants' immediate explanations.

By this method the question of symbolic meaning is shifted out of the exclusive realm of the conscious intentions of actors; with the systematic application of contextual analysis "meanings" become chains of culturally patterned associations embedded in symbolic vehicles, or in the lexicon of the cultural code. Therefore, the analysis of meaning requires the examination of the "hooked imageries" of the cultural code.

This point has been well understood in certain types of literary criticism that use a parallel method. For instance, in discussing the relationship between the writer's intentions and the "associational clusters" (nodes of complex meaning focused in particular images) of his production, Kenneth Burke (1957:18) states:

Now the work of every writer contains a set of implicit equations. He uses "associational clusters." And you may, by examining his work, find "what goes with what" in these clusters. . . . And though he be perfectly conscious of . . . selecting a certain kind of imagery to reinforce a certain kind of mood, etc., he cannot possibly be conscious of the interrelationships among all these equations.

In cultural analysis, as in literary analysis, the conscious "intentions" of the actors must be analytically distinguished from the objective system of meanings organized by the symbols that the anthropologist attempts to analyze through a variety of social and cultural data (see also V. Turner 1964a:21f).[14]

SYMBOL "POLYSEMY" AND THE CULTURAL CODE

I have pointed out that the generalizing power of ritual symbolisms lies in their capacity to free a wide range of meanings from their primary matrices in particular situational contexts and to make them into a condensed coinage that can circulate as a social communication. As Victor Turner (1967a:285) has put it, symbols are "quintessential custom."

While Radcliffe-Brown did not emphasize this synthesizing aspect of ritual symbolism, the problem was early highlighted in W. L. Warner's *A Black Civilization* (1958), a study of the north-Australian Murngin. Warner's data on this subject involved a group of

---

[14] This is not to minimize the importance of exegesis as *part* of the data. Moreover, the extent and nature of exegesis available in any given case is an important part of the ethnographer's problem in interpreting the way in which symbols are comprehended and function in the imaginations of their users (in this regard, see Fernandez 1965); his problem is not only what the cultural meanings may be, but also how symbols are "cognized." The contextual method, on the other hand, also makes it possible to probe symbolic meanings where native exegesis is minimal or nonexistent; see, for example, Forge 1966, T. Turner 1969, Westcott and Morton-Williams 1962.

complex ceremonies that Murngin treat as dramatizations of two major myths. Warner showed that certain key events of the myths (which he called "myth symbols") telescoped a range of complex meanings referable to the socionatural order; since each "myth symbol" was reiterated through representation in a variety of ritual acts, this mythic construct could be seen as articulating the ritual action with a wider complex of sociocultural meanings. For example, the myth symbol "the snake swallowing the women," which is central to the myth of the two Wawilak sisters, is expressed by many ritual acts, such as a man jumping from a forked pole, carrying off a circumcision novice, circumcision itself, and a number of others. Warner shows that the mythic event condenses meanings referable to the male age-grading system on the one hand and the seasonal cycle on the other. For instance, the imagery of the snake is meshed, in Murngin thought, with the storms and floods of the rainy season, and consequently with food scarcity, while the two women are associated with the dry season of food plenty; the snake is essentially a male figure and is thus linked with the masculine age-grading system; the women represent feminine sexuality and the uninitiated (outside the masculine age-grading system), etc. The image of the snake swallowing the women condenses the shift from the rainy to the dry season; the social purification of the uninitiated through initiation into the male age-grading system; sexual intercourse; and so on. According to Warner's thesis, these meanings then enter into the ritual through the conscious representation of the myth symbols in the ritual acts and objects.

The particular complexity of the Murngin material derives from the articulation of two types of message systems, those of myth on the one hand and rite on the other. Since the myth provides the native "hermeneutics" for the rites, Warner treats the myth symbol as the fundamental unit programming the links between the ritual action and the underlying complex of cultural meanings. But in actuality, both the myths and the rites are message systems that manipulate a common cultural code of binary oppositions and associational clusters. For instance, in the Wawilak myth, the women's menstrual and afterbirth blood falling into the well arouse the snake, who swallows them and then later vomits them up again. This set of events is one formulation of certain binary oppositions of considerable importance in Murngin thought: water versus blood, male versus female, animal (snake) versus human (women), swallowing (incorporation connected with "insideness") versus vomiting (externalization connected with "outsideness"). Each of these categories also carries complex meanings linked with wider associational clusters and meaning contexts. For example, the snake brings into play the associational cluster of snake-lightning-thunder-flooding, elements linked with the masculine role in sexual intercourse.

Similarly, major scenes in the associated rituals create their messages out of these (and other) major code categories. For instance, in one section of the Gunabibi ceremonies (Warner 1958: 302f) two poles are covered with paper bark and painted with blood drawn from the men's arms; white feathers are attached to the blood and representations of snakes are painted with blood over this background. In the Murngin view, both poles contain the snake's potency, and their dangerousness is attributed to the fact that the snake's "totemic spirit" is "outside of the waterhole" and within the humanly constructed artifact (Warner 1958:305). Men carry the poles into the ceremonial ground, where novices are lying by the side of a crescent-shaped trench representing the female genitals. As the men bring in the poles, novices are told that the snake is coming out of the water and the poles are used to frighten as well as to instruct them.

Here we have a plethora of categories in complex interplay condensed within a few objects and acts: blood/water; red/white; male (poles)/female (trench)/novices (a mediating category between male and female); outside (the water)/inside (the water). The ritual formulation involves the creation of an artifactual snake in which water (the snake) and blood, red (blood) and white (feathers, possibly semen?) are among the categories expressed in the single symbol.

In the myth, female blood mingling with (male) water arouses the snake, who goes outside his waterhole to eat the women. In the ritual, the pole condenses the mingling of blood and water and the emergence of the snake outside his hole into a single symbol; in addition, the bringing of this artifact to the novices represents in action the snake's emergence from the water. The two message systems do not convey identical messages; in addition to the differences of formulation there are certain other critical differences. For instance, in the rite the source of the blood is masculine rather than feminine, and the snake is a humanly controlled artifact, rather than a creature outside human control (the two women of the myth are unable to control the snake). I have argued elsewhere (Munn 1969) that features of this sort are important aspects of the ritual message relating to a wider pattern of reversals that connect the message system of the Wawilak myth to the rituals; these reversals indicate the rites do not simply restate the same meanings as the myth, but in certain respects act upon the myth messages to transform them.

We can see from these brief examples that both the myth and the ritual messages create a specific organization of the Murngin cultural code. In a complex situation such as this, determination of the messages carried by the myth-ritual construct requires analysis of the ways in which each subsystem handles the relevant categories (with their load of meanings) and of the underlying patterns of similarities and differences between the two message systems. Problems of this sort in the relationship between myth and ritual require considerably more exploration in anthropology.[15]

POLYSEMY AND THE "LOGICAL" REINTEGRATION OF MEANING

I should like to turn now to an aspect of symbol semantics that has recently been given a wider airing: the capacity of symbols to channel and reintegrate the meanings referable to specific contexts at a new level of "logical" synthesis. This subject is part of the more general topic of the abstract,

_____

[15] In many instances, the vexed myth-ritual problem is still conceptualized outside anthropology by simplistic generalizations derived largely from the Cambridge school of anthropology with its Frazerian perspectives. For a review and critique of the ritual theories of myth, see Fontenrose 1966. Within anthropology, a number of recent studies have been concerned with Australian aboriginal rite and myth. The most extensive of these is Maddock's (1969) excellent (but at this writing unpublished) thesis on the Jabuduruwa, a northern Australian ritual. Maddock reviews the literature on the myth-ritual problem, and deals directly with the issue of interrelationships between the two message systems. Stanner's (n.d.) earlier study of Murinbata (northwestern Australian) initiation myth and rite set an important precedent for studies such as Maddock's, although it leaves much to be desired in terms of method. In addition to my restudy of Warner's Murngin material (Munn 1969), in which I set up a model relating the Wawilak myth and rites, Layton (1970) has attempted a brief review of some of the Murngin data that asks questions about the myth-ritual relationship. The problem is also raised by Leach (1972).

logical functions of concrete, qualitative imageries (Lévi-Strauss 1966).

To exemplify one way in which this sort of reorganization may take place I shall draw upon Victor Turner's (1967a) description of the forked branch used in ancestral shrines associated with Ndembu hunting ritual. Turner discusses the multiple meanings of this symbol in some detail, and I can comment here on only a small part of them, so my account is much simplified. The Ndembu forked-branch shrines are dedicated to hunter ancestors by a man who wishes to ensure good luck in hunting. The branch is tied with a plait of grass and a termitary is placed at its base. All the meanings carried by the object itself (irrespective of the Ndembu names for it, which also convey related meanings) refer to desirable qualities in the hunting situation. For example, the grass connotes the fact that the animals hide in the grass while the hunter stalks them. The grass plait is meant to bring about the reverse situation: to prevent the animals from becoming invisible. The termitary is connected with the burial of hunters, who are laid with small termitaries at their heads. Dome-shaped termitaries found in the woods and plains have phallic meaning, and the ants swarming over them convey procreation (the hunter's kill is a masculine form of procreation in Ndembu thought). In addition, properties such as the whiteness of the wood and the sharpness of the prongs carry meanings referring to perceptual qualities: for example, whiteness refers to pureness, clearness (something visible and known), and the sharp prongs convey the hunter's desired sharpness of perception in spotting game. Whiteness also has other meanings, such as seminal fluid.

We can see from all this not only that the forked-branch shrine is a kind of semantic bundle that ties together various categories, each with its complex meanings drawn from varied domains of experience, but that the bundle has an internal patterning involving redundancy: certain meanings overlap others, and these overlaps construct generalized themes, abstract meanings, which emerge implicitly through reiteration at the concrete level. Thus the sharp prongs, the grass plait, and the whiteness of the wood convey messages about visibility, each giving a slightly different or complementary perspective on this common theme. For instance, the reference to the hunter's acuity of vision (the prongs) is the reciprocal of the desired visibility of the animal (the grass). Similarly, the hunter's fertility (equivalent to his luck in killing game) is conveyed by the white symbolism (seminal fluid) and by the termitaries. We might diagram this pattern as follows:

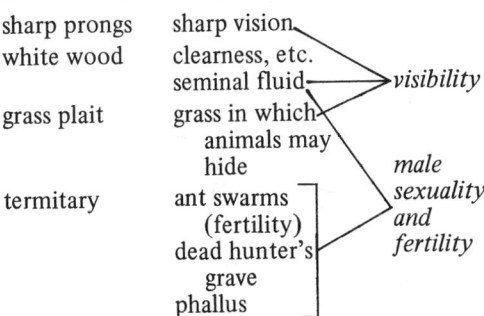

Through patterning of the various specific meanings, the shrine communicates more general notions (male fertility and visibility); both of these themes, as Turner tells us, are important Ndembu values.[16]

---

[16] V. Turner has discussed the pervasiveness of these and other related themes in Ndembu ritual symbolism. As he points out (n.d.:25), "Not every referent of a symbol . . . may be the plenary expression of a theme, but may only convey one aspect or phase of it. The full expression of that theme may only be expressed by a number of symbols, either in

It is notable that some of the symbol vehicles (the termitary and the grass plait) are drawn directly from the situational contexts to which they refer: they are, in effect, "pieces" or metonymic parts of those contexts. In this respect the bonds between symbolic reorganization and the concrete situations are especially tightly maintained, since the Ndembu hunter is presented with objects drawn *directly* from these contexts. Yet at the same time these situational meanings can be seen as reorganized in the context of the shrine into more abstract meanings. As Lévi-Strauss (1966:178f) has stressed, the poising of iconic symbolisms between the concrete and the abstract is central to the affective-cognitive potency of this type of communication.

In their synthesizing capacities ritual symbols are among the mechanisms through which a "second order objectivation of meaning" (Berger and Luckmann 1967:92)—i.e., an objectivation relating lower-level orderings of meaning into higher-level integrations—takes place. Second-order objectivations make lower-level ones "subjectively plausible" to the individual—they put them together into coherent frames. Integration making for increased plausibility or meaningful order can then be fed back into the more specific operative levels of daily action. As, indeed, it is the aim of the Ndembu hunting shrine to ensure the hunter's luck, the shrine feeds back symbolically reintegrated experience into the particular pragmatic operations of hunting to which the symbols refer. This feature is, as we shall see later, an important aspect of the instrumental effectiveness of symbols.

In sum, the condensation of meanings within the vehicles of symbolic action creates the communicative economy and generalizing power of ritual, putting a multiplicity of meanings into social circulation in manageable form. But accounts of multiple meanings do not exhaust the semantic problem; indeed, they constitute no more than the ethnographic beginning of analysis. Not only are meanings structured in the cultural code, but in addition, the message system organizes the categories into particular arrangements within the context of social action. The creativity or "productivity" of ritual symbols with respect to the wider culture lies in their varied manipulation of the cultural code according to implicit principles and requirements of the message system.

SYMBOLIC INSTRUMENTATION

Symbolic instrumentation—the connection of ritual symbols with specific aims and immediate imperatives in the sociopsychological situations of the actors—was treated by classical anthropological theory as "magic," an irrational or mistaken means of attempting to achieve specified ends that presupposed a false relation of identity or substance between symbols and the objects to which they refer. In this view the instrumental use of symbols assumes "that things act on each other through a secret sympathy, the impulse being transmitted from one to the other by means of what we may conceive as a sort of invisible ether" (Frazer 1905: 40). Anthropologists and others interested in symbolism presumed that behind magical behavior lay a particular set of false semantic presuppositions constituting the core of a magicomythical world view. As the philosopher Ernst Cassirer (1955:67f) put it:

... for myth every perceptible similarity is

---

discrete clusters or dispersed through the whole ritual system. As a corollary, any given symbol may represent a semantic complex made up of partial expressions of a variety of themes."

an immediate expression of an identity of *essence*. This similarity is never a mere concept of relation . . . but is a real force. . . . All so-called analogy magic–i.e., homeopathic magic that works through likenesses–reveals this basic mythical view . . . but where we see a mere relation, myth sees immediate existence and presence.

Much of this earlier concern with the instrumental uses of symbols focused on actions that appeared to be aimed at bringing about changes in the physical world, such as aiding crop growth, curing, killing, and so on. Theories of magic were not concerned with the instrumentation in symbolic acts such as marriage and initiation rites, which aim at changing social statuses. However, all symbolic action is instrumental with respect to some class of ends, and the general theory that accounts for instrumentation in one sphere must encompass the others as well.

Current anthropological studies of symbolic instrumentation suggest another hypothesis to take the place of the outdated earlier assumptions. These studies (for example, Douglas 1966: 58f; Geertz 1966; Lévi-Strauss 1967, chap. 10); Fernandez 1967; Lienhardt 1961; Munn 1969; Peacock 1968; Tambiah 1968; V. Turner 1967*b*) point to the view that symbolic acts operate through their capacity to map changed or adjusted perceptions of the possibilities inherent in a situation onto the actor's orientation to it. In other words, ritual action influences the actor's experience of immediate aspects of his situation by creating messages that reconstruct them in a manner modeling the problem and/or the desired ends. Societies variously define the classes of ends for which symbolic action is deemed useful, but no special preconceptions about the nature of the sign-meaning relationship are necessarily implied in the use of symbols to achieve any of these ends. Rather, as Tambiah

(1968) has stressed, certain semantic principles inherent in linguistic operations generally are all that need be presupposed by the instrumental use of symbols.

In general, the effectiveness of symbols derives from the properties I have discussed as intrinsic to symbolic action: (1) the iconicity of the symbol vehicles (these properties make it possible for symbols to present images or expressive plans of desired ends in direct sensual form rather than merely to make statements *about* them); (2) the actualization of the cultural code of shared meanings in forms external to the subjective experience of the individual; i.e., as parts of objective events within the level of action.

Ritual symbols release the relevant shared meanings embedded in the cultural code into the level of ongoing social process; through this objectification they can come to "work back" upon the individual imagination with the authority of external reality. The individual's experience of the situation is to be reordered through the mobilization of shared cultural meanings in iconic plans or "models" and the synthesis of these imaginative forms with the pragmatics of objective social process and immediate reality.

TROBRIAND RITUAL

In his discussion of Trobriand spells, Tambiah (1968:188) asserts that "primitive magic is based on true relational metaphorical thinking." He suggests that the spells transfer desired qualities to the yam garden through the use of metaphorical likenesses and metonymic reconstructions.

In the Trobriand garden spell that asserts (Malinowski 1935:98):

> The belly of my garden grows to the
> size of a bush hen's nest . . .

The belly of my garden grows like an
ant hill . . .

we can see metaphoric processes at
work verbally transferring to the garden
the swelling form characteristic of
other objects and domains, such as the
bush hen's nest and the ant hill (see
also Munn 1971). The desired growth
of yams in the garden is directly pictured in the spell. Metonymic procedures are exemplified by Trobriand
prosperity magic, which aims to "anchor"[17] the yam house and the village.
Spells for this anchoring repeatedly assert that each part of the house (the cor-
nerstone, the floor, the gables, and so
on) shall be anchored. It is as if the
house were being constructed from the
ground up with the desired property. In
both instances we see how the imagery
of the spells symbolically reorganizes
the situation along the lines desired: a
plan of what the garden or house structure "should" be like is created and
used as part of the actual procedures of
planting and house building. As Malinowski himself recognized, the spells
"forecast the images of the wished-for
results" (1954:80).

Metonymy also operates in the selection of material vehicles that accompany the verbal spell; the spell is, in
effect, secreted within these vehicles by
the ritual specialist. For instance, soil
from a bush hen's nest may be brought
into contact with an adze utilized in
the garden planting as the magician re-
cites, "The belly of my garden grows to
the size of a bush hen's nest" (Tambiah
1968:194). Tambiah suggests that this
procedure gives "an air of operational
reality" to the "mental comparison" of

the verbal spell, but one may perhaps
phrase this idea more strongly: by this
means the verbal symbolism is entered
precisely into the technological nexus
of material acts and physical chains of
relationships involved in gardening. The
immediate, pragmatic problems of gardening are thus infused with the wider
cultural meanings and premises covered
by the symbols.

The Trobriand garden symbolism
may be compared with the visual assemblage of the Ndembu hunting shrine
discussed earlier. The hunting shrine also presents an image of the desired ends
(good luck in hunting) through its condensation symbolism. Basic mechanisms of redundancy, metaphor, and
metonymy are variously utilized in
both symbolic forms. In both cases, the
ritual specialists are, in effect, "constructing an image of the environment,
running the model faster than the environment, and predicting that the environment will behave as the model
does" (Galanter and Gerstenhaber,
quoted in Geertz 1964:61).

Native users themselves may explicitly recognize the essential importance
of the metaphoric ingredients to the
effectiveness of the spells. Fortune
(1963:125f) reports that a Dobuan discussing spells for keeping yams anchored in the gardens explained to him,
"We compare one thing to another";
the yams (which Dobuans regard as
"people") are expected to hear these
comparisons and act accordingly. Similarly, the highland New Guinea
Mbowamb (Strathern and Strathern
1968:180f) explain that they "call
upon" certain objects with the desired
qualities to achieve their ends through
spells. "The purpose of this calling-
upon is explained in terms of similes:
e.g., 'as the white marsupial gleams so
the man's skin will shine. . . .' The
more successful the person is at saying

[17] Anchoring is compared to "taking deep root"
and "being like an immovable rock" (Malinowski
1935:22). Like other elements in the spells, anchoring codes a complex of multiple meanings (see Munn
1971).

spells, the more elaborate and imaginative his imagery."

CURING

In symbolic curing, a reconstruction of disturbed situations is made by operations with models that mobilize fundamental cultural meanings; here the situation to which the symbols apply is the patient's body rather than an inanimate object, as in the previous example.

Symbolic curing involves a double procedure: models of disorder are created through a diagnosis defining the symbolic arena of the curer's operation. These models relocate the patient's suffering in external images and events that, as Lévi-Strauss (1967:189f) has suggested, are variously equated (e.g., by metaphor) with the individual's own body and person. Such images provide an expressive cultural "language" for suffering which formulate the patient's experience in objective terms that at the same time refer back to the body and the self.

For example, the highland Maya of Zinacantan (Vogt and Vogt 1970) diagnose illness as due both to soul loss and to a correlative dislocation of the patient's "animal companion" from his corral in the sacred mountain where he is watched over by the ancestors. It is said that the animal has gotten out of its corral and is wandering on the dangerous, wild slopes of the mountains, where it might be killed. Since the animal companion is a kind of alter ego that was born at precisely the same time as his human counterpart (Vogt and Vogt 1970:382), there is a built-in equation of the symbolic imagery with the subject's own person. What happens to the individual happens also to his animal companion (and vice versa). In addition, the image of the animal safe within its corral connotes the safety of the individual within the family: "the ancestral deities' role in the 'corraling' and 'embracing' [guarding] of his wild animal spirit companion . . . is comparable to the 'embracing' of a child by his parents and to the controlling of an individual's unruly behavior by the social rules in Zinacanteco society" (Vogt and Vogt 1970:389). In this respect, the animal companion, corral, and ancestor symbolism provides a recasting of personal experience at the cosmic-symbolic level.

We may observe, however, that in this instance, the negative symbolic programming of experience occurs in the message forms of myth rather than ritual (see my definition of myth in note 2). The second part of the curative process then involves the readjustment or transformation of the disorder in the "mythic" sphere through beneficial ritual action undertaken by the curer with other members of the community. I shall not discuss these rites, but merely point out that by these means the animal companion is returned to its corral and so to the zone of safety, where it is guarded by the ancestors. The illness is "cured" through a ritual reordering of terms in the symbolic programming of the illness in myth (hence a reordering of the patient's subjective experience).[18]

As in much symbolic curing, *zinacanteco* illness is ultimately ascribed to the patient's conflicts with other members of the community or failure to conform to social norms: these con-

---

[18] Symbolic curing need not necessarily use the vehicle of myth in the sense in which I have defined it, but when it does, the problem falls into the wider category of myth-ritual relationships (see note 15). The programming of disturbance or disorder in the mythic sphere and its reorganization through ritual action appear to be a widespread pattern, which needs further investigation and analysis.

flicts are the primary cause of the ancestors' anger, which makes it possible for the animal companion to get out of the corral. Conflict resolution is therefore one of the implicit aims of the cure.

This feature of symbolic curing has been abundantly illustrated by Victor Turner's accounts of Ndembu rites of affliction; here the explicit aims of the rites are the alleviation not only of the patient's illness, but also of specific social disturbances in the community. In his case study of an Ndembu doctor at work, Turner (1967b) demonstrates how the political troubles of a community can become symbolically focused in the illness of a member of the community, while, conversely, the individual's own psychosocial conflicts can find their social projection in the specific structure of community disturbances. Turner's conclusion sums up the process through which the patient's illness becomes the medium of social purification (1967b:392):

It seems that the Ndembu "doctor" sees his task less as curing an individual patient than as remedying the ills of a corporate group. The sickness of a patient is mainly a sign that "something is rotten" in the corporate body. The patient will not get better until all the tensions and aggressions in the group's interrelations have been brought to light and exposed to ritual treatment. . . . The doctor's task is to tap the various streams of affect associated with these conflicts . . . and to channel them in a socially positive direction. The raw energies of conflict are thus domesticated in the service of the traditional social order. Once the various causes of ill feeling against the patient . . . and of his ill feeling against others had been "made visible" . . . the doctor . . . was able, through the cultural mechanism of *Ihamba,* with its bloodlettings, confessions, purifications, prayers to the traditional dead, tooth drawings and build-up of expectations to transform the ill feeling into well wishing.

From the perspective of the community, the curer's diagnosis, consisting primarily in the identification of the particular ancestral shade that has caused the affliction, symbolically locates a source of general political distress in terms that focus it in an individual illness. The patient himself functions as a symbol, a scapegoat for political troubles, and indeed, the curing has in part the air of a sacrifice (consider, for example, the bloodlettings). (In sacrifice, as we shall see later, the victim may also condense disordering meanings that the sacrificial process dissolves.)

From the perspective of the patient, on the other hand, Turner shows that the particular ancestral shade that is diagnosed as causing the trouble provides a social condensation point for personality problems faced by this particular individual. The curative process provides him with an external, social medium for the symbolic resolution of these problems.

In this example, Turner provides us with evidence suggesting more than a culturally defined linkage of the symbolic definitions of illness with the body or person of the patient; he convincingly marshals evidence from the patient's life history that suggests how, in this particular case, the specific diagnosis appears to provide a projective system for the patient's intrapsychic conflicts. In a more general sense, the paper raises the fundamental question of how cultural symbol systems may function in any given instance as projective systems for individual concerns and unconscious conflicts.

The Ndembu study also points to the fact that symbolic action focusing on the solution of one type of problem (here individual illness) may be linked to wider concerns with the regulation or transformation of relationships in the sociopolitical sphere. Indeed, it seems possible that much symbolic action that has as its proximal aim action upon some specific physical situation or object has distal aims that refer to the sociopolitical sphere. Tambiah (1968:201f) argues this point in connection with the Trobriand magic for anchoring yam storehouses:

The Trobriand logic is that a rite conducted realistically to make the storehouse endure is really a metaphoric analogy urging the human belly to restrain its hunger and greed for food. It is the belly that "hears" and "understands" the rite which is externally performed on an inanimate object. ... Thus it is possible to argue that all ritual, whatever the idiom, is addressed to the human participants ...

From this perspective it becomes clear that symbolic acts in which the proximal aims refer directly to the psycho-social and/or socio-political spheres, such as, for example, rites of passage like marriage, cult initiation, and installation in office, are simply one end of a continuum with symbolic actions that have proximal aims referring to the physical order. In rites of passage like initiation, for instance, the aim is to transform the publicly recognized social identity or status of the individual and at the same time to pin the transformation to the individual's own sense of personal identity (Schwartz and Merten 1968, V. Turner 1964a). The symbolic mechanisms are similar to those I have already discussed. For example, in certain parts of the contemporary American high school sorority rituals described by Schwartz and Merten (1968), the pledges are required to wear clothes reflecting the kind of gaucherie associated by these girls with "hoodies," young people whom they regard as social undesirables. Dressed in such garb, the novices undergo ridicule and mockery. The ini-

tiation thus includes the creation of public images or models of what one should *not be* in order to become a sorority member, and these images of "negative identity" are then symbolically detached from the novice through mockery and humiliation. Later the novice is publicly identified with the desired social behavior in the final candlelight ceremonies. Since the girl has been chosen as a pledge because sorority members feel she has the potential for becoming a "socie," the ritual action objectivates this potential to herself and the other girls by giving external form to both negative and positive social identities, separating the novice from one and identifying her with the other.

In sum, whether we are dealing with rites of passage, curing, or rituals of garden growth, symbolic action achieves its ends through its capacity to create expressive-iconic models within which the restructuring of a situation can take place. Both negative and positive models may be created; in the beneficial rites we have discussed, the negative images are dissolved or transformed through the ritual process.

CODE LOGIC AND RITUAL MODALITIES: ASPECTS OF ORDER AND DISORDER

As I have indicated, the cultural code manipulated in ritual action is logically patterned. Symbol analysis must take this logic into account without reducing the study of ritual action to that of cultural systems of thought.

A relatively early isolated work pointing in this direction is Gregory Bateson's (1958) *Naven*, which first appeared in 1936.[19] Bateson developed

---

[19] Rassers' (1959) *Panji the Culture Hero*, which first appeared in Dutch in 1925, is another early

the notion of "cultural structure" as part of his attempt to create frameworks for explaining the sex reversals of Iatmul congratulatory rituals (the "Naven" ceremonies of the title). He defined "cultural structure" as "a term for the coherent 'logical' scheme which may be constructed by the scientist, fitting together the various premises of the culture" (1958:25). By "premise" it appears that Bateson meant a standardized role relationship or the cultural conception of that relationship; therefore the categories to which he is referring are confined to the social domain.[20]

In applying the idea of "cultural structure" to the interpretation of Naven ceremonies, Bateson is concerned with the logical scheme of oppositions between certain Iatmul role relationships; he saw these oppositions as providing a partial explanation for some features of the clothing reversals in the rites. For example, he sums up the "father-child" and "mother-child" (mother's brother-sister's child) relationships by contrasting the competitive character of the former with the noncompetitive character of the latter. Since an individual's notable acts are regarded as the achievements or triumphs of his mother and her patrilineal clan, the individual and his mother's brother cannot be considered to compete with each other (Bateson 1958:48).

Bateson then used this logical opposition as part of his explanation as to why a youth's maternal male relatives (actually, classificatory maternal kin) are Naven congratulators, who put on feminine attire for the occasion: i.e., congratulation comes from maternal kin and is epitomized by the attributes of the mother-child relation; hence the mother's brother takes on feminine role behavior to congratulate a youth. Although Bateson's account is inchoate, it points to the necessity of examining a logical organization of cultural concepts in order to interpret ritual symbolism such as the sex-role reversals of Naven ceremonies.

OPPOSITIONS AND THEIR MEDIATION

In recent ritual studies, concern with the internal logic of the cultural code has become a distinctive trend (e.g., Beidelman 1966a, 1966b, 1968; Cunningham 1964; Douglas 1957, 1966; Leach 1964; Peacock 1967; Rigby 1968; Strathern and Strathern 1968; V. Turner 1966). The focal interest of many of these studies, however, is not simply the code logic as such, but rather the connection between it and experiences of order and disorder, safety and danger, purity and pollution, etc.

Thus, Douglas (1957; 1966:167f) explains the Lele use of the pangolin as a sacrificial animal by examining Lele categories pertaining to man-animal relationships. The pangolin is found to combine attributes distinctive of opposed categories in the cosmology: those of forest creatures as opposed to creatures of the streams; those of humans as opposed to animals. As a paradoxical combination of attributes from all these spheres, it constitutes both a disordering anomaly and a means of mediation between the opposed categories. The sacrifice and consumption of the pangolin in ritual operates, in Douglas' view (1966:167), as a kind of

---

study that attempts to deal with symbolic action in terms relating it to a pattern of logical oppositions in the sociocultural code.

[20] Actually, Bateson deals only with kin and descent categories in this way; his treatment of sex roles, for instance, is subsumed under another model. Despite the many shortcomings of this study, it is still in my estimation one of the most stimulating and suggestive books on ritual symbolism available. In the present commentary I treat only a small part of it.

revitalization process in which a "hybrid monster, which in secular life one would expect them to abhor, is reverently eaten by initiates and taken to be the most powerful source of fertility. . . . That which is rejected is ploughed back for a renewal of life."

The ritual function of the pangolin is to be explained, then, on the basis of its disturbing relationship to the boundary-building properties of the cultural code. Both creative potency and danger may be ascribed to phenomena that are anomalous. As we shall see, sacrifice can provide a way of utilizing and at the same time dissolving such potent but dangerous condensations.

Beidelman's ritual studies are also pivoted on the relation of categorical patterning to ritual operations. In defining ritual as a "manipulation of symbolic objects from . . . various categories" (1966a:387), he states that ritual manipulations take "two antithetical forms: (1) a mixing or confounding of categories which is both potent and dangerous . . . (2) a separation out, a reordering or check upon the existing order of categories, which should be kept apart" (1966a:388).

During the Swazi Incwala, for example, the king is treated with various medicines that make him into a symbol of extreme potency: at the finale he emerges fantastically costumed, wearing black plumes over his head and face, with a lion-skin headband under the feathers; his body is covered with green grass; parts of the sacrificial ox are attached to him, and he also wears a silver monkey skin. These and other objects attached to his body create a mixture of categories (black-green, ox-monkey-lion, etc., each with complex meanings in Swazi culture), and the mixture in the Swazi view is one of great potency, danger, and "darkening" (Beidelman 1966a:389). To return the king to his ordinary state, he must be purged of this complexity, an end achieved in part by discarding the demonic costume and hurling away a green gourd (acts of separation that detach these objects from the body of the king and so separate the categories they represent from each other again).

Beidelman's approach differs from Douglas' in that he conceives of a dynamic relationship between the code structure and the ritual process. The latter appears as the operational mode through which the static category oppositions of the cultural code are transformed, dissolved, or maintained. Similarly, in his analysis of Nuer concepts of nakedness and nudity, Beidelman (1968:127) views Nuer ritual prohibitions on nakedness as attempts "to control and restrict the powerful processes by which objects and persons may pass from one . . . categorization to another, be transformed and thus jeopardize the categorical identities and values and norms attached to themselves." Conversely, Nuer "prescriptions for nudity" (as, for instance, during a rite of passage) are "concerned with the temporary dissolution of such categorization so that some new ordering may be achieved" (1968:130). Beidelman relates both types of regulation to "a more basic sociological problem, viz. the institutionalized processes by which persons symbolically define their social categories."

Ritual reversals, such as, for example, sex-role reversals, have also been discussed from the perspective of the binary "logic" of the cultural code (see especially the recent discussion of Gluckman's [1954, 1963:17f] interpretation of reversal: Beidelman 1966a, Ortiz 1971, Rigby 1968). On the basis of an anlysis of bipolar classifications in Gogo thought, Rigby (1968:169f) argues that certain Gogo rituals in which women take the roles of men symbolically reverse a disturbed temporal state back to its normal, ordered condition. In this case, the ritual manipulation of the sex-role categories, involving the creation of a symbolic disorder through role reversal, is seen as a mechanism for reversing temporal disorder (itself a "reversed" temporal state). In this view, these rites fall in line with much ritual designed to deal with disturbance: disordering symbolism is employed in the process of dispelling disorder and renewing the sense of an ordered state of existence.

In general, then, the questions raised here have to do with the governance of experiences of order and disorder, power and danger, etc., through the ritual manipulation of category oppositions in the cultural code. Beidelman in particular implies that symbolic governance of these experiences is effected through the ritual dissolution, reorganization, or maintenance of boundaries set out in the code.

These contemporary concerns with category polarization and anomaly, while most immediately derived from the ideas of Lévi-Strauss, are continuous with the general notion of boundary mediation that has been a persistent basis for model building in the anthropology of ritual. The sources of what I shall call the boundary mediation model lie in the nineteenth-century concepts of taboo and related ideas of the sacred as a bounded, prohibited space demarcated from its profane surroundings, which Durkheim developed into his theory of an underlying category opposition between the sacred and the profane.

We find in work as early as that of Fustel de Coulanges, for instance, the concept of a sacred area isolated and prohibited to strangers;[21] the group itself is conceived of as a kind of isolated monad with its internal relationships ordered by religion and unity, its external ones defined negatively by strangerhood and exclusion. Hence Fustel (1956:42f) prefigures Van Gennep's later "rites of passage" schema in his interpretation of marriage ritual as a process of separating the bride from her paternal sacred hearth and incorporating her into the sacred hearth of her husband; i.e., the marriage ritual effects a transition across otherwise closed sociospatial boundaries.

SACRIFICE

The earliest application of the boundary mediation model as a framework for describing the underlying structure of a ritual process appears to be in Hubert and Mauss's (1964:97) analysis of sacrifice as a "procedure [which] consists in establishing a means of communication between the sacred and profane worlds through. . . . a victim, that is, a thing that is in the course of the ceremony destroyed." Hubert and Mauss stress the necessary separation of the two spheres (men and gods, profane and sacred), for through their mingling, the power of the gods would destroy men. As a result, the transaction necessary to adjust the relationship between the two spheres must take place through the creation of a mediating entity that condenses elements from both categories in itself and is destroyed in the sacrificial

---

21 The sacred area viewed as subject to prohibition is set apart—in this sense, taboo. See Steiner's (1956:87f) account of Frazer's 1875 essay on taboo for the *Encyclopaedia Britannica*: "Frazer then describes Polynesian *tabu*. First he gives the etymology . . . *ta* to mark; *pu*, adverb of intensity, hence *taboo*: something marked thoroughly. . . . It is by this etymology that he can say that the 'vow of the Nazarite . . . presents the closest resemblance to the Polynesian taboo,' for it means 'one separated or consecrated'—precisely the meaning of taboo. Then he tries to elucidate the meaning of *tabu* by showing its relation to the concept of *noa*. Here he falls into the very common error . . . of regarding *noa* as 'profane' and thus as opposed to 'sacred' and 'taboo.'"

process. The sacrifice paradoxically brings together by keeping apart, and in this way safely opens the circuits for a transaction.

The interstitial properties of the sacrifice may be illustrated from the accounts of Nuer sacrifice (Evans-Pritchard 1956, Beidelman 1966*b*). Evans-Pritchard (1956:202 and *passim*) discusses the close identification of Nuer cattle with men, and suggests that Nuer oxen (the ox being the "sacrificial animal *par excellence*") are connected with masculine identity. During a sacrifice an ox is consecrated to the god, so that the sacrificer (who is always a man) and the deity are united in the ox. The death of the beast adjusts the relationship, ensuring that the dangerous potency of the deities will be kept apart from the human sphere.

Nuer distinguish between two broad cosmic categories: "creation" (the material world) and "spirit" (deity). Building on the significance of this category opposition, Beidelman (1966*b*) has recently expanded the analysis of the interstitial qualities of the Nuer ox, and examined the significance of its castration. He concluded that the desexing of the sacrifice expresses the ideal moral order with its locus in the domain of spirit, since for Nuer, sexuality embodies the "ambiguity of human actions, their vitality, but also their tendency toward morbid conflict" (1966*b*: 462). In addition, he points to the association of spirit with the lineal continuity of agnatic relationship, and creation (sexuality) with uterine relationships. In this view, Nuer sacrifice is transacted through the death of a beast that combines the sacrificer's sexuality with the agnatic ideal of social order; the destruction of the ox separates out the material, "created" aspect of the sexual self (Beidelman 1966*b*:465): "In the spearing of an ox a Nuer expresses a kind of transfiguration, through im-molation of his sexual self and an anticipation of his own transformation, through death, which his own living domestic, sexual self cannot wholly be and, indeed, cannot wholly accept."

Nuer man is, so to speak, caught on the horns of a dilemma: he must somehow synthesize the disordering aspect of the "created," sexual being, involving uterine and domestic loyalties, with the ideal ordering of the norms and bonds of agnation. Only death can resolve the dilemma and release the contradictory life composition. The sacrificial victim, like the sacrificer himself, embodies this contradiction, and therefore its death symbolically dissolves it. It would seem that Nuer sacrifice not only enables a Nuer man "to see a dimension of his own subjectivity" (as Geertz [1972:28] has put it in referring to the Balinese cockfight), but also to "see" the way in which this subjectivity is bound up with the objective social order.

In any given case, Nuer sacrifice is set in motion by a particular disturbance such as illness, drought, etc., regarded by Nuer as due to the intrusion of spirit into the created order (Evans-Pritchard 1956:275 and *passim*; Beidelman 1966*b*:454). The sacrifice of the victim, an icon of the problematic state betwixt and between, functions to establish anew the separation of the two spheres. Thus a disturbance or affliction, interpreted as a breakdown in boundaries between major cosmic spheres set out in the cultural code, initiates the sacrificial process; this process both expresses and destroys disorder by separating the spheres and yielding a temporary resolution of disturbance (redemption and reordering).

Here we see, from a different perspective, symbolic processes similar to those discussed earlier, in the section on "Symbolic Instrumentation." The sacrificial action synthesizes the specific disturbances referable to particular events and individual biographies with nonspecific, pervasive contradictions inherent in the Nuer life situation, encapsulated in the sacrificial symbolism. This synthesis makes it possible to dissolve disorder at different levels (the individual or unique and the sociocultural), and to act on a particular problem by bringing to bear upon it the sociocultural meanings built up in Nuer life situations.

PASSAGE

Probably the best known early use of the boundary mediation model is Van Gennep's (1960) *Les rites de passage*, introduced in 1909.[22] Van Gennep saw the dynamic processes of ritual and social life as if they were projected on a stage set of static social and temporal categorizations yielding fixed boundaries much like "a house divided into rooms and corridors" (1960:26). The dynamism of life processes requires transition across the boundaries (e.g., from one status to another, from one temporal category or phase to another, etc.); this can be effected primarily by ritual action that dramatizes transition and thus articulates the various life processes requiring change with the static, positional ordering of sociocultural categories. In effect, ritual is seen as a kind of adjustive procedure for settling the disturbance caused by the diachronic play of life as change or movement across the backdrop of a structurally compartmented sociocultural space. Van Gennep recognized that the ritual acts did not merely shift the individual or group from one category to another, but in themselves were expressive, symbolic enactments of the transformations. He generalized the mean-

ings of this passage symbolism in his well-known schema, "separation," "transition," and "incorporation," suggesting, for instance, that symbolic acts such as washing express separation, others like crossing doorways express transition, and acts such as sharing meals express incorporation (1960: 20).[23]

Recently V. Turner (1964*a*, 1969*b*) has again drawn attention to the symbolism of the interstitial phase, suggesting that bizarre imageries associated with this phase in initiation ceremonies are related on the one hand to the novice's interstitial status and on the other to the socialization process central to this transitional phase. Thus the state of the novice himself may be metaphorically assimilated to basic biological processes such as death (the imagery of corpses and dissolution) and birth (the imagery of gestation and bodily reconstitution). These physiological images may express the state of the novice as, respectively, "no longer classified" and "not yet classified" (1964*a*: 6). Similarly, novices may be regarded as "either sexless or ambisexual" or "as undifferentiated raw material" (1964*a*: 18). Through these and related imageries the novice himself becomes a symbol of transition, condensing anomalous attributes.

In addition, participants' senses may be flooded with various symbolic representations displaying contradictory categories combined within a single image (for example, mixtures of the human and nonhuman), or distorted representations of ordinary phenomena. Turner (1964*a*:14f) suggests that

---

[22] For recent commentaries on Van Gennep, see Gluckman 1962, Goody 1962, Kimball 1960.

[23] Van Gennep recognizes the possible context dependence of these general meanings (i.e., that a particular rite might mean separation in one context, incorporation in another; see Van Gennep 1960:24, 166), but he also suggests that certain rites tend toward one type of meaning rather than the other (e.g., Van Gennep 1960:54-55).

these disturbing images cause the novice to reflect on aspects of life experience by reducing familiarity and creating surprising paradoxes that lift experience out of its ordinary molds and reassemble it in a novel fashion.

Similarly, Crumrine (1969:18f) has recently hypothesized (following the psychological studies of Berlyne) that the stimulus ambiguity and complexity of images created by impersonators such as the ritual clowns of the Mexican Mayo, whose masks and behavior contradict or reverse norms of everyday life, may arouse curiosity and conflict, causing the individual to refocus on the norms themselves.

A further attempt to build on Van Gennep's ritual framework is Leach's (1961) account of ritual sequence as a mechanism ordering time into a "discontinuity of repeated contrasts" (1961:134). According to Leach's argument, time is ritually segmented by a sequence of contrasting role behaviors arranged in binary pairs: formality of dress and behavior (with its emphasis on status differentiation) and masquerade (which disguises "social personality") appear in the ritual phases of separation and incorporation; role reversals (transvestitism, sacrilege, and so on) appear in the transitional phase, and are in binary opposition to the secular roles of nonritual time. Since either formality or masquerade will be succeeded by transitional or secular behavior, there are two possible sequential chains: secular roles—formality—role reversal—masquerade—secular roles, or secular roles—masquerade—role reversal—formality, etc. Although Leach does not develop the point, his scheme implies that two interlocking cycles—a temporal alternation of pairs and an alternation of the terms of each pair—form the underlying, abstract structure of ritual time.

One of the difficulties with this over-ly simplified but suggestive scheme is that role reversal and even formality often involve masquerade; thus the three modes do not constitute mutually exclusive categories. Nevertheless, the model has interest because it points to the conception of ritual process as a temporal ordering of experience into repetitive segments.

TABOO

The concept of taboo was one of the notions fundamental to the boundary mediation model developed in the anthropology of ritual. Taboos, of course, are prohibitions that do not mediate boundaries, but ritually maintain them. They assert the necessity of separation, inhibition, or regulative control in the form of a prohibition (temporary or permanent) on possible or feasible acts, or on communication (as, for instance, through contact or incorporation) between an actor and certain phenomena in his social field (see Leach 1964; Rappaport 1968:208). Thus taboos artificially place aspects of the environment, or certain relationships, under an "embargo of impossibility" (Freud 1950:27).

A taboo commonly consists of two parts: a type of action or relationship that is prohibited (e.g., eating or touching) and an object of the action (e.g., particular foods that are not to be eaten). Certain types of acts are common taboo media: these are the fundamental points of anchorage for the body in the external environment—for example, eating and sexual intercourse; speaking and acts of perception (seeing, hearing, touching). As Steiner (1956: 116) has put it in his commentary on rites of passage, "the greater number of taboos are indeed concerned with the various delimitations of our spheres and boundaries . . . with the passings of things into the body and out of it; they guard the body's orifices." By mapping control in the fundamental transactions between the body and the external physical world, such taboos express the necessity of developing an interior self-control in which the individual will or desire is subordinated to social will or authority (see Fortes 1967:11, who defines taboo as "authoritative command-ment that is internalized"). From this perspective, taboo appears as the symbolic modality epitomizing the categorical imperative; i.e., taboos provide the fundamental social forms for the communication of this imperative.

Recently, Douglas (1966) has considered taboos on body emissions like blood and semen from the perspective of their relationship to body boundaries; in addition, as an offshoot of Lévi-Strauss' (1963, 1966) studies of totemism and animal categories, much recent attention has turned to taboos focused on animals, especially food taboos. In these latter studies (e.g., Douglas 1957, 1966; Leach 1964; Tambiah 1969), attempts have been made to explain the reason for a particular taboo focus by reference to the classifications of animals in the cultural code. Here again the notions of anomaly, disorder, and "matter out of place" have played important parts.

In her influential commentary on Leviticus, Douglas (1966:41f) has suggested that the creatures that were the focus of Hebrew food taboos had attributes that made them anomalous with respect to the prevailing category system. For example, pigs are anomalous because they have some but not all of the critical attributes of ungulates (see also the earlier example drawn from the Lele). In this view, the appropriateness of these food prohibitions as moral symbols is explained as a way of keeping moral order through keeping logical order in the universe. One literally "keeps out" (prohibits the incor-

poration of) those things that connote disorder, and so expresses symbolically a fundamental adherence to the correct order of existence. If the taboo focus is a center of disorienting experiences, then the form of the ritual taboo can be seen as projecting a model of proper order through the separation of the subject from objects representative of implicitly disordering categories in the cultural code. In effect, the ritual taboo models the boundary that the taboo focus negates. A state of danger can then result from collapsing the protective spacing created by the taboo and so identifying oneself with some of the disturbing qualities that are located in these anomalous things.

Because ritual taboo is not itself a positive action, but a verbalized or verbalizable prohibition of certain actions, it seems particularly necessary to stress that taboos, like other ritual modalities, are components of social action systems. As such they are temporally defined (e.g., they may be temporary, activated only in certain social contexts) and socially segmented (e.g., they may apply to women and not to men, or they may apply to the whole community). The model for handling taboos in a particular ritual system must include within it this sociotemporal phrasing.

In sum, it is possible to consider symbolic action as providing different modalities for the manipulation of category oppositions in the cultural code. From this perspective, ritual processes can be viewed as procedures for creating or emphasizing oppositions (separations and boundaries) between code categories and syntheses or mediations of cultural oppositions and contradictions. These logical processes are thought to have emotional implications relating to the governance of experiences of purity and danger (or correlative attitudes). Tentative and partial as these hypotheses may be, empirical research is currently demonstrating the utility of a model that directs anthropological attention to the relationship between ritual structure and cultural systems of thought.

CONCLUSION AND PROSPECTS

The foundations for an anthropology of ritual symbolism were laid when ritual was perceived as being, in effect, a meta-social form for expressing the social relationships of the actors, mediating these relationships to them in the shape of concrete images or symbols. As we have seen, this framework did not accommodate the complex cultural meanings that symbols channel into a communication currency, but tended to confine meaning to the social co-implicates of the symbols. The broad, descriptive model I have set out in the Introduction is an attempt to adjust this framework in terms more amenable to semantic theory and to the implications of contemporary ritual studies with their emphasis on the area of meaning and the logical organization of the cultural code. My thesis has been that ritual should be viewed as a societal control system, a generalized medium of social interaction, linking the individual to a community of significant others through the symbolic mobilization of shared life meanings. Using selections from a cultural lexicon that condenses or codes these meanings, the ritual message system reintegrates them at a new symbolic level in a social currency of communicative forms. Not only are situational meanings drawn from a diverse range of contexts and condensed into specifiable currencies that can be transacted between actors, but in addition, these meanings are given form outside the subjective experience and apprehension of the actor, as elements in social relationships.

In this process the iconic-expressive qualities of ritual symbolism are very important, since these qualities, in effect, bind the symbols (and meanings) to the wider life contexts at the same time that they make it possible to convert the meanings of these contexts into a communication medium. This feature of iconicity is central to the role of ritual in the regulation of subjective experience: on the one hand, it maintains within the communication the sensuous, spatiotemporal formations through which all life experience is built up; on the other hand, it enables the symbols to convey, with varying degrees of directness, some of the sensuous properties relevant to the particular meaning domains being transacted in any given instance.

At one level, ritual may be seen as an instrument for achieving specific ends involving the immediate interests and situations of the actors. These ends are obtained through programming the immediate situation or problem in terms of a symbolic language that condenses critical cultural meanings relevant to the problem at hand. By this transposition of one order into the terms of another, actors can, in effect, work within the symbolic sphere to achieve ends in the nonsymbolic, immediate life situation.

At another, less overt level, ritual functions in the regulation of experience. Thus it achieves its instrumental aims through its capacity to reorganize the actor's experience of the situation. From this perspective, symbolic forms provide external templates for inner experience, and operations within the external, symbolic sphere are aimed (implicitly or explicitly) at adjusting internal orientations. In this respect, ritual action may create images expressive of order and disorder that provide external templates for their regulation in individual experience. Recent studies have pointed to the manipulation of oppositions in the cultural code as a central mechanism in the ritual creation and regulation of these ordering and disordering experiences.

Finally, at a still more fundamental level, ritual symbols may be said to regulate and affirm a coherent symmetrical relationship between individual subjectivity and the objective societal order. For, as I have suggested, ritual symbols co-imply normatively defined social relationships of internal significance and value. Here we reach the widest level of discourse about the regulative functions of ritual symbols and the definition of the framing notions of ritual symbolism as a system of social action.

PROSPECTS

At the present time, our understanding of ritual symbolism is still in the formative stage. Theory and analysis in this field are less developed than in comparable studies of myth and cosmological classification. Indeed, if functional approaches have tended to absorb symbolic action into its social background, contemporary concerns with cosmology and cultural classification have tended to reduce it to its cultural background; i.e., to treat ritual as part of the evidence for classifications in the cultural code (see, for instance, the influential work of Rodney Needham 1960, 1962). Ritual may, of course, be examined from either perspective, but the nature and function of ritual as a particular kind of sociocultural form cannot be adequately grasped in these reductionist terms.

Almost any aspect of ritual study can be singled out as one requiring further empirical and theoretical work. In some respects, the study of the message structures of ritual has hardly begun; for instance, we are particularly in need of accounts of ritual sequences that attempt to integrate cultural code and symbol analysis with analysis of the temporal structuring of the rites.

Another important problem area is the relationship between the sociocultural level of ritual symbolism and the idiosyncratic, individual level of symbolism, or between public and private symbolism (Leach 1958). Little systematic attention has been given to this issue, although a number of the authors I have cited (notably Beidelman 1966*a*, Leach 1958, V. Turner 1961, Warner 1961) have been influenced by Freudian thinking in their general ideas about the grounds of ritual symbols or the properties of symbolic meanings. Victor Turner (1964*b*:50) has even gone so far as to suggest that the subject is beyond the scope of anthropological competence; nevertheless, he himself has demonstrated how the judicious use of life-history data combined with studies of sociopolitical and symbolic processes may suggest hypotheses concerning the nexus of individual conflicts and culturally available symbolic currencies. The case study method might well be adapted to aid in the development of hypotheses along these lines.

Still another topic in need of exploration from the perspective of symbol analysis is that of ritual change and its relation to aspects of societal change.[24] An exception to the general paucity of studies in this field is Peacock's (1968) full-length account of Javanese Ludruk theater as a "ritual of modernization." Peacock argues that the expression of traditional Javanese category oppositions of *alus* (refined) and *kasar* (crude), each with complex associations in the culture, is being replaced in Ludruk dramatizations by the expression of a new

[24] Two papers in *The Interpretation of Ritual*, a collection published after this chapter had gone to press, are also concerned with this issue. See Southall 1972, Wilson 1972.

opposition, *madju* (progressive) and *kuna* (conservative), with a set of attendant associations referable to the emerging modern society (Peacock 1968:8):

Ludruk gives expression—in puns, songs, stories, speeches, and dances—to both alus-kasar and madju-kuna symbolism. But . . . madju-kuna oppositions are replacing alus-kasar ones in ludruk performances. . . . Alus-kasar cosmology served to make sense out of a traditional society that is no more, while madju-kuna ideology imbues the process of modernization with meaning and legitimacy.

Finally, one can readily compile a list of rituals in our own society that merit the attention of anthropologists concerned with symbol analysis: for example, domestic rituals like Christmas; the political rituals of youth and various forms of avant-garde theater and multimedia art that are part of the same complex; the highly specialized type of symbolic transaction that takes place in the context of an art museum. All of these activities constitute varieties of ritual action in the sense used here: they employ a generalized media for social interaction involving iconic message vehicles that function to convert complex sociocultural meanings into communication currencies.

A cursory look at the dominant symbolism of the American Christmas—gift exchange—may suggest some ideas about the amenability of these rites to symbol analysis similar to that applied to other rituals, primarily those of traditional societies, in the earlier sections of this discussion. I am referring especially to gift exchange in the nuclear family, as this is the core of the gift-giving complex, although the rite is, of course, generalized in varying degrees beyond the family to include extended kin, close friends, business associates, and others in an ego-focused network of contacts.

The gift itself has two aspects: the glittering, festive wrapping, and the utilitarian material good it covers. As Barnett (1954:83) has pointed out in his study of the American Christmas, there is an "informal, but stringent demand that presents be wrapped and addressed. Convention requires that they be prepared, at least in a token manner, before presentation. This item of usage underscores the fact that a gift expresses personal regard and also symbolizes the social relations of donor and recipient." The festive wrapping of packages is a standard practice in American culture in other domestic rites like birthday parties and weddings, or more generally whenever an item is to be provided for someone else without direct cash return. An important feature of this wrapping is that it is regarded as "decoration," for it is through this decorative, nonutilitarian dimension that the donor explicitly communicates affection or personal concern for the recipient. The wrapping, in other words, translates a "purchase" into a "present." From this perspective, the wrapped gift appears to mediate between two important categories that are in binary opposition in our cultural code: the decorative or aesthetic-expressive and the pragmatic or utilitarian. Each of these categories has complex associations: for example, decoration conveys personal and emotional dimensions of experience, and is connected with the feminine sex role;[25] utility connotes qualities of depersonalization, monetary value, and the hardcore realities of business and daily life, and is connected with masculine roles.

If we consider the gift as a ritual

[25] Wrapping packages is itself regarded as an essentially feminine task, although men may also wrap them. In general, the associations of women and the feminine sex role with the decorative-aesthetic dimension is a marked feature in middle-class American culture.

mediation of these opposed categories, we can see that it is a fitting expression of relationships between individuals who are expected to have bonds of personal affection combined with obligations of mutual aid.[26] In the context of the nuclear family, the Christmas gift thus appears as a testament to the ideal synthesis of affection and material support that should bind family members.

Another function of the wrappings, in addition to that of decoration, is to provide a way of covering the gift so that it comes as a "surprise." If we consider the sequence of preparations in the ritual process involved in the family exchange, the importance of secrecy and revelation becomes apparent. Packages are wrapped and privately hidden by individual family members, or by one segment of the family (e.g., parents who keep the presents secret from the children). On Christmas Eve, however, the Christmas tree is set up in the living room or "family room"—that is, in an area where the family ordinarily gathers as a group—and packages are brought out from their hiding places and arranged around this focal symbol. It is in this centralized group context that the packages are unwrapped (usually on Christmas morning) and the separately created "surprises" revealed. In this way, individuality and personal identity, epitomized by the wrapping and hiding of presents, are translated into a social, group relationship through the revelation of individual secrets in the public context of the whole family. Each donor is, it would seem, giving

something of himself, as in the classical type of gift exchange (Mauss 1954:10), and this feature is dramatized by the sequential pattern of individualized secrecy (separation) and group revelation (incorporation). These brief comments will suffice to draw attention to a few interesting aspects of Christmas ritual that anthropologists might explore.

In conclusion, it may be suggested that symbol studies should eventually provide the field theory for the whole area of logico-aesthetic problems in social anthropology. Since the interpretation of ritual must bring together examinations of social process and of the complex meanings in the cultural code, it gives us a particularly important vantage point for viewing these fundamental problems.

---

26 It is also possible, of course, to play on gift-giving to create a fiction that relationships of this sort exist. In addition, qualitative changes in significance can be rung through varying the utility, expense, etc. of the object inside the package. As Fortes (1967:16) has put it in another connection: "A scale is here available for the expression and symbolisation of different social requirements and cultural norms."

REFERENCES

Barnett, J.
1954 *The American Christmas.* New York, Macmillan.
Bateson, G.
1958 *Naven.* Stanford: Stanford University Press. Originally published 1936.
Bateson, G., and M. Mead
1942 *Balinese Character: A Photographic Analysis.* New York: Academy of Science.
Beidelman, T.
1966a Swazi Royal Ritual. *Africa* 36:373-405.
1966b The Ox and Nuer Sacrifice. *Man* 1:453-67.
1968 Some Nuer Notions of Nakedness, Nudity, and Sexuality. *Africa* 38:114-31.
Belo, J.
1949 *Bali: Rangda and Barong.* American Ethnological Society Monographs no. 16. New York: J. J. Augustin.
Berger, P., and T. Luckmann
1967 *The Social Construction of Reality.* New York: Doubleday.
Burke, K.
1957 *The Philosophy of Literary Form.* New York: Vintage.

Cassirer, E.
1955 *The Philosophy of Symbolic Forms,* vol. 2. New Haven: Yale University Press.

Chapple, E., and C. Coon
1942 *An Introduction to Anthropology.* New York: Holt, Rinehart & Winston.

Cohen, A.
1969 Political Anthropology: The Analysis of the Symbolism of Power Relationships. *Man* 4:215-35.

Crumrine, N.
1969 Čapakoba the Mayo Easter Ceremonial Impersonator: Explanations of Ritual Clowning. *Journal for the Scientific Study of Religion* 8:1-22.

Cunningham, C.
1964 Atoni Borrowing of Children: An Aspect of Mediation. In *Symposium of New Approaches to the Study of Religion: 1964 Proceedings of the American Ethnological Society,* ed. J. Helm. Seattle: University of Washington Press.

Douglas, M.
1957 Animals in Lele Religious Thought. *Africa* 27:46-58.
1966 *Purity and Danger.* London: Routledge & Kegan Paul.

Durkheim, E.
1954 *The Elementary Forms of the Religious Life.* London: Allen & Unwin. Originally published 1911.

Evans-Pritchard, E.
1940 *The Nuer.* London: Oxford University Press.
1956 *Nuer Religion.* London: Oxford University Press.

Fernandez, J.
1965 Symbolic Consensus in a Fang Reformative Cult. *American Anthropologist* 67:902-29.
1967 Revitalized Words from "The Parrot's Egg" and "The Bull That Crashes in the Kraal": African Cult Sermons. In *Essays on the Visual and Verbal Arts: 1966 Proceedings of the American Ethnological Society,* ed. J. Helm. Seattle: University of Washington Press.

Firth, R.
1940 *The Work of the Gods in Tikopia.* London School of Economics Monographs in Social Anthropology nos. 1 and 2.

1967 *Tikopia Ritual and Belief.* London: Allen & Unwin.

Fontenrose, J.
1966 *The Ritual Theory of Myth.* Berkeley and Los Angeles: University of California Press.

Forge, A.
1966 Art and Environment in the Sepik. In *1965 Proceedings of the Royal Anthropological Institute.*

Fortes, M.
1967 Totem and Taboo. In *1966 Proceedings of the Royal Anthropological Institute,* pp. 5-22.

Fortune, R.
1963 *Sorcerers of Dobu.* New York: Dutton.

Frazer, J.
1905 *Lectures on the Early History of Kingship.* London: Macmillan.

Freud, S.
1938 The Interpretation of Dreams. In *The Basic Writings of Sigmund Freud.* New York: Random House.
1950 *Totem and Taboo.* London: Routledge & Kegan Paul.

Fustel de Coulanges, N. D.
1956 *The Ancient City: An Anthropological View of Greece and Rome.* New York: Anchor, Doubleday. Originally published 1864.

Geertz, C.
1964 Ideology as a Cultural System. In *Ideology and Discontent,* ed. D. Apter. New York: Free Press, Macmillan.
1966 Religion as a Cultural System. In *Anthropological Approaches to the Study of Religion,* ed. M. Banton. London: Tavistock.
1972 Deep Play: Notes on the Balinese Cockfight. *Daedalus* 101:1-37.

Gluckman, M.
1954 *Rituals of Rebellion in South-east Africa.* Manchester: Manchester University Press.
1962 Les rites de passage. In *Essays on the Ritual of Social Relations,* ed. M. Gluckman. Manchester: Manchester University Press.
1963 Introduction. In Gluckman, *Order and Rebellion in Tribal Africa.* London: Cohen & West.
1965 *Politics, Law, and Ritual in Tribal Society.* Chicago: Aldine.

Goody, J.
1962 *Death, Property, and the Ancestors.* Stanford: Stanford University Press.

Hubert, H., and M. Mauss
1964 *Sacrifice: Its Nature and Function.* Chicago: University of Chicago Press. Originally published 1898.

Kimball, S.
1960 Introduction. In A. Van Gennep, *The Rites of Passage.* London: Routledge & Kegan Paul.

Layton, R.
1970 Myth as Language in Aboriginal Arnhem Land. *Man* 5:483-97.

Leach, E.
1958 Magical Hair. *Journal of the Royal Anthropological Institute* 88:147-64.
1961 Two Essays Concerning the Symbolic Representation of Time. In Leach, *Rethinking Anthropology.* London: Athlone Press.
1964 Anthropological Aspects of Language: Animal Categories and Verbal Abuse. In *New Directions in the Study of Language,* ed. E. Lenneberg. Cambridge: M.I.T. Press.
1968 Ritual. In *International Encyclopedia of the Social Sciences*, vol. 13. New York: Crowell Collier, Macmillan.
1972 The Structure of Symbolism. In *The Interpretation of Ritual,* ed. J. La Fontaine. London: Tavistock.

Lévi-Strauss, C.
1963 *Totemism.* Boston: Beacon Press.
1966 *The Savage Mind.* Chicago: University of Chicago Press.
1967 The Effectiveness of Symbols. In *Structural Anthropology.* New York: Doubleday.

Lienhardt, G.
1961 *Divinity and Experience.* London: Oxford University Press.

MacIntyre, A.
1958 *The Unconscious.* New York: Humanities Press.

Maddock, K.
1969 The Jabuduruwa: A Study of Rite and Myth in an Australian Aboriginal Society. Unpublished Ph. D. dissertation, University of Sydney.

Malinowski, B.
1935 *Coral Gardens and Their Magic.* New York: American Book Co.
1954 *Magic, Science, and Religion.* New York: Doubleday.

Mauss, M.
1954 *The Gift.* London: Cohen & West. Originally published 1925.

Munn, N.
1969 The Effectiveness of Symbols in Murngin Rite and Myth. In *Forms of Symbolic Action: 1969 Proceedings of the American Ethnological Society,* ed. R. Spencer. Seattle: University of Washington Press.
1971 The Symbolism of Perceptual Qualities: A Study in Trobriand Ritual Aesthetics. Paper presented at the Institute on the Arbitrariness of Symbols, meetings of the American Anthropological Association.

Needham, R.
1960 The Left Hand of the Mugwe. *Africa* 30:20-33.
1962 *Structure and Sentiment.* Chicago: University of Chicago Press.

Nisbet, R.
1966 *The Sociological Tradition.* New York: Basic Books.

Ortiz, A.
1971 The Pueblo Indian World. In *Perspectives on the Pueblo,* ed. A. Ortiz. Albuquerque: University of New Mexico Press.

Parsons, T.
1963a On the Concept of Influence. *Public Opinion Quarterly* 27:37-62.
1963b On the Concept of Political Power. *Proceedings of the American Philosophical Society* 107:232-62.
1964 Some Reflections on the Problem of Psychosomatic Relationships in Health and Illness. In Parsons, *Social Structure and Personality.* New York: Free Press, Macmillan.

Peacock, J.
1967 Javanese Clown and Transvestite Songs: Some Relations Between "Primitive Classification" and "Communicative Events." In *Essays on the Verbal and Visual Arts: 1966 Proceedings of the American Ethnological Society,* ed. J. Helm. Seattle: University of Washington Press.
1968 *Rites of Modernization: Symbolic and Social Aspects of Indonesian Proletarian Drama.* Chicago: University of Chicago Press.

Radcliffe-Brown, A.
1952a Taboo. In *Structure and Function in*

Primitive Society. London: Cohen & West. Originally published 1939.

1952*b* Introduction. In N. Srinivas, *Religion and Society Among the Coorgs of South India.* London: Asia Publishing House.

1957 *A Natural Science of Society.* New York: Free Press, Macmillan.

1964 *The Andaman Islanders.* New York: Free Press, Macmillan. Originally published 1922.

Rappaport, R.
1968 *Pigs for the Ancestors.* New Haven: Yale University Press.

Rassers, W.
1959 *Panji the Culture Hero.* The Hague: Martinus Nijhoff. Originally published 1925.

Richards, A.
1956 *Chisungu: A Girl's Initiation Ceremony Among the Bemba of Northern Rhodesia.* London: Faber & Faber.

Rigby, P.
1968 Some Gogo Rituals of Purification. In *Dialectic in Practical Religion,* ed. E. Leach. Cambridge: At the University Press.

Rosaldo, R.
1968 Metaphors of Hierarchy in a Mayan Ritual. *American Anthropologist* 70:524-36.

De Saussure, F.
1966 *Course in General Linguistics.* New York: McGraw-Hill. Originally published 1916.

Schwartz, G., and D. Merten
1968 Social Identity and Expressive Symbols: The Meaning of an Initiation Ritual. *American Anthropologist* 70:1117-31.

Smith, W. Robertson
1956 *The Religion of the Semites.* New York: Meridian. Originally published 1889.

Southall, A.
1972 Twinship and Symbolic Structure. In *The Interpretation of Ritual,* ed. J. La Fontaine. London: Tavistock.

Srinivas, M.
1952 *Religion and Society Among the Coorgs of South India.* London: Asia Publishing House.

Stanner, W.
1967 Reflections on Durkheim and Ab-

original Religion. In *Social Organization: Essays Presented to Raymond Firth,* ed. M. Freedman. Chicago: Aldine.

n.d. *On Aboriginal Religion.* Oceania Monograph no. 11 (republished from *Oceania,* 1959-1961).

Steiner, F.
1956 *Taboo.* London: Cohen & West.

Strathern, A., and M. Strathern
1968 Marsupials and Magic: A Study of Spell Symbolism Among the Mbowamb. In *Dialectic in Practical Religion,* ed. E. Leach. Cambridge: At the University Press.

Tambiah, S.
1968 The Magical Power of Words. *Man* 3:175-206.

1969 Animals Are Good to Think and Good to Prohibit. *Ethnology* 8:423-59.

Turner, T.
1968 Parsons' Concept of Generalized Media of Social Interaction and Its Relevance for Social Anthropology. *Sociological Inquiry* 38:121-34.

1969 Tchikrin: A Central Brazilian Tribe and Its Symbolic Language of Body Ornament. *Natural History* 78:50-59, 70.

Turner, V.
1961 Ritual Symbolism, Morality, and Social Structure Among the Ndembu. *Rhodes Livingstone Journal,* no. 30. Manchester: Manchester University Press.

1962 Three Symbols of Passage in Ndembu Circumcision Ritual. In *Essays on the Ritual of Social Relations,* ed. M. Gluckman. Manchester: Manchester University Press.

1964*a* Betwixt and Between: The Liminal Period in *Rites de Passage.* In *Symposium on New Approaches to the Study of Religion: 1964 Proceedings of the American Ethnological Society,* ed. J. Helm. Seattle: University of Washington Press.

1964*b* Symbols in Ndembu Ritual. In *Closed Systems and Open Minds,* ed. M. Gluckman. Edinburgh and London: Oliver & Boyd.

1966 Colour Classification in Ndembu Ritual. In *Anthropological Approaches to the Study of Religion,* ed. M. Ban-

ton. London: Tavistock.
1967a Themes in the Symbolism of an Ndembu Hunter's Ritual. In *A Forest of Symbols*. Ithaca: Cornell University Press.
1967b An Ndembu Doctor in Practice. In *A Forest of Symbols*. Ithaca: Cornell University Press.
1969a Introduction. In *Forms of Symbolic Action*, ed. R. Spencer. Seattle: University of Washington Press.
1969b *The Ritual Process*. Chicago: Aldine.
n.d. Themes and Symbols in an Ndembu Hunter's Burial. Mimeo.
Urban, W.
1951 *Language and Reality*. New York: Macmillan.
Van Gennep, A.
1960 *The Rites of Passage*. London: Routledge & Kegan Paul. Originally published 1909.
Vogt, E. Z., and C. Vogt
1970 Lévi-Strauss Among the Maya. *Man* 5:379-92.

Warner, W.
1958 *A Black Civilization*. New York: Harper. Originally published 1937.
1961 *The Family of God*. New Haven: Yale University Press.
Westcott, J., and P. Morton-Williams
1962 The Symbolism and Ritual Context of the Yoruba Laba Shango. *Journal of the Royal Anthropological Institute* 92:23-37.
Wilson, M.
1957 *Rituals of Kinship Among the Nyakyusa*. London: Oxford University Press.
1959 *Communal Rituals Among the Nyakyusa*. London: Oxford University Press.
1972 The Wedding Cakes: A Study of Ritual Change. In *The Interpretation of Ritual*, ed. J. La Fontaine. London: Tavistock.

CHAPTER 14 Narrative

BENJAMIN N. COLBY
JAMES L. PEACOCK

Although the study of narrative was central to early anthropology, in recent years it has been peripheral to the discipline. This chapter sketches the early origins and development of the anthropological study of narrative, the period of its submersion if not decline, and some directions of revival.

One seminal source of narrative studies is largely neglected in this paper: the folklore journals. Excellent orientations to traditional studies of folk narrative have already been written by Thompson (1946), Greenway (1964), Dundes (1965), and others, so that the reader may easily refer to these sources to gain knowledge of the traditionally defined discipline of narrative studies in folklore. More difficult is the tracing and synthesizing of scattered contributions in anthropology, psychology, literary criticism, and other fields. Though Fischer (1963) did extremely well in this area in a review of writings that existed a decade ago, theoretically interesting developments have appeared with increasing frequency in the time since his paper was

written, and it seemed that drawing together some of these contributions would be a useful service. In our selection of sources and studies, the guiding motive is not the coverage of a conventionally defined discipline, but the illustration and assessment of what appear to be the most useful and promising approaches toward scientific understanding of that phenomenon deemed narrative. In a concluding section, we assess the contributions that the study of narrative can make to the study of man.

ORIGINS AND EARLY DEVELOPMENT OF THE ANTHROPOLOGICAL STUDY OF NARRATIVE

Myth had a great fascination for scholars of the nineteenth century, when evolution, biblical scholarship, and the growth of scientific interest in primitive man created a keen curiosity about man's origins. Language and myth were thought to be keys to this puzzle and thus were subjects of great attention. The studies of the young Danish scholar Rasmus Christian Rask on the relation of Icelandic to Latin, Greek, Sanskrit, and other Indo-European languages sparked the interest of Jakob Grimm, who looked for regularities of language development from primeval Indo-European origins. But even before the linguistic studies, Jakob and his brother, Wilhelm, were collecting fairy tales and other folk traditions as part of this same historical quest. Among their most influential publications was the 1815 edition of *Kinder- und Hausmärchen* (1884), which included a comparison of plots and plot elements in the narratives of other cultures. The Grimms mistakenly thought it was possible to deduce that most of the resemblances found in their collections were due to a common Indo-European ancestory. Although they recognized that narratives could be borrowed in their entirety by alien cultures, they felt that so many similar elements existing together in the same story implied a genetic relationship.

Whether for linguistic or other reasons, the attention of many nineteenth-century scholars turned toward India, home of Sanskrit and, as was then thought, the hypothetical Indo-European parent language. Theodore Benfey (1859) considered that, with the exception of Aesop's fables and their derivatives (which he thought the Hindus borrowed from the Greeks), most European folktales and in fact folktales throughout the world originated in India. Much of the dissemination was thought to have begun in the tenth century through translated manuscripts rather than oral traditions. Benfey conjectured that Buddhists had earlier spread the same stories from India to China, Tibet, and Mongolia. This hypothesis elicited dispute and subsequent scholarly investigation; but except for details and questions such as whether India was the exclusive source, an inter-mediary of an earlier single source, or one of many centers of dissemination, it stood as a major formulation of the last century.

Late in the nineteenth century, evolutionism, which had enjoyed a brief period of development in the previous century, replaced diffusionism as a focus of scholarship. Endorsed by Darwin (whose *Origin of Species* was not the first evolutionary theory published), social and cultural evolutionism, represented by such figures as Comte (1896), Tylor (1871), Frazer (1890), Morgan (1877), Maine (1861), and McLennan (1865), was the trademark of late nineteenth-century anthropology. Regarding the role of myth in sociocultural evolution, Tylor's theory may be cited as an example.

Tylor theorized that belief in ancestral souls derived from dreams about dead relatives, which provided evidence of the dead's continuing existence. Ancestor worship evolved into animism as the idea of spirit was transferred to inanimate objects, and myth developed as a mode of explaining a world filled with spirits. From this state, culture progressed from polytheism to monotheism. Tylor proposed two types of myths representing the succeeding stages. The first was the scientific myth, which explained observed natural phenomena. The second was the historical and philosophical myth, which explained customs. Tylor believed, along with John Stuart Mill and other English writers, that early man was capable of reflective thought, and only faulty reason and inaccurate observation held him back.

In 1912 Émile Durkheim (1961) supplied an alternative to Tylor's view. Utilizing a detailed analysis of a single culture, that of the Australian aborigines, Durkheim concluded that myth was not derived from rational and inductive observation of natural phenomena, but rather was part of a body of tradition handed down to the individual by the community in which he was submerged. Though neglecting to explain just how the traditions themselves emerged, Durkheim was able to present powerful arguments that the patterns and figures of mythology reflect not natural phenomena but social experience. Though Durkheim could well be regarded as the father of modern British social anthropology, he was misunderstood and neglected by the Americans, whose history is central to our subsequent discussion.

American anthropology began in earnest with Franz Boas. Working mainly with Tsimshian (1902) and Kwakiutl (1910) folktales and myths from the west coast of the United States, Boas set standards for ethnographic research which have been matched only by isolated individuals of the past, such as the Spaniard Sahagún, who described the Aztecs of Mexico. By carefully recording texts in the native language, Boas was able to contradict the more fantastic evolutionary theories of the day, such as Müller's notion that myth was primitive astronomy. Boas accepted the proposition that myths often explained nature, but he considered this to be only one of its many functions. Folktales and myths are created by wishes, exaggerations, transformations, desires for the humanly impossible, hopes for restoration of life (Boas 1938:611): "The onesided emphasis laid upon the intimate relations between religion and mythology obscures the imaginative play that is involved in the formation of myths."

From his extensive studies of narrative culture, Boas concluded that the invention of new motifs is infrequent and that, in fact, current forms of folktales act to restrict such invention (1938:612). Boas thought that dissemination more than independent invention accounts for the similarity of folktales, but that though lines of diffusion can be traced, place of origin cannot. He stressed that, although a tale element may be universal, its meaning differs according to context and culture. In addition to such particularist and humdrum conclusions, Boas hazarded some generalizations; for example, that as cultural life becomes more systematic, so does mythology, and where social organizations are loose, mythology is full of contradictions.

In the 1920s such intellectual descendents of Boas as Robert Lowie, Paul Radin, and Alfred Kroeber made their collections and studies of folktales and myths. Of this group, Radin (1927, 1956) has had the greatest influence on later students of narrative. His long-term study of the Winnebago Indians provided the basis for the major part of his theoretical writings. Radin distinguished between folktale and myth according to native criteria (the Winnebago terms *waika* and *worak*). He found stereotyped formulae to be associated with specific *dramatis personae* (for example, the boasting of the turtle), and he analyzed myths by themes or motifs (for example, overcoming obstacles). He discovered that Winnebago myths bore little resemblance to social ethics, but that folktales did. He is perhaps best known for his position, now championed by Lévi-Strauss (and earlier by Tylor and Mill), that primitives can be philosophical and are not genetically inferior in their ability to think. Part of this stance derived from Radin's belief that literacy is not a requirement for true literature. Some of the world's greatest epics and most beautiful song-poems were not created as fixed texts. Radin (1955) referred to traditional prose narratives as dramas "in which the reciter, the raconteur, impersonates the various characters of the tale or novelette he is narrating. His role as an actor is here more important than his role as a transmitter of specific traditional text, for it is by his skill and excellence as an actor that his audience judges him."

YEARS OF SUBMERSION

Although the tendency is by no means absolute, one may speak of a trend, beginning in the thirties in the English-speaking countries, to submerge the study of narrative within the study of societies and cultures as wholes. Bronislaw Malinowski in Britain and Ruth Benedict in America were major pioneers in this trend.

Malinowski ridicules those "moonstruck" Germanic scholars, such as Müller, Ehrenreich, and Kuhn, who regard myths as primitive astronomical calculations that, by means of "personified rapture," endeavor to explain the character of the heavenly bodies. He generously concludes (1954:97) that "this theory seems to me to be one of the most extravagant views ever advanced by an anthropologist or humanist—and that means a great deal."

Malinowski goes on to assert that, far from being prescientific intellectual speculation, primitive myth is a "hard working" social force that serves a practical function in "savage" life—governing the faith and controlling the conduct of the savage. Myth, proclaims Malinowski (1954:101), is "not an intellectual explanation or an artistic imagery, but a pragmatic charter of primitive faith and moral wisdom." This argument Malinowski supports by such analysis of Trobriand mythology as that of origin myths, which by narrating a clan's origin testify to its claim to property at the place of origin. In conclusion, Malinowski, the flamboyant Slav whom the Trobrianders called the "man of songs," deploys his argument to provoke his staid British colleagues

into spontaneously entering into full participation in native life. Only through such participation can the social role of myth be understood.

By shifting the emphasis from text to context, Malinowski hoped to undermine the scholar's speculation in dusty studies about some isolated text of a tale and to goad him into observing it at work in the full activity of life. Though the emphasis was doubtless salutary for British anthropology by encouraging the excellent fieldwork of that tradition, it did discourage the careful analysis of text or performance itself. To this day, the typical social anthropological analysis concerns itself only with those facets of narrative that can be fitted into the wider analysis of community organization. (For examples from British social anthropology to support this point, see Peacock 1969.)

Like Malinowski, Ruth Benedict emphasized the study of cultures as wholes and the weaving of narrative analysis into such holism. She objected to the view of folktales as survivals from a distant past which do not tally with the rest of a culture. She suspected that the great attention given to survivals was partly caused by the fact that so many folktales in Europe and America had been collected from old people, often the sole survivors of a dying culture. With Malinowski (and Boas), Benedict stressed the importance of context, and although she recognized that a lag between tale and context could exist, she emphasized that the lag was short unless it was useful as a special dramatic device or served some other psychological function. For example, in Zuñi tales the men come courting with bundles of gifts. They did not do so when Benedict was there; but she felt that this and other narrative elements showed a tendency to idealize which indicated a real need in Zuñi society (1969:xv).

Benedict's influence on American anthropology is more diffuse than Malinowski's on the British, but one specific field that reflected her perspective is that of national character studies. In her own studies of Japan and Thailand, and in studies by Margaret Mead and others, as in Mead and Metraux's (1953) *Study of Culture at a Distance,* much use was made of narrative and other expressive materials and texts, for the anthropologists could not observe such cultures up close. Yet, by and large, the investigators of culture at a distance employ narrative materials only to abstract broad themes and to reconstruct total sociocultural gestalts. Rarely do they exhaustively analyze the form and thrust of the narrative itself.

Significant analyses of narrative per se have certainly been made by anthropologists and linguists since the thirties (e.g., Jacobs 1959; Spencer 1957; Sebeok and Ingemann 1956; Fischer 1958, 1963), but the major schools in American anthropology, even those oriented around symbolic and ideological facets of life, have dealt with narrative only peripherally or impressionistically, if at all. During the fifties and sixties those anthropologists who study "ethnoscience" have derived their formulations of native thought structure from native terms isolated from discourse sequences and contexts rather than from the more cohesive elements that compose narrative forms.

PATHS OF REVIVAL

Although the "submersion" tendency has been dominant in anthropology, several paths toward revival of the study of narrative per se can be discerned both within and without anthropology. Illustrating some of the major tendencies, we shall move from narrow to broad units, from text to total performance to the broadest contexts of personality, society, and culture. Though unusual analytical schemes and new interpretations such as those offered by Claude Lévi-Strauss and Kenneth Burke do not fall within the category of science, they may well encourage the production of scientifically validated findings by others; hence considerable attention is given to these creative theorists as well as to methods that at least aim at scientific validity.

TEXTUAL ANALYSIS

The Statistical Approach

The easiest thing an investigator can do is to count words or other text elements. Though counting may sound prosaic and unproductive, a great variety of possible techniques, hypotheses, and experiments can be based on simple word counts. Now that the computer can do the counting, the analyst's energies are saved for creative interpretation.

To date, conventional assumptions rather than any elaborate theory underlie the methodology of word counting. Indeed, the theory of information (Shannon and Weaver 1949) cannot apply to narrative studies unless one makes unrealistic qualifications and hypothetical assumptions. Information theory is based on the notion that if the number of possible choices among a given set of messages is finite, the amount of information carried by a particular message selection can be quantified. Grammars of narrative and language can generate an infinite number of words, sentences, or narrative sequences, each capable of differing totally from all preceding ones. It is not possible to measure the amount of semantic information produced by such grammars without severe contextual and other restrictions. Thus Shannon's method seems inapplicable. Generally, all one can really say is that the more frequently a word is *expected* to appear, the less information it contains when it does appear. If the word "elephant" appeared in an Eskimo folktale, it would cause more surprise and hence carry more information than in a Hindu tale. In English high-frequency words such as "of," "for," and "is" embody less information in folktales than "giant" or "treasure."

These examples ignore the distinction between a normal communication among members of a group and the analysis of such communication by someone outside that group. Conceivably medium-frequency words (i.e., common nonfunction words) can be so overused that they cease to carry punch to members of the group, but they may be highly novel and striking to the analyst from outside.

The signaling of a novel stimulus is a basic function of the nervous system. Changing state receptors send bursts of nerve impulses to various parts of the brain whenever unexpected events occur. Some of these signals show up as distinctive patterns on an electroencephalogram. As the event is understood and occurs repeatedly, the novelty wears off, and the changing state receptors cease their firing. After the individual becomes habituated to a stimulus, the unexpected cessation of that stimulus can start new patterns of nerve impulse issuing from the receptors.

So also in narrative; we can assume that a word or theme used frequently is part of a culture-using group's expectancy pattern. To this group its appearance in narrative may carry little information or novelty. But this is not to say that the group's members are indifferent to such a theme. In fact, its omission may even be disturbing to them. Because of its very frequency and familiarity they may have invested strongly in the domain of thought and feeling represented by the wide variety

of message forms that delineate distinctions in meaning and usage that are lost on the outside observer. To the natives, fine-grained distinctions provide novel stimuli reactions, while to the outside analyst the forms seem redundant.

From all this two notions emerge: first, messages used infrequently may transmit a great deal of information when they are used, thereby inciting strong response; second, messages used frequently may set up a kind of stable field in which psychic investment is strong, so that their unexpected cessation or contradiction incites strong response. Counting either the frequency with which a given message form occurs or the variety of forms developed to express a given message may indicate the degree of psychic investment in the message. To date, this type of counting has dominated statistical studies of narrative.

An early study by Colby illustrates some of the simpler things that can be done to measure the salience of given themes or attitudes in a text. The basic process is to count, by means of a computer, the number of words that represent a given theme. Which theme is represented by which words is formulated in a "thesaurus" of 4,331 words called the Santa Fe Dictionary. Thus the theme "communication" is defined as represented by such words as *said, told, say, story, dream, letter, call, voice, sent,* and *exclaim.* The thesaurus, developed in the course of studying folktales from more than twenty cultures, instructs the computer to count and label as to theme every word in a text (Colby 1970). Such a procedure has often been referred to as content analysis.

Colby went beyond the usual forms of content analysis, however, to discover sequential patterns of themes as they emerged in the unfolding of a tale (Colby 1966*a*, 1966*b*, 1970). To do this, he divided each tale into equal segments. The frequency counts were then performed on all the first segments of the sample's tales, all second segments, and so forth. Statistical tests were run to find which patterns were most significant.

When Japanese and Eskimo folktales were analyzed in this fashion, it was found that in Japanese tales certain of the themes group together as stagesetters, as in "long, long ago in a certain place." Thus high frequencies of name, community, place, time units, and time references were discovered at the beginning of the tales. Dialogue is at a high point in the middle, as reflected in *you* and *your* incidence and a high frequency of conversation themes and of words such as *said, told*, and *say*.

On the assumption that those areas showing the clearest, most definite patterns are also areas of cultural importance, one can make a number of general statements about the Japanese and Eskimo cultures that can then be examined further: The Japanese seem to be more oriented toward concern with external, usually social, situations, while the Eskimo are more oriented toward concern with the abilities and capabilities (mainly physical) of the individual. The Japanese folktales show a distinct pattern in the conceptual category "dimension," which is used to describe objects and people in a pictorial mode of representation, while the Eskimo folktales reveal a pattern in the physical position or "posture" of both the protagonist and others in an enactive or kinesthetic mode of representation. In the Japanese stories the limitations on action tend to be external domination or instruction from other individuals, whereas in the Eskimo stories the limitations on action are limitations of strength or scarcity of game.

The precision of modern computers highlights many problems that were previously difficult to study. With computers one can systematically examine conceptual oppositions, make up indices for testing hypotheses, and quantitatively elucidate contexts and criteria. Large masses of material can be quickly and thoroughly processed, and the procedure can be replicated. Although the computer's lack of human sensitivity does cause problems, as in the failure to perceive meaning in terms of context (though with increasingly sophisticated programming even this is possible to a limited extent), that "vice" can be a virtue in that it allows the computer relentlessly to classify and count *all* the material according to the specified and programmed criteria and no other. Human beings are incapable of this degree of methodical action with large amounts of data.

The use of predetermined categories of content is valid if those categories have been derived from a theory that can be tested by their operationalization, or if they are derived in such a way as to lay some valid claim to being a universal set (which, however, might be used differently in different culture-using groups). In the study just discussed they merely disprove the null hypothesis (which states that no statistically valid correlation or differences exist in the narrative corpus); patterns such as those just described can be considered only the roughest approximations to culturally formed units.[1] If, on the other hand, computers could be used to reveal the logic underlying correlations and differences (i.e., to reveal structures), the analysis would ascend to an entirely new level.

The Structural Approach

During the thirty years between the first edition of Vladimir Propp's *Morfo-*

---

[1] Colby suspects that a number of the categories in the Santa Fe Dictionary (see Colby 1970 for a complete list of the categories) represent universal categories, but experiments to test this possibility have not yet been undertaken.

logija skazki in 1928 and its English translation, *Morphology of the Folktale* (1958), Propp's method received little attention from anthropologists. His work became known to the English-speaking world mainly through the Russian linguist Roman Jakobson, and more recently through the work of the French anthropologist Claude Lévi-Strauss, who was influenced by both Jakobson and Propp. *Morphology of the Folktale* represents an imaginative effort to find regularities in a large body of Russian narratives through a thoroughly operational procedure. Propp's analysis is an important scientific advance.

Morphology (Propp 1958:19) is "the description of the folktale according to its component parts and the relationship of these components to each other and to the whole." To create his morphology, Propp first distinguished between the variables and "invariants" of his system of tales. The characters and their attributes are the variables. In one action, for instance, a friendly person gives the hero a gift that transports him to another kingdom. The friendly person could be a king, an old man, a sorcerer, or a princess; the hero could be called Ivan or Sučenko; and the gift could be an eagle, a horse, or a magic ring.

The actions, or what Propp calls "functions," are the invariants. A function cannot be defined apart from its place in the narrative, and its sequence is subject to special laws. Identical actions (functions) appear in corresponding places of numerous tales, although they are performed in a variety of ways by a variety of characters. Propp (1958:26-64) lists thirty-one functions, following the initial situation: (1) absence (one of the members of a family is absent from home); (2) interdiction (an interdiction is addressed to the hero); (3) violation (the interdiction is violated); and so on, through (31) wedding (the hero is married and ascends the throne).

According to Propp, "one function develops out of another with logical and artistic necessity." Propp is able to define "moves," each of which consists of progression from a lack or a villainy through intermediate functions to some terminal one, such as marriage. He then defines the folktale as a form employing one of eight patterns: the entire folktale may consist of one move, or it may consist of two moves, one of which ends positively and the other negatively, and so on. All other possibilities involve two or more folktales.

Propp has based his functions firmly on the data in his body of tales, struggling to avoid imposing outside criteria. The result is an impressively elegant and consistent analysis lacking only a clear and developed theoretical account of the phenomenon he discovered. Anthropologists who are concerned with purpose and personality may be disappointed to note that to Propp (1958: 68) these aspects "belong among the most inconstant, unstable elements of the folktale" and are hard to classify and define. Conceivably, if not merely the tale text but the entire experience of narrating and hearing the tale were the unit of analysis (see next section), some ambiguities would be resolved, and the psychological categories could be more easily validated. This is, however, mere speculation. What Propp did he did well, though his explanation of what he did has drawn fire and distracted many from a full appreciation of the analysis.

Important and useful as Propp's study is, anthropological interest in structural methods has been inspired almost entirely by the eloquent savant Claude Lévi-Strauss, reputed usurper of Sartre's position as France's leading intellectual. Synthesizing strands of such diverse influences as Propp himself, Marx, Durkheim, Mauss, Piaget, the linguists De Saussure and Jakobson, Lévi-Strauss calls his approach "structural." He expounds myths as permutable ensembles constituting a structure of compatibilities and oppositions. A brief but classic example of Lévi-Strauss' work, written and published in English (1960), is a study of Winnebago myths originally collected and interpreted by Paul Radin. Here is a brief outline of the myths:

1. Two young friends, one of them the son of a chief, join a war party. The friends become the heroes of a victorious battle. In revenge, the enemy tribe retaliates by later ambushing the two. The friends are killed, but after undergoing a series of tests in the netherworld, they are reincarnated. The cycle of their lives begins again.

2. A husband sacrifices his life for his beloved wife, then both husband and wife are reincarnated.

3. Members of a religious society die and undergo tests in the netherworld in order to be reincarnated.

4. The daughter of a chief loves an orphan who is an exceptionally fine hunter. She dies of a broken heart. The orphan brings her back to life by undergoing tests in the lodge where she dies. Later he dies. He is reincarnated in the form of a wolf. The girl, similarly transformed, joins him.

The unifying theme of the first three myths is self-sacrifice and subsequent reward. According to Lévi-Strauss, a fundamental opposition is expressed in the myths between ordinary lives that unfold toward natural death and heroic life, self-abridged. The gain in the latter is a supplementary life quota for others as well as for oneself (1960:357). Myth 4 does not exactly correspond to the other myths or to Winnebago culture, past or current. This noncorrespondence, which Radin explained by surviv-

als and borrowings, Lévi-Strauss explains as a "transformation." Whereas in the first three myths ordinary persons were opposed to positively (heroic) extraordinary people, in the fourth myth negatively extraordinary people form the opposition to the norm. The social standing of the orphan is too low, that of the chief's daughter too high; so they are negatively extraordinary, and the fourth opposition is "upside down." If the basic problem is formulated "upside down," that is, *ab absurdo,* then the rest of the myth content is modified accordingly to express an inverted image of the social pattern actually present in the consciousness of the native (1960:356). Thus a nonstratified society, such as the Winnebago, can produce a myth with a setting of social stratification.

From the four myths Lévi-Strauss (1960:359) draws the following conclusions:

A. Ordinary people live (their full lives) and die (their full deaths).
B. Positive extraordinary people die (earlier) and live (more).
C. Negatively extraordinary people (the chief's daughter, the orphan) are able neither to live nor to die.

Obviously proposition C offers an inverted demonstration of the truth of A and B. Hence, it must use a plot starting with protagonists (here, men and women) in inverted positions. This leads us to state that a plot and its component parts should neither be interpreted by themselves nor relative to something outside the realm of myth proper, but as substitutions given in, and understandable only with reference to the group made up of all the myths of the same series.

Impressive, indeed dazzling, as Lévi-Strauss' tour de force of analytical reasoning is, one may raise some simple questions about its validity. For example, by what criteria do the four myths form a series? Radin collected the myths from different informants and grouped them together solely "because they are part of a collection of ethnographic and linguistic data referring to one tribe" (Lévi-Strauss 1960:352). Lacking a clear functional relationship, the myths could still be considered a group if they displayed a compelling logical unity, and Lévi-Strauss' analysis does seem to reveal an elegant progression from myths 1 to 4. Yet this progression is not convincing. To a French intellectual, but perhaps not to a Winnebago, the chief's daughter appears negatively extraordinary because she is so high on the social scale "that she is cut off from the rest of the group," and therefore is "defective." And though the orphan is a great hunter in a hunting society and therefore also enjoys high prestige, Lévi-Strauss emphasizes his lack of relatives as a social "defect." In this, as in other Lévi-Straussian analyses, the terse logic, enhanced by such terms as "structural level," "deep unity," "transformation," "double oppositon," "system," "series," and "precisely," often projects a misleading image of closure, exhaustiveness, and structure. If, in fact, one does subject his interpretation to the test of formal logic, it fares badly. For instance, his claim that proposition C is an inverted demonstration of the truth of A and B is meaningless if rephrased in formal logic. Lévi-Strauss is invariably suggestive and plausible; but because his interpretations are often ambiguous or arbitrary and his documentation selective, he does not approach the degree of validity of Propp, who strove to account for every element of every folktale in his corpus.

A second type of validity employed by Propp, which actually is a subtype of the criterion of "exhaustive accountability," is what we might deem "sequential accountability." Propp pays attention to the sequence organization of all elements in the narrative. Lévi-Strauss throws this requirement to the winds and transforms that weakness into an apparent strength by making it central to the methodology of structuralism. Thus in his analysis of the Oedipus myth, Lévi-Strauss (1963: 213-18) evokes metaphors ranging from music and language to the French Revolution to say that myth, as a story, has both sequential (narrative) and structural (logical) dimensions. He then claims to take the narrative dimension into account by producing a chart in which mythical events are arranged both in columns and in rows, so that if the rows are read from left to right and the columns from top to bottom, the Oedipus narrative is told. In this way Lévi-Strauss slyly pretends to take account of the narrative sequence, but his analyses and conclusions are based solely on the classification of structurally similar events into columns (e.g., "Oedipus kills his father, Laios" and "Eteocles kills his brother, Polynices" both go under the column heading "Underrating of blood relations"). Structural analysis in this instance means classification of narrative events while disregarding the narrative itself.

In his penchant for depicting static, nonaction scenery as well as in his love for boundaries, structures, and oppositions, Lévi-Strauss is distinctly French. Like his rival Sartre, he has provided us with a biography revealing of his inner philosophy, and he is moving into the role of philosopher. One may suspect that idolization by his French public encourages his tricky if enticing rhetoric. Whatever his analytical contributions to narrative studies may be, the effectiveness of his literary style alone has drawn this field from the sidelines into the center of the current anthropological arena.

Among recent studies of narrative structure may be distinguished those inspired primarily by Lévi-Strauss and those inspired primarily by Propp. Pursued largely by literary critics or by social anthropologists of the Anglo-French tradition, the Lévi-Straussian productions are typically as witty, provocative, and insightful as they are incomplete and intuitive in scientific methodology (for example, see Leach 1965).

Those who emulate Propp have attempted to duplicate his systematic methodology but have not always enjoyed Propp's good fortune in discovering operational narrative units and scientifically defensible procedures for delineating their relationships. Alan Dundes' (1964:58f) analysis of North American Indian folktales, for example, sought units similar to Propp's "functions," distilling "motifemes" such as "lack, lack liquidated, interdiction, violation, consequences, attempted escape, deceit and deception" (1964: 61f). Though defined by some criterial attributes of Propp's functions—similarity of content and importance of position in the narrative system—Dundes' motifemes suffer from their abstractness, which renders them so ambiguous that in many cases an incident from the text can be regarded as, say, lack or interdiction with equal ease. Doubtless the abstractness was a result of Dundes' breadth of concern: he attempted to account for divergent cultures located over the entire North American continent. Similar difficulties, however, trouble the work of Horner (1967), who, though confining himself to a single culture and body of tales—Bulu— uses units similar to those of Dundes. Horner himself notes difficulty in deciding to which "motifeme slot" certain text portions should be assigned (e.g., 1967:20: "Task [or Lack?], Task Accomplished [or Lack Liquidated?]"). It is fair to state that the work of Dundes and Horner, as well as that of Jason (1967, 1968a, 1968b, 1968c, 1968d, 1969), falls short of the criterion of defining units of analysis operationally and sharply enough so that subsequent investigators working with the same materials can replicate the original analysis. Their methodologies are at an entirely different level of precision, however, from those of such statistically and globally oriented researchers as McClelland (1967), who, while achieving operational methods of classifying and rating elements of folktales such that separate raters agree, is grotesquely inattentive to basic features of narrative structure and plot. Studies that promise to combine structural precision with statistical replicability are those of Powlison (1965), and particularly Mathiot (n.d.), whose work, unfortunately, has not yet been published. A nonstructural methodology also working toward this end is that pursued by Colby under the name "eidochronic analysis."

Eidochronic Analysis

Colby's underlying assumption, which is being borne out, is that myths, folktales, and other genres of a culture have unique grammars. Whereas both Propp and Lévi-Strauss maintain that fairy tales and myths possess a single universal structure, regardless of the social group that produces them, Colby (1973) argues that, just as each language has a unique grammar (though with constituent elements similar to those in many other languages), each traditional genre of narrative culture— i.e., each body of tales told by a particular group—has its own grammar, or at least a "recall system" that approximates a grammar in the current linguistic sense. Less like language, though, a narrative grammar is differentially internalized by the various members of the group. The differences in understanding, performance, and competence are much greater for many members of a narrative community than for the speakers of a language.

Particularly influential in Colby's approach to folk narrative have been the scholarly studies of Lord (1960), whose fieldwork with south Slavic epic singers has yielded data of great significance for understanding the generation of folk productions, particularly with regard to the poetic component of a narrative grammar. It is curious that Lord's work has been overlooked by anthropologists and folklorists, though a notable exception has recently appeared (Rosenberg 1970).

The theory behind eidochronic analysis does not deny the universality of certain aspects of narrative, just as language grammars do not preclude universal features of languages, but it provides unusually stringent criteria for judging any claim of universal narrative structure. Eidochronic analysis requires that a narrative grammar should successfully and exhaustively apply to new or as yet unexamined narratives produced by members of the group from which the grammar was derived. Followers of Lévi-Strauss and Propp, by contrast, present *a priori* schemes, not grammars, in the sense that they do not test their derived rules by applying them to new materials from the population originally studied. One hesitates to accept their claims of showing a single psychologically real structure for tale types such as the Oedipus or the Trickster as they appear in widely differing and dispersed social groups because every new story brought into the sample is selected to fit the very scheme that is to be tested.

Eidochronic analysis takes its name from *eidos,* meaning idea or form. Some of the units of analysis are similar to Propp's functions, others represent higher level syntactic units. The word

"function" is not used, however, because of the importance of distinguishing Propp's analytical procedure from his theory, inasmuch as the theory differs from the procedure, particularly in its claim to reveal universal structures. Use of the word "function" may also confuse a research team working with computers, linguistics, and mathematics in folktale research, since it frequently assumes other meanings in these fields.

Performance Analysis

Moving from the neat confines of the narrative text, we confront the performance as a totality encompassing not only the verbal story but the entire narrative experience, auditory and visual, of spectator and actor. Studies of narrative performance in their total context are rare. An excellent recent example, although of a traditional folkloristic approach, is by Dégh (1969), about the storytellers of Kakasd, Hungary. Such studies, however, are more useful if they go beyond a merely descriptive treatment and delve into the principles and dynamics of narrative and dramatic events. Though an analysis by an anthropologist will be presented as an example, the basic frame of reference is best expounded by a literary critic, Kenneth Burke.

William Rueckert (1963), following the southern poet John Crowe Ransom, aptly classes Burke as a "maw" rather than a "wam" type of critic. "Wam" is "maw" spelled backward and pronounced with the mouth primly closed. Burke is definitely the open-mouthed maw. From his orifice has poured a flood of puns, polemic, and endless classifications, all designed to spin out a perspective for the understanding of symbolic action.

Content, for Burke, is always to be viewed in relation to the performance and medium through which it is expressed, and he ridicules (1953:169) the "savants" who would "catalogue for us the 'thoughts' of a stylist like Milton, by stating them simply as precepts divorced from their stylistic context." In Burke's view (1953:36), the artist's work is not so much expressing his own thoughts or feelings as manipulating the "blood, brain, heart, and bowels" of his audience to evoke their response by symbolic action that arouses and satisfies their appetites.

This action of arousing and fulfilling desires or appetites invariably requires guilt, scapegoat, and catharsis. The three elements interlock in any symbolic performance, since (1961:123) "if there is a cleansing, there must be persons or things that do the cleansing (agencies) and there must be offscourings that result from the cleansing." And these must be disposed of, neutralized. To carry away the filth there must appear a scapegoat who, after covering himself with it, is eliminated.

One of Burke's many classifications distinguishes three types of scapegoats or "sacrificial victims" (Burke 1952: 369-75; Rueckert 1963:146): (a) the true scapegoat, the polluted victim who is sacrificed because he is polluted, (b) the sacrificial agent, the unpolluted victim who is sacrificed because he is unpolluted, and (c) the mixed victim who, after killing another, kills himself. The evil offender, such as Iago, exemplifies type a. He deserves what he gets. Type b is too good for the world; b is exemplified by Christ or Thomas Mann's Hanno Buddenbrooks. Oedipus, Othello, and Hamlet all fit c.

The a and c types appear most central to Burke's theory of the dynamics of catharsis. Tragic catharsis calls for steps like the following: A character is elevated, as by exaggerating his natural endowments, and he is depicted as proud. The audience resents him. The character is then made to suffer. The audience pities him. The pity bears several relations to the pride; e.g., that stated, as Burke puts it, in the "language of the body," as when a proud man turns his back, displaying his bottom ("the higher the ape climbs, the more he shows his tail"). To balance the anal-retentive pride, pity permits a diuretic release—the warm outpouring of tears. The tears are like urine in motive as well as substance, since pity is partly an expression of the audience's sympathy with an individual whom it fears might be itself; accordingly, its tears are like Coleridge's "soft flowing daughter of fright." Semen as well as urine is symbolized by the tears, according to Burke's notion that the tragic catharsis is sexually arousing; if the audience cannot copulate on the spot, it merely weeps (1961, 1959).

Burke is an ethnographer of communications in his insistence on the necessity of relating all performances to their contexts. As he puts it (1957:3): "Let us suppose that you ask me: 'What did the man say?' And that I answer: 'He said "Yes."' You still do not know what the man said." On this ground, Burke urges critics to delineate the situations to which symbols are strategic responses and adaptations. Thus he suggests that the sublime and the ridiculous are complementary ways of confronting and encompassing a situation. The *Decameron* should be read "not as a series of hilarious stories, but as a series of hilarious stories *told during a plague*" (1957:53).

Though concerned with total context and the relationships between act and scene, Burke focuses on the structure of the act, the form of the performance (1957:vii). It is this structure that Burke would emphasize in his view of symbolic action. Regardless of the particular situational tensions they confront, all symbolic actions cope with them by transforming them into orderly form and sequence. Thus (1959:364) "the symbol-using animal experiences a certain kind of 'relief' in the mere act of converting any articulate muddle into the orderly terms of a symbol system."

In agreement with Dell Hymes (1964), we would view Burke's perspective as important for anthropology in that it highlights the full dynamic of both the "communicative event" and its situational context. As an example partially applying the Burkean viewpoint in an anthropological study of narrative, Peacock's (1968) analysis of *ludruk* may be cited.

Ludruk is a kind of psychodrama performed in the city of Surabaja, Indonesia, located on Java's northeast coast. There is no script; the actors, who in daily life work at ordinary jobs as bricklayers or cooks, improvise speech and action to fit whatever characters they decide to play. The audience, proletarian like the actors, are very vocal, screaming and cursing at the actors throughout the play. The plays are extremely popular and are also rather long, lasting from five hours to all night, featuring songs, dances, and stories.

The focus here is on *ludruk* narratives of the type called by the actors themselves "domestic stories." These stories fall into two types. One is increasing in popularity, the other decreasing. It happens that the stories increasing in popularity are by various criteria "modern," so are appropriately labeled *M*. Stories of declining popularity may be labeled *T*, for "traditional."

Ludruk's increasing emphasis on *M* stories involves many changes from the traditional story lines. In *T* stories, the main proletarian character (almost always a heroine, played by a male transvestite) fails at climbing socially, but in *M* stories she succeeds; she marries an elite male. *T* stories are dominated by comic twists of chance that block characters' plans, but *M* characters achieve their plans by rationally exploiting sex. Songs and jokes that accompany *T* stories classify characters according to their refinement, but those accompanying *M* stories classify characters according to their progressiveness. *T* story climaxes center around solidification of family ties, but *M* story climaxes focus on violent punishment of a scapegoat that results in the smashing of family ties. The *T* story encompasses a time span of twenty-five years or so, but the *M* story covers only a few weeks.

Not only is the content of the stories changing, but the form is changing as well. Form and empathy are more fragmented in *T* stories than in *M* stories. This is partly because clowns interrupt the narrative more often in *T* stories (approximately 70 percent of *T* story scenes are thus interrupted, only 23 percent of *M* story scenes). *M* stories sustain a narrative that concludes by unleashing violent aggression as spectators scream at a scapegoat.

When *T* stories conclude, they return to the state of equilibrium that prevailed at their beginning. The last scene is calm like the first, and when the play is over spectators say, "Now the situation is again secure and calm [*slamet dan aman*]." *M* stories, in contrast, having carried spectators through a relatively sustained series of climaxes, end with an action that is unfinished. *M* stories end as hero and heroine have married, but have not yet produced a child, which is to say, in Javanese thought, have not yet consummated their marriage. One might suggest that the *M* participants, having been clutched for several hours in empathy with *M* action, feel frustrated by not being permitted to consolidate their success on stage. The frustration perhaps evokes a drive to finish outside the theater what one cannot inside—an itch to consummate in reality what one cannot in fantasy.

Unfortunately, *ludruk* participants are not promising candidates for the consummation of this drive toward success. They are largely semiliterate workers between the ages of twenty and fifty, married, with children, stuck at their occupational level and past the age of schooling, which, in Indonesia, is the main path to social achievement. Those who take part in *ludruk* are unlikely to move into elite houses, produce elite children, and thus cure the mental itch that *M* stories appear to induce.

If this assessment is correct, *ludruk* can be seen as one of several symbolic devices in Indonesia that build into Javanese personalities drives that are not consummated. Lack of consummation creates tension. One mode of easing that tension is the displacement of social aspirations onto one's children. *Ludruk* participants see the children as doing what they cannot, as "building the bridge from Banjuwangi to Gilimanuk," which they have failed to do. Case studies show that in fact the children of *ludruk* participants are succeeding where their parents failed. Furthermore, some of the *ludruk* participants are changing their child-rearing methods to ensure that their children succeed. The hypothesis, then, is that *ludruk* helps create a drive. To fulfill that drive, parents identify with their successful children. To create successful children with whom they can identify, parents are changing their methods of child-rearing.

Several arguments are employed in support of this rather speculative hypothesis. For example, the socioeconomic constraints on *ludruk* participants are such that if they are to choose any mode of expressing the activist drives projected by *ludruk*, they might well choose to change their children. Since they are proletarian, they control little else in society except their children.

A second argument is that the condition of *ludruk* participants is such that *ludruk* might have a stronger effect on the children than on the participants themselves. The participants are parents; few children attend the performances. The parents' personalities are already formed, crystallized. Chances are, even repeated exposure to *ludruk* will not deeply and permanently restructure their psyches. The children's psyches are still soft and malleable. Therefore, if a parent were to frequent *ludruk*, and if each time he goes he is motivated to respond in a new way to his child, these repeated patterns of modified parental response might have deep and permanent effects on the *child*. Thus an amplifying effect would occur in that *ludruk's* repeated temporary effect on the parent has a permanent effect on the child.[2]

Obviously this analysis is moving beyond the performance into the broader sphere of psychological and social effects on participants. In grappling

---

[2] During the course of research in Indonesia in 1970, Peacock revisited the *ludruk* play and players for one week. Several interesting and systematic changes have occurred since the events that followed the original investigation—the fall of Sukarno, the massacre of hundreds of thousands of communists and other Indonesians in 1965, and the rise of Islamic and military powers. Since the 1965 upheaval, the modernizing tendency in *ludruk* has been reversed. *M* plots are being replaced by *T* plots. Plots are increasingly fragmented as clowns increasingly dominate the scenes. And there has been a marked revival of animistic and magical themes accompanying the decline of *M* plot themes emphasizing individual initiative and opportunism. These regressive tendencies may reflect several conditions, among them the death or imprisonment of *ludruk's* most creative figures, and political restraints imposed on the *ludruk* players now that they are tightly controlled ("gripped" and "bitten") by the present military rule. The absolute number of *ludruk* troupes and theaters is greater now than in 1963, but their arenas are now predominantly the urban shantytowns rather than the bustling marketplaces of 1963.

with this problem, the analysis of *ludruk* suffers from the vices and difficulties that are characterized in the next section.

PSYCHOLOGICAL, SOCIAL, AND CULTURAL ANALYSIS OF NARRATIVE

How does a narrative performance relate to the system of interacting roles and groups that compose the participants' society? To the system of logically interlocking and shared values, ideas, and symbols that compose the participants' culture? To the total system of behavioral components that forms the personality of each participant?

All of these questions pose difficult problems of analysis. Consider, by way of illustration, the directness with which a legal prescription, a written law, by contrast to a narrative form, might be related to society, culture, and personality.

First, it is easier to arrive at a statement of what the law "says"—what behavior it explicitly describes and prescribes—than to formulate what the narrative says. Like any expressive form, narrative says things about behavior indirectly—by metaphor, allusion, and symbol. Therefore, it is probably easier to formulate the values and norms of the law that define its place in the wider culture, the shared system of values, ideas, and symbols, than to formulate the cultural meaning of the narrative.

Second, to trace the behavioral implications of the narrative performance—the ways in which it influences behavior in contexts outside the performance—the analyst must dissect the myriad emotional and cerebral responses to the narrative. On the basis of intuition and introspection, he may suspect that audiences harbor deep and profound feelings regarding the story. To record those feelings is difficult. The listener rarely shouts his innermost emotions, and even if he is made to lie on a psychiatrist's couch, only a portion of his emotional reactions comes to light. Indeed, if the artist is more articulate than the audience, it seems unlikely that even the most probing query could draw from audience members as rich and elegant an expression of emotion and thought as that distilled in the narrative itself.

Some might protest that it is just as difficult to record inner feelings concerning legal laws. But much of the influence of the laws on individual and social behavior can be demonstrated by merely recording the patterns they directly enforce. Since narrative forms ordinarily do not directly enforce a pattern of social organization, it is only through a labyrinthine psychosocial analysis (such as that attempted with *ludruk*) that these influences are uncovered. The investigator must somehow dissect the subjective experience derived from participation in the narrative performance, then trace the effects of this experience on participants' behavior in nonperformance contexts. Especially in complex society such analysis is difficult because the nonperformance contexts—economic, political, and familial—are differentiated from the performance contexts and connections between the two are not binding (in the legal sense that court-enforced decisions are binding on the behavior of defendants away from court). The social and psychological consequences of narrative may be great, but it is empirically a staggering task to trace their ramifications.

John Roberts and Brian Sutton-Smith (1962; Roberts 1964; Roberts et al. 1963) have imaginatively and productively employed a method very different from that used in the case of *ludruk* to explore such ramifications. They have demonstrated that narrative and similar cultural productions (songs, dances, poems, riddles, games, and dramas) covary cross-culturally with numerous social and psychological patterns. For example, games of strategy (as opposed to chance) are largely found in societies with high gods and jurisdictional levels above the local community. To explain the correlations, Roberts and Sutton-Smith treat games and other forms as models that both teach behavioral patterns—how to take a chance, how to show skill, how to deceive—and assuage conflicts derived from the patterns and their wider sociopsychological environment. They suggest an evolutionary sequence; strategy concern is characteristic of the most politically and technologically complex societies.

Like all cross-cultural and correlational approaches, the evolutionary hypothesis assumes that myriad subtle processes converge to produce gross relationships of patterning. That such relationships exist even within the delicate and intricate sphere of narrative and society is at least suggested in Peacock's (forthcoming) speculative attempt to link the evolution of narrative form to one of the many schemes of social evolution, in this instance one adapted from the work of Robert Bellah (1964). The form considered is the dramatic performance.

The first stage, which Bellah calls "primitive," is characterized by dramatic ritual performances of the type Gluckman names "rites of social relations" (1962). Such rites are distinguished by, among other things, the extremely diffuse bond uniting the ritual participants. Not only are they coritualists, but they are also neighbors, colandholders, and kinsmen, and they share other roles as well. Their empathy with one another during the rite is therefore along a wide band, tapping a number of social relationships. Owing to the diffuseness of the bond uniting primitive ritual (dramatic) participants, the ritual ordering of the bond is perceived by primitives as affecting a wide range of phenomena—not only the community, but nature and the cosmos. And participants believe that performing the rite is itself sufficient to effect desired changes in these spheres— in the case of the Australian aborigine, to help the witchetty grub flourish.

The primitives contrast with modern participants in drama, who relate to one another daily by specialized bonds and during performances along narrow and specific bands (such as paid actor and paying audience), and who do not believe that manipulating their social relations on the stage will automatically affect society, nature, or cosmos. Since moderns do not expect the performance itself to change the world to fit its symbolism, they are forced to do it themselves. According to this notion, the narrative form of the "modern drama" type tends, regardless of its content, to evoke a more innovative and activistic attitude toward reality than does the ritual of social relations rife in primitive society.

Combining Bellah's second and third stages, one might speak of "archaic-historic" societies (e.g., medieval southeast Asian kingdoms, such as Java, Malaya, and Thailand, some medieval European kingdoms, and some areas of middle America). Characteristic dramatic themes are the comedy of manners and the legend of royalty, often combined into a single performance that features a hero-king endowed with supernatural powers and a clown who lampoons him. The larger society is characterized by social relations that are diffuse, in the primitive sense, but also hierarchical: father and son, master and servant, king and subject. Because the relationship is diffuse, disturbance of it would produce deep and wide ramifications in the lives of the community members. To avoid such drastic ramifications, to harmonize and preserve the relationship, elaborate manners are developed. To sanctify and to satirize these manners, comedies of manners emerge. Interwoven with the legends of royalty, such comedies are staged as drama, such as the *wajang wong* and *wajang kulit* of Java. In such comedies, plot line counts less than periodic jokes or maudlin episodes. The jokes satirize kings and aristocrats. The episodes depict a helpless creature, such as a pregnant woman or orphan child, suffering passively at the hands of a cruel aristocrat or king. Since plot line is not crucial, the performances often run for hours, perhaps all night, with the audience frequently recessing to eat, sleep, excrete, and socialize. Since custom, beginning with child-training, teaches not identification with superiors' personalities but imitation of their manners, performances feature little psychological analysis of the heroes, but rather imitation of their manners and mien by clowns. The dance, which is markedly developed in the southeast Asian archaic-historic societies, is especially suited for mocking and glorifying refined manners. Clowning, dancing, and stereotyped symbols are much more prominent in archaic-historic drama than psychological exploration of character development.

Bellah's fourth stage, "early modern," may be divided into two variants, the collectivist and the individualist. Characteristic performances in early modern collectivist societies (e.g., Nazi Germany, the Soviet Union, and certain new nations) are the nationalist film, play, or ceremony that depicts individuals as relentlessly (but enthusiastically) swept along by forces of history toward a collective goal. Horror tales,

in which individuals are moved by dark spiritual forces and destinies, may also be popular (Kracauer 1959). Political stories are often moralistic and didactic to teach nationalist and revolutionary ideals. Heroes are charismatic and superior to onlookers but lack the supernatural powers of archaic-historic kings. Enemy scapegoats are prominent. Unlike archaic-historic kingdoms, the larger society produces a youth culture, oriented around nationalism. The archaic-historic stress on manners and hierarchy is lost and with it the emphasis on both ultrarefined dancers and ultracrude clowns. With the declining importance of jokes and dance interludes and the increasing spirit of nationalist thrust toward goals, dramatic performances become shorter and more tightly organized toward a climax.

In early modern, individualistic society (e.g., prewar America), the Hollywood films depicting success and romance are characteristic. Such films are neither didactic nor moralistic, since they depict doing for the sake of doing rather than glorifying loyalty as an abstract, collective ideal. Plots are fast-moving and light with hustle and pep. The stories emphasize heterosexual love instead of homosexual comradeship, unlike collectivistic, nationalistic stories, for comradeship may aid collectivistic military-nationalistic struggle and revolution, but it can disrupt the climb to personal success. The climber prefers romance leading to a mobile nuclear family unit that climbs with him. Early modern, individualistic performances tend to be even shorter than collectivist performances, partly in order to depict as clearly and compactly as possible the connection between characters' initial ambition and final success, partly in order not to take too much time from the job. Youth is geared into the fantasy and art of early modern society, but not into its political system, with the result that the popular art, including film, is often silly and trivial.

It is interesting to note that in order to formulate linkages between social and narrative patterning, it seemed necessary to emphasize narrative features that are grosser and more abstract than those employed in the careful textual analyses mentioned earlier. How to achieve both relevance and precision is, of course, always a problem, and it is a prominent one for the analyst who would remain true to the text yet sketch the connections between narrative and the wider forces of society.

There is no need to illustrate here the wealth of psychological researches by such figures as Freud, Jung, and Murray and their followers in the anthropological field of culture and personality. Obviously such researches into the personality traits and needs that are expressed and codified by narrative can greatly illuminate the workings of the mind. One caution that the psychologists have sometimes ignored should be mentioned, however. Instead of generalizing directly from text to mind, the psychologist would be well advised to take account of the total performance context and experience. Otherwise he may treat as expressive of deep psychological states symbolic expressions that can be shown to be merely stylistic devices employed by the narrator to serve specific requirements of a form and audience. Kenneth Burke sets an excellent example in preceding psychological analysis with stylistic analysis of Shakespeare's plays in order to argue that certain expressions that *cannot* be explained as logical and natural devices to serve requirements of audience and form must be present to serve Shakespeare's purely personal needs. (See Burke's comments on *Hamlet*, Act 2, Scene 2, in Burke 1953:102, 196.)

One way toward understanding some of these highly complex relations between artists (or their productions) and their wider psychosocial ramifications is the experiment. Unfortunately very little has been done with narrative experiments, and nothing at all with any kind of experimental anthropology. Bartlett's classic study of narrative recall in Africa, published in 1932, was followed in 1937 by Nadel's study of Nupe and Yoruba responses to artificially constructed narratives. In recalling one story, one tribe "laid stress on logical and rational elements while the other showed distinct appreciation of situational facts and connections of time and place" (Nadel 1937:211). Nadel was able to distinguish three different types, one for the Yoruba and two for the Nupe, which he associated with other cultural characteristics. So many different variables operate in studies of this kind that it is difficult to maintain controls—perhaps one reason anthropologists have failed to follow up these studies. However, as we begin to discover underlying cultural grammars that can be tested and confirmed, an experimental approach may be indicated. For example, it is quite possible to introduce a number of artificially constructed stories with both native and alien eidochronic structures. The use of these eidochronic structures should permit the prediction of recall failure and thus validate the eidochronic structure.

CONCLUSION: THE IMPORTANCE OF NARRATIVE STUDIES

Anthropology would seem to be increasingly turning its attention from cultural stasis and structuralism to social process (as in the studies of modernization and political conflict) and psychological process (as in the studies of language learning and ethnological adaptation). As this focus on psychosocial process becomes paramount, the search for cultural or symbolic correlates of such process might well turn to narrative. Of all the cultural forms, narrative is most clearly designed to portray action and process vividly. Laws and theologies may formulate ideals and goals, but narrative concretely portrays characters in the process of struggling toward those ideals and goals. The study of narrative should therefore yield information crucially important for the new endeavors in anthropology.

The study of the process of mental and personality development would be enriched by narrative studies. Psychologists may uncover neurological and biochemical correlates of mental growth, but anthropologists are equipped to formulate the culturally codified and socially shared models that men employ in carrying out their own and their children's development. The application of structural and statistical narrative-analysis techniques to biographies, as perhaps the most important such narrative model, should yield insights missed by the typical frames of psychiatry and psychology.

Narrative should lend itself well to the comparative study of forms of thought. Narrative is virtually universal in history and among contemporary societies. Narratives are easily compared because, in the broadest definition, all narratives are structurally similar and in a more specific definition tend (we suspect) to fall into a limited number of systems in the same way that kinship systems are repeated throughout the world. Because narrative forms compose compact, condensed units constructed according to intrinsic principles of logic and artistic necessity, their analysis can be brought to a high level of precision.

A hope that spurs the compulsive preoccupation with the intricacies of narrative textual analysis is that since narrative forms possess a clarity of defi-nition similar to linguistic forms, with the development of new canons of excellence, replicability, and exhaustiveness, the study of narrative can be brought to a scientific par with the study of language. As models of narrative and language converge, we may draw nearer to a defensible theory encompassing these and other symbolic forms, such as those of music, the analysis of which is already at quite a high level. At present, however, the use of linguistic models in narrative analysis is mainly metaphorical. Indeed, too naive a usage of the linguistic models is dangerous, since narrative is clearly constructed of units different from those composing languages (Fischer 1960: 442).

One may note a bias in anthropology and social science generally against the study of the social implications of expressive form, including narrative. Insofar as any symbolic forms are given prominence in social analysis, these are evaluative forms—the decrees, doctrines, sermons that serve primarily as vehicles for moral conceptions (whereas expressive forms may be defined as regarded more for their formal qualities, their sensuous surfaces, than for any moral or cognitive conceptions they happen to express). The assumption, especially in social anthropology and sociology, seems to be that if any symbolic forms are crucial for the integration and survival of society, these are the evaluative ones that directly express do's and don'ts and are directly geared to organizations that administer sanctions (e.g., see Parsons 1951, 1961). Expressive forms do not muster such machinery of direct social control.

On the other hand, one can ask whether the frivolous weapons of narrative—its devices with power to thrill, move, and amuse—do not possess advantages over the more obviously powerful evaluative symbols. Because sermons and decrees are often pompous, obvious, and rude, they put people on their guard and arouse their resistance. The subtle and undercover techniques of narrative as art, which do not so obviously aim to control, may seduce people into letting their guard down. Thus narrative expression possesses at least one type of control potential that evaluative forms do not. Furthermore, in this day of reaction against moralistic postures and their supernaturalist base, the traditional control power of evaluative culture is weakened. At the same time, the rise of the mass media, which lend themselves more to stories than to sermons, strengthens the position of expressive culture. Expressive forms, including narrative forms, might well assume increasingly important roles in social control. Should this occur, the study of narrative will become increasingly relevant to the student of society.

REFERENCES

Bartlett, Frederic Charles
  1932 *Remembering: A Study in Experimental and Social Psychology.* Cambridge: At the University Press.
Bellah, Robert N.
  1964 Religious Evolution. *American Sociological Review* 29:358-74.
Benedict, Ruth
  1969 Zuñi Mythology, vol. 1. New York: AMS Press.
Benfey, Theodore
  1859 *Pantschatantra: Fünf Bücher Indischer Fablen, Märchen, und Erzählungen,* 2 vols. Leipzig.
Boas, Franz
  1902 *Tsimshian Texts.* Bureau of American Ethnology Bulletin no. 27. Washington, D.C.: Smithsonian Institution.
  1910 *Kwakiutl Tales,* vol. 2 of *Contributions to Anthropology.* New York: Columbia University Press.
  1938 Mythology and Folklore. In *General Anthropology,* ed. F. Boas. Boston: D. C. Heath.

Burke, Kenneth
  1952 Thanatopsis for Critics: A Brief Thesaurus of Deaths and Dyings. *Essays in Criticism* 2:369-75.
  1953 *Counter-Statement.* Los Altos, Calif.: Hermes Publications.
  1957 *The Philosophy of Literary Form: Studies in Symbolic Action.* New York: Vintage Books.
  1959 On Catharsis, or Resolution, with a Postscript. *Kenyon Review* 21:337-75.
  1961 Catharsis: Second View. *Centennial Review of Arts and Sciences* 5:107-32.
Colby, Benjamin N.
  1966a Cultural Patterns in Narrative. *Science* 151:793-98.
  1966b The Analysis of Culture Content and the Patterning of Narrative Concern in Texts. *American Anthropologist* 68:374-88.
  1970 The Shape of the Narrative Concern in Japanese Folktales. In *Mathematical Anthropology,* ed. Paul Kay. Cambridge: M.I.T. Press.
  1973 A partial Grammar of Eskimo Folktales. *American Anthropologist* 75, no. 3.
Colby, Benjamin N., and Michael Cole
  1970 Culture, Memory, and Narrative. In *Modes of Thought: Festschrift to Evans-Pritchard,* ed. R. Horton and R. Murray. London: Faber & Faber.
Comte, Auguste
  1896 *The Positive Philosophy,* trans. H. Martineau. London: G. Bell.
Dégh, Linda
  1969 *Folktales and Society: Story-Telling in a Hungarian Peasant Community.* Bloomington: Indiana University Press.
Dundes, Alan
  1964 The Morphology of North American Indian Folktales. *FF Communications* 195:1-134.
  1965 *The Study of Folklore.* Englewood Cliffs, N.J.: Prentice-Hall.
Durkheim, Émile
  1961 *The Elementary Forms of the Religious Life,* trans. J. W. Swain. New York: Crowell-Collier. Originally published 1912.
Fischer, John L.

1958 Folktales, Social Structure, and Environment in Two Polynesian Outliers. *Journal of the Polynesian Society* 67:11-36.

1960 Sequence and Structure in Folktales. In *Men and Cultures,* ed. Anthony F. C. Wallace. Philadelphia: University of Pennsylvania Press.

1963 The Sociopsychological Analysis of Folktales. *Current Anthropology* 4:235-95.

Frazer, James George
1890 *The Golden Bough: A Study in Comparative Religion,* 2 vols. London: Macmillan.

Gluckman, Max
1962 Les Rites de Passage. In *Essays on the Ritual of Social Relations,* ed. M. Gluckman. Manchester: Manchester University Press.

Greenway, John
1964 *Literature Among the Primitives.* Hatboro, Pa.: Folklore Associates.

Grimm, Wilhelm, and Jakob Grimm
1884 *Grimm's Household Tales,* trans. Margaret Hunt. London: G. Bell.

Horner, George R.
1967 A Structural Analysis of Bulu (Africa) Folktales. Paper presented at the annual meeting of the American Folklore Society, Toronto.

Hymes, Dell H.
1964 Directions in (Ethno-)Linguistic Theory. In *Transcultural Studies in Cognition,* ed. A. K. Romney and R. G. D'Andrade. *American Anthropologist* 66, no. 3, pt. 2 (special issue).

Jacobs, Melville
1959 *The Content and Style of an Oral Literature: Clackamas Chinook Myths and Tales.* New York: Viking Press.

Jason, Heddy
1967 Oral Literature and the Structure of Language. Paper presented at the annual meeting of the American Anthropological Association, Washington, D.C.

1968a *The Jew and the Barber: About the Particular and the General.* Santa Monica, Calif.: Rand Corporation.

1968b *The Narrative Structure of Swindler Tales.* Santa Monica, Calif.: Rand Corporation.

1968c *The Russian Criticism of the "Finnish School" in Folktale Scholarship.* Santa Monica, Calif.: Rand Corporation.

1968d *Structural Analysis and the Concept of the "Tale-Type."* Santa Monica, Calif.: Rand Corporation.

1969 A Multidimensional Approach to Oral Literature. *Current Anthropology* 10:413-27.

Kracauer, Siegfried
1959 *From Caligari to Hitler.* New York: Noonday Press.

Leach, Edmund
1965 Lévi-Strauss in the Garden of Eden. In *Reader in Comparative Religion,* ed. W. A. Lessa and E. Z. Vogt, 2nd ed. New York: Harper & Row.

Lévi-Strauss, Claude
1960 Four Winnebago Myths: A Structural Sketch. In *Culture in History: Essays in Honor of Paul Radin,* ed. S. Diamond. New York: Columbia University Press.

1963 The Structural Study of Myth. In *Structural Anthropology,* trans. C. Jacobson and B. G. Schoepf. New York: Basic Books.

Lord, Albert B.
1960 *The Singer of Tales.* Cambridge: Harvard University Press.

McClelland, David C.
1967 *The Achieving Society.* New York: Free Press, Macmillan.

McLennan, John Ferguson
1865 *Primitive Marriage.* Edinburgh: A. & C. Black.

Maine, Henry Sumner
1861 *Ancient Law: Its Connection with the Early History of Society and Its Relation to Modern Ideas.* London: J. Murray.

Malinowski, Bronislaw
1954 Myth in Primitive Psychology. In *Magic, Science, and Religion and Other Essays.* Garden City, N.Y.: Doubleday.

Mathiot, Madeleine
n.d. Cognitive Analysis of a Myth: An Exercise in Methodology. Unpublished MS, State University of New York, Buffalo.

Mead, Margaret, and Rhoda Metraux, eds.
1953 *The Study of Culture at a Distance.* Chicago: University of Chicago Press.

Morgan, Lewis Henry
1877 *Ancient Society.* New York: World.
Nadel, S. F.
1937 A Field Experiment in Racial Psychology. *British Journal of Psychology* 28:195-211.
Parsons, Talcott
1951 *The Social System.* Glencoe, Ill.: Free Press.
1961 Introduction to Part 4. In *Theories of Society: Foundations of Modern Sociological Theory,* ed. T. Parsons et al. New York: Free Press, Macmillan.
Peacock, James L.
1968 *Rites of Modernization.* Chicago: University of Chicago Press.
1969 Society as Narrative. In *Forms of Symbolic Action: Proceedings of the 1969 Annual Spring Meetings, American Ethnological Society,* ed. Victor Turner. Seattle: University of Washington Press.
forth- Expressive Symbolism. In *Festschrift*
coming *to Talcott Parsons,* ed. Andrew Effret et al. New York: Free Press, Macmillan.
Powlison, Paul S.
1965 A Paragraph Analysis of a Yagua Folktale. *International Journal of American Linguistics* 31:101-18.
Propp, Vladimir
1958 *Morphology of the Folktale,* trans. L. Scott. Austin: University of Texas Press. Originally published 1928.
Radin, Paul
1927 *Primitive Man as Philosopher.* New York: Appleton-Century-Crofts.
1955 The Literature of Primitive Peoples. *Diogenes* 12.
1956 *The Trickster: A Study in American Indian Mythology.* London: Routledge & Kegan Paul.
Roberts, John M.
1964 The Self-Management of Cultures. In *Explorations in Cultural Anthropology,* ed. W. H. Goodenough, pp. 433-54. New York: McGraw-Hill.
Roberts, John M., and Brian Sutton-Smith
1962 Child Training and Game Involvement. *Ethnology* 1:166-85.
Roberts, John M., Brian Sutton-Smith, and Adam O. Kendon
1963 Strategy in Games and Folktales. *Journal of Social Psychology* 61:185-99.
Rosenberg, Bruce A.
1970 The Formulaic Quality of Spontaneous Sermons. *Journal of American Folklore* 83:3-20.
Rueckert, William Howe
1963 *Kenneth Burke and the Drama of Human Relations.* Minneapolis: University of Minnesota Press.
Sebeok, Thomas A., and Frances J. Ingemann
1956 *Studies in Cheremis: The Supernatural.* New York: Wenner-Gren Foundation.
Shannon, C. E., and W. Weaver
1949 *The Mathematical Theory of Communication.* Urbana: University of Illinois Press.
Spencer, Katherine
1957 *Mythology and Values: An Analysis of Navaho Chantway Myths.* Philadelphia: American Folklore Society.
Thompson, S.
1946 *The Folktale.* New York: Holt, Rinehart & Winston.
Tylor, Edward B.
1871 *Primitive Culture: Researches into the Development of Mythology, Philosophy, Religion, Language, Art, and Custom.* London: J. Murray.

CHAPTER 15 The Structural Anthropology of Claude Lévi-Strauss

BOB SCHOLTE

> The wall of Paradise is built of contraries,
> nor is there any way to enter but for one who
> has overcome the highest spirit of reason who
> guards the gate.
>
> —Nicholas of Cusa

INTRODUCTION

The purpose of this essay is to review, discuss, and assess the ethnological contributions, scientific procedures, and future prospects of structural anthropology.[1] Structuralism is an intellectually complex, historically evolving, and academically successful movement (it is so fashionable and chic that in some circles the mere mention of Lévi-Strauss' name seems more important than what is actually said about him; see Pouillon 1966a:769). As a result, the various topics for discussion and the relevant references for citation have grown to enormous and forbidding proportions. Serious students of structuralism run a risk similar to Van Gennep's *jeune homme*: eventually to die in vain at the age of ninety just keeping their bibliographies up to date (see Needham 1967:143). In this situation, some discrimination and careful selection are obviously necessary and unavoidable.

Though the sociohistorical reasons for structuralism's recent prominence are themselves of great anthropological interest (e.g., Bourdieu and Passeron 1967, Furet 1967, Hughes 1968, Lanteri-Laura 1967), my aim here is not to explain or justify this remarkable success. Nor can I possibly hope to account for all of structuralism's intricate

[1] Substantial portions of this essay are based on my Ph.D. dissertation: "The Ethnology of Anthropological Traditions: A Comparative Study of Anglo-American Commentaries on French Continental Structuralism," University of California, Berkeley, 1969. I would like to thank my thesis advisers, Alan Dundes and Dell Hymes, for their patience and support. I am also grateful to the Social Science Research Council and to the Wenner-Gren Foundation for their financial assistance. Above all, thanks to my wife Pamela, who helped in countless ways.

themes and complex variations.[2] Instead, I would like to propose the following criteria for both the substantive contents and the bibliographic itemization of this essay. First of all, I shall limit myself almost exclusively to structural anthropology proper. I shall mention other structuralist studies only when and where they serve to illuminate or complement ethnographic materials and ethnological results. Second, I shall assume that Lévi-Strauss' work is ideal-typical of structural anthropology as a whole. I shall therefore mention other "structuralists" only by way of contrast and comparison. Finally, I shall restrict my discussion to those methodological premises and substantive conclusions that best serve to ex-

plain Lévi-Strauss' anthropological position as a whole. I shall not consider either his detailed ethnographic examples or his specific ethnological theories except insofar as they expressly contribute to the description and understanding of more general propositions.[3]

THE INTELLECTUAL-HISTORICAL CONTEXT OF STRUCTURAL ANTHROPOLOGY

Lévi-Strauss' intellectual-historical background has been the subject of considerable controversy and confusion (e.g., Dyson-Hudson 1970:222, Sahlins 1966:131). While some have insisted on a respectable heritage (e.g., Hughes 1968:264f), others have found only unsavory origins (e.g., Harris 1968:464f). Still others have either expressed genuine confusion (e.g., Schneider 1965: 39f) or simply changed their minds (e.g., Leach 1969:317). Comparatively few authors have proceeded inductively; that is, have tried to reconstruct an intellectual-historical background on the specific textual bases provided by Lévi-Strauss' own writings. I shall try to do so here.

There is one eighteenth-century social philosopher whose intellectual-historical importance cannot be exag-

---

[2] Numerous introductions to structuralism generally are readily available. There are, first of all, the essential works of some of its most prominent spokesmen; e.g., Althusser 1965a, 1965b; Barthes 1964, 1970; Foucault 1966, 1969; Lacan 1966, 1968; and Lévi-Strauss (see Hayes and Hayes 1970 for a recent bibliography). Second, a number of journals and periodicals have devoted special issues to Lévi-Strauss, structuralism, and semiotics: *Aletheia* 4 (1966), *Annales* 6 (1964), *Cahiers pour l'analyse* 4 (1966), *Communications* 4 (1964) and 8 (1966), *Esprit* 322 (1963) and 360 (1967), *Kursbuch* 5 (1966), *Nouvelle critique* 24 (1969), *La pensée* 135 (1967), *Revue internationale de philosophie* 73-74 (1965), *Social Science Information* 6 (1967), *Temps modernes* 246 (1966), and *Yale French Studies* 36-37 (1966). Third, there are many secondary sources and interpretations of structuralism as a whole. Among the most informative I would include the following: Auzias 1967; Barthes 1967; Bastide 1962; Boudon 1968; Caws 1968; Corvez 1969; Fagès 1967; Jaeggi 1969; Lane 1970; Lepenies 1968; Macksey and Donato, eds., 1970; Mudimbe 1968; Parain-Vial 1969; Piaget 1969, 1970; Pouillon 1966a; Runciman 1969; Schiwy 1969; Sebag 1964; Viet 1965; and Wahl et al. 1968. Finally, there are literally hundreds of books and articles on Lévi-Strauss and structural anthropology proper. I shall have occasion to cite many of these in the course of this paper. Suffice it to mention the most interesting interpretations here: Backès-Clément 1970; Hayes and Hayes, eds., 1970; Leach 1965a, 1970; Lepenies and Ritter, eds., 1970; Maranda and Pouillon, eds., 1970; Pouillon 1956; Paz 1970; and Simonis 1968a.

[3] There are three practical reasons for making these selective choices: First, an adequate discussion of structuralism in its entirety would require several volumes. I hope the list of references at the end of the chapter will prove extensive enough to allow those anthropologists interested in structuralism as a whole to pursue these interests individually. Second, since even Lévi-Strauss' most vocal critics will surely grant that his anthropological writings are among the most prominent and dramatic in the literature, a summary review article devoted to him exclusively does not seem unwarranted or inappropriate. Third, I am sure that the specific details of Lévi-Strauss' contributions to the fields of kinship studies, mythology, folklore, and so on will be more than adequately covered elsewhere in this volume. My own selectivity will therefore merely complement these other contributions.

gerated: Jean Jacques Rousseau (see especially 1962*a*).[4] In fact, any analogies between Lévi-Strauss and Vico (e.g., Leach 1969, Merquior 1970) or between structural anthropology and the Enlightenment generally (e.g., Diamond 1964, Steiner 1967) are derivative by comparison. Lévi-Strauss hails Rousseau as "our master and our brother" (1955*a*:389), and he considers him the prophetic founder of cultural anthropology (1962*a*:11). Not only is Rousseau's Second Discourse *On the Origin and Foundations of Inequality* "the first anthropological treatise in French literature" (1962*b*:99; see also Diamond 1964:xxii); Rousseau's intellectual contributions and ethnological insights surpass those of his predecessors (like Descartes), his contemporaries (such as Diderot), and even his beneficiaries (for example, Bergson).

What are the ostensible reasons for this lavish praise? One clearly stands out: Rousseau was the first thinker to have posed one of history's most important ontological problems—man's passage from animality to humanity, from instinct to intellect, from the literal to the figurative, from the continuous to the discrete, and from nature to culture. Rousseau is credited with "an extraordinary modern view" of this crucial transition, one based on "the emergence of a logic operating by means of binary oppositions and coinciding with the first manifestations of symbolism" (1962*b*:101). This same argument underlies most of Lévi-Strauss' own deliberations on such diverse topics as social organization (1969), totemism (1962*b*), mythology (1964*a*), and primitive logic generally (1962*c*). Each of these intellectual creations and

their attendant social institutions must be understood as more or less successful cognitive means and organizational efforts to mediate the multiplex and fundamental passage from the naturally given to the culturally created. In fact, Lévi-Strauss' usage of this transition in the scientific explanation and subsequent reduction of human circumstance is so pervasive and characteristic that one can quite legitimately conclude that structuralism's intellectual contribution will ultimately have to be judged in accordance with the ethnological viability or philosophical impasse created by this paramount and inclusive distinction between nature and culture (see Ortiques 1963 and especially Simonis 1968*a*).

Among the many "efficient causes" involved in this crucial passage is a psychic quality Rousseau called "pity." He held this uniquely human attribute responsible for allowing men to make the singular transition to the state of culture. Pity is defined as man's capacity to identify with his fellow human beings and with all living creatures. Only this initial identification and its resultant understanding of both man and animal make a subsequent systematization of both the differences and the resemblances between them possible (totemic systems are concrete cultural examples of this intellectual process; see 1962*b*:77f).

Even more significantly, the same epistemological emergent constitutes the initial foundation for anthropological activity generally. Prior to any comparative or ethnological differentiation, pity is the fundamental condition for intersubjective and ethnographic understanding. Pity or empathy entails a "desire for identification with others" and a "total refusal of identification with [oneself]." There is no doubt that such capacities are circumscribed by the ethnographer's own per-

---

[4] Since I shall be referring to Lévi-Strauss' writings quite frequently, I shall not preface each reference with his name. Should a given bibliographic item refer to anyone else, I will, of course, revert to naming the specific author in question.

sonal circumstances. Yet he can learn to use himself "as his own instrument of observation." He can "learn to know himself objectively and at a distance as if he were another person." To do so, he must identify with "his" essential humanity—what Rousseau called the humble third-person "he" within himself. Only this "other" person within him can empathize with (or pity) the concomitant others within those the anthropologist observes. In this self-mediated and intersubjective context, ethnographic identification, subsequent communication, and eventual objectification are possible. In this sense, "the principle of 'confessions,' written or unacknowledged, is . . . basic to the work of every anthropologist." In this scene, too, Rousseau's celebrated formula "the me is another" heralds both the emergence of "unconditional objectivity" and the resolution of the epistemological schism between self and other, outside observer and native participant (1962a:11-12).[5]

Lévi-Strauss draws yet another conclusion from Rousseau's argument. Humility of self and identification with others have ethical or moral consequences. If psychologically "I am not 'me,' but the weakest and humblest of 'others,' " then sociologically my own culture is always partial; that is, "it is in no way a privileged form of society but only one of countless 'others' . . ." (1962a:13). Since such an unequivocal affirmation of cultural relativism is a necessary but not a sufficient condition for an anthropological theory of social values, Lévi-Strauss further echoes

Rousseau's demand for the ethnological discovery of an "unshakable basis of human society" (1955a:389). Cultural anthropology is specifically charged with the scientific delineation of a "new humanist revolution" (1953a: 350), with the spread of this humanism to all mankind (see 1960a:52), and with its concrete implementation (see 1961a:13).

In working out this ethical program, Lévi-Strauss again turns to Rousseau. While for some, like Diderot, the answer lies in the glorification of a state of nature, for both Rousseau and Lévi-Strauss such a vision is impossible and inadequate. Since the human condition neither predates nor transcends social organization, we must construct an ideal model of man's *culture* and therein discover what is original to man and what is artificial (see 1955a:391f). To find "natural man," we must seek *"the society of nature in order to mediate the nature of society"* (1962a: 13).

Though such a pristine society may never have existed and never could exist, we can infer some of its ideal-typical characteristics from Lévi-Strauss' criticisms of contemporary civilizations and from his obverse praise of primitive societies. The latter correspond to "authentic" societies while the former are considered "unauthentic" (1954:367). Primitive cultures are largely democratic and harmonious while civilized societies are generally repressive and exploitive (see 1961b:45). Most importantly, civilized societies are obsessed with historical progress while primitive cultures have resisted temporal change (see 1960a:46f). The so-called progressive outlook has not only led to the exploitation and colonization of native peoples and territories; it has also proven unproductive, if not disastrous: "ninety percent of the progress we make mainly serves to counter-

<hr>

[5] We shall have more to say about these important issues later on. Let me here merely mention the degree to which Lévi-Strauss' praise for Rousseau precludes any facile comparison between structuralism and Cartesianism. Descartes's *cogito* passes directly from the interiority of man to the exteriority of the world, whereas Rousseau's epistemology (like the anthropologist's) also takes the mediating function of the social world into account (1962a:12f).

balance the disastrous effects of the remaining ten percent" (Lévi-Strauss in Dreyfus 1970:237). In fact, civilizations are akin to overheated steam engines, which generate the infinite waste associated with an entropic technology. Primitive societies are by comparison like pendulum clocks. They have generally sustained a measured ecology and a telic balance with nature. Their cultural concepts of reversible time and cyclical change have tended to preserve ideological symmetries and social equilibria (see 1961b:21f). More than any other life style, primitive cultures still exhibit that "crystalline structure" which corresponds to a "permanent hope for mankind" (1960a:49). Anthropology's mission is to preserve these societies from the "cannibal instincts of the historical process" (1955a:43) and to recall, if possible, "the ring of bygone harmonies" (1952a:117).

Lévi-Strauss' anthropological humanism and his visionary quest for a transhistorical society are severely compromised by his acute awareness of the ever present contingencies of historical change and temporal vicissitudes. Actual societies can to some extent survive the ravages of time, but "a cracked bell . . . will never give forth the ring of bygone harmonies" (1952a:117). Only at the point of origin, at the time of the initial transition between nature and culture, was man truly creative and reconciled. But "that indefinable grandeur which is the mark of true beginnings" (1955a:392) disappeared forever with the Neolithic (we are reminded of Rousseau's similar thoughts on the period). Historical and contemporary civilizations, in choosing time and progress, have also chosen violence, exploitation, and destruction. Lévi-Strauss' understanding of man's predicament is a tragic and somber one: while sociohistorical circumstances certainly demand a new humanism, we are in real-

ity incapable of giving it much credence.

The distinct ambiguity and obvious frustration inherent in Lévi-Strauss' humanism must in part be held responsible for the pessimism and resignation one detects in many of his writings (see especially 1955a:393f). Even more significantly, the ultimate result he envisages is a reductive materialism that endangers not only his avowed humanism, but the very distinction between nature and culture itself. Departing entirely from Rousseau's original argument, Lévi-Strauss considers a final reduction incumbent upon a social scientific enterprise: "the reintegration of culture in nature and finally of life within the whole of its physico-chemical conditions" (1962c:247).

This epistemic reduction of human life to "inert matter" (1962c:248) is not merely scientific and methodological; it also generates a concomitant metaphysics and ontology. In one of *Tristes tropiques*'s most disturbing passages, Lévi-Strauss gives the following description of the philosophical implications of the second law of thermodynamics (1955a:397):

The world began without the human race and it will end without it. . . . Man has never–save only when he reproduces himself–done other than cheerfully dismantle millions upon millions of structures and reduce their elements to a state in which they can no longer be reintegrated. . . . "Entropology," not anthropology, should be the word for the discipline that devotes itself to the study of this process of disintegration in its most highly evolved forms.

If there is any hope, it lies in either a resigned mysticism (see 1955a:394) or an aesthetic moment (see 1955a:398). It certainly does not seem to lie in either the understanding of man's unique qualities or the scientific study of his cultural products. The latter two, in fact, have contradictory aims: ontological comprehension entails a qualitative passage from nature to culture, while scientific explanation demands a final reduction of culture to nature. The resultant impasse is absolutely fundamental: if scientific epistemology cannot bear witness to man's cultural uniqueness but only to his material reducibility, how can a social science possibly account for its own ontological preconditions as a cultural artifact and a human activity? Anthropological discourse itself seems reduced to the ethical indifference and entropic demise of the physical and chemical universe (see Simonis 1968a:294f).

Since I shall be in a better position to explain the ethnological consequences of this critical impasse after examining Lévi-Strauss' concept of scientific anthropology, let me discuss now two historical predecessors who are in part responsible for shaping that concept: Émile Durkheim and Marcel Mauss. Lévi-Strauss' indebtedness to them, as to Rousseau, is profound (e.g., 1950, 1960a; see also Bender 1965, Harris 1968:483f, Schneider 1965:38f, Steiner 1967:241). It is sometimes overlooked, however, that there are equally significant differences between Lévi-Strauss' structural anthropology and the French sociological tradition.[6] Both the similarities and the divergencies can be clarified by a textual analysis of Lévi-Strauss' writings.

As early as 1946 Lévi-Strauss' basic

affinities and essential misgivings had been formulated and articulated. French sociology is praised for its scientific conception of anthropological inquiry but condemned for the remnants of nineteenth-century historicism and idealism that still pervade its theoretical framework. Lévi-Strauss considers the French school's interest in human cognition, the total social fact, and the phenomena of exchange especially praiseworthy. At the same time, these substantive interests are compromised by an outmoded psychology and an inadequate awareness of recent developments in such fields as linguistics and cybernetics. Finally, there is a laudable interest in ethnography and ethnology (especially on the part of Mauss), but never the concrete realization of a comparative and rational anthropology (see 1946a).

Lévi-Strauss would concur with Durkheim that "the principal objective" of the social sciences "is to extend scientific rationalism to human behavior" (Durkheim 1895:xxxiv).[7] In fact, the social sciences are "of the same type as the other sciences"; in all cases, the "ultimate end lies in the discovery of general relations between phenomena" (1946a:504). But in the subsequent explanation of the logical genesis of these general relations, Lévi-Strauss' position diverges significantly from Durkheim's. Durkheim's interpretations are often confusing, contradictory, and problematic. At times, general relations are "*socio*-logical," that is, they reflect "domestic relations" (Durkheim and Mauss 1903:84). At other times, they are "socio-*logical*," that is, social relations are the end products of a categorical mind (see

---

[6] There are laudable exceptions to this oversight. For example, Schneider's cogent comparison between Lévi-Strauss and Durkheim includes the important differences as well as the obvious continuities (Schneider 1965:39-40). Similarly, Murphy stresses significant differences between the two (Murphy 1963:18). Most comparisons, however, are between Lévi-Strauss and the French sociological tradition on the one hand and anthropologists of the Anglo-American tradition on the other (e.g., the familiar and long-standing debate between alliance and descent theorists; see especially Berting and Philipsen 1960, Homans and Schneider 1955, and Needham 1962).

[7] Many but not all of Lévi-Strauss' remarks are applicable to both Durkheim and Mauss. I shall single out one or the other only where Lévi-Strauss' comments are specifically directed to either Durkheim or Mauss.

Durkheim 1912:260, Parsons 1938: 445). Lévi-Strauss can accept the latter interpretation, but only with serious reservations. Though Durkheim was correct in equating sociology with psychology and in reducing social relations to intellectual ones, his psychology is inadequate to the task of studying social institutions as "systems of representations" (1949a:3). Durkheim's failure is not merely due to the gap between his sociological speculations on the one hand and "the lack, or insufficiency, of concrete data" (1946a:503) on the other. More importantly, his psychology "oscillates between a dull empiricism and an aprioristic frenzy" (1946a: 503). Durkheim's sociology is in danger of being drawn into behaviorism (Malinowski's interpretation; see 1946a: 534) or naturalism (Radcliffe-Brown's error; see 1962b:61). His psychology (a remnant of his Kantianism) can only result in "an external mysticism which shall later turn back against rational thought itself" (1946a:534). ("This is Lévy-Bruhl's story" [1946a:535].) Worst of all, Durkheim's psychology (and herein lies its irony) must in the final analysis have recourse to an instinctive tendency or a vague sentiment to explain both social phenomena and their intellectual bases. Even when pragmatism and utilitarianism are avoided (e.g., Durkheim and Mauss 1903:81), social facts are in the end nevertheless explained by affective and instinctual causes (see Durkheim and Mauss 1903:85-86, Needham 1963: xxiii). Lévi-Strauss will not accept this type of reduction (1962b:71):

Impulses can explain nothing: they are always *results*, either of the power of the body or the impotence of the mind. In both cases they are consequences, never causes. The latter can be sought only in the organism, which is the exclusive concern of biology, or in the intellect, which is the sole way offered to psychology, and to anthropology as well.

In sum, Lévi-Strauss definitely shares the scientific aspirations of Durkheim's sociology, but he has serious reservations about his substantive explanations. Durkheim is at his best when "admitting that all social life, even elementary, presupposes an intellectual activity in man of which the formal properties, consequently, cannot be a reflection of the concrete organization of the society" (1962b:96). Durkheim is at his worst when he "affirms the primacy of the social over the intellect" (1962b: 97). When he further tries to explain the "domestic relations" responsible for these mental categories, he "finds at his disposal no more than sentiments, affective values, or vague ideas such as contagion or contamination." Lévi-Strauss simply cannot consider this "call upon the inarticulate" an adequate explanation for sociocultural phenomena.

Despite his reservations, Lévi-Strauss continues to trace many of his anthropological assumptions to the French sociological school. Rarely does his respect for this tradition waver. *Structural Anthropology* (1958) is still dedicated to Durkheim, since he, more than anyone else, "incarnates the essence of France's contribution to social anthropology" (1960a:8). Similarly, *The Savage Mind* (1962c) "merely [takes] up again certain themes . . . put forth by Durkheim and Mauss in their essay on primitive classification" (1962d: 217).[8] At the same time, Lévi-Strauss clearly seeks to transcend some of Durkheim's limitations and to arrive at a truly significant anthropology of his own. It is to the works of Marcel Mauss (the Newton of ethnology; see 1956a: 162) that he turns for many additional answers. Implicitly or explicitly, wholly or in part, Mauss's notion of the total

---

[8] The English translations of all bibliographic items cited in their original languages are mine.

social fact and his principle of reciprocity provide Lévi-Strauss with the theoretical and practical keys to a scientific and structural anthropology.

The notion of a total social fact first of all assures the ethnologist of both a concrete and encompassing anthropology. A truly comprehensive study of *"the whole man"* (1963*m*:358) demands "a system of interpretation [which simultaneously renders] account of the physical, physiological, psychic and social aspects of behavior" (1950: xxv). Conversely, only the empirical study of the concrete can bear witness to the whole (see Mauss 1925:78). In this sense, anthropology is the scientific study of the "concrete universal" (see Mauss 1924:304). This definition has two distinct advantages. First, an emphasis on the synthetic nature of social phenomena points to the larger necessity of an interdisciplinary social science (see 1946*a*:536). Mauss himself was acutely aware of the sociological importance of such emerging disciplines as structural linguistics (see 1950:xxxi) and psychoanalysis (see 1946*a*:528-29). Second, Mauss's insistence on a concrete and "down-to-earth sociology" (1960*a*:13) serves to rid the Durkheimian tradition of some of its "metaphysical phantoms," "icy winds of dialectic," "thunder of syllogisms," and "lightning flashes of antinomies" (1960*a*:10). Mauss's empirical attitude also helps to counterbalance Durkheim's "repugnance" (1960*a*:12) for ethnographic investigation and to solidify the intimate and necessary relationship between sociology and anthropology. A certain interest in ethnography had always been a part of French sociology (see 1946*a*:511-12), but an awareness of its crucial importance progressed slowly, until, with Mauss, the anthropological influence becomes dominant (see 1946*a*:512). Only in this specifically ethnological context do the notion of total social fact and the principle of exchange gain their concrete and universal significance.

There are a number of additional advantages to Mauss's concept of the total social fact, ones that again clarify Lévi-Strauss' own position. For instance, Mauss's contribution allows us to assess the proper explanatory role of a psychodynamic psychology (as distinct from an intellectualist one). Mauss was aware of the ethnological importance of psychological theories, especially psychoanalysis. In fact, he anticipated the largely American school of "culture and personality" by nearly a decade (see 1950:xi-xvi). At the same time, he never made the mistake that Benedict, Dubois, Linton, Mead, and others made: he never became embroiled in a meaningless and circular argument about the priority of culture or personality. The dispute is fictitious since the actual relation between the two is always dialectical, never merely causal. "A psychological formulation is no more than the translation on the [level of the] individual psyche of an essentially sociological structure" (1950: xvi). Such allegedly irreducible manifestations of psychodynamic singularity as pathology, neurosis, sorcery, and shamanism are in reality the concrete and particular transformations of a more fundamental and collective symbolism (see 1949*b*, 1949*c*, 1950: xvixxii). The collective symbolism, not its individualistic manifestations, is the proper domain of both psychology and anthropology.

The epistemological value of understanding the relation between social and psychic phenomena dialectically can be illustrated in a related way. As we know, social facts are concrete as well as systematic; that is, "they are lived by men, and subjective consciousness is as much a form of their reality as their objective characteristics" (1960*a*:14). As a result, "all valid interpretation must make the objectivity of historical or comparative analysis coincide with the subjectivity of lived experience" (1950:xxvi). In other words, a comprehensive understanding of social facts as total phenomena in part requires a phenomenological (or emic?) perspective: "*contra* the theoretician, the observer should always have the last word; and against the observer, the native" (1960*a*:12). But since an ethnological perspective also demands a systematic awareness of objective determinants, a mere phenomenological (or empirical) interpretation is always inadequate. Existential or lived experience may simply consist of "the rationalized interpretations of the native—who often makes himself into an observer and even a theoretician of his own society" (1960*a*:12). Such conscious beliefs may be important—even factual and scientific—but they may also be fictitious and ideological. To assess their scientific validity and ethnological importance, the anthropologist must determine their dialectical relation to the systematic and the collective. This latter domain, as we shall see, is not governed by the singular, subjective, and phenomenally given, but by a universal, collective, and hidden reality that underlies and generates all appearances: the unconscious brain (see 1946*a*:528).[9]

With the introduction of the concept of the unconscious, we come to one of structural anthropology's most important premises: phenomenal realities, including cultural artifacts, are always reducible to a common infrastructure. Whether we place this scientific reduction in the general context of the epistemological passage from culture to nature or in the specific domain of the substantive explanation of social relations by their intellectual genesis, the unconscious and universal human brain invariably sustains and always accounts for observed ethnographic data and inferred ethnological realities.[10]

What is the nature of this unconscious reality to which Lévi-Strauss attributes such importance and to which all anthropological reduction aspires? Its definition is in part derived from Mauss's concept of reciprocal exchange (see especially *The Gift*, 1925). Mauss had argued that the exchange of gifts—a total social fact—is a synthetic, relational, and systematic process. Lévi-Strauss adds that this process is in turn made possible by and mirrors the structure of the unconscious. This infrastructural brain consists of three universal principles (1969:84):

[1] the exigency of the rule as a rule; [2] the notion of reciprocity regarded as the most immediate form of integrating the opposition between the self and others; and finally [3], the synthetic nature of the gift, i.e., that the agreed transfer of a valuable from one individual to another makes these individuals into partners, and adds a new quality to the value transferred.

These three principles of the unconscious are the *a priori* assumptions upon which structural anthropology rests. They are latent in all sociocultural phenomena and every cultural artifact is explainable in terms of them. Communication, economic, and kinship

---

9 The reality of the unconscious must for the moment remain a gratuitous assumption. I shall detail Lévi-Strauss' argument in the context of my discussions of Freud, Marx, linguistics, and cybernetics.

10 Though we cannot go into details, it should be noted that the function of the unconscious proposed here also applies to Rousseau's formula "the me is another." Only the unconscious can mediate the opposition between self and other, subjectivity and objectivity (1950:xxx). Ethnographic understanding, consequently, is also made possible by the unconscious structure of the human mind (1950:xxvii-xxxi).

systems are privileged examples (see 1953b:296f). However different, each of them requires specific rules to govern their operations; each establishes reciprocal relations between distinct groups or individual persons; and each engenders a meaning, value, or cohesion not previously present. Each of them, in other words, results from and bears witness to the *a priori* structure of the unconscious brain.

In equating the notion of exchange with the structure of the unconscious, Lévi-Strauss departs from the French sociological tradition in a significant way. Neither Durkheim nor Mauss had posited the *a priori* necessity of a regulatory, reciprocating, and synthetic unconscious. On the contrary, they had reversed the proper order and had derived intellectual and psychological principles from social and instinctual ones (e.g., 1946a:517-18, 1950:xxii-xxvi). Given the crucial role of the unconscious mind in structural explanation, many have understandably argued that much of Lévi-Strauss' intellectual heritage must therefore lie elsewhere: perhaps with Kant (e.g., Ricoeur 1963a:24), Hegel (e.g., Murphy 1963:13), Marx (e.g., Goddard 1965:412f), or even Freud (e.g., Schneider 1965:39f). Does Lévi-Strauss indeed have a concept of mind, infrastructure, or unconscious reality similar to those of any of these thinkers?

To ask this question requires some prior justification. After all, Lévi-Strauss himself has remained relatively indifferent to the philosophical issues raised by such comparisons (e.g., 1955a:55; 1963a:61; 1964a:10-11; see also Furet 1967). One could argue, of course, that the very neglect of philosophical bases implies a definite theoretical and positivistic stance (see Goldmann 1966:120). Structuralism should certainly not be considered aphilosophical. Rather, it tends to subordinate philosophy to science. Such a position does not necessarily deny the presence of philosophical issues, but it does filter their anthropological relevance through the paradigmatic sieve of contemporary scientism.

With this in mind, what, first of all, is the specific nature of the alleged affinity between structuralism and Kantianism? Lévi-Strauss himself disclaims any direct relation. He certainly does not feel obliged to address himself to one of Kant's central problems: the question of the *a priori* grounds of the possibility of science. The anthropologist's task is not epistemological or reflexive in that sense; rather, it is empirical and comparative (see 1963a:59). But isn't Lévi-Strauss really skirting the issue here (see Lacroix 1968:194)? Aren't the affinities between structuralism and Kantianism more profound than Lévi-Strauss is willing to admit? For example, isn't the epistemological underpinning of structural ethnography (Rousseau's "the me is another") closely akin to a neo-Kantian position ("understanding is the rediscovery of the I in the Thou" [Dilthey in Rickman 1967:39])? Similarly, doesn't Lévi-Strauss' ultimate goal for anthropology—"a sort of *super-rationalism* in which sense perceptions are integrated into reasoning and yet lose none of their properties" (1955a:61)—closely resemble Kant's transcendental method—an idealism that brings the concept of understanding into essential relation with sensuous intuition and thus makes the materials of experience intelligible to us? And finally, doesn't Lévi-Strauss' anthropological achievement closely mirror Kant's philosophical contribution: a theory of science that has both a rational and an empirical component, an analytic and a formal epistemology in which the synthetic, relational, necessary, and *a priori* concepts make the particular, empirical, contingent, and *a posteriori* materials possible and intelligible?

There is probably some truth in these analogies, but one must place them in the specific context of Lévi-Strauss' own remarks to assess their accuracy. For example, the principle of empathy is present in both idealism and structuralism, but with distinctly different foundations and consequences. Unlike the idealists, Lévi-Strauss considers the distinction between *Natur-* and *Geisteswissenschaften* (the substantive result of the epistemology of empathy) irrational and mystical (see 1960a:16). He prefers to found his own method on a naturalistic basis. Reducing reflexive thought itself to a natural object (1955a:59), Lévi-Strauss has turned Kant's transcendental idealism into a transcendental materialism (see 1962c:246) or, at most, a Spinozan intellectualism (see Lefort 1951:1410). Lévi-Strauss' naturalistic aims also entail a radically different concept of mind from that implied by Kant's notion of the transcendental subject. The self-objectifying, systematic-relational, and synthetic *a priori* intellect posited by structuralism is a neurological and unconscious entity. One can, of course, characterize this entity as "a Kantian unconscious," that is, "a categorical, combinatory unconscious" (Ricoeur 1963a:9; see also Ricoeur 1964:85). But unlike Kant's notion of mind, the structural unconscious is "a categorical system without reference to a thinking subject; that is why structuralism, qua philosophy, develops a kind of intellectualism [which is] thoroughly antireflexive, anti-idealist, and antiphenomenological. This unconscious spirit may also be said [to be] homologous to nature; perhaps it even is nature" (Ricoeur 1963a:10). It is only with this naturalistic modification that Lévi-Strauss can accept the characterization of structuralism as a form of Kantian-

ism (see 1964a:19). This modification is, of course, crucial. Lévi-Strauss rightly concludes that "whereas in the public mind there is frequent confusion between structuralism, idealism, and formalism, structuralism has only to be confronted with true manifestations of idealism and formalism for its own deterministic and realistic inspiration to become clearly manifest" (1964a:27).

Any comparisons between Hegel and Lévi-Strauss are similarly precarious, since Lévi-Strauss never mentions Hegel and prefers to discuss such important issues as dialectical and analytical method, infra- and superstructure, synchronic system and diachronic event, etc. in the context of Marxism or by reference to Sartre. If a comparison can be made at all, Hegel's rationalism must again be "scientized." Lévi-Strauss himself has not done so, but the structuralist Lucien Sebag did in his *Marxisme et structuralisme* (1964; see also Scholte 1966a). As in the case of the naturalization of Kant's transcendental subject, we here find Hegel's objective spirit materialized by means of a scientific rationalization (see Sebag 1964: 197f; see also Pouillon's critique [1966b:105] of Leach's interpretation [1965b]). The difference between this position and orthodox versions of Hegelian rationalism could not be more striking: instead of an idealization or spiritualization of nature, we have a naturalization or mechanization of the spirit. If Sebag is correct (see Castel 1964 for a Marxist critique), Lévi-Strauss, like Marx, also stood Hegel on his head.[11]

---

11 Before leaving Hegel, one other comparison should be mentioned: that of Goethe, Hegel, *Gestalt* psychology, *Strukturforschung*, and structural anthropology (Nodelman 1966). Whatever systematic similarities may or may not be found among these various scholars and schools, they seem largely peripheral to the anthropological significance of Lévi-Strauss' intellectual-historical ancestry as such.

This brings us to the complex relation between structural anthropology and Marxist sociology, a far more important and informative topic than any comparison between Kant or Hegel and Lévi-Strauss. For one thing, Marxism has been the battleground par excellence for many recent French intellectual quarrels (see Hughes 1968:168f). It is therefore "no exaggeration at all to claim that the intellectual life of Paris since the war is incomprehensible to anyone who is ignorant of the internal controversies of continental Marxists" (Hobsbawn 1966:34; see also Furet 1967). For another, the substantive issues raised in the debate over Marx are crucially important, both philosophically and ethnologically (e.g., Terray 1969). Finally, the Marxist critique of structural anthropology is among the most significant made in the past two decades.

Let me start with the last of these points. The Marxist attack on Lévi-Strauss was initiated in the mid- and late 1950s by Rodinson (1955a, 1955b) and Revel (1957). They characterized structural anthropology as a bourgeois reactionary and intellectually idealist philosophy. Lévi-Strauss replied with a rather obvious, if rhetorically well-aimed, counterthrust: both authors are guilty of the paramount sins of Marxist revisionism and deviationism (see 1958:337-41). Since then, the intellectual warfare has not only continued (especially in *L'homme et la société, La pensée,* and *Les temps modernes*), but has intensified with the appearance of critiques by Lucien Goldmann (1966, 1969), Henri Lefebvre (1963, 1966a, 1966b), and Jean-Paul Sartre (1960, 1966). In the case of Sartre, and aside from the very real and important anthropological issues involved (see Piquet 1965, Pouillon 1965, Verstraeten 1963), the socio-intellectual context is also worth mentioning.

Lévi-Strauss' incredibly harsh dismissal of Sartre's belated appeal to the social sciences is total and devastating: Sartre is denied his philosophical, Marxist, and historical legitimacy; he is accused of ego- and ethnocentricity; and his *Critique* (1960) is reduced to a "first-class ethnographic document" exemplary of "the mythology of our time" (1962c: 249). All this indicates that in France competing schools of thought tend to be exclusive and that the entire social and intellectual leadership has changed. The prominence that once belonged to men like Merleau-Ponty and Sartre now belongs to structuralists like Althusser, Foucault, Lacan, and especially Lévi-Strauss (see Bourdieu and Passeron 1967, Lacroix 1968).

This sociohistorical change in intellectual fashions has not, of course, either silenced the Marxist critics or taken the sting out of their counter-critiques. The latter are, in fact, numerous and varied. They range from detailed and empirical critiques of structural anthropology proper (e.g., Makarius 1970, Makarius and Makarius 1967, Verstraeten 1963) to philosophical and political critiques of structuralist "ideology" generally (see especially Goldmann 1966, Lefebvre 1966a). Goldmann's and Lefebvre's criticisms are especially significant since they take the entire *Weltanschauung* of structuralism to task.[12] Lefebvre traces all of structuralism to the rationalism, absolutism, fetishism, and antihistoricism of Eleatic philosophy. In its contemporary version, this "new" Eleaticism adds to the assumptions of the older philosophy those reactionary values associated with technocratic scientism, cybernetic formalism, and bureaucratic

---

[12] Recent phenomenological criticisms are complementary, though they generally do not incorporate a specifically political dimension (see Dufrenne 1967, 1968; Ricoeur 1963a, 1963b, 1964, 1967a, 1967b, 1969).

conservatism. Panstructuralism (from which Lévi-Strauss, however, is in part excused) has become a transcendental metaphysics and disguised ideology parading as bourgeois materialism and scientific nihilism. Its premises are anti-Heraclitian, anti-Marxist, and anti-humanist. Structuralism constitutes the ultimate destruction of existential, historical, and political meaning (see Lefebvre 1966a). Goldmann's critique is similarly motivated. Echoing Sartre's (1966) contention that structural anthropology simply reflects and sustains a bourgeois ideology, Goldmann specifically relates the ahumanistic, ahistorical, and aphilosophical premises of structuralist thought to the "organized capitalism" of our "current technocratic society" (Goldmann 1969:11, 13). He condemns structuralism for overlooking the axiological dimension, for denying the importance of critical praxis, and for dismissing the notion of historical becoming (see Goldmann 1966:119).

Lévi-Strauss himself dismisses these politically inspired attacks: "I see absolutely no link between structuralism and any political system" (Lévi-Strauss in Gramont 1968:40). To trace structural anthropology to a capitalist system is simply untenable. Such a denial, however, still leaves the question of the intellectual-historical relationship between structuralism and Marxism unanswered. Since Lévi-Strauss often refers to Marx in support of his enterprise, some comparison is clearly in order.

We shall here consider only Lévi-Strauss' work. It should be mentioned, however, that the invocation of Marx and the issue of the propriety of such an appeal extends beyond the boundaries of structural anthropology and involves the social sciences in general and Althusser's writings in particular.

Lévi-Strauss places two important strictures on the applicability of Marxist concepts to structural anthropology: the limited historical domain to which Marxist thought is applicable and the encompassing understanding of total man, to which Marxism contributes only one among many relevant perspectives. This second stricture is, as we saw, derived from Mauss's notion of the total social fact and the principle of exchange. Neither can be reduced to a mere economic interpretation; "the general phenomena of exchange is first of all a total exchange, including food, manufactured objects, as well as those most precious items: women" (1964b: 44). In other words, the fact of exchange precedes its empirical modalities and it cannot be explained by any of its specific contents; see, for example, Lévi-Strauss' critique of Frazer's economic theory of marriage alliance (1949a:138). The total social fact of exchange certainly includes Marx's *Homo oeconomicus* (1955b:535), but he must be encompassed within the larger framework of a scientific anthropology viewed as a "general theory of relationships" (1958:95; see also Simonis 1968b).

The other stricture placed on the ethnological relevance of Marxist analyses concerns the issue of historical time and the attendant distinction between primitive and civilized societies. Let us take only the second point for the moment. Lévi-Strauss claims that "Marx, quite consciously, said that he was not concerned with so-called primitive culture" (Lévi-Strauss in Steiner 1966:34) because historical materialism is applicable only to capitalist societies. Marx understood the fact that concepts derived from "cumulative history" could not be applied to societies in a state of "stationary history" (1958: 336). Lévi-Strauss is therefore infinitely closer to Marx than those "vulgar materialists" who mistakenly do apply the principle of economic determinism to primitive societies: "Marx and Engels frequently express the idea that primitive, or allegedly primitive, societies are governed by 'blood ties' (which, today, we call kinship systems) and not by economic relationships" (1958: 337).[13]

How do the strictures placed on the applicability of Marxism to ethnology affect such crucial issues as the nature of social determinism, historical analysis, and dialectical method? The last of these need not concern us here, since we will be discussing the problems of binarism and dialectics in the context of Lévi-Strauss' debate with Sartre and structuralism's indebtedness to linguistics and cybernetics. Suffice it to point out that in Lévi-Strauss' estimation, Marx was as concerned with scientific or analytical method as he was with historical and dialectical reason. In a truly Marxist orientation, both are equally necessary and "the opposition between the two sorts of reason is relative, not absolute" (1962c:246). Dialectical reason may be constitutive, but only in a derivative sense. It is the dynamic part of analytical reason's effort to account for social reality. Any distinction between the two rests only on "the temporary gap separating analytical reason from the understanding of life" (1962c:246). Here again Lévi-Strauss scientizes Marxist thought to enable him to use both analytical rea-

son (especially binary oppositions) and dialectical reason—"analytic reason in action" (1962c:251)—without thereby contradicting Marx's method (see 1956b:240; also Piquet 1965).

Related to the issue of dialectical and analytical reason is the problem of history and historical method. I previously called attention to Lévi-Strauss' antihistoricism and his search for a transhistorical society (see also Parain 1967). Lévi-Strauss' stance affects his relation to Marxism in a curious way. Even if we grant that dialectical materialism is applicable only to capitalist societies, this does not alter the fact that for Marx history is the privileged domain of man's potential freedom and progressive self-realization (e.g., Furet 1967, Lefebvre in Bastide 1962:145). For Lévi-Strauss, on the contrary, history and historical progress are relative and circumstantial, if not downright destructive and antithetical to human happiness. Little wonder that Lévi-Strauss, who sees the ideal-typical society as one of bygone harmonies and social equilibria, expresses only lukewarm interest in Marx's historical prediction of a future utopia (see 1955a: 61). Even in Lévi-Strauss' analyses of the twin enemies of human progress— bourgeois capitalism and colonialist imperialism (see 1952b and 1961b)—we find no reference to political or revolutionary Marxism, only an abstract and formal analogy between social evolution and game theory (for Marxist critiques, see Rodinson 1955a, 1955b; Revel 1957). For Lévi-Strauss, history is not an evolving and progressive political process at all; "it consists wholly in its method" and can lead to something "provided we get out of it" (1962c: 262). Clearly it is not to Marx the providential, even messianic, political moralist that Lévi-Strauss refers in his famous remark: "Rarely do I tackle a problem in sociology or ethnology

---

[13] Both strictures are definitely in keeping with at least one important tradition in Marxist interpretation: that of Georg Lukacs. He claims, for example, that "it is not the predominance of economic causes in explanation . . . which distinguishes Marxism from bourgeois science in a decisive way, it is the perspective on totality" (Lukacs 1923:47). Lukacs further argues that "historical materialism cannot be applied to precapitalist systems in the same way as those with a capitalist evolution." Analysts who do apply it in this way mistake "mere historical categories— categories of capitalist societies—for eternal categories" (Lukacs 1923:274-75; see Terray 1969 for an interesting and contrasting interpretation).

without having first set my mind in motion by reperusal of a page or two from *18 Brumaire of Louis Bonaparte* or the *Critique of Political Economy*" (1955*a*:61).

What about the explanatory role of structural or synchronic analysis on the one hand and historical or diachronical analysis on the other? Marx's own deliberations on structure and history are controversial (e.g., Pouillon 1956:172). Some interpreters argue for the primacy of a diachronic perspective (e.g., Viet 1965:16: "Marxist structure is essentially diachronic"), while others stress the priority of a structural understanding (e.g., Godelier 1966:839: "The study of the genesis of a structure can only be made if 'guided' by a prior knowledge of that structure"; see also Sebag 1964:83f). Though Lévi-Strauss' position derives from linguistics rather than from Marxism as such, he would doubtless agree with those interpretations that stress the synchronic in Marx at the expense of mere "historicism or eventualism" (Godelier 1966:839). He might go even further and suggest, as some have done, that Marx's position anticipates structural linguistics' subsequent rejection of historicism and evolutionism (see Godelier 1966:843, Sebag 1964:94; see also Lefebvre 1966*b* for an extensive critique). The historical and scientific continuity of Marxism, structural linguistics, and Lévi-Strauss' anthropology would thereby be assured.[14]

Lévi-Strauss' attitude toward Marx's understanding of history must also be placed in the context of their common search for a hidden logic or disguised meaning behind the surface manifestations of man's mental and cultural products (see 1955*a*:61; Steiner 1966: 33). In the work of both Lévi-Strauss and Marx, this hidden logic is said to guide historical and empirical reality. Both therefore posit "the priority of the study of structures to that of their genesis and their evolution" (Godelier 1966:832). In this sense even "economic history is, by and large, the history of unconscious processes" (1949*a*: 23). It is an infrastructural history exhibiting the unconscious and dialectical unfolding of analytic reason. Structural dialectics, therefore, complements historical materialism (see 1956*b*:240). Similarly, "the famous statement by Marx, 'Men make their own history, but they do not know that they are making it,' justifies, first, history and, second, anthropology. At the same time, it shows that the two approaches are inseparable" (1949*b*:23).[15]

Even if we agree with Lévi-Strauss that he and Marx seek to reduce the historical variations of empirical events to an underlying unconscious theme, the nature of this hidden logic is not the same in both cases. Whereas structuralism invariably defines infrastructure in terms of the unconscious, teleological, and synchronic logic of the human brain, Marxism is customarily as-

---

[14] Others have traced Lévi-Strauss' understanding of language to Hegel rather than to Marx. Dufrenne argues that in both Hegel and Lévi-Strauss the idea of language implies a formal ontology "in which language manifests a *logos* that is the dialectical structure of nature, the rationality immanent in nature, and in such a way that the universe of discourse becomes at the same time the discourse of the universe" (Dufrenne 1963:16).

[15] Lévi-Strauss' use of Marx's remark is a peculiar one. The entire quotation reads: "Men make their own history, but they do not make it under circumstances chosen by themselves, but under circumstances directly encountered, given and transmitted from the past" (Marx 1852:15). Marxists have generally interpreted the quote quite differently than Lévi-Strauss. Makarius and Makarius (1967: 199-200), for example, say: "Whereas for Marx men do not know that they make their own history because the latter is determined by material forces which escape their consciousness, for Lévi-Strauss, if history escapes the consciousness of men, it is because [history] is ruled by the unconscious determinants foreshadowed in their minds."

sociated with a definition based on the material, dialectical, and historical facticity of socioeconomic circumstances. One can argue that the two concepts of infrastructure are complementary rather than contradictory (see especially Simonis 1967, 1968b). After all, Lévi-Strauss' understanding of the human mind is ultimately a materialistic one: "Its initial conditions must be given in the form of an objective structure of the psyche and brain without which there would be neither *praxis* nor thought" (1962c:263-64). Similarly, Marx's understanding of economic materialism may have been conceptual: "The development of the 'material forces of production' is in the last analysis only the development of the knowledge of nature under another name. Hence it appears that the deepest foundation of the 'real' basis of the 'material substructure' of human ideology is a spiritual process, that of the perceptive penetration of nature" (Marx in Stark 1958:230). If this is characteristic of Marx's position, his historico-economic definition of infrastructure is merely the particularized and limited result of a more fundamental and universal logico-mental, albeit material, definition of the mind. We can then conclude—with both Marx and Lévi-Strauss—that "nothing is ever really infrastructural except by a decision of the mind . . ." (Sebag 1964:190). This also explains Lévi-Strauss' conception of the primacy of infrastructure by analogy to both the material distribution of the cards in a card game and the intellectual "rules of the game and rules of tactics" (1962c:95). Even if the actual substance of the social game is determined by its technoeconomic substratum and sociohistorical circumstances, its unfolding and actualization as a total social phenomenon is a question of the synchronic and universal

intellect that governs its entire, if latent, meaning.

To have created a definite place for the human intellect in the explanation of social reality without thereby renouncing a materialistic perspective constitutes Lévi-Strauss' main contribution to Marxism (see 1962c:130f, Simonis 1968b). That both the human mind and the economic substratum should be considered in the explanation of human praxis and social reality is again evident when structuralism is compared with Marxism on the issue of social determinants. Here too we detect a distinctive structuralist characteristic: the intellectualization of the dialectic. We rarely find in Lévi-Strauss' work the "mere" political and economic analyses of social phenomena for which Marx's later writings are so justly famous. Lévi-Strauss does claim to have made such analyses (1958:334), and indeed, the genesis and function of writing are specifically seen in exploitive and class-conscious terms (see 1955a:292; 1961b: 32f). But few if any other social phenomena are reducible to such explanations. Even though Lévi-Strauss asserts that Marx himself did not have a mere one-to-one theory of social transformation or determinism (see 1958:333), one cannot help thinking that his own intellectualist ontology is quite distinct from Marx's. The infrastructural determinant Lévi-Strauss invariably invokes is the human brain; e.g., Schneider's (1965:79) paraphrase of his correspondence with Lévi-Strauss. This, of course, is typical of structural explanation: conscious ideologies and social organizations are always the dialectical and transformed expressions of a hidden infrastructural logic that is neither socioeconomic nor even historical, but relational, symbolic, synchronic, systematic, universal, and ultimately neurological. Is this at all consistent with

Marxism? I doubt it, and I certainly concur with Lévi-Strauss when he informs us that he is not a Marxist "in the ordinary sense" of the term (Lévi-Strauss in Steiner 1966:34). Others might wish to add the question: "Can Lévi-Strauss be considered a Marxist in any sense of the term?"

If Lévi-Strauss' intellectualist interpretation of the unconscious infrastructure behind or beneath phenomenal reality is neither Hegelian nor Marxist (let alone Kantian), is it perhaps Freudian? Not really. Anticipating what I hope to detail later on, let me first point out that Lévi-Strauss' understanding of the unconscious is derived from structural linguistics rather than from Freudian psychology. The structure of the unconscious mirrors the logic of language; it is certainly not filled with Freud's *Trieben*.[16] As Boas asserted some time ago (Boas 1920:289; see also Lévi-Strauss 1949a:19-20), there is little if any similarity between a linguistic and a psychoanalytic concept of the unconscious. Instead of being a psychodynamic and libidinal id, the linguistic unconscious is logicosynchronic and neurological. Rather than being a reservoir for idiosyncratic and sexual drives, the structural unconscious is collective and symbolic (e.g., 1949c:202-203). Even if these crucial differences do not as such preclude comparative inferences (e.g., Leach 1965a:17, Schneider 1965:39-40), it seems significant that on the very points where Lévi-Strauss specifically expresses his intellectual indebtedness to Freud (transcending static antinomies and reducing phenomenal reality), Freud merely taught him what he already knew from De Saussure and Marx (see 1955a:59f). In fact, the contrasts rather than the similarities provide the more illuminating grounds for a comparison of Freud and Lévi-Strauss.

Lévi-Strauss' criticisms of Freud are varied and numerous. Let me here mention only the most important. For one, Freud failed to transcend the historicist and individualistic premises of both his psychology and his concept of the unconscious, e.g., his explanation of the incest taboo (see 1969:490-91). For another, Freud's ultimate resort to the instinctual and libidinal foundations of cultural and social phenomena involved him in the same paradoxical dilemma as Durkheim (see 1962b:69-70). Most important of all, a concept of the unconscious that is based on content rather than form—whether libidinal drives (Freud) or archetypal images (Jung)—is unacceptable to a properly symbolic and linguistic theory (1962c:55, Steiner 1966:35). The latter teaches us that it is precisely because the unconscious is "empty"—i.e., logical rather than substantive—that it can organize elements of content and give logical meaning and positional significance to them (e.g., 1950:xxxii; 1962i:218).

Lévi-Strauss' distinctive interpretation of Freud has led to considerable confusion, especially since his psycho*logical* intellectualism entails a rejection of emotive, dynamic, and instinctual factors. This exclusiveness has been fervently debated, especially in the area of kinship studies (see Buchler and Selby 1968a for a recent assessment) and in the literature on myth and totemism (e.g., various articles in Leach, ed., 1967).[17] Let me therefore briefly review Lévi-Strauss' understanding of the

---

16 The consequences of this position for psychoanalytic interpretation are especially evident in the work of Jacques Lacan (see Lacan 1968).

17 To review this intricate debate in specific terms is simply beyond my competence. Relevant material is especially abundant in the area of kinship studies since the Homans-Schneider (1955) versus Needham (1962) debate. In addition to the Buchler

psychological dimension in terms of two important and related structuralist premises: the ontological subordination of the individual and the subjective to the collective and the systematic and the methodological priority of logical and objective explanations to emotional and utilitarian ones.[18]

The first of these premises we have already encountered in the context of Lévi-Strauss' guarded approval of the position of the French sociological school. From an anthropological point of view, psychological formulations are particularized transformations of prior sociological conditions. Man's very situation is such that idiosyncratic and personal experiences "remain intellectually diffuse and emotionally intolerable unless they incorporate one or another of the patterns present in a group's culture. The assimilation of such patterns is the only means of objectivizing subjective states, of formulating inexpressible feelings, and of integrating inarticulated experiences into a system" (1949b:171-72). Even the respect for and reliance upon individual sentiments are in the final analysis a socially conditioned and collectively sanctioned ideology (see Lévi-Strauss' analysis of American individualism, 1946b). As we know, the same priority applies to the least "socialized" members of a culture: the child, the shaman, the·psychotic. Psychological factors are neither autonomous nor primary, but derivative and secondary (see 1950:xvi-xvii), because "the dynamics of subjectivity are incomprehensible without reference to a signifying system *which is encountered, not engendered*" (Sebag 1964:134).[19]

The importance of this premise can be illustrated in a number of ways. Note, for example, the way in which Lévi-Strauss uses such terms as "motivation" and "preference" in the study of kinship and elsewhere. They invariably occur in a logical and systematic context rather than in a psychodynamic or subjective one (e.g., 1962c: 159; 1969:395). The term "choice" is especially instructive in this regard. As I pointed out elsewhere (Scholte 1966b: 1197):

"The word 'choice' in English takes as its focus the individual's action . . . and [the] structure is treated as given" [Schneider 1965:67]. The structuralist [however] is primarily concerned with systematic models composed of logico-mathematical choices among logico-structural alternatives. He is *not* concerned with models "within which actors choose among alternative courses of action," but with the rules and regulation that structure a given system.

Lévi-Strauss' instructive reflections on the anthropological use of communications theory must be similarly read. He discounts the possibility that anthropology, by using such theories, would "get hopelessly involved in individual psychology." Rather, in adopting a communications theoretical perspective, anthropology would "consist exclusively in the study of *rules* and have little concern with the nature of the partners (either individuals or

---

and Selby (1968a) reference cited, helpful bibliographic guides can be found in Siegel's *Biennial Review(s) of Anthropology* from 1959 to the present.

[18] Some might legitimately question the validity and propriety of these priorities. Is a utilitarian explanation any less "objective" than an intellectual one? Or again, is an ethnologic any less "subjective" than individual sentiments? We should point out that Lévi-Strauss is in part speaking of substantive and methodological prerequisites rather than of absolute and irrevocable antinomies (1955a:309; 1962c:38). That he may nonetheless and inadvertently have raised these "relative" choices to the level of unassailable "truths" is, of course, possible.

[19] Since Sebag's point is crucial, let me cite the original French: "La subjectivité dans son movement est incompréhensible sans référence à une ordination signifiante *qui est rencontrée et non pas engendrée*" (Sebag 1964:137).

groups) whose play is being patterned after these rules" (1953b:298). The term "choice" in this approach would refer exclusively to numerical and positional alternatives within the confines of the rules of the game; they would refer to the motivational and preferential acts of groups or individuals only incidentally. Here again behavioral acts are the results of social structures, not vice versa (see 1953b:310-11 or 1965a: 14 for specific examples in kinship systems). What is principally required is a structural and sociological perspective, not an atomistic and behaviorist one. The latter is a frequent mistake made by Anglo-American anthropologists since Radcliffe-Brown: "Instead of seeing in kinship systems a sociological means to achieve a sociological result, [they] rather treat them as sociological results deriving from biological and psychological premises" (1953b:309).

Lévi-Strauss repeats the same argument in regard to myth and totemism, both of which are intellectual systems of collective representations par excellence. As such, they are the expressions of a sociologic rather than a psychodynamic. Their essence is intellectual rather than emotional, symbolic rather than utilitarian. Myth and totemism attest to the inherent value of classifying (see 1962c:9) and to the fact that "the universe is an object of thought at least as much as it is a means of satisfying needs" (1962c:3). In totemism, for instance, "animals and plants are not known as a result of their usefulness, they are deemed to be useful or interesting because they are first of all known" (1962c:9). Totemic relationships "are conceived, not experienced. In formulating them, the mind allows itself to be guided by a theoretical aim rather than a practical aim" (1962b: 63). A totemic relation represents an "objective analogy," not one based on "subjective utility" (1962b:77); "nat-ural species are chosen not because they are 'good to eat' but because they are 'good to think' " (1962b:89). The reality of totemism, like that of any other cultural system, can be reduced to "a particular illustration of certain modes of thought. Sentiments are also involved, admittedly, but in a subsidiary fashion, as responses of a body of ideas to gaps and lesions which it can never succeed in closing" (1962b:104). Totemism, in sum, "pertains to the understanding, and the demands to which it responds and the way in which it tries to meet them are primarily of an intellectual kind" (1962b:104).

The methodological consequences of Lévi-Strauss' intellectualism are important. If social and religious phenomena are the results of cognitive rather than utilitarian interests, if their nature is logical and collective rather than emotional and subjective, then we must replace pragmatic and psychodynamic explanations with logical and structural ones. Failure to do this will merely hamper our progress, as is the case with the psychological school of myth interpretation (see 1955c:207) and with Malinowski's account of totemism (see 1962b:68-69). Only a properly structural explanation—one rooted in an intellectual psychology and mirrored after the principles of structural linguistics and cybernetic logic—can do full justice to the cultural themes and variations of the human brain.

Before detailing the linguistic and cybernetic logic upon which Lévi-Strauss' encompassing understanding of the human brain rests, one final intellectual-historical influence should be mentioned: his indebtedness to the Anglo-American tradition. There are, of course, many substantive reasons for Lévi-Strauss' awareness of and interest in Anglo-American anthropology. For one, he is primarily an Americanist and has devoted much of his time and effort to the structural study of North and South American cultures. Most of his work on comparative mythology, for example, pertains to the American continent (see 1960c, 1960d, 1964a, 1966a, 1968a). Similarly, his theory of totemism is informed by the work of both American and British scholars (1962b:4-8, 33-35). His work on comparative social organization—no matter how different in principle from that of the Anglo-American tradition (see Leach 1965a:13, Lounsbury 1962: 1303-1304, Scheffler 1970, Schneider 1965:15, Wagner 1970)—is still indebted to and part of the continuity of that tradition (e.g., Nutini 1965: 707-708). *The Elementary Structures of Kinship,* for instance, was dedicated to Morgan, introduced with a quote from Tylor, and prepared with the assistance of Kroeber, Linton, and Lowie (see 1969:xiii). More recently, Lévi-Strauss expressed a similar indebtedness to such scholars as Leach, Lounsbury, and Needham (see 1965a, 1962e:10). Finally, we should mention that it was Lowie's *Primitive Society* that first inspired Lévi-Strauss' own interests in cultural anthropology (see 1955a:63) and that it was none other than Franz Boas that was praised as the founder of anthropology's practical and theoretical bases (see 1960a:8).[20]

Let me quickly add that Lévi-Strauss' praise for Anglo-American scholarship is far from uncritical. The French sociological tradition remains uppermost in his mind (see 1960a:8) and Rousseau is still the main inspiration for his present undertakings (see 1962a). His reply to those who accuse him of being "in fief to Anglo-Saxon thought" (1955a:63) is unequivocal: "What imbecility! ... It is to a historical situation, not an intellectual tradition, that I am paying homage" (1955a:63-64). The reasons for Lévi-Strauss' disenchantment are many. For one, functionalism is tantamount to the destruction of all anthropology (e.g., 1962b:58). For another, the arguments surrounding kinship are so futile and abstract that it makes "even a 'preposterous Frenchman' shudder ..." (1965a:18)! All in all, it is the behaviorism of the Anglo-American tradition that is to blame: it can lead only to a "curious combination of dogmatism and empiricism" (1949b:15). The mistake of dogmatism is made by Homans and Schneider (see 1953b:322; 1965a: 14-15; 1967:394) and by Needham in his interpretation of the distinction between prescriptive and preferential marriage exchange (see 1969:389).[21] Empiricism is an especially common and important error among Anglo-American ethnologists. It underlies Radcliffe-Brown's failure to distinguish between social structure and social relations (see 1953b:303, 1962f:143); it accounts for Murdock's psychodynamic reductionism (1953b:306) and his fallacious historicism (1962g); and it explains Maybury-Lewis' total misunderstanding of structuralist method (1960e:52-53).

Even those who assisted in the preparation of *The Elementary Structures of Kinship* do not escape Lévi-Strauss' criticisms. Kroeber, Lowie, and Linton are all wanting in one significant way or another. Linton's approach to culture

---

[20] Lévi-Strauss' interest in the contributions of his Anglo-American colleagues is no doubt in part due to his stay in the United States and to his participation in both American and British scholarly events. He was, for example, present at the important 1952 Wenner-Gren conference and took an active part in its subsequent assessment (see Lévi-Strauss in Tax 1953). Similarly, his 1965 Huxley Memorial Lecture helped to clarify his relation to Anglo-American colleagues. (Lévi-Strauss delivered yet another lecture in Britain in the fall of 1970. I have no access to this lecture at the time of writing.)

[21] To my knowledge only Schneider has taken note of Needham's inflexibility on this score (Schneider 1965:70-71).

and personality is, as we know, incommensurate with structuralism. Lowie's contributions to a "total" anthropology are needlessly compromised by his famous " 'shreds and patches' statement on culture" (1953b:309). Kroeber's efforts in the domain of a structural history are praiseworthy (see 1953b:290), but his understanding of a truly systematic social science is frail (e.g., 1946a:523-24). Even Boas is wanting in those very areas where structuralism finds its own unique place: he never transcended a precarious historicism (see 1949a:6-9, 1960a:24), and his recognition of the importance of the unconscious is severely curtailed by his failure to go beyond "the categories of individual thought" (1949a: 20).

In sum, Lévi-Strauss' understanding and use of the Anglo-American anthropological tradition are—like the others we have examined—selective and critical. This is certainly not surprising: the paradigmatic differences between structuralism and empiricism, rationalism and behaviorism, intellectualism and pragmatism are absolutely fundamental and perhaps irreconcilable (see Goddard 1965, Scholte 1966b). They are the kind of "cultural" and operational differences we will want to keep in mind in our examination of the systematic nature of the structuralist enterprise.

THE SYSTEMATIC NATURE OF STRUCTURAL ANTHROPOLOGY

We have already gained some insight into many of the assumptions and procedures of structural anthropology from our examination of its intellectual-historical precedents. Nevertheless, a number of issues have not as yet been mentioned, or, if they have, still require elaboration.[22]

The intimate ties that have existed and continue to exist between cultural anthropology and linguistics in both Anglo-American and French-continental social science are well known (e.g., Hymes 1964a).[23] In the case of the French tradition, we should mention that Durkheim's sociology provided an important stimulus to De Saussure's linguistics (see Dinneen 1967: 192), while the French sociological tradition was in turn influenced by developments in structural linguistics (see 1946a:506-508). This interdisciplinary interest has continued to flourish, culminating in the recent work of Lévi-Strauss. (For a critique, see Mounin 1970.) It is no exaggeration to say that for Lévi-Strauss "linguistics furnishes a primary model for a general anthropological theory" (Ruwet 1963:564) and that his structuralism may be con-

---

22 Let me repeat here what I said in the Introduction: I must restrict my discussion to those premises and conclusions that best serve to characterize Lévi-Strauss' position as a whole. To detail or specifically illustrate each and every point would simply be prohibitive. As always, I shall try to refer to the relevant literature and to concrete examples in the bibliography.

23 Despite this common interest in linguistics, we should also note that the Anglo-American and French traditions differ significantly in their respective use and understanding of linguistic materials and methods. As in the case of other paradigmatic differences, it is once again primarily a question of empirical behaviorism on the one hand and deductive rationalism on the other (Buchler and Selby 1968b: 24f; Hymes 1967; S. Levin 1965; Scholte 1966b). This is one reason, for example, why the distinction between *la parole* and *la langue* was never a major influence in shaping American anthropological linguistics, while it is crucial to the understanding of the French tradition. Such men as Bloomfield and Malinowski viewed language as a *"mode of action"* while Durkheim and subsequently Lévi-Strauss see language as a *"counter-sign of thought"* (Firth 1964: 94). These substantive differences entail methodological consequences as well. For structuralism, "the signifieds [i.e., ethnological materials] are signs among others [and] semantics must be part of structural linguistics, whereas for American mechanists, the signifieds are substances which must be expelled from linguistics and left to psychology" (Barthes

sidered as "part of a semiotic with linguistics at its heart" (Hymes 1964b: 13).[24]

Lévi-Strauss explicitly seeks to mirror the methodological principles and substantive aims of cultural anthropology after those of structural linguistics. As early as 1945 he took note of the "privileged position" of linguistics and considered it the science "in which by far the greatest progress has been made" (1945a:31). In the same article he predicts a uniquely important role for linguistics in the social sciences, one akin to that played by nuclear physics in the development of the physical sciences (see 1945a:33). Not only that,

linguistics and anthropology are virtually identical in method and object of study (see 1969:492f). Language, according to Lévi-Strauss (1961b:150-51), is "the cultural phenomenon *par excellence*," since it

is the most perfect of all those cultural manifestations which, in one respect or another, constitute systems, and if we want to understand art, religion or law, and perhaps even cooking or the rules of politeness, we must imagine them as being codes formed by articulated signs, following the pattern of linguistic communication.

In keeping with this same spirit, Lévi-Strauss (in Gramont 1968:29) recently described his efforts as follows:

Just as the discovery of DNA and the genetic code led biologists to use a linguistic model to explain a natural phenomenon, I use a linguistic model to explain cultural phenomena other than language. I try to show that the basic structure of language observed by linguists exists in a great many other activities.[25]

What does Lévi-Strauss find in the nature of language and the method of linguistics to warrant such a commitment? Again the reasons were stated as early as 1945 (1945a:33) and continue to be relevant today (see Scholte 1969a:101f):

First, structural linguistics shifts from the study of *conscious* linguistic phenomena to

---

1964:39). In the Anglo-American tradition, language is generally viewed as part of a more encompassing and dynamic psychology, whereas in French structuralism an intellectualist psychology is modeled after a more universal semiotics (de Huesch 1965:9). Let me quickly add that there are also important exceptions to these general differences. For example, Sapir clearly did not share Bloomfield's position (Sapir 1933:9). Similarly, "Kluckhohn's view of linguistics was independent of any narrow behaviorist outlook, not only in virtue of his personal regard for Sapir, but also in virtue of his relationship with the Prague School as mediated through Roman Jakobson and Lévi-Strauss, a structural outlook in a spirit kindred to that of Sapir (Kluckhohn returned from the 1952 conference on Anthropology Today with the report that the one person who had something really important to say was Lévi-Strauss; and that he hoped to have Lévi-Strauss at Harvard)" (Hymes 1967:19). Finally I should add that American linguistics has recently been invaded by Chomsky's transformationalism and that paradigmatic changes are likely to occur as a result (Grace 1969). In fact, I would venture the guess that if any convergence between continental structuralism and Anglo-American anthropology is forthcoming, it may well take place in the context of the assessment of the relation between Chomsky and Lévi-Strauss; this despite Chomsky's own reservations (Chomsky 1968:65) or the use of transformationalism in the critique of structuralism (Ricoeur 1967b). Such comparisons have already begun to appear (e.g., Buchler and Selby 1968b, Nutini 1968a) and will doubtless continue to be made.

[24] I shall not deal here with semiotics as such. Those interested may wish to consult two recent journals devoted to semiotic studies: *Communica-*

tions and *Semiotica*. I would also recommend the following: Barthes 1964, Benveniste 1969, Derrida 1967, De Saussure 1915, Greimas 1970, Jakobson 1960, Kristeva 1969, Metz 1967, Mounin 1970, Sebeok 1964, Wells 1967.

[25] This apparent equation between language and culture or linguistics and anthropology has been subject to both severe criticism (e.g., Dundes 1964, Moore and Olmstead 1952, Shankman 1969) and guarded approval (e.g., Kroeber and Kluckhohn 1952:242, Sommerfelt 1965). I shall mention some of these assessments in the context of specific arguments (see Sperber 1968 for a critical yet sympathetic overview of the issue).

the study of their *unconscious* infrastructure; second, it does not treat *terms* as independent entities, taking instead as its basis of analysis the *relations* between terms; third, it introduces the concept of system . . .; finally, structural linguistics aims at discovering *general laws*, either by induction, or . . . by logical deduction, which would give them an absolute character.

What is the relevance of these points to structural anthropology? We have already encountered the importance of the unconscious in the context of Mauss's concept of exchange and Freud's psychoanalytic perspective. Its role in linguistics and anthropology is no less dramatic (see 1950:xxxi). If linguistic science can hope to discover "fundamental and objective realities consisting of systems of relations which are the products of unconscious thought processes . . . is it possible to effect a similar reduction in the analysis of other forms of social phenomena?" (1951a:58). If it is, can we further conclude that "all forms of social life are substantially of the same nature—that is, do they consist of systems of behavior that represent the projection, on the level of conscious and socialized thought, of universal laws which regulate the unconscious activity of the mind?" (1951a:59). Lévi-Strauss concludes that this is in fact the case: various cultural modalities such as kinship, totemism, and myth are akin to language precisely because they, like language itself, are the products of "identical unconscious structures" (1951a: 62). In this sense, too (1953c:68-69),

language can be said to be the condition of culture because the material out of which language is built is of the same type as the material out of which the whole culture is built: logical relations, oppositions, correlations, and the like. Language, from this point of view, may appear as laying a kind of foundation for the more complex structures which correspond to the different aspects of culture.

Before turning to the second point—anthropology and linguistics as relational sciences—let me emphasize that Lévi-Strauss' argument is not linguistically reductionist. The substance of language does not provide the ultimate explanation for cultural phenomena; rather, both language and culture are the products of the unconscious brain (see 1953c:71, 80). Lévi-Strauss' reductionism is intellectual rather than linguistic, and cultural modalities are reduced to mental structures rather than to language behavior (see Sebag 1964: 169, Simonis 1968a:31). The difference is important not only because some have mistakenly characterized Lévi-Strauss' argument as a "linguistic fallacy" (Dundes 1964:44), but also because his position is far more subtle and heuristic than many critics have led us to believe (e.g., Leach 1970). Lévi-Strauss certainly assumes that there are "substantial comparabilities" (1951a: 61) between language and culture, but these are neither unequivocal nor simple (see 1953a:73). As his criticisms of Whorf and metalinguistics make clear (see 1953c:72f), the *de facto* correlation between language and culture is one of forms, homologies, contradictions, and transformations (see 1958: 85f). The question is not to search for one-to-one correspondences between semiological and cultural phenomena; rather, it seems likely that "some kind of correlation exists between things on certain levels, and our main task is to determine what these things are and what these levels are" (1953c:79). In sum, "to derive from language a logical model which, being more accurate and better known, may aid us in understanding the structure of other forms of communication [and culture], is in no sense equivalent to treating the former as the origins of the latter." If we are entitled to treat cultural systems as symbolic domains at all (without reductionist intent, at least on this level), it is certainly legitimate "to seek homologies between them and to define the formal characteristics of each type considered independently and of the transformations which make the transition possible from one to another" (1958: 83).

Given Lévi-Strauss' guarded attitude toward the role of language, his procedure for anthropological analysis obviously does not entail an uncritical or maniacal imitation of linguistic methods either. Not only does structuralism invoke cybernetic and mathematical models in addition to related methods in linguistics, "a too literal adherence to linguistic method actually betrays its very essence" (1945a:36). Linguistic methods themselves are not without logical problems (see 1962c:66), and we must accept the limitations as well as possibilities of its models (see 1945a: 36). To repeat, Lévi-Strauss reduces neither culture to language nor anthropology to linguistics. He does seek to formulate relations between conscious cultural givens and their unconscious mental infrastructures. To do so, he adopts a linguistic model, among others, to elucidate these universal structures of the human brain. One certainly cannot deny the importance of either language or linguistics, but they are significant precisely because they, too, point to the human spirit and to the need of an "intellectualist" psychology (see Sebag 1964, Scholte 1966b:1256). As if to emphasize the point, Lévi-Strauss maintains that it will not be the ethnologist, linguist, or psychologist who will someday "unravel the intricacies of the human mind." In view of his ultimate reduction of mind to brain, it will be the anatomist and biologist (Lévi-Strauss in Dreyfus 1970:324).

Lévi-Strauss maintains that structural linguistics, like structural anthropology, deals not with terms, but with the relations between them.[26] Anthropology itself is defined as "a general theory of relationships" in which "it will be possible to analyze societies in terms of the differential features characteristic of the systems of relationships which define them" (1958:95-96). As in linguistics, atomism must be rejected (see 1945a:34). Since "the logical principle is always to be *able* to oppose terms" (1962c:75), the contents of the terms themselves matter much less, as in the case of kinship systems (see 1945a:48, Scheffler 1966:80) or mythological texts (see 1955c:208f). This same relationalism, of course, underlies the crucial concepts of exchange and communication.[27] As working assumptions of ethnological inquiry, they demand an anthropology that is relational and holistic rather than atomistic and mechanical.

The most immediate and important consequence of a relational anthropology (I shall discuss a few other points in a moment) is its concern with structures or systems. Here again, linguistics provides a precedent: the concept of language as a system having been De Saussure's essential contribution, while the term "structure" was introduced by the Prague circle (see Benveniste 1963). In both cases, they are used to convey the idea of interdependence and relationship (see Lalande in Benveniste 1962:37f). In Lévi-Strauss' anthropol-

----

[26] The change from atomism and historicism to relationalism and structuralism seems to have been a general one in European intellectual history at the turn of the century (Cassirer 1945, Jakobson 1962). The transition is specifically evidenced in both De Saussure's and the Prague school's opposition to neo-grammarian linguistics (Jakobson 1962:632, Waterman 1963:64).

[27] Recent transformationalist criticisms of structuralism's alleged atomism have simply overlooked the generative implications of minimal elements conceived as part of an ongoing communicative network (Rastier 1967:105).

ogy, "structure" and "system" are similarly used. The preliminary question is always: "Is the system (or structure) systematic?" That is, is it structured like language? (1945a:48). If so, sociocultural systems can be studied as more or less integrated symbolic structures of language itself, marriage rules, economic relations, and artistic, scientific, and religious systems (see 1950:xix). Here again it is the human brain that is the source of the symbolic function (and hence of cultural systems) and which provides the pivotal ontological basis for structural anthropology.

Before turning to the final point raised in Lévi-Strauss' 1945 quotation, we should discuss the controversial role of the binary, oppositional, and phonological model that he uses to arrive at the constituent units that are then combined and systematized to form the structures whose rules the ethnologist seeks to determine (see 1962c:131, Sebag 1964:146). Lévi-Strauss accepts an assumption made in both linguistics and cybernetics (see Jakobson in Tax 1953:312; Jakobson 1962:649), that distinctive oppositions are inherent in the structure of language and that binary logic is characteristic of the human mind (see 1958:92; 1962b: 101).[28] Does this assumption entail a reduction of anthropological analysis to phonological method or, conversely, does it posit an identity between mental, phonological, and social reality? There is certainly no question that structural analysis is intimately tied to phonological method. Binarism seems

---

[28] This assumption is by no means universally shared, even among structuralists (e.g., Barthes 1964:80-81). Others question the supposed identity between the structure of the mind and phonemic systems (e.g., Scheffler 1966:64). Still others object to what appears to be a phonological reductionism in structuralist method (e.g., Lefebvre 1966b:89). Finally, there are numerous empirical objections to Lévi-Strauss' usage of binarism (e.g., Hymes 1964b: 16).

to operate on every level of structuralist discourse (e.g., Greimas 1966a) and appears to apply to the analysis of every sociocultural domain (see Pouillon 1966b:100, Simonis 1968a:212). But as in the case of language generally, we should never assume a one-to-one correspondence between phonological and social systems (e.g., 1945a:35f). Constituent binary elements are preliminary analytical units; their isolation is an initial step in a more comprehensive quest for structured intelligibility. In fact, the constituent units are dialectical means to a synthetic end: they are used "to elaborate a system which plays the part of a synthesizing operator between ideas and facts, thereby turning the latter into *signs*. The mind thus passes from empirical diversity to conceptual simplicity and from conceptual simplicity to meaningful synthesis" (1962c:131). We might add that Lévi-Strauss' criticism of dialectical humanism is similarly motivated: binarism and dialectics are analytical reason in action and refer to "the perpetual efforts analytical reason must make to reform itself if it aspires to account for language, society, and thought; and the distinction between the two forms of reason . . . rests only on the temporary gap separating analytical reason from the understanding of life" (1962c:246). Oppositional logic, in other words, must either lead to an integrated superrationalism (see 1955a:61) or be explained by its physicochemical conditions (see 1962c:247).

According to Lévi-Strauss, "structural linguistics aims at discovering *general laws* . . ." (1945a:33).[29] Structural anthropology also seeks to establish such general laws. For the moment, let

---

[29] As the original quotation indicates, Lévi-Strauss continues by saying that these laws may be arrived at inductively or deductively. I shall discuss these discovery procedures separately.

me discuss just one characteristic of these laws (a trait that will again emphasize the continuity between anthropology and linguistics): their essentially synchronic nature (see also Jakobson in Tax 1953:313). As far as linguistics itself is concerned, we should remember that Jakobson and other members of the Prague school had rejected De Saussure's radical distinction between historical and descriptive questions and had instead proposed that "one can analyze changes in terms of a synchronic pattern just as one does with its static constituents" (Jakobson in Tax 1953:314; see also Greimas 1966*b*: 819f). They added that any diachronic theory of language should therefore be structural, mutational, and teleological (see Jakobson 1962:110, 218). Linguistic determinism, in sum, is considered to be mechanical rather than statistical, i.e., morphological, topological, and teleological (see Jakobson in Tax 1953: 310-11, Rastier 1967:99).

Lévi-Strauss follows a similar path in his delineation of anthropological laws. He too rejects De Saussure's cleavage between the diachronic and the synchronic (see 1960*a*:28-29) and even quotes Jakobson in support of his position (see 1958:89). He also introduces a structural concept of teleological change (e.g., 1945*a*:34) akin to Troubetzkoy's and Jakobson's synchronic explanation of phonological change (e.g., 1969:492-93). Most importantly, if in linguistics *la langue* reveals the mechanical determinants of language behavior while the manifestations of *la parole* are understandable only as a calculus of probabilities (see 1955*b*:527), so in ethnology an unconscious logic exhibits a morphological and qualitative determinism while conscious representations are merely the results of "a sort of 'dialectical average' among a multiplicity of unconscious systems" (1960*e*:29).

This structuralist concept of determinism is important in yet another language-related context: Lévi-Strauss' modification of De Saussure's theory of the arbitrariness of the linguistic sign (see also Benveniste 1939).[30] For Lévi-Strauss, the linguistic sign is arbitrary *a priori*, but "ceases to be arbitrary *a posteriori*" (1958:91). The moment a sign is placed in either the context of its linguistic aggregates or its neurological infrastructure, a systematic, relational, and deterministic conception of its nature and function becomes possible (see 1958:94). In the same way, anthropological elements are reducible to a topological and motivated (in the linguistic sense of the term) determinism rather than to a mere statistical and arbitrary (linguistically speaking) correlation. In this sense, linguistics and anthropology (as well as mathematics and cybernetics) join in an overall structural investigation of the lawful determinants of the sociocultural universe: "the study of those qualitative properties that are invariant under isomorphic transformations" (Jakobson in Tax 1953:311).

The various issues raised by Lévi-Strauss' comparisons of linguistics and anthropology may be further detailed in the context of mathematics and cybernetics. There are, in fact, intimate historical and systematic continuities between these disciplines, and the specific problems raised in one will almost invariably relate to similar issues in another.[31] In addition, the theoretical

---

[30] This is not, of course, the only other context in which the structuralist conception of determinism is relevant. We shall encounter it again, for example, in our discussion of "mechanical" and "statistical" models.

[31] The historical and systematic continuities linking anthropology, linguistics, cybernetics, and mathematics are cogently summarized in Jakobson's important, albeit dated, remarks in Tax's *An Appraisal of Anthropology Today* (1953:310-12). Lévi-Strauss himself has also commented on the close

and practical ties between structuralism and mathematics or cybernetics will, like those between structuralism and linguistics, again reveal those paradigmatic principles that hold the entire structuralist enterprise together in a consistent (if problematic) way. Lévi-Strauss' use of mathematics, for example, involves questions of methodological feasibility and scientific rationalism generally. Similarly, his understanding of information theory again raises problems in binary logic and neurological reductionism. Let me elaborate.

Lévi-Strauss is interested in mathematical thought for both theoretical and practical reasons. Theoretically, its importance may be understood in the context of structuralism's intellectualism—a characteristic we have encountered before and will meet again. According to Lévi-Strauss, "mathematics reveals the intrinsic properties that manifest, in its purest form, the functioning of the human mind" (1968b:10). Mathematical thought further evidences the intellect's universal and natural bases;[32] it "reflects the free functioning of the mind, that is, the activity of the cells of the cerebral cortex, relatively emancipated from any external constraint and obeying only its own laws. As the mind too is a thing, the functioning of this thing teaches us something about the nature of things: even pure reflection is in the last analysis an internalization of the cosmos" (1962c:248). Mathematical thought can hope to provide us with

the ultimate key to "the as yet unmapped universals of the brain and of genetic potentiality" (Anon. 1967:522). In this sense, too, mathematical thought reflects the activity of the unconscious brain (see 1953a:62)—a fact that makes the mathematical study of linguistic phenomena possible and the mathematical treatment of social reality modeled after linguistics so suggestive and important (see 1951:56-57).[33] Not surprisingly, Lévi-Strauss calls for the progressive mathematization of the social sciences on numerous occasions (e.g., 1950:xxxvii; 1953d:30; 1955b: 533; 1958:329; 1960e:53; 1968b:10). One critic even goes so far as to suggest that structural anthropology is reducible to merely another and contemporary version of Leibniz' *mathesis universalis* (see Gurvitch 1963:421); another wonders if Lévi-Strauss hasn't mistakenly equated two entirely different concepts: mathematization and profundity (see Viet 1965:71).

What are some of the ways in which Lévi-Strauss uses mathematical procedures and what is their importance for the structuralist method as a whole? We should first of all mention the analytical advantage of using mathematical notations and logical calculi in the study of classificatory systems. As early as 1949 Lévi-Strauss had asked André Weil for assistance in the study of Murngin kinship in the hope that it would show "how a certain type of marriage laws [could] be interpreted algebraically, and how algebra and the

---

relationship of these various disciplines in a number of articles and books (1952c, 1953b, 1955b, 1961b, 1962c, 1964a, 1965a, 1969).

[32] If Lévi-Strauss is correct, the ethnocentricity of mathematical praxis is secondary to the natural, unconscious, and hence universal foundation of mathematical concepts themselves (see the interesting exchange between Northrop and Lévi-Strauss in Tax 1953:315-16; also 1952b:27).

[33] Although we cannot go into details here, we might recall that De Saussure (1915:168) conceived of *la langue* as an algebra. Interestingly enough, Hjelmslev, in following De Saussure's suggestion, is criticized by none other than Jakobson (1962:475). Even more significantly, Jakobson makes his criticism in the context of the nature-culture distinction and with reference to music. Given Lévi-Strauss' own deliberations on these issues (e.g., 1953a:61-62), this raises some interesting problems. I'll discuss some of these in the third section of this essay.

theory of groups of substitutions [could] facilitate its study and classification" (1969:221). Subsequent to 1949, Lévi-Strauss himself applied similar techniques to various studies of sociocultural transformations and mythic variants. For example, the analysis of "mythemes" "furnishes rules of transformation which enable us to shift from one variant to another by means of operations similar to those of algebra" (1956b:235). In this way, myth variants can be shown to be related and to be analyzable by means of group theory (see 1960c:360). Similarly, the analysis of hierarchical variants and the use of Guttmann scalograms can assist in the structural study of social organization (see 1955b:536f; see also Buchler 1964:781-82; Cuisinier 1963, 1967).[34]

What is especially important to note about most of these mathematical techniques is their relational, combinatory, and qualitative character. The use of this kind of mathematics reflects an important structuralist principle: "It is not things that matter, but the relation between them" (Jakobson in Tax 1953:312; see also 1953a:66 for Lévi-Strauss' comments on the Murngin case, and 1954a:33 for his remarks on phonological method). As a result, Lévi-Strauss is primarily (though by no means exclusively) interested in the "new qualitative approach of mathematics in topology and group theory" (1953a:118). The consequence of this preference is important: the use of statistical methods in structural analyses is always of secondary importance, since

for a relational and qualitative mathematics, quantification and measurement have no necessary or intrinsic connection to structure and meaning (see 1958:329-30). This also means that a deductive manipulation of mathematical symbols is both possible and desirable, irrespective of their quantitative ties to the empirical referents derived from the level of observation. We can go even further: a logical manipulation of the phenomenal data may actually "bring out properties not immediately apparent to the empirical observer" (1960e:53).[35]

In considering the relation between structuralism and cybernetics, we should again be mindful of the historical and systematic continuity between anthropology, mathematics, linguistics, and information theory. In Lévi-Strauss' estimation, all these disciplines may one day be integrated into a vast and encompassing science of communications (see 1950:xxxvi, 1952c). Little wonder, then, that Lévi-Strauss' delib-

---

[34] This is, of course, a very brief, highly selective, and—given the enormous amount of recent literature—probably dated review. White's article elsewhere in this volume will doubtless provide the reader with additional information. Let me here single out only a few sources of special interest to structuralists: Buchler and Selby 1968a, 1968b; Flament 1963; Granger 1960, 1968; Hoffmann 1970; Maranda 1967, 1968; White 1963.

[35] Lévi-Strauss' position has been subject to much criticism (see Maybury-Lewis 1960 for a typical example), especially since the use of mathematical formalism and deductive method often seems incompatible with empirical and inductive approaches. I shall be more specific about these issues later on; let me here merely make a few parenthetical remarks about formalism and deduction. Formalism is certainly not an intended result of structuralism; in fact, it specifically seeks to resolve the distinction between form and content (e.g., 1960f: 122). Furthermore, the mere use of mathematical symbols is not in itself either abstract or formalistic (Barbut 1966:800). It does, however, facilitate ethnological procedures, especially in the case of comparative analysis (Leach 1961a:2, 19). One could also argue that the use of qualitative methods assures a greater degree of objectivity than a mere quantitative analysis of empirical data (e.g., Ingemann and Sebeok 1956:265). As far as deduction is concerned, we should at least entertain the possibility that it can be of significance to anthropology; it already has proven its value in structural linguistics (1950:xxxi, Benveniste 1954). In anthropology, for example, deduction can be used on the "experimental level" (1953b:280) of model construction or in the discovery of the laws of permutation (1962b:16).

erations on information theory should again involve crucial epistemological premises and major ontological assumptions: the use of binary logic, cybernetic models of social reality, the nature of teleological change, and the problem of neurological reductionism. Most important of all, the specific use of cybernetic imagery points to structuralism's bias toward the syntactic and—by implication—to the paradoxes of its humanism and of its reductive discourse (see Simonis 1968a; Scholte 1969a, 1969b, 1969c). Since we shall address ourselves to the latter issue in the next section, let me here confine myself to an explication of Lévi-Strauss' specific use of information theory.

The most inclusive definition of cybernetics' importance to structural anthropology is found in the last few pages of *The Savage Mind* (see also Leach 1965a for an excellent summary). Here we discover the kinship between human thought (both "primitive" and "civilized") and information theory; we find that the human world and the physical cosmos are closed systems of communicative signals (see 1962c:267-69). This cybernetic characterization of the human and the physical, the primitive and the civilized, also entails a specific definition of human society as an information-processing mechanism[36] and, underlying it all, of the brain as a computer. The constraints of classificatory systems can be measured cybernetically; the logic of the unconscious corresponds to that of a binary or analogue computer; the ul-

timate mystery of the human condition—the emergence of the symbolic function (i.e., language and culture)—may someday be resolved by information theory (see 1961b:153-55). The continuity and consistency of Lévi-Strauss' premises are noteworthy: the genetic origins of the symbolic function and the unconscious teleology of the human brain coincide, necessitate, and produce the binary logic and split representation inherent in human thought and language; these, in turn, underlie and define the nature of society as a mechanism of exchange, reciprocity, and communication.

If information theory can be used to describe so much of the human condition, it can certainly assist in the description of particular social organizations. We can, for example, compare primitive and civilized societies in cybernetic terms, the former corresponding to mechanical machines or "cold societies," the latter resembling thermodynamic machines or "hot societies" (1961b:32-33). We can also use this cybernetic model to characterize a community's attitude toward historical time (see 1961b:38-40) and to differentiate between the social and the cultural domains (1961b:40). We may even look forward to the possibility of using information theory to resolve the historical and ethical predicament of contemporary "entropic" civilizations (see 1961b:40-42).[37]

Information theory can in addition assist in the specific analysis of anthropological issues; for example, myth

---

[36] Lévi-Strauss echoes Wiener's celebrated definition of society: society "can only be understood through a study of the messages and communication facilities which belong to it" (Wiener 1954:16). According to Lévi-Strauss (1953a:321), "It can be said that society is, by itself and as a whole, a very large machine for establishing communication on many different levels between human beings."

[37] I cannot here detail Lévi-Strauss' disturbing analysis of the plight of contemporary civilizations or his use of cybernetics to suggest possible resolutions to both the destruction of primitive communities and the condition of modern civilizations. I briefly touched on these issues in my discussion of Rousseau and will do so again in the next section. *Race and History* (1952b) constitutes Lévi-Strauss' most complete statement on the problem.

(1964*a*, Buchler and Selby 1968*b*), totemism (1962*b*, 1962*c*) and kinship. The last of these provides an especially informative example. As we know, social organization as a whole can be defined in communicative terms (see also Flament 1963, Buchler 1964). Such social communication can occur on several levels; for example, "the communication of women, communication of goods and services, [and] communication of messages" (1953*b*:296). Kinship systems and their attendant marriage rules can be interpreted as "the outward expression of a mechanism which 'pumps' women out of consanguine families to redistribute them among conjugal families, i.e., families based on affinity instead of consanguinity" (1952*c*:3). According to Lévi-Strauss, "this amounts to saying that social organization (limited for the purpose of this [example] to kinship systems, descent groups and marriage rules) refers to a level of communication where the objects to be communicated are women, while men—or rather consanguine groups consisting of male kin—are engaged in the process of exchanging these objects among themselves" (1952*c*:7).[38] In sum, as in the case of linguistic messages, anthropology is entitled to treat "marriage regulations and kinship systems as a kind of language, a set of processes permitting the establishment, between individuals and groups, of a certain type of communication" (1951:61).

Even this cursory description of cybernetic methods raises a number of additional issues. For instance, what about the value of using quantitative methods in addition to the qualitative ones mentioned earlier? Using quanti-

tative methods can in part be justified on practical grounds (e.g., 1953*c*:70); that is, in cases of vast amounts of empirical data or extremely complex classificatory systems (e.g., 1962*c*: 151). To the extent that they are complementary to qualitative techniques, they may even be of theoretical value in ethnological analysis (e.g., 1962*c*: 89). The study of kinship again provides an example: differing types of social organization can be ordered along a numerical scale measuring their respective information content. We can thereby hope to supplement "mechanical" data on kinship terminology with "statistical" data on actual marriage choices (see 1952*c*). In that case, we can also hope eventually to utilize mathematical procedures for "prediction and control" (1953*b*:299).[39]

An important function of information theory in structural anthropology is to legitimize the concept of purpose or teleology. One cannot discuss these concepts merely in the context of a final-cause theory or an alleged normative bias in structuralism (as is done, for example, by Coult 1963, Dundes 1964, and Homans and Schneider 1955). We should also take into account the cybernetic basis for these notions (as is done, for instance, by Buchler and Selby 1968*b*, Köngäs and Maranda 1962, and Needham 1962). Few of Lévi-Strauss' critics seem to realize that from a cybernetic point of view, the concept of purpose or teleology is both scientifically legitimate and anthropologically useful. In fact, in anthropology, linguistics (see 1945*a*:24), and other

---

[38] This must seem like a cocky argument. I should point out, however, that even if Lévi-Strauss is incorrect in assuming that men exchange women— if instead the reverse is the case—this would not in itself change the basic argument.

[39] If both statistical and mechanical models can be used in analyses of kinship systems, Needham is mistaken in characterizing Lévi-Strauss' position as one in which statistical and intensive analyses are mutually exclusive (Needham 1962:72). For a similar reason, Moore and Olmstead are incorrect in saying that Lévi-Strauss refuses to use mathematical procedures predictively (Moore and Olmstead 1952: 18).

disciplines, it is imperative to inquire into the general purpose of human activity (e.g., Ruhemann 1967:84). Hence the concept of teleology is integral to any structural explanation of cultural domains—especially if the latter are defined as self-regulatory devices (see 1964c:68f; Brown 1963:111f; Buckley, ed., 1968; Sebag 1964; Spencer 1965). A teleological concept of social reality does not necessarily entail a notion of normative or extraneous finality; it is and can be mechanical as well as purposeful (see Piaget in Goldmann 1965: 18; Simonis 1968a:183f; Sluckin 1960: 231). If, in sum, we grant that cultural systems are communicative mechanisms, "the objection that a teleological outlook is distasteful to modern science need not alarm us, for it is obviously false" (1965a:14). Instead, anthropology should assist in the overall task of exorcising the "ghost of teleology" by helping to explain it "as a special case of determinism capable of feed-back operations" (1964a:14).

Before we conclude this summary account of the relation between cybernetics and structuralism, two other issues deserve mention: the problem of binary logic and the question of cybernetic reductionism. Since we have already mentioned the linguistic basis for an oppositional logic, we need here to add only the reminder that the human brain generally functions digitally and that the prevalence of binary logic is neurologically and cybernetically founded (see also Yalman 1961). This does not preclude the use of analogue models (see Lévi-Strauss' reply [1966a:74] to one of Leach's criticisms [Leach 1964, Steiner 1967:242-43]), though binary analyses obviously constitute a privileged part of structuralist method. Let me add, however, that this digital logic can be and has been put to extremely subtle and complex use. That this also reflects Lévi-Strauss' personal

ingenuity and/or reduces his substantive conclusions to self-fulfilling prophecies are fairly familiar accusations, which I shall consider in due course.[40]

As far as the important issue of cybernetic reductionism is concerned, let me merely repeat what I have said before and will discuss more fully later on: the paradoxical result of Lévi-Strauss' cybernetically inspired arguments (see especially Simonis 1968a). Structuralism's emphasis on a "codal" or syntactic perspective (how the brain is "programmed") leads to a concomitant minimization of the symbolic. This, in turn, entails an epistemic reductionism that endangers the very distinction between the natural and the cultural upon which the entire structuralist enterprise depends. The philosophical paradox is fundamental, implying the irreconcilable ambiguity or impasse of structuralist discourse itself. Before we turn to this crucial problem, however, several other important topics require an explanation: Lévi-Strauss' understanding of social scientific models, the comparative method, and anthropological verification.

Since Lévi-Strauss' understanding of scientific activity has been an especially controversial topic, I would like to make it clear that my sole purpose here is to explain the basic assumptions of structuralist activities as best I can. I am not interested in criticizing Lévi-Strauss' procedures on empirical, dialectical, or phenomenological grounds. This is not to deny that Lévi-Strauss can and should be criticized; I merely refuse to have these purely de-

---

40 The essential questions here are ones of empirical verifiability and of the ontological status attributed to the binary distinctions used. While some anthropologists have expressed guarded approval (e.g., Douglas 1967, Leach 1962, Yalman 1961), others have been severely critical of Lévi-Strauss' binarism (e.g., Geertz 1965; Leach 1967; Leach, ed., 1967; Sahlins 1966; Shankman 1969; Worsley 1967).

scriptive efforts compromised by pre-judgmental interpretations that can on-ly detract from a proper understanding of Lévi-Strauss' intentions. I have read far too many critical assessments of structural anthropology which, while pretending to be descriptively accurate, are in fact grossly ethnocentric and mis-leading. I therefore want my purpose to be clear: to offer a selective but unprej-udiced account of Lévi-Strauss' posi-tion. Since the topics I am about to discuss have been subject to much mis-understanding and criticism, I think a "mere" descriptive effort is entirely warranted.[41]

Turning to the first issue of concern here—the nature of ethnological models

---

[41] A descriptive or "ethnographic" empathy to-ward differing anthropological traditions is especially difficult to retain in instances of paradigmatic de-bates (Scholte 1966b, 1970). The Anglo-American assessment of Lévi-Strauss' work is a case in point; the 1966 quarrel between Köbben and Pouwer in *Bijdragen* is another example (Köbben 1966; Pouwer 1966a, 1966b). I should add that this is not surpris-ing, since the basic difference between Lévi-Strauss and his empiricist critics couldn't be more striking. To simplify: structuralism is primarily an experi-mental and transempirical activity guided by ethno-graphic observation and deductive reasoning; most Anglo-American anthropology (despite enormous internal variability) is basically an inductive and em-pirical enterprise informed by descriptive accounts and inductive analyses. The former tends to consider the final aim of cultural anthropology as one of explanation and intelligibility based on principles of logical order; the latter is generally more interested in empirical facts and behavioral predictions based on observation and quantification. Structuralism's appeal is beyond a merely factual truth to "a truth of reason" (1960a:34); empiricism demands a more immediate factual reference in the phenomenal world. For the one, anthropology most aspire to transcend the observational state (Rastier 1967: 107); for the other, such transcendence is precarious if not outright "metaphysical." In the case of struc-turalism, the creation of scientific facts and their deductive manipulation are considered entirely legiti-mate and objective; empiricism usually labels such procedures arbitrary, subjective, and unscientific (see also Goddard 1965 and Scholte 1966b; for a critique of "paradigmatic" analyses of anthropological tradi-tions see Nathhorst 1969:11f; Orans 1970:175f; Shank-man 1969:75).

and their relation to ethnographic reali-ty—I should emphasize that the con-struction and utilization of scientific models are part and parcel of the gener-al aims of a structuralist enterprise:[42] "in the first place, to observe and to describe; secondly, to analyze and to classify; finally, to isolate constants and formulate laws" (1953d:90). The im-portance of models is especially evident in the case of the final aim of struc-turalism: the discovery of "invariants beyond the empirical diversity of human societies" (1962c:247). Here models have both a practical and a theoretical function. Practically, they can help to reduce the multiplicity of empirical observations to a small num-ber of manageable variables (e.g., 1962f:159). In this way they help to show us "a way out of the confusion resulting from too much acquaintance and familiarity with concrete and empir-ical data" (1953c:70).[43] If we "wish to derive constants which are found at various times and in various places from an empirical richness and diversity that will always transcend our efforts at ob-servation and description" (1958:82-83), we require an analytical device that will "reduce the concrete complex-ity of the data ... into more simple and elementary structures" (1946a: 525). A scientific model is precisely such a device: it is "an object that can be easily isolated, with well defined outlines, whose different states as re-vealed by observation can be analyzed

---

[42] The problem of scientific models is intimately associated with those of ethnological comparison and anthropological verification. I am separating them here for organizational purposes only.

[43] This is certainly a blunt statement and one that has been subject to considerable criticism: e.g., Maybury-Lewis 1960:35 and Nutini 1965:727 (Nutini has since reversed his position: Nutini 1968b). We should note that such a statement is justified in the context of purely deductive scientific procedures; e.g. Mouloud 1965, 1966.

by reference to only a few variables" (1964*b*:544). Only on the level of such models are the complex tasks of defining social phenomena and of analyzing their invariant properties feasible at all (e.g., Lévi-Strauss' deliberations on the universality of the human family [1956*c*:266f]).

The advantages of models are not merely practical, but theoretical as well: they render the observed ethnographic data intelligible and manageable, and also allow for the delineation of structures and for the logical experimentation with, or deductive manipulation of, scientific facts. Models, therefore, are not merely descriptive devices, as Nadel (1957:150f) would have it; they are genuinely explanatory. Most importantly, the construction of models allows for the delineation of structures. As such, "the term 'social structure' has nothing to do with empirical reality but with models which are built up after it" (1953*b*:279). Social structures consist of ethnological models whose characteristics render them scientifically manipulable; i.e., they are systematic, transformational, predictive, and exhaustive (1953*b*:279-80; see also Miguelez 1969, Mouloud 1965).

How do these four crucial characteristics of structures *qua* models make scientific explanation possible? How, in other words, do they contribute to the ultimate aim of cultural anthropology: "the discovery of relations between phenomena" (1946*a*:504)? The definition of structures in systematic terms allows for the initial classification of social morphologies or types (e.g., 1945*b*:524). This is an important analytical step, since "a morphological study is the basis of all scientific investigation" (1960*f*:6; see also the discussion on the comparative method below). Further, the transformational changes characteristic of the constituent elements of structured systems reveal their essential interconnectedness. As a result, cultural anthropology must regard social life as a system of which all aspects are organically connected" to form a "*total social phenomenon*" or "*pattern*" (1954*a*:365).[44] This latter characteristic complements the former one, since "there is a close relationship between the concept of transformation and the concept of structure" (1960*a*: 30). It follows that

no science today can consider the structures with which it has to deal as no more than haphazard arrangements. That arrangement alone is structured which meets two conditions: that it be a system, ruled by an internal cohesiveness; and that this cohesiveness, inaccessible to observation in an isolated system, be revealed in the study of transformations, through which the similar properties in apparently different systems are brought to light [1960*a*:31; see also 1960*e*:54].

The third and fourth characteristics of anthropological models (their predictive value and their exhaustiveness) bring us to Lévi-Strauss' concept of scientific activity: a transempirical epistemology that has been especially subject to intensive criticism in the Anglo-American literature. (E.g., Goddard 1965:426-27; Maybury-Lewis 1960:35;

---

[44] We've discussed the notion of system before and will do so again in the context of the comparative method. Its importance should be stressed, since it marks the substantive and historical transition from atomistic historicism to synthetic structuralism in a number of disciplines at the turn of the twentieth century. As Lévi-Strauss himself remarks (1951*b*:825): "In contrast to the analytical trend of the nineteenth century, to which Marxism was the first reaction, social psychology, sociology, and, above all, social anthropology have taught us during the past thirty years that human society, with its beliefs, customs, and institutions, is not, as has been alleged, 'a thing of shreds and patches,' but that its components are all part of a whole. We now realize that economic life, technology, legal and political institutions, the arts, morals, and religion all belong together, and that we can know nothing of any of them unless we have discovered in what way it combines with the others to form a pattern."

Nutini 1965:727; Zimmerman 1968: 59. There are exceptions, of course; e.g., Nutini 1968a, 1968b; Shapiro in Tax 1953:113.)[45] The third requirement introduces the concept of experimentation, i.e., a "set of procedures aiming at ascertaining how a given model will react when subjected to change and at comparing models of the same or different types" (1953b:280). In the case of the analysis of totemism, for example, experimentation on the model allows us "to construct a table of possible permutations" between structural elements and to "take this table as the general object of analysis which, at this level only, can yield necessary connections, the empirical phenomenon considered at the beginning being only one possible combination among others, the complete system of which must be reconstructed beforehand" (1962b:16).

Experimentation leads directly to the final characteristic of models: they render the empirical data scientifically intelligible by exhaustively accounting for both their actuality and their potentiality. A social structure with its attendant model "has no value except to the extent that it allows for the explanation of the facts considered and permits [us] to put them together, to predict their previous and subsequent states, [and] to explain their adjacent forms by means of a series of transformations" (1962f:157). The analytic units of a structural model are scientifically exhaustive precisely because they need not stand in a one-to-one correspondence to the empirical data. In fact, models would be useless if they did not tell us something more about the data than would be apparent on the level of observation alone (see 1960e:51). A

structural model is said to embody an "efficacy" (*puissance*) by means of which we can transcend the empirical object as such and construct "a kind of super-object," that is, "*a system of relations*" (1962f:144). Only on the level of such models can we eventually discover the actual and potential relations between empirical phenomena and the invariant properties of such relations. It is in this context that we must understand Lévi-Strauss' (1955a:61) important observation that

social science is no more based on events than physics is based on sense-perceptions. Our object is to construct a model, examine its properties and the way it reacts to laboratory tests, and then apply our observations to the interpretation of empirical happenings: these may turn out very differently from what we had expected.

The construction of models and the attendant discovery of social structures have a number of additional consequences for anthropological inquiry. We can best understand these by first recalling one of structuralism's most characteristic premises: "Exploration is not so much a question of covering the ground as of digging beneath the surface" (1955a:50). Structuralism "is the search for unsuspected harmonies. It is the discovery of a system of relations latent in a series of objects" (Lévi-Strauss in Gramont:28). As we know, this search is in turn supported by the assumption that the unconscious brain constitutes the irreducible ontological essence of human nature. The importance of these complementary premises cannot be underestimated; they sustain the entire structuralist enterprise. Let me quote one of Lévi-Strauss' most succinct statements (1949a:21) on their practical significance:

If, as we believe to be the case, the unconscious activity of the mind consists of imposing forms upon content, and if these forms

---

[45] For excellent discussions of the complex issues involved in deductive reasoning in science and the attendant problem of the use of empirical referents in such activity, see Northrop 1960, 1964.

are fundamentally the same for all minds— ancient and modern, primitive and civilized (as the study of the symbolic function, expressed in language, so strikingly indicates)—it is necessary and sufficient to grasp the unconscious structure underlying each institution and each custom, in order to obtain a principle of interpretation valid for other institutions and other customs, provided of course that the analysis is carried far enough.

How does this statement affect the question of models? Quite directly: the ultimate function of structural models is to uncover the unconscious and relational reality underlying empirical and ethnographic phenomena (see Simonis 1968a:170-71). Structural models (and their social correlates) may be defined in terms of their degree of distance from and/or proximity to the unconscious structures of the human brain. This is most obvious in the case of the difference between a culture's "homemade" models (1953b:282) and the scientific models of the ethnologist. An indigenous and conscious model "permits us to grasp the natives' own conception of their social structure; and, through our examination of the gaps and contradictions, the real structure, which is often very different from the natives' conception, becomes accessible" (1958:322). Though we should never minimize the ethnographic importance of indigenous theories (e.g., 1953b:282), we should always remember that "conscious models, which are usually known as 'norms', are by definition very poor ones, since they are not intended to explain the phenomena but to perpetuate them" (1953b:281). Even when native explanations are more or less accurate, we are still faced with a "strange paradox": "the more obvious social organization is, the more difficult it becomes to reach it because of the inaccurate conscious models lying across the path which leads to it" (1953b:281). In sum, "native conscious representations, important as they are, may be just as remote from unconscious reality as any other" (1953b:282). It follows that the ethnographer should never confuse conscious models with their unconscious reality (see 1952d:121, 130f; see Nutini 1965 for a critique). He should instead seek to reduce conscious models to the unconscious basis that is said to underlie them and which determines their manifest reality (e.g., 1950:xxxix).

The relation of mechanical and statistical models to infrastructural reality is somewhat more difficult to determine than that of unconscious and conscious models. The problem derives in part from Lévi-Strauss' definitions: the latter models are largely defined in ontological terms, while the former are primarily characterized by their epistemological function.[46] Thus mechanical and statistical models are distinguished in terms of "the relation between the scale of the model and that of the phenomena" (1953b:283). When the elements of the model are on the same scale as the phenomena, the model is mechanical; when they are on a different scale, it is statistical. Similarly, the ethnological purpose of both statistical and mechanical models is epistemological, i.e., to recognize and isolate levels of reality from a strategic point of view (see 1953b:284).[47]

---

[46] I tend to agree with Parain-Vial (1969:195f) that Lévi-Strauss often seems to vacillate between a substantive definition of scientific models on the one hand and an epistemological one on the other. I don't think, however, that these different uses are irreconcilable.

[47] I should add that the distinction between statistical and mechanical models is far less radical or significant than some commentators have apparently assumed (e.g., Korn 1969a, 1969b; Nadel 1957: 147f; Nutini 1965:720f). Lévi-Strauss readily conceives of translating "statistical models into mechanical models and *vice versa*" (1953b:299). The differences between them are relative rather than "in-

We can further clarify the nature of statistical and mechanical models by comparing them to conscious and unconscious structures. To do so, we should recall two oppositions we previously encountered: statistical versus mechanical time and "civilized" versus "primitive" societies. Let me add the reminder that anthropological explanation tends to proceed from statistical prediction to mechanical determinism and from conscious superstructures to their infrastructural foundations. If we now combine these "relative" oppositions, we have a fairly obvious continuity between anthropology's privileged object of study: primitive cultures; its preferred epistemological tool: mechanical models; its ultimate explanatory aim: topological determinism; and its irreducible ontological basis: unconscious structures.[48] In this context we can also determine the differences and similarities of history, sociology, ethnography, and ethnology. History and ethnography "are based upon the collection and arrangement of documentary material," while sociol-

ogy and ethnology "are more concerned with the study of the models constructed on the basis, or by means of that documentary material" (1964c: 542). Further, ethnography and ethnology seek to construct mechanical models and to examine the unconscious foundations of collective phenomena, while history and sociology tend to work with statistical models and to organize their data "in relation to conscious expressions of social life" (1949a:18; see also 1964c:541f). Though these methods and definitions are by no means mutually exclusive, they do in part serve to illuminate the question of the nature of models. Statistical models seem to be the epistemological correlates of conscious structures, while mechanical models appear to be the means toward discovering unconscious systems.

One crucially important issue remains to be discussed: the relation of social structures and ethnological models to empirical and ethnographic reality. The argument about models and reality derives in large measure from Radcliffe-Brown's definition of social structure and from his failure (from a structuralist point of view) to distinguish between social structures and social relations. Radcliffe-Brown conceived a social structure as a "continuing network" (Radcliffe-Brown 1952: 11) of "actually existing relations" (Radcliffe-Brown 1940:190). Lévi-Strauss, on the contrary, maintains that social structure can never "be reduced to the ensemble of social relations . . . in a given society" (1953b: 279). Rather, social structures consist of those formal characteristics of social models that make social relations possible in the first place. In this sense, kinship systems consist of *both* empirical relations *and* social structures; that is, "the actual workings of the system within a given society on the one hand,

---

trinsic," i.e., "defined in relation to the person of the donor and that of the bearer" (1962c:187). This same relativity extends to the much discussed distinction between prescriptive and preferential marriage systems. Both are models, the one mechanical, the other statistical. But here too, "the extremes always allow for a continuous series of intermediate applications" (1969). The rather violent debates on the issue (from the Needham versus Homans and Schneider confrontation on) do not even seem warranted in Lévi-Strauss' estimation. He says: "If . . . I have used rather loosely the terms 'prescriptive' and 'preferential,' it is because I am unable to consider this distinction as important as the far more fundamental one between 'elementary structures' and 'complex' ones" (1965a:18); i.e., the problem of "the extension of the ethnological theory of kinship to contemporary societies" (1969:397).

[48] It is important to remember that these oppositions are relative, not absolute. Structural anthropology obviously can study "civilized" societies, does use statistical models, must observe conscious phenomena, and may be predictive as well as explanatory.

and on the other, a model, that is a set of rules" (1965a:16). The nature of these structures or models is such that their study "should be given logical priority over [their] empirical application" (1965a:16; see also the earlier discussion on deduction and experimentation). To that extent "the study of kinship systems should remain first and foremost a study of models rather than of empirical realities" (1965a:17).

How does Lévi-Strauss' argument affect the issue of the substantive reality of structures or models? Structural models are as "real" as social relations, though the latter are manifest on the level of empirical reality while the former are expressive of logical necessity (see 1953a:115, Viet 1965:204).[49] Structural models, then, are "real" —though their proximity to or distance from manifest and latent reality, conscious and unconscious truth, and so on may vary from one ethnographic instance or ethnological analysis to another. The important point is always to experiment on the model and thereby determine its infrastructural reality. We can even go so far as to argue that in this sense a structural model is "more real" than the phenomenal reality from which it is initially derived (see 1953a:115, Godelier 1966:835).

---

[49] This has been an especially difficult distinction for most Anglo-American commentators to accept; as early as 1953, Murdock and Nadel expressed their doubts (see their comments in Tax 1953:109f), and even Nutini's (1968b) cogent distinction between deductive or etic models and inductive or emic paradigms is still confusing on this score. Lévi-Strauss himself is fully aware of the scientific and cultural problems: ". . . in English it is difficult to distinguish between reality and concrete reality. I do not know how you would quite qualify it. In my mind, models are reality, and I would even say they are the only reality. They are certainly not abstractions, as was suggested by Professor Nadel [in Tax 1953:113], but they do not correspond to the concrete reality of empirical observation. It is necessary, in order to reach the model which is the true reality, to transcend this concrete-appearing reality . . ." (1953a:115).

This discussion of scientific models brings us back to an important structuralist assumption, one to which I have referred on previous occasions and to which I shall return again in a moment: structural anthropology presupposes that ethnological models and unconscious structures have an analytical priority and an ontological predominance over mere descriptive observations and conscious representations. Contrary to most tenets of empirical anthropology, Lévi-Strauss maintains that one must first illuminate the role of these latent and unconscious structures before one can hope to shed light on empirical reality (see Simonis 1968a:174). Let us, then, turn to a discussion of the comparative method and of scientific verification to illustrate once again the crucial importance of this epistemological and ontological premise.

Let us divide our specific discussion of the comparative method into three interrelated parts: the question of structural form and empirical content, the issue of the systematic relations between and/or relative autonomy of sociocultural domains, and the problem of "concrete universals" in the search for ethnological generalities. The relation of the first of these issues to the comparative method may not at first seem apparent, though we should remember that structuralism has often been accused of formalism (e.g., Burridge 1967:111, Dundes 1964:57, Worsley 1967:155), and that its comparisons are therefore said to be based on formal models rather than concrete relations (e.g., Davenport 1963:216). We should perhaps clarify this controversial issue before we actually turn to a discussion of the comparative method proper.[50]

---

[50] The charge of formalism has not, of course, been limited to Anglo-American critics alone. It is also characteristic of Marxist critics in France (e.g., Goldmann 1966, Lefebvre 1966a). Among those in

The question of form and content is complicated by structuralism's historical background, especially by its ties to linguistics. If one stresses structuralism's indebtedness to phonology—an area in which formal and relational analyses tend to take precedence over substantive and atomistic ones (see Rastier 1967:101)—one could conclude with Todorov that "one finds . . . among structuralists, traces of a 'formalist' influence in [their] general principles as well as in certain of [their] techniques of analysis" (Todorov 1965:81). This impression is reinforced by structuralism's preferred use of logico-deductive, mathematical, and cybernetic models (e.g., Buchler and Selby 1968b). There is, of course, an intimate relation between mathematics, cybernetics, and linguistics—even as far as formalism is concerned. As Benveniste points out: "If the science of language must choose models, it will be [from those] mathematical disciplines which completely rationalize their object [of study] by reducing it to an ensemble of objective properties defined by invariables. In other words, [linguistics] becomes more and more 'formal' . . ." (Benveniste 1954:8).

But structuralism's historical ties to linguistics can also lead to an entirely different conclusion. We could argue that Lévi-Strauss, like De Saussure and Jakobson before him, ultimately seeks to integrate both form and content into a unifying concept of "meaning" (see 1956b:241). It has been said that in phonemics, as in linguistics and semiology generally, the integrative concept is neither form nor content, but "signification": the unification of signifier and signified (see Barthes 1961:155, Jakobson 1962:658).[51] It is perhaps for this reason that Lévi-Strauss rejects Propp's distinction between grammatical form and lexical content (see 1960f). The separation between form and content is only temporary and is definitely transcended once we reach the level of structural analysis proper (see 1962b:86). Structuralism, then, cannot be equated with formalism: it "refuses to oppose the concrete to the abstract and to attribute to the latter a privileged status. A *form* is defined by opposition to a content which is exterior to it; but a *structure* does not have a distinct content, it is content itself, realized in a logical organization considered characteristic of reality" (1960f:3). As in the case of the relation between model and reality, "form and content are of the same nature, vindicated by the same analysis. The reality of content is derived from its structure and what one calls form is a 'structuralization' ['*mise en structure*'] of localized structures, of which content consists" (1960f:21-22).

We should add that Lévi-Strauss' rejection of ontological formalism obviously does not entail a concomitant rejection of transempirical procedures. At certain stages in scientific discovery, formal abstractions or models are both required and productive. But it is equally important to remember that any such formal devices must always retain a dialectical, complementary, and necessary relation to their empirical contents. Anthropologists should never forget that their specific data are human beings (see 1969:114) and that their final goals are ethnographic and concrete (see 1960a:16).

France who have, along with Lévi-Strauss, denied these charges, I would single out Pouillon (1966b), Sebag (1964), and Simonis (1968a). Among Anglo-American authors, Yalman has defended structuralism against the charge of formalism (Yalman 1964:1121; see also Sahlins 1966:132, Scholte 1969a:111f).

[51] As we shall see in the next section, Lévi-Strauss' best intentions remain problematic. The concepts of meaning and of the symbolic are in constant danger of being reduced to the codal or the syntactic (see also Simonis 1968a).

The complementarity between form and content is characteristic of structural analysis as a whole: it moves from content to form and then to structure (see 1960f:4, 1964a:98, Simonis 1968a:211). From one point of view, we can say that in any structural system a relational logic takes precedence over the particular contents. To that extent, only a "formal" analysis can make the empirical data intelligible (e.g., 1966a:133). But from another point of view, a formal analysis is justifiable only to the extent that it encompasses and explicates each and every ethnographic detail (e.g., 1964a: 147). The value of a structural analysis lies precisely in combining these two requirements (the formal and the substantive) in a complementary and dynamic way and in thereby explaining the ethnographic data in intelligible, systematic, and exhaustive terms.[52]

How do these reflections on the relation between form and content affect the nature of the comparative method? To answer this question, let me draw a parallel between comparative analysis and model construction—processes that are related and complementary. Ethnological comparison, like anthropological analysis generally, depends on the initial construction of structural models. The diversity of ethnographic data would simply defy systematic analysis without such models. Comparisons between models are, like the construction of models, genuinely structural processes, i.e., dialectical movements from particulars to generalities and from contents to forms without losing the concrete and empirical reference any structural activity demands (see Sebag 1964:174f).[53] The process may be summarized as follows: The initial classification must be representative and fundamental (i.e., based on an ethnographic description of conscious representations from which their rela-

---

[52] Empiricist criticisms notwithstanding, a structuralist analysis is not meant to be either "abstract" or "arbitrary." I might quote Lévi-Strauss on both these alleged shortcomings of structuralism. As far as the issue of abstractness is concerned, Lévi-Strauss claims (quite correctly, it seems to me) that he—as compared with many other ethnologists—has been exceptionally attentive to "the concrete aspects of human life." Referring to his work in comparative mythology, he says: "I try to show that it is impossible even to start interpreting a myth unless one is perfectly informed about the slightest ethnography detail of the society in which it exists. I would say that there is more concrete ethnology in my books than in any other theoretical works in the field" (Lévi-Strauss in Gramont 1968:38). With regard to the question of "arbitrariness," Lévi-Strauss quite specifically points out (again in the context of myth analysis) that "the method I am following is legitimate only if it is exhaustive: if we allowed ourselves to treat apparent divergencies among myths, which are at the same time described as belonging to one and the same set, as the outcome either of logical transformations or historical accidents, the door would be thrown wide open to arbitrary interpretations: for it is always possible to choose the most convenient interpretation and to press logic into service whenever history proves elusive, or to fall back on the latter should the former be deficient. Structural analysis would, as a result, rest entirely on a series of begged questions, and would lose its only justifica-

tion, which lies in the unique and economical coding system to which it can reduce messages of a most disheartening complexity, and which previously appeared to defeat all attempts to decipher them. Either *structural analysis succeeds in exhausting all the concrete modalities of its subject, or we lose the right to apply it to any one of the modalities*" (1964a:147; italics mine).

[53] Pouwer's noteworthy defense of structural comparisons may nonetheless be mistaken in characterizing the process as simply one in which we progressively abstract at the expense of concrete reality (Pouwers 1966a, 1966b). Though I think he is entirely correct in pointing out the transempirical requirements for all social scientific comparison and explanation (see also Miguelez 1969 and Van Loon 1964:181), I don't think that this amounts to doing "violence to reality to get a grip on it" (Pouwer 1966a:139). To get "behind" or "beyond" empirical reality we must certainly experiment "on" it, but I don't think this is tantamount to violating the data (see the discussion on scientific verification below). Nor, by the way, do I think that it means that all empirically and contextually sensitive procedures are necessarily ideological—as Nutini (1971) seems to imply.

tional properties have been extracted); the subsequent comparison must be systematic and structural (i.e., based on taxonomic models "the formal properties of which can be compared independently of their elements" [1953*b*: 284]); the final step of scientific verification must rejoin the initial descriptive effort (i.e., assure that the analytic and comparative reduction did not "impoverish" the "distinctive richness and originality" of the empirical data [1962*c*:247]).

Structural comparison, like structural analysis, is clearly neither merely formal nor simply empirical, though it contains both these procedures as elements in a total process. It can best be termed systematic and positional (see Miguelez 1969): "based on a systematic comparison, that is to say, on an ensemble of elements between which relations exist" (Richard 1967:122). The comparative method is therefore an integral part of structuralism's stance toward the ultimate task of anthropological inquiry generally: "the discovery of general relations between phenomena" (1946*a*:504). Let me illustrate the importance of this principle by turning to a discussion of the comparative analysis of intracultural domains.

The subject of intracultural comparisons raises several significant issues: the concept of relation generally, the comparative study of sociocultural domains in particular, the possible existence of relatively autonomous sociocultural domains, and the crucial notion of structural variants or transformations. Let me try to tie some of these together, since they complement each other in several ways. We have encountered the issue of relationalism before and should here recall its indispensable role in structuralist activity generally. As Lévi-Strauss points out: ". . . the function of science is not so much to anticipate as to explain" (1964*c*:538), to define sci-

entific facts and determine their systematic relations.[54] Only the latter part of this statement needs to concern us here (the creation of scientific facts will be taken up separately). Structural relations are determined by means of a scientific reduction: isolating the distinctive features and constant relations that are said to underlie the particular data to be explained (see 1950:xxxv, 1953*a*:293f). Experimenting on the models resulting from this reduction will in turn permit us to discover the invariant laws that govern the permutations and transformations characteristic of the structural relations previously determined (e.g., 1955*c*:228, Pouillon 1966*a*:775). Having arrived at this point, we can claim to have explained the empirical data with which we began.

Discovering and explaining systematic relations between empirical phenomena are primary goals of structural anthropology. We should quickly point out, however, that such relations between data may be more or less intimate, that their presence cannot be assumed on an *a priori* basis, and that their reality can be determined only ethnographically. To presuppose otherwise can only lead to the "intolerable abuses of functionalist interpretation" (1943:139). This is why the relations between, say, myth and society are transformational (e.g., 1960*c*:356) and dialectical (e.g., 1956*b*:233) rather than monolithic and mechanical. Only by retaining this flexibility can we hope to arrive at a point where different types of cultures and cultural domains can be justly characterized "in terms of the types of transformations which occur within [and between] them" (1958:334). After having accomplished this task, we can begin the reductive

_____
[54] Explanation and anticipation are not mutually exclusive; but neither are they synonymous.

search for the unconscious and invariant properties that are assumed to underlie and to determine these permutations and transformations.[55]

The ethnological assumption that sociocultural domains are functionally related and contextually situated does not necessarily mean that some of these domains may not at times function relatively autonomously. Mythic structures, for example, are not constrained by external demographic and internal sociological factors in the same way that kinship systems and marriage rules are. Myths are primarily limited by the neurological and unconscious constraints of the human brain. To that extent, "myths signify the mind that evolves them by making use of the world of which it is itself a part. Thus there is simultaneous production of myths themselves, by the mind that generates them, and, by the myths, of an image of the world which is already inherent in the structure of the mind" (1964a:341). Mythic structures, in other words, are ultimately intelligible in terms of internal psychological principles, not merely in terms of the ethnographic context from which they must clearly draw their lexical contents. In this sense, "Lévi-Strauss' structural studies of myths represent the first successful attempt to formulate a mythical metalanguage within which

myths may be translated into one another" (Buchler and Selby 1968b:44; see also Köngäs and Maranda 1962: 188). Lévi-Strauss' position is justified by the very nature of mythic discourse. It, too, is a kind of metalanguage: "it is a language which is subject to certain rules that are not consciously given to people but which they nonetheless utilize; it is on its own proper level that these rules are discovered" (Sebag 1964:127).

What repercussions do the context-sensitive and/or relatively autonomous status of mythic domains have for the main problem at issue here: that of structural comparisons? The result is certainly not, as some would have it, a retreat into "the Land of the Lotus Eaters" (Leach 1967:10).[56] Lévi-Strauss has made it abundantly clear on any number of occasions that structural analyses must always remain comparative and contextual. They must appeal both to a mythic domain and to other ethnographic contexts, regardless of the specific nature or extent of the relation between them. In *The Raw and the Cooked*, for example, he

---

[55] As I mentioned at the beginning of this essay, lack of space prevents me from illustrating most of these points. In the case of the various relations and transformations that Lévi-Strauss in fact draws, the lack of concrete examples is especially unfortunate and gives a falsely "abstract" impression. I would urge anyone who has any doubt about the concreteness and variability of Lévi-Strauss' analyses to consult any of his works, especially those on comparative mythology (see also Richard 1967 and Scholte 1969a). While on the subject of Lévi-Strauss' alleged abstractness, may I also add that Yalman seems quite right when he contrasts structuralism and functionalism precisely on the grounds that the former is able to bring sociocultural domains together in a uniquely concrete and satisfactory way (Yalman 1964:1182,

1965:442; see also Schneider 1965:78-79). I would also suggest that Yalman is again correct in criticizing Maybury-Lewis (1960:41) for having completely misunderstood the criteria of empirical exhaustiveness in structural analysis (Yalman 1965:442). Finally, a parenthetical remark about the related issue of the autonomy of certain cultural domains as compared to the functional integration of others. The alternatives are best described by Leach: a symbolist position on the one hand, a functionalist one on the other (Leach 1961b:386f). Yet Leach himself is curiously ambivalent on the issue. Sometimes he favors a symbolist argument (e.g., Leach 1961b:395, 1965a:14), but at other times he adheres to a functionalist position (e.g., Leach 1965b:779, 1970:2). What is remarkable about Lévi-Strauss is the fact that he seems to have been able to combine the two alternatives (Scholte 1969a:107f).

[56] Pouillon's brilliant critique of Leach's misunderstanding of Lévi-Strauss' position should be singled out (Pouillon 1966b; see also Sperber 1967 and Scholte and Simonis, forthcoming).

says (1964*a*:173): "It is never possible to postulate an interpretation: it must emerge from the myths themselves or from the ethnographic context, and as far as possible from both." The same is true for mythic symbols themselves; they too are relationally determined and contextually understood. They "have no intrinsic and invariable significance; they are not independent in relation to the context. Their significance is primarily *positional*" (1964*a*: 56). By the same token, "the syntax of mythology is never absolutely free within the confines of its own rules. It is inevitably affected by the geographical and technological substructure" (1964*a*:245). Despite all this, mythic structures may at times elaborate a relatively autonomous syntax (see 1964*a*: 245). The extent of a myth's immediate relation to its ethnographic context is one of degree; it is not a distinction of kind as implied in the radical separation between a purely symbolist or an irrevocable functionalist position.

Lévi-Strauss retains a comparative and relational perspective even in the structural study of those mythic systems that are to some extent "transcontextual" and autonomous. He does so by using the concepts of myth transformations and myth variants.[57] This is especially evident in the first three volumes of *Mythologiques*, where Lévi-Strauss' primary aim is to show how a "key" Bororo myth (*mythe de référence*) is "simply a transformation, to a greater or lesser extent, of other myths originating either in the same society or in neighboring or remote societies" (1964*a*:2). In one sense all of the *Mythologiques* comprise a series of variations on a theme. In most cases, the transformations simply bear witness to the baroque-like quality of an under-

lying and common logic. Though there are transformations within transformations (e.g., 1966*a*:290), metagroups (e.g., 1966*a*:256), and even archmyths (e.g., 1966*a*:324), they are ultimately tied together, either to one myth in one society or to a common theme that spreads over several continents (e.g., 1966*a*:326f). Mythic variants and their contents may be entirely contextual or they may be progressively engendered by the logic of myth itself. In all cases, however, they remain comparative and relational, either within the specific confines of their respective ethnographic settings or in those relatively autonomous instances when myths "reflect upon themselves and their interrelation" (1964*a*:12). Most importantly, the logic of transformations which governs these diverse myths again attests to structuralism's eventual goal: to find the invariant relations behind the diversity of empirical phenomena by means of a systematic, relational, comparative, and scientific method.

There is one issue in the comparative method that remains to be discussed: that of the role of "concrete universals" in the search for ethnological laws. The complexity of the problem is brilliantly outlined by Hymes (see Hymes 1964*b*) and entails a number of crucial questions: What is the relation between particular ethnographic phenomena and general ethnological analyses? (See also Schneider 1965:25f.) What is the role of the anthropological observer and the universal unconscious in the search for ethnological invariants? Is the reduction of sociological facts to their distinctive and contrastive features adequate to the task of delineating cultural universals? Finally, can we arrive at concrete universals without counting particular cases? [58]

---

[57] Other than Lévi-Strauss' own work, Buchler and Selby's (1968*b*) study of myth provides an excellent example.

[58] Two parenthetical remarks seems in order here. First, the significance of the concept of "concrete universals" for anthropological investigation

Although we cannot go into every one of these questions in equal detail (we've discussed some of them before and I will attend to several others later on), Lévi-Strauss' position should at least be indicated, however briefly.

As we already know from our discussion of mathematical procedures, the counting of cases—though sometimes possible and desirable—cannot solve the predicament of the comparative method: either to amass examples by "isolating them from their context" or to analyze only a few cases in context from which generalizations cannot legitimately be drawn (1969:xxv). Of the two alternatives, the first is the least satisfactory: it can result only in "superficial" and "ineffective" studies (1958:288). The latter is preferable and may prove that "in the last analysis one well-done experiment is sufficient to make a demonstration" (1958:288). This does not mean that counting cases cannot at times lead to the formulation of statistical models or prove helpful in illustrating a given point (see 1969: xiii), but it does imply that only the second alternative can eventually lead to the delineation of mechanical models and therefore to the discovery of necessary and universal principles.[59]

Lévi-Strauss, then, argues that comparative analyses require the selection of "a small number of cases, judiciously chosen as representing clearly defined types" (1946a:527). Counting particu-lar cases will simply not ensure their comparability (see 1958:315). We need "typical cases," i.e., those that contain "as many of the conditions of the problem as reasoning [can] determine" (1969:xxvi). Such cases ideally correspond to total social facts whose study is as concrete as it is complete (see 1950:xxv). Total social facts, in other words, are "concrete universals" par excellence. The general principle of sociocultural reciprocity is a perfect example. It is both universally present and concretized in such institutions as cross-cousin marriage. In this sense the latter constitutes "a *special case* [*un cas privilégié*] showing particularly clearly that reciprocity is present behind all marriages" (1969:143). In this sense, too, the analysis of cross-cousin marriage systems is a "veritable *experimentum crucis* in the study of marriage prohibitions" (1969:123).

As we know, structural anthropology is defined as a science of relationships. This means that concrete universals are also defined relationally. If so, we clearly face a problem with regard to the invariant properties that supposedly govern these relationships. Can the latter be defined at one and the same time by discontinuities or differences and by invariants or commonalities? If, "as in linguistics, it is the *discontinuities* which constitute the true subject matter of anthropology" (1958:328), how are cultural universals and ethnological generalities possible? (See Hymes 1964b:18f.)[60] Only by an appeal to an infrastructural foundation that lies

---

should be stressed. As Hymes says, "the concreteness of universals . . . is the stock in trade with which anthropology as a discipline must stand or fall" (Hymes 1964b:21). Second, the questions mentioned in the main text are my paraphrase of what I understand to be the central issues raised by Hymes in connection with the problem of concrete universals in structural anthropology.

[59] The priority of intensive analysis can be understood in yet another way. As Needham points out, "you cannot compare, or attempt to explain, what you do not first understand" (Needham 1962: 72).

[60] We might add here that De Saussure's definition of language suffers from the same ambiguity vis-à-vis the status of linguistic universals. He too defines language in exclusively differential terms (De Saussure 1915:166). Hymes has argued that Jakobson's concept of distinctive features transcends the dilemma: "it is a brilliant indication of how a structural perspective and principle can be maintained on the levels of both individual systems and the universe of systems" (Hymes 1964b:19).

beyond the confines of cultural anthropology proper: those preconstituted and fundamental truths that are the preserve of the biological and natural sciences. These invariants are part and parcel of the unconscious structures that are said to inhere in the physicochemical composition of the human brain. The ethnologist must simply take these universals for granted. His own task is more modest: to describe, analyze, and explain the relational and differential features that derive from this infrastructure (see 1949*a*:21; see also Hymes 1964*b*:45f, Miguelez 1969:55f, Simonis 1968*a*:95).[61]

Since I shall examine the problematic implications of Lévi-Strauss' argument in some detail in the next section, let me here merely stress its importance for structuralism generally. Conscious, empirical, and ethnographic phenomena are assumed to be the concrete and comparable realizations of unconscious, structural, and ethnological systems. These, in turn, are said to be the results of neurological, cybernetic, and physicochemical universals. Not only does structuralism as a discipline stand or fall on the basis of this premise, but it also provides the paradigmatic closure for the enterprise as a whole: an encompassing movement from the empirical description of ethnographic details to the analytical construction of ethnological models on to their final reduction to unconscious, comparable, and universal structures. If we accept these premises, procedures, and conclusions, we must at the very least conclude that the aesthetic elegance and logical coherence of Lévi-Strauss' anthropology is both indisputable and consistent. But whether, in addition, his arguments are scientifically defensible has been the subject of considerable debate.

In discussing the nature of structural investigation in relation to scientific verification, we shall have to consider at least three important issues: the creative aspect and concomitant limitation of scientific construction, the methodological possibilities of a deductively verifiable anthropology, and the tensional ties between ethnographic reality and ethnological analysis. We have, of course, considered most of these questions before in one context or another. Here I merely want to try to bring them all together in terms of scientific adequacy and anthropological validity.

Let me first of all discuss the role of ethnographic fieldwork in structural analysis. Though Lévi-Strauss' ethnographic respectability has often been questioned (e.g., Leach 1970:18f), there is no doubt about his avowed commitment to ethnographic research. He explicitly states that "the teaching of anthropology should be reserved for *eyewitnesses* . . . no one should be entitled to teach anthropology unless he has carried out considerable field-research" (1954*a*:372).[62] In response to Gurvitch's attack on structuralism's allegedly lifeless abstractions (see Gurvitch 1963:420), Lévi-Strauss again appeals to his ethnographic experiences, to the tribes he has studied, and to the

---

[61] A statement by Evans-Pritchard represents an interesting variant of this position: ". . . any claim to universality demands in the nature of things a historical or psychological, rather than sociological, explanation, and thereby defeats the sociological purpose, which is to explain differences rather than similarities" (Evans-Pritchard 1963:16).

[62] I suppose one could argue that Lévi-Strauss' own ethnographic experience is quite limited. He himself has confessed that "it is because I feel the inadequacy of my own field experience so acutely that I would like my pupils and collaborators to avoid it" (Lévi-Strauss in Gramont 1968:38). This limitation has not, however, interfered with Lévi-Strauss' detailed use of ethnographic materials or with his sensitive appraisals of the nature of fieldwork (e.g., 1962*a*). I might add that he has also contributed enormously to the expanded range of French ethnographic activities generally (Guiart 1965).

peoples with whom he has lived: "all these names [and places] are associated with men and women of whom I have been fond, whom I have respected, whose faces remain in my memory. They remind me of joys, hardships, weariness, and, sometimes, dangers. They are my witnesses, the living link between my theoretical views and reality" (1958:332). Ethnographic experience must obviously be considered as one of the most immediate and significant means "for obtaining that final empirical satisfaction" (1960a:16) which attends an anthropological investigation. It is a satisfaction "based on the sincerity and honesty of the person who can say, like the explorer bird of the fable, 'I was there; such-and-such happened to me; you will believe you were there yourself,' and who in fact succeeds in communicating that conviction" (1960a:26-27).

How does ethnographic experience relate to ethnological analysis; how can the anthropologist translate "the most intimate subjectivity into a means of objective demonstration" (1960a:26)? In part, he does so by means of a process of mutual reciprocity between observer and observed (see 1963:62) and a subsequent objectification of himself (see 1950:xxix). This process alone, however, does not offer any guarantees. There is, for instance, always the possibility that the ethnographer may distort or misunderstand the native's intentions (see 1950:xxx). Under the circumstances, Lévi-Strauss invokes a characteristic structuralist argument: only the unconscious mind can mediate a mutual understanding and transcend a subjective bias (see 1950:xxx). The ethnographic dilemma "would be unresolvable . . . if the opposition between self and other were not surmountable on one level, a level where objectivity and subjectivity also meet—that is, the unconscious" (1950:xxx).

Here again we encounter a fundamental structuralist assumption: the "unconditional objectivity" (1962a:12) of the unconscious mind. As far as Lévi-Strauss is concerned, no human discourse, whether between observer and observed or between peoples generally, would be possible without this assumption. It even underlies those areas of inquiry to which structural anthropology turns for its own inspiration: Marxism, linguistics, cybernetics, etc. If Lévi-Strauss' premise is correct, any criticism of his alleged subjectivity in analysis becomes largely irrelevant. The kind of question posed by Leach with regard to *The Raw and the Cooked*, for example (" . . . does this book really tell us something about South American mythology or only something about the complexities of La Pensée Lévi-Straussienne?" [Leach 1965b:776]), is answerable precisely in terms of the dialectical relation between self and other which Rousseau's "the me is another" and its unconscious foundations make possible. As Lévi-Strauss points out (1964a:13):

If the final aim of anthropology is to contribute to a better knowledge of objectified thought and its mechanisms, it is in the last resort immaterial whether in this book the thought processes of the South American Indians take shape through the medium of my thought, or whether mine take place through the medium of theirs. What matters is that the human mind, regardless of the identity of those who happen to be giving it expression, should display an increasingly intelligible structure as a result of the doubly reflexive forward movement of two thought processes acting upon the other, either of which can in turn provide the spark or tinder whose conjunction will shed light on both.[63]

---

63 We are reminded again of Lévi-Strauss' objectivistic critique of neo-Kantianism and the latter's distinction between *Natur-* and *Geisteswissenschaften* (1955a:59, 1960a:15f).

There is yet another issue we should consider here: that of the relation between so-called emic and etic reality. The issue is an especially urgent one, since many critics have accused Lévi-Strauss of caring little for the native point of view and of substituting his own theoretical biases for those indigenous to the ethnographic data.[64] As far as the initial descriptive task is concerned, Lévi-Strauss certainly does not reject an emic perspective: "One aim is to recreate a culture in its own terms and to make everybody feel how the people themselves experience it" (1953a:320). In and of itself this perspective is inadequate, however. As we know from our previous discussion of conscious models, the indigenous point of view may be far removed from the actual or unconscious reality that underlies collective representations. Native peoples—and we too, of course—do have systematic explanations for their behavioral patterns and social institutions. But this does not mean that any such system can claim, "on pretext of its native origin, to be a faithful representation of a reality which is just as likely to be revealed, in its unconscious and collective aspect, to the subject's as to the observer's analysis" (1969:110). We need to place any emic or indigenous reality in its proper context; not by destroying or mutilating its empirical reality, but by going beyond or behind such phenomenal manifestations. Remember Lévi-Strauss' premise: "*Contra* the theoretician, the observer should always have the last word; and against the observer, the native. Finally, behind the rationalized interpretations of the native . . . one [must] look for the 'unconscious categories' which . . . are determinants 'in magic, as in religion, as in linguistics' " (1960a:12).

Remember too that the relation between the emic and the etic parallels in a significant way the relation between *la parole* and *la langue*.[65] As in the

---

[64] I would like to make several parenthetical remarks here. With regard to Lévi-Strauss' allegedly arbitrary and subjective procedures, Hymes's criticism is typical: you cannot use the cognitive system of the analyst as warrant for the validity of structural contrasts within another system (Hymes 1964b:16). Interestingly enough, Joiner and Robinson have recently indicated that even a subjectively arbitrary determination of distinctive features does not necessarily interfere with an objective analysis of the underlying structure of a given system (Joiner and Robinson 1968). Other authors have discussed the emic-etic issue with regard to the categories used in Lévi-Strauss' analyses. Fischer, for example, suggests that Lévi-Strauss' "levels of mythic discourse" in "The Story of Asdiwal" (1960d) are to some extent akin to the "paradigmatic systems" used in componential analysis (Fischer 1963:252). Sturtevant has similarly compared Lévi-Strauss' "gustemes" (1958:99f) to emic units used elsewhere (Sturtevant 1964:103). At the same time, Sturtevant argues that Lévi-Strauss, unlike the ethnoscientists, has failed to use "rigorous, replicable procedures for identifying units without the application of criteria foreign to the culture analyzed" (Sturtevant 1964:107). Davenport has also contrasted componential analysis with structural method: "The former is based on establishing contrasting dimensions of meaning while the latter rests upon the concepts of contrast, complementation, and analogy conceived of as epistemological processes." Davenport adds that "Lévi-Strauss comes close to applying dimensional analysis (in *Totemism*), but does not fully achieve it. Applied comparatively, dimensional analysis can yield both qualitative comparisons of contrastive dimensions of meaning and comparisons of purely taxonomic models" (Davenport 1963:217; see also Scheffler 1966:75-76). Finally, I would like to suggest that a careful study comparing and contrasting ethnoscience with structuralism would be most enlightening for anthropological theory in general. Such an analysis might commence with the shared interest of componential analysts and Lévi-Strauss in such works as Simpson's *Principles of Animal Taxonomy* (1961) (see 1963b and Sturtevant 1964:100). We might also wish to take into consideration the differences between the two methods that have been suggested (e.g., Nutini 1968b:11) or the comparison between ethnoscience and phenomenology rather than structuralism that has been advocated (Psathas 1968).

[65] Given the rather specific usage of these terms in De Saussure's linguistics, I prefer not to translate them into what could only be partial English equivalents. For a discussion of their meaning in De Saussure's work, see Dinneen 1967:196f.

reduction of manifest or emic reality to a latent or etic infrastructure, so the intentionality of *la parole* must be understood as a conscious expression of an underlying structure proper to *la langue*. This reduction is not merely methodological; the very nature of reality demands it. *La parole* is quite literally made possible by *la langue,* just as conscious models are the results of infrastructural determinants. The task of the anthropologist, like that of the linguist, is to document the substantive role of this preconstituted, regulatory, codal, and unconscious infrastructure by explaining the diversity of empirical phenomena in terms of it. One could argue that having reached this level of reduction, the analyst can cease talking in terms of emic and etic altogether. What he has left is "simply and solely a CODE-GIVEN Truth" (Jakobson 1962: 650).[66] As I have stressed throughout, Lévi-Strauss effects a similar reduction.

These reflections bring us to an issue that has quite literally obsessed the vast majority of Anglo-American commentators on structural anthropology: the problem of scientific verification. In his review of Lévi-Strauss' *Mythologiques II: Du miel aux cendres* (1966), Maybury-Lewis expresses a view typical of these critics: "The problem of validation is the central difficulty, not only in Lévi-Strauss' analyses of myth, but in all of his structuralism" (Maybury-Lewis 1969:119). Indeed, how could Lévi-Strauss' ethnological explanations carry any weight if they were merely the results of a "highly sophisticated conjuring trick" (Leach 1967:6) based on a "decidedly cavalier attitude towards the facts of history

and ethnography" (Leach 1961a:77)? What if Lévi-Strauss' anthropological analyses were simply indicative of a self-fulfilling, albeit ingenious, prophecy (see Harris 1968:497, Shankman 1969:59)? If all this is true, the kindest thing we can possibly say is that structural analyses are exciting and fascinating (see Maybury-Lewis 1968: 136f), much like Magister Ludi's Bead Game—intriguing, but hardly verifiable.

To some extent the danger of subjectivism is certainly present in structural anthropology—even in structural linguistics.[67] Even those most sympathetic to structuralism's cause have felt called upon to warn against the dangers of inventing rather than discovering latent structures (see Gennette 1965:37). Are scientific criteria of verification therefore irrelevant in judging the validity of structural analyses? Are only aesthetic and intuitive criteria applicable (see Leach, ed., 1967:xviii)?[68] Certainly not as far as Lévi-Strauss is concerned; his aim is definitely to be scientific and objective (e.g., 1954a:363-64). But this is more easily said than done. In fact, among the social sciences and the humanities, only structural linguistics has fully attained to the level of a true science (and must for this reason be emulated by anthropologists). Only in linguistics is the object of study universal, the method homogeneous, and the analysis based on a few fundamental principles (see 1964c:543). In anthropology, however, the object of

---

[66] If we accept the logical or syntactical bias of this argument, the much discussed issue of the psychological and/or structural reality of contrastive categories becomes largely irrelevant. Psychological reality is reducible to structural reality, structural reality to logical reality (Buchler and Freeze 1966:84).

[67] A.-J. Greimas told me in conversation that critics of structural linguistics are especially prone to use Martinet's empirical criticism of Jakobson's work and to extend Martinet's argument to Lévi-Strauss' efforts as well. (For a summary of Martinet's critique and Jakobson's reply, see Rastier 1967:106f).

[68] I find the assumption that there are no "legitimate" criteria of viability in aesthetic interpretation as unwarranted and prejudicial as the obverse premise that aesthetic factors do not (or should not) enter into scientific explanation (see Scholte 1971b).

study is not always clear-cut, methods are by no means uniform, and procedures may be based on any number of assumptions. Though this should not detract from anthropology's scientific goals, it does make their realization far more difficult (1964a:7):

[In disciplines like ours] scientific knowledge advances haltingly and is stimulated by contention and doubt. Unlike metaphysics, it does not insist on all or nothing. For [structuralism] to be worthwhile, it is not necessary in my view that it should be assumed to embody the truth for years to come and with regard to the tiniest details. I shall be satisfied if it is credited with the modest achievement of having left a difficult problem in a rather less unsatisfactory state than it was before. Nor must we forget that in science there are no final truths. The scientific mind does not so much provide the right answers as ask the right questions.

Lévi-Strauss' remarks, important though they are, do not themselves resolve the issue of scientific verification. What will, then? Those criteria proper to two related but separate scientific activities: the theoretical or deductive and the observational or empirical (see 1960a:26f). Even though their integration constitutes the final aim of anthropology, they and their respective criteria of verification must be kept distinct. On the level of observation and description, empirical or factual verification is imperative. Take, for example, the case of describing a native classificatory system. Here as elsewhere "the principle underlying a classification can never be postulated in advance. It can only be discovered a posteriori by ethnographic investigation, that is, by experience" (1962c:58). Similarly, in the case of the frequent opposition between the raw and the cooked in South American myths, Lévi-Strauss appeals to the corroborative and empirical evidence of a fellow ethnographer to demonstrate that this distinction is not a figment of his own imagination, but one that actually occurs in the myths themselves (see 1967b:30). Or again, in response to Leach's allegation that in The Raw and the Cooked he chose to consider only myths with animal characteristics in order to bolster the distinction between nature and culture (see Leach 1965b: 780), Lévi-Strauss replies (in a personal communication):

It would be difficult indeed to discover myths with no animal characteristics in tropical South America. Besides, there is in the whole field of American mythology, both North and South, a widespread assumption that in mythical times, the distinction between men and animals did not exist as yet. Finally, in Mythologiques III [1968a], I handle numerous myths with no animal characteristics.

In sum, on the observational and descriptive levels, empirical and factual criteria are both necessary and related to the ethnological results we can hope to derive from ethnographic materials. It is precisely because empirical evidence is always required that Lévi-Strauss pays "such intense, almost compulsive attention to details" (1958:327). Those who do not do so cannot be considered structuralists (see 1965b:127). If, on occasion, Lévi-Strauss advances a hypothesis that does not meet the empirical proof he himself demands, he willingly stands corrected (see 1964a:15). That empirical errors or limitations can and always will be found (if not by our fellow anthropologists, then by the next generation) goes without saying. Any social science—structural, functional, formal, empirical, or what have you—is an ongoing and partial enterprise.[69] One might even call it a heroic,

---

[69] To the extent that all anthropological knowledge is mediated knowledge (Scholte 1971a and 1971b), none of these alternative social scientific par-

if not impossible, enterprise (consider Lévi-Strauss' pessimism in *Tristes tropiques*, 1955a:394).[70] This does not, of course, detract from the empirical requirement—at least not on the observational and descriptive levels.

There is yet another aspect to scientific activity—one not bound by the merely apparent and empirical. This is the level of the theoretical or deductive—a level characterized by such transempirical values as exhaustiveness, consistency, intelligibility, reconstruction, and the creation of possibilities (see Barthes 1963, Bourdieu 1968:686f, Granger 1965:254f, Miguelez 1969: 53f, Mouloud 1965:323f). Our descriptive activities already prepare the way for such theoretical analyses; that is why structural models should be characterized by simplicity, generality, and exhaustiveness (see Rastier 1967:102). The subsequent experimentation on these models is a transempirical and deductive process (see 1962b:16-18 for a good example). It is important to note, however, that the empirical basis for both the construction of and experimentation on structural models is inviolate. Only a factual correlate to our theoretical activities can assure

a direct relationship between the detail and concreteness of ethnographic description and the validity and generality of the model which is constructed after it. For, though many

models may be used as convenient devices to describe and explain the phenomena, it is obvious that the best model will always be that which is *true*, that is, the simplest model which, while being derived exclusively from the facts under consideration, also makes it possible to account for all of them [1953b: 280-81].

We should remember that the relation between the empirical and the theoretical is genuinely dialectical; though structural models are based on descriptive evidence, the explanation of ethnographic data is in turn made possible by deduction and experimentation. In the face of the overwhelming diversity of kinship systems, for example, only a theoretical construct such as generalized exchange can bring some order to the facts (see 1969:220). In cases such as these, "the system must be understood and interpreted in terms of the total structure (and a structure like the one which we have first deduced and then experimentally verified)" (1969:367; see also Lévi-Strauss' analysis of Crow-Omaha [1969:402-403]). It is also important to realize that these deductive and theoretical analyses are neither subjective nor arbitrary (see Bourdieu 1968: 699f, Mouloud 1965:323-24). Not only are they based on principles of symbolic logic; objective evidence is provided whenever and wherever possible. In Lévi-Strauss' transformational analyses of myth structures, for example, "external" factors are almost invariably invoked—cosmological or natural events (see 1964a:333-34), ethnographic and historical facts (see 1966a:380), and even biological or neurological principles (see 1964a:240).

If empirical evidence cannot be explicitly provided, Lévi-Strauss appeals to a characteristic rationalist assumption: the premise that there is "a truth of reason" (1960a:34) in addition to a "truth of fact." In that case, the empir-

---

adigms—empiricism included—can escape a partial and selective "center of interest" (Miguelez 1969: 42f).

[70] Let me quote from one of Lévi-Strauss' letters to me in which he responds to some of the empirical criticisms of *Du miel aux cendres* (1966) and *The Raw and the Cooked* (1964a): "What most people don't seem to realize is that a scientific study of myths (or any other domain) cannot be a one-man work, but will need a great many students and a great many years—if not centuries. . . . I have tried to start something that will take generations to achieve. And it will never be really achieved, no more than physics, chemistry, or biology will be."

ical validity or falsity of the point in question is, of course, indeterminable. Nor would Lévi-Strauss ever claim that under these circumstances his analysis was factually "true" (something that is obviously impossible to determine). He would assert rather that such exclusively logical and deductive analyses can at least hope "to explain more things, and explain them better, than other approaches [might]" (personal communication). Since anthropological analysis cannot always tie its logical explanations directly to empirical predictions (see 1964c:538-39), we may at times be able to do no more than replace "a less intelligible complexity by one that is more so" (1962c:248). These limitations are simply part and parcel of anthropology's overall effort to arrive at "economy of explanation; unity of solution; and ability to construct the whole from a fragment, as well as later stages from previous ones" (1955c: 211). To deny the legitimacy of theoretical experimentation merely because the scientific ideal of a logically and empirically integrated anthropology is not always realizable "is surely more sterile from the viewpoint of scientific progress than the formulation of hypotheses. Even if these should prove to be unacceptable, they will elicit, precisely because of their inadequacy, the criticism and research that will one day enable us to progress beyond them" (1945c:248).

The anthropological function of deductive procedures is substantial as well as methodological. As we have previously seen, "models would be useless, if they did not tell us something more and differently from the data" (1960e: 51). What they eventually tell us, of course, is the fact that conscious phenomena are the transformational outcomes of an unconscious infrastructure. However we phrase this reduction, its ontological import is clear: "be-

tween the system taken in its entirety and any given empirical phenomenon, the relation is one of possibility to actuality; but from its inception, the Mind contains within itself the complete gamut of possibilities" (Sebag 1964:36; see also Mouloud 1965). It is this rationalist assumption that once again sustains and legitimizes both the substantive underpinnings of structural anthropology and its methodological procedures. As I shall try to show in the next section, this assumption and its consequences also make the structuralist enterprise a profoundly problematic one.

How can we best summarize and integrate this discussion on scientific method? We might turn to the work of a man who understood structuralism as well as anyone—the late Lucien Sebag.[71] Sebag realized that Lévi-Strauss, from the very beginning of his intellectual career, was disenchanted with a mere "boldness of theoretical premonitions" at the expense of "concrete data" (1946a:503). At the same time, Lévi-Strauss has known that a blind empiricism is also inadequate. Our ultimate aim should never be merely "to add facts together, but to reach scientific facts under the level of the unscientific" (1946a:521). Both to resolve this dilemma and to assure a concrete and universal anthropology, we require a truly dynamic concept of scientific praxis, one based on the ethnologist's capacity to create scientific facts and to deduce logical explanations that will still meet strict criteria of empirical verifiability and rational consistency (see Sebag 1964:202f). The only

[71] It is a tragic and ironic fact that the young author of one of structuralism's most brilliant defenses against Marxist and existentialist criticism should have died by his own hand. Sebag's suicide must have been a deep personal and intellectual loss for Lévi-Strauss and others. (See Lévi-Strauss' tribute to him in Sebag 1965a; see also Axelos 1966.)

discipline in which such a resolution has in fact been effected is structural linguistics. Only in this field has a truly integrative and scientific revolution taken place (Sebag 1964:165):

Conceptualizing a linguistic system assumes that all possible languages can, at least in principle, be related to it. This process of correlation implies an *empirical* stage (analysis of a sufficient number of languages so that all the elements that constitute the domain where linguistic activity unfolds can be known to me) and a properly *deductive* stage: starting with these fundamental elements, I can *a priori* realize all possible types of combinations. I can then anticipate further discoveries which concrete reality can never furnish me. Moreover, once this enterprise has proven successful, actual languages will appear as so many realizations of a preexisting logical system. Empirical analysis is certainly first, but it actualizes its own claim only when reversibility becomes possible, that is, when I can deduce empirical reality on the basis of a formal treatment of the phenomena thus obtained. Each language [will then] appear as actualizing in a specific way the properties that define the very concept of language.

By taking our cue from structural linguistics, we can hope eventually to unite theoretical conceptualization with empirical realization (see Mouloud 1965:393f). By transcending the phenomenally given while still retaining a concrete basis, anthropology can aspire to become a truly creative and scientific enterprise. Though this transempirical step is perhaps controversial, it can also be argued that it is precisely the one that constitutes structuralism's most significant contribution to anthropological inquiry (Sebag 1964:206):

To experiment is to create that which didn't exist: it is to integrate being within the gamut of its possible transformations; in every experience, the imagination is at work; it is to the latter that this capacity to tear oneself away from appearances accrues. This "process of creating diversity" [*faire varier*] is not pure fiction; it is positive work; the new object obtained is not illusionary, it exists as a corollary to the earlier one. Science discovers only on condition that it creates.

I realize that many cultural anthropologists must find this an impossible position to accept. Yet it may also be the one incumbent upon any science since Einstein (see Nutini 1968b). In the natural sciences, imbued as they are with logico-mathematical and logico-deductive methods, the philosophical rationalism of a structuralist paradigm finds its clearest justification and most dramatic realization. As Sebag well knew and cybernetics confirms (e.g., Bateson 1970), "what characterizes scientific construction is the priority of method to substance, or, more precisely, of conceptualization to that which is conceptualized. Being is only defined in terms of the means for conceptualizing it ..." (Sebag 1964:217). Only if we accept this intellectualist premise can a structural anthropology make sense. And in making this assumption, we also provide for paradigmatic closure; for an integration of epistemology and ontology within the infrastructural reality of the human brain. As Lévi-Strauss himself points out (1962b:91):

In every one of its practical undertakings, anthropology ... does no more than assert a homology of structure between human thought in action and the object to which it is applied. The methodological integration of essence and form reflects, in its own way, a more necessary integration—that between method and reality.

A CRITICAL ASSESSMENT OF STRUCTURAL ANTHROPOLOGY: ITS LIMITATIONS, CONTRIBUTIONS, AND PROSPECTS

We can in part discuss the limitations, possibilities, and prospects of structural anthropology in terms of the assessments made by some of its most important critics. These fall into roughly three broad categories: empirical criticisms, phenomenological or dialectical ones,[72] and structuralist critiques proper. Of these three, the first will concern us least, since we have already covered most of the basic reservations of empirical critics, and since most of them are abundantly represented in the Anglo-American literature and are more widely known than the others. Let me, then, merely summarize what I understand the empiricists' main misgivings to be.

As I have detailed elsewhere (Scholte 1966b) and have implied here as well, I think the empirical critique of structuralism can best be understood in the light of the philosophical and scientific assumptions that separate the two paradigms. In the case of structuralism, these premises are fairly clear: the relational logic of the synchronic, universal, and unconscious mind are said to generate the empirical givens of historical, particular, and conscious circumstances. We can document the underlying and syntactical operations of this generative and tranformational logic by means of inductive, descriptive, or empirical procedures *and* by means of deductive, manipulative, or experimental methods. The paradigmatic key, in other words, is scientific rationalism. An empiricist paradigm takes exception to almost every one of these premises (or at the very least to Lévi-Strauss' specific use of them). Scientific rationalism (in this version, in any case) is considered gratuitous, if not actually metaphysical (e.g., Leach 1965b:779). The attendant procedures are judged to be viciously circular, if not actually false (e.g., Leach 1970:117). The resul-

tant judgment of structural anthropology couldn't be more unequivocal: it is subjective (e.g., Burridge 1967:106, Leach 1965b:778), selective (e.g., Leach 1965a:20, Leach 1967:6), arbitrary (e.g., Harris 1968:497, Leach 1961a:77), merely clever (e.g., Leach 1965b:776, Leach 1970:54), even specious (e.g., Hymes 1964b:16). It is abstract (e.g., Leach 1965a:13, Maybury-Lewis 1960:35), rigid (e.g., Leach 1967:8; Leach, ed., 1967:xiif), and dogmatic (e.g., Leach 1970:117). It may even be meaningless (e.g., Korn 1969b: 9) and incomprehensible (e.g., Leach, ed., 1967:xvii). It is certainly unverifiable and unempirical (e.g., Colby 1966: 381, Dundes 1964:47, Goddard 1965: 426, Leach 1967:6f, Leach 1970:97f, Maybury-Lewis 1968:139, Nathhorst 1969:37, Shankman 1969:63f, Willis 1967:519). In sum, structuralism is at best an aesthetic experience (e.g., Leach, ed., 1967:xviii), at worst a self-fulfilling prophecy (e.g., Leach 1970:117).[73]

What is there to say? Would it serve to reiterate Lévi-Strauss' attentiveness to the empirical and the concrete? Would it be helpful to stress the scientific viability of transempirical procedures? Would it matter if I were to point out that no social scientific paradigm—empiricism included—could ever hope to be presuppositionless? Finally, would it make any difference if I were to reaffirm the partiality and relativity of any and all anthropological activity? I doubt it. Any critique external to the paradigm itself can never be satisfactorily answered unless, of course, one takes a partisan position. I would certainly not deny that structuralism can be subjected to empirical criticism (so can empiricists themselves) and that such

---

[72] The basic thrust of these criticisms is similar but by no means identical. For the sake of brevity I have lumped them together and overlooked their significant differences.

[73] Some of these criticisms refer only to a part rather than to the whole of Lévi-Strauss' work. I would also like to stress that this is a partial and selective list of critics.

criticism might prove helpful and in part justified. Still, it seems rather partial and even secondary compared to what I, for one, consider to be equally serious and more encompassing critiques: the phenomenological or dialectical one and the structuralist critique from within.

Before turning to the current debate between structural anthropology and phenomenological or dialectical philosophy (again, these are by no means the same; see footnote 72), I should perhaps justify this comparatively lengthy discussion of a relatively local dispute that has not attracted sustained interest among Anglo-American anthropologists. My reasons for devoting this much space to the debate are quite simple: it involves crucial insights into the limitations of structuralism and prepares the way for an internal critique of the very foundations of Lévi-Strauss' enterprise. The neglect of this dispute is lamentable, though not without cause. There has never been a very intimate relation between the Anglo-American anthropological or philosophical traditions and French-continental ones (e.g., Dufrenne 1963:11). It is not surprising, therefore, that someone like Leach, in reviewing the debate between Lévi-Strauss and some of his French critics, should find it "extremely difficult to pin down what all the pother is all about" (Leach 1967:8). Since the debate makes no sense to Leach in "plain English," it simply reminds him of "Lewis Carroll's account of the non-battle between Tweedledum and Tweedledee" (Leach 1970:14).[74] As we shall see, Leach's dismissal of the issues involved in the dispute is premature: it does entail fundamental alternatives (e.g., Dufrenne 1968; Lefebvre 1966a, 1966b) which have a direct relevance for anthropological praxis (see Ricoeur 1969, Verstraeten 1963).

The debate between structural anthropology and phenomenological or dialectical philosophy revolves around two sets of related issues: the nature of history and the use of diachronic explanations on the one hand and the definition of meaning and the applicability of linguistic methods on the other. Each of these issues entails a number of derivative problems: the irreducible objectivity and/or sociocultural mediation of scientific activity, the necessity for and/or the subordinate status of a self-reflexive stance, the intentional and/or structural reality of human discourse, and so on. Though we have encountered many of these questions before and will again later on, they can be most fruitfully discussed in the specific context of the debate between Lévi-Strauss, Ricoeur, Sartre, and other representatives of the structuralist, phenomenological, and dialectical points of view.

Lévi-Strauss' confrontation with structuralism's phenomenological and dialectical adversaries is not, of course, of recent origin, though the most avid disputes have certainly occurred in the past few years. In the 1930s and 1940s relations between the then embryonic alternatives seemed rather cordial. Lévi-Strauss not only befriended Merleau-Ponty and Beauvoir (see 1962c: xi), but even wrote an extensive and laudatory appraisal of Gurvitch's phenomenological sociology (see 1946a: 532f); and his first major publication, *The Elementary Structures of Kinship* (1969), received immediate and favorable attention in *Les Temps Modernes* (see Beauvoir 1949). By the late 1950s,

---

[74] As is often the case with Leach's deliberations on Lévi-Strauss, he isn't entirely consistent (Sperber 1967 and Scholte and Simonis, forthcoming). Despite his dismissal of the issues involved in the debate between phenomenologists and structuralists, Leach doesn't hesitate to invoke Ricoeur's hermeneutic stance in one of his own studies on comparative mythology (Leach 1966; see also Buchler and Selby 1968b:91).

however, the intellectual atmosphere had definitely changed. Where he had once praised Gurvitch, Lévi-Strauss now summarily dismissed his sociological contributions and cryptically asserted that he understood Gurvitch "less and less each time I happen to read his works" (1958:324). Similarly, Sartre's *Critique de la raison dialectique* was a text in one of Lévi-Strauss' seminars at the École Pratique des Hautes Études during the 1960-1961 academic year and subsequently received a devastating assessment in *The Savage Mind* (1962c:245f). The intellectual camaraderie cooled further in the next few years. As Bourdieu and Passeron point out: "What Simone de Beauvoir saw in [*The Elementary Structures of Kinship*] in 1949 expresses the intellectual expectations of the period much more than the intrinsic truth of the work, and is diametrically opposed to what Ricoeur and Sartre are able to read into it today" (Bourdieu and Passeron 1967:197). Merleau-Ponty's praise of Lévi-Strauss in 1960 may have been the last sympathetic word from the phenomenological or dialectical tradition. Since then structuralism has been the target for extensive and intensive critiques from a host of phenomenologists and Marxists.

To some extent this turn of events was inevitable. During Lévi-Strauss' formative intellectual period in the 1930s, the fundamental differences between the scientific and the phenomenological approaches were already evident to him. In his reminiscences about the period he says (1955a:61-62): "Phenomenology I found unacceptable, in so far as it postulated a continuity between experience and reality. ..." The resultant "illusions of subjectivity" are incommensurable with a truly scientific mission: "to understand Being in relation to itself, and not in relation to oneself. Phenomenology and existen-

tialism did not abolish metaphysics: they introduced new ways of finding alibis for metaphysics." This initial reservation is pivotal: to sever the ties between experience and reality and thereby assume that the understanding of being transcends the existential limits of human praxis minimizes the intentional thrust of human discourse and the mediating role of historical circumstance. Most important of all, it seems to discontinue the critical relation between self-reflection and scientific labor (see Derrida 1970:251f, Scholte 1971a and 1971b, Simonis 1967:27f). Structuralism is then entitled to make a fundamental assumption: reflection, discourse, and historicity are reducible to a universal infrastructure that is objective, systematic, and synchronic. Let me explain the implications of this premise.

Already implicit in Lévi-Strauss' critique of the Marxist-Hegelian tradition is a definitive rejection of any notion of homogeneous and continuous temporality (see Lacroix 1968:192). This also entails a concomitant rejection of any phenomenological or dialectical concept of a progressively cumulative and subjectively totalizing historical consciousness. Any such totalization is considered impossible, even useless (see Derrida 1970:260, Gaboriau 1963: 585). But for Sartre and many others, some notion of "chronological, cumulative, and irreversible development" is the irreducible key to self-realization and human totalization (Lantéri-Laura 1967:131). For Lévi-Strauss, however, this notion is merely peculiar to our own unique sense of history and historicity. As such, it simply reflects an egocentric, ethnocentric, and pedestrian insensitivity to the "prodigious wealth and diversity of habits, beliefs, and customs" (1962c:249) in existence. As far as Lévi-Strauss is concerned, Sartre's reification of historical consciousness amounts to a doctrine "that man has taken refuge in a single one of the historical or geographical modes of his existence, when the truth about man resides in the system of their differences and common properties" (1962c:249). No wonder Sartre's attitude toward primitive societies is prejudicial; "indeed what can one make of peoples 'without history' when one had defined man in terms of dialectic and dialectic in terms of history?" (1962c:248). From Lévi-Strauss' point of view, historical consciousness is neither cumulative nor dialectical; it is either a consequence of a given society's "conduct" (1952b:40) vis-à-vis other societies (see especially 1952a) or the result of an analyst's intentional perspective toward a certain society (see 1952b:24). To choose cumulative and progressive history as a means of characterizing self-realization and social viability is simply "pre-determined by the [vested] interests of the observer" (1952b:38). It is a reflection on the nature of a society only in so far as that society, like the observer, "wills" a dialectical perspective toward historical contingencies (see 1952b:40, 1961b: 42). Like any other chronological decision, such a choice pertains to the synchronic domain of myth rather than to the diachronic events of history proper (see 1962c:254). Sartre's historicism (and other philosophies like it) is a "first-class ethnographic document" precisely because it is exemplary of "the mythology of our time" (1962c: 249).

Lévi-Strauss' rejection of Sartre's argument still leaves unclear the proper relation between history and anthropology. The issue can be resolved if we recall that ethnography and ethnology deal largely with so-called primitive societies—that is, those that are characterized by "an obstinate fidelity to the past conceived as a timeless model,

rather than [as] a stage in the historical process" (1962c:236). This obstinacy is expressed by virtually every institution in these societies. Though they are "borne along on the flux of time," they always seek "to steer a course between the contingencies of history and the immutability of design and remain, as it were, within the stream of intelligibility. They are always at a safe distance from the Scylla and Charybdis of diachrony and synchrony, event and structure, the aesthetic and the logical. . ." (1962c:73-74). This effort, of course, is not always successful. Even a passionate desire for timeless harmonies must still confront the concrete and "fundamental antithesis between history and systems of classifications" (1962c:232). It may well be that history inevitably upsets "the plans of the wise" and that diachrony will always "emerge victorious" (1962c:155). But this does not take away from the fact that the ideal and the quest are always for a timeless past and an eternal present. In sum, "in theory, if not in practice, history is subordinated to system" (1962c:233).

This ideal goal of a timeless system pervades all of primitive society, but the mythic domain (and by extension Sartre's historicism!) constitutes an especially dramatic example (e.g., 1955c:209). In this regard myth is akin to music: both are "instruments for the obliteration of time" (1964a:16). Though myths may not be victorious in their "never ending struggle with diachrony" (1962c:231), their aspirations at least are clear: to provide a structured intelligibility for contingent events (see 1962c:69). As Lévi-Strauss concludes, "the characteristic feature of the savage mind is its timelessness; its object is to grasp the world as both a synchronic and a diachronic totality . . ." (1962c:263). To this extent primitive societies—not historical civilizations—constitute a privileged domain for the structuralist quest for a synchronic, universal, and unconscious essence.

If Lévi-Strauss is correct, his phenomenological and Marxist critics have reversed the proper order of investigation. If "the whole of human history" is merely "a set of attempts to organize differently the same means, but always to answer the same questions" (1962e: 10), then the resolution to the question of human existence cannot lie in a unique historical consciousness or a dialectical epistemology. We must instead seek the answer in a structured rationality and an unconscious essence that precede and explain intersubjective reality and historical circumstance (see Bourdieu 1968:690f, Sebag 1964:9f). To arrive at these essential structures we require a scientific perspective, one that radically severs the "habitual" relation between lived experience and objective reality (see Granger 1965:282-83, Sebag 1964:228-29; see also Dufrenne 1968:9-12 and Verstraeten 1963:78 for countercritiques).

Does structuralism's critique of phenomenological or dialectical alternatives preclude the possibility of encompassing the lived reality and intersubjectivity of human praxis? Are Bourdieu and Pouillon correct in suggesting that structural anthropology merely seeks to complement comparative objectivity with existential reality, to mediate—not eliminate—the relation between objective necessities and subjective plans? (See Bourdieu 1968: 705f, Pouillon 1956:165.) There certainly is no doubt that Lévi-Strauss does not entirely reject the existential and subjective dimension of human experience. He specifically points out that any objective and comparative analysis must coincide with "the subjectivity of lived experience" (1950:xxvi). He even invokes Sartre's name in this context

(1955d:1216). Similarly, he argues that anthropology's ultimate goal "is—to borrow a formula from a recent work of Sartre—an effort at totalizing a historical becoming at the heart of an individual experience" (1961c:17). But the crucial factors here are the concepts of totalization and individuality to which Lévi-Strauss addresses himself. Individuality is certainly not conceived of in irreducible terms. Anthropology itself can succeed only as an effort toward self-objectification, as "making the most intimate subjectivity into a means of objective demonstration" (1960a: 26). Nor is totalization understood in dialectical or historical terms. It is realizable only as a reductive movement toward the universal and unconscious laws that govern the partial expressions of existential and historical "totalities."

In sum, the paradigmatic differences between structural anthropology and phenomenological or dialectical philosophies could not be more unequivocal. Pouillon (1965:59) has very aptly summarized them as follows:

For Lévi-Strauss, [anthropology] is a question of discovering "mental circuits," universal laws about the functioning of the spirit which, in the final analysis, would depend upon certain cerebral mechanisms; in short, it is a question of finding the matter behind man and not a freedom in him. One is therefore dealing with two radically opposed concepts of the relation of consciousness to reality. For Sartre, consciousness of oneself and of things discovers itself in praxis and, for this reason, it is an understanding of reality: dialectics is constitutive. For Lévi-Strauss, consciousness, whether pure intellect or practical consciousness, has no such privilege; it thinks it understands the real but its truth is merely functional: reason is always constituted. In the first case the relationship to the real is before me and the real is contemporaneous with me; in the second this relationship is behind me and the real is less the object I think than the condition of the fact that I think it. In the first case the relationship is established by praxis; in the second it is revealed by structure.

Before we elaborate on some of these differences (especially the crucial notion of praxis),[75] we should discuss one other aspect of the problem of history: that of the nature of diachronic explanation. As far as Lévi-Strauss is concerned, the explanatory models of historical studies simply echo the substantive logic of temporal intentionality. That is, the historian "chooses" a chronology of events in the same way that a society "wills" its own historicity. Historical explanations, like historicist ideologies, are consequences of codal choices and of structural systems; they are not "successions, but families of events, each one considered in its structure, its internal composition, its totality" (1955d:1196).

Lévi-Strauss' interpretation of historical understanding obviously precludes any progressivistic bias in the explanation of historical events (such as Sartre, following Hegel, had sought to impose). For Lévi-Strauss, cultural evolution is mythic; there are only continuities and discontinuities in time (see 1962f:150). Historical explanation always requires a code—that is, a chronologic (see 1962c:258)—in which events can be understood as a relation between before and after, not as a continuous development (see 1962c:260). To this ex-

tent, historical explanation proceeds in the same way that mythic explanations do (see 1966a:304-305). They can be progressive and totalizing only to the extent that the historian or agent of history "wills" them so.

Since historical explanation "consists wholly in its method" (1962c:262), it cannot possibly provide a critical epistemology for the social sciences. The reality of history is not the "object of an apodictic experience" (1962c: 256), and a preference for it is merely the result of a post hoc choice determined by the ideological commitment of the historican. Even if we grant that history "can serve as a point of departure for any quest of intelligibility" (1962c:262), the best thing for the anthropologist to do is to accept the suggestion and depart from it (see Simonis 1968a:199).[76]

Does this mean, as many critics have claimed, that structuralism amounts to "a one-sided abstract logical analysis of cultural phenomena, with a neglect of

---

[75] Since I cannot possibly detail the implications of each and every one of the important contrasts suggested by Pouillon, let me at least take this occasion to cite some of the most relevant secondary literature (excluding the debates surrounding Althusser and other "structuralists"): Abel 1966; Castel 1964; Domenach 1967; Dufrenne 1968; Edmond 1965; Furet 1967; Goldmann 1966; Granger 1965; Green 1963; Greimas 1966b; Lefebvre 1963, 1966a; Lefort 1951, 1952; D. Levin 1968; Lyotard 1965; Makarius and Makarius 1967; Morawski 1969; Mouloud 1965; Parain 1967; Piquet 1965; Pouillon 1965; Rodinson 1955a, 1955b; Ruyer 1961; Sartre 1960, 1966; Sebag 1964; Simonis 1967, 1968a, 1968b; Verstraeten 1963; Wald 1969; Ziegler 1965.

[76] Lévi-Strauss' position is based on a number of additional considerations. For example, in the specific context of ethnological concerns, the comparative dimension of geographical space is as important—if not more so—than that of historical time (see 1962c:259). This is why ethnography and ethnology are primarily concerned with mechanical rather than statistical models (see 1953b:285). We can go even further: a synchronic method can often assist in the resolution of historical problems (e.g., 1947). In many cases, "if history, when it is called upon unremittingly (and it must be called upon first), cannot yield an answer, then let us appeal to psychology, or the structural analysis of forms; let us ask ourselves if internal connections, whether of a psychological or a logical nature, will allow us to understand parallel recurrences whose frequency and cohesion cannot possibly be the result of chance" (1945c:248). Finally, one could even argue that a structural analysis must of necessity precede a diachronic one (see 1963a:65, Sebag 1964:175f). As Lévi-Strauss says (1960a:11): "It is impossible to discuss an object, to reconstruct the process of its coming into being without knowing first *what it is*; in other words, without having exhausted the inventory of its internal determinants." (See also my discussion of Marxism.)

their proper social dynamics . . ." (Slamet-Velsink 1958:298)? Is it true that Lévi-Strauss' position is neither diachronic nor even synchronic, but panchronic (see Locher 1961:209)? Lévi-Strauss himself would undoubtedly disclaim such a conclusion. He realizes that in the final analysis "everything is history: What was said yesterday is history, what was said a minute ago is history. . . . [Certainly] a little history—since such, unfortunately, is the lot of the anthropologist—is better than no history at all" (1949b:12). The issue is not one of rejecting historical studies and diachronic explanations outright, but one of assessing their proper relation to anthropological inquiries and synchronic methods (see Sebag 1964: 193). This is an exceptionally complex and difficult task. Not only do primitive cultures tend to hide their historical circumstances behind the timeless logic of their ideological inventions; the anthropologist is faced with a methodological "uncertainty principle" as well (Lévi-Strauss in Steiner 1966:36). He cannot at one and the same time study "process" from within and "structure" from without (see 1962g:45, Steiner 1966:36).[77]

Since Lévi-Strauss cannot deny the obvious presence of historical contingencies, how can they be understood and accounted for in anthropological terms? By using a transformational method, one that encompasses the temporal and the dynamic while still assuring the priority of a structural perspective. Following the lead of structural phonology (see 1958:89), Lévi-Strauss adopts "a transformational rather than a fluxional method"

(1960a:31). This allows him to show that, in Goethe's words, "all forms are similar, and none are the same, so that their chorus points the way to a hidden law" (cited in 1960a:31). Cultural anthropology becomes the scientific study of logical transformations, concrete universals, and empirical variations on an unconscious and infrastructural theme. Any recourse to historical events can be considered only as derivative; that is, history is important only to the extent that it makes it possible to "abstract the structure which underlies [its] many manifestations and [which] remains permanent throughout a succession of events" (1949a:21).

Here again we meet with a crucial paradigmatic assumption of a structuralist enterprise: the dialectics of historical consciousness and constituting praxis are derived from and explained by the analytics of a preconstituted and unconscious infrastructure (see also Pouillon 1965:57). As before, the fundamental difference between structuralism and phenomenology or dialectics is clear: for structuralism, intellect precedes praxis—not vice versa. From a structuralist point of view, the infrastructural priority of unconscious laws precludes "the possibility of a historical genesis or [a] logic of an entire society derived from the constitutive praxis of individuals and groups [Sartre's position] since [any] such praxis is developed in a presymbolized universe, and no prior transcendence [surgissement] of this symbolization is possible" (Sebag 1964:129).

The mention of a symbolic a priori provides a convenient bridge to a second major set of issues involved in the current debate over structuralism: that of the nature of meaning and the use of linguistic method. Combined with our knowledge about the issues surrounding the nature of history and the use of diachronic explanation, the ensuing dis-

---

[77] How this concession to history differs from a phenomenological and dialectical point of view! For Lévi-Strauss, a structural determinism grudgingly admits to the fact of historical contingency; for Sartre and others, consciousness of time constitutes man's only hope for freedom.

cussion should provide us with an introduction to one of structuralism's most vexing dilemmas: How is a self-reflexive and critical discourse possible when, as in the case of structuralism, such an enterprise is, on the basis of its own inner logic, itself reducible to the collective silence and synchronic syntax of an unconscious essence or infrastructural "program"?

Before we detail this crucial dilemma, let us first discuss the related issues of meaning and linguistics. Historically, the divergencies between structuralism and phenomenology or dialectics were already evident in the late 1930s (e.g., Pos's informative critique of semiology in 1939), though the actual involvement of structural anthropology seems to date primarily from Ricoeur's numerous critiques (see Ricoeur 1963a, 1963b, 1964, 1967a, 1967b, 1969) and from his exchange with Lévi-Strauss himself (see 1963a). The many issues involved in the dispute are complex and important: the specific nature and proper analysis of symbolism, the relation of language to human consciousness and of speech to subjective experience, the status of la langue and of la parole in linguistic science and in anthropological explanation, the consequences of defining the human sciences in terms of semiological disciplines, and—tied to these issues—the aforementioned problem of history, historical consciousness, and diachronic explanation. Though I cannot hope to detail each and every one of these points with equal care, let me at least summarize what I understand to be the major bones of contention.

One way to approach the dispute is to consider the relation between la langue and la parole. Both the structuralists and their critics would agree on at least one thing: "A language is at the same time the product and the instrument of speech; their relation is therefore a genuinely dialectical one" (Barthes 1964:16). But in their respective assessments of the ontological and epistemological priority of the one or the other, they would certainly diverge. The difference is already apparent in one of the earliest phenomenological critiques of structural linguistics (Pos 1939). Pos rejects the structuralist emphasis on empirical and objective science and argues instead that internal and subjective knowledge is privileged and absolute (see Pos 1939:364). As far as the study of language is concerned, this means that the intentional act of speaking is never entirely reducible to mere linguistic knowledge (see Pos 1939:359). We should always remember that "the linguist is a linguist thanks to the fact that there is a speaking subject, not despite this fact" (Pos 1939:365).

Such a concern with the phenomenology of subjective consciousness and the attendant emphasis on the intentionality of the spoken word leads to quite different results from the structuralist preoccupation with the unconscious laws of la langue and the underlying logos of a relational system. Even if we assume that the two interests are to some extent complementary (e.g., Benzon in Dyson-Hudson 1970:243-44, Ricoeur 1967b:819-20),[78] phenomenologists would still object to structuralism's persistent tendency to subsume the intentionality of la parole —the je veux dire (Ricoeur 1967a:

---

[78] Merleau-Ponty's attempt to reconcile phenomenological philosophy with structural linguistics is of some interest here (see Merleau-Ponty 1960). In this regard he differs significantly from Sartre (see Hughes 1968:208). We should not forget, however, that Merleau-Ponty nonetheless retained an essentially intentional concept of language activity. La parole parlante still takes precedence over la parole parlée (Lewis 1966:33); the diachronic and subjective still envelop the synchronic and objective; the symbolic still retains an irreducible reservoir of meaning.

806)—to the *logos* of *la langue*—the *je suis parlé* (Domenach 1967:772). Let me try to explain what is involved here.

Lévi-Strauss claims that "language, as unreflecting totalization, is human reason which has its reasons and of which man knows nothing" (1962c: 252). Phenomenologists, on the other hand, would argue that "*la parole* has its reasons which are not [those] of *la langue*" (Verstraeten 1963:86). They insist that the study of "spoken or living language" (Ricoeur 1967b:13) is not reducible to a study of *la langue* or even signification alone (see Dubois 1967). As Dufrenne observes (1963: 39):

Before one goes to the length of invoking an unconscious *logos*, at work alike in the spoken word and the institution, one should perhaps first clarify the lived meanings that are experienced by men speaking the language. In any case, one should join to any logic of the language a phenomenology of the spoken word.

As far as the structuralists are concerned, this objection is simply misguided. They are concerned with *Homo significans* (Barthes 1963:78), with the mechanisms of making or creating sense. The structuralist hopes to determine the characteristics of the "place" where meaning is made and coded; he is not so such concerned with the message or meaning itself (see Barthes 1963: 78). The apparent fact that the linguistic system makes semantic meaning possible in the first place (see Ladrière 1967) is yet another indication that "the dynamics of subjectivity [or *la parole*] are incomprehensible without reference to a signifying system [or *la langue*] *which is encountered, not engendered*" (Sebag 1964:134). What requires an explanation is not *la parole* in its intentional unfolding, but the fact that *la parole* exists at all (see Lacroix

1968:224), that man "*is* one who speaks" (1962c:252; italics mine).

As we know, the explanation of *la parole* lies in the mechanical (as opposed to statistical) and relational (as contrasted to substantive) structure of *la langue*. In *la langue*—as in all unconscious activities of the human mind—we find the following structural laws: regulatory principles as such, the necessity for exchange, and the synthetic integration of transferred values (see 1969: 84). These laws also define the symbolic function—an unconscious reality that cultural anthropology must take for granted as an *a priori* faculty of the human mind (e.g., 1946a:517-18). One is tempted to suggest that the importance attributed to this symbolic function is also responsible for Lévi-Strauss' definition of anthropology as a "semiological science," a discipline that "takes as a guiding principle that of "meaning" and which studies "meaningful wholes" (1954a:364, 380). More important, however, is the fact that semiology tends to reduce symbols to signs, meanings to codes, and paradigmatic chains to syntagmatic ones. Anthropology is a semiology to the extent that it, too, studies "the life of *signs* at the heart of social life (1960a:16; italics mine). It deals primarily with signification, with the transformations between differing codes and social rules (see 1960a:18). In sharp contrast to a phenomenological point of view, symbolic meaning is here understood in a relational or functional context without any apparent reference to a mediating intention (see Ricoeur 1967b:16) or even a semantic reference (see Derrida 1970:256-57). As Barthes makes clear, this is tantamount to substituting a "sociology of *signs*" for a "sociology of *symbols*" (Barthes 1962:120). The idea that there might be symbolic images or contents sufficient to mediate the nature of reality and experience is simply replaced by a notion of differential signs in which meaningful symbols are defined solely in terms of their logical position within paradigmatic systems and syntagmatic chains of associative and oppositional features. The syntactical or logical biases of structural anthropology couldn't be more evident.

Since those sympathetic to structuralism's cause have expressed distinct reservations about this "grammatical" reductionism (e.g., Sperber 1968:218f), it is not surprising that Lévi-Strauss' critics should also have made this an important point of contention. Some feel that the obvious emphasis on the codal and systematic can lead only to a partial and inadequate interpretation. Even if we grant that "the structure brings the symbol into play, it does not confer upon it a sense or meaning" (Dufrenne 1963:39). Meaning cannot be derived solely from a *text*, i.e., from "a *corpus* already constituted, arrested, closed, and—in this sense—dead" (Ricoeur 1967a:801). Meaning is also created in *context*, i.e., in the creative act of discourse, "of saying something, of returning the sign to a thing" (Ricoeur 1967a:808). One cannot legitimately replace the living praxis of speech with a merely combinatory syntax (see Lefebvre 1966b:218-19). Any choice in favor of the syntactic at the expense of the semantic (see Ricoeur 1963b:607) falsely reduces the referential to the differential (see Dufrenne 1968:64-65). As Hymes and others have pointed out (see Hymes 1964b:15), the logical outcome is paradoxical as well: not only are cultural invariants impossible, but structuralist discourse is itself forced to differentiate *ad infinitum*. This "stated abandonment of all reference to a *center*, a *subject*, to a privileged *reference*, to an *origin*, or to an absolute *archè*"

(Derrida 1970:256-57) is at the heart of the structuralist impasse.

As far as Lévi-Strauss' own stance on the issue of syntactics and semantics is concerned, he does not see it as one of favoritism or choice at all. For Lévi-Strauss, meaning "is always reducible" (1963a:64).[79] From a methodological point of view, at least, "the recovery of meaning is secondary and derivative compared with the essential work, which consists of taking apart the mechanisms of an objectified thought" (1963a:66). But what is this "objectified thought" if not syntagmatic, relational, differential, and digital? Even the symbolic can be understood only within the context of this positional logic; it has no meaning outside its underlying and combinatory syntax (see 1964a:56, Steiner 1966:35). Only a functional definition of symbolic forms—never a substantial one—allows for a deterministic science of anthropological laws. This is why Lévi-Strauss argues that the unconscious structures of the symbolic function "are not only the same for everyone and for all areas to which the function applies, but . . . they are few in number; we [can thus] understand why the world of symbolism is infinitely varied in content, but always limited in its laws" (1949d:203).

Lévi-Strauss' concept of the symbolic function makes him less and less capable of dealing with substantive meaning and semantic domains and involves him more and more in problems of logical construction and syntactic rules (see Simonis 1968a:307). The human mind is defined and understood in cybernetic terms and a universe of signals replaces that of symbols (see 1962c:268-69). As if to emphasize the

---

79 The translation of this particular word is mine, since I cannot concur with the *New Left Review*'s rendition of *réductible* as "phenomenal."

syntactical bias of this already mechanistic universe, Lévi-Strauss seems to
prefer digital to analogical processes.[80]
Little wonder that those symbolic
forms that are said to exhibit the grammar of the human intellect most dramatically—preeminently music and
myth—become privileged areas of anthropological inquiry. In both of them
the syntactical seems to predominate
(see Fleischmann 1966:41).

Some critics have argued that the
entire movement from meaning to
grammar, from message to code, and
from the semantic to the syntactic will
prove fatal to the structuralist enterprise as a whole. Not only does Lévi-
Strauss reduce the mind to a computer
and human culture to its physicochemical conditions (see 1962c:247; see also
Foucault 1966:390f); he even endangers the very possibility of a structuralist discourse itself. For if, on the one
hand, Lévi-Strauss' own reflections on
the human condition are also reducible,
he will eventually be forced to become
a merely silent listener to the hidden
workings of the unconscious brain. If,
on the other hand, structuralist discourse is not subject to this reduction,
it finds itself in the paradoxical position of being able to speak only metaphorically about an infrastructural essence to which all else is presumed to
be metonymically related (see Simonis
1968a:305f, Scholte 1969a).

Before I detail this crucial impasse,
let me briefly discuss some of the ways
in which these important criticisms of
structural anthropology can affect the
actual analysis of ethnographic materials. The recent debate over the proper
approach to comparative mythology

provides a relevant example.[81] As is to
be expected, the dispute revolves in
part around the issue of history and
historical explanation. We are already
familiar with the structuralist position
on the issue: historicist arguments and
diachronic explanations are either rejected or at least minimized. Whereas for
"historicism, to understand is to find
the genesis, the previous form, the
sources, the meaning of evolution," for
structuralism it is "the schemes, the
systematic organizations in a given state
which are intelligible first" (Ricoeur
1963a:8).

What is even more significant about
this rejection of historicism (at least for
our present purposes) is structuralism's
attendant avoidance of the "hermeneutic circle"; that is, a reflexive epistemology in which the historically situated and contextually conscious interpreter "intends" the mythic text or
object of analysis in the context of its
current and immediate relevance, e.g.,
kerygmatic models for the "re"-interpre-
tation of traditional Christian mythology (see Ricoeur 1964:93f).[82] The hermeneutic approach considers a tie between historical consciousness and
ethnological understanding—between
experience and reality—to be fundamental to any textual interpretation,
the analysis of myths included. Structur-

---

[80] We might add the reminder that "what the
analog gains in semantics it loses in syntactics, and
what the digital gains in syntactics it loses in semantics" (Wilden 1970:6).

[81] As is the case in the dispute between structural anthropology and phenomenological philosophy generally, there was a considerable degree of
mutual understanding and congenial respect at the
very beginning (see Ricoeur 1963a:7). A few years
later, however, the antagonists were forced to conclude that their differences were irreconcilable and
their approaches mutually exclusive (see Ricoeur
1967a:11).

[82] I cannot possibly detail the assumptions and
procedures of hermeneutic interpretation here (let
alone the rich historical tradition that may have
given rise to its recent prominence in some social
scientific circles). For an introductory study, I can
recommend Palmer 1969; for a concrete application,
I would suggest Ricoeur's work (1965 or 1969).

alism, however, extends its disenchant-ment with historical context to the temporally situated and historically conscious interpreter: "The ethnologist may consider this mediating conscious-ness as a simple variant of [the] initial myth (Sebag 1965b:1612), e.g., Freud's psychoanalytic version of the Oedipus myth (see 1955c:217-18). Un-like the hermeneutic interpreter, the structural analyst "seeks to cancel out his own subjectivity . . . and, above all, never to interpret a symbol [or myth] on the basis of the efficacy it may have for him as a historically situated individ-ual" (Sebag 1965b:1611-12). Any such intentional or motivated interpre-tation can hope to be only another variant of the myth in question. As such, it can be no more than another transformation or version of a more important, underlying, and relational syntax. Why this argument should not equally apply to the intentional (albeit scientific) praxis of the structuralist himself is, of course, a very legitimate question (e.g., Sartre in Kahn 1967:41; see also Scholte 1971a and 1971b).

The mention of syntax again raises the issue of meaning and linguistic method. As before, the phenomenolog-ical critique[83] and the structuralist re-sponse are predictable (compare, for example, Fialkowski 1966 and Funt 1969). The phenomenologist is con-cerned with preserving the semantic rich-ness of myths, the kinds of meanings that generate and allow for historically

novel and contextually relevant reinter-pretations (see Ricoeur 1963a:21). The structuralist is concerned with uncover-ing the syntactic logic of myths; the kind of logic that is often hidden and is reached only by "a semantic impover-ishment" (1962c:105). Since he is pri-marily interested in signification—that is, in the logic of a given sign system "which plays the part of a synthesizing operator between ideas and facts" (1962c:131)—he is correspondingly less attentive to the semantic contents to which these sign systems ultimately refer. To proceed otherwise would in-evitably lead to a typical (and phenom-enological) fallacy: putting the se-mantic-laden cart before the functional-ly operative horse. Even if we assume that the most important function of myth is to "indicate areas of meaning [*signifier la signification*]" (1964a: 340), we can never hope to understand this function by a one-sided appeal to lexical content or symbolic meaning. Only a structural study of the relational grammar that underlies the semantic content will allow us to understand the fact of symbolic meaning at all. The reverse procedure is simply impossible (see Sebag 1965b:1616f). As always, it is structuralism's distinctive concept of the human mind that is said to legiti-mize these procedures and priorities. According to Sebag, "structuralist re-search reveals the unity of the human spirit and the systematic character of all forms of intellectual activity, [which] opens the way to a morphol-ogy of types of discourses, founded not on considerations exterior to the intellect, but on the diverse combina-tions of their constituent elements" (Sebag 1965b:1622). The ontological rationalism and epistemological reduc-tionism that inform the structuralist paradigm as a whole should again be evident. Let me, therefore, turn to

---

[83] I am restricting myself to the phenomenolog-ical critique here, though I suspect that a dialectical position would be critical of structural anthropology for similar reasons. In fact, in this regard Lefebvre seems to have gone even further than Ricoeur. Le-febvre's critique undermines the entire language-oriented approach. His concern is to understand lan-guage in terms of a sociological model rather than to explain society by means of a linguistic paradigm (see Lefebvre 1966b:173f).

some of the paradoxes that these premises and methods seem to imply.[84]

At the very beginning of this essay, I claimed that structuralism's contribution will ultimately have to be judged in accordance with the credibility of the distinction between nature and culture or the impasse created by it. Let me explain what I had in mind when I made that statement. As you will recall, Lévi-Strauss considers the transition from animality to humanity, from instinct to intellect, from the literal to the figurative, from the continuous to the discrete, and from nature to culture the single most important historical and ontological "event" in human evolution.[85] Most, if not all, of man's intellectual creations and attendant social institutions can be understood as more or less successful means of mediating this multiple passage from the naturally given to the culturally created. The incest prohibition, for example, is one such mediation, "because of which, by which, and above all in which the transition from nature to culture is accomplished" (1969:24). The incest prohibition mediates between the universal biological fact of sexual reciprocity and the specifically cultural fact of marital alliance. Whereas nature imposes such alliances without determining them, culture defines their concrete modalities (see 1969:31). The incest taboo, in other words, "results from a social reflection *upon* a natural phenomenon" (1969:13); it is a cultural and institutional "intervention" (1969:32) in a natural and biological domain. The incest prohibition thereby "affirms, in a field vital to the group's survival, the pre-eminence of the social over the natural, the collective over the individual, organization over the arbitrary" (1969:45). To that extent, it is the condition for and the promise of cultural life itself (see Simonis 1968a: 48).[86]

But how is this cultural life to be explained by the scientific anthropologist? In answering this question, we begin to get a glimpse of the structuralist paradox. Though human intelligibility and ontological realization proceed from the naturally confronted to the culturally constituted, anthropological explanation and scientific closure proceed in reverse: from cultural forms to their natural foundations. In the case of the incest prohibition, for example, the diverse cultural manifestations that attend it are made possible and explained by an underlying grammar (the exchange of women *qua* signs), which is in turn the product of "certain funda-

---

[84] The ensuing critique of structuralism is in large part derived from Yvan Simonis' *Claude Lévi-Strauss ou la "passion de l'inceste": Introduction au structuralisme* (1968a; see also Scholte 1969b). Since I obviously cannot give this brilliant and important book its due credit here, let me at least take this opportunity to recommend it to anyone interested in structural anthropology. To my mind, Simonis' description and assessment of Lévi-Strauss' work is far superior to any other currently available.

[85] Two parenthetical remarks seem in order. First, I am not concerned here with proving or disproving the ethological or even ethnological accuracy of the distinction between nature and culture (see Kortmulder 1968 and Leach 1970 for recent assessments). I am far more concerned with explaining what I consider to be the illogical implications of Lévi-Strauss' argument. Second, I should add that Lévi-Strauss at one point denies that his original formulation of the distinction between nature and culture (in 1949) was of any substantive value and that his argument must now be considered as having primarily a methodological importance (see 1962c: 247). With all due respect to Lévi-Strauss, I cannot see how he has, in fact, effected any significant change in his initial position. The entire *Mythologiques* is based on the assumption that the distinction between nature and culture is true and viable. As recently as 1970 he argued that "there are no natural phemonena in an uncultured state [à l'état brut]: for man, the latter exist only conceptually and are filtered through logical and affective norms amenable to culture" (1970a:12).

[86] Many equally informative examples of the transition from nature to culture could, of course, have been given. Though I shall give several other examples in the course of this discussion, I would again like to refer the interested reader to Simonis' book (1968a) for additional material.

mental structures of the human mind" (1969:75). These regulatory, reciprocal, and synthetic infrastructures are, as we know, in the final analysis unconscious and universal (e.g., 1969:84). As such, they pertain to the natural and biological domain (e.g., 1969:8-9). In sum, the culturally specific expressions to which the incest prohibition gives rise are of necessity rooted in the infrastructural domain proper to the natural order. Simonis quite rightly characterizes the epistemological process as follows: "We go from culture toward nature, we seek to understand how the cultural is anchored in the natural, we thereby seek to render it intelligible" (Simonis 1968a:54). Whereas Lévi-Strauss talks about the substance of culture as if it were an emergent order of reality, he speaks about its subsequent explanation as if it were an integral part of nature itself (see Simonis 1968a:66). The resultant dilemma constitutes a permanent ambiguity in structural anthropology: "The explanatory direction invariably goes from culture to nature, [while] the movement toward intelligibility goes the other way around" (Simonis 1968a:77-78). If culture mediates the natural, nature in turn explains the cultural.

How does this paradoxical situation affect the paradigmatic intellectualism so characteristic of structural anthropology? Could we argue that the distinction between nature and culture is in turn the result of the *a priori* activity of the symbolic function? If we phrase the problem in this way, we can show how all of man's intellectual efforts are directed toward resolving the passage from the naturally given to the culturally constituted. The various ethnologics of sociocultural institutions stand as witnesses to this mediation. As such, they entail a more or less successful unification of reason and intuition, form and content, structure and event, etc. Art, for example, constitutes just

such a unification (see 1962c:24f). Music may even be considered a "hypermediation" (1964a:27). Language, of course, is one of the most dramatic and prevalent systems of mediation and signification in this sense (see 1955a:25f). It, like the others mentioned, is a testimony to the unification of system and meaning, nature and culture.

At the very point where an intellectualist reconstruction of the distinction between nature and culture seems to provide some sort of resolution to the reductionist impasse, we again confront that uncompromising materialism which attends Lévi-Strauss' understanding of scientific explanation. Conscious systems of classification are made possible by a symbolic function that is itself explained by an unconscious infrastructure. In the final analysis, cognitive efforts at mediating or unifying the natural and the cultural result from the workings of a universal, biological, and determining mechanism inherent in the human brain. If at first we were led to believe that man's intellectual creations might bear witness to his consciously deliberate and semantically constitutive capacities to resolve and to explain his passage from the state of nature to the state of culture, we are now forced to conclude that all these efforts are determined by unconscious and structural mechanisms that are part and parcel of the natural or biological order itself. In culture, as in nature, the same unconscious structural laws are operative (see Simonis 1968a:115). In the end, men can be studied in the same way as ants, and like them can be reduced to their physicochemical conditions (see 1962c:246-47).[87]

If cultural phenomena do constitute

---

[87] This analogy between men and ants—one to which Sartre had objected (see 1962c:246)—is precarious even by cybernetic standards (see Wiener 1954: 51-58).

a distinct order of reality, as Lévi-Strauss so often implies (indeed, most of his ethnological arguments depend on the assumption that they do), is a natural reductionism at all legitimate or consistent? In many ways we are once again confronted with the enormous question that faced the protagonists of the *Natur-* and *Geisteswissenschafft* debate at the turn of the century: Is man's circumstance unique or is it not? If it is, do the social sciences require a distinctive and irreducible epistemology? If it is not, can man and culture be explained in biological and scientific terms? As we know, Lévi-Strauss opts for a reductive naturalism and a radical scientism. This choice involves him in the same paradox to which other versions of this position have led: an explanation in these terms renders the human condition inexplicable. It dissolves and nullifies man (the "zero degree" of the natural sciences; see Simonis 1968a:79), and with him the ethical humanism to which structural anthropology at one time aspired. As Simonis (1968a:344) remarks:

Structuralism is interested in the workings of the human spirit, in its natural condition. It has the ability to restore us to our basic finitude, to still our sense of "transcendence," hoping even to suppress it. Structuralism yields to this finitude, it makes it the truth about man and tries to reverse the direction of human intelligibility by founding it on an unconscious system which remains beyond our influence. It constitutes the negation of all anthropology.

As you may recall from our discussion of Lévi-Strauss' pessimism, there seems to be precious little hope for man or, for that matter, for the restoration of anthropology. If a dim ray of hope may be said to exist at all, it seems to lie in a kind of cerebral mysticism (see 1955a:394) or an aesthetic moment (see 1955a:398). If we then ask which human activity or cultural

domain most closely approximates this cosmic or sensuous experience, we find that it is art itself and, even more specifically, music. Music, says Lévi-Strauss, is "the supreme mystery of the science of man, a mystery that all the various disciplines come up against and which holds the key to their progress" (1964a:18). Why? Because music "hyper-mediates" the distinction between nature and culture, unconscious and conscious! It does so by integrating two "grids": one external, historical, and cultural, the other internal, organic, and natural (see 1964a:16f).[88] And how is this "hyper-mediation" explained? That is, how is an integration between the externally symbolic and the internally syntactic effected? The answer should not surprise us: by a reduction to the infrastructural reality of the human brain.

As always, the results are paradoxical, even tragic. Man's valiant efforts at mediating and resolving the passage from nature to culture are largely inadequate and illusionary. In a very real sense they are obstacles in the path to unconscious truth as much as means for arriving at it. Even musical works (and, by analogy, myths) can hope to do no more than "bring man face to face with potential objects of which only the shadows are actualized, with conscious approximations (a musical score and a myth cannot be more) of inevitably unconscious truths, which follow from them" (1964a:17-18). Predictably, behind man's conscious, creative, and cultural activities looms the deterministic and entirely mechanical reality of a se-

88 I cannot here detail Lévi-Strauss' remarkable explanation of the meaning and workings of music. These reflections are all the more interesting because of the apparent ties between musicology, linguistics, and mathematics (see Ruwet 1967). The interested reader may wish to consult some of the literature on structural aesthetics generally (e.g., Dorfles 1965) or some of the articles on Lévi-Strauss and music in particular (e.g., Deliège 1965a, 1965b).

mantically reducible and infrastructural unconscious. One is tempted to ask: Why, in view of the futility of these Penelopean efforts, the quest for mediation and intelligibility in the first place? (See Scholte 1969a, Verstraeten 1963:517f.)

If we take Lévi-Strauss' search for a transcending "super-rationalism" (1955a:61) seriously (and I obviously believe that we must), and if we also recall that neither music nor any other human creation (including language) is ever able to realize this ideal, then we must conclude that structural anthropology—like myth and music—will never approximate, let alone realize, an integrative dialogue with an inexplicable unconscious truth. The result is to place the structuralist in an impossible predicament: as he tries to understand and explicate the mysterious workings of an inexplicable brain, he must also be the silent listener to what can be only derivative appearances of those syntactic rhythms and physiological pulsations that characterize structuralism's hidden infrastructure. In this regard the anthropologist is in the same position as the social initiate vis-à-vis his mythic tradition or the concert audience vis-à-vis the musical performance: "The myth and the musical work are like conductors of an orchestra, whose audience becomes *the silent performers*" (1964a:17; italics mine). Simonis (1968a:298-99) comments:

... emotion in the inexplicable silence of music, pure logic and sensuous emotion joined. . . . Structuralism advocates silence in order to enjoy our silent and musical bonds with the cosmos. Let us appreciate it like a fragile flower. . . . And since, unfortunately, we are condemned to exchange in virtue of the "symbolic," let us beware of being seduced by its charms. . . .

And what if the anthropologist is seduced by these very charms of the symbolic? What, in other words, if he is asked to *speak* about the human condition? His efforts may be an illusion; as conscious and deliberate symbols, words certainly cannot be metonymically related to the silent and unconscious essence that constitutes the determining reality of his subject matter.

If cultural phenomena are mere appearances, indirect expressions of a more fundamental infrastructure, and if man can talk about this unconscious essence only metaphorically, then the structuralist himself can do no more: he too is forced to speak in conscious metaphors about an unconscious reality. Perhaps this is why Lévi-Strauss' "book on myths is itself a kind of myth" (1964a:6). But we should go even further. The creator whose metaphors most successfully mediate between the natural silence of the unconscious and the cultural discourse of conscious awareness is the artist, especially the composer. If this is so, we are forced to a remarkable and, from Lévi-Strauss' point of view, paradoxical conclusion: structuralism is only part science; the closer it comes to realizing its own inner logic, the more it becomes an aesthetic metaphor. Structural anthropology, "even assuming that it begins in science, can only terminate as art" (Simonis 1968a:314).

As we know, this is hardly the conclusion to which Lévi-Strauss himself would subscribe. If anything, he seeks to explain metonymically and scientifically what "primitive" thought and artistic activity try to create metaphorically and aesthetically. But if we consider the previous argument valid, we should conclude instead that on the basis of its own ontological premises and epistemological assumptions, structuralism must eventually arrive at either an aesthetic logic or an inexplicable silence. If Lévi-Strauss chooses the latter course, he will never be able to articulate the anthropological humanism to which structural anthropology in principle aspires. If he chooses the former alternative, he will have to become a poet-musician, a creator of metaphors. Whatever his choice, he can never hope to realize explicitly the scientific and reductionist aims that have always been the intended purpose of his enterprise.

What of the future of Lévi-Strauss' enterprise? Where is structuralism likely to go from here? I venture no definite predictions, but I can offer a few tentative hypotheses. First, I suspect that structural anthropology will continue to revitalize and to stimulate a previously lethargic and involutional French social scientific tradition (see Guiart 1965, Hughes 1968). Structuralism will be especially effective in expanding the geographic range of French ethnographers and in providing French ethnologists with a cosmopolitan and interdisciplinary scientific approach.[89] Second, I think (and hope) that the theoretical depths, refined sensibilities, and encompassing aims of Lévi-Strauss' efforts will—despite their paradoxes, frailties, and limitations—continue to attract many of those who consider cultural anthropology a personal quest as well as a rigorous discipline. Third, I am sure that Lévi-Strauss' concrete contributions to such diverse fields as the study of social organization, comparative religion, scientific method, anthropological theory, and all the rest will continue to inspire productive debates and to generate novel insights.[90]

[89] This is not meant to disparage French social science. I merely wish to point out that Lévi-Strauss has broadened the scope of post-World War II French social thought enormously and that his contributions have revitalized discussions on all levels of social scientific activity.

[90] As I pointed out in my introduction, I elected not to detail this aspect of structuralism. In this regard I am following in the footsteps of many French commentators on Lévi-Strauss: discussing structuralist philosophy rather than structuralist praxis (see Cuisinier 1967:825-26).

What, finally, about the prospects of structural anthropology in view of the major criticisms that have been leveled against it? As far as the empirical critique is concerned, I am sure that Lévi-Strauss' contributions will be subjected to continued scrutiny. As a result, some of his analyses will probably be dismissed, others will no doubt be revised, and still others may be corroborated. I am also hopeful, though far less sure, that Lévi-Strauss' valuable critique of Anglo-American empiricism will someday be properly appreciated.

As far as the phenomenological, dialectical, and "internal" critiques are concerned, I am convinced that all of them call attention to structuralism's most urgent task: to develop a critical and reflexive stance (see Derrida 1970:251; Diamond, in press; Dufrenne 1968:57f; Scholte 1971a and 1971b; Simonis 1968a:349f). Unless Lévi-Strauss is able to rescue structuralist praxis from the paradoxes created by a reductive science, the entire enterprise will be checkmated by its own syntagmatic bias. Lévi-Strauss should realize that consciousness is *not* "the secret enemy of the human sciences" (1964c: 537), that what is said about man is always said by a man, and that human thought is in the final analysis the conscious product of a thinking person (see Dufrenne 1968:126). Even an irrevocable and unconscious infrastructure cannot change the fact that "in all the universe, man cannot find a well so deep that, leaning over it, he does not discover at the bottom his own face" (Kolakowski 1968:66).[91]

REFERENCES

Abel, Lionel
    1966 Sartre vs. Lévi-Strauss. *Commonweal* 24:364-68.

[91] After completing this essay, two important works came to my attention: Maranda and Pouillon, eds., *Exchange and Communications* (1970) and

Althusser, Louis
1965a *For Marx.* New York: Vintage Books (1970).
1965b *Lire le Capital.* Paris: Maspero.
Anon.
1967 Matrix and Myth. *Times Literary Supplement* 66:521-22.
Auzias, Jean-Marie
1967 *Clefs pour le structuralisme.* Paris: Sèghes.
Axelos, Kostas
1966 Lucien Sebag entre le Marxisme, le Freudianisme, et le structuralisme. *Aletheia* 4:237-41.
Backès-Clément, Catherine
1970 *Lévi-Strauss.* Paris: Sèghes.
Barbut, Marc
1966 Sur le sens du mot structure en ma-thématique. *Temps modernes* 22:791-814.
Barthes, Roland
1961 La littérature aujourd'hui. In *Essais critiques,* pp. 155-66. Paris: Du Seuil.
1962 Sociologie et socio-logique: À propos de deux ouvrages récentes de Claude Lévi-Strauss. *Social Science Information* 1:114-22.
1963 L'activité structuraliste. *Lettres nouvelles,* February, pp. 71-81. (The Structuralist Activity. *Partisan Review* 34 [1967]:83-88.)
1964 *Elements of Semiology.* London: Cape.
1970 *L'empire des signes.* Geneva: Skira.
Bastide, Roger, ed.
1962 *Sens et usages du terme structure dans les sciences humaines.* The Hague: Mouton.
Bateson, Gregory
1970 Form, Substance, and Difference. 19th Annual Alfred Korzybski Memorial Lecture, New York, January 9.
Beauvoir, Simone de
1949 Les structures élémentaires de la pa-renté. *Temps modernes* 49:943-49.
Bender, Donald
1965 The Development of French Anthropology. *Journal of the History of the Behavioral Sciences* 1:139-51.
Benveniste, Émile
1939 Nature du signe linguistique. In *Pro-blèmes de linguistique générale,* pp. 49-55. Paris: Gallimard.
1954 Tendences récentes en linguistique générale. In *Problèmes de linguistique générale,* pp. 3-17. Paris: Gallimard.
1962 "Structure" en linguistique. In *Sens et usages du terme structure dans les sciences humaines,* ed. R. Bastide, pp. 31-39. The Hague: Mouton. (Reprinted in *Problèmes de linguistique générale,* pp. 91-98. Paris: Gallimard [1966].)
1963 Saussure après un demi-siècle. In *Pro-blèmes de linguistique générale,* pp. 32-45. Paris: Gallimard (1966).
1969 Sémiologie de la langue, pts. 1 and 2. *Semiotica* 1:1-12, 127-35.
Berting, J., and H. Philipsen
1960 Solidarity, Stratification, and Sentiment: The Unilateral Cross-Cousin Marriage According to the Theories of Lévi-Strauss, Leach, Homans, and Schneider. *Bijdragen tot de Land-, Taal-, en Volkenkunde* 116:55-80.
Boas, Franz
1920 The Methods of Ethnology. In *Race, Language, and Culture,* pp. 281-304. New York: Free Press, Macmillan (1966).
Boudon, Ray R.
1968 *À quoi sert la notion de "structure"?* Paris: Gallimard.
Bourdieu, Pierre
1968 Structuralism and Theory of Sociological Knowledge. *Social Research* 35:681-706.
Bourdieu, Pierre, and Jean-Claude Passeron
1967 Sociology and Philosophy in France since 1945: Death and Resurrection of a Philosophy Without Subject. *Social Research* 34:162-212.
Brown, Robert
1963 *Explanation in Social Science.* Chicago: Aldine.
Buchler, Ira R.
1964 A Formal Account of the Hawaiian- and Eskimo-Type Kinship Terminologies. *Southwestern Journal of Anthropology* 20:286-318.
Buchler, Ira R., and R. Freeze
1966 Measuring the Development of Kinship Terminologies: Scalogram and Transformational Accounts. *American Anthropologist* 66:765-88.
Buchler, Ira R., and Henry A. Selby

Lévi-Strauss' *Mythologiques IV: L'Homme nu* (1971). I regret not having had time to integrate them in the present text.

1968a *Kinship and Social Organization: An Introduction to Method and Theory.* New York: Macmillan.

1968b *A Formal Study of Myth.* Monograph Series 1. Austin: Center for Intercultural Studies in Folklore and Oral History, University of Texas.

Buckley, Walter, ed.
1968   *Modern Systems Research for the Behavioral Scientist.* Chicago: Aldine.

Burridge, K. O. L.
1967   Lévi-Strauss and Myth. In *Structural Study of Myth and Totemism,* ed. Edmund R. Leach, pp. 91-115. ASA Monograph no. 5. London: Tavistock.

Cassirer, Ernst
1945   Structuralism in Modern Linguistics. *Word* 1:99-120.

Castel, R.
1964   Méthode structurale et idéologies structuralistes. *Critique,* November, pp. 963-78.

Caws, Peter
1968   What Is Structuralism? *Partisan Review* 35:75-91.

Chomsky, Noam
1968   *Language and Mind.* New York: Harcourt, Brace & World.

Colby, Benjamin N.
1966   The Analysis of Culture Content and Patterning of Native Concern in Texts. *American Anthropologist* 68:374-88.

Corvez, Maurice
1969   *Les structuralistes.* Paris: Aubier-Montaigne.

Coult, Alan D.
1963   Causality and Cross-Sex Prohibitions. *American Anthropologist* 65:255-77.

Cuisinier, Jean
1963   "La pensée sauvage" et le structuralisme. *Esprit* 31:545-63.

1967   Le structuralisme du mot, de l'idée, et des outils. *Esprit* 35:825-42.

Davenport, William
1963   Social Organization. In *Biennial Review of Anthropology 1963,* ed. Bernard J. Siegel. Stanford: Stanford University Press.

Deliège, Céléstin
1965a La musicologie devant le structuralisme. *L'arc* 26:45-52.

1965b Sur quelques motifs de l'ouverture aux mythologiques. *L'arc* 26:69-76.

Derrida, Jacques
1967   *L'écriture et la différence.* Paris: Du Seuil.

1970   Structure, Sign, and Play in the Discourse of the Human Sciences. In *The Languages of Criticism and the Sciences of Man: The Structuralist Controversy,* ed. R. Macksey and E. Donato, pp. 247-72. Baltimore: Johns Hopkins Press.

Diamond, Stanley
1964   Introduction: The Uses of the Primitive. In *Primitive Views of the World,* ed. S. Diamond. New York: Columbia University Press.

in   Anthropology in Question. In *Reinventing Anthropology,* ed. D. H. Hymes. New York: Pantheon.
press

Dinneen, Francis P.
1967   *An Introduction to General Linguistics.* New York: Holt, Rinehart & Winston.

Domenach, J. M.
1967   Le système et la personne. *Esprit* 35:771-80.

Dorfles, Gillo
1965   Pour ou contre une esthétique structuraliste? *Revue internationale de philosophie* 73-74:409-41.

Douglas, Mary
1967   The Meaning of Myth. In *The Structural Study of Myth and Totemism,* ed. Edmund R. Leach, pp. 49-69. ASA Monograph no. 5. London: Tavistock.

Dreyfus, Catherine
1970   An Interview with Lévi-Strauss. *Mademoiselle,* August, pp. 236-37, 324.

Dubois, Jean
1967   Structuralisme et linguistique. *La pensée* 135:19-28.

Dufrenne, Mikel
1963   *Language and Philosophy.* Bloomington: Indiana University Press.

1967   La philosophie du néo-positivisme. *Esprit* 35:781-800.

1968   *Pour l'homme.* Paris: Du Seuil.

Dundes, Alan
1964   *The Morphology of North American Folktales.* Helsinki: Tiedeakatemie.

Durkheim, Émile
1895 *The Rules of Sociological Method.*
New York: Free Press of Glencoe,
Macmillan (1962).
1912 *The Elementary Forms of the Religious Life.* New York: Collier
(1961).
Durkheim, Émile, and Marcel Mauss
1903 *Primitive Classification.* London:
Cohen & West (1963).
Dyson-Hudson, Neville
1970 Structure and Infra-Structure in Primitive Society: Lévi-Strauss and Rad-
cliffe-Brown. In *The Languages of
Criticism and the Sciences of Man:
The Structuralist Controversy,* ed.
R. Macksey and E. Donato, pp. 218-
46. Baltimore: Johns Hopkins Press.
Edmond, Michel-Pierre
1965 L'Anthropologie structuraliste et
l'histoire. *La pensée* 123:43-50.
Evans-Pritchard, E. E.
1963 *The Comparative Method in Social
Anthropology.* London: Athlone.
Fagès, J.-B.
1967 *Comprendre le structuralisme.* Paris:
Privat.
Fialkowski, Aldine
1966 Structuralisme et herméneutique.
Esprit 34:16-30.
Firth, J. R.
1964 Ethnographic Analysis and Language
with Reference to Malinowski's
Views. In *Man and Culture: An Evaluation of the Work of Bronislaw Ma-
linowski,* ed. J. R. Firth, pp. 93-118.
New York: Harper & Row.
Fischer, John L.
1963 The Psychosocial Analysis of Folk-
tales. *Current Anthropology* 4:235-
95.
Flament, C.
1963 *Applications of Graph Theory to
Group Structure.* Englewood Cliffs,
N.J.: Prentice-Hall.
Fleischmann, Eugene
1966 L'esprit humain selon Claude Lévi-
Strauss. *Archives of European Sociology* 7:27-57.
Foucault, Michel
1966 *Les mots et les choses: Une archéologie des sciences humaines.* Paris:
Gallimard. (*The Order of Things: An

Archaeology of the Human Sciences.
New York: Pantheon [1970].)
1969 *L'archéologie du savoir.* Paris: Gallimard.
Funt, David P.
1969 The Structuralist Debate. *Hudson
Review* 22:633-46.
Furet, François
1967 Les intellectuels français et le struc-
turalisme. *Preuves,* February, pp.
3-12. (The French Left. *Survey* 62:
72-83.)
Gaboriau, Marc
1963 Anthropologie structurale et histoire.
Esprit 31:579-95. (Reprinted in
Structuralism: A Reader, ed. Michael
Lane, pp. 156-69. London: Cape
[1970].)
Geertz, Hildred
1965 Comment. *Journal of Asian Studies*
24:294-97.
Genette, Girard
1965 Structuralisme et critique littéraire.
L'arc 26:30-44.
Goddard, David
1965 Conceptions of Structure in Lévi-
Strauss and in British Anthropology.
Social Research 32:408-27.
Godelier, Maurice
1966 Système, structure et contradiction
dans "Le Capital." *Temps modernes*
22:828-64. (Reprinted in *Structuralism: A Reader,* ed. Michael Lane,
pp. 340-58. London: Cape [1970].)
Goldmann, Lucien
1965 Introduction générale. In *Entretiens
sur les notions de genèse et structure,*
ed. Maurice de Gandillac et al., pp.
7-22. The Hague: Mouton.
1966 Structuralisme, Marxisme, existentia-
lisme. *L'homme et la société* 2:
105-24.
1969 *The Human Sciences and Philosophy.*
London: Cape.
Grace, George W.
1969 Notes on the Philosophical Background of Current Linguistic Controversy. Working Papers in Linguistics, no. 1. Honolulu: University of
Hawaii.
Gramont, Sanche de
1968 There Are No Superior Societies.
New York Times Magazine, January

28, pp. 28-40.

Granger, Gilles G.
1960 *Pensée formelle et sciences de l'homme*. Paris: Aubier.
1965 Objet, structure, et significations. *Revue internationale de philosophie* 73-74:251-90.
1968 *Essai d'une philosophie du style*. Paris: Colin.

Green, André
1963 Le Psychoanalyse devant l'opposition de l'histoire et de la structure. *Critique* 19:649-62.

Greimas, A.-J.
1966a *Sémantique structurale*. Paris: Larousse.
1966b Structure et histoire. *Temps modernes* 22:815-27.
1970 *Du sens: Essais sémiotiques*. Paris: Du Seuil.

Guiart, Jean
1965 Survivre à Lévi-Strauss. *L'arc* 26:61-64.

Gurvitch, Georges
1963 Le concept de structure sociale. In *Le vocation de la sociologie*, pp. 403-46. Paris: Presses Universitaires de France.

Harris, Marvin
1968 *The Rise of Anthropological Theory: A History of Theories of Culture*. New York: Crowell.

Hayes, Nelson E., and Tanya Hayes, eds.
1970 *Claude Lévi-Strauss: The Anthropologist as Hero*. Cambridge: M.I.T. Press.

Hobsbawn, E. J.
1966 Review of George Lichtheim's *Marxism in Modern France*. *New York Review of Books* 7:34-36.

Hoffmann, Hans
1970 Mathematical Anthropology. In *Biennial Review of Anthropology 1969*, ed. Bernard J. Siegel, pp. 41-79. Stanford: Stanford University Press.

Homans, George G., and David M. Schneider
1955 *Marriage, Authority, and Final Causes: A Study of Unilateral Cross-Cousin Marriage*. Glencoe, Ill.: Free Press.

Huesch, Luc de
1965 Situations et positions de l'anthropologie structurale. *L'arc* 26:6-16.

Hughes, H. Stuart
1968 *The Obstructed Path: French Social Thought in the Years of Desperation 1930-1960*. New York: Harper & Row.

Hymes, Dell H.
1964a *Language in Culture and Society: A Reader in Linguistics and Anthropology*. New York: Harper & Row.
1964b Directions in (Ethno-)Linguistic Theory. In *Transcultural Studies in Cognition*, ed. A. K. Romney and R. G. D'Andrade, pp. 6-56. *American Anthropologist* 66, no. 3, pt. 2 (special issue).
1967 Linguistic Method in Ethnography. MS. (Revised version published in *Method and Theory in Linguistics*, ed. Paul L. Garvin, pp. 249-325. The Hague: Mouton.)

Ingemann, Francis J., and Thomas A. Sebeok
1956 *Studies in Cheremis: The Supernatural*. Viking Fund Publications in Anthropolgy, no. 22. New York: Wenner-Gren Foundation.

Jaeggi, Urs
1969 *Ordnung und Chaos: Strukturalismus als Methode und Mode*. Frankfurt: Suhrkamp.

Jakobson, Roman
1960 Concluding Statement: Linguistics and Poetics. In *Style in Language*, ed. T. A. Sebeok, pp. 350-73. New York: Wiley.
1962 *Selected Writings I: Phonological Studies*. The Hague: Mouton.

Joiner, L. E., and M. S. Robinson
1968 An Experiment in the Structural Study of Myth. Unpublished MS.

Kahn, Jean-François
1967 La Minutieuse conquête du structuralisme. *L'express* 844:39-40.

Köbben, A. J. F.
1966 Structuralism versus Comparative Functionalism: Some Comments. *Bijdragen tot de Taal-, Land-, en Volkenkunde* 122:145-50.

Kolakowski, Leszek
1968 Karl Marx and the Classical Definition of Truth. In *Toward A Marxist Humanism: Essays on the Left Today*, pp. 38-66. New York: Grove Press.

Köngäs, Elli-Kaija, and Pierre Maranda
1962 Structural Models in Folklore. *Midwest Folklore* 22:133-92.

Korn, Frances

1969a The Logic of Some Concepts of Lévi-Strauss. *American Anthropologist* 71:70-71.

1969b An Analysis of the Use of the Term "Model" in Some of Lévi-Strauss' Works. *Bijdragen tot de Taal-, Land-, en Volkenkunde* 125:1-11.

Kortmulder, K.
1968 An Ethological Theory of the Incest Taboo and Exogamy: With Special Reference to the Views of Claude Lévi-Strauss. *Current Anthropology* 9:437-49.

Kristeva, Julia
1969 *Sémiologie: Recherches pour une sémanalyse.* Paris: Du Seuil.

Kroeber, A. L., and Clyde Kluckhohn
1952 *Culture: A Critical Review of Concepts and Definitions.* New York: Vintage (1963).

Lacan, Jacques
1966 *Écrits.* Paris: Du Seuil.
1968 *The Language of the Self: The Function of Language in Psychoanalysis.* Baltimore: Johns Hopkins Press.

Lacroix, Jean
1968 *Panorama de la philosophie française contemporaine.* Paris: Presses Universitaires de France.

Ladrière, Jean
1967 Sens et système. *Esprit* 35:822-24.

Lane, Michael, ed.
1970 *Structuralism: A Reader.* London: Cape.

Lanteri-Laura, G.
1967 History and Structure in Anthropological Knowledge. *Social Research* 34:115-61.

Leach, Edmund R.
1961a *Rethinking Anthropology.* London: Athlone.
1961b Lévi-Strauss in the Garden of Eden: An Examination of Some Recent Developments in the Analysis of Myth. *Transactions of the New York Academy of Sciences* 23:386-96.
1962 Genesis as Myth. In *Genesis as Myth and Other Essays*, pp. 7-24. London: Cape.
1964 Anthropological Aspects of Language: Animal Categories and Verbal Abuse. In *New Directions in the Study of Language,* ed. Eric H. Lenneberg, pp. 23-63. Cambridge: M.I.T. Press.

1965a Claude Lévi-Strauss: Anthropologist and Philosopher. *New Left Review* 34:12-27.
1965b Review of Claude Lévi-Strauss' *Mythologiques: Le cru et le cuit. American Anthropologist* 67:776-80.
1966 The Legitimacy of Solomon: Some Structural Aspects of Old Testament History. *Archives of European Sociology* 8:58-101.
1967 Brain Twister. *New York Review of Books* 9, no. 6:6-10.
1969 Vico and Lévi-Strauss on the Origins of Humanity. In *Giambattista Vico: An International Symposium,* ed. G. Tagliacozza, pp. 309-18. Baltimore: Johns Hopkins Press.
1970 *Lévi-Strauss.* London: Fontana/Collins.

Leach, Edmund R., ed.
1967 *The Structural Study of Myth and Totemism.* ASA Monograph no. 5. London: Tavistock.

Lefebvre, Henri
1963 Réflexions sur le structuralisme et l'histoire. *Cahiers internationaux de sociologie* 10:3-24.
1966a Lévi-Strauss et le nouvel eléatisme. *L'homme et la société* 1-2:21-31, 82-103.
1966b *Le langage et la société.* Paris: Gallimard.

Lefort, G.
1951 L'échange et la lutte des hommes. *Temps modernes* 6:1400-17.
1952 Sociétés sans histoire et historicité. *Cahiers internationaux de sociologie* 7:91-114.

Lepenies, Wolf
1968 Der französische Strukturalismus: Methode und Ideologie. *Soziale Welt* 3-4:301-27.

Lepenies, Wolf, and Hans H. Ritter, eds.
1970 *Orte des wilden Denkens: Zur Anthropologie von Claude Lévi-Strauss.* Frankfurt: Suhrkamp.

Levin, David M.
1968 On Lévi-Strauss and Existentialism. *American Scholar* 38:69-82.

Levin, Samuel R.
1965 Langue and Parole in American Linguistics. *Foundations of Language* 1:83-94.

Lévi-Strauss, Claude
1943 Guerre et commerce chez les Indiens

de l'Amérique du Sud. *Renaissance* 1:122-39.

1945a Structural Analysis in Linguistics and in Anthropology. In *Structural Anthropology*, pp. 31-54. New York: Basic Books (1963).

1945b L'oeuvre d'Edward Westermarck. *Revue de l'histoire des religions* 129:84-100.

1945c Split Representation in the Art of Asia and America. In *Structural Anthropology*, pp. 245-68. New York: Basic Books (1963).

1946a French Sociology. In *Twentieth Century Sociology*, ed. Georges Gurvitch and W. E. Moore, pp. 503-37. New York: Philosophical Library.

1946b La technique du bonheur. *Esprit* 127:643-52.

1947 The Serpent with Fish Inside His Body. In *Structural Anthropology*, pp. 269-73. New York: Basic Books (1963).

1949a Introduction: History and Anthropology. In *Structural Anthropology*, pp. 1-27. New York: Basic Books (1963).

1949b The Sorcerer and His Magic. In *Structural Anthropology*, pp. 167-85. New York: Basic Books (1963).

1949c The Effectiveness of Symbols. In *Structural Anthropology*, pp. 186-205. New York: Basic Books (1963).

1950 Introduction à l'oeuvre de Marcel Mauss. In Marcel Mauss, *Sociologie et anthropologie*, pp. ix-lii. Paris: Presses Universitaires de France.

1951a Language and the Analysis of Social Laws. In *Structural Anthropology*, pp. 55-66. New York: Basic Books (1963).

1951b Avant-Propos: Les sciences sociales au Pakistan. *Bulletin international des sciences sociales* 3:825-29.

1952a "The Concept of Archaism in Anthropology." In *Structural Anthropology*, pp. 101-19. New York: Basic Books (1963).

1952b *Race and History*. Paris: UNESCO.

1952c Toward a General Theory of Communication. Paper presented to the International Conference of Linguists and Anthropologists, University of Indiana.

1952d Social Structures of Central and Eastern Brazil. In *Structural Anthropology*, pp. 120-31. New York: Basic Books (1963).

1953a Comments. In *An Appraisal of Anthropology Today*, ed. Sol Tax. Chicago: University of Chicago Press.

1953b Social Structure. In *Structural Anthropology*, pp. 277-323. New York: Basic Books (1963).

1953c Linguistics and Anthropology. In *Structural Anthropology*, pp. 67-80. New York: Basic Books (1963).

1953d Panorama of Ethnology, 1950-1952. *Diogenes* 2:69-92.

1954 The Place of Anthropology in the Social Sciences and Problems Raised in Teaching It. In *Structural Anthropology*, pp. 346-81. New York: Basic Books (1963).

1955a *Tristes Tropiques*. New York: Atheneum (1967).

1955b Les mathématiques de l'homme. *Bulletin international des sciences sociales* 6:643-53. (Reprinted in *Esprit* 24 [1956]:525-38.)

1955c The Structural Study of Myth. In *Structural Anthropology*, pp. 206-31. New York: Basic Books (1963).

1955d Diogène couché. *Temps modernes* 10:1187-1220.

1956a Do Dual Organizations Exist? In *Structural Anthropology*, pp. 132-63. New York: Basic Books (1963).

1956b Structure and Dialectics. In *Structural Anthropology*, pp. 232-41. New York: Basic Books (1963).

1956c The Family. In *Man, Culture, and Society*, ed. H. L. Shapiro, pp. 261-85. New York: Oxford University Press.

1958 *Structural Anthropology*. New York: Basic Books (1963).

1960a *The Scope of Anthropology*. London: Cape (1967).

1960b Ce que l'ethnologie doit à Durkheim. *Annales de l'Université de Paris* 30:47-52.

1960c Four Winnebago Myths: A Structural Sketch. In *Culture in History: Essays in Honor of Paul Radin*, ed. S. Diamond, pp. 351-62. New York: Columbia University Press.

1960d The Story of Asdiwal. In *The Structural Study of Myth and Totemism*, ed. E. R. Leach, pp. 1-47. ASA monograph no. 5. London: Tavistock.

1960e On Manipulated Sociological Models. *Bijdragen tot de Taal-, Land, en Volkenkunde* 116:45-54.

1960f Le structure et la forme. *Cahiers de l'Institute de Science Économique Appliquée* 99, no. 7:3-36.

1961a Today's Crisis in Anthropology. *UNESCO Courier* 14, no. 11:12-17.

1961b *Conversations with Lévi-Strauss* (with G. Charbonnier). London: Cape (1969).

1961c Le métier d'ethnologue. *Annales* 129:5-17.

1962a Rousseau: The Father of Anthropology. *UNESCO Courier* 16 (1963): 10-14.

1962b *Totemism.* Boston: Beacon Press (1963).

1962c *The Savage Mind.* London: Weidenfeld & Nicolson (1966).

1962d Sur le caractère distinctif des faits ethnologiques. *Revue des travaux de l'Académie des Sciences Morales et Politiques* 115:211-19.

1962e The Bear and the Barber. *Journal of the Royal Anthropological Institute of Great Britain and Ireland* 93 (1963):1-24.

1962f Comments. In *Sens et usage du terme structure dans les sciences humaines et sociales,* ed. R. Bastide. The Hague: Mouton.

1962g Les limites de la notion de structure en ethnologique. In *Sens et usage du terme structure dans les sciences humaines et sociales,* ed. R. Bastide, pp. 40-44. The Hague: Mouton.

1963a Confrontation over Myths (with Paul Ricoeur). *New Left Review* 62 (1970):57-74.

1963b Review of George G. Simpson's *Principles of Animal Taxonomy. L'homme* 3:140.

1964a *Mythologiques I: The Raw and the Cooked.* New York: Harper & Row (1969).

1964b Reciprocity: The Essence of Social Life. In *The Family: Its Structure and Function,* ed. R. L. Coser, pp. 36-48. New York: St. Martin's Press.

1964c Criteria of Science in the Social and Human Disciplines. *International Social Science Journal* 16:534-52.

1965a The Future of Kinship Studies. In *Proceedings of the Royal Anthropological Institute of Great Britain and Ireland,* pp. 13-22.

1965b Réponses à une questionnaire sur le structuralisme. *Paragone* 16:125-28.

1966 *Mythologiques II: Du miel aux cendres.* Paris: Plon.

1967 A Contre-courant (with G. Dumur). *Nouvel observateur* 115:30-33.

1968a *Mythologiques III: L'origine des manières de table.* Paris: Plon.

1968b Hommages aux sciences de l'homme. *Social Science Information* 7, no. 2: 7-11.

1969 *The Elementary Structures of Kinship,* 2nd ed. London: Eyre & Spottiswoode. First French edition 1949.

1970a Les champignons dans la culture: À propos d'un livre de M. R.-G. Wasson. *L'homme* 10:5-16.

1970b Confrontation over Myths (with Paul Ricoeur). *New Left Review* 62:57-74.

1971 *Mythologiques IV: L'homme nu.* Paris: Plon.

Lewis, Philip E.
1966 Merleau-Ponty and the Phenomenology of Language. *Yale French Studies* 36-37:19-40.

Locher, G. W.
1961 De Anthropoloog Lévi-Strauss en het probleem van de Geschiedenis. *Forum der Letteren,* November.

Lounsbury, Floyd G.
1962 Review of Rodney Needham's *Structure and Sentiment. American Anthropologist* 64:1302-10.

Lukacs, Georg
1923 *Histoire et conscience de classe.* Paris: Minuit (1960). *(History and Class Consiousness.* Cambridge: M.I.T. Press [1970].)

Lyotard, J. F.
1965 Les Indiens ne cueillent pas les fleurs (à propos de Cl. Lévi-Strauss). *Annales* 1:62-83.

Macksey, Richard, and Eugenio Donato, eds.
1970 *The Languages of Criticism and the Sciences of Man: The Structuralist Controversy.* Baltimore: Johns Hopkins Press.

Makarius, Raoul
1970 Parenté et infra-structure. *La pensée* 149:51-55.

Makarius, Raoul, and Laura Makarius
1967 Ethnologie et structuralisme. *L'homme et la société* 3:187-200.
Maranda, Pierre
1967 Formal Analysis and Inter-Cultural Studies. *Social Science Information* 6:7-36.
1968 *Calcul et formalisation dans les sciences de l'homme.* Editions du Centre National de la Recherche Scientifique.
Maranda, Pierre, and Jean Pouillon, eds.
1970 *Exchange and Communications.* The Hague: Mouton.
Marx, Karl
1852 *The 18th Brumaire of Louis Bonaparte.* New York: International Publishers (1963).
Mauss, Marcel
1924 Questions posées à la psychologie. In *Sociologie et anthropologie,* pp. 304-308. Paris: Presses Universitaires (1950).
1925 *The Gift: Forms and Functions of Exchange in Archaic Societies.* Glencoe, Ill.: Free Press.
Maybury-Lewis, David P.
1960 The Analysis of Dual Organization: A Methodological Critique. *Bijdragen tot de Taal-, Land-, en Volkenkunde* 116:17-44.
1968 Science by Association. In *Claude Lévi-Strauss: The Anthropologist as Hero,* ed. N. E. Hayes and Tanya Hayes, pp. 133-39. Cambridge: M.I.T Press.
1969 Review of Claude Lévi-Strauss' *Mythologiques: Du Miel aux Cendres. American Anthropologist* 71:114-20.
Merleau-Ponty, Maurice
1960 De Mauss à Claude Lévi-Strauss. In *Signes,* pp. 143-57. Paris: Gallimard.
Merquior, José G.
1970 Vico et Lévi-Strauss. *L'homme* 10:81-93.
Metz, Christian
1967 *Essais sur la signification au cinéma.* Paris: Klincksieck.
Miguelez, Roberto
1969 L'explication en ethnologie. *Social Science Information* 8, no. 3:27-58.
Moore, O. K., and David L. Olmstead
1952 Language and Professor Lévi-Strauss. *American Anthropologist* 54:116-19.
Morawski, Stefan

1969 Le Marxisme et ses rivages possibles. *L'homme et la société* 13:145-68.
Mouloud, N.
1965 La logique des structures et l'épistémologie. *Revue internationale de philosophie* 73-74:314-34.
1966 L'esprit des sciences structurales et la philosophie de la raison. *Revue de métaphysique et de morale* 71:339-58.
Mounin, Georges
1970 *Introduction à la sémiologie.* Paris: Du Seuil.
Mudimbe, Valentin Y.
1968 Structuralisme, événements, notions, variations, et les sciences humaines en Afrique. *Cahiers économiques et sociaux* 6:3-70.
Murphy, Robert F.
1963 On Zen Marxism: Filiation and Alliance. *Man* 21:17-19.
Nadel, S. F.
1957 *The Theory of Social Structure.* Glencoe, Ill.: Free Press.
Nathhorst, Bertel
1969 *Formal or Structural Studies of Traditional Tales: The Usefulness of Some Methodological Proposals Advanced by Vladimir Propp, Alan Dundes, Claude Lévi-Strauss, and Edmund Leach.* Stockholm Studies in Comparative Religion, no. 9. Stockholm: Almqvist & Wiksell.
Needham, Rodney
1962 *Structure and Sentiment: A Test Case in Social Anthropology.* Chicago: University of Chicago Press.
1963 Introduction. In Emile Durkheim and Marcel Mauss, *Primitive Classification,* pp. vii-xlviii. London: Cohen & West.
1967 Terminology and Alliance. *Sociologus* 16-17:141-57, 39-54.
Nodelman, Sheldon
1966 Structural Analysis in Art and Anthropology. *Yale French Studies* 36-37:89-103.
Northrop, F. S. C.
1960 *Philosophical Anthropology and Practical Politics.* New York: Macmillan.
1964 Toward a Deductively Formulated and Operationally Verifiable Comparative Anthropology. In *Cross-Cultural Understanding: Epistemol-*

ogy in Anthropology, ed. F. S. C. Northrop and H. H. Livingston, pp. 194-222. New York: Harper & Row.

Nutini, Hugo
1965 Some Considerations on the Nature of Social Structure and Model Building: A Critique of Claude Lévi-Strauss and Edmund Leach. *American Anthropologist* 67:707-31.
1968a A Comparison of Lévi-Strauss' Structuralism and Chomsky's Transformational Generative Grammar. Unpublished MS.
1968b On the Concepts of Epistemological Order and Coordinative Definitions. *Bijdragen tot de Taal-, Land-, en Volkenkunde* 124:1-21.
1971 The Ideological Basis of Lévi-Strauss' Structuralism. *American Anthropologist* 73:537-44.

Orans, Martin
1970 Social Organization. In *Biennial Review of Anthropology 1969*, ed. B. J. Siegel, pp. 132-90. Stanford: Stanford University Press.

Ortiques, Edmond
1963 Nature et culture dans l'oeuvre de Lévi-Strauss. *Critique* 189:142-57.

Palmer, Richard E.
1969 *Hermeneutics: Interpretation Theory in Schleiermacher, Dilthey, Heidegger, and Gadamer.* Evanston, Ill.: Northwestern University Press.

Parain, C.
1967 Structuralisme et histoire. *La pensée* 135:38-52.

Parain-Vial, Jean
1969 *Analyses structurales et idéologies structuralistes.* Paris: Privat.

Parsons, Talcott
1938 *The Structure of Social Action.* New York: Free Press, Macmillan (1961).

Paz, Octavio
1970 *Claude Lévi-Strauss: An Introduction.* Ithaca: Cornell University Press.

Piaget, Jean
1969 Le structuralisme. *Cahiers internationaux de symbolisme* 17-18:73-85.
1970 *Structuralism.* New York: Basic Books.

Piquet, Jean-Claude
1965 Les conflits de l'analyse et de la dialectique. *Annales* 20:547-57.

Pos, H. J.
1939 Phénoménologie et linguistique. *Re-*

vue internationale de philosophie 1: 354-65.

Pouillon, Jean
1956 L'oeuvre de Claude Lévi-Strauss. *Temps modernes* 12:150-73.
1965 Sartre et Lévi-Strauss. *L'arc* 26:55-60. (Sartre and Lévi-Strauss. *Critical Anthropology* 1 [1970]:34-39.)
1966a Présentation: Un essai de définition. *Temps modernes* 22:769-90.
1966b L'analyse des mythes *L'homme* 6: 100-105.

Pouwer, J.
1966a The Structural and Functional Approach in Cultural Anthropology. *Bijdragen tot de Taal-, Land-, en Volkenkunde* 122:129-44.
1966b L'analyse des mythes. *L'homme* 6: A Rejoiner. *Bijdragen tot de Taal-, Land-, en Volkenkunde* 122:151-57.

Psathas, George
1968 Ethnomethods and Phenomenology. *Social Research* 35:500-20.

Radcliffe-Brown, A. R.
1940 On Social Structure. In *Structure and Function in Primitive Society*, pp. 188-204. New York: Free Press, Macmillan (1965).
1952 Introduction. In *Structure and Function in Primitive Society*, pp. 1-14. New York: Free Press, Macmillan (1965).

Rastier, François
1967 Sur les études phonologiques de Jakobson. *L'homme* 7:94-108.

Revel, Jean-François
1957 *Pourquoi des philosophes?* Paris: Julliard.

Richard, Phillippe
1967 Analyses des mythologiques de Claude Lévi-Strauss. *L'homme et la société* 4:109-33.

Rickman, H. P.
1967 *Understanding in Human Studies.* London: Heineman.

Ricoeur, Paul
1963a Symbole et temporalité. *Archivie di filosofia* 1-2:5-41.
1963b Structure et herméneutique. *Esprit* 31:596-627.
1964 Le symbolisme et l'explication structurale. *Cahiers internationaux de symbolisme* 4:81-96.
1965 *De l'interprétation: Essai sur Freud.* Paris: Du Seuil.

1967a New Developments in Phenomenology in France: The Phenomenology of Language. *Social Research* 34:1-30.

1967b La structure, le mot, l'événement. *Esprit* 35:801-21. (Structure, Word, and Event. *Philosophy Today* 12 [1968] :114-29.)

1969 *Les conflits des interprétations: Essais d'herméneutique*. Paris: Du Seuil.

Rodinson, Maxime

1955a Racisme et civilisation. *Nouvelle critique* 66:120-40.

1955b Ethnographie et relativisme. *Nouvelle critique* 69:46-63.

Ruhemann, Barbara

1967 Purpose and Mathematics: A Problem in the Analysis of Classificatory Kinship. *Bijdragen tot de Taal-, Land-, en Volkenkunde* 123:83-124.

Runciman, W. G.

1969 What Is Structuralism? *British Journal of Sociology* 20:253-65.

Ruwet, Nicolas

1963 Linguistique et sciences de l'homme. *Esprit* 31:564-78.

1967 Musicology and Linguistics. *International Social Science Journal* 19:79-87.

Ruyer, R.

1961 Le mythe de la raison dialectique. *Revue de la métaphysique et de morale* 66:1-35.

Sahlins, Marshall D.

1966 On the Delphic Writings of Claude Lévi-Strauss. *Scientific American* 214:131-36.

Sapir, Edward

1933 Language. In *Selected Writings of Edward Sapir in Language, Culture, and Personality*, ed. D. G. Mandelbaum, pp. 7-32. Berkeley: University of California Press.

Sartre, Jean-Paul

1960 *Critique de la raison dialectique*. Paris: Gallimard.

1966 Jean-Paul Sartre répond. *L'arc* 30: 87-96.

Saussure, Ferdinand de

1915 *A Course in General Linguistics*. New York: Philosophical Library (1959).

Scheffler, Harold W.

1966 Structuralism in Anthropology. *Yale French Studies* 36-37:66-88.

1970 *The Elementary Structures of Kinship* by Claude Lévi-Strauss: A Review Article. *American Anthropologist* 72:251-68.

Schiwy, Günther

1969 *Der französische Strukturalismus: Mode, Methode, Ideologie*. Reinbeck bei Hamburg: Rowohlt Taschenbuch.

Schneider, David M.

1965 Some Muddles in the Model: Or, How the System Really Works. In *The Relevance of Models for Social Anthropology*, ed. Max Gluckman and Fred Eggan, pp. 25-85. ASA Monograph no. 1. London: Tavistock.

Scholte, Bob

1966a Review of Lucien Sebag's *Marxisme et Structuralisme*. *American Anthropologist* 68:1255-56.

1966b Epistemic Paradigms: Some Problems in Cross-Cultural Research on Social Anthropological History and Theory. *American Anthropologist* 68:1192-1201.

1969a Lévi-Strauss' Penelopean Effort: The Analysis of Myth. *Semiotica* 1:99-124.

1969b Review of Yvan Simonis' *Claude Lévi-Strauss ou la "Passion de l'inceste": Introduction au structuralisme*. *American Anthropologist* 71: 503-505.

1969c Lévi-Strauss' Unfinished Symphony: The Analysis of Myth. *Natural History* 78:24-26, 100-101.

1970 Toward a Self-Reflexive Anthropology: An Introduction with Some Examples. *Critical Anthropology* 1, no. 2:3-33.

1971a Toward a Reflexive and Critical Anthropology. In *Reinventing Anthropology*, ed. D. H. Hymes. New York: Pantheon.

1971b Discontents in Anthropology. *Social Research* 78:777-807.

Scholte, Bob, and Yvan Simonis

forth- Lévi-Strauss and la pensée leach-
coming ienne. *Semiotica*.

Sebag, Lucien

1964 *Marxisme et structuralisme*. Paris: Payot.

1965a Le chaminisme Ayoreo. *L'homme* 5: 5-32, 92-122.

1965b Le mythe: Code et message. *Temps modernes* 20:1607-23.

Sebeok, Thomas A., ed.
1964 Approaches to Semiotics: Cultural Anthropology, Education, Linguistics, Psychiatry, Psychology. The Hague: Mouton.

Shankman, Paul
1969 Le rôti et le brouilli: Lévi-Strauss' Theory of Cannibalism. American Anthropologist 71:54-69.

Siegel, Bernard J., ed.
1959- Biennial Review(s) of Anthropology.
1970 Stanford: Stanford University Press.

Simonis, Yvan
1967 Marxisme et structuralisme. Frères du monde 45:7-35.
1968a Claude Lévi-Strauss ou la "passion de l'inceste": Introduction au structuralisme. Paris: Aubier-Montaigne.
1968b Échange, "praxis," code et message. Cahiers internationaux de sociologie 45:117-29.

Simpson, George G.
1961 Principles of Animal Taxonomy. New York: Columbia University Press.

Slamet-Velsink, Ina E.
1958 Les organisations dualistes existent-elles? Het historisch Perspektief. Bijdragen tot de Taal-, Land-, en Volkenkunde 114:292-305.

Sluckin, W.
1960 Minds and Machines. Baltimore: Penguin.

Sommerfelt, Alf
1965 Linguistic Structures and the Structures of Social Groups. Diogenes 51:186-92.

Spencer, Robert
1965 The Nature and Value of Functionalism in Anthropology. In Functionalism in the Social Sciences, ed. Don Martindale, pp. 1-34. Philadelphia: American Academy of Political and Social Sciences.

Sperber, Dan
1967 Edmund Leach et les anthropologues. Cahiers internationaux de sociologie 43:123-41.
1968 Le structuralisme en anthropologie. In François Wahl et al., Qu'est-ce que le structuralisme?, pp. 167-238. Paris: Du Seuil.

Stark, Werner
1958 The Sociology of Knowledge: An Essay in Aid of a Deeper Understanding of the History of Ideas. London: Routledge & Kegan Paul.

Steiner, George
1966 A Conversation with Claude Lévi-Strauss. Encounter 26:32-38.
1967 Orpheus and His Myths. In Language and Silence: Literature and the Inhuman, pp. 239-50. Chicago: Aldine.

Sturtevant, William C.
1964 Studies in Ethno-Science. In Transcultural Studies in Cognition, ed. A. K. Romney and R. G. D'Andrade, pp. 99-131. American Anthropologist 66, no. 3, pt. 2 (special issue).

Tax, Sol, ed.
1953 An Appraisal of Anthropology Today. Chicago: University of Chicago Press.

Terray, Emmanuel
1969 Le Marxisme devant les sociétés "primitives." Paris: Maspero.
1971 Marxism and Primitive Societies. New York: Monthly Review Press.

Todorov, Tzvetan
1965 L'héritage méthodologique du formalisme. L'homme 5:64-83.

Van Loon, J. F. Glastra
1964 Language and the Epistemological Foundations of the Social Sciences. In Report of the Fifteenth Annual (First International) Round Table Meeting on Linguistics and Language Studies, ed. C. I. J. M. Stuart, pp. 171-85. Washington, D.C.: Georgetown University Press.

Verstraeten, Pierre
1963 Lévi-Strauss ou la tentation du néant. Temps modernes 19:66-109, 507-552.

Viet, Jean
1965 Les méthodes structuralistes dans les sciences humaines. The Hague: Mouton.

Wagner, Roy
1970 Review of Claude Lévi-Strauss' The Elementary Structures of Kinship. Journal of the Polynesian Society 79:245-52.

Wahl, François, et al.
1968 Qu'est-ce que le structuralisme? Paris: Du Seuil.

Wald, Henri
1969 Structure, Structural, Structuralism. Diogenes 66:15-24.

Waterman, John T.

1963   *Perspectives in Linguistics.* Chicago: Phoenix.

Wells, Rulon
1967   Distinctively Human Semiotic. *Social Science Information* 6:103-24..

White, H.
1963   *An Anatomy of Kinship: Mathematical Models for Structures of Cumulated Roles.* Englewood Cliffs, N.J.: Prentice-Hall.

Wiener, Norbert
1954   *The Human Use of Human Beings: Cybernetics and Society.* Garden City, N.Y.: Doubleday-Anchor.

Wilden, Anthony
1970   Analog and Digital Communication. Unpublished MS.

Willis, R. G.
1967   The Head and the Lions: Lévi-Strauss and Beyond. *Man* 2:519-34.

Worsley, Peter
1967   Groote Eylandt Totemism and "Le totemisme aujourd'hui." In *The Structural Study of Myth and Totemism,* ed. E. R. Leach, pp. 141-59. ASA monograph no. · 5. London: Tavistock.

Yalman, Nur
1961   On Some Binary Categories in Sinhalese Religious Thought. *Transactions of the New York Academy of Sciences* 24:408-20.
1964   Review of Claude Lévi-Strauss' *La pensée sauvage. American Anthropologist* 66:1179-82.
1965   Dual Organizations in Ceylon? Or the Goddess on the Tree-Top. *Journal of Asian Studies* 24:441-57.

Ziegler, Jean
1965   Sartre et Lévi-Strauss. *Nouvel observateur,* May 6, pp. 22-23.

Zimmerman, Robert L.
1968   Lévi-Strauss and the Primitive. *Commentary* 45:54-61.

CHAPTER **16** Network Analysis

NORMAŃ E. WHITTEN, JR.
ALVIN W. WOLFE

FROM RULES TO STRATEGIES

Social network analysis in the 1970s is one important expression of a theoretical trend in all the social sciences since the 1940s, a trend away from concepts implying relatively static cultural patterns or fixed social institutions and toward concepts implying adaptation and adaptability. Nothing could express the theoretical watershed in social anthropology better than Raymond T. Firth's (1951:39-40) contrast of the concept of social organization with the then prevalent conception of social structure:

There are structural elements running through the whole of social behaviour, and they provide what has been metaphorically termed the social anatomy, the form of a

The authors have been discussing the nature of social systems from both theoretical and methodological perspectives for some six years, during which both of us have engaged in field and library research. We came to the subject of network analysis independently, and have followed our own paths of interest and scholarship. Interestingly enough, while we have influenced each other, we seem to represent opposite poles in contemporary trends. Because of this, we undertook this joint venture enthusiastically, seeing it as an opportunity to help us and others to resolve productively whatever opposition exists.

Whitten wishes to thank Ronald Stutzman, Ann Rynearson, James Pierson, Shulamit Decktor, Sylvia Rudy, Roy Behnke, Barbara Behnke, Mark Levine, and Douglas Midgett for many clarifying and provocative discussions about the nature of network analysis. Dorothea S. Whitten read and commented critically on two drafts of this paper. His research for this chapter began under NIMH Program No. 1 PO1 MH 15567-01.

Wolfe wishes to thank especially two students, Fred Schenk and Nancy Hooyman, for their continually thoughtful input during the preparation of this paper. He has also benefited from the comments, on an earlier but related paper (Wolfe 1970), of numerous colleagues at the University of Wisconsin-Milwaukee and elsewhere; among these are J. A. Barnes, A. L. Epstein, Mark Granovetter, Kenneth Little, Adrian Mayer, Philip Mayer, J. Clyde Mitchell, Robert Scheurell, Charles Tilly, and Edward Wellin. Thanks also are due to the University of Wisconsin-Milwaukee Graduate School, which made some of this work possible through financial and other assistance.

Needless to say, both of us have benefited from attempting to coordinate our own divergent views in order to communicate to our readers not only where social network analysis stands, but also where it might go. If we have failed in any way the fault is certainly ours and not that of any of the many who have helped.

society. But what is this form? It consists really in the persistence or repetition of behaviour; it is the element of continuity in social life. The social anthropologist is faced by a constant problem, an apparent dilemma—to account for this continuity, and at the same time to account for social change. Continuity is expressed in the social structure, the sets of relations which make for firmness of expectation, for validation of past experience in terms of similar experience in the future.... At the same time there must be room for variance and for the explanation of variance.

This is found in the social organization, the systematic ordering of social relations by acts of choice and decision. Here is room for variation from what has happened in apparently similar circumstances in the past. Time enters here. The situation before the exercise of choice is different from that afterwards.... Time enters also as a factor in the development of the implications of decision and consequent action. Structural forms set a precedent and provide a limitation to the range of ... alternative that makes for variability. A person chooses, consciously or unconsciously, which course he will follow. And his decision will affect the future structural alignment.

In sociology as well as in anthropology, post-World War II scholars called for a redressing of earlier structural concepts. Peter Blau argued in *Bureaucracy in Modern Society* (1956:35) that the then prevailing view of bureaucracy was misleading. "Weber's decision to treat only the purely formal organization of bureaucracy implies that all deviations from these formal requirements are idiosyncratic and of no interest for the student of social organization." Blau properly interpreted such theory (see Weber 1947, 1958) as asserting a primacy of perpetuated structural relations (groups, offices, institutions). In his general critique of Weber's work, Blau (1956:19) notes the obvious, that "actual operations [of people in formal organizations] do not exactly follow the formal blueprint. To

understand how bureaucracy functions *we must observe them in action*" (emphasis added).

Like Firth in anthropology, Blau (1956:53) turned his attention to the "patterns of activities and interactions that cannot be accounted for by the official structure," but "which find expression in a network of social relationships and in prevailing practices." Some eight years later Blau was still interested in the phenomena he had begun to adumbrate in 1956, but he had shifted his focus to the mechanisms of informal relations within social systems. His thinking is clearly spelled out in *Exchange and Power in Social Life* (1964; see especially pages 88-114).

Social anthropology, we submit, has entered a phase of development analogous to that of industrial sociology in the 1950s, illustrated here by the work of Blau (for more recent surveys, see Caplow 1964, Turk 1970). "Descent theory" in kinship analysis seems to be social anthropology's analogue to bureaucratic theory in sociology. Such theory, which focuses attention on models of perpetuating, definable, discrete, "corporate" *groups* (see Fortes 1953; Goody, ed., 1962, 1969; Gluckman 1950; M. G. Smith 1956; Mair 1965), is under fire (see Schneider 1965) by those espousing exchange or "alliance" theory (Lévi-Strauss 1969, Needham 1962, Dumont 1961, Maybury-Lewis 1967, Leach 1962). Unfortunately, debates over the relative merits of descent and alliance theory in kinship (Schneider 1965, Lévi-Strauss 1969, Josselin de Jong 1952, Harris 1968:501-13) have not yet moved in the direction indicated by the work of Blau in sociology. Rather, the core of debate is still frequently centered on the identifiable mechanisms for the perpetuation of definable, discrete groups (see Schneider's comment, 1965:73-74).

With increasing frequency the analysis of structural relationships and of the models of their perpetuity is being undertaken together with analyses of "categorical relationships" and "personal networks" (for general statements, see Mitchell 1966; Wolf 1966; Southall, ed., 1961; Boissevain 1968; and Banton 1967). Those who are now interested in and contributing to social network analysis owe greater debts to earlier writers, and certainly we recognize the relevance of work done in the 1930s: the analysis of observations in the Western Electric plant reported by Roethlisberger and Dickson (1939), the sociometry of Moreno (1934), the interaction studies of Chapple and Arensberg (1940), the cliques-in-classes studies of Warner and Lunt (1941). But Firth, Blau, and the others serve as useful markers for a sort of tipping of the balance, from concern with group or "formal" structure and inert individuals to concern with active individuals generating patterns by their own decisions in all contexts of interaction.

In the 1940s the keen analyses of both Fortes (1949a, 1949b) and Lévi-Strauss (1969), different as they were, put such emphasis on the intricacies of social structural relationships that some adumbration of network theory can be discerned in them. Concerned about the variability that was too often overlooked in structural studies, Fortes, in "Time and Social Structure" (1949b: 84), presented a dynamic conception of structure as "an arrangement of parts brought about by the operation, through a period of time, of principles of social organization which have general validity in a particular society." Fortes is but a step from describing social structure as the complex outcome of the strategies of many players subject to some common ground rules. And in a totally different mode, Lévi-Strauss led the trend away from the conceptualization of groups as fixed structures and toward a view of social structure as transformation possibilities inherent in certain crucial exchange and alliance relationships. Like Fortes, Lévi-Strauss (1967:45) recognized that even "kinship is not a static phenomenon; it exists only in self-perpetuation... thus, even the most elementary kinship structure exists both synchronically and diachronically." Neither Lévi-Strauss nor other alliance theorists have themselves contributed concepts or methods to network analysis, but they have certainly helped to increase the awareness of relationships of reciprocity, of strategies of relationships, and of transformations in relational systems. "But as soon as the various aspects of social life—economic, linguistic, etc.— are expressed as relationships, anthropology will become a general theory of relationships. Then it will be possible to analyze societies in terms of differential features characteristic of the systems of relationships which define them" (Lévi-Strauss 1967:95-96).

We have deliberately mentioned some of the literature in organizational anthropology and sociology by specific reference to the study of formal groups (kinship corporations and modern bureaucracies) to make the point that networks, or informal social relations, are not excluded by the existence of any formal apparatus. Rather, network analysis provides the investigator with pathways into the heart of social systems, whether or not the social systems have pronounced formal, perpetuating structural arrangements with corporate, exclusive characteristics. (For an early demonstration that this is so, see Fortes 1949a, 1953.) We shall have more to say about this later.

Recognition of some inadequacies in group structural theories has been a source of discomfort in the social sciences for some years. Some, like S. F.

Nadel (1957) and Robert K. Merton (1949, 1957), have felt that answers lie largely in improvement of theories of roles and role relationships. Others, such as George M. Foster (1961, 1963, 1969) and Eric Wolf (1966), have sought to correct the imperfections of group theory by elaborating our understanding of dyadic, patron-client, and brokerage contracts. And others, like Thibault and Kelly (1959), George Homans (1961), and Peter Blau (1964), have tried to develop an interpersonal exchange model that sees most, if not all, social behavior as subject to the principles of marginal economic theory. Responding to this same uneasiness over structural analysis, some, like J. Van Velsen (1964), have developed what they call "situational analysis," while others, such as Barth (1963, 1966), Bailey (1968), Boissevain (1968), Nicholas (1965), and A. Mayer (1966), have generated what Abner Cohen (1969) calls "action theory." These approaches arise from a common concern about the insufficiency of group-oriented theory, but they may differ from network analysis in that they sometimes focus on the individual in interaction, while network analysis follows the interaction as it ramifies throughout the social context. Indeed, the subject of network analysis *is* the social context, not individual behavior per se, or even the dyadic link per se.

THE NATURE OF THE PROBLEM IN 1970

Current attempts by many social, economic, and political anthropologists to conceptualize networks, to do network analyses, and to construct network theory and network models often seem to represent deliberate efforts to cut across domains of politics, kinship, formal groups, economics, ethnic categories, and even dimensions of cognition in order to get at a *relevant series of linkages existing between individuals which may form a basis for the mobilization of people for specific purposes, under specific conditions.*

Since linkages in any network must be focused if analysis is to have a concrete basis, the concepts of "center" and "ego" necessarily arise. Since a link is not a link unless it connects something to something else, concepts of "connectedness" (the frequency with which members of one person's network interact independently of that person) sometimes creep in (e.g., Luce 1950, Bott 1957, Boissevain 1968: 457). Because of ego-centeredness, paths of linkages "charted" by an investigator may have at least a superficial resemblance to models developed to deal with cognatic kinship systems or with small control groups. Some investigators pay much attention to their charts (Barnes 1954:43, 1969a, 1969b) while others scarcely mention charts at all (Whitten 1970a, 1970b).

FROM RESIDUE TO PHENOMENON

In the course of regular ethnographic research, anthropologists have described many segments of the networks of social relations of the peoples they have studied. Still, the concept of network remained for some time a rather vague notion. For example, Radcliffe-Brown (1965:190) wrote in the early fifties that "human beings are connected by a complex network of social relations. I use the term 'social structure' to denote this network of actually existing relations." J. A. Barnes (1954: 43) gave the concept of network graphic meaning in his study of "Class and Committees in a Norwegian Island Parish":

The image I have is of a set of points some of which are joined by lines. The points of the image are people, or sometimes groups, and the lines indicate which people interact with each other. We can, of course, think of the whole of social life as generating a network of this kind.

The concept, so defined, was picked up shortly by Robert Redfield (1956) and by Elizabeth Bott (1955), whose studies of the family and social network were not only widely read but also widely reprinted (Bott 1955, 1957, 1960, 1964). The meanings Bott gave to social network varied among her own writings and differed somewhat from the meaning Barnes (1954) had intended, and several subsequent analysts did still more to widen the range of meaning. Unfortunately, not all of those to whom the idea appealed felt a responsibility to provide it with the precise definition that would help to locate it in relation to other general concepts. They could not know, as each worried over his own particular problem—conjugal roles and social networks (Bott 1957), migration and social network (P. Mayer 1961, Phillpott 1968), urbanization and social network (Epstein 1961), music and networks (Whitten 1968), politics and network (A. Mayer 1962), the nature of "horizontal segments" (Steward et al. 1956)—that the scholarly world would be straining to use the concept much more generally, in an expansion of specific propositions.

Barnes (1969b:53) recently responded to pressures resulting from what he took to be growing confusion in the literature:

I must take some of the responsibility for this, for what I wrote seems not to have been clear. . . . I did not distinguish between the distinctive features of all networks (in contrast to dyadic relationships, groups, categories, and the like) and those features that happened to be present in the Norwegian network I described. Some readers assumed that these specific and local features must be present in all networks, and have introduced

modifications to fit empirical situations where these features are absent. Other readers have misunderstood what I meant by the total network, perhaps because I did not give any reference to Radcliffe-Brown, from whom I had taken this idea.

Barnes proceeds to clarify the language of discussion about networks by drawing heavily on mathematical concepts from graph theory. Descending in abstract space, as represented by diagrams on a piece of paper, Barnes (1969b:57) moves from the total network of social relationships to the partial network, which he defines as "any abstract of the total network *based on some criterion applicable through the whole network*" (emphasis added). This criterion could be based in economics, kinship, marriage system, politics, or some other domain of society and culture. Because he defines "total network" as coincident with "society" and "partial network" as coincident with a particular domain of society, Barnes must develop further concepts to refer to ego-centered social sets.

He finds "stars" of a "first order" radiating from any ego, anywhere, with whom he chooses to begin. He represents the ego by a dot, and with lines radiating from this dot he forms an analogue of a "star subgraph" (Ore 1962:12). Drawing subsequent concepts from graph theory, he derives a notion of density from the abstract concept that "alpha" (any ego) in interaction with a "contact" (alter) may find that his "contact" is also in interaction with another of his contacts. In that case, the two contacts (or alters) are said to be *adjacent* in the star. All of the relationships among a given ego and his alters, adjacent and nonadjacent, make up what he calls a "zone" (Barnes 1969b:58-60); and by logical extension, zones are conceived of as being "first order," "second order," and so on.

If this sort of mathematical presentation sometimes seems overly abstract, the situation is in no way improved by another tendency found in Barnes (1954) and in too many works since then: the tendency to view social networks as somehow *residual*—the relationships that remain after the major structural relationships are dealt with. A short series of excerpts, chronologically ordered to provide perspective, will give some idea of the pervasiveness of the notion of network as residual, a notion that we feel has actually hindered development of network analysis. First, Barnes again (1954:42-43):

The third social field has no units or boundaries; it has no coordinating organization. It is made up of the ties of friendship and acquaintance which everyone growing up in Bremnes society [the total network of the Norwegian community where he conducted his study] partly inherits and largely builds up for himself. . . . I find it convenient to talk of a social field of this kind as a *network*.

Redfield (1956:50):

Barnes . . . thinks in particular of that part of the total network that is left if the relationships of the territorial and the industrial systems are removed. To distinguish this residual part of the network, and to give it a name suggestive of its presence in every society that is more than the imagined primitive isolate, let us call it the "countrywide network."

Southall, ed. (1961:29-30):

It has been suggested that . . . [face-to-face] relationships may usefully be distinguished as structural, categorical, or egocentric according to the basis upon which persons intuitively classify one another on meeting. Face-to-face relationships of a structural type are aspects of roles defined within the structure of an institution. . . . Categorical relationships are those in which persons meet in an informal context yet without knowing one another very well, and consequently begin to act on the basis of intuitively assigning one another to various type categories as an empirical approach towards appropriate behavior. Egocentric relations are those in which people know one another sufficiently intimately as persons to base their mutual expectations of one another's behavior directly on this personal knowledge.

Wolf (1966:2):

We thus note that the formal framework of economic and political power exists alongside or intermingled with various other kinds of informal structure which are interstitial, supplementary, parallel to it. . . . I should like to focus on three sets of such parallel structures in complex societies: kinship, friendship, and patron-client relations. . . . The informal structures of which I have spoken are supplementary to the system: they operate and exist by virtue of its existence, which is logically, if not temporally, prior to them. . . .

Boissevain (1968:542):

There is a range of social phenomena which have received little attention from social anthropologists and even less from cultural anthropologists and sociologists. These are the forms of social organization that lie somewhere between interacting individuals, on the one hand, and formal corporate groups, on the other. . . . I refer of course to the networks of relatives, friends, and acquaintances, and to the more intimate but often temporary coalitions which are formed out of these; the cliques, interest groups, and factions of which all persons are members.

The tendency, initiated by Barnes and fostered by so many others, to see network as residual rather than focal, must have turned away many potential analysts of network processes. Who wants to study mere residues? Fortunately, the full story is more positive and less simplistic.

FROM METAPHOR TO MODEL

If network analysis is to be developed, networks must be conceptualized as the phenomena of primary concern, not simply as social leftovers after the groups are extracted or as links that fill the interstices between formal structures. Boissevain (1968) intended something like this, but he was distracted by several other issues at the same time and ultimately failed to produce a clear statement of his focus. He did, however, delineate a number of salient issues, to which we shall return. Adrian Mayer came closer to an appropriate view in his "System and Network" (1962) than he did in his more recent paper on "quasi-groups" (1966), although the latter is a remarkable synthesis of several perspectives. Srinivas and Béteille (1964) refer to the possibility of conceptualizing the whole social system as a set of interlocking networks, and in recent statements J. Clyde Mitchell (1969; ed., 1969) demonstrates an appreciation of the problem.

On the one hand, Mitchell (1969:7) writes that the three orders of relationship that he (1959, 1966), Southall (ed., 1961), and Epstein (1962) had separated independently (the structural, the categorical, and the personal) "should not be looked upon as three different *types* of actual behavior, but rather as three different ways of making abstractions from the same actual behavior so as to achieve different *types of understanding and explanation*." He continues, "By this argument, therefore, there can be no opposition of structural and personal links but only different ways of subsuming the data into explanatory frameworks." And in his conclusion he states (1969: 22):

The upshot of my argument then must be that the distinction between social relationships seen as social networks as against corporate groups (or as quasi-groups) is primarily a matter of the level of abstraction at which we are able to operate in summarizing the regularities that we can discern in social relationships as a whole.

Yet, on what must be the other hand, Mitchell (ed., 1969:41) writes in the same year, "But people who have lived in a town for any period build up relationships with people in many different social contexts and these people *may* become part of a social network" (emphasis added).

Peter Gutkind (1965:59-60) appears to have been less inclined than most to view networks as residual categories:

For the Ganda [of Africa], urbanism as a way of life has not resulted in an abrupt break with the past. For urban Ganda, the model of the desirable society continues to be the traditions of the main features of Ganda life and culture. The urban non-Ganda, however, must construct for himself a pattern of social life and organization designed specifically for urban, and thus non-traditional, conditions. To achieve his ends he must participate in a network of contacts and associations which are radically different from those of his kin-based rural environment. As he progressively stays for longer periods in town, urban life presents itself as a more desirable social model and, presumably, a more clearly structured social order.

...I have tried to point to a distinction between kin-based and association-based networks. These two models of social organization should not, however, be seen as mutually exclusive. They meet and overlap at numerous points. They are designed to meet different conditions. A kin-based network is designed to meet, flexibly, new situations to which role responses are yet uncertain....

I believe that the social network concept allows for the documentation of how in practice the individual and the group manipulate various roles both simultaneously and separately. In this respect social network analysis points to the way in which role performance is a part of a system, or a series of systems. To achieve a better understanding of how participation in various types of networks determines and structures specific roles, i.e. ethnic, kin, political, economic or recreational roles, microanalysis is likely to point the way.

In working toward the development of a theory of social networks, Wolfe

(1970:229) focuses directly on networks per se:

On theoretical grounds, we are persuaded that relationships structured in categorical terms and those structured in role systems can profitably be dealt with in the same mode as interpersonal relationships that are not so structured. Links that persons have as members of groups or categories are certainly a part of their total social network. The differences among various kinds of "sets," as we call limited portions of networks (personal sets, categorical sets, action sets, role system sets, field sets) should become fully evident in the process of network analysis as we envision it.

He also presents what he calls a "taxonomy of network concepts," a modified version of which is presented in Figure 1.

Wolfe, then, does not conceptualize a dichotomy between "structures" and "networks," but sees the infinite network of social relations as structured in sets of various kinds. When networks are viewed in this way, one seeks to understand the relationships among these sets and to understand the consequences of operating in one kind of set or another. Methods for such descriptions and comparisons are discussed especially by J. A. Barnes (1969a, 1969b) and Wolfe (1970).

Whitten (1970a, 1970b), building upon A. Mayer (1966) and Boissevain (1968), does find it convenient to contrast structural relations, categorical relations, and personal or egocentric sets or networks. In considering egocentric sets, however, he argues that an effective analysis, after locating a strategic ego node, must go on to explore the categorical, structural, and personal resources of the node, his personal network, and the broker and patronage relations between his network and those of other strategic and ancillary actors. Obviously, network analysts of the 1970s, while agreeing not to treat interpersonal linkages as residual phenomena, have still not agreed on any specific path on which to proceed.

We shall return to these issues after

SOCIAL NETWORK

A model in which links are seen as relating persons in social situations

Limited Network (Set) Any extract of the total network based on some criterion applicable throughout the whole network					Unlimited Network
Personal Set	*Categorical Set*	*Action Set*	*Role-System Set*	*Field Set*	The social network conceived without application of limiting criteria
Set limited to the links of one person	Set limited to links involving persons of a certain type or category	Set limited to links purposefully used for a specific end	Set limited to links involved in an organized role system or group	Set limited to links with a certain content (e.g., economic, political, etc.)	

Figure 1. Taxonomy of social network concepts. (Adapted from Wolfe 1970.)

we have considered more of the relevant contemporary and historical literature. Here it should be sufficient to note a difficulty that has long plagued analysis of kindreds in kinship systems (see Murdock 1949, Davenport 1959, Freeman 1961, Whitten 1965, Schneider 1965, Douglass 1969): every person in every social system can, from some perspectives, be regarded as an egocentric system unto himself; at the same time, *some* egocentric networks in the same social order may teach us little or nothing. Network analysis implies that something about a natural social order can be learned by an analysis of strings of associations (or transactions), but it does not (and cannot) tell us where to begin. Upon what egocentric network should an investigator focus? The question has been raised by a number of investigators, and we shall return to this too.

SOME ISSUES IN NETWORK ANALYSIS

Whether or not one is interested in the morphological characteristics of networks (or portions of networks) themselves, considerable precision is called for in describing the social phenomena with which an investigator will work. The metaphor alone is not sufficient; some parameters must be defined.

So much is being written right now on the subject, and so much revision is taking place simultaneously, that we cannot expect to summarize it all in this brief paper. We shall discuss only certain issues that have been particularly troublesome or which are, in our view, crucial to current understanding or for future development of network analysis. For the rest, we recommend several publications that help to review the field: Jay (1964), Mitchell (1966, 1969; ed., 1969), Boissevain (1968), Barnes (1969*b*), Wolf (1966), Y. A.

Cohen (1969), Crissman (1969), Emerson (1969), Aronson (ed., 1970).

THE ISSUE OF LIMITING NETWORKS

In its most expansive sense, the network metaphor or model refers to an unbounded mass of relationships of all kinds among an infinite number of persons stretching back to the beginning and forward into the future. But nobody has tried to make statements that apply to network in this largest sense. One of the issues in network analysis has to do with the ways in which the total, infinite, unbounded, everlasting network can be given some useful focus and limitation.

Adrian Mayer (1966) is one of those who have found it convenient and efficient to suggest limiting criteria for network analysis. In so doing he turned to Radcliffe-Brown (1965:190) and to Barnes (1954), and so defined a network as synonymous with "social structure." A "set" then became the first limitation: a personal network—any system of ties radiating from an identifiable ego locus (see A. Mayer 1966:98-99). However, he notes that Barnes's sets were "classificatory"—that is, related to people's *concepts* of the class framework of Bremnes. This makes the reader again wonder if the Radcliffe-Brown–Barnes model is the most appropriate for Mayer's own work. It may possibly be a red herring dragged across an otherwise relatively simple definitional problem involving aggregates of people connected by series of interpersonal exchanges.

To differentiate Barnes's early concept of "sets" from those with which he would be dealing, Mayer turned to Chapple and Coon (1947:283) and separated Barnes's "classificatory sets" from Chapple and Coon's "interactive sets." He writes (1966:99), ". . . both types of set are similar in that they are ego-centered and may contain intermediaries between ego (the originator) and the terminal individuals." What he seems to mean by ego-centeredness is that, in the realm of *classificatory sets*, the anthropologist studies social structure by learning how the informant (ego) classifies and stereotypes people as similar to or different from himself, at various degrees, according to various categorical criteria. With the *interactive set* the anthropologist studies the exchanges that take place around a given ego locus, together with those exchanges that take place between alters that are connected in some manner to a particular ego. Mayer is obviously interested in the latter process, as is Boissevain (1968), but perhaps the definitional problem involved in using Barnes as interpreter of Radcliffe-Brown led to some confusion.

Mayer makes clear progress, though, pointing to acknowledged ambiguities in usage, and thereby providing a firm basis for reexamination. He suggests a model of a nongroup, nonassociational sector of society which might be diagrammed as in Figure 2. In this scheme, "bounded" refers to the finite extent of known interaction from the standpoint of a given ego or network nucleus, such as a family (see Bott 1957, A. Mayer 1966), and "unbounded" re-

fers to unlimited series of possible interaction strings. Most significantly, Mayer (1966:100) refers to bounded networks (sets) as those known to ramify from a given ego:

... at any given time the component units of a set have a known boundary; it is not one of group membership ... but of their common connection to the central ego. It is this common link which enables Bott to treat her networks as unit entities which can be analysed and compared.

In an attempt to clarify what he took to be misunderstanding of his earlier position, Barnes (1969b:68) wrote:

There are a limited number of persons in a finite network, and this fact is significant for the flow of interaction going on in the network.... Second, the network is either bounded or unbounded.... If it is unbounded, everyone in the social universe is in the network and there are no persons outside it.

But Barnes (1969b:57) sees another way of limiting the total number of relationships that must be considered in a network: a "partial" network is "any extract from the total network based on some criterion applicable throughout the whole network." Thus, he says, the cognatic web of kinship forms a partial network, and a political network would also be a partial network.

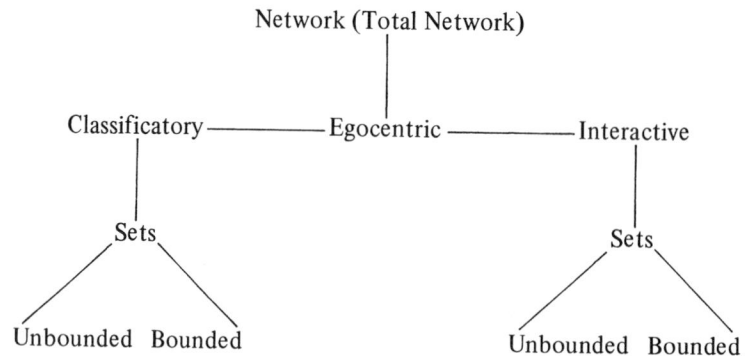

Figure 2. Paradigmatic representation of A. Mayer's network schema.

Thus any network about which we can make statements is qualified by some combination of characteristics. It is either bounded or unbounded, finite or infinite, partial or total. Figure 3 is a paradigmatic representation of Barnes's types of "networks."

The eight types of sets defined analytically vary all the way from a set composed of *certain kinds of links only* (partial), connecting a *limited number of people* (finite), in a universe in which *some persons exist who are not included in the network* (bounded), to a set composed of *all kinds of links* (total), connecting an *unlimited number of persons* (infinite), in a universe in which everyone is included in the network and there are *no persons outside it* (unbounded). Each of these theoretically possible types appears also to be an empirical possibility. A problem of importance would be the mapping of transformation possibilities among the types. Perhaps one needs to be reminded that each of the three contrasts is relative in the sense that sets are more or less bounded depending on the criteria used, that sets are finite or infinite depending on where one decides to stop counting, and that the more narrowly one defines a "kind of link," the more "partial" the set can be.

There can be no doubt that Barnes's three network characteristics are distinct, orthogonal, and important dimensions. The scheme is analytically more elegant than the related "taxonomy of network concepts" (Figure 1) suggested by Wolfe (1970). Wolfe, after deciding to call any extract of the total network a "set," classified sets according to the nature of the linkages to which they are limited: links of one person only (personal set), links involving persons of a certain type (categorical set), links involved in a role system or group (role-system set), links purposefully used toward a specific end (action set), and links with a certain content (field set).

Wolfe's *infinite network* would be, in Barnes's terms, total, infinite, unbounded; Wolfe's *personal* and *categorical sets* would be total, finite, and bounded, except that the category involved might be such that the set would be infinite. A *field set* would be partial, but could be finite or infinite and bounded or unbounded. A *role-system set* and an *action set* are both partial (but to different degrees), both finite, and both bounded (but again to different degrees). There is little advantage to be gained from arguing about these details at the moment, in the abstract. As empirical work proceeds, that which is useful will become clear.

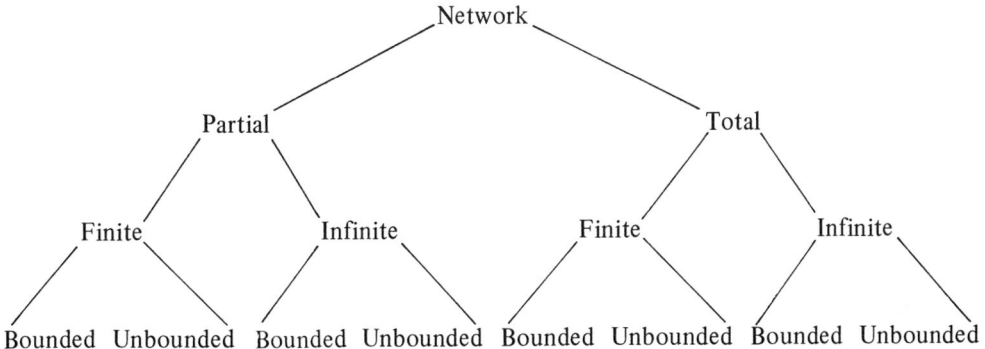

Figure 3. Paradigmatic representation of Barne's types of networks.

As the analyst begins to work with real data rather than abstractly conceived relationships, he discovers once again that relationships exist in time and change through time. For theory, then, one must add time as a fourth dimension by which the total network is limited, for as we noted at the beginning of this section, social relationships link us backward in time and ultimately forward into the future.

Adrian Mayer (1966:116) suggests a dynamic view of a sequence from quasi-group to group: ". . . when the more constant members of an action set are at the same time those directly linked to ego, one can characterize them as the 'core' of the quasi-group. This core may later crystallize into a formal group. . . ." By bringing his notion of "core" to bear on specific action sets, Mayer (1966:115-17) attempts to link group theory with nongroup theory and to a large degree is successful. He carefully points out that when a core begins to coalesce around a particular ego, the core itself may become a group or clique, and then the node in a network or set; the individual ego locus then becomes obscure, and the set radiates from what is now a "group." Such analytical skill should help bridge the group-nongroup hiatuses and move toward the more sophisticated theory of society for which Boissevain has recently called, a theory based on a continuum from individual to group. Whitten's scheme of the relationships of groups, categorical sets, networks, and cores, which will be discussed in the following section, draws directly and heavily upon the work of both Mayer and Boissevain.

Wolfe attempts to deal with the problem of structural time, or developmental cycle, by differentiating "phases" for any link in a set of links. His "codebook" appended to Wolfe (1970:240) reads, in part:

Neither a set as a portion of a network nor a link as a constituent of a set can be considered invariant through time. As a relationship between two persons, a link is established, develops through experiences of the individuals, adapts to all sorts of conditions, and ends (at least when death does them part), and it is easy to conceive of these changes as differentiating *phases*. Even in the absence of specific hypotheses about regularities in the developmental cycles of links or in the developmental histories of sets, recognition of phases is appropriate.

Too little attention has been given to the problem of delimiting networks chronologically, although some efforts have been made in that direction (Leeds 1964; Foster 1969; Whitten 1965, 1969; Whitten and Szwed, eds., 1970*a*). If network analysis is to make some contribution to the understanding of adaptation and adaptability, this issue must be high on the agenda.

THE ISSUE OF INTIMACY AND EXTENSION

If one is talking about a personal network, an egocentric set of links focusing on one person, then one must decide how far outward from that ego the set extends, and must distinguish among members of the set according to some measures of social distance. Epstein (1961) differentiated "effective" (close) and "extended" (distant) parts of an egocentric network. Boissevain (1968:546-47) adds another component, which he labels "intimate."

At least three important ranges or zones can be distinguished within which the relations are qualitatively different. They form concentric zones which centre on ego. The first is composed of those persons, whether relatives or friends, with whom ego is on closest terms. These persons form what may be called ego's *intimate network*. The second range may be called the *effective network*. It consists of persons whom ego knows less well and from whom he can expect less (and who expect less or nothing of him) than from the members of his intimate network. These may include relatives, friends and other acquaintances of various sorts. The third zone is made up of persons whom ego does not know personally but of whom he knows and whom he very easily can get to know. These are for the most part members of the intimate networks of the persons in his own intimate network. These persons constitute ego's *extended network*.

It seems quite unlikely to us that consensus could ever be reached on any set of criteria that could universally discriminate among intimate, effective, and extended relationships or intimate, effective, and extended zones. This being the case, we need hardly do more here than identify the issue. There must be some quite different approach to its resolution. If the analyst keeps this problem always in mind, then distinctions will be made only when they are heuristic; for example, when they permit the investigator to reach a level of generalization allowing for *comparison* of adaptive strategies or styles (or both).

THE ISSUE OF CONNECTEDNESS

"Connectedness" or something like it (density, close-knit/loose-knit, large mesh/small mesh, etc.) has been more frequently cited as a significant characteristic of networks than any other type of measure or limitation. (For example, see the section on "Applications," below.) It is one of those variables that many talk about though few have measured. Barnes (1969a, 1969b) has recently given the subject systematic treatment. He reviews the use of such concepts not only in social science, but in mathematics as well. One of his observations (1969a:224) shows the gravity of the problem:

... in five papers, derived over a period of fifteen years in sequence from one another as shown by their footnote references, the term "connectivity" is applied to six distinct measures, each writer apparently introducing changes to suit his own convenience without reference to contemporary common usage in his own and related fields of inquiry.

Barnes's aim is not to provide an authoritative glossary of terms or typology of related measures, but rather to caution against loose usage and to encourage attention to the measures other analysts are using. He himself (1969a: 225) has used a measure he calls density, "the number of lines present in the vicinity of any given point as a fraction of the maximum possible number." Charles Tilly (n.d.a) and Wolfe have used a very similar measure. Wolfe (1970:18) writes, "For any set, the density index represents the percentage of potential links that are actualized."

We wholeheartedly endorse Barnes's warnings, and are optimistic that once analysts appreciate the magnitude of variance around such issues as connectedness and density, greater care will be exercised.

NETWORK ANALYSIS: OTHER THEORETICAL BASES

During the decade of the 1960s, what agreement there was among interested scholars centered around notions of "action sets" (A. Mayer 1962, 1966; Jay 1964; Boissevain 1968; Barnes 1968). Whitten puts emphasis on network analysis as a strategy for studying social systems by focusing on ramifying relationships. One can justifiably focus on personal interaction, on characteristics of reciprocity or exchange, instead of on characteristics of sets. Instead of trying to develop network theory as such, one can seek the theoretical bases for network analysis in role theory or exchange theory or action theory. We have already referred to Blau (1956, 1964), Homans (1961), and Thibault and Kelly (1959), all important contributors toward a theory of social behavior as exchange.

If we accept the proposition that exchange is at least implicit in the notion of social network (see Heider 1969), then it behooves us to examine closely the relationships between network analysis and theoretical models. It is interesting to find that those scholars who have delineated such crucial concepts as the "dyadic contract" (Foster 1961, 1963), "patronage" (Campbell 1964, Wolf 1966), and "clientage" (Nadel 1935, 1942) have often not explicitly noted that *series* of exchanges can define a network (notable exceptions are Boissevain 1966 and, to a lesser extent, Foster 1969). Whitten feels that the theoretical underpinnings for network analysis not often specified by writers on the subject seem to derive from three sources: role theory, exchange theory, and action theory. Of these three, the position of role theory has yet to be effectively used as a theoretical basis (for an argument that it *should* serve in this capacity, see Crissman 1969).

ROLE THEORY

Many of the authors we have mentioned, and others we shall discuss below, refer to role theory in their discussions of network analysis (see especially Barnes 1954, Bott 1957, A. Mayer 1966:101-102, Epstein 1958, Boissevain 1968, Mitchell 1966, Crissman 1969). Usually, however, the way in which role theory can establish a conceptual foundation for the analysis of social networks is unclear. This is probably because role theory is commonly applied in situations where the analysis of groups is a productive way to study

social relations. For example, in commenting on the analyses of Epstein (1958) and Barnes (1954), J. Clyde Mitchell (1966:57-58) writes:

The unit of observation at the first level of abstraction out of which first of all the sets, and subsequently the fields, are constructed is the role, and the sort of data which Barnes and Epstein present could be cast in terms of roles and role-performance. *A role, however, pertains to behaviour in a structural position.* Thus while we may speak of the role of a person A *vis-à-vis,* say, a person B in *his* personal network and of B's role towards C in B's network, we cannot speak of A's role *vis-à-vis* C because he is not in A's network. Since we need to delineate the mechanism whereby behavior between people in one set of roles may affect the behavior of a different set of people in another set of roles ... it seems that we need the concepts of "field" and "network" as well as role. [Emphasis added.]

Because of Mitchell's insistence on refining concepts such as field and network in addition to the concept of role, we shall seek theoretical constructs for a basis of network analysis elsewhere, leaving to others the task of appropriately linking role theory with the underpinnings of network analysis. In passing, however, it should be noted that the most common work on role theory cited by writers on networks is S. F. Nadel's *The Theory of Social Structure.* Early in this book (1957:12) Nadel makes this statement: "We arrive at the structure of a society through abstracting from the concrete population and its behavior the pattern or network (or 'system') of relationships obtaining 'between actors in their capacity of playing roles relative to one another.'" (Nadel is quoting from Parsons 1949:34.) Suffice it here to note that this is *not* the sense in which most writers use the concept of network, though references to this statement creep into a number of otherwise divergent approaches. It is with exchange and action theory that we find the theoretical basis for network analysis.

EXCHANGE THEORY

Exchange theory in anthropology, though not in sociology, is grounded in attempts to relate the material and social life of people in natural settings. Marshall Sahlins (1965:139) reviews the literature from Mauss (1954) in the twenties to the 1960s, and specifies the core of the theory at the outset of his paper: "... the connection between material flow and social relations is reciprocal. A specific social relation may constrain a given movement of goods, but a specific transaction—'by the same token'—suggests a particular social relation. If friends make gifts, gifts make friends."

Exchanges may symbolize opposition, as when two actors "exchange torts," or cooperation, as when people compliment one another or exchange some acceptable tokens. Structurally speaking, exchanges between individuals may merely link the individuals into a dyadic relationship, or they may symbolize ramifying cooperation and/or competition between groups or aggregates of individuals. The concept of reciprocity is at the heart of exchange theory, and this concept has been conveniently treated by Sahlins (1965:147-48), developing ideas from Mauss (1954) and Malinowski (1922), Firth (1951) and Gouldner (1960), as a continuum from "generalized reciprocity" through "balanced reciprocity" to "negative reciprocity":

"Generalized reciprocity" refers to transactions that are putatively altruistic, transactions on the line of assistance given and, if possible and necessary, assistance returned. The ideal type is Malinowski's "pure gift." ... "Balanced reciprocity" refers to direct exchange ... and "negative reciprocity" is the attempt to get something for nothing with impunity, the several forms of appropriation, transactions opened and conducted toward net advantage. Indicative ethnographic terms include "haggling" or "barter," "gambling," "chicanery," "theft," and other varieties of seizure.

For network analysis, the important aspect of exchange theory, with its concept of reciprocity, is its demonstration that any exchange can forge an interpersonal link, and interpersonal links can connect individuals in series of communicative, economic, manipulative, and other types of strands. Without exchange theory the notion of network would appear quite abstract, divorced from the realities of human life in specific social and cultural settings. From the vantage point of exchange theory, a social network may also be viewed as a mechanism of distribution. Its functioning provides a means of moving goods and services from person to person, both horizontally and vertically (Greenfield 1966:7, Heider 1969). Another theoretical position, called "action theory," usefully employs exchange theory to summarize the specific aspects of a particular network in a stated context.

ACTION THEORY

Action theory in anthropology, according to Abner Cohen (1969:223), may be regarded as "a reaction against the emphasis placed by earlier anthropological studies on 'collective representations' ... This school of thought tends to sweep the theoretical pendulum towards an orientation emanating from Weberian 'action theory.' " Cohen goes on to describe as "action theory" a developing approach in anthropology which eschews analysis in terms of group and group symbols, and sees instead social (or political) life as a game involving continuous "scheming, struggling, and making decisions." Among works representing this school of thought he cites Bailey (1968), Barth (1963, 1966), Boissevain (1968), A. Mayer (1966), and Nicholas (1965). This school concentrates, according to Cohen (1969:223), on "the activities of 'political man' who is ever impelled to the pursuit of power." He takes no action without contemplating the relative gains and losses in a transaction.

Although Cohen exaggerates the picture painted by action theorists, and inaccurately implies that action theory imputes to *all* individuals in a social order the sort of behavior dealt with by game theory, he nevertheless correctly identifies many of the theoretical positions that adhere to those who propose to carry out network analysis of a social system. It is not necessary to assume that all men are following the model of Cohen's "political man," however. All we need assume is that so long as *some people* in any particular system do behave as Cohen describes, then the ramifications of their behavior vis-à-vis others may require us to study the interpersonal, minimaxing exchanges that take place between individuals linked to one another in effective personal networks owing to their common relationship to a *socially significant ego*. The more the socially significant ego maneuvers for social position, the more important becomes an analysis of his exchanges and their ramifying consequences on individuals caught up in his maneuvers. A convenient way of identifying socially significant egos is to analyze the political economy of a given system. Work along such lines has been carried out by Whitten (1965, 1970a), Adams (1966), and Phillpott (1968), among many others. Although Whitten (1970a) feels justified in generalizing about cultural content and action styles, and in infer-

ring general properties of particular subcultures on the basis of research into a few strategic networks, there are others who do not. For example, Swift (1967:311) writes:

The field worker will form impressions based on the networks of his closest informants, but when he wishes to translate these impressions into general statements about the nature of networks in the society it seems to me he faces research problems more difficult than those arising from the essentially normative analysis of role and group.

The relationship between fieldwork, informant relationship, measures of consistency, and theoretical bases for generalization need much more careful examination before we take such polarity as significant, however. Freilich (ed., 1970) recently has pointed up the value of such examination.

TOWARD A SYNTHESIS OF ROLE, EXCHANGE, AND ACTION THEORIES

An important aspect of Boissevain's (1968:549-50) review concerns the careful attention given to what he calls "social catalysts," defined as "brokers and other manipulators." Such brokers wheel and deal through interpersonal linkages, forming, transforming, and using interpersonal relationships for some perceived advantage, and in the process affect the social relationships within the direct and indirect spheres of their maneuvers. "Network specialists," Boissevain says, "provide important links in networks viewed as a series of communication channels. They transmit, direct, filter, receive, code, decode, and interpret messages." Such "strategically placed" persons, if fortunate or adept, may turn their skills as brokers in social capital into personal power; their ability to manipulate networks enables them to make social events turn out to their advantage.

Boissevain uses his concept of network specialist (broker) to bridge the gap in his continuum from individuals to groups with a halfway step of "quasi-groups." Following A. Mayer (1966) and Pospisil (1964), and in specific opposition to Ginsberg (1934:40), Bottomore (1962:92), Dahrendorf (1959:236), and Nadel (1951:188f), who use "quasi-group" in the sense of categorical social relationships, Boissevain (1968:550) defines a quasi-group as "a coalition of persons, recruited according to structurally diverse principles by one or more existing members, between some of whom there is a degree of patterned interaction and organization."

Although personal networks centered on a socially, economically, or politically important ego may coalesce into a clique, faction, gang, action set, or other grouplike, short-run, nonperpetuating cluster, the ego-centeredness of such a cluster may begin to disappear as the groupness appears. This is sticky theory, and at the moment we can consider it only a useful device in structuring Boissevain's concept of a *continuum* of social forms from the individual to the corporate group. Studies of a quasi-group forming out of a personal network, and even of a group forming out of a quasi-group, would seem necessary to illustrate the value of some of these concepts. This underscores, once again, the need for a developmental, temporal perspective in such studies.

One way of gaining a developmental perspective is through the study of factions that form as a result of conflict between "leaders" (see Bailey 1965, Nicholas 1965, Schwartz 1969, Boissevain 1964). If we substitute "network broker" for "leader" and assume that a network broker's skills in organization may be used to muster social capital in opposition to similar actions on the part of an alter broker, then we can see how the analysis of social conflict can be furthered through factional studies, and how network analysis can perhaps give us a more dynamic view of complementary and contrastive conflict and solidarity in social systems.

Another way to study the relationship of individuals to quasi-groups and of quasi-groups to group formation is through developmental sequence studies such as those of Goody (ed., 1958) on family and household, Leeds (1964) on Brazilian careers, and Whitten (1965, 1969) on Colombian-Ecuadorian mobility strategies. Whitten suggests that action sets in the form of personal kindreds become stem kindreds, and that stem kindreds can evolve into an ambilineal ramage over four or more generations of socioeconomic mobility.

By reviewing and suggesting directions for study of dynamic linkages that can account for the coalescing and dispersing of action sets in times of conflict, Boissevain clearly demonstrates the methodological value of network analysis as a means of understanding a social order. We suggest, however, that the strategy of network analysis is as important in formal settings as in settings where corporate groups do not exist. Although we agree with Boissevain (1968:553) that analyses of individual brokers, ego-centered networks, and quasi-groups are of great importance in the analysis of a social structure, we cannot agree with his conclusion that they are *more* important than analyses of extant formal groups in a particular social system. If one is to understand the nature of the social capital brought into an exchange relationship in a natural social order, then it is imperative to comprehend something of the formal system of economic, political, and social groupings, as well as the ramifying ego-centered networks.

By analyzing political process in the Dewas district of the state of Madhya

Pradesh in India, A. Mayer (1966:102-108) shows the value of action concepts. Taking a candidate for political office as his ego, Mayer shows how such a strategic locus in the political economy initiated action series in the development of an action set. The generation of the concept of action set brings us to the heart of Mayer's contribution (1966:108): ". . . action-sets . . . are formed of links derived from many social fields; but because they are purposive creations by an ego, this purpose gives all the links a common feature, without which the action-set could not be classed under the quasi-group rubric." But Mayer is careful not to oppose quasi-group formation to the existence of groups. When he analyzes quasi-groups in the form of action sets, he is analyzing the *moves* of a strategic figure (a candidate for office) who is in the process of mobilizing his set (network) for action. Any such analysis must include the social functions of mobilization, involving a wide range of brokerage, group, and dyadic relationships. If an anthropologist can begin "anywhere" in a social order to study networks, still he must begin somewhere, and the decision is not always easy to make. By talking about specific actors who are mustering social help by building or activating a set of interpersonal ties ramifying in and out of groups, categories, and brokerage nodes, Mayer avoids the problem.

A. Mayer sees the action set as bounded, but denies its existence as a "group," for the basis of membership is specific to each linkage, and there are no rights or obligations that bring all these members into relationships with each other. Moreover, "the action-set could not exist without the ego around whom it is formed" (A. Mayer 1966: 109). For Mayer, one must study the action set only while the social relationships of which it is composed are being activated by the (then) central ego.

In considering the comparison of action sets, Adrian Mayer stimulates a number of possibilities for the study of social change through the methodology of network analysis. For example, within a society an investigator can focus on the differential patterns of linkage of complementary and contrasting sets and tie such patterns to "campaign strategy" (see A. Mayer 1966:110-11). Reliance on action theory leads Mayer (1966:111) to an important consideration: "We must distinguish between the *potential material of network links, and those links which are actually used* [i.e., "carry transactions"] in the action-set's constitution" (emphasis added). By subclassifying "transactions" in terms of ethnographically induced roles, Mayer (1966:113-14) distinguishes patronage and brokerage roles:

In the first [patronage roles], the transactor has the power to give some benefit which the respondent desires; upon fulfillment of the latter's part the benefit is made available. . . . Patronage is an unambiguous transaction, in which the responsibility for any failure to redeem a promise can be clearly put down to the patron. A broker is a middle-man, and the transaction is one in which he promises to obtain favours for the respondent from a third person . . . the broker can enter into more transactions, in relation to his resources of power, than can the patron.

The problem with such classification is that, as Mayer himself notes (1966: 114), such transactions may overlap in practice, making differentiation of patronage and brokerage roles difficult. It would seem preferable to note the exchange mechanisms between transacting nodes rather than to impose (or even infer) analytical types unless the types themselves can be described as contrastive or complementary within particular sociocultural environments.

The definitions and concepts sketched here and in the preceding section may be seen to form certain relationships, which Whitten conceptualizes in the model shown in Figure 4.

APPLICATIONS OF
NETWORK CONCEPTS

We are not in full agreement about how far we should go in thinking of developing a set of statements that might become, formally, "network theory." Barnes (1968), the principal network theoretician, has some comments on uses of network concepts. After referring to his own work in Bremnes (Barnes 1954), Bott's use of network (1955, 1957), and Adrian Mayer's review and application (1966), Barnes writes (1969*b*:52):

These and other reports show that the concept is useful in describing and analyzing political processes, social classes, the relationship of a market to its hinterland, the provision of services and the circulation of goods and information in unstructured social environments, the maintenance of values and norms by gossip, structural differences between tribal, rural, and urban societies, and so on.

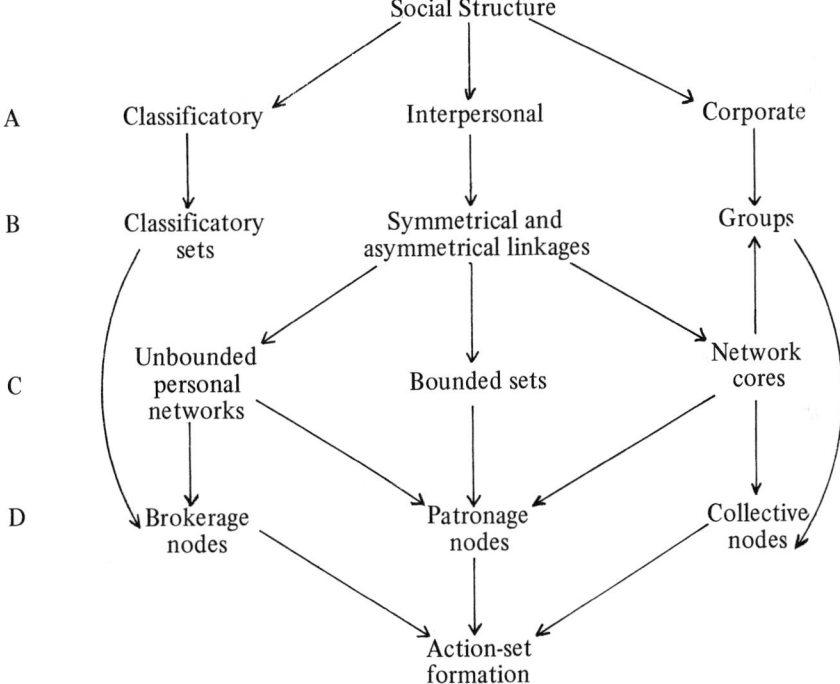

KEY: A = bases for social organization
      B = forms of social relationship
      C = social relations described by network analysis
      D = social activators
      → = may transform to

Figure 4. A paradigm of network concepts in action and exchange theory.

A decade earlier, in reviewing social anthropological contributions to the study of complex societies, Eisenstadt wrote (1961:209):

It is perhaps only the concept of network that to some extent provides a potentially new analytical tool. It clearly describes or points out the existence of some differential interrelation between different people who are not organized in corporate groups; and it may help in the analysis of the relation of different persons, acting in such a network, to different types of social roles and institutional frameworks.

The tracing through of networks of people involved in diverse activities has always gone on in the analysis of social systems, but such tracing is now becoming more specific as a technique and more fashionable as a subject for discussion. In many studies (Fortes 1949*a*, 1969; Whyte 1953; Fallers 1956; Leeds 1964; Whitten 1965) network analysis is implicit, while in some monographs and articles (Aronson, ed., 1970; Barnes 1954; Bott 1957; Greenfield 1966; Plotnicov 1967; Mitchell, ed., 1969; Whitten 1970*a*) pains are taken to explicate a working concept of network, and to define classes of network phenomena for analytical scrutiny. A few authors write about network *theory,* but some of these mean an elaboration of role theory. Lawrence Crissman (1969:80), for example, says:

Personal networks, when elucidated, provide an inventory of the dyadic roles individuals have accumulated according to the rules, or structure, of their culture and society, and serve to place them in its organization. A personal network should, then, be described in terms of the roles it contains, the roles being studied as roles. . . . By tracing personal networks in the field, the structure of a culture can be elucidated and the workings of the society seen in operation.

In Crissman's statement we can clear-

ly see a yearning toward synthesis of field strategy and theoretical foundation, a yearning in which we share.

It would probably be helpful to have a more systematic description of the range, actual and possible, of network analysis tendencies. For a beginning, we can separate the situations in which network characteristics are considered from the standpoint of role theory, exchange theory, and action theory from those in which network characteristics themselves are part of the theoretical model. Within the latter category Wolfe chooses to separate the theoretical situations in which network characteristics are treated as dependent variables from those in which network characteristics are treated as independent variables. This tripartite classification may appear more systematic than the literature warrants; nonetheless, the writings of various network analysts seem to support it, when viewed *ex post facto.*

Let us turn our attention first to those who use network characteristics as part of their theoretical model—or would do so if they developed a formal model. And within that broad category, let us look first at those who see network characteristics as affecting something.

NETWORK VARIABLES AS INDEPENDENT

Bott hypothesizes quite straightforwardly that the kind of network in which a family is involved affects in a very direct manner the conjugal role relations in that family: close-knit network leads to conjugal role segregation. There is, of course, criticism of Bott's definition, of her measures, of her sample, of her findings, and of the general validity of the hypothesis (Turner 1967, Platt 1969). But from the theoretical perspective we take here there can be no doubt about the stance Bott takes (1957:60): "The degree of segregation in the role-relationship of husband and wife varies directly with the connectedness of the family's social network."

Network characteristics are also conceptualized as independent variables in models intended to explain individual behavior. One such study, by Robert P. Scheurell and Irwin D. Rinder, deals with deviancy, specifically "incest offenders" (n.d.: 8-9):

From this analysis, the following process seems to occur in incest cases. The offender's values or orientation toward household tasks is one of relative isolation, which means the offender cannot rely on external sources to maintain the segregated pattern. Instead, the segregation of household tasks is maintained through the use of children with neither spouse assuming some of the tasks. This process [and its results] . . . [increases] the probability of incestuous behavior.

The issue here is not the validity of the analysis but the fact that network characteristics are directly involved as independent variables in the model.

We can see Adrian Mayer conceptualizing a model with network characteristics (in his case action-set characteristics) as independent variables affecting outcomes. After differentiating "hard" and "soft" election campaign strategies as appropriate in different situations, Mayer says (1966:111): "Now it is possible to argue that an action-set with shorter paths will be more appropriate to a harder campaign. . . . The long-pathed set, on the other hand, would seem to be better for a softer campaign." A similar perspective using other network characteristics is found on the succeeding page of his paper.

Another theoretical situation in which network characteristics are clearly used as independent variables is a study of the diffusion of a medicinal drug through the medical profession.

Coleman, Katz, and Menzel (1957:253) concerned themselves with the effectiveness of networks of interpersonal relations at each stage of the diffusion process. Friendship sets, advisory sets, and discussion sets, they found (1957: 266), "did not behave identically. The discussion network and the advisor network showed most pair simultaneity [the presumed effect of network characteristics] at the very beginning and then progressively declined. The friendship network shows initially less pair-simultaneity than the other two, but . . . appears to reach its maximum effectiveness later."

A significant number of studies have tended to demonstrate effects of networks or network characteristics on migration or adaptation of migrants (P. Mayer 1961, 1964; Abu-Lughod 1961; Phillpott 1968; Gans 1962; Tilly n.d.*b*; Parkin 1969). Philip Mayer (1961, 1964) sees the close-knit networks of certain Xhosa urban migrants (called the "Reds") "encapsulating" them in city enclaves, protecting them from extensive change and reinforcing tribal values even in the city. These contrast with another category of Xhosa in town (the "School Migrants"), whose loose-knit networks encourage modernization both in town and in the rural areas. Similarly, in recent work in the United States, Mark Granovetter (n.d.) has argued that close-knit networks inhibit the movement of people into large-scale social systems and thereby help to maintain a sense of alienation, whereas loose-knit networks of social relations permit the establishment of an elaborate communication system that furthers the integration of individuals within the wider social order. Comparing two kinds of newcomers to Kampala, Uganda, David Parkin (1969) arrives at a general conclusion not far removed from Philip Mayer's and Granovetter's. Network characteristics are, then, being suggested as independent variables to help explain phenomena of migrant adaptation. They are invoked as independent in other contexts as well (such as participation in voluntary associations), but our purpose here is to illustrate this use of network variables, not to provide comprehensive documentation.

NETWORK VARIABLES AS DEPENDENT

Other investigators present network characteristics as dependent variables in their theoretical models. There are those (Lesser 1961, Wirth 1938) who see a general evolutionary trend from one form of network to another— usually from a narrow, close-knit form to a loose-knit form of wider scale. The point here is only that one can easily postulate that network form is the result, not the cause, of some general active forces in social life.

Not far removed from the evolutionary view is the one that sees network characteristics as differing according to "culture." Parkin (1969:145-47) provides a neat statement along these lines in a comparison of the cultural characteristics of two "super-tribal cultural types" of populations, both of which have taken up residence in Kampala, Uganda. The people he calls "Migrants" (e.g., Luo, Luhya, Acholi, Lango) are involved in an effective "brotherhood" network, which, while sometimes imposing onerous obligations on individuals, can be easily mobilized to resolve domestic crises, and proves effective in the cities as well as in the villages. In contrast, the culture of those he calls "Hosts" (e.g., Ganda, Soga, Nyoro, Toro) does not include the ideology of brotherhood and the kind of network that goes along with it, so that a "Host" network "may thus be highly extended without being effective." This sort of reasoning (and it is

fairly common) suggests that differences in network forms are the results of general cultural differences.

In numerous studies specific social conditions have been identified as independent variables that affect network characteristics. Turner (1967:126-29), reexamining Bott's ideas about social network, finds that his data from a Pennine parish suggest that geographic mobility affects network connectedness. Such a finding is compatible with a theoretical model used in sociometry, although its strictest theoreticians speak of groups and cliques rather than networks. J. L. Moreno (1953:715-17) suggests a number of hypotheses relevant to a model of network characteristics as dependent on other social conditions, such as "original affinity" and "physical propinquity." Also, Festinger, Schachter, and Back (1950:151f) present conclusions about the ways in which social and housing conditions affect "what friendships will develop and what social groupings will be formed." These could be translated directly into network terms.

NETWORK ANALYSIS BASED ON ROLE, EXCHANGE, AND ACTION THEORY

Finally, we again call attention to those situations in which the field investigator (as network analyst) sees the social network in terms of other theoretical models, and uses ramifying series of exchanges and role relationships to gain deeper understanding of the workings of a social or cultural system (see Whitten 1968, 1970a). The concern of such network analysis is to deal with observable human interaction (not merely the norms, rules, representations, etc.) and to avoid the "disorganization model" of social systems, in which bounded, corporate, interactive sets (groups) either are not apparent or are unintelligible to the investigator (see Liebow 1967; Hannerz 1969, 1970; Gerlach and Hine 1970). The active elements in such theoretical models are not network characteristics per se, but the data that can be gained by effecting a network analysis.

We discussed three theoretical bases for network analysis in the previous section, and noted tendencies suggested by Boissevain (1968) and A. Mayer (1966) as particularly fruitful. The contributions to several recent symposia, in particular "Urban Social Networks: International Comparisons" at the 1969 meetings of the Central States Anthropological Society in Milwaukee and the "Experimental Session on Patronage, Clientage, and Power in Latin America" at the meetings of the American Anthropological Association in New Orleans, also in 1969, indicate that much current interest in network analysis is of this nature. The argument on which such work is based is that network analysis is the product of general ethnographic concerns, and that an analytic approach based on action and exchange theory will therefore yield a more dynamic and relevant view of the lifeways of particular peoples than can be achieved by models that employ network characteristics as merely a means to an understanding of networks themselves.

In natural settings, people have their own ideas about strategy, power, and interpersonal linkages. They place themselves in their own system through categorical contrasts, and in a political-economic matrix through strategic social and economic exchanges. Network analysis conducted from this perspective demands a technique that cuts through such models, and suggests a socioeconomic reality that may give rise to various folk models.

A folk model of Trobriand social structure, long held by Trobrianders and by anthropologists, for example,

included a "paramount chief" (Malinowski 1922). Singh Uberoi (1962) has exploded this "Piltdown myth" of social anthropology by demonstrating, by means of Malinowski's own writing, that networks of exchanges in the famous *kula* ring link individuals together. These individual linkages cut across antagonistic corporate groups, and give father and son a strategic advantage (father helps son establish his *kula* exchange partners) in the wide-flung political economy of the Massim area. This series of exchanges between trade partners (which Malinowski described, but which his theoretical stance was inadequate to explicate) binds the region together, socially and economically, against the counterforce of segmentary, corporate, matrilineal clans, the linkages within which ideally and jurally separate father and son. The paramount chief of Omarakana becomes, according to this analysis, merely a local officeholder in a village that has fortuitously become a strategic point in its ecosystem because the highest number of exchange relationships often cluster there.

The concept of chief becomes, then, an ideal precipitate of ramifying, cross-cutting networks, not an authority figure in corporate holdings. Another way of explaining this is to suggest that the Trobriand folk model of "paramount chief" represents a cultural capacity of the Trobriand exchange system to adhere via series of cross-cutting trade networks. Adherence, from the perspective of an ideology of descent, generates an image of apical control, which becomes crudely translated as "paramount chief." When it is clear that the apical figure of the folk model lacks power, then his role and status are projected into the past. People simply suggest he used to have such power, or that his predecessors had such power. Exchange theory suggests that he need never have had power. The power view fits a cognitive, jural model of matrilineal kinship. According to exchange theory, the system adheres through a series of linked trading partners and the reciprocal flow of goods.

This system, which integrates the kinship domain and the exchange partner domain, is best described in terms of ramifying and overlapping exchange networks, with internal clusters of people who manipulate jural rules based on membership in corporate descent groups. Group structural and network relationships complement one another, so that both descent theory and exchange theory are necessary for a clear statement of Trobriand *de jure* and *de facto* social relationships.

WHERE DO WE BEGIN?

We began this essay with tendencies in organizational anthropology and industrial sociology, and we conclude with a few remarks on network analysis in large-scale and small-scale societies. We have referred to research undertaken in the field, and to research that reexamines published literature from a previous era. The message is obvious: network analysis provides a convenient, efficient, and, most importantly, *productive* way of penetrating to the heart of various social orders.

This brings us back to an original question: *Where do we start in a network analysis?* For personal networks, the question is: *What ego do we choose?* One strategy is to begin with an ego strategic to action in a particular natural setting. Finding the ego is dependent on the resources of the ethnographer, the nature of the particular culture, and that culture's setting within the broad economic, political, and cultural pressures of the contemporary world. Questions then of social capital, human and economic resources, the nature of activation of social capital, and

the exchanges that maintain a pool of capital in times of nonactivation loom large to the ethnographer who undertakes network analysis. This is particularly true when, by his very presence, the ethnographer himself becomes a significant ego locus, around whom ties begin to form, cluster, and have sociopolitical effect.

No one has suggested that the task is simple, or that the most strategic starting point is easily identified, or that the analyst will necessarily be able to begin at this point even if he succeeds in identifying it, or that it will retain its strategic character after he has made a promising start. Situations change, groups form and dissolve, interrelationships shift; networks remain. The important thing is to begin.

REFERENCES

Abu-Lughod, Janet
1961 Migrant Adjustment to City Life: The Egyptian Case. *American Journal of Sociology* 67, no. 1:22-32.

Adams, Richard N.
1966 Power and Power Domains. *América latina* 9, no. 2:3-21.

Aronson, Dan R., ed.
1970 *Social Networks. Canadian Review of Sociology and Anthropology* 7, no. 4 (special issue).

Bailey, F. G.
1965 Decisions by Consensus in Councils and Committees: With Special Reference to Village and Local Government in India. In *Political Systems and the Distribution of Power*, ed. Michael Banton. ASA Monograph no. 2. New York: Praeger.
1968 Parapolitical Systems. In *Local-Level Politics*, ed. Marc Swartz. Chicago: Aldine.

Banton, Michael
1967 *Race Relations.* New York: Basic Books.

Barnes, John A.
1954 Class and Committees in a Norwegian Island Parish. *Human Relations* 7, no. 1:39-58.
1968 Networks and Political Process. In

Local-Level Politics, ed. Marc Swartz. Chicago: Aldine.

1969*a* Graph Theory and Social Networks: A Technical Comment on Connectedness and Connectivity. *Sociology* 3, no. 2:215-32.

1969*b* Networks and Political Process. [Revised version of Barnes 1968.] In *Social Networks in Urban Situations,* ed. J. C. Mitchell. Manchester: Manchester University Press.

Barth, Fredrik
1966 *Models of Social Organization.* Occasional Papers of the Royal Anthropological Institute no. 23. London: Royal Anthropological Institute.

Barth, Fredrik, ed.
1963 *The Role of the Entrepreneur in Social Change in Northern Norway.* Bergen: Norwegian Universities Press.

Blau, Peter M.
1956 *Bureaucracy in Modern Society.* New York: Random House.
1964 *Exchange and Power in Social Life.* New York: Wiley.

Boissevain, Jeremy
1964 Factions, Parties, and Politics in a Maltese Village. *American Anthropologist* 66, no. 6:1275-87.
1966 Patronage in Sicily. *Man: Journal of the Royal Anthropological Institute of Great Britain and Ireland* 1, no. 1:18-33.
1968 The Place of Non-groups in the Social Sciences. *Man: Journal of the Royal Anthropological Institute of Great Britain and Ireland* 3, no. 4: 542-56.

Bott, Elizabeth
1955 Urban Families: Conjugal Roles and Social Networks. *Human Relations* 8, no. 4:345-84.
1957 *Family and Social Network.* London: Tavistock.
1960 Conjugal Role and Social Network. In *A Modern Introduction to the Family,* ed. N. Bell and E. Vogel. New York: Free Press of Glencoe, Macmillan.
1964 Family, Kinship, and Marriage. In *Man in Society: Patterns of Human Organization,* ed. Mary Douglas et al. London: MacDonald.

Bottomore, T. W.
1962 *Sociology: A Guide to Problems and Literature.* London: Allen & Unwin.

Campbell, J. K.
1964 *Honour, Family, and Patronage: A Study of Institutions and Moral Values in a Greek Mountain Community.* London: Oxford University Press.

Caplow, Theodore
1964 *Principles of Organization.* New York: Harcourt, Brace & World.

Chapple, Eliot D., and Conrad Arensberg
1940 Measuring Human Relations: An Introduction to the Study of Interaction of Individuals. *Genetic Psychology Monographs* 22, no. 1:3-147.

Chapple, Eliot D., and C. S. Coon
1947 *Principles of Anthropology.* New York: Holt.

Cohen, Abner
1969 Political Anthropology: The Analysis of the Symbolism of Power Relations. *Man: Journal of the Royal Anthropological Institute of Great Britain and Ireland* 4, no. 2:215-35.

Cohen, Yehudi A.
1969 Social Boundary Systems. *Current Anthropology* 10, no. 1:103-26.

Coleman, James, Elihu Katz, and Herbert Menzel
1957 The Diffusion of an Innovation Among Physicians. *Sociometry* 20, no. 4:253-70.

Crissman, Lawrence W.
1969 On Networks. *Cornell Journal of Social Relations* 4, no. 1:72-81.

Dahrendorf, Ralf
1959 *Class and Class Conflict in Industrial Society.* London: Routledge & Kegan Paul.

Davenport, William
1959 Nonunilinear Descent and Descent Groups. *American Anthropologist* 61, no. 4:557-72.

Douglass, William A.
1969 *Death in Murélaga: Funerary Ritual in a Spanish Basque Village.* Seattle: University of Washington Press.

Dumont, L.
1961 Descent, Filiation, and Affinity. *Man* 61, no. 11:24-25.

Eisenstadt, S. N.
1961 Anthropological Studies of Complex Societies. *Current Anthropology* 2, no. 3:201-22.

Emerson, Richard M.
1969 Operant Psychology and Social Exchange Theory. In *Behavioral Sociology*, ed. Robert Burgess and Donald Bushell. New York: Columbia University Press.

Epstein, A. L.
1958 *Politics in an Urban African Community*. Manchester: Manchester University Press.
1961 The Network and Urban Social Organization. *Rhodes-Livingstone Journal* 29:129-62.
1962 Immigrants to Northern Rhodesian Towns. Paper presented to section N (sociology) of the British Association for the Advancement of Science, Manchester, August 31.

Fallers, Lloyd A.
1956 *Bantu Bureaucracy: A Study of Integration and Conflict in the Political Institutions of an East African People*. Cambridge: Heffer.

Festinger, Leon, Stanley Schachter, and Kurt Back
1950 *Social Pressures in Informal Groups: A Study of a Housing Project*. New York: Harper.

Firth, Raymond T.
1951 *Elements of Social Organization*. New York: Philosophical Library.

Fortes, Meyer
1949a *The Web of Kinship Among the Tallensi: The Second Part of an Analysis of the Social Structure of a Trans-Volta Tribe*. London: Oxford University Press.
1949b Time and Social Structure: An Ashanti Case Study. In *Social Structure*, ed. M. Fortes. Oxford: Clarendon Press.
1953 The Structure of Unilineal Descent Groups. *American Anthropologist* 55, no. 1:17-41.
1969 *Kinship and the Social Order: The Legacy of Lewis Henry Morgan*. Chicago: Aldine.

Foster, George M.
1961 The Dyadic Contract: A Model for the Social Structure of a Mexican Peasant Village. *American Anthropologist* 63, no. 6:1173-92.
1963 The Dyadic Contract in Tzintzuntzan II: Patron-Client Relationships. *American Anthropologist* 65, no. 6: 1280-94.
1969 Godparents and Social Networks in Tzintzuntzan. *Southwestern Journal of Anthropology* 25, no. 3:261-78.

Freeman, J. D.
1961 On the Concept of Kindred. *Journal of the Royal Anthropological Institute of Great Britain and Ireland* 91, no. 2:192-200.

Freilich, Morris, ed.
1970 *Marginal Natives: Anthropologists at Work*. New York: Harper & Row.

Gans, Herbert
1962 *The Urban Villagers*. New York: Free Press, Macmillan.

Gerlach, Luther P., and Virginia H. Hine
1970 The Social Organization of a Movement of Revolutionary Change: Case Study, Black Power. In *Afro-American Anthropology: Contemporary Perspectives*, ed. N. E. Whitten, Jr., and J. F. Szwed. New York: Free Press, Macmillan.

Ginsberg, M.
1934 *Sociology*. London: Butterworth.

Gluckman, Max
1950 Kinship and Marriage Among the Lozi. . . and Zulu. In *African Systems of Kinship and Marriage*, ed. A. R. Radcliffe-Brown and D. Forde. London: Oxford University Press.

Goody, Jack, ed.
1958 *The Developmental Cycle in Domestic Groups*. Cambridge: At the University Press.
1962 *Death, Property, and the Ancestors*. Stanford: Stanford University Press.
1969 *Comparative Studies in Kinship*. Stanford: Stanford University Press.

Gouldner, Alvin
1960 The Norm of Reciprocity: A Preliminary Statement. *American Sociological Review* 25, no. 2:161-78.

Granovetter, Mark
n.d. The Strength of Weak Ties: Alienation Reconsidered. Mimeographed.

Greenfield, Sidney
1966 Patronage Networks, Factions, Political Parties, and National Integration in Contemporary Brazilian Society. Mimeographed.

Gutkind, P. C. W.
1965 African Urbanism: Mobility and Social Network. *International Journal of Comparative Sociology* 6, no. 1:48-60.

Hannerz, Ulf
1969 *Soulside: Inquiries into Ghetto Culture and Community.* New York: Columbia University Press.
1970 What Ghetto Males Are Like: Another Look. In *Afro-American Anthropology: Contemporary Perspectives,* ed. N. E. Whitten, Jr., and J. F. Szwed. New York: Free Press, Macmillan.

Harris, Marvin
1968 *The Rise of Anthropological Theory.* New York: Crowell.

Heider, Karl G.
1969 Visiting Trade Institutions. *American Anthropologist* 71, no. 3:462-71.

Homans, George C.
1961 *Social Behavior: Its Elementary Forms.* New York: Harcourt, Brace & World.

Jay, Edward J.
1964 The Concepts of "Field" and "Network" in Anthropological Research. *Man in India* 44, no. 177:137-39.

Josselin de Jong, J. P. B.
1952 *Lévi-Strauss's Theory on Kinship and Marriage.* London: E. J. Brill.

Leach, Edmund R.
1962 *Rethinking Anthropology.* London: Athlone Press.

Leeds, Anthony
1964 Brazilian Careers and Social Structure: A Case History and Model. *American Anthropologist* 66, no. 6, pt. 1:1321-47.

Lesser, A.
1961 Social Fields and the Evolution of Society. *Southwestern Journal of Anthropology* 17, no. 1:40-48.

Lévi-Strauss, Claude
1967 *Structural Anthropology.* Garden City, N.Y.: Anchor Books, Doubleday.
1969 *The Elementary Structures of Kinship.* Boston: Beacon Press. Originally published 1949.

Liebow, Elliot
1967 *Tally's Corner: A Study of Street Corner Men.* Boston: Little, Brown.

Luce, Robert Duncan
1950 Connectivity and Generalized Cliques in Sociometric Group Structure. *Psychometrika* 15, no. 2:169-90.

Mair, Lucy
1965 *An Introduction to Social Anthropology.* Oxford: Clarendon Press.

Malinowski, Bronislaw
1922 *Argonauts of the Western Pacific.* London: Routledge & Kegan Paul.

Mauss, Marcel
1954 *The Gift,* trans. I. Cunnison. Glencoe, Ill.: Free Press. Originally published 1924.

Maybury-Lewis, David
1967 *Akwẽ-Shavante Society.* London: Oxford University Press.

Mayer, Adrian C.
1962 System and Network: An Approach to the Study of Political Process in Dewas. In *Indian Anthropology: Essays in Memory of D. N. Majumdar,* ed. T. Madan and G. Sarana. Bombay: Asia Publishing House.
1966 The Significance of Quasi-Groups in the Study of Complex Societies. In *The Social Anthropology of Complex Societies,* ed. Michael Banton. ASA Monograph no. 4. New York: Praeger.

Mayer, Philip
1961 *Townsmen or Tribesmen: Conservatism and the Process of Urbanization in a South African City.* Cape Town: Oxford University Press.
1964 Labour Migrancy and the Social Network. In *Problems of Transition,* ed. J. F. Holleman et al., pp. 21-34. Proceedings of Social Sciences Research Conference, University of Natal, Durban, July 1962. Pietermaritzburg: Natal University Press.

Merton, Robert K.
1949 *Social Theory and Social Structure.* Glencoe, Ill.: Free Press.
1957 The Role-Set: Problems in Sociological Theory. *British Journal of Sociology* 8, no. 2:106-20.

Mitchell, J. Clyde
1959 The Study of African Urban Structures. In *International Conference on Housing and Urbanization, 2nd Ses-*

sion, Nairobi. London: Scientific Council for Africa South of the Sahara.

1966   Theoretical Orientations in African Urban Studies. In *The Social Anthropology of Complex Societies,* ed. Michael Banton. ASA Monograph no. 4. New York: Praeger.

1969   Norms, Networks, and Institutions. Paper delivered at Seminar on Network Approaches, Leiden University.

Mitchell, J. Clyde, ed.
1969   *Social Networks in Urban Situations.* Manchester: Manchester University Press.

Moreno, J. L.
1934   *Who Shall Survive?* Washington: Nervous and Mental Disease Publishing Co.
1953   *Who Shall Survive? Foundations of Sociometry, Group Psychotherapy, and Sociodrama.* Beacon, N.Y.: Beacon House.

Murdock, George P.
1949   *Social Structure.* New York: Macmillan.

Nadel, S. F.
1935   Nupe State and Community. *Africa* 8, no. 3:257-303.
1942   *A Black Byzantium: The Kingdom of Nupe in Nigeria.* London: Oxford University Press.
1951   *The Foundations of Social Anthropology.* Glencoe, Ill.: Free Press.
1957   *The Theory of Social Structure.* Glencoe, Ill.: Free Press.

Needham, Rodney
1962   *Structure and Sentiment.* Chicago: University of Chicago Press.

Nicholas, R. W.
1965   Factions: A Comparative Analysis. In *Political Systems and the Distribution of Power,* ed. Michael Banton. ASA Monograph no. 2. New York: Praeger.

Ore, Oystein
1962   *Theory of Graphs.* Providence: American Mathematical Society.

Parkin, David
1969   *Neighbors and Nationals in an African City Ward.* Berkeley and Los Angeles: University of California Press.

Parsons; Talcott
1949   *Essays in Sociological Theory.* Glencoe, Ill.: Free Press.

Phillpott, Stewart B.
1968   Remittance Obligations, Social Networks, and Choice Among Montserratian Migrants in Britain. *Man: Journal of the Royal Anthropological Institute of Great Britain and Ireland* 3, no. 3:465-76.

Platt, Jennifer
1969   Some Problems in Measuring the Jointness of Conjugal Role Relationships. *Sociology* 3, no. 3:287-97.

Plotnicov, Leonard
1967   *Strangers to the City: Urban Man in Jos, Nigeria.* Pittsburgh: University of Pittsburgh Press.

Pospisil, Leopold
1964   *The Kapauku Papuans of West New Guinea.* New York: Holt, Rinehart & Winston.

Radcliffe-Brown, A. R.
1965   *Structure and Function in Primitive Society.* New York: Free Press, Macmillan. Originally published 1952.

Redfield, Robert
1956   *Peasant Society and Culture: An Anthropological Approach to Civilization.* Chicago: University of Chicago Press.

Roethlisberger, F. J., and W. J. Dickson
1939   *Management and the Worker.* Cambridge: Harvard University Press.

Sahlins, Marshall D.
1965   On the Sociology of Primitive Exchange. In *The Relevance of Models for Social Anthropology,* ed. Michael Banton. ASA Monograph no. 1, New York: Praeger.

Scheurell, Robert, and Irwin Rinder
n.d.   Conjugal Roles in Lower Class Incest. Mimeographed.

Schneider, David M.
1965   Some Muddles in the Models: Or, How the System Really Works. In *The Relevance of Models for Social Anthropology,* ed. Michael Banton. ASA Monograph no. 1. New York: Praeger.

Schwartz, Norman B.
1969   Goal Attainment Through Factionalism: A Guatemalan Case. *American*

Anthropologist 71, no. 6:1088-1108.

Singh Uberoi, J. P.
1962 *Politics of the Kula Ring: An Analysis of the Findings of Bronislaw Malinowski.* Manchester: Manchester University Press.

Smith, Michael G.
1956 On Segmentary Lineage Systems. *Journal of the Royal Anthropological Institute of Great Britain and Ireland* 86, no. 2:39-80.

Southall, Aidan, ed.
1961 *Social Change in Modern Africa.* London: Oxford University Press.

Srinivas, Mysore N., and André Béteille
1964 Networks in Indian Social Structure. *Man* 64, no. 212:165-68.

Steward, Julian H., et al.
1956 *The People of Puerto Rico.* Urbana: University of Illinois Press.

Swift, R. G.
1967 Review of *Social Anthropology of Complex Societies,* ed. M. Banton. *Oceania* 37, no. 4:310-11.

Thibault, John, and Harold T. Kelly
1959 *The Social Psychology of Groups.* New York: Wiley.

Tilly, Charles
n.d.*a* Community, City, Urbanization. Mimeographed. Stanford: Center for Advanced Study in the Behavioral Sciences.
n.d.*b* On Uprooting, Kinship, and the Auspices of Migration. Mimeographed.

Turk, Herman
1970 Interorganizational Networks in Urban Society: Initial Perspectives and Comparative Research. *American Sociological Review* 35, no. 1:1-18.

Turner, Christopher
1967 Conjugal Roles and Social Networks: A Reexamination of an Hypothesis. *Human Relations* 20, no. 2:121-30.

Van Velsen, J.
1964 *The Politics of Kinship: A Study in Social Manipulation Among the Lakeside Tonga of Nyasaland.* Manchester: Manchester University Press.

Warner, W. Lloyd, and Paul S. Lunt
1941 *The Social Life of a Modern Community.* New Haven: Yale University Press.

Weber, Max
1947 The Theory of Social and Economic Organization, trans. A. M. Henderson and T. Parsons. Glencoe, Ill.: Free Press.
1958 Bureaucracy. In *From Max Weber: Essays in Sociology,* ed. and trans. H. H. Gerth and C. Wright Mills, pp. 196-244. New York: Oxford University Press.

Whitten, Norman E., Jr.
1965 *Class, Kinship, and Power in an Ecuadorian Town: The Negroes of San Lorenzo.* Stanford: Stanford University Press.
1968 Personal Networks and Musical Contexts in the Pacific Lowlands of Colombia and Ecuador. *Man: Journal of the Royal Anthropological Institute of Great Britain and Ireland* 3, no. 1:50-63.
1969 Strategies of Adaptive Mobility in the Columbian-Ecuadorian Littoral. *American Anthropologist* 71, no. 2:221-42.
1970*a* Network Analysis and Processes of Adaptation Among Ecuadorian and Nova Scotian Negroes. In *Marginal Natives: Anthropologists at Work,* ed. M. Freilich, chap. 8. New York: Harper & Row.
1970*b* Network Analysis in Ecuador and Nova Scotia: Some Critical Remarks. *Canadian Review of Sociology and Anthropology* 7, no. 4:269-80.

Whitten, Norman E., Jr., and John F. Szwed, eds.
1970*a* *Afro-American Anthropology: Contemporary Perspectives.* New York: Free Press, Macmillan.
1970*b* Introduction. In *Afro-American Anthropology,* ed. N. E. Whitten, Jr., and J. F. Szwed, pp. 23-62. New York: Free Press, Macmillan.

Whyte, William F.
1953 *Street Corner Society.* Chicago: University of Chicago Press.

Wirth, Louis
1938 Urbanism as a Way of Life. *American Journal of Sociology* 44, no. 1:1-24.

Wolf, Eric R.
1966 Kinship, Friendship, and Patron-Client Relations in Complex Soci-

eties. In *The Social Anthropology of Complex Societies,* ed. Michael Banton. ASA Monograph no. 4. New York: Praeger.

Wolfe, Alvin W.
1970 On Structural Comparisons of Networks. *Canadian Review of Sociology and Anthropology* 4, no. 7:226-44.

CHAPTER 17 Kinship, Descent, and Alliance

HAROLD W. SCHEFFLER

The line of descent runs through the males. As it was put to me, "The child comes from the man, and the woman only takes care of it." Berak said in regard to this, "I remember what old Boberi . . . said at Dandenong, when some of the boys were grumbling and would not listen to him. The old man got vexed, and said to his son, 'Listen to me! I am here, and there you stand with my body.' "

—Howitt 1904:255

So also the Afghan poet, complaining of his traitorous sons, writes: "My hand could reach them even now. But I would not destroy my own soul."

—Hearn 1879:165

I. INTRODUCTION

Subsystems[1] of social relations may be isolated for analytical and comparative purposes in either of two ways: by reference to the various kinds of rights and duties, or privileges and obligations, that comprise "what they are about," or by reference to the culturally defined kinds of actors (social persons or social identities[2]) to whom vari-

---

[1] As Beattie (1959:46) has observed, "social anthropologists do not study or compare 'whole' societies . . .; such a thing would be impossible." They must study subsystems of social relations and then attempt to determine whether or not, how, and to what degree these subsystems are related to one another. A critical task is to isolate social and cultural subsystems in a way that is "natural" to the object of study.

[2] Goodenough (1965:3) defines a social identity as "an aspect of self that makes a difference in how one's rights and duties distribute to specific others." As Goodenough notes, Linton (1936:113-15) and Merton (1957:368-70), among others, "tend to treat

ous rights, duties, and so on are ascribed or otherwise allocated (see Beattie 1959). Since the same kinds of rights and duties may be determined by different kinds of criteria in different societies, and different rights and duties may be prescribed by the same criteria in others, it is not usually possible to focus on both the actors and the rights and duties at the same time (see Goodenough 1970:397).

Relations of genealogical connection are widely (probably universally) posited and also accorded social significance as criteria for the allocation of rights and duties. Thus we may isolate, analyze, and compare subsystems of social relations on these grounds; that is, in terms of the genealogically defined kinds of social identities of which they are composed and between which their more or less distinctive right- and duty-statuses are distributed. Of course, the normative content of these social subsystems (i.e., "what they are about") is highly variable, as is their "importance" (however that may be measured) relative to the other subsystems of social relations with which they combine in particular cases. Such differences in the normative content and relative importance of genealogically ordered subsystems of social relations, as well as intersocietal differences in their inherent organization or structure and their modes of articulation or integration with other social subsystems, may be regarded as problems for sociological, ecological, or other forms of explanation.

That is to say, given an adequate analysis of the content and structure of any particular social or cultural subsystem (institution), we may then attempt to account for the occurrence of that institution in contrast to another (or others) of the same general sort in one or more of several (not necessarily mutually exclusive) ways. Such forms of explanation consist for the most part in further and progressively broader contextualization of the institution whose existence we wish to explain (see Gellner 1962).[3] Unfortunately, many anthropological attempts to account for the occurrence of particular institutions or for their differential distribution have rested on highly unsatisfactory concepts of the nature of the institutions themselves—that is, on inadequate structural analysis of them; or they have simply conflated structural analysis with other forms of "explanation" and thus foreshortened understanding of both the institutions and their "causes." This is nowhere more evident than in the study of systems of kinship, descent, and alliance.

II. GENEALOGICAL CONNECTION

The first and most important issue that has to be dealt with is what we mean, or what it is most useful to intend, by the term "genealogical connection." The sociological concern is with a criterion for the allocation of rights and duties that has currency across a

---

a social category together with its attached rights and duties as an indivisible unit of analysis, which they label a 'status' or 'position' in a social relationship." In so doing they fail to distinguish between the formal or *defining* characteristics of a social category and the more or less distinctive set of rights and duties (a "right- and duty-status," in Goodenough's terms) that attaches to it. It is clear from the examples given by Goodenough (1965:2) that this distinction must be made, for a great many otherwise highly laudable analyses have been muddled by failure to make it (see, e.g., Fortes 1969:50f, Witherspoon 1970). In this essay the term "status" is often employed as a brief designation for what Goodenough terms a "right- and duty-status."

---

[3] Gellner (1962:153) states that his argument "is concerned with the application of Functionalism to the interpretation of concepts and beliefs," but his argument applies equally to any sort of social system.

fairly broad range of societies.[4] There-fore, one of the things the term should *not* be taken to mean is relations of biological or genetic connection as such relations are understood in the science of biology, because such relationships are unknown to (i.e., not posited by) the vast majority of the world's peo-ples, and so they could not possibly serve for those peoples as criteria for the ordering of their social relations. Of course, this does not preclude use of the term to designate relationships such as "consanguinity" and the like, which *are* posited in various folk-cultural systems and which *do* serve as "grounds for assigning specific rights and duties, membership and status, to specific per-sons" (Barnes 1967*a*:101).

As Lévi-Strauss (1963:50) has ob-served, "A kinship system does not exist in the objective ties of descent or consanguinity between individuals: It exists only in human consciousness. . . ." In other words, the "kinship relations" of interest to the social or cultural an-thropologist are those "genealogical" connections whose existence is pre-sumed by or "known" to any people, not those posited by or known to any scientific discipline. Thus the founda-tion of any kinship system consists in a folk-cultural theory designed to ac-count for the fact that women give birth to children; i.e., a theory of hu-man reproduction. So far as we know, no human society is without such a theory. Of course, such theories are highly variable: notions about how women become pregnant, and about whether or not offspring share some physical or metaphysical substance

with their genetrices, are quite diverse. Yet it is reasonable to assert that, so far as we know, there is no society in which the identity "genetrix" is not posited. The Australian aboriginal cases cited by Montagu (1937) do not consti-tute evidence to the contrary, for al-though many peoples (not just some Australian aborigines) do not suppose that the "female parent contribute[s] anything whatsoever of a physical or spiritual nature to the being of the child," no culture denies the simple fact, accessible to the observation of all men, that women give birth to children after a period of gestation of the fetus in the womb. The unique relationship of bearer-offspring is everywhere ac-knowledged or, more accurately, posited, and the local language terms designating the two poles of this rela-tionship may be glossed as "genetrix" and "offspring." Of course, the forms of social significance attributed to this relationship are quite diverse, but this should not be allowed to obscure the fact that the relationship itself is a cul-tural universal.

The possibility that there might be some societies in which "the role of sexual intercourse in reproduction is unknown," and therefore in which the identity "genitor" (the male comple-ment of the female identity "genetrix") is not posited, greatly excited the imag-inations of early anthropologists. In-deed, Malinowski (1937:xxiii) once described "the question of primitive nescience of paternity" as "the most exciting and controversial issue in the comparative science of Man." Reports of "ignorance of paternity" were at one time quite common (see Frazer 1910; Malinowski 1930*a*, 1963; Montagu 1937 for reviews of these reports) and were often cited in support of diverse (and sometimes mutually contradicto-ry) "evolutionary," sociological, and psychological theories. By and large,

---

[4] Although I have suggested that this criterion is a cultural universal, insofar as the ethnographic rec-ord permits such an assertion about any element of culture, it should be obvious that the sociological interest of the criterion is not contingent on its pos-sible universality. It is an important element where it exists, and that is what matters here.

however, such reports have been proven distorted, false, or at least open to serious question on a number of grounds, including reliability of evidence and the facile ethnocentric assumption that many "savages" are not just ignorant but also intellectually inferior and thus incapable of making the observations or inferences that would lead them to posit the existence and necessity of genitors (see Read 1918).

Of course there are a number of peoples who posit no "physical" connection between presumed genitor and offspring in the sense that they do not suppose that genitor and offspring share any physical substance such as blood, bone, or flesh. But all of these peoples do posit the existence and necessity of genitors: they may suppose that genitor and offspring share some metaphysical substance such as their souls (Lahontan 1905:461-67, Malinowski 1963:180); or that semen functions to activate or vivify the fetus, which owes its physical substance solely to the genetrix (Richards 1950:222); or that semen or copulation functions to form or shape the fetus so that offspring may be presumed necessarily to resemble their genitors in some aspect of their appearance (Malinowski 1929a: 207-208, Austen 1934, Powell 1969b:603, Thomson 1933:506-507).[5] In these cases, as in others (see Leach 1961:10f), certain qualities of paternal genealogical connection are held to contrast with certain qualities of maternal genealogical connection, but in other respects both kinds of genealogical connection are held to be the same: both are regarded as necessary and complementary products of reproductive processes[6] and both are regarded as inalienable; that is, once they are es-

tablished they cannot be undone, and they cannot be established in any other way.

In a few cases it has been reported that the existence and necessity of genitors is not presumed, for it is not presumed that pregnancy is a consequence of a specific act, or even of repeated acts, of sexual intercourse; it results instead from the activities of certain spiritual entities (Frazer 1910; Malinowski 1916, 1929a, 1963; Montagu 1937). Recent clarification of the most famous cases of this sort has shown that these early reports were based on a misunderstanding: the spiritual agents are held to be responsible for *vivification* of the fetus rather than for its conception per se, which is held to result from sexual intercourse and the conjunction of substances from the bodies of the genitor and genetrix (Meggitt 1962:270f; Powell 1956:277-78, 1968; cf. Frazer 1910, iv:57f). Meggitt's and Powell's observations suggest that where spiritual agents are alleged to play a part in reproduction, and especially where those entities have marked ritual significance, male informants (upon whom ethnographers have tended too strongly to rely) may emphasize them in their accounts of reproduction. The men perceive no contradictions between their accounts and the straightforward sexual accounts typically offered by female informants, not because their knowledge of the latter is "repressed" (Malinowski 1927; Montagu 1937) or because the

---

[5] See Singer (1959:505) on a somewhat similar theory formulated by Aristotle.

[6] Folk-cultural "knowledge" of these processes is seldom if ever sufficiently similar to the scientifically

known "biological facts" to merit the rather grand label "physiological," and thus of course most peoples, including most Europeans, are "ignorant of the facts of physiological paternity" in some sense. The precise sense given to the term "physiological" is particularly critical to the arguments for or against "primitive nescience of paternity," and most anthropological discussions of this matter have been insufficiently clear about just what it is that a people would have to "know" about "the facts of procreation" in order to be described as knowledgeable rather than ignorant.

account commonly given by the men[7] is a "religious dogma" appropriate to certain social contexts (see Leach 1967a, Dixon 1968, Spiro 1968), but because the two accounts are only complementary parts of a larger whole.

The few remaining reports of ignorance of paternity, because of an alleged failure to attribute to sexual intercourse a necessary part in the reproductive process, at least in human beings (see Schneider 1968a:127-28), may rest on similar failures of communication between ethnographers and informants. While these cases cannot fairly be dismissed out of hand, or on the basis of inferences from apparently similar cases, the evidence concerning them *is* equivocal (see especially Schneider 1968a:128, and cf. Malinowski 1932; Rentoul 1931, 1932), and it is probably safe to conclude (tentatively) that the relationships of genetrix-offspring and genitor-offspring are complementary cultural universals.

If each individual is assumed to be immediately genealogically connected to two other individuals, it follows that he is less immediately related to many others, those who are so connected to his parents and children, if he has any. In many societies all individuals presumed to be genealogically connected to a given other individual, though perhaps only within a limited range, are conceptually aggregated into a single category. The verbal label for this category, where such a label exists, is appropriately glossed as "kin" or "kindred."

III. THE CONCEPT OF SOCIAL KINSHIP

It has often been argued that a cross-culturally useful definition of kinship cannot rest exclusively on the notion of genealogical connection; a broadly relevant concept of kinship must take account of and be defined by social and not only genealogical relationships (Malinowski 1930a, 1963; Radcliffe-Brown 1950:4; Beattie 1964; Schneider 1969). Insofar as the argument rests on the presumption that there are societies in which the identity "genitor" is not posited, it now seems quite unnecessary; and even if a few such societies did exist, it might just as well (perhaps better) be said that paternal kinship is a concept that is alien to them. It would rob these societies (if any such societies really do exist) of one of their most interesting and distinctive cultural features to attempt to redefine kinship in such a way that they too could be said to "recognize" (i.e., posit) relations of paternal kinship. Insofar as the argument rests on the presumption that there are some, perhaps many, societies that posit genealogical connections but ascribe little or no social significance to them, it is somewhat more difficult to refute, though no less unnecessary and misleading (see Scheffler 1970a).

The issue here is the necessity and sociological utility of Malinowski's (1930a) "principle of legitimacy" and of his and Radcliffe-Brown's concept of "social kinship" as something greater than, though inclusive of, social relations ascribed on the basis of genealogical connection.

Malinowski argued (1930a [1962: 65]) that although the existence of genitors is not always posited, and although it may confer no rights or duties on the reputed genitor even when it is posited, it still is possible to maintain that

---

[7] That is, given by male informants to anthropologists. Powell (1956:278) notes that he was told that the Trobriand sexual theory of reproduction "was 'women's and children's talk' . . . what *fathers* or their sisters told children as they became old enough to take more than a childish sexual interest in the opposite sex" (emphasis added).

kinship is universally bilateral, for in every society we find the "moral and legal rule ... that no child should be brought into the world without a man—and one man at that—assuming the role of ... guardian and protector, the male link between the child and the rest of the community." This "role," he noted, is often ascribed to the genitor, but it is often the case that if the genitor is to claim his rights as such he must be married to the genetrix, and if he is not these rights may be claimed by her husband. Even in the Trobriand Islands, he argued, where the existence of genitors is not posited, conception and birth out of wedlock are disapproved for the simple reason that the child then has no mother's husband to serve as its "social father," and every child must have a "social father." Similarly, Radcliffe-Brown (1950:4) argued that "social fatherhood is usually determined by marriage," as though it were generally the case that a man who is not married to the genetrix of his offspring has no rights in respect of them as their genitor, and if the genetrix is married to another man, that man is entitled to claim the offspring as his own for any and all social purposes. As Radcliffe-Brown understood them, proverbs such as "Children belong to the man to whom the bed belongs" (W. R. Smith 1963:132-33) express this legal or jural arrangement. More recently, Goodenough (1970:385, 396) has argued that "we cannot deal with jural fatherhood without reference to marriage," because "although fatherhood may be conceived as the rights a man has in the children he has begotten, his only sure claim to being their begetter derives from his being their mother's husband."

Now it is quite generally the case that establishing genealogical connections (i.e., engendering and bearing children) out of wedlock is disapproved

and subject to strong negative sanctions. Where this is so, premarital and adulterine genitors and genetrices and their offspring may be deprived of certain (but not necessarily all) rights and duties in respect of one another, and in respect of their kin, which would be theirs if the genealogical relationship had been established in wedlock. However, the role of marriage in conditioning entitlement to the rights and duties of parentage, and of any other social identities and statuses that might be determined by reference to one's parentage, can be (and often has been) considerably overemphasized and misrepresented.

It is essential to distinguish between at least two kinds of rights that a man may or may not acquire by marriage to a woman, and which are pertinent, though in quite different ways, to rights and duties in respect of her offspring. These are rights *in uxorem* (i.e., rights of exclusive[8] sexual access) and rights *in genetricem* (i.e., rights in the reproductive capacity of the woman and therefore entitlement to certain rights in respect of her offspring, such as custody or possession regardless of their presumed paternity). The former rights are perhaps a universal feature of the marriage contract (Goodenough 1970:395); the latter certainly are not.

It is often taken as a legal presumption (but as a rule of evidence, *not* a rule of substantive law) that a woman's

---

[8] It might be better to say more or less exclusive, for there are many societies in which certain kinsmen (usually brothers) of a man have rights of sexual access to his wife, but it is usually only by virtue of the woman's marriage to the man that other men acquire such lower priority rights of sexual access to her (Goodenough 1970:395). However, in societies (such as Siriono; see Holmberg 1950) where men have rightful claims over particular kinds of kinswomen as potential wives, sexual relations prior to marriage are often permitted between such kin, and the privilege may continue after marriage to other persons.

husband (i.e., the man who holds the right of exclusive sexual access to her) is the genitor of her offspring. But this presumption, which is sometimes expressed in proverbs like the one cited above, is widely regarded as rebuttable. It rests on the further assumptions that the husband has been exercising his marital (sexual) rights and that they have not been infringed by another man; and where there is evidence that these assumptions are false and the husband did not engender his wife's offspring, the identity of genitor and the rights and duties entailed by it may be claimed by or ascribed to the man who is the presumptive genitor (see Nokes 1957:158, James 1957, Kay 1965, Forde 1950:291-93, and Gluckman 1950:187-89). In some cases the rights of adulterine or premarital genitors extend to custody of their offspring (Forde 1950:291-93; Leach 1954:166; Goswami 1960:87, 1963; Parry 1928:21f; Bender 1970:84), and thus in some cases the genitor who is not the mother's husband may successfully claim his offspring even though the mother's husband may not wish to disclaim them.[9] To claim these rights a man must of course acknowledge that he is the genitor, and this he may have to do formally by paying a fine or compensation to the husband or the father of the genetrix. In some cases, however, the testimony of the genetrix is regarded as sufficient to establish the identity of the genitor for whatever legal purposes may be relevant (van Velsen 1964:122, 124).

The rebuttable legal presumption that a woman's offspring is also the offspring of her husband is, again, a pre-

sumption concerning the evidence for paternity, not the legal definition of "paternity" or "fatherhood," as Malinowski, Radcliffe-Brown, and others appear to have supposed. This presumption serves to prevent arbitrary disinheritance through arbitrary disavowal of paternity, and it is designed at least as much to protect the interests of offspring and their mothers as it is to protect the interests of men in their wives (W. R. Smith 1963:139). Thus it is not surprising that an adulterine or premarital genitor may be ascribed certain duties but largely prohibited from claiming extensive rights in respect of his offspring, and his offspring may be fully entitled to certain rights and duties in respect of him, his kin, or his descent group (see, e.g., Fortes 1949a:27). In many cases, of course, adulterine and premarital children may effectively be prevented from claiming their rights in respect of their genitors and their genitors' kin by the fact that their "illegitimacy" and/or their genitors' identities may be kept secret from them, or by the stigma that may attach to "illegitimacy" and the consequent reluctance to acknowledge the relationship publicly. It is sometimes necessary to acknowledge it, however, as when individuals who are closely related by extramarital genealogical ties, not heretofore known to them, contemplate marriage—for it is generally the case (though often overlooked by ethnographers and theoreticians) that incest taboos apply to extramarital as well as to "legitimate" kinship relations. In any event, pragmatic limitations do not change the fact that in many societies men may claim rights or be ascribed duties in respect of their offspring, and their offspring in respect of them and their kin, regardless of the fact that the men in question were not entitled to engender those offspring to begin with, and even though other men may hold

---

[9] Of course, the burden of proof is usually on the one who would upset the rebuttable claim of the mother's husband. In some cases, however, an extramarital genitor who may not wish to claim custody of his child may still have to acknowledge his paternity for "ritual" reasons (see, e.g., Fortes 1950:266).

rights of sexual access over the genetrices of those children.

Among some peoples a man may acquire rights *in genetricem* in respect of his wife, in which case any children born to her while he holds those rights are regarded as his for whatever legal purposes may be involved, even if he himself should acknowledge that he is not their genitor. In some societies, such rights are dependent on the payment of a bride-price or on the size of the bride-price (Rehfisch 1960, Williamson 1962).

Among the Nuer a child belongs to the lineage of the man who holds rights *in genetricem* over its genetrix,[10] whether or not he is presumed to be the genitor, and in many cases he is not. In some cases the man in question is deceased and rights of sexual access to his wife have passed to his brother or lineage mate, and in others he is sterile and has chosen another man to engender a child for him. In the extreme case, a woman may acquire rights *in genetricem* in respect of another woman and choose a man to engender a child for her, and she then has the legal or jural status of "father" of that child. That is to say, she is regarded as the genitor of that child for many social purposes, but of course she is not regarded as its genitor in the literal sense. Here too the normal and ideal situation is regarded as that in which genitor and mother's husband are one and the same man, and it is only a legal fiction, with a limited range of relevance, that the mother's husband is the genitor regardless of any evidence to the contrary. The known genitor, in any case, is accorded certain rights and duties in re-

---

[10] In many African societies (e.g., Zande) a child belongs to the lineage of its genitor regardless of marital status, and there are many societies in which lineage or clan affiliation cannot be altered or transferred by acts of adoption; that is to say, this identity is inalienable.

spect of his offspring: when a man's daughter marries he is entitled to receive a set portion of her bride-price, regardless of the condition of his paternity, and the prohibitions on sexual intercourse and marriage based on genealogical propinquity are applicable whether or not the relationship is "legitimate" (Evans-Pritchard 1951).

None of this is to deny that it is generally true that, where genitor-offspring (or genetrix-offspring) relations are created out of wedlock, the parties to them are deprived of *some* (perhaps even the majority) of the rights and duties they would otherwise enjoy in respect of one another or in respect of their kin or descent groups. Yet the ethnographic record offers little if any reliable evidence that genealogical relations established out of wedlock are ever totally discounted–i.e., regarded as wholly immaterial to social relationships of any kind. Thus it seems unwarranted to suggest (as some anthropologists have) that only "legitimate" genealogical connections (i.e., only those established in wedlock) are acknowledged or recognized for social purposes, or to conclude (as some anthropologists have) that "the unit of structure from which a kinship system is built up is the . . . 'elementary family,' consisting of a man, his wife and their child or children, whether or not they are living together" (Radcliffe-Brown 1941 [1952:51]; cf. Lévi-Strauss 1963:50-51). The qualification "whether or not" they are living together dissociates the definition of the elementary structures (relations) of kinship from the "elementary" or "nuclear" family as a *domestic* unit, and this is surely necessary, but it does not dissociate that definition from the criterion of "legitimacy," which dissociation is also necessary. After all, social relations based on "illegitimate" genealogical connections *do* exist, and so far no good reasons have been advanced to justify treating them as though they were somehow not part of the kinship systems of the societies in which they occur.

Furthermore, there are some societies in which a domestic union between a man and a woman does not become fully established as a marriage until the couple has produced offspring (see Radcliffe-Brown 1950:49). Among the Siriono, for example, it appears that individuals become related as "spouses" only *after* they have become related as cocontributors to the being of another individual (see Scheffler and Lounsbury 1971). Of course, even in this case it is not the simple fact of having jointly begotten offspring that makes a man and woman husband and wife, for it seems that they must also have entered previously into a contract whereby they entitled each other to certain domestic rights and duties in respect of one another and jointly to beget offspring. Yet this contract is insufficient to make them husband and wife; only offspring jointly produced within the context of a domestic union can do that. It might reasonably be argued that in this society one cannot "legally" be a husband or wife without first being a parent, rather than vice versa. Of course, even where this may not be the case, a woman's fecundity may be so highly prized that her bearing of a child prior to marriage may be regarded as a demonstration of her potential value as a wife, rather than as a stigma (see Malinowski 1929*b* [1962:7], 1930*a* [1962: 63-64]; Riviere 1969:166).

The elementary relations of any kinship system are best defined as those of genitor-offspring and genetrix-offspring per se (Malinowski 1927:vii; cf. Lévi-Strauss 1963:46). While these relations are universally conceived as inalienable, as "in the nature of things," the relationship of husband and wife, in con-

trast, is typically regarded as a purely social or contractual one that may be undone and which may or may not exist between the genitor and genetrix of any particular individual, no matter how strongly it may be felt that it should exist between them. It is a source of considerable concern to most of the world's peoples that it is possible to create relations of genealogical connection out of wedlock. But rather than simply ignore or discount any relations that may be so established, people tend to impose many of the duties normatively entailed by them while at the same time depriving the genitors or genetrices of many or all of their "natural" rights. While it is important to note that a man's entitlement to some or most of his rights and duties as genitor of his offspring may be denied him if he did not have the right to engender them in the first place, he remains their genitor whether he had that right or not, and this fact is never totally discounted for social purposes.

According to Rivers (1915:700) and Radcliffe-Brown (1950:4), there are societies in which, though the existence and necessity of genitors and genetrices are posited, the relationships count for little or nothing unless ratified by some social process such as adoption. Radcliffe-Brown asserted: "The complete social relationship between parent and child may be established not by birth but by adoption as it was practiced in ancient Rome and is practiced in many parts of the world today." (Unfortunately, Radcliffe-Brown neglected to specify any of the other cases he had in mind.) The falsity of this argument has been demonstrated elsewhere (Scheffler 1970*a*) and need not be demonstrated again here. It may be noted, however, that the practices in question are not aptly described as adoption; they are rather customary means (rites) whereby a man acknowledges his acceptance of his presumptive paternity, and it is the presumptive genitor who has the right (sometimes the duty) to perform them.

Legitimate or not, parentage in the strict genealogical sense—not in the metaphorical sense given to the term by Malinowski (1930a) and others—remains an irreducible element in all cultural and social systems and is everywhere ascribed moral, if not legal, significance as the basis of some irreducible and binding set of rights and duties. There appears to be no need to define "jural fatherhood" as anything other than the rights and duties a man has in respect of the children he has begotten, though of course there are many situations in which most of these rights and duties may be allocated to another man, who is then, by legal fiction, treated as though he were the genitor.

IV. KINSHIP SYSTEMS VS. DESCENT SYSTEMS

If a society is to order social relations among its members by reference to presumed relations of genealogical connection, it may do so in either or both of two ways; and it is highly important for the anthropologist to keep them conceptually distinct, since they are always distinguished in the cultures that employ both of them. The failure to keep them distinct or to recognize the necessity of the distinction has led to a great deal of difficulty in ethnographic description and comparison (see Wake 1967, Radcliffe-Brown 1929, Malinowski 1930a, Fortes 1969 for discussions of the history of the problem).

The first of these ways is egocentrically, by focusing on each person individually and subdividing the totality of persons considered to be genealogically connected to him (his kindred) into a number of lesser categories—categories of kin.[11] If each of these categories is

ascribed a more or less distinctive set of rights and duties with respect to Ego, and vice versa, each person is then the center or hub of a system of social relations. (To the extent that some of Ego's rights in respect of alter are rights *in rem*,[12] the constituent social relations of this subsystem are not simply dyadic.)

The other way in which social relations may be ordered by reference to relations of genealogical connection is in terms of common descent. By focusing on a few (usually deceased) individuals, all persons recognized as descendants or as some specified type of descendant of each of these selected individuals may be deemed to constitute a distinct set. Again, distinctive statuses may be ascribed to members of these sets vis-à-vis one another, or with respect to nonmembers in general or special types of nonmembers (e.g., individuals who are related genealogically to the putative founder or apical ancestor of the set but not in the way required for inclusion in the set).

In the following discussion the egocentric systems of social identities and statuses are described as *kinship systems*, and the ancestor-oriented as *descent systems*. Although these terms are used here to designate systems of social identities *and* their associated right- and duty-statuses, it should be kept in mind that these systems are defined and are most clearly distinguishable by the foci of their respective subcategories: the

---

[11] These categories are not necessarily labeled by the single lexeme forms usually described as kinship terms. See pt. V for further discussion of this point.

[12] Rights *in personam* are "rights over a person imposing some duty or duties upon that person"; rights *in rem* are rights over a person or a "thing" as against the world, i.e., "imposing duties on all other persons in respect of that particular person [or thing]" (Radcliffe-Brown 1952:32-33). See Hoebel (1954:46-63) for an important discussion of various kinds of rights and duties.

subcategories of a kinship system are egocentric; those of a descent system are ancestor-oriented.

The distinction being made here may be illustrated by brief reference to certain Tallensi categories; e.g., *soog* (plural, *saaret*). Goody (1961:11) describes this as an "unnamed complementary [noncorporate] uterine [matrilineal] descent group." Although Fortes (1949a: 31-32; 1969:54-55) states that the concept *soog* "involves the idea of matrilineal descent in contrast to that of patrilineal descent," he also describes *saaret* as "uterine kin"; that is, as an egocentric category consisting of persons related consanguineally but only through women. There are as many sets of *saaret* in Tallensi society as there are women who have borne surviving offspring. The fact that individuals who are *soog* to one another may trace their genealogical connection through a common maternal ancestress (as opposed to a common female parent or mother)[13] does not make *soog* a descent category, for *soog* is egocentrically defined; this is clear from the fact that the *saaret* of the ancestress in question include all of her uterine kin, not just her uterine descendants. Moreover, no set of *saaret* ever forms a group by virtue of its common ancestry; as Fortes puts it, "uterine descent [i.e., kinship] is maintained as a purely personal bond."

Thus, in the terms used in this essay, *soog* is a category belonging to the kinship system of Tallensi society (but cf. Scheffler 1966:543). The Tallensi designate the categories of their (patri-

lineal) descent system generically by means of terms derived from other realms of discourse (Fortes 1949a: 10-11); i.e., a lineage of any order may be described as the "house" (*yir*) of the founding ancestor, a metaphor common to many societies in Africa and elsewhere, and, continuing with the metaphor, Tallensi designate any segment of a more inclusive lineage as a "room" (*dug*). (The designation employed is relative to the context of discourse; any lineage but the most inclusive is either a "house" or a "room," depending on whether it is being considered independently or as a subunit of a higher order unit.) Lineages may also be described as the "children" (*biis*) of the founding ancestor; no doubt the term is here used in the sense of "offspring" or "descendants." Thus coordinate segments of a lineage group may be described as "brother" (*sunzo*) lineages, and their rights and duties with respect to one another are modeled on the mutual relations of brothers. Further still, lineages may be described as related to one another as "mother's brother" to "sister's son." That is, the Tallensi employ kinship terms (by extension) to describe genealogical and social relations between lineages as such.

Similar applications of kinship concepts and terms to describe relations between units of descent systems have often been misconstrued by anthropologists who argue that these are not simple extensions of kinship terms; the so-called kinship terms are really words that designate subcategories of descent groups and relations between individuals as members of such groups (see, e.g., Beattie 1958, 1964; Needham 1962). Systems of kin classification are discussed in Part V; it will be sufficient to note here that the falsity of this interpretation is demonstrated by cases like the following.

---

[13] On the distinction between "filial" (or parent-child) and "descent" (ancestor-descendant) relations, see Fortes (1959:206-207; 1969:280-81). In the terms employed here the minimal ancestor-descendant relationship is that of grandparent to grandchild; that is, a child is not here described as a descendant of his or her parent except within the context of a discussion of relations of common descent (see also Forde 1963).

The Nuer (Evans-Pritchard 1951) distinguish between *mar* and *buth*, relations of genealogical connection between individuals and patrilineages (*thok dwiel*) respectively. The individuals classified by any Nuer under one or another Nuer kinship term are more specific kinds of *mar*; they are *not* kinds of *buth*, though in the Nuer case, as in the Tallensi, relations between lineages as such are often described by means of kinship terms. Similarly, in the Baniata language (Scheffler 1972a), one distinguishes between *ia finomo*, kinsmen, and *rana*, which may be employed egocentrically to designate one's uterine kin or with reference to a specific ancestor to designate a matriclan. However, individuals classified under one or another Baniata kinship term are more specific kinds of *ia finomo*; they are not describable as kinds of *rana*. In the Varisi language of Choiseul Island (Scheffler 1965), people distinguish between *onotona* and *sinangge. Onotona*, an egocentric term, may be glossed as "kin," and persons referred to by this term are subdivided into a number of specific kin categories. *Sinangge* refers to relations of common cognatic descent, to genealogical relations between individuals (or sets of individuals) as comembers of one or another cognatic descent category or group. Whereas each person's *onotona* are divided into a number of lesser categories, each *sinangge* is divided into only two categories, defined and distinguished by the type of genealogical connection that relates their members to the putative founder of the unit: *popondo valeke* and *popondo nggole,* i.e. patrilineal and nonpatrilineal descendants of that apical ancestor. Incidentally, of course, two individuals who are patrilineal descendants of the putative founder of a *sinangge* are also agnatic kin of one another, but the Choiseulese do not distinguish this relationship either categorically or jurally[14] as a special type of *kinship* relation. That is, there are no special agnatic *kinship* categories or statuses; though patrilineal descent from the founder of the group does entitle one to certain special rights over the estate of the group, this does not entail any distinct status relationships between agnatic kin as such (see Scheffler 1965).

To all appearances, all societies have kinship systems (as defined above), and a great many have descent systems as well. Of course, the kinship and descent systems of different societies may differ markedly in their normative content, in their significance (however that may be measured) relative to one another and to other social subsystems, and in the precise ways in which they

---

[14] "Jural" is here used as a general cover term for rights and duties in general, regardless of their mode of sanction, as per Radcliffe-Brown (1935 [1952:32f]). Later, however, in an apparent attempt to deal with some of the difficulties presented by his faulty conceptualization of the relationship between kinship and descent systems, Radcliffe-Brown (1950:77-78) began to distinguish jural relations as a special class of social relations whose sanctioning somehow involves a notion of "justice," though he did not explicate what he meant by justice. For a similar distinction see Fortes (1969:87f). Without denying the validity of the distinction that may have to be made between kinds of social relations on the basis of the kinds of sanctions to which they are subject, we may still acknowledge, as Radcliffe-Brown did, that notions of right and duty may be involved in what he termed "personal relations" sanctioned by "affection, esteem and attachment." In his later position Radcliffe-Brown tended too much in the direction of Malinowski, who, in his treatment of the Trobriand case, described the norms (rights and duties) of paternal kinship as though they were wholly emotional or sentimental reactions to the failure of the society to give any legal recognition to the "natural" interests of men in their offspring (see Malinowski 1926:100f)—that is, as though they involved no concepts of right and duty at all. But it is clear from his ethnographic descriptions that they do. Powell's (1956) distinction between the "formal" and "informal" structures of Trobriand society is of the same order; it is merely a distinction between the Trobriand kinship and descent systems.

complement one another. Formal similarities between the kinship or descent systems of different societies (i.e., similarities in the ways in which their respective subcategories are defined) are not necessarily indicative of any functional similarities. It is not unusual to find more than one of each type of genealogically ordered system in the same society. A society may have multiple systems of kin classification (vocative and referential systems being the most obvious examples), or more than one type of descent group (e.g., patrilineal and matrilineal groups, as in so-called double-descent systems).

The present conceptualization of kinship and descent systems should be compared with that of Radcliffe-Brown, Malinowski, and others (see, e.g., Lowie 1920, Schneider 1961:3-4, 1967). Radcliffe-Brown (1929) defined kinship as "genealogical connection recognized for social purposes and made the basis of the customary organization of social relations." By descent he referred to "kinship" traced "through males" or "through females" exclusively and "given more importance [than other kinds of genealogical connection] for social purposes," specifically group affiliation—"the entrance of an individual into a certain social group as being the child of a member of that group" (see also Radcliffe-Brown 1952:39). Malinowski, with obvious reference to relations of common descent, wrote of societies in which there is a "legal overemphasis on one side of kinship" (1929c, 1930b). That is to say, both failed to distinguish between the postulation of relations of genealogical connection as such and the ascription of social significance to these cultural constructs (and conflated the two in their definition of kinship). Both then went on to conceptualize the descent system of a society as a subsystem of its kinship system, which was held to consist

in the totality of social relations ascribed on the basis of genealogical connection. Relations of descent were conceived as a special class of relations of kinship, differentiated from the larger class principally by the kind and degree of "social emphasis" put on them.

Wake in 1889 and Thomas in 1906 argued similarly, but they used the terms "kinship," "descent," and "relationship" somewhat differently. Wake (1967:254f) used "relationship" to refer to the "fact" of genealogical connection per se and without regard to any possible attribution of social significance. He argued that relationship in this sense is probably universally bilateral. By "kinship" he referred to a "special" kind of social relationship based on one or another kind of acknowledged genealogical connection, and he argued that "kinship, as distinguished from mere relationship," is "restricted to one line of descent"—i.e., to one of the two "lines" of parent-child relationship. It is clear that he was using "kinship" in the same way in which Rivers (1924:85f) was later to employ "descent": to refer to the status of group affiliation as determined by relationship of genealogical connection. This usage of "kinship" seems curious today, but it is quite understandable and probably was not idiosyncratic. It seems to rest on the etymological relationship of "kin" to "kind," by virtue of which a relationship of kinship may be construed as "being of the same kind," in the restricted sense of belonging to the same social group.

Two objections to conceiving of descent systems as subsystems of kinship systems may be noted here. First, egocentric and ancestor-centered systems, where found together, are not in fact two subsystems of any larger genealogically defined system. Certainly, both types of system are constructed of relations of genealogical connection, and the two systems necessarily overlap because individuals related by common descent are also related as kin. (Thus, as we have seen, kinship terms may be extended and used to describe relations between members of the same or different descent units or between the units themselves.) But the respective foci of the categories of the two systems are quite different, and so the two systems are related only as complementary subsystems of the larger social system, not as the two parts of a larger genealogically constituted system. Conceiving of their interrelations as Radcliffe-Brown, Malinowski, and others did may lead to conceiving of one as somehow (historically, structurally, or in some other way) "primary" and the other as "derivative" of it. Attempts to refute arguments to this effect have led in turn to arguments that the distinction between kinship and descent systems is itself spurious (at least in certain cases), and that what we have to deal with in fact is a single genealogically constituted system (see, e.g., M. G. Smith 1956, Lévi-Strauss 1969, Needham 1962).[15] In these latter arguments it is usually the kinship system that suffers.

The second difficulty is that conceiving of kinship and descent systems as subsystems of a larger genealogically constituted system may lead the analyst to minimize, ignore, or otherwise misconstrue the fact that in many cases the same individuals have identities and statuses relative to one another in *both* the kinship and descent systems (as defined above). Most often this miscon-

struction has taken the form of a description in which the descent-conferred identities and statuses of two individuals are treated as their sole genealogically defined identities and statuses in relation to one another, and their identities and statuses as kinds of kin are either overlooked or analytically merged with their identities and statuses conferred by common descent. Thus, for example, with reference to a society featuring matrilineal descent groups, social relations between men and their sisters' sons have often been described as though they were of only one sort, the sort ascribed between lineage or clan mates, whereas in fact we may (and usually do) have to distinguish between their social relations as mothers' brothers and sisters' sons (i.e., as types or kinds of kin) *and* as lineage or clan mates. Similarly, social relations between men and their offspring may be described as though they were of only one sort, the sort ascribed between men and the lineage or clan mates of their wives (see Malinowski's [1935] and Powell's [1956, 1969a, 1969b] accounts of Trobriand society; but cf. Robinson [1962], Sider [1967]); but, again, what we really have to deal with are two different identity and status relations between the same individuals. It so happens that the particular genealogical connection that makes them particular kinds of kin also places them relative to one another in the descent system, but in the descent system their mutual kinship identities and statuses may be quite irrelevant.

The formal difference between relations of kinship and relations of common descent entails certain functional differences. Kinship relates or opposes *individuals* to one another; one's jural status as a kind of kinsman is necessarily a status with respect to another individual who is one's kinsman of the reciprocal category, though where rights

---

[15] Needham goes so far as to deny that relations of genealogical connection are significant structural components of societies he claims are ordered by concepts of "prescriptive alliance." While the concept of a descent group is critical to his theory of alliance systems, Needham has yet to explain what a descent group is if it is not a group of persons related by common ascendant genealogical connections.

in rem are at issue (as in the case of a Trobriand man's right to bestow his daughter in marriage; see Robinson 1962), third parties may also be involved, but as "private persons." Relations of common descent, in contrast, necessarily relate or oppose *sets* of individuals to one another or to other sets of the same structural order (see Schneider 1967; Fortes 1959, 1969; Barth 1966:22f). Thus one's jural status as a member of a descent category is necessarily a status shared with or by others who are also descended from the putative founder of the unit in the same way as oneself. Such statuses are of two general sorts: those having to do with relations between comembers of the same unit and those having to do with relations between members of different descent-ordered units. Of course, these two kinds of statuses are often closely related, for the rights and duties of comembers as such may well involve obligations to one another in social relations with members of different units.

Social units whose boundaries are set by relations of common descent exhibit a wide range of additional (and, formally speaking, secondary) features, depending on the nature and the specific mode of distribution of the rights and duties that constitute the benefits of membership (see, e.g., Barth 1966:22f). They may therefore exhibit few, if any, of the features that have led various sociologists and anthropologists to speak of "groups" as distinct from other kinds of social units (see, e.g., Goffman 1961:7-14; Schneider 1961:10, n. 6; Sprott 1958:9-22).[16] The functional

contrast between relations of kinship and relations of common descent is nonetheless clear. Although the totality of any individual's kin is sometimes described as a "bilateral kin group" (see, e.g., Lowie 1920:64), it is true, as has often been observed, that relations of kinship cannot be employed to define groups in the same way as relations of common descent (see, e.g., Freeman 1960, Barnes 1967a, Service 1962). As Fortes (1953:29) puts it, "kinship is used to define and sanction a personal field of social relations for each individual." In some cases, however, relations of kinship provide the basis for the formation of temporary, ad hoc "action groups" such as "kindreds" in Freeman's (1960) sense (see also Radcliffe-Brown 1950:15-18).

The functional differences between kinship and descent systems, and the fact that in some societies relations of common descent provide the framework for most political relations (and therefore the most dramatically sanctioned social relations), should not lead us to overemphasize the significance of relations of common descent. While it might be possible to argue from one or another theoretical perspective—e.g., the functionalist perspective that focuses on "the institutions that are indispensable for the continuity through time without which there can be no ongoing society" (Fortes 1969:309)—that the descent system of some society is more "important" than, say, its kinship system, it would still remain true, as Fortes (1959:209) has observed, that

---

[16] For some examples of descent units that are not groups, by some definitions of the term, see Service (1962) on sodalities. In many such cases the sole "corporate property" of the unit is its name, and, aside from the right *in rem* to the use of this name, rights conferred by membership of such a unit are entirely rights *in personam* over other members of the group and consist largely in claims to hospitality and other services of the same general sort.

a social stucture based on an association of exogamous, corporate unilineal descent groups is not likely to hold together in a permanent political system unless it is either subject to some form of overriding, centralized government, or is knit together in a field of dyadic social relations by a web of kinship ties that counterbalance the centrifugal tendencies of the descent groups. . . .

That is to say, even where the descent groups are highly multifunctional and constitute the principal political units, even to the extent that an individual may have no political or "legal" status except as a member of a descent group (see Fortes 1953:26), the kinship system may be no less significant for the maintenance of the social order in its present form. The two subsystems are simply complementary parts of a larger whole (the total social system), which obviously would not be "the same" if either were altered. Of course, it might well be argued that the patrilineal or matrilineal aspects of some particular society constitute its most distinctive features in contrast to some other society, but that is another matter.

Two final points here: First, Fortes has recently (1959, 1969) argued that, in general, different types of sanction are associated with social relations of kinship and common descent. Kinship relations, he argues, are sanctioned "internally" by reciprocities built into the social relations themselves; one fulfills his duties to his kinsmen because only in this way can he be assured that they will fulfill their duties to him. But the rights and duties constituting statuses conferred by relations of common descent are sanctioned "externally"; i.e., relations of common descent unite sets of individuals vis-à-vis the world at large (including other such sets), and these sets may act as groups to ensure the rightful claims of their members and to protect them from injury by members of other groups. The contrast drawn by Fortes is most clearly applicable within societies in which we find both kinship and descent systems and in which the principle of joint or corporate responsibility applies in certain relations between members of different descent groups. But as Fortes (1953:26) notes, that principle is not an invariant feature of the organization of unilineal descent groups, and Barth (1966:22f,

1953:72f) has suggested some of the conditions under which it does and does not apply. Moreover, although Fortes' distinction between "internal" and "external" (or "moral" and "jural") sanctions is not easy to interpret or apply, his generalization seems to take insufficient account of the modes of sanction sometimes available to individuals to enforce their rights (or others' duties) *in rem* as ascribed on the basis of kinship (see, again, Robinson 1962:127f on a Trobriand man's right to bestow his daughter in marriage). In any event, it is not the nature of their respective systems of sanction that is at issue when we distinguish between kinship and descent systems; it is rather the formal structure of the categories of relationship per se.

Finally, we must consider rules of succession and inheritance,[17] which have often been described in terms of matrilineal or patrilineal descent, though quite often the rule in question is that one's "estate" (be it an office or some item or items of property) devolves on one's children (or some one of them—e.g., the eldest). Fortes, however (1959:208; see also 1969:267-68), has argued that

where a sibling succeeds or inherits "in preference to," i.e., by priority of right over, a child, descent is the critical factor; for a sibling is closer to the source of the deceased's "estate"—a common ancestor—than is a son or daughter. But where succession and inheritance devolve on sons or daughters "in preference to" siblings, this is governed by the rule of filiation.

Moreover, Fortes (1969:282) generalizes as though, in succession to offices within or held by unilineal descent

---

[17] For a useful discussion of the use of these terms in anthropology see the entry under "succession" (by B. E. Ward) in Gould and Kolb, eds. (1964:699-700), and also Goody (1966). See also Freedman on descent and kinship in Gould and Kolb, eds. (1964:192-94, 366-68).

groups, preference is usually given to a sibling, and as though filial succession is characteristic of succession to offices "outside" such groups. Goody (1966), however, cites a number of examples that show quite clearly that this is not the case, and he describes both filial and sibling succession as "lineal," whether or not the office is within or held by a descent group. Goody (1966:33) also describes filial and sibling succession as "next-of-kin systems"—in contrast, for example, to systems of "circulating" or "rotational" succession, in which preference is given to a fairly remote kinsman of the previous incumbent.

From the perspective of the distinction made here between kinship and descent systems, the apparent disagreement between Fortes and Goody may be resolvable as follows: Rules governing the transmission of rights in offices may be components of either the kinship or the descent system of a society, but the rules themselves are best described simply as rules of filial or sibling succession. Where an office is within or held by a descent group as its corporate property, as in African "royal descent groups" (Goody 1966: 26-27,), that office is part of the descent system of the society, and succession to it is governed "by descent," at least insofar as the successor must be related to the previous incumbent by common descent from the putative founder of the group. (This need not imply that all members of the group are entitled to succeed to the office.) Some order of priorities has to be established among the potential successors, and this may be done by giving preference to a son (or a sister's son in the matrilineal case) or to a sibling of the incumbent.[18] From the perspective of the

actors in the system (i.e., culturally), either rule may be a "rule of descent"—that is, a rule stating "what serial combination of forms of filiation shall be utilized in establishing pedigrees recognized for social purposes" (Fortes 1959:207). For, after all, both sons and brothers of the incumbent are patrilineally related to him *in a society where patrilineal descent is posited or conceptualized as a special kind of genealogical relationship.*[19]

In contrast, where the office in question is *not* within or held by a descent group, then rules of filial or sibling succession are components of the kinship system of the society, though of course they apply only to the kinsmen of the incumbent. They are therefore solely "next-of-kin" rules; they take no account of relations of common descent (except insofar as common descent implies relations of ascendant genealogical connection or kinship).

There is, of course, the special case of so-called dynastic descent groups, many of which are hardly groups in any particularly meaningful sense of the term (see Goody 1966:26; Fortes 1969:282f). Where an office such as a kingship is a "corporation sole" (Fortes 1969:283), the rule of succession to it may also establish and define the boundaries of a class of "nobles" or persons of "royal ancestry," all members of which are entitled (though not equally eligible) to succeed to the office. In some cases (see, e.g., Schapera 1937, Southwold 1966) this set consists of all descendants of the putative original officeholder through males or through females exclusively, and it is thus a patrilineal or matrilineal descent group of sorts. This is the sole such "group" in the society, and it is clearly best understood as an artifact of the rule of suc-

---

[18] Goody (1966) discusses some of the organizational benefits and liabilities entailed by these and other forms of succession.

[19] It appears to be so conceptualized among the Maori, whose descent groups (*hapu*) do not have patrilineal constitutions. For a brief discussion of succession among the Maori, see Scheffler (1966:545).

cession; the rule of succession is not an aspect of the internal structure of the "group."

Ethnographers have often spoken of individuals as "inheriting" certain jural statuses that are in fact associated with membership of descent groups, but a clear distinction must be drawn between the intergenerational transmission of rights (*in rem* or *in personam*) held successively by single individuals and those held simultaneously by sets of individuals. The latter, if allocated "on the basis of birth or genealogical position" (Barth 1966:24), are held and transmitted by common descent. Therefore, we shall speak of rules of inheritance only when the rights in question are held successively by single individuals; that is, when the rights are noncorporate. In some societies (e.g., Tallensi; see Fortes 1949*a*) a man does not attain full jural status within his descent group until the death of his father, but it is not that he "inherits" his position in the group from his father; it is rather that full jural status is restricted to "adult" members of the group, and a man is not defined as "adult" until his father is deceased.

From this perspective it is clear that rules of inheritance must be regarded as components of a society's kinship system. (Again, it is immaterial whether preference is given to sons, sisters' sons, or siblings.) We may restrict the terms "patrilineal" and "matrilineal" to forms of genealogical connection recognized within the descent systems of societies (see also Bohannan 1963:59, 132), and describe rules of inheritance (or succession) as agnatic or uterine, using these terms to describe forms of genealogical connection recognized within the kinship systems of societies. Inheritance by sisters' sons is a form of uterine inheritance; it is just that the property in question is held by males and transmitted through females (the

mothers of the heirs). Where preference is given to siblings, we may speak of leviratic or sororal inheritance (though this too may involve considerations of agnatic or uterine connection, as when preference is given to an agnatic rather than a uterine sibling).

The term "levirate" is often used more specifically to denote the special case of transmission of rights (*in personam* or *in rem*) in a man's widow to his brother "or some other one of his close kinsmen" (Lowie 1920:33). Lowie remarks on the diversity of the "customs" so labeled, but concludes (1920:33-34) by agreeing with "Tylor's view that the levirate results from the notion of marriage as a compact between groups rather than individuals." (The "groups" may be families or descent groups.) "From this principle," he argues, "it follows that when a union terminates by the death of one of the mates a substitute is automatically supplied by the group of the deceased." However, Lowie notes (1920:36), if this were true, "we should expect the levirate and the sororate to coexist"; that is, if a man's wife dies, her "group" should be obliged to replace her, perhaps with her sister or classificatory sister. But, as Lowie notes, no such neat correlation exists. He explains away the lack of strong correlation by arguing that if the ethnographic data were fuller, the correlation would be better than it appears, and a few clearly negative cases are dismissed as "not frequent enough to interfere with the conception of the levirate and the sororate as two closely connected institutions."

The facts of the matter appear to be that the levirate is sometimes a component of a society's kinship system and sometimes a component of its descent system. That is to say, in some cases a man inherits certain of his brother's rights in his wife (and failing a brother, these rights may devolve on a more distant collateral kinsman); in not a few cases it might be more appropriate to say that a man succeeds to his brother's statuses as a kinsman, for rights and duties in respect of his brother's children may also devolve on him. In other cases, however, possibly where bride-price is paid by a lineage, the woman is in some limited sense the corporate property of the group as a whole, and on the death of her husband certain rights in respect of her devolve on the group as a whole, then to be reallocated to one of the men of the group, or perhaps transferred to another group. The society may, of course, establish a system of priorities among the members of the groups, and it may give preference to a brother of the deceased. From this perspective the so-called levirate and sororate are *not* simply converse aspects of the same jural relationship (i.e., marital alliance between "groups"; see Part VII). "Leviratic" transmission of one's (or a group's) marital rights in a woman does not imply, as its logical corollary, any obligation on the part of the "group" (if any) that supplied the women as a wife to begin with. If "groups" are involved at all, it is only where rights in the woman as a wife (and possibly mother) are acquired by her husband's group and reallocated by it on his death. This does not necessarily entail a further or continuing lien on the group that supplied the woman. This interpretation of the levirate also accounts (formally) for those cases in which men inherit rights in their fathers' wives (though usually only those who are not also their mothers).

V: SYSTEMS OF
KIN CLASSIFICATION

The study of systems of kin classification has occupied a prominent place in ethnological theory at least since the publication of Morgan's *Systems of Consanguinity and Affinity of the Human Family* in 1871. Morgan's work was and still is criticized for a variety of reasons, but surely the most important objection leveled against it is that many of the systems he dealt with are not in fact systems of *kin* classification (see, e.g., Westermark 1891, Lang 1903, Thomas 1906, Lowie 1920). The debate over whether certain classificatory systems are systems of kin classification or some other kind of system, and over the sociological implications of either interpretation, has continued to the present (see, e.g., Radcliffe-Brown 1930-1931; Malinowski 1929c, 1930b; Leach 1961; Needham 1962; Schneider 1968b; Firth 1968; Fortes 1969). In the early years the controversy was considerably muddled by a tendency to confuse questions of what the terms might "originally" have meant with what they now mean and by an unwarranted assumption that each term has but a single meaning. The former confusion has largely disappeared as the emphasis in anthropological studies has shifted away from questions of culture history and toward "structural analysis" of one sort or another, but many arguments based on it are still widely accepted.[20] Moreover, the assumption of monosemy (one word: one meaning), though often disguised by inarticulate semantic theory (see, e.g., Needham 1962, Leach 1967b), continues to misinform many discussions of the meanings of kinship terms.[21]

---

[20] For a case in point, note Needham's (1962:37) comments on Hocart's (1937) unsupported contention that the "belief" in extensions of meaning rests on nothing more than a naive ethnocentric prejudice on the part of western European anthropologists and philologists.

[21] In the following discussion I use the phrase "kinship terms" to indicate words that designate categories of kin. This remark may seem pointless, but it is necessitated by the unfortunate practice of

Early writers on the subject often argued that the central fallacy in Morgan's work was his assumption that the terms he translated as "father," say, are "synonymous in the native mind with 'procreator'" (Lowie 1920:58). They pointed out that in those systems that Morgan described as "classificatory" (see also White 1958, Scheffler 1972b), other kinsmen, such as one's father's brothers, are also denoted by the same term; the evidence, they argued, indicates not that these other kinsmen are called "father," but that they and one's presumed genitor "are designated by a *common term* not strictly corresponding to *any* in our language" (Lowie 1920:59). In other words, they argued that it is not a matter of the extension (by sense attenuation) of the "father" term to kinsmen of other types, but of the existence of a term that designates a single, structurally undifferentiated category of which one's father and certain of his kinsmen are *equal* members. Such a category might be defined, it was argued, by reference to generational status relative to Ego, perhaps within a "social group," or by reference to social statuses such as marriageability, sexual distance, etc. In some quarters this line of argument has hardened into the dogma that many so-called kinship terms are in fact the names of jural statuses (i.e., "social categories") which are ascribed or allocated on a variety of nongenealogical grounds (see, e.g., Beattie 1958, Leach 1958, Needham 1962).

This interpretation is almost wholly erroneous. First, "social category" interpretations of systems of kin classification often leave unexplained just how the alleged social statuses are allocated if not by reference to relations of genealogical connection, or they make use of genealogical criteria (e.g., generation, "side," descent, etc.) without acknowledging that these are in fact matters of genealogy. Second, the plausibility of the antigenealogical, antiextensional, antimetaphorical "social category" theories rests largely on a failure to go beyond the most immediately apprehensible linguistic surface features of the systems with which they deal (Malinowski 1929c [1962:137]; Lounsbury 1965, 1969; Scheffler 1972a). In the Hawaiian system, for example,[22] father, father's brother, mother's brother, etc., are *not* equal denotata of the term *makua,* "parent." The Hawaiian language distinguishes between *luaui makua,* a "true, own, or proper parent," and *makua hanauna,* a "collateral or classificatory parent" (see Pukui and Elbert 1965). Similar distinctions are made for all Hawaiian kinship terms, and they are reported for most systems of kin classification that are at all well documented.[23] Thus, despite frequent repetition of the observation, it is quite untrue that various peoples do not distinguish terminologically between their fathers and other men they call or refer

---

some anthropologists to describe as "kinship terms" words that they argue have no genealogical reference (see Beattie 1964). Thus they argue (somewhat cryptically) that kinship terms have no necessary reference to relations of genealogical connection, when it might more sensibly be argued that certain alleged kinship terms are not in fact kinship terms. For further discussion of this matter, see Scheffler and Lounsbury (1971) and Scheffler (1972b, 1972c).

[22] I choose the Hawaiian system as an example because it was dealt with in some detail by Lowie (1920:58-60). Interestingly enough, Lowie, like so many others who have taken the same line, then went on to describe other types of systems of kin classification in terms of primary meanings and extensions, but apparently without being aware that this was what he was doing.

[23] For a detailed account of the general semantic theory needed to deal with these data, see Scheffler and Lounsbury (1971). See also Greenberg's (1966) account on the highly important distinction between the unmarked and marked members of an opposition (but cf. Scheffler 1972c).

to by the same terms, and fail to make other terminological distinctions of the same kind (cf. Fox 1967:240).

Though often reported, verbal distinctions of this sort have been widely misinterpreted. The most common misinterpretation is that the distinction being made is not between the primary and extended senses of a term, but between two (or more) subcategories of a broad "social category" that is the primary designatum of the term (see, e.g., Hocart 1937, Leach 1958, Beattie 1958, Powell 1969b). While this interpretation has a certain superficial plausibility, it leaves unexplained why it is that the closest kin type(s) denoted by a term is so often designated as its "true" denotatum, its denotatum par excellence. Hocart (1937) and others have suggested that this is because Ego usually has a "special" and "close" social relationship with persons of the kin type(s) so designated, and so they are treated as "special cases" of relatives of the kind designated by the term. Thus, the argument continues, a term may appear to be used to denote one's father, for example, but the reference is not to the genealogical relationship as such. This argument is unsatisfactory on at least two counts. First, it suffers from faulty logic. Leach (1958), for example, would have us believe that the "primary sense" of Trobriand *tama* is "domiciled male of my father's subclan hamlet," and that one's father is but a special case of this general class of relatives and thus marked as the "true *tama*." Note, however, that the broader and alleged primary sense not only includes Ego's father, but is defined by reference to Ego's father. The category that includes only Ego's father is logically prior to the more inclusive category defined by reference to Ego's father. Therefore, we must conclude that the narrow sense of *tama* (marked "true *tama*") is its logical or structural primary sense, to which the broader sense is related by widening or expansion (see also Scheffler 1972c). The second objection is that the argument overlooks the fact that the kin type FB, for example, may be described as "father's brother," i.e., by a two-term relative product in which "father" occurs in its narrow or specific sense, or designated simply as "father." This, too, shows that "father" is polysemous, and that its narrow, specific sense is logically or structurally prior to any of its broader or more inclusive senses. It shows that the terminological status of FB is reckoned by reference to that of one's own or true father.

Once an adequate range of linguistic and semantic facts is taken into account, it is obvious that most alleged kinship terms are in fact kinship terms, and that most kinship terms are not unlike many other words in all languages in that they, too, are often polysemic: each term serves to designate not just one but perhaps several structurally related categories, the broader of which is derived from the primary designatum of the term by certain genealogical rules of terminological extension.[24] As noted in Part IV, kinship terms may be used to signify relations between individuals as members of descent groups or of different but genealogically related descent groups. These extensions of kinship terms are no less genealogically based than their uses to designate classes of kin. This fact has sometimes been obscured by somewhat cryptic arguments to the effect that descent groups are not conceived by the people who belong to them as genealogically constituted units (see, e.g., Beattie 1958, Needham 1962; but cf. Scheffler and Lounsbury 1971). To recognize

---

[24] For a general discussion of such rules, see Scheffler and Lounsbury (1971).

these simple, if rather attenuated, extensions of kinship terms for what they are is not to "reduce" systems of intra- and intergroup relations to relations of kinship, for all that such extensions imply is a degree of structural isomorphism (not structural identity) between systems of kin classification and systems of descent-ordered groups.

Of course, many kinship terms have semantic functions in addition to their category-designating functions. As Rivers noted long ago (1907; see also Schneider and Roberts 1956), they are often used to refer to (i.e., connote) statuses or social relationships *ascribed between Ego and kinsmen of the kinds designated by the terms*. Here, too, distinctions may be made between the two (or more) categories designated by the same term; the status connoted by a term in its extended category-designating sense may be an attenuated version of the status connoted by the term when used in its primary category-designating sense. For example, the Banyoro (Beattie 1958) designate father's brother and father's sister as kinds of fathers ("little father" and "female father" respectively), and the right- and duty-statuses ascribed to them consist of only a few of the rights and duties ascribed to fathers in respect of their children. As the father term (*ise*) is further extended to more remote collateral kin of the father, the statuses connoted by it become even more attenuated. But among the Banyoro, as in many other societies, the use of a kinship term in one of its extended category-designating senses and along with the lexical marker (e.g., "little") indicating explicitly that it is being so used may be construed by the designated kinsman as connoting an individious status distinction—as drawing unnecessary attention to the fact that, since he is not the prime denotatum of the term (its central referent), Ego does

not owe him or her the same degree of deference and so on that he owes his own father. Therefore, Banyoro regard it as impolite to employ the terms in their marked forms, at least in direct address (see also Scheffler 1972*a*).

The dual semantic function of kinship terms—to designate categories of kin and to connote social statuses or relationships ascribed to kin of those categories—has led some anthropologists to argue that terminological distinctions between different kinds or classes of kin are always socially motivated; that is, that coclassification implies similarity of status and, conversely, that classification under different terms implies dissimilarity of status (see Lowie 1920, 1929; Radcliffe-Brown 1941 [1952:52]; Murdock 1949:106f; Lévi-Strauss 1963:37-38; Eggan 1968; Fortes 1969:45-59). The argument is not simply functional but causal: terminological equations and distinctions of kin types are held to follow (sometimes as mere accidents [Needham 1962]) from equivalence or nonequivalence of social status, or both terminological and jural status are held to be dependent "on the group structure of the society" (Firth 1968:31-32), or on other abstract "structural principles" such as Radcliffe Brown's "principle of the solidarity of siblings" or of "the unity of the lineage group."

While it may be true in some cases that coclassification implies similarity of status and, conversely, that classification under different kinship terms implies dissimilarity of status, this is far from being a nonexceptionable arrangement (Murdock 1949:107). In many societies the statuses associated with kin classes are differentiated hardly at all, and in many others statuses are ascribed to specific types (not terminological categories) of kin, or to categories of kin that receive no single lexemic designation (see, e.g., Opler 1937, Tax

1955, Goodenough 1965). Moreover, most ethnographic reports of a neat correlation between terminological and jural statuses rest on little more than casual observation, not on rigorous independent structural analyses of the terminological and jural status systems, and so it may well be that the correlation is less common than a superficial examination of the ethnographic literature would suggest.

In any event, the assumption that such a correlation exists must be treated as a heuristic assumption, as pointing to an arrangement known (or at least reported) to exist in some cases and to be looked for as a possibility in others. It must not be treated, as it often has been (see, e.g., Radcliffe-Brown 1941; Fortes 1969:45-59; Leach 1970:95), as a principal tenet of analysis and used as an excuse for shortcutting the analytical process by failing to provide *first* a satisfactory structural analysis of the system of classification as such. The two systems (the system of classification and the system of kin statuses) must not be fused *a priori* into a single system; they must be analyzed independently and their structures then compared to determine whether or not, and if so to what extent, they are isomorphic. Otherwise, the analyst runs the risk of purporting to demonstrate (anecdotally) nothing more than what he presumed had to be the case to begin with.

Formal or structural semantic analyses of systems of kin classification[25] have been widely, though inappropriately, criticized for not taking status-relationship connotations and some forms of extension (metaphorical) into

account, and therefore for failing to provide a complete account of the meanings and uses of the terms under analysis (see, e.g., Guemple 1965, Fortes 1969:45-59). Inasmuch as no one, to the best of my knowledge, has argued that the genealogical significata of kinship terms are their only meanings, this objection is misplaced because it amounts either to a denial that the terms have different kinds of meanings or, if it is acknowledged that they do, to an assertion that the two or more kinds of meanings cannot be satisfactorily analyzed independently of one another. Whether or not any particular kinship terms do have status connotations in addition to their genealogical significata (by virtue of which we may describe them as kinship terms to begin with) is, of course, an empirical question. But when they do, it is obvious that the two kinds of meanings must be described independently of one another, and analysis of the genealogical significata must precede analysis of the status connotations. We must distinguish between structural analyses of different kinds or domains of meaning and usage and the full account of meaning and usage that can be provided only

---

terms, but he did not deal explicitly with the polysemy of the terms of these systems. Kroeber (1909) attempted the first "componential analyses," but he too failed to reckon with the polysemy of the terms with which he dealt. Later attempts by Davis and Warner (1937) and Greenberg (1949) suffer from the same limitation and, in the former case, from unnecessary complexity. Papers by Goodenough (1956a) and Lounsbury (1956) added considerable semantic sophistication to the endeavor but also paid insufficient attention to the possibility of polysemy within the domain of kin classification. A great deal of subsequent discussion (Wallace and Atkins 1960, Wallace 1965) of the "psychological" or "cognitive" reality of "componential analyses" deals (rather ineffectively) with the host of problems (or pseudoproblems) raised by this failure to take adequate account of the relevant ethnographic and linguistic facts. For further discussion see Scheffler and Lounsbury (1971: chaps. 3, 7) and Scheffler (1972c).

---

[25] It is not generally realized that the structural analysis of systems of kin classification has an "ancient history." Morgan (1871) attempted structural analyses and comparisons of Iroquois- and Dravidian-type systems, largely in terms of definitional and extension rules phrased as relative products of other

by integrating the former. So far, structural semantic analyses of kinship terminological systems have been concerned largely with the genealogical significata of the terms, and their status connotations (if any) have been ignored for a variety of reasons.[26] One of these is that adequately detailed and systematic data concerning status connotations are generally lacking in ethnographic reports, and another is that status connotation constitutes a different kind of meaning that need not and *should not* be considered in analysis of category designation (see also Scheffler 1972c).

Morgan (1871:12-13) distinguished between two general types of systems of kin classification, which he labeled the "descriptive" and the "classificatory." Briefly, "descriptive systems" are those in which the "primary terms" (the parent, child, sibling, and grandkin terms, if any) are not subject to collateral extension; "classificatory systems" are those in which some or all of these terms are subject to collateral extension. Morgan's "descriptive" category, however, contains many systems in which some or all "primary terms" are extended "lineally" (intergenerationally) rather than collaterally (intragenerationally). Thus, while Morgan's distinction is valid enough (even though he applied it inconsistently), the distinction between systems that do not extend their terms and systems that do is logically and therefore typologically prior to it.

All systems of kin classification feature special parent, child, and sibling terms.[27] Therefore, the structurally simplest systems are those that feature only these terms and do not subject

them to extension. The Estonian system (Morgan 1871:62-64) provides one example. In this system, more remote kin types are designated by relative products of the parent, child, and sibling terms; i.e., as Morgan put it, kin such as FF and FFB are "described" by means of the "primary" terms. Many other systems (see Morgan 1871 on Scandinavian and Semitic systems) have special grandkin terms and/or special uncle, aunt, nephew, niece, and perhaps even cousin terms. Again, these terms are not subject to inter- or intragenerational extension, but they make possible other kinds of relative-product designations; for example, when there is a special uncle term, FFB may be described as "father's father's brother" or "father's uncle."

The general category of systems with extension rules may be divided into two broad categories: (1) those whose sole or principal extension rules establish structural equivalences between kin types of different generations and (2) those whose sole or principal extension rules establish structural equivalences between kin types of the same generation. There are several simple varieties of the first type, and these types may be rank-ordered according to the relative strength (i.e., pervasiveness) of their respective extension rules. The strongest such rule is that found in the

---

[26] For some notable exceptions see Pospisil (1964) and Goodenough (1965).

[27] The question of whether or not Ego should be included in the system has been the subject of some

discussion (see Romney and D'Andrade 1964, Pelto 1966), but this is a pseudoproblem generated largely by the use of inappropriate dimensions of contrast in the analysis of "American" kin classification. Also, some analysts seem to have been misled by the nature of the diagrams they use to display the data on systems of kin classification. The terms of a kinship system designate classes of "poles" in genealogical relationships, and each term has a certain other (or others) as its consistent reciprocal(s). Ego is always and necessarily included in any analysis, but "disguised," as it were, as a member of *all* of the classes; or, in other words, as a member (or potential member) of each one of the classes when considered as the designated kinsman.

Magyar system (Morgan 1871:64-65), in which the parent, child, and sibling terms are extended to all other kin (at least within the second degree of collaterality) via the rule "Let anyone's parent as a linking kinsman be regarded as structurally equivalent to that person himself or herself; conversely, let any linking kinsman's child be regarded as structurally equivalent to that linking kinsman himself or herself." Thus grandparents are designated by the parent terms, grandchildren by the child terms; parents' and grandparents' siblings and Ego's elder cousins are designated by the elder sibling terms, and siblings' children and grandchildren and Ego's younger cousins are designated by the younger sibling terms. English features a weaker version of the same rule, i.e., "Let anyone's parent's parent be regarded as structurally equivalent to that person's parent," etc. Thus, grandparents and grandchildren are designated by the parent and child terms (the extensions are obligatorily marked by the prefix grand-). The closest collateral kin types are invariant to the rule and are designated by special terms. However, these terms are extended by the rule; e.g., uncle is extended from parent's brother to parent's parent's brother (again, the extension is marked, though not obligatorily, by a prefix, in this case great-). In some systems the rule is further weakened by the presence of special grandkin terms; parent's parent is regarded as structurally equivalent to parent only as a linking kinsman. Aside from the fact that they do not extend the parent and child terms to grandparents and grandchildren, these systems are much like the English system. Some systems feature the rule "Let parent's parent as a designated kinsman be regarded as structurally equivalent to parent as a designated kinsman," etc. This very weak version of the rule has relatively little effect in the systems in which it occurs, and seems to occur only in systems whose major overt features are given by collateral or intragenerational extension rules (see below).

The intergenerational extension rules noted so far establish structural equivalences between kin types *lineally* related to one another in *adjacent* generations. Another type of intergenerational extension rule establishes a structural equivalence between *lineally* related kin types in *alternate* generations; e.g., a man's father and his son, a woman's mother and her daughter. A third type establishes a structural equivalence between kin types *collaterally* related to one another; e.g., a woman's brother and her son, a man's sister and his daughter (Lounsbury 1964a, 1965). To the best of my knowledge, these latter two types of rules do not occur as the sole extension rules of any system; they are always supplemented by, or supplementary to, collateral extension rules. Systems that feature both inter- and intragenerational extension rules are in a sense structural hybrids; they are discussed below, after systems featuring only collateral extension rules.

Collateral extension rules may also be ranked according to their relative strength. Empirically, the strongest such rule is that found in the so-called Hawaiian-type systems (Murdock 1949:223): "Let anyone's parent's sibling be regarded as structurally equivalent to that person's parent," etc. Systems with such rules have no special collateral categories (other than sibling, of course); they extend the parent, child, and sibling terms and their special grandkin terms (if any) to all collateral kin of the same generations as the class foci. Some of these systems lack special grandkin terms and extend the parent and child terms to grandkin via the weakest of the intergenerational extension rules noted above. Clearly, collateral extension dominates over lineal extension in these systems—the former is much more general—and so these systems are best placed in the general category of systems with collateral extension rules. The weakest form of collateral extension is that found in the so-called Eskimo-type systems (Murdock 1949:223). The rule is "Let parent's parent's sibling be regarded as structurally equivalent to parent's parent," etc. This leaves the first-degree collateral kin types in the first ascending and first descending generations and the cousin types invariant, and they are labeled by special terms. Thus on superficial inspection these systems may appear rather like the English system. However, the extension rule has the effect of extending the special collateral terms collaterally, not intergenerationally, as in English.

Finally, there is a collateral extension rule of intermediate strength: "Let anyone's parent's sibling of the same sex as that parent be regarded as structurally equivalent to that parent," etc.; in other words, the same-sex sibling merging rule (Lounsbury 1964a). Where this rule occurs it may be supplemented by one or more of a large number of additional extension rules, by reference to which a variety of subtypes and subsubtypes of systems may be defined.

In the simplest of these subtypes, parents' opposite-sex siblings, cross-cousins, and the children of opposite-sex siblings are marked by special terms, and these, along with the parent, child, and sibling terms, are extended collaterally in one of three ways. The variation in the ways in which the parallel versus cross-collateral distinction is extended cannot be described here, but examples of the three types of system may be found in (1) the Iroquois, (2) the Dravidian and Kariera, and (3) the Kuma and Siane of the highlands of

New Guinea (see Scheffler 1971, 1972b).

The other main subtype consists of systems that employ the same-sex sibling merging rule *plus* one or another of the additional types of intergenerational extension rules noted above. The so-called Arunta-type systems of Australia and the Ambrym system (Scheffler 1970b) employ intergenerational extension rules that establish structural equivalences between lineally related kin in alternate generations, thus often evacuating some of the grandkin categories. Systems that employ rules that establish structural equivalences between collateral kin in different generations may be divided into two subtypes: those with rules of uniform and nonuniform transmission of kin-class statuses. The Crow- and Omaha-type systems (Lounsbury 1964a, 1965) provide examples of the former subtype. So far as I know, there is only one type of nonuniform intergenerational extension rule: the "parallel transmission" rule of the Siriono and a few other South American systems of kin classification (Scheffler and Lounsbury 1971).

Since this structural typology of systems of kin classification has yet to be applied in a broad comparative study designed to account for the differential distribution of types of such systems, little can be said in general terms about the sociological or other possible correlates of one or another type of basic terminological system or of one or another type of extension rule. Moreover, the construction of a general theory purporting to account for the differential distribution of types of systems or simply types of extension rules presupposes the existence of a number of valid specific explanations. As I have already noted, anthropologists have tended to look to jural status distinctions, factors of group affiliation, marriage rules, and the like for explanations of terminological equations and distinctions among kin types; but as Firth (1968) and Schneider (1968b) have observed, this practice has not been informed by any general theory specifying why our attention should be so directed. It has simply been assumed that terminological equations and distinctions *must* be socially motivated, and especially that coclassification implies similarity of jural status in relation to Ego. The formal inadequacies of most purported demonstrations of the validity of this assumption have been overlooked, casually dismissed, or explained away by appeal to a variety of ingenious but ad hoc pseudohistorical, sociological, or semantic speculations. Since many attempts at sociological explanation of particular systems or kinds of systems of kin classification have not been preceded by adequate structural analyses of the systems of classification as such (often because it was erroneously supposed that they are not in fact systems of kin classification), many such explanations attempt to account for the existence of properties that the system or systems in question do not possess. (For a case in point, see the extensive literature on Ambrym kinship terminology and Scheffler 1970b).[28]

Lounsbury (1964b, 1965) has observed that there are certain formal similarities between one or another form of the Crow- and Omaha-type skewing rules and one or another form of jural-status transmission, at least in certain societies, and that, in general, rules of

---

[28] Both the weaker and stronger versions of the unity of the lineage theory of the structure of Crow- and Omaha-type systems are subject to this criticism (see Radcliffe-Brown 1952:70f, Beattie 1958; and cf. Tax 1955, Lounsbury 1964a), as is the theory of so-called prescriptive alliance systems, since it is, for the most part, little more than a minor permutation of the former theory (see Lévi-Strauss 1969, Needham 1962, Dumont 1968; but cf. Scheffler 1970c).

terminological extension may correlate with rules of status succession. The specific hypotheses presented by Lounsbury have yet to be checked against a broader range of data, and so their general validity remains to be demonstrated. It should be noted, however, that this conceptualization of the possible correlations between terminological and jural-status systems is rather different from that criticized above. Lounsbury's hypothesis does not require that all kin types denoted by the same term occupy the same jural status relative to Ego, but only that at least one of the more distant types denoted by the term *potentially* occupy the same status as the primary denotatum. Thus, for example, in a Crow-type system many kin types designated as "father's sister," such as father's sister's daughter, may well be ascribed rights and duties in respect of Ego that are quite different from those to which the father's sister herself is entitled; but on the death of the father's sister her daughter may succeed to her jural status in respect of Ego. It may be this (genealogical) principle of status succession that is expressed in the Crow skewing rule, at least in some cases. Lounsbury's hypothesis should not be taken to suggest that all more distant kin labeled by a given term are regarded as potential successors to the status ascribed to the primary denotatum; for the more distant kin types, designation by a given term may have no social implications. Further, Lounsbury's hypothesis does not rest on an assumption of uniform causation (cf. Lévi-Strauss 1965); the same extension rule may have different social structural correlates in different societies, and rules of status transmission are only one of the social structural variables that may be reflected in rules of terminological extension (see Scheffler and Lounsbury 1971).

Finally, it should be noted that just

as there are no good reasons to suppose that the structurally primary senses of kinship terms are necessarily their historically most prior senses, neither are there any good reasons to suppose that they are the first-learned senses.[29] There may be some interesting relations between the semantic structures of systems of kin classification and the semantic etymology of their terms or the order in which the various senses of polysemic terms are learned by the individual, but these are largely unexplored, and indeed cannot be explored satisfactorily unless questions of structure of meaning are clearly distinguished from questions of etymology and learning.

VI: DESCENT AND RESIDENCE

The literature on descent systems is truly vast, and any attempt to survey it could easily turn into a survey of the sociology of "tribal" society. Although not all such societies feature descent units or groups of one sort or another, much of this sociology has taken its form and central preoccupations from the study of societies with such units, and societies without them were long treated as somewhat aberrant and unusual (see Radcliffe-Brown 1950, 1952; Lévi-Strauss 1969:104; Leach 1970: 105). Fortunately, there are now a number of fairly comprehensive surveys of this literature (Forde 1947; Radcliffe-Brown 1950; Fortes 1953, 1959, 1969; Middleton and Tait 1958; Schneider and Gough, eds., 1961; Sahlins 1968; Fox 1967; Goody 1968), and so no survey need be attempted here. The focus in this section is on the much discussed problem of the relation between descent and residence, or between descent groups and "local groups," with particular reference to the problem of the so-called patrilineal descent groups of the New Guinea highlands.

In the course of one of his important contributions to the study of residence rules, Goodenough (1962:5) notes that "it is common for local groups to be organized as descent groups," and he implies that it is more conventional "to think of them as descent groups which have been 'localized.'" Goodenough here alludes to a problem that has plagued anthropology from its very beginnings: the relative importance in the organization of "tribal" societies of ties of common residence or "locality," on the one hand, and ties of kinship or descent on the other. It was once fashionable (Morgan 1877, Lowie 1920), and still is to some extent (see Goodenough 1955, Fox 1967), to phrase the issue in "historical" terms and to argue that unilineal descent groups have had their "origins" in the practice of consistent unilocal (virilocal or uxorilocal) postmarital residence. Although this argument has a certain "logical" appeal and may appear to be useful for didactic purposes, it cannot be confirmed or disconfirmed and is of no scientific interest. Nowadays the argument tends to be cast in sociological terms. At the two extremes, the debate is between those who argue that comparison of social systems must begin with a local group of people and proceed by viewing different forms of kinship and descent systems as means of ordering rela-

---

[29] Although it is debatable whether Malinowski would have argued for such a simple relationship, he is widely credited with having argued that the structure of the process of acquiring one's knowledge of the structure of the terminological system parallels the structure of the system itself, and that the child learns to extend kinship terms as he learns to extend the sentiments and social relationships he associates with their primary denotata. This has led many anthropologists to reject his arguments for terminological extensions, since it is widely supposed that to accept them one must also accept his argument about the extension of "sentiments," etc., which is of course quite false.

tions within and between such groups (Leach 1961:104) and those who argue that any tendency for a descent group to be identified with a local group is simply a function of the degree to which the rights and duties of descent group affiliation have a spatial referent and require common residence for their effective exercise (Firth 1959:214-15).

Some proponents of the former view suggest that residence is a structural variable comparable to kinship and descent; others attempt to reduce the common conceptualization of local groups and relations between them in terms of descent groups and relations between them (see Evans-Pritchard 1940, Middleton 1958) to a mere "rationalization" or "expression" of ties of common residence in terms of ties of common descent (see Kroeber 1938, Lepervanche 1967). However, as Fortes (1953:36; 1969:220f) has pointed out, we have no well-documented cases in which residence with a group is jurally free and is itself a source of rightful claims over the properties and members of the group. Rather, residence is typically a right or duty conferred by one or another kind of genealogical connection, and in many cases so-called rules of residence may be reduced, it seems, to rights or duties to reside or associate with the family or lineage or a particular type of kinsman of one spouse or the other (see Goodenough 1956b, 1962). In most cases there is no single postmarital residence rule, but a range of choices open to a couple (or an individual) both at marriage and afterward. The relative frequencies of the various choices within the normative range may shift from time to time and place to place within the same society; and so the overall genealogical composition of its residential units (be they domestic groups, lineages, or whatever) may vary without the occurrence of any change in the "rules" or criteria employed by

the actors when making their residential choices (see Fortes 1949b and Goody, ed., 1958, on the important concept of "developmental cycles").

Although anthropologists sometimes seem to lose sight of the fact (see Sahlins 1965, Lepervanche 1967, Strathern 1968), it makes sense to think of local groups and relations between them in terms of descent groups and their interrelations only when there is a systematic relationship between local and descent groups. This does not mean that local groups that are spoken of as though they were unilineal descent groups must be composed exclusively or even predominantly of patrilineal or matrilineal descendants of the putative group founder (insofar as their adult male members are concerned). But it does necessitate at least "a compact nucleus ... to act as the local center" (Fortes 1953:36) for a descent group that may be widely dispersed, with many of its members living in association with the local nuclei of other such groups. Observations by Forde (1947), Firth (1959:214-15), and Goodenough (1963) suggest that there is a tendency for descent groups to be "localized" and for relations between local groups to be expressed in terms of relations between descent groups under the following conditions: some of the rights claimed by virtue of membership of the descent groups must have a spatial referent; i.e., they must require some particular location for their exercise. Where these are rights in some primary productive resource—land, for example—members of the group will tend to live together on or near that resource so long as they have no comparable rightful interests in comparable resources elsewhere. This tendency will be particularly strong where the resource is of such a nature that its effective exploitation demands that rights in it remain joint and undivided and requires the cooperation of a number of individuals, and where the overall political organization of the society is such that the resource and those who exploit it may have to defend it or themselves from other such groups. Where these factors are operative, the adult male members of the descent units tend to reside together on or near their estates and to form solidary units that exhibit a number of additional organizational features (internal status differentiation, offices, etc.) not found among descent units whose rights of membership have no spatial referents.

Under conditions such as these, provision is usually made for individuals to have access to the resources of groups other than their own, and to associate themselves with these other groups, typically by allocating rights of usufruct (not ownership) to nonlineal descendants of the groups' founders (i.e., sisters' children in patrilineal systems, brothers' children in matrilineal systems). While it was once supposed that such rights represent the vestiges or survivals of previously different forms of descent system, it is far more probable that they represent adaptive responses to the sorts of general organizational problems discussed by Goodenough (1963). As Sahlins (1965:105) has noted, a social system "would need perfect freedom at its borders, a demographic moratorium, or else the capacity to intensify production at any and all locations" in order to maintain political-territorial segments with 100 percent patrilineal or matrilineal composition (again, at least insofar as their adult male members are concerned). Therefore, it is only to be expected that any tendencies for unilineal descent groups to be localized will seldom be fully realized in the form of a society whose local groups bear simple one-to-one relationships to its descent groups (though insofar as adult male members are concerned, approxima-

tions to this condition are probably not uncommon). Again, this need not prevent conceptualization of local groups and relations between them as descent groups and relations between them, even if the discrepancy between local and descent group composition is sometimes rather large. The important variable, it seems, is some "legal" basis for supposing an association between the two.

It should be made clear, however, that even where there is a strong correlation between the composition of local and descent groups, nonresidence with the local nucleus of one's own group never entails automatic loss of one's identity as a member of that group or, conversely, automatic identification as a member of the descent group with whose local nucleus one does reside—otherwise we would have no justification for speaking of *descent* groups to begin with.[30] Typically, sisters' children (in a patrilineal system) or broth-

---

[30] This is not to suggest that I agree with Fortes (1959, 1969) that groups such as the Maori *hapu* and the Choiseulese *sinangge* are not in fact descent groups. Fortes argues that these groups are like "joint stock companies," in which an individual's right of membership rests on the acquisition of stock, by purchase or otherwise, with the difference that "title to 'stock' derives from filiation." Here, I think, Fortes is mistaken. In the case of the Choiseulese *sinangge,* anyway, entitlement to affiliate with the local nucleus of a cognatic descent category (a cognatic descent group) consists in demonstrated or accepted descent from the putative founder of the category and group, who is also the putative original "owner" of the estate occupied by the group (Scheffler 1965). Of course, one's identity as a descendant of that man involves one's identity as the child of one's father or mother (i.e., filiation), but an individual is entitled to affiliate with groups with which neither of his parents were affiliated but with which their parents were. If I understand Fortes correctly, he would describe this as an instance of "cumulative filiation," which he describes as the "analog" of descent (1969:281). It is not clear to me why Fortes refuses to describe this genealogical criterion as cognatic descent. The only apparent reason is a functional one—cognatic descent does not and cannot define the boundaries of mutually exclusive

ers' children (in a matrilineal system) reside with the local nucleus of the group only on sufferance and are not incorporated into the descent group itself (though outsiders may not feel constrained to pay much attention to the distinction between resident members and nonmembers). It does happen in such societies that individuals who are not lineal descendants of the putative founder of the descent group are incorporated into the group; again, this seldom happens to sisters' or brothers' children, but rather to their lineal descendants who remain associated with the lineage nucleus over a long span of time (see Mayer 1949 and Winter 1956 for descriptions of this process). But even these individuals may not be incorporated into the lineage; they may become identified as a separate and merely "associated" or "attached" lineage (see Fortes 1945, 1949a).

When such incorporation occurs, it is probably not because of any need to keep the apparent facts of local group composition in line with the "ideology" of local group constitution (cf. Langness 1964, Sahlins 1965). It is more likely a function of the fact that, where there is a legal basis for supposing an association between local and descent group affiliation, long-term resident nonmembers tend eventually to assume the duties of descent group membership in order to secure their positions within the local group, and they may be rewarded for assuming these duties by being accorded the concomitant rights. As time passes it becomes easy to assume that those who exercise the rights of membership are in fact fully members of the group and lineal descendants of the putative founder. In other words, where rights

in spatially fixed resources are allocated by descent but are acquirable by other means (e.g., effective allocation by legitimate holders of those rights, who may allocate them sparingly and only to certain close kin), it may be useful or necessary to justify the possession of such rights by fabricating genealogical charters. We should not lose sight of the fact that this is possible and reasonable only to the extent that such rights are normally allocated by descent. It is nowhere the general case that those who somehow come to share interests in a local estate merely rationalize or justify this sharing in terms of common descent; this is done only in exceptional cases (which may be fairly frequent) where shared interests are normally ascribed by descent to begin with.

This brings us to the so-called patrilineal descent groups of the New Guinea highlands. Although one might think it an easy matter to determine whether or not a group is a patrilineal descent group, ethnographers working in the highlands have not always found it so, and it is widely debated whether certain groups in this area are patrilineal or, for that matter, whether they are any kind of *descent* group. Brown (1962:57), for example, states: "We may be hard put to decide . . . whether [the] groups are mainly agnatic with numerous accretions, or cognatic with a patrilineal bias." Barnes (1962) speaks of "cumulative patrifiliation" rather than patrilineal descent, and Salisbury (1964:170) claims that among the Siane group affiliation is not "acquired" by descent, "in the usual definition of the term," and that intergroup relations are conceptualized in terms of "corporate affinity" (as is alleged to be the case in some areas of southeast Asia; see Part VII) rather than in terms of "agnation" (as in much of Africa).

The groups in question are all more or less compact residential units, and

---

groups—but it seems to me that the significant question concerns the nature of the genealogical construct itself, not its social functions (see Scheffler 1966, 1967).

the difficulty is that ethnographers find some reasons to believe that these groups are regarded by their members as patrilineal descent groups but other reasons to suppose that patrilineal descent is not the only criterion of entitlement to membership. For example, it is commonly reported that members of the groups are described as "brothers" or "like brothers," the "sons of one father," but it is very common for men to associate themselves with groups of which their mothers were identified as members, and, unlike the situation in so many African societies, they appear to suffer no jural disadvantages when they do so (see, e.g., Meggitt 1965; Barnes 1962, 1967b; Strathern and Strathern 1969). Moreover, although these groups commonly maintain lengthy genealogical charters, these charters are not always strictly patrilineal; nonpatrilineal descendants of the putative founder are identified as members and, again, suffer no jural disadvantages with respect to the rights of groups affiliation (though as Strathern and Strathern [1969] observe, they may suffer certain practical disadvantages by not living with their close paternal kin). Barnes (1962, 1967b) notes many other ways in which highland New Guinea "descent groups" and "descent group systems" differ from apparently comparable units and systems of units in Africa.

There are a number of sources of confusion in this literature, but one of the most significant is the failure to distinguish between simple parent-child and ancestor-descendant relations, or what Fortes (1959, 1969) terms filiation and descent (cf. Barnes 1962, 1967b). Assertions that these groups have patrilineal "ideologies" and descriptions of them as lineages, clans, or descent groups apparently rest quite often on an assumption that native descriptions of the groups as composed of

"brothers," the "sons of one father," imply a patri*lineal* constitution and, further, that only patrilineal descendants of the founder are properly members of them. If this is assumed, then, of course, it is quite puzzling that nonpatrilineal descendants of the founder suffer no jural disadvantages, and to resolve this puzzle one may have to resort to notions of a widespread "discrepancy between ideology and statistical norms" and even to denigration of the significance of kinship or genealogical connection as a structural variable (see, e.g., Langness 1964). But such native descriptions need not imply patrilineal constitutions; they may imply nothing more than a right or duty of sons to reside with and support their fathers, or of brothers, the sons of one father, to reside with and support one another. If so, men may tend to affiliate with the groups their fathers were identified with and there may be a cumulative tendency ("cumulative patrifiliation" [Barnes 1962]) for the men of a group to be related to one another through their fathers, their fathers' fathers, etc. It would be appropriate, as Barnes has suggested (1967b; see also Bulmer 1966 and Glasse 1969), for the people to order social relations within and between groups on the model of social relations between men and their fathers and brothers and to use paternal and fraternal kinship (not descent) analogically to describe the current state of social relations within and between groups, regardless of their specific composition.[31]

That many highland so-called descent groups do not have patrilineal

---

[31] Unfortunately, Barnes himself continues to use the terms "agnatic" and "patrilineal" as virtual synonyms and to describe the Enga "indigenous model for relations of logical inclusion, exclusion, superordination and subordination of sets" as agnatic or patrilineal. But he uses "agnatic" and "patrilineal" to modify kinship, not descent (1967b:39).

constitutions is demonstrated by the following: We have already noted that it often happens that men are associated with groups with which their mothers were identified and appear to suffer no jural disadvantage as a consequence (at least insofar as the rights and duties of group membership are concerned). By and large, the so-called nonagnatic members of highland "patrilineal descent groups" are the sons of women who were born into those groups, married out, and then after being widowed or divorced or for some other reason returned to those groups. According to Strathern and Strathern (1969), who provide one of the few accounts of the pertinent folk categories, the Melpa distinguish between two classes of lineage member: those who are attached through their fathers (*wua-nt-mei*) and those who are attached through their mothers (*amb-nt-mei*). Sons of men of the latter category are identified as members of the former, and it appears that from 20 to 50 percent of the adult male members of a lineage may belong to this capacity ("born of a woman"). In contrast to the Choiseulese distinction between group members who are "born of a man" and those who are "born of a woman" (Scheffler 1965), this is quite clearly not a distinction between patrilineal and nonpatrilineal descendants of the group founder. It is plainly a distinction between patrifiliation and matrifiliation, between those whose entitlement to membership rests on paternity (not patrilineal descent) and those whose entitlement rests on maternity (see also Strathern 1972: 18-19). The distinction appears to be of little jural consequence.

This, however, does not justify a description of these groups as cognatic descent groups. Though cognatic descent groups may be found in some areas of the New Guinea highlands (Glasse 1968) and genuine patrilineal descent groups in others, the idiom used to describe the internal and external relations of many highland political-territorial groups is one of paternal and fraternal *kinship*. To all appearances, the principal jural bases for the use of this idiom are patrifilial *inheritance* of rights in land or a duty incumbent on men to reside with and support their fathers and brothers.[32] Not surprisingly, most "change of affiliation" in the highlands occurs after the death of one's father.

In most areas of the New Guinea highlands, groups at one or another level of segmentation are corporate with respect to land; the group is said to own the land on which it resides and the land may be regarded as an inalienable property. In some areas it is only the so-called clan that is corporate with respect to land; its component subgroups are not, and there is a good deal of interlocal mobility within the clan's region (see Langness 1964). In other areas, however, rights in estates at all levels are divided rather than joint, and brothers or classificatory brothers have reversionary interests in one another's parcels. In these cases men may affiliate with their mothers' groups only if their mothers' brothers are able to provide them with land. Where land is relatively scarce, even though a mother's brother may wish to make a grant of land and may have the right to do so, he may effectively be prevented from making it by his brothers and classificatory brothers who have reversionary interests in his land and who may not wish to imperil their or their sons' interests in it. Thus, in highland areas in which land is relatively scarce, ceding of land to sisters' sons may be relatively uncommon, interlocal mobility may be relatively re-

---

[32] Such groups might therefore be described as patrifilial *kin* groups rather than as patrilineal descent groups.

stricted, and local groups may tend strongly to be composed of men related to one another through their fathers, their fathers' fathers, etc. This tendency is not, however, a consequence of more rigid adherence to a patrilineal group constitution, for, it seems, no such norm is present (see Meggitt 1965, Kelly 1968).

There appears to be little justification for the arguments that in the highlands there are wide discrepancies between "ideology" and practice and between jural and statistical norms, and that genealogical connection or kinship is nothing more than an idiom used merely to express or conceptualize the solidarity of local groups, whose members are more concerned with factional allegiance than with genealogy as such (see Langness 1964, Lepervanche 1967, Strathern 1968). The genealogical and social relations of paternal and fraternal *kinship* provide the principal structural framework of many highland societies.

VII: ALLIANCE

All societies prohibit sexual relations and marriage between certain kinds of relatives, but not always the same ones; in some societies sexual relations between certain kinds of kin are at least tolerated, while marriage between the same individuals is flatly prohibited. Therefore, we must distinguish between rules prohibiting *sexual relations* between kin or certain kinds of kin (usually described as incest tabus) and rules prohibiting marriage between kin or members of the same descent or kin group (rules of exogamy). On the positive side, some societies are reported to complement their incest tabus and rules of exogamy with "prescriptive" or "preferential" marriage rules. These rules usually specify one or another type of cross-cousin (the child of a parent's opposite-sex sibling) as one's most

appropriate spouse (preferential rule) or as his only appropriate spouse (prescriptive rule), or so it is reported. A great deal of anthropological ingenuity has been demonstrated in various attempts to account for the existence and differential distribution of these rules of cross-cousin marriage, the most elaborate of which is now widely (though some would argue misleadingly) known as "alliance theory" and is principally identified with Lévi-Strauss, Dumont, and Needham.[33]

Dumont (1968:19) notes that in the expression "marriage alliance," alliance "refers to the repetition of intermarriage between larger or smaller groups" (specifically, descent groups), and that the expression as a whole "denotes what amounts to a special theory of kinship." Although the theory, as Dumont also notes, was developed—principally by Lévi-Strauss—to deal most specifically with societies featuring cross-cousin marriage rules, Lévi-Strauss insists that the theory expounded in his *Elementary Structures of Kinship* (1969) is a general theory of systems of kinship and marriage (i.e., systems of ordering social relationships, including marriage, by reference to relations of kinship), not a special theory about the functions of cross-cousin marriage in a special type of society (see also Lévi-Strauss 1956).

At the risk of oversimplification and misrepresentation, the theory may be briefly stated like this: The prohibition of incest, though variable in its range, is a universal rule and, though often rationalized on "biological" grounds, is in fact a social rule designed to preclude marriage within the family and thereby to establish a mutual dependency be-

---

[33] Lévi-Strauss (1969) provides an extensive review and critique of earlier theories. See also Meggitt (1968:177f) for some enlightening observations on the history of the study of Australian "marriage classes."

tween families (i.e., to create society) by compelling men to exchange their sisters and daughters in marriage with the men of other families. The rule to "marry out" is but the converse of the rule not to "marry in," and both rules have the same function: to establish relations of exchange between families. In some societies this integration of families into a larger social system is accomplished by the exchange of women for other kinds of "property," as in the payment of so-called bride-price, but in others women are exchanged, directly or indirectly, for one another. The various forms of cross-cousin marriage may be interpreted, Lévi-Strauss argues, as special cases of this general phenomenon of "marriage by exchange."

Glossing over the essential distinction between rules governing sexual relations and those governing marriage, Lévi-Strauss notes that cross-cousins, often singled out as particularly appropriate spouses, are no more distant relatives than parallel cousins (the children of a parent's same-sex siblings), who are usually prohibited as spouses. Thus, he argues, degree of kinship can have nothing to do with their different jural statuses. Assuming that cross-cousins must be the preferred or prescribed spouses for the same reason that parallel cousins (along with siblings) are prohibited as spouses, he argues that the categorical and jural distinction between the two arises from the simple fact that, where "families" (read lineages) exchange their women as wives over several generations, all of anyone's parallel kin will be members of one's own "family" and all of his cross kin will be members of the other "family." Thus, he argues, the prohibition on marriage between parallel cousins is but one aspect of the general prohibition on marriage between members of the same group and, conversely, the prescription

of or preference for marriage with a cross-cousin is but an aspect of the more general positive requirement to take one's spouse from another group.

Lévi-Strauss distinguishes, however, between at least two general forms of intergroup exchange of women in marriage. In systems of restricted exchange, two groups exchange their women directly; bilateral cross-cousin marriage is one result. In systems of generalized exchange, no group may take its wives from the same group to which it gives its own women; rather, the system requires at least three (or three types of) groups: "own group," "wife-taking groups," and "wife-giving groups." One result of this sort of intergroup exchange is unilateral cross-cousin marriage; that is, the marriage of a man to his mother's brother's daughter (MBD) but not to his father's sister's daughter (FZD), or vice versa. For various reasons that need not be gone into here, Lévi-Strauss argues that patrilateral cross-cousin marriage cannot be part of an effective system of indirect intergroup exchange; attempts to practice it usually break down or lead to systems of direct exchange.

In Lévi-Strauss' view, then, rules of cross-cousin marriage are nothing more than aspects of systems of intergroup exchange; when they are phrased prescriptively, they express no more than a generalized obligation between descent groups in terms of more particular obligations between specific members of such groups. It should be noted, however, that Lévi-Strauss acknowledges that some societies in which bilateral cross-cousin marriage is prescribed or preferred lack any kinds of descent or kin groups that could be described as exchanging units. These cases he tends to dismiss as "primitive" attempts to institutionalize the principle of exchange; his final summation of his general theory of systems of cross-cousin marriage (1969:493) takes no account of them.

There are a number of difficulties with this theory and with the several extended attempts to modify it and make it more acceptable.[34] For example, at the outset Lévi-Strauss defines an elementary structure of kinship as a society that requires its men to marry women of a particular kin type, kin category, or kin group, and in which this rule is reflected in the system of kin classification—in the absence of any strictly affinal categories and the apparent terminological identification of all affinal relatives with categories of kin. But many of the cases he deals with do not exhibit this latter feature (consider his treatment of the Miwok case [1969:359f], and see Scheffler [1970c] for a detailed critique). Needham (1958, 1962) attempts to deal with this and other difficulties by arguing that Lévi-Strauss should have distinguished more rigorously between prescriptive and preferential marriage rules, for his theory deals only with prescriptive rules and systems founded on them. That is, only prescriptive rules have the terminological effects characteristic of an "elementary structure." Prescriptive rules, Needham argues, specify a particular "category of relationship" from which a man must choose his spouse; all other categories of women are forbidden as spouses. The categories are not kin categories, but "social categories" defined by "relations of descent and alliance"; i.e., by relations of formal marital alliance between unilineal descent groups.[35] According to Need-

ham, MBDs or FZDs are nowhere the prescribed spouses, though in societies that have prescriptive marriage rules (prescriptive alliance systems) they may happen to belong to the prescribed category and they may be the preferred spouses (or they may be prohibited as spouses).

There are at least three major difficulties with this revision of Lévi-Strauss' theory. First, there is extensive evidence that the systems of classification the theory purports to explain are in fact systems of kin classification, not systems of social categories, as the theory maintains, and that the terms of these systems are polysemic (i.e., they have structurally primary senses that are subject to extension), which the theory flatly denies (see Scheffler 1970c, Scheffler and Lounsbury 1971 for extensive reviews of this evidence). Second, in the most frequently cited cases of "prescriptive alliance systems" the kind of marriage rule specified by the theory does not exist. Leach (1969) notes that the Kachin, frequently cited as an indubitable case of asymmetric prescriptive alliance (a system of generalized exchange in Lévi-Strauss' terms), do not prescribe marriage with a woman of any kin category, nor do they flatly prohibit marriage with a woman of the category containing the FZD, though marriage with the FZD herself is forbidden. Similar arrangements are found in most well-documented cases of alleged prescriptive alliance, though in some (e.g., the Purum) there is no separately designated category of "potential spouse" (in this case MBD is classified as "sister," or probably as "sister-in-law"). Third, the theory fails to account for cases like the Siriono (Scheffler and Lounsbury 1971), Yaruro, and many others in which the sys-

---

[34] See, e.g., Needham 1962; Fox 1967; Dumont 1966, 1968 for some attempted modifications, and Josselin de Jong 1952, Schneider 1965, Scheffler 1970c, and Leach 1970:95f for some of the criticism.

[35] Needham has recently dispensed with the requirement that the exchanging units should be corporate unilineal descent groups, but this amounts to

a considerable modification and "weakening" of the theory as a whole. For further comment, see Scheffler and Lounsbury 1971.

tem of kin classification clearly meets the requirements of the theory—insofar as there are no strictly affinal categories and affines are classified as though each man had married his MBD or, in the bilateral cases, either his MBD or FZD—but the society features no unilineal descent groups or categories that could be engaged in the exchange of women in marriage. In some of these societies marriages are arranged solely by the would-be spouses, and it is therefore difficult to see how the notion of marriage as exchange applies to them.

Lounsbury (1962) has suggested that the major fallacy of alliance theory is its preoccupation with the notion of prescription. Although ethnographers have often used the term "prescription" (or "preference") to describe the marriage rules of societies allegedly organized as prescriptive alliance systems, their reports often reveal that a man is not obliged to marry one or another type of cross-cousin (or, if no such woman is available, a woman of the same kin category), but that men have *rightful claims* over such kinswomen as wives, or that men have rightful claims over their ZSs as potential DHs. This is particularly clear in the case of so-called asymmetric prescriptive alliance systems. In societies allegedly so organized it seems that these rightful claims are given expression in the systems of kin classification in the form of a rule of kin class or terminological extension, which equates Ego's *rightful* spouse (his MBD, her FZS) with his or her spouse or spouse's sibling of the same sex as a linking relative. By this rule, a man's MBD's child, for example, is treated as structurally equivalent to his wife's or his wife's sister's child, and thus as equivalent terminologically to his own child (see again Scheffler and Lounsbury 1971). In societies allegedly organized as symmetric

alliance systems (systems of restricted exchange in Lévi-Strauss' terms), it appears that a man may have an obligation (duty) to marry a woman (of no particular kin type) of the cross-cousin category, and this rule may be expressed in the system of kin classification in the form of a rule of terminological extension which requires the classification of all of anyone's affinal relatives as though they were the appropriate kinds of consanguineal relatives (see Scheffler 1971).

It seems clear from the ethnographic record that, where unilineal descent groups are present and where marriage between the members of different groups *may* be regarded as entailing a broader political alliance between the groups themselves, rights or duties in marriage in respect of particular types or categories of kin may serve to ensure the perpetuation of the political alliance. Such an alliance may be (but is not necessarily) established by any marriage, but once it is established, its perpetuity may rest not only on a generalized obligation to continue it, but also on the rights of men to claim, say, their MBDs as wives, or their ZSs as DHs. Since the members of the descent groups involved in a political-marital alliance are (or may be presumed to be) kin of one another, genealogical and social relationships between the groups as such may be (and often are) expressed in kinship terms.[36] There is, then, no necessary contradiction between rules of cross-cousin marriage and their expression in systems of kin classification

---

[36] Lévi-Strauss (1965:17) notes that Needham's revision of his theory, in particular Needham's exclusion of virtually "all consideration[s] of marriage preferences expressed in terms of kinship degrees," results in an "empty and tautological" definition of "the social structure." Lévi-Strauss here alludes to the fact that Needham's theory provides no description of the criteria by which certain groups are related as wife-givers and wife-takers in a "prescriptive alliance system." Thus to say, as Needham does, that

and systems of intergroup political-marital alliance (see Needham 1962). However, neither is there any necessary relationship between them. The existence of such rightful marital claims or duties in respect of particular types or classes of kin is not necessarily dependent on the existence of any other social structural features, and especially not on the existence of unilineal descent groups or categories, as cases like the Siriono clearly demonstrate (Scheffler and Lounsbury 1971).

It has been a popular anthropological misconception since the time of Tylor (and perhaps before) that marriage in "primitive society" is a family or group affair, that "the union of individuals is often largely symbolic of an alliance of groups" (Lowie 1920:35). Such assertions (see also Lévi-Strauss 1956:269, 281) confuse definitions of marriage with generalizations about marriage, which are often either too broad or simply false. It is more accurate to assert, as Radcliffe-Brown (1950:51) did of marriage in Africa, that marriage is often *not simply* a union of a man and a woman, but *may* have jural implications for social relations between their kin or their descent groups. The total complex of institutionalized social relationships centering on marriage varies from society to society. In some the union that constitutes marriage is solely the result of an agreement between the man and the woman concerned (although, as in our own society, it may be sanctioned by the state) and only informally entails any social relationships between the families or other kin of the principals. This is also the case

certain groups are "defined" as "wife-givers" and "wife-takers" in relation to one another is merely to describe an aspect of their social relations but not to say anything about what underlies and, in a sense, prescribes their continuing marital relationship. It is easy to see, however, that this underlying variable consists in the relations of genealogical connection presumed to exist between their respective members.

among peoples like the Siriono, although a Siriono man has rightful marital claims over particular kinds of kinswomen (MBDs) and privileged sexual access to them before and after marriage, even when both he and they have married others. It remains to be explained why certain kinds of kinswomen and not others are designated as rightful spouses by the culture,[37] but it seems that such jural arrangements represent a recurrent adaptation (though) only one of many possible forms of adaptation) to the stresses of social life in small-scale, isolated, and, almost of necessity, pragmatically endogamous communities in which conflict over women tends to be endemic.

In societies of larger scale where social life is nevertheless still regulated predominantly by norms of kinship and descent, marriage seldom (if ever) involves the transfer of *all* rights in a woman to her husband or his kin, and affines are necessarily implicated to one degree or another in one another's affairs because they have divided rights in respect of the same individuals. Under such circumstances it is hardly surprising that social relations between affines as such are often subject to jural control, or that marriages between members of two groups are sometimes regarded as having implications for relations between those groups as such. Nor is it surprising that parents or their siblings should be granted rights to arrange marriages or to veto marriages contemplated by their children. It is rarely the case, however, that such rights are granted to descent groups in respect of their members (but cf. Needham 1962:43). Perhaps this is because it is neither possible nor regarded as the "ideal" in any society for any two or three groups to intermarry exclusively

[37] For a suggested explanation in cultural terms, see Scheffler and Lounsbury 1971: chap. 8.

with one another (but cf. Lévi-Strauss 1965:17); it is, instead, both necessary (for demographic reasons, for example) and expedient (for political reasons) for any group to have its members married to members of many other groups. Depending of course on the nature of the intergroup relationships normatively entailed by a marriage, not all political-marital intergroup alliances can be cultivated equally, and not all marriages can be or are of equal political significance. Therefore, not all marriages need be regarded as concerning the group as such; there is simply no need for descent groups to have the authority to arrange marriages between their members in order to establish and maintain a system of intergroup political-marital alliance.

There is, it seems, a structural continuity between what some anthropologists (e.g., Needham 1966) have distinguished as three major and structurally noncomparable "types of society": cognatic systems, unilineal descent systems, and prescriptive alliance systems. In varying degrees, all societies order social relations among their members on the basis of culturally posited relations of genealogical connection presumed to exist among them, in some by relations of kinship alone, in others by relations of common descent as well. In societies where social relations based on common descent become institutionalized, their systems of social relations based on kinship will differ to some degree from those found in societies in which relations of common descent are not recognized. But this is merely a matter of the necessary mutual adaptation of two genealogically defined subsystems of social relations, and such mutual adaptation in no way entails total insignificance for relations of kinship. In all societies there is some tendency for marriage to be regarded as establishing social relations between the

kin or the descent groups of the principals, probably because, as we have already noted, marriage nowhere entails the transfer of all rights in a woman to her husband or to his kin or descent group, and because individuals related only through marriage soon become related, at least indirectly, as kin of the offspring of that marriage.

Marriage, as Radcliffe-Brown often noted (e.g., 1950:43), entails "a rearrangement of social structure," or perhaps it would be more accurate to say it entails reorganization of the systems of social relations focusing on the principal parties to the marriage; where they are members of descent groups, this reorganization must include adjustment of the rightful interests that other members of those groups have in the principals, and some provision must be made for the complementary division of interests in their offspring. It is a common notion that marriage between the members of two descent groups relates the groups as such and that it is desirable to continue this relationship indefinitely. In some societies this continuity is formally conceptualized in notions of intergroup marital alliance, but not, as Lehman (1963, 1970), Yalman (1967), Hiatt (1965), and Meggitt (1962) have observed, in holistic cultural systems of the sort posited by proponents of alliance theory. The kinship systems of societies featuring formal concepts of intergroup marital alliance are adapted to their descent systems by means of the allocation to men of rights or duties to claim kinswomen of a particular type or category as their wives.[38] Thus so-called prescriptive alli-

---

[38] For emphasis it should be stated again that such rights and duties are not necessarily associated with concepts of political-marital alliance between unilineal descent groups. They are widely distributed in North and South America in societies that feature no such groups, and they are prevalent in India in societies with and without such groups. In many of

ance systems differ from simple unilineal descent systems only in the addition of a further structural principle—intergroup alliance—which is itself little more than a formalization of a much more common notion about the concomitants of individual marriage.

REFERENCES

Austen, L.
1934 Procreation Among the Trobriand Islanders. *Oceania* 5:102-13.
Barnes, J. A.
1962 African Models in the New Guinea Highlands. *Man* 62:5-9.
1967*a* Genealogies. In *The Craft of Social Anthropology*, ed. A. L. Epstein. London: Tavistock.
1967*b* Agnation Among the Enga: A Review Article. *Oceania* 38:33-43.
Barth, F.
1953 Principles of Social Organization in Southern Kurdistan. *Universitetets Etnografiske Museum Bulletin* (Oslo), no. 7.
1966 *Models of Social Organization.* Royal Anthropological Institute, occasional paper no. 23. London.
Beattie, J. H. M.
1958 *Nyoro Kinship, Marriage, and Affinity*. International African Institute Memoirs, no. 28.
1959 Understanding and Explanation in Social Anthropology. *British Journal of Sociology* 10:45-60.
1964 Kinship and Social Anthropology. *Man* 64:101-103.

these cases their sole function is to regulate individual marriage. According to Hiatt (1965, 1967) and many other anthropologists who have worked in Australia, many aborigines entertain no notions of prescribed intergroup affinal alliance, though they do occasionally describe the interesting though structurally insignificant relations established between descent groups by virtue of practice of their "rules" of individual marriage. See Fox (1969), who mistakes this description of the consequences of individual marriage for a description of an "ideal" model of the structure of the total society. The same mistake has been made by many ethnographers, but more often by theoreticians with no firsthand ethnographic experience in Australia.

Bender, D. R.
1970 Agnatic or Cognatic? A Re-evaluation of Ondo Descent. *Man* (n.s.) 5:71-87.
Bohannan, P.
1963 *Social Anthropology*. New York: Holt, Rinehart & Winston.
Brown, P.
1962 Non-agnates Among the Patrilineal Chimbu. *Journal of the Polynesian Society* 71:57-69.
Bulmer, R.
1966 Review of M. J. Meggitt's *The Lineage System of the Mae-Enga of New Guinea. Man* (n.s.) 1:127-29.
Davis, K., and W. L. Warner
1937 Structural Analysis of Kinship. *American Anthropologist* 39:291-313.
Dixon, R. M. W.
1968 Correspondence: Virgin Birth. *Man* (n.s.) 3:653-54.
Dumont, L.
1966 Descent or Intermarriage? A Relational View of Australian Descent Systems. *Southwestern Journal of Anthropology* 22:231-50.
1968 Marriage Alliance. *International Encyclopedia of Social Science* 10: 19-23.
Eggan, F.
1968 Kinship. *International Encyclopedia of Social Science* 8:390-401.
Evans-Pritchard, E. E.
1940 *The Nuer.* Oxford: Clarendon Press.
1951 *Kinship and Marriage Among the Nuer*. Oxford: Clarendon Press.
Firth, R.
1959 *Social Change in Tikopia*. London: Allen & Unwin.
1968 Rivers on Oceanic Kinship. Commentary in W. H. R. Rivers, *Kinship and Social Organization*. London Shool of Economics Monographs on Social Anthropology, no. 34.
Forde, C. D.
1947 The Anthropological Approach in Social Science. *Advancement of Science* 4:213-24.
1950 Double Descent Among the Yako. In *African Systems of Kinship and Marriage*, ed. A. R. Radcliffe-Brown and C. D. Forde. London: Oxford University Press.
1963 On Some Further Unconsidered As-

pects of Descent. *Man* 63:12-13.

Fortes, M.
1945 *The Dynamics of Clanship Among the Tallensi*. London: Oxford University Press.
1949a *The Web of Kinship Among the Tallensi*. London: Oxford University Press.
1949b Time and Social Structure: An Ashanti Case Study. In *Social Structure: Studies Presented to A. R. Radcliffe-Brown*, ed. M. Fortes. Oxford: Clarendon Press.
1950 Kinship and Marriage Among the Ashanti. In *African Systems of Kinship and Marriage*, ed. A. R. Radcliffe-Brown and C. D. Forde. London: Oxford University Press.
1953 The Structure of Unilineal Descent Groups. *American Anthropologist* 55:17-51.
1959 Descent, Filiation, and Affinity. *Man* 59:193-97, 206-12.
1969 *Kinship and the Social Order*. Chicago: Aldine.

Fox, R.
1967 *Kinship and Marriage: An Anthropological Perspective*. Harmondsworth: Penguin Books.
1969 Alliance and the Australians. *Mankind* (Sydney) 7:15-18.

Frazer, J. G.
1910 *Totemism and Exogamy*. London: Macmillan.

Freeman, J. D.
1960 On the Concept of the Kindred. *Journal of the Royal Anthropological Institute* 91:192-220.

Gellner, E.
1962 Concepts and Society. In *Transactions of the Fifth World Congress of Sociology* 1:153-83.

Glasse, R. M.
1968 *Huli of Papua: A Cognatic Descent System*. Paris: Mouton.
1969 Marriage in South Fore. In *Pigs, Pearl-Shells, and Women*, ed. M. J. Meggitt. Englewood Cliffs, N.J.: Prentice-Hall.

Gluckman, M.
1950 Kinship and Marriage Among the Lozi of Northern Rhodesia and the Zulu of Natal. In *African Systems of Kinship and Marriage*, ed. A. R. Radcliffe-Brown and C. D. Forde. London: Oxford University Press.

Goffman, E.
1961 *Encounters*. Indianapolis: Bobbs-Merrill.

Goodenough, W.
1955 A Problem in Malayo-Polynesian Social Organization. *American Anthropologist* 57:71-83.
1956a Componential Analysis and the Study of Meaning. *Language* 32:195-216.
1956b Residence Rules. *Southwestern Journal of Anthropology* 12:22-37.
1962 Kindred and Hamlet in Lakalai, New Britain. *Ethnology* 1:5-12.
1963 Review of *Social Structure in Southeast Asia*, ed. G. P. Murdock. *American Anthropologist* 65:923-28.
1965 Rethinking "Status" and "Rule." In *The Relevance of Models for Social Anthropology*, ed. M. Banton. New York: Praeger.
1970 Epilogue: Transactions in Parenthood. In *Adoption in Eastern Oceania*, ed. V. Carroll. Honolulu: University of Hawaii Press.

Goody, J.
1961 The Classification of Double Descent Systems. *Current Anthropology* 2:3-25.
1966 Introduction to *Succession to High Office*, ed. J. Goody. Cambridge Papers in Social Anthropology, no. 4. Cambridge: At the University Press.
1968 Kinship II: Descent Groups. *International Encyclopedia of Social Science* 8:401-408.

Goody, J., ed.
1958 *The Developmental Cycle in Domestic Groups*. Cambridge Papers in Social Anthropology, no. 1. Cambridge: At the University Press.

Goswami, B. D.
1960 Kinship System of the Lushais. *Bulletin of the Anthropological Survey of India* 9:81-88.
1963 A Note on the Lushai Family. *Eastern Anthropologist* 16:201-207.

Gould, J., and W. L. Kolb, eds.
1964 *A Dictionary of the Social Sciences*. New York: Free Press, Macmillan.

Greenberg, J. H.
1949 The Logical Analysis of Kinship.

Philosophy of Science 16:58-64.

1966 Language Universals. In *Current Trends in Linguistics*, vol. 3: *Theoretical Foundations*, ed. T. A. Sebeok. The Hague: Mouton.

Guemple, D. L.
1965 Saunik: Name Sharing as a Factor Governing Eskimo Kinship Terms. *Ethnology* 4:323-35.

Hearn, W. E.
1879 *The Aryan Household*. London: Longmans, Green.

Hiatt, L. R.
1965 *Kinship and Conflict*. Canberra: Australian National University Press.
1967 Authority and Reciprocity in Australian Aboriginal Marriage Arrangements. *Mankind* (Sydney) 6:468-75.

Hocart, A. M.
1937 Kinship Systems. *Anthropos* 32: 345-51.

Hoebel, E. A.
1954 *The Law of Primitive Man*. Cambridge: Harvard University Press.

Holmberg, A.
1950 *Nomads of the Long Bow*. Institute of Social Anthropology Publications, no. 10. Washington, D.C.: Smithsonian Institution.

Howitt, A. W.
1904 *The Native Tribes of Southeast Australia*. London: Macmillan.

James, T. E.
1957 The Illegitimate and Deprived Child: Legitimation and Adoption. In *A Century of Family Law, 1857-1957*, ed. R. H. Graveson and F. R. Crane. London: Sweet & Maxwell.

Josselin de Jong, J. P. D. de
1952 *Lévi-Strauss's Theory on Kinship and Marriage*. Mededelingen van het Rijksmuseum voor Volkenkunde (Leiden), no. 10.

Kay, H. H.
1965 The Family and Kinship System of Illegitimate Children in California Law. In *The Ethnography of Law*, ed. L. Nader. *American Anthropologist* 67, no. 6, pt. 2 (special publication).

Kelly, R. C.
1968 Demographic Pressure and Descent Group Structure in the New Guinea Highlands. *Oceania* 39:36-63.

Kroeber, A. L.
1909 Classificatory Systems of Relationship. *Journal of the Royal Anthropological Institute* 39:77-84.
1938 Basic and Secondary Patterns of Social Structure. *Journal of the Royal Anthropological Institute* 68: 229-309.

Lahontan, Baron de
1905 *New Voyages to North America*, ed. R. G. Thwaites, 2 vols. Chicago: A. C. McClurg. Originally published 1703.

Langness, L.
1964 Some Problems of Conceptualization of Highlands Social Structure. In *New Guinea: The Central Highlands*, ed. J. B. Watson. *American Anthropologist* 66, no. 4, pt. 2 (special publication).

Leach, E. R.
1954 *Political Systems of Highland Burma*. Cambridge: Harvard University Press.
1958 Concerning Trobriand Clans and the Kinship Category Tabu. In *The Developmental Cycle in Domestic Groups*, ed. J. Goody. Cambridge Papers in Social Anthropology, no. 1. Cambridge: At the University Press.
1961 *Rethinking Anthropology*. London School of Economics Monographs on Social Anthropology, no. 22.
1967a Virgin Birth. *Proceedings of the Royal Anthropological Institute* 1967:39-50.
1967b The Language of Kachin Kinship. In *Social Organization: Essays Presented to R. Firth*, ed. M. Freedman. Chicago: Aldine.
1969 "Kachin" and "Haka Chin": A Rejoinder to Lévi-Strauss. *Man* (n.s.) 4:277-85.
1970 *Lévi-Strauss*. Fontana Modern Masters Series. London: William Collins.

Lehman, F. K.
1963 *The Structure of Chin Society*. Illinois Studies in Anthropology, no. 3. Urbana: University of Illinois Press.
1970 On Chin and Kachin Marriage Regulations. *Man* (n.s.) 5:118-25.

Lepervanche, M. de

1967 Descent, Residence, and Leadership in the New Guinea Highlands. *Oceania* 38:134-68.

Lévi-Strauss, C.
1956 The Family. In *Man, Culture, and Society*, ed. H. L. Shapiro. New York: Oxford University Press.
1963 *Structural Anthropology*. New York: Basic Books. First published 1958.
1965 The Future of Kinship Studies. *Proceedings of the Royal Anthropological Institute* 1965:13-22.
1969 *The Elementary Structures of Kinship*. Boston: Beacon Press. Originally published 1949, revised 1967.

Linton, R.
1936 *The Study of Man*. New York: Appleton-Century.

Lounsbury, F. G.
1956 A Semantic Analysis of the Pawnee Kinship Usage. *Language* 32:158-94.
1962 Review of R. Needham, *Structure and Sentiment*. *American Anthropologist* 64:1302-1310.
1964a A Formal Account of the Crow- and Omaha-Type Kinship Terminology. In *Explorations in Cultural Anthropology*, ed. W. Goodenough. New York: McGraw-Hill.
1964b The Structural Analysis of Kinship Semantics. In *Proceedings of the Ninth International Congress of Linguists*, ed. H. G. Hunt. The Hague: Mouton.
1965 Another view of Trobriand Kinship Categories. In *Formal Semantic Analysis*, ed. E. A. Hammel, *American Anthropologist* 67, no. 5, pt. 2 (special publication).
1969 Language and Culture. In *Language and Philosophy: A Symposium*, ed. S. Hook. New York: New York University Press.

Lowie, R.
1920 *Primitive Society*. New York: Boni & Liveright.
1929 Relationship Terms. In *Encyclopaedia Britannica*, 14th ed., 19:84-90.

Malinowski, B.
1916 Baloma: The Spirits of the Dead in the Trobriand Islands. *Journal of the Royal Anthropological Institute* 46:353-430.

1926 *Crime and Custom in Savage Society*. London: Kegan Paul.
1927 *The Father in Primitive Psychology*. New York: Norton.
1929a *The Sexual Life of Savages in Northwestern Melanesia*. London: Routledge.
1929b Marriage. In *Encyclopedia Britannica*, 14th ed., 14:940-50. Reprinted in Malinowski 1962.
1929c Kinship. In *Encyclopaedia Britannica*, 14th ed., 13:403-409. Reprinted in Malinowski 1962.
1930a Parenthood: The Basis of Social Structure. In *The New Generation*, ed. V. F. Calverton and S. D. Schmalhausen. London: Allen & Unwin. Reprinted in Malinowski 1962.
1930b Kinship. *Man* 30:19-29. Reprinted in Malinowski 1962.
1932 Pigs, Papuans, and Police Court Perspective. *Man* 32:33-38.
1935 *Coral Gardens and Their Magic*, 2 vols. New York: American Book Co.
1937 Foreword to M. F. A. Montagu, *Coming into Being Among the Australian Aborigines*. London: Routledge.
1962 *Sex, Culture, and Myth*. New York: Harcourt, Brace & World.
1963 *The Family Among the Australian Aborigines*. New York: Schocken Books. Originally published 1913.

Mayer, P.
1949 *The Lineage Principle in Gusii Society*. International African Institute Memoirs, no. 24. London: Oxford University Press.

Meggitt, M. J.
1962 *Desert People*. Sydney: Angus & Robertson.
1965 *The Lineage System of the Mae-Enga of New Guinea*. Edinburgh: Oliver & Boyd.
1968 "Marriage Classes" and Demography in Central Australia. In *Man the Hunter*, ed. R. B. Lee and I. De Vore. Chicago: Aldine.

Merton, R. K.
1957 *Social Theory and Social Structure*, rev. and enlarged ed. Glencoe: Free Press.

Middleton, J.

1958 The Political System of the Lugbara of the Nile-Congo Divide. In *Tribes Without Rulers*, ed. J. Middleton and D. Tait. London: Routledge & Kegan Paul.

Middleton, J., and D. Tait
1958 Introduction to *Tribes Without Rulers*, ed. J. Middleton and D. Tait. London: Routledge & Kegan Paul.

Montagu, M. F. Ashley
1937 *Coming into Being Among the Australian Aborigines*. London: Routledge.

Morgan, L. H.
1871 *Systems of Consanguinity and Affinity of the Human Family*. Smithsonian Contributions to Knowledge, no. 17. Washington, D.C.: Smithsonian Institution.
1877 *Ancient Society*. New York: Henry Holt.

Murdock, G. P.
1949 *Social Structure*. New York: Macmillan.

Needham, R.
1958 A Structural Analysis of Purum Society. *American Anthropologist* 60:75-101.
1962 *Structure and Sentiment*. Chicago: University of Chicago Press.
1966 Age, Category, and Descent. *Bijdragen tot de Taal-, Land-, en Volkenkunde* 122:1-35.

Nokes, G. D.
1957 Evidence. In *A Century of Family Law, 1857-1957*, ed. R. H. Graveson and F. R. Crane. London: Sweet & Maxwell.

Opler, M. E.
1937 Apache Data Concerning the Relation of Kinship Terminology to Social Classification. *American Anthropologist* 39:201-12.

Parry, N. E.
1928 *A Monograph on Lushai Customs and Ceremonies*. Shillong: Assam Government Press.

Pelto, P. J.
1966 Cognitive Aspects of American Kin Terms. *American Anthropologist* 68:198-202.

Pospisil, L.
1964 Law and Societal Structure Among the Nunamiut Eskimo. In *Explorations in Cultural Anthropology*, ed. W. Goodenough. New York: McGraw-Hill.

Powell, H. A.
1956 Trobriand Social Structure. Ph. D. dissertation, University of London.
1968 Correspondence: Virgin Birth. *Man* (n.s.) 3:651-52.
1969*a* Genealogy, Residence, and Kinship in Kiriwana. *Man* (n.s.) 4:177-202.
1969*b* Territory, Hierarchy, and Kinship in Kiriwana. *Man* (n.s.) 4:580-604.

Pukui, M. K., and S. Elbert
1965 *Hawaiian-English Dictionary*. Honolulu: University of Hawaii Press.

Radcliffe-Brown, A. R.
1929 A Further Note on Ambrym. *Man* 29:50-53.
1930- The Social Organization of the Australian Tribes. *Oceania* 1:34-63, 1931 206-46, 322-41, 426-56.
1935 Patrilineal and Matrilineal Succession. *Iowa Law Review* 20:286-303. Reprinted in Radcliffe-Brown 1952.
1941 The Study of Kinship Systems. *Journal of the Royal Anthropological Institute* 71:1-18. Reprinted in Radcliffe-Brown 1952.
1950 Introduction to *African Systems of Kinship and Marriage*, ed. A. R. Radcliffe-Brown and C. D. Forde. London: Oxford University Press.
1952 *Structure and Function in Primitive Society*. Glencoe: Free Press.

Read, C.
1918 No Paternity. *Journal of the Royal Anthropological Institute* 48:146-54.

Rehfisch, F.
1960 The Dynamics of Multilineality on the Mambila Plateau. *Africa* 30:246-60.

Rentoul, A. C.
1931 Physiological Paternity and the Trobrianders. *Man* 31:152-54.
1932 Papuans, Professors, and Platitudes. *Man* 32:274-76.

Richards, A.
1950 Some Types of Family Structure Amongst the Central Bantu. In *African Systems of Kinship and Marriage*, ed. A. R. Radcliffe-Brown and C. D. Forde. London: Oxford University Press.

Rivers, W. H. R.

1907 On the Origin of the Classificatory System of Relationships. In *Anthropological Essays Presented to E. B. Tylor*, ed. N. W. Thomas et al. Oxford: Clarendon Press.

1915 Kin, Kinship. In *Encyclopedia of Religion and Ethics*, ed. J. Hastings, 8:700-707. New York: Scribner.

1924 *Social Organization*. London: Kegan Paul.

riviere, P.
1969 *Marriage Among the Trio*. Oxford: Clarendon Press.

Robinson, M. S.
1962 Complementary Filiation and Marriage in the Trobriand Islands: A Re-examination of Malinowski's Material. In *Marriage in Tribal societies*, ed. M. Fortes. Cambridge Papers in Social Anthropology, no. 3. Cambridge: At the University Press.

Romney, A. K., and R. G. D'Andrade
1964 Cognitive Aspects of English Kin Terms. In *Transcultural Studies in Cognition,* ed. A. K. Romney and R. G. D'Andrade. *American Anthropologist* 66, no. 3, pt. 2 (special publication).

Sahlins, M. D.
1965 On the Ideology and Composition of Descent Groups. *Man* 65: 104-107.
1968 *Tribesmen*. Englewood Cliffs, N.J.: Prentice-Hall.

Salisbury, R. F.
1964 New Guinea Highlands Models and Descent Theory. *Man* 64:168-71.

Schapera, I.
1937 *A Handbook of Tswana Law and Custom*. London: Oxford University Press.

Scheffler, H. W.
1965 *Choiseul Island Social Structure*. Berkeley: University of California Press.
1966 Ancestor Worship in Anthropology: Or, Observations on Descent and Descent Groups. *Current Anthropology* 7:541-51.
1967 On Concepts of Descent and Descent Groups. *Current Anthropology* 8: 506-509.
1970*a* Kinship and Adoption in the Northern New Hebrides. In *Adoption in Eastern Oceania*, ed. V. Carroll.

Honolulu: University of Hawaii Press.

1970*b* Ambrym Revisited: A Preliminary Report. *Southwestern Journal of Anthropology* 26:52-66.

1970*c* The Elementary Structures of Kinship by C. Lévi-Strauss: A Review Article. *American Anthropologist* 72:251-68.

1971 Dravidian-Iroquois: The Melanesian Evidence. In *Anthropology in Oceania: Essays in Honor of H. I. Hogbin*, ed. C. Jayawardena and L. Hiatt. Sydney: Angus & Robertson.

1972*a* Baniata Kin Classification: The Case for Extensions. *Southwestern Journal of Anthropology* 28, no. 4 (Winter).

1972*b* Systems of Kin Classification: A Structural Semantic Typology. In *Kinship Studies in the Morgan Centennial Year*, ed. P. Reining. Washington, D.C.: Anthropological Society of Washington.

1972*c* Kinship Semantics. In *Annual Review of Anthropology, 1972*, ed. B. J. Siegel, vol. 1. Palo Alto, California: Annual Reviews, Inc.

n.d. Baniata Kin Classification: The Case for Extensions. Unpublished papers.

Scheffler, H. W., and F. G. Lounsbury
1971 *A Study in Structural Semantics: The Siriono Kinship System*. Englewood Cliffs, N.J.: Prentice-Hall.

Schneider, D. M.
1961 Introduction to *Matrilineal Kinship*, ed. D. M. Schneider and K. Gough. Berkeley: University of California Press.
1965 Some Muddles in the Models: Or, How the System Really Works. In *The Relevance of Models for Social Anthropology,* ed. M. Banton. New York: Praeger.
1967 Descent and Filiation as Cultural Constructs. *Southwestern Journal of Anthropology* 23:65-73.
1968*a* Correspondence: *Virgin Birth*. Man (n.s.) 3:126-29.
1968*b* Rivers and Kroeber in the Study of Kinship. Commentary in W. H. R. Rivers, *Kinship and Social Organization*. London School of Economics Monographs on Social Anthropology, no. 34.

1969 Kinship, Nationality, and Religion in American Culture: Toward a Definition of Kinship. In *Forms of Symbolic Action: Proceedings of the 1969 Annual Meeting of the American Ethnological Society,* ed. R. F. Spencer. Seattle: University of Washington Press.

Schneider, D. M., and K. Gough, eds.
1961 *Matrilineal Kinship.* Berkeley: University of California Press.

Schneider, D. M., and J. Roberts
1956 *Zuñi Kin Terms.* Laboratory of Anthropology, Notebook no. 3, Monograph no. 1. Lincoln: University of Nebraska.

Service, E.
1962 *Primitive Social Organization: An Evolutionary Perspective.* New York: Random House.

Sider, K. B.
1967 Affinity and the Role of the Father in the Trobriands. *Southwestern Journal of Anthropology* 23:90-109.

Singer, C.
1959 *A History of Biology to About the Year 1900,* 3rd ed. New York: Abelard-Schuman.

Smith, M. G.
1956 On Segmentary Lineage Systems. *Journal of the Royal Anthropological Institute* 86:39-79.

Smith, W. R.
1963 *Kinship and Marriage in Early Arabia,* 2d ed., rev. Boston: Beacon Press. This edition first published 1903.

Southwold, M.
1966 Succession to the Throne in Buganda. In *Succession to High Office,* ed. J. Goody. Cambridge Papers in Social Anthropology, no. 4. Cambridge: At the University Press.

Spiro, M. E.
1968 Virgin Birth, Parthenogenesis, and Physiological Paternity: An Essay in Cultural Interpretation. *Man* (n.s.) 3:242-61.

Sprott, W. J. H.
1958 *Human Groups.* Hammondsworth: Penguin Books.

Strathern, A.
1968 Descent and Alliance in the New Guinea Highlands: Some Problems of Comparison. *Proceedings of the Royal Anthropological Institute* 1968: 37-52.

1972 *One Father, One Blood: Descent and Group Structure Among the Melpa People.* Canberra: Australian National University Press.

Strathern, A., and M. Strathern
1969 Marriage in Melpa. In *Pigs, Pearl-Shells, and Women,* ed. M. J. Meggitt. Englewood Cliffs, N.J.: Prentice-Hall.

Tax, S.
1955 The Social Organization of the Fox Indians. In *Social Anthropology of North American Tribes,* ed. F. Eggan, enlarged ed. Chicago: University of Chicago Press.

Thomas, N. W.
1906 *Kinship Organizations and Group Marriage in Australia.* Cambridge: At the University Press.

Thomson, D. F.
1933 The Hero Cult, Initiation, and Totemism on Cape York: The Knowledge of Physical Paternity. *Journal of the Royal Anthropological Institute* 63:505-10.

Van Velsen, J.
1964 *The Politics of Kinship.* Manchester: Manchester University Press.

Wake, C. S.
1967 *The Development of Marriage and Kinship,* ed. R. Needham. Chicago: University of Chicago Press. Originally published 1889.

Wallace, A. F. C.
1965 The Problem of Psychological Validity of Componential Analyses. In *Formal Semantic Analysis,* ed. E. A. Hammel. *American Anthropologist* 67, no. 5 pt. 2 (special publication).

Wallace, A. F. C., and J. Atkins
1960 The Meaning of Kinship Terms. *American Anthropologist* 62:58-80.

Westermark, E.
1891 *The History of Human Marriage.* London: Macmillan.

White, L.
1958 What Is a Classificatory Kinship Term? *Southwestern Journal of Anthropology* 14:378-85.

Williamson, K.
1962 Changes in the Marriage System of

the Okrika Ijo. *Africa* 32:53-60.

Winter, H.
1956 *Bwamba: A Structural-Functional Analysis of a Primitive Society*. Cambridge: Heffer.

Witherspoon, G.
1970 A New Look at Navajo Social Organization. *American Anthropologist* 72:55-65.

Yalman, N.
1967 *Under the Bo Tree: Studies in Caste, Kinship, and Marriage in the Interior of Ceylon*. Berkeley: University of California Press.

CHAPTER 18 Economic Anthropology: Problems in Theory, Method, and Analysis

SCOTT COOK

THE SCOPE OF ECONOMIC ANTHROPOLOGY

AN OVERVIEW

In just over four decades the field of study now known as economic anthropology has evolved from a nameless embryonic idea to a recognized and quasi-revolutionary subdiscipline of social and cultural anthropology. In the 1920s few scholars devoted special attention to the general problems common to economics and anthropology (Gras 1927:10); today there is considerable debate among its sectarianized practitioners as to whether the term "economic anthropology" should continue to denote its original meaning (Frankenberg 1967; Le Clair and Schneider, eds., 1968:5-13, 455-73). In his seminal essay N. S. B. Gras (1927:10), an economic historian, coined the term "economic anthropology" and conceived of it as a "synthesis of anthropological and economic studies" which entailed "the study of the ways in which primitive peoples ob-

tained a living." Gras distinguished economic anthropology from "anthropological economics," which he defined as "a study of the ideas that primitive peoples held about economic matters." Among his suggestions for future research was collaboration between anthropologists and economists so that "anthropologists could provide those in the economic field with facts in return for ideas and the fundamental issues involved in getting a living" (1927:22).

In retrospect, Gras's contribution seems to have had relatively little impact upon anthropologists in comparison with the works of Malinowski (1921, 1961), Mauss (1954), and Leroy (1925). This was unfortunate, since Gras's well-reasoned arguments would have provided effective alternatives to three negative aspects of Malinowski's dominant contribution: his "anti-economics," his inconsistent handling of the separate analytical operations distinguished by Gras under the rubrics of economic anthropology and anthropological economics, and his neglect of the diachronic-evolutionary perspective in the name of synchronic-functionalist inquiry. Only during the last two decades, under the influence of scholars like Polanyi, White, and Godelier, has economic anthropological inquiry systematically focused on diachronic evolutionary problems, which, with the important exception of Thurnwald's work (1932), had been essentially ignored since Malinowski's day. It was not until the 1960s, in accordance with the spirit of the so-called new ethnography and ethnoscience movement in cultural anthropology, that Gras's notion of anthropological economics (with some modifications) was reemphasized by Salisbury (1968a:479-85) under the label of "ethno-economics."

The anti-economics posture of Malinowski (Le Clair and Schneider, eds., 1968:3-5; cf. Raymond Firth 1964a) prevailed among anthropologists until 1939-1940, when important books by Firth (1965a), Goodfellow (1939), and Herskovits (1940) were published, each in its own way advocating the position that anthropologists could benefit analytically by studying and applying selected aspects of conventional economics to primitive and peasant economies. While Malinowski's early works—their anti-economics notwithstanding—did first present the possibility of an empirically based anthropological study of economic relations, it was Firth's work (1959, 1965a, 1966) that first dealt with problems and provided data of equal value to anthropology and economics (see Belshaw 1967:25). However, a version of Malinowski's anti-economics reappeared in economic anthropological discourse as a basic tenet of the so-called substantivist revolution (Le Clair and Schneider, eds., 1968) that emerged in the 1950s under the leadership of Karl Polanyi (Cook 1968, Zeisel 1968, Dalton 1968, Humphreys 1969). This rather anachronistic development, which was largely ignored by

British economic anthropologists, engendered a protracted scope-and-method controversy in the 1960s between the followers of Polanyi and various other scholars (sometimes lumped together as "formalists") who for various reasons opposed the substantivist doctrine of the nonapplicability of conventional economic theory to the study of nonwestern, nonindustrial economies (Cook 1966a, 1966b, 1969; Frankenberg 1967:65-70; Dalton 1969; Le Clair and Schneider, eds., 1968:9-11).

It now appears, more than forty years after the publication of Gras's essay, that economic anthropology is finally following a Grasian path of development, with a majority of anthropologists conceding that conventional economics is at least potentially relevant and applicable to the study of primitive and peasant economies. Only Polanyi's followers still deny this, adamantly arguing *a priori* that economic theory is applicable only to the market-oriented, price-governed economic systems of modern industrial capitalism (e.g., Sahlins 1965b:225-26, 1969; P. and L. Bohannan 1968; Dalton 1969). This resuscitated anti-economics orientation is reinforced by a dominant interest among its advocates in describing the qualitative institutional context of economic behavior, as opposed to analyzing the quantitative results of that behavior (see Goldschmidt 1967:11).

ANTHROPOLOGY AND ECONOMICS

The mainstream of work in economic anthropology today is characterized by a growing spirit of cross-fertilization and collaboration between economists and anthropologists—a spirit that has been concretely manifested in a series of publications (e.g., Firth and Yamey, eds., 1964; Raymond Firth, ed., 1967; Le Clair and Schneider, eds., 1968;

Wharton, ed., 1969; Brookfield, ed., 1969; McLoughlin, ed., 1970). This spirit is a relatively recent phenomenon, especially from the standpoint of economics. In an incisive essay comparing the scope and method of economics and anthropology written in 1960, the economist Joseph Berliner (1962) was apologetic for the constricted perspective of his colleagues, who, when engaging themselves in the study of "comparative economic systems," habitually considered only the variant forms of Western-industrial economic systems; nevertheless, he argued (1962: 53) that this habit did not merit the stigma of being categorized as ethnocentrism but rather was simply a natural intellectual response by economists to the analytical complexities and possibilities of the Western institutional field. Berliner reasoned that economists of a decade ago were willing to forgo knowledge about relations between changes in economic variables and changes in other cultural variables, as well as about culturally specific versus universal properties of economic systems, in order to acquire a more intensive and precise understanding of the "systematic regularities among economic variables themselves."

From today's perspective, however, it is clear that many economists—especially those involved in problems of agricultural and industrial development in modernizing peasant societies—have decided that the complexities of the nonwestern institutional field also offer intellectual challenges and possibilities for mensurational ingenuity. In fact, what is emerging through the collective efforts of these economists is a tradition of comparative, empirical microeconomics—a long overdue development, clearly envisaged by Veblen (1948) in 1898, which offers the possibility of promoting a process of cumulative feedback into the received wisdom of conventional economic theory. This process will be nourished by a continuing series of analytical excursions by economists into the "far-flung territories, underworlds, and hinterlands" of economics, and by economically more sophisticated excursions by anthropologists.

This trend toward increased cross-fertilization should not be interpreted as indicating that the basic problems in epistemology and method of the economics/anthropology relationship have been resolved. On the contrary, as more empirical cases are examined with the tools of formal theory, and as more scholars seek to adapt their analytical operations to a selective alternation between anthropological inductionism and economic deductionism, we can anticipate more, not fewer, problems of applicability and relevance. The burden here falls squarely upon the individual economic anthropologist, who must be ultimately responsible for operationalizing the concepts and propositions of formal theory in the study of empirical economies. Moreover, it is in the results of the operationalization process that the explanatory value of formal concepts and propositions in anthropology will be determined (see Godelier 1967a; Joy 1967a; Salisbury 1968a; Kaplan 1968; Le Clair and Schneider, eds., 1968:455-73, 486-87; Cook 1969: 389-91).

Given the inevitability of problems and contradictions in method which arise in the application of the economist's tools to the study of economic phenomena in nonindustrial societies, why should anthropologists invest their time and effort in the study of economics—especially in view of the proliferating complexities of their own discipline? The answer to this question must be prefaced by a retrospective note. As Raymond Firth has observed (1967:2), the recognition of a discrete analytical sphere that could be labeled "economic" came slowly to anthropologists, since they tended to take economic phenomena for granted (much as economists have taken noneconomic phenomena for granted via the assumption of *ceteris paribus*) and concentrated mainly on the social framework of economic activity. In contrast to their forerunners, many contemporary economic anthropologists realize that the absence of what may be classed as specifically "economic" institutions or structures in nonindustrial societies does not indicate the absence of economic process in those societies (see Firth 1965*b*:7). Now that this realization has come, they are turning to economics to acquire a general understanding of the economic process; general ideas about allocational and decision-making processes entailed in reaching hypothetical optimums differentially operative within various economic units; a basic understanding of the technical forces and social relations of production; and knowledge of sources of inequality in the ownership, use, and distribution of wealth in complex societies, as well as mechanisms for perpetuating this inequality.

In addition, the study of economics can provide the anthropologist with some understanding of the ways in which quantitative data may be analyzed through the application of such tools as supply and demand analysis, time series analysis, matrix analysis, game theory analysis, input-output analysis, and so on. More broadly, the anthropologist, trained as he is in empirical-inductive method, can expect his study of economics to bring him a basic understanding of the nature and significance of deductive model-building as a heuristic tool. He can expect to learn to appreciate, as the economic theorist does, the explanatory possibilities of a method that is based on the assumption that knowledge of what *might* occur (i.e., problematic) or of what *must* occur (i.e., apodictic) can lead the investigator to a more comprehensive knowledge of what is actual or occurring (i.e., assertoric) in a given situation (see Godelier 1967*a*:258). Finally, and more pragmatically, the study of economics provides the anthropologist with increased awareness of the need and rationale for collecting systematic quantitative (or quantifiable) data, especially data focused on the *frequency* of observed activity and on its *representativeness* (Epstein 1967).

For the anthropologist, of course, economic values and facts reflect cultural norms, and every economic statement is a shorthand account of human behavior and relationships between individuals and groups. He is never interested in quantities and their relationships as ends in themselves. This orientation applies to the laws of supply and demand, to investment and saving, to time series, and to all the rest (see Steiner 1957:113).

There is a very healthy trend in economic anthropology away from argument in favor of the applicability of formal economics and toward its actual application to hypothetical and real situations. For example, Lee (1969) has adapted the transactional models of input-output economics to the analysis of !Kung Bushman subsistence; Edel (1967) has utilized econometrics to measure variations in the adoption of cooperatives by Jamaican fishing villages; Joy (1967*b*) has applied matrix analysis to Barth's data on the division of labor and exchange in the mountain fur economy; Orans (1968) has used the maximization principle to formulate a model of caste relations in India, Pakistan, and Ceylon; Cook (1970) has employed time series and supply and demand analysis in a study of price and output variability in a peasant-artisan stoneworking industry in the valley of Oaxaca, Mexico; and Schneider (1970) has analyzed economic relations among the Wahi Wanyaturu as a competitive decision-making process.

This trend is represented in the scope-and-method literature by a sophisticated essay by Edel (1969), who focuses on certain methodological problems that emerge from the application of economic analysis to a variety of hypothetical and real anthropological cases. He restricts his view of economic analysis to only two basic problem-solving strategies (i.e., ways for determining the unknown values of selected quantifiable variables): the "maximization" strategy, which defines a problem in terms of the allocation of limited resources to alternative ends, and the "fixed target" strategy, which seeks to find out whether certain fixed targets can be attained from the available means (1969:422). Edel's concise and explicit elucidation of these two strategies in anthropological problem-solving provides an illustration of economic analysis as "a system for organizing information in a framework amenable to the manipulation of mathematical functions and values" (1969: 428). Moreover, it supports his conclusion that "in very society the physical means of subsistence and means for the provision of other wants must be fitted to the ends of subsistence, and there must be some degree of satisfaction" which is another way of saying that economic analysis will be applicable to some extent in all societies.

Unlike many other formalists, Edel (1969:428-29) emphasizes three special requirements and limitations of economic analysis: (1) There are three elements that must be stipulated before such an analysis can be begun (a) pref-erence function—a mathematical representation of the things actors in the economic process desire to obtain or maximize; (b) resources—availability and ownership patterns; and (c) technical production or exchange possibilities (see Le Clair and Schneider, eds., 1968:457-59). (2) There is no way to deal with the diachronic dimension of the functions; i.e., economic analysis is purely synchronic. (3) The economic process may not be the only system relating values, technology, and resource ownership; consequently, complementary types of analysis are required to provide complete coverage of relevant relationships. Because of these requirements and limitations, Edel contends, economic analysis cannot cannibalize the traditional domains of other social sciences. Quite the contrary, he argues that the field of economic anthropology is necessary and viable precisely because economic analysis cannot cope effectively with interpersonal relations and relations between customs, which are the focus of anthropology. Edel concludes his essay (1969:430) by proposing that economic anthropology deal with the "economic process of matching resources to targets with reference to the social milieu to which it is fitted." A growing number of economic anthropologists share this view of the scope of their discipline.

FORMALISM AND SUBSTANTIVISM

The relationship between economics and anthropology cannot be resolved without considering the larger issue of the scope of economic anthropology. Two separate tendencies in this regard are found in the literature. On the one hand, there are scholars who argue that economic anthropology is best conducted within the framework of comparative political economy (i.e,, economic history + institutionalism or Marxian economics), with its scope encompassing the description and analysis of all economic systems of record (i.e., extinct and extant preindustrial and industrial systems) or of hypothetical construction (e.g., Godelier 1967a, Dalton 1969). On the other hand, there are those who are impressed with the success of neoclassical economics in formulating principles to explain and predict processes of resource utilization in general, and who accordingly conceive of economic anthropology as the study of social relations concomitant to the process of resource utilization (i.e., economizing), and as entailing the description and analysis of the specific ways in which this process is patterned in various sociocultural settings (e.g., Firth 1961; Nash 1961, 1966; Salisbury 1962, 1968a; Belshaw 1969, 1971). The first view is essentially historical, relativistic, and substantive in orientation, relies heavily on a taxonomic/typological method, and is concerned primarily with the structure and functioning of contrasting institutional and organizational types. The second view is essentially ahistorical (synchronic), analytic and formal in orientation, relies heavily on a method of applying general abstract (logico-deductive) principles, and is concerned primarily with the systematic analysis of the conditions and dynamics of social performance in contrasting cultural settings.

As it turns out, both of these approaches involve analysis encompassing a field of study that goes beyond the bounds of the economic sphere proper. This occurs in substantive analysis because a majority of its practitioners deny, even for heuristic purposes, the existence of a discrete economic sphere and emphasize the ways in which economic activity articulates with its institutional matrix in a given social system. According to this approach, no preindustrial social system has an exclusively economic institution, but the noneconomic institutions comprising such a system have economic aspects. In formal analysis, on the other hand, the economy is conceived as a boundless field of economizing (i.e., rational decision-making), which is an object of study wherever it occurs in a social system (which, of course, is everywhere). The dilemma arising from this situation is that neither the substantive nor the formal approach clarifies the object of its study; both purport to study the economy but neither provides precise criteria for delimiting an economic field of study as distinct from any other field within the social system under analysis (see Godelier 1967a:247-53).

Maurice Godelier, an erudite and articulate spokesman for the position that economic anthropology should be conducted as an extension of political economy, bases his argument on the necessary role that anthropology must play in renovating the ethnocentric notion of economic rationality which has been central in economic thought since the days of the physiocrats. From its inception the major task of Western economic inquiry, according to Godelier, has been that of explaining scientifically the structure and functioning of two different historical systems—the mercantile-machine economies of urban European origin and the exotic, preindustrial economies of non-European origin which existed on the flanks of the former—and of ideologically justifying the superiority of the former system over the latter, as well as the inherent rationality of the former (contrasted with the "irrationality" of the latter). He interprets the anthropological record as demonstrating unequivocally that rationality is a relative concept, and as a principle operative in social reality has sociocultural as well as economic aspects. With an infusion of this anthropological knowledge, Godelier reasons (1967*a*:247-313 and *passim*), economic science (neoclassical and Marxist) will abandon its ethnocentric view that Western capitalism, with its institutionalized economizing behavior, is the locus of rationality in past and present human societal development and will replace it with a more truly comparative view of rationality. To assure its validity, however, the comparative anthropological view must guard against "reverse ethnocentrism" or the tendency to ignore behavior patterns or norms (e.g., economizing) in nonwestern societies simply because they are so prominent in Western societies.

The formalists, on the other hand, are more inclined to accept the contributions of neoclassical economics toward an understanding of economizing behavior as valid tools for the analysis of a much wider range of decision-making situations than those customarily dealt with by economists. From their perspective the principal analytical task of economic anthropology is to pursue systematically the various implications of the economizing process in different spatio-temporal settings, and they employ the logically precise and mensurationally versatile concepts of neoclassical economics whenever appropriate. Their goal is to achieve a more complete and accurate understanding of variation and complexity of observed social performances. In working toward this goal they concern themselves less with formulating explanations of historical diversity than with constructing models that are predictive of future performances in various social settings. In sum, they share with all anthropologists an interest in the unique proper-

ties of economic situations at particular times and places, but their overriding analytical concern is to isolate generalizable properties in those situations.

UNIFYING THEMES IN CONTEMPORARY INQUIRY

Much of the discussion in preceding sections suggests that the discipline of economic anthropology has not yet reached a stage in its development conducive to a concise, integrated, and uniformly accepted definition of its scope. Nevertheless, if it is true that the unity of a science shows itself in the unity of the problems it successfully solves, and that such unity emerges only when the relationship among its explanatory principles is established (see Robbins 1935:2), then it appears that economic anthropology is rapidly approaching the threshold of scientific unity. While there is still substantial controversy and disagreement among economic anthropologists over a variety of issues, there are also certain unifying themes in the contemporary literature.

First, there is the use of a comparative strategy that consists of both a synchronic and a diachronic search for relationships between (1) economic organization/performance in two or more social situations in the same society or in two or more different societies; (2) economic organization/performance and noneconomic organization/performance (e.g., political, religious, kinship) in one society or in two or more societies; and (3) economic organization/performance in a given sample of societies and noneconomic organization/performance in the same sample.

The typical problem in economic anthropology deals with the multiple relationships between economic and noneconomic organization/performance in one small-scale society (e.g., Trobriand

Islands, Tikopia, Siane, Panajachel, Kapauku Papua). The typical search is for regularities in the relations between the economy of a society and other fields of activity in that society. Or the search is expanded to encompass regularities in the relations between the economies (or some aspect thereof) and other activity fields (e.g., political, religious) in those societies. Sometimes the search is for systematic regularities in economic organization/performance in a wider sample of societies, so that ideally the investigator could, on the basis of only partial information about the economy of a society and culture previously unfamiliar to him, predict other attributes of it with some degree of accuracy.

In their comparativism, then, economic anthropologists have not deviated significantly from the cultural and social anthropological strategies formulated earlier in this century by Malinowski and Radcliffe-Brown. In accordance with Malinowski's position, they agree that all cultural (including economic) phenomena must be considered in their relationship to other aspects of the culture under study; and they agree with Radcliffe-Brown that all social phenomena must be considered in their relationship to the corresponding phenomena in other societies (see Berliner 1962:53). It is only in a recent exploratory statement by Belshaw (1969) that we find an incisive reappraisal of the comparative strategies of the past together with programmatic outlines of new strategies for the future. More specifically, Belshaw argues (1969:6) that the elaboration of a more scientifically relevant theoretical framework in economic anthropology will require, among other things, that the "elements which enter into the system of analysis should be capable of continuous comparison from one social system to another." This will enable us, he main-

tains, to talk of the degree to which the element is present or operative in any society, but will require that those elements we select as relevant for analysis be expressible in quantified terms.

A second unifying theme in contemporary economic anthropological inquiry is "functional contextualization." Whether or not the investigator consciously employs a comparative strategy in a given study, he will discover and analyze the interrelationships of the economic and other fields of activity in the sociocultural system under study. This reflects an adherence to the functionalist strategy that has been applied in economic anthropological studies since the contributions of Malinowski, Mauss, and Thurnwald, which emphasized the holistic, interdependent nature of human social life. In recent years there has been considerable debate among economic anthropologists about how to conceptualize and analyze economy/noneconomy articulation in a social system. Yet even in those studies that analyze the economy in its own terms, the wider sociocultural context of economic activity is delineated and the multiple modes of economic articulation with it are specified (e.g., Raymond Firth 1966, Tax 1953, Pospisil 1963).

A final unifying theme that characterizes contemporary economic anthropology is the quest for verifiable and verified propositions about economic structure, performance, and process. This common goal of analysis is reflected in such interests as model-building, conceptual clarification, and the elaboration of general theoretical frameworks. By and large, economic anthropologists are now exercising considerable care in defining basic terms and in following operationally sound heuristic and analytical procedures, and are seeking to clarify and refine their taxonomies and typologies (e.g., Steiner 1957; Le Clair 1962; Neale 1964; Sahlins 1965*b*; Cancian 1966; Cook 1966*b*; Godelier 1967*a*; P. S. Cohen 1967; Epstein 1967; Le Clair and Schneider, eds., 1968; Dalton 1969; Belshaw 1969). This is an unmistakable sign of the increasing scientific maturity of the discipline.

PROBLEMS IN EPISTEMOLOGY AND METHOD

SCIENCE AND IDEOLOGY

Paradoxically, from its inception the discipline of economics has evolved as a "dismal" science and a "passionate" one. From the economic discourses of Aristotle and later of St. Augustine and St. Thomas Aquinas, on through those of the physiocrats and the classical political economists, to the emergence of the neoclassical school and the various "unorthodox" reactions to it (e.g., the Marxists, the historicalists, the institutionalists) and down to the present day, economic and moral-ethical issues have been intertwined in economic thought (Schumpeter 1954, Robinson 1964). Schumpeter has distinguished the "analytic or scientific aspects of economic thought" from those aspects that are neither scientific nor analytic (Cook 1966*a*:329-30); and it is a result of his efforts, together with those of other scholars (e.g., Fraser 1947, Eucken 1950, Merton 1957, Jones 1961, Mannheim 1964, Lowe 1965, Lichtheim 1967), that a principal strategy for eliminating the unhealthy aspects of sectarianism in academic discourse is to seek to understand how it arises.

One of the root causes of sectarian conflict in economic discourse in general and in economic anthropology in particular is a genuine difference in the epistemologies (explicit and implicit) of its contributors. Two dominant and opposing orientations, alluded to earlier,

may be isolated: materialism and idealism. The proponents of materialism (substantivism) emphasize the spatial, corporeal, sensuous, nonvaluational, empirical, and deterministic in their studies, whereas the idealists (formalists) stress the supra- or nonspatial, incorporeal, suprasensuous, normative or valuational, and indeterministic. The formalists in economic anthropology find that the method of conventional economic theory is compatible with their idealistic epistemology (which in some cases was itself formulated through the intensive study of economics). Their approach is formal in that it is (1) conducted in accordance with procedures that are designed to ensure validity (i.e., in strict logical form with an attempt to justify every step), (2) pertains to or emphasizes constituent elements (i.e., is analytic), and (3) pertains to the form, shape, or mode of that slice of phenomenal reality being studied as distinct from its substance (i.e., form is perceived separately from subject matter or content). On the other hand, the substantivists in economic anthropology deny the applicability of economic theory to anthropological inquiry because the method of neoclassical economics contradicts their materialist epistemology. Their approach is substantive because it implies that the object of investigation (i.e., the "embedded" or "social" economy) has independent existence, that it somehow belongs to the real nature or essential content of its empirical context.

The process of categorizing individual scholars as either formal or substantive conceptualizers may involve, at some point, a set of "temperamental biases" that are "deep-seated in the personality" and are nonrational; that is, are not reached as a direct result of a reasoning process (Jones 1961:15-16). For example, an extreme formal conceptualization of the economy like

Lionel Robbins' (as a relationship between ends and scarce means that have
alternative uses [1935:16]) or an extreme substantive conceptualization
like Polanyi's (which sees the economy
as "an instituted process of interaction
between man and his environment,
which results in a continuous supply of
want satisfying material means"
[1957:248]) may be explained at one
level (and ex post facto) as representing
its conceptualizer's position on philosopher W. T. Jones's hypothetical "in-
ner/outer" axis of bias. This axis contrasts the value attitudes of those "who
are satisfied with a relatively external
relation to the objects of their experience and those who are satisfied only if
they can . . . get inside them, i.e., who
want to experience them as they experience themselves" (1961:25). Thus in
economic anthropology it can be said
of the substantivist that he wants somehow to get inside of the object of his
experience; paradoxically, he wants to
conceive of the abstract whole (which
is the object of study) in the same way
he perceives its more concrete aspects.
If anthropological inquiry is uniquely
characterized, as Lévi-Strauss (1967:
26) has asserted, by "making the most
intimate subjectively into a means of objective demonstration," then it appears
that in economic anthropology the substantive method may overemphasize
subjectivity at the expense of objective
demonstrability.

Apart from these proposed differences in epistemology, another set of
the implications of sectarianism in economic anthropology lies more strictly
within the province of the sociology of
knowledge. One of the major theses in
the latter field of study is that a particular scholar's views may be considered
as manifesting an ideological content
when we "sense in his total behavior an
unreliability which we regard as a function of the social situation in which he
finds himself" (Mannheim 1964:61).

This "social situation" might consist of
any combination of several factors, including real or imagined socioeconomic
class affiliation, real or imagined affiliation with a particular political party or
faction external or internal to one's
profession, informal but enduring personal friendships or loyalties to another
scholar or scholars, and so on. Needless
to say, any particular scholar's views on
central issues in economic anthropology are not exclusively or even necessarily explainable as functions of these or
other aspects of his social situation.
Moreover, it can be argued that each
scholar's work stands or falls solely on
its success or failure in satisfying recognized canons of scientific procedure
(which are sometimes ambiguous in anthropology), the evaluative process itself neutralizing intruding biases. The
obvious polarization of views in contemporary economic anthropology,
however, presents us with a series of
contradictions that should be better resolved if we systematically pursued the
implications of a postulated distinction
between the "objective" and "subjective" aspects of our field of study.
Among other things, this strategy implies that anthropologists must accept
the thesis that just as economy and society are parts of economic anthropology (as objects of study), so economic
anthropology itself is part of an economy and a society (as intellectual
pursuit and specialized mode of livelihood) (see Lévi-Strauss 1967:51; Robinson 1964:14).

More specifically, given the rather
unique course of its development, the
field of economic anthropology provides an excellent case study in the relations between personal and collective
knowledge and other existential factors
in the society and culture of its practitioners. The formal-substantive bifurcation in contemporary economic anthropological thought, while paralleled by
developments in other subareas of an-

thropology as well as in other disciplines, has been accompanied by the formation of two separate spheres of discourse, each challenging the validity and legitimacy of the other. In this context of reciprocal negation and distrust, the independent scholar must continue to adapt by inquiring into the content of beliefs and assertions of his colleagues to determine their validity (e.g., by confronting their assertions with relevant evidence, critically examining terminology), but he must also pose a new question: How do such views originate and how are they perpetuated? If properly conducted by capable scholars, the pursuit of answers to this question need not lead to the total func-tionalization of economic anthropological thought—i.e., its interpretation exclusively on the basis of its psychological, economic, social, or ethnic sources and functions (see Merton 1957:457). But it will lead to a greater awareness of the relations of personality, society, and culture in economic anthropology in particular and in social and cultural anthropology in general. At the very least, it should demonstrate conclusively that no single scholar or group of scholars is the exclusive purveyor of scientific truth, that none is free of influence from beliefs, attitudes, and viewpoints originating outside the immediate research situation.

In short, given the present state of

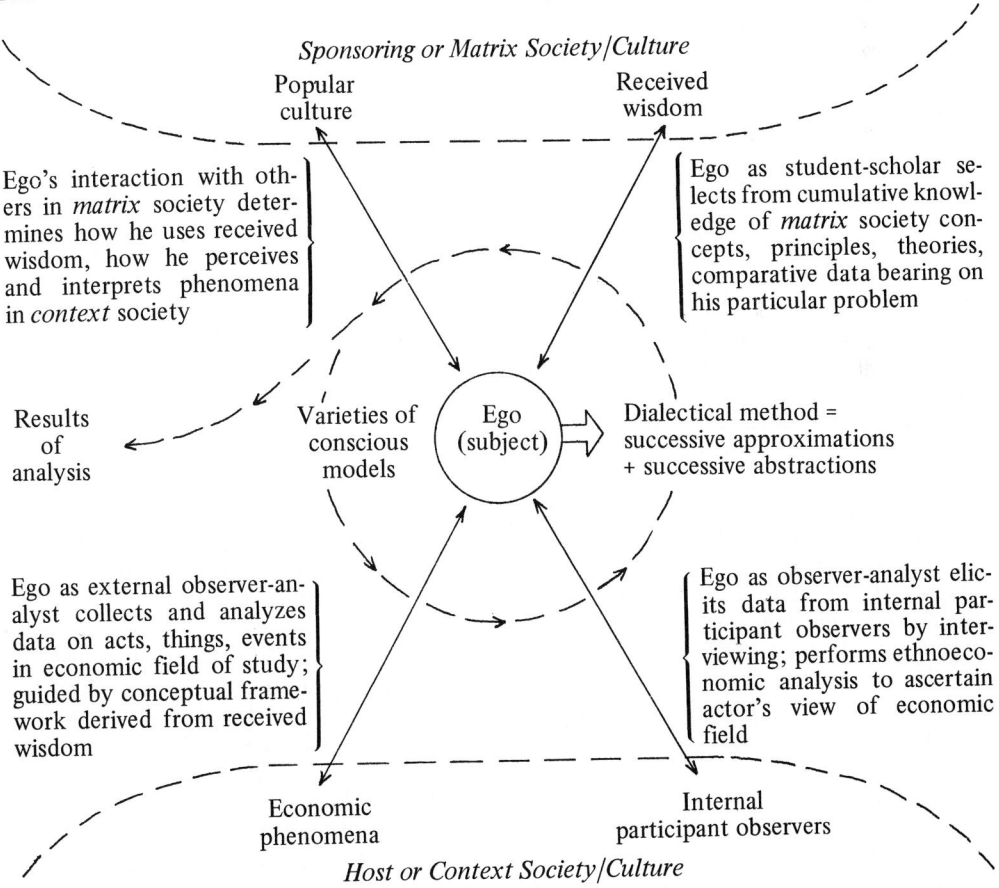

Figure 1. The epistemological situation of the economic anthropologist.

our knowledge, excursions into the philosophy of science and the sociology of knowledge do not explain why scholar X is a substantivist or a formalist. They simply enable us to comprehend more clearly the broader implications of discipline-specific controversies and indicate one direction future inquiry must take if it hopes to arrive at valid and comprehensive explanations.

THE EPISTEMOLOGICAL SITUATION
OF THE ECONOMIC ANTHROPOLOGIST

At this stage in its development the basic problems of economic anthropology lead into the area of epistemology (i.e., theory of the process of interaction between an observer-analyst and phenomenal reality through which he putatively achieves knowledge of the latter) and method (i.e., strategies and tactics by which the field of study is approximated and abstracted to facilitate understanding, explanation, and/or prediction). The epistemological/methodological situation of the economic anthropologist may be depicted schematically as shown in Figure 1. This tentative scheme is designed to facilitate discussion about the multiple roles of the economic anthropologist as he observes, collates, catalogs, describes, analyzes, and interprets things, events, and ideas relating to a particular object of inquiry. In other words, it delineates the salient attributes of the processual field of intellectual operation of the economic anthropologist, in both its subjective and its objective dimensions. The ensuing discussion will emphasize certain methodological implications of the thesis that the economic anthropologist studies society/ economy (or an aspect thereof) as an object but is also within society/economy as a subject (see Godelier 1967a: 313 and *passim*).

It may be inferred from the diagram that the economic anthropologist oc-cupies an intermediate zone between two object societies (and cultures)—the *matrix* society, which enculturates and sponsors him, and the *context* society, which is his object of study and his host. His occupancy of this hypothetical zone does not disengage him from interaction processes; in past and present he interacts both subjectively and objectively in a wide variety of social and cultural situations within his matrix-context environment.

The two principal kinds of interaction between the economic anthropologist (as ego or subject) and his matrix society/culture are (1) scientific and (2) ideological. Through the process of scientific interaction he studies, evaluates, and selects from the received wisdom of his matrix society/culture (i.e., cumulative knowledge organized into and conveyed through academic disciplines) for the purpose of organizing, analyzing, and interpreting phenomena selected for study and observed systematically in the context society/culture. This process is scientific insofar as it results in some contribution toward the cumulative growth of a discipline-specific body of systematically articulated, analytically productive concepts and principles, and to the extent that it is organized around a series of well-defined criteria for evaluating the relevance of the various links in the chain of mental steps that lead from what the scientist observes, perceives, or imagines to what he concludes about "what is" (see Rapoport 1965:22).

Through the process of ideological interaction our hypothetical economic anthropologist acquires a set of values, beliefs, attitudes, biases, etc., which inevitably reflect his background, status, and total social situation in the matrix society. These values, beliefs, and attitudes—to the extent that they remain out of the subject's awareness and are not eliminated from or controlled in his performance of scientific roles—are essentially counterscientific and tend to inhibit the cumulative growth of knowledge. This is not to deny the possibility of ethnocentric or unobjective elements in "science," but it does imply that ideology is, by definition, more infused with ethnocentrism and subjective bias. Finally, these two interaction processes, the scientific and the ideological, tend to be mutually influential rather than mutually exclusive, especially in a field of study like economic anthropology, which includes in its subject matter the phenomena of caste and class and the inequitable allocation of political power and access to scarce and strategic material means invariably associated with them.

As Figure 1 indicates, the two principal modes of interaction between the economic anthropologist (ego as external observer-analyst) and the context society are the anthropological economic or ethnoeconomic mode and the economic anthropological mode. The ethnoeconomic mode entails a relationship between the economic anthropologist and one or more informants (internal participant observers) which enables the investigator to elicit from his informants ideas, propositions, taxonomies, models, etc. dealing with the structure and function of economic processes or entities in the context society. The economic anthropological mode, on the other hand, involves the anthropologist in the collection and analysis of quantitative and nonquantitative data dealing with acts, events, and things in the economic field of study in accordance with strategies and tactics derived mainly from the study of relevant portions of the accumulated knowledge of the matrix society. More specifically, this knowledge consists of concepts, propositions, principles, generalizations, models, etc. accumulated from many separate studies conducted in a wide variety of societies and cultures and collectively identified as belonging to the discipline of economic anthropology for transmittal from one generation of practitioners to another.

In Figure 1, we see that Ego is conceived as relating to the four separate modes of interaction in his field through a dialectical process of perception and cognition. This process implies that the economic anthropologist employs a strategy of alternation between two methods, each with its own rhythm: the deductive and the inductive or empirical (see Lévi-Strauss 1967:25-26; Le Clair and Schneider, eds., 1968:471-73). The method he employs to begin analysis is either one of "successive approximations to reality" (Cook 1966a:335-36) or of "successive abstractions from reality" (inputs) for the purpose of constructing a variety of conscious models (outputs). For example, he might initiate a study of peasant householding with a model derived from the economist's theory of the firm, which he successively modifies to fit the realities of the empirical situation being analyzed (i.e., method of successive approximations). Or he might initiate his study with no specific model as a departure point, and later, after accumulating and categorizing a corpus of data on peasant householding, proceed to isolate principles that apply to a progressively larger percentage of the total household sample until a series of principles of widest applicability are combined into a descriptive model (i.e., method of successive abstractions). Ideally the analyst will employ both methods in a complementary fashion.

This analytical process is dialectical because the analyst assumes that phenomenal reality is not what it appears to be, and that this reality can be approximated only if abstract-deductive theories or propositions are continuously revised, clarified, and refined in the light of new empirical data (Selsam and Martel, eds., 1963:94-96, 138-40, and *passim*). This strategy derives its analytical strength from the assumption: that abstract principles and concepts lead to the approximation of the concrete object of study in the course of reasoning. It assumes the validity of Marx's thesis that the "method of advancing from the abstract to the concrete is but a way of thinking by which the concrete is grasped and is reproduced in our minds as a concrete" (1904a:292).

What this means for contemporary economic anthropology is that the economic anthropologist can usefully apply, for example, the formal economic notion of "market" as a tool to approximate an understanding of marketing organization and process in economies not usually studied by economists. He can employ many of the economist's concepts and principles in the study of primitive and peasant economies so long as he does not assume *a priori* that the phenomena under study are necessarily explainable by them. More broadly, it implies that the economic anthropologist must be eclectic in his knowledge and use of the received wisdom of his matrix society/culture, and that he should not restrict the scope and method of his inquiry without seeking to narrow the limits of his naiveté in other disciplines that have a bearing on his field of study.

PROBLEMS IN THE THEORY AND ANALYSIS OF ECONOMIC PHENOMENA IN PREINDUSTRIAL SOCIETIES

TOWARD A DEFINITION OF THE ECONOMIC FIELD

Among what Godelier (1967a:247) refers to as that "chain of questions as imposing as they are inevitable" which confront all students of economics and economic anthropology, the first and

most formidable is: "What is the field of human activities that constitutes the proper object of economic science?" Economic anthropologists, together with other students of economics, have tended to take either of two contrasting positions in answer to this question: that the "economy" is (1) a field of specific activities or (2) a field encompassing a specific aspect of all human activity. In this section the views of various scholars on the economy issue will be discussed, and a composite set of criteria by which any anthropologist can designate a particular field of human activities (or identify particular aspects of activities in other fields) as economic will be proposed.

There is agreement among economic anthropologists that the anthropological perspective precludes their describing and analyzing a particular economy without simultaneously demonstrating its ties with noneconomic elements in a given social system. Perhaps as a consequence of this functionalist orientation, they have been slow to recognize the analytical value of positing the economic field of study as an aspect of social reality both internal and external to the social system. Such a conceptual delimitation of the analytic area of inquiry (e.g., Parsons and Smelser 1956, Godelier 1967) is a valuable point of departure for any study in economics and is compatible with the aims of anthropological explanation.

The most persevering and vocal proponents of the conceptualization of the economy as wholly internal to or "embedded" in society are, as we've noted, Polanyi and his followers—the substantivist group. In their approach the economy is viewed as the process of provisioning society or the sociocultural system. No social relation, institution, or set of institutions is considered to be economic; it can only serve economic purposes (e.g., Polanyi 1957:243-70;

Sahlins 1965b:225-26; Dalton 1968). While this view reinforces the traditional functionalism of anthropology, it is not clear from the substantivists' writings precisely what meaning they attribute to the term "economic." They persistently contend that it is a process of materially provisioning society but fail to delineate the specific components of the process. They define economics as an aspect of everything that provisions society but nothing that provisions society is defined as economic. Paradoxically, then, it appears that the economic anthropology advocated by the proponents of the substantivist approach is a study without an empirically ascertainable field of inquiry. Thus in negating the "market mentality" (Polanyi) and the "Business Outlook" (Sahlins) together with the thesis that economics = economizing, and by replacing the latter with their counterthesis that economics = provisioning, the Polanyi group has deprived itself of an objective field of study.

The other major approach in contemporary economic anthropology, the formalist (i.e., economics = economizing), is, on the other hand, no more successful in delimiting a specific, discrete, empirically distinguishable field of inquiry. When an economic anthropologist defines the scope of his study as encompassing all decision-making behavior generated by the relationship between ends and scarce means with alternative uses, as the formalists do, it follows that the study deals by definition with everything in society, but in fact with nothing. In other words, hypothetically to identify as "economic" a nebulous universe of mutually alternative ends in which choice is exercised by maximizing scarce means (e.g., Robbins 1935, Raymond Firth 1961, Burling 1962, Belshaw 1967) is conceptually to dissolve the empirical (i.e., substantive or material) economic into the hypothetical (i.e., formal or ideal) noneconomic. This implication emerges clearly from the statement of Le Clair and Schneider (eds., 1968:455), apropos of the heuristic status of the "scarcity" definition of economics, which they accept in principle, that "if the terms are defined as broadly as they need to be defined, almost every human action can be seen as involving a decision concerning the allocation of scarce resources among alternative ends; every human act is then an economic act." To those economic anthropologists who feel uncomfortable with such a broad conception of the scope of the economic field, this analytical focus on economizing is acceptable only when it is circumscribed by an economic field delimited by other criteria; i.e., all acts within the economic field involve economizing but not all economizing acts are within the economic field (e.g., Edel 1969:430-31).

Given these theoretical and methodological shortcomings in the approaches of the two major groups of contemporary economic anthropologists, it is not surprising to find some critics who are skeptical of the whole enterprise. Andrew Vayda, for example, has expressed frustration with his own and others' attempts to define the "economy" for purposes of exposition and analysis. It seems that each time he examines an ethnographic case to find and study the economy, the latter invariably dissolves into a mix of other human activities and structures. This has led him to conclude that the economy rubric is a holdover from an "earlier stage of social scientific inquiry" and that "more fruitful categorizations of phenomena" are possible (1967:86). Vayda obviously believes that these "more fruitful categorizations" can be derived from the field of ecology, presumably because it leads "into much broader areas of inquiry than those normally intended in attempts to demarcate the *economy* for investigation" (1967:90). More recently, he has carried the argument one step further by questioning the viability of economic anthropology as a subfield within cultural anthropology and would apparently replace it with ecological anthropology (1969:95).

While it is currently unfashionable to place limitations on the uses of ecology in anthropology, one of them is that it is not economics. The ecosystem does not contain the economy any more than the economy contains the ecosystem. The real problem is one of their articulation, and here ecology (ecological anthropology) and economics (economic anthropology) must collaborate. Perhaps through collaboration the tendency toward psychological reductionism present in formal economic anthropology will counterbalance the tendencies toward biological-environmental reductionism in ecological anthropology, thereby creating conditions conducive to major contributions to our understanding of economic behavior as sociocultural process (see "Limitations and Possibilities of the Ecological Approach," the final section of this chapter).

A more positive reaction than Vayda's is represented in the attempts by Godelier (1967*a*), Frankenberg (1967), Le Clair and Schneider (eds., 1968), Cook (1969), and others to establish a minimum set of criteria that can profitably serve as departure points in any anthropological study of the economic field and which will facilitate the operationalization of concepts, propositions, and models. The motivation behind these efforts is not to impose still more personalized views of the economy on other colleagues, but rather to work toward a clarification and synthesis of the two currently prevailing views to establish a genuine "substantive formalism" or "formal substantivism" (see Kaplan 1968, Cook 1969).

The criteria sought by these writers are intended to cope with an epistemological-methodological problem in economic anthropology which has plagued scientists since the days of Galileo and Newton: the "bifurcation of nature into the 'immediately sensed' and the 'postulated-but-not-sensed'—that is, nature as sensed, and nature as conceived by scientific theory" (Nutini 1968:6). Le Clair and Schneider (eds., 1968:461) go directly to the heart of this problem in elaborating on their suggestion that an "economy" and an "economic system" might very well be two different things, the former referring to whatever it is in the real world that economic anthropologists are concerned with and the latter referring to the description or model of the real-world phenomenon. What is important here is not the issue of terminology but the implicit emphasis on the need for operationalizing the linkage between formal constructs and empirical reality to avoid reification. Also, what Le Clair and Schneider and others are emphasizing is that there is no real-world phenomenon or entity that can be labeled "economy" or "economic system"; there are only phenomena that can be observed, measured, and analyzed in an economic context or field—which is a hypothetical, heuristic construct, not a real, substantive entity.

Preliminary to any attempt to delimit the economic field of inquiry in a specific way, it is necessary to express a notion of the general contours of that field. Here is such a notion: *The economy is a culturally mediated field of a human population's activity in which its members interact with their physical and social environment in the calculated attempt to aquire, directly or indirectly, a living.* The phrase "directly or indirectly" implies a contrast between subsistence/acquisitive activity involving production for consumption within a single management unit (with an absence or minimum of interunit exchange), and subsistence/acquisitive activity involving production both for consumption and for exchange within separate management units (with regularized interunit exchange). Such a distinction is applicable to the study of economic activity at any level of sociocultural integration, but it is especially relevant to the study of so-called complex preindustrial societies, in which "market principles" operate through marketplaces to facilitate complementary exchange between mutually interdependent and specialized production-consumption units organized on a household/interhousehold—village/intervillage—town/city basis (Belshaw 1965: 6-9, 53-83; Nash 1966:59-89; Wolf 1966:1-59).

The phrase "acquire . . . a living" implies that the individual actor, usually as a member of a discrete management unit, comes into possession of material wealth to satisfy subsistence/acquisitive needs through his own productive efforts. It is not intended to convey the incorrect idea that the distribution process in all societies always allocates products on the basis of work, or that wealth is everywhere appropriated by its producers or nonproducers solely for the purpose of keeping them alive. In other words, the emphasis is on such activities as are life-sustaining or directly related to the reproduction of the population as a viable social unit, but not to the exclusion of activities involving the production, transfer, or use of material wealth for prestige, religious, or other nonsubsistence purposes.

"Calculated attempt" implies that economic activity entails either a rational weighing of alternative courses of action or a rational readjustment of

given means to obtain certain minimal ends, and is purposeful—its intended purposes being appropriation, transformation, exchange, and utilization to attain the immediate goals of subsistence or acquisition. "Rational" as employed here does not imply that actors are making decisions in accordance with any universally operative maximization principle, but simply that they are pursuing ends coherent among themselves and are employing means appropriate to the ends pursued (Godelier 1967: 12). In preindustrial societies such calculated attempts and rationality operate often in the context of "scheduling," which, according to Kent Flannery (1968:74), is a "cultural activity which resolves conflict between procurement systems." It must also be emphasized that economic process is not always or everywhere the result of conscious design or intention; the economic process, like any social process, also involves the unintentional and the unplanned. The aggregate, system-wide effect of a multitude of intentional, calculated, goal-oriented economic acts by individuals cannot be ascertained merely by projecting the individual act onto the societal screen (see Sahlins 1969).

Finally, the definition as a whole is designed to emphasize process, not stasis; it seeks to convey the notion that at a particular time and place economic activity occurs only on the basis of movement, exertion, and interaction (i.e., energy expenditure). In short, the economic field is process—empirically reducible to flows of materials, energy, commodities, and information—in which human actors, singly and in groups, calculate and act to acquire and/or dispose of wealth.

Given this general view of the economic field, it is appropriate to specify its component processes. The activities within this field are empirically identifiable in a given society. The individual members of a population perform roles in a social structure and behave in the economy through (1) the appropriation of materials from the natural environment, (2) the transformation of these appropriated materials into utilizable products by the use of tools and labor power, and (3) the transfer and use of these products. The plans, choices, and calculations that are considered or made with direct regard to these acts of appropriation, transformation, transfer, and utilization are also within the economic field of study. The investigator cannot, of course, observe this field as a concrete totality (i.e., in the same way that the biologist observes an organism); nor can he assume that the specified acts will necessarily occur in the sequence given above, much less that every individual actor will perform all of these acts. But he can observe the performance of such acts when they occur, and he can count or measure their concrete results. Finally, he can question actors about their activities.

What emerges from the preceding discussion is a sectoral model of the economic field comprising three separate yet interdependent event sectors: production (appropriation plus transformation), transfer, and utilization (see Le Clair 1962). Distribution, in the sense of the process of reward or allocation of product to the factors of production, can be posited as the process that integrates these sectors as a circular flow system and articulates this system with the larger sociocultural system. It is this distribution process that regulates the circulation of wealth in a given society, and underwrites the structure and dynamics of its allocation among the various status groups of the social system.

The production event sector includes those acts or series of acts whose actual or intended results is the "purposeful alteration and combination of physical material until it reaches some desired empirical state" (Udy 1959:2)—usually as a finished or semifinished good that is then available for utilization. The utilization event sector includes "consumption events" involving the utilization of goods or services for the direct satisfaction of human wants, and "capital consumption events," which involve the utilization of goods or services for further production (Le Clair 1962: 1192). Lastly, the transfer sector includes all those acts or series of acts that shift control over or rights in an economic good from one individual to another—giving, borrowing, lending, selling, buying, bartering.

Before we proceed into a discussion of these three sectors as separate areas of inquiry in economic anthropology, a few additional general comments are in order. The economic field as defined above may be considered methodologically as a pigeonholing device to facilitate systematic data collection by the fieldworker, and theoretically as a subsystem within a social system. As a systemic entity, each sector is mutually interrelated with every other and the subsystem as a whole is in mutual interaction with every other activity field in the total system. The nature of these systemic relationships has been a concern of many scholars from Marx (1904a) and Weber (1949) to Parsons and Smelser (1956), Le Clair (1962), and Godelier (1967a), and it will continue to concern scholars in the future.

Once the economic field as delimited above is accepted as the proper object of economic anthropological inquiry, we are faced with certain questions of method and priority. In the past some anthropologists have studied one or another aspect of this field without operating within any systematic theoretical framework; others have been influenced, explicitly or implicitly, consciously or unconsciously, by theories that either select out particular sectors as primary or focus on the articulation of the field (or aspects of it) with its total sociocultural matrix, to the exclusion of relationships internal to the field; still others have followed an eclectic approach, drawing upon several disciplines to analyze the structure and functioning of the economic field and its social system synchronically, or have used concepts like multilinear evolution, human ecology, energy, and analogies borrowed from the biological sciences to analyze the field and its social system diachronically.

Finally, anthropologists have shown less theoretical concern with phenomena that are conceived of as predominantly economic than they have with regard to what Max Weber (1949) called "economically relevant" and "economically conditioned" phenomena. As "economically relevant" phenomena anthropologists have studied, for example, religious or political activities, which are not of primary economic interest but which do acquire economic significance because they have consequences that are of interest from an economic point of view. And as "economically conditioned" phenomena, anthropologists have studied activities that do not qualify as economic by the definition presented above and whose economic effects are not of particular interest (e.g., medical beliefs and practices), but which in particular cases are strongly influenced by economic factors (e.g., the differential use of modern medical facilities and techniques by different socioeconomic groups in a stratified society) (see Weber 1949: 64-65). In short, the economic field, when not the direct object of economic anthropological inquiry, is always an indirect object of inquiry.

And then there is the evasive and frustrating problem of articulation—the relations between the economic field and other activity fields such as kinship, religion, and politics. Godelier (1967a:253), in a subtle and incisive treatment of this problem, views the economy as constituting both a field of specific activities (production, distribution, and consumption of material goods) and a specific aspect of all human activities that are not within this field but whose functioning involves the exchange and/or use of material means. Therefore, the economy is a specific field of relations both external and internal to other fields of social activity. Given this framework, the task of the economic anthropologist is to analyze the external and internal aspects of his field of study until his analysis leads him to other social realities that give economic phenomena meanings that are not discernible apart from their sociocultural context. Godelier appropriately warns anthropologists that their method of contextualizing economic phenomena in order to understand them must not foster the delusion that the economy, at any time or place, is reducible to noneconomic structures and processes, or that it can be fully understood by using these latter alone as points of departure for analysis.

This conception of the internal/external nature of economy/society articulation represents a major breakthrough in economic anthropological theory and now awaits operationalization in specific empirical studies. It neatly resolves, on the one hand, the formalist dilemma of equating economics with economizing with all behavior and, on the other hand, the substantivist dilemma of substituting the study of social phenomena (e.g., institutions) for the study of economic phenomena. Godelier would agree in spirit with Neale, a supporter of Polanyi, who asserts (1964:1305) that "the element needed to define 'economic' operation-

ally is materiality," but he would clearly not agree that the concept of "em-
beddedness" is a valid tool for identifying phenomena as economic. In fact,
Godelier criticizes Polanyi for arguing
that there are societies in which the
economy is not embedded in social
structure (i.e., is "disembedded"), an
argument derived from Polanyi's acceptance of the nineteenth-century
myth that the industrial capitalist economy is ruled totally by its own laws.
As Godelier (1967a:264) points out in
rejecting this view, "in the last analysis
'disembedded' suggests an absence of
internal relations between the economic and the noneconomic, when in reality this relation exists in all societies."
The converse of this statement is equally true: that "embedded" suggests an
absence of relations within the economic field which are external to noneconomic fields, when in reality this relation exists in all societies.

THE ECONOMIC FIELD OF STUDY:

THEORETICAL CATEGORIES

AND SUBSTANTIVE PROCESSES

The General Relation of Production to Distribution, Exchange, and Utilization

Economics and economic anthropology are characterized by a lack
of clarity in the theory and analysis
of the relations between production,
distribution, exchange, and utilization.
Among other things, this situation
reflects the fact that each of these
categories is a component of one
process, a distinct aspect of one system
(see Marx 1904a:291). These categories
are postulated as separate by the analyst, yet the results of empirical analysis
invariably demonstrate their interre-
latedness. The fact that these categories
do not exist ontologically as self-contained, independent spheres of phenomenal reality does not imply that

they do not exist epistemologically, nor
does it invalidate their heuristic utility
as abstract theoretical categories. The
problem is not whether these categories
themselves represent empirical reality,
but whether as heuristic tools they enable the analyst to arrive at progressively
more accurate approximations of that
reality.

The nature of the relations between
these categories may be briefly described as follows: production is the
process by which the members of a society appropriate and transform natural
resources to satisfy their needs and
wants; distribution determines the extent to which the individual participates in this production; exchange
enables him to acquire the particular
products into which he wishes to convert the quantity allocated to him
through distribution; and through consumption products are individually appropriated as objects of use and enjoyment. Marx (1904a:274-75; cf. 1971:
22) is the author of the most concise
statement of this conventional scheme:

Production yields good adapted to our needs;
distribution distributes them according to social laws; exchange distributes further what
has already been distributed, according to individual wants; finally, in consumption the
product drops out of the social movement,
becoming the direct object of the individual
want which it serves and satisfies in use. Production thus appears as the starting point;
consumption as the final end; and distribution
and exchange as the middle; the latter has a
double aspect, distribution being defined as a
process carried on by society, while exchange,
as one proceeding from the individual.

These relationships are not without
their ambiguities. For example, production implies consumption in the sense
of using up the means of production
just as consumption implies production
in the sense of the nutritive process
through which men consume foodstuffs

so as, in effect, to produce their own bodies (Marx 1904a:276-77). Yet these ambiguities can lead to new insights and may reinforce the validity of the categories as a general framework of analysis. This seems to be true in those instances when they have been systematically applied in the analysis of economic life in preindustrial societies (e.g., Firth 1965a; Foster 1942; Godelier 1967a; Marx 1965, 1971: 16-22).

Production

Under the stimulus of a critical reappraisal of the contributions of Marx and Engels, and a convergence with cultural ecological and cultural materialist inquiry, the formal versus substantive problem in economic anthropology can be redefined as a production problem. In essence, this problem is to determine how basic environmental, ecological, and technological processes relate to economically productive social activities (i.e., those involving labor power and other energy expenditure), together with flows of material resources and information, in calculated and planned acts of appropriation, transformation, transfer, and utilization. In essence, this is the problem of ecosystem/economy differentiation and articulation, which has proved elusive to contemporary social scientists. There are indications, however, that empirical and theoretical efforts focused on the production process by economic anthropologists, ecological anthropologists, archaeologists, and cultural geographers will contribute significantly to our understanding of this problem (e.g., Wagner 1960; Douglas 1962; Lee 1969; Vayda 1968; Vayda, ed., 1969; Rappaport 1969; Flannery 1968; Y. Cohen 1968; Hole and Heizer 1969, chap. 14).

It is not oversimplifying to argue that economic anthropologists have been very much concerned with production activities and organization in their ethnographic and analytic work, but that with few exceptions their general theoretical views have been framed in terms of distribution and exchange. I need cite only the three most prominent figures in the development of economic anthropology—Malinowski, Thurnwald, and Firth—to document this generalization. Production activities are included within the scope of their work, yet each has made his major contribution to the development of economic anthropological thought in the realm of exchange and distribution: Malinowski (1922, 1926) with the *kula* and other forms of ceremonial, utilitarian, and gift exchange among the Trobrianders, and reciprocity as a generalized social mechanism; Thurnwald (1932) with political economic processes and relations, linked to reciprocity and redistribution mechanisms, in various preindustrial economies; and Firth (1961, 1967) with a transactional or exchange view of social organization, showing how decision-making and economizing in the disposition of scarce means are systematically patterned in every society. In short, all of these major contributors to the development of economic anthropology share a common view that exchange processes and relations, not production processes and relations, are fundamental in human economy and society (see Frankenberg 1967:83-84).

Nor does this emphasis change in the contributions of Polanyi and his followers—which of course is paradoxical in view of their great concern with the material provisioning of society; this concern logically entails a focus on production processes and organization, which in fact is not present in their work. Transactional modes, not production modes, emerge as the dominant concern of the substantivist writers.

They do not analyze or theorize about the forces and relations of production or about the creation of commodities, but invariably restrict themselves to the circulation and destination of commodities already produced. Polanyi's tripartite scheme of reciprocity, redistribution, and market exchange presupposes production modes but does not link up with them; the social concomitants of transactional modes, not of production modes, are of dominant concern to him and his followers (e.g., Polanyi et al., eds., 1957; Dalton 1968, 1969; Sahlins 1965a, 1965b).

Ironically, the following statement by Firth (1967:4), the founder and major figure in neoclassical economic anthropology (Frankenberg 1967), serves as well to characterize his approach as it does that of the Polanyi group: ". . . while the material dimension of the economy is regarded as a basic feature, the significance of the economy is seen to be in the transactions of which it is composed and therefore in the quality of relationships which these transactions create, express, sustain, and modify." In both approaches, then, the focal concern has been with the transaction, the exchange or transfer aspect, which often serves to link the economic with another field of activity, rather than upon production, the appropriating and transformative aspect, which directly links the economic field with its natural environment.

If Marvin Harris had included the economic anthropological literature within the scope of his *Rise of Anthropological Theory* (1968), he would no doubt have noted the contradiction of an economic anthropology that has developed almost in negation of systematic concern with the material substratum of the economy and its ties with economic and other social relations. The separate trajectories of economic anthropology and "cultural

materialism" (Harris 1968:4-5, 643-87) certainly merit the attention of the historian of anthropological thought; their divergent courses of development were set by 1900, and only seventy-odd years later, under the impetus of a general antiempiricist, antidogmatic Marxist trend of thought, do they show signs of converging.

That this convergence is rooted in a critical revival of the Marxist tradition—generated in part by the recent availability of the *Grundrisse* (Marx 1965, 1971; Nicolaus 1968; Hobsbawm 1965; Godelier 1967a; McLellan 1971) —is not surprising. There is no need to dwell here on Marx's historical materialist approach, which assigns priority, but not exclusive causality, to modes of production in relation to the social and political structure and ideological superstructure of any sociocultural system. The incorrect views that Marx advocated a simplistic, unilateral causal relationship from base to structure to superstructure (e.g., Harris 1968:217-49) and posited a rigid unilineal evolutionary scheme are, fortunately, now being laid to rest in the structuralist-Marxist dialogue, which emphasizes infrastructure/superstructure correspondences and multilineal evolutionism (e.g., Godelier 1967b; 1969a:176-82 and *passim*).

Less well known to economic anthropologists are Marx's views on the role of production within the economy. In certain passages of *Capital* (1904b: 367), for example, he seems to anticipate a cultural ecological perspective when he refers to "natural technology, i.e., in the formation of . . . plants and animals, as instruments of production for sustaining life," and continues, "Technology discloses man's mode of dealing with nature, the process of production by which he sustains his life." Statements like these throughout Marx's writings reflect a genuinely substantive conception of the economy as a process of interaction between men and their environment, a process through which men as producers "integrate the use of natural resources and techniques and assure continuous cooperation in the provision of material goods" (Dalton 1961:6). Within this total process, it is clear that Marx assigned production the key role; it is the process out of which all others in the economy are generated and around which they tend to revolve (Marx 1904*a*:291-92; 1971:16-43). This emphasis is also reflected, in a broader social evolutionary context, when Marx (1956:53) argues that men "begin to distinguish themselves from animals as soon as they begin to *produce* their means of subsistence," by which they "indirectly *produce* their actual material life" (cf. Debetz 1961, Engels 1963*b*, Trigger 1967). It must be emphasized, however, that Marx (and Engels) was not interested in production or the economy as static or separate entities per se; rather this focus served as a point of departure for analyzing wider political-economic forces and, ultimately, the structure of society itself. Engels expressed this concisely (Selsam and Martel, eds., 1963:201-202):

What we understand by the economic conditions which we regard as the determining basis of the history of society are the methods by which human beings in a given society produce their means of subsistence and exchange the products among themselves (in so far as division of labor exists). Thus the *entire technique* [original italics] of production and transport is here included. According to our conception this technique also determines the method of exchange and, further, the division of products, and with it, after the dissolution of tribal society, the division into classes also and hence the relations of lordship and servitude and with them the state, politics, law, etc. Under economic conditions are further included the geographical basis on which they operate and those remnants of earlier stages of economic development which have actually been transmissed and have survived . . . also of course the external milieu which surrounds this form of society.

Interestingly enough, a societally detached, synchronic version of the Marxian production focus has been thoroughly absorbed into bourgeois or neoclassical economics. "Economists seem to agree," say Parsons and Smelser (1956:20), "that the paramount goal of economic activity—and hence of an economy as a system—is best defined as production." There are, nevertheless, several influential economic theorists like Kenneth Boulding (1966:3-30) who consider exchange processes, not production, as central in any economic system. Many economic anthropologists support this position because, as Belshaw (1965:4) states, ". . . all enduring social relations involve transactions which have an exchange aspect." To study exchange, then, is to study social behavior, and an economic strategy becomes—in this formalist or transactionalist approach—a general strategy for the study of all social relations (see Homans 1958, Burling 1962, Blau 1964, Barth 1967, Belshaw 1969, Schneider 1970:4). In contrast, it is precisely this ubiquitousness of exchange that suggests to some economic anthropologists that production must serve as the principal criterion for differentiating between the economy and other subfields of a sociocultural system. This, incidentally, is the position favored by Parsons and Smelser, as is implicit in their assertion (1956:24) that "when the process of production is completed the economy has 'done its job.' "

In economic anthropology Maurice Godelier argues persuasively for the concept of production as a departure point for synchronic and diachronic analysis. Defining production as the "totality of operations which supply a society with its material means of existence" (1967a:259), he argues that it encompasses all operations of this type regardless of the specific societal context in which they are performed. Thus hunting, gathering, and fishing economies, in which man occupies nature and exploits it without transforming it, as well as more advanced agricultural and industrial economies, in which material necessities are produced by transforming nature, are included within the same analytical framework. In a formal sense the modes of production in these societies are reducible to an identical series of relationships: to produce in all cases entails a combination of certain technical rules (T_r), raw materials or resources (R_s), tools (T_s), and human labor (H_l) to obtain a product (P) that is socially beneficial. This is, in essence, what economists call the production function—a functional mix of the factors of production which takes different forms according to the nature of the variables and the possible ways of combining them in a given society (Godelier 1967a:259-65).

Retrospectively, it is the adaptive aspect of production that has explained its role in empirical and theoretical analysis in cultural anthropology and which has overshadowed its formal economic attributes in such analysis. Cultural anthropologists, including the evolutionists, conceptualize culture as the *sapiens*-specific means for adaptation, and view adaptation as the process by which men in societies make effective productive use of energy potentials in their natural environment (see Y. Cohen 1968). But they have emphasized the diverse elements of production systems (i.e., technologies) which correspond to sociocultural variations, not the invariant elements of the production process which cross-cut contrasting sociocultural systems. This

approach to the study of culture and society with its technoecological notion of production dates at least from the publication of Morgan's (1963) *Ancient Society* in 1877 and Engels' (1963a) *Origin of the Family, Private Property, and the State* in 1884. Engels' interpretation of Morgan's evolutionary scheme emphasized the modes of production and their relationship to population reproduction. According to Engels (1963a:5), "the determining factor in history is the production and reproduction of the immediate essentials of life," a dual process consisting of the "production of the means of existence . . . of food and clothing, dwellings, and of the tools necessary for that production" and of "the production of human beings themselves, the propagation of the species." It was not until the development of Leslie White's (1949, 1959) unilineal evolutionary-energy approach and of Julian Steward's (1955:30-42) multilineal evolutionary "method of cultural ecology" that this nineteenth-century "cultural materialist" strategy reentered the mainstream of cultural anthropological inquiry (Harris 1968, chaps. 22-23). But it reentered in a way in which the substantive economic field was embedded to the point of dissolution into its institutional matrix; and the quest of base/superstructure correspondences, especially in the work of the Stewardians, usually led to results negating the materialist intellectual foundation of the cultural ecological method. It was not, then, with the rebirth of cultural materialism from its nineteenth-century Marxist cradle that ecological and economic anthropological inquiry converged through a common production focus.

In its contemporary technoeconomic determinist version (e.g., Harris 1969), this view holds that the development of technology (i.e., techniques of environmental exploitation involving the mobilization and control of energy) is the prime mover in societal evolution (Service 1968); that it operates on the social level through changing population density, settlement patterns, material wealth, sociopolitical integration, etc.; and that this evolution not merely is a matter of fixed stages or levels (i.e., a universal, unilineal process), but generates infinite degrees of development that are influenced by factors internal and external to the sociocultural system. From the longer term diachronic perspective (i.e., millennia), technoeconomic factors seem to yield the only coherent sequence of societal transformations of a cumulative and directional nature. But shorter term analyses—especially of specific societies or regional populations—reveal "many situations in which the action of a technological factor is conditioned by social constrictions and advanced or retarded by ideological factors" (Ribeiro 1970:428).

One corollary of this view, which is evoking criticism from a growing number of scholars (e.g., Le Clair and Schneider, eds., 1968:469-70; Harner 1970), is the thesis that an economic surplus is necessary before cultural development can occur. According to this argument, some members of a society must produce a surplus of food above their own needs to enable other members to specialize in non-food-producing activities (see Steward 1955, Service 1968).

If this view is modified by eliminating the elusive surplus concept, analysis can be focused on the following question: "As the average productivity of a society rises, what forms will the increased product take?" (Le Clair and Schneider, eds., 1968:470). This provides a formal theoretical rationale for the view that hinges on the concept of "product mix"—the problem, faced by every economic system, of determining what goods are to be produced and in what relative quantities (Le Clair 1962:1190 and *passim*). The product mix of any economic system is influenced in various ways by environmental and technological factors. More specifically, the natural environment of any society embodies a set of opportunities and associated limits; through the availability or unavailability of natural resources (e.g., exploitable plants and their seasonal regime; the location, quantity, and habits of utilizable animal species; the occurrence of utilizable minerals and potable water; the climate, water supply, soil, and biota as they influence the growth of utilizable plants) the production of certain goods is made possible or impossible (Wagner 1960:61). For example, the peoples of the Siberian tundra could not organize their subsistence around taro, just as the Polynesian peoples could not hunt or herd reindeer. Similarly, the environment might demand certain responses: the survival of the Arctic Eskimo depends upon their producing a material culture that protects them against the severe cold (Forde 1963).

These environmental requirements, limits, and opportunities are not mutually independent, nor are they absolute. For example, the occurrence of two raw materials together may facilitate the production of some good that could not be produced if either were not present. It is the technological aspect of any cultural system that plays a key role in transforming environmental potentialities into economic realities. The Mesoamerican *metate*, or grinding stone, cannot be manufactured if suitable stone is unavailable; and the availability of such stone in sufficient quantities does not assure that it will be quarried, much less that *metates* will be manufactured from it. A classic ethnographic example of the operation of such factors is the acquisition of the horse by the Plains Indians of North America (Wissler 1914; Lowie 1963:42-46) and by the Patagonian Indians of South America (Steward and Faron 1959:408-13), which enabled them to exploit indigenous animals (bison in North America, rhea and guanaco in Patagonia) more efficiently than before. This represents in microcosm what has been happening throughout human history: the development of new, increasingly efficient technologies—and the consequent harnessing of higher concentrations of energy—to exploit recognized environmental potentialities. Through such progressive technical improvements in the utilization of energy the individual worker is, other things remaining equal, able to produce increasingly large quantities of processed materials or goods per working hour (Thurnwald 1932, chaps. 1, 29; Chapple and Coon 1942: 73-276; White 1949, 1959; Childe 1951a; Goldschmidt 1959; Y. Cohen 1968; Watson and Watson 1969).

By submerging the social-economic concept of production in the cultural-adaptive concept of technology, the cultural materialist approach has prevented itself from recognizing the role of production as a means for integrating cultural ecological and evolutionary interests with the study of economic anthropology and the economic field proper. What is there about production that enables it to serve this integrative purpose? On the one hand, production integrates the ecological and economic fields through its intimate relationship with technology: it is the direct processual link between the economic field and the natural environment. On the other hand, production, through its intimate linkage with work organization and ideology, is a principal nexus of articulation between the ecological/economic field and the sociocultural system. And, of course, men's relationship to the production process—via control over its scarce material means or actual participation as producers—determines their relationship to each other in society, as well as their relative share in the total product.

It is precisely here that Marx's contribution becomes indispensable to the problem of the integration of economic and ecological studies in anthropology. Marx, as is well known, proposed that in every society the economic base or mode of production has two essential components: (1) the forces of production, the physical and technological arrangement of economic activity, and (2) the social relations of production, the interpersonal and intergroup relationships that men must establish with one another as a consequence of their roles in the production process (Marx 1904a:11; Smelser 1963:7).

In a given society the forces of production can be minimally defined as relationships among tools, time, and tasks that emerge from the concrete, observable technical features of any work situation. The social relations of such a work situation can be observed and related directly to a series of determinants such as the size or other physical features of the work place, seasonal and cyclical stability of production patterns, technical attributes of tools, etc. (see Chapple and Coon 1942:138-41; Smelser 1963:70). However, work organization is not synonymous with the social relations of production of a society. Rather it is best understood as a particular division of labor within a more general societal division of labor. For example, I have studied Mexican peasant-artisan stoneworkers and can document the ways in which tool type and distribution relate to the type of quarry being exploited, the organization of the quarry workers, and their sharing out of the total output of raw stone (Cook 1968, 1970). In this context I am describing aspects of the social relations of *metate* production, not how the *metate* makers as a productive group within the village and regional division of labor relate to other groups—that is, how the resources and products they use, control, and produce articulate them in a sociopolitical sense with other resource-using, controlling, and/or producing groups (e.g., with other peasant-artisans, landlords, wage-earners, and so on). Work organization, accordingly, is best conceived as mediating between the forces and social relations of production of a given society; it is synonymous with neither of these but is encompassed by both. From the political economic perspective, the social structure of a society—in this case a Mexican village—dissolves into the social relations of production among its people; and work organization—in this case relations among *metate* makers—is but one dimension of these social relations, by which our *metate* makers are joined in interaction with the landowning agriculturists, the storekeepers, the moneylenders, and so on.

When we consider the matter of operationalization, we see that production is empirically measurable as inputs (e.g., man-hours, man-days, caloric expenditures, capital costs) and outputs (i.e., number of units produced expressed in monetary or caloric equivalents). Also, the relative ease with which production results lend themselves to empirical measurement facilitates market analysis employing supply and demand concepts, time series analysis, etc. Perhaps the key to an integrated ecological/economic anthropological analysis is this possibility of alternating between production as a substantive process and production reduced to output, a statistical abstraction.

Nevertheless, it is important not to allow an empiricist concern for operationalization to eliminate a consideration of fundamental issues of political economic analysis. From this latter perspective, the production focus dovetails directly with problems of access to and/or control over the means of production in a given society; and, most importantly, shows how the total product of that society is allocated among various groups within the population. With the exception of certain simple band or tribal societies, this kind of inquiry inevitably leads into a study of the political power structure and social ranking or stratification (e.g., Fried 1967; Sahlins 1960a, 1960b, 1968: 74-95).

Up to this point our discussion has dealt with production as a theoretical category, and with the general role of the production process in the environment/technology/culture relationship. However, economic anthropology is also concerned with identifying and analyzing various types of production modes, and with demonstrating how these modes are organized and operate in different nonindustrial societies. Accordingly, seven basic types of nonindustrial production are recognized by economic anthropologists: tillage or cultivation, animal husbandry, fishing, hunting, collection or gathering, construction, and manufacturing (see Chapple and Coon 1942, chap. 6; Udy 1959, chap. 2; Wagner 1960, chap. 6). The problem of subsistence or food procurement and the temporal sequencing of modes of food production in human societal development have been the focus of considerable attention.

It has long been recognized that all complex societies acquire their food supply by cultivation, by animal husbandry, or by a combination of the two, whereas in "simpler" societies the population is sustained by various combinations of hunting, gathering, and/or fishing. This societal dichotomy is con-

sidered to have cross-cultural diachronic significance, since cultivation and
animal husbandry invariably appear after hunting, gathering, and fishing
(Lowie 1938:282)—i.e., hunting and
gathering (foraging) represent the earliest level of cultural adaptation in human evolution (Y. Cohen 1968:48).

Construction and manufacture characterize all production modes in all societies; the creation of productive
capital (i.e., tools and equipment)
through these two processes is perhaps
the chief distinguishing trait of human
societies and is a functional prerequisite
of any nonindustrial economic system
(Wagner 1960:89). There is still insufficient data to support cross-culturally
valid generalizations about the relative
proportions of total available labor
time and energy expended in food-
yielding as opposed to non-food-yield-
ing productive activities in societies at
various levels of cultural adaptation.
What is clear, however, is that the absolute level of capital input (and concomitant complexity of division of
labor and specialization) required by
horticulture is considerably higher than
that required by foraging, just as the
level required by agriculture is higher
than that required by horticulture.

In any given economy, a major problem of economic anthropological analysis is to understand the relationships between these various productive activities from the standpoint of allocation
of labor time, division and organization
of labor, amount and nature of goods
produced, and productive efficiency
(input versus output)—i.e., the variables
of complexity, work load, outlay, and
uncertainty (Udy 1959, chap. 2). These
relationships are best observed and
analyzed in the context of management
units, where the focus of attention is
the circulation and transformation of
value arising out of the exercise of
choices by the individual members of

the unit in the utilization of scarce resources (see, e.g., Barth 1967, Schneider 1970).

A minority of contemporary economic anthropologists object to the application of the formal theory of choice
to the analysis of productive behavior
in nonindustrial economies because in
these societies, as they argue, "constraints on individual choice . . . are extreme, and are dictated not only by
social obligation but also by primitive
technology and by physical environment" (Dalton 1969:67). According to
this view, for example, the Tikopian is
born into a taro- and coconut-growing
economy and does not weigh the advantages of planting these crops rather
than lettuce and cabbage; he chooses
between cultivating taro and coconuts
on the one hand and engaging in non-
food-producing activities on the other.
What this argument ignores is that all
human choices are subject to similar
kinds of constraints. Thus the Kansas
farmer does not decide to plant wheat
rather than mangos solely because he
happens to participate in a wheat-grow-
ing economy; his decision is as surely
conditioned by environmental factors
as the Tikopian's (see Nash 1969, Le
Clair 1969). As Le Clair (1969) has
noted, "the only thing that is involved
here is that the parameters of choice
are different. It is important to study
the differences in . . . [these] parameters . . . but whatever . . . [they] may be
in a particular situation, presumably the
principles of choice remain the same."
For example, whenever choices are made
between complementary, substitute, or
supplementary productive activities,
the principle of opportunity cost (i.e.,
the sacrifice of the alternatives forgone
in producing a particular good or service) is operative; the cost of building a
house is the canoe or baskets or nets
that might have been built in its place.
This view finds support in the archaeo-

logical literature in the concern with "scheduling" as a cultural activity that resolved conflict between procurement systems in the mixed economies of pre-agricultural populations (Flannery 1968).

Distribution and Exchange

This section includes separate discussions of two processes that anthropologists often lump together: distribution and exchange. As we saw earlier, distribution determines the proportion of total output that the individual will receive, whereas exchange determines the specific products into which the individual wants to convert the share allocated to him by distribution. Distribution implies a reward system (Udy 1959, chap. 6) in which produce is channeled out among individuals or groups by reason of their control over the factors of production or for the labor they expended in the productive process. Exchange, on the other hand, refers to the various processes by which goods (and services) move between individuals or groups, as, for example, between producer and consumer, buyer and seller, donor and recipient. From the standpoint of functional analysis, these two processes are closely interrelated in all societies, but there is a higher degree of correspondence between them in band and tribal societies than in more advanced preindustrial and industrial societies.

In every society the producer-product relation, once the product is finished, is not necessarily or immediately one of possession; the return of the product to the individual depends on his relations to other individuals. More precisely, the distribution process intervenes between the producer and his product to establish his share (i.e., to transfer rights of possession) in total output according to prevailing norms.

Every society has explicit or implicit norms governing the way its total pool of products is to be shared out among its members (see Marx 1904a:283; Udy 1959, chap. 6; Le Clair 1959). It is analytically important, however, to remember that sharing-out behavior is a process guided only partly by norms, not simply a series of acts in response to norms. It may turn out that the producer of a given product has a primary claim on it—but this always depends on the prevailing distribution system. Thus the "primary claimant" (Le Clair 1959:20) might be a nonproducer who is trustee or steward, administrator, owner-boss, lineage head, a reluctant distributor of largess, or a benevolent despot. Whatever the outcome of a given distribution process, it must revolve around some person or persons. In hunting societies, for example, when a number of hunters cooperate to kill a utilizable animal, there are strict rules for ascribing ownership of that animal to only one hunter, who distributes its parts among the others, again in accordance with recognized norms (Dowling 1968:502). Likewise, in fishing societies when a number of fishermen work together on a fishing expedition, it is the owner of the boat and/or net who usually distributes the catch (see, e.g., Raymond Firth 1965a, chap. 8; 1966, chap. 8).

Aside from producer claims (i.e., some individual as producer of a good has a primary claim on it) and claims arising out of some relation of the claimant to the productive process (as in the cases of hunting and fishing cited above), at least two other kinds of claims to output operate in primitive and peasant societies: those arising out of some nonproductive relationship between producer and claimant (e.g., real or fictive kinship) and those arising out of some relationship of the claimant to his community as a whole, of which the individual producer's obligation represents a portion of the whole, as in the case of a tribal village chief (Le Clair 1959:20-21).

The system of distribution in primitive and peasant economies must incorporate mechanisms for dealing with two major problems: (1) the division of a joint product among the members of cooperative groups, and (2) the compensation of the factors of production, especially labor, from a source other than their immediate product. In dealing with the first problem, it is necessary to discover the principles that guide the sharing-out process; the second problem entails a determination of the source of compensation (i.e., money or goods in kind), and the basis for equation of the services of labor and other productive factors with goods of a kind other than those immediately produced (Firth 1965a:279; Udy 1959, chap. 6).

Firth's (1965a:313) summary of his analysis of the principles of distribution in the Tikopia economy applies to many primitive economies: there is a "definite concept that all participants in a productive activity should receive a share of the product, but that social considerations do not make it necessary for this share to be exactly proportionate to the contribution in time, labor, or skill that each individual has made." Underlying this lack of emphasis on differential performance as a criterion for allocation is the concept of "total contribution." To place one's labor at the disposal of another is a social, not merely an economic, service; what is important is not simply the provision of labor power to be converted into material products, but the fact of participation, of assistance and moral support in the activity (Firth 1965a:303). In contrast, among the Malay fishermen, where the system of distributing earnings involves monetization, Firth

(1966:256) found that "proportionate returns to capital and labor . . . tend to correspond to the degree to which each contributes to the total yield."

A proper understanding of the role of distribution in an economic system cannot be achieved by focusing only on the methods and operations by which individual rewards are determined and allocated; it is also necessary to study the results of allocation, which are expressed as lists of quantities of goods apportioned to various status occupants or groups (see Le Clair 1962:1195). Through this dual focus on the system of distribution and the pattern of distribution, the noneconomic ramifications of the control and use of material wealth in a given society emerge more clearly. Societies at the band level of adaptation are usually characterized as egalitarian; fundamental inequalities between different sets of persons unequivocally emerge in tribal and peasant societies, where social and/or political achievement entitle some individuals to more than an equal share of material reward. Thurnwald (1932: 107), one of the pioneers of the systematic comparative study of political economy, observed that "in graded and stratified societies distribution is the function of powerful families of influential men, of the ruling aristocracy, or of the administrative bureaucracy; and it is often abused [by] . . . distributors of any political power [who] reserve a percentage of the profits for themselves."

As Thurnwald's statement implies, there is a difference between inequality and exploitation in preindustrial societies; the fact that certain individuals and groups in such societies regularly acquire rights of ownership or control over disproportionate shares of material wealth does not necessarily make them exploiters of their fellows. This is true even when the most favored individuals or groups are nonproducers (in the material sense) and the least favored are producers, since such a situation often involves an exchange between manual workers and intellectual workers, the goods produced by the former being apportioned to the latter in return for services rendered (Godelier 1967a: 272). Sahlins (1968, chap. 5) has analyzed the mechanisms through which the relationship between chief and followers in tribal societies generates a circulation of goods and services according to the principle of generalized reciprocity; he implies that genuine political economic exploitation might not appear in human society until the Industrial Revolution and the rise of a capitalistic class system. But the functional origins of property-based exploitation in precapitalist societies remain elusive. "As a general rule," warns Godelier (1967a), "it is extremely difficult to determine where the power of function (i.e., services rendered to the community) ceases and the power of exploitation begins in societies where social contradictions and group conflicts are little developed" (see also Godelier 1969a: 132-82). It is clear that the search for political economic exploitation of man by man cannot be restricted to those societies transformed by industrialization.

It was noted earlier that distribution and exchange processes are closely interrelated in all societies. For purposes of analysis, the distribution system can in effect be conceived as consisting of norms regarding certain transfer events (i.e., from production unit to consumption unit or between consumption units), the norms stipulating those conditions under which particular transfer events must or should occur (Le Clair 1962:1196). Two distinct kinds of transfer events are objects of anthropological analysis: physical transfers and jural transactions. The first involves lo-cational movement and physical control; the second involves the transfer of culturally defined ownership and use rights. In a typical transfer situation one individual physically exchanges one thing for another and in so doing relinquishes physical control over that thing to another individual. It must be emphasized that in such a situation the individual actor does not himself transfer ownership or use rights; his culture in effect "transfers ownership by reading intentions into the minds of participants in a transaction" (Commons 1954:562). In other words, cultural norms (i.e., the exchange system) intervene between transacting parties and their goods (or services) to determine the course and consequences of their mutual transfer.

The transfer aspect of the economic process has long been a major topic of anthropological inquiry. In the 1920s both Malinowski and Mauss made major contributions to the study of transfer phenomena, Malinowski concentrating on the varieties of trade and gift-giving among the Trobriand islanders (1961) and Mauss making the first systematic comparative study of gift exchange (1954), in which he emphasized its function in articulating the social system (via the concept of "total prestation"). While Malinowski and Mauss were first in demonstrating how gift exchanges create, symbolize, and maintain status relations, it was Raymond Firth, in his classic 1929 study of the Maori economy, who first dealt analytically with the theoretical economic problems of gift exchange (1959, chap. 12).

A later comparative contribution to the systematic understanding of transfer processes was made by Polanyi et al. (eds., 1957). This group of scholars made a basic distinction between goods-handling and goods-receiving processes, and asked the following basic questions of the ethnographic cases analyzed (1957:vii): "Who passed on goods to whom, in what order, how often, and with what response among those listed under whom?" As a result of their synthesis, three basic types of transfer were isolated (1957:vii-ix): (1) reciprocative sequence among fixed partners (AB/BA or AB/BC/CA); (2) redistributive sequence between a central actor and many peripheral actors (BA/CA/DA/EA/FA, followed by A/BCDEF); (3) random market sequence (A/BCDEF or B/ACDEF or F/ABCDE, etc.). Their inquiries led them well beyond the limits of economic exchange into the realm of related institutions; and they regarded reciprocity, redistribution, and market exchange as mutually exclusive sociocultural processes that characterized total economies or integrated total societies (e.g., Polanyi 1957, Codere 1968). Most contemporary economic anthropologists agree with Salisbury's judgment (1968a:480) that these "are not terms that characterize 'entire economies' or 'modes of integration,' nor are they terms which fit economies into a unilineal progression from 'primitive' to 'archaic' to 'market,'" as is so often implied in the writings of Polanyi and others. For example, John Bennett (1969), departing from the position that we are essentially ignorant about the nature and role of reciprocity behavior in market economies, has described and analyzed reciprocal economic exchanges among North American farmers, who of course are completely committed to market economic operations.

Sahlins (1965b) has reduced Polanyi's three types of transfer activity into two broader types, which he calls "reciprocity" or "vice-versa" movements between two parties (A⇄B) and "pooling" or "redistribution"—centralized movements involving "collection from members of a group, often under one hand, and redivision within this group," as follows (1965b:141):

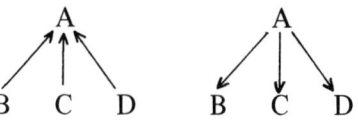

Sahlins points out that redistribution is a system of reciprocities associated with collective action within a social unit, as distinct from the reciprocity system, which is associated with individual action between parties. The redistribution system implies social unity and centricity; the reciprocity system implies social duality and symmetry (see also Polanyi 1957).

As the economic anthropologist examines the ethnographic record, he finds that a few fundamental forms of physical transfer are multiplied into a wide variety of transactional systems through the operation of cultural, social, and situational circumstances. It is now recognized that the differences among these various kinds of exchange system are not adequately clarified by efforts to describe the total systems with which they articulate. Rather, as Salisbury expresses it (1968a:481), "they are better understood through closer analysis of the specific situations, in both monetary and tribal societies, where it is mutually advantageous to use recurrent rather than isolated exchanges, or where imbalances in volumes tendered can be, or must be, tolerated for long periods."

Sahlins (1965b:145-49) has sought to impose order on this ethnographic diversity of transactional modes through a "scheme of reciprocities"—a continuum that takes as its major criterion the stipulation of material returns; i.e., the "spirit of exchange" moves from disinterested concern for the other party to mutuality to self-interest. This is essentially a descriptive synthesis of insights from works of Malinowski, Mauss, Thurnwald, and Polanyi. The continuum is defined by poles and midpoint as follows: (1) generalized reciprocity, the solidary extreme (A$\rightleftharpoons$B), involving unstipulated reciprocation; (2) balanced reciprocity, the midpoint (A$\rightleftharpoons$B), involving direct reciprocation with time and equivalency stipulations; and (3) negative reciprocity, the unsociable extreme (A$\rightleftharpoons$B), involving a two-party confrontation in which each party seeks to maximize utility at the other's expense. Sahlins (1965b:149-74) also proposes a relationship between types of reciprocities and kinship distance, suggesting that reciprocity is inclined toward the generalized extreme by close kinship and toward the negative extreme in proportion to a diminution in kinship propinquity, and that it varies with other factors such as social rank, relative wealth and need, and type of goods.

As the results of more and more specific ethnographic case studies accumulate, it appears that two-party (viceversa) transactions are, with few exceptions, unbalanced and engender conflict as one party seeks to gain as much advantage over the other as possible, short of terminating the relationship and initiating another with a new partner (see, e.g., Dole 1956, Salisbury 1960). Thus while reciprocity incorporates elements of conflict, bargaining (haggling) also incorporates elements of cooperation (Khuri 1968:698; Salisbury 1968a: 480-81). From the conceptual standpoint, this implies that any economic transaction involving a two-party transfer of goods may be considered as generating a market situation and may be analyzed accordingly (see Belshaw 1965; Salisbury 1968b; Schneider 1970, chap. 5)—the market being defined not as a location or as an allocational system, but as an institutional

arena created by regular transactions of goods between a multitude of transactors (see Raymond Firth 1967:5-6; Salisbury 1968b:118).

Given this framework of analysis, five basic types of economic transactions (i.e., interpersonal and/or intercommunity encounters involving the transfer of material goods) have been dealt with by economic anthropologists: (1) those occurring in the marketplace; (2) those involving partnerships between two individuals; (3) those between two discrete communities; (4) those between an individual distributor and many receivers within a single community; and (5) those that involve the giving of gifts in a ceremonial context (see Herskovits 1952; Polanyi 1957; Belshaw 1965; Nash 1966, 1968; Salisbury 1968b). It must be emphasized that these "types" are taxonomic conveniences for purposes of analysis, and that in any given ethnographic case they are by no means mutually exclusive or unrelated. For example, among the Australian aborigines of the Daly River the *merbok* system involved deferred gift exchanges between partners in the same community and, ultimately, between networks of partners in different communities—thus combining transactional types 2, 3, and 5 (Stanner 1933-1934).

Marketplace Systems. Marketing and marketplace systems in tribal and peasant societies are central topics of concern in a large corpus of literature in economic anthropology (summarized in Belshaw 1965, chap. 3; Nash 1966, chap. 4; Wolf 1966:40-48; and Salisbury 1968b). This includes studies in Africa (e.g., Bohannan and Dalton 1962; P. and L. Bohannan 1968, chaps. 12-15; Stanner 1969; Hill 1969), China (e.g., Skinner 1964), Malaya and Indonesia (e.g., Raymond Firth 1966, Dewey 1962, Geertz 1963), South

America (e.g., Ortiz 1967, Forman and Riegelhaupt 1970), Mesoamerica (e.g., Redfield 1962; McBryde 1945; Foster 1948; Tax 1953; Nash 1961, 1966; Kaplan 1965; Beals 1967; Cassady 1968; Diskin 1969; Waterbury 1970) and the Caribbean (e.g., Mintz 1955, 1957, 1959, 1960a, 1960b, 1967; Katzin 1959, 1960).

Marketplace exchange, as described and analyzed in this literature, has three separate yet interdependent processual dimensions—locational, interactional, and allocational (see Raymond Firth 1967:5; Belshaw 1965:6-9; Le Clair 1962:1185-86)—and two distinct yet often coexistent institutional forms—"sectional" and "network" (Wolf 1966:40-41). Analytically, the locational dimension of marketplace exchange is closely related to sectional organization, whereas the interactional and allocational dimensions are more closely related to network organization. In the first case, the focus of analysis is the spatial flow of goods from place of production to place of exchange or sale to place of consumption; the resulting market area may be viewed, as in highland Mesoamerica, as a solar system combining central marketplace towns and a series of mutually interdependent, product-specialized satellite villages or, as in China, as a configuration of central places or distribution centers (cities or towns) and their web of dependent territories (rural hinterland) (Skinner 1964). In the second case, the foci of analysis are the social relations of transactors (buyers and sellers), the dynamics of bargaining, and its outcome as measured in quantifiable economic values; this market arena is a model-building concept that postulates price as the principal integrative factor in regional marketing systems. Accordingly, as analysis progresses, the relevant analytic units are no longer marketplaces inhabited by flesh-and-blood peasant traders, but markets inhabited by fleshless and bloodless categories of buyers and sellers; the system analyzed is not a landlocked series of marketplaces, but a nonlocational network of transactional markets; the relevant parameters at this level of analysis are no longer time and place, but price and quantity, supply and demand (Nash 1961, Cassady 1968, Cook 1970).

Implicit in the distinction between sectional and network forms of market organization is a contrast between a system in which production and exchange are closely circumscribed by regionally operative social, cultural, and ecological factors that sharply limit the range of alternatives open to the individual actor, and a system in which these activities and alternatives are more loosely circumscribed and defined. Thus, in the marketplace systems of highland Mesoamerica, the Andes, and West Africa, the various sections (e.g., corporate peasant villages) are dependent upon each other for different products and this mutual interdependence forces them to produce these products regularly and indefinitely; whereas in the marketing system of a Norwegian fishing community, for example, there is no sectionally organized production and exchange, but rather a series of flexible relationships between individual economic agents (Wolf 1966). The difference between these two systems is one of degree, not of kind, and it is misleading to compare them in a dichotomous typology, ranging personalism (sectional) against impersonalism (network). As Belshaw has warned (1965:80): "There is no such thing as an enduring non-personalistic relationship, and no economy in the world can be based entirely or even largely on non-personalistic relationships, for this would be the negation of continuity and security and would be atomistic group behavior rather than behavior in a society." The fact remains, however, that the typical economic unit in the "open" network system has greater flexibility of choice and action in production and exchange than does its counterpart in the "closed" sectional system (see Wolf 1966:40-41).

What are some of the salient features of marketplace systems and trade which have emerged from contemporary research in peasant-artisan societies? One characteristic of these systems is that they tend to be associated, on the one hand, with rural-based prestation (reciprocity) and subsistence systems and, on the other, with urban-based manufacturing and commercial systems. In Mesoamerica it is common for a peasant artisan to sell his products in the marketplace during one season of the year and immediately spend his earnings on liquor, candles, flowers, fireworks, bread, chocolate, and other customary items for consumption in a festive celebration, while in another season he earns a daily wage as an urban laborer and spends his accumulated income on seed, fertilizer, and other items related to preparing and cultivating his land in the village—thereby integrating both systems (see Belshaw 1965:75-76).

Another feature is that a substantial volume of local and outside products bypasses the marketplace. Among the mechanisms that facilitate this process is a subregional trade based on the operation of comparative advantage coupled with symbiosis between adjacent or neighboring communities, itinerant peddling, trucking, and local stores or other businesses (e.g., *molinos de nixtamal,* or corn-grinding mills, in Mesoamerica). Often the prices involved in transactions in this sphere are not determined by two-party bargaining, but depend on various kinds of fixed pricing, credit sales, and trading

partnerships (e.g., Ward 1967, Mintz 1967, Khuri 1968). Given the scarcity of cash in the typical peasant system, and the fact that cash is usually mobilized in anticipation of or as a result of marketplace trading, it is common for the "bypass" transaction to involve either payment in kind or direct and indirect barter. In the Mesoamerican peasant village, for example, corn, eggs, and fruits in season are accepted in payment for services rendered (e.g., blacksmithing, milling, haircutting, curing) and for manufactured or other articles sold in local stores; and bartering of various goods is common (e.g., fruits for clay pots). Under conditions of expanding monetization in the peasant economies of the world, it is typical for national currency to serve as a standard of value in barter transactions (i.e., the exchange rate between goods is determined by their market price expressed in money terms).

The economic functions of marketplace trade (e.g., bulking of dispersed produce, distribution, storage) are combined with a wide variety of noneconomic ones (see Mintz 1959; Bohannan and Dalton 1962:15-19; P. and L. Bohannan 1968, chap. 14). The typical peasant trader arrives in the marketplace not only to convert his embodied labor power into cash and to acquire complementary goods and services, but also to handle political, legal, or administrative affairs, to attend public meetings, to engage in religious worship or have ritual services performed (e.g., marriage, baptism, confirmation), to seek medical advice or treatment, to visit with friends and relatives, and on through a long list of other activities. To satisfy these multiple needs, the population of a typical marketplace community is characterized by a more highly diversified occupational role inventory than are the population units in its hinterland.

The main price-determining mechanism in marketplaces is negotiation (though price fixing is reportedly practiced in some areas; see Herskovits 1952:220-21), but there is evidence that sellers' calculations and bargaining strategies vary in accordance with the statuses they occupy (i.e., producer, middleman, agent) and the type of goods they sell (e.g., durable or perishable). The typical peasant marketer does act in accordance with an "extremum principle"—i.e., maximizing money receipts as a seller and minimizing money expenditures as a buyer (Lowe 1965:36-37)—but determining the extent to which his decisions follow this principle requires working out the relationships among relevant functions, as well as defining or at least specifying their general characteristics (Le Clair and Schneider, eds., 1968:459). For example, a preliminary analysis of sales data in a Mexican peasant-artisan industry suggests that it is much more difficult to work out these relationships quantitatively in the case of producer-sellers than it is in the case of middlemen-traders, who, unlike the producers, do have a direct money cost basis that enables them to calculate profit margins and serves as a guide in the quotation-bid interaction of marketplace negotiations. In contrast, the producer-seller is limited to an "opportunity cost-plus" formula in calculating returns and negotiating—a formula that entails estimating the value of labor and expenditures for raw materials, tools, transportation to point of sale, etc., and obviously lacks the quantitative simplicity and precision of the trader's money cost formula (Cook 1970). These important differences notwithstanding, it is clear that most peasant marketers practice double pricing (e.g., higher prices for tourists and other non-locals than for locals for the same products), which reflects, among other things, different degrees of market knowledge and haggling skill (Salisbury 1968b:118).

Another characteristic of marketplace systems is the variability of prices and output of local products. While there have been relatively few intensive studies of such variability (e.g., Raymond Firth 1966, Nash 1961, Cook 1970), it is clear that, in addition to price fluctuations generated by supply and demand conditions on any given trading day, prices and output of agricultural and artisan products vary (1) from market day to market day within the same season, (2) from season to season, and (3) from year to year. The causes underlying such variability include (in addition to natural and ecological factors affecting agricultural output) general price levels of a given product, buyer outlay or demand patterns, producer expectations about future market conditions, special household provisioning requirements related to ceremonial or festive cycles, the labor requirements of the agricultural cycle (which determines how much labor time is available for supplementary productive activity), the availability and other conditions of alternative employment opportunities outside the village for the village-based peasant artisan, and the quantity and quality of the annual crop harvest (which determine the amount of cash the peasant cultivator will have availabe for complementary goods and services). The relative influence of these and other factors on aggregate price and output variability can be fully understood only in the context of an analysis of the total economic situation of the houshold unit served by the peasant-artisan producer (see Smith 1955, Nash 1961, Rosemary Firth 1966, Chayanov 1966, Wolf 1966, Cook 1970).

Trade in peasant marketplaces is often portrayed as closely approximating the economist's model of perfect competition, with price established through the interaction of buyers who do not buy enough to set price with sellers who do not control enough of the supply to set price (see Foster 1948; Tax 1953:13-19; Nash 1966:70; Salisbury 1968b:118). There is empirical support for this generalization from many studies; however, by no means sufficient data are available to warrant our considering any variation from this pattern as anomalous. It is quite possible that more intensive studies of single-product markets in peasant-artisan marketplace systems, focusing on the structural relations of buyers and sellers and their interaction through time—preferably during at least one complete annual cycle—will provide data indicating that these market situations are more complicated than the perfect-competition analogy implies, and may be characterized by significant degrees of imperfection (e.g., Cook 1970:786-87). Indeed, given the widespread emergence in peasant marketing systems of entrepreneurs who accumulate substantial funds of capital as a basis for credit and mercantile operations, it is to be expected that significant transformations will occur in traditional, atomistically competitive markets.

Marketplace trade is also characterized by temporal patterning or sequencing, which is evidenced both within and between discrete trading days. While the data are insufficient to support anything beyond tentative generalizations, two basic patterns (inferred from indices like size of trading population, size and variety of product inventories, and volume of transactions) may be discerned in the course of trade on any given market day: (1) a cycle of expansion-peak-contraction, and (2) a series of discontinuous wavelike fluctuations, with each peak comparable to every other. The specific timing of each phase in these cycles varies among marketplaces in the same system but tends to be repetitive from one trading day to the next in the same marketplace, other things remaining equal (e.g., seasonal factors, meterological conditions, cultural factors). Individual marketplaces may operate daily or at fixed intervals of several days (usually not more than seven, though special fiesta markets are also held annually or when conditions merit). The interval between market days is fixed by custom. In areas with multiple-marketplace systems, trading is staggered on a subregional basis, with trade occurring at set intervals in each component marketplace. For example, in the valley of Oaxaca, Mexico, there is a system of rotating or periodic marketplaces, each subregional marketplace being the focus of trading activity once a week on its own day, the same from week to week and from year to year (Malinowski and De la Fuente 1957, Beals 1967, Diskin 1969); among the Tiv of central Nigeria there is a five-day marketing cycle (P. and L. Bohannan 1968, chap. 15); and a four-day cycle is reported for Dahomey (Herskovits 1952:219).

Trading Partnerships. A trading partnership exists when relations between a particular buyer and a particular seller (or giver and receiver) persist beyond a single transaction (Salisbury 1968b: 119). Such partnerships are widespread in nonmarket economies (i.e., those without marketplaces or organized factor and commodity markets, and with no all-purpose money or undergoing monetization), where they are a major trading mechanism involving individual traders in material transactions with real or fictive kinsmen, affines, or friends (Herskovits 1952, chap. 9; Malinowski 1961:91-95; Harding 1967; Brown 1970). They are also found in monetized peasant market economies, where they serve as effective means of adapting to the risks and uncertainties inherent in competitive trading (e.g., Redfield 1962, Mintz 1967, Belshaw 1965:57-58). A common type of partnership in peasant market economies is based on the extension of credit by one of the parties (e.g., Ward 1967). Transactions in the marketplace between partners, whether based on the extension of credit or not, do not preclude haggling, whereas those conducted in nonmarket economies often preclude it in favor of balanced reciprocity or barter according to prevailing notions of "set equivalences" (Sahlins 1965*a*). Even in nonmonetary economies, however, there is evidence to suggest that superior knowledge or skill on the part of one trader may be exercised to considerable material advantage over his partner (e.g., Olson 1936). Finally, it appears that individual trading partner relationships cannot be properly understood without tracing the total network of relationships in which both partners are enmeshed with others in the same group, and that the terms of trade of any one set of traders must be studied in the context of this total network of relationships—much as economists handle international trading relations.

The fact that exchange ratios are customarily not negotiated by trading partners in nonmonetary economies does not mean that all goods *ipso facto* change hands without deviation from the prevailing schedule of equivalences (see Herskovits 1952:210-11). On the contrary, there is a wide indeterminacy in such exchanges, so that similar products change hands at different ratios in different transactions (Sahlins 1965*a*: 96). In specific ethnographic cases this variability of exchange values does reflect sensitivity to forces of supply and demand, but only as these operate throughout the entire network of trad-

ing relations. As a general rule, however, it appears that supply-demand disequilibrium in partnership trade is brought into balance by pressure on trade partners rather than on exchange rates; i.e., the transaction price remains constant and the goods flow in the direction of either the giving or the receiving partner, depending on the nature of the disequilibrium. If the situation becomes intolerable to either partner, the relationship may be renegotiated or terminated, with each partner then entering into new negotiations with new partners (Sahlins 1965*a*:112-13). Given these and other complications of partnership trade, the extent of individual involvement is surprisingly extensive in some instances; Malinowski (1961:276) cites one Trobriander who had more than a hundred individual partners dispersed among several localities, although he notes that the typical individual had only four to six partners.

Trade partnerships in preindustrial, nonmonetary societies are also characterized by a potential for converting dyadic relationships into links in a system of intergroup relationships. In his study of the *merbok* system of the Daly River tribes in northern Australia, Stanner (1933-1934:164-65) shows how trade did not set individual partner against individual partner so much as family or closely related kinship group (all of whom traded with each other) against an individual partner in another horde or tribe.

Trade partnerships in peasant market economies assume two general forms: asymmetrical (partners of unequal socioeconomic and/or ethnic status) and symmetrical (partners of equal socioeconomic and/or ethnic status). In the former, the terms of trade (prices) habitually favor the partner of higher status (who is buyer) in comparison with open market prices at the expense of the partner of lower status (who is seller). This occurs, among other places, in Mesoamerica (e.g., Mixtec highlands of Oaxaca, Chiapas highlands), where peasant-Indian hinterland populations are dominated by *mestizo* (*ladino*) populations in towns and cities, and where buyers who specialize in bulking and reselling on a wholesale basis (*acaparadores*) are invariably recruited from the dominant *mestizo* class (see Marroquín 1957, Stavenhagen 1965:62-63). This relationship may be reinforced through the extension of loans (cash advances) by the buyer to the seller, and persists, among other reasons, because of a series of market conditions that create a structure characterized by quasi-atomistic competition and relatively undifferentiated production on the supply side, and by minimal competition and relatively few big-lot buyers (i.e., quasi-oligopsony) on the demand side. There are, on the other hand, asymmetrical quasi-partnerships in other areas of Mesoamerica (e.g., Oaxaca valley), where the bargaining advantages of the big-lot buyer are partially offset by the fact that the sellers are representatives of closed production units (corporate villages) with natural monopolistic aspects (though without conscious, coordinated planning and control of output and pricing). In this market situation the big-lot buyer who habitually abuses his superior bargaining power risks the possibility of antagonizing the sellers—perhaps with the consequence of eliminating his only viable, direct, and regular supply source for specialist products (Cook 1970: 786-87).

Symmetrical partnerships result in terms of trade (prices) that do not regularly favor one partner in comparison with going market prices; market prices, together with the value placed on maintaining the partnership, form a basis for settling each transaction. A classic ethnographic example of this type is the *pratik* relationship of Haiti, in which the participants are equals for trading purposes (Mintz 1967:100). This relationship may link together producer and middleman, middleman and middleman, or middleman and consumer. But whatever the specific linkage may be in any given case, the *pratik* relationship operates on the same principle as other varieties of symmetrical partnership: partner A accepts whatever goods partner B offers, on the understanding that partner B will either accept whatever partner A offers later or continue to supply him when goods are scarce. Stipulations as to the class or type of goods traded are specified in each situation (e.g., in Haiti various kinds of fruits and vegetables are the principal trade goods). The important thing is that the relationship reduces mutual risk, since both partners ensure against total failure to sell or total stoppage of supplies (see Salisbury 1968*b*: 119).

The extension of credit is an important basis for both asymmetrical and symmetrical trade partnerships between middlemen of various types and producers of agricultural and artisan goods. In most cases the creditors in such arrangements have very limited capital, which limits the number of potential borrowers they can serve. Such arrangements are customarily established on a foundation of mutual personal trust between the partners, and even if a creditor may have a relatively large stock of capital, he will not know enough individuals well enough to justify his establishing a significantly larger number of credit-reinforced partnerships than he would otherwise (Ward 1967:138). The most common arrangement is for a peasant producer-seller (agriculturist, fisherman, artisan) to borrow from a middleman-buyer (e.g., shopkeeper), who also provisions him with consumer goods or cash for capital replacement purposes (e.g., repair or purchase of tools and equipment, purchase of seed). An interesting variation is reported from Java, where farmers extend credit to middlemen by giving up a portion of their crop harvest in exchange for a claim on the sales returns to the middleman, either at a predetermined price or at a price geared to the actual sale price (Dewey 1964:245-46). Considered from the perspective of economic development, trade generated through credit relationships is significant, since it facilitates the risky transition from subsistence production to a cash economy (Salisbury 1968b). On the other hand, from the perspective of political economy, trade arising out of asymmetrical credit relationships may, as a functional equivalent to debt peonage, operate to perpetuate economic underdevelopment and class exploitation.

Intercommunity Trade. Intercommunity trade involves the acquisition of products (foodstuffs, raw materials, or manufactured goods) which are unavailable in the importing community. Such trade often reflects permanent intercommunity and/or interregional production specializations and always arises through mutual interest in comparative advantage, each trading unit gaining materially or symbolically. Since this trade customarily requires traveling considerable distances across political or ethnic boundaries, the potential for hostility and conflict is high, thus creating a need for peacekeeping or solidarity-promoting mechanisms. Various modes of intercommunity trade are found in the ethnographic record, including "silent trade," "visiting trade" (i.e., extension of generalized reciprocity to the intercommunity sector [Heider 1969]), "administered trade" (Polanyi et al., eds., 1957), and extension of market systems with or without

itinerant middlemen. Archaeological research yields no evidence of regular intercommunity trade before the end of the Pleistocene, but scattered data suggest the existence of sporadic trade in nonsubsistence goods during the late Pleistocene and early post-Pleistocene (Gabel 1967:51-55; Hole and Heizer 1969:292-96).

The so-called silent trade or dumb barter was an exotic mode of trade in which goods were transferred at customary rates without any meeting or discussion. Representatives of one group would deposit goods to be traded at a customary place, retreat some distance, and give a signal, perhaps a shout or a stroke on a gong; then the representatives of the second group would bring their trade goods to the same place and retreat. The first group then returned and removed the newly deposited goods (assuming these met the established criteria of equivalences), the second group took the original goods, and everyone went home. A classic example of this kind of trade between the Carthaginians and African tribesmen was recorded by Herodotus; subsequent reports indicate that it also was operative in Siberia, Lapland, West Africa, Timor, Sumatra, India, Ceylon, New Caledonia, New Guinea, and aboriginal California. It usually occurred where relatively primitive people regularly traded with people of a more technologically advanced culture; in Africa, for example, the Bambuti pygmies gave bananas for meat from the neighboring agricultural Bantu. Unfortunately, we may never achieve a more complete understanding of this now extinct institution and its social and economic ramifications for lack of an extant detailed statement of what was traded, when, under what conditions, and how often (Thurnwald 1932:149-50; Herskovits 1952:185-87; Raymond Firth 1970).

Visiting trade is commonly, but not

exclusively, found among relatively un-specialized tribal societies with clearly demarcated boundaries. It is closely articulated with ceremonial, ritual, and kinship spheres of behavior, and may involve the transfer of token, symbolic, or utilitarian objects that are given as gifts (rather than bartered). When this is the case, the trading activity is based on the principle of deferred (rather than immediate) reciprocation. In other words, it extends the rules and norms of a kinship-based, generalized reciprocity system (see Sahlins 1965*b*) operating within a given community into a transactional system operating between communities. Instances of visiting trade culled from the ethnographic record can be classified and compared in two dimensions: (1) content of transactions—e.g., regional specialties, like Turkish obsidian or Guatemalan quetzal feathers or Amphletts pottery; permanent, like stone quarries; or occasional and shifting, like food during times of shortage and surplus in California and on the Northwest Coast; symbolic, as in the transfer of *kula* tokens, ritual patterns (Navaho-Ute dances), or social patterns (Yap Empire kin ties, Arapesh trading partnerships); and (2) mode of transaction—e.g., alternating visits between equals, as in *kula* voyages; unilateral trips, like those of the "tribute bearers" of the Caroline Islands; rendezvous, as in Australian aborigine regional ceremonies (Heider 1969).

"Administered trade" (Polanyi 1957:262 and *passim*) is typically conducted in "ports of trade" (Polanyi et al., eds., 1957; Polanyi 1963, 1966) between political agents of the trading societies. Goods are traded on a long-term set equivalency basis, with haggling restricted to nonprice matters like measures, quality, or means of payment (Polanyi 1957:262). In such trade the import interest of both communities is dominant over their export interest, and goods typically move long distances in fleets or caravans through unpoliced areas to a neutral port, which has not always been a coastal or river site; such "ports" have often been located in an ecological border area between highlands and lowlands, desert and jungle, or forest and savannah (Chapman 1957:115-16). This form of trade was operative in many areas of the world as an aspect of preindustrial state organization. Ports of trade are known to have existed in the Aztec and Maya regions of Mesoamerica; on the Malabar coast, in Madras, Calcutta, Rangoon, Colombo, Batavia, and in China; on the north Syrian coast and in certain Greek city-states of Asia Minor and the Black Sea; and, finally, in the African kingdoms of Whydah-Dahomey on the upper Guinea coast and of Angola on the lower Guinea coast.

Intercommunity trade conducted outside of (or alongside) systems of partnerships and/or elaborate ritual, and not subject to administered pricing or set equivalences, is best understood in the context of market principles. In areas like Mesoamerica, Africa, and Melanesia, which yield classic examples of nonmarket forms of trade, we also find substantial evidence from aboriginal times of market forms of trade. The Aztec trading class (*pochteca*) included sixty-nine separate special trader categories, and there is documentation showing that many of their trading operations, involving the marketing of goods between separate regions and communities in Mesoamerica, not only were conducted on the principle of buying cheap and selling dear, but also often entailed complex sequential exchange transactions calculated to yield material profit (León Portilla 1962; Katz 1966, chap. 6). On the frontier between the eastern Sudan and Uganda, and in highland-lowland border zones in Mesoamerica, specialized intertribal or intercommunity production, together with reinforcing ecological conditions, promoted intertribal trade, with certain groups dominating as middlemen. Thus the Kokir and the Didinga made yearly profits from their trade in grain, goats, and metal products with other tribes (Herskovits 1952:221-23). A similar situation occurred in Melanesia, where the Sinaketans served as intermediaries between Trobriand and Dobuan production centers.

Intracommunity Distribution. Economic transactions between an individual distributor and many receivers within a single community—insofar as they occur regularly and involve the circulation of a significant proportion of total goods produced—characterize band and tribal societies. Such distributions typically are restricted to foodstuffs and, like ceremonial gift exchanges, usually (though not explicitly or necessarily) generate a deferred counterflow of equivalent goods. Thus the circulatory process in this type of intracommunity distribution approximates the general pattern of economic exchange: goods changing hands through an initial act of distribution result in a return flow (to the distributor) of goods different from yet equivalent to those originally given. In other words, the distributor disposes of goods that he can't or won't consume himself (goods that are often products of his own labor) and obtains in return a claim on the future output of others. Distributive acts of this kind, while not occurring under conditions of prolonged, anomalous food shortage, do serve to even out the impact of temporary shortages or differences in output between households, which to greater or lesser degree characterize all primitive and peasant economies (Thurnwald 1932:106-108; Richards 1964:79-83, 89, and *passim*; Malinowski 1935; Henry 1951; Herskovits 1952:169-74; Service 1966:14-21; Salisbury 1968b:120-21). Sharing through distributive acts, however, is by no means a culturally imperative mode of adaptation to conditions of food scarcity (e.g., Holmberg 1950). In many societies it appears to be one advantageous way of coping with inadequate technology for the storage and preservation of perishable foodstuffs.

The ethnographic record clearly shows that intracommunity distributive activities have kinship and political aspects (Sahlins 1960a, 1960b). Typically, food distributions are made along kinship lines; even when consanguineal or affinal ties are not the sole basis for such distributions, there is often a concomitant political process in which the putative generosity of the giver is a display of his power and may be associated with his occupancy of chiefly status. This is true not only of redistributive systems based on networks of tribute and/or taxation in kind, but also of less elaborate systems in which the most efficient or successful producers tend to be net givers (Henry 1951). In all of these systems a continuous series of one-way transactions between two individuals serves to differentiate their positions in the social hierarchy (Sahlins 1960a:496).

Ceremonial Gift Exchange. Like nonceremonial distribution, ceremonial gift exchange consists of an initial transfer of goods which in the short run appears as a one-sided give-away, but in the long run leads to a deferred counter-transfer. Unlike nonceremonial distribution, however, ceremonial gift exchange often involves ritual items not intended or suitable for consumption (e.g., shells in Melanesia, copper disks among the Kwakiutl), and gives rise to symbolic or incorporeal returns (e.g., political support, esteem, courtesy, fealty, friendship). Indeed, the term "prestation" is preferable to "gift" in this context, because an initial ceremonial transfer—circumscribed as it is by various religious, political, and ritual sanctions—often is not voluntary and always creates the obligation to return (Mauss 1954:3; Belshaw 1965:46-49). As Mauss (1954) emphasized in his seminal essay on the relationship between gifts and return gifts (see also Panoff 1970), the most compelling force toward reciprocation by the recipient of a given donation is the fact that he is *minister* to the *magister* donor until such time as he reciprocates (Raymond Firth 1967:8-17). Failure to reciprocate results in social disapproval and loss of prestige (Herskovits 1952: 155).

Ceremonial prestations regularly occur in all societies, but quantitatively (e.g., volume of goods traded) and functionally (i.e., role in the economy and elsewhere) they are considerably more important in primitive and peasant societies, where they are often associated with life cycle celebrations or feasting related to other social or political events. Mauss's study, for example, includes illustrative cases of ceremonial prestations in Samoa, New Zealand (Maori), the Andaman islands, Melanesia, northwest North America (Kwakiutl, Tlingit, Haida), ancient Rome, the Hindu classical period, and feudal Germanic societies.

In any society a prestation cycle is based on three kinds of obligations: to give, to receive, and to repay or return (see Mauss 1954:37-40; Raymond Firth 1967:8-17; Baric 1970:407-408). In primitive and peasant societies, various cultural and situational pressures encourage the individual to give gifts to others. For example, among the Zapotec-speaking peoples of the valley of Oaxaca, where an ancient reciprocity

system known as *guelaguetza* still operates (Beals 1970), individuals occupying certain social statuses vis-à-vis Ego (consanguineal or affinal kinsmen, fictive kinsmen, neighbors, friends) will suffer disapproval or loss of prestige if they fail to cooperate when he asks them for a donation. The obligation to give, on the other hand, carries with it an obligation to accept a donation when it is offered. A refusal of the donation is tantamount to a rejection of social relations, and might be interpreted as a declaration of hostility. Finally, the obligation to return the donation closes the prestation cycle. In the Zapotec case, the recipient is required to reciprocate in kind when the donor requests him to do so. This requirement is reinforced by an accounting procedure according to which the exact specifications of the donation are measured and recorded in an account book, which is consulted when the counterdonation is subsequently offered. Failure to reciprocate with an equivalent donation when requested to do so may result in the intervention of local political or judicial authorities and the levying of a fine on the reneging party. However, the usual pattern in Zapotec society is for any donation to be reciprocated with "interest" or on an incremental basis (e.g., a turkey weighing ten pounds is reciprocated with one turkey weighing twenty pounds or two turkeys weighing more than ten pounds; ten dozen eggs are reciprocated with twenty dozen eggs and four kilograms of chocolate). This practice can be viewed not only as a response to the prestige associated with generosity but as a means of saving, as well as a means of extending the interhousehold donor/recipient-recipient/donor relationship indefinitely. Of course, when a donation is reciprocated equally (without increment) the former economic equilibrium between the two households is restored and the future prestation potential is maintained.

Utilization

As a theoretical category the utilization process encompasses two general types of activities: those leading to further production and those involving direct, immediate consumption; or, more specifically, those employing resources as capital and those employing resources for the direct satisfaction of current wants (see Herskovits (1952: 298-309; Le Clair 1962:1192). For purposes of analysis, "capital" may be defined as the stock of resources (i.e., existing assets) at a particular time available to increase the volume of consumption in future periods, either directly or indirectly, through production (see Raymond Firth 1964b:18). There are three major ways in which capital is utilized in the economic process: as a productive asset; as a means of facilitating control over purchasing power; and as a fund for investment (Firth 1964b:19). While some scholars have expressed skepticism over the applicability of the capital concept to preindustrial economies (e.g., White 1959, chap. 9; Dalton 1969; Sahlins 1969), there have been several studies that have identified and analyzed each of the three functions of capital in such economies (e.g., Firth 1965a; Firth and Yamey, eds., 1964; Foster 1942).

In the 1930s, when Firth was conducting his study of Polynesian economy (1965a), Tikopia had only recently begun to use Western money. Assets like canoes, paddles, nets, digging sticks, and adzes represented productive equipment utilized in cultivating and fishing. Also in this category were certain fixed assets, such as arable land that had been improved and worked by generations of Tikopians. Goods like foodstuffs, lengths of bark cloth, pandanus mats, coconut sinnet cord, and wooden bowls, employed as "gifts" to obtain or reciprocate various kinds of goods and services, provided control over purchasing power. The Tikopians also utilized goods of this type as funds for investment by stockpiling them for a period prior to recirculating them through one act of distribution. This distribution might be made when a man commissioned the construction of a canoe or had to fulfill obligations occasioned by an initiation or funeral ceremony. The canoe operation added to the stock of productive assets that could be expected to provide a future yield; the ceremonial operation obligated the recipient to reciprocate later with appropriate goods and services. Indeed, a considerable proportion of the food, bark cloth, and the rest was produced and stockpiled months in advance in conscious anticipation of such obligations (Raymond Firth 1965a, chap. 7, 1964b:19; Herskovits 1952: 300-301).

One problem in this functional classification and analysis of goods is presented by the relatively high liquidity or ease of convertibility of many goods in primitive and peasant economies from one use to another. Again, Firth (1965a:237-38) notes that pandanus mats, on which the Tikopians slept, and bark cloth, used for blankets and clothing, were also utilized in the manufacture of objects like canoes, troughs, and sinnet cord—thereby serving both production and consumption purposes. Among the Zapotec peasants of the valley of Oaxaca and other Indian populations of Mesoamerica the *metate* is obviously a durable consumer good, the basic kitchen grinding implement in the peasant household, used principally, though not exclusively, to grind boiled maize for the making of *tortillas*; in a highly elaborated form, however, it is also a prestige good presented ritually by godparents to bride in a ceremonial wedding context; and when it is employed by a professional *tortillera* (a woman who makes *tortillas* for sale), it clearly becomes a producer's good. Maize itself provides a similar illustration in Mesoamerican peasant economies: during the harvest period it is accumulated in the peasant's storage bins to be subsequently utilized in the preparation of food for his family and as feed for his poultry, and also to be exchanged (directly or indirectly) for a wide range of complementary goods and services that he needs and does not produce himself (see Foster 1942:40). It is clear, then, that a variety of material assets in primitive and peasant societies may or may not be categorized as capital, depending upon the way they are utilized.

When we turn to the utilization of wealth in direct consumption, the focus is upon goods and services as they become objects of use and enjoyment and/or of appropriation by individuals acting singly or in groups. From the theoretical perspective of the circular flow of goods and services in an economic system, consumption may be conceived as the process by which the finished product "drops out of the social movement, becoming the indirect object of the individual want which it serves and satisfies in use" (Marx 1904*a*:275). In consumption things are embodied in persons (as opposed to production, in which the labor power of persons is embodied in things), and it provides direction to and represents the culmination of the economic process.

A key concept in the study of consumption processes is the consumption unit, a kin-based income-pooling or household unit that typically incorporates males and females of varying ages and is found in all preindustrial societies ranging from Bushman bands (Lee 1969) to Malay fishing villages (Rosemary Firth 1966). For purposes of analysis the individual unit member is assumed to follow the preference scales of his culture as he acts to satisfy his perceived needs and wants. Intraunit variation in needs and wants (i.e., demand) occurs on the basis of age and sex differences; interunit variation occurs on the basis of status and occupational differences (e.g., Raymond Firth 1965*a*:33-35; Salisbury 1962, chap. 7; Rosemary Firth 1966; Epstein 1967:160-61).

On the macro level of analysis, preference scales and consumption norms have been shown to be culture-specific, although the rapid spread of Western goods, technology, and money—and the concomitant operation of a "demonstration effect" (Duesenberry 1949: 27; Nurkse 1955:58-65)—is inevitably creating an increasingly predictable uniformity in preference scales and consumer demand in nonwestern cultures. The patterned way in which a primitive or peasant consumer makes his consumption decisions over time represents his standard of living. Many of the values of a given sociocultural system are directly expressed in consumption behavior—through food prohibitions, for instance (Herskovits 1952:271; Godelier 1967:274). Also, different standards of living within a given population are invariably correlated with inequality in the control, ownership, and distribution of wealth, as well as with some degree of sociopolitical stratification.

The typical primitive or peasant culture is characterized by a relatively limited inventory of material artifacts, and foodstuffs constitute the most important objects of consumption; small wonder, then, that nutrition and food utilization are salient topics of concern in the anthropological literature (e.g., Richards 1964; Foster 1942, chap. 7; Tax 1953:133-207; Pospisil 1963:361-

80; Rosemary Firth 1966; Epstein 1968, chap. 5; Lee 1969). One of the directions this concern has taken is toward the determination of a nutritional base line (i.e., subsistence minimum), above which a food "surplus" can be said to exist in a given society. This has proved to be a rather elusive and frustrating task because human wants are culturally mediated and socially circulated, are not limited to nutrition, and must be balanced to yield a valid schedule of preferences.

Nevertheless, definitional refinements and the use of increasingly precise caloric measures have made the surplus concept operational, especially on the micro level of analysis (see Pearson 1957; Harris 1959; Dalton 1960, 1963; Orans 1966). For example, in his recent study of the !Kung Bushmen, Lee (1969:89-90) calculates the daily per capita energy requirement of the camp member at about 1,975 calories, and estimates that food output exceeds energy requirements by about 165 calories per capita daily. The consensus of previous studies was that the caloric minimum required to sustain human life fell roughly between 2,000 and 3,000 calories per capita daily (Wolf 1966:4), but such estimates must always be qualified by the fact that subsistence level implies cultural as well as uniform biological species requirements. The economic question, of course, is not what constitutes "minimum subsistence," but rather what people do with their time when they have solved the problem of feeding themselves; i.e., how many man-units of time are devoted to what kinds of activities (see Le Clair and Schneider, eds., 1968:470).

The mediating role of culture in organizing human wants into preference schedules has been systematically analyzed in Salisbury's study of the Siane (1962:171-74). On the basis of their purchases from five categories of goods (valuables, luxuries, soap, hard goods, cash)—the goods in each category being competitive or mutually substitutable —he found that the demand behavior of Siane consumers was significantly correlated with degree of Europeanization: the least Europeanized groups displayed an unbalanced demand for valuables (more than half of total purchases) and the most Europeanized groups displayed a balanced demand for all types of goods, especially luxuries (one-quarter of total purchases). These two broad patterns were accompanied by significant individual differences in demand which tended to cluster around native categories of social status (e.g., village officials, "big men," young childless married men) or reflected experience with indentured labor. The extent to which demand patterns among the Siane are predictive of those in other cultures cannot be determined until more studies of the type conducted by Salisbury are made.

FURTHER ISSUES OF
THEORY AND ANALYSIS

Labor and Services

The problem of the specific role of labor and services in the economic process cannot be resolved outside of the broader context of economy/society articulation and of the delimitation of the economic field. In the history of economic thought this problem has been approached from the assumption that it is both possible and desirable to distinguish between those forms of labor that contribute to production and those that are not strictly productive. There has been agreement among economic thinkers that "productive" labor must create or assist in creating wealth. But there has been considerable variance among them on the definition of wealth, which in turn has led to a diversity of views on distinguishing productive from unproductive labor. While one critic has dismissed this entire problem as the "most enormous red herring of economics" (Steiner 1957), it is recognized as important by many of those scholars who are concerned with resolving the issues of the formal-substantive debate in economic anthropology (e.g., Godelier 1967a:247-53).

Adam Smith, the founder of the classical school of economic thought, argued that all labor that operated to "fix or realize itself in some permanent object or vendible commodity"was productive—a view that implicitly excluded all services not directly related to the extraction and/or transformation of material resources from the category of "productive" (i.e., economic) activities (Robbins 1935:7-8). This view was elaborated by David Ricardo, and later was adopted by Karl Marx as the central thesis in his labor-cost theory of value. In this theory Marx attempted to show the difference between three concepts: the amount of labor power (measured in time) expended during the production of a commodity (i.e., its real value), the subsistence minimum required to maintain the worker while the commodity is being produced, and the difference between these and the market price of the commodity (relative value) under given historical conditions (see Raymond Firth 1967:21). Several anthropologists have found this approach analytically rewarding. Salisbury (1962:144), for example, has concluded that "time . . . is the Siane measure of cost," and Godelier (1971) has measured the labor time component of the value of salt in analyzing this product's dual role as commodity and currency among the Baruya of New Guinea.

In later nineteenth-century neoclassical economic thought, production was defined not as making or creating *things,* but as creating *utility* (i.e., ability to satisfy wants as measured in salability); however, there was substantial variation among neoclassical economists as to which kinds of utility were in fact productive. A few emphasized "form" utility (i.e., that which is created through manufacturing or the transformation of raw materials into finished products) as the essence of production, while others emphasized "space," "time," and "possession" utility (Knight 1965:49-50). This latter emphasis implies that merchandising, storage, finance, middleman, and transportation activities are just as "productive" as extractive and transformative actitivies; and, most important, it enables the economist to include all services for which payment is made under the rubric of "productive services."

In anthropological analysis this utility perspective of neoclassical economics means, for example, that the ritual performance of a priest or shaman, which is compensated by payment in money or goods, is just as productive as the work performance of a peasant-artisan in quarrying stone and manufacturing *metates* from it, or plowing, sowing, and harvesting a field. Such an implication has been vigorously criticized by Neale (1964), who argues that services and labor are not easily forced into a utilitarian mold outside the market economy, since neither service nor labor is necessarily *paid for.* Opler (1968), on the other hand, has presented ethnographic evidence and cogent arguments in criticism of Aberle's (1967) contention that the market concepts "pay" and "fee" are inappropriate in an analysis of the economic aspects of performances by Apache shamans, which take the form of reciprocal prestations. According to Opler (1968:389),

. . . it can be established for the Navaho, as for the other Apachean tribes, that a distinction is

made between ritual offerings to the gods . . .
and the payments in cash, cloth, animals, and
other economically valuable "goods" given to
the ritualist. . . . "Prestation" is an inappropriate label for either the ritual payment or the
practical payment, for . . . no obligation exists
until after the ritual payment is accepted by
the shaman or singer. . . .

Given our earlier delimitation of the
economic field in formal-substantive
terms, the problem of ascertaining
which activities and performances (labor and services) are within this field is
manageable. Its solution can proceed
according to the following formula:
*Those performances are "economic" or
have "economic" aspects which entail
the production, transfer, or utilization,
directly or indirectly, of material goods
with use or exchange value, as well as
those performances that involve the
transfer or utilization of services, re-
munerated in cash or kind, for the purpose of satisfying wants and/or contributing to subsistence.*
Systematically applied, this formula
enables the analyst to handle within a
common analytical framework both
materially productive activities (labor)
and activities that render services but
do not yield material products, so long
as they elicit remuneration in money or
kind. For example, within the category
of services, the performance of a Pres-
byterian minister in preaching a sermon
to his congregation (for which he is
paid a salary) is of comparable economic relevance to the performance by an
Apache shaman of certain rituals for his
clients in return for a bundle of goods.
Both performers exchange specialized
services for material compensation by
their clientele, and consequently are
economically involved. They have, in
essence, performed ritual services with
economic aspects; their performances
are within the economic field of analysis but are simultaneously internal to the
religious-ceremonial field of their sociocultural systems.

Rationality and Maximization

Beginning with Malinowski's prece-
dent-setting polemical attack in 1922
on the notion of "primitive economic
man," who, according to him
(1961:60), was "prompted in all his actions by a rationalistic conception of
self-interest, and achieving his aim directly and with the minimum of effort"—a notion he mistakenly attributed to the economists of his day (Le
Clair and Schneider, eds., 1968:4)—anthropologists have been concerned with
determining to what degree (if any)
preindustrial tribesmen and peasants
"economize," "maximize," and are "rational" in their economic conduct.
Born in the context of Melanesian studies, this concern has been carried by
anthropologists to a multitude of culture areas and countries, including Polynesia (Raymond Firth 1965a), Africa
(Goodfellow 1939; Miracle 1962;
Schneider 1964a, 1964b, 1970; Goldschmidt 1967), Mesoamerica (Redfield
1962, Tax 1953, Nash 1961, Issac
1965, Cook 1970), and Colombia (Ortiz 1967), and back to Melanesia (Pospisil 1963). Salisbury (1968a:478),
who has recently summarized the results of a number of these and other
studies, states that "currently the major issue in economic anthropology
is . . . to what extent different formal calculuses of rationality or of 'economizing' can be isolated in non-Western
conditions" (see also P. S. Cohen 1967;
Belshaw 1967; Godelier 1967a; Le Clair
and Schneider, eds., 1968:456-59).
The general consensus of contemporary studies focused on this issue seems
to be that preindustrial tribesmen and
peasants, together with men in industrial societies who earn their living in the
market economy, are "rational" in

their economic conduct. Of course, the kind of conduct in tribal and peasant societies described by many anthropologists is by no means so precisely rational in the formal sense as the double-entry bookkeeping of Max Weber's capitalist cost accountants. But it must be remembered that cost accountants are not the principal decision-makers in capitalist business firms; day-to-day business decisions in the real world deviate substantially from the conditions assumed in the economist's decision models—evaluation of risk, certainty, complete information, and so on (see Ortiz 1970:622). The problem in both precapitalist and capitalist contexts is to arrive at a minimal definition of rationality which emphasizes the basic logic of choice without positing situation-specific responses as rational or irrational.

Perhaps the most significant aspect of Godelier's contribution to economic anthropological thought is his convincing demonstration that rationality as a principle of behavior neither is rooted in a particular economic system nor operates only in the economic sector of a society. More specifically, he argues that neither the capitalist nor the socialist economies are the pinnacles of economic rationality institutionalized in human history, and that Western industrial-mercantile economies are not intrinsically more rational than nonwestern preindustrial economies.

Two important questions pertaining to economic rationality are dealt with in the anthropological literature, according to Godelier (1967a:11): (1) In what form should the economic actors in a given economic system behave to achieve their proposed objectives? (2) What is the rationality of an economic system and how can it be compared to that of other systems? The first question implies an intentional rationality pursued by individual actors (i.e., pursuing ends coherent among themselves and employing means appropriate to the ends pursued), whereas the second implies an unintentional rationality characterizing a total system—for example, the capacity of assuring the renewal and/or growth of the means of production, the raising of living standards, and so on (Godelier 1967a:11-12). Godelier summarizes his position on the issue of economic rationality this way (1967a:21):

> ... All ethnological and historical information shows us that in all societies, individuals or groups try to achieve the maximum determined ends whose content and ranking express the predominance of certain social relations (kinship, religion) over others, and are based in the internal structure of each type of society. For example, in primitive societies competition for the control of women is not explained by sexual or other needs or preferences of individuals, of the men, but by the important place which kinship occupies in these societies. To analyze the reason why this structure (kinship) occupies a central place with regard to others is to undertake to discover a "social rationality" of which economic rationality is simply one aspect.

In other words, all fields of social activity (including the economic) in all known societies require the acting individual to make choices between alternative ends that usually are of different importance to him. Again, regardless of the specific social field of action in which the choice-making individual is involved or the particular group he represents, he will habitually make choices that are contextually appropriate—that is rational or logical.

Marshall Sahlins (1969) has recently used Godelier's discussion as a point of departure for examining the formal versus substantive rationality issue (see Weber 1947:184-86) from the culturological/cultural ecological perspective. It is "substantive rationality" (Godelier's "unintentional system rationality") that Sahlins equates with ecological selection or adaptation, and which he contends is most appropriate in economic anthropology. He argues that the problem of rationality is cultural (i.e., is related to the adaptiveness of a society or population through its culture), not psychological or behavioral (i.e., relating to the adaptiveness of individual actors through their plans and choices). The economy, according to this approach, is properly conceived for comparative analysis as implying minimal rather than optimal processes or activities; its job is to keep a population or society provisioned for survival (i.e., the achievement of a subsistence minimum), not to enable the members to acquire surplus or profit (i.e., the achievement of an optimum) to satisfy abstract acquisitive needs. Sahlins rejects the use of maximization models or economizing concepts in attempts to understand provisioning processes in preindustrial societies; to Sahlins, applying such models to these societies is tantamount to turning them into bourgeois social orders.

It seems to me that Sahlins, while making a useful ecological interpretation of substantive rationality, overstates the case for the incompatibility of the formal and substantive approaches; that optimization models, contrary to his arguments, can be used as means for approximating and understanding of performance in any empirical economy without inhibiting understanding of how a given society achieves a survival minimum. Indeed, the knowledge that formal optima are not achieved or even approached by economic actors or units in particular situations and, more specifically, the degree of such "underperformance" is important in understanding the nature of their actual adaptation. No empirical economy, preindustrial or otherwise,

has ever achieved optimal resource use; whether the analyst prefers to examine processes of "constraining optima" or "achieving minima" among a given population will not alter the realities of less than optimum performance. Of course, this position assumes that one of the central problems of economic anthropological inquiry is to understand the interplay between microprocess and macroprocess, between the movement of individual actors or units and the movement of the total population or system (see Cook, in press).

That an individual actor chooses rationally need not imply that he chooses in accordance with any universally operative extremum principle, always seeking to maximize gain and minimize loss optimally (Lowe 1965:36-37). Anthropological studies of economic decision-making in preindustrial societies invariably suggest that an extremum principle operates relatively (situationally) rather than absolutely (uniformly). Tribesmen and peasants do not always choose the best or least costly alternative, but rather as good or as appropriate an alternative as is possible under the circumstances. The fact that these circumstances often include illiteracy and ignorance or misinformation about Western procedures (e.g., double-entry bookkeeping, simple arithmetic) does make the economic performance of many peasant peoples appear irrational when measured against standards operating under more favorable circumstances. But more than one anthropologist concludes his study impressed with the evidence that the reasoning and calculations involved in economic decision-making among his tribal or peasant informants are essentially the same as those that a member of his own society would use if he had to make decisions under comparable circumstances.

Even before Malinowski's criticism

of the economic man construct, economists had begun to revise it to make it more relevant to empirical situations, which are always pervaded by uncertainty and imperfection. This revisionist pattern has been accelerating ever since (see P. S. Cohen 1967), with Herbert Simon's theory of "satisficing" representing one of the more contemporary and comprehensive efforts. According to Simon (1959:274), "economic man is a satisficing animal whose problem-solving is based on search activity to meet certain aspiration levels, rather than a maximizing animal whose problem solving involves finding the best alternatives in terms of specified criteria." Defining rationality as the "selection of preferred behavior alternatives in terms of some system of values whereby the consequences of behavior can be evaluated," Simon (1965:75, 76) proposes three aspects of the principle:

A decision may be called "objectively" rational if *in fact* it is the correct behavior for maximizing given values in a given situation. It is "subjectively" rational if it maximizes attainment relative to the actual knowledge of the subject. It is "consciously" rational to the degree that the adjustment of means to ends is a conscious process.

Finally, Simon (1965:80-84) suggests that rationality is always limited by incomplete knowledge of consequences and by the inability of the actor to anticipate all future values or to consider all possible alternatives.

Kenneth Boulding, another economist, has presented what is perhaps the most original and anthropologically relevant restatement of the formal theory of economic choice. The impetus for his rethinking of the economic man theory was his realization that economists "have badly neglected the impact of information and knowledge structures on economic behavior and proces-

ses" (1961:82), a neglect that he attributes to the fact (often overlooked) that economists are primarily concerned with the behavior of commodities rather than with the behavior of men.

Given the impact of uncertainty and market imperfections upon human economic behavior in empirical, real-world situations, Boulding (1961:86-87) reformulates the three standard propositions in maximization theory (i.e., behavioral alternatives, value ordering, and selection of best alternative) in two revised rules of economic conduct: (1) we will do today what we did yesterday unless there are very good reasons for doing otherwise, and (2) the good reasons that are necessary if we are not to do today what we did yesterday are derived mainly from dissatisfaction with what we did (or what happened to us) yesterday. A "day" in this context means the "period of regular cyclical activity" in the system being studied; it might be a day, a week, a month, a season, a festive period—any span of time encompassing any regularly recurring activity. According to Boulding, it is important for the student of economic behavior to consider not only the quantity and proportion of man-unit time (hours, days, weeks, whatever) allocated to various productive activities, but also "the primitive image of time as an essentially cyclical phenomenon, a time for this and a time for that."

In economic anthropology, we must match our concern with the objective results of economic decisions with a concern for the structure and dynamics of economic alternative perceptions, information flows, and the circulation and transformation of subjective economic knowledge; this is a necessary prerequisite to explaining, for example, cyclical variation in economic quantities (e.g., price, output) on the micro and macro levels of analysis in the context of small-scale peasant-artisan societies. It should, in retrospect and in prospect, be encouraging to anthropologists that economic theorists of the stature of Simon and Boulding are formulating research strategies that imply that crucial problems in the revision and operationalization of neoclassical theory can be dealt with meaningfully in the empirical context of anthropological inquiry.

Limitations and Possibilities of the Ecological Approach

Those among us who are segregating their economics from their ecology, or who emphasize divergences rather than convergences between the economic and ecological fields, do not find support from etymology. There is a common Greek root for the terms "economics" and "ecology"—*oikos* (house) connoted the integration of society with its natural environment as expressed in the domicile centered in a sacred hearth (see chapter 5 of this volume). This common Greek root implies that economics (discourse on the household) and ecology (household management) should be similar sciences. In earlier usages "ecology" was interchangeable with "economy" (in 1870 Haeckel defined ecology as a body of knowledge concerning the economy of nature; in 1927 Elton referred to ecology as "scientific natural history dealing with the sociology and economics of animals"); the subtitle of Marston Bates's *Man in Nature* (1964) is "A Look at the Economy of Nature and the Ecology of Man."

There are various reasons why the economy-ecology bifurcation is perpetuated in anthropology. An important one is that a growing number of practitioners of ecological anthropology are relying heavily on biological or animal ecology; this approach reinforces the thesis that man is simply another species operating in an interspecies ecosystem and reduces culture to a species-specific mode of adaptation (e.g., Vayda and Rappaport 1968). The major error of this approach, from the perspective of social science, is that in its eagerness to emphasize *Homo sapiens'* role as just another species in nature's floral and faunal array, it glosses over the crucial evolutionary fact that *Homo sapiens* is the only species that produces its own means of subsistence by directly manipulating and transforming the physical environment through organized social activity. In other words, the forces and social relations of *production* are unique to human adaptation, and make man's adaptation a process substantially unlike that of any other species in the natural order. Only *Homo sapiens*, among the earth's living species, has achieved an adaptation in which its populations transform nature's materials into life-supporting products and whose social relations are not genetically programmed but rather are culturally transmitted from one generation to the next and reflect relationships to and participation in the production process. This is both the fundamental ontological feature of human society and the epistemological departure point for approximating an understanding of the structure and functioning of its contrasting modes and processes.

Since it has been through his economic or productive activity that man has succeeded diachronically in progressively alienating himself from nature, economics itself becomes antithetical to the interests of those naturalists who wish to demonstrate above all else the underlying dependence of man on nature. While the founders of nineteenth-century historical materialism did emphasize the extent to which man's technoeconomic rationality separated him from other primates and animals and gave him the capacity to transform nature through production, they were not necessarily guilty of blatant anthropocentrism, as some idealist critics would have us believe. Engels, for example, in his seminal essay on "The Part Played by Labour in the Transition from Ape to Man" (1963b:291-92), warns his readers against flattering themselves unduly on account of the historically progressive human conquest of nature, and presents a clear statement of what we now call "ecological degradation" in elaborating on the thesis that each conquest takes its revenge on man. Ironically, it was an earlier political economist, Thomas Malthus, who in his *Essay on the Principle of Population* apparently laid the foundation for the development of animal ecology by conceiving of populations and their environments without distinguishing human beings from other organisms in any fundamental way (Vayda and Rappaport 1968:478-79). Yet, as we have seen, the undeniably crucial message of the premier nineteenth-century materialist thinkers, Marx and Engels, is that it is a mistake to allow an interspecific population focus to displace a concern with intraspecific relations and processes that facilitate man's un-animal-like manipulation and transformation of his natural environment.

From the formal theoretical or general systemic perspective, the ecological system and economic system models have much in common. Both of them emphasize circularity of process or the cyclical nature of transactions or flows; both are dynamic and transactionalist. The following paradigm of Otis Dudley Duncan (1964:41) for approaching the ecosystem, with few modifications, serves equally well as an approach to the economic system. According to Duncan, the flow of materials, energy, or information can be studied from the standpoint of:

1. Entry into the system.
2. Transformation during the flow through the system.
3. Transfer from one unit or level of the system to another.
4. Accumulation of storage at some point within the system, followed by retrieval and resumption of the flow.
5. Application to the advantage of some (living) unit part of the system.
6. Dissipation, or temporary or ultimate loss to the system.

Raw materials, for example, enter the economic system through acts of appropriation and are transformed into useful or exchangeable products during the production process; transfer occurs both during and after production, with the flow of the finished product perhaps being interrupted by accumulation or storage as a necessary step in the marketing process (depending on the type of economy being analyzed). The finished product, in becoming an object of use, either by its manufacturer or another for direct consumption or further production purposes, is both applied to the satisfaction of wants and begins its dissipation in economic destruction or obsolescence.

These two systems, the ecological and the economic, are analogous not to organisms, but to servomechanisms; they are characterized more by positive and negative feedback than by manifest and latent function. Both tend toward optimal states of equilibrium but in reality never achieve such equilibrium. A description and analysis of flows in either system includes spatiotemporal patterning and the volume or quantity of flows in each sector. But, depending upon the particular problem focus (materials, energy, information, commodities, values) and the kind of subsystem under scrutiny (organism-environment system, interspecies community system, technoeconomic system), description and analysis require specialized terminology.

Whether or not one prefers to consider the economic system as a subsystem of the ecosystem or of the social system or of both, or prefers to abandon the system approach in its entirety, the fact remains that the disciplines of economics and ecology do diverge in their scope and analytical aims. Lee (1969:73) has neatly summed up these divergences:

Ecologists take as their unit of study a species which has energy relations with other species within an ecosystem. A population is maintained by the energy absorbed in the course of food-getting activities of its members. The focus here is on interspecific trophic exchanges.... Economists, by contrast, focus on the exchange relations within a single species. A productive unit ... is maintained by the inputs from other productive units, and in turn its outputs are allocated to other like units or to the "final demand" sector of the economy.... Viewed ecologically, these transactions can be considered as a highly evolved form of intraspecific exchange.

Obviously a basic problem for those interested in economy/ecosystem articulation is to find or formulate concepts that mediate between ecological and economic, technological and organizational, actor-specific and population-specific relational contexts. One concept that is promising in this regard is "scheduling," as formulated by Kent Flannery for his analysis of procurement systems among preceramic populations in Mesoamerica. According to Flannery (1968:75), scheduling decisions (i.e., those weighing the relative merits of two or more courses of action in resource procurement and relating to the allocation of time and labor) "are made constantly by all human groups

on all levels of complexity, often without any awareness that a decision is being made." One of the great advantages of this concept is that it enables us to include decision-making in our field of study without positing scarcity of means or maximization; if I interpret Flannery correctly, scheduling is actually necessitated by a relative abundance (rather than scarcity) of provisioning opportunities. It implies a derandomization of production activities to promote survival despite seasonality in the food supply. How does this concept apply to contemporary peasant-artisan populations in Mesoamerica, whose ancestors long ago moved from food collecting to incipient cultivation to sedentary agricultural civilization with a highly elaborated division of labor and production organization? One way in which scheduling is facilitated is through the pricing mechanism. In the regional marketing systems operating today in areas that include remains of Flannery's cave-dwelling hunters and gatherers, price as negotiated in the marketplace emerges as a key information input that influences peasant-artisans' decisions on allocating their time and effort, and thus has an impact on the ecosystem by altering the flows of materials and energy. The schedule of the preceramic Mesoamerican was keyed to the seasonal availability of certain wild plants and animals; the schedule of today's preindustrial peasant-artisan is keyed to the seasonal availability of crop yields from domesticated plants, not to speak of wage-paying jobs and cash-raising activities (i.e., the availability of alternative cash-raising pursuits). Most important, his schedule today is no longer structured around local natural environmental and informational inputs; rather it is structured to a large degree around inputs that are increasingly sociocultural, not natural environmental, and are of regional, national, and international origin (see

Bennett 1969:9-25 and *passim*; Adams 1970:30-123).

Thus just as cultural ecology has provided us with increased understanding of human social organization and behavior by studying the behavior of the flora and fauna that man exploits as predator, so economic anthropology can provide us with increased understanding of human economic organization and performance by studying the behavior of the commodities he produces, exchanges, and utilizes. The concept of scheduling, for example, offers the possibility of considering price as an ecological as well as an economic variable in a peasant-artisan market economy.

It is obvious, however, that scheduling is simply one manifestation of a more basic process that is operative in all extant human societies: adaptation. John Bennett (1969:9-25, 306-34), in his cultural ecological study of a region in the Canadian northern plains, has recast this much used and abused concept to emphasize its dynamic behavioral implications. Specifically, he identifies the adaptive process with "coping" behaviors—problem-solving, decision-making, consuming or not consuming, inventing, migrating, staying—and conceives of it as encompassing two components (1969:14):

... first, the notion of adaptive strategies, or the patterns formed by the many separate adjustments that people devise in order to obtain and use resources and to solve the immediate problems confronting them; second, the idea of adaptive processes, or the changes introduced over relatively long periods of time by the repeated use of such strategies or the making of many adjustments.

These conceptual distinctions provide the investigator with a frame of reference for linking conscious private decisions of the members of a society with standardized group patterns of resource use (which are not recognized as such by the actors themselves). Bennett demonstrates, for example, how the sedentary Euro-American population effectively coped with the extreme variability of natural resource distribution in the northern plains by developing, through a trial-and-error procedure, intraregional specialization of production—an adaptive process that contrasts with the nomadism of the aboriginal Indian population. Incidentally, he achieves his integrated analysis of cultural ecological and economic phenomena without using the ecosystem concept, to which he objects on the grounds that it is mechanically equilibrating (1969:23-24). Perhaps this decision to avoid the ecosystem and related concepts is responsible for his unfortunate lack of concern with population/resource balance in the plains region and his casual treatment of demographic factors.

From the perspective of economic anthropology, one of the most frustrating tendencies in the ecological anthropology literature is the implicit reduction of economics to nutrition and of production to the creation of calories rather than the creation of use and exchange values through the appropriation and transformation of natural resources. Thus in a recent general textbook by Marvin Harris (1971:203-204, 222-24) we find topical headings like "Energy and the Factors of Production" and "Production and Reproduction," which suggest an integration of economic and ecological perspectives. Yet in Harris' discussion the "factors of production" are conceived as labor power expended in the form of calories, and "production" itself is reduced to the process of provisioning of nutritional requirements among a given population. Similarly, Sahlins (1968: 85-89, 1972:chap. 1) speculates that the Bushmen and other hunting-gathering peoples may be representative of the "original affluent society" because they work at food acquisition only a few hours daily, spending the rest of their time in leisure.

Admittedly nutrition is universally recognized as one of the functional prerequisites of society, but for some reason it is often overlooked that men must produce more than calories if calories are to be produced; and that calories, to be meaningful in economic analysis, must be converted or at least related to use and/or exchange values. Malinowski (1960:95-99) dealt with the nutritive need in elaborating his theory of culture, as well as with cultural response to this need among human populations, under the rubric of "commissariat." But he avoided "nutritional reductionism," as is evident from the following statement (1960:98):

In short, the whole series of processes designated here as commissariat puts on the list of derived but indispensable necessities an extensive inventory of physical utensils, devices, or machines. These in turn have to be renewed to the extent that they deteriorate or are used up. We can see that one of the inevitable consequences already to be inferred from the working of the organized commissariat is that it imposes a by-play of constant *productive* activities, both in the preservation of food and in the *production* of all the implements for the primary food-producing, food-providing activities [italics added].

In other words, production in the human economy/ecosystem is not reducible exclusively to nutritional output, or the means of production to nutrition-providing labor inputs. Moreover, it is through their organized productive effort in a given natural environment that human populations provision themselves with the material means of social reproduction; and it is through the forces and organization of production that the "rationality" of ecological selection operates in the process of sociocultural adaptation.

Transferring the interspecific concept of trophic exchange into the realm of intraspecific (human) relations may throw light on the emergence of the human economy from prehominid origins; and when this transference is applied to the study of hunting-gathering groups like the Bushmen, it may increase our understanding of one aspect of an elementary form of human economy (which Lee [1969:74] describes as one in which the "relation between the production and consumption of food is immediate in space and time"). What this approach excludes is the fact that construction and manufacture of material means characterize all production modes in all societies; and that the production of tools and equipment, however crude, is perhaps the chief distinguishing trait of human societies (Wagner 1960:89). It is clear that at the point in the evolutionary process where the cooperatively organized human economy separated itself from the organismic realm of animal energetics, the construction and manufacture of equipment and tools for future use were present. And it is certainly plausible to propose that the origins of commodity exchange—i.e., the production of material goods for utilization by a unit other than that which produced them—lie in this nonfood sector. The trend in the evolution of the economy leading to an "increasing separation in space and time between the production of food and its final allocation in consumption" (Lee 1969:92) is useful for distinguishing different types of economic organization; but it is dependent upon prior changes in the forces and social relations of production, and cannot be fully understood unless these are considered also.

The point that must be emphasized in concluding a review article such as this is that the ecological and economic branches of anthropology should be viewed as complementary rather than contradictory. As social scientists, anthropologists should be concerned, up to a point, with, for example, man/pig/ land ratios among Melanesian horticultural populations, with man and pig being considered as competitors for scarce food and land resources (Rappaport 1968). But we must also be concerned with related questions such as the distribution of pigs among the human population; why some households or social units have more pigs than others, some have fewer, and some have the same number; the reasons underlying this distribution, and the mechanisms whereby pigs circulate as property among their human consumers. It's useful to know how many units of energy pigs extract from human beings or otherwise consume in the local ecosystem, as opposed to the number of energy units they yield as nutritional objects. But it's crucial that we understand the reasons why pigs are commodities (i.e., combine value in use and value in exchange) and what their commodity status implies for the total circulation of wealth among such horticultural populations, in terms of the allocation of labor power, time, etc., and of the production, exchange, and utilization of other commodities. In essence, it is incumbent upon those of us who view the relationships between human populations, environment, organization, and technology as encompassing an integrated transactional systemic process to aim at the formulation of a conceptual framework and a set of explanatory principles that integrates, rather than segregates, the ecological and economic branches of anthropological inquiry.

REFERENCES

Aberle, D. F.
1967   The Navaho Singer's "Fee": Payment or Prestation. In *Studies in Southwestern Ethnolinguistics*, ed. D. Hymes and W. E. Bittle, pp. 15-32. The Hague: Mouton.
Adams, R. N.
1970   The Study of Complex Societies. In R. N. Adams, *Crucifixion by Power*. Austin: University of Texas Press.
Baric, Lorraine
1970   Gift Exchange. In *Encyclopaedia Britannica*.
Barth, Fredrik
1956   Ecologic Relationships of Ethnic Groups in Swat, North Pakistan. *American Anthropologist* 58:1079-89.
1960   Nomadism in the Mountain and Plateau Areas of Southwest Asia. In *Problems of the Arid Zone*, pp. 341-55. Paris: UNESCO.
1967   Economic Spheres in Darfur. In *Themes in Economic Anthropology*, ed. R. Firth, pp. 149-74. London: Tavistock.
Bates, Marston
1964   *Man in Nature*. Englewood Cliffs, N.J.: Prentice-Hall.
Beals, Ralph L.
1967   The Structure of the Oaxaca Market System. *Revista mexicana de estudios antropológicos* 21:333-42.
1970   Gifting, Reciprocity, Savings, and Credit in Peasant Oaxaca. *Southwestern Journal of Anthropology* 26: 231-41.
Belshaw, Cyril S.
1965   *Traditional Exchange and Modern Markets*. Englewood Cliffs, N.J.: Prentice-Hall.
1967   Theoretical Problems in Economic Anthropology. In *Social Organization: Essays Presented to Raymond Firth*, ed. M. Freedman, pp. 25-42. London: Cass.
1969   *The Conditions of Social Performance*. London: Routledge & Kegan Paul.
1971   Economic Systems, Primitive. In *Encyclopaedia Britannica*.
Bennett, John W.
1969   *Northern Plainsmen*. Chicago: Aldine.
Berliner, Joseph
1962   The Feet of the Natives Are Large: An Essay on Anthropology by an Economist. *Current Anthropology* 3: 47-61.
Blau, Peter M.
1964   *Exchange and Power in Social Life*. New York: Wiley.

Bohannan, Paul, and Laura Bohannan
1968 *Tiv Economy*. London: Longmans.
Bohannan, Paul, and George Dalton
1962 *Markets in Africa*. Evanston, Ill.: Northwestern University Press.
Boulding, Kenneth
1961 *The Image*. Ann Arbor: University of Michigan Press.
1966 *Economic Analysis*, vol. 1: *Microeconomics*. New York: Harper & Row.
Brookfield, H. C., ed.
1969 *Pacific Market-Places: A Collection of Essays*. Canberra: Australian National University Press.
Brown, Paula
1970 Chimbu Transactions. *Man* 5:99-117.
Burling, Robbins
1962 Maximization Theories and the Study of Economic Anthropology. *American Anthropologist* 64:802-21.
Cancian, Frank
1966 Maximization as Norm, Strategy, and Theory: A Comment on Programmatic Statements in Economic Anthropology. *American Anthropologist* 68:465-70.
Cassady, Ralph
1968 Negotiated Price-Making in Mexican Traditional Markets: A Conceptual Analysis. *América indígena* 28:51-78.
Chapman, Anne
1957 Port of Trade Enclaves in Aztec and Maya Civilizations. In *Trade and Market in the Early Empires*, ed. K. Polanyi et al., pp. 114-53. Glencoe, Ill.: Free Press.
Chapple, Eliot D., and Carleton C. Coon
1942 *Principles of Anthropology*. New York: Holt.
Chayanov, A. V.
1966 *The Theory of Peasant Economy*. Homewood, Ill.: Irwin. Originally published 1925.
Childe, V. Gordon
1951a *Man Makes Himself*. New York: Mentor Books.
1951b *Social Evolution*. Cleveland: World.
Codere, Helen
1968 Exchange and Display. In *International Encyclopedia of Social Sciences*, vol. 5, pp. 239-45. New York: Free Press, Macmillan.
Cohen, Percy S.
1967 Economic Analysis and Economic Man. In *Themes in Economic An-*

thropology, ed. R. Firth, pp. 91-118. London: Tavistock.
Cohen, Yehudi A.
1968 Culture as Adaptation. In *Man in Adaptation: The Cultural Present*, ed. Y. Cohen, pp. 40-60. Chicago: Aldine.
Commons, John R.
1954 Institutional Economics. In *Source Readings in Economic Thought*, ed. Newman et al., pp. 557-74. New York: Norton.
Cook, Scott
1966a The Obsolete "Anti-market" Mentality: A Critique of the Substantive Approach to Economic Anthropology. *American Anthropologist* 68:323-45.
1966b Maximization, Economic Theory, and Anthropology: A Reply to Cancian. *American Anthropologist* 68:1494-98.
1968 Review of *Primitive, Archaic, and Modern Economies: Essays of Karl Polanyi*, ed. G. Dalton. *American Anthropologist* 70:966-69.
1969 The "Anti-market" Mentality Reexamined: A Further Critique of the Substantive Approach to Economic Anthropology. *Southwestern Journal of Anthropology* 25:378-406.
1970 Price and Output Variability in a Peasant-Artisan Stoneworking Industry in Oaxaca, Mexico: An Analytical Essay in Economic Anthropology. *American Anthropologist* 72:776-801.
in press Production, Ecology, and Economic Anthropology: Notes Toward an Integrated Frame of Reference. *Social Science Information*.
Dalton, George
1960 A Note of Clarification on Economic Surplus. *American Anthropologist* 62:483-90.
1961 Economic Theory and Primitive Society. *American Anthropologist* 65:1-25.
1963 Economic Surplus, Once Again. *American Anthropologist* 65:389-94.
1968 Introduction to *Primitive, Archaic, and Modern Economies: Essays of Karl Polanyi*, ed. G. Dalton, pp. ix-liv. Garden City, N.Y.: Doubleday-Anchor.
1969 Theoretical Issues in Economic An-

thropology. *Current Anthropology* 10:63-102.

Debetz, G. F.
1961 The Social Life of Early Paleolithic Man as Seen Through the Work of the Soviet Anthropologists. In *Social Life of Early Man*, ed. S. L. Washburn, pp. 137-49. Chicago: Aldine.

Dewey, Alice
1962 *Peasant Marketing in Java*. New York: Free Press, Macmillan.
1964 Capital, Credit, and Saving in Javanese Marketing. In *Capital, Saving, and Credit in Peasant Societies*, ed. R. Firth and B. S. Yamey, pp. 230-55. Chicago: Aldine.

Diskin, Martin
1969 Estudio estructural del sistema de plaza en el valle de Oaxaca. *América indígena* 29:1077-99.

Dole, Gertrude E.
1956 Ownership and Exchange Among the Kuikuru Indians of Mato Grosso. *Revista do Museu Paulista* (n.s.) 10:125-33.

Douglas, Mary
1962 Lele Economy Compared with the Bushong: A Study of Economic Backwardness. In *Markets in Africa*, ed. P. Bohannan and G. Dalton, pp. 211-36. Evanston, Ill.: Northwestern University Press.

Dowling, John H.
1968 Individual Ownership and the Sharing of Game in Hunting Societies. *American Anthropologist* 70:502-507.

Duesenberry, James S.
1949 *Income, Saving, and the Theory of Consumer Behavior*. Cambridge: Harvard University Press.

Duncan, Otis Dudley
1964 Social Organization and the Ecosystem. In *Handbook of Modern Sociology*, ed. R. E. L. Harris, pp. 36-82. Chicago: Rand McNally.

Edel, Matthew
1967 Jamaican Fishermen: Two Approaches in Economic Anthropology. *Social and Economic Studies* 16: 432-39.
1969 Economic Analysis in an Anthropological Setting: Some Methodological Considerations. *American Anthropologist* 71:421-33.

Engels, Friedrich
1963a *The Origin of the Family, Private Property, and the State*. Eastbourne: New World Publications. Originally published 1884.
1963b The Part Played by Labour in the Transition from Ape to Man. In F. Engels, *Dialectics of Nature*, pp. 279-96. New York: International Publishers.

Epstein, T. S.
1967 The Data of Economics in Anthropological Analysis. In *The Craft of Social Anthropology*, ed. A. L. Epstein, pp. 153-80. London: Tavistock.
1968 *Capitalism, Primitive and Modern*. East Lansing: Michigan State University Press.

Eucken, Walter
1950 *The Foundations of Economics*. London: Hodge.

Firth, Raymond
1959 *Economics of the New Zealand Maori*, 2nd ed. Wellington, N.Z.: R. E. Owen, Government Printer. Originally published as *Primitive Economics of the New Zealand Maori*, 1929.
1961 The Social Framework of Economic Organization. In R. Firth, *Elements of Social Organization*, pp. 122-54. Boston: Beacon Press.
1964a The Place of Malinowski in the History of Economic Anthropology. In *Man and Culture: An Evaluation of the Work of Bronislaw Malinowski*, ed. R. Firth. New York: Harper Torchbooks. Originally published 1957.
1964b Capital, Saving, and Credit in Peasant Societies: A Viewpoint from Economic Anthropology. In *Capital, Saving, and Credit in Peasant Societies*, ed. R. Firth and B. S. Yamey, pp. 15-34. Chicago: Aldine.
1965a *Primitive Polynesian Economy*, 2nd ed. London: Routledge & Kegan Paul. Originally published 1946.
1965b Problems of Economic Anthropology. In R. Firth, *Primitive Polynesian Economy*, 2nd ed., pp. 1-31. London: Routledge & Kegan Paul.
1966 *Malay Fishermen: Their Peasant Economy*, 2nd ed. London: Routledge &

Kegan Paul. Originally published 1946.

1967 Themes in Economic Anthropology: A General Comment. In *Themes in Economic Anthropology*, ed. R. Firth, pp. 1-28. London: Tavistock.

1970 Trade, Primitive. In *Encyclopaedia Britannica*.

Firth, Raymond, ed.

1967 *Themes in Economic Anthropology*. London: Tavistock.

Firth, Raymond, and B. S. Yamey, eds.

1964 *Capital, Saving, and Credit in Peasant Societies*. Chicago: Aldine.

Firth, Rosemary

1966 *Housekeeping Among Malay Peasants*, 2nd ed. London: Athlone Press.

Flannery, Kent

1968 Archaeological Systems Theory and Early Meso-America. In *Anthropological Archaeology in the Americas*, ed. B. Meggers, pp. 67-87. Washington, D. C.: Anthropological Society of Washington.

Forde, Daryll

1963 *Habitat, Economy, and Society*. New York: Dutton. Originally published 1934.

Forman, Shepard, and Joyce F. Riegelhaupt

1970 Market Place and Marketing System: Toward a Theory of Peasant Economic Integration. *Comparative Studies in Society and History* 12:188-212.

Foster, George

1942 *A Primitive Mexican Economy*. American Ethnological Society Monographs, no. 5. Seattle: University of Washington Press.

1948 The Folk Economy of Rural Mexico with Special Reference to Marketing. *Journal of Marketing* 13:153-62.

Frankenberg, Ronald

1967 Economic Anthropology: One Anthropologist's View. In *Themes in Economic Anthropology*, ed. R. Firth, pp. 47-89. London: Tavistock.

Fraser, L. M.

1947 *Economic Thought and Language*. London: Black.

Freilich, Morris

1967 Ecology and Culture: Environmental Determinism and the Ecological Approach in Anthropology. *Anthropological Quarterly* 40:26-43.

Fried, Morton

1967 *The Evolution of Political Society*. New York: Random House.

Gabel, Creighton

1967 *Analysis of Prehistoric Economic Patterns*. New York: Holt, Rinehart & Winston.

Geertz, Clifford

1963 *Peddlers and Princes: Social Change and Economic Modernization in Two Indonesian Towns*. Chicago: University of Chicago Press.

Godelier, Maurice

1967a *Racionalidad e irracionalidad en la economía*. Mexico City: Siglo Veintiuno Editores. Originally published 1966.

1967b System, Structure, and Contradiction in *Capital Socialist Register*, pp. 91-119.

1969a *Las sociedades primitivas y el nacimiento de las sociedades de clases según Marx y Engels*. Medellín, Colombia: Editorial La Oveja Negra.

1969b La "monnaie de sel" des Baruya de Nouvelle-Guinée. *L'homme* 9, no. 2:5-37.

1971 "Salt Currency" and the Circulation of Commodities Among the Baruya of New Guinea. In *Studies in Economic Anthropology*, ed. G. Dalton, pp. 52-73. Anthropological Studies, no. 7. Washington, D.C.: American Anthropological Association.

Goldschmidt, Walter

1959 *Man's Way*. New York: Holt, Rinehart & Winston.

1967 The Economic Transactions of an African Herdsman and the Market Rationality in Primitive Behavior. Paper presented at annual meeting of the American Anthropological Association, Washington, D. C.

Goodfellow, D. M.

1939 *Principles of Economic Sociology*. Philadelphia: Blakiston.

Gras, N. S. B.

1927 Anthropology and Economics. In *The Social Sciences and Their Interrelations*, ed. W. F. Ogburn and A. A. Goldenweiser, pp. 10-23. Boston: Houghton Mifflin.

Harding, Thomas G.
1967   *Voyagers of the Vitiaz Strait: A Study of a New Guinea Trade System.* American Ethnological Society Monographs, no. 44. Seattle: University of Washington Press.

Harner, Michael J.
1970   Population Pressure and the Social Evolution of Agriculturalists. *Southwestern Journal of Anthropology* 26:67-86.

Harris, Marvin
1959   The Economy Has No Surplus. *American Anthropologist* 61:185-200.
1968   *The Rise of Anthropological Theory.* New York: Crowell.
1969   Monistic Determinism: Anti-Service. *Southwestern Journal of Anthropology* 25:198-206.
1971   *Culture, Man, and Nature.* New York: Crowell.

Heider, Karl G.
1969   Visiting Trade Institutions. *American Anthropologist* 71:462-71.

Helm, June
1962   The Ecological Approach in Anthropology. *American Journal of Sociology* 67:630-40.

Henry, Jules
1951   The Economics of Pilaga Food Distribution. *American Anthropologist* 53:187-219.

Herskovits, Melville J.
1940   *The Economic Life of Primitive Peoples.* New York: Knopf.
1952   *Economic Anthropology.* New York: Knopf.

Hill, Polly
1969   Hidden Trade in Hausaland. *Man* 4: 393-409.

Hobsbawm, Eric J.
1965   Introduction to Karl Marx, *Pre-Capitalist Economic Formations,* pp. 9-65. New York: International Publishers.

Hole, Frank, and Robert Heizer
1969   *An Introduction to Prehistoric Archaeology,* 2nd ed. New York: Holt, Rinehart & Winston.

Holmberg, Allan R.
1950   *Nomads of the Long Bow.* Institute of Social Anthropology Publications, no. 10. Washington D.C.: Smithsonian Institution.

Homans, George
1958   Social Behavior as Exchange. *American Journal of Sociology* 63:597-606.

Humphreys, S. C.
1969   History, Economics, and Anthropology: The Work of Karl Polanyi. *History and Theory* 8:165-212.

Issac, Barry L.
1965   "Rational" and "Irrational" Factors in Southern Mexican Indian "Capitalism." *América indígena* 25:427-36.

Jones, W. T.
1961   *The Romantic Syndrome.* Hague: Martinus Nijhoff.

Joy, Leonard
1967a One Economist's View of the Relationship Between Economics and Anthropology. In *Themes in Economic Anthropology,* ed. R. Firth, pp. 29-46. London: Tavistock.
1967b An Economic Homologue of Barth's Presentation of Economic Spheres in Darfur. In *Themes in Economic Anthropology,* ed. R. Firth, pp. 175-89. London: Tavistock.

Kaplan, David
1965   The Mexican Marketplace Then and Now. In *Essays in Economic Anthropology: Proceedings of the 1965 Annual Spring Meeting of the American Ethnological Society,* ed. J. Helm, pp. 80-94. Seattle: University of Washington Press.
1968   The Formal-Substantive Controversy in Economic Anthropology: Reflections on Its Wider Implications. *Southwestern Journal of Anthropology* 24:228-51.

Katz, Friedrich
1966   *Situación social y económica de los aztecas durante los siglos XV y XVI.* Mexico City: Universidad Nacional Autónoma, Instituto de Investigaciones Sociales.

Katzin, Margaret
1959   The Jamaican Country Higgler. *Social and Economic Studies* 8:421-35.
1960   The Business of Higglering in Jamaica. *Social and Economic Studies* 9:297-331.

Khuri, Fuad I.
1968   The Etiquette of Bargaining in the Middle East. *American Anthropolo-*

gist 70:698-706.

Knight, Frank H.
1965 *The Economic Organization.* New York: Harper Torchbooks. Originally published 1931.

Le Clair, Edward E., Jr.
1959 *A Minimal Frame of Reference for Economic Anthropology (Revised).* Troy, N.Y.: Rensselaer Polytechnic Institute.
1962 Economic Theory and Economic Anthropology. *American Anthropologist* 64:1179-1203.
1969 Comments on Dalton's review article. *Current Anthropology* 10:86.

Le Clair, Edward E., Jr., and Harold K. Schneider, eds.
1968 *Economic Anthropology: Readings in Theory and Analysis.* New York: Holt, Rinehart & Winston.

Lee, Richard
1968 What Hunters Do for a Living, or How to Make Out on Scarce Resources. In *Man the Hunter,* ed. R. Lee and I. De Vore, pp. 30-48. Chicago: Aldine.
1969 !Kung Bushman Subsistence: An Input-Output Analysis. In *Contributions to Anthropology: Ecological Essays,* ed. D. Damas. Ottawa: National Museums of Canada bulletin no. 230, Anthropology Series no. 86.

León Portilla, Miguel
1962 La institución cultural del comercio prehispánico. *Estudios de cultura nahuatl* (Mexico) 3:23-55.

Leroy, Olivier
1925 *Essai d'introduction critique a l'étude de l'économie primitive.* Paris: Guenther.

Lévi-Strauss, Claude
1967 *The Scope of Anthropology.* London: Jonathan Cape.

Lichtheim, George
1967 *The Concept of Ideology and Other Essays.* New York: Vintage.

Lowe, Adolph
1965 *On Economic Knowledge.* New York: Harper & Row.

Lowie, Robert H.
1938 Subsistence. In *General Anthropology,* ed. F. Boas, pp. 282-326. Boston: D. C. Heath.
1963 *Indians of the Plains.* Garden City,

N.Y.: Natural History Press.

McBryde, Felix Webster
1945 *Cultural and Historical Geography of Southwestern Guatemala.* Institute of Social Anthropology publication no. 4. Washington, D.C.: Smithsonian Institution.

McLellan, David
1971 Introduction to Karl Marx, *The Grundrisse,* pp. 1-15. New York: Harper & Row.

McLoughlin, Peter F. M., ed.
1970 *African Food Production Systems.* Baltimore: Johns Hopkins University Press.

Malinowski, Bronislaw
1921 The Primitive Economics of the Trobriand Islanders. *Economic Journal* 31:1-16.
1926 *Crime and Custom in Savage Society.* London: Routledge.
1935 *Coral Gardens and Their Magic,* vol. 1. New York: American Book Co.
1960 *A Scientific Theory of Culture.* New York: Galaxy Books, Oxford University Press. Originally published 1944.
1961 *Argonauts of the Western Pacific.* New York: Dutton. Originally published 1922.

Malinowski, Bronislaw, and Julio de la Fuente
1957 La economía de un sistema de mercados en México. *Acta antropológica* (n.s.) 1, no. 2.

Mannheim, Karl
1964 *Ideology and Utopia.* New York: Harvest Books. Originally published 1936.

Marroquín, Alejandro
1957 *La Ciudad mercado: Tlaxiaco.* Mexico City: Imprenta Universitaria.

Marx, Karl
1904a *A Contribution to the Critique of Political Economy.* Chicago: Kerr.
1904b *Capital,* vol. 1. London: Sonnenschein.
1956 *Selected Writings in Sociology and Social Philosophy,* ed. T. B. Bottomore and M. Rubel. London: Watts.
1965 *Pre-Capitalist Economic Formations.* New York: International Publishers.
1971 *The Grundrisse,* ed. and trans. D. McLellan. New York: Harper & Row.

Mauss, Marcel
1954 *The Gift: Forms and Functions of*

Exchange in Archaic Society, trans. Ian Cunnison. London: Cohen & West. Originally published 1925.

Merton, Robert K.
1957 *Social Theory and Social Structure*. Glencoe, Ill.: Free Press.

Mintz, Sidney
1955 The Jamaican Internal Marketing Pattern. *Social and Economic Studies* 4:95-103.
1957 The Role of the Middleman in the Internal Distribution System of a Caribbean Peasant Economy. *Human Organization* 15:18-23.
1959 Internal Market Systems as Mechanisms of Social Articulation. In *Proceedings of the Annual Spring Meetings of the American Ethnological Society*, pp. 20-30. Seattle: University of Washington Press.
1960a A Tentative Typology of Eight Haitian Marketplaces. *Revista de ciencias sociales* 4:15-57.
1960b Peasant Markets. *Scientific American* 203:112-18.
1967 Pratik: Haitian Personal Economic Relationships. In *Peasant Society: A Reader,* ed. J. M. Potter et al., pp. 98-109. Boston: Little, Brown.

Miracle, Marvin P.
1962 African Markets and Trade in the Copperbelt. In *Markets in Africa*, ed. P. Bohannan and G. Dalton, pp. 698-738. Evanston, Ill. Northwestern University Press.

Morgan, Lewis Henry
1963 *Ancient Society*. Cleveland: Meridian Books, World Publishing Co. Originally published 1877.

Nash, Manning
1961 The Social Context of Economic Choice in a Small Society. *Man* 219:186-91.
1966 *Primitive and Peasant Economic Systems*. San Francisco: Chandler.
1968 Economic Anthropology. In *International Encyclopedia of Social Sciences*, vol. 4, pp. 359-65. New York: Free Press, Macmillan.
1969 Comments on Dalton's review article. *Current Anthropology* 10:87-88.

Neale, Walter
1964 On Defining "Labor" and "Services" for Comparative Studies. *American*

Anthropologist 64:1300-1307.

Nicolaus, Martin
1968 The Unknown Marx. *New Left Review*, April.

Nurkse, Ragnar
1955 *Problems of Capital Formation in Underdeveloped Countries*. Oxford: Blackwell.

Nutini, Hugo G.
1968 On the Concepts of Epistemological Order and Coordinative Definitions. *Bijdragen Tot de Taal-, Land-, en Volkenkunde* 124:1-21.

Olson, Ronald L.
1936 Some Trading Customs of the Chilkat Tlingit. In *Essays in Anthropology Presented to A. L. Kroeber*, ed. R. H. Lowie, pp. 211-14. Berkeley: University of California Press.

Opler, Morris
1968 Remuneration to Supernaturals and Men in Apachean Ceremonialism. *Ethnology* 7:356-93.

Orans, Martin
1966 Surplus. *Human Organization* 25: 24-32.
1968 Maximizing in Jajmaniland: A Model of Caste Relations. *American Anthropologist* 70:875-97.

Ortiz, Sutti
1967 The Structure of Decision-Making Among Indians of Colombia. In *Themes in Economic Anthropology*, ed. R. Firth, pp. 191-228. London: Tavistock.
1970 Review of *Economic Anthropology: Readings in Theory and Analysis*, ed. E. E. Le Clair and H. K. Schneider. *American Anthropologist* 72:622-24.

Panoff, Michael
1970 Marcel Mauss's *The Gift* Revisited. *Man* 5:60-70.

Parsons, Talcott, and Neil J. Smelser
1956 *Economy and Society*. Glencoe, Ill.: Free Press.

Pearson, Harry W.
1957 The Economy Has No Surplus: Critique of a Theory of Development. In *Trade and Market in the Early Empires,* ed. K. Polanyi et al., pp. 320-41. Glencoe, Ill.: Free Press.

Polanyi, Karl
1957 The Economy as Instituted Process. In *Trade and Market in the Early*

Empires, ed. K. Polanyi et al., pp. 243-70. Glencoe, Ill.: Free Press.

1963 Ports of Trade in Early Societies. *Journal of Economic History* 23: 30-45.

Polanyi, Karl, with Abraham Rotstein

1966 *Dahomey and the Slave Trade: An Analysis of an Archaic Economy*. Seattle: University of Washington Press.

Polanyi, Karl, et al., eds.

1957 *Trade and Market in the Early Empires*. Glencoe, Ill.: Free Press.

Pospisil, Leopold

1963 *Kapauku Papuan Economy*. Yale University Publications in Anthropology, no. 67. New Haven: Yale University Press.

Rapoport, Anatol

1965 *Operational Philosophy*. New York: Wiley. Originally published 1953.

Rappaport, Roy A.

1968 *Pigs for the Ancestors*. New Haven: Yale University Press.

1969 Some Suggestions Concerning Concept and Method in Ecological Anthropology. In *Contributions to Anthropology: Ecological Essays*, ed. D. Damas, pp. 184-88. Ottawa: National Museums of Canada bulletin no. 230.

Redfield, Robert

1962 Primitive Merchants of Guatemala. In *Human Nature and the Study of Society: The Papers of Robert Redfield*, vol. 1, ed. M. P. Redfield, pp. 200-210. Chicago: University of Chicago Press. Originally published 1939.

Ribeiro, Darcy

1970 Reply. *Current Anthropology* 11: 426-34.

Richards, Audrey I.

1964 *Hunger and Work in a Savage Tribe*. Cleveland: World Publishing Co. Originally Published 1932.

Robbins, Lionel

1935 *An Essay on the Nature and Significance of Economic Science*. New York: St. Martins Press.

Robinson, Joan

1964 *Economic Philosopy*. Garden City, N.Y.: Doubleday-Anchor.

Sahlins, Marshall D.

1958 *Social Stratification in Polynesia*. American Ethnological Society monograph. Seattle: University of Washington Press.

1960*a* Production, Distribution, and Power in a Primitive Society. In *Men and Cultures*, ed. A. F. C. Wallace, pp. 495-500. Philadelphia: University of Pennsylvania Press.

1960*b* Political Power and the Economy in Primitive Society. In *Essays in the Science of Culture*, ed. G. Dole and R. L. Carneiro, pp. 390-415. New York: Crowell.

1962 *Moala: Culture and Nature on a Fijian Island*. Ann Arbor: University of Michigan Press.

1965*a* Exchange Value and the Diplomacy of Primitive Trade. In *Proceedings of the 1965 Annual Spring Meeting of the American Ethnological Society*, ed. J. Helm, pp. 95-129. Seattle: University of Washington Press.

1965*b* On the Sociology of Primitive Exchange. In *The Relevance of Models for Social Anthropology*, ed. M. Banton, pp. 139-227. London: Tavistock.

1968 *Tribesmen*. Englewood Cliffs, N.J.: Prentice-Hall.

1969 Economic Anthropology and Anthropological Economics. *Social Science Information* 8:13-33.

1972 *Stone Age Economics*. Chicago: Aldine-Atherton.

Salisbury, Richard F.

1960 Ceremonial Exchange and Political Equilibrium. *Proceedings of the Fifth International Congress of Anthropological and Ethnological Sciences* (Paris) 2:255-60.

1962 *From Stone to Steel*. Melbourne: University of Australia Press.

1968*a* Anthropology and Economics. In *Economic Anthropology: Readings in Theory and Analysis*, ed. E. E. Le Clair and H. K. Schneider, pp. 477-85. New York: Holt, Rinehart & Winston.

1968*b* Trade and Markets. In *International Encyclopedia of Social Sciences*, vol. 16, pp. 118-22. New York: Free Press, Macmillan.

Schneider, Harold K.

1964*a* A Model of African Indigenous Economy and Society. *Comparative Studies in Society and History* 7:37-55.

1964b Economics in East African Aboriginal Societies. In *Economic Transition in Africa*, ed. M. J. Herskovits and M. Harwitz, pp. 53-75. Evanston, Ill.: Northwestern University Press.

1970 *The Wahi Wanyaturu: Economics in an African Society*. Viking Fund Publications in Anthropology, no. 48. New York: Wenner-Gren Foundation.

Schumpeter, Joseph A.
1954 *History of Economic Analysis*. New York: Oxford University Press.

Selsam, Howard, and Harry Martel, eds.
1963 *Reader in Marxist Philosophy*. New York: International Publishers.

Service, Elman R.
1966 *The Hunters*. Englewood Cliffs, N.J.: Prentice-Hall.
1968 The Prime Mover of Cultural Evolution. *Southwestern Journal of Anthropology* 24:396-409.

Simon, Herbert A.
1959 Theories of Decision-Making in Economics and Behavioral Science. *American Economic Review* 49:253-83.
1965 *Administrative Behavior*. New York: Free Press, Macmillan.

Skinner, William G.
1964 Marketing and Social Structure in Rural China. *Journal of Asian Studies* 24:3-43.

Smelser, Neil J.
1963 *The Sociology of Economic Life*. Englewood Cliffs, N.J.: Prentice-Hall.

Smith, M. G.
1955 *The Economy of Hausa Communities of Zaria*. Colonial Research Studies, no. 16. London: Her Majesty's Stationery Office.

Stanner, W. E. H.
1933- Ceremonial Economics of the Mulluk
1934 Mulluk and Madngella Tribes of the Daly River, North Australia. *Oceania* 4:156-75, 458-71.
1969 The Kitui Kamba Market, 1938-39. *Ethnology* 8:125-38.

Stavenhagen, Rodolfo
1965 Classes, Colonialism, and Acculturation. *Studies in Comparative International Development* 1, no. 6. St. Louis: Social Science Institute, Washington University.

Steiner, Franz

1957 Towards a Classification of Labor. *Sociologus* 7:112-29.

Steward, Julian H.
1955 *Theory of Culture Change*. Urbana: University of Illinois Press.
1968 Cultural Ecology. In *International Encyclopedia of Social Sciences*. New York: Free Press, Macmillan.

Steward, Julian H., and Louis C. Faron
1959 *Native Peoples of South America*. New York: McGraw-Hill.

Tax, Sol
1953 *Penny Capitalism: A Guatemalan Indian Economy*. Institute of Social Anthropology Publications, no. 16. Washington. D.C.: Smithsonian Institution.

Thurnwald, Richard
1932 *Economics in Primitive Communities*. London: Oxford University Press.

Trigger, Bruce
1967 Engels on the Part Played by Labour in the Transition from Ape to Man: An Anticipation of Contemporary Anthropological Theory. *Canadian Review of Sociology and Anthropology* 4:165-76.

Udy, Stanley H., Jr.
1959 *Organization of Work: A Comparative Analysis of Production Among Nonindustrial Peoples*. New Haven: HRAF Press.

Vayda, Andrew P.
1967 On the Anthropological Study of Economics. *Journal of Economic Issues* 1:86-90.
1968 Economic Systems in Ecological Perspective: The Case of the Northwest Coast. In *Readings in Anthropology*, ed. M. H. Fried, vol. 2, pp. 172-78. New York: Crowell.
1969 Comments on Dalton's review article. *Current Anthropology* 10:95.

Vayda, Andrew P., ed.
1969 *Environment and Cultural Behavior: Ecological Studies in Cultural Anthropology*. Garden City, N.Y.: Natural History Press.

Vayda, Andrew P., and Roy A. Rappaport
1968 Ecology, Cultural and Noncultural. In *Introduction to Cultural Anthropology*, ed. J. A. Clifton, pp. 477-97. Boston: Houghton Mifflin.

Veblen, Thorstein
1948 Why Is Economics Not an Evolutionary Science? In *The Portable Veblen*, ed. M. Lerner, pp. 215-40. New York: Viking Press.
Wagner, Philip A.
1960 *The Human Use of the Earth*. New York: Free Press, Macmillan.
Ward, Barbara E.
1967 Cash or Credit Crops? An Examination of Some Implications of Peasant Commercial Production with Special Reference to the Multiplicity of Traders and Middlemen. In *Peasant Society: A Reader,* ed. J. M. Potter et al., pp. 135-53. Boston: Little, Brown.
Waterbury, Ronald
1970 Urbanization and a Traditional Market System. In *The Social Anthropology of Latin America: Essays in Honor of Ralph Leon Beals,* ed. W. Goldschmidt and H. Hoijer, pp. 126-56. Los Angeles: Latin American Center, University of California.
Watson, R. A., and Patty Jo Watson
1969 *Man and Nature: An Anthropological Essay in Human Ecology*. New York: Harcourt, Brace & World.
Weber, Max

1947 *The Theory of Social and Economic Organization*. Glencoe, Ill.: Free Press.
1949 *The Methodology of the Social Sciences*. Glencoe, Ill.: Free Press.
Wharton, Clifton, ed.
1969 *Subsistence Agriculture and Economic Development*. Chicago: Aldine.
White, Leslie A.
1949 *The Science of Culture*. New York: Grove Press.
1959 *The Evolution of Culture*. New York: McGraw-Hill.
Wissler, Clark
1914 The Influence of the Horse in the Development of Plains Culture. *American Anthropologist* 16:1-25.
Wittfogel, Karl
1955 Developmental Aspects of Hydraulic Societies. In *Irrigation Civilization: A Comparative Study*, ed. J. Steward, pp. 43-52. Washington D.C.: Pan American Union.
Wolf, Eric
1966 *Peasants*. Englewood Cliffs, N.J.: Prentice-Hall.
Zeisel, Hans
1968 Polanyi, Karl. In *International Encyclopedia of Social Sciences*, vol. 12, pp. 172-74. New York: Free Press, Macmillan.

RONALD COHEN

INTRODUCTION

Why do people agree, or act as if they agree, not to kill, maim, steal, or loot? How is it that they abide by rules ordering their social lives? Where do these rules come from and how do they change? These are universal and time-worn questions dealing with the essence of social life, its ordering and adaptation to its own needs and to changing conditions. Because these questions and others dealing with power, authority, and the distribution of valued means and ends are so basic to man's nature itself, men have been asking questions about such things for a very long time. Because a main focal point of all such questions has to do with "valued ends and means," the topic really deals with human desires and the way people seek to satisfy them in a sociocultural context. In other words, politics is to man as form is to content; it packages his desires, individual and collective, and shapes them into a process for achieving some degree of satisfaction from the social, cultural, and physical

world he lives in. Without such a form, social life is impossible, and it is with this form and its activity that political anthropology is concerned.

I shall try to show where and how these questions emerged and developed through time. Then when these roots are understood we shall look in summary fashion at what political anthropology is today, what it has accomplished, and what it may try to do if its present trends continue into the future.[1]

EARLIER APPROACHES TO COMPARATIVE POLITICS

It is logically impossible to inquire beyond the level of origin myths into the origin and function of politics without asking comparative questions. Why should "we" order our social life as we do? One answer is the cosmological

---

[1] There are excellent review articles on the subject already available (Easton 1959, Winckler 1970), and therefore this article attempts a more interpretive approach to the subject.

one: Because that's the way its always been; that's the way the world was created at the beginning. Therefore our modes of behaving express the will of God, which means, of course, that other systems do not express the divine purpose—and are to that extent less legitimate or good.

It is this line of reasoning that underlies or leads to the morally ethnocentric view of comparative politics, which is deeply embedded in Western traditions and American political culture. Basically this line of thought suggests that "our" way of doing things is best—the American system of government is the best ever devised by man. Ergo, another kind of government is less good and should be avoided at all costs. Since government is a means by which people in whole societies organize the authoritative distribution of wants, this statement is in fact true, and we shouldn't change governments or systems unless we change our system of wants and/or their distribution as well.

However, there is a more fundamental reason for looking at political systems from a morally ethnocentric point of view. This has to do with a view of human nature itself. From one Western theological position, man is seen as inherently evil, a creature who must be constrained from expressing his wickedness in society. Thus progress in government is the development of a "social contract" in which men agree to restrain their innate evil for the greater benefits of civilization. The proof that such a contract does have positive functions, the argument goes, can be seen by looking at nonwestern societies, where in a "state of nature" man allows himself to act out his evil will. Thus Hobbes noted that American Indians have no government at all, even within the family, "the concord of which dependeth upon natural lust . . . and they live at this day [early seventeenth cen-

tury] in that brutish manner" (Curtis 1955:301).

Such views led many in the West to see nonwestern man in the New World as the embodiment of unconstrained evil. As a social force Indians were viewed as wreaking havoc upon the civilized Westerner, and therefore must be constrained and "civilized" or killed so that proper and enlightened human existence might not be impeded. This theme is seen again in the classic Western movie, in which the Indian is evil personified, individually and collectively threatening the higher culture of the white man. Such views fit in with those of the early missionaries, who depicted "natives" as depraved, cruel, and desperately in need of an enlightened, ordered Christian existence. Colonialism too absorbed this view of man, and its adherents spoke of the civilizing obligations of the West toward "native races"—the so-called white man's burden. All of these ideas—the social contract, the classic Hollywood movie image of the Indian, the obligations of the missionary and the colonizer—bring to comparative analysis important elements of their ideology from the deeply ingrained Western Christian tradition of original sin and a psychocultural view of man in society that defines goodness as social-governmental restraint of the dominant human proclivity toward evil.

The other side of the moralist coin is a minority view in Western intellectual history. The dominant view is, as we have seen, that man is essentially bad and therefore must be constrained by political systems. The minority view of man in nature—man without Western culture—sees him as good, unsullied, noble, and natural." In this "uncivilized" state, the evil generated by human interactions and the compromises necessary to oil the wheels of society, thereby weakening natural goodness, are absent. Thus society itself or the social contract seen as devolution becomes the corrupting force that demoralizes man.

This theme underlies many philosophical and cultural symbols. Asceticism teaches that purity of spirit can be achieved only by leaving society and its temptations. Sodom and Gomorrah are biblical symbols of the belief that town life is corrupt, and this theme is present in the images of the city slicker and the cowboy. The lone cowboy-hero stays away from society, coming to the evil saloon-infested towns only grudgingly, to redress serious crimes and wrongdoings. Having gallantly gunned down the villain, he returns to the sagebrush to refrigerate his morality and Samson-like strength.

This view is associated in evolutionary terms with devolution or antiprogress. Man the good becomes even more social and complexly so, therefore even more corrupt. In the past, in Eden or Atlantis, things were better, but they have been getting progressively worse ever since, *because of the conditions under which men have to live.* The last point is crucial. Writers like Rousseau and Engels were not simply putting nonwestern man on a pedestal of pre-civilized nobility. They were essentially reformers and environmentalists. Things *are* bad, they said. In the past, before men had been corrupted by society, things were better. Therefore let's create conditions in which things could in fact get better rather than worse. In other words, underlying the idea of the noble savage is the idea of contemporary social criticism and social reform, which informs and motivates this early form of political anthropology.

The difficulty with both the pessimistic view (man is a beast and must be controlled) and the optimistic one (man is noble and conditions must be created that will allow this goodness to

be freely expressed) is their manufactured imputations that morality is the essence of sociopolitical existence. If, by chance or fact, this assumption is untrue, then the moralist view of comparative politics is unsound and unfruitful. And so it is in fact. For to do research on comparative political systems when one already has an answer as to why the systems are different is to destroy the possibility of understanding what creates or conditions these differences. Yet the moralists did by assumption create answers that cut off further research and understanding. Men were different (*a*) because of the differential expression of their essential evil, or conversely (*b*) because of the progressive corruption by society.

Methodologically this approach uses what I would call armchair functionalism to show that *they* are different from *us* because they lack our political institutions. In other words, these writers created or accepted an image of man and his essential nature in their own society and then attempted to create a model of society without the familiar structures of European polities; this they called the "state of nature." It represented man unprotected and unencumbered by a social contract, and the empirical referent was supposed to be nonwestern man and his society. Logically it was simply the result of a two-society comparison in which little heed was paid to the actual details of nonwestern social life. Instead these writers projected onto that world the opposite of their images of and assumptions about their own political systems in order to show the positive or negative qualities (depending upon their viewpoints) of Western institutions.

Can such assumptions tell us why one political system is segmentary in form while another uses village councils? Or can it tell us anything about the differential responses and effects such systems will experience upon incorporation into larger nation states in the modern world? No, it can't. For moralism produces ready-made answers or at least policies instead of research, polemic instead of logic, and a call to political action instead of an attempt to delineate carefully the known and the unknown.

The position that ultimately did win out to become the ongoing intellectual approach for political anthropology was that of empiricism and comparative study. This was based on the assumption that variability must be explained by reference to a multitude of social, environmental, political, psychological, and economic forces rather than man's moral nature.

Like that of the moralists, the materialistic and scientific tradition threads its way far back in time—in this case to scholars like Aristotle, Ibn Khaldun, and Montesquieu. These men saw variability in types of systems (Aristotle) or in types of ecological adaptation (Ibn Khaldun), and attempted to explain such differences on the basis of social forces present in the contexts they were describing. Instead of a two-society comparison—primitive versus civilized—the empiricists used other societies as cases of variation adapted to local conditions of time and place. Thus for Montesquieu government is the result of complex combinations of environmental and psychological forces and a whole way of life; that is, a culture.

Up to the nineteenth century the empiricist tradition was in all likelihood the less interesting, for the moralists pointed the investigation not at politics per se, but at the nature of man and the ethical nature of society—a far more interesting and apparently more profound topic. But as data and information on nonwestern peoples accumulated, as comparative studies became more acceptable for their own sake, the moralists lost ground. Museums were founded in mid-century, and Darwinism gave scholars a means of organizing and understanding these materials that seemed more satisfying than moralism. Finally by the end of the century writers like Sir Henry Maine (*Ancient Law,* 1891:115-16) argued that the moralists really did not know nonwestern man at all and therefore invented him to suit their own purposes!

Basically, the empirical approach is tidy and simple. There are differences among men in the way they order their lives, and our job is to try to understand and explain these differences. Political anthropologists differ in their modes of explanation, their attempts to define units of analysis, and the scope of their studies, yet ultimately all are united in the desire not to illustrate a moral "principle" but to understand empirical variety among political institutions and behavior.

VARIETIES OF POLITICAL ANTHROPOLOGY

NINETEENTH-CENTURY EVOLUTIONISTS

Once Darwinism had changed the intellectual climate of the nineteenth century, then, along with everything else, political phenomena were viewed in evolutionary perspective. Such ideas were not new. As Voget points out in Chapter 1, they are part and parcel of the Western intellectual tradition. However, never had they been so widely accepted or with such sweeping effects upon all branches of knowledge. Man's political systems were most advanced in the country of the scholar doing the writing and least advanced among those peoples judged to be analogous to the lowest rungs of the evolutionary ladder. Politics in this sense was not studied for itself but as part of the evolutionary whole—the society, which was evolving.

This sort of thinking is fine if there is a perfect Guttman scale in which political complexity is exactly correlated with the complexity and change in the indicators chosen to represent societal evolution. However, the more the data that turned up, the less likely it was that such perfect correlations among the traits of a particular type of society at any one stage would be corroborated. And ultimately these complex schemas of unilineal evolution fell by the wayside from too much deductiveness and not enough facts.

However, a legacy was created that is still useful. Political systems did develop one out of the other. How did this occur? What general typology of systemic evolution will account for the growth and development of man's political organization? This latter question assumes that a general typology that separates early from later forms of social life is possible, and this assumption is still basic to anthropology as a discipline. These were the questions and assumptions of the nineteenth century. The answers were ineffective, but the questions still inform the conduct of inquiry.

FUNCTIONALISTS

When fieldwork and the attempt to make sense of field data began turning up much more detailed accounts of other cultures as well as many more cases than had been available earlier, anthropologists turned to functionalism as the answer. Functionalism is the attempt to study phenomena on the basis of general categories of activity that must be carried out if the phenomena are to survive. It is, I believe, a general intellectual response to any new spurt of variance in one's object of study, since it provides easily defined pigeonholes into which data can be sorted. In more formal terms, if research on some

variety of system activity has in the past isolated a specific set of cases or types, and suddenly many more cases with greater detail or many more types are discovered, then one of the few possible ways of joining new and old material together into one corpus is to turn to functionalism. This approach assumes that any systemic phenomenon X that is a type of A must carry out a specified set of functions. And this in turn provides a valid and initial means of doing comparative analysis. Thus functionalism is a normal but somewhat preliminary means of deriving knowledge about systems from data.

Following their nineteenth-century precursors, the early twentieth-century anthropologists were, with a few notable exceptions, interested in *whole* societies. Thus politics—leadership, the settling of disputes, and so on—became for them one among a variety of functional categories of analysis on which their holistic accounts of these societies could be based. In functional terms, political organization was seen as an important device for helping to maintain social order; but the central problem for analysis was the society and its culture. Politics was an "independent" category, like religion, kinship, and socialization; it helped to explain the society, but politics itself was not yet a separate interest. Indeed, to have such a specialized interest would be a contradiction of the functionalist-holistic creed.

One major exception to this general trend is R. H. Lowie, who in his book *The Origin of the State* (1927) tries to focus the comparative analysis of anthropology on an old but still open question. Without clearly saying so, Lowie implies that for him the "state" is in fact political organization or government per se, and he centers his attention on the way governments operate and develop in human social evolution. He therefore examines a series of critical independent variables—population size, stratification, sovereignty (i.e., authority), and territorialism— across a variety of societal types representing a scale from quite simple to complex. Unlike Sir Henry Maine, he concludes that no simple progression from "status" to "contract"—i.e., kin to non-kiṇ association—can explain the development of political systems. He does acknowledge a positive correlation between territorialism and non-kin association, but this does not mean any simple one-to-one relationship. Lowie was too wise to make such a claim, for he knew of peoples, such as the Mongols, whose organizational form consisted of little but kinship groupings, but who nevertheless had founded states and empires.

Lowie can be said to be the founder of contemporary political anthropology, on a number of grounds. He used political institutions as a problem for investigation, and he saw that the sociocultural context in combination with comparative analysis would produce correlative evidence leading to theoretical interpretations.

PRIMITIVE STRUCTURALISTS

As I have already noted, functional analysis is an initial or preliminary way to handle variation. The unit is the whole phenomenon—e.g., a whole culture—and the parts of the unit are the functional categories. When much of the variance is studied, then "types" of systems can be isolated: similar ways of *carrying out* the same functions are classed together as structural types. At this later stage the focus of analysis then shifts to an attempt to understand why these structures are similar to or different from one another, how they work, originate, and change. This approach I would call structuralism—the study of the relationship of parts to one another and the conditions under which they persist and change in predictable directions.

The first major attempt at this type of structural analysis, and the first serious attempt to define a field of political anthropology, was the work that went into *African Political Systems* (Fortes and Evans-Pritchard, eds., 1940). In this volume a simple dichotomy of political structures (states and nonstates) is delineated and the way in which political functions are performed is described and correlated with the political structure. Many of these generalizations provided the base line for future developments. For example, thinking of politics as a function of corporate lineages was an important advance that led to a large corpus of research on the politics of kinship, especially unilineally organized descent groups. On the other hand, to claim that traditional political theory has little to offer anthropology, or to claim on the basis of very little research that population density is unrelated to political structure, is misleading, even though the general thrust of the book is to depict economic and ecological variables as major determinants of the political system of a society.

The structural differences isolated in *African Political Systems* were of such a gross nature, however, that more precise insights and generalizations were impossible. The obvious refinement has been the restriction of comparisons within a more limited set of differences in order to control for gross distinctions of political structure. Such an analysis is carried out by Middleton and Tait in their edited symposium *Tribes Without Rulers* (1958). By restricting comparisons to acephalous societies, the editors are able to correlate a series of sociopolitical variables with differences in lineage depth among African polities.

In this early period Radcliffe-Brown (1940) set up a model for political analysis that became, roughly, the theoretical base line for people in the field. For him politics is social action concerned primarily with the maintenance of order, the legitimate use of violence, and the occupation and rights to a territory. The job of the anthropologist is to ferret out those actions and roles that deal with these functions, show how they are interrelated into a political system, and then indicate how this structure of roles works in the social life of a people. The model has become both a methodological and a theoretical guide to the cross-cultural study of politics.

Yet it lacks behavioral depth and complexity. The way the system works turns out to be the way it *should* work. Thus structure in the hands of these early workers turns out to be the *constitutional* arrangements of a political system. To know the politics of the United States by studying only its constitution is to concentrate solely on the obligatory and moral underpinning to politics, which operates in a clearly delineated set of structures such as the Senate, the House of Representatives, and so on. The primitive quality of nonwestern politics is therefore to some extent an invention by primitive theorists whose balanced political systems are constitutionally correct but behaviorally emasculated. Political man is hidden from view by structurally balanced systems in which morally correct behavior is the only kind allowed and automatic sanctions keep deviants from disturbing the status quo.

Reenter the noble savage! Nowhere to be seen is the power seeker, the political strategem, intrigue, factionalism, the desire to win, and the effects of both winning and losing. Are these universal aspects of all politics or only of Western systems? The early structuralists did not address the question, and it would seem from their work that the everyday striving for power of Western politics is simply absent in nonwestern systems. But is this really true? Since these primitive structuralists gave us only the rules of the game and very little on how the game is in fact played, we cannot really answer the question. In other words, because of an insufficient view of political systems and political process, the early structuralists gathered good data on the constitutional formats of nonwestern societies but not on the actual behavior of political actors in real political systems. The new noble savage was simply assumed to be locked into his own constitutional framework, operating in perfect or almost perfect consonance with his own social contract. By methodological fiat historical development of this constitution was considered unknowable in the nonwestern context. So two of the most important questions of political analysis, (a) "How does the system operate?" and (b) "How did it develop?" were either insufficiently answered or not answered at all.

CONFLICTS, EVENTS, AND BEHAVIORISM

One of the first challenges to the oversimplified approach of early structuralism was that of Gluckman (1963), who introduced conflict into the anthropological perception of nonwestern man. In Hegelian-Marxian terms, Gluckman sees conflict in all human affairs— every "thesis" must have an "antithesis." But unlike Marx, Gluckman sees the synthesis—that is, the outcome of conflict—to be the restoration and strengthening of the status quo ante. If there is a monarch, then there must be antagonism to his power. This antagonism is expressed in rituals of rebellion that help to maintain the system. This idea is an important contribution, but the conclusion leads to an unfounded equilibrium theory in which the denouement of the conflict is always the maintenance of the system, aided by the very rituals designed to change or overthrow it. In Gluckman's political anthropology, the outcome of conflict is never a revolution or palace coup, but, happily, the restoration of order by some institutionalized catharsis of the forces of conflict inherent in society. It is as if his common sense and his Marxism told Gluckman to look for conflict, while his antihistorical approach forced him to postulate the political system's unchanging continuation as a problem to be explained. Ultimately this hypothesis produces a parody of conflict analysis: conflict is not an engine of change, but a mechanism of equilibrium in political and social systems. Since conflict has almost always been seen as an instrument and stimulus for change rather than for stability, this idea of the function of conflict had something salutary to contribute to the social sciences in general, but unfortunately it deterred political anthropology from engaging in serious historical analysis and from investigating the problem of change.

Gluckman's other major reaction to primitive structuralism is more important, for it has stimulated others to enlarge upon it, refine it, and generally carry it forward as an intellectual thrust in political anthropology. The idea is basically methodological but it has some serious theoretical implications as well. Gluckman (1940) noticed that structure (the rules of the game) can never be seen by an observer *in vacuo*, as it were. The fieldworker in fact participates in situations that are parts of events. Gluckman reasons further that instead of focusing on kinship or politics or religion or whatever, the ethnographer should in some cases use these events or situations themselves as units of study. Basically this is a behaviorist idea. To Radcliffe-Brown and his followers, the actual situation is only a rather muddy reflection of a more important Platonic reality—structure. Gluckman is saying that there are many rules and many games all being played at once by actors who may or may not understand the games and their own roles. Thus he has encouraged research in culture contact situations, such as that of the modern chief caught between sets of conflicting rules. The anthropologist has then to use the situation as the "real" unit to be analyzed and the structure as an independent variable *among others* for understanding the behavior of the actors who carry out the event.

To show how powerful a tool this approach is, we have only to look briefly at the work of one of Gluckman's students with the Cyrenaica Bedouin (Peters 1967). According to their own reports, the Bedouin have a classic segmentary system like that of the Nuer, Tiv, Somali, and others who reckon all politically important interpersonal relationships by unilineal (agnatic) descent. Thus informants quickly corroborate ideas of complementary opposition, indicating that political alliances are a direct function of structural proximity as delineated by the lineage system itself. In order to know who supports whom, one merely plots the lineage system; political allies then become apparent—or should—since they are determined by degree of proximal lineage ties. Peters points out that, like the early structuralists, the people themselves really believe that this is their political system. However, when he actually plotted out who was most closely allied to whom in real-life situations, he found that ecology, trade, and other factors determined that political alliances were more often and more advantageously made with distant lineages and kin rather than with close ones. Thus the constitutional framework (structure) is in conflict with political and economic reality. The people make up stories to explain the many exceptions *as if* the constitution governed their behavior, but in doing so they are as truthful as anyone anywhere whose traditions do not fully apply to the exigencies of their existence.

This was an important step forward and it has led other followers of Gluckman, especially V. W. Turner (1957), and more drastically Turner's colleague Swartz (1968), to carry situational analysis even further into a form of typology and theoretical depiction of events. During his fieldwork Turner was struck by the fact that structural rules applied to events could not predict regularities. He decided that if real situationally based behavior was to be understood, analysis should appropriately be based on a feedback model that (*a*) divided a conflict event into phases and then (*b*) showed how a number of alternatives can occur at each changeover to a new phase (Swartz, Turner, and Tuden, eds. 1966:18-19). These then in turn feed back upon the flow of events to determine the course of conflict and its resolution. To this idea Swartz, Turner, and Tuden have added ideas about political supports and demands as well as the idea of arena and field as the locus of the political event. Structure is only one aspect of such an analysis, while the course of events themselves, outside political forces, the personalities of the participants, indeed almost anything, can determine which way things will go as political action moves forward. To these analysts, as to Peters (1967), the situation—that is, behavior—is the dependent variable, and structure is an independent variable that helps to determine it. The entire process is depicted as occurring in a progression that has feedback mechanisms and a flow chart effect in which

political activity is an output of forces directed at actors operating in time.

But there are several shortcomings to this approach. First of all, it seems to generate no general propositions or hypotheses. It does seem to be an efficient and sensible way of gathering field data on political phenomena; its open-ended quality as to sources of variance require the researcher to record all possible supports, demands, and actions of political actors in an arena and in the field. But it doesn't tell why one set of supports or demands would or should operate in a specific situation. For this information and level of generalization we must look elsewhere.

Furthermore, this event-process analysis can inform only a limited set of data, thus impairing comparative research—the very source of the anthropological perspective. There are many political systems now defunct (Aztec, Inca, Tokugawa, Cherokee . . .) for which such data as this approach requires are not available. Are they to be dropped from the realm of anthropological inquiry because we have no data on their political events? It is in this sense that event analysis becomes technique rather than theory. It is a good way of obtaining information on living systems, but it cannot serve as a general plan for the comparative analysis of all political systems. It should also be remembered that there are literally millions of political events. Some way, not yet clear, must be devised to classify such events so that variance can be seen from a proper level of abstraction out of which theory can be constructed.

An interesting development of the behavioral approach in political anthropology has been the attempt to focus attention on uninstitutionalized political groupings. A good example has been the research emphasizing factions. A faction is a nondurable grouping, mobilized rather loosely under a leader who uses his social contacts in many spheres, both kin and non-kin, to obtain support in order to further his own interests or those of his group interests (Firth 1957). Why some factions remain unstructured while others become more clearly and permanently organized; whether they are disruptive or contribute to social order, or both; whether factions include many or only a limited variety of conflicts and competition—none of this is yet clear in the literature. Thus Firth (1957) feels that factions can and do contribute to social order, while Beals and Siegal (1966) argue for the opposite point of view.

Taken as far as it will go, the behaviorist position reduces politics and political anthropology to the study of "strategems and spoils" (see Bailey 1969). It views politics as the study of political man or as a game in which players are motivated to win and therefore act in a manner calculated to bring them whatever values they are pursuing (see Riker 1962). Why political systems should differ from one another is a question left unasked and unanswered, since it is political man acting to win the game that is being studied, and presumably he will be quite the same wherever we find him, even though the details of his behavior will vary with the system. Furthermore, there is no attempt to separate government of the society from family, economic organization, or any other institution. This means that relations between the political aspects of all institutions—authority in the family compared to authority in government, for example—cannot easily be studied from such an approach.

NEOSTRUCTURALISTS

In the last few decades the structuring of political action by rules governing the authority relations of a society has remained the dominant focus of inquiry within the discipline of political anthropology. As the behavioral challenges of Gluckman and others have come to be heard, however, the emphasis has shifted away from the simplicity of early structuralism to a more complex rendering of political activity in which structure is only one element, albeit a very important one. In other words, process among contemporary structuralists is seen not as the functioning of structure, but as the complex result of many facets of sociocultural, economic, political, and psychological systems, all of which condition political action.

Structure, the rules governing political behavior or the constitutional framework, is seen by structuralists as a means of classifying the political systems of mankind into a finite set of classes that will encompass the variety of political experience invented by men to give order to their lives. The assumption here is that the classificatory criteria separate different kinds of political life and merge similar ones. The weakness of this idea, as we have seen, is that though political systems may differ significantly, political man may be essentially the same in all of them; and it is this regularity and its causes that we ought to investigate. There is, in other words, the perfectly good "psychic unity" kind of argument for assuming that political behavior is the same no matter where you find it. However, this is not a zero-sum game, so we cannot say that one approach is either all wrong or all right. It is probably most useful at present to say that for some purposes the strictly behavioral approach may be more suitable, while in others a combination of behavioral and structural approaches will produce the best results.

Another weakness of the structural approach is its seeming lack of time depth. Structures of political action are often seen as repetitive acts that exist in a temporal vacuum into which time progression is not allowed, because it would, theoretically, contaminate the abstract working of the model. This was certainly true of the primitive structuralists, but it is much less so today for a number of reasons. First of all, many of the newer structuralist writers are also evolutionists (e.g., Fried 1967), and are thus very much concerned with the relation of macrotime to structures and their development. Second, it is quite easy to add input-output analysis to ordinary structural analysis, as Easton (1959) does, thereby incorporating microtemporal operations and change into the structural model.

In my view, the strengths of the structural approach outweigh many of its supposed weaknesses. As an overall approach it provides anthropology *and* political science with a periodic table of political systems. Differences and similarities among these systems have to be explained. The level of generality among the systems is such that internal variability within any one type can encompass differences in time. Thus hunting and gathering polities can be used to construct a model to represent all such systems, thereby throwing open the question of evolution and development within types and between them.

Although this may sound overly conjectural at first, it is much less so in practice. For example, hunting and gathering polities operate as a type within an ascertainable degree of scarcity in the natural environment, which produces common and to some degree variable features in their political systems. Beyond a certain point, as exemplified by the Northwest Coast of North America, the ecology and associated sociopolitical organization resemble very closely those associated with the harvesting and storing of food. In operational terms, then, we can draw the parameters of our model of hunting and gathering polities to exclude the Northwest Coast, including it in another type but realizing that it represents one among several possibilities of transition from one model to another.

In all of this the structure of the political system is seen as a dependent variable in which the structure itself is the major problem to be explained. However, that is only a small portion of the approach, albeit an important and intriguing one. We can look, conversely, at the structure of political systems as an independent variable, and ask what can be seen from this perspective. In what way, for example, does a person who has lived all his life under a certain political system differ from a person who has known only some other political system? I believe there are already enough data available to allow us to begin making some generalizations about personality and political system. Certainly there has been a deep interest in the subject ever since Fromm's *Escape from Freedom* (1941) and Benedict's *The Chrysanthemum and the Sword* (1946), but little systematic synthesis and research have been carried out. And what is the effect of political structures upon one another? This question is especially relevant to the process of building new nations, in which many types of structures are being incorporated. Is this process the same no matter what, or are there serious differences that depend upon the nature of the political systems involved?

All of this means that neostructuralism has a full and varied program of empirical research and theory construction inherent in its approach. This is probably a major reason that it is still of major importance to political anthropology, and will be for the foreseeable future.

But there is another reason. Political anthropology is the "natural" development of a refined or sharpened interest in social structure. Nadel (1957) saw this and pointed toward political studies as a natural development for those primarily concerned with social structures. Nadel analyzed the logical and epistemological bases of the concept of social structure, and in effect declared that political activity is its most important and determinative aspect. This conclusion follows, he says, from the fact that the most important criteria for identifying positions in a society are the actors' command over the actions of others and/or command over existing benefits and resources. In other words, power and authority relations underlie and are major determinants of interrole relationships. In this sense politics can be said to be the core of social structural studies.

The Neostructuralist View of Politics

Following Nadel (1957), the neostructuralist view of politics assumes that political activity is a part of all social relations. Thus Fried (1967:20-21) talks of political organization as a "portion of social organization," and Easton (1959), Smith (1960), and Cohen (1970a) all define political activity as an *aspect* of social relations. If this view is taken, then, as Easton (1959) points out, we must operationally define *the* political system as the widest scaled set of authority relations in society, and it is to this system of relations we give the name political system, whereas political activity within this unit takes place at the subsystem level among structural components of the overall system. In other words, politics can be studied anywhere—in the family, the lineage, a religious or economic organization, or any other social institution. However, if some authority system can be said to include all of these constituent organi-

zations or at least is congruent with them, then we call this the political system or, in Smith's words, the government.

To all neostructuralists, then, the authority structure of a society is one of the most important features of the political life of the society. Authority is the recognized right of superiors to allocate scarce values. This means that authority is legitimated power; a recognized right is a prerogative that no individual or group successfully opposes. Polity members may agree, disagree, or be noncommittal about these prerogatives, but as long as nothing is actively done to take such rights away from their owners, the authority distinction exists and will persist. Indeed, such rights are often protected by sanctions that prescribe punishment for would-be usurpers. When this is not the case, authority is the result of some set of personal achievements and is open on a competitive basis to all members of a particular group in the polity. Such would be the case in what Fried (1967:33) calls egalitarian societies, where there are no "means of fixing or limiting the number of persons capable of exerting power."

Once authority relations exist, however, there is no reason to assume or theorize that they will persist in some stable or equilibrated fashion. Authority may increase or decrease with respect to the amount of power available to the role occupant attempting to use it. The increase or decrease of power may be due to his own actions, those of superiors or subordinates, or both. It may also result from role changes in the society, if new roles that take away or add to his power are created. Finally, authority may change because of changes in the interpolity environment. Thus an independent ruler can lose much of his power if he becomes subjected to colonial rule.

Power, the generic category of which

authority is one part, is the ability or capacity to influence valued action. Influence is the capacity of an actor to have his or her wishes carried out when these wishes differ from those deemed desirable by others. Smith (1956) points out that power is "segmentary"; that is, it can never by contained within an authority structure, since everyone, no matter what his or her own position in the system, can attempt to gain more power than is legitimate under the constitutional arrangements—the authority structure. Political activity involves among other things the competition of individuals and groups for such increases of power. And although observations in many systems bear out this generalization, why it should be so is not too clear and usually requires assumptions about human nature. One such assumption is that there is a basic motivation or drive for power that serves as the fuel that propels the political structure into action. Riker (1962:22) assumes that there is such a thing as *politically rational man*—one who would rather win than lose. The point is that such a motive or energizing core is necessary to make a political system work. How universal such motives are, what shape they take, how they are acquired and develop in comparative terms—all this is simply unknown at present. The point is that for the structuralist to create any theory he must assume the existence of certain psychological traits that we do not as yet fully understand cross-culturally.

As the discussion of change in authority has already hinted, the sources of power can vary from society to society and within any one society over time. First of all, as Fried (1967), Lenski (1966), and others point out, power is closely related to social stratification. Those attributes that raise persons in the eyes of their fellows are values, and people of high status have ipso facto more control and influence over such values than others. Thus the avenues to high social status are by definition the avenues to political power. Personal success, wealth, powers of adjudication, success in the food quest, physical appearance, and a host of other qualities may qualify as status determinants (Cohen 1970b). Whatever the list for any particular society, the person who measures high on these status dimensions must have power to achieve such status, and he has power because he is high in the status scale; that is, he commands, in the opinion of others, more of a scarce resource than other people.

Second, power varies with the political skills of actors. This can be seen when two actors occupy comparable political offices and one succeeds brilliantly, becoming in the process a very powerful man, while his colleague simply carries on his duties without enhancing his power. The reasons for such differences vary to some extent from one society to another. However, a determination to win and a deep understanding of the political system and its culture are probably essential ingredients, besides other qualities not so well known at present.

An important point follows from this discussion. The authority structure and the power structure are very different orders of social phenomena. One can discover the authority structures in any society quite easily and simply by asking who has the recognized right to command what specific influence over persons, things, and services. The *structure* of authority is then simply the relationship of the authority aspects of the role sets in any society. The word "sets" indicates, as Nadel (1957) has pointed out, that there may be many social structures not necessarily totally interconnected within the same society. When we move the discussion to power, however, the possibility of structuring becomes much more amorphous and difficult. How are the people and/or roles that wield influence in a society connected with one another? Is there really a power elite or merely an ideological position that claims that such a structure *should* or *must* exist? I don't really know the answer to these questions, but they can't be answered on ideological or moral grounds alone. Whether such a thing as a power *structure* does exist in a society, or whether there are many unrelated and shifting centers of power, is a matter for empirical research, not moralistic posturing. If such structures do exist within or outside of the formal authority system, they must have some stable access to power, and what this is and the relationship of these power-holders to one another will constitute a power structure. It must be remembered, however, that the sources of power are very broad and not easily confined within a system. Thus power is always "leaking" into new persons and groups who use political skill to get it. It might be well to ask in this context whether anthropologists should not speak of formal and informal authority structures rather than a power structure, which in itself may be a contradiction in terms, given the amorphous nature of power in human affairs.

THE POLITICAL PROCESS

In general, the neostructuralist sees the political realm as stemming from the operation of authority structures, just as the classic structuralists before him have done. Fried (1967:18) therefore speaks of "rank" societies as being warlike. In other words, one of his structural types has as a behavioral correlate variable but noticeable degrees of warfare. On the other hand, it *is* variable, not constant, and he theorizes that density per settlement is an important determinant of such warfare. Thus

structure is modified in its relation to behavior by a set of ecological, demographic, and other intervening variables that determine the final behavioral output as well as the history and development of the political system itself.

M. G. Smith (1960) sees power and authority in tension with the overall process that he calls "governmental." This process he breaks down into two parts. First there is the operation of authority features, which he labels administrative action—the carrying out of legitimate governmental demands. Then there is "political" action, which consists of attempts to influence policy, shape it, or determine how it shall be carried out. Political action reflects the search for power in the system and cannot be confined to the authority system alone, since anyone may try to influence policy. Although this is a simplified view, Smith sees political process as stemming from the tension and interaction of the forces of "politics" and "administration" as he has defined them.

In my own work (Cohen 1970*a*) I have followed Smith in viewing political process as stemming from the relationship of power to authority. Political process has two sources, first the breakdown or decrease of authority, second the legitimization of power resulting in new authority roles and/or the enhancement of power available to old ones.

But political process is not simply an abstracted relationship between power on the one hand and authority on the other. As an output of the relationship or tension we can observe policies and behaviors all encompassed in the behavioral category of decisions. Decisions are choices or sets of choices (policies) among various possible alternatives. In Easton's (1959) terms, I see decisions as outputs resulting from demands (inputs) upon the political structure. Such demands stimulate activity of various types, which produce variance among types of decisions. All political structures must cope with demands, but the way they handle them and therefore the way they associate decision-making with various roles help to determine differences among authority structures. Who and what are involved in decisions are important features of political systems.

There are two types of political decisions: routine, which have an everyday quality, and crisis decisions, in which the vital interests of persons and groups are involved. Most administrative decisions deal with the ordinary playing or acting out of public policy. They are decisions made under normal circumstances about normal activities—the food quest, distributing and overseeing the use of land, and so on. When things that vitally concern an individual or a group are involved, then that individual or group is generally fully mobilized to participate in resolving the crisis and to affect the direction of the decision. When crisis decisions must be made, the political process surfaces so as to be available for study. Such occasions, often surrounding succession to office, are excellent times to study a political system *qua* system (Cohen 1966; Goody, ed., 1966).

In addition to power, authority, and decision-making, I suggest that political socialization creates an important support for the political system by producing individuals who know and are sympathetic to the political culture of the group. Political culture consists of the set of ideals and symbols that describe the aims and goals of political life in any society. In practice this means the way in which power and authority are conceived and carried out in the culture as a whole. Le Vine (1966) has done possibly the most interesting work in this area by relating personality

components and socialization to differences in political system. But the field is still an underdeveloped one in anthropology, although political science has had something of a social psychological bias ever since the 1920s.

Finally, the political system itself must be seen to operate in an inter-polity environment in which authority sets are related to one another. This is also an extremely underdeveloped part of anthropology, yet one that will, I would guess, grow the fastest in the next few years. Concepts of the plural society and plural structures (Kuper and Smith, eds., 1969) and of incorporation processes (Cohen and Middleton, eds., 1970) are attempts to deal with this level of structural analysis.

In summary form, these are some of the major ideas of neostructural analysis in political anthropology. Its strength lies in its programmatic attack on the subject, which can produce systematic additions to our knowledge of the political realm of society. On the other hand, politics, as Swartz and his colleagues note (1966), has an event-like and situationally based quality that can be overlooked by the structuralist. Very likely structuralists will have to face this problem and solve it. My own solution has been to add behavioral elements—political skills, decision-making, socialization, and others—to a structural model of the political system in order to encompass structure and behavior in one generalized conception of the polity which will explain the operation of the system over time. However, this raises as many questions as it answers. For example, if authority is defined as legitimated power, what is legitimacy? Is it a consensually recognized or unchallenged right to influence and control behavior and resources? Does it rest on coercion, mutually recognized utility, shared values, or combinations of these that vary across cultures and types of systems? These questions emerge from the nature of the basic concepts in any model of the political system and therefore serve as major growing points for research.

TYPES OF POLITIES

As we have already seen, the neo-structuralist position requires that a periodic table or classification of political systems be set up so that the full range of variance can be examined. But as I have said elsewhere (Cohen 1965), taxonomy is not theory. It is necessary as a beginning and may point the way to theorizing, but in and of itself it simply stipulates the criteria that most usefully indicate the variance in the phenomena being studied. Thus if a phenomenon X varies consistently and in agreed-upon ways with regard to Y we may classify X by using Y as our criterion of differentiation. In evolutionary study, however, X may be a complex of things, and significant features at one end of its variance may not be present at the other end. Thus criteria of classification may have to shift or change as we go from one end of an evolutionary sequence to the other. This is not inconsistency, merely coming to grips with the empirical facts.

Societies that have no centralized government to control activities across settlements or bands are divided into two great classes, band or Pleistocene polities on the one hand and Neolithic varieties or agricultural polities on the other. Obviously these represent the evolutionary facts in that one type developed out of the other. Band polities vary according to the group's available food supplies, which also cause variations in population density, the size of the band, and the amount of suprafamilial political activity. Because the ultimate social unit, the family, is self-sufficient except for getting wives,

food supplies can increase or decrease over time with correlative changes in the political system, and the group continues to adapt to its environment. I assume that family, patrilocal, and composite bands are in that order progressively more complex and populous, but that each may develop out of any of the others, depending on the resource base of the society. Which came first, if any, is impossible to tell at present. In my view, the possibility exists that many varieties of bands have always been present, and emerged or developed their roots from a wide range of variance in prehominid social and political life.[2] This seems likely because of the wide variety of social organizational forms known among nonhuman primates (Jay, ed., 1968).

At this stage man's social organization is so close to being completely determined by the food quest that it is quite conceivable that important changes could take place easily and quickly. For example, northern Athapascans traditionally spent part of their yearly round on the Mackenzie River and part of the year in small family groups in the hinterland. On the river they formed composite bands living off the available fish and game. If the river ever failed, they were already preadapted to family-level existence elsewhere, since they carried it on anyway part of the year. If the river could support them all year round, they could give up their segmented family organization and live along the river in larger and more permanent settlements—which is precisely what has happened in the last hundred years. Neither step represents a sharp break with the past; both are merely outgrowths of what was already there.

Political life follows correlatively.

------

[2] For a reexamination of this variance, see Steward (1968).

Greater ecological emphasis upon family organization makes the family the primary political unit. Knowledge and practice of communal hunts and other activities can produce concepts of shamans and hunt leaders, but only with situation-specific powers. On the other hand, greater population density can produce gerontocracy (Hart and Pilling 1960), the need for more permanent headmen to adjudicate disputes, and so on. In either case, individual success and skill at politics are widely valued.

The Neolithic invention of crops and herds produced enormous potential for variation in human society and in political systems as well. It is at this level that the greatest variance among types of systems emerges. Unlike later systems whose organizational features limit variation, at the Neolithic level there are many quite different solutions to the sociopolitical problems created by advances in technology. In organizational terms the basic problem was to develop ways of relating human beings to specific resources—plots of land and herds of cattle or other animals—which as food-producing capital assets actually persisted beyond the life span of individuals. Band peoples who conceived of certain territories as their own (not all of them did) had this same problem; but now individuals and small family groups had to be related to concentrated, sustained, and persisting phenomena in some way that allowed for an orderly social life in a local group that could be many times larger than a simple band.

There are a number of interrelated and overlapping ways of solving this common problem, and these solutions are reflected as well in the differences among political systems at the Neolithic level. If relationships between group members and persistent resources are to be established and the resources allocated authoritatively, corporate bodies that last beyond the term of office of the corporate officeholders must be instituted. At this level of complexity a number of such bodies develop—lineages (with or without clans), councils, age-grade societies—along with the idea that a powerful man and his followers provide stable means of organizing political power in an acephalous community. The seeds of all of these systems are present in most polities of the Neolithic type, but usually one of them tends to dominate the political system; that is, to become the widest scaled authority structure in the society. In mobile pastoralist societies or ones that have for other ecological reasons been moving or expanding, deep lineages and clans perform this function. In more stable societies with permanent village units, the stimulus of living in one place produces community-wide political organization in the form of a village cult group or a council. These groups may be composed of lineage elders or others, but the main idea is that stable residence in the village produces the basis for political life. In East Africa, age-grade societies provide such services at the widest scale level, although, again, lineages are present and perform functions for their members. In New Guinea, although other structures are present, the "big man" and his following tend to represent the widest scaled organization of legitimated power.

For reasons that are not altogether clear, authority relations expand beyond the local group to encompass a number of groups. This may occur through the differentiation of one descent group into a high-status ruling class whose leadership cuts across many groups. It also occurs when a group migrates into an area where another group is already established; if the newcomers are to stay, they must acknowledge the higher status and hence the authority of the earlier settlers. Or it may result from constriction of space (Carneiro 1970); that is, increased population densities (Stevenson 1968). Whatever the reason, the result is the same: chieftaincy; and from chieftaincy grow ideas of more concentrated centralization, in which one clan or a lineage within that clan becomes royal while close kin and associates form a bureaucracy to help run the state. The difference between states and chieftaincies results from that quality of chieftaincy which I would call para-statism. This is an incapacity to centralize organization without producing a constant tendency for the state to break up into a number of self-governing units. Barnes (1954) calls this a snowball social structure. Each subordinate looks and acts like his superior, and minor chiefs can hope to break away and form their own polities. In such a system (a) differentiation of political functions is still minimal and (b) each subleader can become a leader if he does not carry out his debt or promise of fealty to his lord. Chieftaincies, then, are fissiparous centralized governments whose centrifugal forces are greater than their centripetal forces, so that the system is constantly breaking into similar pieces. In such systems a minimal amount of centralized bureaucracy aids in the tasks of centralized government, since few specialized political functions are performed at the center.

From such beginnings, and possibly others such as diffusion, centralized states evolve. They differ from one another in the degree of autonomy given to local groups. This quality is generally inversely associated with levels of subordination from the center outward and with the degree of ascribed status necessary for filling political offices. In other words, the more levels of hierarchy there are in a state, the greater is the tendency for control to be central-ized in order that the state remain in one piece. Similarly, ascribed status as a means of recruitment to office means that persons appointed to positions in the government hierarchy need not demonstrate any particular loyalty to the central government, thereby weakening its power (Cohen 1966).

States also differ in degree of oligarchy. The more oligarchic the society, the more diffuse and less specific the relations between superiors and subordinates. This tendency in turn depends upon the absence of money salaries for bureaucrats, as well as some degree of social insecurity. Without money to pay for the loyal service of subordinates or to influence directly or indirectly the decisions of his superiors, a man can hope for security and social mobility only if he can rely on the unqualified subservience of those beneath him in the social scale and is equally subservient to those above him. The degree to which such states are centralized is dependent upon other factors noted above, especially the mode of recruitment to office.

Finally, states vary in degree of industrialization in the modern sense. Such a large leap in the productivity, and therefore wealth, of the society requires such enormous changes in the scale of coordinating economic and political organization that we can justifiably speak of the industrialized states as having a qualitatively distinct form of polity. The complexities of an industrialized economy and its educational, social, and cultural correlates are quite similar whether one is in Japan, Russia, or the United States, or observing the emergence and development of the institutions of an industrial economy in a recently independent state in Africa. Such an economy is correlated with a rising status for women, and this holds for all societies that undergo industrial development. What does vary among these societies, for the present at least, is the degree to which their various constituent institutions are or are not under the regulatory control of the central government. From the perspective of anthropological time, however, fully industrialized societies are so recent that their ultimate convergence toward a common political structure is one among a number of evolutionary possibilities to be considered by political anthropologists.

All states have the capacity through citizenship concepts to be multi-ethnic, and most are at one time or another. In expanding to include new peoples, or in developing a central government, states incorporate Neolithic rural polities that become peasantry in the state. That is, peasantry is a group of nonstate or conquered state people who have become absorbed into a dominant state structure. There is some interface contact between the peasantry and the state, but peasants also continue to develop and maintain their own rural culture. They therefore assimilate slowly after their incorporation into the state, even though some of their members go off to join the "Great Tradition" at the center. They provide the basic reason for cultural heterogeneity in the young states.

All of these polities have political cultures and all exist in an interpolity environment, and we still know very little about either of these aspects of their existence. We also know very little about the relationship of authority systems within political systems to one another and to the system as a whole. Thus the nature of the university and its relations to this overall polity are not clearly understood either in our own society or in others, and yet this is a key question. There are many more of these interpolity relations to which political anthropology must address itself in the next few years as it develops

into a special branch of social science on its own. Possibly the most important of these questions concerns the relationship of the traditional polity to that of the modernization process that is transforming these polities into modern nation states. I have described this process elsewhere (Cohen and Middleton, eds., 1970) and intend to expand this treatment for future publication. Suffice it to say here that (a) the incorporation process has been going on for a very long time and (b) the structure of traditional systems is an important determinant of the modernization process.

CONCLUSION

In conclusion we can say that political anthropology has emerged only recently in terms of academic time but already shows signs of developing into a healthy and mature science. This can best be seen in the kinds of questions it has undertaken to ask:

1. What is politics?
   (a) What are political "process" and political "action"?
   (b) Are political actions the same in whatever context they appear?
2. What is a political system?
3. How many kinds of political system have there been in human history, and how did they develop?
4. What effect (if any) do differences among political systems have on political action?
5. What is the effect of the political system upon its constituent individuals and their culture?
6. What is the effect of the nonindustrial political system upon the modernization process in the contemporary world?

These are the main questions we ask. When we discover the answers they will provide us with part of the solution to that most basic of all social science puzzles: What is man? And in so doing they will allow us to understand what helps and what hinders us in our search for a better life.

REFERENCES

Bailey, F. G.
1969 *Stratagems and Spoils: A Social Anthropology of Politics.* Oxford: Blackwell.

Barnes, J. A.
1954 *Politics in a Changing Society.* London: Oxford University Press.

Beals, A. R., and B. J. Siegal
1966 *Divisiveness and Social Control.* Stanford: Stanford University Press.

Benedict, R.
1946 *The Chrysanthemum and the Sword.* Boston: Houghton Mifflin.

Carneiro, R.
1970 A Theory of the Origin of the State. *Science* 169:733-38.

Cohen, R.
1965 Political Anthropology: The Future of a Pioneer. *Anthropological Quarterly* 38:117-31.
1966 The Dynamics of Feudalism in Bornu. In *Boston University Papers on African History*, ed. J. Butler, vol. 2. Boston: Boston University.
1970a The Political System. In *Handbook of Method in Cultural Anthropology*, ed. R. Naroll and R. Cohen. Garden City, N.Y.: Natural History Press.
1970b Social Stratification in Bornu. In *Social Stratification in Africa,* ed. A. Tuden and L. Plotnicov. New York: Free Press, Macmillan.

Cohen, R., and J. Middleton, eds.
1970 *From Tribe to Nation in Africa.* San Francisco: Chandler.

Curtis, M.
1955 *The Great Political Theories.* New York: Harcourt Brace.

Easton, D.
1959 Political Anthropology. In *Biennial Review of Anthropology, 1959,* ed. B. Siegal. Stanford: Stanford University Press.

Firth, R.
1957 Introduction to *Factions in Indian and Overseas Indian Societies,* ed. R.

Firth. *British Journal of Sociology* 8, no. 4:291-342 (special issue).

Fortes, M., and E. E. Evans-Pritchard, eds.
1940 *African Political Systems.* London: Oxford University Press.

Fried, M. H.
1967 *The Evolution of Political Society.* New York: Random House.

Fromm, E.
1941 *Escape from Freedom.* New York: Farrar & Rinehart.

Gluckman, M.
1940 Analysis of a Social Situation in Modern Zululand. *Bantu Studies* 14.
1963 *Order and Rebellion in Tribal Africa.* New York: Free Press of Glencoe, Macmillan.

Goody, J., ed.
1966 *Succession to High Office.* Cambridge Papers in Anthropology, no. 4. Cambridge: At the University Press.

Hart, C. W. M., and A. R. Pilling
1960 *The Tiwi of North Australia.* New York: Holt, Rinehart & Winston.

Jay, P. C., ed.
1968 *Primates: Studies in Adaptation and Variability.* New York: Holt, Rinehart & Winston.

Kuper, L., and M. G. Smith, eds.
1969 *Pluralism in Africa.* Berkeley: University of California Press.

Lenski, G.
1966 *Power and Privilege: A Theory of Social Stratification.* New York: McGraw-Hill.

Le Vine, R.
1966 *Dreams and Deeds.* Chicago: University of Chicago Press.

Lowie, R. H.
1927 *The Origin of the State.* New York: Harcourt Brace.

Maine, Sir Henry
1891 *Ancient Law.* London: Murray.

Middleton, J., and D. Tait, eds.
1958 *Tribes Without Rulers.* London: Routledge & Kegan Paul.

Nadel, S. F.
1957 *The Theory of Social Structure.* London: Cohen & West.

Peters, E.
1967 Some Structural Aspects of the Feud Among the Camel-Herding Bedouin of Cyrenaica. *Africa* 37:260-82.

Radcliffe-Brown, A. R.
    1940 Preface to *African Political Systems*, ed. M. Fortes and E. E. Evans-Pritchard. London: Oxford University Press.
Riker, L. H.
    1962 *Theory of Political Coalitions*. New Haven: Yale University Press.
Smith, M. G.
    1956 On Segmentary Lineage Systems. *Journal of the Royal Anthropological Institute* 86:39-80.
    1960 *Government in Zazzau*. London: Oxford University Press.
Stevenson, R. F.
    1968 *Population and Political Systems in Tropical Africa*. New York: Columbia University Press.

Steward, J. H.
    1968 Causal Factors and Processes in the Evolution of Prefarming Societies. In *Man the Hunter*, ed. R. B. Lee and I. De Vore. Chicago: Aldine.
Swartz, M.
    1968 *Local-Level Politics*. Chicago: Aldine.
Swartz, M., V. W. Turner, and A. Tuden, eds.
    1966 *Political Anthropology*. Chicago: Aldine.
Turner, V. W.
    1957 *Schism and Continuity in an African Society*. Manchester: University of Manchester Press.
Winckler, E. A.
    1970 Political Anthropology. *Biennial Review of Anthropology, 1969*, ed. B. Siegal. Stanford: Stanford University Press.

CHAPTER 20 On Studying the Ethnography of Law and Its Consequences

LAURA NADER
BARBARA YNGVESSON

INTRODUCTION

The anthropological study of law is only slowly gaining momentum in spite of the fact that today there is an almost obsessive concern with law in the United States. Several government comissions have been designated to investigate riots (Kerner 1968), protest politics (Skolnick 1969), crime in general (Wolfgang 1967), and the administration of justice (Overby 1967). In recent years major political speeches have been riddled with talk of law and order, and much attention is given to the new weaponry and surveillance techniques that may be used to maintain law and to enforce order. We are experiencing a time when the poor and underprivileged are no longer the major focus of law enforcement, which is increasingly concerned with a more affluent group—young adults from middle-class backgrounds. The use of the law is spreading. Minorities—ethnic groups, women, homosexuals—are actively seeking legal means to improve their civil status. Young lawyers are voicing the view that law enforcement should apply not only to the lower and middle classes, but also to the more powerful in this country, whose known violations of the law have a widespread effect on American society (e.g., Cox, Fellmeth, and Schulz 1969). At the same time that the call for law enforcement has spread across classes, the problem of access to the legal system is ever more acute (Main 1970). Young law professionals participating in the major movement to change the system from within seize upon the law as a tool for structural change. We are living at a time when citizens are awake to the hope that they can protect themselves by means of the law, defend themselves by means of the law, and change the system by means of the law.

In the world of developing nations there is also much talk of law—as an instrument of social engineering, as a vehicle for consolidating nationalist movements and homogenizing heterogeneous populations, and as a means of entrenching power positions, both indigenous and foreign. The populations of these new nations have been experiencing and will continue to experience the difficulties of using conflicting and changing systems of law, often imported wholesale, often based on an alien value system. Those who regularly profit from sudden changes in the law are the growing classes of legal and paralegal professionals (Muratorio n.d.; Buxbaum 1961:26-43), and the political entrepreneurs responsible for the policy of the sometimes devastating melting-pot approach to nation-building through the law. Those who often suffer are the preliterate, the illiterate, the common people closest to urban centers—people whose indigenous systems of law are sabotaged under modernization pressures and for whom the imposition of centralized, professionalized law has decreased traditional access to law, at least until they learn by various means how to manipulate or use the newly introduced system.

It is against this backdrop of social ferment that we wish to discuss the more academic concerns of the anthropological study of law. We do this in the belief that it is healthy at least occasionally to assess the more traditional arguments and priorities in this field with some perspective stemming from a world wider than professional anthropology. Anthropology has developed a perspective that is useful in understanding something about the plasticity of human beings, and in this case about the myriad solutions needed to deal with problems such as the maintenance of continuity and predictability. Anthropologists of law in the past have developed their perspective by means of describing other cultures and by means of the generalizations they have been able to derive from their descriptions. Today we are still concerned with problems of description in our attempts to improve our knowledge of cross-cultural diversity in the field of law, of the con-

ditions underlying law, and of the consequences of alternative modes of law. In this, as in most young fields, we do not know much. We have hypotheses (intelligent hunches), loosely related minitheories, and some good descriptive data—all useful in problem-solving, all needed in building scientific knowledge. Therein lies the challenge.

Previous articles (Nader 1965b, Moore 1969) survey the literature and stress major themes in the study of law by anthropologists. The present essay will discuss selected themes and selected literature relevant to the interrelationship of law and other aspects of culture and society. It will attempt to explore a variety of issues thought to be important because they point toward questions of description, analysis, field techniques, function, and diversity that have not yet been mined.

ORGANIZING IDEAS

What constitutes an adequate ethnographic description of law? How do we measure this adequacy? What techniques do we use to acquire various kinds of descriptive materials? How is comparison used to reach more general levels of understanding? These are perennial questions, but the perspective from which they are now being asked has shifted along with the general trend in anthropology to focus on process rather than the organization and structure of institutions, on the network rather than the group. When old points of view are no longer productive, it's time to look at data from new vantage points.

Our discussion of descriptive approaches and techniques emphasizes a perspective on the anthropological study of law that may be labeled *ethnographic* rather than legalistic. A legalistic description of judicial decision-making might, for example, include a discussion of legal procedure, codes or statutes, and concepts like that of the reasonable man (March 1956). An ethnographic description of judicial decision-making would, *in addition*, include such factors as ascribed attributes of the users of the "court": whether the user is Indian or *Ladino*, black or white; whether he is born a citizen of one town or another; whether the participants are drunk or sober, rich or poor, educated or uneducated, numerous or few; whether the users are individuals or corporate groups; whether the court is congested or functionally suited to its case load; and whether the structure of the present case is related to past cases. These kinds of information are ethnographically crucial for an understanding of judicial decision-making, and they are critical for understanding the sociolegal consequences of a decision and the process through which it is achieved. As Gulliver (1969*b*:17) remarks, "The 'overly legalistic viewpoint among social scientists' in part explains that there should have been so little interest in the concern for the consequences of dispute settlement and legal action." Every good practicing lawyer uses a broad kind of ethnographic knowledge rather than the strictly legal in his attempt to win a case, simply because he knows this knowledge is relevant to the decision that is being made. Such data are, for the most part, traditionally ignored in jurisprudential theories of judicial decision-making, and it is not difficult to understand why. Llewelyn and Hoebel (1941:289) explained it this way:

Philosophers dealing with a particular society at a particular time may well hesitate to call anything "law" which does not meet their own standard of the just, lest by giving it a fair name they give it standing. But, sociological analysis must see legal institutions as they are: a result of the eternal interplay of interest and justice; a structured machinery which, however, at any given moment, is whatever it is, smoothly designed and lovely or a creaking semi-wreck. The test of its value lies in the work it accomplishes upon the law-jobs; but the test of its reality is what it is. . . .

Thurman Arnold (1935:70), irreverent but analytical, earlier pointed out that "the writings of jurisprudence should be considered as ceremonial observances rather than as scientific observations."

Malinowski (1942:1237), viewing the legal profession as a trade or craft, distinguishes the work of the sociologist or ethnographer from that of the lawyer in the following ways:

It is clear that this approach to primitive law and law in general is wider than that of the lawyer who is merely a craftsman in our modern legal system. The lawyer *qua* craftsman must primarily be interested in law breaking, in guiding of the clients' conduct so as to prevent punishment if not breach, in framing contracts and effecting compromises. All this brings about his professional involvements and his financial emoluments. The sociologist and the ethnographer on the other hand must primarily be interested in the working of social control, that is, in the maintenance of order. I would like to suggest that today jurisprudence must also take the deeper as well as the more comprehensive view of the problems of law.

It might in all fairness be added that the more profound legal thinkers would not be satisfied with Malinowski's description. They would argue that the study of law should go beyond ceremonial observances, and that such a study should contain something more than descriptions of an ideal self-contained system of handling lawbreakers. Willard Hurst (1960:521) has rejected the model of law as defined by many of his legal brethren as at the least unproductive:

Anglo-American law men are by tradition

and training biased toward equating law with what judges do, to the neglect not only of legislative, executive, and administrative activity, but also to the neglect even of the out-of-court impact of the work of lawyers, let alone the additions or subtractions made in legal order by lay attitudes and practices affecting legal norms.

And more specifically, regarding analyses (1960:522):

The bulk of legal history writing has been about topics defined by legal categories . . . there is some rather formal history of property law, but little history for the significance of fee simple title for types of land use, for the private and social accounting of income and costs of alternative land uses, or for the political and social balance of power. . . . Though better than a generation has gone by since we heard the call for a sociological jurisprudence, legal history writing has made little response, but continues content on the whole to let the formal headings of the law fix its subject matter. . . . It is odd that for so many states we have writing which with care, sometimes verging on antiquarian enthusiasm, traces the beginnings of territorial and state courts . . . but little good is the writing on such basic themes as law's relation to the creation of transportation networks, the law's response to the business cycle, or the relation of tax policy to the fortunes of agriculture and other extractive industries.

We have quoted from the works of both anthropologists and professors of law to indicate that in the fields of both law and anthropology leading scholars have thought it important to point out the intellectually debilitating consequences of studying law in terms of topics defined strictly by legal categories. Our bias here is apparent: anthropologists have been overly influenced by a model of law as defined by the legal profession, a model that tends, most obviously, to produce works that focus on legal codes, legal procedure, and legal concepts, with minimal attention to contextual data. Anthropologists (e.g., Moore 1969) often talk about their work on law as being contextual in orientation—as recognizing the relation between law and society, as seeing law as part of social life—but in fact we seem to do this mainly when we are dealing with gross classifications (e.g., Maine 1963), very little when we make explications of particular societies. All of this makes it very difficult to use monographic data to test refined propositions dealing with functional relations and processual patterns.

The legalistic model also influences work in anthropology of law in more subtle ways. Moore (1969:295) describes the goals of the anthropology of law as being "to understand more about the way in which legal institutions, rules, and ideas function as part of the framework within which ongoing social life is carried on, and how the processes of social life affect that very framework." Investigations of the effects of things legal on social life and of social life on things legal are, of course, significant aspects of anthropological law studies, yet in this particular way of focusing on law and society there is an implicit assumption that legal rules, institutions, and ideas are a realm unto themselves, affected by and affecting, but not in fact an aspect of, ongoing social life. This assumption underlies several outstanding contributions to the study of judicial institutions in a variety of societies, but the viewpoint based upon it is only one of many possibilities; if we are to develop an adequate ethnography of law, the angle of vision of the ethnographer needs to be broadened.

What, then, are the aims today of an ethnography of law, of any contextually descriptive anthropological study of law? What significant trends can be pointed to and in what previous works are these trends rooted? Ethnographic descriptions illustrative of the wider angle of vision we have mentioned have been available for some time; Malinowski 1926, Colson 1953, Gulliver 1963, Bailey 1960, and Turner 1957 are only a few, and there are several newer studies: Cicourel 1968, Gulliver 1969a, Graburn 1969, Spradley 1970. These studies indicate that an ethnography of law is not simply a description of "the law," a framework for social life, but rather a description of social processes deeply embedded in social contexts.

In addition, the ethnography of law, like other forms of ethnographic description, is a mapping of certain shared modes of perceiving, the behavioral referents of which are the law ways of the particular groups or collections of persons observed. The real value of such an ethnography is an understanding of the underlying rules of the game and of models of behavior. This approach implies that main emphasis is placed not on describing an "outside structure"—the legal framework within which ongoing social life is carried on—but on describing, so to speak, an "inside structure," which, if we assume its use by the people under investigation, will explain observed behavior. The focus of the study is on people interacting and not on a formalized legal system or the formal actors in that system, although the latter may comprise part of the shared perceptions the anthropologist is attempting to describe. The concept of an ethnography of law oriented toward a definition of the shared "legal perceptions" of the persons being studied directs the focus of research away from the legal system of a territorially or politically definable group—a group that may, but often does not, share legal and other social concepts. Such an ethnography would instead focus research on a network of persons that in its own terms and in those of its social context is defined as a unit, what Barth (1969) would call an

"ethnic group." This approach, as we shall see later on, necessarily directs the focus away from monolithic use of the "case approach." The unit for observation will be the network of involved persons, which would include a judge but not as the exclusive focus of attention (Nader 1969c, Yngvesson n.d.).

An "ethnic group," in Barth's (1969:11) sense of the term, is a group that "has a membership which identifies itself, and/or is identified by others, as constituting a category distinguishable from other categories of the same order." The cultural characteristics of an ethnic category are those the actors regard as significant. Such cultural features include overt signals and signs (dress, language, etc.) and basic value orientations (1969:15):

The identification of another person as a fellow member of an ethnic group implies a sharing of criteria for evaluation and judgment. It thus entails the assumption that the two are fundamentally "playing the same game." . . . On the other hand, a dichotomization of others as strangers, as members of another ethnic group, implies a recognition of limitations on shared understandings, differences in criteria for judgment of value and performance, and a restriction of interaction to sectors of assumed common understanding and mutual interest.

Applying Barth's analysis to the domain of law, one could ask how persons who define themselves as falling within the boundaries of a particular category resolve issues involving conflict and the maintenance of social order—both within that category or "ethnic group" and across ethnic boundaries. Studies by Cox (1968) among the Hopi, by Starr (1969) in Turkey, and by Collier (1970) on Zinacantan Indian law in Mexico address themselves implicitly to this question, as does Yngvesson's dissertation (1970) on dispute settlement in a Scandinavian community. Yngvesson describes a situation in which one set of rules (stressing tolerance, nonassertive behavior, consensus decisions regarding sanctions, and community-wide sanctioning mechanisms) is applied within the "ethnic group," and a quite different set (calling for immediate response by the offended party and extracommunity third-party resolution mechanisms) when interethnic relations are involved.

In Spradley's *You Owe Yourself a Drunk* (1970), issues that are implicitly dealt with in the studies cited above are treated explicitly. Spradley asks (1970:184): "How do members of the group dealt with [Seattle urban nomads] classify and define themselves and the social identity of those with whom they interact?" He is particularly concerned with the interaction of tramps with institutions of law enforcement, and concludes that "the legal system of America and the criminal justice practice are based on norms and values which are in contrast to those of the urban nomad. Judges are socialized into the dominant society and learn to dispense justice on the basis of those values." Much of Spradley's book is devoted to an analysis of the way drunks structure their interaction with this system and their forced passage through it, and he concludes that incarceration, intended as punishment for public drunkenness, becomes a cause of public drunkenness. The book lends support to Barth's (1969) contention that interethnic social encounters—in this case, encounters over law—are as much structured and subject to rules as are relations within an ethnic group.

Cahn and Cahn's (1966) article "What Price Justice?" which discusses the possibility and usefulness of establishing neighborhood corporation-type courts in the United States, makes similar assumptions, utilizing an economic model to measure the quality of prod-

ucts "merchandized by the legal system." The authors assume the existence of subgroups with values and needs different from those held by the larger society, and suggest that we should create a legal system responsive to these, on the assumption that shared criteria for evaluation and judgment are essential components of a just administration of the law. The creation of such a system requires research leading to the definition of boundaries of shared models for behavior—legal and otherwise—and of rules of the game patterning behavior within and across boundaries (see Goodenough 1957, Geertz 1965, Barth 1969).

Studies like those cited relate to the questions of how law should be administered in a polyethnic society and whether local problems can in fact be satisfactorily dealt with through a national legal system that is unresponsive to local norms and that does not operate according to the local rules of the game. More attention to such aspects as cultural boundary zones, disparate models and rules, and variations in use patterns leads us away from the view that this or any other nation has "a" legal system. It fosters instead, as we noted above, an emphasis on networks of persons sharing values and principles regarding dispute resolution. As Aubert (1969*b*:277) has suggested, these may reflect pervasive structural features of the society being studied and point toward an inquiry into other social factors that may correlate with the particular kinds of law models defined. There may be far greater similarities in the conceptual models—relating both to law and to other aspects of social life—of a community in Apalachia, a small mountain tribe in New Guinea, a fishing village in Scandinavia, and a business firm in the United States than between any of these networks of persona and the larger political units of which they are a part. Nader (1969c) documents similarities in the conceptual models relating to styles of dispute settlement in such diverse locales as a Norwegian administrative agency, the indigeneous courts of northern India, an African tribal group, a California small claims court, and a village court among the Zapotec Indians of Mexico, and suggests that the compromise model of dispute settlement is generated by interactions that flow from particular patterns of social relations.

Although it is not our intention here to go into an extended treatment of descriptive studies in the anthropology of law, a few key works that have made significant contributions to our present interests merit special discussion. The aim here is to place these works in the context of a discussion of the ideas to which they have contributed: (1) a stress on law as a process rather than a framework—on the settlement of a conflict and the mechanisms through which this is achieved, rather than on the definition of legal rules and the identification of particular agencies or parties formally backed by force and endowed with authority; (2) an interest in the social context of dispute resolution and in the influence of this context on the process; (3) (as implied in part by 2) an interest in the litigants and in their relationships to each other as well as to all other persons involved in settlement procedures; (4) an interest in multiple systems within one society and in the bases for and strategies involved in choosing one resolution mode over another; (5) the use of an extended case, or a sequence of related cases, to illustrate in detail the processes and strategies involved. At least one of these is a central focus in each of the works discussed below.

In his conclusion to *Crime and Custom in Savage Society*, Malinowski (1926:125) notes:

Throughout our discussion we found the real problem not in bald enumeration of rules, but in the ways and means by which these are carried out. Most instructive we found the study of the life situations which call for a given rule, the manner in which this is handled by the people concerned, the reaction of the community at large, the consequences of fulfillment or neglect. All this, which could be called the cultural context of a primitive system of rules, is equally important, if not more so, than the mere recital of a fictitious native *corpus juris*.

Although Malinowski has been much maligned for the stress he placed on reciprocity and "binding obligations," and his corresponding lack of emphasis on legal rules and formal legal institutions, his approach set the stage for a needed reappraisal of the place of law in social life. In spite of this, the three decades following publication of his work produced few anthropological works on law bearing the imprint of his views. The students of the ethnography of law during this period—Hoebel (1940, 1954), Gluckman (1955, 1956), Bohannan (1969), Pospisil (1958b, 1969), Schapera (1938, 1969), Richardson (1940), to name a few—are strongly oriented toward the view that law, in the guise of legal rules and institutions, is a framework within which social life is carried out. Furthermore, they evidence a corresponding neglect of the analysis of legal processes as social processes that go on prior to, following, and at times to the exclusion of any "formal" law procedures in the society in question. The continuing influence of these writers is discussed in a number of recent articles, including two survey articles by Nader (1965b) and Moore (1969).

Writers of ethnographic studies of law who stress the importance of function rather than form are beginning to have more weight, and it is time to discuss the important and neglected contributions of these scholars, who set guidelines for the study of law as the study of those social processes that come into operation when a prescribed rule is violated (Nader 1965a:6). Hogbin (1934), who was heavily influenced by Malinowski, is an example. Colson's 1953 article, "Social Control and Vengeance in Plateau Tonga Society," although in no way similar to the works of the Malinowski-Hogbin type, reflects some of the concerns expressed by Malinowski and represents a major early contribution containing in a condensed form the principal elements characterizing the best work in the field today. It is significant that the article ignores the issue of whether "law" is present or absent among the Plateau Tonga. Rather, by focusing on one detailed case of homicide, the author shows how members of the society concerned handle a breach of prescribed rules, and demonstrates through careful analysis how a complex network of cross-linkages serves to hold in check a potentially escalatory situation. She also touches on considerations of strategy, pointing to the choices open to parties involved, given the structural situation she has defined. Colson's emphases on (1) the processes of control, (2) the relation of these processes to structural considerations, (3) the importance of litigants' strategies for manipulating the structure, and (4) the use of detailed case materials to illustrate the relationship between these three elements have become prominent features of much current work in this field.

Turner's *Schism and Continuity in an African Society* (1957) picks up many of the threads of analysis found in Colson's article. Here the operation of social control processes is demonstrated through a detailed analysis of five cases, each of which involves some of the same principals and all of which

are part of a developing sequence portraying shifts in the balance of power between key individuals and groups in an Ndembu community. Turner calls this sequence of cases a "social drama." The analysis of litigant strategies is an important feature of the monograph, which documents the problems faced by individuals caught up in structural, as well as interpersonal, conflict situations in their quest for power. Turner's analysis of conflict among the Ndembu is in essence an analysis of political process in a particular Ndembu community; in this work, then, the dichotomy between "law process" and social process is nonexistent.

Schwartz's article "Social Factors in the Development of Legal Control: A Case Study of Two Israeli Settlements" (1954), while primarily addressed to the question of legal development, also deals in some detail with social control process in two Israeli communities and documents the degree to which the social and the legal merge in one of the settlements. Schwartz relates this merging to features of social organization in one of the settlements, and contrasts this situation with that of the other community, in which separate legal institutions are in evidence. Schwartz straddles the fence between the two general approaches to law that have been discussed; he is primarily interested in pinpointing criteria that will account for the presence or absence of certain forms of law, but to accomplish this he must investigate social control processes and their social correlates, at a more general level.

A third important work indicating concerns similar to those of Colson and Turner is Bailey's *Tribe, Caste, and Nation* (1960). Here also, as in Turner's work, the development and resolution of disputes are closely tied to political processes. In a chapter entitled "A Dispute in Baderi," Bailey analyzes in detail the strategies used by parties to the dispute, placing them in the context of competition for power within the town and showing how this competition takes the form of the manipulation of the different kinds of social system of which the disputants are a part. In Bailey's work, to a greater degree than in Turner's and Schwartz's studies, social control and dispute resolution are reduced to a "pure process," so to speak, in which "structures" are simply tools to be used in maximizing the benefits of individual litigants. The significant rules in such a situation are rules of the game, not jural or cultural postulates that act as moral constraints on behavior, although these are present. Cases are used as data for the analysis of strategies and as indices of changing alignments, rather than as sources for legal (or other social) norms or as evidence of the presence or absence of a particular "legal" institution or its functional equivalent.

While Bailey does not relate his discussion of political structure and political process to the question of multiple systems of conflict resolution (or "legal levels"), his work points to the importance of considering such multiple systems, or structures, in any ethnography of law (Bailey 1960:197):

We can describe "the structure" standing by itself; but if we are to describe the "structure in action," we have to think no longer of *the* structure, but rather of several structures, which together set a limit to the possible ways of behaving, but at the same time permit the individual to pursue his own ends by choosing to use whatever relationship he finds most advantageous at that particular time.

Gulliver's *Social Control in an African Society* (1963) is another significant contribution in the trend toward analysis of law processes as social processes, subject to other social, as against specifically "legal," constraints and incen-

tives. His work provides an excellent analysis of the way social control processes function at various levels of the social system, here the parish and age-group system, the patrilineal descent system, and the modern local government among the Arusha in northern Tanganyika. Gulliver (1963:173) describes the role of these systems in effecting social control:

Firstly, two of them provide a set of corporate groups or established categories of people, which largely determine both the kind and the strength of support and constraint to which men are subject when disputes occur and settlement of them is attempted. Secondly, each of these sub-systems identifies a number of particular roles of influence and leadership, the occupants of which, *inter alia*, play a permanent part in the arrangement for and the carrying out of dispute procedures as advisors, advocates, conciliators. Thirdly, each sub-system provides regularized means for dealing with overt conflict and dispute between individuals.

In a section entitled "Processes of Dispute Settlement," Gulliver explains how the three subsystems are used, stating rules governing choice between one system and another, discussing strategies, and giving a detailed account of settlement processes operating in each system. As in Bailey's work, the emphasis is on several systems operating within one society. Bailey places greater emphasis on the actors and views the systems as limiting factors on their actions; Gulliver stresses the functioning of the systems themselves throughout most of his book, but in the final chapter he reverses the viewpoint and considers the use of the systems from the perspective of the actors involved.

The concern with multiple systems of social control within one society is again demonstrated in an article by Nader and Metzger, "Conflict Resolution in Two Mexican Communities"

(1963). Here again the viewpoint is on law as seen from below: What strategies do husbands and wives use in each of the two towns when deciding how to resolve a conflict? Within what limits are these choices confined—that is, what is the range of remedy agents available to the disputants? What aspects of social organization and demography are correlated with choice patterns in each of the towns? The focus is on the means by which conflicts are resolved and on the underlying reasons for the resolution patterns. When conflict resolution is viewed from this perspective, a whole range of remedy agents must be considered, rather than simply a formal legal system.

The idea that several social control systems operate within one society and that each of these functions within a specific domain or at particular levels of the society is further discussed by Pospisil in his article "Legal Levels and Multiplicity of Legal Systems in Human Societies" (1967). This article develops in greater detail the implications of an approach to social control found in several of the works previously discussed. Pospisil approaches the problem from above, asking what legal institutions are present in a society rather than how people in this society resolve their conflicts. Yet both approaches build on the evidence that many modes of dispute settlement are available and lead to considerations of social context and its relationship to social control mechanisms. The initial focus on people in conflict, people disputing, rather than on the institutional framework for resolution, generates in addition studies oriented toward considerations of process, with particular emphasis on patterns of choice and strategies. This focus on the dispute process should reveal how and to what degree disputes or conflicts are shaped by the presence of specific dispute-resolving mechanisms.

Most of the works discussed above have focused on the ways in which people handle grievances, as functions of the kinds of relationships in which they are involved, and correspondingly have deemphasized legal rules and law as functions of authority. The rules defined in most of these works are rules of the game, related to strategies and goals sought by the litigants. Frequently the concept of law dealt with in a work encompasses not one but a multiplicity of systems available as alternatives for conflict resolution.

AN EVALUATION OF
THE CASE METHOD

Perspectives on what should go into a description are, of course, intimately related to methods used, and vice versa. In part because anthropologists, like lawyers, have invested their energies principally in understanding dispute settlement and litigation in general, we have for the past several decades found the case method particularly useful. Or it may be that as a result of concentrating on cases we developed an interest in dispute settlement. Of course, all ethnographic fieldworkers collect cases, no matter what the focus of interest, simply in the process of examining particulars prior to or as part of generalization. In the anthropological study of law, the word "case" has usually referred to the gathering of materials about disputes. We have used the case method in the search for systemic aspects of procedural and substantive law, for uncovering important jural postulates, for abstracting values important to a society. These cases have been varied in form and content and even in the names anthropologists have given them: the trouble case, the extended case. They have varied in their sources; there are cases that have been observed, cases taken from recorded materials such as archival records, cases taken from memory, and hypothetical cases. Very often these distinctions are not recognized as important, and memory cases, for example, may be treated as equivalent to observed cases, with little attempt to differentiate the principles underlying memory patterns and those underlying direct observation by the ethnographer (see Berndt 1962).

By focusing our attention on "the case" as a framework for data collection, we have tended to ignore much information that might have added to our knowledge, not only about the cases themselves, but about other aspects of law in the society we are investigating. The use of interviews, questionnaires, and dockets, participant observation, and the observation of what Malinowski refers to as "law-abiding" patterns, all can provide us with other kinds of information than that usually classified in a "case" format. A new perspective might be provided by asking the question: What are we missing by so concentrating our attention on the case approach, extended or not? In this section on techniques, the use of cases as a framework for data collection will be discussed and critically evaluated; in addition we shall suggest the form future explorations might take by discussing the importance of using techniques such as interviews, participant observation, and so on as a means of collecting a wider range of data pertinent to law than cases alone. To a large extent, the relevance of these types of data becomes evident only when the concept of "ethnography of law" has been redefined along the lines we suggested above.

As we have mentioned earlier, the emphasis on process, choice, motivation, and the like give rise to ever more sophisticated use of the case method (Gulliver 1969b:13):

The prime concern in the general field of anthropology of law is the study of processes, and in particular, the processes of dispute settlement. . . . Here the fundamental unit of study is the case, the empirical dispute, and its mode of treatment. The thorough examination of detailed case material is likely to be the most rewarding procedure, as it already has been in the best literature. But, of course, it must be an examination within the full socio-cultural context of the dispute cases.

As Gulliver (1969b) points out, use of the case method is hardly new in this field. It is not simply the use of cases, however, but the way they are used that marks a change in the anthropology of law in the last decade or so. Llewelyn and Hoebel (1941), for example, viewed a case as a means for discovering the "law jobs" of a society and the "administrative machinery" available for attacking them; their interests were directed toward the ways devised by a particular society for handling problems that they considered of a universal nature. Barton (1919, 1949), who utilized the case method considerably earlier than did Llewelyn and Hoebel, used cases to provide data on offenses, on sanctions, and on the elements of "modern legal mechanisms" employed by the Ifugao and the Kalingas. He also used case materials (particularly in *The Kalingas* [1949]) as sources for rules of substantive law in the society he was studying. A more recent example of the use of cases to a similar end is Pospisil's *Kapauku Papuans and Their Law* (1958a). In all these examples the authors emphasized the use of the case method to describe "law" as a domain in its own right in the societies they studied.

Cases have also been used, of course, and are currently being used, as sources specifically for data on the interrelationship of law and particular features of social organization: Gluckman (1965) uses case materials from his earlier (1955) work to show how the ideas about law held by the Barotse are related to status relationships in Barotse society; Nader (1964a) analyzes sixty Zapotec law cases with a view to discovering what they reveal about Zapotec social organization; Nader (1965a) examines the relation between types of social grouping (such as dual organization) and legal procedure; Nader and Metzger (1963) investigate the relation between family structure and use of the courts for resolving marital conflicts; Burridge (1957) uses case materials to illustrate the relationship between law and political authority; Gibbs (1962) analyzes case materials to establish a relationship between a society's judicial procedures and results, on the one hand, and the existence of a strong and unchallenged respect for authority in the society, on the other. Many other such studies could be cited. They have in common the use of case material primarily as sources for a variety of data regarding law *and* society; for example, the relation of a particular form of social system to a given type of legal system, the social correlates of grievance behavior, the functions of law in a particular society, and so on.

In the Introduction to *Law in Culture and Society* (1969a:10), Nader remarks on the increasing "reluctance to draw tight boundaries around the domain of law," and cites Professor Lon Fuller (Nader 1969a:8): "By speaking of law *and* society we may forget the law is itself a part of a society, that its basic processes are social processes, that it contains within its own internal workings social dimensions worthy of the best attentions of the sociologist." While excellent work continues, and should continue, in investigating law *and* society relationships, the "reluctance to draw tight boundaries" is generating new interest in, and new approaches to, the study of anthropology of law.

As we have mentioned, an integral aspect of this approach involves what Epstein (1967:230) refers to as a resetting of the dispute case "in the framework of the on-going social process from which it was abstracted." Stemming from work by Colson (1953), Mitchell (1956), Turner (1957), Bailey (1960), and Van Velsen (1964), there is a growing tendency now in studies of the anthropology of law to view the core of a dispute case as simply one stage in a developing process that may have begun many years earlier, with consequences that may continue for some time to affect social relations in the unit under study. A series of interrelated cases may be involved concerning some or all of the same actors (Gulliver 1969a, Turner 1957), or there may be one or more separated but extended cases (Colson 1953, Bailey 1960); in each instance one sees developments and alterations in the balance of power between the individuals involved. In this use of the case method the "law process," as embodied in the dispute event, and the "social process," as seen throughout the developing case, are not viewed as separate. The case becomes an arena in which various structural principles are brought into play through the operations or transactions of the principal actors involved. Thus utilized, cases may become diagnostic tools for pinpointing stress areas in the social structure of the community studied (Turner 1957), illustrating which issues the people involved perceive to be conflict-engendering and the relationships into which conflict is structured in that society. Cases utilized in this way have been called "extended cases" (Gluckman 1961, Van Velsen 1967). An extended case may comprise a series of related cases through time, involving some or all of the same actors; or it may comprise one detailed case followed over a period of months or years. In each instance, the dispute in question is viewed within the social context in which it develops and is played out, allowing the analyst to trace developments and alterations in the balance of power between the individuals involved. Bailey (1960), Turner (1957), Starr (1969), and Yngvesson (1970) have used extended dispute cases in this way, focusing on the description and analysis of strategies used by litigants and the remedy agents sought in obtaining a desired end.

Bailey's work, particularly, illustrates the manipulation of different systems by individuals in achieving a particular aim-Metzger (1960) wrote a classic, though rarely cited, essay that utilized coalition theory to document the relation between balance of power, outcome, and classes of individuals involved in conflict. Yngvesson's dissertation points to similar developmental patterns underlying social processes in various domains of social life, similarities that were discovered through the "situational" analysis of behavior in the various domains. The similarities in process pointed further to pervasive (and often nonexplicit) values and norms governing social interaction in the community, irrespective of whether the persons were involved in law relations, political relations, or economic relations. For example, the norm that "each adult person in the village must treat others as equals," and the structural implications of this rule, affected conflict resolution, political decision-making, and the distribution of economic returns in business.

Cases may also be useful as tools for isolating conceptual boundaries that separate one group from another. In the analysis of dispute cases, a choice of settlement mechanisms that consistently results in differential treatment of certain persons can point the ethnographer to a more extended investigation of the relationship between these

persons and the sanctioning group. In Yngvesson's (1970) research, accurate definition of the conceptual boundary separating "insiders" from "outsiders" in the Scandinavian community under study was facilitated by such an analysis. This research, and that of others, suggests that methods of dispute settlement—and often the very recognition of a situation as a dispute—depend on the degree to which parties to the dispute consider themselves to be operating within or across ethnic boundaries.

It is interesting that the most avid users of the situational (Van Velsen 1964) or extended case approach have for the most part reported from societies where courts are not present; and where courts are present, or at least recently introduced, these same ethnographers collect few cases from the courts to report on, and then do not use the extended case approach in dealing with the cases (see Gulliver 1963, chaps. 9 and 10). As has been discussed earlier, there is (1) *process* to be described in the connections between the court system and other dispute-settling mechanisms in any society, and also (2) *process* within the court system as well. Unfortunately, recorded cases, whether from U.S. or Zambian files, normally do not contain information on process, which then has to be observed or elicited, and which should contain descriptions of informal (extralegal) procedures as well as judicial procedures and also descriptions of the interactions and transactions important to understanding the process.

Cases taken from memory are frequently used, but they are ethnographically useful only if the ethnographer has compared enough cases collected by various means (memory, observation, use of hypothetical situations, records, and so on) to understand the principles that are disclosed by the patterns of selectivity underlying memory cases (or, in another area, underlying the choice of material to be placed in the record). Koch (1967) collected both memory and observed cases. Nearly all of his memory cases contain greater amounts and degrees of violence and bloodshed than the observed cases. Berndt's *Excess and Restraint* (1962) consists almost entirely of memory cases reported by New Guinea men in their living quarters, and nearly all of the cases are characterized by excess rather than restraint. The use of the memory case collected in this way is comparable to the conclusions that might be reached by a foreign ethnographer who visited a U.S. college town and collected case materials from a fraternity house, or based a description of the American legal system on a reading of something like the *New York Daily News*.

Jan Vansina's *Oral Tradition: A Study in Historical Methodology* (1965) is very helpful on these points. He reminds us (1965:95) that "a major source of error and falsification is the influence exerted on the contents of a testimony by the functions of the testimony, and the purposes of the informant. Functions and purposes ultimately derive from the social structure of the society being studied." He further instructs us in methods of analyzing the structure of a testimony so that we may be able to discern the various possible sources of distortions and falsifications made by the informant. He cautions us (1965:53) to distinguish between individual and group testimonies, those resulting from disputes and those from questioning: "It is imprudent to interpret a testimony without first knowing its structure." These are all methodological dos and don'ts that have not received much attention, certainly not from those who collect and analyze law cases in preliterate societies. Lack of attention to such problems at the appropriate time leads to

controversies later on, such as those discussed by Graburn (1969) in his account of variant behavior among the Eskimos, and the varied interpretations of these behaviors by anthropologists.

Gluckman (1955:52-53) cautions us on the differences between cases observed by a trained observer and those collected by a native aide. And anyone who knows how court cases are recorded by officials in most societies knows the pitfalls of interpreting such materials as if they were comprehensive descriptions. We are not suggesting here that the only useful case materials are those observed and recorded *in situ* by the anthropologist. We are saying that each type of case has its uses and limitations, and that each type of case needs to be systematically examined to determine exactly what those uses and limitations are.

Richard Abel (1969), in his study of the customary law of wrongs in Kenya, discusses the relative values of the case method and the interview for eliciting a sophisticated statement of substantive rules. He argues (1969:577) that by the criteria of specificity, comprehensiveness (the full range of legal prescriptions), and representativeness, the case-method approach is far superior to the interview for collecting a body of substantive rules. "When research focuses on actual cases it is immediately clear whether a stated rule is evidenced by numerous, mutually confirming, applications, or is merely the reflection of isolated, and therefore suspect happenstance." (See Goldschmidt 1967 for an example of rule-directed interviews.)

Barton (1919) devoted about two-thirds of his book to substantive rules, which are often presented without case materials and with little discussion of the means by which he arrived at his laws or decided a rule could be labeled as law, except insofar as the rule falls within a class of Western legal concepts: family, property, penalty, and the like. Sometimes it is clear he is deriving legal rules from case material. But the problem of how one distinguishes substantive law from all other rules in a society—such as those dealing with residence, marriage, inheritance, borrowing, and the like—other than through the case approach is not clarified by Barton's work, nor, in spite of various attempts, has it been clarified by anyone else.

Pospisil (1965) analyzes inheritance rules among the Kapauku. But by means of what assumptions and with what evidence can we call these rules, so elegantly analyzed by Pospisil, law? The case method scores high in usefulness, but it may be that the exploration of rules governing the *definition of infractions* is due for a revival. Given the headway in methodological orientation that ethnoscientific eliciting has afforded us, we may do better than Barton (1919) or Dundas (1915) or Goldschmidt (1967) at rule-directed interviews.

Let us take another example of type case material and its possible use—that most abridged form of case recording, the docket. At most, dockets may record the names of the litigants (and usually thereby their sexes), their places of residence, and the cause for action. Such data alone would not be useful in the same way that extended case materials are. Nader (n.d.) is using docket materials from the district court of Villa Alta, Oaxaca, Mexico, as a way of determining the range of complaints accepted by the district court, a starting point in understanding the relationship between the municipal courts of the Villa Alta district and the district court itself. In using docket materials, one can ask specific questions aimed at verifying or disproving hypotheses: What is the frequency of cases per village and the percentage distribution by

class, age, and so on? What are the number of "crimes" recorded per capita? What is the relative rate per village of each type of crime that is brought before the district court and accepted for adjudication? Where do intervillage disputes occur and to what degree of seriousness? From these data we can make summary statements that will allow us to predict *what* and *how much*, although the data will not allow us to answer *why* questions. For instance, it was noted that some villages refer mainly homicide cases, others mainly theft and property cases, others mainly rape and sex cases. But we don't know why. The statements themselves suggest the kind of questions the investigator might wish to pursue in a more ethnographic fashion (see Hunt and Hunt 1967). At any rate, dockets could be useful in the early stages of research as introductory probes. However, we need to be appropriately cautious in the use of criminal statistics, as is well illustrated by Black's article (1970) on "Production of Crime Rates." It is clear that the dockets Nader is analyzing define the domain of social control of the Villa Alta court more closely than they define the deviance that actually occurs. Many cases, such as those initiated by children against their parents, are simply not accepted as legal cases under Mexican law. As Black notes (1970: 733), "Theory has not directed inquiry to the principles and mechanisms by which some technically illegal acts are recorded in that official ledger of crime while others are not."

In addition to case type materials, most anthropologists use other techniques, such as loosely structured or open-ended interviews. If anthropologists who study law have used more tightly structured interviews, they have rarely published them. One form of interview—eliciting—has been used by Black and Metzger (1965) to produce information about the terminology used by American lawyers to distinguish various types of lawyers, as well as to elicit native categories of crime, procedure, and the like among the Tzeltal Indians of Chiapas. Nader (n.d.), in exploring a number of subjects with Zapotec judges, used an extensive form of interview, which yielded a variety of information elucidating the range of options and conditions available in a court. These options permit the judge to decide the guilt or innocence of an accused person, fine him, jail him, or all three. The interviews also disclosed a range of characteristics that define good and bad judges. A good judge may "have a head," a bad judge may "have no head" or "have a hot head." A good judge "judges" (that is, he hears a case out rather than fining without judgment, is patient rather than impatient, and so on). The interviews defined the various types of cases (light or heavy, long or short), the types of sanctions (correction or shame), the types of litigants (good or stubborn, drunk or sober, and so on), and the degrees of seriousness and their characteristics. Much of the information elicited by the interviews could be eked out of case materials, and so in some sense the interviews increase the validity of hypotheses generated from case materials. Case materials, however, do not often tell us crucial facts—for example, about the organization of the court, recruitment of personnel, attitudes of the litigants, and the like. Intensive interviews reveal this sort of information rather quickly, and are particularly useful if the specific questions and answers are reported.

Although our heavy concentration on the case method for the past couple of decades has been productive for our study of forms of dispute settlement as they relate to patterns of social relationships, the case method leaves a number of other interesting questions

of culture unexplored: Why do people obey laws? Under what conditions do violations of the rules, go unsanctioned? How are people socialized in regard to the legal rules of a particular society? What are the processes of cultural labeling? What are popular attitudes toward the law, and what, indeed, are the manifold functions of law? These paths need exploring.

In earlier portions of this essay we have drawn attention to some of these lacunae. Malinowski's *Crime and Custom in Savage Society* (1926) stressed the need to understand something about the reasons people obey laws and the principles on which these reasons are based, and he viewed a study of obedience to law as complementary to the study of lawbreaking, which focuses on the dispute or trouble case. It is very important that such complementary studies be carried out if we are to avoid the mistaken belief that it is law and only law that keeps people law-abiding. Law is but one form of social control (Nadel, 1953), and in most societies in the world not even the most important one. In fact, when people begin to assume that law is the major form of social control, we can *ipso facto* deduce that the society is not in a healthy state or that it is in a state of very rapid change, which can be tolerated or managed only by totalitarian legal order. Jane Jacobs (1968:214-15) observes the maintenance of order in this way: "We must understand that the public peace—the sidewalk and street peace—of cities is not kept primarily by the police, necessary though they are. It is kept primarily by an intricate, almost unconscious, network of voluntary controls and standards among the people themselves." It is this "intricate network of voluntary controls and standards" that interested Malinowski, and such a subject can hardly be studied by means of the situational or extended case method, but rather by an understanding of the total social and cultural system. It was by means of a systemic focus that anthropologists first discovered the existence of societies that were viable and stable even though they lacked central government (Colson 1953, Evans-Pritchard 1940). By viewing society as a whole, anthropologists recognized the roles played by gossip, public opinion, segmental opposition, conflicting loyalties, rituals of rebellion, and the like as mechanisms of social control (see Gluckman 1956 for useful summary examples of these mechanisms at work). It was through a study of descent and affiliation patterns that the degree or intensity of marital conflict, as symbolized by divorce, was discovered to be related to the type of affiliation pattern, patrilineal or matrilineal, of the society. These mechanisms, crucial for developing an understanding of law-abiding patterns, were not discovered by the case-method approach. Furthermore, as Muir (1967) has shown in his study of *Prayer in the Public Schools*, compliance with the law cannot always be measured by recorded violation; Muir heavily utilizes questionnaires to get at the reasons for compliance or noncompliance with the Supreme Court decision on school prayer. In addition to compliance studies by political scientists, we have sociological experiments such as the one carried out by Schwartz and Orleans (1967), who explored the ways in which compliance and noncompliance with tax laws are influenced by popular attitudes toward various types of sanctions.

Closely related to the study of law-abiding patterns and compliance studies are works such as that by Stirling (1957). He examines citizens' motives for using or avoiding newly instituted legal codes in Turkey, and in the process discovers that their use patterns

stem from their perspective on a set of valued personal relations (1957:26-27):

First, when a landowner dies, the people most nearly involved are all on the spot, living in his household, or at least in the same village or group of villages. These people have a multiplicity of relationships and of formal and informal rights and duties to each other. The readjustments which the removal of the head of a kinship group requires are considerable, and it is better to take these slowly, and work out the redistribution of property rights *ad hoc*, than to call in officials who will ruthlessly apply the legally correct rules, and force all the permanent and final rearrangements of ownership to be made at once.

Hahm, in his paper "Korea's Initial Encounter with Western Law," attempts to account for general disrespect for and avoidance of the law among Koreans (1968:93):

It is the tragedy of modern Korean legal history that every step of the "reforms" and "modernization" was accompanied by a progressive loss of national independence. It was not so much that the initial encounter with international law was unpleasant or even humiliating. It was the fact that even the loss of judicial sovereignty was justified in the name of modernization of the judiciary or the possible termination of extraterritoriality. Henceforth, the Westernized legal system of Korea was to labor under the weight of tremendous amounts of ill-will built up against it among the populace.

Compliance with the law, acceptance and use of the legal system, respect for the law, obedience to the law, all are part of the study of popular attitudes toward the law, but we do not yet have in anthropology, which claims to be the study of culture, a comparative study of such phenomena, nor have we studied, in any systematic way, concepts comparable to the Western concept of justice. In other words, anthropology has focused on social structure rather than on cultural structure. As L. H. Friedman (1969:28) has so aptly put it, "The legal culture provides fuel for the motor of justice; social values and attitudes fill in the missing elements needed to explain uses, nonuses, misuses, and abuses of legal process and the legal system."

There are some exceptions in the sociological literature, such as L. H. Ross (1961) on "Traffic Law Violation: A Folk Crime." Such topics, surprisingly underexplored by anthropologists, need to make use of an eclectic methodology—the case approach, participant observation, native eliciting procedures, and the like. Spradley's work (1970) is a pioneer attempt by an anthropologist to get at the culture structure that regulates interaction between tramps and the legal system with which they have intimate contact. Hahm (1969a) speaks of popular attitudes toward law and legal institutions; in studying a culture such as that of Korea, in which people conscientiously avoid the law—a culture Hahm describes as alegal in comparison with the legalistic West—he resorts to interviews and survey questionnaires for data on attitudes (1967:218-38; 1970:1-23), on history (1969b), and on patterns of social interaction (1967: 187-204). As pointed out earlier, Hurst (1960) sees popular attitudes as important in molding the future development of law in America, as does Pound (1906:399), when he notes that ordinarily legal precepts change because public opinion has changed. If legal precepts do not change along with public opinion, the consequences is a law out of step with the citizenry. Such a law is vividly portrayed by Massell (1968) for Soviet Central Asia.

Other areas, such as the selective enforcement of the law, have been virtually ignored by anthropologists. How does one study the cases that never get prosecuted? There is a paucity of data on this topic in ethnographies of law, in part because the focus on the case method leads us to study the actual enforcement of the law rather than patterns of selectivity. Such questions as why large corporations sue when they have no intention of going to court are not answered by an analysis of case records, since the "case" never gets to court. Similarly, if we were to investigate violations of laws enforced by administrative agencies in this country, we would find that, owing to the informal means of dealing with such cases, few violations are on the record. How can we record a latent function of the law—the law as threat—used by the litigant who has easy access to the court by virtue of having ample time and money?

The ethnographic study of the law should be a study both of what happens *and* of what doesn't happen in enforcement (which would include sanctions) and use patterns. Criminologists and sociologists in the United States have pointed out that certain forms of deviance are unequally distributed in society, that the incidence of violence is not random, and that the recorded distribution of crime implies that the economically underprivileged somehow have a monopoly on certain criminal behavior. For example, one researcher notes, "These data may suffice to substantiate the view that lower position in the status hierarchy of American society and the frustrations which lower position brings in its wake lead to higher homicide rates" (Coser 1968:74). The data on such rates come from cases recorded by enforcement officers, but, as has been pointed out, criminality can be produced or virtually ignored by law-enforcement officials (Sax 1967). Cicourel's work of 1968 is illustrative; he shows that juvenile offenders from low-income families and from middle-to-high-income families are treated differentially by law-enforcement officers, by teachers, and by members of their kin groups, and concludes that middle-to-upper-class delinquents, like white-collar criminals, enjoy a historical advantage within the legal system. In exploring how a juvenile comes to be labeled delinquent, Cicourel leads us again to question the police statistics on delinquent acts, which indicate that most crime is committed by ghetto residents.

It is most important, particularly for anthropologists who study stratified societies, to devise methods for discovering patterns of selective enforcement. In smaller, nonstratified societies, this kind of information is usually learned through channels of public opinion. One way to explore selective enforcement in complex societies is by examining what sociologists describe as the process of labeling—what behavior is labeled as "criminal" and "violent," what violent behavior goes unlabeled, and how all this relates to the kinds of individuals who are more generally prosecuted (L. H. Ross 1961. Quinney 1970, Black 1970, Schur 1969). Ethnoscientific techniques may be useful here, but so would the comparative method. It would have been useful for a study such as Coser's, for example, if he had done his study across classes. Would his theory of relative deprivation, used to explain why some low-status groups show high homicide rates and others do not, have explained the pattern of white-collar crime or corporation violence?

We could cite a number of interesting studies, past and present, that have utilized methods other than the case approach. Stewart Macaulay (1963), professor of law at Wisconsin, discovered the attitudes of businessmen toward contracts by means of interviews. James Gibbs (1969:184-207) is using psychological tests to explore types of personalities prone to contentiousness. The general position being emphasized here stems from an appreciation of the productivity of the case method, whether extended or not, as well as from a concern that overuse of this method may lead the anthropology of law to become too narrowly focused on dispute settlement. Let anthropology avoid what has happened in the law profession as a result of overdependence on the use of cases (Friedman 1969:44-45): "Academics study case law and teach from it. They derive their sense of what is important from what they read . . .: casebooks. A 'problem' is therefore a case law problem. . . . Few professors take their ideas of what is legally important from what actually goes on in the outside world." Friedman points out that this situation created a certain myopia in the law schools. Until only quite recently, questions dealing with poverty law and consumer-protection issues were almost totally neglected by legal scholars. "Commercial cases that get to an appellate court are big cases, in money terms. Hence, the little man's woes rarely reached the treshold of scholarly consciousness."

Again, Spradley's book on urban nomads (1970) is a pioneering example; he does not utilize any such method as the trouble case or extended case approach, mainly because he wishes to describe a different portion of the "law" than that usually documented by social scientists. He is interested in culture—how these drunks categorize, codify, and define their own experience. He is interested in the victims of the legal system rather than its personnel. He describes his methodological approach as follows (1970:1):

The foundation for *all* ethnography lies in the complex relationship between the researcher and his informants. In this study, research was begun by months of *listening* to men talk about their experiences with law enforcement agencies in order to *discover* which questions could be appropriately asked of informants and, further, to ascertain the wording of these questions. The initial data were gathered through participant observation in a criminal court, an alcoholism treatment center, and on Skid Row. Subsequently, a lengthy questionnaire was administered to a sample of 100 men who had been in jail for public drunkenness and, finally, many hours of formal ethnographic interviewing were carried out with a smaller number of informants.

Spradley's taxonomic analysis of terminological systems (types of roles recognized by men in the "bucket") or behavioral patterns (taxonomy of ways to beat a drunk charge) cannot be compared with any traditional study of the anthropology of law simply because most such studies have focused, by means of the most sophisticated methodology we have at hand, on social structure and social relations rather than upon culture. Although Gluckman (1965) attempted admirably to get into Barotse jurisprudential ideas, we believe he was hampered by the field methodology he used originally, which yielded no taxonomy but only interpretation of isolated Barotse words (or concepts).

Thus far we have discussed description and the concomitant methodological techniques relevant to approaches to the study of law in particular societies. Anthropologists who believe their intellectual responsibility does not stop at describing the particular should also consider exercises in comparison, so that their findings may reach beyond society-specific generalizations.

Comparison, or the comparative method, as it is often termed, is dear to the image anthropologists have of what they do. Comparison is indeed crucial to our stated aims of searching for empirical and explanatory generalizations. However, although some form of "the comparative method" has been with us for more than a century, there is still much debate over what constitutes comparison and what conditions are necessary to enable us to compare—very often by anthropologists who themselves do little in the way of what Eggan calls controlled comparison (1954) or what J. W. M. Whiting describes as cross-cultural comparison (1954).

In recent contributions to law that use a controlled or cross-cultural comparative method in making and presenting findings (Cohn 1965; Roberts 1965; Nader and Metzger 1963; Nader 1964*b*, 1965*a*, 1969*c*; B. B. Whiting 1965; Yngvesson n.d.), there is minimal armchair discussion of what should constitute comparison or what terminology should be used. If problems with this use of comparison arise, if criticisms of this work develop, empirically based questions can be raised with regard to specific problems or ideas, questions that will in part depend on whether the comparison has been carried out within a society, within a region, or cross-culturally. Presumably the degree of control over what is being compared decreases with the crossing of cultural boundaries.

Anthropologists who study law, however, have done very little in the way of comparison. As a result, their discussions of comparison are less than sophisticated and their contribution to general anthropological explanatory theory based on comparison is minimal. Bohannan (1969) speaks of "casual" as well as "controlled" comparison. "Casual" comparison, which Bohannan also calls "selected counterilluminative information" and Gluckman (1969) "implicit comparison," we would not class as comparative method. It is rather a kind of expository technique specifically mentioned by Van Velsen (1969) as "false comparison," which has been used by anthropologists at least since the nineteenth century. The comparative studies we are interested in promoting and encouraging, instead of beginning with polemics involving units and terminological debates, would start with questions such as these: What kinds of social bonds are compatible (incompatible) with a win-or-lose system of dispute resolution (Nader 1969*c*, Yngvesson n.d., 1970)? Under what circumstances are minimax (compromise) systems of dispute settlement found (Bohannan 1965)? What are the effects of and what affects the use patterns of a particular system? What are the potentials and limitations of specific types of law-enforcement agencies? What is the relation between coalition formation and the frequency of disputes (Cohn 1965)? Under what conditions do people resort to recognized legal authority for resolution of disputes or grievances (Gulliver 1963, 1969*a*; Yngvesson 1970)? What factors generate situations in which only selected acts of physical aggression result in legal wrongs or in which the selective emphasis on certain kinds of physical aggression varies within the same society (Skolnick 1969)? What is the consequence of the fact that in the so-called developed nations *the* law is intelligible only to a professional priesthood (Aubert 1966)? Why does the number of lawyers per capita vary so greatly between Korea and Japan, on the one hand, and India, the Philippines, and the United States, on the other? What is the relation between membership in a particular group (e.g., the American middle class) and the mode of legal redress used by and on its members (Sutherland 1961, Ross 1961, Macaulay 1963)? What principles govern the patterns of selective administration of justice (Carlin and Howard 1965)? What are the social (including legal) factors that form the basis of judicial decision-making (Gluckman 1956, Schubert 1959, Metzger 1960)? The questions

that are asked will determine the specific methodological approaches that need to be considered—the kind of comparative techniques that will be useful in the testing of findings from descriptive studies in single societies.

Whether we choose to do comparison through time or within or across cultures, the result will be to clarify and to increase explanations of uniformities and differences. As Nader has emphasized (1965*b*:22), problems inherent in comparison have not been insoluble in other domains of anthropological study, but to solve them in this area one does have to start with certain assumptions about the regularity of law forms and functions. There is a large body of literature on various methodological aspects of comparative methods, and there is a great deal of accumulated experience in anthropology. We who are interested in the anthropological study of law need not start cold in discussing or doing comparison. We do need to find out what the interesting questions about law are, thereby ascertaining if the method of approach, whether historical or synchronic comparison, can then be developed to suit the problem. Problems of method cannot be solved in a vacuum, and the many earlier attempts to solve them thus have created in-group polemics that will be uninteresting, for the most part, to future generations.

TWO PROBLEM AREAS: PLURALISM AND DRIFT

Interesting problem areas and new questions are sometimes discovered in the process of studying particular societies. Let us take the example of pluralism. The focus on process and networks by means of the extended case method has forced upon us the observation that all societies are plural in composition and that this pluralism is reflected in legal systems. Societies are plural in role differentiation, in status (rank) differences, and in other variables responsible for providing alternatives in the society. We wish here to call attention to the questions that are raised if we note that in any one political system we have a variety—indeed in any complex society a plethora—of legal levels and/or legal systems. As Pospisil (1967:25) points out, "any penetrating analysis of law of a primitive or civilized society can be attained only by relating it to the pertinent societal structure and legal levels, and . . . by a full recognition of the plurality of legal systems within a society." There are at least two positions on the question of pluralism in the literature. The first position is that represented, in part, by Pospisil, who would argue that all societies are plural by virtue of the various kinds of social groups found within them; for example, nuclear family, lineage, clan, or various ethnicities. The challenge from this viewpoint is not to distinguish between plural and nonplural societies, but rather to distinguish between various types of pluralism. A second point of view, elaborated by M. G. Smith (1965:7,18), argues that the plural society is a special type of society to be distinguished from the homogeneous society. "In the homogeneous society, members share the same basic institutions—political, economic, religious, familial, and educational. In plural societies, there is a combination of structural pluralism and cultural pluralism, the former term describing cleavage between groups, and the latter term, their use of different institutions." These divergent points of view indicate the preference of the anthropologist to see society either as a continuum of components or in terms of polar or ideal types.

Anthropologists have perhaps made a bit too much of homogeneity, as is in-

dicated by improved fieldwork of the sort mentioned earlier, which concentrates heavy effort on intrasociety variation. In all cultures there are alternatives and various uses of "the system" based on such biological factors as sex and age and a variety of ascribed and achieved variables. Perhaps it will be productive to follow Dan Lev's suggestions (in a personal communication) to explore the simplest types of pluralism—horizontal and vertical. Essentially Pospisil (1967:24) is speaking about vertical pluralism when he refers to "legal levels that are superimposed one upon the other, the system of a more inclusive group being applied to members of all its constituent subgroups." M. G. Smith is more concerned with horizontal pluralism, which in the main reflects dominant-subordinate relations between the nation and the various groups of which it is composed. Recognition of both types of pluralism is important.

Much of the "trouble in administering the law" has arisen from a total ignorance or avoidance of the question of pluralism. Indeed, it is not unusual for the prejudices of the dominant ruling class to prevail over a society as law. As Pound (1906:399) stated the problem:

Justice, which is the end of the law, is the ideal compromise between the activities of each and the activities of all in a crowded world. The law seeks to harmonize these activities and to adjust the relations of every man with his fellows so as to accord with the moral sense of the community. When the community is one in its ideas of justice, this is possible. When the community is divided and diversified, and groups and classes and interests, understanding each other none too well, have conflicting ideas of justice, the task is extremely difficult.

This ignorance or avoidance of pluralism is also intimately related to misuses and nonuses of the law that result in widespread negativism and disrespect for the law or in conflict between systems (as evidenced in the United States or in any young nation in which the law is in a "developmental state"). Hahm (1967:146-66; 1968) discusses the development of attitudes of disrespect for the law in Korea as a result of traditional expectations of the political structure as well as of Korea's initial encounters with foreign law. In China (Van Der Sprenkel 1962:119) such negative attitudes toward the law and law courts resulted in village "antilitigation societies," even though in China

...the major control over individuals is in the hands of the immediate groups to which they belonged. ... Matters would first be dealt with by those best able to know both the facts of the case and the local law, and the majority of cases would go no further. This was one way of providing for the great diversity of custom throughout the area of China, whereas to have charged the official courts with the whole burden of applying law would have required much more costly administration and given rise to problems of elaborate codification.

Antonio Pigliaru (1959) describes the conflicting systems of law found in Sardinia, where the vendetta is a legal system in competition with the state. The traditional system does not incorporate laws of the state that are not coherent with its system. It behooves the anthropologist to ask under what conditions diversity is tolerated by the state. Ehrlich (1936:14) provides us with one hypothesis: "It is only when the state has grown extremely powerful and has begun to tend towards an absolute form . . . [that the idea arises] of making the state the authoritative, and in course of time the sole, source of law."

The simple recognition of pluralism has helped us in some cases toward a better understanding of behavior defined as deviant by the state. Whyte's early study (1943) makes sense of gang behavior by viewing the gang not so much as deviant, but rather as a subculture whose members are conforming to its norms. In a similar vein Sutherland (1961) develops his theory of crime by means of the concepts of homogeneity and vertical pluralism: ". . . criminal behavior is learned in association with those who define such behavior favorably and in isolation from those who define it unfavorably . . . a person engages in such criminal behavior if, and only if, the weight of the favorable definitions exceeds the weight of the unfavorable definitions."

The greatest bulk of the literature on pluralism and law has dealt with the "problem" of pluralism in the new nations—societies whose legal systems reflect their former colonialism. After the demise of the colonies and the creation of new states, the power supporting plural legal order was replaced, for the most part, by centralized government that explicitly aimed at using the law as a means of resolving the "pluralism problem." Under colonialism pluralism was considered a way to block or control by dividing and conquering. And the various social, ethnic, and religious groups had little to do with each other. As Dan Lev has noted (in a personal communication), "Colonial governments were intent upon distinguishing not only between European élites and governed peoples, usually on racial grounds, but between the constituent population groups of the colony. It was not merely divide and rule that promoted this approach, it was simply easier to administer native populations so that their natural distinctions were heeded." Although Lev's experience is principally with Indonesia and Malaysia, his position applies more generally.

The motivation of new states is of a different sort from that of the colonial powers and has its roots deeply planted in a hypothesis that, although largely untested, is treated as if it were God's truth. The hypothesis is that national success (which usually means economic development)—indeed, national existence—depends on creating a homogeneous people, and that the best way to do this is by means of the law, usually imported from the West. There is also something that smacks of sympathetic magic here, the idea that if these nations import a legal system or code from a progressive country, they too will have at least the seeds of progress and modernity. Friedman (1969) presents a challenging critique of this position, which is based largely on "belief" rather than evidence.

It has not been uncommon for scholars to accept the premise that a society must have one law controlling the behavior of all its members (in spite of the fact that no society does, and most emphatically not the societies from which these scholars come). Pospisil (1967) comments on the history and validity of this idea. There is very little in the literature, however, on the consequences of such an idea, on the epidemiological impact that it has had on attempts to deal with practical problems in the new nations or even here in the United States. The validity of the notion that homogeneity, the state, success, and progress all go hand in hand can be challenged only by charting the consequences in particular case studies. In a stratified society the ruling elite has much to gain by invoking homogeneity, since it is the culture of the elite, or that to which its members have adapted, that sets the standard for homogenization.

The question of what constitutes illegal behavior becomes debatable in societies where peoples of differing ways of life, with differing expectations and priorities, live under one center of legitimate political authority. One part of the population of such a society is usually attempting to assert its authority over others. The situation we have described for colonies or new nations is not unlike that in the more technologically "advanced" countries. In any society, then, we have subcultures with their own systems of law, and the various subcultures may be in conflict with one another, one segment usually imposing or trying to impose its values on others who are forced to conform to them (Barnes 1961). It is not, as Hoebel (1954) would have it, that in a society some individual or group is recognized socially—that is, by the society as a whole—as having the privilege of applying physical force. There is no better example of the problems inherent in such a view as Hoebel's than the situation in the United States (Skolnick 1969).

In the development of law, at least that part that is consciously engineered, the "realities" of the situation are most often *not* absorbed as part of the data crucial to realistic planning. It is one thing to recognize that law is not, in fact, a monopoly of the state; it is another matter, and one that desperately requires cognizance of the "realities," to agree on the consequences that an attempt at centralized state monopoly has for stated objectives; for example, the assurance of the speed of justice, the access of the people to the law, and so on.

The interest in solving or resolving pluralism has given birth to a large literature on legal development. As Friedman points out (1969:14) in discussing the social engineering aspects of development, "Legal development abroad and law reform in this country rest on one simple basic assumption: some legal systems are better than others with respect to a particular dimension called modernity." It may well be that in a more realistic view the engineering of legal development would be seen as a dominant-subordinate acting out of conflict resulting from disparate values and from competition for power. In the new nations new loci of power are developing and consolidating, and the law is often used as a means to consolidate power positions. As Friedman (1969: 47) points out, "Importation of law is sometimes part of a political revolution." Some anthropologists have studied the consequences of new law; not many have explored the behind-the-scenes motivation for legal development or reform.

Other aspects of legal change are not "engineered," but are best explainable in terms of drift and of lay attitudes toward and use of the law (Llewelyn and Hoebel 1941, Hurst 1960). Here we need more effort in developing fact-based theories of legal change, and there has been a beginning in this direction in the recent concentration of scholarly effort on the determinants and consequences of choice and alternatives. In Macaulay's work on "Noncontractual Relations in Business" (1963) we observe that the choice of using or not using a contract will determine the forms of settlement that will be used should a dispute develop. Bailey, after pointing out that his *Tribe, Caste, and Nation* (1960) is not about the political *structure* of the Konds of India, but about political activity in *several structures*, underlines the importance of studying choice patterns (1960:12):

When we consider a man as a locus of several roles which occur in different systems, all of which claim to do the same job, we must take into account choice. In some cases this element is not going to affect the continuance of the social system. . . . But where the choice lies between different types of relationship, the continuance of a social system may be affected. . . . People can, so to speak, when there are several systems of political relationship between which to choose, opt out of one system and into another.

In order to illustrate this process, Bailey analyzes one case of dispute in detail. The analysis makes clear how choices made in the course of the dispute evidenced the inefficacy of one structure and demonstrated the greater viability of an alternate system of alliances. Bailey suggests that by analyzing a series of such cases one can demonstrate a process of social change. Turner (1957) had carried out just such an analysis, employing the "social drama" to illustrate how power changes in an Ndembu village were effected during a series of five interrelated conflict cases. Barth, in his 1966 article "Models of Social Organization," pointed to the trend suggested by these and other works and stated that the "central problem" for anthropology should be the investigation of constraints and incentives determining choice (1966:1). The emphasis in Barth's article was on the step beyond the description of choice, toward a systematic analysis of the factors patterning choice in a particular social situation. A recent study (Yngvesson 1970) attempts such an analysis, investigating the choice of dispute-settling mechanisms in a Scandinavian community. Two main mechanisms are described for the community, and cognitive models are defined that appear to be linked to the choice of one or the other of these alternatives. The study isolates the changes in the natural and social environments of the community that create pressures toward an increasing use of one of the models, thus changing the pattern of choice in favor of one over the other mode of decision-making and dispute settlement.

These studies are pertinent, as we have suggested, to understanding "drift" in contrast to engineered change. To illustrate the concept of drift we would rather paraphrase Sapir (1921:155) on linguistic drift than attempt to translate Llewelyn's rather garbled version of the concept. The drift of a legal system is constituted by the unconscious selection on the part of its users of those individual variations that are cumulative in some special direction. This direction may be inferred, in the main, from the past history of the system. In the long run any new feature of the drift becomes part and parcel of the common, accepted law, but for a long time it may exist as a mere tendency in the legal system. As we look about us and observe current usage, it is not likely to occur to us that our legal system has a "slope," that the changes of the next few years are in a sense prefigured in certain obscure tendencies of the present, and that these changes, when consummated, will be seen to be but continuations of changes that have already been initiated. We tend to feel, rather, that our legal system is virtually a fixed system and that what slight changes are destined to take place in it are as likely to move in one direction as another. The feeling is fallacious.

Students interested in exploring the concept of drift in systems of law must focus a great deal more attention than our predecessors did on the concepts of *use and users*, and upon *patterns of access* to the system. Theories of legal change will ultimately develop from a study of a particular culture and society through time or from the comparative study of various cultures. (See Buxbaum 1967 and Moore 1970 for recent contributions to the data bank necessary for developing theories of legal change.) However, we have yet to produce adequate descriptions of the inter-

action between those having formal legal roles and the users of the system of law. We must complement the view from above with that from below.

THE PURPOSE, CONSEQUENCE, AND FUNCTION OF LAW

An interest in the use and the users of legal systems and of particular legal institutions will bring us into questions dealing with the purpose, consequence, and function of law, which in turn might help us develop a theory of functions of law. It is true, as Swett (1969) notes, that "despite what seems to be general agreement among anthropologists concerning the systemic nature of law as a cultural institution having a complexity of functions, the relationship between elements of the system and their functions remains unclear." We are sorely in need of a theory on the function of law. And we need to develop such a theory not in terms of the universe of possibilities usually defined as "legal" (i.e., what *the* legal system has stated as its *legal* functions, which is then generalized for all legal systems), but in terms of the consequences of the law for segments of a specific society. In their descriptions and analyses of particular legal systems as they operate in particular societies, anthropologists have not attempted to describe the full range of functions of law. Upon closer observation, this may be found to be related to the extensive use of the case method, which stems, as we have noted, from a traditional legal interest in litigation. The function of the law as a mechanism for dispute settlement seems rather obvious when we gather case materials, as does its related function "to create conformity with norms." Yet when we are willing to admit the "reality" to which Llewelyn refers, anthropologists as well as lawyers would admit law a myriad of functions.

Much of the ethnographic data reported by anthropologists on the question of function was reviewed in Nader (1965*b*) and will not be reviewed again in this essay; since 1965 there has not been very much that is new in the way of either data or theory. We do still know, however, that the law does not function solely to control. It educates, it punishes, it harasses, it protects private and public interests, it provides entertainment, it serves as a fund-raising institution, it distributes scarce resources, it maintains the status quo, it maintains class systems and cuts across class systems, it integrates and disintegrates—all these things in different places, at different times, with different weightings. It may be a cause of crime; it plays, by virtue of its discretion, the important role of definer of crime. It may encourage respect or disrespect for the law, and so forth. We have assumed that there was probably a cross-cultural difference in the content and form of a legal system, and at the same time we have ignored the variety of functions (sometimes referred to as extralegal, latent, or unintended) that a legal system may or in fact does have. We have concentrated in the main on law as a system of social control and have not even opened up the possibility that law might at times function as a system of social discontrol.

In 1958 Harold Berman organized his text on *The Nature and Functions of the Law* around what he calls the "social functions of the law." He includes under social functions the "purposes of law as well as its important tendencies to produce unintended consequences." His book is organized around four purposeful functions of the American legal system: (1) law as a process for resolving disputes, with the court as the model dispute-settling institution; (2) law as a process for maintaining historical continuity and doctrinal consistency by means of legal reasoning and reasoning by analogy; (3) law as a process for facilitating and protecting voluntary arrangements—men must be able to rely on the expectations created by the words or acts of others; and (4) law as a process for resolving acute social conflict (with specific illustrations from labor law). It is upon the fourth and the first purposive functions that anthropologists have put the greatest effort; like the law professors, we have spent little time on the "important tendencies to produce unintended consequences."

We have a large and very good body of cross-cultural materials on formally recognized institutions of dispute settlement (for examples, see Hoebel 1954). Anthropologists have written about judges, councils, go-betweens, crossers, duels, and so forth. We have also contrasted third-party intervention with direct confrontation, and we have contrasted mediation, arbitration, and adjudication. We have a pretty fair idea of the range of variation in patterns of formally recognized institutions of dispute settlement, and we know a good deal about how formally recognized roles or institutions contribute to the settlement of disputes in specific societies. The most dominant theme at the second Wenner-Gren conference on the anthropology of law (Nader, ed., 1969) was the topic of dispute settlement, and attempts were made there to distinguish types and the conditions underlying them. Gulliver (1969*b*:17) distinguishes two structurally different modes, negotiation and adjudication. In negotiations,

each party seeks to exert what strength it can against the other, such strength ranging from forensic argument and skill to the threat of physical force, from moral pressures to offers to denials of other advantages. Here the result, the settlement, is in effect some mutually acceptable, tolerable resolution of the matter in dispute based on the assessed or demonstrated strengths of the parties. . . . [In adjudication] a binding decision is given by a third party with a degree of authority. Such a decision is in some way coercive in that the adjudicator (judge or the like) has not only both the right and obligation to reach and enunciate a decision but also power to enforce it.

Aubert (1963, 1969*b*) has also addressed himself to the problem of classifying dispute-settlement forms, as has Nader (1969*c*). On the whole, the criteria used in these works for distinguishing modes of settlement are related to the general distinction between non-zero-sum and zero-sum games. In the former, the relationship between the parties is such that it is possible to effect a settlement in which a basic consideration is to minimize the risk of maximal loss for each side. In the latter, the relationship between the parties is such that a gain for one side is necessarily a loss for the other, and there is little chance of reaching a settlement in which one party does not suffer a total loss.

Both Gulliver (1969*b*) and Aubert (1969*b*) develop at some length the specific implications of these two settlement models. Gulliver (1969*b*:18) discusses aspects of the social context in which each is likely to be found and suggests the hypothesis that "there is greater reliance on, appeal to, and operation of rules, standards, and norms where adjudication rather than negotiation is the mode of dispute settlement." Aubert relates each form of settlement to a cluster of other elements; for example, the "legal model" or "either/or" type of decision is related to a marked orientation toward the establishment of guilt, toward the establishment of matters of fact, toward the determination of which norms should be applied, and it usually involves the presence of a third party. And, according to Aubert, in settlements in which

negotiation is predominant, it is not necessary to agree regarding the factual origin of the conflict or regarding applicable norms, and the settlement may be reached between the two litigants without the intervention of a third party. Yngvesson (n.d.) and Nader (1969*c*) relate each form of settlement to a general expectation underlying interaction between parties to litigation. If continued relations are favored by the litigants, then give-a-little, get-a-little is preferred to zero-sum or win-or-lose, whereas zero-sum is favored if continuing relations are not desired. So, for example, we should not be surprised to find the give-a-little, get-a-little style of settlement in labor-management disputes.

There have been a number of studies of dispute settlement using one or both of the two models. Aubert (1967, 1969*a*) has studied conflict resolution in Norway and notes the diminishing importance of the "legal model" and of court resolutions of conflict, whereas bargaining and negotiation in other resolution agencies are becoming more common. Gulliver, in a study of the Ndendeuli of southern Tanzania (1969), analyzes negotiation as a means of dispute settlement in a society without courts. Nader (1969*c*) analyzes dispute-settlement processes in several unrelated institutions and points out that style of settlement may be viewed independently of the institutional form within which it occurs, indicating the need for studies aimed at discovering the social and cultural factors that determine or generate a style. Starr (1969) discusses dispute settlement in a Turkish village, concentrating particularly on the use of informal (in contrast to court) settlement techniques, and the social correlates of these with the nature of the grievance and the relative status of the parties. Others too (Metzger 1960, Yngvesson 1970) discuss noncourt dispute-settlement processes as they relate to the type of grievance and the relationship between the litigants. Metzger was particularly interested in the use of coalition theory to document the relations between balance of power, outcome, and classes of individuals involved in conflict. In all these studies, negotiation and bargaining procedures are found when the parties to the dispute are kinsmen or neighbors or residents of the same community. The same principle has been observed in complex societies; Macaulay (1963) describes the avoidance of the law as a way of building and keeping good business relations, and the literature provides other such examples of avoidance of the law, particularly when zero-sum operations would militate against solutions allowing continuing relations (Van Der Sprenkel 1962:112-23; Hahm 1967:19-20).

Implicit—and at times explicit—in many of these studies is a concern with the way persons who share a concept of community deal with disputes among themselves. In other words, an important focus in these works is the question of how people who have vested interests in the preservation of a valued relationship will deal with disruptions or threatened disruptions to this relationship. The literature indicates that persons in such relationships will frequently try to resolve conflict or to handle criminal activity in such a way that reconciliation, or at least the continuance of relations between the parties, is possible. As we see in Hahm's (1967) and Van Der Sprenkel's (1962) work on Korean and Chinese culture, in Cox's (1968) study of the Hopi, in studies of some Scandinavian communities, and in Starr's (1969) study of a Turkish village, these attempts take the form of avoidance of court settlements, and in fact the avoidance of any settlement forms involving officials of the

formal legal system, such as the police. Another recent thesis (Collier 1970) lends support to those observations. Collier (1970:6) suggests that among the Mexican Zinacantans, litigants who wish to preserve a valued relationship will seek a settlement procedure that will promote reconciliation, and she notes that although these Indians use *ladino* legal procedures, a decision to take another *zinacanteco* to a *ladino* court is "like a decision to go to war." Avoidance of the law may also function to maintain close relations between specific interest groups and the state, as is described in Sutherland's work on *White Collar Crime* (1961).

The law may function not only to resolve disputes between specific parties, but also to resolve social conflict. In many societies the practices used in resolving social conflict are inseparable from those used in dispute settlement. Berman (1958) separates the two by noting that the first deals with disputes between individuals and the latter with disputes or conflict between classes of individuals. Societies vary in their dependence on law for handling class conflict, but all societies have devised some methods for resolving, or at least controlling, preventing, or avoiding social conflict. Man is distinctive among primate groups in the degree to which he may escalate conflict. By virtue of the use of language and the development of technology in human society, the degree to which a violent incident among humans may escalate is theoretically limitless. Today, for example, an incident could escalate into worldwide warfare. Language, communication, and technology all make this possible. At the same time, culture and social structure and such available controls as force, compromise, and passivity make such escalation improbable.

What happens when a society depends too heavily on an institution such as a court for handling class conflict? If we use the United States as an example, we find that American society has been unable to handle the social conflicts of the mid-twentieth century through the law alone. Berman (1958) points to the limitations of the American court system in its attempt to handle labor problems in the earlier part of the century; the administrative agencies that were created then were more flexible than the courts in their handling of class cases. Today we find it increasingly difficult to handle through the court system such collective acts as civil disobedience, riots, and the delinquency of corporations. Anthropologists (see Gluckman 1956) have described a wide variety of mechanisms used in other societies to deescalate social conflict, mechanisms such as segmental opposition, conflicting loyalties, rituals of rebellion, and compromise mechanisms, all of which are weak, underdeveloped, absent, or unacceptable in American society at large.

In the anthropological literature we often speak about multiplex societies. In these societies contentious behavior usually involves closely related persons, and any settlement necessarily becomes involved in a close-knit network of relations. Such societies are in sharp contrast with our own, in which most individuals are related to others in a single linking relationship. By virtue of multiplicity, most small-scale societies (and this would include small-scale societies within larger societies) are constantly aware of the possibility that any one act may escalate, and they prepare for escalation, or possible escalation, by consciously or unconsciously utilizing some of the mechanisms mentioned above. When the law is used in such societies as an important mechanism for deescalation, legal procedures are usually based on the compromise prin-

ciple; the philosophy of give-a-little, get-a-little predominates over the absoluteness of a win-or-lose solution, over the guilty-not-guilty syndrome, over an emphasis on fault. Internal problems of escalation face some societies, such as the United States, only occasionally. Escalation is not an everyday possibility in the United States, as it is in most face-to-face societies, and we have not developed any institutional frameworks specifically designed to deescalate violence, to handle interclass conflicts such as riots and consumer complaints. Our courts are either too rigid in procedure or too powerless to handle escalation adequately. Fuller (1968:108) has noted the limitations of systems of adjudicative law in respect to their use as instruments of social order in dealing with certain problem areas. However, mechanisms of social control outside the law have not been adequately measured or described, and escalation is rarely discussed as a problem that concerns the law. To return again to questions of method, we reiterate that the topics that social scientists choose for study of the law should not be determined by the place accorded the court and the case in the folk system of thought. Berman's illustrations from labor law indicate that when the courts have failed us in the past, we have explored alternatives rather than remodeled our courts and procedures (1958:474-75):

It is the failure to utilize legal institutions to create new forms and new concepts of cooperation between labor and management which is the most discouraging aspect of the early history of labor law in America.

The inadequacy of the judicial response to this challenge led eventually to important legislative restrictions upon the powers of the judiciary in labor cases, as well as to the creation of a system of administrative regulation of collective bargaining. It is an explicit function of the newer labor legislation, and of the administrative controls which it established, to encourage new attitudes of cooperation between labor and management.

At the moment, it appears that the judicial response to the crises of the 1960s and 1970s has led to increasing police powers rather than to the development of new legal institutions (Skolnick 1969). We may ask what are the concomitant variables affecting legal choices in these different periods of American history.

It is interesting that sanctions, often mentioned when definitions of law are in question, are rarely discussed in the recent ethnographies. In the context of our earlier discussion of ethnic group boundaries, Radcliffe-Brown's (1934: 533-34) comments on the function of sanctions reflect his experience in nonstratified, relatively homogeneous societies:

It is not the effects of the sanctions upon the person to whom they are applied that are the most important but rather the general effects within the community applying the sanctions. For the application of any sanction is a direct affirmation of the social sentiments by the community and thereby constitutes an important, possibly essential, mechanism for maintaining these sentiments. . . . The sanctions are thus of primary significance to sociology in that they are reactions on the part of a community to events affecting its integration.

Radcliffe-Brown is stressing the point of view that sanctions are a reaction *on the part of the community* to disruptive events and that the effects of the sanctions *within the community applying them* are of primary importance; sanctions should act to strengthen shared values within the community. What this suggests is that sanctions applied across ethnic boundaries—that is, sanctions that are not the reactions of the community in question but rather of an alien group—may function coun-

ter to the goals intended by the sanctioning group or authority. Such sanctions may in fact act to strengthen shared values within the group to which they are applied, but they may thus further polarize values between the sanctioning and the sanctioned communities.

Packer (1968) addresses himself to some of these problems in considering the question of possible alternatives to the use made of the criminal sanction in the United States. He suggests that sanctions that are a reflection of morality or that aim at reinforcing morality are appropriate only to homogeneous systems—that is, within ethnic boundaries, rather than across them. In posing the question of whether morals and their reinforcement are appropriate issues for polyethnic sanctioning mechanisms, Packer emphasizes that the deterrent function of sanctions is more important than that of "affirming social sentiments," which Radcliffe-Brown stressed as more basic. Packer is also concerned with the consequences of indiscriminate resort to the criminal sanction (1968:365):

The criminal sanction is the best available device we have for dealing with gross and immediate threats of harm. It becomes less useful as the harms become less gross and immediate. It becomes largely inefficacious when it is used to enforce morality rather than to deal with conduct that is generally seen as harmful. Efficacy aside, the less threatening the conduct with which it is called upon to deal, the greater the social costs that enforcement incurs. We alienate people from the society in which they live. We drive enforcement authorities to more extreme measures of intrusion and coercion.

Packer is arguing that we have depended too heavily on the criminal sanction as a way of controlling antisocial behavior. His work is an important contribution to the theory of sanctions as well as to the argument about the preventive functions of the law, and the use that can be made of control mechanisms outside the law proper. Van Der Sprenkel (1962) provides useful ethnographic data on the preventive functions of nonlegal institutions.

The latent or "unintended" consequences of the law are often, but not always, discussed anecdotally by law scholars. Thurmond Arnold (1935) wrote a serious book about the latent functions of the law that was read by many of the legal professionals (when it was read at all) as anecdotal. If Lawrence Friedman were to write a serious book expanding his comments on the function of law reform (1969:42-44), it would probably be dismissed as muckraking:

Justification is one of the major functions of law reform. Whatever value it has for society, law reform is useful to the legal profession. It is part of the demonstration that what the bar is and does is good for society. On the whole, the public image of the profession is not as strong as the profession would like. Lawyers have been denounced as lackeys, parasites, tools of big business, shysters, and worse.... Law reform makes it possible for the top of the profession to strike poses of nobility and rectitude, to go before the public in an attitude of high public spirit. ... Modern law reform . . . tends to be socially innocuous. Through it, the profession advertises to the world at large how earnestly it cleans its house, how diligently it strives for rationality.

The degree to which law reform functions as advertisement for the legal profession is an important question to all scientists, as well as to the general citizenry. In an unpublished paper Blanca Muratorio describes some of the consequences of law reform for peasants in Bolivia. Peasants were made legally equal to the whites and *mestizos* through political revolution. Because of their poverty, a corrupt judiciary, and questionable police practices, they were forced to defend their equal rights by means of traditional patron-client bonds and the use of street-corner lawyers. These practices served to reinforce their status as an unprivileged ethnic group. Muratorio's essay emphasizes the relationship between the law and class structure; reform in the law was not enough to change the status quo unless the traditional access to law for peasants was drastically modified.

Social evaluations of the law are not uncommonly made by leading Scandinavian sociologists of law. Aubert, in his article "Some Social Functions of Legislation" (1966), asks what functions a particular piece of legislation was meant to have: Was it meant to influence the behavior of the public (i.e., the function of communicating norms and achieving conformity with them) or was it meant to facilitate communication among lawyers when a breach of law occurred? It is important to ask such questions if we are interested in understanding the conditions under which citizens comply with new or old legislation. The Nader reports, such as the F.T.C. report (Cox, Fellmeth, and Schulz 1969), are contributions to the description of the functioning of specific administrative agencies, comparing the intended and the unintended consequences of such institutions. It was proposed in the introduction of Hahm's 1967 work that "unrealistic law can only lead to disrespect for the legal process with a resultant decline in the efficiency of law. No government can use law as a propaganda tool nor as a scapegoat for inefficient administration without deterioration in the legal climate for which it stands." It is clear that expression of dissatisfaction with the law is often included in descriptions of systems of law, but it is often unclear how the dissatisfaction expressed by authors relates to the expectations and attitudes of the various users or potential users of the system.

Van Der Sprenkel (1962:123) suggests one viewpoint: "Among the most frequent motives for an action being brought into court were mischief or malice on the part of those who had little to lose—either to damage an enemy or to pay off an old score. To involve someone in a lawsuit was a way of ruining him." Hahm (1967:19) describes the Korean view of law, which contrasts with the general American view: "Law . . . was an unpleasant necessity prescribed by the failure of reason in politics. . . . Litigation and lawsuit meant that there was discord that required the power of the state for solution. They also signified the failure of politics." The quality of social science literature on the purpose, consequence, and function of law signifies the failures of social scientists to do more than barely reveal surface phenomena in their studies of law in social and cultural contexts.

CONCLUDING REMARKS

The first major contributions of this century to the anthropological study of law were written during the period from 1920 to 1941. Prior to that time the majority of works on law in nonwestern societies were written by colonial administrators, missionaries, and the like, rather than by anthropologists. The 1950s produced a series of important anthropological monographs on the law of particular nonwestern societies, but to date less than half a dozen articles and one monograph deal directly with the Anglo-American legal system. The 1960s were a time when anthropologists began to reorganize their thinking on law in terms of choice of problem, methodological approach, and the manpower problem. Anthropologists have made a less uniquely anthro-

pological contribution to social science knowledge in law than in other areas of study.

In this essay we have attempted to formulate an approach that will be fruitful in dealing with questions to which we assign high priorities. The ethnography of law should become something more than the sociological study of judicial institutions, and something more than a study of how specific formal institutions settle disputes, as we increase our numbers and broaden our angle of vision. Many, but not all, of our deficiencies are related to the manpower question. There are few more than two dozen contemporary anthropologists who specialize in law (international sample). In the United States, some thirty-one universities and colleges offer courses on the anthropology of law, and only two or three graduate schools are supporting training programs for anthropologists in this field. This is true in spite of the fact that the subject matter has great relevance and potential application to major national problems. A few examples will suffice:

Successful implementation of new laws in a pluralistic society. Laws are often formulated without due consideration of the subcultures to which they are meant to apply. West Virginia game laws, for example, might have been more successful if the lawmakers, for whom hunting is a sport, realized that for some West Virginians it is subsistence activity.

Congestion in the courts. Some have said that the law is a princess, but if we want to increase our understanding of court congestion we would do better to think of the law as an octopus. As there are limitations to the criminal sanction, so there are limitations to the use of courts, and congestion may be reduced by means other than the needed expansion of an overburdened court system, as is illustrated by the ethnographic data on delegalization and the uses of public opinion, for example.

Alternative institutions. Again anthropological data can be viewed as laboratory examples for such innovations as the family court programs. The same may be said for neighborhood courts. Both these institutions have their counterparts in many societies throughout the world.

In short, we should begin to make important findings on important questions. More anthropologists will be drawn to the study of law as they discover that it requires them to be social scientists first and foremost, and as they realize that a legal education is not a necessary requirement for the social study of law. What is necessary is the identification of important problem areas, the raising of imaginative questions, and a curiosity about a segment of twentieth-century life that is increasingly affecting the choice patterns of women and men in cultures around the world.

REFERENCES

Abel, R. L.
  1969 Studies in Law and Modernization: Customary Laws of Wrongs in Kenya; an Essay in Research Method. *American Journal of Comparative Law* 17:573-626.
Arnold, T.
  1935 *The Symbols of Government.* New Haven: Yale University Press.
Aubert, V.
  1963 Competition and Dissensus: Two Types of Conflict and of Conflict Resolution. *Journal of Conflict Resolution* 7:26-42.
  1966 Some Social Functions of Legislation. *Acta Sociologica* 10:98-120.
  1967 Courts and Conflict Resolution. *Journal of Conflict Resolution* 11:40-51.
  1969a Law as a Way of Resolving Conflicts: The Case of a Small Industrialized

Society. In *Law in Culture and Society,* ed. L. Nader, pp. 282-303. Chicago: Aldine.
  1969b Introduction: Case Studies of Law in Western Societies. In *Law in Culture and Society,* ed. L. Nader, pp. 273-81. Chicago: Aldine.
  1969c *Sociology of Law.* Harmondsworth: Penguin Books.
Bailey, F. G.
  1960 Tribe, Caste, and Nation: A Study of Political Activity and Political Change in Highland Orissa. Manchester: Manchester University Press.
Barnes, J. A.
  1961 Law as Politically Active: An Anthropological View. In *Studies in the Sociology of Law,* ed. Geoffrey Sawer, pp. 167-96. Canberra: Australian National University.
Barth, F.
  1966 Models of Social Organization. Occasional paper no. 23, Royal Anthropological Institute of Great Britain and Ireland.
  1969 *Ethnic Groups and Boundaries.* Boston: Little, Brown.
Barton, R. F.
  1919 Ifugao law. *University of California Publications in American Archaeology and Ethnology* 15:1-186.
  1949 *The Kalingas: Their Institutions and Custom Law.* Chicago: University of Chicago Press.
Berman, H. J.
  1958 *The Nature and Functions of Law.* Brooklyn: Foundation Press. 3rd ed. 1972.
Berndt, R. M.
  1962 *Excess and Restraint: Social Control Among a New Guinea Mountain People.* Chicago: University of Chicago Press.
Black, D. J.
  1970 Production of Crime Rates. *American Sociological Review* 35:733-48.
Black, M., and D. Metzger
  1965 Ethnographic Description and the Study of Law. In *The Ethnography of Law,* ed. L. Nader, pp. 141-65. *American Anthropologist* 67, no. 6, pt. 2 (special issue).
Bohannan, P.
  1965 The Differing Realms of Law. In *The*

Ethnography of Law, ed. L. Nader, pp. 33-42. *American Anthropologist* 67, no. 6, pt. 2 (special issue).
1969 Ethnography and Comparison in Legal Anthropology. In *Law in Culture and Society*, ed. L. Nader, pp. 401-18. Chicago: Aldine.

Burridge, K. O. L.
1957 Disputing in Tangu. *American Anthropologist* 59:763-80.

Buxbaum, D. C.
1967 *Traditional and Modern Legal Institutions in Asia and Africa.* International Studies in Sociology and Social Anthropology, vol. 5. Leiden: Brill.

Cahn, E. S., and J. C. Cahn
1966 What Price Justice? The Civilian Perspective Revisited. Symposium, Justice and the Poor. *Notre Dame Lawyer* 41:927-60.

Carlin, J. E., and J. Howard
1965 Legal Representation and Class Justice. *UCLA Law Review* 12:381-437.

Cicourel, A. V.
1968 *The Social Organization of Juvenile Justice.* New York: Wiley.

Cohn, B. S.
1965 Anthropological Notes on Disputes and Law in India. In *The Ethnography of Law*, ed. L. Nader, pp. 82-122. *American Anthropologist* 67, no. 6, pt. 2 (special issue).

Collier, J.
1970 Zinacanteco Law: A Study of Conflict in a Modern Maya Community. Ph. D. dissertation, Tulane University.

Colson, E.
1953 Social Control and Vengeance in Plateau Tonga Society. *Africa* 23:199-212.

Coser, L. A.
1968 Violence and the Social Structure. In *Violence in the Streets*, ed. S. Endlemen, pp. 71-101. Chicago: Quadrangle Books.

Cox, B. A.
1968 Law and Conflict Management Among the Hopi. Ph. D. dissertation, University of California, Berkeley.

Cox, E. F., R. C. Fellmeth, and J. E. Schulz
1969 *The Nader Report on the F.T.C.* New York: Grove Press.

Dundas, C.
1915 The Organization and Laws of Some Bantu Tribes. *Journal of the Royal Anthropological Institute* 45:234-306.

Eggan, F.
1954 Social Anthropology and the Method of Controlled Comparison. *American Anthropologist* 56:743-63.

Ehrlich, E.
1936 *Fundamental Principles of the Sociology of Law. Harvard Studies in Jurisprudence,* vol. 5. Cambridge: Harvard University Press.

Epstein, A. L.
1967 The Case Method in the Field of Law. In *The Craft of Social Anthropology*, ed. A. L. Epstein, pp. 153-80. London: Tavistock.

Evans-Pritchard, E.
1940 *The Nuer: A Description of the Modes of Livelihood and Political Institutions of a Nilotic People.* Oxford: Clarendon Press.

Friedman, L. H.
1969 On Legal Development. *Rutgers Law Review* 24:11-64.

Fuller, L.
1968 *The Anatomy of the Law.* New York: Praeger.

Geertz, C.
1965 The Impact of the Concept of Culture on the Concept of Man. In *New Views of the Nature of Man*, ed. J. R. Platt, pp. 93-118. Chicago: University of Chicago Press. Reprinted in *Man Makes Sense*, ed. E. A. Hammeland, W. S. Simmons, pp. 47-65. Boston: Little, Brown, 1970.

Gibbs, J. L., Jr.
1962 Poro Values and Courtroom Procedures in a Kpelle Chiefdom. *Southwest Journal of Anthropology* 18:341-50.
1969 Law and Personality: Signposts for a New Direction. In *Law in Culture and Society,* ed. L. Nader, pp. 176-207. Chicago: Aldine.

Gluckman, M.
1955 The Judicial Process Among the Barotse of Northern Rhodesia. Manchester: Manchester University Press.
1956 *Custom and Conflict in Africa.* Glencoe, Ill.: Free Press.

1961 Ethnographic Data in British Social Anthropology. *Sociological Review* (n.s.) 9:5-17.

1965 *The Ideas in Barotse Jurisprudence.* New Haven: Yale University Press.

1969 Concepts in the Comparative Study of Tribal Law. In *Law in Culture and Society*, ed. L. Nader, pp. 349-73. Chicago: Aldine.

Goldschmidt, W.
1967 *Sebei Law.* Berkeley: University of California Press.

Goodenough, W.
1957 Cultural Anthropology and Linguistics. In *Report of the Seventh Annual Round Table Meeting on Linguistics and Language Study*, ed. Paul L. Garvin. Monograph Series on Language and Linguistics, no. 9. Washington. D.C.: Georgetown University Press.

Graburn, N. H. H.
1969 Eskimo Law in Light of Self- and Group-Interest. *Law and Society Review* 4:45-60.

Gulliver, P. H.
1963 *Social Control in an African Society: A Study of the Arusha, Agricultural Masai of Northern Tanganyika.* Boston: Boston University Press.

1969a Dispute Settlement Without Courts: The Ndendeueli of Southern Tanzania. In *Law in Culture and Society*, ed. L. Nader, pp. 24-68. Chicago: Aldine.

1969b Introduction: Case Studies of Law in Non-Western Societies. In *Law in Culture and Society*, ed. L. Nader, pp. 11-23. Chicago: Aldine.

Hahm, Pyong-Choon
1967 *The Korean Political Tradition and Law.* Seoul: Hollym.

1968 Korea's Initial Encounter with Western Law: 1866-1910 A.D. *Korea Observer* 1:80-93.

1969a The Decision Process in Korea. In *Comparative Judicial Behavior,* ed. G. Schubert and D. J. Danelski, pp. 19-47. London: Oxford University Press.

1969b Religion and Law in Korea. *Kroeber Anthropological Papers*, no. 41, pp. 8-53.

1970 Law and Justice in Korea. Unpublished paper, Yonsei University, Seoul, Korea.

Hoebel, E. A.
1940 *The Political Organization and Lawways of the Comanche Indians.* American Anthropological Association memoir no. 54. *Contributions from the Santa Fe Laboratory of Anthropology,* vol.4.

1954 *The Law of Primitive Man: A Study of Comparative Legal Dynamics.* Cambridge: Harvard University Press.

Hogbin, H. I.
1934 *Law and Order in Polynesia: A Study of Primitive Legal Institutions.* London: Christophers.

Hunt, E., and R. Hunt
1967 The Role of Courts in Rural Mexico. In *Peasants in the Modern World*, ed. P. Bock, pp. 109-39. Albuquerque: University of New Mexico Press.

Hurst, W.
1960 The Law in United States History. *Proceedings of the American Philosophical Society* 104:518-26.

Jacobs, J.
1968 Violence in the City Streets. In *Violence in the Streets*, ed. S. Endleman, pp. 214-26. Chicago: Quadrangle Books.

Kerner, O.
1968 *The Kerner Report: Report of the National Advisory Commission on Civil Disorders.* New York: New York Times Co.

Koch, K. F.
1967 Conflict and Its Management Among the Jalé People of West New Guinea. Ph.D. dissertation, University of California, Berkeley.

Llewelyn, K. N., and E. A. Hoebel
1941 *The Cheyenne Way: Conflict and Case Law in Primitive Jurisprudence.* Norman: University of Oklahoma Press.

Macaulay, S.
1963 Non-contractual Relations in Business: A Preliminary Study. *American Sociological Review* 28:55-66.

Main, J.
1970 Only Radical Reform Can Save the Courts. *Fortune*, pp. 111-13, 152-54.

Maine, Sir H. S.
1963 *Ancient Law: Its Connection with*

the *Early History of Society and Its Relation to Modern Ideas*. Boston: Beacon Press. Originally published 1861.

Malinowski, B.
  1926 *Crime and Custom in Savage Society*. London: Kegan Paul, Trench, Trubner.
  1942 A New Instrument for the Interpretation of Law—Especially Primitive. *Yale Law Journal* 51:1237-54.

March, J. G.
  1956 Sociological Jurisprudence Revisited: A Review (More or Less) of Max Gluckman. *Stanford Law Review* 8:499-534.

Massell, G. J.
  1968 Law as an Instrument of Revolutionary Change in a Traditional Millieu. *Law and Society Review* 2:179-228.

Metzger, D.
  1960 Conflict in Chulsanto: A Village in Chiapas. *Alpha Kappa Deltan* 30: 35-48.

Mitchell, J. C.
  1956 *The Yao Village: A Study on the Social Structure of a Nyasaland Tribe*. Manchester: Manchester University Press.

Moore, S. F.
  1969 Law and Anthropology. In *Biennial Review of Anthropology, 1969*, ed. B. J. Siegel. Stanford: Stanford University Press.
  1970 Politics, Procedures, and Norms in Changing Chagga Law. *Journal of the International African Institute* 60: 321-43.

Muir, W. K.
  1967 *Prayer in the Public Schools: Law and Attitude Change*. Chicago: University of Chicago Press.

Muratorio, Blanca
  n.d. The Tinterillos: An Ethnographic Approach to the Street Corner Lawyers. Unpublished paper, University of California, Berkeley.

Nadel, S. F.
  1953 Social Control and Self-Regulation. *Social Forces* 31:265-73.

Nader, L.
  1964*a* An Analysis of Zapotec Law Cases. *Ethnology* 3:404-19.
  1964*b* Talea and Juquila: A Comparison of Zapotec Social Organization. *University of California Publications in American Archaeology and Ethnology* 48:195-296.
  1965*a* Choices in Legal Procedure: Shia Moslem and Mexican Zapotec. *American Anthropologist* 67:394-99.
  1965*b* The Anthropological Study of Law. *American Anthropologist* 67, no. 6, pt. 2:3-32.
  1969*a* Introduction. In *Law in Culture and Society*, ed. L. Nader, pp. 1-10. Chicago: Aldine.
  1969*b* Preface. In *Law in Culture and Society*, ed. L. Nader, pp. vii-ix. Chicago: Aldine.
  1969*c* Styles of Court Procedure: To Make the Balance. In *Law in Culture and Society*, ed. L. Nader, pp. 69-91. Chicago: Aldine.
  n.d. To Make the Balance: Essays in Zapotec Law. In preparation.

Nader, L., ed.
  1969 *Law in Culture and Society:* Chicago: Aldine.

Nader, L., and D. Metzger
  1963 Conflict Resolution in Two Mexican Communities. *American Anthropologist* 65:584-92.

Overby, A. L.
  1967 *Discrimination Against Minority Groups in the Administration of Justice*. U.S. President's Commission on Law Enforcement and Administration of Justice. Washington, D.C.: U.S. Government Printing Office.

Packer, H. L.
  1968 *The Limits of the Criminal Sanction*. Stanford: Stanford University Press.

Pigliaru, Antonio
  1959 *La vendetta barbaricina come ordinamento giuridico. Publicazioni dell' Istituto di Filosofia del Dritto dell' Università di Roma*, ed. A. Giuffrè, vol. 13. Milan.

Pospisil, L.
  1958*a Kapauka Papuans and Their Law*. Yale University Publications in Anthropology, no. 54. New Haven: Yale University Press.
  1958*b* Social Change and Primitive Law. *American Anthropologist* 60:832-37.
  1965 A Formal Analysis of Substantive Law: Kapauku Papuan Laws of In-

heritance. In *The Ethnography of Law*, ed. L. Nader, pp. 166-85. *American Anthropologist* 67, no. 6, pt. 2 (special issue).

1967 Legal Levels and Multiplicity of Legal Systems in Human Societies. *Journal of Conflict Resolution* 11: 2-26.

1969 Structural Change and Primitive Law: Consequences of a Papuan Legal Case. In *Law in Culture and Society*, ed. L. Nader, pp. 208-29. Chicago: Aldine.

Pound, Roscoe
1906 The Causes of Popular Dissatisfaction with the Administration of Justice. *Reports of the American Bar Association* 29, pt. 1:295-417.

Quinney, Richard
1970 *The Social Reality of Crime*. Boston: Little, Brown.

Radcliffe-Brown, A. R.
1934 Social Sanctions. In *Encyclopedia of the Social Sciences* 13:531-34. New York: Macmillan.

Richardson, J.
1940 *Law and Status Among the Kiowa Indians*. American Ethnological Society, monograph 1.

Roberts, J. M.
1965 Oaths, Autonomic Ordeals, and Power. In *The Ethnography of Law*, ed. L. Nader, pp. 186-212. *American Anthropologist* 67, no. 6, pt. 2 (special issue).

Ross, L. H.
1961 Traffic Law Violation: A Folk Crime. *Social Problems* 8:231-41.

Sapir, E.
1921 *Language*. New York: Harcourt, Brace.

Sax, J. L.
1967 Civil Disobedience. *Saturday Review*, September 28, pp. 22-25, 56.

Schapera, I.
1938 *A Handbook of Tswana Law and Custom*. New York: Oxford University Press.

1969 Uniformity and Variation in Chief-Made Law: A Tswana Case Study. In *Law in Culture and Society*, ed. L. Nader, pp. 230-44. Chicago: Aldine.

Schubert, G. A.
1959 *Quantitative Analysis of Judicial Behavior*. New York: Free Press of Glencoe, Macmillan.

Schur, E. M.
1969 *Our Criminal Society: The Social and Legal Sources of Crime in America*. Englewood Cliffs, N.J.: Prentice-Hall.

Schwartz, R. D.
1954 Social Factors in the Development of Legal Control: A Case Study of Two Israeli Settlements. *Yale Law Journal* 63:471-91. Reprinted in *Law and the Behavioral Sciences,* ed., L. M. Friedman and S. Macaulay, pp. 509-22. Bobs-Merrill, 1969.

Schwartz, R. D., and S. Orleans
1967 On Legal Sanctions. *University of Chicago Law Review* 34:274-300.

Skolnick, J. H.
1969 *The Politics of Protest*. Task Force on Violent Aspects of Protests and Confrontations. Washington, D.C.: U.S. Government Printing Office.

Smith, M. G.
1965 The Sociological Framework of Law. In *African Law: Adaptation and Development*, ed. H. Kuper and L. Kuper, pp. 24-48. Berkeley: University of California Press.

Spradley, J. P.
1970 *You Owe Yourself a Drunk: An Ethnography of Urban Nomads*. Boston: Little, Brown.

Starr, J.
1969 Mandalinci Köy: Law and Social Control in a Turkish Village. Ph.D. dissertation, University of California, Berkeley.

Stirling, P.
1957 Land, Marriage, and the Law in Turkish Villages: Pt. 1, The Reception of Foreign Law in Turkey. *International Social Science Bulletin* (UNESCO) 9:21-33.

Sutherland, E. H.
1961 *White Collar Crime*. New York: Holt, Rinehart & Winston. Originally published 1949.

Swett, D. H.
1969 Cultural Bias in the American Legal System. *Law and Society Review* 4:79-110.

Turner, V. W.
1957 *Schism and Continuity in an African Society: A Study of Ndembu Village*

Life. Manchester: Manchester University Press.

Van Der Sprenkel, S.
1962 *Legal Institutions in Manchu China: A Sociological Analysis.* London School of Economics Monographs on Social Anthropology, no. 24. London: Athlone Press.

Vansina, J.
1965 *Oral Tradition: A Study in Historical Methodology*, trans. H. N. Wright. Chicago: Aldine.

Van Velsen, J.
1964 *The Politics of Kinship.* Manchester: Manchester University Press.
1967 The Extended-Case Method and Situational Analysis. In *The Craft of Social Anthropology*, ed. A. L. Epstein, pp. 129-49. London: Tavistock.
1969 Procedural Informality, Reconciliation, and False Comparisons. In *Ideas and Procedures in African Customary Law*, ed. M. Gluckman, pp. 137-52. London: Oxford University Press.

Whiting, B. B.
1965 Sex Identity Conflict and Physical Violence: A Comparative Study. In *The Ethnography of Law,* ed. L. Nader, pp. 123-40. *American Anthropologist* 67, no. 6, pt. 2 (special issue).

Whiting, J. W. M.
1954 The Cross-Cultural Method. In *Handbook of Social Psychology,* ed. G. Lindzey, vol. 1, pp. 523-31. Reading, Mass.: Addison Wesley.

Whyte, W. F.
1955 *Street Corner Society: The Social Structure of an Italian Slum,* rev. ed. Chicago: University of Chicago Press. Originally published 1943; paperback ed., 1966.

Wolfgang, M. E.
1967 *Crimes of Violence.* President's Commission on Law Enforcement and Administration of Justice. Washington, D.C.: U.S. Government Printing Office.

Yngvesson, B.
1970 Decision-Making and Dispute Settlement in a Swedish Fishing Village: An Ethnography of Law. Ph.D. dissertation, University of California, Berkeley.
n.d. Berkeley-Albany and Oakland-Piedmont Small Claims Courts: A Comparison of Role of Judge and Social Function of the Courts. Unpublished paper.

CHAPTER 21 The Anthropology of War

KEITH F. OTTERBEIN

While many anthropologists have devoted attention to phenomena variously designated as warfare, feuding, armed conflict, or armed combat, they seldom attempt to define what they are describing. Warfare is defined by Malinowski (1941*b*:522) as "an armed contest between two independent political units, by means of organized military force, in the pursuit of a tribal or national policy." A year earlier Mead (1940:402) had defined warfare as a "recognized conflict between two groups *as groups*, in which each group puts an army (even if the army is only fifteen pygmies) into the field to fight and kill, if possible, some of the members of the army of the other group. . . ."

Recently Mead (1968:215) stated: "Warfare exists if the conflict is organized and socially sanctioned, and the killing is not regarded as murder." Her criteria for this definition (1968: 215-16) are "organization for the purpose of a combat involving the intention to kill and the willingness to die, social sanction for this behavior, which distinguishes it from murder of members of its own group, and the agreement between the groups involved on the legitimacy of the fighting with intent to kill."

Other anthropologists are concerned with the distinction between warfare and feuding. Naroll (1964*a*:286) defines warfare as "public lethal group combat between territorial teams. (N.B. Thus blood feuds between nonterritorially defined kin groups are not considered warfare.)" A territorial team is "a group of people whose membership is defined in terms of occupancy of a common territory and who have an official with the special function of announcing group decisions—a function exercised at least once a year." My own distinction between warfare and feuding is based upon Naroll's definition of a territorial team. In my definitions the term "political community" has the same meaning as Naroll's "territorial team." Warfare is "armed combat between political communities," while feuding is "a type of armed combat occurring within a political community, in which if a homicide occurs, the kin of the deceased take revenge through killing the offender or any member of his kin group" (Otterbein 1968*b*:93). Armed combat is fighting with weapons. The fighting is performed by military organizations (Otterbein 1970:3-5).

Schneider (1950:777), a sociologist, is critical of those anthropologists who consider "fighting which occurs among primitives who live in exogamous clans or local residence groups" as warfare. For Schneider, such fighting is a "matter of crime and punishment within populations where systems of public justice are undeveloped." Although he does not explicitly say so, Schneider seems to imply that fighting between exogamous kinship groups is feuding. In a review article on feuding, Pospisil (1968) takes issue with Schneider. Pospisil's definition (1968:392)

sets feud apart from war and external self-redress because the last two terms refer to acts of violence committed by members of politically unrelated groups: in war both combat groups act as units in the organized fighting; in external self-redress members of two subgroups only, each belonging to a different, politically unrelated group, participate in the hostilities.

Feud itself consists of a series of acts of violence—injury, revenge, and counterrevenge—"usually involving killings, committed by members of two groups related to each other by superimposed political-structural features . . . and acting on the basis of group solidarity. . . ."

From three basic concepts—warfare, political community, and cultural unit—I have derived three types of warfare (Otterbein 1968*a*, 1970). The first two concepts have been defined above; the third is derived from Malinowski (1941*b*). "A cultural unit is composed of contiguous political communities that are culturally similar" (Otterbein 1968*a*:277). Internal war is "warfare between political communities within

the same cultural unit." External war is "warfare between culturally different political communities, i.e., political communities which are not members of the same cultural unit." I distinguish two types of external war (Otterbein 1968*a*:277; 1970:84-92): offensive external war (external war—attacking) and defensive external war (external war—being attacked). The two types of external war can be combined to produce a third measure of external war (Otterbein 1968*a*:286-87). Ember and Ember (1971) make a similar distinction between internal and external war.

WARFARE IN ANTHROPOLOGICAL LITERATURE

Although many ethnographies contain brief but adequate descriptions of warfare, there are actually few anthropological books and articles that are devoted primarily to the analysis of warfare. There are adequate ethnographies for comparative research (Otterbein 1970:11). In order to have a fifty-society probability sample for a cross-cultural study, I needed to peruse the sources for seventy-four societies. Thus two-thirds of the randomly chosen ethnographic accounts examined had sufficient information on warfare to be included in the study. On the other hand, the theoretical anthropological literature dealing with warfare is scant compared to the thousands of books and articles devoted to such topics as kinship, religion, and technology. The list of references at the end of this article, which attempts to be comprehensive, includes fewer than 250 items, and not all the items listed are written by anthropologists or discuss warfare. A few books are included, primarily those noted for their sections on warfare (e.g., Barton 1919, Berndt 1962, Evans-Pritchard 1940, Karsten 1923, Keiser 1969, Mariner 1820, M. E. Opler 1938, and Warner 1958). A substantial number of articles are included which deal solely with warfare, but from a descriptive point of view (e.g., Beemer 1937; Bell 1935; Fortune 1939, 1947, 1960; Glasse 1959; Goldschmidt, Foster, and Essene 1939; Grinnell 1910; Hasluck 1967; Hill 1936; Hocart 1931; Jeffreys 1956; Kroeber 1928; Landes 1959; M. K. Opler 1939; Padden 1957; Skinner 1911; Slobodin 1960; K. M. Stewart 1947; Van der Kroef 1952; Warner 1931; and Zegwaard 1959). Several historical and ethnohistorical studies are listed (e.g., Adcock 1962, Ajayi and Smith 1964, Bram 1941, Follett 1932, Oman 1960, Peckham 1961, Russel 1957, Wales 1952, Wintringham 1943, Wolf 1959, Woolley 1965, and Yamada 1916). Recently Divale (1971*b*) has compiled a comprehensive bibliography on warfare which lists many descriptive studies not cited above.

There are few review articles on war. Regional reviews cover Oceania (Wedgewood 1930), highland New Guinea (Berndt 1964), and the northeastern woodlands of the United States (Hadlock 1947). Vayda and Leeds (1961) present a brief introduction to three articles that appear in one issue of the journal *Anthropologica*. Two review articles dealing with the anthropology of conflict scarcely touch upon the subject of warfare (Siegel and Beals 1960, LeVine 1961). Pope (1962) describes a series of experiments with the bow and arrow and draws a number of conclusions concerning the efficiency of various weapons, and Klopsteg (1963) discusses various types of bows and arrows used in the New World. Carneiro (1970*b*:865-66), who is undertaking cross-cultural studies of cultural evolution, has recently published his comprehensive trait list: 57 out of 618 traits deal exclusively with warfare. The evidence for warfare and "intrahuman killing" in the Pleistocene is surveyed by Roper, who concludes (1969:448) that "although there seems to be sound evi-

dence for sporadic intrahuman killing, the known data is not sufficient to document warfare."

Collections of papers and readings include only a limited number of selections by anthropologists dealing with primitive warfare. One volume titled *War: Studies from Psychology, Sociology, Anthropology* (Bramson and Goethals, eds., 1964) contains twenty-one selections, only two by anthropologists—Malinowski (1941*b*) and Mead (1940). Three other selections, by McDougall (1964), Sumner (1911), and Schneider (1950), deal with primitive war. (The revised edition includes an article by a third anthropologist, Vayda [1968*b*].) A reader titled *Law and Warfare: Studies in the Anthropology of Conflict* (Bohannan 1967) contains twenty-three selections; only six are case studies of primitive war. At the 1967 annual meetings of the American Anthropological Association a symposium devoted solely to warfare was held. While all but two of the sixteen papers are by anthropologists, nine of the contributions scarcely deal with primitive war. (Twelve of the items are listed in the bibliography to this article.) This group of papers has since been published (Fried, Harris, and Murphy, eds., 1968). Reviews of the collection have not been favorable (Fürer-Haimendorf 1968, Fox 1969). Fox's review (1969:315) in the *American Anthropologist* concludes. "Somehow I don't think this is the book on WAR that the world has been waiting for."

Few textbooks in anthropology make more than passing mention of warfare. A perusal of many anthropological textbooks reveals only five that include sections or chapters on warfare. Keesing (1958:295-97) has a brief chapter. The second edition of Hoebel's (1958:508-22) textbook contains a substantial chapter. Honigmann (1959:504-507) provides a brief section. Bohannan (1963:301-306) has a section on diplomacy and warfare. And Turney-High, who is the author of a book on primitive war (1949), devotes part of a chapter of his *Man and System* (1968:381-88) to warfare. I include three sections on warfare and one on feuding in my textbook (Otterbein 1972).

Why have anthropologists been so little concerned with the study of warfare? Only a tentative answer can be given. If one is willing to accept the assumption that most of the major problems and research areas in anthropology have been set forth and delineated by great anthropologists, an answer is available. A scanning of the references listed at the end of this article reveals few articles and no books written by the major figures in anthropology. Not one important anthropologist has devoted more than a small fraction of his professional life to the study of warfare. This is still, however, not a satisfactory answer to our initial question. It raises a further question: Why were the great anthropologists not interested in studying warfare? There are several possible answers: (1) The peoples studied by most anthropologists, even in the nineteenth century, had ceased to engage in war long before the anthropologists arrived on the scene; hence warfare was not an ongoing phenomenon while they were conducting their fieldwork. (2) Many anthropologists have been morally opposed to war. Two of the founding fathers, Tylor, a Quaker, and Boas, a German expatriate, were pacifists. Currently many anthropologists oppose specifically the war in southeast Asia. In most instances this opposition, for reasons that seem sufficient to them, precludes their studying war in general. Those who participated in the 1967 symposium are notable exceptions. (3) Early anthropologists failed to appreciate the important role that warfare can play in the affairs of primitive societies. Although these an-

thropologists were omnivorous readers, many of them focused their attention upon the humanities rather than upon the writings of historians and political scientists. Thus they were more likely to "discover" the importance of, for example, folklore and mythology among primitive peoples than military organization and warfare.

The situation is changing today. In the past decade or two a number of anthropologists have begun to turn their attention to the study of war. In 1964 the profession was treated to a film that shows actual battle scenes taken among the Dani of highland New Guinea (Gardner 1964). A book version' of the film (Gardner and Heider 1968), a popular account (Matthiessen 1962), and an ethnographic account of the Dani (Heider 1970) are available. And one anthropologist (Wolf 1969) has recently turned his attention to the study of peasant wars. Many of the publications reviewed in this paper have been written in the last fifteen years. Since many of these publications are not well known, more space will be devoted to these contributions than to better known works published in the first half of this century.

APPROACHES TO WARFARE

Warfare, when it has been analyzed by anthropologists, has been treated as a topic, not a theoretical approach. That is, it is a topic to be studied in the sense that kinship, religion, or technology is a topic, rather than a theoretical approach such as evolutionism, functionalism, or structuralism. Many studies of warfare, as we have seen, are purely descriptive; many other studies are primarily descriptive, but have theoretical approaches injected into them. As a rule, these studies reflect the theoretical interests of the period at which they were written. Thus in the nineteenth century warfare was viewed from an evolutionary perspective and now it is seen from an ecological perspective. Hence it seems appropriate to review the literature dealing with primitive war according to the theoretical approach employed, since warfare is a topic rather than a theory per se.

Sixteen approaches are used to classify the various studies of primitive warfare. Since half of the approaches treat war as a dependent variable (i.e., as a phenomenon to be explained by independent variables) and the other half treat war as an independent variable (i.e., as a phenomenon that explains certain dependent variables), the theories can be grouped into two major categories: (1) causes of war and (2) effects of war. However, rather than first discuss the eight approaches that purport to explain the causes of war and then the eight approaches that purport to describe the effects of war, it is possible to pair the approaches and discuss first a cause-of-war approach and then an effect-of-war approach, then another cause-of-war approach and another effect-of-war approach, and so on until all eight pairs of approaches have been described. The paired theoretical approaches are these:

Causes of War (Dependent Variable)	Effects of War (Independent Variable)
Innate aggression	On species
Frustration-aggression	Ethnocentrism
Diffusion	Acculturation
Physical environment	Ecological adaptation
Goals of war	Patterns and themes
Social structure	On social organization
Military preparedness	Survival value
Cultural evolution	Origin of the state

The logic behind pairing the approaches is simple. For each pair, the variable that is responsible for warfare (first column) is essentially the same variable that is affected by warfare (second column). For example, the "innate aggression" approach finds in biological

man the cause of war, while the "effects on species" approach examines the effects of war upon man viewed biologically. The following variables appear to be common to each pair of remaining approaches: hatred of enemy, spread of invention, natural environment, values of men, social groupings, efficient military organization, and level of sociopolitical complexity. There is no inherent logic to the order in which the pairs are presented. "Cultural evolution" and "origin of the state" could just as well be the first pair as the last.

INNATE AGGRESSION

An instinct of pugnacity or aggression is used by some nonanthropologists to explain fighting not only between individual men, but between groups of men. The instinct is viewed as an innate, genetically based drive. For McDougall (1926), a psychologist who conducted ethnographic fieldwork in Oceania, it is an inherited predisposition that can be activated by some instigating frustrating condition. For Freud (1959) it is a constantly operating force continually seeking release. Warfare, for instinct theorists, is rooted in man's psychobiological heritage.

McDougall's theory is of interest in part because he finds support for it in his field research. He assumes that the "races of men certainly differ greatly in respect to the innate strength of this instinct," which may be directed from one's fellow villagers to members of other villages (1964:33):

The replacement of individual by collective pugnacity is most clearly illustrated by barbarous peoples living in small, strongly organized communities. Within such communities individual combat and even expression of personal anger may be almost completely suppressed, while the pugnacious instinct finds its vent in perpetual warfare between communities whose relations remain subject to no law.

Intergroup warfare selected men not only for their pugnacity, but for their "moral qualities." Those groups that had warriors who, because of a "more developed self-consciousness," obeyed the commands of leaders were the groups that were successful in war. Thus the instinct of pugnacity impelled primitive societies to war, which in turn led to the defeat of those societies whose warriors were deficient in "fundamental social attributes." The victors had "superior moral qualities," which McDougall believes were related to a strengthening of the "gregarious instinct" and the "instincts of self-assertion and subjection." The tribes of Borneo which McDougall studied provide support for his theory. The more warlike tribes of the interior were superior to their neighbors living in the coastal regions. They built better houses, their "domestic morality" was superior, they were "mentally more active," they were "more trustworthy," and their social organization was "more efficient." "Yet all these tribes are of closely allied racial stocks, and the superior moral qualities of the central tribes would seem to be the direct result of the very severe group-selection to which their innate pugnacity has subjected them for many generations" (1964:39). Perry (1917), a British diffusionist, provides a refutation of the theory by pointing to McDougall's own fieldwork. McDougall claims that the Punan of the central highlands are among the finest of the peoples of Borneo; he also describes the Punan as going to war only seldom, and never going to war to take heads.

In 1966 two books that attribute warfare to innate aggression were published. These books, one by an ethologist, Konrad Lorenz (1966), and the other by a writer, Robert Ardrey (1966), have—one is tempted to say—evoked the aggressive instinct in many anthropologists. Critical reviews of Lorenz' and Ardrey's theories are to be found reprinted in a volume edited by Ashley Montagu (1968a). Reviewers include Gorer (1968a, 1968b), Holloway (1968a, 1968b), La Barre (1969), Leach (1968), Montagu (1968b), and Sahlins (1968). Since Lorenz includes a discussion of Ute aggression in his book, Montagu's edited volume includes two previously unpublished articles by Beatty (1968) and O. C. Stewart (1968) that refute Lorenz' contentions with ethnographic data. Three criticisms can be leveled against the innate aggression theories of Lorenz and Ardrey: (1) Their theories are simplistic to the point of being tautological: Men go to war because they are compelled to go to war. Why are they compelled to go to war? Because they possess an aggressive instinct. (2) Fighting between two men is not warfare. None of the definitions of warfare quoted above asserts that personal combat per se is war. They all contain the notion that the fighting is between groups of men. Lorenz and Ardrey do not—as McDougall, for instance, does—explain how fighting between men of a single social group becomes curbed and rechanneled toward other groups. Nor do their theories explain why some groups are more warlike than others, or why different groups wage war differently. (3) There is no physiological evidence that man possesses an aggressive instinct. Men fight, it seems to me, because they stand upright and have two free hands that can hold tools or weapons. The tools can be used to strike other men as easily as they can be used to kill animals.

Effects on Species

Warfare can have a biological effect upon particular cultures and upon mankind as a whole. The outline followed here is adapted from Hulse's review article (1961). Warfare, through deaths in battles, can alter the age and sex composition of a particular culture. Divale (1970) assembles a massive array of census data to demonstrate that in many primitive societies the sex ratio is frequently three boys to two girls. This discrepancy is attributed to female infanticide. Yet the adult sex ratio for the same societies is approximately one man to one woman. He attributes this drop to battlefield deaths. Divale's (1971a) case study of Ibo warfare provides further support for the theory. Warfare, for various reasons, increases disease rates, which in turn lead to higher death rates. Disease rates increase because of crowded conditions, poor sanitation, malnutrition, and new contacts between peoples with different susceptibilities to communicable diseases. Alland (1968) describes how destruction of forested regions can force diseased animals into contact with domestic animals. The stricken domestic animals then transmit the diseases to man. Paul (1968) concurs with Alland's analysis. Warfare, through differential death rates, alters the sizes of populations relative to each other. Livingstone (1968) argues that many primitive societies have had a much higher proportion of deaths due to war than modern nations. A reviewer of Livingstone's paper agrees (Thieme 1968). Divale's census data (1970) also supports this interpretation. Cook (1946) describes the effects of warfare and sacrifice upon the population of the Valley of Mexico just prior to the Spanish conquest.

According to Hulse (1961), warfare, for a number of reasons, may result in stimulating or impeding shifts in gene frequencies. The extinction of genetically distinct groups will produce a shift. Returning warriors may bring home diseases that have a selective influence upon the population, and captured females may introduce new genes into the population. Warriors may spread their genes among the peoples in whose lands they are fighting. Conquerors who establish themselves as aristocracies may, by taking multiple wives, concubines, and mistresses, contribute many genes to the conquered population. Migrations and dispersions of populations may create new genetic mixtures. The genes that Hulse considers are not ones that would give their bearers an advantage in battle. Livingstone (1968) speculates that size, strength, and hair (which makes a warrior look fierce) may have been selected because of their relationship to fighting ability. Perhaps intelligence could be added to this list. However, Brues (1959:467) argues that a "dominant weapon or tool may alter the average physique of a race using it over the course of time by giving a selective advantage to individuals of a body build best adapted to its use." She speculates that spearmen developed linear builds, while archers developed lateral builds and strong shoulders. Those who used blunt crushing implements developed heavily built physiques. There is no evidence, as I have said, that fighting or warfare has produced or contributed to the development of an aggressive instinct in man.

FRUSTRATION-AGGRESSION

The frustrations of everyday life create an aggressiveness that is often channeled into warfare. This is not to say that frustration actually causes war; frustration-aggression theorists, at least among anthropologists and psychologists, have been careful not to make this claim. Their theories do imply, however, that once military organizations exist, the more frustrated a people becomes, the more likely it is to go to war. The classic formulation of this theory comes from psychology (Dollard et al. 1939:1): "This study takes as its point of departure the assumption that *aggression is always a consequence of frustration*. More specifically the proposition is that the occurrence of aggressive behavior always presupposes the existence of frustration and, contrariwise, that the existence of frustration always leads to some form of aggression." Dollard's monograph concludes with a case study of the Ashanti of West Africa, which contains a discussion of warfare. Ashanti warriors were expected to commit suicide rather than submit to capture. This custom is interpreted as stemming from the frustrations aroused in the individual warrior by battle conditions. These frustrations in turn arouse aggression directed against the king and his authority. Capture and desertion are manifestations of this aggression, which is prohibited. On the other hand, warfare itself is an outlet for aggression. Aggressive manifestations "are enjoined in war where the expression of aggression serves a socially useful end" (Dollard et al. 1939:190). The present status of frustration-aggression theory in psychology is reviewed by Berkowitz (1962).

Frustration-aggression theory is used by Murphy (1957) to explain the ferocity of Mundurucu warfare. These Amazon-dwelling Indians did not war with each other, but conducted long-distance raids of annihilation upon enemy tribes. Intervillage matrilocality distributed Mundurucu males throughout the culture, producing a social structural situation in which related male kinsmen resided in different communities with their affines. If overt conflicts were to occur, Mundurucu villages would be torn to pieces. This did not occur because men repressed their grievances, since they could not rely

upon the support of their kinsmen residing elsewhere. Fraternal interest group theory had its genesis in this part of Murphy's theory (see "Social Structure"). (This repressed hostility achieves release through warfare.) The article led to an exchange between Wilson (1958) and Murphy (1958), Wilson arguing that societal needs account for Mundurucu warfare and Murphy arguing that psychological needs are responsible. Ellis (1951:199), in a review of Pueblo Indian warfare, concludes that "warfare served to provide legitimate outlet for the frustrations and aggressions arising from unpermitted competition or suspicions thereof among peoples of the same general culture." And Steward and Faron (1959:325-30) suggest that the need for social harmony in crowded Tupinamba villages resulted in frustrations that found expression in warfare. Historical accounts describe these Indians of coastal Brazil as engaging in relentless warfare and in extremely cruel torture of captives.

(When I began this review I expected to find more examples of the use of this theory. Possibly I have overlooked some, since the theory can be subtly applied in a descriptive study without any overt reference to frustration-aggression theory.)

Ethnocentrism

A consequence of war is hatred of the enemy. Complementing this sentiment is love of one's own people. Over fifty years ago Sumner gave the technical name "ethnocentrism" to this phenomenon. He states (1906:12-13): "The relationship of comradeship and peace in the we-group and that of hostility and war towards others-groups are correlative to each other. . . . Loyalty to the group, sacrifice for it, hatred and contempt for outsiders, brotherhood within, warlikeness without—all grow together, common products of the same situation." What this situation was, Sumner (1911) describes in greater detail elsewhere. It was the "competition of life": When men as members of groups "extort from nature the supplies they need," a conflict of interests arises. If supplies are large and the number of men is small, the conflict may be mild; if there are many men striving for a small supply, the conflict may be violent. The competition of life is responsible for war. Sumner's theory is undergoing long-term analysis and testing by Campbell and LeVine (1961, 1965), and results of their study have just recently begun to become available (LeVine 1970).

Support for the ethnocentrism approach of Sumner can be found in Gorer's study of the Lepcha of the southern slopes of the Himalayas. Gorer (1938:163, 446-49) states that Sumner's theory does not hold true for these people, because they are not aggressive toward other groups and internal conflict is at a minimum; however, the reasons he gives for the Lepcha's failure to develop any pattern of external aggression are in accord with Sumner's theory. The reasons include "their isolation, their low material development, and the difficulties of wresting a livelihood from their environment." Thus the "competition of life" is at a minimal level. Gorer also attributes the lack of internal conflict to child-rearing practices that place few demands upon children and to strong social sanctions against quarreling. If Gorer had written his study after the publication of Dollard's classic monograph, he might have pointed out that the Lepcha do not provide support for frustration-aggression theory, since their lives are frustrating and they do not war with neighbors. However, frustration-aggression

theorists would probably see evidence for their theory in the high rate of Lepcha suicide and their projection of fear upon malevolent deities.

Two anthropological studies are congruent with the ethnocentrism approach, although neither was designed to test Sumner's theory. Wallace (1968) describes the process of mobilization that occurs when a political community in a "relaxed state" transforms itself into a "mobilized state" in preparation for war. He argues that fear and hatred of the enemy are not prerequisites for war, but develop once mobilization is achieved. Diamond (1968) is critical of Wallace's theory, for, as he points out, wars may occur when political communities are not mobilized. Leach (1965), in describing the nature of primitive warfare, argues that most people who can be called primitive conceive of the world "out-there" as composed of three categories: near, intermediate, and far. The near out-there consists of home, the local village, kinsfolk, friends, tame animals, and witches. The intermediate out-there consists of village fields, neighboring villages, affinal relatives with whom "we" exchange wives, enemies against whom "we" make war, wild animals, and ghosts. (The far out-there need not be described here). For Leach (1965:175), "killing is a classifying operation. We kill our enemies; we do not kill our friends."

DIFFUSION

Warfare is regarded by a few anthropologists as an invention peculiar to man. Once invented, war, or rather the institution of war, diffused from its point of origin to other peoples. An early and extreme statement of this approach is to be found in the writings of the British diffusionists of the early twentieth century. Perry, a member of the diffusionist school, argues that warfare was invented in and spread from Egypt (1917:14):

The hypothesis that warfare originated among a sun-worshipping aristocracy is therefore in accordance with the facts. . . . It can be shown that the motive which led the 'children of the sun' to the ends of the earth, was that of the exploitation of wealth, and examples could be quoted of the manner in which they enslaved whole populations to work in their mines.

A more sophisticated version of the approach is Mead's (1940) treatment of war as "only an invention." She states (1940:272-73): "So simple peoples and civilized peoples, mild peoples and violent, assertive peoples, will all go to war if they have the invention. . . . Warfare is just an invention known to the majority of human societies. . . ." Mead does not discuss the diffusion of the institution of war.

Several scholars concern themselves with the development and spread of warfare from central Eurasia. Schneider (1952:69) regards "war as an invention of relatively late origin." Although he cautiously states that "warfare did not begin with the battle-axe people" of Europe (1952:71), he nevertheless concludes that the civilizations of the Old World were "inundated by invasions of peoples generally in possession of war chariots and using weapons of bronze" (1952:74). Thus for Schneider, warfare—and he apparently means efficiently waged war—diffused from central Europe throughout the Eastern Hemisphere. Childe (1941), in a study of war in prehistoric societies, provides evidence for a drastic upsurge in warfare which occurred in Europe in late Neolithic times. Childe is also explicitly opposed to the theory of the British diffusionists. The devastating effectiveness of barbarian invaders upon complex civilizations has been discussed by Downs (1960), who attributes their success to well-equipped cavalry and hit-and-run tactics. An interpretation of the cause of such invasions is to be found in Teggart's (1939) study of Rome and China. This historian argues that wars in particular locations disrupted trade routes that were supplying peoples beyond the periphery of the civilized world. When these peoples no longer received the goods to which they had become accustomed, they invaded the great civilizations in order to obtain them.

Acculturation

Acculturation is an approach that, while taking diffusion for granted, examines the influence of the diffused practice or culture trait upon warfare itself and upon the way of life of the members of the recipient culture. One need not know when or where war was invented, or even be concerned with the matter, in order to employ an acculturational approach. Knowles (1940), in a study of the torture of captives by the indians of eastern North America, delineates three torture patterns—frame, pole and stake, and platform—which had specific geographical distributions. Frame torture was located in the lower Mississippi region, pole and stake torture in the Southeast, and platform torture among the Iroquois. Knowles describes the manner in which these methods of torture were integrated into the warfare practices of the Indians of these regions. Although diffusion is not a basic focus of his study, Knowles does suggest that frame torture diffused from Middle America, that pole and stake torture had a European origin, and that platform torture was an Iroquoian practice that diffused to tribes with whom the Iroquois fought. Linton (1944), in a study of the fortified villages of the Pueblo peoples (Anasazi culture) of the Southwest, argues that warfare itself could have been responsible for the construction of their elaborate fortifications, many in virtually inaccessible places. He believed that "the building of fortifications by one group would necessitate similar action by other groups..." (Linton 1944:31). A typology of defensive systems of archaeologically known groups in the Southwest can be found in Farmer's review (1957).

Weapons and horses are traits that have received considerable attention in studies employing an acculturational approach. The most important of these studies is Secoy's (1953) analysis of changing military patterns on the Great Plains. Secoy shows how the diffusion of horses northward from the Southwest influenced aboriginal warfare practices in western North America. Warriors became mounted while continuing to use their traditional weapons. Next he shows how the diffusion of firearms westward from the Atlantic seaboard influenced Indian warfare east of the Mississippi River. Fighting from ambush, with the warriors often deployed in long lines, was the most efficient way of using the slow-loading muskets. The Post-horse–Pre-gun pattern and the Post-gun–Pre-horse pattern, as Secoy calls them, met in the eastern Great Plains and a new mode of warfare developed, called the Horse and Gun pattern. Warriors equipped with firearms went to war mounted on horseback. One gains the impression from reading Secoy's analysis that this new pattern entailed cavalry battles consisting of warriors, equipped with firearms, fighting from horseback. Secoy does not describe the pattern as such, but his overall argument implies it. Actually cavalry battles rarely occurred. Horses were usually used simply to transport war-

riors to and from the scene of battle. Small-scale battles with firearms continued. Both the battles described by Secoy and descriptions of battles in ethnographic accounts, such as Ewers' (1955) and Grinnell's (1956) treatment of Blackfoot and Cheyenne warfare, support this interpretation. Thus it can be argued that the Horse and Gun pattern was an elaboration of the Post-gun–Pre-horse pattern, rather than a new pattern that emerged from a synthesis of the Post-horse–Pre-gun pattern and the Post-gun–Pre-horse pattern.

Other studies also show the influence of weapons on warfare. I have described elsewhere (Otterbein 1964) how the Iroquois altered their tactics to accommodate the use of newly acquired firearms. At first the muskets were used as shock weapons in charges upon enemy lines and fortifications, and later they were used in sniping from behind forest cover. In another study (Otterbein 1967) I have shown how the invention of the short stabbing spear and envelopment tactics by Shaka, a Zulu chief, resulted in an increase in casualty rates for the Zulu and for the neighboring Nguni tribes of South Africa. Changes in the military organization and in the goals of war were also responsible for the increase. The study also shows how rapidly the new weapons and tactics diffused to enemy tribes—three years, to be exact (Otterbein 1967:354). Gluckman (1960) and Ritter (1957) have also described Zulu warfare. According to Kiefer (1967), when modern firearms diffused to the Tausug, who live on the island of Jolo in the Philippines, four major effects occurred: (1) a lessening of the number and significance of large political alliances, (2) a lessening of the ethical basis of self-help as a legal institution, (3) an increase in cash-crop production in order to purchase guns, and (4) an immediate increase in the death rate. Kiefer discusses Tausug armed combat in greater detail in two other papers (1968, 1970) and in an unpublished monograph (1969).

PHYSICAL ENVIRONMENT

Few anthropologists argue that the physical environment or a culture's mode of adaptation to its environment is responsible for warfare. Gorer (1938:447), for one, believes that war is correlated with subsistence technology:

People dependent entirely or chiefly on vegetable food, whether gathered or cultivated, will have less obvious cause for aggression outside the group than those dependent on animals; however many domestic animals you possess, stolen animals can still constitute a useful addition to your property; if you have as much land as you can cultivate, extra land is merely an added burden.

No one has actually substantiated this argument. Ekvall (1961, 1964), while not claiming that the possession of large herds is a cause of Tibetan warfare, demonstrates that the nomadic way of life of these people serves as preparation for war. Vayda (1961), in a comparative study of Iban and Maori warfare, argues that these Borneo and New Zealand peoples, because of their mode of agriculture (shifting cultivation), have traditionally been in constant need of new land. Warfare permitted them to expand territorially. Through warfare, central political units forced peripheral units to expand into either uninhabited or inhabited territory. Thus Vayda found both the Iban and the Maori expanding into regions of virgin forests. But since second-growth land is easier to use, frequently the expansion was at the expense of other peoples. This was often the case

for the Iban, who, unlike the Maori, shared their island with culturally different native populations. Elsewhere Vayda has discussed Iban (1969) and Maori (1960, 1970) warfare in detail.

Ecological Adaption

A view that has gained recent popularity is the ecological approach. In the broad sense, ecology deals with the relationship of men and other animals to each other and to the physical environment. For those anthropologists who subscribe to this approach, an equitable distribution of resources is viewed as ecologically desirable—for man, that is—since it makes for greater utilization of natural resources. Since a possible consequence of warfare is the reallocation of resources, either land or animal, ecologists have been interested in the effects of war. Leeds (1963:76-78), in a survey, lists a number of ecological effects that war can produce. Resources may be augmented, as in the case of territorial aggrandizement; resources may be used more intensively during and after wars; and "warfare may lead to the exploitation of new resources or of old resources in new ways." Internally, warfare "reorders the allocation of rewards within the society," and it leads to the "redistribution of labor both quantitatively among old uses and qualitatively among new labor uses." Externally, warfare produces the "immediate or delayed movement of resources," and it sets into motion "cultural diffusion, producing, in the long run, an ever larger trait content in warring entities from which to select responses."

In a review article Vayda places the ecological study of war into a functional framework and sets forth a series of hypotheses concerning the functions of primitive war in maintaining or regulating certain economic, demographic, and psychological variables (1968a:88-89):

(1) A diminishing per capita food supply and increasing intra-group competition for resources generate intense domestic frustrations and other in-group tensions; (2) when these tensions reach a certain level, release is sought in warfare with an enemy group; (3) a result of the warfare is reduction of the pressure of people upon the land, either because of heavy battle mortality or because of the victorious group's taking its defeated and dispersed enemy's territory; (4) the reduced pressure on the land means that the diminution of per capita food supply and the increase of intra-group competition over resources are arrested and that domestic frustrations and other in-group tensions can be kept within tolerable limits.

Vayda has been criticized by Lesser (1968) and by others attending the meeting at which he read his paper (Fried, Harris, and Murphy, eds., 1968:97-102) for using only an equilibrium model in his attempt to understand war. In a similar article Vayda (1968b) further discusses warfare as a regulating variable.

Two ecological hypotheses have received tentative support. In a study that classifies animal and human fighting into types, Suttles (1961:161) suggests that "warfare in those primitive societies where numerous small groups live in a state of actual or potential hostility . . . has the same spacing-out function that reproductive fighting has among other animals." Comments on this article have been provided by Scott (1961). Vayda's (1961) study of the Iban and the Maori can be seen as providing support for this hypothesis (see "Physical Environment"). The hypothesis that one function of warfare is to redistribute resources has received support in Sweet's (1965) case study of camel raiding among north Arabian Bedouin. She shows that groups with the greatest number of camels become the victims of the raiding activities of enemy groups with fewer camels. Sweet believes that this raiding is a "mechanism of ecological adaptation," since it results in more equitable distribution of animals vital to life in the desert.

GOALS OF WAR

One approach to the causes of war which has found favor among many anthropologists stems from the notion that wars are caused by men who are attempting to obtain certain goals at the expense of other men. When men employ armed combat to achieve these goals, they are engaged in warfare. Some analysts believe that the goals exist within the minds of individual warriors, while other analysts believe that the genesis of the goals is the culture itself.

Those subscribing to the view that the goals pursued by means of warfare are to be sought in the minds of the warriors include Fathauer (1954:115), who argues that the Mohave of the American Southwest were motivated to go to war to satisfy magico-religious beliefs that were integral to their culture; Vayda (1969:219), who believes that to understand the early phase of Iban head-hunting satisfactorily, one must consider the thoughts and feelings of these Borneo warriors; and Naroll (1966:17), who in a cross-cultural study of primitive war concerns himself with "what the members of a war party in a particular culture have in mind when they set out for the attack."

Those who believe that the goals of war spring from the culture itself include White (1949:132), who eschews psychological explanations and argues for a culturalogical explanation of war; Newcombe (1950:329), who contends that Plains Indians went to war because their sociocultural systems obliged them to; and Wilson (1958:1195), who sees in Mundurucu warfare a cultural imperative requiring these South American Indians to recruit new members.

For empirical purposes it does not seem critical to maintain this cultural-psychological dichotomy, as Vayda labels it (1969:212). A similar point of view is expressed by Smith (1951:359). When a goal is a part of the culture of a people, it is a value; when the goal becomes internalized in individuals, it is a motive. Thus a value and a motive are the same; the difference between them lies in the mind of the analyst. If he focuses upon the culture, he calls the goal a value; if he focuses upon individuals, he calls the goal a motive. A succinct statement of this approach is to be found in my recent cross-cultural study of primitive war (Otterbein 1970:63-64):

The approach to the causes of war utilized in this study assumes that wars are caused by military organizations which go to war in order to obtain certain goals. These goals may vary from war to war, and they may change over time. Thus for any political community there will probably be several goals of war. At any given period in the history of the political community, if sufficient data are available, the order of importance of these goals can be ascertained. Whether the officials of the political community determine the goals and send the military organization to war in order to achieve these goals, or whether the leaders of the military make the decision as to the goals does not alter the nature of this approach. Thus the approach assumes that wars are caused by the decisions of men as members of organizations, whether they are military organizations or governing bodies. Six reasons for going to war are delineated in this study: subjugation and tribute, land, plunder, trophies and honors, defense, and revenge. These six represent a classification scheme for grouping a wide range of possible goals.

I have applied this approach in a field study of the Mwecika Higi of northern Nigeria (Otterbein 1968c).

The particular Higi political community I studied fought with five other Higi political communities. The number of goals of war and the order of their importance to the Mwecika Higi varied from one political community to the next. Ideally, the study could have been more comprehensive. I should have focused upon not just one Higi political community, but several, and I should have enumerated the various battles between the political communities and listed their particular causes. One study that does list causes for particular battles is Pospisil's study of the Kapauku (1958), a highland New Guinea people who were still waging war when he conducted his fieldwork.

Several general studies of primitive war provide lists of the various goals of war found in various cultures. Swanton (1943:7-17), who regards revenge as the leading war motive among primitive peoples, lists in addition social advancement, excitement, religious obligation, capture of women and slaves, plunder, appropriation of territory, trade, defense, and fear. Turney-High (1949: 141-204) discusses these same goals and others at length under the headings of sociopsychological motives, the economic motive, and military values. Smith (1951) groups causes of American Indian warfare into "four major sets of distributions": feud or simple reprisal, social contests, shame-aggression, and mourning-war. In an earlier article Smith (1938) discusses the goals of Plains Indian warfare in terms of a war complex that contains ingredients of the above "distributions." Speier (1941) describes three types of war: absolute, in which the object is to annihilate the enemy; instrumental, in which the object is to gain access to political, economic, and religious values controlled by the enemy; and antagonistic, in which the object is to achieve glory. In a recent paper Tefft (1969) hypothesizes that if political communities fight for goals that are nonnegotiable, they are unlikely to develop systematic peacemaking procedures; whereas if they fight for negotiable goals, they are likely to develop such procedures. Thus Tefft implies that goals that meet social and psychological needs are less likely to be negotiable than economic and political goals. The hypothesis remains to be tested.

Several case studies of specific tribal groups emphasize the importance of the goals of war in their descriptions of warfare. Mishkin (1940), although not directly disagreeing with Smith (1938), stresses the importance of economic goals in understanding Plains Indian warfare, particularly Kiowa warfare. The Nootka of the Northwest Coast, as shown in an analysis by Swadesh (1948) of texts collected by Sapir, fought for multiple reasons, including revenge, slaves, plunder, heads, status, and occasionally territorial rights. Codere (1950:105) contrasts the warfare of the Kwakiutl with that of the Nootka, their close neighbors, and concludes that "it is impossible to discover in Kwakiutl warfare an underlying economic motivation." Evans-Pritchard (1957a) points out the greater importance of pride and prestige over plunder and destruction in a description of the raiding of the Azande of the southern Sudan. Additional detail on Azande warfare is to be found in a companion article published by Evans-Pritchard in the same year (1957b). Kiefer (1970) analyzes Tausug armed combat in terms of Max Weber's distinction between affectual, traditional, means-rational, and ends-rational modes of action, and he concludes that the members of this Moslem state in the Philippines engaged in armed combat that was both affec-

tual and means-rational, but seldom traditional or ends-rational. By affectual combat Kiefer means warfare motivated by human emotions such as fear, rage, and hatred; in means-rational combat the goal is taken for granted and means for bringing about the desired goal are chosen among several alternatives.

The study of Iroquois warfare has divided opinion on the goals that motivated these woodland Indians. Hunt (1940), a historian, argues that the desire to control the fur trade after 1640, when the beaver supply in New York State had been depleted, was a powerful motivating factor. Although Snyderman (1948) emphasizes the social factors in Iroquois warfare, Scheele (1950) subscribes to Hunt's economic interpretation. A recent analysis of the sources utilized by Hunt has cast doubt upon the validity of his interpretation (Trelease 1962). Tooker (1963), who is not satisfied with Trelease's reanalysis, reviews the various reasons that the Iroquois were able to defeat their northern neighbors, the Hurons. More recently Forbes (1970) has taken issue with Hunt's analysis and with those Iroquoian specialists who have been strongly influenced by him. (For a blow-by-blow account of the critical battle that took place in 1649, see Thwaites, ed., 1896-1901, 34:122-37.) In a similar study, Trigger (1967) lists three attributes of Iroquois and Huron warfare: the desire of warriors to acquire personal prestige, blood revenge for previous killings, and the need to sacrifice prisoners through prolonged torture. Knowles (1940) has described the methods of torture in detail. Elsewhere Trigger (1962) has described early Iroquois warfare. I have described changes in Iroquois weapons and tactics during the seventeenth century (Otterbein 1964). Naroll (1969b) has described an Iroquois war with the French which began in 1657. The definitive work on the causes of Iroquois warfare has yet to be written.

Patterns and Themes

Particular goals of war can become so important to the members of a culture that they influence and dominate many other aspects of life. The more general version of this approach received its major theoretical elaboration from Benedict (1934). Voget (1964) applies the patterns-and-themes approach directly to the study of warfare. He argues (1964:486) that warfare may be the "primary institutionalized pattern" of a culture, by which he means that the pattern effects integration in two ways: "(1) by structuring roles and (2) by spreading its substance through other aspects of the culture." The major portion of his article shows that warfare was the primary focus for the integration of Crow Indian culture. In a similar study, Spicer (1947) demonstrates that the "warlike" Yaqui of northern Mexico integrated warfare into their culture in a fashion resembling Pueblo Indian Apollonianism. Yaqui militarism was strongly influenced by the teachings of Jesuits during the seventeenth and eighteenth centuries. According to Spicer (1947:46), "military forms of organization, military titles, and military concepts of a war between good and evil pervaded their teachings to the Yaquis." With the emergence of revolutionary movements in the nineteenth century, the Yaquis refocused their "ceremonial-military orientation" on practical warfare. The result was the subordination of individual interests to the supernaturally sanctioned goals of the group. In another study, Dobyns, Ezell, Jones, and Ezell (1957) show thematic changes in the warfare of the Yuman tribes of the Southwest. They contend (1957:50) that these tribal peoples "acquired technical means—horses, knives and spears—to maintain their independence at the same time that they acquired new cultural themes and elaborated aboriginal themes—cavalry warfare, ethnic insult and economic raiding—which strengthened their will to resist being overwhelmed." Ethnic insult expressed itself in torture and execution of prisoners of war, as well as in ceremonial cannibalism. Economic raiding consisted of horse seizure and slave raiding. These three "cultural themes reinforced the basic postulate of ethnic superiority held by each tribe." The study concludes with the following general hypothesis (1957: 50): "We suggest that this basic postulate of moral superiority is a functional prerequisite for any tribal society plagued with hostile neighbors. Without such a basic postulate, and the expression of cultural themes to reinforce it constantly, members of a tribal society probably could not resist conquest."

(When I began this review I expected to find many more examples of the use of this approach. Possibly I have overlooked some examples, since the approach can be subtly applied in a descriptive study without making reference to the writings of Benedict.)

SOCIAL STRUCTURE

Social structural factors that can be considered responsible for war are encompassed within an approach known as fraternal interest group theory. This approach was first developed by van Velzen and van Wetering (1960) to explain why the local groups of some cultures are peaceful internally while others are rife with internal dissension. They explain the difference in terms of a single independent variable—fraternal interest groups. Such groups are localized aggregates of related males who can resort to aggressive measures when the interests of their members are threatened. Since related males can more easily support each other in conflicts if they reside together, van Velzen and van Wetering employ patrilocal residence as an index of the presence of fraternal interest groups. The absence of fraternal interest groups is indexed by matrilocal residence, a social structural condition that results in the scattering of related males over a large region, making it difficult for them to support each other's interests. In a cross-cultural study using five measures of peacefulness/nonpeacefulness, including the presence or absence of blood feuds, van Velzen and van Wetering demonstrate that the presence of fraternal interest groups is responsible for the conflicts that occur within local groups. My wife and I obtained similar results in a cross-cultural study of feuding (Otterbein and Otterbein 1965)—a study that shows that polygyny may also be employed as an index of the presence of fraternal interest groups, since polygyny usually produces a situation in which men have a number of unmarried sons living with them. The study also demonstrates that the level of political integration of the cultures has no influence on the relationship between fraternal interest groups and feuding.

Fraternal interest group theory is used to explain not only feuding, but warfare as well. I have shown in a cross-cultural study (Otterbein 1968a, 1968b) that internal war (i.e., warfare between political communities within the same culture) can be explained by the presence of fraternal interest groups. Such groups form small-scale military organizations that attack enemies who are members of other political communities. The study demonstrates, moreover, that it is only in uncentralized political systems (i.e., bands and tribes) that fraternal interest groups explain internal war. Apparently, in centralized political systems (i.e., chiefdoms and states) political leaders can prevent the raiding of these small-scale military organizations. On the other hand, external war (i.e., warfare between political communities that are not members of the same culture) cannot be explained by the presence of fraternal interest groups. The distance that separates the political communities probably explains why the presence of fraternal interest groups predicts internal but not external war; that is, the farther the political communities are from each other, the more difficult it probably is for small-scale military organizations to operate successfully.

Four recent case studies of warfare lend support to fraternal interest group theory. Chagnon, in his studies of the Yanomamö (1967, 1968a, 1968b, 1968c), a warlike tribe of South American Indians, shows that what he calls "local descent groups" (small groups of related men) defend their mutual interests to the point of feuding and warfare. Kiefer, in his study of the Tausug (1969), a Moslem culture in the southern Philippines, describes the composition of feuding groups and attributes the armed conflict that occurs to their structure. They are fraternal interest groups. Koch, in a study of the Jalé (1970), a highland New Guinea people, suggests that the cannibalistic revenge that occurs between neighboring Jalé political communities can be attributed to the activities of fraternal interest groups. And I have discovered fraternal interest groups among the Higi of Nigeria (Otterbein 1968c).

A social structural theory that has elements in common with fraternal interest group theory, and perhaps can be subsumed under that theory, is Sahlins' analysis (1961) of the expansionary tendency of segmentary lineage systems. Using the Nuer and Tiv, tribal peoples of Africa, as examples, he argues that the opposition and conflict between the units of a segmentary lineage system force the units to expand geographically. When the segments come in contact with other peoples, they unite militarily and defeat those they oppose. When not in contact with other peoples, the segments fight among themselves. The units of a segmentary lineage system are fraternal interest groups, since cultures with such lineage systems are patrilocal and usually polygynous. Sahlins' argument that opposing cultures will be defeated would be more convincing if he described actual military engagements between his two sample cultures and their neighbors. From his analysis one cannot be certain that it is the structural features of the lineage systems rather than the military abilities of the Tiv and Nuer that are responsible for their geographical expansion.

Closely related to fraternal interest group theory is Mead's discussion (1968) of the requirements that need to be met if war between modern nations is to be prevented. She argues that a system of divided loyalties needs to be created in order to prevent the formation of groups that provide "mutually exclusive self-identifications." In other words, war can be abated if nations can develop social structures in which units resembling fraternal interest groups are absent. Elsewhere, Mead (1963) discusses the problems that will face man if he ever achieves a warless world.

Effects on Social Organization

War may have three quite different effects on social organization: it may produce cohesion, stratification, or disorganization. Sociologists and social psychologists argue that intergroup conflict creates internal cohesion. The literature dealing with this theory is adequately reviewed by Coser (1956). Of the sixteen propositions that Coser culls from various sources, several are germane to anthropological interests. Conflict serves to establish and maintain the identity and boundary lines of societies and groups. Conflict with outgroups increases internal cohesion. Conflict, either intense or mild, with another group defines group structure in terms of size and degree of involvement of members. Groups may hunt for real or unreal enemies without or within, with the deliberate purpose or the unintentional result of maintaining unity and internal cohesion. Conflict reaffirms dormant norms while at the same time creating new norms and modifying old ones. Conflict makes possible a reassessment of relative power and thus serves as a balancing mechanism that helps to maintain and consolidate societies. Coalitions will result from conflicts in which primarily pragmatic interests of the participants are involved. Sherif (1961), in a controlled field study of two competing boys' groups at a summer camp, tests and substantiates several hypotheses. For example, "the course of relations between two groups which are in a state of competition and frustration will tend to produce an increase in in-group solidarity" (Sherif 1961:48).

Basing our research on the conflict-cohesion theory, my wife and I (Otterbein and Otterbein 1965) tested the hypothesis that cultures that frequently engage in war are less likely to have feuding than cultures that have peaceful external relations. Although this hypothesis is not supported by data from the total sample in our cross-cultural study, we did demonstrate that the hypothesis holds for cultures characterized by a high level of political integration. On the other hand, we found that cultures with a low level of political integration which frequently engage in war are also characterized by a high degree of feuding. The results, we believe, indicate that it is only in cultures with officials who have the power to intervene in feuds that warfare leads to internal cohesion through the suppression of feuding. In another cross-cultural study (Otterbein 1968a, 1968b) I have shown that warfare between culturally similar political communities (i.e., internal war) is not curtailed if the political communities war with culturally different political communities (i.e., external war). I conclude that it is the absence of any official who speaks for the warring political communities that accounts for the failure of the political communities to unite in the face of a common enemy. It thus appears from these cross-cultural studies that for social cohesion to increase there must be an official who can control internal conflicts.

Further cross-cultural support for the conflict-cohesion theory is to be found in Young's study of initiation ceremonies (1965:71). He tests and finds support for the hypothesis that "local warfare predicts in some measure the highly institutionalized types of male solidarity, and if community conflict is absent solidarity is also likely to be absent."

Additional support for the conflict-cohesion theory is to be found in two case studies. Chagnon (1968a), in his study of the Yanomamö, describes how village headmen strive at all times to reduce internal conflicts in order to prevent their villages from splitting into smaller villages, which would be more vulnerable to attack. His analysis shows that warfare and the threat of war are the major factors motivating the headmen's attempts to reduce conflicts

within their villages. In a controlled comparison study of the Asmat of New Guinea, Eyde (1966) shows that warfare leads to an increase in community size, that it causes kinship groups to band together, and that it increases solidarity through the establishment of men's houses.

Although a subject of interest primarily to sociologists, the effect of war upon the development of stratification is an important topic. Oppenheimer (1914), who is known primarily for his conquest theory of the origin of the state, in actuality sets forth a theory of stratification that argues that castes and hereditary social classes come into being through the subjugation of one group by another. Another European sociologist, Andrzejewski (1954), in a volume describing the military organizations of both primitive and historical peoples, devotes a major section to a detailed analysis of the influence of the military on social stratification. Andrzejewski argues that a warrior class may arise through conquest or through gradual differentiation from the rest of the population. Eclectic in his approach, he argues that in some cases war may increase stratification by elevating the military to a position of supremacy, and in other cases it may lead to a decrease in stratification through the need to grant various privileges to the masses in order to enlist their support.

Deriving his argument from this tradition, Goldman (1955) argues that status rivalry, usually involving warfare, was a major factor in the evolution of stratification in Polynesia. Fried (1961, 1967), who devotes considerable attention to the origins of stratification, agrees that warfare and stratification are correlated, but argues that stratification must already be present in the society and that warfare serves only to heighten its development (1961:134): "Warfare serves to institutionalize stratification only when the social orders of one or more parties to the warfare have already become stratified." Fried expands upon this argument in a larger work (1967).

Warfare may lead to social disorganization. Benedict (1959:374), in a posthumously published article written in 1939, describes the fighting of many primitive peoples as being of the "non-lethal species of warfare," since their wars do not "drag to ruin the civilization of both tribes." In contrast to this warfare is the "lethal variety of the genus War"; this is the species of warfare in which modern nations of the twentieth century engage. Although Benedict's article is essentially a plea that mankind stop short of annihilating itself, it nevertheless sets forth the notion that the warfare of primitive peoples is not destructive to their cultures, but that the warfare of complex civilizations is.

This same theme is echoed throughout Toynbee's *A Study of History*. In the preface to a collection of excerpts from this work, Toynbee states (1950:vii) that "war has proved to have been the proximate cause of the breakdown of every civilization which is known for certain to have broken down. . . ." Service would probably agree with Toynbee, but certainly not with Benedict. In a comparative study of primitive social organization, Service (1962) argues that hunting and gathering bands are patrilocal when their neighbors are likewise bands, but that when they come into contact—the contact is usually hostile—with cultures that are structurally more complex, such as tribes, chiefdoms, and states, the patrilocal social structure of the band collapses and a bilateral grouping results which Service calls a composite band. More recently Service (1968) has described the intense disorganization that usually occurs when European civilizations, equipped with firearms, intrude into regions occupied by primitive peoples.

MILITARY PREPAREDNESS

Military readiness can itself be considered a cause of war. That is to say, if a culture is well prepared militarily, it is more likely to become involved in wars than if it were not so well prepared. If in fact military readiness does cause war, two possible reasons can account for the relationship: (1) The possession of an efficient military organization may tempt leaders of the political community or of the military organization itself to attack neighboring political communities that they believe are militarily less prepared. An attack even upon a weak neighbor may result in retaliatory attacks, and thus the militarily well-prepared political community becomes embroiled in war. (2) The mere possession of an efficient military organization, one that is in readiness for operations but not actually engaged in them, may provoke a neighboring political community to attack, since it fears it may be suddenly attacked and wishes to have surprise on its side. Although this theory is testable, anthropologists have chosen to test the converse of it; namely, that military readiness decreases the likelihood that a political community will become involved in war. This is the theory of deterrence, which is commonly accepted in professional military and governmental circles. Advocates of this theory argue that possession of an efficient military organization will deter would-be aggressors from attacking. Naroll and I have tested deterrence theory rather than the theory of military preparedness.

In a cross-cultural study of primitive war, Naroll (1964b, 1966) tests the deterrence theory by correlating a series of measures of military orientation with the frequency of war. The rationale behind the development of this measure of war frequency is to be found in Tatje (1970:694-95). Naroll did not find that cultures that scored high on his various measures had a lower frequency of war than did cultures that scored low. Thus his data do not support deterrence theory. On the other hand, they provide only slight support for the military preparedness theory, since only low positive correlations were found between the frequency of war and some of the measures of military orientation. In a cross-historical study, using pairs of warring states, Naroll (1969a) tests deterrence theory by correlating various types of defensive stance with war frequency, with the same results: low positive correlations, which provide no support for deterrence theory and only weak support for military preparedness theory. Naroll, Bullough, and Naroll (n.d.) discuss the results of this study at length elsewhere.

The theory of deterrence was tested in another cross-cultural study (Otterbein 1970), in which I constructed a scale of military sophistication composed of eleven efficient military practices. If all practices were present in a culture, the culture received the highest scale score possible; the fewer the number of efficient practices, the lower the scale score. Since I distinguished between three types of warfare—internal war, offensive external war, and defensive external war—I was able to test deterrence theory with a refined measure of war frequency. The relationship between the military sophistication scale and defensive external war yields a low positive correlation that is not statistically significant. Thus I, like Naroll, find no support for deterrence theory. However, I also implicitly tested the military preparedness theory. (Actually I tested what I call a trial-and-error theory, a theory that a political community that frequently goes to war will utilize the most efficient military practices.) I find absolutely no relationship between my scale and internal war, and thus I conclude that culturally similar political communities are likely to engage in frequent warfare regardless of the efficiency of their military organizations. Elsewhere I show that the frequency of internal war can be explained by the presence of fraternal interest groups (see "Social Structure"). I also tested for a relationship between my scale and offensive external war. (I tested for this relationship because I had already tested and found strongly confirmed the hypothesis that cultures that rank high on the military sophistication scale are cultures with expanding territorial boundaries.) I find a significant positive correlation. Thus I conclude that political communities with efficient military organizations are likely to engage in frequent warfare with culturally different political communities. Therefore, a theory of military preparedness as a cause of one type of war finds empirical support.

Survival Value

Warfare—that is, warfare that is efficiently waged—confers a survival advantage upon a political community and upon any customs or practices that are part of its culture. Thus militarily efficient groups, and the cultures they bear, will be the survivors in intersocietal struggles. This line of reasoning was initiated in the nineteenth century by Tylor (1888:267) in his famous statement on exogamy:

Exogamy, enabling a growing tribe to keep itself compact by constant unions between its spreading clans, enables it to overmatch any number of small intermarrying groups, isolated and helpless. Again and again in the world's history, savage tribes must have had plainly before their minds the simple practical alternative between marrying-out and being killed out.

This approach is referred to as a survival-value theory (Harris 1968:198, 491); that is, the practice is of value to the culture in enhancing its chances for survival. Survival-value theory receives theoretical elaboration at the hands of Keller (1915:62-63): "War, resulting in the annihilation of one group by another, is the primordial agency of selection in the mores, and probably the most efficient that has ever existed." Keller goes on to argue that only the customs of those societies that prevailed in intersocietal conflicts would be found widely distributed among human groups. More recently, White (1949: 313) has argued that the existence of the incest taboo can be explained by Tylor's theory of exogamy. Service (1962) contends that warfare selects societies for social and political integration. When two societies engage in war, the more highly integrated society will be the winner. Carneiro (1970a) has pointed out that when societies war, two types of "cultural selection" operate: (1) "In intrasocietal selection, two or more variants of a trait compete for the same 'cultural slot' with the more efficient one eventually displacing the less efficient." (2) "In intersocietal selection . . . the unit on which selection operates is not the culture trait as such, but the society bearing it."

I employed the survival-value approach in a recent cross-cultural study of war (Otterbein 1970), in which I evaluated a series of pairs of contrasting military practices and ascertained the more efficient practice of each pair. I then combined eleven of these practices into a military sophistication scale. They include a professional military organization, a high degree of subordination, war being initiated only by officials, the presence of diplomatic negotiations, a complex tactical system based upon lines and ambushes, shock weapons, body armor, field fortifications, cavalry, fortified villages, and war being fought for political control. Each of the fifty cultures in my sample is ranked according to its degree of military sophistication. Each efficient military practice is shown to be associated with a high level of political centralization (i.e., chiefdoms and states), and of course the scale itself is highly correlated with degree of political centralization. The scale is used to test the hypothesis that "the higher the degree of military sophistication, the more likely that the political communities of a cultural unit will be militarily successful" (Otterbein 1970:94). Military success is measured in terms of expanding territorial boundaries. The hypothesis is strongly confirmed. I also test for a relationship between level of political centralization and military success, and find only a low positive nonsignificant correlation. Therefore, I am able to show that political communities with sophisticated military organizations are militarily successful, while at the same time refuting any possible argument that the success is due to the level of centralization of the political communities (1970:102): "A cultural unit whose political communities wage war in a sophisticated manner has an increased advantage in intersocietal struggles in comparison with cultural units whose political communities do not wage war in a sophisticated manner."

CULTURAL EVOLUTION

A substantial number of scholars relate the type of war fought by a people to the evolutionary level of their culture. Inherent in this approach is the notion that it is the sociopolitical complexity or the political centralization of the culture that is responsible for the manner in which people fight their wars. Sumner (1911) discusses the development of war and peace as social institutions from the lowest to the most advanced levels of society. A student of his, Keller (1915), argues that war and military organization, while serving a selective function upon a lower stage of culture, have become counterselective in the last two centuries. Davie (1929), another social evolutionist, traces the course of development of warfare from the earliest evidence of its existence. For him warfare had its origin in cannibalism. In a cross-cultural study, Hobhouse, Wheeler, and Ginsberg (1930) demonstrate that as technology developed, the killing of captives taken in war declined. Childe (1941), while taking issue with the order of technological levels of Hobhouse, Wheeler, and Ginsberg, describes the increase in warfare that occurred at successive archaeological periods in the Old World. Although not an evolutionist, Benedict, in a 1939 paper, describes the fighting of many primitive peoples as being of the "nonlethal species of warfare," while modern warfare is described as being of the "lethal variety" (1959:374). Similarly, Chapple and Coon (1942) argue that the warfare of tribal peoples is more closely related to game behavior than to warfare waged by modern nations. Wright (1965) demonstrates in a cross-cultural study that with increasing political centralization the type of warfare waged changes from defensive to social, to economic, and then to political. Broch and Galtung (1966), in a reanalysis of Wright's data, show that not only is political centralization a determinant of the type of war fought, but so is the extent of intercultural contact between the culture and its neighbors.

A nonevolutionist who took an evolutionary perspective is Malinowski (1941b), who argues that warfare only slowly evolved as a mechanism of organized force for the pursuit of national policies. He describes six types of armed contest: (1) fighting between group members—the prototype of criminal behavior; (2) fighting as a juridical mechanism for the adjustment of differences; (3) armed raids for sport; (4) warfare as the political expression of early nationalism; (5) military expeditions of organized pillage; (6) war as an instrument of national policy. Each type is an entirely different "cultural phase" in the development of organized fighting. This article is an expanded version of an earlier presentation (Malinowski 1941a). Turney-High (1949) argues that most tribal peoples have not reached the "military horizon"; that is, they do not wage war efficiently. Only societies that have evolved beyond the tribal level have reached the "military horizon." Many of Turney-High's examples, however, are tribal peoples who wage war efficiently. Thus he contradicts his theory by describing cultures at the tribal level that have reached his "military horizon." In a study not of warfare but of diplomacy, Numelin (1950)—using a voluminous number of examples, as does Turney-High—describes what he calls its beginnings by listing various types of primitive diplomats and the tasks they perform for their societies.

An avowed cultural evolutionist, White (1949) argues that as man's cultural heritage increases, economic and political goals become the causes of war. According to White (1949:131), "warfare is virtually non-existent among many primitive tribes." When cultures have progressed to the point where it is worth fighting over hunting or fishing grounds, grazing lands or fertile valleys, warfare emerges. Newcombe (1960), building upon White's analysis, delineates four types of warfare, corresponding closely to Wright's types. Type 1 warfare consists of brief skirmishes between hunting and gathering bands. Type 2 warfare is designated as primitive warfare (Wright's "social war"). Type 3 warfare is "true" warfare involving economic causes. And finally, Type 4 warfare constitutes world wars based upon the industrial revolution. Another evolutionist, Service (1962), describes the type of warfare that occurs at each of five levels of sociopolitical development—band, tribe, chiefdom, state, and empire. He differs from the above evolutionists in that he believes that warfare was frequent and intense at all levels, although waged differently and for different reasons. More recently, Fried (1967) has taken exception with Service and expounded the commonly accepted point of view that warfare occurs less frequently and is of a different nature among band and tribal peoples than among peoples organized into states. Vayda (1956), in a comparative study of three Oceanic cultures—the Maori, the Marquesans, and the Hawaiians—shows that the more complex culture of the Hawaiians is related to a manner of waging warfare that is more efficient than that waged by the Maori or the Marquesans.

Nonanthropologists are concerned with the actual frequency of warfare and casualty rates of wars. Sorokin (1937:282) examines "three quantitative elements of war: the strength of the army, the number of casualties (killed and wounded), and the duration of each of the wars studied" (italics omitted). He is able to draw only a few conclusions from his statistical analysis of wars that are predominantly European. For example, Sorokin (1937:364) found that "there is no continuous linear trend in the evolution of the magnitude of war in the course of time,

either toward increase or decrease of war, in the life history of all the nations studied." In this and in an earlier study (1928), he attributes warfare to a breakdown in intergroup relations. Richardson (1960), a physicist, collects casualty rates for both wars and violent conflicts on a global basis and plots total casualty rates century by century. He demonstrates that there has been a rapid increase in casualty rates in the past few centuries. For a comprehensive review of Richardson's theories, one should consult Rapoport (1957, 1960).

In a cross-cultural study (Otterbein 1970) I test a series of hypotheses that relate level of political centralization to various aspects of warfare. Some of these aspects are listed elsewhere (see "Survival Value"). In most instances efficient military practices are associated with centralized political systems. Eleven of the practices are combined into a military sophistication scale, with which I test and find substantial support for the hypothesis that "the higher the level of political centralization, the higher the degree of military sophistication" (Otterbein 1970:75). However, the study does show—contrary to what most of the evolutionists have argued—that uncentralized political systems (i.e., Service's bands and tribes) may wage war efficiently. Twenty percent (six out of thirty) of the societies in my sample which had uncentralized political systems rated high on the military sophistication scale. I also find that level of political centralization is not significantly related to military success, as measured by expanding territorial boundaries. Elsewhere (Otterbein 1968a:283) I have shown that the frequency of internal war is not significantly related to level of political centralization. And in another place (Otterbein 1971) I show that offensive external war is not significantly related to level of political centralization. My findings are thus at complete variance with the arguments of those evolutionists who have held that primitive peoples are not warlike, in the sense that they infrequently engage in warfare. Abrahamson (1969), in a cross-cultural study, demonstrates that external threat, while not significantly related to political complexity, does lower the correlations between political complexity and both social differentiation and demographic complexity. In commenting upon this article (Otterbein 1971), I have shown that defensive external war has a significant inverse relationship to level of political centralization. That is, centralized political systems are less likely to be attacked than uncentralized political systems.

Origin of the State

Some scholars are less concerned with the influence of different types of societies upon the manner in which war is waged than with the influence of warfare upon the development of political centralization. Spencer (1896), an evolutionist, argues that leadership and subordination developed first in the military and were then transferred to the political system. Thus an increase in the efficiency of the military resulted in an increase in political centralization. The "conquest theory of the state" is developed by Gumplowicz (1899:119): "States have never arisen except through the subjection of one stock by another, or by several others in alliance.... No state has arisen without original ethnical heterogeneity ...." Conquest theory is further developed by Oppenheimer (1914:55-81), who bases his work upon the research of Frederick Ratzel, a German geographer. "In the genesis of the state, from the subjection of a peasant folk by a tribe of herdsmen or by sea nomads, six stages may be distinguished": (1) robbery and killing in border fights; (2) the peasants, through thousands of unsuccessful attempts at revolt, accept their fate; (3) the peasants regularly bring their surplus to the tents of the herdsmen as tribute; (4) the union on one strip of land of both ethnic groups; (5) lords assume the right to arbitrate, and in case of need to enforce their judgment; (6) the two groups, at first merely residing next to each other, are scattered indiscriminately throughout the area.

Lowie (1962), in reviewing Oppenheimer's conquest theory, points out that his theory is in fact a treatise on the development of castes or social stratification. For Lowie, the state had its genesis in associations that established territorial ties, which later came to take precedence over blood ties. Park (1941), in discussing what he calls the social functions of war, restricts himself primarily to a treatment of warfare at the state level of political complexity. He states (1941:551): "The function of war has been (1) to extend the area of peace, (2) to create within that area a political power capable of enforcing it, and (3) to establish an ideology which rationalizes and a cult which idealizes the new political and social order." Both Gluckman (1960) and I (Otterbein 1967) have described the development of statehood for the Zulu of South Africa. An extensive review of the literature dealing with the origin of the state is to be found in Krader (1968).

Other studies, more modest in scope, attempt to explain the development of the state in particular regions. Barton (1949) argues that the Kalinga of northern Luzon in the Philippines had advanced along the road to statehood by developing the institution of the peace pact. Their neighbors, the Ifugao, who did not have the peace pact, were not, in Barton's view, so politically advanced as the Kalinga. Recently Dozier (1964, 1967) has argued that the peace pact was not a device for the formation of statehood for two reasons: first, it was not conceived by the Kalinga as such; second, among the southern Kalinga political units were larger and the population was denser, yet in the south the peace pact was much less effective than in the north and more intraregional killings occurred. Gearing (1961, 1962), in a case study of the Cherokee in the late eighteenth century, describes the rise of war leaders that occurred in response to intersocietal struggles with neighboring Indians and colonists. The tribal councils expanded to include the war leaders in order to prevent them from carrying out unauthorized raids; political centralization resulted. Gearing calls this process the "Mesopotamian career to statehood," since he detects the same conditions existing in the Tigris-Euphrates valley as existed in the Southeast during the colonial period. According to Kurtz (1969), similar conditions existed for the Canyoncito Navaho in the eighteenth century, but the external threat to these Navaho was not great enough to force the "war chanters," the traditional war leaders, to cease raiding on their own initiative. Rosenfeld (1965) argues that the process of state formation began in the Arabian Desert region when ruling groups gained power over rival lineages by conquering towns and converting them into tribute states and trade centers. Further conquest was made possible by incorporating slaves, mercenaries, and townsmen into the military organization. Tribute and taxes supported the military.

Although Steward (1955), in advancing his theory of irrigation civilizations, does not argue that warfare is instrumental in producing statehood, he does consider warfare to be an integral part of his conceptual scheme. The first four stages of his scheme—Hunting and Gathering, Incipient Agriculture, Formative, and Regional Florescent—culminate in the state. Warfare then becomes vitally important. Population expansion, resulting in the need for more land by each state, triggers wars of conquest, which result in a fifth stage known as Initial Empire. Civil wars lead to a breakup of the empire, a stage known as the Dark Ages. Success in war creates new empires that in turn break up, a stage referred to as Cyclical Conquests. Similar in some respects to Steward's theory is Carneiro's (1961, 1970c) theory of the origin of the state. Specific ecological conditions pertain. There must be an area of restricted arable land and dense population. Carneiro states (1970c:735), "With increasing pressure of human population on the land, however, the major incentive for war changed from a desire for revenge to a need to acquire land." Because the defeated cannot withdraw, "the consequences of defeat under these conditions would generally be, first, the payment of tribute, and at a later stage, outright incorporation into the territory of the victor" (Carneiro 1961:61). Integrated territorial units transcending individual villages, referred to as chiefdoms, begin conquering each other. The resultant complex political unit Carneiro calls a state or kingdom. Carneiro's theory differs from Steward's in that warfare is viewed as instrumental to the development of statehood. In his more recent article, Carneiro (1970c) modifies his "circumscription theory" to include not only restricted arable land, but also concentration of resources and social circumscription (meaning a high density of population). These three ecological conditions, singly or in conjunction, are responsible for the origin of the state.

REFERENCES

Abrahamson, Mark
1969 Correlates of Political Complexity. *American Sociological Review* 34: 690-701.

Adcock, F. E.
1962 *The Greek and Macedonian Art of War.* Berkeley: University of California Press.

Ajayi, J. F. Ade, and Robert S. Smith
1964 *Yoruba Warfare in the Nineteenth Century.* New York and London: Cambridge University Press in association with the Institute of African Studies, University of Ibadan.

Alland, Alexander, Jr.
1968 War and Disease: An Anthropological Perspective. In *War: The Anthropology of Armed Conflict and Aggression*, ed. M. Fried, M. Harris, and R. Murphy, pp. 65-75. Garden City, N.Y.: Natural History Press.

Andrzejewski, Stanislaw
1954 *Military Organization and Society.* London: Routledge & Kegan Paul.

Ardrey, Robert
1966 *The Territorial Imperative.* New York: Dell.

Barton, Roy F.
1919 *Ifugao Law.* University of California Publications in American Archaeology and Ethnology, no. 15.
1949 *The Kalingas.* Chicago: University of Chicago Press.

Beatty, John
1968 Taking Issue with Lorenz on the Ute. In *Man and Aggression*, ed. M. F. Ashley Montagu, pp. 111-15. New York: Oxford University Press.

Beemer, Hilda
1937 The Development of the Military Organization in Swaziland. *Africa* 10:55-74, 176-205.

Bell, F. L. S.
1935 Warfare Among the Tanga. *Oceania* 5:253-79.

Benedict, Ruth F.
1934 *Patterns of Culture.* Boston: Houghton Mifflin.
1959 The Natural History of War. In *An Anthropologist at Work*, ed. M. Mead, pp. 369-82. Boston: Houghton Mifflin.

Berkowitz, Leonard
1962 *Aggression: A Social Psychological Analysis.* New York: McGraw-Hill.

Berndt, Ronald M.
1962 *Excess and Restraint: Social Control Among a New Guinea Mountain People.* Chicago: University of Chicago Press.
1964 Warfare in the New Guinea Highlands. *American Anthropologist* 66, no. 4, pt. 2:183-203.

Bohannan, Paul
1963 *Social Anthropology.* New York: Holt, Rinehart & Winston.
1967 *Law and Warfare: Studies in the Anthropology of Conflict.* Garden City, N.Y.: Natural History Press.

Bram, Joseph
1941 *An Analysis of Inca Militarism.* American Ethnological Society monograph no. 4.

Bramson, Leon, and George W. Goethals, eds.
1964 *War: Studies from Psychology, Sociology, Anthropology.* New York: Basic Books. (Rev. ed. 1968.)

Broch, Tom, and Johan Galtung
1966 Belligerence Among the Primitives: A Re-analysis of Quincy Wright's Data. *Journal of Peace Research* 1:33-45.

Brues, Alice
1959 The Spearman and the Archer: An Essay on Selection in Body Build. *American Anthropologist* 61:457-69.

Campbell, Donald T., and Robert A. LeVine
1961 A Proposal for Cooperative Cross-Cultural Research on Ethnocentrism. *Journal of Conflict Resolution* 5:82-108.
1965 Propositions About Ethnocentrism from Social Science Theories. Unpublished MS. (An expanded and revised version will be published under the title *Ethnocentrism: Theories of Conflict, Ethnic Attitudes, and Group Behavior.*)

Carneiro, Robert L.
1961 Slash-and-Burn Cultivation Among the Kuikuru and Its Implications for Cultural Development in the Amazon Basin. In *The Evolution of Horticultural Systems in Native South America: Causes and Consequences*, ed. J. Wilbert, pp. 47-67. Caracas: Sociedad de Ciencias Naturales La Salle.

1970a Foreword to Keith F. Otterbein, *The Evolution of War: A Cross-Cultural Study*. New Haven: HRAF Press.
1970b Scale Analysis, Evolutionary Sequences, and the Rating of Cultures. In *A Handbook of Method in Cultural Anthropology*, ed. R. Naroll and R. Cohen, pp. 834-71. Garden City, N.Y.: Natural History Press.
1970c A Theory of the Origin of the State. *Science* 169 (3947):733-38.
Chagnon, Napoleon A.
1967 Yanomamö–The Fierce People. *Natural History* 76:22-31.
1968a *Yanomamö: The Fierce People*. New York: Holt, Rinehart & Winston.
1968b Yanomamö Social Organization and Warfare. In *War: The Anthropology of Armed Conflict and Aggression*, ed. M. Fried, M. Harris, and R. Murphy, pp. 109-59. Garden City, N.Y.: Natural History Press.
1968c The Feast. *Natural History* 77, no. 4:34-41.
Chapple, Eliot, and Carleton S. Coon
1942 *Principles of Anthropology*. New York: Henry Holt.
Childe, V. Gordon
1941 War in Prehistoric Societies. *Sociological Review* 33:126-38.
Codere, Helen
1950 *Fighting with Property: A Study of Kwakiutl Potlatching and Warfare, 1792-1930*. American Ethnological Society monograph no. 18.
Cook, S. F.
1946 Human Sacrifice and Warfare as Factors in the Demography of Pre-colonial Mexico. *Human Biology* 18:81-102.
Coser, Lewis A.
1956 *The Functions of Social Conflict*. Glencoe, Ill.: Free Press.
Davie, Maurice R.
1929 *The Evolution of War: A Study of Its Role in Early Societies*. New Haven: Yale University Press.
Diamond, Stanley
1968 War and the Dissociated Personality. In *War: The Anthropology of Armed Conflict and Aggression*, ed. M. Fried, M. Harris, and R. Murphy, pp. 183-88. Garden City, N.Y.: Natural History Press.

Divale, William T.
1970 An Explanation for Tribal Warfare: Population Control and the Significance of Primitive Sex-Ratios. *New Scholar*, Fall, pp. 173-92.
1971a Ibo Population Control: The Ecology of Warfare and Social Organization. *California Anthropologist* 1:10-24.
1971b *Warfare in Primitive Societies: A Selected Bibliography*. Los Angeles: California State College, Center for the Study of Armament and Disarmament.
Dobyns, Henry F., P. H. Ezell, A. W. Jones, and G. Ezell
1957 Thematic Changes in Yuman Warfare. In *Cultural Stability and Cultural Change*, ed. V. F. Ray, pp. 46-71. Seattle: American Ethnological Society.
Dollard, John, et al.
1939 *Frustration and Aggression*. New Haven: Yale University Press.
Downs, James F.
1960 Thoughts on Cavalry, Guerrilla Warfare, and the Fall of Empires. *Kroeber Anthropological Society Papers*, no. 23 (fall).
Dozier, Edward P.
1964 The Kalinga Peacepact Institution. *VIe Congrès International des Sciences Anthropologiques et Ethnologiques* 2:315-19.
1967 *The Kalinga of Northern Luzon, Philippines*. New York: Holt, Rinehart & Winston.
Ekvall, Robert B.
1961 The Nomadic Pattern of Living Among the Tibetans as Preparation for War. *American Anthropologist* 63:1250-63.
1964 Peace and War Among the Tibetan Nomads. *American Anthropologist* 66:1119-48.
Ellis, Florence H.
1951 Patterns of Aggression and the War Cult in the Southwestern Pueblos. *Southwestern Journal of Anthropology* 7:177-201.
Ember, Melvin, and Carol R. Ember
1971 The Conditions Favoring Matrilocal versus Patrilocal Residence. *American Anthropologist* 73:571-94.
Evans-Pritchard, E. E.

1940   *The Nuer.* Oxford: Clarendon Press.
1957a Zande Warfare. *Anthropos* 52:239-62.
1957b Zande Border Raids. *Africa* 27:217-31.
Ewers, John C.
1955   *The Horse in Blackfoot Indian Culture.* Bureau of American Ethnology bulletin no. 159. Washington, D.C.: Smithsonian Institution.
Eyde, David B.
1966   Cultural Correlates of Warfare Among the Asmat of South-West New Guinea. Ph.D. dissertation, Yale University.
Farmer, Malcolm F.
1957   A Suggested Typology of Defensive Systems of the Southwest. *Southwestern Journal of Anthropology* 13:249-66.
Fathauer, George H.
1954   The Structure and Causation of Mohave Warfare. *Southwestern Journal of Anthropology* 10:97-118.
Follett, Prescott H.
1932   War and Weapons of the Maya. *Middle American Research Series* 4:373-410.
Forbes, Allan, Jr.
1970   Two and a Half Centuries of Conflict: The Iroquois and the Laurentian Wars. *Pennsylvania Archaeologist* 40:1-20.
Fortune, Reo F.
1939   Arapesh Warfare. *American Anthropologist* 41:22-41.
1947   The Rules of Relationship Behaviour in One Variety of Primitive Warfare. *Man* 47:108-10.
1960   New Guinea Warfare: Correction of a Mistake Previously Published. *Man* 60:108.
Fox, Robin
1969   Review of *War: The Anthropology of Armed Conflict and Aggression,* ed. M. Fried, M. Harris, and R. Murphy. *American Anthropologist* 71:314-15.
Freud, Sigmund
1959   Why War? In *Collected Papers,* ed. J. Strachey, 5:273-87. New York: Basic Books. Originally published 1932.
Fried, Morton H.
1961   Warfare, Military Organization, and the Evolution of Society. *Anthropologica* 3:134-47.
1967   *The Evolution of Political Society.* New York: Random House.
Fried, Morton H., Marvin Harris, and Robert Murphy, eds.
1968   *War: The Anthropology of Armed Conflict and Aggression.* Garden City, N.Y.: Natural History Press.
Fürer-Haimendorf, Christoph von
1968   Review of *War: The Anthropology of Armed Conflict and Aggression,* ed. M. Fried, M. Harris, and R. Murphy. *Saturday Review,* June 1, pp. 27-29.
Gardner, Robert
1964   *Dead Birds* (16-mm. film, 83 min.). Cambridge: Peabody Museum, Harvard University.
Gardner, Robert, and Karl G. Heider
1968   *Gardens of War: Life and Death in the New Guinea Stone Age.* New York: Random House.
Gearing, Fred
1961   The Rise of the Cherokee State as an Instance in a Class: The "Mesopotamian Career to Statehood." *Bureau of American Ethnology Bulletin* 180:125-34.
1962   *Priests and Warriors.* American Anthropological Association memoir no. 93.
Glasse, Robert M.
1959   Revenge and Redress Among the Huli: A Preliminary Account. *Mankind* 5:273-89.
Gluckman, Max
1960   The Rise of a Zulu Empire. *Scientific American* 202 (April):157-68.
Goldman, Irving
1955   Status Rivalry and Cultural Evolution in Polynesia. *American Anthropologist* 57:680-97.
Goldschmidt, Walter, George Foster, and Frank Essene
1939   War Stories from Two Enemy Tribes. *Journal of American Folk-Lore* 52:141-54.
Gorer, Geoffrey
1938   *Himalayan Village: An Account of the Lepchas of Sikkim.* London: Michael Joseph; New York: Basic Books, 1967.
1968a Man Has No "Killer" Instinct. In *Man and Aggression,* ed. M. F. Ashley Montagu, pp. 27-36. New York:

Oxford University Press.

1968b Ardrey on Human Nature: Animals, Nations, Imperatives. In *Man and Aggression*, ed. M. F. Ashley Montagu, pp. 74-82. New York: Oxford University Press.

Grinnell, George B.
1910 Coup and Scalp Among the Plains Indians. *American Anthropologist* 12: 296-310.
1956 *The Fighting Cheyennes*. Norman: University of Oklahoma Press.

Gumplowicz, Ludwig
1899 *The Outlines of Sociology*. Philadelphia: American Academy of Political and Social Science.

Hadlock, Wendell S.
1947 War Among the Northeastern Woodland Indians. *American Anthropologist* 49:204-21.

Harris, Marvin
1968 *The Rise of Anthropological Theory*. New York: Crowell.

Hasluck, Margaret
1967 The Albanian Blood Feud. In *Law and Warfare*, ed. P. Bohannan, pp. 381-408. Garden City, N.Y.: Natural History Press.

Heider, Karl G.
1970 *The Dugum Dani: A Papuan Culture in the Highlands of West New Guinea*. Chicago: Aldine.

Hill, William W.
1936 *Navajo Warfare*. Yale University Publications in Anthropology, no. 5.

Hobhouse, L. T., G. C. Wheeler, and M. Ginsberg
1930 *The Material Culture and Social Institutions of the Simpler Peoples*. London: Chapman & Hall.

Hocart, A. M.
1931 Warfare in Eddystone of the Solomon Islands. *Journal of the Royal Anthropological Institute of Great Britain and Ireland* 61:301-24.

Hoebel, E. Adamson
1958 *Man in the Primitive World: An Introduction to Anthropology*. New York: McGraw-Hill.

Holloway, Ralph L., Jr.
1968a Human Aggression: The Need for a Species-Specific Framework. In *War: The Anthropology of Armed Conflict and Aggression*, ed. M. Fried, M.

Harris, and R. Murphy, pp. 29-48. Garden City, N.Y.: Natural History Press.
1968b Territory and Aggression in Man: A Look at Ardrey's Territorial Imperative. In *Man and Aggression*, ed. M. F. Ashley Montagu, pp. 96-102. New York: Oxford University Press.

Honigmann, John J.
1959 *The World of Man*. New York: Harper & Row.

Hulse, Frederick S.
1961 Warfare, Demography, and Genetics. *Eugenics Quarterly* 8:185-97.

Hunt, George T.
1940 *The Wars of the Iroquois*. Madison: University of Wisconsin Press.

Jeffreys, M. D. W.
1956 Ibo Warfare. *Man* 56:77-79.

Karsten, Rafael
1923 *Blood Revenge, War, and Victory Feasts Among the Jibaro Indians of Eastern Ecuador*. Bureau of American Ethnology bulletin no. 79. Washington, D.C.: Smithsonian Institution.

Keesing, Felix M.
1958 *Cultural Anthropology: The Science of Custom*. New York: Holt, Rinehart & Winston.

Keiser, R. Lincoln
1969 *The Vice Lords: Warriors of the Streets*. New York: Holt, Rinehart & Winston.

Keller, Albert G.
1915 *Societal Evolution*. New York: Macmillan.

Kiefer, Thomas M.
1967 Power, Politics, and Guns in Jolo: The Influence of Modern Weapons on Tao-Sug Legal and Economic Institutions. *Philippine Sociological Review* 15:21-29.
1968 Institutionalized Friendship and Warfare Among the Tausug of Jolo. *Ethnology* 7:225-44.
1969 Tausug Armed Conflict: The Social Organization of Military Activity in a Philippine Moslem Society. Philippine Studies Program, Research Series no. 7. Chicago: Department of Anthropology, University of Chicago.
1970 Modes of Social Action in Armed

Combat: Affect, Tradition, and Reason in Tausug Private Warfare. *Man* 5:586-96.

Klopsteg, Paul E.
1963 Bows and Arrows: A Chapter in the Evolution of Archery in America. In *The Smithsonian Report for 1962,* pp. 567-92. Washington, D.C.: Smithsonian Institution.

Knowles, Nathaniel
1940 The Torture of Captives by the Indians of Eastern North America. *Proceedings of the American Philosophical Society* 82:151-225.

Koch, Klaus-Frederich
1970 Cannibalistic Revenge in Jalé Warfare. *Natural History* 79, no. 2:41-50.

Krader, Lawrence
1968 *Formation of the State.* Englewood Cliffs, N.J.: Prentice-Hall.

Kroeber, Alfred L.
1928 A Kato War. *Festschrift d'hommage offerte à P. W. Schmidt,* ed. W. Koppers, pp. 394-400. Vienna: Mechitharisten-Congregations-Buchdruckerie.

Kurtz, Ronald J.
1969 Headmen and War Chanters: Role Theory and the Early Canyoncito Navaho. *Ethnohistory* 16:83-111.

La Barre, Weston
1969 Review of *Man and Aggression*, ed. M. F. Ashley Montagu. *American Anthropologist* 71:912-15.

Landes, Ruth
1959 Dakota Warfare. *Southwestern Journal of Anthropology* 15:43-52.

Leach, Edmund
1965 The Nature of War. *Disarmament and Arms Control* 3:165-83.
1968 Don't Say "Boo" to a Goose. In *Man and Aggression*, ed. M. F. Ashley Montagu, pp. 65-73. New York: Oxford University Press.

Leeds, Anthony
1963 The Functions of War. In *Science and Psychoanalysis*, ed. J. Masserman, vol. 6: *Violence and War: With Clinical Studies*, pp. 69-82. New York: Grune & Stratton.

Lesser, Alexander
1968 War and the State. In *War: The Anthropology of Armed Conflict and Aggression,* ed. M. Fried, M. Harris,

and R. Murphy, pp. 92-96. Garden City, N.Y.: Natural History Press.

LeVine, Robert A.
1961 Anthropology and the Study of Conflict: An Introduction. *Journal of Conflict Resolution* 5:3-15.
1970 An Anthropological Study of War and Peace. Paper delivered at the 69th annual meeting of the American Anthropological Association, November 19-22.

Linton, Ralph
1944 Nomad Raids and Fortified Pueblos. *American Antiquity* 10:28-33.

Livingstone, Frank B.
1968 The Effects of Warfare on the Biology of the Human Species. In *War: The Anthropology of Armed Conflict and Aggression,* ed. M. Fried, M. Harris, and R. Murphy, pp. 3-15. Garden City, N.Y.: Natural History Press.

Lorenz, Konrad
1966 *On Aggression.* New York: Harcourt, Brace & World.

Lowie, Robert H.
1962 *The Origin of the State.* New York: Russel & Russel. Originally published 1927.

McDougall, William
1926 *An Introduction to Social Psychology*, rev. ed. Boston: Luce.
1964 The Instinct of Pugnacity. In *War: Studies from Psychology, Sociology, Anthropology,* ed. L. Bramson and G. W. Goethals, pp. 33-43. New York: Basic Books.

Malinowski, Bronislaw
1941a War—Past, Present, and Future. In *War as a Social Institution: The Historian's Perspective*, ed. J. Clarkson and T. Cochran, pp. 20-30. New York: Columbia University Press.
1941b An Anthropological Analysis of War. *American Journal of Sociology* 46:521-50.

Mariner, William
1820 *An Account of the Natives of the Tonga Island in the South Pacific Ocean.* Boston: Charles Ewer.

Matthiessen, Peter
1962 *Under the Mountain Wall.* New York: Viking Press.

Mead, Margaret

1940 Warfare Is Only an Invention—Not a Biological Necessity. *Asia* 40:402-405.

1963 The Psychology of Warless Man. In *A Warless World*, ed. A. Larson, pp. 131-42. New York: McGraw-Hill.

1968 Alternatives to War. In *War: The Anthropology of Armed Conflict and Aggression*, ed. M. Fried, M. Harris, and R. Murphy, pp. 215-28. Garden City, N.Y.: Natural History Press.

Mishkin, Bernard
1940 *Rank and Warfare Among the Plains Indians*. American Ethnological Society monograph no. 3.

Montagu, M. F. Ashley, ed.
1968a *Man and Aggression*. New York: Oxford University Press.
1968b The New Litany of "Innate Depravity," or Original Sin Revisited. In *Man and Aggression*, ed. M. F. Ashley Montagu, pp. 3-17. New York: Oxford University Press.

Murphy, Robert F.
1957 Intergroup Hostility and Social Cohesion. *American Anthropologist* 59:1018-35.
1958 Reply to Wilson. *American Anthropologist* 60:1196-99.

Naroll, Raoul
1964a On Ethnic Unit Classification. *Current Anthropology* 5:283-312.
1964b Warfare, Peaceful Intercourse, and Territorial Change: A Cross-Cultural Survey. Unpublished MS.
1966 Does Military Deterrence Deter? *Trans-action* 3:4-20.
1969a Deterrence in History. In *Theory and Research on the Causes of War*, ed. D. G. Pruitt and R. C. Snyder, pp. 150-64. New York: Praeger.
1969b The Causes of the Fourth Iroquois War. *Ethnohistory* 16:51-81.

Naroll, Raoul, Vern L. Bullough, and Frada Naroll
n.d. *Military Deterrence in History*. Albany: State University of New York Press. In press.

Newcombe, William W., Jr.
1950 A Re-examination of the Causes of Plains Warfare. *American Anthropologist* 1950:317-30.
1960 Toward an Understanding of War. In *Essays in the Science of Culture*, ed.

G. Dole and R. Carneiro, pp. 317-35. New York: Crowell.

Numelin, Ragnar J.
1950 *The Beginnings of Diplomacy: A Sociological Study of Intertribal and International Relations*. London: Oxford University Press.

Oman, C. W. C.
1960 *The Art of War in the Middle Ages*. Ithaca: Cornell University Press.

Opler, Marvin K.
1939 The Ute Indian War of 1879. *El Palacio* 46:255-62.

Opler, Morris E.
1938 *Dirty Boy: A Jicarilla Tale of Raid and War*. American Anthropological Association memoir no. 52.

Oppenheimer, Franz
1914 *The State: Its History and Development Viewed Sociologically*. Indianapolis: Bobbs-Merrill. Originally published 1908.

Otterbein, Keith F.
1964 Why the Iroquois Won: An Analysis of Iroquois Military Tactics. *Ethnohistory* 11:56-63.
1967 The Evolution of Zulu Warfare. In *Law and Warfare* ed. P. Bohannan, pp. 345-49. Garden City, N.Y.: Natural History Press.
1968a Internal War: A Cross-Cultural Study. *American Anthropologist* 70:277-89.
1968b Cross-Cultural Studies of Armed Combat. Studies in International Conflict, Research Monograph no. 1, *Buffalo Studies* 4:91-109.
1968c Higi Armed Combat. *Southwestern Journal of Anthropology* 24:195-213.
1970 *The Evolution of War: A Cross-Cultural Study*. New Haven: HRAF Press.
1971 Comment on Mark Abrahamson, "Correlates of Political Complexity." *American Sociological Review* 36:113-14.
1972 *Comparative Cultural Analysis: An Introduction to Anthropology*. New York: Holt, Rinehart & Winston.

Otterbein, Keith F., and Charlotte Swanson Otterbein
1965 An Eye for an Eye, a Tooth for a Tooth: A Cross-Cultural Study of

Feuding. *American Anthropologist* 67:1470-82.

Padden, Richard C.
1957 Cultural Change and Military Resistance in Araucanian Chile, 1550-1730. *Southwestern Journal of Anthropology* 13:103-21.

Park, Robert E.
1941 The Social Functions of War. *American Journal of Sociology* 46:551-70.

Paul, Benjamin D.
1968 The Direct and Indirect Biological Costs of War. In *War: The Anthropology of Armed Conflict and Aggression*, ed. M. Fried, M. Harris, and R. Murphy, pp. 76-80. Garden City, N.Y.: Natural History Press.

Peckham, Howard H.
1961 *Pontiac and the Indian Uprising*. Chicago: University of Chicago Press.

Perry, W. J.
1917 An Ethnological Study of Warfare. *Manchester Memoirs* 61, no. 6:1-16.

Pope, Saxton T.
1962 *Bows and Arrows*. Berkeley: University of California Press.

Pospisil, Leopold
1958 *Kapauku Papuans and Their Law*. Yale University Publications in Anthropology no. 54.
1968 Feud. In *International Encyclopedia of the Social Sciences*, ed. D. L. Sills, 16:389-93.

Rapoport, Anatol
1957 Lewis F. Richardson's Mathematical Theory of War. *Journal of Conflict Resolution* 1:249-99.
1960 *Fights, Games, and Debates*. Ann Arbor: University of Michigan Press.

Richardson, Lewis F.
1960 *Statistics of Deadly Quarrels*. Pittsburgh: Boxwood Press.

Ritter, E. A.
1957 *Shaka Zulu: The Rise of the Zulu Empire*. New York: Putnam.

Roper, Marilyn Keyes
1969 A Survey of the Evidence for Intrahuman Killing in the Pleistocene. *Current Anthropology* 10:427-59.

Rosenfeld, Henry
1965 The Social Composition of the Military in the Process of State Formation in the Arabian Desert. *Journal of the Royal Anthropological Institute* 95:75-86, 174-94.

Russel, Carl P.
1957 *Guns on the Early Frontiers*. Berkeley: University of California Press.

Sahlins, Marshall D.
1961 The Segmentary Lineage: An Organization of Predatory Expansion. *American Anthropologist* 63:322-45.
1968 African Nemesis: An Off-Broadway Review. In *Man and Aggression*, ed. M. F. Ashley Montagu, pp. 116-40. New York: Oxford University Press.

Scheele, Raymond
1950 Warfare of the Iroquois and Their Northern Neighbors. Ph.D. dissertation, Columbia University.

Schneider, Joseph
1950 Primitive Warfare: A Methodological Note. *American Sociological Review* 15:772-77.
1952 On the Beginnings of Warfare. *Social Forces* 31:68-74.

Scott, J. P.
1961 Commentary on "Subhuman and Human Fighting." *Anthropologica* 3:164-72.

Secoy, Frank R.
1953 *Changing Military Patterns on the Great Plains*. American Ethnological Society monograph no. 21.

Service, Elman R.
1962 *Primitive Social Organization: An Evolutionary Perspective*. New York: Random House.
1968 War and Our Contemporary Ancestors. In *War: The Anthropology of Armed Conflict and Aggression*, ed. M. Fried, M. Harris, and R. Murphy, pp. 160-67. Garden City, N.Y.: Natural History Press.

Sherif, Muzafer
1961 Intergroup Conflict and Cooperation: The Robbers Cave Experiment. Norman: University of Oklahoma, Institute of Group Relations.

Siegel, Bernard J., and Alan R. Beals
1960 Conflict and Factionalist Dispute. *Journal of the Royal Anthropological Institute of Great Britain and Ireland* 90:107-17.

Skinner, Alanson
1911 War Customs of the Menomini Indians. *American Anthropologist* 13:229-312.

Slobodin, Richard
  1960 Eastern Kutchin Warfare. *Anthropologica* 2:76-94.
Smith, Marian W.
  1938 The War Complex of the Plains Indians. *Proceedings of the American Philosophical Society* 78:425-64.
  1951 American Indian Warfare. *Transactions of the New York Academy of Sciences* 13:348-65.
Snyderman, George S.
  1948 *Behind the Tree of Peace: A Sociological Analysis of Iroquois Warfare.* Philadelphia: University of Pennsylvania Press.
Sorokin, Pitirim A.
  1928 Sociological Interpretation of the "Struggle for Existence" and the Sociology of War. In *Contemporary Sociological Theories*, pp. 307-56. New York: Harper.
  1937 *Social and Cultural Dynamics,* vol. 3: *Fluctuation of Social Relationships, War, and Revolution.* New York: American Book Co.
Speier, Hans
  1941 The Social Types of War. *American Journal of Sociology* 46:445-54.
Spencer, Herbert
  1896 *The Principles of Sociology*, vol. 2. New York: Appleton.
Spicer, Edward H.
  1947 Yaqui Militarism. *Arizona Quarterly* 3:40-48.
Steward, Julian H.
  1955 Development of Complex Societies. In *Theory of Culture Change*, pp. 178-209. Urbana: University of Illinois Press.
Steward, Julian H., and L. C. Faron
  1959 *Native Peoples of South America.* New York: McGraw-Hill.
Stewart, Kenneth M.
  1947 Mohave Warfare. *Southwestern Journal of Anthropology* 3:257-78.
Stewart, Omer C.
  1968 Lorenz/Margolin on the Ute. In *Man and Aggression*, ed. M. F. Ashley Montagu, pp. 103-10. New York: Oxford University Press.
Sumner, William G.
  1906 *Folkways*. Boston: Ginn.
  1911 *War and Other Essays*. New Haven: Yale University Press.

Suttles, Wayne
  1961 Subhuman and Human Fighting. *Anthropologica* 3:148-63.
Swadesh, Morris
  1948 Motivations in Nootka Warfare. *Southwestern Journal of Anthropology* 4:76-93.
Swanton, John R.
  1943 *Are Wars Inevitable?* Washington, D.C.: Smithsonian Institution.
Sweet, Louise E.
  1965 Camel Raiding of North Arabian Bedouin: A Mechanism of Ecological Adaptation. *American Anthropologist* 67:1132-50.
Tatje, Terrence A.
  1970 Problems of Concept Definition for Comparative Studies. In *A Handbook of Method in Cultural Anthropology*, ed. R. Naroll and R. Cohen, pp. 689-96. Garden City, N.Y.: Natural History Press.
Tefft, Stanton K.
  1969 Warfare Resolution Among Primitive Peoples: Some Preliminary Observations. Paper delivered at the 68th annual meeting of the American Anthropological Association, November 20-23.
Teggart, Frederick J.
  1939 *Rome and China: A Study of Correlations in Historical Events*. Berkeley: University of California Press.
Thieme, Frederick P.
  1968 The Biological Consequences of War. In *War: The Anthropology of Armed Conflict and Aggression*, ed. M. Fried, M. Harris, and R. Murphy, pp. 16-21. Garden City, N.Y.: Natural History Press.
Thwaites, Reuben G., ed.
  1896- *The Jesuit Relations and Allied Documents . . . 1610-1791*, 73 vols. Cleveland: Burrows.
Tooker, Elisabeth
  1963 The Iroquois Defeat of the Huron: A Review of Causes. *Pennsylvania Archaeologist* 33:115-23.
Toynbee, Arnold J.
  1950 *War and Civilization.* New York: Oxford University Press.
Trelease, Allen W.
  1962 The Iroquois and the Western Fur Trade: A Problem in Interpretation.

Mississippi Valley Historical Review 49:32-51.

Trigger, Bruce G.
1962 Trade and Tribal Warfare on the St. Lawrence in the Sixteenth Century. *Ethnohistory* 9:240-56.
1967 Settlement Archaeology—Its Goals and Promise. *American Antiquity* 32:149-60.

Turney-High, Harry H.
1949 *Primitive War: Its Practice and Concepts.* Columbia: University of South Carolina Press.
1968 *Man and System: Foundations for the Study of Human Relations.* New York: Appleton-Century-Crofts.

Tylor, Edward B.
1888 On a Method of Investigating the Development of Institutions; Applied to Laws of Marriage and Descent. *Journal of the Royal Anthropological Institute of Great Britain and Ireland* 18:245-70.

Van der Kroef, Justus M.
1952 Some Head-Hunting Traditions of Southern New Guinea. *American Anthropologist* 54:221-35.

Van Velzen, H. U. E. Thoden, and W. van Wetering
1960 Residence, Power Groups, and Intrasocietal Aggression. *International Archives of Ethnography* 49:169-200.

Vayda, Andrew P.
1956 Maori Warfare. Ph.D. dissertation, Columbia University.
1960 *Maori Warfare.* Maori monograph no. 2. Wellington, N.Z.: Polynesian Society.
1961 Expansion and Warfare Among Swidden Agriculturalists. *American Anthropologist* 63:346-58.
1968a Hypotheses About Functions of War. In *War: The Anthropology of Armed Conflict and Aggression,* ed. M. Fried, M. Harris, and R. Murphy, pp. 85-91. Garden City, N.Y.: Natural History Press.
1968b Primitive War. In *International Encyclopedia of the Social Sciences,* ed. D. L. Sills, 16:468-72.
1969 The Study of the Causes of War, with Special Reference to Head-Hunting Raids in Borneo. *Ethnohistory* 16:211-24.

1970 Maoris and Muskets in New Zealand: Disruption of a War System. *Political Science Quarterly* 85:560-84.

Vayda, Andrew P., and Anthony Leeds
1961 Anthropology and the Study of War. *Anthropologica* (n.s.) 3:131-33.

Voget, Fred W.
1964 Warfare and the Integration of Crow Indian Culture. In *Explorations in Cultural Anthropology,* ed. W. H. Goodenough, pp. 483-509. New York: McGraw-Hill.

Wales, Horace G. Q.
1952 *Ancient South-east Asian Warfare.* London: B. Quaritch.

Wallace, Anthony F. C.
1968 Psychological Preparations for War. In *War: The Anthropology of Armed Conflict and Aggression,* ed. M. Fried, M. Harris, and R. Murphy, pp. 173-82. Garden City, N.Y.: Natural History Press.

Warner, W. Lloyd
1931 Murngin Warfare. *Oceania* 1:457-94.
1958 *A Black Civilization: A Study of an Australian Tribe.* New York: Harper & Row.

Wedgewood, Camilla H.
1930 Some Aspects of Warfare in Melanesia. *Oceania* 1:5-33.

White, Leslie A.
1949 *The Science of Culture.* New York: Grove Press.

Wilson, H. Clyde
1958 Regarding the Causes of Mundurucu Warfare. *American Anthropologist* 60:1193-96.

Wintringham, Tom
1943 *The Story of Weapons and Tactics: From Troy to Stalingrad.* Boston: Houghton Mifflin.

Wolf, Eric R.
1959 *Sons of the Shaking Earth.* Chicago: University of Chicago Press.
1969 *Peasant Wars of the Twentieth Century.* New York: Harper & Row.

Woolley, C. Leonard
1965 *The Sumerians.* New York: Norton.

Wright, Quincy
1965 *A Study of War,* 2nd ed. Chicago: University of Chicago Press. Originally published 1942.

Yamada, Nakaba
1916 *Ghenkō: The Mongol Invasion of*

Japan. New York: Dutton.

Young, Frank W.
1965 *Initiation Ceremonies: A Cross-Cultural Study of Status Dramatization.*

Indianapolis: Bobbs-Merrill.

Zegwaard, Gerald A.
1959 Headhunting Practices of the Asmat of Netherlands New Guinea. *American Anthropologist* 61:1020-41.

CHAPTER 22 Pluralism

PIERRE L. VAN DEN BERGHE

The term "pluralism" in social science has been used in two different senses, which overlap sufficiently to compound the confusion. The older tradition traces its ancestry to Alexis de Tocqueville (1835-1840) and counts among its modern representatives a number of American and French political scientists and sociologists (Aron 1950, Kornhauser 1960, Lipset 1963, Polsby 1960, McCord 1965, Simpson and Yinger 1953). To this school pluralism is first and foremost a property of the political system, and more specifically a necessary condition for democracy in highly complex and differentiated polities. These authors have compared "democratic" societies, principally the United States and western European states, either with *anciens régimes* of the aristocratic variety (as did Tocqueville) or with modern totalitarian states. The pluralistic democracies, they claim, are characterized by the division of effective decision-making power among a wide variety of autonomous groups and institutions in competition with each other.

This situation is contrasted with the more monolithic autocracies of the traditional or modern variety, in which specialized institutions (such as churches, labor unions, voluntary associations, artisan guilds, and trade organizations), if they are allowed to exist at all, are not independent centers of decision-making. In the more autocratic regimes (of which modern totalitarianism of right or left represents the purest form), power is centralized in the hands of a small ruling class and exercised over an atomized mass of impotent citizens who may be "mobilized" in a political party or in party-controlled organizations, but who are not allowed to develop any sources of power that might rival the monolithic state.

In pluralistic societies (of which the American lobby system provided the archetype), the existence of a wide variety of competing interest groups vying with each other for participation in and influence over the state machinery is regarded as both a consequence and a cause of democracy. In much the same way as laissez-faire economists see in "free enterprise" the basic mechanism protecting the economic interests of the consumers, the political theorists of pluralism see in the multiplicity of competing interest or power groups the necessary and sufficient condition for the preservation of the citizens' freedom. Organized interest groups (e.g., political parties, churches, labor unions) are held to interpose themselves between the power of the state and the mass of otherwise unorganized citizens; conflicts of interest among these groups are supposed to result in the greatest political good for the greatest number in a way that the theorists have not clearly specified, but which seems to be somewhat akin to the notion that competition among business firms is good for the consumer.

In fairness to the contemporary proponents of this school of pluralism, it should be stressed that scarcely any of them takes quite as naive and sanguine a view of the political process in complex industrial societies as this highly schematized presentation of the theory suggests. Before turning to the second usage of the term "pluralism," however, I should spell out my criticisms of this first usage.

1. The theory is based on an extremely narrow range of societies, specifically on Western states of the eighteenth, nineteenth, and twentieth centuries, with heavy emphasis on the United States as the archetype of the pluralistic society, in sharp contrast to European aristocratic, fascist, and communist regimes. The model is thus of very limited use in comparative analysis.

2. This first model of pluralism fails to distinguish between functional differentiation and "true" pluralism as I shall define it presently. Thus, for example, the existence of an American Medical Association, a Republican party, an American Federation of Labor,

an American Association of Manufacturers, and so on is simply a case of functional differentiation, not of pluralism. Each of these associations has specific aims and is based on the specialized interests of a particular group operating in its own institutional sphere. On the other hand, the simultaneous existence of competing organizations in the same institutional sphere and with duplicatory functions is an instance of pluralism. For instance, the fact that there exist in the same society both a white and a black medical association, or a Republican and a Democratic party, or a Catholic and a Baptist church, or a socialist and a communist labor federation, is indeed an instance of pluralism as I define it. The processes of differentiation—i.e., of increasing complexity of interdependent structures and of increasing specialization of function—are quite different from those that arise from the segmentation of societies into replicatory, parallel groups and institutions. The failure of the first school of pluralism to distinguish between these two types of phenomena obscures fundamental differences both within and among societies. A society may be highly differentiated but fairly monistic, or, conversely, it may be highly pluralistic but not very differentiated. The two phenomena are at least partly independent of one another. It should be noted here that there is a partial overlap in meaning between the two usages of pluralism, and that this leads to misunderstandings unless the area of overlap is clearly specified.

3. The data examined by the first school of pluralism invalidate the conclusion that pluralism and democracy are linked in any necessary way. It is indeed remarkable that most analysts of the American polity have failed to note that the most pervasive and enduring aspect of pluralism in the United

States is the chasm that separates its white and nonwhite inhabitants, and that this is precisely the issue on which the American political and social systems have been most glaringly undemocratic. Indeed, nearly all groups that have remained distinct, either racially or culturally, from the dominant group have been treated quite undemocratically: Indians, Afro-Americans, Mexicans, Puerto Ricans, Chinese, Japanese, and to a lesser degree the Jewish and Catholic immigrants from southern and eastern Europe. Of those groups, the ones that were defined as white were allowed, indeed expected, to become assimilated in the Anglo-Saxon melting pot, but the ones that were considered racially distinct were prevented from becoming socially assimilated, and were thus reduced to permanent pariah castes.

Let us now turn to the second usage of "pluralism." This tradition goes back only some thirty years, to Furnivall (1939, 1948) and Boeke (1953), and the concept gained widespread currency only in the 1960s. Even today its use is still mostly limited to anthropologists and to sociologists specializing in nonwestern and nonindustrial societies. Although different authors have given somewhat different definitions of pluralism, there is nevertheless a common denominator of meaning. Pluralism, in this sense, refers to a property, or set of properties, of societies wherein several distinct social and/or cultural groups coexist within the boundaries of a single polity and share a common economic system that makes them interdependent, yet maintain a greater or lesser degree of autonomy and a set of discrete institutional structures in other spheres of social life, notably the familial, recreational, and religious.

It is still premature to speak of a "theory of pluralism," and indeed it is doubtful that any such distinct body of theory will ever emerge, for pluralism is nothing more than a set of basic characteristics common to a great many of the world's societies. Pluralism is simply a sensitizing concept, calling attention to an important and hitherto neglected aspect of societies. The notion of pluralism is thus not an alternative social theory, but rather an additional tool in the existing analytical kit of anthropologists, sociologists, and other social scientists.

Historically, the concept of pluralism grew out of the growing unease, both within and outside the anthropological profession, with anthropology's conventional focus on the "society-culture" as a relatively homogeneous, integrated, independent, self-regulating whole; in short, as what functionalists have called a "closed system." Until two decades ago, the vast bulk of the anthropological literature was devoted to the study of various aspects of the "way of life," the "culture," or the "social structure" of "a people," the unit of analysis being defined by a criterion of relative cultural homogeneity. The conventional analytical boundaries of the systems under study were *culturally* determined, with special emphasis on a mutually understandable language, a common system of religious and secular values, common principles of kinship organization and marriage, a consensual system of legal norms, common educational principles, and so on.

For certain limited purposes of ethnographic description, and indeed also for the development of models dealing with well-defined classes of phenomena (notably in linguistic and kinship analysis), the conventional approach worked well enough. Yet from the very first faltering steps of anthropology in the late nineteenth century it was obvious that social evolution, unlike biological evolution, was not primarily a divergent and intraspecific process of selective adaptation to an external environment, but in good part a process of limitless (though not random) cross-fertilization by which even totally unrelated cultures could and did give rise to perfectly viable hybrids.

Early theories of diffusionism and unilinear evolution, which were in fact little more than highly schematized and partly erroneous descriptions of historical processes, gave way in the 1930s to the theory of acculturation as a model for the analysis of culture change. Associated with eminent names like Malinowski, Linton, Herskovits, and Redfield, the theory represented the most systematic attempt to date to deal with the dynamics of exogenous change resulting from contact between different "culture groups." The focus, however, was still predominantly cultural. The questions asked were aimed at discovering what was happening to the culture of group X as a consequence of contact with group Y. Refinements were introduced into the analysis, such as the notions of cultural selectivity and "reinterpretation," but the unit of study was still the "cultural group," and hence cultural contact was still viewed largely as an exogenous process disturbing the integration or equilibrium of the cultural system.

While the anthropological vanguard was acutely concerned with cultural dynamics and culture contact by the 1930s, the rear guard was still busy with ethnographic description of "cultural isolates," or, worse yet, with dubious reconstruction of a pristine past before the pollution of Western contact. Ironically, the anthropologist who was himself a representative of a militantly expansionist civilization, and a witness to an obtrusive colonial system, often retreated to an ethnological Garden of Eden, pretending that Adam and Eve had not yet bitten into the apple of Western knowledge.

The pluralist approach was, in a sense, a predictable response to the great gap between the mainstream of anthropological concerns and the important social processes taking place all over the world, and especially in the very areas that had become the *chasse gardée* of anthropologists. The limitations of treating the world as if it consisted of some two thousand Tikopias that could be cross-tabulated as independent cases drawn from the Human Relations Area Files became increasingly obvious. The analytical focus shifted in part from the culture group to the much larger multiethnic society, which, for most political and economic purposes, had become the independently viable unit.

Two of the earliest studies of plural societies that broke away from the tradition as early as the thirties are Redfield's *The Folk Culture of Yucatan* (1941) and Gluckman's *Analysis of a Social Situation in Modern Zululand* (1958). While neither author uses the word "pluralism," both stress the importance of relating the local community to the larger society (and, in the case of Gluckman, to the colonial system). In this respect, Redfield was already abandoning his own much more conventional approach in his Tepoztlán study (1930), begun in 1926, and refining his famous folk-urban dichotomy to include a third "peasant" type, a rural population living symbiotically with an urban one.

By the 1940s and 1950s an ever growing number of social scientists became increasingly concerned about the special properties of multiethnic societies, and began to use a variety of labels to describe them. Thus Radcliffe-Brown (1940) spoke of South Africa as a "composite society"; the Dutch economist Boeke (1953) spoke of Indonesia as a "dual society"; Little (1955) referred to "social dualism" in Sierra

Leone; Van Lier (1950) mentioned the "segmental societies" of the West Indies; and Nash (1957, 1958) described Guatemala and Mexico as "multiple societies" and as "non-national states" marked by the presence of "two societies within one political network" (Nash 1958:65). This period also saw a growing number of anthropologists and sociologists like Hilda Kuper (1947), Tumin (1952), and Wagley (1960, 1964) turn their attention to the systematic field study and description of interethnic or interracial relations from the holistic perspective of total systems of interaction. Such studies became even more common in the 1960s (Benedict 1961; Colby and van den Berghe 1961, 1969; Crowder 1962; Despres 1967; Hilda Kuper 1969; Leo Kuper 1965a; Maquet 1961; A. C. Mayer 1961; P. Mayer 1961; M. G. Smith 1965a, 1965b; van den Berghe 1964a, 1965a).

At a more applied level, the earlier formulations of Redfield, Malinowski, and the acculturation school of anthropology led a number of Mexican anthropologists, especially Julio de la Fuente (1955), Alfonso Villa Rojas, and Gonzalo Aguirre Beltrán (1957), to develop what they called the "regional integration" framework. Concerned with implementing the Mexican policy of noncoercive integration of the indigenous population into the mainstream of the national culture, they looked at the various regions of their country as systems of interaction between interdependent Indians and *ladinos*, and attempted to introduce planned social change by influencing the total situation and not simply by acting on the Indians. More recently, the Mexican sociologist Pablo González Casanova (1963) explicitly applied the concept of pluralism to Latin America.

Somewhat independently of the Mexicans, a group of French Africanists, mostly sociologists, led by Georges Balandier, developed an analytical framework similar in most respects to that of the largely English-speaking pluralists (Balandier 1955b, 1965; Mercier 1965). Through his now classic statement of the "colonial situation," Balandier helped to reorient much of Africanist scholarship away from conventional ethnography and toward the study of the dynamics of change and conflict growing out of the colonial experience.

The main intellectual source of the modern school of pluralism is Furnivall (1939, 1948), who was among the first to use the term extensively in its more recent sense. As initially used by Furnivall, "pluralism" was not a cross-culturally applicable concept referring to a set of properties common to a wide range of societies, but rather a term describing what Furnivall conceived of as societies of a unique historical type: the multiracial colonial societies created by the political expansion of Europe in the tropics. M. G. Smith (1969c:429) takes Furnivall to task for restricting the scope of the concept and thus reducing its analytical value. There is certainly nothing uniquely tropical, colonial, or European about pluralism, nor is pluralism confined to multiracial situations, argues Smith, whose 1960 article "Social and Cultural Pluralism" is perhaps the most important of the more recent writings of the school.

That article has become a common basis of departure or disagreement for subsequent writings in the same broad orientation. In it Smith argues that pluralism is distinct from "other forms of social heterogeneity such as class stratification in that it consists in the coexistence of incompatible institutional systems." While many plural societies are multiracial, Smith says, it is a mistake to "conceive the conditions and problems of pluralism directly in terms of race relations," because "to do so is to mistake the social myth for reality." All modern societies are culturally heterogeneous and hence show some variability in their institutions. Occupational specialization and social class are two common bases of differentiation, but they are not sufficient to constitute pluralism. If this heterogeneity remains anchored in a common system of basic institutions embracing "kinship, education, religion, property and economy, recreation and certain sodalities," then there is no pluralism. While pluralism is often accompanied by a hierarchy of cultural groups, stratification can exist without pluralism, and pluralism must not be confused with pure and simple stratification. Cultural difference and class stratification vary independently.

If the institutions of the various groups in a plural society are incompatible, what, according to Smith, holds the plural society together? "The monopoly of power by one cultural section is the essential precondition for the maintenance of the total society in its current form." Thus in his 1960 formulation Smith defines pluralism as a condition in which each of several cultural groups has a set of mutually incompatible institutions in every major sphere of life except the political, in which the institutions of one of the cultural groups dominate the entire society. Smith further restricts the term "plural society" to those in which the politically dominant group is a numerical minority.

In his later formulations, Smith (1969a, 1969b, 1969c) somewhat shifts the emphasis of his argument. He now tends to put greater stress on the political factor and to deemphasize cultural incompatibilities. What Smith calls "differential incorporation"—that is, the political domination of one group over the others—is now the key defining characteristic of plural societies.

The second type of political incorporation is "consociation," a system such as that of Switzerland, in which institutional pluralism may exist but rights and privileges are shared equally by the various groups. Finally, in the case of "uniform incorporation," individual citizens are incorporated directly into the public domain without reference to any sectional identification that may or may not exist. Pluralism, then, defined in terms of unintegrated institutional structures, is a much more widespread condition than "plural societies," which must satisfy the additional criterion of "differential incorporation."

Smith goes on to distinguish three associated levels of pluralism. *Cultural* pluralism, by itself, consists solely in institutional differences without any corporate social distinctions. Cultural pluralism is compatible with "uniform incorporation." *Social* pluralism is present if institutional differences coincide with the sharp division of a society into closed corporate groups. This condition is compatible with consociation. Finally, *structural* pluralism prevails in plural societies; i.e., in differentially incorporated ones. Structural pluralism presupposes both social and cultural pluralism, and social pluralism presupposes cultural pluralism.

The recently published symposium *Pluralism in Africa* (L. Kuper and M. G. Smith, eds., 1969) reveals a general agreement among the various contributors that culturally and structurally heterogeneous societies do represent a special type of social system to which the consensus and equilibrium models derived from sociological and anthropological functionalism do not apply. Most of the authors address themselves to the problem of social integration in those societies, and most conclude that political coercion by one of the corporate groups in the society is frequently one of the main elements holding the society more or less precariously or unstably together. Beyond this underlying agreement, however, some diversity of views is apparent, especially on the breadth of the definition of pluralism and plural societies, and hence on the scope of the empirical phenomena to be subsumed under these concepts.

Several of the authors disagree with Smith that political coercion by the one group (often a minority) that monopolizes the means of power is a sufficient basis of integration for plural societies. I have put equal stress on political coercion and economic interdependence (often of an exploitive nature) as necessary, sufficient, and *mutually reinforcing* bases of social integration in plural societies (van den Berghe 1967:139). In their earlier treatments, both Boeke (1953) and Furnivall (1939) also stressed the integration of plural societies through market mechanisms, an essential feature of plural societies to which Smith devotes scant attention. Plural societies that lack the powerful bond of economic ties tend to be ephemeral conquest empires that fragment almost as quickly as they are formed. Oppression and exploitation are the two complementary sides of minority-group domination in what Smith calls systems of "differential incorporation." Other authors, especially Max Gluckman (1969a, 1969b), Hilda Kuper (1969), and Leo Kuper (1965a, 1965b, 1965c, 1969b; H. and L. Kuper, eds., 1965) suggest that notwithstanding sharp cleavages between ethnic communities in plural societies, there also exists a whole network of links between groups, and that even a measure of cooperation and consensus may exist on the desirability of certain common aims. Gluckman (1969b:374-75), for example, relates how, having started with a conflict model, he was led by his Zululand fieldwork to ask and try to answer the question of why, despite

clashes and oppositions, blacks and whites could go about their daily business so easily and routinely. "The South African social system was then, and has become increasingly, a horrible one, morally. But it worked and works, in total and in its parts." This was the central problem of Gluckman's classic monograph (1958) referred to earlier. In reference to a biethnic area in highland Guatemala, Colby and I (1969) describe a situation in which Indians and *ladinos*, in addition to being joined by what we regard as the minimum integrative ties of politics and economics, are also linked by important ties between their partly overlapping religious systems.

On balance, it seems that if plural societies are to show any stability, they have to be held together by more than sheer political coercion. For one thing, the cost of coercion for the dominant group is too high unless it is accompanied by economic exploitation; and exploitation is a form of interdependence, however asymmetrical the economic relationship may be. In addition to these minimum conditions, the constituent groups in a plural society may have other areas of institutional overlap, and it seems that Smith's rigid criterion of incompatible institutions in every sphere except the political is too restrictive an ideal type to have much empirical application. The very criterion of incompatibility is often difficult to operationalize. It is clear, for example, that prescriptive monogamy is incompatible with preferential polygyny, but is Buddhism incompatible with Christianity? Christians may think so, but not many Buddhists.

Another point needs clarification. Some authors have implied that the sharpness of group cleavages is a function of the relative absence of interaction between members of the groups. It seems rather that *quality* of interaction is at least as important as quantity. More precisely, pluralism is a function of the *qualitative differential* between intra- and intergroup relations. A society is pluralistic to the extent that relations *between* groups are segmental, utilitarian, nonaffective, and functionally specific, and to the extent that relations *within* groups are total, nonutilitarian, affective, and diffuse.

Smith, as we have seen, restricts the concept of pluralism to societies where different groups have culturally incompatible institutions, and he makes a sharp analytical distinction between pluralism on the one hand and functional differentiation and social stratification on the other. Mazrui (1969) adopts a much broader and eclectic definition of pluralism which includes both differentiation and stratification, and Leo Kuper (1969a), while admitting that ethnic and racial cleavages are very special cases, also includes class stratification as a form of pluralism. I have taken an intermediate position, trying to distinguish between pluralism and functional differentiation and also between pluralism and societies, such as segmentary lineage societies, divided between corporate groups that have substantially identical institutional structures. Thus I am excluding from the definition of pluralism societies characterized by the sheer presence of specialized bodies (the American Dental Association, the American Federation of Labor, the American Association of Manufacturers) and those that are primarily held together by what Durkheim rather misleadingly termed "mechanical solidarity." Also, like Leo Kuper and unlike Smith, I prefer not to regard the plural society as a distinct ideal type of society, but rather to consider pluralism a set of characteristics exhibited *in greater or lesser degree* by a great many of the world's societies, and to treat the sovereign polity, the

colonial territory, or some political subdivision thereof as the most convenient unit of analysis.

More formally, I call a society pluralistic if it possesses the following two basic features: (1) segmentation into functionally similar corporate groups, whose members frequently, though not necessarily, belong to different cultures or subcultures, and (2) a social structure compartmentalized into analogous, duplicatory, parallel, noncomplementary, but distinguishable (if only in terms of subcultural variation) sets of institutions. Admittedly, the borderline between very rigid types of stratification such as the Hindu caste system and multiethnic or racial societies is not clear cut, as witnessed by the use of the term "caste" to describe both types of societies.

Since definitions are in the last analysis arbitrary, it is important not to reify them. The main contribution of the pluralist orientation is not the classification of societies into yet another taxonomy, but the systematic reorientation of anthropology and comparative sociology away from the allegedly homogeneous, insular, integrated, consensus-based "society-culture" as the basic unit of analysis. For certain purposes, it may be useful to treat the society-culture as a closed system in equilibrium; but unless some of the analysis is shifted to the more complex level of the plural society—the interplay between the corporate segments of the society, the articulation of its diverse institutional structures, the movement of individuals between these groups and structures, and the dynamics of change arising out of these processes of interaction—a good deal of the most important phenomena taking place in most of the world's societies will necessarily elude analysis.

Another central concern of a number of writers of the pluralist school has been the relationship between cultural and social or structural pluralism. For M. G. Smith (1969c) the cultural aspect (in the sense of coexistence of incompatible institutions) is the least common denominator of pluralism. If the society is also segmented into well-defined corporate groups, then you have what Smith calls social pluralism. Finally, if these corporate groups are differentially incorporated, then you have structural pluralism. Others, such as Leo Kuper (1967, 1969c) and I (van den Berghe 1967, 1969), have accepted the validity of the distinction between the institutional and the group levels of analysis, but have suggested a more complex relationship between cultural and social pluralism. While, in the vast majority of cases, the most fundamental lines of cleavage in a plural society are based on ethnicity (or some specific aspect thereof, such as religious or linguistic distinctions), there is not always a one-to-one correspondence between cultural and social differences. Thus in racially stratified societies such as the United States and South Africa, ethnic (i.e., cultural) and racial (i.e., social) lines coincide only very imperfectly. Cultural distinctiveness between racial groups may disappear almost entirely (as between most white and black Americans and white and "Coloured" South Africans) and yet the racial cleavages become increasingly deep.

In the American case, for example, it is not correct to say that the racial chasm is simply the structural aspect of the preexisting cultural differences. (Nor, obviously, is it an intrinsic product of physical differences, for "race" is very clearly a *socially* defined category.) What happened, rather, was that slavery "deculturated" Africans and acculturated them into an impoverished outcaste subculture of the dominant group, and then that Afro-Americans, as a result of segregation and their pari-

ah status, developed a limited kind of secondary cultural pluralism through a process of cultural drift. "Black culture" in the United States, so far as its objective characteristics are concerned, is overwhelmingly a variant of the dominant Anglo-Saxon culture; its special characteristics are a result of pariah status, not survivals of African culture.

The very concept of ethnicity raises important analytical problems that cannot be solved by regarding cultural pluralism as simply a function of the existence of objective cultural differences between institutions or groups. Ethnicity is not a static concept, as anthropologists are increasingly discovering, but an extraordinary fluid composite of objectively identifiable cultural characteristics and subjectively perceived differences. New situations such as urbanization or political conflicts can in a relatively short time give rise to the creation of new ethnic groups or the merging of old ones. A mystique of nationalism may in time accentuate ethnic distinctiveness, or alternatively merge a multiplicity of local particularisms into a larger cultural entity. Different issues in the same society may activate different lines of "ethnic" cleavage. There may be wide discrepancies between out-group and in-group definitions of cultural cleavage. Objectively very diverse groups may feel very close, and, more frequently, objectively very similar groups may feel very far apart. In short, there is much more to cultural pluralism than objective differences in institutions, and social pluralism is not always the expression at the group level of cultural pluralism at the institutional level.

If one accepts the notion that pluralism is a matter of degree rather than an all-or-none phenomenon, then it becomes important to spell out the dimensions along which it varies. Certainly the number of groups in a society makes a difference. Numerous authors, for example, have stressed the similarities in the positions of "middlemen" groups (such as overseas Chinese and Indians) in tripartite societies, and the ways in which these situations differ from the dynamics of political conflict in bicultural countries like Canada and Belgium. The relative size of the groups is also important, though probably not so overwhelmingly so as to justify making a sharp distinction between societies in which the dominant group is a majority and those (at least as numerous) where it is a minority. M. G. Smith (1960, 1969a), for example, reserves the term "plural society" for the dominant minority situation without, however, convincingly demonstrating that a drastic change occurs in the structure of the society when a dominant group passes from 49 to 51 percent of the total.

Apart from the number of groups and their ratios vis-à-vis each other, the degree of geographical concentration of these groups is of considerable importance. A spatially dispersed minority, such as black Americans, cannot hope to pursue a policy of nationalism so successfully as, say, French-Canadians, who have a strong territorial basis in which to anchor their political demands. In that respect, Canada is a more pluralistic society than the United States.

When we look at societies from the standpoint of degree of structural segmentation, a wide range of pluralism is also observable. The lines of cleavage between groups can be sharp and impermeable, as between castes or "racial" groups, or alternatively they can be so loose as to elude definition. The more pluralistic societies will exhibit such phenomena as complete ascription of group membership and a corresponding lack of mobility from one group to another, strict prescriptive group endog-

amy, commensality rules, a rigid, differential (and deferential) etiquette of intergroup relations, and sometimes, when the more symbolic and social lines of cleavage have failed or are breaking down, sharp and invidious spatial segregation as well. By contrast, minimally pluralistic or nonplural societies will have situations approximating the "open class" model, with considerable lack of consensus as to who belongs to which group, a good deal of social mobility, and an absence of any rule of prescriptive endogamy and of any overt norms of differential interaction.

Shifting the analysis from the structural to the cultural aspect of pluralism, one may distinguish several degrees of *objective* cultural pluralism; i.e., of observable cultural differences between groups. Groups can show maximal cultural pluralism when they come from unrelated traditions (e.g., the Bakongo and the Portuguese, the Navaho and the Anglo-Americans); they can exhibit intermediate pluralism by belonging to well-differentiated but related ethnic groups (e.g., the French-Swiss, Italian-Swiss, and German-Swiss); or they can be minimally pluralistic by showing only minor subcultural variants of the same tradition (e.g., white and black Americans, white and "Coloured" South Africans).

As ethnicity, however, is not only a function of objective cultural differences, it is also important to take into account the subjective perceptions of cultural differences by members of various groups. Thus two groups that are objectively very close, so close that they exhibit only minor dialectal differences in language, such as black and white Americans, may subjectively magnify the significance (and hence the reality) of these cultural differences, and perceive each other as culturally very distant. This subjective perception of objectively minimal differences may in time accentuate the objective differences, and a myth of "nationalism" may eventually give rise to the objective reality of it. However, even when ethnicity is still a myth, the very existence of the myth makes for a greater degree of pluralism than would otherwise be the case. A myth is simply a different level of social reality. One must also allow for the complication that the subjective perceptions of various groups are not necessarily congruent with each other. Thus for a long time most white Americans viewed their black fellow countrymen as very different from themselves, while most blacks insisted that since they had been in America longer than most whites, as a group they were more American than the whites. Now the subjective perceptions of these two groups are in the process of being reversed: more whites view blacks as culturally like themselves, while Afro-Americans are busily developing a mystique of African heritage. As Barth (1969:32-33) notes: ". . . a drastic reduction of cultural differences between ethnic groups does not correlate in any simple way with a reduction in the organizational relevance of ethnic identities, or a breakdown in boundary-maintaining processes."

Another key dimension of variability in the amount of pluralism is the *range of shared institutions* among groups in a plural society. Minimally, as I have suggested, groups have to share political and economic institutions. This is not to say that they have to share *all* their political and economic institutions. There may exist side by side a market economy and a subsistence one, or a parliamentary democracy for the ruling group and a colonial system for the subject peoples (as in South Africa). However, as a minimum basis of societal integration, all the constituent groups have to be incorporated, however differentially, in a single supreme

polity, and these groups must be linked by ties of economic interdependence. When no ties other than relations of power and of production exist between groups, the society can be said to be maximally pluralistic at the institutional level. Many plural societies, however, fall short of this degree of institutional compartmentalization. Thus *ladinos* and Maya Indians in southeastern Mexico and Guatemala share, in addition to common political and economic institutions, a complex set of religious ties, including ties of ritual kinship, which are an additional focus of social integration (Colby and van den Berghe 1961, 1969). Or, very commonly, ethnic groups may be linked by systems of hypergamous polygyny or of unidirectional, "hypergenous" concubinage.

So far, I have suggested that the analysis of plural societies must be conducted primarily at two levels, that of institutions and that of groups. The lack of a simple one-to-one correspondence between institutional differences and cleavages between groups makes this analytical distinction essential, even though, in many cases, corporate ethnic groups may indeed "share a culture" that, notwithstanding minor internal variations, sets them clearly apart from other similarly constituted groups in the same plural society. In short, there is considerable empirical overlap between the institutional structure and the group structure, but not enough to dispense with the analytical distinction.

In conclusion, I should like to add a third major level of analysis of plural societies: that of individuals. As a number of anthropologists and sociologists concerned with the dynamics of acculturation and of intergroup contacts have noted (Barth 1969, P. Mayer 1961, van den Berghe 1968), numerous individuals in many plural societies are constantly moving between groups, despite the fact that the lines of cleavage between groups may often remain quite sharply drawn. Thus we frequently find a superficially paradoxical situation in which individuals can "pass" with relative ease between groups that remain nevertheless quite stable in terms of relative size or cultural characteristics. In Belgium and Canada, for example, countervailing trends of natality differentials and cultural assimilation keep the ratio of Flemings and Walloons and French- and Anglo-Canadians nearly constant, thereby hiding the fact that many individuals and even family units shift their group membership over time.

The acculturation of individuals who shift from one group to another is of course a problem that has occupied anthropologists for at least forty years. More recent, however, is the realization that, in addition to this long-range and often irreversible movement of individuals from one group to another, persons can also shuttle between cultural systems, simultaneously or in quick succession operating in two or more groups or cultures. In the same sense as persons can be fully bilingual, they can also be bicultural and biethnic, as a number of studies of African migrant workers in towns have illustrated.

There is therefore a danger, when stressing the structural analysis of institutions and groups, of underrating the actual degree of fluidity and dynamism that often characterize plural societies. After all, groups and institutions are nothing but analytical abstractions and shorthand devices for describing *interacting individuals*. The pluralist approach has been under fire for being simply another form of static structuralism. In my view, it is nothing of the sort, although I can see that the present essay may give some support to this criticism. Indeed, in trying to define the main dimensions of plural societies, I have stressed mostly problems of

structure as distinct from process, but at no point have I assumed that plural societies are stable or in equilibrium. Some are clearly more stable than others (e.g., Switzerland compared to Nigeria, South Africa compared to Israel), but, by and large, plural societies seem more dynamic than their polar opposites, which, for lack of a better term, we may call "monistic" societies. For one thing, it appears that the very segmentation of the society into groups that almost invariably have an unequal share of political and economic resources creates an additional source of endemic conflict, and often of revolutionary change.

The pluralist approach is thus not a static framework for the structural description of multiethnic societies. Nor is it, to be sure, a theory of social change. Indeed, it is not a theory at all, but simply a set of sensitizing concepts to aid us in studying the complex reality of multiethnic systems and to steer us away from our concern with the "society-culture" as a closed system. The pluralist framework is presented as a step toward the understanding of change and conflict in a great many of the world's large-scale societies. Furthermore, the concept of pluralism deals with the macroscopic level of analysis, which has the most far-reaching relevance to our very survival as a species. If anthropology is to remain relevant it must be able to account as well for language riots in Bombay, religious upheaval in Belfast, black power in America, and civil war in Nigeria as it does for the elegant symmetry of unilateral cross-cousin marriage among the dualistically organized societies of the Amazon basin. At the cost of passing for a philistine sociologist, may I suggest that, intellectually, both types of problem may be equally enthralling, but that there are pressing reasons why anthropology should not remain the arcane fief of urbane collectors of exotica. Happily anthropology never was purely that, but it sometimes came perilously near.

REFERENCES AND SUGGESTED READINGS

Aguirre Beltrán, Gonzalo
1957 *El Proceso de aculturación*. Mexico City: Universidad Nacional Autónoma de México.

Alexandre, Pierre
1969 Social Pluralism in French African Colonies and in States Issuing Therefrom: An Impressionistic Approach. In *Pluralism in Africa*, ed. L. Kuper and M. G. Smith. Berkeley: University of California Press.

Aron, Raymond
1950 Social Structure and the Ruling Class. *British Journal of Sociology* 1:1-16.

Balandier, Georges
1955a *Sociologie des Brazzavilles Noires*. Paris: Colin.
1955b *Sociologie actuelle de l'Afrique noire: Dynamique des changements sociaux en Afrique centrale*. Paris: Presses Universitaires de France.
1965 The Colonial Situation. In *Africa: Social Problems of Change and Conflict*, ed. P. L. van den Berghe, pp. 36-57. San Francisco: Chandler.

Banton, Michael
1967 *Race Relations*. New York: Basic Books.

Barth, Frederick, ed.
1969 *Ethnic Groups and Boundaries*. Boston: Little, Brown.

Beals, Ralph L.
1953 Social Stratification in Latin America. *American Journal of Sociology* 57:327-39.

Benedict, Burton
1961 *Indians in a Plural Society: A Report on Mauritius*. London: Her Majesty's Stationery Office.
1962 Stratification in Plural Societies. *American Anthropologist* 64: 1235-46.

Berry, Brewton
1951 *Race Relations: The Interaction of Ethnic and Racial Groups*. Boston: Houghton Mifflin.

Blood, Sir Hilary
1957 Ethnic and Cultural Pluralism in Mauritius. In *Ethnic and Cultural Pluralism in Intertropical Countries*, pp. 356-62. Brussels: INCIDI.

Boeke, J. H.
1953 *Economics and Economic Policy of Dual Societies, as Exemplified by Indonesia*. New York: Institute of Pacific Relations.

Braithwaite, L.
1960 Social Stratification and Cultural Pluralism. In *Social and Cultural Pluralism in the Caribbean*, ed. V. Rubin, pp. 816-31. *Annals of the New York Academy of Sciences* 83.

Broom, Leonard
1960 Urbanization and the Plural Society. In *Social and Cultural Pluralism in the Caribbean*, ed. V. Rubin, pp. 880-91. *Annals of the New York Academy of Sciences* 83.
1962 *Caribbean Studies: Special Report*. San Juan: Caribbean Scholars' Conference, Institute of Caribbean Studies, University of Puerto Rico.

Colby, Benjamin N., and Pierre L. van den Berghe
1961 Ethnic Relations in South-Eastern Mexico. *American Anthropologist* 63:772-92.
1969 *Ixil Country: A Plural Society in Highland Guatemala*. Berkeley: University of California Press.

Crowder, Michael
1962 *Senegal: A Study in French Assimilation Policy*. London: Oxford University Press.

Crowley, Daniel J.
1957a Plural and Differential Acculturation in Trinidad. *American Anthropologist* 59:817-24.
1957b Urbanization and the Plural Society. *American Anthropologist* 59:880-91.
1960 Cultural Assimilation in a Multiracial Society. In *Social and Cultural Pluralism in the Caribbean*, ed. V. Rubin, pp. 850-54. *Annals of the New York Academy of Sciences* 83.

Dahl, Robert A.
1967 *Pluralist Democracy in the United States: Conflict and Consent*. Chicago: Rand McNally.

Dahrendorf, Ralf
1959 *Class and Class Conflict in Industrial Society*. London: Routledge & Kegan Paul.

Davidson, Basil
1969 Pluralism in Colonial African Societies: Northern Rhodesia and Zambia. In *Pluralism in Africa*, ed. L. Kuper and M. G. Smith. Berkeley: University of California Press.

De la Fuente, Julio
1955 *Relaciones interétnicas*. Mexico City: Instituto Nacional Indigenista.

Despres, Leo A.
1964 The Implications of Nationalist Policies in British Guiana for the Development of Cultural Theory. *American Anthropologist* 66:1051-77.
1967 *Cultural Pluralism and Nationalist Politics in British Guiana*. Chicago: Rand McNally.
1968 Anthropological Theory, Cultural Pluralism, and the Study of Complex Societies. *Current Anthropology* 9: 3-26.

Dobby, E. H. G.
1952 Resettlement Transforms Malaya: A Case-History of Relocating the Population of an Asian Plural Society. *Economic Development and Cultural Change* 1:163-89.

Fallers, Lloyd
1963 Equality, Modernity, and Democracy in the New States. In *Old Societies and New States: The Quest for Modernity in Asia and Africa,* ed. C. Geertz, pp. 158-219. New York: Free Press of Glencoe, Macmillan.

Frankel, Charles
1962 *The Democratic Prospect*. New York: Harper & Row.

Freedman, M.
1966 The Growth of a Plural Society in Malaya. In *Social Change: The Colonial Situation*, ed. I. M. Wallerstein, pp. 278-89. New York: Wiley.

Furnivall, J. S.
1939 *Netherlands India: A Study of Plural Economy*. Cambridge: At the University Press.
1948 *Colonial Policy and Practice: A Comparative Study of Burma and Netherlands India*. Cambridge: At the University Press.

Gann, L. H.
1958 *The Birth of a Plural Society: The Development of Northern Rhodesia under the British South Africa Company, 1894-1914*. Manchester: Manchester University Press.

Gann, L. H., and Peter Duignan
1962 *White Settlers in Tropical Africa*. Harmondsworth: Penguin Books.

Geertz, Clifford, ed.
1963 *Old Societies and New States: The Quest for Modernity in Asia and Africa*. New York: Free Press of Glencoe, Macmillan.

Gitlin, Todd
1965 Local Pluralism as Theory and Ideology. *Studies on the Left* 5, no. 3:21-45.

Gluckman, Max
1958 *An Analysis of a Social Situation in Modern Zululand*. Manchester: Manchester University Press.
1969a Tribalism, Ruralism, and Urbanism in Plural Societies. In *Profiles of Change: The Impact of Colonialism on African Societies*, ed. V. W. Turner. Cambridge: At the University Press.
1969b The Tribal Area in South and Central Africa. In *Pluralism in Africa*, ed. L. Kuper and M. G. Smith. Berkeley: University of California Press.

González Casanova, Pablo
1963 Sociedad plural, colonialismo interno, y desarrollo. *América Latina* 6, no. 3:15-32.

Gordon, Milton
1954 Social Structure in Group Relations. In *Freedom and Control in Modern Society*, ed. M. Berger, T. Abel, and C. H. Page, pp. 141-57. New York: Van Nostrand.
1961 Assimilation in America: Theory and Reality. *Daedalus* 90:263-85.

Green, Thomas F.
1966 *Education and Pluralism: Ideal and Reality*. Syracuse: Syracuse University Press.

Gusfield, Joseph R.
1962 Mass Society and Extremist Politics.

American Sociological Review 27: 19-30.

Gutkind, P. C. W.
1957 Some African Attitudes to Multi-Racialism from Uganda, British East Africa. In *Ethnic and Cultural Pluralism in Intertropical Countries*, pp. 338-55. Brussels: INCIDI.

Haug, M. R.
1967 Social and Cultural Pluralism as a Concept in Social System Analysis. *American Journal of Sociology* 73:294-304.

Hazeersingh, K.
1966 The Religion and Culture of Indian Immigrants in Mauritius and the Effect of Social Change. *Comparative Studies in Society and History* 8: 241-57.

Heard, Kenneth A.
1961 *Political Systems in Multiracial Societies*. Johannesburg: South African Institute of Race Relations.

Hellman, Ellen
1957 Culture Contact and Change in the Union of South Africa. In *Ethnic and Cultural Pluralism in Intertropical Countries*, pp. 363-73. Brussels: INCIDI.

Hoetink, H.
1967a The Concept of Pluralism as Envisaged by M. G. Smith. *Caribbean Studies* 7:36-43.
1967b *The Two Variants in Caribbean Race Relations: A Contribution to the Sociology of Segmented Societies*. London: Oxford University Press.

Hoselitz, Bert
1966 Interaction Between Industrial and Pre-industrial Stratification Systems. In *Social Structure, Social Mobility, and Economic Development*, ed. N. J. Smelser and S. M. Lipset. Chicago: Aldine.

Hsiao, Kung-chuan
1927 *Political Pluralism: A Study in Contemporary Political Theory*. London: Kegan Paul, Trench, Trubner.

Hutton, J. H.
1946 *Caste in India: Its Nature, Function, and Origins*. Cambridge: At the University Press.

Institut International des Civilisations Différentes (INCIDI)

1957 *Ethnic and Cultural Pluralism in Intertropical Countries*. Brussels.

Kagame, Alexis
1957 Le Pluralisme ethnique et culturel dans le Rwanda-Urundi. In *Ethnic and Cultural Pluralism in Intertropical Countries*, pp. 268-93. Brussels: INCIDI.

Kirkwood, Kenneth
1957 Ethnic and Cultural Pluralism in British Central Africa. In *Ethnic and Cultural Pluralism in Intertropical Countries*, pp. 294-324. Brussels: INCIDI.

Klass, Morton
1960 East and West Indian: Cultural Complexity in Trinidad. *Annals of the New York Academy of Sciences* 83:855-86.

Kornhauser, W.
1960 *The Politics of Mass Society*. London: Routledge & Kegan Paul.

Kuper, Hilda
1947 *The Uniform of Colour*. Johannesburg: Witwatersrand University Press.
1969 "Strangers" in Plural Societies: Asians in South Africa and Uganda. In *Pluralism in Africa*, ed. L. Kuper and M. G. Smith. Berkeley: University of California Press.

Kuper, Hilda, and Leo Kuper, eds.
1965 *African Law: Adaptation and Development*. Berkeley: University of California Press.

Kuper, Leo
1965a *An African Bourgeoisie: Race, Class, and Politics in South Africa*. New Haven: Yale University Press.
1965b Religion and Urbanization in Africa. In *International Yearbook of Religion: Religious Pluralism and Social Structure*, pp. 213-33. Cologne: Westdeutscher Verlag.
1965c Sociology: Some Aspects of Urban Plural Societies in Africa. In *The African World: A Survey of Social Research*, ed. R. A. Lystad, pp. 107-30. New York: Praeger.
1967 Structural Discontinuities in African Towns: Some Aspects of Racial Pluralism. In *The City in Modern Africa*, ed. H. Miner. New York: Praeger.
1969a Plural Societies: Perspectives and Problems. In *Pluralism in Africa*, ed. L. Kuper and M. G. Smith. Berkeley:

University of California Press.
1969*b* Some Aspects of Violent and Nonviolent Political Change in Plural Societies. In *Pluralism in Africa*, ed. L. Kuper and M. G. Smith. Berkeley: University of California Press.
1969*c* Ethnic and Racial Pluralism: Some Aspects of Polarization and Depluralization. In *Pluralism in Africa*, ed. L. Kuper and M. G. Smith. Berkeley: University of California Press.

Kuper, Leo, and M. G. Smith, eds.
1969 *Pluralism in Africa*. Berkeley: University of California Press.

Lewis, W. Arthur
1965*a* Beyond African Dictatorship: The Crisis of the One-Party State. *Encounter* 25, no. 2:3-18.
1965*b* *Politics in West Africa*. London: Allen & Unwin.

Lipset, Seymour Martin
1963 *The First New Nation: The United States in Historical and Comparative Perspective*. New York: Basic Books.

Little, Kenneth
1955 Structural Change in the Sierra Leone Protectorate. *Africa* 25:217-34.

Lloyd, P. C., ed.
1966 *The New Elites of Tropical Africa*. London: Oxford University Press.

Lofchie, Michael
1969 The Plural Society in Zanzibar. In *Pluralism in Africa*, ed. L. Kuper and M. G. Smith. Berkeley: University of California Press.

McCord, William
1965 *The Springtime of Freedom: Evolution of Developing Societies*. New York: Oxford University Press.

McKenzie, H. I.
1966 The Plural Society Debate: Some Comments on a Recent Contribution. *Social and Economic Studies* 15:53-60.

Magubane, B.
1969 Pluralism and Conflict Situations in Africa: A "New" Look. *African Social Research* 7:529-54.

Maquet, J. J.
1961 *The Premise of Inequality in Ruanda*. London: Oxford University Press.

Marriott, McKim
1963 Cultural Policy in the New States. In *Old Societies and New States: The*

Quest for Modernity in Asia and Africa, ed. C. Geertz, pp. 27-56. New York: Free Press of Glencoe, Macmillan.

Mason, Philip
1957 The Plural Society in Kenya. In *Ethnic and Cultural Pluralism in Intertropical Countries*, pp. 325-37. Brussels: INCIDI.

Mayer, Adrian C.
1961 *Peasants in the Pacific: A Study of Fiji Indian Rural Society*. London: Routledge & Kegan Paul.

Mayer, Philip
1961 *Townsmen or Tribesmen*. Cape Town: Oxford University Press.

Mazrui, Ali A.
1969 Pluralism and National Integration. In *Pluralism in Africa*, ed. L. Kuper and M. G. Smith. Berkeley: University of California Press.

Mercier, Paul
1965 On the Meaning of "Tribalism" in Black Africa. In *Africa: Social Problems of Change and Conflict*, ed. P. L. van den Berghe. San Fransisco: Chandler.

Mills, C. Wright
1956 *The Power Elite*. New York: Oxford University Press.

Mitchell, J. C.
1956 *The Kalela Dance: Aspects of Social Relationships Among Urban Africans in Northern Rhodesia*. Manchester: Manchester University Press.
1960 *Tribalism and the Plural Society: An Inaugural Lecture Given in the University College of Rhodesia and Nyasaland on 2 October, 1959*. London: Oxford University Press.
1966 Aspects of Occupational Prestige in a Plural Society. In *The New Elites of Tropical Africa*, ed. P. C. Lloyd, pp. 256-71. London: Oxford University Press.

Morris, H. S.
1956 Indians in East Africa: A Study in a Plural Society. *British Journal of Sociology* 7, no. 3:194-211.
1957 The Plural Society. *Man* 57, no. 8:124-25.
1967 Some Aspects of the Concept Plural Society. *Man* 2, no. 2:169-84.

Nash, Manning

1957 The Multiple Society in Economic Development: Mexico and Guatemala. *American Anthropologist* 59: 825-38.

1958 Political Relations in Guatemala. *Social and Economic Studies* 7:65-75.

1959 Some Social and Cultural Aspects of Economic Development. *Economic Development and Cultural Change* 7:137-49.

1964 Southeast Asian Society: Dual or Multiple. *Journal of Asian Studies* 23:417-31.

Padilla, Elena
1960 Peasants, Plantations, and Pluralism. In *Social and Cultural Pluralism in the Caribbean*, ed. V. Rubin, pp. 837-42. *Annals of the New York Academy of Sciences* 83.

Perrow, Charles
1964 The Sociological Perspective and Political Pluralism. *Social Research* 31:411-22.

Polsby, N. W.
1960 The Pluralist Alternative: How to Study Community Power. *Journal of Politics* 22:474-84.

Quermonne, Jean-Louis
1961 Le Problème de la cohabitation dans les sociétés multi-communautaires. *Revue française de science politique* 11:29-59.

Radcliffe-Brown, A. R.
1940 On Social Structure. *Journal of the Royal Anthropological Institute* 70.

1952 *Structure and Function in Primitive Society: Essays and Addresses.* London: Cohen & West.

Ratnam, K. J.
1961 Constitutional Government and the "Plural Society." *Journal of South-East Asian History* 2, no. 3:1-10.

Redfield, Robert
1930 *Tepoztlán, a Mexican Village: A Study of Folk Life.* Chicago: University of Chicago Press.

1941 *The Folk Culture of Yucatan.* Chicago: University of Chicago Press.

Rex, John
1959 The Plural Society in Sociological Theory. *British Journal of Sociology* 10, no. 2:114-24.

Riesman, David, Reuel Denney, and Nathan Glazer

1950 *The Lonely Crowd: A Study of the Changing American Character.* New Haven: Yale University Press.

Rheinstein, Max
1963 Problems of Law in the New Nations of Africa. In *Old Societies and New States: The Quest for Modernity in Asia and Africa*, ed. C. Geertz, pp. 220-46. New York: Free Press of Glencoe, Macmillan.

Rose, Peter I.
1964 *They and We: Racial and Ethnic Relations in the United States.* New York: Random House.

Rubin, Vera
1962 Culture, Politics, and Race Relations. *Social and Economic Studies* 11, no. 4:433-55.

Rubin, Vera, ed.
1960 Social and Cultural Pluralism in the Caribbean. *Annals of the New York Academy of Sciences* 83:761-916.

Rubin, V., R. A. J. van Lier, and L. Braithwaite
1962 Pluralism in the Caribbean. In *Caribbean Studies: Special Report 1962*, pp. 9-18. San Juan: Caribbean Scholars' Conference, Institute of Caribbean Studies, University of Puerto Rico.

Schiller, A. Arthur
1965 Law. In *The African World: A Survey of Social Research*, ed. R. A. Lystad, pp. 166-98. New York: Praeger.

Shils, Edward A.
1956 *The Torment of Secrecy: The Background and Consequences of American Security Policies.* London: Heinemann.

1963 On the Comparative Study of the New States. In *Old Societies and New States: The Quest for Modernity in Asia and Africa*, ed. C. Geertz, pp. 1-26. New York: Free Press of Glencoe, Macmillan.

Simpson, George E., and J. Milton Yinger
1953 *Racial and Cultural Minorities: An Analysis of Prejudice and Discrimination.* New York: Harper.

Sjoberg, Gideon
1952 Folk and "Feudal" Societies. *American Journal of Sociology* 58:231-39.

Skinner, Elliott P.

1960   Group Dynamics and Social Stratifi-
       cation in British Guiana. In *Social
       and Cultural Pluralism in the Carib-
       bean*, ed. V. Rubin, pp. 904-16. *An-
       nals of the New York Academy of
       Sciences* 83.

Sklar, Richard L., and C. S. Whitaker, Jr.
1966   The Federal Republic of Nigeria. In
       *National Unity and Regionalism in
       Eight African States*, ed. G. M. Car-
       ter, pp. 7-150. Ithaca: Cornell Uni-
       versity Press.

Smith, M. G.
1955   A Framework for Caribbean Studies.
       In *Caribbean Affairs*. Kingston, Ja-
       maica: University of the West Indies.
1957   Ethnic and Cultural Pluralism in the
       British Caribbean. In *Ethnic and Cul-
       tural Pluralism in Intertropical Coun-
       tries*, pp. 439-47. Brussels: INCIDI.
1960   Social and Cultural Pluralism. In *So-
       cial and Cultural Pluralism in the Car-
       ibbean*, ed. V. Rubin, pp. 763-77.
       *Annals of the New York Academy of
       Sciences* 83.
1961   The Plural Framework of Jamaican
       Society. *British Journal of Sociology*
       12, no. 3:249-62.
1963   *Dark Puritan*. Kingston, Jamaica:
       University of the West Indies.
1965a *Stratification in Grenada*. Berkeley:
       University of California Press.
1965b *The Plural Society in the British West
       Indies*. Berkeley: University of Cali-
       fornia Press.
1969a Institutional and Political Conditions
       of Pluralism. In *Pluralism in Africa*,
       ed. L. Kuper and M. G. Smith. Berke-
       ley: University of California Press.
1969b Pluralism in Precolonial African Soci-
       eties. In *Pluralism in Africa*, ed. L.
       Kuper and M. G. Smith. Berkeley:
       University of California Press.
1969c Some Developments in the Analytic
       Framework of Pluralism. In *Pluralism
       in Africa*, ed. L. Kuper and M. G.
       Smith. Berkeley: University of Cali-
       fornia Press.

Smith, Raymond T.
1962   *British Guiana*. London: Oxford Uni-
       versity Press.
1963   Culture and Social Structure in the
       Caribbean: Some Recent Work on
       Family and Kinship Studies. *Compar-*

       ative Studies in Society and History
       6, no. 1:24-46.

Speckman, J. D.
1963   The Indian Group in the Segmented
       Society of Surinam. *Caribbean
       Studies* 3:3-17.

Thompson, Leonard
1969   Historical Perspectives of Pluralism in
       Africa. In *Pluralism in Africa*, ed. L.
       Kuper and M. G. Smith. Berkeley:
       University of California Press.

Tocqueville, Alexis de
1835- *Democracy in America*, trans. Henry
1840   Reeve, 4 vols. London: Saunders &
       Otley.

Tumin, Melvin
1952   *Caste in a Peasant Society*. Prince-
       ton: Princeton University Press.

Van den Berghe, Pierre L.
1964a *Caneville: The Social Structure of a
       South African Town*. Middletown,
       Conn.: Wesleyan University Press.
1964b Toward a Sociology of Africa. *Social
       Forces* 43:11-18.
1965a *South Africa: A Study in Conflict*.
       Middletown, Conn.: Wesleyan Uni-
       versity Press.
1965b Introduction to *Africa: Social Prob-
       lems of Change and Conflict*, ed.
       P. L. van den Berghe, pp. 1-11. San
       Francisco: Chandler.
1967   *Race and Racism*. New York: Wiley.
1968   Ethnic Membership and Culture
       Change in Guatemala. *Social Forces*
       46:514-22.
1969   Pluralism and the Polity: A Theoreti-
       cal Exploration. In *Pluralism in Afri-
       ca*, ed. L. Kuper and M. G. Smith.
       Berkeley: University of California
       Press.
1970   Pluralism and Conflict Situations in
       Africa: A Reply to B. Magubane. *Af-
       rican Social Research*.

Van Lier, R. A. J.
1950   *The Development and Nature of So-
       ciety in the West Indies*. Amsterdam:
       Royal Institute for the Indies.
1953   Culture Conflict in de Heterogene
       Samenleving. *Sociologisch Jaarboek*
       8:36-56.

Wagley, Charles
1960   Discussion of Social and Cultural Plu-
       ralism. In *Social and Cultural Plural-
       ism in the Caribbean*, ed. V. Rubin,

pp. 777-80. *Annals of the New York Academy of Sciences* 83.

1964 *Amazon Town: A Study of Man in the Tropics*. New York: Macmillan.

Wagley, Charles, and Marvin Harris
1958 *Minorities in the New World: Six Case Studies*. New York: Columbia University Press.

Wallerstein, Immanuel, ed.
1966 *Social Change: The Colonial Situation*. New York: Wiley.

Wertheim, W. F.
1959 *Indonesian Society in Transition: A Study of Social Change,* 2d rev. ed. The Hague: W. van Hoeve.

Wittermans, Elizabeth
1964 *Inter-ethnic Relations in a Plural Society*. Groningen: J. B. Wolters.

Yinger, J. M.
1962 Integration and Pluralism Viewed from Hawaii. *Antioch Review* 22: 397-410.

Zinkin, M.
1951 *Asia and the West*. London: Chatto & Windus.

CHAPTER 23 Urban Anthropology

JOHN GULICK

INTRODUCTION

SOME CAUTIONS

Since I am a North American anthropologist who studied in the United States and am a member of the faculty of a university in the United States, this review of the present condition of urban anthropology is written from a North American professional perspective. This means that it is organized primarily around the urban research that has been done by North American anthropologists, although work done by English and British Commonwealth anthropologists (chiefly in African cities) and some others has not been neglected.

I have not intentionally slighted any works that are relevant, but I may have done so unintentionally, and, if so, this may have been due to my North American perspective. Some readers may detect other signs of a North American bias, and I wish to make it clear at the start that I am aware of the possibility of it.

There is another reason for the North American point of view from which this paper is written: my concern about the present condition of North American sociocultural anthropology in general. I am troubled and perplexed by it. I think that urban anthropology in its present state may be part of the problem, but at the same time I think that, properly developed, urban anthropology could greatly strengthen the rest of sociocultural anthropology. While it would be presumptuous of me to discuss the professional problems of another nation's anthropology, I feel obligated to discuss those of my own.

For reasons that should become apparent in due course, some of the very important work in urban anthropology (as I, and I believe many others, conceive it) has been done not by professional anthropologists, but by sociologists, psychologists, political scientists, social workers, city planners, geographers, and others. Urban research is one of the aspects of the behavioral sciences in which the arbitrariness of distinctions between the subdisciplines becomes especially acute. The reader should be prepared, therefore, for references to the contributions of nonanthropologists to urban anthropology.

"Urban anthropology" is a succinct term that I shall use often but in different contexts, and essentially with different meanings. An increasing number of anthropologists are doing research in and on cities, but their objectives and methods are many, varied, and not always clear cut; their disagreements on basic concepts are as profound as they are at times acrimonious (see Valentine 1969). Urban anthropology is not a subdiscipline in the sense of intellectual system and coherence that the term implies. Rather, it consists of a number of new directions that some anthropologists are taking. From some of these activities may be forged significant new cutting edges for the science of mankind, but that is for future observers to decide. In the meantime, I shall review the present-day action and some of its precedents.

HISTORICAL NOTES

The idea of urban anthropology seems to have taken most American anthropologists unawares.

In his 1950 presidential address to the American Anthropological Association, Ralph Beals (1951) dealt explicitly with the contributions that anthropology might and should make to urban theory, thereby also strengthening acculturation theory. However, his emphasis was mostly on theoretical collaboration with sociology and not particularly on anthropological fieldwork in cities. *Anthropology Today* (Kroeber et al., eds., 1952:854), an encyclopedic inventory published some twenty years ago, referred to urban studies only in terms of the urban phases of Old World and New World archaeology, plus a brief reference to increasing interest in urban and migrant populations in Africa.

As late as 1956, David Mandelbaum (1956:214) published a major review paper on anthropological studies of complex cultures in which attention to urban research was limited to a single brief reference to Lloyd Warner's (1963) *Yankee City* studies. Apparently Mandelbaum did not perceive the considerable research that had already been done in African cities as pertaining to complex cultures. His orientation was more toward anthropological delineations of complex-cultures-as-wholes, based on extrapolations from village studies to whole cultures that included cities, though the extrapolations did not, in fact, take the cities into account.

Actually, significant accomplishments in urban fieldwork were being made at that time, but there is only a hint of them in these three major pronouncements. Some years later there wasn't even a hint in Maurice Stein's (1960) interpretive survey of American community studies. Stein devotes a chapter to "Anthropological Perspectives on the Modern Community," but in it he says nothing about urban fieldwork by anthropologists. Rather, taking off from Sapir's characterization of modern culture as "spurious," he invokes Radin and Redfield, and recommends to sociologists these anthropologists' findings on small or primitive communities, where "important human potentialities are fulfilled in a fashion peculiarly alien to present-day America" (Stein 1960:250).

The beginnings were indeed fitful. Between 1925 and 1929, when the Chicago urban sociologists were doing some of their greatest work, Margaret Mead, W. Lloyd Warner, and Helen and Robert Lynd were also doing important pioneering work. Mead and Warner were doing "classic anthropological" research among primitive peoples in New Guinea, Samoa, and Australia. The Lynds, neither of them anthropologists, were studying by participant observation the city of Muncie, Indiana. In 1929 they published *Middletown: A Study in American Culture* (1956), which had an appreciative foreword by the anthropologist Clark Wissler. In one sense, *Middletown* was the beginning of urban anthropology in the United States. But in another sense it was not, for it did not, so far as I know, inspire any anthropologists to do research among what have become known as "middle Americans" in urban communities. Despite its explicit identification as an anthropological study, *Middletown*, as well as its sequel, *Middletown in Transition* (1937), became absorbed into American sociology, where for a while there was some vogue for community studies.

In 1930 Lloyd Warner, having returned to the United States, began, with many associates, the series of studies of the small city of Newburyport, Massachusetts, that have become known as the *Yankee City* series (1963). The findings of this project, too, became part of the corpus of American sociology—not anthropology—particularly by establishing one of the basic models of the American social class system. Warner became, in effect, a sociologist.

Margaret Mead, in contrast, became in the ensuing forty years the epitome of anthropology for many people in the United States and elsewhere in the world. But though many of her ideas are directly concerned with the problems of modern United States culture, she has not contributed very much to urban anthropology per se. She has, in effect, bypassed urban anthropology by combining the old culture-as-a-whole anthropology with her intense professional interest in the contemporary cul-

tural problems of the United States. Mead communicates in terms of American culture in general (most of its people being urban), but she does not elucidate the specific phenomena of urbanism and urbanization—perhaps because she is so much immersed in them herself.

In 1934 the British-trained sociologists Ellen Hellmann and Monica Hunter did research by participant observation in, respectively, Rooiyard (a soon-to-be-demolished slum in Johannesburg) and East London, South Africa. These research efforts did lead directly to further urban anthropology in Africa, eventually putting it well ahead of that of any other area of the world in this respect.

In the United States, on the other hand, William F. Whyte's (1943) field study on the Italian North End of Boston, though it was clearly anthropological in method, seemed to inspire only sociological and social psychological research. And even earlier works, such as Wessel's study of ethnic groups in Woonsocket, Rhode Island (Wessel had been trained at Columbia both by sociologists and by anthropologists like Boas and Benedict [Simmons 1970: 557-571]), do not seem to have led directly to any further North American urban anthropology.

Nevertheless, it was in the early 1940s that the first unmistakable beginnings of American urban anthropology can be discerned.

In 1941 Robert Redfield published what is the definitive anthropological presentation of the folk-urban polar model. Using four settlements in Yucatan as illustrations, he set forth the well-known characterization of sacred-secular, organized-disorganized, etc., which had long been current in sociological thinking (Redfield 1941:338f). Redfield seems to have been primarily interested in characterizing whole societies, but by doing it in terms of community types, he produced a formulation that is relevant to specific local-level research.

In 1940 Horace Miner did a field study in the fabulously remote African town of Timbuctoo. Already aware of Redfield's ideas concerning folk and urban cultures, and of the very similar ideas of urban sociologists like Louis Wirth, Miner wanted to test their applicability in the field. Not published in its first edition until 1953, and subsequently republished in a revised edition (1965), Miner's Timbuctoo study has been embellished by a considerable amount of thinking that was developed long after he did his fieldwork. Nevertheless, his basic conclusion about Timbuctoo is important: Timbuctoo's culture conforms to the urban model only in some respects; in others, it conforms to the folk model (Miner 1965:305). This conclusion raises more questions than it answers, questions for which answers have been sought ever since by urban anthropologists.

In the years immediately following World War II, many anthropologists turned their attention away from "primitive" cultures and toward complex but mostly preindustrial ones, and some of them were confronted by the same problem as Miner's in Timbuctoo. The fact was that Redfield's urban ideal type was not found to be predominant in the urban phenomena they were observing. This proved to be a stimulus for more urban fieldwork.

Oscar Lewis' early career is an excellent and important illustration of and central element in the development of urban anthropology. Lewis had done a field study of Tepoztlán, Mexico (1951), which Redfield had presented to the world in 1930 as a type case of the folk community. Lewis' conclusions differed sharply from Redfield's, partly because he took account of the many connections that Tepoztecans had with Mexico City. From there it was a short step to a study of Tepoztecans who had moved to Mexico City. Lewis' purpose was to test the folk-urban theoretical stereotype that migration to the city causes breakdown of the family and other damage to primary relationships (Lewis 1952:31-32). Presented very cautiously and with qualifications as a preliminary report, this paper is an early example of a type of urban research that was soon being conducted by other anthropologists in other parts of the world, mostly regions already established as areas for ethnographic research, such as South America, Southeast Asia, and Africa.

One important area in which urban anthropology did not develop so rapidly in the late 1940s and 1950s was India. The considerable energies that anthropologists devoted to Indian research at that time were channeled into village and institutional studies (see Marriott 1955; Rowe, ed.,1963). Out of these efforts there developed such concepts as the "great" and "little" traditions of Hindu culture, but the former was not so systematically associated with certain urban subcultures as it could have been (Marriott 1955:172-73 and *passim*).

William Rowe has since turned to urban research in India, and other anthropologists have studied rural and urban differences (or the lack of them) in certain Indian institutions (e.g., Freed and Freed 1969). Urban anthropology in India has also recently been greatly furthered by the publication of a symposium volume whose contents range, as the editor points out, from "etic" to "partially emic" to "wholly emic" analyses (Fox 1970:xi). However, urban research in India—and there has been much of it—has been done mostly by Indian nationals trained in Western sociological survey techniques.

Their publications consist predominantly of statistical tables with relatively little discussion. Unfortunately, however, facts do not always speak for themselves (for examples, see Dhekney 1959 and Bulsara 1964).

Meanwhile, Lewis refined and applied his methods of intensive family analysis among his Tepoztecan migrants in Mexico City, and in so doing began to develop his idea of the "culture of poverty" (Lewis 1959:2). Applied later to Puerto Ricans living in San Juan and New York City (Lewis 1966), the concept of the culture of poverty established some central hypotheses for much of the urban research that is now being done in the United States.

PRINCIPAL ARENAS
OF URBAN ANTHROPOLOGY

From the North American professional vantage point, urban anthropology is being conducted in two principal arenas. One of these is comprised of the various ethnographic areas of the world in which American and European anthropologists have automatically been foreigners studying cultures exotic to their own enculturation. Urban anthropology conducted in these areas is essentially an extension of traditional sociocultural anthropology, though adapted to various problems and phenomena peculiar to the contemporary scene.

The other arena consists of Western industrial cities, principally American. Moving into this type of environment, anthropologists are faced with certain epistemological and ethical matters that are not traditional and in which the very identity of anthropology is at stake. There are a number of factors involved in this that will be discussed later.

These two arenas will be dealt with in turn in later sections. First, however, I must examine the question of what it is that urban anthropologists are studying.

URBAN DOMAINS: ENVIRONMENTS
THAT DEFY CLOSE DEFINITION

BIASES

No one, it seems, is indifferent to cities. There are city-lovers and city-haters, and there are those whose feelings about cities are ambivalent and contradictory—but not indifferent. One reason for this lack of indifference is, I think, that cities are, to a large extent, manmade environments. City life therefore involves not only constant interactions with other human beings, but also constant coping with other human beings' physical designs, arrangements, and artifacts. This kind of coping is not wholly absent from village life, but in a village the natural environment constitutes an ever present counterelement to the manmade one. For many people the natural environment provides an escape or release from the impingements on their lives of other human beings. It is difficult to be indifferent to such impingements, and the larger a city is, the more intense they are, either through other people directly or through the manmade physical environment or both. It would be interesting to establish at what points in the range of size of human settlements and under what conditions the manmade environment begins to be predominant in the inhabitants' perceptions, but no one, to my knowledge, has done so.

And yet for at least two thousand years people have been trying to define just what the urban environment is, as distinct from other environments. Many have convinced themselves or others that they had the answer, but all of the answers so far have been found wanting. Lack of objectivity—often unrecognized or unacknowledged—seems to have been one factor in this lack of agreement. Another is the vast variety, in size and other features, of settlements that have been considered urban.

QUALITATIVE MODELS

Many people feel intuitively that a relatively large population is an important factor in determining whether a settlement can be considered urban. Since population size can be measured with fair accuracy, it should be a valuable objective index of urbanism. But it is not, and the reason is that there is no agreement on what the minimum size of an urban place is. The United States Bureau of the Census says 2,500; the United Nations says 20,000 (Breese, ed., 1969:23); and Kingsley Davis, the renowned demographer, says 100,000 (Breese, ed., 1969:5f). Since there is no agreement on a minimum population size that will qualify a settlement as urban, there cannot, objectively speaking, be agreement on any qualitative phenomena that might be variables dependent on size. However, this lack of objective criteria of judgment has never stopped people from inventing qualitative characteristics of urban life.

In fact, a traditional model of urban life has accumulated. Contributed to by many people, it has had its systematizers, Robert Redfield among them. The model is bipolar and primarily moralistic, reflecting the partisan feelings that apparently dominate most people's thinking about cities.

Items 12 through 15 will be recognized as the core elements in the folk-urban distinction of Redfield. Redfield has been credited with refining this distinction from a crude dichotomy into a more sophisticated continuum; but this was really a minor modification, for the distinction is that of polar opposites in either case. Louis Wirth, who was himself a major contributor to this model, in one of his last papers (1964:223) expressed chagrin at the way in which these arbitrary, ideal-typical polar concepts have so often been taken for established facts, rather than for what they are, merely bases for hypotheses to be tested.

The Moralistic Bipolar Model

	Rural		Urban
0r	Country (village)	0u	Town (city)
1r	Community (*Gemeinschaft*)	1u	Noncommunity (*Gesellschaft*)
2r	Folk	2u	Urban
3r	Primitive	3u	Civilized
4r	Natural ("true")	4u	Spurious, superficial, artificial
5r	Simple	5u	Sophisticated
6r	Provincial	6u	Cosmopolitan
7r	Tribal society	7u	Mass society
8r	Moral	8u	Corrupt
9r	Inherently stable	9u	Inherently changing
10r	Human in scale	10u	Dehumanized
11r	Particularistic	11u	Universalistic
12r	Homogeneous	12u	Heterogeneous
12rx	Few alternative modes of behavior	12ux	Many alternative modes of behavior
13r	Personal	13u	Impersonal (anonymous)
13rx	Constrained	13ux	Free
14r	Integrated	14u	Disintegrated (anomic)
14rx	Conformist	14ux	Nonconformist
15r	Sacred	15u	Secular
15rx	Superstitious, myth-oriented	15ux	Rational

On the whole, this model is antiurban. Items 1u, 4u, 7u, 8u, 10u, and 13u-15u have usually been employed in pejorative contexts, whereas their opposite numbers in the rural series have been used as positive terms. Items 3u, 5u, 6u, 9u, and 12u are ambiguous as far as moralistic import is concerned, but they are not neutral terms, any more than are 3r, 5r, 6r, 9r, and 12r.

Many observers have discerned distinctions among the phenomena represented by the 12-15 series besides those implied in the polar pairs. I have made an attempt to identify these distinctions by items labeled x. Thus an aspect of impersonal relationships ($13u$) is freedom ($13ux$) from various kinds of interference. This freedom contrasts with the constraints ($13rx$) that are inherent in many personal relationships ($13r$). Items $13ux$, $14ux$, and $15ux$ seem most often to be used in positive terms and their opposite numbers in pejorative ones, resulting in a reversal of the generally predominant preference for the rural items. (That urban life lacks constraining personal relationships is one of the many easily refutable implications of the model.)

Some social scientists continue to think explicitly in terms of this model or some version of it. Kahl (1959) is a good example, one that puts relative stress on the pro-urban interpretation to which I have just alluded. Frankenberg's (1966) review of communities in Britain is a more extended exposition that generally expresses the traditional anti-urban point of view. So, too, is a very recent anthropological textbook (Oswalt 1970) that idealizes man the noble hunter (p. 121) and refers to urbanites as "enslaved by an artificial environment" (p. 121), to Timbuctoo as similar to American urban culture in its money emphasis, crime, cheating, and dishonesty (p. 127), and to the "dehumanized and unnatural city" (p. 144). Many others assume the validity of the model but express this assumption implicitly.

The bipolar model has been thoroughly criticized, but I am not sure how effective these attacks really have been, at least so far, in discrediting it. For one thing, the critics have not yet been able to work out a sufficiently comprehensive substitute model that has equal appeal.

And the appeal of the bipolar moralistic model is great, for it is a system of stereotypes that encapsulates a great number of prejudices that camouflage the oversimplifications and inconsistencies of the system. A major fallacy of the model is its assumption that "rural" represents a single, uniform type of settlement, and that "urban" does also.

Another fallacy is the glaring internal inconsistency among the urban traits. Cultural heterogeneity is one of the few traits (perhaps the only one) that all observers agree is characteristic of cities. (Whether and to what extent city dwellers are able to participate in this heterogeneity in their individual experiences is an interesting question but one that need not be pursued at this point.) If heterogeneity is in fact characteristic of cities, it should follow by logic alone that the other traits—for example, anonymity and anomie—cannot be assumed to characterize all city-dwellers. This and related points have been made very effectively by Oscar Lewis (1965:496) in a short paper that is one of the most succinct and comprehensive critiques of the moralistic bipolar approach in print. It is paired with a paper by Philip Hauser (1965) that demonstrates that when the moralistic bipolar traits are taken at face value and applied to cross-cultural data, a very poor fit is revealed between the stereotype and known facts.

Gideon Sjoberg's *The Preindustrial City* (1960:13-16) criticizes the bipolar moralistic model in general and finds particular fault with its failure to apply to preindustrial and nonindustrial cities. Sjoberg's own model of preindustrial cities is based on an assumption of various cross-cultural uniformities. This model should be taken as the basis of hypotheses to be tested by fieldwork where possible.

Since some of Sjoberg's data pertain to past conditions that no longer exist, it is now impossible to test these hypotheses in some cases, but it is still possible in others. For example, Windle and Sabagh (1963:436), using a census of 19,000 employees of the Iranian National Oil Company, set about to test Sjoberg's generalization that preindustrial urban upper-class parents have more children who reach adulthood than do lower-class parents, not because of higher fertility but because of lower mortality. They discovered that the professional and staff employees did indeed have more children than the skilled and unskilled workers, but that the foremen had even more children than the professional and staff employees. They concluded (1963: 441-42):

While the findings of this study do not contradict Sjoberg's generalization, they suggest that it may no longer be sufficient to describe the situation when the preindustrial city is beginning to experience industrialization and modernization. One should consider the possible effect of this new process on the willingness or desire to adopt fertility control practices. A white collar upper status class . . . may be most ready to accept such practices. If they do, then this is likely to counteract the effect of declining infant and child mortality. Other classes and groups more imbued with tradition but benefiting also from the quickening tempo of economic growth [e.g., the foremen] may use their newly acquired wealth to maximize the size of their families.

Windle and Sabagh, demographers, thus conclude their hypothesis-testing by in effect proposing another hypothesis, one to which urban anthropologists could well address themselves. Inadvertently, perhaps, they also point up the dangers inherent in so many publications about the process of industrial urbanization in the world, which assume the established factual truth of the bipolar model (e.g., having a small number of children is automatically the

rational pattern—item 15*ux*—of all urbanites).

It is because of such persistent and pervasive thinking that the bipolar moralistic model cannot be ignored. If, as Sjoberg claims, most of its elements are not applicable to the preindustrial city, we are still left with the question of what the central qualities of industrial cities are, and therefore what the effects of urban industrialization are, and the only available answer so far is the bipolar moralistic model. Yet its inadequacies have been demonstrated in the most highly industrialized cities as well as in preindustrial ones. The problem is not that the human characteristics itemized in the model are imaginary, for they are real enough. But the model expresses them in an overly abstract fashion and asserts a pattern of distribution that does not fit reality.

The question remains: What are the essential characteristics of urban environments that distinguish them from nonurban environments? If, in search of answers, we look only at the largest cities in the world, we may succeed only in begging the question. In 1960 there were twenty-five cities in the world that had more than 2.5 million inhabitants each (Breese, ed., 1969:33). Surely the sheer immensity of these cities must result in consequences that are similar in all and could be identified as essentially urban? Perhaps, but there are also differences despite size, though sometimes related to it. Let us consider three similarly sized pairs of these cities. Moscow is relatively free of smog; Los Angeles is choking on it. Cairo has no suburbs to speak of and therefore no suburbia-related commuter problem; Detroit has both. Rio de Janeiro, despite its enormous size (four to five million), is famous for its spirit of relaxation, gaiety, and traditional charm; São Paulo, just as big and just as surely Brazilian, is known for its competitiveness and its emphasis on modernity and hardheaded business (Leeds 1968:37). The differences between these pairs of cities can be accounted for by amount and type of industrialization, size of gross national product, and history; but this is just another way of saying that the effects of size alone are themselves affected by other factors.

As for any demonstration of the validity of the bipolar model that the world's largest cities can offer, one needs only to consider three studies done in Tokyo (Dore 1958, Norbeck 1965, and Vogel 1967) to see that in the heterogeneity of big cities one can discover *all* of the elements in the model, both "rural" and "urban."

This statement also holds true when one considers smaller cities like Ibadan, Nigeria, population about 900,000, whose inhabitants include (1) Westernized office workers living in single-family suburban houses and dependent upon the private automobile for the maintenance of their social life, (2) various "ethnic" groups living in circumscribed quarters, and (3) "inner city" residents who live in lineage compounds and commute to the countryside each week for farmwork (Lloyd et al., eds., 1967). Or Oshogbo, Nigeria, population about 120,000, whose cultural patterns range from "universalism and achievement" to the traditional kinship system (Schwab 1965:109). Or Timbuctoo, Mali, population 7,000, whose combination of "folk" and "urban" patterns was Miner's major discovery (Miner 1965). Largely on the basis of African materials, Bascom (1968:91) seems to despair of associating any behavioral traits definitively with urbanism; "cities should be defined strictly in terms of demographic factors: relative size, density and permanence." Since relative size is such a demonstrably elastic concept, I do not see that such reductionism can be very helpful in either

the building or the testing of hypotheses.

URBAN ESSENTIALS IN SIX SMALL TOWNS

If the "essential urban" characteristics elude us in the complexities of the largest and some of the not so large cities, perhaps we can make greater progress if we consider some of the smallest settlements with which the words "city" and "urban" have been associated, either by the inhabitants or by observers.

Charles Wagley's (1953) study of Itá, a Brazilian community on the Amazon River, is not concerned with definitions of the city but with the problems of underdevelopment in the tropics. Itá's status as an urban community must be deduced from scattered remarks that Wagley makes on the subject.

Itá was founded as a community early in the seventeenth century. By the middle of the nineteenth century it had a population of about seven hundred people and was divided into two sections, one called the "village" (inhabited by the Indians and their descendants), the other called the "city" (inhabited by Europeans and *mestiços*— merchants, government officials, landowners, and artisans) (Wagley 1953: 45). Growing up around a fort, it became an important river port and government control station. From about 1890 to 1912 it shared in the prosperity of the rubber boom that affected the whole Amazon valley, but from 1912 to 1942, during the collapse of the rubber market, its population declined to only three hundred. At the time of Wagley's study it had begun to recover.

Itá has a gridiron street plan, with the town hall (which would have been a monumental structure if the rubber boom had not suddenly ended) and the new public health post fronting on the main square. The public health post serves a large area for which Itá is an excellent center of communication. Itá is the administrative center of a "municipality" consisting of jungle and small hamlets situated on subsidiary streams flowing into the Amazon.

Wagley refers to Itá variously as a "city" (p. 23), a "backward, decadent, and isolated community" (p. 58), a "rural" community (p. 148), and "essentially" a "farming" community (p. 276). These designations are quite contradictory in terms of the standard rural-urban model, but Wagley is not concerned with that. He devotes much attention, however, to the social class structure of Itá and its hinterland, identifying four classes in ranked order: first class (local upper class), second class (lower-class town dwellers), farmers, and collectors (mostly of rubber) (p. 105). Of a sample of ninety-eight men in Itá town whom he interviewed systematically, Wagley classified fourteen as first class, forty-six as second class, twenty-nine as farmers, and nine as collectors, categorizing the first class as upper class and the other three as lower class (p. 132). Wagley's comments are significant (1953:104-105).

To the outsider ... Itá may appear to be a homogeneous society of rural peasants, of people who differ little from one another in social rank. In Belém upper class people are apt to classify the people of Itá, with the exception of a few government officials stationed there, as caboclos. ... Yet, as one lives and participates in Itá social life, it soon becomes apparent that people, within the confines of the community itself, are quite sensitive to differences in social rank. ...

Such present-day distinctions ... result from the class system of colonial Amazon society, from the former servitude of Indians and imported African slaves, and from the social ascendancy of the Portuguese colonials. They also reflect the economic and social position of the various groups who inhabit Itá today ....

As the city folk tend to view Itá as a homogeneous society of small-town peasants, the First Class people of Itá are apt to view the people below them in the social hierarchy as simply "the people," or as "caboclos." In turn, the town-dwelling Second Class indicate their superiority to all the rural population by speaking of them as "caboclos," and the farmers reserve this term for the Island collectors, to whom they feel superior. And finally, the Island collectors would be slightly offended if they were called "caboclos," for they make little distinction between themselves and the farmers.

With a population of six hundred, Itá is no larger than hundreds of thousands of farmers' settlements throughout the world that no one (native or foreign observer) would be tempted to call cities or urban or urbanized. In fact, it is smaller than many of them. Since Wagley does not discuss the matter, we can only infer the reasons for Itá's being considered, by some people at least, to be a city. My inferences are that Itá, small as it is, is larger than surrounding settlements over which certain inhabitants of Itá have political and economic control; that Itá as a community is the location of linkages between different segments and levels of a national society; that the localization of these linkage functions is an important factor in the social status heterogeneity of its population; that Itá is considered urban only in relative terms—by its inhabitants, yes, but not by people in much larger coastal cities of Brazil. If, by at least some people's standards, Itá is urban, this does not mean that it exhibits all of the supposedly definitive urban characteristics. For instance, the natural environment is of overwhelming importance in daily life, and Wagley's chapter "From Magic to Science" makes it clear that items $13r$, $15r$, and $15rx$ in the bipolar moralistic model are at least as important in the life of the place as are their opposite numbers. Perhaps there is a gradient of characteristics that define "urban" that we should seek to discover and describe in detail, and then test.

Unlike Wagley, Rubén Reina, in his study of Flores, Guatemala (1964), is primarily interested in the definition of urbanism. Flores appears to be similar to Itá in a number of respects. Though its population is more than twice that of Itá (1,500), it is nevertheless very small. It is located on an island in Lake Petén-Itzá, and one can walk around the island's perimeter in half an hour (Reina 1964:268). Like Itá, Flores has a colonial-Iberian-Indian ethnic history; is the economic, administrative, and communications center of a district that is remote from the big urban centers of its society; subsists on the extractive economy of its region (rubber, lumber, chicle), which links it with the world market; and has a clearly distinct structure of social classes.

> Upon first acquaintance with Flores, it is rather difficult to recognize social differences. ... Differences in terms of wealth, leadership, intellectualism, or 'cultura' aquire very particular social meanings. But all these attributes are not apparent at first because of the even degree of sophistication across all social groups which is consciously upheld [Reina 1964:269].

People of every social class in Flores apparently share a pride in their collectively heterogeneous background and in their city's "civilization" in the midst of the forest.

The social classes are (Reina 1964:270):

1. Upper: about half a dozen families of wealth, owning property in Guatemala City and interacting largely with each other.
2. Upper middle: politically active professional people who aspire to greater affluence and intellectualism.

3. Middle: artisans, shopkeepers, and minor officials extremely intent on upward mobility, especially through the education of their children.
4. Poor: wage laborers, including chicle collectors, with a low level of education; interested in but fearful of upward mobility through the education of their children.

Reina proceeds to describe the "city style" of festivals and ceremonies, and the "impersonalization" of the Florentinos' business behavior. He ascribes this impersonalization to the precariousness of the market and the exploitiveness that it generates, rather than to any lack of personal familiarity among the inhabitants, for "everyone knows the biographical details of everyone else's life." Reina concludes 1964: 274-75):

> The important point emerging from this material is the strong urban world view held by only a handful of people who know each other intimately. It presents us with a large number of the elements of the city discussed by Redfield, Wirth ... namely, individualization, emotional atomization, secularization, blasé attitudes, rationalism, cosmopolitanism, differentiation, and self-criticism. ... But the most important fact ... is that this image appears ... in an environment largely dominated by the forces of nature. The outstanding social feature of Flores is the exaggerated degree to which the ideal of living in a "city" and being urban has become the core of their general cultural orientation.

The idea that urbanism is a set of attitudes, values, and behavioral patterns that is not necessarily a direct adaptation to an immediate city environment was not originated by Reina, but he has pursued it further than others. A corollary idea, which I did not originate either, is that "nonurban" behavior can exist in the midst of a city environment. Perhaps *some* of the stereotypic urban characteristics are dependent upon the city environment while others are not, and one of the tasks of urban anthropology should be to factor out which ones are which. However, we are still begging the question of what a city is, and therefore general assertions about the "process of urbanization" remain ambiguous and meaningless.

Frobisher Bay is a settlement of 1,600 people located about a hundred miles north of the Arctic Circle on Baffin Island, Canada. Except for its size and the fact that it is an administrative center for a sparsely settled region, a remote outpost of a national society, it has little in common with Flores. The forces of nature are overwhelming in both places, but in one they are tropical and in the other arctic.

Unlike Flores (and Itá), Frobisher Bay has a very short history, which began in 1942 with the construction of a U.S. Air Force airstrip. In 1955 Frobisher Bay became a transshipment point for supplies and personnel to the eastern end of the U.S.-Canada Distant Early Warning Radar Defense Line (DEW Line). Flores and Itá were originally creatures of Spanish and Portuguese preindustrial imperialism; Frobisher Bay is a creature of the twentieth-century North American military-industrial complex.

John and Irma Honigmann (1965) studied Frobisher Bay in 1963, by which time its population consisted of about nine hundred Eskimos and about seven hundred "Eurocanadians." The Honigmanns' basic aim was to study the adaptations of the aborigines of the area—the Eskimos—to life in this "instant town" (my phrase, not theirs), much of that life being the Eskimos' own. Since all the inhabitants of Frobisher Bay are recent immigrants, this is not an urban-migrant adaptation study

so much as it is a study of Eskimos' adaptation to Eurocanadian material culture, work patterns, and sociopolitical organization. The Honigmanns consistently refer to Frobisher Bay as a "town" (never, I believe, as a "city") and do not concern themselves explicitly with urbanism as a concept. They refer to it as an "urban setting" (p. 100) but without specifying what is meant. The relatively large number of organized groups is said to be consistent with its "urban character" (p. 118), and the "urban impersonality" of the Eurocanadians is mentioned (p. 5).

Implicitly, however, this study is concerned with the definition of urbanism. In the first place, it was very much stimulated by reports that social disorganization (a classic stereotypic trait of urbanism) was conspicuous in the life of the town (Honigmann and Honigmann 1965:3). This stereotype is refuted in the study (p. 152). The Eskimos' shyness and "the town's impersonality" were facts with which the Honigmanns had to cope (p. 5). They also refer to its "large" population (p. 6) in comparison with other Eskimo settlements, a relative statement comparable to the idea that Itá is large in comparison with hamlets in its administrative district. However, Frobisher Bay is not a dense settlement, even relatively speaking, for it consists of at least three widely separated subsettlements. Transportation between these subsettlements consists of bus and taxi service, which is essential for the daily life of the inhabitants and bears all the earmarks of urban, "impersonal" transportation (pp. 49-51). One of the uses to which these buses and taxis is put is visiting among the members of relatively restricted circles of kinsmen whose members' homes are often scattered in different subsettlements, rather than concentrated in one place (p. 102). Although the Honigmanns do not say so, such nonlocalized networks are often considered to be characteristically "urban."

Other facilities in Frobisher Bay are clearly characteristic of North American industrial cities (though not of preindustrial ones). Electricity, fuel oil, gasoline, and water are delivered to the consumer. Most of the food and beverages are imported from afar and sold in packaged form. Housing is prefabricated and standardized in a limited number of styles. Having been totally self-sufficient before the town existed, Eskimos frequently find an adjustment problem in all this provision of necessities (p. 153), particularly with regard to identity formation and self-esteem (p. 170).

The Honigmanns point out, however, that many Eskimos came to Frobisher Bay voluntarily and have remained there by their own choice (p. 161), and that the typical Eskimo, "while not reared for routine and repetition" (p. 231), is "venturesome, optimistic, independent and resourceful . . . eager to try and able to change" (p. 234). Such a person obviously has advantages as a migrant to a town, or in any new situation.

This introduces the topic of predispositions for urban adjustment, which will be discussed later; it is an important corrective to the widespread idea that the urban environment inevitably simply imposes itself on the hapless newcomer.

The Honigmanns make much of the fact that the Eskimos in Frobisher Bay are under the tutelage of the Eurocanadians and their institutions. Among other things, this situation involves the maintenance of clear social distance between the two populations. The Honigmanns insist, however, that among the Eskimos there is nothing more than an incipient social class differentiation (p. 248), if that (p. 101).

Though it is a new town, characterized by "incessant built-in change" (p. 231), and with an uncertain future, Frobisher Bay cannot be dismissed as an aberrant case. Many now long-established cities began in similar fashion, and its lines of dependent communication with the parent culture to the south are really no longer than those of Flores and Itá with their parent cultures. Missing from Frobisher Bay, apparently, is a strong sense that the town is a carrier of cultivation and civilization, a sense that is very strong in Flores and in the Latin and Islamic Mediterranean urban traditions in general. Perhaps this is because Frobisher Bay is a carrier of twentieth-century industrialism. This would, I think, be the reaction of urban theorists like Lewis Mumford. Some people might argue that the school curriculum, as directed toward the Eskimo children (pp. 173-74), is evidence of such a tradition in Frobisher Bay, though I am doubtful about that.

In any case, what is clearly remarkable about Frobisher Bay, from the viewpoint of current notions of cultural evolution, is that in it are juxtaposed one group of people inured to twentieth-century industrial technology and another group of people many of whom were enculturated in a preneolithic technology. Yet the stresses being undergone by the Eskimos do not appear to be excessive, and they are not so great as those experienced by many nonurban groups in the world who are adapting to urban situations to which they are much closer, as far as cultural history is concerned, than are the Eskimos and the Eurocanadians in Frobisher Bay. This should, once again, alert us to the existence of predispositions toward urban adaptation and to the fact that "urban situations" are many and varied.

San Lorenzo is a port town on the

northern coast of Ecuador. It was founded in the nineteenth century when the Ecuadorian government granted exploitation rights in the region, chiefly exploitation of forest products, to two foreign companies, one English and the other German (Whitten 1965:25). Negroes, who now constitute most of the population of the town, were from the beginning the major source of labor in the region. Linked as it was to national policies first by commercial exploitation and then literally by a railroad connecting it with Quito, the national capital, San Lorenzo has continually been subject to changes originating in the larger society of which it is a part.

San Lorenzo has an upper class of forty-eight white or *mestizo* persons, whose wage-earners are professional people none of whom is native to the town. There is a middle class of about three hundred persons, somewhat less than half of whom are *mestizos* and the majority Negroes. All the rest of the population are lower class and almost entirely Negro (Whitten 1965:45).

Whitten (1965:195) points out that between 1942 and 1963 San Lorenzo changed from being a "predominantly Negro village with a population of between 500 and 700 into an ethnically and culturally heterogeneous town with a population approaching 3,000."

Aq Kupruk is a settlement in Afghanistan that had about 300 households in 1965 (Dupree 1966:11). Estimating an average of 6 persons per household, the place should have a population of about 1,800, but this figure would evidently be too small, in view of Dupree's remark that about 70 percent of the 1,500 men are landowners (p. 18). Dupree categorizes Aq Kupruk as intermediate between a "true village" and a "true town" (p. 51), for which, together with "city," he provides some very handy (somewhat too

handy, in my opinion) definitions (p. 10).

Dupree's main point about Aq Kupruk is that it is becoming "de-urbanized," owing to two recent events outside the control of anyone in the settlement: (1) a major trade route that had gone through it was diverted and (2) it was made the administrative center of a less significant region than the one of which it had previously been the center.

Nevertheless, at the time of study it had many features that are associated with urbanness: it was still an administrative and trading center with a bazaar of almost a hundred shops (p. 44); it was ethnically heterogeneous (p. 24) and the ethnic groups were rank-ordered hierarchically (p. 48); gangs of youths and young men were recruited on a multiethnic basis, growing out of work groups, suggesting "incipient unionism" (p. 49); and little sense of loyalty to Aq Kupruk or identification with the town as a whole was felt by its inhabitants (p. 50) because, as an organized settlement, it largely represented the government (that is to say, the police, tax collection, and conscription), whose locale is characteristically thought of in the Middle East as being urban. Thus elements of urbanism are clearly present in Aq Kupruk, despite the facts that most of its inhabitants are farmers and that it is a small place compared to what most Middle Eastern people would call a city.

The same statement can be made about the sixth and last example I shall present. Daghara, a town in southern Iraq, has a population of about 3,000 and serves as the administrative center of a district with a population of about 26,000 (Fernea 1970:17). It has a bazaar whose specialists attract customers from the surrounding hamlets of farmers; it adjoins a main road that connects it with two of the major cities of the country; and it has government facilities (police station, irrigation office, infirmary, schools, and general administrative offices). Many of the functionaries connected with these offices are outsiders whose residence is temporary, but there are also resident merchants and farmers who are native to Daghara. Also living there is a tribal chief to whom many townsmen and farmers in the hamlets owe allegiance, and whose guesthouse is an important institution in the town (Fernea 1970:18-20).

Fernea sometimes refers to Daghara as a village and sometimes as a town, but never as a city. In a footnote (p. 198) he writes the following, which is of some interest:

I have reserved the use of the term "hamlet" to refer to the many small settlements of cultivators scattered throughout the countryside. These settlements contain no specialized buildings other than those associated with a household, or mudhifs which are meeting places for men and where male guests are entertained. Daghara village could, because of its size and local importance, be as well called "Daghara town." I have heard local people call it both *qariya* (village) and *madina* (city). I am unaware of a term in Arabic for a collectivity of intermediate size such as is usually meant by the term "town" in English. By long tradition "madina" has usually been reserved to refer to a center which has a market place, a mosque, and a public bath. Daghara lacks a public bath. Except for these minor considerations, the use of the term "village" to refer to Daghara is entirely arbitrary and probably reflects the urban background of the writer. As an administrative and market center, Daghara village might be similar to county seats in some sections of rural America.

URBAN ESSENTIALS GENERALIZED

It is my impression that these six small and in many respects very different settlements have certain characteristics in common which led each of the anthropologists who studied them, and

some of the inhabitants as well, to perceive them as urban. The common characteristics are these:

1. There are local residents and institutions that serve as brokers between the larger society of which the settlement is a part and the immediate region that the settlement dominates by reason of the brokerage functions located in it. The brokerage functions are concerned primarily with governmental administration, transportation, communication, and commerce.

2. In connection with these brokerage functions, persons considered to be strangers or outsiders to the settlement regularly visit it. The presence of these strangers and outsiders is a normal condition of life in the settlement.

3. There is a distinct system of social classes among the inhabitants. Members of the different classes tend to behave toward each other in terms of a categorical order of social relationships. In other words, they tend to treat each other in terms of stereotypes (Mitchell, ed., 1969:10).

4. Members of the uppermost class, in particular, have various personal connections and associations in other, larger cities. These connections impart prestige and probably usually imply power. They may also be accompanied by behavior and attitudes that are, in the context of the particular culture, sophisticated, cosmopolitan, cultivated, universalistic, and urbane. However, the fact that the majority of lower-class city dwellers do not exhibit such traits has, often mistakenly, been seen as a reason for considering these people's life style as separate and different from the urban way of life (Richardson and Bode 1969:2).

5. Impersonal, rationalistic, goal-oriented, or single-stranded interpersonal relationships characterize much, though not all, of the behavior involved in items 1, 2, and 3. *However*, the same

people who are involved in such relationships are also involved in intensely personal, multiplex, or many-stranded relationships with friends, relatives, neighbors, and others.

6. Many aspects of life in the settlement are subject to change as a consequence of changes in the larger society over which the inhabitants have no control. This tendency to change can intensify the impersonal aspect of social interaction in some instances. It also tends to make the inhabitants change-oriented. Though change orientation may be actively negative or passive, as well as actively positive, it nevertheless is conscious (see King 1967:513). Drastic vicissitudes have been the lot of many cities and their inhabitants (for just one example, see Gulick 1967a: 36).

7. Cultural heterogeneity, in various forms, is a factor in all of the above six characteristics.

That these characteristics can be present in very small settlements, that their presence is not dependent on large size alone, has been demonstrated. I believe it could also be demonstrated that in the vast number of small rural tribal or peasant villages in the world—villages that no one would think of calling urban—these characteristics are not present at all or are present in only rudimentary form, and that it is for this very reason that they are excluded from the urban category by their inhabitants and outsiders alike. When I speak of characteristics that may be present in rudimentary form, I have in mind a situation that is common in Middle Eastern peasant villages, for example, where absentee landlords' agents or schoolteachers—outsiders—may be resident and where there are status differences between landowning farmers and landless laborers. Though these characteristics are suggestive of urban characteristics 1 and 3, they do not by

any stretch of the imagination make such villages urban.

On the other hand, it is not true that the urbanness of Itá, Flores, Frobisher Bay, San Lorenzo, Aq Kupruk, and Daghara is purely a state of mind that has no causal connection with large cities. Though none of them is itself a large city, each one exhibits urbanness by reason of its linkages with at least one city that *is* large. None of these six little towns would exist in its present form, and some of them would not exist at all, if there were no large city somewhere within the larger society of which it is a part.

In general terms, any city of any size "is a behavioral product of a larger socio-cultural system," and the larger system must be understood if the city itself is to be fully understood (Richardson and Bode 1969:3).

The urban elements that have been abstracted from the cultures of these six small settlements are also present, of course, in larger settlements. There are exceptions, notably some of the peasant villages in very densely populated areas such as the Nile Delta and Java, which may have populations as large as 25,000, but the likelihood is that settlements of more than a few thousand will have at least some urban elements. An important reason is that some institutions of regional political and economic power are likely to be located in them. The localization of such institutions of power, even on a very small scale, may, it has been suggested, be the crucial determining element of urbanism (Miner, ed., 1967:6). At the smallest scale level, as illustrated by each of the six cases reviewed above, regional political power is most likely to be discerned in formal administrative structures and personnel. There are hierarchies of such formal administrative localizations that are useful as indices of urbanism, especially in preindustrial societies, but less so in industrial ones.

At what point in the size and industrialization scales do the manmade-environment aspects of urban life become significant? For reasons already discussed, these aspects of urbanism were not accounted for in my analysis of the six small towns, and for the present I believe the question must remain open —a serious problem unresolved.

For the time being, I propose that the seven characteristics that I have abstracted from the work of seven other anthropologists be considered phenomena that constitute the urban human environment in which urban anthropologists do their research. The idea is similar to that of the "external" factors of which Mitchell has written (1966:48-49):

The factors that determine the context in which town-dwellers interact we call external because . . . we are able to take them for granted and to examine instead the behaviour of individuals within the social matrix created by these factors. These are what Southall . . . refers to as "extrinsic factors" and what I earlier called "external imperatives."

Mitchell goes on to list six factors, four of which, though phrased differently, coincide with mine, while the other two are chiefly relevant only to African cities.

The aim of all this is not to split hairs, but to see to what extent urban anthropological work so far enables us to reach agreement on what our common subject of interest is. Unless we can reach such agreement, we shall not be able to develop any very powerful hypotheses concerning the effects of urbanization or to test them very convincingly.

URBAN ANTHROPOLOGY IN ETHNOGRAPHIC AREAS

In an introductory chapter to a book largely concerned with nonanthropological social science research in American cities, Schnore and Lampard (1968:29-32) note the interest of urban anthropologists in comparative studies and specifically in studies of the effects of urbanization on family life and the adaptation of migrants to the city. I think that the specific interests of urban anthropologists are more extensive than Schnore and Lampard indicate, but I also think that the contributions of anthropologists to comparative urban studies are less than these authors imply they are. The major synthetic works—Hauser 1957, Sjoberg 1960, Hauser, ed., 1961, Hoselitz and Moore, eds., 1963, Moore 1965, and others— though sometimes reflecting anthropological views, are not basically anthropological. The same is true of the major comparative urban readers (Breese, ed., 1969 and Fava, ed., 1968, for example). However, the balance is beginning to be redressed with the publication of an urban anthropological symposium (Eddy, ed., 1968) and a reader (Mangin, ed., 1970). Part of the reason for the infrequency of urban anthropological systematizers and collectors is the recency and miscellaneousness of much of their research.

The big exception to this is the urban anthropology of Africa south of the Sahara. It has been a going concern continuously and cumulatively for over thirty-five years. In addition to innumerable "standard" ethnographies, there are pioneering conceptual works (e.g., G. and M. Wilson 1945) and pragmatic, policy-oriented studies like those of Hallenbeck (ed., 1955) and Southall and Gutkind (1956). Beginning with the monumental general symposium volume edited by Daryll Forde (1956), there are symposium volumes on a number of topics, such as change in general (Southall, ed., 1961), urban migration (Kuper, ed., 1965), cities in general (Miner, ed., 1967), one city in particular (Lloyd et al., eds., 1967), and methodology (Mitchell, ed., 1969); there are substantial review papers such as those of Mayer (1962), Mitchell (1966), and Epstein (1967); there is even a trilogy of books on migrants in a single city (Reader 1961, Mayer 1963, and Pauw 1963); and there are many bibliographies, including monographic, annotated ones like that of Simms (1965).

Among the positive results of all this work is the fact that the African urban anthropologists have wrestled so hard with some phenomena (such as the adaptations of rural migrants to cities) that no one studying these phenomena in other areas has any need to replicate the simplistic concepts with which the Africanists, like everyone else, began.

For the very reason that the African urban anthropologists have their own systematizations and their own scholarly in-groups working on more systematization, I shall not attempt to review African urban anthropology per se. Because there is little such systematization of urban studies in other ethnographic areas, I shall not attempt to review any of them, as such, either. Rather I shall discuss the various ethnographic areas compositely in the context of certain subjects that have been of recurrent interest to urban area specialists.

RURAL-URBAN DIFFERENCES

On the whole, anthropologists have avoided being trapped into thinking in terms of extreme and artificial rural-urban differences. The bipolar moralistic model is, of course, the most conspicuous example of this type of thinking, but anthropologists seem to have been somewhat less bemused by it than many other social scientists and philosophers.

True, the rhetoric of the bipolar model is not infrequently employed, as in this quotation, for example (Barclay 1964:270):

Urbanism as such is nothing new in the Middle East. Indeed, it is a Middle Eastern invention which has characterized the area for five thousand years, but it is, however, a pre-industrial type of urbanism, sharing with the peasant village and the folk community a more sacred orientation and so contrasting with the more "rationalized" social structure and secular world view of the industrial city originating in nineteenth-century Europe and America.

Yet in the book from which this quotation is taken (a study of Buuri al-Lamaab, a settlement in the Sudan that is changing from a peasant village to a truck-garden settlement to a bedroom suburb of Khartoum), the ethnographic facts are presented in such detail that the reader can reach his own conclusions concerning them.

Consciously rebutting the concept of rural-urban polarities is Willems' (1970) study of the village of Neyl in the industrial lower Rhineland of Germany. Neyl occupies an ecological position in relation to the city of Cologne somewhat comparable to that of Buuri al-Lamaab in relation to Khartoum.

While apartment houses were mushrooming all over the fringe area, at least half the village land was still being used for subsistence and truck farming, the profits from which were exceedingly small in comparison with the income the villagers could have derived from nonagricultural use of their land. This apparently irrational attitude can be understood only in light of an unyielding adherence to the core value of landownership and farming [Willems 1970:538-39].

Yet in many other ways, the people of Neyl were adopting city styles of life. Willems (1970:539) sees this current situation not as anomalous but as one phase in a long tradition of adaptive continuity between the village and the city.

The social structure of preindustrial Cologne contained a peasant segment whose way of life flowed, without meeting a distinguishable line of demarcation, into that of the urban lower classes. The great tradition of the city expressed itself on various levels of which only the lowest, the culture of the parish and marketplace, was accessible to the lower classes, including the city peasantry. Neyl . . . was but an outlying dependency of the city . . . its way of life was, in a number of significant aspects, continuous with that of the lower classes of the city, and the villagers participated in the "great tradition" on the same level with them.

This quotation strikes a note that is wholly compatible with my own analysis of cultural continuities between Middle Eastern villages and cities (Gulick 1969). There has been a long history of two-way influences between Middle Eastern villages and cities, resulting in a culture in which village life and city life are both similar and different. This mutual influence is illustrated by a series of trait complexes arranged in a gradient from most rural to most urban: farming, patrilineal segmentary kinship structure, factionalism, sexual alienation, household size and domestic family structure, individualized and personal style of social relationships, commercialism, religion and sectarian institutions, and elite social classes (Gulick 1969:122f). None of the trait complexes is assumed to be wholly urban or wholly rural, for the idea of "pure" types and polar opposites is rejected in the formulation of the gradient. All of the trait complexes can be found in villages and cities, but there are important differences among them in style and degree.

A basically similar point of view is to be found in Kenny's (1961) study of a rural *pueblo* and an urban parish in Spain. Marked differences, continuities, and subtle differences in style and degree are intermingled. For example, while Kenny notes many instances in which rural life is more "personal" than urban life, he notes the importance in both milieux of personal patronage *and* of a certain kind of impersonal attitude (1961:137): "The *ensimismadismo*, or sense of being wrapped up in oneself, of the pueblo, easily becomes in town an indifferent attitude of the 'couldn't care less' variety; one minds one's own business, and, incidentally, that of one's favored group."

Lieban's (1967) study of sorcery in the Philippines is based on studies done in a rural area and in Cebu City, both located in the same ethnic area, that of the Cebuano. Lieban presents almost all of his data without distinguishing between rural and urban patterns, presumably because there are few such differences. However, he did discover that sorcery cases attributed to economic disagreements were more numerous in the rural area than in the city. He attributes this difference to the fact that mutual economic aid is more expected in the rural area than it is in the city, and that therefore when it is withheld, the reaction is more bitter—resulting in more sorcery—in the rural area than in the city (Lieban 1967:141-42). The distinction in this case is one of significant degree but not of contrast between any all-or-nothing absolutes. Somewhat similar in significance are the findings of De Vos and Miner (1959) in a study comparing rural and urban Algerians largely on the basis of Rorschach protocols. After noting considerable differences, they say (1959:346) that these differences "are far overshadowed by similarities in personality that are part of a modal configuration. These modalities suggest the effects of certain culturally widespread experiences in psychosexual development."

Complexity and subtlety of distinction are also noticeable in Geertz's (1965) analysis of change in the Javanese town of Modjokuto. Identifying ten "first-order social groupings" (six urban, four rural) in the town and its hinterland, he successively regroups them according to five distinctions (Javanist-Islamic, politically responsive-politically unresponsive, elite-mass, urban-rural, modern-traditional). The Javanist-Islamic traditions cross-cut all the urban and rural groups; while all of the urban groups are politically responsive, some of the rural ones are, too. While none of the village groups is elite, some of the urban groups are not elite either. While all of the rural groups are traditional, most of the urban groups are also traditional (Geertz 1965:130-40). Such an analysis defies recasting in the clichés and truisms of the bipolar model, a matter of which Geertz is well aware (1965:145):

> The prewar Modjokuto village was never the favorite image of the romantic ethnographers—a seamless superorganic unit within whose collective embrace the individual simply disappeared into a cloud of mystic harmony. But neither was it that equally favorite image of alienated sociologists—an anomic mass of *lumpen* torn loose from their social and cultural moorings. On the contrary it maintained its over-all form both while filling up with people and while coping as best it could with the powerful effects of colonial capitalism.

To argue against simplistic distinctions between urban and rural environments is not to argue that there are no distinctions between them at all. Indeed, the migration and adaptation of rural people to cities has been, as Schnore and Lampard (1968) correctly noted, one of the major research interests of urban anthropologists.

MIGRATION TO CITIES

Predispositions

A recurrent theme in the literature is that the primary reason for migration from rural areas to cities, or from smaller cities to larger ones, is economic necessity. People may be pushed by economic difficulties at home or pulled by supposed economic advantages to be found in urban settlements, but in either case the motive force is economic.

I do not question the great importance of this motive for migration. Many studies document it very clearly. However, I do question an apparently basic assumption that underlies the emphasis on this motive to the exclusion of all others, and some of its implications. The basic assumption is that all normal rural people are reluctant to migrate to cities and that they do so only because they are forced by dire necessity. One implication of this is that rural people are not in any way predisposed toward urban life and that therefore all migrants are equally ill-prepared for it.

There is some anthropological evidence to the contrary. Writing about the development of towns in the western Pacific, Belshaw (1963:20) says, "When towns undergo rapid spurts of growth based upon immigration, the motivation for the immigration is not based entirely, and perhaps not even primarily, upon job-hunting in a simple sense. The primary motivation is to share in a new and exciting way of life."

This is an unusual statement. I wonder how many other urban anthropologists would be moved to make similar ones if they began looking for evidence on which to base them. Goodman (1967) reports on a study of migrants in the city of Skopje, Yugoslavia, which found that while improvements in their income and housing were perceived, they also felt the environment to be stimulating, vivid, with better possibilities for everything including intellectual growth and improved knowledge of self. The "self-enhancing possibilities" of life in cities are mentioned. However, to keep a balanced view, it is necessary to mention that some of the migrants to Skopje became anomic (Goodman 1967:180-81). Heiss (1967: 267), in his study of Italian migrants in Australia, emphasizes the importance of the influence of attitudes toward assimilation over the nature of their neighborhood. In a direct refutation of the implications of the bipolar model, Goldrich (1964:328), in his study of peasants' sons enrolled in city vocational schools in Central America, concludes that they were already predisposed toward political participation (possibly linked to perceived social advancement) before they migrated.

The prior experiences and expectations of migrants have been noted by some authors. A case in point is a comparative study (Khuri 1967) of two groups of migrants to Beirut, Lebanon, one Shi'a Muslim, the other Christian. Already educated for middle-class occupations before coming to the city, the Christian men and their families did not cluster together in the city; a number of the women, after having been housebound in the villages, went out and got jobs; many of the Christians in Beirut emigrated to foreign countries because of greater occupational opportunities there. The Muslims, on the other hand, were not highly educated before coming to the city and did cluster together there; the men's occupations were concentrated in certain service jobs; none of the women worked outside the home, since they had been taught to prefer home life, and now genuinely welcomed the opportunity to make it a fact rather than the fiction it had been in the villages, where many of them had had to work in the fields; and they did not emigrate abroad, finding all the religious and occupational enhancements of life that they wished in Beirut (Khuri 1967:212-13).

Great differences in urban adaptation, partly related to different predispositions, have been recorded by Pons (1969) in his study of the Congolese city of Stanleyville (now Kisangani). These differences are particularly noticeable in such matters as the maintenance of rural ties, the stability of marriage, and women's work patterns (Pons 1969:244-45).

Probably the most extensively and intensively known case of this kind is Mayer's (1963) study of the "Red" and "School" migrants in the city of East London, South Africa. The "Red" migrants bring to the city a whole subculture centered on many generations of resistance to the intrusive culture of the whites. The "School" migrants, on the other hand, bring to the city a subculture oriented toward acceptance and assimilation with the culture of the whites. Mayer devotes most of his book to a discussion of the contrasting adaptations that result from these two different migrant predispositions.

Since much of our knowledge of predispositions comes from hindsight, it is often difficult to differentiate between predispositions brought to the city and adaptations made subsequently. The point is, however, that the existence and importance of predispositions, so often ignored, has been demonstrated by anthropologists.

Styles of Adaptation

Much of the urban anthropological literature on marriage, kinship, neighborhoods, quarters, and associations is presented in the context of migrants' adaptation to cities. Since I shall deal with each of these subjects separately, I shall discuss in this section only certain general, though important, concepts concerning adaptation.

When the bipolar moralistic model is applied to rural-to-urban migrant adaptations, its predictions are basically of two kinds. One is that the migrants will lose their rural characteristics and adopt urban ones—with generally negative results, the model being what it is. The other is that the migrants will manage to retain certain of the traits they brought with them (largely positive), and to the extent that they do, they will be considered to remain nonurban in character even though they are city-dwellers.

Such rigid thinking, predicated on putative antitheses, has been struggled with by several of the British anthropologists working in Africa, as is admirably shown in Mayer (1962) and Epstein (1967). One of the earliest working concepts of the Africanists was "detribalization," which meant primarily the anomie of migrants whose rural patterns were undermined by urban life. Mayer (1962:589) objects to the concept because it implies "synchronized change of the whole man," whereas in reality many migrants adopt changes in some aspects of their lives but not in others. The concept has been refined by the alternation model of Gluckman (1961), according to which the migrant behaves according to rural patterns when in rural settings and urban ones when in urban settings. This model in turn has been further refined by Epstein (1967) and Mitchell (ed., 1969). In sum, the individual "can switch back and forth between urban and tribal behavior according to the immediate situation" (Mayer 1962:579).

The literature on these alternation models is too extensive to permit recapitulation of all the arguments here. The point I wish to make is that they constitute an important corrective to assumptions about adaptation derived from the bipolar model.

Migrants' Associations and Quarters

Formal associations of recent migrants in cities have been reported from all over the world (Fallers, ed., 1967). In Peru, "practically every town of over 1,000, and many of less, seems to have a club in Lima, and virtually every district has a club" (Mangin 1959:27). Chinese immigrants in the towns of the Society Islands, in the Pacific, have them (Moench 1963:83f); "ethnic" immigrants to the United States have had thousands of them (Glazer and Moynihan 1963:194 and *passim*); village-of-origin mutual aid societies in Cairo are distributed in various parts of the city in significant relation to the points of entry into it (Abu-Lughod 1961); tribal migrants' societies are a significant aspect of the social structure of Freetown, Sierra Leone (Banton 1957) and of West Africa generally (Little 1965). As in the case of the "ethnic" clubs in the United States, an important question, but one difficult to answer, is to what extent these societies are organized to help newly arrived immigrants and to what extent they serve other needs. Little and Epstein have argued, rather inconclusively, about the extent to which very recent immigrants to West African cities really are "joiners" (Epstein 1967:287). Nevertheless, I think the evidence is such that one can responsibly risk the generalization that wherever there are recent migrants to cities, there probably are migrants' organizations that exist primarily for the purpose of mutual aid.

Furthermore, repeated observations in preindustrial cities, where socially distinctive quarters are typical (Sjoberg 1960:100), show that among such quarters are those resulting from the clustering together of people recently come from somewhere outside of the city. I have illustrated this in the case of Baghdad, Iraq (Gulick 1967*b*:246), where three tribal-migrant quarters are clearly identified by name, preserved in their locations of initial settlement by extremely rapid city growth in recent decades. One of the most notable among studies of such phenomena is Abner Cohen's (1969) book about the Hausa quarter in Ibadan, Nigeria; and this community is only one of many like it in various West African cities.

Squatter Settlements

Of all the types of migrants' quarters in cities, squatter settlements have perhaps attracted the greatest amount of attention. Occurring all over the world, they are known by various names, some of which have themselves become famous: *favelas* (Brazil), *barriadas* (Peru), *ranchos* (Venezuela), *bidonvilles* (French-speaking North Africa), *gecekondu* (Turkey), *sarifas* (Iraq).

Despite many local differences and variations, there are some general characteristics of squatter settlements. The dwellings are built by their occupants, who initially use the cheapest, most easily obtainable materials—frequently materials discarded by others. The land is most often government-owned, expropriated rent-free by the squatters. Public sanitation and other facilities are minimal or absent, and the settlements can be very dense and extensive. There is general agreement that squatter settlements are the result of mass migration to cities where low-cost housing is in short supply. Very frequently they are a conscious, deliberate response to this condition; many settlements have been set up literally overnight in accordance with organized plans.

In many cities squatter settlements are so extensive that their inhabitants constitute a major segment of the total population; for example, 45 percent in Ankara, Turkey, and 50 percent in Maracaibo, Venezuela (Abrams 1964:13). This fact, combined with typically very unhygienic conditions and the inhabitants' willingness to work for minimal wages (often underbidding longer term poor residents of the city), has meant that squatter settlements are typically regarded as a menace to law and order. Though Abrams (1966) occasionally shows some compassion for the squatters, his worldwide survey for the U.S. State Department repeatedly emphasizes the illegality of land occupation by squatters (Abrams 1966:1, 15, 33, 34, 37) and makes resettlement of these people merely the means to achieve the goal of "squatter clearance" (pp. 11-12). To be fair, Abrams does say that clearance should not be undertaken without providing alternative places for the squatters to live, but he shows little awareness of what the squatters' real needs are. For example, he notes (p. 9) that one can anticipate that they will settle near industries if they can (implication: prevent them from doing so in the first place); the fact that of course they will settle as close as possible to places where they can find work apparently does not suggest to him that suitable low-cost housing might appropriately be provided in industrial areas, only that available land in such areas be safeguarded against the encroachments of people desperate for jobs.

Impressed by their outward appearance ("chaotic" jumble of ramshackle dwellings amid great filth), outside observers, including policy-makers, are inclined to project their impressions onto the interior life of the settlements, of which they actually know little. The Iraqi government regarded as a generalized menace the vast *sarifa* settlements that developed in and around Baghdad up until 1963. Despite the fact that they were well organized internally according to the tribal structures of their inhabitants, who were making a major contribution to the labor force of the city, they were bulldozed down in 1963 and their inhabitants moved to less conveniently located and probably less comfortable housing (Gulick 1967b:252). Such a move is typical of what governments do or would apparently like to do.

Anthropologically speaking, the greatest amount of interest in squatter settlements seems to center in Latin America. Indeed, Latin American urban research in general seems to be concerned with them to a major degree (Morse 1965). A rather lively discussion has developed in regard to the quality of life in Latin American squatter settlements, a discussion relevant to the controversy that swirls around the concept of the culture of poverty, though this concept was not generated out of research in squatter settlements.

Early in the 1960s, research that had been done in the 1950s, which provided some counterweight to the popular image of absolute, desperate misery that was then current, began to be published. In 1961, Bonilla published the results of a survey in the *favelas* of Rio de Janeiro, which, though revealing considerable discouragement among the inhabitants, nevertheless yielded this conclusion (Bonilla 1970:81):

Despite the conflict, frequent aggression, exploitativeness, and insecurity of personal relationships that according to the accounts of all observers are commonplace in the *favela*, the *favelado* himself feels that he is part of a fairly cohesive, solidary group. It is vis-a-vis the world outside the *favela* that he feels bypassed, forgotten, and excluded.

Also in 1961 were published several articles (in Hauser, ed., 1961) dealing with squatter settlements or other aspects of urban adaptations in Latin America. Among these, Pearse 1961: 195) points out that the ownership and occupation of a house in one of Rio's *favelas,* for all its many faults, is often an improvement over rural conditions. He gives considerable emphasis to the importance of family ties (local and rural) but also mentions the avoidance of extrafamilial obligations and the lack of a sense of neighborhood (Pearse 1961:200). Two articles on Lima, Peru, extend our horizons. Matos Mar (1961:181) emphasizes the internal organization of the *barriadas*—thirty associations and twenty-six more being formed, plus two thousand shops and workshops. He also mentions that many *barriadas* in Lima are settled not by immediate migrants from the country, but by people who have already spent some time in other parts of the city (Matos Mar 1961:190). In contrast to the squatters around Lima, slum dwellers inside the city were reported to have very high delinquency rates and no social organization, and to be very distrustful and eager to get out of their present neighborhoods (Rotondo 1961:250-53). That all is not well in the mental health of squatters either, however, has been documented by Fried (1959).

This general theme is repeated in a study of La Parada, the wholesale marketing area of Lima, which is explicitly contrasted with the *barriadas* (Patch 1967:178). La Parada is a place of disintegrated families, thieves' markets, con men who take advantage of people's distress, and very high valuation of *machismo* (with corresponding transsexuals and homosexuals), reflected in gangs that attack new migrants—in sum, "pervasive amoral individualism" (Patch 1967:219 and *passim*). *Barriada* residents, by contrast, are well organized to achieve various goals. This is not to imply that life in the *barriadas* is utopian or even particularly pleasant; no one claims that it is. The point is that there is evidence that it is less desperate than life in the slums in the interior of the city, and that personal and emotional problems are no more severe among the *barriada*-dwellers than they are in the rural areas they came from (Mangin 1960:913-14).

Safa's study (1968) of a squatter settlement in San Juan, Puerto Rico, yields information that is consistent with many of the findings on the *favelas* and *barriadas* of South America. The people are well organized into committees that have solved some problems, such as bringing electricity and piped water to the settlement (Safa 1968:339). There are frequent visiting and reciprocal aid and many highly personal, nonutilitarian relationships within the settlement. "Los Peloteros is a very friendly neighborhood" (Safa 1968:347). With outside institutions, however, relations tend to be subservient and impersonal (Safa 1968:341), resulting in a sort of isolation that would seem similar to that of the *favelados* in Rio as described by Bonilla.

At least three general statements on squatter settlements (other than Abrams') have been written: Mangin 1967, Ray 1969, and Turner 1969. Mangin reviews the standard myths about them (they are chaotic, an economic drain, nonparticipatory, breeding grounds for discontent, etc.) but emphasizes that all authorities agree on distinguishing between them and slums. Primarily he sees them as attempts at solutions to problems through popular initiative, not as problems themselves (Mangin 1967:67), although he does not claim that they are free of problems or that there is not conflicting evidence on the amount of distress within them. Ray's book, though primarily concerned with the *ranchos* of Venezuela, also ranges far beyond

them. It is rich in details and very effectively makes clear the complexity of such issues as goal-oriented organization and what is actually involved in it. Ray agrees with Mangin that Lewis' "culture of poverty" may apply better to slum dwellers in more settled lower-class parts of cities than it does to squatters, among whom an atmosphere of hope prevails (Ray 1969:156). He sees among the squatters personal freedom and mobility, bustling activity, and a sense of real if limited control over one's destiny, all of which are largely lacking among slum dwellers, who for various reasons are trapped in overpriced rental quarters where there are no possibilities of control or initiative. This situation produces a mental set that he calls the "industrialized urban mentality," which began to appear among the inhabitants of the *superbloques* of Caracas not long after they were moved into them. The *superbloques* are thirty-eight apartment buildings, each fifteen stories high and two hundred yards long, into which between 100,000 and 125,000 people were moved. The result was "an atmosphere of destitution unknown in most barrios" (Ray 1969: p. 155). A typology of the land tenure of squatters has been provided by Turner (1969:514), making it very clear that squatter settlements in themselves are highly diverse.

Without question, squatter settlements constitute a great opportunity for many kinds of anthropological research based on sophisticated hypotheses, for much systematic thinking has already been done on them.

FAMILY AND KINSHIP

Research on urban family and kinship has very often been done in conscious reaction to the sociological myth of the "breakdown of the urban family." Though an aspect of the bipolar moralistic model, this myth has led a long and active life of its own. The results of the many reactive studies are, basically, that it usually is difficult, and often impossible, to demonstrate any "breakdown" of urban families unless breakdown is defined as any deviation from a preconceived rural model whose correspondence with reality is subject to dispute. One of the clearest and most thoroughly documented critical reviews of this whole matter is Gutkind's short monograph on African urban family life (Gutkind 1963:154-60).

The composition and emotional atmosphere of the household is a subject of obvious importance to the vast majority of mankind. Studies that have now been done all over the world make safe the generalization that individual households are most likely to consist of the nuclear family, whether urban or rural and regardless of what the ideal household, as variously perceived in different cultures and subcultures, may be. Holding type of composition and social class (as much as possible) constant, we find that urban households are likely to be somewhat smaller than rural ones.

My own research has shown that in some Arab countries it is impossible to demonstrate any consistent differences in the sizes of urban and rural households (Gulick 1969:130-35). A number of experts on India have shown that in that country there is a similar lack of significant rural-urban differences (Freed and Freed 1969; Sovani 1966: 72). Kapadia (1966:279) makes the important point that the slight increase in the number of nuclear families observed in Indian cities (in comparison with villages) masks the continuing importance in the cities of nonresidential extended family patterns. The following distribution of household composition in India is worthy of note (Kapadia 1966:296):

	Nuclear	*Extended*
Rural	32.16%	67.84%
Urban	38.01%	61.99%

This shows a much higher incidence of residential extended families (rural and urban) than occurs in most other areas, a phenomenon worthy of study in itself. But the importance of extended family patterns amid prevailing nuclear family residence has been demonstrated elsewhere, for example in Farsoun's study of families in Beirut, Lebanon (Farsoun 1970:306). On the other hand, idealization of the nuclear family household (both rural and urban) is also found (e.g., Hammel 1961:1001).

An insufficiently recognized fact is that household and other familial arrangements vary significantly even within the same city, let alone the same culture. Though wholly consistent with the idea of urban heterogeneity, this fact has not prevented most people from making simplistic comparisons between "urban" and "rural" in general. Five household types, cross-tabulated with three social classes, have been identified in Cebu City, Philippines (Liu et al. 1969:395). Four household types among Hindus in the city of Bangalore have been identified (Ross 1961:303) and discussed at length. Amid the great changes they are experiencing, the people of a central city ward in Tokyo exhibit a variety of household types and behavioral patterns (Dore 1958:122 and *passim*) that offers great contrasts as well as continuities with those of "salarymen" in suburban Tokyo (Vogel 1967). In Ibadan, Nigeria, the "Victorian" and "egalitarian" families of the suburbanites (Lloyd et al. 1967:143) contrast with the traditional extended families that are found in town despite the literal breakup of many of their house compounds (Mabogunje 1968:226), and with the Hausa families in Ibadan, where the role of wife often alternates, as an adaptation to pioneering mobility, with that of prostitute (Cohen 1969:61-62). The psychodynamic differences between the suburbanites and the traditional central city-dwellers of Ibadan, with respect to father-child relationships, have been examined at length and with great sophistication by Le Vine et al. (1967). Among working-class people in Isfahan, Iran, there are nuclear families living alone, nuclear families living in their own households within compounds shared by various combinations of relatives, including extended families, and nuclear families sharing households with various relatives, including extended families. In one-quarter of the cases of extensions of the simple nuclear family, the primary linkages are through the wife rather than the husband, and the core groups include not only sets of married brothers, but also sets of married sisters and sets of married brothers and married sisters (Gulick and Gulick 1974).

It should also be noted that nonfamilial households, in relatively small numbers, have been observed in some cities, including Port Said (Gulick 1969:135) and Singapore. Among the Chinese in Singapore, the *kongsi*, or residential club, is an important institution (Murphy 1959:294).

In part, such variations in pattern merely reflect different stages in diachronic phases of family histories, but they also reflect subcultural differences. The latter include relatively static patterns and dynamic adaptations to changing conditions. This point emerges from a study done in Papeete, Tahiti (Kay 1963:66-67) and is emphasized by Gutkind (1963:157-58) in his efforts to counteract the stereotype of urban breakdown of the family. Of more importance to Kay, however, is the frequency of woman-centered households in Papeete, and his interpretation (entwined with the idea of disorganization!) of this coincidence of household type with that of many North American Negroes (Kay 1963: 70-71). Adaptational variations in response to changes due to rural-urban migration and various urban situations, presented in microscopic detail and in the context of certain overall similarities, are significant in Oscar Lewis' first extensive exercise in delineating the culture of poverty in Mexico (Lewis 1959:11-19).

Concern with demonstrating that the statistically typical nuclear family household is not an isolate in a sea of anomie has been a specific interest of some anthropologists. The point was well demonstrated in a study among working-class people in London, which also demonstrated, however, the importance of selectivity in the maintenance of extended kin ties among these people (Firth, ed., 1956:44, 59). Similar findings, amid some differences, have emerged from a more recent study of upper-middle-class families in London (Firth et al. 1970:458-60).

More important is a family study that demonstrates the stable matrifocal and neighboring patterns of working-class Londoners and the disruption of these patterns that resulted from moving to a new housing project (Young and Willmott 1957). This is a pivotal study in urban research. At the same time that it helps counteract the stereotype of urban family disorganization, it also documents the disorganization that can and does result, not from "urbanization," but from certain changes imposed on city-dwellers. A direct development of this research in London is a study of the structure and ecology of families in central Lagos (Nigeria) and the severe emotional and economic hardships visited upon most of them by slum clearance and their removal to a suburban housing project

(Marris 1962). The influence of Young and Willmott's study can also be seen in that of Herbert Gans in a physically deteriorated section of Boston, Massachusetts, which had already been condemned to destruction in the interest of urban "renewal." The book that resulted from this study, *The Urban Villagers* (Gans 1962), had a powerful impact on social scientists and city planners, and it raised the issue, which I shall discuss later on, of whether urban anthropologists should involve themselves professionally in matters of public policy—in this case, urban renewal. Awareness of all the considerations that are involved in the application of anthropological insights to urban renewal policies and plans is very clearly illustrated in a recent study in Ibadan, Nigeria (Onibokun 1970).

The maintenance in cities of kinship ties more extensive than those of the kindred and the extended family has been recorded, and it is impossible to generalize except to say that large-scale kinship structures do exist in cities. In Africa, where tribal identity is based on some unilineal kinship system, this issue is entangled with that of tribalism in cities. And despite the many changes that have occurred, the continuation of tribal-ethnic-lineal ties is a matter of fact, as for example in the cases of the Hausa in Ibadan (Cohen 1969) and the Lokele in Stanleyville (Pons 1969: 244-45). In the Middle East, the importance of lineages in urban political and social prestige affairs has been noted (Gulick 1967a).

One of the most explicit presentations on this subject is to be found in three articles by E. M. Bruner (1959; 1961, 1963) concerning the Toba Batak in the city of Medan, Sumatra, Indonesia. The Toba Batak are very much aware of being a single kinship community (Bruner 1963:4), and their sense of identity is heightened in the city,

where they are surrounded by so many other groups (Bruner 1961:520). Of particular interest and importance is Bruner's emphasis on the flexibility with which they maintain these kinship ties, a crucial element in their continuance (Bruner 1959:124). Kinship sentiments are not equally intense by any means, and in some cases may even be rather impersonal, but the point is that the urban Toba Batak has at his disposal an extensive system of kin alliances (Bruner 1963:6-7). Quite similar in principle, it would seem, is the ideology of "brotherhood" that is an important element in the lives of Kenyan migrants in Kampala, Uganda (Parkin 1969:118). And there is the *tungka* relationship among overseas Chinese town-dwellers in the Pacific islands, which is one of mutual trust for commercial advantage, based on either friendship or kinship, and often developing into further kinship ties (Moensch 1963:87-89).

The point that urban anthropologists are beginning to demonstrate is that there is no inherent incompatibility between extensive kinship organization and city life so long as the organization is flexible enough to be adapted to the needs of city life. Political and economic alliances are among those needs, and kinship is adaptable to serving them.

LOCALIZED AND DISPERSED GROUPS

The spatial distribution of population aggregates has long been an interest of urban ecologists. Anthropologists are not uninterested in urban ecology, and certainly such studies as Whiteford's (1964:28-29, 82-83), which includes the spatial distribution of residential areas of different social classes in two Latin American cities, and Abu-Lughod's (1969:174-75), which shows the spatial distribution of the residences of rural-oriented, traditional urban, mixed traditional and modern urban, and modern urban people in Cairo, are important contributions to urban anthropology.

Urban anthropologists are not content, however, with studies of the localization of aggregates; they want also to know about the localization of self-aware groups of people—in other words, about quarters (or *barrios*) and neighborhoods. The classic instance of the urban quarter was the Jewish ghetto of medieval European cities, but Sjoberg (1960:100-102) has clearly shown that many such segregative localizations have been typical of preindustrial cities. They occur also in modern preindustrial cities, as for example the Zoroastrian quarter of Kirman, Iran (English 1966:49). However, it is questionable whether there are now any cities completely subdivided into quarters each of which is clearly distinctive culturally and also constitutes a definite community. That some cities of considerable size—Tripoli in Lebanon, for example—are replete with named sections has been shown (Gulick 1967a:153-62), but usually only some of these seem to have the ethnic distinctiveness and/or tightness of internal structure (e.g., of an occupational or kinship group) that conveys the aura of community. However, the research that has been done on this so far has not been thorough enough to allow any conclusive statements.

The conceptual distinction between quarter and neighborhood is not clear. Sections of cities that have been identified as quarters vary greatly in size, and one cannot systematically define neighborhoods as being subdivisions of quarters. The word "neighborhood" seems to have different connotations for different people, ranging from the idea of a small number of adjacent households rather intimately associated with each other to something indistinguishable

from the quarter as Sjoberg conceives it.

One way of approaching this whole problem has been to use census or survey data to plot the residential distribution of known groups, such as tribal groups in African cities. One such case is the distribution of tribal groups in Jos, Nigeria, where nearly everyone has migrated from somewhere else and tribal voluntary associations are extremely important. What the distribution reveals is one or two tribal groups predominant in particular wards of the city, but nowhere constituting more than 76 percent of the population (Plotnicov 1967:62). Fieldwork in depth (focusing on individual case histories) reveals that within this general picture some tribal groups are much more tightly localized and corporate in structure than others (Plotnicov 1967:271).

Pons, in his study of Stanleyville (now Kisangani), Congo, used a multiphased survey method for identifying various concentrations of the fifteen tribal groups resident in the city. He found a general pattern of significant concentrations in small neighborhoods but an overall picture of heterogeneity. Absolute majorities of particular groups in any survey area were rare (Pons 1969:67). After a general random survey, he concentrated his analysis on four so-called neighborhoods (population range: 2,500-4,800), and demonstrated highly varied cultural patterns in them (Pons 1969:108-22). He then focused his attention as a participant observer on the seventy households of one particular street. This analysis of "Avenue 21" is a remarkable presentation of the adaptations of members of a mobile population to each other under circumstances where anonymity and privacy are difficult to maintain. Constant readjustments in relationships are combined with stable networks of kin, tribal "brotherhood," and proximity of residence (Pons 1969:169).

Another research approach is to concentrate on a section that is already locally identified by name and/or reputation. Such concentration sometimes results in accusations that the urban anthropologist is trying to study an unrepresentative urban population as if it were an isolated village. Such an accusation would certainly not be justified in the case of Peattie's (1968) study of La Laja, a *barrio* in the new industrial city of Ciudad Guayana, Venezuela, or in the case of Cohen's (1969) study of Sabo, the Hausa quarter in Ibadan, Nigeria.

La Laja is a working-class area in a distinctive physical location with a population of 490. With a highly mobile population, it nevertheless has a core of long-term residents. There is no single institution in the *barrio* to which all residents belong, everyone has personal connections outside the *barrio*, and at no time does each resident know all the others personally. Peattie (1968:40) refers to this situation as "typically urban." At the same time, the kinship networks of the inhabitants are very important in the *barrio* itself as well as outside it. Peattie sees this as an adaptation of kinship to the necessities of urban life, but such are the habits of professional thought, evidently, that she also refers to it as "folkish" (p. 41). There is considerable neighborly sociability in the *barrio* (p. 56) and a number of voluntary groups exist, but none of them provides any cohesion for the *barrio* as a whole (p. 57). Neighbors tend to leave each other alone, informal social controls are weak, and therefore when there is trouble, outside agents of control (the police) are usually called in (pp. 58-59). Just the same, Peattie calls La Laja "a neighborhood." Such weakness of concerted "communal" action has been observed in other poor Latin American neighborhoods (B. Roberts 1970: 27-28), although purposeful as-

sociations of some kind have also been observed among the Latin American poor, as witness the approximately two hundred permanent carnival clubs in the city of Recife, Brazil (Real 1967).

Sabo is far more unified than La Laja. Clearly identified as Hausa and having its own chief, it has a corporate identity. However, its population of 3,400 is internally differentiated into three overlapping types: old-timers (who seem the most interested in maintaining ethnic exclusiveness, since economic advantages are perceived in doing so), recent migrants (most of whom are single males still uncertain whether they will stay or not), and a continuous stream of temporary visitors (Cohen 1969:38). The social structure of the quarter is dominated by the businesses of about thirty "landlords," who maintain long-distance trade relationships in the country. In some senses tightly knit and exclusivist, Sabo exists because of the widely ramified interests of its inhabitants.

With such studies now at our disposal, it is impossible to indulge in simplistic generalizations about "localization"—which is not at all to say that locally significant behavior does not exist in cities.

It is in the interest of introducing some system and objectivity into the study of local and nonlocal relationships that network analysis is being developed. That it calls for highly intensive field observations is made clear by Mitchell (ed., 1969), while the mathematical complexities that can become involved are well illustrated by Wolfe (1970). An interesting attempt to combine a form of network analysis with urban ecology is the study that Caplow and his associates (1964) carried out in San Juan, Puerto Rico. Picking twenty-five diversified locales (they call them neighborhoods) in each of which resided twenty contiguous households, they tried to define different neighborhood behavior types in terms of extensity and intensity of interaction (Caplow et al. 1964:73-75). The results raise some interesting questions, but they are limited by the fact that the analysis is set in terms of arbitrary samples, thus omitting many of the potential relationships of the households.

Though the general emphasis is on the sociability of urban neighbors, absence or weakness of neighborhood relationships has been discussed by some observers. Two cases in point are of particular interest because the contexts in which they occur are so different.

Among the suburban salarymen of Tokyo, neighborhoods are very weak, though there are vestiges of certain rural patterns. The men's associations are primarily with relatives elsewhere to whom they have obligations and in the companies where they work. The women's are primarily with their relatives and former schoolmates. The neighborhood is not the locale where one expects to make friends (Vogel 1967: 109). Among the reasons for this appear to be the intensive obligations that most people owe to people outside the neighborhood and the intense concern for the competitive success of their children in school, which may discourage their comparing notes with others in the same situation.

Concentration of concerns within the immediate family is one factor that "contributes to the atomistic nature of the neighborhood" among Chicanos in a small Texas city on the Rio Grande (Rubel 1966:55). Neighbors are assumed to be malicious, envious, and therefore dangerous, and the closer they are, the more they are avoided (Rubel 1966:86). However, these attitudes seem to have been brought from rural Mexico and are not associated with the pressures for upward mobility that drive the Japanese salarymen.

Suspiciousness and hostility of other kinds do generate some forms of localized urban social organization, however. Particularly notable in this connection are the juvenile gangs that have been observed in places other than Western industrial cities—Baghdad, for example (Gulick 1967b:251, 1969:128), and the cities of Taiwan (Lin 1959:258).

There is, in short, ample evidence of the existence of spatially significant organized social behavior in cities all over the world, and urban anthropologists have contributed in important ways to this knowledge. At the same time, urban anthropologists are generally aware, too, that localized and nonlocalized behavior patterns exist together in the same population, and that their studies must comprehend both in interrelationship with each other. Two good examples, among many, are Meillassoux's (1968) study of voluntary associations in Bamako, Mali, and Parkin's (1969) study of "neighbors and nationals" in Kampala. Jacobson (1971), drawing principally on North American and African ethnographic materials, presents a very useful review of the conceptual and methodological problems connected with the discontinuities and tenuousness that characterize many nonlocalized urban relationships.

CITIES AS CONTEXTS

The fact of urban heterogeneity should warn people away from generalizing too simply about any particular city and from insisting too much on any city's being a "system." Nevertheless, certain generalizations have been made that are chiefly useful in raising important questions for further study, and some macroscopic studies of cities have been done that may be useful in putting the more usual anthropological microscopic materials into context.

I have already referred to Leeds' (1968) generalized contrast between

Rio de Janeiro and São Paulo. There are others. Whiteford (1964) has devoted a book to showing the differences, in social class structure and adaptations to modernization, between two moderate-sized Latin American cities as wholes. Similar in scope, though not couched in terms of Warner's social class types, is Geertz's (1963) comparative study of two small cities in Indonesia. A demographic study of Mexican cities, categorized into types by size, has attributed to them different patterns of attitude toward contraception, suggesting some interesting hypotheses about the influence of city size on culture (Leñero Otero 1968:871-72). The city of Medellín, Colombia, has been the subject of a study of city-wide resistance to family planning (Jaramillo Gómez 1968). All of these are efforts to weave together various facets of the cultures of particular cities in order to explain certain phenomena.

Less specialized in focus, perhaps, are a few studies that attempt to comprehend certain cities as somewhat systemic social fields. The need to study cities as sets of subsystems has been noted by Gluckman (1961:80). I have contributed a one-man study of Tripoli, Lebanon (Gulick 1967a). Lloyd et al. (1967) present the work of several people who studied Ibadan, Nigeria, as comprehensively as possible. English (1966) presents a study of Kirman, Iran, which puts particular emphasis on the city and its hinterland, a dimension of urbanism that urban anthropologists too often ignore. The case for holistic urban anthropological research has been strongly presented by Fox (1971).

URBAN ANTHROPOLOGY IN NORTH AMERICAN INDUSTRIAL CITIES
THE INTELLECTUAL CLIMATE

A professor of classics at the University of Texas has expressed feelings that are undoubtedly shared by many professors of anthropology in the United States (Arrowsmith 1970:46):

The overwhelming frustration and rage everywhere felt, the erosion of responsibility in the loss of community, the numbing sense that all our customary means of coping with chaos are obsolete, the daily bile of impotence and defeat, the awful torpor of affluence and the prevalent selfishness of American life, the doubts increasingly felt about the American republic itself—to these things the university seems to have nothing to say.

If we substitute "urban anthropology" for "the university," to what extent will there then be professional agreement with this statement? Anthropology has certainly had something to say on the "loss of community," but what of the other miseries of soul and culture that Arrowsmith mentions?

As if in echo, one of the most recent additions to the urban anthropology of the United States opens with "The American city is convulsed with pain . . . is being rent asunder. Our sense of community is being shattered" (Spradley 1970:1). But reading on, one finds it a little difficult to see what community it was that we lost sense of, for Spradley almost immediately refers to the "myth of the melting pot"; that is, to the illusion that the United States has not been a congeries of distinct subcultures for a long time. Any senses of community that might have existed in such a congeries would presumably have been ethnospecific within each subculture. Who, then, are "we," and the sense of *what* community is it that we have lost?

While individual urban anthropologists (including myself) might be able to answer this question (doubtless in a great variety of ways), the corpus of urban anthropological literature on the United States has not, so far, done so. One reason is that "loss of sense of community" has long since been recognized as too loose a concept to be useful as an analytic variable. Nevertheless, people keep on reiterating it, presumably because it evokes feelings of generalized social distress that are indeed real, as Arrowsmith and Spradley make very clear.

Another reason is that most urban anthropological research in the United States has addressed itself to specific communities, or to specific subcultures within communities, at quite descriptive or particularistic levels, only some of which may be directly pertinent to the problems and feelings Arrowsmith expresses so succinctly. Those problems and feelings pertain to national culture and national character. Should the urban anthropological research of the near future, while done in specific local environments, be addressed primarily, somewhat, or barely at all to these problems of United States national culture and character?

Different urban anthropologists will presumably give different responses to this question. The point I wish to make is that I believe that no urban anthropologist who plans to do research in the United States can evade this question. I cannot predict what general direction United States urban anthropology will take on this matter, but my personal preference is for research that will elucidate the lives of particular people and at the same time help us to find cures for our present national agonies.

A major challenge that remains to be met is how to articulate our professional concerns about the problems of our national culture and character with specific, manageable urban research situations involving practicable problem-solving.

Jules Henry's polemical book *Culture Against Man* (1963) is a good example of the lack of such articulation. The title really signifies "American Industrial Culture Against Man," and the book is a vehement documentation of this point, but Henry has virtually nothing to say about what might be done about the conditions he deplores, and the book ends lamely on a note of "perhaps this too shall pass away."

A somewhat different kind of disjunction (but one having similar results) has been noted by Friedenberg (1970: 1, 25) in a review of Margaret Mead's book *Culture and Commitment*. He emphasizes that the fact that the current intergenerational conflict is worldwide

relieves her of the necessity ... of considering specifically American aspects of the conflict; while the fact that she speaks as an anthropologist permits her to couch her argument solely in terms of conflicting patterns of culture without looking behind those patterns to examine the social and economic processes that generate them. Since Canadian, French and Japanese youth are as disaffected as our own, she can eliminate the Vietnam war and the draft as fundamental sources of conflict. ... The result is wholly non-controversial and makes no specific demands ... offering no explanation of or response to, the despair of the young that the world has become as loveless, commercial and tawdry as Christmas itself.

In fairness, it should be noted that elsewhere Mead has made many specific suggestions about changes that need to be introduced in American culture, but precisely how those changes are to be accomplished is a challenge with which most anthropologists seem unprepared to cope. This is presumably a reflection of a sentiment, still strong in the discipline, that an anthropologist's job is to study and clarify patterns of culture, not to try to change them. As I have already suggested, I do not believe that urban anthropology will develop significantly unless it recruits more people who are positively inclined toward research that seeks understandings that *will* facilitate responsible change. Ironically, there are anthropologists who are temperamentally opposed to applied anthropology yet suggest that only total change of the system will suffice to cure the ills of American culture. Presumably this attitude represents a rejection of American middle-class culture rather than a proposal for professional action, for such action would mean full-scale revolution and all the coerced suffering that goes with it. On the other hand, human beings everywhere have always tinkered with their cultures in the hope of improving them; why should not anthropologists participate in such tinkering on an informed, professional basis? If they don't, other behavioral scientists surely will. In fact, they are already doing so . This is particularly true in regard to city life, in which certain satisfactions are to be found that could be maximized.

It would be interesting to know what a sample of anthropologists would make of the following quotation taken from a published diary for the month of February 1970 written by a twenty-one-year-old American university student (Haracz 1970:19):

I'm glad I came out here to school [Michigan State University at East Lansing], because a kid who's spent all her life within thirty miles of New York City needs to know there are other ways of thinking and feeling and acting besides those you get over WNBC . . . but I really get homesick for New York sometimes. I like that rush and constant excitement; I know who I am, and being alone in the middle of eight million people doesn't make me feel lost, like it does some of my friends who visit there—I'm me and the impersonality of New York can't take that away from me, and I like having to choose between things I want to do, rather than what I'll settle for, like I do here. Most of all it's home, I'm a city person at heart, and I always will be. I love the freedom I find there; it's my turf, despite all the things that are wrong with it, and I love it; it's me.

Surely anyone whose sentiments are so much at variance with the conventional wisdom concerning the identity crisis supposedly engendered by impersonal city life must be a person complacently satisfied with the "system" and the "establishment." The rest of Kate Haracz' article makes it very clear that this is not the case; she feels despairing and disaffected in just the ways Friedenberg mentions, and more. She is, however, apparently a person of middle-class background, and perhaps this has something to do with her particular articulation of the qualities of urban life and the problems of national culture. But how many anthropologists would be willing to do the kind of middle-class urban research that might deepen our understanding of this articulation? Not many, I believe, for I think that middle-class American culture is probably the last culture in the world that most American anthropologists would be willing to study objectively by participant observation. This is because most of them are emotional refugees from this very culture. (Is there just one middle-class American culture?)

So far, most urban anthropologists have concentrated their efforts not on the American middle classes—which presumably encompass most of the people in the culture—but on people who are disadvantaged in middle-class terms.

ETHNOGRAPHY OF THE DISADVANTAGED

Who Is Disadvantaged?

Glazer and Moynihan's (1963) analysis of five ethnic groups in New York City discusses at length the continued distinctiveness of the Jews, the Italians, and the Irish Catholics from each other and from the "white-Anglo-Saxon Protestants," but it also shows how to a considerable degree they have taken on some of the characteristics of the WASP middle-class culture. For the most part, this is not true of the Puerto Ricans and the Negroes in New York City, and the reasons for this are also discussed at length.

By middle-class standards, most of the Puerto Ricans and Negroes are disadvantaged people, and it is to the study of these people and others like them, such as American Indians, that much of the urban anthropological research in the United States has been devoted.

As we have seen, Oscar Lewis has proposed that such people have developed a culture (learned and self-perpetuating) that he calls the "culture of poverty," which can be described in terms of about seventy traits. He sees it as an adaptation and a reaction of the poor to "their marginal position in a class-stratified, highly individuated, capitalistic society" (Lewis 1966:xliv). The hypothesis is, then, that the culture of poverty is a cross-societal, international phenomenon. For two reasons, I shall not discuss the culture of poverty any further. First, though it has been discussed mostly in urban settings, it also occurs in rural areas, as Lewis notes, and so far it has not been proved to be urban-specific. Second, Valentine's (1968) review and critique of the concept is readily available, as is a lengthy exchange between Valentine and various supporters and critics (Valentine 1969). Greaves (1971) presents a brief but very thoughtful and informative discussion of the concept, focusing on the interpretive problems that are raised by a critical comparison of Lewis (1966), Liebow (1967), and Hannerz (1969).

I do wish to make two comments on Valentine (1969). First, Lewis' rebuttal to Valentine's criticism that he does not make it clear whether he conceives of the "culture of poverty" as a culture or a subculture (Valentine 1969:189) is a reflection on the pitiful state of imprecision of anthropology's central concept. Perhaps further research in urban anthropology will result in some improvement because of the inescapable fact of varied, and at the same time juxtaposed, life styles in cities. Second, the venomous personal tone of many of the exchanges in Valentine (1969) is very noticeable. My guess is that it can partly be accounted for by the fact that many American anthropologists hate American middle-class culture and therefore react emotionally to such questions as whether the culture of poverty is middle-class culture manqué or whether it is a viable culture in its own right.

If my guess is correct, then we are faced with the very serious question of whether American anthropology as presently constituted is qualified to study American cultures reasonably objectively. If it is not, then we must face the possibility that would-be recruits to professional anthropology who want to study their own culture would be best advised by anthropologists to become political scientists, psychologists, or sociologists, since these professionals for a long time have claimed to have objective techniques for studying their own culture. This is the crisis of professional identity to which I referred at the beginning of this paper. Personally, I still believe that anthropologists have much to contribute as objective analysts of their own culture in their favorite roles as visualizers and participators (Gulick 1963:454), but I wish to emphasize that these roles, to be properly played, require great intellectual discipline.

The Blacks

Anthropological depictions of American urban blacks range from the single-minded to the many-stranded. The urban "bluesman" is a "stereotype of the stud, the hustler" (Keil 1966:152), and soul music, which is his forte, is a central symbol of the reality of black cultural identity (Keil 1966:189; also Haralambos 1970:382). The stud image has been noted as characteristic of others besides black culture heroes; for example, the "street corner man" (Liebow 1967:118, 120):

... the man is always careful to attribute his inadequacies as a husband to his inability to slough off one or another attributes of manliness such as independence of spirit, a liking for whiskey, or an appetite for a variety of women. They trace their failures as husbands directly to their weaknesses as men, to their manly flaws. . . .

... quite apart from his desire to exploit women, the man seeks them out because it is his nature to do so. This "nature" that shapes his sex life, however, is not human nature but rather an animality which the human overlay cannot quite cover. The man who has a wife or other woman continues to seek out others because he has too much "dog" in him.

A similarly exploitive male personality, but more in the context of physical violence than sexuality, has been depicted by Keiser (1969:54 and *passim*) in connection with gang members in Chicago. And Hannerz (1969:177) discusses at length the "ghetto-specific male role . . . including . . . toughness, sexual activity, and a fair amount of liquor consumption." Hannerz, however, has also identified four different personality types—perhaps indicative of four different subcultures—all living together in the same area of Washington, D.C. They are the mainstreamers (who approximate the general American middle class), the swingers, the street families, and the street-corner men (equivalent to those identified by Liebow, also in Washington, D.C.).

A comparable range of personalities has been found among blacks in New Orleans, leading to an important conclusion: "We find reason to doubt that such a thing as '*a* Negro personality' exists at all" (Rohrer and Edmonson 1960:77). Four personality types of male residents, to some extent comparable to those of Hannerz, have been identified in a single federal housing project in a midwestern city (William Moore 1969:89-105). However, Moore also includes "forced masculinity" as a general trait, and comments (1969:82): "All the techniques employed by disadvantaged boys have the same objective: the development of masculine behavior conceived primarily in terms of aggression and detachment from emotionality." Accompanying this male image is that of the matrifocal household, but increasingly studies are showing that this, too, is an oversimplified version of a reality that is actually much more varied (Stack 1970:303).

Disputes over varied interpretations of the realities of life and the needs of blacks in the culture of poverty render the subject quite inconclusive at present. Padfield (1970:34-35) points to the ethnocentrism of the concept of the culture of poverty and emphasizes that we must get the rationale for the phenomena concerned from the participants themselves. Parker and Kleiner (1970:525-26) say that, given certain adjustive functions of the culture of poverty, the imposition of middle-class patterns upon it might be disastrous and that perhaps the whole economic system should be changed. Valentine and Valentine (1970:412) emphasize the great amount of organizational activity among the poor blacks they are studying, the correspondingly strong goal orientation among them, and the imperative need for those who study them to recognize and empathize with these pressures.

The Spanish Americans

The Puerto Ricans in New York City have excited great interest. Oscar Lewis' study of the Rios family in San Juan and in New York, *La Vida* (1966), is a major contribution to this subject, and the long introduction to the book is an extended exposition of the culture of poverty. Lewis (1968) has published a companion volume to *La Vida* which discusses data on the larger samples from which he drew his intensive materials on family life. A number of points from this study are of interest. The migrants to New York complained that "the impersonality and anonymity of living in New York" had a bad effect on their own morality, specifically encouraging them to cheat more (Lewis 1968:128-29). Migrants moved in with relatives—a typical pattern all over the world—and they frequently visited relatives with whom they were not living (p. 191), but the feeling of benevolent mutual aid seemed to deteriorate (p. 193). On the other hand, some informants felt that life was less tense in New York than in Puerto Rico because of less gossip and interference from relatives and neighbors (p. 179). Elsewhere I have pointed out that it is all but inevitable that such qualities of life should occur together (Gulick 1967a: 197). The Puerto Ricans in New York lived in "neighborhoods that formed little islands within the city, perpetuating their native language and many of their customs" (Lewis 1968:204).

Such neighborhoods tend to be dear to the hearts of anthropologists, but Patricia Sexton, in her book on Spanish Harlem, has a very important word of warning on the subject (Sexton 1965:172):

Organized communities tend to be exclusionist. The closer people are to each other, it seems, the more resistant is their response to suspicious [suspect?] or undesired outsiders. The Irish and Polish working class community organized by Saul Alinsky in Back of the Yards, for example, became so tightly organized that it is now an oasis of segregation and racial exclusion in central Chicago. Unless contrary forces are brought to bear—religious, educational, moral—the organized community may itself become a walled ghetto.

Of course, such organized communities long ago did literally become walled ghettoes in Middle Eastern and European cities, and I shall not belabor the point that in urban life, overweening ethnic identities can result in ethnic stereotypes, reactions to which can in turn lead to genocide, as happened in Nazi-dominated Europe.

In rather sharp contrast to the discordant image of the family in the culture of poverty is the "remarkable solidarity" of most of the households and the "happy tranquility" of the children in a Mexican neighborhood in Houston, Texas (Goodman and Beman 1968:96). This neighborhood is so tightly knit that even Mexican-American newcomers have difficulty becoming integrated into it (Goodman and Beman 1968:91). This is a different picture of neighborhood life from that of Mexicans in a small Texas town who were studied, as I have previously noted, by Rubel (1966). Are these differences merely artifacts of different styles of research (e.g., the use of children as informants in the Houston study) or could they objectively be demonstrated and, if so, how would they be explained? A more mature urban anthropology should be able to answer such questions.

A less serene picture of Mexican-American life in southwestern cities is conveyed by such studies as Spicer's (1970), which delineates the clienteles revolving around certain non-Mexican *patrones*, and Waddell's (1968) application of cognitive dissonance theory to the difficulties of Mexican-Americans on probation.

Of methodological interest are the efforts of Hanson, Simmons, and McPhee (1968) to apply refined statistical techniques to the understanding of migration patterns and other experiences of Mexican-Americans in cities.

The North American Indians

One of the few studies of urban Indians that was not done in a western or southwestern U.S. city is that of Freilich (1970) on the Mohawks in Brooklyn, New York. Well known for their specialization in "high steel" construction work, Mohawk men, Freilich concluded (1970:202-203), equated being steelworkers with being warriors, in either case fearless heroes, thus achieving a continuity between aboriginal patterns and urban industrial ones. It would be interesting to know how many Mohawks were among the "hard hat" construction workers who gained notoriety by attacking antiwar demonstrators in New York City in 1970. Even in the 1950s, Freilich (1970:204) observed "hard hat" symbolic behavior among the Mohawks in Brooklyn.

A recurrent theme in North American Indian urban studies is predispositions for urban life, a subject I have already discussed in connection with other people. The general impression is that the reasons for successful adaptation to city life (as indicated by steady employment and protracted residence in the city) and unsuccessful adaptation (as indicated by problems rooted in excessive drunkenness and by retreat from the city) have primarily to do with predispositions that have nothing to do with city life per se. This point has been made concerning various Indian migrants in the San Francisco Bay area (Ablon 1964:298) and the Navahos in Denver (Graves 1970:47). Graves

(1970:51-52) sees the problems of these people as being structural and psychological rather than attributable to the fact that they are Indians, but other investigators may not agree with this. Hodge (1969:20), for example, in his monograph on the Navahos in Albuquerque, says that the majority of urban Indians would prefer to live on their reservations, despite material advantages to be gained in the city, because of the emotional support of their fellows and the more relaxed work patterns to be found on the reservations. And Graves himself has noted the strong pull of the reservation on urban Indians, especially when their economic fortunes are not faring well (Graves 1966:296; Graves and van Arsdale 1966:307). (This makes one wonder whether the frustrations of urban blacks, who have no reservations to return to, may not be much more acute than those of the Indians. However, reservation life is far from idyllic, as many anthropological studies have shown.) In any case, the existence and availability of the reservation are aspects of Indianness, and have effect on urban adaptations (Hodge 1969:25). In other words, there are predispositions that are Indian-specific and others that apparently are not.

On the whole, urban Indians do not appear to cluster together or organize very much on the basis of tribes. But pan-Indian feelings may be heightened by residence in the heterogeneous city with its Anglo-controlled institutions, and pan-Indian enclaves and organizations have been observed in Los Angeles (Price 1968:174) and in San Francisco (Ablon 1964:303).

SPATIALLY FOCUSED STUDIES

Studies of this type are unusual, and none of the four I shall discuss was done by an anthropologist, or by an urban geographer either.

New and May (1966) are concerned with reactions to neighborhood renovation in Pittsburgh. Their major conclusion is that groups concerned with innovation and renovation are not in communication with each other (New and May 1966:356-57). Ways of overcoming the structural barriers between such groups are needed—a worthy subject of study for urban anthropologists, but one that would involve them in policy matters, which many of them prefer to avoid.

Gans (1962:104) notes that the West Enders of Boston were not particularly conscious of their area as such until they became aware of the threat of redevelopment and relocation. Nevertheless, much of his book is devoted to showing the kinds of neighborhood behavior that occurred among them. Spatial elements were important in their lives, though there were no strong sentiments attached to them. While the communal elements in the West Enders' lives seem anomalous in the context of the bipolar moralistic model, the noncommunal elements, particularly "amoral familism," were primarily carryovers from rural Italy (Gans 1962:200-203) and not products of the urban industrial environment of Boston.

This study is a breaker of stereotypes, and so is Gans's (1967) study of Levittown, New Jersey, a housing-tract suburb of Philadelphia. This book is a conscious attack on city planners who impose their schemes on clients whose motivations they do not comprehend (Gans 1967:393-94 and *passim*) and intellectuals who use suburbia as a scapegoat for their disaffection with the predominantly nonintellectual traits of United States culture. Gans says that his purpose is not to eulogize Levittown but to counteract the prevalent antisuburban stereotypes. His general conclusions, presented in great detail, are that most of the Levittowners are neither bored nor isolated in their environment of standardized housing, although he discusses very perceptively the ones who are. Three-quarters of the Levittowners are "lower middle class" in culture (Gans 1967:27), and there are Catholic, Protestant, and Jewish residents.

Although Gans does not stress the point, this is a study of a segment of "mainstream America," not in the abstract, but in a particular physical location in which the investigator himself lived for two years.

The range of subcultures that Gans studied in Levittown generally comprises values systems that, as I have suggested earlier, most American anthropologists personally dislike or find uncongenial. Gans claims that most of the Levittowners are reasonably contented in their suburban environment and criticizes city planners for presuming that they know ways in which that environment should be improved.

How many American anthropologists would be willing to undertake comparable suburban studies in order to discover whether Gans's findings are generally applicable, and if so to what extent? How many of them would find themselves tempted to side with the planners, in spite of their suspicion of "applied" social science, in connection with proposed changes that would improve this particular set of subcultures? My guess is that few American anthropologists would be willing to undertake replications of Gans's study of Levittown. If I am correct, then the urban anthropology of the United States is in danger of failing to become "relevant" in an extremely important way. If anthropologists are unwilling to study mainstream urban United States culture, they can hardly contribute, responsibly and professionally, to the reordering of that culture's priorities that many people feel is needed. "The anthropological perspective," according to two reform-minded educators, "allows one to be part of his own culture and, at the same time, to be out of it" (Postman and Weingartner 1970:4). The irony is that middle-class American anthropologists are apparently unable or unwilling to apply this perspective in participant-observer research of the sort undertaken by Gans. North American urban anthropology is part of anthropology's general identity problem—as I noted at the beginning of this paper—because it brings this paradoxical situation to the fore. The opportunity, however, for it to establish its relevance by recruiting professionals who *are* willing to undertake such research is obvious, as is the likelihood that the character of anthropology would undergo some changes as the result of such a development.

The "Addams area" is a physically deteriorated residential area immediately west of the new University of Illinois campus at Chicago Circle. Its inhabitants are Italians, Puerto Ricans, Mexicans, and Negroes, the Italians being the longest established and now being displaced somewhat by the others. Suttles' (1968) study of this area is a remarkable combination of territorial and social-psychological observations. The residents perceive clearly their own spatial distributions by ethnic group (p. 17) and yet have a certain sense of unity because of their awareness of the area's bad reputation among outsiders (p. 35). An important aspect of their social life is the acting out of patterns of reassurance that their neighbors are not as bad as their stereotypes imply (pp. 26-27). Street life is an intense form of sociability that is enjoyed for its own sake, but it also protects each household from intrusions on its interior privacy (pp. 76-77). Those who do not share very much in this life are the

Negroes, most of whom live in a public housing project that its residents cannot alter in any way—by turning the street floor of a house into a shop, for example—thereby frustrating efforts at economic betterment and restricting opportunities for becoming involved in the local community. This book is one of the best single refutations of the bipolar model as applied to American industrial cities.

EXPERIMENTS AND NEW DIRECTIONS

A certain amount of experimentation, more or less problem-oriented, is taking place with various kinds of urban groups.

Studies of hitherto neglected groups constitute one type. A comparative study of the Syrian and Lebanese communities in Detroit and Toledo, for example, analyzes some clear-cut distinctions between them in occupational patterns, religious observance, localization of residence, and so on (Elkholy 1966). A study of the Samoans in San Francisco shows the way in which their funerals promote continuity and solidarity, enhancing their generally successful adaptations to the city (Ablon 1970). Less conventional is the study by John Roberts et al. (1956) of the small-business highway culture in Nebraska, which is interpreted as having both rural and urban characteristics.

These are studies of people who, on the whole, are successful and do not present society with "social problems." This is not true of Spradley's (1970) ethnography of public drunkards in Seattle. Spradley's purpose in presenting his material is to point the way toward increased recognition by Americans of the dignity of subcultural differences in their midst. In picking a group of people whose dignity is probably the least recognized of any, he tries to show how their condition is in part perpetuated by certain institutions in the society (Spradley 1970:4-5).

Studies of a more pinpointed problem orientation include Polgar's (1966) investigation into the most effective means of involving people in family planning in New York City, and various studies of city schools and teaching. "Population anthropology" and "education anthropology" are new fields of interest in the discipline. Their scope of inquiry by no means needs to be restricted to North American industrial cities, but some important beginnings have been made there.

A brief critical review of the participant-observer technique in educational research concludes Wolcott's paper on school administrators (Wolcott 1970: 120-21). Other anthropological studies in urban education concentrate on behavior in the classroom in the context of the communicability (or lack of it) of classroom materials, weighing such variables as teacher-pupil interactions and the relevance of "white middle-class" materials to blacks (see, for example, Leacock 1969 and Talbert 1970). The literature on the deficiencies of American education is enormous, and anthropologists who are interested in the subject need to think very carefully about precisely what contributions they can best make.

They also need to be wary. For example, cultural compatibility between teacher and pupils (often insufficient) is a highly desirable objective from the point of view of theories of acculturation (and formal education is a type of acculturation). Dissonances related to the relationships of boys to predominantly female teaching staffs have excited great and polemical interest. Such dissonances occur not only in "ghetto" schools, but also in those catering to upper-middle class pupils—for example, those in an upper-middle-class section of Toronto (Seeley et al. 1956:97).

Urban anthropologists should be sensitive to the fact that it is one thing to observe carefully and think in precise terms about the availability of a variety of role models for specific types of behavior, but it is quite another to invent dichotomous "basic female" and "basic male" "natures" and to interpret any personal deviation from either ideal type as a contamination of one by the other. According to this kind of thinking, the "feminized male" is by definition a defective person who is, among other things, unfit to be a teacher of boys (Sexton 1970:67). Conversely, the "masculinized female" is also a defective personality. This kind of thinking—and it has been promoted by many behavioral scientists—is rigid, dogmatic, and stereotypic. It is the same kind of thinking as that which lies behind the bipolar moralistic model, and it is equally appealing to many people for the same reasons. The fact that it is prevalent in the culture at large should not recommend it to social scientists as a valid theory of behavior; racial prejudice is prevalent too. Urban anthropologists need to be alert to the fact that the "feminized male" and "masculinized female" are figments of semantic manipulation, and that they deny the possibility of the normality of a wide range of personality variables among people who are biologically male and among those who are biologically female—a normality that is especially consistent with the heterogeneity of cities.

The ideal male personality, as depicted by Sexton and others, bears a strong resemblance to the "ghetto-specific" male personality I have discussed earlier. Educational anthropologists would do well to bear in mind that efforts (through teacher selection, for example) to maximize the actual prevalence of this personality might also maximize tendencies, already widespread in the culture as a whole, toward the acceptance of destructiveness, exploitive violence, and militarism as normal and desirable (Komisar 1970).

Violence is not an exclusively urban phenomenon, as the lynch mobs in the rural United States and countless tribal feuds all around the world have plainly demonstrated. Nevertheless, it has rapidly become one of the truisms of the new ecology that overcrowding (particularly in cities) is a direct cause of violence. The evidence comes almost entirely from contrived, extreme situations inflicted upon laboratory animals.

Crowdedness, or population density, is very difficult to measure. Available statistical abstractions such as number of people per unit of area or per room of dwellings appear to be too gross to discriminate causal factors, given the cultural differences in tolerance of crowdedness among human beings. Edward Hall (1966) has contributed some suggestive ideas on different cultural reactions to space, though they are not specifically relevant to the crowdedness of cities. A study of mental health in midtown Manhattan, which revealed a high percentage of more or less impaired people, seems to discount the high population density of the area as a causal factor (Srole et al. 1962:261).

Studies bearing on this aspect of urban life are in progress, mostly as pioneering ventures. Alexander (1967:99) reviews work that indicates that "those social disorders apparently caused by density are in fact caused by low income, poor education, and social isolation." Alexander's plea is for more housing and other spatial arrangements that will counteract what he feels is excessive autonomy and withdrawal on the part of many city families. He presents a convincing case, at least up to a point; but Milgram (1970) has also presented a convincing case for what he calls urban "overload," a term borrowed from systems analysis. The basic idea is that metropolitan urbanites often react in noncooperative ways ("impersonal," "dehumanized") toward strangers because they have had to adapt themselves to more interactions than they can cope with. These remarks of Milgram's (1970:1465) are particularly pertinent to matters that have been discussed in this paper:

However, the absolute level of cooperativeness for urban subjects was quite high, and does not accord with the stereotype of the urbanite as aloof, self-centered, and unwilling to help strangers . . . I suggest that contrasts between city and rural behavior probably reflect the responses of similar people to very different situations, rather than intrinsic differences in the personalities of rural and city dwellers.

As far as spatial adaptations are concerned, Sommer (1969) has reviewed some of the recent research that has been done, observing spatial behavior in minute detail. Such research would, I suggest, be particularly compatible with the interests and favorite research methods of many anthropologists.

Stagner (1970:60), an industrial psychologist, makes a basic assumption: that the major "output" of city life should be its inhabitants' satisfaction with life. He warns against reliance on generalities based on aggregate statistics and insists on the necessity of learning about city-dwellers' perceptions of satisfaction directly from them, not from the researchers' projections. He notes that the Wayne State University Urban Studies Center is working on achieving some precision in these matters (Stagner 1970:61-62, 67). What more obvious invitation to cultural anthropologists to involve themselves in urban research on life problems of central importance could be asked for?

CHALLENGE AND OPPORTUNITY

I see the central challenge to urban anthropology in North America to be the search for research problems connected with the central concerns of society, and the study of these problems in the major subcultures of society. Anthropology offers the general willingness of its professionals to work directly with the people being studied, in their native habitats; but anthropology has no copyright on this approach, and others, as I have documented, are beginning to adopt it in North American urban studies. If anthropologists wish to continue to participate in North American urban studies and become more deeply involved in them, they must overcome their prejudices, such as the general antipathy to the middle class.

If it is true that the opportunities for anthropological research in the traditional ethnographic areas are contracting, then it is imperative for the survival of the discipline that this North American challenge be met. In doing so, urban anthropologists must help the discipline as a whole to sharpen its concepts and divest itself of its favorite stereotypes if it is to work fruitfully (as it must) with representatives of other disciplines who are already active in the urban field. I personally have always felt that the achievement of a general behavioral science that would do away with the present artificial, vested-interest-inspired distinctions between the various disciplines is a desirable goal. If it is ever achieved, I hope that anthropology's contribution will consist of clearer, more powerful concepts than we now have to offer. The opportunities to strengthen our concepts are all about us; not least of the rewards is the strengthening of the science and the society in which we participate.

REFERENCES

Ablon, Joan
  1964 Relocated American Indians in the San Francisco Bay Area. *Human Organization* 23:296-304.
  1970 The Samoan Funeral in Urban America. *Ethnology* 9:209-27.

Abrams, Charles
  1964 *Man's Struggle for Shelter in an Urbanizing World*. Cambridge: M.I.T. Press.
  1966 *Squatter Settlements: The Problem and the Opportunity*. Washington, D.C.:HUD.

Abu-Lughod, Janet
  1961 Migrant Adjustment to City Life: The Egyptian Case. *American Journal of Sociology* 41:22-32.
  1969 Varieties of Urban Experience: Contrast, Coexistence, and Coalescence in Cairo. In *Middle Eastern Cities*, ed. I. M. Lapidus, pp. 159-87. Berkeley: University of California Press.

Alexander, Christopher
  1967 The City as a Mechanism for Sustaining Human Contact. In *Environment for Man: The Next Fifty Years*, ed. W. R. Ewald, Jr., pp. 60-109. Bloomington: Indiana University Press.

Arrowsmith, William
  1970 Toward Universities of the Public Interest. *Current*, no. 118, pp. 46-51.

Banton, Michael
  1957 *West African City: A Study of Tribal Life in Freetown*. London: Oxford University Press.

Barclay, Harold B.
  1964 *Buurri al-Lamaab: A Suburban Village in the Sudan*. Ithaca: Cornell University Press.

Bascom, William
  1968 The Urban African and His World. In *Urbanism in World Perspective*, ed. S. F. Fava, pp. 81-93. Originally published 1963.

Beals, Ralph L.
  1951 Urbanism, Urbanization, and Acculturation. *American Anthropologist* 53:1-9.

Belshaw, Cyril
  1963 Pacific Island Towns and the Theory of Growth. In *Pacific Port Towns*

and Cities, ed. A. Spoehr, pp. 17-24. Honolulu: Bishop Museum Press.

Bonilla, Frank
1970   Rio's Favelas: The Rural Slum Within the City. In *Peasants in Cities*, ed. W. Mangin, pp. 72-84. Boston: Houghton Mifflin. Originally published 1961.

Breese, Gerald, ed.
1969   *The City in Newly Developing Countries*. Englewood Cliffs, N.J.: Prentice-Hall.

Bruner, Edward M.
1959   Kinship Organization Among the Urban Batak of Sumatra. *Transactions of the New York Academy of Sciences* 22:118-25.
1961   Urbanization and Ethnic Identity in North Sumatra. *American Anthropologist* 63:5C8-21.
1963   Medan: The Role of Kinship in an Indonesian City. In *Pacific Port Towns and Cities*, ed. A. Spoehr, pp. 1-12. Honolulu: Bishop Museum Press.

Bulsara, Jal F.
1964   *Problems of Rapid Urbanization in India*. Bombay: Popular Prakashan.

Caplow, Theodore, Sheldon Stryker, and Samuel E. Wallace
1964   *The Urban Ambience: A Study of San Juan, Puerto Rico*. Totowa, N.J.: Bedminster Press.

Cohen, Abner
1969   *Custom and Politics in Urban Africa*. Berkeley: University of California Press.

De Vos, George, and Horace Miner
1959   Oasis and Casbah: A Study in Acculturative Stress. In *Culture and Mental Health*, ed. M. K. Opler, pp. 333-50. New York: Macmillan.

Dhekney, B. R.
1959   *Hubli City: A Study in Urban Economic Life*. Karnatak University.

Dore, R. P.
1958   *City Life in Japan: A Study of a Tokyo Ward*. Berkeley: University of California Press.

Dupre, Louis
1966   *Aq Kupruk: A Town in North Afghanistan*. In *City and Nation in the Developing World*. AUFS Readings, vol. 2, pp. 9-61. New York: American Universities Field Staff.

Eddy, Elizabeth M., ed.
1968   *Urban Anthropology: Research Perspectives and Strategies*. Athens: University of Georgia Press.

Elkholy, Abdo A.
1966   *The Arab Moslems in the United States*. New Haven: College and University Press.

English, Paul W.
1966   *City and Village in Iran*. Madison: University of Wisconsin Press.

Epstein, A. L.
1967   Urbanization and Social Change in Africa. *Current Anthropology* 8: 275-95.

Fallers, Lloyd A., ed.
1967   *Immigrants and Associations*. The Hague: Mouton.

Farsoun, Samih K.
1970   Family Structure and Society in Modern Lebanon. In *Peoples and Cultures of the Middle East*, ed. L. Sweet, 2:257-307. Garden City, N.Y.: Natural History Press.

Fava, Sylvia, ed.
1968   *Urbanism in World Perspective: A Reader*. New York: Crowell.

Fernea, Robert A.
1970   *Shaykh and Effendi: Changing Patterns of Authority Among the El Shabana of Southern Iraq*. Cambridge: Harvard University Press.

Firth, Raymond, ed.
1956   *Two Studies of Kinship in London*. London: University of London.

Firth, Raymond, Jane Hubert, and Anthony Forge
1970   *Families and Their Relatives: Kinship in a Middle-Class Sector of London*. New York: Humanities Press.

Forde, Daryll, ed.
1956   *Social Implications of Industrialization and Urbanization in Africa South of the Sahara*. Paris: UNESCO.

Fox, Richard G.
1971   Rationale and Romance in Urban Anthropology. Paper presented at the 70th annual meeting of the American Anthropological Association, November 19.

Fox, Richard G., ed.
1970   *Urban India: Society, Space, and Image*. Monograph no. 10, Program in Comparative Studies on Southern

Asia. Durham, N.C.: Duke University Press.

Frankenberg, Ronald
1966   *Communities in Britain: Social Life in Town and Country*. Baltimore: Penguin Books.

Freed, Stanley A., and Ruth S. Freed
1969   Urbanization and Family Types in a North Indian Village. *Southwestern Journal of Anthropology* 25: 342-59.

Freilich, Morris
1970   Mohawk Heroes and Trinidadian Peasants. In *Marginal Natives: Anthropologists at Work*, ed. M. Freilich, pp. 185-250. New York: Harper & Row.

Fried, Jacob
1959   Acculturation and Mental Health Among Indian Migrants in Peru. In *Culture and Mental Health*, ed. M. K. Opler, pp. 119-37. New York: Macmillan.

Friedenberg, Edgar Z.
1970   Review of Margaret Mead's *Culture and Commitment*. *New York Times Book Review*, March 8, pp. 1, 25-29.

Gans, Herbert J.
1962   *The Urban Villagers: Group and Class in the Life of Italian-Americans*. New York: Free Press of Glencoe, Macmillan.
1967   *The Levittowners: How People Live and Politic in Suburbia*. New York: Pantheon Books.

Geertz, Clifford
1963   *Peddlers and Princes: Social Change and Economic Modernization in Two Indonesian Towns*. Chicago: University of Chicago Press.
1965   *The Social History of an Indonesian Town*. Cambridge: M.I.T. Press.

Glazer, Nathan, and Daniel Patrick Moynihan
1963   *Beyond the Melting Pot: The Negroes, Puerto Ricans, Jews, Italians, and Irish of New York City*. Cambridge: M.I.T. Press.

Gluckman, Max
1961   Anthropological Problems Arising from the African Industrial Revolution. In *Social Change in Modern Africa*, ed. A. Southall, pp. 67-82. London: Oxford University Press.

Goldrich, Daniel
1964   Peasants' Sons in City Schools: An Inquiry into the Politics of Urbanization in Panama and Costa Rica. *Human Organization* 23:328-33.

Goodman, Mary Ellen
1967   *The Individual and Culture*. Homewood, Ill.: Dorsey Press.

Goodman, Mary Ellen, and Alma Beman
1968   Child's-Eye Views of Life in an Urban Barrio. In *Spanish-Speaking People in the United States*, ed. J. Helm, pp. 84-103. Seattle: University of Washington Press.

Graves, Theodore D.
1966   Alternative Models for the Study of Urban Migration. *Human Organization* 25:295-99.
1970   The Personal Adjustment of Navajo Indian Migrants to Denver, Colorado. *American Anthropologist* 72:35-54.

Graves, Theodore D., and Minor van Arsdale
1966   Values, Expectations, and Relocation: The Navaho Migrant to Denver. *Human Organization* 25:300-307.

Greaves, Thomas C.
1971   Is There a Culture of Poverty? *Expedition* 14:10-13.

Gulick, John
1963   Urban Anthropology: Its Present and Future. *Transactions of the New York Academy of Sciences* (ser. 2) 25:445-58.
1967a *Tripoli: A Modern Arab City*. Cambridge: Harvard University Press.
1967b Baghdad: Portrait of a City in Physical and Cultural Change. *Journal of the American Institute of Planners* 33:246-55.
1969   Village and City: Cultural Continuities in Twentieth-Century Middle Eastern Cultures. In *Middle Eastern Cities*, ed. I. M. Lapidus, pp. 122-58. Berkeley: University of California Press.

Gulick, John, and Margaret E. Gulick
1974   Varieties of Domestic Social Organization in the Iranian City of Isfahan. In *City and Peasant: A Study in Socio-Cultural Dynamics*, ed. A. L. LaRuffa et al. New York: Annals of the New York Academy of Sciences, Vol. 220, Article 6, pp. 441-469.

Gutkind, Peter C. W.
1963   *African Urban Family Life*. The Hague: Mouton.

Hall, Edward T.
1966 *The Hidden Dimension*. Garden City, N.Y.: Doubleday.
Hallenbeck, Wilbur C., ed.
1955 *The Baumannville Community: A Study of the Family Life of Urban Africans*. Durban: Institute for Social Research, University of Natal.
Hammel, E. A.
1961 The Family Cycle in a Coastal Peruvian Slum and Village. *American Anthropologist* 63:989-1005.
Hannerz, Ulf
1969 *Soulside: Inquiries into Ghetto Culture and Community*. New York: Columbia University Press.
Hanson, Robert C., Ozzie G. Simmons, and William N. McPhee
1968 Quantitative Analyses of the Urban Experiences of Spanish-American Migrants. In *Spanish-Speaking People in the United States*, ed. J. Helm, pp. 65-83. Seattle: University of Washington Press.
Haracz, Kate
1970 The Education of Kate Haracz: Journal of an Undergraduate. *Change in Higher Education* 2, no. 3:12-26.
Haralambos, Michael
1970 Soul Music and Blues: Their Meaning and Relevance in Northern United States Black Ghettos. In *Afro-American Anthropology*, ed. N. E. Whitten, Jr., and J. F. Szwed, pp. 376-83. New York: Free Press, Macmillan.
Hauser, Philip M.
1957 *Urbanization in Asia and the Far East*. Calcutta: UNESCO.
1965 Observations on the Urban-Folk and Urban-Rural Dichotomies as Forms of Western Ethnocentrism. In *The Study of Urbanization*, ed. P. M. Hauser and L. F. Schnore, pp. 503-17. New York: Wiley.
Hauser, Philip M., ed.
1961 *Urbanization in Latin America*. New York: Internat. Docs. Service.
Heiss, Jerold
1967 Factors Related to Immigrant Assimilation: The Early Post-Migration Situation. *Human Organization* 26: 265-72.
Henry, Jules

1963 *Culture Against Man.* New York: Random House.
Hodge, William H.
1969 *The Albuquerque Navajos*. Tucson: University of Arizona Press.
Honigmann, John J., and Irma Honigmann
1965 *Eskimo Townsmen*. Ottawa: Canadian Research Centre for Anthropology, University of Ottawa.
Hoselitz, Bert F., and Wilbert E. Moore, eds.
1963 *Industrialization and Society*. Paris: UNESCO-Mouton.
Jacobson, David
1971 Mobility, Continuity, and Urban Social Organization. *Man* 6:630-44.
Jaramillo Gómez, Mario
1968 Medellín: A Case of Strong Resistance to Birth Control. *Demography* 5:811-26.
Kahl, Joseph A.
1959 Some Social Concomitants of Industrialization and Urbanization. *Human Organization* 18:53-74.
Kapadia, K. M.
1966 *Marriage and Family in India*, 3rd ed. Bombay: Oxford University Press.
Kay, Paul
1963 Urbanization in the Tahitian Household. In *Pacific Port Towns and Cities*, ed. A. Spoehr, pp. 63-74. Honolulu: Bishop Museum Press.
Keil, Charles
1966 *Urban Blues*. Chicago: University of Chicago Press.
Keiser, R. Lincoln
1969 *The Vice Lords*. New York: Holt, Rinehart & Winston. Winston.
Kenny, Michael
1961 *A Spanish Tapestry: Town and Country in Castile*. New York: Harper & Row.
Khuri, Fuad I.
1967 A Comparative Study of Migration Patterns in Two Lebanese Villages. *Human Organization* 26:206-13.
King, Arden R.
1967 Urbanization and Industrialization. In *Handbook of Middle American Indians* 6:512-36.
Komisar, Lucy
1970 Violence and the Masculine Mystique. *Washington Monthly* 2, no.

5:39-48.

Kroeber, A. L., et al., eds.
1952 *Anthropology Today*. Chicago: University of Chicago Press.

Kuper, Hilda, ed.
1965 *Urbanization and Migration in West Africa*. Berkeley: University of California Press.

Leacock, Eleanor B.
1969 *Teaching and Learning in City Schools: A Comparative Study*. New York: Basic Books.

Leeds, Anthony
1968 The Anthropology of Cities: Some Methodological Issues. In *Urban Anthropology*, ed. E. Eddy, pp. 31-47. Athens: University of Georgia Press.

Leñero Otero, Luis
1968 The Mexican Urbanization Process and Its Implications. *Demography* 5:866-73.

Le Vine, R. A., N. H. Klein, and C. R. Owen
1967 Father-Child Relationships and Changing Life-Styles in Ibadan, Nigeria. In *The City in Modern Africa*, ed. H. Miner, pp. 215-56. New York: Praeger.

Lewis, Oscar
1951 *Life in a Mexican Village: Tepoztlán Restudied*. Urbana: University of Illinois Press.
1952 Urbanization Without Breakdown. *Scientific Monthly* 75:31-41.
1959 *Five Families: Mexican Case Studies in the Culture of Poverty*. New York: Basic Books.
1965 Further Observations on the Folk-Urban Continuum and Urbanization with Special Reference to Mexico City. In *The Study of Urbanization*, ed. P. M. Hauser and L. F. Schnore, pp. 491-503. New York: Wiley.
1966 *La Vida: A Puerto Rican Family in the Culture of Poverty–San Juan and New York*. New York: Random House.
1968 *A Study of Slum Culture: Backgrounds for La Vida*. New York: Random House.

Lieban, Richard W.
1967 *Cebuano Sorcery: Malign Magic in the Philippines*. Berkeley: University of California Press.

Liebow, Elliott
1967 *Tally's Corner: A Study of Negro Streetcorner Men*. Boston: Little, Brown.

Lin, Tsung-yi
1959 Two Types of Delinquent Youth in Chinese Society. In *Culture and Mental Health*, ed. M. K. Opler, pp. 257-71. New York: Macmillan.

Little, Kenneth
1965 *West African Urbanization: A Study of Voluntary Associations in Social Change*. Cambridge: At the University Press.

Liu, William T., Arthur J. Rubel, and Elena Yu
1969 The Urban Family of Cebu: A Profile Analysis. *Journal of Marriage and the Family* 21:393-402.

Lloyd, P. C., A. L. Mabogunje, and B. Awe, eds.
1967 *The City of Ibadan*. Cambridge: At the University Press.

Lynd, Robert S., and Helen Merrill Lynd
1937 *Middletown in Transition*. New York: Harcourt, Brace.
1956 *Middletown: A Study in Modern American Culture*. New York: Harcourt, Brace. Originally published 1929.

Mandelbaum, David G.
1956 The Study of Complex Civilizations. In *Current Anthropology*, ed. W. L. Thomas, Jr., pp. 203-25. Chicago: University of Chicago Press.

Mabogunje, Akin L.
1968 *Urbanization in Nigeria*. London: University of London Press.

Mangin, William
1959 The Role of Regional Associations in the Adaptation of Rural Migrants in Peru. *Sociologus* 9:23-36.
1960 Mental Health and Migration to Cities. *Annals of the New York Academy of Sciences* 84:911-17.
1967 Latin American Squatter Settlements: A Problem and a Solution. *Latin American Research Review* 2:65-98.

Mangin, William, ed.
1970 *Peasants in Cities: Readings in the Anthropology of Urbanization*. Boston: Houghton Mifflin.

Marriott, McKim, ed.

1955 *Village India: Studies in the Little Community.* American Anthropological Association Memoir, no. 83.

Marris, Peter
1962 *Family and Social Change in an African City: A Study of Rehousing in Lagos.* Evanston, Ill.: Northwestern University Press.

Matos Mar, José
1961 The Barriadas of Lima: An Example of Integration into Urban Life. In *Urbanization in Latin America,* ed. P. M. Hauser, pp. 170-90. New York: International Documents Service.

Mayer, Philip
1962 Migrancy and the Study of Africans in Towns. *American Anthropologist* 64, no. 3, pt. 1:576-92.
1963 *Townsmen or Tribesmen,* vol. 2 of *Xhosa in Town,* ed. P. Mayer. Cape Town: Oxford University Press.

Meillassoux, Claude
1968 *Urbanization of an African Community: Voluntary Associations in Bamako.* Seattle: University of Washington Press.

Milgram, Stanley
1970 The Experience of Living in Cities. *Science* 167, no. 3924:1461-68.

Miner, Horace
1965 *The Primitive City of Timbuctoo,* rev. ed. Garden City, N. Y.: Anchor Books, Doubleday.

Miner, Horace, ed.
1967 *The City in Modern Africa.* New York: Praeger.

Mitchell, J. Clyde
1966 Theoretical Orientations in African Urban Studies. In *The Social Anthropology of Complex Societies,* ed. M. Banton, pp. 37-68. London: Tavistock.

Mitchell, J. Clyde, ed.
1969 *Social Networks in Urban Situations.* Manchester: University of Manchester Press.

Moench, Richard
1963 A Preliminary Report on Chinese Social and Economic Organization in the Society Islands. In *Pacific Port Towns and Cities,* ed. A. Spoehr, pp. 75-89. Honolulu: Bishop Museum Press.

Moore, Wilbert E.

1965 *The Impact of Industry.* Englewood Cliffs, N.J.: Prentice-Hall.

Moore, William, Jr.
1969 *The Vertical Ghetto: Everyday Life in an Urban Project.* New York: Random House.

Morse, Richard M.
1965 Recent Research on Latin American Urbanization: A Selective Survey with Commentary. *Latin American Research Review* 1:35-74.

Murphy, H. B. M.
1959 Culture and Mental Disorder in Singapore. In *Culture and Mental Health,* ed. M. K. Opler, pp. 291-316. New York: Macmillan.

New, Peter King-Ming, and J. Thomas May
1966 Alienation and Communication Among Urban Renovators. *Human Organization* 25:352-58.

Norbeck, Edward
1965 *Changing Japan.* New York: Holt, Rinehart & Winston.

Onibokun, Gabriel A.
1970 Sociocultural Constraints on Urban Renewal Policies in Emerging Nations. *Human Organization* 29:133-39.

Oswalt, Wendell H.
1970 *Understanding Our Culture: An Anthropological View.* New York: Holt, Rinehart & Winston.

Padfield, Harland
1970 New Industrial Systems and Cultural Concepts of Poverty. *Human Organization* 29:29-36.

Parker, Seymour, and Robert J. Kleiner
1970 The Culture of Poverty: An Adjustive Dimension. *American Anthropologist* 72:516-27.

Parkin, David
1969 *Neighbours and Nationals in an African City Ward.* Berkeley: University of California Press.

Patch, Richard W.
1967 La Parada, Lima's Market: A Study of Class and Assimilation. In *City and Nation in the Developing World,* AUFS Readings 2:177-223. New York: American Universities Field Staff.

Pauw, B. A.
1963 *The Second Generation,* vol. 3 of *Xhosa in Town,* ed. P. Mayer. Cape Town: Oxford University Press.

Pearse, Andrew
1961 Some Characteristics of Urbanization in the City of Rio de Janeiro. In *Urbanization in Latin America*, ed. P. M. Hauser, pp. 191-205. New York: International Documents Service.

Peattie, Lisa Redfield
1968 *The View from the Barrio*. Ann Arbor: University of Michigan Press.

Plotnicov, Leonard
1967 *Strangers to the City: Urban Man in Jos, Nigeria*. Pittsburgh: University of Pittsburgh Press.

Polgar, Steven
1966 The PPFA Mobile Service Project in New York City. *Studies in Family Planning*, no. 15, pp. 9-15.

Pons, Valdo
1969 *Stanleyville: An African Urban Community Under Belgian Administration*. London: Oxford University Press.

Postman, Neil, and Charles Weingartner
1970 *Teaching as a Subversive Activity*. New York: Delacorte Press.

Price, John A.
1968 The Migration and Adaptation of American Indians to Los Angeles. *Human Organization* 27:168-75.

Ray, Talton F.
1969 *The Politics of the Barrios of Venezuela*. Berkeley: University of California Press.

Reader, D. H.
1961 *The Black Man's Portion*, vol. 1 of *Xhosa in Town*, ed. P. Mayer. Cape Town: Oxford University Press.

Real, Catarina
1967 *O Folclore no carnaval do Recife*. Rio de Janeiro: Ministerio da Educação e Cultura.

Redfield, Robert
1930 *Tepoztlán, a Mexican Village: A Study of Folk Life*. Chicago: University of Chicago Press.
1941 *The Folk Culture of Yucatan*. Chicago: University of Chicago Press.

Reina, Rubén E.
1964 The Urban World View of a Tropical Forest Community in the Absence of a City: Peten, Guatemala. *Human Organization* 23:265-77.

Richardson, Miles, and Barbara Bode

1969 *Urban and Societal Features of Popular Medicine in Puntarenas, Costa Rica*. Working Paper no. 3, ser. 1. Latin American Studies Institute, Louisiana State University.

Roberts, Bryan
1970 Urban Poverty and Political Behavior in Guatemala. *Human Organization* 29:20-28.

Roberts, John M., Robert M. Kozelka, Mary L. Kiehl, and Thomas M. Newman
1956 The Small Highway Business on U.S. 30 in Nebraska. *Economic Geography* 32:139-52.

Rohrer, John H., and Munro S. Edmonson
1960 *The Eighth Generation: Cultures and Personalities of New Orleans Negroes*. New York: Harper & Row.

Ross, Aileen D.
1961 *The Hindu Family in Its Urban Setting*. Toronto: University of Toronto Press.

Rotondo, H.
1961 Psychological and Mental Health Problems of Urbanization Based on Case Studies in Peru. In *Urbanization in Latin America*, ed. P. M. Hauser, pp. 249-57. New York: International Documents Service.

Rowe, William L., ed.
1963 *Contours of Culture Change in South Asia. Human Organization* 22, no. 1 (special issue).

Rubel, Arthur J.
1966 *Across the Tracks: Mexican-Americans in a Texas City*. Austin: University of Texas Press.

Safa, Helen I.
1968 The Social Isolation of the Urban Poor: Life in a Puerto Rican Shanty Town. In *Among the People: Encounters with the Poor*, ed. I. Deutscher and E. J. Thompson, pp. 335-51. New York: Basic Books.

Schnore, Leo F., and Eric E. Lampard
1968 Social Science and the City: A Survey of Research Needs. In *Social Science and the City: A Survey of Urban Research*, ed. L. F. Schnore, pp. 21-48. New York: Praeger.

Schwab, William B.
1965 Oshogbo—an Urban Community? In *Urbanization and Migration in West Africa*, ed. H. Kuper, pp. 85-109.

Berkeley: University of California Press.

Seeley, John R., R. Alexander Sim, and Elizabeth W. Loosley
1956 *Crestwood Heights: A Study of the Culture of Suburban Life.* New York: Basic Books.

Sexton, Patricia Cayo
1965 *Spanish Harlem: Anatomy of Poverty.* New York: Harper & Row.
1970 How the American Boy Is Feminized. *Psychology Today* 3, no. 8:23-29, 66-67.

Simmons, Leo W.
1970 Obituary of Bessie Bloom Wessel, 1888-1969. *American Anthropologist* 72:555-57.

Simms, Ruth P.
1965 *Urbanization in West Africa: A Review of Current Literature.* Evanston, Ill.: Northwestern University Press.

Sjoberg, Gideon
1960 *The Preindustrial City, Past and Present.* New York: Free Press, Macmillan.

Sommer, Robert
1969 *Personal Space: The Behavioral Basis of Design.* Englewood Cliffs, N.J.: Prentice-Hall.

Southall, Aidan W., ed.
1961 *Social Change in Modern Africa.* London: Oxford University Press.

Southall, Aidan W., and Peter C. W. Gutkind
1956 *Townsmen in the Making: Kampala and Its Suburbs.* Kampala: East African Institute of Social Research.

Sovani, N. V.
1966 *Urbanization and Urban India.* New York: Asia Publishing House.

Spicer, Edward H.
1970 Patrons of the Poor. *Human Organization* 29:12-19.

Spradley, James P.
1970 *You Owe Yourself a Drunk: An Ethnography of Urban Nomads.* Boston: Little, Brown.

Srole, Leo, T. S. Langner, S. T. Michael, M. K. Opler, and T. A. C. Rennie
1962 *Mental Health in the Metropolis: The Midtown Manhattan Study,* vol. 1. New York: McGraw-Hill.

Stack, Carol B.
1970 The Kindred of Viola Jackson: Residence and Family Organization of an Urban Black American Family. In *Afro-American Anthropology,* ed. N. E. Whitten, Jr., and J. F. Szwed, pp. 303-11. New York: Free Press, Macmillan.

Stagner, Ross
1970 Perceptions, Aspirations, Frustrations, and Satisfactions: An Approach to Urban Indicators. *Annals of the American Academy of Political and Social Science* 388:59-68.

Stein, Maurice R.
1960 *The Eclipse of Community: An Interpretation of American Studies.* Princeton: Princeton University Press.

Suttles, Gerald D.
1968 *The Social Structure of the Slum: Ethnicity and Territory in the Inner City.* Chicago: University of Chicago Press.

Talbert, Carol
1970 Interaction and Adaptation in Two Negro Kindergartens. *Human Organization* 29:103-14.

Turner, John F. C.
1969 Uncontrolled Urban Settlement: Problems and Policies. In *The City in Newly Developing Countries,* ed. G. Breese, pp. 507-34. Englewood Cliffs, N.J.: Prentice-Hall.

Valentine, Charles A.
1968 *Culture and Poverty: Critique and Counter-Proposals.* Chicago: University of Chicago Press.
1969 Culture and Poverty: Critique and Counter-Proposals. *Current Anthropology* 10:181-200.

Valentine, Charles A., and Betty Lou Valentine
1970 Making the Scene, Digging the Action, and Telling It Like It Is: Anthropologists at Work in a Black Ghetto. In *Afro-American Anthropology,* ed. N. E. Whitten, Jr., and J. F. Szwed, pp. 403-18. New York: Free Press, Macmillan.

Vogel, Ezra F.
1967 *Japan's New Middle Class: The Salary Man and His Family in a Tokyo Suburb.* Berkeley: University of California Press.

Waddell, Jack O.
1968 From Dissonance to Consonance and

Back Again: Mexican Americans and Correctional Processes in a Southwest City. In *Spanish-Speaking People in the United States*, ed. J. Helm, pp. 134-44. Seattle: University of Washington Press.

Wagley, Charles
1953 *Amazon Town: A Study of Man in the Tropics*. New York: Macmillan.

Warner, W. Lloyd, ed.
1963 *Yankee City*, abr. ed. New Haven: Yale University Press. Originally published in 5 vols., 1941, 1945, 1947, 1959.

Whiteford, Andrew H.
1964 *Two Cities of Latin America: A Comparative Description of Social Classes*. Garden City, N.Y.: Anchor Books, Doubleday.

Whitten, Norman E., Jr.
1965 *Class, Kinship, and Power in an Ecuadorian Town*. Stanford: Stanford University Press.

Whyte, William F.
1943 *Street Corner Society: The Social Structure of an Italian Slum*. Chicago: University of Chicago Press.

Willems, Emilio
1970 Peasantry and City: Cultural Persistence and Change in Historical Perspective, a European Case. *American Anthropologist* 72:528-44.

Wilson, Godfrey, and Monica Wilson
1945 *The Analysis of Social Change*. Cambridge: At the University Press.

Windle, Charles, and Georges Sabagh
1963 Social Status and Family Size of Iranian Industrial Employees. *Milbank Memorial Fund Quarterly* 41, no. 4, pt 1:436-43.

Wirth, Louis
1964 Rural-Urban Differences. In *On Cities and Social Life,* ed. A. J. Reiss, pp. 221-25. Chicago: University of Chicago Press.

Wolcott, Harry F.
1970 An Ethnographic Approach to the Study of School Administrators. *Human Organization* 29:115-22.

Wolfe, Alvin W.
1970 On Structural Comparisons of Networks. *Canadian Review of Sociology and Anthropology* 7, no. 4:226-44.

Young, Michael, and Peter Willmott
1957 *Family and Kinship in East London*. Glencoe, Ill.: Free Press.

CHAPTER 24 Medical Anthropology

RICHARD W. LIEBAN

INTRODUCTION

Health and disease are measures of the effectiveness with which human groups, combining biological and cultural resources, adapt to their environments. The fact that health and disease are related to cultural as well as biological factors underlies the convergence of medical and cultural anthropological interests.

Modern medicine has had a primarily biological orientation (Jaco 1958), but basic concern with social and cultural aspects of the maintenance of health and the etiology of disease is deeply rooted in medical history. Ever since the earliest medical systems of which we have historical knowledge, variations in health have been connected with variations in social circumstances and habit patterns. (For example, see

I am extremely grateful to the late William Caudill and to John Honigmann, Ruth Lieban, Leonard Pearlin, and Charles Wright for reading an earlier version of this chapter, and for their helpful comments and suggestions. Responsibility for the contents of the chapter is, of course, solely mine.

Rosen 1963, Dubos 1965, Veith 1966.) Interest in social and cultural dimensions of illness reached a peak in the West during the nineteenth century, stimulated by public health problems associated with the Industrial Revolution (Dubos 1959). This was the period of an impressive development of social medicine, led by such figures as Villerme in France and Virchow in Germany (Dubos 1959, 1965; Rosen 1963). Virchow and others conceived of medicine as a social science, both in a basic and an applied sense. That is, they not only emphasized the need for scientific investigations of the impact of social and economic conditions on health and disease, but they also stressed that a society had the obligation to assure the health of its members, and they advocated social intervention to promote health and combat disease (Rosen 1963). In that perspective, Virchow referred to politics as "nothing but medicine on a grand scale."

Beginning in the latter part of the nineteenth century, modern medicine came to be increasingly preoccupied with specific microorganic agents as the causes of disease (Galdston 1963, Dubos 1959, Polgar 1968). With attention concentrated so heavily on direct, immediate causes of disease, such as the effect of microbes on body tissue, interest in the social and cultural context of medicine declined (Galdston 1959). In recent years, however, this has changed, and there has been a marked upsurge in research by both medical and social scientists on social and cultural aspects of health and disease.

In anthropology this development has been stimulated by problems connected with Western medical programs in developing areas and by current trends in Western medicine itself (Scotch 1963). Undoubtedly changes that have occurred in the relative importance of certain threats to health have increased the need for medically related research in anthropology and other social sciences. Galdston (1963) discusses the point: "The infectious diseases have been all but 'conquered.' Now there is emergent a new pathodemography. The disorders and diseases now dominant are due not to specific pathogens, but rather to economic, social, political, and cultural factors. The resultant pathology is manifest in physiological, functional, behavioral, and psychological disorders." Under the circumstances, Galdston sees the need for more anthropological knowledge in medicine, which will be "increasingly confronted by pathogenic forces that are ecological, social, and cultural in nature."

Much of the development of medical anthropology has occurred since World War II. The beginnings of major anthropological involvement in medical problems were cogently reviewed by Caudill (1953) in his landmark paper on applied anthropology in medicine. Prior to that time, descriptions of etiological beliefs and medical practices in simpler societies had been important components of certain ethnography (e.g., Evans-Pritchard 1937, Gillin 1948), and Rivers (1924) and Clements (1932) had produced substantial works on the worldwide distribution of etiological concepts. But even in 1945 Ackerknecht could write about the serious neglect of medicine in much of the ethnographic literature available up to that time, and when Caudill (1953) wrote his review, involvement of anthropologists and other social scientists in health programs and medical research and education was still something of a novelty. Since then the situation has changed considerably, and there has been a marked increase in work by anthropologists and other social scientists in medicine and medically related areas. A good idea of the scope and volume of research during what might loosely be considered the first decade of substantial growth in medical anthropology can be gained from excellent review articles by Polgar (1962) and Scotch (1963). A cogent summary and analysis of developments in subsequent years is provided by Fabrega (1972).

The rapid emergence of substantial interest in social and cultural aspects of medicine among anthropologists of diverse training, theoretical and methodological orientations, and particular problem interests has created something of an identity problem for medical anthropology. The field has been viewed from a wide range of perspectives. For example, Weaver (1968) sees it as a branch of applied anthropology; Alland (1966, 1970) emphasizes its potential contribution to basic research on human evolution. One way of approaching a definition could be on a purely operational basis, in terms of what those who consider themselves engaged in medical anthropology do. A spectrum of activities could be spelled out, such as those represented by various committees of the recently organized Society for Medical Anthropology, including anthropology and epidemiology, community medicine, medical education, nursing, pediatrics, population planning, and traditional medical systems (*Medical Anthropology Newsletter* 1969). But a circular definition of this kind avoids epistemological issues that go beyond the question of what's in a name, and it is these issues that concern us at this point. In considering them, let us return momentarily to the basis for the intersection of medical and anthropological interests.

Physicians and anthropologists have intersecting interests because health and disease are related not only to biological factors, but also to people's cultural resources and the social behavior that utilizes these resources. As Ackerknecht (1947) defines the situation, "disease and its treatment are only in the abstract purely biological processes ... such facts as whether a person gets sick at all, what kinds of disease he acquires and what kind of treatment he receives depend largely on social factors."

In the junction of physicians' interests with those of anthropologists, the physician's primary concern is likely to be with the ways in which human behavior affects the maintenance of health and the occurrence and control of disease (Roemer 1959). Medical anthropologists have a major involvement in research on these problems, primarily in applied anthropology and etiological and epidemiological studies. But there is another side of the picture, in which problems are defined not by the effects of human behavior on the states of health and disease, but by the indications about human behavior that can be discerned in responses to the states of health and disease. Health and disease are fundamentally connected with the reproduction, quality, preservation, and loss of life. In view of the significance of these phenomena for human societies, it is not surprising that an anthropological study of health and the occurrence and means of coping with disease can involve one deeply in the manner in which people perceive their world, in the characteristics of human social systems, and in social values. In this perspective, medical anthropology is not only a way of viewing the states of health and disease in society, but a way of viewing society itself.

These two dimensions of medical anthropology may be compared to the distinctions drawn by Straus (1957) and Kendall (1963) in the field of medical sociology, which they see as composed of two branches: sociology *in* medicine and sociology *of* medicine. As Kendall describes them, the first of these distinctions emphasizes the contributions of sociological knowledge to the diagnosis and treatment of disease, while the second "concerns itself with sociological study of the medical profession." She says, "Put most succinctly, in the first type of medical sociology, physicians and related health personnel are the actual or potential *consumers* of sociological information, while, in the second, they are the *subjects* of sociological inquiry" (Kendall's italics).

The two aspects of medical anthropology with which we are concerned are more broadly conceived. Thus the anthropological study of social and cultural influences on health and disease includes not only subjects of immediate therapeutic relevance, but phenomena that have special interest because of their effects on human ecology and the course of human evolution; and it is not only medical personnel that is the subject of medical anthropology, but society at large, as it relates to health and medical problems.

Furthermore, Kendall finds sociology in medicine and sociology of medicine usually unrelated branches of endeavor, and Straus believes they actually tend to be "incompatible" activities. In contrast, distinctions made here between the study of social and cultural influences on medical phenomena and the study of society via medical phenomena do not refer to unrelated or incompatible domains of medical anthropology. The same behavior, pivotal from the standpoint of medical anthropology, can be studied as it affects the state of health or disease in a society, and as a response to a medical situation that is revelatory of the attitudes, beliefs, and customary actions of a group.

Indications are that the stressful reactions of individuals who are convinced that they are the victims of sorcery, witchcraft, or axiomatic punishment for violations of taboos can lead to their illness and death (Cannon 1942, Lester 1972). In such cases, culture is pathogenic. And regardless of the causes of an illness, once it is attributed to magical attack, this diagnosis can determine such matters as the kind of practitioner who will be consulted for treatment and the therapy that will be used (Lieban 1967). In these respects, behavior based on certain cultural beliefs can be studied in relation to its effects on the medical situation. But such behavior can also be studied for its wider social implications.

When members of a society regard illness as a sanction, for example, attributions of incidences of illness to the work of enemies or to punishment for deviation from norms reflect strains and conflicts in the social system (Evans-Pritchard 1937; Middleton and Winter, eds., 1963; Marwick 1965). And such attributions can indicate deficiencies in or the absence of other sanctions when strains and conflicts occur (B. Whiting 1950, Swanson 1960, Lieban 1967). Here medical phenomena become the means of understanding social phenomena rather than vice versa.

In such cases, the wider ramifications of medical phenomena may illustrate human behavior under conditions of conflict and inadequate social sanctions. But in cases of this kind the findings of medical anthropology are more than illustrative. For the ways in which medical phenomena are linked to behavior in these social circumstances, and the reasons they are linked as they are, are in themselves significant aspects of such behavior.

Medical anthropology, then, encompasses the study of medical phenomena as they are influenced by social and cultural features, and social and cultural phenomena as they are illuminated by their medical aspects. These distinctions may be seen as two facets of a set of interrelated phenomena. But depending on the nature of the study and the interests of the investigator, one or the other at times may receive greater emphasis or be the focus of attention.

I shall not try to provide an exhaustive survey of the voluminous literature pertinent to medical anthropology within the limited scope of this chapter (useful bibliographies may be found in Caudill 1953, Rosen and Wellin 1959, Polgar 1962, Pearsall 1963, Simmons 1963, Scotch 1963, Mechanic (1968), and Fabrega (1972). Rather than attempt the very condensed synthesis that such a strategy would require, I shall discuss somewhat selectively four major areas of medical anthropology— ecology and epidemiology, ethnomedicine, medical aspects of social systems, and medicine and culture change —the problems encountered in these areas, approaches to these problems, and relevant research findings.

Inasmuch as there are other chapters in this volume on cultural psychiatry and psychological anthropology, I shall give relatively limited attention to the etiology and treatment of mental illness and to psychological dimensions of medical anthropology in general. While in this respect the scope of coverage is reduced, it is enlarged by the fact that in what follows I have not confined myself to discussion of work done by anthropologists, but have also included pertinent studies by other social scientists and by physicians and biologists. I hope that inclusion of references to their work in a chapter entitled "Medical Anthropology" will not be regarded by colleagues in other fields as disciplinary poaching, but rather as recognition of convergent interests across boundaries that are not always logical, and of contributions made by scientists in other fields to the study of problems of concern to growing numbers of anthropologists.

ECOLOGY AND EPIDEMIOLOGY

In the study of medical aspects of the adaptation and maladaptation of human groups to their environments, cultural factors are of major importance. Consider Jacques May's (1960) experience as an epidemiologist in a village in China before World War II. May observed that some of the villagers were seriously affected by a heavy infestation of hookworm, while others were not. An investigation showed that almost all the hookworm patients were rice growers; there were no rice cultivators among those not ill with the malady. The rice cultivators worked in mud mixed with night soil, which helped explain the infestation of hookworm larvae. The other villagers were engaged in silkworm farming, and spent their working days on ladders tending mulberry leaves. Here disease boundaries and cultural distinctions virtually coincided. In a case such as this, the effects of culture on the prevalence of disease are striking, but it is also apparent that the hookworm infestation was part of a complex ecosystem involving relationships between human and nonhuman organisms and their environments.

The influence of culture on occurrences of disease in ecosystems that include human beings is contingent on a variety of factors with which culturally oriented behavior is linked. An interesting exploration of the intricacies of such linkages is provided by John Whiting's (1964) analysis of the parts that postpartum sexual taboos and late weaning may play in protecting infants against kwashiorkor. Whiting notes that kwashiorkor is largely confined to areas of high temperatures and humidity, conditions conducive to the growing of root and fruit crops low in protein. In societies dependent on such foods, he observes, a lactating mother may help prevent the reduction of the already low protein values of her milk—a reduction that could lead to illness for her nursing child—so long as she avoids another pregnancy. He also points out that the prevention of pregnancy in such societies, without alternative means of contraception, generally is accomplished by abstinence from sexual intercourse. In essence, as Whiting sees it, in these circumstances prolonged postpartum taboos are cultural practices that could have the effect of reducing the frequency of kwashiorkor both by prolonging the nursing period and by ensuring that the protein content of the lactating mother's milk is not lowered below the danger point. Here cultural practices are seen as prophylactic in an ecological situation produced by the interrelationship of certain cultural, biological, and physical variables.

The ecological approach, characterized by comprehensive attention to the mutual relations between organisms and their environment, brings to medicine and public health a concern with multiple causes (Gregg 1956, Gordon 1958). It also focuses attention on multiple effects of human actions that alter the relationship between people and their environment, often with important medical consequences. This, of course, is a central contemporary issue in industrial societies, where various forms of environmental modification threaten health. It also can be a paramount consideration in assessing the net value of economic growth projects in developing societies. The construction of new irrigation systems in arid areas such as Egypt has augmented food production, but it also has increased the incidence of schistosomiasis (bilharziasis), a disease carried by a water-borne fluke (Read 1966, Dubos 1965, Alland 1966). Schistosomiasis has been endemic in the Nile Valley for centuries, and in view of the opportunity for spread of the disease afforded by the new irrigation works, it has been predicted that the new Aswan High Dam may prove to be a liability rather than an asset (van der Schalie 1969).

Health ramifications are important criteria of the effects of cultural practices on the adaptation of human groups to their environments. The adaptive value of human behavior is not determined simply by assessing the advantages this behavior offers a population in its relationship with its environment, but also by looking for detrimental consequences of the behavior and weighing gains against losses (Alland 1966, 1967, 1970). Health figures significantly when such an ecological balance sheet is calculated, as the spread of schistosomiasis associated with the spread of irrigation agriculture in certain areas has shown. (For other examples of increases in the prevalence of disease as the results of development, see Hughes and Hunter 1970.)

Changes in the relationship between human populations and disease parasites have been brought about by a combination of cultural and biological processes. Concentrated populations, for example, are more vulnerable to epidemics than dispersed ones (Alland 1969, 1970; Kunstadter 1969). It seems unlikely that parasites capable of producing epidemics could have maintained themselves with man as their sole host before the development of agriculture, since in relatively small, scattered hunting and gathering societies there would be few, if any, potential hosts available once the disease had run its course within a group (Polgar 1964). The development of agricultural communities, accompanied by an increase in trade, greatly enlarged the supply of potential victims. A related example is to be found in unbroken tropical forests, which offer an inhospitable environment for the malaria vector, *Anopheles gambiae*, since the mosquito cannot breed in very shaded water. The introduction of agriculture into West Africa necessitated clearing the tropical forest, and the consequent open swamps afforded breeding places for malarial mosquitoes, with a resulting increase in disease incidence (Livingstone 1958). And cultural developments that led to the concentration of populations in preindustrial cities and intercontinental contacts between peoples also provided the opportunity for widespread epidemics (Polgar 1964, Armelagos 1967).

Through their effects on changes in the relationship between human populations and disease parasites, cultural evolutionary developments such as these can be linked to biological evolutionary changes in both hosts and parasites. A number of observers have pointed out that since parasites require hosts, parasites deleterious enough to threaten elimination of hosts also threaten to eliminate themselves (Dubos 1959,

1965; Polgar 1964; Gordon 1958; Alland 1966). Under these circumstances, when a highly virulent parasite is introduced into a human population, there are selective pressures on the parasitic population to produce a less destructive strain able to live in accommodation with its hosts while serving its own needs (Dubos 1959). As far as evolutionary changes in the host population are concerned, exposure to the parasite will exercise selective pressure in favor of genetic endowments resistant to pathogens. Livingstone (1958) has impressively analyzed a case in point, relating the increase of malaria in West Africa, discussed above, to the spread of the sickle-cell gene among populations of the area, since the heterozygote for this gene is resistant to falciparum malaria. In a later analysis of data from sixty societies in both East and West Africa, Wiesenfeld (1967) found that increased dependence on agriculture, accompanied by increased exposure to malarial parasitism, was associated with rising frequency of the sickle-cell trait.

Some individuals homozygous for the sickle-cell gene die young from sickle-cell anemia, but in malarial areas this pernicious effect of the gene on a population's adaptation to its environment is offset by the immunity to malaria that heterozygous individuals possess (Medawar 1960). When malaria is eradicated, however, the advantage of the gene for the population that possesses it is lost, while for those homozygous for the gene the negative consequence, sickle-cell anemia, remains.

The loss of selective advantage of genes under changed environmental conditions is a problem that has interested the geneticist Neel (1962), who believes it likely that in this respect the gene (or genes) responsible for diabetes mellitus has undergone effects similar to those of the sickle-cell gene. Neel calls the genotype for diabetes "thrifty" because there is evidence that in the early years of life the diabetes genotype is exceptionally efficient in the intake and/or utilization of food. Neel feels that such a genotype would have been advantageous when all human groups consisted of hunters and gatherers whose supply was variable, since in times of temporary abundance of food it would enable individuals who had it to store up extra adipose reserve against periods of acute food shortage. (Recent data on contemporary hunter-gatherers indicate that Neel may have overestimated earlier food supply fluctuations [Dunn 1968].) Neel sees indications that this capability of the diabetic genotype is due to the fact that it is distinguished at the outset by greater than normal availability of effective circulating insulin at some stage in the cycle of responses that follow food intake. He then asks, "How to reconcile this with the relative insufficiency of later years?" His hypothesis is that the normal metabolism of glucose balances insulin and anti-insulins.

In keeping with the usual mechanisms operative in physiologic balances, we may theorize that in the individual predisposed to diabetes, the postulated increased ability in the early years of life to release insulin provokes in time a relative overproduction of its antagonist. There is initially in those genetically predisposed to diabetes a balance between increased insulin production and an increased production of antagonist. Not until this balance is overcome by excessive antagonist production does clinical diabetes develop.

In Neel's view, civilization has brought an increased frequency of diabetes associated with increased mean caloric intake and/or decreased physical activity, resulting in increased stimulation of insulin and its antagonist. According to this hypothesis, then, cultural evolution has had the effect of transforming a genetic advantage into a serious liability (see Smith 1970).

SOCIAL AND CULTURAL ASPECTS
OF EPIDEMIOLOGY

Thus far we have been considering certain medical aspects of the adaptation and maladaptation of human populations to their environments. The etiology, frequency, and distribution of disease have been important parts of the discussion; but we have been less interested in the causes and occurrences of disease per se than as illustrations of ecological processes in which social and cultural factors affecting health figure prominently. Now let us turn to social and cultural aspects of epidemiology as a subject in its own right.

Epidemiology is essentially devoted to selective distributions of disease and their meanings (Francis 1959). Epidemiological units of investigation are populations and samples of populations rather than clinical samples (Mechanic 1968). Epidemiology is both descriptive and analytic (Scotch 1963), and the field has become increasingly concerned with the origin and cause of disease rather than with its distribution alone (Suchman 1968). In this connection, some observers feel that the significant contributions made by epidemiology have stemmed from analytical rather than descriptive studies, and they are critical of the dichotomy made by some between "epidemiological" and "etiological" investigations (Cassel, Patrick, and Jenkins 1960).

Epidemiology has a close relationship to ecology. It has been defined as a branch of ecology (Suchman 1968), as the "ecology of disease" (Bates 1953), and · as "medical ecology" (Gordon 1958). In discussing the epidemiology of ailments such as hookworm, kwashiorkor, schistosomiasis, and malaria, we have considered the relationship between the behavior of human groups and their physical and biotic environments. As we have seen, social and cultural factors play an important part in these ecological relationships. Such factors may be causally. connected with disease occurrences either indirectly, as in the case of poverty linked to malnutrition, or directly, as in the case of mental illness occasioned by emotional disturbance (Suchman 1968). Social and cultural factors, then, may help determine disease etiology and distribution through their influence on the relationship between a human population and its natural environment, or through their direct influence on the health of the population.

Social and cultural distinctions associated with differences in age, sex, occupation, class, ethnicity, and community can have significant effects on epidemiological phenomena.

Age Differences

The incidence of numerous acute infections is highest in childhood, indicating that as people grow older they develop immunities that decrease their vulnerability to these diseases (Francis 1959). Death rates are clearly related to age; they are relatively high in infancy, low between the ages of five and fourteen, begin rising in the age period of fifteen to nineteen, and continue to increase with age after that (Mechanic 1968). Obviously these epidemiological patterns reflect biological variations in vulnerability to sickness and death associated with age differences, but the patterns are also subject to social and cultural influences, as exemplified by significant group contrasts in infant mortality rates (Anderson 1958), depending on such factors as nutrition, sanitation, and medical care.

Sex Differences

Indications are that biological factors play a large part in sexual differences in mortality, with females having longer life expectancy. Madigan (1957) compared mortality rates among Catholic nuns and monks, whose similar styles of life provided an excellent opportunity to minimize the effects on health of the different life experiences of men and women in the general population. Madigan found that the difference between male and female mortality rates under these circumstances was comparable to that in the population at large. Yet, as Mechanic (1968) points out, although biological factors account for part of this difference, they do not explain why the difference has increased so substantially in recent years. Here medical phenomena influenced by cultural changes help to account for the trend: reductions in the risk of childbearing; the increasing significance of cardiovascular and renal diseases, which afflict men more than women; improvement in the detection and treatment of exclusively female cancers, such as those of the breast and uterus, as compared with lung cancer, which is the most frequent form of cancer among men.

The picture with respect to morbidity differences between the sexes is complex. In the United States, a nationwide survey in 1963-1964 of 42,000 households, containing approximately 134,000 persons, showed that the rate of visits to physicians was higher for females than for males, even when prenatal and postnatal care were excluded (U.S. National Center for Health Statistics 1965). However, it is difficult to say whether these data mean that women actually have a higher frequency of illness than men, that they are more likely to seek medical assistance when they are ill, or both. Apropos of this problem, indications of the influence of socialization on the illness behavior of children comes from a study conducted in the midwestern

states by Mechanic (1964), who found that children's reports of "fear of getting hurt" and "attention to pain" indicated that boys were more stoical than girls. But if male and female role distinctions can influence differences in response to illness, they can also influence differences in the development of illness as well, particularly if the culture emphasizes such role distinctions. Read (1966), for example, points out that osteomalacia, a disease characterized by softening of the bones and caused by a lack of sunshine or a deficiency of vitamin D in the diet, occurs with greatest frequency in parts of the world where sunshine is abundant. Speaking of the Bedouin area of Niger, she says, "These Bedouins live in black tents made of goat hair. Men, youth and children go freely, but married women spend most of their lives in tents, wearing a white shawl indoors, but outside a heavy black cloak completely covering head and body, leaving a merest slit for the eyes." The diet of the Bedouins is poor in vitamins A and D and in calcium, and osteomalacia is mainly found "among child-bearing women, who are sometimes immobilized by their pains, need a cane for support in walking and cannot mount or ride a donkey."

Occupational Differences

Studies of the effects of occupation on disease have been an important part of the epidemiological literature since the nineteenth century, when studies of social aspects of pathology indicated that susceptibility to disease varied in accordance with means of gaining a livelihood. When Snow (1936) investigated the occurrence of cholera in the area of the Broad Street pump in London in 1854, he discovered that the incidence of cholera was high among workers in a percussion cap factory where water from the Broad Street pump was drunk, while workers at the Broad Street brewery, where beer was served instead of water, were not similarly affected.

A good deal of epidemiological attention has been paid to the effects on cardiovascular diseases of physical and mental activity characteristic of certain occupations in contemporary industrial society. A study of mortality from arteriosclerotic heart disease among men working in different kinds of railroad jobs in the United States disclosed that mortality during the period of the study was 5.7 per thousand for clerks, 3.9 for switchmen, and 2.8 for section hands, indicating a correlation between mortality from the disease and amount of physical activity during working hours (Dubos 1965). These data are consistent with others obtained in England, showing that bus conductors, who are constantly moving while collecting fares, have a lower mortality from heart disease than bus drivers (Dubos 1965). Occupations that entail a good deal of social psychological stress and relatively little physical activity have been linked in some studies with a relatively high occurrence of coronary heart disease (Morris 1964). Severe occupational stress among tax accountants was shown to be associated with increases in both serum cholesterol and blood clotting time (Friedman, Rosenman, and Carroll 1958; Friedman and Rosenman 1959). Although a number of investigations have shown correlations between emotional factors and cardiovascular diseases (for useful reviews of such studies, see Syme and Reeder 1967), several cautionary notes seem to be in order. First, as King (1963) points out, such diseases probably can be accounted for only by a compound etiology, involving the interaction of diet, stress, exercise, and hereditary factors. Second, while the study of tax accountants apparently indicated that specific increases in stress preceded specific physiological reactions, it is sometimes difficult to disentangle correlational from causal evidence. It has been noted that when attempts are made to establish associations of occupation with coronary artery disease, "both the disease and the occupational choice could logically result from a third variable, e.g., personality type" (Wardwell, Hyman, and Bahnson 1964).

Hughes (1963) points out that although there has been considerable research on occupational hazards to health in the epidemiology of industrial society, similar studies among primitive groups have been relatively rare. He shows how significant this aspect of health can be in simpler societies by citing the prevalence of hydatid disease, whose vector is canine feces, among the St. Lawrence Island Eskimos. In this group, "the men's occupational habit of attempting to unravel frozen dog harness by using their teeth contributes to transmission of the disease, for the harnesses often have been soiled by excreta, in which eggs of the minute tapeworm *Echinococcus multilocularis* are found" (see also Foster 1962).

Status and Ethnic Differences

A substantial part of epidemiological research has been devoted to the influence of social stratification and ethnic differences on disease prevalence and etiology. This influence can be particularly significant in nutritional maladies and in certain infectious diseases whose spread is affected by the material conditions of life. The following figures on numbers of deaths per million population during an outbreak of plague in India, which reflect caste differences in combination with ethnic differences, graphically illustrate the point: low-caste Hindus, 53.7; Brahmans, 20.7; Moslems, 13.7; Eurasians, 6.1; Jews,

5.2; Parsees, 4.6; Europeans, 0.8 (Sigerist 1961).

As the importance of infectious diseases has decreased, epidemiological interest in the effects of socioeconomic differences on the prevalence and etiology of degenerative diseases has grown. But here the influence of socioeconomic variables is not so readily apparent, and in some cases, such as studies of the relationship between social class and coronary heart disease, research findings have been contradictory (Graham 1963; Wardwell, Hyman, and Bahnson 1964). Mechanic (1968) sees certain methodological problems that can skew results of such studies of chronic illnesses. These include very selective samples that do not reflect the broader range of socioeconomic differences, biases in reporting that stem from the difficulty of securing adequate information from the lowest socioeconomic groups, and crude categorizations of socioeconomic distinctions. On the last point, Rogers (1968) finds that the concept of social class, as employed in epidemiological studies, has been too composite and diffuse.

The practical question is whether or not there might be other more precise, identifiable, and, hopefully, isolable elements contained within these more diffuse categories. For example, while there is nothing very much that public health could be expected to do about the phenomenon of social stratification, or about 'social class' as a causative element, there might be a good deal it could do about some of the characteristics of social class which serve to cause disease or to facilitate its occurrence, were they but pinpointed.

Differences in disease rates of ethnic groups have been an important problem in epidemiology, and a number of studies have explored possible relationships between ethnic styles of life and degenerative pathologies. Various forms of cancer have been investigated in this light, and intergroup variations in prevalence have been found. In comparing groups in Hawaii, for example, Quisenberry (1960) found the highest frequency of cancer of the stomach among the Japanese, primary cancer of the liver among Filipino men, cancer of the breast among white women, cancer of the intestines among whites, cancer of the nasopharynx among Chinese, and cancer of the uterine cervix among Hawaiian women. But while such differences in prevalence exist, etiological explanations for them must still be speculative. Disease rates for cancer of the cervix are a case in point. They are especially low for Jewish women, and this seems to be uniform in various areas of the world (Wynder et al. 1954). The rates are also low among Moslem and Parsee women. Male circumcision is practiced by all these peoples, and much attention has been given to this factor in attempts to account for the low prevalence of the disease among women of these groups. Graham (1963) points out that when hygiene is poor, uncircumcised males may introduce a substance, smegma, into contact with the cervix, and since smegma has been found to be carcinogenic to the cervix of mice, the possible relationship between circumcision, smegma, and prevalence rates for cancer of the human cervix have attracted epidemiological interest. However, as Graham notes, studies investigating the problem have not produced mutually consistent results, and he questions methods employed in the research. Graham also raises the possibility that a genetic factor may be involved in differential group rates for cervix cancer.

Community Differences

Associations of disease frequency with contrasting community settings have formed another focus of epidemiological interest. As part of this interest, social correlates of rural-urban distinctions and their implications for health have been significant problems for investigation. Scotch (1960, 1963) found that when rural and urban Zulu were compared, high blood pressure was found to occur more frequently among the urbanites, regardless of sex or age. Scotch observes that urban Zulu are subject to greater frequency and severity of social stress than rural Zulu, and he sees this stress as an important factor in the difference in rates of hypertension between the two populations. He points out that while acculturation proceeds slowly in the countryside, a considerable breakdown of traditional Zulu culture has occurred in the city; yet "acculturation to European modes of life is blocked except for piecemeal adoptions of simpler European technologies" (Scotch 1960). In his analysis, Scotch emphasizes that he does not regard urbanization in itself, or even culture change in general, as stressful enough to have a significant effect on hypertension; it is social conditions conducive to behavior that is not adaptive to the demands of urban living that do the damage.

Thus the urban hypertensive was likely to live in an extended family, have a lower income, resort to bewitchment to explain illness and misfortune, retain traditional religious beliefs, and have a large number of children. In general the reverse was true of the nonhypertensive. In addition, the nonhypertensive was likely to attend the European clinic more frequently, and for women, to belong to the Christian church, both adaptive patterns.

Scotch's analysis is consistent with the view of Cassel, Patrick, and Jenkins (1960) that a culture adapted to rural life may increase rather than decrease stress in an urban situation because of the incongruity between the culture of the migrant and the social situation in which he lives. But there are also indications that the persistence of traditional cultural traits in situations of change need not exacerbate stress and actually may ameliorate it or its effects. For example, Jahoda (1961) found relatively little mental illness in Ghana under the stresses accompanying change there, and attributed this situation to the influence of traditional healers and similar institutions that have adapted to new circumstances. In general, there is substantial evidence that old cultural patterns are not necessarily incompatible with new institutions (see Abegglen 1958, Dore 1958, Geertz 1963, Lloyd 1968). Studies such as those of Scotch (1960) and Jahoda (1961) raise the problem of identifying circumstances when old cultural patterns are adaptive to new conditions and when they are not, and the implications of this difference for health.

ETHNOMEDICINE

MODERN VS. TRADITIONAL PRACTICES

The domain of ethnomedicine is indigenous medical features, those to which Hughes (1968) refers as "not explicitly derived from the conceptual framework of modern medicine." This does not mean that traditional medical systems are impervious to the influence of modern medicine. In the Philippines, for example, it is not unusual to hear local healers refer to "TB" or "germs." But despite such accretions, distinctive traditional qualities persist in these systems; and even when modern medical features are borrowed, they function in an alien context and can carry different connotations than they do in modern medicine (Lieban 1967; see also Halpern 1963).

In addition to "ethnomedicine," various other terms have been used to refer to the domain under discussion or parts of it: "folk medicine," "popular medicine," "popular health culture," "ethnoiatry" (Scarpa 1967), "ethno-iatrics" (Huard 1969).

Polgar (1962) has distinguished the "professional health culture" of medical practitioners from the "popular health culture" of unspecialized lay practitioners. He would include folk healers among health professionals so long as they are recognized as specialists by others in their society.

Leslie (1967) contrasts professional and popular health cultures on a different basis. He has taken a special interest in highly sophisticated indigenous medical systems that are rooted in ancient civilizations, particularly those of South Asia, and which persist today alongside modern medicine. He uses "professional health culture" to refer to the realms of practitioners in both systems, but would not include the medical sphere of folk specialists:

A distinction should be made at the outset between *professional health cultures* and *popular health cultures*. The first term refers to the institutions, roles, values, and knowledge of highly trained practitioners of the indigenous medical systems of South Asia, as well as practitioners of cosmopolitan scientific medicine. *Popular health cultures* include the health values and knowledge, roles and practices of laymen, of specialists in folk medicine, and of laymen-specialists such as the avocational practitioners of homeopathic medicine.

Leslie also points out that while these sophisticated indigenous medical systems appeal to ancient texts, they combine modern institutional forms—hospitals, colleges and schools of medicine, pharmaceutical companies, and so on—as well as certain modern medical concepts with those of traditional civilizations. And in a later paper (1969b) Leslie observes that students of the modernization process have neglected

indigenous scientific traditions, "apparently assuming that the only scientific knowledge and institutions relevant to modernity are Western."

Leslie's point about the distinction between great and little medical traditions in societies such as India and China, which are the present heirs of major ancient civilizations, is well taken. (Polgar [1963] also notes the significance of this distinction.) But in view of the connections between great and little traditions generally (see, for example, Redfield 1956 and Marriott 1955b), it does not seem unreasonable to consider their medical aspects as contrastive but interdependent manifestations of indigenous medicine. My use of the term "modern medicine" is not intended to belittle traditional practices; I use it simply to refer to medical concepts and practices that are based on modern developments in the sciences.

DISEASE CLASSIFICATIONS

Modern medicine classifies diseases in terms of a single taxonomy of universal categories. From the standpoint of this taxonomic system, a recognized disease retains its identity wherever it occurs, regardless of the cultural context. Therefore, as the use of the system has spread, it has increasingly served as a transcultural reference for diagnosis of disease.[1]

In contrast, the disease classifications of indigenous medical systems, much more limited in the reach of their influence, tend to be confined within cultural boundaries, and in ethnomedicine there is often marked variation in dis-

---

[1] There is opinion that this would not hold true for certain mental disorders, which are seen as culturally relative (e.g., see Wittkower and Fried 1959). For a discussion of differences of viewpoint on this question, see Kiev (1964).

ease entities recognized from culture to culture.

To begin with, in some instances phenomena considered to be symptoms of disease by some groups may be regarded as signs of health or without medical significance by others. A classic case in point is *pinta* (dyschromic spirochetosis), which is so common among northern Amazonian Indians that those whose skins are blotched with the disease are regarded as normal; a similar situation obtains with respect to yaws among the Mano of Africa (Ackerknecht 1946). Read (1966) quotes an Egyptian physician to the effect that since Egyptian villagers believe that illness must be associated with pain, bilharziasis and certain other parasitic infections are not considered to be illnesses or to require treatment. Intestinal worms are so endemic among the Thonga of Africa that they consider them necessary for digestion (Ackerknecht 1946). The same is true of Yap islanders (Saunders 1954). Some Mayan Indians in Guatemala regard worm infestation as an unpleasant but fairly normal condition, recognizing it as a problem that requires treatment only when the worms emerge through the esophagus and cause vomiting or choking (Adams 1953).

These examples do not mean that diagnosis in indigenous medical systems in general is less sensitive to or less concerned about signs of morbidity. than modern medical diagnosis. It may be more or less, depending on the phenomena perceived and the significance attached to them in a particular cultural context. In his elegant analysis of disease categories among the Subanun of the southern Philippines, Frake (1961) describes a system that in some respects makes finer discriminations between symptoms of skin disease than modern medicine. The Subanun often make significant distinctions between lesions on

the hands and feet and those on other parts of the body, and when it comes to certain skin diseases that they regard as extremely disfiguring, lesions hidden by clothing are categorized differently than those visible on a clothed body.

Referents of a disease taxonomic system such as that of the Subanun include signs of morbidity that are empirically comparable to those that occur among other groups. But the significance given to these signs and the syndromes in which they appear, as classified indigenously, are subject to intercultural variation and distribution within the boundaries of particular areas or cultural systems, such as a series of distinctive disease taxa found widely in Latin America and among Spanish-speaking groups of the United States: e.g., *susto, empacho, ojo,* or *mal ojo* (Adams and Rubel 1967; Rubel 1960, 1964; Clark 1959; Saunders 1954, 1958; Simmons 1955).

ETHNOMEDICAL THERAPY

Therapy in ethnomedicine is a vast subject that can be touched on only lightly here. It includes both magicoreligious and mechanical and chemical procedures. Laughlin (1963) has made the point that the success of the human species is in no small measure due to the ability to cope with medical problems; and an assessment of indigenous medical systems, including those of nonliterate societies, shows an impressive array of practices that demonstrate empirical therapeutic knowledge, including trephining, bonesetting, removal of ovaries, obstetrics including caesarean section, laparotomy, uvulectomy, comparative anatomy, autopsy, cautery, inoculation, baths, poultices, inhalations, laxatives, enemas, ointments, and cupping (Ackerknecht 1942, Simmons 1955, Laughlin 1963, Huard 1969). Laughlin (1963) lists among the medical skills of Eskimo-Aleut groups in the Arctic

... suturing, removal of stone points, amputation, ligation, opening of the abdominal cavity; acupuncture, including both the use of fixed points and those determined by the individual case; blood letting ... delivery of malposed foetuses, breach deliveries ... massage applied commonly and rigorously ... the use of herbal hotpacks, sometimes in the sweat bath; and the use of a variety of herbals. These achievements are associated with true comparative anatomy, practiced on the sea-otter, done to permit the practitioner to become and remain skillful for practice on humans; the manufacture of mummies by means of evisceration and drying; and the dissection of dead humans to discover why they died.

The pharmacopoeia of ethnomedicine is copious and includes such proven drugs as quinine, opium, coca, cinchona, copaiba, curare, chaulmoogra oil, ephedrine, and rauwolfia. Quisumbing (1951) lists more than eight hundred known medicinal plants in the Philippines alone, including flora efficacious in the treatment of a number of maladies, such as asthma, diarrhea, dysentery, malaria, diabetes, and kidney ailments, to mention only a few.

As the great medical traditions of the Mediterranean, South Asia, and China developed, they became based on secular scientific theories (Sigerist 1961, Leslie 1969b, Croizier 1968, Needham and Lu 1969), and simpler indigenous medical systems appear to vary in the extent to which they depend on magic and religion. Laughlin (1963) finds a relative minimization of magic in the pragmatic orientation of Eskimo-Aleut culture, yet in many cultures medical practices and religious practices are often fused (Glick 1967); and even when mechanical or chemical therapy is employed, magicoreligious elements may also be an essential part of the prescription, or the treatment may be regarded as incomplete without attention to mystical factors involved in the etiology of the illness. Shiloh (1961) describes indigenous Middle Eastern medical beliefs that attribute a burn or a fall from a high place, such as a housetop or a tree, to an evil spirit or the evil eye. In such cases the bruised or torn flesh is dressed with curative preparations and bandaged, and broken bones are set; but concurrent with such straightforward mechanical treatment there will be a search for the evil spirit or evil eye responsible for the accident. Herbalist-surgeons in Ethiopia employ pragmatic means to treat illness, including an elaborate pharmacopoeia, but mysticism is mixed with *materia medica*; the name of a curative plant may not be said aloud, for instance, because this would enable the spirit causing the disease to defend itself against the therapy (Messing 1968). In the Philippines, healers may prescribe a simple decoction of certain plants for illness—but the leaves will have been picked from the east side of the plant, because that is the direction in which the sun rises, and the healer may have learned the prescription itself from a spiritual benefactor who conveyed it to him in a dream or vision (Lieban 1967).

Preventive Measures

Although preventive medicine has been seen as less important in most traditional medical systems than in modern medicine (e.g., Foster 1962), studies such as that of Colson (1969) indicate how significant preventive measures can be in a traditional medical system, and the literature shows that prophylactic practices are widely prevalent in indigenous medicine. These include both mechanical and magicoreligious measures, such as bathing, massage, and rapid rewarming to prevent hypothermia, dietary restrictions, surgery, inoculation, incantations, amulets, and prayers at shrines (Laughlin 1963, Hughes 1963).

In indigenous medical systems as in modern medicine, prophylaxis is geared to etiology. Thus in many areas of the world, including Latin America and South and Southeast Asia, one finds prevalent notions, derived from Hippocratic humoral theory or comparable ideas of Indian medicine, that health depends in part on a proper balance between "hot" and "cold" (Foster 1953, 1967; Jelliffe 1956; Polgar 1962; Nash 1965; Hart 1969). (For interpretations relating this etiology in Mexican communities to the social outlook of peasants, see Foster 1967 and Ingham 1970.) Associated with this theory is the prescription of detailed precautions to maintain the equilibrium of health, such as measures to prevent chilling in a Guatemalan Mayan community: keeping oneself covered, avoiding cold water and foods that are classified as "cool," and not getting caught in the rain (Adams 1953).

Vulnerability to illness may be shielded in many ways. Thus, in some groups the name of a child is changed after someone in the family has suffered a deadly affliction, in the belief that a new name will disguise the soul of the child against attack by spirits who cause disease (Hughes 1963). With the idea that the evil eye is drawn to what is attractive, Turkish villagers protect their children by hanging unattractive objects on their clothing (Oztürk 1964). While the health value of mechanical procedures such as these may be readily apparent on an empirical basis, undoubtedly in many situations magical resources may also be prophylactically effective. In a society where belief in magical attacks may induce severe stress that can lead to illness and death (Cannon 1942), reliance on the protection of an amulet may be psychically hygienic.

Ethnomedical Specialists

When illness occurs, it may be ignored, or treated without the help of a specialist (Polgar 1962). If treatment is sought from a medical practitioner, various types of specialists may be available, including herbalists, diviners, shamans, midwives, and masseurs (e.g., Nurge 1958, Lieban 1962b, Maclean 1969). Therapists may specialize in only one type of skill or calling, or they may combine several in their practice (Lieban 1962b). While there is considerable material on distinctions among traditional therapists based on variation in specialization, there is relatively little regarding distinctions based on variation in reputation for therapeutic success. Yet this factor, as well as the perceived appropriateness of the specialization for the illness to be treated, plays an important part in determining the choice of therapists. Romano (1965) finds that some folk healers have achieved considerable fame and devoted followings among Mexican-Americans of southern Texas, while other folk healers practice in comparative obscurity. Blum and Blum (1965) describe a comparable situation with respect to folk healers in Greece. In one Philippine city, healers differ significantly in the number of patients they attract, and the most successful among them may treat up to a hundred patients a day (Lieban 1967).

Qualifications for folk medical roles vary considerably. In some cases, no formal training may be required for practitioners (Metzger and Williams 1963); in others, a long apprenticeship may be customary (Maclean 1969). In the great medical traditions of Asian civilizations, with a sophisticated literature going back beyond the beginning of the Christian era, training was comprehensive. In India the student of Ayurvedic medicine entered into a spiritual relationship with his guru; he learned how to diagnose illness by observing his teacher, and he memorized medical texts that were explicated by the guru (Leslie 1969a). In China, the teaching of medicine under state supervision goes back at least to the seventh century (Huard and Wong 1968), perhaps to the fifth century (Needham and Lu 1969). Chinese medicine spread to Japan in the early centuries of the Christian era, and by the eighth century a medical program was established by the Japanese. "Seven years of training were required for medicine, five years for pediatrics and surgery, and four years for eye, ear, nose and throat, or dentistry" (Bowers 1965).

Spiritual accreditation is frequently an attribute of indigenous medical roles. But this does not necessarily mean that spiritual backing obviates medical knowledge. They tend to be interrelated, as in the case of Tzeltal practitioners in Chiapas, Mexico (Metzger and Williams 1963). These practitioners are principally distinguished by their ability to "pulse," a skill that comes to the curer only as a "gift of God." Curers as a class are divided into two groups, "master curers" and "junior curers." One of the ways in which the two differ is in extent of knowledge. It is said of the junior curer that "not all is given into his hands by God," of the master curer that "all is given into his hands."

CULTURAL ASPECTS OF ETHNOMEDICINE

Up to this point we have discussed characteristics of indigenous medical systems, but we have not yet concentrated our attention on ways in which medical beliefs and behavior relate to and illuminate the cultural contexts in which they appear. The relationship between medicine and the rest of culture has been noted by Ackerknecht (1942),

who said, "Medicine is nowhere independent and following its own motivations. Its character and dynamism depend on the place it takes in every cultural pattern; they depend on the pattern itself."

Concepts of disease are cultural classifications of adversity. They do not, of course, cover the whole range of misfortune a society may face, but they can reflect its members' view of misfortune in a general sense (Maclean 1969), or their specific outlook on disease and its place in their lives. Thus Frake (1961), in discussing the problem of why finer distinctions are made between certain folk disease categories than others, offers the hypothesis that "the greater the number of distinct social contexts in which a particular phenomenon must be communicated, the greater the number of different levels of contrast into which that phenomenon is classified." In the Subanun culture, Frake finds that skin maladies, which are differentiated more elaborately than any other diseases, are involved in a wide variety of social situations, where they can influence bride-price calculations (because of concern over the attractiveness of the bride as well as the contagiousness of the disease), justification for failure to perform an expected task (in which case the disabling properties of the disease must be communicated), and behavior in competitive joking and maligning, in which skin-disease terms figure prominently (it is often essential to speak at just the level of generality that specifies what is pertinent and still leaves ambiguous other information that could be embarrassing).

The reactions of an ill person to his symptoms may express important cultural values of his society. Clark (1959) found that men in a Mexican-American community tend to be especially Spartan in responding to illness. "A man who admits to illness is not *macho* (tough and rugged). . . . Relatives and friends commend him for endurance and sometimes criticize him when he yields to an infirmity before it becomes acute." Although the relationship between responses to pain and cultural factors has been a relatively neglected subject in anthropology, work that has been done on it indicates that ethnic groups do vary in their reactions to pain, and the differences appear to reflect cultural contrasts (Wolff and Langley 1968). The work of Zborowski (1952, 1969) has been of special interest. In a well-known study (1952) he found that Jews, Italians, and "Old Americans" differed in their reactions to pain. Although medical personnel advised Zborowski that Jews and Italians were similar in their "exaggerated" emotional responses to pain, he found important differences in the responses of the two groups. The Italian patients studied called for relief from pain and were principally concerned with the analgesic effect of drugs given them; once the pain was relieved, they tended to forget it quickly. Jewish patients, on the other hand, were often reluctant to take drugs, were apprehensive that a drug might be habit-forming, felt that it only masked pain temporarily and did not remedy the condition that caused the pain, and often continued to show depressed behavior after the pain was gone because they were apprehensive that it might recur as long as the disease was not completely cured. In general, Zborowski found that the Italian patients were characterized by a present-oriented apprehension concerning the sensation of pain, while the Jewish patients tended to show a future-oriented anxiety with respect to the symptomatic and general meaning of the pain experience. The findings of a later study by Sternbach and Tursky (1965) were consistent with Zborowski's.

Etiology and Diagnosis of Disease

The etiology of disease is central to any discussion of the connection between medical phenomena and their cultural settings. To begin with, in most indigenous medical systems the primary consideration in the diagnosis of disease is its cause (Glick 1967; see also Adams 1953, Alland 1964). And causality in these systems usually is sought in the relationship between the victim of illness and his surroundings as this relationship is culturally interpreted. While traditional etiologies may attribute illness to mechanical and emotional as well as magical and religious causes (Polgar 1962), and, as I have mentioned previously, the great medical traditions of ancient civilizations underwent secularization, in general magic and religion play important parts in indigenous explanations of the occurrence of disease (Hughes 1968), and in many indigenous medical systems ideas about illness and religious beliefs are all but inseparable (Glick 1967). Numerous etiologies illustrate the significance of magic and religion in traditional medical systems. To take just a few examples, the Abron of the Ivory Coast attribute illness to some power, good or evil, that has acted against the victim (Alland 1964); indigenous etiologies of the Middle East attribute illness to personal behavior or the actions of someone or something possessed with power (Shiloh 1961); the Gimi of New Guinea attribute most illness to sorcerers or to malevolent little troll-like beings (Glick 1967). As Glick notes, in such settings the ethnographer who asks about the causes of illness "hears about competition, jealousy, greed and lust; witches, sorcerers and demons; mother's brothers and grandfathers recently deceased." Since etiology is so inextricable from its sociocultural context, explanations of the occurrences of illness are at the same time representations of the world as it is experienced and comprehended by members of the society.

Thus far, I have been discussing etiologies as emic phenomena; that is, as they are perceived by the members of a group who utilize them to explain why illnesses occur. But etiological interpretations linking the causes of illness to the culture of the group in which they occur may also be etic, made by observers who see connections between phenomena that are not necessarily perceived by anyone in the group studied. For example, Rubel (1964) has offered a hypothesis concerning the etiology of a syndrome frequently known as *susto*,[2] which occurs among Indians and non-Indians in Latin America and among Spanish-speaking peoples of the United States.

As this syndrome is described, victims lose their appetites, are listless, disinterested in dress and personal hygiene, weak, depressed, and introverted, and sleep restlessly. In the areas where the syndrome occurs, it is believed due to some loss or detachment of the soul, which in turn is attributed variously to capture by spirits or to fright. On the basis of an analysis of cases of individuals who contracted *susto*, Rubel postulates that this syndrome will appear as a consequence of a stressful situation in which an individual is unable to meet the role expectations of his own society. Taking Rubel's analysis as a point of departure, O'Nell and Selby (1968) studied differential susceptibility to *susto* among males and females in two Zapotec communities, in which women must conform to a tighter set of role expectations and have fewer ways of reducing anxiety over role performances

than men. In consonance with this pattern and Rubel's hypothesis, O'Nell and Selby found a markedly higher incidence of *susto* among women than among men.

This problem of the relationship between illness and role expectations is a central one in the following section, where social systems are viewed from a medical perspective.

MEDICAL ASPECTS OF SOCIAL SYSTEMS

ILLNESS AS SANCTION

The belief that illness is a punishment for wrongdoing is widespread in human society. Where it occurs, the social order is identified with the moral order of a universe in which health depends on virtue.

The attribution of illness to misconduct may have been a very early form of social control in the development of human society (Hallowell 1963), and in Paul's view perhaps the most important latent purpose of indigenous concepts of etiology and curing is to provide sanction and support for moral and social systems (Paul 1963). The idea of punitive sickness is, of course, no stranger to Western traditions; it has been a feature of Judeo-Christian beliefs concerning the consequences of sin (Polgar 1968, Crombie 1969). And today in many nonwestern societies illness is a major social sanction.

Where illness is a sanction, etiology is a stringent guide to social expectations. Hospitality, for example, is an important value in Ojibwa society, and this is underscored by the belief that failure to share generously with guests exposes the host to the threat of illness (Hallowell 1963). Among the Ganda of East Africa there is a belief that a disease called *obuko*, the symptoms of which are swelling of the cheeks, limbs, and

[2] In some areas the term *susto* may refer to other syndromes, and conversely other labels may be used for the syndrome here referred to as *susto* (Seijas 1969, Rubel 1970, O'Nell 1970).

genitals and body tremor, is caused by the violation of certain taboos (Bennett and Mugalulu-Mukiibi 1967). In this society, social proscriptions such as those forbidding parents-in-law to share prepared food with their children-in-law, or a boy to touch his female cousin, are linked to the etiology of disease. Among the Irigwe of Nigeria, men who preside over shrine houses have important authority and ritual obligations upon which Irigwe welfare depends. These obligations are also related to the etiology of disease, for it is believed that if the shrinekeepers do not fulfill their obligations, they will provoke the displeasure of ancestors and nature spirits and be subject to illness and untimely death (Sangree 1970). In this case, there are epidemiological data that can be related to etiology. Sangree was told of numerous men who had become shrinekeepers and died shortly afterward, supposedly because they had mishandled one or another ritual and had been killed by spirits. He also had access to an earlier medical survey of sleeping sickness that showed that its prevalence was highest among males in the southern part of the Irigwe territory, where Irigwe lineages that have the major ritual responsibilities are located. The survey report stated that this distribution of the disease was probably due to women's exclusion from sacred groves, which were the main areas of tsetse fly infestation, and in which a large number of southern Irigwe men were obliged to hold rituals. Given this combination of epidemiology and Irigwe etiology, the prevalence of disease would have the effect of showing how dangerously exacting the shrinekeeper's role is, and demonstrating the failings of men.

Since the belief in punitive sickness is a traditional sanction of traditional social roles, it is frequently a force for conservatism when societies are subject to pressures for change (Messing 1958, Lieban 1962a, Adams and Rubel 1967). And in situations where etiologies defend the existing social system, they also indicate where there are strains on the system under the impact of change. In Sibulan, a rural Philippine municipality as in other lowland areas of the Philippines, there is a belief in ingkantos, spirits that can appear in human form, both male and female (Lieban 1962a). People usually see ingkantos of the opposite sex in dreams or visions, and frequently describe them as handsome or beautiful, often Caucasian in appearance. Sexual motifs are frequently expressed in relationships with ingkantos, sometimes to the point of intercourse. Ingkantos are not only physically attractive; they also are rich and powerful, and they can offer a dazzling style of life to their protégés; but contact with them can be dangerous and lead to illness and death. In considering the social implications of this etiology, we begin with the fact that in rural communities such as Sibulan, most people are poor and live simply. But the poor of Sibulan are aware of people with standards of living substantially higher than their own: owners and managers of plantations; a small professional, official, and business class in a nearby city, where there is also a university that has Americans on its staff and attracts others as visitors. In addition to their awareness of these local contrasts with their own standards of living, the people of Sibulan have impressions of wealth from those among them who have traveled to Manila and other Philippine cities and from mass communications media, such as motion pictures, which are shown in the nearby city and by mobile units in the countryside, and newspapers and magazines, which circulate in limited quantity. In this setting, ingkantos—who are described by those who see them as dwelling in imposing houses or mansions, driving magnificent cars, wearing beautiful watches, and in general living luxuriously—appear to represent, *inter alia*, alluring wealth that is inaccessible to those in the rural *barrios* of Sibulan. Through fantasy people may interact with *ingkantos*, use their luxuries, and be promised wealth of their own. But these relationships are apt to be perilous and end in illness or death for the human beings involved.

Ingkantos appear to be a symbolic focus of ambivalence about tantalizing outside influences on the local community. They represent highly desirable and unsettling goals that could divert or weaken adherence to traditional roles in the community. At the same time, the etiology of illness attributed to *ingkantos* dramatizes the danger of these basically unattainable goals and thereby supports reconciliation to the customary limitations and realities of *barrio* life. (Beliefs in dangerous spirits that bear some similarity to *ingkantos* are found in other areas, such as Burma [Spiro 1967]; for a psychiatric interpretation of a patient's experience with such a spirit in Liberia, see Wintrob 1966.)

In discussing punitive sickness, it is well to point out that victim and transgressor need not be one and the same person. Thus Clark's (1959) study of a Mexican-American community describes how a husband who abuses his pregnant wife may be accused of subjecting his unborn child to *susto* by his actions. The individual who violates Ojibwa food taboos endangers not only his own health, but that of his family as well (Hallowell 1963). Among the Ixil of Guatemala, displeased ancestral spirits may cause illness, and Colby and van den Berghe (1969) describe how a young man's cramps were ascribed to the fact that his mother had had an argument with his grandmother ten or

more years earlier. Adams and Rubel (1967), discussing diagnosis in some Middle American Indian communities, report that if the patient himself has not been guilty of any social or ritual misdemeanor, the lives of his parents and even grandparents will be explored. An etiology of this kind, which states that others may suffer punishment for one's own transgressions, fosters the value of social interdependence. Beyond that, it widens the range of incidences of illness that are potentially attributable to proscribed conduct and thereby increases the applicability of this kind of sanction.

The notion that the actions of one individual may result in illness or death for another can function as a sanction on the behavior of both persons in societies that subscribe to belief in sorcery and witchcraft. Kluckhohn (1962) points out that in Navaho society, a troublemaker tends to be talked about as a probable witch. The fact that the individual who "acts mean" may be accused of being a witch acts as a deterrent to hostile acts, as does its corollary: an offended person may use witchcraft to avenge himself. Similarly. Hallowell (1963) has shown how aggression in Ojibwa society is constrained by the prospect of retaliation through sorcery.

Recourse to the risk of illness as a sanction seems to carry with it certain implications about the availability or effectiveness of other means of social control in a society. The problem may be looked at in relation to cross-cultural comparative studies of witchcraft and sorcery. In an analysis of the prevalence of witchcraft in primitive societies, Swanson (1960) sees the frequent use of witchcraft in a society as indicative of a serious lack of legitimate means of social control and moral bonds. He offers the hypothesis that witchcraft will be prevalent in situations where there are intimate but "un-legitimate" social relations, "situations in which people must interact closely with one another for the achievement of common ends" and "in which the relations among people were not developed with the consent, tacit or explicit, of all concerned; or in which persons with conflicting objectives cannot resolve their differences through commonly agreed upon means such as the courts or community councils." Swanson finds strong statistical confirmation of his hypothesis in a sample of forty-nine societies. Consistent with these findings are the results of a cross-cultural study of sorcery in societies with coordinate and superordinate social controls (B. Whiting 1950). Societies with coordinate controls lack special authorities to settle disputes or punish offenders, so that the primary means of social control is retaliation by peers; in societies with superordinate controls, certain individuals possess authority to settle disputes and enforce punishment. Whiting hypothesizes that sorcery as a means of retaliation will be more important in societies with coordinate rather than superordinate social controls, and her hypothesis is statistically confirmed in a comparison of fifty non-western societies.

These studies provide evidence that the relative prevalence of attributions of illness to magical attacks is an indicator of a society's capacity to avoid disputes and settle them when they arise through legitimate authority. Whiting approaches the problem structurally and provides important evidence that the development of political authority with jurisdiction over disputants is associated with a reduction in the importance of sorcery. But the existence of such institutionalized authority in itself does not necessarily obviate or mitigate reliance on sorcery as an explanation of illness. The effectiveness of the authori-

ty must also be considered. In rural lowland areas of the Philippines, for example, the majority of cases in which illness is ascribed to sorcery involve disputes over the ownership or use of land (Lieban 1960, 1967). As a nation-state, the Philippines has formal legal mechanisms—land titles, courts, and so on—through which it can exercise authority when land problems arise. But these mechanisms are often ignored, and even when they are not bypassed, they frequently are still ineffective and do not prevent or resolve numerous land disputes that can lead to the practice or accusation of sorcery. Marwick (1965) has described similar ways in which sorcery marks failings in the exercise of legitimated authority among the Cewa of East Africa.

When illness is interpreted as a sanction, medical diagnosis is frequently also a diagnosis of the relationship of patients with those believed to be responsible for attacks against them. And if restoration of health is believed to be contingent on removing the ultimate cause of the illness, medical therapy can consist of social repair. Adams and Rubel (1967) discuss "socio-ritual curers" in Middle American Indian societies and their concern with the social rectitude of the patient, whom they tend to see as the victim of his own misbehavior. The general pattern is epitomized in Vogt's (1969) description of Zinacantan curing ceremonies. In this Indian society of Chiapas, Mexico, most illnesses are attributed to witchcraft, which is a consequence of social disturbances, or to divine punishment for the patient's transgressions. The shaman who officiates at curing both expresses and influences social relations among the participants. In rural hamlets of this area, the curing ceremony apparently mediates and settles conflicts that occur in daily life. The convergence of medical therapy and the healing of social breaches is emphasized by Turner in his discussion of curing rituals in an East African society that sees illness as punishment for violation of moral or customary rules (1964: 262):

It seems that the Ndembu "doctor" sees his task less as curing an individual patient than as remedying the ills of a corporate group. The sickness of a patient is mainly a sign that "something is rotten" in the corporate body. The patient will not get better until all the tensions and aggressions in the group's interrelations have been brought to light and exposed to ritual treatment. . . . The sick individual, exposed to this process, is reintegrated into his group as, step by step, its members are reconciled with one another in emotionally charged circumstances.

In situations of this kind, the practitioner plays a key role in the influences of the medical system on social control. For if a medical case reveals that the risk of illness has not been an effective sanction in preventing or ameliorating social difficulties, the intervention of the healer to influence the outcome of the illness can still be a persuasive social sanction.

ILLNESS AS DEVIANCE

We have seen that when illness is considered a social sanction, its occurrence is a sign that someone has deviated from social norms. But illness can also be seen as a form of deviance in its own right.

The position that in certain respects illness may be viewed as a type of deviance subject to social control is especially associated with the work of Parsons (1951, 1953, 1958, 1964; Parsons and Fox 1952). He points out that a high incidence of illness is dysfunctional for a social system. Therefore, a society has a functional interest in exercising whatever controls it can to minimize illness. This would be true even if illness were in no sense an expression of motivated behavior. But in fact in various ways motivation is involved in the etiology of numerous illnesses and in receptivity to therapeutic influence. This fact increases the significance of illness for the social system, which requires its members to have the capacity and be motivated to perform social roles that may be necessary for the maintenance or development of the system. Although Parsons (1958) has tended to emphasize mental or psychosomatic illnesses as forms of deviance, he has also made it clear that his thesis is applicable to other illnesses as well: "As we have already emphasized, illness is very often motivational in origin. Even in those instances where the *etiology* of the disorder is primarily physiochemical, the nature and severity of symptoms and the rate of recuperation are almost invariably influenced by the attitudes of the patient."

Parsons has particularly directed his attention to the "sick role" in the United States, which he sees defined by the following characteristics: (1) The incapacity is interpreted as involuntary; the patient is not held responsible for his condition. (2) The incapacity is regarded as a legitimate basis for exempting the sick individual from normal role obligations. (3) This waiving of obligations is conditional; it depends on recognition by the sick person that to be ill is undesirable and that he has an obligation to try to get well. (4) The sick person and those responsible for his welfare have an obligation to seek competent assistance, principally the assistance of a physician.

Parsons' approach to illness as a form of deviance and to reactions of society to the sick person has been the subject of criticism that will be considered shortly. However, he provides a valuable theoretical framework for the analysis of facets of the relationship between illness and social control, and his thesis appears to be consonant with behavior that occurs in certain kinds of medical situations. For example, Schneider (1947) found that in basic army training, at the beginning of the training period those who developed disabilities that did not hospitalize them but did exempt them from normal duties were considered to be incapacitated through no fault of their own and were not resented or condemned. But if these individuals persisted in the sick role, they received less and less sympathy, and eventually were cut off from the rest of the group, which had made its adjustment to the demands of army life. In Schneider's view, the sick role supported a major goal of army culture by draining off deviants and allowing the group to become more homogeneous, while providing the individual soldier an opportunity to escape from a situation that was psychologically intolerable for him.

Parsons (1958) sees the complexity of life produced by the development of modern industrial society as making great demands on the capacity of the individual. As a consequence, "the motivation to retreat into ill health has been accentuated and with it the importance of effective mechanisms for coping with those who do retreat."

The favorable reception of Parsons' analysis of the sick role by western European writers indicates that it makes sense in terms of middle-class European experience (Freidson 1961-1962), and Fox (1968) points out that in at least one respect—the threat posed by dependence and the retreat from obligations and tasks—the concept of the sick role has particular pertinence for the Soviet Union, where maximum effort and productivity are expected at all times to meet the needs of collective industrial and agricultural development, as well as for the United States, with its emphasis

on values of responsibility, activity, achievement, and independence. The problem of malingering in the Soviet Union, the severe sanctions that have been enforced against it, and the strategic role of the Soviet physician in legitimating illnesses of persons absent from their jobs are instructive (Field 1957).

Yet although the sick role as conceptualized by Parsons is obviously a useful tool for analyzing medical aspects of social control in certain contexts, its applicability, as Parsons recognizes, is variable. This becomes apparent even if we concentrate on American society, which has been the focus of Parsons' analysis, and note the influence of class differences on responses to illness. For example, syndromes that are regarded as incapacitating and requiring medical treatment by upper- and middle-class families are less likely to be seen in this way by lower-class families, at least in the town in New York State studied by Koos (1954). In a Hawaiian community, men with lower incomes are reticent about their health; indications are that although they often believe they have serious health problems, they will not go to a physician for fear of losing their jobs if they are found to be ill, an apprehension that seems to be realistic (Heighton 1968). It is apparent that socioeconomic factors can have an important influence on readiness and opportunity to play the sick role as Parsons defines it. Freidson (1961-1962), who has emphasized the limitations of Parsons' thesis when the broad range of behavior surrounding illness is considered, finds it of little relevance to illnesses such as those not considered serious enough to warrant a significant reduction in activity; those considered incurable and adjusted to as such; those that do not lead the sick person to consult a physician; and those that occur among working-class, peasant, and nonwestern populations, among at least some of which being ill in a socially acceptable manner does not require professional legitimation or consultation.

ILLNESS AS AN INDICATOR OF SOCIAL SYSTEM PERFORMANCE

In a good part of our discussion so far we have seen how illness and responses to it can be related to the structure and maintenance of a social system, a system of interactions among the members of a society and a system that is linked to its environment. But medical phenomena also can be indicative of the performance of a social system.

The health of its population is one significant test of the effectiveness with which a society functions. Certain philosophers of the ancient world believed that physicians would not be in great demand in a society that was well governed, and Plato considered the need for many hospitals and doctors as a sign of a bad city (Dubos 1959). Soon after the Russian Revolution, when a typhus epidemic severely threatened people weakened by hunger and without soap and fuel, Lenin told the Seventh Congress of the Soviets, "Either the louse defeats socialism or socialism defeats the louse" (Field 1957). Contemporary approaches to the problem of social indicators in the United States, indexes of the state of American society, include health as one of the major areas of pertinent evidence (e.g., Bauer 1966; U.S. Department of Health, Education, and Welfare 1969).

The use of health as a gauge of a society's effectiveness in meeting the needs of its members confronts major conceptual problems. The World Health Organization (1946) defines health as "a state of complete physical, mental and social well-being and not merely the absence of disease or infirmity." The highly abstract criteria of this definition are difficult to operationalize. More specific, measurable criteria, such as life expectancy or morbidity, may be used to determine the state of health in a society. But this does not obviate complex questions of value. For, as Bates (1959) points out, health connotes an optimal state, and this may differ in accordance with one's goal. Is the goal length of life, maximum happiness, or maximum productivity? Beyond this there are cognitive problems, as similar mental or physical states can have dissimilar health significance for people of different groups or in different circumstances.

Given these difficulties, adequate utilization of health as a social indicator appears to be a complex, long-range objective. But steps in this direction are needed as part of a general effort to improve the means of evaluating the performance of social systems. Short of that, attention to the problem of such evaluation in its health dimensions can in itself provide a useful cross-cultural perspective for viewing "supernatural" and "natural" etiologies of illness. For when the prevalence of illness is attributed to the action of spirits, sorcerers, witches, or the manifestation of some other extraordinary power, this belief may be seen as a mystical interpretation of a society's shortcomings, the supernatural counterpart of natural interpretations that also perceive the prevalence of illness as reflective of deficiencies of the social system.

MEDICINE AND CULTURE CHANGE

Under the impact of modern technology, and the industrial societies dependent on it, profound cultural changes are taking place throughout the world. In the developing areas, modern health and medical practices have been among the most important changes introduced. Yet despite the increasing utilization of modern medicine in these areas, with consequent reduction in morbidity and mortality, traditional medical systems still persist and exert a significant influence on the state of health and on medical decisions and outcomes in developing societies.

The fact of the matter is that modern medicine generally has been established in these societies not so much by displacing indigenous medicine as by increasing the medical options available to their populations. Saunders (1958) observes that for Spanish-speaking people of the southwestern United States, adoption of modern medicine does not necessarily mean giving up old medical ways, and the observation could be extended to the peoples of many areas. To be sure, numerous individuals in developing societies, particularly those of a relatively high socioeconomic level and educational background, may utilize modern medicine more or less exclusively. But most of the population depends on indigenous medicine, either exclusively or in part.

In these pluralistic medical situations, one medical system may be influenced by the other. White medical beliefs have been incompletely assimilated into the medical system of the eastern Cherokees, and in some cases the older Cherokee beliefs and modern white disease theory show some fortuitous correspondence, providing reinforcement for Cherokee beliefs (Fogelson 1961). I have previously mentioned other examples of the influence of modern medicine on indigenous medical systems. It has been argued that modern medicine can more effectively serve populations in developing areas by utilizing certain of the resources of indigenous medical systems (e.g., Shiloh 1965, Kiev 1966). Yet for the most part both practitioners and the population at large dichotomize the medical situation in developing societies; competition between local healers and physicians is often intense, invidious distinctions abound, and differences that people perceive in the two kinds of medical systems can have a significant effect on the medical choices they make. Knowledge of the reasons for these choices not only has practical value for efforts to improve local, regional, and world health, but also can contribute to a general understanding of human behavior in relation to culture changes.

COGNITIVE INFLUENCES ON CHOICE OF MEDICAL TREATMENT

Definition of Disease

One cognitive approach to the problem of alternation between modern medicine and indigenous medicine has emphasized the importance of the type of disease as an influence on the choice made. Observers have pointed out that people in developing areas tend to distinguish the kinds of illnesses that can be cured by the physician from those that will respond only to the therapy of local healers (e.g., Erasmus 1952; Simmons 1955; Foster 1958, 1962; Goodenough 1963). Gould (1957) made a systematic analysis of the nature and effects of this kind of dichotomy in a community in northern India. There he discovered that modern medicine tended to be utilized for critical incapacitating dysfunctions (such as pneumonia, typhoid fever, and very severe hernia), while patients were inclined to go to indigenous healers for treatment of chronic nonincapacitating dysfunctions (such as enlarged liver, asthma, and rheumatism). Leslie (1967) found evidence in India corroborating the kind of distinction found by Gould in the village he studied. In a later paper based on subsequent research in this community, Gould (1965) modified some of his original conclusions. For one thing, he noted that since people make different etiological interpretations of the same disease, and since the disease may vary in its manifestations, it is not possible to give a name to a malady and on that basis assign it a single place in a precise classification scheme along the lines he first proposed. He also found that he had originally underestimated the influence of personal relationships on medical choices made by the people of the community.

There is ample evidence that people who utilize both modern and indigenous medical systems tend to place illnesses in two broad categories: those more likely to be cured by a physician and those more likely to respond to the ministrations of a healer. But considerable allowance must be made for flexibility in such perceptions. The course of an illness, the outcome of previous treatment for the same condition, and a variety of other factors may cause the patient to redefine it and shift from one medical system to the other (Lieban 1967). While it is true that modern and indigenous disease names are guides to the sort of practitioner a patient will consult, a label is not necessarily fixed for the duration of an illness. The patient may begin to doubt that he really has whatever it was he thought he had, and the label of the illness may be changed if the practitioner is changed. Thus Erasmus (1952) observes that in poorer districts of Quito, Ecuador, people have more confidence in a physician's treatment of illnesses with modern names, but they do not always classify their symptoms according to those names until a physician is consulted at an advanced stage of the illness.

Gratifications of Treatment

Another cognitive approach to the utilization of modern and indigenous medicine emphasizes the contrastive but complementary gratifications the two types of systems may offer to patients. Gonzalez (1966) distinguishes two categories of healing techniques: medicines and practices. She defines medicine as "any substance applied to or introduced into the body, which is believed by some specialist and/or the sick person to change the existing state of the body in the direction of better health," while a medical practice is "any act undertaken by either the sick one or someone else, which may or may not directly involve the body, but which is believed to have an effect on the health." In Gonzalez' view, people in developing or nonwestern areas have utilized modern therapy primarily for the effectiveness of its medicines, which are widely recognized as superior to indigenous medicines. But such Western therapeutic practices as rest, exercise, exposure to fresh air or a change of climate, and reduced smoking or drinking seem either inappropriate or unconvincing to people in these areas. At the same time, Gonzalez points out that indigenous medical practices, in which ritual usually plays a key role, still have considerable popular appeal. Gonzalez (1966) finds that in the Guatemalan groups she has studied, people very often seek help for the same illness from both the indigenous curer and the physician.

It is not so much a question of either/or, as it is *what* shall be sought from each specialist. I strongly believe that the power of scientific medicine in relieving symptoms is what is sought from the doctor, while the practices suggested by the curer for relieving the basic cause of the disease, plus the hope he gives the patient, lead the ill to him.

Gonzalez' thesis, based on her Guatemalan data, receives substantiation from findings made in other areas (e.g., Maclean 1966). In light of her definitions of "medicine" and "practices," her view that people are drawn to physicians for medicine and to curers for their practices does not accommodate cases that are brought to physicians for physicomechanical procedures such as surgery or obstetrics. Nor does it account for the positive value that physicians' acts, as such, can assume for their patients. I particulary have in mind here injection, which has been given something approaching a ritualistic significance by people in many areas. They expect it as part of therapy, and may even lose confidence in the practitioner if they do not receive it (Foster 1958, Alland 1964; for a discussion of the importance of injection in medical treatment in rural Thailand and the role there of unlicensed, private "injection doctors," see Cunningham 1970). However, Gonzalez' point about the importance of ritual in the persistence of indigenous medicine appears to be well taken, and her ideas are consistent with the widespread observation that people will utilize modern medicine on the basis of its demonstrated successes while still retaining their traditional beliefs about disease causality (Simmons 1955; Erasmus 1952, 1961; Newell 1957; Foster 1958). With its emphasis on the complementary services that modern medicine and indigenous medicine offer patients, Gonzalez' thesis is more applicable to cases of illness that are taken to both kinds of practitioners than to cases of illness that are treated throughout their duration exclusively by physicians or by healers.

The Influence of Tradition

As I have mentioned before, the prevalence of indigenous medical beliefs has not prevented the utilization of modern medicine where its effectiveness has been shown. This fact has been particularly accentuated by Erasmus (1961) as part of his theory of culture change, including its medical facets.

Erasmus has stressed that traditions are not blinders that keep individuals from seeing advantages in changing their behavior, and he has been highly critical of the weight that some writers 'have given to prior cultural conditioning as an impediment to modernization. In his words, ". . . even uneducated and illiterate people are not simple tradition-bound puppets of their culture. Given adequate opportunity to measure the advantages of a new alternative, they act to maximize their expectations."

Erasmus extends this view to culture change as a whole, but an important part of his argument is based on medical phenomena, such as the large numbers of people who voluntarily sought treatment at injection centers in Colombia and Ecuador following the spectacular initial success of public health programs to eradicate yaws by treating victims with penicillin injections, and the ability of a new charity maternity hospital in Ecuador to establish a substantial clientele among lower-class mothers in a very short time, despite minimal concessions by the hospital to indigenous beliefs about childbirth, because of the clear evidence that women had a better chance to survive childbirth in the hospital than they did at home following traditional practices (see also Maclean 1966).

Positions similar to Erasmus' have been maintained by public health personnel. Roemer (1954) states that some anthropologists tend to exaggerate the grip of tradition and to underestimate the receptivity of people to change in their medical behavior if they experience new measures that help them.

There is no doubt that perceptible accomplishments of modern medicine have won it an increasing following in the face of entrenched traditions. This is shown not only in sudden acceptances of modern medicine on the basis of dramatic demonstrations of positive results (as in the case of penicillin treatment of yaws), but also in phased growth of reliance on modern therapy as a response to manifest increases in its competence. Thus, when bed rest and custodial treatment were all that modern medicine had to offer the tuberculosis patient, the Navaho regarded these practices and the techniques of Navaho medicine men as alternative therapies for the disease. More recently, as a consequence of therapeutic developments in modern medicine and Navaho experiences with them, they have accepted chemotherapy and surgery as the proper means of curing tuberculosis (Adair 1963).

But while demonstrated therapeutic advantages of modern medicine have gained it widespread and growing adherence in developing areas, it is also true that the personal experiences of many people prevent them from perceiving these advantages, and in these circumstances, their traditions may dominate what they see and do. Although Erasmus (1961) emphasizes people's readiness to discard their old customs for new ones if they can readily perceive the benefit of doing so, he also points out that when cognitive situations are not conducive to such perceptions, it is not surprising that people continue their traditional activities, or add new practices while still retaining their old ones. This has perhaps particular relevance for medical situations, in which appearances can so frequently be deceptive, and Foster (1958) notes that convincing demonstration is relatively more difficult in health programs than in other forms of technical aid. Perception of medical realities can be obfuscated by a number of factors in situations where modern medicine is effective and/or indigenous medicine is not.

1. Most illnesses eventually end in spontaneous recovery (Beck 1961). When this occurs and the patients have been treated by local healers, confidence in indigenous medicine may be bolstered by cures with which it is only fortuitously connected. (For a specific example, see Kiev 1966.)

2. When therapy for an illness is sought from both a physician and a healer, the physician may cure the patient and the healer get the credit. (Again, see Kiev 1966.)

3. Purposes as well as results of modern medicine may be misperceived. Measures that the physician may take to diagnose an illness are often thought to be the treatment; the patient may believe he should expect to see results as soon as a blood sample has been taken (Lebeuf 1955).

When the advantages of modern medicine are not convincingly apparent, traditional medical beliefs provide a ready frame of reference. These beliefs are linked to other ideas and patterns of behavior (Firth 1959). They are particularly interwoven with magic, religion, and traditional social values, and they serve multiple cognitive functions (Hughes 1968). They can also focus multiple cognitive sources of resistance to change in medical behavior. This is graphically illustrated by an incident described by Cassel (1955) involving a doctor at a health center in South Africa and a part-time Bantu healer. Pulmonary tuberculosis was prevalent in the area when the health center was opened in 1940, but local people were very resistant to modern medical therapy for the disease, attributing it to malign magic, and they were particularly fearful of hospitalization. The daughter of the healer had contracted the disease after marriage, and she returned to her parents' home. In subsequent years eight members of that household became afflicted. Eventually the healer agreed to consult with the center doctor about the medical crisis in his household, and after prolonged discussion the doctor finally persuaded him that the patients in the family should be hospitalized. Then, during further discussion of the course of the disease in the family, the physician explained that the daughter must have introduced it when she returned home. At that the healer became completely uncooperative and withdrew his permission for hospitalization. When the physician had suggested that the daughter had started the disease in the family, he unwittingly had as much as accused her of sorcery or witchcraft, for it was the indigenous belief that the disease was caused by malign magic. Only after the physician completely withdrew his earlier identification of the daughter as the source of the disease did the healer again grant permission for hospitalization.

OTHER INFLUENCES ON
MEDICAL BEHAVIOR

Fatalistic Attitudes Toward Illness

Medical efforts may be impeded if an individual believes that the outcome of his illness is inevitable, unalterable by any human action (Foster 1958, Erasmus 1961). However, a distinction should be made here between passive reactions to morbid signs that the sick person does not regard as marks of illness (Read 1966) and reactions to symptoms that are perceived as manifestations of illness but are believed to be beyond human ability to affect. In addition, in some cases fatalistic views may be only *post factum* explanations of the outcomes of illnesses; they may not necessarily persuade the sick person that remedial action would be futile while the illness is in progress (Lieban 1966).

Symbolic Significance of Medical Phenomena

People may respond to medical systems on the basis of what they represent as well as what they do. Different associations may be contradictory in their effects. On the one hand, utilization of modern medicine is often regarded as enlightened or sophisticated behavior, and this fact can be an inducement when social status is a consideration (Foster 1958, 1962; Lieban 1967). On the other hand, when ethnic pride comes into play, traditional medical beliefs and practices can be valued as distinctive resources of the group (Halpern 1963). "Loyalty" may even be shown to certain illnesses considered beyond the competence of modern medicine (Schwartz 1969). In contemporary China and India, considerable intellectual and political support has been given indigenous medical systems, not only because of their therapeutic accomplishments, but also as manifestations of cultural creativity and the national identity of these countries (Crozier 1968; Leslie 1967, 1969b).

Therapeutic Styles

The manner of therapy as well as its substance may influence people's choice of practitioners. Marriott (1955a) found that in a rural community of northern India, Western medical practice was handicapped by the villagers' perceptions of such things as its emphasis on privacy and individual responsibility, its utilization of written prescriptions, and the democratic nature of its expectation of interpersonal trust—all features incongruent with village experience and attitudes. Marriott argues that a distinction must be made between "Western" and "scientific" medicine, and that medical practices could be divested of many Western cultural accretions to make them more compatible with the local scene without impairing their technical effectiveness.

An interesting example of a way in which the form of modern medicine might literally be adapted to local expectations with an increase in effectiveness and no loss of technical efficiency is provided by Buchler (1964). He discovered that people of Grand Cayman in the West Indies have been conditioned by their traditions to expect the administering of liquids when they become ill, and he suggests that when the physician in that area thinks of prescribing pills, he would be well advised to consider whether there is a liquid that might achieve approximately the same effect.

There is ample evidence to show that certain Western medical procedures are not necessarily based on logico-empirical considerations, or may contravene them (e.g., Roth 1956, 1957). Sorting out what is intrinsically therapeutic from what is not and distinguishing features that can be variably modified to make medicine more responsive to views, wants, and needs of patients is a problem in both basic and applied science. Attention to this problem can help balance the tendency of some public health scientists to emphasize consumers rather than providers of health services (see Hochstrasser and Tapp 1970).

Social Factors

The importance of knowledge of social organization to effective intercultural health programs has been stressed by British social anthropologists (Firth 1957; Freedman 1956, 1957). Freedman (1956) notes that for the health worker this means both "a clear picture of the structure of the community in which he has to carry out his duties and the study of health workers and institutions in relation to the public they set out to serve."

The effects on medical behavior of social relationships within groups being served by health and medical programs are found in such factors as patterns of power and authority, which permit those in dominant positions to facilitate or impede acceptance of medical changes by others (Freedman 1956, Lewis 1955, Foster 1958); class and caste differences, which affect access to and utilization of health and medical facilities (Simmons 1958, Foster 1958, Erasmus 1961, Lieban 1967); factionalism, which can have a differentiating effect on responses of antagonists to health and medical programs (Foster 1958); and family, kinship, and other solidary social factors, which in themselves can influence or link people in medical decisions: for example, Kunstadter (1960) found that the stronger the bond of solidarity between Mescalero Apache parents and their children (twenty years and older), the greater the likelihood of similarity in their use of the Public Health Service clinic. Weaver (1970) describes a general pattern among Spanish-Americans of the southwestern United States: when illness occurs, members of the nuclear family of the afflicted individual are the first to perceive and validate the situation; after that, if the symptoms are severe and/or persistent, the family turns for consultation and minor medication first to the kin group, then to neighbors and important persons of the community, and only after that to an indigenous healer or scientifically trained practitioner.

Much of the literature on social relationships between medical personnel and the groups they serve has emphasized the effects of the social distance that separates modern medical professionals from patients of lower status, both in developing and in industrial societies (Simmons 1958, Foster 1958). Simmons states that mutual trust, respect, and cooperation vary inversely with the social distance between practitioner and patient, and various observers find that difficulties of rapport between the two can hamper utilization of modern medicine (Polson and Pal 1956, Freedman 1956, Clark 1959, R. J. Wolff 1965). Yet professional behavior that may be regarded as intimidating or supercilious and may disaffect patients in some cultural settings can be the expected and approved model in others. Marriott (1955a) reports that when a Western doctor in an Indian village tried to ignore status differences between his patients and himself, and adopted a friendly, equalitarian bedside manner, his patients regarded his behavior as threatening rather than reassuring, because it denied them the subordinate relationship in which they felt secure when interacting with persons of authority. Furthermore, the physician's inquiries about the patients' problems undermined faith in his competence, since the villagers expected to be told what their trouble was; all their experience with indigenous healers had taught them that practitioners are supposed to know what is wrong without asking questions. Comparable expectations regarding the behavior of practitioners are reported to be characteristic of most villagers in Greek communities studied by Blum and Blum (1965).

It seems apparent that in social situations in which deference to authority is stressed, maintenance of social distance may enhance rather than diminish confidence in the practitioner.

Socioeconomic and Technical Factors

In developing societies, as in our own, the state of health is pervasively affected by social inequalities and associated privations. The impact of socioeconomic conditions on nutrition and health of underprivileged peoples in Latin America has been emphasized by Bonfil Batalla (1966) in a critique of applied anthropology. He criticizes what he calls the "psychological em-

phasis" in applied anthropology's concentration on such subjects as ideas and beliefs about health and illness and communication problems due to differences in cultural traditions, with relative neglect of basic causes of public health and malnutrition problems. He states that it is such factors as basic social structure and inadequate technology that underlie health problems in Latin American societies, and that improvement of life conditions depends on their alteration rather than concern with local ideas about health, welfare, and the causes and treatment of illness, which he regards as psychological manifestations of a problem rather than its causes.

Bonfil Batalla's argument is, of course, pertinent to areas other than Latin America, and there is no gainsaying the fundamental importance of the factors he cites. The risk of disease is greater for the poor than for others, and generally good medical care is less accessible to them (Kosa, Antonovsky, and Zola, eds., 1969). Even when they receive effective therapy, their living conditions combined with their limited medical knowledge may defeat the purposes of treatment. Parasitosis, for example, is endemic in the slums of Bogotá, Colombia; according to an outpatient physician, the poor take their medicine with polluted water and pathology persists (Press 1969).

But while poverty is the matrix of many serious health problems, and general improvement in health in developing countries is basically contingent on improvement in the living standard of the majority of the population, in several respects the other factors we have been discussing also play very important roles in both the current and the future health status of these societies. In the first place, improved health and medical practices do exist and do reach the poor. Such efforts are relatively limited in their range and effectiveness under present social and economic conditions, but they have significantly reduced morbidity and mortality in many areas. Therefore, factors that induce people to utilize the facilities, personnel, and practices of modern medicine now available can and do reduce suffering and save lives. Second, increased understanding of medical realities can motivate as well as result from social change. Growing awareness by the poor of the health implications of their standard of living, and of the advantages of expanding the availability of modern medicine, can increase pressures for social change that would make improvement possible. Taylor and Hall (1967) point out that successful health programs are inclined to produce recognition that change is possible, and improvements in health and other social and economic changes tend to be synergistic. The point is that health can be an aspiration of people, as well as a consequence of social process. Increased awareness of ways to improve it can contribute constructively to social action.

Complexities of Technological Development

We have been concerned here with what is essentially a distributional problem: factors that facilitate or impede utilization of modern medicine. In developing societies the benefits of such utilization are fairly clear-cut: lowered morbidity and mortality rates among groups with substandard health. But in areas where modern medicine is most highly developed, it has become apparent that new technical achievements in medical science make the relationship between the utilization of modern medicine and the welfare of human populations increasingly complex.

This complexity is clearly seen in problems with which physicians increasingly must deal: weighing the prolongation of the life of the aged and ailing or the hopelessly injured against the hardships this may entail for the patient and others (Dubos 1965, Solomon 1969); deciding who among those needing it to stay alive will receive therapy such as renal dialysis when funds, the number of machines, and staff to operate them are limited (Hubble 1969); deciding precisely when death has occurred for potential transplant donors—a situation in which timing is crucial (Solomon 1969).

Dubos (1965:427) finds modern medicine facing a paradox unprecedented in history:

On the one hand, science can eventually solve the technical aspects of almost any medical problem. On the other hand, the application of medical knowledge to the prevention and treatment of disease will be necessarily limited by economic and other social factors. Choices have to be made among all the possibilities for medical care and disease prevention, but there is no agreement as to the social or ethical bases on which to make choices.

And the situation promises to become even more complicated in the years to come. Prospective developments in curative and preventive medicine through "genetic engineering" presage not only dramatic new medical achievements but also new questions concerning society's response to increasing opportunity for human control of biological processes (Lederberg 1970). It is apparent that medicine, in its social, cultural, and biological dimensions, will continue to share in the central problem of our age: how to use our rapidly expanding knowledge wisely and humanely.

REFERENCES

Abegglen, James G.
1958 *The Japanese Factory*. Glencoe, Ill.: Free Press.

Ackerknecht, Erwin H.
1942 Problems of Primitive Medicine. *Bulletin of the History of Medicine* 11:503-21.
1945 On the Collecting of Data Concerning Primitive Medicine. *American Anthropologist* 47:427-32.
1946 Natural Diseases and Rational Treatment in Primitive Medicine. *Bulletin of the History of Medicine* 19:467-97.
1947 Primitive Surgery. *American Anthropologist* 49:25-45.

Adair, John
1963 Physicians, Medicine Men, and Their Navaho Patients. In *Man's Image in Medicine and Anthropology*, ed. I. Galdston, pp. 237-57. New York: International Universities Press.

Adams, Richard N.
1953 *An Analysis of Medical Beliefs and Practices in a Guatemalan Indian Town*. Guatemala City: Pan American Sanitary Bureau.

Adams, Richard N., and Arthur J. Rubel
1967 Sickness and Social Relations. *Handbook of Middle American Indians* 6:333-56. Austin: University of Texas Press.

Alland, Alexander, Jr.
1964 Native Therapists and Western Medical Practitioners Among the Abron of the Ivory Coast. *Transactions of the New York Academy of Sciences* 26:714-25.
1966 Medical Anthropology and the Study of Biological and Cultural Adaptation. *American Anthropologist* 68:40-51.
1967 *Evolution and Behavior*. Garden City, N.Y.: Natural History Press.
1969 Ecology and Adaptation to Parasitic Diseases. In *Environment and Cultural Behavior*, ed. A. P. Vayda, pp. 80-89. Garden City, N.Y.: Natural History Press.
1970 *Adaptation in Cultural Evolution: An Approach to Medical Anthropology*. New York: Columbia University Press.

Anderson, Odin W.
1958 Infant Mortality and Social and Cultural Factors. In *Patients, Physicians, and Illness*, ed. E. G. Jaco. Glencoe, Ill.: Free Press.

Armelagos, George J.
1967 Man's Changing Environment. In *Infectious Diseases: Their Evolution and Eradication*, ed. A. Cockburn, pp. 66-83. Springfield, Ill.: Charles C. Thomas.

Bates, Marston
1953 Human Ecology. In *Anthropology Today*, ed. A. L. Kroeber, pp. 700-713. Chicago: University of Chicago Press.
1959 The Ecology of Health. In *Medicine and Anthropology*, ed. I. Galdston, pp. 56-77. New York: International Universities Press.

Bauer, Raymond A., ed.
1966 *Social Indicators*. Cambridge: M.I.T. Press.

Beck, William S.
1961 *Modern Science and the Nature of Life*. London: Penguin Books.

Bennett, F. J., and A. Mugalulu-Mukiibi
1967 An Analysis of People Living Alone in a Rural Community in East Africa. *Social Science and Medicine* 1:97-115.

Blum, Richard H., and Eva Blum
1965 *Health and Healing in Rural Greece*. Stanford: Stanford University Press.

Bonfil Batalla, Guillermo
1966 Conservative Thought in Applied Anthropology: A Critique. *Human Organization* 25:89-92.

Bowers, John Z.
1965 *Medical Education in Japan*. New York: Harper & Row.

Buchler, I. R.
1964 Caymanian Folk Medicine: A Problem in Applied Anthropology. *Human Organization* 23:48-49.

Cannon, Walter B.
1942 Voodoo Death. *American Anthropologist* 44:169-81

Cassel, John
1955 A Comprehensive Health Program Among South African Zulus. In *Health, Culture, and Community*, ed. B. D. Paul, pp. 15-42. New York: Russell Sage Foundation.

Cassel, John, R. Patrick, and D. Jenkins
1960 Epidemiological Analysis of the Health Implications of Culture Change: A Conceptual Model. *Annals of the New York Academy of Sciences* 84, no. 17:938-49.

Caudill, William
1953 Applied Anthropology in Medicine. In *Anthropology Today*, ed. A. L. Kroeber, pp. 771-806. Chicago: University of Chicago Press.

Clark, Margaret
1959 *Health in the Mexican-American Culture*. Berkeley: University of California Press.

Clements, Forrest E.
1932 Primitive Concepts of Disease. *University of California Publications in American Archaeology and Ethnology* 32:185-252.

Colby, Benjamin N., and Pierre L. van den Berghe
1969 *Ixil Country: A Plural Society in Highland Guatemala*. Berkeley: University of California Press.

Colson, Anthony C.
1969 The Prevention of Illness in a Malay Village: An Analysis of Concepts and Behavior. Ph. D. dissertation, Stanford University.

Croizier, Ralph
1968 *Traditional Medicine in Modern China*. Cambridge: Harvard University Press.

Crombie, Aliston
1969 Discussion. In *Medicine and Culture*, ed. F. N. L. Poynter. London: Wellcome Institute of the History of Medicine.

Cunningham, Clark E.
1970 Thai "Injection Doctors": Antibiotic Mediators. *Social Science and Medicine* 4:1-24.

Dore, Ronald P.
1958 *City Life in Japan*. Berkeley: University of California Press.

Dubos, René
1959 *Mirage of Health*. New York: Harper & Row.
1965 *Man Adapting*. New Haven: Yale University Press.

Dunn, Frederick L.
1968 Epidemiological Factors: Health and Disease in Hunter-Gatherers. In *Man the Hunter*, ed. R. B. Lee and I. De Vore, pp. 221-28. Chicago: Aldine.

Erasmus, Charles J.
1952 Changing Folk Beliefs and the Relativity of Empirical Knowledge. *Southwestern Journal of Anthropology* 8:411-28.

1961 *Man Takes Control*. Minneapolis: University of Minnesota Press.

Evans-Pritchard, E. E.
1937 *Witchcraft, Oracles, and Magic Among the Azande*. Oxford: Clarendon Press.

Fabrega, Horacio, Jr.
1972 Medical Anthropology. In *Biennial Review of Anthropology, 1971*, ed. B. J. Siegel, pp. 167-229. Stanford: University Press.

Field, Mark G.
1957 *Doctor and Patient in Soviet Russia*. Cambridge: Harvard University Press.

Firth, Raymond
1957 Health Planning and Community Organization. *Health Education Journal* 15:118-25.
1959 Acculturation in Relation to Concepts of Health and Disease. In *Medicine and Anthropology*, ed. I. Galdston, pp. 129-65. New York: International Universities Press.

Fogelson, Raymond D.
1961 Change, Persistence, and Accommodation in Cherokee Medico-Magical Beliefs. In Symposium on Cherokee and Iroquois Culture, ed. W. N. Fenton and J. Gulick. *Bureau of American Ethnology Bulletin* 180:215-25.

Foster, George M.
1953 Relationships Between Spanish and Spanish-American Folk Medicine. *Journal of American Folklore* 66: 201-17.
1958 *Problems in Intercultural Health Practice*. Pamphlet no. 12. New York: Social Science Research Council.
1962 *Traditional Cultures and the Impact of Technological Change*. New York: Harper & Row.
1967 *Tzintzuntzan: Mexican Peasants in a Changing World*. Boston: Little, Brown.

Fox, Renée
1968 Illness. *International Encyclopedia of the Social Sciences* 7:90-96. New York: Free Press, Macmillan.

Frake, Charles O.
1961 The Diagnosis of Disease Among the Subanun of Mindanao. *American Anthropologist* 63:113-32.

Francis, Thomas, Jr.
1959 The Epidemiological Approach to

Human Ecology. *The American Journal of the Medical Sciences* 237: 677-84.

Freedman, Maurice
1956 Health Education: How It Strikes an Anthropologist. *Health Education Journal* 14:18-24.
1957 Health Education and Self-Education. *Health Education Journal* 15: 78-83.

Freidson, Eliot
1961- The Sociology of Medicine. *Current*
1962 *Sociology* 10-11:123-92.

Friedman, M., and R. H. Roseman
1959 Association of Specific Overt Behavior Pattern with Blood and Cardiovascular Findings. *Journal of the American Medical Association* 169: 1286-96.

Friedman, M., R. H. Roseman, and V. Carroll
1958 Changes in the Serum Cholesterol and Blood Clotting Time in Men Subjected to Cyclic Variation of Occupational Stress. *Circulation* 17:852-61.

Galdston, Iago
1959 Introduction. In *Medicine and Anthropology*, ed. I. Galdston, pp. 7-10. New York: International Universities Press.
1963 Retrospect and Prospect. In *Man's Image in Medicine and Anthropology*, ed. I. Galdston, pp. 521-25. New York: International Universities Press.

Geertz, Clifford
1963 *Peddlers and Princes*. Chicago: University of Chicago Press.

Gillin, John
1948 Magical Fright. *Psychiatry* 11:387-400.

Glick, Leonard B.
1967 Medicine as an Ethnographic Category: The Gimi of the New Guinea Highlands. *Ethnology* 6:31-56.

Gonzalez, Nancie Solien
1966 Health Behavior in Cross-Cultural Perspective: A Guatemalan Example. *Human Organization* 25:122-25.

Goodenough, Ward H.
1963 *Cooperation in Change*. New York: Russell Sage Foundation.

Gordon, John E.
1958 Medical Ecology and the Public Health. *American Journal of the Medical Sciences* 235:337-59.

Gould, Harold A.
1957 The Implications of Technologic: Change for Folk and Scientific Med cine. *American Anthropologist* 59 507-16.
1965 Modérn Medicine and Folk Cognitio: in Rural India. *Human Organizatio* 24:201-208.

Graham, Saxon
1963 Social Factors in Relation to th Chronic Illnesses. In *Handbook o Medical Sociology*, ed. H. E. Free man, S. Levine, and L. G. Reeder pp. 65-98. Englewood Cliffs, N.J. Prentice-Hall.

Gregg, Alan
1956 The Future Health Officer's Respon sibility: Past, Present, and Future *American Journal of Public Health* 46:1384-89.

Hallowell, A. Irving
1963 Ojibwa World View and Disease. I *Man's Image in Medicine and Anthro pology*, ed. I. Galdston, pp. 258-315 New York: International Universitie Press.

Halpern, Joel M.
1963 Traditional Medicine and the Role o the Phi in Laos. *Eastern Anthropolo gist* 16:191-200.

Hart, Donn V.
1969 *Bisayan Filipino and Malayan Hu moral Pathologies: Folk Medicin and Ethnohistory in Southeast Asia* Southeast Asia Program, data pape no. 76. Ithaca: Department of Asiar Studies, Cornell University.

Heighton, Robert H., Jr.
1968 Physical and Dental Health. Ir *Studies in a Hawaiian Community. Na Makamaka O Nanakuli*, ed R. Gallimore and A. Howard, pp. 118-37. Honolulu: Bernice P. Bishop Museum.

Hochstrasser, Donald L., and Jesse W. Tapp, Jr.
1970 Social Anthropology and Public Health. In *Anthropology and the Behavioral and Health Sciences*, ed. O. von Mering and L. Kasden. pp. 242-71. Pittsburgh: University of Pittsburgh Press.

Huard, Pierre
1969 Western Medicine and Afro-Asian Ethnic Medicine. In *Medicine and Culture*, ed. F. N. L. Poynter, pp. 211-37. London: Wellcome Institute of the History of Medicine.

Huard, Pierre, and Ming Wong
1968 *Chinese Medicine*. New York: McGraw-Hill.

Hubble, Douglas
1969 Discussion. In *Medicine and Culture*, ed. F. N. L. Poynter, pp. 154-77. London: Wellcome Institute of the History of Medicine.

Hughes, Charles C.
1963 Public Health in Non-Literate Societies. In *Man's Image in Medicine and Anthropology*, ed. I. Galdston, pp. 157-233. New York: International Universities Press.
1968 Ethnomedicine. *International Encyclopedia of the Social Sciences* 10:87-92. New York: Free Press, Macmillan.

Hughes, Charles C., and John M. Hunter
1970 Disease and "Development" in Africa. *Social Science and Medicine* 3: 443-93.

Ingham, John M.
1970 On Mexican Folk Medicine. *American Anthropologist* 72:76-87.

Jaco, E. Gartly
1958 Introductory: Medicine and Behavioral Science. In *Patients, Physicians, and Illness*, ed. E. G. Jaco, pp. 3-8. Glencoe, Ill.: Free Press.

Jahoda, G.
1961 Traditional Healers and Other Institutions Concerned with Mental Health in Ghana. *International Journal of Social Psychiatry* 7:245-68.

Jelliffe, D. B.
1956 Cultural Variation and the Practical Pediatrician. *Journal of Pediatrics* 49:661-71.

Kendall, Patricia L.
1963 Medical Sociology in the United States. *Social Science Information* 2:1-15.

Kiev, Ari
1964 The Study of Folk Psychiatry. In *Magic, Faith, and Healing*, ed. A. Kiev, pp. 3-35. New York: Free Press, Macmillan.

1966 Obstacles to Medical Progress in Haiti. *Human Organization* 25:10-15.

King, Stanley H.
1963 Social Psychological Factors in Illness. In *Handbook of Medical Sociology*, ed. H. E. Freeman, S. Levine, and L. G. Reeder, pp. 99-121. Englewood Cliffs, N.J.: Prentice-Hall.

Kluckhohn, Clyde
1962 *Navaho Witchcraft*. Boston: Beacon Press. Originally published 1944.

Koos, Earl L.
1954 *The Health of Regionville*. New York: Columbia University Press.

Kosa, John, Aaron Antonovsky, and Irving K. Zola, eds.
1969 *Poverty and Health: A Sociological Analysis*. Cambridge: Harvard University Press.

Kunstadter, Peter
1960 Culture Change, Social Structure, and the Use of Medical Care by the Residents of the Mescalero Apache Reservation. Paper presented at annual meeting of the American Anthropological Association, Minneapolis.
1969 Fertility, Mortality, and Migration of Hill and Valley Populations in Northwestern Thailand. Paper presented at annual meeting of the American Anthropological Association, New Orleans.

Laughlin, William S.
1963 Primitive Theory of Medicine: Empirical Knowledge. In *Man's Image in Medicine and Anthropology*, ed. I. Galdston, pp. 116-40. New York: International Universities Press.

Lebeuf, J. P.
1955 Sociology as the Basis of Health Education. *Health Education Journal* 13:232-36.

Lederberg, Joshua
1970 Government Is Most Dangerous of Genetic Engineers. *Washington Post*, July 19.

Leslie, Charles
1967 Professional and Popular Health Cultures in South Asia: Needed Research in Medical Sociology and Anthropology. In *Understanding Science and Technology in India and Pakistan*, ed. W. Morehouse, pp.

27-42. N.p.: University of the State of New York.

1969a Modern India's Ancient Medicine. *Trans-action* 6, no. 8:46-55.

1969b Traditionalism and Modernization in Asian Health Cultures. Paper presented at annual meeting of the American Anthropological Association, New Orleans.

Lester, David
1972 Voodoo Death: Some New Thoughts on an Old Phenomenon. *American Anthropologist* 74:386-90.

Lewis, Oscar
1955 Medicine and Politics in a Mexican Village. In *Health, Culture, and Community*, ed. B. D. Paul, pp. 403-34. New York: Russell Sage Foundation.

Lieban, Richard W.
1960 Sorcery, Illness, and Social Control in a Philippine Municipality. *Southwestern Journal of Anthropology* 16:127-43.

1962a The Dangerous Ingkantos: Illness and Social Control in a Philippine Community. *American Anthropologist* 64:306-12.

1962b Qualification for Folk Medical Practice in Sibulan, Negros Oriental, Philippines. *Philippine Journal of Science* 91:511-21.

1966 Fatalism and Medicine in Cebuano Areas of the Philippines. *Anthropological Quarterly* 39:171-79.

1967 *Cebuano Sorcery*. Berkeley: University of California Press.

Livingstone, Frank B.
1958 Anthropological Implications of Sickle Cell Distribution in West Africa. *American Anthropologist* 60:533-62.

Lloyd, P. C.
1968 *Africa in Social Change*. New York: Praeger.

Maclean, Catherine M. U.
1966 Hospitals or Healers? An Attitude Survey in Ibadan. *Human Organization* 25:131-39.

1969 Traditional Healers and Their Female Clients: An Aspect of Nigerian Sickness Behavior. *Journal of Health and Social Behavior* 10:172-86.

Madigan, Francis C.
1957 Are Sex Mortality Differentials Bio-logically Caused? *Milbank Memorial Fund Quarterly* 35:202-23.

Marriott, McKim
1955a Western Medicine in a Village of Northern India. In *Health, Culture, and Community*, ed. B. D. Paul, pp. 239-68. New York: Russell Sage Foundation.

1955b Little Communities in Indigenous Civilization. In *Village India*, ed. M. Marriott, pp. 171-222. Memoir no. 83, American Anthropological Association.

Marwick, M. G.
1965 *Sorcery in Its Social Setting*. Manchester: Manchester University Press.

May, Jacques M.
1960 The Ecology of Human Disease. *Annals of the New York Academy of Sciences* 84, no. 17:789-94.

Mechanic, David
1964 The Influence of Mothers on Their Children's Health Attitudes and Behavior. *Pediatrics* 33:444-53.

1968 *Medical Sociology*. New York: Free Press, Macmillan.

Medawar, Peter B.
1960 *The Future of Man*. New York: Basic Books.

Medical Anthropology Newsletter
1969 Vol. 1, no. 3.

Messing, Simon D.
1958 Group Therapy and Social Status in the Zar Cult of Ethiopia. *American Anthropologist* 60:1120-26.

1968 Interdigitation of Mystical and Physical Healing in Ethiopia. *Behavior Science Notes* 3:87-104.

Metzger, Duane, and Gerald Williams
1963 Tenejapa Medicine I: The Curer. *Southwestern Journal of Anthropology* 19:216-34.

Middleton, John, and E. H. Winter, eds.
1963 *Witchcraft and Sorcery in East Africa*. New York: Praeger.

Morris, Jeremy N.
1964 *Uses of Epidemiology*, rev. ed. Edinburgh: Livingstone.

Nash, Manning
1965 *The Golden Road to Modernity*. New York: Wiley.

Needham, Joseph, and Lu Gwei-djen
1969 Chinese Medicine. In *Medicine and Culture*, ed. F. N. L. Poynter, pp.

255-84. London: Wellcome Institute of the History of Medicine.

Neel, James V.
1962 Diabetes Mellitus: A "Thrifty" Genotype Rendered Detrimental by "Progress"? *American Journal of Human Genetics* 14:353-62.

Newell, Kenneth W.
1957 Medical Development Within a Maori Community. *Health Education Journal* 15:83-89.

Nurge, Ethel
1958 Etiology of Illness in Guinhangdan. *American Anthropologist* 60: 1158-72.

O'Nell, Carl W.
1970 Letter in Across the Editor's Desk. *Medical Anthropology Newsletter* 2, no. 2.

O'Nell, Carl W., and Henry A. Selby
1968 Sex Differences in the Incidence of Susto in Two Zapotec Pueblos: An Analysis of the Relationship Between Sex Role Expectations and a Folk Illness. *Ethnology* 7:95-105.

Oztürk, Orhan M.
1964 Folk Treatment of Mental Illness in Turkey. In *Magic, Faith, and Healing*, ed. A. Kiev, pp. 343-63. New York: Free Press, Macmillan.

Parsons, Talcott
1951 *The Social System.* Glencoe, Ill.: Free Press.
1953 Illness and the Role of the Physician. In *Personality in Nature, Society, and Culture*, ed. C. Kluckhohn and H. A. Murray, 2nd ed., pp. 607-17. New York: Knopf.
1958 Definitions of Health and Illness in the Light of American Values and Social Structure. In *Patients, Physicians, and Illness*, ed. E. G. Jaco, pp. 165-87. Glencoe, Ill.: Free Press.
1964 *Social Structure and Personality.* New York: Free Press, Macmillan.

Parsons, Talcott, and Renée Fox
1952 Illness, Therapy, and the American Family. *Journal of Social Issues* 8:2-3, 31-44.

Paul, Benjamin D.
1963 Anthropological Perspectives on Medicine and Public Health. *Annals of the American Academy of Political and Social Science* 346:34-43.

Pearsall, Marion
1963 *Medical Behavioral Science: A Selected Bibliography of Cultural Anthropology, Social Psychology, and Sociology in Medicine.* Lexington: University of Kentucky Press.

Polgar, Steven
1962 Health and Human Behavior: Areas of Interest Common to the Social and Medical Sciences. *Current Anthropology* 3:159-205.
1963 Health Action in Cross-Cultural Perspective. In *Handbook of Medical Sociology*, ed. H. E. Freeman, S. Levine, and L. G. Reeder, pp. 397-419. Englewood Cliffs, N.J.: Prentice-Hall.
1964 Evolution and the Ills of Man. In *Horizons of Anthropology*, ed. S. Tax, pp. 200-211. Chicago: Aldine.
1968 Health. *International Encyclopedia of the Social Sciences* 6:330-36. New York: Free Press, Macmillan.

Polson, Robert A., and Agaton P. Pal
1956 *The Status of Rural Life in the Dumaguete Trade Area, Philippines.* Southeast Asia Program, data paper no. 21. Ithaca: Department of Asian Studies, Cornell University.

Press, Irwin
1969 Urban Illness: Physicians, Curers, and Dual Use in Bogotá. *Journal of Health and Social Behavior* 10: 209-18.

Quisenberry, Walter B.
1960 Sociocultural Factors in Cancer in Hawaii. *Annals of the New York Academy of Sciences* 84, no. 7: 795-806.

Quisumbing, Eduardo
1951 *Medicinal Plants of the Philippines.* Republic of the Philippines Department of Agriculture and Natural Resources, Technical Bulletin no. 16. Manila: Republic of the Philippines Bureau of Printing.

Read, Margaret
1966 *Culture, Health, and Disease.* London: Tavistock.

Redfield, Robert
1956 *Peasant Society and Culture.* Chicago: University of Chicago Press.

Rivers, W. H. R.
1924 *Medicine, Magic, and Religion.* New York: Harcourt, Brace.

Roemer, Milton I.
1954 Health Service Organization as a Task in Applied Social Science. *Canadian Journal of Public Health* 45:133-45.
1959 Social Science and Organized Health Service. *Human Organization* 18:75-77.

Rogers, Edward S.
1968 Public Health Asks of Sociology . . . *Science* 159:506-508.

Romano, Octavio Ignacio V.
1965 Charismatic Medicine, Folk-Healing, and Folk-Sainthood. *American Anthropologist* 67:1151-73.

Rosen, George
1963 The Evolution of Social Medicine. In *Handbook of Medical Sociology*, ed. H. E. Freeman, S. Levine, and L. G. Reeder, pp. 17-61. Englewood Cliffs, N.J.: Prentice-Hall.

Rosen, George, and E. Wellin
1959 A Bookshelf on the Social Sciences and Public Health. *American Journal of Public Health* 50:441-54.

Roth, Julius A.
1956 What Is an Activity? *Etc.: A Review of General Semantics* 14:54-56.
1957 Ritual and Magic in the Control of Contagion. *American Sociological Review* 22:310-14.

Rubel, Arthur J.
1960 Concepts of Disease in Mexican-American Culture. *American Anthropologist* 62:795-814.
1964 The Epidemiology of a Folk Illness: Susto in Hispanic America. *Ethnology* 3:268-83.
1970 Letter in Across the Editor's Desk. *Medical Anthropology Newsletter* 2, no. 2.

Sangree, Walter H.
1970 Tribal Ritual, Leadership, and the Mortality Rate in Irigwe, Northern Nigeria. *Southwestern Journal of Anthropology* 26:32-39.

Saunders, Lyle
1954 *Cultural Differences and Medical Care*. New York: Russell Sage Foundation.
1958 Healing Ways in the Spanish Southwest. In *Patients, Physicians, and Illness*, ed. E. G. Jaco, pp. 189-206. Glencoe, Ill.: Free Press.

Scarpa, Antonio
1967 Introduction. *Ethnoiatria* 1:2-4.

Schneider, David M.
1947 The Social Dynamics of Physical Disability in Army Basic Training. *Psychiatry* 10:323-33.

Schwartz, Lola R.
1969 The Hierarchy of Resort in Curative Practices: The Admiralty Islands, Melanesia. *Journal of Health and Social Behavior* 10:201-209.

Scotch, Norman
1960 A Preliminary Report on the Relation of Sociocultural Factors to Hypertension Among the Zulu. *Annals of the New York Academy of Sciences* 84, no. 17:1000-1009.
1963 Medical Anthropology. In *Biennial Review of Anthropology, 1963*, ed. B. J. Siegel, pp. 30-68. Stanford: Stanford University Press.

Seijas, Haydée
1969 Algunos aspectos de la etnomedicina de los indios Sibundoy de Colombia (Some Aspects of the Ethnomedicine of the Sibundoy Indians of Colombia). *Boletín Informativo*, no. 6, pp. 5-15. Abr. and trans. Clarissa Scott, *Medical Anthropology Newsletter*, January 1970.

Shiloh, Ailon
1961 The System of Medicine in Middle East Culture. *Middle East Journal* 15:277-88.
1965 A Case Study of Disease and Culture in Action: Leprosy Among the Hausa of Northern Nigeria. *Human Organization* 24:140-47.

Sigerist, Henry E.
1961 *The History of Medicine*. New York: Oxford University Press.

Simmons, Ozzie G.
1955 Popular and Modern Medicine in Mestizo Communities of Coastal Peru and Chile. *Journal of American Folklore* 68:57-71.
1958 *Social Status and Public Health*. Pamphlet no. 13. New York: Social Science Research Council.
1963 Social Research in Health and Medicine: A Bibliography. In *Handbook of Medical Sociology*, ed. H. E. Freeman, S. Levine, and L. G. Reeder,

pp. 493-581. Englewood Cliffs, N.J.: Prentice-Hall.

Smith, Charline G.
1970 Culture and Diabetes Among the Upland Yuma Indians. Ph. D. dissertation, University of Utah.

Snow, J.
1936 *Snow on Cholera*. New York: Commonwealth Fund.

Solomon, Joan
1969 Academy Conference on Human Research, pt. 2. *The Sciences* 9:10-14.

Spiro, Melford E.
1967 *Burmese Supernaturalism*. Englewood Cliffs, N.J.: Prentice-Hall.

Sternbach, R. A., and B. Tursky
1965 Ethnic Differences Among Housewives in Psychophysical and Skin Potential Responses to Electric Shock. *Psychophysiology* 1:241-46.

Straus, Robert
1957 The Nature and Status of Medical Sociology. *American Sociological Review* 22:200-204.

Suchman, Edward A.
1968 Epidemiology. *International Encyclopedia of the Social Sciences* 5:97-101. New York: Free Press, Macmillan.

Swanson, Guy E.
1960 *The Birth of the Gods*. Ann Arbor: University of Michigan Press.

Syme, S. Leonard, and Leo G. Reeder, eds.
1967 Social Stress and Cardiovascular Disease. *Milbank Memorial Fund Quarterly* 45, no.2, pt. 2.

Taylor, Carl E., and Marie-Françoise Hall
1967 Health, Population, and Economic Development. *Science* 157:651-57.

Turner, Victor W.
1964 An Ndembu Doctor in Practice. In *Magic, Faith, and Healing*, ed. A. Kiev, pp. 230-63. New York: Free Press, Macmillan.

U.S. Dept. of Health, Education, and Welfare
1969 *Toward a Social Report*. Ann Arbor: University of Michigan Press.

U.S. National Center for Health Statistics
1965 *Volume of Physician Visits: By Place and Type of Service, United States, July 1963-June 1964*. Series 10-18. Washington, D.C.: U.S. Government Printing Office.

Van der Schalie, Henry
1969 Control in Egypt and the Sudan. *Natural History*, February special supplement, pp. 62-65.

Veith, Ilza
1966 *The Yellow Emperor's Classic of Internal Medicine*. Berkeley: University of California Press.

Vogt, Evon Z.
1969 *Zinacantan*. Cambridge: Belknap Press, Harvard University Press.

Wardwell, Walter I., Merton Hyman, and Claus B. Bahnson
1964 Stress and Coronary Heart Disease in Three Field Studies. *Journal of Chronic Diseases* 17:73-84.

Weaver, Thomas
1968 Trends in Research and Medical Education. In *Essays on Medical Anthropology*, ed. T. Weaver, pp. 1-2. Southern Anthropological Society. Athens: University of Georgia Press.
1970 Use of Hypothetical Situations in a Study of Spanish American Illness Referral Systems. *Human Organization* 29:140-54.

Whiting, Beatrice B.
1950 *Paiute Sorcery*. New York: Viking Fund Publications in Anthropology, no. 15.

Whiting, John
1964 Effects of Climate on Certain Cultural Practices. In *Explorations in Cultural Anthropology*, ed. W. Goodenough, pp. 511-44. New York: McGraw-Hill.

Wiesenfeld, Stephen L.
1967 Sickle Cell Trait in Human Biological and Cultural Evolution. *Science* 157:1134-40.

Wintrob, R. M.
1966 Psychosis in Association with Possession by Genii in Liberia. *Psychopathologie Africaine* 2:249-58.

Wittkower, Eric D., and Jacob Fried
1959 Some Problems of Transcultural Psychiatry. In *Culture and Mental Health*, ed. M. K. Opler, pp. 489-500. New York: Macmillan.

Wolff, B. Berthold, and Sarah Langley
1968 Cultural Factors and Response to Pain: A Review. *American Anthropologist* 70:494-501.

Wolff, Robert J.
　1965 Modern Medicine and Traditional Culture: Confrontation on the Malay Peninsula. *Human Organization* 24: 339-45.

World Health Organization
　1946 *Constitution of the World Health Organization*. Geneva: World Health Organization.

Wynder, Ernest L., Jerome Cornfield, P. D.

Schroff, and K. R. Doraiswami
　1954 Study of Environmental Factors an Cancer of the Cervix. *American Jour nal of Obstetrics and Gynecolog* 68:1016-52.

Zborowski, Mark
　1952 Cultural Components in Response to Pain. *Journal of Social Issue* 8:16-30.

　1969 *People in Pain*. San Francisco: Jos sey-Bass.

CHAPTER 25 Psychological Anthropology

ERIKA BOURGUIGNON

INTRODUCTION

In its broadest sense, psychological anthropology comprises the entire area of overlapping interests of the disciplines of psychology and anthropology. Indeed, if culture, the central concept of cultural anthropology, is defined in terms of behavior, and psychology is defined as the study of behavior, the two might appear to the unwary to be synonymous. The area of overlap is indeed broad, ranging from comparative studies of animal behavior, particularly of primates, to developmental studies of children, to normal and abnormal personality functioning, individual and collective behavior, studies of perception and cognition, learning, memory, dreams, altered states of consciousness, and much more. Viewed from this perspective, what is sometimes called the American school of culture and personality studies is seen as only a segment of a larger field. This larger field has been variously described and delimited. Honigmann (1959:68) differentiates between "traditional culture and per-

sonality research" and "psychocultural studies," which represent a broader "interdisciplinary viewpoint." Harris (1969:395-96) has recently characterized, in a critical vein, most ethnography, even that of the British social anthropologists, as being afflicted by a "mentalistic" cast.

When one considers the many topics common to psychology and anthropology, it is clear that they represent much of the classical subject matter of the field of psychology. What, then, is the distinguishing mark of psychological anthropology? There are, it seems to me, two such marks: fieldwork, whether ethological or ethnological, and the comparative perspective, whether evolutionary or cross-cultural. For example, most of the work that psychologists have carried out with primates has been in the nature of experimental laboratory studies, rather than in the observation of free-ranging animals in their own habitats, and most of it has not been concerned with the development of evolutionary sequences. This statement is not meant as a criticism of the frequently highly innovative and revealing work of the best of the comparative psychologists. It is made here merely to emphasize the differences between the two disciplines in the formulation of research problems and the strategies of research utilized. The basic question of psychological anthropology—and, it appears to me, of anthropology in general—is twofold: What in human behavior is both uniquely and generically human? That is, first, in what ways is man distinct from other primates—wherein lies his uniqueness? And second, what are the universal characteristics underlying the great evident variations in the behavior of human groups? The first question requires an evolutionary perspective of the kind most fully expressed in the work of A. I. Hallowell. The second requires a comparativist perspective transcending the traditional anthropological emphasis on variation and relativity.

The evolutionary perspective implies this, for the features that make men different from other primates are of necessity and by definition those shared by men as a species, not those characteristic of only some groups of men. Some other approaches on the current anthropological scene also stress the underlying universalities, although their statements of the problem and their methods of attack differ widely. The search for linguistic universals by Chomsky and his group constitutes a search for fundamental laws of the human mind, as does, in a different way, the structuralism of Lévi-Strauss. The search for regularities in human societies pursued by the statistical approach of large-scale cross-cultural studies similarly represents an attempt to find a way to make statements about human societies, and thus about the behavior of human groups in general, rather than to stress the unique, the contingent, the relative. Perhaps these

may be seen as current aspects of the old anthropological dialectic, once phrased as history (the unique) versus science (the generalizing). The emphasis on the unique also has taken new forms, particularly in the recent development of ethnoscience and the study of cognitive structures. I shall return to these matters later. Here I merely refer to them to present a context for the discussion that follows.

Although psychological anthropology is usually treated as a separate area of subject matter within cultural anthropology, it may profitably be regarded as an approach to, or a perspective on, most of the standard anthropological subjects. I have already referred to behavioral evolution. This represents a psychological dimension of the study of human evolution, a study that is generally carried out by physical rather than cultural anthropologists. With respect to language, there is also an evolutionary dimension to be considered, which has important psychological ramifications, involving as it does the definition of a psychological capacity for the invention and development of language. In addition, the questions of the relation of language and thought and of the linguistic relativity of cultural reality have long been subjects of anthropological discussion and research. The question of underlying shared structures and of the universal aspects of language acquisition in children all have importance for a psychological anthropology that sees language as a crucial aspect of culture.

With respect to material culture, we must again confront the evolutionary question of the development of man's capacity to invent as well as to fashion and utilize tools. In the synchronic study of material culture as well, however, we deal not only with economic and technological issues, but also with questions of motor habits and skills perception, cognition, and values. In that area of material culture generally labeled "art"—i.e., the plastic and graphic arts—the evolutionary aspects of symbolization, cognition, and perception, of values and attitudes, are even· more evident than in the more strictly utilitarian types of objects of human manufacture. Music, dance, and folklore tend to be generally seen in symbolic rather than technological terms. The arts, in a major facet of their functioning, lead us to the most symbolic dimension of human behavior: ritual and religion. Here the psychological dimension has long been under investigation, whether within a Freudian or a Durkheimian framework. Similarly the family, which generally carries prime responsibility for the socialization of the next generation, has long been seen as the crucial psychological agent of society. And the political structure, the organization of authority, has often been seen as a major object for the projection of emotions and attitudes generated within the family. That these views have sometimes been stated as contradictory or as complementary need not concern us for the moment.

It is perhaps not necessary to continue this list—to specify the psychological dimensions of economics and warfare, of ethnomedicine and ethnopharmacology, of sanctions and values operative in human societies, of processes of cultural change and cultural continuity, and so forth—in order to demonstrate that there is a psychological dimension to all of the various universal aspects of human culture (Herskovits 1948). Psychological anthropology, then, may be seen as a point of view, an approach to the understanding of human behavior. While it may appear to some as competitive and exclusive, it is perhaps better viewed as complementary to other approaches. Also, as will become evident in the following pages, while psychological anthropology can be distinguished from other approaches, such as those represented by structuralism or cultural materialism, among others, it does not constitute a unified position or school. Indeed, even the so-called American school of culture and personality contains many divergent and at times conflicting tendencies. These matters will be explored below. Here I shall stress one further point, specifically with reference to the culture and personality movement: However its contribution to general anthropology may finally be evaluated, it has left cultural anthropology two well-established rubrics of investigation: the study of socialization and education and that of cultural psychiatry.

HISTORICAL BACKGROUND

While no full-scale history of psychological anthropology exists to date, a number of historical reviews of various aspects of this interdisciplinary field have been published. Most extensive and broadly based is the survey of the multiple relationships between psychology and anthropology by Hallowell (1954), beginning with the work of the German psychologist Herbart (1776-1841) and that of the early nineteenth-century German anthropologists Theodor Waitz and Adolf Bastian. Tracing the mutual relations between the two disciplines in several countries for approximately a century, Hallowell finds many exchanges and cross-fertilizations along a broader front than might be suspected from a narrower view, which tends to limit the interaction between the two fields to the American culture and personality movement. Such a narrower field is surveyed by several authors, such as Singer (1961), Harris (1969, chaps. 15, 16, 17), and, specifically with respect to

North American Indians, Honigmann (1972).

Some of the basic problems of psychological anthropology have long been present in the intellectual history of man. One such question concerns the definition of man, of the essentially human. Once this metaphysical question was reformulated as an empirical one, attempts could be made to arrive at empirical answers through comparative studies of animal behavior on the one hand and of human groups on the other. A second question, present in one form or another among all human groups, concerns the differences among human societies, and how these differences are to be accounted for. One aspect of this topic is the apparently universal ethnocentrism, ranging from the ancient Egyptians' belief that they were the only truly human beings (Frankfort 1946:33) to the Eskimo, who call themselves *inuit* (men), and the Navajo, who speak of themselves as *diné* (the people). Over the centuries, various explanations for group differences have been offered, such as climate, race, *Zeitgeist,* the genius of a people, national character, and culture. Several of these proposed explanatory concepts show a confusion between environmental factors, factors of biology, and factors of learning. Unfortunately, in much contemporary writing outside of anthropology, particularly on the issue of race, much of this confusion is still very much with us.

In view of the persistence of these questions, we may claim Aristotle and Herodotus as ancestors of at least certain aspects of our discipline. However, it was the great voyages of discovery of the fifteenth and sixteenth centuries that brought the issue of human identity into sharp focus at the beginning of the modern period. Questions concerning newly contacted human groups were asked: Were American Indians and African blacks fully human? Did the have souls? The echoes of these ques tions and the actions justified by th philosophical answers of the period st haunt our lives today. The shock these encounters with radically differ ent ways of life was to have a majo impact on social thought. J. J. Rou seau, whom Lévi-Strauss (1963) h claimed as the father of cultural anthro pology, found a major source of refle tion on the state of society and th state of nature in the very existence the American Indian. In his though about the relationship between educa tion and society we may well see a m jor source of our current concerns wit socialization and enculturation.

Anthropology was formalized as discipline in the latter part of the nin teenth century. Hallowell (1960a) h shown the importance of the intelle tual problems posed by the very exi tence of the American Indian for th development of anthropology in th United States. Here the Indian was living reality for those who wished t study him. In contrast, the developin European anthropology was of a mor speculative nature. And in many re spects, it was a psychological anthro pology. As an example, we may tak Tylor's (1871:1) classic definition the concept of culture. He tells us tha it is "that complex whole which in cludes knowledge, belief, art, law, cu tom and any other capabilities and hat its acquired by man as a member society." A number of the terms in thi definition are clearly psychological i character: concepts such as "know edge" and "belief" involve cognitiv processes, "capabilities and habits ac quired" imply learning, and since thos who acquire them are specified a "members of society," the learning im plied is of the kind now generally re ferred to as enculturation. Indeed, th psychological process of learning is cen tral to the concept of culture, which is, as a rule, contrasted with unlearned, inherited, "instinctive" behavior traits, such as those found in animal behavior or those thought by some to characterize human races. Furthermore, the problems with which Tylor concerned himself were to a large extent psychological. Thus he defined religion as a belief in spirits; that is, he defined it as a cognitive phenomenon. He thought its origin could be found in primitive man's explanations of death, dreams, and trance states. He was concerned, thus, with explanation, again a cognitive process, dealing, in the case of dreams and trances, with subjective experiences of altered states of consciousness. His explanation of the origin of religion is a psychological explanation, endowing primitive (i.e., early) man with curiosity and rationality in confronting an intellectual problem (Evans-Pritchard 1965:24-26).

The classical evolutionists, of whom Tylor was one, addressed themselves to essentially unanswerable questions about the origins of various human institutions, and then proceeded to trace the evolution of mankind from these earliest hypothesized beginnings to its lofty state in the nineteenth-century Western world. Contemporary primitives were equated, to a greater or lesser extent, with early societies or "races" of men. The Australian aborigines were generally thought to be representative of the earliest groups extant. In investigating the evolution of human institutions, these writers were fundamentally concerned with the evolution of the human mind. This involved the growth of knowledge and of skills, of man's capacity to free himself from irrationality and superstition. Magic and, at times, religion were included in the latter terms.

The evolutionary perspectives of nineteenth-century anthropology had a

profound effect on Freud, who read widely in the literature of anthropology and who incorporated some of its features in his own theories. And when an encounter occurred between twentieth-century American anthropology and Freudian thought, it was these relics of anthropology's own past that formed the greatest stumbling block to mutual cooperation.

Freud (1956:5) tells us that he wrote *Totem und Tabu* (1912-1913) as a response to Wundt's nonpsychoanalytic *Völkerpsychologie* (1900-1920) and to Jung's attempt to solve "problems in the psychology of the individual through the utilization of ethnographic materials." In contrast to Jung, he says, he attempted to explain ethnographic phenomena, specifically totemism and the incest taboo, by means of findings from the psychoanalytic investigation of individuals. He saw the concept of taboo as a familiar one, present in European society, while totemism was an archaic phenomenon that had long since disappeared from European life and left survivals only in the development of children. Totemism is seen by Freud as characteristic of a stage in the evolution of society. The development of the modern child recapitulates the stages of the psychological evolution of human society. The idea that institutions found today only in some primitive societies were typical of mankind at a given stage of its evolution, to be abandoned when higher stages were reached, was part of the intellectual climate of the day and seemed self-evident. That the childhood of the modern individual recapitulates the stages of the development of mankind similarly appeared reasonable and self-evident. Nor was it unreasonable to believe that the origins of institutions, in this case totemism and the incest taboo, could be reconstructed. These attempts, however fanciful they may seem to us, were entirely in keeping with the practices of the times, although in the United States, in particular, a reaction against unilineal classical evolutionism had already set in.

Freud was widely criticized by American anthropologists for his evolutionist views, his attempts at imaginative historical reconstruction, and the notion of the inheritance of acquired psychological characteristics which he built into his system (e.g., Kroeber 1958a, 1958b; Du Bois 1937). It is therefore of some interest to note that more recently Fox (1967) has argued that Freud's understanding of the operation of Australian kinship groups anticipated that of contemporary social anthropologists.

While criticizing Freud's approach to the search for the origins of the incest taboo in the primal horde hypothesized by Darwin and Atkinson, Kroeber (1958a:53) is not ready to reject this search outright, and he expresses the hope that an understanding of present-day institutions among primitives may yet "gradually lead to a partial reconstruction of origins." Du Bois (1937) finds most objectionable in Freud's work the very features he borrowed from the anthropology of an earlier period: the identification of contemporary primitives with early peoples on the one hand and with the concept of the simple on the other; the so-called comparative method; the notion of recapitulation, which allows the identification of the institutions of primitive societies with the behavior of Western children on the one hand and neurotic patients on the other; the explanation of cultural developments in terms of psychological formulations; and, finally, the belief in the inheritance of acquired characteristics. This last item is implicit in the idea that the psychological traces of the events of the primal horde—the killing and eating of the

father by the sons and the resultin guilt followed by the institution of th incest taboo and of the rituals of sacr fice and the totemic feast—account fc the presumed universality of the Oed pus complex in modern individual Hallowell (1939) subjected the recapi ulation thesis to a most searching re view and found it totally without sup port. Yet Kroeber (1958a, 1958b), D Bois (1937), and Hallowell (1939 among others, found much of value fc anthropology in the work of Freuc The reflections and speculations b Freud and his associates on specificall anthropological subjects about whic they had generally only secondhan knowledge were rejected by most ar thropologists. Abraham (1913), for ex ample, published a study of mytholog entitled *Dreams and Myths: A Study i Race Psychology*, with the chief objec tive of showing how Freud's wish theo ry of dreams could be applied t myths. Anthropologists, who were re ceptive to psychoanalytic ideas on th whole, saw in psychoanalysis a dynami theory of human behavior, which coul help to shed light on the recurring fea tures in the actions and attitudes c contemporary, living human being. For example, Kroeber (1958a:52) says

However much cultural anthropology ma come to lean more on the historical instead c the psychological method, it can never ult mately free itself, nor should it wish to, fron the psychology that underlies it. To thi psychology the psychoanalytic movement in tiated by Freud has made an indubitably sig nificant contribution.

And he goes on to mention as example the correspondence noted by Freud be tween taboo and compulsion neurosis as well as the ability of the theory o ambivalence to account for the combi nation of mourning for the dead witl fear of the dead.

The year 1912, which saw the publi

cation of the first portions of *Totem und Tabu*, was also the year of the publication of another study of the origin and function of primitive religion: Émile Durkheim's *Les formes élémentaires de la vie religieuse: Le système totémique en Australie (The Elementary Forms of the Religious Life: A Study in Religious Sociology*, 1915). Like Freud, Durkheim turned to the Australian aborigines for his materials, since presumably they were the most primitive human groups in existence. And like Freud, he held totemism to be the earliest form of religion. However, Durkheim viewed both the origin and the function of religion in sociological rather than psychological terms. For Durkheim, society was a thing *sui generis*, which must be explained in its own terms. In 1895 he had written in *The Rules of Sociological Method* (1938; as quoted in Pierce 1964:160), "The determining cause of a social fact must be sought among the antecedent social facts, and not among individual states of consciousness." And "The function of a social fact must always be sought in the relationship the fact sustains with some social ends." Durkheim appears to do away with a need for psychological explanations, indeed to reject them, a point of view widely shared among British social anthropologists. Yet a variety of psychological concepts enters into Durkheim's scheme, although these concepts are phrased as statements of collective rather than individual psychology. For example, as Evans-Pritchard (1965:68) puts it, "No amount of juggling with words like 'intensity' and 'effervescence' can hide the fact that he derives the totemic religion of the Blackfellows from the emotional excitement of individuals brought together in a small crowd, from what is a sort of crowd hysteria."

To Durkheim, the god of the Austra-lians was the clan itself, and more generally, God is society divinized. The rules of religion are thus the rules of society and the object of worship is the society itself. As Durkheim (1964:335, 336, 337) himself has phrased it in a commentary on his book on religion:

... sacred things are simply collective ideals that have fixed themselves on material objects. The ideas and sentiments that are elaborated by a collectivity, whatever it might be, are invested by reason of their origin with an ascendancy and an authority that cause the particular individuals who think them and believe in them to represent them in the form of moral forces that dominate and sustain them ... the particular virtues that we attribute to these ideals ... are ... the effects of that singularly creative and fertile operation ... by which a plurality of individual consciousnesses enter into communion and are fused into a common consciousness.

For it is only by expressing their feelings, by translating them into signs, by symbolizing them externally, that the individual consciousnesses, which are, by nature, closed to each other, can feel that they are communicating and are in unison.

There are in [man] two classes of consciousness ... One class merely expresses our organisms and the objects to which they are directly related ... The states of consciousness of the other class ... come to us from society: they transfer society into us and connect us with something that surpasses us.

A whole series of psychological concepts are operative here: ideals and sentiments, individual and common consciousness, and perhaps most importantly, symbolization and its reciprocal, the transfer of society into man. This latter idea, as T. Parsons (1964:144) has pointed out, strongly resembles the concept of internalization developed by Freud and, in the United States, by C. H. Cooley and G. H. Mead. The process of symbolization, by which gods are created, however, is not further analyzed by Durkheim.

While Freud and his associates attempted to apply principles derived from the psychoanalytic study of neurotic individuals to the analysis of cultural phenomena, and Durkheim sought to understand how society, made up of individuals, could be explained in terms of its own laws rather than those of the psychology of individuals, quite a different psychological enterprise was also in progress. And this, too, yielded an important publication in the year 1912: Richard Thurnwald presented a special supplement to a prominent German psychological journal devoted to proposals for psychological research among primitives (Stern and Lipmann, eds., 1912). The problem areas covered by various eminent psychologists and anthropologists dealt with such topics as the optic sense of space, color sense, memory and understanding, suggestibility, concept of time (determination and estimation), counting, expression and language (including a passage from Darwin), drawing and art, convictions and style of thought, sociology, and, finally, world view. Thurnwald himself supplied an introduction and an appendix on the "practice of ethnopsychological research, particularly by means of linguistic studies." The following year, Thurnwald (1913) continued this activity with the publication of "Ethnopsychologische Studien an Südsee Völkern" (Ethnopsychological Studies Among South Sea Peoples), reporting on his work in the Solomon Islands.

Even earlier, however, as part of the Cambridge Torres Straits Expedition of 1898, which reflected the teachings of Wundt in Germany, extensive investigations were carried out among native peoples. Rivers (1901), as a member of this expedition, carried out experiments with respect to various aspects of vision, including color vision and reac-tion to visual illusions. He later pursued this work further among the Todas of southern India (Rivers 1905).

The early studies of color vision are notable in several respects: the observation, based first on the literature of ancient societies and later on work with nonliterate groups, that color vocabularies in these societies differ from those of modern Western languages was generally interpreted as indicative of differences in the actual perception of color among human groups. Furthermore, these differences in color perception were thought to be innate. The fact that the experimental results obtained by Rivers depended to some extent on the tests he used was shown by the subsequent work of Woodworth, who tested 1,100 persons from various parts of the world at the St. Louis World's Fair in 1904. He found in a matching test that lack of specific color terms did not imply inability to perceive colors. The history of the study of color vision, as traced by Segall, Campbell, and Herskovits (1966) as a background for their own study of the relation between cultural factors and visual perception, represents a fascinating case study of the interdependent evolution of theory and method of investigation. Moving from a notion of innate differences between human groups, presumably revealed by differences in vocabulary, we now have come to a diametrically opposite position. Human groups are now thought to be roughly similar in innate capacity. Differences in behavior are attributed to differences in the availability of categories. These, as expressed in differences in vocabulary, in turn are attributed to differences in the cultural evaluation and utilization of the phenomena in question (e.g., Conklin 1955).

In the early studies, as we have seen, differences between groups were interpreted as innate, and the groups were referred to as "races" rather than as societies, cultures, or language communities. There even was talk of "race psychology." Clearly the term "race" was used much more loosely than modern physical anthropology would justify. Race and society were treated largely as synonymous. The age of genetics was yet to come. "Instinct" was another word used loosely and often without biological specification. Gradually, as modern anthropology and psychology have grown out of the theoretical and empirical work of the late nineteenth and early twentieth centuries, a great transformation has taken place in our popular as well as technical vocabularies, in our writing style as well as in our concepts and hypotheses. To some extent, then, reading the earlier literature of these disciplines resembles an expedition into a foreign language and an alien culture, requiring often enough a careful and difficult translation into modern equivalents. The earlier writings, whether of Tylor, Freud, or Rivers, are therefore easily taken out of their cultural context and misread, projecting modern notions of "race," for example, backward on writers of seventy-five or a hundred years ago.

As we look back we can see that a modern conception has required major developments in both the biological and the sociocultural researches on which contemporary theories are built. Genetics and a redefinition of race, a separation of culture from biology, of the learned from the innate, a redefinition of the relationship between the two and consequently a redefinition of the concept of "instinct," a renewed perspective on human evolution—all these and more have been necessary contributions to whatever gains we have made toward a psychologically informed anthropology. Since the turn of the century we have moved from race to culture as key concepts for the explanation of human behavior. In so

doing we have moved from a focus on evolution as a theory accounting for the presumed changes in capacity from so-called primitive man to civilized (i.e., Western) man to a broader view of evolution. We now conceive of it as a development of a capacity for culture from primates to *Homo sapiens*. In the earlier period, differences in the behavior of human groups were seen as based on an evolution of human institutions, reflecting, in turn, the evolution of human biological capacities. In reaction against such a biologically deterministic position, a radical cultural relativism developed in the United States under Boas and his students. Today this relativism in its extreme form is being replaced by a concern with an underlying common human nature, accompanied by a search for principles, more often ecological and sociological than psychological in nature, to account for the varieties of human institutions. To some extent, these transformations in anthropology can be understood as due to the inherent dynamics of the discipline, the testing and rejecting of theories, the accumulation of data, the influence of neighboring fields. Yet an investigation along the lines of a sociology of knowledge might be expected to reveal the influence of the societal context within which these changes in theoretical orientation have taken place.

BEHAVIORAL EVOLUTION

A concern with the evolution of human behavior was foreshadowed in the writings of A. I. Hallowell as early as 1937, placing culture and personality studies on a firm biological evolutionary footing. With his presidential address to the American Anthropological Association in 1949, Hallowell (1950) essentially presented a challenge to the profession: while in the nineteenth century human evolution was viewed as an inclusive process, it now appeared that the enemies of evolutionary thought had won the day. Modern anthropologists seemed to have abandoned any concern with "other orders of continuity and differentiation" than those of a strictly morphological nature. In a dozen important papers since then, Hallowell has outlined what he has called a "conjunctive approach" that brings together "organic, psychological, social and cultural dimensions of the evolutionary process . . . as they are related to the underlying conditions that are necessary and sufficient for a human existence" (1963:440). Adapting a term from Roe and Simpson (1958), he has called this approach one of behavioral evolution.

We may differentiate several types of exploration relevant to the study of behavioral evolution. On the one hand, there is the investigation of antecedents of human behavior and the foreshadowing of human institutions in animal behavior, particularly among primates. On the other, there is the ever more precise definition of the "human level of existence," in Hallowell's words (1961: 236), by means of primate studies together with the "development of psychoanalytic theories, culture and personality studies and the conceptualization of the nature of culture by twentieth century cultural anthropologists." With this more precise definition we strive for a better understanding of the sufficient as well as the necessary factors making for such a level of existence. This specification of the human level requires a definition of a generic human nature and the identification of the factors that make it distinctive as a level of adaptation.

In some respects, Hallowell's challenge appears to have been well heeded. In the last twenty years there has been a spate of studies, many by physical anthropologists, of primate behavior in the animals' natural habitat (e.g., studies included in Washburn, ed., 1961; De Vore, ed., 1965; Poirier, ed., 1972). While the picture that has emerged from these studies is in many ways rather different and more complex than that which was available earlier, primarily on the basis of studies in zoos and laboratories, it is possible to discern some underlying regularities. A variety of aspects of the behavior of primates has come under scrutiny: ecological and territorial adaptation, use of tools, learning and transmission of learned behavior, group organization, defensive and aggressive behavior, communication, mothering and socialization, and so on.

Looking at primate behavior, Hallowell (1960b, 1961) hypothecates a "protocultural phase in hominid evolution." From a beginning in 1942 (Hallowell and Reynolds 1942), preceding most of the field studies of primates, he has pursued these leads in a series of papers (1950, 1953, 1954, 1956, 1959, 1960b, 1961, 1963, 1966). I shall attempt to summarize briefly, as far as possible, the salient points: The protocultural level involves a series of necessary and preadaptive conditions for the development of a cultural level. Among these are the very fact of social life characterized by groups consisting of adults of both sexes and immature young at various stages of development. The young are thus reared in a complexly differentiated social group; this differentiation includes an experientially established dominance gradient and a differentiation of roles along lines of sex, age, maturation, and dominance. Group life involves patterns of communication and the social transmission of acquired behavior. This last, of course, implies not only the individual's capacity to learn, but also some degree of innovation. Learning, communication, transmission of learned behavior, and role differentiation within the group all are involved in the process of the socialization of the young. Another important aspect of protoculture appears to be an ecological adaptation involving patterns of territoriality, which control the· internal as well as the external relations of the group, a terrestrial habitat, and some utilization of implements.

These features are easily recognized as underlying regularities in the various problem areas all human societies must confront, whether these problem areas be formulated as "universal aspects of culture" (Herskovits 1948) or as the "functional prerequisites of a society" (Aberle et al. 1950). In human societies, however, they appear modified in major ways from their protocultural antecedents, and their forms vary from culture to culture. Where the underlying protocultural constants are expressed among nonhuman primates in ways that vary from species to species, but are generally constant within species, in man there is a great intraspecific variation from culture to culture. Infrahuman as well as human social groups, as we have already seen, are composed of males and females, and the young are socialized in association with individuals of both sexes and varying maturational stages. The composition of such groups, based on patterns of mating, varies from species to species among primates, from the special mating patterns among howlers, sometimes referred to as "sexual communism," to the monogamous matings of gibbons and the polygynous mating patterns of other primate species. Among humans, mating and thus familial patterns vary from society to society; and one of these patterns, polyandry, is a novel form that does not occur among other species. Yet underlying these variations in social forms, whether species-specific or culturally variable, there remains the psychological fact that all primates are socialized into a sexually and maturationally diversified social group.

Wallace (1970a) has attempted to link the evolutionary development from a protocultural to a cultural level to the expansion of the cerebral cortex, as shown in the paleontological record. Hallowell (1960b:339f), however, points also to the importance of neoteny, a matter that had been stressed earlier by La Barre (1954:303f). Hallowell's primary concern, however, is with the "psychological restructuralization" (1960b:360) that must have taken place in the course of hominid evolution and which makes possible a human—that is, a cultural—level of adaptation. One essential aspect of this process, of course, is the development of symbolic forms and specifically of language. It is important to make a distinction here between intrinsic symbolic processes of a private character and extrinsic (i.e., arbitrary) and explicit shared symbolic processes. Private implicit symbolism may be assumed to exist in some form in mammals in general, as it is probable that dreaming, a symbolic process, is a general mammalian phenomenon. This probability is suggested by the observation that all mammalian species tested exhibit periods of REM (rapid eye movement) sleep, which we know to be associated with dreaming in man (Dement 1966:100). On the other hand, extrinsic shared symbolic processes are unique to man. The most familiar and best investigated of these, of course, is language.

One important consequence of these symbolic processes is the development of self-awareness, of self-objectification. There are many ramifications to this matter of self-awareness. Dobzhansky (1965), for example, has pointed out that it is a necessary condition for the universal fact of man's awareness of his own future death, with all the implications this has for the development of religions and philosophies. Hallowell (1953, 1959, 1960*b*) has stressed the importance of self-objectification to the existence of normative orientations in all human societies, ranging from incest avoidance to attitudes toward property to notions of etiquette and correct forms of speech. Without reflexivity and the social sanctions operating through the mechanisms of guilt and shame, human societies as we know them could not exist. It is interesting to note that Hallowell is in fact dealing here with the problems that both Freud and Durkheim considered and which were reviewed earlier. To Freud, guilt originated in the events of the primal horde, events of the distant past that presumably occurred over and over again until their traces were established in human heredity. To Durkheim, the states of consciousness derived from society "transfer" society into man and connect the individual with this larger whole. Neither of these accounts helps us to come to grips with the problem at hand. Hallowell, in his concern with self-awareness and self-objectification, views these individual psychological phenomena as emergents of hominid evolution, and relates them on the one hand to the organization of human social structures and on the other to the ontogenetic development of the individual, in whom we can study the growth of reflexivity.

I have mentioned the symbolic processes of dreaming. Hallowell (1966: 269) points out how, with the development of complex symbolic means of communication and the development of self-awareness in the course of evolution, the private world of dreams could assume not only an individual but also a social significance:

Unconscious psychological forces, hitherto latent in hominid evolution, but now mediated through dreams, visions, and other imaginative processes, intruded themselves upon man, because of his evolving capacity for self-awareness and the knowledge he could acquire of the inner life of other persons. Dream experiences could become the object of reflective thought and become socially significant.

These and related matters are developed with a great deal of relevant documentation by Hallowell (1953, 1959, 1960*b*, 1963, 1966), and their implications and ramifications are explored widely. Here it should be noted that he specifically ties the contributions of culture and personality research into his review of the psychological implications of the observable data of behavioral evolution as they are expressed in the behavior of primates, in the remains of prehistoric human behavior discovered in the archaeological record, and, crucially, in what we know of the behavior of living human groups. Thus to understand the relationship between learning and culture, he points out (1960*b*:361), learning must be "considered in relation to the development of personality structure. . . . The only way in which a culture can be perpetuated is through the characteristic psychological structuralization of individuals in an organized system of social action." Without the development of culture and personality studies, providing psychoanalytically informed comparative ethnographic research, therefore, understanding of the distinctively human level of adaptation could not have been formulated. Yet, by comparing this human level of functioning with the protocultural level of the primates, Hallowell (1960*b*:361) points to yet another major point of comparison: "The psychological basis for culture lies not only in a capacity for highly complex forms of learning but in a capacity for transcending what is learned: a potential for innovation, creativity, reorganization and change."

While Hallowell has been interested in the development of personality structure in the course of human evolution, Jules Henry (1959) has considered the continuing relationship between culture, personality, and evolution. Reviewing certain evidence concerning psychosomatic disease and in particular the relationship between personality disorders, stress arising from the social system, and reproductive dysfunctions in women, he suggests that these disorders may appear only in the presence of genetic susceptibility. The stress situations, by affecting reproduction, would thus lead to the failure to pass on this susceptibility. This suggests a linkage of personality factors, "sociosymbolic stress," genetic factors, and evolutionary trends.

Personality factors, specifically the ability for displacement activities—that is, "the capacity to discharge impulse over substitute pathways" (Henry 1959:221, after Tinbergen 1951)—are seen as having major importance in social adaptation. Furthermore, if this capacity for displacement varies on the basis of genetic factors, an evolutionary implication is quite clearly indicated. On the other hand, this formulation also points to the possibility that it may be feasible to rate societies on the basis of the amount and types of sociosymbolic stress they impose on their members, thus not only provoking psychosomatic disorders but also accelerating evolutionary pressures. However, these speculations go beyond Henry's provocative statements of the issues.

Personality, then, may be seen as directly related not only to the evolution and continuity of culture; it may also be seen as a mediating factor in the processes of biological evolution of a species exposed to the sociosymbolic stresses of a cultural environment.

THE PSYCHIC UNITY OF MANKIND AND THE NATURE OF HUMAN NATURE

The nineteenth-century German anthropologist Adolf Bastian (1881) spoke of a "psychic unity of mankind." On this hypothetical unity he based his opposition to the then fashionable theories of broad cultural diffusion, for, by a general law, human beings everywhere must produce similar fundamental ideas (*Elementargedanken*), which account for the recurrence of similar inventions and institutions. Boas (1940: 272-73) phrased this point of view succinctly: "Bastian denies that it is possible to discover the ultimate source of inventions, ideas, customs, and beliefs which are universal of occurrence.... The human mind is so formed that it invents them spontaneously or accepts them whenever they are offered to it." To Bastian, then, the psychic unity of mankind was a hypothetical entity used to account for supposedly independent inventions. The extension of this notion to imply that the same phenomena are always due to the same causes was roundly rejected by Boas in favor of detailed historical reconstructions, which might point toward convergence rather than to an identical sequence of events. Far from being an analytic or descriptive statement of psychological structures or processes, capacities, or tendencies shared by men, the psychic unity of Bastian was a *deus ex machina*. It did not attempt to account for human behavior as such, only for the apparently independent recurrence of inventions and ideas. The point might be of no more than passing historic interest were it not for the fact that the term is now often used as synonymous with "human nature" (e.g., Mead 1964:367).

The concept of a generic human nature has passed through a series of vicissitudes. Introductory sociology texts, for example, have tended to make short shrift of it, rejecting the notion as either platitudinous or ethnocentric, attributing the values of the speaker's culture to mankind in general (e.g., Bennett and Tumin 1949:204). Spiro (1954:19-20) has documented the rejection of a concept of human nature, as distinct from the nature of other animals, by experimental psychologists and by some social psychologists as well. And anthropologists were then so fascinated by the diversity of cultures that they too denied the existence of a "universal human nature" (Spiro 1954:21). More recently J. J. Clarke (1970) has carried this rejection to a rather extreme position that appears to deny the possibility of defining underlying common "needs" or "problem areas" of human societies. Yet all comparative studies and all searches for generalizations about human societies are predicated on the possibility of finding comparable dimensions.

On the other hand, Fischer (1965: 221-25) has noted an increased interest in the subject of human nature in recent years. Hallowell, as we have seen, identified several interrelated psychological factors basic to a human level of adaptation: extrinsic shared symbolic processes, reflexivity, a normative orientation, imaginative processes, defense mechanisms, cumulative learning, and the ability to transcend learning through creativity and innovation.

Spiro (1954) identifies three aspects of the psychological dimension of a universal human nature: the capacity for symbolization, basic motives, and the common personality factor. With respect to basic motives, he strongly and cogently argues against the customary distinction between biological (or primary) and acquired (or secondary) drives. He points out that they interpenetrate each other and cannot be distinguished in the concrete instance. This very fact is distinctive of human nature (Spiro 1954:25): "... since man's acquired drives constitute his uniquely *human* motivations, and since they are as *natural* as his biological motivations . . . man's acquired drives [constitute] another psychological dimension . . . of an uniquely human nature" (italics in original). Concerning the common personality factor, he identifies four dynamic principles of personality functioning: needs (id), values (superego), ego processes (learning, perception, and cognition), and the defense mechanisms for the preservation of self-esteem (projection, rationalization, sublimation, and so on). Having rejected the differentiation between basic and acquired needs, Spiro cites the existence of a "world view" in every human society as an example of a type of need.

In one way or another, all comparative psychological research, whether of cognitive and perceptual processes or of personality functioning, can be seen as testing explicit or implicit assumptions about a generic human nature. Thus Mead's (1928) pioneering study of Samoan adolescent girls explicitly tested G. Stanley Hall's theory of adolescence as a biologically caused, thus necessarily universal, period of storm and stress, and found the theory contradicted by her data. A universal statement is disproved by a single negative instance. Freud postulated a universal latency period in prepubescent children. Róheim (1932) found it absent among the central Australians, and on this basis argued for a modification of the theory.

Perhaps the best known example of a disputed psychoanalytic universal is the Oedipus complex. Freud claimed it to be a universal stage in the life of small boys. Malinowski (1927) claimed that among the matrilineal Trobriand Islanders a boy's incest wishes are directed toward his sister—not, as in Freud's model, toward his mother—and his hostility is directed against his mother's brother rather than against his father. Róheim (1932, 1941), studying the equally matrilineal Normanby Islanders, challenged Malinowski's findings and reported an Oedipus complex of classical form. Ernest Jones (1925) disputed Malinowski's findings on theoretical grounds. Among other things, Jones pointed out that Malinowski's data did not deal with small children but with adults and adolescents. Among the Trobriand Islanders, no less than among Europeans, the father is the mother's lover, and the jealousy underlying the Oedipus hostility would thus be provoked in a matrilineal society as well as in a patriarchal one of the type Freud observed. Erich Fromm (1949), criticizing Freud's preoccupation with sex and his neglect of the issue of authority, has argued that the hostility between sons and fathers that Freud saw was real enough, but it was directed against the father as an authoritarian figure rather than as a sexual rival. This confusion was possible because in the European instance the father combined two roles, that of the authoritarian and that of the mother's lover. We might then suggest that in the case of the matrilineal Trobriand Islanders these two roles are separated and assigned to two different persons: the mother's brother as the authoritarian, the father as the sexual rival. In this sense, the Trobriand data represented the test case to distinguish between a Freudian (sexual) and a Frommian (authority) view of the father-son hostility in the Oedipus com-

plex. In the Frommian view, then, one might expect Malinowski's findings in a matrilineal society; in a Freudian view, Róheim's. Campbell and Naroll (1972), without referring to Fromm, also see a separation of the sexual and disciplinarian roles of the father in Trobriand society, thus permitting a decision in favor of an authority theory of the Oedipus complex. Thus "Malinowski's work helps to integrate personality theory with learning theory" (Campbell and Naroll 1972:437). However, the issue of a shift from infancy to adolescence and thus of the possible meaning of the Oedipus complex is not mentioned by Campbell and Naroll. Róheim (1934:248) has sought the source of the Oedipus complex not in learning, as Campbell does, but in biology: in a human development of a genital sexuality that is premature in relation to the development of the body as a whole and to the development of the individual's ego.

Marie-Cécile and Edmond Ortigues, in their important book *Oedipe africain* (1966), formulate the problem of the possible variations of the Oedipus complex in still different terms. Their theoretical formulations are derived from those of the French structuralist psychoanalyst Jacques Lacan (1966a, 1966b; Miel 1966). Working in Dakar as a practicing psychoanalyst among Africans (primarily Wolof, Lebu, and Serer), Mme Ortigues is able to draw on her own rich clinical materials. These authors also make an important distinction between the kinds of information obtained by the anthropologist and by the clinician, due to their manner of acquiring their data, a matter that is directly relevant to their severe critique of Malinowski.

While they recognize an "oedipal problem" among their African patients, they are primarily interested in the manner in which this problem is resolved, and it is here that they find the greatest difference between Senegalese and Europeans. Unlike the European, the African child does not arrive at a resolution of the Oedipus complex through identification with the father. Unconscious rivalry with the father is displaced on brothers and members of the peer group, and this displaced rivalry is strongly overcompensated by expressions of solidarity. The group of brothers is the central concern: it is toward this group that strivings for recognition are addressed, and it is this group's rejection that is the greatest source of anxiety. These differences are seen in the context of the particular social organizations of the Senegalese groups and also of the varying degrees of Westernization found among the individuals studied. A great role in the life of the individual, as seen by the authors, is played by the dramatization of various psychological themes in ritual and myth.

Anne Parsons (1964) has reviewed the Malinowski-Jones argument and has considered the question of the Oedipus complex in relation to south Italian data. Here she finds a still different "nuclear complex." Among the south Italians, the strongest tie of family life is the relationship of the son to the mother; highly sublimated, it is basic to the Madonna complex, with virginity as its central symbol. The hostility between son and father finds open expression and, unlike that of the Freudian model, is not transcended by an eventual identification of the son with the father. The key "triangle" of the south Italian family consists of the relationship between father and daughter and prospective son-in-law. Thus, while there is indeed a family triangle, the individuals involved and the manner in which hostility and attraction are managed are crucially different from both the Freudian and the Malinowskian patterns. It

should be noted also that the *direction* of the emotions is reversed, from senior to junior generation.

Such a phenomenon is also found by Herskovits and Herskovits (1958) in their discussion of Dahomean mythology. In this body of data they discover little evidence of the son's hostility toward the father, but much rivalry between brothers and a strong expression of the father's fear of being replaced by the son. They explain these findings on the basis of the structure of the Dahomean polygynous household.

Again, A. Parsons' reference to the mother-son relationship as the strongest tie in the family structure is reminiscent of Hsu's (1972; ed., 1970) analysis of kinship systems dominated by a single structural relationship. Hsu finds the mother-son tie, incidentally, to be the primary relationship in the kinship system of India. It would therefore be of some interest to compare the implications of this relationship for Hsu's Indians and Parsons' south Italians.

We have come some distance from the original question concerning the universality of the Oedipus complex, and an answer does not appear to be forthcoming. Somehow, the ground appears to have shifted. Freud dealt with a phase in the development of the male child. The anthropologists I have cited appear to be dealing with variations in the structure of the family—patriarchal, matrilineal, polygynous, as the case may be—and the implications of these variations for interpersonal relationships within it. As A. Parsons (1964: 328) has phrased it in her concluding remarks:

For the original question of whether the Oedipus complex is universal or not, we would sum up by saying that it is no longer very meaningful in that particular form. The more important contemporary question would rather be: what is the possible range within which culture can utilize and elaborate the instinctually given human potentialities, and what are the psychologically given limits of this range?

This is indeed an excellent question, and a great deal of work remains to be done before the answer is found. Yet in reviewing the history of the treatment of that other question about the universality of the Oedipus complex, one is tempted to wonder whether, in the course of the search for the answers to it, the question might not be some so transformed that no answer will, in fact, ever to be forthcoming!

COMPARATIVE STUDIES OF PERCEPTION AND COGNITION

As we have seen, comparative studies of perception, particularly visual perception, were begun before the turn of the century with the work of the Cambridge Torres Straits Expedition. There have been scattered studies in this area ever since then, but no continuous and truly cumulative effort until recent years. Interest in this area was stimulated in the 1950s and 1960s when a series of studies was undertaken, many in Africa. A number of publications have now appeared reviewing this branch of comparative studies in varying detail (French 1963; Triandis 1964; Segall, Campbell, and Herskovits 1966; Price-Williams 1968, ed. 1970). The relative neglect of such studies for so many years seems to be due in part to the fact that comparative research on perception tends to fall between two areas of specialization: they tend to be too technical and laboratory-oriented for the anthropologist, and to require too much research among exotic groups for the psychologist. In terms of the theoretical issues of psychology, however, such comparative studies speak directly to the argument between nativists (those who hold that universal laws of sensory perception are governed by the constancy of the human nervous system) and empiricists (those who argue that previous experiences influence perceptual responses). The psychological literature dealing with this issue in regard to individual differences in visual perception is reviewed by Segall, Campbell, and Herskovits (1966:77-82). In a cross-cultural context, the empiricist position would lead to an expectation of differences in perception among groups with different experiences, i.e., different cultures.

Earlier students, as already indicated, spoke of the differences they had found as "race differences." No differences have in fact been identified which can be explained in terms of the biological, hereditary differences among human *racial* groups (Klineberg 1935). On the other hand, there is strong evidence that differences in the perceptual performance of human groups do exist, and these require interpretation.

Segall, Campbell, and Herskovits (1966:24-25) have pointed out that the term "perception" is used with somewhat varying meanings by psychologists and anthropologists, ranging from processes "bordering on sensation" among psychologists to "processes bordering on cognition" by anthropologists. This lack of consistency in the use of terms adds to the difficulty of surveying and evaluating the findings in this field. It is in the area of visual perception that most experimental work has been carried out and that differences have been most clearly established. These experimental studies, mostly conducted by psychologists or in cooperation with psychologists, deal with a variety of aspects of visual perception: color perception, susceptibility to various types of optical illusions, depth perception in two-dimensional materials (drawings, photographs), perceptual dominance, testing of the *Gestalt* laws of perception (e.g., experiments on closure), eidetic imagery, judgment of sizes at distance, spatial acuity, interpretation of unstructured stimuli, and so on.

The most ambitious and best controlled comparative study of visual perception was conducted by Segall, Campbell, and Herskovits (1966). It involved thirteen African groups, one Philippine group, one group of Europeans in South Africa, and two North American groups. In several of these instances separate samples of adults and children were tested, so that a total of twenty-eight samples was studied. Two kinds of optical illusion were used, and it was found that Westerners were a great deal more susceptible than nonliterates to one kind of illusion (Müller-Lyer and Sandler parallelogram) and less susceptible than many of the nonwestern groups to optical illusions of another kind (horizontal-vertical illusions). These findings are held to support the two hypotheses on which this study was based: that both cultural factors (the so-called "carpentered world" of the Westerner) and ecological factors (the presence or absence of "broad horizontal vistas") affect susceptibility to the illusions. The authors argue that the findings support their hypotheses and replicate the findings of Rivers half a century earlier. The bidirectionality of the findings suggests that some experiential factors favor susceptibility to one kind of illusion and others to the second kind, and that these experiences vary from society to society. Some additional studies have produced supporting evidence among other cultural groups. For example, Gregor and McPherson (1965) found that more acculturated groups of Australian aborigines were more susceptible to the Müller-Lyle and Sandler illusions than less acculturated groups. Other studies fail to confirm or only partially confirm these findings (Jahoda 1966, Mundy-

Castle and Nelson 1962). Price-Williams (1968:312) argues that while the findings of Segall, Campbell, and Herskovits do indicate that "previous habits of perceptual inference tend to influence the perception of space thus portrayed," he finds less agreement on the nature of these habits. The question of interpreting the findings, then, appears to be at least partially unsolved.

Kilbride and Robbins (1969) have reviewed some of the literature, particularly with reference to Africa, concerning two other problems of visual perception—depth perception and recognition of objects in photographs and drawings—and report on their findings in an experimental study of these aspects of perception among the Baganda. Comparing rural and urbanized (i.e., more highly acculturated) Baganda in performances on a series of drawings, they find the acculturated "more successful in pictorial perception." If acculturation modifies pictorial perception, it is clear that learning and previous experience play important roles in such performance.

Two further studies are of interest here: Berry (1965) compared Temne of Sierra Leone and Baffin Island Eskimo with respect to several perceptual tests and found the Eskimo not only superior in performance but also less "group-reliant" and "field-dependent" in regard to perception. Dawson (1967) tested Temne as well as Mende. In respect to depth perception in drawings, she found that field-independent individuals of both groups performed better than field-dependent persons. Both Dawson and Berry relate differences between field-dependent and field-independent individuals to differences in socialization practices. Berry makes cross-cultural comparisons in this regard, while Dawson's comparisons are concerned with intragroup differences. Both of these studies are related to the work of Witkin et al. (1954), who studied the relationship of personality variables to performance in space orientation tests, differentiating between field-dependent and field-independent types.

If we consider the relationship between cultural factors and perception in what has been said so far, it is clear that there is a variety of such factors involved. Segall, Campbell, and Herskovits (1966) speak of the "carpentered world"; the cultural factor involved here refers to a series of features of material culture, based on inventions of certain types of tools. It is characterized by straight lines and right angles. The ecological factor that they hypothesize (broad horizontal vistas) operates in the context of cultural adaptation to such an environment. Spatial acuity for the Eskimo appears to involve adaptation not only to an environment of broad vistas but also to skills in hunting. Such perceptual adaptation is also illustrated by Winters' (1964) study of the Kalahari Bushmen, who exhibit great accuracy in the perception of the size of distant objects.

The work of Berry (1965) and Dawson (1967), however, adds another dimension to studies of visual perception by introducing as correlates of perceptual performance personality factors (relative field dependence) and variations in socialization practices, which are used to account for these personality differences. On the basis of this work, then, it would appear that certain types of perceptual performance not only are adaptive in some ecological and cultural settings, but also have broader psychological and cultural ramifications. Optimum performances of certain types, it would seem, are not simply acquired by practice and experience, but are associated with and expressive of certain personality features. These features are likely to be expressed in other types of behavior as well—self-reliance, for example, which also may be adaptive in the particular eco-cultural setting, as among hunters. Furthermore, it is claimed that these personality features are associated with and the results of certain socialization practices. Barry et al. (1959) have related dependence and independence training to subsistence practices of societies, and have found hunting societies in particular to train for independence.[1] We arrive, then, at a tentative series of hypotheses postulating a connection between socialization, personality, and perception as a first step, and perception and ecological adjustment as a second. The circle is closed by a third step linking socialization and subsistence economy, i.e., ecological adaptation. (Since we are dealing with a circle, we might equally well start with this third hypothesis and work through the other relationships from there.)

The assumption of a connection between perception and personality is basic to the Rorschach psychodiagnostic test (Rorschach 1921). In this test, which has been widely used cross-culturally, it is the manner of utilizing the perceptual field—that is, the unstructured shapes of the inkblots—that is employed as an indicator of personality features. The manner of perception revealed by the subject is of as much or greater importance to the analyst than the content of what is perceived.

As I have noted, a great deal of research has been carried out concerning various aspects of visual perception. In contrast, little work has been conduct-

---

[1] Barry et al. (1957) have shown, in their cross-cultural study of sex differences in socialization, that girls are generally taught to be more dependent than boys. It is interesting to note that Witkin et al. (1954) find women more field-dependent than men in their perceptual performance.

ed with respect to auditory perception. Rivers (1901) carried out some experiments in this area, but there has been only scattered work since then. Most of our information in this area comes from linguistics (e.g., Sapir 1949; Brown, Black, and Horowitz 1955) and musicology (e.g., Merriam 1967). Both language and music represent, of course, highly patterned and characteristic uses of sounds, varying from one musical or linguistic system to another.

Following Hall (1968), Kilbride and Robbins (1969:299) suggest that Western societies focus on the development of "visual perceptual skills," while others, such as African societies, may focus more strongly on "auditory-proprioceptive skills." Perhaps the research emphasis on visual rather than auditory perception that I have noted is itself a reflection of the culture of the researchers.

If cultures do indeed structure, emphasize, and utilize various sensory modalities differently, this represents an area of research that is as yet virtually untapped. Williams (1966) has discussed tactile behavior among the Dusun of northern Borneo, and has urged the study of tactility. Kinesthetic patterns and spatial orientation offer another challenge to research (Kurath 1960). For example, dizziness, which is likely to produce anxiety and fear of loss of control in Americans (e.g., Fenichel 1945), is interpreted by Haitians as a sign of the onset of spirit possession (Métraux 1959), as it is by Brazilian members of the Umbanda cult (Esther Pressel, personal communication). Dizziness in Americans may be an expected part of fear of heights. Fear of the heights is said to be absent among the Iroquois (Wallace 1951: 64-65).

When language intervenes as a structuring and ordering agent in the perceptual process, we are presumably dealing with matters closer to cognition than to perception. Thus the use of color terms may affect performance on tests of color perception (e.g., Rivers 1901). Through language, cultural factors intrude directly into the perceptual process. It both furnishes and reveals principles of organization that influence behavior. Such organization has been studied by several anthropologists among different cultures; for example, with respect to orientation in time and space (e.g., Hallowell 1937b, Evans-Pritchard 1940, Bohannan 1953).

It is striking to note the differences between experimental psychologists' and cultural anthropologists' approaches to studies of perception. The psychologist develops hypotheses by analyzing the implications of preliminary data in the light of his theories of human behavior, and then constructs experiments designed to confirm or disconfirm these hypotheses. He compares the behavior of two or more samples with regard to the same stimulus materials. He attempts to control the behavior of his respondents in the experimental situation. Much of the work on perception by anthropologists, on the other hand, is essentially contextual, with respect to a single society, rather than a comparison of statistical findings from two or more groups. It is the cultural context the anthropologist attempts to "control" by investigating its various ramifications. Evans-Pritchard (1940), for example, relates the terminology of time orientation of the Nuer to a cycle of seasons and their connections with subsistence activities and ritual activities. The "culturally constituted behavioral environment" (Hallowell 1955:87) in which members of a society live may be reconstructed by the anthropologist on the basis of observations of this sort. From such descriptive accounts the perceptual processes—that is, the subjective experiences of individuals—may then be inferred on the basis of observed behavior. In both cases, that of the psychologist and that of the anthropologist, there is a need for inference and there is a degree of control. But what is inferred and what is controlled varies importantly.

In his contextual studies the anthropologist traditionally seeks not only specific categories and terminologies of classification, but also the relationship of these categories to other aspects of the culture. Research on systems of classification has recently been formalized by the work of ethnoscientists. Sturtevant (1964:100), for one, has characterized the traditional anthropological practice as an attempt to "describe the universe in which a group of people live," in contrast with the "new" ethnography of the ethnoscientists, who attempt to "describe the principles by which these people classify their universe." While these studies tend to be highly formalized, they are relevant to psychological anthropology, at least in theory, in that they speak to the issue of cognition.

In either case, whether contextual or ethnoscientific, studies of the relativity of behavioral universes tell us about a group's alertness to certain cues and possibly lack of concern for certain others, and they indicate also the apparent immediacy of experiences based on such conventional cues. The major system of conventional cues is, of course, language, and here we can study the shifting meanings embedded in the system by investigating the responses of bilingual or multilingual individuals. For example, Doob (1957) found that subjects in three groups of Africans (Ganda, Luo, Zulu), under controlled test conditions, agreed significantly more often with statements in their native languages than with the same statements expressed in English. Doob (1957:96) comments that "use of one language rather than another may make a difference in evoked attitude." The findings suggest also that to a multilin-

gual person, each language represents a system of cues capable of evoking different sociocultural contexts and different cognitive and perceptual systems. A similar implication is carried by the work of Ervin (1964), who administered a projective test (TAT) to French-English bilinguals and found significant differences in the themes of stories told by the same individual when the language in which the test was administered was changed. Since this is a personality test, different responses from language to language imply two somewhat different personality profiles for a single individual. With respect to cues, we may note that certain beliefs about the universe and the entities within it predispose an individual toward certain perceptions or pseudoperceptions. This is illustrated by Hallowell's (1942) account of a Saulteaux Indian who "heard" a *windigo* monster, i.e., who apparently experienced an auditory illusion (Hallowell 1955:57-58, discussed at length in Segall, Campbell, and Herskovits 1966:28-32). Indeed, the pseudoperceptions characteristic of the guardian spirit complex and its associated vision quest, so widespread among North American Indian societies (Benedict 1923), illustrate this point, as do pseudoperceptions ("hallucinations") experienced by persons under the influence of hallucinogenic drugs, *when there exists a set of cultural expectations concerning such experiences* (La Barre 1969, Castañeda 1968, Bourguignon 1970). However, pseudoperceptions are too distinct from sensory perceptions to be treated in this context in further detail.

PERSONALITY

In our discussion of behavioral evolution, we encountered the concept of personality as an emergent of that process. We also found personality differences among individuals referred to as variables significant in the operation of biological evolution. Personality and personality processes were seen as central concerns, furthermore, in generalized discussions of human nature. And personality factors turned up again as possibly significant variables in our review of studies of perception, both as intragroup differences and as intergroup differences.

Personality has, in fact, been the central psychological concern of psychological anthropology for the past forty years. Yet as late as 1937, Du Bois (p. 247) could say that little was known about the "individual behavior and attitudes" of primitive people, and that discussions of primitive psychology were for the most part "based on social factors rather than upon knowledge of the individuals involved." By 1968, Honigmann could assemble a list of fifty "primitive societies for which major studies of personality are available" (pp. 266-67). Most of these studies had appeared in the interim, and their distribution strikingly reflects the geographic interests of American anthropologists, who are the primary contributors to this list. About half the societies listed are in North America and more than a quarter in the Insular Pacific, while only a handful are to be found in Africa, South America, and East Eurasia, in that order. The "primitives" involved, furthermore, represent various stages of acculturation and Westernization. Indeed, certain societies have been studied at several levels of acculturation.

It should be noted that in this period, in addition to conducting research among primitive societies, anthropologists also carried out personality investigations among numerous peasant groups in Europe, South America, and Asia, and contributed to the literature of national character studies. (There exist various excellent reviews of this literature. See for example, Barnouw 1963; Honigmann 1967; Inkeles and Levinson 1954, 1968; Inkeles 1972.)

The approaches to the broad subject of culture-personality interactions utilized by the contributors to this sizable body of materials are strikingly varied. For example, taking the first three societies from the list of fifty presented by Honigmann, we find such contrasts as these: The Dogon were studied by a team of Swiss psychoanalysts (Parin, Morgenthaler, and Parin-Matthey 1963) by means of what the authors refer to as psychoanalytic conversations, from which a picture of Dogon personality was constructed. Field (1960), an ethnographic research worker turned psychiatrist, studied the operations of therapeutic shrine cults in Ghana, in a multitribal setting, investigating both the dissociational states of the priest-therapist and the types of psychopathologies presented by the patient population. The LeVines (LeVine 1962, LeVine and LeVine 1963), a husband-wife team of American anthropologists, report on child training among the Gusii on the basis of ethnographic fieldwork, observations, and interviews. Admittedly there may be greater homogeneity among various studies of North American groups by American anthropologists. Still, it would be difficult to define the common terms of these studies and to construct a comparative analysis based on them, in view of the variations in the types of data presented and in the theoretic frameworks within which they are cast.

Yet in spite of these reservations, it must be recognized that there exists one central question with which the culture and personality research of the past forty years has been concerned. This question deals with what Wallace (1970a:84) terms "the cultural distribution of personality characteristics." However, before taking a closer look at the issues involved in the study of this central question, we must first note certain background factors that have significantly influenced the development of formulations and approaches in this area.

Venturing into the psychological field, anthropologists soon found themselves enmeshed in certain conceptual and terminological problems. The terminology of personality description they employed, whether applied to individual personalities or whole cultures, was largely borrowed from the clinical field. For example, in her famous and path-breaking book, *Patterns of Culture*, first published in 1934, Benedict (1961:238) could speak of the "aggressive, paranoid tendencies of Dobu and the Northwest Coast." The very terminology used thus had an evaluative tone and pressingly urged questions of normality and pathology. Yet Benedict's emphasis was strongly on the relative nature of culture. While she pointed to the similarity between the culturally developed "paranoia" of the Kwakiutl on the one hand and that of the American psychiatric patient on the other, for example, she also argued that, because the behavior of the Kwakiutl was in conformity with cultural standards and expectations, it was not clinically pathological. She argued that, instead of looking at a list of symptoms, psychiatrists must look to the degree of cultural fit of a set of behaviors.

Much later, the psychiatrist A. H. Leighton (Leighton and Hughes 1961: 381) stated that in cross-cultural studies "no existing form of diagnosis is usable." Furthermore, he urged:

One has to get rid of the built-in etiological preconceptions that exist in most diagnostic acts. Where studies are concerned with exploring the etiological influences of cultural factors, the psychiatric phenomena for study have to be defined in terms of symptom patterns. The question of whether they are patho-

logical or not should be set aside. In short, one has to study the distribution of selected types of human patterns, and only later ask what the functional effect and consequences of these are. The determination of pathology is the last thing to be done rather than the first.

This wise counsel, however, was not anticipated. Benedict and others did speak of "normal" and "abnormal" behavior, saying the "abnormals are those who are not supported by the institutions of their civilization" (Benedict 1961:258).

The term "normal," however, had its own semantic load, being variously interpreted as "statistically average" and as synonymous with "healthy" (Wegrocki 1939). If, furthermore, the statistical norm of a given society was in fact behavior that might be argued to be pathological on other than contextual grounds, could it then be said that an entire society was insane (e.g., Devereux 1939, Brickner 1943)? Or, on the contrary, did one have to maintain that a society develops its own standards and the statistical norm does represent mental health for its members?

It must be remembered that these were not purely academic questions, with consequences only in some rarefied field of ideas. The culture and personality movement developed in the 1930s, a period of economic depression and questioning of age-old values, of the rise of dictatorships and preparations for war, and it reached its most active period of publication during and shortly after World War II. And during that war, and the cold war that followed, anthropologists produced national character studies, many of them of enemy nations (for example, Benedict 1946; Gorer 1943; Gorer and Rickman 1949; Mead and Métraux, eds., 1953). In 1934, *Patterns of Culture* was a plea for tolerance and understanding of other cultures and for deviants in one's own society. To Benedict, "social relativity" was "a doctrine of hope, not despair."

For Harris (1969, chap. 15), culture and personality grew out of "Boasian particularism," the emphasis on the uniqueness of each culture. Aberle (1960) pointed to the strong influence of linguistics on the emerging research orientation, through the work of Sapir, who was himself a linguist, and through Sapir's influence on Benedict. The significance of the growth of psychoanalysis in the United States at the time and of the development of a neo-Freudian orientation for psychological anthropology must not be underestimated. Academic psychology appears to have had little influence, except perhaps in Benedict's references to the *Gestalt* school. Clinical psychology, however, somewhat later provided the great impetus for the use of personality tests. Yet the historic context of economic and political facts must surely not be overlooked.

The central questions that have occupied students of culture and personality, then, might be generalized as follows: Do members of a single society, living within the bounds of a single culture, share a common cognitive orientation, a common world view, a common basic or modal personality, a social or national character? How is one to discover whether or not this is so?

Two basic strategies have been developed to deal with these questions: (1) The isomorphism between "culture" and "personality" is assumed. Thus personality can be investigated by analyzing culture. (2) Methods must be developed to assess personality, independent of cultural analysis, to discover (*a*) whether shared personality characteristics do exist among the members of the group under investigation and (*b*) whether a fit exists between "personality" so described and "culture" investigated and described in its own terms.

The first strategy is that used by Benedict, who stated (1932:24) that one may consider cultures to be "individual psychology thrown large upon the screen, given gigantic proportions and a long time span." It is the strategy she adopted in *Patterns of Culture*, in which a single dominant configuration is identified for each culture. Two points in particular should be noted. First, the pattern that characterizes each culture is the result of selectivity: "The cultural pattern of any civilization makes use of a certain segment of the great arc of potential human purposes and motivations" (Benedict 1961:237). But the reasons that might exist for particular choices are not elucidated. Some patterns are well integrated, others are not; indeed, lack of integration is a hallmark of Northwest Coast culture. Second, there is little discussion of individuals as such to be found in the book; acts of individuals serve only as illustrations for cultural forms. However, individual differences are recognized, and some people, because of their "temperaments," are said to be at ease in a given culture while others, a minority, are not. But the misfits of one society—the meek Dobuan, the aggressive Zuñi, the peaceful Kwakiutl—may have "temperaments" that would be well suited to the pattern of another. In spite of the existence of such deviants, it is possible to study culture as "personality writ large" because culture molds personality (Benedict 1961: 236):

If we are interested in human behavior, we need first of all to understand the institutions that are provided for in any society. For human behavior will take the forms those institutions suggest, even to extremes of which the observer, deep-dyed in the culture of which he is a part, can have no intimation.

The second strategy involves the utilization of various methods to assess adult personality, such as the collection of life histories, dreams, and projective tests. This has given rise to an extensive literature, which has been reviewed in several publications. For example, Langness (1965) has accumulated an impressive list of studies based on life histories, for the most part among primitive peoples. However, he points out that relatively little analytic use has been made of the wealth of information contained in these publications, and he presents various suggestions for tapping this storehouse of cultural and psychological data.

Studies of dreams have been reviewed several times (e.g., D'Andrade 1961, Bourguignon 1972). Dreams have been used for several kinds of analysis and some examples may be cited here. Honigmann (1961) presents a case study of the dream of a Cree Indian, relating it, together with the dreamer's associations both to the life of the dreamer and to the culture of his society. Eggan (1955, 1961, 1966) collected several hundred dreams among the Hopi over a period of many years, and shows how the cultural materials of myth and ritual are used and transformed by the subjects in their dreams. Schneider (Schneider and Sharp 1969) analyzes the manifest content of a series of 149 dreams collected by Sharp among the Australian Yir Yoront with respect to several content categories, and also cites some comparative results from the analysis of 1,500 dreams from 75 societies culled from the literature. He finds both culturally specific and pan-human trends. Thus Schneider reports finding in all societies of his sample "a higher proportion of dreams of aggression than of death or coitus" (p. 55), and that furthermore, in dreams of aggression the dreamer is more likely to be the victim than the aggressor. On the other hand, Yir Yoront culture is reflected, for example, in the finding that

when men dream of sexual relations, their women partners tend to be members of a social category with whom such relations are permitted. If not, the obstacles encountered in the dream tend to correspond in difficulty to the degree of severity of the taboo involved.

Lindzey (1961) reviews the extensive literature on the use of projective tests in cross-cultural research,[2] analyzing problems and assets in the use of these devices. On the basis of this review, he arrives at an important series of generalizations (1961:311-12):

1. "There is enormous variation in personality even within apparently homogenous, nonliterate societies."

2. ". . . varying degrees or levels of acculturation are accompanied by varying personality attributes and perhaps by variation in general level of adjustment."

3. ". . . individuals representative of different socialization practices and different cultural backgrounds respond differently to most projective techniques."

4. ". . . personality inferences based upon the widely used projective techniques appear consistent with parallel inferences derived from ordinary field work methods."

He observes further that "a very large number of modal or typical personality descriptions for particular cultures have been derived from projective test findings." However, he concludes on a note of caution (p. 328). Praising

---

[2] In the United States, Hallowell (1941a, 1941b) pioneered in the use of the Rorschach test among American Indians in 1938, stimulating its later widespread cross-cultural use. It is primarily the American literature that is reviewed by Lindzey (1961). Among Japanese anthropologists, Fujisawa first used the Rorschach in 1930 in a study of Formosan aborigines, although this study was not published until 1953. Huzioka (1968) summarized some of the Japanese Rorschach literature in connection with his own study of the East African Hadzapi.

the "studies involving the most sophisticated use of these instruments in this setting (for example Gladwin and Sarason 1953, Spindler 1955, Wallace 1952) . . ." he finds them "vastly outnumbered" by studies "in which these devices do not appear to have made a legitimate investigative contribution." After the passage of almost a decade, these conclusions still hold true. Part of the difficulty, as in the case of the life history materials mentioned above, resides in the complexity of the analytic methods, and indeed the specialized training required in designing and carrying out such studies.[3]

If personality is assessed by methods independent of those of cultural analysis, we may or may not find homogeneity within a given society and a fit between personality descriptions and cultural descriptions. Lindzey (1961), as we have seen, tells us that on the basis of projective test results, much variation in personality is found "even within apparently homogeneous nonliterate societies." Yet he also observes a fit between cultural descriptions and personality assessment based on projective tests. How are such findings to be accounted for? Benedict (1961), as we have seen, tells us that personality is molded by social institutions. We must therefore study the process of "molding," primarily, that is, the processes by means of which the newborn of a society are turned into functioning members of that society. An extensive literature on child training in different societies has developed over the last thirty-five to forty years, and we shall consider some aspects of this literature presently.

Another answer to the question of fit between personality and culture is found in the contrary claim that a particular culture is the expression of a particular personality type. In its most extreme form, this has been the answer suggested by Róheim (1943) in his formulation of an "ontogenetic theory of culture." This theory attributes crucial importance to a single typical infantile trauma, which characterizes a given culture and which differs from the typical trauma of some other culture. The pattern of life having been set by infantile experiences, all adult activities are sublimations of these, or their acting out, either in reality or on a fantasy level.

An interpretation that to some extent incorporates both of these somewhat extreme views appears to have wider support. Kardiner (1939:12) formulated the concept of "basic personality structure," which he defined as "that group of psychic and behavioral characteristics derived from contact with the same institutions." This is distinct from the total personality of the individual; it constitutes the shared element of personality within a society. The individual is exposed to a series of "primary institutions" (family structure and basic disciplines relating to food, sex, and elimination), which produce certain attitudes. These are projected[4] by the individual and result in secondary institutions such as religion

---

[3] A more recent review of projective tests and the challenge they present to anthropologists has been published by Spain (1972), who also presents an impressively long bibliography on the subject, indicating its continued attraction.

---

[4] It should be noted that at least three different uses of the term "projection" are to be found in the culture and personality literature: (1) The Freudian usage refers to a defense mechanism in which the individual assigns to others ("projects" on them) certain of his own unconscious attitudes and strivings. (2) Kardiner sees mythology and religion as areas ("projective screens") which permit the expression of unconscious fantasies; e.g., spirits are seen as having certain of the perceived characteristics of parents, (3) In personality tests referred to as "projective techniques," the subject's perceptions of the forms express ("project") aspects of his personality.

and mythology. Thus culture (or some portion of it) molds personality, and itself is molded, either wholly or in part, by the personalities of its members.

This formulation was first modified by Whiting and Child (1953) and later was more fully elaborated by B. Whiting (ed., 1963:4-5). In this more complex view, ecology is seen as giving rise to the maintenance system of a society, i.e., its economy and social structure. This system in turn affects child rearing practices. These practices of child rearing lead to child personality, which may be inferred from child behavior and childhood culture. Child behavior may be considered to include work and games, while cultural products of childhood include such matters as fantasy, sayings, recreation, and concepts of the world. In time, adult personality arises from child personality. It in turn may be inferred from such aspects of adult behavior as crime rates, suicide rates, leisure-time activities, and the like, and from adult cultural products such as religious beliefs, theories of disease, and folk tales. In this scheme part of culture gives rise to personality, which, since it cannot be observed directly, is inferred from other shared cultural aspects, which are treated as reflections of personality.

There are a number of differences between Kardiner's and Whiting's schemes, beyond the obviously greater complexity and sophistication of the latter. Kardiner (1939, 1945) utilized anthropological descriptions of various fieldworkers to arrive at his formulation of primary institutions and inferred the resulting basic personality structure, which he then also saw reflected in the "projective screens" of the secondary institutions. In the case of the Alorese, he derived pictures of individual personalities from life histories and dreams reported by Du Bois

(Kardiner 1945, Du Bois 1944). These, however, as Wallace (1970a:86-87) has pointed out, did not necessarily conform to the basic personality model.

Whiting's scheme, on the other hand, is presented as a framework for the comparative study of child training. However, ". . . the causal relationships implied in this scheme are open to discussion" (B. Whiting, ed., 1963:5).

Both Kardiner's and Whiting's schemes are in fact linear. There is, however, reason to argue that we are dealing with a set of circular relationships, or better, a system in which various types of feedback may be observed. We may cite just two such relationships. For example, is there not a connection between parental personality and child rearing practices? Kardiner (1945:27) does include "maternal attitudes" among the significant factors to be observed. Earlier, we discussed field-independent types of perception as attributes of personality, resulting from certain socialization practices. But, as we have seen, this behavior in turn is adaptive to the society's maintenance system.[5]

Another criticism of these schemes is that they represent static models. Studies of culture change and acculturation therefore represent crucial tests for such a model. We shall consider some of the psychological implications of processes of cultural dynamics below.

The Kardiner-Whiting model suggests that one may study the effects of culture on personality, of personality on culture, or both. Spiro (1972:583) has stated that ". . . the documentation of the importance of cultural determi-

---

[5] In their most recent review of the relevant literature, Harrington and Whiting (1972) have also introduced feedback into their model.

nants in personality formation was a major—though not exclusive—intellectual achievement of culture-and-personality studies, and it represents the major contribution of anthropology to personality theory." However, since this enterprise has been so successful and since, indeed, it is "the study of culture and social systems [that] *is* the focal concern of anthropology" (1972:584), he suggests a reorientation to transform personality into an explanatory concept. Thus, he states (1972:605), the "important theoretical goal is to discover the ways in which personality systems enable social and cultural systems to serve their social functions." It is necessary to study not only their existence but also their operation, which is, "in the last analysis, a motivational problem." In his book *Burmese Supernaturalism* (1967), Spiro did indeed follow through with this program, showing cognitive, perceptual, and motivational explanations not only for the individual's acquisition of beliefs in certain traditional spiritual entities, but also for the maintenance of these beliefs. And he clearly shows that various types of "explanations" of societal phenomena (historical, political, psychological) are not contradictory but indeed necessary complements for a total causational account.

Underlying the Kardiner-Whiting scheme, Spiro's analysis, and most work in the whole culture and personality field is the assumption that members of a particular group do in fact share some elements of personality, because they share their group's culture, or some aspects of it. Although the importance of individual differences is recognized, this assumption means concern with some hypothetical central tendencies, variously phrased as "basic personality structure" (Kardiner 1939, 1945), "modal personality" (Du Bois 1944, Wallace 1952), "modal personali-

ty type" (Hallowell 1951), "social character" (Fromm 1941, Riesman et al. 1950), and so on. The concept of a shared culture goes back, as we have seen, to Tylor's (1871) classic definition. Wallace (1961, 1970*a*; Wallace and Atkins 1960) has vigorously questioned this basic assumption, on both empirical and theoretical grounds. Rather than uniformity, Wallace sees diversity. In his Rorschach study of the Tuscarora Indians, for example, Wallace (1952) found that a modal personality defined on the basis of twenty-one dimensions of the test included only 37 percent of his sample. That is, by these criteria, almost two-thirds of the sample fell outside the modal type and thus were "deviant." Rather than "replication of uniformity" within a society and from generation to generation, Wallace sees the principal problem of culture as the "organization of diversity," so that the work of the society can be accomplished. Cognitive sharing, for example, cannot be demonstrated, or cognitive maps according to which members of a society operate, since several models may predict behavior with equal accuracy. Furthermore, he argues (1970*a*:35), "cognitive non-sharing" may be a "functional desideratum" of society because "(1) it permits a more complex system to arise than most, or any, of its members can comprehend; (2) it liberates the participants in a system from the heavy burden of knowing each other's motivations."

A comparison between the positions of Spiro (1967, 1972) and Wallace (1970*a*) suggests that they see both the achievements and the goals of culture and personality studies in very different terms indeed. Spiro sees the aim as the investigation of a "motivational problem" and Wallace argues that motivations (as part of the cognitive orientation of the individual) are unknowable. Yet Wallace is no less interested than

Spiro in the effects of personality on social systems (e.g., Wallace 1956*a*, 1956*b*).

CHILD TRAINING, SOCIALIZATION, ENCULTURATION

As we have seen, one of the major problems of psychological anthropology has been the question of how the personality type characteristic of a given culture is developed in each new generation. This question has led to a great interest in the manner in which children are taught their culture and come to internalize its values, its characteristic way of perceiving the world—literally and figuratively—and become the kinds of people they turn out to be as adults. The focus has been on the observation of interactions between children and parents or parent surrogates and on interviewing adults, testing children, and so on. The broad literature in this area has been reviewed recently and most extensively by Williams (1972).

From birth to maturity a variety of interacting and interdependent processes are at work, which may be differentiated for analytic purposes but which in fact constitute a single living stream: growth and maturation, personality development, language acquisition, learning of aspects of culture, including the learning of social roles. Some of these processes may be subsumed under the term "education," particularly where formal institutions for the teaching and training of the young exist (Henry 1960; Spindler, ed., 1963).

For the broader area of study, anthropologists have used several terms, often with some bewildering inconsistency. Psychologists, sociologists, and sometimes anthropologists have used the term "socialization." J. W. M. Whiting (1968) has pointed to some dissatisfaction with this term both for

its ambiguity and for its apparent limitation to the learning of social roles. Herskovits (1948) coined the terms "enculturation," "enculturative process," and "enculturative experience." He distinguishes enculturation from socialization, which he defines (1948:38) as "the process by means of which an individual is integrated into his society," and points out that men are not the only animals that are socialized. In contrast, he notes (1948:39):

The aspects of the learning experience which mark off man from other creatures, and by means of which, initially, and in later life, he achieves competence in his culture, may be called *enculturation*. This is in essence a process of conscious or unconscious conditioning, exercised within the limits sanctioned by a given body of custom. [Italics in original.]

And again (1948:640):

The enculturative process includes the whole of that aspect of adjustment of the newly-born individual to the group of which he is to become a member, and more. . . . The enculturative experience, however, also includes those reactions to aspects of life that, as expressions of the creative drive, are only secondarily reactions to the social structures which make of society an organized unit.

And Herskovits goes on to enumerate music, art, dancing, and philosophical speculation among the patterns to which the individual is enculturated.

Margaret Mead (1963:185), who also uses both "socialization" and "enculturation," defines the terms quite differently. Socialization is said to mean "abstract statements about learning as a universal process" and enculturation "the actual process of learning as it takes place in a specific culture. . . ." Williams (1969, 1972) follows this usage. A recent discussion by Shimahara et al. (1970) eloquently demonstrates the lack of terminological precision in this area. In view of this, "child training" has been used by some as an alternate term (Whiting and Child 1953; B. Whiting, ed., 1963). Regardless of which terms one favors, the literature is variable in aims and methods. In recent years, psychologists and psychiatrists have also contributed to studies of nonwestern, often nonliterate, societies in this respect.

We may broadly distinguish four types of field studies, admitting, however, that this classification is to be considered merely as a possible rough and ready guide to the area:

1. The search for possible regularities in child development. Examples are found in the work of Géber and in Ainsworth's (1967) excellent and detailed study of Ganda infants. Ainsworth seeks to add to our understanding of how the child's attachment to the mother develops. The weaning practices of the Ganda add interest to the choice of this population for study, but it is child development in general that offers the focal point of investigation. Géber (1956, 1958; Géber and Dean 1957) have reported psychomotor development of African children (Ganda and several other samples) much accelerated over European and American standards. These findings are supported by Ainsworth (1967:310-30), who concludes "that the course of sensory motor development of the Ganda child is influenced by child-care practices" (p. 329). The questions here are not: What is Ganda culture like? What kind of people are the Ganda? but: How are Ganda infants cared for? How do they develop in comparison with children in countries where standardized rates have been established for various aspects of development?

2. How do children learn their culture in a particular society? How are children "enculturated"? Williams (1969) has presented a description of the enculturation of Dusun children, analyzed in terms of traits and trait complexes

and synthesized as a series of "ten separate patterns of Dusun enculturation." Each of these patterns includes a number of traits and trait complexes, and together they form a configuration within Dusun culture. Explicitly no attempt is made to project a relationship between this configuration and other configurations of Dusun culture or between it and Dusun adult personality.

3. The relationship between child training and other aspects of culture. J. W. M. Whiting et al. (eds., 1966) have published a detailed guide for a comparative study of socialization in six cultures. This guide seeks information not only on child rearing, through observation and interviews, but also on cultural antecedants and cultural consequents of socialization, following the scheme outlined by B. Whiting (ed., 1963) and discussed above. The descriptive materials presented by B. Whiting represent the most fully comparable series of data from several different cultures available at present.

Mead (1963:184) has stated emphatically, "Everything that has been patiently accumulated on the subject of child rearing in different cultures has demonstrated the most minute correspondence between the over-all patterns of a culture and the patterns of child rearing in that culture."

Thus, quite aside from the effects of training practices on children, child rearing may be seen as one pattern (or as a group of patterns) among other congruent patterns that make up a culture. This does indeed presuppose a certain view of culture, which appears to differ from that of the Whiting scheme (and its antecedent in Kardiner's version), in which child rearing is seen not as a microcosmic model of a culture but as a factor within a causal chain. However, most of the studies that have attempted to establish such correspondences are largely concerned with personality as a described rather than as an inferred entity, as is the case in the studies by Whiting and his group.

4. The relationship between child training and adult personality. Most anthropological studies of child training appear to belong in this category. For the majority of these, the basic explanatory theory is Freudian or, more frequently, neo-Freudian. This approach is best exemplified in the work of Kardiner (1939, 1945), mentioned earlier, which was highly influential in the development of studies of this type. As a psychoanalyst, Kardiner did not himself conduct fieldwork, but arrived at this view of the relationship between culture and personality through the cooperation of anthropologists, notably Linton. His approach focuses on the general description of child training by the cooperating anthropologists, and on available life history data. He is less concerned with biological drives than with the "integrational units" by means of which these drives are consummated. He attempts to identify successive integrational units by following the life cycle of the individual. In spite of the influence exerted by Kardiner for a time, only two field studies were carried out within his frame of reference, by collecting detailed life histories and projective test materials as well as general cultural background data and information on child training: Du Bois's (1944) study of the Alorese and its somewhat refined replication among the Trukese by Gladwin (Gladwin and Sarason 1953).

These psychoanalytically oriented studies attempting to link child training and adult personality have been criticized on several scores. Orlansky (1949), in a frequently cited paper, attacked the Freudian, or supposedly Freudian, hypotheses on which much of this work is based. Axelrad (1962) has presented a systematic point-by-point rejoinder, in which he claims that not only Orlansky but also the neo-

Freudians and many of the anthropological contributors to the culture and personality literature have misunderstood or distorted Freud's hypotheses. In fact, his condemnation of anthropological and neo-Freudian attempts to link child training and personality is, if anything, more sweeping than Orlansky's, for he states (1962:92): "We are not really in possession of a firm theory that specifies the relationships between personality and culture. Psychoanalysis does have a theory of personality. Certain anthropologists have a theory of culture. But we have not really a viable theory of *culture and personality*." (Italics in original.)

Several other difficulties have been noted in this group of studies, some of which have already been mentioned. The model, which relates childhood to adult personality, is essentially static. By the 1950s concern had developed over the relationship between what was represented as an essentially fixed personality type, replicated from generation to generation, and the realities of cultural change. In part because of the nature of anthropological fieldwork, the assumption appears to have been built into these studies that the adults whose personalities can be assessed today are the products of the training they can be observed providing for (or imposing on) their children. This assumed synchronicity is a radical flaw of the approach.

Another flaw is found in the apparent arbitrariness of the aspects that are selected for emphasis both in child training and in adult personality. It is noteworthy, for example, that Du Bois (1944) does not quite agree with Kardiner's (1945) analysis of her data, and there has been considerable controversy over the role to be assigned to swaddling in the development of Russian personality (Gorer and Rickman 1949, Mead 1954, Barnouw 1963:128-34).

And finally, the method of eliciting

quasi-psychoanalytic data in life histories in a nontherapeutic situation—in fact with paid informants—has been questioned by Powdermaker (1945) and Ortigues and Ortigues (1966).

CULTURE CHANGE

The literature dealing with psychological aspects of culture change has been reviewed by G. and L. Spindler (1963), Barnouw (1963), and Wallace (1970a). The Spindlers point to a major concern with psychological materials by anthropologists dealing with problems of culture change during the period 1929-1952 and a marked decrease in the use of such materials in the decade 1952-1962.

Culture change may be seen as having a variety of psychological dimensions: the psychology of innovation (Barnett 1953); the motivation to accept innovations, whether from within a society or from without, in a situation of culture contact or acculturation; the learning processes or processes of "re-enculturation" involved in such acceptance or rejection (Herskovits 1945, Hallowell 1945, Gillin 1942); the psychological dimension of such acculturational processes as reinterpretation and synchretism (Herskovits 1948, Bourguignon 1954), and so on. Acculturation, or culture change, requires not only the acceptance of new items in a cultural inventory, but, as we have seen earlier, a modification of the various psychological processes; for example, the learning of new forms of perception, such as depth perception in two-dimensional representations. Some of the literature has been concerned with the practical problems of motivating people to accept change (e.g., Foster 1969).

The central problem of the relationship between personality and culture reappears here: What is the relationship between culture change and personality change? Can culture change while personality remains unchanged? How is adult personality affected by culture change? Is child rearing modified as other aspects of culture are altered?

As I pointed out earlier, the model that derives adult personality from child training techniques, with personality in turn giving rise to various aspects of culture, is essentially a static model for which situations of culture change represent a test. In some situations of this type, family structure and child training are altered intentionally so as to give the new generation childhood experiences and attitudes different from those with which their parents grew up. The classic case of such a planned modification is that of the kibbutzim of Israel, where education is a collective undertaking and attempts have been made to abolish the traditional forms of the family (Spiro 1958a, 1958b; Bettelheim 1969).

Two studies of situations in which personality is seen as affected by acculturative changes, but with apparently quite different results, may be cited. Hallowell (1951) compares three levels of acculturation among Ojibwa Indians on the basis of samples of Rorschach protocols. He asks on the one hand whether there is a psychological continuity from the least acculturated to the most, and on the other hand whether there are differences in personal and social adjustment among these levels. The three levels are indeed found to be psychologically distinct, although even among the most acculturated some continuity with the old personality type exists. However, where acculturation has proceeded slowly, at level 2 there has been a notable personality readjustment to the new situation. At level 3 there is much maladjustment, and what remains of the traditional personality structure is inadequate to cope with the problems of life. In Hallowell's words (1955:352), "There is a kind of frustration of maturity."

Mead (1956) reports on a 1953 restudy of the Manus, whom she had investigated twenty-five years earlier (Mead 1930). In 1928 the children led happy, carefree, relatively independent lives, forming friendships and learning a variety of skills with a high degree of self-confidence and alertness, with none of the "animism" of childhood postulated by Piaget. The happy period of childhood, however, was followed by arranged marriage, accompanied by strains and hostilities. Marriages had to be financed, and they put young men into debt. Brides went to live with their husbands' families and were obliged to observe various rules of propriety for which they were ill prepared. The debts and the scarcity of resources made childhood friends hostile competitors. Property values were of greatest importance. Nonpayment of debts and sexual offenses were punished by supernatural sanctions. In Benedict's (1938) terms, Manus "cultural conditioning" was "discontinuous," the demands on adults being harsh and those on children virtually nonexistent. A happy, carefree childhood was followed by a tense and guilt-ridden adulthood; friendly children turned into hostile adults. When Mead returned to Manus in 1953, she found that, as a result of World War II (during which Manus had been a major staging area) and the powerful innovative force of a charismatic leader, Manus society had been radically transformed: arranged marriages with their heavy financial burdens had been abandoned, and gone, apparently, was the concern with property and guilt. The children whom Mead had studied as youngsters were now adults who were able to maintain friendships with their peers, and who had not acquired the unpleasant personalities of

their elders. Instead of discontinuity, they had, in fact, experienced continuity in their lives.

A possible interpretation of these findings suggests itself: if the parents of the 1928 children had indeed had the same early experiences as their offspring, the discontinuity of adolescence or the lack of it appears to loom important in the development of adult personalities. A single type of child training may thus give rise to two different adult personality types if the cultural contexts differ.

Manus culture was changed in part by a conscious effort of the people to develop a different way of life from the kind they had known. Wallace (1956a, 1956b) has termed such efforts "revitalization movements." He sees them as responses by some individuals to the disorganization of their sociocultural system, which causes them to suffer personal disorganization as well. The response to such disorganization may be an (unconscious) attempt at regeneration by one or several individuals. Often such regeneration involves the development of a leader, or prophet, who synthesizes his view of a new life in a visionary trance state. Such an experience, called "mazeway resynthesis" by Wallace (1956a) and "conversion" by Sargant (1959), has the potential for individual and cultural renewal only if the person who experiences it can develop a following. The usual supernatural interpretation of such an experience lends it great conviction where belief or potential belief is strong, but in a secular society it may carry the stigma of psychosis. A great many examples of such leaders can readily be cited: the Iroquois prophet Handsome Lake (Wallace 1970b), Paliau in Manus (Mead 1956, Schwartz 1962), and Anne Lee, who founded the Shakers (Bourguignon and Haas 1965), among others. In some of these instances, only the prophet experiences trance states, once or several times. In others, conversion experiences are undergone by new members of the movement, marking their changed state, and in still others, trance states are ritualized and engaged in over and over again. While a typology of revitalization movements with respect to their utilization of trance states has not been worked out, it is important to note here that an apparently universal psychological potential—the ability to experience altered states of consciousness of a patterned type—can be utilized for social ends in a society where persons have not necessarily been enculturated for such experiences. For example, Goodman (1972) has noted that among Maya peasants, where a traditional cultural pattern of trance states does not exist, Pentecostal Protestant missionaries have introduced such behavior generally and very effectively. I noted above Benedict's comment concerning the selective cultural use of only a "certain segment of the great arc of potential human purposes and motivations." Perhaps this might now be rephrased to the effect that a given society at a given time makes use of only some of the latent potentials in the personalities of its members. When culture changes, other potentials may receive selective opportunities for development, stimulation, or frustration, presenting the people in a new light.

CROSS-CULTURAL STATISTICAL STUDIES

The major event in psychological anthropology of the recent past has been the development of comparative studies designed to test specific hypotheses by means of statistical techniques. While most of the research reviewed so far has involved the collection and analysis of primary field data, comparing a handful of cultures at most, these studies require a sample of cultures. And while most anthropological research has been primarily holistic and descriptive, whatever the theoretical framework, these studies deal with a small number of variables designed to test one or more hypotheses. The pioneering study of this type was Whiting and Child's *Child Training and Personality,* first published in 1953. Recently O'Leary (1969) was able to list some sixty studies of this type, many by students and associates of Whiting.

Because Whiting and Child's study constitutes the pioneering effort in this field, highlighting both the strengths and the weaknesses of this approach, it may be considered in some detail. The aim of the study is to relate child training practices to adult personality, which is indirectly represented by explanations of illness and therapeutic methods, since these elements are considered to reflect the typical personality of each culture. The study utilizes a sample of seventy-five societies for which data on child training and on medical theories and therapies could be located. The major hypotheses represent a learning theory restatement of psychoanalytic concepts concerning the nature of fixation. Whiting and Child differentiate between two types of fixation: "positive" and "negative." They seek to correlate explanations of illness with severity of socialization (high socialization anxiety) in one of five systems of child training (oral, anal, sexual, dependence, and aggression); these explanations are themselves classified under the same five headings. Therapeutic measures, on the other hand, similarly classified, are expected to confirm the existence of positive fixations, and correlations are sought with initial satisfaction in the same five systems of socialization. Thus ten hypotheses are tested, five relating theories of illness to socialization anxiety and five relating therapies to initial satisfaction in a given behavior system. Three of the hypotheses concerning "negative" fixations were statistically confirmed, and only one concerning "positive" fixations.

J. W. M. Whiting (1966:vii-viii) has himself listed some shortcomings of this study: the original data were limited and often inadequate; there is no room for intrasocietal variation in practice within the coding scheme; intergenerational stability had to be assumed, while in some instances the behavior relating to illness might reflect results of the socialization of an earlier generation; no independent personality assessment was available to corroborate the judgments based on cultural features (behavior related to illness).

Some of these difficulties may indeed be inherent in studies of this type. Yet there is a further difficulty that, so far as I know, has not been discussed, and which bears on the nature of the coding categories. In devising such categories, an investigator must draw on his knowledge of the ethnographic literature to foresee, as much as possible, the cultural variations to be encountered and provide for them in his scheme. It is the unpredicted variations that may make it difficult to apply the coding system or may lead to distortion of the data in attempts to fit them into a predesigned Procrustean bed. Applying the Whiting and Child scheme to my own data concerning Haitian peasant culture may serve to illustrate the point. It should be noted, however, that Haitians are not included in the Whiting and Child sample.

Haitian peasants take a great interest in medicines, both native and foreign. Many of these are taken orally.[6] An-

other type of therapy, however, rather than involving ingestion of some materials by the patient, involves feeding the gods, to calm their anger over some neglect. Since food is involved (and consumed by someone, sometimes the patient himself, impersonating the spirit in a state of possession trance), is this to be coded as oral therapy? We must either stretch the category or omit the item. Emphasis on oral therapy leads us to look at initial satisfaction with regard to nursing. Haitian infants are nursed eighteen months or less, whereas the median age at weaning of the Whiting and Child sample is two and a half years. The Haitian peasant child is nursed when it cries, but the crying may be due to some discomfort other than hunger, and often the child may not be nursed if it does not cry. On the other hand, weaning is relatively harsh and abrupt, leading us to expect high socialization anxiety and thus a negative rather than a positive fixation, expressed in oral explanations of illness. Such explanations do exist, as well as some nonoral ones. One example of an oral method of causing illness is found in the process of making a zombi, explained alternately as due to poisoning (ingestion) or an oral spell (Bourguignon 1959). A key question, however, concerns the definition of "illness." A psychotic considered a zombi is "ill" by scientific standards, but in Haitian terms he is something else altogether. Furthermore, zombis are not only partially resuscitated dead persons; some are turned into animals. How is this information to be coded?

In addition, we find prominent among Haitian theories of illness the idea of being eaten. While this explanation clearly involves oral aggression, Whiting and Child make no provision for this in their oral category. (They do, however, find fear of others correlated with oral socialization anxiety as

---

[6] See Huxley (1969) for a list of Haitian plant remedies.

well as with initial anxiety in the aggression training system.)

In sum, we find an overall pattern of oral concerns: oral remedies, including feeding of spirits, and oral causes of illness, including being eaten by spirits. The coding scheme necessarily fragments this pattern.

The issue here is not so much a criticism of the Whiting and Child study as a difficulty inherent in the setting up of categories in comparative research. In such studies assumptions must be made about the comparability of social phenomena. These must be based on ethnographic data as well as on theoretical expectations. And the variability of cultures complicates the issue in ways not readily apparent from an analysis of theoretical positions and statistical methodology.

The large number of cross-cultural psychological studies now published has confirmed a variety of hypotheses about relations between subsistence economy, household structure, and aspects of child training on the one hand and aspects of child training, religious beliefs, art forms, fantasy, and games on the other. An issue of particular debate has concerned the correlates of harsh male initiation rites prevalent in some parts of the world. Whiting, Kluckhohn, and Anthony (1958) related them to exclusive mother-infant son sleeping arrangements, linked in turn to a prolonged postpartum sex taboo. Young (1962) has preferred to see such initiation rites associated with the existence of exclusive male organizations, while Cohen (1964) has linked them to the presence of unilineal descent groups and to the existence of joint liability. As Wallace (1966) has pointed out, these explanations are complementary rather than contradictory, as claimed by the participants in the debate.

It should be noted that in most of these studies, personality variables appear only by inference. The statistical correlations and comparisons are established between initiation ceremonies and one group of societal practices (institutions, customs), such as child training practices, household organization, polygyny, postpartum sex taboo, and unilineal descent groups. A study by Slater and Slater (1965), however, introduces into this argument such specific psychological attributes as maternal ambivalence and narcissism. They develop a score for narcissism and find it related to a distant marital relationship (as exemplified in prolonged postpartum sex taboo and polygyny) and suggest a feedback from strong male narcissism to a weak marital relationship and from a weak marital relationship to the mother's relationship with the child. Being deprived (sexually), the mother is both depriving and demanding toward the child. Rather than a linear causal chain, we have a circular scheme with two types of feedback.

Among the methodological difficulties in a number of these studies is the lack of rigorous sampling procedures. Furthermore, worldwide samples are used, without concern for regional variations. Yet a number of recent publications (e.g., Bourguignon and Greenbaum 1968, Driver and Schuessler 1967, Barry 1968, Murdock and White 1969) have pointed to the importance of such variations for comparative studies. For example, Greenbaum and I (Bourguignon and Greenbaum 1968: 55) have shown, on the basis of the Ethnographic Atlas (Murdock 1967), that of 304 societies in all parts of the world, only 38 percent have a postpartum sex taboo of over one year, yet 67 percent of all societies in sub-Saharan Africa do. Similarly (1968:57), male genital mutilation, a factor in the coding of initiation rites, occurs between the ages of twelve and fifteen in only

10 percent of the 815 societies coded, but it is present in 25 percent of African societies and is totally absent in South America. Segregation of adolescent boys, another factor in the coding of initiation rites, is shown to be absent in 61 percent of 611 societies distributed throughout the world (p. 56); however, when these factors are analyzed by regions, we find it absent in 75 percent or more of the societies in all regions except two: Sub-Saharan Africa (22 percent absent) and Insular Pacific (37 percent absent). Such variations may be expected to affect the results of such worldwide comparative studies, for averaging the differences among regions distorts the real nature of these variables.

This expectation is confirmed in a study of dissociational states, in which I found significant differences not only in the distribution of these states in institutionalized form among the major regions of the world (Bourguignon 1968:40-41), but also in their variation by societal characteristics. Thus, on a worldwide basis, trance states interpreted as due to spirit possession are significantly more likely to be found in societies that have or have recently had slavery than in those that do not. However, such a difference is not statistically significant among South American societies (pp. 65-68).

In summary, it can be stated that:

1. It is not the aim of these statistical studies to draw psychological portraits of human societies or to establish causal relations among variables.

2. There are methodological difficulties of varying degrees which remain to be overcome.

3. Few correlations have been established, but a number of significant differences among societies appear to have been identified which have a bearing on the relationships between a series of psychologically relevant variables.

4. Few studies deal directly with psychological factors, but a large number point inferentially toward confirmation of psychological hypotheses.

With methodological refinements, the approach does hold promise of developing an organized body of theoretical propostitions, tested empirically, about the functioning of human societies, thus avoiding the frequently ad hoc nature of explanation in holistic descriptive studies.

CONCLUDING COMMENT

In some sense, we appear to have come full circle. Benedict's *Patterns of Culture* inferred psychological characteristics of persons from the institutions of their societies. The statistical studies reviewed demonstrate relations between societal variables and use psychological hypotheses to account for them. The contrasts between the two approaches are great: from humanistic to quantitative, from descriptive and intuitive to statistical and empirical. Yet the behavior and attitudes of individuals, individuals as actors in their societies, are essentially absent in both of these types of studies. It is true that the descriptive studies of behavior must furnish the raw material for statistical studies. And it is to be hoped that such "traditional" field studies in culture and personality will be conducted with greater sophistication, rather than abandoned in favor of the lure of the "scientific" analysis, which can never be more than a second, generalizing step, based on the particulars provided by fieldwork. Fieldwork and comparison are both essential to the anthropological enterprise, and the overwhelming and often unanticipated variability of culture must not be lost sight of as the pendulum swings toward the search for regularities. Mankind, psychologically, is both one and many, and both of these complementary facts must be kept in mind simultaneously if psychological anthropology is to fulfill its promise.

REFERENCES

Aberle, David
1960   The Influence of Linguistics on Early Culture and Personality Theory. In *Essays in the Science of Culture: In Honor of Leslie A. White,* ed. G. E. Dole and R. L. Carneiro. New York: Crowell.

Aberle, David, et al.
1950   The Functional Prerequisites of a Society. *Ethics* 6:100-111.

Abraham, Karl
1913   *Dreams and Myths: A Study in Race Psychology.* Nervous and Mental Disease Monograph Series, no. 15

Ainsworth, Mary D. Salter
1967   *Infancy in Uganda.* Baltimore: Johns Hopkins University Press.

Axelrad, Sidney
1962   Infant Care and Personality Reconsidered: A Rejoinder to Orlansky. *Psychoanalytic Study of Society* 2:75-135.

Barnett, Homer
1953   *Innovation: The Basis of Culture Change.* New York: McGraw-Hill.

Barnouw, Victor
1963   *Culture and Personality.* Homewood, Ill.: Dorsey Press.

Barry, Herbert III
1968   Regional and Worldwide Variations in Culture. *Ethnology* 7:207-217.

Barry, Herbert III, M. K. Bacon, and I. L. Child
1957   A Cross-Cultural Survey of Some Sex Differences in Socialization. *Journal of Abnormal and Social Psychology* 55:327-32.

Barry, Herbert III, I. L. Child, and M. K. Bacon
1959   Relation of Child Training to Subsistence Economy. *American Anthropologist* 61:51-63.

Bastian, Adolf
1881   *Der Völkergedanke im Aufbau einer Wissenschaft vom Menschen und seine Begründung auf ethnologischen Sammlungen.* Berlin.

Benedict, Ruth
1923   *The Concept of the Guardian Spirit in North America,* Memoir no. 29, American Anthropological Association.
1932   Configurations of Culture in North America. *American Anthropologist* 34:1-27.
1938   Continuities and Discontinuities in Cultural Conditioning. *Psychiatry* 1:161-67.
1946   *The Chrysanthemum and the Sword.* Boston: Houghton Mifflin.
1961   *Patterns of Culture.* Boston: Houghton Mifflin. Originally published 1934.

Bennett, John, and Melvin Tumin
1949   *Social Life: Structure and Function.* New York: Knopf.

Berry, J. W.
1965   *A Study of Temne and Eskimo Visual Perception: Preliminary Report.* Psychological Laboratory report no. 28. Edinburgh: University of Edinburgh.

Bettelheim, Bruno
1969   *The Children of the Dream: Communal Childrearing and American Education.* New York: Macmillan.

Boas, Franz
1940   The Limitations of the Comparative Method of Anthropology. In F. Boas, *Race, Language, and Culture,* pp. 270-80. New York: Macmillan. Originally published 1896.

Bohannan, Paul
1953   Concepts of Time Among the Tiv of Nigeria. *Southwestern Journal of Anthropology* 9:251-56.

Bourguignon, Erika
1954   Reinterpretation and the Mechanism of Culture Change. *Ohio Journal of Science* 54:329-34.
1959   The Persistence of Folk Belief: Some Notes on Cannibalism and Zombis in Haiti. *Journal of American Folklore* 72:36-46.
1968   *A Cross-Cultural Study of Dissociational States: Final Report.* National Institute of Mental Health, PHS MH 07463. Columbus: Ohio State University Research Foundation
1970   Hallucination and Trance: An Anthropologist's Perspective. In *Origin and Mechanisms of Hallucinations,*

ed. W. Keup. New York: Plenum Press.

1972 Dreams and Altered States of Consciousness in Anthropological Research. In *Psychological Anthropology*, ed. F. L. K. Hsu, new ed. Cambridge, Mass.: Schenkman.

Bourguignon, Erika, and Lenora Greenbaum
1968 Diversity and Homogeneity: A Comparative Analysis of Societal Characteristics Based on the Data of the Ethnographic Atlas. Occasional Papers in Anthropology, no. 1. Columbus: Ohio State University.

Bourguignon, Erika, and Adolf Haas
1965 Trans-Cultural Research and Culture Bound Psychiatry. Paper presented at the seventh western divisional meeting of the American Psychiatric Association, Honolulu.

Brickner, R. M.
1943 *Is Germany Incurable?* Philadelphia: Lippincott.

Brown, R. W., A. H. Black, and A. E. Horowitz
1955 Phonetic Symbolism in Natural Languages. *Journal of Abnormal and Social Psychology* 50:388-93.

Campbell, Donald T., and Raoul Naroll
1972 The Mutual Methodological Relevance of Anthropology and Psychology. In *Psychological Anthropology*, ed. F. L. K. Hsu, new ed. Cambridge, Mass.: Schenkman.

Castañeda, Carlos
1968 *The Teachings of Don Juan: A Yaqui Way of Knowledge.* Berkeley: University of California Press.

Clarke, J. J.
1970 On the Unity and Diversity of Cultures. *American Anthropologist* 72: 545-54.

Cohen, Yehudi A.
1964 *The Transition from Childhood to Adolescence: Cross-Cultural Studies of Initiation Ceremonies, Legal Systems, and Incest Taboos.* Chicago: Aldine.

Conklin, Harold C.
1955 Hanunóo Color Categories. *Southwestern Journal of Anthropology* 11:339-44.

D'Andrade, Roy G.
1961 Anthropological Studies of Dreams. In *Psychological Anthropology*, ed.

F. L. K. Hsu. Homewood, Ill.: Dorsey Press.

Dawson, J. L. M.
1967 Cultural and Physiological Influences upon Spatial-Perceptual Processes in West Africa. *International Journal of Psychology* 2:115-28, 171-85.

Dement, W.
1966 The Psychophysiology of Dreaming. In *The Dream and Human Societies*, ed. G. E. von Grunebaum and R. Callois. Berkeley: University of California Press.

Devereux, George
1939 Maladjustment and Social Neurosis. *American Sociological Review* 4: 844-51.

De Vore, Irven, ed.
1965 *Primate Behavior: Field Studies of Monkeys and Apes.* New York: Holt, Rinehart & Winston.

Dobzhansky, Theodosius
1965 Religion, Death, and Evolutionary Adaptation. In *Context and Meaning in Cultural Anthropology: In Honor of A. Irving Hallowell*, ed. M. E. Spiro. New York: Free Press, Macmillan.

Doob, L. W.
1957 The Effect of Language on Verbal Expression and Recall. *American Anthropologist* 59:88-100.

Driver, H. E., and K. F. Schuessler
1967 Correlational Analysis of Murdock's 1957 Ethnographic Sample. *American Anthropologist* 69:332-52.

Du Bois, Cora
1937 Some Anthropological Perspectives on Psychoanalysis. *Psychoanalytic Review* 24:246-63.

1944 *People of Alor.* Minneapolis: University of Minnesota Press.

Durkheim, Emile
1915 *The Elementary Forms of the Religious Life: A Study in Religious Sociology.* New York: Macmillan. Originally published 1912.

1938 *The Rules of Sociological Method.* Chicago: University of Chicago Press. Originally published 1895.

1964 The Dualism of Human Nature and Its Social Conditions, trans. C. Blend. In É. Durkheim et al., *Essays on Sociology and Philosophy*, ed. K. H. Wolff. New York: Harper Torchbooks. Previously published in Émile Durkheim *1858-1817: A Collection of Essays, with Translations and a Bibliography*, ed. K. H. Wolff. Columbus: Ohio State University Press, 1960. Originally published 1914.

Eggan, Dorothy
1955   The Personal Use of Myths in Dreams. In Myth: A Symposium, ed. T. Sebeok. *Journal of American Folklore* 68:445-53.
1961   Dream Analysis. In *Studying Personality Cross-Culturally*, ed. B. Kaplan. New York: Harper & Row.
1966   Hopi Dreams in Cultural Perspective. In *The Dream and Human Societies*, ed. G. E. von Grunebaum and R. Callois. Berkeley: University of California Press.

Ervin, Susan
1964   Language and TAT Content in Bilinguals. *Journal of Abnormal and Social Psychology* 68:500-507.

Evans-Pritchard, E. E.
1940   *The Nuer*. London: Oxford University Press.
1965   *Theories of Primitive Religion*. London: Oxford University Press.

Fenichel, Otto
1945   *The Psychoanalytic Theory of Neurosis*. New York: Norton.

Field, M. G.
1960   *Search for Security: An Ethno-Psychiatric Study of Rural Ghana*. Evanston, Ill.: Northwestern University Press.

Fischer, J. L.
1965   Psychology and Anthropology. In *Biennial Review of Anthropology*, ed. B. J. Siegel. Stanford: Stanford University Press.

Foster, George
1969   *Applied Anthropology*. Boston: Little, Brown.

Fox, Robin
1967   Totem and Taboo Reconsidered. In *The Structural Study of Myth and Totemism*, ed. E. Leach. London: Tavistock.

Frankfort, Henri
1946   *The Intellectual Adventure of Ancient Man*. Chicago: University of Chicago Press.

French, David

1963   The Relationship of Anthropology to Studies in Perception and Cognition. In *Psychology: A Study of a Science*, ed. S. Koch, study 2, vol. 6. New York: McGraw-Hill.

Freud, Sigmund
1956   *Totem und Tabu*. Frankfurt: Fischer-Bücherei. Originally published 1912-1913.

Fromm, Erich
1941   *Escape from Freedom*. New York: Farrar & Rinehart.
1949   The Oedipus Myth and the Oedipus Complex. In *The Family: Its Function and Destiny*, ed. R. N. Anshen. New York: Harper.

Fujisawa, S.
1953   A Psychological Study of the Formosan Aborigines. *Japanese Journal of Ethnology* 18, nos. 1-2 (in Japanese). Cited in Y. Huzioka, The Personality of the Hadzapi, *Kyoto University African Studies* 2 (1968):147-210.

Géber, Marcelle
1956   Développement psychomoteur de l'enfant africain. *Courrier* 6:17-29.
1958   L'enfant occidentalisé et de niveau social supérieur en Uganda. *Courrier* 8:517-23.

Géber, Marcelle, and R. F. A. Dean
1957   Gesell Tests on African Children. *Pediatrics* 6:1055-65.

Gillin, John
1942   Acquired Drives in Culture Contact. *American Anthropologist* 44:550-51.

Gladwin, Thomas, and S. B. Sarason
1953   *Truk: Man in Paradise*. Viking Fund Publications in Anthropology, no. 20. New York: Wenner-Gren Foundation for Anthropological Research.

Goodman, Felicitas D.
1972   *Speaking in Tongues: A Cross-Cultural Study of Glossolalia*. Chicago: University of Chicago Press.

Gorer, Geoffrey
1943   Themes in Japanese Culture. *Transactions of the New York Academy of Sciences*, ser. 2, 5:106-124.

Gorer, Geoffrey, and John Rickman
1949   *The People of Great Russia: A Psychological Study*. London: Cresset Press.

Gregor, A. J., and D. A. McPherson
1965   A Study of Susceptibility to Geomet-

ric Illusions Among Cultural Subgroups of Australian Aborigines. *Psychologia Africana* 11:1-13.

Hall, E. T.
1968 Proxemics. *Current Anthropology* 9:83-109.

Hallowell, A. I.
1937a Handbook of Psychological Leads for Ethnological Fieldworkers. Prepared for the Committee on Culture and Personality, National Research Council, Division of Anthropology and Psychology. Mimeographed. Published in *Personal Character and the Cultural Milieu*, ed. D. G. Haring. Syracuse: Syracuse University Press, 1948.
1937b Temporal Orientation in Western Civilization and in a Preliterate Society. *American Anthropologist* 39: 647-760. Reprinted in A. I. Hallowell, *Culture and Experience*, 1955.
1939 The Child, the Savage, and Human Experience. *Proceedings of the Sixth Institute on the Exceptional Child.* Longhorne, Pa.: Woods School. Reprinted as The Recapitulation Theory and Culture, in A. I. Hallowell, *Culture and Experience*, 1955.
1941a The Rorschach Method as an Aid in the Study of Personalities in Primitive Societies. *Character and Personality* 9:235-45.
1941b The Rorschach Test as a Tool for Investigating Cultural Variables and Individual Differences in the Study of Personality in Primitive Societies. *Rorschach Research Exchange* 5: 31-34.
1942 Some Psychological Aspects of Measurement Among the Saulteaux. *American Anthropologist* 44:62-77. Reprinted in A. I. Hallowell, *Culture and Experience*, 1955.
1945 A Social-Psychological Aspect of Acculturation. In *The Science of Man in the World Crisis*, ed. R. Linton. New York: Columbia University Press. Reprinted in A. I. Hallowell, *Culture and Experience*, 1955.
1950 Personality Structure and the Evolution of Man. *American Anthropologist* 52:159-73.
1951 The Use of Projective Techniques in the Study of the Sociopsychological Aspects of Acculturation. *Journal of Projective Techniques* 15:27-44. Reprinted in A. I. Hallowell, *Culture and Experience*, 1955.
1953 Culture, Personality, and Society. In *Anthropology Today*, ed. A. L. Kroeber. Chicago: University of Chicago Press.
1954 Psychology and Anthropology. In *For a Science of Social Man*, ed. J. Gillin. New York: Macmillan.
1955 *Culture and Experience.* Philadelphia: University of Pennsylvania Press. (Reprinted by Schocken Books, New York, 1967.)
1956 The Structural and Functional Dimensions of a Human Existence. *Quarterly Review of Biology* 31, no. 2.
1959 Behavioral Evolution and the Emergence of the Self. In *Evolution and Anthropology: A Centennial Appraisal*, ed. B. J. Meggers. Washington, D.C.: Anthropological Society of Washington, D.C.
1960a The Beginnings of Anthropology in America. In *Selected Papers from the American Anthropologist, 1888-1920*, ed. F. de Laguna. New York: Harper and Row.
1960b Self, Society, and Culture in Phylogenetic Perspective. In *The Evolution of Man*, ed. S. Tax, vol. 2: *Evolution After Darwin*. Chicago: University of Chicago Press.
1961 The Protocultural Foundations of Human Adaptation. In *Social Life of Early Man*, ed. S. L. Washburn. Viking Fund Publications in Anthropology, no. 31. New York: Wenner-Gren Foundation for Anthropological Research.
1963 Personality, Culture, Society in Behavioral Evolution. In *Psychology: The Study of a Science*, ed. S. Koch, study 2, vol. 6. New York: McGraw-Hill.
1966 The Role of Dreams in Ojibwa Culture. In *The Dream and Human Societies*, ed. G. E. von Grunebaum and R. Callois. Berkeley: University of California Press.

Hallowell, A. I., and E. L. Reynolds

1942 Biological Factors in Family Structure. In *Marriage and the Family*, ed. H. Becker and R. Hill. Boston: Heath.

Harrington, Charles, and J. W. M. Whiting
1972 Socialization Process and Personality. In *Psychological Anthropology*, ed. F. L. K. Hsu, new ed. Cambridge, Mass.: Schenkman.

Harris, Marvin
1969 *The Rise of Anthropological Theory*. New York: Crowell.

Henry, Jules
1959 Culture, Personality, and Evolution. *American Anthropologist* 61:221-26.
1960 A Cross-Cultural Outline of Education. *Current Anthropology* 4:267-305.

Herskovits, M. J.
1945 The Processes of Culture Change. In *The Science of Man in the World Crisis*, ed. R. Linton. New York: Columbia University Press.
1948 *Man and His Works*. New York: Knopf.

Herskovits, M. J., and F. S. Herskovits
1958 *Dahomean Narrative*. Evanston, Ill.: Northwestern University Press.

Honigmann, J. J.
1959 Psychocultural Studies. In *Biennial Review of Anthropology*, ed. B. J. Siegel. Stanford: Stanford University Press.
1961 The Interpretation of Dreams in Anthropological Field Work: A Case Study. In *Studying Personality Cross-Culturally*, ed. B. Kaplan. New York: Harper & Row.
1967 *Personality in Culture*. New York: Harper & Row.
1968 The Study of Personality in Primitive Societies. In *The Study of Personality: An Interdisciplinary Approach*, ed. E. Norbeck, D. Price-Williams and W. M. McCord. New York: Holt, Rinehart & Winston.
1972 North America. In *Psychological Anthropology*, ed. F. L. K. Hsu, new ed. Cambridge, Mass.: Schenkman.

Hsu, F. L. K.
1972 Kinship and Ways of Life: An Exploration. In *Psychological Anthropology*, ed. F. L. K. Hsu, new ed. Cambridge, Mass.: Schenkman.

Hsu, F. L. K., ed.
1970 *Kinship and Culture*. Chicago: Aldine.

Huxley, Francis
1969 *The Invisibles: Voodoo Gods in Haiti*. New York: McGraw-Hill.

Huzioka, Yosinaru
1968 The Personality of the Hadzapi: An Approach to the Evolution of Personality. *Kyoto University African Studies* 2:147-210.

Inkeles, Alex
1972 National Character and Modern Political Systems. In *Psychological Anthropology*, ed. F. L. K. Hsu, new ed. Cambridge, Mass.: Schenkman.

Inkeles, Alex, and D. J. Levinson
1954 National Character: The Study of Modal Personality and Sociocultural Systems. In *Handbook of Social Psychology*, ed. G. Lindzey, vol. 1. Reading, Mass.: Addison-Wesley.
1968 National Character: The Study of Modal Personality and Sociocultural Systems. In *Handbook of Social Psychology*, ed. G. Lindzey and E. Aronson, 2nd. rev. ed., vol. 4. Reading, Mass.: Addison-Wesley.

Jahoda, Gustav
1966 Geometric Illusions and Environment: A Study in Ghana. *British Journal of Psychology* 57:193-99.

Jones, Ernest
1925 Mother Right and the Sexual Ignorance of Savages. *International Journal of Psychoanalysis* 6:109-130.

Kardiner, Abram
1939 *The Individual and His Society*. New York: Columbia University Press.
1945 *The Psychological Frontiers of Society*. New York: Columbia University Press.

Kilbride, P. L., and M. C. Robbins
1969 Pictorial Depth Perception and Acculturation Among the Baganda. *American Anthropologist* 71:293-361.

Klineberg, Otto
1935 *Race Differences*. New York: Harper.

Kroeber, A. L.
1958a Totem and Taboo: An Ethnologic Psychoanalysis. In *Reader in Comparative Religion*, ed. W. A. Lessa and E. Z. Vogt, 2nd ed., pp. 48-53.

New York: Harper & Row. Originally published 1920.

1958b Totem and Taboo in Retrospect. In *Reader in Comparative Religion,* ed. W. A. Lessa and E. Z. Vogt, 2nd ed., pp. 53-56. New York: Harper & Row. Originally published 1939.

Kurath, G. P.
1960 Panorama of Dance Ethnology. *Current Anthropology* 1:233-54.

La Barre, Weston
1954 *The Human Animal.* Chicago: University of Chicago Press.
1969 *The Peyote Cult.* New York: Schocken Books.

Lacan, Jacques
1966a *Écrits.* Paris: Éditions du Seuil.
1966b The Insistence of the Letter in the Unconscious. *Structuralism: Yale French Studies* 36/37:112-47.

Langness, L. L.
1965 *The Life History in Anthropological Science.* New York: Holt, Rinehart & Winston.

Leighton, A. H., and J. H. Hughes
1961 Cultures as Causative of Mental Disorders (with Discussion). In "Causes of Mental Disorders: A Review of Epidemiological Knowledge." *Milbank Memorial Fund Quarterly* 39.

Lévi-Strauss, Claude
1963 Jean Jacques Rousseau: The Father of Anthropology. *Courier* 16:10-15.

LeVine, Robert A.
1962 Studying Child Rearing and Personality Development in an East African Community: Anthropology and Africa Today. *Annals of the New York Academy of Sciences* 96:620-28.

LeVine, Robert A., and B. B. LeVine
1963 Nyansongo: A Gusii Community in Kenya. In *Six Cultures,* ed. B. Whiting. New York: Wiley.

Lindzey, Gardner
1961 *Projective Techniques and Cross-Cultural Research.* New York: Appleton-Century-Crofts.

Malinowski, Bronislaw
1927 *Sex and Repression in Savage Society.* London: Kegan Paul, Trench, Trubner.

Mead, Margaret
1928 *Coming of Age in Samoa.* New York: Morrow.

1930 *Growing Up in New Guinea.* New York: Morrow.
1954 The Swaddling Hypothesis: Its Reception. *American Anthropologist* 56:395-409.
1956 *New Lives for Old.* New York: Morrow.
1963 Socialization and Enculturation. *Current Anthropology* 4:184-88.
1964 *Continuities in Cultural Evolution.* New Haven: Yale University Press.

Mead, Margaret, and R. Métraux, eds.
1953 *Studies of Culture at a Distance.* Chicago: University of Chicago Press.

Merriam, A. P.
1967 *Ethnomusicology of the Flathead Indians.* Viking Fund Publications in Anthropology, no. 44. New York: Wenner-Gren Foundation for Anthropological Research.

Métraux, Alfred
1959 *Voodoo in Haiti.* New York: Oxford University Press.

Miel, Jan
1966 Jacques Lacan and the Structure of the Unconscious. *Structuralism: Yale French Studies* 36/37:104-111.

Mundy-Castle, A. C., and G. K. Nelson
1962 A Neuropsychological Study of the Knysna Forest Workers. *Psychologia Africana* 9:240-272.

Murdock, G. P.
1967 Ethnographic Atlas: A Summary. *Ethnology* 6, no. 2.

Murdock, G. P., and D. R. White
1969 Standard Cross-Cultural Sample. *Ethnology* 8:329-69.

O'Leary, Timothy
1969 A Preliminary Bibliography of Cross-Cultural Studies. *Behavior Science Notes* 4:95-115.

Orlansky, Harold
1949 Infant Care and Personality. *Psychological Bulletin* 46:1-48.

Ortigues, Marie Cécile, and Edmond Ortigues
1966 *Oedipe africain.* Paris: Plon.

Parin, P., F. Morgenthaler, and G. Parin-Matthey
1963 *Die Weissen denken zuviel: Psychoanalytische Untersuchungen bei den Dogon in Westafrika.* Zürich: Atlantis.

Parsons, Anne
1964 Is the Oedipus Complex Universal?

The Jones-Malinowski Debate Revisited and a South Italian "Nuclear Complex." In *The Psychoanalytic Study of Society*, ed. W. Muensterberger and S. Axelrad. New York: International Universities Press.

Parsons, Talcott
1964 Durkheim's Contribution to the Theory of Integration of Social Systems. In Emile Durkheim et al., *Essays on Sociology and Philosophy*, ed. K. H. Wolff. New York: Harper Torchbooks.

Pierce, Albert
1964 Durkheim and Functionalism. In Émile Durkheim et al., *Essays on Sociology and Philosophy*, ed. K. H. Wolff. New York: Harper Torchbooks.

Poirier, F. E., Jr., ed.
1972 *Primate Socialization*. New York: Random House.

Powdermaker, Hortense
1945 Review of *People of Alor* by Cora Du Bois. *American Anthropologist* 47: 160.

Price-Williams, Douglass R.
1968 Ethnopsychology I: Comparative Psychological Processes. In *Introduction to Cultural Anthropology*, ed. J. A. Clifton. Boston: Houghton Mifflin.

Price-Williams, Douglas E., ed.
1970 *Cross-Cultural Studies*. Baltimore: Penguin Books.

Riesman, David, et al.
1950 *The Lonely Crowd*. New Haven: Yale University Press.

Rivers, W. H. R.
1901 Vision. In *Reports of the Cambridge Anthropological Expedition to the Torres Straits*, ed. A. C. Haddon, vol. 2, pt. 1. Cambridge: At the University Press.
1905 Observations on the Senses of the Todas. *British Journal of Psychology* 1:321-96.

Roe, Anne, and George Simpson
1958 *Behavior and Evolution*. New Haven: Yale University Press.

Róheim, Géza
1932 Psychoanalysis of Primitive Culture Types. *International Journal of Psychoanalysis* 13, pts. 1 and 2.

1934 *The Riddle of the Sphinx*. London: Hogarth Press.
1941 Play Analysis with Normanby Island Children. *Journal of Orthopsychiatry* 11:524-30.
1943 *Origin and Function of Culture*. Baltimore: Nervous and Mental Disease Monographs.

Rorschach, Hermann
1921 *Psychodiagnostik*. Bern: Verlag Hans Huber.

Sapir, Edward
1949 The Psychological Reality of the Phoneme. In *Selected Writings of Edward Sapir in Language, Culture, and Personality*, ed. D. G. Mandelbaum. Berkeley: University of California Press.

Sargant, William
1959 *Battle for the Mind*, rev. ed. London: Pan Books.

Schneider, David, and Lauriston Sharp
1969 *The Dream Life of a Primitive People: The Dreams of the Yir Yoront of Australia*. Anthropological Studies, no. 1, ed. W. Goodenough, American Anthropological Association. Ann Arbor, Mich.: University Microfilms.

Schwartz, Theodore
1962 The Paliau Movement in the Admiralty Islands, 1946-1954. *Anthropological Papers of the American Museum of Natural History*, no.49, pt. 2.

Segall, M. H., D. T. Campbell, and M. J. Herskovits
1966 *The Influence of Culture on Visual Perception*. Indianapolis: Bobbs-Merrill.

Shimahara, Nobuo, et al.
1970 Enculturation: A Reconsideration. *Current Anthropology* 11:143-54.

Singer, Milton
1961 A Survey of Culture and Personality Theory and Research. In *Studying Personality Cross-Culturally*, ed. B. Kaplan. New York: Harper & Row.

Slater, P. E., and D. A. Slater
1965 Maternal Ambivalence and Narcissism: A Cross-Cultural Study. *Merrill-Palmer Quarterly of Behavior and Development* 11:241-59.

Spain, D. H.
1972 On the Use of Projective Tests for

Research in Psychological Anthropology. In *Psychological Anthropology*, ed. F. L. K. Hsu, new ed. Cambridge, Mass.: Schenkman.

Spindler, George
1955 Sociocultural and Psychological Processes in Menomini Acculturation. *University of California Publications in Culture and Society*, vol. 5.

Spindler, George, ed.
1963 *Education and Culture: Anthropological Approaches,* New York: Holt, Rinehart & Winston.

Spindler, George, and Louise S. Spindler
1963 Psychology in Anthropology: Applications to Culture Change. In *Psychology: A Study of a Science*, ed. S. Koch, study 2, vol. 6. New York: McGraw-Hill.

Spiro, M. E.
1954 Human Nature in Its Psychological Dimensions. *American Anthropologist* 56:19-30.
1958a *Children of the Kibbutz*. Cambridge: Harvard University Press.
1958b Is the Family Universal? In *A Modern Introduction to the Family*, ed. N. W. Bell and E. Z. Vogel. Glencoe, Ill.: Free Press.
1967 *Burmese Supernaturalism*. Englewood Cliffs, N.J.: Prentice-Hall.
1972 An Overview and a Suggested Reorientation. In *Psychological Anthropology*, ed. F. L. K. Hsu, new ed. Cambridge, Mass.: Schenkman.

Stern, Wilhelm, and Otto Lippmann, eds.
1912 Vorschläge zur psychologischen Untersuchung primitiver Menschen. *Zeitschrift für angewandte Psychologie und psychologische Sammelforschung* 5, pt. 1 (supplement).

Sturtevant, W. C.
1964 Studies in Ethnoscience. *American Anthropologist* 66:99-131.

Thurnwald, Richard
1913 Ethnopsychologische Studien an Südsee Völkern. *Zeitschrift für angewandte Psychologie und psychologische Sammelforschung* 6 (supplement).

Tinbergen, N.
1951 *The Study of Instinct*. Oxford: Clarendon Press.

Triandis, H. C.

1964 Cultural Influences upon Cognitive Processes. In *Advances in Experimental Social Psychology*, ed. L. Berkowitz, vol. 1. New York: Academic Press.

Tylor, E. B.
1871 *Primitive Culture*. London: J. Murray.

Wallace, A. F. C.
1951 Some Psychological Determinants in Culture Change in an Iroquoian Community. In *Symposium on Local Diversity in Iroquois Culture*, ed. W. N. Fenton. Bulletin no. 149, Bureau of American Ethnology. Washington. D. C.: Smithsonian Institution.
1952 *The Modal Personality Structure of the Tuscarora Indians, as Revealed by the Rorschach Test*. Bulletin no. 150, Bureau of American Ethnology. Washington, D. C.: Smithsonian Institution.
1956a Mazeway Resynthesis: A Bio-cultural Theory of Religious Inspiration. *Transactions of the New York Academy of Sciences* 18:626-38.
1956b Revitalization Movements. *American Anthropologist* 58:264-81.
1961 The Psychic Unity of Human Groups. In *Studying Personality Cross-Culturally*, ed. B. Kaplan. New York: Harper & Row.
1966 *Religion: An Anthropological View*. New York: Random House.
1970a *Culture and Personality*. New York: Random House.
1970b *The Death and Rebirth of the Seneca*. New York: Knopf.

Wallace, A. F. C., and John Atkins
1960 The Meaning of Kinship Terms. *American Anthropologist* 62:58-80.

Washburn, S. L., ed.
1961 *The Social Life of Early Man*. Viking Fund Publications in Anthropology, no. 31. New York: Wenner-Gren Foundation for Anthropological Research.

Wegrocki, H. J.
1939 A Critique of Cultural and Statistical Concepts of Abnormality. *Journal of Abnormal and Social Psychology* 34:166-78.

Whiting, Beatrice, ed.

1963   *Six Cultures*. New York: Wiley.

Whiting, John W. M.
1966   Preface. In *Field Guide for a Study of Socialization*, ed. J. W. M. Whiting et al. Six Culture Series, vol. 1., New York: Wiley.
1968   Socialization. *International Encyclopedia of Social Science*. New York: Macmillan.

Whiting, John W. M., and I. L. Child
1953   *Child Training and Personality*. New Haven: Yale University Press.

Whiting, John W. M., R. Kluckhohn, and A. S. Anthony
1958   The Function of Male Initiation Ceremonies at Puberty. In *Readings in Social Psychology*, ed. E. E. Maccoby, T. Newcomb, and E. Hartley. New York: Holt.

Whiting, John W. M., et al., eds.
1966   *Field Guide for a Study of Socialization*. Six Culture Series, vol. 1. New York: Wiley.

Williams, T. R.
1966   Cultural Structuring of Tactile Experiences in a Borneo Society. *American Anthropologist* 68:27-39.
1969   *A Borneo Childhood: Enculturation in Dusun Society*. New York: Holt, Rinehart & Winston.
1972   *Human Culture Transmitted: An Introduction to Study of the Socialization Process*. St. Louis: C. V. Mosby.

Winters, W.
1964   Recent Findings from the Application of Psychological Tests to Bushmen. *Psygram* 6:42-55.

Witkin, H. A., et al.
1954   *Personality Through Perception*. New York: Harper.

Wundt, Wilhelm
1900- *Völkerpsychologie: Eine Untersuchung der Entwicklungsgesetze von Sprache, Mythus, und Sitte,* 10 vols.
1920   Leipzig: Engelmann.

Young, Frank W.
1962   The Function of Male Initiation Ceremonies: A Cross-Cultural Test of an Alternative Hypothesis. *American Journal of Sociology* 67:379-96.

CHAPTER 26 Cultural Psychiatry

JOHN G. KENNEDY

INTRODUCTION

The problem of the relationships between sociocultural factors and emotional disorder was not one that could be phrased in these terms until the social sciences had developed some degree of theoretical sophistication, until such concepts as society and culture had become useful tools. Neither was such a relationship likely to be posited when what are now regarded as mental problems either were considered to be inexplicable organic malfunctions or remained undistinguished within the range of tolerable human idiosyncrasies. Propitious circumstances for seeing relationships between such variables had developed by the 1930s and 1940s, when Freudian ideas reached a peak of influence in American psychiatry, and when the culture-and-personality approach of anthropology was most popular.

It was really only a decade or so prior to the beginning of this century that psychiatrists began to awaken to the potential theoretical importance of materials from other cultures. Kraepelin, "the great classifier," who traveled to Southeast Asia and other areas of the world in the 1890s, began to write of the differences in symptomatology that he found, and it was he who established the concept of "comparative psychiatry" (1904). Freud also was aware of the significance of comparative data, and used available ethnological reports to construct and confirm his theories, as seen particularly in *Totem and Taboo* (1950).

Kluckhohn (1956:490-91), noting that American anthropology largely ignored or rejected the growing body of psychiatric theory and data up until 1928, remarks that this rejection may have been a reflection of the personality types that chose anthropology as a career. As he points out, the integration of psychiatric findings into anthropo-

Assistance in gathering the references for this paper was rendered by Dagmar Gunderson, Donald Sutherland, and especially by Robert Schoenman. All are graduate students in the Department of Anthropology, U.C.L.A.

1119

logical studies was initiated primarily by Ruth Benedict, Margaret Mead, and Edward Sapir in the early thirties, "though these three tended always to rephrase psychiatric insights in cultural terms." Scarcely less important in influence, and certainly more analytical and more explicitly psychiatric, were such writers as Kluckhohn himself, A. I. Hallowell, M. E. Opler, M. K. Opler, George Devereux, Scudder McKeel, Margaret Mead, Cora Du Bois, J. J. Honigmann, and Ralph Linton.

Armed with evidence from nonliterate peoples, nineteenth- and early twentieth-century anthropology mounted a drastic attack on ethnocentrism in social science, demonstrated the immense formative influence of culture on individuals, and documented the tremendous variability of patterns of social life around the globe. During this same period dynamic psychiatry was evolving the position that many disorders were psychogenic—that is, produced by noxious environmental factors, particularly in early childhood. By the 1930s many psychiatrists were aware of the potential usefulness of the cross-cultural laboratory, and such eminent figures as Harry Stack Sullivan, Abram Kardiner, and Eric Erikson were among the psychiatrists and psychoanalysts working with anthropologists and pointing out the need for a cultural dimension in the study of individual psychodynamics.

After the relative moratorium on research during World War II and its aftermath, work toward the integration of psychiatric and anthropological data and theory seemed to floresce. Psychiatrists with long residences in colonial territories began to report findings, and a number of anthropologists described what seemed to be unique syndromes of disordered behavior. In the 1950s two large-scale epidemiological studies attempting to test some of the ideas re-lating culture to mental disorder were under way (reported in Leighton, Clausen, and Wilson 1957; Leighton and Hughes 1959; Leighton et al. 1963; Srole et al. 1962), and several others of smaller scope were also yielding apparently interesting results (Eaton and Weil 1955, Lin 1953, Ödegård 1952, Malzberg and Lee 1956, and others). By the end of the decade a number of syntheses of the previous literature had appeared (P. R. Benedict and Jacks 1954, Honigmann 1954, Linton 1956, M. K. Opler 1956, Wittkower and Fried 1959), and a journal specifically concerned with the field (Transcultural Psychiatric Research Review) had made its appearance. After this outburst of activity, however, enthusiasm died down somewhat, and the integration called for by Edward Sapir in "Why Cultural Anthropology Needs the Psychiatrist" (1938) has never been developed to its potential.

The social scientific and cross-cultural approach has perhaps had more impact on psychiatric theory than the reverse, but much of the present espousal of social and cultural viewpoints in psychiatry appears to be lip service rather than the reflection of any deep understanding of social process or culture. Nevertheless, scattered studies and findings have proliferated. It is clear that the field where anthropology and psychiatry intersect has now outgrown its previous secondary place as a category of "culture and personality" or psychological anthropology, and demands separate and equal treatment.

Transcultural psychiatry (Wittkower and Fried 1959), cross-cultural psychiatry (J. M. Murphy and Leighton 1965), and ethnopsychiatry (Devereux 1961a) are among the most popular terms now in use to designate the general field, but none of these labels is adequate to describe it. There are many areas where the concerns of psychiatry and anthropology overlap, and there is not space enough to discuss them all here. My inevitably selective presentation of materials is intended only to highlight the main interests and the methodological and theoretical problems of the field.

EPIDEMIOLOGY

Much of the involvement of the social sciences with the investigation of "mental illness" stems from three bases: (1) the observation that "insanity" is not evenly distributed among populations, (2) the apparent shifts of the frequencies of disturbances within populations over time, and (3) the fact that much psychiatric disorder has no proven link to physiological or biochemical causes. Even "the schizophrenias" still evade the search for biochemical keys, while the neuroses and character disorders are generally conceded to be largely products of faulty or warped socialization. These three sets of circumstances, in conjunction with the very successful uses of population statistics in the epidemiology of known organic diseases, have provided impetus for psychiatric epidemiology.

The basic methodological mandate of epidemiology is disarmingly simple: "Count the frequency of disorders in a given population." Tsung-yi Lin, a leading social psychiatrist, has defined psychiatric epidemiology as "the study of the distribution of a disease in space and time within a population, and of factors which influence this distribution" (Lin and Standley 1962:10). The primary goal is thus to ascertain the *rates* of various types of disease or disorder in populations that are defined by certain properties, such as geographical location, social class, ethnic group, and separate culture. Once such rates have been established, inferences can be made and hypotheses tested regarding these variables and their relationship to mental disorder. Rational plans also can be made by responsible agencies for distributing facilities and aids in accordance with needs. Epidemiology thus promises much on both theoretical and practical grounds.

During the decades since 1930, the epidemiological approach to the study of mental illness has had numerous trials at great expense, with the participation of many excellent minds, yet the results are contradictory, inconclusive, and generally disappointing. Such studies have helped spread the ideology of the mental health movement in the United States and Europe and have thus stimulated the construction of mental health facilities, but they have provided little progress toward solution of major etiological questions. We still have no firm idea of the frequencies and intensities of psychiatric problems in large populations.

In support of this harsh judgment we may cite a number of authors who have tried to compare epidemiological studies. In the best summation of such research, Dohrenwend and Dohrenwend (1969:12-13) tabulated forty-four field studies of prevalence by thirty-five investigators or teams:

... the range in the rates reported in these studies is from less than 1 percent to over 60 percent, suggesting that variation in rates may be associated with social factors that differ between studies. As we see, however, when the studies are grouped according to the geo-political areas in which they are conducted and according to whether the study site was rural or urban, these contrasts in setting do not account adequately for the variation in rates.

These findings confirmed the results of earlier comparisons of different sets of studies. The authors of these studies attributed the vast differences to widening definitions of mental disorder and differences in study design and classification systems (Plunkett and Gordon 1960:91, Lin and Standley 1962:15).

After reviewing the cross-cultural data, Wittkower and Fried remarked (1959:491) that "on methodological grounds there are no existing statistics which permit valid statistical transcultural comparisons of incidence and prevalence in mental illness."

Mishler and Scotch (1963:340) came to similar conclusions in their survey of epidemiological research on schizophrenia, and the eminent authors of a recent psychiatric textbook bluntly generalize: "There are no reliable estimates of the incidence and prevalence of schizophrenia" (Redlich and Freedman 1966:461). Thus there is much evidence to corroborate H. B. M. Murphy's comment (1965:303): "The past failure of psychiatric epidemiology is quite obvious if one considers how much has been done and how rarely the findings have contributed to psychiatric theory or even to the application of that theory and the planning of services."

Nevertheless, past failure is not an adequate reason for discarding such a promising approach. If we were able to ascertain true rates of psychiatric disorder in discrete populations, we could be well on our way to solving many basic theoretical and practical problems. An examination of a few illustrative studies may reveal their potential as well as the areas of difficulty. However, before looking at some specifics, it is necessary to make a few general statements about epidemiological surveys.

The two principal types of measure used in these surveys are called *prevalence* and *incidence*. Prevalence refers to the amount of illness or disorder (i.e., number of cases) existing in a specific population at a given time (point prevalence) or during a given period of time (period prevalence). Incidence refers to the number of *new* cases occur-

ring in a population during a specified period of time. Most investigators admit that incidence is a much more sensitive indicator of etiology because it can be much more clearly tied to the independent variables. However, incidence is extremely difficult to measure in field studies, a fact that has made practically all investigators in this field select prevalence as the dependent variable. Incidence studies have been made, but almost all of them have used first admissions to hospitals as the indicator of new cases. Thus they are all unreliable and questionable.[1] On the other hand, a general drawback of the prevalence concept, apart from the great difficulties in measurement, is the fact that any count is an accumulation or pile-up of old and new cases—a product of incidence plus duration of illness. Since prevalence surveys are cross-sectional and generally use sampling methods, they are unable to tell with certainty the circumstances under which disorders of variable and long duration (such as schizophrenia) arose. They also tend to overweight the types of problems that tend to be of long duration and to underweight the short-term ones.

The etiological hypotheses of most surveys of mental disorders are based upon differences in rates of disorder. Such differences are usually attributed to one or more of four general sets of variables:

1. *Heredity and inbreeding.* Members of racial groups, cultural groups, and

---

[1] Areas differ in the numbers, types, and availability of services; usage of facilities varies with knowledge and attitudes related to such problems; diagnostic and admission criteria have been shown to vary immensely—not only from one to another country, cultural group, state, and city, but among local hospitals and within them. These criteria also vary through time in all such groups. In addition to all these, differences in the efficiency of record-keeping make attempts to compare such data absurd (Dunham 1969:131, Lin and Standley 1962:14).

social classes may form a relatively closed gene pool that could contain a high proportion of the genes potentially causing the disorders.

2. *Differential stresses* to which groups are exposed. Members of lower socioeconomic classes are expected to be·exposed to more pervasive and noxious influences than members of higher ones. Other frequently considered situations of stress are poverty, migration, and endemic disease.

3. *Social selection*. Differential social demands, attitudes toward disorder, and so on might result in shifts in the distribution of disturbed people. Most common here is the reasonable notion that in stratified societies those falling prey to mental disorder will tend to drift down the social pyramid and pile up at the bottom, thus accounting for the greater frequencies typically found there. Other examples of selection are cultural patterns of extrusion or infanticide of defectives, by which groups can reduce the frequencies of these types. Conversely, attitudes of acceptance might result in a selective accumulation of such individuals from other groups.

4. *Differences in treatment,* including both facilities and methods. Poor treatment could result in higher rates, while effective treatment might lower them (Hollingshead and Redlich 1958).

SOME ILLUSTRATIVE EXAMPLES

The Midtown Manhattan Study

Since the famous Midtown Manhattan study (L. Srole et al. 1962) is among the most influential, costly, and carefully planned studies done to date, let us first discuss some of its aspects. Much of my comment also applies to other large studies, such as that made in Stirling County, Nova Scotia (A. Leighton 1959, D. C. Leighton et al. 1963).

The core of the Midtown study consisted of interviews with 1,660 out of a total sample of 1,911 people between the ages of twenty and fifty-nine, randomly selected from a district of Manhattan's East Side. The study used a specially designed questionnaire administered by well-trained nonmedical professionals, and the data they gathered were then rated by one of two psychiatrists. "Symptoms" in each protocol were classified according to the seriousness of their psychiatrically impairing character and degree of interference with life adjustment.[2]

The well-known and striking results of this study run contrary to common opinion. A major finding was that less than one-fifth of the Midtown population was "well." About three-fifths were assessed as suffering from some kind of mental problem that would benefit from psychiatric help, and more than one-fifth (about 23.5 percent) were judged so incapacitated that they should have been hospitalized. There are many other interesting findings in the Midtown study, particularly those relating to social class. In my opinion, however, they are all questionable because of certain aspects of methodology.

The most obvious source of error in such an approach is the complete absence of contact between the clinician and the interviewee. Some recognition of this difficulty is evidenced in the gross "intensity" categories that were used instead of diagnostic groupings, but in view of the notorious unreliability of psychiatric judgments, even with the patient in front of the examiners, diagnosis of paper protocols seems like utter folly (Stoller and Geertsma 1963, Kreitman et al. 1961,

---

[2] The main categories used were: mild symptom formation, moderate symptom formation, and impaired (marked, severe, incapacitated).

Beck 1962). This problem cannot be explained away by pointing to the high degree of agreement on judgments among the rating psychiatrists; this agreement is suspect, since the raters aided in developing the criteria for rating. Even if we could accept this built-in agreement, we would still have to recognize that the raters were consistent only in rating the extremely impaired and the extremely unimpaired; regarding the middle three categories, Gruenberg (1964:86) remarks:

... I believe that calculations based on these discriminations, judging from the limited data presented or their reliability ... are not worthy of interpretation. However, the cutting point selected for analysis is where the raters themselves thought themselves weak, i.e., between *moderate* and *marked* symptom formations. *Most of the published data depends on this discrimination.* (Italics added.)

Another source of potentially serious error lies in the sampling methods. Gruenberg points out that by the study's criteria of residence, neither transients of various kinds nor family members living away from home in institutions such as colleges, prisons, hospitals, military organizations, and nursing homes were counted in the research population. Also important are the 251 "unknowns" (13 percent of the actual sample who were not included). The assumption that this is a small percentage and that the distribution of characteristics of interest among these unknowns was similar to the distribution among those interviewed seems extremely dubious for this type of investigation. It might well be that a large percentage of the unknowns included those so mentally healthy that they threw out the pestering interviewer; those so extremely impaired—aggressive psychotics—that the truth-seeking interviewer, like jesting Pilate, would not stay for an answer; or perhaps depressed individuals who did not want to be bothered. If these 13 percent happened to fall heavily in one or two categories, the total results of the study would have been quite different.

Possible biases and errors also inhere in the instrument used to elicit symptoms. The Midtown as well as the Stirling County schedules placed heavy reliance upon the interviewees' reports of their own psychophysiological symptoms as indicators of disorder. A difficulty here is the inability to get at disorders that are not indexed by physiological disturbances, as well as the possibility that in many cases a physiological symptom may not indicate psychiatric disorder. The Midtown researchers stated that they were attempting to tap "such symptoms as would demonstrably represent the most salient and *generalized* indicators of mental pathology" (Srole et al. 1962:41), though they themselves admitted that their instrument tended to miss disorders such as alcoholism, sociopathic traits, and the early stages of paranoid schizophrenia (1962:65, 269). Such deficiencies in instrument sensitivity are important because these are among the most widespread and most socially incapacitating emotional problems.

Dohrenwend and Dohrenwend (1969:95-109) examined the problem of instrument validity, with special focus upon the Midtown and Stirling County studies, and their critique (p. 100) is devastating:

Thus, in the absence of systematic sampling of items, no argument can be made for the content validity of the Midtown measure of psychological disorder. The same is true of the Stirling and Yoruba studies in which items were taken from the N.S.A. (Neurological Screening Adjunct) and other test sources without explicit specification of the selection procedures.

As for "predictive validity," they say

(p. 101), "Typically conducted at one point in time, the studies have thus not tested their assessments of disorder against criteria of future psychiatric condition, admission to treatment or social functioning."

The Dohrenwends also found the Midtown researchers' claim of "concurrent validity" unsubstantiated. Their test of the interview items discriminated a group of 139 diagnosed neurotic and remitted psychotic patients from 72 persons judged well by a psychiatrist, but (p. 101)

Although the Midtown psychiatrists reported that, in rating cases well or not well, they gave special weight to eight of the 22 items that discriminated at the .01 level, they also paid particular attention to 6 items that failed to discriminate at this level. Thus in the Midtown study, although the data from which the psychiatrists worked had been tested for concurrent validity in the manner described above, *this test did not determine the use of these data* by the psychiatrists in making their ratings of cases.

In addition, by pointing out the lack of public steps of inference in these studies, the Dohrenwends show that the studies lack "construct validity." Their general assessment of the rating process in both the Midtown and Stirling County studies is that "there is considerable ambiguity about the relations between the Midtown and Stirling judgmental ratings of untreated disorder" (p. 104).[3]

Aside from the problematic character of the instruments themselves, there is also evidence that these studies failed to deal with possible errors arising from the interviewer-interviewee relationship. The problem is one of gathering valid data, and the questionable assumption is that the survey instruments are so well constructed that a *nonprofessional* interviewer can elicit significant information for diagnosis of mental disorder.

The Midtown and Stirling County studies depend almost exclusively on *self-reports* of the respondents, elicited by nonpsychiatrists at one point in time. Such uncontrolled factors as differences in interview skills, degree of psychiatric sophistication, ethnic group attitudes of interviewee and interviewer, variable conditions in the home, previous experience with solicitors or with institutions of various kinds, attitudes toward strangers or toward middle-class persons, all could bias results significantly. These variables might even consistently characterize significant numbers of people in the same socioeconomic stratum and thus produce spurious class ("SES") differences.

One such variable, "response-style," was examined by the Dohrenwends. They took their cue from a study suggesting that respondents may have modified their answers to the twenty-two items in the Midtown scale[4] in their desire to be discharged from the hospital, and from studies showing that some populations tend to "yea-say" or "nay-say" to questions regardless of content. After performing a number of tests, the Dohrenwends concluded (p. 88) that members of various New York ethnic groups do tend to respond differently to an expanded version of the Midtown twenty-two item scale according to cultural *evaluation* of the items; Puerto Ricans, for example, do not attach any negative significance to many of the "symptoms" and readily admit to them, while other groups are more reticent.

---

[3] The interested reader should refer to Dohrenwend and Dohrenwend 1969 for detailed elaboration of these critiques.

[4] This scale consists of 22 of the original 252 items that were found to discriminate in the same way the long version did (Langner 1962).

This is only one of the kinds of thing that can go wrong at the point of data collection. Anyone who has done anthropological fieldwork knows the avoidance, indirection, misunderstanding, and even outright lying that may greet any kind of questioning, and is highly suspicious of studies using one-shot interviews on any but the most obvious of subject matters. The effects of interviewers' personalities, male-female effects, laziness of fieldworkers, and so on are unbelievably difficult to control. Sociologists may be overly fond of criticizing "observer effects" of anthropologists in the field, but the one-shot interview is a situation in which these are not only maximal but uncorrected.

Another of the many sources of error in this study, as in many other survey studies of mental disorder, is the questionable assumption that symptoms reported at one point in time index the types of persistent stereotyped malfunctioning that are typical of serious mental disorders as they are known to clinicians. However, "...Tyhurst... suggested that the presence of symptoms was not necessarily an indication of the presence of disorder. Rather, symptoms reported might be transient responses to life crises" (Dohrenwend and Dohrenwend 1969:171).

Since the conditions of life typical of slum dwellers and members of some other subcultures can consistently produce the kinds of stresses that can induce these temporary adaptive responses, a higher frequency of high symptom scores can be expected among such groups than among persons of middle-class life styles. Thus, even if we accepted the questionable survey data at face value, the high frequencies of severe impairment reported in such studies as Midtown are suspect.

The Midtown survey is often cited as among the most thorough that have been done. I leave it to the reader to judge what reliance can be placed on its findings. With this study as a background illustration of where the methodological difficulties lie, let us now look at some evidence from the nonwestern world.

Nonwestern Studies

Because of the potential fruitfulness of epidemiology, many studies of mental disorder in nonwestern societies contain estimations of prevalence or incidence. Most of these are of little value and have failed to contribute to a cumulative body of comparable knowledge. A few examples will suffice to illustrate the kinds of information upon which the epidemiological generalizations of transcultural psychiatry are based.

A great number of these studies are based purely upon hospital statistics; and in view of the obvious drawbacks of such data, it is amazing to see the continuing flow of articles, complete with charts containing numbers and percentages of patients in various diagnostic categories, divided by age, sex, tribe, race, and so on. Usually one finds an opening qualifying statement as to generalizability, yet the writer proceeds to compare admission figures with population statistics, as if meaningful estimations of incidence or prevalence are possible with this kind of data.

Carothers' (1953) study of 609 admissions to the Mathari mental hospital in Kenya has been quoted perhaps as much as any study in Africa, yet from an epidemiological point of view, it is completely worthless. He calculated rates of mental disorder for his African population and arrived at an incidence figure of 3.4 per thousand per year, which he then went on to compare with rates in England (57 per thousand per year) and the United States (161 per thousand per year). Though he was convinced that Africans suffered less mental illness than Europeans, he felt something might be wrong with this calculation, so he went to the local chiefs to get their estimations. Adding these data to his hospitalized population, he arrived at a rate of 10.37 per thousand of population, which is still much lower than for Europeans (Carothers 1953:558). He then went on to make all kinds of comparisons of "the Africans" with American blacks, with general hospitalization rates for the state of Massachusetts, and so on. This would not be so bad were it not for the fact that he makes numerous casual interpretations of this flimsy epidemiological evidence to account for differences and similarities in the sets of figures.

Mishler and Scotch (1963:339) comment similarly on Carothers' conclusions regarding culture change:

... a study from East Africa by Carothers, which attempts to demonstrate that culture change does lead to higher rates of mental illness, is also highly questionable on a number of counts, not the least of these being that the data consist of hospital admissions in a country where such admissions cannot seriously be taken as representative, subject as they are to any number of biases.

Mishler and Scotch also make a more detailed critique of the epidemiological aspect of Geoffrey Tooth's (1950) widely cited study on the Gold Coast, singling it out because of Benedict and Jacks' (1954) statement that it is "the most nearly complete of any study for Africa." Tooth located his cases by asking chiefs and census enumerators about "mad" persons, and Mishler and Scotch cite his own statements about the erratic nature of this case-finding process. They criticize the fact that he did not include hospitalized patients in his prevalence figures, and call attention to the inadequacy of his sample.

Tooth collected 400 cases in a two-year period, yet the data were so incomplete that only 173 of them could be analyzed; the remaining 227 were never mentioned again (Mishler and Scotch 1963:335).[5]

Similar methodological problems afflict other African studies that attempt to estimate frequencies of disorders in populations. One of the best *general* studies of mental disorder in a nonliterate population was made by M. J. Field (1960), who was trained in both anthropology and psychiatry. She interviewed more than 2,500 visitors to therapeutic religious shrines among the Akan peoples of Ghana. Her analysis is generally very enlightening, but she too could not refrain from attempting to estimate prevalence.

Field found her cases of disorder through inquiring among local village headmen. After excluding some questionable cases, some epileptics, two cases of late-treated trypanosomiasis, and a cranial nerve-damaged youth, she emerged with an exceptionally low rate of chronic schizophrenics (41 in twelve Ashanti country towns and villages with an estimated total population of 4,283) (Field 1960:445, 449). Any field anthropologist must empathize with her account, but, as M. K. Opler points out, higher rates would be expected in the rapidly changing Ghanaian scene. Furthermore (Opler 1967:453):

The Achilles Heel of this book is the astounding number of cases (over 2500) diagnosed by *one* person. In this light when I read that she located 41 chronic schizophrenics among them representing a population estimated in 1948 at 4,283 (almost a 0.10 per cent incidence) and then read, "In Europe and America the expectation of schizophrenia in the general population is 0.8 per cent," I for one cannot jump on the bandwagon.

---

[5] Tooth's findings have considerable interest in other connections, as we shall see.

Knowing what we do about the difficulties of diagnosing schizophrenia in even the most favorable circumstances, it is unlikely that Field's methods revealed all the cases, or that in her single interviews she was able to differentiate the many organic problems that can simulate the condition. It is also probable that the distributions were skewed by the fact that whole villages had to be eliminated because of uncooperative headmen.

Another such example is a Ghanaian study by the well-known British anthropologist Meyer Fortes and his wife, psychiatrist Doris Mayer (1965). The empirical content of this research is interesting, but again unwarranted epidemiological conclusions are drawn from unsatisfactory data. During the two and a half years in the 1930s when Fortes was conducting his classic study of the Tallensi, he noted only one clearly psychotic person out of a population of "thirty to forty thousand" (Fortes and Mayer 1965:19). However, in 1963, almost thirty years later, his wife found no fewer than 13 cases of psychosis in the same group, which had now grown to 50,000. Fortes and Mayer tentatively ascribe the higher frequency to stressful social changes in the intervening years.

The question of whether some cases might have been missed in 1934 is disposed of by saying that, owing to Tallensi attitudes, madmen are not hidden from view, and that because they are cared for they do not die off. Also, "mad Tallensi are like madmen anywhere," and "only the latent or borderline cases need identification by a psychiatrist" (1965:23). Such statements are questionable at best, and in Africa organic problems and diseases so often confuse the picture that in the absence of physical examinations and neurological testing, the early estimate of prevalence cannot be taken seriously.

In discussing examples of transcultural epidemiology, special attention should be devoted to the Cornell study *Psychiatric Disorder Among the Yoruba* (A. Leighton et al. 1963). The purpose of this study was to replicate the methods of the Canadian Stirling County study in Africa, producing for the first time really comparable sets of data from two cultural settings. It was engineered by Alexander Leighton and his group, and based upon more than fifteen years of previous experience in mental illness surveys.

The authors of the Cornell-Aro study stated their goals as being primarily methodological. They were concerned with "ways and means for identifying and estimating disorder prevalence among the Yoruba people" and "with ways and means for identifying, describing, and counting Yoruba cultural and subnational factors of maximal relevance to the origin, course, and outcome of psychiatric disorders." They intended to improve sampling methods, to reduce the time required for epidemiological studies of this type, and to illuminate theory relating to the connection of sociocultural factors and mental health (A. Leighton et al. 1963:6-7).

The project was carried out in a period of three months by a research team of four psychiatrists and three social scientists, aided by medical personnel. The location was a group of villages around the Nigerian city of Abeokuta, as well as within the city itself. The sample consisted of 406 individuals, who were interviewed with the aid of interpreters for about one and one-quarter hours each. The psychiatrists then jointly evaluated the schedules, using the categories of the American Psychiatric Association as a guide, and classified each individual as (*a*) a clear psychiatric "case," (*b*) a probable case, (*c*) a possible case, or (*d*) free of psychiatric disorder.

The major causal assumption was that sociocultural disintegration produces relatively high frequencies of mental disorder, and thus one of the jobs of the social scientists was to select villages representing varying degrees of integration within which to sample frequencies of disorder. Indicators such as poverty, secularization, family instability, poor leadership, migration, "cultural confusion," and so on were used to rate a number of villages as "integrated," "intermediate," and "disintegrated."

A contact team of workers was sent to each selected village to prepare the officials and the sampled respondents, and a few days later the research teams descended to do the interviews. The following day a final team of social scientists interviewed a subsample of the same respondents. The data so gathered were then analyzed and the results compared with those from Stirling County, Nova Scotia. The authors felt that they were able to demonstrate that sociocultural disintegration is associated with high frequencies of disorder, that their methods are applicable in a cross-cultural context, and that meaningful comparisons with the Stirling County findings could be made.

Many of the criticisms one might make of this study are commendably anticipated in chapters entitled "The Problem of Cultural Distortion" and "The Question of Bias" as well as by the tentative way in which most findings are discussed. Still, a careful reader finds that major questions are not resolved. There is not space here for a detailed critique of the Yoruba study, but because it is so well known, and because it might be thought by the nonspecialist to be more meaningful than it actually is, a few of its more instructive difficulties should be mentioned.

In the first place, the Cornell-Aro study is subject to all of the pyramiding possibilities of error inherent in methodologies depending on self-reported symptoms of a predominantly psychophysiological nature, recorded by nonpsychiatrists on interview schedules at one point in time, then diagnosed at second remove from the patient before being finally again translated into scores of degrees of relative impairment. All of these possibilities of compounded error are greatly increased when the research team moves into an alien culture.

The question of organic disease and other physiological problems often related to symptoms of emotional disorder was another source of possible error not adequately dealt with. As the investigators themselves state (p. 88), "Despite earlier plans, the respondents in our sample were not given a routine medical check." Anumonye (1966:97) has noted in this connection that the researchers themselves state: "Where there is so much infection, parasitic, and nutritional disease, it is to be expected that some of the symptoms registered in the psychophysiological category could be discarded as not indicative of psychiatric disorder." Anumonye's own experience with the group leads him to point out how cross-cultural mistranslation probably biased results. For example, he shows how many kinds of psychiatric and organic problems are classified together in some of the Yoruban words used by the interviewers, leading to unpredictable inflations of symptoms reported (Anumonye 1969:99). This comment is important in view of the fact that most of the authors' discussions of possible error argue that mental disorder was probably *under*reported.

In a similar vein is the criticism of Raymond Prince (1964*b*:51), who also worked among the Yoruba. He feels that a serious blind spot in the study was a

... lack of awareness of the emotional symptoms of malnutrition. . . . When the Yoruba subject spoke of weakness, burning in the skin, insomnia, dimness of vision, tearfulness and despair, the psychiatrist from the affluent society would immediately list these under "disorders of psychogenic origin or without clearly defined physical cause." But they are equally symptoms of malnutrition and may occur in the absence of physical signs.

The dubious sampling of the Yoruba study also makes any generalizations of questionable value. The authors note that sampling was done at three levels: selection of villages, selection of households, and selection of individuals within households. But it turned out that they went to places where they were welcome; thus "A truly random selection of villages and city sections might show some differences in prevalence from those we report" (A. Leighton et al. 1963).

T. A. Lambo, one of the principal investigators on the Cornell team, in another context reveals skepticism about the sampling in his answer to a question regarding the prevalence of schizophrenia in Nigeria (Lambo 1965*a*:715): "The only information that we have at present comes from the work which Professor Leighton and his team did in Nigeria. . . . I would be extremely cautious in using this data because his study is confined to a fairly homogeneous section of the population." Anumonye (1966:97) also comments on the sampling: "There is yet another source of error: the authors indicate that the sample used in Abeokuta City was rather small (64) as compared with

the villages (262) and also that there were no cross-check informants equivalent to the headmen used in the villages."

The authors themselves note a number of problems of interpretation arising from the loss of respondents from the samples and from differential male-female response to questioning. None of these questions are resolved satisfactorily (see A. Leighton et al. 1963:163-72).

The reliability of the findings are further put in doubt by the fact that a five-week follow-up study of many of the same families by another investigator got very different results (A. Leighton et al. 1963:173-74): "Men continued to report far more symptoms for themselves than did women for themselves, but the numbers of symptoms given by both groups dropped drastically from the previous survey." The authors attach little importance to this check. "The most probable explanation for this would seem to be resistance to repeated interviews, but it could also be related to differences in interviewer, interpreter, preparation for the visits, or changing factors within the village itself." Not discussed is the fact that in addition to the implied lack of reliability, all of these differences could also have been operative in the original study. Would an interviewee have given the same responses to a different interviewer in the first study, or to the same interviewer working with a different interpreter? The authors' "explanation" itself points to a huge unknown factor and thus to a source of possible error.

In addition to these problems with the primary mental health data, there are severe problems with specifying the independent variable—the degree of sociocultural disintegration. The Cornell investigators made the dubious assumption that such indicators as secularization, poverty, and so on are culture-free, but there is a great question as to whether the "indicators" actually mean the same things in Nigeria as they do in Nova Scotia. Second, the social data that provide the evidence for disintegration and integration rest on an inadequate base: "It can thus be seen that the groups of respondents supplying data for the social science questionnaire are small. On this account we must hesitate to make definitive statements" (A. Leighton et al. 1963:214). Third, many of the data from this questionnaire are equivocal or contradictory to the thesis; for example, data on migration (pp. 221-22), on leadership (p. 226), on membership in associations (p. 227), and on law and order (p. 229). Fourth, the descriptions of the three types of village (integrated, intermediate, disintegrated) raise questions as to whether the conditions described are permanent or temporary, recent or of long standing. How long would a village have to be disintegrated, dilapidated, and poverty-stricken before the prevalence of symptoms increased? Finally, these indicators of disintegration are at such a general level that it is difficult to see how they specifically affect mental health. It is not evident that the symptoms of any of the respondents rated as "impaired" were directly related to poverty, "cultural confusion," or the like.

In light of these and other methodological and theoretical problems, what degree of confidence can we have in the comparisons and generalizations offered by the authors? They suggest, for example, that depressive symptoms and compulsive traits are more prevalent in Stirling County than among the Yoruba (pp. 132, 137), and that paranoid features are more common among the Nigerians. What can we make of the statement that the findings suggest a higher prevalence of sociopathic traits in Stirling County when we are told that in

Yoruba villages the information on this question was obtained from headmen, who may have wanted to make their villages look good (p. 133)? Can we place any reliance on the figures showing higher total frequencies of disorder in Stirling than in Yoruba? Our already tottering confidence is not strengthened by the authors' own acknowledgment (p. 132) that

... the Yoruba stand out for apparently having more headaches, respiratory difficulty, genitourinary disturbance, and skin trouble. Most of this we can attribute to the generally higher prevalence of organic disorder which affects percentage figures in this whole major symptom category. *Also pertinent is the fact that the questionnaire used in the Nigerian study investigating those topics is more detailed than was the case in Stirling.* [Italics added.]

Finally the authors devastatingly admit (p. 124) that "the differences and similarities between the Yoruba and Stirling figures are to an unknown degree under the influence of differences in the procedures employed in the two studies."

While the candor with which these investigators admit to methodological shortcomings is admirable, it is all too evident that this study was an ill-conceived attempt to tackle a complex subject in far too short a time. I have taken some time to review it here because it has been extensively quoted and because it is an instructive example of methodological problems in this field. Perhaps its main virtue is the drastic lesson it offers in the general inappropriateness of American sociological survey techniques in cross-cultural contexts. But cross-cultural epidemiology is not as hopeless as it might seem at this point. An interesting study of modest scope, which grew out of the Cornell-Aro study in Nigeria, was conducted by Robert Collis (1966). Many commentators have remarked on the part played by disease and dietary deficiencies in mental disorders in Africa, and Collis' study was designed to investigate the relationship of poor health to mental disorder. A subsample of people who showed degrees of functional impairment not associated with epilepsy, encephalitis, and other organic disorders was drawn from the larger Cornell-Aro epidemiological survey sample and was compared with a control group of respondents judged as "well." The original sample of "psychiatric cases" numbered 65, but only 33 of these finally consented to the research program; the control group of "wells" numbered twenty.

After first being interviewed in depth, each subject had his history taken and was given a thorough physical examination, which included blood tests for hemoglobin and white cell counts and for malaria, microfilms of fecal smears for amoeba, ova, cysts, and so on, urinalysis, and a Kahn test. In the second stage of the study the "cases" were divided into three groups. Group X was given "total push" physical therapy, consisting of various medications, vitamins, proteins, and so on, all designed to enhance physical strength and health; group Y was given one placebo tablet three times a day; and group Z was treated with psychiatric drugs such as thorazine. After three months of treatment each patient was examined, assessed for improvement, and placed in one of three categories: "the same," "improved," or "greatly improved." Improved social functioning as well as reduction of "symptoms" was considered in the evaluation.

In the second phase of this part of the study a different type of treatment was given for eight weeks to those who had failed to improve under the first conditions: those from the "physical treatment" (X) group who had not improved were given psychiatric drugs;

those on placebo who remained the same were divided into two groups, one receiving physical treatment and the other psychiatric treatment; and so on. The third and final stage of the study was an assessment for rate of relapse three months after cessation of all treatment. The laboratory results indicated no significant differences between the controls and the "cases"—all were to a certain extent suffering from hookworm, iron deficiency, and other disorders related to environment and life style. However, the physical examination differentiated the groups clearly. The controls were strong in physique and vigorous, while almost half of the "cases" suffered from marked nutritional deficiencies, strongly suggesting that continued research should be directed to the relationship of malnutrition and psychiatric disorder.

Among the results of the treatment experiment were the following: (1) Many of the patients experienced a placebo effect, which faded about the fifth week of treatment. One patient treated with placebos maintained his improvement. (2) Psychiatric drug treatment gave a significantly higher improvement rate overall than physical treatment. (3) There were, however, numerous patients who improved significantly on physical treatment, and these tended to maintain their improvement better than those on psychiatric drugs alone. (4) Almost two-thirds of the patients who showed initial improvement relapsed to some extent. (5) All of the patients who improved under either treatment method and who did not relapse were able to perform sexually to their satisfaction: the men were potent and the women were able to conceive. (It had been discovered that impotence and infertility were among the most severe anxiety-producers among the Yoruba.)

There were a number of methodological difficulties. For one thing, the spread of "cases" was not as wide as could be desired; there were few psychoses, hysterias, or other extreme disorders. There were possibilities of error through failure of patients to take medicine, and there was some disruption of the sampling by an unfriendly chief, among other problems. Nevertheless, this study gives one some sense of confidence in the findings. One reason for this, in addition to the fine design, is the fact that the investigator was in repeated contact with the patients over a period of months. Other good features are the detailed descriptions of many cases and of the research procedures. The subjects are not presented as "symptom patterns" or "ridits,"[6] but as suffering individuals. For these reasons we have some confidence in the psychiatric classification of the patients. Collis does not claim conclusiveness for his pilot study and suggests how other factors might account for his results. This study is a pioneer for a type that should be carried out on a larger scale and with better facilities in the future. It is not epidemiological, but it illustrates the kind of intensive work that will be necessary for good epidemiology.

An impressive and interesting epidemiological study on a large scale is the set of surveys carried out on Taiwan by Tsung-yi Lin and his associates (1969). From 1946 to 1948 they made a complete psychiatric census in three differing population units—a rural area, a small town, and a section of a large city—with a total of 19,931 inhabitants. The cases were located by consulting the census registers, examining reports of leaders and physicians in the

selected communities, inquiring of neighbors concerning suspected cases, and conducting personal interviews with *every inhabitant* of each area. Each case found by the psychiatric teams was then reinterviewed by the principal investigators themselves. Altogether they located 214 cases of mental disorder, making a total prevalence rate of 10.8 per thousand. Only 60 percent of these cases had been previously reported in official or hospital records.

Schizophrenia was reported at prevalence rates of 1.8 per thousand in the village, 2.5 in the town, and 2.1 in the city, and tended to cluster in the most densely populated part of each area. There were also slightly higher rates in the upper and lower classes than in the middle class, as these strata were rated by Lin. Manic-depressive psychosis and especially depression turned out to be very rare (0.7 per thousand). Among other notable findings, in view of the intensity of the case-finding methods, was the extremely low percentage of psychoneuroses (0.1).

This research is unique in one other respect: a follow-up study was made fifteen years later in the same three areas, with the same research design and the same basic research team. Identical case-finding methods and diagnostic criteria were used, and since continuing contact with officials and medical people had been maintained over the years, no difficulties were encountered (Lin et al. 1969:67). This time the first stage (information from officials, census records, doctors, teachers, and police) lasted four to six months; the second stage, consisting of searching out the actual cases, took two to three months; and the final stage of household interviews took seven months. Provisional diagnoses were followed up by intensive examinations before final diagnostic decisions were made.

Since the population of the area had

---

[6] The "ridit" is a statistical score that was used as a composit index of the various ratings used in the Midtown Manhattan, Stirling County, and Yoruba studies.

grown in the meantime, the number of people screened in the second survey was 29,184, indicating a 46.4 percent rise. The age structure had changed because of historical factors, education had increased, the occupational structure and other factors had changed. The investigators took account of all these changes in their analysis.

Among the interesting findings was an overall increase in prevalence of total mental disorders, from 10.8 per thousand in 1946-1948 to 17.2 per thousand in 1961-1963.[7] This significant increase was found to be entirely in the psychoneuroses rather than in the psychoses, the rate of which actually declined, from 3.6 per thousand in 1946-1948 to 3.1 per thousand in 1961-1963.

The authors have not, to my knowledge, offered much to explain these and many other interesting findings. They do point out that the results support the notion that psychoses are less affected by environmental changes than neuroses, but carefully note (Lin et al. 1969:90):

It is also possible that the span of 15 years was too short a period for environmental factors to provoke a psychotic process in sufficient numbers of persons within a population to affect the prevalence rating. This finding may also be taken to support the fairly widespread view that some innate genetic or organic factors play a more important role in the etiology of psychotic disorders than in that of neurotic disorders. . . .

These studies are in many ways models of what epidemiological studies can be. It is regrettable that there are so few surveys that are comparable to them. Nevertheless, even the Taiwan study is not immune to criticism. For instance, Mishler and Scotch (1963:337) have remarked that in Lin's initial study the psychiatric variables were better conceived and researched than the sociological ones:

Lin did not make it clear exactly how these class categories were established, mentioning only that a number of factors such as wealth, education, occupation, and appearance of house and furniture were taken into consideration. Even in this careful study, the independent variables used to study the relation of schizophrenia prevalence to social factors reflect the general poverty of the field, consisting only of sex, ecological distribution, and social class.

For my own part, I would also have liked to know what happened to the original cases in the fifteen years between studies. It would be interesting to know precisely what psychoneuroses were found, and to have precise indicators of stress. Also, in view of what we now suspect about the relationship of mental disorder to disease, malnutrition, and other factors, these aspects could be investigated with the resources available to the Taiwan group. In addition it would be useful to employ independent psychiatric raters from different countries, but perhaps that is asking too much at this stage of transcultural research development. We owe thanks to Lin and his group for providing us with one of the most thorough epidemiological studies on record.[8]

DRUG USE

Though little more can be done here than to indicate the importance of drug use, we should not leave the discussion

---

[7] In their 1969 report they state the 1946-1948 figure as 9.4 per thousand (pp. 74-75). It is not clear where they got this figure, as the earlier report gives a rate of 10.8 (Lin 1953:325-27 and *passim*).

[8] For readers interested in epidemiological research, the following instructive studies are additionally recommended: Bremer 1951 (a Norwegian village), Helgason 1964 (Iceland), and Aall-Jilek 1965 (a useful study of epilepsy in a Tanzanian tribe).

of epidemiology without mentioning the problem in various cultural contexts. Brevity is required by the unfortunate lack of systematic epidemiological data[9] on this topic, a deficiency brought about in part by differing cultural attitudes toward drug use. Many societies regard the use of various drugs as normal and valuable, and there is no justification for imposing Western notions of pathology upon them even if by our standards they use drugs to excess.

The subject of drug use, like that of sexual deviation, is probably theoretically closer to problems of deviance and social control than to mental disorder strictly considered, though certainly no sharp line can be drawn between the two. The area where psychiatric concerns seem most pertinent is the subject of "drug abuse," a slippery concept in the cross-cultural context. For example, many groups such as the Tarahumara Indians of Mexico (J. G. Kennedy 1963), encourage frequent drunkenness but have no alcoholism problems. Other groups habitually use cocaine, powerful snuffs, hashish, and so on and still maintain a viable economic and social life (e.g., see Efron et al. 1967). Such facts should be of great interest to research psychiatry but are as yet little studied.

Most cross-cultural data on drug use are given in accounts not dedicated to specific study of the phenomenon and certainly are not epidemiological. A recent attempt by Blum and his associates to cull the available data from

the 247 societies in the Human Relations Area Files disclosed the paucity of information and unevenness of quality of the reports from other societies (Blum et al. 1969:140-41): "Lack of attention by ethnographers, travelers, and other observers of drug behavior is coupled with the already-noted unreliability among them where there has been observer interest. In consequence, there is no drug for which adequate descriptions exist for the majority of societies in our sample."

Of all drugs, alcohol has received by far the most attention in cross-cultural writing. Viewed in its totality, the body of data on alcohol use reveals tremendous differences in patterns of consumption, attitudes toward alcohol, and behavior under its influence.

In a well-known cross-cultural study, Horton (1943) attempted to link high and low frequencies and intensities of alcohol use with levels of anxiety and sanctions against drinking in the society. This study is obviously an interesting beginning at bringing some order out of the chaos, but it is based on the same inadequate data cited by Blum, and in addition has been criticized as oversimple. For instance, it does not take account of the many positive attributes of the euphoric state that alcohol can induce. Also, in attempting to corroborate his thesis, Horton had to construct some unsatisfactorily indirect indices of anxiety level, such as "subsistence insecurity" and "acculturation," which he then correlated with alcohol use. Honigmann (1967:354) notes that Horton does not allow for the simple fact that "recent contact may have introduced alcohol to people who don't appreciate its potency and lack established drinking conventions. Therefore they frequently drink to the point of terrible drunkenness." This is what happened to the Frobisher Bay Eskimo, as well as to the Navajo and other Ameri-

---

[9] A recent article by Blum on the "Social and Epidemiological Aspects of Psychopharmacology" (1968) is largely devoted to research methods and researchable problems; little is offered on *results* of research. Collections and summary writings on drugs, such as those by Efron et al. (1967), Blum et al. (1969), and M. K. Opler (1970), review various aspects of the cross-cultural evidence and should be consulted by the interested student.

can Indians (Honigmann 1967:354, 388).

Peter Field (1962) investigated Horton's hypothesis with more emphasis on social organization. Some variables correlating with *sobriety* over time were patrilocal residence at marriage, approach to a clan-community organization, presence of bride-price, and a village settlement pattern (rather than nomadism).

Blum's conclusion in his case study of Greek drinking (Blum et al. 1969) contains a more inclusive summary of the cross-cultural facts and is epidemiological, at least in implication. His study supports a number of writers who contend that in societies where drinking is an integral part of social custom and religious rites, where the place and manner of consumption are regulated by traditional rules, and where values support self-control, sociability, and ability to hold one's liquor, "alcoholism problems are at a minimum, provided no other variables are overriding." He finds drinking problems and alcoholism to be associated with societies where the introduction of alcohol is recent and has not been integrated into preexisting institutions, where there are no prescribed patterns for behavior "under the influence," where alcohol has been used by a dominant group to aid in exploiting a subject group (as among some American Indian tribes), and where controls and laws regarding drinking are new and conflict with older ones. "In cultures where ambivalant attitudes toward drinking prevail, incidence of alcoholism is also high" (Blum et al. 1969: 226-27).

None of these studies is explicitly epidemiological, though their conclusions often depend on impressionistic assumptions of high or low frequencies and relative intensity of drinking. Good epidemiology would certainly help to resolve many of the questions posed. However, inconclusive as the cross-cultural alcohol studies are, they are far better than those dealing with other drugs—perhaps because these other drugs are less common and often must be used clandestinely.[10]

Cannabis, known in its various derivatives as hashish, hemp, *kif, ganja, charas*, marihuana, and other names, is another widespread drug whose use merits epidemiological study in conjunction with clinical and biochemical analysis. In contrast to such powerful psychoactive hallucinogenic substances as the various mushrooms, the South American snuffs, cocaine, and peyote, cannabis seems to be relatively rarely used among nonliterate peoples. There are some reports from Nigeria (e.g., Asuni 1964, Lambo 1965b), but even there it seems to be a lately diffused item from the Middle East and southern Asia, where of course it has been known since at least 500 B.C. (Blum et al. 1969:62-63).

There have long been reports of cannabis "psychosis" in the Middle East and India, and Warnock reported that about one-sixth of his mental hospital admissions in Cairo were due to this (Blum et al. 1969:73). Benabud (1957) found about 49 percent of the psychiatric admissions in Morocco in 1956 to be due to cannabis, with 27 percent suffering from cannabis psychosis. Sig, also reporting on Morocco, stated that cannabis psychoses accounted for 30 percent of the admissions he studied

---

[10] Though not epidemiological, MacAndrew and Edgerton's recent book (1969) should be consulted by those interested in the cross-cultural study of drinking. By systematically marshaling cross-cultural literature step by step, they impressively challenge the assumptions of conventional wisdom on the effects of alcohol, particularly the notion that it not only impairs sensorimotor function, but disinhibits moral functioning, dissolves the superego, and all the rest.

(Blum et al. 1969:74). Dhunjibhoy (1930:261-63) also reported such psychoses in India. Such findings are quite contrary to recent opinion in this country, based upon clinical observation that cannabis may precipitate psychoses in unstable premorbid personalities but cannot induce it in "normal" individuals (e.g., Allentuck and Bowman 1942, Solomon 1966). One complicating factor in evaluating such reports as well as in doing research is the fact that often other drugs, such as opium derivatives and alcohol, may be mixed or alternated with cannabis, and thus may be implicated in the psychiatric statistics. For example, Dhunjibhoy (1930:263) reported that much of the violent crime, running amok, and similar behavior in India is due to mixing cannabis with datura, a powerful hallucinogen.

Sig also estimated that of eight million inhabitants of Morocco in 1956, one million were users of cannabis, and that 4 percent of the national income was spent on the drug. When the government attempted to destroy the crop and ban the use of cannabis in 1946, an epidemic of cocaine use was threatened and the order was rescinded. In Tunisia and Algeria more effective programs against cannabis resulted in a tremendous compensatory rise in alcohol use, with no improvement in public health (Blum et al. 1969:74).

The use of cannabis has apparently spread most rapidly in recent times in areas where disadvantaged, rootless, migrant, or acculturating populations come together in urban conglomerates, though my personal experience indicates that it is also widespread in poverty-stricken villages in Egypt, and this is probably true elsewhere in the rural Middle East. After a very thorough world survey, H. B. M. Murphy (1963) felt that heavy chronic use with deleterious effects was generally most widespread among males under thirty-five who were poor, unstable, deprived, and without strong relations to others.

An interesting epidemiological-like study that might be profitably replicated elsewhere is Carstairs' (1954) comparison of the uses of *daru*, a powerful alcoholic beverage, and *bhang*, a type of Indian hemp or *Cannabis indica*. In a large village in Rajasthan, India, he found that two top caste groups that differ in their value systems and role requirements exhibit corresponding contrasts in choice of intoxicants. The Rajputs, a caste of warriors and landlords, are violent, chivalrous, and outgoing. They eat meat and drink *daru*, and frequently engage in wild drinking bouts. On the other hand, the high-caste Brahmins, who are the spiritual aristocracy, enhance the depth of their devotional trances and feats of asceticism by drinking cannabis in infusions of *bhang*. Rajputs disdain the inward experience induced by cannabis, while "a Brahmin who gets drunk will be outcasted [and] condemned to associate with the lower castes of society" (Carstairs 1954:234).

What I would like to see in studies of this kind are chemical analyses of the intoxicants, some figures on frequency and intensity of usage (and nonusage), sex, age, and other differentials, and detailed case data on individuals. With that kind of information, better assessment of such intriguing cultural differences would be possible.

Other natural stimulants that should warrant further epidemiological collaboration of anthropologists, psychiatrists, and biochemists are coca, cocaine, and *ayahuasca* of South America, *kava* of the Pacific, betel or areca nut of India and Southeast Asia, and *qat* in East Africa and South Arabia. Of these, cocaine may be the most potent and dangerous. It has been implicated in the exploitation of Indian labor at high altitudes in the Andes, where for centuries it has been used to help the inhabitants adapt to the difficult environment (Blum et al. 1969:103).

Among the most psychoactive of drugs discovered and used by nonwestern peoples are the hallucinogenic mushrooms, particularly the Mexican psilocybe ("magic mushroom") and the fly agaric of Asia and Europe. These powerful trance-inducing plants are apparently used mostly by shamans or old men in many of the groups and in some societies are restricted to sacred occasions. The evidence on extent of use and effects, however, is conflicting. For example, as Blum notes, Kennon attributes the general "degradation" of the Koryak to the "toadstool habit." Such disagreements are due in part to the fact that historically observers of varying degrees of acuteness noticed and described the phenomena at many stages of contact between the aboriginal and European cultures (Blum et al. 1969:121-22). Again, good epidemiological data on the use of these mushrooms would be most welcome.

The use of hallucinogenic peyote by several tribes of American Indians, particularly for religious purposes and healing, has been studied more extensively (e.g., Slotkin 1956, La Barre 1938, Aberle 1966, Lumholtz 1902, Furst 1972). These studies have been concerned with peyote use primarily as a social and cultural phenomenon, though research with biochemical and psychiatric orientations has continued on mescaline, the hallucinogenic chemical of the mescal cactus (see La Barre 1960 for a partial bibliography). Research is still needed on the long-term psychological and social effects of such substances on groups that regularly use them.

As in the case of alcohol, there is great variability in the effects of peyote and mescaline, and these differential re-

sponses appear to be tied to cultural conditioning and attitude. Wallace (1959a) has presented a graphic illustration of these effects by comparing the reactions of white persons to mescaline with Indian reactions to peyote. The whites reacted with mood shifts, breakdown of inhibitions, suspiciousness, depersonalization, idiosyncratic hallucinations, and no therapeutic benefit. The general Indian response to peyote, in contrast, included relative stability of mood, increased reverence, maintenance of orderly behavior, *no* suspiciousness, patterned hallucinations, and marked therapeutic benefit.[11]

I have not tried to review the large field of drug use, but only wish to suggest the relevance of the topic to cultural psychiatry. Much important collaborative research could be carried out on the long-term physiological and psychological effects of various drugs. The natural experiments carried out by thousands, even millions, of people with different cultures, different constitutions, and different attitudes, generation after generation, are impossible to replicate in the laboratory. Studies of peoples that constantly induce "temporary psychoses" by means of various drugs could add a considerable dimension to this branch of psychiatric study. So could studies designed to reveal the relationships, if any, between massive use of various drugs and the types and frequencies of mental disorders in populations using them. Are any of these substances therapeutic under conditions of stressful living? If so, regular

---

[11] Such a comparison should be taken cautiously in view of the fact that pure mescaline is a much more powerful drug than its counterpart in the peyote button, which is mixed with other alkaloids and inert substances. Nevertheless, the contrast generally holds, and is consistent with later findings that cultural attitudes, values, and specific environmental factors such as interpersonal support do strongly condition the beneficent and harmful effects of various drugs.

use might be found to keep incidence rates down. Does such use exacerbate present stress or precipitate psychoses at increased rates? Might the same drugs not act in contrary ways in different segments of a population? These are only a few of the questions still to be answered.

The relationship between drug use, deviance, and psychological disorder could be explored in ways that could help resolve the fruitless debates based upon scattered evidence from Euro-American societies. Information from so-called primitive and ancient societies is often cited in these debates by those who recognize the importance of cross-cultural data for their arguments. Yet the kind of epidemiological and clinical evidence needed to illuminate such questions is just not available. The cross-cultural study of drug use is an area where interdisciplinary cooperation is essential, and where anthropology can provide research relevant to the problems of our time.

CULTURAL FACTORS IN MENTAL DISORDER: THE VIEW FROM WESTERN PSYCHIATRY

Among the principal stimuli for early studies of mental disorders in other cultures was the belief fostered by travelers, missionaries, and some social scientists that primitive peoples are free of the mental disorders that burden modern industrial man (e.g., Faris 1934, Seligman 1929). However, there is agreement among most modern scholars who have looked closely at the subject that though there probably are important variations in frequency and form, the major psychotic patterns known in Western psychiatry are found throughout the world (e.g., P. R. Benedict and Jacks 1954; Honigmann 1953, 1969; Kiev 1969; Mishler and Scotch 1963; Sanua 1969; Wallace 1961*b*).

There is, of course, considerable discomfort with the rigidity and culture-bound nature of existing psychiatric categories, and the need for revised nomenclature has been expressed numerous times (e.g., M. K. Opler 1963, 1967; Yap 1969). The problems in classifying the "ethnic disorders," which I shall discuss later on, are further evidence of the necessity of such revision. Recent reworking of such important classification systems as that found in the American Psychiatric Association manual indicates that until we know much more about etiology and process, all classifications remain provisional.

I can only touch on the problems of a field as vast as this, so I shall discuss the ways in which the two major Western psychotic categories, schizophrenia and depression, have been handled cross-culturally. Some of the neuroses will be mentioned in passing, but I shall steer away from the "character disorders," which are controversial in our own systems and rarely mentioned in the cross-cultural literature.

DEPRESSION

It seems that depression would be a particularly good subject for the testing of theory in the light of cross-cultural variation, yet so far little information has come from this source. Some of the earliest reports established the notion that depression was rare in "primitive societies" as compared with "civilized" ones. Kraepelin (1904), who coined the hybrid term "manic-depressive," noted that in Southeast Asia depressive features were absent in schizophrenics, and "well-marked states of depression lasting for some time, such as fill the observation wards at home, I could not find at all." He then added a comment that has been repeated by many others: "To this corresponds the absence of sin and suicidal tendency." Another medical observer of the Javanese scene, P. M. van Wulfften Palthe, also noted the infrequency of depression among the Javanese as compared with the resident Chinese in Java (both cited in Stainbrook 1954:44). The notion that "simple" people are free of depression was seemingly supported by these and other reports, reinforcing the idea that the stong feelings of guilt and responsibility derived from Christian and Judaic teachings have played vital roles in producing depression in Western and Westernizing societies.

The widespread opinion that "Africans" are generally free of depression was given impetus by a number of influential studies. Carothers (1948) diagnosed only 24 cases (1.6 percent) of depression out of 1,508 African hospital patients in Nairobi, Kenya, during a ten-year span. In the same period he diagnosed 22 percent of 222 hospitalized Europeans as depressives. Gordon (1934, 1936) claimed never to have seen a true manic-depressive among Africans at the same hospital. Laubscher (1937) also reported that severe depressions were extremely rare at his hospital in South Africa, and remarked on the extremely low suicide rate among the Bantu (one per 100,000). In a nonhospital survey in Ghana, Tooth (1950:52-53) diagnosed a relatively high 34 "affective states" out of 173 disturbed individuals, but of these, 28 were either chronically "manic" or "hypomanic," and only one exhibited the extreme mood swings of the manic-depressive. Smartt's (1956) report from Tanganyika is similar; 51 of 252 admissions (about 20 percent of these cases) were "predominantly affective." Again, however, manics outnumbered depressives more than two to one.

Reports of low frequencies of depression have apparently had a much greater influence than they deserve,

since a number of other writers present contrary data. For example, Forster (1958), also working in Ghana, categorized 36.4 percent of 1,286 hospital patients as manic-depressive. H. Aubin reported that depressive states were the commonest medical disorder suffered by West African soldiers, and H. Collomb and J. Zwingelstein found that in Senegal 16.3 percent of 1,600 patients were depressive (all cited in Collis 1966:27).

One nonhospital study reporting high rates of depression in Africa is M. J. Field's (1960) study of visitors to healing shrines in Ghana. She observes that "depression is the commonest mental illness of Akan rural women," and that it is quite frequent among men. Her findings have caused some consternation because she presents detailed clinical evidence that depression is common, and, unlike most investigators of African societies, describes depressions characterized by self-accusation, feelings of unworthiness, guilt, remorse, and regret (like the Western model). Field points out that depressed people are not regarded as mentally ill among the Akan, and states (1960:149):

The depressive personality is, in sickness and health, self-effacing and is seldom a disturbing nuisance. She is therefore the last type of patient who would ever find her way to any kind of European hospital unless she had some concurrent conspicuous physical trouble such as a retained placenta or pneumonia. It is not surprising, therefore, that psychiatrists and other doctors who see patients only in hospitals and clinics should have the idea that depression in Africa hardly exists.

Other evidence that there may be more depression in Africa than has been thought comes from the survey of A. Leighton et al. (1963) among the Yoruba of Nigeria, where clear depressive symptoms were detected in 46 percent of the hospital cases, 19 percent of the urban respondents, and 23 percent of the village respondents.[12] Despite the methodological limitations of the study, such high rates are notable. The Cornell-Aro researchers discovered that depression was not categorized or recognized as a problem by the Yoruba, yet the people were familiar with individual depressive symptoms such as continuous crying, extreme worry, loss of appetite, loss of interest in life, and so on (A. Leighton et al. 1963:112). Savage and Prince (1963), on the other hand, found little depression among hospitalized Yoruba. They felt that the discrepant opinions concerning African depression might be accounted for by "an excessively narrow definition," along with "a tendency to generalize from the lunatic asylum populations and neglect the patients who remain at home or who receive treatment in the centers of the indigenous healers" (1963:83-84).

Even Lambo, a Yoruban psychiatrist working among his own tribe, seems to be unsure about the question of depression in the group. He states, for example (1956:1390-91), that there is a "real absence of reactive depression, which may be accounted for by faith in magical defenses." Yet he reports that he has treated almost classical depressive psychoses of both endogenous and organic types (among "Westernized" Yoruba), and that the absence of depression (or classical psychotic depression) in Africa as a whole "seems to be more apparent than real." Yet he also says, "Whether depressions are rare, nobody knows. The only fact known is that they are rarely seen by doctors and the native therapists." However, like many other workers in Africa, he noted

a lack of ideas of guilt, self-reproach, and unworthiness in his depressed patients.

Prince (1968b) has recently tried to bring some order out of the somewhat confused findings on depression. Surveying twenty-one reports of seventeen observers, he was able to note a shift in the frequencies with which depressions were reported in the colonial period (prior to independence of most African states) and the "era of independence" (after 1957). Observers before 1957, with the exception of M. J. Field, reported depression as rare, with little or no self-castigation. In the period since independence, observers tend to report that it is common.

Prince ventures four reasons for these differences (1968b:186-90): (1) "The prestige factor" caused an ethnocentric attitude among doctors. "In the Colonial era depressions should not be seen and named because Africans were not responsible [on the theory that depression is related to strong superego and consequent guilt]; in the era of Independence depressions should be seen because Africans are responsible and aware." (2) Colonial doctors did not recognize depression in many cases that would now be called "masked depression." (3) Depressed patients were not regarded as "sick" in African societies, and therefore they did not find their way to the custodial type of hospital typical of the colonial era; but "more recently observations have been made in open hospital settings, out-patient clinics, sample surveys and indigenous treatment centers," and depressions are thus seen much more often. (4) The actual incidence of depression may have been increased by Westernization, literacy, and so on.

The arguments advanced by Prince seem plausible, but much more research is needed to establish them as more than hypotheses, and to assess their rel-

---

[12] These figures refer to the individuals rated as having a high probability of being psychiatric cases (Leighton et al. 1963:140).

ative importance. In his first three reasons he implies that Africans probably always suffered as much depression as any other group, but his last reason allows that there may actually have been less depression among Africans in the past than at present. Of course, there may have been less, and also depressions that existed could have gone undetected. Prince has clarified the issues, but they are still unresolved.

Much of the evidence buttressing the notion of the rarity of affective disorders among primitives comes from Africa, but there are scattered data from other areas as well. For example, Kardiner (1945:246-47) comments on the infrequency of suicide and depression among the Alorese, which he attributes to their mother-child relationships. He feels that their lack of strong maternal attachment and mother idealization prevents the development of strong superegos and thus the consequent self-punitive guilt reactions of depression. This idea of the lack of a strong superego among primitives (or sometimes of any superego at all) is still widespread among psychoanalytic thinkers.

American blacks from the South have long been known for low rates of depression in comparison with both whites and northern blacks (e.g., Lemkau, Tietze, and Cooper 1942; Prange and Vitols 1962). Lin and his associates found low rates of psychotic depression among both the Chinese in Taiwan (0.7 percent; Lin 1953) and the Taiwan aborigines (0.9 percent; Rin and Lin 1962: 138). Nonpsychotic depressions were not counted there. Sorensen and Stromgren (1961:65) reported 3.9 percent depression of both psychotic and neurotic types in a Danish town, while Helgason (1964:88) reported 8.2 percent in a sample population from Iceland.

While most rates given for depressive illness tend to be low, there are a few reports of high rates. In the Midtown Manhattan study, 24 percent of the population "showed some notable symptomatology of depressive states," and three times as many of them were in the lower class as in the upper class (M. K. Opler and Small 1968:263-64). This difference contrasts with Stainbrook's (1952, 1954) observations in Bahia, Brazil, where little depression was seen in a lower-class state hospital, whereas in a private hospital for middle- and upper-class patients, depression with guilt and self-punitive behavior "were not infrequent" (1954:45).

Findings of high rates that aroused particular interest were contained in studies of the Hutterite Anabaptist religious sect of the north-central United States and Canada, a group that had long been reported to be amazingly free of mental disorder in general. A careful search for cases, of course, proved the tale to be untrue, but a surprising finding was the exceptionally high rate of manic-depressive psychosis diagnosed within the sect. Among ten populations surveyed in the United States, Europe, and Taiwan, the Hutterites ranked third in total frequency of "lifetime expectancy" of psychosis (Eaton and Weil (1955:75), and they were highest in manic-depressive psychoses.[13] The researchers also found that there were four times as many persons with depressive reactions as there were schizophrenics among the Hutterites, and these rates were three times as great as comparable Swedish and Formosan figures (Eaton and Weil 1955:84-85). This high rate was attributed to religious values and child-rearing practices that foster intense repression of impulses with consequent heavy guilt, coupled with acceptance of depressive symptoms in the nonstigmatizing cultural belief pattern of *Anfechtung* (temptation of the

---

[13] Because of differing methods and definitions, the comparability of these ten studies is questionable.

devil). In this idea system, what we view as depressive behavior is interpreted as a trial by God (Eaton and Weil 1955: 103; Kaplan and Plaut 1956).

Consistent with the evidence for cultural variations in depressive reactions is the evidence that over the past decades a decline in manic-depressive psychosis has been observed in the United States. During the decade 1940-1950 alone, hospital admissions for this disorder dropped from 7.6 per 100,000 to 4.7 per 100,000—a decrease of 38 percent (Kramer, Pollack, and Redick 1961:69-70). Similar but even more drastic decreases have been noticed in certain states and hospitals. It is still not known whether such decreases in admission rates reflect real changes in incidence or simply changes in diagnostic styles, but the latter is suspected (Hoch and Racklin 1941).

While it is probable that much of the reported variability of depression is due to various methodological artifacts, the evidence still suggests that there probably exist some real differences in the frequencies of depressive states. One idea proposed to account for differences is the "social cohesion" hypothesis. An illustration of this hypothesis is Eaton and Weil's (1955:85-89) proposal that the high prevalence of depression among the Hutterites is due to the tight cohesion of the sect—an interpretation that fits well with the relatively low rates of schizophrenia and character disorders, both of which are frequently associated with disintegrated social conditions. Related to high cohesion of the group is the Hutterites' emphasis on religion, on duty to God and society, and on self-control, conformity, and responsibility. All of these factors might make for the intense guilt feelings and the self-punitive turning inward of anger that are characteristic of depression.

The cohesion hypothesis was elaborated by Yehudi Cohen (1961:483-84), who proposed that the more cohesive the group, the more the member will tend to identify with it. He will then be unable to act out, either consciously or unconsciously, his aggressive and sexual feelings toward other group members, and will thus tend to feel worthless, guilty, and self-critical in comparison with group standards. Norman Chance (1964:20) reformulated the hypothesis this way: "depression will be found with more than average frequency (a) in societies characterized by highly traditionalized and tightly knit social groupings, (b) in the higher socio-economic strata, (c) among professional and executive groups exhibiting strong group affiliations and feelings of reciprocal dependency."

Unfortunately, Chance could test this hypothesis only with questionnaire data from psychiatrists who worked in various countries, each of whom reported the symptom frequencies of patients he saw. Chance subjectively cross-classified the cultural groups as to high and low cohesion and reported incidence of depression, and his findings gave the cohesion hypothesis tentative support.

Yap (1965a:102) objected that this evidence is unsatisfactory, and pointed out that the cohesion hypothesis is "a diametrically opposite view from that of ethnologists who associate tradition-oriented societies with shame sanctions and absence of intrapunitive sanctions, and therefore with less guilt and presumably less depression." Yap also noted that the social cohesion theory runs counter to Durkheimian suicide theory, which posits strong social integration and social restraints as conditions *nonconducive* to suicide.

Stainbrook (1954:47) seems to have arrived earlier and independently at a contrary hypothesis for some of the same types of society used by Chance:

... societies with an extended family structure tend to have lower incidence of depressive reactions than do societies with the more restricted conjugal family. .... The experience of infancy and childhood in the extended preliterate family would appear, in general, to be characterized by less intense frustration in relation to objects. This may be due both to characteristics of basic mothering and the much greater opportunities to seek rewards and avoid punishments in a multi-mothering group. Similarly, object loss should be less threatening to security and less evoking of guilt because of the generalization of object-interest to several family members. Moreover, in later life, an enduring multiple external source of esteeming and affirming family members is maintained.

Though they are suggestive, it appears that neither the social cohesion hypothesis nor Stainbrook's formulation contains variables refined enough to account for group differences in depressive reactions. Social structural variables are perhaps too remote and simple to be predictive of such behaviors, since intervening variables might produce different types of emotional response patterning within the same social structural type, and vice versa. Religious and ethical values suggest themselves as forces of this type. It may be that Judeo-Christian beliefs *are* positively correlated with incidence of depression. This possibility is consistent with P. R. Benedict and Jacks' notion (1954) that the high frequencies of confusion disorders and low frequencies of depression among primitives may be due to their emphasis of shaming sanctions and external social control. Modern Western societies, in contrast, emphasize guilt sanctions, which cause aggression to be turned inward, with resulting higher frequencies of depression.[14]

These notions, though somewhat

crude, generally fit such facts as Funkelstein and Hitson's (1959) findings that depressed Boston patients tended to be people who had been taught to be responsible for their own actions and to anticipate the needs of others, in contrast to paranoid patients, who had learned to accept authority passively. Such theories have never been put to any real test, probably because such independent variables as shame and guilt sanctions are too inexact, and thus do not clearly differentiate groups. Yap (1965a:100) even argues with some cogency that the distinction between shame and guilt sanctions is "intellectually arbitrary and without empirical justification."

Another interesting untested suggestion of Stainbrook's is that the cultural provision or lack of provision of esteem-sustaining roles, along with the social generation of stresses at various stages of the life cycle, could have a bearing on frequency of depression. As he points out (1954:47): "Our own society fails lamentably in status provisions for the adolescent, the postmenopausal woman and the aged of both sexes." Savage and Prince (1963) similarly document the particular stresses upon other social categories in Nigeria —barren women, menopausal women, and students, all of whom apparently are particularly susceptible to depression. In addition, Yoruba students fall prey to a related condition that they call "brain fag" (Prince 1960b).

Freudian theory relating mourning to melancholia has inspired the suggestion that the elaborate mourning ceremonies of some societies might provide the action patterns for a working through or allaying of guilt for hostile feelings toward the deceased, thus preventing many depressions that would otherwise occur (Stainbrook 1954:48; Yap 1965a:99). This same basic idea has been suggested to account for the rela-

---

[14] Five years later Leighton and Hughes (1959:350) restated the same hypothesis more clearly.

tive lack of obsessive-compulsive disorders reported for primitive societies, but I know of no study that has put these ideas to the test.

A problem with most theories of the causes of depression is that they are oversimple; their formulators enthusiastically hope that they have found the one factor that indexes or determines all the others. It seems more probable that a multiplicity of variables may interact in various combinations to produce total sets of conditions that lead to high or low frequencies of depressive reactions. Variables that suggest themselves include dietary deficiences, disease, mortality rates, cultural insulation from death and from belief in an afterlife and other religious formulations, existence and saliency of expiatory ritual forms, level of economic development, basic personality variables, structural variables such as family type, degree of security afforded by group affiliations, and life-cycle stresses such as adolescence and menopause.

SCHIZOPHRENIA

Many workers in nonwestern cultures have not hesitated to use the Western category of schizophrenia, the term for the most common psychotic disorder diagnosed in European and American societies. The Transcultural Psychiatry group at McGill University (H. B. M. Murphy et al. 1963) sent questionnaires to psychiatrists in many parts of the world, seeking information about frequencies and characteristics of mental disorders in their countries, and schizophrenia was everywhere reported as "frequent." Four of the twenty-six diagnostic symptoms on the questionnaire were *never* reported as infrequently seen: (1) social and emotional withdrawal, (2) auditory hallucinations, (3) delusions in general, and (4) flatness of affect. Since this study relied only on doctors' reports, it tells us nothing about the regional epidemiology of schizophrenia, but it is useful in indicating the probable universality of the malady at the most general level. Many of the remaining twenty-two symptoms in the survey seemed to vary among cultural or social groups; depersonalization was reported more commonly in urban populations, for example, while delusions of grandeur appeared more commonly in rural populations. (See also Wittkower et al. 1960, Murphy 1968.)

The current opinion of many psychiatrists is that about 1 percent of the population everywhere in the world will suffer from schizophrenia at some time in their lives (e.g., Mishler and Scotch 1963:318). However, the evidence upon which this assumption is founded is slim indeed, since it comes principally from hospital studies in urbanized nations such as England (Norris 1959) and the United States. If this constancy were an established fact it would have considerable implications for theories of etiology, since present psychogenic and sociogenic hypotheses relying on notions of environmental stress would probably be ruled out. Also difficult to sustain would be many genetic hypotheses, owing to the great differences in human gene pools. However, such a conclusion at this time is unwarranted. Questions of variations in frequency, in quality of symptomatology, and in reversibility of the affliction still remain unanswered. As we have seen, the difficulties of identifying cases of any mental disorder in other cultures are very great, and even in Western societies schizophrenia poses particularly knotty diagnostic problems.

A disease that is defined with reference to varying degrees of impairment in any one of several major and different psychological functions—impairment which must be shown to be not attributable primarily to organic causes—is certain to create difficulties for diagnosis, theory and research. One would expect the reliability of the diagnoses to be relatively poor [Mishler and Scotch 1963:321].

Other major diagnostic difficulties are the frequently insidious onset of the disorder and the fact that psychotic episodes may occur only intermittently between long periods of normal activity. In cross-cultural studies the doctor often does not have full fluency in the native language, rendering the diagnostic process suspect in cases where sensitivity to slight nuances of meaning is essential to detection. Added to these problems are the abilities of some organic diseases to produce schizophrenic-like symptoms, and the fact that diagnosing physicians come from many differing psychiatric traditions. Thus it is not difficult to see why there are few reliable or comparable data on schizophrenia, or indeed on any mental disorder, in developing countries.

Nevertheless, there are a number of suggestive findings, particularly from Africa, which indicate directions for future research. Most of the major opinions about African mental disorder were promulgated by three colonial psychiatrists working in hospitals for a number of years in Kenya (Carothers 1948, 1953), South Africa (Laubscher 1937), and the Gold Coast (Tooth 1950).

Laubscher's study was conducted in a hospital serving a number of Bantu-speaking tribes near Queensland, South Africa, and in a ten-year period he examined 1,089 seriously disordered patients. Here again is a study that is of no use for epidemiological purposes, since we have no idea how many variables have influenced admission rates, but among 554 patients from eight of the tribes he diagnosed 325 schizophrenics (194 males, 131 females). The rest of the group were manic-depressives (10 males, 12 females), epileptics (73 males, 19 females), idiots and imbeciles (47 males, 9 females), and other psychoses (35 males, 24 females). Laubscher (1937) generalized: "The triad of schizophrenia, epilepsy and feeblemindedness always predominate. The schizophrenics all conform to the classical paranoid, catatonic and hebephrenic types . . . the picture of mental confusion stands out clearly above any other syndrome." He also noted that hallucinations involve native spirits or God among the Christians, and that ideas of "influence" (forces operating from a distance), which are common among Western schizophrenics, were completely absent. Delusions of persecution were extremely frequent, as were delusions of grandeur (Laubscher 1937:282-87). These features suggest that the frequency of paranoid schizophrenia was rather high, though P. R. Benedict and Jacks (1954) felt that Laubscher's patients "are of a type approximating more clearly the hebephrenic than any other category."

Carothers (1953) presented data on 558 natives of Kenya admitted to Mathari Mental Hospital. During a five-year period he diagnosed 28.6 percent as schizophrenic, dividing them into the four common classes: simple (23 cases), hebephrenic (87 cases), catatonic (32 cases), paranoid (11 cases—6.3 percent). He also found another 11 cases of pure "paranoia" that he felt were not schizophrenic, and observed that paranoid features appeared in only 14 percent of his uneducated patients, while they appeared in 15 of 30 in the educated group. This finding supported his conclusion that paranoid dynamics in schizophrenia are associated with Westernization.

The third of these influential studies, by Geoffrey Tooth (1950), recorded two years of surveys and investigations of mental illness on the Gold Coast. I have already pointed out some of the methodological problems of this study. However, Tooth's study has been influential for other than epidemiological reasons. He calls attention to the near identity of the symptoms of some phases of sleeping sickness (trypanosomiasis) and schizophrenia, and supports some of the African hospital findings by a nonhospital study. Tooth reports that of his 173 studied cases of mental pathology, 20.8 percent (36) exhibited delusional states, 19.1 percent (33) schizophrenia, 19.7 percent (34) neurosis, and 4.6 percent (7) unclassified psychotic states. It is difficult to say what these categories mean except that they illustrate the difficulties of diagnosis in environments characterized by endemic diseases and cultural contexts vastly alien to the investigator.

Benedict and Jacks (1954:332) unhesitatingly state that in these three studies (Laubscher 1937, Carothers 1953, and Tooth 1950), "schizophrenia was the most frequent diagnosis for all of the populations studied, whether hospitalized or not." Though there is no justification for rediagnosing another investigator's cases from a distance, as Benedict and Jacks do, the patients exhibiting "delusional states" as well as the "psychopaths" and unclassified psychotics reported by Tooth do seem suspiciously like schizophrenics.[15] Consistent with other African findings, of the 33 patients Tooth did diagnose as schizophrenic, only 6 were classified as paranoid (1950:51). His 34 "affective states," which were predominantly "manic," may also include some schizophrenics.

Perhaps the most interesting part of Tooth's report, however, is the discussion and description of trypanosomiasis, or sleeping sickness. He reports that this terrible disease of the bloodstream produces schizophrenic-like symptoms, particularly in its late phases, in about 8 percent of the cases treated in Gold Coast medical centers. In a specific comparison of the two disorders he states that syndromes representative of simple dementia and of paranoid and catatonic schizophrenia may be seen in trypanosomiasis. Delusions, hallucinations, "mixed thoughts, mutism, greasy skin, etc. all occur in various combinations" (Tooth 1950: 6-14).

Linton (1956:70-75) feels that such close similarities support theories of an organic etiology for schizophrenia, and Wallace (1960:712) is of the opinion that since apparently the only diagnostic feature differentiating trypanosomiasis from schizophrenia is the trypanosome microorganism in blood samples, it can reasonably be postulated that "the trypanosomiasis psychosis is a *variety of schizophrenia whose organic etiology is known.*" Whatever the justice of this inference, Tooth's study does alert us once again to the importance of organic factors and the necessity for caution in appraising cross-cultural diagnoses where neurological and other clinical tests have not been possible.

Lambo (1955; 1956:1390; 1965a: 62), who has taken pains to refute Carothers' ethnocentric statements about the "African mind" and so on, has also challenged the notion that paranoid schizophrenia is rare among Africans. However, even he has recognized differences between the paranoid qualities of his Nigerian patients and those of European paranoid schizophrenics, and notes that in Nigeria such

---

[15] "The clinical characteristics of this group were: the presence of more or less systematized delusions combined with hallucinosis but, on the whole, a paucity of content and shallowness of affect; the lack of psychogenic precipitating factors and of gross dilapidation of habits" (Tooth 1950:46).

symptoms are found almost exclusively among acculturated and detribalized people (1965a:63). Lambo's description of the process among the nonliterate Yoruba (1965a:69) approximates those of Carothers, Laubscher, and Tooth: "Thus, the schizophrenic psychosis in the non-literature Yoruba is ill-defined, punctuated with multiple pathoplastic features and, on the whole, the picture of mental confusion is the most prominent feature. Hence its form, especially in the early phase, is essentially amorphous." Other familiar African features listed by Lambo are the frequency of aggressive frenzy (1965a: 72), the general difficulties of differentiating these cases from "borderline states" (1965a:73), the generally shorter duration of psychotic episodes among rural Yoruba in comparison with urban Yoruba, and the lesser prevalence of chronicity in rural areas (1960:1696; 1965a:82).

Smartt (1956:450) was aware of Lambo's remarks on differences between Yoruba literates and nonliterates, yet he found *no* differences between these categories in Tanganyika, and no cases at all resembling European paranoid schizophrenia. He stated that schizophrenia was the most common serious disorder, and diagnosed all his cases as hebephrenic or catatonic. Parallel results are reported by Collomb (1964:130), Fortes and Mayer 1965: 40), and Tewfik (1958:66-67), among others.

Infrequency of paranoid or other systematized symptoms, in conjunction with frequent diagnoses of catatonic and hebephrenic states, excited confusions, comparative shortness of psychotic episodes, and higher remission rates, is not confined to Africa. In their survey of doctors in various parts of the world, H. B. M. Murphy et al. (1963) found that large percentages of simple and catatonic varieties were reported in Asian countries, and, like Lambo in Africa, they note that the percentages of paranoid types tend to be more frequently reported in the cities and in the middle classes. Rin and Lin (1962:143) found less schizophrenia among Formosan aborigines than among the more educated and urbanized Chinese of the same island. They also report (1962: 145): "A large number of cases had an acute onset, the duration of the episode tended to be short, relapse was not frequent, except in the case of the manic-depressive psychosis, and a very small number of cases became seriously deteriorated."

Schmidt (1964) reports that most of the schizophrenics admitted to the hospital in Sarawak are of the hebephrenic or simple types, and that paranoid symptoms are rare. Pfeiffer (1963) and Kline (1963) both found the hebephrenic types the most frequent in Indonesia, and Kline reports higher frequencies of paranoid schizophrenia among city dwellers than among Bedouins in Kuwait. Although Munoz et al. (1966: 1206) used a somewhat different system of classification in comparing hospital records of Mapuche Indians and urban dwellers in Chile, the results of their interesting study seem to be comparable.

Al-Issa, comparing literate and illiterate patients in Iraq, presents some contrary evidence (1968:149): "It is interesting to note that contrary to prediction from cross-cultural studies, paranoid delusions were not significantly related to literacy."

Related to these findings, but at a perhaps less fundamental level, are the reported "pathoplastic" effects of culture on the forms of symptoms. Most common are reports of passivity or withdrawn behavior in psychotics of some areas, as opposed to loud, aggressive, and abusive qualities in psychotics of other regions. Falling toward the quiet, nonaggressive end of the continuum appear to be patients from India (Wittkower and Rin 1965), the Hutterites (Eaton and Weil 1955), and the Irish (M. K. Opler 1959b). Toward the noisy, aggressive side would probably come the Africans, Americans, and Japanese (e.g., Schooler and Caudill 1964). It would be useful to be able to compare cultural groups empirically on these and more precise dimensions, and to relate these variables to treatment outcome, etc. A model of a study that might be expanded into a more comprehensive effort is M. K. Opler's comparison of Irish-American and Italian-American schizophrenics in a New York hospital (1967:282-303).

Such differences as we have been discussing illustrate cultural shaping of disorder, but they support those writers who have suggested that the label "schizophrenia" probably does not denote a single disease process. According to Al-Issa (1968:148):

It appears from different surveys of symptoms of schizophrenia that it is hebephrenic or catatonic rather than the paranoid type which is found by investigators in non-Western cultures. However, it should be noted that the reliability of all these observations must be in doubt because of the doubtful reliability of the psychiatric classification system even when used in the West. The description of the African "schizophrenic," for instance, makes one wonder whether it is true schizophrenia at all.

One recent distinction seems to conform with Western-nonwestern differences: the subclassification of schizophrenia into "process" and "reactive" types. As Chapman and Baxter put it (1963:352):

Briefly, a process (or "typical") schizophrenic is said to be characterized by a poor premorbid adjustment reflecting inadequate interest in other people and the activities of life. The disorder gradually worsens, frequently becoming identifiable in late adolescence. Symptoms usually include affective flattening; the prognosis is poor, and the disorder typically follows the deteriorating course described by Kraepelin for *dementia praecox*. The reactive (or "typical") schizophrenic, on the other hand, is characterized by a fairly normal prepsychotic adjustment with relatively adequate social, sexual, and occupational participation prior to the onset of the disorder. The psychotic symptoms appear suddenly, usually later in life and in response to severe stress. Symptoms include a clouded sensorium and marked affective display, sometimes with considerable overt aggression. The prognosis is good.

If this distinction is meaningful, it would appear that many of the schizophrenics reported from nonwestern countries belong in the "reactive" category, and if differential distribution of these two types could be established, we might be able to learn a great deal more about the interaction of heredity, biochemistry, and stress in producing various pathological outcomes.

SHAMANS

A suggestive feature of the "reactive" schizophrenic syndrome is the good prognosis, and Silverman (1967) has used new findings to throw light on the old anthropological controversy over the primitive shaman: is he a psychotic, a recovered psychotic, or a gifted "normal" individual who can control a self-induced trance (Ackerknecht 1943; Devereux 1956, 1961b; Boyer 1962, 1964a; Boyer et al. 1964; M. K. Opler 1959a, 1961; Honigmann 1967)?

There seems no reason why all shamans should have similar personalities in all societies (or even within the same society) simply because they perform similar roles. Shamans are traditionally distinguished from priests by their demonstrations of direct contact with spirits through "possession" in trance or dreams. It seems clear that their dissociated states can be achieved by autohypnosis, drugs, fasting, sleep deprivation, severe pain, and other strategies. There is evidence that both hysteric dissociation and schizophrenic hallucination are also often interpreted as spirit contact. Thus, both sides of the debate are undoubtedly right in specific cases, and there is no reason to conclude that shamans as a group possess similar personality structures, or that they are *either* "deranged" or "normal."

It is an interesting fact, however, that in a large number of societies shamans and other types of folk healers and religious leaders are described as being at the unstable end of the personality spectrum. Several of the practitioners of Zar ceremonies in Egyptian Nubia (J. G. Kennedy 1967) recounted episodes in their earlier years which were undoubtedly psychotic breaks. A psychotic history seems characteristic of many of the California Indian curers (Kroeber 1940), Siberian shamans (Czaplicka 1914:172), and New Guinea cargo-cult prophets (Burton-Bradley 1970), as well as practitioners in many other groups (Devereux 1956).

Wallace, a keen student of the cross-cultural evidence, has overgeneralized the situation, yet his remark has cogency in many cases (1966:145): "The potential shaman is often a sick human being, suffering from serious mental and physical disorders which spring from and involve a profound identity conflict." He feels that the ritual of becoming a shaman often resolves such identity conflicts and theorizes that community support saves the troubled individual from lapsing into a "wildly disturbed schizophrenic state" (1966: 151). Wallace proposes the interesting hypothesis that the hallucinatory "possession" behavior of the shaman is often a kind of salvation ritual for a premorbid personality type under stress, a process enabling him to achieve a personality with more than one stable identity (1966:144-45).

Many writers who have described shamans as mentally disturbed have more cautiously proposed that they suffer from hysterical neuroses rather than psychoses. One reason for this diagnosis is that a shaman is usually able to control his dissociated behavior, can play a useful social role, and is distinguished by the people from "insane" persons in the group. For example, Nadel (1965), trained both as a psychologist and as an anthropologist, found no epileptics or "lunatics" among the shamans of the Nuba tribes. He distinguished real fits and trances from simulated attacks, and stated (1965:477) that "the majority of the shamanistic performances are genuine cases of hysterical dissociation."

As we would suspect, the few objective data on nonwestern healers and shamans do not support any single diagnosis. John Gillin (1948:396) administered Rorschach tests to six curers of this type in Guatemala and concluded that in a clinical sense all were "schizoid," revealing a predominance of "primitive drives" and poor comprehension of common everyday problems. One even showed schizophrenic characteristics, but in general, they surpassed others of the community in intelligence and lack of tension and rigidity. Lantis found that one of the two Eskimo shamans whom she Rorschach-tested showed signs of personality disorder (1960).

Boyer (1961, 1962, 1964*a*, 1964*b*) has presented Rorschach and psychiatric interview data showing that thirteen Apache shamans suffered from hysterical personality disorders with attributes of the "imposter" and dominant fixations in the oral and phallic phases. On this basis he argues against the notions of Ackerknecht (1943) and Devereux (1956) that shamans in general are remissed schizophrenics. However, Boyer has never claimed that all Apache shamans are "abnormal," and he has explicitly stated (1964a:254) that some of them "may be innately creative individuals who have more capacity than their cultural mates to use regression in the service of the ego."

Sasaki (1969:237) psychiatrically examined fifty-six shamans from two areas of Japan, all of whom worked in states of "possession," and concluded that eighteen were suffering from psychiatric disorder while thirty-eight were not. Of those so affected, eight were diagnosed as schizophrenic or otherwise psychotic, while ten had "personality deviations"; some of these ten had histories of psychotic episodes.

In an interesting recent study, Fabrega and Silver (1970) used a Holtzman inkblot technique to test twenty h'ilo letik (shamans) in comparison with a control group of twenty-three males of other occupations in Zinacantan, in southern Mexico. The results were somewhat equivocal. On many variables of personality and social role performance the shamans were indistinguishable from the others, but "there is some evidence to suggest that psychologically, h'ilo letik when compared to non-h'ilo letik show greater evidence of anxiety, hostility, and deviant verbalization or pathological thinking" (1970):483). In their discussion of these differences, however, the authors cautiously conclude that some of the differences may be due to aspects of the shamans' role in Zinacantan or to the testing situation (1970:484-85).

These scattered findings certainly do not prove Devereux's extreme view that "the shaman is mentally deranged"

(1956:28-29), since many other data are available on shamans with stable, strong personalities and no evidence of disordered episodes or deviance (e.g., Handelman 1967, 1968; M. K. Opler 1959a). The impression that comes through from some shamans' accounts, such as that of Don Juan, described by Castañeda (1968), is of great strength of character. I agree with Honigmann, who points out (1967:341): "To resolve the problem calls for nothing less than good, clinical data secured from shamans themselves." However, one of the most interesting conclusions arising from the cross-cultural data is the considerable evidence to support Eliade's statement (1964:27) that "the primitive magician, the medicine man, or the shaman is not only a sick man; he is, above all, a sick man who has been cured, who has succeeded in curing himself."

The descriptions of shamanistic behavior and the frequency and consistency of reports of the intense confusional and temporary types of psychoses in nonwestern societies tie in with some recent research on reactive and process schizophrenia. Silverman (1968, 1970) cites data that suggest that paranoid schizophrenia is an *incomplete* process of resolution of the reactive psychotic process, and proposes that nonparanoid or acute schizophrenia may be a problem-solving process, which, if allowed to run its course under benign and supportive conditions, may result in a reintegrated, socially functioning personality. He even suggests that the new phenothiazine drugs may be detrimental in such cases, because they interfere with the natural reconstitutive process. In many societies the shamans' experience fits the description of the holistic problem-solving process of reactive schizophrenia. Citing various evidence on shamans, Silverman outlines five stages of this schizophrenic process by which the supportive environment and prestige accorded the shaman may aid in the successful resolution of his profound personality upheavals.

CULTURAL FACTORS IN MENTAL DISORDER: THE QUESTION OF CULTURE-SPECIFIC SYNDROMES

The nineteenth century, the period when psychiatry was developing into a respectable subspecialty of medicine, was also the period when colonialism was at its peak. Doctors, missionaries, and travelers in many parts of the world brought back reports of the "strange customs" of "natives" with "primitive minds." It was a period of avid scientific collecting and classifying of newly discovered animal, plant, and mineral forms, and like other scientists, doctors enthusiastically searched for exotic diseases to which they could attach their names with appropriate Greek suffixes.

These early observers noticed curious kinds of bizarre behavior that seemed different from those familiar in their homelands, and a number of exotic terms began to appear in the medical journals of Europe and America. Some of these have remained in the literature, while new ones continue to be added from time to time. Among the best known of these exotic syndromes are *koro*, an obsessive fear among Chinese males that the penis will withdraw into the abdomen (Yap 1965*b*); *imu*, a Japanese fright reaction to snakes (Kumasaka 1964, Winiarz and Willawski 1936); *amok*, a frenzied killing spree in Southeast Asia; *latah*, an uncontrolled imitative reaction to being startled (Yap 1952); *windigo* (or *witiko*), a cannibalistic obsession of northeastern American Indians (Parker 1960); *pibloktoq* or "arctic hysteria" among the Eskimo (Wallace 1961*a*); "wild man"

behavior, a frenzied, antisocial attack in New Guinea (Newman 1964); *susto*, a kind of depressive-anxiety attack common in Latin America (Rubel 1964, Sal y Rosas 1958); "frenzied anxiety" among East Africans (Carothers 1947); "malignant anxiety" among West Africans (Lambo 1962); the "jumping disease" among French-speaking inhabitants of Maine (Stevens 1965); the *"Puerto Rican syndrome"* (Mehlman 1961, Fernández-Marina 1961), and on through a long list.

Most modern scholars tend toward the opinion that these exotic maladies are not clinically distinct syndromes, but are simply the old familiar psychiatric syndromes of the West called by different names and shaped by different cultures (e.g., Brill 1913, Honigmann 1969, Kiev 1969, M. K. Opler 1956, Wallace 1961*b*, Yap 1951, 1969). However, the problems posed by the anomalous aspects of these disorders do not appear to be completely resolved, and a continued study of them may be of considerable benefit to both psychiatry and anthropology. To illustrate common issues, I am selecting two of these syndromes for extensive discussion, and present limited descriptions of several others.

PIBLOKTOQ

So much has been written about "arctic hysteria," or *pibloktoq* (*piblokto*), that it almost appears gratuitous to discuss it once again. Yet reconsideration may be useful because the great volume of commentary has not yet decided the questions involved, and because the subject illustrates some general features of the problem of "culture-specific" disorders. Is "arctic hysteria" identical with *latah*, as is often alleged? Is it hysteria, or some type of schizophrenia? Why is it so common in the arctic regions (if it actually is)?

What relationship does it bear to culture? This Eskimo example portrays the common features of "arctic hysteria" (Whitney 1911:83-84):

At half-past one that night, I was awakened from a sound sleep by a woman shouting at the top of her voice—shrill and startling, like one gone mad. I knew at once what it meant—someone had gone *piblokto*. I tumbled into my clothes and rushed out. Far away on the driving ice of the Sound, a lone figure was running and raving. The boatswain and Billy joined me, and as fast as we could struggle through three feet of snow, with drifts often to the waist, we gave pursuit. At length I reached her, and to my astonishment discovered it was Tongwe. She struggled desperately and it required the combined strength of the three of us to get her back to the shack, where she was found to be in bad shape—one hand was frozen slightly, and part of one breast. After half an hour she became rational again, but the attack left her very weak.

Very similar accounts are given by Peary (1907), Rasmussen (1915), and many others, and Wallace (1961b:263) has abstracted the following stages from the early reports:

1. *Prodrome*. In some cases a period of hours or days is reported during which the victim seems mildly irritable or withdrawn.
2. *Excitement.* Suddenly with little or no warning, the victim becomes wildly excited. He may tear off his clothing, break furniture, shout obscenely, throw objects, eat feces, or perform other irrational acts. Usually he finally leaves shelter and runs frantically onto tundras or ice pack, plunges into snow drifts, climbs onto icebergs, and may actually place himself in considerable danger, from which pursuing persons usually rescue him, however. Excitement may persist for a few minutes up to half an hour.
3. *Convulsions and Stupor*. The excitement is succeeded by convulsive seizures, in at least some cases by collapse, and finally by stu-porous sleep or coma lasting for up to twelve hours.
4. *Recovery*. Following the attack, the victim behaves perfectly normally. There is amnesia for the experience. Some victims have repeated attacks, others are not known to have had more than one.

In addition to the basic pattern, a number of other types of aberrant behavior have also been termed "arctic hysteria." One of these is an involuntary imitative reaction. The person may be induced by onlookers to put some snow under his clothes, go out into dangerous places, and so on (Czaplicka 1914:312). Similar behavior is called *amurakh* in the Yakutsk and Amur provinces of Siberia. *Amurakh* is a kind of startle reaction in which sudden movements or sounds precipitate the individual into moans and cries, and into automatic imitation of the gestures and speech of those around him (Novakovsky 1924:114). These characteristics are so similar to those of *latah* that Aberle classified arctic hysteria and *latah* as the same phenomenon (1952). Other types of behavior sometimes subsumed under the term "arctic hysteria" are frenzied homicidal (*amok*-like) outbursts triggered by unexpected sudden actions, crying and howling like a dog for hours, singing while asleep, erotic mania (Czaplicka 1914:313, 309, 316-17); and clairvoyance and vaginal cramps (Novakovsky 1924:116).

P. M. Yap, who has specialized in culture-specific disorders, does not include arctic hysteria in his latest classification of reactive psychoses, because it is, in his opinion (1969:40), "only a vague generic term for mental illness, or denotes only unspecialized hysterical reactions. Such terms should not be allowed to creep into the psychiatric literature." But can these behaviors be dismissed so easily as manifestations of hysteria, as the early explorers thought? If so, what makes for the high frequencies in this part of the world? What accounts for differences in frequency and manifestation by ethnic group, age, sex, and season? Czaplicka, who brought together the available evidence in 1914, was of the opinion (p. 320) that

. . . nearly all cases described can be regarded as instances of hysteria. . . . There is no question that the economic and geographical conditions of the Arctic region lead to the development of nervous diseases, but since such ailments are met with in other geographical areas, it is clearly incorrect to class them as distinctively "Arctic."

This parallels Brill's (1913) psychoanalytic interpretation of the behavior as hysteria, and seems close to Yap's (1969) present position. Early writers were impressed with the frequency of these behaviors in arctic regions and tended to look for their causes in race, heredity, primitive mentality, or climate, alone or in combination. Nearly all the early travelers were convinced that the long, dark, gloomy winters, with consequent isolation and difficult living conditions, were an important determinant of these reactions. However, their geographical distribution makes any of the older single-factor theories of causation difficult to accept. For example, the Eskimo and other arctic groups of North America apparently do not exhibit such a behavior pattern, leading Novakovsky (1924:118) to suggest that the name be changed to "Hysteria Siberica." Also there seem to be variations within the Siberian and Greenland areas, though there are no sound epidemiological data.[16]

In keeping with the regional diversity are apparent differences in behavioral subtype. I have found no descriptions of the *amurakh* (or *latah*) manifestation among polar Eskimos in areas where *pibloktoq* (or *menerik*) seems to be frequent (e.g., eight of seventeen women associated with Peary's expedition were afflicted during one winter season). This differential distribution may be much greater than the scanty evidence indicates, and when this is considered together with the Eskimo's practical accommodation to winter conditions (Gussow 1960:212), it becomes even more difficult to accept a simple theory of climate as cause. Reports of Russian settlers affected by similar hysteria-like disorders after living in the proximity of Siberian natives (Novakovsky 1924:120) and of *pibloktoq* among whites in Greenland in the 1850s (cited in Wallace 1961*b*:264) similarly argue against a racial explanation.

After reading Admiral Peary's accounts of *pibloktoq* and discussing individual cases with Peary's lieutenant, Donald B. MacMillan, the psychoanalyst Brill (1913) was impressed by the analogies with hysteria in Western society, and wrote a paper on that theme. He made the diagnosis on the basis of the prevalence of *pibloktoq* among women, evidence of their frustrated and dominated lives, and in some cases evidence of repressed sexual wishes.

In a more recent paper, Gussow (1960:229-35) also diagnosed it as hysteria and pursued the psychoanalytic explanation by inferring that such phenomena are manifestations of Eskimo basic personality, which he regards

---

[16] ". . . hysteria is not developed to the same degree among the various tribes of Siberia. This fact is especially obvious in the Northeastern portion. Among the Chuckchee and Koryak it comes more seldom and in milder form than among the Yakut and Tungus. Among the Yukagir and Lamut, hysteria sometimes acquires an acute epidemic form. The same is observed in the Western portion. Here among those least susceptible are the Tartar tribes" (Novakovsky 1924:118-19).

as hysterical in type. He feels that such behavior is related to the dangers of Eskimo daily life and the threats of starvation, with the sex differential stemming from the subservient position of women. He views the flight across ice and snow, accompanied by screams guaranteed to bring pursuit, as a seductive, manipulative, and regressive maneuver of a person under stress, and thus in need of an infantile type of assurance in the face of profound fear and anxiety.

Such a psychoanalytic interpretation is also buttressed by Parker (1960, 1962), who contrasts the flamboyant, acting-out, nonaggressive hysterical disorder of the Eskimo with the morbid depressions, anorexia, and abusive and paranoid ideation common in the *windigo* disorder of the Algonkian tribes. He attributes the differences between these groups to contrasting socialization and consequent personality structures. Parker (1962:85) proposes the hypothesis that hysterical symptoms tend to prevail in societies that provide relatively high satisfaction of dependency needs, and cites evidence to show that this is characteristic of Eskimo societies but not of the Ojibwa, who frustrate them.

Such hypotheses carry us beyond the original formulations and should be field-tested. A difficulty with the argument is that Parker draws evidence for socialization and personality type from literature on the Eskimo of both Greenland and the North American continent, but the behavior he is trying to explain is reported only for the Greenland Eskimos. Furthermore, he does not take account of the almost identical behavior among the many non-Eskimo Siberian groups of varying cultures and socialization practices (Honigmann 1967:403).

A. F. C. Wallace (1961*b*) also accepts the hysteria diagnosis for *pibloktoq*. However, he criticizes his fellow an-

thropologists for sticking with outdated "functional notions of mental disorder," and advocates an organic explanation. He proposes the hypothesis that *pibloktoq* is a form of hypocalcemia, a condition resulting from calcium deficiency and manifesting itself in a neuromuscular condition called tetany. He notes that medical research would be necessary to establish his case, but argues it on the basis of considerable evidence that (1) the diet resources of the area are low in calcium and low in the vitamin D needed for efficient utilization of calcium (1961*b*: 267-68) and (2) the dietary habits of the Greenland Eskimo do not make maximum use of foods rich in vitamin D and calcium; pregnant and lactating women, for example, are subject to food taboos that deprive them of calcium-rich foods just when they need them most (1961*b*:266, 270).

This is a suggestive hypothesis, but Wallace himself notes that with calcium deficiency one would expect a high prevalence of rickets, which is not found. To get around this he proposes the ingenious evolutionary hypothesis that natural selection has produced a hyperthyroid physiology among Eskimos, with tetany rather than rickets being the disease response to vitamin D and calcium deficiency (with rickets they could not have survived).

Wallace does not hesitate to go even further out on the limb (1961*b*: 271-74): he proposes that the reason for the relative rarity of hysteria in the Western world today may be due to the fact that most cases previously diagnosed as hysteria were in reality tetany. If this were the case, the disappearance of the disorder might be the result of improved diet, housing, and working conditions.

The intellectual daring of such thinking is refreshing, but it seems questionable that this simple hypothesis could account for the widespread manifesta-tions of hysterical behavior in many different variations and environments. It has not even been demonstrated that the symptoms of tetany and hysteria are identical (Wallace actually states on-ly that the symptoms of the two are "compatible" [1961*b*:266]). The ser-vice Wallace has rendered is in showing the necessity of reevaluation of in-grained notions and in calling attention to an important dimension requiring in-clusion in any future study.

Even though Czaplicka (1914:315) called the phenomenon "hysteria," she noted that there are probably several different mental disorders lumped un-der the name "arctic hysteria." Even psychiatrically inexpert explorers in arctic Asia distinguished at least two types: the *menerik* type (the frenzied outburst of activity that seems identical to *pibloktoq*) and the *amurakh* type (which appears identical to *latah*); both are Yakut terms. The *menerik* type was noticed to be most frequent among young girls and young men (especially those being trained as shamans), while the *amurakh* type was most often found in women between thirty-five and fifty years of age (Czaplicka 1914:319). It seems that there is also a possibility that epileptic seizures were included in some of the accounts, as well as some postpartum psychoses. Schizophrenias may also have occasion-ally been included, though at least some groups (Yakut, Yakagir, Tungus) differentiated "crazy persons" from those with *menerik*-type behavior, and the Chuckchee also distinguished epi-lepsy (Czaplicka 1914:316).

Thus while the hypocalcemia hypoth-esis is appealing in its simplicity, it suffers from the maladies common to all the unicausal theories in cultural psychiatry. It assumes that the folk or accepted diagnostic categories do de-note single syndromes of what are prob-ably several types of disorder, and it relies on simple etiological hypotheses when the causes of most mental dis-orders are in all probability multifactor-ial. This problem, like the others we have considered, calls for further re-search by psychiatrically and medically expert investigators along with anthro-pologists. The old theories should not be disregarded, but reconsidered *in combination* in the light of new knowl-edge and techniques. The complex in-teraction of climate, diet, heredity, so-cialization practices, basic personality structure, and cultural stresses must now be reassessed in relation to each of the several behavior disorder syndromes lumped within the folk categories.

WINDIGO

Windigo, wendigo, witigo, wittigo —all these terms denote a form of ob-sessively cannibalistic derangement among the northern Algonkian-speak-ing Indians, particularly the Ojibwa and the Cree. The first phase of the disor-der, which usually affects unsuccessful hunters or people who have spent long periods alone in the frozen wilderness, consists of depressively morbid feelings, nausea, and distaste for food. This syndrome is generally followed by feel-ings of being bewitched and by homi-cidal thoughts. The individual has a morbid desire to eat his companions and attributes this to the fact that he is possessed by the mythological *windigo* monster, a giant cannibalistic being with a heart of ice. In the final stage the afflicted one either carries out his murderous compulsions or is executed by the group when he tries to do so (Parker 1960:603, Teicher 1960).

Does such a set of feelings and be-havior constitute a separate diagnostic category that should be included in psychiatric texts as *windigo* psychosis? Wallace (1961a:175) does not think so:

Windigo psychosis with its common pattern of somatic delusions, ideas of reference, persecution complex, and "cannibalistic panic" is a precise image of paranoid schizophrenia as observed in Western man, except that the overt ideas of persecution or influence of Western man are apt to be oriented toward different supernatural beings or even toward other humans (such as "the men in the Kremlin" or "the FBI"), and to emphasize sex rather than food (the cannibalistic panic being replaced by homosexual panic).

However, this may be a premature judgment, since observers who have had the closest acquaintance with the cultures involved all state that the term *windigo* and its equivalents actually refer to a number of differing disorders. Most of these scholars see the *windigo* culture pattern as providing a general "insane role" that, once defined, sets in motion a chain of self-fulfilling and frequently fatal social actions and reactions.

For example, Hallowell, a psychiatrically sophisticated anthropologist, describes how the initial symptoms of repugnance to food and anxiety raise the fear of bewitchment in the individual and the group, along with fear that he may be falling victim to the *windigo* monster. His companions begin to treat him differently, thus accentuating his own fear (Hallowell 1934:7-8):

Individual experience is immediately shunted into a vicious circle of belief pattern from which there is no escape. The individual affected is usually watched day and night by some relative, and in former times, a medicine man would probably be consulted. If there were no improvement, the afflicted one would often ask to be killed and this desire was usually gratified.

Many sufferers apparently sought surcease from their obsessional desire to eat human flesh, to them the greatest sin (Landes 1938:26). Hallowell continues (1934:9), "My point is that all reported cases of this "psychosis' may not be pathological, and even those which are may be, perhaps, of varying psychiatric classification on closer inspection."

Fogelson (1965:81), in discussing Hallowell's cases, points out that most of them involved only the initial phases of the *windigo* process: "Such cases, perhaps, more closely approximate severe anxiety neuroses than full blown psychoses. Hallowell calls for the collection of additional case data to demonstrate that disorders labeled as windigo do not share a common etiology and should be differentially diagnosed."

Ruth Landes, a student having firsthand experience with the Ojibwa, also states that several types of clinical diagnosis are covered by the term *windigo*. She notes (1938:25-26) that to the Ojibwa the syndrome has two phases. In the first, the individual withdraws into a moody depression, neither eating nor sleeping, and ignoring his surroundings. During this period he frequently communicates his cannibalistic fantasies to the group. "His family around him looks to him like luscious beavers heavy with fat. In his lucid moments he describes himself as sad because he wants to eat them, but is not motivated strongly enough to get them." The depressive stage is followed by a homicidal cannibalistic outburst unless some kind of intervention takes place. "With non-shamans assiduous nursing and loving care during the period of melancholia will persuade the sufferer to face life again." She also notes that despite the stereotype, some persons by-pass the depressive phase, some exhibit depressive symptoms but do not signal their fantasies before executing them, and some recover after the initial depression.

Fogelson (1965) thoroughly analyzed a number of *windigo* cases by means of a process model, emerging with five completely different courses of this folk syndrome. It is unfortunate that he could not associate these processual types with psychiatric categories, but his cautious conclusion seems entirely justified (1965:98): " . . . it does seem evident that the native windigo category incorporates several different disorders recognized in Euro-American psychiatry. It is suggested that these disorders probably range from mild and severe episodes of anxiety neurosis to full-blown psychoses."

Teicher's (1960:112) careful analysis of seventy case reports of *windigo* also supports the contention that many different disorders are shaped by the *windigo* "insane role." In addition, he states (1960:110) that in twenty-five of the cases there was no sign of mental aberration at first; the cannibalistic behavior was motivated purely by threat of starvation. Once a person had eaten human flesh, however, he believed himself possessed, and lived out the role expectations of the *windigo* pattern until he was dispatched.

To me the evidence does not lead to a conclusion that *windigo* is a single syndrome in Western terms, and attempts to classify it as one or to explain "its" causes thus appear ill founded. Even such an acute observer of the cross-cultural scene as P. M. Yap (1969:41) must be challenged when he attempts to pigeonhole the *windigo* phenomenon as an "atypical syndrome" of the "reactive psychoses," subtyping it as "Primary Fear Reaction: Trance Dissociation."

There have not been many attempts to explain *windigo* behavior, but early writers tended toward the opinion that it was related to conditions of food scarcity and hunger (e.g., Landes 1938). Later Seymour Parker (1960) presented a psychoanalytic interpretation of *windigo*, deriving it from a character structure shaped by childhood experiences that produced unsatisfied dependency cravings. He was careful to avoid the implication that the considered these conditions to *cause* the disorder; his plausible analysis was offered rather as an explanation of one of the forms that severe mental disorder can assume in particular societies.

A modern revival of the hunger hypothesis based on new scientific findings has recently been presented by Vivian Roehrl (1970:97-101). She cites published and unpublished evidence indicating the importance of anorexia (pathological loss of appetite) with consequent nutritional deficiency in *windigo* conditions, and evidence that some recoveries have apparently been related to the fact that sufferers were induced to eat bear fat—a folk remedy considered specific for *windigo* possession. Noting findings on the vitamin content of similar meats and new data on the relationship of these vitamins as well as blood sugar levels to mental illness and health, Roehrl infers that the famine conditions and dietary deficiencies of the Indian economy could have played a role in both the psychosis and its cure.

It seems plausible that food deprivation might well play a role in *some* of the states called *windigo*, as might also sleep deprivation (Dement 1966, Gove 1970), another regular feature of the condition. Social isolation, panic induced by fearful cultural beliefs, genetic factors, diseases, and biochemical disorders of various kinds might all be implicated in differing degrees in various cases. What is so exasperating about this, as about all the discussions of the "exotic disorders," is the vast amount of interesting speculation on the basis of such slender evidence. Since Fogelson, Kiev, Linton, Parker, Roehrl, Teicher, Wallace, and Yap have never reported observing an actual case of *windigo*, and have made their diagnoses, classifications, and analyses from fragmentary accounts, most of the discussion amounts only to speculative hypotheses that may now be untestable.

LATAH

In many developing countries a similar set of symptoms has been described. The syndrome has become known by the Malay name *latah*, since it was in Malaysia that it was first described. The main symptoms, usually precipitated by shock or fright or tickling, are echolalia (echoing or imitating speech), echopraxia (imitating actions), command automatism (automatic obedience to commands), and coprolalia (uncontrollable utterance of obscene or taboo words). After an attack the patient is usually quite conscious of what he has done, and is ashamed of it.

Yap (1952), who has made by far the most exhaustive study of this phenomenon, claims that it is identical with *imu* among the Ainus of Japan, *myriachit* and *ikota* among Siberian tribes, *mali-mali* in the Philippines, and the affliction of the "jumping Frenchmen" of Maine, among others. Aberle (1952) believes it is the same as arctic hysteria.

Among the Malay and most other groups in which *latah* is manifested, it appears chiefly in women, particularly those of the lower economic classes. Linton (1956), following Kraepelin, considers it a Malay female form of hysteria. Adelman (1955:75) also believes it is a "traumatic hysteria," but Van Loon (1927), who saw many patients at an earlier period, carefully distinguished *latah* from hysteria on the basis of his observation that it involves much more profound loss of conscious control. In his opinion it is a female psychosis.

It is interesting that this malady is not found among the Chinese of the Southeast Asian area, except among those brought up by Malayans. Its widespread and uneven distribution in the world also points to cultural rather than racial roots (Yap 1952, 1969). Yap (1969:41-42) now apparently agrees with Van Loon that *latah* is a kind of psychosis. Previously (1952: 556-57) he had listed a number of explanations that had been offered and rejected them all (an organic disease, hypnotism, hysteria, fright reaction, a special neurosis). At that time he cautiously concluded (1952:560): ". . . the *latah* reaction is a special form of fright *neurosis*, with minimal hysterical features, culturally maintained, and to be found only in persons whose powers of mastery and defense are limited by the level of their own cultural development." (Italics added.) He pointed out that *latah* appears in weakly integrated personalities in cultures of low technological development that provide poor means of organizing fear, making a relatively large proportion of people in these societies tend to react to fright with ego-disorganizing symptoms.

Aberle, who observed three cases, similarly stressed the defensive nature of the symptoms and related them to Anna Freud's concept of "identification with the aggressor." He noted also (1952:296) that *latah* victims are primarily women of "submerged" social position, that they often experience fantasies of sexual attack, and that the precipitating events are sudden powerful stimuli, such as shocks or tickling.

In an interesting paper reviewing the historical evidence for *latah* and *amok* in Southeast Asia, H. B. M. Murphy (1972) has inferred that *latah* is generally a by-product of social change, particularly colonialization. From the evidence he was able to dig up it seems that

... latah appeared relatively suddenly during the second half of the nineteenth century, spread quite rapidly among the populations most exposed to European influence, and has moved in wave fashion away from these centers so that today it is virtually absent in the locations where it was first observed, but present in more distant locations from which it was previously absent. Throughout this period its symptoms have remained relatively stable, but the earlier form in males has disappeared, the intensity of the attacks has declined, and in areas from which it is disappearing the residual subjects seem less intelligent than the earlier ones.

In view of this historical pattern, ". . . in one sense the syndrome can be seen as the pathological pole of an attitude which was socially useful at that juncture": the felt need for rapid imitative learning of "initially incomprehensible customs." This attitude was characteristic of Japanese and Malays "who sought a more modest advancement and security by serving Europeans or the modern leaders of their own people." As Murphy sees it:

For this type of learning there is an advantage in an ability to imitate automatically and to subordinate one's individuality and personal inclinations to the orders of a superior; and for both these abilities hypersuggestibility is an aid. An increased suggestibility was thus likely to be encouraged or elicited in certain strata of society by the introduction of beneficial but little understood changes that had to be rapidly learnt, and this increased suggestibility, I propose, prompted the development of the latah syndrome, which then died away again as rapid rote learning could be replaced by an understanding of what was being learnt.

Murphy proposes no diagnosis for the *latah* condition, but seems to imply that it is a form of hysteria. His hypothesis is an interesting one, and it would be interesting to test it in other areas and with clinical data. It is not inconsistent with my previous suggestion that many of these exotic syndromes may have hysterical understructures, and it has the virtue of partially accounting for similarities of symptoms in culturally dissimilar areas. The idea also is consistent with the general notion of these "folk illnesses" as cultural roles for psychic stress, since individuals with schizophreniform illnesses, epilepsies, and other confused states could conceivably react with such behavior.

Though Murphy probably has not accounted for all the relevant variables in the colonial situation, the set of conditions created by the imposition of the customs and goods of powerful Western nations upon peoples of the Third World has had certain uniformities. We might expect that where similar contact conditions match significantly similar underlying personality processes, the "insane roles" too would resemble one another. The *latah*-like *amurakh* behavior of the Siberians, the anxiety behaviors of East and West Africans, the "jumping Frenchman" phenomenon in Maine, the *imu* behavior of the Ainu, and other exotic syndromes might usefully be studied in this light.

AMOK

The *amok* behavior pattern, which entered the literature from Southeast Asia, has been called "the classical rage reaction" (Wittkower and Dubreil 1969:292). It is generally confined to males who have withdrawn, quiet personalities prior to onset. The attack itself is usually preceded by frustrating stress, which brings about further withdrawal and loss of contact, accompanied by rage and ideas of persecution. At some point these individuals leap up, often with a terrifying scream, lay hold of a *kris* (dagger), and maniacally attack anyone or anything they meet. They may be captured and calmed, but frequently continue their frenzied attacks until they are killed or severely wounded. If they survive, the attack is usually followed by amnesia and depression.

Kraepelin (1904), one of the earliest trained European observers of *amok*, considered it an epileptic dream state, but few later writers have concurred. For example, Van Loon (1927:436-38), who worked in the psychiatric hospital in Batavia for some years, differentiated *amok* from epilepsy but claimed that the aggressive reaction was the Malay response to the "infectious deliriums" of malaria, syphilis, and "*dementia praecox*." He believed it was a terror reaction of people with childlike, primitive minds in the face of organically based hallucinatory states.

Linton (1956:116) classified *amok* as a form of hysteria, largely on the basis of reports that the Dutch authorities in Southeast Asia had stamped it out by capturing *amok*-runners and sentencing them to lives of hard labor, thus taking the glory and suicidal drama out of it.

In his most recent assessment, Yap (1969:45) places *amok* among the reactive psychoses, defining it as a specific clinical entity:

I have defined amok as a strictly psychogenic reaction based on hyperidism ["a state of indifferentiated, morbid hostility"]. It is therefore to be placed alongside the acute psychopathic reactions described in constitutionally predisposed or intellectually subnormal persons under stress, familiar to psychiatrists everywhere, and should not be confused with apparently similar behavior caused by schizophrenia, epilepsy, or acute brain lesion resulting from toxic, exhaustive, or infective causes.

Previously he was more cautious (1951:319-320): "Perhaps the more correct view is that of van Wulfften Palthe, who called *amok* a standardized form of emotional release accepted by the community, and indeed expected of the individual who is placed for some reason or other in an intolerably embarrassing or shameful situation."

Yap's later conclusion that *amok* warrants a separate diagnostic category is apparently based upon Philippine data gathered by Dr. J. C. Zaguirre (1957). But it is difficult to see how he reached this conclusion, since Zaguirre, who saw and treated the *amok* patients he described (Yap did not), proposes a thesis contrary to Yap's (Zaguirre 1957:1138): ". . . 'amuck' is not a disease entity, and it can be a precipitate of various stressing factors, an acute reaction manifestation of a susceptible individual affected with any one of the various psychiatric disorders." This is similar to Yap's earlier opinion, and is consistent with my own general assessments of other folk categories, given above.

Burton-Bradley (1970) reports that he has treated *amok* cases of nearly identical dynamics among people of three different levels of technological development and distinct cultures: Melanesians of New Guinea, Chinese in Singapore, and Europeans of Australia. He therefore rejects the idea that it is culture-bound (1970:1). He seems basically to agree with Yap that *amok* should be classified as a psychogenic psychosis (1970:11-12). He rejects the notion of organic pathology as primary, though he agrees that the commonly implicated factors—betel intoxication, malaria, syphilitic meningo-encephalitis, hypoglycemia, schizophrenia, cannabis addiction—may be associated with it in secondary roles (e.g., by lowering the threshold of reaction). Burton-Bradley (1970:3, 12) points to the idea of "unrelieved insult in a context of culturally determined group expectancies" as the basic etiological feature of *amok*.

H. B. M. Murphy's (1972) historical research on *amok* has revealed that the behaviors associated with the word have undergone considerable change from the mid-sixteenth century, when it apparently was first used, up to the present. From a term initially referring to groups of exceptionally courageous men who had taken a vow to sacrifice themselves in battle against the enemy, it evolved into a word for persons who preferred a fighting death to slavery and other degrading fates. By 1850 the syndrome was defined as a pathological state, much as it is now, and, except in remote areas, had lost any connotation of a conscious attempt to avoid an ignominious situation. The frequency of *amok* seems to have increased to epidemic proportions by the mid-nineteenth century, then died down before 1900. The decline in frequency has continued up to the present.

As it became increasingly rare, the cases of *amok* that were seen by psychiatrists were usually associated with some organic condition—malaria or other sources of febrile delirium in the early twentieth century, and often with schizophrenia, organic brain syndrome, and so on in the 1930s and 1940s. In a recent series of twenty-four cases studied by Schmidt (1964) in Sarawak, "a history of familial mental illness was uncovered in all but six" (H. B. M. Murphy 1972).

Murphy interprets the history of *amok* much as he does the history of *latah*. He relates the changes in the *amok* syndrome, as he sees them, with social change (Murphy 1972):

Amok . . . can hardly be called a psychiatric syndrome before the nineteenth century, since it is only then that one meets cases where the conscious intent to attack is absent, and where social provocations seem insufficient to explain the behavior. The syndromes [*latah* and *amok*] are thus best conceived not as offshoots from Malaysian cultural tradition but as transitional products of that tradition and certain modernizing influences. . . .

. . . In its original, conscious form it was a recognized instrument of social control, restricting the abuse of power by chiefs and the wealthy . . . sanctioned by proverbs . . . and endorsed by the hero-worship of the man who went amok and escaped the consequences. . . .

. . . When less drastic forms of social control were demonstrated in the European settlements and when it proved more profitable to collaborate with the European trader than to pursue traditional methods of warfare and piracy, however, recourse to amok become not only unnecessary but repulsive, and most individuals rejected it as something they themselves might undertake. It is at this point and in this setting that the pathological syndrome first appears, with the provocation (physical sickness, domestic troubles) being quite insufficient by traditional standards and with the art of being dissociated from consciousness, but with the same underlying meanings of escaping distress into death while at the same time taking revenge on the society that has permitted this distress. And as other means of escaping these distresses are learnt, and the amok tradition grows fainter in men's minds, this pathological unconscious or insane recourse to the behavior dies away also.

This again is a provocative hypothesis linking *amok* with cultural features and change, but at this point it is not possible to assess the evidence upon which it is based. It may be that the apparent changes of incidence and quality to which Murphy points simply reflect the advent of European physicians and psychiatrists on the scene, with their particular biases and changes of diagnostic fashion. However, in contrast to Burton-Bradley, Murphy seems to agree with the view presented here that present manifestations of *amok* are probably cultural shapings of various pathological states. Again, his ideas concerning the psychosocial dynamics involved provide insightful leads for more complete analyses in the future.

An African counterpart to *amok* which has received a great deal of attention is "frenzied anxiety," a condition that Carothers diagnosed in twenty-one of his patients (nineteen male, two female) in the Mathari hospital in Kenya. Carothers (1947:576) considered it a psychoneurosis, a kind of psychopathic episode with hysterical elements:

In this condition the onset is associated with some real source of anxiety (perhaps only real to an African), but the anxiety is not sustained, and is soon replaced by a state of frenzy in which the patient is excited, noisy, incoherent, and perhaps filthy, aggressive and dangerously violent. The violence often results in homicide but is apt to be ill-directed and generalized and the supposed author of the patient's anxiety may not be among the victims. Recovery usually occurs within a few hours or days and is as complete as it is rapid—but 4 of these cases on recovering from the frenzy developed hysterical symptoms, 2 deaf-mutism, 1 deafness and 1 aphasia. The subject subsequently denies all memory for the period of frenzy.

In addition to similar syndromes in the Philippines and Kenya, other parallels to *amok* have been described elsewhere in Africa (Gelfand 1964, Smartt 1956, M. J. Field 1960, Tewfik 1958) and in many parts of the world: New Guinea (Burton-Bradley 1968, 1970), Puerto Rico (Rubio et al. 1955), Australia (Cawte 1966), and other regions. This type of behavior has been called pseudo *amok* (Yap 1969), hysterical psychosis (Langness 1967:146), and an atypical form of schizophrenia (P. R. Benedict and Jacks 1954). Much clinical and anthropological work needs to be done to establish whether the apparently parallel forms of these syndromes represent actual identities of process, and to ascertain the true role of cultural and social influences.

"WILD MAN" BEHAVIOR IN NEW GUINEA

A number of fieldworkers have reported a type of behavior in various New Guinea tribal groups which superficially resembles *amok*. The debate as to whether it is psychopathological or a culturally patterned deviant role illustrates several points concerning allegedly culturally specific disorders. Frequent features of the "wild man" syndrome are sudden onset with feelings of coldness, partial deafness (or feigned deafness), apparently uncontrolled behavior such as inappropriate dressing, open thievery, aggressive gestures, and sometimes trembling and loss of muscular control. The people's explanation is that a spirit has possessed the person (Salisbury 1968).

While this New Guinea wild-man behavior does bear some resemblance to *amok* in Malaysia, it seems quite different in its total configuration, and particularly in its quivering and thievery. No initial depression is described, and although the behavior occurs in quite warlike groups, the aggressive outbursts are more threatening than homicidal. They do not culminate in the death of the victim, and are not followed by amnesia.

Salisbury takes a rather straightforward, anthropological position with regard to these attacks, viewing them as hypnotic trances within the "normal" range of behavior. He notes that they appear at times of individual stress, and that they are often anticipated by the group. Salisbury (1968:93) interprets them as manipulative means of coping with the stresses inherent within tightly knit societies with limited role opportunities.

Langness (1965, 1967, 1969) has taken issue with Salisbury, holding that such behavior indicates a type of "hysterical psychosis." Citing data from his own New Guinea study, Langness presents evidence that among the Bena Bena these episodic behaviors are *not* anticipated or consciously sought, but are responses to a high degree of psychic stress, and involve disorders of consciousness of the extreme type that we call psychotic.

Phillip Newman has not entered this controversy, but in an excellent paper on similar behavior among the Guramumba (1964) he proposes that it may be a form of hysteria. Noting that the behavior, rather than arousing fear, has a quality of public entertainment, he considers it a way for a person under stress to signal his inability or lack of desire to fulfill expected roles, and thus a way of changing the group's image of him without loss of social support (Newman 1964:17).

Each of these three anthropologists, all of whom have witnessed similar types of behavior, has a different diagnosis: Salisbury claims it is purposefully induced trance behavior, "possession" in normal individuals; Langness claims it is a type of temporary psychosis; Newman tentatively speaks of hysteria. Each of the arguments is cogent, each may be correct for the group described, and each may have some applicability to the wider New Guinea pattern. The published evidence makes it difficult for the reader to come to any conclusion. A major part of the difficulty appears to revolve around the use of a native category (in this case "possession") as opposed to an analysis based on Western understandings of "mental disorder." Again it seems that a number of clinical entities may be grouped together under a folk label ("possession") to which a set of region-wide cultural role expectations is attached. However, all three authors (as well as Glick 1968) make it clear that not *all* types of what we term pathological behavior in these groups are regarded by the groups themselves as part

of the wild-man pattern. Thus many questions arise which can be settled only by future psychiatrically oriented research. Among the Kuma, one of the groups included in Salisbury's review, there is even a possibility that this type of behavior may be induced by mushrooms that are hallucinogenic at only one period in the year (Reay 1960, 1965). Although it seems unlikely, drugs or diseases might also be sometimes implicated in the other New Guinea societies.

SUSTO

Susto, also known as *espanto, masmo,* and a number of other names that vary from region to region, is a folk illness widespread in Latin American subcultures. It is a syndrome traditionally attributed to fright or shock resulting from the loss of one's soul or its capture by a spirit (Rubel 1964:270). Gillin (1948:388) describes the case of a sixty-three-year-old Guatemalan Indian woman, which he states is typical:

She was in a depressed state of mind, neglected her household duties and her pottery making, and reduced her contacts with friends and relatives. Physical complaints included diarrhea, "pains in the stomach," loss of appetite, "pains in the back and legs," occasional fever. Ventilizations were wheedling and anxious. She alternated between moods of timorous anxiety and tension, characterized by tremor of the hands and generally rapid and jerky movements, and moods of profound *though conscious* lethargy. Orientation was adequate for time and place, and normal reflexes were present.

The general features, as abstracted by the two scholars who have studied *susto* most closely, are these: ". . . during sleep the patient evidences restlessness, during working hours patients are characterized by listlessness, loss of appetite, disinterest in dress and personal hygiene, loss of strength, depression and introversion" (Rubel 1964:271). "In both the Mexican-Central American locus and in Peru, the symptoms as described by various writers suggest a psychic upset usually accompanied by somatic symptoms, suggestive of hysteric, depressive or anxiety states" (Gillin 1948:388). Rubel also mentions one case in which epileptic attacks were ascribed to *espanto* (1964:272).

Kiev (1969:108) points to Rubel's description of *susto* to buttress his argument that acceptance of native categories, particularly by anthropologists, has contributed to what he considers the erroneous notion of culture-bound syndromes:

A case in point is Rubel's (1964) suggestion for an epidemiological study of *susto* or magical fright among Mexican-Americans, which he defines as they do, in terms of the situation in which it occurs. In this way it is not possible to determine whether, in fact, this is really a distinct clinical entity, since the presumed social etiological factors are already built into the diagnoses. That is to say, the diagnosis is made on the basis of the situation in which it occurs, the presence of which is considered as essential to the definition of the syndrome. The implementation of such a study would lead to obtaining information about the social and cultural situations in which depressive-anxiety attacks occur—a useful approach in the study of the epidemiology of social causes, but not for studying the depressive-anxiety attack itself.

This critique seems misdirected. Why could not the study of social categories and clinical symptoms proceed together usefully, without confusion? Rubel obviously does not accept the native term as a clinical diagnostic category, but draws together available data on the distribution and characteristics of a "folk illness." He well recognizes, as apparently Kiev does not, that *susto* does not correspond to any one Western clinical syndrome, and he thus does not claim that it is a distinct form of psychopathology. The fact that a set of similar symptoms is linked with similar causal beliefs in a number of distinct Indian and *mestizo* or *ladino* cultures is interesting in itself and invites study.

In view of these considerations as well as the variety of symptom patterns reported, it is difficult to see how Yap (1969) could classify *susto* as a "reactive psychosis." It again seems plain that a number of greatly differing psychiatric conditions, mainly depression, psychosomatic pains, and anxiety, but sometimes also epilepsy and psychosis, are included under one magicoreligious folk concept.

Like other native categories, the *susto* complex of beliefs and sick-role expectations evidently provide a means by which people suffering from a variety of anxieties, conflicts, and somatic complaints can legitimately be released from the role pressures of everyday life. The rationale of supernatural fright provides a believable cause within the Catholic-Indian belief system, and a curing institution (the *curandero*) is available to provide support, attention, and relief.

DISCUSSION

Several points emerge from the brief look at so-called culture-specific disorders. First, the general diagnostic confusion of the field is manifest. As we have seen, each ethnic disorder has been labeled many different ways by different scholars. They have been called culturally unique syndromes, hysterical neuroses, psychoses, and a number of other things. Second, it seems evident that in most cases, to the people involved, the ethnic label generally indicates a set of cultural role behaviors that allows the individual under psychic stress certain prerogatives, and prescribes a sequence of culturally defined responses from the group. Devereux (1956) has perhaps expressed this idea as well as anybody. However, it must be pointed out that these exotic syndromes are never the *only* form of the "insane role" in these societies.

The exotic character of the so-called ethnic psychoses has focused more attention upon them than they deserve and obscured the fact that "crazy" people are known and dealt with in every society. A recent study by Edgerton (1966) calls our attention again to this fact. He interviewed 505 respondents from four East Africa tribes under standardized conditions. He also administered some projective tests, and supplemented these techniques with depth interviews of native doctors.[17] A major finding of interest was that the basic pattern of symptoms recognized was "remarkably similar for all four tribes, no tribe presents a catalogue of behaviors that is at marked variance with any other tribes."

Also significant was the finding that the perceived psychotic behaviors corresponded to kinds of behaviors that lead to hospitalization in East Africa, and they also are remarkably like western European concepts of psychoses. Some interesting differences of emphasis were noted, such as that all the tribes seemed to emphasize nudity, violence, and excitement as criteria for madness to a greater extent than Europeans would, but hallucinations, one of our main diagnostic signs, were practically never mentioned. But in general, "what is psychotic for them would be psychotic for us." My reading of the literature indicates that this probably is true of the most extreme psychoses in all groups.

A third observation is that there appear to be strong underlying similarities in many of these disorders across a broad range of nonwestern cultures, perhaps related to level of economic development. M. K. Opler (1967:133) is of the opinion that:

The lack of delusional systematizations in a wide variety of mental disorders of nonliterate peoples: the "running wild" of Fuegian tribes (Cooper), the Greenland Eskimo *pibloktoq* (women running about naked–Cooper), the "Arctic hysteria" of Lapps, Eskimos, and Northeast Siberian tribes (Cooper and Yap), and the similar forms of psychosis, latah of Malays and imu of the Ainu tribes of Hokkaido (Yap and Aberle), all point to atypical forms of schizophrenia varying from the Western standard. Like the "frenzied anxieties" with hysterical elements of Carothers and Aubin, they remind us of schizo-affective disorders as discussed by Adolph Meyer, but more loosely organized, more episodic, and more bound to action modes of emotional expression than to fantasy.

In view of the analysis here, it seems unlikely that there is a one-to-one correlation of any of the exotic disorders and schizophrenias. However, many schizophreniform problems do seem to be included in these native categories, and the statement draws our attention to some of the underlying commonalities.

A possible synthesizing idea here is the concept of "hysterical psychosis." Hollender and Hirsch (1964) recently reviewed the use and meaning of this term, and Langness (1965, 1967) has pointed out its applicability to much of the cross-cultural data. As he summarizes its features (Langness 1967:143):

... an hysterical psychosis begins suddenly and dramatically. The onset is temporarily related to an upsetting event or circumstance. The manifestations may take the form of hallucinations, delusions, depersonalization, or grossly unusual behavior. Affectivity, when altered, is in the direction of volatility rather than flatness. Thought disorders, when they occur, are circumscribed and very transient.

---

[17] Edgerton's study is unique in its combination of focus upon *native* conceptions of psychosis and methodological rigor. Let us hope it will be emulated in other areas, and in conjunction with clinical and epidemiological studies.

The acute episode seldom lasts longer than one to three weeks, and the process recedes as suddenly and dramatically as it began, leaving practically no residue. Second and third episodes may, and do, occur.

It will be noticed that this description is remarkably similar to the qualities of the "schizophrenias" and other psychotic episodes of nonwestern peoples. Hollender and Hirsch (1964) also propose that "hysterical psychosis" is the best diagnosis for such phenomena as the "brief schizophrenia" of soldiers under stress, the disordered states of victims of auto accidents, and so on, as well as for many of the exotic syndromes, and they suggest in passing that *amok, witiko, pibloktoq, latah,* and *imu* might be forms of it. Langness (1967:148-50) reviewed the cross-cultural literature and concluded that each of those five particular ethnic disorders differed from hysterical psychosis on some important dimensions, but he found a number of other descriptions that fitted the pattern very closely. Among these were the wild man behavior of some of the New Guinea tribes, Devereux's (1961a) description of brief psychotic episodes among the Mohave Indians, Smartt's (1956) depiction of "unclassified psychoses" in East Africa, Harris' (1957) account of *saka* in Kenya, which she called "possession hysteria," the "transient psychoses" described by M. J. Field (1960) in Ghana, and the so-called Puerto Rican syndrome (Rubio et al. 1955, Langness 1967:145-46).

Langness' proposal that hysterical psychosis is broadly applicable to many of the diverse descriptions and conflicting diagnoses in the cross-cultural literature merits attention and research. His paper also raises an important question that relates to a theme running through almost all the literature on mental disorder among nonwestern peoples: Are there high frequencies among these peoples of the general personality type known to psychiatrists as the "hysterical personality," and if so, could this personality structure underlie the many apparent similarities of dynamics found in the disorders of the nonwestern world?

One observation pointing toward such a conclusion comes from Hollender and Hirsch (1964:1072), who have noted that the states they designate as hysterical psychosis, which are so similar to many of the apparently diverse syndromes of the nonwestern world, seem to arise in people whose premorbid personality was of the hysterical type. The term "hysterical personality" is not defined in the APA manual, though the term is in common use among psychiatrists. Occurring primarily in women in the West, it is generally characterized by vanity, egocentricity, emotional lability and excitability, dramatic attention-seeking and sexually provocative, demanding, and dependent behavior, and a tendency to live for the immediate situation (Chodoff and Lyons 1958). Hollender and Hirsch propose that this personality type is highly susceptible to being overwhelmed by stress, with ego functions being temporarily disrupted, thus presenting the symptoms of hysterical psychosis as they define it.

Another source of evidence suggesting the possibility of a widespread frequency of hysterical personality types in these parts of the nonwestern world is the near unanimity of professional opinion that hysteria is much more common among nonliterate, nonurban peoples than among urban and literate ones. This conforms with the widely held opinion that the decrease in hysterias seen in European and American psychiatric practice in this century is related to the rise of literacy and urbanization, changes in women's status and in attitudes concerning sex, and so on.

Evidence supporting such a conclusion has been manifest throughout my discussion of cultural factors in mental disorder. There are many data in favor of it, not all of which can be reviewed here, but the following should be mentioned: (1) there is a high frequency of possession cults characterized by hysterical, dissociated behavior in these societies (Bourguignon 1965, Lewis 1966, Zaretsky 1966). (2) It is in these low-technology societies that we find such manifestations of mass frenzy as cargo cults (Williams 1923, Worsley 1957) witch-finding cults (Andersson 1958), the tarantism of the late Middle Ages, and so on. Most experts in psychiatry regard this type of behavior as hysterical. (3) Almost all scholars who have described disorders in these societies have found it expedient to speak of the "hysterical features" of these disorders (e.g., Yap 1952 [latah], Carothers 1947 [frenzied anxiety], Brill 1913, Grygier 1948, Parker 1960, Gussow 1960, Wallace 1961a (arctic hysteria).[18]

These kinds of findings suggest the hypothesis that there may be in many societies a type of basic personality structure that has a number of features in common with the "hysterical personality," and they raise a number of theoretical and empirical questions that cannot be pursued here. I can only suggest that among the variables that might account for this character structure, where it is shown to exist widely, are permissive child-rearing practices with

minimal repression of dependency needs, communalistic values, a high degree of face-to-face interaction, lowly esteemed female roles, beliefs in supernatural possession along with "hysterical-like" behavior models (Parker 1962:81), magical modes of thinking (Langness 1967:147), and illiteracy (Carothers 1959). Any or all of these factors, combined with malnutrition, frequent high fevers in infancy, general life insecurity, and so on, might well produce high frequencies of the labile, histrionic personality processes typical of hysterics.

It would seem that whatever their origin, such "hysterical" processes may condition the kinds of mental disorder that we see in many parts of the nonwestern world, making them both similar to one another and bizarre and difficult to classify by our standards. If there actually are lower frequencies of schizophrenia, depression, obsessive-compulsive neuroses, and psychopathy, and if it is true that most psychopathological disorders in these societies have a better prognosis than those in our own society, such a basic structure might be their conditioning foundation. In any case, it seems certain that definitive answers are not yet in.

NONWESTERN PSYCHIATRIC PRACTICES

Human beings suffering from pain, fear, and stress have universally sought out certain of their fellows for reassurance and aid, creating in every society the reciprocal roles of doctor (or shaman-priest or folk healer) and patient (supplicant). Practitioners were thus created by universal needs, and though they have often known how to maximize the rewards of their positions by shrewd exploitation of such needs, they have flourished because of the relief they have provided through consum-

---

[18] Related support for such inferred personality features comes from such statements as this (De Vos and Hippler 1969:375-76): "There are reports on the use of psychological tests that suggest the apparently normative appearance in some cultures of relatively immature control over impulses and emotional processes. For example, data on Alorese (Du Bois 1944) and the Algerian Arabs (Miner and De Vos 1960) reveal the widespread presence of immature personality processes which appear to be normative to the forms of social adaptation manifested within these cultures."

mate skills. The ways in which peoples outside the modern Euro-American tradition deal with sufferers of what we term mental disorders is a subject of considerable importance in cultural psychiatry which has not yet received the careful study it deserves. As Ari Kiev (ed., 1964) has recently pointed out in his excellent collection of essays on nonwestern psychiatric practices, it may well be that Western psychiatry could learn a considerable amount from indigenous psychotherapies.

Kiev (1964:5) notes that despite great expenditures of money and research effort, Western psychiatry itself has not been able to prove its effectiveness unequivocally: "Most statistical studies show that 65-70% of neurotic patients and 35% of schizophrenic patients improve after treatment regardless of the type of treatment received. Long-term follow-up studies of treated patients have also demonstrated no differences among various treatments." The eminent psychologist Hans Eysenck (1966:40) carefully surveyed the literature on treatment efficacy and stated, "The results do show that whatever effects psychotherapy may have are likely to be extremely small." The disarray of the psychotherapy field is also reflected in the great number of "schools" and methods, all claiming efficacy, from which the often bewildered patient must choose.

The relative chaos of the field is perhaps one reason that recent psychopharmacological discoveries appear to be viewed as salvation by many psychiatrists. The phenothiazines, lithium, and the antidepressants, among others, have produced amazing results for many suffering individuals, and though some of the early optimism is waning, much more is promised from this direction. Thus research on drugs used by folk practitioners is another area in which collaboration of anthropology and psychiatry is desirable. It is well known, for example, that reserpine from the shrub *Rauwolfia serpentina* has been effectively used for centuries by folk curers in India, Java, Malaysia (Kline 1954, Horden 1968), and West Africa (Prince 1960*a*). Research also continues on therapeutic uses of mescaline, the active ingredient of peyote, and is being initiated on related substances such as *Banisteria caapi* or *ayahuasca*, a South American vine whose roots are powerfully hallucinogenic; its principal psychoactive ingredient is harmine (Dobkin de Rios 1969-1970, 1972). Much more research should and can be done on drugs known to folk medicine, but effective therapy for many psychiatric disorders must still include interpersonal interventions of various kinds, even in cases where psychiatric drugs are effective. It still would seem wise to study also apparently effective nondrug techniques in other cultural traditions.

Jerome Frank (1961:61-64) has emphasized the common factors in all therapies, and has focused attention upon the emotional roles of such activities as the arousal of faith and hope of relief, the heightening of self-esteem, group support and attention, reaffirmation of shared cultural assumptions, and the organizing effect of a plan of action on the bewildered patient. Anthropological authors, too, have often noticed similarities between "primitive" and "modern" therapeutic techniques. For example, Wallace (1958) has detailed the remarkable parallels between the Iroquois and the psychoanalytic theories of dreams. Similarities between modern and traditional practices have also been pointed out among the Apache (M. E. Opler 1936), the Ute (M. K. Opler 1959*a*), the Navajo (Pfister 1932), the Mohave (Devereux 1961*a*), and the Puerto Ricans (Seda-Bonilla 1969). This use of the cross-cultural data, deemphasizing differences between systems, is very valuable in calling attention to universals, since psychiatrists need to understand the common principles underlying all psychic healing and to realize their very real kinship with healers and priests. But what about differences between systems? What may make one set of practices more efficacious than another? The unique characteristics of specific nonwestern psychiatric practices and the limitations of our own methods might well be brought into strong relief if they could be spotlighted against the many-textured patterns of variant cultural systems.

THE DRAMATIC HEALING RITUAL

Among the outstanding differences between primitive and Western therapies is the employment of dramatic means and powerful symbolism. As a means of indicating some of the variables that may have therapeutic significance in various traditions, I am going to contrast some general features of trance curing ceremonies with the common Western patient-therapist model of treatment. I do not want to imply that all or even most nonwestern societies utilize the curing pattern I shall outline. Edgerton (1971) has recently described an African practitioner who uses quite a rational and quasi-scientific approach to problems of mental disorder. Though such cases are rare in the literature, undoubtedly there are many more such individuals among the healers of the nonwestern world. In many areas there are curers who dispense or prescribe herbal preparations and other folk remedies, usually in some religious or magical context (see Chapter 24). Some are quite legitimate; others are charlatans. But the dramatic ritual frequently involving trance states is also very widespread and presents perhaps the sharpest contrast to our own styles of dealing with emotional problems.[19]

Rather than being a private encounter of two individuals, the trance ritual is a semipublic event made up of at least three elements—patient, therapist, and audience—all of whom actively participate. Frequently there are auxiliary helpers such as assistants, musicians, and masters of ceremony; and in the audience are people who know the patient and curer in their daily life roles. In sessions of this type, "therapy" generally is attempted in one session that ranges from several hours to a night or day or many days. For example, a Nubian *zar* ceremony may last seven days, a Navajo sing nine days. Sessions may be repeated several times if recovery is not effected, but each performance is a special ceremonial event, not a regular routinized transaction. The setting for treatment is generally symbolically marked off in some way. Usually protective and "good" symbols are found in abundance, and a special stagelike arrangement of the room contributes to an emotionally charged atmosphere. The lighting and special clothing of the

---

[19] For reasons of space I cannot here quote extensively from the detailed accounts of these frequently dramatic rituals, but the reader may consult the following as an introduction: Anisimov 1963 on the Evenks and Bogoras 1907 on the Chuckchee of Siberia; Freeman 1967 on the Iban of Borneo; Firth 1967 on the Malays; Lee 1966 on the !Kung Bushmen of South Africa; M. J. Field 1960 and 1968 on the Akan of Ghana; Calloway 1870 on the Amazulu; R. H. Prince 1964*a* and 1968*b* on the Yoruba; J. G. Kennedy 1967 on the Nubians; Messing 1957 on Ethiopia; Seda-Bonilla 1969 on Puerto Rico; Kiev 1961, Bourguignon 1965, Ravenscroft 1965, Wittkower 1964, and Wolff 1956 on Haiti; Leighton in Prince, Leighton, and May 1968 on the Navajo; White 1928 and Fox 1964 on Keresan pueblos; Rasmussen 1929:123-29 and J. M. Murphy 1964 on the Eskimo; Gillin 1948 and Holland and Tharp 1964 on Guatemalan Indians; Surya et al. 1965 and Obeysekere 1970 on India; Obeysekere 1970 on Ceylon.

participants clearly set the event off from daily life situations.

After preliminaries, the practitioner initiates a many-dimensioned attack against the evil forces believed to be causing the problem, often through ritual reenactment of a well-known myth. It is a dramatic performance in which mysterious feats of prestidigitation, clairvoyance, and ventriloquism may be accomplished, while the audience reacts with vocal enthusiasm or awestruck silence.

Much of the activity assaults the sensory system of the designated patient and to a lesser degree has a similar effect on the audience. The room may be hot, dark, and filled with smoke or incense. Drums are frequently throbbing. Sometimes the patient is given drugs or revoltingly foul medicines. He may also participate in exercises inducing hyperventilation, have dangerous weapons brandished near him, be frightened by terrifying masked dancers, be dunked in cold water, or have his body rubbed with various objects and substances.

Physical manipulation and violent body movement are frequent means of stimulating the sufferer and involving him in the ritual. In the Nubian *zar*, for example, the patient is smoked with incense, smeared with sacrificial blood, has dates dropped on his head, is bathed in the Nile, and so on (Kennedy 1967). In other societies patients are whipped, burned with hot irons, cut with knives, given emetics, struck sudden blows, or given other shocks, such as having liquid spat into their faces. The healer often physically manipulates various parts of the afflicted one's body as he chants powerful spells. He may suck out sorcery substances or pains by means of tubes or directly with his mouth. In addition to having to maintain an uncomfortable position, the patient may be given little to eat and drink and be permitted little sleep for a prolonged period.

An important recurrent aspect of these ceremonies is what may be called symbolic bombardment. Protective and purificatory symbolic acts are constant; symbolic numbers, colors, shapes, and substances with powerful latent and overt meanings are everywhere in evidence. Dramatic ritual sacrifices sometimes climax the ceremony, or several sacrifices may be interspersed throughout. Frequently the content of the myth and ritual consists of a prolonged battle between the shaman and powerful spirits that are symbolic of illnesses, evil deeds, and perhaps parts of the body. As Leighton has noted (Prince, Leighton, and May 1968), this dramatic battle is usually made to culminate with victory over the evil spirits. Role reversals sometimes take place: individuals mock sacred symbols, indulge in obscenities, burlesque secular leaders, and so on.

Such active sensory assaults frequently aid in inducing the possession trance, a state of dissociation during which patients may act out all kinds of ordinarily repressed impulses and wishes. These actions are done at the behest of entering spirits, who may kill the occupied body if they are not satisfied, effectively absolving the patient of responsibility for his disapproved behavior. The patient not only receives attention but may be given desirable goods designed to placate the spirits, while receiving supportive response from the audience. Often he cries like a baby, barks like a dog, or exhibits glossolalia.

It is frequently reported that near the end of such exciting and prolonged rituals patients collapse from exhaustion and drop into deep sleep. Falling unconscious in a ritually constructed world of spirits, fantasy, and death, they awaken in the world of ordinary reality, usually surrounded by family and friends. They often feel a mild euphoria, and sometimes are free of their symptoms. Amnesia concerning their former symptoms as well as about their trance behavior is commonly reported. Sometimes the practitioner decrees a number of taboos to be observed or rituals to be carried out by the patient for some prescribed time after the ritual.

This treatment method is obviously different from the rationalized Western model of two-person therapy or any form of group therapy. People with many types of mental disorders are subjected to powerful stimuli, and are purposefully induced into a temporarily altered state of consciousness, from which they emerge improved or cured.

It is possible to see how hysteria, anxiety states, and perhaps some depressions might benefit from such treatment, but for many other disorders such a process would appear on the surface to be highly dangerous. Such phenomena as hyperventilation syndrome (deadening of extremities), pain in the chest, sweating and fear of impending death, and sleep deprivation experiences (misperceptions, confusion, paranoid phenomena, hallucinations) are themselves pathological, and can be dangerous in combination with existing symptoms. The extreme regressions and dissociative behavior would not be recommended treatment for most psychotics or many neurotic patients. Ludwig (1966) lists a number of possible maladaptive effects of such altered states of consciousness, yet a peculiar thing about the literature on these intensive trance rituals is that one looks in vain for any evidence of such acute stress reactions. On the contrary, many investigators end their descriptions with a list of possible reasons for the apparent therapeutic effects of the rituals (e.g., Kiev 1968:147).

SOME DIMENSIONS OF VARIATION IN TREATMENT

Patients

Good descriptions of patients and their symptoms are extremely rare in cross-cultural studies of healing. Sometimes no symptoms at all are reported. A few notable exceptions are some reports by psychiatrically trained observers (e.g., Prince 1964a, M. J. Field 1960, Kiev 1968, Wallace 1959b, 1960), but in no study reviewed is a large sample of patients systematically examined and diagnosed by a qualified observer, their native therapy chronicled, and follow-ups of their outcomes made. Much of the best cross-cultural material we have on patients is in some of the cases used to illustrate general curing methods (e.g., Prince 1964a, M. J. Field 1960, Fox 1964, Hes 1964, Madsen 1964, Wallace 1958). A number of reports also give general accounts of the *types* of symptoms exhibited by people being treated, but these are unsatisfactory bases for conclusions regarding effectiveness of therapy.

Western and nonwestern cultural beliefs and attitudes about mental disorder vary in at least two respects, both of which are significant in determining the outcome of such a disorder. These are (1) natural versus supernatural concepts of cause, and (2) differences in normative evaluations of "abnormal" behavior (i.e., states of feeling are defined as good or bad, valid or invalid, dangerous or beneficial, etc.). These two related sets of values and attitudes set the conditions of the patient's role in any society.

In Western psychiatric thought the disease model of natural causation, accompanied by assumptions of mind-body duality, has been dominant for some time. It has become extremely complicated by the confusion of involuntary deviance with voluntary types of crime and misbehavior, and through uncertainty as to the effects of environmental and other influences on both crime and mental disorder. Many more people than previously now define themselves as in need of treatment, yet acceptance of treatment labels one as "sick," with the persisting underlying fear that the cause is organic, and thus perhaps hereditary and unmodifiable by treatment. Thus the sick role is itself stressful and symptom-producing.

Edgerton (1969) has recently reminded us, with a series of interesting cases from four East African tribes, that the process by which people with various kinds of behavioral problems come to be "recognized" as suffering from mental disorder is a topic badly in need of cross-cultural study. He directs our attention to the fact that this process is a complex one, involving acts of perception, labeling, and treatment, which is seldom clear-cut and always involves considerable negotiation.

The labels applied to deviant behavior in nonwestern societies appear much broader, less fixed, more negotiable, and less productive of fear and anxiety then our own. Some reasons we may adduce for this are: (1) Many more behavior patterns labeled neuroses or "character disorders" in the West are in other societies regarded as within the normal range. (2) Many subjective feeling states, such as hallucinations and illusions, are positively valued or viewed as nonthreatening, and therefore go unlabeled and untreated. If these experiences produce fear, it is fear of spirits, which can be handled, rather than the fear of permanent incompetence or crippling nonspecific anxiety (Wallace 1959a). When neurotic symptoms such as hysteria or obsessions are manifested, they are frequent-

ly controlled within prescribed ceremonial contexts in which such behaviors are valued. (3) Concepts of causation such as spirit intrusion, sorcery, and breach of taboo offer more comprehensive theories of curing than do Western etiologies. (4) Generally nonwestern systems offer only one theory of causation and one or two types of healers, reducing choice, and therefore uncertainty and doubt, to a minimum. (5) What we view as separate physical and emotional symptoms are regarded in many nonliterate societies as a general malfunction of the whole organism, not of the "mind" or "body" alone. Emotional conflicts tend to manifest themselves somatically, and the whole person is generally treated. Thus psychological aspects of organic disease are also automatically and effectively treated. The possible importance of such "whole person" treatment for Western psychiatry has recently been pointed out by Frank (1965).

Therapists

In contrast to the empathic, nonjudgmental, personal model of the West,[20] the nonwestern therapist cloaks himself in a powerful impersonal role. Attributes that frequently occur in descriptions of nonwestern healers are authority, charisma, skills of legerdemain, instability of personality, ability to dissociate at will, and knowledge of herbs and rituals. Shamans and other folk healers who claim supernatural powers often have atypical histories and personalities for their societies. Frequently they have undergone

---

[20] Some studies have shown that unconditioned regard for the patient is positively related to judgments of therapists' effectiveness. "From the standpoint of personality, the good psychotherapist has qualities such as self-confidence, energy and controlled emotional warmth" (Frank 1961:111).

lengthy apprenticeships to learn their craft, but most nonwestern curers of this type have traits that set them apart and communicate an aura of special supernatural connection. These seem instrumental to their abilities to invoke awe, mystery, admiration, and faith. The nonwestern practitioner often appears as a powerful master of the spirits, and he tends to relate to the patient impersonally, through a respected and feared role. The potential use of his miraculous power for evil or death enhances respect, induces fear, and commands obedience. Not only this, but traditionally the nonwestern shaman is a generalist. He treats all bodily and mental complaints, combining skills and roles that have become specialized in the evolution of Western medicine. On behalf of the patient, he uses his power to achieve contact with the sickness-producing forces of evil and to do battle against them. He psychologically detaches himself from the mundane world by various techniques, such as dissociated spirit possession, symbolism, and dress, or by the fact that he is a stranger. He frequently comes from another ethnic group, class, or area that is reputed to have more knowledge of magic. Separateness is also increased by the fact that so many of them have passed through the crisis of madness, a period of contact with the world of death.

Another contrast is seen in the relationship between patient and practitioner. The Western therapist is expected to maintain a "professional" nonjudgmental stance, not to "get involved," and so on, yet paradoxically he must also be "warm" and "human." The nonwestern therapist is not generally faced with this dilemma. Though he may know the patient well, during treatment he moves into an impersonal role dimension. He rarely encounters the typical complex interpersonal or "transference" involvements that are discussed in psychiatric journals. Such role differences may have considerable implications for therapy.

Goals of Therapy

In Western psychiatry the goals of therapy range from the removal of specific "symptoms," such as tics and phobias, to massive personality overhauls. Generally, however, all therapies have in common the interrelated notions of relief from subjective feelings of pain, anxiety, and so on and the improvement of social functioning through improved use of energy, improved reality testing, attitude change, and new independence.[21] Often noted therapeutic goals are "ego-strengthening," instilling self-esteem, and so on. Western therapies are thus basically reeducative processes in which recovery is correlated with the degree to which the patient alters his behavior in the direction of the therapist's values (Hobbs 1962, Kiev 1964:5).

Developing in more stable social systems where child socialization and adult role requirements are more closely coordinated, nonwestern therapies are generally less concerned with the goal of ego-strengthening or education. Frank (1968) has noted that the faith-arousing techniques of these groups may often have educative consequences such as enhancement of self-worth through group support and "organization" of vague feelings of distress, but these seem to be unintended side effects. In this regard, nonwestern therapies are directed more to restoration of

---

[21] Redlich and Freedman (1966:272) state what appears to be a generally accepted position: "Psychotherapeutic techniques must enable the patient to correct his pathological and undesirable habits and help him replace them with useful and gratifying attitudes and behavior. . . . Put simply, psychotherapists treat misfits."

temporarily lost self-confidence than to construction of a new self-concept.

In keeping with their theories of causation, nonwestern psychotherapeutic goals are generally pragmatic and aim toward immediate results. The major goal is almost always relief from painful symptoms, and rarely do we encounter any effort to alter the personality radically. There is often some counseling of a moral or ritual nature, but there is no effort to change values or to aid the patient to "find his values," "establish realistic goals," or anything of the sort. Generally values are taken for granted and are subject to very little choice.

The holiest of Western therapeutic goals is insight, a kind of enlightened understanding of past events, with sudden awareness of underlying conflicts. Insight seems particularly meaningful to our Western rationality-worshiping societies. Many other societies emphasize proper ritual performance to achieve harmony with dangerous and helpful forces, and stress ecstasy instead of insight. The apparent success of many of these techniques raises a serious question as to the meaningfulness of insight as a therapeutic goal.

Treatment Setting

In Western psychiatry, overwhelming and perhaps exaggerated therapeutic significance is attributed to the interaction process itself, and details of the settings in which treatment takes place are almost invariably missing from psychiatric reports. This may be because there are general similarities in therapeutic practice, and settings are therefore taken for granted, but it appears that little curative import is attached to them. However, studies of the subliminal impact of media used in motivational research (e.g., Klein 1970, chaps. 8 and 9) and of the influence of settings (Hall 1966, Maslow and Mintz

1956, Mintz 1956, Sommer 1965) make it clear that people respond consciously and unconsciously to cues from their entire environment. Therefore, it would seem reasonable that many features of the surroundings may have a profound psychological impact on hypersensitive patients. This has been realized to a limited extent in recent concerns with hospital design, the uses of color, and so on.[22] In Western psychotherapy the most frequent purpose of environmental manipulation, in the instances when it does occur, seems to be to reduce tension. These attempts seem haphazard and ad hoc, and it seems clear that most prison and hospital-like institutional settings depress and disorient many patients rather than benefit them.

Much more attention is generally paid to the treatment setting in nonwestern therapeutic situations, and often the setting is designed to intensify anticipation and to arouse and sustain such emotions as fear, wonder, and general excitement. Another world is created through symbolism, drama, costume, color, and music. The many ways by which this is accomplished, and their differential effects on specific types of patients, deserve a great deal of study. In ancient Greece, for example, the method of "incubation" was used for the psychiatrically distressed. The patient slept within a sacred temple chamber for a prescribed length of time (Meier 1967). Another interesting example of attention to setting is found in Ari Kiev's description (1968:129-30) of a Mexican-American *curandero's* treatment room:

In general the curandero sees patients in a part of his home set aside for treatment.

---

[22] Freud's method of reducing competing sensory impact by placing the patient on a couch facing away from the therapist in a dimly lighted room was a very insightful innovation along this line.

These rooms, even in poor slum homes, are distinctive because of the great number of religious objects contained in them. The presence of numerous pictures and statues of the Virgin Mary and Jesus, of various sized crosses and religious candles, which are often arranged around an altar in the corner of the room, creates an atmosphere of religious solemnity which makes one forget the poverty of the slum or the humble shack of the curandero. Indeed, in such treatment rooms one feels as if in a church, and cannot help but view the curandero with awe and respect.

A principal feature of all such settings is the symbolic separation from daily life, the creation of an extraordinary world that is believed to be subject neither to the laws of the physical world nor to the laws of men. This otherworldly atmosphere is usually intensified by special props and an assortment of devices—smoke, perfume, incense, darkness, special lighting—all of which may distort sensory perception and cognition. Though some attempts to manipulate the environment are used in Western psychiatry (e.g., Frank 1961:129), the general lack of focus upon them and misunderstanding of them render their potential effects relatively inoperative.

TREATMENT PROCESSES AND TECHNIQUES

The Verbal Dimension

"All schools [of Western psychotherapy] regard the therapist's verbal reactions as of particular importance. They represent his tools" (Mann 1965:27). In most nonwestern psychotherapies, action, including the manipulation of nonverbal symbols, is the main treatment modality, not talk. This does not mean that no verbal communication occurs; only that it is not stressed, is generally much less frequent, has a different quality and timing, and has a different kind of significance to the patient.

However, two kinds of verbal interaction found frequently in nonwestern therapies bear considerable resemblance to their Euro-American counterparts: the diagnostic interview and confession. For the troubled person, the diagnostic interview is a verbal interchange during which the practitioner systematically gathers information about the patient's symptoms and life conditions. This talking part of the process is usually carried on not only with the patient, but also with the family and interested friends. It generally differs from its Western counterpart in its frequent focus upon bodily discomforts, strained social relations, and moral breaches, and in its lack of attention to earlier life experiences or subjective feelings or conflicts. It also differs in its immediate activism.

The diagnostic interview is often a faith-inducing initiation of therapy itself.[23] For example, in addition to gathering information, the therapist may use a divination procedure that can have potent effects (e.g., Prince, Leighton, and May 1968:1173; J. G. Kennedy 1967:187). This procedure generally determines the type of illness that is to be treated and the ceremonial treatment necessary, and sometimes indicates that the patient is to be assigned to a special cult group. A line of action is laid down, reducing tensions and increasing expectations of help.[24]

Confession is another kind of verbal behavior common to many Western and nonwestern therapeutic processes. It is a cathartic discharge of affect, experi-

---

[23] Recent experimental evidence indicates that in our society the therapeutic interview often has an anxiety-reducing effect that may be as beneficial as the therapy that follows. Patients who are prepared for therapy by specially designed role-induction interviews have been found to respond to treatment better and more quickly than unprepared patients (Frank 1961).

[24] See Devereux 1956 and Edgerton 1969 for useful discussions of some of the cross-cultural complexities relating to diagnosis.

enced as a purging of guilts and tensions, which is recognized in all quarters as being of frequent therapeutic benefit (La Barre 1947, 1964). However, there are probably considerable differences in confession to a single practitioner or priest, to a small private group, and to a "public," and differential effects between confession followed by penance and confession alone; if penance is imposed, the kind of acts required will introduce further differences in effect. While such a process must almost always have some therapeutic effect, this must vary with the degree to which norms are internalized, with the degree of guilt important in the culture, and with the ways the person is handled after his confession. Particular therapeutic effects of these variables in different disorders are unknown, as are the possible antitherapeutic results of confession.

Another variable is the direction in which most communication flows. In nonwestern therapies most verbal messages flow from healer to patient. They are more authoritative and less subject to question than the Western therapists' messages. When the healer speaks not to the patient but to spirits and the audience, receiving other messages from them in return, he is in effect communicating with the patient indirectly; the patient is not required to make any immediate response, or to deal with the therapist as a person.

Another means of indirect communication is through the trance mechanism, which removes responsibility for instructions and interpretations from patient and therapist alike and transfers it to a respected and feared spirit. When both patient and practitioner are in trance the situation is analogous to mutual hypnosis. Studies of this phenomenon are recent and few (Tart 1969), but they suggest that with such techniques communication can take place on deep subconscious levels, with one

person participating in the other's mental processes and fantasies. Under such conditions it is possible that the shaman may be in much more direct touch with the patient's unconscious, with perhaps greater healing effects for some types of conditions, than is the case in most Western therapies.

Indirect communication is also achieved through divination procedures in which culturally standard interpretations of chance events (subject to some manipulation by the practitioner) are specifically applied to the patient's case (e.g., see Dobkin de Rios 1969-1970, 1972; Prince 1964a). The indirect quality of much communication in nonwestern therapies may be a very important curative element. This technique is also used to some extent in Euro-American group therapy, but to many the idea seems to imply deception and is contrary to values of openness and frankness.

A final general contrast that we should note lies in the nature of the communication between therapist and patient. Since curing is an integral part of religion in nonwestern societies, the therapeutic language is *ritual* language. Much of it has a formalized, stereotyped, highly symbolic character, with profoundly meaningful mythical themes linking the situation to all the mysteries of the cosmos (Wallace 1966:238; Prince, Leighton, and May 1968). I will discuss this later; here I only want to note that this level of symbolic communication is relatively minimal in typical Western psychotherapy.

POSSIBLE THERAPEUTIC ATTRIBUTES OF NONWESTERN CURING

Faith, Suggestion, Group Support, and Catharsis

Among the most common ideas advanced to account for the effectiveness of native curing practices is that most of it is due to complete emotional commitment to treatment efficacy. Frank (1961) has stressed the ways in which these techniques arouse hope and faith, and has discussed how the "placebo effect" (i.e., psychological relief provided by a substance that is inert or a treatment that is nonspecific to the illness) operates to make *all* therapies successful to some degree. "The intensity of hope that can be elicited by psychotherapy must be but a pale shadow of that evoked by religious healing" (Frank 1961:72).

Prince (1964a:110-11) likewise feels that "suggestion is the most important element of all primitive psychotherapies," and points out that this element is more effective in nonwestern societies than in the Western world because it is unashamedly recognized and utilized through a "continuous barrage of suggestions at all levels from the most intellectual to the most concrete and primitive." Such interpretations often carry the implication that the problems most likely to be relieved by ritual suggestion are those created by the culture—anxiety states or psychosomatic ills that may have been previously induced or exacerbated by belief in sorcery and witchcraft, fear of spirits, and so on.

Many authors likewise mention that the rallying of the group around the individual, providing attention and visible support, is therapeutic. A few have noted how conflictual and anxiety-producing social relations may be realigned by the healer during the ceremonies in ways seldom achieved in our own society. Particularly insightful in developing this theme are Turner's (1964) analysis of a Ndembu ritual, Freeman's (1967) description of the Dayak, and Fox's (1964) presentation of Cochiti therapy. Fox tells of an especially interesting case in which the cure was effected through adoption into another clan, thus providing the patient with a supportive social group. Prince (1964a: 113) also mentions healers who move Yoruba patients to new compounds, and Madsen (1964:430-37) describes how a Mexican-American *curandero* helps a patient resolve value conflicts clearly due to culture change by beneficially realigning her social relations.

Temporary indulgence of wish fantasies and acting out of forbidden desires have been often singled out as effective kinds of abreaction or catharsis (e.g., Harris 1957, Kiev 1961, J. G. Kennedy 1967, Messing 1957, Mischel and Mischel 1958, Prince 1964a). The reasonable assumption is that this safety-valve function for repressed impulses is beneficial, helping individuals in unrewarding social positions to maintain a functioning equilibrium.

The generally unelaborated invocation of the notions of faith, suggestion, group support, and catharsis is generally about as far as most writers go in explaining the apparent effectiveness of native curing methods, but these processes do not appear to describe all that is happening in many cases.

Some Suggestive Leads

In his book *Battle for the Mind*, Sargant (1957) calls attention to the similarities of physiological overstimulation in these curing ceremonies and conditions of sudden abreaction and personality change after battle fatigue, features of brainwashing, and Pavlovian experiments in which dogs are subjected to stresses sufficient to induce neurological collapse. He suggests that such collapse occurs in trance ceremonies, and that in this condition suggestibility is increased so that some learned patterns may be disrupted and new convictions and patterns implanted. Some experiments by Neher (1961, 1962), which have apparently never been followed up, also show that certain patterns of drumming (five to nine cycles per second) produce electroencephalographic patterns in the auditory cortex which are similar to the dissociative effects of photic driving with flashing lights. If such studies were continued they might aid us to understand how these stimuli cause certain kinds of general physiological changes correlated with behavioral dissociation; but it is doubtful that such studies alone could fully explain how faith, suggestion, and catharsis, interacting with these stresses, produce symptom change or personality transformation, and why the added stress is not pathogenic.

One of the persistent attributes of these curing rituals is the production of altered states of consciousness, one feature of which is deep regression to infantile modes of cognition and action. At one end of the range of effects is complete personality change resembling conversion. As Leighton says (Prince, Leighton, and May 1968:1178), "It is as if the whole procedure brought about a situation in which the structure of the patient's personality becomes soft, and then after the emotional crisis, resets in a new form."

The similarities of this change to some effects of psychedelic drug therapy are striking; for example, ". . . creative or revelatory experiences involve a *temporary* and *voluntary* breaking up of perceptual constancies, permitting one to shake free from dead literalism, to recombine the old familiar elements into new, imaginative, amusing, or beautiful patterns" (Mogar 1969:389). The analogy to shock treatments, which can have similar effects for equally unknown reasons, is also evident. But whatever may be the specific processes involved, it appears that an essential feature of breaking up the "sick" pattern in trance curing is the

inducement of a profound regression. In our society degrees of regression are purposefully induced in the controlled settings of psychoanalysis and hypnotherapy, but outside of these contexts such behavior is regarded as a sign of pathology. However, recent research on psychedelic drugs, meditation, peak experiences, mystic enlightenment, and altered states of consciousness have enlarged our understanding of regression.

The phrase "regression in service of the ego," coined by Ernest Kris (1958), has been invoked in many quarters to describe the beneficial qualities of "altered state" experiences. For example, Maupin (1969) speaks of "adaptive regression" in Zen mediation, and Pahnke and Richards (1969:423), describing experiments with psychedelic drugs, use "regression in service of the ego" for the salutary effects noted (see also McGlothlin 1967). Bourguignon (1965) extends this idea in her analysis of Haitian voodoo (*vodun*) ceremonies. She suggests that in conditions of environmental restriction and daily life impoverishment, such activities may release creative forces. Dissociative trance behavior may operate to enlarge the field of action for the self, rather than to restrict it. She therefore views it as a healthy, positive "dissociation in service of the ego."

What we know about the beneficial effects of a supportive environment as opposed to a nonsupportive one in psychedelic experiments and peyote ceremonies, as well as what is known about controlled regression in psychotherapy, suggests that the *environment* and *meaning* of the "altered state" experience may be critical factors in producing therapeutic effects. Such effects thus seem related to the uses of symbols, rituals, and myths, and it is probable that more is happening than provision of a background of meaning and the heightening of self-esteem through identification with spiritual powers or cosmic forces in a group setting (Frank 1961; Prince, Leighton, and May 1968).

Wallace (1966:233-42) has provided some helpful ideas concerning this process. He defines ritual as stereotyped communication, which through the concentration of combined meanings packed into symbols can communicate several messages simultaneously to different levels of the participants' consciousness. The overt message content of rituals can have a conscious therapeutic intention—ideological, salvational, or whatever—while at the same time, on a deeper level, the ritual makes a statement about the nature of the world. "The stereotype of ritual is orderliness raised to an extraordinary degree; rituals are predictable, the contingent probabilities in claims or ritual events are near unity; the myth upon which the ritual is based describes a world in which chaos is being or is to be replaced by order" (Wallace 1966:238).

A ritual structure may thus communicate some of the most potent metamessages of "order" known to man. We may hypothesize that in the altered state of consciousness typical of trance ceremonies, the ritual communicates its multileveled therapeutic messages of profound meaning more directly to the unconscious of patients and participants than is possible in a state of ordinary awareness. The direct suggestions of the curer, together with the support, disapproval of symptoms, and urging to get well expressed by the audience, are more specific therapeutic messages. In conjunction with the powerful symbolic statements of meaning and order, they have a powerful impact upon the "open" consciousness of the patient in an "altered state." Some of the personality changes that take place under these conditions can be described as a special kind of *relearning*, and Wallace (1966:239-43) has provided us with a

suggestive outline of "trance learning" that should be consulted by those interested in this topic.

Lévi-Strauss's (1963) brilliant analysis of a South American Indian curing ceremony for a woman in difficult childbirth amplifies these ideas. A shaman enacts a mythical journey and battle with a demon who has captured the woman's spiritual double. In recounting the myth he symbolically identifies each of the dramatic events with specific bodily organs and functions of the woman. By a powerfully evocative oscillation of mythical and physiological themes, the problem organs of the patient are symbolically translated into the setting and actions of the myth. This "psychological manipulation of the sick organs" is brought to a climax when the shaman symbolically penetrates the womb and frees the captive soul, and the woman delivers.

Such a method is obviously very suggestive for psychosomatic ailments, but Lévi-Strauss also points out parallels with some work with schizophrenics by psychoanalyst Marie Sechahaye. Sechahaye became aware that the symbolic system of speech was not powerful enough to reach these patients, and was convinced that only symbolic *actions* could reach the deeply buried complexes. Results were obtained when she acted out symbolic events, such as the weaning of a regressed patient whose conflicts stemmed from the period of breast feeding.

Lévi-Strauss's (1963:200) interpretation parallels Wallace's analysis of the levels of ritual symbolism: "The symbolic load of such acts qualifies them as a language. Actually, the therapist holds a dialogue with the patient, not through the spoken word, but in concrete actions, that is, *genuine rites* which penetrate the screen of consciousness to carry their message directly to the unconscious."

These curing ceremonies bear some

resemblance to such Western treatment modalities as psychodrama, hypnotherapy, and their derivatives (*Gestalt* therapy and so on). J. L. Moreno (1959: 1376), the originator of psychodrama, claimed such a similarity, and Seda-Bonilla (1969:493) has recently pointed out some interesting parallels between psychodrama and the curing practices of a Puerto Rican spiritualist healer. It is obvious that psychodrama does incorporate certain aspects of the primitive healing drama. It stresses staging, acting, the interpersonal context of the problem, social support, and the indirect communication of intermediaries ("auxiliary egos"). It also uses suggestion, produces catharsis, and so on. However, psychodrama lacks critical ingredients of the trance healing ceremony, such as the production of altered states of consciousness and the employment of powerful transcendent symbolism and ritual, which I have indicated may be keys to the effectiveness of ritual healing.

Primitive therapy is an area where comparative study may be very productive, both in practical values and in human behavior theory. It seems clear that despite its apparent diversity, Western psychiatry still works within a relatively narrow range of assumptions, which restrict its ability to utilize the inventions of other societies. On the other hand, the cross-cultural data we now have, though very suggestive, is inadequate. The provocative clues must be followed up with detailed studies of patients, therapeutic and antitherapeutic interventions, and outcomes. Modern technology provides some means of studying these phenomena in new ways. For example, newly developed portable EEG equipment may be used to follow up Neher's pioneer experiments with auditory drives under field conditions (Prince 1968*a*:121-37). Such equipment could also be used to study various kinds of trance states in

healers and patients (Kasmatsu and Hirae 1969, Kamiya 1969), and to diagnose differentially such conditions as epilepsy, hypoglycemia, and others. This type of study can be accomplished only by the cooperation of imaginative anthropologists and psychiatrists who understand each other's languages, and are willing to spend the necessary time and effort.

ADDITIONAL TOPICS IN CULTURAL PSYCHIATRY

Though the topics discussed above are those that have received the most attention in cultural psychiatry, I have not meant to imply that they are the only ones of interest to the field. For reasons of space, I have not discussed the perenially sticky concepts of "deviance" and "normality," for example. It has probably been apparent that my pragmatic working position is fairly close to that of Honigmann (1968) and Wegrocki (1939), who distinguish intrapsychic conflicts and "psychiatric abnormality," characterized by measureable cognitive and emotional deficits and distortions, from "social abnormality," which is characterized by normative deviance and is culturally defined. A few other specific topics that may hold promise for future united research efforts of anthropologists and psychiatrists are the following.

MENTAL RETARDATION

Our knowledge of mental deficits, their distributions, the effects of various attitudes and practices upon them, and their social significance is small enough for the Western industrialized societies, but for the Third World it is practically nonexistent (Edgerton 1970). Despite the lack of data, several assumptions about such handicapped individuals in "primitive" societies are common: (1) that the severely retarded are typically killed, (2) that the mildly retarded may not be seen as anything out of the ordinary, (3) that the mildly retarded, if they are recognized as such, are not stigmatized, and (4) that the mildly retarded do not constitute a social problem. Edgerton (1970) reviewed the small amount of data available in the Human Relations Area Files and made an independent search of the ethnographic literature on these topics. What evidence he could glean indicated that though there are isolated data supporting each of the four common assumptions, they are generally incorrect. The evidence, scant as it is, showed a great range of variation of response to the mentally retarded. A further search for correlations between environmental difficulty and stress also indicated that there is a little evidence to support the hypotheses of economic determinism in this regard. Many peoples in the most harsh environments, under great stress of periodic food deprivation, are quite kind and gentle toward retardates, whereas cruelty and stigma are sometimes found among groups in much richer and more supportive environments.

It seems evident that here is a great neglected area of research, one that could tell us something about general processes of social stigmatization and provide badly needed contrastive data for those working with these problems in American and European contexts. I know of only two serious attempts by anthropologists to consider problems of this type. Sarason and Gladwin (1958) have produced an excellent study of psychological and cultural problems in mental subnormality, and Edgerton (1967) made a fine field study of the social adaptation of low-IQ individuals after discharge from a large California hospital. Sarason and Gladwin's work indicates how study of the subnormal can throw light on general problems of socialization and cultural transmis-

sion, while Edgerton's book reveals insights into general processes of deviance and stigma through examination of the coping behaviors of these handicapped individuals. Much could be learned by carrying these research interests in subnormality into other cultural contexts.

DRUG RESPONSE

For some time it has been reported that members of different cultural groups differed in their response to psychotropic drugs. For example, Divry, Bobon, and Collard, working in Europe, reported strong antipsychotic reactions to Ri625-haloperidol (cited in Collard 1962), but these results could not be duplicated in the United States. Later Collard (1962:S118) carefully compared the reaction thresholds of a group of Belgian psychotic patients with a group of Americans of identical diagnosis, and found that the Americans needed about ten times the Belgians' dose of haloperidol to get the same results. In other studies U.S. patients could tolerate twice the amount that German patients could.

Along with scattered reports, like that by Aall-Jilek (1965) citing relatively low dosages of phenobarbital used to suppress epileptic attacks among the Wapagoro of Tanzania, findings such as Collard's induced H. B. M. Murphy (1969a) to conduct a survey on the subject. The impressionistic reports he received from forty-six doctors in all parts of the world gave mixed assessments, but several cross-cultural differences seemed to exist: between European and American schizophrenics exposed to disinhibiting neuroleptics, between Malay and Euro-American schizophrenics exposed to chloropromazine, and between Anglo-Protestant and Irish-Catholic geriatric patients exposed to weak doses of a stimulant and a sedative.

There are obviously many methodological difficulties in research in this area, in addition to problems of diagnosis and experimental conditions. Cultural variables related to socialization, personality type, anxiety levels, and so on may be confounded with physiological factors of genetics, race, and diet. Nevertheless, this is a potentially promising area of cross-cultural psychiatric research.

THERAPEUTIC COMMUNITIES

One outcome of the increased psychiatric understanding of social factors in mental disorder has been the attempt to create milieus or communities that are more therapeutic than traditional hospitals (e.g., Jones 1953, Rappaport 1960, Kraft 1966). Though these programs constitute experiments, often with rather vague notions of psychosocial process, they emphasize the therapeutic aspects of more natural, meaningful environments than traditional institutions can provide. They stress activity, involvement, creation of natural human relationships, and independence, as opposed to the passivity, withdrawal, dependence, and constricted pattern of relationships that often seem to add an extra layer of pathology to a hospital patient's existing problems.

These ideas were given impetus by studies of hospital milieus by anthropologists (e.g., Caudill 1958, Salisbury 1962) and sociologists (e.g., Stanton and Swartz 1954, Goffman 1961), which have documented the psychologically impairing social processes inherent in much of traditional mental hospital treatment. These researches show that what constitutes "good mental health" has been largely taken for granted, and that treatment has been hampered by the controlled artificiality of hospital structures. However, studies of natural therapeutic communities could be even more fruitful in develop-

ing criteria for future positive action. The most famous of such natural communities is the colony at Gheel in Belgium, whose citizens have been receiving people with mental problems into their community and homes for centuries (Sano 1930, Kilgour 1936). Another such community with almost as long a history has been reported in Japan (Kumasaka 1967:666-67). There may well be other such communities in Third World countries, and detailed field research in such natural experiments might be expected to throw light upon the still obscure principles upon which an effectively therapeutic environment is actually based.

One of the most interesting approaches in this area is Lambo's attempt to integrate modern treatment methods with a village therapeutic community in Nigeria (Lambo 1961, 1964; Osborne 1969). He uses modern drugs and therapeutic techniques in conjunction with native rituals and cooperation with indigenous healers in a natural setting in which villagers are trained to handle people with psychiatric problems. It is to be hoped that Lambo's innovations will be picked up and expanded elsewhere, and that social scientists will grasp the unique opportunities for study that such experiments provide.

ANTITHERAPEUTIC SOCIAL MILIEUS

Perhaps of even greater significance is the related set of questions regarding what constitutes a "sick society" or disordered social system. Ruth Benedict (1934) raised this issue by her use of psychiatric labels, such as "paranoid" and "megalomaniac," to characterize typical personality types of such societies as the Dobu and Kwakiutl. This rather indiscriminate labeling of whole groups with the implicitly pejorative language of psychiatry was rightly decried in many quarters (e.g., M. K. Opler, ed., 1959, Wallace 1961*b*). The widespread reaction against such ethnocentrism, however, seems to have directed attention away from the importance of the possible contribution that may be made by study of culturally patterned systems of psychic stress or pathology-producing institutions.

It would be absurd, of course, to assert or imply that large numbers of any society are psychotic. However, there is good theoretical and empirical reason to suppose that neuroses and many other emotional disorders may be regularly produced in high frequencies in some social groups. This follows from our knowledge of the ways in which early socialization processes and later stresses may produce many such patterns. The findings on social, psychological, and physical stress in situations of war, poverty, disease, and disaster, combined with the growing understanding of the processes of socialization and mental functioning, indicate that it is time to reopen this whole area of inquiry. Erich Fromm (1955) has made a contribution to this subject in his discussion of "culturally patterned defects" and his attempts to grapple with the difficult problem of what constitute "healthy" social milieus. No matter how critical we may be of such efforts, we should seriously attempt to overcome some of our relativistic-functional biases and deal with the apparent empirical reality of pathogenic differences in societies and cultures. Gruenberg's provocative article on "socially shared psychopathology" (1957) is suggestive, and I have recently given some preliminary consideration to some aspects of this problem with regard to witchcraft systems and war (J. G. Kennedy 1969, 1970). Despite the obvious conceptual, methodological, and moral difficulties in such analyses, concentration of thinking and research on this topic could be of great practical and theoretical significance.

CONCLUSION

I have tried to portray a potentially rich field of social research, one that is beset with extraordinary conceptual and methodological difficulties. The examples I have chosen were selected not only to illustrate these difficulties, but also to indicate the promise that the collaboration of psychiatry and anthropology may offer. In spite of formidable obstacles, this is an exciting area of research. Much more intensive and prolonged multidisciplinary attacks on these problems seem called for. Short-term surveys, studies of hospital populations, and impressionistic accounts of therapeutic rituals cannot fill the bill.

The methodological Achilles' heel of many studies is in the diagnosis and appraisal of cases of mental disorder. As we have seen, much of this difficulty is due to lack of etiological knowledge, the multifactorial nature of mental disorder, differential cultural appraisal of similar behaviors (i.e., differential definitions of normality), and problems of cross-cultural communication.

One of the most promising approaches toward solution of the diagnostic problem is the development of culture-free tests, i.e., biochemical, neurophysiological, and behavioral indicators of psychic vulnerability. So far biochemical studies have failed to find any critical chemical elements in body fluids that may distinguish psychotics from normals, but Zubin and Kleitzman (1966) report a number of neurophysiological studies that hold some promise for distinguishing these groups. Differences between schizophrenics and normals in perception of time, in startle responses, in pupillary reaction, in ability to tap in synchrony with a repetitive click, and in elicited EEG patterns have been reported. If validated, such tests could provide culture-free diagnoses of at least the most severe psychoses. Such leads are still tentative and untested in the cross-cultural crucible, and it seems that we still must rely on what Zubin and Kleitzman (1966:497) call "culture dependent" techniques of interviewing and observation for the foreseeable future. Along this line, Brody (1966), Prince and Mombour (1967), and H. B. M. Murphy (1969*b*) have made recent contributions to methods of cross-cultural interviewing, while De Vos (1965) has pointed out the continuing usefulness of the Rorschach in cross-cultural diagnosis.

It appears that the best approaches will combine the intensive long-term techniques of anthropological observation of groups with the clinical methods of psychiatry. In epidemiology much more systematic attention must be devoted to each case of a sample and long-term follow-ups made. Prospective and retrospective studies of selected cohorts of individuals who are followed throughout long segments of their lives may be one of the most effective methods of overcoming the research problems in this field. The important long-term studies of Douglas on premature infants (1960), Terman and his group on gifted children (Terman and Oden 1947, Oden 1968), and the newer methods of getting at life history data reported by Roff and Ricks (1970) are suggestive of the kinds of techniques that should be utilized in cross-cultural work. We need more rigorous studies of perception and attitude of population to mental disorder of the kind pioneered by Edgerton (1966), and more rigorous studies of shamans and curers like those of Fabrega and Silver (1970) and Sasaki (1969).

Another suggestive line of research would be cross-cultural studies of family process in relation to mental disorder. Excellent techniques for observing families and groups have been developed, but to my knowledge they have not been used in the diverse family structures found outside the Western world.

The theories of the research groups led by Gregory Bateson, Theodore Lidz, John Spiegal, L. C. Winne, and others would benefit from testing in very contrasting family types. (See Mishler and Waxler 1966 and Handelman 1967 for reviews and examples of this work.)

More experimental studies of the type pioneered by Collis (1966) should be undertaken on a large scale. Just as it is obvious that psychiatrists working in these countries need an anthropological background, it is evident that medical expertise is required for cross-cultural psychiatric studies, since much more attention must be devoted than heretofore to the physiological variables related to mental disorder. Only by massive, concentrated, and sophisticated cross-disciplinary efforts can the theoretical riches latent in the cross-cultural approach to mental disorder be discovered. Young anthropologists and psychiatrists have a unique opportunity to contribute to the understanding of man as well as to the alleviation of his pain if they rise to this research challenge.

REFERENCES

Aall-Jilek, L. M.
    1965   Epilepsy in the Wapagoro Tribe in Tanganyika. *Acta Psychiatrica Scandinavica* 41:57-86.
Aberle, David F.
    1952   Arctic Hysteria and Latah in Mongolia. *Transactions of the New York Academy of Sciences,* ser. 2, 22: 291-97.
    1966   *The Peyote Religion Among the Navajo.* Chicago: Aldine.
Ackerknecht, Erwin H.
    1943   Psychopathology, Primitive Medicine, and Primitive Culture. *Bulletin of the History of Medicine* 14:30-67.
Adelman, F.
    1955   Toward a Psycho-Cultural Interpretation of Latah. *Davidson Journal of Anthropology* 1:69-75.
Al-Issa, Ihsan
    1968   Cross-Cultural Studies of Symptoma-

tology in Schizophrenia. *Canadian Psychiatric Association Journal* 13: 147-58.

Allentuck, S., and K. Bowman
1942 Psychiatric Aspects of Marihuana Intoxication. *American Journal of Psychiatry*, September.

Andersson, E.
1958 *Messianic Popular Movements in the Lower Congo*. Uppsala, Sweden: Studia Ethnographica Uppsalensia.

Anisimov, A. F.
1963 The Shaman's Tent of the Evenks and the Origin of the Shamanistic Rite. In *Studies in Siberian Shamanism*, ed. H. N. Michael. Toronto: University of Toronto Press.

Anumonye, A.
1966 A Critical Discussion of the Findings of "Psychophysiologic Symptoms" in the Cornell-Aro Survey. *Journal of Psychosomatic Research* 10:95-100.

Asuni, T.
1964 Socio-Psychiatric Problems of Cannabis in Nigeria. *Bulletin on Narcotics* 16:17-28.

Beck, Aron
1962 Reliability of Psychiatric Diagnosis: A Critique of Systematic Studies. *American Journal of Psychiatry* 119:210-16.

Benabud, A.
1957 Psychopathological Aspects of Cannabis Use in Morocco: Statistics for the Year 1956. *Bulletin on Narcotics* 9:1-8.

Benedict, P. R., and I. Jacks
1954 Mental Illness in Primitive Societies. *Psychiatry* 17:377-89.

Benedict, Ruth
1934 Culture and the Abnormal. *Journal of Genetic Psychology* 1:60-64.

Blum, R. H.
1968 Social and Epidemiological Aspects of Psychopharmacology. In *Psychopharmacology: Dimensions and Perspectives*, ed. C. R. B. Joyce, pp. 243-82. London: Tavistock.

Blum, R. H., et al.
1969 *Society and Drugs*, vol. 1. San Francisco: Jossey-Bass.

Bogoras, W.
1907 The Chuckchee Religion. *Memoirs of the American Museum of Natural History* 11, no. 2.

Bourguignon, Erika
1965 The Self, the Behavioral Environment, and the Theory of Spirit Possession. In *Context and Meaning in Cultural Anthropology*, ed. M. Spiro. New York: Free Press, Macmillan.

Boyer, L. Bryce
1961 Notes on the Personality Structure of a North American Indian Shaman. *Journal of the Hillside Hospital* 10:14-33.

1962 Remarks on the Personality of Shamans, with Special Reference to the Apaches of the Mescalero Indian Reservation. In *The Psychoanalytic Study of Society*, ed. W. Meunsterberger, vol. 2. New York: International Universities Press.

1964a Further Remarks Concerning Shamans and Shamanism. In *Israel Annals of Psychiatry and Related Disciplines* 2:235-57.

1964b Folk Psychiatry of the Apaches of the Mescalero Indian Reservation. In *Magic, Faith, and Healing*, ed. A. Kiev. New York: Free Press of Glencoe, Macmillan.

Boyer, L. Bryce et al.
1964 Comparison of the Shamans and Pseudo-Shamans of the Apaches of the Mescalero Indian Reservation: A Rorschach Study. *Journal of Projective Techniques and Personality Development* 28:173-80.

Bremer, J.
1951 A Social Psychiatric Investigation of a Small Community in Northern Norway. *Acta Psychiatrica*, supplement 62.

Brill, A. A.
1913 Piblokto or Hysteria Among Peary's Eskimos. *Journal of Nervous and Mental Disease* 40:514-20.

Brody, Eugene B.
1966 Recording Cross-Culturally Useful Psychiatric Interview Data: Experience from Brazil. *American Journal of Psychiatry* 123:446-56.

Burton-Bradley, B. G.
1968 The Amok Syndrome in Papua and New Guinea. *Medical Journal of Australia* 1:252.

1970 The Amok Runner in Cross-Cultural

Perspective. Paper presented at meetings of the Anthropological Association of the Pacific, Honolulu.

Calloway, Henry
1870 *The Religious System of the Amazulu*. London: Folk-Lore Society.

Carothers, J. C.
1947 A Study of Mental Derangements in Africans. *Journal of Mental Science* 93:548-97.
1953 *The African Mind in Health and Disease*. Monograph no. 17. Geneva: World Health Organization.
1959 Culture, Psychiatry, and the Written Word. *Psychiatry* 22:307-20.

Carstairs, G. M.
1954 Daru and Bhang: Culture Factors in the Choice of an Intoxicant. *Quarterly Journal Studies of Alcohol* 15:220-36.

Castañeda, Carlos
1968 *The Teachings of Don Juan*. Berkeley: University of California Press.

Caudill, William
1958 *The Psychiatric Hospital as a Small Society*. Cambridge: Harvard University Press.

Cawte, J. E.
1966 Australian Aborigines in Mental Hospitals. *Oceania* 36:264-82.

Chance, Norman
1964 A Cross-Cultural Study of Social Cohesion and Depression. *Transcultural Psychiatric Research Review* 1:19-21.

Chapman, L. J., and J. Baxter
1963 The Process-Reactive Distinction and Patients' Subculture. *Journal of Nervous and Mental Disease* 136:352-59.

Chodoff, Paul, and Henry Lyons
1958 Hysteria, the Hysterical Personality, and Hysterical Conversion. *American Journal of Psychiatry* 114:734-40.

Cohen, Yehudi
1961 *Social Structure and Personality*. New York: Holt, Rinehart & Winston.

Collard, J.
1962 Drug Responses in Different Ethnic Groups. *Journal of Neuropsychiatry* 3, supplement 1:S114-21.

Collis, R. J.
1966 Physical Health and Psychiatric Disorder in Nigeria. *Transactions of the American Philosophical Society* 54.

Collomb, H.
1964 Psychosomatic Conditions in Africa: Summary. *Transcultural Psychiatric Research Review* 1:130.

Czaplicka, Marie
1914 *Aboriginal Siberia: A Study in Social Anthropology*. Oxford: Clarendon Press.

Dement, William
1966 Psychophysiology of Sleep and Dreams. In *American Handbook of Psychiatry*, ed. S. Arieti, 3:290-332. New York: Basic Books.

Devereux, George
1956 Normal and Abnormal. In *Some Uses of Anthropology: Theoretical and Applied*. Washington, D.C.: Anthropological Society of Washington.
1961a *Mohave Ethnopsychiatry and Suicide: The Psychiatric Knowledge and the Psychic Disturbances of an Indian Tribe*. Ethnology Bulletin no. 175. Washington, D.C.: Smithsonian Institution.
1961b Shamans as Neurotics. *American Anthropologist* 63:188-90.

De Vos, G.
1965 Transcultural Diagnosis of Mental Health by Means of Psychological Tests. In *Transcultural Psychiatry*, ed. A. V. S. De Reuck and R. Porter. Boston: Little, Brown.

De Vos, G., and A. Hippler
1969 Cultural Psychology: Comparative Studies in Human Behavior. In *Handbook of Social Psychology*, ed. G. Lindzey and E. Aronson, 2nd. ed. Reading, Mass.: Addison-Wesley.

Dhunjibhoy, J. E.
1930 A Brief Résumé of the Types of Insanity Met With in India, with a Full Description of "Indian Hemp Insanity" Peculiar to the Country. *Journal of Mental Science* 76:254-64.

Dobkin, Marlene
1968 Trichocereus Pachonsi: A Mescaline Cactus Used in Folk Healing in Peru. *Economic Botany* 22:191-94.

Dobkin de Ríos, Marlene
1969- Folk Healing with a Psychedelic Cactus in North Coastal Peru. *International Journal of Social Psychiatry* 15.
1970

1972 *Visionary Vine*. San Francisco: Chandler.

Dohrenwend, Bruce P., and Barbara Dohrenwend
1969 *Social Status and Psychological Disorder*. New York: Wiley.

Douglas, J. W. B.
1960 Premature Children in Primary Schools. *British Journal of Medicine* 1:1008.

Du Bois, Cora
1960 *The People of Alor*. Cambridge: Harvard University Press. Originally published 1944.

Dunham, H. Warren
1969 City Core and Suburban Fringe: Distribution Pattern of Mental Illness. In *Changing Perspectives in Mental Health*, ed. S. C. Plog and R. B. Edgerton. New York: Holt, Rinehart & Winston.

Eaton, Joseph, and Robert Weil
1955 *Culture and Mental Disorders*. Glencoe, Ill.: Free Press.

Edgerton, R. B.
1966 Conceptions of Psychosis in Four East African Societies. *American Anthropologist* 68:408-25.
1967 *The Cloak of Competence*. Berkeley: University of California Press.
1969 On the "Recognition" of Mental Illness. In *Changing Perspectives in Mental Illness*, ed. S. C. Plog and R. B. Edgerton. New York: Holt, Rinehart & Winston.
1970 Mental Retardation in Non-Western Societies: Toward a Cross-Cultural Perspective on Incompetence. In *Social and Cultural Aspects of Mental Retardation*, ed. H. C. Haywood. New York: Appleton-Century-Crofts.
1971 A Traditional African Psychiatrist. *Southwestern Journal of Anthropology* 27:259-78.

Efron D., et al
1967 *Ethnopharmacologic Search for Psychoactive Drugs*. U.S. Department of Health, Education, and Welfare. Washington D.C.: U.S. Government Printing Office.

Eliade, Mircea
1964 *Shamanism: Archaic Techniques of Ecstasy*. London: Routledge & Kegan Paul.

Eysenck, H.

1966 *The Effects of Psychotherapy*. New York: International Science Press.

Fabrega, Horatio, Jr., and D. Silver
1970 Some Social and Psychological Properties of Zinacanteco Shamans. *Behavioral Science* 15:471-86.

Faris, Robert
1934 Some Observations on the Incidence of Schizophrenia in Primitive Society. *Journal of Abnormal and Social Psychology* 29:30-31.

Fernández-Marina, Ramón
1961 The Puerto Rican Syndrome: Its Dynamics and Cultural Determinants. *Psychiatry* 24:79-82.

Field, M. J.
1960 *Search for Security: An Ethnopsychiatric Study of Rural Ghana*. Evanston, Ill.: Northwestern University Press.
1968 Chronic Psychosis in Rural Ghana. *British Journal of Psychiatry* 114:31-33.

Field, Peter
1962 A New Cross-Cultural Study of Drunkenness. In *Society, Culture, and Drinking Patterns*, ed. D. J. Pittman and C. R. Snyder. New York: Wiley.

Firth, Raymond
1967 Ritual and Drama in Malay Spirit Mediumship. *Comparative Studies in Society and History* 2:190-207.

Fogelson, R. D.
1965 Psychological Theories of Windigo "Psychosis" and a Preliminary Application of a Models Approach. In *Context and Meaning in Cultural Anthropology*, ed. M. E. Spiro. New York: Free Press, Macmillan.

Forster, E. F. B.
1958 A Short Psychiatric Review from Ghana. In *Mental Disorders and Mental Health in Africa South of the Sahara*. Commission de Cooperation Technique en Afrique au Sud du Sahara, publication no. 35. Geneva: World Health Organization.

Fortes, Meyer, and Doris Mayer
1965 Psychosis and Social Change Among the Tallensi of Northern Ghana. *Cahiers d'études africaines* 6, no. 21:5-40.

Fox, Robin
1964 Witchcraft and Clanship in Cochiti

Therapy. In *Magic, Faith, and Healing*, ed. A. Kiev. New York: Free Press of Glencoe, Macmillan.

Frank, Jerome D.
1961 *Persuasion and Healing*. Baltimore: Johns Hopkins University Press.
1965 The Role of Cognitions in Illness and Healing. In *Research in Psychotherapy*, vol. 2, ed. H. H. Strupp and L. Luborsky. Washington, D.C.: American Psychological Association.
1968 The Role of Hope in Psychotherapy (with Critical Commentary). *International Journal of Psychiatry* 5: 383-412.

Freeman, Derek
1967 Shaman and Incubus. In *The Psychoanalytic Study of Society*, ed. W. Muensterberger and S. Axelrad, vol. 4. New York: International Universities Press.

Freud, Sigmund
1950 *Totem and Taboo*. New York: Norton

Fromm, Erich
1955 *The Sane Society*. New York: Rinehart.

Funkelstein, D. H., and H. Hitson
1959 Family Patterns and Paranoidal Personality Structure in Boston and Burma. *International Journal of Social Psychiatry* 5:182-90.

Furst, Peter
1972 *Flesh of the Gods*. New York: Praeger.

Gelfand, M.
1964 Psychiatric Disorders as Recognized by the Shona. In *Magic, Faith, and Healing*, ed. A. Kiev. New York: Free Press of Glencoe, Macmillan.

Gillin, John
1948 Magical Fright. *Psychiatry* 11:387-400.

Glick, L. B.
1968 Comment on "Possession in the New Guinea Highlands." *Transcultural Psychiatric Research Review* 5:200-205.

Goffman, E.
1961 *Asylums*. New York: Anchor Books, Doubleday.

Gordon, H. L.
1934 Amentia in the East African. *Eugenics Review* 25:223-35.
1936 Inquiry into the Correlation of Civili-

zation and Mental Disorder in the Kenya Native. *East African Medical Journal* 12:327-35.

Gove, Walter
1970 Sleep Deprivation: A Cause of Psychotic Disorganization. *American Journal of Sociology* 75:782-99.

Gruenberg, Ernest M.
1957 Socially Shared Psychopathology. In *Explorations in Social Psychiatry*, ed. A. Leighton et al. New York: Basic Books.
1964 Review of L. Srole et al., *Mental Health in the Metropolis: The Midtown Manhattan Study*. In *The Study of Abnormal Behavior*, ed. M. Zax and G. Stricker. New York: Macmillan.

Grygier, Tadeusz
1948 Psychiatric Observations in the Arctic. *British Journal of Psychiatry* 39:84-96.

Gussow, Z.
1960 Pibloktoq (Hysteria) Among the Polar Eskimos: An Ethnopsychiatric Study. *Psychoanalytic Study of Society* 1:218-36.

Hall, Edward
1966 *The Hidden Dimension*. New York: Doubleday.

Hallowell, A. I.
1934 Culture and Mental Disorders. *Journal of Abnormal and Social Psychology* 29:1-9.

Handelman, Don
1967 The Development of the Washo Shaman. *Ethnology* 6:444-64.
1968 Shamanizing on an Empty Stomach. *American Anthropologist* 70:353-56.

Harris, Grace
1957 Possession "Hysteria" in a Kenya Tribe. *American Anthropologist* 59:1046-66.

Helgason, Tómas
1964 Epidemiology of Mental Disorders in Iceland. *Acta Psychiatrica Scandinavica*, supplement 173:1-258.

Hes, Josef
1964 The Changing Social Role of the Yemenite Mori. In *Magic, Faith, and Healing*, ed. A. Kiev. New York: Free Press of Glencoe, Macmillan.

Hobbs, Nicholas
1962 Sources of Gain in Psychotherapy. *American Psychologist* 17:741-47.

Hoch, P., and H. L. Racklin
1941 An Evaluation of Manic-Depressive Psychosis in the Light of Follow-up Studies. *American Journal of Psychiatry* 97:833-34.

Holland, W. R., and Roland G. Tharp
1964 Highland Maya Psychotherapy. *American Anthropologist* 66:41-52.

Hollender, M. H., and S. J. Hirsch
1964 Hysterical Psychoses. *American Journal of Psychiatry* 120:1066-74.

Hollingshead, A., and F. Redlich
1958 *Social Class and Mental Illness.* New York: Wiley.

Honigmann, John J.
1954 *Culture and Personality.* New York: Harper.
1967 *Personality in Culture.* New York: Harper & Row.
1968 Toward a Distinction Between Psychiatric and Nonpsychiatric Judgments of Abnormality. In *Readings in the Psychology of Adjustment*, ed. L. Gorlow and W. Katkovsky. New York: McGraw-Hill.
1969 The Study of Personality in Primitive Societies. In *The Study of Personality: An Interdisciplinary Appraisal*, ed. E. Norbeck, D. Price-Williams, and W. McCord. New York: Holt, Rinehart & Winston.

Horden, A.
1968 Psychopharmacology: Some Historical Considerations. In *Psychopharmacology: Dimensions and Perspectives*, ed. C. R. B. Joyce. London: Tavistock.

Horton, D.
1943 The Function of Alcohol in Primitive Societies: A Cross-Cultural Study. *Quarterly Journal of Studies in Alcohol* 4:199-320.

Jones, Maxwell
1953 *The Therapeutic Community: A New Treatment Method in Psychiatry.* New York: Basic Books.

Kamiya, J.
1969 Operant Control of EEG Alpha Rhythm and Some of Its Reported Effects on Consciousness. In *Altered States of Consciousness*, ed. C. T. Tart. New York: Wiley.

Kaplan, B., and Thomas Plaut
1956 *Personality in a Communal Society:* *An Analysis of the Mental Health of the Hutterites.* Social Science Studies. Lawrence: University of Kansas Press.

Kardiner, Abram
1945 *The Psychological Frontiers of Society.* New York: Columbia University Press.

Kasmatsu, A., and T. Hirae
1969 An Electroencephalographic Study on the Zen Meditation (Zazen). In *Altered States of Consciousness*, ed. C. T. Tart. New York: Wiley.

Kennedy, John G.
1963 Tesguino Complex: The Role of Beer in Tarahumara Culture. *American Anthropologist* 65:620-40.
1967 Nubian Zar Ceremonies as Psychotherapy. *Human Organization* 26:185-94.
1969 Psychosocial Dynamics of Witchcraft Systems. *International Journal of Social Psychiatry* 15:165-78.
1970 Ritual and Intergroup Murder: Comments on War, Primitive and Modern. In *War and the Human Race*, ed. M. Walsh. The Hague: Elsevier Press.

Kiev, Ari
1961 Spirit Possession in Haiti. *American Journal of Psychiatry* 118:133-38.
1964 The Study of Folk Psychiatry. In *Magic, Faith, and Healing*, ed. A. Kiev. New York: Free Press of Glencoe, Macmillan.
1968 *Curanderismo: Mexican-American Folk Psychiatry.* New York: Free Press, Macmillan.
1969 Transcultural Psychiatry: Research Problems and Perspectives. In *Changing Perspectives in Mental Illness*, ed. S. C. Plog and R. B. Edgerton. New York: Holt, Rinehart & Winston.

Kiev, Ari, ed.
1964 *Magic, Faith, and Healing.* New York: Free Press of Glencoe, Macmillan.

Kilgour, A. J.
1936 Colony Gheel. *American Journal of Psychiatry* 92:959-65.

Klein, G.
1970 *Perception, Motives, and Personality.* New York: Knopf.

Kline, N. S.
1954 The Use of Rauwolfia Serpentina

Benth. in Neuropsychiatric Conditions. *Annals of the New York Academy of Science* 59:107-32.

1963 Psychiatry in Indonesia. *American Journal of Psychiatry* 119:809-815.

Kluckhohn, Clyde
1956 The Influence of Psychiatry in Anthropology in America During the Past One Hundred Years. In *Personality and Cultural Milieu*, ed. D. Haring. Syracuse, N.Y.: Syracuse University Press.

Kraepelin, E.
1904 *Psychiatrie*, 7th ed. Leipzig: Bund Barth.

Kraft, Alan M.
1966 The Therapeutic Community. In *American Handbook of Psychiatry*, ed. S. Arieti, 3:543-51. New York: Basic Books.

Kramer, M., E. S. Pollack, and R. Redick
1961 Studies of the Incidence and Prevalence of Hospitalized Mental Disorders in the United States: Current Status and Future Goals. In *Comparative Epidemiology of Mental Disorders*, ed. P. H. Hoch and J. Zubin. New York: Grune & Stratton.

Kreitman, N., et al.
1961 The Reliability of Psychiatric Diagnoses: An Analysis. *Journal of Mental Science* 107:887-908.

Kris, Ernest
1958 *Psychoanalytic Explorations in Art.* London: Allen & Unwin.

Kroeber, A. L.
1940 Psychosis or Social Sanction. *Character and Personality* 8:204-215.

Kumasaka, Y.
1964 A Culturally Determined Mental Reaction Among the Ainu. *Psychiatric Quarterly* 38:733-39.
1967 Iwakuya: Early Community Care of the Mentally Ill in Japan. *American Journal of Psychotherapy* 21:666-76.

La Barre, W.
1938 *The Peyote Cult.* Yale University Publications in Anthropology no. 19. New Haven: Yale University Press.
1947 Primitive Psychotherapy in Native American Cultures: Peyotism and Confession. *Journal of Abnormal and Social Psychology* 42:294-309.
1960 Twenty Years of Peyote Studies. *Current Anthropology* 1:45-60.
1964 Confession as Psychotherapy in American Indian Tribes. In *Magic, Faith, and Healing*, ed. A. Kiev. New York: Free Press of Glencoe, Macmillan.

Lambo, T. A.
1955 The Role of Cultural Factors in Paranoid Psychosis Among the Yoruba Tribe. *Journal of Mental Science* 101:239-66.
1956 Neuropsychiatric Observations in the Western Region of Nigeria. *British Medical Journal* 2:1388-94.
1960 Further Neuropsychiatric Observations in Nigeria. *British Medical Journal* 2:1696-1704.
1961 A Form of Social Psychiatry in Africa. *World Mental Health* 13, no. 4.
1962 Malignant Anxiety. *Journal of Mental Science* 108:256-64.
1964 Patterns of Psychiatric Care in Developing African Countries. In *Magic, Faith, and Healing*, ed. A. Kiev. New York: Free Press of Glencoe, Macmillan.
1965a Schizophrenic and Borderline States. In *Transcultural Psychiatry*, ed. A. V. S. De Reuck and R. Porter. Boston: Little, Brown.
1965b Medical and Social Problems of Drug Addiction in West Africa. *Bulletin on Narcotics* 17:3-13.

Landes, Ruth
1938 The Abnormal Among the Ojibwa Indians. *Journal of Abnormal and Social Psychology* 33:14-33.

Langner, T. S.
1962 A Twenty-Two Item Screening Score of Psychiatric Symptoms Indicating Impairment. *Journal of Health and Human Behavior* 3:269-76.

Langness, L. L.
1965 Hysterical Psychoses in the New Guinea Highlands: A Bena Bena Example. *Psychiatry* 28:258-77.
1967 Hysterical Psychosis: The Cross-Cultural Evidence. *American Journal of Psychiatry* 124:143-52.
1969 Possession in the New Guinea Highlands. *Transcultural Psychiatric Research Review* 6:95-100.

Lantis, Margaret
1960 *Eskimo Childhood and Interpersonal Relationships*. Seattle: University of

Washington Press.

Laubscher, B. J. F.
1937 *Sex, Custom, and Psychopathology: A Study of South African Pagan Natives.* London: Routledge & Kegan Paul.

Lee, R. B.
1966 The Sociology of !Kung Bushman Trance Performances. In *Trance and Possession States,* ed. R. Prince. Montreal: R. M. Bucke Memorial Society.

Leighton, A. H.
1959 *My Name Is Legion.* New York: Basic Books.

Leighton, A. H., and J. Hughes
1959 Culture as Causative of Mental Disorder. In *Causes of Mental Disorders: A Review of Epidemiological Knowledge,* pp. 341-83. Proceedings of round table held at Arden House, Harriman, N.Y. New York: Milbank Memorial Fund.

Leighton, A. H., et al.
1963 *Psychiatric Disorder Among the Yoruba.* Ithaca: Cornell University Press.

Leighton, A. H., John Clausen, and Robert N. Wilson, eds.
1957 *Explorations in Social Psychiatry.* New York: Basic Books.

Leighton, D. C., et al.
1963 *The Character of Danger: Psychiatric Symptoms in Selected Communities.* New York: Basic Books.

Lemkau, P., C. Tietze, and H. Cooper
1942 Mental Hygiene Problems in an Urban District. *Mental Hygiene* 26:100.

Lévi-Strauss, Claude
1963 The Effectiveness of Symbols. In C. Lévi-Strauss, *Structural Anthropology.* New York: Basic Books.

Lewis, I. M.
1966 Spirit Possession and Deprivation Cults. *Man* 1:307-29.

Lin, Tsung-yi
1953 A Study of the Incidence of Mental Disorder in Chinese and Other Cultures. *Psychiatry* 16:313-36.

Lin, Tsung-yi, and C. C. Standley
1962 *The Scope of Epidemiology in Psychiatry.* WHO Public Health Paper no. 16. Geneva: World Health Organization.

Lin, Tsung-yi, et al.
1969 Mental Disorders in Taiwan and Fifteen Years Later: A Preliminary Report. In *Mental Health Research in Asia and the Pacific,* ed. W. Caudill and T. Lin. Honolulu: East-West Center Press.

Linton, Ralph
1956 *Culture and Mental Disorders.* Springfield, Ill.: Charles C. Thomas.

Ludwig, A.
1966 Altered States of Consciousness. In *Trance and Possession States,* ed. R. Prince. Montreal: R. M. Bucke Memorial Society.

Lumholtz, Carl
1902 *Unknown Mexico,* vol. 1. New York: Scribner.

MacAndrew, Craig, and Robert B. Edgerton
1969 *Drunken Comportment: A Social Explanation.* Chicago: Aldine.

McGlothlin, W. H.
1967 Social and Para-Medical Aspects of Hallucinogenic Drugs. In *The Use of LSD in Psychotherapy and Alcoholism,* ed. H. A. Abramson. Indianapolis: Bobbs-Merrill.

Madsen, William
1964 Value Conflicts and Folk Psychotherapy in South Texas. In *Magic, Faith, and Healing,* ed. A. Kiev. New York: Free Press of Glencoe, Macmillan.

Malzberg, Benjamin, and Everett Lee
1956 *Migration and Mental Disease.* New York: Social Science Research.

Mann, J.
1965 *Changing Human Behavior.* New York: Scribner.

Maslow, A. H., and N. L. Mintz
1956 Effects of Esthetic Surroundings: I. Initial Effects of Three Esthetic Conditions upon Perceiving of "Energy" and "Well Being" in Faces. *Journal of Psychology* 41:247-54.

Maupin, Edward
1969 Individual Differences in Response to a Zen Meditation Exercise. In *Altered States of Consciousness,* ed. C. T. Tart. New York: Wiley.

Mehlman, R. D.
1961 The Puerto Rican Syndrome. *American Journal of Psychiatry* 118:328-32.

Meier, C. A.
1967 *Ancient Incubation and Modern*

Psychotherapy. Evanston, Ill.: Northwestern University Press.

Messing, S.
1957 Group Therapy and Social Status in the Zar Cult of Ethiopia. *American Anthropologist* 60:1120-26.

Miner, Horace M., and George De Vos
1960 *Oasis and Casbah: Algerian Culture and Personality in Change*. Museum of Anthropology Papers no. 15. Ann Arbor: University of Michigan.

Mintz, N. L.
1956 Effects of Esthetic Surroundings: II. Prolonged and Repeated Experience in a "Beautiful" and an "Ugly" Room. *Journal of Psychology* 41: 459-66.

Mischel, Walter, and Frances Mischel
1958 Psychological Aspects of Spirit Possession. *American Anthropologist* 60:249-60.

Mishler, E. G., and N. A. Scotch
1963 Sociocultural Factors in the Epidemiology of Schizophrenia. *Psychiatry* 26:315-51.

Mishler, E. G., and N. Waxler
1966 Family Interaction Process and Schizophrenia. *International Journal of Psychiatry* 2:375-415.

Mogar, R. E.
1969 Current Status and Future Trends in Psychedelic (LSD) Research. In *Altered States of Consciousness*, ed. C. T. Tart, pp. 381-97. New York: Wiley.

Moreno, J. L.
1959 Psychodrama. In *American Handbook of Psychiatry*, ed. S. Arieti, 2:1375-96. New York: Basic Books.

Muñoz, D. V., et al.
1966 Cross-Cultural Definitions Applied to the Study of Functional Psychoses in Chilean Mapuches. *British Journal of Psychiatry* 112:1205-15.

Murphy, H. B. M.
1963 The Cannabis Habit: A Review of Recent Psychiatric Literature. *Bulletin on Narcotics* 15:15-23.

1965 The Epidemiological Approach to Transcultural Psychiatric Research. In *Transcultural Psychiatry*, ed. A. De Reuck and R. Porter. Boston: Little, Brown.

1968 Sociocultural Factors in Schizophrenia: A Compromise Theory. In *Social Psychiatry*, ed. J. Zubin and F. Freyhan. New York: Grune & Stratton.

1969a Ethnic Variations in Drug Response: Results of an International Survey. *Transcultural Psychiatric Research Review* 6:5-23.

1969b Handling the Cultural Dimension in Psychiatric Research. *Social Psychiatry* 4:11-15.

1972 History and the Evolution of Syndromes: The Striking Case of Latah and Amok. In *Psychopathology: Contributions from the Biological, Behavioral, and Social Sciences*, ed. M. Hammer, K. Salzinger, and S. Sutton. New York: Wiley.

Murphy, H. B. M., E. Wittkower, and N. A. Chance
1964 Cross-Cultural Inquiry into the Symptomatology of Depression. *Transcultural Psychiatric Research Review* 1:5-18.

Murphy, H. B. M., et al.
1963 A Cross-Cultural Survey of Schizophrenic Symptomatology. *International Journal of Social Psychiatry* 9:237-49.

Murphy, Jane M.
1964 Psychotherapeutic Aspects of Shamanism on St. Lawrence Island. In *Magic, Faith, and Healing*, ed. A. Kiev. New York: Free Press of Glencoe, Macmillan.

Murphy, Jane M., and Leighton, A.
1965 *Approaches to Cross-Cultural Psychiatry*. Ithaca: Cornell University Press.

Nadel, S. F.
1965 A Study of Shamanism in the Nuba Mountains. In *Reader in Comparative Religion*, ed. W. A. Lessa and E. Z. Vogt. New York: Harper & Row.

Neher, Andrew
1961 Auditory Driving Observed with Scalp Electrodes in Normal Subjects. *Electroencephalography and Clinical Neurophysiology* 13.

1962 A Physiological Explanation of Unusual Behavior in Ceremonies Involving Drums. *Human Biology* 34:151-60.

Newman, Phillip
1964 Wild Man Behavior in a New Guinea Highlands Community. *American Anthropologist* 66:1-19.

Norris, Vera
1959 *Mental Illness in London*. New York: Oxford University Press.
Novakovsky, S.
1924 Arctic or Siberian Hysteria as a Reflex of the Geographic Environment. *Ecology* 5:113-27.
Obeysekere, Gananth
1969 The Ritual Drama of the Sanni Demons: Collective Representations of Disease in Ceylon. *Comparative Studies in Society and History* 11:174-216.
1970 Ayurveda and Mental Illness. *Comparative Studies in Society and History* 12:292-96.
Ödegärd, O.
1952 The Incidence of Mental Diseases as Measured by Census Investigations versus Admission Statistics. *Psychiatric Quarterly* 26:212-18.
Oden, Meliba H.
1968 The Fulfillment of Promise: Forty-Year Follow-up of the Terman Gifted Group. *Genetic Psychology Monographs* 77:3-93.
Opler, M. E.
1936 Some Points of Comparison and Contrast Between the Treatment of Functional Disorders by Apache Shamans and Modern Psychiatric Practice. *American Journal of Psychiatry* 92:1371-87.
Opler, M. K.
1942 Psychoanalytic Techniques in Social Analysis. *Journal of Social Psychology* 15:91-127.
1956 *Culture, Psychiatry, and Human Values*. Springfield, Ill.: Charles C. Thomas.
1959a Dream Analysis in Ute Indian Therapy. In *Culture and Mental Health*, ed. M. K. Opler. New York: Macmillan.
1959b Cultural Differences in Mental Disorders: An Italian and Irish Contrast in the Schizophrenias—U.S.A. In *Culture and Mental Health*, ed. M. K. Opler. New York: Macmillan.
1961 On Devereux's Discussion of Ute Shamanism. *American Anthropologist* 63:1091-93.
1963 The Need for New Diagnostic Categories in Psychiatry. *Journal of the National Medical Association* 55:133-37.

1967 *Culture and Social Psychiatry*. New York: Atherton.
1970 Cross-Cultural Uses of Psychoactive Drugs. In *Principles of Psychopharmacology*, ed. W. G. Clark and J. del Guidice. New York: Academic Press.
Opler, M. K., ed.
1959 *Culture and Mental Health*. New York: Macmillan.
Opler, M. K., and S. M. Small
1968 Cultural Variables Affecting Somatic Complaints and Depression. *Psychosomatics* 9:261-66.
Osborne, Oliver H.
1969 The Yoruba Village as a Therapeutic Community. *Journal of Health and Social Behavior* 10:187-200.
Pahnke, W. N., and W. Richards
1969 Implications of LSD and Experimental Mysticism. In *Altered States of Consciousness*, ed. C. T. Tart. New York: Wiley.
Parker, Seymour
1960 The Witiko Psychosis in the Context of Ojibwa Personality and Culture. *American Anthropologist* 62:603-23.
1962 Eskimo Psychopathology in the Context of Eskimo Personality and Culture. *American Anthropologist* 64:76-96.
Peary, Robert E.
1907 *Nearest the Pole*. New York: Doubleday.
Pfeiffer, W. M.
1963 Comparative Psychiatric Studies of Different Population Groups in West Java. *Archiv für Psychiatrie und Nervenkrankheiten* 204:404-14.
Pfister, O.
1932 Instinctive Psychoanalysis Among the Navahos. *Journal of Nervous and Mental Disease* 76:234-54.
Plunkett, R. J., and John E. Gordon
1960 *Epidemiology and Mental Illness*. New York: Basic Books.
Prange, A. J., and M. M. Vitols
1962 Cultural Aspects of the Relatively Low Incidence of Depression in Southern Negroes. *International Journal of Social Psychiatry* 8:104.
Prince, Raymond H.
1960a The Use of Rauwolfia by Nigerian Native Doctors. *American Journal of Psychiatry* 118:147-49.
1960b The "Brain Fag" Syndrome in Ni-

gerian Students. *Journal of Mental Science* 106:559-70.

1964a Indigenous Yoruba Psychiatry. In *Magic, Faith, and Healing*, ed. A. Kiev. New York: Free Press of Glencoe, Macmillan.

1964b Review of Leighton et al., *Psychiatric Disorder Among the Yoruba. Transcultural Psychiatric Research Review* 1:48-51.

1968a Can the EEG Be used in the Study of Possession States? In *Trance and Possession States*, ed. R. Prince. Montreal: R. M. Bucke Memorial Society.

1968b The Changing Picture of Depressive Syndromes in Africa: Is It Fact or Diagnostic Fashion? *Canadian Journal of African Studies* 1:177-92.

Prince, Raymond H., A. Leighton, and R. May
1968 The Therapeutic Process in Cross-Cultural Perspective: A Symposium. *American Journal of Psychiatry* 124:1171-83.

Prince, Raymond H., and W. Mombour
1967 A Technique for Improving Linguistic Equivalence in Cross-Cultural Surveys. *International Journal of Social Psychiatry* 13:229-37.

Rappaport, Robert
1960 *Community as Doctor*. Springfield, Ill.: Charles C. Thomas.

Rasmussen, K.
1915 *Foran Dagans Øje*, vol.1.: *Grønland*. Copenhagen.

1929 Report of the Fifth Thule Expedition, 1921-24. *Intellectual Culture of the Iglulik Eskimos* 7, no. 1. Copenhagen: Gyldendalske Boghandel, Nordisk Fortag.

Ravenscroft, Kent, Jr.
1965 Voodoo Possession: A Natural Experiment in Hypnosis. *International Journal of Clinical and Experimental Hypnosis* 13:157-82.

Reay, M.
1960 Mushroom Madness in the New Guinea Highlands. *Oceania* 31:135-39.

1965 Mushrooms and Collective Hysteria. *Australian Territories* 5:18-28.

Redlich, F. C., and Daniel X. Freedman
1966 *The Theory and Practice of Psychiatry*. New York: Basic Books.

Rin, H., and T. Lin
1962 Mental Illness Among Formosan Aborigines as Compared with the Chinese in Taiwan. *Journal of Mental Science* 108:134-46.

Roehrl, Vivian J.
1970 A Nutritional Factor in Windigo Psychosis. *American Anthropologist* 72:97-101.

Roff, Merrill, and David F. Ricks, eds.
1970 *Life History Research in Psychopathology*. Minneapolis: University of Minnesota Press.

Rubel, A. J.
1964 The Epidemiology of a Folk Illness: Susto in Hispanic America. *Ethnology* 3:268-83.

Rubio, M., M. Undaneta, and J. L. Doyle
1955 Psychopathologic Reaction Patterns in the Antilles Command. *U. S. Armed Forces Medical Journal* 6:1767.

Salisbury, Richard F.
1962 *Structures of Custodial Care*. University of California Publications in Culture and Society, vol. 8. Berkeley: University of California Press.

1968 Possession in the New Guinea Highlands: A Review of Literature. *International Journal of Social Psychiatry* 14:85-94.

Sal y Rosas, F.
1958 El mito del jani o susto de la medicina indígena del Perú. *Revista de la Sanidad de Policía* 18:167-210.

Sano, F.
1930 The Case of the Insane Outside of Institutions. In *Proceedings of the First International Congress of Mental Hygiene* 1:379-91. Washington, D.C.

Sanua, Victor D.
1969 Socio-Cultural Aspects of Schizophrenia. In L. Bellak et al., *The Schizophrenic Syndrome*. New York: Grune and Stratton.

Sapir, E.
1938 Why Cultural Anthropology Needs the Psychiatrist. *Psychiatry* 1:7-12.

Sarason, S. B., and T. Gladwin
1958 *Psychological and Cultural Problems in Mental Subnormality: A Review of Research*. Genetic Psychology Monographs. Provincetown, Mass.: Journal Press.

Sargant, W.
1957 *Battle for the Mind*. London: Heinemann.

Sasaki, Yuji
  1969 Psychiatric Study of the Shaman in
        Japan. In *Mental Health Research in
        Asia and the Pacific*, ed. W. Caudill
        and T. Lin. Honolulu: East-West Cen-
        ter Press.
Savage, C. H., and R. Prince
  1963 Depression Among the Yoruba. Pa-
        per presented at scientific meeting of
        the American Psychoanalytic Asso-
        ciation, St. Louis.
Schmidt, K. E.
  1964 Folk Psychiatry in Sarawak: A Ten-
        tative System of Psychiatry of the
        Iban. In *Magic, Faith, and Healing*,
        ed. A. Kiev. New York: Free Press of
        Glencoe, Macmillan.
Schooler, C., and W. Caudill
  1964 Symptomatology in Japanese and
        American Schizophrenics. *Ethnology*
        3:172-78.
Seda-Bonilla, Eduardo
  1969 Spiritualism, Psychoanalysis, and
        Psychodrama. *American Anthropolo-
        gist* 71:493-97.
Seligman, C. G.
  1929 Sex, Temperament, Conflict, and
        Psychosis in a Stone Age Population.
        *British Journal of Medical Psycholo-
        gy* 9:187-202.
Silverman, Julian
  1967 Shamans and Acute Schizophrenia.
        American Anthropologist 69:21-31.
  1968 A Paradigm for the Study of Altered
        States of Consciousness. *British Jour-
        nal of Psychiatry* 114:1201-18.
  1970 When Schizophrenia Helps. *Psycholo-
        gy Today* 4, no. 4:63-65.
Slotkin, J. S.
  1956 *The Peyote Religion: A Study in In-
        dian-White Relations*. Glencoe, Ill.:
        Free Press.
Smartt, C. G. F.
  1956 Mental Maladjustment in the East
        African. *Journal of Mental Science*
        102:441-66.
Solomon, David
  1966 *The Marijuana Papers*. Indianapolis:
        Bobbs-Merrill.
Sommers, R.
  1965 Further Studies of Small Group Ecol-
        ogy. *Sociometry* 28:337-48.
Sorensen, A., and E. Stromgren
  1961 Frequency of Depressive States With-

in Geographically Delimited Popula-
        tion Groups. *Acta Psychiatrica Scan-
        dinavica* 37, supplement 162:62.
Spiro, M. E.
  1950 A Psychotic Personality in the South
        Seas. *Psychiatry* 13:189-204.
  1959 Cultural Heritage, Personal Tensions,
        and Mental Illness in a South Sea
        Culture. In *Culture and Mental
        Health*, ed. M. K. Opler. New York:
        Macmillan.
Srole, Leo, et al.
  1962 *Mental Health in the Metropolis: The
        Midtown Manhattan Study*. New
        York: McGraw-Hill.
Stainbrook, E.
  1952 Some Characteristics of the Psycho-
        pathology of Schizophrenic Behavior
        in Bahian Society. *American Journal
        of Psychiatry* 109:330-35.
  1954 A Cross-Cultural Evaluation of De-
        pressive Reactions. In *Depression*, ed.
        P. H. Hoch and J. Zubin. New York:
        Grune & Stratton.
Stanton, A. H., and M. S. Schwartz
  1954 *The Mental Hospital: A Study of In-
        stitutional Participation in Psychiat-
        ric Illness and Treatment*. New York:
        Basic Books.
Stevens, H.
  1965 Jumping Frenchmen of Maine. *Ar-
        chives of Neurology* 12:311-14.
Stoller, Robert J., and R. Geertsma
  1963 The Consistency of Psychiatrists' Clin-
        ical Judgments. *Journal of Nervous
        and Mental Diseases* 137:58-66.
Surya, N. C., et al.
  1965 Ayurvedic Treatments in Mental Ill-
        ness: A Report. *Transactions of the
        All India Institute of Mental Health*
        5:28-39.
Tart, Charles T.
  1969 Psychedelic Experiences Associated
        with a Novel Hypnotic Procedure,
        Mutual Hypnosis. In *Altered States
        of Consciousness*, ed. C. T. Tart. New
        York: Wiley.
Teicher, Morton I.
  1960 *Windigo Psychosis: A Study of a Re-
        lationship Between Belief and Behav-
        ior Among the Indians of Northeast-
        ern Canada*. Seattle: American Eth-
        nological Society.
Terman, L. M., and Oden, M. H.

1947 *Genetic Studies of Genius*, vol. 4: *The Gifted Child Grows Up*. Stanford: Stanford University Press.

Tewfik, G. I.
1958 Problems of Mental Illness in Uganda. In *Mental Disorders and Mental Health in Africa South of the Sahara*. Commission de Cooperation Technique en Afrique au Sud du Sahara, publication no. 35. Geneva. World Health Organization.

Tooth, G. C.
1950 *Studies in Mental Illness in the Gold Coast*. Colonial Research Publication no. 6. London: Her Majesty's Stationery Office.

Turner, V. W.
1964 An Ndembu Doctor in Practice. In *Magic, Faith, and Healing*, ed. A. Kiev. New York: Free Press of Glencoe, Macmillan.

Van Loon, F.
1927 Amok and Latah. *Journal of Abnormal and Social Psychology* 21: 434-44.

Wallace, A. F. C.
1958 Dreams and Wishes of the Soul: A Type of Psychoanalytic Theory Among the Seventeenth-Century Iroquois. *American Anthropologist* 60, no. 2, pt. 1:234-48.
1959a Cultural Determinants of Response to Hallucinatory Experience. *American Medical Association Archives of General Psychiatry* 1:58-69.
1959b The Institutionalization of Cathartic and Control Strategies in Iroquois Religious Psychotherapy. In *Culture and Mental Health*, ed. M. K. Opler. New York: Macmillan.
1960 The Biocultural Theory of Schizophrenia. *International Record of Medicine* 173:700-714.
1961a *Culture and Personality*. New York: Random House.
1961b Mental Illness, Biology, and Culture. In *Psychological Anthropology*, ed. F. Hsu. Homewood, Ill.: Dorsey Press.
1966 *Religion: An Anthropological View*. New York: Random House.

Wegrocki, H. J.
1939 Critique of Cultural and Statistical Concepts of Normality. *Journal of Abnormal and Social Psychology* 34:166-78.

Weinberg, S. K.
1965 Cultural Aspects of Manic-Depression in West Africa. *Journal of Health and Human Behavior* 6:247-53.

White, L. A.
1928 A Comparative Study of Keresan Medicine Societies. *Proceedings of 23rd International Congress of Americanists*.

Whitney, Harry
1911 *Hunting with the Eskimo*. New York: Century.

Williams, F. E.
1923 The Vailala Madness and the Destruction of Native Ceremonies in the Gulf Division. Anthropology Report no. 4. Port Moresby, Territory of Papua.

Winiarz, W., and J. Willawski
1936 Imu: A Psychoneurosis Occurring Among Ainus. *Psychoanalytic Review* 23:181-86.

Wittkower, E. D.
1964 Spirit Possession in Haitian Vodun Ceremonies. *Acta Psychotherapeutica et Psychosomatica* 12:72-80.

Wittkower, E. D., and G. Dubreil
1969 Cultural Factors in Mental Illness. In *The Study of Personality*, ed. E. Norbeck, D. Price-Williams, and W. McCord. New York: Holt, Rinehart & Winston.

Wittkower, E. D., and Jacob Fried
1959 Some Problems of Transcultural Psychiatry. In *Culture and Mental Health*, ed. M. K. Opler. New York: Macmillan.

Wittkower, E. D., and H. Rin
1965 Recent Developments in Transcultural Psychiatry. In *Transcultural Psychiatry*, ed. A. V. S. De Reuck and R. Porter. Boston: Little, Brown.

Wittkower, E. D., et al.
1960 A Cross-Cultural Inquiry into the Symptomatology of Schizophrenia. *Transcultural Research in Mental Health Problems Review and Newsletter*, December, pp. 2-17.

Wolff, M. S.
1956 Notes on the Vodun Religion in Haiti with Reference to Its Social and Psychodynamics. *Revue internation-*

ale d'ethnopsychologie normale et pathologique 1:209-40.

Worsley, Peter
1957 *The Trumpet Shall Sound.* London: Macgibbon & Kee.

Yap, P. M.
1951 Mental Diseases Peculiar to Certain Cultures: A Survey of Comparative Psychiatry. *Journal of Mental Science* 97:313-27.

1952 The Latah Reaction: Its Pathodynamics and Nosological Position. *Journal of Mental Science* 98-515-64.

1965a Phenomenology of Affective Disorder in Chinese and Other Cultures. In *Transcultural Psychiatry*, ed. A. V. S. De Reuck and R. Porter. Boston: Little, Brown.

1965b Suk Yeong or Koro: A Culture-Bound Depersonalization Syndrome. *British Journal of Psychiatry* 111: 43-50.

1969 The Culture-Bound Reactive Syndromes. In *Mental Health Research in Asia and the Pacific*, ed. W. Caudill and T. Lin. Honoulu: East-West Center Press.

Zaguirre, J. C.
1957 Amuck. *Journal of the Philippine Federation of Private Medical Practitioners* 6:1138-49.

Zaretsky, I.
1966 Bibliography on Spirit Possession and Spirit Mediumship. Berkeley: University of California, Department of Anthropology.

Zubin, J., and M. Kleitzman
1966 A Cross-Cultural Approach to Classification in Schizophrenia and Other Mental Disorders. In *Psychopathology of Schizophrenia*, ed. P. H. Hoch. New York: Grune & Stratton.

CHAPTER 27 Identity, Culture, and Behavior

RICHARD H. ROBBINS

The need to know who one is appears to be one of the most deep-rooted in our humanity.
—R. D. Laing

... The individual is only himself by virtue of being at the same time something other than himself.
—Lucien Lévy-Bruhl

INTRODUCTION

It has been the wont of social and cultural anthropologists to appropriate theoretical concepts from other scientific domains, and to utilize these concepts as tools in interpreting social and cultural phenomena. As a result, anthropologists have been treated by their colleagues to commentaries on subjects ranging from thermodynamics to psychodynamics, from topology to cognitive theory. My purpose here is also to review the uses to which anthropologists can and have put a conceptual framework that received its major theoretical emphasis in other areas of scientific specialization: the concept of self or identity.

In the past decade anthropologists have shown renewed interest in three theoretical issues, all of which bear upon the utilization of the identity concept in anthropological interpretation: the issue of the usefulness of the culture concept (Voget 1960), the problem of the place of the individual in culture theory (Opler 1964), and the consequences of utilizing theoretical concepts from other fields (Gluckman, ed., 1964).[1] Devons and Gluckman (1964) deal with the last issue by em-

---

I wish to express my thanks to Eunice Holt, Jeffrey Abare, and Gloria Bushey for their assistance in the research for and preparation of this manuscript.

[1] These issues have, of course, long been of interest to social scientists, going back at least as far as Durkheim (1938) and Kroeber (1917).

phasizing the importance of drawing limits on what they call one's naivety concerning theoretical formulations developed in disciplines outside one's own. Ignoring the limits of one's naivety, they say, impedes the interpretation of those aspects of reality which are the concern of the investigator's field of study, and threatens to draw the scientist into errors of interpretation (1964: 166-167).[2] However, it is difficult to find a theoretical scheme in anthropology—or an anthropologist, for that matter—that indeed draws such limits, for virtually all explorers of social and cultural phenomena have made use of some concept to link up the abstraction "culture" to human behavior or nature. This concept may be biological and used in the context of human needs (Malinowski 1944), or it may be ecological, relating cultural forms to the need for environmental adaptation (Harris 1966, Steward 1955). The concept may come from physics, relating cultural development to basic thermodynamic processes (White 1949, 1959), or it may be psychological, linking culture to psychodynamic processes (Honigmann 1968), to man's "impulse to order" (Douglas 1966:4-5), or to his propensity to associate (Lévi-Strauss 1963:90). In fact, one of the few anthropologists who have truly recognized the limits of his naivety was Alfred Kroeber (see Kroeber 1944:7), and he apparently was dissatisfied with the result (Harris 1968:330). Gluckman and Devons recognize that failure to draw from other disciplines limits the social scientist's understanding of

social or cultural events. However, I suggest the only reason anthropologists so infrequently abstain from trespassing on the fields of others is that the culture cept in itself is inadequate for a satisfactory understanding of social processes and human behavior. This is the point Voget (1960:943) makes when he states that psychological concepts are vital to anthropological theory. Yet this issue seems to involve more than just a choice between culture and psychology; it involves the fact that the culture concept lacks a theory of human motivation—motivation that must be accounted for if culture is to be viewed as a product of human behavior and social life or as a concomitant of human nature rather than solely as a determinant of behavior. In other words, if the human animal is to be viewed not only as a carrier of culture but as its propagator as well, the anthropologist must account for that propensity to socialize, symbolize, and create gods, potlatches, and initiation rituals. Whether the motivating concept allowing a satisfactory depth of understanding is drawn from physics, biology, or psychology is irrelevant, except to the problem being studied. What is important is that the motivation to cultural behavior be accounted for in some manner.

The identity concept is presented here as such a motivating concept (see Foote 1951). It is assumed that human awareness and concern for self can explain much about social and cultural processes, that the application of the identity concept is well within the bounds of anthropological interpretation, and that while the identity concept represents a theory of personality, it is also, in a wider sense, a theory of human nature. This discussion will primarily concern itself with the ways in which the identity concept has been utilized in anthropology, and will dem-

---

[2] Devons and Gluckman, to demonstrate their thesis, compare the approach taken to witchcraft by Evans-Pritchard (1937) and Clyde Kluckhohn (1967), and conclude that the latter, directly utilizing constructs from psychology, is the lesser study. Kennedy (1967), however, has taken issue with them, and stated that Evans-Pritchard is at least as psychological in his analysis as Kluckhohn.

onstrate its usefulness in generating hypotheses about social and/or cultural events.

APPROACHES TO THE IDENTITY CONCEPT

Since the identity concept converged on anthropology from a number of disciplines, it is natural that various anthropologists have utilized that concept from the diverse perspectives developed in these disciplines. Three such perspectives or models will be examined here: the identity-health model, the identity-interaction model, and the identity-world view model.[3]

The identity-health model entered anthropology primarily through the works of such writers as Erik Erikson (1968), Carl Rogers (1959), and Harry Stack Sullivan (1953). This model emphasizes the relationship of identity to the well-adjusted or maladjusted personality, examining those conditions of self that make for "optimal psychological adjustment" (Rogers 1959:206). From this perspective, identity tends to be equated with a coherent sense of self (Wheelis 1958:19) or a feeling on the part of the individual of sameness and continuity (Erikson 1968:87). It is to this usage of the identity concept that Lerner (1958:403) appears to subscribe when he speaks of the quest for a stable identity among nations in the Middle East (see also Chance 1965, Wintrob 1968).

The identity-interaction model is most often associated with the works of Charles H. Cooley (1956), early in the twentieth century; George Herbert Mead (1934); and, more recently, Erving Goffman (1959, 1961). Rather than

viewing identity as it relates to psychological adjustment, this model emphasizes the importance of a person's conception of self as a guide to his interaction with others. Identity, in this perspective, tends to be equated with social position, with the prime interest centering upon the relationship between identity and the distribution of rights and duties among identity relationships (Goodenough 1965a:8; Goffman 1956:474-75). It is from this perspective that Goodenough (1965a) views the social structure of Truk, Spradley (1970) the world of the tramp, and Schwarz and Merten (1968) the social life of high school sororities.

The identity-world view model is most rooted in anthropological interpretation, and, as Wallace (1968:47) points out, is related to such traditional anthropological concepts as value, theme, and ethos. Redfield, for example, treating world view as the "structure of things as man is aware of them" (1953:86), states that "every world view starts from the man who is the viewer and includes the idea of a self" (1953:91); and Hallowell, who most fully developed the identity or self concept from a world view perspective, states (1955:76):

The nature of the self, considered in its conceptual component, is a culturally identifiable variable. Just as different people entertain various beliefs about the nature of the universe, they likewise differ in their ideas about the nature of the self. And just as we have discovered that notions about the nature of beings and powers existent in the universe involve assumptions that are directly relevant to an understanding of the behavior of the individual in a given society, we must likewise assume that the individual's self-image and his interpretation of his own experience cannot be divorced from the concept of self that is characteristic of his society. For such concepts are the major means by which different cultures promote self orientation in the kind of meaningful terms that make self-awareness

---

[3] Wallace and Fogelson (1965:380) also point out the various usages of the identity concept, labeling them the psychoanalytic, the sociocultural, and the psychological traditions.

of functional importance in the maintenance of a human social order.

While these three perspectives on the identity concept differ, none excludes the assumptions made by the others. Psychologists have combined the identity-health model with an identity-interaction model (Sullivan 1953, Laing 1962), and health aspects have been incorporated into the identity-world view model (Hallowell 1955:95). What unites these three models is the assumptions all make about the nature of the individual. What differentiates them, on the other hand, is the stress each model places on the different assumptions. Five such assumptions or propositions will be of concern here:[4]

First, and most basic, is the proposition that the way an individual conceives of his self or identify will have an effect on his behavior and beliefs.

The second proposition holds that a conception of self is a prerequisite to human social life, or that a conception of self is necessary to orient the individual to others and to his physical environment. It is this proposition that is central to the identity-world view model. Hallowell, for example, sees a self concept as one of those indispensable conditions that made the cultural adaptation of *Homo sapiens* possible (1959:50): "The functioning of a social system as a moral order implies a capacity for self objectification, self identification and appraisal of one's own conduct, as well as that of others, with reference to socially recognized and sanctioned standards of behavior."

The third proposition, and the one that is most stressed by the identity-interaction approach, is that an individual's identity is formed and maintained in the course of interaction with others.

In other words, it is through social interaction that one pieces together information obtained from others which results in a picture of one's self or identity (Miller 1963:671).

The fourth proposition maintains that individuals need to have communicated to them by others information that confirms, validates, or reinforces their particular view of self (Erikson 1959:111; Laing 1962:88). This is basically what Rogers refers to when he speaks of the "need for positive regard" (1959:208, 223), and what Goldschmidt (1959) speaks of as a need for "positive affect." It is this proposition that is central to the identity-health model, since one assumes that a lack of identity confirmation has an adverse effect on psychological adjustment (Laing 1962:75).

Fifth is the proposition that individuals are constantly striving to obtain from others confirmation of their view of self. Wallace calls "identity work" this attempt to "gain from others a favorable testimonial as to one's identity" (1967:67).

Implicit in all these propositions is the assumption that an individual's identity is never static, that an individual's conception of self is in a constant state of flux.[5] In the course of this discussion we shall develop other propositions relating to the identity concept, but all are, to one degree or another, derived from these five key propositions.

HISTORICAL ANTECEDENTS OF THE IDENTITY CONCEPT IN ANTHROPOLOGY: SOUL AND SELF

The seventeenth- and eighteenth-century philosophers treated the self as an object of awareness by relating it to hu-

---

[4] These propositions or axioms are by no means the only ones important to the identity construct (see, e.g., Kinch 1963, Wallace 1967).

[5] It is this assumption on the constant flux of identity that most differentiates identity theory from role theory.

man consciousness;[6] but William James (1952), late in the nineteenth century, was the first to explore systematically the relationship of the self concept to human behavior. His work, in fact, contains virtually all the perspectives of identity theory outlined above. His use of the term "personal identity" (1952:213) is much the same as Erikson's, while he also treated the interaction aspects of self later developed by Cooley and Mead. To what extent James's work influenced the works of early twentieth-century anthropologists is unknown, although at least one writer to be dealt with her, Lucien Lévy-Bruhl, was aware of his work (1966:15).

To trace the development of the identity concept in anthropology one must indulge in an examination of early classics, and risk reading unintended meanings into the works of past masters. The approach taken here is to attempt to link up the identity concept with a concept long of concern to anthropologists, the concept of soul. That the folk concept of soul is somehow akin to the scientific concept of self has been hinted at by a number of writers (Hallowell 1955:77; Diggory 1966:1). Edward Tylor, for example, in offering his "minimum definition of religion" more than a hundred years ago, hinted at such a relationship when he equated the soul with a "second self" (1958:12). It was perhaps this mention of self that led George Herbert Mead (1934:149) to write:

Among primitive people ... the necessity of distinguishing the self and the organism was recognized in what we call the double: the individual has a thinglike self that is affected by the individual as it affects other people which

is distinguished from the immediate organism in that it can leave the body and come back to it. This is the basis for the concept of soul as a separate entity.

Thus to Mead, and perhaps to Tylor, it is the concept or awareness of self that gives rise to and is symbolically represented in the concept of soul.

Among the early writers on soul, however, it was Lucien Lévy-Bruhl that most fully, though indirectly, developed the idea of a relationship between the soul and identity. To Lévy-Bruhl the soul is an appurtenance, as are excreta, footprints, and virtually all things owned by the individual.[7] These appurtenances are, as he puts it, "extensions of the personality" (1966:122), and "are inseparable from the personality; they are part of it, they are the man himself" (1966:121). Thus the individual is given symbolic representation by his appurtenances, while "a complete collection of certain appurtenances is the equivalent of the individual himself" (1966:125). If one then views the soul as an appurtenance, it becomes a representation of the individual's social personality or identity. Lévy-Bruhl's "law of participation" apparently states, in fact, that the self, or soul, is represented, reflected, or imbued in a person's possessions (1966:201-202):

Since an individual's appurtenances are himself, and his double, reproduction, reflection are also the man himself ... *the individual is only himself by virtue of being at the same time something other than himself.* Viewed in this fresh aspect, far from being one unit, as we conceive him to be, he is one and yet several at the same time. Thus he is ... a veritable "centre of participation." [Emphasis added.]

The major criticism of Lévy-Bruhl's work is that his distinction between primitive and civilized modes of thinking

---

[6] Hegel (1910:31), for example, states that the "being of the mind is its act, and its act is to be aware of itself." (See Diggory 1966 for an excellent review of the historical antecedents of the self concept.)

[7] Lévy-Bruhl's appurtenances bear some resemblance to what Nadel (1951:67) refers to as "diacritical signs."

is unwarranted (see Evans-Pritchard 1965:86-87). That is, one would assume that the psychic attribute of representing the self in material objects is universal.[8] Yet Dorothy Lee (1959: 136-37) takes much the same tack as Lévy-Bruhl in her analysis of the Wintu concept of self. In deducing the Wintu self concept from linguistic materials, Lee contrasts it with the Western concept of self, which, she says, has clear boundaries and is a distinct unit and can be named and defined; the Wintu concept of self does not have clear boundaries and is not opposed to the other. Thus "on most occasions it participates to some extent in the other, and is of equal status to the other."

The question raised by both Lévy-Bruhl and Lee as to whether there is a cross-cultural difference in the degree of participation between the self and other persons or things is beyond the scope of this discussion. Nor is it of paramount interest that the equation of soul with self increases the historical depth of the identity concept in anthropology. What is important is that the identity or self concept bears a striking resemblance to the folk theory of soul, thus providing a model for behavior that closely approximates the folk model. This is clearly pointed out by Rubel's (1964) and Wallace's (1967) interpretation of the Latin American *susto* syndrome. *Susto* is an illness traditionally believed to be caused by the loss of one's soul or its capture by a spirit. Rubel (1964:281), in questioning Gillin's (1948) interpretation of a case of *susto* as "libidinal frustration," ascribes the illness to the inability of the person to live up to the expectations of role performance. Wallace (1967:63) goes further and interprets

the illness as self loss, giving an analysis that even more closely coincides with the traditional exegesis of the illness.

THEORETICAL FORMULATIONS

For a theoretical scheme to be relevant to a specific field of social inquiry it must be formulated in such a way that the scheme itself suggests problems to be studied or generates hypotheses about social or cultural phenomena. More specifically, the theory should be presented in such a way as to stimulate the researcher to ask the right questions. Let us examine those aspects of identity theory that most suggest problems of anthropological interest.

CONSTITUENTS OF IDENTITY

William James was one of the first to segregate aspects or constituents of identity. He speaks, for example, of a "material self" (1952:189), or that aspect of self that includes the body of the individual, his family, clothes, and home; a "social self" (1952:190), meaning recognition obtained from others, honor, and fame; and a "spiritual self" (1952:192) consisting of a "man's inner, subjective being, his psychic faculties or dispositions." Other schemes for dividing constituents of identity have been developed, a fact that has made for more confusion than clarification. One source of theoretical disarray is the use of a variety of terms to label what are apparently the same constituents, or of the same terms to label constituents that have different meanings for different investigators. Erikson, as well as James, uses the term "personal identity" to denote the individual's feeling of selfsameness and continuity in time and space, while others (Goodenough 1963:182; McCall and Simmons 1966:64-65) speak of personal identity as that aspect of self which

---

[8] See Veblen's (1931) treatment of status symbols.

represents the unique way an individual identifies himself, or the style with which he carries out his rights and duties. To Goodenough (1963:182) an individual's personal identity is linguistically represented in such labels as "nice," "mean," and "lazy." The person's social identity, on the other hand, is the way he sees his rights and duties distributing to others (Goodenough 1963:182; 1965a:3), an aspect of self that Miller (1963:673) refers to as "subjective public identity." Miller refers to the way others actually view the individual as his "objective public identity," while Goffman (1963:2) refers to this aspect as "actual social identity."

While there is substantial disagreement on terminology to be used in defining identity constituents, there is general accord on those aspects of self that make a difference in behavior and beliefs. There is, first, an individual's self-identity, a term that corresponds generally to the self concept (Miller 1963:673). It is the view the individual has of his own identity, or, as Allport (1960:34) puts it, "the self as known to the individual." It includes the person's conception of his physical appearance, social status, skills, and so on. Social identity, on the other hand, refers to the conception a person has of others' view of his identity or the way he believes they view his physical appearance, social status, and so on. An individual's public identity represents the way others actually view him, or, as Miller (1963:673) puts it, "a person's patterns or traits as they appear to the members of the group." Finally, a person's personal identity is his view of what makes him unique and unlike any other person. It is assumed that there is never a perfect fit or total consistency among these aspects of self, so that a person's social identity is unlikely to be identical with his public or self identity. In fact, the delineation of identity

constituents derives its importance from the assumption that the striving of an individual to attain consistency between the self he would like to be and the self he believes is attributed to him by others is the prime motivation for social behavior.[9] Hence, while a perfect fit between constituents is unlikely, one may speak of a strain toward consistency (Burton and Whiting 1965:612), with each constituent influencing the formation of the others. In other words, a person's public identity, which influences the way others act toward him, will align or realign his social and self identities, as his social identity, which influences the way he acts toward others, will influence his public identity. It is this inconsistency and interrelationship of identity constituents that account for the flux in a person's identity. This has the further implication of obviating the need to speak of fixed or ascribed identities, since, as open as it is to change from so many directions, it is never fixed or permanent.

The delineation of identity constituents presents to the anthropological investigator the problem of seeking those cultural processes that contribute to this trend toward consistency, and in ensuing pages we shall examine the ways in which a lack of consistency among aspects of the self relates to such anthropological concerns as witchcraft, initiation rituals, and potlatches.

---

[9] It is in this respect that identity theory most differs from ego psychology, for where the latter sees human behavior, as well as culture (Róheim 1950), deriving from the interaction of the id, superego, and ego, the identity construct sees behavior as being motivated by the interaction of identity constituents, or the strain toward consistency of self, social, public, and personal identities. Also, in the Freudian framework, culture is a less direct result of the conflict between personality aspects, being, in a sense, a compensation for the conflict. From the viewpoint of identity theory, culture acts directly to resolve the discrepancy between personality aspects.

IDENTITY DIMENSIONS

A person's identity is fabricated from his and others' perception of those relevant characteristics or features of the person that make him like or unlike others (Goodenough 1963:179). These relevant features comprise identity dimensions such as physical appearance, age, sex, personal name, ethnic group membership, skills, social rank, and so on (Wallace 1967:65). For example, in a given society the terms "handsome," "ugly," "pretty," "cripple," and "tall" may partly comprise the identity dimension of physical appearance, while the terms "executive," "boss," "laborer," and "lackey" may be included in the dimension of social rank. As Miller (1963:676) suggests, identity dimensions are frequently bipolar. A recent American television advertisement defined a desirable woman as "thin and rich," thus defining one end of the identity dimensions of physical appearance and economic status, and implying that the other extreme must be "fat and poor." As Wallace (1967:65) points out, each dimension may further be divided into four points. At one end of the scale is the ideal attribute of that dimension, at the other end the feared attribute. In between are the attribute claimed by the individual and the attribute he actually possesses. Thus a desirable or ideal economic status may be represented by earnings in excess of $30,000 a year, and a feared status by earnings under $5,000. An individual may then claim an income of $20,000 while his real income is $10,000. One assumes that the degree of similarity between the self one would like to be and the self one sees oneself as being constitutes a measure of the individual's self-esteem (Rogers 1959:122; Coopersmith 1967:4-5).

The delineation of those dimensions that determine an individual's social position has long been a concern of anthropologists, although usually outside the context of identity theory. Kin status, of course, has received the major emphasis (Kroeber 1909, Murdock 1949, Goodenough 1956, Lounsbury 1956), but such dimensions as body image (Postal 1965), social rank (Goodenough 1965a), ethnic group membership (Barth 1969), and personal names (Goodenough 1965b; Strauss 1959:15) have, among others, been treated from an identity perspective.

It would be profitable here to review some of the issues posed by the delineation of identity dimensions and the way the issues have been and may be approached within anthropology. The first and most basic issue is the investigation of those criteria or features of identity dimensions in given societies that make a difference in the way the individual views himself and is viewed by others. The identity concept assumes that individuals have a propensity to divide and classify (Lévi-Strauss 1963, 1966), and to seek in themselves and others features that either differentiate or unite them. The first question, then, involves getting the "natives'" view of these significant features. Spradley (1970:65-96), for example, states that tramps utilize such criteria as geographic mobility, mode of travel most frequently used, and home base to differentiate identities among themselves. Barth (1969:119) shows how Pathans utilize the criteria of patrilineal descent, adherence to Islam, and acceptance of Pathan custom in defining their ethnic identity. Schwartz and Merten (1968:1121) contrast two life styles that are significant in forming the identity of high school sorority members: the life style of socialites or "socies" and that of hoods or "greasers." Each of these identities is distinguished by such attributes as modes of speech, hair style, and attitudes toward authority.

A second area of investigation regarding identity dimensions involves explaining why in a given society certain dimensions or attributes are significant for distinguishing identities while others are not. Related to this question is the issue of the adaptive value of a given trait. In presenting this issue one assumes that to the extent that individuals strive to maintain or attain an identity they see as desirable, they will strive to develop or acquire those skills, possessions, or personal attributes that in their society define a desirable identity. For example, to the degree that a society requires ordered behavior, adherence to group norms will be adaptive as an ideal or desired identity feature. In a hunting society both hunting skill and the personal attribute of generosity are adaptive in defining an ideal identity, since they ensure motivation for obtaining food and sharing it. Among the Beaver Indians of British Columbia a person's identity is in part defined by the amount of supernatural power he possesses, a power that is validated or demonstrated by successful hunting and the sharing of the meat with others (Ridington 1968:1153). Thus by striving to attain a favorable identity the individual is also ensuring the survival of the group. Tramps, according to Spradley (1970:254), define a desired identity in part by physical mobility: the more mobile the individual, the greater his prestige. This trait is adaptive since it prevents individuals from accumulating long criminal records; the longer an individual stays in a given area, the more times he will be arrested and the more time he must serve in jail.

While these characteristics are adaptive, one may also investigate the degree to which a trait is nonadaptive. The American automobile, long a sign of a desirable identity, is hardly consistent with the need for clean air; and a large family, usually a sign of desired fertility or sexual prowess, is also nonadaptive in an era of excessive population growth. Here, as opposed to hunting skill among the Beaver and mobility among tramps, one finds a lack of consistency between the things or behaviors toward which society motivates an individual and those things or behaviors necessary for the survival of that society.

A third issue suggested by the identity formulation is the problem of specifying that dimension which is given prime importance in a given interaction. One assumes that we base our interactions with others not on a total identity configuration, but on that dimension which, for whatever reason, is of high saliency in a given interaction. When an individual interacts with another whom he defines as "father," it is obvious that it is the kin dimension that is of utmost importance in that interaction, and not physical appearance. Anthropologists who have worked in small-scale societies are familiar with the experience of being fitted into the natives' scheme of social relations as a kinsman, so that the natives can utilize the kin dimension in guiding their interaction with the fieldworker. One may ask, for example, at what point in culture change such dimensions become inadequate in guiding interaction with outsiders. In fact, what has variously been called the search for identity (Spindler 1968:335) and identity conflict (Wintrob 1968:93; Trent 1965) may be only the loss of one identity dimension (e.g., ethnic identity) rather than the loss or destruction of a total identity. In other words, while a Menomini may have doubts about his ethnic group membership as a consequence of culture contact (Spindler 1968:336), he may still be certain about his kin status. Thus in studying culture change from an identity perspective one needs to investigate the effect of the disruption of one identity dimension on an entire identity structure.

In studying the relationship between identity dimensions, or, as Miller (1963:682) calls it, the degree of centrality between dimensions, one assumes that no one identity dimension acts in isolation from any other, that social rank may be influenced by physical appearance, and that even the view others have of an individual's physical appearance (e.g., height) may be influenced by his social rank (Wilson 1968).

IDENTITY PROCESSES IN CULTURE

Identity processes have to do with those aspects of culture that directly relate to the formation and maintenance of identities. If any society is to survive, it must have some institutionalized means of inculcating in its members knowledge of behaviors and symbols appropriate to given identities, and must periodically ensure that those identities are confirmed or reinforced. It must have means to ensure that individuals believe that they are what they are supposed to be, and means to facilitate identity transformations. These means are what we have called identity processes. A number of such processes will be treated here, with the understanding that any given cultural phenomenon may involve some or all of them. Nor do such processes necessarily occur independently of one another. Thus identity change may, and usually does, involve identity diffusion, and identity struggles may relate to identity confirmation.

IDENTITY FORMATION AND CHANGE

Identity formation has to do with the way an individual learns his identi-

ty, the way he knows what is a desirable or undesirable identity, and, more importantly, the way he comes to believe he is what he is supposed to be or wants to be, or what others want him to be. If the use of the identity concept in anthropology has done nothing else, it has focused interest in socialization away from exclusive concern with early childhood and shifted it toward adolescence and later life. One result has been a revived interest in rites of passage, especially as they concern identity formation or change. This concern with initiation ceremonies has also led to an interesting debate between John Whiting and his associates (Burton and Whiting 1965), on the one hand, and Yehudi Cohen (1964) on the other— a debate that points up a number of interesting problems and issues concerning the identity concept (see also Whiting, Kluckhohn, and Anthony 1958; Young 1962; Abrahamson 1966; Wallace 1966).

As Erikson (1959:112) points out, one of the most important aspects of identity formation is the process of identification. One of the questions with which Burton and Whiting (1965) deal is: What is it that makes a person identify with another? They introduce what they term the "status envy hypothesis" (1965:611):

If there is a status that has privileged access to a desired resource, the incumbent or occupant of such a status will be envied by anyone whose status does not permit him control of, and the right to use, the resource. Status envy is then a motivational component of status disability, and such motivation leads to learning by identification.

They also state that there are primary identification processes (those that occur in infancy) and secondary identification processes (those that occur in childhood) (1965:612). Utilizing the status envy hypothesis and primary and secondary identification stages, they then examine the relationship between sleeping arrangements in infancy (primary identification) and male initiation rituals (secondary identification). When a male infant sleeps with his mother and the father sleeps elsewhere, the mother will represent the envied status, and it is with her that the infant will identify. However, when such a sleeping arrangement exists in a patrilocal society, where the men traditionally have access to desired resources and hence are also envied, there will develop a conflict in the sexual identity of males. Burton and Whiting (1965:614) hypothesize that in such a situation male initiation ceremonies will be used to resolve this conflict by "brainwashing the primary feminine identity" and establishing the secondary male identity. They further hypothesize that when exclusive mother-son sleeping arrangements exist in matrilocal societies, and it is with females that the male identifies even after infancy, the *couvade* will exist to allow the male an opportunity to act out his feminine identifications.

Cohen (1964) has taken issue with Burton and Whiting on a number of points. First, he states that initiation rituals function not to resolve conflict in sexual identity, but to establish a "sense of social-emotional anchorage" (1964:533), and he states further that Burton and Whiting fail to show that conflict in sex identity actually exists in societies with exclusive mother-son sleeping arrangements and patrilocal residence. The disagreement on this point appears to hinge on the identity dimension that is formed by initiation rituals, with Burton and Whiting emphasizing the sex dimension and Cohen focusing on the group membership dimension. In other words, to Cohen the question is not whether a person will identify with the male or female sex, but whether he will identify with a nuclear family or extended family group; initiation ceremonies exist in those so-cieties where "joint responsibility" among extended family groups is the rule.

A second area of disagreement centers on mechanisms of identification. To Burton and Whiting it is status envy, while to Cohen (1964:536-37) a person will identify with those individuals who take prime responsibility for educating him. Thus in societies where children are "brought up for anchorage and identification in the wider kin group outside the family they will be brought up and taught by members of the child's descent group and by their parents," but in societies where anchorage is with the nuclear family they will be brought up by parents and nonmembers of the child's descent group.

A third area in which the two approaches differ is in their treatment of stages of identification and in the emphasis placed on initiation ceremonies as shapers of identity. While Burton and Whiting are concerned with infancy (primary identification) and childhood (secondary identification), Cohen is concerned with preadolescence and adolescence. Societies, says Cohen (1964:539), are more likely to take formal and explicit steps to facilitate identity formation in the former stage than in the latter, since biochemical and hormonal changes that take place in the first stage of puberty make the child more vulnerable to identity change. These steps taken in the first stage of puberty may take the form of separating the boy from the nuclear family (extrusion), or they may take the form of brother-sister avoidance. Cohen hypothesizes that in societies where a boy's social and emotional anchorage is the extended family, there will be some rite of extrusion, and there may be a "further disruption in the child's relationship to his family in the form of an initiation ceremony" (1964:543). To Cohen, then, the initiation ceremony functions not to resolve conflict in sex identity, but to reinforce a process already begun in the first stage of puberty.

In a number of respects the debate between Whiting and Cohen, as well as that between Whiting and Young (Young 1962), is superfluous. Most importantly, it is unlikely that an initiation ritual functions only to reinforce one identity dimension, be it sex or group membership. Rather, such rituals are multidimensional, aiding the formation of many different aspects of self. If such rituals changed or formed only one dimension, they would probably lead to a loss of centrality (see above).

The approach taken by Cohen and Whiting in examining rites of passage is followed by Kiefer (1970) in her study of the Japanese educational system, by Schwartz and Merten (1968) in their study of high school sorority initiation rites, and by Spradley (1970) in his examination of the process by which an individual becomes a tramp, or, as he calls it, an urban nomad. School examinations, called "examination hell," function in Japan, according to Kiefer, as rites of extrusion, avoidance, and initiation to anchor the Japanese youth in a specific group. It is school experiences, and most importantly the examinations, that serve to facilitate what Kiefer calls "conversion-through-suffering" (1970:72), by which a Japanese learns the attitudes appropriate to his role in a bureaucratic organization and by which he extends the emotional habits learned in the family to his age mates.

Schwartz and Merten focus their attention on the part that high school sorority initiation rites play in identity formation. Girls join sororities, according to Schwartz and Merten, to demonstrate their "coolness," "coolness" being synonymous with prestige. Sorority members recognize two distinct social groups, the socialites or "socies"

and the hoods or "greasers," with a third nonexclusive category, the "out-of-its," including hoods and all others lacking the attribute of "coolness" (1968:1121). Socie girls are those who "subscribe to the adolescent version of a middle-class way of life" that to them is morally acceptable, while greasers are those who subscribe to a working-class way of life and are viewed by sorority girls as promiscuous, sloppy, stupid, and unfriendly; "in short, they were seen as perversely unfeminine" (1968:1127). Schwartz and Merten view the initiation ritual as a means by which a girl's identity as a socie is formed and confirmed. The ritual facilitates this process by vividly contrasting, through the use of expressive symbols, the desirable identity of socie and the negative or feared identity of hood. During the initiation period the initiates are made to dress in ridiculous fashion, smear lipstick on their faces, and have eggs broken in their hair to mark them symbolically with the negative identity of hood, hoods being persons who dress undesirably, use too much makeup, and wear elaborate (unacceptable) hair styles. Thus the initiation ceremony functions to establish a contrast between desirable and undesirable identities, to emphasize the attributes that mark off these identities, and finally to confirm or validate the desirable identity of socie (Schwartz and Merten 1968:1129-30).

Spradley (1970:132-70) treats the arrest process as a rite of passage that symbolically marks the identity transition to tramp. "Making the bucket," as the tramp calls it, involves eight steps by which he is "stripped of his former identity and should believe the truth about himself: that he is a common drunkard, a bum" (1970:133).

It is a thin line that separates the processes of identity formation and change represented by rites of passage and the type of identity transition that takes place as a result of culture change. Peacock (1968:6), in fact, draws a parallel between rites of passage and culture change in his analysis of the role that Javanese drama plays in the modernization process (see also Goodenough 1963:216). Thus the process of identification with which Burton and Whiting deal (the "status envy hypothesis") is also relevant in the study of culture change (see Berreman 1964), as are those factors that either encourage or hinder identity change. Goodenough (1963), for example, has outlined those conditions necessary in a community development program to facilitate the change from one identity to another, conditions that also apply to rites of passage. There must be, he says, a desire for change, a commitment to change, an understanding of the things to be changed, recognition by others of the change, and a belief on the part of the individual that he in fact has a new identity (1963:216). Whether or not such conditions can be met in the process of culture change is an open question, although anthropologists have dealt with the problems that arise when the conditions are not met. Chance (1965:377), for example, found that Alaskan Eskimos who desired to change their identity—that is, who wanted to abandon Eskimo clothing, food and so on in favor of Western apparel, food, and forms of recreation—but who did not have access to Western goods or services were more likely to develop symptoms of mental disorder than those who either had access to such goods or did not care to identify themselves as Westerners (see also Parker and Kleiner 1970). In other words, where you have both a commitment and a desire to change an identity, but where there is no recognition from the reference group or no access to "proof" of the identity change, rates of mental ill-

ness will increase. Graves (1967) found that a similar situation among the Navajo resulted in increased incidence of alcohol use, and Berreman (1964: 240-41) discovered in his study of the Aleuts that "when identification with a dominant group is unsuccessful it leads to overt rejection of the [dominant] group and glorification of the membership group such as one finds with revitalization movements of the nativistic type" (see also Goodenough 1963:287; Wallace 1966:157; Burridge 1969). Parker (1964:338) comes to much the same conclusion when he states that

minority group members attracted to Western society are more likely to develop negative attitudes toward their own and the dominant ethnic group when they perceive barriers to their newly acquired aspirations. A devalued self-image and hostility toward Western society emerge from a situation where individuals set new goals which they then perceive they cannot reach.

Thus one finds that when the desire and effort to change one's identity are unsuccessful, and the distance increases between the self a person wants to be (his ideal identity) and the self he does not want to be (his feared identity), the result may be mental disorder, excessive use of alcohol, or alienation from one's own and the reference group.

Peacock's (1968) study of Javanese drama suggests not only a parallel between culture change and rites of passage, but also the importance that such areas of culture as folklore, drama, literature, and art play in presenting identity models (see also Bruner 1959). Bronowski (1965:58), in fact, states that all the arts function to tell the individual something about his self. Postal (1965) has compared Kwakiutl and Hopi folktales in an effort to delineate the way these two societies conceptualize body image. While her interest is primarily in analyzing folktales to arrive at world view, her work suggests that folktales or literature (see Merrill 1961) may serve as an important vehicle by which the individual learns the appropriate behaviors or symbols that characterize identities in his society. It is perhaps more than a stylistic device that makes such writers on identity and self as Lynd (1958), Goffman (1959), and Laing (1962) draw so heavily on literature for examples of identity processes.

IDENTITY DIFFUSION OR DISSOLUTION

Identity diffusion[10] is a term introduced by Erik Erikson to denote a splitting of self-images, a loss of center, or a dispersion of identity. When viewed from the perspective of the identity-health model, identity diffusion connotes a psychopathic state in which the individual suffers from a lack of identity confirmation and alienation (Erikson 1968:212-16). However, when viewed from the perspective of the identity-interaction model, identity diffusion is a process that facilitates identity formation or change. Phenomena such as shame (Lynd 1958) and "mortification of the self" (Goffman 1960:454) function, in this sense, to dissolve the old identity and open the person to experiences involved in the formation of a new identity. Schwartz and Merten (1968:1129) view the ritual hazing of a sorority pledge as a preparation for her transformation of identity by serving to raise questions about her self, which "thereby opens her to the expe-

rience of a radical reintegration of self." Goffman (1960) speaks of the same process in discussing the "initiation" of inmates into total institutions. They enter the new social situation with already established identities, as do the sorority initiates. The inmates are then systematically stripped of their old identities. First, all identity equipment—personal possessions signifying the old identity—are taken from the inmate. After this defacement process the inmate is then stigmatized, called such names as "fish" and "swab," and given demeaning tasks (Goffman 1960:456); all sources of confirmation of the old identity are removed. Then the inmate begins to learn the "house rules" (1960:457), and to reorganize his self around the new situation. The military inductee in a democratic society also enters his new situation with an identity formed around values different from those of the new life. He also is stripped of his old identity by having his clothing removed and his hair shorn, and then is given the paraphernalia of his new identity. As Vidich and Stein (1960: 499) put it, "Through a multiplicity of such processes, the recruit was enjoined to participate in the world of military symbols and to reshape or drop previous identities, while picking up new self-images consistent with the terms and framework of the military community."

Identity diffusion as a process used to facilitate identity transformation may also be seen in the procedure by which individuals become shamans (Wallace 1966:145). Such things as fasting, trance, drug use, and removal from the community may be viewed as behaviors that aid in the dissolving of the old identity preparatory to the acceptance of the new. Wallace (1966: 150) states:

___

[10] Erikson (1968:212) later replaced the term "identity diffusion" with the term "identity confusion," because, he says, the former term connotes a spacial concept. The term "identity diffusion" is retained here because the author believes it better expresses the phenomenon in question, and because it has already attained usage in anthropology (see Schwartz and Merten 1968:1129).

The general process of becoming a shaman is . . .

remarkably similar throughout the world: a phase of schizoid identity dissolution is followed by a phase of paranoidal identity restitution, the new identity being that of shaman, and with community support and encouragement for the development of controlled hysterical dissociability during which the shaman is able to visit, speak to, see, or be entered by his alter ego.

The question arises as to the effectiveness of identity diffusion in accomplishing the transformation from one identity to another. It is relevant, therefore, that research suggests that the more severe the rite of passage, or the greater the amount of culturally induced identity diffusion, the more the individual is committed to the group into which he is being initiated, or the greater his commitment to his new identity (Abrahamson 1966:115).

IDENTITY MANAGEMENT AND WORK

Identity management, or, as Wallace (1967:67) calls it, "identity work," is the effort a person makes to present an image of himself, or "stage a character" (Goffman 1959:252), with the aim of eliciting from others information that will confirm or validate the desired image or identity. Identity management may entail specific behaviors on the part of the individual designed to elicit identity-confirming information, or it may entail the adoption of certain material goods or insignia designed to elicit such responses (Goffman 1956). Such identity work may be done for the purpose of confirming an already established identity, of rectifying a spoiled or stigmatized identity, or of defending an identity that has been challenged.

Barth (1969) treats as a "forum" those situations where a Pathan may act out behavior that exhibits his claim to the ethnic identity of Pathan. By being hospitable, for example, the host is given an opportunity to "exhibit his competence in management, his surplus and the reliance others place on him. More importantly, it shows the ease with which he assumes responsibility, and implies authority and assurance—basic male Pathan virtues" (1969:121). The Pathan political council also serves as a forum where a man is able or permitted to demonstrate courage, judgment, dependability, and morality, all basic attributes of a desired Pathan identity (1969:122). In such forums, or by such behavior, a Pathan is given the opportunity to prove to others that he does indeed possess the attributes of the identity he claims. Barth also points out that in changing situations, where such attributes do not define a favorable identity, the behavior associated with the Pathan identity is discontinued (1969:129).

Eidheim (1969) gives an excellent account of identity work in the behavioral mechanisms used by Lapps to rectify the stigmatized identity they believe is attributed to them by Norwegians (see also Goffman 1963). Norwegians view Lapps as inferior, so, as Eidheim points out, if Lapps are to participate in the Norwegian life to which they aspire, they must publicly deemphasize their "Lappishness" to qualify themselves as "full participants in the Norwegian society" (1969:48). Thus they work toward demonstrating their competence in modern fishing and agriculture, or pretend to be well traveled, or dwell on their cleanliness and fine housing, and speak Norwegian in an effort to present an identity they believe will qualify them for Norwegian life and to deemphasize an identity they believe would disqualify them from such a life. Eidheim (1969:51) gives a vivid illustration of that process:

Five or six [Lapp] men were engaged in the work together with the Norwegian crew of three, whose main job was trimming the vessel. The spacial setting was a boat alongside the quay with a relatively big storehouse on the shoreside where the fish was kept. On the quay among themselves and in direct interaction with the crew on the quay edge, the [Lapp] men used Norwegian, inside the storehouse they used Lappish; they switched every time they passed the door.

A third type of identity management is that done by a person whose identity has been threatened or challenged. The Kwakiutl potlatch represents such an example of identity work (see Wallace and Fogelson 1965:388). Codere (1950: 63) makes explicit in her discussion of the potlatch that it involves the maintenance or confirmation of a social position, that by the ostentatious display and distribution of wealth the person is validating his identity and defending it against the rivalrous claims of others. Thus the giver of the potlatch not only would give away goods, but would also boast of his exploits and ridicule those who would threaten his identity (see Benedict 1959:272).

IDENTITY STRUGGLES

Wallace (1967:78) calls an identity struggle those interactions in which there is a discrepancy between an individual's claimed identity and the identity attributed to him by others. Perhaps one of the best examples of an identity struggle in the anthropological literature is the "medicine fight" of the Beaver Indians of British Columbia (Ridington 1968). The Beaver, as mentioned above, believe that an individual's power or status (identity) is determined by the amount of supernatural power he possesses, a power confirmed in part by his hunting prowess or personal fortunes. Any lack of success in hunting or any personal misfortune is seen by others as a loss of that power, and hence a loss of prestige (Ridington

1968:1155). The person experiencing the misfortune, however, does not interpret his lack of success in this light; to him his misfortune is not caused by his loss of supernatural power, but is a result of an attack by someone who is using his power against him. In other words, the identity he claims to have—a person possessing a high degree of supernatural power—is different from the identity attributed to him by others, who see his failures as a loss of power. The protagonist in this drama then dreams to establish the identity of the person who he believes is directing this supernatural assault upon his person, and publicly accuses that individual. This begins the "medicine fight": a series of accusations and counteraccusations that occasionally lead to physical violence (Ridington 1968:1155).

The identity struggle concept also enhances our understanding of certain withcraft practices. Middleton (1966), for example, in his analysis of conflict resolution among the Lugbara, treats as separate phenomena ghost invocation and witchcraft, although the Lugbara term for both is identical (1966:147). When viewed from the perspective of identity theory, however, the two practices become complementary aspects of the same phenomenon. When a Lugbara feels that he should have a status (identity) higher than that recognized by others, this claim is passed on to the elders in the community. The elders, through the use of oracles, invoke the ghosts of the dead ancestors, who must validate or invalidate the claim. If someone's claim to a more desirable identity is confirmed, then it follows that those individuals of once equal status, or those to whom the individual was subordinate, lose status relative to the person who has had his new identity validated. They in turn resolve their loss of prestige by claiming that he obtained oracular confirmation through the use of witchcraft. If they are able to convince others of this charge, the man is "cast out from the everyday system of authority" (Middleton 1966:148). In other words, the person who seeks oracular confirmation is attempting to resolve a discrepancy between his claimed identity and his public identity; if such a claim is validated it infringes on the identity of others, who may then attempt to rectify the discrepancy between *their* claimed and attributed identities through accusations of witchcraft. Thus both ghost invocation and witchcraft are complementary aspects of a process of identity struggle.

Identity struggles need not always be couched in supernatural terms. The entire potlatch process is, in effect, a series of identity struggles, as are most types of ceremonial exchange (see Salisbury 1962).

One additional phenomenon that the concept of identity struggle may help us understand is the effect of economic change on interpersonal relations within a society. When new goods are introduced into a society and these goods have identity value—that is, status-conferring qualities—but the means of access to these prestige goods are different from the avenues of access to goods previously considered to confer status, there appears to be an increase in the frequency of identity struggles (see Salisbury 1962, Robbins 1973). Before the introduction of wage labor among the Kwakiutl, a person could potlatch or make an identity claim only if he had the appropriate inherited social rank. With wage labor, however, anyone with money could purchase potlatch goods from the Hudson's Bay Company store, give potlatches, and hence claim a more desired identity. The result, as Codere (1950:96) points out, was an increase in potlatching. Among the Lugbara, a similar sequence of events led to an increase in witchcraft accusations (Middleton 1960:228; 1962).

IDENTITY CONFIRMATION

Identity confirmation involves those cultural processes that function to permit or aid the individual in attaining consistency between his self and his social and public identities. Rites of passage, ceremonial exchanges, or gift-giving in dyadic relations all serve this function. Ceremonies in total institutions, as Goffman (1960:472) suggests, serve to confirm identities, and Erikson (1968:51) sees the Yurok sweat ceremony as a way in which "male self-esteem and inner security are restored by ritual atonement." Two cultural processes that have been viewed from the standpoint of identity theory will be examined here as mechanisms that confirm identities: curing rituals (see Wallace 1967:63) and trance states.

The Ndembu *Isoma* ritual is performed when a woman has not been able to conceive children. The Ndembu believe that such an affliction occurs when a woman has been caught or entered by a "shade" or ancestral ghost because she has forgotten her matrilineal ancestors (Turner 1969:11). The Ndembu are a matrilineal society but practice virilocal residence. As a result, a woman's loyalty is torn between her matrilineal kin, who are responsible for her children, and her husband, in whose village she resides (Turner 1969:12). When viewed from the perspective of the identity framework, the affliction is caused by a fading of the woman's identity or by a lack of definiteness of the group membership aspect of her identity. The curing ritual itself serves to reconfirm her identity as a member of a specific descent group, as well as to reconfirm the identities of all others in the ceremony vis-à-vis each other.

Wallace (1966) and Bourguignon (1965) have analyzed possession or trance states utilizing the identity concept. Wallace contends that possession allows the individual to lapse into alternative identities, a lapse precipitated by "profound identity conflict" (1966: 145). Salvation by possession, he says,

... involves the acceptance of two (or even more) mutually contradictory identities, each being permitted or even encouraged to take exclusive control of the body at certain times, with more or less mutual ignorance or indifference. The possession allows the acting out of an identity that on other occasions would be disallowed.

Bourguignon's study of trance in Haiti takes Wallace's analysis a step further. To Wallace, the identity conflict leading up to the possession is resolved by the acting-out process. Bourguignon, on the other hand, sees the resolution springing from the reaction of others to the trance victim. In Haiti trance occurs when a person is mounted by a spirit or *loa*, who itself is ranked in a status hierarchy. Others react to the individual in trance not according to his identity, but according to the identity of the possessing spirit. One case cited by Bourguignon (1965:53) is illuminating:

A. C.'s father . . . is a mild-mannered man, generally ignored and pushed around by his kin. Yet he has one of the most powerful deities of the family, and when possessed, he is given great deference by his wife, who has left him, by his children, by his successful half-brother, and by others. Significantly his possession on ceremonial occasions appears to linger on longer than most others.

In other words, while the possession ceremonial allows the individual to cloak himself in a new identity, one that is more desirable than his everyday identity, his self-esteem (the distance between his ideal and actual identity) is restored not only by the acting out of the new identity, but by the recognition received from others of the validity of the new identity.

One may deduce from the propositions enumerated earlier, and from the above analysis, that every society must periodically set aside a time during which the identities of its members are confirmed or reconfirmed to ensure the smooth working of everyday social interactions (see Wallace 1966:138). These periods bear some resemblance to what Erikson (1968:156) has called a "psychosocial moratorium," except that they are not limited to one specific time in the life cycle, but must recur throughout the life of the person.

IDENTITY METHODOLOGY

The effectiveness of any ethnographic method may be measured not only by its ability to generate useful data, but also by the time and finances involved in applying it and by the cooperativeness of informants in submitting to it. As such, methods of obtaining information on identity may be viewed in terms of ease of application, ranging from such inferential techniques as the "good man" method (see below) to the more complex self-report interviews, such as Kelly's (1955) "Role Construct Repertory Test." The aim of this section will be to examine the techniques utilized by anthropologists in obtaining information on identity, and to appraise the usefulness of such techniques.

INFERENTIAL METHODS

The "good man" method has the virtue of allowing the researcher to deduce the identity structure of a society from existent ethnographic materials. It entails the delineation of those attributes that a society uses to define a desirable person, and the assumption that persons in that society are striving to attain those attributes. The identity structure of a society may also be arrived at through observation of behavior or by the examination of such expressive areas of culture as religion or myth. Chance (1965:379) was able to infer the ethnic identity of Eskimos from the way they dressed, their food preferences, and their choice of recreational activities, and Postal (1965) inferred the body image of the Kwakiutl and Hopi from their folktales.

While such methods are attractive for their ease and range of application, they have the disadvantage of assuming much. In Chance's study, for example, one may ask whether the adoption of Western clothing, food, and recreation actually represented a change in ethnic identity, or whether it represented a new way of symbolically representing old identities.

PICTURE TESTS

Two picture tests have been developed that aim toward gathering information on identity. Parker (1964) utilized five pictures depicting situations, objects, and persons from Western and Eskimo society in an effort to elicit stories from Eskimo informants relevant to ethnic identity. He was able to show that hostility directed toward Western persons in such stories was a measure of what he calls "inter-ethnic social distance" (1964:332). From a picture of a pilot and an airplane he elicited either interest in what the pilot was doing or overt hostility with comments expressing the wish that "the pilot would go away and not come back anymore" (1964:333).

The "Instrumental Activities Inventory Test" developed by George and Louise Spindler (1965) can also be used for gathering data on ethnic identity. With this technique individuals are shown pictures of persons engaged in various activities intended to represent either traditional pursuits, contemporary native activities, or activities associated with the dominant group. The activities used by the Spindlers on a Blood reservation include carpentry, farming, branding calves, and chicken dancing, among others (1965:319). Informants were then asked to choose those activities they valued most highly, and an equal number of those most disliked. The Spindlers' aim was to find out how the choices of activities related to such variables as sex, schooling, and socioeconomic status, to arrive at cognitive orientations, and to reveal how persons viewed themselves in relation to such activities.

Picture tests have the advantage of eliciting data on self-image in a more direct way than the inferential methods listed above. Their major drawbacks are in cross-cultural application, where the investigator must be aware of much of the value system of the culture being studied. The Spindlers point out, for example, that while a Blood Indian might in fact wish to be an office worker, the pragmatism of these people prevents them from choosing an activity that is not actually available to them (1965:326).

SELF-REPORT TECHNIQUES[11]

Self-report methods involve directly eliciting from informants what they think about themselves. They may entail asking informants "how they would like to be" as compared to "how they would not like to be" (Wallace 1967:80); they may involve getting information on how the individual thinks his rights and duties distribute to specific others (Goodenough 1965a); or

---

[11] For a review of self-report techniques, see Wylie 1961.

they may involve the more elaborate triadic sorting technique developed by George Kelly (Spradley 1970:75).

Goodenough (1965a) used a scalogram to discover how persons perceived their duties vis-à-vis others. With this method one takes a set of duties ("must bow to," "must avoid," etc.) appropriate to the society being studied, and elicits from informants whether or not such duties apply to them in relation to specific others. By utilizing this method with various dimensions (e.g., "deference") one can arrive at the total identity structure of a society.

Spradley (1970:75) used the triadic sorting technique in his analysis of the attributes that define various types of tramps. Informants were given terms for three kinds of tramps ("bindle stiff," "airedale," "boxcar tramp") and asked to show which two were alike and which one was most different from the other two. Informants were then asked the criteria by which such distinctions were made.

Self-report methods are preferable to either inferential or picture test techniques since they involve the informant's own perception of his and others' identity. Their major weakness is that they are highly time consuming, making it difficult for informants to devote either the time or concentration necessary for the task. This is especially true when informants are unaware of the reasons they are being asked such questions.

CONCLUSIONS

This paper has been an attempt to review and evaluate the use of the identity concept in anthropology. It has attempted to demonstrate that the identity framework can enlarge our understanding of such phenomena as initiation rituals, possession states, and ceremonial exchanges, as well as to il-luminate much about the process of cultural change. It has presented issues that can be profitably pursued within the identity framework, and shown how such a framework complements the culture concept.

It would be useful to review briefly some of the advantages of the identity concept in anthropology as it has been presented here. First, the theory involved is relatively simple. Second, it relates to such traditional anthropological concerns as ethos, value, and theme, as well as to such supernatural concerns as soul. Third, it forms a bridge between folk and scientific theory to the extent that most, if not all, societies have implicit in their belief system some idea or construct of self and identity. Finally, as Wallace (1967) points out, it relates directly to cognitive theory, involving, as it does, getting the "natives' point of view" on the ways in which they differentiate, define, and give meaning to identities within their society. In this instance it has the additional virtue of supplying cognitive theory with a motivational dimension.

One last point: In an earlier section some basic propositions were listed relating to the identity construct. They imply a view of the human animal that may best be summed up in William James's (1952:198) phrase "self-seeking"; that is, the prime motivation for human behavior may be sought in the efforts of the person to bring within his orbit behaviors, objects, or persons that reflect to him the image of himself he desires. It is perhaps not amiss to say that the vitality of identity theory must rise or fall on the acceptance or rejection of this proposition.

REFERENCES

Abrahamson, Mark
    1966 *Interpersonal   Accommodation*. Princeton, N.J.: Van Nostrand.

Allport, Gordon W.
1960 *Personality and Social Encounter.* Boston: Beacon Press.
Barth, Fredrik
1969 Pathan Identity and Its Maintenance. In *Ethnic Groups and Boundaries,* ed. F. Barth, pp. 117-34. Boston: Little, Brown.
Benedict, Ruth
1959 Anthropology and the Abnormal. In *An Anthropologist at Work,* ed. M. Mead, pp. 262-83. Boston: Houghton Mifflin.
Berreman, Gerald D.
1964 Aleut Reference Group Alienation, Mobility, and Acculturation. *American Anthropologist* 66:231-50.
Bourguignon, Erika
1965 The Theory of Spirit Possession. In *Context and Meaning in Cultural Anthropology,* ed. M. E. Spiro, pp. 39-60. New York: Free Press, Macmillan.
Bronowski, J.
1965 *The Identity of Man.* Garden City, N.Y.: Natural History Press.
Bruner, Jerome S.
1959 Myth and Identity. *Daedalus* 88: 349-58.
Burridge, Kenelm
1969 *New Heaven, New Earth: A Study of Millennarian Activities.* New York: Schocken Books.
Burton, Roger V., and John W. M. Whiting
1965 The Absent Father and Cross-Sex Identity. In *Reader in Comparative Religion,* ed. W. A. Lessa and E. Z. Vogt, pp. 610-14. New York: Harper & Row.
Chance, Norman
1965 Acculturation, Self-Identification, and Personality Adjustment. *American Anthropologist* 67:372-93.
Codere, Helen
1950 *Fighting with Property.* American Ethnological Society monograph, no. 18. Seattle: University of Washington Press.
Cohen, Yehudi A.
1964 The Establishment of Identity in a Social Nexus: The Special Case of Initiation Ceremonies and Their Relation to Value and Legal Systems. *American Anthropologist* 66:529-52.

Cooley, Charles H.
1956 *Human Nature and the Social Order.* Glencoe, Ill.: Free Press. Originally published 1909.
Coopersmith, Stanley
1967 *The Antecedents of Self-esteem.* San Francisco: W. H. Freeman.
Devons, Ely, and Max Gluckman
1964 Conclusion: Modes and Consequences of Limiting a Field of Study. In *Closed Systems and Open Minds: The Limits of Naivety in Social Anthropology,* ed. M. Gluckman. Chicago: Aldine.
Diggory, James C.
1966 *Self-Evaluation: Concepts and Studies.* New York: Wiley.
Douglas, Mary
1966 *Purity and Danger: An Analysis of Concepts of Pollution and Taboo.* New York: Praeger.
Durkheim, Émile
1938 *The Rules of Sociological Method.* Glencoe, Ill.: Free Press.
Eidheim, Harald
1969 When Ethnic Identity Is a Social Stigma. In *Ethnic Groups and Boundaries,* ed. F. Barth, pp. 39-57. Boston: Little, Brown.
Erikson, Erik H.
1959 The Problem of Ego Identity. In *Psychological Issues* 1:101-164.
1968 *Identity, Youth, and Crisis.* New York: Norton.
Evans-Pritchard, E. E.
1937 *Witchcraft, Magic, and Oracles Among the Azande.* London: Oxford University Press.
1965 *Theories of Primitive Religion.* Oxford: Clarendon Press.
Foote, Nelson N.
1951 Identification as the Basis for a Theory of Motivation. *American Sociological Review* 16:14-21.
Gillin, John
1948 Magical Fright. *Psychiatry* 11:387-400.
Gluckman, Max, ed.
1964 *Closed Systems and Open Minds: The Limits of Naivety in Social Anthropology.* Chicago: Aldine.
Goffman, Erving
1956 The Nature of Deference and Demeanor. *American Anthropologist*

58:473-502.

1959   *The Presentation of Self in Everyday Life*. New York: Doubleday.

1960   Characteristics of Total Institutions. In *Identity and Anxiety*, ed. M. Stein et al., pp. 449-79. New York: Free Press of Glencoe, Macmillan.

1961   *Asylums*. New York: Doubleday.

1963   *Stigma: Notes on the Management of a Spoiled Identity*. Englewood Cliffs, N.J.: Prentice-Hall.

Goldschmidt, Walter

1959   *Man's Way*. Cleveland: World.

Goodenough, Ward H.

1956   Componential Analysis and the Study of Meaning. *Language* 32:195-216.

1963   *Cooperation in Change*. New York: Russell Sage Foundation.

1965a Rethinking Status and Role. In *The Relevance of Models for Social Anthropology*. Monograph no. 1, pp. 1-24. London: Tavistock.

1965b Personal Names and Modes of Address in Two Oceanic Societies. In *Context and Meaning in Cultural Anthropology*, pp. 265-76. New York: Free Press, Macmillan.

Graves, Theodore D.

1967   Acculturation, Access, and Alcohol in a Tri-Ethnic Community. *American Anthropologist* 69:306-321.

Hallowell, A. Irving

1955   *Culture and Experience*. Philadelphia: University of Pennsylvania Press.

1959   Behavioral Evolution and the Emergence of the Self. In *Evolution and Anthropology: A Centennial Appraisal*, pp. 36-60. Washington, D.C.: Anthropological Society of Washington.

Harris, Marvin

1966   The Cultural Ecology of India's Sacred Cattle. *Current Anthropology* 7:51-66.

1968   *The Rise of Anthropological Theory*. New York: Crowell.

Hegel, G. W. F.

1910   *The Phenomenology of Mind*, trans. J. B. Baillie. London: Allen & Unwin.

Honigmann, John J.

1968   The Study of Personality in Primitive Societies. In *The Study of Personality: An Interdisciplinary Appraisal*, ed. E. Norbeck et al., pp. 246-76. New York: Holt, Rinehart & Winston.

James, William

1952   *The Principles of Psychology*. Chicago: Encyclopaedia Britannica. Originally published 1891.

Kelly, George

1955   *The Psychology of Personal Constructs*, 2 vols. New York: Norton.

Kennedy, John G.

1967   Psychological and Social Explanations of Witchcraft. *Man* 2:216-25.

Kiefer, Christie W.

1970   The Psychological Interdependence of Family, School, and Bureaucracy in Japan. *American Anthropologist* 72:66-75.

Kinch, John W.

1963   A Formalized Theory of the Self-Concept. *American Journal of Sociology* 68:481-86.

Kluckhohn, Clyde

1967   *Navaho Witchcraft*. Boston: Beacon Press.

Kroeber, Alfred L.

1909   Classificatory Systems of Relationship. *Journal of the Royal Anthropological Institute* 39:77-84.

1917   The Superorganic. *American Anthropologist* 19:162-213.

1944   *Configurations of Culture Growth*. Berkeley: University of California Press.

Laing, R. D.

1962   *The Self and Others*. Chicago: Quadrangle Books.

Lee, Dorothy

1959   *Freedom and Culture*. New York: Prentice-Hall.

Lerner, Daniel

1958   *The Passing of Traditional Society*. Glencoe, Ill.: Free Press.

Lévi-Strauss, Claude

1963   *Totemism*. Boston: Beacon Press.

1966   *The Savage Mind*. Chicago: University of Chicago Press.

Lévy-Bruhl, Lucien

1966   *The "Soul" of the Primitive*. New York: Praeger. Originally published 1927.

Lounsbury, F. G.
1956 A Semantic Analysis of the Pawnee Kinship Usage. *Language* 32:158-94.
Lynd, Helen Merrell
1958 *On Shame and the Search for Identity*. London: Routledge & Kegan Paul.
McCall, George J., and J. L. Simmons
1966 *Identities and Interactions*. New York: Free Press, Macmillan.
Malinowski, Bronislaw
1944 *A Scientific Theory of Culture*. Chapel Hill: University of North Carolina Press.
Mead, George H.
1934 *Mind, Self, and Society*. Chicago: University of Chicago Press.
Merrill, Francis E.
1961 Stendhal and the Self: A Study in the Sociology of Literature. *American Journal of Sociology* 66:446-53.
Middleton, John
1960 *Lugbara Religion*. London: Oxford University Press.
1962 Trade and Markets Among the Lugbara of Uganda. In *Markets in Africa*, ed. P. Bohannan and G. Dalton, pp. 561-78. Evanston: Northwestern University Press.
1966 The Resolution of Conflict Among the Lugbara of Uganda. In *Political Anthropology*, ed. M. Swartz et al., pp. 141-54. Chicago: Aldine.
Miller, Daniel R.
1963 The Study of Social Relationships: Situation, Identity, and Social Interaction. In *Psychology: A Study of Science*, ed. S. Koch, 5:639-737. New York: McGraw-Hill.
Murdock, George Peter
1949 *Social Structure*. New York: Macmillan.
Nadel, S. F.
1951 *Foundations of Social Anthropology*. Glencoe, Ill.: Free Press.
Opler, Morris E.
1964 The Human Being in Culture Theory. *American Anthropologist* 66:507-528.
Parker, Seymour
1964 Ethnic Identity and Acculturation in Two Eskimo Villages. *American Anthropologist* 66:325-39.

Parker, Seymour, and Robert J. Kleiner
1970 The Culture of Poverty: An Adjustive Dimension. *American Anthropologist* 72:516-27.
Peacock, James L.
1968 *Rites of Modernization*. Chicago: University of Chicago Press.
Postal, Susan Koessler
1965 Body-Image and Identity: A Comparison of Kwakiutl and Hopi. *American Anthropologist* 67:455-62.
Redfield, Robert
1953 *The Primitive World and Its Transformations*. Ithaca: Cornell University Press.
Ridington, Robin
1968 The Medicine Fight: An Instrument of Political Process Among the Beaver Indians. *American Anthropologist* 70:1152-60.
Robbins, Richard H.
1973 Alcohol and the Identity Struggle: Some Effects of Economic Change on Interpersonal Relations. *American Anthropologist* 75:99-122.
Rogers, Carl R.
1959 A Theory of Therapy, Personality, and Interpersonal Relationships, as Developed in the Client-Centered Framework. In *Psychology: A Study of Science*, 3:184-256. New York: McGraw-Hill.
Róheim, Geza
1950 *Psychoanalysis and Anthropology*. New York: International Universities Press.
Rubel, Arthur J.
1964 The Epidemiology of a Folk Illness: Susto in Hispanic America. *Ethnology* 3:268-83.
Salisbury, Richard
1962 *From Stone to Steel*. Melbourne University Press.
Schwartz, Gary, and Don Merten
1968 Social Identity and Expressive Symbols: The Meaning of an Initiation Ritual. *American Anthropologist* 70:1117-31.
Spindler, George D.
1968 Psychocultural Adaptation. In *The Study of Personality: An Interdisciplinary Appraisal*, ed. E. Norbeck et al., pp. 326-47. New York: Holt,

Rinehart & Winston.

Spindler, George D., and Louise Spindler
 1965 Researching the Perception of Cultural Alternatives: The Instrumental Activities Inventory. In *Context and Meaning in Cultural Anthropology*, ed. M. E. Spiro, pp. 312-37. New York: Free Press, MacMillan.

Spradley, James P.
 1970 *You Owe Yourself a Drunk: An Ethnography of Urban Nomads.* Boston: Little, Brown.

Steward, Julian
 1955 *A Theory of Culture Change.* Urbana: University of Illinois Press.

Strauss, Anselm L.
 1959 *Mirrors and Masks: The Search for Identity.* New York: Free Press of Glencoe, Macmillan.

Sullivan, H. S.
 1953 *The Interpersonal Theory of Psychiatry.* New York: Norton.

Trent, Richard D.
 1965 Economic Development and Identity Conflict in Puerto Rico. *Journal of Social Psychology* 65:293-310.

Turner, Victor W.
 1969 *The Ritual Process.* Chicago: Aldine.

Tylor, Edward B.
 1958 *Religion in Primitive Culture.* New York: Harper & Row. Originally published 1871.

Veblen, Thorstein B.
 1931 *The Theory of the Leisure Class.* New York: Random House.

Vidich, Arthur J., and Maurice R. Stein
 1960 The Dissolved Identity in Military Life. In *Identity and Anxiety*, ed. M. Stein et al., pp. 493-506. New York: Free Press, Macmillan.

Voget, Fred W.
 1960 Man and Culture: An Essay in Changing Anthropological Interpretation. *American Anthropologist* 62:943-65.

Wallace, Anthony F. C.
 1966 *Religion: An Anthropological View.* New York: Random House.
 1967 Identity Processes in Personality and in Culture. In *Cognition, Personality, and Clinical Psychology*, ed. R. Jes-

sor and S. Feshback, pp. 62-89. San Francisco: Jossey-Bass.
 1968 Anthropological Contributions to the Theory of Personality. In *The Study of Personality: An Interdisciplinary Appraisal*, ed. E. Norbeck et al., pp. 41-53. New York: Holt, Rinehart & Winston.

Wallace, Anthony F. C., and Raymond D. Fogelson
 1965 The Identity Struggle. In *Intensive Family Therapy*, ed. I. Boszormenyi-Nagy and J. L. Framo, pp. 365-406. New York: Harper & Row.

Wheelis, Allen
 1958 *The Quest for Identity.* New York: Norton.

White, Leslie
 1949 *The Science of Culture.* New York: Farrar, Straus.
 1959 *The Evolution of Culture.* New York: McGraw-Hill.

Whiting, John W. M., Richard Kluckhohn, and Albert Anthony
 1958 The Function of Male Initiation Ceremonies at Puberty. In *Readings in Social Psychology*, ed. E. Maccoby et al., pp. 359-70. New York: Holt, Rinehart & Winston.

Wilson, Paul R.
 1968 Perceptual Distortion of Height as a Function of Ascribed Academic Status. *Journal of Social Psychology* 74:97-102.

Wintrob, Ronald M.
 1968 Acculturation, Identification, and Psychopathology Among Cree Indian Youth. In *Conflict in Culture: Problems of Developmental Change Among the Cree*, ed. N. A. Chance, pp. 93-104. Ottawa: Canadian Research Centre for Anthropology.

Wylie, Ruth C.
 1961 *The Self Concept: A Critical Survey of Pertinent Research.* Lincoln: University of Nebraska Press.

Young, Frank W.
 1962 The Function of Male Initiation Ceremonies: A Cross-Cultural Test of an Alternative Hypothesis. *American Journal of Sociology* 67:379-96.

CHAPTER 28 Anthropology and Education

FREDERICK O. GEARING

Sciences are not legislated; they just grow. This was historically true of anthropology and its major subdisciplines. It remains true and becomes evident whenever a substantial number of anthropologists find themselves discovering new interconnections among old curiosities and concerns, and become increasingly intrigued by them. When such curiosities and concerns fall into some common realm, these men begin to find one another. To all appearances a momentum of that sort is now building in the very broad and seemingly heterogeneous realm suggested by the phrase "anthropology and education."

Over the last thirty years many anthropologists have intermittently engaged themselves in this realm in the hope that the "anthropological message" might reach more people, and have looked to matters of curriculum in schools and colleges. Other anthropologists have been led to the same realm by ethnographic and theoretical interests in behaviors that unfold in and around the schools and colleges, at home or in other contexts remote in

place or time. Interests in spreading the anthropological message and in producing ethnography or theory have usually seemed most dissimilar and have typically been kept separate. In recent years, however, when anthropologists have chanced to engage themselves in education for some substantial period of time, it has become evident to many of them that the first interest leads quite inevitably to the second. The anthropological message has competition. In a trivial sense that message competes with messages from other realms of scholarship for scarce curriculum space. In a fundamental and more interesting sense it competes with processes of cultural transmission in the changing society at large, and thus competes directly with the pivotal aspects of those processes as they unfold in the schools, less through purposeful instruction than through reenactments, unawares, of cultural values, beliefs, and forms of organization. In short, any nontrivial interest in the anthropological message leads quite inevitably to an interest in the seemingly distinct ethnographic and theoretical enterprise. The reverse is also true, not inevitably perhaps, but with marked frequency.

Of course, interconnections within each of these two areas have also emerged; for example, some of the ways in which cultural transmission in formal educational settings differs from cultural transmission in familial settings have become apparent, as well as continuities and discontinuities between these two aspects of socialization. The behaviors in the schools, in those societies that have them, reveal to the oncoming generation a great deal about the shape of the wider social structure (its statuses) and a great deal more about the variety of entailed behavioral expectations (its roles), but these things are revealed in distorted form, probably systematically distorted form. "Schools," remarked Bud Khleif, one of the wittier anthropologists involved in this realm, "are museums of virtue." In a word, schools comprise a major scene of one aspect of socialization—socialization to large groups.

It is not yet clear what the recent interest in interconnections of this sort in the general realm of anthropology and education portends for the future. A subfield is perhaps best defined sociometrically: those who engage in it are in more frequent communication with each other than with others in other subfields. By that measure the realm of anthropology and education is conspicuously not a subfield today, though it may soon become one. Nor is "anthropology and education," as of today, a body of theory. Rather it consists of an array of research and intervention-research interests bearing on the nature of those institutions called schools—on the ways schools daily recreate themselves and change, on the patterning of behaviors that occur in and around them, and on the parts played by those behaviors in the trans-

mission of culture to oncoming generations. Anthropologists tend to view schools in broad social contexts and comparatively, the most heuristically powerful comparisons being perhaps those with processes of cultural transmission in small-scale societies that traditionally have had no schools. Such writings by anthropologists to date have been almost exclusively in the language of "first-draft" ethnography, with only minimal press toward both the careful derivation of emic language, as in ethnoscience, and the careful generation of etic language required for worldwide cross-cultural studies.

It might follow, and does seem to be true, that the net deliverable result to date is a taxonomy of major human situations and some characteristics of processes of cultural transmission in those situations. Such a taxonomy is not much, but it sets the stage for a wide array of research and intervention-research and thereby invites such activity, some of which is under way and much more of which appears imminent.

ANTHROPOLOGY AND EDUCATION IN HISTORICAL PERSPECTIVE

During the two decades beginning in 1930, a remarkable number of anthropologists were moved to write on matters explicitly related to education. Earlier, in 1904 and 1905, E. L. Hewett wrote critically about the parochial nature of curricula, recommending the broader perspective of anthropology; Boas, in 1928, after research on the variability in rates of maturation, wrote about maturation and other matters as well, as these seemed to him to bear on the work of the schools; also in 1928 Margaret Mead wrote the first of a distinguished series of studies on cultural transmission and schools. The list of writers from 1930 to 1950, even in the absence of a serious attempt at systematic coverage, reads like an anthropological who's who: in 1930 Mead again; in 1931, Hogbin; in 1932, Rattray; in 1936, Firth, Malinowski; in 1937, Keesing; in 1938, Raum, Fortes, Herskovits; in 1939, Goldenweiser; in 1941, Morris Opler, John Whiting; in 1942, Nadel; in 1943, Erikson, Redfield, Malinowski, Mekeel, Benedict, Embree, Powdermaker, Watkins; in 1944, Thompson and Joseph, Du Bois, Lloyd Warner et al.; in 1945, Goldfrank; in 1946, Pettit; in 1947, Leighton and Kluckhohn, Ehrich; in 1949, Joseph, Spicer, and Chesky. Almost all these writings drew upon the authors' own ethnographic data; almost half dealt with traditional educational systems, and an equal number dealt with Western schools in nonwestern settings. In all these studies it is possible to read messages for schools generally, and in several those messages are made explicit. The literature is "early" only in the time sense; for example, Fortes' 1938 study, "Social and Psychological Aspects of Education in Taleland," must surely be one of the very best works in this realm to date. Much of this early work has been ingested in the body of anthropological theory and method.

It is evident that the attention of these anthropologists, once drawn to educational matters, was as quickly drawn away. Margaret Mead is of course the most conspicuous exception. Perhaps ten of these thirty-odd persons wrote two to four additional items; probably none wrote more than that except Mead and perhaps Warner. That patterned sequence of attention and inattention is not remarkably different from the way in which anthropologists, over total careers, have treated such topics as technology, economic systems, political organization, religious ritual, and so on. Teaching-learning behaviors have been treated as one in the series of separable and more or less obligatory "chapters" that together constitute the table of contents of the usual monograph, which seems plausible enough in the context of a genre of holistic, ethnography-based research. This handling of *this* topical heading, though, points to a history-of-ideas puzzle of some possible interest.

In that genre of anthropological research, a perceptual screen selectively made one phenomenon but not another into a datum, and that screen is clear: learned behaviors became data, which is to say that one studied culture. Within that mind-set, "education" was but another category of learned, customary practices—how they do that—and in the main was treated as such. However, if learned behavior is the subject matter, then things learned and the learning itself are opposite sides of the same coin. In the historical flip of that coin— which is the intellectual history of these particular ideas—culture fell up and cultural transmission down. Perhaps anthropology could as easily have become a science in which the ethnographic monographs were organized under such topical headings as cultural transmission before two years, from two to twelve, at marriage, and so on; or cultural transmission inside the family, inside the village, beyond; and with either or both, there would be a longish chapter at the end entitled "Things Learned: A Recapitulation." How is it that the coin did not fall that way? This is the puzzle. I have no answer.

Historically anthropology and education studies have usually sought to have some impact on human practice—principally an impact on the schools. Perhaps paradoxically, the most instructive early career is that of an adoptive colleague, Maria Montessori. She was a physician, but she is reported to have studied anthropology and psychology intensively over some seven postgraduate years. She was half scientist and inquirer, half mystic and prophet, which brings her within the range, at least, of certified practioners of the anthropological enterprise. She appears to have studied no tribal or peasant peoples, but she worked most intensively with the urban poor, worked in fact with the often homeless gamins of the Roman slums, and in all probability no one's culture could be more exotic than that. More importantly, at all crucial points she acted like an anthropologist: in her insistence that the human animal learns not with tongue and ear and brain alone but with all its parts, not through transactions between adult and child alone but through interaction with the total physical and human environment as well. It is as if she had closely scrutinized the processes of cultural transmission in a host of tribal societies, and had inferred that since these are the prevailing patterns in such societies, and since *Homo sapiens*, living in such societies through virtually all of the human career and across all continents, seems to have kept "reinventing" these same processes of cultural transmission, there must be something to be learned there. But most centrally, Maria Montessori behaved like an anthropologist in this: She insisted that, however "true" such general principles may prove to be, there must be ethnography—that one must see the general in the rich particularized detail of good ethnography. She required this disciplined constraint of herself, and, even more, she insisted that the workers in the schools (she did not like the word "teacher") incessantly do ethnography as well. She has been described as "the woman who looks at children as a naturalist looks at bees."

Montessori wrote extensively, including *Pedagogical Anthropology* in 1913; three of her works have been recently reissued under the titles *The Montessori Method* (1964), *Spontaneous Activity in Education* (1965a), and *Dr. Montessori's Own Handbook* (1965b).

Montessori's career is instructive if one looks not principally at Montessori, but at how she was received in this nation. We briefly look back in order perhaps to see ahead. Montessori invested her total energies in intervention-research in educational settings. The educational practices she said would work did in fact dramatically work in the slums of Rome. That living exhibit was tangibly there for men to inspect, and many prominent men from around the world, notably including the United States, did inspect it, and most were astounded. The questions are: To what effect? And why that effect?

After an initial period of curiosity and some support, Montessori was soundly rejected by the scientific community (essentially psychology). Psychologists simply determined that her theory was wrong, though they were divided as to precisely how. According to a recent review of those years by J. McV. Hunt (1964), the rejection was based on some five prevailing notions, all five of which seem today to have been quite wrong. (It does not follow, of course, that Montessori was necessarily right.) Of those five notions then prevailing in the scientific community, four were fully congruent with the then-building momentum in a related realm, instrumented measurement, testing. For example, one notion, that of fixed intelligence, was closely related to the growing interest in IQ testing.

In the schools, the reaction was similar. Public interest in Montessori began in this country in 1909, and there was a grace period of some five years before there was concerted expression of opposition from the psychologists. But in a complex of interlocking bureaucracies, almost nothing happens in five years. When the chorus of theoretical opposition began, the schools—in some relief, one imagines—opted out.

Perhaps there is an American cultural pattern of some pervasiveness and power evident in this. It has to do with social structure, with expectations as to conduct according to social position, and specifically with shared notions about who gets information and who passes it on to whom. One sees a hierarchy of structural positions; from top down: the scientific community, a hinge population of once-removed scientists who interpret and certify new knowledge, school administrators at various levels, teachers, students. If one then looks at the notion of fixed intelligence, and at the designing and use of its (then) counterpart, IQ testing, and if one imagines those informations flowing through the hierarchy, one fact is reasonably evident: in each of the dyadic pairs of the hierarchy, *initiatives* are always reserved by one who is "up" (who acts) vis-à-vis one who is "down" (who is acted upon)—initiatives in putting in motion the behaviors that yield information, initiatives in deriving meaning from the information, and initiatives in using the meanings derived.

Montessori's work quite literally implied the reverse placement of two of the three kinds of initiative. She structured classroom environments mainly in the form of a cafeteria-like array of "didactic apparatus" among which the child moved, selected, manipulated. But her main task, and her teachers', was ethnographic: to watch what the children did. When it became evident that an item was not working for the child, the task then was to devise some modification or some alternative device on the spot, or later if necessary, and

the new device in turn became part of the cafeteria.

Now, by that procedure, some initiatives flow upward through the hierarchy instead of down. Now student-initiated behaviors yield information to teacher, and teacher-initiated behaviors yield information to administrator, and so on up the line. Initiatives in deriving meaning from such information would seem to flow downward, following the old pattern; Montessori was not proposing some mindless laissez-faire. But initiatives in using the new information would seem again reversed, to flow upward: the child opts, in the first instance, to be engaged by the new or modified device, or not to be engaged. There is abundant evidence in hosts of diverse situations that persons at all levels of such hierarchies have found such reversals most difficult to accept.

Ethnography is the art and discipline of watching and listening, and of trying inductively to derive meaning from behaviors initiated by others. We tend, like Montessori, to recommend it widely. The presumption is strong that it was not Montessori the theorist who was rejected after all. It was Montessori the ethnographer. Let anthropologists stick by their guns, but let them beware.

CHARACTERISTICS OF CULTURAL TRANSMISSION

Given the emergent nature of anthropology and education, an attempt to characterize the area is especially subject to idiosyncratic interpretation. What follows will unavoidably be so. Four analogous attempts are readily available, and the reader is well advised to consult them. The American Educational Research Association's *Review of Educational Research* periodically publishes reviews of research by people in various disciplines, including anthropology. In 1961 Theodore Brameld and Edward B. Sullivan prepared such a review. Subsequent reviews have been published by Harry Wolcott (1967a) and Peter Sindell (1969).

In 1955 George D. Spindler edited *Education and Anthropology*, a volume based on a 1954 conference of anthropologists and educators, and in 1963 he edited a second collection of essays, *Anthropology and Culture*, by anthropologists and educators. These two volumes serve well to suggest the variety of anthropological interests and concerns in this realm at those two points in time. More recently, two readers have appeared: Harry M. Lindquist's *Education: Readings in the Processes of Cultural Transmission* (1970) and John Middleton's *From Child to Adult: Studies in the Anthropology of Education* (1970). Finally, a volume of essays edited by Murray Wax et al., *Anthropological Perspectives on Education* (1971), is derived from a series of conferences organized by Stanley Diamond and later by Murray Wax and me. These two readers and the last collection, like the earlier volumes, serve to suggest the variety of anthropological interests.

In an emergent realm no very distinct defining limits are visible, nor can such limits be now drawn, except capriciously. My purpose here is to exemplify and in that sense to characterize the substantive knowledge about cultural transmission. What can be offered is a gross taxonomy of human situations, and some of the characteristics of cultural transmission as these vary among large classes. Those large classes are merely these: studies of cultural transmission in little societies versus studies in big ones, and within the latter category studies of cultural transmission in one-culture situations versus studies in multicultural situations.

The boundary of any society is of course not simply "there," but must be found, and for these and many other purposes boundaries seem best drawn by political criteria; that is, a "society" here is the largest politically autonomous grouping (in acephalous structures this means the village or other units *within* "peace groups" or "jural communities"). The division that seems most predictive, as far as size is concerned, is between communities of less than 1,500 population and those of more than 10,000; the middle range of communities of 1,500 to 10,000 population is better examined separately, in view of the variability to be anticipated there. Within the class of large societies, the distinction between one-culture and multiculture situations must be somewhat arbitrary, for in all big societies there are divergent career lines, urban centers and rural hinterlands, and other pervasive distinctions that necessarily generate divergent life styles. Sometimes such divergences are relatively minor and thus there are big one-culture societies, though these are relatively rare. The more common multicultural situations in big societies are evidenced in markedly contrasting life styles based on rural-urban differences, ethnic differences, differences based on economic class and/or sociological race, and so on.

These three large categories of human situation were not generated, of course, by studies of cultural transmission, but by the wider traditions of anthropological thought or habit. Often some such similar categories are held in mind by the scholars whose works are now to be viewed; if not, I shall impose them in the interest of finding or creating a measure of order.

CULTURAL TRANSMISSION
IN SMALL SOCIETIES

What can be said of a general nature, first, about cultural transmission in small societies?[1] In 1938 Meyer Fortes, crediting Hoernlé (1931), Firth (1936), and Malinowski (1936), summarized what was then known about education in "preliterate" societies (Fortes 1938:5-6):

[We know that] the training of the young is seldom regularized or systematized, but occurs as a "by-product" . . . of the cultural routine; that the kinsfolk, and particularly the family, are mainly responsible for it; that it is conducted in a practical way in relation to the "actual situations of daily life." It has been observed that manners and ethical and moral attitudes are first inculcated within the family circle in association with food and eating and with the control of bodily functions. A good deal of discussion has been devoted, also, to what appear to be overtly educational institutions, such as initiation schools and ceremonies, age grades, or secret societies. It has been proved that direct instruction in tribal history, sexual knowledge, and ritual esoterica is promoted by these institutions.

Fortes then notes that while those earlier studies provided much information about what is transmitted and about the circumstances and framework of the transmission, very little is known about how the transmission occurs, and he proceeds to address the question: How does a member of a younger Tallensi generation come to be "transformed from a relatively periph-

eral into a relatively central link in the social structure; from an economically passive burden into a producer; from a biological unit into a social personality irretrievably cast in the habits, dispositions, and notions characteristic of his culture"? In regard to the circumstances and framework of that transformation, Fortes records, much as others had earlier for other peoples (1938:9):

. . . As between adults and children in Tale society, the social sphere is differentiated only in terms of relative capacity. All participate in the same culture, the same round of life, but in varying degrees, corresponding to the stage of physical and mental development. Nothing in the universe of adult behaviour is hidden from children or barred to them. They are actively and responsibly part of the social structure, of the economic system, the ritual and ideological system. Psychological effects of fundamental importance for Tale education follow from this. For it means that the child is from the beginning oriented towards the same reality as its parents and has the same physical and social material upon which to direct its cognitive and instinctual endowment. The interests, motives, and purposes of children are identical with those of adults, but at a simpler level of organization. Hence the children need not be coerced to take a share in economic and social activities. They are eager to do so. This does not mean that Tale children are altogether passive in the hands of their parents. Temperamental idiosyncrasies in children strike the observer at a glance. Tantrums, disobedience, destructiveness, and other aggressive outbursts occur sometimes. Among youths and adults misfits and incompetents can be found. But even they live for the same ends and have the same objective values and interests as the majority.

That the Tallensi education system quickly and most powerfully does its task Fortes illustrates by a series of anecdotes, the most astonishing perhaps being this (1938:11):

I was playing with [two boys] (8-9 years), sons of the same joint family, and their

---

[1] Studies of cultural transmission in small societies defy extrication from the established realm of culture and personality. Contrasts in emphasis are apparent. Culture and personality studies are usually concerned with the affective dimensions of teaching-learning transactions and with the affective aspects of things learned, while education studies tend to treat teaching-learning transactions as cognitive transactions concerned with beliefs and values and organizational forms. This and other such contrasts are artifacts, observer-borne to the scene. I have no license or inclination to legislate. I am talking now about cultural transmission in small societies; I shall invoke the territoriality implicit in the table of contents of this volume (and, in any event, the territoriality ascribed by my own spotty competence) and shall try to avoid culture and personality.

friends. We were discussing parents. [They], speaking together, told me the story of the latter's mother. Three or four years ago she had run away from their father to marry another man. They said, in the very words that an adult member of the family would use, speaking seriously: "She ran away and took our belly and went and bore over there, so our child is there. Then she bore another child there. When our child is big enough we will separate it and bring it home." These two were thus identifying themselves completely with the family, mother-child attachments notwithstanding.

In part, Fortes continues, the Tallensi teaching-learning behaviors are consciously and purposefully pointed to the perpetuation of Tallensi culture. Rituals are recognized to contain specific educational functions; in this patrilineal society genealogical knowledge is critical, and children learn the identities of critical ancestors at sacrifices: "Our ancestor shrines are our books," said a chief. The education functions of imitative play with hoe or bow are recognized, and such play is encouraged. Rebuke or physical punishment occurs when a child fails in some responsibility that by Tallensi judgment may reasonably be expected of him.

Everyone except infants and the very old is simultaneously a teacher of others younger and a student of others older. The age differences may be great or small and the relationships may exist among play groups or within the family or beyond, according to the situation. Fortes sees these educating relationships forming a "social space" that expands as the child grows (1938:17):

. . . An individual's social space is a product of that segment of the social structure and that segment of the habitat with which he or she is in effective contact. To put it in another way, the social space is the society in its ecological setting seen from the individual's point of view. The individual creates his social space

but is himself in turn formed by it. On the one hand, his range of experiences and behaviour are controlled by his social space, and on the other, everything he learns causes it to expand and become more differentiated. In the lifetime of the individual it changes *pari passu* with his psycho-physical and social development.

He traces the widening circles of that social space as the child grows to adulthood and traces what is learned in both incremental and differentiating (as by sex) terms.

But Fortes' concern is not only with what is learned and the circumstances of the learning, but how it is learned. Intertwined, he says, and in Taleland closely correlated, are four facets of maturation: the physiological, the psychological, the social, and the cultural. The Tallensi imagine these to unfold together naturally, at rates that vary from child to child, into an array of learned interests, skills, and observances (right conduct and obligations, ethical values, ritual requirements, and so on), from childhood into adulthood. This learning, Fortes suggests, proceeds by the gradual addition of detail to "schemas" (1938:42-43):

These total patterns which constitute the texture of Tale cultural behaviour are not built up bit by bit, by addition, during the course of a child's life. They are present as *schemas* from the beginning. My observations suggest that the course of development is somewhat as follows: at first the child acquires a well-defined interest associated with a postural diagram of the total pattern. The postural diagram is, as it were, a contour map, extremely simplified and crude but comprehending the essential elements and relations of the full pattern. Further experience strengthens and amplifies the interests at the same time as it causes the details of the postural diagram to be filled out, making it more and more adaptable and controllable, producing more discriminatory responses to real situations, and linking it up with other patterns of behaviour and with norms of observance. The total pattern is not built up brick by brick, like a house, but evolves from the embryonic from.

Fortes provides illustrative examples, including the following, in respect to kinship (1938:43-44):

... The schema, rudimentary and unstable as yet, can be detected in the 3-4-year-old. He or she discriminates kinsfolk from non-kinsfolk, equating the former mainly with people living in close proximity. He knows his own father and mother precisely, but already calls his mother's co-wives "mother." Similarly, he knows that "father" is his own father, but that other men—in the first instance those of the same joint family—are also "fathers," and he knows that the other kinsfolk frequently seen are brothers, sisters, grandfather, grandmother. But he is still incapable of discriminating genealogical differences; he groups people by generation and by spatial proximity. Thus an adult brother may be described as a "father." A child learns the fundamental kinship terms and has the idea of distinguishing its relatives according to generation and genealogical distance long before it can couple this knowledge accurately with differential behaviour towards kinsmen. The 6-year-old knows the correct terms and appropriate behaviour defining its relations with the members of its own paternal family and has grasped the principle of classification according to descent. But in practice he still confuses spatial proximity and relative age with kinship, beyond the limits of his own family. The 10-12-year-old has mastered the schema, except for some collateral and affinal kinsmen, the terms for whom are known though he cannot describe the relationships.

Biological drives and cultural motives combine to produce variations in the rates of evolution of different schemas. I have not the experimental data to give accurate or even sample norms, but a rough indication is possible. If the 6-year-old is compared with the 12-year-old in respect to e.g. knowledge of the kinship structure, of agricultural processes, of ritual, and of sex life, the 6-year-old is least advanced in knowledge of the kinship structure and ritual, and most advanced in his or her knowledge of sex life, while knowledge of agricultural processes could fall somewhere between these two levels.

Finally, Fortes names imitation, identification, and cooperation as the main learning processes among the Tallensi; provides ethnographic data suggesting how these operate; and gives a detailed account of the variations of imitative play according to age and sex.

As ethnography, the report has rarely been equaled, and it would well serve other ethnographers as an "outline of cultural materials" in regard to cultural transmission. Fortes asks, in effect: In any small society, how many persons take it upon themselves to correct or instruct a child? Who are these persons specifically? Which behaviors do they imagine require attention and which do they expect will simply "come along" in due time? If a behavior requires attention, when does one intervene in the lifetime of child and adult? What are the frequency and kinds of rewards and punishments? When is the person imagined to be educationally "finished," if ever? And of course what is transmitted—the culture itself in this small society?

As generalizing theory, Fortes' study is thought-provoking and at no point easy to dismiss. There is one point of special interest. The notion of "schemas" (not original with Fortes, as he notes) may be a powerful heuristic, or it may be more; Piaget would insist on an unfolding series of more basic schemas, differentiated as to cognitive form, as a controlling matrix that would in turn shape a congruent series of schemas specific to the content of any particular realm; he would, that is, very probably interpret Fortes' kinship example differently.

It is unclear whether Fortes intends the three named learning processes to be specific to the Tallensi or universally basic by the nature of the human psyche.

Firth (1936), upon whom Fortes drew in his 1938 study, provides particulars about the educational system of the Tikopia, which differs in no fundamental way from that of the Tallensi.

Pettit (1946) summarizes ethnographic tendencies in cultural transmission systems of North American Indians, and concludes that: (1) corporal punishment is rare; (2) otherwise discipline is common and is typically relegated to specific kinsmen or other specific individuals, to cult groups, to the society at large through ridicule, and especially to supernatural powers; (3) spontaneous imitation is not "the basic motive" for learning; avoiding ridicule and seeking praise or other reward are; (4) the giving of personal names, frequently in a series, acts as an effective stimulus to learning; (5) training in economic pursuits is not slighted nor, relatively, is religious training emphasized; (6) where the vision quest is found, it is generally accessible to most persons (males, females, or both, variously from society to society) and is a quest for "inner conviction of social and economic competency and spiritual security"; (7) myths, folktales, biographies, and autobiographies all serve nontrivial educational purposes, and indeed seem to have been "influenced in their development" by those purposes.

Williams (1958) describes the cultural transmission system of the Papago in terms of the "six major structural features": the Papago pattern of reward and punishment, which has an unusual degree of indulgence before puberty; their pattern of social deference to relative age, in small increments, pervasively; their pattern of sharing family work, which is extensive, beginning with small tasks very early; their pattern of use of supernatural sanctions for disruptive and personally dangerous behavior, extensively; their pattern of expecting similar behavior of children and adults, with one set of norms, which the child is expected slowly to approximate; their pattern of treating the child as a person, thus permitting him the same opinions and free choices as adults, qualified by the requirement that before acting he first consult someone older.

Two studies may be mentioned, in part as illustration of the capriciousness of any attempt to separate cultural transmission studies in anthropology and education from culture and personality studies. Dorothy Eggan (1956) has described traditional Hopi instruction. Her special focus on the affective components in teaching-learning transactions puts the study at or over that arbitrary boundary. Yet she found that those affective elements "continued to operate throughout the entire life span of each individual as a *reconditioning* factor . . . [and this helped maintain] stability both in the personality structure of the individual and the structure of the society." Similarly Spindler (1963) has described the traditional Menominee personality formation and cognitive learning process, which gives special attention to religious ritual and storytelling.

As cultural facts, initiation rites have an honored tradition of their own in anthropology, going back to Van Gennep's *Rites of Passage*. Hart (1955) is perhaps to be credited with bringing these institutions into full focus in the context of the analysis of cultural transmission. Hart badly overstates his case in one respect: he attempts to argue that all instruction by kinsmen and neighbors—that is, *all* instruction other than "postpubertal" instruction—amounts to random behaviors (*within* any community) and has inconsequential effect; this is, he says, "an area of cultural laissez faire." Nevertheless, in his analysis of postpubertal instruction, principally initiations, Hart does hit upon four ethnographic facts of apparently wide generality and significance: (1) at the point of initiation, educational responsibility shifts into the hands of strangers or near strangers or disguised, unrecognizable intimates; (2) initiations are frightening and often painful, generally traumatic; (3) initiations enact and convey through taboos the boy's separation from home; (4) the "curriculum" at initiations does not focus on basic food-getting skills, but rather "includes such things as the learning of the myths, the tribal account of the tribe's own origin and history, and the performance, the meaning, and the sacred connections and connotations of the ceremonials."

Hart says (1955:141):

In doing this, society is asserting and underlining its rights in the child. . . . Clearly in every society there is always a family and there is always a state, and equally clearly both have rights in every child born into the society. And no society yet—Western or non-Western—has found any perfect way or equal way of adjudicating or harmonizing public rights and private rights. The state's rights must have priority when matters of citizenship are involved, but the assertion of the state's rights is always greeted with wails of anguish from the family. "I didn't raise my boy to go off and get subincised," wails the Australian mother, but he is carried off and subincised just the same. . . . It is an inevitable conflict, because it arises from the very structure of society, as long as society is an organization of family units, which it is universally. The only solution is to abolish the family or abolish the state, and no human group has been able to do either.

The point can be restated. The cultural transmission processes in these small societies are not random or otherwise dormant prior to the time of initiation; that they have done their cultural transmission job well is indeed

evidenced by the insistence on separation at the point of initiation. "Separation" reads, in structural terms, "change roles," as we have long known. Additionally, in more narrowly educational terms, separation does not read, as Hart suggests, "Now let us get started"; rather it reads, "There is something else." That something else is an additional system of symbols (myths, rituals, and so on), precisely those symbols that embody the initiate's widest identity, as tribesman or whatever, as may be required by the social structure of his community and of its wider social environs. In these small politically autonomous societies that wider structure is often the patterned system of alliance and apposition called the peace group or jural community.

All this is ethnographic, of whatever generality. Hart also speaks of "inevitable conflict" between the claims of the family and the wider community, and he implies that that inevitable conflict is inevitably handled by initiations. But the Tallensi do not practice initiations (except narrowly, as inductions into one kind of cult grouping—this with no other educational function). The structure of the wider Tallensi society is unusual—the lineages with their ancestor shrines, these joined in clans with their rituals, which variously overlap and complement each other in Fortes' "fields of clanship." In such a system, perhaps, there is no structural need for the form of exclusive, unifying identity that appears to be a critical educational function of initiations. This is a theoretical matter that requires investigation. It speaks to continuity and discontinuity in cultural transmission, to the conditions under which each occurs, which is to say, to two educational tasks and the purposes they both serve.

Finally, a document of an entirely different nature needs special mention:

Ruth Underhill's *Autobiography of a Papago Woman* (1936). Everything said above is revealed there, and poignantly so, for here was a woman temperamentally ill suited to receive the transmission, yet the Papago educational system accomplished its work—imperfectly but adequately, as is so often the case in this class of human condition, these small societies.

CULTURAL TRANSMISSION
IN LARGE SOCIETIES

Big societies abound. But big societies with some reasonable measure of cultural homogeneity seem extremely rare. Lawrence Wylie (1957) has described the educational system of one good candidate for this class of human circumstance—a village in France. I have seen, but have not studied with this focus of attention, another, a village in Greece. Perhaps the bush schools among the Mende as described by Little (1951) provide another. Wylie notes several cultural matters that are transmitted in the French school, matters broader than the information and technical skills taught. One of these is a general intellectual stance: it is conveyed to students that particular facts are shifting and meaningless in themselves; that general principles are enduring and "given"; that the task of intellect is to derive the correct principle from facts, or to seek appropriate facts based on principle. It is further conveyed that this stance is deemed appropriate in science and morals alike. Besides transmitting culture, the French school serves a gatekeeping function; through examinations at junctures over the years the student is moved into one or another track that in turn sets his future career choices. This of course points to the commonly perceived function of the schools, to transmit knowledge and develop skills,

which is what the examinations purport to measure; and in these homogeneous situations, they probably do measure them reasonably well.

If one includes in this class of circumstance a modest increment of cultural heterogeneity, there is Warren's (1967) study of the school system in a German farming village newly affected by industrialization, and Singleton's (1967) study of education in a Japanese village similarly affected. In both, the gatekeeping functions of these schools are conspicuous, in the form of a series of formal examinations, nationally prepared, which fully determine the educational and career futures of the students. In both, the career option between agricultural and urban pursuits is of course evident to students and their families; there is some effort on the part of some agricultural families to keep sons in agricultural pursuits, apparently more so in Germany than in Japan; but the options are invidiously ranked by the schools and the society at large and by the agricultural families themselves.

In both schools, matters of cultural transmission, beyond information and skill, are evident. One such matter is an area of minor dispute in Japan: many parents wish the schools to teach "morals" as in prewar years, but to the teachers that connotes the prewar militaristic nationalism, and most of them refuse or evade the issue. In any event, it is an empty dispute, as Singleton's data make evident (though it is not treated explicitly in the analysis); for while moral precepts may not be talked about much, the moral rule, obedience to hierarchical authority, is enacted with virtually total consistency throughout the day, by the school staff in relation to each other, by students in relation to teachers (with some stylistic variation), and by younger students in relation to older students.

Analogous cultural matters are transmitted in the German context. Warren's study contains much ethnographic detail of classroom behaviors, on the basis of which he gives this summary of the first weeks of the child's introduction to school (1967:28).

The first month was an impressive introduction to a pattern of school life sharply characterized by structure and order. From an institutional point of view, the first grader experienced a process of social incorporation which not only had a central focus on authority but which also allowed few alternatives or deviations. The incorporation process was experienced directly—particularly through the style and intensity of discipline imposed by the teacher and indirectly through, for example, academic channels of expression which imposed minimal possibilities for freely chosen responses.

The use of language was especially significant. Pupils were encouraged to render thought patterns, simple emotional reactions, ideas about proper conduct in the classroom, and ideas about basic social and personal relationships with family members and peers, in a mode of expression that had literally a poetic form and rhythm. More attention was given to an appropriate verbal rendition of this form and rhythm than to a free, relatively unstructured exploration of its content . . .

In all these cases, French, German, Japanese, there is a strong sense of common identity and common purpose between the villages and the urban centers to which they attach—in general, cultural homogeneity.

When children in larger societies enter school, they leave one site of cultural transmission, the home and neighborhood, and enter a new one. In this new site new kinds of cultural content are conveyed, including the codes by which the people of the society relate to one another in large groups. This is clearly evident in the German and Japanese cases; the German classroom conveys the rationalized bureaucratic order of the wider German society and the Japanese classroom conveys the more personalized hierarchical order of the wider Japanese society. These wider structures are replicated, reenacted, in the classrooms. In part this is accomplished through purposeful plan. Probably in larger part it is accomplished without conscious intent, for the teachers themselves are socialized to behave in a manner that projects the cultural code.

This aspect of cultural transmission, socialization to large groups, requires future ethnographic scrutiny. We know almost nothing about the selectivity that must necessarily occur. What, from the totality of the wider code, is selectively replicated? We know still less about the "language" of replication. Does the plethora of little poems in the German classroom really read "bureaucratic order" to the children? We suspect there is cultural lag in the classroom as compared to cultural change in the wider community, but we know little about lag with any exactness. Big societies are prone to accelerated social change, but when a child learns about behavioral codes in the wider society, and when that child-become-adult-become-teacher reenacts that code in the classroom, and then those children in the classroom grow up and move into that wider society, how much lag are we talking about? And are there recurrent processes in the selection and training of teachers and in organizational adaptation of the school which tend to increase the lag or decrease it?

Further, when we exercise the heuristic of comparison, two additional ethnographic questions emerge. First, in the small societies earlier in view, technical training occurred in the context of kinsmen; now it has shifted in large measure to the school. In those small societies technical achievement was presumably measured by performance; now it is measured indirectly by examinations. Bias of some kind is necessarily introduced in the gatekeeping function of these schools, but we know almost nothing about precisely how such examinations get made, administered, evaluated—by what array of selected persons with what array of prior socializations? And thus, even in these culturally homogeneous societies, with what systematic bias? Second, in small societies initiations are often found to be the occasion for the mobilization of symbols that embody men's widest identities. In large societies these would be national identities. Salutes to the flag and the like are rather different from subincision, and one suspects rather beside the point. What are these larger symbols? How are they mobilized in schools, if they are?

Homogeneous Isolates Within Heterogeneous Societies

Beyond these large and culturally homogeneous societies, there are homogeneous "parts" of otherwise heterogeneous societies where the cultural transmission systems seem little affected by heterogeneity. For analytic purposes these homogeneous isolates can be considered apart from the heterogeneous societies of which they are part. Henry (1957) has described middle-class students with middle-class teachers in schools in this nation; he has analyzed in good ethnographic detail how, through interactions between teacher and students—interactions not in the curriculum and only subliminally in anyone's mind—attitudes get organized, such as docility, a readiness for confession, a "witch hunt syndrome." Again (1959) Henry describes how teachers' attempts to let these children be "free," as those efforts are worked through and "handled" in the social structure of the classroom, in fact serve

to dampen rather than enhance creativity. Burnett (1969) has looked at high school ritual (homecoming) and recognizes there some of the processes of cultural transmission that anthropologists have usually found in solidarity rituals. Atwood (1964) describes interactional patterns in the bureaucracy of a school as an innovation is introduced and resistances develop. West's classic study *Plainville, U.S.A.* (1945) describes the educational process in a culturally homogeneous rural setting.

Studies of these homogeneous isolates tend to emphasize an ethnographic fact often seen in the earlier studies on homogeneous societies—the very large role, in the overall task of cultural transmission, played by unconscious enactment, as against conscious "teaching"—and with the same implications as to selectivity of replication of the wider social order, the language of that replication, and lag in cultural transmission.

CULTURAL TRANSMISSION IN HETEROGENEOUS SOCIETIES

Surprisingly, perhaps, more anthropologists have done educational studies in heterogeneous societies than in all others combined.

Margaret Mead (1942) observes that there are "learning cultures" and "teaching cultures." By the first she means the small societies viewed earlier; the phrase is misleading, but the intended contrast is well taken. By "teaching cultures" she means culturally large and heterogeneous societies. When she calls these societies teaching cultures she means that all cultural transmission of which adults are consciously aware requires that those who know tell those who do not know, and she sees this mind-set as generated by the fact of cultural heterogeneity, especially by the various colonialisms that follow cross-cultural contact; in teaching cultures that mind-set is further extended to apply to one's own children as well.

The overview, from this point, must be extremely selective. One form of cultural heterogeneity derives from ethnic history. The study by Wax and his associates (1964) of "country Sioux" in their federally run school and later in high school traces the emergence of student-teacher conflict at about grade two, and the further perfection of coordinated warfare by each year's "generation" of students against their teachers; these are wars the students win "but in winning lose." The conflict is put in motion by, among other things, teachers' insistence on competitive individualism in classroom behavior (as in reciting), which is alien to the students; the teachers enact and exact that individualism, but do not purposefully teach it. Wolcott (1967b) reports parallel phenomena from his participant observation as teacher in a Kwakiutl school. Sindell (1968) has observed Cree students in school and out, and has focused on contrasting notions about aggression, a closely parallel matter. Parmee (1968) has looked at Apache schools. King (1967) reports on a church-run Canadian boarding school for Indians. Among other things, he describes the staff organization of the school itself, the role sets, especially as these appose Indian and white, adult and child; as an ethnographer he was especially fortunate that a role discrepancy was introduced to that organization—two Indian women were hired as counselors, a status previously held by whites—and he watched as the organization "righted itself" by extruding the discrepant element. La Flesche (1963) has described his own student life in an Indian school.

Hobart and Brant (1966) compare schools for Eskimos in Greenland and Canada in regard to organization, the selection of teachers, and the language and content of instruction. Honigmann and Honigmann (1965) include a chapter on the schools in their ethnography of a mixed Eskimo-Canadian town.

In all these bicultural situations, schools are by definition hinge institutions. If they are indeed hinges, they have consistently become rusted, for they do not do well any of the tasks that any of the involved parties intend. Why? Perhaps for two reasons, operating singly or together. First, the cultural differences at issue are in fact large. It seems improbable, however, that contrasts in world view, great as these often are in such cases, would necessarily prevent teacher and student from jointly accomplishing their recognized "core" task of transmitting and learning essentially technical skills (the three Rs). On the other hand, these observers note repeatedly items from another facet of culture: individualism and communality, contrasting definitions of aggression in interpersonal relations, and other conflicting states. These reflect contrasting systems of role expectations, and, as the writers have noted, they indirectly block the work at hand by precluding functional relationships between teacher and student and throughout the classroom generally. About this we have abundant ethnographic detail.

Here, however, studies come to rest, for no very good reason other than some habitual anthropological sense of closure. The ethnographic question is: Under what conditions and in what ways do teachers simply alter their own role behavior, or the students alter theirs? There do not seem to be ideological resistances involved, at least at a conscious level. We deal, no doubt, with problems of cross-cultural perception in the first instance (see Du Bois 1955, Gearing 1970a). We deal also with problems of role retransaction, the way it occurs, the conditions under which it occurs and fails to occur; that is, we deal with social change in bureaucratically organized institutions, to which we shall return below.

A further array of studies in analogous multicultural settings is at hand. Theodore Parsons (1965) has studied the reenactment in the classroom of the caste structure of a Chicano-Anglo community in California, and Madsen (1964) and Rubel (1966) have included school phenomena in their studies. Gans (1962) includes a section on education in his study of an urban Italian-American community. Studies in English from other continents exist in smaller numbers. Philip Foster (1965) analyzes the national educational system in Ghana, including higher education, especially as it affects spatial and social mobility. Lindquist (1970) has assembled a series of readings dealing for the most part with educational phenomena in Africa, Asia, and Europe. Other studies include Fischer (1961) on Japanese schools on Truk, Redfield (1943) on Indian-*ladino* schools in Guatemala, and Nash (1961) on a village school in Burma.

Studies bearing directly on cultural transmission in the schools are now emerging with some frequency from linguistics and cognitive anthropology. In Liberia Gay and Cole (1967) have studied the strong predilection of the Kpelle to conform intellectually to information they deem traditional and to reject discovery itself, and more particularly the Kpelle mathematical operations; the problems and prospects of both areas have been analyzed in relation to Western schools in the region. There have been studies of black dialects and related matters by Bailey (1969), Bernstein (1964), Dillard (1967, 1968, 1969), Gumperz (1969), Kochman (1969), Labov (1969), Stewart (1969), Talbert (1969), and Wolfram (1969). Maccoby and Modiano (1969a, 1969b) have studied contrasting cognitive styles in Mexico.

It is evident that the contrasts we have noted between processes of cultural transmission in small societies and those in big and homogeneous societies are to be found within large multicultural societies. Here again, in the realm of socialization to large groups, transmission seems to move by enactment as much as or more than by conscious instruction. Hence the same implications follow: questions as to selectivity in classroom replication of codes from the wider social structure, questions as to the language of replication, questions as to lag in the codes replicated. But here, in these multicultural settings, those problems are confounded by the ethnographic question: Whose codes? The answer seems clear, though published ethnographic detail is almost wholly lacking: The codes of those segments of the larger societies that enjoy economic and political power. Similarly, questions about the language of replication are confounded by other questions: Whose language? And does it carry the message? The answers seem clear, but the ethnographic data are missing. And the matter of generational lag may become confounded to the degree that shifts occur in the selection of teachers from the various cultural segments of the total population.

The gatekeeping function of the schools still obtains, with the entailed problems of measurement of achievement. And both are dramatically confounded in these multicultural situations. Finally, there remain the ethnographic questions about the nature of symbols that convey to students their widest (i.e., national and other) identities, and whether these significantly enter the classrooms. These questions are confounded by the confounding of identity questions generally in multicultural societies; i.e., whose identity is to be celebrated, adopted, deferred to, whatever?

All these dimensions of incremental ethnographic questioning refer to the fact of differential power, which in many of the situations reviewed above becomes virtually polarized, all the power versus none at all. Power and its exercise raise of course another whole series of questions as to ethnographic fact.

Finally, hinge institutions seem often to work poorly in these multicultural situations, and schools have been conspicuous in this regard. That in turn raises questions as to organizational change. King's (1967) study of the Canadian boarding school for Indians included good ethnographic detail of the structure of the school and of the processes of change and resistance to change that operated there. Eddy (1969) has provided a good corpus of data gathered by interviews with teachers in inner-city schools during their first year as teachers.

I had occasion, in the context of the generally abortive relations between teachers and students in Indian schools, to raise the question as to the conditions under which people do reciprocally retransact roles. Retransaction of role may be the growing tip of all organization change, and the two problems may thus be facets of a single problem. Atwood's (1964) study, briefly alluded to earlier, views the matter in this way. It may therefore not seem surprising that the most concerted current examination by anthropologists of the ethnography and theory of role transaction is not found among the research activities reviewed here, but in the context of curriculum-making—i.e., in intervention-research in the schools—to be reviewed below.

One final study demands separate consideration. Throughout this overview of studies in complex societies we have been caused repeatedly to note that teachers, being themselves the products of earlier cultural transmission, will enact that cultural content in classrooms, consciously or unawares; in the school now in view, teachers seem dramatically to have shifted their patterns of behavior from an individualistic to a markedly cooperative orientation. It has not been frequently noted here, but it is often evident in the studies that what teachers hope to do and imagine themselves doing in their classrooms often diverge from what they are in fact doing; in this school, aspiration and behavior seem highly congruent. I refer to Spiro's (1955) study of the school in one kibbutz in Israel.

CROSS-CULTURAL STUDIES: A BEGINNING

What the result of research to date can offer, I have said, is a gross taxonomy, and a taxonomy is not much, a mere invitation to do research. But as net result there is a bit more. Perhaps a score of anthropologists have done relevant and instructive studies of large samples of human societies. These scholars usually treat selected child-rearing practices (and the affective psychological states presumably resulting from those practices) as independent variables, and selected other practices that are clearly "educational," such as initiations or games, as dependent variables. By the tenuous criteria suggested earlier (footnote 1), these are "culture and personality" studies and also "anthropology and education" studies. I shall arbitrarily pick one (Herzog 1962) to serve as illustration. Herzog addresses questions as to the conditions under which societies practice some form of "instruction," principally by nonkinsmen—both instruction within the community and instruction that requires the student to take up residence outside his home community (the last includes most initiations). Herzog reasons (on the basis of work by Whiting et al.) that different forms of household organization (extended family, nuclear family, mother-child households) generate different psychological hurdles or proclivities for the maturing child (respectively dependency, early achievement striving or dependency, sex identity for boys). His data, analyzed in those terms and with additional reference to the size of the society (determined by political boundaries), indicate (1) that instruction inside the community correlates well with extended households, apparently serving to get the child over those dependency needs; (2) that instruction outside the community (often initiations) correlates well with mother-child households, apparently assisting male children in establishing male identifications; (3) that instruction inside the community is very probable in large societies where the nuclear family prevails and women are freed from major subsistence activities, thus apparently serving to get the child over dependency needs created by indulgent mothers. This study points to the possibility of moving beyond the gross taxonomies suggested by anthropological habit, and of course it moves beyond heuristic comparison.

Two papers by Yehudi Cohen (1969, 1971) employ cross-cultural analysis to address questions raised by this review. Cohen finds that schools emerge with state societies. And he sees the state attempting to undercut local loyalties by generating national loyalties, the school being one institution in which symbols of universalistic ideology are invoked and national loyalties generated.

Jules Henry has provided "A Cross-Cultural Outline of Education" (1960) which should prove useful in studies of cultural transmission generally, and especially in cross-cultural analysis of cultural transmission.

INTERVENTION-RESEARCH IN THE SCHOOLS

The results of anthropological research efforts are easily made visible; fieldwork leads to writings that can readily be retrieved. There remains, however, another long-standing anthropological interest: the desire, shared by most anthropologists and intermittently expressed by some, that the anthropological message reach more persons. Instances of pursuit of this interest are not at all visible, nor is there at this time any established means by which they can systematically be made visible. One hears, usually by chance association, of curriculum-oriented efforts by Nancy Gonzales in Iowa City, by Robert Kiste in Minneapolis, by Wilfrid Bailey in Athens, Georgia, by Henry Burger in Albuquerque, by Paul Bohannan in Evanston, Illinois, by Sherwood Washburn in Berkeley; I too have engaged in such activities in Riverside, California. But no one seems in a position to make even a gross estimate as to whether these efforts can be taken as examples of recent and current attempts to affect curricula by twenty anthropologists, or fifty, or five hundred.

Three recent efforts have gained a measure of visibility, each for a special and different reason. Efforts organized by David Mandelbaum, Gabriel Lasker, and Ethel Albert took place during the years 1960-1963; these addressed a variety of questions bearing on the teaching of anthropology in the colleges, mainly at the undergraduate level. This program was initiated through the American Anthropological Association and the two resulting publications were distributed to all members of the association; thus the efforts became widely known, and the results, as guidelines, have been frequently and widely consulted. *The Teaching of Anthropology* (Mandelbaum, Lasker, and Albert, eds., 1963*a*) contains essays by some fifty prominent anthropologists from this country and abroad. The companion volume, *Resources for the Teaching of Anthropology* (1963*b*), is a bibliographic work.

Two other major and well-known efforts undertook the creation of curriculum materials for the schools. The first is the Anthropology Curriculum Study Project, directed by Malcolm Collier, generally known to anthropologists because it is a program of the American Anthropological Association. The second is the principal social studies effort, currently directed by Peter Dow, of the Education Development Center of Cambridge, Massachusetts; this is known to anthropologists through the involvement of Asen Balikci, Irven De Vore, and other anthropologists, and also through the considerable national attention earned by the excellent results.

These two activities bear brief comment, for the curriculum materials they have produced provide guidelines and a good foundation for the sort of curriculum that anthropologists seem to have in mind when they speak of the broader dissemination of the anthropological message: they seem to wish the schools and colleges to be deeply permeated, throughout the years, by what might be termed an empirical "Mankind curriculum." I recently wrote (1970*b*):

The essential content of a Mankind curriculum is a single empirical fact: the discovered fact that all men are Man, members of the single species *Homo sapiens*. A Mankind curriculum is a concerted, empirical study throughout the grades of the nature of that discovered entity, Man. . . .

In such a curriculum, the persisting orienting questions are: What is human about all humans? How does any people, whoever, wherever, whenever they are, uniquely express that common humanity? These are empirical questions, to be handled empirically.

But also another empirical question: How does any people uniquely abuse and thwart their own humanness or that of their neighbors? A Mankind curriculum is a study of, not a romance with, that entity, Man.

A Mankind curriculum is essentially a grand exercise by the student in empirical comparison used as heuristic. *Homo sapiens* is most readily seen, as a single entity, in comparisons of similarities and differences with behavior in other species, especially other primates, with special attention to learning, including of course the uniquely human capacity for symbolically mediated learning. The entity *Homo sapiens* is further made tangible through comparison of sameness and difference among human societies. The student observes a culturally alien people and most readily sees himself by noting differences: I am not-he. But through empirical work, the student can also come to see apparently bizarre behavior transformed in his perception into personally meaningful behavior, through the addition of new data and well-known modes of fundamentally simple analysis. By this the student discovers he can vicariously enter the experience of that people in some approximation, which is to say, he discovers sameness: I am he, simply because I can enter his experience.

This sort of experience is seeing Man empirically, as intended by a Mankind curriculum as here defined. These glimpses of Man, not some attempt at abstract characterization of human nature, are what are intended as answers to the orienting question, "What is human about all humans?"

The products of the Anthropology Curriculum Study Project and the social studies effort of the Education Development Center make generally available to the schools a firm foundation for such an empirical Mankind curriculum. EDC's "Man: A Course of Study" can provide that foundation and establish the general shape of such a curriculum for the upper elementary grades.

"Man: A Course of Study" explicitly asks: What is human about all humans? It guides student inquiry through a wide-ranging and unhurried look at the life of one small human community, the Netsilik Eskimo, mainly through unnarrated film with natural sound.

The course opens with a series of comparative examinations of animal behavior—salmon, gulls, baboons—with special attention to troop organization and vocal communication among baboons; it moves then to the examination of Eskimo life. Throughout, the data provided are unusually rich, evocative, engaging, contained in a wide variety of wisely selected media, including strategy "games" (a caribou hunt, a seal hunt) which seek to help the student get inside the culturally informed, calculating head of the Eskimo hunter as he pursues these life-and-death subsistence activities.

At any point from grades eight or nine through twelve, ACSP's "Patterns in Human History" can also provide the foundation for a Mankind curriculum. This course too addresses the question: What is human about all humans? But where "Man: A Course of Study" treats extensively one human community, "Patterns in Human History" looks analytically at an array of human communities both familiar and strange, selected for their contrasts in size and form—which seems appropriate treatment at this grade level.

The course begins with the past experience of the students and on that basis helps them develop a working command over the concept of role. It traces then the interconnected biological and cultural career of ancient man. The course then returns to the concept of role, which provides the main analytic tool by which selected human communities are compared in their diversity as the course looks at the overall shape of the long human career, the major turning points in that career, and the resulting contemporary diversity of human communities seen as very general types—tribal, peasant, urban. Finally, the course turns to the contemporary problem of "economic development," viewed from the perspective of the village peasant. The data provided are quite rich, contained in a variety of media.

But serious curriculum interests such as these lead inevitably back to theoretically oriented research interests. The staffs of ACSP and EDC were caused to concern themselves with the social systems that are the classrooms and schools, and to look at the ways those systems are congruent and incongruent with the teaching-learning activities entailed by the curriculum purposes at issue.

This is an area usually referred to by educators and educational psychologists as "pedagogy" or "process," but to anthropologists those matters seem subsumed by wider curiosities about how a social system forms and sustains itself and, conversely, how it changes or can be made to change by intervention. It is thus not surprising that the work of other anthropologists, who started from wholly theoretical concerns, have come to intersect the above curriculum-oriented work.

Parsons (1965) undertook the ethnography of a small town of mixed Anglo and Chicano population, and particularly addressed the question of how the caste system of the community was reenacted in the major socializing institutions of the community, particularly the schools; that is to say, he was asking how that social system at large daily re-created itself through cultural transmission. He discovered, and reported in good ethnographic detail, activities in the schools, such as the practice of asking some elementary grade children to be "helpers" to their fellow students at junctures where this seemed to serve simple instructional purposes; but he also discovered how such innocent-appearing (and probably innocently intended) activities were assimilated to the caste system of the wider community, so that helpers were always Anglos, the helped almost always Chicanos.

From these and other foundations people have moved to similar curiosities about the structure of classrooms generally. It has seemed to some that all actors in a classroom, teachers and students, have learned from infancy and relearn throughout life two gross equations: big equals strong equals informed, and little equals weak equals uninformed; and that in our society these equations are further assimilated with the structural images we attach to expertise, as in the relations between doctor and patient, lawyer and client, and so on. These together appear to help form and strongly reinforce the folk images of teacher and student held by students and teachers alike: a teacher is a conveyor of information; a student is a receptacle for that information.

I said earlier that a Mankind curriculum implies, among other things, that "the student discovers he can vicariously enter the experience of [Netsilik Eskimos or any culturally alien] people in some approximation, which is to say, he discovers sameness: I am he, simply because I can enter his experience." It will be evident that a conveyor of information simply cannot convey information of that kind to a receptacle, that the classroom social system runs directly against the grain of that particular curriculum purpose: the anthropological message competes most directly at this juncture and many others with aspects of the very cultural transmission processes of the society.

Several anthropologists, including Fred Erickson, Gearing, and Parsons, thinking in a somewhat analogous vein, turned to intervention-research: By what devices may teachers and students be helped to retransact new classroom roles? The answer has seemed to lie in clinical ethnography, especially self-observation when that is sharply focused.

According to preliminary evidence, behavioral changes so induced are impressive.

Clearly all organizational change entails role retransaction. When some roles change in any role system, effects usually follow in others: the retransaction of teacher-student roles will have inevitable effects on principal-teacher roles. What effects precisely is an ethnographic question, in the first instance.

This intervention-research appears to be among the most concerted current efforts of anthropologists bearing directly on the theoretical question, pivotal in studies of cultural transmission in schools and in urban anthropology generally: How do large bureaucratic organizations daily re-create themselves and how do they change?

And so the two sets of activity meet, the one starting from curriculum concerns, the other starting from theoretical curiosities. But it should finally be noted that anthropological curriculum-making in turn will generate new research questions. I said earlier that the anthropological message *competes* with the processes of cultural transmission in the society at large: a Mankind curriculum is "out in front" of the culture, anticipating and perhaps generating culture change. This appears to raise theoretical problems as yet unimagined.

TRENDS AND CONDITIONS

That the realm of anthropology and education is not today by any reasonable definition a subfield seems clear. As to whether it should be one I have no opinion. Certain trends, moving toward and away from that eventuality, may briefly be mentioned.

Foremost, from within the discipline there is the creation in 1968 of the Council on Anthropology and Education, an association of persons, predominantly anthropologists, who share interests in research and development activities in the schools. The council members have formed a series of standing committees, according to their several special interests: research in schools and communities, research training, curriculum development and the preparation of school personnel, minority affairs, museums in education, and cognitive and linguistic research. The level of activity of the members of these committees is reflected in the fact that, at the two annual meetings of the American Anthropological Association since the creation of the council, a total of ten symposia were presented by the several committees. The council publishes an occasional newsletter.

The variety of well-recognized anthropological forces, both theoretical and pragmatic, which press toward increased attention to urban studies by anthropologists seem also to press toward increased focus on schools in particular. Urban schools, like many other urban institutions, are large, bureaucratically organized bodies of interacting persons. Among the central questions in urban studies are those bearing on how such structures form, how they re-create themselves daily and thereby persist, how they change; these questions can be addressed in school research, and in some respects more readily there than in other institutional settings. Additionally, as I noted earlier, schools are often the major loci of a critical facet of cultural transmission, socialization to large groups; it would

follow in principle that here the growing tip of urban continuity and change can be made evident.

On the other hand, "pure" research remains highly ranked, at the expense of "applied" research, in the eyes of most anthropologists, and many of them recognize that research in the schools typically gets caught up with other distracting involvements, regardless of initial intent. Additionally, it no doubt appears to some that schools, to confound the matter further, are typically beyond redemption.

From without the discipline, the educational demand for anthropologists appears to be considerably greater than the supply. Virtually all educators are aware of the great and increasing need for cross-cultural awareness, though virtually all imagine that this is a problem of inculcating in students "tolerant" mind-sets; most are therefore mystified as to how to proceed, and many look to anthropology for help, as they should. Conversely, many educators are rightly persuaded that various ethnic studies are needed, though many imagine that ethnic studies have to do with redressing imbalances in the study of history, which is only tangentially so; primarily such studies are exercises in charter-making. Most educators are mystified here as well, and many look to anthropology for help, as they emphatically should not, for no one can make another man's charter. Finally, very few educators are aware that questions might be put to anthropologists about the nature of classrooms and schools and the communities that surround them, and about the nature of the transactions that occur and fail to occur in those settings. So the demand is large, but to date it is ill defined and partly ill conceived.

Some of these trends and conditions point toward a future subfield, and others point in the opposite direction;

both contain ambiguities. The outcome will necessarily be determined by results that emerge or fail to emerge from work in the schools, insofar as these results are of theoretical interest to anthropologists and scientists generally.

What is now conspicuously missing is a resynthesis of diverse behavioral theories, anthropological and otherwise, into a theory of cultural transmission of universal human applicability, or perhaps several such theories in competition with each other. I hazard the prediction that the theoretical parts are at hand and that the key term that will permit resynthesis will prove to be "transaction," meaning those processes by which any two actors in any encounter, including actors in those kinds of encounters called education, transact or fail to transact "equivalent meanings" (Wallace 1970) as to the salient parts of the universe about them, as to who each is vis-à-vis the other, and as to the situation they therefore face, their agenda.

REFERENCES

Atwood, Mark S.
  1964 Small-Scale Administrative Change: Resistance to the Introduction of a High School Guidance Program. In *Innovation in Education*, ed. M. B. Miles. New York: Teachers College Press.
Bailey, Beryl L.
  1969 Language and Communicative Styles of Afro-American Children in the United States. *Florida FL Reporter* 7, no. 1.
Benedict, Ruth
  1943 Transmitting Our Democratic Heritage in the Schools. *American Journal of Sociology* 48:722-27.
Bernstein, Basil
  1964 Elaborated and Restricted Codes: Their Social Origins and Some Consequences. *American Anthropologist* Special Publication 66:55-69.
Boas, Franz
  1928 *Anthropology and Modern Life*. New York: Norton.
Brameld, Theodore, and Edward B. Sullivan
  1961 Anthropology and Education. *Review of Educational Research* 31:70-79.
Burnett, Jacquetta H.
  1969 Ceremony, Rites, and Economy in the Student System of an American High School. *Human Organization* 28:1-10.
Cohen, Yehudi
  1969 Schools and Civilizational States. In *The Social Sciences and the Comparative Study of Educational Systems*, ed. J. Fischer. New York: International Textbooks.
  1971 The Shaping of Men's Minds: Adaptations to Imperatives of Culture. In *Anthropological Perspectives on Education*, ed. M. Wax, S. Diamond, and F. Gearing. New York: Basic Books.
Dillard, J. L.
  1967 Negro Children's Dialect in the Inner City. *Florida FL Reporter* 5.
  1968 Non-Standard Negro Dialects: Convergence or Divergence. *Florida FL Reporter* 6.
  1969 How To Tell the Bandits from the Good Buys, or What Dialect To Teach? *Florida FL Reporter* 7, no. 1:84-85.
Du Bois, Cora
  1944 *The People of Alor*. Minneapolis: University of Minnesota Press.
  1955 Some Notions on Learning Intercultural Understanding. In *Education and Anthropology*, ed. G. Spindler. Stanford: Stanford University Press.
Eddy, Elizabeth
  1969 *Becoming a Teacher*. New York: Teachers College Press.
Eggan, Dorothy
  1956 Instruction and Affect in Hopi Cultural Continuity. *Southwestern Journal of Anthropology* 12:347-70.
Ehrich, Robert
  1947 The Place of Anthropology in a College Education. *Harvard Educational Review* 17:57-61.
Embree, Edwin R.
  1943 The Educational Process as Applied in America. *American Journal of Sociology* 48:759-65.

Erikson, Erik H.
  1943 *Observations on the Yurok: Child-hood and World Image*. University of California Publications in American Archaeology and Ethnology 35, no. 10.
Firth, Raymond
  1936 *We, the Tikopia*. London: Allen & Unwin.
Fischer, J. L.
  1961 The Japanese Schools for the Natives of Truk, Caroline Islands. *Human Organization* 20:83-88.
Fortes, Meyer
  1938 Social and Psychological Aspects of Education in Taleland. *Africa* 11, no. 4 (supplement).
Foster, Philip
  1965 *Education and Social Change in Ghana*. Chicago: University of Chicago Press.
Gans, Herbert J.
  1962 *The Urban Villagers: Group and Class in the Life of Italian Americans*. New York: Free Press of Glencoe, Macmillan.
Gay, John, and Michael Cole
  1967 *The New Mathematics in an Old Culture*. New York: Holt, Rinehart & Winston.
Gearing, Frederick O.
  1970a *The Face of the Fox*. Chicago: Aldine.
  1970b Mankind, Empirically. Notes presented to the Wenner-Gren symposium on relevance in anthropology, May 1970. Proceedings in preparation.
Goldenweiser, Alexander
  1939 Culture and Education. In *Stanford Education Conference*. New York: Social Education.
Goldfrank, Esther
  1945 Socialization, Personality, and the Structure of Pueblo Society. *American Anthropologist* 47:516-39.
Gumperz, John J.
  1969 Social Differences in Verbal Strategies. Paper presented at the annual meetings of the American Anthropological Association, New Orleans.
Hart, C. W. M.
  1955 Contrasts Between Prepubertal and Postpubertal Education. In *Education and Anthropology*, ed. G. Spind-

ler. Stanford: Stanford University Press.
Henry, Jules
  1957 Attitude Organization in Elementary School Classrooms. *American Journal of Orthopsychiatry* 27:117-33.
  1959 The Problem of Spontaneity, Initiative, and Creativity in Suburban Classrooms. *American Journal of Orthopsychiatry* 29:266-79.
  1960 A Cross-Cultural Outline of Education. *Current Anthropology* 1:267-305.
Herskovits, Melville J.
  1938 *Dahomey*. New York: Knopf.
Herzog, John D.
  1962 Deliberate Instruction and Household Structure: A Cross-Cultural Study. *Harvard Educational Review* 32:301-342.
Hewett, Edgar L.
  1904 Anthropology and Education. *American Anthropologist* 6:574-75.
  1905 Ethnic Factors in Education. *American Anthropologist* 7:1-16.
Hobart, C. W., and C. S. Brant
  1966 Eskimo Education, Danish and Canadian: A Comparison. *Canadian Review of Sociology and Anthropology* 3:47-66.
Hoernlé, A. W.
  1931 An Outline of the Native Conception of Education in Africa. *Africa* 4: 145-63.
Hogbin, H. Ian
  1931 Education at Ontong-Java. *American Anthropologist* 33:601-614.
Honigmann, John J., and Irma Honigmann
  1965 *Eskimo Townsmen*. Ottawa: Canadian Research Centre for Anthropology.
Hunt, John McV.
  1964 Introduction. In M. Montessori, *The Montessori Method*. New York: Schocken Books.
Joseph, Alice, Rosamond Spicer, and Jane Chesky
  1949 *The Desert People*. Chicago: University of Chicago Press.
Keesing, Felix M.
  1937 *Education in Pacific Countries*. Shanghai: Kelly & Walsh.
King, A. Richard
  1967 *The School at Mopass: A Problem of*

Identity. New York: Holt, Rinehart & Winston.

Kochman, Thomas
1969 "Rapping" in the Black Ghetto. *Trans-action* 6, no. 4:26-34.

Labov, William
1969 *The Logic of Non-Standard English*. Georgetown Monograph Series on Languages and Linguistics, no. 22.

La Flesche, Francis
1963 *The Middle Five: Indian Schoolboys of the Omaha Tribe*. Madison: University of Wisconsin Press.

Leighton, Dorothea, and Clyde Kluckhohn
1947 *Children of the People*. Cambridge: Harvard University Press.

Lindquist, Harry M., ed.
1970 *Education: Readings in the Processes of Cultural Transmission*. Boston: Houghton Mifflin.

Little, K. L.
1951 *The Mende of Sierra Leone*. London: Routledge & Kegan Paul.

Maccoby, Michael, and Nancy Modiano
1969a Cognitive Style in Rural and Urban Mexico. *Human Development* 12: 22-32.
1969b The Intellectual Style of Mexican Peasant Children. Paper presented at the annual meeting of the National Association for the Education of Young Children, Salt Lake City.

Madsen, William
1964 *The Mexican-Americans of South Texas*. New York: Holt, Rinehart & Winston.

Malinowski, Bronislaw
1936 Native Education and Culture Contact. *International Review of Missions* 25:480-517.
1943 The Pan-African Problem of Culture Contact. *American Journal of Sociology* 48:649-65.

Mandelbaum, D., G. Lasker, and E. Albert, eds.
1963a *The Teaching of Anthropology*. American Anthropological Association Memoirs, no. 94. Berkeley: University of California Press.
1963b *Resources for the Teaching of Anthropology*. American Anthropological Association Memoirs, no. 95. Berkeley: University of California Press.

Mead, Margaret
1928 *Coming of Age in Samoa*. New York: Morrow.
1930 *Growing Up in New Guinea*. New York: Morrow.
1942 Educational Effects of Social Environment as Disclosed by Studies of Primitive Societies. In *Symposium on Environment and Education*, ed. E. W. Burgess et al. Chicago: University of Chicago Press.

Mekeel, Scudder
1943 Education, Child-Training, and Culture. *American Journal of Sociology* 48:674-87.

Middleton, John, ed.
1970 *From Child to Adult: Studies in the Anthropology of Education*. Garden City, N.Y.: Natural History Press.

Montessori, Maria
1913 *Pedagogical Anthropology*. New York: Stokes.
1964 *The Montessori Method*. New York: Schocken Books.
1965a *Spontaneous Activity in Education*. New York: Schocken Books.
1965b *Dr. Montessori's Own Handbook*. New York: Schocken Books.

Nadel, S. F.
1942 *A Black Byzantium*. London: Oxford University Press.

Nash, Manning
1961 Education in a New Nation: The Village School in Upper Burma. *International Journal of Comparative Sociology* 2:135-43.

Opler, Morris
1941 *An Apache Way of Life*. Chicago: University of Chicago Press.

Parmee, Edward A.
1968 *Formal Education and Culture Change: A Modern Apache Indian Community and Government Education Programs*. Tucson: University of Arizona Press.

Parsons, Theodore W.
1965 Ethnic Cleavage in a California School. Ph. D. dissertation, Stanford University.

Pettit, George A.
1946 Primitive Education in North America. *University of California Publications in American Archaeology and Ethnology* 43:182.

Powdermaker, Hortense
  1943 The Channeling of Negro Aggression by the Cultural Process. *American Journal of Sociology* 48:750-58.
Rattray, R. S.
  1932 The Education of Girls. In *The Tribes of the Ashanti Hinterland*. Oxford: Clarendon Press.
Raum, Otto
  1938 Some Aspects of Indigenous Education Among the Chaga. *Journal of the Royal Anthropological Institute* 68:209-221.
Redfield, Robert
  1943 Culture and Education in the Midwestern Highlands of Guatemala. *American Journal of Sociology* 48:640-48.
Rubel, Arthur J.
  1966 *Across the Tracks: Mexican-Americans in a Texas City*. Austin: University of Texas Press.
Sindell, Peter S.
  1968 Some Discontinuities in the Enculturation of Mistassini Cree Children. In *Conflict in Culture*, ed. N. A. Chance. Ottawa: Canadian Research Centre for Anthropology.
  1969 Anthropological Approaches to the Study of Education. *Review of Educational Research* 39:593-605.
Singleton, John
  1967 *Nichū: A Japanese School*. New York: Holt, Rinehart & Winston.
Spindler, George D.
  1955 *Education and Anthropology*. Stanford: Stanford University Press.
  1963 *Education and Culture*. New York: Holt, Rinehart & Winston.
Spiro, Melford E.
  1955 Education in a Communal Village in Israel. *American Journal of Orthopsychiatry* 25:283-92.
Stewart, William
  1969 On the Use of Negro Dialect in the Teaching of Reading. In *Teaching Black Children To Read,* ed. J. Baratz and R. Shuy. Washington, D.C.: Center for Applied Linguistics.
Talbert, Carol
  1969 A Sociolinguistic Analysis of Spoken Black-American English in a Classroom, Related to Pupil Patterns of

Centrality and Peripherality. Paper presented at the annual meetings of the American Anthropological Association, New Orleans.
Thompson, Laura, and Alice Joseph
  1944 *The Hopi Way*. Indian Education Research Series, no. 1. Lawrence, Kans.: Haskell Institute.
Underhill, Ruth
  1936 *Autobiography of a Papago Woman*. American Anthropological Association Memoir no. 46.
Van Gennep, Arnold
  1960 *Rites of Passage*. Chicago: University of Chicago Press. Originally published 1909.
Wallace, A. F. C.
  1970 *Culture and Personality*, 2nd ed. New York: Random House.
Warner, W. Lloyd, R. J. Havighurst, and M. B. Loeb
  1944 *Who Shall Be Educated?* New York: Harper.
Warren, Richard L.
  1967 *Education in Rebhausen*. New York: Holt, Rinehart & Winston.
Watkins, M. H.
  1943 The West African "Bush School." *American Journal of Sociology* 48:666-75.
Wax, Murray, R. Wax, and R. V. Dumont, Jr.
  1964 Formal Education in an American Indian Community. *Social Problems* 2, no. 4 (supplement).
Wax, Murray, Stanley Diamond, and Frederick Gearing, eds.
  1971 *Anthropological Perspectives on Education*. New York: Basic Books.
West, James
  1945 *Plainville, USA*. New York: Columbia University Press.
Whiting, John
  1941 *Becoming a Kwoma*. New Haven: Yale University Press.
Williams, Thomas R.
  1958 The Structure of the Socialization Process in Papago Indian Society. *Social Forces* 36:251-56.
Wolcott, Harry F.
  1967a Anthropology and Education. *Review of Educational Research* 37:82-92.
  1967b *A Kwakiutl Village and School*. New

York: Holt, Rinehart & Winston.

Wolfram, Walter A.
1969 *A Sociolinguistic Description of Detroit Negro Speech.* Washington,
D.C.: Center for Applied Linguistics.

Wylie, Lawrence
1957 *Village in the Vaucluse.* New York: Harper & Row.

Credits and Acknowledgments

Acknowledgment is made to the following for their kind permission to reprint material from copyrighted sources:

Chapter 1

Cambridge University Press (*The Andaman Islanders* by A. R. Radcliffe-Brown, 1922); Routledge & Kegan Paul, Ltd. (*The Foundations of Social Anthropology* by S. F. Nadel, 1951); Beacon Press (*The Elementary Structures of Kinship* by Claude Lévi-Strauss, translation copyright © 1969 by Beacon Press; published first in France under the title *Les Structures élémentaires de la parenté* in 1949); The Macmillan Company (*Social Structure* by George P. Murdock, copyright © 1949); The Free Press, a Division of The Macmillan Company (*The Andaman Islanders* by A. R. Radcliffe-Brown, copyright © 1964); McGraw-Hill Book Company (*Toward a Science of Mankind* by Laura Thompson, copyright © 1961).

Chapter 4

Oxford University Press (*Man, Culture, and Society*, edited by H. Shapiro, 1960); Basic Books, Inc. (*New Roads to Yesterday*, edited by Joseph R. Caldwell, 1966); Kent V. Flannery and the American Association for the Advancement of Science ("The Ecology of Early Food Production in Mesopotamia" by Kent V. Flannery, *Science*, March 12, 1965, vol. 147, pp. 1247-56); *Southwestern Journal of Anthropology* ("Population Pressure and the Social Evolution of Agriculturists" by M. J. Harner, 1970, vol. 26, pp. 67-86).

Chapter 5

The Regents of the University of California (*Cultural and Natural Areas of Native North America* by A. L. Kroeber, University of California Press, 1939); University of Chicago Press (*The Little Community* by Robert Redfield, copyright © 1960 by The University of Chicago); Duke University Press ("Language Analysis and the Concept 'Environment' " by H. L. Mason and J. H. Langenheim, *Ecology*, 1957, vol. 38, pp. 325-40); Columbia University Press (*Culture in History*, edited by S. Diamond, 1960); Charles Scribner's Sons (*So Human an Animal* by René Dubos, 1968); *American Scientist* ("The Ecological Approach to the Social Sciences" by F. Fraser Darling, 1951, vol. 39, pp. 244-54); Harper & Row, Publishers, Inc. (*The Meaning of the Twentieth Century* by K. E. Boulding, 1964; *Modern Theories of Development* by L. von Bertalanffy, 1933, Harper Torchbooks 1962).

Chapter 6

Tavistock Publications, Ltd. (*The Craft of Social Anthropology*, edited by A. L. Epstein, 1967); Houghton Mifflin Company (*Introduction to Cultural Anthropology*, edited by James Clifton, 1968); Holt, Rinehart and Winston, Inc. (*Stress and Response in Field Work*, edited by F. Henry and S. Saterwal, 1969; *The Study of the Lugbara* by John Middleton, 1970; *Being an Anthropologist*, edited by George Spindler, 1970; *Yanomanö: The Fierce People* by Napoleon Chagnon, 1968; *Understanding an African Kingdom* by John Beattie, 1965); Little, Brown and Company, Inc. (*Tally's Corner* by Elliot Liebow, 1968); Harper & Row, Publishers, Inc. (*Marginal Natives*, edited by Morris Freilich, 1970); HRAF Press (*Kapauku Papuans and Their Law* by Leopold Pospisil, 1964); University of Pittsburgh ("An Analysis of Zapotec Law Cases" by Laura Nader, *Ethnology*, 1964, vol. 3, pp. 404-419); The Macmillan Company (*Custer Died for Your Sins* by Vine Deloria, Jr., copyright © 1969); Evans Brothers, Ltd. (*The Savage and the Innocent* by David Maybury-Lewis, 1965); E. P. Dutton & Co., Inc. (*Argonauts of the Western Pacific* by Bronislaw Malinowski, Preface by Sir James G. Fraser, 1961); Aldine-Atherton, Inc. (*Women in the Field*, edited by Peggy Golde, 1970).

Chapter 7

Basic Books, Inc. (*Structural Anthropology* by Claude Lévi-Strauss, 1963); Routledge & Kegan Paul, Ltd., and Humanities Press, Inc. (*Man and Culture: An Evaluation of the Work of Malinowski*, edited by Raymond Firth, 1957); The Free Press, a Division of The Macmillan Company (*The Nerves of Government* by Karl Deutsch, copyright © 1963).

Chapter 9

The Macmillan Company (*Kinship and Social Organization* by I. R. Buchler and H. A. Selby, copyright © 1968); John Wiley & Sons, Inc. (*Theory of Games and Economic Behavior* by J. von Neumann and O. Morgenstern, 3rd ed., 1964); Society for General Systems Research ("Wheat on Kilimanjaro: The Perception of Choice Within Game and Learning Model Frameworks" by P. Gould, *General Systems*, 1965, vol. 10, pp. 157-66); *Current Anthropology* ("Theoretical Issues in Economic Anthropology" by G. Dalton, 1969, vol. 10, pp. 63-101); *Southwestern Journal of Anthropology* ("Changing Emphases in Social Structure" by George P. Murdock, 1955, vol. 11, pp. 361-70; "American Kinship Terms Once More" by Robbins Burling, 1970, vol. 26, pp. 15-24); Prentice-Hall, Inc. (*An Anatomy of Kinship* by Harrison C. White, copyright © 1963); Gordon and Breach Science Publishers, Inc. ("Structural Equivalence of Individuals in School Networks" by F. Lorrain and H. White, *Journal of Mathematical Sociology*, 1971, vol. 1, pp. 49-80); Royal Anthropological Institute of Great Britain and Ireland (*Models of Social Organization* by F. Barth, occasional paper no. 23, 1966).

Chapter 10

Holt, Rinehart and Winston, Inc. (*Cognitive Anthropology*, edited by Stephen Tyler, 1969; *Cultural and Biological Man* by Eliot D. Chapple, 1970); Harvard University Press (*The Navaho* by Clyde Kluckhohn and Dorothea Leighton, 1946, rev. ed. 1972); American Association for the Advancement of Science ("The Science of Human Learning, Society, Culture, and Personality" by George P. Murdock, *Scientific Monthly*, December 1949, vol. 69, pp. 377-81); Chicago University Press (*New Views of the Nature of Man*, edited by John R. Platt, copyright © 1965 by The University of Chicago; *Prehistoric Man in the New World*, edited by Jesse D. Jennings and Edward Norbeck, copyright © 1964 by The University of Chicago; *Meaning and Necessity* by Rudolf Carnap, copyright © 1956 by The University of Chicago); The M.I.T. Press (*Word and Object* by Willard van Orman Quine, copyright © 1960 by The Massachusetts Institute of Technology; *Language, Thought, and Reality: Selected Writings of Benjamin Lee Whorf*, edited by John B. Carroll, copyright © 1956 by The Massachusetts Institute of Technology); University of Michigan Press (*The Structure of Complex Words* by William Empson, 1967); The Regents of The University of California (*Selected Writings of Edward Sapir in Language, Culture, and Personality*, edited by David G. Mandelbaum, University of California Press, 1949); *International Journal of American Linguistics* ("Navajo Phonology and Hoijer's Analysis" by Zellig S. Harris, 1945, vol. 11, pp. 239-46; Review of Zellig S. Harris' *Methods in Structural Linguistics* by Margaret Mead, 1952, vol. 18, pp. 257-60; Review of C. F. Hockett's *A Manual of Phonology* by Noam Chomsky, 1957, vol. 23, pp. 223-34); *International Journal of American Linguistics* and Madeleine Mathiot (*An Approach to the Cognitive Study of Language* by Madeleine Mathiot, 1968, vol. 34, no. 1, publication no. 45); *International Journal of American Linguistics* and Fred W. Householder, Jr. (Review of Zellig S. Harris' *Methods in Structural Linguistics*, 1952, vol. 18, pp. 260-68); *Southwestern Journal of Anthropology* ("Hanunóo Color Categories" by Harold C. Conklin, 1955, vol. 11, pp. 339-44); Mouton & Co., Publishers (*Proceedings of the Ninth International Congress of Linguistics, Cambridge, Mass., 1962*, edited by Horace G. Lunt, 1964).

Chapter 11

The Free Press, a Division of The Macmillan Company (*Religion in Java* by Clifford Geertz, copyright © 1960); Language-Behavior Research Laboratory ("Sociolinguistics and Communication in Small Groups" by John J. Gumperz, 1970, working paper no. 33); Aldine-Atherton, Inc. (*Man in Adaptation* by Yehudi Cohen, 1968).

Chapter 12

Holt, Rinehart and Winston, Inc. (*Communication and Culture*, edited by Alfred G. Smith, 1966); Prentice-Hall, Inc. (*Stigma* by Erving Goffman, copyright © 1963); *Ethnology* ("Statistical Models and Decision Models of Social Structure: A Kwaio Case" by Roger W. Keesing, 1967, vol. 6, pp. 1-16); Roy G. D'Andrade ("Categories of Disease in American-English and Mexican-Spanish," unpublished paper by Roy G. D'Andrade et al.).

Chapter 15

Atheneum Publishers (*Tristes Tropiques* by Claude Lévi-Strauss, 1967); Basic Books, Inc. (*Structural Anthropology* by Claude Lévi-Strauss, 1963).

Chapter 16

Plenum Publishing Corp. ("Class and Committees in a Norwegian Island Parish" by John A. Barnes, *Human Relations*, 1954, vol. 7, pp. 39-58; Institute for African Studies, University of Zambia, and John A. Barnes ("Networks and Political Process" by John A. Barnes, in *Social Networks in Urban Situations*, edited by J. C. Mitchell, Manchester University Press for Institute for Social Research, University of Zambia, 1969); International African Institute, London (*Social Change in Modern Africa*, edited by Aidan Southall, Oxford University Press, 1961); Clarendon Press ("Graph Theory and Social Networks" by John A. Barnes, *Sociology*, 1969, vol. 3, pp. 215-32); C. A. Watts & Co., Ltd. (*Elements of Social Organization* by Raymond Firth, 1951); Tavistock Publications, Ltd. (*The Social Anthropology of Complex Societies*, edited by Michael Banton, 1966); Royal Anthropological Institute of Great Britain and Ireland ("The Place of Non-Groups in the Social Sciences" by Jeremy Boissevain, *Man*, 1968, vol. 3, pp. 542-56); York University, Ontario ("African Urbanism: Mobility and Social Network" by P. C. W. Gutkind, *International Journal of Comparative Sociology*, 1965, vol. 6, pp. 48-60); *Canadian Review of Sociology and Anthropology* ("On Structural Comparisons of Networks" by Alvin W. Wolfe, 1970, vol. 4, pp. 226-44); *Oceania* (Review of *Social Anthropology of Complex Societies*, ed. M. Banton, by R. G. Swift, 1967, vol. 37, pp. 310-11); *Current Anthropology* ("Anthropological Studies of Complex Societies" by S. N. Eisenstadt, 1961, vol. 2, pp. 201-222); *Cornell Journal of Social Relations* ("On Networks" by Lawrence W. Crissman, 1969, vol. 4, pp. 72-81).

Chapter 17

Royal Anthropological Institute of Great Britain and Ireland ("Descent, Filiation, and Affinity" by Meyer Fortes, *Man*, 1959, vol. 59, pp. 193-97, 206-212).

Chapter 20

University of Oklahoma Press (*The Cheyenne Way* by Karl N. Llewellyn and E. Adamson Hoebel, copyright © 1941); American Philosophical Society and Willard Hurst ("The Law in United States History by Willard Hurst," *Proceedings of the American Philosophical Society*, 1960, vol. 104, no. 5);

Chapter 21

Chapter 23

Chapter 24

Chapter 25

Chapter 26

Chapman and J. Baxter, *Journal of Nervous and Mental Disease*, 1963, vol. 136, pp. 352-59); Francis L. K. Hsu (*Psychological Anthropology*, edited by Francis L. K. Hsu, Dorsey Press, 1961); *British Journal of Psychiatry* ("A Study of Mental Derangements in Africans" by J. C. Carothers, *Journal of Mental Science*, 1947, vol. 93, pp. 548-97); Holt, Rinehart and Winston, Inc. (*Changing Perspectives in Mental Illness*, edited by Stanley C. Plog and Robert B. Edgerton, 1969); American Psychiatric Association and L. L. Langness ("Hysterical Psychosis: The Cross-Cultural Evidence" by L. L. Langness, *American Journal of Psychiatry*, 1967, vol. 124, pp. 143-52); The Free Press, a Division of The Macmillan Company (*Curanderismo: Mexican-American Folk Psychiatry* by Ari Kiev, copyright © 1968); Addison-Wesley Publishing Company, Inc. (*Handbook of Social Psychology*, edited by Gardiner Lindzey and Elliot Aronson, 2nd ed., vol. 4, 1969).

Chapter 27

Random House, Inc. (*Religion: An Anthropological View* by Anthony F. C. Wallace, 1966); The Free Press, a Division of The Macmillan Company (*Context and Meaning in Cultural Anthropology*, edited by Melford E. Spiro, copyright © 1965).

Chapter 28

International African Institute, London ("Social and Psychological Aspects of Education in Taleland" by Meyer Fortes, *Africa*, 1938, vol. 11, no. 4 [supplement]); Holt, Rinehart and Winston, Inc. (*Education in Rebhausen* by Richard L. Warren, 1967).

Name Index

Subject Index

Acculturation, 43, 46, 119, 197, 205, 306, 932–34, 962, 970, 1104. *See also* Culture change.
Action theory, 731
Adaptation, 90, 143ff, 180, 184, 187, 191, 192, 197, 211
  in ecological anthropology, 846ff, 934–35
  urban, 999ff
Address systems, 421ff
Affective disorders. *See* Depression; *Susto.*
Age, determination of, in fieldwork, 298–300
Age class, 25
Age grade, 376
Aggression, 927ff. *See also* War.
Agriculture, 199, 351–52
Alcohol, use of, 1135ff
Alcoholism, 360
Alliance theory, 41–42, 780ff
Amok, 1160ff
Analysis, 206, 371ff. *See also* Theory.
Animism, 614
Anthropology:
  Anglo-American, 655–57, 689
  applied, 46–48, 883–84, 1033, 1061–62. *See also* Intervention research.
  behavioral, 868–70
  British social, 3, 35, 39, 47–48, 119, 121–23. *See also* Enthnology, British.
  cognitive, 447–78, 510, 520, 547
  configurational, 516
  ecological, 179–239
  economic. *See* Economic anthropology.
  education and, 1223–49
  evolutionary, 818
  fields of, 1–2
  goal of, 212

  government and, 46–47
  historical approach in, 111–41
  history of, 1–88, 89ff, 113ff, 241ff, 293ff, 329–30, 454–67, 865ff, 889–90, 915, 926, 980ff, 1075ff, 1109, 1120ff, 1202ff, 1223ff
  humanistic, 245–46
  industrial, 47
  legal, 52–53, 275–76, 883–921
  linguistic. *See* Linguistic anthropology; Sociolinguistics.
  mathematical. *See* Mathematical anthropology.
  medical, 1031–72
  objectivity in, 1013
  pedagogical, 1226
  political. *See* Political anthropology.
  psychological. *See* Psychological anthropology.
  relational, 660
  scientific, 642
  social, 26ff, 371. *See also* Anthropology, British social.
  structural, 520, 539, 547, 637–704
  Urban. *See* Urban anthropology.
Anthropology Curriculum Study Project, 1241ff
Archaeology, 12–13, 59, 91–93, 126–29, 196
Archetype, 543
Art, 24, 357
Associations, 1000ff
Authority, 872–74
Avoidance, 355–56. *See also* Taboo.

Balance theory, 411ff
Behavior and belief, 525–26

1285